# Poetry
# Criticism

# Guide to Gale Literary Criticism Series

| For criticism on | Consult these Gale series |
| --- | --- |
| Authors now living or who died after December 31, 1999 | *CONTEMPORARY LITERARY CRITICISM (CLC)* |
| Authors who died between 1900 and 1999 | *TWENTIETH-CENTURY LITERARY CRITICISM (TCLC)* |
| Authors who died between 1800 and 1899 | *NINETEENTH-CENTURY LITERATURE CRITICISM (NCLC)* |
| Authors who died between 1400 and 1799 | *LITERATURE CRITICISM FROM 1400 TO 1800 (LC)*<br><br>*SHAKESPEAREAN CRITICISM (SC)* |
| Authors who died before 1400 | *CLASSICAL AND MEDIEVAL LITERATURE CRITICISM (CMLC)* |
| Authors of books for children and young adults | *CHILDREN'S LITERATURE REVIEW (CLR)* |
| Dramatists | *DRAMA CRITICISM (DC)* |
| Poets | *POETRY CRITICISM (PC)* |
| Short story writers | *SHORT STORY CRITICISM (SSC)* |
| Black writers of the past two hundred years | *BLACK LITERATURE CRITICISM (BLC)*<br><br>*BLACK LITERATURE CRITICISM SUPPLEMENT (BLCS)* |
| Hispanic writers of the late nineteenth and twentieth centuries | *HISPANIC LITERATURE CRITICISM (HLC)*<br><br>*HISPANIC LITERATURE CRITICISM SUPPLEMENT (HLCS)* |
| Native North American writers and orators of the eighteenth, nineteenth, and twentieth centuries | *NATIVE NORTH AMERICAN LITERATURE (NNAL)* |
| Major authors from the Renaissance to the present | *WORLD LITERATURE CRITICISM, 1500 TO THE PRESENT (WLC)*<br><br>*WORLD LITERATURE CRITICISM SUPPLEMENT (WLCS)* |

ISSN 1052-4851

# Poetry Criticism

*Excerpts from Criticism of the Works of the Most Significant and Widely Studied Poets of World Literature*

## Volume 29

*Linda Pavlovski*
**Editor**

GALE GROUP

**Detroit**
**New York**
**San Francisco**
**London**
**Boston**
**Woodbridge, CT**

# STAFF

Lynn M. Spampinato, Janet Witalec, *Managing Editors, Literature Product*
Kathy D. Darrow, *Product Liaison*
Linda Pavlovski, *Editor*
Mark W. Scott, *Publisher, Literature Product*

Justin Karr, *Associate Editor*
Rebecca J. Blanchard, Vince Cousino, Debra A. Wells, *Assistant Editors*
Patti A. Tippett, Timothy J. White, *Technical Training Specialists*
Deborah J. Morad, Kathleen Lopez Nolan, *Managing Editors*
Susan M. Trosky, *Director, Literature Content*

Maria L. Franklin, *Permissions Manager*
Shalice Shah-Caldwell, *Permissions Associate*

Victoria B. Cariappa, *Research Manager*
Tracie A. Richardson, *Project Coordinator*
Tamara C. Nott, *Research Associate*
Scott Floyd, Timothy Lehnerer, Ron Morelli, *Research Assistants*

Dorothy Maki, *Manufacturing Manager*
Stacy L. Melson, *Buyer*

Mary Beth Trimper, *Manager, Composition and Electronic Prepress*
Carolyn Fischer, *Composition Specialist*

Michael Logusz, *Graphic Artist*
Randy Bassett, *Image Database Supervisor*
Robert Duncan, Dan Newell, *Imaging Specialists*
Pamela A. Reed, *Imaging Coordinator*
Kelly A. Quin, *Editor, Image Content*

Library of Congress Catalog Card Number 88-641014
ISBN 0-7876-3077-2
ISSN 1052-4851
Printed in the United States of America

10 9 8 7 6 5 4 3 2 1

# Contents

Preface vii

Acknowledgments xi

**Thomas Carew 1595?-1640** ................................................................ 1
*English poet and masque writer*

**Donald Davie 1922-1995** ..................................................... 91
*English poet, critic, editor, memoirist, and translator*

**Li Po 701-763** ...................................................... 131
*Chinese poet*

**John Milton 1608-1674** ...................................... 192
*English poet, essayist, dramatist, and historian*
*Entry devoted to* Paradise Lost

**Marge Piercy 1936-** .................................... 295
*American novelist, poet, and essayist*

**Lizette Woodworth Reese 1856-1935** ........................... 328
*American poet, prose writer, and short story writer*

**Angelos Sikelianos 1884-1951** ........................... 356
*Greek poet and dramatist*


Literary Criticism Series Cumulative Author Index 377

*PC* Cumulative Nationality Index 451

*PC* Cumulative Title Index 453

# Preface

*P*oetry Criticism (*PC*) presents significant criticism of the world's greatest poets and provides supplementary biographical and bibliographical material to guide the interested reader to a greater understanding of the genre and its creators. Although major poets and literary movements are covered in such Gale Literary Criticism series as *Contemporary Literary Criticism (CLC)*, *Twentieth-Century Literary Criticism (TCLC)*, *Nineteenth-Century Literature Criticism (NCLC)*, *Literature Criticism from 1400 to 1800 (LC)*, and *Classical and Medieval Literature Criticism (CMLC)*, *PC* offers more focused attention on poetry than is possible in the broader, survey-oriented entries on writers in these Gale series. Students, teachers, librarians, and researchers will find that the generous excerpts and supplementary material provided by *PC* supply them with the vital information needed to write a term paper on poetic technique, to examine a poet's most prominent themes, or to lead a poetry discussion group.

## Scope of the Series

*PC* is designed to serve as an introduction to major poets of all eras and nationalities. Since these authors have inspired a great deal of relevant critical material, *PC* is necessarily selective, and the editors have chosen the most important published criticism to aid readers and students in their research. Each author entry presents a historical survey of the critical response to that author's work. The length of an entry is intended to reflect the amount of critical attention the author has received from critics writing in English and from foreign critics in translation. Every attempt has been made to identify and include the most significant essays on each author's work. In order to provide these important critical pieces, the editors sometimes reprint essays that have appeared elsewhere in Gale's Literary Criticism Series. Such duplication, however, never exceeds twenty percent of a *PC* volume.

## Organization of the Book

Each *PC* entry consists of the following elements:

- The **Author Heading** cites the name under which the author most commonly wrote, followed by birth and death dates. Also located here are any name variations under which an author wrote, including transliterated forms for authors whose native languages use nonroman alphabets. If the author wrote consistently under a pseudonym, the pseudonym will be listed in the author heading and the author's actual name given in parenthesis on the first line of the biographical and critical introduction. Uncertain birth or death dates are indicated by question marks. Single-work entries are preceded by the title of the work and its date of publication.

- The **Introduction** contains background information that introduces the reader to the author and the critical debates surrounding his or her work.

- A **Portrait of the Author** is included when available.

- The list of **Principal Works** is ordered chronologically by date of first publication and lists the most important works by the author. The first section comprises poetry collections and book-length poems. The second section gives information on other major works by the author. For foreign authors, the editors have provided original foreign-language publication information and have selected what are considered the best and most complete English-language editions of their works.

- Reprinted **Criticism** is arranged chronologically in each entry to provide a useful perspective on changes in critical evaluation over time. All individual titles of poems and poetry collections by the author featured in the entry are printed in boldface type. The critic's name and the date of composition or publication of the critical work are given at the beginning of each piece of criticism. Unsigned criticism is preceded by the title of the source in which it appeared. Footnotes are reprinted at the end of each essay or excerpt. In the case of excerpted criticism, only those footnotes that pertain to the excerpted texts are included.

- Critical essays are prefaced by brief **Annotations** explicating each piece.

- A complete **Bibliographical Citation** of the original essay or book precedes each piece of criticism.

- An annotated bibliography of **Further Reading** appears at the end of each entry and suggests resources for additional study. In some cases, significant essays for which the editors could not obtain reprint rights are included here. Boxed material following the further reading list provides references to other biographical and critical sources on the author in series published by Gale.

## Cumulative Indexes

A **Cumulative Author Index** lists all of the authors that appear in a wide variety of reference sources published by the Gale Group, including *PC*. A complete list of these sources is found facing the first page of the Author Index. The index also includes birth and death dates and cross references between pseudonyms and actual names.

A **Cumulative Nationality Index** lists all authors featured in *PC* by nationality, followed by the number of the *PC* volume in which their entry appears.

A **Cumulative Title Index** lists in alphabetical order all individual poems, book-length poems, and collection titles contained in the *PC* series. Titles of poetry collections and separately published poems are printed in italics, while titles of individual poems are printed in roman type with quotation marks. Each title is followed by the author's last name and corresponding volume and page numbers where commentary on the work is located. English-language translations of original foreign-language titles are cross-referenced to the foreign titles so that all references to discussion of a work are combined in one listing.

## Citing *Poetry Criticism*

When writing papers, students who quote directly from any volume in the Literary Criticism Series may use the following general format to footnote reprinted criticism. The first example pertains to material drawn from periodicals, the second to material reprinted from books.

Sylvia Kasey Marks, "A Brief Glance at George Eliot's *The Spanish Gypsy*," *Victorian Poetry* 20, no. 2 (Summer 1983), 184-90; reprinted in *Poetry Criticism*, vol. 20, ed. Carol T. Gaffke (Detroit: The Gale Group), 128-31.

Linden Peach, "Man, Nature and Wordsworth: American Versions," *British Influence on the Birth of American Literature*, (Macmillan Press Ltd., 1982), 29-57; reprinted in *Poetry Criticism*, vol. 20, ed. Carol T. Gaffke (Detroit: The Gale Group), 37-40.

## Suggestions are Welcome

Readers who wish to suggest new features, topics, or authors to appear in future volumes, or who have other suggestions or comments are cordially invited to call, write, or fax the Managing Editor:

Managing Editor, Literary Criticism Series
The Gale Group
27500 Drake Road
Farmington Hills, MI 48331-3535
1-800-347-4253 (GALE)
Fax: 248-699-8054

# Acknowledgments

The editors wish to thank the copyright holders of the excerpted criticism included in this volume and the permissions managers of many book and magazine publishing companies for assisting us in securing reproduction rights. We are also grateful to the staffs of the Detroit Public Library, the Library of Congress, the University of Detroit Mercy Library, Wayne State University Purdy/Kresge Library Complex, and the University of Michigan Libraries for making their resources available to us. Following is a list of the copyright holders who have granted us permission to reproduce material in this volume of *PC*. Every effort has been made to trace copyright, but if omissions have been made, please let us know.

## COPYRIGHTED EXCERPTS IN *PC*, VOLUME 29, WERE REPRODUCED FROM THE FOLLOWING PERIODICALS:

## COPYRIGHTED EXCERPTS IN *PC*, VOLUME 29, WERE REPRODUCED FROM THE FOLLOWING BOOKS:

# Thomas Carew
## 1595?-1640

English poet and masque writer.

## INTRODUCTION

Carew is closely associated with the Cavalier Poets, an informal group of early seventeenth-century English lyricists. All of these writers—Carew, Robert Herrick, Sir John Suckling, and Richard Lovelace—valued urbane wit and precise diction in their poems, and most—Herrick is the exception—had intimate ties with the court of Charles I. Carew is best known for his courtly masque *Coelum Britannicum*, love poetry, a small group of songs, several elegies, and erotic verse, most notably "A Rapture." Overall, Carew is viewed as a significant transitional figure in English lyric poetry whose work epitomizes the light, elegant Cavalier style and features a witty rejuvenation of conventional forms in the period between the English high Renaissance and the subsequent Restoration era.

## BIOGRAPHICAL INFORMATION

Carew was born in 1594 or 1595, probably in West Wickham, Kent. His father, Matthew Carew, was a master in Chancery; his mother, Alice Ingpen Ryvers, was the daughter and granddaughter of lord mayors of London. Nothing is known of Carew's boyhood and early schooling until he entered Merton College, Oxford, in June 1608 at age thirteen. He took his bachelor of arts degree in January 1611. The following year he was admitted to the Middle Temple, presumably to be trained for a legal career. Around this time Carew's father suffered devastating financial reverses, prompting Carew to leave the Middle Temple and enter the service of Sir Dudley Carleton, English ambassador to Venice, in 1613. In Venice, Carew was exposed to Italian literature and began learning European languages. He traveled with Sir Dudley's embassy to The Hague in March 1616 but returned to London several months later, having been relieved of his duties. By late 1616, Carew had begun to make his way at the court of Charles I. In 1619 he traveled with Sir Edward Herbert (later Lord Herbert of Cherbury) to Paris, where he wrote several poems, acquired fashionable manners, and apparently came to know Italian poet Giambattista Marino, whose lyrics Carew may have used as models for some of his own. Around this time Carew likely met "Celia," the subject and addressee of many of his love poems. By the early 1630s Carew's place at court was firmly fixed. He was named Gentleman of the Privy Chamber Extraordinary and later made Sewer ("Cup-Bearer") in Ordinary to Charles I. His masque, *Co-*

*elum Britannicum*, was performed at court in 1633. Many anecdotes survive concerning Carew's "life scandalous" as a courtier. He evidently cared little for religion and certainly endured painful bouts of syphilis. Meanwhile, he continued to write poetry, acquiring a reputation as a gifted lyricist. In 1639 Carew accompanied Charles on his expedition against Scotland. He died early in 1640, possibly as a result of hardships he suffered during the northern winter. His only collection of poetry appeared posthumously in the year of his death.

## MAJOR WORKS OF POETRY

*Poems. By Thomas Carew, Esquire* is a collection of lyrics, songs, pastorals, poetic dialogues, elegies, addresses, and occasional poems. Most of the pieces are fairly short—the longest, "A Rapture," is 166 lines, and well over half are under 50 lines. The subjects are various: a number of poems treat love, lovemaking, and feminine beauty. Several of the poems, including "An Elegie upon the death of the Deane of Pauls, Dr. Iohn Donne" are memorial tributes; others, notably "To Saxham," celebrate country-house life; and a few record such events as the successful production of a play ("To my worthy Friend, M. D'Avenant, upon his Excellent Play, *The Iust Italian*") or the marriage of friends ("On the Marriage of T. K. and C. C. the Morning Stormie"). Many of the songs and love poems are addressed to the still-unidentified "Celia," a woman who was evidently Carew's lover for years. The poems to Celia treat the urgency of courtship, making much of the *carpe diem* theme. Others commend Celia through simile, conceit, and cliché. The physical pleasures of love are likewise celebrated: "A Rapture" graphically documents a sexual encounter through analogy, euphemism, and paradox, while "Loves Courtship" responds to the early passing of virginity. A number of Carew's poems are concerned with the nature of poetry itself. His elegy on John Donne has been praised as both a masterpiece of criticism and a remarkably perceptive analysis of the metaphysical qualities of Donne's literary work. English poet and playwright Ben Jonson is the subject of another piece of critical verse, "To Ben. Iohnson, Upon Occasion of His Ode of Defiance Annext to His Play of *The New Inne*." This poem, like the elegy on Donne, is concerned with both the style and substance of the author's literary works as well as with personal qualities of the author himself. Among Carew's occasional, public verse are his addresses to ladies of fashion, commendations of the nobility, and laments for the passing of friends or public figures, such as Gustavus Adolphus, King of Sweden.

## CRITICAL RECEPTION

Carew has long been recognized as a notable figure in English literary history. His earliest critics—chiefly other poets—evidently knew his work from the many manuscripts that circulated. Among many others, two of the most celebrated writers of the age, Sir John Suckling and William Davenant, paid tribute to Carew, playfully admiring his poetic craftsmanship. Carew's reputation, however, experienced a slow but steady decline during the second half of the seventeenth century. Despite some interest in Carew in subsequent years, not until the twentieth century did critics offer a reexamination of Carew's place in English literary history. F. R. Leavis wrote in 1936: "Carew, it seems to me, has claims to more distinction than he is commonly accorded; more than he is accorded by the bracket that, in common acceptance, links him with Lovelace and Suckling." More recently, Carew's place among the Cavalier Poets has been examined, as have his poetic affinities with Ben Jonson and John Donne; "A Rapture" has been scrutinized as both biography and fantasy; the funerary poetry has been studied as a subgenre; evidence of Carew's views concerning political hierarchy has been found in his occasional verse; and love and courtship have been probed as themes in the "Celia" poems. By the end of the twentieth century, Carew has been recognized as an important poet representative of his time and a master lyricist. According to Edmund Gosse, "Carew's poems, at their best, are brilliant lyrics of the purely sensuous order. They open to us, in his own phrase, 'a mine of rich and pregnant fancy.'"

## PRINCIPAL WORKS

### Poetry

"To my Honoured friend, Master Thomas May" 1622
"To my worthy Friend, M. D'Avenant" 1630
"In Celias face a question did a rise" 1632
"An Elegie upon the death of the Deane of Pauls, Dr. Iohn Donne" 1633
"To the Reader of Master Davenant's Play" 1636
"To my worthy friend Master Geo. Sands" 1637
"To my honoured friend, Henry Lord Cary of Lepington, upon his translation of Malvezzi" 1638
"To Will. Davenant my Friend" 1638
"Song. Conquest by Flight" 1639
*Poems. By Thomas Carew, Esquire* (poetry and masque) 1640
*The Poems of Thomas Carew with His Masque Coelum Britannicum* (poetry and masque) 1949

### Other Major Works

*Coelum Britannicum: A Masque at Whitehall in the Banqueting-House, on Shrove-Tuesday-Night, the 18. of February, 1633* (masque) 1634

## CRITICISM

### Bruce King (essay date 1964)

SOURCE: "The Strategy of Carew's Wit," in *A Review of English Literature*, Vol. 5, No. 3, July, 1964, pp. 42-51.

[*In the following essay, King probes Carew's use of "conventional poetic rhetoric for unconventional purposes" and explores "Carew's attempt to impose a civilized order upon the desperate chaos of man's inner realities" through his poetry.*]

Thomas Carew is often praised for his sophisticated gallantry, his urbane assurance, and for the way in which he seems to express the best values of a rich civilization.[1] However, if we try to put our finger on what is mature, firm, or civilized in Carew's poetry we find ourselves circling around his wit. This means that a study of Carew's wit is a study in what distinguishes him from other poets. Wit may serve a poet in several ways. There is, for example, the wit of a *double entendre* which allows the speaker to mention what is socially hidden. Donne's early poems offer obvious examples of this. There is also the wit of Dryden's satires which mocks its victims by comparing the lesser to the greater. And there is the wit of Hamlet's irony which, in its implications, reveals a personality caught between conflicting demands of conscience and society. Wit usually serves both a psychological and social purpose. It relieves psychic tensions while enabling the speaker to deal with matters that would otherwise be socially forbidden for discussion.[2] What is of literary interest is how the basic psychological functions of wit are shaped into rhetorical strategies that attempt to deal with social realities. Even the light irony of Dryden's satires has a strategic purpose; it suggests that his victims are beneath contempt and that they are not worth taking seriously. It is in the shaping of a literary strategy that a poet reveals his personality and the values he holds in relation, or opposition, to society.

What is the basic attitude behind Carew's wit? What causes us to feel that we are dealing with a personality of superior intelligence and of a high complexity of values? This is easier to answer if we examine the social function of his wit. Carew's poems deal with courtship and the suasion of seduction. For many writers this would mean smallness of theme and pettiness of interest. However, Carew treats courtship as a battlefield upon which most problems of human relations are presented in microcosm. His poems attempt more intimate communication between people than manners allow. Carew's wit is often aggressive since it must not only break through social rhetoric, but it must offer him protection in his manoeuvres. For this reason he twists conventional poetic rhetoric into a means of saying the unconventional. His urbanity is a pose which allows him to use social graces for self-protection, while it offers him a claim to disregard the limits which manners impose upon individuals.

The majority of Carew's poems in Grierson cleverly invert traditional poetic compliments to threaten, or to pretend to threaten, some woman.[3] **'To my inconstant Mistris'**, **'A deposition from Love'**, **'Ingratefull beauty threatned'** and **'To a Lady that desired I would love her'** are sophisticated poems of courtship, but they also threaten retaliation if the poet is injured by his mistress. I have, of course, singled out one theme from Carew's works, but it is a basic theme, and it is common to his best poems. Take, for example, **'Ingratefull beauty threatned'**, in which the wit functions to keep someone at disadvantage while protecting the speaker against injury. Behind the gallantry of the poem lies a struggle for dominance. Carew warns his mistress that she is merely an average woman whom he has picked from the crowd, and that the qualities attributed to her do not exist except in his verse. Having given her social prestige through his poetry, he can also 'uncreate' her if she causes him to doubt her fidelity. Notice that the concluding four lines of the poem, which are derived from Donne's 'Elegie XIX', use the imagery of mysticism for sexual advances. Donne inverts the conventions of such imagery to expose, to say what he knows about woman's sexual organs and desires:[4]

> . . . all women thus array'd;
> Themselves are mystick books, which only wee
> (Whom their imputed grace will dignifie)
> Must see reveal'd. Then since that I may know;
> As liberally, as to a Midwife, shew

> Thy self: cast all, yea, this white lynnen hence,
> [Here] is no pennance, much less innocence.

Carew, however, appropriates the rhetoric to gain a position of mastery:[5]

> Let fooles thy mystique formes adore,
>    I'le know thee in thy mortall state:
> Wise Poets that wrap't Truth in tales,
> Knew her themselves, through all her vailes.

The poetic strategy depends upon the power of a poet in a small courtly society where, like newspaper gossip, verses make and unmake reputations. Carew's claim is that his mistress is foolish to think that he will allow himself to be used for her social advancement, or that he will allow conventions of courtship to be used as a means to dominate over him. It does not matter whether this poem was written about a real woman since the problems with which it deals are basic. Like devices of modern warfare, Carew's poetry is perhaps more useful when threatening aggression than when employed. The literary value lies in the ease and sophistication with which the problem is handled.

Given this as the basic strategy of Carew's wit, many of his best poems are variations upon it. Some poems threaten; others, such as **'A deposition from Love'**, injure. The opening stanza of **'A deposition from Love'** at first sounds similar to any petrarchan complaint about a pitiless mistress; however, it only appears petrarchan since key words ('fortresse', 'within', 'paradise', 'gate') are *double entendres*:

> I was foretold, your rebell sex,
>    Nor love, nor pitty knew;
> And with what scorne, you use to vex
>    Poore hearts, that humbly sue;
> Yet I believ'd, to crowne our paine,
>    Could we the fortresse win,
> The happy lover sure should gaine
>    A Paradise within:
> I thought loves plagues, like Dragons sate,
>    Only to fright us at the gate.

The poem is not, as are some of Donne's early poems, merely a pyrotechnical display of hidden sexual meanings. We are told that the speaker 'did enter, and enjoy what happy lovers prove'. Now he is cast off by his mistress and his complaint is that having 'once possest' her his pain is greater than before. The strategy is very clever. Carew has taken the petrarchan convention of the lamenting lover and has used it as a form of revenge. The poem pretends to elicit sympathy for the rejected lover; however, the originality of the poem is the public disclosure that the poet has sexually enjoyed his mistress, and that she has now given herself to another man. The poem is neither a lover's lament, nor is it simply a poem of sexual frankness. In its description of sexual looseness, it is close to satire. Carew's genius is the way in which the satiric elements of the poem are carefully balanced and controlled by traditional Renaissance conventions, so that what is being said comes as a surprise and draws attention to itself.

The second stanza with its bold 'But I did enter, and enjoy' is meant to shock; that it is understated and put casually only makes the effect greater:

> But I did enter, and enjoy,
>     What happy lovers prove;
> For I could kisse, and sport, and toy,
>     And tast those sweets of love;
> Which had they but a lasting state,
>     Or if in *Celia's* brest,
> The force of love might not abate,
>     *Jove* were too meane a guest.
> But now her breach of faith, far more
> Afflicts, then did her scorne before.

Even the beautiful final conceit of **'A deposition from Love'** plays its part in reminding us of the disclosure:

> If the stout Foe will not resigne,
>     When I besiege a Towne,
> I lose, but what was never mine;
>     But he that is cast downe
> From enjoy'd beautie, feeles a woe,
> Onely deposed Kings can know.

It would be a mistake to see these poems as merely exercises in anti-petrarchanism. The inversion of Elizabethan amatory imagery was old-hat by the early seventeenth century, and it no longer had interest in itself except as a means within more complicated poetic strategies. Carew works within poetic conventions so that he may seem to speak with detachment and high self-control. The purpose is to avoid injury by keeping personal emotion at a distance. Carew uses poetic conventions to organize personal emotions for social warfare. Even the controlled stanzaic forms, the purity of diction, and the cold logic of the poems are means to deal with the social and personal realities of courtship while pretending that one does not care. A good part of what is best in Carew derives from this strategy of nonchalance. T. S. Eliot's famous phrase for it is 'a tough reasonableness beneath [a] slight lyric grace'. The genealogy of this strategy probably derives from Donne's early libertine poems with their exuberant delight in sexual frankness. However, the distance in sophistication and caution between, say, Donne's 'Indifferent' and Carew's poetry is great. Even Donne's later poems to Mary Herbert, such as 'The Blossom' and 'The Relic', only lightly play with the ironies of courtship and sexual aggression.[6] Donne's wit in this mode is mostly teasing. The serious use of embarrassing another as a poetic device is, in English poetry, primarily Carew's discovery. Nor is it a minor discovery; embarrassment and aggression may be a means to break through the rhetoric of social manners to establish contact with others. Fights sometimes make friends. What Carew attempts to achieve is a realistic relationship between man and woman.

**'To a Lady that desired I would love her'** bears out the usefulness of Carew's pose of worldliness in a sophisticated society. The poem is clearly an attempt to gain what chess players call equality. The situation is that the speaker has been offered the position of poet-courtier for a lady's affections. Carew realizes, however, that playful attitudes often camouflage a battle for dominance. The poem rejects the ploy of playful courtship, with its subservience to the lady's whims, and insists that the situation be seen in terms of mutual needs. The poet will write no laments and will not whine for love. He knows that his mistress is mortal and that she has 'dishevell'd hayre'. If she wants compliments and the glamour that poetry can bring, she must realize that the poet's terms are equality and sexual fulfilment. Thus the subject of the poem is one of mastery, of jockeying for position. Even in the stanzas where the lady is complimented there is a threat not only of aggression ('Each pettie beautie can disdaine') but also of the rejection of the whole game.

The dialectic of Carew's poetry does not turn inward and attempt to track the movements of the mind, as Donne's images do, but rather it attempts to justify the poet's attitudes. Carew pretends to be reasonable, he ironically appeals to the reader to see the justness of his point of view. The fourth stanza of the poem cleverly argues that the images a poet creates are related to how he feels. The petrarchan subservient lover will create a 'puddle' of 'griefe' which will not reflect the lady's beauty:

> Griefe is a puddle, and reflects not cleare
>     Your beauties rayes,
>   Joyes are pure streames, your eyes appeare
>     Sullen in sadder layes,
> In chearfull numbers they shine bright with prayse.

There is a threat of latent aggression in the next stanza with its grotesque perversion of petrarchan imagery. If satisfied with the lady's love, he will not mention 'Stormes in your brow, nets in your haire', 'betray' or 'torture'. The imagery not only parodies petrarchanism but becomes progressively more unflattering:

> Which shall not mention to express you fayre
>     Wounds, flames, and darts,
> Stormes in your brow, nets in your haire,
>     Suborning all your parts,
> Or to betray, or torture captive hearts.

**'To a Lady that desired I would love her'** is, however, a less aggressive poem than **'To my inconstant Mistris'**; here Carew claims to play the part of a petrarchan lover not to win his mistress's affections but to use her in gaining another woman. The strategy is particularly complicated since it presumably courts the woman by belittling her. It is a naked display of superiority in gaining social, and therefore personal, dominance in the battle between the sexes. As in many of Carew's poems the main strategy involves a manœuvre to appropriate conventional poetic rhetoric for unconventional purposes. In this poem Donne's favourite analogy between sacred and profane love is transformed into a social weapon. In Donne's love poems religious imagery is used to express a state of mind similar to that of devotion, while in Donne's religious poems, amatory imagery suggests the direct sensuousness of spiritual experience. Carew however is not interested in investigating the various implications of this analogy. Instead he uses the images to injure. His demonstration of constancy ('strong faith') will achieve greater conquests ('The full reward, and glorious fate') with other women: 'A fayrer hand then thine, shall cure That heart, which thy false oathes did wound.' His mistress is mistaken if she thinks that because he has cried over her she has him in her power. His demonstration of love is a superior means to advertise himself to women of finer sensibilities ('a soule more pure Than thine').

There are of course many non-aggressive poems on standard themes among Carew's works. Carew, like Donne, often played at creating strikingly original compliments. **'Ask me no more where *Jove bestowes'*** is perhaps the most beautiful song of its period. Few poets have ever created such purely lyrical lines where the logic of analogy is so completely compressed that the statements are untranslatable into prose paraphrase. The lyrical songs, however, are the minor side of Carew. Carew is too realistic, and perhaps too self-protective, to make many flights into irrational beauty. But the lyric poems do reveal an intense emotional warmth which Carew otherwise keeps under control, and which would seem to explain his need to establish clear, secure personal relationships.

Carew's poetry deals with the side of reality that is often hidden from public discussion: sexual appetites, the desire to dominate over others, the need for warmth and security, and the need to protect oneself against harm. While these are usually thought of as psychological drives, we are often aware of their existence; our social values recognize a delicate system of checks and balances in the give and take between people. Manners are the common means to legislate over this potential battlefield. However, manners are too slipshod to rule over all areas of society where clashes between personalities occur. Individuals or social groups often manage to appropriate manners for their own use, and then injustice occurs. What was meant to be flexible becomes rigid; what was meant to give rights leads to serfdom. The great themes of literature often derive from this border area between social values and psychological needs. In the modern novel there is a constant search for some superior organization of personality which will enable us to respond to this personal side of reality. Lawrence's novels record, when he is not being self-willed and didactic, a constant oscillation between the assertion of the ego, with its desire to be independent, and the search for warmth and security, which results from the weakening of the ego and its fusion with others. While Lawrence was unable to solve this problem, he had a heightened awareness that both the constant assertion of personality and the annihilation of individuality lead to psychic sickness.

Nor is the concern with the proper relationship of individuals to others a peculiarly modern literary theme. The supposed immorality of Restoration comedy derives from its naked acceptance of the view that man is appetitive matter in motion seeking satisfactions. It proposes as morally superior the man who clearly understands human na-

ture, and who manages to control it to his own advantage.[7] The heroes and heroines of Restoration comedy continually seek to discover what others are really like so that they may live on rational terms with them. This is the theme of *The Man of Mode* and the significance of the brilliant proviso scene in *The Way of the World*. The 'honesty' of Wycherley is that he refuses to play the game and insists upon a more rigorous moral code.

The attitude of Restoration comedy has its origins in the wit of Carew. Carew's achievement is to have created a social pose of urbane worldliness which opens communication between the sexes but which threatens retaliation if one is injured. It is a means of mastering reality so that one may live within society without being a dupe or a cad. Essentially this is a problem of love. Since courtship is a matter of personal relations, it provides us with a microcosm of the tensions between the individual and society. In love we desire union with another person, by which we may feel at once secure in our giving and taking of affections, and yet self-sufficient in the completeness of our personality in relation to the external world. There is, however, a masochistic perversion of this in which, through self-hate, the ego is totally extinguished. There is also an aggressive attitude in which the ego is never extinguished, but attempts to appropriate or possess others without returning affection.[8] Courtship creates both possibilities at once: the overly compliant person who sacrifices his identity to become part of the other's narcissistic universe. While Carew's poems may seem to injure others, they are actually attempts to correct the unequal relationship implicit within the petrarchan rhetoric of courtship. If Carew's poems do not speak, as some of Donne's do, of a fusion of personalities, they at least have the value of creating situations where the fullness of love is possible. It is a razor-sharp position from which slight deviations can result in a disagreeable toughness. However, there is in Carew's best poetry a rich awareness of the complexity of our relations with others.

I think that I can illustrate the many dimensions of Carew's awareness by using Sir John Suckling as a foil. I have no wish to devalue Suckling; in an age of excellent poets he is superior to most. However, Suckling has less insight into the complexities of life; he reduces a valuable part of existence to a few simple ideas. In 'Of thee (kind boy)' the themes are that man is merely appetite and that beauty is relative. Love is a pleasing folly ('Make me but mad enough') and a product of the fancy (''tis love in love that makes the sport'). Even Suckling's libertinism is grossly literal (''tis the appetite Makes eating a delight'), and lacks the intense philosophical scepticism that makes Rochester an important poet. Suckling's talent is in his technique. He is a master of the manipulation of syllabic rhythms, the use of tonal modulation within a poem, and the modification of rhyme patterns. However, he never comes to grips with the substance of reality. Carew's poems are less simple, and describe life's essential battles. In a sense each of Carew's poems has a double existence: there is the poetry of the brilliantly finished surface of the poem itself; and there is the poetry of Carew's attempt to impose a civilized order upon the desperate chaos of man's inner realities.

### Notes

1. F. R. Leavis, *Revaluation* (1936), p. 16.

2. See S. Freud, *Jokes and their Relation to the Unconscious,* transl. J. Strachey (1960), pp. 140-58. Since I am concerned with the social purpose of Carew's poetry, my essay ignores the sadistic element that Freud finds in aggressive wit.

3. Four of the seven love lyrics which represent Carew in Grierson's *Metaphysical Lyrics and Poems* are aggressive or threatening. In the *Oxford Book of Seventeenth Century Verse,* seven out of nine love poems are aggressive. I include among these 'Good Counsell to a Young Maid', which is a warning against mistaking man's sexual desires for love. The proportion is somewhat less in Carew's total works; but I am concerned with the attitude behind Carew's best poems.

4. Donne's 'Elegie XIX', lines 40-6. Also see Clay Hunt, *Donne's Poetry,* New Haven (1954), pp. 18-21.

5. All quotations of Carew are from *The Poems of Thomas Carew,* ed. R. Dunlap, Oxford (1949).

6. See Hunt, pp. 44-50.

7. Recent studies that take this point of view include N. N. Holland, *The First Modern Comedies,* Cambridge, Mass. (1959); and D. Underwood, *Etherege and the Seventeenth-Century Comedy of Manners,* New Haven (1957).

8. A useful discussion of this is N. O. Brown, *Life Against Death,* New York (1959), pp. 40-54.

### G. A. E. Parfitt (essay date 1968)

SOURCE: "The Poetry of Thomas Carew," in *Renaissance and Modern Studies,* Vol. XII, 1968, pp. 56-67.

[*In the following essay, Parfitt contends that Carew should not simply be categorized as a Cavalier poet and instead emphasizes Carew's association with Jonson and Donne and his revitalization of poetic conventions.*]

### I

No-one seems really sure what to do with Carew, partly perhaps because no fully adequate account of English poetry in the first half of the seventeenth century has been written. In *Revaluation,* Dr. Leavis suggested an approach which makes Carew an important link between Johnson and Marvell, thus giving his work a greater prominence than it usually has, but Leavis's remarks have not been followed up and so the traditional view of Carew, linking him vaguely with 'the Cavalier poets', is still dominant.

One reason why this traditional view matters is that, insofar as it follows Jonson, Cavalier poetry shows a narrowing of range of reference and interest, becoming courtly in a sense which suggests a decisive split between 'court' and 'country' and a consequent concentration upon relatively few areas of emotional experience and, more specifically, upon narrowly circumscribed facets of society. One result is cynical knowingness and surface sophistication; another is that reactions to experience become conventional and simplified. Leavis, in linking Carew with Jonson and Marvell, is implying that Carew, like these greater poets, has a width of reference and variety of response which distinguishes him from Suckling, Lovelace, or even Herrick. This essay is an attempt to demonstrate that implication, to show that Carew can react to a wide range of experiential stimuli; and has something of that varied awareness of what is involved in being human which is one of the marks of major poetry.

Although Carew is primarily thought of as a love poet, his work is perhaps best approached by some consideration of his writing in other *genres.* **'Obsequies to the Lady Anne Hay'** is an elegy on a distant cousin of the poet's and these are its opening lines:

> I heard the Virgins sign, I saw the sleeke
> And polisht Courtier, channell his fresh cheeke
> With reall teares; the new-betrothed Maid
> Smild not that day; the graver Senate layd
> Their business by; of all the Courtly throng,
> Griefe seald the heart, and silence bound the tongue.

The poet, obviously, is praising the dead woman by asserting that her death had a national impact; a theme which could easily seem empty hyperbole. But we will dismiss these lines as such only if we allow stock resistance to public elegy to block our awareness of their real poetic activity. For Carew is seldom obviously original; he works instead by revitalising a conventional *genre* or attitude. Here, for example, 'I heard' and 'I saw' in the first line give, through the repetition, an effect of factual statement as well as a sense of verisimilitude. Then there is the precision of the adjectives describing the courtier: 'sleeke' and 'polisht' suggest superficiality and an artifice hostile to true emotion, while 'fresh' checks this implication, without destroying it, and yet adds the complementary idea of inexperience of deep feeling. So when Carew says that this courtier's tears were 'reall' the impact comes from the surprise: 'sleeke' and 'polisht' courtiers should weep tears of feigned feeling. Anne Hay's worth was such as to break the smooth surface and touch the man beneath the rôle. Finally, we should note how the solemn subordinate sense-units build up to the balanced and assured abstractions of 'Grieft seald the heart, and silence bound the tongue', where the strongly active verbs give the personifications force and point.

In this passage, working within a conventional *genre,* Carew's verse is fully alive: he is using language precisely to re-enliven the human situation which lies behind all conventions but which repetition so easily deadens. The concluding lines of **'To my worthy friend Master Geo. Sands'**—written within the convention of the verse-compliment—show Carew again re-animating the tradition. The poet has been comparing his love poetry with Sands' religious verse:

> Perhaps my restlesse soule, try'de with persuit
> Of mortall beauty, seeking without fruit
> Contentment there, which hath not, when enjoy'd
> Quencht all her thirst, nor satisfi'd, though cloy'd;
> Weary of her vaine search below, Above
> In the first Faire may find th' immortal Love.
> Prompted by thy example then, no more
> In moulds of clay will I my God adore;
> But teare those Idols from my heart, and write
> What his blest sprit, not fond love shall indite;
> Then, I no more shall court the verdant Bay,
> But the dry leavelesse Trunke on Golgotha;
> And rather strive to gaine from thence one Thorne,
> Then all the flourishing wreaths by Laureats worne.

Carew is here aware of the conflict between divine and secular love, a conflict generally recognized and always implicit in love poetry of the Christian era but seldom used to real effect. Usually—one thinks of Donne and Vaughan—poets who explicitly bring the two together reject sexual love outright, but, although Carew aims at such rejection, its glibness is avoided, for his 'Perhaps' suggests uncertainty and self-awareness, while the statement that 'mortall beauty . . . hath not, when enjoy'd / Quencht all her thirst, nor satisfi'd though cloy'd' contains an awareness of both the value and limitations of human love. Similarly, while the imagery of the last four lines sets the 'dry leavelesse Trunke on Golgotha' and the 'Thorne' against 'the verdant Bay' and 'the flourishing wreaths' mainly to stress the paradox that Christ's humiliation and death is more fruitful for the Christian than the glory of earthly achievement, the images do at the same time give weight to the richness of secular experience.

Carew, then, can demonstrate in his verse both an exact sense of language and an alert, sensitive mind. These qualities, with the independence which springs from them, enable him to use conventional *genres* without being inertly conventional himself. The independence of Carew's mind can be very clearly seen in the poem **'To Ben Jonson Vpon occasion of his Ode of defiance annext to his play of the new Inne'**. As is well known 'The New Inn' was hissed from the stage when, in 1629, it was first produced, and when Jonson published it in 1631 it was accompanied by a powerful 60-line attack on popular taste, a poem magnificently vituperative but narrow in tone and outlook. Carew's poem is part of the considerable literary and sub-literary activity caused by Jonson's attack, and its beginning is perhaps what we should expect from a friend of Jonson:

> Tis true (deare Ben) Thy just chastizing hand
> Hath fixt upon the settled age a brand
> To their sworne pride, and empty scribbling due,
> It can nor judge, nor write . . .

But Carew was no sycophant, and he goes on

> and yet 'tis true
> Thy commique Muse from the exalted line
> Toucht by thy Alchymist, doth since decline . . .

The rest of the poem is a judicious mixture of praise and advice, making clear that Carew both knew where Jonson's greatness lay and what dangers were inherent in the sarcastic rage of the attack on the playgoers. Like the better-known elegy on Donne, **'To Ben Jonson'** is primarily an achievement of critical intelligence, but it is also one of honesty. Both features suggest an intelligence which, when we turn to the love poems, should make us hesitate before we dismiss them as elegantly conventional.

But before we look at the love poems we should briefly take account of Carew's country-house poems, **'To Saxham'** and **'To my Friend G. N. from Wrest'**. The *genre* owes its establishment in England mainly to Jonson and Carew's two poems show clearly the influence of 'To Penshurst'. At Saxham the disadvantages of winter are overcome, because, addressing the house,

> thou within thy gate,
> Art of thy selfe so delicate;
> So full of native sweets, that blesse
> Thy roof with inward happinesse;
> As neither from, nor to thy store
> Winter takes ought, or Spring addes more.

Like 'To Penshurst' Carew's poem is about generosity, openness and hospitality, being relevant to, and gaining weight from, the environment of contemporary legislation and concern about the gentry's social function. At Saxham nature delights in supplying food, guests are welcomed ungrudgingly and the welcome does not depend on wealth or rank. The qualities celebrated and enacted relate to society in a way which makes **'To Saxham'** relevant and responsible to an extent beyond anything in Suckling or Lovelace. Nevertheless, one can see a narrowing of range in Carew's poem, in the way that hyperbole is dangerously near to over-balancing into absurdity:

> The scalie herd, more pleasure tooke,
> Bath'd in thy dish, then in the brooke,

and, the final couplet,

> And as for Thieves, thy bounties such,
> They cannot steale, thou giv'st so much.

Carew's limitations can be measured by comparing this ending with the conclusion of 'To Penshurst': Jonson's rich sense of the family as an humane unit working for the wider good and his more general feeling for its civilizing influence are both lacking. But Carew remains aware of this kind of influence and his control of moral overtone is found in the detail of his lines (in 'delicate' and 'inward' in the lines already quoted) and in the effective use of paradox here:

Thou hast no Porter at the doore
T'examine, or keep back the poore;
Nor locks, nor bolts; Thy gates have bin
Made only to let Strangers in.

Neither **'To Saxham'** nor **'To my friend G. N. . . .'** is a great poem, although there is greatness in the opening part of the latter, but both indicate Carew's concern with a full and satisfying life, reaching towards Jonson rather than reminding us of Suckling's posturing or Herrick's elegance.

II

The seriousness and range of matter which characterize the poems discussed so far both link Carew with Jonson, in a way which suggests that, as Leavis hints, it is more fruitful to approach Carew by way of Jonson than to lump him with the Cavaliers, a term as vague and deceptive as most of its kind. The discussion of Carew's work outside love-poetry should also help to make us alert to the revitalization of conventions which is almost always going on in the love poems.

It is, for example, going on in the couplet lyric called **'The Spring'**, which has received little attention from critics. Its theme—that the poet's mistress is at odds with Nature in being unresponsive to the poet-lover—is common enough, used by, for example, Weelkes in his madrigal 'Now every tree renews his Summer green', by Drummond in the sonnet 'With flaming hornes the Bull . . .', and by Petrarch in 'Zefiro torno . . .'. Carew, however, makes more effective use of the theme than any of these men, comes closest, that is, to realizing its potential.

At first we may be bothered by our post-romantic difficulty in really accepting that here, as in most pre-romantic verse, natural description is not primarily used objectively, that the poem is not concerned with nature itself so much as with natural description as a way of making a point against a human being. If we take a quietly humorous detail of description such as 'wakes in hollow tree the drowzie Cuckow' as the norm we may be puzzled by the artificiality of the opening lines or of such a couplet as:

Now doe a quire of chirping Minstrels bring
In tryumph to the world, the youthful Spring.

But if we suppress preconceptions we become gradually aware that formalizing Nature serves a purpose, to isolate the mistress against the whole force of Nature. More precisely, Nature is formalized in the sense that it is described in human terms, because the poem's success necessitates a relationship being established between Nature and Mistress such as to make poetically valid conclusions drawn from the analogy between them. 'Robes' (l. 2), 'tender' (l. 6), 'drowzie' (l. 8) all have human connotations, while the language used to describe winter ('Candies', 'ycie', 'silver', 'Chrystall') establishes a kind of beauty which—and these connotations become relevant later—includes a sense of inhumanity and, perhaps, superficiality. This frozen Nature is aspiring to the condition of Art of an almost

Byzantine kind: its immediate appropriateness is in the contrast made with the description of Spring which follows, where we find this sequence of key words: 'warms . . . thawes . . . benummed . . . tender . . . sacred birth . . . dead . . . wakes . . . drowzie' (ll. 5-8). Something fluid and alive is replacing Winter's icy beauty.

The description of life replacing death in Spring reaches its climax at lines 11 and 12; immediately an exception is stated:

Now all things smile; only my Love doth lowre:
Nor hath the scalding Noon-day Sunne the power,
To melt that marble yce, which still doth hold
Her heart congeald, and makes her pittie cold.

'Now' sums up the progress of all things to life in Spring and 'smile' has strong human connotations: for both reasons the reversal of the movement in 'only my Love doth lowre' is—even if expected—a shock. By implication the woman's behaviour is inhuman, unnatural, as we realize that she is being associated with the winter of the opening lines, an association stressed by the overlap of vocabulary. But Carew has suggested that winter is dead and unnatural, and that its natural movement is towards spring; now, speaking of the woman, he takes the full effect of associating her with winter, for the verb 'hold' implies that woman's heart is not naturally hard, while 'pittie' is said to be part of her make-up, even if it is 'cold'. The suggestion is that the natural and the human is being denied expression by this woman.

Instead of ending here, having demonstrated the isolation of his mistress from natural rhythms, Carew turns to further illustration. Structurally, this enacts the woman's unnatural isolation, stressing her exception to the norm by surrounding her with it. Further, the pastoral episode of Amyntas and Chloris acts as an explicit statement that the woman is by human standards unnatural. Carew concludes with a summary:

all things keepe
Time with the season, only shee doth carry
June in her eyes, in her heart January.

The statement mimes in syntax the gap between appearance and reality.

Competent, exact use of language, clarity and neatness of structure, accuracy of detail are the basic virtues of successful poetry, and **'The Spring'** has these. But I have analysed it closely to show that Carew's lyrics repay close reading: the detail of his writing activates his work, giving a conventional theme here new energy and life. The relationship claimed between woman and the seasons is artificial, but it functions significantly in allowing Carew to emphasize the woman's unnaturalness by indicating it as the sole exception to a natural rhythm. The patterning of language contrasting the frozen with the fluid, the dead with the alive, works to revitalize the worn idea of the cold-hearted mistress, and in so doing re-emphasizes a

connection between life and 'literary love' such as the poets of the Elizabethan sonnet tradition had tended to blur.
We may also note that insofar as court-centred poetry of
the early seventeenth century draws on a more limited
range of experience than does that of Donne and Jonson,
Carew is at least partially an exception; for if his attitude
to Nature is basically formal and 'courtly' (such terms as
'silver' and 'Chrystall' imply the art-language of a social
élite) he is, nevertheless, using rather than simply applying
this attitude and is still able to introduce the ox and a
number of closely-observed details ('benummed',
'drowzie').

It is this ability to work within and to re-animate convention that gives originality to much of Carew's love-poetry.
Sometimes, in a sense, this originality is itself conventional, as in poems like **'To my inconstant Mistris'** and
**'Ingratefull Beauty Threatned'** where the poet-lover becomes aggressively demanding rather than humbly submissive. Here the attitude reminds us of Donne, but antedates him, and the emphasis it receives in Carew reminds
us of his concern to anchor love in the range of normal
human behaviour. The process—often one of restating a
convention's relation to life—can be seen clearly in **'A Divine Mistris'**, which starts with the routine claim that the
mistress is perfect in beauty and of divine origin:

> my faire love
> Who fram'd by hands farre more divine;
> For she hath every beauteous line . . .

This is followed at once by the qualification:

> Yet I had been farre happier
> Had Nature that made me, made her;

and the poem concludes bluntly:

> Shee hath too much divinity for mee,
> You Gods teach her some more humanitie.

In what is scarcely a complex poem Carew simultaneously
feels and renders the traditional urge to write hyperboli-
cally about his mistress while yet introducing a more complex poet-persona than usual. The stress on the earth-
bound limitations of the poet's nature is in part the
conventional pose of the poet's inferiority, and as such a
compliment to the mistress, but Carew also reminds us
that the attitude his persona adopts has validity, hyperbole
is being held in check by a kind of realism. So 'humanitie'
does more than make the obvious contrast with 'divinity';
it also reminds us that idealisation of the mistress can de-
humanise a situation. Although this poem lacks the precise
'placing' through vocabulary which **'The Spring'** has, the
presentation of the lady as perfect beauty carries an element of criticism in 'humanitie' and the direct common-
sense of the poet's attitude. Carew is not, as Donne often
is, rejecting the conventional machinery, but, more like
Jonson, is restating its relationship with life.

In some cases, as in **'A Divine Mistris'**, the process is one
of emphasizing the human basis implied by conventional

attitudes to love; but often it is more a question of anima-
tion, less by adapting or augmenting a convention than by
precision of diction. **'Vpon a Ribband'** is a trivial poem,
opening with these lines:

> This silken wreath, which Circles in mine arme,
> Is but an Emblem of that mystique charme,
> Wherewith the magique of your beauties binds
> My captive soule, and round about it winds
> Fetters of lasting love; This hath entwin'd
> My Flesh alone, That hath empalde my mind:
> Time may weare out These soft weak bands; but These
> Strong chaines of brasse, Fate shall not discompose

This development of a single syntactical unit is controlled
and clear, its articulation shaped by the marked antitheses.
Variety and liveliness of sense-units re-animate the conventional 'Fetters of lasting love', while the antitheses
bring out strongly the contrasts in the argument. Words in
their placing, like 'entwin'd', 'empalde', and 'discompose',
enforce attention on what exactly is being said. Constantly
this re-establishment of some traditional idea as living currency happens, as in these magnificent lines from **'A beautifull Mistris'**,

> If thou but show thy face againe,
> When darknesse doth at midnight raigne,
> The darkness Flyes, and light is hurl'd
> Round about the silent world.

But one important aspect of Carew's love poetry has not
yet been mentioned, the erotic element. This links Carew
with Cavaliers like Suckling, Lovelace and Randolph
rather than with Jonson or with Donne's main emphases.
It is a striking, if seldom noticed, fact that while overt
eroticism is largely absent from personal love poetry in
the sixteenth century, it emerges strongly in the early decades of the seventeenth. The possible reasons for this
cannot be discussed here, but the main one may be that as
Puritanism gained strength it drove a wedge between the
religious and less religious, isolating the latter by its extremism and pushing them to react with another type of
extremism. Certainly in the erotic poetry of Cleveland,
Cartwright, Lovelace and Suckling there is a hectic, over-
wrought quality, suggestive of immaturity and moral uncertainty. Both the exclusion of, and undue emphasis on,
the physical in love-poetry is immature in the sense of being insufficient to give a full sense of love; and if the
Cavaliers reduce love to a set of physical contacts a lot of
Elizabethan poetry suffers from thin-blooded pseudo-
spirituality. Between 1500 and 1650 few non-dramatic poets face up to the problem of sexuality in a Christian society. Donne sometimes, usually obliquely, manages to do
so and Marvell in 'To His Coy Mistress' bombards the dilemma with an intense awareness of Time's inexorability.
But in some senses Carew comes closer than either to
bringing into contact an awareness of the delights of sex
and a sense that this can scarcely be expressed within the
traditional framework of Christian thought.

If this is so the linking of Carew with the Cavaliers because his verse has an overt erotic element must be super-

ficial, hiding more than it reveals. When Professor Kermode describes Carew's most successful erotic poem, **'A Rapture'**, as one of 'the libertine versions of sensual innocence' (together with pieces by Randolph and Lovelace) he reveals an inadequate awareness of the poem and, for him, an unusual deadness in relation to tone. Carew's use of direct eroticism is confined to relatively few poems but these are not isolated from the main body of his work, because the human 'realism' which anchors so many of his lyrics, preventing both inert conventionality and any over-spiritual stress, involves an implicit awareness of the importance of sex and an unwillingness to pretend that love is either just a game or just a matter of the union of souls. This does not necessarily mean that when Carew writes directly of sex he will manifest the reconciliation of physical and spiritual demands which we can call mature: **'The Second Rapture'**, with its nymphet theme and deadness of sympathy, is as unpleasant as anything in Suckling or Lovelace. Nor, when Carew writes erotically, is he necessarily taking direct account of the religio-erotic tension which is constantly implicit in love-poetry of the Christian era. **'An Eddy'**, for example, is a success principally because of the richly erotic suggestion projected on to the image of the river, a success of strategy and of beauty rather than of moral awareness. But in **'To A. L. Perswasions to Love'** there is an attempt to take account of this tension by stressing that the poet's 'perswasion' of the lady involves fidelity and a kind of love which can survive the decay of beauty:

> . . . wisely chuse one to your Friend,
> Whose love may, when your beauties end,
> Remaine still firme . . . (ll. 49-51)
> Cull out amongst the multitude
> Of lovers, that seeke to intrude
> Into your favour, one that may
> Love for an age, not for a day . . . (ll. 55-58)

In this poem Carew stresses the importance of sex and is also aware that other values bear upon sexual relationships. The poem's value is that it takes account of more factors of human existence than persuasion poems commonly do, although it stops short of direct confrontation between opposing ideals. This is the area in which **'A Rapture'** is important. The poem is long and complex, too much so to discuss here, but it comes nearer perhaps than any other poem written between 1500 and 1650 to evoking a full sense of the erotic while accepting and giving expression to the conflict between this and accepted Christian moral standards. The normal Elizabethan tactic, when expressing overt eroticism, is to condemn what is being expressed or to use some kind of pre-Christian setting; the usual Cavalier device is to ignore the Christian code, to pretend that poet and mistress are somehow exempt from it, or to emit a smoke-screen of pseudo-argument. Carew, however, not only acknowledges a conflict between Christianity and the erotic but suggests that such a clash is inevitable, while his embodiment of the erotic has such force and beauty that it makes the erotic-moral opposition a real

factor in the poem, makes the poem a disturbing phenomenon, puzzling and extending our experience as poetry should do.

## III

I have claimed for Carew a sensitivity to language and have argued that this presupposes and reveals an alert and enquiring mind. Neither quality makes Carew a major poet, for both are surely pre-requisites of any real success as a poet at all. Nor does either quality necessarily distinguish Carew and the Cavaliers, for both qualities appear in the best of Suckling and Lovelace, and more consistently in Herrick. The distinction is more a matter of scope, sympathy and complexity.

Because Donne's influence on seventeenth-century poetry has been more fully discussed than Jonson's and because the latter's influence is usually dealt with in relation to his own love lyrics, the fundamental nature of Carew's affinity with Jonson has been obscured. Yet Carew's fondness for the couplet, his range of material, and his ability to work effectively within conventional frameworks all remind us of Jonson. Although Carew can and does make use at times of fairly complex stanza forms (as indeed Jonson also does) his normal manner is simple in a way which resembles Jonson's formal simplicity and reminds us of the latter's stress on matter above manner. The similarity is most clearly seen, perhaps, in the country-house poems, but throughout his work Carew returns constantly to a human base: his criticism of his mistress is of failures of humanity; his concern with sex arises from an awareness of the body-soul paradox which, in **'A Rapture'** especially, he will not sublimate or suppress; his concern over Jonson's attack on the public is about the dangers it has for Jonson's own personality; and his involvement over Anne Hay is, in part, a desire to demonstrate human virtue breaking through the armour of artifice. Carew lacks Jonson's firm moral base and seldom follows him in developing a moral attitude satirically, but he has the same basic humanity, which allows moral distinctions to be drawn and gives his writing a sense of involvement with the real world. Broadly speaking, the cynicism of Suckling, the coarseness of Cleveland's sensibility, Herrick's restricted prettiness, and Lovelace's odd dissociation (he shows at times a sense of ideals, stated but seldom embodied in his verse) are all lacking in Carew. The negatives become positives because Carew's linguistic awareness reveals when examined that for Carew the conventions and pretensions of art must constantly be related to human life, and that life for Carew is something fuller—more complex, less abstract and simplified—than it is for, say, Suckling. Insofar as Carew draws upon Jonson and Donne he does simplify, as lesser poets following greater commonly do, reducing Jonson's range of concern and his moral firmness, smoothing Donne's intense verbal attacks on experience, his ability to make words think. But this is only a degree of simplification, involving Carew neither in the sacrifice of his individuality nor in that abandonment of an adequate range of experience which thins so much Cavalier verse. By pretending that Carew is in any serious sense Cavalier we reduce the homogeneity of the term, stress peripheral rather than central aspects of Carew's work, and ultimately distort the picture of early seventeenth-century poetry.


**Louis L. Martz (essay date 1969)**

SOURCE: "Thomas Carew: The Cavalier World," in *The Wit of Love*, University of Notre Dame Press, 1969, pp. 60-110.

[*In the following essay, Martz surveys Carew's poetry, noting its "Cavalier elegance, its Mannerist styling." Martz continues by observing Carew's wit, influences, critical capacity, and relationship to his age.*]

In the cold spring of 1639, Thomas Carew, the favorite poet of the Court of Charles I, joined his King's army in an ill-conceived and ill-prepared expedition against the Scots. It was the same expedition for which Carew's friend and fellow poet, Sir John Suckling, had beggared himself in order to provide a beautifully clothed and plumed troop of cavalrymen—but whether they could fight was another matter. The King's hope was to quell the rebellious Scots, who had refused to abide by the rules of the Church of England; but he found the Scottish army much too strong for his own forces, stronger in motivation, bound together by religious zeal, and therefore stronger in military capacity. Charles did not dare to invade Scotland, and indeed hardly a shot was fired. Instead Charles made a humiliating, temporary peace, and planned to bide his time until, as he hoped, his power would grow stronger. Instead he grew steadily weaker. The Scottish expedition was the beginning of the end of Charles I's regime, an open revelation of the weaknesses that beset his state both in England and in Scotland; thus began a swift decay of royal power that reached its end when, in 1649, the Parliamentary army beheaded the King and abolished his monarchy.

Thomas Carew did not live to see the death of this "brave Prince of Cavaliers," as Robert Herrick called him, for Carew died in March, 1640—a symbolic date, for that was the very spring when Charles was forced to reconvene Parliament after his eleven years of personal rule. Thus began in November, 1640, the Long Parliament which utterly destroyed the King's power.

In the year 1640, shortly before Thomas Carew's death, it seems, he composed a poem in which memories of the Scottish campaign form a dark opening that fades away before an overwhelming appreciation of a way of life that represents the best of the Cavalier ideal: **"To my friend G. N. from Wrest"**—a country estate in Bedfordshire.

> I Breathe (sweet *Ghib:*) the temperate ayre of *Wrest*
> Where I no more with raging stormes opprest,
> Weare the cold nights out by the bankes of Tweed,
> On the bleake Mountains, where fierce tempests breed,

And everlasting Winter dwells; where milde
*Favonius,* and the Vernall windes exilde,
Did never spread their wings: but the wilde North
Brings sterill Fearne, Thistles, and Brambles forth.
Here steep'd in balmie dew, the pregnant Earth
Sends from her teeming wombe a flowrie birth,
And cherisht with the warme Suns quickning heate,
Her porous bosome doth rich odours sweate;[1]

We should note how, unlike Donne, Carew has a warm appreciation of the natural vigor of the earth. He goes on to admire the simple mansion, not erected "with curious skill" or with "carved Marble, Touch, or Porpherie." This is a house built for hospitality, without Doric or Corinthian pillars; it is designed for service, not for show. In the center of the poem he draws an active picture of the Lord and Lady at the head of "their merry Hall" filled with people of all ranks, servants, tenants, women, steward, chaplain, all eating at various tables in appropriate but flexible hierarchy. Meanwhile "others of better note"

>                    freely sit
> At the Lords Table, whose spread sides admit
> A large accesse of friends to fill those seates
> Of his capacious circle, fill'd with meates
> Of choycest rellish, till his Oaken back
> Under the load of pil'd-up dishes crack.

Although he praises the house for not being showy with statuary and extravagant artifice, the whole estate nevertheless reveals itself to be a work of art on the outside where nature and art have combined to direct the waters flowing from the local spring. Art, says Carew,

>                    entertaines the flowing streames in deepe
> And spacious channels, where they slowly creepe
> In snakie windings, as the shelving ground
> Leades them in circles, till they twice surround
> This Island Mansion, which i' th' center plac'd,
> Is with a double Crystall heaven embrac'd . . .

The whole view of the estate, then, is one in which simple dignity and generous hospitality combine with art to create an atmosphere of natural fertility and bounty. This theme reaches a climax in the finale as Carew sees the landscape and the fountain of waters mingled with pastoral and mythological figures out of Ovid's *Metamorphoses* and Vergil's *Georgics:*

> With various Trees we fringe the waters brinke,
> Whose thirstie rootes the soaking moysture drinke,
> And whose extended boughes in equall rankes
> Yeeld fruit, and shade, and beautie to the bankes.
> On this side young *Vertumnus* sits, and courts
> His ruddie-cheek'd *Pomona, Zephyre* sports
> On th'other, with lov'd *Flora,* yeelding there
> Sweetes for the smell, sweetes for the palate here.
> But did you taste the high & mighty drinke
> Which from that Fountaine flowes, you'ld cleerly think
> The God of Wine did his plumpe clusters bring,
> And crush the Falerne grape into our spring;
>                    · · · · ·

Thus I enjoy my selfe, and taste the fruit
Of this blest Peace, whilst toyl'd in the pursuit
Of Bucks, and Stags, th'embleme of warre, you strive
To keepe the memory of our Armes alive.

Thus the poem is framed by memories of the war, as
though the threat of destruction had led Carew to appreciate the values of this ancient, traditional way of noble
country life—a way of life celebrated long before by
Carew's poetical master and father, Ben Jonson, in his
similar poem "Penshurst," and by Jonson's own masters,
Vergil, Horace, and Martial.

And indeed had such a way of life really been honored
and followed by King Charles and his Court, the monarchy would never have come to its disaster. But by the year
1640 Charles and his Court had lost touch with the common people, unlike the Lord and Lady in their crowded
hall at Wrest. Charles and his Court lived more and more
a life apart, charmed by art and music, led by a King of
impeccable artistic taste, whose collection of works of art,
gathered in his palaces, represented one of the greatest art
collections in all of Europe. Inigo Jones, that architect of
rare ability, was in charge of all the King's buildings;
Jones's new banqueting house at Whitehall, built in the
latter years of King James's reign, had its ceiling painted
by Rubens during Charles's reign; and Van Dyck came
from Antwerp to live as the resident painter of King
Charles and his Court. But by the year 1640 this era of
courtly elegance and art was near its end.

That end may be seen as symbolized in two more events
of this climacteric year: by the publication, in May or
June, 1640, a few months after Thomas Carew's death, of
his volume of collected poems, containing a world of
Cavalier ideals; and secondly, by the presentation, in January, 1640, of the last of the great Court masques, *Salmacida Spolia,* composed jointly by Inigo Jones and by
Carew's good friend and fellow poet, Sir William Davenant. The masque was based upon a curious allegorical
interpretation of the myth of Salmacis, which is here interpreted as representing "Salmacian spoils," that is to say,
rewards gained by peace and not by destructive war. It is
the climax and epitome of the great series of Court masques that had flourished during the reign of James I on a
relatively simpler scale, and then gradually rose to a scale
of greater and greater extravagance after the reign of
Charles I began in 1625. The masques of the Caroline era
were glorious, expensive spectacles that called upon all
the Court's immense artistic resources, for scene design-
ing, for costume, for music, for dancing, and for poetry.
All these resources were brought together for the last time
in *Salmacida Spolia,* to give a moral allegory of the times,
as the published version of the entertainment describes it:[2]

*The Subject of the Masque*

Discord, a malicious Fury, appears in a storm and by
the invocation of malignant spirits, proper to her evil
use, having already put most of the world into disorder
[a reference to the Thirty Years' War then raging on the

Continent], endeavours to disturb these parts, envying
the blessings and tranquillity we have long enjoyed.

These incantations are expressed by those spirits in an
Antimasque; who on a sudden are surprised and
stopped in their motion by a secret power, whose wisdom they tremble at; and depart as foreknowing that
wisdom will change all their malicious hope of these
disorders into a sudden calm, which after their departure is prepared by a dispersed harmony of music.

This secret wisdom, in the person of the King attended
by his Nobles and under the name of Philogenes or
Lover of his People, hath his appearance prepared by a
Chorus, representing the beloved people, and is in-
stantly discovered environed with those Nobles in the
Throne of Honour.

Then the Queen personating the chief heroine, with her
martial ladies, is sent down from Heaven by Pallas as a
reward of his prudence for reducing the threatening
storm into the following calm.

Thus, after a series of fantastic scenes representing various
aspects of discord and disorder, the King makes his appearance in great magnificence:

Then the further part of the scene disappeared, and the
King's Majesty and the rest of the masquers were discovered sitting in the Throne of Honour, his Majesty
highest in a seat of gold and the rest of the Lords about
him. This throne was adorned with palm trees, between
which stood statues of the ancient heroes. In the under
parts on each side lay captives bound, in several postures, lying on trophies of armours, shields, and antique
weapons, all his throne being feigned of goldsmith's
work. The habit of his Majesty and the masquers was
of watchet, richly embroidered with silver; long stockings set up of white; their caps silver with scrolls of
gold and plumes of white feathers.

Then, after a song in praise of the King's virtues, particularly his patience and mercy in view of "those storms the
people's giddy fury raise," the Queen descends in an even
more magnificent scene.

Whilst the Chorus sung this song, there came softly
from the upper part of the heavens a huge cloud of
various colours, but pleasant to the sight; which, descending to the midst of the scene, opened, and within
it was a transparent brightness of thin exhalations, such
as the Gods are feigned to descend in; in the most eminent place of which her Majesty sat, representing the
chief heroine, environed with her martial ladies; and
from over her head were darted lightsome rays that illuminated her seat; and all the ladies about her participated more or less of that light, as they sat near or further off. This brightness with many streaks of thin
vapours about it, such as are seen in a fair evening sky,
softly descended; and as it came near to the earth the
seat of Honour by little and little vanished, as if it gave
way to these heavenly graces. The Queen's Majesty
and her ladies were in Amazonian habits of carnation,
embroidered with silver, with plumed helms, baldrics
with antique swords hanging by their sides—all as rich
as might be; but the strangeness of the habits was most
admired.

Thus with song and dance and extravagant splendor the King and the Queen and the Court persuaded themselves that peace was still at hand and that the Court would prevail.

One assumes that Thomas Carew must have been present at this gorgeous spectacle, for he loved these masques and had himself composed the libretto for a very expensive and elaborate show entitled *Coelum Britannicum,* presented at Court in 1634. Of this splendid show, Sir Henry Herbert reports: "It was the noblest masque of my time to this day, the best poetrye, best scenes, and the best habitts. The kinge and queene were very well pleasd with my service, and the Q. was pleasd to tell mee before the king, 'Pour les habits, elle n'avoit jamais rien vue de si brave.'"[3] The praise was well deserved, for Carew's book for the masque is one of the most thoroughly written that we have for any masque of the day. Indeed the proportion of poetry to scenery appears to be larger than that found in any other masque of the time except for Milton's Ludlow masque. It consists of an extravagant hymn of praise for the virtues of the royal pair whose destiny it is to rout all the vices and disorders of the day and to bring into the three kingdoms of England, Scotland, and Ireland a perfect peace derived from perfect morality. Thus after a long series of anti-masques have been performed, representing the several disorders of existence, the Genius of the three kingdoms appears and foresees the future:

> Raise from these rockie cliffs, your heads,
> Brave Sonnes, and see where Glory spreads
> Her glittering wings, where Majesty
> Crown'd with sweet smiles, shoots from her eye
> Diffusive joy, where Good and Faire,
> United sit in Honours chayre.
> Call forth your aged Priests, and chrystall streames,
> To warme their hearts, and waves in these bright beames.[4]

Then after a series of such songs of praise, the noblemen appear, gorgeously arrayed, to begin the defeat of evil:

> At this the under-part of the Rocke opens, and out of a Cave are seene to come the Masquers, richly attired like ancient Heroes, the Colours yellow, embroydered with silver, their antique Helmes curiously wrought, and great plumes on the top; before them a troope of young Lords and Noblemens sonnes bearing Torches of Virgin-wax, these were apparelled after the old British fashion in white Coats, embroydered with silver, girt, and full gathered, cut square coller'd, and round caps on their heads, with a white feather wreathen about them; first these dance with their lights in their hands: After which, the Masquers descend into the roome, and dance their entry.[5]

And then after several harmonious songs, the masque concludes by the appearance of seven magnificent allegorical figures: Religion, Truth, Wisdom, Concord, Government, Reputation, and lastly, Eternity, all joining in praise of the glorious virtues of Britain's King and Queen.

The fatal separation of this gorgeous world of art from the world of political actuality is clearly evidenced in a superb poem that Carew had written, probably in January of 1633, to his friend and fellow poet of the Cavaliers, Aurelian Townshend. Townshend had written a poem to Carew, urging him to write a poetical tribute in honor of Gustavus Adolphus, who had been killed at the battle of Lützen, November 6, 1632. Thus Carew writes **"In answer of an Elegiacall Letter upon the death of the King of Sweden from Aurelian Townsend, inviting me to write on that subject"**:[6]

> Why dost thou sound, my deare *Aurelian,*
> In so shrill accents, from thy *Barbican,*
> A loude allarum to my drowsie eyes,
> Bidding them wake in teares and Elegies
> For mightie *Swedens* fall? Alas! how may
> My Lyrique feet, that of the smooth soft way
> Of Love, and Beautie, onely know the tread,
> In dancing paces celebrate the dead
> Victorious King, or his Majesticke Hearse
> Prophane with th'humble touch of their low verse?
> *Virgil,* nor *Lucan,* no, nor *Tasso* more
> Then both, not *Donne,* worth all that went before,

(Notice his extraordinary admiration for the poetry of Donne.)

> With the united labour of their wit
> Could a just Poem to this subject fit,
> His actions were too mighty to be rais'd
> Higher by Verse, let him in prose be prays'd,
> In modest faithfull story, which his deedes
> Shall turne to Poems:

It sounds like an honest tribute to a great military leader, and yet as the poem continues a certain ironic tone appears to arise in the following lines:

> And (since 'twas but his Church-yard) let him have
> For his owne ashes now no narrower Grave
> Then the whole *German* Continents vast wombe,
> Whilst all her Cities doe but make his Tombe.

That is to say, Gustavus has made all of Germany a graveyard; therefore let him lie there. If we doubt the irony here the rest of the passage will bear it out:

> Let us to supreame providence commit
> The fate of Monarchs, which first thought it fit
> To rend the Empire from the *Austrian* graspe,
> And next from *Swedens,* even when he did claspe
> Within his dying armes the Soveraigntie
> Of all those Provinces, that men might see
> The Divine wisedome would not leave that Land
> Subject to any one Kings sole command.

It is clear that Carew is finding no great virtues in military conquest, and quickly he turns his mind to things upon which he places a much higher and indeed a supreme value:

> But let us that in myrtle bowers sit
> Under secure shades, use the benefit
> Of peace and plenty, which the blessed hand
> Of our good King gives this obdurate Land . . .

By the word "obdurate" Carew recognizes that the King is having some difficulty with his subjects, but the passage breathes not the slightest doubt that the King will prevail:

> Let us of Revels sing, and let thy breath
> (Which fill'd Fames trumpet with *Gustavus* death,
> Blowing his name to heaven) gently inspire
> Thy past'rall pipe, till all our swaines admire
> Thy song and subject, whilst they both comprise
> The beauties of the *SHEPHERDS PARADISE:*

Carew is referring here to a pastoral comedy written by his friend Walter Montagu, played (with splendid scenery and costumes) by Queen Henrietta Maria and her Ladies on January 9, 1633, and apparently repeated on February 2, 1633.[7] But the production that Carew now proceeds to describe in his poem is not *The Shepheards Paradise* as we know it from the printed text of 1659; instead, as Dunlap has pointed out,[8] Carew's description suggests the masque *Tempe Restord,* which Aurelian Townshend and Inigo Jones had presented in February, 1632. Carew urges his friend to continue writing works in the pastoral genre, "For who like thee," Carew asks,

> In sweetly-flowing numbers may advance
> The glorious night? When, not to act foule rapes,
> Like birds, or beasts, but in their Angel-shapes
> A troope of Deities came downe to guide
> Our steerelesse barkes in passions swelling tide
> By vertues Carde, and brought us from above
> A patterne of their owne celestiall love.

With that echo of the concluding lines of Donne's "Canonization," Carew seems to be describing the elaborate descent of "Divine Beauty" and the "Stars," in *Tempe Restord,* as the Queen and her Ladies descended in one of Inigo Jones's miraculous machines and brought home to earth the meaning of true virtue as opposed to Circean corruption.[9] And this resemblance is borne out by Carew's reference to "the divine *Venus*" and "her heavenly *Cupid*" in the following lines, for in *Tempe Restord* the appearance of the Queen and her Ladies is praised for creating an "Ayre" "Where faire and good, inseparably conioynd, / Create a *Cupid,* that is never blind."[10] Thus Carew continues:

> Nor lay it in darke sullen precepts drown'd
> But with rich fancie, and cleare Action crown'd
> Through a misterious fable (that was drawne
> Like a transparant veyle of purest Lawne
> Before their dazelling beauties) the divine
> *Venus,* did with her heavenly *Cupid* shine.
> The stories curious web, the Masculine stile,
> The subtile sence, did Time and sleepe beguile,
> Pinnion'd and charm'd they stood to gaze upon
> Th'Angellike formes, gestures, and motion,
> To heare those ravishing sounds that did dispence
> Knowledge and pleasure, to the soule, and sense.

So far the parallel may seem to fit; but the conclusion of Carew's account describes two events for which there is no real correspondence in *Tempe Restord.* At the close of this masque Cupid simply flies up into the air,[11] but Carew

describes a much more elaborate action that suggests the Platonizing theme of Montagu's play:[12]

> It fill'd us with amazement to behold
> Love made all spirit, his corporeall mold
> Dissected into Atomes melt away
> To empty ayre, and from the grosse allay
> Of mixtures, and compounding Accidents
> Refin'd to immateriall Elements.

And finally, Carew makes the Queen's own singing the climax of his account, whereas in *Tempe Restord* the Queen does not sing:

> But when the Queene of Beautie did inspire
> The ayre with perfumes, and our hearts with fire,
> Breathing from her celestiall Organ sweet
> Harmonious notes, our soules fell at her feet,
> And did with humble reverend dutie, more
> Her rare perfections, then high state adore.

In the fifth Act of *The Shepheards Paradise,* however, a song of twenty lines is sung by the Queen in her role as Bellesa, chosen for her beauty as "Queen" of this pastoral retreat. Immediately after this she falls asleep, being alone, and Moramente enters, "sees her here lie sleeping and stands wondering," with the following speech:

> Was it the rapture my soule was allwayes in, when she contemplates the divine *Bellesa,* that did present her voyce unto me here in heaven? Sure it was: her soul, uselesse now unto her body, is gon to visit heaven, and did salute the Angels with a song.[13]

These words of Moramente seem to "comprise" the subject for a song that appears in Townshend's collected works, with the title "On his Hearing her Majesty sing":

> I have beene in Heav'n, I thinke,
> For I heard an Angell sing,
> Notes my thirsty ears did drinke.
> Never any earthly thing
> Sung so true, so sweet, so cleere;
> I was then in Heav'n, not heere.
>
> But the blessed feele no change,
> So I may mistake the place,
> But mine eyes would think it strange,
> Should that be no Angels face;
> Pow'rs above, it seems, designe
> Me still Mortall, her Divine.
> Till I tread the Milky way,
> And I lose my sences quite,
> All I wish is that I may
> Hear that voice, and see that sight,
> Then in types and outward show
> I shall have a Heav'n below.[14]

It seems possible that this song may have formed a part of some adaptation of *The Shepheards Paradise.* And there is evidence that such an adaptation was made. A manuscript in the Folger Library represents an acting version of *The Shepheards Paradise,* with a prologue and certain songs between the acts which do not appear in the printed text of the play.[15] This prologue makes it plain that some kind of masque is being presented in coordination with Montagu's play, certainly at the beginning, and possibly between the acts as well. The prologue presents Apollo and Diana in conversation; Apollo tells Diana that the Gods have agreed to appear on this occasion in the form of stars:

> Soe now by this they all consented are,
> Each one to put himselfe into a starre:
> And thus in Gallantry each brings a light,
> And waites with it a servant to this night,
> They'le give the light & leave you to preside
> In vertue, but as you are Deifide;

Perhaps the Gods then, later in the evening, descended from their Heaven and appeared in the manner described in Carew's lines above:

> When, not to act foule rapes,
> Like birds, or beasts, but in their Angel-shapes
> A troope of Deities came downe to guide
> Our steerelesse barkes in passions swelling tide
> By vertues Carde . . .

Certainly these lines accord much better with the Gods and stars of the prologue than they do with the descent of the Queen and her Ladies as stars in *Tempe Restord*. Has Townshend perhaps used some of the themes, along with the costumes, settings, and machinery, from his masque of the previous year, in order to enhance the beauties of *The Shepheards Paradise?*[16] It seems likely, all considered, and such a conclusion would resolve the puzzle of Carew's account, which seems to describe a production related to *The Shepheards Paradise*, and yet devised in some manner by Townshend as well. In any case, such are the "pastimes" that Carew asks his friend to celebrate, as he ends the poem to Townshend with these most significant and revealing lines:

> These harmelesse pastimes let my *Townsend* sing
> To rurall tunes; not that thy Muse wants wing
> To soare a loftier pitch, for she hath made
> A noble flight, and plac'd th'Heroique shade
> Above the reach of our faint flagging ryme;
> But these are subjects proper to our clyme.
> Tourneyes, Masques, Theaters, better become
> Our *Halcyon* dayes; what though the German Drum
> Bellow for freedome and revenge, the noyse
> Concernes not us, nor should divert our joyes;
> Nor ought the thunder of their Carabins
> Drowne the sweet Ayres of our tun'd Violins;
> Beleeve me friend, if their prevailing powers
> Gaine them a calme securitie like ours,
> They'le hang their Armes up on the Olive bough,
> And dance, and revell then, as we doe now.

The whole situation of the Cavalier world, as glimpsed in this poem, and indeed the full impact of Carew's poetry, may be seen as symbolized in a great Mannerist painting by Bronzino, of which I was reminded by reading *The Nice and the Good* by Iris Murdoch, who has given this painting a symbolic place in her book. It is Bronzino's allegory known as "Venus, Cupid, Folly, and Time," where

the graceful, harmonious, beautifully posed figure of Venus forms the center of the picture, while her grace is threatened from all sides by corrupting forces. Her son, Cupid, kneels beside her on the left in a distorted posture, embracing her indecently. Old Father Time holds over the head of Venus a threatening muscular arm. On the right side dances the figure of Folly or Pleasure, a young boy with a glint of madness in his eyes. In the background, darkened in shadows, lurk three sinister figures: one in the upper left corner may represent the figure of Truth, who seems to be turning her face away in horror from the scene; down lower on the left one sees clearly the tormented face of a figure that must be Jealousy; and in the background on the right side lurks a strange composite monster who must be the figure of Deceit, for the bland, pretty face does not square with the animal lower parts that we can see in the corner of the painting; moreover, as critics point out, her left and right hands are misplaced.[17] Can the Queen of Love and Beauty survive these threats?

Thomas Carew is not wholly unaware of these dangers, for his poems deal incessantly with time, infidelity, and death. Many of his finest poems are funeral tributes or poems written to the King or to noble ladies when they are suffering illness. Here, for example, is a poem where the images of red and white common to love-poetry are turned gracefully to deal with the paleness of a young lady suffering from some anemic disease:

> Stay coward blood, and doe not yield
> To thy pale sister, beauties field,
> Who there displaying round her white
> Ensignes, hath usurp'd thy right;
> Invading thy peculiar throne,
> The lip, where thou shouldst rule alone;
> And on the cheeke, where natures care
> Allotted each an equall share,
> Her spreading Lilly only growes,
> Whose milky deluge drownes thy Rose.
>
> Quit not the field faint blood, nor rush
> In the short salley of a blush,
> Upon thy sister foe, but strive
> To keepe an endlesse warre alive;
> Though peace doe petty States maintaine,
> Here warre alone makes beauty raigne.

But sometimes Death will win, as Carew shows in a poem on the death of a young girl, Lady Mary Villers, where all the symbols of Love and Beauty are delicately brought together in balanced, measured form to pay a tribute to the death of youth:

> This little Vault, this narrow roome,
> Of Love, and Beautie is the tombe;
> The dawning beame that 'gan to cleare
> Our clouded skie, lyes darkned here,
> For ever set to us, by death
> Sent to enflame the world beneath;
> 'Twas but a bud, yet did containe
> More sweetnesse then shall spring againe,
> A budding starre that might have growne
> Into a Sun, when it had blowne.

This hopefull beautie, did create
New life in Loves declining state;
But now his Empire ends, and we
From fire, and wounding darts are free:
His brand, his bow, let no man feare,
The flames, the arrowes, all lye here.

It seems appropriate to call this poem a work of Mannerist art, if we do not use the term Mannerist in a derogatory sense. I will use it as many art historians do, when they seek to describe certain aspects of late Renaissance culture, during the last seventy years or so of the sixteenth century, the period after the death of the two great masters, Raphael and Leonardo. But we must define closely the term Mannerist, as John Shearman has tried to do in his recent book on this subject.[18] As he and many others have pointed out, "Mannerism" is derived from the Italian word *maniera,* meaning simply, *style.* A Mannerist painter is a painter with high style, with so strong an emphasis on style that it stands out as the figure of Venus stands out in Bronzino's painting among the threatening gestures of the other figures in the scene. A Mannerist painter has learned all that can be learned from the earlier great masters and he now proceeds to turn their art and craft toward other ends, creating a different kind of art in which the high style stands at the front, taking the eye with its elegance and its sophistication. Such art can, of course, be mere imitation in the bad sense of that word, but it may also be creative imitation—that is, imitation of the manner of the great masters which moves into a different era of sensibility and creates a new world of art. Now transferring cautiously this term into the poetic realm, perhaps we might say that Carew is a Mannerist because he imitates so skillfully the works of the great masters who preceded him and yet brings their art into a different dimension, celebrating values different from those presented by Donne and Jonson and other poets to whom Carew is obviously indebted. The short epitaph that I have just read inherits the Jonsonian form as displayed in many of Jonson's own epigrams and epitaphs, but carries beyond Jonson its elegance and perfection of form, its delicacy of sympathetic admiration for dead Beauty.

Carew's admiration for his master, Ben Jonson, is no empty adulation, as we may see from the remarkable poem that Carew wrote to Ben on the occasion of his poetical father's outrageous exhibition of bad temper when the public hissed his play, *The New Inn,* off the stage in 1629.[19] In 1631 Jonson published the play with a title-page in which he blames everybody but himself for the failure:

A Comoedy. As it was never acted, but most
negligently play'd, by some, the Kings Servants.
And more squeamishly beheld, and censured by
others, the Kings Subjects. 1629. Now, at last,
set at liberty to the Readers, his Majesties
Servants, and Subjects, to be judg'd.

He appends to the play a very bad-tempered poem in which he denounces the English audience in these words:

Come leave the lothed stage,
And the more lothsome age:

Where pride, and impudence (in faction knit)
Usurpe the chaire of wit!
Indicting, and arraigning every day
Something they call a Play.
Let their fastidious, vaine
Commission of the braine
Run on, and rage, sweat, censure, and condem'n:
They were not made for thee, lesse, thou for them.

Carew pays his master Ben the ultimate tribute by judging this outburst of temper in strict accordance with the master's own principles. Carew's poem acts as a tacit reminder that Jonson has urged the use of reason and proportion, that he has represented the values of balance and self-control—the virtues of Roman poetry and of Roman morality. The poem is friendly, but judicious, gentle, but firm:

Tis true (deare *Ben*:) thy just chastizing hand
Hath fixt upon the sotted Age a brand
To their swolne pride, and empty scribbling due,
It can nor judge, nor write, and yet 'tis true
Thy commique Muse from the exalted line
Toucht by thy *Alchymist,* doth since decline
From that her Zenith, and foretells a red
And blushing evening, when she goes to bed,
Yet such, as shall out-shine the glimmering light
With which all stars shall guild the following night.

We should notice that Carew is paying a brilliant tribute to his master here by writing his poem in the style of Jonson's verse epistles, a style sufficiently end-stopped to keep the couplet form alive, and observing the caesura frequently, in good classical form with an effect of balance and proportion, and yet with a movement flexible enough to allow for the colloquial idiom of a good verse-letter. At the same time Carew reveals here his fine critical sense, recognizing that Jonson had reached the peak of his power in the *Alchemist,* produced nearly twenty years before. He chides his father by saying that of course an author may very well bind "In equall shares thy love on all thy race;" nevertheless it is the reader's duty to "distinguish of their sexe, and place;"

Though one hand form them, & though one brain strike
Soules into all, they are not all alike.
Why should the follies then of this dull age
Draw from thy Pen such an immodest rage
As seemes to blast thy (else-immortall) Bayes,
When thine owne tongue proclaimes thy ytch of praise?

And he urges his master to continue his learned use of materials from ancient authors, and says that no one should

thinke it theft, if the rich spoyles so torne
From conquered Authors, be as Trophies worne—

thus defending Jonson against the charge of plagiarism from ancient authors, a charge often leveled against him. In one phrase he sums up the essence of Jonsonian technique:

Repine not at the Tapers thriftie waste,
That sleekes thy terser Poems . . .

*Terser* is the exact word to describe the essence of Jonsonian art, for *terse* means not simply concise and compact,
but it means, in Elizabethan English, polished, brilliant,
sleeked, burnished by careful craftsmanship.

Such then is Carew's critical admiration for one of the old
masters, even in that master's declining years. But there
were other masters. One of them has inspired what is perhaps Carew's greatest poem: **"An Elegie upon the death
of the Deane of Pauls, Dr. John Donne."** Here Carew
sums up Donne's achievement with a critical acumen never
surpassed in later critical writings: if we grasp the poem
we grasp Donne. Carew saw, as well as T. S. Eliot,
Donne's power of feeling his thought as immediately as
the odor of a rose; he saw as well as Grierson Donne's
immense power of "passionate ratiocination" where image
and argument are compressed in one dramatic moment:

But the flame
Of thy brave Soule, (that shot such heat and light,
As burnt our earth, and made our darknesse bright,
Committed holy Rapes upon our Will,
Did through the eye the melting heart distill;
And the deepe knowledge of darke truths so teach,
As sense might judge, what phansie could not reach;)
Must be desir'd for ever.

And we note that Carew here surpasses all other critical
essays on Donne by creating his essay in Donne's own
style, with the enormous suspension of syntax over-riding
the couplet form in the manner of Donne's long passionate
utterances. He praises Donne for refusing to imitate ancient authors and for using the English language in a remarkably original fashion that enabled Donne to excel poets who were born to speak languages more musical than
English—languages such as Latin or Italian, "whose tun'd
chime / More charmes the outward sense."

Yet thou maist claime
From so great disadvantage greater fame,
Since to the awe of thy imperious wit
Our stubborne language bends, made only fit
With her tough-thick-rib'd hoopes to gird about
Thy Giant phansie, which had prov'd too stout
For their soft melting Phrases.

Here the phrase "imperious wit" strikes to the very center
of Donne's achievement, for Carew is using *wit* here in
the broad seventeenth-century sense, meaning creative intellect, along with all the other associations that wit has in
our own day. Donne's *imperious* intellect, his indomitable
reason, bends our stubborn language into forms unprecedented in earlier ages, creating those extraordinary stanza
forms that Donne used for one poem and one poem only.
We should note here that Carew is praising Donne in a
way that seems to castigate himself, for Carew well knows
that he himself is a writer of "soft melting Phrases" and
that he himself has brought back into poetry the kind of
mythological imagery which he praises Donne for having
banished from English verse:

But thou art gone, and thy strict lawes will be
Too hard for Libertines in Poetrie.
They will repeale the goodly exil'd traine
Of gods and goddesses, which in thy just raigne
Were banish'd nobler Poems, now, with these
The silenc'd tales o'th' Metamorphoses
Shall stuffe their lines, and swell the windy Page,
Till Verse refin'd by thee, in this last Age
Turne ballad rime, Or those old Idolls bee
Ador'd againe, with new apostasie;

And Carew then concludes by lines that celebrate the end
of an era, appropriately echoing both Shakespeare and
Donne,[20] as his Elegy proclaims

The death of all the Arts, whose influence
Growne feeble, in these panting numbers lies
Gasping short winded Accents, and so dies:
So doth the swiftly turning wheele not stand
In th'instant we withdraw the moving hand,
But some small time maintaine a faint weake course
By vertue of the first impulsive force:

Thus Carew, writing shortly after Donne's death in 1631,
grasps both the style and the deep significance of Donne's
poetical achievement. Carew is indeed one of the great
critics of English literature; if he had been writing in our
own day he would undoubtedly be known as one of the
"new critics."

The extraordinary Mannerist quality that Carew has, in
imitating to perfection the style of the great masters, is
shown with equal strength in another "critical essay" that
he wrote, **"To my worthy friend Master Geo. Sands, on
his translation of the Psalmes,"** as the title reads in
Carew's collected poems. Here is another poem in pentameter couplets, but we notice that the style does not display either the moderate, flexibly end-stopped movement
of Jonson's verse epistles, nor the passionate rush of
Donne's over-riding Muse:

I presse not to the Quire, nor dare I greet
The holy place with my unhallowed feet;
My unwasht Muse, polutes not things Divine,
Nor mingles her prophaner notes with thine;
Here, humbly at the porch she listning stayes,
And with glad eares sucks in thy sacred layes.
So, devout penitents of Old were wont,
Some without dore, and some beneath the Font,
To stand and heare the Churches Liturgies,
Yet not assist the solemne exercise:
Sufficeth her, that she a lay-place gaine,
To trim thy Vestments, or but beare thy traine;
Though nor in tune, nor wing, she reach thy Larke,
Her Lyrick feet may dance before the Arke.

These couplets are completely end-stopped, each couplet
standing as a perfect unit, somewhat anticipating the Augustan manner in caesura, balance, and antithesis. Carew
is presenting here a superb imitation of the couplet style
that George Sandys had achieved in his famous translation
of Ovid's *Metamorphoses,* published in 1626, and widely
regarded by modern scholars as a very important step in

the creation of the couplet form mastered by Dryden and Pope.[21] Equally important, one should note that exactly this kind of closed couplet also covers many pages in the volume, *A Paraphrase Upon the Divine Poems,* by George Sandys, in which Carew's poem first appeared, in 1638, headed simply **"To my worthy friend Mr. George Sandys."** Carew is not thinking only of the Psalms here, although Sandys did translate eighteen of the Psalms in this volume into pentameter couplets; but the volume also contains enormous paraphrases of other books of the Bible, such as the fifty-five-page paraphrase of the Book of Job with which the volume opens, done in the closed couplet form. As usual, Carew is fitting the style of his essay to the form of the poetry that he is celebrating.

What we see then in these three poems to three early masters, Jonson, Donne, and Sandys, is Carew's critical ability to enter into the very world created by other poets, to absorb them, understand them, and recreate them in his own mind—surely the basic quality that one expects in any good critic. But Carew's critical sense is best shown by his realization of the limitations of his own Muse, which, as he says, is made to sing the cause of Love and Beauty, as indeed he has done for the whole Cavalier Court. A great many of Carew's poems are entitled "Song" and rightly so, for dozens of them were set to music by the best musicians at the Court of Charles I. Some sixty musical settings for his Songs have been discovered[22]—most of them by Henry Lawes, the chief composer of the day in England, the man who composed the music for Milton's masque in 1634, who in fact directed the masque and played the part of Thyrsis in it. In 1634, Carew and Milton were both participating in the Mannerist art of the Cavalier Court; and indeed the two Egerton boys, who played in Milton's masque, had played only a few months before in Carew's masque *Coelum Britannicum.* The great divisions that were soon to split all England had not yet appeared within the world of art.

In these love songs Carew is working in the great European tradition of the courtly love-lyric, inspired by all the Italian love-poets from Petrarch down to Carew's contemporary Marino, and also inspired by many French poets of the sixteenth century.[23] It is important to remember that Charles's Queen, Henrietta Maria, was a Frenchwoman, the daughter of a Medici, and that she brought with her into England an affection for the graceful beauty of French and Italian art-forms, from which the Court masque indeed derives. These European courtly analogues outweigh any echoes that may be assembled from Donne or even from Jonson. Certainly Carew owes something to Donne and distinct echoes of Donne's poems can easily be found, as in his poem, **"Upon a Ribband,"** in which he echoes Donne's famous conceit, "A bracelet of bright haire about the bone," used by Donne in "The Funerall" and in "The Relique." But significantly, this macabre image, combining a symbol of physical love with a symbol of death, is turned by Carew into a graceful compliment. The bracelet here is no longer a "wreath of haire," but is simply a ribbon, a "silken wreath," tied gracefully about the poet's wrist. It is

a symbol of what happened to Donne's inspiration when it entered into Carew's realm celebrating the Queen of Love and Beauty:

> This silken wreath, which circles in mine arme,
> Is but an Emblem of that mystique charme,
> Wherewith the magique of your beauties binds
> My captive soule, and round about it winds
> Fetters of lasting love; This hath entwind
> My flesh alone, That hath empalde my mind:
> Time may weare out These soft weak bands; but Those
> Strong chaines of brasse, Fate shall not discompose.
> This holy relique may preserve my wrist,
> But my whole frame doth by That power subsist:

Appropriately, the first five lines of the poem have something of the run-on movement of Donne's dynamic rhythms, but in the last five lines above, we notice that the verse-form gradually modulates into the courtly, Jonsonian mode of the pentameter couplet. The extravagant preoccupation with Donne's influence that marked literary criticism in the earlier years of the twentieth century has led to the listing of Carew in standard bibliographies and anthologies of "The Metaphysical Poets;" yet, as the above poem indicates, the word "metaphysical" will apply only to some of the surface aspects of Carew's work, and even then in only a few of his poems. Songs such as **"Ingratefull beauty threatned"** or **"To my inconstant Mistris"** clearly show the accent and the rigorous realism of Donne's dramatic addresses to his Lady:

> Know, *Celia,* (since thou art so proud,)
>     'Twas I that gave thee thy renowne:
> Thou hadst, in the forgotten crowd
>     Of common beauties, liv'd unknowne,
> Had not my verse exhal'd thy name,
> And with it, ympt the wings of fame.
>
>                 . . . . .
>
> Tempt me with such affrights no more,
>     Lest what I made, I uncreate;
> Let fooles thy mystique formes adore,
>     I'le know thee in thy mortall state:
> Wise Poets that wrap't Truth in tales,
> Knew her themselves, through all her vailes.

It has the ring of Donne about it, and yet the Lady's name, Celia, used in many of Carew's poems, links the poem also with the tradition of the Sons of Ben Jonson. The examples of both Donne and Jonson are present in this poem; both poets cooperated in giving Carew's lyrics this quality of terse, colloquial speech. But such a poem as this is quite unusual in Carew's work—there are only four or five other songs which might be found thus to combine the movement of Donne and Jonson. Most of Carew's lyrics are drawn from the courtly world of the whole European Renaissance. This is especially true of Carew's famous erotic poem, **"A Rapture,"** where he urges his Celia in cadences that strongly echo Donne in many places, and yet the total effect of the poem does not at all create the world that we know from Donne's Elegies. Carew's poem achieves success and even a sense of purity, through

Carew's delicate use of traditional pastoral images, all imbued with a sense of nature's deep vitality:

> Meane while the bubbling streame shall court the shore,
> Th'enamoured chirping Wood-quire shall adore
> In varied tunes the Deitie of Love;
> The gentle blasts of Westerne winds, shall move
> The trembling leaves, & through their close bows breath
> Still Musick, whilst we rest our selves beneath
> Their dancing shade; till a soft murmure, sent
> From soules entranc'd in amorous languishment
> Rowze us, and shoot into our veines fresh fire,
> Till we, in their sweet extasie expire.
>    Then, as the empty Bee, that lately bore,
> Into the common treasure, all her store,
> Flyes 'bout the painted field with nimble wing,
> Deflowring the fresh virgins of the Spring;
> So will I rifle all the sweets, that dwell
> In my delicious Paradise, and swell
> My bagge with honey, drawne forth by the power
> Of fervent kisses, from each spicie flower.

Thus it seems appropriate that the editor of Carew's volume of 1640 should have chosen as the first poem **"The Spring"** (and we might remember and contrast it with Donne's "Spring" poem "Loves Growth"). Here in Carew's poem is none of Donne's passionate reasoning, none of Donne's philosophical argumentation and racy wit. Carew's poem is composed in courtly cadences with a perfection of Mannerist elegance, in couplets marked with strong caesurae; indeed the whole poem is poised upon a major caesura in the center, for it is a poem of twenty-four lines which pauses and gracefully turns in another direction exactly in the middle of its thirteenth line. In its Cavalier elegance, its Mannerist styling, with all its subtle harmonies of sound, it draws together themes celebrated in dozens of French, Italian, and English poems of the earlier Renaissance, pastoral, and Petrarchan. But here is the poem in all its perfection:

> Now that the winter's gone, the earth hath lost
> Her snow-white robes, and now no more the frost
> Candies the grasse, or castes an ycie creame
> Upon the silver Lake, or Chrystall streame:
> But the warme Sunne thawes the benummed Earth,
> And makes it tender, gives a sacred birth
> To the dead Swallow; wakes in hollow tree
> The drowzie Cuckow, and the Humble-Bee.
> Now doe a quire of chirping Minstrels bring
> In tryumph to the world, the youthfull Spring.
> The Vallies, hills, and woods, in rich araye,
> Welcome the comming of the long'd for May.
> Now all things smile; onely my *Love* doth lowre:
> Nor hath the scalding Noon-day-Sunne the power,
> To melt that marble yce, which still doth hold
> Her heart congeald, and makes her pittie cold.
> The Oxe which lately did for shelter flie
> Into the stall, doth now securely lie
> In open fields; and love no more is made
> By the fire side; but in the cooler shade
> *Amyntas* now doth with his *Cloris* sleepe
> Under a Sycamoure, and all things keepe

> Time with the season, only shee doth carry
> *Iune* in her eyes, in her heart *Ianuary*.

But whether the mistress represents June or January, it appears that she is equally beautiful, since the beauty of the winter is clearly being presented in a lovely manner in the first few lines, and certainly the appreciation of nature suggests the natural vitality that lurks within the Lady's eyes. And the same is true of the entire poem: it is a graceful creation in which a few touches of natural vigor suffice to prevent the Mannerist perfection from falling into frigidity.

Finally, we may find all these forces, love-songs of the European Renaissance, the craftsmanship of Jonson, and something even perhaps of the metaphysical note of Donne, in Carew's most famous poem, properly entitled simply **"A Song"**:

> Aske me no more where love bestowes,
> When Iune is past, the fading rose:
> For in your beauties orient deepe,
> These flowers as in their causes, sleepe.

As readers have often pointed out, the word *causes* adds to the poem a metaphysical note that carries the poem beyond the range of the usual Cavalier lyric, for it evokes Aristotle's doctrine of the four causes: formal, material, efficient, and final (purposive), all of which are contained in the Lady's beauty.

> Aske me no more whether doth stray,
> The golden Atomes of the day:
> For in pure love heaven did prepare
> Those powders to inrich your haire.
>
> Aske me no more whether doth hast,
> The Nightingale when May is past:
> For in your sweet dividing throat,
> She winters and keepes warme her note.
>
> Aske me no more where those starres light,
> That downewards fall in dead of night:
> For in your eyes they sit, and there,
> Fixed become as in their sphere.
> Aske me no more if East or West,
> The Phenix builds her spicy nest:
> For unto you at last shee flies,
> And in your fragrant bosome dyes.

We notice how these stanzas move from the "golden Atomes" of daylight through the wintering song of the nightingale and into certain suggestions of death and falling in the third stanza—a movement from light to dark, from life to death, summed up in the final stanza where the Phoenix image provides a symbol of both death and resurrection. Thus the poem has, after all, something of the metaphysical movement from the Many toward the One. Here, of course, all is treated in a tone of courtly compliment, but nevertheless with something of Donne's manner of turning all transient images of the Many toward the Oneness that he seeks in his love. The sense of change and death is controlled by turning all things toward the *causes* of his love, and this in miniature is Donne's effect.

In miniature, Carew displays a perfection of form and manner that Donne and Jonson themselves never quite achieved with their more robust and wide-ranging powers; thus Carew's whole volume of 1640 may be said to represent the ideals of the Cavalier world in a series of poetical miniatures, graceful, elegant, perfectly crafted, perfectly absorbing the lessons of the earlier masters. It is a world of art-forms, too fragile to sustain the violent pressures of the times. But in the paintings of Van Dyck, in the drawings of Inigo Jones, and in the poetry of Carew and his friends, those forms of art survive the ashes of political disaster.

*Notes*

1. Quotations from Carew's poetry are taken from *The Poems of Thomas Carew, with his Masque Coelum Britannicum*, ed. Rhodes Dunlap, Oxford, Clarendon Press, 1949; I am throughout this lecture indebted to Dunlap's introduction and commentary.

2. The text of *Salmacida Spolia* (ed. T. J. B. Spencer) is available in *A Book of Masques, in Honour of Allardyce Nicoll* (Cambridge University Press, 1967), pp. 337-70; for my quotations see pp. 347, 357-8. Many of Inigo Jones's drawings for *Salmacida Spolia* are handsomely reproduced in *Festival Designs by Inigo Jones: Drawings for Scenery & Costume from the Devonshire Collection, Chatsworth*, Introduction and Catalogue by Roy Strong, Foreword by Thomas S. Wragg (International Exhibitions Foundation, 1967), plates 90-103. See the full catalogue of the Jones drawings at Chatsworth: Percy Simpson and C. F. Bell, *Designs by Inigo Jones for Masques & Plays at Court* (Oxford, 1924), Walpole Society, vol. 12; with many illustrations. Also Allardyce Nicoll, *Stuart Masques and the Renaissance Stage*, New York, Harcourt, Brace and Co., 1938; with many illustrations.

3. *The Dramatic Records of Sir Henry Herbert*, ed. Joseph Quincy Adams (New Haven, Yale University Press, 1917), p. 55. For extracts from contemporary documents concerning the production of Carew's masque see Gerald Eades Bentley, *The Jacobean and Caroline Stage*, 7 vols. (Oxford, Clarendon Press, 1941-68), III, 106-10. For Inigo Jones's drawings for this masque see Simpson and Bell, *Designs*, Nos. 191-209.

4. *Poems of Carew,* ed. Dunlap, p. 177.

5. *Ibid.*, pp. 178-9.

6. Townshend's poem to Carew is printed in *Poems of Carew*, ed. Dunlap, pp. 207-8. My dating of Carew's poem depends upon the reference to Montagu's *Shepheards Paradise*, produced on January 9, 1633. Of course, the elaborate preparations for this play

were discussed at Court throughout the preceding Fall: see Bentley, *op. cit.,* IV, 917-21; the Queen and her Ladies were reported as already "practising" their parts by September 20, 1632. Carew may well have seen rehearsals; but his poem seems to be describing a full-scale performance of some kind. Townshend's verse-letter speaks of how "the windes from every corner bring / The too true nuse of the dead conquering king." Allowing several weeks for this "news" to reach England, one might wish to date Carew's answer in late November or in December, 1632. On the other hand, if Townshend was writing around to his friends to collect a group of elegies, he might well have been doing this in January. A collection of ten elegies on Gustavus Adolphus was in fact published in *The Swedish Intelligencer,* Third Part, London, 1633; all of these are printed anonymously, except for one by Henry King.

7. See Bentley, *op. cit.,* IV, 918; Simpson and Bell, *Designs,* Nos. 163-79.

8. *Poems of Carew,* ed. Dunlap, p. 252.

9. See *Aurelian Townshend's Poems and Masks,* ed. E. K. Chambers (Oxford, Clarendon Press, 1912), pp. 90-91:

> In the midst of the ayre the eight *Spheares* in rich habites were seated on a Cloud, which in a circular forme was on each side continued unto the highest part of the Heaven, and seem'd to have let them downe as in a Chaine.

> To the Musicke of these Spheares there appear'd two other Clouds descending, & in them were discovered eight Stars; these being come to the middle Region of the skie, another greater Cloud came downe above them; Which by little and little descending, discovered other glistering Stars to the number of sixe: and above all in a Chariot of gold smithes workes richly adorned with precious Iemmes, sat divine Beauty, over whose head, appear'd a brightnesse, full of small starres that inviron'd the top of the Chariot, striking a light round about it. . . .

> This sight altogether was for the difficulty of the Ingining and number of the persons the greatest that hath beene seene here in our time. For the apparitions of such as came downe in the ayre, and the *Choruses* standing beneath arrived to the number of fifty persons all richly attired, shewing the magnificence of the Court of *England.*"

See Simpson and Bell, *Designs,* Nos. 139-62.

10. Townshend, *Poems and Masks,* ed. Chambers, p. 93.

11. *Ibid.,* p. 96: "the *Eagle* with *love* flew up, and *Cupid* tooke his flight through the Ayre, after which the Heavens close."

12. The whole fourth Act of *The Shepheards Paradise* is full of abstract conversation about the pure and spiritual nature of Love, and at the beginning of the fifth Act, Genorio exclaims:

> "Me-thinks I find my mind on wing, loose from my senses, which like limed twigs held it till now. It is so light, and so ascensive now, it meanes to work it selfe above *Martiroes*. I am already so farre towards it, as the beliefe that I did never love till now. O how I was deceived, while I conceived that Love was so Materiall it could be touched, and grasp't! I find it an undepending ayrinesse that both supports, and fills it selfe, and is to be felt by what it nourisheth, no more then aire, whose virtue onely we discerne."

*Shepheards Paradise* (1659), p. 110.

13. *Ibid.,* p. 112. Bentley (*op. cit.,* IV, 918) quotes a contemporary as reporting that the Queen, in her performance of *The Shepheards Paradise,* "is said to have herself excelled really all others both in acting *and singing*" (my italics).

14. Townshend, *Poems and Masks,* ed. Chambers, p. 13; taken from Henry Lawes, *The Second Book of Ayres and Dialogues,* 1655, where the song is attributed to Townshend.

15. Folger ms. 4462: see Bentley, *op. cit.,* IV, 920; and G. Thorn-Drury, *A Little Ark, Containing Sundry Pieces of Seventeenth-Century Verse* (London, Dobell, 1921), pp. 4-7, where Thorn-Drury prints the Prologue and four songs that occur between the acts; the Folger ms. was then in Thorn-Drury's possession.

16. Thus Townshend's work might be said to "comprise" (comprehend, contain, sum up) "the beauties of the *SHEPHERDS PARADISE.*" In this connection, Erica Veevers has called attention to the existence in the Huntington Library of a printed fragment or synopsis of a pastoral masque by Townshend that seems to bear a close relation to *The Shepheards Paradise.* She suggests that Townshend may have written this entertainment "to complement a performance of Montagu's play." See *Notes and Queries,* 210 (1965), pp. 343-5. (The fragment by Townshend is also described by Bentley, *op. cit.,* V, 1231.) See also the rejoinder by Paulina Palmer (*Notes and Queries,* 211 [1966], pp. 303-4), who calls attention to Townshend's poem in praise of the Queen's singing. Since there appear to have been at least two performances of *The Shepheards Paradise,* there is room to conjecture several occasions on which Montagu's play may have been enhanced by Townshend's aid.

17. See the interpretation of this painting by Erwin Panofsky, *Studies in Iconology,* Harper Torchbooks (New York, Harper and Row, 1962), pp. 86-91 (originally pub. by Oxford University Press, 1939).

18. John Sherman, *Mannerism* (London, Penguin Books, 1967), pp. 15-30.

19. See the analysis of this poem by Edward I. Selig, *The Flourishing Wreath. A Study of Thomas Carew's Poetry* (New Haven, Yale University Press, 1958), pp. 150-60; this whole book has many fine insights into Carew's poetry. See also the excellent series of articles by Rufus Blanshard: "Carew and Jonson," *Studies in Philology,* 52 (1955), pp. 195-211; "Thomas Carew and the Cavalier Poets," *Transactions of the Wisconsin Academy,* 43 (1954), pp. 97-105; "Thomas Carew's Master Figures," *Boston University Studies in English,* 3 (1957), pp. 214-27. See also the chapter by George Williamson, "The Fringe of the Tradition," in *The Donne Tradition,* Cambridge, Harvard University Press, 1930; and the classic essay by F. R. Leavis, "The Line of Wit," in *Revaluation* (London, Chatto and Windus, 1936), esp. p. 38, with its witty summation of the eclectic effects of Carew's epitaph on Maria Wentworth: "It opens in the manner of Ben Jonson's Epitaphs. The conceit in the second stanza is both Jonson and Donne, and the third stanza is specifically Metaphysical. After the Augustan passage we come to the Caroline wit of the 'chaste Poligamie.' And we end with a line in Marvell's characteristic movement. . . ."

20. Dunlap (*Poems of Carew,* p. 251) notes the echo of the opening lines of *I Henry IV:* ". . . Finde we a time for frighted Peace to pant, / And breath shortwinded accents of new broils . . ." One should note too the echo of Donne's *First Anniversary* (67-73), esp. of Donne's phrase "A faint weake love of vertue" (71). See also Donne's *Second Anniversary* (6-7): "But as a ship which hath strooke saile, doth runne / By force of that force which before, it wonne."

21. See Ruth C. Wallerstein, "The Development of the Rhetoric and Metre of the Heroic Couplet, Especially in 1625-1645," *PMLA,* 50 (1935), pp. 166-209; esp. pp. 186-93 for the influence of Sandys's Ovid and paraphrase of Job.

22. See Dunlap's "Note on the Musical Settings of Carew's Poems," in his edition of Carew, pp. 289-93.

23. See Dunlap's many analogies in the notes to his edition of Carew.

## D. F. Rauber (essay date 1971)

SOURCE: "Carew Redivivus," in *Texas Studies in Literature and Language,* Vol. XIII, No. 1, Spring, 1971, pp. 17-28.

[*In the following essay, Rauber examines the qualities that distinguish Carew from the other Cavalier poets, calling him "the most purely intellectual poet of the early seventeenth century."*]

Among the small mysteries of seventeenth-century poetry is the curiously checkered reputation of Thomas Carew. While modern critics have frequently separated him from Pope's "mob of gentlemen who wrote with ease," he has never secured a proper niche of his own. After a brief flurry of attention, he falls back into the mob again. It is possible, of course, that Carew is not quite good enough a poet to assert a position of individual importance, but the uncertainty of critical opinion concerning him justifies a fresh examination.

The mixed feelings of the critics toward Carew appear initially in the writings of Sir Herbert Grierson. He first praises Carew highly as "the poetic ornament" of the Caroline court and as "a careful artist with a deeper vein of thought and feeling in his temperament than a first reading suggests." But then he takes away much of what was awarded by making the destructive comparison, "in some of the higher qualities of man and artist Carew is as inferior to Wyatt or Spenser as Vandyke is to Holbein."[1]

In the 1930's both of these directions were followed. George Williamson saw Carew as merely one of the Cavalier trio—Carew, Suckling, Lovelace—all of whom he relegated to "the fringe of the Donne tradition," a region not readily distinguishable from limbo.[2] On the other hand, the upward swing in reputation acquired new impetus from F. R. Leavis' influential "The Line of Wit" in *Revaluation*. Not only does the line of wit run "from Ben Jonson (and Donne) through Carew and Marvell to Pope," but Leavis singled out Carew for special notice: "Carew, it seems to me, has claims to more distinction than he is commonly accorded; more than he is accorded by the bracket that, in common acceptance, links him with Lovelace and Suckling. He should be, for more readers than he is, more than an anthology poet." But, as with Grierson, this is closely followed by a strong qualification: "To say this is not to stress any remarkable originality in his talent; his strength is representative, and he has individual force enough to be representative with unusual vitality." Leavis also introduced a certain element of acrimony into the argument by using Carew as a stick with which to beat Herrick and his admirers: "without Jonson behind him what would Herrick (still an overrated figure) have been? The point of the instance lies in the very triviality of Herrick's talent, which yet produced something not altogether negligible (beside him Carew looks like a major poet)."[3]

Quite possibly in reaction to Leavis, typical opinions in the 1940's were unfavorable. Douglas Bush discussed Carew in the usual Donne-Jonson terms but with noticeable coolness: "He could use Donne's ideas and phrases, and he could give to the poetry of love a half-metaphysical tone and edge through realistic, cosmic, and religious images, but he had very little of Donne's glancing wit, intensity, learning, and intellectual pressure. Carew was essentially—and mainly at second-hand, through Jonson—a classical amorist." Tucker Brooke, writing a few years later, is even less impressed. He puts Carew back among the other Cavaliers, adding a little waspishly that "his

reputation was not high even in those indulgent circles." About the most that Brooke will allow Carew is that he "appears to have given his poems a care that he did not bestow upon his conduct" and that in some few poems "he shows more than respectable critical powers."[4]

Finally, as an example of more recent opinion, A. Alvarez, writing in 1961, treats Carew as representative of the court poets but singles him out as "the most original of the Cavaliers." Like Leavis and others, Alvarez is mainly interested in these poets, with their "courtly stance of formal, polished detachment," as precursors of "the elegant and more social wit of the Augustans."[5]

It is not my purpose to explore further the history of the criticism. It may be mentioned in passing, however, that a review of the literature suggests that Carew and many other seventeenth-century poets have suffered greatly from the critical convention of measuring them directly against Donne or Jonson. This is a habit that inhibits us from seeing these lesser poets as having aims, techniques, and successes quite different from those of the masters.[6]

Be this as it may; the main intent of my catena is merely to support the claim that many critics have felt that Carew is somehow out of the ordinary run of courtly gentlemen, that there is something about him which jars with the generalized picture we have of these poets. This feeling was expressed even in Carew's lifetime, by Sir John Suckling, who—at least half seriously—in his rollicking "A Session of the Poets" separated him from the easy poets of the common mold:

> Tom Carew was next, but he had a fault
> That would not well stand with a laureate;
> His Muse was hard-bound, and th'issue of's brain
> Was seldom brought forth but with trouble and pain.
>           And
> All that were present there did agree,
> A laureate muse should be easy and free . . .[7]

Is it possible to determine precisely what distinguishes Carew from his fellows? The best clue is, I think, the one given by Geoffrey Walton, a follower of Leavis', who has observed: "His poems on Donne and Jonson show not only his immense admiration for them but also his critical intelligence and power of sustained thinking in verse. *This intelligence is the controlling force in his lyrics*" (italics mine).[8] The distinguishing mark of a controlling intelligence is compatible with Suckling's mainly social sneer against his friend, especially in light of the very pronounced anti-intellectual strain in Suckling. That intelligence is the portal into the world of Carew's art is further evinced by the fact that most critics who are impressed by him are led to that appreciation through a study of the critical poems. Especially important in this context is the **"Elegy upon the Death of . . . Dr. John Donne,"** one of the finest and most subtle pieces of Donne criticism ever penned. Surely it is reasonable to expect that the discriminating intelligence that finds play there would manifest itself elsewhere in the poetry.

The difficulty is that intelligence is an imprecise concept, not sufficient in itself to locate Carew uniquely. Indeed, my feeling is that Carew has not been properly evaluated because no study has yet been made of the quality of his intelligence. In crude form, my thesis is simply that Carew was the most purely intellectual poet of the early seventeenth century. The distinction I have in mind can be made clearer by contrasting Carew with Donne and Jonson, both of whom can certainly be called intellectual poets. However, the intellectualism of Donne is impure in the sense that his intellectual and logical structures are in large measure only the carriers of a passionately felt direct experience. That is, Donne uses logic, but he fills his logical forms with a highly charged emotional content. On the other hand, the intelligence of Jonson is exhibited in a tireless paring away of the accidental to reveal in the end the quintessence of beauty. Carew shares this Jonsonian impulse toward a refining away of dross, but his interest is not in isolating the essence of beauty, which is an aesthetic aim. Rather he is interested in revealing the essence of the intellect itself. By Carew's pure intellectualism I mean that he is a man dominated by a passion for thought itself and for the logical forms in which abstract thought is expressed.

This special orientation of Carew, and the ways in which he differs from both Donne and Jonson, can be illustrated from the opening section of **"To A. L.: Perswasions to love."**[9] This poem is a particularly good test case, since it also allows us to measure Carew's individuality against the background of the hoary *carpe diem* tradition. The poem begins:

> Thinke not cause men flatt'ring say,
> Y' are fresh as Aprill, sweet as May,
> Bright as is the morning starre,
> That you are so . . .

This, while perhaps not unique, is quite different from the usual opening of a *carpe diem* poem. Compare it, for example, with Shakespeare's Sonnet 2:

> When forty winters shall besiege thy brow
> And dig deep trenches in thy beauty's field,
> Thy youth's proud livery, so gaz'd on now,
> Will be a tatter'd weed, of small worth held.[10]

Carew audaciously denies what poets of direct frontal attack readily and even anxiously grant, the reality of the woman's beauty. Carew is more devious. The abrupt, almost rude, opening is meant to suggest a blunt honesty that cuts through convention: "Everyone says this of you, my dear, but let's examine it. Is it really true?"

Carew also takes pains to set himself apart from "flatt'ring men," though he does so unobtrusively. He succeeds perfectly, however, in creating with a single stroke the impression of a detached objectivity and bluntness, which establishes from the start a dominant tone of analysis and, even more important, is meant to shock deeply a woman who has probably never had the fact of her beauty ques-

tioned. Carew thereby gains an immediate tactical advantage—the woman is thrown off balance. Once this has been accomplished, the battle plan is to maintain the advantage by preventing the woman from gathering together her scattered forces. This plan is executed with great skill:

> . . . or though you are
> Be not therefore proud, and deeme
> All men unworthy your esteeme.

The "or though you are" is superb. It maintains the tone of being completely fair and open, while at the same time it is deliberately cloudy and confusing. The phrase can be taken to mean "but, just for the sake of argument, let us assume that you are beautiful, still. . . ." Or it can be taken as a dramatic reversal of the earlier denial of beauty, a confession that in reality her beauty is so great that a tribute to it is wrenched from the lover, breaking its way irresistibly through his pose of objectivity.

Carew has also taken into account the possibility that the woman may attempt to resolve her confusion by questioning the objectivity and sincerity of the lover. Consequently, he places fresh emphasis on his separateness from the crowd of flatterers by the stress upon "all" in "deeme / All men unworthy your esteeme," a line which shifts attention to the woman's discrimination and her implied regality.

The major device employed by Carew in the whole development is speed; things are so arranged that the woman is not allowed to linger upon any one point. Carew hurries her along. The woman allows herself to be led because she feels that she *must* follow the argument and is deluded into believing that she *is* following it. The purpose of the highly argumentive structure is to produce in her a state of undetected confusion. This can best be demonstrated by putting the whole section (including the lines next to be quoted) in skeleton form: Think not, because of A, that B is true; or, even granting B to be true, do not therefore conclude C and D; for believing C and D results in E, but the purpose of B is non-E, so E is clearly incompatible with B.

This relentless pressure is strikingly evident in the next lines of the poem:

> For being so, you lose the pleasure
> Of being faire, since that rich treasure
> Of rare beauty, and sweet feature
> Was bestow'd on you by nature
> To be enjoy'd, and 'twere a sinne,
> There to be scarce, where she hath bin
> So prodigall of her best graces.

Notice also that the pretense of doubting her beauty, having served its purpose, is here abandoned entirely. Not only is her beauty assumed, but assumed with such finality it seems impossible that it could ever have been questioned. Carew conceals this shift, not only by his supremely confident tone, but also by combining it with a deliberately distracting change of emphasis from direct consideration of her beauty to the theme of enjoyment of beauty. The latter immediately gives rise, however, to a new accusation—that of betraying nature, of sinning against the very source of beauty. But no sooner does Carew introduce the image of sin, than he converts it into something less profound: her implied refusal of her lover is presented in strongly social terms as a kind of cheapness and frugality, qualities appropriate perhaps to middle-class women but not to great court ladies.

Carew then brings this whole continuous movement of thought to a definite conclusion:

> Thus common beauties, and meane faces
> Shall have more pastime, and enjoy
> The sport you loose by being coy.

Again, the strongly stressed "thus" is fine; it gives the argument the tone of completeness and certainty appropriate to an Euclidian demonstration. There was some possibility that the argument from nature and sin would create too serious an emotional context. As shown above, Carew dropped this dangerous theme very quickly, substituting the notion of aristocratic pride. Here he drops a notch lower, from the somewhat noble theme of social pride to the level of a woman's fear of being outwitted by her less gifted sisters in the "game" of love. Then, coldly and without personal interest, the poet observes that as a simple matter of fact she is playing the game badly and is losing.

What I mainly want to show in this analysis is the enormous care and thought Carew put into the poem. Surely it is one of the most complex *carpe diem* poems in the literature, comparing very favorably with Marvell's "To His Coy Mistress." Carew is deeply involved, but what produces the energy behind the poem, what motivates its writing?

The key lies in the fact that the poem has an intellectual quality and value much greater than required by the theme. It exhibits the kind of intellectual interest one associates with, say, chess. It is as though Carew had taken *carpe diem* as a problem and were trying to construct, in an almost geometrical sense, the perfect solution. By perfect solution I do not mean anything narrow or simple; obviously Carew marshals every resource of logic, psychology, tone shifts, ambiguity, and so on. He carefully balances these elements one against the other, devoting special attention to overall effect and to the masking of his various deceptions. What gives the poem life is ultimately our sense of the total involvement of the poet in the intricacies of his work. In developing his strategy and in executing it Carew responds fully; he glows, not with ardor for the woman, but with delight in the flawless functioning of his own mind and in the pure beauty of his solution.

An even more revealing poem, again in the *carpe diem* mold, is **"Perswasions to enjoy."**

> If the quick spirits in your eye
> Now languish, and anon must die;

> If every sweet, and every grace,
> Must fly from that forsaken face:
>> Then (Celia) let us reape our joyes,
>> E're time such goodly fruit destroyes.
> Or, if that golden fleece must grow
> For ever, free from aged snow;
> If those bright Suns must know no shade,
> Nor your fresh beauties ever fade:
> Then feare not (Celia) to bestow,
> What still being gather'd, still must grow.
>> Thus, either Time his Sickle brings
>> In vaine, or else in vaine his wings.

The content and imagery of this poem are quite ordinary, although there are several fine rhetorical strokes such as the double meaning of "aged snow." Yet we do not, I think, experience the poem as being ordinary; what gives it special force and attractiveness is the strong emphasis on logical form. Here Carew employs and investigates the hypothetical syllogism, using successively the forms "If A, then B—A—Therefore B" and "If not A, then B—not A—Therefore B." (Or, one can look upon the whole pattern as a constructive dilemma: If either A or B, then C—Either A or B—Therefore C.) But what gives the form its logical power is that the two conditions are produced by dichotomous division (A and non-A, mortal and nonmortal). But every dichotomous division is exhaustive, so that the form has a very high degree of formal validity. Indeed, so great is the contrast between the invincible logical form and the triviality of content that we cannot help feeling that content is here only an occasion for admiration and even examination of the form itself.[11]

The importance of the logical form is emphasized by the striking summary conclusion: "Thus, either Time his Sickle brings / In vaine, or else in vaine his wings." Each member of this disjunctive conclusion must refer to one of the two hypothetical conditions developed earlier. Time bringing his sickle in vain refers to the condition that the woman's beauty is mortal, with Time defeated because the lovers "reape" their joys before he can apply his dread sickle to them. But if her beauty is immortal, Time brings in vain his wings, symbols of the passage of time, for time is destroyed in that eternity where no beauties "fade," where there is "no shade." The force of the logic is obviously that of "heads I win, tails you lose." No matter which of the two all-embracing conditions is accepted, great pressure is exerted on the woman to surrender: either "Then (Celia) let us reape our joyes" or "Then feare not (Celia) to bestow."

Of considerable importance is the fact that there are signs in the poem of a wry critical examination of the logical form. For example, having established his clear and strong logical pattern, Carew proceeds to distort it by crossing references. That is, in the "if mortal" section, the *flying* of the graces from the woman's face is connected not with Time's sickle but with his wings; just as in the "if nonmortal" section, the strong growth imagery—"golden fleece must grow / For ever" and "What still being gather'd, still must grow"—is connected with sickle and not wings. Here the intellect of the poet is playing ironically with the inability of logical form to contain the complexities and interrelations of real language or of real life. The poet also contrasts ironically the logical form with its rhetorical effect. The obviously false condition that the woman's beauty is immortal is treated as fully and as solemnly as the true condition that it is mortal and transitory. Both conditions have the same logical status and weight. But rhetorically things are quite different; we are never more struck by the fleeting nature of beauty than in the immortality passage.

Furthermore, while these logical concerns seem to be at the heart of the poem, this does not mean that they are unrelated to the overt theme. On the contrary, the perfection of the logical form serves as a symbol for the eternal and unchanging, while the problems introduced by the cross references and considerations of logic versus rhetoric represent the transitory and changing. The transitory is seen by Carew to infect even the most perfect and abstract of human constructions, the forms of pure logic. In other words, Carew has completely intellectualized the *carpe diem* assumption.

One would expect, then, that Carew would go beyond logical form into the realm of philosophical problems; and so he does, in an unprofessional but far from naive way. A good example is **"Mediocritie in love rejected"**:

> Give me more love, or more disdaine;
>     The Torrid, or the frozen Zone,
> Bring equall ease unto my paine;
>     The temperate affords me none:
> Either extreame, of love, or hate,
> Is sweeter than a calme estate.
> Give me a storme; if it be love,
>     Like Danae in that golden showre
> I swimme in pleasure; if it prove
>     Disdaine, that torrent will devoure
> My Vulture-hopes; and he's possest
> Of Heaven, that's but from Hell releast:
>     Then crowne my joyes, or cure my paine;
>     Give me more love, or more disdaine.

This poem clearly is based upon a paradoxical rejection of the Aristotelian doctrine of the mean, and I think we err if we take it as merely courtly play or as paradox for its own sake. The philosophical issues raised in the poem seem genuine and subtle. Carew's argument is basically that the doctrine of the mean is defective in being too static, in failing to take into account psychological process. His reinterpretation of the principle is highly relativistic and places its emphasis upon actual human experience. Carew insists that psychologically the mean can be viewed as the most unstable, the most torn and divided state of all, because of its indeterminancy. In point of fact, says Carew, the goal of calm is attained only through the turbulence, and then release, of extreme psychological states. It is, in brief, what might be called a romantic as over against a classical psychology.

Carew opens with a standard geographical figure, in which the mean is represented by the temperate zone, and the ex-

tremes of love and hate by the torrid and frozen zones. By use of the respectable but puzzling principle of *coincidentia oppositorum* Carew virtually equates the two opposites, and in this also he is quite close to modern psychologies.

Having established his scheme, Carew converts his geographical figure into a meteorological one, to introduce movement into the model. The mean is not changed; all that is required is the change of adjective from "temperate" to "calm," which gives an extremely smooth transition and is illustrative of Carew's great technical competence. The now joined extremes are represented by storm. The storm of love, the golden shower—Carew has brilliantly interpreted the Danae in sexual terms—totally engulfs the participant. He swims in pleasure, and this image beautifully combines the notions of exertion and psychological calm and contentment. Conversely, the torrent of hate also engulfs the victim to "devoure," or destroy, him. But this process also ends ironically in calm, the calm of extinction. And extinction can relativistically—"he's possest / Of Heaven, that's but from Hell releast"—be presented as a heaven (with probably some play on "haven").

With the extremes both characterized by calm and represented by Heaven, the storm and its analog Hell can only pertain to the mean. We have, in other words, a complete reversal: the apparent turbulence of the extremes has become a calm; the apparent calm of the mean, a turbulent Hell. This is more than an elegant or playful construction. It is not, of course, necessarily true, but neither is it obviously false. Carew's picture of the mean as an instability is no more unreasonable than the classical view of it as a balance, and the poet's treatment does emphasize the important but often neglected fact that, in either view, the mean is a tensional state.

Lest I have given the impression that there is nothing more to Carew than a coldly brilliant intellect masquerading under courtly trifles, I would like to conclude by looking at the song **"Celia singing."** The examination will not contradict what has preceded, but it should add new dimensions to our appreciation of this sophisticated and certain artist.

> You that think Love can convey,
>     No other way,
> But through the eyes, into the heart,
>     His fatal dart:
> Close up those casements, and but heare
>     This Syren sing;
>     And on the wing
> Of her sweet voyce, it shall appeare
> That love can enter at the ear:
> Then unvaile your eyes, behold
>     The curious mould
> Where that voyce dwels, and as we know
>     When the Cocks crow,
>     We freely may
>     Gaze on the day;
> So may you, when the Musique's done
> Awake and see the rising Sun.

At first glance, this seems to be ordinary courtly poetry. The first stanza is entirely conventional in both thought and imagery. The dart of love shot from the eyes is out of Petrarch or the Courts of Love; singer as siren, the wings of song, and the rest are hackneyed and dull. At best, it would appear, we have here only a highly polished surface.

The reason for this almost excessive conventionality becomes clear in the second stanza. We have been listening, with closed eyes, to Celia singing, purportedly to prove by experiment the truth of the momentous thesis that indeed love can enter at the ear as well as through the eyes. This is the setting. But then something happens. With "Then unvaile your eyes" we are snapped out of the drowsy mood induced by the first section; the tone has changed abruptly and we are aware of a greater seriousness and a new intensity. "Unvaile" is the first word of power in the poem, and it marks the falling away of the haziness of habit that controls our ordinary seeing. It is as though we were seeing the world (or Celia at least) for the first time, with an Eden-like freshness. This impression is bolstered by the dramatic "behold," which by its terminal position in the line is taken first in isolation—"behold" in the sense of the Authorized Version. Then, "behold / The curious mould," where "curious" adds to the new atmosphere of wonder; and finally, "curious mould / Where that voyce dwels," which is still more potent in its suggestion that the voice is somehow separate from the singer and is an entity in its own right.

Carew next elaborates this induced wonder in a different context. Suddenly we are transported into the crisp freshness of a dawn, with the sharp trumpet of a cock crowing the sun to birth. The poem opens up expansively as we "freely may / Gaze on the day." Then, at the height and pitch of awareness, everything is coalesced and drawn together swiftly in the terse precision of the concluding couplet: "So may you, when the Musique's done / Awake and see the rising Sun." Ostensibly the emphasis here is on the elegant comparison of Celia to the sun rising in splendor, but I would argue that the real point is in the surprising "Awake." We have already unveiled our eyes and seen, but "awake" operates to transform the whole experience, giving it the quality of a dream or, better, a vision.

This simple lyric is far from ordinary. Its formal subject, a minor point in the mechanics of love, was only a pretext. The second subject, praise of Celia, seems equally pretextial.[12] The true subject of the poem is the transforming power of music, not stated but exemplified. It is important to remember that this is a song, for in the course of the singing itself we are invited to contemplate the experience of listening to song—song almost completely disembodied and abstracted from its means of production. And it is this, the power of song to reveal new worlds, which is here being both celebrated and proved upon our pulses.

Carew has not been completely honest with us. The first section was a trap, and poor Celia was merely an occasion. Yet we have no grounds for complaint, for he has manipulated us into a direct experience of art, tricked us into a vision of beauty, unveiled our eyes to our great profit. This, it hardly needs saying, is more than elegant verse, though its elegance is great. It is poetry simply and without qualification. And yet, to return to the main theme, this pure poetry is born in the mind of Thomas Carew, a mind accustomed to reflective abstraction and capable of a pure intellectual power unique in a highly intellectual age.

*Notes*

1. *Metaphysical Lyrics and Poems of the Seventeenth Century,* ed. Herbert J. C. Grierson (Oxford, 1921), p. xxxvi.

2. George Williamson, *The Donne Tradition* (Cambridge, 1930), p. 206.

3. F. R. Leavis, *Revaluation* (1936; London, 1953), pp. 29, 15, 36.

4. Douglas Bush, *English Literature in the Earlier Seventeenth Century* (Oxford, 1945), p. 116; Tucker Brooke, *The Renaissance* in *A Literary History of England*, ed. A. C. Baugh (New York, 1948), p. 657.

5. A. Alvarez, *The School of Donne* (1961; New York, 1967), pp. 53 and 55. For a more complete analysis of Carew's reputation, from his own day to modern times, see Edward Selig, *The Flourishing Wreath: A Study of Thomas Carew's Poetry* (New Haven, 1958), pp. 1-15. Selig finds that a great many critical evaluations of Carew merely repeat what had been said earlier and show no signs of direct examination of the poetry.

6. Selig reaches almost the same conclusion: "Undoubtedly, Carew profited from the work of his predecessors. This does not mean that his achievement is entirely to be explained in terms of theirs. Particularly wrong, it seems to me, is the idea that we must regretfully banish Carew to the fringe of the Donne tradition, where we may preserve and at the same time dismiss him according to the rule of metaphysical poetry" (p. 174).

7. In *Poetry of the English Renaissance 1509-1660,* ed. J. W. Hebel and H. H. Hudson (New York, 1929).

8. Geoffrey Walton, "The Cavalier Poets" in *Pelican Guide to English Literature,* ed. Boris Ford, III, 160-172. The citation is from p. 165.

9. All Carew quotations are from *The Poems of Thomas Carew,* ed. Rhodes Dunlap (Oxford, 1949). In the portion of the poem I am concerned with Carew owes nothing to Marino, though the latter portion of the poem is a free translation of *Belleza caduca.*

10. *The Complete Plays and Poems of William Shakespeare,* ed. W. A. Neilson and C. J. Hill (Cambridge, Mass., 1942).

11. Carew would not be the first logician to use trivial content, as the perusal of logic book shows. There is actually a tradition of unimportant content, for the purpose of not distracting from the forms.

12. Selig agrees that the poem is "extravagant, commonplace, and trivial only on the surface" (p. 24). He does not agree, however, that Celia is a pretext; rather he sees her as central and reads the poem as a carefully controlled exhibition of decorum: In *Celia Singing,* the poet avoids the extremes of Ovidian irony and Petrarchan adoration, and strikes a balance between nature and art" (p. 25). I believe that this is true but it is not as important as the isolation of music itself for purposes of contemplation.

## Paula Johnson (essay date 1976)

SOURCE: "Carew's 'A Rapture': The Dynamics of Fantasy," in *Studies in English Literature, 1500-1900,* Vol. XVI, No. 1, Winter, 1976, pp. 145-55.

*[In the following essay, Johnson analyzes Carew's erotic poem "A Rapture."]*

**"A Rapture"** was in its day a very shocking poem. Not only did it provoke rebuttals from poets as small as Habington and as great as Marvell, but it even drew upon Carew a reproof in Parliament.[1] Its reputation has persisted to our own times: until recently it has been regularly omitted from anthologies of seventeenth-century verse, and as regularly included in collections of erotica.[2] Carew's editors have been reticent or disapproving in their annotations, and literary historians have usually shied away with the briefest of ambivalent remarks. **"A Rapture"** is "the most daring and poetically the happiest of the imitations of Donne's clever if outrageous elegies"; it "has great interest as a libertine version of the Golden Age theme," but is Carew's "longest, best, and least printable poem," his "most notoriously licentious verses."[3] Edward Selig, author of the only full-length critical study of Carew's work, ignores **"A Rapture"** altogether. The only more extended comments I know of are buried in studies that few are likely to consult.[4]

Gradually and recently, however, a few critics have begun, if not to discuss the poem, at least to acknowledge its existence less coyly. Howarth, to be sure, felt bound to allude to it obliquely by calling Carew "a moral theorist occupied with the problem of abstract sanctions and restraints upon human conduct";[5] but this appeal to a justifying high seriousness has come to seem less necessary. Skelton's honest delight in Carew's "high spirits and witty use of sexual imagery" puffs away the moralistic haze, but he simplifies too much, I think, when he goes on to classify the poem as a "witty exercise," one of those jeux d'esprit that do no more than "amuse us as accurate portrayals of masculine sexuality."[6] Martz, in a graver vein, judges that **"A Rapture"** "achieves success and even a sense of purity, through Carew's delicate use of traditional pastoral images, all imbued with a sense of nature's deep vitality."[7] And Parfitt, in a finely perceptive essay on Carew, brings

the re-evaluation a step farther along: in **"A Rapture"** Carew "not only acknowledges a conflict between Christianity and the erotic but suggests that such a clash is inevitable, while his embodiment of the erotic has such force and beauty that it makes the erotic-moral opposition a real factor in the poem, makes the poem a disturbing phenomenon, puzzling and extending our experience as poetry should do."[8] In view of the change in cultural climate that these successive comments reflect, I believe it is now possible to give this chef d'oeuvre of a considerable minor poet the attention it deserves and demands. Deserves, for its position in literary history; demands, because it *is* puzzling and disturbing, and because like all good erotica, it's fun. It's too late in the day of this world not to admit, with Eric Partridge, that "a dirty mind is a constant joy."

Though Dunlap properly refers the reader to Tasso, Marino, Ovid, and Donne, he does not suggest any single poem of which **"A Rapture"** is translation or imitation; nor can I. Probably it is better to think in terms of analogues rather than sources for poems like this one so thoroughly inmeshed with poetic traditions, conventions, and fashions; but even a list of analogues tends to infinity. One might add to Dunlap's list Saint-Amant's *La Jouyssance;* Venus' garden in Fletcher's *Venus and Anchises* and the garden of touch in Marino's *L'Adone;* voyages to a pleasure-isle in the latter poem, the *Gerusalemme Liberata,* and the second book of *The Faerie Queene;*[9] the influence of the blason, perhaps via Sidney's "What tongue can her perfections tell," but also from innumerable other poets; the dilemma of the classical lovers in Elysium that Donne suggests in "Loves Deitie" and Suckling makes explicit in "Oh for some honest lover's ghost"; the far-off but also very near context of the *Song of Songs,* the *Amores* and *Ars Amatoria,* and the *Greek Anthology.* The catalogue is limited only by one's reading experience and one's patience, and tells us in the end only what we knew already: that Carew is not, in the modern sense, very "original." But let us turn to the poem.

Any poem is, in the reader's experience, both a simultaneous system and a patterned series of events. In neither of these aspects is **"A Rapture"** wholly consistent; whether we begin at the beginning, go on to the end, and then stop, or we bring together parts of the poem that temporal sequence separates, there are frustrations as well as satisfactions. Though I cannot always offer a way out of these difficulties, there are a couple of small guideposts that will direct us into them.

The first indicator is the word *there:* "There, shall the Queene of Love" (25); "there I'le behold" (27), "No curtaine there" (31), "There, a bed" (35); and then the word becomes unnecessary until 99: "There, no rude sounds," "All things are lawful there" (111), "The Roman Lucrece there" (115)—this is as close to an exhaustive listing as we need. Most of the time, "there" is clearly Love's Elysium (in line 31 it may also be the woman's body); but why should its there-ness need to be underlined in just these passages, and what enables the poet to dispense with it in others? As soon as the lovers are comfortably settled in the happy garden, we need no longer be reminded that this is far, far away; in fact, to remind us would be to rupture the illusion. But after the moment of ultimate bliss, the reminders come back, and with doubled force, because at the same time appears our second indicator. Carew shifts from the future tense, which has governed the entire poem until this point, and (with a brief respite in 147-150) remains until the end in the grammatical present. The first corollary of this change is an exorcism: "no affright . . . no jealous cares . . . no envious eyes"—don't let the practical difficulties of a real assignation tarnish the elysian joys. *There* must be contrasted as strongly as possible with the *here* that one dare not mention as such. And the indicators take us still further: Celia never exists in the present; she belongs entirely to the mode of "I will enjoy thee." The intentional force of that initial "will" does not, however, persist; "there, a bed / Of Roses, and fresh Myrtles shall be spread" is obviously not a statement of intent or command; rather, it is a use of non-present as a means of creating the sense of distance. Children playing make-believe sometimes use past tense to similar purpose ("Pretend I was a robber and you came walking by not noticing anything"), to clarify to each other that this *is* make-believe. In Carew's poem, since the poem is itself an imaginative construction, this use of the non-present produces a fantasy within a fantasy, at a safe distance from the self that ordinary life demands we maintain. Only when the poet turns his attention away from Celia to the procession of the repentant chaste, where the legendary or literary nature of the characters removes them automatically into the fantastic realm, can he afford present verbs. The tenses also draw our attention to the first and last sections of the poem, the arguments against honor. In the beginning honor "is but a Masquer" that the "wise" lovers can in fancy elude—"mounted on the wings of love / Wee'le cut the flitting ayre." But at the end, honor becomes a tyrant and usurper, who "Bids me fight and kill." It no longer merely "is" a pageant that one can scorn, but it acts, fetters, dispenses, commands, makes. The general meaning, then, of *there* and *shall* is that of any-time-but-now-any-place-but-here, the realm of fantasy, untrammeled by problems or probabilities, by repressions or restraints, a land freer even than our dreams.

And the dream-poem is one obvious kind of analogue with **"A Rapture."** From the *Roman de la Rose* to Petrarch to Sidney to Herrick, one of the accepted ways for a poet to describe the yielding of his mistress is to say that "it was only a dream," thus to disimplicate her and excuse himself, while saying nevertheless what he most desires to say. The crucial difference between the analogues and Carew's poem is that in the latter the poet neither goes to sleep nor wakes up. Cleveland begins "The Senses Festival" by confessing unreality ("I saw a Vision yesternight"), and Suckling ends *His Dream* with the broken line, "and then—I awak'd"; not so Carew. One is not always sure whether this poet knows he is dreaming. Nor would it be accurate to explain this peculiarity by saying that Carew dramatizes an ego-ideal in a wished-for situation, like

Donne in "Going to Bed." Donne's hypothetical mistress is actualized, as everyone knows, by the imperatives that relate the speaker to her while they indirectly describe her movements; Carew abandons imperatives after the first paragraph, where, except perhaps for "draw neere" they indicate no action at all; and in the broad center of the poem he attributes to the lady not so much as a gesture. The bedtime partners of Ovid, Donne, and Marino are always present, making signs to the lover, stepping into bed, scolding, resisting, acquiescing. Celia must be the most completely passive female in erotic literature—what other lady was ever compared to a "sea of milke"? "The consequence," as Skelton puts it, "is that we feel Carew is greatly enjoying his poem and kicking over the moral traces; but we are not convinced that a real Celia is in question."[10] Skelton, it is fair to say, attributes this consequence to Carew's "fanciful dexterity"; but there's more to it than that. In order to understand what's really going on, we'll need a play-by-play account (for clarity, leaving all the arguments about honor to the end of the discussion).

Carew's Celia is doubtless from *Volpone*—"Come my Celia, let us prove / While we may, the sports of love"—but for Carew, "I will enjoy" is the first thought, and the command "come" is its incidental result. The immediacy of "now" does not outlast the opening line, though the mutuality implied by "with me" does, as in line 14 the poet adroitly places himself with the lady, sharing her scruples but relegating them to the past. But the concomitant singular "thou" further implies that the poet is a little more sophisticated than the lady; he has learned the truth about honor and is eager to share his discovery. "Come then," he invites for the second time, and the lovers are on their way to where Venus is queen not only of love and beauty but also of nature and innocence. "Our close Ivy twines" refers to later action; first, the subject changes from "we" to "I" and Celia only remains as the possessive pronoun before metaphorized parts of a female body bared, unbraided, naked, exposed. The lover's first act is to "behold"; even his "enfranchiz'd hand" merely "slides" without response over an ivory figurine. The poet may be using a flexible version of the five-senses scheme of Chapman and Marino, with some rearrangement and redistribution of emphasis. In any case this section is chiefly visual and primarily distinguished for its artistry. The stock epithets *snowy* and *golden* become nouns, on the mannerist assumption that we already know the conventions and expect the poet to show how skillfully he can manipulate them: "Thy bared snow and thy unbraided gold." Unlike these witty metaphorizings, "ivory" takes us definitely away from the human body, a movement which is consonant with the intent of the poem. Carew draws aside the curtain that hides the picture, to show that although honor is manmade and delusive, art, also manmade, is the revelation of invention and craft. This snow-gold-ivory figure, the virginity of whose treasure multiplies its price, is the product of the poet's ars amatoria, which thus obliquely confirms the high value of body and art and of the poet's experience of both. But unfortunately (from one viewpoint) this success of ingenium makes for a human failure, since in transforming the woman's body into precious artifice, Carew denies to it any possibility of response, any interior. It slips paradoxically into the same category as the "vast Idoll," having no value and no life in itself, but only the value the poet imputes to it, which rests in turn only on his own enjoying and beholding.

At the end of this section, unexpected aptness refreshes the hackneyed conceit of coining. The poet admits that the sexual act is reproductive, but plays down this reality, as one must in a poem of fruition. The lovers—Celia has temporarily been recalled in "we"—will produce not off-spring but Cupids, cupiditates, ever-renewed desires. Their "faint respites" suggest that consummation has already taken place; "may" in line 42 is future by implication, and in relation to that future the lovers dream of "past plea-sures." Their dreams and waking experience merge, just as fantasy and reality have done in the poem. The natural surroundings—the "enamoured chirping Wood-quire," the "trembling leaves," and the "dancing shade"—engage in active play while the humans are quiescent. So thorough is the merging that the "soft murmure" in line 51 may come either from within or outside the lovers; all is "entranc'd in amourous languishment." A closed couplet of beauti-fully paired lines rounds off the paragraph: the promised heats appear like lightning—"Rowze us, and shoot into our veins fresh fire." The sudden shock exhilarates us the more for following a lull, and the forceful succession of monosyllables electrifies the senses "Till wee, in their sweet extasie expire," as the repeated prefix and downward-turning inflection breathe out, linger, and relax. Though the actual consummation can only be described once without risk of redundancy, the poem's movement represents multiple climaxes and releases of tension. The transparent image of "the empty Bee, that lately bore / Into the common treasure, all her store" gives us, if we need it, confirmation that the poet has just treated us to orgasm-by-analogy.

When after the formal simile the "I" returns to "rifle all the sweets" after the bee's "Deflowering the fresh virgins of the spring," we may well wonder just how "common" the treasure really is. Even the woman's body becomes for the lover "*my* delicious Paradise"; as a person she has van-ished again, leaving the poet alone with his amorous imag-ery. Not the couple now, but only the mistress merges with the painted fields. This is not a place to which "we" will fly, but which "I will enjoy"—Celia *is* love's Elysium. Carew's autocentricity here is, to the best of my knowl-edge, rivalled only by Lovelace, who at the end of "To Chloris: Love made in the first age" roundly declares. "Enjoying of myself I lie." But where Lovelace is crude, the poet of **"A Rapture,"** by the loving care he expends on the work of nimble fancy, reminds one of Mozart's Cherubino: "Ogni donna mi fa palpitar . . . E se non ho chi m'oda, Parlo d'amor con me." It is the wish-fulfiling dream of an adolescent, graceful, charming, and utterly self-absorbed.

And this helps to account for one of the poem's difficul-ties. Carew alters the poem's mode without warning, and the reader may have an uneasy feeling that the ground un-der his feet isn't quite steady. Perhaps we can discover why this is so. The poet addresses his first argument to his mistress in the time-honored fictive way. We are not given any reason, at that point, for believing that Celia's manner of being is different from Laura's, Stella's, Delia's, or that of Spenser's inamorata. Any of the poems written "to" these more or less illusive ladies could in fact be sent to a real woman. They are socially plausible, as indeed are Marino's "La Pastorella" and "Trastulli estivi," and Donne's "Going to Bed," despite the difference in implied social effect. This interpersonal aspect is important, be-cause any real reader has to be able to imagine a fairly definite *implied* reader, so as to know what stance toward the poem he should adopt. Among the poet's subtlest and most crucial masteries is the art of putting the reader where he would have him. Love poets, as Empson remarked, "are wooing the reader even if they are not trying to se-duce a mistress";[11] thus the model for the reader's transac-tion with a love-poem can only be the projected inter-personal relation of the fictive lovers. But in what socially—or indeed humanly—credible attitude can one imagine Celia?

Through line 28 the poet is making a standard libertine plea, and it is always assumed in such cases that the lady's refusal precedes, succeeds, and is concurrent with the po-et's address. But once we have moved into the middle of the poem, Carew must imply the lady's consent, and that implication belongs only to certain genres other than the suasoria—the epithalamium for instance (which is why Grierson was able to read "Going to Bed" as a nuptial poem). Consent is also decorous if the poet has not attrib-uted to the lady any present scruples: thus parts of the *Amores*, Catullus' "Vivamus mea Lesbia," and a few of Donne's *Songs and Sonets*. Carew, whose social sensitiv-ity is elsewhere exquisite—in, for example, **"To A. D., unreasonable distrustfull of her owne beauty"**, and in the green-sickness poems[12]—has here misjudged the effect of combined conventions. The poet's shift from one set of implications about the lady to a quite different set, without transition, warning, or even recognition of the shift, leaves the reader wondering just where he is. Nor is one's puzzle-ment much mended by Celia's penchant for melting into the landscape. There is no *a priori* reason why she shouldn't do this; only before we interpret her as Spens-erian fecundity, we need to be given some clue as to the relation between the actualized shy social creature of lines 13-16 and the metamorphosed body of 63-90.

Carew's symbols, Selig says, have "a power to suggest connaturality between mind and matter, between inner and outer atmospheres which are wholly transparent, and through which rays of pure sunlight shine down upon a precious world."[13] But when the lover, following the bee, carries out his oral exploration of the garden that Celia's body has become, the symbolism is by no means wholly transparent. One can visualize the metaphoric vehicles, and one can visualize the woman's alluring nakedness, but the relation between them is problematical. In his excitement the lover calls up one delicious metaphor after another, regardless of whether a less heated imagination can combine them intelligibly or not. With the "ripned Cherry" he evidently begins a love's progress downward along the route of the blason, but seems to lose and recover his way in phantasmagoria of flowers, geography, and partial glimpses of female anatomy. Although the code in this passage seems oddly vague and inconsistent, Carew is subtle and precise about the consummation, which makes it the more strange that he should be imprecise here. The alchemical conceit that follows is clearer. "Then bring the great Elixar to thy hive" surely represents yet another analogical consummation (this would be the third), but it occurs, I believe, by analogy and not actually. Though most of the body-symbols are decipherable anatomically, they are interesting and enriching because they are more than mere anatomy. Thus "Elixar" is best taken as the potency that intimate contact with his mistress' body awakens in the lover. He, then, is the source of highest good; it is he who, poet-like, transforms the material. But because the poet has completely replaced the mistress by his art, he can as lover offer the "one soveraigne Balme" only, in effect, to his own imagination. Similarly, in lines 79-80, he can identify only his own limbs, and only he can act; the landscaped lady is deactualized to a mere "thine." Even the lover's Jovian tempest evokes no response from the "smooth, calme Ocean," but by now this radical split between passive and active is no longer surprising. The dreamer's godlike omnipotence is characteristic of fantasy, and Carew throughout the poem underlines this absolute power by terms of seemingly unnecessary violence: "rifle," "seize," "ravisht," "storme," "unrip." And we remember that the poem's title can mean *rape* as well as *ecstasy.* Fantasy's obverse characteristic is isolation: though in this realm one can do everything, there is no testing actuality to bump against. In fantasy, one is omnipotent, invulnerable, and all, all alone.

The lady does at last begin to fade back into the picture; and although her disappearance taints Carew's lushness with hints of frustration, her reappearance and the return to considerations of the real world are managed with—forgive me—consummate skill.

Carew obscures the action a little by using three different phallic symbols, and by the proleptic "Ride safe at Anchor." Again, as in lines 63-74, the speaker in his excitement abandons realistic sequence and consistent imagery. But this time intercourse not foreplay is in question and the mistress's actuality can no longer be forgotten. The lover needs the help of her "bold hand" and the evidence of his prowess in the "bounding waves" of her response.[14] That response is irrelevant to sensations of the lover's own body only until he can feel her involuntary movement. Then she once again becomes real and active, with an embrace and kisses. But when her presence, however hypothetical, forces itself on the dreamer, it wedges open the closed world of fantasy, evoking a remembrance of all the sordid and uncomfortable circumstances of an assignation in the real world, a remembrance that the change to present

verbs dramatizes. The ship that was to convey the lovers safely between Honor's giant legs may have come to port, but the mental voyage does not end peacefully. The poet reacts to his unwelcome recollection by denial: "There, no rude sounds shake us with sudden starts." Elysium continues to exist, but precariously, as a negation, "there."

Ears and eyes, so fully rejoiced in Elysium, are in the real world "jealous" and "envious." The luscious garden of the body is reduced to "midnight Arbors and darke groves," furtively sought. The names "Of husband, wife, lust, modest, chaste, or shame" are hated as much in Elysium as they are respected in the world. Elysium, we suddenly realize, has inverted all values; there, "We only sinne when Loves rites are not done." In Elysium "Aretine" rhymes with "divine," the traditional opposites Lucrece and Lais merge, and the mighty voyages of Ulysses are merely "dull dreames of the lost Traveller." Though the poet insists that "All things are lawfull there," what he really means is that laws are turned around; one is under command to do exactly what the world forbids. Thus those who lived in chastity must when they reach Elysium "Pay into Loves Exchequer double rent." But the inversion contains ambiguity, too, since the line "Like, and enjoy, to will, and act, is one," which could be a motto for the whole poem, is susceptible of opposite readings: every impulse is immediately translated into act, *and* there are no acts, only private impulses. This ambiguity is connected with the difficulties in Carew's argument against honor.

When the lover, in lines 1-20, first exhorts Celia to disregard honor, he does not try very hard to develop a logical case. Honor is a chimera; the best people aren't fooled by it; to respect it is a kind of false religion—such are his grounds of persuasion. Of these only the last merits any allusion in the interior of the poem: "Th' enamoured chirping Wood-quire shall adore / In varied tunes the Deitie of Love"; and the perfume of Celia's kisses

> Like a religious incense shall consume,
> And send up holy vapours, to those powers
> That blesse our loves, and crowne our sportfull hours.

Such is the true faith. At the end of the poem, however, Carew symbolizes honor, as we have seen, in political terms—the tyrant, usurper, false impostor, whose commands run counter to religion. But the religion is now Christianity, which although it "bids from bloodshed flye," is on honor's side in supporting chastity. Despite this incongruence, the poet's argument in lines 151-164 is effective. He asks, in summary, how one can do what is right when one's culture insists with equal vehemence on two incompatible kinds of behavior.

It is not so easy, though, to argue in favor of an inversion of values, because the conventional values are embedded in the language; his very words often betray the libertine. So do they our poet. He cannot have religion both for and against him, nor can he have it both ways in the language. We may recall that among the names hated in Elysium was "lust," which unlike the other terms is hated in the real world too. And it was not possible to turn impulse into act without turning act into impulse. Now at the poem's end, the betrayal is yet more damaging—in fact, completely destructive. Honor makes men "Atheists"—despisers of religion, bad people; so, asks the poet, why shouldn't it make women bad people too? The inversion has failed. For the analogy to work, one would have to find a term for unchaste women that would carry positive overtones. As the last line stands, the word "whores" suddenly re-inverts the whole moral world that the poet has been so carefully setting upside-down. However wryly, we must admit that honor wins in the end, that all the lovely sensations were delusive, that there is no way to withdraw finally from the ungracious demands of the hypocritical world.[15] We understand at last the full meaning of the verb tenses: so far from establishing a still point of the turning world, they confessedly distinguish between what is, what may be postulated as fiction, and what, though we can wish it and dream it, is not and can never be.

*Notes*

1. A. F. Allison, "Some Influences in Crashaw's Poem, 'On a Prayer Book sent to Mrs. M. R.,'" *RES*, 33 (1947), 34-42; James E. Ruoff, "Thomas Carew's Early Reputation," *N & Q*, 202 (1957), 61-62; Douglas Bush, *Mythology and the Renaissance Tradition in English Poetry*, rev. ed. (New York, 1963); Paulina Palmer, "Lovelace: Some Unnoticed Allusions to Carew," *N & Q*, 212 (March, 1967), 96-98; Paul Delany, "Attacks on Carew in William Habington's Poems," *SCN*, 24 (1968), 36; cf. also David Foxon, *Libertine Literature in England, 1660-1745* (New Hyde Park, N.Y., 1965).

2. "A Rapture" is included in *Seventeenth Century Poetry*, ed. Hugh Kenner (New York, 1964); *The Anchor Anthology of Seventeenth Century Verse*, 2, ed. Richard S. Sylvester (New York, 1969); *The Cavalier Poets*, ed. Robin Skelton (London, 1970); *Literature of the English Renaissance*, ed. Frank Kermode and John Hollander (New York, 1973); and, most recently, in *Ben Jonson and the Cavalier Poets*, ed. Hugh Maclean (New York, 1974); *Poetica Erotica: A Collection of Rare and Curious Amatory Verse*, ed. T. R. Smith (New York, 1921); *A Treasury of Ribaldry*, ed. Louis Untermeyer (Garden City, N. Y., 1956); and *Erotic Poetry: The Lyrics, Ballads, Idyls and Epics of Love—Classical to Contemporary*, ed. William Cole (New York, 1963). Smith and Cole use Ebsworth's text (see below); Untermeyer omits the first and last sections of the poem.

3. Editors: J. W. Ebsworth, *The Poems and Masque of Thomas Carew* (London, 1893); Arthur Vincent, *The Poems of Thomas Carew* (New York, 1899); Rhodes Dunlap, *The Poems of Thomas Carew* (Oxford, 1949). My quotations from Carew conform to Dunlap's text. Literary historians: H. J. C. Grierson, ed., *Metaphysical Lyrics and Poems of the*

*Seventeenth Century* (1921; rpt. New York, 1959), p. xxvi; Frank Kermode, ed., *English Pastoral Poetry, from the Beginnings to Marvell* (London, 1952), p. 251; Rufus A. Blanshard, "Thomas Carew and the Cavalier Poets," *Transactions* of the Wisconsin Academy of Sciences, Arts, and Letters, 43 (1954), 98; and Allison's article cited in note 1.

4. Edward Selig, *The Flourishing Wreath: A Study of Thomas Carew's Poetry* (New Haven, 1958); Werner P. Friederich, *Spiritualismus und Sensualismus in der Englischen Barocklyrik* (Vienna, 1932), pp. 51-54. Friederich argues that erotic poems, of which he uses "A Rapture" as chief instance, are artistically negligible because they do not result from an inner struggle; he cites a comparative discussion of "A Rapture" and Donne's "The Extasie" in B. C. Clough's "The Metaphysical Poets," diss. Harvard, 1920, pp. 138ff. Friederich's general attitude is also that of J. B. Broadbent, *Poetic Love* (New York, 1965); my dissent will be apparent. See also Earl Miner, *The Cavalier Mode* (Princeton, 1971), pp. 80-82, 251-252.

5. R. G. Howarth, ed., *Minor Poets of the Seventeenth Century: Suckling, Lovelace, Carew, and Herbert* (London, 1931), p. xiv.

6. Robin Skelton, *Cavalier Poets*, Writers and their Work, 117 (London, 1960), pp. 11-12; cf. p. 18.

7. Louis L. Martz, *The Wit of Love* (London and Notre Dame, 1969), p. 104.

8. G. A. E. Parfitt, "The Poetry of Thomas Carew," *RMS*, 12 (1968), 56-67.

9. On possible influences see David O. Frantz, "Leud Priapians' and Renaissance Pornography," *SEL*, 12 (1972), 157-172. For a comprehensive review of the garden topos, see A. Bartlett Giamatti, *The Earthly Paradise and the Renaissance Epic* (Princeton, N. J., 1966); also, and more particularly, Frank Kermode, "The Argument in Marvell's 'Garden,'" *EC*, 2 (1952), 225-241.

10. Skelton, *Cavalier Poets*, p. 12.

11. William Empson, *Some Versions of Pastoral* (1935; rpt. Norfolk, Conn., 1960), p 132.

12. Cf. Selig, pp. 87-90. An even more glaring example of incompatible conventions is Carew's "An Elegie" (Dunlap, p. 19).

13. Selig, p. 82.

14. It is possible that the lovers are practicing a primitive method of contraception similar to coitus interruptus. If so, the chronological sequence of entry *after* ejaculation may be literal. Poetic couplings, however, tend to be straightforward, no matter how elaborately they may be allegorized. Cf. Steven Marcus, *The Other Victorians* (New York, 1964), pp. 271-273, 280.

15. Ebsworth's rewriting of the couplet: "This goblin 'Honour', whom the world enshrined, / Should

make men Atheists, and not women kind?" has therefore the curious effect of eliminating not only an offensive word, but the clearest indication that the poet does, after all, know where he is.

### Ada Long and Hugh MacLean (essay date 1978)

SOURCE: "'Deare *Ben*,' 'Great DONNE,' and 'my Celia,': The Wit of Carew's Poetry," in *Studies in English Literature, 1500-1900*, Vol. XVIII, No. 1, Winter, 1978, pp. 75-94.

[*In the following essay, Long and MacLean summarize Carew's verse in order to evaluate his wit and poetic talent.*]

Thomas Carew's literary reputation has undergone some reassessment in recent years. For a long time Clarendon's estimate provided the pattern for critical opinions of the man and his work: Carew "was a Person of a pleasant and facetious Wit, and made many Poems (especially in the amorous Way) which for the Sharpness of the Fancy, and the Elegancy of the Language, in which that Fancy was spread, were at least equal, if not superior to any of that Time."[1] Often cited by students of Carew's verse, the passage anticipates Rhodes Dunlap's comment that, "unlike Donne's, Carew's wit does not usually spring from the establishment or discovery of new and pregnant relationships within the world of experience; it relies instead on skilful hyperbole and logically extended metaphor."[2] Jonson's influence on Carew has been recognized from the first; but most critics have been content, in that regard, to point out Carew's "classicism," or his habit of painstaking revision. Consequently, the effort to anatomize Carew's wit often relapses into admiration of his ability to "weave conceits into a context of easy hyperbole," while the poet is apt to be distinguished merely by his "disciplined professionalism" from the gentlemanly mob of "Cavalier poets."[3]

F. R. Leavis knew better. Jonson, after all, "was as robustly interested in men and manners and his own talk as in literature and the poetic art"; the Jonsonian mode (which Leavis remarks in Carew) "may be described as consciously urbane, mature, and civilized."[4] Following Leavis, G. A. E. Parfitt links Carew with Jonson primarily by virtue of their "basic humanity, which allows moral distinctions to be drawn and gives [Carew's] writing a sense of involvement with the real world."[5] Earl Miner, for whom Carew's poetry eminently exemplifies the several aspects of "the Cavalier mode," observes that the complexities of that mode "are essentially those of social relations interwoven with personal relations, and it is just this that distinguishes the aesthetic mode of the Cavaliers from that of the Metaphysicals."[6]

In the light of these hints, an examination of the poet's particular use of decorum and his related concern with time and change leads to some new suggestions about the character of Carew's wit. The large majority of Carew's poems, whatever their particular genre, fall into three categories. The first includes those poems which explicitly or by implication, but always with due regard for decorum, acknowledge the continuity of tradition in literary or social contexts: these poems, affirming the authority of the past, include such lyrics as **"Mediocritie in love rejected," "To my inconstant Mistris,"** and **"The Complement,"** as well as the first and third of the epitaphs on Lady Mary Villiers. The prime example in this kind is Carew's response **"To Ben. Johnson. Upon occasion of his Ode of defiance annext to his Play of the new Inne"**. The poems of a second group, often recalling the witty manner of Donne, reflect Carew's recognition of time's power over law and custom. The controlling decorum of these pieces is subtly modified, even challenged, by a variety of unexpected elements, which anticipate those changes that the future must bring. This second category includes the second epitaph on Lady Mary Villiers, together with that on Maria Wentworth, and (for choice) the lyric, **"Disdaine returned."** Chiefly, of course, one thinks of the elegy on Donne. Finally, in some of his most intriguing poems, Carew plainly confronts his age, his time. In these pieces, decorum may be neglected or repudiated; in any event, one feels that it is not of much moment for the poet, who is chiefly concerned to come to grips with "the way we live now." Among the lyrics, **"Ingratefull beauty threatened"** is especially to the point. Poems in this group are often exercises in self-examination, reflecting the author's gloomy concern to discover where felicity is to be found: **"A Rapture"** gives early promise of its author's determination to reassess the exhausted codes of a society beset by uncertainty and hazard. One group of Carew's poems, then, is marked by a relatively easy and confident wit, which celebrates enduring values and attitudes; a distinctly more passionate note is struck by another group, where wit typically illustrates the inevitability of change; in the poems of a third group, wit serves at once to temper and ironically comment upon the process of adjustment from a stance of comfortable assurance to one of bleak realism.

While a good many of the more familiar love lyrics fall into the first of these categories, and a significant number of the occasional pieces into the third, the three groupings do not reflect chronology. It is probable that **"A Rapture"** was written early,[7] while the three epitaphs on Lady Mary Villiers were presumably composed in the fall of 1630.[8] Available evidence does not lend much support to the hypothesis that Carew's vision of men and manners steadily darkened with the years. What matters is that his wit, taken in the round, need not be measured chiefly in terms of "skilful hyperbole and logically extended metaphor," and that this poet's originality extends well beyond the capacity to "revitalize a conventional genre or attitude."[9]

To speak of decorum in Renaissance verse is, of course, to attend to the degree of propriety in the poet's matching of image, style, and genre, within the context of "'the cause and purpose he hath in hand'—the poetic subject, be it high invention or lightly considered trifle, commendatory or satirical in intent, grave or fanciful in nature."[10] But this is not to imply that the poet's care for decorum is narrowly "literary." For Jonson and his followers especially, the conditioning influence of personal and social relationships on the criterion of decorum requires some emphasis. According to Puttenham,

> By reason of the sundry circumstances that mans affaires are, as it were, wrapt in, this *decencie* [i.e., decorum] comes to be very much alterable and subject to varietie, in [so] much as our speach asketh one maner of *decencie* in respect of the person who speakes, another of his to whom it is spoken, another of whom we speake, another of what we speake, and in what place and time and to what purpose. And as it is of speach, so of al other our behaviours. . . . there is a decency to be observed in every mans action and behaviour aswell as in his speach and writing. . . .[11]

Jonson knew that language "most shewes a man. . . . It springs out of the most retired, and inmost parts of us, and is the Image of the Parent of it, the mind"; extending Hoskyns' observations on epistolary style to writing in general, he can agree that brevity, perspicuity, and vigor are all subsumed, at length, by "*Discretio* . . . respect to discern what fits yourself, him to whom you write, and that which you handle."[12] The poet's language, which reflects his mind, and answers fitly to the matter in hand, ought properly also to speak to the mind of the person addressed: it is governed by an idea of decorum that takes account of personal and social relationships in all their demanding variety. Thus, Jonson's several poems to friends, together with those on the theme of friendship, as a rule exemplify the plain, "free" manner appropriate to expressions bearing on this subject.

> Sonne, and my Friend, I had not call'd you so
> To mee; or beene the same to you; if show,
> Profit, or Chance had made us: But I know
> What, by that name, we each to other owe,
> Freedome, and Truth; with love from those begot.
> Wise-crafts, on which the flatterer ventures not.[13]

Again, the clarity and order of those lines in Jonson's epistle to Lady Aubigny (*The Forest,* XIII) that describe the even tenor and single purpose of her life, a model for other "great wives," reflect the "even, and unalter'd gaite" of one "that can time and chance defeat"; when the poet considers the directionless course of those who, "giddie with change," inhabit "the maze of custome, error, strife," the rhythms of his verse stagger and halt, mired in a welter of complex constructions.

Decorum, finally, as E. B. Partridge remarks, is rooted in "what is natural. Jonson clearly anticipated that sense of 'nature' which became a central dogma in the neo-classic age: that is, the natural is the normal and the universal."[14] Jonson's Lady Aubigny is a "faire tree," for whose "ripe and timely issue" the future reserves high honor; but for those others who blush at her, no emblem serves so well as the "maskes" worn by a society careless of "truthes

complexion," and quite unable to perceive "right, the right way." As for Selden's decorously seasoned style, notably his artful pairing of "Newnesse of Sense, Antiquitie of voyce,"

> Nothing but the round
> Large claspe of Nature, such a wit can bound.[15]

The wit of Jonson's poetry, then, is regularly dimensioned by the poet's care for a decorum much more than narrowly literary.[16] Carew's poetry is also marked by this concern for a "larger" decorum; but with a difference. Jonson's poems, even those of the later years, bravely continue to set the decorum of virtue, nature, right, against their indecorous opposites: misfortune and neglect scarcely disturb the poet's certitude. But Carew, making poetry chiefly in the sinister twilight of those decades just preceding an era of social change and upheaval, is evidently struck by time's power to transform established moral codes, even to render decorous what in an earlier age might well be decorum's antithesis. And the wit of his verse is affected accordingly.

Although the greater number of Carew's love lyrics answer to the demands of a decorum sufficiently conventional and familiar in this mode, these poems include some instructive examples of the directions his wit may take, in terms of the three categories proposed in this essay. Bruce King draws attention particularly to the "aggressive attitude" regularly on view in the lyrics;[17] the degree and kind of aggressiveness, however, are not everywhere identical. For instance, the song, **"To my inconstant Mistris,"** thematically recalling odes by Catullus and Propertius,[18] in no sense starts away from an established decorum. Generations of Renaissance poets had composed verses in which a betrayed lover appeals, by way of theological conceits, to a controlling God of Love from whom an appropriate response may reasonably be expected. This is not to say that Carew's wit is altogether commonplace, for he expertly matches the oaths and vain tears of the inconstant lady (excommunicate and damned) with those of the constant lover (crowned in glory), while slyly acknowledging that the speaker's real reward is the love of another than she to whom he has remained constant. By virtue of its wit, in fact, the poem aptly enough exemplifies Carew's talent for "revitalizing a conventional genre or attitude." But the dimensions of its governing decorum—the manner of its imagery, the speaker's stance, the implicit recognition that Love is supreme appellate judge—essentially conform to those of an established tradition.

With another "aggressive" lyric, **"Disdaine returned,"** the case is somewhat altered. Properly speaking, the first two stanzas, of six lines each, are not witty at all; employing the familiar epithets of minor Elizabethan verse, Carew rather lifelessly rehearses a Renaissance commonplace: only that love which reaches past sense-experience may expect to baffle time's power. In the final stanza of eight lines, however, sententious generalization gives way to particular experience, aptly couched in direct address.

No teares, *Celia,* now shall win,
　　My resolv'd heart, to returne;
I have searcht thy soule within,
　　And find nought, but pride, and scorne;
I have learn'd thy arts, and now
　　Can disdaine as much as thou.
Some power, in my revenge convay
That love to her, I cast away.[19]

If Celia's "pride, and scorne" parody the ideal of a "stedfast mind," the speaker can at least be sure of his own "resolv'd heart," wittily proposing to complete a bitter exchange: his love for the lady's disdain. It is worth noting that he should appeal at last, not to an explicitly identified God of Love, but to "Some power" that employs "conveyance"[20] to satisfy this lover's desire for revenge. Given that the final stanza makes an ironic comment, in the light of actual experience, on the bland antitheses of established theory, Carew may well be inviting the reader to associate this "power" with that of time itself. In any event, while the poem preserves the facade of a decorum usual in these cases, doubt and disenchantment have evidently undermined the easy assumptions of old orthodoxy.

If the world of **"To my inconstant Mistris"** is controlled by a familiar God of Love, and that of **"Disdaine returned"** implicitly subject to powers other than those directly exercised by men and women, the scene of **"Ingratefull beauty threatned"** is dominated by the speaker himself, who acknowledges no other power than his own, to create, know, destroy.

Know *Celia,* (since thou art so proud,)
　　'Twas I that gave thee thy renowne:
Thou hadst, in the forgotten crowd
　　Of common beauties, liv'd unknowne,
Had not my verse exhal'd thy name,
And with it, ympt the wings of fame.

That killing power is none of thine,
　　I gave it to thy voyce, and eyes:
Thy sweets, thy graces, all are mine;
　　Thou art my starre, shin'st in my skies;
Then dart not from thy borrowed sphere
Lightning on him, that fixt thee there.

Tempt me with such affrights no more,
　　Lest what I made, I uncreate;
Let fooles thy mystique formes adore,
　　I'le know thee in thy mortall state:
Wise Poets that wrap't Truth in tales,
Knew her themselves, through all her vailes.

In this poem, all to brave clearness is indeed reduced, as the speaker, explicitly asserting absolute rule over the lady's beauty, power, and reputation, employs an idiom that is plain, abrupt, and at length brutally realistic.[21] Celia's "sweets," her graces and her killing beauty, are no more than noticed: their sphere is after all a borrowed one. The poet's wit, ranging through degrees and kinds of knowing, bears on wisdom and folly at various levels; to "know" proud-foolish Celia in her "mortall state" (as her bemused admirers cannot) is to claim kinship with those truly "Wise

Poets" whose knowledge speaks through the fictions they made. And by implication, when time has worn the tapestry of social decorum to shabby and threadbare posturing, to recognize its inadequacy is to reaffirm that truth of nature which decorum should steadily reflect.[22]

Other such "sets" might be cited to illustrate the particolored character of Carew's wit, as it operates in decorously various contexts.[23] But it is in his occasional verse that the larger dimensions of his wit may most fruitfully be observed, notably the verse-letter to Jonson and the elegy on Donne; and **"A Rapture"** must make a third, for if it is not precisely an "occasional poem," the piece is distinguished less for its extravagantly sensuous imagery than for the bold challenge to conventional decorum that informs its wit.

The verse-letter to Jonson has been sensibly analyzed by Edward Selig, who shows that the poem aptly illustrates the principle of decorum "according to the kind or genre": as he observes, "the speaking voice and the epistolary style coincide," and his supportive discussion of the poem's colloquial idiom makes the points that matter.[24] Selig also attends to the decorous requirement "that one consider carefully to whom he [writes]," noticing the witty combination of "supreme compliment, and . . . supreme rebuke" that brings the poem to a close; he adds that "the theme of time seems to underlie the entire poem, and to coordinate the images, which ring variations upon the theme."[25] These latter areas of Selig's discussion, however, are touched on rather than explored: the full range of decorum in this poem, and the reach of its wit, are therefore in some degree obscured. That "the wiser world holds Jonson in the highest possible esteem"[26] may be granted; but Carew is addressing Jonson in the contexts of art and of friendship, and those contexts chiefly determine the poem's decorous expression. For Jonson, the marks of a poet include a capacity for "Exercise of [one's wit], and frequent"; a talent for imitation, especially of "one excellent man above the rest, and so to follow him, till [one] grow very *Hee*"; and that art of crafty revision which alone confers perfection upon nature.[27] Carew draws attention to just these matters.

Repine not at the Tapers thrifty waste,
That sleekes thy terser Poems, nor is haste
Prayse, but excuse; and if thou overcome
A knottie writer, bring the bootie home;
Nor thinke it theft, if the rich spoyles so torne
From conquered Authors, be as Trophies worne.

He addresses a poet held in universal esteem, no doubt; but he speaks to the particular qualities considered by that poet to be principal elements of his art. Again, while the poem is undoubtedly decorous "according to the person addressed," it is so also "in respect of the person who speaks": effectively, its decorum is that appropriate to friends. This is in fact to say that Carew's sensitive response to the value set by Father Ben on friendship, and to the special character of that Jonsonian virtue, accounts for the poem's tone, by turns affectionate and sharp. Indeed,

Jonson might be said to have given the informing principle for Carew's epistle in *Underwood*, XXXVII:

> Little know they, that professe Amitie,
>     And seeke to scant her comelie libertie,
>     How much they lame her in her propertie.

Another passage (in *Underwood*, XXVI) might have served as text:

> Yet doth some wholsome Physick for the mind,
>     Wrapt in this paper lie,
> Which in the taking if you mis-apply,
>     You are unkind.

In this poem to "deare *Ben*," Carew has fulfilled the two basic responsibilities of a friend: loyal support, frank advice. And he has gracefully maintained a delicate balance between admiration and honesty: praise keeps criticism from impudence, criticism checks praise this side of flattery.[28]

If the poem's wit reflects the author's concern for decorum of genre, style, and person addressed, its character answers to a larger vision: Carew's confidence in a traditional ideal of friendship (made flesh by way of the Tribe), and in enduring principles of art that time cannot erode. In this regard, the allusions to time are subtler than Selig's analysis would allow. The poem begins and ends by drawing attention to the limits imposed by nature, but also to its room and promise. It is altogether natural that poets, being men, should rise to a zenith of accomplishment, then decline, and yield their place in time: that is "what happens." Yet the apt and measured use of time, the patient labor by one's "watchfull Lampe," conforms to the deliberate rhythms of nature just as hasty impatience, eager after variety and difference, runs counter to them. "Time devoures" and cancels the trivial malice of a "detracting world"; Jonson's art, in its causes and methods linked to a "*Nature* [that] is always the same, like her selfe," "shall outshine the glimmering light / With which all stars shall guild the following night."[29]

Carew's stance in this poem, then, consistently reflects his reliance on an established and natural order of things that is proof against mutability, that contains and controls each kind of change. To adopt this standpoint is to adopt a "larger" decorum: that "sense of the harmonious whole which . . . implies that harmony is natural to man and that man is more than the sum of his activities."[30] The wit of Carew's poem accords best, perhaps, with *OED* 11.7: "Quickness of intellect or liveliness of fancy, with capacity of apt expression. . . ." Yet its character is, at bottom, relatively sober and restrained: it surely implies, even turns on "wisdom, good judgment, discretion, prudence" (*OED* 11.6). Certainly the wit that consists in "the apt association of thought and expression, calculated to surprise and delight by its unexpectedness" (*OED* 11.8) has not much place in this traditionally oriented celebration of values that, defying time's changeful vicissitudes, remain still themselves.[31]

That the elegy on Donne is couched "very much in the style that Donne himself affected"[32] has been recognized by several critics. Decorum "according to the person addressed" governs and directs the play of flashing wit that has earned for the poem its special renown. The shocking figure with which the elegy opens, the rugged syntax of those rhetorical questions that follow, in particular the rapid movement of suggestive images in 11. 25-60: all are calculated to evoke the polymorphic figure of "great DONNE," who planted, mined, wrought, but chiefly "redeem'd" the literary sins of an age. Carew's association of Donne with Prometheus and Christ at once is, after all, not very extravagant in a poem that celebrates "*Apollo's first, at last, the true Gods Priest*"; while the range of imagery inevitably recalls the language of Donne's tenth Holy Sonnet: "bend / Your force, to breake, blow, burn, and make me new." Further, since "praise is the essential element of the [funeral elegy],"[33] one would expect that a poet of Jonson's train, schooled in decorous tradition, would undertake to point and adorn his wit especially in lines given over to praise.

In a related aspect, however, the poem breaks sharply with established decorum: that of genre. "Praise, lament, and consolation," as Hardison notes, "are the three major components of funeral elegy."[34]

> A natural progression of *mood* imposes itself on most funeral poetry, as Scaliger's instructions show. The poem that Scaliger describes will have a definite movement from dejection to consolation. It will open with a brief summary of the greatness of the individual (*praise*) and then develop the same material in much more detailed form (*demonstration of loss*) through biographical detail heightened by the devices of amplification. Recalling the deeds of the dead person intensifies the grief of the survivors and leads to a lament. Grief is then consoled, and the poem ends on the exhortation that the audience imitate the virtues of the subject of the poem.[35]

Finally, while the consolation of immortality is "frequently mentioned [but] not heavily stressed" in classical elegy, "the Christian consolation of immortality . . . is one of the distinguishing features of Christian funeral poetry."[36] From this established pattern the structure of Carew's elegy on Donne significantly diverges. In effect, the poem consists almost entirely of praise and lament. An introductory passage (11. 1-24) artfully combines these elements; then follow thirty-six lines of praise and twenty-five of lament; at length the poet, unwilling and unable to do more, summarily returns to the *topos* of praise in the concluding epitaph. In short, there is no hint of *consolatio* or of an "exhortation that the audience imitate the virtues of the subject of the poem." That is at the least unexpected, even indecorous (in the context of genre), given that this is an elegy on "the Deane of Pauls."

Yet in another sense the omission is quite appropriate.

> I will not draw the envy to engrosse
> All thy perfections, or weepe all our losse;

These are too numerous for an Elegie,
And this too great, to be express'd by mee.

"Great DONNE," after all, broke traditional molds, "And fresh invention planted"; his wit and his alone could bend "Our stubborne language"; the form itself of elegy is inadequate to mark his passing. And there are grounds more relative even than this. The poem to Jonson sturdily affirms that the artist's constancy to his purposes, disparaged by a "dull age," is finally at one with nature and time, and will be justified in "after dayes." The elegy (making every allowance for the wide-ranging implications of Donne's affinity with *natura naturans*) emphasizes instead the failure of a mission. Time at last will put an end to the influence of that "first impulsive force," and re-establish the incongruous rule of "those old Idolls," in whose name "poetique rage" is made "A Mimique fury." Donne gone, the world cannot hope for a successor in whom his spirit will be re-animated. By inference, to trust that time, and harmonious universal law, will confirm the insight of those who teach "deeper knowledge of darke truths," is an illusion. Still, if change tears at the fabric of established tradition, and soon cancels the influence of bright stars like Donne, it recurrently brings new vitality to art and life. The counterpoint of stylistic decorum "according to the person addressed," and of structural indecorum "according to the kind or genre," is, then, quite appropriate to this ambivalent poem. While Carew could see the point of Jonson's remark that Donne "for not being understood would perish," he must needs also agree that Donne was "the first poet in the world in some things."[37]

The poem's wit matches this balance. The brilliant play of imagery informing the central passage of praise is familiar; but the poem is witty also by virtue of its structure. Essentially, the elegy responds to four rhetorical questions (posed in the opening lines), each somewhat wider in scope than that preceding it, thus:

(a) Can we not produce one elegiac poem to memorialize Donne?

(b) Can we not produce even an elegiac memorial in fitting prose?

(c) Has our capacity for song been quite cut off by his death?

(d) Was Donne in fact the "dispenser" of language itself?

Lines 11-24 respond to the second of these questions, confirming its inference. Lines 25-70 respond affirmatively to the third ("nobler Poems" and "Verse refin'd by thee" give way to "windy Page" and "ballad rime"); and lines 71-87 return an emphatic affirmative to the fourth question: only by "dumbe eloquence" may those who remain acknowledge "The death of all the Arts." This being so, there can be but one response to that first and immediate question: Donne's "perfections" and other men's limitations (together with those of art) effectively deny the possibility of elegy. All that can be managed is an epitaph.[38] The

witty transmutation of elegy to epitaph finally confirms the truth of Carew's tribute to Donne. As its structural indecorum fittingly recalls Donne's capacity to discard "The lazie seeds / Of servile imitation," its structured movement toward a point of wit emphasizes the incapacity of lesser men. "We are time's subjects, and time bids begone."[39]

The elegy on Donne, an undoubted *tour de force*, has some claim to be considered the most remarkable poem in the canon of Carew's verse. As a rule (to speak generally), the poet's wit is honed to a finer edge in the poems that chiefly reflect Donne's influence than in those that recall Jonson's style and outlook. Nonetheless, it is arguable that the poems of a third group are of special interest, for in these pieces Carew is clearly his own man. **"Obsequies to the Lady Anne Hay"** makes one of this group, together with (for example) the second elegy on Buckingham, and the lines to George Sandys, "on his translation of the Psalmes"; as well as **"A Rapture,"** which probably antedates the other pieces. Here, typically, the poet acknowledges that decorum demands a particular stance or mode; then he goes his own way, in effect declaring his independence of literary decorum. And the break from formal tradition is in each poem matched by an expression of Carew's disenchantment with a variety of orthodox attitudes which for his society have the force of established truths. Striking through the mask of literary decorum, Carew is thereby enabled to speak his mind in larger social contexts. All these poems are in some degree ironic, but the character of each poem's wit is distinct and individual. The witty exuberance of **"A Rapture"** is certainly "calculated to surprise and delight by its unexpectedness"; in the other poems, while one perceives "quickness of intellect or liveliness of fancy, with capacity of apt expression," their elegiac tone ensures that wit shall be somewhat more solemn sad, expressing thoughtful wisdom and good judgment. These poems find Carew neither justifying universal harmonies nor bringing decorum to the bar of change, but seeking rules to live by in a dangerous world; anticipating, in effect, the view of Henry Thoreau (who admired Carew's art): "Say what you have to say, not what you ought. Any truth is better than make-believe."[40]

**"A Rapture"** appears to have been composed about 1624. By that time, the emphasis of English poems informed by the "carpe diem" theme had altered from that of such pieces composed in Spenser's day. The "lovely lay" chanted in Acrasia's bower (*FQ*, II.xii.74-75) may serve to epitomize the older tradition of this genre: the singer advocates an enjoyment of love while youth and beauty are at the full, since time must at length destroy all that. One seizes the day, therefore, with a certain poignancy of mood. Among seventeenth-century poems, Herrick's "Corinna's going a Maying" and "To the Virgins, to make much of Time" continue this tradition, together with such relatively minor efforts as "Cupids Call," by James Shirley, or Waller's "Goe lovely Rose," not to mention Carew's own **"Perswasions to enjoy."** But the genre also developed in quite another way, one that (curiously enough) emphasizes precisely those elements in the title of Carew's lyric: persuasion, enjoyment. Examples include "Upon Love fondly refus'd for Conscience sake," by Thomas Randolph; Shirley's "Love for Enjoying"; and William Cartwright's "Beauty and Deniall." Poems of this kind seem to have three characteristics. Looking not to Spenser but to Marlowe's *Hero and Leander,* especially to the rhetorical brilliance of Leander's persuasive analogies, the authors who adopt this approach are primarily concerned, it seems, to parade their wit, chiefly by the play of intellectualized analogy. Again, while the end of all (in the context of a given poem) is certainly sexual pleasure, the speaker's posture is one of cool sophistication; explicitly sexual allusions are either absent or (as in the poems by Shirley and Cartwright) reserved until the very end. Finally, the dimensions of the lovers' world have perceptibly narrowed from those that obtain in poems attuned to the Spenserian mode. Time threatens, no doubt; but that matters less than the collocation of natural examples to justify the lover's urgent need for his lady's favors. If Elizabethan poems in this kind are apt to place the lovers within a larger time-span than their own, the emphasis in Jacobean and Caroline examples of the genre falls rather on the immediacy of present desire. If the one charms by way of its meditative and thoughtful cast, the other relies on quick wit and dramatic surprise to arrest attention. By the time of Charles I's accession, in fact, an established decorum of style and kind in this regard has very generally given place to decorous standards of another sort.

The originality of **"A Rapture"** consists primarily in the fact that, while it reflects in some degree the features of each position, it exemplifies neither one.[41] Intellectually witty (and not at all poignant or wistful) in the fashion congenial to so many of Carew's contemporaries, the poem quickly launches into a frank exposition of sexual pleasure; coy hints and arch reserve have no place in this boldly explicit account of love-play. Supportive analogies are not drawn simply from the realm of external nature, but from the most familiar instances of love's power in classical and Renaissance song and story; yet the force of these analogies depends in each case on the poet's impudent reversal of orthodox tradition. What gives the poem its special mark (even beyond the splendid shock of its sensuality) is the pattern of thought, developed throughout in terms of man's faculties and, finally, of moral values. To examine the structure of the poem is to perceive that **"A Rapture"** is a witty discourse about the proper uses of time, directed to a society that has lost its sense of moral equilibrium.

The poem is clearly divided into four parts. Opening in the present, it turns at line 21 to an elaborate account of the delights awaiting these lovers. With line 115, the speaker, turning to the past, undertakes to re-interpret various legends of constancy. At line 147, finally, the poem returns to the present, emphasizing now the larger issues implicit in the encounter of this lover, this lady. Against the panoramic backdrop of time future, past, and present, four faculties receive successive emphasis: the will, the sense, imagination, reason.[42] That the will should take first place

is quite in keeping with Carew's purpose: the poem's title in fact anticipates this. The title of Donne's "The Extasie" retroactively achieves witty surprise as the interpenetration of sense and spirit is progressively revealed. The bearing of Carew's title in that regard is soon clear, but it is witty in another way: if a religious is enraptured, this lover undertakes actively to enravish (inviting the lady to respond kindly, to be sure). That initial emphasis echoes in the assertive confidence of the opening, "I will enjoy thee now my *Celia*," and especially in the injunction to "be bold, and wise," which effectively informs the poem as a whole.[43] The prime function of these first twenty lines is to sound a call to action, here and now, in the light of a distinction between truth and falsehood. Since honor is "not as we once thought / The seed of Gods," a traditional dichotomy of pure spirit and corrupt nature will not serve. Instead, man's natural courage, the instrument of his will in his fallen state: timidity, greed, and the demon holdfast. To these the "Gyant, Honour, that . . . is but forme, and onely frights in show," owes its borrowed being; one is therefore wise to be bold, challenge the "stalking Pageant," and emancipate the natural man.

Will having made a way, it is the senses' turn. Again, boldness is true wisdom. To explore, in love, the full potential of every sense is to perceive their power to instruct fancy (l. 42), allow the soul a share in pleasure quite beyond its proper reach (42-44), and at length call down from "those powers / That blesse our loves" a condition of "Halcion calmenesse" that will "fix our soules / In steadfast peace, as no affright controules" (95-98). Further, "the Queene of Love" who presides over these ceremonies counts in her train both "Innocence . . . and Nature." Concealment, deceit, hypocrisy are banished; absolute candor holds sway in this realm, where

> All things are lawfull . . . that may delight
> Nature or unrestrained Appetite;
> Like, and enjoy, to will, and act, is one,
> We only sinne when Loves rites are not done.

Again, therefore, to be bold is at once to realize the full range of sense's potential, and to sweep away those tired forms that bind and limit men and women.[44]

The imagination is by its nature free; yet Carew very well understands that the artist's imagination, blending myth and history in persuasive poetry, exerts in despite of time a singular power over the imaginations of other men. That fancy may resume its naturally active role, a boldly creative stroke is required: nothing less than a fresh reading of traditional story. Some slight authority exists, of course, for a Penelope that "doth . . . display / Her selfe before the Youth of Ithaca."[45] But Carew, consistently with his practice throughout the poem, breaks away from authoritative tradition in two ways. The gods who balked Apollo's pursuit of Daphne were not kind but "angry"; implicitly, then, perhaps not gods at all. Certainly they fix and fetter men: by contrast, "artfull postures, such as be / Carv'd on the barks of every neighbouring tree / By learned hands," instruct and encourage fullness of being. Nature and art, that is to say, combine that men and women may be in every way "enlarg'd." More than this: if mankind might ordinarily be thought to accumulate wisdom by gradual progression, in the course of time's passage, the expertise of Carew's Lucrece, matched as it is with that of Renaissance artist and Greek courtesan, reminds a reader that the vital energies of nature need not await the slow labors of men in their generations, but in every era may be tapped, known, and rifled by those who have nerve enough to thrust past ancient authority. By the boldly imaginative revaluation of past record, long-hidden wisdom may be revealed.

After all this excitement, the concluding section of **"A Rapture"** may seem to be something of an anticlimax; but these final twenty lines complete the poem's pattern in more than one sense. Returning to the present and to the matter at hand, the speaker reaffirms his initial determination, the more confidently now for having presented the case with such persuasive eloquence. Yet these last lines assign an equal emphasis to the principles implicit in this meeting: the passage, in fact, identifies those larger values (beyond the lovers' immediate satisfaction) for which men and women are to be made free. This final section provides the poem with its real point.

Carew began with an arrogant expression of male dominance: "I will enjoy thee now my *Celia*." But as the poem turns to its conclusion, that language is modulated: "Come then my *Celia,* wee'le no more forbeare / To taste our joyes. . . ." In the light of that gentle allusion to "your soft sex" (held fast in fetters), and especially of the question that brings the poem to a close, one may think that if Carew is not quite proposing absolute equality of the sexes, he is at the least advocating a considerably increased degree of mutual responsiveness and regard; certainly also a candid recognition, and reappraisal, of male and female roles in social converse. It appears, further, that men and women ought to keep the "lawes" of "humane Justice, and . . . sacred right." Given Carew's persistent appeal to "Nature" throughout the poem, coupled with his repudiation of "th'angry Gods" and of codes that claim an authority more than natural, the allusion to "sacred right" may appear disingenuous. But the demand that concludes the poem throws light on this matter. To paraphrase these lines: by serving the monstrous idol called "Honour" (which supplants true justice by its wild parody, revenge, and the duellers' code, condemned by the church), men effectively turn atheistical; by the same token, why should not women (whose desire for gain or power matches and urges on male lust, thus permitting revenge to thrive) be recognized equally for the whores they are? Strict logic governs one possible response to the cruelly cynical wit of this poser: men *are* atheists, women whores. It follows then that theirs can be only a brutish equality, and that "humane Justice" or "sacred right," in the context of Carew's courtly society, must be meaningless. But the carefully developed structure of the poem invites another response, one that is surely Carew's own. To repudiate

"Goblin Honour," together with its logical cage of custom that confines those who adore the giant, is to free human reason. And that in turn is to enable the new-building of a just and equal society, where human rights are in fact as sacred as old religion thought its idols were. In that society, men and women are neither atheists nor whores: they are free to be themselves.[46]

**"A Rapture,"** then, in some sense provides a model for those later occasional poems in which Carew typically thrusts past formal decorum, employing a relatively plain idiom for the serious effort to challenge change. These pieces have wit enough, but to be witty is not now the poet's special care. To speak of his "philosophy" is to fly too high; still, in these compositions it appears that his chief concern is the identification of an enduring system of values that need not collapse in course of time. These poems really call for a separate essay, which would deal with their formal art in the context of Carew's troubled career, not forgetting Clarendon's statement that the poet "died with the greatest Remorse for that License [of earlier years], and with the greatest Manifestation of Christianity that his best Friends could desire."[47] Given their various occasions and genres, one can at the least say that these pieces consistently disappoint expectation. While the elegiac lines "On the Duke of Buckingham," for instance, manage to combine praise, lament, and consolation, and to bring all to a gracefully witty conclusion, the companion piece, "An other," is very different. The extended passage of praise that makes up the greater part of this poem depends on a wistfully conditional fancy ("If Fate / Could constant happinesse create"); noting that the stars, for good or ill, govern our conditions, Carew gloomily concludes that universal justice and the happiness even of one individual are, by nature's law, denied to mankind. The first poem is decorously elegiac; the other, in spite of that encomiastic catalogue, permits sorrow to burst its formal bonds and reach on to desperate conclusions that would effectively cancel the idea itself of elegy.

**"Obsequies to the Lady Anne Hay"** illustrates the point in another way. Three-fifths of the poem is given over to disavowals by Carew of his competence to undertake this task, and to repudiation of the usual patterns to which the poem might conform; he notices too, with a touch of impatience, that time, by cutting short the lady's life, has rendered the elegist's assignment especially difficult. When the poet does at length turn directly to his object, he is clearly less interested in praising her beauty or virtue than in developing an aptly paradoxical fancy. If "sleeke / And polisht" courtiers can weep "reall teares," and grief can unite "all the Courtly throng," no ordinary elegiac convention will answer: a trial by her envious rivals must confirm this lady's quality. The poet's wit, brushing frankly past established conventions of style and kind, is freshly decorous for the occasion and his time. This is not quite to say that its unexpectedness is calculated to surprise and delight; rather it expresses the full irony of the fact that, to disturb the complacency of enamelled sophisticates, and stir their hearts, virtue must needs die.

As for the lines to Sandys, their occasion would seem to have called for some considered praise of his friend's art as translator, an acknowledgement that *A Paraphrase upon the Divine Poems* everywhere bears witness to God's directive inspiration, and (perhaps) a gracefully turned reminder that God employs the several talents of men for His divine ends. In short, complimentary verses in this kind might be expected to dwell on Sandys' art and its place in a divine scheme of things. But Carew breaks away from these familiar patterns, chiefly in that the poem becomes a vehicle for the expression of his own uncertainties, doubts, fears. It is true that he briefly pays court (ll. 29-32) to the exemplary power of Sandys' art; but these expressions of conventional piety are relatively unconvincing, for unease, apprehension, wanhope even, inform the poem's mood, and speak through its conditional verbs. Most striking in this regard is that allusion to "the dry leavelesse Trunke on *Golgotha.*" It is, at the least, a singularly unapt figure in this context, one that all but obscures the bright promise of new dedication. One recalls Shakespeare's Claudius, kneeling hopelessly before a shrine that holds no absolving promise for him. Carew has turned the genre (and its decorum) inside out: the poem is by no means a formal and witty acknowledgement of Sandys' inspired art, but a realistic and plain-spoken, yet strangely diffident, confession of his own natural inadequacies.

This essay has been concerned to enlarge the dimensions of the critical context within which Carew's wit is ordinarily taken under consideration. A good many lyrics in the canon have perforce been passed over; yet those singled out for comment include the most significantly representative of Carew's poems. On the evidence they provide, the critic who would take the true measure of this poet's accomplishment must recognize that Carew's witty manner (through its full range of modes) consistently reflects a determination to explore and chart the effects of "times trans-shifting" on the character of those decorous considerations that govern social converse as well as the poet's art.

*Notes*

1. *The Life of Edward Earl of Clarendon,* 2 vols. (Oxford, 1760), I, 28.

2. *Poems of Thomas Carew,* ed. Rhodes Dunlap (Oxford, 1949), liv-lv.

3. *Seventeenth Century Poetry: The Schools of Donne and Jonson,* ed. Hugh Kenner (New York, 1964), p. 332; Robin Skelton, *The Cavalier Poets* (London, 1960), p. 23.

4. F. R. Leavis, *Revaluation: Tradition and Development in English Poetry* (London, 1962), pp. 21, 19.

5. G. A. E. Parfitt, "The Poetry of Thomas Carew," *Renaissance and Modern Studies,* 12 (1968), 56-67.

6. Earl Miner, *The Cavalier Mode from Jonson to Cotton* (Princeton, N. J., 1971), p. 12. Cf. also Hugh Richmond, *The School of Love: The Evolution of the Stuart Love Lyric* (Princeton, N. J., 1964), pp. 217, 301.

7. *Poems of Thomas Carew,* p. 236.

8. *Poems of Thomas Carew,* pp. 239-240.

9. Parfitt, p. 57.

10. Rosemond Tuve, *Elizabethan and Metaphysical Imagery* (Chicago, 1961), p. 192.

11. George Puttenham, *The Arte of English Poesie,* in *Elizabethan Critical Essays,* ed. G. G. Smith, 2 vols. (London, 1904), II, 175, 181.

12. *Ben Jonson,* ed. C. H. Herford, Percy and Evelyn Simpson, 11 vols. (Oxford, 1925-1952), VIII, 625, 633.

13. *Underwood,* LXIX. Cf. also *Underwood,* XVII, XXVI, XXXVII; and Geoffrey Walton, "The Tone of Ben Jonson's Poetry," in *Seventeenth Century English Poetry: Modern Essays in Criticsim,* ed. W. R. Keast, 2nd edition (New York, 1971), pp. 152-173.

14. E. B. Partridge, *The Broken Compass: A Study of the Major Comedies of Ben Jonson* (London, 1958), p. 171. Cf. H. S. Wilson, "Some Meanings of 'Nature' in Renaissance Literary Theory," *JHI,* 2 (1941), 430-448.

15. *Underwood,* XIV.

16. One might argue that, as Thomas Kranidas asserts of Milton, Jonson's concept of decorum is also "in its highest sense an ideal of unity. . . . at once the tool and ideal for adjusting proportions, relationships, colors to achieve a radiant whole" (*The Fierce Equation: A Study of Milton's Decorum* [The Hague, 1965], p. 48).

17. Bruce King, "The Strategy of Carew's Wit," *REL,* 5 (1964), 42-51.

18. Catullus, viii, 12-19; Propertius, II, iii, 25.

19. Joseph Haslewood thought the last stanza "not of the same highly poetic turn" with the first two (*Poems of Thomas Carew,* p. 222). But the form and tone of these lines certainly suggest deliberate calculation on Carew's part.

20. The term in this context seems to have the primary force of *OED* 11b: "Cunning management or contrivance; underhand dealing, juggling, sleight of hand."

21. Although Dunlap cites Propertius, II, xi, for its anticipation of Carew's theme, the austere and rueful irony of the Latin ode has not much in common with the threatening tone of the English poem, nor with the brusque impatience informing its conclusion.

22. Cf. also the discussion of "Disdaine returned," and of "Ingratefull beauty threatned," by Hugh Richmond, pp. 205-207.

23. For instance, "An Hymeneall Song on the Nuptials of the Lady Ann Wentworth, and the Lord Lovelace," "On the Mariage of T. K. and C. C., the morning stormie," and "A married Woman," thematically linked by the topic of marriage, are sharply distinguished by virtue of Carew's stance in each poem.

24. Edward Selig, *The Flourishing Wreath: A Study of Thomas Carew's Poetry* (New Haven, Conn., 1958), 150-160.

25. Selig, pp. 150, 160.

26. Selig, p. 156.

27. *Ben Jonson,* VIII, 637-639.

28. Cf. Hugh Maclean, "Ben Jonson's Poems: Notes on the Ordered Society," in *Essays in English Literature from the Renaissance to the Victorian Age,* ed. Millar MacLure and F. W. Watt (Toronto, 1964), 46-51.

29. Cf. *Ben Jonson,* VIII, 567.

30. Joseph Summers, *The Muse's Method* (Cambridge, Mass., 1962), p. 21.

31. In this connection, "To the Reader of Master William Davenant's Play" may usefully be contrasted with "To my worthy Friend, M. D'avenant, Upon his Excellent Play, the Just Italian." The first of these occasional pieces, which appeals to a traditional, even elite, standard of wit, falls clearly in the first of those categories outlined above; the other (and earlier) poem in some measure anticipates the very different standpoint of the elegy on Donne.

32. J. W. Draper, *The Funeral Elegy and the Rise of English Romanticism* (New York, 1929), p. 35. Cf. also Louis Martz, *The Wit of Love: Donne, Carew, Crashaw, Marvell* (Notre Dame, Indiana, 1969), pp. 97-100, esp. p. 97: "If we grasp the poem we grasp Donne."

33. O. B. Hardison, *The Enduring Monument: A Study of the Idea of Praise in Renaissance Literary Theory and Practice* (Chapel Hill, N. C., 1962), p. 114.

34. Hardison, p. 22.

35. Hardison, p. 114.

36. Hardison, p. 114. Cf. Thomas Wilson, *The Arte of Rhetorique,* ed. R. H. Bowers (Gainesville, Fla., 1962), pp. 83-105.

37. *Ben Jonson,* I, 138, 135.

38. Cf. Puttenham, *Arte,* II, 58-59: "an inscription such as a man may commodiously write or engrave upon a tombe in few verses, pithie, quicke, and sententious."

39. Carew's handling of the formal epitaph is relevant in this regard. The first and third of those on Lady Mary Villiers, classically chiselled and restrained, demonstrate his mastery of the Jonsonian manner, but the complex figure that informs the second ("The purest soule that e're was sent") indicates some concern to enliven the mode. As for the epitaph on Maria Wentworth, the witty first, second, and sixth stanzas contrast very curiously with the weary catalogues that make up the rest of the poem. This epitaph might well stand as an ironic parody of the genre.

40. H. D. Thoreau, *Walden* (New York, 1950), p. 292. Cf. *The Journal of Henry David Thoreau,* ed. B. Torrey and F. H. Alden, 2 vols. (New York, 1962), I, 134.

41. That particular lines and expressions reflect the influence of Donne, and that the denunciation of Honour recalls a passage in Tasso's *Aminta* (I. 656-723), may readily be granted (*Poems of Thomas Carew,* 237-239). What is at issue here is Carew's combining of variegated elements to make a poem quite his own.

42. Memory is subsumed and effectively re-cast by the creative power of the imagination: cf. lines 115-146.

43. While one cannot be sure that Carew means to recall Spenser's Britomart, adjured to "*Be bold, be bold . . . Be bold . . . / Be not too bold*" (*FQ,* III.xi.54), the relish of a traditional wisdom that tempers boldness with caution (not to mention the contrast of virginal Britomart with pliable Celia) is quite apt in the world of "A Rapture," where for all practical purposes boldness *is* wisdom.

44. For a perceptive commentary on this section of the poem, cf. Miner, pp. 80-82.

45. Cf. Pausanias, *Description of Greece,* VIII.xii.

46. This article was accepted for publication before the appearance of "Carew's 'A Rapture': The Dynamics of Fantasy," by Paula Johnson (*SEL,* 16 [1976], 145-155). While we are generally in agreement that the poet's use of shifting tenses is significant (and also with Ms. Johnson's remark that, "like all good erotica," the poem is "fun"), our reading of the poem differs from hers chiefly on three counts. "A Rapture" is not, after all, about any kind of real Celia but rather about the evolution of the poet's attitude. In earlier stages of the poem Celia may well be "the most completely passive female in erotic literature" (Johnson, p. 149), but by the end, when the poet has broken through into a redefinition of social customs and values, he responds to her in different terms: she is no longer an object but a partner. Secondly, the dominantly directive role of the will in lines 1-20 effectively undercuts Ms. Johnson's view of the poem as "the wish-fulfilling dream of an adolescent, graceful, charming, and utterly self-absorbed" (p. 151). Finally, her statement that the concluding analogy could work only if one found "a term for unchaste women that would carry positive overtones" (p. 155) is puzzling; there is, after all, no such *term* provided for a man either.

The analogy works precisely because "whores" balances "atheists." Far from relapsing into conventional morality, then, the concluding terminology suggests the inadequacy of that morality and hints at an option. The very crudity of the word "whore" in this context signals the inadequacy of the moral assumptions implied by that term.

47. Clarendon, *Life,* I, 36.

## Michael P. Parker (essay date 1982)

SOURCE: "'To my friend G. N. from Wrest': Carew's Secular Masque," in *Classic and Cavalier: Essays on Jonson and the Sons of Ben*, University of Pittsburgh Press, 1982, pp. 171-91.

[*In the following essay, Parker analyzes Carew's "To my friend G. N. from Wrest," maintaining that the poem "represents the crucial middle term between Jonson's initial essays in the English country-house poem and Marvell's transformation of the genre in the 1640s and 1650s."*]

Despite the upsurge of interest in the English country-house poem during the past twenty-five years, critics have largely ignored Thomas Carew's two contributions to the genre, **"To Saxham"** and **"To my friend G. N. from Wrest"**. The neglect of **"To Saxham"** is attributable in part to Carew's patterning of his poem on "To Penshurst"; despite its occasionally ingenious conceits and felicitous phrasing, we might argue that **"To Saxham"** can be dismissed as no more than a good imitation of a Jonsonian original. But the poem to G. N. from Wrest is a different piece altogether. Composed in late 1639 or early 1640, Carew's poem diverges consciously from the Jonsonian model.[1] For Jonson, Penshurst not only mirrors the larger social and moral hierarchy but is an integral part of that hierarchy: the incident of King James's impromptu visit to the Sidney estate establishes that duty to sovereign, duty to dependents, and duty to self are complementary and inseparable. In **"To G. N. from Wrest"**, however, Carew abandons the Jonsonian ideal of the ordered cosmos. The primary attraction of Wrest is its isolation from the macrocosm: the sovereign has come to represent a threat to the ideals of the country house, rather than their fulfillment. Employing techniques borrowed from the court masque, Carew invests the congenial company gathered at Wrest Park with the mythology traditionally reserved for the monarch and his immediate circle. In a number of respects, **"To G. N. from Wrest"** foreshadows the treatment and themes of "Upon Appleton House." Carew's piece represents the crucial middle term between Jonson's initial essays in the English country-house poem and Marvell's transformation of the genre in the 1640s and 1650s.

To appreciate Carew's poem, it is necessary to have some knowledge of Wrest Park, its proprietor, and his circle of friends. Unfortunately, a scholarly blunder in the early twentieth century has until now impeded such investigation. In the detailed history of Wrest Park in *The Victoria History of the County of Bedfordshire,* M. R. Manfield remarks that the manor and the title of earl of Kent passed to Anthony de Grey, an aged and obscure Leicestershire clergyman, on the death of his cousin Henry in 1631.[2] In fact, Henry de Grey did not die until the close of 1639, and it is undoubtedly during the residence of Henry and his fascinating countess, Elizabeth Talbot, that Carew visited Wrest.[3] Rhodes Dunlap, editor of the standard edition of Carew's poetry, perpetuates the error of the *Victoria History;* only the general excellence of his commentary appears to have prevented subsequent editors and critics from rectifying his mistake.[4] The error is of significance, however, since it deterred Dunlap from pursuing the clues to the remarkable cultural life that flourished at Wrest Park during the 1630s.

Wrest Park had been in the possession of his family for almost three hundred and fifty years when Henry de Grey, eighth earl of Kent, succeeded to the title in 1623.[5] The family fortunes, ailing for over a century, greatly improved with Kent's marriage in 1601 to Elizabeth Talbot, granddaughter of the redoubtable Bess of Hardwick and, with her two sisters, coheiress to the vast Shrewsbury land holdings. The de Greys were in constant attendance at court during the reign of James I, maintaining a house in Whitefriars; in 1617 Lady Kent succeeded the countess of Roxborough as chief lady-in-waiting to Queen Anne. With the accession of Charles I, however, the earl and countess appear to have lost what influence they commanded at court. In 1627 Kent resisted the king's attempt to extract a forced loan from the nation; as one of the so-called Refusers, he was stripped of the lord-lieutenancy of Bedfordshire, a position he had held since 1621.[6] Although the earl regained his office by December 1629 and occasionally thereafter attended important court ceremonies—the baptism of the duke of York in 1633 and the Garter installation the following year—from the late 1620s, he and his wife retired more or less permanently to Wrest Park.

Retirement from London, however, did not entail abandoning all courtly pleasures: Wrest became the gathering place for many of the most brilliant men and women of the Caroline period. From 1628, the jurist John Selden was a constant house guest of the de Greys and may have acted as legal adviser to the family.[7] The relationship between Selden and his hosts was intimate, to say the least. John Aubrey reports that the "Countesse, being an ingeniose woman and loving men, would let him [Selden] lye with her, and her husband knew it. After the Earle's death he maried her. . . . I remember my Sadler (who wrought many years to that Family) told me that Mr. Selden had got more by his Prick than he had done by his practise."[8] Although Selden's biographers have traditionally discounted Aubrey's steamy relation (on what ground is unclear), the jurist's contemporaries wrote of the connection in a vein that corroborates the account in *Brief Lives.* In an anonymous parliamentary satire of the 1640s (Osborn MS. PB VII/30 in the Beinecke Library at Yale University), the royalist author snipes at "Grave M^r Selden, who doth now repent / He ever searcht y^e Antiquities of Kent." Both Selden and the countess, it should be noted, were in their sixties at the time the satire was written. Selden was not the only writer to find the company at Wrest Park congenial. Samuel Butler served as a page in the countess's household sometime during the late twenties or early thirties; there, Aubrey reports, Butler "employed his time much in painting and drawing, and also in Musique," and may have met the miniaturist Samuel Cooper under the countess's auspices.[9] Sir John Suckling also appears to have known the de Greys well. In a 1639 letter to Selden, he inquires after the countess's health and remarks the esteem he holds for her "conversation."[10]

The company of poets and wits apparently whetted Lady Kent's literary aspirations, although her own efforts were on a more modest scale. She was the authoress of *A Choice Manuall of Rare and Select Secrets in Physick and Chyrurgery,* which went through nineteen seventeenth-century editions, and of *A True Gentlewoman's Delight, wherein is contained all manner of Cookery,* a collection of recipes perhaps got up with the aid of the French-trained cook she had inherited from Lord Montague.[11] Although the society at Wrest had a strong literary coloring, life there does not seem to have been so learned as to exclude all else. In a letter from Wrest dated January 21, 1638/39, Madam Ann Merrick writes her friend Mrs. Lydall to discuss the latest plays, to ask what cut of sleeve is currently in vogue at court, and to lament the impending Scottish campaign, "lest all the young gallants should go for soldiers, and the ladies should want servants to accompany them."[12] The evidence, though slim, suggests that the family and guests at Wrest Park pursued a lively round of cultural activities. Such a surmise is supported by the countess's family ties to the two most important aristocratic patrons of art and literature in early seventeenth-century England: one of her two sisters married William Herbert, third earl of Pembroke, the other Thomas Howard, second earl of Arundel. The de Greys' not altogether friendly relations with their wealthy brothers-in-law may, in fact, have spurred the countess to literary hobnobbing. Financially unable to compete with Arundel and Pembroke in reedifying country seats or acquiring choice objects d'art, the earl and countess contented themselves with cultivating the friendship of the choice wits of the age.

The most prominent literary figure associated with Wrest Park, however, is Thomas Carew. **"To my friend G. N. from Wrest"**, probably his last poem, is also one of his best. Although Carew again employs many of the country-house topoi that he used in **"To Saxham,"** he organizes them according to an utterly different structural principle borrowed from the court masque. Stephen Orgel describes how, in Jonson's hands, the masque "separated into two sections. The first, called the antimasque, . . . presented a world of disorder or vice, everything that the ideal world of the second, the courtly main masque, was to overcome and supersede."[13] The physical structure of the Jacobean and Caroline stage underlined the cosmic implications of

the conflict: by means of machinery, the antimasque figures were customarily banished to "hell," the space beneath the stage, when the deities of the main masque descended from the "heavens" above it. The shift from order to disorder was conveyed not only through the dramatic action but through the use of "scenes"—architectural and landscape tableaux painted on curtains or shutters. In **"To G. N. from Wrest,"** Carew translates the vertical geography of the masque into a horizontal frame. The three regions of the stage—"heavens," stage proper, and "hell"—are echoed in the poem by the three regions of the hall, the garden, and the world outside the estate, respectively. As in the masque, the drama stems from the poet's efforts to unite the first two regions as he separates them from the third. Carew integrates hall and garden by dissolving the architectural frame of the house; he divides the unified estate from the disorder of the external world by elevating another barrier, the moat, into an encompassing zodiac. Wrest, "i' th' center plac'd," becomes a world in its own right.

Carew's structural innovation is illuminated by a comparison with "To Penshurst." Jonson presents the Sidney estate in terms of the natural and social hierarchy: he begins with the four elements, works his way up the scale through beasts and men, and concludes with the king—God's anointed—and God himself. The first half of **"To G. N. from Wrest"** reproduces the Jonsonian structure through geographical movement. The poet proceeds from the world outside the estate through the meadows to the house and its inhabitants. From the hall, however, he retraces his steps through the grounds to the moat; in the final movement, the poet again reverses his path, bringing the tutelary gods of the garden into the house itself through the emblematic marriage of Ceres and Bacchus. This peripatetic progress, which foreshadows the speaker's mental and physical perambulations in "Upon Appleton House," echoes the regular alternation between order and disorder in the tableaux of the court masques. With the poet's "beating of the bounds," Wrest is closed off from the ruder world outside; the daimonic forces of the estate are released, and the gods emerge from the landscape to mingle with men.

While other country-house poems address an estate itself—Penshurst, Saxham, Appleton House—or the estate's owner—Sir Robert Wroth, Sir Lewis Pemberton—Carew writes this poem from inside Wrest to the world outside, to the G. N. (perhaps Gilbert North) of the title. As the poet describes it, that external world is not appealing:

> I Breathe (sweet *Gbib:*) the temperate ayre of *Wrest*
> Where I no more with raging stormes opprest,
> Weare the cold nights out by the bankes of Tweed,
> On the bleake Mountains, where fierce tempests breed,
> And everlasting Winter dwells; where milde
> *Favonius,* and the Vernall windes exilde,
> Did never spread their wings: but the wilde North
> Brings sterill Fearne, Thistles, and Brambles forth.
>
> (1-8)

"Bankes of Tweed" and "the wilde North" undoubtedly allude to the unsuccessful military expedition of 1639, in which Charles I sought to bring the convenanting Scots to heel. In Carew's mention of the hardships of the campaign and the sterility of the landscape, it is difficult to overlook an oblique criticism of the king's imprudent Scottish policy—criticism that the presence of the opposition leader Selden at the de Grey estate would make all the more pointed.[14] The retrospective viewpoint provided by the pleasures of the "temperate ayre" of Wrest renders the horrors of the border country striking. Carew builds up the disparate details of his experience—the "raging stormes," "cold nights," "bleake Mountains," "fierce tempests"—into a fully realized, almost fantastic description of the realm of "everlasting Winter."

The technique is painterly: in fact, Carew's landscape closely resembles the tableau designed by Inigo Jones for the first scene of *Salmacida Spolia,* the last masque of the Caroline period. Performed on January 21, 1639/40, during the month in which Carew may have added final touches to his poem, Davenant's masque opens with

> a horrid scene . . . of storm and tempest; no glimpse of the sun was seen, as if darkness, confusion, and deformity, had possest the world, and driven light to heaven, the trees bending, as forced by a gust of wind, their branches rent from their trunks, and some torn up by the roots: afar off was a dark wrought sea, with rolling billows, breaking against the rocks, with rain, lightning and thunder.[15]

Davenant retains a belief in the power of royal example to tame discord and to put a permanent end to political unrest. In the final song of *Salmacida Spolia,* an address to the monarchs, the chorus proclaims:

> All that are harsh, all that are rude,
> Are by your harmony subdu'd;
> Yet so into obedience wrought,
> As if not forc'd to it, but taught.
>
> (5-8)

In **"To G. N. from Wrest,"** however, Carew abandons this faith in monarchs to seek a solution in a more limited sphere. In *Salmacida Spolia,* the opening landscape of darkness and confusion is dispelled by divine intervention:

> the scene changed into a calm, the sky serene, afar off Zephyrus appeared breathing a gentle gale: in the landskip were corn fields and pleasant trees, sustaining vines fraught with grapes, and in some of the furthest parts villages, with all such things as might express a country in peace, rich, and fruitful. There came breaking out of the heavens a silver chariot, in which sate two persons, the one a woman . . . representing Concord; somewhat below her sate the good Genius of Great Britain. (2. 313)

The change of scene in Carew's poem is no less dramatic: as in the masque, the wintry landscape cedes to a bucolic vision of peace and plenty. But the transformation is effected, not by deus ex machina, but through the poet's physical retreat to a private estate—to "here," at Wrest. The de Greys' country seat contrasts with the bleak northern mountains in every respect—in its warmth, in its light, but especially in its fertility.

Carew's transition, theatrical in its suddenness, departs from the technique of gradual intensification that Jonson employs to distinguish the Sidney home from the surrounding landscape. Whereas Jonson portrays Penshurst as a working estate, replete with farmers, clowns, and grazing stock, Carew describes Wrest in a manner usually reserved for an earthly paradise such as Eden or "Loves Elizium":

> Here steep'd in balmie dew, the pregnant Earth
> Sends from her teeming wombe a flowrie birth,
> And cherish with the warme Suns quickning heate,
> Her porous bosome doth rich odours sweate;
> Whose perfumes through the Ambient ayre diffuse
> Such native Aromatiques, as we use
> No forraigne Gums, nor essence fetcht from farre.
>
> (9-15)

Jonson's "better markes, of soyle, of ayre, / Of wood, of water" (7-8) undergo exuberant expansion; as G. R. Hibbard remarks, Carew depicts Wrest in "terms appropriate to a court beauty."[16] Indeed, the personification inverts the topographical blazon that Carew so often employs in his lyrics: it is not hard to connect the "Arromatick dew" and "Balmy sweat" that the poet celebrates in **"Upon a Mole in Celias bosome"** with the Ovidian luxuriance of the earth at Wrest. Carew's description of the grounds at Wrest, however, is no mere purple patch; the passage provides a neat transition between the opening rejection of the military life in the northern hills and the introduction of the theme of good housekeeping. The portrayal of the estate as a *locus amoenus* intensifies the reader's sense of Wrest's isolation from the bleak external world; insistence on the use of only "native Aromatiques," an echo of the "native sweets" celebrated in **"To Saxham,"** anticipates the themes of economy and self-sufficiency that govern the treatment of the house proper.

The first architect of Wrest, Carew asserts, "built a house for hospitalitie" (24). The audible similarity between "house" and "hospitality" posits a like relation between the concepts the words represent: Wrest indeed seems completely devoted to the "ancient and laudable" tradition of housekeeping that the Stuart monarchs had vainly tried to revive during the first decades of the century.[17] If Carew's account of the earl's openhanded hospitality is accurate, the de Greys were among the last to practice a dying custom; by the 1630s, Lawrence Stone observes, "most noblemen had adopted a more modest manner of rural living."[18] Feasting in the hall at Wrest recalls the similar passage in "To Penshurst," but Carew orchestrates the details very differently. At the Sidney's "liberall boord," all gradations of rank are laid aside; there, no guest comes

but is allow'd to eate,
Withoute his feare, and of thy lords owne meate:
Where the same beere, and bread, and selfe-same wine,
That is his Lordships, shall be also mine.

(61-64)

Jonson's insistence on sharing the "lords owne meate" perhaps glances at the snub administered him by the earl of Salisbury, who once invited him to dine, but seated him at a lower table.[19]

If Jonson's account of the freedom of Penshurst is not merely literary embellishment, Carew's description of the meal at Wrest displays a marked shift in social mores. The guests are carefully segregated by rank, and the poet presents them in descending social order. This hierarchy is subtly underlined by the progression from positive to superlative degree in the adjectives modifying the foods on which the banqueters dine. The tenants, servants, and neighbors, seated at "large Tables," eat "wholesome meates"; the women, household officers, and neighbors of the better sort dine on "daintier cates"; at the summit of the social hierarchy,

Others of better note
Whom wealth, parts, office, or the Heralds coate
Have sever'd from the common, freely sit
At the Lords Table, whose spread sides admit
A large accesse of friends to fill those seates
Of his capacious circle, fill'd with meates
Of choycest rellish, till his Oaken back
Under the load of pil'd-up dishes crack.

(39-46)

The earl's "capacious circle" is the emblem of the convivial society of aristocrats and commoners that Carew celebrates at Wrest. Though hardly democratic, this inner circle does recognize the claims of "wealth" and "parts"; Selden, whose father was of yeoman stock, could never have found entrée at Wrest if it did not. To this small group belong not only the "choycest" viands but the freedom of the estate. The modern reader may blanch at the inequities on which this freedom is based; to Carew, however, the careful distinctions preserved in the hall at Wrest reflect a stable, smoothly functioning society. In a period of increasing social rigidity, the generosity of the de Greys was striking; by the 1630s, housekeeping of this sort was largely a thing of the past.[20] The poetic emphasis is on the sense of fellowship that the communal meal symbolizes. All those linked to the earl by ties of love or duty can be sure of a place at his board.

The readiness of the de Greys to fulfill the responsibilities adhering to their social rank is reflected by the architecture of Wrest Park—or, rather, by the lack of architecture.[21] Carew brackets the central scene of feasting in hall with two passages of negative definition in which the claims of "reall use" balance those of "outward gay Embellishment." The very phrasing of the alternatives forecasts the way the beam will fly: the simple solidity of "reall use" outweighs the polysyllabic fussiness of its opponent. Instead of elaborate but unused fireplaces, Wrest offers "cheereful flames"; in place of "Dorique" and "Corinthian Pillars," the house boasts a "Lord and Lady" who "delight / Rather to be in act, then seeme in sight"; instead of antique statuary, "living men" throng the hall (25-34). In Carew's design, the two passages describing false architecture function as antimasques. In a movement that parallels the climactic dramatic incident of the court masque, the unmasking that reveals the revelers' true identities, the poet calls forth the realities—fire, lord and lady, men—that in other houses remain frozen in architectural disguises. The poet banishes the perverted emblems of hospitality to evoke the spirit of hospitality itself.

Employing negative definition to make his point, Carew draws what seems a forced dichotomy between elaborate architecture and good housekeeping; the one, after all, does not necessarily preclude the other. On a limited income, however, a large expenditure on building could entail retrenchment in other areas of consumption.[22] The de Greys' failure to remodel Wrest may in fact have been due to economic considerations: although the countess's personal fortune augmented it, the earl's income was not large.[23] While G. R. Hibbard reads Carew's rejection of "Dorique" and "Corinthian" pillars as an attack on the neo-Palladian architecture introduced into England by Inigo Jones, more recent research indicates that such an intent is unlikely.[24] Examples of English Palladian architecture were few and far between in 1639; the cultured and widely traveled Carew, moreover, was hardly the man to attack them. It is more likely that the poet has made a virtue of necessity, and that his depreciation of elaborate architecture is an attempt to salve his hosts' vanity rather than an artistic manifesto. That the de Greys' vanity needed salving is, of course, only speculation. Nevertheless, the fact that the earl's two brothers-in-law, the earls of Pembroke and Arundel, were among the few English noblemen engaged during this period in large-scale rebuilding or artistic acquisition suggests that familial rivalry between the countess and her two sisters may have in part determined the course of Carew's poem. Lady Kent had taken legal action against her brothers-in-law in 1630, alleging that they had shortchanged her in the division of the Talbot inheritance; it is unlikely that the bad blood arising from the suit had entirely abated with the 1635 settlement in Lady Kent's favor.[25] Carew's immediate audience among the household at Wrest may have read the attack on Corinthian pillars as a subtle glance at Pembroke's embellishment of Wilton, the reference to a hall thronged with statuary as an allusion to the marbles that lined the main gallery of Arundel House.[26] The de Greys might conceivably have grown incensed at artistic display financed with income they regarded as rightfully theirs. Although the precise identities of Carew's satiric targets have been lost with time, the moral point of his satire remains clear. The poet praises the decision *not* to build, and the old-fashioned homeliness of Wrest becomes, paradoxically, a negative monument to the owner's virtue.

Aesthetic considerations, however, are as influential as personal concerns in determining Carew's poetic procedure. Negative definition is a complex strategy. By describing architectural embellishment in detail—"carved marble," "sumptuous" mantels, pillars, statues, "Piramides," and "Exalted Turrets"—the poet captures the devices of the enemy. Each detail is specifically named, each excoriated in turn: the itemized list functions as ritual exorcism in which the poet expels every lurking expectation from the reader's mind. But the device functions in the opposite way as well. Most readers would be surprised to learn that Carew gives no description at all of the house at Wrest; in remembrance, the proscribed details of the "prouder Piles" fuse with the description of the festivities in the hall to create a much grander vision of Wrest than reality would warrant. By evoking, then dismissing, these visually striking forms of misdirected architecture, Carew effectively dissolves the boundaries between the house and the garden that surrounds it. The spirit of good fellowship flows out from the hall to embrace the estate; the gods of grove and field enter into the moral economy that centers on the lord and his guests. The house as a self-contained architectural fabric disappears, unimportant to the larger structure.

The entry into the garden is marked by another series of negative definitions. In a passage that balances the exorcism of the pillars, mantels, and statuary, Carew dismisses fashionable garden ornaments of the type that Pembroke recently installed at Wilton.[27] The de Greys' estate boasts no "Effigie" of Amalthea's horn, no stone statue of Ceres, and no "Marble Tunne" carved with the figure of Bacchus, since

> We offer not in Emblemes to the eyes,
> But to the taste those usefull Deities.
> Wee presse the juycie God, and quaffe his blood,
> And grinde the Yeallow Goddesse into food.
>
> (65-68)

Again, the rhetorical device produces a double effect. The detailed visual imagery evokes the deities in concrete form; transcending that form is the appeal to another sense to confirm the reality of the experience. The high-spirited sacramental parody, which recalls the transformation of gore into wine in Carew's verses welcoming the king to Saxham, insists on the real presence of the gods at Wrest. Carew quite literally presses the pagan deities into the service of the rites of hospitality: nature and the gods who rule it impart their conjoined power to the human inhabitants of the estate through the communal meal.

In the passages of the poem that deal with the house and housekeeping, Carew denounces art which separates man from nature. Within their estate, the de Greys achieve a perfect integration of the natural and human worlds; no art interferes with the process. But the statement is deceptive in its simplicity. The housekeeping of the de Greys evinces more skill than any amount of architectural embellishment. In subordinating display to use, they practice an art

that caters to all the senses, rather than to one. In its total effect, their art becomes indistinguishable from nature.

Carew demonstrates the proper application of art in the lively description of the moat surrounding the estate, a passage that provides the second focal point of the poem:

> Yet we decline not, all the worke of Art,
> But where more bounteous Nature beares a part
> And guides her Hand-maid, if she but dispence
> Fit matter, she with care and diligence
> Employes her skill, for where the neighbor sourse
> Powers forth her waters she directs their course,
> And entertaines the flowing streames in deepe
> And spacious channells, where they slowly creepe
> In snakie windings, as the shelving ground
> Leades them in circles, till they twice surround
> This Island Mansion, which i' th' center plac'd,
> Is with a double Crystall heaven embrac'd,
> In which our watery constellations floate,
> Our Fishes, Swans, our Water-man and Boate,
> Envy'd by those above, which wish to slake
> Their starre-burnt limbes, in our refreshing lake,
> But they stick fast nayl'd to the barren Spheare,
> Whilst our encrease in fertile waters here
> Disport, and wander freely where they please
> Within the circuit of our narrow Seas.
>
> (69-88)

The theory that art is the "Hand-maid" of nature is utterly conventional: Carew blazes no critical trails here. The syntax of the sentence, however, redefines the simple distinction that the poet seems to make. Amid the wealth of modifying phrases and clauses, the precise antecedent of the repeated "she" is lost. The confusion is singular in Carew's oeuvre and probably should not be attributed to shoddy craftsmanship. Instead, Carew graphically indicates that at Wrest art and nature have become indistinguishable: their interdependence is so perfect as to transcend the facile rules that still hold in the world outside. The sinuous windings of the sentence, moreover, answer another purpose as well, for they nicely recreate the scene that they describe. "Serpentine" or "snaky" is an epithet commonly applied to the natural movement of streams; in the genre of the country-house poem, one can cite the "serpent river" in "To Sir Robert Wroth" (18), or the "snake" that curls in "wanton harmless folds" through the meads surrounding Appleton House.[28] The "snakie windings" of the river at Wrest, however, are directed by art; they are designed to surround the estate in the circles of the double moat, isolating it completely from the external world. The happy conjunction of epithet and topography assumes emblematic significance: the serpent turning back on itself is a common Renaissance image of eternity or perfection.[29] The poet emphasizes this conquest of time in his characterization of the encircling moat as another "Crystall heaven," replete with its own cast of constellations. The moat both reflects and surpasses the circle of the zodiac. The contrast between "fertile waters" and "barren Spheare," in its return to the polarities introduced in the opening lines of the poem, boldly reaffirms the superiority of Wrest to the larger but bleaker world outside. The re-animated signs of the zodiac, whose procession marks the change of the seasons, mix in lively confusion in the "narrow seas," freeing Wrest from the ordained temporal cycles that regulate less happy climes.

Although William A. McClung views this episode as a "pretty but somewhat purposeless *divertissement*,"[30] the transformation of the moat into a new zodiac signals an important shift for Carew and for the whole genre of the country-house poem. The aquatic free-for-all in the outer "circles" of the moat constitutes a masque of the natural world that complements the human celebration of the "circle" around the earl's table within. The renovation of the zodiac, moreover, forms the basic conceit of Carew's one masque, *Coelum Britannicum;* in **"To G. N. from Wrest,"** the conceit is transferred from the public setting of the court to the private world of an estate. Eternity, the demigod whose appearance concludes *Coelum Britannicum,* no longer extends his protection solely to the court; the mythological regalia that traditionally invest the monarch have found a new and safer home. While the king and court pursue military adventures in the bleak northern hills, Carew strives to preserve the Caroline ideal of peace and plenty that he helped to create in his masque. In attempting to isolate Wrest from the impending political struggle, Carew echoes, on a smaller scale, his advice in the epistle to Aurelian Townshend, given some seven years earlier, that England steer clear of the embroilments of the Thirty Years' War. This separation of the estate from the turmoil outside looks forward to Marvell's celebration of Appleton House as "heaven's center, Nature's lap, / And paradise's only map" (767-68). The "Island Mansion" of Wrest, "i' th' center plac'd," could merit the same description.

By demarcating the boundaries of Wrest, Carew releases the daimonic powers within. The natural forces of fertility and abundance, described in the introduction to the estate, assume vital, anthropomorphic form. In the grove bordering the moat,

> On this side young *Vertumnus* sits, and courts
> His ruddie-cheek'd *Pomona, Zephyre* sports
> On th'other, with lov'd *Flora,* yeelding there
> Sweetes for the smell, sweetes for the palate here.
>
> (93-96)

Carew presents the deities as actually present: no disclaimer, such as Denham's "quick Poetic sight," mediates the vision. The paired couples are mythological emblems of autumn and spring, respectively; in pictorial tradition, Vertumnus and Pomona are crowned with fruits, while Flora, attended by the blossom-garlanded Zephyr, wears a robe embroidered with flowers.[31] In their complementary arrangement, the couples recall the allegorical figures that often flanked the proscenium in Jones's masque designs. For *Salmacida Spolia,* Jones created a frieze on which were painted, among others, "Commerce, with ears of corn," and "Felicity, with a basket of lilies," figures meant to express the benefits that the masque both celebrates and

aims to effect. Carew's deities play a like role, but they also assume a tutelary function. Zephyr and Flora, Vertumnus and Pomona, are the guardians of Wrest, stationed at the estate's border to mark the gentle extremes of the perpetual summer that reigns within.

The moment of intense vision fades as Carew again turns to his correspondent. But, while the deities are no longer visible, their influence continues to be felt:

> But did you taste the high & mighty drinke
> Which from that Fountaine flowes, you'ld cleerly think
> The God of Wine did his plumpe clusters bring,
> And crush the Falerne grape into our spring;
> Or else disguis'd in watery Robes did swim
> To *Ceres* bed, and make her big of Him,
> Begetting so himselfe on Her: for know
> Our Vintage here in *March* doth nothing owe
> To theirs in Autumne, but our fire boyles here
> As lustie liquour as the Sun makes there.
>
> (97-106)

What begins as a celebration of Wrest's water supply shades, without warning, into a paean to the estate's home-distilled spirits—the "lustie liquour" that "our fire boyles here." The consummation of Ceres and Bacchus crowns the series of fertility images that runs throughout the poem; the fruit of their union, brought forth with the aid of a little mechanical midwifery, is a drink that surpasses the most prized of classical vintages. Again, the activity emphasizes the estate's independence of seasonal time: like the "suns within" of Saxham, the kitchen fires of March at Wrest re-create the mild southern autumn. The blurred geography of the scene—is it set in the garden or in the house cellars?—and the conflation of miracle and technology underscore the integration of the human and natural worlds of the estate into a unified, divinely favored whole.

The secular masque Carew composes for the de Greys culminates in the marriage of Ceres and Bacchus. The marriage also provides a fitting climax to Carew's poetic quest for the "Paradise within" (**"A deposition from Love,"** 8). In Carew's lyrics, the adverb "there" invariably designates an unattained spiritual or physical ideal, "here" the disappointing reality that the poet is compelled to accept.[32] But in this last poem, and only in this last poem, the signification of the two adverbs is reversed: the poet at last achieves the ideal for which he has so long searched "here," on a private estate in Bedfordshire.

A sense of personal fulfillment suffuses the envoi of **"To G. N. from Wrest"**; with pointed brevity, the poet contrasts his own lot with that of his addressee:

> Thus I enjoy my selfe, and taste the fruit
> Of this blest Peace, whilst toyl'd in the pursuit
> Of Bucks, and Stags, th'embleme of warre, you strive
> To keepe the memory of our Armes alive.
>
> (107-10)

The opposition sets the retired against the active life, peace against war. The verbs reinforce the polarity. In contrast to the sensual relaxation of the poet, who can "enjoy" and "taste the fruit" of his hours, G. N. must "strive." The participial modifier, "toyl'd," suggests not only exhaustion but entanglement. G. N. is a prisoner of his own activity; the poem implicitly invites its addressee to relinquish his fruitless pursuits to share the "blest Peace" that, in a matter of three years, would survive only on isolated country estates like Wrest. The image of the chase—"th'embleme of warre"—may well comment on the actual political situation at the time Carew was writing. The Treaty of Berwick, which ended the Scottish campaign, was a makeshift agreement that resolved none of the religious and political questions behind the dispute; sensible observers realized that it was only a matter of time before war erupted again in earnest. In G. N.'s effort "To keepe the memory of our Armes alive," the poet glances both at the recent military failure and the threat of more serious conflict to come. The view of England that Carew sketches in the last lines of the poem is even darker than the stylized bleakness of the opening landscape would lead one to expect.

The magic circle that Carew traces encompassed a select company that did not endure the coming winter. Henry, eighth earl of Kent, died during the night of November 20/21, 1639; Edward Nicholas related on December 12 that the countess "so much laments the death of her husband that Mr. Selden cannot comfort her."[33] Selden and Lady Kent moved permanently to her house in Whitefriars soon after. The title and Wrest Park passed to a distant cousin, Anthony de Grey, the eighty-three-year-old parson of Aston Flamville in Leicestershire. Thomas Smith reported to Sir John Pennington that the new earl "is a minister, and has divers daughters, some married to farmers and some to mercers, who will be much troubled to know how to carry themselves like ladies."[34] The succession of an aged clergyman with Puritan sympathies broke up the cultured circle at Wrest; almost overnight, the estate moved from the golden age to the more practical world of Jane Austen. Thomas Carew did not long outlive the transition, dying in March 1640. In Clarendon's words, "after fifty Years of his Life spent with less Severity or Exactness than it ought to have been, He died with the greatest Remorse for that Licence, and with the greatest Manifestation of Christianity, that his best Friends could desire."[35]

Unlike their illustrious brothers-in-law, the earl and countess of Kent are scarcely remembered today. The de Greys played no crucial role in the politics of the period. They assembled no lasting collections of objects d'art, as did Arundel; they constructed no architectural monument to their glory, as did Pembroke at Wilton. Their chief accomplishment was to gather at Wrest a coterie of writers and intellectuals and to provide a congenial atmosphere in which their protégés could work and unwind—quiet accomplishments no less important for the arts and letters in Caroline England than those of Arundel and Pembroke. Aside from the scattered bits of information given by Aubrey and contemporary correspondence, **"To G. N. from Wrest"** is the only surviving testimony to the de Greys' interests and hospitality. Since those interests were primarily literary and social, Carew's poetic tribute to the conviviality of Wrest is a fitting memorial.

The masquelike elements Carew employs in **"To G. N. from Wrest"** suggest the central position the de Greys and their estate had come to hold in the poet's own system of values. Through their proper ordering of Wrest, the earl and countess re-create, on a limited scale, that golden age when the gods feasted and visited with men. As befits a lord and lady who "delight / Rather to be in act, then seeme in sight" (31-32), the de Greys relinquish the center stage in the poem to the deities—Vertumnus and Pomona, Zephyr and Flora, Ceres and Bacchus—whose presence at Wrest is both the proof and the fruit of the proprietors' virtue. The celebration of peace and plenty, the expulsion of false forms of order, and the use of scenic tableaux and a detailed iconographic program echo *Coelum Britannicum* and the series of Jonsonian masques that preceded it. In **"To G. N. from Wrest,"** however, Carew translates these themes and techniques to a less ambitious, more personal sphere.

The innovations Carew brings to the country-house poem prefigure the transformations the genre would undergo in the hands of Marvell. The comprehensive vision of social harmony that Jonson expresses in "To Penshurst" becomes, in **"To G. N. from Wrest,"** an ideal attainable only by a chosen few; Carew associates the country-house poem with the ideal of rural retirement that became increasingly prominent in English poetry during the 1630s. In "Upon Appleton House," Marvell simultaneously intensifies the significance of this vision and restricts its scope even further. Like Wrest, Appleton House becomes a world complete in itself, detached from outside disorder. Unlike the de Greys, however, the Fairfax family retires for a higher end, and their retreat is only temporary: In the course of time, the young Maria will emerge from the demiparadise and turn the lessons she has learned there to "some universal good" (741). Carew's poem from Wrest lacks this meditative, at moments almost messianic, strain. The speaker of Carew's poem is a gregarious reveler rather than a haunter of meadows and woods; his emphasis falls on the pleasures of society rather than on those of solitude. But, in spite of their differences, the two poems share much—a new emphasis on the role of the poet, the isolation of the estate from a larger hierarchy, the playing with masque conventions—that distinguishes them from "To Penshurst." The line of development seems clear. Carew's retirement on the eve of civil war anticipates the retreat of the Fairfaxes and their poet from the frustrations and disappointments of interregnum politics ten years later. It was on estates such as Wrest and Nun Appleton, removed from the immediate conflicts of midcentury, that the ideals of Charles I's court would bear their last, late fruit.

Granted some latitude in definition, **"To G. N. from Wrest"** might be dubbed Carew's "Secular Masque": "secular" in the sense that it celebrates a private family rather than the public, semidivine persons of the monarchs, and "secular" inasmuch as the poem addresses the question central to so much Cavalier verse—how to escape the ravages of time. Like Dryden's "Secular Masque," Carew's poem constitutes a farewell, in part disillusioned, in the main elegiac, to a court and a culture whose time was past. And as Dryden's verses, presumably the last he wrote, sum so well his entire career, so the poetic and personal concerns of Thomas Carew coalesce in **"To G. N. from Wrest."** Abandoning the court in which he spent so much of his life and the elusive "Celia" on whom he spent so much of his verse, the poet finally discovers what Jonson might call his "center" in a new setting and in a different genre. The "secure repose" and "steadfast peace" for which Carew yearns in lyrics like **"An Eddy"** and **"A Rapture"** are realized at last in the attainment of **"Wrest."**

*Notes*

1. For the dating of the poem, see *The Poems of Thomas Carew with His Masque "Coelum Britannicum,"* ed. Rhodes Dunlap (Oxford: The Clarendon Press, 1949; rpt. 1970), pp. xli-xlii. All citations of Carew's poetry follow Dunlap's edition.

2. "Flitton cum Silsoe," in *The Victoria History of the County of Bedfordshire,* ed. H. Arthur Doubleday and William Page (Westminister: A. Constable, 1904-14), vol. 2, p. 327.

3. G. E. Cokayne, in *The Complete Peerage of England, Scotland, Ireland, Great Britain, and the United Kingdom* (London: St. Catherine, 1910-59), vol. 7, pp. 173-74, and the *Dictionary of National Biography,* hereafter cited as *DNB,* concur in placing Henry's death on November 21, 1639; the former cites his will and two contemporary notices to confirm the date. The burial register of Flitton Parish records the following entry for November 28, 1639: "The right Honorable Lord Henry Grey, Earle of Kent; he died upon Wednesday night beeing the 20th day of November." Reprinted in F. G. Emmison, ed., *Bedfordshire Parish Registers,* (Bedford: County Record Office, 1938), vol. 18, B-65.

4. In view of the earl's death in November 1639, Dunlap's tentative dating of the poem to March 1640 should probably be revised to the summer or autumn of the preceding year.

5. Because two of the sixteenth-century earls of Kent held their title only de jure (the fourth earl of Kent declined the peerage, "by reason of his slender estate"), the numerical sequence of the various earls is hopelessly confused. I follow Cokayne in designating Henry de Grey, who held the title from 1623 to 1639, the eighth earl.

6. Thomas Birch, ed., *The Court and Times of Charles I* (London: Henry Colburn, 1848), vol. 1, p. 241; letter of June 15, 1627, to the Reverend Joseph Mead. A number of peers who refused to help

collect the loan were removed from local office; see Conrad Russell, *Parliaments and English Politics, 1621-29* (Oxford: The Clarendon Press, 1979), pp. 332-33.

7. "John Selden," *DNB,* vol. 17, pp. 1150-62.

8. *Brief Lives,* ed. Oliver Lawson Dick (London: Secker and Warburg, 1949; rpt. 1950), p. 271.

9. Ibid., p. 45. Although Aubrey's notes are ambiguous concerning Butler's meeting with Cooper, Edmund Gosse believes that it came through the countess ("Samuel Butler," *DNB,* vol. 3, p. 526).

10. The letter is reprinted in *The Works of Sir John Suckling: The Non-Dramatic Works,* ed. Thomas Clayton (Oxford: The Clarendon Press, 1971), pp. 150-51.

11. "Elizabeth de Grey," *DNB,* vol. 8, pp. 624-25; Lawrence Stone, *The Crisis of the Aristocracy, 1558-1641* (Oxford: The Clarendon Press, 1965), p. 560.

12. *Calendar of State Papers Domestic, 1638-1639,* p. 342; hereafter cited as *CSPD.*

13. *The Illusion of Power: Political Theater in the English Renaissance* (Berkeley and Los Angeles: University of California Press, 1975), p. 40.

14. The earl himself paid a fine rather than accompany the king on the expedition, although the cause may have been ill health rather than opposition to royal policy (*CSPD, 1638-1639,* pp. 621-22).

15. *The Dramatic Works of Sir William D'Avenant,* ed. James Maidment and W. H. Logan (Edinburgh: William Paterson, 1872-74), vol. 2, p. 312. Subsequent references to Davenant's works are given parenthetically in the text.

16. "The Country House Poem of the Seventeenth Century," *Journal of the Warburg and Courtauld Institutes* 19 (1956), 167.

17. Between 1614 and 1627, the government issued no fewer than nine proclamations ordering gentlemen in London to return to their country estates to "keepe hospitality." That eight of the nine proclamations were issued in the months immediately preceding Christmas suggests royal authorites' concern not only to remind the gentry to attend to their Hilary Term responsibilities but to head off a crush at the court's annual Christmas festivities. The texts of the proclamations are reprinted in R. R. Steele, ed., *A Bibliography of Royal Proclamations of Tudor and Stuart Sovereigns and of Others Published Under Authority, 1485-1714,* in *Biblioteca Lindesiana* (Oxford: The Clarendon Press, 1910), vol. 5.

18. *The Crisis of the Aristocracy,* p. 187.

19. William A. McClung, *The Country House in English Renaissance Poetry* (Berkeley and Los Angeles: University of California Press, 1977), pp. 9-10.

20. Stone, *The Crisis of the Aristocracy,* p. 187. If Carew's account is accurate, the earl was also

singular in taking his meals in the hall; as early as the fourteenth century, it had become customary for the lord and his family to dine in the great chamber or parlor, relinquishing the hall to the servants and household officers; see Mark Girouard, *Life in the English Country House: An Architectural and Social History* (New Haven: Yale University Press, 1978), pp. 46-47. Yet the practice of the entire household's dining in the hall during the warm summer months apparently survived on some estates well into the 1700s (Girouard, p. 136); perhaps Carew's poem describes this custom.

21. Almost no information remains on the character of the manor house at Wrest Park. McClung, supplementing the work of Sir Nikolaus Pevsner, suggests that it was probably a fifteenth-century structure with sixteenth-century additions (*The Country House in English Renaissance Poetry,* p. 111 n.).

22. The Sidneys confronted precisely this choice between remodeling and "keeping hospitality" at Penshurst some thirty years earlier. In "Jonson, Lord Lisle, and Penshurst," *ELR* 1 (1971), 250-60, J. C. A. Rathmell draws on the correspondence between Lord Lisle and his wife to suggest that Jonson's celebration of the bounty of Penshurst is a gentle exhortation to dissuade the family from embarking on a building project that undoubtedly would embarrass them financially. "To my friend G. N. from Wrest" differs from Jonson's poem inasmuch as the de Greys had already made the decision not to build before the time of the poem's composition.

23. See Stone, *The Crisis of the Aristocracy,* appendix 8c. In 1641 the de Greys received less than £1100 in gross annual rents. In Stone's stratification of the peerage into eight income levels, the earl of Kent is included in the lowest group. Edward Nicholas, writing to Sir John Pennington on December 12, 1639, reported that the earldom was worth only £500 a year (*CSPD, 1639-1640,* p. 158).

24. "The Country House Poem," p. 167. McClung discounts this hypothesis (*The Country House in English Renaissance Poetry,* pp. 99-103).

25. Cokayne, *The Complete Peerage,* vol. 7, p. 174. Cokayne cites brief parts of the bill of complaint filed by the countess; the complete deposition, however, remains unpublished. David Berkowitz of Brandeis University, who is working on a biography of Selden, informs me that he has been unable to locate the file in the Public Record Office. He adds that the suit "was undoubtedly embarrassing to Selden, who had been aided by Herbert and was on excellent terms with Arundel, who was soon to grant him an annuity and had been instrumental in changing the king's hostility to Selden" (letter of July 24, 1979, to the author). William Herbert, third earl of Pembroke, died on April 10, 1630; Lady Kent amended her suit to include his brother and heir, Philip, as well as her sister Mary.

26. For an account of the Herbert brothers' rebuilding of Wilton, see John Summerson, *Architecture in Britain, 1530-1830,* 5th ed. (Harmondsworth, Middlesex: Penguin, 1970), pp. 142-44; and see Roy Strong, *The Renaissance Garden in England* (London: Thames and Hudson, 1979), pp. 147-65. The famous gallery of statues at Arundel House is depicted in the portrait of the earl by Daniel Mytens.

27. Wilton did in fact possess a statue of Bacchus (Strong, *The Renaissance Garden,* pp. 149-52); the gardens of Arundel House in London contained 32 statutes, 128 busts, and 250 other assorted fragments in the mid-1630s (Strong, p. 170). Both gardens were innovative in their use of sculptural ornament.

28. Lines 632-33. All citations of Marvell's poetry follow *Andrew Marvell: The Complete Poems,* ed. Elizabeth Story Donno (Harmondsworth, Middlesex: Penguin, 1972).

29. Edgar Wind, *Pagan Mysteries in the Renaissance,* 2nd ed. (New York: Barnes and Noble, 1968), p. 266. Wind notes the emblem as commonly illustrated "by the serpent biting its own tail, but known also in the form of a circular loop on the serpent's back."

30. *The Country House in English Renaissance Poetry,* p. 145.

31. Vincenzo Cartari, *Le imagini . . . degli dei,* intro. Stephen Orgel (Venice, 1571; rpt. New York: Garland, 1976), pp. 262, 267-68. Although Carew may have consulted Cartari or some other mythological handbook, it is just as likely that he drew his descriptions from the major classical sources themselves: for Vertumnus and Pomona, *Metamorphoses,* 14. 623 ff., and Propertius, 4.1; for Zephyr and Flora, Ovid's *Fasti,* 5. 193 ff.

32. A partial catalogue of poems in which Carew employs this distinction would include "A Rapture," "To my Mistresse in absence," "Upon a Ribband," "On a Damask rose," and "A prayer to the Wind." For a full discussion of this issue, see Paula Johnson, "Carew's 'A Rapture': The Dynamics of Fantasy," *SEL* 16 (1976), 148.

33. *CSPD, 1639-1640,* p. 158; letter to Sir John Pennington.

34. Ibid., p. 128; letter of November 28, 1639.

35. *The Life of Edward Earl of Clarendon, Lord High Chancellor of England and Chancellor of the University of Oxford* (Oxford: The Clarendon Press, 1759), vol. 1, p. 36.

**Raymond A. Anselment (essay date 1983)**

SOURCE: "Thomas Carew and the 'Harmelesse Pastimes' of Caroline Peace," in *Philological Quarterly*, Vol. 62, No. 2, Spring, 1983, pp. 201-19.

*[In the following essay, Anselment interprets Carew's qualified and at times ironic praise of Gustavus Adolphus in his poem "In answer of an Elegiacall Letter upon the death of the King of Sweden."]*

Thomas Carew's occasional poem **"In answer of an Elegiacall Letter upon the death of the King of *Sweden* from *Aurelian Townsend*, inviting me to write on that subject"** has not received the critical attention it deserves. Although his response to the death of Gustavus Adolphus has been characterized "a superb poem," the more typical judgment criticizes a "fatal separation" between the worlds of art and politics.[1] Literary, historical, and art scholars alike sense in the poem a "mood of make-believe and play-acting which was to be the undoing of King Charles."[2] For some, Carew's apparent unconcern about the plight of Protestant forces embattled in the Thirty Years War reflects a "cultural self-consciousness" masking, perhaps, a "sense of false security"; more negative critics dismiss his attitude as the "ignoble passivity" of "silken dalliance" or the "pusillanimous hedonism" of a "narrow snobbery and an effete indulgence."[3] While these reactions are understandable responses to isolated lines of the poem, they contain several unwarranted premises. When these premises are recognized and the work is seen in its original context, Carew's stance reveals a complexity and sensitivity at least as worthy of notice as the common notion of his decadence.

Literary discussions of the Caroline decades, particularly the years of so-called personal rule between 1629 and 1640, have long assumed that political revolution was inevitable. Recent historians, however, have begun to warn against imposing a teleological view on the period; though Charles's reign ended in disaster, they point out that the social, political, and religious conflicts demonstrate no preordained movement towards revolution.[4] Revisionist interpretations of Charles and his policies further suggest that he is a far more complicated monarch than portrayed by Whig historians and that the years between the 1629 Parliament and the Short Parliament are more benign than the fashionable tag "eleven year tyranny" suggests.[5] The biases of Royalists or Whigs notwithstanding, modern scholars are also beginning to accept the Venetian ambassador's assessment of the economic advantages England enjoyed during this time.[6] Analysis of Charles's eleven year rule between parliaments is still incomplete, but study of his early reign suggests he was not in conflict with a disaffected nation. Contrary to popular impressions, the king was not unalterably opposed to the institution of Parliament nor was the country completely unwilling to go along with his ship-money levies; in reality a king faced with a number of difficult problems did not shirk them: "In peacetime his reign was perhaps stronger than has been thought."[7] When Carew, therefore, refuses in 1633 to disturb "Our *Halcyon* dayes" and to heed the alarms of a continental war, he should not be faulted outright for laziness or self-delusion. He deserves to be judged whenever possible in relation to the 1630s.

This judgment should also eschew any bias against pacifism. Readers critical of Carew's position find most disturbing his conclusion:

> what though the German Drum
> Bellow for freedome and revenge, the noyse
> Concernes not us, nor should divert our joyes;
> Nor ought the thunder of their Carabins
> Drowne the sweet Ayres of our tun'd Violins.[8]

Disdain for this "low and debased feeling" or this "vitious ease"[9] seems to assume that peace fosters idleness and decadence while war promotes heroism and virtue. Since this attitude already figures prominently in seventeenth-century accounts of the civil war which link the peace and prosperity of the 1630s with the aftermath of violence,[10] the attractiveness of this point of view seems all the more irresistible. But the premise must be resisted, or Carew's preference for pacifism, the central issue of the poem, will be condemned before it is properly understood.

Carew meets both the issue and the premise in Aurelian Townshend's familiar address to "Tom Carew."[11] Presuming upon the liberty of his friendship, Townshend asks Carew to put aside his lyric devotion to Celia and to compose a suitable memorial for "the dead conquering king." The ease and tact Townshend exhibits from the outset contain neither the abrasiveness nor the stridency of John Saltmarsh and of John Russell when they deride "those soft *Poets*, who have dipt their brains / In am'rous humours" and those "Amorettoes" who have "become like to the *Sybarite*."[12] Townshend also avoids the chiding in Dudley North's similar challenge:

> Is brave *Gustavus* of too solid stuffe,
> His great exploits, for your sleight vein too tuffe?
> That like poor falsifyers you despair,
> To profit from a piece so rich and fair:
> Whil'st from more trivial subjects you will drive
> A trade, shall make your reputation thrive.[13]

He appeals, instead, to "a sperritt that full mans it all," and he alludes to Carew's elegy on Donne, encouraging his friend to produce still another poetic triumph. Without dismissing the lyric accomplishments or disdaining their lesser stature, Townshend turns from a graceful compliment to their "Lirique feete" and an ambiguous reference to their sincerity to a long, somewhat forced version of the tribute Carew might render Gustavus Adolphus. The poem leaves no doubt about the direction Townshend believes his fellow poet should take, and even though it does not overtly raise the issues of poetic seriousness pressed in poems such as Dudley North's "Incentive to our Poets," the request implies the elegy is a more substantial inspiration for the muse than the lyric.

Carew acknowledges this tacit criticism of his poetic dalliance at the outset of his answer to Aurelian Townshend. As in his earlier response to Ben Jonson, an occasional piece which also takes its direction from the poem it answers, the opening lines establish an intimate but not uncritical relationship. Their characterization of Townshend's tone and their introduction of his phrases recall his poem though in slight distortion:

> Why doest thou sound, my deare *Aurelian*,
> In so shrill accents, from thy *Barbican*,
> A loude allarum to my drowsie eyes,
> Bidding them wake in teares and Elegies
> For mightie *Swedens* fall? Alas! how may
> My Lyrique feet, that of the smooth soft way
> Of Love, and Beautie, onely know the tread,
> In dancing paces celebrate the dead
> Victorious King, or his Majesticke Hearse
> Prophane with th'humble touch of their low verse?
>
> (1-10)

Exaggerated impressions of the militant Townshend and the lackadaisical Carew convey a characteristic lightness and grace. At the same time the jest playfully reproves the officiousness of his friend and concedes the implicit criticism of his own silence. With studied indifference Carew assumes an urbane pose which must not be confused, however, with the serious views the poem develops.

Carew's real attitude begins to emerge in his conventional disavowal of all attempts to praise Gustavus Adolphus. The mock modesty in his concern about profaning the dead king with "humble" and "low verse" is less evident in his contention that no poet

> Could a just Poem to this subject fit,
> His actions were too mighty to be rais'd
> Higher by Verse, let him in prose be prays'd,
> In modest faithfull story, which his deedes
> Shall turne to Poems.
>
> (14-18)

That words are futile is, of course, a standard topos in elegiac literature, and the same idea in Robert Gomersall's elegy to Gustavus Adolphus provides remarkably similar phrases: "he who writeth his History, shall be thought to write a Poem, and he that would write a Poem of him, cannot but write a History. It is impossible, that invention should exceed his actions or that a Penne should dare more than *Sweden*."[14] In other poems Carew remains somewhat sceptical about the power of poetry, but the reservations he may have about the poet's ability to capture truth do not necessarily imply doubt about Gustavus Adolphus. Carew also follows the other elegists when he entrusts the "grave Chronicler" with Gustavus's "too-briefe storie" and asserts

> his Journals may
> Stand by the *Cæsars* yeares, and every day
> Cut into minutes, each, shall more containe
> Of great designement then an Emperours raigne.
>
> (27-30)

Contemporary news reports, sermons, and elegies devoted to the Swedish king seldom miss the opportunity to discuss the anagram Gustavus / Augustus, and they often ex-plain at great length how Adolphus in less time, against stronger enemies, and with higher ideals surpassed even the greatest of ancient military rulers.[15] They concur, moreover, with Carew that "Hee / Gain'd after death a posthume Victorie" both in mortal battle and in heavenly reward.[16]

Differences begin to arise only when Carew places Gustavus at greater distance. In the first of a series of imperatives designed to alter the focus, the poem proposes an alternative to Townshend's elaborate memorial:

> And (since 'twas but his Church-yard) let him have
> For his owne ashes now no narrower Grave
> Then the whole *German* Continents vast wombe,
> Whilst all her Cities doe but make his Tombe.
>
> (31-34)

Carew buries the monarch with wit, decorum, and grim humor. Gustavus's greatness was, after all, achieved through terrible devastation, and Carew refuses to obscure this reality. His recognition that the vitality of Gustavus and the fecundity of Germany are now equally ashes or dead things implies a futility underscored in Carew's view of "supreame providence." While other elegies on the death of Gustavus Adolphus routinely attribute his destiny to the inscrutable designs of providence, the fate of Gustavus and the course of the Thirty Years War illustrate for Carew the folly in believing that a single man or faction can triumph. Certain that "Divine wisedome would not leave the Land / Subject to any one Kings sole command" (41-42), Carew finds the choice between warring sides immaterial. The momentum of the passage's logic and syntax gives forcefulness to the final imperatives and their disjunction:

> Then let the Germans feare if *Cæsar* shall,
> Or the Vnited Princes, rise, and fall,
> But let us that in myrtle bowers sit
> Vnder secure shades, use the benefit
> Of peace and plenty.
>
> (43-47)

Carew turns his back on the continent out of conviction and not cowardice. The reason may well be in large part a general realism or even pessimism about temporality evident in some of his earlier occasional pieces. Although in these poems Carew is ambivalent about the destructive power of time, he emphasizes in his response to Jonson that decline is inevitable. The belief that Jonson's greatest accomplishments will be remembered is a consolation Carew cannot always assert with confidence. In the first of the two elegies on the Duke of Buckingham the memory of the country's most powerful political figure depends upon whether "Truth's hand / Incize the story of our Land" (3-4, p. 57). One of the very few poets to mourn the loss of Charles's favorite, Carew bitterly contends in the second poem, "the vaine pursuit / Of humane Glory yeelds no fruit, / But an untimely Grave" (3-5, p. 58). The fate of Buckingham, counterpointed with the relentless repetition of the word "safe," demonstrates that no refuge offers protection from the malevolent powers of "the starres." Like the bullet shot into Gustavus's back, the knife plunged into Buckingham's breast brings with an ignominious death the knowledge that even the "Darlings" of fate are doomed. While the unrelieved bleakness conveys a sense of personal loss and a strain of cynicism unmatched in his other poems, the tenor is atypical of neither Carew nor his age. The English minister and the Swedish king each exemplify in parallel fashion the mutability that preoccupies writers unusually sensitive to the uncertainties of time.[17]

Carew's reservations about the fate of Gustavus may also reflect the independence of judgment seen in his support of the unpopular Buckingham. For most followers of his exploits, Gustavus Adolphus was "one of the Iewels of the *Protestant* Princes" whose "matchlesse and imparalell Heroike Acts and Expeditions" had seized contemporary imaginations.[18] Hailed the "lion of the North" and the "Northern star," the Swedish king appeared to writers in the early 1630s the "Divine future operation" foretold in the new star discovered in 1572.[19] Successive triumphs detailed at great length in the weekly accounts of Butter, Bourne, and the other writers of corantos inflamed the desire to destroy the triple crown of popedom; and eulogists of the warrior-king's piety, magnanimity, courage, and valor proclaimed Gustavus the new Joshua, Josiah, or Moses who would lead the Protestant nations to their promised destiny. Detractors foolhardy enough to have "railed at the king of Sweden, and called them worse than puritans, that doe praye for him" ran the risk of official punishment,[20] yet moderate criticism of Gustavus did occur. In a letter written to Henry Vane hinting at the monarch's arrogance and ambition, the courtier Toby Matthew voices an attitude current outside the court as well. Diaries and letters of the period record that Gustavus "was tax'd to be over-ventrous and headstrong" and that he had become "puffed up too much with his own victories."[21] While this characterization does not appear in the elegiac tributes which followed his unexpected death, the suggestion of the overreacher remains tacit in Carew's criticism of Gustavus's doomed attempt to defy "Divine wisedome" and to establish "sole command."

A personal desire for peace also explains the poem's qualified view of Gustavus Adolphus. Carew recognizes the carnage none of the other poems admits, because he will not obscure "the benefit / Of peace and plenty" in a glorification of military grandeur. Central to the poem is the hope expressed a year earlier in **"A New-yeares gift. To the King,"**

> Circle with peacefull Olive bowes,
> And conquering Bayes, his Regall browes.
> Let his strong vertues overcome,
> And bring him bloodlesse Trophies home:
> Strew all the pavements, where he treads
> With loyal hearts, or Rebels heads;
> But *Byfront,* open thou no more,
> In his blest raigne the Temple dore.

(27-34, p. 90)

The wish for the "great continued festivall" possible in Charles's reign if the doors of war remain shut is not an isolated compliment. However much contemporaries chose to flatter Charles with his father's famous label "The Peace-Maker," recent events gave urgency to the exhortation, "And you all you, the flower of English blood; that doe enjoy these fruits of peace: quailes and manna in every field, nectar and ambrosia under every vine; the marrow of the land, and oile of seas, Neptune your foole, and Ceres your servant is, the gods of the heathen are become your slaves; whilest the God of gods is become your friend, and gives you Kings of peace, by whom you live and die in peace."[22] After the disastrous wars of the early Caroline years, the English appear in general to have lost some of their taste for conflict and to have accepted the peace with France and Spain concluded in 1629 and 1630. During the next several years of Gustavus's triumphant rise, Englishmen volunteered with varying degrees of enthusiasm for the regiments sent to aid the Protestant cause, and some seemed prepared to give the Swedish king financial support, but the realities of war were not entirely lost on a country at peace. As William Gouge reminds the listeners of a sermon praising Gustavus Adolphus, "We here in *England* doe still enjoy the great blessing of *peace,* together with that farre greater blessing the *Gospell of peace*. . . . At this time this blessing ought to be the more highly esteemed, because it is in a manner proper to us. For most of the parts of Christendome are now, or lately have beene exceedingly annoyed with bloudy warre."[23]

Carew's emphasis, however, on the use as well as the "benefit / Of peace and plenty, which the blessed hand / Of our good King gives this obdurate Land" (46-48) has about it an insistence and even a defensiveness. The juxtaposition of the "good King" with the "obdurate Land" and the overbalancing of the lines on Gustavus with those on the revels of peace may well reflect a personal belief that "men great and good, / Have by the Rabble beene misunderstood."[24] Any policy of nonintervention in the Thirty Years War ran the additional risk of upsetting popular support for Frederick, who claimed the crown of Bohemia, and his wife Elizabeth, Charles's sister. Frederick's thwarted right to the Palatinate in particular vexed militant English Protestants throughout the 1620s and early 1630s; and even when his death soon after the loss of Gustavus diminished the Palatinate issue and when attention shifted towards Charles's own coronation in Scotland, the king was urged to sound the alarm and "vindicate the wrong / Of thy deare Sister, and her Children young."[25] Charles needed little reminder of his sister's plight, for he had already tried unsuccessfully to win the support of Gustavus on the Palatinate issue. There is reason to believe, however, that the king was reluctant to involve the nation in war. The common view of a passive king influenced by the pro-Spanish faction within the court overlooks the Venetian ambassador's remark, "He is pacific, but by necessity."[26] The ambassadorial reports during this period and the arguments of recent historians emphasize the reality that a successful war depended upon extensive funding. Charles had learned from his struggles with the parliaments that apparent sentiments for war did not always have the necessary will or means to pursue a successful military venture. With neither adequate financial nor political support, the king had to make a virtue of necessity; he had learned the wisdom of his father's efforts to avoid military entanglements.[27] When the exploits of Gustavus made his own neutrality seem unattractive to some of his subjects, the king through the Star Chamber imposed a censorship on all news of the continental war,[28] a supporter of Charles, Carew also offered his poetical talents on the king's behalf.

Carew's answer to Aurelian Townshend, then, cannot be easily simplified. Outwardly refusing to grieve for Gustavus Adolphus, the poem actually expresses qualified praise. Admitting the achievements celebrated in other elegies and, indeed, adopting much of their conventional tribute, Carew yet recognizes the limitations inherent in Gustavus's military and political greatness. His assessment of the ill-fated attempt to wage religious war seems to anticipate a modern judgment that Gustavus's death marks the end of an era in which religion could unify large areas of the continent.[29] The reservations about Gustavus's purpose and the refusal to romanticize the realities of his victories, in any case, value peace far more than any foreign venture. The insularity Carew advocates surely reflects the bitter experience of England's recent military fiascos, and he will not obscure this lesson in a conflict which appears at a distance attractive. An England at peace, quite simply, promises much more than a Europe at war, and Carew proposes to celebrate this potential in the revels seriously considered in the poem's second movement.

A deliberate inversion of the first forty-four lines, the next forty-four turn Townshend's request back upon itself. The "just Poem" which cannot "fit" the subject of Gustavus can "comprise" the celebration of peace provided its author is Aurelian Townshend. Returning compliment for compliment, Carew urges his friend to forget "Fames trumpet" and to pick up his "past'rall pipe":

> For who like thee (whose loose discourse is farre
> More neate and polisht then our Poems are,
> Whose very gate's more gracefull then our dance)
> In sweetly-flowing numbers may advance
> The glorious night?
>
> (55-59)

Despite the slightly exaggerated tone in which Carew recalls Townshend's impression of his friend's "sweete" wit and "Lirique feete," this description and the subsequent allusions to Townshend's specific accomplishments are not mere flattery. The praise defends the masque as a serious art form, one especially suited to the Caroline world and the cause of peace.

Controversy about the extent to which Carew bases his comments upon Townshend's *Tempe Restored* or upon the poet's masque version of Walter Montague's *The Shepheards Paradise* need not obscure the qualities Carew ad-

mires.[30] When he praises the "neate and polisht" discourse of his friend and encourages him to capture in "sweetly-flowing numbers" the beauty of *The Shepheards Paradise,* Carew emphasizes traits valued among members of the Caroline coteries and the followers of Ben Jonson. They are the same qualities he observes in his occasional piece **"To my Honoured friend, Master *Thomas May,* upon his Comedie, *The Heire*":** "words in order meet, / And softly stealing on with equall feet" which "Slide into even numbers, with such grace / As each word had beene moulded for that place" (13-16, p. 92). The carefully crafted yet seemingly natural style is, in a word, the terseness Carew stresses in Jonson's "terser Poems" and "terser *Beaumonts*" verse.[31] The same "Masculine stile" in Townshend's earlier work together with its "subtile sence" and "stories curious web" provides an ideal which is demanding as well as entertaining. Unwilling to concede Francis Bacon's criticism, "These things are but toys,"[32] Carew argues that the desired masque should illuminate a "misterious fable" through "rich fancie, and cleare Action." Again, as in his poems on John Donne and William Davenant, he acknowledges the power of poetic fancy, and he emphasizes the poet's obligation to seize the "soule, and sense" with "Knowledge and pleasure."[33] He agrees, in principle, with Bacon's essay "Of Masques and Triumphs" that "those things which I here set down are such as do naturally take the sense and not respect petty wonderments"; but in practice Carew believes the elegance and grace, the "strong and manly," Bacon desires demand the same poetic skill displayed in the best contemporary poetry.[34]

An equally demanding moral seriousness justifies the poet's greatest efforts. Although the "rurall tunes" he urges are admittedly below the "loftier pitch" of the elegy, Carew admires the high seriousness in his friend's courtly entertainment. Throughout the flattering account of the earlier masque and its court participants, Townshend is seen to fulfil the ideals of enlightenment expressed in *Tempe Restored.* The center of the masque, the descent of Queen Henrietta Maria and the ladies of the court in the form of Divine Beauty and her constellation, represents a triumph in stagecraft which in the words of its creator Inigo Jones "was for the difficulty of the Ingining and number of persons the greatest that hath beene seene here in our time";[35] but Carew stresses the meaning and not the mechanics of the spectacle. Fancy, action, style, and sense overcome the distractions of time and sleep:

> Pinnion'd and charm'd they stood to gaze upon
> Th'Angellike formes, gestures, and motion,
> To heare those ravishing sounds that did dispense
> Knowledge and pleasure, to the soule, and sense.
>
> (73-76)

The power of the masque appropriately possesses the ability of Townshend's Divine Beauty to "amaze, / And send the senses all one way"; in Carew's recollection,

> It fill'd us with amazement to behold
> Love made all spirit, his corporeall mold

Dissected into Atomes melt away
To empty ayre, and from the grosse allay
Of mixtures, and compounding Accidents
Refin'd to immateriall Elements.

(77-82)

This memory of the performance more than coincidentally reaffirms the importance of the defeat of Circe at the arrival of Divine Beauty;[36] a similar confirmation of the masque's success also lies behind the final tribute Carew pays to Townshend's creativity:

But when the Queene of Beautie did inspire
The ayre with perfumes, and our hearts with fire,
Breathing from her celestiall Organ sweet
Harmonious notes, our soules fell at her feet,
And did with humble reverend dutie, more
Her rare perfections, then high state adore.

(83-88)

Carew derives his impression of the Queen's influence partly from the assurance of Townshend's Chorus that the presence of the Queen of Beauty affects a unique enthrallment:

The Musick that yee heare, is dull,
But that ye see, is sweete indeed:
In euery Part exact, and full,
From whence there doth an Ayre proceed,
On which th'Intelligences feed,
Where faire and good, inseparably conioynd,
Create a *Cupid,* that is neuer blind.[37]

Stated more prosaically in the final paragraph of the masque's allegorical commentary, the attractiveness of the queen's perfection illustrates how "Corporeall *Beauty,* consisting in simmetry, colour, and certaine vnexpressable Graces, shining in the Queenes Maiestie, may draw vs to the contemplation of the *Beauty* of the soule, vnto which it hath analogy."[38] Either version makes obvious the thrust of Carew's praise: he might expect his friend to catch some irony in his paraphrase of the masque's ideals, and his compliment about Townshend's ability to arrest time and sleep may be a gibe at the incipient boredom of court functions, but a playful tone does not undermine the overriding theme that a successful masque is motivated by high moral seriousness.

The movement of the poem's second section further illustrates Carew's recognition of the central role royalty assumes in this moral enlightenment. All Caroline masques share the poem's awareness of the actual and abstract natures simultaneously embodied in the rulers; and they similarly celebrate transformations of the real into the ideal; Carew, however, adds a dimension of wit. Structurally and thematically the Queen displaces Gustavus Adolphus. She becomes, as Carew argues in another poem,

Thou great Commandresse, that doest move
Thy Scepter o're the Crowne of Love,
And through his Empire with the Awe
Of Thy chaste beames, doest give the Law.

(1-4, p. 90)

A manifestation of the power to liberate human potential from its Circean bonds of lust, Henrietta also embodies in the masques of the 1630s the promise of domestic tranquillity. Jonson's *Love's Triumph* and *Chloridia* and Townshend's *Tempe Restored* establish in their elaborate mythology the transcendent position Carew accords the Queen: she is in the figure of love a guarantor if not a creator of "Our *Halcyon* dayes."[39]

Thus the inspiration of Townshend's previous poetry is, he concludes, "proper to our clyme." Carew recommends it to Townshend not because he doubts his friend's ability to eulogize Gustavus—in fact he assures him that his muse has, indeed, "made / A noble flight, and plac'd th'Heroique shade / Above the reach of our faint flagging ryme" (91-93), but because it is among "harmelesse pastimes." Overshadowing his final compliment are both the refusal to glorify a war that has destroyed much of Europe and a reaffirmation of the peaceful life:

Beleeve me friend, if their prevailing powers
Gaine them a calme securitie like ours,
They'le hang their Armes up on the Olive bough,
And dance, and revell then, as we doe now.

(101-04)

The casualness and even disdain with which Carew turns a deaf ear to heroic glory are meant to be provocative. Certain that the "Rowte" and "vulgar trade" of this "sullen Age" cannot appreciate anything beyond the superficial, he often encourages his friends to draw together and ignore misguided criticism.[40] This appeal to the "wiser world," so memorably apparent in his poem to Ben Jonson, explains his scorn for the "Bellow for freedome" and his smugness about "calme securitie." Rhetorically the overstated conclusion also challenges Townshend and any other reader not to ignore the choice others would surely take if given the chance.

Its sense of national well being is not the delusion of a court sycophant unwilling to accept portents of civil catastrophe. Although economic data about the Caroline decades are still uncertain, some historians now take seriously Clarendon's view in *The History of the Rebellion,* "there quickly followed so excellent a composure throughout the whole kingdom, that the like peace, and plenty, and universal tranquillity for ten years was never enjoyed by any nation; and was the more visible and manifest in England, by the sharp and bloody war suddenly entered into between the two neighbour crowns, and the universal conflagration, that, from the inundation of the Swedes, covered the whole empire of Germany."[41] While England may not have been "the Garden of the world" or Charles "the most indulgent to his Subjects, and most solicitous for their Happiness and Prosperity,"[42] Carew still had reason to celebrate the peaceful rule of "our good King." His motive may have been the belief that Englishmen of the 1630s "wanted that sense, acknowledgment, and value of our own happiness, which all but we had; and took pains to make, when we would not find, ourselves miserable.

There was in truth a strange absence of understanding in most, and a strange perverseness of understanding in the rest."[43] One of the few who did understand, Carew attempts to illuminate others in his answer to Townshend.

The scope of Carew's understanding and artistry is further apparent in his contribution to "harmelesse pastimes," *Coelum Britannicum*. The longest and greatest Caroline masque, this Shrove Tuesday production of 1634 confirms the high seriousness of the form Carew praises. Its glorification of unbounded peacefulness and prosperity depends again upon the talents of Inigo Jones, but the poet assumes a supremacy unrivalled in other court productions. The verve and imagery of the masque's long descriptive passages, its witty dialogue and ingenious arguments, and the cynical as well as idealistic dimensions of its tone characterize the best Caroline poetry. For the performance at Whitehall Carew develops an Italian work of Giordano Bruno into an impressive vision of British grandeur. Surpassing anything that Townshend had ever attempted, he allies the ideals of Jonson and Jones in a celebration of the monarchy and its policy of peace that does, indeed, "dispence / Knowledge and pleasure, to the soule, and sense."

Its success depends, paradoxically, upon a self-conscious realism which tempers the masque's celebration. In triumphant hyperbole Carew redefines the position of those "Bright glorious Twins of Love and Majesty," Henrietta Maria and Charles. Reversing traditional movement towards apotheosis, the opening image of the king and queen anticipates the final vision: they are the end to which everything celestial and temporal aspires. The flattering description of the first one hundred lines is not, however, unqualified. With the entrance of Momus Carew introduces a satirical voice. Momus' recognition of his audience acknowledges the artificiality of the occasion, and his long lament about the new reforms in heaven parodies both specific Caroline reforms and the masque's basic conceit. The urbane manner with which Carew mocks his own hyperbole in slightly ludicrous accounts of the gods' attempts to become Charles and Henrietta Maria is even more apparent in his ridicule of the notion that mortals will displace the gods. Again Momus breaks the illusion of the masque and asks his audience, "Doe not you faire Ladies acknowledge your selves deeply engaged now to those Poets your servants, that in the height of commendation have rais'd your beauties to a parallel with such exact proportions, or at least rank'd you in their spruce society" (308-13, p. 161)? And later he promises any "Lady not competently stock'd" with virtue "shall not on the instant utterly despaire, if shee carry a sufficient pawne of handsomenesse; for however the letter of the Law runnes, *Jupiter* notwithstanding his Age and present austerity, will never refuse to stampe beauty, and make it currant with his owne Impression" (319-24). Carew, quite obviously, has no illusions about the poetic game played for the entertainment of the court, yet despite this sophistication, or perhaps because of it, he succeeds in adding meaning to its conventions.

The idealization of the peaceful Caroline era, in fact, derives much of its impact from its triumph over the pervasive realism. Momus brings to the world of masquing lords and ladies political comment and topical satire, but the major threat to the vision of a celestial Britain remains the contenders for the places vacated when the constellations are purged of their former occupants. The rival claims of Riches, Poverty, Fortune, and Pleasure advanced in the middle section of the masque tax the wit and logic of both Momus and Mercury with a seriousness unusual in traditional antimasque figures. Although Mercury assures his audience that their "forc'd reasons, and strain'd arguments, / Vrge vaine pretenses," the Four Figures press their arguments for domination and will not be dismissed out of hand with Mercury's rejoinder, "but we advance / Such vertues onely as admit excesse" (659-660). These ideals of magnificence, prudence, magnanimity, and "Heroick vertue" become the proper focus of the masque only when Riches, Poverty, Fortune, and Pleasure are shown to have no substance.

Once they are driven from the stage, the poetry and spectacle of *Coelum Britannicum* manifest true worthiness in the magnificent metamorphosis of the masque's conclusion. In contrast to the vociferous arguments of the four contenders, the king has no need to break his silence. Charles, as the embodiment of England's greatness, is the center of a vision of past, present, and future glory whose changing songs and scenes involve all of the senses in celebration. In the wonder of the final movement self-consciousness about the artificiality of the occasion disappears and everyday reality is forgotten. Through the magic of Jones's mechanical illusions and the power of Carew's poetical ones, the masque gives substance to its emblem of England's Genius, "a young man in a white embroidered robe, upon his faire haire an Olive garland with wings at his shoulders, and holding in his hand a Cornucopia fill'd with corne and fruits" (893-95).

The kingdoms, druids, and rivers this Genius of England calls forth and the group of ancient heroes who emerge from the rock upon which the three kingdoms sit help confirm an alternative to the destructiveness of war which envisions a heroism surpassing that of Gustavus Adolphus. Unlike the memorial Carew proposes for the slain Swedish king, his final image of Charles celebrates in far greater proportions the unparalleled creativity of the English monarch. Visually and poetically Charles and his wife are the focus of the audience and design; gone is the masque's opening scene of ancient Roman or British ruins: "In the firmament about him, was a troope of fifteene starres, expressing the stellifying of our British Heroes; but one more great and eminent than the rest, which was over his head, figured his Majesty. And in the lower part was seene a farre off the prospect of *Windsor* Castell, the famous seat of the most honourable Order of the Garter" (1080-1086). Surrounded by his subjects on the masquing floor of Whitehall and the six allegorical representations of his reign. Charles literally and figuratively embodies England's civilizing forces. Emblematically the troop of stars and the prospect of Windsor Castle insist upon the heroic magnitude of his efforts to realize a harmonious, prosperous government where "Religion, Truth, and Wisdome" can flourish. The greatest of the stars, greater even than Arthur or St. George, he is visually placed in a tradition of heroism symbolized in the Order of the Garter and its commitment to the greatest religious and national ideals of England.[44] The chivalric king of Rubens' *Landscape with St. George and the Dragon* and of Van Dyck's *Charles I on Horseback,* in Carew's conception the pacific king becomes the heroic defender of Caroline civilization.

Although Gustavus Adolphus received the Order of the Garter from the British nation, none of the English elegies following the Battle of Lutzen gives this champion of European Protestantism comparable praise. Most of these poems remain lifeless, even perfunctory compared with Carew's imaginative revitalization of the masque. His Shrove Tuesday performance transforms misgivings about the artificiality of the form into an assertion of English greatness which captures in Caroline terms the idealism and grandeur of the most exultant Elizabethan celebrations of nation and monarchy. The title page of *Coelum Britannicum* implies through a quotation from Ausonius that the masque was written at the command of the king, but its inspiration must surely be the desire to celebrate peace. While much of the nation was caught up in the news of Gustavus Adolphus, Carew could share the vision of Rubens. "This Island," he would agree with him, "seems to me to be a spectacle worthy of the interest of every gentleman, not only for the beauty of the countryside and the charm of the nation; not only for the splendor of the outward culture, which seems to be extreme, as of a people rich and happy in the lap of peace."[45] And he obviously wanted others to value their tranquillity. In the early 1630s, when civil turmoil was not an imminent possibility and when England was the envy of a war-ravaged Europe, Thomas Carew knew the wisdom of the Virgilian line which concludes Clarendon's eulogy of a lost era: "*O fortunati nimium, bona si sua norint!*"[46]

*Notes*

1. In the one analysis of the poem, Louis Martz observes in *The Wit of Love* (U. of Notre Dame Press, 1969), "The fatal separation of this gorgeous world of art from the world of political actuality is clearly evidenced in the superb poem that Carew had written, probably in January of 1633" (p. 73). F. R. Leavis, who also apparently admired the poem, thought it should have been included in the *Oxford Book of Seventeenth Century Verse;* see "The Line of Wit" in *Revaluation* (London: Chatto & Windus, 1936), p. 15. The poem now appears in the fourth edition of *The Norton Anthology of English Literature* but not in Thomas J. Clayton's fine Oxford edition, *Cavalier Poets* (New York: Oxford U. Press, 1978). Brief, interesting references to Carew's poem also occur in Isabel Rivers' *The Poetry of Conservatism* (Cambridge: Rivers Press,

1973), Per Palme's *Triumph of Peace* (Stockholm: Almqvist & Wiksell, 1956), and Lynn Sadler's *Thomas Carew* (Boston: G. K. Hall & Co., 1979).

2. C. V. Wedgwood, *Poetry and Politics under the Stuarts* (Cambridge U. Press, 1960), p. 44.

3. L. C. Knights, "The Social Background of Metaphysical Poetry" in *Further Explorations* (London: Chatto & Windus, 1965), p. 118; Margaret Whinney and Oliver Millar, *English Art 1625-1714* (Oxford: Clarendon Press, 1957), p. 72; Ethel Seaton, *Literary Relations of England and Scandinavia in the Seventeenth Century* (Oxford: Clarendon Press, 1935), p. 85; P. W. Thomas, "Two Cultures? Court and Country under Charles I" in *The Origins of the English Civil War,* ed. Conrad Russell (London: Macmillan Press, 1973), pp. 179, 175. None of these observations, however, is developed.

4. G. R. Elton, "The Unexplained Revolution" in *Studies in Tudor and Stuart Politics and Government* (Cambridge U. Press, 1974), II, 183-89; Conrad Russell, "Introduction" in *The Origins of the English Civil War,* pp. 1-31.

5. Hugh F. Kearney, *The Eleven Years' Tyranny of Charles I* (London: Routledge & Kegan Paul, 1962); J. P. Kenyon, *Stuart England* (New York: St. Martin's Press, 1978); Conrad Russell, *Parliaments and English Politics 1621-1629* (Oxford: Clarendon Press, 1979).

6. *Calendar of State Papers Venetian, 1636-1639,* ed. Allen B. Hinds (London: His Majesty's Stationery Office, 1923), XXIV, 499.

7. Conrad Russell, *Parliaments and English Politics 1621-1629,* p. 426. Other studies which recognize the era of peace include J. H. Elliott, "England and Europe: A Common Malady?" in *The Origins of the Civil War,* pp. 246-57; G. M. D. Howat, *Stuart and Cromwellian Foreign Policy* (London: Macmillan, 1974); J. S. Morrill, *The Revolt of the Provinces* (London: Allen and Unwin, 1976); J. P. Kenyon, *Stuart England.*

8. Thomas Carew, "In answer of an Elegiacall Letter upon the death of the King of *Sweden* from *Aurelian Townsend,* inviting me to write on that subject" in *The Poems of Thomas Carew,* ed. Rhodes Dunlap (1949; rpt. Oxford: Clarendon Press, 1970), 96-100, p. 77. Hereafter cited in the text.

9. Samuel R. Gardiner, *History of England 1603-1642* (London: Longmans, Green, and Co., 1884), VII, 208; Rhodes Dunlap's citation of W. J. Courthope, *A History of English Poetry* (London: Macmillan and Co., 1903), III, 244, in *The Poems of Thomas Carew,* p. 253.

10. Royce MacGillivray surveys this attitude in "The Surfeit of Peace and Plenty" in *Restoration Historians and the English Civil War* (The Hague: Martinus Nijhoff, 1974), pp. 237-42.

11. Aurelian Townshend's poem "Aurelian Tounsend to Tho: Carew vpon the death of the King of Sweden" is included in Appendix D of Dunlap's edition, pp. 207-08.

12. John Saltmarsh, "To his ingenious *Friend* Master *Russell,* upon his Heroick Poem"; John Russell, *The Two Famous Pitcht Battles of Lypsich, and Lutzen* (Cambridge, 1634), sig. ¶¶3v, p. 32.

13. Dudley North, "An Incentive to our Poets upon the Death of the victorious King of *Swedeland*" in *A Forest Promiscuous* (London, 1659), p. 72.

14. Robert Gomersall, "To the Reader" in *Poems* (London, 1633), sig. 01r. Other variations include *The Great and Famous Battel of Lutzen . . . Faithfully translated out of the French Coppie* (London, 1633), p. 31; Frederick Schloer, *The Death of the Two Renowned Kings of Sweden and Bohemia* (London, 1633), p. 37.

15. John Russell, p. 34; Gomersall, sigs. 03r-v; William Camden, *Remaines Concerning Britaine* (London, 1637), p. 399; *The Swedish Intelligencer. The Third Part* (London, 1633), pp. 155, 184, and the following poems in this issue: Henry King, "An Elegy," sig. ¶4r; Anon., "On the King of Sweden," sig. ¶¶2v; Anon., "Upon the King of Sweden," sigs. ¶¶¶3r-v.

16. But none rivals Richard Love's conclusion, "He is not cannon'd: no, Hee's canonized" in *The Swedish Intelligencer,* sig. ¶¶1v. More straightforward examples include Thomas Roe, "Upon the glorious King of Sweden," in *The Swedish Intelligencer,* sig. ¶2r and Robert Monro, *Monro His Expedition* (London, 1637), II, 165.

17. Among the poems on Gustavus Adolphus, John Russell's long narrative of the battles of Lypsich and Lutzen is particularly sensitive to the vulnerability of valor in an uncertain world. Ada Long and Hugh Maclean consider some of Carew's other responses to time in "'Deare *Ben,*' 'Greate DONNE,' and 'My *Celia*': The Wit of Carew's Poetry," *SEL,* 18 (1978), 75-94.

18. Schloer, p. 27.

19. Alexander Gil, *The New Starr of the North* (London, 1632), p. 22.

20. John Pory notes this fate of Doctor Coniers in the letter of October 13, 1632 in *Letters and Other Minor Writings,* ed. William S. Powell (U. of North Carolina Press, 1977), p. 306.

21. *Calendar of State Papers, Domestic Series, Charles I. 1631-1633,* ed. John Bruce (London: Her Majesty's Stationery Office, 1862), V, 293-94; James Howell, *Dodona's Grove, or the Vocall Forrest* (London, 1644), p. 117; Simonds D'Ewes, *The Autobiography and Correspondence of Sir Simonds D'Ewes,* ed. James Halliwell (London: Richard Bentley, 1845), II, 85.

22. John Randol, *Noble Blastus* (London, 1633), p. 28.

23. William Gouge, *The Saints Sacrifice* (London, 1632), p. 276.

24. Carew, "To my worthy Friend M. *D'avenant,* Vpon his Excellent Play, *The Iust Italian,*" p. 96.

25. Walter Forbes, "A Panegyricke To the High and Mighty Monarch Charles" in *The Entertainment of the High and Mighty Monarch Charles* (Edinburgh, 1633), p. 35.

26. *Calendar of the State Papers Venetian, 1636-1639,* ed. Allen B. Hinds (London: His Majesty's Stationery Office, 1923), XXIV, 296-97.

27. Conrad Russell develops this interpretation in *Parliaments and English Politics 1621-1629* (Oxford: Clarendon Press, 1979); see particularly pp. 70-84.

28. A Star Chamber decree on October 17, 1632 prohibited the printing of all English newspapers. Folke Dahl suggests in "Amsterdam—Cradle of English Newspapers," *The Library,* 5th series, 4 (1949-50) that Charles imposed the censorship because he felt reports about Gustavus "were, in a way, tacit reproaches to his policy and his person" (p. 174).

29. Michael Roberts suggests in *Gustavus Adolphus: A History of Sweden 1611-1632* (London: Longmans, Green, and Co., 1958), "The end of his life heralded the closing of an epoch: the epoch which had begun with the Reformation; and though England was still to produce, in Cromwell, Gustav Adolf's epigone, on the continent the influence of religion upon politics was waning fast" (II, 773).

30. Rhodes Dunlap suggests in his edition of Carew that "the description which follows . . . fits exactly Townshend's masque *Tempe Restord*" (p. 252). Erica Veevers uses a fragment of a masque in the Huntington Library to argue that Carew actually had in mind "A masquing accompaniment to *The Shepherds Paradise*" Townshend wrote for a performance of Montague's play; while Paulina Palmer counters with the suggestion that Carew "may be referring equally well to Townshend's poem 'On hearing her Majesty sing'"—see their exchange "A Masque Fragment by Aurelian Townshend," *N&Q,* 12 (1965), 343-45 and "Thomas Carew's Reference to 'The Shepherd's Paradise,'" *N&Q,* 13 (1966), 303-04. Unable to match all of Carew's description with *Tempe Restored,* Louis Martz develops the suggestion of a masque intended for Montague's play: "Has Townshend perhaps used some of the themes, along with the costumes, settings, and machinery, from his masque of the previous year, in order to enhance the beauties of *The Shepheards Paradise*" (p. 89)? But the link between Montague's play and Townshend's poems remains, at best, conjectural; and the passages Martz cannot fit into *Tempe Restored* are not out of place if they are interpreted figuratively.

31. "To Ben. Ionson," p. 65; "To my worthy Friend, M. *D'avenant*," p. 96.

32. Francis Bacon, "Of Masques and Triumphs" in *The Works of Francis Bacon,* ed. James Spedding, et al. (London: Longman and Co., 1858), VI, 467.

33. Carew seems to have in mind Jonson's strictures on the masque and its appeal to the body and soul. Jonson's attitude is discussed by D. J. Gordon in "Poet and Architect: The Intellectual Setting of the Quarrel between Ben Jonson and Inigo Jones," *Journal of the Warburg and Courtauld Institutes,* 12 (1949), particularly 154 ff.

34. Bacon, VI, 467-68.

35. Aurelian Townshend, *Aurelian Townshend's Poems and Masks,* ed. E. K. Chambers (Oxford: Clarendon Press, 1912), p. 91.

36. The masque's prose commentary argues that the defeat of Circe signifies "a divine Beame comming from aboue, with a good inclination, and a perfect habit of vertue made, by the *Harmony* of the Irascible and concupiscible parts obedient to the rationall and highest part of the soule. Making man onely a mind vsing the body and affections as instruments, which being his true perfection, brings him to all the happinesse, which can bee inioyed heere below" (pp. 98-99).

37. Townshend, p. 93.

38. Townshend, p. 99.

39. See the discussion of this theme in Stephen Orgel and Roy Strong, *Inigo Jones The Theatre of the Stuart Court* (U. of California Press, 1973), I, 52ff.

40. "To Ben. Ionson," "To the Countesse of *Anglesie*," "To my worthy Friend, M. *D'avenant*," "To my much honoured friend, *Henry* Lord *Cary*," "To the Reader of Master *William Davenant's* Play," and "Obsequies to the Lady *Anne Hay*."

41. Edward Hyde, Earl of Clarendon, *The History of the Rebellion* (Oxford: Clarendon Press, 1849), I, 94.

42. Edward Hyde, Earl of Clarendon, *The Life of Edward Earl of Clarendon* (Oxford: Clarendon Press, 1759), I, 71.

43. Clarendon, *The History of the Rebellion,* I, 108.

44. Orgel and Strong also emphasize the significance of the Order of the Garter in *Inigo Jones,* I, 69-70.

45. Peter Rubens, *Letters,* trans. and ed. Ruth Saunders Magurn (Harvard U. Press, 1955), p. 320.

46. Clarendon, *The Life,* I, 71.

## James Fitzmaurice (essay date 1985)

SOURCE: "Carew's Funerary Poetry and the Paradox of Sincerity," in *Studies in English Literature, 1500-1900,* Vol. 25, No. 1, Winter, 1985, pp. 127-44.

[*In the following essay, Fitzmaurice studies Carew's poetic thoughts on death and the artificiality of language.*]

Sincerity, inasmuch as it is allied with or derived from intention, is likely to occupy a controversial position in current critical discussion. For what might be called the traditionalists in the evaluation of literature, it is at the root of all creative activity and is especially a criterion in funerary verse. Allowances may be made for poetry which appears mortuary but is not so in the strictest sense, for example, Donne's "First Anniversary," or, for what is both mortuary and concerned with other matters, as in Tennyson's *In Memoriam.* But that which is truly involved with the death of an individual human being, is directly from our selves and untainted by "slavish" attention to such relative incidentals as style or precedent in form. Style and formal precedent have important places, but are only crucial insofar as they are successfully transcended. Art is not art, as Henri Peyre writes, "unless the artist has committed himself heart and soul to his metier."[1] Those who write against the grain of this established manner of dealing with sincerity call into question the possibility of intentionality for a number of reasons. For some, the reader makes the text or, as Wolfgang Iser suggests, performs it, and is hence responsible for all or much of its sincerity. For others, the old new critics, the intentional fallacy was long ago exploded. For still others, the unraveling of codes or the interrogation of textuality is the business of the critic. Individual presence is an ever-present *ignis fatuus.* Ironically, in the work of these last, the poststructuralists, a closely related concept, authenticity, is claimed as a decisive test. Regardless of approach, some call for "congruence between avowal and actual feeling," as Lionel Trilling puts it, often asserts itself openly or covertly as a criterion.[2]

Carew as a courtier would, of course, be expected to take a keen interest in sincerity and its simulation, no doubt studying and using what he found in Bacon and Machiavelli. But for Carew the poet, sincerity is paradoxical and exists in a realm where theory and praxis intersect, where problem and problematics coincide. Poetry is inescapably artifice, and even in its most sincere and direct evocation of emotion, the sense of loss which accompanies death, it is something other than direct pronouncement and hence at a distance from a hoped-for pure evocation of feeling. For many of Carew's predecessors indirect expression did not need to entail falsehood. Ruth Wallerstein sums it up thus: "For all these writers poetry is a mediate expression of truth to the imagination in sensuous terms, through a richly elaborated beauty."[3] But there is a second, and, perhaps, more pervasive tradition, one which Jonas Barish traces to Plato. "To change, clearly is to fall, to reenact the first change whereby Lucifer renounced his bliss and man alienated himself from the Being in whose unchanging image he was created."[4]

The substitution of inarticulate statements of loss or the infusion of gesture into a vacuum created by the supposed inadequacy of language is no answer. Sighs and tears are merely an alternative form of language and any limitation on their range of expression is no guarantee of unfeigned feeling. Crocodile tears are a Renaissance commonplace. Silence may or may not be an indicator of true emotion, but its existence outside of caesura within a context, lifetime aphasia, say, has so many possible interpretations as to be no expression at all. Rimbaud may have given in to the "temptation of silence," as Peyre suggests, but that silence would be less forceful if it were not preceded by literary production.[5] Poetry, then, is no more necessarily a matter of deceit or indirection than other emotive forms. But if it is open about its nature, it is always, and in funerary poetry especially, in a position akin to what is encountered in the Cretan liar paradox. The paradox states, "All Cretans are liars. I am a Cretan." Funerary poetry which is forthright must state either directly or by implication, "All sincerity is fabricated. This poem expresses sincere loss." Fabrication here is intended to convey both the senses of "put together" and "foisted off deceitfully." It is no accident that Margaret Ferguson runs into an analogous situation in her study of jest and earnest in *The Unfortunate Traveller,* since intention is fundamental in both cases.[6] Carew certainly, and Nashe probably, are in the position of Chaucer's Pardoner. They disclose the trick and call for the audience to kiss the relics, and while Chaucer's Host refuses, when these authors are successful, we do not. The position of the traditionalists and that of those who offer critiques of the standard approach are each essential to a half of the paradox. The one stresses the truth without really being able to disprove the lie and the other shows the lie without negating the truth. Carew's mortuary poetry asserts, with varying degrees of stress on each part according to the piece in question, the truth of sincerity as truth and the truth of it as lie.

To complicate matters further, the term elegy, which Carew uses in several cases, and the practice of writing verses on the deaths of individuals had a number of meanings and associations in England in the early parts of the seventeenth century. "Elegy" was firmly established as a designation for funerary poetry and had been so used for a hundred years, but on the Continent elegiac poetry was more frequently amorous, following the tradition of Ovid and Propertius, and the term could refer to any poem in the elegiac mode, that is, having a distich of hexameter and pentameter. Perhaps using this Continental practice as a basis, there appeared a number of poems in English which laid claim to being elegy or elegiac without any substantial connection to the theme of death. Gascoigne's *Complaynt of Phylomene, an Elegye* (1576) does not even use hexameters and is simply a mythological poem. Most famous, of course, are Donne's elegies, which are mainly erotic. To this looseness of generic specificity may be added the difficulties connected with a newly popularized form, the stigma, it might be said, of fad. The poetry occasioned first by the death of Sidney and later by that of Prince Henry made verses on the deaths of individuals, particularly individuals of note, a very modish phenomenon. The sincerity, or truth of feeling, of a poet might be called into question, hence, for either of two reasons. He might be writing on the subject simply to show that he

could compose funeral elegy, or he might be writing to flatter influential relatives. The charge of flattery, of course, is always a danger with writing on this sort of topic and critical reception often turns out either very positive or very negative. Chaucer's motive for composing *The Book of the Duchess* is often taken to be a key issue in the evaluation of the poem and is generally held to be laudable. He wrote the poem, it is said, to express true feeling, and its power comes from its movement away from artificiality towards the direct. At the end of the piece the man in black drops all ornateness from his style and says simply, "She ys ded." "At a stroke," John Fisher tells us, "this converts the insincere language and sentimental imagery of dying for love into poignant reality."[7] Spenser's *Daphnaida,* on the other hand, often has been taken to be artificial and therefore unfelt. In the words of Renwick, otherwise one of Spenser's admirers, the poem is probably "the payment of a social—for all we know a material—debt."[8] But Chaucer is more detached than he is often given credit for being and is more acutely aware of the problems of sincerity. Likewise, Spenser is more involved than might seem to be the case. The death of Lady Douglas Howard is more than an excuse for an ornamental and unfelt poem.

In any case, criticism in the last twenty or thirty years has gone a long distance towards a revaluation of Carew's poetry as a whole, an effort perhaps started by a small remark in F. R. Leavis's now-famous essay.[9] But the poems on the subject of the deaths of individuals have largely been ignored. Edward Selig's *The Flourishing Wreath* is for the most part confined to the amorous verse, and Lynn Sadler's *Thomas Carew,* while more complete, shows a preference for the funerary poems (aside from the poem on Donne) which have traditionally received attention, those on the deaths of children or young people. **"Maria Wentworth"** and the three pieces on Mary Villiers are, as she says, reminiscent of Jonson's poetry on the deaths of his children and on Solomon Pavey.[10] The corpus of Carew's mortuary verse, however, tells a fuller and, I believe, a more interesting story.

***"Obsequies to the Lady* ANNE HAY"** provides a good place to start with the poetry itself. It appears to be a simple, uncomplicated poem on the death of a worthy lady, but is much more. "ANNE HAY" is a treatment of the problems that face the poet because of the inadequacy of language to express loss and it is also a poem which immediately and convincingly conveys a sense of that loss. In the opening lines a "sleeke / And polish Courtier" shed "reall tearse," the strength of the image coming, as G. A. E. Parfitt suggests, from our association of the court with deceit.[11] The speaker of the poem goes on to claim his personal involvement in the lady's death by contrasting his current profound feelings with his previous superficial emotional experiences, encounters with "private sorrow" which were no more than what resulted from the frowns of his froward mistress. He now adduces his desire to write from the heart and in a direct fashion. He will not use the mechanics of art to evoke the beauty of his subject. He will eschew the techniques of Apelles. He will not "here a feature, / There steale a Grace" in describing her physical being. Nor will he plunder the vast store of material on virtuous women to describe her character. Such is the province of "base pens," who appropriate "holy Dittyes" to the hearses of common strumpets. His refusal to follow Apelles, known as the premier painter of antiquity for his composite Venus and for his Calumny (later imitated by Botticelli), is a refusal of all artificiality in his expression of sorrow.

Apelles' eclecticism is, in fact, much a part of Carew's method, and obviously so. Apelles culled classical beauties for a composite Venus while Carew proposes to collect a group of contemporary "Virgins of equall birth, of equall yeares," who, in aspects of their physical and moral beings, will each represent a part of Anne Hay's perfection. Equal, of course, refers to equal to Anne Hay, but in a second sense it recalls the classical precedents of Apelles, creating a *paragone* of women as well as arts. One of the English girls will exemplify her eyes, another her teeth, and so on with the result that a living blazon will be created. The transformation of this temporal event into a permanence like that of art will not be through "bribed pens" or "partiall rimes" but by the presumably continuous word of mouth of peers, "partners of [her] youth," from generation to generation. The point of this poem is that it, itself, is not the real poem. Still it is the only indication of Anne Hay's passing that has had an importance for following generations. Pope's piece "On General Henry Withers" owes no debt to Anne Hay or any putative collection of virgins. It may take some inspiration from "ANNE HAY" [12]

A circumstance which adds to the undercutting of the claim of unfeigned grief and praise is to be found in the poet's casual but repeated reference to the fact that he has never met Anne Hay. How can one feel the absence of someone who has not been present and can never be? How can one be at pains to describe the delicate beauty of someone one has never seen in the flesh? In a less forthright situation, these references would be omitted. Because they are included it is clear that we are being told that the poet's knowledge of Anne Hay is an artificiality, a creation of her reputation and, as is specifically indicated, the renown of her family. When the poet tells us of her lineage, we get the most honest admission that superficialities are involved. When he switches from "noble *Carlil's* Gemme" and "the fayrest branch of *Dennye's* ancient stemme" to the "white and small / Hand," we may get the false impression that he has had direct contact with the lady. But in either case the poet has no claim to firsthand knowledge of his subject. "ANNE HAY" is, in short, a funerary poem that claims not to be what it is, even as Dylan Thomas's "Refusal to Mourn" is not really a refusal. It is a composite which rejects composites and a poem based not on actual observation of anyone but solely on authorial imagination and family connection, a poem which at the same time disdainfully ridicules the report of "engag'd kindred." As Thomas Cain has made clear, the praise of *gens* was conventional in epideictic poetry, so Carew is under no obligation to distance himself from Anne Hay's family.[13] That

Carew need not question the propriety of mentioning family makes his questioning of it especially significant. This is, however, one of the funerary poems we, as audience, are liable to accept as a genuine expression of loss. The honesty about never seeing the girl fits in with the various indications of artificiality, frank admissions that poetry can only go so far. Smoothness of line and appropriateness of diction both serve to convey the impression of real emotion because they indicate care in composition. We must either give in and say that this poem shows sincere feeling or at least admit to the poet's power to feign it. The piece has it both ways. It is an expression of sorrow and loss and it is an examination of the problems of expression.

> Or shall I, to the Morall, and Divine
> Exactest lawes, shape by an even line,
> A life so s raight, as it should shame the square
> Left in the rules of *Katherine,* or *Clare,*
> And call it hers, say, so she did begin,
> And had she liv'd, such had her progresse been?
>
> (pp. 67-68)

The answer is both yes and no.

**"To the Countess of *Anglesie* upon the immoderately-by-her lamented death of her Husband"** is a funerary piece cast in the form of a poem of advice. It is a more complicated poem that "ANNE HAY" in the sense that it is about the reaction of one person to the death of another. It is also a poem that deals with feeling emotion and with dissimulation. The Countess is admonished not to continue her elaborate grief over the loss of her husband because the appearance of excessive mourning indicates insincerity. Those "Whose love was doubted" may pour out their tears, but such zeal is inappropriate for her "whose whole life / In every act crown'd [her] a constant Wife." The assumptions on the part of the speaker are all wrong, for if the lady is sincere about her grief, no concern with public reception should come into play. Further, acting in the role of a woman of the time, she might be expected to indulge herself. But, most importantly, the poet does not bother to take his own advice. Convinced of her sincerity by the "surfet" of her grief, as others would be inclined to doubt it, according to the system he proposes, he proceeds to "tell the world, upon what cates [she] sit[s] / Glutting [her] sorrows. "What follows is the epitome of hyperbole, sincere or insincere.

> In motion, active grace, in rest, a calme
> Attractive sweetness, brought both wound and balme
> To every heart. He was compos't of all
> The wishes of ripe Virgins, when they call
> For Hymen's rites, and in their fancies wed
> A shape of studied beauties to their bed.
> Within this curious Palace dwelt a soule
> Gave lustre to each part, and to the whole.
>
> (p. 70)

The husband is in all ways perfect, and only the thought that the Countess will further sorrow by hearing the catalog of virtues stops the poet from continuing to list them.

The details of the poem's stated reason for its encomium of the husband further point up the difficulties inherent in distinguishing sincere and insincere manifestations of grief. In line twenty-seven the reader is brought into the poem as if he were present. The speaker seems convinced that the lady, who still has not stopped crying, has come to appear ridiculous to the audience. Certainly the image of the Countess stirring her tears with her husband's dust in order to keep it from flying away in the storm of her sighs is bizarre, but it is a creation of the poem and scarcely a reference to life. The poet is projecting a fiction in which the reader does not hear the expostulation to the lady and only sees her gestures, misinterpreting them according to the conventions of the time, when, in fact, the reader knows only what he has read on the page before him. Any intervention to put things straight can only make matters worse because it calls into question what otherwise might have been accepted. Further, the shift of "you" from lady to reader between lines twenty-six and twenty-seven interrupts the illusion of unseen audience presence as the reader adjusts to his direct participation in the poem. The reader suddenly finds himself an important figure in what he is reading, even as what he is asked to believe is called into question by further protestations of the genuine, claims that point to an infinite regress of further and less convincing claims. Using the terms of the poem itself, it may be said that the breath of the poet neither fans the flames of old sorrows nor blows away the funerary ashes. The piece is about the vicissitudes of art, not life. Nevertheless, the impression that the figure of the poet and, perhaps, beyond the poet, the author, both feel unfeigned grief can function in a legitimate reading of the poem. An audience may well be convinced the feeling expressed is true by the very kinds of artificiality it has been told to suspect, smoothly polished lines and unabashed overstatement.

> Then let him rest joyn'd to great *Buckingham,*
> And with his brothers, mingle his bright flame:
> Looke up, and meet their beames, and you from thence
> May chance derive a chearfull influence.
> Seeke him no more in dust, but call agen
> Your scatterd beauties home, and so the pen
> Which now I take from this sad Elegie
> Shall sing the Trophies of your conquering eye.
>
> (p. 71)

The countess is admonished to take heart from her husband's spirit, is told his memory will help her to live life.

The poem **"On the Duke of *Buckingham,*"** like that to the Countess of Anglesie, involves a dead man and a mourning wife. The piece on Buckingham contains a set of statements designed to give the impression of complete and unmitigated sincerity. But the poem shows that it is really a kind of filter through which the audience receives an account of his life and death. Writing, according to many poststructuralists, has been less privileged than speech because it has been taken to be secondary, less immediate. It does not give the impression of direct feeling as does the spoken word. The figure of the wife in the poem puts it succinctly, "His Actions let our Annals tell: /

Wee write no Chronicle" (p. 57). The poem in fact suggests that even speech is suspect. But, in an image reminiscent of that in which the Countess of Anglesie mixes her tears with her husband's ashes, the wife's tears are cooled by her sighs and, compounded, make a piece of stone. The artificiality of the image may serve to undercut the poem's claims to be taken solemnly, and other factors operate along these lines as well. A record of the wife's lament is fashioned by a stonecarver from the rock that her tears have made. The poet downgrades the importance of the carver, "So he the fashion onely lent," and elevates the unverbalized feelings of the lady, "Whilst she wept all this Monument." Still, it is clear that without the poet as carver or carver as poet all that would remain to remind us of Buckingham would be an inchoate block. The hand of the carver, it turns out, is the hand of hands, the hand which records the "desperate hand, thirstie of blood" that belongs to the murderer and the hand that causes "Truth's hand / [to] Incize the story" of Buckingham's virtue. Further, Buckingham himself is less the subject of the poem than are the patronage of two kings, the barbarity of the murderer, and the grief of the widow. The poem purports to be a record of immediacy unadulterated by language, but language, of course, is always present. It is clearly there in the punning phrase that speaks of sincerity showing the "chast Wifes pregnant eyes." Still, the smoothness of line and apparent straightforward praise can serve to convince the audience of the sincerity of feeling, which might be said to be "behind" the poem.

> This Pile
> Weares onely sorrowes face and stile,
> Which, even the envie that did waite
> Upon his flourishing estate,
> Turn'd to soft pitty of his death,
> Now payes his Hearse.
>
> (p. 57)

The second of the poems on Buckingham's death consists by and large of unadulterated praise, but the opening lines invert the idea of the first, that stones rather than words are eloquent. This reversal may be a veiled reference to the ugliness of the monument later recorded in the *DNB.*[14]

**"An Elegie on the La: *PEN:* sent to my Mistresse out of France"** compounds the problem of sincerity in funerary poetry with its counterpart in love lyric, and it goes a step in complication beyond **"To the Countess of Anglesie"** by inserting a hostile audience, the mistress, into the poem. This unlikely combination has elicited the reasonable suggestion that the poem is simply witty erotic verse.[15] But the piece may be treated as mortuary poetry equally well, part of a virtuoso performance in which the poet demonstrates the difficulties of sincerity in any mode by trying to serve two masters. He must praise the dead lady but not diminish his position with his mistress, and again sincerity is rendered problematic. In the opening lines the mourner-lover appears to abandon the audience of the title and addresses a fictional rejected lover, a comrade in suffering. He admonishes this lover to "forbid /

His eyes to weepe that losse" and rather to turn his sorrow to a fit object, making good use of tears "which else would be but brine." He goes on to argue the topos of the precedence of public sorrow over private. The original audience, the mistress, though not addressed, is still present, and presumably would take offense at this reordering of emotional priority. But insult, direct or indirect, is a characteristic mode in Carew's love poetry, as Selig has shown, and may, itself, be taken to be a sign of sincere feeling. Indifference, it is said, cannot elicit a barbed attack. Still, difficulties in interpretation must follow as we, the audience, or the mistress as audience, think through the consequences of this argument. If the lover says he loves the mistress, he may or may not be sincere. If he says or even suggests he doesn't, presumably he may love and may only be fooling himself or trying to fool others. An infinite and ridiculous regress is possible, for the lover may simply be pretending to be bitter at rejection in order to convince the mistress of what is really feigned sincerity, or he may not know that behind this is real sincerity, and so on. In any event, the mourner-lover in **"La: *PEN*"** changes course and apologizes directly to the subject of his poem, a third audience, for shedding only one tear at her grave, a tear which is singularly meaningful. It writes on the earth of her burial plot. Apparently fearful that even this small token will enrage the mistress, he immediately apologizes to her, too. The pair of apologies could set off a whole string, but the mourner-lover, in the manner of Donne, explains that the tear for the lady is really a tear for the mistress, since the death of the lady indicates that the mistress is also mortal.

The resolution of the conflict between mistress and lady is achieved in the remainder of the poem not through this sort of wit, though there is plenty of it present, but by a pairing of the two women in religious reference. Although religious imagery is in evidence from the beginning (tears become manna), the first connection of it to the women comes when the lady is designated "faire soul" and the mistress "sweet Saint" in the apology sequence. The terms are then exchanged as the lady becomes a saint taken from the earth, leaving a few "good soules" behind. The lady goes to heaven and there the mourner-lover fears she will experience the envy of other saints, a fate more appropriate to an amorous than to a religious situation.

> But what can heaven to her glory adde?
> The prayses she hath dead, living she had,
> To say she's now an Angell, is no more
> Praise then she had, for she was one before;
> Which of the Saints can shew more votaries
> Then she had here? even those that did despise
> The Angels, and may her now she is one,
> Did whilst she liv'd with pure devotion
> Adore and worship her; her vertues had
> All honour here, for this world was too bad
> To hate, or envy her: these cannot rise
> So high, as to repine at Deities.

> (p. 21)

The imagery remains religious as the mourner-lover writes of his martyrdom and addresses the mistress as "Idoll of

my soule." Until the last lines of the poem the women are brought together in imagery and kept distinct in syntax. This separation collapses in the phrase "Rest then blest soule," which syntactically looks backward to the mistress and forward to the lady. The mistress may rest because the poem, her competition with the lady, is over, and the lady may rest because her song of praise is finished. Ironically, the very last word, promised a few lines before to the mistress, is given to the lady. The reason for collapsing the two women together is clear enough. Funerary poetry and love lyric are remarkably similar, and vary, as the poem says, mostly in superficialities of "stile." Sincerity in both cases can be problematic and the intricate confusion of the women simply underscores the importance of illusion or impression and the relative unimportance of individual people as subjects. While the poem has variously been interpreted as being on Lady Pennington and on Lady Peniston, it is also, and perhaps most interestingly, as the abbreviated title suggests, on the Lady Pen, that is, on writing. At the beginning of the poem the fellow rejected lover is told to "take off his pen, and in sad verse bemone." This is the essential paradox of mortuary poetry. It must be both unartificial and artificial, though the strength of **"La: *PEN*"** lies less in an audience being impressed by the poet's sense of sorrow and more in its awareness of his urbane ability to juggle two commitments to two women.

> for as ghosts flye away,
> When the shrill Cock proclaims the infant-day,
> So must I hence, for loe I see from farre,
> The minions of the Muses comming are,
> Each of them bringing to thy sacred Herse,
> In either eye a teare, each hand a Verse.

> (p. 21)

The image of the stampede of completely sincere poets fully given over to the lady contrasts humorously with the more controlled and hence more sophisticated figure of the mourner-lover.

**"Epitaph on the Lady S. Wife to Sir W. S."** and the first of the set of short pieces on Mary Villiers are more traditionally funerary than the preceding poems in that sincerity in them is more evidenced than it is questioned. But in both cases an evocation of the deceased is combined with allusion to the difficulty of direct, and hence sincere, knowledge. The praise of Lady S. is based on the concept of the correspondence between inside and outside beauty, another Renaissance topos. Although the "darke Vault" of burial has no such connection with its contents, the lady when alive displayed an external beauty that matched the inner beauty of her virtue. Since the inward virtue is what really counts and since it is hidden, the observer has only her outward traits as signs of what must be praised. Appropriately, the detailed list of the lady's qualities, wisdom, devotion, cheerfulness, gravity, and seriousness, are all described as jewels on a coat, a coat that recalls, as the poem tells us, "*Aaron's* Ephod." In Aaron, as the *Geneva Bible* attests, the priest-hood is initiated and his robe is its visible sign.[16] The poet's knowledge of the lady's exemplary soul, sure as the poem indicates it is, is a matter of understanding at a distance, even as the priestly class provides contact with God (perhaps necessarily) in an indirect form. Despite these admitted problems of indirection the poem is able to provide a touching picture of its subject.

> The harmony of colours, features, grace,
> Resulting Ayres (the magicke of a face)
> Of musicall sweet tunes, all which combind,
> To crown one Soveraigne beauty, lies confind
> To this darke vault. Shee was a Cabinet
> Where all the choysest stones of price were set;
> Whose native colours, and purest lustre, lent
> Her eye, cheek, lip, a dazling ornament:
> Whose rare and hidden vertues, did expresse
> Her inward beauties, and minds fairer dresse.
>
> (p. 55)

The contrast of past fullness of life and present loss is similar to, though more violent than, the pairing of the image of the snow-cloud of geese and the picture of the little girl propped with pillows to receive a last look before burial in Ransom's "Bells for John Whiteside's Daughter." The compliment is also paid in terms of biblical typology, since the urim and thummim of the ephod are transformed in the lady, as in the New Testament, into the Pearl of Great Price.

The second and third of the epitaphs on Mary Villiers along with the short poem on the death of Maria Wentworth are essentially unmixed in their mortuary evocation. That is, they contain virtually no analysis of the problems of this sort of verse. The "chaste Poligamie" of Maria Wentworth, the virgin married to "every Grace," has justly been singled out as a memorable figure.[17] More characteristic of the three poems is simple, direct, controlled statement.

> And here the precious dust is layd;
> Whose purely-tempered Clay was made
> So fine, that it the guest betray'd.
>
> Else the soule grew so fast within
> It broke the outward shell of sinne,
> And so was hatch'd a Cherubin.
>
> (p. 56)

The first epitaph on Mary Villiers presents a different picture. Not the virtue of the girl herself, but a possible connection between the reader and her family is stressed. Failing this connection, the reader is given an even more tenuous tie. He, too, may have a loved one and when he returns home he may find his "Darling in an Urne." It is the brutality of this last image, most distanced of all from the death of Mary Villiers, that testifies to the strength of feeling of the poet even while it shocks the audience. If the three epitaphs on Mary Villiers are taken as a group (as we take Herrick's three short poems "To his Booke," "Another," and "Another"), it is possible to see a movement from confrontation of the fact of death in a blunt, almost crude fashion, to an increasingly literary treatment.

In the final poem in the set we are told we are free of the tyranny of love now that Mary is dead. The thought, borrowed from Ronsard,[18] is out of place in a poem on the death of a child and attracts the criticism of Sadler for its artificiality. "The more Carew draws on conventional imagery—no matter how well he may convert images of love to the rites of death—the less sincere he seems in the elegies."[19] Still, there is no compelling reason that art cannot be the terminus of sorrow.

**"An Elegie upon the death of the Deane of Pauls, Dr. John Donne"** has long been singled out as the finest of the tributes to that poet contained in the 1633 volume of his poetry and as one of Carew's best pieces. It is also, unlike the poems treated so far, a tribute to a fellow poet and to a major literary figure of the age. Hence the task Carew sets himself is anything but trivial. It is widely accepted that much of the force of the tribute comes from Carew's ability to deliver a poem in praise of Donne in Donne's style.[20] That correspondence provides a key to the poem in a variety of ways. Certainly Carew's poem displays the qualities of Donnean wit and Donne's characteristic roughness of syntax,[21] and in so doing it demonstrates "masculine expression" while avoiding "servile imitation," to use the language of the poem itself. It performs the same sort of illusion as we find in the master, because the indirect (the feminine) and the copied (that contaminated by previous use) appear to be shunned. The reader as a consequence is likely to feel a strong sense of the sincere involvement of both poets. Nevertheless, that impression cannot be achieved without indirection and imitation, not necessarily servile but imitation just the same. It is the sort of *imitatio* Greene attributes to Erasmus's *Praise of Folly*, "parody," in which a later author interacts with an earlier one.[22]

The first line of the poem introduces the theme of the masculine in poetry as rape, in both its senses as sexual assault and as seizure. Now that Donne is dead, times will be difficult for poets, who will have to "force from widdowed Poetry" their verse, including the poem presently being composed. This is precisely what the poem tells us Donne has had to do because the Greeks and Romans were there first to claim all the smooth and pleasing subjects with "their soft melting Phrases." Likewise Latin and Greek are mellifluous languages while English has a harshness demanding the rough, direct expression which is the hallmark of Donne. Many poetasters, unsuccessful imitators of the ecstasies attributed to Anacreon and Pindar, once abounded but were put to shame and hence silenced by Donne. In his absence, they may appear again. Missing in Carew's poem is any reference to the tradition of the shocking and unpleasant to be found in Juvenal and Martial or in the imagery and action of the English stage as it ultimately derives from Seneca.

Several aspects of this poem, however, show just how much Carew is aware of the illusions about which he writes and which he, as funerary poet, embodies in his own writing. At the beginning of the poem and later on, the silence of poets in the absence of Donne is stressed, even though its end makes manifest that this funerary poem is one of several by several hands. The poet stops writing and concludes his praise, he says, to give others the opportunity to have their say on the subject. Dumbness in the face of death is normal and conventional (it is a case of the inexpressibility topos described by Curtius),[23] but Carew's invocation of it along with his purported rejection of the classics are in the category of "holy Rapes upon our Will." We know better than to let him get away with it but because of the affectionate spirit of the poem we do so anyway. Similarly, the suggestion that Donne has purged English poetry, which had become rife with allusion to classical myth, is not quite consistent with the praise which compares Donne to Prometheus and makes the poet inspirer of the "Delphique quire" and weeder of the Muse's garden. The assertion that an English poet is on a par with or better than all prior and contemporary practitioners is reminiscent of Jonson's poem on Shakespeare, and the appeal to British audiences, regardless of sincerity one way or the other, probably is the same. Donne's poetry, Carew goes on to tell us, gains its strength from the immediacy of its visual reality. Through the eye the heart is made liquid. "Sense might judge, what phansie could not reach" is part of an elaboration on this visual power. Sense is imagery not simply taken as imagery but felt as if by the senses. It is fancy accepted as fact. In the reader this acceptance must take place regardless of whether he knows that transformation is involved. It is Donne's "Giant phansie" changed in the audience into giant sense that gives the feeling of reality which, in turn, adds to the impression of sincerity. The conspicuous irrelevance, to borrow a term from Harry Berger, Jr., of the title, and the irony of form of the last line enclose the poem in contradictions, confirm it in its dominant mode. The piece is not, as the title implies, primarily about the death of the Dean of Paul's and only incidentally about the poet John Donne, here rendered distant from the poetic audience by the title of doctor. That such titles and church offices are dry as dust is immediately adduced in the passage on the "uncisor'd Churchman" who will speak at Donne's graveside and in the reference to the pulpit with "her plaine / And sober Christian precepts." The poem's title is pointedly the reverse of descriptive and the last line is simply one more instance of contradiction between stated criteria and practice. The poem says it abhors classical precedent but ends with an echo of a common and respected classical form, chiasmus, "*Apollo's first, and last, the true Gods Priest.*"

Although the poems mentioned thus far in this essay do not by any means exhaust Carew's thinking on death or artificiality in language in poetry, they do, with one exception, cover what he has to say about the deaths of specific people. The remaining poem, that written in reply to Aurelian Townsend's letter on the death in battle of Gustavus Adolphus, starts out with praise for the fallen king, "His actions were too mighty to be rais'd / Higher by Verse," but it rapidly turns against that subject and even, as Louis Martz has observed, suggests that the king's wars are not

admirable.[24] He might as well be buried in Germany rather than Sweden, since he has turned Germany into a graveyard. The poem goes on to expatiate on the place of art in a peaceful society and ignores Gustavus Adolphus for the remainder of its length. Carew's vision in this poem is, as Earl Miner tells us, one which depicts a good king presiding over the *vita beata.*[25] This, the last of the funerary poems in *Poems* of 1640, is, finally, what Carew has sometimes claimed in pieces which precede it. It is a mortuary poem which is not a mortuary poem.

Lionel Trilling and Henri Peyre, each quoted earlier in this essay, come to opposite conclusions about the course of sincerity in literature. Peyre believes that sincerity in the twentieth century is "a proud and royal way," that what in earlier literature was bypath is now main highway.[26] To Trilling the obvious ridiculousness of statements that imply reference to authorial earnestness make the current era one in which sincerity is no longer a viable standard.[27] Taken together, the two positions evoke a strong pair of emotions which coexist in many scholars today, love for and hatred of sincerity as a critical standard. Simultaneously we want to embrace what has been called "presence," the direct and unadulterated emanations of another human being, and to reject as illusory such contact. We desire complete sincerity while skeptically denying that any sort of sincerity either is possible or makes sense as a concept. It is true that many scholars don't hold much with the quiddities of any theory which would "deconstruct" individual consciousness. Still, these scholars might find themselves a little embarassed by the excesses of writers too fully committed to expression of Wordsworth's "essential passions of the heart." Perhaps one of the strengths of the poetry of G. M. Hopkins is that he can take us so close to the edge of maudlin and unconvincing sentimentality in, say, "Binsey Poplars," and not ask us to descend into it. Sincerity has distinct limits as a criterion. But there are only a few critics, perhaps Paul de Man the most notable among them, who would go so far as to reject it altogether. If it is an illusion, it is persistent, strong, and, I would say, indispensable.

*Notes*

1. Henry Peyre, *Literature and Sincerity* (New Haven: Yale Univ. Press, 1963), p. 1.

2. Lionel Trilling, *Sincerity and Authenticity* (Cambridge, Mass.: Harvard Univ. Press, 1973), p. 2.

3. Ruth Wallerstein, *Studies in the Seventeenth-Century Poetic* (Madison: Univ. of Wisconsin Press, 1950), p. 26.

4. Jonas Barish, *The Antitheatrical Prejudice* (Berkeley: Univ. of California Press, 1981), p. 105.

5. Peyre, p. 312.

6. Margaret Ferguson, "Nashe's *The Unfortunate Traveller:* The 'Newes of the Maker' Game," *ELR* 11 (Spring 1981):165ff.

7. John Fisher, *The Complete Poetry and Prose of Geoffrey Chaucer* (New York: Holt, Rinehart and Winston, 1977), p. 543.

8. William L. Renwick, *Edmund Spenser, An Essay on Renaissance Poetry* (London: E. Arnold, 1925), p. 63, rpt. in *The Works of Edmund Spenser: A Variorum Edition,* ed. Edwin Greenlaw et al., 11 vols., *The Minor Poems* (Baltimore: Johns Hopkins Press, 1943), 1:432.

9. F. R. Leavis places Carew above Herrick in stature. *Revaluation: Tradition and Development in English Poetry* (New York: George W. Stewart, 1947), p. 36.

10. Lynn Sadler, *Thomas Carew* (Boston: Twayne, 1979), p. 125.

11. G. A. E. Parfitt, "The Poetry of Thomas Carew," *RMS* 12 (1968):57.

12. See *The Poems of Thomas Carew,* ed. Rhodes Dunlap (Oxford: Clarendon Press, 1949), p. 248, hereafter referred to as Dunlap. All quotation from Carew in the present essay follows this edition. References are given by page number.

13. Thomas Cain, *Praise in "The Faerie Queene"* (Lincoln: Univ. of Nebraska Press, 1878), p. 6.

14. Dunlap, p. 244.

15. Dunlap, p. 223.

16. Exod. 28:41.

17. Leavis, p. 38. See also Rufus A. Blanshard, "Carew and Jonson," *SP* 52 (April 1955):207.

18. Dunlap, p. 240.

19. Sadler, p. 125.

20. Rufus Blanshard, p. 195; Lynn Sadler, p. 87; and Louis L. Martz, *The Wit of Love* (Notre Dame: Univ. of Notre Dame Press, 1969), p. 98. Martz, however, recognizes the irony of the poem and points out that "Carew well knows that he himself is a writer of 'soft melting Phrases,'" p. 99.

21. Edward I. Selig, *The Flourishing Wreath* (New Haven: Yale Univ. Press, 1958), p. 165.

22. Thomas M. Greene, *The Light in Troy: Imitation and Discovery in Renaissance Poetry* (New Haven: Yale Univ. Press, 1982), p. 45.

23. Ernst R. Curtius, *European Literature and the Latin Middle Ages,* trans. Willard B. Trask, Bollingen Series 36 (Princeton: Princeton Univ. Press, 1973), p. 159.

24. Martz, p. 78.

25. Earl R. Miner, *The Cavalier Mode from Jonson to Cotton* (Princeton: Princeton Univ. Press, 1971), pp. 83-84.

26. Peyre, p. 306.

27. Trilling suggests that Leavis's standard of seriousness is "engagingly archaic," p. 6.

## Renée Hannaford (essay date 1986)

SOURCE: "Self-Presentation in Carew's 'To A. L. Perswasions to Love'," in *Studies in English Literature, 1500-1900,* Vol. 26, No. 1, Winter, 1986, pp. 97-106.

[*In the following essay, Hannaford discusses the complex dramatic pose of the speaker in Carew's "To A. L. Perswasions to Love."*]

A concern for fashioning the self as a dramatic character or performer may be found in many seventeenth-century poets, and is insistently displayed in the poetry of Thomas Carew. The modes of personation characteristic of Carew's dramatic love lyrics create an assemblage of poetic activity recording the complexities of courtship rites and ceremonious social form in an increasingly skeptical and scientific age. These modes display Carew's profound awareness of the conflict between private personality and public role in a society which placed a high value on sociability (or good courtiership). Techniques of self-presentation both reflect and create a deliberative personality, one for whom Hamlet's "to be or not to be" is a continual act of choice from among a variety of roles, revealing an understanding of personality (akin to Montaigne's) as fluid, changeable, volitional, subject to occasion—in short a self-fashioned artifact, rather than something fixed and constant. It is not surprising, therefore, that the various speakers in Carew's love poems act out roles and explore attitudes often frankly antithetical, since the experience of contradiction was recognized by many seventeenth-century writers and artists as an essential human *donné.*

Carew's poems, taken as a whole, show an interest in extreme attitudes of social behavior usually within the context of courtship, and analyze the constraints of social behavior that limit or inhibit human interaction. Carew's reputation as the "Oracle of Love" certainly tells us that he earned the literary homage of a highly competitive and critical group of fellow poets and courtiers (poetry being after all a gentleman's pursuit, and as such a gentleman's proving ground in the larger game of advancement at court), but it also tells us how his contemporaries viewed the relationship between poetry and the forces that shape identity. The fictive selves projected in Carew's lyrics inhabit and construct a particular social world; in a work of art, the artist creates an image that seems to embody in a relatively coherent system and style some of the pressures and problems which a given society is experiencing in everyday life.[1]

While it can be said that all poems represent a poetic voice of the poet, there are different kinds of poetic voice. A rather impersonal poetic voice may be found in some of Carew's commendatory poems such as **"To my much honoured Friend, Henry Lord Carey of Lepington, upon his translation of Malvezzi."** In some of Donne's holy sonnets the speaker assumes a more biographical voice, thus standing in closer relation to the poet as maker. It is, however, a more stylized poetic voice—the performing self—that I wish to consider here. The performing speaker that occurs in a lyric such as Carew's **"To A. L. Perswasions to love"** suggests a fragmentation of self that results from a process of self-definition, an attempt to project an inquiring self out of conflicting systems of belief or social practices. Also, Carew's lyric clearly exposes the necessity of role-playing and inventive improvisation by the gentleman-courtier which encouraged the creation of self as a work of art.[2]

The social and literary tradition of the gentleman-courtier, growing out of Castiglione and reinforced by the numerous rhetorical handbooks and conduct books of the period, already showed how the self could be transformed by selecting various socially "fashionable" qualities or components from appropriate areas of human discourse and behavior. A different self would be constructed when asking for preferment from one's superior in rank and authority (since this entails a deliberately affected submissive role) than when wooing a mistress, a situation involving primarily the projection of domination or the affectation of submission ironically to assure domination. When the speaker in Carew's **"Obsequies to the Lady Anne Hay"** remarks "I saw the sleeke / And polish Courtier, channell his fresh cheeke / With reall, teares" (lines 1-3), he is attempting to distinguish between artful mimicry and genuine self-manifestation.

The process of self-definition depends upon the ability to modify identity through "theatricality" or "improvisation." "Theatricality" has long been adduced by art-historians as an element of baroque style. "Theatrical" implies an actor, who is, consciously and overtly, artificial and affected, who willingly assumes another identity or "fashions" an appropriate role for a particular occasion. In Carew's lyric, not only is the interaction of the poem's rhetorical members (speaker, audience, and reader) dynamic, but tension exists between the poet's act of self-fashioning and the "fashionable" qualities he chooses to project. In this context, poetic performance may be viewed as the activity of a poem's speaker during a period marked by his continuous presence in the poem before a particular audience, and which has some influence over that audience.[3]

The self-image projected by the speaker in a courtship or seduction poem such as **"To A. L. Perswasions to love"** provides a convenient starting point for an examination of Carew's performing speakers, his treatment of inherited conventions and borrowed literary models, and his consciousness of self as style. As a seduction poem, the colloquial "first move" in the game of love, it is interesting that the techniques of self-presentation in the poem draw our attention to the speaker rather than to the woman addressed. The speaker's style in the poem, not his prospective mistress, is the poem's actual subject: his mastery of persuasive rhetorical delivery and subtle argument, his treatment of themes and conventions appropriate to poetic courtship, and his psychological manipulation of the woman addressed. The speaker adopts a relaxed, unsenti-

mental, and worldly attitude toward love and courtship that will win applause from the poem's wider audience attentive, and perhaps sympathetic, to his aggressive psychological realism, while simultaneously, on the level of the poem's immediate audience, he will ironically conquer a reluctant beauty. Even if the speaker fails to win his ostensible purpose, the seduction of "A. L.," the poem will have displayed his successful performance, since the speaker's negative implications throughout the poetic argument expose only a passing interest in "A. L." anyway. He is merely "playing" with her in an accepted social and literary form as he delights in and adorns the role of seducer. Carew's poem exhibits a sophisticated yet playful awareness of audience and a desire to achieve social status through poetic competition; Carew as poet is intensely aware that a courtier's survival at court depends upon his ability to manipulate signs.[4]

The opening lines of the poem (lines 1-26) move rapidly through a tightly structured sequence of persuasive argument founded upon the traditional *carpe diem* theme, but differing sharply from the conventional horizon of expectations usually invoked by this theme. The speaker is no lovesick, worshipful, idealizing boy who hears the harmony of the spheres at the sight of his beloved; he is no amateur at love, but a master player already fully initiated into the subtleties of the game. The forceful, audacious negative that begins the poem already shows the speaker exerting his desire for dominance over a prospective mistress in a rhetorical situation he fully intends to control.

> Thinke not cause men flatt'ring say,
> Y'are as fresh as Aprill, sweet as May,
> Bright as the morning starre,
> That you are so, or though you are
> Be not therefore proud, and deeme
> All men unworthy your esteeme.[5]

The speaker immediately separates himself from "flatt'ring" men who indulge in the traditional homage of Petrarchan compliment; he does not intend to flatter her. The rudeness of his opening remark he quickly counterpoises with "or though you are"; psychologically this operates as a witty ploy to attract and keep the attention of a woman accustomed to receiving artful compliments. The speaker, however, will not give her the satisfaction of an unmitigated compliment, since even if she really is "fresh" and "sweet" and "bright" she would be wrong to separate herself from others by being "proud" and finding "all men unworthy" of her. The speaker has already clearly indicated his separateness from "all," since he refuses to flatter her.

The speaker's argument then glibly grants her provisional status as a beauty, but only by focusing upon her negative quality of proudness. By emphasizing her needs and her "pleasure," the speaker implies a desire to please characteristic of the verse compliment, but he is not an enthralled Petrarchan lover. Arguing that beauty, as nature's bounty and gift, must be enjoyed to be fully appreciated (both by her and by the speaker), the speaker cleverly plays upon the verbal echoes of the "sweet saynt" of Neoplatonic love theory to accuse her of "sinne," which he defines in social terms. If the lady refuses to share her "best graces" so graciously given to her by "prodigall" nature, she will demean herself, since "common beauties" and "meane faces" will have more socially productive pleasures. Behind the *carpe diem* theme, the speaker contrives to project himself as an amorous realist. His compliment on the lady's "best graces," conjoined with the "common beauties" and "meane faces" she may choose to move among, deliberately employs the language of physical advantages, of superficial, although glittering, appearances. The apparent tension between the deceptiveness and disillusionment of the social ritual of compliment and the lady's own artful fashioning of herself, as well as the speaker's awareness of the pragmatic motives that lie beneath the surface of acceptable conduct, strikes a vibrant note of disenchanted wit and a desire for moral directness that echoes throughout the poem.

The implied ethics of dress or costume arising from the speaker's argument not only leads to a fuller discussion of typical *carpe diem* motifs such as time the enemy of beauty and *sic transit gloria mundi,* but also manages in passing to comment on the Neoplatonic and Petrarchan convention of idealizing physical beauty, of equating a beautiful woman with a beautiful soul. The speaker's recognition that even "common beauties" and "meane faces" enjoy "the sport" of love exposes his awareness of amorous pursuit and courtship as elaborate social games, but even more importantly, his belief that women are players too.

> Did the thing for which I sue
> Onely concern my selfe not you,
> Were men so fram'd that they alone
> Reap'ed all the pleasure, women none,
> Then had you reason to be scant;
> But 'twere a madnesse not to grant
> That which affords (if you consent)
> To you the giver, more content
> Then me the beggar; Oh then bee
> Kinde to your selfe if not to mee.
>
> (lines 17-26)

Thus the speaker effectively appeals to "A. L."'s vanity, her sense of exclusion, of being left out of the game, of not being asked again to play. As long as she consciously chooses to set herself apart, she remains, according to the poem's logic, a very poor player. In the context of the speaker's argument and his poetic performance, the lady is worth pursuing only if she is as adept a player as he is; thus the speaker accords her a predominantly social value.

Carew's poem suggests that seduction or courtship play can originate from rather complicated psychological motives, and that such motives influence love's progress. Women, like men, asserts the speaker, are creatures of pleasure, and the pleasure is a shared one, a mutual act of accommodation. Again, this emphasis on sharing echoes the earlier invocation of scantiness in social behavior as a "sinne." "But," posits the speaker, since in granting her

sexual favors to him she is actually guided by her own self-interest, she ought to emulate beneficent nature, and be "prodigall" of herself: "Which affords to the giver . . . *more* content." The implied negative of "if you consent" certainly leaves the speaker not much worse off than the "beggar" he now plays, and he will have the satisfaction of watching her endure her chosen self-denial, or what passes socially for a kind of "madnesse." The speaker's ironic, slightly mocking self-detachment in "Oh then bee / Kinde to your selfe if not to mee" exhibits a frank directness of motives, an admission that his motives are without sentiment although enacted within the context of the appropriate social rites. The successful lover (as a typical role) adopts as a mask or disguise the accepted social or stylized code of behavior appropriate to courtly *amours,* a form of personation that Bacon finds inherent in all public behavior.[6] Men and women may share similar attitudes toward conventions of courtship behavior; the speaker projects a profound sense of displacement from social codes by a blunt recognition of what lies beneath socially prescribed forms. The problem of courtly restraint in human discourse necessitates the ability to read gestures and inflections (social signifiers) properly, since acceptable social conduct involved to a high degree the suppression or reduction of expressivity or genuine self-manifestation.[7]

The couplet in lines 27-28 provides a transition into the lengthy remainder of the poem, which is Carew's free translation of Marino's canzone "Belleza caduca." James V. Mirollo had called Marino's "Belleza caduca" "a dull poem," but Carew's careful reworking of Marino's original is anything but dull.[8] Samuel Daniel, the first translator of Marino into English, in 1623 published his own version of "Belleza caduca," "A Description of Beauty, translated out of Marino," the same model used by Carew in **"To A. L. Perswasions to love."** Reworked in Daniel's hands, "A Description of Beauty" would almost seem to rely on another literary model, so strikingly does it differ from Carew's poem; it lacks the argumentative structure, incisive metaphor, ironic humor and detachment, and persuasive psychological manipulation found in **"To A. L."** Carew commends the *carpe diem* theme, but like Marino, his manner of describing sexual desire and consummation in this poem and others dealing with this theme exhibits a pervasive sense of irony almost bordering on satire.

The remainder of the poem continues its appeal to the woman's "wiser thoughts," her own self-interest, since to forsake such thoughts she would, alas, only be injuring herself. The speaker views the progress of their interaction quite simply, reducing external controls in the open recognition of his physical attraction and his desire for a successful performance in his chosen role. The real sexual warfare, he asserts, is taking place within "A. L." Although he urges her to "starue not your selfe," his tone of ironic detachment, that she may or may *not* make him "pine away," continues to make the speaker the poem's real subject. Against the backdrop of *natura naturans,* time and age hasten toward their end: "Tis gone while wee but say 'tis here" (line 36). The speaker quite frankly tells her that she doesn't have much time left to enjoy herself, for age will bring desertion by mere "flatt'ring" lovers. The seasonal imagery in the poem, with its suggestions of procreation, fecundity, and sexual activity, links the Petrarchan conventions of seasonal change and the lady's participation in natural, cyclical rhythms with the appeal to her "wiser thought." The speaker accords her the capacity to make rational decisions, "And thinke before the summers spent / Of following winter" (lines 52-53), acknowledging that she, like him, has the ability to see beneath conventional rhetoric which only enforces a dogmatic pattern that eliminates her free choice. It is her free choice to submit to the speaker's domination, which he represents as entirely in her own self-interest. In the social roles and contrived performances that constitute human interaction, the psychological complexities that motivate action (or seduction) he attributes to both sexes. However, more important to the speaker's conception of his role is his desire for dominance. He is the poem's subject, and the detached, ironic attitude toward "A. L." throughout the poem makes his adoption of the conventional role of the eternal lover ("one that may / Love for an age, not for a day" [lines 57-58]) morally suspect but stylistically appropriate, and offers the speaker another opportunity to embellish his role.

The speaker desires "A. L." to learn "natural" behavior from the hierarchy of created things he invents and from which she has separated herself: the morally emblematic "Ant" that uses the present time of "plenty" to hoard for the inevitable time of "scant," and the snake, eagle, and rose that together observe time's cycle of death and renewal. "A. L." too has her season of freshness and beauty, but unlike the regenerative seasons of creatures and plants, she is warned that "if your beauties once decay / You never know a second *May*" (lines 77-78). Her "lives short houre" can only be used wisely if her "beauties flower" is shared and enjoyed by both of them. The coordinate verbs in the closing line of the poem prefaced by "both" create a structural antithesis suggestive of time's destruction and renewal, of existence viewed in terms of this continual process.[9]

> Oh, then be wise, and whilst your season
> Affords you dayes for sport, doe reason;
> Spend not in vaine your lives short houre,
> But crop in time your beauties flower:
> Which will away, and doth together
> Both bud, and fade, both blow and wither.
>
> (lines 79-84)

As a seduction poem, **"To A. L. Perswasions to love"** employs the conventional *carpe diem* theme of the transience of love and beauty pitted against time and change, but Carew as poet revitalizes the generic conventions by presenting in the poem's speaker a tension between social ceremony and self-governance. Against the classical antecedents of *carpe diem*, devouring Time, and *sic transit gloria mundi* appropriate to the genre, the speaker imposes himself upon the poem's particular and immediate audi-

ence through his projection of urbane equipoise, mastery of persuasive rhetorical argument, and psychological realism. In performing his role as seducer, the speaker belies hostility and aggression; beneath the playful façade of courtship behavior and social ritual that he artfully exploits exist real needs and desires that must be kept constantly in check. Hostility and aggression represent attitudes of social warfare that the poem's wider audience could doubtless fully appreciate at a time when reputations at court could be won or permanently damaged by verses.

The speaker's own attitude of self-regard throughout the poem also functions for him as a means of self-protection, since he refuses to suffer any loss of self-esteem in this staged social encounter. The poem's argumentative structure and rhetorical strategy also present the speaker's self as a linguistic device. In this sense, then, self as style seizes upon the word as power to embellish and define the speaker's role, traditionally in seduction poems a persuasive one. When the identity of the self is primarily the experience of control over one's powers, then to present an infallible self is to present one which has control over the verbal context of action, such that the proper word or phrase, properly delivered or performed, is the highest attainment of human interpersonal power.[10] By using a variety of strategies then, the speaker maintains strict control of the rhetorical situation, and his subtle expression of antagonism toward the woman in the poem, reinforced by his role distance, serves to sustain his desire for dominance and power in the poem, the realm of art.

**"To A. L. Perswasions to love"** explores the role-playing and psychological motives that underlie social ritual, and Carew's performing speaker offers us one point of view on the proper relationship between men and women. As poetic performance, the concern for interaction between the poem as social and aesthetic artifact and the poem's coterie audience demonstrates a double movement of display and recognition. As social behavior, courtship is primarily concerned with manners, with those attributes of social behavior commonly accepted and legitimized by a particular group. The style of self projected in this poem reflects a preoccupation with the manners of a cultural elite; this style of self may serve as a mask or disguise regularly adopted and discarded by Carew's poetic personae, an activity that permeated every moment of the splendid baroque stage that was life at the court of Charles I. Carew's performing speaker strives for poetic *sprezzatura* as well as sophistication in handling a poetic problem to capture audience interest and to swing the focus of the poem away from the subject addressed to the speaker's own artfully fashioned self.

*Notes*

1. Jean Duvignaud, *The Sociology of Art,* cited in Judith Hook's *The Baroque Age in England* (London: Thames and Hudson, 1976), p. 105.

2. The social and literary tradition of the gentleman-courtier, growing out of Castiglione's *The*

*Courtier,* was reinforced by the numerous popular rhetorical handbooks such as Puttenham's *Arte of English Poesie* (1589); Henry Peacham (the Elder), *The Garden of Eloquence* (1577 and 1593); Angel Day, *The English Secretorie* (1592); and John Hoskins, *Directions for Speech and Style* (ca. 1599); or conduct books such as Henry Peacham's *The Compleat Gentleman* (1634). See also Domna C. Stanton, *The Aristocrat as Art: A Study of the Honnête Homme and the Dandy in Seventeenth- and Nineteenth-Century French Literature* (New York: Columbia Univ. Press, 1980).

3. See Erving Goffman, *The Presentation of Self in Everyday Life* (New York: Doubleday, 1959), p. 22.

4. Norman Bryson, *Word and Image: French Painting of the Ancien Régime* (Cambridge: Cambridge Univ. Press, 1981), p. 40.

5. *The Poems of Thomas Carew, with his Masque Coelum Britannicum,* ed. Rhodes Dunlap (Oxford: Clarendon Press, 1970). All subsequent references to Carew's poetry are taken from this edition.

6. See Bacon's "Of Great Place" and "Of Simulation and Dissimulation" in his *Essayes.* In the former, Bacon expounds upon the need for self-fashioning to prospective social climbers at court; a man must constantly examine himself as to his motives, reflecting upon his successful maneuvers as well as his failures to know how best to conform to what is necessary for social advancement. The gentleman-courtier must become familiar with the role-models attached to his "place," for "imitation is a globe of precepts." An even more revealing preoccupation with techniques of interpersonal strategy and the manipulation of identity can be found in the latter essay, where he identifies three modes of personation common to all human interaction, "Closenesse, Reservation [or] Secrecy," "Dissimulation," and "Simulation." On dissimulation in French baroque court life see Arnold Hauser, *The Social History of Art,* 4 vols. (New York: Vintage Books, 1957), 2:189.

7. Bryson, p. 44.

8. James V. Mirollo, *The Poet of the Marvelous: Giambattista Marino* (New York: Columbia Univ. Press, 1963), ch. 13, "The Marinesque Current in England," p. 251. Dunlap cites evidence from manuscript sources to indicate that lines 1-26 of Carew's poem may have been intended to stand alone as a separate piece; also, the numerous manuscript variants suggest that the poem as a whole (Carew's original 26 lines and the adopted material from Marino) received long and careful polishing. See Dunlap, p. 216.

9. Edward I. Selig, *The Flourishing Wreath: A Study of Thomas Carew's Poetry* (New Haven: Yale Univ. Press, 1958), p. 135.

10. Ernest Becker, "Social Encounters: The Staging of Self-Esteem" in James E. Combs and Michael W.

Mansfield, eds., *Drama in Life: The Uses of Communication in Society* (New York: Hastings House, 1976), p. 105.

## Reid Barbour (essay date 1988)

SOURCE: "'Wee, of th'adult'rate mixture not complaine': Thomas Carew and Poetic Hybridity," in *John Donne Journal,* Vol. 7, No. 1, 1988, pp. 91-113.

[*In the following essay, Barbour assesses Carew's relationship to the poetic values of the Caroline era.*]

This essay explores three related constituents of Thomas Carew's poetry. The first is the poet's uncertainty about the value of what he proclaimed his favorite poetic activity—lyric love poetry. Carew's pronounced ambivalence about this vein emerged from general Renaissance debates about the place of lyric in the literary hierarchy, but it has also influenced the conflicting assessments of his career. He is labelled, on the one hand, a poet of ease, a natural, a "privileged scoffer," and, on the other, a critical poet of "trouble and pain," a poet who almost wrote important verse and only inexactly qualifies for any school or tribe of poetry.[1] Thus, Carew's readers seem to choose between two positions: a satisfaction with his polished lyrics; and a suspicion that Carew's wit does not rest so easily on such a severely limited place in the history of seventeenth-century verse. Rather than take sides, I shall argue that Carew's aesthetic stems in part from this very conflict in his appraisal of the lyric.

Second, Carew represents his unstable valuations of poetry—be it love lyric, verse panegyric, or even prose—as a dialogue between fixity and dispersion. For Carew and his coterie, fixity entails on the "good" side an ideational or truth-telling poetry, a socially conservative poetry, a rhetorically ordered and generically regimented poetry. On the "bad" side it spells "fixation": the poet's own limitations and redundancies, the monotony or obsession which Carew sometimes associates with his beloved "lyric feet." Accordingly, Carew sometimes wonders—and leads critics to ask—about what he might have written. Dispersion on the "bad" side indulges in the dissolute pleasure and empty rhetoric of those same lyric feet, constitutes the punishment which God (in the Psalms translated by Carew) metes out for such dissolution, and unleashes the flux threatening all centers of order—social, religious, and literary. But on the "good" side, Renaissance justifications of dispersion allow pleasure, mixed genres, and playful rhetoric, yield the exhilaration of the multiplex self (Montaigne), and facilitate the saving work of the Reformation.[2] In Carew's poetry, seventeenth-century motives of fixity and dispersion interact in many guises. Further, they find an important measure of value in the poet's adoption of those metaphors for poetic "covers" so traditional in the medieval and exegetical inheritances of the seventeenth century, namely, the so-called integuments or veils under which truth—fixed or dispersed—is putatively secure.[3] In essence, Carew's elegies and lyrics provide a site at which Caroline culture can display, yet also revaluate its reliance on ornamental surfaces.

Finally, and this is third, Carew's unstable literary values provoke him to seek a utopian or privileged discourse that will reconcile, in one hybrid genre, the grandeur of a socially committed poetry, the pleasure of lyric, and the plain fidelity sometimes associated with prose in the early seventeenth century. As the poet explores his media, especially in the masque, he becomes, in A. J. Smith's words, a "superior artist because he admits contrary impulses to his poems and holds them in tense balance, when his associates are happy to fall back upon cliches of sentiment or party loyalties."[4] As in Marvell's poetry, however, "style will not resolve a real clash of interests."[5] Thus, Smith's "balance" resembles the elusive ideals of hybrid discourse and *concordia discors* which Carew proposes but must always refashion.

I

Carew's unstable valuation of the love lyric may readily be placed in context. In *De Sapientia Veterum*, Francis Bacon epitomizes the Renaissance indecision about love's fixity and dispersion. In his interpretation of "Pan," Bacon reads the battle between Pan and Cupid as that between nature's "certain inclination and appetite to dissolve the world and fall back into ancient chaos" and the "overswaying concord of things [which] restrains its will and effort in that direction and reduces it to order."[6] But if Cupid controls the atomistic flux of nature, he also allegorizes that very flux; in his essay on Cupid, Bacon calls the blind archer the "natural motion" of the atom; though the atoms "come together," they also undo everything "fixed and immovable."[7] Both sides of Cupid are imperilled in what Bacon feels to be the obvious interpretation of the dangerous Sirens—the pleasure whose obsession (fixation) leads to dissolution.[8]

In his short lyric, **"A Fancy,"** Carew suggests the ambivalent value of lyric pleasure in terms of the poetic surface and its coterie readers.

> Marke how this polisht Easterne sheet
> Doth with our Northerne tincture meet,
> For though the paper seeme to sinke,
> Yet it receives, and bears the Inke;
> And on her smooth soft brow these spots
> Seeme rather ornaments then blots;
> Like those you Ladies use to place
> Mysteriously about your face:
> Not only to set off and breake
> Shaddowes and Eye beames, but to speake
> To the skild Lover, and relate
> Vnheard, his sad or happy Fate:
> Nor doe their Characters delight,
> As carelesse workes of black and white:
> But 'cause you underneath may find
> A sence that can enforme the mind;
> Divine, or moral rules impart

> Or Raptures of Poetick Art:
> So what at first was only fit
> To fold up silkes, may wrap up wit.[9]

Majorie Donker and George M. Dulbrow have summarized the problems faced by Renaissance theorists who sought to place lyric on the literary hierarchy. Although "lyric" refers, for the most part, to "expressions of praise and persuasion," it ranges from the highest (lauding God, truth, virtue, honor) to the "middle" (according to Puttenham), to the "ignoble" (indulging in human love and pleasure).[10] The same goes for the value of the love lyric in Carew's **"A Fancy."** Although the convening of ink and paper[11] can depict any occasion of writing or printing which in some cases may be channelled into "Raptures of Poetick Art," the first twelve lines also figure the specific vein of silken wit, the smooth and amorous lyrics so persistently issued from Carew's pen, and proclaimed by Carew and his contemporaries as his typical activity—his fixation. As a result, the location (above, "underneath") and agenda ("delight," "impart") of "Raptures" are more elusive than the clear divisions of the poem lead us to believe.

Robert S. Kinsman has argued that qualities akin to fixity and dispersion are mutually associated with Renaissance "fancy." This faculty "is conceived of as an analytical and combinative power," and in music, the "fantasia" thrives on an improvisatory energy which, nonetheless, serves religiously to captivate the auditor: "[i]t is surely of interest that a form acknowledging the force of fancy, that skittery inward sense so frequently rebellious to reason, should have ultimately tamed unruly affections as it added its own entrancing 'free' vigor to the restraints of a musical *ratio*."[12] **"A Fancy,"** the first few images underscore orthodox assets of determinacy in writing. The opening two couplets offer a clever tribute to form-giving powers; the moment when the pen touches paper is both the literal occasion and the metaphorical explanation of ordered expression. Sinking, or excessive absorption of ink so as to produce indefinite shapes,[13] is only a superficial, though pleasing, illusion: the paper surprisingly "bears the Inke"; the contrary qualities of North and East seem resolved; and vague "blots" appear clarified for the "marking" spectator.

"Polisht" and "smooth" are, however, epithets frequently associated by Carew with his typical poetry, his amorous "Lyrique feet, that of the smooth soft way / Of Love, and Beautie, onely know the tread" (Dunlap, 74.6-7). Couched in terms of praise for writing in general, the series of figures beginning "and on her smooth soft brow" gestures toward the amorous conventions that Carew and his contemporaries, even Parliament,[14] agreed to be his type (though they disagreed at times on its merits). The connection between poetic ornament and female adornment has a long history and finds important Elizabethan expression in Puttenham.[15] So too Carew's contemporaries, especially dramatists, compare women's faces to the purity of blank paper, so that writing in schemes and tropes ranges in association from the signs of courtship to the expense of contamination and domination.[16] In Carew's lyric, the indefinite spots secretly appeal to a coterie audience in a fashion at once mysterious and clear. The inky ornaments connecting writing and amours are fancied as a lover's language which must function under the duress of social rules and fickle privilege. Thus figures on the face (paper) inflect, deflect, and reflect at the surface, addressing their special audience, "the skild Lover" (reader), so that the words are "unheard" and yet articulate. Only the initiated reader can decipher such signs.

But the poem does not stop here; rather, it commits itself, though tentatively, to the truth-value of these ornaments. Throughout the first twelve lines, the status of the spots, poetic or otherwise, is elusive. Prior to their becoming witty "characters" in the latter part of the poem (and with that change the authorized vehicles for significant poetry), they waver on a threshold between non-language and ornamented language. The facial ornaments are both fixed in their meaning (they "relate") and dispersive in their activities (they "set off and breake / Shaddowes and Eye beames"): they are at once secure and indirect, powerful and pleasurable.

Yet the alternatives of the final eight lines focus on the validity of these "spots," and raise a central issue for Carew's career; that is, the poet's full participation in the lyrics of courtly fantasy intensifies his recurring criticism of the same in poems, say, to **"La: *Pen*,"** Donne, and Sandys. In the final eight lines, we move from "spots" to "characters," from figurative indirection to statement "underneath" the traditional shell of poetry, and from the analogy of love-games and writing to the potential morality and truth securing language—a movement qualified by "can" and "may." Officially, all worthy poetry has something beneath its surface, and so, in line with traditional hierarchies, the "Raptures of Poetick Art"—potentially, though not necessarily didactic—come almost as an afterthought. They are also, as we have seen, a forethought. In Horatian terms of delight and instruction, then, such "Raptures" are situated somewhere between "carelesse" delights and imparted truth, between amours and morality. Delight itself is tentatively defined; either all delights are careless (including the "spots"), or some, the "Raptures," are "careful" in their alignment with "sence." In sum, Carew's valuation of lyric poetry wavers where one dichotomy (non-poetic and poetic) collides with another within poetry itself (smooth, amorous lyric and serious wit).[17]

The final couplet epitomizes this uncertainty about love lyrics, even as it completes the marshalling activity of logic ("so") and parallelism ("may wrap up wit" matching "underneath may find"). Either the paper was fit to fold silk (or fish) before it received any kind of fancy, or one kind of fancy, silken love poetry, compromises language in its dissolute pleasure.[18] If Carew's poetry is consistent about the terms in which he characterizes his "prophaner" verse ("smooth," "soft," "polisht"), it explores, in turn, the inconsistencies in the linguistic status and value of pro-

faneness—alternately full and empty, fixed and dispersed, useful and fruitless, and sometimes all these qualities at once.

## II

In Carew's **"Ingratefull beauty threatned"**, the speaker's anger at his arrogant mistress disturbs the skill which he has acquired in reading the integuments of love. Unlike Donne's confident elitist in "To his Mistris Going to Bed,"[19] Carew's speaker, having "fixt" the woman in his realm, finds only a troubled analogy with the priestly poets who wrap truth in veils and yet continue to see it:

> Let fooles thy mystique formes adore,
>     I'le know thee in thy mortall state:
> Wise Poets that wrap't Truth in tales,
> Knew her themselves, through all her vailes. (18.15-18)

The truth which the love poet sees beneath his own fiction is now flawed and common; he has flattered his mistress in order to manipulate her, and now struggles with the discrepancies between the shells of "Wise Poets" and his own.

But the most brilliantly disturbing analogy between writing and rapture is **"A Rapture."**[20] Its main strategy is parodic, displacing and mixing resources to upset any systematic or pure poetics. As the speaker evades "[t]he huge Collosses legs," pities Penelope's "dull dreames," and calls for a total revision of love's elegiac and otherwise lyric traditions, he creates a proximity between supposedly serious and dissolute kinds of poetry. That Carew learned much from Donne in this poem ("*more* subtle wreathes") yet provided resources for Crashaw's ecstasy over the prayerbook[21] concurs with this strategy. So do its title (**"Rapture"**)—the ambivalence of which we saw in **"A Fancy"**—and genre (elegy)—the Renaissance range of which spans from the exalted praise of dead aristocrats to the erotic seduction of a mistress. Throughout the poem, Carew figures the analogy between writing and sex in images of fixing and unfixing.

The speaker of **"A Rapture"** calls for a freedom from traditional values—shams, he says, akin to economic abuse. Yet attempting to obtain his own mastery over the silent mistress—one which coins, rifles, and collects double rent—he makes the sexual writerly ("wearing as I goe / A tract for lovers on the printed snow" [51.71-72]) and the literary grotesquely sexual: the raped Lucrece proves to enjoy pornographic lectures, and so imitates art along the lines of those mangled orgies fancied by "Loves great master, Aretine" (52.116). Thus, "to quench the burning Ravisher, she hurles / Her limbs into a thousand winding curles, / And studies artfull postures, such as be / Caru'd on the barke of every neighbouring tree / By learned hands" (52.119-23). Both "plyant" and "caru'd," Lucrece's dissolution is somehow controlled by the obsessions of love's master: fixation and dispersion interlock. Indeed, several images in the poem depict unfixing: for example,

Ovid's "Daphne hath broke her barke, and that swift foot, / which th'angry Gods had fastned with a root / To the fixt earth, doth now unfetter'd run" (52.131-33). But Daphne's release—and the speaker's release from the tyranny of tradition and honor—become fixed in an alternative tradition, with its own "fixt earth," isolated paradise, and abuses. Of course, her status has literary relevance: Daphne, secured again in the "embraces of the youthfull Sun," is comparable to the god's poetic instrument, "his Delphique Lyre" (52.135).

Along with the sexual merger of fixity and dispersion, social and literary codes converge in **"A Rapture."** Social codes of revenge dictate writerly requirements "to carve out . . . revenge, upon that word" and brand "[w]ith markes of infamie," both subsumed at last in a Donnean paradox about "[t]his Goblin Honour" (53.160-66). Sex and "sweet" poetry coincide in a single gesture: "Laura lyes / In Petrarchs learned armes, drying those eyes / That did in such sweet smooth-pac'd numbers flow" (52.139-41). And it is the same for the inspired poet: Daphne, "[f]ull of her God . . . sings inspired Layes, / Sweet Odes of love, such as deserve the Bayes, / Which she her selfe was" (52.137-39). Thus, the poem recalls the analogy between amorous and rhetorical schemes in **"A Fancy."** Also, in **"A Rapture,"** love's discourse is unheard by "jealous eares," and the phallic bark, having sailed the "sea of Milke" and "smooth, calme Ocean," plays upon the sinking and "bounding" waves that give way to "Halcion calmnesse" wherein the gods "fix our soules" (51.85-98). Such sexual "fancies" subvert the Jonsonian tradition in which only poetasters "deformed their mistress" (poetry) while true poets steer souls by their rudder, the moral pen.[22] With the enraptured "Rudder" steering "into Loves channell," Carew's conjunction of eroticism and poetry establishes new standards for his typical poetry, yet leaves them as questionable as the old "cancell'd lawes."

### III

If the convergence of poetic resources can subvert traditional values, their reconciliation in one mixed genre offers an idealized revision of these values. Carew's search for the ideal mixture—the goal always deferred—is most extensive in his masque, but it operates in several of his other poems. The construction of what Terence Cave calls a Utopian text[23]—one which generates, yet circumscribes every resource imaginable—is analogous to Carew's enterprise of locating a hybrid genre which resolves the conflicts of fixity and dispersion. Yet Carew's "resources of kind," as Rosalie Colie might call them,[24] must be interpreted in terms of the poet's typical assumptions and critical questions about poetry, found especially in his social panegyrics and versified literary criticism.

That seventeenth-century poets organized verse by types or "veins" directs any such search for an ideal mixture of resources. Whereas our anthologies tend to use Carew as a case study of a poet who eludes any simple "tribe," Carew and his contemporaries were more reductive with his po-

etry. Shirely declared Carew to be the headmaster, before Stanley's arrival, of love's poetic school, "the Oracle of Love" whose "numerous language" would "steer every genial soul." Another poet considered Carew ever sweet, never satirical, though this is patently untrue. Parliament reduced his poems to pornography.[25]

Carew's own typifications sometimes work in his favor. In **"To My Rivall,"** his "smooth soft language" (41.10) is also full and powerful, in contrast to the rival's dissolute "empty words" (41.5). With something presumably "underneath" their soft textures, Carew's words can even allow dispersion in pleasure: "Such pearlie drops, as youthfull May / Scatters before the rising day" (41.8-9). The rival is a "vaine intruder" whose "unhallowed brine" is excluded from the speaker's rituals of love.

Yet Carew's address to Sandys "on his translation of the Psalmes" finds his own "smooth" words "unhallowed," "unwasht," and outside the temple (93.1-4). Carew's Muse, with her "Lyrick feet," is "restlesse" and empty, though obsessed and "cloy'd" with secular love (94.23-28). Carew fears that his advertisement for Sandys's Psalms will contaminate their purity, yet he dwells on his own poetic possibilities—on what his verse "may" be, either as a secular handmaid to, or as the equivalent of, Sandys's Muse.[26] Unfixing his poetry from its dissolute obsessions "may"—and the modal recalls **"A Fancy"**—be a first step in transforming it into something securely meaningful. As in **"A Fancy"** or his verse letter to Townsend, Carew considers "higher" verse in the subjunctive mood; he expresses loyalty to Sandys in terms of what he himself might write. We shall see that Carew's contrast between his lyric obsessions and unfulfilled potential recurs in the more persuasive elegies to **"La: Pen,"** Townsend, and Donne.

When Carew does translate Psalms, he dutifully conveys the stark dichotomy between the righteous with "Soe fixt a state" and the sinful, "like the light dust / That vpp and downe the Emptie Ayre / The wilde wynd driues, with various Gust" (135.16-19). Sandys's own translation of this passage includes a metaphor which, applied to poetry, resembles that of the veil—"dispers'd like chaff." In poems like the one to Sandys, Carew makes it clear that chaffy poetry—however pleasurable—can become a tiresome fixation. In turn, the religious "tractes" written by God's "Law giueing finger" (135.6-7) provide an alternative to the sexual "tracts" of **"A Rapture"**. But Carew's poetry dwells less on a new (spiritual) "fixt . . . state," and more on possibility; consequently, his application at the "Alters" of Psalm 51—where the unlikely conversion might occur—is more permissive and urgent than Sandys's.[27]

But rival claims for his loyalty give Carew the occasion to parody the instability of poetic values. Consider the rivalry between the lover and the funeral elegist in that strange **"Elegie on the La: Pen: sent to my Mistresse out of France."** Put simply, the poet would write on either side of the titular colon—of the dead patron or of the quick mistress—if he had a longer attention span. Writing love poetry on a regular basis, he admits, invites monotony: "My Muse must back to her old exercise, / To tell the story of my martyrdome" (21.70-71). More than in the Sandys poem, Carew suggests the mechanical procedures by which the courtly poet can versify love's conventions. Yet the distracted poet is also dispersed, "as ghosts flye away," by the "minions of the Muses" who come with the single purpose of praising the dead patron with tears of manna (21.75-78). Suddenly, the lover faces the possibility that his attentions are at once too fixed and not fixed enough.

With this divided purpose, the speaker's private obsessions and public obligations confront one another. He finds himself apologizing to the mistress:

> Though you are only soveraigne of this Land,
> Yet universall losses may command
> A subsidie from every private eye,
> And presse each pen to write; so to supply,
> And feed the common griefe; if this excuse
> Prevaile not, take these teares to your owne use,
> As shed for you; for when I saw her dye,
> I then did thinke on your mortalitie. (20.25-32)

As in some of Donne's verse letters,[28] the strategy and aim of the elegy are fractured—its tears have uncertain application and value. In fact, the "praise" for the dead Lady virtually desires her death as well as a return from funeral elegy to love lyric: "[I] began to feare lest Death, their [the gods'] Officer, / Might have mistooke, and taken thee [the mistress] for her" (20.41-42). Having attempted to negotiate between his two "subjects," the speaker eventually stops weighing the "losse i'th' change 'twixt heav'n and earth," and settles for the security his customary "chanell": "But I must weepe no more over this urne, / My teares to their owne chanell must returne; / And having ended these sad obsequies, / My Muse must back to her old exercise" (21.67-70). In the end, he chooses "ignoble" regularity over the fullness of virtue.

The choice, however, is not so clear. The assumption of virtue beneath the elegiac veil is threatened by the potential scandal of the dead "subject." Lady Peniston, one candidate, was reputedly an adulteress whose epitaph roughly resembles Donne's holy sonnet on the church: Lady Peniston, "love'd / By the most worthy of her time," may in heaven "love all that love hir, and not sinne" (Dunlap, 223). As Howard Bloch has shown about other texts,[29] sexual scandal figures a scandal for poetry itself—presumed to be a garment that, fitting true, cohesive nature without tear or excess, never achieves such a match, and never really has such a subject to cover. So too the elegiac confusion of purpose thrives in a coterie which generates tension between one gesture (praise) and another (desire). **"La: *Pen*"** is a flawed subject, not just because society deemed her disreputable, but because Stuart poetry reappraises the value of poetic surfaces, and intensifies the struggle between constraint and license in its coterie verse. Carew's "chanell," then, flows in what one critic calls "the difficult channels of Jacobean society."[30]

Even "proper" subjects for mournful elegy—the Countess of Anglesie and her deceased husband—engage Carew's wit in the paradoxes of fixity and dispersion. Again, love lyric and funeral elegy become rivals in their claims for fullness. To begin with, the elegy admires the marvelous ways in which the couple wards off atomism, not unlike the Lady in **"Song: Aske me no more":**

> You, that behold how yond' sad Lady blends
> Those ashes with her teares, lest, as she spends
> Her tributarie sighes, the frequent gust
> Might scatter up and downe the noble dust,
> Know when that heape of Atomes, was with bloud
> Kneaded to solid flesh, and firmely stood
> On stately Pillars, the rare forme might move
> The froward Juno's, or chast Cinthia's love.
>
> (69-70.27-34)

The widow's tears and the husband's "kneaded" body perform the same task of preventing the otherwise unrestrained dispersion of the husband's ashes and charms. In turn, the poet follows convention in asking the Countess to unfix her obsession with the dead; in suggesting new loves for her, the poet declares all mournful utterance to be "hollow Echoes." By implication, amorous poetry is full, and the poet offers to make her loves his regular subject—"the Trophies of your conquering eye" (71.86). The husband's solidity, after all, was constituted by the fancies of scattered women: "He was compos'd of all / The wishes of ripe Virgins, when they call / For Hymens rites, and in their fancies wed / A shape of studied beauties to their bed" (70.37-40). Ironically, the Countess's new loves will coincide with her redemption from the dust of her husband: "Seeke him no more in dust, but call agen / Your scatterd beauties home" (71.83-84). In allowing the Countess new desires, the poet opts to return to his "old exercise."

IV

The realization that Carew's "typical" lyrics of desire and praise involve a troubled dialogue between fixity and dispersion, fullness and emptiness, is only a first step. This dialogue, to repeat, situates Carew's lyric career in the context of seventeenth-century reconsideration of many guarantors of order—in the self, in political rule, in worship, in the book of nature, and in language. But we must also reconstruct Carew's proposals for a stable textual concourse or hybrid genre from his query of literary possibilities. Such a *concordia discors* would presumably transform the separate resources—lyric and prose, for example—into an ideal text ensuring the order and purity of "the Caroline autocracy."[31] Poetry in general, whether epideictic or amorous, becomes questionable in regard to its truth-value. That prose might play a role in the posing of ideal texts gains reinforcement from Carew's success with prose in his masque. Yet his inclination toward the "kneaded" discourse appears in several poems, where prose is cited as firm, linear, and plainly true. Its quotidian plainness spells, however, its limits, so that prose must appropriate the grandeur of an idealizing poetry and the pleasures of the love lyric.[32]

In **"Obsequies to the Lady Anne Hay"**, Carew associates "the sleeke / And polisht Courtier" with the monotony of his own lyric activities:

> I that ne're more of private sorrow knew
> Then from my Pen some froward Mistresse drew,
> And for the publike woe, had my dull sense
> So sear'd with ever adverse influence,
> As the invaders sword might have, unfelt,
> Pierc'd my dead bosome, yet began to melt. (67.7-12)

Not only is the poet's customary "channell" (cf. 67.2) irresponsibly private and empty—his are no "reall teares"—but it is "artlesse," for all its sophistication. Art requires, therefore, some access to truth; but it needs guidance, because the subject is unseen as well as unheard: "But who shall guide my artlesse Pen, to draw / Those blooming beauties, which I never saw?" (67.19-20). And simply following the lyric conventions of fulsome praise and "learned" conceits ("rifling so whole Nature / Of all the sweets a learned eye can see" [67.26-27]) will earn the poet little credit from "posterities."

The poet has recourse from the "dull wayes" of ornamentation in his resolve that Lady Anne Hay is "the Theame of Truth, not Poetrie" (68.46). This creed of linguistic fidelity to the truth echoes Daniel's *Civil Wars* which, as Jonson bluntly put it, contributed to the emerging prosaics of poetry.[33] Yet the poet, having suggested that Anne Hay cannot be measured by the "Exactest lawes" of saints, must not simply write as if her life were dull fact for chronicle or annals. He cannot simply oppose the fact of her existence against the polish of tropes and figures. Thus, although there is something recurringly attractive for Carew in the plain fidelity and linearity of prose, he makes it one facet of a hybrid genre which is also exalted and full in its poetic grandeur. This is subtly figured in Anne Hay's peers, who will continue her noble line as the "glorious journall of [her] thrifty dayes, / Like a bright starre, shot from his sphaere, whose race / In a continued line of flames, we trace" (68.64-66). In such a living elegy, the prose chronicle of everyday life or of a journey merges with the glorious force (*energia*) of exalted poetry. But, as Carew has remarked, the courtier's amorous "lyric feet" usually lack force as well—Sidney would agree—and must be strengthened as part of the hybrid. For the mixture of exalted elegy, honest prose, and smooth, amorous lyric prevails as Carew's ideal poem.

So Carew completes his hybrid when he includes the staples of Petrarchan lyric, presumably refined beyond desire, in his praise for Anne Hay:

> One shall enspheare thine eyes, another shall
> Impearle thy teeth; a third, thy white and small
> Hand, shall besnow; a fourth, incarnadine
> Thy rosie cheeke, untill each beauteous line,
> Drawne by her hand, in whom that part excells,
> Meet in one Center, where all beautie dwells.

> (68.51-56)

It is such a resourceful "Center" that the poet would find, and yet it is distant from him, in his poems as it is in Anne

Hay's noble survivors. The poet's own status is ambivalent, caught between dull courtly poets and those poets who see in Anne Hay's death "just cause" for grief.

Carew's hybrid ideal is most clearly articulated in his critical praise of other poets (Townsend, Donne, Jonson, and Davenant). These poems are defined by loyalty on the one hand, and by analysis on the other; as such, they clarify Carew's position in his culture's heightened confrontation with fixity and dispersion—in politics and religion, in psychology and science, and in literature.[34] In his fashioning of ideals, however, Carew is notoriously critical or "honest."[35] He refuses to posit a final escape from the conflicts and impurities which disturb his mixture of resources.

Carew's manifesto for the national segregation of English verse—**"In answer of an Elegiacall Letter upon the death of the King of Sweden from Aurelian Townsend"**—dictates that the English poets dwell on careless pleasure—"the smooth soft way / Of Love, and Beautie" (74.6-7). What results is a conservative reversal of poetic hierarchies—all to ensure the poet's total disengagement from European politics. Amid the complexities of this "answer," the poet offers his hybrid text of exalted elegy, prose chronicle, and lyric.[36] Lyric is the primary consideration. Despite his performance of a funeral elegy, Carew suggests that venturing thus "beyond the pale" of his customary lyrics will imbroil him, as it would English society, in contaminating political issues. The "smooth soft way" of his "Lyrique feet" secures Carew in a social and textual domain, so that his reluctance about amorous verse in **"A Fancy"** converts into a halcyon satisfaction "In answer."

But a secure lyric vein is one face of a Janus whose other face is dull complacence, a "drowsiness" which recalls the "dullness" of courtly lyric in **"Anne Hay,"** and anticipates the "lazie seeds" of the Donne elegy. Although love poetry is exalted to the status of national epic, the poet's ambition to write "glorious journalls" still intrudes. These "Journals" (75.27) would stretch impressively, yet unsafely out of the light of English calm and into the "Heroique shade," improper yet transcendent "[a]bove the reach of our faint flagging ryme" (77.92-93). In showing loyalty to Townsend's poetic "wing," Carew's Muse hovers between the inside and outside of the prescribed circle. But the inside—lyric pleasure—entails a legislated fixity while the outside—the "loftier pitch"—spells dispersion into the political and literary beyond.

Carew answers these ironies with a literary hybrid of heroic elegy, "faithful" prose, and silken lyric. There are two reasons why prose is required: poets from Virgil to Donne cannot invent "a just Poem to this subject fit" (75.14), and their poems in any event would be superfluous, unable to elevate the King any "higher." The prose "Journal" should be "modest faithfull"—the work of some "grave Chronicler"—yet its quotidian nature is transformed "to Poems" by the romantic text of the King's heroic life. The results

of this mix are paradoxical: as the prose finds its fulfillment in the poem of the King's life, this poem resembles
an outrageous fiction, "things rather feign'd then done /
Like our Romances of the Knight o'th' Sun" (75.23-24).
Both historical prose and romantic poetry divide in their
status between emptiness and fullness, so that the projected fruits of the hybrid are at once apt and incredible.
This mixture includes the poem's basic commitment to
smooth, amorous lyric which itself vacillates between an
apt, yet "flagging" revelry and the national "plenty" on
which such "prophane" or "low" verse is based (74-77.10,
47, 93).

This confluence of literary channels asserts an ideal *concordia discors* against what seems the inevitability of textual and political impurity. Renaissance poets often expose
the problematics of mixed genre, the complex criteria of
historical writing, and the impossibility of literary segregation from the "world."[37] Yet in a poem to Davenant, Carew
affirms the validity of his hybrid in the very terms of contamination which seem so threatening to it:

> What though Romances lye
> Thus blended with more faithfull Historie?
> Wee, of th'adult'rate mixture not complaine,
> But thence more Characters of Vertue gaine;
> More pregnant Patterns, of transcendent Worth,
> Than barren and insipid Truth brings forth:
> So, oft the Bastard nobler fortune meets,
> Than the dull Issue of the lawfull sheets. (98.13-20)

Suddenly Carew enters the domain of Sidney's *Apology*
and of Greville's biography of Sidney with their claim that
"Characters of Vertue" and "pregnant Patterns, of transcendent Worth" are superior to mere fact. Like Sidney,
who sometimes chafes at the contamination of literary
mixtures (for example, tragicomedy), Carew assumes that
*sprezzatura,* if not morality, legitimates the bastard. At
least, the social consensus is said to permit the "adult'rate
mixture." "Faithfull Historie" is still a partner, but incurs
the charge of infidelity in admitting a glorious romantic
presence. Indeed, Carew is clearer about the status of these
sheets—paper and bedclothing—than he is about the face /
paper of **"A Fancy"**; but he must also admit that the purity and lawfulness of poetry are undone. The "pregnant
Patterns"—however true and full—have no ultimate control over the strange "Issue" emerging from underneath
poetry's "sheets."

## V

Eventually, the masque offers Carew's most comprehensive forum in which to propose a reconciliation between
glory, fidelity, and pleasure. In the poem to Townsend,
Carew refashions one of Townsend's masques, using both
description and typification to suggest the masque's hybrid
nature and its avoidance of the contextual problems surrounding all masques.[38] This reconstructed masque, to
which I will return, is clarified in its hybridity by Carew's
other poems of critical allegiance.

**"An Elegie upon the death of the Deane of Pauls, Dr.
Iohn Donne"** attempts to resolve the exalted, lyrical, and

prosaic constituents of Donne's works. As usual, Carew
scolds bad poets and prose writers on two counts: they
"force" or attempt what is beyond their abilities (that is,
they are limited to a single poetic vein), and their rhetoric
is insipid, "lazie" (72.26), "dry" (71.7), and "fading"
(71.6). As he begins to examine Donne's resources, Carew
treats Donne's prose as a faithful premise, an anchor. Yet
the sermons are not merely records of faith and doctrine;
rather they are fired with glorious significance, a "journal
of deep mysteries" as Vaughan says in another context.[39]
Other prose lacks both the passion and depth of Donne's
prose: such unworthy stuff is incomplete, "dowe-bak't"
(71.4). By contrast, Donne's prose is transformed by the
poet's soul into the kind of complete amalgam that the
King of Sweden's life makes from a chronicle of events.

If glory and pregnancy expand the "kneaded" material of
prose, Donne's poetry, with its "rich and pregnant phansie" or "Giant phansie," becomes the scene of a necessary
struggle with linguistic restraints. The "tough-thick-rib'd
hoopes" are distinguished from the "soft melting Phrases"
of much lyric poetry (73.51-53); as "hoopes," Donne's inventive language is somehow tougher, more colloquial
than "the jugling feat / Of two-edg'd words" (72.34-35).
The credibility of poetry resides in its "line / Of masculine
expression," in qualities which redeem language from
emptiness, duplicity, and remoteness. After all, Donne's
"Giant phansie" might prove as insubstantial as the Donnean masquer in **"A Rapture"** and the romantic heroes of
"An Answer." Grounding fancy in linguistic fact, Donne
offers the best prosaic poetry, just as he bequeaths the best
poetic prose.

Although such hybridity already accounts in part for
Donne's lyric revolution, Carew addresses directly what
amounts to Donne's failure to cure the deficiencies of lyric
in any lasting way. Such failure serves to celebrate
Donne's achievement, but it also affirms the degeneration
of the lyric tradition into plagiaristic monotony—the typical "soft melting Phrases" mindlessly imitative of Anacreon. Donne's work in "the Muses garden" has "throwne
away" the "lazie seeds" of lyric monotony and "servile
imitation," but these seeds are disseminated, if fruitless
(72.25-27). Above all, they are empty: "with these /
The silenc'd tales o'th' Metamorphoses / [the poets] shall stuff
their lines, and swell the windy Page" (73.66-67). For all
Donne's efforts, inauthenticity prevails, while the justification of lyric still eludes.

In his ode to Ben Jonson, whose utmost toil "sleekes . . .
terser Poems," Carew edges closer toward what justifies
an obsession with lyric. It is the very labor—the "trouble
and pain"—with which one creates, yet also questions and
challenges, the lyric. Lazy versifiers feel no guilt about
their "hired" conventions; but Jonson, says Carew, grows
"pale with guilt" about the derivative nature of his poems
(65.36). If amorous lyrics in particular expose a troublesome proximity between fixity and dispersion in Stuart literary values, they also reveal what is imperfect, yet productive about the hybrid, the *concordia discors,* or the

resolution of materials. Indeed, "resolve," in the seventeenth century, ranges in meaning from utmost fixity to utter dispersion; but, as Owen Feltham defined it in the 1620s, to resolve is above all to revise.[40] Accordingly, Carew's elegy for Donne situates the living poet between the "panting numbers" or "gasping short winded Accents" of an easy, courtly lyric unaccustomed to labor, and the dis-eased sense of inadequacy with which painstaking poets like Jonson "dispense / Through all our language, both the words and sense" (71.9-10). Although Donne—his influence flagging—must "spit disdaine" on Carew's efforts (74.85), these very efforts confirm the significance of Donne's hybridity.

In his criticism of plays, particularly Davenant's, Carew finds ideal texts in special need of protection from impurity. In the case of drama, however, contamination derives from the "marking" spectator, so that Carew elevates the objective constituents of the text over the tastes of the audience. With the masque, the protected audience of King and court offers no such threat to the mixed virtues of the masque's own text, architecture, and performance. We see the hybrid constituents of a masque in Carew's recreation of what may be Townsend's *Tempe Restord*. In his "answer" to Townsend, Carew reports some facets of the plot, devices, and characters of *Tempe Restord*, yet calls it the *Shepherds Paradise*.[41] Carew's conflation signals what the passage itself suggests, that he is offering an idealized type as well as a report. Thus, the "glorious night" of the masque (76.59) is both historical and utopian—as surely as is Anne Hay's "glorious journal." The agenda of the masque, as stated by Carew, redacts the familiar Spenserian / Jonsonian metaphor for controlling virtue, given new meaning in **"A Rapture"**: "to guide / Our steerelesse barkes in passions swelling tide / By vertues Carde" (76.61-63). But this purpose, resembling the autocratic aims of the Caroline masque in general,[42] also offers to rectify the now familiar facets of Carew's favorite hybrid. Thus, "sweetly-flowing numbers" interact with a "Masculine stile" and "ravishing sounds" (76.58, 71, 75). The story, both complex and profound, and the spectacle, both "celestiall" and mythological, represent to all faculties the stable fusion of "Knowledge and pleasure . . . [and] amazement" (76.76-77). Carew's tribute echoes his elegy to Donne, insofar as Townsend is said to transcend the "darke sullen precepts" of other writers, and to "dispense / Knowledge and pleasure, to the soule, and sense" (76.65, 75-76). Furthermore, Townsend confirms the interaction of prose and poetry found in Donne's works: Townsend's "loose discourse is farre / More neate and polish then our Poems are" (76.55-56). For lesser poets, whose texts fail to achieve *concordia discors,* Carew resorts to the national legislation limiting their activity in the "answer" to Townsend. His own status, we already know, is uncertain.

In Townsend's masque, Carew claims, dispersion is simply wonderful. With the advancement of the night, the pleasure of "dance . . . and revel" and other "harmlesse pastimes" dissipate the ethereal mysteries of the masque in the very act of filling the elite audience with them, and of riveting that audience to them:

> It fill'd us with amazement to behold
> Love made all spirit, his corporeall mold
> Dissected into Atomes melt away
> To empty ayre, and from the grosse allay
> Of mixtures, and compounding Accidents
> Refin'd to immateriall Elements. (76.77-82)

As the ornaments of **"A Fancy"** are unstable in their linguistic status, so too the pure refinement of "mixtures" does not clearly separate ideality from dispersion into "empty ayre." In both works, the ornaments and staging are deceptive, with so much unseen and unheard. The ideal literary concourse, as Carew defines it, seems necessarily constituted by the impure channels that feed it: in the materials of his texts, Carew promotes Caroline ideals of ethereal virtue in terms of their "grosse allay / Of mixtures."

## VI

The masque, like the lyric, elicited radically different valuations from its seventeenth-century creators and audiences—from royal excess and empty spectacle to "more removed mysteries."[43] Above all, masques attempted to reconcile pleasure and virtue, text and architecture, disorder and order. But the status of the masque was questioned, and the artists themselves located their creations somewhere between the contingencies of occasion and the permanence of Forms.[44] As Jennifer Chibnall has explained, the Caroline masque staged such negotiations in "continual attempts to deal with uncertainties and social realities";[45] in other words, resolution and reform were problematic for the aristocracy:

> [w]here Jonson sought to reconcile the elements, to re-order the disorder and vitality of the anti-masque, the Caroline masque attempts only to contain it. Spectacle more readily both encompasses the flux of creative revel and transcends it. To attempt resolution is to risk failure.[46]

Still, in *Coelum Britannicum,* Carew tries to "argue a resolution of the contradictory ideologies" of aristocratic stasis—their superior place given to them—and aristocratic reform—their places compromised by social change and by personal vice. As Chibnall says of the aristocracy, their "place cannot be static yet must be stable."[47]

Carew's masque proposes, then, to reconcile the values conflicting at all Caroline thresholds—at the surface of the love lyric, at the revelry joining masquers and audience, at the fruition of hybrid ideals. Not surprisingly, *Coelum Britannicum* offers a powerful amalgam of blank verse, plain-speaking prose, and lyric. Moreover, in representing political reform, it reiterates the ultimate fixity of the Caroline rulers—they are "ever-fixed"—yet not at the expense of their graceful movements and gracious dispensations on earth. With the unfettered Hedone banished from Caroline heavens, Carew's lyrics pray for an aristocratic security transcending the toilsome activities of the lower ranks:

> Eternitie:
> Brave Spirits, whose adventrous feet

> Have to the Mountaines top aspir'd,
> Where faire Desert, and Honour meet,
>   Here, from the toyling Presse retir'd,
> Secure from all disturbing Evill,
> For ever in my Temple revell. (184.1115-20)

But much insecurity remains for Carew's Muse to charm away. Beneath the temple of "Apollos quire," where the aristocracy are circumscribed in space, the ascending "Rout" resist "the resistlesse influence" of their superiors (184.1125). In Carew's heretical source, Bruno's *Spaccio de la Bestia Trionfante,* the Truth and Virtue of celestial reform must reckon with Bruno's contention that there are infinite worlds, and that Jupiter is irreducibly protean.[48] For all its obsession with the centrality of Charles and Maria, Carew's masque is itself a complex symbolic act which has no ultimate control over the values of dispersion in seventeenth-century culture. Nevertheless, the ornaments of Carew's poetry, like much drama of his time, offer critical allegiance to a status quo seeking, though in halcyon days, for acceptable terms in which to revise itself.[49]

If there is truth in John Suckling's parody, invention did not come easily for Thomas Carew. But even if Suckling's accusation of "trouble and pain" has no basis in fact, it clinches Carew's importance for our understanding of Caroline aesthetics. Michael P. Parker has shown that Suckling's charge locates Carew outside the privileged circle of natural and, therefore, careless wits, whose *sprezzatura* carried the day over the fever and fret of studied composition.[50] It is safe, I think, to reverse Suckling's defensive claims and to suppose that Carew's pursuit of the hybrid genre gives us a glimpse at the motives of Caroline ethereality and carelessness. Other glimpses are available, say, in the dreams recorded in Laud's diary, or in the "resolve" with which John Ford's protagonists vainly attempt to change themselves. In each case, we see the toil of legitimation in Caroline discourse, for all its feckless calm and abundant glory. Not unlike Milton's pastoral garden, Carew's hybridity—which one critic likens to pastoral[51]—reckons the value of the labor itself.

*Notes*

1. The paradoxes invading Carew's status and potential as a poet of many slight, though skillful, lyrics and a few great elegies may be found in appraisals by the poet himself, by the poet's contemporaries, and by twentieth-century critics. For the Carew whose poetic "preference" for smooth lyrics was "determined by the nature of his poetic gift," see Leah Jonas, *The Divine Science* (New York: Columbia Univ. Press, 1940), p. 245. For the poet of "trouble and pain" who could not quite escape his self-claimed limitations, see Joseph H. Summers, *The Heirs of Donne and Jonson* (Oxford: Oxford Univ. Press, 1970), pp. 62-64, 72-75; Michael P. Parker, "'All are not born (Sir) to the Bay': 'Jack' Suckling, 'Tom' Carew, and the Making of a Poet," *English Literary Renaissance* 12 (1982), 362-63. For

Carew as the "privileged scoffer," see Annabel Patterson, *Censorship and Interpretation* (Madison: Univ. of Wisconsin Press, 1984). Other studies of Carew's reputation include James E. Ruoff, "Thomas Carew's Early Reputation," *Notes and Queries* 202 (1957), 61-62; Lynn Sadler, *Thomas Carew* (Boston: Twayne, 1979), ch. 7; and Rhodes Dunlap, ed., *The Poems of Thomas Carew with his Masque "Coelum Britannicum"* (Oxford: Clarendon, 1970), pp. xlvi-li.

2. According to John Jewel (1562), the "majesty and Godhead of Christ be everywhere abundantly dispersed," thanks to the Reformation. Against the fragmentation of the Church, however, Jewel insists that Christ is "in one place." See *Apologia Ecclesiae Anglicanae,* ed. J. Ayre (Parker Society), p. 59.

3. For allegory whose truth is dispersed beneath the veil, see Henry Vaughan, "Monsieur Gombauld" (ed. Alan Rudrum [New Haven: Yale Univ. Press, 1976], 81,41-44): "Nor are they mere inventions, for we / In the same piece find scattered philosophy / And hidden, dispersed truths that folded lie / In the dark shades of deep allegory." Gombauld's romance is also called a "commended mixture" of "Fables with truth, fancy with history," for which see the discussion of Carew's mixed genres below.

4. A. J. Smith, *The Metaphysics of Love* (Cambridge: Cambridge Univ. Press, 1985), p. 238.

5. Smith, p. 238.

6. Francis Bacon, *De Sapientia Veterum,* in *The Works,* ed. by James Spedding et. al., vol. 13 (Boston: Brown and Taggard, 1860), 99. Another good place to look for the Renaissance struggle to contain the very desires which it permits are the epithalamia of the period, for example, Spenser's lyric and also Jonson's in *Hymenaei.*

7. Bacon, pp. 122-25.

8. Bacon, pp. 169-72.

9. Dunlap, p. 117. Carew's poems are quoted in this edition by page and line numbers.

10. See their *Dictionary of Literary-Rhetorical Conventions of the English Renaissance* (Westport, CT: Greenwood, 1982), pp. 134-38.

11. The "Eastern" quality of the paper seems generic, though one auditor has suggested that this refers to "rice paper."

12. *The Darker Vision of the Renaissance: Beyond the Fields of Reason,* ed. with an introduction by Robert S. Kinsman (Berkeley: Univ. of California Press, 1974), pp. 7-8.

13. Thus the OED defines "sink."

14. See Ruoff's article, cited above.

15. See Puttenham, *The Arte of English Poesie* (Kent, OH: Kent State Univ. Press, 1970), pp. 149-50.

16. See, for example, Dekker, *Satiromastix* (in *The Dramatic Works,* ed. Bowers [Cambridge: Cambridge Univ. Press, 1953], I, ii, 225-27): "Say that you have not sworne unto your Paper, / To blot her white cheekes with the dregs and bottome / Of your friends private vices"; and Congreve, *Love for Love* (in *The Complete Plays,* ed. Davis [Chicago: Univ. of Chicago Press, 1967], IV, i, 634-39): "You're a Woman . . . [y]ou are all white, a sheet of lovely spotless Paper, when you first are Born; but you are to be scrawl'd and blotted by every Goose's Quill."

17. With its heightened analysis and criticism of nature and of language, the seventeenth century is especially interesting in its views toward integuments. A scene in Townsend's *Albion's Triumph* resolves the problems surrounding allegorical "veils" and the hieroglyph of nature into comedy, with Platonicus speaking for Caroline ideals:

> Platonicus: . . . For I will goe with thee [to the amphitheater], if it be but to teach thee to Reade in thy owne Booke. Outsides have Insides, Shells have Kernells in them. And under every Fable, nay (almost) under every thing, lyes a Morall. What art thou doing Publius?
>
> *Publius stumbles at a stone, and stoops to take it up.*
>
> Publius: Lifting up the stone I stumbled at.
>
> Platonicus: To what ende?
>
> Publius: To see what lyes under it.
>
> Platonicus: What should lye under a stone, but a Worme, or a Hoglouse?
>
> Publius: If there lye not a Morall under it, then have you taught me false Doctrine.
>
> Platonicus: Such thankes have they that teach such Schollers.
>
> (*The Poems and Masques,* ed. Brown [Reading: Whiteknights Press, 1983], 82)

Lynn Sadler (74-75) has commented on "A Fancy" that this "slight, rather strange little poem . . . also makes a strong case for the worthwhileness of poetry beneath its mere surface texture," and that it implies an elite, "fit" audience. Yet Sadler does not pursue the poem's strangeness.

18. Puttenham compares poetic ornaments to "silkes or tyssewes and costly embroderies" (150). Cf. Berowne's rejection of the lover's "Taffeta phrases, silken terms precise" in *Love's Labour's Lost,* V, ii, 406 (in the Arden edition, ed. Richard David [Cambridge: Harvard Univ. Press, 1966], p. 160). Carew refers to a "Ribband" as the "silken wreath" which is "an Emblem of that mystique charm" of his mistress's beauty (29.1-2).

19. Like pictures, or like bookes gay coverings made
For layment, are all women thus arraid;
Themselves are mystique bookes, which only wee
Whom their imputed grace will dignify
Must see reveal'd.

(ed. Gardner [Oxford: Clarendon, 1965], 16.39-43).

20. For a less sophisticated version of the relationship between "vaine" rapture and poetic rape, see "A Divine Love" (in Dunlap's Appendix A, "Poems of Uncertain Authorship," pp. 188-90).

21. A. F. Allison, "Some Influences in Crashaw's Poem, 'On a Prayer Booke Sent to Mrs. M. R.,'" *The Review of English Studies* 23 (1947), 41-42.

22. Cited by Jonas (23) from Jonson's preface to *Volpone* and prologue to *The Staple of News.*

23. See Terence Cave, *The Cornucopian Text* (Oxford: Oxford Univ. Press, 1979), passim.

24. Rosalie L. Colie, *The Resources of Kind: Genre-Theory in the Renaissance* (Berkeley: Univ. of California Press, 1973).

25. For Shirley's remarks, see G. M. Crump's introduction (p. xxxiv) to his edition of Stanley's works (Oxford Univ. Press, 1962). Townsend separates Carew from satire in a verse letter to him; yet Carew is satirical in several poems: for example, "To my worthy Friend, M. D'avenant, Upon his Excellent Play, 'The Just Italian,'" and the Donne elegy. For the charge of pornography, see Ruoff's article, cited above.

26. For the secular Muse as a handmaid to the religious Muse, cf. "Mr Robert Hericke his farwell vnto Poetrie" (ed. L. C. Martin [New York: Oxford Univ. Press, 1965], 412.99-102): "Knowe yet (rare soule) when my diuiner Muse / Shall want a Hand-mayde, (as she ofte will vse) / Bee readye, then In mee, to wayte vppon her / Though as a seruant, yet a Mayde of Honor."

27. In Psalm 51, Carew has the altar "prest / With many a sacrificed beast," while Sandys (*The Poetical Works* [London, 1872]) has "lay" for "prest." Sandys will not let sinners "approach th'assemblies of the pure," where Carew would not let them "stay." Carew's thresholds are often dynamic, just as his mood is often subjunctive—dwelling in possibility. Joseph Summers, who pauses to consider what kind of poet Carew might have been, underscores the poet's limitations by remarking on the unlikelihood of Carew's becoming a religious poet (*Heirs of Donne and Jonson,* pp. 72-74).

28. In an epistle to the Countess of Salisbury, Donne must justify those epistles written for other ladies: "And if things like these, have been said by mee / Of others; call not that Idolatrie" (*The Satires, Epigrams and Verse Letters,* ed. W. Milgate [Oxford: Clarendon, 1967], 108.37-38).

29. R. Howard Bloch, *The Scandal of the Fabliaux* (Chicago: Univ. of Chicago Press, 1986).

30. Graham Parry, *Seventeenth-Century Poetry: The Social Context* (London: Hutchinson, 1985), p. 11. For further discussion of this shifty elegy, see James Fitzmaurice, "Carew's Funerary Poetry and the Paradox of Sincerity," *Studies in English Literature* 25 (1985), 136-39.

31. Stephen Orgel, *The Illusion of Power* (Berkeley: Univ. of California Press, 1975), p. 83: "Thomas Carew's and Inigo Jones's *Coelum Britannicum* was the greatest theatrical expression of the Caroline autocracy. Carew's allegory is about the radical reformation of society, the purifying of the mind and passions, the power of language and apparitions to exorcise the rebellious spirit; it even undertakes to create a new body of poetic symbolism, as if to redeem through its imagery the imperfect nature that art imitates."

32. Cf. the classification of two kinds of bad poetry in Dryden's *An Essay of Dramatick Poesie,* in *The Works* (Berkeley: Univ. of California Press, 1971), 16, 11; one kind of bad poet "affects plainness, to cover his want of imagination."

33. "I versifie the troth; not Poetize" (*The Civil Wars,* ed. L. Michel [New Haven: Yale Univ. Press, 1958], I, vi, 8). "Poetizing" intermixes "fictions, fantasies" with the historical truth. Daniel eventually left the poem unfinished and turned to writing prose history.

34. A few well-known examples may suffice. In politics and religion, so-called Parliamentarians and Puritans were held responsible for dissolving the traditional unities of State and Church, yet they held fast to precedent (legal, scriptural) and the monarch; the King, on the other hand, was accused of excess, dissolution, and innovation (for which, see Martin Butler, *Theatre and Crisis, 1632-1642* [New York Cambridge Univ. Press, 1984]). In anatomizing melancholy, Burton resists the atomistic implications of his project and pseudonym, yet has Democritus Jr. admit his multiform self. Indeed, the word most commonly associated with the formation of the self—"resolve"—can mean anything from utter fixity to careful revision to utter dispersion. In science, William Harvey announced the circulation of the blood in terms of the system of correspondences, while Bacon worried over the status of the Forms to be discovered by induction. For literature, Carew's elegy for Donne illustrates the heightened conflict between entrenched convention and outright experimentation; this must be considered next to the fear, expressed by Waller, Sprat, and others, that the English language was utterly un-fixed and dispersive (and, therefore, in need of reform).

35. Beyond the evidence of the poetry, Carew's honesty is recorded in anecdotes (Howell's report about Carew's criticism of Jonson) and in modern assessments of his political status as a "privileged scoffer" (Patterson).

36. Michael P. Parker has demonstrated the political strategies of the poem with reference to Virgilian pastoral. Parker expands upon Martz's suggestion of the irony directed toward the fallen King of Sweden, who in the poem compares unfavorably with Charles. I find especially suggestive Parker's treatment of pastoral: as a favorite genre for the Caroline status quo, it not only eludes any set position on the generic hierarchy (hence epic is preceded by *and* precedes it), but also represents an inclusive hybrid: for pastoral "incorporates heroic and lyric strains and integrates them into a pleasing, harmonious whole" (101). The pastoral has "elasticity and capaciousness." Parker notes the culturally specific function of pastoral, and argues that Carew too anticipates its demise. See Michael P. Parker, "Carew's Politic Pastoral: Virgilian Pretexts in the 'Answer to Aurelian Townsend,'" *John Donne Journal* 1 (1982), 101-16.

37. Sidney's *Apology* illustrates the problems of mixed genre; Daniel's *The Civil Wars* and Drayton's *Poly-Olbion* with Selden's commentary suggest a turning point in historical poetry; and Nashe's *Lenten Stuff* dramatizes one writer's vexed attempt to segregate his inventions from political responsibility.

38. For contextual problems confronting masque creators, see Stephen Orgel, *The Jonsonian Masque* (New York: Columbia Univ. Press, 1981); and David Lindley, ed., *The Court Masque* (Manchester: Manchester Univ. Press, 1984).

39. "Monsieur Gombauld" (ed. Rudrum, 80.7).

40. "Resolutions may often change, sometimes for the better; and the last ever stands firmest . . . I will resolve oft, before I vow once." See John L. Lievsay, ed., *The Seventeenth-Century Resolve* (Lexington: Univ. of Kentucky Press, 1980), p. 105.

41. See Dunlap's annotations, p. 252. Louis L. Martz has commented at length on Carew's recreation of Townsend's masque. Martz believes that Carew's description fits *Tempe Restord* to some degree, yet diverges from that masque in two respects: Carew's emphasis on the Platonized transformation of love into ethereality and on the Queen's triumphant singing suggests the ending of *Shepherd's Paradise*. Martz argues that an actor's text, housed at the Folger, and a lyric found in Townsend's collected works support the possibility that Carew is recounting an adaptation of *Shepherd's Paradise,* one enhanced by features from the other masque. For the evidence, see Martz's *The Wit of Love* (Notre Dame: Univ. of Notre Dame Press, 1969), pp. 84-89. Whether this is so, or Carew has simply confused the masques, the point remains that the masque is Carew's best repository for mixed resources.

42. See Orgel, *The Illusion of Power* and *The Jonsonian Masque,* passim; and Jennifer Chibnall, "'To that

secure fix'd state': the function of the Caroline masque," in Lindley, pp. 78-93.

43. See Jonson's preface to *Hymenaei* in Stephen Orgel, ed., *Ben Jonson: Selected Masques* (New Haven: Yale Univ. Press, 1970), p. 48; and Orgel's commentary on this in *The Jonsonian Masque*, pp. 103-09.

44. This relates to the conflict between masque as glorious type or truth and masque as a nocturnal occasion. Even in the description of the spectacle of *Hymenaei,* there is a lament "that is lasted not still, or, now it is past, cannot by imagination, much less description, be recovered to a part of that spirit it had in the gliding by" (Jonson's *Selected Masques,* p. 66).

45. Chibnall, p. 79.

46. Chibnall, p. 81.

47. Chibnall, p. 87. Cf. my "John Ford and Resolve," "John Ford and Resolve," *SP* 86 (1989), 341-66.

48. Bruno's text contains the core of Carew's masque—the reform plot—but Carew deflects the crisis of authority by making Charles and Henrietta Maria the models for reform in a Ptolemaic cosmos. Cf. Bruno's emphasis on crisis and on infinite worlds, and his explanation of Jove as "something variable, subject to the Fate of Mutation . . . in one infinite entity and substance there are infinite and innumerable particular natures" (*The Expulsion of the Triumphant Beast,* trans. and ed. by Arthur D. Imerti [New Brunswick, NJ: Rutgers Univ. Press, 1964], p. 75). The gods themselves "take delight in the multiform representation of all things and in the multiform fruit of all minds" (p. 160). Nonetheless, Bruno's text connects Jove's many shapes with his former lusts; sees reform as a way to reconvene the "undeservedly dispersed" virtues in heaven; and grounds its pantheistic disseminations in "the one material principle, which is the true substance of things, eternal, ingenerable, and incorruptible" (75). Douglas Brooks-Davies sees Bruno's text as crucial for the Renaissance conception of the "mercurian monarch"—priest, magus, and ruler—which the Stuarts continue. This notion affects Carew's masque in its "obsession with purgation," in the presence of British heroes, and obviously in Bruno's Mercury. See *The Mercurian Monarch: Magical Politics from Spenser to Pope* (Manchester: Manchester Univ. Press, 1983), pp. 1-3, 99-106.

49. See Martin Butler's *Theatre and Crisis, 1632-42,* passim.

50. See the Parker article cited in note 1 above.

51. See note 36 above.

## Diana Benet (essay date 1988)

SOURCE: "Carew's Monarchy of Wit," in *"The Muses Common-Weale": Poetry and Politics in the Seventeenth Century*, edited by Claude J. Summers and Ted-Larry Pebworth, University of Missouri Press, 1988, pp. 80-91.

[*In the following essay, Benet contends that Carew appropriated the absolutist rhetoric of Kings Charles and James in envisioning himself as sole arbiter of aesthetic judgment.*]

Nothing seems further from reality than poetic compliments whose extravagance time has exposed as pure friendship. Beyond the poet's affability, however, some of Thomas Carew's poems to or about fellow authors disclose important aspects of his cultural perspective. Reading these poems in the context of the writings and speeches of Kings James and Charles, one has the sense of witnessing a new social phenomenon resulting from the convergence of political and cultural currents. These currents are complex, but the immediate effect of their confluence seems startlingly simple: the populace has discovered its voice and is using it as never before. Though this development sounds innocuous, neither Thomas Carew, courtier and coterie poet, nor the Stuart kings are pleased to hear the murmurings from below. To the kings and the poet, the new voice signals social upheaval: they see a conflict emerge between an authoritative voice and a dissident voice raised to usurp its hegemony.

James and Charles reacted to this phenomenon by reiterating certain principles, convictions arising from a master idea and meant to silence their people and, especially, their parliaments. In the political context, such a reaction, though repressive, is not surprising; in the literary domain, however, it is remarkable. A number of Thomas Carew's poems transfer his monarchs' principles into the world of letters, reflecting the royal attitude that the public voice threatens the usurpation of rightful authority. Consistently in these poems, Carew appropriates the language and the categories of the existing political and social orders, reorienting them to construct a monarchy of wit based on absolutist Stuart principles. Imitation is supposed to be a sincere form of flattery: Carew's appropriation of James's and Charles's rhetoric and political strategies would seem to be a valorization of their state. However, since the kings' absolutist stance depends on their claims of being unique sources of authority, imitating them produces a challenge to, rather than an affirmation of, their rank and governance. Covertly, Carew's poems subvert the state of his Stuart kings by positing an alternate order of authority governed by poet-kings.

In the realm of literature, two of the major factors that contributed to the emergence of a diverse public ready to express its views are well known: the growth of the popular theater and the increasing readiness of authors to publish their work made everyone a potential commentator. Even King James realized that the publication of *Basilikon Doron* made the royal book "subject to every mans censure, as the current of his affection leades him."[1] In the political world, also, the general public gained access to materials bound to provoke discussion. The first coranto was published in December 1620 and, though the publication of domestic news was illegal during this period, ways of leaking State information were devised. Parliamentary deliberations were supposed to be secret, but members circulated manuscripts of their own speeches. When these were pirated and offered for sale, they achieved a wider circulation, as did summaries of debates and other parliamentary business. Given such stimulation, it is hardly surprising that the "rabble," as Thomas Carew styled it, seemed to grow loquacious. In 1621, James twice issued proclamations intended to stop public discussion of state affairs, complaining, "There is at this tyme a more licentious Passage of lavish Discourse and bould Censure in matters of State than hath been heretofore or is fitt to be suffered."[2]

The freedom and limitation of speech had long concerned the English monarchy, inspiring Henry VIII in the 1530s to extend "the definition of treason to cover the spoken word."[3] Elizabeth and James expected their parliaments to speak only on subjects they specified and prohibited parliamentary discussion of foreign affairs and religion. James especially emphasized the impropriety, not to say the illegality, of discussion of his regal power: "As to dispute what God may doe is Blasphemie. . . . So it is sedition in subjects to dispute what a King may do in the height of his power." At different times, he reminded his people of God's law that "Thou shalt not rayle upon the Judges, neither speak evill of the ruler of thy people" and told a parliament that "Men should bee ashamed to make shew of the quicknesse of their wits here, either in taunting, scoffing, or detracting the Prince of State in any point."[4] Charles was as attentive as his predecessors to the liberties and limits of his subjects' speech, but the three rulers faced a losing battle. In Elizabeth's day, the House of Commons "moved from a position of asking to speak their minds on issues put before them without fear of punishment, to a position of demanding the right to initiate discussion and influence policy on any issue they chose." Lawrence Stone remarks that by the 1620s the House of Commons had progressed from the desire to moot particular subjects to the basic question of freedom of speech.[5] It is no wonder that, as James and Charles heard their subjects encroaching on territory they deemed their own, they articulated a full complex of attitudes about speech in relation to authority.

Regardless of the issues that elicited them, the statements of the kings from whose courts Carew wrote reveal some consistent assumptions about speech and authority. These are implicit in the ancient political metaphor of head and body, which James used in *The Trew Law of Free Monarchies:* "As the discourse and direction flowes from the head, and the execution according thereunto belongs to the rest of the members, every one according to their office: so it is betwixt a wise Prince, and his people."[6] Since only the head has a tongue, only the head is gifted with the power of genuine speech. And "direction" as well as discourse belongs to the head of the body politic, again, because the mind resides in the head. As far as James and Charles are concerned, authority in the State belongs only

to the voice of the king; secondarily, authoritative speech belongs to those officials whom the king empowers with his singular authority. Occasionally, he empowers a group such as parliament to discuss certain topics; but such discussion in the absence of royal authority he regards as political insubordination. It seems as perverse to him as if talk were to issue suddenly from his leg. From this self-serving cluster of kingly ideas followed the corollaries whose aim was to silence the free and unwelcome expression of popular and parliamentary views: the denial that unauthorized voices are based on understanding or vital knowledge and the charge that they subvert a hierarchy based on the indisputable power and wisdom of the king.

Fundamental to the royal view of authoritative speech is the equation of comprehension with rank; explicitly or implicitly, the Crown maintained that understanding and, therefore, responsible discourse are related to status in the government hierarchy. King James's insistence on his subjects' inability to understand the essence of his power is well known: "If there fall out a question that concerns my Prerogative or mystery of State, deale not with it," he ordered the judges in the Star Chamber, "for they are transcendent matters." Charles's attitude echoed his father's. Responding to a parliamentary remonstrance in 1628, he claimed that the ability to understand key issues belonged to him alone: "Now I see you are fallen upon points of state which belong to me to understand better than you, and I must tell you that you do not understand so much as I thought you had done."[7] The equation of rank with understanding is given a clever twist and translated into the world of letters by Carew in **"To my much honoured friend Henry Lord Cary of Lepington upon his translation of Malvezzi."**

This poem elicits little attention today since neither Malvezzi's *Romulus and Tarquin* nor Henry Cary himself is of interest to literary criticism. Indeed, even in his own day the poet believed the translator could hope only for a small audience. It seems, at first, that in his poem Carew attributes the limited appeal of his friend's translation to its subject: Malvezzi had to learn "vulgar Italian," the demotic idiom, before he wrote his book. Even so, his material is "so sublime," his mode of expression "so new," that he is "by a good / Part of his Natives hardly understood." It stands to reason that an excellent translation will duplicate the sublimity and novelty that puzzled the Italian public and have the same effect on the English.

But Carew's consoling explanation to his friend is more complex, and typical of his attitude toward the public world at large:

> You must expect no happier fate, 'tis true
> He is of noble birth, of nobler you:
> So nor your thoughts nor words fit common eares,
> He writes, and you translate, both to your Peeres.
>
> (ll. 13-16)[8]

At first it seems that the poet locates the problem of the work's reception in the social class of its author and translator. With considerable cleverness, he seems to have "proved" that understanding is a function of social rank: the English lord, because he is a peer, understood the Italian marquesse while most of his compatriots did not, though he condescended to write in their ordinary speech. Similarly, Lord Cary's translation will not be generally understood; because of his social status he, like Malvezzi, speaks a language different from the language of common people. Only his peers, for whom the poet speaks, can understand him.

But the latter statement brings us up short, of course, and apprises us of the poet's covert agenda: he appropriates the terminology that defines the existing social system to posit a rival, challenging system. As one who understands Malvezzi and Henry Cary, Thomas Carew speaks for their "Peeres"; obviously, then, peerage in this system of aristocracy is not a matter of social rank. The true nobility of Malvezzi and Cary, the poet suggests, consists of the novelty, sublimity, and elegance of their thoughts and words; his own nobility consists of his understanding and appreciation. Their important titles are not *lord* or *marquesse,* but *translator* and *author*—titles that Thomas Carew, as *poet* or *author,* can match. The lower classes in the caste system the poet creates are all those, titled or untitled, who do not understand, at least, the talents or achievements of their superiors: certain "thoughts and words" are too large, literally, for ears of congenital smallness. Initially, it seems as if the poet's emphasis on nobility is a crude compliment to Henry Cary's social rank; in fact, it is a subtle compliment to his native talent and to his accomplishment as a translator.

The common public will not praise Lord Cary's work because they will not understand it, but this judicious discretion was not typical in state affairs. More often, Carew's kings stressed their subjects' ignorance as a compelling argument for their silence. James sought to control his people's discussion of political business because it was "of high Nature unfit for vulgar Discourse," "Matter above the Reach and Calling that to good and dutiful Subjects appertaineth."[9] Charles tried to stop the impeachment of Buckingham in the House of Commons by arguing his superior knowledge against the members' supposed ignorance: he "himself doth know better than any man living," he declared, the character of the Duke.[10] When dissidence persisted, the kings protested, as an offense against the reasonable established order, the lifting of unqualified voices against those invested with authority. James warned one of his parliaments that they should "not meddle with the maine points of Government; that is my craft. . . . I must not be taught my office." Charles complained in 1626 that eminent state counselors had been "censured and traduced in this house [of Commons], by men whose years and education cannot attain to that depth." Three years later, he professed astonishment that "young lawyers" in the House "take upon them to decry the opinions of the Judges."[11] This kind of hierarchical transgression, a topsy-turvy state of affairs wherein ignorance questions or contradicts wisdom, figures significantly in Carew's poems to Ben Jonson and to William Davenant.

Carew's poem to Jonson, **"Upon Occasion of his Ode of defiance annext to his Play of the new Inne,"** opens with an image of authority and points to its attempted usurpation:

> Tis true (deare *Ben:*) thy just chastizing hand
> Hath fixt upon the sotted Age a brand
> To their swolne pride, and empty scribbling due,
> It can nor judge, nor write.

By virtue of his "just chastizing hand," Jonson is a judge who has fairly deliberated and meted out punishment. His decision to mark the offenders by branding discloses their status, since that form of punishment was reserved for criminals of the lowest class. The crimes that revealed their true nature (despite the status they might claim in society) and merited the humiliating chastisement are obvious: they attempted the usurpation of functions properly undertaken by their superiors. Empty scribblers have presumed to write, and "sotted" heads, minds "foolish, doltish, and stupid" (*OED*), have presumed to judge. If Charles was shocked that young lawyers offered their opinions against experienced judges, we can only imagine his consternation if convicted malefactors had spoken out to judge their judges. Such an instance of insubordination Carew perceives in Jonson's situation. The entire age has meddled in matter above its reach and calling. The populace has tried to usurp the authority belonging only to those who can judge and write.

Carew's contempt for the public voice is evident in the way he hides his agreement with its appraisal of *The New Inn.* The age cannot judge or write,

> and yet 'tis true
> Thy commique Muse from the exalted line
> Toucht by thy *Alchymist,* doth since decline
> From that her Zenith, and fortells a red
> And blushing evening, when she goes to bed.

(ll. 4-8)

As far as the poet is concerned, the benighted public has no right to express its views even if, as it happens, they coincide with his own and are, therefore, correct. Carew cleverly manages not to identify his evaluation with that of the incompetent public: by not commenting at all on *The New Inn,* he avoids echoing the voice he has discredited. In spite of this maneuver, however, his criticism of Jonson's entire dramatic work aims at its present nadir, his reference to a "blushing evening" clearly indicating the shame of a humiliating failure, despite the compliments that follow.

Carew's magisterial remarks on the "sotted Age," his confident overview of Jonson's work, and the reasonable distinctions he perceives among his friend's plays all declare an authority equal to the "just chastizing hand" of Jonson. But when he suggests that he is a better judge than the emotionally involved father of the works under discussion, his claim to power is complete. He urges Jonson to accept from his superior a version of what he would not accept (quite properly) from his inferiors: that his plays, "though one brain strike / Soules into all . . . are not all alike. "Having asserted his authority, Carew proceeds to judgment:

> Why should the follies then of this dull age
> Draw from thy Pen such an immodest rage
> As seemes to blast thy (else-immortall) Bayes,
> When thine owne tongue proclaimes thy ytch of praise?
> Such thirst will argue drouth. No, let be hurld
> Upon thy workes, by the detracting world
> What malice can suggest.
>
> (ll. 23-29)

If the thickheaded public tried to usurp the judicial office, Jonson's fault was to acknowledge the decision handed down from a kangaroo court. Worse, his "ytch of praise" ceded to the "dull age" the power to grant or withhold something he prized. In effect, and for all his "defiance," Jonson submitted to a body whose judicial capacity he and the poet deny.

Carew goes on to demonstrate that Jonson can never hope to be justly valued by the pugnacious crowd: while the mob scorns the playwright as a plagiarizer, the poet honors him as a conqueror of foreign powers bringing home "rich spoyles" (ll. 33-42). Carew's language, making Jonson a king winning trophies, demonstrates that in thought, language, and discrimination, a major chasm separates the general public and true poets. Since the chasm exists, Carew advises Jonson to look to the future. "Let others glut on the extorted praise / Of vulgar breath, trust thou to after days":

> Thou art not of their ranke, the quarrell lyes
> Within thine owne Virge, then let this suffice,
> The wiser world doth greater Thee confesse
> Then all men else, then Thy selfe only lesse.
>
> (ll. 47-50)

He enjoins Jonson to acknowledge the distinctions separating him from vulgar writers, and "the wiser world" from vulgar audiences. A surfeit of praise is available to scribblers of the hastily written trash enjoyed by the ignorant public. But the hunger for commendation that Jonson revealed in his "Ode" should be satisfied by the esteem of the "wiser world." How the elder poet must have hated Carew's imitation of his own manner: the seamless combination of criticism, praise, and advice is delivered in accents as measured, deliberate, and conclusive as any of Jonson's.

In Carew's view, there can be no such thing as universal acclaim: the gap between the vulgar and the wiser worlds is so wide that they cannot approve or applaud the same things. He concedes that the louder voice belongs to the witless rout. But ultimately, he asserts, the truly powerful voice belongs to Jonson's (and his own) small class, whose authority will be upheld by "after dayes," long after the applause of the mob has been forgotten. The poet stresses

the ignorance of the public and its incapacity to judge, not to suggest that Jonson is above appraisal, but to assert his own claim to deliver the authoritative verdict. Displacing the public voice that would usurp the privilege of making literary judgments, he claims a unique authority for those who can judge and write, for true poets.

When Charles ordered the House of Commons to stop prying into Buckingham's affairs, he suggested that in a well-ordered state, people who do not understand should acknowledge their limitation and allow themselves to be guided; therefore, he told the Commons to "cease [its] unparliamentary inquisition" and to "commit unto his Majesty's care, and wisdom, and justice" any necessary reformations.[12] In **"To my worthy Friend, M. D'Avenant, Upon his Excellent Play, *The Just Italian*",** Carew exalts as desirable a similar popular docility in literary affairs and appropriates his monarch's all-knowing and angry paternalism. He dispatches quickly with the great merit of Davenant's play to concentrate on his real subject, the public who disliked it. The age, Carew believes,

> Requires a Satyre. What starre guides the soule
> Of these our froward times, that dare controule,
> Yet dare not learne to judge? When didst thou flie
> From hence, cleare, candid Ingenuitie?
> I have beheld, when pearch'd on the smooth brow
> Of a faire modest troope, thou didst allow
> Applause to slighter workes; but then the weake
> Spectator, gave the knowing leave to speake.
> Now noyse prevailes, and he is tax'd for drowth
> Of wit, that with the crie, spends not his mouth.
>
> (ll. 4-14)

From the beginning, the poem's diction suggests political confrontation: though "Garlands" "crowne" Davenant's "triumphant worke" (ll. 2-4), the times "dare" to criticize it. The age's preference for satire is only one indication of its contentious nature. Calling the times "froward," Carew accuses his obtuse contemporaries of being refractory or ungovernable, a trait whose relevance to theater-going is not immediately clear. The people challenge and criticize freely, without any knowledge of standards for judgment, as a consequence merely of their malevolent disposition to belittle and censure. This verbal aggressiveness Carew describes as a new attitude, contrasting the present public with a past audience characterized by "Ingenuitie." The word means "straightforwardness" and "sincerity," but in the seventeenth century, its primary sense was related to social class. The first definition the *OED* cites is "the condition of being free-born; of honourable extraction or station." As he did in the poem to Jonson, Carew implies that the public behaves like the social dregs. The vanished audience he misses was "a faire modest troope," its gentility and modesty evident in the applause it gave to plays "slighter" than Davenant's. But primarily the audience was genteel and modest, as far as Carew is concerned, because it knew and kept its humble place; the "weake Spectator," acknowledging his limitations, deferred to the opinion of the "knowing." Meekly accepting the judgment of his betters, he kept his lowly mouth shut.

But now the public forgets its well-deserved modesty, pretends to have wit, and produces "noyse"—an annoying and meaningless eruption of sound. Carew expatiates on the public ignorance and tastelessness with a zest exceeding the "scorne, and Pity" he declares it merits (ll. 15-32). In the final consolation he offers Davenant, he explains his vehemence:

> Repine not Thou then, since this churlish fate
> Rules not the stage alone; perhaps the State
> Hath felt this rancour, where men great and good,
> Have by the Rabble beene misunderstood.
> So was thy Play; whoose cleere, yet loftie straine,
> Wisemen, that governe Fate, shall entertaine.

Obviously, Carew wishes he could organize his world according to the ideal scheme also favored by his monarchs: a public accepting the guidance of a few "understanders," trusting the judgment of that overclass entirely. It is against this ideal hierarchy that the "froward" audience of Davenant's play rebelled. Perhaps the unspecificity of Carew's remarks about the "great and good" statesmen reflects a necessary discretion; certainly, it facilitates his equation of literary and governmental affairs. The criticism of Davenant's play as an "impious reach" or conception (l. 23) is the equivalent of the criticism of blameless state officials when their "reach" or "policy" *(OED)* has been misunderstood. As the weak spectator tries to usurp the critical function of the knowing in the theater, the rabble tries to usurp the evaluative capacity of men able in governmental matters. Carew makes the acts of rebellion seem equal. But, as if the elevation of literary affairs to the level of government were not subversive enough, he suggests that the authorities facing the insurrections are not equal. "Men great and good" may be on a par with "Wisemen"; but the first rule only the State while the second "governe Fate." The stage, a relatively small and insignificant sphere, is left to the churls. In this poem, Carew almost admits that the theater is part of the only state whose power concerns him; he almost declares the supremacy of the literary domain governed by wise men like himself.

James objected to his subjects' unrestricted speech as a direct challenge to his authority, as a "breach of prerogative royal," and Charles was equally alert to the threat: "under the pretense of privilege and freedom of speech . . . [the Commons] take liberty to declare against all authority of Council and Courts at their pleasure."[13] But ultimately, as dissidents insisted on their ability to understand and their right to speak, Charles could respond only with renewed and more specific restrictions. When the parliament of 1628-1629 persisted in discussing the Church's Articles, he had them printed with a declaration stating his intention to silence "any unnecessary disputations, altercations, or questions . . . which may nourish faction both in the Church and Commonwealth." To avoid the peril of faction, the king restricted all deliberation on the Articles to authorized Convocation. His aim, he explained later, was to "tie and restrain all opinions to the sense of those Articles, that nothing might be left for private fancies and innovations."[14] Like his monarchs, Carew saw danger in the expression of "private fancies." Imitating the autocratic urge to control unauthorized interpretation, in **"To the Reader of Master William Davenant's Play"**, he reveals a desire to impose his judgment that parallels his monarchs' desire to rule absolutely.

Addressing the member of the public, the poet takes the talkative bull by the horns to instruct him on how to read Davenant's *The Witts:*

> It hath been said of old, that Playes are Feasts,
> Poets the Cookes, and the Spectators Guests,
> The Actors Waitors: From this Simile
> Some have deriv'd an unsafe libertie
> To use their Judgements as their tastes, which chuse
> Without controule, this Dish, and that refuse:
> But Wit allowes not this large Priviledge,
> Either you must confesse, or feele it's edge.

Carew substitutes, for an image of unrestricted sociability, an image of political power. The trouble with Ben Jonson's simile, according to him, is that it inspired some people to confuse taste with judgment; it caused them to confuse a social situation in which compulsion is irrelevant with an intellectual situation in which certain strictures must apply. This misunderstanding has resulted in "an unsafe libertie." Carew's use of "unsafe," surely a word too strong in this context, may hint at a concern with a situation far more important than current approaches to the stage; it suggests that he sees liberty "without controule" in any sphere as a threat to desirable order. Against the potential anarchy of individual freedom, he introduces the powerful figure of a monarch. Wit is personified as a stern king who does not grant individuals the right to deny his power. He demands that it be acknowledged, if not appreciated. The phrase "feele it's edge" suggests that too much liberty is "unsafe" because this king has a sharp punishment for rebels who resist his control.

It is the poet, of course, who tries to curb the excessive freedom assumed by incompetent readers who think they can judge literary work as they judge sausage. As the dictator of rules for aesthetic judgment, Carew insists that everything is not open to individual interpretation but has a character or quality that is indisputable, given perceptive powers acute enough: "Things are distinct, and must the same appeare / To every piercing Eye, or well-tun'd Eare" (ll. 11-12). He will permit individual taste and personal preference only so long as "the Good / And Bad, be by your Judgment understood" (ll. 19-20). Finally, after devoting twenty lines to these stern, restrictive cautions to the reader, Carew turns to the play that occasioned the poem:

> But if, as in this Play, where with delight
> I feast my Epicurean appetite
> With rellishs so curious, as dispence
> The utmost pleasure to the ravisht sense,
> You should professe that you can nothing meet
> That hits your taste, either with sharpe or sweet,
> But cry out, 'tis insipid; your bold Tongue
> May doe it's Master, not the Author wrong;

For Men of better Pallat will by it
Take the just elevation of your Wit.

(ll. 21-30)

Claiming superior powers of discrimination, Carew assures the reader that even if he exercises only his taste, he will find something in Davenant's play to his liking. The reader need not concern himself with evaluation; the poet gives him the authorized judgment. In spite of the dicta of Wit, the reader may still think he has the freedom to judge the merit of this work published to the world at large. But Carew "allowes not this large Priviledge" and threatens accordingly. The reader is free only to agree with him, the monarch whose authority in the domain of wit is unquestionable. The bold tongue that dares to disagree can hurt only its own master by revealing his dim-witted inferiority. Using his "edge" to threaten readers with their exposure as tasteless and indiscriminate, Carew devises a way to "controule" public liberty.

The writings of James and Charles suggest that, in spite of how often they were challenged, they assumed a society divided into two classes: the small elite they headed, whose power and authority derived from the royal rank, knowledge, and wisdom; and a huge underclass, whose submissiveness should logically follow from their station and their presumed ignorance. Such a perspective came naturally to men who believed they ruled by divine right. When dissident voices angered the Stuarts, subjecting them to criticism, hampering their freedom to act, or trying to define and therefore circumscribe their power, the kings tried to suppress them as threats to their authority. The poems I have discussed suggest that Thomas Carew also assumed a two-class division: the small elite of fine authors that he headed (in his own estimation), king-authors endowed with knowledge, wisdom, and taste; and the rest of the populace, good subjects when they permitted themselves to be guided, bad when they expressed their own unfounded opinions.

Assuming that authority should be the natural right of a talented and intellectual elite, Carew responded to, or even anticipated, the popular voice raised in criticism against his friends. Jealously protecting the hegemony in literary affairs that he believed should belong to himself and his artistic peers, he wrote poems that are political statements as much as they are consolations or compliments. These reveal a strong contempt for a socially heterogeneous public expressing its views despite its supposed ignorance; simultaneously, they disclose a covert hostility toward the Stuart sociopolitical system. Two opposed groups confront each other in Carew's poems: the commons and the peers; those who cannot judge or write and the wiser world; the weak and the knowing spectators; the rabble and the wisemen; the indiscriminate and the men of better palate. The poet points to the attempted overturning of the hierarchical distinctions implied by *inferior* and *superior, ignorant* and *wise, the rabble* and *the great* with images of social insubordination that are themselves gestures of rebellion: low-class offenders censure their judge, the mob criticizes men

"great and good," and libertines defy a king. But for Carew, the rout and the rabble who rebel against their betters are the ignorant and indiscriminate in every social echelon. Their superiors are the talented authors.

The complex reasons why Carew would wish to undermine, in however abstract a fashion, the social structure on which he depended cannot be determined fully. But we know that he was dismissed in 1616 by Sir Dudley Carleton, his patron, for having "foolishly put to paper certain aspersions" on the character of Carleton and his wife. At least once, in other words, Carew had responded with a form of verbal aggression to a situation in which he felt at a disadvantage. He was certainly at a social disadvantage as a courtier. He "came of good family," but the recent knighthoods of his father and his elder brother would have been unimpressive at the Stuart court. The poems discussed above suggest that he was very conscious of the difference between the superiority he assumed for himself as a poet and the inferiority others assumed for him in the social hierarchy. The poems also demonstrate that, between the time Carleton dismissed him and the time he wrote these poems, Carew improved his "talent for adroitly managing his own repressed competitiveness, for making gestures that covertly challenge the powerful, even while they gratify them."[15] It must have delighted Carew to flout the intellectual and aesthetic inferiority of people who assumed social superiority to himself, and to get away with it.

Speaking for his author-peers, the wiser world, and the discriminating, Carew claimed absolute authority in the world of letters. In this regard, he was bound to be more successful than his rulers. Carew appropriated the absolutist rhetoric of his kings to create a monarchy whose power surpasses theirs. As James's and Charles's repeated complaints and warnings show, a king cannot always control his subjects. But a poet, it seemed to Carew, can control his subjects absolutely: against the rebellious outbursts directed at his friends, he triumphed. He managed in his poems to discredit his subjects' dissenting voices and to supplant their unauthorized views with his own. Against their usurping clamor, he managed to have the last word. It is appropriate that Carew reserved his highest praise for John Donne. As Carew described Donne's kingdom, the poet-king did as he liked and not a peep was heard from the passive subjects upon whose wills he "Committed holy Rapes." Whatever the reality, in the elegy Carew made Donne's dominion total: only after his death do libertines dare to rebel against his "strict lawes," using stories that Donne had "silenc'd" absolutely. Carew appreciated that kind of power, especially because he could create and wield it himself. Manners and good sense forced him to suggest that his author-friends share his status, but one feels that theirs are courtesy-titles. Carew's poems exalt and preserve his taste, his judgment, his word, his authority. His compliments notwithstanding, Thomas Carew is the king, the sole and absolute ruler of the monarchy of wit that he created.

*Notes*

1. *The Political Works of James I. Reprinted from the Edition of 1616,* intro. by Charles Howard McIlwain (Cambridge: Harvard University Press, 1918), 5. In quotations from this text, typographical conventions are modernized.

2. Perez Zagorin, *The Court and the Country: The Beginning of the English Revolution* (New York: Atheneum, 1970), 108, 106.

3. Lawrence Stone, *The Causes of the English Revolution, 1529-1642* (London: Routledge & Kegan Paul, 1972), 59.

4. *James,* 310, 60, 289.

5. *Causes of Revolution,* 93.

6. *James,* 65.

7. *James,* 332; Conrad Russell, *Parliaments and English Politics: 1621-1629* (Oxford: Clarendon Press, 1979), 385.

8. All quotations of Carew's poems are from *The Poems of Thomas Carew, With His Masque Coelum Britannicum,* ed. Rhodes Dunlap (1949; rpt. London: Oxford University Press, 1970).

9. Zagorin, *Court and Country,* 107.

10. Samuel Rawson Gardiner, ed., *The Constitutional Documents of the Puritan Revolution,* 1625-1660, 3d ed. (Oxford: Clarendon Press, 1906), 4.

11. *James,* 315; *Constitutional Documents,* 5, 93.

12. *Constitutional Documents,* 5.

13. Russell, *Parliaments and Politics,* 135; *Constitutional Documents,* 94.

14. *Constitutional Documents,* 75, 89.

15. Rhodes Dunlap, "Introduction," in *The Poems of Thomas Carew,* xxi, xiii. The remark about "repressed competitiveness" I appropriate from Katharine Eisaman Maus's discussion of Ben Jonson, Mosca, and Jeremy in *Ben Jonson and the Roman Frame of Mind* (Princeton: Princeton University Press, 1984), 9.

## Renée Hannaford (essay date 1989)

SOURCE: "'My Unwashed Muse': Sexual Play and Sociability in Carew's 'A Rapture'," in *English Language Notes,* Vol. XXVII, No. 1, September, 1989, pp. 32-39.

[*In the following essay, Hannaford describes "A Rapture" as "a kind of miniaturized masque" that "reveals tensions in [the] aesthetic, social, and cultural values" of Carew's day.*]

> For Kings and Lovers are alike in this
> That their chief art in reign dissembling is.
>
> —Sir John Suckling

The relationship between art and social life in the earlier seventeenth century is particularly fascinating to a study of Carew's poetry, which has so often been cursorily cited by critics to condemn him to the status of merely an anthology poet. From his biographical facts (scanty but not veiled in obscurity) as well as his literary artifacts, it is clear that Carew was both a participant in and observer of court life. It is impossible to dismiss the likely influence of his travels abroad on the formation of Carew's literary tastes. Carew left the Middle Temple and his law studies to enter the service of Sir Dudley Carleton, who in 1613 was Ambassador to Venice. In March of 1616, Carew was a part of Dudley's embassy to The Hague. A letter, dated 1616, speaks of the languages he acquired while in Carleton's service.[1] In November of 1616, Carew attended the installation of Charles as Prince of Wales. After a period of vainly seeking court preferment, Carew attained his object, accompanying Sir Edward Herbert (later Lord Herbert of Cherbury) on his embassy to Paris. Much later, during the period 1630-33, Carew became Gentleman of the Privy Chamber Extraordinary, then Sewer in Ordinary to the King. Consequently, Carew's rise from the multitude seeking court preferment to the status of a "successful" courtier at the Caroline court itself exposes the hazards of patronage resulting from a social system founded upon status. His dismissal from Carleton's service not only allows us a glimpse of his social character out of character, as it were, but also suggests to us the predominant concern for status, social ritual, and ceremony that characterized court life, particularly the court of Charles I.

In a social system based on status, where by law and by common practice a man is known not only by his name alone but also by his title or rank, status conditions a man's social awareness and enforces at its most basic level the distinction between those who are gentlemen and those who are not.[2] Revolving around the center of power, a courtier must always be forced to feel an acknowledged dependence (and therefore social inferiority) upon a patron, his superior in rank and authority. Therefore, the cultivation of manners, polite deportment, civil conversation, and social ritual were essential to participation in that world, and a successful public performance of his role was the courtier's way of defining himself as an acceptable social being—a gentleman. The poise, sophistication, and self-possession characteristic of the successful courtier's "working" role is supremely reflected in Van Dyck's court portraits of the 1630s. In a society saturated with dramatic forms of expression (in behavior, in dress, and in the visual arts) and in which style and manner were elevated to an art-form, sociability, "the play form of social interaction,"[3] was a collective game functioning to validate and confirm certain cultural assumptions. As Peter Berger has pointed out:

> The world of sociability is a precarious and artificial creation that can be shattered at any moment by someone who refuses to play the game . . . pure sociability is rarely possible except among equals since otherwise the pretence is too strenuous to maintain.[4]

Many of Carew's lyrics and occasional poems deliberately and often outrageously play with literary conventions or sources and, by doing so, reflect an aspiring courtier-poet's erudition and poetic gifts to an equally self-conscious and culturally sophisticated audience of both competitors and potential patrons. Essential to these poems is Carew's penchant for exploring opposites, whether of things or ideas, a concern for playful exaggeration and diminution or distortion that exposes a pattern of perception and a particular vision of social order. This need to expand and reduce objects and ideas, always determined by the poetic context, as a characteristic mode of poetic activity offers a vision of self as contained and limited, existing in opposition to larger, external forces and social institutions.

Among his contemporaries, Carew's reputation as a witty amorist who "speaks raptures"[5] was largely due to his infamous **"A Rapture,"** a poem probably composed "in wisdomes nonage and unriper yeares"[6] that circulated widely in manuscript and earned for Carew the sobriquet "The Oracle of Love." What Rhodes Dunlap has called "the obvious and magnificent licentiousness"[7] of **"A Rapture"** that so captivated and shocked Carew's contemporaries also earned him a Parliamentary reproof; as early as 1640 with the publication of the first edition of his *Poems,* his verses were so notorious that they were used as a rhetorical device in a political address.[8] Aside from its obvious eroticism (which has in fact encouraged modern interest in the poem), **"A Rapture"** has received critical plaudits from several quarters. Although Edward I. Selig doesn't mention **"A Rapture"** in his book *The Flourishing Wreath* (perhaps considering it too hot to handle), Earl Miner has called it "the most genuinely poetic of all the erotic poems of the century."[9] Ada Long and Hugh Maclean trace the poem's thematic and generic tradition and perceptively analyze its structure and argument, reading the poem as "a witty discourse about the proper uses of time, directed to a society that has lost its sense of moral equilibrium."[10] Paula Johnson contends that the poem is essentially the "wishfulling dream of an adolescent, graceful, charming, and utterly self-absorbed."[11] In this erotically charged "perswasion to love," the speaker's advocacy of moral libertinism constitutes a kind of heroic activity (reminiscent of the miniature mock-heroics of Carew's **"A flye that flew into my Mistris her eye"**); to seize the moment is "bold, and wise," so "valiant lovers" act upon their desires, a form of behavior generally acceptable only in the realm of art.[12] The speaker's theatrical exploitation of his theme, his insistent "I," and his skillful manipulation of literary conventions through which he continually reverses audience expectations constitutes a virtuoso poetic performance for connoissuers of "love's rites." However, the poem's twin contexts of sexual play and sociability and its deployment of political language suggests a concern for social order / disorder that moves beyond a witty display of sexual politics.

The use of allegory, symbol, remythologized history, and a facility for sensuous description and theatrical effects resembling elaborate set designs link **"A Rapture"** with the masque and that genre's expression of political and social values, but its eclectic blending of genres also shows the influence of French *conversatie* paintings depicting gallant and fashionable men and women making "civilized" love in a natural setting. The speaker's analogical re-creation of Celia as a landscape or garden thematically reflects the Renaissance humanist enthusiasm for metamorphosis that Renssalaer Lee has noted in Ariosto, and echoes Elizabethan song lyrics and the erotic pastoralism of Marlowe's *Hero and Leander.* The speaker's argument in this poem often relies upon his subtle mingling of myth and history by offering equations and equivalencies that conjoin art and nature. The speaker's exemplum of Daphne's amorous pursuit of Apollo inverts the action of the myth (Daphne "doth now unfetter'd run" after *him*), but like Bernini's *Apollo and Daphne,* shows a preoccupation with a moment of transformation. Elise Goodman, in discussing how contemporary ideas about fashion and etiquette are reflected in Ruben's *Conversatie à la Mode,* suggests that "the ideal social conversation is to blend fantasy and reality,"[13] and the ideal location for such *bonne société* is the baroque garden, the amorous grove where water jokes, amusing parterres, *allés,* and attendant classical deities provoke and stimulate the senses. In **"A Rapture,"** the speaker argues for "Loves free state" (also coveted by the speaker in "Upon my Lord Chiefe Justice") and against the constraints of social conventions that make lovers hypocrites. Finally, this appeals to the poem's wider audience through Carew's lengthy sensuous pictorial and analogical description of Celia's body as a baroque garden created for fashionable recreation. If in **"A Rapture"** the speaker attacks social forms and customs through a witty erotic discourse on love's alchemy, his evocation of the real world outside "Elysium" and its threatening, destructive power ensures that his voyage will not end peacefully, despite his "sportfull houres."

Within the "libertine pastoralism"[14] of the poem, the speaker projects a series of tableaux embellished with elegant and ornamental detail in a grand mock-historical manner. In the poem's context of sexual politics, although the speaker is not particularly hostile or antagonistic toward Celia, neither is he very interested in social interaction with her, since the speaker remains the focus of the poem. "Celia" provides little more than a metaphoric touchstone for erotic fantasy, her body abstracted into a backdrop of luxuriant landscape which the speaker wanders through as the attendant *genius loci.* "Elysium," Celia's metamorphosed body, is guarded by "The giant, Honour," whom the lovers must evade if they wish to pass into the annals of heroic legend. That "Honour" is "but a masquer" intentionally puns upon the theatrical nature of the speaker's role, and offers by its liminal emphasis perhaps another perspective on the poem's dramatic affinities: the expansion of experience through vivid sensual description, the emphasis on physical movement in intensely realized space, and the baroque interest in spectacle which culminated in the masque. Although much of the poem traces the speaker's highly inventive wishfull thinking (as Paula Johnson has suggested by her examination of tense changes in the poem), the affinity of this poem with masque, with a specifically courtly entertainment of obvious interest to Carew (his *Coelum Britannicum* was performed at Whitehall on 18 February 1633) raises issues that illumine, I think, the capacious handling of themes and literary eclecticism so apparent in the poem and that point toward the vision of social and political order contained in it.

**"A Rapture"** is more than a witty dream-poem, an idealized "inspired laye" from which the speaker draws poetic inspiration. The poem's opening image of "Honour" as a "masquer" is balanced structurally by the poem's closure with the same image and its worldly power, showing a playful and sophisticated awareness of the resolution of the ideal (fantasy or daydream artfully transposed) and the real (the speaker's indictment of social conventions taken as external truths) that exists in the masque. The presence of allegory, myth, and symbol throughout the poem are qualities also associated with the masque, and the speaker's appearance as courtier / lover / hero depends, as in the masque, on the ability of the audience to read appropriately the signs of the performance. The speaker's real power in the poem arises from his ability to project vividly and intensely what his audience would recognize as an illusion. As a kind of miniaturized masque (remembering Carew's fondness for the hyperbole of reduction) with appropriate tailoring to the requirements of lyric, the poem fulfills what Stephen Orgel views as Johnson's conception of the masque:

> . . . masques were the vehicles of the most profound ethical statements, creating heroic roles for the leaders of society, and teaching virtue in the most direct way, by example. Every masque moved toward the moment when the masquers descended and took partners from the audience, annihilating the barrier between the ideal and the real, and including the court in its miraculous transformation.[15]

With playful exuberance and youthful high spirits, the speaker in **"A Rapture"** cuts a heroic role for himself as a "valiant lover" rewarded by "the Queene of Love," where "all things are lawful that may delight"; indeed, "We only sin when love's rites are not done." The speaker's masterful depiction of love's progress as he analogically tends his garden, the "delicious paradise" that is Celia's body, qualifies him as an authoritative voice in pursuit of "virtue" or wisdom, the happy lover's reward after delightful interludes of "active play"; his lessons *do* teach by direct example. Finally, the poem moves toward ethical statement in its insistence upon the reappraisal of social codes that inhibit and restrict authentic behavior. The poem attempts to build a new social order founded on reason and not bullied by custom that encourages role-playing, dissimulation, and hypocrisy. Ada Long and Hugh Maclean conclude that:

> To repudiate "Goblin Honour," together with its logical cage of custom that confines those who adore the giant, is to free human reason. And that in turn is to enable

the new-building of a just and equal society where human rights are in fact as sacred as the old religion thought its idols were. In that society, men and women are neither atheists nor whores; they are free to be themselves.[16]

In the concluding stanza of the poem, the speaker invites Celia to help him defeat the tyrant and "proud usurper" Honour, an allegorical figure whom the speaker sees in moral and political terms. He identifies the larger values of "human justice" and "sacred right" that exist beyond the lover's immediate sexual gratification, and he criticizes the moral assumptions of a society in which doing what is right (the expression of private values) is incompatible with imposed social expectations. Men and women cannot conscientiously serve what society and religion define as "Honour," because conventional morality encourages disguise and artifice which diminishes private experience. In terms of the poem's argument, Celia must learn that unquestioning acceptance of a concept like Honour (or "vaine and empty words") petrifies human interaction and can result in aggression and hostility. This realization, although relatively common to the sexual warfare taking place in many Cavalier *carpe diem* poems, because of this poem's use of political language and its generic eclecticism, suggests a vision of social order that moves beyond the relationship between the sexes. As in so many of his verse compliments, Carew as poet deliberately makes lyric bear the weight of profounder reflections about social behavior and cultural assumptions than such vehicles usually carry.

The epigraph to this essay from Suckling, Carew's fellow wit and admirer, exposes the analogy to public structures of authority that define human relationships in a hierarchical society supremely conscious of rank and the serious consequences of successful "play-acting" or sociability, and points toward the nature or power as a dialectic of domination and submission. Carew's fondness for an hyperbole of reduction as a poetic tool is also a way of perceiving, and certainly **"A Rapture"** exemplifies Carew's proficiency with this poetic strategy. The miniature world he creates itself reveals a need for control, for a miniature world, as Gaston Bachelard has suggested, is a dominated world. While it can be said that **"A Rapture"** firmly established among his contemporaries Carew's reputation as an urbane and witty amorist, the poem also reveals tensions in aesthetic, social, and cultural values, tensions that exceed in scope initial physical and psychological motivations in which an individual most fully confronts the often antithetical demands of private and public values.

*Notes*

1. Rhodes Dunlap, *The Poems of Thomas Carew with his Masque Coelum Britannicum* (Oxford, 1970) xx.

2. Perez Zagorin, *The Court and the Country: The Beginning of the English Revolution* (New York, 1970) 73.

3. Peter Berger, "Society as Drama," *Drama in Life: The Uses of Communication in Society,* ed. James E. Coombs and Michael W. Mansfield (New York, 1976) 39.

4. Berger 39.

5. Dunlap xlvi.

6. Dunlap xlix.

7. Dunlap lii.

8. James E. Ruoff, "Thomas Carew's Early Reputation," *Notes & Queries* 202 (1957):62.

9. Earl Miner, *The Cavalier Mode from Jonson to Cotton* (Princeton, 1970) 81.

10. Ada Long and Hugh Maclean, "'Deare Ben,' 'Great DONNE,' and 'my Celia,': The Wit of Carew's Poetry," *Studies in English Literature 1500-1800* 18 (1978):89.

11. Paula Johnson, "Carew's 'A Rapture': The Dynamics of Fantasy," *Studies in English Literature 1500-1800* 16 (1976):151.

12. Dunlap. All references to the poem cite this edition.

13. Elise Goodman, "Ruben's Conversatie à la Mode: Garden of Leisure, Fashion, and Gallantry," *Art Bulletin* (June 1982):251.

14. Douglas Bush, *Mythology and the Renaissance Tradition in English Poetry* (New York, 1963) 235.

15. Stephen Orgel, "The Poetics of Spectacle," *New Literary History* 2 (1971):367.

16. Ada Long and Hugh Maclean 94.

---

# FURTHER READING

## Biography

Holliday, Carl. "Thomas Carew (1598-1639)." In *The Cavalier Poets: Their Lives, Their Day, and Their Poetry*, pp. 79-88. Plainview, N. Y.: Books for Libraries Press, 1911. Reprint 1974.

> Describes Carew's life as a gallant, calling him "one of the most successful court poets of his day."

## Criticism

Altieri, Joanne. "Responses to a Waning Mythology in Carew's Political Poetry." *Studies in English Literature, 1500-1900* 26, No. 1 (Winter 1986): 107-24.

> Maintains that Carew exploited cultural myths in his poetry in an effort to play down political events considered unfavorable in Britain.

Dunlap, Rhodes. *The Poems of Thomas Carew with His Masque Coelum Britannicum*. Oxford: Clarendon Press, 1949, 297 p.

> Comprises Carew's poetic writings preceded by an account of his life, reputation, and literary achievement.

Jungman, Robert E. "The Ending of Thomas Carew's 'The Spring'." *Concerning Poetry* 8, No. 2 (Fall 1975): 49-50.

> Evaluates the motif of Carew's mistress acting out of tune with Nature in "The Spring."

——. "Carew's 'To Ben. Ionson'." *Explicator* 40, No. 1 (Fall 1981): 17-18.

> Comments on Virgilian echoes in Carew's laudatory poem to Ben Jonson.

——. "Carew's 'The Spring,' Lines 22-23." *Explication* 40, No. 4 (Summer 1982): 17-18.

> Observes Carew's indirect quotation of Ecclesiastes 3:1 as part of his effort to persuade his mistress to make love in "The Spring."

Leavis, F. R. "The Line of Wit." In *Revaluation: Tradition & Development in English Poetry*, pp. 10-41. London: Chatto & Windus, 1956.

> Contains a seminal reconsideration of Carew's poetic stature, elevating him above the other Cavalier poets and associating him more closely with Ben Jonson and John Donne.

Lyon, John. "Jonson and Carew on Donne: Censure into Praise." *Studies in English Literature, 1500-1900* 37, No. 1 (Winter 1997): 97-118.

> Explores seventeenth-century views of John Donne and calls into question what is ordinarily perceived as Carew's unequivocal praise of Donne's poetry in his "An Elegie upon the death of the Deane of Pauls, Dr. Iohn Donne."

Malekin, Peter. "Love, Sex and Attitudes to Women in the Poetry." In *Liberty and Love: English Literature and Society 1640-88*, pp. 134-48. London: Hutchinson, 1981.

> Mentions Carew's "A Rapture" as part of a survey of seventeenth-century courtly love poetry.

McFarland, Ronald E. "Some Observations on Carew's 'Song' and Robinson's 'For a Dead Lady'." *The Markham Review* 10 (Fall-Winter 1980-81): 29-32.

> Analyzes Carew's "Song: Ask Me No More," observing its possible influence on E. A. Robinson's "For a Dead Lady."

McGuire, Mary Ann C. "The Cavalier Country-House Poem: Mutations on a Jonsonian Tradition." *Studies in English Literature, 1500-1900* XIX, No. 1 (Winter 1979): 93-108.

> Includes a reading of Carew's "To Saxham," locating the poem within an English literary tradition of celebrating country-house life.

Parker, Michael P. "'All are not born (Sir) to the Bay': 'Jack' Suckling, 'Tom' Carew, and the Making of a Poet." *English Literary Renaissance* 12, No. 3 (Autumn 1982): 341-68.

> Describes the relationship of Carew and Sir John Suckling as one of "complementary opposition" in

matters concerning poetry. Parker suggests that the poets must be viewed as representatives of two poles, not one, in Cavalier poetry.

————. "Carew's Politic Pastoral: Virgilian Pretexts in the 'Answer to Aurelian Townsend'." *John Donne Journal* 1, Nos. 1-2 (1982): 101-16.

Closely examines pastoral language and imagery in Carew's "In Answer of an Elegiacall Letter upon the Death of the King of Sweden from Aurelian Townsend, Inviting Me to Write on That Subject."

Sharpe, Kevin. "Cavalier Critic? The Ethics and Politics of Thomas Carew's Poetry." In *Politics of Discourse: The Literature and History of Seventeenth-Century England*, edited by Kevin Sharpe and Steven N. Zwicker, pp. 117-46. Berkeley: University of California Press, 1987.

Argues that Carew, rather than epitomizing the Cavalier profligacy of the Caroline courtier, should be aligned with the humanism and morality of Ben Jonson and his followers.

Todd, Richard. "Carew's 'crowne of Bayes': Epideixis and the Performative Rendering of Donne's Poetic Voice." *John Donne Journal* 10, Nos. 1-2 (1991): 111-27.

Views Carew's "Elegie" to John Donne "as a rendering or burning down of elegy to epitaph."

Walton, Geoffrey. "The Cavalier Poets: Thomas Carew (1595?-1639?)." In *From Donne to Marvell*, edited by Boris Ford, pp. 210-14. *The New Pelican Guide to English Literature, Vol. 3:* Harmondsworth, England: Penguin Books, 1982.

Approaches Carew as both a literary heir of Ben Jonson and a precursor of the English Augustan poets.

# Donald Davie
## 1922-1995

English poet, critic, editor, memoirist, and translator.

## INTRODUCTION

Davie is well respected for both his creative and his critical contributions to contemporary literature. His belief that the poet "is responsible to the community in which he writes for purifying and correcting the spoken language" is manifested by the classical formalism of his verse. Although his work is often considered overly academic, it is also recognized as both elegant and compressed.

## BIOGRAPHICAL INFORMATION

Davie was born in Barnsley, Yorkshire, England on July 17, 1922. In 1941 he enlisted in the Royal Navy. After World War II he attended Cambridge, receiving his doctoral degree in 1951. In the 1950s Davie was associated with the Movement, a group of poets that included Philip Larkin, Kingsley Amis, and Thom Gunn. In contrast to English poets of the 1940s who were influenced by imagism and symbolism, the Movement poets emphasized restrained language, traditional syntax, and the moral and social implications of poetic content. In the late 1950s Davie spent several years teaching in Ireland. Disillusioned with what he viewed as a declining English culture and feeling himself alienated from English academics who emphasized the separateness of poetry and criticism, Davie moved to the United States. He taught several years at Stanford University and Vanderbilt University before moving back to England. He continued to write poetry and criticism until his death in 1995.

## MAJOR WORKS

Davie has described himself as a poet for whom intellectual concerns take precedence over expressions of sensual experience. Some critics, however, note a sensuous attraction to nature in several poems in *A Winter Talent and Other Poems* which became more pronounced and deliberate in *Events and Wisdoms*. Many of Davie's poems deal with his ambivalent feeling toward England. Several poems from *In the Stopping Train* illuminate this tension as Davie attempts to come to terms with the England of his childhood and the England of today. *The Shires* is comprised of forty poems, one for each county in England, in which Davie contemplates the past, present, and future of his native country. His *Collected Poems* and *Selected Po-*

*ems* are collections of verse that display the directness and aesthetic control for which Davie has been commended throughout his career.

## CRITICAL RECEPTION

It has been asserted that many of Davie's most successful poems are suffused with a sense of place and a sense of history associated with place. Among these, *Essex Poems* considers the differences between England and America. Other commentators have underscored the role of Ireland and Canada in his work. It has also been noted that Davie's critical interest in other poets often affects his own poetic style. He has written critical works on Boris Pasternak, Ezra Pound, and Thomas Hardy; it follows that commentators attribute his experimental use of metaphor, symbolism, and loosely-structured verse forms to the influence of these poets. Stylistically, analyses have focused on Davie's adherence to the aesthetic considerations of the Movement poets: prose-like syntax, formal structures, and the conservative metaphors of the eighteenth-century Augustan poets. Finally, recent critical commentary has identified and discussed the importance of religious and political issues in Davie's work.

---

# PRINCIPAL WORKS

## Poetry

*(Poems).* 1954
*Brides of Reason* 1955
*A Winter Talent and Other Poems* 1957
*New and Selected Poems* 1961
*A Sequence for Francis Parkman* 1961
*Events and Wisdoms: Poems 1957-1963* 1964
*Essex Poems 1963-1967* 1969
*Poems* 1969
*Six Epistles to Eva Hesse* 1970
*Collected Poems, 1950-1970* 1972
*Orpheus* 1974
*The Shires: Poems* 1974
*In the Stopping Train and Other Poems* 1977
*Three for Water-Music* 1981
*Collected Poems, 1970-1983* 1983
*To Scorch or Freeze: Poems about the Sacred* 1988
*Collected Poems* 1991
*Poems and Melodramas* 1996
*Selected Poems* 1997

## Other Major Works

*Purity of Diction in English Verse* (criticism) 1952
*Articulate Energy: An Enquiry into the Syntax of English Poetry* (criticism) 1955
*The Heyday of Sir Walter Scott* (criticism) 1961
*The Language of Science and the Language of Literature, 1700-1740* (criticism) 1963
*Ezra Pound: Poet as Sculptor* (criticism) 1964
*Thomas Hardy and British Poetry* (criticism) 1972
*Pound* (criticism) 1975
*The Poet in the Imaginary Museum: Essays of the Two Decades* (criticism) 1976
*A Gathered Church: The Literature of the English Dissenting Interest, 1700-1930* (criticism) 1978
*Trying to Explain* (criticism) 1979
*These the Companions* (memoirs) 1982
*Czeslaw Milosz and the Insufficiency of Lyric* (criticism) 1986
*Under Briggflatts: A History of Poetry in Great Britain, 1960-1988* (criticism) 1989
*The Eighteenth-Century Hymn in England* (criticism) 1993
*Older Masters: Essays and Reflections on English and American Literature* (criticism) 1993
*Essays of Discontent: Church, Chapel, and the Unitarian Conspiracy* (essays) 1995

# CRITICISM

### Bernard Bergonzi (essay date 1962)

SOURCE: "The Poetry of Donald Davie," in *The Critical Quarterly*, Vol. 4, No. 4, Winter, 1962, pp. 293-304.

[*In the following essay, Bergonzi examines stylistic and thematic aspects of Davie's early work.*]

Donald Davie's first book was a cool, rather tough work of literary criticism, *Purity of Diction in English Verse,* published in 1952. This was ostensibly an academic study of the procedures of various minor eighteenth century poets, together with reflections on later poetry; it contained some admirable literary history, and was full of worthwhile hints for the student of Augustan verse. But *Purity of Diction,* despite its bland scholarly guise, had a barely concealed polemical purpose. It represented Davie's reaction against the dominant assumptions of twentieth century poetics: that the essence of poetry lay in metaphor, and particularly in the bold or violent collocation of images, and that syntax must inevitably be distorted or broken in the interests of poetic immediacy. The minor Augustans whom Davie admired had used metaphor sparingly, and 'arresting' images hardly at all; they preserved in their diction a tone that was carefully balanced between cultivated speech and literary usage (and which Davie saw as closely related to desirable moral qualities of poise and balance); and they employed a compressed, energetic syntax which, though based on the syntax of prose, was capable of a wide range of poetic effects: Davie's interest in syntax was to be expanded in his next critical work, *Articulate Energy* (1957). Occasionally the contemporary relevance of his scholarly investigations was made overt; in *Purity of Diction* he remarked, 'there is no denying that modern poetry is obscure and that it would be less so if the poets adhered to the syntax of prose'.

When Davie's first collection of poems, ***Brides of Reason,*** came out in 1955 it was apparent that he had learnt the lessons presented in *Purity of Diction* with almost unnerving thoroughness. It was more than a book of verse, it was a manifesto in favour of poetic conservatism. It showed that verse could with advantage be written in the tightest of strict forms (though these sometimes tumbled over into merely mechanical regularity and a metronomic thump), and that vivid metaphor wasn't essential for poetic effect. The diction showed a calculated conventionality, and Davie's subdued tone of voice was described by G. S. Fraser as 'the lecturer's, calmly stressing our common involvement but not especially dramatizing his own'. The syntax, though deployed with subtlety and finesse, was rooted in the word-order of prose, without symbolist dislocations (though this, one might add, didn't wholly exempt Davie from the obscurity he had complained of in *Purity of Diction;* his characteristic kind of obscurity has always stemmed from a combination of ellipsis and extreme allusiveness). A common reaction to this wilfully antidionysiac book was to dismiss it as 'flat' or 'dull', particularly from those who had grown up with the heady romanticism of the Dylan Thomas era. This, I think, was unjust, though one could see why the book failed to appeal widely. It contained a handful of very fine poems, but it was also marked by a variety of irritating mannerisms.

One thinks above all of Davie's habit of uncontrolled literary quotation and reference. He has argued that our experience of a poem or other work of art is just as valid a starting point for a poem as our experience of a landscape or of falling in love. I can accept this in principle, and I am extremely sympathetic with Davie's desire to align himself with the Classical and Renaissance concept of poetry as something that must inevitably draw on the work of other writers—as exemplified by all English poets from Chaucer to Pope—rather than with the Romantic view of a poem as the transcript of a unique and original experience, where any kind of 'literariness' is an unwelcome dilution. Still, there is a question of degree: a recent reviewer has remarked that the names of over thirty writers are mentioned in *Brides of Reason*. A rapid check of my own suggests that the number is in fact nearly forty; and this can surely be described as hammering home a point, valid in itself, with somewhat insolent emphasis. Allusions apart, many of the poems are about writing poetry, and the words 'poem', 'poet', and 'poetic' occur with some frequency. This inward-looking preoccupation was one that Davie shared with other poets of the Movement; and indeed it can be found in some of the greatest symbolist and post-symbolist poets. In this respect Davie, though conservative, was still fundamentally 'modern'.

There is a sense in which the extreme literariness of much of *Brides of Reason* might be called a mark of Davie's personal honesty. He was, by vocation, a scholar and teacher of literature, for whom the classics of English literature were as alive as the Greek and Latin classics had been for the Augustans, and who was keenly interested in problems of poetic process. Why, then, shouldn't he use them as valid poetic material? I'm half-convinced by this argument; but I still prefer those poems which are not primarily literary, but which present a marvellously exact and painful formulation of a moral dilemma. One of the best is **'The Evangelist'**:

'My bretheren . . .' And a bland, elastic smile
Basks on the mobile features of Dissent.
No hypocrite, you understand. The style
Befits a church that's based on sentiment.

Solicitations of a swirling gown,
The sudden vox humana, and the pause,
The expert orchestration of a frown
Deserve, no doubt, a murmur of applause.

The tides of feeling round me rise and sink;
Bunyon, however, found a place for wit.
Yes, I am more persuaded than I think;
Which is, perhaps, why I disparage it.

You round upon me, generously keen:
The man, you say, is patently sincere.

Because he is so eloquent, you mean?
That test was never patented, my dear.

If, when he plays upon our sympathies,
I'm pleased to be fastidious, and you
To be inspired, the vice in it is this:
Each does us credit, and we know it too.

One notices here things derived from Davie's study of the Augustans: the personified abstraction in the second line, and, more significantly, the way in which, at the beginning of the third stanza, the subdued metaphor of the 'tides of feeling', very nearly a cliché, is revivified by careful syntactical placing, governing the kinetically vigorous verbs, 'rise and sink'. But, more than these details, one is aware of the implacable mask of ironic good-breeding, and the way in which the gentle modulations of the verbal surface enact a quiet intellectual drama, giving us, first, the inner debate of the speaker, then moving into open dialogue with his interlocutrix; and culminating finally with the whip-lash of the seemingly flat last line. One finds here the economy of means which Davie so much admired in the Augustans. Only a singularly imperceptive reader could, I think, dismiss this poem as merely cerebral, as so much of Davie's early poetry was dismissed. There is, it seems to me, an under-current of intense feeling, almost of anguish, flowing strongly beneath the decorously rippling surface. The subject of Dissent, or Nonconformity, is clearly one with which Davie felt an extreme personal involvement from his early years, and it is reflected in several other poems, notably the sequence called **'Dissentient Voice'** from his next collection, *A Winter Talent* (1957).

One of the few poems from *Brides of Reason* in which Davie allows himself a directly rather than obliquely personal utterance is **'The Garden Party'**. It's quite well-known and is extremely skilful, though some of its appeal may come from the way in which it conveys, delicately and honestly, a sense of its period. But this may well be true of much more literature than we imagine, perhaps in some measure of all, as Lionel Trilling has persuasively argued in his essay, 'The Sense of the Past'. The early fifties saw the emergence of a sensibility acutely aware of the painfulness of social uprooting and the blurring of traditional class patterns. One finds these themes enacted in a number of celebrated works: *Lucky Jim*, *Room at the Top*, *Look Back in Anger*, *The Uses of Literacy* (as much a work of autobiography as of social criticism). But in the twenty lines of this poem Davie has captured the essence of this state of feeling with great economy and precision:

Above a stretch of still unravaged weald
In our Black Country, in a cedar-shade,
I found, shared out in tennis courts, a field
Where children of the local magnates played.

And I grew envious of their moneyed ease
In Scott Fitzgerald's unembarrassed vein.
Let prigs, I thought, fool others as they please,
I only wish I had my time again.

To crown a situation as contrived
As any in 'The Beautiful and Damned',
The phantom of my earliest love arrived;
I shook absurdly as I shook her hand.

As dusk drew in on cultivated cries,
Faces hung pearls upon a cedar-bough;
And gin could blur the glitter of her eyes,
But it's too late to learn to tango now.

My father, of a more submissive school,
Remarks the rich themselves are always sad.
There is that sort of equalizing rule;
But theirs is all the youth we might have had.

As in **'The Evangelist'**, the sting of the poem is reserved for the final line, a sad, rebellious outcry.

**Brides of Reason,** for all its limitations, was an important and accomplished collection. In a sense, it was *too* accomplished: it showed that Davie had discovered precisely the kind of poetry he wanted to write, could write it skilfully, and might go on writing into the foreseeable future. Some of the other Movement poets have done just that, with no noticeable development. But Davie's next book of verse, **A Winter Talent,** was something of a surprise. Several of the poems in it were in much the same style as those in **Brides of Reason,** and were probably written at about the same time. But others showed an opening up of technique and an unexpected movement towards symbolism. In *Purity of Diction* Davie had shown a rather prim distaste towards symbolism and its derivatives, a distaste which seemed as much moral and even political as literary; he had remarked of Pound, for example, that 'the development from imagism in poetry to fascism in politics is clear and unbroken'. But in 1955, in a note contributed to D. J. Enright's anthology, *Poets of the 1950's,* published in Tokyo, Davie referred to Pound as a poet 'who has influenced me more deeply and more constantly than any other poet of the present century'. In the same year, *Articulate Energy,* though still manifesting a conservative bias in favour of prose syntax in poetry, and in favour of a Wordsworthian openness to the aspirations of ordinary humanity rather than a closed symbolist system, had also shown a remarkable sympathy to individual poems that were undoubtedly symbolist in their methods. Looking at Davie's subsequent poetry and criticism, one can only conclude that he had succumbed to the strange magnetic attraction that symbolism has for those who attempt to study it in a spirit of detachment or even suspicion.

*A Winter Talent* opens with a very beautiful love poem, **'Time Passing, Beloved'**, which shows how interestingly Davie had developed from the manner of **Brides of Reason**:

Time passing, and the memories of love
Coming back to me, carissima, no more mockingly
Than ever before; time passing, unslackening,
Unhastening, steadily; and no more
Bitterly, beloved, the memories of love
Coming into the shore.

How will it end? Time passing, and our passages of love
As ever, beloved, blind
As ever before; time binding, unbinding
About us; and yet to remember
Never less chastening, nor the flame of love
Less like an ember.

What will become of us? Time
Passing, beloved, and we in a sealed
Assurance unassailed
By memory. How can it end,
This siege of a shore that no misgivings have steeled,
No doubts defend?

The subject of the poem strikes more deeply than those of the brilliant, ironic, moral investigations in the earlier book. The formal devices show an equally startling change. The syntax is not that of prose; unlike the earlier poems, this doesn't move inexorably forward from a calm opening to the painful flick of the last line. Instead, there is not progression but a kind of solemn revolution; the poem seems to rotate slowly round the verbal participles of the first two stanzas before coming quietly to rest in the murmured questions of the final stanza. If I have understood correctly the discussion of 'syntax as music', in *Articulate Energy,* then **'Time Passing, Beloved'** certainly seems to belong to that category.

Frequently in **A Winter Talent** one is reminded of the enlightening analyses of *Articulate Energy,* particularly of Davie's demonstration of the way in which verbs impart a vital energy to a poem. As, for instance, in **'The Wind at Penistone'**, which opens:

The wind meets me at Penistone.
                    A hill
Curves empty through the township, on a slope
Not cruel, and yet steep enough to be,
Were it protracted, cruel.

In an excellent review of **A Winter Talent,** (*Listen,* Winter, 1958) Thom Gunn noted that Davie was now attempting to use conceptual language, which he had recommended in *Purity of Diction* and employed in **Brides of Reason,** in a symbolic fashion. In **'The Wind at Penistone'**, for instance, Davie uses the words 'edge' and 'reserves' as symbolic concepts. Certainly the most ambitious attempt to combine the conceptual and the symbolic is to be found in **'Under St. Paul's'**. In this dense, elaborate poem, which I continue to find rather baffling, we begin with explicitness and an Augustan personification of Candour; but at the conclusion we have moved on to quintessentially symbolist imagery:

Across the dark face of the water
Flies the white bird until nothing is left but the water.

**'Under St. Paul's'**, which I can't really consider a success, is perhaps an early example in Davie's work of something he has frequently favoured in his later criticism; the 'open-ended' poem, which doesn't neatly return at the end to the starting point, but moves onward and outward, far away from its origin, like a river flowing into the sea.

Parallel with the changes in technique, the poems in *A Winter Talent* show a steadily widening range of themes. *Brides of Reason* had presented a tight-lipped, sharp-eyed provincial of nonconformist origins, whose main allegiances were to literature and, perhaps, to Cambridge:

> Those Cambridge generations, Russell's, Keynes' . . .
> And mine? Oh mine was Wittgenstein's, no doubt.

But in *A Winter Talent* Davie turns further afield; partly to Ireland, where he was then living—I note in passing the incisive elegance of such a poem as **'North Dublin'**—and, more significantly, to Italy. The set of poems on Italian art and landscape show an extension of sensibility and a breakaway from insular confinement; one of them, **'Via Portello'**, is surely among Davie's finest achievements:

> Rococo compositions of decay,
> Each a still-life, the fruity garbage-heaps
> Teem by themselves. A broad and cobbled way,
> Tiepolo's and Byron's thoroughfare
> Lies grand and empty in its sullied air,
> And watches while the rest of Padua sleeps . . .

But though Davie continued to take in a wider vision, it was not the well-trodden shores of the Mediterranean that were to arouse his imagination most deeply, but territory less familiar to English poets: Eastern Europe, and North America. One of the most strange and beautiful poems in *A Winter Talent* was **'The Mushroom Gatherers'**, subtitled 'After Mickiewicz', and this pointed to an interest that was to be amplified in his next book, *The Forests of Lithuania* (1959).

Although *A Winter Talent* contained an admirable body of work, and showed a welcome development both in themes and treatment from *Brides of Reason,* my feeling when it appeared was that the contents, excellent though they were, seemed to be buttressing a major composition which hadn't, so far, been written. *The Forests of Lithuania,* though it wasn't what one might have expected, did suggest that Davie was making an attempt on the long poem. This composition was made up of a series of extracts adapted from the long epic poem, *Pan Tadeusz,* composed in exile by the Polish national poet Adam Mickiewicz in the eighteen-thirties. *Pan Tadeusz* is set amongst the Polish gentry in Lithuania during the days of Napoleon's invasion of Russia, when they enjoyed a short-lived hope of liberation. Like other readers, I was spurred on by Davie's versions to read *Pan Tadeusz,* in G. R. Noyes' prose translation, and was grateful for the experience. Even in Noyes' rather pedestrian prose one does have the sense of reading a great poem; an authentic epic rooted in the *mores* of a wholly feudal society that had astonishingly survived into the nineteenth century; and yet strangely combined with the conventions of romantic fiction (see Davie's useful discussion of the work in his latest critical book, *The Heyday of Sir Walter Scott*).

Davie's adaptation contains some magnificent verse, but gives rather little of the broad epic sweep of the original. In fact, it is Davie's most avowedly symbolist work. The publisher suggests that *The Forests of Lithuania* represents a revival of the long poem; but what Davie has done is to reduce Mickiewicz's lengthy and fully articulated epic to a series of six sections which present the 'gists' or 'piths' of the poem, with the narrative links suppressed. Syntax has become ideogram, in precisely the manner which called forth Davie's sternest disapproval in his early criticism. Similarly the characters of the epic, who are carefully introduced in the original, are flung in with the abruptness of Eliot's Hakagawa or Mr. Silvero, or the personages of the *Cantos*. Much as I admire *The Forests of Lithuania,* it is, I think, a weakness of the poem that rather a lot of it is unintelligible unless one has first read *Pan Tadeusz.* Davie's intention was to make an adaptation rather than a straight translation, but in the event he hasn't made his own composition sufficiently self-contained. And Davie wanted, I'm sure, to write what could be regarded as an English poem, just as much as Pope's Homer or Fitzgerald's Omar Khayyam.

*The Forests of Lithuania* has an interesting relation to the work of Pound. It couldn't have been written, I feel, without the example of *Homage to Sextus Propertius,* though one imagines that Davie is closer to Mickiewicz than Pound was to Propertius. The work is prefaced with a poem in the manner of the *Cantos,* which takes the opportunity mildly to rebuke Pound and those other defenders of Latin culture who have restricted European civilization to the shores of the Mediterranean, and have refused to recognise that the ideal Europe is a community embracing East as well as West, a reminder perhaps timely today, though one would hesitate to describe *The Forests of Lithuania* as a political poem. The point is made explicit in section IV of the poem, where the 'happy skies of Italy' are contrasted with the impenetrable Lithuania forest, full of wild creatures, and the source of legends:

> Who has plumbed Lithuania's forest,
> Pressed to the thicket's core?
> As the sea-floor is known to the fisherman
> Meagerly, even inshore,
> So the hunter can know of the forest
> Only the face of its waters
> Never their bed.

I have described *The Forests of Lithuania* as ideogrammatic, and comparing it with *Pan Tadeusz* this is, I think, true; yet it is only relatively true. There are many vigorously kinetic passages, employing all Davie's skill in manipulating syntax, where the contrast with the verbless juxtapositions of the *Cantos* is complete as possible. Perhaps the finest of these passages occurs at the conclusion of the hunt sequence, when the Seneschal breaks off his triumphant performance on the horn:

> But now his arms were thrown
> Wide, and the horn
> Fell, swung on a thong;

As, cruciform
And swollen-faced, his eyes
Lifted, still he tried
To catch the last and long
Long-drawn
Note from the skies,

As plaudits came to drown
The horn.

The superb kinetic and aural onomatopoeia of these lines might, of course, be dismissed as 'mere' technique. For me, however, they remain as evidence that Davie can do more things with language, and has more powers in reserve, than any other post-war poet.

In **The Forests of Lithuania** he was attempting to recreate a mode of sensibility as far removed as possible from contemporary England and the ironic, bourgeois, academic pre-occupations of his early poetry. The epical simplicities of Mickiewicz's feudal world gave Davie an opportunity to hint at, if not to formulate, heroic gestures of a kind that would be impossible in a modern setting. And an aspiration towards the heroic, though customarily frustrated, has recurred in his subsequent poetry. The pursuit of remote territory and states of feeling was continued in Davie's next sustained poetic work, a set of poems called **A Sequence for Francis Parkman,** published in 1961. Here Davie re-enacts a number of incidents or characters from the early history of the United States and Canada, as described in Parkman's various volumes. I admire these poems very much, though Davie may find this admiration something of an embarrassment, as he regards the sequence as rather a sport or poetic luxury, quite apart from what he sees as the line of his true development. Certainly they are rhetorical, and Davie's latest work has been consciously anti-rhetorical. Yet it is a rhetoric that works well and has the traditional and nearly forgotten poetic virtue of memorability, as in the splendid conclusion of **'Lasalle'**:

He loved solitude and he loved power
And lonely as when born of chaos, bright
Voiceless, sail-less, without sign of life
The great Gulf opened, tossing—but what for?
Not for the Faith, for glory, or for France,
Whirled on the miry vortex of his need,
The light canoes of Indian nations foundered.

Another poem, **'Montcalm'**, has the evocative refrain, 'In Candiac by Nîmes in Languedoc', which was lately dismissed by a reviewer in a Leavisian stock-response as 'Bellocian'. This moves me to protest; there is nothing *necessarily* wicked about using musical or evocative language in poetry, and in any case Belloc was not as bad a poet as all that. In the final poem of the sequence, a letter to an American friend, Davie shows what attracts him in American history:

Man with man
Is all our history; American,
You met with spirits. Neither white nor red

The melancholy, disinherited
Spirit of mid-America, but this,
The manifested copiousness, the bounties.

He envies the largeness of scale, the possibilities, of the mainly empty American landscape, feeling restricted by the cluttered and antique civilization in which he has grown up: in a sense Davie is reversing the famous complaint made by Henry James in his book on Hawthorne, that America had none of the institutions and social density of Europe that made life possible for a novelist. Davie sees America as offering more possibilities to the poet.

Apart from these two sequences, Davie has written many individual poems since **A Winter Talent** came out in 1957, but as they have not yet been collected it's difficult to form a coherent picture of his recent work; though a representative selection appeared in the May 1962 number of the American monthly, *Poetry*. Certainly one of the finest of his later poems (reprinted in *The Guinness Book of Poetry 1959-60*) is **'To a Brother in the Mystery'**, to which Mr. Lucie-Smith justly drew attention in the last issue of the *Critical Quarterly*. In this and other poems Davie has returned, though more profoundly, to the preoccupation of his early work with the art of poetry. But now the stress is much more on the art. As this poem implies, the poet's primary responsibility is to his medium, which is obdurate like stone, and the act of composition is like carving or chiselling: Davie has given a fuller exposition of these views in a broadcast talk, 'Two Analogies for Poetry' (*Listener,* 5 April 1962). The whole stress of Davie's recent criticism has been against the notion—which underlay *Purity of Diction*—that the primary concerns of poetry are moral and social; instead he sees the central business of poetry as being to contemplate the world, to understand its inmost meaning, rather than busily attempt to change it. There are passages from Rilke, from the *Duino Elegies,* which, so far as I can grasp them in translation, seem to be doing just this; it is, I think, a noble aim for poetry, even if far removed from the assumptions of modern English criticism. But as Davie has implied, to explain and defend such poetry would require a religious and metaphysical frame of reference rather than an ethical one. Thomism, for instance, can find a place for poetry as contemplation; but I do not think Davie has yet moved so far.

This new direction in Davie's thinking has been marked by a resolute turning away from the characteristics and indeed the strengths of his earlier poetry; in a recent letter to me Davie remarked of the style he is aiming at, 'The new one should be, yes, celebratory; but I hold it in my mind rather as a series of negative prescriptions, e.g. NO irony; NO literary allusions; NO backward-looking historical nostalgias'. A number of Davie's recent poems, written since **'To a Brother in the Mystery'**, appear transitional rather than successful in their own right; they are limpid and obviously close to experience, but a certain vitality has gone out of them, perhaps because Davie is eschewing the rhetoric that gave so much energy to his earlier work. It may well be that he is employing a principle of organization that I have totally failed to grasp. At all events, a poem such as **'Right Wing Opinions'**, published in *The Review* No. 1, (April-May 1962) seems, to employ a convenient oxymoron, to possess a kind of limpid opacity; I have read it many times, but cannot understand it. Not all of Davie's late poems are like this. Several of those published in *Poetry* are undoubtedly successful, most particularly **'New York in August'**, which is as fine as anything he has written; though in view of his recent stand against literary allusions, it may be significant that this poem takes its point of departure in Pasternak's 'Storm in the City' (very beautifully translated by Davie in *Listen*, Autumn 1962). Here is **'New York in August'**:

> There came, for lack of sleep,
> A crosspatch, drained-out look
> On the old trees that keep
> Scents of Schiedam and the Hook
>
> In Flushing, as we picked out, past
> Each memorised landmark,
> Our route to a somnolent breakfast.
> Later, to Central Park,
>
> UNO, and the Empire State.
> A haven from the heat
> Was the Planetarium. We got back late,
> Buffeted, dragging our feet.
>
> Clammy, electric, torrid,
> The nights bring no relief
> At the latitude of Madrid.
> Never the stir of a leaf
>
> Any night, as we went
> Back, the children asleep,
> To our bed in a loaned apartment,
> Although I thought a deep
>
> And savage cry from the park
> Came once, as we flashed together
> And the fan whirled in the dark,
> For thunder, a break in the weather.

Davie has come a long way in the last ten years, but the bulk of his poetry has shown him to be, so far, a poet whose best work has emerged from a fairly close dependence on literature or history; and in this he resembles Pound. And like Pound or Joyce, or, for that matter Picasso or Stravinsky, he is an Alexandrian, who has moved energetically from place to place or period to period in search of the materials of his art. And this, perhaps, in our present phase of cultural development, is inevitable for a serious artist whose vision is not permanently blinkered by the provinciality in which Davie began his career. Yet he wishes to return to English themes, but in a celebratory way, not with the ironic, deprecating stance of a Larkin or a Betjeman; 'There *must* be more life in England than this,' he has written, 'there must be some light other than this flickering glancing one in which England is still beautiful'. He has expanded this idea in a note, 'England as Poetic Subject' (*Poetry*, May 1962). It is an intention which I admire and applaud, and hope to see realised. Ex-

trapolating from this intention, and from the open, limpid, non-rhetorical, non-ironical, non-allusive nature of Davie's latest poetry, it seems not unreasonable to suggest that if he does succeed in celebrating the positive qualities of English life it may be rather in the manner of William Carlos Williams' writings about America. And for an Englishman to do this in our time is something I find, not impossible, but unimaginable. But Davie may succeed: certainly I entertain higher hopes of him than of any other English poet of his generation.

**Donald Greene (essay date 1973)**

SOURCE: "A Breakthrough into Spaciousness: The 'Collected Poems' of Donald Davie," in *Queen's Quarterly*, Vol. LXXX, No. 4, Winter, 1973, pp. 601-15.

[*In the following essay, Greene emphasizes the importance of Canada to Davie's verse.*]

I

> Eight hours between us, eight
> hours by the clock between us,
> eleven hours flying time.

Canada nowadays is what you fly over when travelling non-stop between California and Europe. The plane takes off, circling over the blue Pacific water and white sand beaches of Venice (California) and Malibu, dotted with surfboarders and scuba divers; then over the rugged mountain chain surrounding the Los Angeles basin, then across the Mojave and Nevada and Utah deserts (on the right route and a clear day you get a fine view of the Grand Canyon). Then the snow-capped immensity of the Rocky Mountains. But then, hour after hour of flat, monotonous prairie, dotted with towns, smaller and larger, their streets repeating the checkerboard pattern of the farms. Drinks are served, dinner is consumed, boredom sets in. After a while you look down: the checkerboard towns and farms are gradually disappearing; the flatness begins to be dotted by innumerable small lakes, and someone says, "I suppose we're over Canada now"—northern Saskatchewan or Manitoba. It is time to show the movie. Later, bored by it, you raise your window blind and see beneath you, in the slowly fading twilight, an unbounded stretch of water; if you are inexperienced, you may think you have reached the Atlantic. But a glance at your watch and a little calculation tells you that this cannot be—it must be Hudson Bay. After a while, the conjecture is confirmed, for you are over land again—Baffin Land, or Ungava, or the shiny icy tip of Greenland. About this time boredom merges into sleepiness. You take your shoes off, wad a pillow under your head, wrap a blanket around you and drop into unconsciousness for a few hours. The noise of activity wakens you; you look down and see beneath you the greenery and the smoke of the Midlands. You join the queue at the washrooms for a hasty shave, and, refreshed and expect-

ant, get out of the plane at Heathrow to encounter the excitement of a London morning.

> This is the country we fly
> over, over the Pole
> from Los Angeles to London
> or Leningrad. This is where
> the Hare Indian squaw or whatever
> co-ed from Oregon in
> Haight-Ashbury dumps her baby.

The historical allusion in the last sentence (from Davie's
long, scarifying poem, **"England"**) is to an observation
made by Thomas Simpson (Sir George's kinsman) about
the family customs of the indigenous dwellers in the Mackenzie River valley in the early nineteenth century. The
contemporary allusion doesn't need glossing.

This volume—almost all the poetry Davie has written for
publication, beginning some twenty years ago—ought to
be of interest to Canadians, for Canada plays a surprisingly large part in it. Not that Davie himself has spent
much time in Canada. Born, fifty years ago, in the Yorkshire industrial town of Barnsley, he completed his grammar school education there in time to serve the last four
years of World War II in the Royal Navy, on rugged con-
voy duty to northern Russia, and in Ceylon and India. After the war he entered Cambridge, obtaining his Ph.D. in
1951 with a thesis on the reception of the Russian novel in
England and America. He taught at Trinity College, Dublin, where he published his first, brilliant book of criticism,
*Purity of Diction in English Verse,* and later at Cambridge
and the newly established University of Essex.

When, in 1968, Davie moved to the United States, holding
appointments first at the University of Southern California
and later at Stanford, where he now teaches, his action
was the subject of some vicious criticism in British literary and academic circles. Why, it is hard to say, given the
long-established tradition of migration by the creative artist—James, Eliot, Joyce, Auden, Pound, to name the most
obvious. The event is of considerable importance in
Davie's later poems. Referring to Pound (on whom Davie's
book, *Ezra Pound: Poet as Sculptor,* is regarded by many
as the best critical work that has been done) and to Landor,
an earlier émigré, Davie writes of

> Ole Uncle Ez, the crustiest sort
> Of Yankee at King Arthur's court.
> Both poets, relishing the state
> Of mortified expatriate. . . .
>                     Self-banished bards
> Who never lack for occupation
> Each hectoring his relinquished nation
> Even as they exemplify
> The prepossessions they decry.

There is a good deal of this tone of self-mockery throughout the volume: a tone for which Davie entered a notable
apologia in perhaps the best known of his earlier poems,
**"Remembering the Thirties,"** a comment in the Fifties
on the "classics" of the youth of his generation, Auden,
Isherwood, MacNeice—

> They played the fool, not to appear as fools
> In time's long glass. A deprecating air
> Disarmed, they thought, the jeers of later schools;
> . . .

> A neutral tone is nowadays preferred.
> And yet it may be better, if we must,
> To praise a stance impressive and absurd
> Than not to see the hero for the dust.

Yet *coelum non animam mutant qui trans mare currunt* is
insisted on in the statement that appears on the dust jacket
of the British-Canadian edition of the volume: "The book
. . . has been written in the faith that there are still distinctively English—rather than Anglo-American or
'international'—ways of responding imaginatively to the
terms of life in the twentieth century." Did Davie autho-
rize it? One supposes so, although one can't always tell
with such blurbs. It will be curious to see whether it appears in the American edition. I should like to think that
the statement is no more than a riposte, not very effective
perhaps, to the critics of Davie's emigration, or—more
likely—a challenge to the "neutral tone" and characterless
content of the "Anglo-American" poetry of his contemporaries. At any rate, I'm glad to say that I can detect no
"distinctively English" way of responding imaginatively to
twentieth-century life in these poems—nor an Anglo-
American or international way: only a Davian way, no
more distinctively English than Joyce's way of responding
was distinctively Irish or Eliot's distinctively American.
The fine artist—Davie is unquestionably that—has nothing
to fear from the "melting pot" of jet-assisted international
travel: it doesn't subtract from the individuality of his response, but adds to, strengthens, diversifies it.

Canada, in the latest (and most impressive) poems of the
volume, becomes a kind of bridge for Davie between his
old and new homes—but, as in the air crossing, a symbol,
a concept, rather than something tangible in the here and
now. Davie's is the Canada of the seventeenth, eighteenth,
and early nineteenth centuries: Indeed, he uses the word
only in his early *A Sequence for Francis Parkman,* and
there only for the country around the St. Lawrence: very
properly, for the country of Sir George Simpson and Captain George Vancouver was not Canada. The Parkman sequence, Davie tells us, "unlikely as it may seem . . . represents my response to North America on my first visit
there, from September 1957 to August 1958." Not really
unlikely: where could a visitor to North America better
start than with Parkman? (Davie mischievously reports
that his poetic contemporary Philip Larkin "in an amiable
review speculated that Francis Parkman was 'one of Mr.
Davie's American friends'." Amusing; yet one is thankful
that Davie has advanced beyond such "distinctively English" provinciality.) These are, I think, the weakest and
most conventional group of verses in the volume. The responses to Parkman are the ones to be expected from a
newcomer, but Davie presumably had no means of knowing how thoroughly Parkman—the heroic Jesuit martyrs,
LaSalle, Frontenac, Montcalm—had been worked over by
writers like Sir Gilbert Parker and Marjorie Pickthall (if

Davie has never heard these names, no need for him to look them up).[1] Readers of *Queen's Quarterly* involved in the celebrations of the tercentenary of the founding of Fort Frontenac will be able to make use of Davie's

> What's to be seen of old Fort Frontenac?
> The British fortress, by a hundred years
> More recent, but still Old
> Fort Henry, draws the Buicks,

and others besides Davie have got mileage out of the discrepancy between the career of Chief Pontiac and his eponymous automobile. Is there an anniversary coming up for the city of Vancouver? Davie concludes his volume with a (much better) poem about the strange man after whom it is named.

In **"Los Angeles Poems"** and **"Recent Poems"** the North American historical experience has matured, in a way it perhaps never has for even the best of the North American writers who have tried to work with it. Parkman was an *echt*-Romantic, throwing a veil of New England Romanticism over events which took place a century or more before he was born into Brahmin affluence. For his later poems Davie has gone to the primary sources—the harsh day-to-day narratives of the explorers and hard-bitten fur traders who wrested an empire out of the Northwest for that prototype of the great twentieth-century conglomerate, the Governor and Company of Gentlemen Adventurers Trading into Hudson's Bay—and comes to the conclusion

> Heroic comedy, I suggest,
> Fits American history best.

"Why rehearse," he now asks (in the brilliant *Six Epistles to Eva Hesse,* 1970), "What Parkman has, though not in verse, / Recounted nobly? Why go on / About La Salle, son of Rouen, / Or Tonty, his most faithful creature?" Instead, we get

> In 1831
> "Robertson brought his bit
> of Brown with him
> to the Settlement this spring . . ."
> That is to say, his squaw.
> And that was Governor Simpson,
> got Betsy Sinclair with child,
> whose mother had been a Swampy
> Cree. The permafrost
> spins out a skein of wings
> that sting to a sexy heat

and

> Donald Smith of Forres
> finished up Lord Strathcona
> (strath of the coffee-machine?
> Glen of Conan)

and

>                    the bastard
> able diminutive George

> Simpson was later Sir George,
> a small inflexible pin
> on which the unwieldy engine
> of the Hudson's Bay Company turned . . .
> A holy terror. What
> a bastard . . .
>                    the driving, the king-
> pin, does it have to be Lenin
> on whom the unwieldy engine
> turns?

All this, strictly speaking, is much more Scotch than English, as, to be sure, the history of the country always has been (the main street of the allegedly most English city in Canada, Victoria, is "Douglas Street")—"Scots on the make / who gave their names to forts / on the Coppermine River or / headlands in Arctic seas." One of Davie's most useful critical works is his *The Heyday of Sir Walter Scott* (1961), an appreciative study of that great novelist and some of his European contemporaries. In his later poems, however, one wonders whether Davie has not come to feel about Scott somewhat as Mark Twain—a crucial figure in any discussion of North American history and ethics—came to:

> Shortbread tartans, a voice
> for the voiceless and lachrymose English,
> our kings implausibly kilted,
> we all came out of the author
> of *Waverley.* "Sir Walter
> Scott is no more," wrote George
> Simpson, who had not envisaged
> a teen-age culture. "Our
> universally admired,
> respected fellow-
> countryman is gone."
> Gone, gone as the combo
> starts in digging the beat
> and the girls from the nearest College
> of Further Education
> spread their excited thighs.

(All those quotations are from the astonishingly witty and bitter *tour de force* **"England"**). Another Scotch vignette of past and present:

> Or there's the unco' guid with
> a brutal difference. "My
> father was in the Asquith
> tradition, and pro-Boer.
> Which is a pity because
>                 *I wish they'd killed the lot.*"
> Scotswoman on the make
> at 70 plus . . .[2]

All this will not appeal of course to patriotic Canadians proud of their heritage, any more than it will to those to whom this fine love-hate poem is addressed. But, as Davie warns its addresses,

> This is a poem not about you
> But FOR you, for
> your delectation, lady.

## II

To try, in the course of even a longish review, to give the reader a very clear idea of the contents of this important volume, three hundred pages of some of the most competent poetry of our time, is an almost hopeless task. Perhaps the best strategy will be to take up Mr. Davie's challenge in his "Foreword" to see whether we can "discern a movement from first to last" in this chronologically arranged collection, "which in some way parallels a development over the same period which they [the readers] can discern in themselves." Waiving the question of this reviewer's possible development (and politely ignoring Davie's addressing his request to "some of my English readers in particular"), we can certainly see a development "which is more than a sterile alternation or an eclectic snatching and grabbing, more too than nervous response to the winds of fashion." The history of second-rate verse throughout the ages has been the history of response to the winds of fashion: in the late sixteenth century, feeble Petrarchan love lyrics; in the mid-seventeenth, decadent metaphysical poetry; in the late eighteenth, slack heroic couplets and weak-tea Miltonics; in the late nineteenth and early twentieth, the dregs of Romanticism. In the fifties and sixties, it was solipsistic symbolism and imagism, pseudo-Eliot and pseudo-Pound, of which Davie has been an increasingly outspoken enemy. One would like to think that this volume may prove as effective a breakthrough as Donne's (and Shakespeare's) poetry was against the tyranny of pseudo-Petrarch, as Dryden's against pseudo-Donne, Wordsworth's against pseudo-Pope, and Eliot's against pseudo-Wordsworth.

Like earlier revolutionaries (see Dryden's elegy on Lord Hastings and Coleridge's "Lines to a Beautiful Spring in a Village") Davie's apprenticeship was in the accepted idiom of his day. Take, for instance, the first poem in *A Winter Talent* (1957), **"Time Passing, Beloved"**:

> Time passing, and the memories of love
> Coming back to me, carissima, no more mockingly
> Than ever before; time passing, unslackening,
> Unhastening, steadily; and no more
> Bitterly, beloved, the memories of love
> Coming into the shore.
>
> How will it end? Time passing and our passages of love
> As ever, beloved, blind
> As ever before; time binding, unbinding
> About us; and yet to remember
> Never less chastening, nor the flame of love
> Less like an ember.
>
> What will become of us? Time
> Passing, beloved, and we in a sealed
> Assurance unassailed
> By memory. How can it end,
> This siege of a shore that no misgivings have steeled,
> No doubts defend?

If (to quote Johnson) one abandons one's mind to it, a vague, nostalgic personal emotion is communicated, cer-

tainly. And in its incantatory way, it sounds well—Davie has the ear, the command of rhyme, consonance, rhythm that is the poet's *sine qua non.*

Yet before long Davie is going to refer slightingly to

> the Swinburnian instruments of alliteration, consonance and assonance, terminal and internal rhyme and chime and half-rhyme. . . . After all, what is Swinburnian is not this array of devices (since they are used by every poet one can think of), but only a degree of coarseness and lack of subtlety in their deployment. . . . It is Milton's "linked sweetness long drawn out," not any Sitwellian or Swinburnian "vowel-music" which we should bear in mind when we consider Valéry's insistence on the musicality of poetry, on the duty it has to the ear as well as to the intelligence.[3]

And (a little earlier) he complains that Dylan Thomas, Swinburne's twentieth-century heir, "exploits a pseudo-syntax. Formally correct, his syntax cannot mime, as it offers to do, a movement of the mind. . . . That the metaphors could in fact be broken down into successive meanings is irrelevant; even when the breaking down has been done for us, we cannot hold on to it when we return to reading the poem."[4] (Consider the syntax, or the absence of it, in the above poem.) Syntax, syntax, syntax, Davie preaches indefatigably: imagery can never be a substitute for it, nor can "Vowel-music"—or rather, as Davie argues in his most illuminating critical essay, the "musicality of poetry . . . immediately issues, not in manipulation of vowels and consonants, but in manipulation of syntax."[5] The discussion of these matters involves Davie, in this and other critical works, in long, complex debates with other poets and critics about fundamental matters of linguistics and epistemology. (My own suspicion is that these difficulties stem from the dualism of I. A. Richards, and many before him—the dualism between discursive and emotive language—and could easily be resolved if some critic or philosopher were bold enough to abandon it. Davie, in 1970, begins to take a healthy sardonic attitude toward it, describing his *Six Epistles to Eva Hesse,* "Sparkle, sparkle, little verse, / Not poetry, nor yet discourse.") And he ends by courageously weighing the two gods of his fellow practitioners and finding them wanting:

> In Pound's verse the rhythm steps out alone and we must follow it in blind faith, with no metrical landmarks to assist us. Every reader must decide for himself whether he can make this act of faith. I confess for my part I cannot, and it seems to me that after scrapping the contracts traditionally observed between poet and reader, a poet like Pound substitutes a contract unjustly weighted against the reader. . . .
>
> Having banished syntax from their poetry, they [Pound and Eliot] do not pretend anything else. They do not mislead their readers by retaining even the empty shells of syntactical forms . . . [unlike Rimbaud, whose] pseudo-syntax . . . appears to me radically vicious; in the sense, at least, that where it appears poetry flies out of the door. . . .

Systems of syntax are part of the heritable property of past civilization, and to hold firm to them is to be traditional in the best and most important sense. This seems ungracious to both Pound and Eliot, who have both insisted upon the value of the European civilized tradition, and have tried to embody it in their poems. Nevertheless, it is hard not to agree with Yeats that the abandonment of syntax testifies to a failure of the poet's nerve, a loss of confidence in the intelligible structure of the conscious mind, and the validity of its activity.[6]

Poetry, in short, if it is to be poetry, must communicate, and if it is to communicate it must use public, not private, language.

And, in the end, it must deal with public experience—it must have, as Pound said Joyce's *Ulysses* has, "ubiquity of application. Art does not avoid universals, it strikes at them all the harder in that it strikes through particularities." Sadly enough, it is Pound whom Davie accuses of having through his own poetry (and life) encouraged the public to keep poetry and public experience in separate compartments. The award to Pound of the Bollingen prize for poetry in 1949, while Pound still lay under a charge of treason, Davie says,

> meant in effect that American society accepted and recognized an absolute discontinuity between the life of the poet and the life of the man. Ever since, in British and American society alike, this absolute distinction has been sustained, and upheld indeed as the basic assumption on which society must proceed in dealing with the artists who live in its midst. . . . To be on the safe side, society will treat him [the poet] from the first as pathologically irresponsible in everything beyond mere connoisseurship and expertise in his craft. . . . Pound has made it impossible for any one any longer to exalt the poet into a seer.[7]

Of course, it is highly unfair to blame Pound for this state of things, which originated long before Pound. Few Americans (and fewer Canadians) have ever taken seriously what their poets have tried to say to them. As far back as Tiresias the seer has had difficulty in finding a receptive audience, though it is perhaps only in the past hundred years that poets have consciously abdicated the role—and critics have attempted to prove its impossibility. One of Davie's sharpest critical comments is his rebuttal of Northrop Frye's conception of the poem as a bloodless and ingenious "construct," a *ding an sich:*

> The appeal of theories such as Mr. Frye's is manifest in the loaded words that their promoters use in recommending them. A poetry in which the syntax articulates only "the world of the poem" is said to be "pure," "absolute," "sheer," "self-sufficient." Wordsworth's poems are "impure" because they have about them the smell of soil and soiled flesh, the reek of humanity. Their syntax is not "pure" syntax because it refers to, it mimes, something outside itself and outside the world of its poem, something that smells of the human, of generation and hence of corruption. It is my case against the symbolist theorists that, in trying to remove

the human smell from poetry, they are only doing harm. For poetry to be great, it must reek of the human, as Wordsworth's poetry does. This is not a novel contention; but perhaps it is one of those things that cannot be said too often.[8]

Except to those who have professionally narrowed their tastes and interests to a fashionable coterie of contemporary poets and critics, all the above (a highly simplified version of Davie's criticism, of course) will seem the most obvious truth about poetry, stated in earlier times by such poet/critics as Dryden, Johnson and Wordsworth. It is "traditional" doctrine; "conservative," Davie does not hesitate to call it; "reactionary" some of his contemporaries have stigmatized both his poetry and his teaching. It is well known, of course, that one of Davie's earliest and most enduring interests has been the poetry of the eighteenth century, analysis of which occupies many pages in his critical writings and of which he has edited an interesting anthology. "I have sought," he concludes a chapter in his *Articulate Energy,* "only to make these assumptions [about syntax, by modern poets] explicit, so that we may know just what we are doing, and what we are turning our backs upon, when we agree with the symbolists that in poetry syntax turns into music. Is Pope's handling of poetic syntax really so irrelevant to the writing of poetry today? And are we really so sure of ourselves that we can afford to break so completely with the tradition he represents?"[9] A poet who preaches "Back to Pope," and then, in the 1970s, has the audacity to publish his **Collected Poems**? What in the world is the reader to expect there?

Odd as it might seem, the analogy with Pope is far from useless. How very few of the great English poets have had a "third period," in the sense that the phrase is often applied to Beethoven—a clear development, in their forties or fifties, of a new, mature style, a style more rugged yet more precise, more richly varied in effect, often more colloquial in diction and more audacious (yet never careless) in syntax.[10] One thinks readily of only three, Shakespeare, Pope and Yeats. (Is Milton, in *Samson Agonistes,* a candidate? Most Miltonists would disapprove. I should like to nominate the Christopher Smart of the *Psalms,* the *Hymns,* and the verse translation of Horace; but this bizarre-seeming thesis would take a long time to expound.) The great majority never seem to get beyond a "second period," usually reached at a comparatively early age. Certainly this is true of Wordsworth, Tennyson, Browning, Eliot, Pound, Auden—or, if one segregates a "third period" in them, it is a falling back rather than an advance.

Pope summarized his own development toward his "third period," that of the 1742 *Dunciad* and the *Epilogue to the Satires,* as "Not in Fancy's maze he wandered long, / But stooped to truth, and moralized his song." Davie's nonconformist conscience is in his book from the very beginning, and there are some moving poems on his dissenting heritage: the charming **"A Baptist Childhood"** and the impressive **"A Gathered Church."** Yet the "moralizing" is not as passionate as it is to become: the poem he entitles **"The Nonconformist,"** though (as often in the early Pope) more serious than its surface indicates, is light-hearted:

> X, whom society's most mild command,
> For instance evening dress, infuriates,
> In art is seen confusingly to stand
> For disciplined conformity, with Yeats.
>
> Taxed to explain what this resentment is
> He feels for small proprieties, it comes,
> He likes to think, from old enormities
> And keeps the faith with famous martyrdoms.
>
> Yet it is likely, if indeed the crimes
> His fathers suffered rankle in his blood,
> That he finds least excusable the times
> When they acceded, not when they withstood.
>
> How else explain this bloody-minded bent
> To kick against the prickings of the norm;
> When to conform is easy, to dissent;
> And when it is most difficult, conform?

A great many of the earlier poems are vignettes—*paysages moralisés*—of Ireland, Italy, the United States, East Anglia, Yorkshire, the Midlands: The latter ones often tenderly autobiographical. Here is **"Barnsley, 1966"**:

> Wind-claps of soot and snow
> Beat on the Railway Hotel's
> Tall round-headed window;
> I envy loquacious Wales.
>
> Taciturn is the toast
> Hereabouts. Were this Wales,
> My father had ruled this roost,
> Word-spinner, teller of tales.
>
> If he missed his niche
> I am glad of it today.
> I should not have liked him rich,
> Post-prandial, confident, bawdy.
>
> He was rinsed with this town's dirt
> For seventy wind-whipped years,
> Chapped lips smiling at hurt,
> Eyes running with dirty tears.

And the movingly lyric **"Stratford on Avon"**:

> I look a long way back
> To a house near Stratford.
> You had come out of our black
> Barnsley, a girl, to Oxford.
>
> Beautiful, boys pursued you.
> In dusk and the overgrown
> Garden, I, as you knew,
> Watched you sitting alone
>
> On the creosoted stair
> To the girl's dormitory.
> No one else was there.
> You slept on the first storey.

> Lanes crept by the riverside.
> We had said Goodnight too soon,
> Strange to that countryside
> Famous under the moon.
>
> And yet within the echo
> Of our lame exchanges
> No grasses ceased to grow,
> No apple pair turned strangers.
>
> And that was the summer of nineteen
> Forty, the war still slack.
> Twentyfive summers since then.
> I look a long way back.

There is much more in the first two-thirds of the volume that deserves comment: the adaptations of Mickiewicz and the versions of the *Dr. Zhivago* poems: a number discussing the poet's craft, such as the Browningesque (or Rilkean?) soliloquy, **"To a Brother in the Mystery"** (addressed to Charles Tomlinson, we are told), using the metaphor of decorative sculpture in a medieval cathedral. In all these the craftsmanship is richly varied and satisfying; there is always a "point" and generally a novel point. But it is in the latter part of the volume that we begin to explore exciting new territory. There is the long—what? meditation? (at one point Davie calls it a "Rosciad") mentioned at the beginning of this article, a coldly furious denunciation of the "life-style" of England of the 1970s—

> Chill and slack as you are,
> the torrid is what you affect;
> the slipway of greasy Anne
> at Shottery launched more keels,
> you think, than cleanly Helen.

I am not quite sure how the Canadian Northwest fits into it; perhaps somehow it is intended to recall the British to an earlier heroism—though that seems too simple in view of the bastard Sir George Simpson and others like him. Perhaps what it boils down to is Auden's "You shall love your crooked neighbour / With your crooked heart." I don't know; the poem will take a good deal of pondering. But few patriotic (or anti-patriotic, if one prefers) poems of such passion have been written since Book IV of *The Dunciad* and the *Epilogue to the Satires*.

The even longer *Six Epistles to Eva Hesse*—published as a separate book in 1970—originated, Davie tells us, as an expression to Miss Hesse, translator of Pound and editor of a collection of essays about him, of some of his "reservations" about the views found there, and it drifts, to continue the Popean analogy, into an *Essay on Criticism* or perhaps an *Art of Poetry* (as Pope's *Essay* really is)—indeed, a "Defence of Rhyme" as Davie amusingly puts it. When did we last have good verse epistles, another form Pope excelled in? The Auden-MacNeice *Letters from Iceland?* There is certainly nothing obsolete about the genre, and Davie deserves thanks for reviving it. It is written, with Swiftian skill, in Hudibrastics, a difficult form, as Davie points out—

And so with rhyme: the Hudibrastic
Form of it's the least elastic—

in case there are those who still think Swift was only a
"minor poet." As in **"England"** Davie draws parallels and
moral lessons from the eighteenth-century explorers, extending his scope now to those of the Pacific: for instance,
that great Yorkshireman Captain Cook, the "marmoreal
paragon"—"Did when he died, the Age of Reason, / Learn
the irrational was in season? / There, on the black sand,
hacked, dismembered / Worshipfully.. . ." Was his famed
imperturbability, his stiff upper lip

A mask, perhaps; the shy, self-made
Provincial hides behind his trade.
If so, it works: the self-respecting
Yorkshireman there's no detecting.

And this sends Davie into a reminiscence of an encounter,
when a boy, with a famed local cricketer who scowled and
retreated when he was applauded:

It was a poor
Cramped nobility, to be sure,
That disdainful dourness which
Had the globe for cricket-pitch
Once—which now, if it survives
At all, informs the sullen lives
Of Yorkshire bards who take perverse
Pride in writing metred verse,
All their hope invested in
One patent, brilliant discipline.

There have been few since Pope and Swift who could
make such easy transitions among the historical, the contemporary and the intensely personal. Byron and Auden
worked at it, but I'm not sure that Davie's craftsmanship
isn't sometimes more polished than theirs.

Still another new—or old—form: **"Trevenen,"** which
Davie says he thought he might write as a "closet drama,"
but which instead became a long, Crabbesque narrative biography of the young Cornish naval officer, James
Trevenen (1760-1790; see *DNB*), who, after serving with
distinction in the Pacific under Cook and his successor
James King, found himself at home unemployed because
(he thought) of intrigues at the Admiralty. Burke (according
to Davie) encouraged this paranoia, and, resigning his
commission in protest, Trevenen joined the Russian navy,
where he was killed fighting the Swedish fleet at the Battle
of Viborg. "Or Hero-Worship" Davie suggests that Crabbe
would have subtitled the piece. If Davie is a poetic "reactionary," one hopes that the reaction will spread to give us
more such poetry as this excerpt (apropos of Fox and
Burke's political oratory):

Apart from that, it can be shown
To have been an age much like our own;
As lax, as vulgar, as confused;
Its freedoms just as much abused;
Where tattle stole a hero's thunder,
His death a thrill, and nine days' wonder;

Where personalities were made,
And makers of them plied a trade
Profitable and esteemed;
Where that which was and that which seemed
Were priced the same; where men were duped
And knew they were, and felt recouped
By being town-talk for a day,
Their Gothic follies on display;
Where (and here the parallel
Comes home, I hope, and hurts as well)
Few things met with such success
As indignant righteousness.

And this (Trevenen's death):

Cold and pain in the breast
Fatigue drives him to rest.
Rising, "to open a new
Source of comfort to you"
(Writing to his wife
The last night of his life),
Captain Trevenen, sick,
Wears on no other tack,
Aware man's born to err,
Inclined to bear and forbear.

Pretence to more is vain.
Chastened have they been.
Hope was the tempter, hope.
Ambition has its scope
(Vast: the world's esteem);
Hope is a sickly dream.
And seeking, while they live,
Happiness positive
Is sinful. Virtue alone—
This they have always known—
Is happiness below.
Therefore, she is to know,
Whatever is, is right.
That solid, serious light
Shall reconcile her to
Candidacy below
For where his sails are furled,
Far from fame and the world.

Auden, I think, seldom wrote with greater competence;
and this is the reward for following the example of Auden
and Yeats rather than that of Pound and Eliot. "Following
the example" may alarm some readers, who may also be
alarmed by the occasional echo (chiefly syntactic and
chiefly in the earlier poems) of Auden (this from a poem
about Piranesi)—

Seeing his stale vocabulary build
The same décor—observe this "gloomy vault"—
We tire of this good fellow, highly skilled
No doubt, but pertinacious to a fault—

or Yeats (appropriately, in the Irish poems)—

"Dissenter" and "tasteful" are contradictions
In terms, perhaps, and my fathers
Would ride again to the Boyne
Or with scythes to Sedgemoor, or splinter
The charming fanlights in this charming slum
By their lights, rightly—

or Eliot—

> . . . children's voices singing
> *rou-cou* under the drum
> of language where the dung-fed
> pigeon rhymes with love . . .
> When I read the British
> contemporaries I
> admire, I am abashed
> by the levelness of their tone.
> They are saying how all children
> are, whenever they are
> flustered, unkind, however
> mild and soaring their voices
> under the drum. I have
> a reading knowledge of English—

or (dare one say it?) Betjeman—

> Judy Sugden! Judy, I made you caper
> With rage when I said that the British Fascist
> Sheet your father sold was a jolly good paper—

and, of course, in the later poems, Byron and Crabbe. They may also be alarmed at Davie's statement, in the fine opening poem of the collection, **"Homage to William Cowper,"**

> A pasticheur of late-Augustan styles
> I too have sung the sofa and the hare.

Pasticheur? Not to worry, as the English say. The good craftsman learns his predecessors' techniques (as Auden and Yeats did) and, if he is also a good artist, assimilates them to his own. That very fine critical work, Reuben Brower's *Pope: The Poetry of Allusion* shows in detail how, at every stage of Pope's poetry, one can trace the influence of Virgil here, of Milton, or Spenser, or Dante there—and the end result is always something new, something distinctively and satisfyingly Pope. But it is in connection with Pope's great teacher, Dryden, that Brower best sums up the process:

> Dryden did something else for his generation that Marvell and Milton, much less Cowley, could not do: he reaffirmed the public role of the poet. . . . Thanks to Dryden the tone of Augustan poetry is less parochial than it might have been: it is resonant with echoes of other literary worlds, of larger manners and events. Minor Augustan poetry is dead for modern readers not because it was too "general," but because it was too local. . . . Dryden's achievement matters because the verse through which he draws on the European tradition satisfies us as other poetry does by offering concentrated and surprising richness of relationship: we feel that language is being "worked" for all its worth. . . . But Dryden's use of tradition satisfies also a condition of another sort. In the act of writing poetry that was far from provincial in implication, Dryden engaged the most active political and intellectual interest of his immediate audience. The particular issues are of little concern for us at present; but we can recognize their importance in the late seventeenth century, and see that the general issues involved were of a sort that is central in any conceivable society.[11]

It is not an exaggeration to say that something of this kind is what Davie, in his poetry—and his criticism; Dryden too combined poetry and criticism—is trying to do for the present generation. The last lines of his **Six Epistles to Eva Hesse** are ostensibly about the Lewis-Clark expedition to Oregon; but Davie is also talking about the poet's vocation:

> A breakthrough into spaciousness,
> New reaches charted for the mind,
> Is solid service to mankind.

*Notes*

1. In fact, Davie tells me, as a boy he read Sir Gilbert Parker.

2. For the sake of historical accuracy, it should be noted that Asquith was no pro-Boer; on the contrary, he was one of the leaders of the opposing Liberal Imperialist wing of his party. Yet somehow the name seems dramatically more plausible here than that of Lloyd George, the leading "pro-Boer," would have been.

3. "The Relation Between Syntax and Music in Some Modern Poems in English," in *Poetics* (Proceedings of the First International Conference of Work-in-Progress Devoted to Problems of Poetics), (Warsaw: Państwowe Wydawu, 1961; The Hague: Mouton, 1971), pp. 204-05.

4. *Articulate Energy: An Inquiry into the Syntax of English Poetry* (London: Routledge & Kegan Paul, 1955), p. 126.

5. "The Relation Between Syntax and Music," p. 205.

6. *Articulate Energy,* pp. 128-29.

7. *Ezra Pound: Poet as Sculptor* (New York: Oxford, 1964), p. 242.

8. *Articulate Energy,* p. 165.

9. *Articulate Energy,* pp. 63-64.

10. In *Epilogue to the Satires: Dialogue I,* the "friend" complains to Pope, "You grow correct, that once with rapture writ." It would be interesting to know what Pope meant here by "correct." The diction in the poem is much more colloquial, the syntax much less conventional than in, say, the *Essay on Man,* which is the kind of poetry the friend pleads with Pope to go back to writing.

11. *Pope: The Poetry of Allusion,* (Oxford: Clarendon Press, 1959), p. 12.

**Augustine Martin (essay date 1983)**

SOURCE: "Donald Davie and Ireland," in *Donald Davie and the Responsibilities of Literature,* edited by George Dekker, Carcanet New Press, 1983, pp. 49-63.

*[In the following essay, Martin analyzes Davie's complex relationship to Ireland and how it affects his poetry.]*

In February 1980 Donald Davie published two poems side by side in the San Francisco journal *Inquiry* and coupled them beneath the caption, 'English in Ireland'. The caption is subtle, because it refers, I think, to language as well as to people and history. The collocation of the two poems, one written eight years later than the other, marks and defines a significant phase in the English poet's dialogue with Ireland, its people, landscape, historical remains, literary traditions, its tragic politics. This dialogue which has, over twenty-five years, been mostly tender and contemplative, has once or twice taken on the violence and rudeness of a lover's quarrel. The first of these two poems, **'1969, Ireland of the Bombers'**, is the most dramatic of these collisions. I took personal offence when it appeared in the *Irish Times* of that year, and as I am curiously implicated in the genesis of the second, reconciliatory poem, **'1977, Near Mullingar'**, I think I may explain some of the passion and complexity that lies behind both literary utterances. To understand that psychological relation is to glimpse not only the Irish dimension to the poet's consciousness but to apprehend something of how he encounters experience.

To begin with, the title of the first poem travesties a self-gratulatory Irish cliché—'Ireland of the Welcomes'; the offences that follow in the body of the text are elaborate and subtle in ways that only an Irish reader—especially an Irish reader of Davie—could properly appreciate:

> Blackbird of Derrycairn,
> Sing no more for me.
> Wet fields of Dromahair
> No more I'll see
>
> Nor, Manorhamilton,
> Break through a hazelwood
> In tufted Leitrim ever.
> That's gone for good.
>
> Dublin, young manhood's ground,
> Never more I'll roam;
> Stiffly I call my strayed
> Affections home.
>
> Blackbird of Derrycairn,
> Irish song, farewell.
> Bombed innocents could not
> Sing half so well.
>
> Green Leinster, do not weep
> For me, since we must part;
> Dry eyes I pledge to thee
> And empty heart.

The poem is in a traditional Irish genre, the lament for exile, whose popular ballad form is echoed in the line 'Never more I'll roam' which could be lifted from one of a hundred songs of emigration. Its more venerable ancestor, the song of self-exile, goes back to early Irish Christian po-

etry, specifically in this case I suspect to St Columba's lament on leaving Ireland for Iona:

> There is a grey eye
> That will look back on Erin:
> It shall never see again
> The men and women of Erin.
>
> I stretch my glance across the brine
> From firm oaken planks:
> Many are the tears of my soft grey eye
> As I look back upon Erin.[1]

Every phrase and cadence of Davie's poem is witness to his strenuous involvement in the Irish scene during his residence in Dublin during the 1950s. Its metre is adapted with great ease from an Irish bardic form, and it employs tactfully a range of sonal devices which the poet probably derived in the first place from Austin Clarke, and which are far more operative in Davie's middle and later poetry than critics seem to acknowledge. Though in the present instance there are not strictly six syllables in the first and third lines of each stanza, and five in the second and fourth, that pattern is sufficiently established in the first quatrain and approximated in the others to assure an educated Irish eye that the metre he is using is based on an Irish syllabic model.[2] This form employs assonance as an acceptable alternative to rhyme—Derrycairn/Dromahair—and involves a pattern of internal assonantal echoes with the end rhymes: 'me' / 'fields' / 'see'. The form, the rhythm, the conventional epithets 'tufted Leitrim', 'Green Leinster'— with their personalizing of the Irish landscape ('the pleasant land of Ireland') are adapted with apparent innocence from Gaelic poetry, and then coldly thrown into counterpoint against the particularity of phrase and sudden enjambment which ram home the reproach at the ends of stanzas three and four. It is cruel strategy and it does not end there.

The injury is compounded by the invocation of the 'Blackbird of Derrycairn', one of Austin Clarke's most splendid poems, a radiant version of the medieval nature lyric from that same body of Irish poetry, *The Colloquy of the Old Men*, from which Yeats quarried 'The Wanderings of Oisin', and which dramatises the disputes between the old pagan values represented by Oisin and those of the new religion represented by St Patrick. A glance at Clarke's first stanza establishes a sense of Davie's designs, prosodic and satirical:

> Stop, stop and listen for the bough top
> Is whistling and the sun is brighter
> Than God's own shadow in the cup now
> Forget the hour-bell. Mournful matins
> Will sound, Patric, as well at nightfall.

Donald Davie was the first—he may still be the only—non-Irish poet to recognize and benefit from Clarke's astonishing metrical inventiveness, his adaptation of Gaelic metres to English verse. The melodic variety of that single stanza involves not just the subtle assonance of 'brighter' and 'nightfall' and the reversed echo of 'bough top' with 'cup now' but a whole web of delicate correspondences: 'whistling' with 'listen', 'shadow' with 'matins' with 'Patric', the serpentine progress of the diphthong in 'bough'—like a Celtic design—down to 'hour-bell' and 'sound' in the last line. This lyric appeared in Clarke's *Ancient Lights* which Davie reviewed in *Irish Writing* of Spring 1956 when he was a lecturer at Trinity College, Dublin, his 'young manhood's ground'.

His review, regarded since as a watershed in the revival of Clarke's reputation, shows an acute awareness of what Clarke was about—despite Davie's lack of Irish. He draws attention to Clarke's 'use of a device traditional in poetry in Irish, of interlacing assonance and—a corollary of that—rhyming off the beat' which in Clarke 'changes the pivotal movement of the lyric stanza' and which, if the poems were better known, 'could be a momentous innovation in the whole tradition of Anglo-American verse'. I hope to show that these prosodic patterns begin to enter Davie's own poetry—with interesting selectivity—in *A Winter Talent* published the following year, and eventually to show how the English poet gleefully out Clarkes Clarke in that hilarious *tour de force*, **'Commodore Barry'**. For the moment, however, I cite the review to establish how well the poet knew the literary coin he was dealing in when he issued **'Ireland of the Bombers'**.

The poem seemed to raise so many other interesting questions involving the relation between man and poet, poet and subject matter, technique and literary convention. How serious was the vow and the interdict? Could an urbane, modern English poet assume the voice and idiom of a traditional Irish satirist to indict a whole people? Perhaps there was a *persona* somewhere at work? After all were not the universities everywhere teaching that a poem was really an arrangement of words on a page? Could the poet who had written so vividly and affectionately of Glendalough, the Corrib, the waterfall at Powerscourt, Sutton Strand, the Boyne, and of Meath in May actually forswear—even figuratively—these places which had once so animated his vision and language? If so what were the possible consequences to his own sensibility? And surely the poet who had written that chilling and prophetic poem on the Orange Parade in **'Belfast on a Sunday Afternoon'** must understand better than most those 'passionate intensities' which his own ancestors, the English Protestant dissenters had helped to build into Irish history over the centuries. Through all of my ruminations, however, there was a nagging acknowledgment that this particular English poet had, uniquely, somehow earned the right to talk to us like that. That his emotions were deeply engaged and that above all his poem—so curiously wrought of intimacy and rejection—was a great deal more than an arrangement of words on a page. (If I seem to be making too much of my own feelings—which may not after all be very representative—it should be recalled that Irish people north and south were just then sick with anguish at the escalating atrocity on both sides of what seemed an insoluble conflict and of the simplistic judgments of many outside commen-

tators. Poetic reproofs from Englishmen in California were not especially appreciated.) However, when I became Associate Director of the Yeats International Summer School at Sligo six years later, my first invitation was to Donald Davie to lecture there the following August. I don't recall in what terms I referred to his poem, but it was that reference which persuaded him to come. And there was, of course, no doubt about the seriousness of his former interdict, nor indeed, I suspect, about the relief with which he absolved himself from it. The second poem records his feelings as he returns from Sligo across the same landscape that he had laid 'Under this private ban'.

The poetic convention is the same as in the former poem, but there is a wry nod to Yeats's Jack the Journeyman—and perhaps to all those tinkers with their tin cans and soldering irons that he had met in Synge, or in the flesh on the Irish roads of the fifties—in the poet's self-image:

> I thought: a travelling man
>     Will come and go, here now
> And gone tomorrow, and
>     He cannot keep a vow.
> Forworn, coming to Sligo
>     To mend my battered past,
> I thought: it must be true;
>     The soldier cannot last.

The stanzas that follow are startling for a writer who has been so unequivocal in his hatred of violence, and in his suspicion of those who had used art to condone or glamorise atrocity:

> But, dear friends, I could weep.
>     Is it the bombs have made
> Old lesions knit, old chills
>     Warm, and old ghosts be laid?
> Atrociously, such changes
>     The winning gentleness
> Gentler still, and even
>     The poets not so reckless.

The interpenetration of technique and feeling is just as effective as when he wanted to register the force of indignation. We note how much the mood of questioning compunction is assisted by the whisper of those vowel correspondences, 'dear' / 'weep' / 'lesions', settling on the emotive words in the first stanza; and the truly 'articulate energy' of the quiet verbs through the last three lines. Nor is there doubt of the balance and tension achieved in the next stanza between that powerful, two-edged adverb 'atrociously' as it resonates against 'gentleness' and 'reckless'—a perfect Clarkean chime with assonance augmented by consonance off the beat.[3]

The final stanzas provide another kind of balance. What looks at first glance merely an unfavourable, and perhaps conciliatory, comparison of England with Ireland—which of course it is primarily—may perhaps be more deeply interpreted as an act of faith in the heart's affections amid the very pessimism through which Davie in his public voice interprets the contemporary world. Meeting old friends *has* 'mended' his battered 'past'. Ireland of the Bombers has become—if the phrase is bearable—Ireland of the Welcomes. Again the Yeats connection provides a comparison and a contrast. The contempt that Yeats felt for 'this foul world in its decline and fall' is shared in part by Davie; but the English poet has no apocalyptic system of destruction and renewal to console him; nor would he have any truck, I suspect, with an impersonal, and to that extent irresponsible, posture of 'tragic joy' at the 'irrational streams of blood' or the mire of cultural barbarism that threaten reason and order. It is with dismay that the second poem acknowledges that violence and atrocity can and do intensify love and friendship, perhaps by bringing out the tears of things—'dear friends, I could weep'. It is a distraught recognition of something that his Dissenting Christianity may have implanted in him at an earlier time—that out of evil can come good, atrociously. That amid the clashing armies on the darkling plain we can still, as communities as well as individuals, be 'true / To one another'. Or so it seems for the two climactic stanzas before the scope widens and the mood resolves itself in that poised ambiguity of the final line.

I have begun with these two poems, and written in such a personal—and what may well appear self-indulgent—way because I believe that the poems and their motivations exemplify so many features of Donald Davie's stance and sensibility. The first is quite simply that he means what he says; if he is occasionally obscure he is never evasive. I think he writes to change men's hearts. The second is that he is seldom for long a mere tourist in his adopted cultures—a 'travelling man' is the very antithesis of a tourist. He has the curiosity, the concern and at times the necessary bad manners to get involved, to test cultural difference, to savour atmosphere, to criticise and react and accuse. Thus his remarkable 'sense of place' is seldom merely descriptive, though on the surface it sometimes seems so, as in the grossly deceptive **'The Wearing of the Green'** where I certainly would have been lost without the political hint in the title. I am sure this holds true for his North American poems, lyrical, narrative and historical as well as for his Irish ones. The third is the protean suppleness with which his technique adjusts and changes to meet different thematic and emotional challenges.

The final feature is his stubborn fight for reason and civilisation against certain forms of violence and mass passions—what his urbane Augustans would have derided as Enthusiasm. He identifies this Dionysiac adversary more readily, and deals with it more assuredly, in its North American manifestations,

> a mass public, swayed by it knows not what, capable of responding only to the grosser stimuli, at once fickle and predictable, exacting as only the undirected can be. . . . And the 1960s, that hideous decade, showed what was involved: the arts of literature were enlisted on the side of all that was insane and suicidal, without order and without proportion. Charles Olson in his last years was appalled by the stoned and bombed out zombies who flocked to hear him read and lecture.[4]

Davie's integrity, rigour and strength is never more manifest than in his defiance and denunciation of this cultural rabble, just as his tact and magnanimity is never more eloquent than in his superb poem on Helen Keller and Anne Sullivan Macy.

With Ireland it was different. Dublin was a peaceful and relaxed city in the fifties and Davie loved it. The young poet was sufficiently exercised trying to introduce modern critical methods to his students and to the far less educable ranks of Dublin's critical literati. Indeed it could be said that Denis Donoghue at University College, Dublin, and Donald Davie at Trinity, in that decade dragged Irish literary study into the modern age. I recall the unexampled spectacle of undergraduates, myself among them, moving back and forth between the universities as one or other of these two happened to be lecturing. Sectarian tension in Northern Ireland seemed comfortably below the surface, though it emerged sporadically as a theme in the work of Louis MacNeice and W. R. Rogers. But it was in his Dublin years that his first volume, ***Brides of Reason,*** was published. And in the midst of that elegant, classical book, this Dionysian force erupts in a poem deceptively titled **'Belfast on a Sunday Afternoon'**.

It is difficult to determine how deliberate its placing in the volume is—I suspect Davie takes a Yeatsean care with the arrangement of poems within a volume—but I recall the shock of coming upon it in a first consecutive reading as being rather like the shock administered to the poet and his companion when they stumbled on the Orange Parade. The first 'Irish' poem in the volume **'Demi-Exile. Howth'** was an urbane discussion of English identity abroad wherein the poet declined overt commitment to either country, 'Hands acknowledging no allegiance, / Gloved for good against brutal chance' exploiting a possible ambiguity on the phrase 'for good'. Four poems on there was a tranquil mood piece on the Boyne which seemed quite innocent of any reference to the political connotations of that river. Next there was a brutal short poem, **'Thyestes'**, about the persistence of mythic enormities in everyday life. Then with extraordinary vividness and violence the air was full of bands, **'Sashes and bearskins in the afternoon'**:

> And first of all we tried to laugh it off,
> Acting bemusement in the grimy sun;
> But stayed to worry where we came to scoff,
> As loud contingents followed, one by one.
>
> Pipe bands, flute bands, brass bands and silver bands,
> Presbyter's pibroch and the deacon's serge,
> Came stamping where the iron Mænad stands,
> Victoria, glum upon a grassy verge.
>
> Some brawny striplings sprawled upon the lawn;
> No man is really crippled by his hates.
> Yet I remembered with a sudden scorn
> Those 'passionate intensities' of Yeats.

The form is neoclassical; the metre, iambic; the tone, civilised incomprehension: in the Augustan echoes of 'scoff' and 'scorn' one has the sense of the eighteenth century suddenly confronted with and embarrassed by the archaic fervour of the Cromwellians. Yet the Maenad Victoria may well echo the infanticidal women of the Thyestes myth, and there may be fear as well as scorn in the invocation of Yeats's apocalyptic reading of signs and portents and a terror to come. An added eeriness is perhaps in the technical precision with which the poet, an heir as well as a scholar of the Dissenting tradition, picks out 'Presbyter's pibroch and the deacon's serge'.

What is certain is that one poem later he is looking with less than rapture at **'The Evangelist'** and his 'mobile features of Dissent'; in **'An English Revenant'** he is at pains to locate himself elaborately in the golden mean, the temperate zone of the human condition, before launching on two sombre and scrupulous meditations on the atrocities of his time. In the first **'Hawkshead and Dachau in a Christmas Glass'** he pronounces: 'At Dachau Yeats and Rilke died'; and in **'Eight Years After'** he enunciates a view of art and violence from which he is really to deviate very little for the rest of his career:

> For fearsome issues, being squarely faced,
> Grow fearsomely familiar. To name
> Is to acknowledge. To acquire the taste
> Comes on the heels of honouring the claim.

> 'Let nothing human be outside my range.'
> Yet horrors named make exorcisms fail:
> A thought once entertained is never strange,
> But who forgets the face 'beyond the pale'?

The position thus set out in measured antithesis lights the slow-burning fuse that sets off the explosion of outrage fourteen years later in **'Ireland of the Bombers'**; which in turn leads to the self-questioning, reappraisal and reconciliation eight years further on in **'Near Mullingar'**. The progress also entails a pilgrimage from Augustan pentameter to Gaelic cross-rhyme, from Enlightenment directness to Celtic intricacy, as if to demonstrate not just the need for answerable style but also the complexity and hazard of being 'English in Ireland'.

It falls outside my brief to consider more than one side of the astonishing rhythmic change and liberation that invests Davie's next volume, *A Winter Talent.* His criticism of the previous years points clearly to the example—I think this a much safer word than 'influence' when speaking of such a deliberate artist as Davie—of Pound and Stevens, though whoever may have mediated such remarkable lyric achievements as **'Time Passing, Beloved'** and **'The Wind at Penistone'** has been elided without trace in the originality of the performance. Most of the poems in the *England* section of the book adhere, though with greater flexibility, to the Augustan iambic. But the five poems that make up the *Ireland* suite have clearly absorbed the example of Clarke. **'The Priory of St Saviour, Glendalough'** takes the fight into Clarke country, the medieval, monastic world of the Irish Romanesque which constitutes so much of the Irish poet's symbolic land-

scapes, and **'North Dublin'** fastens—though this is no doubt fortuitous—on a part of the city often explored by Clarke, not least in *Ancient Lights.* **'North Dublin'**, is subtly continuous both with the 'Dissenter' theme of the earlier, English poems and **'Belfast on a Sunday Afternoon'**. I give the poem in full to emphasize the consistency of its rhythmic method:

> St George's, Hardwicke Street,
> Is charming in the Church of Ireland fashion:
> The best of Geneva, the best of Lambeth
> Aesthetically speaking
> In its sumptuously sober
> Interior, meet.

> A continuous gallery, clear glass in the windows
> An elegant conventicle,
> In the Ionian order
> What dissenter with taste
> But would turn, on these terms
> Episcopalian?

> 'Dissenter' and 'tasteful' are contradictions
> In terms, perhaps, and my fathers
> Would ride again to the Boyne
> Or with scythes to Sedgemoor, or splinter
> The charming fanlights in this charming slum
> By their lights, rightly.

The only two iambic lines in the structure are the second and the penultimate, and the poem owes much of its force to that deliberate and ironic symmetry. One has to look harder—ideally read aloud—to discover the prosodic pattern of the rest. But if one begins with the cadence which 'Episcopalian' makes with 'taste' and the assonance of 'contradictions' with 'splinter' the secret of the poem's undeniable melody becomes clear. If it were mere verbal music the game would not be worth the candle, and an admirer of Alexander Pope would hardly settle for less than the sound becoming an echo to the sense. Thus the first of these echoes is bland and funny, the second disputatious and violent. Having taken the hint, therefore, one becomes more conscious of the assonance that dominates the first stanza, winding its way through 'Street', 'Geneva', 'speaking', 'Interior', 'meet'. In the supporting correspondences of 'Hardwicke', 'charming', 'fashion' and 'Lambeth' the sound and the sense enter into remarkable alliance. The alliterations, also an integral part of the Gaelic prosody, reinforce the pattern throughout the three stanzas.

In the second, the sound effects are even more elaborate, beginning with the frank internal harmonies of the first line through the intricate accords of 'elegant', 'conventicle', 'dissenter', 'term'. In the last stanza 'Dissenter' and 'Sedgemoor' form an alliance of sound and sense similar to the Anglican locutions of stanza one. The vigorous beat of 'ride', 'scythes', 'fanlights', 'lights', 'rightly' gives us the yeoman Dissenters on the move to a music of lumination, fervour and righteousness.

The historical implication is finely complex, as is the poet's personal psychology. The Boyne has lost its pastoral innocence. It was the defeat of the Catholic cause by William of Orange there in 1689 that was being celebrated by the marchers who had made Davie shudder in the earlier poem. As he stands amid the cool elegance of this Anglican church in Dublin he realizes the multiple ironies of his own identity. The neutrality of **'Demi-Exile. Howth'** is no longer easy. I would go so far as to say that in this poem we see the first maturity of a historical imagination in Davie's poetry. And by this I don't mean an imagination that can handle historical themes, or deal in the history of ideas or exploit the possibilities of genealogy or myth—we have already seen him do these things well—but an imagination which enables the poet to locate himself meaningfully in time and space so as to feel and witness to the complexities that have shaped his consciousness of the world. This historical imagination expands throughout his later work, especially in *The Forests of Lithuania, A Sequence for Francis Parkman,* the *Epistles to Eva Hesse,* **'Trevenen','Vancouver'** and **'Commodore Barry'** where it goes riotously on shore-leave.

It is clear that the essence of this Gaelic prosody is verbal interweave. The poet in English takes it from there and makes his own of it. Generations of Anglo-Irish poets have experimented with it, notably Callanan, Larminie, MacDonagh—who wrote a book on it and entitled it the 'Irish mode'—contemporary Irish poets such as Farren, Montague and Kinsella. Apart from the last two I suspect that these names are unknown to most readers of the present article. Some of these writers attempted to take over the Gaelic syllabic mode radically into English. The curious may wish to look at Austin Clarke's 'The Scholar' to see a sample of the result. Successful experiments in radical formal translation into English are more rare than successes with strict *terza rima* in English. It is significant that Davie himself has brought off such a coup in **'The Year 1812'**. It is also characteristic of him that in one of his most illuminating essays on Yeats, 'Yeats, the Master of a Trade',[5] he confines himself to matters of technique. And in giving such attention to his metrics here I am encouraged by the fact that in his 'Modern Masters' book on Pound he devotes almost one third of the text to a discussion of the great poet's prosody.

What is most impressive about Davie's use of the Irish mode is his selectivity in employing it, and the apparent ease with which he can adapt and vary it. Two further examples from *A Winter Talent* help to make the point. **'The Wearing of the Green'** is a poem that broods passionately on the Irish landscape through three still, symmetrical stanzas, as if waiting for the scene to deliver up the heart of its mystery. The stillness, the stasis, is achieved by means of a recurrent phrase which is not so much a refrain as an incantation, a sort of druidic summoning, and by means of the verbal interweave which the subject obviously calls for. The mystery reveals itself in historical, even political terms in this, its last stanza:

> Imagination, Irish avatar,
> Aches in the spring's heart and in mine, the stranger's

> In Meath in May. But to believe there are
> Unchanging Springs endangers,
> By that fast dye, the earth;
> So blood-red green the season,
> It never changes
> In Meath in May.

Without worrying the life out of a poem that so obviously wishes to keep its counsel, one might offer as thematic annotation the fact that in the early years of the century Yeats, A. E. and others more nationalistically minded had been looking for a Celtic avatar or saviour, that the Easter Rising had behind it a doctrine of blood sacrifice—the 'green earth will be warmed by the blood of martyrs'—that green is the national colour, that the poem's title is also that of a nationalist ballad. What is more to our purpose is the sonal pattern that guarantees the slowness of the pace and impels us into harmony with the poet's mood. It derives primarily from the vowel sounds in the refrain, 'Meath' and 'May'. The more dominant is the latter, occupying heavily the positions of metrical stress— 'Imagination', 'Aches', 'stranger's', 'Unchanging', 'endangers', 'changes', 'May'; the other acts as a sort of descant on the melody in 'Meath', 'believe', 'green', 'season', 'Meath'. There is no poem like this in the Gaelic tradition, either in the stressed or syllabic metres. There is nothing quite like it in Clarke either. And it is possible that there are technically similar poems in modern English that owe nothing to Irish metrics. Yet I must record my conviction that much of its effectiveness derives from a way with rhymes and assonances that Davie adapted from an Irish source. Such provenance can be more firmly claimed and demonstrated in the second example.

**'The Priory of St Saviour, Glendalough'** is a cunning blend of Gaelic assonance and the metaphysical conceit. It begins with a technical formulation from a guidebook:

> A carving on the jamb of an embrasure,
> 'Two birds affronted with a human head
> Between their beaks' is said to be
> 'Uncertain in its significance but
> A widely known design.' I'm not surprised.

The assurance with which the quotations are accommodated to the metrical form deserves almost more attention than sound effects, though the internal rhyme of 'head' with 'said' is worth noting. The second stanza is remarkable for its accurate and particular sense of the scene— anyone who has been to Glendalough will receive a shock of recognition—also for the kinetic power of the verbs which is sustained into the final stanza, enforcing the sense of search and mystery that arises from the static enigmas of the opening stanza. Here, unhampered by the language of the guidebook, Davie can deploy the Celtic mysteries of his prosody, in a stanza of rare texture.

> For the guidebook cheats: the green road it advises
> In fact misled; and a ring of trees
> Screened in the end the level knoll on which
> St Saviour's, like a ruin on a raft,
> Surged through the silence.

The tonic vowel sound with which the first line opens in 'guidebook' consolidates its authority in 'advises' at the end, goes underground to announce its re-emergence in 'like' and closes the sequence—like the serpent's tail in a Celtic design—in 'silence' at the end. Its junior partner weaves its path through 'cheats' and 'green', 'trees' and 'screened'. The drama of the last two lines is then shrewdly reinforced by the emphatic alliterations. I allow the final stanza to speak for itself:

> I burst through brambles, apprehensively
> Crossed an enormous meadow. I was there.
> Could holy ground be such a foreign place?
> I climbed the wall, and shivered. There flew out
> Two birds affronted by my human face.

There is a temptation to end on that image of the poet, facing the strangeness of a foreign place, sensing the old paganness beneath the equally exotic monasticism of the 'holy ground', yet determined to follow his hunch through to the end. But for the sake of completeness two points need briefly to be made. The first concerns Davie's use of his Gaelic prosody in poems unconnected with his Irish experience, the second is a mandatory glance at **'Commodore Barry'**, the last poem in his collected edition of 1972.

In the first place it is important to note that he often encounters Irish themes without recourse to Irish metres. **'The Waterfall at Powerscourt'** employs an impressive range of rhythmic devices, assonance, dissonance, alliteration, without suggesting an Irish model other than Joyce's metamorphic dog on Sandymount Strand in the Proteus episode in *Ulysses*. But its real counterpart is Davie's **'The Wind at Penistone'**. Similarly the two **'Dublin Georgian'** poems and **'Killala'** are highly successful poems which sit securely within an English metrical tradition.

But *Events and Wisdoms*, so instinct with a sense of place, so determined upon atmosphere and stasis, so struck with the strangeness of America, seems constantly to demand the effects of muted rhythm and covert echo that this syllabic verse can deliver. **'New York in August'** deploys the rhyme off the beat with striking effect:

> Clammy, electric, torrid,
> The nights bring relief
> At the latitude of Madrid.
> Never the stir of a leaf
>
> Any night, as we went
> Back, the children asleep,
> To our bed in a loaned apartment,
> Although I thought a deep . . .

In **'Cypress Avenue'**, **'Humanly Speaking'**, **'The Feeders'**, **'Love and the Times'**, **'Across the Bay'**, **'Agave in the West'**, **'Viper-Man'** and **'In Chopin's Garden'** the same device is used without drawing attention to itself; assonance is as frequent as rhyme, blank endings are quietly reinforced by occult internal echoes, a

sense of freedom from the tyranny of rhyme is reinforced by a subtle web of correspondences which control emphasis in a new variety of ways. Sometimes these effects, when they become visible, are intrinsically striking. The first stanza of **'Viper-Man'** is marvelously textured:

> Will it be one of those
> Forever summers?
> Will the terrace stone
> Expand, unseal
> Aromas, and let slip
> Out of the cell of its granulations
> Some mid-Victorian courtship?

It was inevitable, however, that Davie would test his virtuosity against the master himself, Austin Clarke. This he does in **'Commodore Barry'**, a poem which decides to take literally the assertion that Barry was 'Father of the American Navy'. As background it is worth remembering that the Gaelic poet Owen Roe O'Sullivan, invoked in Davie's first line, had written a poem in English called 'Rodney's Glory' which Davie had included in his *Augustan Lyric*. O'Sullivan had sailed with Rodney and had hoped to buy himself out with his eulogy of the admiral. Davie's poem subsumes some of O'Sullivan's style, but his real model, and perhaps target, is Clarke. I suspect that these lines from Clarke's 'Song of the Books' may have been the English poet's point of departure:

> Lightly, Red head O Sullivan
> Who fought with Rodney, jolly jacktar
> Too much at sea, thin as a marlin
>         Spike, came and went,
> Poet, schoolmaster, parish clerk.
> He drank his Bible money at Mass time
> A moll upon his knee, bare arsed.

This is not an extreme example of Clarke's virtuosity with metrical exercise. In more extreme examples one has the impression of the meaning trying to hold on to the sound like a man trying to control a powerful fire hose. The temptation to add *double entendre* to vocallic antiphony is hardly resistable, and the result is often one of exquisite irresponsibility. Davie's third stanza is a fair sample of his skill with the idiom:

> A flurry of whitecaps off
> The capes of the Delaware!
> Barry, the Irish stud,
> Has fathered the entire
> American navy! Tories
> Ashore pore over the stud-book,
> Looking in vain for the mare,
> Sovran, whom Jolly Roger
> Of Wexford or Kildare
> Claims in unnatural congress
> He has made big with frigates.

His last is nonsense brought close to the pitch of genius:

> *My* sovereign,' said saucy
> Jack Barry, meaning Congress;
> And yes, it's true, outside

The untried, unstable recess
Of the classroom, every one has one:
A sovereign—general issue,
Like the identity-disc,
The prophylactic, the iron
Rations. Irony fails us,
Butters no parsnips, brails
No sail on a ship of the line.

It is perhaps the best note of all on which to end a discussion of Davie's relation with Ireland, evincing as it does a sense of earned and intimate ease with its subject, delighting in its feeling for history and literary tradition, elated by the intricacies of language, which alone can make such themes and interests speak in the idiom of poetry.

*Notes*

1. See *1,000 Years of Irish Poetry,* Kathleen Hoaglund (ed.) (New York: Devin-Adair 1947) p. 101.

2. The actual Irish metre involved is called 'freslige ar dechnaid'; its Gaelic intricacies are described in Kuno Meyed, *A Primer of Irish Metrics* (Dublin, 1909) p. 23.

3. This device in Clarke's theory 'takes the clapper from the bell of rhyme' with the result that 'lovely and neglected words are advances to the tonic place and divide their echoes.' See Austin Clarke, *Collected Poems* (Dublin: Dolmen Press 1974) p. 574.

4. *Articulate Energy,* postscript to 1976 edition, p. xiv.

5. *The Poet in the Imaginary Museum,* p. 125.

## Gregory A. Schirmer (essay date 1983)

SOURCE: "This That I Am Heir to: Donald Davie and Religion," in *Donald Davie and the Responsibilities of Literature,* edited by George Dekker, Carcanet New Press, 1983, pp. 129-42.

[*In the following essay, Schirmer considers the role of religion in Davie's work.*]

Even a casual reading of the poetry and criticism of Donald Davie must notice the important place that religion, specifically the Dissenting tradition in England, has always held in his work. Most obviously, a number of the poems in the *Collected Poems 1950-1970* concern the Dissenting tradition in general, while others express Davie's own ambiguous response to the particular, Baptist faith in which he was brought up. Moreover, the aesthetic principles that have guided and informed both Davie's poetry and criticism—such 'classical' standards as restraint and sparseness, for example—clearly owe something to the rigorous ethical and aesthetic principles of Nonconformity.

In recent years, Davie's concern with religion has become altogether more urgent and personal. Not only are more and more of his poems concerned with religion, but also they have become decidedly religious in nature, informed by—or indeed intent on expressing—a firm sense of religious belief. And in his criticism, Davie has turned increasingly towards religious writers, especially those working within the Dissenting tradition. This new direction in Davie's writing, and the reasons for it, cannot be overlooked in any estimation of Davie's current work, and certainly not in any attempt to project where Davie is likely to go during the next few years.

Davie was born into a family in which Dissent was deeply ingrained. His paternal grandfather was a Baptist deacon and lay preacher, and his father, although less fervent than his grandfather, was an active and regular member of the Sheffield Road Baptist Church in Barnsley, taking his son to chapel with him each Sunday. Davie's mother's family also was Nonconformist. Nevertheless, Davie did not go through with the important adolescent ritual of Believer's or Adult Baptism, and drifted, in his late teens, into various shades of unbelief. (While an undergraduate at Cambridge he did, however, join the Robert Hall Society, an association of Baptist students.) By the time he came back, in 1946, from a tour of duty in the Royal Navy, he had lost his religious faith altogether, and for the next twenty years vacillated between agnosticism and an extremely tepid Anglicism (the religion practised by his wife). In the late 1960s, partly because of the death of his parents and of some close friends, Davie began re-evaluating his spiritual life, and in 1969, while at Stanford University, he began attending Christchurch Episcopalian Church in Los Altos Hills, California. He was baptized into the American Episcopalian Church in 1972.[1]

Davie's response to his upbringing as a Baptist, at least as it is recorded in his poetry, is coloured by social as well as religious feelings. (Davie's grandfather was a railway signalman, both his grandmothers had been domestic servants, his father was a shopkeeper, and his mother was, in his own words, 'born in a colliery cottage'.[2]) The class associations of the Dissenting tradition clearly lie behind such lines as these from **'Barnsley and District'** (*Events and Wisdoms*):

The parish primary school where a mistress once
Had every little Dissenter stand on the bench
With hands on head, to make him out a dunce;

Black backs of flourmills, wafer-rusted railings
Where I ran and ran from colliers' boys in jerseys,
Wearing a blouse to show my finer feelings—

These still stand. And Bethel and Zion Baptist,
Sootblack on pavements foul with miners' spittle
And late-night spew and violence, persist.[3]

When Davie addresses the religious, as distinct from the social, dimensions of his Dissenting background, he does so with the subtlety, irony, and intellectual reserve that characterize much of his earliest poetry. An example is- **'The Evangelist'**, published in Davie's first book of poems, *Brides of Reason*:

'My brethren . . .' And a bland, elastic smile
Basks on the mobile features of Dissent.
No hypocrite, you understand. The style
Befits a church that's based on sentiment.

Solicitations of a swirling gown,
The sudden vox humana, and the pause,
The expert orchestration of a frown
Deserve, no doubt, a murmur of applause.

The tides of feeling round me rise and sink;
Bunyan, however, found a place for wit.
Yes, I am more persuaded than I think;
Which is, perhaps, why I disparage it.

You round upon me, generously keen:
The man, you say, is patently sincere.
Because he is so eloquent, you mean?
That test was never patented, my dear.

If, when he plays upon our sympathies,
I'm pleased to be fastidious, and you
To be inspired, the vice in it is this:
Each does us credit, and we know it too.

This is the side of Dissent that Davie finds unpalatable. Indeed, in *A Gathered Church,* a study of the Dissenting tradition, he argues strenuously that this emotional strain in Dissent is, in fact, merely a strain, and that, contrary to conventional wisdom, figures like Isaac Watts and Charles Wesley were closer to the intellectually rigorous Augustan temperament of Alexander Pope than to the decidedly anti-intellectual evangelicalism portrayed in this poem.[4] And **'The Evangelist'** is clearly the work of a poet who finds the temperament of Alexander Pope congenial; the poem's tightly controlled metric and stanzaic regularity, the complex syntax of the final, revealing stanza, and the tendency toward qualification ('Deserve, *no doubt,* a murmur of applause' and 'Which is, *perhaps,* why I disparage it') all bespeak a strong intellectual presence. But **'The Evangelist'** is more than a sceptic's view of evangelicalism. What is most striking about the poem, in fact, is its honesty—the narrator's admission of being affected by this blatantly emotional appeal and the recognition that his fastidious response (felt in the rhythm and syntax of the poem) must itself be counted, at least in part, a vice.

The four-poem sequence **'Dissentient Voice'** (*A Winter Talent*) expresses Davie's response to the religion of his upbringing in a more thorough and more personal way than does **'The Evangelist'**. The first poem, **'A Baptist Childhood'**, deliberately echoes Dylan Thomas's 'Fern Hill' to emphasize the strong streak of puritanism in Dissent:

When some were happy as the grass was green,
I was as happy as a glass was dark,
Chill eye beneath the chapel floor unseen
Most of the year, a mystery, the Ark.

Aboveboard rose the largely ethical
Glossy-with-graining pulpit; underground

The older Scriptures trembled for the Fall
And lapped at Adam with a sucking sound.

Grass-rooted goodness and a joy unmixed
Parch unbaptized inside a droughty head;
Arcadia's floor is not so firmly fixed
But it must tremble to a pastor's tread.

This view of Dissent as a religion intent on denying the inherent goodness and beauty of human existence is reinforced in the second and third poems of the sequence, which describe the tension between Nonconformity and the arts. But this is by no means **'Dissentient Voice'**'s last word on religion. A much more complex and ambiguous attitude surfaces in the fourth poem, **'A Gathered Church'**. Addressed to Davie's grandfather, the Baptist deacon and lay preacher, it opens by drawing a distinction between Davie the poet and his grandfather the man of religion:

Deacon, you are to recognize in this
The idlest of my avocations, fruit
Of some late casual studies and my need
(Not dire, nor much acknowledged as a claim
Upon your known munificence) for what
You as lay preacher loved and disavowed,
The mellow tang of eloquence—a food
I have some skill in rendering down from words
Suppose them choice and well-matured. I heard
Such from your bee-mouth once. A tarnished sun
Swirling the motes which swarmed along its shaft
Mixed soot with spices, and with honey, dust;
And memories of that winning unction now
Must countenance this application. For
I see them tumbled in a frowzy beam,
The grains of dust or pollen from our past,
Our common stock in family and church,
Asking articulation. These affairs
Touched you no doubt more nearly; you are loath
To see them made a gaud of rhetoric. But, sir,
I will deal plainly with you. They are past,
Past hoping for as you had hoped for them
For sixty years or more the day you died,
And if I seem a fribble in this case
No matter. For I will be eloquent
And on these topics, having little choice.

As a poet, Davie writes not to assert the religious values held and preached by his grandfather—values that are now 'Past hoping for as you had hoped for them'—but rather with a purely aesthetic aim ('The mellow tang of eloquence'), something that his grandfather, because of his religious convictions, had to disavow. Religion, from this point of view, is so much grist for the mill:

So here I take the husk of my research,
A form of words—the phrase, 'a gathered church',
A rallying cry of our communions once
For you perhaps still stirring, but for me
A picturesque locution, nothing more
Except for what it promises, a tang.

Moreover, as an unbeliever, Davie sees his grandfather's religion as fundamentally anti-humanistic:

'A gathered church.' That posy, the elect,
Was gathered in, not into, garden-walls;
For God must out of sheer caprice resect
The jugular stalks of those He culls and calls.

The reference to the church body as protected by garden-walls recalls (partly by means of the change from blank verse to alternating rhyme) Isaac Watts's 'The Church the Garden of Christ', the first stanza of which sets forth this metaphor:

We are a Garden wall'd around,
Chosen and made peculiar Ground;
A little Spot inclos'd by Grace
Out of the World's wide Wilderness.[5]

The distinction that Davie's poem insists on between the flowers of the elect being gathered *in* rather than *into* the garden walls reflects the view of the Dissenting tradition expressed in the three earlier poems of **'Dissentient Voice'**; rather than being brought into the desired protection of a 'Chosen and peculiar Ground', the flowers are cut and collected, torn away from their roots in the world of human affairs. Moreeover, this is done by God apparently 'out of sheer caprice'.

In a note included in his *Collected Poems,* Davie describes **'A Gathered Church'** as a poem in which he works through to 'an apprehension of Dissent as embodied and made concrete in the personality of my grandfather'. And here is where Davie's poem becomes complex and ambiguous. The vivid and very human memory of his grandfather that surfaces in the final stanza of the poem tempers the hostile view of religion expressed, in various ways, from the beginning of **'Dissentient Voice'**, and in the closing lines of the poem, the generous and affectionate nature of his grandfather is set against the life-denying qualities that Davie earlier attributes to the garden of Dissent:

Now all the churches gathered from the world
Through that most crucial bottleneck of Grace,
That more than hourglass, being waspish, waist
Where all the flutes of love are gathered in,
The girdle of Eternity, the strait
Too straitened for the sands and sons of Time,
More mean and private than the sticking-place
Of any partial loyalties—all these
In you, dear sir, are justified. Largesse,
Suppose it but of rhetoric, endears,
Disseminated quite at large to bless
The waste, superb profusion of the spheres.

But these lines do more than simply reject the confining 'waist' of Grace's bottleneck for the munificence of Davie's grandfather and for the quality of 'Largesse' in general (including the rhetorical largesse of the poet); they also recognize, especially in the ambiguous word 'justified', that the very qualities that Davie finds so admirable in his grandfather depend, to some extent at least, on the religious convictions that he held. To the degree that, as Davie says in his note, his grandfather embodies his own perception of Dissent, **'Dissentient Voice'** does not merely attack the institution and doctrines of Nonconformity, but rather sees through the abstraction to its human manifestations, and finds there the very qualities of life that Davie himself, as a poet and unbeliever, cherishes.

Notwithstanding the respect that Davie expresses for the Dissenting tradition as embodied in his grandfather, **'Dissentient Voice'** disavows any religious conviction on Davie's part, and hints at no spiritual void in his own life. In his poems of the late 1960s and after, however, this apparent complacency about religion—as about many other matters—is called into question. One poem that reflects the wavering between unbelief and belief that Davie experienced in the years before his conversion is **'The North Sea'** *(Essex Poems)*. As such, it marks a transition between poems like **'Dissentient Voice'** and Davie's recent religious poetry:

North Sea, Protestant sea,
I have come to live on your shore
In the low countries of England.
            A shallow gulf north-westward
Into the Isle of Ely
And the Soke of Peterborough
Is one long arm of the cold vexed sea of the North.

Having come to this point, I dare say
That every sea of the world
Has its own ambient meaning:
The Mediterranean, archaic, pagan;
The South Atlantic, the Roman Catholic sea.

But somewhere in mid-America
All of this grows tiresome,
The needles waver and point wildly

And then they settle and point
Somewhere on the ridge of the Andes
And the Rocky Mountains
True to the end of the world.

Pacific is the end of the world,
Pacific, peaceful.

And I do not know whether to fear
More in myself my bent to that end or
The vast polyp rising and beckoning,
Christ, grey-green, deep in the sea off Friesland.

The poles in this poem are not merely the old world and the new, Essex and California, although this dichotomy surely lies behind the poem. (It was written while Davie was at the University of Essex, some time after he had spent a year at the University of California, Santa Barbara, and just before he went to Stanford.) Davie is struggling here between the easy secularism that had defined most of his spiritual life as an adult—the kind of secularism in which all thought of religion merely 'grows tiresome' and which is associated, in Davie's mind at least, with California—and a religious faith that, especially as expressed in the poem's final image, threatens to disrupt the rather effortless unbelief that he had drifted into and had come to accept as natural.

It is more than coincidence that finds **'The North Sea'** in *Essex Poems.* That collection, along with **'More Essex Poems 1964-1968'** and the long poem entitled **'England'** written about the same time, reflect the general crisis of identity and allegiance that Davie experienced in the late 1960s, especially through four troubled years as Pro-Vice Chancellor of the University of Essex. And if one can argue that the sense of national disaffection and loss expressed in many of the Essex poems (and in Davie's decision to leave England in 1968) helped crystallize Davie's political and social views—his conservative rejection of socialist England, for example, and his often strident attacks on the libertine and liberal tendencies of the late 1960s in general—then one might also suggest that those feelings may well have had something to do with Davie's movement during this period towards the fixed principles of religious orthodoxy, culminating in his conversion to the American Episcopalian Church in 1972.

In any event, the religious poems that Davie has written since the 1960s, and particularly since joining the Episcopalian Church, stand decidedly apart from his earlier poems about religion, having at their centre deeply felt religious convictions. And yet they are not, in style and attitude, wholly unlike **'Dissentient Voice'**. As a poem like **'Having No Ear'** (published in 1979[6]) makes clear, Davie's recent religious poetry does not propose to abandon a belief in human intellect for a mystical, anti-intellectual religious faith:

> Having no ear, I hear
> And do not hear the piano-tuner ping,
> Ping, ping one string beneath me here, where I
> Ping-ping one string of Caroline English to
> Tell if Edward Taylor tells
> The truth, or no.
>
> Dear God, such gratitude
> As I owe thee, for giving, in default
> Of a true ear or of true holiness,
> This trained and special gift of knowing when
> Religious poets speak themselves to God,
> And when, to men.
>
> The preternatural! I know it when
> This perfect stranger—angel-artisan—
> Knows how to edge our English Upright through
> Approximations back to rectitude,
> Wooing it back through quarter-tone
> On quarter-tone, to true.
>
> Mystical? I abjure the word, for if
> Such faculty is known and recognized
> As may tell sharp from flat, and both from true,
> And I lack that capacity, can I say
> That Edward Taylor's Paradise was seen
> By other light than day?

This poem is certainly religious in a way that **'Dissentient Voice'** is not. For one thing, it takes a different view of religious art; the poet's concern here is not merely aesthetic ('the mellow tang of eloquence'), but, rather, pointedly re-

ligious. All the deliberately self-conscious playfulness of the first stanza, for example—itself a kind of poetic tuning-up, with its numerous rhymes and echoes—comes to rest on the question of whether a Christian poet like Edward Taylor 'tells / The truth or no'. But although 'Having No Ear' is religious in what it has to say, and in the assumptions that inform it, it is, after all, extraordinarily intellectual in manner; in fact, the poem rests on a fairly complex logical argument: if the piano-tuner, unlike the narrator, can know the true note on a musical scale and, moreover, can find it by rational, measured means ('Approximations to rectitude'), and if the critic can know, also through rational means, 'when / Religious poets speak to God, / And when to men', then who is to say that the truth of religion, even of a religion as seemingly anti-rational as that of the strict Calvinist Edward Taylor, cannot be known by other than mystical means, cannot exist, that is, in the light of human rationality? If this paraphrase seems overly syllogistic, that is only to call attention to the poem's insistence, through its very structure, on logical coherence, and to its insistence that rationality and religious faith can co-exist.

Nonetheless, a poem that expresses deeply felt religious convictions is not likely to manifest the kind of ironic distancing and intellectual qualifications that characterize a poem like **'The Evangelist'**. And several of Davie's recent poems depend on personal voice and emotional intensity in a way quite alien to much of his earlier work dealing with religion. An example is **'Devil on Ice'**:

> Called out on Christmas Eve for a working party,
> Barging and cursing, carting the wardroom's gin
> *To save us all from sin and shame,* through snow,
> The night unclear, the temperature subzero,
>             Oh I was a bombardier
>             For any one's Angry Brigade
> That Christmas more than thirty years ago!
>
> Later, among us bawling beasts was born
> The holy babe, and lordling Lucifer
> With Him alas, that blessed morn. And so
> Easy it was I recognize and know
>             Myself the mutineer
>             Whose own stale bawdry helped
> Salute the happy morn, those years ago.
>
> Red Army Faction could have had me then—
> Not an intrepid operative, but glib,
> A character-assassin primed to go,
> Ripe for the irreplaceable though low
>             Office of pamphleteer.
>             Father of lies, I knew
> My plausible sire, those Christmases ago.
>
> For years now I have been amenable,
> Equable, a friend to law and order,
> Devil on ice. Comes Christmas Eve . . . and lo!
> A babe we laud in baby-talk. His foe
>             And ours, not quite his peer
>             But his Antagonist,
> Hisses and walks on ice, as long ago.[7]

The poem draws on Davie's experiences in the north of Russia during his service in the Royal Navy and, in its sharply self-accusing tone, is of a piece with the recent and justly admired **'In the Stopping Train'**.[8] But **'Devil on Ice'** is quite explicitly about the religious problem of sin, and depends less on psychological insight and reflection than on conventional religious distinctions between good and evil.

Davie has said that the one religious doctrine that he held to, even in his unbelief, was that of original sin and man's innate depravity.[9] This belief, which is quite in keeping with Davie's affinities for classical restraint rather than romantic afflatus, surfaces in much of his recent poetry, including, of course, **'Devil on Ice'**. Another example is **'Livingshayes'**, a poem much closer than **'Devil on Ice'** to Davie's own definition of Christian poetry as that which 'appeals, either explicitly or by plain implication (and in whatever spirit—rebelliously for instance, or sardonically, as often with Emily Dickinson) to some one or more of the distinctive doctrines of the Christian church: to the Incarnation pre-eminently, to Redemption, Judgment, the Holy Trinity, the Fall.'[10] The Christian doctrine that 'Livingshayes' is concerned with is that of sin and redemption:

> 'Live-in-ease', and then to wash
>     Their sins in Lily Lake
> On Holy Thursday, for their own
>     And their Redeemer's sake.
> Easy living, with that clear
>     And running stream below;
> First contract the harm, and then
>     Wash it white as snow.
> Not altogether. Chris Cross first,
>     The top of a high hill'.
> Living it up and easy needs
>     Him hung and bleeding still.

Like many of Davie's poems, **'Livingshayes'** is rooted in a specific place. (The poem includes a note indicating that the ritual of bathing on Holy Thursday in Lily Lake, a small pond near the village of Silverton in Devon, is historically real, and Chris Cross is, in fact, the name of a hill overlooking the village and the lake.) But the poem quite obviously transcends its locale to make a statement about the doctrine of redemption. Moreover, as the final stanza and especially the final line insist, the poem emphasizes man's sinful part in the redemptive process far more than it does God's saving part; **'Livingshayes'** calls attention not just to the notion that Christ's death saved man, but also to the related idea that man's sins caused and, more important, continue to cause Christ's suffering ('Him hung and bleeding *still*').

As might be expected of a writer whose criticism and poetry have always gone hand in hand, the preoccupation with religion found in Davie's poetry of the past few years has a marked, though somewhat differently focused, corollary in his recent criticism. In contrast to his earlier critical support for the work of Ezra Pound and Thomas Hardy—

one a non-Christian theist and one a non-believer—Davie has spent much of his critical energy recently investigating the literature that has come out of the Dissenting tradition, and arguing, characteristically, for a reevaluation of it.

The central document here is *A Gathered Church*. In this book, Davie argues that writers like Isaac Watts and Charles Wesley were essentially men of reason, not emotion and intuition, and that the Dissenting tradition, at its best, was not hostile to the arts.[11] In fact, Davie argues, Dissent worked in and advanced the admirable aesthetic tradition of '*simplicity, sobriety,* and *measure*':

> Just here, in fact, is where negative virtues become positive ones. And this is true not just of Calvinist art but of all art, not just of Calvinist ethics but of all ethics. The aesthetic *and* the moral perceptions have, built into them and near to the heart of them, the perception of licence, of abandonment, of superfluity, foreseen, even invited, and yet in the end denied, fended off. Art *is* measure, *is* exclusion; is therefore simplicity (hard-earned), is sobriety, tense with all the extravagances that it has been tempted by and has denied itself.[12]

And in his introduction to *The Oxford Book of Christian Verse*, Davie argues that this aesthetic is especially appropriate for religious poetry, John Donne and Gerard Manley Hopkins notwithstanding:

> For when a poet chooses a style, or chooses *between* styles, he is making a choice in which his whole self is involved—including, if he is a Christian poet, that part of himself which is most earnestly and devoutly Christian. The question is, for him: what sort of language is most appropriate when I would speak of, or to, my God? And it is not only the puritans among poets who appear to have decided that the only language proper for such exalted purposes is a language stripped of fripperies and seductive indulgences, the most direct and unswerving English. To speak thus plainly has the additional advantage that it ought to be meaningful to plain men and women, the poet's fellow-Christians; but the main reason for choosing it is that when speaking to God, in poetry as in prayer, any sort of prevarication or ambiguity is unseemly, indeed unthinkable.[13]

The connection between Davie's defence of Watts and Wesley and the aesthetic principles that he has upheld in his own writing is obvious. More specifically, the criterion advanced here for religious poetry—that it be written in a plain rather than ornate or ambiguous style—also describes Davie's own recent religious poetry. Although poems like **'Having No Ear'**, **'Devil on Ice'** and **'Livingshayes'** are clearly less 'direct and unswerving' than the hymns of Watts and Wesley, they are nonetheless more immediately accessible, less subtly ambiguous, and less self-consciously eloquent than poems like **'Dissentient Voice'** or **'The Evangelist'**.

The difference that Davie's religious convictions have made to his work can perhaps best be gauged by comparing two poems, one early and one late, addressed to a Christian woman. The first, entitled **'Selina, Countess of**

**Huntingdon'**, appeared in Davie's first published book of poems, ***Brides of Reason.*** It describes an historical figure—Selina Hastings, who in the eighteenth century founded a group of Calvinist Methodists, opened a Methodist seminary that was later closed by court order, and spent a large part of her life trying to bring Methodism to the upper classes:

> Your special witness, as I recollect,
> Was, in your fervour, elegance; you yearned
> For Grace, but only gracefully, and earned,
> By sheer good taste, the title of 'elect'.
>
> So perfectly well-bred that in your hands
> All pieties were lavender, that scent
> Lingered about your college, where you spent
> Your fragrance on the burly ordinands.
>
> In your communion, virtue was uncouth;
> But now that rigour lost its cutting edge,
> As charm in you drove its schismatic wedge
> Between your church's beauty and its truth.

This poem does not in any way assert religious faith; rather, it relies on the kind of historical and ironic distancing ('All pieties were lavender' and 'you yearned / For Grace, but only gracefully') found in several of Davie's early poems about religion to express an ambiguous attitude toward Dissent as a religious and cultural institution.

Far different is **'An Anglican Lady: in memoriam Margaret Hine'**, written recently:[14]

> Flattered at having no
> less an authority than
> Richard Hooker named
> for my correction, I
> had drawn, before I knew it, the
> notepaper towards me for
> the reference (Book Five;
> 60, 3) when, live,
> you sprang before me, Margaret.
>                               I had chanced,
> brought perhaps by sortilege or some
> diviner leading, on
> a sheet of your, the secretary's,
> notepaper. Oh my
> poor Margaret, after how many
> years, and since Hooker how
> many centuries, does this
> sad clod encounter, not in books but in
> East Anglian blowing mornings, his
> And Hooker's and your own, your decorous, God!

Although this poem uses allusion in a way that a Watts hymn would not, the reference to Richard Hooker, the great Elizabethan theologian, is not essential—as the reference to Selina Hastings in **'Selina, Countess of Huntingdon'** is—to an apprehension of the poem's meaning or feeling. **'An Anglican Lady'** ends, after all, with a perfectly direct and forceful expression of religious conviction. Moreover, whereas the complex syntax of **'Selina, Countess of Huntingdon'** tends to underscore the poem's

ironic tone, and thus emphasize the distance between the narrator and what he is describing, in **'An Anglican Lady'**, the syntax works to strengthen the very unambiguous religious feeling that is at the heart of the poem (most noticeably in the delayed syntactical fulfilment that builds dramatic tension at the end of the poem, only to resolve it by coming to rest on the poem's most important word: God).

In **'Bedfordshire'** (*The Shires*), Davie describes a nineteenth century brick chapel, and then adds, 'I have never known / What to do with this that I am heir to'. The statement accurately describes Davie's lifelong ambiguity towards the particular, Dissenting doctrines that were his heritage. But it also describes the ambiguity towards religious belief in general that has marked the greater part of Davie's literary career. To say that in his recent turn toward religious faith, Davie has discovered 'What to do with this that I am heir to' is to risk overstatement. Nonetheless, Donald Davie's writing—both critical and poetic—has been affected markedly by the religious convictions that he has come to during the past decade, and it seems fair to predict that the work that he does in the next decade will be determined, at least as markedly, by those convictions.

*Notes*

1. The biographical information in this paragraph comes from a personal memorandum from Davie to me. 'Winters and Leavis: Memories and Reflections', *Sewanee Review*, 87, (Fall 1979) 4, pp. 608-18, includes several passing references to Davie's religious life. See also *These the Companions,* especially the final chapter, entitled 'Puritans'.

2. 'A West Riding Boyhood', *Prose* 7 (1973); reprinted in *Trying to Explain,* p. 21. Parts of this essay are included in the first chapter of *These the Companions.*

3. Unless otherwise indicated, all citations come from Donald Davie, *Collected Poems 1950-1970.* A passage in 'A West Riding Boyhood' bears comparison with the lines from 'Barnsley and District':

   The only material fear that I can remember is of 'rough boys', who were to be recognized in Barnsley about 1930 because they wore jerseys (and also, the roughest of them, wooden clogs), whereas gentle or gentlemanly or nice boys wore blouses, as I did. But this was not a serious fear, and did not survive a day when my worst tormentor turned out to wear a blouse and to be shod in sandals. Barnsley society, as it was known to a school-boy, was rigorously simplified and, as I see it now, truncated: there were only two classes—proletariat and petty bourgeois. Attorneys, clergymen, doctors (though not dentists) sent their children away to boarding-schools; and so, effectively, in St Mary's School there were only the sons of colliers and the sons of small shopkeepers like my father.

   (*Trying to Explain,* pp. 20-21)

4. Davie also makes an argument for the Augustan nature of Wesley's work in 'The Classicism of Charles Wesley', in *Purity of Diction in English Verse,* pp. 70-81. See also Davie's comments on Isaac Watts in his Introduction, *Augustan Lyric,* pp. 13-17.

5. *Augustan Lyric,* p. 53.

6. *American Scholar* (Autumn 1979) p. 470.

7. *Sewanee Review,* 88 (April-June 1980) 2, p. 177.

8. See *These the Companions,* chapters 3 and 4 for an account of Davie's experience in Russia.

9. Personal memorandum cited in footnote 1.

10. Introduction, *The Oxford Book of Christian Verse* (Oxford University Press 1981), pp. xx-xxi. At the time of writing, 'Livingshayes' had not yet been published.

11. Davie has strong feelings about the conventional disregard, often for reasons of class, of Nonconformist contributions to English culture. In his Introduction to *Augustan Lyric* (p. 15), he says:

> Particularly puerile are attempts to explain English nonconformity, along with brass bands and whippet-racing, as a product of something called (if you please) 'working-class culture'. One looks in vain for any general recognition that the artistic culture of the nation, so far from being repudiated by nonconformists as the product of a ruling class or an alien caste, has been embraced by the best of them in every generation, and enriched (though also at times valuably purged) by their efforts. Isaac Watts is the unavoidable representative of that embrace and that enrichment.

12. *A Gathered Church,* pp. 25-6.

13. *Oxford Book of Christian Verse,* pp. xxviii-xxix.

14. At the time of writing, 'An Anglican Lady' had not yet been published.

## Kieran Quinlan (essay date 1984)

SOURCE: "Donald Davie: The Irish Years," in *The Southern Review,* Vol. 20, No. 1, January, 1984, pp. 29-40.

*[In the following essay, Quinlan explores autobiographical aspects of Davie's Irish poems.]*

Donald Davie was an English don at Trinity College, Dublin, from 1950 until 1957. It was during these years that he published the books on which a substantial part of his reputation both as poet and critic still rests: *Purity of Diction in English Verse* (1952), **Brides of Reason** (1955), *Articulate Energy* (1955), **A Winter Talent & Other Poems** (1957). And it was in Ireland also that he formed many of his opinions as to what the ideal relationship between the artist and his society should be. In fact, in some instances,

Ireland seems to be the hidden criterion by which Davie judges his own country's cultural short-comings. Again, "in Ireland or the United States" is a phrase that recurs in Davie's writings, suggesting that he sees some kind of similarity between these two nations and also that his Irish years were a preparation for his later, more complete, exile from England. Yet one can read critics who have devoted considerable effort to analyzing Davie's career and art—Neil Powell and Blake Morrison for example—without being told that the poet lived in Dublin rather than in England for several years before undertaking his first transatlantic journey in 1957. Calvin Bedient, in *Eight Contemporary Poets,* praises two of Davie's Irish poems without making even passing reference to their origin, in spite of the fact that this information is relevant to the poems' interpretation. Happily Davie himself has recently made good this omission in his recollections, *These the Companions.* There, just when in the normal sequence of things one expects to come upon an account of the Movement poets of the 1950s, one finds instead a chapter entitled simply "Dubliners." But this chapter, excellent though it is, does not quite embrace all the complexity of Davie's poems on Ireland, nor does it draw out the full implications of his experience there; above all, it cannot—of necessity—offer an *Irish* perspective on Davie. This English poet's Trinity period, then, is richly deserving of further investigation.

From the vantage point—or, more correctly, the disadvantage point—of the present, it is difficult to imagine both Donald Davie and Ireland as they each were in the fifties. By this I mean that the sixties marked such a distressing time for Davie in his relationship with his own country—the tension between Englishness and Americanness, his unhappy experience as Pro-Vice-Chancellor at Essex University—that it is now almost impossible to see him as the less embattled Englishman he was in 1950. And, of course, the relationship between England and Ireland, though still infinitely nuanced on both sides, has dramatically altered since the advent of the crisis in Northern Ireland in the late sixties. An effort of historical imagination is therefore called for.

To begin with, it is not clear from Davie's account of his Irish years what his attitude towards that country was before his employment there. There had probably been few if any Irish in his native Barnsley where he was but dimly aware of the "priest-ridden" Roman Catholics, themselves presumably as English as he was. Still, he had been exposed to the melodies of Tom Moore at an early age and was to retain his love of them ever afterwards. His particular interests at Cambridge would have acquainted him with Swift and Goldsmith, and again, his college tutor was the well-known Anglo-Irishman and Yeats scholar, T. R. Henn. It was probably through the latter that Davie first encountered the elegant Peter Allt of Trinity:

> After the war, when I was a research student in Cambridge, there came to my college the Anglo-Irishman Peter Allt, then collaborating with G. D. Allspach in America on the variorum edition of the poems of Yeats.

I was crankily suspicious of all sorts of things in those days, and a certain largeness of manner in Allt, his affecting a silver-knobbed cane, and his elaborately allusive conversation, damned him in my eyes as affected.

This wariness of the proletarian Davie in the presence of the patrician Irishman did not prevent the future poet from accepting a position at Trinity. It would have been quite usual at that time for a young English scholar to consider Trinity a desirable first appointment, especially if he were attached to the comforts of the Oxbridge-style universities. The only rivals at that level would have been Edinburgh and possibly Durham, for Trinity had historical and collegial links with the two ancient British institutions. Though Davie does not appear to have been particularly enamored of such a lifestyle—he records his recurring depression whenever he revisits Cambridge—the change to Trinity was not at all traumatic.

The Dublin in which Davie and his young family arrived in 1950 was very much the down-at-heel capital of the newly declared Republic of Ireland (the country having been a member of the British Commonwealth of Nations until 1949). The country was depressed and emigration to England was at an all-time high. Looking back at the fifties now, however, the period—for all its drabness—seems to have been Dublin's final golden era. The philistine developments of the sixties and seventies in a more prosperous Ireland, the demolition of whole streets of Georgian houses, had not yet begun. Heinrich Böll published his classic *Irisches Tagebuch* in 1957 in which he celebrated the nation's fadedness and thereby attracted whole generations of his fellow countrymen to visit this unspoilt arcadia. In political terms, tension between Ireland and England was probably at its lowest ever, for, in spite of its neutrality and occasional pro-German rhetoric, Ireland had helped England considerably during the war years and had been impressed by that country's courageous defiance of Hitler's armies when all seemed hopeless. For at least another fifteen years it would be quite common for Irish schoolboys to speculate whether they ought to seek a cadetship in the Irish army or write to one of the "Squadron Commanders" that advertised in the popular British weeklies.

On the other hand, the Anglo-Irish circles into which Davie was introduced in 1950 had long been alienated by de Valera's antagonistic attitude towards them and by his general equation of being Irish with being Catholic. Though they still owned a disproportionate number of businesses in the city and still sent their children to English public schools (Anglican or Catholic according to their own persuasion), there was a certain faded elegance in their lifestyle. And Trinity College—which the Catholic archbishop of the city had forbidden his subjects to attend without written permission from him—was still the symbol, if somewhat tattered, of traditional Protestant ascendancy. The college elicited Davie's reserved affections:

> For the first and probably the last time in my life, there in Trinity and for Trinity I felt faintly that loyalty to-

wards institutions—the regiment, the old school, the college, the club—which engaged the emotions of my fellow Englishmen in a way that for the most part I couldn't comprehend. When we were there Trinity, we were told, was as poor as a church-mouse, and certainly under steady hostile pressure from sectarian nationalism in the rival institution, the National University; but there was of course no question of realizing the assets represented by the *Book of Kells* and the *Book of Durrow* and the other ancient *incunabula* held in stewardship for the nation. That sentiment and that principle could not easily be accommodated in universities I have moved in since, factories producing "research" and graduates (very much in that order). The false analogy on which these plume themselves, between their operations and those of industry, is reflected in their architecture, as Trinity's quite different conception of itself is mirrored in the pillared porticoes, not all of them grandiose, which allude insistently to temple and shrine.

This is a typical example of what I mean by saying that Dublin had a formative influence on Davie's artistic and social development.

The background of the time requires a little more filling in. For one thing, Trinity, the symbol of an alien religion and governing class, was—as Davie accurately remarks in *These the Companions*—held high in the affections of Dubliners. The college, in fact, enjoys a paradoxical relationship with the country for it was also the alma mater of Wolfe Tone and Robert Emmet, two of Ireland's most romantic revolutionary heroes, and of Douglas Hyde, the Protestant founder of the Gaelic League which aimed at the "de-anglicization" of Ireland. And yet, Trinity played little part in the Irish Literary Revival and was despised by Yeats and Joyce (though for very different reasons). When Davie was there, it had made up for some of its sins by the rather quixotic gesture of hiring as its Professor of Modern Irish (Gaelic) an extreme nationalist and reputed Communist, Martin Ó Cadhain, who was without any academic credential though he had indeed written the best modern book in the language (*Cré na Cille*). In short, Trinity participated in the general schizophrenia of the nation at large. Davie alludes to some of this complexity in a reference to his not being told by one of the college dons that the playwright Brendan Behan had once been an active member of the IRA:

> To me, as an Englishman, not all could be divulged—least of all by Owen Skeffington who, though a socialist, and protestant, and thoroughly anglicized by his protestant education, was the son of the most authentic martyr to British violence . . . ; who therefore doubtless harboured, though at a level far below his consciously "progressive" agnosticism, anti-British sentiments of perhaps peculiar virulence. (I remember that we disagreed explicitly only once. . . . )

Here Davie's reservations about Skeffington, his use of the word "doubtless," may seem excessive until one recalls that an Irishman is likely to have just as many reservations about the genuineness of his English acquaintances' liberal politics in the matter of British-Irish relations.

Mention of Behan reminds us that there was a minor literary renaissance going on in the city during Davie's tenure there. At its more sober end, it centered around the *Bell,* a literary journal edited by Sean O'Faolain and, later, by Peadar O'Donnell; at its more intoxicated and factious end, it included Behan himself, his arch rival Paddy Kavanagh, and the host of characters described in Anthony Cronin's *Dead as Doornails,* John Ryan's *Remembering How We Stood,* and, fictionally, in J. P. Donleavy's *The Ginger Man.* It is clear from Davie's recollections—and from *their* recollections—that he had little contact with this group:

> I at any rate, trying in my Dublin years to school myself so as to practise verse as a *strict* discipline, could not afford to be indulgent towards a Behan or a Kavanagh. Be they Irish or be they English (and their English associates were mostly worse), they were for me bad news and bad medicine.

Dublin is notorious for the number of its "writers" who have never put pen to paper and here one senses that Davie, though convivial by nature, was quite determined to avoid such time-consuming and unproductive company. After all, the great Yeats himself had paid only a single (well-documented) visit to a pub!

The Irish writers with whom Davie did come into contact were either remnants of an older generation—Joseph Hone, Yeats's biographer, Lord Dunsany, the prolific writer of fairy tales—or members of a more disciplined school. In particular, Davie became an admirer of Austin Clarke, a poet who had attempted to carry over Gaelic meters and assonance into English poetry. What is important here is that Davie was well aware of the *craftsmanship* of the best Irish verse, both in Gaelic and in English: at one point he shows a welcome irritation with Paddy Kavanagh's ignorance of the fact that the lifetime of Shakespeare and Ben Jonson coincided with the last glorious efflorescence of lyric poetry in Gaelic.

T. S. Eliot's trinity of politics, religion, and literature would seem to provide suitable headings for an examination of some of Davie's poems on Ireland. **"Demi-Exile. Howth,"** then, appears to have been his first poem on the country. It is, as one might expect, about "Division of loyalties, dolour of exile." The last four lines suggest that without some kind of loyalty there can be no true experience, though that loyalty can carry in its wake certain painful acceptances:

> Hands acknowledging no allegiances,
> Gloved for good against brutal chance,
> Pluck the shadow and not the substance,
> Grasp no nettle of circumstance.

The poet's own hand, however, is "English" and thus innocent of the above accusation. Overall, there is a quiet reflectiveness in **"Demi-Exile. Howth,"** a detached ruminating, which it would be difficult to evoke in the post-1968 era of British-Irish relations.

Here it is appropriate to make some observations about Davie's attitude towards Irish nationalism. G. K. Chesterton asserts somewhere that it is the English *patriot* who ought to be most understanding of the Irish nationalist. This is a paradoxical statement that would require almost infinite qualification. The basic difficulty is that whereas an Englishman defines his patriotism in terms of his loyalty to the crown, his country, his traditions, without any reference to other nations, it is almost impossible for an Irishman to avoid mention of England in any assertion of his own sense of nationality. Thus, for the most part, Ireland is peripheral to the English consciousness; England, however, is central to Irish preoccupations. Hence, since the Irish national consciousness defines itself—however mildly—in terms of historical opposition to England, it is extremely difficult for an Englishman to feel as benign and understanding towards it as he would towards French or Spanish or even German nationalism. I think that this accounts for a certain ambivalence on Davie's part even prior to the renewed IRA bombings, and for the kind of suspicion evident in the remark on Sheehy Skeffington that was quoted earlier.

But Davie's attitude is more complicated than this. The lines from **"Demi-Exile. Howth"** show how important he considers national loyalty to be and one of his most persistent criticisms of his own country has been of the seeming indifference of its citizens. Davie most heartily approves of Irish nationalists—what else could he expect an Irishman to be?—even as he is grimly aware of the "brutal chance" threatening in the wings. In the concluding lines to "Commodore Barry," written about the fellow seaman who founded the American navy, Davie indicates just how important it is, in his view, to have a central commitment:

> "My sovereign," said saucy
> Jack Barry, meaning Congress;
> And yes, it's true, outside
> The untried, unstable recess
> Of the classroom, every one has one:
> A sovereign—general issue . . .

And if Davie has been critical of what he considers to be the excesses of Irish nationalism, it is well to remember that he has applied no less exacting standards to his own country: Britain's response to the Suez crisis was merely "the imprudent flourish / of kettledrum and cornet."

It is especially interesting nowadays to look at **"Belfast on a Sunday Morning,"** a poem written about Davie's attitude towards those Irish who most loudly proclaim their allegiance to Britain. One finds that Davie is first of all tempted to scoff at them but that his final stance is one of worry (well-founded in retrospect) and scorn:

> Pastmasters pale, elaborately grim,
> Marched each alone, beneath a bowler hat:
> And, catapulted on a crumpled limb,
> A lame man leapt the tram-lines like a bat . . .
>
> Some brawny striplings sprawled upon the lawn;
> No man is really crippled by his hates.

> Yet I remembered with a sudden scorn
> Those "passionate intensities" of Yeats.

Here Davie seems to find the Ulstermen's strident display of "Britishness" more foreign to him than the (then) more genial nationalism of Southern Ireland.

But **"The Wearing of the Green"** belies the above suggestion that Davie was wholly at ease with Irish nationalism in the 1950s. The title itself is the same as that of a well-known song about the aftermath of the United Irishmen's unsuccessful insurrection in 1798, the foundation date of modern Irish republicanism. The song runs:

> Oh, Paddy dear! and did ye hear the news that's goin'
>    round?
> The shamrock's forbid by law to grow on Irish
> ground!
> No more St. Patrick's day we'll keep; his colour can't
> be
>    seen
> For there's a cruel law agin' the Wearin' o' the Green.

Davie's poem begins with a description of the colors of Meath (an Irish county just outside Dublin) in May: "Green more entire must needs be evergreen, / Precluding autumn. . . ." But then he moves on to a more serious reflection:

> Imagination, Irish avatar,
> Aches in the spring's heart and in mine, the strang-
> er's,
> In Meath in May. But to believe there are
> Unchanging Springs endangers,
> By that fast dye, the earth;
> So blood-red green the season,
> It never changes
> In Meath in May.

Throughout this poem, the deadening repetition of the almost banal **"In Meath in May"** suggests the negative effect of the county's (and the country's) "unchanging Springs" and uniform array. Transferring this perception to a political context—a transfer that is justified, I think, by the allusion to the nationalist song—the implication seems to be that "So blood-red green the season," "endangers, / By that false dye, the earth," meaning that an unchanging Irish nationalism is dangerous for all concerned, Irishmen and Englishmen alike. This is an interesting and even disturbing insight, especially since it was written at a time of relative harmony between the sister nations.

In concluding this section, it should be stressed that Davie, both in 1950 and afterwards, attacked not Irish nationalism as such but rather its excesses, and especially its extra-parliamentary excesses as manifested in the activities of the IRA. His criticism here, while undoubtedly influenced by his British background, is really not very different from his criticism of those fellow Englishmen who have lapsed into a narrow preoccupation with their own traditions to the exclusion of wider concerns. Again, more importantly, the day-to-day parliamentary politics of Ireland where neither of the two major parties could be accused of harbor-

ing left-wing, socialist aspirations were very much in tune with Davie's conservative (with small "c") sympathies, sympathies very strongly in the tradition of Edmund Burke, that Irishman from Trinity who opposed the French Revolution and yet argued the legitimacy of American grievances.

Catholicism, Ireland's predoment religion, does not appear to have attracted Davie very much in the 1950s, though the most embarrassing pages of *These the Companions* are devoted to praising Irish priests and nuns for offering "evidence of chastity as a persistently available way of life" in the face of a misguided sexual liberalism. In his Trinity days, however, Davie found something alien in "the sandalled Capuchin's silent stride" through the city. Far more congenial to this lapsed Dissenter's (Baptist) sensibilities was the sober humanism of the Church of Ireland, that is, the Anglican church in Ireland, a denomination that would generally be considered quite "low" by English "high," Anglo-Catholic standards. **"North Dublin,"** a poem about a famous city church that was built sometime after 1802 in the style of London's St. Martin-in-the-Fields and which is alluded to several times in *Ulysses,* conveys a sense of this attraction.

> St. George's, Hardwicke Street,
> Is charming in the Church of Ireland fashion:
> The best of Geneva, the best of Lambeth
> Aesthetically speaking
> In its sumptuously sober
> Interior, meet.
>
> A continuous gallery, clear glass in the windows
> An elegant conventicle
> In the Ionian order—
> What dissenter with taste
> But would turn, on these terms
> Episcopalian?
>
> "Dissenter" and "tasteful" are contradictions
> In terms, perhaps, and my fathers
> Would ride again to the Boyne
> Or with scythes to Sedgemoor, or splinter
> The charming fanlights in this charming slum
> By their lights, rightly.

Episcopalian is what, in fact, Davie turned several years later when he moved to America and became drawn to a communion not unlike that of the Church of Ireland.

Davie describes the Dublin of the 1950s as an "atmosphere charged / with recollection of a brilliant era." *Recollection* is the critical word here for several of his reviews at the time indicate that he saw the local scene in the post Yeatsian years as somewhat provincial and that his own focus was on the wider horizon offered by his native country. He was especially struck by the Irish national proclivity for speaking ill of members of their own race and presents his observation amusingly in **"Dublin Georgian."** The scene is that of a reception given in the Provost's House in Trinity in a room noted for its stucco interior by Robert West:

Were I to move among the talkers here,
I'd soon be disabused
About this artist, hearing him traduced
Wherever laughing malice has the ear
Of Irish wit. But I avert my gaze,
Refuse to know
His marxist and his mystagogic phase,
Or the connubial scandal years ago
Retailed around me. Every Irish master
Must learn to suffer, for the nation's sake,
The national proclivity for plaster,
Mouldings that chip, and pediments that flake.

Anyone acquainted with the biographies of Yeats and George Moore and Joyce will appreciate how true all of this is! Davie himself in some comments on Austin Clarke in *These the Companions* offers what might well serve as a gloss on the middle section of his poem:

> It is likely enough, in any case, that Clarke was "taking a rise" out of the company he was in. For in the corroding malice of his conversation there was always a special place for Yeats. . . . And this was only the beginning of his perversity. The writer of verse like this [Clarke's] which demanded for its appreciation precisely the attention recommended by modern criticism, in his own weekly reviewing for *The Irish Times* mocked with malice every pretension of the vanguard. . . . Clarke's cynicism was complete, and his irony would undercut every position. . . . He was never so happy as when he cut the ground from under his own feet.

**"Dublin Georgian (2)"** is ostensibly about West's own house in Lower Dominick Street, a house that has since been turned into a Catholic orphanage. The poet's companion on the occasion of a visit there

> Admires the moulding, sighs
> "Ah" at the staircase, and extols the chaste
> Ceiling by Stapleton; occupies
> (Thin shoulders raised, a flutter of bony hands)
> The pure *gestalt*
> Of the double arch; expatiates, understands
> How architect and plasterer had felt
> The underpinning of that virile beauty
> In the age's order.

Here the poet seems to be distancing himself from his companion of "instructed taste," and one can see the exaggerated gesturing of the orphan-like "thin" aesthete as he expounds on the happy marriage of art and society in the eighteenth century. But then comes the shock of:

> Later, in the street,
> He held forth to me how the artist's duty
> Is mutiny, evasion, and retreat.

Art no longer exists in harmony with the society that nourishes it and thus the Joycean strategy of silence, exile, and cunning is called for. The poet seems to detach himself from this assertion, however, as though his own situation as an Englishman frees him of the need for such maneuverings. And yet, ironically, it is this same strategy that

Davie himself was to adopt in the years after he left Trinity, years that were to witness his assault on what he considered to be English philistinism.

Donald Davie left Ireland in 1957 to take up an academic appointment in the United States. By then several of the attitudes with which he is now associated had formed themselves so that it is accurate to say that his "demi-exile" in Ireland was a preparation for his greater exile, cultural and intellectual, in America. He continued to visit Ireland annually for the Yeats Summer School until 1969 when the first of the IRA bombings in Northern Ireland provoked him to write **"Ireland of the Bombers,"** a poem which he subsequently sent to the *Irish Times:*

> Dublin, young manhood's ground,
> Never more I'll roam;
> —Stiffly I call my strayed
> Affections home.

To an Irishman, Davie's anger here, his refusal to visit *Southern* Ireland, seems not so much misdirected—honest condemnation of the IRA's tactics ought to be more common among moderate Irishmen than it actually is—but rather a surprising forgetfulness of the complexity of Irish life in which nothing is what it appears to be and in which a friendly tolerance of all traditions continues to prevail. In 1975, however, at the invitation of an Irish senator (who is also, by that happy Irish conjunction which so pleases Davie, a professor of English literature), the poet agreed to visit the country again; and in 1981 he was made Academic Director of the Yeats Summer School in Sligo.

In recent years Davie has continued his attack on British philistinism through the pages of *PN Review.* Sometimes in so doing he has drawn upon his experience of the Yeats Summer School, and of the Irish situation in general, as an example of how art and society ought to relate to one another. He has judged that a similar institution in Stratford has worked far less well and less authentically:

> And where else but in Sligo, in the Republic of Ireland, are the much debated gulfs between poetry and life, or poetry and society, effortlessly surpassed, year after year?

Irish perversity is tempted to argue that perhaps Davie's shorter and more intense visits to the country have rendered his observations less perceptive than they were during his Trinity years, though it is hard to quibble with such enthusiastic praise.

One would like to conclude that Davie has finally reconciled himself with whatever differences he may once have had with Ireland. But such is not at all the case. In fact, the future of Davie's relationship with Ireland is not completely certain. The last observation is not meant to sound ominous but, rather, it is an assertion that his is not the kind of sentimental attachment that precludes reflection, criticism, or even rejection. Nor will every Irishman feel happy with some of the qualities that Davie sees in Ireland. But all this is to say that Davie's interest in Ireland is almost as affectionate, exasperating, intense, confused, clear, and thoughtful as is his interest in his own country.

### Seamus Heaney (essay date 1988)

SOURCE: "'Or, Solitude': A Reading," in *On Modern Poetry: Essays Presented to Donald Davie*, edited by Vereen Bell and Laurence Lerner, Vanderbilt University Press, 1988, pp. 81-87.

[*In the following essay, Heaney deems "Or, Solitude" a "poetic happening" and an "important event in the history of British poetry over the last quarter of a century."*]

An unexpected sensation of furtherance: that is what I remember of my first reading of Donald Davie's poem **"Or, Solitude"** in an issue of *New Statesman* late in 1965. What exactly the poem meant I could not have said, nor could I have formulated my response in the terms I now propose, yet the actual experience of the lines did constitute a poetic "happening." In them, the consensus that usually allows the English imagination to order reality on a domestic scale had been for the moment refused, and English poetry was receiving one of its rare visitations of strangeness. The roof had come off, and the sensibility was being exposed to something both unlimited and adjacent. One might have called the poem visionary, except that it concluded with a rhetorical curtailment which seemed to climb down from that high mode. Or one could have called it evocative, except that it intended something far more declarative than that word would suggest. Even the poet himself had difficulty determining where the poem had got to and what he was to make of it. For example, the first line of the fourth stanza—the point where the turn occurs, where what is being apprehended begins to declare itself—was revised between its first book appearance in *Essex Poems* (1969) and its publication in *Collected Poems 1950-1970*. I will discuss the change later, but I adduce it here as a symptom of the new combination of improvisational process and fastidious wording that made Davie's *Essex Poems* not only the essential volume in his own career, but an important event in the history of British poetry over the last quarter of a century.

**"Or, Solitude"** is, as the poet noted in the 1970 *Collected Poems,* the subtitle of Wordsworth's "Lucy Gray": "Oft had I heard of Lucy Gray: / And, when I crossed the wild, / I chanced to see at break of day / The solitary child." It is not surprising, therefore, that Davie's melody retains a certain intoned pathos, and that his *mise-en-scène* involves a presence who is part genius of place, part a phantom of sentiment:

> A farm boy lost in snow
> Rides his good horse, Madrone,
> Through Iowan snows for ever
> And is called "alone".

> Because gone from the land
> Are the boys who knew it best
> Or best expressed it, gone
> To Boston or Out West,

> And the breed of the horse Madrone,
> With its bronco strain, is strange
> To the broken sod of Iowa
> That used to be its range,

> The transcendental nature
> Of poetry, how I need it!
> And yet it was for years
> What I refused to credit.

In some obvious ways, this is an "American" poem. It is set in Iowa; it has a source in nineteenth-century frontier literature, uses terms like "range" and "farm boy" (not "farmer's boy" or "labourer"), and works with elements that are typical and even expected: snows, prairie, bronco. It is also American in the way it shifts memories of several Frostian winter-pieces from New England to the Midwest, and is susceptible to the idiom of Hart Crane. The "broken sod" has surely been wakened from the dream with which Crane invested the prairie in the closing lines of "Proem: Brooklyn Bridge." But this is at the same time an "Essex poem" in the way that the transition from the third to the fourth stanza involves both disjunction and projection, for such transitions are a feature of many of the lyrics in the volume and mark Davie's admission into his poetic practice of Black Mountain influences. Finally, **"Or, Solitude"** is an "English" poem in the way it confines the spaciousness to which it is genuinely open within a form and cadence deliberately related to *Lyrical Ballads.*

The concerns—Englishness, Americanness, the inner and outer weather of countries and countrysides—constitute a poetic ground from which the individual lyrics in *Essex Poems* do not aspire to detach themselves. On the contrary, as Davie wrote about the poems of Charles Olson and Ed Dorn in relation to their wayward learning, "they emerge from it only to burrow back into it." Similarly, the thematic concerns of these lyrics refuse to melt away and leave the poem orphaned within its linguistic limits. This is partly for biographical reasons, Donald Davie having been on the verge of making his move from England to the United States at the time of their composition. As a result of this impending departure, he was pondering with acute personal urgency not only the physical differences between a North Sea climate and a Pacific one, but also the cultural and psychological consequences of living a committed life in these extremely contrasting milieux. For somebody as bonded to England as Davie was, not just by nurture, speech, and service in wartime, but by an affection consciously deepened and sharpened by literary study and poetic vocation, the prospect of practising his art in a landscape unhallowed by communal association, unsalted by known dialects and pungent place-names, was necessarily fraught with intense self-questioning.

Testing and disturbing as these uncertainties must have been at a private level, there was a further level of questioning to which they were attendant but not subsidiary. This involved the ongoing dialogue and tension in Anglo-American literary culture, the doubt about native English parochialism that had been planted by Ezra Pound fifty years earlier and remained inescapable by anyone alive to the shifts and reverberations of poetic energy in the 1950s and 1960s. That was the era of A. Alvarez's anthology, *The New Poetry,* with its notorious assault on "the gentility principle" in English letters, the debilitating conviction that "life is always more or less orderly, people always more or less polite, their emotions and habits more or less decent and more or less controllable." It was also the era of translation, when the first flush of the new postwar poetry from Eastern Europe was entering the insular consciousness. Davie was alive to it all, translating from Pasternak's Russian "The Poems of Doctor Zhivago" and swerving beyond the usual gentility-bound preference for Anglophile Eliot into the less travelled (in England) realms of Pound. He was still alive to it when he wrote "An Afterword for the American Reader" in *Thomas Hardy and British Poetry* (1972); there he glosses "gentility" as "civic sense" or "political responsibility" and inclines to value these qualities above the liberties and assumptions of American poets who are "rapt and exalted bards together, in a sublime democracy." Three years after *Essex Poems,* six thousand miles away from Essex, Davie was still productively in two minds, except that his corrective example was now drawn from British tradition and it was American practice that was perceived to be in need of correction.

*Essex Poems* is the volume where Davie's poetry jumped ahead of what might have been expected of him. That is to say, the reasonableness, the scrupulous discursive impulses, the acrid relish of landscapes, all of which attained a certain fullness of expression in *Events and Wisdoms* (1964), might have continued to issue in surely based poems of a still traditionally English sort, poems where the voice issued from a well-defined persona, which functioned as statements by that persona, bulletins relayed from a composed intelligence that had claims upon us because of its consistency and intentness. What happened instead was a breakaway by the voice from its recognizably social espousals, its tones of irony, discretion, or severity. The language was now more the vehicle of its own heuristic assays, the poem typically an action rather than an address. Although not all the poems in the volume belong to this "new" mode, whatever unifies the book and gives it an excited feeling of access is the result of some such change in the poetic process itself. One has a great sense of risks being taken, of a poet who is inclined to keep the colt tightly reined-in getting ready to let go and be carried in an unexpected direction. This does not involve abandonment of control, because, at every living moment of the unexpectedness, concentration, alertness, and balance are vitally important. Rather, it involves an abandonment of the self to art, a new stage in what Davie called in 1959 "the long struggle back to English poetry considered by the poet as a way of spiritual knowledge."

That may sound high-flown, but it is typical of the earnestness that enters Davie's writing almost every time he addresses the work of Ezra Pound or ponders its implications for the practice of subsequent poets. It is also consistent with his adducing of Pound as the sponsor of poetry as an art to be thought of in terms of other arts (a making no less than a saying) and his radical pursuit of this conception to the point where he considered we might "sell the pass on poetry from the start by refusing to consider any metaphysical or ontological grounds for the poetic activity." At a more practical and commonsensical level, this "new aesthetic" issued in statements like the one he made in the course of an exchange with Alvarez, printed in the first issue of *the review* (1962): "A man who is emotionally immature can, by dint of the passion he has for literature, transcend his emotional immaturity for the sake of the poem he is writing."

All in all, therefore, by the time he came to write **"Or, Solitude,"** the pressure of the concerns underlying its final stanza was deep and constant:

> The transcendental nature
> Of poetry, how I need it!
> And yet it was for years
> What I refused to credit.

Those boys who best expressed the land have gone from it, and the farm boy lost in snow is thereby already symbolic and late-comerly. He is a manifestation of Lucy Gray, a revenant from the desert places in Robert Frost's poem of that name, which includes another snowbound consciousness intuitively responsive to the links between desolations *in here* and *out there.* But he is also directly sprung from a book to which Davie directs attention in his note in *Collected Poems 1950-1970.* Hamlin Garland's *Boy Life on the Prairie* contains a poem called "Lost in a Norther" where the farm boy rides in a blizzard, for days on end, numbed and solitary:

> Lost on the prairie! All day alone
> With my faithful horse, my swift Ladrone.
> And the shapes on the shadow my scared soul cast.
> Which way is north? Which way is west?
> I ask Ladrone, for he knows best,
> And he turns his head to the blast.

That the horse in Davie's poem is called not Ladrone but Madrone is a lovely waver since it may encompass an oblique *hommage* to the ratiocinative talents of Yvor Winters at the very moment when a Wintersian type of aesthetic is being left behind. Writing of this "great doctor of abstractions" in *These the Companions,* Davie noted with pleasure the unexpected earthiness of the man's conversation, a "halting monologue about the behaviour of Canadian waxwings . . . or the multiple nice distinctions within the botanical family that includes the great madrone." But whatever the reason for the switch of the horse's name, the musical effect remains the same, and as the Madrone / "alone" rhyme tolls, it opens a path into a pristine aural domain, a prairie spaciousness conjured by the after-echo of words like "Iowan snows," "gone from the land," and "range." Yet the terrain is also obstinately physical, thanks to another cluster of harder, more abrupt effects; for example, the rhyming of "need it" and "credit," while it occurs in a sentence that addresses a theme ultimately to be named "metaphysicality," keeps faith at the same time with the bluntness and cloddishness of ploughing. There is a little shudder to it, a sense of coming-up-against, an intimation of the out-thereness of what is being talked about.

In fact, this push toward a reality independent of categories that are primarily psychological and social has been an abiding concern of Davie's poetics, and there is in **"Or, Solitude"** a vindicating energy, a given-from-beyond quality that distinguishes other Essex poems and sets them in special poetic relation both to "the real world" and to the writer's intentions. The writing "goes itself"; it conducts and transmits that ontological neediness to which Davie was alluding in his crucial essay, "Two Analogies for poetry." So it is no surprise that "the transcendental nature / Of poetry" should have been revised later to "The metaphysicality / Of poetry." He needs "metaphysicality" more because, presumably, it represents a more extreme embrace of risk, a more exposed commitment to poetry as a genre that must justify itself not simply "as a way of getting or keeping in touch or practising group therapy."

The phrase "the transcendental nature of poetry" allows for an interpretation of the poem that would go something like this: because of the fetch and persuasiveness of these Iowan absences, I am inclined to credit my knowledge of reality as previous, extensive, and irrational, and I am also inclined to think of poetry as massaging and assisting that not uncomplacent feeling of being a Wordsworthian "inmate of this active universe." But "the metaphysicality of poetry" is much more "sculptured." It insists that there is a divide between the poetriness of poetry and the rest of our experience, that to conceive of poetry as having a conciliatory relation with our nature or an obligation to flatter our humanity is to conceive of it too laxly. The very sounds of "the metaphysicality of poetry" are more faceted and resistant, their hardness stands off, whereas there is something alluring, tenebrous, and perhaps inflationary about "the transcendental nature of poetry."

This reading of **"Or, Solitude"** has permitted itself to be affected by Donald Davie's writings on what he desires for and from poetry because I believe that in this case we are dealing with one of those poems in which poetic action and theoretical effort manage to coalesce. It happens to bridge the gap (perceptible in the sixties to himself and to his readers) between the poems he was given to write and the poems he would have liked to have written; it accrues as the bonus of long meditation on the consequences for English poetry of the achievements of the international modernists. It salutes the immoderacy and exorbitance of the expectations they had from art ("how I need it!"), yet by the constricted means it employs—short lines, a curtailed musicality that finally settles for speech over singing tones—it opts for a poetry that is ultimately more Hardyesque. So, in spite of what I said at the beginning about this being an American poem, and in spite of its obvious reach

beyond the native limits, the final critical emphasis must be placed on its domestic force. Years before the publication of Davie's book on the desirable moderating effect that Hardy's "scientific humanism" might exercise on postmodernist poetry, **"Or, Solitude"** arises involuntarily out of the questions which provoked that book and by its curtailed music enacts the conclusion which the book would proffer:

> Are not Hardy and his successors right in severely curtailing for themselves the liberties that other poets continue to take? Does not the example of the Hardyesque poets make some of those other poets look childishly irresponsible?

### Mark Jarman (essay date 1988)

SOURCE: "A Shared Humanity: 'In the Stopping Train' and 'The Whitsun Weddings'," in *On Modern Poetry: Essays Presented to Donald Davie*, edited by Vereen Bell and Laurence Lerner, Vanderbilt University Press, 1988, pp. 89-101.

[*In the following essay, Jarman contrasts the role of the poet as evinced in Davie's "In the Stopping Train" and Philip Larkin's "The Whitsun Weddings."*]

> These are my customs and establishments.
> It would be much more serious to refuse.
> —Philip Larkin
> "The Importance of Elsewhere"
>     A man who ought to know me
>     wrote in a review
>     my emotional life was meagre.
>
>             —Donald Davie **"July, 1964"**

In his recent collection of lectures, *Czeslaw Milosz and the Insufficiency of Lyric*, Donald Davie argues that, because of twentieth-century history, the lyric poet has lost the privilege of being responsible only to himself and his emotions. Therefore, he must find a way to speak for more than himself. The late twentieth-century search for a more representative self is not peculiar to our era. Keats sought it in his attempts at empathy, in the very negative capability now associated with the self-involved lyric and against which Davie reacts. Davie himself has sought in his poems a larger expression, while at the same time acknowledging the limits of the lyric that make such an expression impossible. **"In the Stopping Train,"** one of Davie's finest poems, is an attempt to understand the insufficiency of lyric by subjecting the poet himself to nearly merciless critical examination.

It is helpful to compare Davie's poem, from his 1977 volume of the same name, with the title poem of Philip Larkin's 1964 collection of poems. **"In the Stopping Train"** seems, in part, a response to "The Whitsun Weddings" and not merely because both record journeys on stopping or local trains, but because the former presents a totally different role for the poet from that of the latter. The irony is that Larkin, in his poem, is not nearly as wrapped up in himself as Davie is in his. Yet Larkin's detachment from his subject has been cause for serious criticism, and quite rightly.

First of all, justifying his own ways to those of his fellow-men has never been the problem for Larkin that it is for Davie, except as Larkin has been too much like other people, letting "the toad work squat" on his life for example, or not enough like them, as in "Annus Mirabilis" where he admits to being a very late bloomer. Larkin is at his best when posing as the curious observer or when absent altogether. His self-effacement has been called smugness, though it might be seen as modesty. Davie's self-examination is not its opposite exactly, but more a search for humility, for atonement. But Davie is a Christian poet, and Larkin is not.

Existential anxiety is not present in "The Whitsun Weddings." Once Larkin boards his train on a hot Saturday afternoon at Whitsuntide, he feels "all sense / Of being in a hurry gone." The windows are down, the cushions are hot, but he pretty much has the car to himself, and after observing the urban landscape giving way to countryside as the train makes its way from Lincolnshire to London, he begins to read. The landscape is important to Larkin, especially as it retains its rural features and as they are lost or marred. Despite the poem's fame, stanza 2 is worth quoting entirely.

> All afternoon, through the tall heat that slept
>      For miles inland,
> A slow and stopping curve southwards we kept.
> Wide farms went by, short-shadowed cattle, and
> Canals with floatings of industrial froth;
> A hothouse flashed uniquely: hedges dipped
> And rose: and now and then a smell of grass
> Displaced the reek of buttoned carriage-cloth
> Until the next town, new and nondescript,
> Approached with acres of dismantled cars.

All of Larkin's strengths are present here, including his love of and doubts about pastoral England: his eye for the telling image—those cattle, that hothouse, those canals—his extraordinary gift for the simple yet perfect imagistic phrase, "the tall heat," and even his way of pointing to a poem's central intelligence, the annoyed reference to "the reek of buttoned carriage-cloth." Yet it is the little drama of the poem, beginning in the third stanza and continuing through the next six until the end, that requires an assessment of Larkin's particular, even peculiar temperament as a lyric poet. It requires one because, in this poem at least, none is offered by the poet himself.

Both American and British critics have noted Larkin's superior air in this poem. Blake Morrison in his book *The Movement* says that Larkin "seems to patronize as well as to pity" the working-class wedding parties he observes at each train depot. Merle Brown in an essay on Larkin's audience published in the *Iowa Review* in 1977 is downright censorious, but he puts his finger on the problem of how much the lyric poet can represent himself and others. Brown writes,

> In "The Whitsun Weddings" . . . Larkin takes on the sovereign privileges of . . . invisible, unnameable observing even though he also presents himself as a visible, existent, individual entity. He should have recognized that such a hybrid is inadmissible in poetry the likes of his. By bringing the act of attending into the scene, he has unknowingly committed an obscenity, in the sense that he has brought on stage what by its nature must occur offstage.

Strong stuff. But what Larkin has done in this poem is no more than what Tolstoy does in *War and Peace,* except that it violates our expectations of the first-person point of view, especially in a poem where we implicitly take that point of view to be the poet's himself.

What Larkin does is to presume to understand what is going on in the minds and hearts of the people he sees. Once he realizes the noise at each stop is not merely workers on the platforms but truly an event—the last weddings of the Whitsun week, portions of festivals that have marked the week for centuries—he is interested.

> Struck, I leant
> More promptly out next time, more curiously,
> And saw it all again in different terms.

Granted, the catalog of Larkinesque caricatures that follows is smugly satirical. On the platforms waving goodbye to the newlyweds are fathers with "seamy foreheads," "Mothers loud and fat," "An uncle shouting smut," and girls in their "parodies of fashion," including "jewellery-substitutes." Yet Larkin's eye is typically English, picking out as it does the limited expectations, the cheapness at the end of empire; what it sees has been a theme of British literature since World War II. But Larkin penetrates the phenomenon more deeply here, understanding it even as he seems to push it away, and to do this he assumes an omniscience based on shared experience. He observes that this event is witnessed in different ways, by children as "dull," by fathers as "Success . . . huge and wholly farcical," by the women as a "secret like a happy funeral," and by the girls themselves as "a religious wounding."

> Free at last,
> And loaded with the sum of all they saw,
> We hurried towards London . . .

Critics of this poem point out that Larkin either fails or refuses to see his place among the dozen marriages that have "got underway" on the train with him, and that he presumes even further to speak for them, when he notes,

>                    none
> Thought of the others they would never meet
> Or how their lives would all contain this hour.

Only he sees this coming together, "this frail / Travelling coincidence," where in fact he is the odd man out. Although we might express irritation with him, to censor him is to deny the emotional accuracy of the poem. His removal from the others, his difference from them, may have resulted in complacent self-regard, but it is not alienation. It does allow him to see the event whole, and his personal affection for it is related to his love for England itself. When he recognizes what is going on, his response is "Yes." This response is an affirmation, too. Larkin affirms the persistence of Whitsun festivities. He also affirms the weddings themselves with the blessing that ends the poem, when he imagines that, after the train stops, what it holds will continue on "like an arrow-shower / Sent out of sight, somewhere becoming rain." Finally, however we may object to the condescending tone of this, it is not an emotion that any of the other passengers—the newly-weds—would have had; rather, it is one felt for them.

**"In the Stopping Train"** may be the poem Larkin's critics are looking for in "The Whitsun Weddings." Davie's train passenger would enjoy Larkin's serene outward look, too, if he believed it would do any good. But Davie's rage is inward and is aimed precisely at what divides him from others, including himself. The rhythm of "The Whitsun Weddings" is unhurried. Its eight ten-line stanzas rhyme *ababcdecde;* five of the eight dovetail with the stanza following them; all but the second line of each stanza is in iambic pentameter; only that second line, in iambic dimeter, registers the jolt of the train's stopping and starting, if it is meant to imitate anything. Davie's poem, in ten unnumbered parts, with stanzas appearing as couplets, tercets, quatrains, does not flow smoothly from strophe to strophe over bright knots of rhyme like Larkin's. Instead, it reflects in its lurching, enjambed, trimeter lines not only the speaker's anguish but the train's frustrating stop and start. Davie's train trip is neither as comfortable nor as magisterial as Larkin's. It lacks, too, Larkin's sweeping way with a metaphor in which he can speak of well-wishers left behind on boarding platforms

> As if out on the end of an event
> Waving goodbye
> To something that survived it.

But Davie's cramped, self-analytical ride does give us a narrative structure that exists as more than a route to an end. It is the mode by which the commonplace event—taking a train somewhere—is invested with the urgency to have understood oneself before the end of the journey. Davie's poem, then, has the greater symbolic and emotional resonance.

Part 1 of **"In the Stopping Train"** gets right to the matter, yet at the same time it begins probing for the heart of the poet's unhappiness.

> I have got into the slow train
> again. I made the mistake
> knowing what I was doing,
> knowing who had to be punished.
>
> I know who has to be punished:
> the man going mad inside me;
> whether I am fleeing
> from him or towards him.

The tone of puritanical self-loathing is quite clear, but is boarding this train "again" a recurrent error or, as he implies, a deliberate punishment? The self divided from the self has to be punished, in part, for his lack of charity.

> He abhors his fellows,
> especially children; let there
> not for pity's sake
> be a crying child in the carriage.
>
> So much for pity's sake.

This is the first of the bitterly humorous remarks made at the speaker's own expense throughout the poem. Is there a crying child on the carriage to which the "So much for pity's sake" has been directed? Or does the wish defeat any notion of pity, even that suggested by the expression "for pity's sake"? The fascination of this poem is the total lack of objectivity. No flowers will be observed, no architecture or landscapes will be noted simply for pleasure as in the Larkin poem. Instead, language about them will be analyzed.

> Jonquil is a sweet word.
> Is it a flowering bush?
> Let him helplessly wonder
> for hours if perhaps he's seen it.

Davie zeroes in on the culprit—it is the artist, the man going mad inside him with a self-involved passion, who "never needed to see, / not with his art to help him." It is this figure, too, who has hatreds and loves, though false. He is the passionate figure who, for reasons not yet clear aside from his selfishness, must be punished.

Meanwhile, he displays for us his various artistic and intellectual strengths as he tries to understand his situation. The play of language, of tones of voice, and of rhythm predominate in Davie's poem, whereas in Larkin's imagery and metaphor are foremost. Part 2 of **"In the Stopping Train"** contains the most moving of Davie's word-play; it is affecting because it touches on the larger symbolism of this ride.

> A stopping train, I thought,
> was a train that was going to stop.
> Why board it then, in the first place?
>
> Oh no, they explained, it is stopping
> and starting, stopping and starting.

Here, "they" are adults; the exchange recalls their voices. In this section there *is* a child in the carriage after all. Having understood the adult assurances, Davie says, "I saw the logic of that; / grown-ups were good at explaining." But the starting and the stopping of the train do not keep it from getting to the end of the line. As broad as the hint becomes here—"even expresses have to do that"—still, there is a power in this internal dialogue, this analysis of memory. The child Davie is not sure the adults understand his anxiety about riding such a train, and the adults show this by ending the conversation.

Well, they said, you'll learn
all about that when you're older.

Of course they learned it first.
Oh naturally, yes.

Is it mortality, then, that has been the source of the inner man's, the artist's madness? The resentful tone of the last lines is mitigated by one of resignation. This is one of the poem's quietest moments.

Davie shows a distinct temperament in part 3; that is, it is distinct from Larkin's ironic detachment. Regarding the reckless traffic on the highway that runs beside the train, the "passing and re-passing" of cars with "a recklessness like breeding," "he is shrieking silently: 'Rabbits!' "To follow this with the refrain "He abhors his fellows" may be seen as an understatement. Yet the British use of the rabbit, despite its cutesified transformation in *Watership Down,* is instructive. Larkin's "Myxomatosis," ostensibly about the disease spread to control the rabbit population in Britain after World War II, ends with lines that could be meant to indict an aspect of the British character,

> You may have thought things would come right again
> If you could only keep quite still and wait.

And there is in *The Wind in the Willows,* of all places, Kenneth Grahame's characterization of the rabbits who never wish to be involved, whose response is "*Do some-thing? Us rabbits?*" Davie's epithet here may carry these connotations, along with the angry one of the sterile condemning the mindlessly procreative. Yet, this dissonance is resolved.

> Yet even the meagre arts
> of television can
> restore them to him sometimes,
>
> when the man in uniform faces
> the unrelenting camera
> with a bewildered fierceness
> beside the burnt-out Simca.

Confronted by the record of urban, probably terrorist violence, in which "his fellows," individuals like those he has been cursing, have been victimized and the representative of order, "the man in uniform," must make sense for the masses watching, Davie is capable of what he claims to lack—pity, perhaps even charity.

Lest we be seduced by this harmonic moment, however, the splenetic voice returns in part 4, growling, "What's all this about flowers?" He observes that "Some people claim to love them." Here the poet is faced with the full power of a word's meaning and the need to justify it to his own intelligence.

> Love *them?* Love flowers? Love,
> love . . . the word is hopeless:
> gratitude, maybe, pity. . . .

> Pitiful, the flowers.

Again, as with the rueful "So much for pity's sake," the notion of pity being misaligned with its object has wit. But "love" is the most important word in the poem, the word the poem resolves on, its last word, in fact. These flowers are pitiful because they are merely words, or merely a word, and the poet "can name them all, / identify hardly any." The madness, the passion, and the spleen here are vented because of an inability or a refusal to apply to reality the names the poet has for it, including "love." Nominalists make for anxious Christians.

Part 5 is interesting for a number of reasons. First, though not the most important, is that in Davie's recent **Selected Poems**, it has been deleted from the poem. Second, and more important, it helps to characterize the speaker, to identify him more closely with Davie. It is subtitled "*Judith Wright, Australian.*" Why would this particular character be thinking about the Australian poet Judith Wright? It would be simple enough to say that, well, Donald Davie is the speaker and he thinks of quite a lot of things to do with English literature, especially contemporary sorts. Has Davie carefully created a fictional self or selves for this poem? We already know the character has a literary bent; here he is giving an opinion that appears first to be gratuitous but, on a closer look, is not. Our speaker is occupying his time with more than internal agony and outward grousing. He is writing or thinking about somebody else.

> Judith Wright, Australian,
> 'has become,' I said,
>
> 'the voice of her unhappy,
> still-to-be-guilty nation.'
>
> Wistfully I said it,
> there in the stopping train.

A literary man can be believed to be writing or thinking about a review, for example, as he takes even the most miserable of rides; after all, he has time, and there is the leisure to work on a train. The greater import here, however, is that Davie has recognized that a poet can be the voice of an entire nation. Though guilt is that nation's inheritance, he assigns Wright's voice to it wistfully, with a melancholy wish. Australia's history has been, though it is no longer, bound up in England's. England has had its voices, but the singular spokesman has faded along with empire. For whom today does the contemporary English poet speak? Here he speaks only for himself and his own guilt.

In part 6 the poem turns and the speaker faces himself.

> The things he has been spared . . .
> "Gross egotist!" Why don't
> his wife, his daughter, shrill
> that in his face?
>
> Love and pity seem
> the likeliest explanations;

another occurs to him—
despair too would be quiet.

These lines look back to the rumination of part 5 and ahead to those to come. What he has been spared is any concern for or obligation to anything besides his profession. Here "Love and pity" are introduced, although this time not as part of a witty self-satire, but as solemn recognitions of his family's indulgence. They are joined by another motive, in a play on Thoreau's famous observation, here personalized and all the more poignant. Our speaker himself is living a life not of quiet desperation but, if his inner turmoil is an indication, of noisy desperation. His self-disgust is partly with the ridiculous figure cut by the ranting inner man. Love, pity, and despair, in the form of those closest to him, regard his anguish sadly and quietly.

Part 7 is the most rhythmically compelling of the poem. At this point, rather than apologize, Davie rears up and justifies his professional activities in martial terms.

> Time and again he gave battle,
> furious, mostly effective;
> nobody counts the wear
> and tear of rebuttal.

He has not shrunk from controversy. He has even been proud of the stands he has taken, although there is some question about their lasting importance. Finally, playing on his favorite metaphor of poetry as sculpture, an art worked in a durable medium, he admits that his intellect and emotions have been "hardened" by his engagements. One can make a list of the many stands Davie has taken in his career, the areas of intellectual and artistic endeavor he has pronounced for—and against—and recognize this as an honest assessment of the man by the man himself. The phrase "Time and again" that begins each of the section's five quatrains and the rhymes in each stanza, rare in this poem, give the section its power. Yet the single most powerful stanza in the poem derives its strength from an apparent disruption.

> Time and again, oh time and
> that stopping train!
> Who knows when it comes to a stand,
> and will not start again.

Once more, the emblematic nature of this train is emphasized; the subject and the form could not be more closely welded.

Part 8 brings a change of tone, one that approaches the second stanza of "The Whitsun Weddings." As I have argued, there is a calmness, even a serenity, to Larkin's point of view that allows him to see the big picture, or what he imagines to be the big picture, without coming himself to any sort of intense self-realization. That is not his point, to be sure. Davie, on the other hand, shows us active and painful self-division. As he recognizes this state for what it is, he detaches himself from it so to speak, and in this section speaks more in Larkin's disinterested tone.

Part 8 is also subtitled, in parenthesis, "Son et Lumière." It is as if the window of the stuffy car were opened for a moment.

> I have travelled with him many times
> now. Already we nod,
> we are almost on speaking terms.
>
> Once I thought that he sketched
> an apologetic gesture
> at what we turned away from.

He describes how his traveling companion's glasses caught the light as he turned away, and comes to the following passage of deft, impressionistic landscape painting.

> I knew they had been ranging,
> paired eyes like mine,
> igniting and occluding
>
> coppice and crisp chateau,
> thatched corner, spray of leaf,
> curved street, a swell of furrows,
>
> where still the irrelevant vales
> were flowering, and the still
> silver rivers slid west.

This is called having your cake and eating it, too. Though the spectacles blind the viewer and though the vales are called "irrelevant," the self-laceration is missing here in words like "crisp," "thatched," "spray," "curved," "swell," "flowering," and "silver." The sounds are gorgeous and forgiving.

Perhaps they hint at a reconciliation not to occur in this poem. An intenser rhythm returns in part 9, albeit with a sprightliness that includes a recognition of the landscape's redemptive properties. Here, too, the play of voices is most apparent and effective. If for this character "words alone are certain good," then admitting this leads to a sort of acclamation of what our fellow can do—play with words.

> The dance of words
> is a circling prison, thought
> the passenger staring through
> the hot unmoving pane
> of boredom. It is not
> thank God a dancing pain,
> he thought, though it starts to jig
> now. (The train is moving.) "This,"
> he thought in rising panic
> (Sit down! Sit down!)
> "this much I can command,
> exclude. Dulled words, keep still!
> Be the inadequate, cloddish
> despair of me!" No good:
> they danced, as the smiling land
> fled past the pane, the pun's
> galvanized *tarantelle*.

This may be the most emotionally complicated section of the poem, since the dull words tie him to the earth ("cloddish"), tend to embarrass him as he grows excitable about their possibilities ("Sit down! Sit down!"), and bring on a "rising panic" with its connotations of terror and the power of Pan. The "dancing pain" becomes a "jig," and the words, despite Davie's demurral, do dance. The landscape smiles, and the hot boredom of the poet's self-examination gives way, as was hinted in the previous section, to a momentary forgiveness in which we can hear not only the immediate wordplay on pane/pain, but reverberations between those words and the words "pun," "panic," and the important initiating circumstance, "punishment." The punishing slow pace of this self-criticism has yielded, despite impending panic, to the play of words, yet still within the prison of language.

Davie is too much the puritan to let himself off on a gaudy note of consolation or to let his poem become a pastoral. The final part, its tenth, is at once the most varied tonally, the most self-revealing, and the most moving. The play becomes self-punishment again as Davie "pummels his temples."

> 'A shared humanity . . .'
> . . . 'Surely,
> surely that means something?'
> He knew too few in love,
> too few in love.
> That sort of foolish beard
> masks an uncertain mouth.
> And so it proved: he took
> some weird girl off to a weird
> commune, clutching at youth.
> Dear reader, this is not
> our chap, but another.
> Catch our clean-shaven hero
> tied up in such a knot?
> A cause of so much bother?
> He knew too few in love.

By the end of Larkin's poem, he knows many in love, e.g., all the newlyweds. But Davie knows, he claims, "too few." Yet detachment like Larkin's could hardly be ascribed to what Davie does know and has observed. In one of the most risky satiric caricatures I can imagine, Davie first skewers what appears to be a contemporary, perhaps the victim of a midlife crisis, "clutching at youth." Then he turns on himself and plays on the doubleness he has presented throughout the poem to emphasize that in no way are we to mistake "our chap" for "another."

> Catch our clean-shaven hero
> tied up in such a knot?
> A cause of so much bother?

What adds to the chill of this portrait is its echo of one in a similarly structured and similarly emotional poem, from Davie's *Events and Wisdoms,* **"After an Accident."**

> Death is about my age,
> Smiling and dark, clean-shaven.

The "shared humanity" that must mean something has been glossed in numerous ways throughout the poem, as

Davie responds to his possible carriage mates, to the remembered wisdom of grown-ups, to the traffic outside the train, to his wife and daughter, to the enviable position of Judith Wright who speaks for her nation, and to himself. Davie may not know what he means, but he does know how it feels to share the humanity of others, to be human. Larkin, on the other hand, does know what a shared humanity means, for others if not exactly for himself.

The most compelling and most ambiguous line in this section is the refrain, "He knew too few in love." Michael Schmidt has read it simply as "He loved too few people." That is the reading that makes the most sense. Yet there are subtler overtones that are compelling, too. In his knowledge of others there was not enough love. Of those he knew, too few were in love—even in love like the foolish bearded man with his weird girl. A commune might, indeed, be the sort of community Davie claims to know nothing of, a weird one as far as he can tell. The reproach implicit in this line is a Christian one. The Christian admonition, to love one's neighbor as oneself, comples Davie in many of his poems. No less does it here.

My distinction that Davie is a Christian poet and Larkin is not might seem strange only because the occasion of Larkin's poem is a Christian holiday. Yet Larkin's interest is in what characterizes the object of his affection; this has little to do with Christianity. In his most famous poem, "Church Going," he affirms the perpetuation of custom much as he does in "Show Saturday"—"Let it always be there." This is his theme in "The Whitsun Weddings" as well. Davie's concerns as a Christian are the salvation of his soul and the fellowship of his fellowmen. It makes sense that as a Christian poet he would be distressed by the self's interference with these aims, especially as it uses language to obstruct them. Furthermore, it follows that he would find the lyric insufficient to express the obligations of a modern poet. **"In the Stopping Train"** tests the limits of the form, whereas "The Whitsun Weddings" goes beyond the form inadvertently and, perhaps, dubiously. What is tantalizing is to imagine a form in which the achievements of both poems—the intensity of self-revelation and the understanding of the experience of others—are shared.

---

# FURTHER READING

### Criticism

Bateson, F. W. "The Analysis of Poetic Texts: Owen's 'Futility' and Davie's 'The Garden Party'." *Essays in Criticism* 29, No. 2 (April 1979): 156-64.
    Compares stylistic aspects of Wilfred Owen's "Futility" and Davie's "The Garden Party."

Bedient, Calvin. "On Donald Davie." *The Iowa Review* 2, No. 2 (Spring 1971): 66-88.

Discusses the defining characteristics of Davie's verse.

Bell, Vereen and Laurence Lerner, eds. *On Modern Poetry: Essays Presented to Donald Davie*. Nashville: Vanderbilt University Press, 1988, 256 p.
    Collection of critical essays on Davie's poetry and literary criticism.

Dekker, George. "Donald Davie: New and Divergent Lines in English Poetry." *Agenda* 14, No. 2 (Summer 1976): 45-57.
    Considers the role of England in Davie's *The Shires* and compares his work to that of another English poet, Philip Larkin.

Dodsworth, Martin. "Donald Davie." *Agenda* 14, No. 2 (Summer 1976): 15-22.
    Traces the development of Davie's verse.

Powell, Neil. "Donald Davie: Dissentient Voice." In *British Poetry Since 1970: A Critical Survey*, edited by Peter Jones and Michael Schmidt, pp. 39-45. New York: Persea Books, 1980.
    Assesses Davie's literary reputation.

Pritchard, William A. "Donald Davie's Poetry." *Poetry* CXXII, No. 5 (August 1973): 289-93.
    Positive review of Davie's *Collected Poems 1950-1970*.

Reed, John R. "Reflexive Poetry: The Winter Talent of Donald Davie." *Western Humanities Review* XIX, No. 1 (Winter 1965): 43-54.
    Contends that Davie "does not merely talk about his own poetry, he presents, in the poetic examination of his own talent, the self-discipline that engenders the poems."

Schmidt, Michael. "The Poetry of Donald Davie." *Critical Quarterly* 15, No. 1 (Spring 1973): 81-8.
    Provides a thematic and stylistic overview of Davie's verse.

Tinkler-Villani, Valeria. "The Poetry of Hell and the Poetry of Paradise: Food for Thought for Translators, Critics, Poets and Other Readers." *Bulletin of the John Rylands University Library of Manchester* 76, No. 1 (Spring 1994): 75-92.
    Analyzes the treatment of Dante in Davie's "Summer Lightning."

# Li Po
## 701-762

(Also transliterated as Li Bo, Li Bai, and Li T'ai Po) Chinese poet.

## INTRODUCTION

Li Po is hailed as one of China's two greatest poets; it is said that he and his T'ang dynasty contemporary Tu Fu together in their poetry cover the whole range of human nature. A rebel and wanderer, Li Po was as much known for his fondness for wine and revelry as for his love of nature and unrestrainedly spirited verses. His boldness and originality come from his capacity to elevate traditional themes and forms to their highest level with unparalleled grace and eloquence. His poems are characterized by an immediacy and spontaneity of feeling, a childlike wonder and playfulness, and a facility for language. Li Po is perhaps best known for his dream poems, many of which invoke subtle Taoist images and powerful emotions of fear and exhilaration. In many of these pieces he promotes the idea that he would rather forget than confront reality, and there emerges from them a picture of a wild, Bohemian artist unfettered by convention. It is generally agreed that, with Tu Fu, Li Po raised the *shih* or lyric form to a height of power and expressiveness that has not since been surpassed in Chinese poetry.

## BIOGRAPHICAL INFORMATION

Most sources agree that Li Po was born around 701 in the far west of China and probably had some knowledge of Central Asian languages and cultures. It is said he was a precocious child and by the age of ten could read the Chinese classics and histories; by the time he was fourteen he was known for his poetical genius. In his youth he also showed an interest in meditation and went to study for a time with the Taoist Master of the Eastern Cliff. As a young man, Li Po, a skilled swordsman, moved to the Szechwan capital to serve the emperor, but his free spiritedness—or unruliness—made him a poor candidate for courtly life. He then began a life of adventure, wandering about the country writing, studying, and drinking. Around 727 he married the daughter of a retired prime minister at An-lu in Hupei, where he stayed for several years. In 742 in Ch'ang An, Li Po was admitted to the court of Emperor Hsüan-tsung and appointed as a member of the newly founded Hanlin Academy. The emperor was said to have delighted in Li Po's genius and literary productions as well as his capacity for wine and love of revelry, and Li Po soon became a court favorite. He wrote some of his

most famous poems or songs for imperial occasions and festivities. During his time in Ch'ang An, Li Po also became interested in the science of alchemy. In 744 he fell out of favor with the emperor and returned to his life of wandering. Around 744, Li Po met Tu Fu in the eastern capital of Loyang. Tu Fu was as yet unknown as a poet, while Li Po's renown was already considerable. The two poets became friends, and over the course of their careers would write poems in each other's honor. In 745, Li Po was initiated into the Taoist religion, and shortly thereafter began his journeys to northern and eastern China, which were to last for ten years. The poems of the next ten years show his growing interest in Taoism. In 755 Li Po moved to the Yangtze region, then in the throes of the An Lu-shan rebellion which was to topple the T'ang empire. He moved next to central China, where he was implicated in an anti-royalist uprising and subsequently banished to the remote southwest interior of the country. He eventually received amnesty and retraced his steps eastward, writing poetry and drinking in his usual fashion. The famous legend of his death in 762 says that while he was travelling in a boat in a state of drunkenness he saw the reflection of the moon in the water and attempted to embrace it, and drowned as a result.

## MAJOR WORKS

Over one thousand poems are attributed to Li Po. However, only a fraction of those have been rendered into English. The first volume devoted entirely to a selection of his work in English translation was Shigeyoshi Obata's *The Works of Li Po* in 1922. Arthur Waley's *The Poetry and Career of Li Po* (1950) combines translation with biography. David Hinton's 1996 *The Selected Poems of Li Po* offers the most comprehensive look in English at the work of the poet. Perhaps best known to Western readers is the poem translated by the modernist writer Ezra Pound under the title "The River Merchant's Wife: A Letter." To most readers educated in Chinese, Li Po's poems are exceedingly popular; many are routinely memorized by schoolchildren. His "Quiet Night Thoughts," in which he lies in bed and watches the bright moon, is perhaps the best known of all Chinese poems. Almost as familiar are his famous lines in an "Old Poem" describing the dream of the sage Chuang Tzu, who upon awakening remarked he did not know whether he had just dreamt he was a butterfly or if he was now a butterfly dreaming it was Chuang Tzu. Some of the more opaque poems in which Li Po uses more obscure Taoist imagery, however, are little known even among Chinese literature scholars. Critics note that most of Li Po's poetry is written in the ordinary verse forms of the day. His great contribution was to transform those forms into verse that was fresh, bold, and exhilarating. His poems are said to possess a river-like quality, with their gushing energy, tumbling fall, and majestic flow. Li Po seemed to have been most fond of the form of lyricism known as *ku-shih,* perhaps because its irregular line lengths allowed him the freedom to create a wild, rhapsodic effect. Some of his most translated works are from the important group of fifty-nine poems called "Old Poems" (or, literally, "Ancient Winds"). These poems most often have political, social, and philosophical themes and express his admiration for the excellent poetry of the past. Other themes that are distinctive in his poetry are Taoism, alchemy, the cosmos, romance, wine, the immortals and their world, and dreaming.

## CRITICAL RECEPTION

It has been said that no other major figure in world literature has been so little written about as Li Po. Part of the reason for this neglect may be that there is a tradition in Chinese literary scholarship of trying to understand a writer's work in relation to the circumstances in which it was written, and with Li Po there has been great difficulty in dating much of his work. That he is not the subject of extensive critical exegesis, however, in no way diminishes his importance to Chinese poetry in general. He was during his day regarded as a "Banished Immortal" because his verse was considered so sublime as to be the work of

an other-wordly being. Today he is ranked, with Tu Fu, as one of the two supreme poets of the Chinese language.

Scholarship in English on Li Po is scant. The earliest discussion in English seems to have been by Obata in the introduction to his translations of Li Po's poetry; these remarks are introductory and touch cursorily on the poet's life and major thematic interests. Waley's 1950 detailed study of Li Po's work and career sought to understand the poet in terms of his character. Waley paints an unsympathetic portrait of Li Po but provides illuminating insights into the poetry from an historical point of view. Most other examinations of Li Po's works in English have generally been in introductory notes to translations. The few more detailed critical pieces on Li Po's works have been concerned with the Taoist imagery employed in the poems, Li Po's originality of style and technique used within the bounds of traditional poetic structure, and the detailed craftsmanship and manipulation of conventional forms required to create poems that appear to be so "immediate" and spontaneous.

---

## PRINCIPAL WORKS

**Poetry**

*Cathay* 1915
*The Works of Li Po* 1922
*The Poetry and Career of Li Po* 1950
*Li Po and Tu Fu: Poems* 1973
*Li Po: A New Translation* 1982
*Poems* 1984
*The Selected Poems of Li Po* 1996

---

## CRITICISM

### Shigeyoshi Obata (essay date 1922)

SOURCE: "Introduction," in *The Works of Li Po, the Chinese Poet*, E. P. Dutton, 1922, pp. 1-22.

[*In the following introduction to the first volume of Li Po's work rendered into English, Obata offers details of the poet's life that informed his verse.*]

I

At the early dawn of medieval Europe China had reached the noontide of her civilization. Indeed, the three hundred years of the Tang dynasty beginning with the seventh century witnessed a most brilliant era of culture and refinement, unsurpassed in all the annals of the Middle King-dom. And the greatest of all the artistic attainments of this period was in literature, and particularly in poetry. There were no dramatists; no romancers; but only poets—and poets there were galore.

"In this age," remarks a native critic, "whoever was a man, was a poet." And this is not satire. The "Anthology of the Tang Dynasty" consists of nine hundred Books and contains more than forty-eight thousand nine hundred po-ems by no less than two thousand three hundred poets. Moreover, since this collection was compiled as late as the eighteenth century by order of a Manchu emperor, it rep-resents only a meager crop from a field that had suffered the ruthless ravages of time for fully a thousand years. Imagine, then, the vast efflorescence of what must have been veritably a tropic jungle of poesy!

Now a person may consider it no distinction to be counted one among these poets when the list is so large; but to be picked out as the greatest of them all—as the leader of this colossal army of immortals, is certainly a singular dis-tinction and honor. And this honor falls to Li Po. He, by almost unanimous consent, is regarded as the greatest poet under the Tangs, and of China of all times. "He is the lofty peak of Tai," proclaims an admirer, "towering above ten thousand mountains and hills; he is the sun in whose pres-ence a million stars of heaven lose their scintillating splen-dor."

Before attempting to follow the poet's career in detail, let us take a glance at China as it was under the Tang dy-nasty, especially under the famous emperor Hsuan Tsung, who was one time patron to Li Po, and whose long and il-lustrious reign, ending with his tragic fall, marks the golden age of Chinese poetry.

## II

The Tangs came to power in the early decades of the sev-enth century when Mahomet was just starting out on his first campaigns. Tai Tsung, the second emperor of the dy-nasty, in the twenty-three years of his reign (627-650) con-solidated the hostile sections of the country and laid a firm foundation for his empire, which he greatly expanded by conquering Tibet and subduing the Tartar tribes of the Mongolian desert. Wu Hu—an empress (684-704)—has been much maligned for usurping the male prerogative of sovereignty; but she was undoubtedly one of China's ablest rulers and did more than uphold the prestige of her land during the last quarter of the century. Then followed shortly Hsüan Tsung, who ascended the dragon throne in 713 and ruled for forty-two years.

It was an age of great political power for China. Her su-zeraignty extended from Siberia to the Himalaya mountain range, and from Korea to the Caspian Sea. Tributes were paid by India and Tonkin. The Caliphs of Medina sent pre-cious stones, horses, and spice. From the Japanese capital, Nara, came envoys and students at frequent intervals, while

once, in 643, from far Greece Emperor Theodosius des-patched a mission to the court of Cathay.

It was an age of prosperity. The fertile valleys of the Yel-low River and the Yangtze-kiang were turned into fields of rice, barley and waving corn, amid gleaming streams and lakes. Peace reigned in China proper—the vast domain that had once been torn up and made desolate by interne-cine wars during the four centuries of the *Three Kingdoms* and the *Six Dynasties*. Even in the remotest rural district, the *wine-pennant,* a tavern sign, was seen flying on the roadside, denoting the presence of tranquillity and good cheer, while large cities like Lo-yang (i.e. Honan-fu, Honan) and Chin-ling (i.e. Nanking, Kiansu) flourished immensely with increasing trade and travel.

Chang-an, the present city of Hsian-fu in Shensi, was the capital and the wonder of the age. The city was never so rich, splendid, and spendthrift. "See ye," proudly sings a poet, "the splendor of the imperial abode, and know the majesty of the Son of Heaven!" Beside the main castle with its nine-fold gates, there were thirty-six imperial pal-aces that reared over the city their resplendent towers and pillars of gold, while innumerable mansions and villas of noblemen vied with one another in magnificence. By day the broad avenues were thronged with motley crowds of townfolk, gallants on horseback, and mandarin cars drawn by yokes of black oxen. And there were countless houses of pleasure, which opened their doors by night, and which abounded in song, dance, wine and pretty women with faces like the moon.

It was also an age of religious proselytism. Buddhism had been in China for centuries before the Tang dynasty, and the country was dotted with monasteries and pagodas. It was in the reign of Tai Tsung that Yuen Tsang, a Buddhist priest, made his famous pilgrimage to India and brought back several hundred volumes of Sanscrit sutras. While Confucianism remained ostensibly the guiding principle of state and social morality, Taoism had gathered a rich in-crustation of mythology and superstition and was fast win-ning a following of both the court and the common people. Laotzu, the founder of the religion, was claimed by the reigning dynasty as its remote progenitor and was honored with an imperial title. In 636 the Nestorian missionaries were allowed to settle in Chang-an and erect their church. They were followed by Zoroastrians, and even Saracens who entered the Chinese capital with their sword in sheath.

Thus Chang-an became not only the center of religious proselytism, but also a great cosmopolitan city where Syr-ians, Arabs, Persians, Tartars, Tibetans, Koreans, Japanese and Tonkinese and other peoples of widely divergent races and faiths lived side by side, presenting a remarkable con-trast to the ferocious religious and racial strife then pre-vailing in Europe. Again, in Chang-an there were colleges of various grades, beside special institutes for caligraphy, arithmetic and music. Astronomy was encouraged by Tai Tsung, who also filled the imperial library with more than two hundred thousand books. Hsuan Tsung saw to it that there was a school in every village in the fifteen provinces of his empire.

Hsuan Tsung himself was regarded as a perfect prince, wise and valiant, a sportsman accomplished in all knightly exercises and a master of all elegant arts. Being a musician, he established in his palace an operatic school, called the "Pear Garden," at which both male and female actors were trained, and in which historians find the prototype of the modern Chinese drama. The emperor surrounded himself with a brilliant court of poets, artists, and beautiful women. Odes were offered him by Li Po and Tu Fu; Li Kuei-nien sang at his bidding, while Yang Kuei-fei, the loveliest of the three thousand palace ladies, ever accompanied his palanquin. Although in his latter years he indulged in all sorts of extravagant revelry, he was never vulgar. It is fitting that he is still remembered by the name of *Ming Huang*—the "Illustrious Sovereign."

But in order to complete the picture of this era there is a darker side, which really brought into full play the spiritual energies of the Chinese race. Within, the court, from the very beginning of the dynasty, was upset more than once by the bloody intrigues of princes and princesses who coveted the imperial crown. Without, China had her Vandals and Goths and Franks, to whom her wealth and splendor offered irresistible temptation to pillage. The border warfare never ceased, and not without many a serious reverse for the imperial forces, which made forays in retaliation, often far into the hostile territories, losing their men by thousands. Tai Tsung's Korean expedition was nothing but a gigantic fiasco, and the conquest of that peninsula was completed by generals of the Empress, Wu Hū. But in her reign the Kitans, a redoubtable foe, appeared on the northern border. In the west the restive and warlike Tibetans could not be wholly pacified by political marriages, in which the imperial princesses were bestowed on the barbarian chieftains from time to time. The armies of Hsuan Tsung were most unfortunate. In 751 thirty thousand men perished in the desert of Gobi; while in the campaigns in Yunnan against the southern barbarians the Chinese lost, it is said, two hundred thousand men. Finally came the rebellion of An Lu-shan, which like a storm swept the mid-imperial plains, drenched them in blood, and left the empire tottering on the brink of ruin.

An Lu-shan was a soldier of the Kitan race, who distinguished himself in fighting against his own tribes, and who won the favor of Yang Kuei-fei and the confidence of Hsuan Tsung. His promotion was rapid. He was ennobled as a duke, and made the governor of the border provinces of the north, where he held under command the best armies of the empire and nursed an inordinate ambition, biding his time. Meanwhile at the court, the blind love of Hsuan Tsung for Yang Kuei-fei was corrupting the government. Her brother Yang Kuo-chung was appointed prime-minister, while eunuchs held high offices of state. At last in the spring of 755, An Lu-shan, under the pretext of ridding the court of Yang Kuo-chung, raised the standard of rebellion. He quickly captured the city of Lo-yang, occupied the entire territory north of the Yellow River, comprising the provinces of Shansi and Chili, and was soon marching eastward on Chang-an. He had proclaimed himself the Emperor of the Great Yen dynasty.

"Is it possible!" exclaimed Hsuan Tsung, now an aged monarch, in amazement at the ingratitude of his vassal and at the impending catastrophe. The defense at the Pass of Tung Kwan collapsed. The emperor was forced to flee from the capital one rainy morning, with his favorite mistress and a handful of his faithful servants. The soldiers escorting Hsuan Tsung blamed Yang Kuo-chung for the disaster, and he and all his kin were massacred. Yang Kuei-fei herself did not escape. She was ruthlessly snatched from the arms of her imperial lover, and was strangled and buried on the roadside without ceremony. The emperor abdicated in favor of his son, and proceeded mournfully to Ssuchuan, the land of Shuh.

The new emperor, Su Tsung, mustered a strong army under General Kuo Tsu-i to oppose the foes. Confusion was added by the revolt of Prince Ling, the sixteenth son of Hsuan Tsung, who challenged the authority of his brother from his stronghold in the southern provinces, though this uprising was promptly suppressed. An Lu-shan was driven from Chang-an in 757, and was shortly murdered by his own son, who was in turn killed by An Lu-shan's general, Shi Ssu-ming, another Kitan Tartar, who assumed the imperial title and retained the northern provinces in his iron grip. But Shi Ssu-ming himself was soon assassinated by his son, and the rebellion came finally to an end in 762. We need not follow the history longer. In that very year the former emperor, Hsuan Tsung, who had returned from exile to a lonely palace in Chang-an, died, broken-hearted.

Such was the era. It had, on the one hand, internal peace, prosperity, cosmopolitan culture, profuse hospitalities and literary patronage; on the other, distant wars, court intrigues and, finally, the national catastrophe with its tragic drama of stupendous magnitude, that brought forth Li Po and his race of poets, kindled their imagination, and touched their heart-strings to immortal song.

## III

The ancestry of Li Po is traced back through the obscurity of many generations to Li Kao of the fifth century, who ruled the Liang State, or the western portion of what is now the province of Kansu. The family dwelt in exile for a period in the Mongolian desert land. The poet himself writes of his being "Originally a cotten-clothed of Lunhsi." That is to say, he was a plain citizen of a district in Kansu. But he was born, according to best authorities, in the adjoining land of Shuh, or the present Ssuchuan—that picturesque western province of mountains and tumbling waters which flow into the great Yangtze-kiang.

As to the year of his birth, biographers again differ. Some maintain it to have been as early as 699, while others would have it as late as 705, with consequent variation in his age, since he died, as all agree, in the year 762. A biographical calendar, compiled by Sieh Chung-yung of the Sung dynasty, places the poet's birth in the second year of the Shen-lung era; while another calendar by Wang-chi of the Ming dynasty, who edited the complete works of Li

Po, fixes the year as the first of the Chang-an era. All evidence seems to favor the latter date, which falls in the year of 701.

On the night of the poet's birth his mother dreamed of the planet of Chang-keng, which is Venus, and which is popularly known in China as the *Tai-po Hsing,* meaning literally the *Great White Star.* Thus it was that he was named Po (the *White* One), and surnamed Tai-po (the *Great White* One). Later he dubbed himself the Green Lotus Man, borrowing the name from a Buddhist saint; and sometimes went by the self-evident designation of the "Old Wine Genius."

When a boy of six Li Po could read, and by the age of ten he had mastered the Confucian books of the *Odes* and the *History* and miscellaneous classics by a hundred writers, and was composing poems of his own. While he was still in his teens, he retired with a recluse by the name of Tunyen-tzu to the mountain of Min in northern Ssuchuan. Here the two men kept strange birds as pets and succeeded in taming them to feed from their hands, the report of which brought to their hermitage the local magistrate, who invited them to enter the government service. But they declined. Our young poet sang contentedly:

> For twenty springs I've lain among the clouds,
> Loving leisure and enamored of the hills.

In 721 he traveled down the Yangtze to Yun-meng, the land of seven moors, that lies to the north of the river and the Tung-ting Lake; here he was married to a granddaughter of a certain ex-minister Hsu, and stayed there for three years.

Then he moved up north to Shantung, and made his home in Jen-cheng and elsewhere. "I am thirty," he wrote to a friend, "I make verses without tiring, while in front of my house carts and horses go by." Years passed without any visible achievement. One cannot blame too harshly his first wife who, impatient of the lack of his promotion, left him with the children. It was during this period that he became one of the "Six Idlers of the Bamboo Valley" who gathered in the mountain of Chu-lai for the jolly fellowship of wine and song. He traveled extensively, too. Once he was in the city of Lo-yang, enjoying the lavish hospitality of Tung Tsas-chiu, who had a special wine house built for the poet at the Tien-tsin bridge-head, where

> Songs were bought with yellow gold, and laughter
> with white white jewels

Later the same host invited the poet to Ping-chou near Taiyuan-fu in Shansi, where Tung's father was stationed as the military commander. Here the two companions went on happy excursions, taking singing-girls out on the river by the dynastic shrine of Chin. It was in Ping-chou that the poet befriended Kuo Tsu-i, who was still a young soldier in the ranks, but who was later to become the savior of the empire as well as of the poet's life. In the year 738 Li Po was back in Shantung when Tu Fu, his one great

and formidable rival in poetic fame, arrived in the province and met him. At once a warm friendship and exchange of poems began that lasted lifelong, and that makes the happiest and most memorable chapter in China's literary history. Tu Fu was the younger of the two. They slept together under one coverlet (so he tells us in one of his poems), and went hand in hand like two brothers.

Li Po traveled south to the lands of Wu and Yueh of old to wander amid the ruins of once glorious palaces and among the lakes of lotus lilies, and chose to sojourn in a district called Yen, in Chehkiang, famous for the beauty of its hills and valleys. Here he met Wu Yun, scholar and Taoist, who on being summoned to court took Li Po with him to Chang-an, the capital of the empire.

It was about the year 742 that Li Po entered Chang-an, the golden metropolis, when the long prosperous years of the Tien-pao era had just begun, and the court of Hsuan Tsung had reached the pinnacle of brilliance. Li Po went to see Ho Chi-chang, a guest of the crown prince, and showed his poems. The jovial courtier was so pleased that he bartered his gold ornament for wine and entertained the new-comer. Moreover, he commended the poet to the emperor. "I have in my house," he said, "probably the greatest poet that ever existed. I have not dared to speak of him to your Majesty because of his one defect, which is rather difficult to correct: he drinks, and drinks sometimes to excess. But his poems are beautiful. Judge them for yourself, sire!" So saying, he thrust in Hsuan Tsung's hand a bundle of manuscript. "Fetch me the author of these poems!" spoke the emperor instantly—so runs one story.

But according to other versions it was Wu Yun, or Princess Yu-chen, who introduced Li Po to the court. At any rate, the poet was given an audience in the Hall of Gold Bells. His discourse and ode at once won the admiration of the emperor, so that he feasted the poet at the Table of the Seven Jewels and assigned him to the Han-ling Academy. That is, Li Po was placed under imperial patronage, without any special duties but to write occasional poems, of which the ninth piece in the present book is an example.

He banqueted with lords and ladies in and out of the court, and sought frequently the taverns of the city. But who were his boon companions? A vivid portrayal of that much celebrated company, the "Eight Immortals of the Winecup," whose revels were the talk of Chang-an, is happily preserved for us in an equally celebrated poem by Tu Fu.

> *Chi-chang* rides his horse, but reels
>     As on a reeling ship.
> Should he, blear-eyed, tumble into a well,
>     He would lie in the bottom, fast asleep.
> *Ju-yang Prince* must have three jugfuls
>     Ere he goes up to court.
> How copiously his royal mouth waters
>     As a brewer's cart passes by!
> It's a pity, he mournfully admits,
>     That he is not the lord of Wine Spring.

Our minister *Li* squanders at the rate
    Of ten thousand *tsen* per day;
He inhales like a great whale,
    Gulping one hundred rivers;
And with a cup in his hand insists,
    He loves the *Sage* and avoids the Wise.
*Tsung-chi* a handsome youth, fastidious,
    Disdains the rabble,
But turns his gaze toward the blue heaven,
    Holding his beloved bowl.
Radiant is he like a tree of jade,
    That stands against the breeze.
*Su Chin,* the religious, cleanses his soul
    Before his painted Buddha.
But his long rites must needs be interrupted
    As oft he loves to go on a spree.
As for *Li Po,* give him a jugful,
    He will write one hundred poems.
He drowses in a wine-shop
    On a city street of Chang-an;
And though his sovereign calls,
    He will not board the imperial barge.
"Please your Majesty," says he,
    "I am a god of wine."
*Chang Hsu* is a caligrapher of renown,
    Three cups makes him the master.
He throws off his cap, baring his pate
    Unceremoniously before princes,
And wields his inspired brush, and lo!
    Wreaths of cloud roll on the paper.
*Chao Sui,* another immortal, elate
    After full five jugfuls,
Is eloquent of heroic speech—
    The wonder of all the feasting hall.

One day in spring Hsuan Tsung with Lady Yang Kuei-fei held a royal feast in the Pavilion of Aloes. The tree-peonies of the garden, newly imported from India, were in full flower as if in rivalry of beauty with the emperor's voluptuous mistress. There were the musicians of the Pear Garden and the wine of grapes from Hsi-liang. Li Po was summoned, for only his art could capture for eternity the glory of the vanishing hours. But when brought to the imperial presence, the poet was drunk. Court attendants threw cold water on his face and handed him a writing brush. Whereupon he improvised those three beautiful songs in rapturous praise of Yang Kuei-fei, which were sung by the famous vocalist, Li Kuei-nien, while the emperor himself played the tune on a flute of jade.

But it was one of these very songs, according to a widely accepted tradition, that helped cut short the gay and prodigal career of the poet at the court. Kao Lishih, the powerful eunuch, who had been greatly humiliated by having been ordered to pull off Li Po's shoes once as the latter became drunk at the palace, persuaded Yang Kuei-fei that the poet had intended a malicious satire in his poem by comparing her with Lady Flying Swallow, who was a famous court beauty of the Han dynasty, but who was unfaithful and never attained the rank of empress. This was enough to turn gratitude to venomous hate, and Yang Kuei-fei interfered whenever the emperor sought to appoint the poet to office. There is another tradition that Li Po in-

curred the displeasure of Hsuan Tsung through the intrigue of a fellow courtier. This story is also plausible. Li Po was not the sort of man fitted for the highly artificial life of the court, where extreme urbanity, tact and dissimulation, were essential to success. He soon expressed a desire to return to the mountains; and the emperor presented him with a purse and allowed him to depart. He was then forty-five years old, and had sojourned in the capital for three years.

Once more Li Po took to the roads. He wandered about the country for ten years, "now sailing one thousand *li* in a day, now tarrying a whole year at a place, enjoying the beauty thereof." He went up northeast to Chinan-fu of Shantung to receive the Taoist diploma from the "high heavenly priest of Pei-hai." He journeyed south and met Tsui Tsung-chi, the handsome Immortal of the Wine-cup, who had been banished from the capitol and was an official at the city of Nanking. The old friendship was renewed, and withal the glad old time. It is related that one moonlight night they took a river journey down the Yangtze from Tsai-hsi to Nanking, during which Li Po arrayed himself in palace robes and sat in the boat, laughing aloud, and rolling his frenzied eyes. Was it the laughter of wanton revelry, or of self-derision, or of haughty scorn at the foolish world that could not fathom his soul? In 754 Wei Hao, a young friend of his, came to meet him at Kuang-ling, Kiangsu Province, and traveled with him a while. To him Li Po entrusted a bundle of his poems, saying, "Pray remember your old man! Surely in the future I'll acquire a great fame."

Next year, in March of 755, we discover him fleeing from the city of Lo-yang amid the confusion of the war of An Lu-shan, whose troops occupied the city and made the waters of the Lo River flow crimson with blood. The poet went down to the province of Chehkiang, and finally retired to the mountains of Luh near Kiu-kiang in Kiangsi Province. When Li Ling, the Prince of Yung, became the governor-general of the four provinces near the mouth of the Yangtze, Li Po joined his staff. But the subsequent revolt and the quick fall of the Prince in 757 lead to imprisonment of the poet at the city of Kiu-kiang, with a sentence of death hanging over him. On examination of the case officials were inclined to leniency. One of them, Sung Ssu-jo, recommended the emperor not only to pardon Li Po but to give him a high place in the government service. But the memorial, which by the way had been written by Li Po himself at Sung's direction, failed to reach its destination. Then Kuo Tsu-i, now a popular hero with his brilliant war record, came to the rescue; he petitioned that Li Po's life might be ransomed with his own rank and title. The white head of the poet was saved, and he was sentenced to perpetual banishment at Yeh-lang—the extreme southwest region of the empire covered by the present province of Yunnan.

He proceeded westward up the river leisurely. There seems to have been little pressure from the central government, certainly no inclination on the part of the poet, to expedite the journey. At Wu-chang he was welcomed by the local governor Wei, with whom he spent months and climbed the Yellow Crane House three times. Further up he encountered Chia-chi, his former companion at Chang-an, and Li Hua, a kinsman of his. These two had also been demoted and dismissed from the capital. The three luckless men now joined in a boat party more than once on the Tung-ting Lake under the clear autumn moon. That these were not so lugubrious affairs after all is attested by their poems. After such delays and digressions Li Po sailed up the Yangtze through the Three Gorges and arrived in Wushan, Ssuchuan, in 759, when amnesty was declared.

> It was as if warmth enlivened the frozen vale,
> And fire and flame had sprung from dead ashes.

The old poet started homeward, resting a while at Yo-chou and Chiang-hsia, and returning to Kiu-kiang again. He visited Nanking once more in 761; and next year went to live with his kinsman, Li Yang-ping, who was magistrate of Tang-tu, the present city of Taiping in Anhwei. Here in the same year he sickened and died.

A legend has it that Li Po was drowned in the river near Tsai-shih as he attempted, while drunken, to embrace the reflection of the moon in the water. This was further elaborated into a tale, which was translated by Théodore Pavie. This story, quoted by d'Hervey Saint Denys, is altogether too beautiful to omit. I retranslate the passage from the French:

> The moon that night was shining like day. Li Tai-po was supping on the river when all of a sudden there was heard in the mid-air a concert of harmonious voices, which sounded nearer and nearer to the boat. Then, the water rose in a great tumult, and lo! there appeared in front of Li Tai-po dolphins which stood on their tails, waving their fins, and two children of immortality carrying in their hands the banners to indicate the way. They had come in behalf of the lord of the heavens to invite the poet to return and resume his place in the celestial realm. His companions on the boat saw the poet depart, sitting on the back of a dolphin while the harmonious voices guided the cortége. . . . Soon they vanished altogether in the mist.

As to Li Po's family and domestic life the curiosity of the western mind has to go unsatisfied. The Chinese biographers never bother about such trivialities of a man's private affairs. The Old and the New Books of Tang are both totally silent. Only in his preface to the collection of the poet's works Wei Hao remarks:

> Po first married a Hsu and had a daughter and a son, who was called the Boy of the Bright Moon. The daughter died after her marriage. Po also took to wife a Liu. The Liu was divorced, and he next was united to a woman of Luh, by whom he had a child, named Po-li. He finally married a Sung.

Hsu, Liu, and Sung are all family names of the women who were successively married to Li Po. Of his several poems extant, addressed to his "wife," it is difficult to tell just which one is meant in each case. From a poem written to his children we learn that the girl's name was Ping-yang, and the son whom Wei Hao refers to by the unusual nickname of the "Boy of the Bright Moon," was called Po-chin. Of the third child, Po-li, mentioned by Wei Hao, there is no reference elsewhere. Po-chin died without having obtained any official appointment in 793. His one son wandered away from home; while his two daughters were married to peasants.

Although Li Po had expressed his desire of making the Green Hill at a short distance southeast of Taiping-fu his last resting place, he was buried at the "East Base" of the Dragon Hill. His kinsman, Li Hua, wrote the inscription on his tombstone. Twenty-nine years after the poet's death a governor of Tang-tu set up a monument. But by the second decade of the ninth century when another great poet, Po Chu-i, came to visit the grave, he found it in the grass of a fallow field. About the same time Fan Chuan-cheng, inspector of these districts, discovered the "burial mound three feet high, fast crumbling away"; he located the two grandaughters of Li Po among the peasantry, and on learning the true wish of the poet, removed the grave to the north side of the Green Hill and erected two monuments in January of 818.

### IV

The Old Book of Tang says that Li Po "possessed a superior talent, a great and tameless spirit, and fantastical ways of the transcendent mind." In modern terminology he was a romanticist.

Like Wordsworth he sought the solitude of hills and lakes. But he was a lover rather than a worshipper of Nature. He was "enamored of the hills," he says. To him the cloud-girt peak of Luh Shan, or the hollow glen of autumn, was not a temple but a home where he felt most at ease and free to do as he pleased—where he drank, sang, slept, and meditated. He spent a large part of his life out of doors, on the roads, among the flowering trees, and under the stars, writing his innumerable poems, which are the spontaneous utterances of his soul, responding, to the song of a mango bird or to the call of far waterfalls. And his intimate Nature-feeling gained him admission to a world other than ours, of which he writes:

> Why do I live among the green mountains?
> I laugh and answer not. My soul is serene.
> It dwells in another heaven and earth belonging to no man—
> The peach trees are in flower, and the water flows on
> . . .

Taoism with its early doctrine of inaction and with its later fanciful superstitions of celestial realms, and supernatural beings and of death-conquering herbs and pellets fascinated the poet. Confucian critics, eager to whitewash him of any serious Taoistic contamination, declare that he was simply playing with the new-fangled heresy. But there is no doubt as to his earnestness. "At fifteen," he writes, "I sought gods and goblins." The older he grew, the stronger became the hold of Taoism on his mind. In fact, the utilitarian principle of Confucian ethics was alien both to his temperament and to the circumstances of his life. The first thing he did after his dismissal from the court was to go to Chinan-fu and receive the Taoist diploma from the high priest of the sect, "wishing only (says Li Yang-ping) to return east to Peng-lai and with the winged men ride to the Scarlet hill of Immortality." Peng-lai is the paradisical land of the Taoist, somewhere in the eastern sea. The poetry of Li Po reflects the gleams of such visionary worlds. His "Dream of the Sky-land," rivaling *Kubla Khan* in its transcendent beauty and imaginative power, could not have been written but by Li Po, the Taoist. Even in superstition and opium there is more than a Confucian philosophy dreams of.

But mysticism and solitude filled only one half of the poet's life. For he loved dearly the town and tavern—so much so that he is censured again by moralists as having been sordid. Li Po not only took too hearty an interest in wine and women, but he was also scandalously frank in advertising his delight by singing their praise in sweet and alluring terms. In this respect Li Po, like so many of his associates, was a thorough Elizabethan. Had the Eight Immortals of the Wine-cup descended from their Chinese Elysium to the Mermaid Tavern, how happy they would have been with their doughty rivals in song, humor, wit, capacity for wine, and ardent and adventurous, if at times erratic, spirit!

Li Po "ate like a hungry tiger," says Wei Hao, who should know; while according to another authority, "his big voice could be heard in heaven." In his early youth he exhibited a swashbuckling propensity, took to errantry, and learned swordmanship, and even slashed several combatants with his cutlass.

"Though less than seven feet in height, I am strong enough to meet ten thousand men," he boasted. It is hardly necessary, however, to point out the rare and lovable personality of the poet, who made friends with everybody—lord or prince, Buddhist or Taoist, courtier or scholar, country gentlemen or town brewer; and addressed with the same affectionate regard alike the emperor in the palace and the poor singing-girl on the city street of Chang-an.

In his mature age Li Po, despite his natural inclination and temperament, cherished the normal Chinese ambition to serve the state in a high official capacity and try the empire-builder's art. It was with no small anticipation that he went to the court and discoursed on the affairs of the government before the emperor. But he was only allowed to write poems and cover his vexations with the cloak of dissipation. Later when amid the turmoil of the civil war he was called to join the powerful Prince of Yung, his aspirations revived, only to be smothered in the bitterness of defeat and banishment. The last few years of his life were pathetic. Broken in spirit and weary with the burden of sorrow and age, but with his patriotic fervor still burning in his heart, he watched with anxiety the sorry plight of his country.

In the middle of the night I sigh four or five times,
Worrying ever over the great empire's affairs.

The rebellion of An Lu-shan and its aftermath were not wholly quelled till the very year of the poet's death.

Then, there was the inevitable pessimism of the old world. The thought of the evanescence of all temporal things brought him solace for life's disappointments, and at the same time subdued his great tameless spirit. The Chinese race was already old at Li Po's time, with a retrospect of milleniums on whose broad expanse the dynasties of successive ages were like bubbles. What Shakespeare came to realize in his mellowed years about the "cloud-capt towers and gorgeous palaces," was an obsession that seized on Li Po early in life. Thus it is that a pensive mood pervades his poetry, and many of his Bacchanalian verses are tinged with melancholy. Even when he is singing exultantly at a banquet table, his saddest thought will out, saying "Hush, hush! All things pass with the waters of the east-flowing river."

### Arthur Waley (essay date 1950)

SOURCE: *The Poetry and Career of Li Po*, George Allen and Unwin, 1950, pp. 31-49.

[*In the following excerpt from his full-length study of Li Po's life and career, Waley examines a selection of verses from the poet's most productive years, most likely 745-753.*]

It will be convenient to discuss here the question of [Li Po's] four successive wives. Wei Hao tells us that by his first wife, Miss Hsü, he had a daughter and a son named Bright Moon Slave. This is a child-name and as Wei Hao does not give his adult name, Bright Moon Slave probably died young. The first wife also died young, and it was perhaps to give Li Po a change of scene after her death that his friend Yüan invited him to stay in the north in 735. He next married a Miss Liu, 'but they parted.' The word used probably implies that they parted by mutual consent, which was legally permissible. His third marriage was with 'a lady of Lu' (i.e. Shantung), whose name is unknown. By her he had a son named P'o-li, who is perhaps the same person as the son Li Pai-ch'in to whom Li Po himself refers in several poems and to whom he was deeply attached. In a poem written round about 750 and addressed to his 'two young children left to be looked after in eastern Lu,' he says:

> To the east of my upstairs drinking-room
>                         there grows
> A peach-tree whose leaves are brushed
>                         by the grey mist.
> That tree I planted with my own hand;
> I have not seen it for almost three years.
> The tree by now must be level with the room,
> And still I am no nearer to getting home.
> My lovely daughter whose name is P'ing-yang

Plucks the blossom, resting her weight on the tree.
She plucks the blossom, but cannot show it to me;
Her tears fall; they are like a flowing spring.
My little boy is called Pai-ch'in;
He is younger than she, but his shoulder
                                touches hers.
The two of them are walking underneath the tree;
There is no one to stroke their hair, to show
                                them love . . .

The poem was written from Nanking at a time when he had left his children at Sha-ch'iu, near the Tortoise Mountain, in southern Shantung, where presumably his wife's family lived. In another poem, written a few months later, he asks a Mr. Hsiao who is going from Nanking to Shantung to look up his family. 'They are living near Sha-ch'iu,' he says. 'I have seen nothing of them for three years and am very sad. If you go there you will easily recognize Pai-ch'in. He rides about in a little cart drawn by a white goat.'

Finally, to pursue Li's marriages to the end, we find him in 756 married to a Miss Tsung, a descendant of Tsung Ch'u-ko, a well-known statesman who, after three times being Chief Minister, finally became involved in a poisoning-plot and was executed in 710. It is probable that Li's last wife survived him.

His new friend Tu Fu who had a brother at Lin-i, not far from where Li Po was living, turned up in Shantung soon after Li Po settled there. Tu left in the autumn, on his way to try his luck for the second time in Ch'ang-an. There is a conventional poem of parting, in which Li Po says little more than 'Let us drink together to the dregs, for who knows when we shall meet again?,' and in a poem sent not long after Tu Fu's departure he complains that since his friend went away 'The wine of Lu does not make me drunk, the songs of Ch'i in vain repeat their appeal. My thoughts are of you and, like the river Wên, in a full flood I send them to join you in the south.' After that there are no more poems addressed to Tu Fu; but some fourteen poems written by Tu Fu during the coming dozen or so years were to Li Po or are about him—'On a winter's day thinking of Li Po,' 'On a spring day thinking of Li Po,' 'Dreaming of Li Po,' 'At the world's end, thinking of Li Po,' 'Twenty rhymes sent to Li Po,' 'A gift to Li Po,' and so on. Sometimes he complains of getting no news:

Those whom death parts manage to swallow
                                their tears;
Those whom life parts sigh and forever sigh.
'South of the River' is a sick and fevered land;
From you since your exile I have not any news.

Li Po did not stay long with his family in Shantung. The greater part of his time from 745 to 753 was spent in north-eastern Honan, between Kaifeng and Kweiteh, with occasional visits to Shantung and other parts of eastern China. [I have said elsewhere] that the *Exile's Letter* belongs to this time. I would hazard the guess that it was Li Po's great productive period and that most of the twenty

or thirty poems on which his fame rests were produced then. Thirteen of them at any rate are earlier than 754, for they figure in an anthology, the *Ho Yüeh Ying Ling Chi,* which consists of poems written between 714 and 753. Most of these thirteen famous poems are not otherwise datable. One or two of them have been mentioned already; I will now say something about the rest.

**'Fighting South of the Ramparts'** is written to an old tune, the original words of which I have translated in *Chinese Poems* (1946) p. 52.

Last year we were fighting at the source
                                of the Sang-kan;[1]
This year we are fighting on the Onion River[2]
                                road.
We have washed our swords in the surf of
                                Parthian seas;
We have pastured our horses among the snows
                                of the T'ien Shan,
The King's armies have grown grey and old
Fighting ten thousand leagues away from home.
The Huns have no trade but battle and carnage;
They have no fields or ploughlands,
But only wastes where white bones lie
                                among yellow sands.
Where the House of Ch'in built the great wall that
                                was to keep away the Tartars.
There, in its turn, the House of Han
                                lit beacons of war.
The beacons are always alight, fighting and
                                marching never stop.
Men die in the field, slashing sword to sword;
The horses of the conquered neigh piteously
                                to Heaven.
Crows and hawks peck for human guts,
Carry them in their beaks and hang them on
                                the branches of withered trees.
Captains and soldiers are smeared on the
                                bushes and grass;
The General schemed in vain.
Know therefore that the sword is a cursed thing
Which the wise man uses only if he must.[3]

In this poem Li Po no longer assumes that soldiers 'come home safe and sound after a hundred victories.' It may well have been written in 751, for in the summer of that year the Chinese suffered two great defeats, one at the Hsi-êrh River near Ta-li, in northern central Yünnan, and the other many thousand miles away on the Talas River in northern Turkestan. In Yünnan, where they were engaged in a punitive expedition against the Nan-chao kingdom, hastily levied untrained soldiers were used, many of whom succumbed to malaria. Of this campaign Li Po wrote that a tremendous call-up of soldiers suddenly happened when the country was supposed to be everywhere at peace:

In Heaven and Earth all was unity;
All was peaceful within the Four Seas.
'I should like to know what this levy means.'
The answer came, 'The troops they have
                                raised in Ch'u
Are to cross the Lü[4] by the end of the fifth month
And are then to march southward into Yünnan.'

They were frightened creatures, not fighting men;
In the hot climate the long marches were hard.

'Of a thousand that went hardly one came back,' he says later in the same poem. A few months afterwards, at the battle of Talas, the Chinese armies were caught between the forces of the Arabs and those of the Karluks, a Turkish tribe. Only a small remnant got back to Kucha. It may well be that Li Po had both these disastrous campaigns in mind when he wrote 'Fighting South of the Ramparts.'

**'The Parting'** is a ballad about the two queens Huang and Ying. They were the daughters of the legendary Emperor Yao, who gave them in marriage to Shun and abdicated in his favour. Shun's ministers conspired against him and set Yü the Great on the throne. A legend says that the spots on the bamboo-stems that grow on the Hsiang River were caused by the tears of the two queens.

> Long ago there were two queens called Huang
>            and Ying.
> They stood on the shores of the Hsiao-hsiang,
>            south of the Tung-t'ing Lake.
> Deep was their sorrow as the waters of the lake
>            that go down ten thousand leagues.
> Dark clouds blackened the sun, apes howled in
>            the mist and ghosts whistled in the rain.
> The queens said, 'Though we speak of it
>            we cannot mend it.
> High Heaven dares not shine on our loyalty;
> The thunder crashes and bellows its anger
> That while Yao and Shun are here they should
>            be crowning Yü.
> When a prince loses his servants, the dragon
>            turns into a minnow:
> When power goes to slaves mice change to tigers.
> Some say that Yao is shackled and hidden away,
> And that Shun has died in the fields.
> But the Nine Mountains of Deceit stand there
>            in a row,
> Each like each and which of them covers the
>            lonely bones
> Of the Double Eyed, our Master?'
> So the royal ladies wept, standing amid
>            yellow clouds,
> Their tears followed the wind and waves, that
>            never return.
> And while they wept they looked in the distance
>            and saw
> Tsang-wu, the deep mountain, and the queens
>            cried:
> 'The mountain of Tsang-wu shall fall and the
>            waters of the Hsiang shall cease
> Sooner than the marks of our tears shall fade,
>            that stain the bamboo-stems.'

The Chinese are fond of bird-fables. In the **'Sparrow Song'** an allegory on the danger of associating with the great, the sparrow is warned against flying in the wake of the kingfisher, which is snared for the sake of its bright feathers, and against nesting near the swallows in the ancient Palace at Soochow, which was burnt down when in 236 B.C. a night-watchman, holding up his torch to look at a swallow's nest, started a fire that spread to the whole building.

> When you fly abroad do not chase the halcyon
>            of Hainan,
> When you need a rest do not perch near the
>            swallows in the Palace of Wu.
> For fire may start in the Palace of Wu and
>            burn the swallows' nest;
> If you follow the halcyon of Hainan you will
>            fall into the fowler's net.
> Stay all alone, with your wings deep down
>            among the daisies of the field.
> Kestrel and kite still may come; nothing will
>            happen to *you!*

**'The Szechwan Road'** is an old song-theme; the original words are lost, but it was presumably a travellers' song, describing the difficulties and dangers of the mountain-road from Shensi to Szechwan. In the hands of at least one previous poet (Yin K'êng, who died about 565) it becomes a political allegory, the dangers of the road symbolizing the difficulties of a statesman's career. Before discussing whether Li Po's poem is an allegory or simply a rhapsodical description of a famous highway, I will attempt to translate it, with the proviso that the effect of the original depends on a splendour of language that is utterly impossible to reproduce in translation:

> Eheu! How dangerous, how high!
> It would be easier to climb to Heaven
> Than walk the Szechwan Road.
> Since Ts'an Ts'ung and Yü Fu ruled the land
> Forty-eight thousand years have gone by,
> And still from the kingdom of Shu to the
>            frontiers of Ch'in
> No human hearth was lit.
> To the west, starting from the great White
>            Mountain, it was said
> There was a bird-track that cut across to the
>            mountains of Szechwan;
> But the earth of the hill crumbled
>            and heroes[5] perished.
> So afterwards they made sky-ladders and hanging-
>            bridges.
> Above, high beacons of rock that turn back
>            the chariot of the sun;
> Below, whirling eddies that meet the clashing
>            torrent and turn it away.
> The crane's wing fails, the monkeys grow weary
>                              of such
> climbing.
> How the road curls in the Pass of Green Mud!
> With nine turns in a hundred steps
>            it twists up the hills.
> Clutching at Orion, passing the Well Star,
>            I look up and gasp;
> Then beating my breast sit and groan aloud.
> I fear I shall never return from my westward
>            wandering;
> The way is steep and the rocks cannot be climbed.
> Sometimes the voice of a bird calls
>            among the ancient trees—
> A male calling to its wife, up and down
>            through the woods;
> Sometimes a cuckoo sings to the moon,
>            weary of empty hills.
> It would be easier to climb to Heaven than

walk the Szechwan Road,
And those who hear the tale of it turn pale
with fear.
Between the hill-tops and the sky there is not
a cubit's space;
Withered pines hang leaning over precipitous walls.
Flying waterfalls and rolling torrents blend
their din,
Pounding the cliffs and circling the rocks they
thunder in a thousand valleys.
Alas, traveller, why did you come
to so fearful a place?
The Sword Gate is high and jagged,
If one man stood in the Pass he could hold it
against ten thousand.
At the sight of a stranger, the guardians of the Pass
leap on him like wolves.
In the day time one hides from ravening tigers,
in the night from long serpents
That sharpen their fangs and suck blood,
wreaking havoc among men.
They say the Damask City[6] is a pleasant place;
I had rather go quietly home.
For it is easier to climb to Heaven than to walk
the Szechwan Road.
I look over my shoulder, gazing to the West,
and heave a deep sigh.

It is usually said that Li Po wrote this poem in order to dissuade the Emperor from fleeing to Ch'êng-tu when An Lu-shan was threatening Ch'ang-an in 756. But as we have seen, it is included in an anthology collected in 753, so that this explanation is impossible to accept. Moreover, the poem itself does not fit such a hypothesis; the situation envisaged is that of some one who, having travelled part of the way to Ch'êng-tu, decides that the discomforts of the journey are intolerable and that he had better 'go home' at once. This seems to have little to do with the situation of the Emperor who had no 'home' to go to; for five days after he left Ch'ang-an, the city was occupied by the rebels. Nor does the poem read as though it were an allegory on the difficulties of political life in general. I cannot help suspecting that this enormously powerful and vivid piece of description served merely the slender purpose of excusing the poet on some occasion when having got as far as northern Szechwan he failed to go on to Ch'êng-tu, where friends or relations were expecting him.

The next poem in the collection, called **'Hardships of Travel,'** is written on a song-theme similar to the last:

The clear wine in my golden cup cost five
thousand a gallon;
The choice meats in my jade dish are worth
a myriad cash.
Yet I stop drinking and throw down my
chopsticks, I cannot bring myself to eat.
I draw my sword and gaze round with mind
darkened and confused.
I want to cross the Yellow River, but ice-blocks
bar my way;
I was going to climb Mount T'ai-hang when
snow filled the hills.
So I sat quietly dropping my hook, on the

banks of a grey stream.
Suddenly again I mounted a ship, dreaming
of the sun's horizon.
Oh the hardships of travel!
The hardships of travel and the many branchings
of the way,
Where are they now?
A steady wind breaks the waves, the time will
soon have come
When I shall hoist my cloudy sail and cross
the open sea.

Here Li Po turns the old song-theme to a mystic purpose. He has grown tired of his profligate existence as a spendthrift aristocrat. He looks round him and feels he must strike a blow to save his country from the dangers that beset it. But the time has not yet come, so he retires from the world and leads a life of calm seclusion. Suddenly he mounts the ship of Taoist mysticism, and the rest of the poem corresponds roughly to Emily Dickinson's

Past the houses, past the headlands
Into deep eternity.

The next poem, closely connected with the one that goes before, is the record of a dream. It is very long, and I will only translate part of it:

On through the night I flew,
High over the Mirror Lake.
The lake-moon cast my shadow on the waves
And travelled with me to the Stream of Shan.[7]
The lord Hsieh's[8] lodging-place was still there;
The green waters rippled, the cry of the apes was
shrill.
I shod my feet with the shoes of the lord Hsieh
And climbed to Heaven on a ladder
of dark clouds.
Half way up, I saw the unrisen sun
Hiding behind the sea,
And heard the Cock of Heaven crowing
in the sky.
By a thousand broken paths I twisted and
turned from crag to crag,
My eyes grew dim, I clutched at the rocks and
all was dark.
The roaring of bears and the crooning of
dragons echoed
Amid the stones and streams.
The darkness of deep woods made me afraid,
I trembled at the storeyed cliffs.
The clouds hung dark, as though they would
rain,
The air was dim with the spray of rushing waters.
Lightning flashed, thunder roared,
Peaks and ridges tottered and broke.
Suddenly the walls of the hollow where I stood
Sundered with a crash.
I looked down on a bottomless void of blue,
Where the sun and moon gleamed on a terrace
of silver and gold.
A host of beings descended,
Cloud-spirits whose coats were of rainbow
And the horses they rode on were the winds . . .

The **Exile's Letter** I have translated [elsewhere]. . . .
Then comes a poem that needs a little explanation, for it is

based on a passage in the Taoist work *Chuang Tzu:* 'Once Chuang Chou dreamt that he was a butterfly. He did not know that he had ever been anything but a butterfly and was content to hover from flower to flower. Suddenly he woke and found to his surprise that he was Chuang Chou. But it was hard to be sure whether he really was Chuang Chou and had only dreamt that he was a butterfly or was really a butterfly, and was only dreaming that he was Chuang Chou.' The poem alludes to two other stories. The fairy Ma-ku said that since she came to Fairyland (P'êng-lai) the sea that surrounded it had become much shallower. It was well on its way to becoming dry land. Finally, the Marquis of Tung-ling, a great figure under the Ch'in dynasty, after the Han overthrew the Ch'in, was found resignedly growing melons on a patch of waste ground outside the Green Gate at Ch'ang-an. Here is the poem:

> When Chuang Chou dreamed he was a butterfly
> The butterfly became Chuang Chou.
> If single creatures can thus suffer change,
> Surely the whole world must be in flux?
> What wonder then if the ocean of P'êng-lai
> Should dwindle into a clear, shallow stream
> Or the man who plants melons at the Green Gate
> Should once have been the Marquis of Tung-ling?
> If wealth and honour indeed be flighty as this
> By our toiling and moiling what is it that we seek?

The next poem is simply a polite note of thanks to a clerk employed at the local prefecture, who had brought round to Li Po's inn two fish and two gallons of wine:

> The wine of Lu is like amber, the fish of Wên River
> Have scales of dark brocade. Noble the spirit
> Of these generous clerks in the province of
>                           Shan-tung.[9]
> With your own hands you brought these things
>                 as a present to a stranger from afar.
> We have found much to agree about and feel
>                       regard for one another.
> The gallons of wine, these two fish are tokens of
>                           deep feeling.
> See how their gills suck and puff, their fins
>                           expand
> Lashing against the silver dish, as though they
>                       would fly away.
> I call the boy to clean the board, to wield
>                       the frosty blade.
> The red entrails fall like flowers, the white
>                   flesh like snow.
> Reeling I fix my golden saddle, mount and ride
>                       for home.

**'Answering a layman's question'** (I give the title as it stands in the anthology) like most short lyric poems is particularly hard to translate satisfactorily. Here is at any rate the meaning of this famous quatrain:

> You asked me what my reason is for lodging in
>                 the grey hills;
> I smiled but made no reply, for my thoughts
>                   were idling on their own;
> Like the flowers of the peach-tree borne by the

stream, they had sauntered far away
To other climes, to other lands that are not
            in the World of Men.

Next comes the poem of farewell[10] to his family, written when he set out for the capital in the autumn of 742, followed by the *Chiang Chin Chiu,*[11] 'About to offer wine,' that is to say **'Song before Drinking.'** This is to the tune of an old song sung to the accompaniment of flutes and drums. The original words, dating perhaps from the 1st century A.D., are still preserved, but they are hopelessly corrupt and almost the only intelligible passage is 'Let us give ourselves up to the old song that the heart made.' Here are Li Po's new words to the tune:

> See the waters of the Yellow River leap down
>                 from Heaven,
> Roll away to the deep sea and never turn again!
> See at the mirror in the High Hall
> Aged men bewailing white locks—
> In the morning, threads of silk,
> In the evening flakes of snow.
> Snatch the joys of life as they come
>                 and use them to the full;
> Do not leave the silver cup idly glinting
>                 at the moon.
> The things that Heaven made
> Man was meant to use;
> A thousand guilders scattered to the wind
>                 may come back again.
> Roast mutton and sliced beef will only taste well
> If you drink with them at one sitting
>                 three hundred cups.
> Great Master Ts'ên,
> Doctor Tan-ch'iu,
> Here is wine, do not stop drinking
> But listen, please, and I will sing you a song.
> Bells and drums and fine food, what are they to me
> Who only want to get drunk and never again
>                 be sober?
> The Saints and Sages of old times are all stock
>                 and still,
> Only the mighty drinkers of wine have left
>                 a name behind.
> When the prince of Ch'ên gave a feast[12] in the
>                 Palace of P'ing-lo
> With twenty thousand gallons of wine he loosed
>                 mirth and play.
> The master of the feast must not cry that his
>                 money is all spent;
> Let him send to the tavern and fetch wine
>                 to keep our tankards filled.
> His five-flower horse and thousand-guilder coat—
> Let him call the boy to take them along
>                 and pawn them for good wine,
> That drinking together we may drive away the
>                 sorrows of a thousand years.

We do not know who Master Ts'ên was. Doctor Tan-ch'iu was Yüan Tan-ch'iu, a Taoist adept to whom Li Po addressed a large number of poems. We know from the inscription that Li Po wrote for the tomb of Hu Tzu-yang, who figures in the *Exile's Letter,* that Tan-ch'iu received his diploma from Hu on the Sung Shan near Lo-yang in 742. The following is one of the poems that Li Po addressed to him:

> My friend is lodging high in the Eastern Range,
> Dearly loving the beauty of valleys and hills.
> At green spring he lies in the empty woods,
> And is still asleep when the sun shines on high.
> A pine-tree wind dusts his sleeves and coat;
> A pebbly stream cleans his heart and ears.
> I envy you who far from strife and talk
> Are high-propped on a pillow of grey mist.

The last poem in the collection is the **'Song of the Crows roosting at night,'** also an old song-theme. It is about the carousals of the King of Wu with the legendary Hsi Shih, the most beautiful of women. Moralists have of course claimed that it is a satire upon the infatuation of the Emperor Hsüan Tsung for his consort Yang Kuei-fei. As we do not know whether it was written before or after 745 (when Yang Kuei-fei became an Imperial Consort) it is impossible to say whether this explanation is true:

> On the royal terrace at Soochow the crows are
>          going to rest;
> The King of Wu sitting in his palace drinks
>          with Hsi Shih.
> With songs of Wu, dances of Ch'u the feast
>          does not lag;
> Half only of the sun sticks out from the jaw of
>          the green hills.
> The silver arrow on the water-clock has marked
>          many hours;
> They rise to watch the autumn moon sink into
>          the river waves.
> What if daylight mounts the east? Need
>          morning end their sport?

That, as I have said, is the last poem in the anthology of 753. I will translate one more undatable poem; it is called **'Waking from Drunkenness on a Spring Day:'**

> 'Life in the world is but a big dream;
> I will not spoil it by any labour or care.'
> So saying, I was drunk all day,
> Lying helpless at the porch in front of my door.
> When I woke up I looked into the garden court;
> A single bird was singing amid the flowers.
> I asked myself, what season is this?
> Restless the oriole chatters in the spring breeze.
> Moved by its song I soon began to sigh
> And as wine was there, I filled my own cup.
> Noisily singing I waited for the moon to rise;
> When my song was over, all my senses had gone.

Li Po, as I have said, is like most great poets known to the general reader by a relatively small number of pieces. The rest are indeed worth studying chiefly because it is only in the context of his work as a whole that the typical and outstanding pieces can be fully understood. But much of his work inevitably consisted of slight, complimentary poems addressed to friends at farewell parties or on other social occasions. They follow set conventions and might in

most cases have been written by any skilful versifier of the day. Among his best-known poems are some of those written to order at Court; but they owe their celebrity, I think, more to the legends that grew up later about the circumstances under which they were written than to their intrinsic merit, and I have not attempted to give an account of them.

The one kind of poetry that he never tried his hand at was the bucolic. There are in his works no farmyard scenes, no idyllic herd-boys piping in the dusk, no jolly woodcutters or philosophic fishermen. It was, above all, the wilder aspects of Nature that attracted him; vast untenanted spaces, cataracts, trackless mountains and desolate ravines. . . .

*Notes*

1. Runs west to east through northern Shansi and Hopei, north of the Great Wall.

2. The Kashgar-darya, in Turkestan.

3. Quotation from the *Tao Te Ching*.

4. The Upper Yangtze.

5. These heroes were five strong men sent by the King of Shu (the old name for Szechwan) to fetch the five daughters of the King of Ch'in. We must suppose that they went via the Yangtze and Han River and perished in attempting to return by land.

6. Ch'êng-tu, the capital of Szechwan.

7. The whole scene is in northern Chekiang.

8. Hsieh Ling-yün (385-433) was a famous mountain climber, who invented special mountain-shoes.

9. Shan-tung in T'ang times meant the whole of N.E. China, including the modern province of Shantung.

10. See above, p. 22.

11. This is No. 42 in the Tun-huang MS. (see below, p. 107), where it bears the title 'Lament for empty wine-jars.'

12. In 232 A.D.

### Burton Watson (essay date 1971)

SOURCE: "Li Po," in *Chinese Lyricism*, Columbia University Press, 1971, pp. 141-53.

[*In the following excerpt from his full-length study of Chinese lyric poetry, Watson discusses several examples of Li Po's work, classifying individual poems according to their traditional form and observing that the poetry is notable "less for the new elements it introduces than the skill with which it handles old ones."*]

The first thing to note about Li Po's poetry, particularly in comparison to that of Tu Fu, is that it is essentially backward-looking, that it represents more a revival and fulfillment of past promises and glory than a foray into the future. In the matter of poetic form critics generally agree that Li Po introduced no significant innovations. He seems to have been content to take over and employ what his predecessors had left him, writing in all the ordinary verse forms of the time, including the *lü-shih* and *chüeh-chü*, though he showed a marked preference for the *ku-shih* or old-style form. The irregular line lengths of the *ku-shih*, the freedom from compulsory tonal and verbal parallelism, and the unlimited length were apparently to his liking, and he used the form to create a kind of wild, rhapsodic quality reminiscent of the poets of the *Ch'u Tz'u*. One of his best-known *ku-shih* poems, for example, the *Shu-tao-nan* or **"Hard Roads in Shu,"** employs lines that range in length from four to eleven characters, the form of the lines suggesting by their irregularity the jagged peaks and bumpy mountain roads of Szechwan depicted in the poem.

In theme and content also, his poetry is notable much less for the new elements it introduces than for the skill with which it handles old ones. Of the approximately 1,000 poems attributed to Li Po, about one sixth are in *yüeh-fu* style, which means that they are reworkings of themes drawn from the folk song tradition of earlier times. Two of his best-known poems, familiar to English readers through Pound's translations as **"The River-Merchant's Wife"** and **"The Jeweled Stairs' Grievance,"** are *yüeh-fu*, dealing with the age-old subjects of the neglected wife and the palace lady who has fallen out of favor. Another important group of 59 poems, meditations on political, social, and philosophical themes, is entitled *ku-feng* or "in the old manner," and expresses his admiration for the poetry of the past, particularly that of the late Han and Wei, and his longing to recapture its excellences.

In treating the traditional themes, Li Po often introduces a freshness of outlook or imagery, a narrative skill, a beauty of diction that make his poem the most memorable and satisfying statement on the subject, replacing in popularity the earlier models upon which he drew. But because his poems, particularly those in *yüeh-fu* style, are conventionalized or impersonal in feeling and rely for so much of their appeal on pure lyricism, they are often less interesting in translation than those of other, perhaps inferior, poets.

The second important characteristic of Li Po's poetry that must be pointed out is the fantasy and note of childlike wonder and playfulness that pervade so much of it. From the time of his youth Li Po was strongly attracted to the *tao-shih,* the Taoist recluses who lived in the mountains and, through alchemy and the practice of various austerities, sought to become *hsien* or immortal spirits. Men who had turned their backs on contemporary society and its values, they are described by Li Po in terms that make them sound like the "beats" of their day,

> sleeping on boulders, all under one quilt,
> chopping through the ice to drink from cold springs,
> three men sharing a single pair of clogs.[1]

It is clear that the life of the *tao-shih* attracted him greatly and many of his poems deal with mountains, often de-

scriptions of ascents that midway modulate into journeys of the imagination, passing from actual mountain scenery to visions of the nature deities, immortals, and "jade maidens" of Taoist lore. In such poems Li Po once more shows his affinities with the past, with the poets of the *Ch'u Tz'u* or the early *fu* tradition who in their writings ranged back and forth freely between the real world and the supernatural.

This same element of fantasy lies behind the hyperboles and playful personifications—rather rare in T'ang poetry as a whole—that have so long delighted readers of Li Po's poetry. His descriptions of nature are particularly rich in such ingenuous fancy, as when he unself-consciously talks to the moon, speaks of a mountain and himself as "looking at each other without either of us tiring,"[2] or tells us that the star T'ai-po or Venus, from which he took his courtesy name, Li T'ai-po, "talked with me,/and opened up for me the barriers of Heaven."[3]

Li Po spent most of his life in travel, part of it exile imposed by the court because of unsavory political connections. Just what kept him so constantly on the move it is difficult to say. The point to note is that, in spite of all this moving about and the hardships and loneliness that it must have entailed, his poetry is remarkably free from expressions of unmitigated woe. Partly this may be due to the fact, already mentioned, that his writing tends to be less personal, less revealing of inner emotion than that of many of his contemporaries. But it is also due to his own inimitable vigor and zest for life. We have noted his fondness for nature, particularly the mountain landscapes with their promise of spiritual delight and emancipation, and his relatively sunny view of a universe in which stars stop to talk to him, the moon is a companion, and, as he declares in a poem to be quoted shortly, "heaven and earth are my quilt and pillow." One more consolation remains to be mentioned, one inseparably linked with his name: the very real and lifelong enjoyment he appears to have derived from drinking. Nearly all Chinese poets celebrate the joys of wine, but none do so as tirelessly and with such a note of genuine conviction as Li Po. Though he wrote in a poetic tradition that condoned, even demanded, the frank expression of sorrow, and he himself often gave voice to such feelings, one imagines that he could never have been entirely desolate so long as he had his wine.

Because of the rather impersonal nature of Li Po's poetry and the relative paucity of biographical data that has been preserved, we are unable to date most of his works with any certainty. For this reason, I have arranged the examples of his work by subject and will discuss them in that manner, beginning with two examples of poems in *yüeh-fu* style. The first is entitled **"Tzu-yeh Song #3"** and uses a 5-character line. . . . This poem deals with autumn, when cloth is customarily fulled to make uniforms to send to the soldiers stationed at the frontier. Jade Pass is in Kansu far to the west.

> Ch'ang-an—one slip of moon;
> in ten thousand houses, the sound of fulling mallets.

Autumn winds keep on blowing,
all things make me think of Jade Pass!
When will they put down the barbarians
and my good man come home from his far campaign?

The second, entitled **"Bring the Wine,"** uses a 7-character line with occasional lines of other lengths. It is a rather strident poem—one can almost hear the poet pounding the table—and hardly original in either ideas or imagery. And yet, like so much of Li Po's work, it has a grace and effortless dignity that somehow make it more compelling than earlier treatments of the same theme.

Have you not seen
the Yellow River waters descending from the sky,
racing restless toward the ocean, never to return?
Have you not seen
bright mirrors in high halls, the white-haired ones lamenting,
their black silk of morning by evening turned to snow?
If life is to have meaning, seize every joy you can;
do not let the golden cask sit idle in the moonlight!
Heaven gave me talents and meant them to be used;
gold scattered by the thousand comes home to me again.
Boil the mutton, roast the ox—we will be merry,
at one bout no less than three hundred cups.
Master Ts'en!
    Scholar Tan-ch'iu!⁴
bring wine and no delay!
For you I'll sing a song—
be pleased to bend your ears and hear:
Bells and drums, foods rare as jade—these aren't worth prizing;
all I ask is to be drunk forever, never to sober up!
Sages and worthies from antiquity—all gone into silence;
only the great drinkers have left a name behind.
The Prince of Ch'en once feasted in the Hall of Calm Delight;
wine, ten thousand coins a cask, flowed for his revelers' joy.
Why does my host tell me the money has run out?
Buy more at once—my friends have cups to be refilled!
My dappled mount,
my furs worth a thousand—
call the boy, have him take them and barter for fine wine!
Together we will wash away ten thousand years of care.

The following two poems, in 7-character *chüeh-chü* form, belong to the category known as *huai-ku* or meditations on the past. . . . The first, entitled **"At Su Terrace Viewing the Past,"** was written when the poet visited the site of the Ku-su Terrace, built by Fu-ch'a, king of Wu, in the region just south of the Yangtze delta. The king's extravagant ways and infatuation with the beautiful Hsi-shih—the "lady" of the poem—weakened his state and led to its overthrow in 472 B.C. by its rival, the state of Yüeh (see the next poem).

Old gardens, a ruined terrace, willow trees new;
caltrop gatherers, clear chant of songs, a spring un-

bearable;
and now there is only the west river moon
that shone once on a lady in the palace of the king of Wu.

**"In Yüeh Viewing the Past,"** Kou-chien was the ruler of Yüeh who overthrew King Fu-ch'a of Wu.

Kou-chien, king of Yüeh, came back from the broken land of Wu;
his brave men returned to their homes, all in robes of brocade.
Ladies in waiting like flowers filled his spring palace
where now only the partridges fly.

Li Po is particularly noted for his mastery of the *chüeh-chü* form. Two examples have been given above, in which the form is used to lament the vanished glories of the past. The following six record scenes that the poet encountered in his travels or sum up his thoughts. **"Autumn Cove Song #5"**; 5-character *chüeh-chü*.

At Autumn Cove, so many white monkeys,
bounding, leaping up like snowflakes in flight!
They coax and pull their young ones down from the branches
to drink and frolic with the water-borne moon.

**"Viewing the Waterfall at Mount Lu"**; 5-character *chüeh-chü*. The second of two poems on the subject of Mt. Lu in Kiangsi; Incense Stone is the name of one of its peaks.

Sunlight streaming on Incense Stone kindles a violet smoke;
far off I watch the waterfall plunge to the long river,
flying waters descending straight three thousand feet,
till I think the Milky Way has tumbled from the ninth height of Heaven

**"Spring Night in Lo-yang—Hearing a Flute"**; 7-character *chüeh-chü*. . . .

In what house, the jade flute that sends these dark notes drifting,
scattering on the spring wind that fills Lo-yang?
Tonight if we should hear the willow-breaking song,
who could help but long for the gardens of home?

**"Still Night Thoughts"**; 5-character *chüeh-chü*.

Moonlight in front of my bed—
I took it for frost on the ground!
I lift my eyes to watch the mountain moon,
lower them and dream of home.

**"Summer Day in the Mountains"**; 5-character *chüeh-chü*.

Too lazy to wave the white plume fan,
stripped to the waist in the green wood's midst,
I loose my headcloth, hang it on a stony wall,
bare my topknot for pine winds to riffle.

**"Presented to Wang Lun"**; 7-character *chüeh-chü*. Written at a place called Peach Flower Pool in Anhwei and given at parting to a friend of the poet, a local wine seller named Wang Lun.

> Li Po on board, ready to push off,
> suddenly heard the tramping and singing on the bank.
> Peach Flower Pool a thousand feet deep
> is shallower than my love for Wang Lun who sees me off.

The following, entitled **"Seeing a Friend Off,"** is an example of a *lü-shih* by Li Po, this one in 5-character lines. It is unusual in that it violates the rule that the two middle couplets of a *lü-shih* must observe strict verbal parallelism, the kind of violation, Chinese critics hasten to add, that is permitted only to a genius like Li Po. Note the richly symbolic use of the nature images "green hills," "white water," "drifting clouds," etc.

> Green hills sloping from the northern wall,
> white water rounding the eastern city:
> once parted from this place
> the lone weed tumbles ten thousand miles.
> Drifting clouds—a traveler's will;
> setting sun—an old friend's heart.
> Wave hands and let us take leave now,
> *hsiao-hsiao* our hesitant horses neighing.

The remainder of the poems to be quoted are all in *ku-shih* or old-poetry form.

**"A Night with a Friend"**; 5-character *ku-shih*.

> Dousing clean a thousand old cares,
> sticking it out through a hundred pots of wine,
> a good night needing the best of conversation,
> a brilliant moon that will not let us sleep—
> drunk we lie down in empty hills,
> heaven and earth our quilt and pillow.

**"Facing Wine with Memories of Lord Ho; Introduction and Two Poems"**; 5-character *ku-shih*, the first of the two.

Lord Ho, a high official in the household of the Crown Prince, on our first meeting at the Tzu-chi Temple in Ch'ang-an at once dubbed me the "banished immortal." Then he took off his golden tortoise and exchanged it for wine for our enjoyment. He is gone now, and I face the wine, wrapped in thought, and write these poems.

> Wild man of Ssu-ming Mountain,
> Incomparable Ho Chi-chen,
> in Ch'ang-an when we first met,
> calling me a "banished immortal"[5]—
> He used to love the "thing in the cup"
>    (now he's dust under the pine tree),
> and traded the golden tortoise for wine—
>    my robe wet with tears, remembering.

**"In Reply When Lesser Officials of Chung-tu Brought a Pot of Wine and Two Fish to My Inn as Gifts"**; 5- and 7-character *ku-shih*.

> Lu wine like amber,
> fish from the Wen, the purple damask of their scales;
> and Shantung's fine officials, in expansive mood,
> their hands bearing gifts for a man from far away.
> We've taken to each other—we hit it off;
> the pot of wine, the pair of fish convey this thought.
> Wine comes—I drink it;
> fish to be carved at parting,
> twin gills that gape and pant, back and body taut-finned,
> they twitch and twitter on a silver plate, all but taking wing.
> I call the boy to clear the cuttingboard; frosty blades whirl—
> red flesh and pale[6]: fallen flowers, a gleam of whitest snow.
> With your leave I dip my chopsticks, eat my fill,
> then climb into the golden saddle, still drunk, to set off home.

**"Poem #19 in the Old Manner;"** 5-character *ku-shih*, nineteenth in the set of fifty-nine poems "in the old manner" mentioned above. Lotus Flower Mountain is the highest peak of Mt. Hua, one of the five sacred mountains of China, on the border between Shansi and Shensi. In a lake on its summit were said to grow lotuses which had the power to transform one into an immortal spirit. Bright Star was a spirit who lived on Mt. Hua. Wei Shu-ch'ing, a man of the Han dynasty who became an immortal by drinking an infusion of mica, lived on Cloud Terrace, another peak of Mt. Hua. The last four lines refer to the forces of the rebel An Lu-shan, who led a body of Chinese and foreign troops west to attack Ch'ang-an in 755.

> West ascending Lotus Flower Mountain,
> far far away I saw the Bright Star maid;
> with pale hands she plucked lotus blossoms,
> with airy steps she walked the great clear void;
> her rainbow skirts, their broad belt trailing,
> dipped and fluttered as she strode up the sky.
> She called me to climb with her to Cloud Terrace,
> to lift hands in salutation to Wei Shu-ch'ing.
> Dazed and enraptured, I went with her;
> mounting a stork, we rode the purple gloom.
> I looked down and saw the Lo-yang River,
> barbarian troops marching in endless files;
> streams of blood that stained the meadow grasses,
> wildcats and wolves wearing the hats of men!

We know little about Li Po's family life. He seems to have married several times, and the following poem is evidence that he had children by at least one of these marriages. At the time it was written, Li Po had left his family in Jen-ch'eng in Shantung (referred to in the poem as Lu), and was traveling in the south (Wu) on his way to the capital. Mt. Kuei and the Wen-yang River are in Shantung, near where his family were living. The poem is entitled **"Sent to My Two Little Children in the East of Lu"** and is in 5-character *ku-shih* form.

> Wu land mulberry leaves grow green,
> already Wu silkworms[7] have slept three times.
> I left my family in the east of Lu;

who sows our fields there on the dark side of Mt.
Kuei?
Spring chores too long untended,
river journeys that leave me dazed—
south winds blow my homing heart;
it soars and comes to rest before the wine tower.
East of the tower a peach tree grows,
branches and leaves brushed with blue mist,
a tree I planted myself,
parted from it these three years.
The peach now is tall as the tower
and still my journey knows no return.
P'ing-yang, my darling girl,
picks blossoms, leaning by the peach,
picks blossoms and does not see me;
her tears flow like a welling fountain.
The little boy, named Po-ch'in,
is shoulder high to his elder sister;
side by side they walk beneath the peach—
who will pat them with loving hands?
I lose myself in thoughts of them;
day by day care burns out my heart.
On this piece of cut silk I'll write my far-away
thoughts
and send them floating down the river Wen-yang.

The last Li Po poem I shall quote is entitled **"Song of a Dream Visit to T'ien-mu: Farewell to Those I Leave Behind."** In *ku-shih* form and using lines that vary in length from four to nine characters, it is noteworthy for its rhapsodic air and easy, rushing rhythms, which conceal the great care and precision with which it is put together. It begins with a reference to the Isles of Ying, fairy islands in the eastern sea where the immortal spirits live, and an assurance that the poet will, by contrast, describe an actual mountain. But his visit to the mountain is made in a dream and, like the journey passages of the *Ch'u Tz'u* and Han *fu*, grows increasingly fantastic until the dream is shattered and the sleeper awakes. The work ends with the poet bidding farewell to the world and declaring his intention to become a recluse, dwelling among the white deer and green bluffs of the wilderness. The subject of the poem, T'ien-mu, or Matron of Heaven, is a mountain near the sea in Chekiang (here referred to by the old name Yüeh), northwest of the more famous Mt. T'ien-t'ai. Lord Hsieh is the Six Dynasties landscape poet Hsieh Ling-yün, who lived in the region. He is supposed to have invented for mountain climbing a special type of clogs with detachable teeth, the front teeth being removed for climbing uphill, the back teeth for coming down. Li Po at one point echoes a poem which Hsieh Ling-yün wrote on the subject of Mt. T'ien-mu, "Climbing the Peak at Lin-hai," particularly the following lines:

> At dawn setting out south of the clear river;
> evening, shelter in the midst of Shan,
> next day to climb T'ien-mu peak,
> high high among clouds and rainbows;
> who can say when I'll return?

Seafarers tell of the Isles of Ying,
shadowy in spindrift and waves, truly hard to seek
out;

Yüeh men describe T'ien-mu,
in clouds and rainbows clear or shrouded, there for
eyes to glimpse;
T'ien-mu touching the sky, surging toward the sky,
lord above the Five Peaks, shadowing the Red Wall;
T'ien-t'ai's forty-eight thousand fathoms
beside it seem to topple and sprawl to south and east.
I longed, and my longing became a dream of Wu-
Yüeh;
in the night I flew across the moon of Mirror Lake;
the lake moon, lighting my shadow,
saw me to the Valley of Shan,
Lord Hsieh's old home there today,
where green waters rush and roil and shrill monkeys
cry.
Feet thrust into Lord Hsieh's clogs,
body climbing ladders of blue cloud,
halfway up the scarps I see the ocean sun,
and in the air hear the cocks of heaven.[8]
A thousand cliffs, ten thousand clefts, trails uncertain,
I turn aside for flowers, rest on rocks—suddenly it's
night;
bear growls, dragon purrs in the din of cliffside torrents
shake the deep forest, startle the piled-up peaks;
clouds blue-dark, threatening rain,
waters soft-seething, sending up mists:
a rent of lightning, crack of thunder,
and hilltops sunder and fall;
doors of stone at grotto mouths
swing inward with a grinding roar,
and from the blue darkness, bottomless, vast and wild,
sun and moon shine sparkling on terraces of silver
and gold.
Rainbows for robes, wind for horses,
whirling whirling, the Lord of the Clouds comes
down,
tigers twanging zithers, *luan* birds to turn his carriage,
and immortal men in files thick as hemp—
> Suddenly my soul shudders, my spirit leaps,
> in terror I rise up with repeated sighs:
> only the mat and pillow where now I woke—
> lost are the mists of a moment ago!
All the joys of the world are like this,
the many-evented past a river flowing east.
I leave you now—when will I return?—
to loose the white deer among green bluffs,
in my wandering to ride them in search of famed hills.
How can I knit brows, bend back to serve influence
and power,
never dare to wear an open-hearted face?

*Notes*

1. "Seeing Off Han Chun, P'ei Cheng, and K'ung Ch'ao-fu on Their Way Back to the Mountains."

2. "Sitting Alone on Mount Ching-t'ing."

3. "Climbing Mount T'ai-po."

4. "Scholar Tan-ch'iu": Yüan Tan-ch'iu, a Taoist friend of the poet; "Master Ts'en" in the preceding line has been tentatively identified as the poet Ts'en Ts'an (715-70).

5. "Banished immortal": implying that Li Po was really an immortal spirit of Heaven who, because of

some offense, had been condemned to take on human form and descend to earth.

"Golden tortoise": badge of high office.

"Ssu-ming Mountain": in Chekiang, where Ho lived after he left court and became a Taoist hermit.

6. "Red flesh and pale": the red and white portions of the raw fish. Like the Japanese today, the Chinese in early times often ate their fish raw.

7. "Wu silkworms": the silkworms sleep and shed their skins four times before they weave their cocoons.

8. "Cocks of heaven": another name for the golden pheasant. "Lord of the Clouds": a deity addressed in the shaman songs of the *Ch'u Tz'u.*

**Arthur Cooper (essay date 1973)**

SOURCE: "Li Po," in *Li Po and Tu Fu: Poems Selected and Translated with an Introduction and Notes,* Penguin Books, 1973, pp. 22-37.

[*In the following excerpt from his translation and study of the poetry of Li Po and Tu Fu, Cooper sketches the details of Li Po's life and provides a general overview of the poet's techniques, style, and artistic concerns.*]

Although nowhere near as fortunate in that respect as Shakespeare, not a great deal is really known about the life of Li Po.[1] Even the place of his birth, information regularly made available in the most minor Chinese biographies, and its date have been, at least until recently, the subjects of much speculation. This seems all the more curious in view of his exceptional fame in his own lifetime; but it is now generally agreed that he was born in 701 and outside present-day China, probably near what is now the frontier of the Soviet Union and Afghanistan. The name of his original home would therefore have meant very little to his contemporaries, who must be excused also for not knowing his place of birth because he spent most of his life travelling and had the romantic habit of speaking of many places he particularly liked as if they were his own home. (There had probably never before been such facilities for tourism, and safety in it; for which Tu Fu, when opportunity allowed, was no less enthusiastic.) Furthermore Li Po, having been praised for his extraordinary talent in early youth as a 'Fallen Immortal' or 'Banished Fairy', was inclined for ever after to adopt this character; to which a fixed earthly abode would have been unsuitable.

Also, though like other poets of his time he wrote many occasional poems, parting from friends, thanking for hospitality and the like, these do not generally contain much information useful for biography; while his major poems, being for the most part dream poems, are seldom informative about the time or circumstances in which they were written. In this they are in marked contrast with those of Tu Fu, which are almost all to some extent historical and autobiographical; so that scholarship has been able to date most of these with remarkable precision, better even than for some of our own poets a thousand years later. . . .

There is a very ancient Confucian literary tradition that would make *all* poetry occasional and moral; and so to be understood properly only in relation to the circumstances of its inspiration, preferably of a political nature. The difficulty found by many Chinese scholars, who nevertheless cannot help loving him, of fitting Li Po into this frame has often been a painful embarrassment to them.

Li Po's family tradition was that an ancestor of about a century earlier had been banished for political reasons, if not at first to the place of the poet's own birth then to some other outlandish Western Region; and that this ancestor was himself a descendent of the autonomous Duke, Li Kao (d. A.D. 417), of a region in what is now Kansu Province in West China. The latter was also claimed as ancestor by the Imperial Family of Li Shihmin who had founded the T'ang dynasty, so that Li Po felt able to address Imperial Princes as 'cousins'. Farther back still, Li Kao was known to be a descendent of General Li Kuang (d. 125 B.C.), a famous scourge of the Huns who had called him 'The Flying General'; and yet farther back, in common with all families of this Li surname, including of course the Imperial Family who favoured Taoism for that reason, they claimed descent from one Li Erh, who was supposed to have been the historical Lao Tzu ('Old Sage') himself in the sixth century B.C.; but this last was undoubtedly mythical.

Against this romantic ancestry, a dark suspicion must be mentioned that Li Po's family were not even Chinese at all, but Turks. That both they and the Imperial Li Family, along with many other leading families of the Empire, had some Turkish connections may be taken as certain; but as far as Li Po's own family is concerned, it is of greater significance than any 'blood' that they had lived for several generations in Turkish-speaking parts (Li Po himself said he could compose poetry in 'another language', probably some form of Turkish) and, like many an Anglo-Irish family without even a 'Mac' or an 'O' in its ancestry, may even have chosen in some respects to go 'more Turkish than the Turks'. One son of the Glorious Monarch (reigned 713-56), obsessed by the Turkishness of the Imperial Family, certainly did this and vacated his palace to live in a tent in his garden.

To be Chinese at that date, however, was, playful fantasies apart, to acknowledge the Emperor's Mandate from Heaven and to be literate in Chinese. By these, the only real criteria, Li Po was certainly Chinese to all his contemporaries. Whatever his true ancestry and however much he may have chosen in a cosmopolitan, outward-looking age to let Turkish, Persian and other foreign influences affect his art, these foreign influences were affecting in various ways all the Chinese arts of his time, without a suspicion of the artists themselves being 'alien'.

To suggest further, as has been done, that his notorious drunkenness was an inherited 'barbarian' trait is certainly beside the point in an age when, among specially talented people, drunkenness was universally recognized as a state of perfect, untramelled receptivity to divine inspiration; with no hint of Turkishness or anything 'barbaric' about it. (A similar view has also, of course, prevailed at times in our own civilization, notably in the Greek Mysteries and the Bacchic or Dionysiac state of ecstasy.) In all, there seems no reason at all to attribute anything in Li Po's character or work to 'foreign blood'.

Li Po's family had come and settled in China proper, in the south-western province of Szechwan, by the time he was five years old, so he is unlikely to have had much direct memory of an exotic past. It is probable, however, that in the remote regions the family had been traders, and that they kept up with foreign trading communities of all races and religions (Zoroastrian, Hindu, Jewish, Nestorian Christian, Muslim) then to be found all over China; and as represented by the obviously un-Chineselooking figures often found in T'ang pottery. If they were themselves traders in a China dominated by a professional class of civil servants, they would (even if rich) not quite have been 'gentry'; but however Chinese or aristocratic their origins may in fact have been, they would anyway not have belonged to the local 'landed gentry' wherever they settled. Such circumstances could have contributed to a number of things: their concern and his with a supposed grand ancestry (Tu Fu, whose ancestry really was grand, says nothing about it); the combination, which helped to make Li Po's work so striking to his contemporaries, of evident foreign influences with equally strong and self-conscious Chinese tradition, but looking back to a distant Chinese past more than to recent movements and fashions; and the un-Confucian, that is to say, not quite gentlemanly, boastfulness and competitiveness of character that he displayed. This background could also help explain his constant wandering; and the great loneliness to be found in all his work, despite his outward high spirits and success. No man was ever more recognized for his genius in his lifetime.

Li Po was not merely un-Confucian in his manners, enjoying or hiding himself in a reputation as an *enfant terrible,* but often explicitly anti-Confucian in his thought. He poured scorn on the moral and intellectual qualities (such as patient literary scholarship) most admired in the Confucian tradition, and expressed his own admiration only for the man of impulse. For a time in his youth he lived as a wandering gallant, whose sword was free to redress wrongs wherever he went.[2] In this character he seems to have had something in common with Cyrano de Bergerac: both the real seventeenth-century man, with his free-thinking, his imaginary journeys to the sun and moon, and his serious studies of physics; and the theatrical one of Rostand's play. Nothing, however, is known of Li Po's prowess (he only says, in a prose letter, that he was keen on swordsmanship at the age of fifteen) or of his achievements in this kind of life. But he is said by contemporaries to have killed several men.

Neither these adventures, however, which certainly did not continue far into his life, nor his drunkenness which did,

nor even his satirizing of Confucian virtues (an accepted sport of the time, played also on occasion by Tu Fu who, by his own account, was a heavy drinker, too)—none of these things has been so shocking ever since to the Confucian outlook as Li Po's refusal, despite the outstanding talents early evident in his poetic compositions, to take the official examinations and serve the Empire in its higher civil service. Poetic genius most of all, but also the other higher arts such as calligraphy, painting and music, which were distinguished from mere crafts, meant in the traditional Chinese view an understanding of the single Tao, such as would be wasted if not given also in other ways to the service of Empire and of people. An ivory tower was suitable to poets only when preparing themselves for such service; or after it, to retreat to nobly instead of accepting wealth and honour; or sometimes when grievously wronged while in service; or for religious ascetics, who might also be poets and, if good enough, should also then be considered for such service.

There have been various speculations about why Li Po did not take the examinations. Perhaps pride was a reason, given uncertainty of coming out first in the list: an acceptable reason, for such pride was fully respected in a brilliant youth of this Renaissance-like age. There was a further excuse because this was before examination papers were handed in on completion with ciphers instead of names, so that influence still counted. But Li Po might have obtained such influence, and none of this could be a lasting excuse. Perhaps he was simply too impulsive and incapable of the necessary self-discipline to get through all the preparation with set books and model questions on government and economics. There is evidence, however, that he was very widely read, spent much of his life in study, and by no means lacked the kind of ambitions for which it was normally necessary to take the examinations.

Among subjects he studied on his own account (and incorporated in his poetry) was what would now be called physics and chemistry. This may point to another reason why, so disconcertingly to his admirers then and since, he did not take the examinations: he might have taken them if the curriculum had been in anything but arts subjects, drawn up by Confucians, with which he was impatient and the relevance of which he did not see. Although his chemistry may have been directed at such things as finding 'elixirs of life', the imagination in his poetry seems essentially one of 'natural philosophy', and as such quite different from Tu Fu's.

Politically, in fact, he remained (like some scientists) always a child; and this political naïvety of his has led to his being charged with lack of concern for the welfare of the people, with being selfish and without compassion in contrast to Tu Fu, especially during the turbulent age which theirs (after beginning in such peace and prosperity) was to become during their lives.[3] That the charge is not altogether just may be seen from some of the poems in this book. Li Po in his own way possessed great sympathy and compassion for his fellow-beings (including an especially sympathetic insight into the minds of women) and was fiercely indignant at all suffering of which he was aware, for instance in war. But he can also give a fatalistic impression because he had little notion of practical solutions; or (again like some scientists) was inclined to regard everybody else's stupidity as the self-evident explanation of all evil. It was enough to see that something was not in harmony with the Tao, and difficult then to take any further interest in it. That, with his impulsiveness and all else in his character (including, I think, an incapability of expecting to be misunderstood, which gives his poems their special spontaneity) was all part of his Taoism.

It was also part of his Taoism that his poems seem to receive rather than to give: to receive the light of the Tao without illumination of their own and to receive, hospitably, the reader's own imagination instead of informing it. The real content of Li Po's best poetry seems to be not in the words but as if it were somehow inbetween them (Lao Tzu's 'teaching without words'); as in the five simple syllables, with those italicized added for English grammar: 'drunk*enly I* rise *to* stalk *the* brook moon'. Li Po has dozed over his wine outdoors in spring until night has fallen: that much we have been told. That the stream he followed on waking and getting up from the ground (there is no harm in imagining a chair, though in China in those days people seldom sat on them) ran between magical wooded slopes, we are not told; and these wooded slopes are made the more magical, their presence is the more felt, *because* we are not told. We are therefore *there,* just as we are where we are now; with nobody telling us where we are or *describing* what is around us.

We know, in fact, by two things that there are wooded slopes: that the moon belongs only to the brook and not also to its banks, as it would if they were open fields; and that it has to be 'stalked', which is a reasonable translation of the Chinese verb used. But we have no need to think in this logical way and no time to do so, before being taken from wherever we may be and placed in that faraway landscape and at that moment more than twelve hundred years ago; bringing nothing but ourselves with us on the flight and so achieving perfect identity with the man Li Po, there and then.

This kind of technique, which is not often subject to such rational analysis as attempted here, belongs, of course, in varying degrees and among other techniques to all the best poetry in the world. But the Chinese language, for reasons which will be seen when we come to discuss it, is particularly suited to it; and Li Po seems to use it with exceptional spontaneity and skill, especially in the very short form of poem of which he is universally acknowledged one of the greatest masters. It not only contributes to the extraordinary visual quality of much Chinese poetry, his in particular, far more than any explicit description could do: it leads to very simple yet profound thoughts, as part of a time and place, such as may never be thought in words at all and can hardly be expressed in them without banality. These are thoughts which, like the Tao itself in the Taoist imagination of it, disappear on illumination.

Unfortunately for the translator, poetry of this kind uses everything in a poem to make a texture, as it were, in order to catch the wavelength of the Tao that it seeks; so that it is even less transferrable than other kinds of poetry from the texture of its own language into another. But if one is at first half-inclined to react to translations of some of these very simple little Chinese poems (also the Japanese equivalent) with a 'So what?', so, it must be admitted, one may often be inclined at first, on reading them in the original: they *do* have very little to say, but even in translation (in which so much of their reflective surface is usually dulled) they may sometimes be found to have a correspondingly great amount to *reflect.* It is because of this that at their best they are infinitely re-readable, never losing their freshness; so that a very short poem may come to seem a great one.

Besides these very short poems and some that are longer but similar in spirit and technique, Li Po is most famous for poems in old ballad styles, called *yüeh-fu.* These may be described as quasi-folksongs. In fact, they have much deeper thought and learning than folksongs but use the folksong model both for its music (to which these poems were sung)[4] and for its tradition, like that of folksongs and ballads all over the world, of allowing quick jumps in time and space and mood, and of avoiding the explicit. The name *yüeh-fu,* often translated 'Music Bureau', derives from the name of a musical academy established in 90 B.C. for collecting folksongs, among other purposes. This was seen in the Confucian tradition as a way of discovering the mind of the people: their needs and aspirations, and their feelings about the government they enjoyed or endured.

Although this academy did not exist for very long, it had a profoundly beneficial influence in after ages for the tradition it created of recording the words of ballads and folksongs, and for counteraction against excessively erudite and rule-bound 'classical' tendencies in a poetry produced by a social class chosen mainly by literary examination.

In much of Li Po's versification he was antiquarian rather than either conservative or modernist. He preferred generally the older, freer metres ungoverned by recently developed rules (rather like those of Malherbe in sixteenth-century France). These new rules served to counterpoint the intrinsic tones of words (as described further below) and were exploited with great effect by Tu Fu. Li Po, however, was often better suited by the very irregular lengths of line in some of the old *yüeh-fu* and by the uninterrupted runs of strong syllables (rather like G. M. Hopkins' 'dappled dawn drawn falcon') that could occur in them; and he seems also to have been more of a spontaneous, natural singer (with such echoes in his mental ear) than a conscious theorist and experimenter as was Tu Fu.

Poetry in the West since the eighteenth century has tended to move from 'rules' to 'freedom', so that one might get an impression that of these two Li Po was more the 'modern poet'; but in their own day it was the other way round.

Tu Fu was more the innovator, and it was he who made the typically 'avant-garde' remark in one of his poems: 'Until death I shall not rest, to make my words startle men!' Li Po nevertheless was also a 'discoverer', particularly of little noticed or remembered poets of earlier centuries; such as one Yin K'eng, who lived some time in the sixth century, significantly also in the Western Regions, and whose few surviving verses have a Li Po vigour and mystery.

Li Po's ear was also without a doubt informed by the 'urban pop music' of his day, in places with food, wine and cabaret, which were the contemporary equivalent of night clubs. Many of the girls in these places were foreign and brought new kinds of song and dance from Central Asia.[5] That the nomadic peoples of this vast area were largely without writing did not mean that they were without culture or that their music was primitive. (Music has had perhaps much more power as a messenger between civilizations than it is generally credited with: Turkish fifes and drums and songs may have carried the seeds of new thought in both directions from one literate civilization to another, even though they had no literate communication, across the mountain ranges and deserts between them.) New Chinese verse-forms, called *tz'u,* for singing to the new popular music and allowing irregular lengths of line to fit the tunes, had their origin at this time, though their own 'classical' age was in the tenth to the thirteenth centuries.[6]

The tune of one of these songs of the T'ang dynasty survives thanks to a twelfth-century musician and poet, Chiang K'uei, who discovered it from an old lutenist at an inn in Nankin in 1198 and printed it with his own words in a song-book in 1202. (The songs usually went out of fashion from generation to generation, surviving only as verse-metres.) With the very kind permission of Dr Laurence Picken of Jesus College, Cambridge, who transcribed it from its old Chinese notation, this beautiful little melody is reproduced below; with a syllable-for-syllable translation I have attempted of the lyric composed to it by Chiang K'uei. Although not by Li Po, this short song seems to have clear affinities with some of the songs translated here; and may therefore, with its music, bring these and the spirit of the age to which he belonged nearer to the reader.

The song is of a girl of the *geisha* kind to her departing noble lover.

"Ancient Air For the Lute"

And so now Spring ends Wil - lows weave
  yel - low strands, Cry - evening crows:
Your gold sad - dle - bow Dreams not words
  fol - low now: Words my lute knows![7]

Li Po may be called a 'romantic' poet in that almost all his poems are to some extent dream-poems; many of his longer ones spirit-journeys, for which he had precedents in ancient poems related to the trances of mediums in early

Chinese religious dances. (Coleridge's *Kubla Khan* is, of course, such a spirit-journey; and more will be said of it concerning a poem of Li Po's which has some affinities with it.) Some scholars who quite approve of such spirit-journeys and find them moving, given that they are in the setting of a 'primitive' society with 'interesting' customs and ways of thought ('interesting' meaning perhaps 'safely remote'), are inclined to label Li Po's 'imitations' as merely escapist; but it was also a Taoist view to regard the reality of imagination and of dreams as no less real than what is usually called reality by contrast. The Taoist philosopher Chuang Chou (latter fourth, early third century B.C.) dreamt he was a butterfly; but when he awoke said he did not *know* whether he had dreamt he was a butterfly, or whether he was not now a butterfly dreaming he was Chuang Chou.

Contemporary descriptions of Li Po speak of his great, flashing eyes and loud, shrill voice. His presence seems to have electrified everyone and the speed at which he could compose, when in drink, to have astonished them. He seems to have been the arch-poet as envisaged by the romantic imagination, and in 'real life'; so much so that his name has become much the best known abroad of any Chinese poet, much like Byron among English poets, to people who may not have read any of his poems even in translation. But in his own country and those that share its script and culture, he has also been the most widely read of poets, and must be one of the most widely read of all great poets in the world's literature; and one of the most influential, although he was no theorist and it is very hard to say what exactly it is in his poetry that captivates.

The well-known legend of his death, in 762, is that he fell drunk from a boat while trying to grasp the reflection of the moon, and was drowned. It might even be true, particularly as death from pneumonia seems to have been described as 'drowning'. It is indeed always difficult to separate fact and fiction about his life; a few further details of which will emerge in the remarks on his poems. . . .

*Notes*

1. Arthur Waley, however, says surprisingly 'Li Po is one of the Chinese poets about whose life we know most'; but must rather mean 'about whom there is the most gossip'. This is in *The Poetry and Career of Li Po* (Allen and Unwin, 1950), a rather unsympathetic study, that one cannot help suspecting was written partly to justify the great translator's often expressed personal lack of appreciation of this poet.

2. This was an old Chinese tradition, found also in Japan and the subject of a number of famous Japanese stories and now films. There is an excellent and scholarly history and description of it in China, in James J. Y. Liu's *The Chinese Knight Errant* (Routledge and Kegan Paul, 1967).

3. Little of what he wrote in this later time may have survived, judging by a statement of a cousin of his that nine out of ten of all his last works were lost.

4. Other poems were chanted rather than said, usually to the accompaniment of a zither. There was no notion of reading poems silently till perhaps a thousand years later.

5. 'Pop' of this kind seems always to have been the origin of new Chinese verse-forms; including, half a millennium earlier, the classical five- and seven-syllable metres of Li Po's and Tu Fu's own day.

6. See *A Collection* and *A Further Collection of Chinese Lyrics* by Alan Ayling and Duncan Mackintosh (Routledge & Kegan Paul, 1965 and 1969).

7. The second verse is more literally: 'Dreams follow your gold saddle, there is a little sweetness my heart does not put into words: my lute understands the language (for that).' Chinese can express such an idea in far fewer words and syllables than English.


**Elling Eide (essay date 1973)**

SOURCE: "On Li Po," in *Perspectives on the T'ang*, edited by Arthur Wright and Denis Twitchett, Yale University Press, 1973, pp.367-403.

[*In the following essay, Eide discusses three neglected poems by Li Po—"My Trip in a Dream to the Lady of Heaven Mountain," "Lu Mountain Song," and "Song of the Heavenly Horse"—and comments on aspects of these poems, including techniques used and facts expressed, that other critics have overlooked.*]

Although Sinology is a field crowded with men and issues still untouched by the hand of modern scholarship, even Sinologists are often astonished to discover how little work has been done on the T'ang poet Li Po. He and his contemporary, Tu Fu, are so closely associated, now so universally famous, that one tends to assume that these two, at least, have surely been "done" adequately for the present time. Yet, the abundance of rather careful Tu Fu scholarship is matched by a striking absence of serious Li Po material, and I suspect that no one in world literature has been so much read and so little analyzed. The fact is that since the commentary by Wang Ch'i (1696-1774), we have only a handful of significant contributions to Li Po studies: Arthur Waley's short and rather unsympathetic biography, Erwin von Zach's admirable but now dated translations, the invaluable though somewhat clumsy Kyoto concordance, the two useful volumes of essays and research material by Chan Ying published in Peking in 1957 and 1958, and now Kuo Mo-jo's fresh and imaginative *Li Po yü Tu Fu* [Li Po and Tu Fu], the first scholarly book published in China since the Cultural Revolution.

It is nice, of course, to have a writer whose appeal can survive the centuries without a mulch of annotation, and the critical neglect of Li Po does tell much about Chinese attitudes toward criticism and the man. In the little that has been written we find, for example, a kind of "homeopathic" critical approach that treats the subject matter in a fashion as carefree and bizarre as Li Po's presumed personality, to give us a certain unlooked for measure of the poet in the critics' eyes.[1] Again, in what is written—and in the critics' failure to write more—there is reflected the Confucian, and now Marxist, moral judgment that while Tu Fu is good for you, Li Po, in all probability, is not. Yet important questions have been neither answered nor asked, and although Wang Ch'i and his two predecessors have identified most of the place-names and allusions, the appreciation of Li Po, as man or poet, is no deeper or more firmly grounded today than it was at the close of the T'ang dynasty.

One of the questions that has long intrigued me—a basic question about the nature of Li Po's accomplishment—is, simply, what was it about Li Po that so excited Tu Fu's admiration? Why, indeed, was he one of the very few Chinese poets to be widely and immediately recognized as a genius by his contemporaries? Needless to say, the traditional view that they admired him because he was a genius and that he was a genius because he was supernaturally inspired is no more helpful than the explanation that his poems seem powerful and spontaneous because he was a passionate man who wrote spontaneously. This, clearly, is mistaking effect for cause, and I am fond of pointing out that "spontaneous" poetry is not written spontaneously any more than fast music is written in a hurry. The publication of Dylan Thomas's workbooks nicely checked our own tendency to make a similar mistake about a Western poet, and Yeats made the point well in "Adam's Curse":

> We sat together at one summer's end,
> That beautiful mild woman, your close friend,
> And you and I, and talked of poetry.
> I said, 'A line will take us hours maybe;
> Yet if it does not seem a moment's thought,
> Our stitching and unstitching has been naught.'

To probe the question of how Li Po achieved effects worthy of Tu Fu's admiration and, further, to identify those effects more clearly, I have been reading Li Po's poems, attempting to use a rigorous philological method while employing the same sensors and permitting myself the same reactions that I would allow when reading English poems. That is to say, I start with my own somewhat simplistic definition of poetry as "the art of putting language under tension to make the pieces vibrate so that the whole will say more than one has any right to expect," and I then look to see what Li Po is doing to get maximum vibration from his language.

Thus far, I am satisfied with the results, for the analysis has in no way fragmented the poems or killed the poetry. On the contrary, it has shown them to be extremely well knit, meaningful, and often moving. Here, I should like to discuss three of the poems that are, I believe, considerably better, more complex, and more meaningful than has generally been supposed. When we see what is said and something of *how* it is said, I think we can also begin to see just what it was that so dazzled Tu Fu and his contemporaries. . . . In what follows I shall not explain every allusion and term; rather, I shall concentrate almost entirely on techniques, relationships, facts, and *speculations* that have not previously been touched upon by the commentators. In the notes Li Po's compositions will be identified by their numbers in the Kyoto concordance, and for my basic text I use the facsimile of the unique Sung edition, also found in the Kyoto index series. For the transcription of ancient Turkish, I follow V. M. Nadeljaev et al., *Drevnetjurkskij slovar'* (Leningrad: Nauka, 1969).

**"My Trip in a Dream to the Lady of Heaven Mountain"** is a good starting point because it is the easiest of the three poems, and because it provides examples of some half-dozen of Li Po's most characteristic devices for getting the most out of his language. David Hawkes has already called attention to the way he enriches the texture of his poem by drawing on Taoist mysticism and other shamanistic or supernatural elements found in earlier poetry.[2] Indeed, with its flight through space theme, it belongs to one of the most venerable traditions in Chinese literature. Most interesting, however, is the way Li Po weaves the supernatural, natural, philosophical, and literary elements into a net that involves the reader in the act of creativity—reflecting that a line can be taken in this way or in that and savoring the embellishments of sound and allusion, he becomes a participant in the performance of the poem.

1 Seafarers tell of a magic island,
2 Hard to find in the vague expanse of mist and towering waves.
3 In Yüeh men talk of the Lady of Heaven,
4 Glimpsed by chance, dissolving and glowing, amid the rainbows and clouds.
5 The Lady of Heaven, joining the heavens, faces the Heavenly Span
6 Her majesty tops the Five Summits and shadows Vermilion Wall
7 Heavenly Terrace rises up forty-eight thousand staves,
8 Yet tips southeast beside her as if it wanted to fall.
9 Wanting to probe the mystery in a dream of Wu and Yüeh,
10 Through a night I flew across the moon on Mirror Lake.
11 The moon on the lake projected my shadow,
12 Escorting me to the River Shan.
13 The place where Duke Hsieh once retired stands to the present day;
14 The lucent waters swiftly purl and shrill-voiced monkeys cry.
15 Duke Hsieh's cleated clogs on my feet,
16 I climbed the ladder of blue clouds.
17 From the slope I could see the sun in the ocean;
18 From space I could hear the Rooster of Heaven.
19 A thousand cliffs, ten thousand turns, a road I cannot define;
20 Dazzled by flowers, I rest on a stone and darkness suddenly falls.
21 Bears grumbling, dragons humming, fountains rumbling on the mountainside

22 Quaking before a deep forest. Frightened by impending spires.
23 Green, green the gum trees. On the verge of rain.
24 Rough, rough the river. Breaking in spray.
25 Flashing, cracking, roaring, clapping,
26 Hills and ridges crumble and fall.
27 The stone gates of the Grotto Heavens
28 Boom and crash as they open wide.
29 The Blue Dark is a rolling surge where bottom cannot be seen,
30 Where sun and moon throw glittering light on platforms of silver and gold
31 Rainbows are his clothing. His horses are the wind.
32 The Lord Within the Clouds appears. All things swirl as he decends
33 Tigers strumming zithers. Coaches phoenix drawn.
34 The immortals now assemble. Arrayed like rows of hemp.
35 With the sudden excitement of my soul, my vital force is roused;
36 I rise distraught and startled, long and drawn my sighs.
37 There is only the pillow and mat on waking;
38 Gone are the mists of a moment ago.
39 The pleasures found within the world are also just this way;
40 Ten thousand affairs out of the past are an easterly flowing stream
41 Parting now I leave you. When shall I return?
42 A white deer will soon be loosed within the blue-green shores;
43 When I must go, I shall ride away to visit the peaks of renown.
44 How could I ever furrow my brow and bend my back in service of rank and power?
45 To hurry the pleasures of love and wine wilts man's youth away.

**"My Trip in a Dream to the Lady of Heaven Mountain: A Farewell to Several Gentlemen of Eastern Lu"**

How shall the poem be read? On how many levels? Li Po delights in playing with levels of meaning, and the technique is particularly appropriate here, where he is also playing with real and unreal worlds. The poem is a technicolor dream and a rhapsody about a real mountain; a frolic with allusions and word magic and an exercise in rejuvenating an ancient theme; a discourse on timeless eternity and the carefully clocked narration of a single day. It is also an essay in Taoist metaphysics, a statement of personal belief, and a magnificent description of a mountain thunderstorm. Probably no one will miss the progression from night to day that parallels Li Po's progress up the mountain. But note also the progression of the storm: sunlight, gathering clouds, wind, rain, thunder and lightning, and finally clearing with rainbows and the reemergence of the animals and birds. The darkening of trees before the storm is nicely observed, and earlier usage gives gum trees special association with rain; just as dragons and tigers have associations with gathering clouds and rising wind. In all, this description of a thunderstorm seems to compare very well with the highly praised storm in the *mu'allaqa* of Imr al-Qays (fl. c. 530), who was apparently also a wanderer addicted to wine, women, and poetry in the Li Po manner.[3]

This blending of levels and blurring of distinctions between real and unreal worlds makes for effective poetry and must have been one of the characteristics to excite Tu Fu's admiration. It is also a reminder that the poem is no mere exuberant outburst of song. Indeed, it is somewhat surprising to discover that Li Po, from whom we might except and accept almost any fantasy, is so careful to maintain a balance between the real and unreal. As if he were providing his reader with justifications for the suspension of disbelief, he often reconciles poetic license with rationality—as he does here by setting his fantasy within a dream and permitting us to explain the flight through space as the water-reflected moon's projection of his shadow.[4] A better appreciation of this characteristic feature may have been one reason that Tu Fu and other good Confucians of the T'ang could accept Li Po more wholeheartedly than could the scholars of later dynasties.

With the main features of the poem in mind, we might look back at the contribution made by literary allusion. The two opening couplets are the first blocks in a structure full of echoes and a sly reminder of an important precedent for one of the dominant themes: the exploration of worlds. Like this poem, "The Rhymeprose on a Trip to the Heavenly Terrace Mountains" by Sun Ch'o (c. 310-97) also opens with reference to mysteries on land and sea:

> Across the sea there are [the islands] of Fang-chang and P'eng-lai,
> On land [the ranges] Ssu-ming and T'ien-t'ai.
> Both these are where the mystic sages roamed and taught,
> Where ghostly sylphs, encaverned, dwelt.[5]

From this, Sun Ch'o proceeds with an exploration of mountains that is at the same time an exploration of Buddhist-flavored Neo-Taoist metaphysics. In the present poem we find Li Po improving upon Sun's lines to introduce his own geometaphysical explorations; and any suspicion that it is all coincidence is removed by line 9, where he again borrows from Sun Ch'o, using the rare and rather technical term *ming-sou,* which I have translated as "to probe the mystery."[6]

Farther along in the poem, the T'ang reader must have been pleased to note the echoes of the poet Hsieh Ling-yün (385-433) and the clickclack consonance . . . in line 15 that underscores the reference to Hsieh's mountain-climbing shoes. He might also have paused over line 6 to remember the opening of Hsiang Yü's famous poem: "My strength could topple mountains, my energy covered the world." But lines 5 and 8 contain the features most characteristic of Li Po and most deserving of our attention here.

I sometimes detect in his poetry what, for want of a better word, might be called a "trigger"—a pun, a bit of strange syntax, or an unexpected word which, when recognized and "activated," sets off a chain of associations alerting the reader to new levels of meaning and camouflaged allusions elsewhere in the poem. Line 5, as usually construed, is taken to say, "The Lady of Heaven, joining the heavens, stretches across the heavens." But this reading requires a syntactic construction that is atypical of Li Po, and I suspect that we have, instead, one of his "triggers." Slowing down to decide whether he likes the line's three repetitions of "heaven," the reader might recall the rather obscure constellation "Heavenly Span," a group of eight stars in Cassiopoeia that is thought of as a bridge across the Milky Way. Just such a bridge would be necessary to reach the magic islands, located, as the *Lieh-tzu* tells us, in a ravine filled with the waters of the earth and the Milky Way.[7] At the same time, the obscurity of this asterism is just what is needed to alert the reader so that he will give proper attention to what follows.

Sun Ch'o's high estimation of those mountains notwithstanding, the Heavenly Terrace reels back and tips southeast before the greater magic of the Lady of Heaven. We are, however, being asked to sense more than magic, for there is also cosmology and allusion here. The "T'ang wen" section of the *Lieh-tzu*, which tells us about the magic islands cut off by the waters of the Milky Way, also tells us about Kung-kung breaking the Pillars of Heaven, the celestial counterpart of the Heavenly Terrace, causing the earth and sky to tilt, with the result that, ever after, heavenly bodies have rolled toward the west, while the waters of the earth flow southeastward into the sea. The reader need not, of course, recall this *Lieh-tzu* story in order to follow the poem on at least one level, but he probably will recall it if he has proceeded with all his sensors out, seeking confirmation of his suspicions about the "Heavenly Span." The recollection, then, will tend to confirm those suspicions, while simultaneously tightening the poem by setting up resonant associations between outwardly unrelated lines. It is, at the same time, noteworthy—and characteristic of Li Po—that these associations should be established by knotting together threads of allusion and reference in a common external source which itself has some more general relevance to the poem.[8] In this case, recollection of the *Lieh-tzu* chapter adds depth to the poem, since, like the poem on one level, it too is concerned with the concept of worlds within worlds. One might note, incidentally, that this cosmology also anticipates and "explains" line 40, thereby pumping a bit of juice back into that tired cliché about life being like an easterly flowing stream. Anticipation is only one of the ways Li Po revives clichés. He does it with parallelism in lines 14 and 15 of the next poem, balancing "green shadows" against "birds flying" to remind us that *this* "green" is *kingfisher* green. As if informed of Roman Jakobson's observation that everything sequent is simile, he does it with juxtaposition in line 4 of the third poem, where the proximity of "orchid-strong jaw sinew"[9] reactivates the sense of "cheeks" in *ch'üan-ch'i,* which is usually regarded simply as a mysterious term meaning "a fast horse."

A final noteworthy aspect of Li Po's craft displayed in this poem is his manipulation of meter, tone, and rhyme to tighten the structure and reinforce the imagery and literary allusion. The usual observation that Tu Fu was a great master of regulated verse, while Li Po preferred a freer and less rigorous style seems to have led to a critical consensus that Li Po did not do anything particularly worthy of analysis in this area. But look at what is happening here:

Immediately obvious are the six two-line stanzas punctuating the poem—all but one of which rhyme in the oblique tones. One also quickly notices lines like 22-24 and 31-34, recalling the patterns (and the word magic) of the "Nine Songs," and others like 25-28 and 35-38, which are reminiscent of, and sometimes actually borrowed from, Han dynasty rhyme prose. At closer inspection, one then discovers the unusual tonic features of the poem, set forth here with "o" for the even tones and "x" for the oblique ones, while the rhyming lines are marked by "R."

```
 1 xx ooo R
 2 oooo xoo R
 3 xo xox R
 4 ooox xxx R

 5 oxoo xoo R
 6 xxxx xxo R
 7 ooxx xox
 8 xxxx ooo R

 9 xxoo xox R
10 xxox xox R

11 ox xxx
12 xx xxo R
13 xoxx oxx
14 xxxx ooo R
15 xx xox
16 oo ooo R
17 xx xxx
18 oo ooo R

19 ooxx xxx R
20 ooxx xxx R

21 oooo xoo R
22 xooo ooo R
23 oooo xx
24 xxxo oo R

25 xxxx
26 oooo R
27 xoxx
28 oooo R
29 ooxx xxx
30 xxxx ooo R

31 oooo oox R
32 oooo ooox R

33 xxxo ooo R
34 oooo xoo R
35 xoxx xx
```

```
36 xoxo oo R
37 oxoo xx
38 xxoo oo R
39 xoox xox R
40 xoxx oox R
41 xoxo ooo R
42 xxxx ooo R
43 ooxo xoo R
44 ooooxo xox
45 xxxx ooo R
```

In tonic poetry, as in music, monotony produces a tension that one seeks to resolve, perhaps unconsciously, by getting on to a contrasting or "resolving" tone as quickly as possible. Here, in lines 6-8, 11-15, and 31-32, for example, the long sequences of words in the same tonic category—particularly those in the less easily sustained oblique tones—are quite extraordinary, and one can hardly doubt that they contribute to the poem's breathless pace, which seems so appropriate to the narration of events in a dream. Neither can one doubt that the effect was intentional, for even and oblique tones would be much more evenly dispersed in a random text, and we shall see Li Po using tones to achieve special but very different effects in the next poem.

```
 1 I am, in fact, the Madman of Ch'u,
 2 Making fun of Confucius with a Phoenix Song.
 3 In my hand I carry a green jade cane
 4 And set forth at dawn from Yellow Crane Hall.
 5 When I search for immortals on the Five Summits, I never complain how far,
 6 For all my life I have liked to roam in the mountains of renown.
 7 Lu Mountain bursts in splendor at the side of Southern Dipper;
 8 The nine panels of Folding Screen covered in cloud brocade;
 9 And shadows fall on the shining lake to grow like indigo eyebrow paint.
10 The Golden Gates before me open with a curtain between two spires,
11 The Silver River upside down hangs across three beams of stone.
12 The Incense Burner and the waterfall look to each other from far away,
13 The winding cliffs and huddled peaks rise in the blue on blue.
14 Green kingfisher shadows and red clouds intensify in the morning sun,
15 And birds fly on but never arrive, and the skies of Wu are long.
16 Climbing the height gives a splendid view of all of heaven and earth;
17 The mighty Yangtse in endless flow departs and never returns.
18 Yellow clouds for ten thousand miles have colored the driving wind,
19 White waves on the nine circuits are flowing mountains of snow.
20 I like to sing about Lu Mountain,
21 With inspiration from Lu Mountain.
22 At rest, I gaze in Stoney Mirror to purify my heart;
23 Green moss obscures the tracks that Duke Hsieh left behind.
```

24 Sublimed cinnabar, taken soon, will throw off worldly care;

25 When the heart is a lute thrice tuned, the Way can be attained.

26 Far above I see the immortals in the midst of luminous clouds,

27 Proceeding to court in the Palace of Jade with lotuses in their hands.

28 I made a promise long ago to meet Boundless above the nine spheres;

29 I wish I could take Lu Drifting along to visit Transcendently Pure.

### "A Lu Mountain Song for the Palace Censor Empty-Boat Lu"

As we turn now to **"A Lu Mountain Song for the Palace Censor Empty-Boat Lu,"** it might be best to stay with the discussion of tonic features, for in this poem, which is also superficially about a mountain, we have an equally lush vocabulary, but a totally different disposition of tones. The striking thing in **"Lu Mountain Song"** is that sequences in the same tonic category are regularly *avoided*—so much so, in fact, that a balance of even and oblique tones before the caesura becomes a dominant pattern throughout the poem:

```
 1 xx xoo
 2 xo xxo R
 3 xo xxx
 4 ox oxo R
 5 xxoo xox
 6 xoxx ooo R

 7 ooxx oxo R
 8 ooxx oxo R
 9 xxoo oxo R
10 oxoo xox
11 ooxx oxo R
12 ooxx oox
13 ooxx ooo R
14 xxoo xox
15 xoxx ooo R

16 ooxo oxo R
17 xooo xxo R
18 ooxx xox
19 xoxx oxo R

20 xo ooo
21 xo oox R
22 ooxx oxo
23 xoox oox R
24 xxoo oxo R

25 ooxx xoo R (and ooox xoo R)
26 oxoo xox
27 xxoo oxo R
28 ooxx xox
29 xxoo oxo R
```

As can be seen, eight of the lines (1, 6, 10, 15, 16, 17, 19, and 26) do not have the balance or "resolution" before the caesura, but the pattern is sufficiently well established by the others so that these departures from that pattern can

themselves make a contribution to the effectiveness of the poem. It is hard to be sure how much of this was intentional on Li Po's part, but it is interesting to observe that in several cases (lines 1, 6, 10, and 15) any weakening of the caesura that one might feel as a result of the imbalance would not be inappropriate to the sense of the line. It is also interesting, and probably more significant, that irregular lines predominate in the third stanza (lines 16-19), setting it off tonically from what precedes, just as it is set off by its shift of focus, anticlimactic imagery, and the double meanings which will be discussed below. It would seem very possible that Li Po counted on this tonic variation to serve as a "trigger" alerting the reader to the special significance of the lines. The peculiar nine-line second stanza, which has always given commentators so much difficulty, may be similarly served by the irregularity of line 10 which tends to "set off" the three opening lines. This slight variation of the pattern (together with the perfect tonic identity of lines 7 and 8 and some balanced expressions in the later couplets) may have made it easier for the T'ang reader to guess that the stanza was, as it turns out, Li Po's own "Phoenix Song" to be construed as a tercet with three rhyming refrains. In any event, the tonic features of this poem like those of the first, must have made an impression on Tu Fu even though he preferred to use tones very differently in his own poetry.

And just as these tonic features stand in sharp contrast to those of the first poem, so does the experience of **"Lu Mountain Song"** proceed in a somewhat different order. In the first poem, the primary intent was conveyed rather quickly through vivid description and fairly obvious multiple levels of meaning, leaving the reader to work out his appreciation of details at leisure. Here, though one is again struck by a rich description of a mountain, the numerous details must sink in first before the poem can burst open to reveal the full range of its intention. (And it is, of course, appropriate that the more difficult poem should have the more regular tonic pattern to sustain the poetry and guide the reader through its complexities). . . .

Gradually, as one rereads, . . . random elements begin to make an impression. How like Li Po to write a **"Lu Mountain Song"** for a Mr. Lu—Wallace Stevens would have made it "A Jamaica Song for Mr. James"—and does not the man-mountain association make it all the more reasonable to associate Li Po with the waterfall, and the Incense Burner Peak ("lu" again) with Mr. Lu, the authority on throne room protocol?[10] Then one pictures Li Po at the mountain top discovering that his elevation so minimizes ground distance that the birds, seen as far-off specks, seem to fly endlessly without getting anywhere. And it is, of course, a "mountain of renown"—one where elixirs can be brewed most satisfactorily. Thus, green shadows and red clouds, the food of would-be immortals who would themselves learn to fly, seem all the more nicely to anticipate the more elaborate elixir, sublimed cinnabar, mentioned in line 24.

From this point, one begins to struggle a bit, especially with the difficulties of line 25; the immediate context suggests the Taoistic interpretation, "making one's heart pure as lute music through breath control concentrated on the three cinnabar fields of the body,"[11] but it is hard to forget that the phrase "lute heart" occurs first and most memorably in the *Shih chi* biography of Ssu-ma Hsiang-ju, where it is recorded that Ssu-ma seduced the young widow Cho Wen-chün by "luting his heart"—that is, conveying his feelings in lute music—as he played his "Phoenix Song." If this is to be the interpretation, then the words *san-tien*, previously construed as "the three cinnabar fields," may be taken in their more usual sense of "three repetitions or refrains,"[12] and one is thereupon drawn back to the second stanza, where Li Po seems to have written his own "Phoenix Song" consisting of a tercet with three refrains. He says he is making fun of Confucius (and therewith the establishment), but he is writing to Mr. Lu. Could it be that when he says "Confucius" . . ., he is also punningly pulling the leg of his friend "Empty-Boat" . . .?

Suddenly it all seems too much, for we have complexity without sufficient form and direction. Everything resonates, but there is no progression. And we may even note that we seem to be left with a very limp stanza in lines 16-19, coming as an anticlimax after the exuberance of what went before.

The answer is that Li Po is trying to make his reader see something more—something that would have been more readily appreciated by Empty-Boat, Tu Fu, or any of their contemporaries. Fortunately, we have the keys to the mystery. Empty-Boat, a native of unreliable Fanyang—which had become the more unreliable since An Lu-shan established his base of power there—was appointed to the post of palace censor sometime shortly after 756, at the height of the An Lu-shan Rebellion.[13] When news of the appointment reached Li Po in 759 or 760, he was no doubt quick to see that a Fan-yang man at court was in a precarious position—especially quick to see it, perhaps, because news of the appointment was probably brought to him by Chia Chih, drafter of Empty-Boat's appointment, a man of considerable influence who had himself fallen from favor and had stopped to visit with Li Po on his way into exile.[14]

With this in mind, we need only the "trigger" of the poem's last line to be convinced of what Li Po is up to here. When he says he would like to take Lu Drifting (Lu Ao) along, we know that he means Empty-Boat Lu, not only because of the general sense of the poem and the identity of the surnames, but also because a palace censor, an authority on protocol, would be precisely the man to take if you were planning to have an audience with the immortals. We can be still the more certain because Empty-Boat's name comes from the *Chuang-tzu,* where the ideal man is likened to an untied boat, both *empty* and *drifting along.*[15] Thus, Li Po has constructed his line so that Lu Ao's name plus the next word become a pun or kenning for Empty-Boat Lu. The ploy is just outrageous enough to send the reader back through the poem to confirm and reorganize his initial impressions.

There is no doubt now that Li Po is having fun, that the dual interpretations and innuendoes are really there, and

that this is, indeed, his "Phoenix Song" In fact, two "Phoenix Songs." One, like the original sung for Confucius, to warn Empty-Boat of political dangers; the other, like Ssu-ma Hsiang-ju's, to seduce Empty-Boat with the attractions of Lu Mountain so that he, too, will run away. And if the warning seems weak in comparison with the praise of the mountain, we need only reexamine the third stanza with an expectant eye. Surveying the world from his lofty perch, Li Po can contemplate the "yellow wind" from the West, stirred up by the Sogdian An Lu-shan. That same height would make it hard to see waves on the "nine rivers" of Kiukiang at the foot of Lu Mountain even if one could conceive of them as "flowing mountains of snow,"[16] but the impossibility is the magic of the line, for it forces us to see instead the social order of the T'ang flowing away like water to the sea. The use of the word *circuit* instead of *channel* or *river* is, then, no accident here as some have assumed. Li Po is reminding us that he is thinking of China's plight by recalling the Nine Circuits into which China was divided by Emperor Yü after he had dug the nine rivers to control the flood. The symbolism is heightened by the evocation of lines from Hsieh Ling-yün:

> But a thousand thoughts torment me day and night,
> Ten thousand passions harass me, dawn till dusk.
> I climbed the cliffs to watch the Stone Mirror shining.
> I pushed through the forest and entered the Gates of Pine.
> Tales of the Three Rivers are mostly forgotten by now,
> Only the names of the Nine Streams still remain.
> The magic things rarely display their marvels,
> The weird people hide their subtle souls.[17]

In his contribution to the present volume, Hans H. Frankel has proposed six *topoi* as characteristic of poems concerned with the contemplation of history: (1) ascent to a high place; (2) looking into the distance in conjunction with viewing the past; (3) the durability of rivers and mountains as a contrast to human transience; (4) reference to historical personalities and extant relics of the past; (5) description of a landscape devoid of historical association; and (6) tears. It is probably no mere coincidence that we can find something of at least five of the *topoi* in this one stanza, where Li Po is contemplating China's past, present, and future.

Admittedly, Tu Fu or a contemporary would have responded to all of this much more readily than we do today. But I suggest that his response would have proceeded more or less in the order I have described, causing him to marvel at the skill and wit with which Li Po had woven his lines together to create a dense and beautiful poem that is also an effective statement about himself and his society. An appreciation of this skill in making statements about himself and his society depends, of course, on knowing as much as possible about Li Po and the T'ang—but properly applying what we do know can also enable us to learn still more. The last poem provides a case in point, for we can see there that the T'ang reader's familiarity with the facts of Li Po's life must have greatly reinforced the impact made by the poem. At the same time, we today can, by careful correlation of the facts at hand, see that Li Po may be telling us more than we have previously known about what it was like to live in the T'ang and to be Li Po.

Before considering the poem itself, I will have to digress to summarize my own position on various questions relating to Li Po's background and ancestry. This is necessary when proposing a correlation of Li Po's life and poetry because one never knows to which group of believers his readers happen to belong: those who feel that Li Po was so surely of foreign origin that there is nothing to discuss; those who feel that he was so thoroughly Chinese that there is nothing to discuss; or those, like Herbert Franke, who feel that the question is meaningless because "Li Po belongs to Chinese literature just as Chamisso does to the German and Joseph Conrad to English."[18] The trouble is that for Franke's analogy to work, we would have to have a Conrad *suspected* by some of Polish birth, protesting his English origin, but often writing about Poland and sometimes composing in Polish at the court of an English king who was uneasy about his own Slavic ancestry and suspicious of all foreigners including Poles.

To draw only the most reasonable conclusions from the most reliable sources—Li Po himself; the writings of Li Yang-ping, Wei Hao, and Liu Ch'üan-po, who knew Li Po; and the inscription by Fan Ch'uan-cheng, who knew Li Po's granddaughters—we ought to be able to agree on the following general propositions, which are sufficient to support the present analysis of his poetry:

1. Li Po was born in 701, somewhere in Central Asia, where his family had been living for a century or more. In a letter datable to 757, Li Po wrote that he was fifty-six years old—thus born in 701.[19] Li Yang-ping and Fan Ch'uan-cheng indicate that the family returned to China no earlier than 705. (He probably died in late 762 or early 763, but we cannot use the Li Yang-ping preface to establish the year of his death as virtually all recent writers have been inclined to do. That preface, dated November 30, 762, says only that Li Po was sick and nothing about his having died.)

2. There is no reason not to accept the claims that while "in exile" the Lis lived in Suyab, now Tokmak in the Kirghiz S.S.R., *and* near T'iao-chih in what is now northern Afghanistan.[20] Both spots were on the trade routes, and it scarcely matters whether the areas were under Chinese control at any given time. Once exiled, the Lis might have gone secretly where they pleased (it is said that they changed their name), and we cannot, for that matter, even be positive that the family was Chinese to begin with. In any event, we know that there were upheavals in the Lis' claimed ancestral home area (near T'ien-shui in Kansu) during the late Sui, when they are said to have fled, and we know that an embassy from northern Afghanistan was able to reach China without difficulty in 705.[21]

3. Much more likely than not, the Li family was engaged in trade both before and after their return to China. That would have been the most usual way to make a living along the trade route, and when they returned to China, the Lis returned to Szechwan, known for its foreign merchant community, rather than to their claimed ancestral home. A merchant background would also account for the fact that Li Po seems always to have had plenty of money without holding land or office; and the double stigma of being a "foreign merchant" might be added to "drink" and "indifference" on the list of possible explanations for his failure to enjoy the usual civil service career. China's ethnocentrism and Confucian disdain of merchants are well known. In fact, Li Po does *not* seem to have been indifferent to a career, and it is questionable whether he really drank more than some successful officeholders.[22]

4. There is no reason not to believe Liu Ch'üan-po and Fan Ch'uan-cheng when they imply that Li Po could compose in a foreign language, and there is at least one poem (no. 945) by Li Po himself with a similar suggestion. It would be strange if the Lis did *not* know Turkish or some other foreign language after living for a century in Central Asia; and many people, including members of the T'ang royal family, are said to have known Turkish. Naturally if they were merchants, there would have been all the more reason to keep the language alive even after their return to China.

5. Regardless of whether he was born to it or whether it was acquired, Li Po shows the marked influence of Central Asian culture. We know, of course, that he writes about Central Asian subjects, as in the poem we are about to consider. We might also note that his elder son Po-ch'in ( . . . a Chinese name that might yet transcribe *begim,* the Turkish for "My Prince") had a second and very unChinese name, "Moon Slave," which is a typically Turkish name for an *eldest* son.[23] His younger son had the equally exotic name P'o-li, a transcription of a foreign word for "rock crystal," which evokes the culture of Central Asia in several ways. During the T'ang dynasty rock crystal most often came to China from that area in northern Afghanistan where the Lis are said to have lived, and P'o-li was also the name of the mountain in that same area containing the cave said to produce the "heavenly horses."[24] We might further observe that P'o-li, taken word for word, means "quite black" and is, therefore, just the opposite of Li Po's courtesy name T'ai-po, meaning "very white," which happens, of course, to be the name of a mountain in China, as well as a perfect translation of the well-attested Turkish personal name "Appaq." We know that black and white mountains held special significance for the Turks, and this suggestion of Turkish cultural influence seems the more compelling when we consider the name of Li Po's father. It has been argued before that he acquired his name K'o, meaning "stranger," when he returned to China. And quite possibly so. But what was he called "back home," and why did he choose to stick with this none too flattering name? Very possibly it was a compromise, for K'o, pronounced *k'vk* in the T'ang, sounds very much like *kök,* the Turkish word for "blue." We know that blue, white, and black were three colors of special significance to the

Turks,[25] and it is curious to find them so easily associated with three successive generations of Lis. Curious also that among close blood relatives for whom names are preserved, it is only his daughter P'ing-yang . . . whose name suggests no immediate association with Turkish culture—and even here it is perhaps not impossible to see a transcription of the Turkish for "thousand echoes." A preoccupation with black and white mountains, a great weakness for wine, and a passion for the moon are reported or detectable characteristics of the Turkish people throughout much of history.[26] We have just spoken of the mountains, and Li Po's love of wine is well known. It only remains to be noted that Li Po mentions the moon approximately 403 times, exclusive of date-time references, in some 1,000 poems. Tu Fu has 167 moons in 1,457 poems; and Yeats, our own most moonstruck poet, refers to the moon 176 times in 448 poems with a total length roughly equal to the Li Po corpus.

The significance of many of these points will, I hope, become more evident when we consider our final poem:

1 From a Scythian cave came the heavenly horse,
2 With tiger-stripe back and dragon-wing bones.
3 Neighing to the blue clouds. Shaking a green mane.
4 Orchid-strong jaw sinew, speed-tokened cheeks, he vanished when he ran.
5 Over the Kunlun. To the West Edge of Earth.
6 His four feet never stumbled.
7 At cockcrow groomed in Yen, at dusk he was foddered in Yüeh,
8 The path of a spirit, a lightning flash, galloping past as a blur.
9 A heavenly horse summons. A flying dragon response.
10 Eyes bright as the Evening Star, his breast a brace of ducks,
11 His tail was like a comet, his neck a sprinkler cock;
12 Red light spewed from his mouth, in his sweat canals were pearls.
13 He once accompanied the Timely Dragon to leap in the heavenly streets,
14 Haltered gold and bridled moon that shone in the City of Stars.
15 A spirit apart, proud and assured, he vaulted the nine domains,
16 A white jade like a mountain that nobody dared to buy.
17 Soon they laughed at this Purple Swallow,
18 Thought to themselves, "How dumb your kind."
19 The heavenly horse dashed forward. He longed for the sovereign's coach.
20 With reins let out he could leap and rear to tumble the passing clouds,
21 But his feet moved in check for ten thousand miles,
22 And he gazed from afar at the gates to the throne.
23 He met no horseman like Master Cold Wind
24 To employ the scion of vanishing light.
25 White clouds in a blue sky,
26 The hills are far away.
27 The salt wagon piled high must climb the precipitous grade,
28 Counter to custom, unmindful of right, fearing the close of day.

29 Po-le's art to curry and clip was lost along the way;
30 In my youth they used my strength, they cast me off in age.
31 I would like to meet a T'ien Tzu-fang
32 That he, in pity, might care for me,
33 But though he had Jade Mountain grain,
34 My flesh could not be healed.
35 A hard frost in the Fifth Month withered the buds on the cinnamon tree;
36 Now in the stall I furrow my brow, the bit of injustice in myteeth.
37 I beg the sovereign to redeem me, send me off to Emperor Mu,
38 That I may yet play with my shadow and dance by the Jasper Pool.

**"Song of the Heavenly Horse"**

If the reader has, however tentatively, accepted my arguments concerning Li Po's background, it should be evident that this poem is far more autobiographical than has been supposed. Look, for example, at the number of terms and references that Li Po has used to underscore his identity with the heavenly horse: the Scythian cave (located in P'o-li Mountain); the Evening Star (also "T'ai-po" in Chinese); and the "white jade like a mountain" (since "Po" means "white," and "T'ai-po" is also the name of a mountain). Thus alerted, one might further note that "haltered gold" is a similar identity, since "gold" (or "metal") is the element associated with the West and with T'ai-po or "whiteness," be it the man, the mountain, or the star. "Bridled moon" in the same line is perhaps even more productive. First, it tightens the poem by "resonating" with the numerous astronomical references; then one might relate it to the other anatomical terms by thinking of the "moon" or "moons" of the horse's forehead and cheeks. But, of course, in this context, the phrase tends, above all, to make us think of Li Po and his passion for the moon. T'ang readers acquainted with Li Po might also have thought of his elder son "Moon Slave," who sometimes traveled with his father and was known to his friends. Finally, we probably need to consider "scion of vanishing light" in line 24 as yet another identity, since "vanishing light" suggests both speed and the West where the light goes when it disappears. At the same time, it is easy to think of T'ai-po, the Evening Star, as scion of the setting sun.[27] It would probably have to have been a rather private joke, but it is just conceivable that Li Po is also suggesting "scion of I Khan," King of the Turks. This khan, whose personal name seems to have been Qara or "Black," would be relevant in a "horse context" because he sent an impressive gift of fifty-thousand horses to China in 553. But regardless of how we construe this identity, there is a nice irony in the fact that this allusion to a "son of the West," who is being badly used in China, is immediately followed by an allusion to a Chinese, the legendary Emperor Mu, who was graciously received in the Western world.

These various identities and affinities do not, of course, make a good poem or even an autobiographical poem in and of themselves. It is important, therefore, to note how well elements of the poem correspond with what we know about Li Po's career: exotic origin (lines 1-8); early evidence of great talent (also 1-8); pride, self-confidence, and ambition (especially lines 6-12, 15-16, 19-20); overnight fame and success at the capital plus association with the emperor and high officials (lines 9-16); rather inexplicable rejection (lines 17-18); desperate efforts to return to service (lines 19-28); disgrace, jail, and exile (lines 31-38); and an old age spent far removed from the splendors he had once known (lines 25-38). In many of his poems Li Po uses "blue clouds" and "cinnamon twigs" as symbols of honors and aspiration to high office.[28] In this poem the progression of this career from youthful ambition to an old age of rejection and neglect seems emphasized by the "neighing to the blue clouds" in line 3 and the "withered buds on the cinnamon tree" in line 35.

It is hard to guess how much this poem may have told a T'ang reader about the reasons for Li Po's frustration, but even now we can pick out a few suggestions. The repeated references to the West and the final couplet with its plea that he be sent back to the West may be a hint that his origins and China's ethnocentrism were, indeed, one source of his discontent. Then, just from the tone of the poem alone, we might suspect that an excess of pride and ambition was another factor. But interestingly, that may be what Li Po is consciously trying to tell us—particularly in line 28. The words which I translate as "counter to custom, unmindful of right" are still used in modern speech as a cliché for "acting irrationally," and it is assumed that the source is the *Shih chi* biography of Wu Tzu-hsü, who beat the corpse of a king who had killed his father and brother.[29] There is, however, another occurrence of the phrase in the *Han shu* biography of Chu-fu Yen (died 127 B.C.).[30] Accused of being overly ambitious and overly familiar with the emperor, Chu-fu Yen replied:

> From youth, I traveled and studied for more than forty years and never enjoyed success. My parents did not regard me as a son, my brothers would not receive me, my colleagues rejected me, my days of distress were long. But if a man cannot dine from five pots in life, then let him be boiled in five pots to die. My day is coming to a close. Thus, I act counter to custom and unmindful of right [i.e. careless about formalities].

It is not impossible that Li Po was aware that his personality could offend as well as charm, and read in the light of the Chu-fu Yen biography, line 28 could be both an apology and a hint of his desperation. Of course, the line might simultaneously evoke the Wu Tzu-hsü biography, so it is also possible to read in a criticism of officialdom for having acted irrationally. Perhaps Li Po meant to leave this point in question.

Thus far, I have talked primarily about *what* Li Po is saying in this poem without having said much about *how well* he is saying it. To some extent, an understanding of what is said is, of course, prerequisite to judging how well it is being said, and we have already noted sufficient correspondences between Li Po's life and the poem to guess

that it must have seemed a powerful personal statement, especially to the T'ang readers who knew Li Po. But before concluding, we might note a few additional features that reinforce the statement and strengthen the poem.

Most obvious among the "strengthening" devices is the elaborate blending of horse imagery, astronomy, anatomy, and references to himself and the West, which fills the poem with echoes and anticipations. And, as noted in the discussion of "bridled moon," the words sometimes cross over to resonate with terms and references in different categories. A similar case is that of Po-le, the great judge of horses, for Po-le is also the star that governs horses, and it was Po-le, the man, who came to the aid of the old horse relegated to pulling the original salt wagon. Still more strengthening or tightening of the poem is provided by lines 25 and 26 which anticipate the final couplet with its references to Emperor Mu and the Jasper Pool. "White clouds in a blue sky, The hills are far away" is a revision of lines from the song for Emperor Mu sung by the Queen Mother of the West when he visited her at the Jasper Pool.[31] Appropriately, a note of despair ("the hills are far away") has been substituted for the optimism of the original song.

By now, any reader familiar with Chinese literature will probably have noticed the numerous echoes of earlier "horse poetry" which serve as another strengthening device. In the Han dynasty sacrificial ode of identical title and in the "Rhymeprose on a Red and White Horse" (*Che-po ma fu*) by Yen Yen-chih (384-456) we have the source of many terms and phrases adapted here: the tiger's double spine, speed-tokened cheeks, the West Edge of Earth, exhaustion of strength in youth, the grooming in Yen and feeding in Yüeh, the gates to the throne, and the nine domains.[32] These special echoes would, I think, help to make an exotic poem seem at the same time familiar to a Chinese reader; and in that, their contribution is not unlike the one made by tone, rhyme, and meter, or other patterning devices which help to bind a complex of imagery so that it will hold a reader until he can work out his personal response.

It is, finally, the contribution of tone, rhyme, and meter that deserves our attention, for in this poem, as in the two previously discussed, Li Po has done more in this area than has been heretofore supposed. This time there is no tonic patterning of any importance, but something rather special has been done with the meter and the rhymes:

```
 1 oxox xox R
 2 xoxo oxx R
 3 ooo xxx R
 4 oooo xxx R
 5 ooo xox
 6 xx oxx R
 7 ooxo xxx R
 8 ooxx xxx R

 9 oxo ooo R RR
10 xooo xoo RR
11 xooo xxo R
```

```
12 xooo xoo R
13 oooo xoo R
14 ooxx xoo R
15 xxoo oxo R
16 xxoo oxo R
17 oo xxx
18 xx xxo R

19 oxo xoo R RR
20 xxox ooo RR
21 xx xxx
22 oo oxo R
23 xo oox
24 ox xxo R

25 xo xoo
26 oox R
27 oooo xxx R
28 xoxo xxx R
29 xxxx oxo R
30 xxox xxo R
31 xo oxo
32 xo xxo R
33 ox xoo
34 xo xxo R
35 ooxx oxo R
36 xxoo oxo R
37 xoxx xox
38 ooxx xoo R
```

Although I have attempted to indicate the internal rhymes only for lines 9 and 10 and 19 and 20, where they reinforce the final rhymes, the superfluity of rhyme is immediately evident from a glance at the above schematization. For a T'ang reader the effect may have been still more striking, since, with the exception of line 37, the nonrhyming lines are always the shorter lines. An equally striking feature of the poem is the irregular meter—in particular, the six-word lines that break into two units of three words with a caesura in the middle. It is easy to speculate that Li Po was striving for a special effect with this manipulation of meter and rhyme, but not so easy to guess what the effect was supposed to be. The abruptness of line 26, which is just three words, seems appropriate to emphasize the gloomy revision of the song by the Queen Mother of the West. And it is true that the Han sacrificial ode "Song of the Heavenly Horse" consists entirely of three-word lines. But one is left with the feeling that for the T'ang reader there was something more.

That "something" was, I think, Li Po's further evocation of the West by elaboration of some hitherto unrecognized verse form that was, in T'ang times, popularly associated with the music and culture of Central Asia—a verse form evolved, perhaps, to suit the requirements of music of Central Asian origin.[33] I suspect that identification of the basic form and a proper understanding of what Li Po has done with it will have to await the future studies of Laurence Picken, whose performance of T'ang music was a highlight of the conference that produced this volume. Nevertheless, I believe we can even now establish that superfluous rhyme and irregular meter were associated with music and Central Asia during the T'ang dynasty. Although

it may not be the basic verse form behind **"Song of the Heavenly Horse,"** we do find *one* basic unit of verse with those features that seems to have been so associated. It appears to be a seven-word verse of six lines, characterized by rhyme in all lines but the fifth and by the optional use of a "broken six-word meter" in one or two of the lines.[34] The following poem, also by Li Po, may be a significant example:

1 Grape Wine.                    Golden bowls.
2 A girl from Wu, just fifteen, bundled on a blooded horse.
3 Indigo blue she paints her brows, red brocade are her shoes;
4 She speaks her words a little askew to tempt when she sings her songs.
5 At the feast on tortoise-shell mats, she gets drunk in your arms,
6 In bed beneath the lotus curtains, what will she do to you?

```
1 OOX OXO R
2 OOXX XXO R
3 OXXO OOO R
4 XXXX OOO R
5 XXOO OXX
6 OOXX XOO R
```

**"Take Wine"**

It would require a separate essay to make the case that this poem represents a distinct verse form and, moreover, a form associated with music and the culture of Central Asia. The main points of that argument can, however, be briefly raised if the interested reader will compare this poem with the two examples by Ts'en Shen (715-70) and T'ang Yen-ch'ien (fl. c. 885), cited in note 40. As one scans lines 1-6 of the three poems, three things are immediately obvious: (1) all three poems have the same rhyme pattern—and, in fact, the same rhyme; (2) all three poems are concerned with music and parties; and (3) all three poems refer in some way to the culture of Central Asia. (At a glance, only the Ts'en Shen poem is *specifically* concerned with Central Asia—written at a military encampment in Chiu-ch'üan ["Wine Spring"], it makes reference to *p'i-p'a* music, barbarian singers, and fricassee of wild camel—but all three use the foreign word *p'o-lo* when referring to "golden wine cups.")[35] The suspicion that three poems so peculiarly similar *do* represent a *distinct* verse form tends to be confirmed when we scrutinize the poem by T'ang Yen-ch'ien. It has, in fact, eight rather than six lines and would therefore seem to upset the argument—until one notices that the last two lines are simply a congratulatory couplet tacked onto the basic form. Such a tacked-on couplet could hardly be effective, unless it were being tacked onto something with an identity of its own. One might argue, of course, that T'ang Yen-ch'ien has merely written a bad poem that collapses at the end, but, happily for T'ang, the Li Ch'i poem that David Lattimore [elsewhere] discusses shows another poet making similar use of this basic form. If one detaches the *clearly detachable* first and last couplets of that ten-line poem, he is again left with a six-line verse rhyming in all lines but the fifth. Again it is a poem about a party and music—indeed, it is even called a "zither song"—and again there is an evocation of Central Asia, for the poet is apparently contrasting frontier hardship with comfortable loneliness back home, and the crows are almost surely the carrion crows of the *frontier* wall.[36]

Regardless of whether I have successfully isolated a significant basic verse form behind Li Po's "Song of the Heavenly Horse," one can, I think, safely assume that the poem would, in any event, have seemed easily associable with *some* special music of the day. The soon to evolve *tz'u* or "lyric" poetry, also distinguished by irregular meter and "superfluous" rhyme, was unquestionably related to music, and it would be strange if Li Po were not equally as much influenced by music as his immediate successors. He writes frequently about parties, dancing, and song, and Wei Hao even thought it relevant to record that "The Waves of Kokonor" *(Ch'ing-hai po)* was one of Li Po's favorite songs. Interestingly, the tune of that title which Picken has reconstructed from the Japanese Tōgaku (T'ang music) repertory, sounds astonishingly similar to the Central Asian music that we know today.[37] This all points, then, to another aspect of Li Po's craftsmanship, another simple, but often overlooked reason for his fame and popularity among his contemporaries: the ability to write dense and evocative yet very singable poems that were exceptionally well suited to the new music of the eighth century.

## Notes

1. There is a measure of Li Po's originality in the *Li shih pien-i* by the Ming scholar Chu Chien, who dismisses many of the best poems, most often finding them deficient in the very respects in which they are most excellent and original. The extent to which he seemed exotic can be judged by another essay, which argues that Li Po must have been a Nestorian Christian because he named one son "P'o-li" ("rock crystal") and there is mention of a rock-crystal goblet in a Nestorian inscription. Similarly, admiration for the poem "The Road to Shu Is Hard" can be measured by the fact that two respected modern scholars, Yü P'ing-po and Li Ch'ang-chih, continue to insist that it must have been written to dissuade the emperor from flight to Shu. A great poem should mark a great occasion.

2. David Hawkes, "The Supernatural in Chinese Poetry," *The Far East: China and Japan* (Toronto: University of Toronto Press, 1961), pp. 311-24. Many of the images in this poem correspond with shamanistic techniques and symbols analyzed by Mircea Eliade in *Shamanism: Archaic Techniques of Ecstasy,* Bollingen Series, no. 76 (New York: Pantheon, 1964), e.g. dream, flight through space, ascending a ladder, entering trance and awakening, journey to the center of the earth, music, confluence of spirits, and the world tree (the Rooster of Heaven perches in a kind of world tree).

3. See A. J. Arberry, *The Seven Odes: The First Chapter in Arabic Literature* (London: Allen and Unwin, 1957), p. 66.

4. Cf. the Kyoto concordance, nos. 502, 578, and 636.

5. Quoted from Richard B. Mather, "The Mystical Ascent of the T'ien-t'ai Mountains: Sun Ch'o's *Yu-t'ien-t'ai-shan fu,*" *Monumenta Serica* 20 (1961): 234-35.

6. Here, I follow the *Ho-yüeh ying-ling chi,* hereafter *Ho-yüeh,* notable for its interesting variants, as I do also for the last line of this poem. All other texts I have seen ignore that variant and write, "It would mean that my heart and face would never be able to smile" *(shih wo pu te k'ai hsin yen).* To my knowledge the *Ho-yüeh* variant is the only instance in polite Chinese literature where the pleasures of wine and sex are mentioned *together* without some sort of reproving noise.

7. See A. C. Graham, *The Book of Lieh-tzü* (London: John Murray, 1960), p. 97.

8. Cf. "The Road to Shu Is Hard" (no. 062), where the totemism of ancient Shu (Szechwan) and the snake and cuckoo symbolism all come to life after one is led back to the *Huayang kuo chih* and the lore of that area.

9. Although jaw sinews could easily be likened to the tough, flat leaves of the orchid (an *Epidendrum*), it is by no means certain that *lan* did mean "orchid" at the time this term was coined. If *lan* does denote a plant and is not simply a phonetic borrowing, it might be better to translate it as "boneset" *(Eupatorium perfoliatum),* or "agrimony" *(E. cannabinum).* It is clear that in many *early* texts *lan* is often a member of the genus *Eupatorium,* perhaps *E. Lindleyanum* (= *E. Chinense* and *E. Kirilowii?*). Still, as Bretschneider notes, the occasional emphasis on great fragrance suggests than *lan* may have sometimes denoted "orchid" even in the Classics.

10. Perhaps one could work out a typology of plays on words in Chinese. Here we have a near identity of both sound and characters; in the last line of this poem something that is more of a pun and nonce kenning; and something else again in poem no. 702, where Li Po says, "T'ai-po Mountain talks with me." Yet another type might be represented by the word *tieh* when used to mean "the three cinnabar fields," as here in line 25; there is even the remote possibility of an interlingual pun in line 24 of the third poem.

11. I am indebted to Professor Nathan Sivin for help with the Taoist interpretation of this line.

12. The most famous "three refrains" are the so-called "Yang-kuan san-tieh" evolved from a poem by Wang Wei (699?-761?). That poem in no way resembles this, but it suggests that songs with three "refrains" or "repetitions" were popular in the T'ang. I am grateful to Professor Laurence Picken for calling to my attention the *Ch'in-hsüeh ju-men* (Shanghai: Chung-hua T'u-shu-kuan, 1881?),

B.16a-19a, where the compiler Chang Ho (fl. c. 1850) gives a score for the "Yang-kuan san-tieh" and shows how, at a late period at least, the words were associated with the music. Professor Ogawa Tamaki discusses the "Yang-kuan san-tieh" briefly in "The Song of Ch'ih-le: Chinese Translations of Turkic Folk Songs and Their Influence on Chinese Poetry," *Acta Asiatica* 1 (1960): 54*n*1.

13. The edict promoting Empty-Boat to the post of palace censor may be found in the *CTW* 367.2a. We know it cannot have been drafted until after its author Chia Chih (718-72) was appointed editor of imperial edicts and proclamations in 756.

14. For that visit, see Li Po's poem no. 378.

15. *Chuang-tzu* 32.1

16. Kiukiang supposedly derives its name ("Nine Rivers") from the "nine channels" Emperor Yü dug to control the floods. It is improbable that there were nine obvious channels, not even commemorative ones, in Li Po's day, so there is all the more reason to see something else in this line.

17. Quoted from J. D. Frodsham, *The Murmuring Stream: The Life and Works of Hsieh Ling-yin (385-433), Duke of K'ang-lo* (Kuala Lumpur: University of Malaya Press, 1967), 1:154.

18. Herbert Franke, *Sinologie* (Bern: A. Francke, 1953), p. 169.

19. No. 1008 in the Kyoto concordance.

20. Waley objects that the T'iao-chih in Afghanistan, which slipped from Chinese control around 680, would have been forgotten by most people in the eighth century. Perhaps so, but people who had lived there would not have forgotten the old name, and Li Yang-ping is probably only recording what he heard from Li Po.

21. See Edouard Chavannes, *Documents sur les Tou-kiue (Turcs) Occidentaux* (Saint Peters-bourg, 1903; reprint Paris: Adrien-Maisonneuve, n.d.), p. 157.

22. Kuo Mo-jo is one of the few to defend Li Po against the charge of alcoholism. On page 196 of the paperback edition of his new book (see Bibliographical Note) he observes that Tu Fu has 300 compositions (21 percent of the total) with references to drinking, while Li Po has only 170 (sixteen percent of his total). One could, however, still come away with the impression that Li Po was the greater drinker. He uses the word "wine" some 210 times in his poems, while for Tu Fu the count is only 176 occurrences. Of course, if Li Po did not drink inordinately, the talk about his drinking could have been a disingenuous way of calling attention to his foreign background. Foreigners, Turks in particular, were generally presumed to be heavy drinkers. There is also some evidence that Li Po may have mocked China's ethnocentrism by

caricaturing the popular image of barbarians both in his poetry and in his personal life. See, for example, poem no. 084.

23. V. V. Radlov (W. Radloff), *Opyt" slovarja tjurkskix" narěčij*, reprint (Moscow: Izdatel'stvo Vostočnoj Literatury, 1963), vol. 1, part 1, pp. 5-6, under *ai*, gives a long list of epic and folk heroes with "moon" in their names: Moon Khan, Moon Wing, Moon Marksman, etc.

24. *HTS* (Po-na-pen) 221b.6a.

25. Interestingly, Li Po wanted to be buried on a *blue* mountain (Ch'ing-shan southeast of Tang-t'u in Anhwei). Of course, it may have been, as generally presumed, simply because the poet Hsieh T'iao (464-99), whom he greatly admired, had once built a villa there. There is data on Turkish color preferences scattered throughout René Giraud's *L'Empire des Turcs Célestes* (Paris: Adrien-Maisonneuve, 1960) and Ilse Laude-Cirtautas's *Der Gebrauch der Farbbezeichnungen in den Turkdialekten*, Ural-altaische Bibliothek, no. 10 (Wiesbaden: Harrassowitz, 1961).

26. I am indebted to Joseph Fletcher for help on many problems relating to Central Asia. Otto Maenchen-Helfen has notes on the moon in Central Asian culture in "The Yüeh-chih Problem Re-examined," *Journal of the American Oriental Society* 65 (1945): 80. Translations of a few dozen Li Po moon passages are provided by Ch'en Ch'in-jen, "The Moon and Li Po's Poems," *Tamkang Journal* 3 (1964): 215-22.

27. Professor Yang Lien-sheng, who has helped in countless ways, has some useful remarks on T'ang denotations of the word *ching* ('sun', etc.) in *Ch'ing-hua hsüeh-pao*, n.s. 7, pt. 2 (1969):262.

28. E.g., no. 427.

29. *Shih chi* (Po-na-pen) 66.6a.

30. *Han shu* (Po-na-pen) 64A.20a.

31. See *Mu T'ien-tzu chuan (SPTK)* 3.15ab.

32. See respectively *Yüeh-fu shih-chi (SPTK)* 1.6b and *Wen hsüan (SPTK)* 14.1a-10a.

33. Professor Ogawa Tamaki is on the trail of this kind of influence in the article cited in note 16. For more material in ancient Turkish see Resid Rahmeti Arat, *Eski Türk şiiri* (Ankara: Türk Tarih Kurumu Basimevi, 1965).

34. I regard it as a "basic" unit because *special* end-rhyme patterning would be impossible in a shorter verse. For two more examples, see "After a Party with the Governor of Wine Spring" (Chiu-ch'üan t'ai-shou hsi-shang tsui-hou tso) by Ts'en Shen, and "Farewell to Finance Minister Hsü" (Sung Hsü hu-ts'ao) by T'ang Yen-ch'ien, *CTShih* (Shanghai: T'ungwen, 1887), 7.49b and 25.18a.

35. There is still no consensus on the *"p'o-lo (p'uâ: lâ)* problem."* Professor E. H. Schafer leaves it as *pala* in *The Golden Peaches of Samarkand* (Berkeley: University of California Press, 1963), p. 256. The dates and geographical contexts of the occurrences suggest to me an association with the Persian *piyāla*, "wine cup," perhaps cognate with Greek *phialē*. The T'ang *p'o-lo* often are of Tibetan provenance. For a suggestive cultural link see the silver bowl reproduced on page 256 of David Snellgrove and Hugh Richardson's *A Cultural History of Tibet* (London: Wiedenfeld and Nicolson, 1968). It is the right size and shape for a *p'o-lo* and has an unmistakable Greco-Bactrian design. My thanks to Professors Herbert Bloch and G. L. Tikku for help with Greek and Persian problems respectively.

36. For another very similar contrast see "Song of the Water-Clock at Night" by Wen T'ing-yün (812?-70?). James J. Y. Liu, *The Art of Chinese Poetry* (Chicago: University of Chicago Press, 1962), p. 44, and the *Hua-chien chi (SPTK)* 1.6a.

37. Laurence Picken, "Central Asian Tunes in the *Gagaku* Tradition," *Festschrift Walter Wiora* (Kassel: Bärenreiter, 1967), p. 550. Two of the poems in which Li Po mentions Kokonor (nos. 234 and 619) have quite unusual rhyme and meter patterns, and in one (no. 234) Li Po speaks of improvising a "Kokonor dance."

## Paul W. Kroll (essay date 1986)

SOURCE: "Li Po's Transcendent Diction," in *Journal of the American Oriental Society*, Vol. 106, No 1, 1986, pp. 99-117.

*[In the following essay, Kroll elucidates some of Li Po's more opaque poems "in light of their precise Taoist diction and imagery." Nearly a hundred substantive footnotes have been excised from this abridged version of Prof. Kroll's article, as have his more technical discussions of linguistic and prosodic matters and all Chinese characters. For the complete article, see* Journal of the American Oriental Society,*Vol. 106, No 1, (1986): 99-117.]*

### I. PROTASIS

Of the several areas of Li Po scholarship still awaiting satisfactory study, perhaps none has been more consistently neglected than the great poet's Taoist connection. Scholars both Asian and Western almost uniformly wink at or miserably misinterpret Li Po's use of Taoist imagery and diction in his poems. It is true that some forays in the topic have been attempted. But in virtually every instance such efforts view the poet's so-called "Taoist" sentiments in the light of politics, as indications of Li Po's "escapist" or "satirical" tendencies, or else they regard as the only "Taoist" statements worth examining the poet's use of allusions to the *Lao tzu* and *Chuang tzu* texts or to supposedly philo-

sophical concepts contained in those works. Studies of this sort, however, quite miss the point. Rarely do they succeed in telling us anything worthwhile about the verbal craft or technique behind Li Po's poetry, and almost never do they result in a fuller critical reading of any individual poem. Most culpably, though, they are not actually concerned with, and do not confront, Taoism as it was known to Li Po himself.

For to Li Po, as to all other T'ang poets, "Taoism" meant the sacred scriptures, solemn practices, and holy mysteries comprehended in the religious sphere of the Shang-ch'ing and Ling-pao traditions—a well-developed and, for the most part, elite spiritual domain that had defined itself during the Six Dynasties period and assumed notable importance in the lives of the medieval literocracy. Indeed Li Po is only one of many poets whose works reveal the immense influence of this hierological realm on T'ang literature. But, although extensive and important studies in various aspects of medieval Taoism have been appearing regularly over the past two decades from French and Japanese scholars, and lately from some Americans as well, very few students of medieval literature have in fact availed themselves of the insights to be gained from an acquaintance with the Taoist culture of T'ang China. While it is axiomatic among sinologists that, if one is fully to understand medieval literature he must be thoroughly versed in the classic texts of the Confucian canon and the more important of the scriptures of medieval Buddhism, a comparable concern has rarely been shown for the writings of medieval Taoism—despite the fact that most poets of the T'ang were well-read in these texts and make much use of phrases and concepts gleaned from them in their verses. Much T'ang poetry has in consequence been misread, misapprehended, and mistranslated, or—when the difficulties of interpretation seem too great—simply ignored altogether. The present paper is an attempt to restore to a few more or less opaque poems of Li Po their intelligibility, in light of their precise Taoist diction and imagery.[1]

We begin with a poem, rather baffling at first glance, entitled **"The Lady of the Highest Prime"** (Shang-yüan fu-jen):

> Shang-yüan is what Lady?
> Specially matching the Royal Mother's loveliness.
> Upborne and apical—her tri-cornered chignon;
> 4 The rest of her hair falling loosely to her waist.
> As outer wrap she wears a blue furred damask,
> And her person is attired in a caftan of red frost.By her hand she leads forward little miss Ying,
> 8 Idly blows with her a phoenix-call on the pipes.
> Conversing with their eyebrows, the two of them laugh freely,
> Then on a sudden they glide away, in the wake of the wind.[2]

Proper identification of the ethereal woman who is the subject of this poem is of course critical for the reader. Shang-yüan fu-jen is one of the most exalted goddesses of medieval Taoism. The equal in beauty of Hsi Wang Mu, as the poet remarks in his second line, she is probably best remembered for her participation with that more famous goddess in the divine banquets hosted by the Royal Mother in 110 B.C., and 66 A.D. for, respectively, the avid ruler Liu Ch'e (i.e. Han Wu Ti, a seeker at that time of Taoist arts; r. 140-86 B.C.) and the three devout brothers Mao (i.e., Mao Ying, Mao Ku, and Mao Chung, major figures in Taoist hagiography). In both instances, according to the texts in which these fêtes are recounted, when Hsi Wang Mu decided to transfer supernal writings and talismans to the fortunate humans, she requested the Lady of the Highest Prime to assist her. The mortal beings, upon asking who this mysterious lady was (cf. the first line of Li Po's poem), are informed that she is a celestial officer, in whose care are the rosters of the jade maidens of the ten regions of heaven. And they further learn, before she appears in person, that Shang-yüan fu-jen is on familiar terms with the great lord of the rising sun, Fu-sang ta ti-chün and is easily capable of crossing vast tracts of sky and sea in a trice. When she does descend from the clouds it is to the accompaniment of unearthly pan-pipes and drums. Her retinue is composed of over a thousand comely young lasses, all in their late teens, wearing raiment of shimmering bright blue. The grand lady herself is described, in the *Han Wu ti nei-chuan,* as follows:

> The Lady's years were possibly a bit more than twenty. Her heaven-endowed figure was pure and radiant, her numinous eyes incomparably bright. She was garbed in a caftan of red frost, shot through with cloud-striated hues—it was neither damask nor embroidered and cannot be described in words. Her head was done up in a tricornered chignon, the rest of her hair falling loosely even to her waist. She wore the cap of Ninefold Numinous Night-shining Light. She was girded with a pendant of six-pointed [snowflakes] and of fire jades, plus a dangling seal-ribbon of phoenix patterns and sapphire flowers. At her waist was the sword of wraith-shaking fluid yellow.[3]

In this dazzling vision we have, quite obviously, the source of Li Po's poem on the Lady—or at least of the first half of it—even to some of the exact wording. (Although the blue fur-trimmed damask worn as an outer wrap does not appear in the *Han Wu ti neichuan* passage, it is present, virtually *ad verbum,* in the analogous passage found in the *Mao shan chih* which likewise reflects a pre-T'ang tradition.) It is important to realize that, in describing the semblance and attire of Shang-yüan fu-jen, Li Po was not free to indulge his private fancy. The outward manifestation, especially the clothing, of the Taoist divinities was carefully particularized in canonical texts: it was imperative to be able clearly to distinguish in one's visualization (or "meditation") practices just which inhabitant of the Taoist heavens one was encountering. Indeed, certain distinctive attributes became emblems of the holy figures to whom they were attached. Simple mention of a "caftan of red frost," for example, was sufficient in T'ang poetry (for those versed in such matters) to identify the presence of Shang-yüan fu-jen. In a composition depicting her, therefore, the poet had no option but to preserve in his verse

her appearance as recognized in canonical sources—as Li Po has done in lines 3 through 6 of his poem.

In the final four lines of his composition, however, Li Po adds a new and playful element to the Lady's portrait. He presents her as genial companion to Lung-yü, "little miss Ying," a girl of noble birth who was supposed to have learned from her husband Hsiao Shih the art of mimicking phoenix-calls on the syrinx and eventually to have soared off with him to the heavens, behind one such divine bird that had come in response to her pipe-playing. Here the poet has Shang-yüan fu-jen communicate gaily but enigmatically (to our benighted eyes) with Lung-yü, finally to leave the scene abruptly, borne away on the wind to realms beyond our ken. The poem is both an exercise in verbal iconography and incomprehensible religious wonderment: who is the Lady? She materializes in her characteristic apparel, brings forth a talented younger acquaintance, then too quickly is gone from sight again, returning to her mystic haunts. Without a knowledge of the specific Taoist texts upon which Li Po is drawing in his references both to Shang-yüan fu-jen and to "little miss Ying" the poem will remain a mystery to the reader. Only by fellow initiates is it to be fully understood.

## II. A PACKET OF POSTILS

Prior to considering other complete works of Li Po in this vein, I propose to survey briefly a selection of phrases culled from various of his poems, all referring to transcendent objects, practices, or regions, and all inadequately treated by traditional commentators. In addition to clarifying a segment of Li Po's Taoist diction, which may occasionally aid us later on, it is hoped that this little clutch of scholia may be of benefit in reading the works of other T'ang poets who wrote on like themes.

*The damask satchel.* In a poem glorifying the peculiar supremacy of Mount O-mei among the many eminent peaks of Shu, Li Po remarks

> Coolly indifferent, prizing the purple auroras,
> Indeed I have gained the techniques of the damask satchel.[4]

And elsewhere, upon bidding farewell to a fellow devotee of the Way, who is setting off on a distant journey, the poet declares

> I do possess the acroama of the damask satchel,
> Which may be used, milord, to maintain your person.[5]

This "damask satchel" (*chin nang*) is one belonging to Hsi Wang Mu. In the *Han Wu ti neichuan* is told how, in consequence of Liu Ch'e's ardent plea, she removes from it and hands over to the sovereign a scroll that had been carefully stored therein. That scroll was the sacred text of the *Wu-yüeh chen-hsing t'u,* the "Plans of the True Forms of the Five Marchmounts." One of the most celebrated periapts of medieval Taoism, known from at least the early fourth century, this document would keep its possessor free from harm (especially—but not only—when entering alpine areas), through the good offices of spiritual emissaries sent by the deities of the Five Holy Mountains. We thus recognize the aptness of Li Po's allusions: in the first instance it is through his knowledge of the "techniques of the damask satchel" that he is able to ascend Mount O-mei and behold its sublime wonders, in the second instance he is generously offering to share these secret teachings with his leave-taking friend so as to ensure the latter's own safety.

*The Book of the Purple Aurora.* In a late work in which he proclaims his readiness to abandon his mortal form, quit this world, and enter the realm of the Infinite (*wu-ch'iung*), the poet says

> Serenely chanting the *Book of the Purple Aurora*,
> I am permitted to open up the Palace of Stamen and Pearl.[6]

*Tzu-hsia p'ien*, the "Book of the Purple Aurora," adverts cryptically to one of the most important of Taoist canonical texts, namely the "Scripture of the Yellow Court" (*Huang-t'ing ching*). This enigmatic work makes reference to the divinities housed within one's body, especially those dwelling in the five viscera, and was to be chanted while visualizing or "actualizing" those corporal deities. The text is in verse, written in rhyming lines of seven words each, and exists in two separate forms—the *wai ching* (or "Outer Scripture") and the *nei ching* (or "Inner Scripture"). We are informed by an early commentator that, if one succeeds in reciting the *Huang-t'ing ching* ten thousand times, one will have so fortified and equipoised one's physical form as to be impervious to disease, one's body will give off an inflorescent sheen, the five viscera will be open to view, and one will have attained the pathway to immortality. Extremely influential and widely known in medieval times among the literate class, the *Huang-t'ing ching* is mentioned often in T'ang poetry. Li Po's allusion to it as the "Book of the Purple Aurora"—and the reference to the "Palace of Stamen and Pearl" (Jui chu kung) is a private coinage, the idiom of an insider, derived from the first stanza of the Inner Scripture, which reads:

> In the purple aurora of Highest Clarity, before the
>     Radiant One of the Void,
> The Most High, Great Tao Lord of the Jade Source
>     of Light,
> Dwelling at ease in the Stamen and Pearl [Palace],
>     composed [verses of] seven words,
> Disposing and transforming the Five Matrices,
>     permutating the myriad spirits:
> This is deemed the *Yellow Court*, known as the
>     *Inner Book*.

We shall encounter the *Huang-t'ing ching* again, in a poem to be considered in the third section of this paper.

*Sounding Heaven's Drum.* A few months before Li Lung-chi (r. 712-756, pht. Hsüan Tsung) ascended the throne in 712, two of his royal sisters took Taoist orders. According to Wei Hao, who wrote the preface to one of the first collections of Li Po's verse, it was on the recommendation—as a fellow adherent of the Way—of one of these women, Yü-chen kung-chu (The Princess Realized in Jade), that our poet later was summoned in 742 to the emperor's increasingly Taoicised court.[7] In a laudatory poem penned in celebration of her, Li Po says of this devout woman

> In the clear morning she sounds the drum of heaven,
> In a flash and a flicker mounts up on a pair of dragons.[8]

The obscure phrase "sounding heaven's drum" (*ming t'ien ku*) refers to the purposeful clacking together of one's four anterior teeth. According to a notice in the *Yün-chi ch'i-ch'ien*, this dental resonance aids in evoking the superbeings and gods in the course of a formal visualization. It is rather fitting, then, that in the second line of the couplet quoted above Li Po should picture the imperial votaress ascending subsequently to the sky behind a brace of heaven-destined dragons.

*Fluid Aurora.* In the first of his hexad of poems on **"Wandering on Mount T'ai."** Li Po receives from a group of celestial maidens a "cup of fluid aurora" (*liu hsia pei*). Such a drink was early noted by Wang Ch'ung (27-91) and later by Ko Hung (283-344) as having been offered to one Hsiang Man-tu, when the latter paid a visit to the heavenly habitation of the "Transcendent Persons" (*hsien jen*); the drink reportedly had the power of banishing all hunger and thirst. As I have remarked elsewhere, one of the basic scriptures of Shang-ch'ing Taoism. *The Purple Text of the Numinous Writ* (*Ling-shu tzu-wen*), contains a section detailing the proper procedures for obtaining this divine beverage. This passage affords us far more insight into the nectar's qualities than do the bare references of Wang Ch'ung and Ko Hung. We learn from it that the "fluid aurora" is a pentachrome pneuma, a draught of solar essence which, when imbibed, suffuses one's person with the energy of the sun. The correct technique for securing a drink of this liquor may be summarized as follows: look upon the sun just as it is rising in the east, clack your teeth nine times,[9] and invoke the names of the sun's *hun*-souls and the five high lords within the sun by silently repeating an incantation that goes

> Cloud-soul of sun, vermilion luminescence,
> Illuminant sheathe, verdant refulgence,
> Red Lad of revolving auroras,
> Shimmering simulacrum of mystic flame!

This done, you must shut tight your eyes and actualize in thought (*ts'un szu*) the five-colored fluid aurora from the sun descending over your body, down to your feet and back again to the top of your head. It will then pass into your mouth. A glittering figure made of purple pneumas—the essence of the aurora—will then appear and will also pass into your mouth. Having taken in the solar liquor, you must gulp down your own circulating pneuma forty-five times, swallow your saliva nine times, and chant in a low voice another, much longer incantation—after which you make a double bow to the sun, concluding the ritual. This practice should be carried out ten times monthly, at dawn on the first, third, fifth, seventh, ninth, thirteenth, fifteenth, seventeenth, nineteenth, and twenty-first days of the month. If performed diligently for eighteen years, it will result in the ultimate refinement of one's physical form, enabling one to travel airborne through the vault of the sky.

In the poem referred to above, Li Po is imparted a cup of fluid aurora by divine grace. The happy consequence of this is that, although he acknowledges he may not be fit material for transcendence, by the end of the piece he confidently declares

> Broad-ranging enough now to make the cosmos dwindle,
> I'll leave this world behind, oh so far away!

Elsewhere, lauding a certain Master White Down, i.e. Master Pekoe (Po-hao Tzu), Li Po states that this lofty recluse "Privately pours a cup of fluid aurora."[10] In two other poems[11] the solar potion becomes an elegant metaphor for fine wine—one assumes a pale rosé.

*The Barrier of Heaven.* The phrase *t'ien kuan,* "Barrier of Heaven," appears three times in Li Po's poems, and commentators uniformly treat it as a casual kenning for the vast sky. However, for Taoist initiates the phrase denoted two specific astronomical referents. It was the secret name of the seventh and brightest star of the Great Dipper (at the tip of the handle, our Alkaid), one of the fiery deiforms constituting that most potent of all constellations. Even more importantly, it designated a discrete asterism— also referred to sometimes as the Heavenly Design (*t'ien t'u*) or the Triple Barrier (*san kuan*)—which was an entranceway to the deathless realms of the highest heavens.

A section of an early Highest Clarity scripture, called in short *The Purple Writ of the Azure Crux,* is devoted to the "Procedure for Spreading Open the Barrier of Heaven."[12] The text begins by identifying the Barrier of Heaven as "the Vital Gate (or Gate of Life) of the Nine Heavens; its sphere resides in the southeast corner of the Nine Heavens." We then learn that

> It is the place that the host of Realized Ones (*chen jen*) traverse, through which the divine transcendents pass, and from which adepts [of the Tao] proceed. It is set off 5,000 *li* from the Golden Pylons[13] and 7,000 *li* from the supernal palaces of Jade Clarity (*Yü ch'ing*).[14] If one is able to spread open the Triple Barrier, he may then immediately ascend on high to the Golden Pylons and saunter and feast in Jade Clarity.[15]

Following this, there is a detailed description of the Barrier itself and elaborate instructions about how to realize a passage through it.[16] Only those who had crossed the Heavenly Barrier could be assured of having their name recorded in the fatidic rosters of immortality, certifying their celestial estate.

It is hard not to believe that Li Po is being doctrinally precise in his verse when, in a poem we shall later consider at greater length, he states that the presiding spirit of holy Mount T'ai-po "grants to me a colloquy, And for my sake opens up the Barrier of Heaven!"[17] Similarly, in a poem centering on the legendary leave-taking of the Yellow Thearch (Huang Ti) from this world, the poet writes "Astride a dragon, scaling heaven, he attains the Barrier of Heaven."[18] And in another composition, when piously praising Li Heng (pht. Su Tsung, r. 756-762) for bringing order again to the nation, out of the chaos into which it had been cast by An Lu-shan's rebellion, Li Po pictures the sovereign as a Taoist superman:

> Lifting high his feet, he trod Purple Tenuity;
> The Heavenly Barrier of its own accord gaped wide.[19]

Thus the monarch of all below also exercises power over the starry kingdoms of space.

*The Golden Pylons.* Commentators are fond of explaining the phrase *chin ch'üeh,* "Golden Pylons," as a simple variation of *chin men,* "Gate of Gold," a familiar reference in poetry to the imperial court; and on three occasions this is indeed the way Li Po employs the phrase. But the "Golden Pylons" is also the proper name of the paradise domain of Li Hung, Tao Lord and Latter-day Sage (*hou-sheng tao-chün*), who during the days of the apocalypse will gather to himself those saints and adepts fated to survive the destruction of the present world.

The scripture mentioned above, which speaks at length about the Barrier of Heaven, also furnishes us with an account of the uranic Palace of the Golden Pylons. Four large gates open into the palace precincts, each gate flanked by a pair of pylons—the left one of gold, the right of jade—nine thousand rods high. Azure dragons and white tigers may be found about the pylons, which are further guarded by "heavenly creatures and giant serpents." These portals enclose a compound 7,000 *li* in circumference. A portion of the ensuing description tells that

> Within [the palace compound] is the Purple Basilica of Golden Radiance and the Jade Chamber of the Rose-gem Abode. They are where the Latter-day Sage, Thearchic Lord of the Golden Pylons, resides. Purple clouds shade the heights; verdant auroras surround the abode. Sun and moon, on either side, shed their glow, and divine candlelight shines diffusely. Jade maidens and golden Realized Ones scatter aromatics. The parvis in the void streams with light, and a wind drums from the Eight Murks. Mystic pennons flap and dance; banners overarch trees of jade. High-pitched tones [proceed] from sapphire branches, piping of their own accord with a hundred resoundings.[20]

Closely associated with Li Hung is the great divinity known as the Azure Lad (Ch'ing t'ung), one of whose epithets is "Supreme Minister of the Golden Pylons" (Chin-ch'üeh shang-hsiang). This important lord is essentially a solar deity of the orient dawn and represents symbolically the principle of growth and enlightenment; he has his own paradise realm—the Azure Palace of the Square Speculum of Eastern Florescence (Tung-hua fang-chu ch'ing-kung)—in the Eastern Sea. When, furthermore, we know that he is sometimes referred to as "the Jade Resplendent One" (Yü huang), we have the final bit of information enabling us to understand what Li Po is getting at in a couplet that reads

> If we do not ramble on to the Golden Pylons,
> I imagine we shall be guests of the Jade Resplendent One.[21]

The poem in which these lines appear takes for topic the compounding of the Nine-cycled Elixir of the Grand Return (*ta-huan chiu-chuan tan*) and abounds in arcane allusions to the alchemical process of creating that storied concoction.[22] In the lines quoted here, which come near the end of the poem, Li Po is declaring hopefully his belief that the successful manufacture of the elixir will result in the ascension of himself, and the Taoist friend to whom the poem is addressed, to the glorious paradise of Li Hung—or, at least, to the only slightly less exalted appanage of the Azure Lad.

One suspects that the transcendent implications of the phrase "Golden Pylons" is also operating, at a metaphorical level, when Li Po elsewhere describes a section of Mount Lu by saying "The Golden Pylons have opened before me—a screen between two peaks."[23]

Finally, in two poems Li Po places golden pylons on the elysian seamounts of the eastern ocean. In one of these pieces, he says "The silver terraces and golden pylons seem as if in a dream";[24] in the other, "Turning for a time to Ying-chou, I shall visit the golden pylons."[25] Owing to an influential line in one of Kuo P'u's (276-324) famous set of "Sauntering to Sylphdom" verses, terraces (*t'ai*) of gold and silver appear often in medieval poems about the three paradise isles of P'eng-lai, Ying-chou, and Fang-chang. But Li Po's pylons of gold surely exhibit in this context a reflected shimmer from the celestial palatinate of the grand deity Li Hung.

*The Jade Capital.* Although medieval Taoist cosmology admits of some variation in detail, according to different scriptures, the general outline of heavenly zones and spheres is tolerably clear. In the Taoist synthesis represented by the Ling-pao canonical tradition, the three hierarchically arranged (and perhaps concentric) heavens of Greatest Clarity, Highest Clarity, and Jade Clarity are surmounted—or rather, enclosed—by the Great Enveloping Heaven (Ta-lo t'ien). The Jade Capital, or to be more exact, the Jade Capitoline Mountain (Yü-ching shan) "is placed in the exact center of the highest heaven," the focal point of the supreme enceinte known as the Mystic Metropolis (Hsüan tu). So states the mid-sixth century Taoist encyclopedia called *The Secret Cruces Without Superior,*[26] which compendium also tells us that "at the time of completion of a Great Kalpa the divine scriptures of the Three Grottoes reside together in the midst [of the Jade Capitoline Mountain in the Great Enveloping Heaven],

where calamities cannot reach them."[27] That is to say, it is in the Jade Capital that the timeless originals of the sacred celestial books are preserved, inviolate even from the disasters attendant upon the annihilation of the world. Thus when Li Po says of a Taoist priest, in a poem to be examined more closely later,

> His disengaged heart is possessed of no "far" or "near";
> For long it has resided poised in the Jade Capital.[28]

we understand that the cleric's serene mind finds its true home in the unassailable shelter of the highest gods and holy writs.

It is also on the Jade Capitoline Mountain, in the Mystic Metropolis, that the divinities of each of the ten directions of space[29] assemble monthly (each group on a particular day and in a particular palace or estrade), to collate the heavenly texts that record the merits or faults of the men or specters over whom they have jurisdiction. And it is here too that, six times yearly, the entire concourse of deities assembles to do reverence to the numinous scriptures housed in the Jade Capital, in a procession complete with music and hymns. Li Po seems in one poem to catch a glimpse of this gathering, when he says

> Far off I see Transcendent Persons in the midst of prismatic clouds;
> Holding lotus flowers in their hands, they attend the levee at the Jade Capital.[30]

In another poem Li Po pays a Taoist friend a most flattering compliment, stating

> It is said as well that, to attend the levee in the heavens,
> you are proceeding to the Jade Capital.[31]

That is, the poet's acquaintance is fit to join in the hallowed celebration of the gods.

This very precise use of the term "Jade Capital" may be seen also in the works of poets, such as Wang Wei (701-761) and Tu Fu (712-770), for example, who are not usually thought of as displaying any discernible leaning toward Taoist imagery in their verse. But this simply reminds us again that the imagery and vocabulary of the Taoist scriptures were common currency for virtually all the poets of T'ang, not only for the devout, and that we must make a special effort to recover this important segment of the poetic lexicon of medieval China.

### III. THE ORDINATION POEMS

A significant event in the spiritual life of the postulant was the receiving of a Taoist "register" (*lu*). The register is a formal patent which certifies the holder as an initiate and verifies his place in the celestial bureaucracy; in this regard, it is a document of ordination. There are several different types and levels of register, but they all usually include—in varying calligraphically artistic forms—a catalogue of the divinities and Realized Ones with whom the adept is now supposed to be on familiar terms, able to invoke these superbeings out of the depths of the sky or (what is essentially the same thing) from out of the microcosm of his own body. A register may only be transferred to the initiate by an accredited Taoist master in a ceremonial ritual. We are told in the *Sui shu*:

> Those who accept the doctrine of the Way first receive the *Register of the Text in 5,000 [Words]*, then the *Register of the Three Caverns*, then the *Register of the Cavern of Mysteries*, and then the *Register of Highest Clarity*. In every case the register is written on white silk. The names of the various celestial administrators and magistrates which are recorded, and [those of] their attached assistants and apparitors, are very numerous. There are also included various talismans placed as ornaments in the midst [of the lists of names and titles]. The composition of the text is selcouth and uncommon, not to be understood by the world. The recipient must first fast and purify himself, after which he presents one gold ring, together with various gifts and donatives, in order to have audience with the master. Accepting his donatives, the master transmits to him the register. At the same time, he cuts in two the gold ring, half to be kept by each of them, saying it is to be deemed [a symbol of] their convenant. The disciple takes possession of the register and, having bound it securely, suspends it from his belt.[32]

This ritual joins together master and disciple in a sacred contract, which is itself the earthly counterpart of the compact holding between the divine denizens of the Taoist heavens (and their revealed scriptures) and the worthy human devotee. Often the ritual also included transferral of holy scriptures from master to disciple—these texts themselves, which can be read by mortals, being but the mundane simulacra of the true, eternal scriptures composed in celestial script and enduring unprofaned in the heavens.

Li Po, we know, participated in such a ritual in the late fall or winter of the year 744, following his two-year stay in Ch'ang-an. His ordination ceremony was held at the Palace of the Purple Culmen (Tzu-chi kung), in Ch'i-chou, in the district of An-ling, county of P'ing-yüan—about forty-five miles northwest of the present city of Chi-nan in Shantung.[33] He has left us two poems commemorating this event. One is a long poem of thirty-two lines, addressed to Kai Huan, the calligrapher who was responsible for writing out the register received by Li Po; the other is an eight-line composition in "regulated verse" addressed to the Taoist prelate Kao Ju-kuei who was the poet's actual preceptor. Both poems are couched largely in the parlance of the insider: they are, we must remember, offerings from pupil to teacher, meant to inspire the approval and applause of Li Po's religious betters. They are, in some measure, self-conscious displays of elite erudition. Neither poem (and especially the longer one) has been adequately handled by traditional commentators, who are silent about some of the more curious verses in these works.

We shall here attempt a closer reading of these poems, giving due attention to their peculiarities of diction and Taoist reference. The longer of the two is titled informatively **"In Quest of the Tao in An-ling, I Met Kai Huan who Fashioned for me a Register of the Realized Ones; [This Poem] Left Behind as a Present When About to Depart."** It reads as follows:

> Clear water gives a view of white rocks;
> Of Transcendent Persons, I am familiar with the Azure Lad.
> Kai, the Great Master of Peaceful Barrow (Anling),
> 4 By his tenth year was in joint communication with Heaven.
> His "precipitant stream" and, too, his subtle words—
> In conversation or discourse, how could they give out?
> He is able to command those paid two thousand piculs,
> 8 Who clap him on the back, amazed at his divine acuity.
> Flourishing his writing-brush, he presents a new poem,
> Of highest value throughout the land East of the Mountains.
> Even till today, a visitor to the Level Plain (P'ing-yüan)
> 12 Is moved and incited, aspiring to his rarified manner.
> I have studied the Way with the North Sea (Pei-hai) Transcendent,
> Who transmitted to me what was written in the Stamen and Pearl Palace.
> Within the cinnabar field I brought the Jade Pylons to completion;
> 16 In the white light of day I long for the cloudy emptiness.
> For my sake you have drawn up a register of the Realized Ones;
> The persons of Heaven are abashed at your miraculous art.
> The Seven Primes penetrate [to me], unhindered in descent;
> 20 And the Eight Cantles now flash forth a starry nimbus!
> The Three Disasters will be purged by Jade-cog and Armil;
> Kraken dragons will enfold the trifling husk of my body.
> Raising a hand, I shall renounce heaven and earth—
> 24 For the nullity of the void equates origin and end.
> Yellow gold fills up the high halls,
> Yet satchels and sacks can in no way be stuffed.
> I laugh down at the gentlemen of the world,
> 28 Whose cloud-souls sink into Lo-feng in the north.
> The cairns of the myriad-chariot lords from days of yore
> Are turned today into one entire sprouting of fleabane!
> —If the words I present may be deemed substantial,
> 32 Truly this will lighten my way over [Mounts] Hua and Sung.[34]

There is much in this poem that requires explanation. We may begin by noting the reference in line 2 to the Azure Lad, whom we have met earlier. He is one of the Taoist divinities most often implicated in the transmission of sacred scriptures, in the transferral of celestial knowledge, and it is fitting for Li Po to begin a poem on the topic of receiving a certificate of initiation with a mention of this helpful deity (whose name and title very likely figured prominently in the register itself; he stands out from the other transcendents like a white rock in clear water). After the opening couplet, the poet devotes the next ten lines to praise of the master calligrapher and Taoist adept Kai Huan. The "precipitant stream" (*hsüan ho*) of line 5 suggests Kai Huan's skill in oral discussion, by means of a characterization once applied to the famous Chin dynasty scholar Kuo Hsiang (d. 312), of whom it was said "When one hears Hsiang converse, it is like a precipitant stream draining its waters—gushing forth, it never dries up."[35] In line 6, "those paid two thousand piculs," who are in awe of Huan, are the influential local officials of the P'ing-yüan area.[36]

In the fourth quatrain the poet himself reappears (this has been neatly prepared for by lines 11-12, the grateful "visitor" of which may well indicate the "aspiring" novice, Li Po). He claims for himself certain accomplishments in his pursuit of the Way, owing to the tutoring of the Taoist master of Pei-hai County—that is, Kao Ju-kuei, who is identified exactly in the second poem we will discuss. Li Po was apparently instructed by Master Kao in the interpretation of the *Huang-t'ing ching,* this being, as we have seen in section two of this paper, the sacred text that "was written in the Stamen and Pearl Palace." Line 15 refers to the poet's practice of the techniques of breath control, refining the vital pneuma of his corporal frame. The "cinnabar field" (*tan t'ien*) is one of the key loci of interior alchemy; here the poet must have in mind the "lower" cinnabar field, found three inches below the navel.[37] As for the "Jade Pylons" (*yü ch'üeh*), a couplet from the ninth stanza of the *Huang-t'ing ching* reveals that

> The palace of the sector of the lungs resembles a
> floriate canopy;
> Beneath it there is a young lad, seated on the Jade
> Pylons.

Liang Ch'iu-tzu, an important early eighth-century commentator on the *Yellow Court Scripture* notes that the "Jade Pylons" betoken the white pneuma of the kidneys, joined to the lungs above. Having brought this inner energy-force "to completion," the poet yearns in the next line to ascend bodily to the heavens "in the white light of day," as the most sublime Transcendent Ones have done.

With line 17, beginning the second half of the poem, Li Po enters on the celebration of the great event itself, the receiving of the register, which marks the culmination of his studies under Kao Ju-kuei and which also represents the perfection of Kai Huan's calligraphic skill. Line 19 refers to the powerful charm known as the "Design of the Unhindered Descent of the Seven Primes" (*ch'i-yüan huo-lo t'u*). This talisman—no doubt included in the text of the bestowed register—enlists for the aid of the adept the salvific powers of the seven visible stars of the Northern Dipper (or, alternatively, the powers of sun, moon, and the five visible planets). Possessed of this sidereal periapt,

one will be able to subdue the demons emanating from the dread Six Palaces of the North (the "Lo-feng" of line 28, see below) and preserve oneself from the tortures of that infernal region. In line 20 the poet pictures to himself the primordial celestial characters in which the heavenly writs were prototypically composed: they radiate a blinding octagonal light which even the Transcendents cannot look upon.

Continuing in the next couplet (lines 21-22) his declaration of the boons accruing to him through his investiture, Li Po devises a pair of lines the precise references of which have long bewildered critics. Their exact meaning can indeed be understood. But to do so we must look rather closely at certain passages in two medieval scriptures.

Now, "Jade-cog" (*hsüan*) and "Armil" (*chi*)[38] are the standard names for the second and third stars, respectively, of the Dipper; and sometimes the two words form a compound used to indicate the group of four stars that form the bowl of the Dipper.[39] As we know, the Dipper is the most potent of constellations. To be able to invoke and control the divinities of its individual stars is to be able to command one's heavenly fate and ensure oneself everlasting life. With the exception of the seventh star (the "Barrier of Heaven"), "Jade-cog and Armil" seem perhaps somewhat more puissant than the others. Certainly that appears to be so for Li Po, who could easily have used the bisyllabic general term "Northern Dipper" (*pei tou*) in his line, had he not wished specially to highlight "Jade-cog and Armil." Indeed, one sacred text states that the astral deity "Jade-cog and Armil" (apparently denoting a single star, as in the passage to be quoted in the next paragraph below) "is the suzerain of the Northern Dipper. Heaven's great baron and king, ruling and constraining the 12,000 divinities, and maintaining the fatidic rosters of men."[40]

In his verse Li Po seems to have been influenced, to begin with, by the important text known as the *Shang-ch'ing t'ien-kuan san-t'u ching* (Scripture of the Three Designs of the Heavenly Barrier, from Highest Clarity), a late fourth or early fifth century revelation, the first part of which deals with a technique for actualizing the attendant lords of the Dipper's seven stars, for apotropaic purposes. This scripture denotes the *fourth* star of the Dipper by the name "Jade-cog and Armil."[41] The adept is instructed to envisage

> the cloud-souls and elemental essences of Jade-cog and
> Armil, Occult Tenebrity, Heaven's Balance-weight,[42]
> the Nine Lords of the Highest Barrens, all garbed in
> volant skirts of purple brocade, with caps of the mystic
> dawn placed on their heads. Make them descend from
> amid the mysterious Dipper into your own person.
> Then, make incantation, saying:
>
> > Cloud-souls and elemental essences of Jade-cog and
> > Armil,
> > Of Occult Tenebrity, of Heaven's Balance-weight,
> > Nine Lords of the Highest Barrens,
> > By integral conjunction and a myriad permutations,

Be made into a single divinity.
Shift and measure out the Seven Stars for my sake,
Fill up and block the Gate of Ghosts.
Stop up and block the pneuma of death.
Make the Northern Dipper revolve on its mysterious pivot,
Measure out the breath of life in the Latency of the West,[43]
Keep me apart from the North's god-king in Feng-tu,
Let me gain a name inscribed in the casements of the south.[44]

But what have "Jade-cog and Armil" to do with the "Three Disasters" (*san tsai*), and what are these latter? They are the cataclysmic calamities of wind (tempest), fire (conflagration), and water (flood) that will accompany the end of the world at the close of this kalpa—the concept is taken over from Buddhist notions of the apocalypse. "Jade-cog and Armil," according to another scripture, has the power to summon forth, and thereby the power to control, the transitional stage between kalpas. Mastery over the Dipper, including mastery over the mighty star "Jade-cog and Armil," will suffice to bring one safely through the epochal catastrophes. Li Po is suggesting that he has now acquired this mastery.

To understand the second line of the couplet in question, we must be familiar with a different text, namely the *T'ai-shang tung-hsüan ling-pao ch'ih-shu yü-chüeh miao-ching* (Marvelous Scripture of the Jade Acroama of the Red Writ of Numen and Gem, from the Cavern of Mysteries of the Most High). This work, one of the original scriptures of the Ling-pao canon, is an apocalyptic text composed of incantations to the divine kings of each of the five directions, to the stars of each direction, the mountains, and the waters. Particularly important for us—and for Li Po in this particular verse—is the section concerned with the supplication of the waters. We are told here that the one way to avoid the dreadful flood that will overwhelm the world at the end of the kalpa is to inscribe the incantation revealed in this text on blue paper, with yellow ink, and to cast it into the waters. This done, one will acquire the services of a "kraken dragon" (*chiao lung*) who will bear one away safely on its back, at the final deluge. Esoteric as these allusions may seem to us now, Li Po fully expected the Taoist recipient of the poem, Kai Huan, to apprehend them rightly and to appreciate their intricate wording.

This rather complex pair of lines, emphasizing the poet's newly won immunity from the ultimate forces of destruction, leads logically to his subsequent renunciation of the things of this world. All distinctions between supposed opposites appear false to him now, and the habitual hoarding of wealth and valuables especially seems a worthless show. Realizing this, he can laugh with cosmic disdain at those whose profane actions ensure their spiritual damnation in the depths of Lo-feng. Lo-feng is the fearsome judgement place and prison of the Six Heavens in the North. Also referred to as Feng-tu, or more graphically as the Citadel of Lasting Night (Ch'ang-yeh ch'eng, it is a domain of ghosts and demons, the spirits of the unholy dead. Located in the

north, it is consequently a dark and dank empire.[45] The "cloud-souls" (*hun*) of the profane, which should properly return at death to their original, airy home in the sky, are here seen by Li Po to "sink" (*ch'en*) into the damp dungeons of Lo-feng, never to be cleansed and perfected. The poet is conscious that he himself, on the other hand, has now become enfranchised as one of the elect. And he accordingly perceives the folly of those temporal rulers who think to conquer time and oblivion through rearing imposing burial mounds as monuments—futile markers that are soon overgrown with weeds. In the concluding couplet of the piece, Li Po expresses his hope for Kai Huan's approval of his words, which will sustain him in his mystical extravagation to the holy alps Hua and Sung, ascension of these peaks symbolizing withdrawal from the moils of mundane activity. The poem is a well-balanced and enthusiastic commemoration of the author's formalized status in the faith, drawing at least partially on language and lore known only to other students of the sacred books.

The second poem indited by Li Po to celebrate his ordination is addressed, as mentioned already, to the Taoist master who directd the ritual and bestowed the consecrated register on the poet. It is titled **"Upon his Returning Home to Pei-hai, I Respectfully Offer a Farewell Banquet to Reverend Master Kao Ju-kuei, Gentleman of the Tao, After He Transmitted to Me a Register of the Way."**

> The Way is hidden, not able to be seen;
> The numinous writings are stored in the grotto heavens.
> The master who is mine, after four myriads of kalpas,
> 4 One age following another, has transmitted and passed them down.
> Departing, he leaves behind a staff of green bamboo;
> Singing as he goes, he treads the purple haze.
> His disengaged heart is possessed of no "far" or "near";
> 8 For long it has resided poised in the Jade Capital.[46]

This is a more sedate effort than the preceding and does not demand quite as much of us in the way of arcane learning. Opening with a bald statement regarding the dighel nature of the Tao,[47] the poet proceeds in line 2 to remark the inaccessibility of the scriptures which he here portrays as cached in the "grotto heavens" (*tung t'ien*)—the hollow worlds, each a discrete universe complete with its own sky, sun, moon, and stars, that spread out below the sacred mountains of the Taoists. It is these scriptures, the successive transferrals of which may take place only once in countless eons, that Kao Ju-kuei has revealed to his pupil Li Po. In the fifth line of the poem, Li Po pictures his master in terms of Fei Ch'ang-fang, an adept of the Latter Han dynasty, who made use of a green bamboo cut exactly to his height to effect his departure from the everyday world. When the bamboo was hung from a tree behind his house, it took on the semblance of Fei's corpse. Amid great lamentation his family members took down the suspended corpse-bamboo and interred it, no one noticing the real Fei who watched alongside (his body had become purified of corporeal dross). He then went off to accompany his occult teacher into the mountains. Li Po has Kao Ju-kuei leaving behind a bamboo staff, emblematic of his terrestrial form, while his true being goes off, back to his celestial home, borne on a "purple haze" (*tzu yin*) from the mystic reaches of the sky. And it is, avers the poet, none other than the cosmic mountain of the Jade Capital—where the highest gods and texts reside (see above)—that is Master Kao's established dwelling place and destination. Li Po offers thus both a conventional poem of farewell and an encomiastic tribute to his revered mentor.

### IV. T'AI-PO ON T'AI-PO

In a writer as conscious as Li Po of the exact attributes and dispositions of words, the knowledge that a prominent feature of the natural landscape bore the same name as he did must certainly have provoked a measure of linguistic—and perhaps even emotive—sympathy. I refer of course to the mountain known as T'ai-po, or "Grand White," an epithet that was also the cognomen of Li Po himself. We are told by the poet's kinsman Li Yang-ping that on the night Li Po was delivered his mother dreamt she was visited by the moving star (or planet) called T'ai-po (our Venus); hence the baby was bestowed the given name Po, "White," and the cognomen T'ai-po, "Grand White." Later in life the poet was fancifully regarded by some contemporaries as the "essential spirit" (*ching*) of that star.[48] Mount T'ai-po, in Wu-kung township (present-day Mei district, in Shensi), on the westernmost spur of the Chung-nan range, was clearly the alpine *doppelgänger* of the star and provided an earthly communication point with it. Indeed, one medieval text states unequivocally that the mountain contained the elemental essence of the star, fallen to earth. This sidereal essence manifested itself as the lovely white stone slabs, resembling fine jade, that were miraculously discovered on T'ai-po Shan in 742 and out of which the emperor ordered carved a 20-foot tall image of Lao Tzu, plus flanking statues of himself and two of his high ministers, to be erected in the temple devoted to the deified Lao Tzu in Ch'ang-an.

The great Taoist teacher and cleric Szu-ma Ch'engchen (647-735), "patriarch" of the Shangch'ing sect in the early eighth century, recorded that Mount T'ai-po concealed the eleventh of the 36 "lesser grotto-heavens"; it was thus an undeniable locus of sacrality. It had, moreover, been the favored retreat of several early T'ang recluses, alchemists, and adepts—most notably Sun Szu-miao (?581-682?) and T'ien Yu-yen (fl. ca. 680). But Li Po seems to have been the first writer to portray the mountain in verse. He has left us two marvelous poems that are set on T'ai-po Shan. In both of them the mountain is an epiphanic site, where the poet is confirmed in his yearning for supramundane existence. . . .

> To the west I ascend the peak of Grand White—
> In dusky sunlight finish with my scrambling and climbing.
> Grand White grants to *me* a colloquy.

> 4 And for my sake opens up the Barrier of Heaven!
> I will mount the cooling wind and be gone
> —Breaking straight out through the floating clouds.
> Lifting my hand, I may draw near the moon;
> 8 Proceeding onward, as if there is no mountain now!
> Once parted and gone away from Wu-kung,
> What time would I come back here again?

> **"Climbing T'ai-po's Peak"**

It is not only an ascent of Mount T'ai-po that is related here; more importantly to the poet, it is an ascent to transcendence. The physical climb itself is of little moment: it is completed in the twilight gloaming of the second line. Then the true ascent begins. The poet is accorded coversation with the mountain itself—or is it with the star after which the peak is named? But in fact there is no real distinction between the two. The singularity of this occurrence is accented by the third line's steady string of words in deflected tones. The wonderful consequence of this interview is the opening, for the poet, of the Barrier of Heaven, giving access to the avenues of the sky (see above). And we note how this entry into the supernal districts is phonetically distinguished from what came before—three successive level-tone words triumphantly capping the seven deflected-tone words (the five words of line 3 and the first two of line 4) preceding.

With the second stanza the poet is released into the upper world, indifferntly harnessing the wind, after the manner of the legendary Lieh Tzu, wafted away, through and out of the clouds—"floating clouds" has here a collateral sense, referring to the flimsy scuddings of mortal life, from which the poet has now broken away. He is propelled close enough to the moon that he may touch it with his hand. (This striking image in the third line of the stanza is emphasized, just as was the third line of the first stanza, by the fact that the verse is entirely constituted of deflected-tone words.) Now the poet has lost all connection with the mountain itself, which seems to have disappeared behind him. In the final couplet, he asserts his disinclination ever to return to that sublunary world in which the physical mountain exists—symbolized by the county of Wu-kung, geographical locale of T'ai-po Shan. One suspects, too, that Li Po may be revivifying in this context the semantic import of the district's name, "Martial Accomplishment"—a range of activity that also is meaningless to him now. This conclusion is a clever variation of one of the customary endings of poems on famous sites—the sad sigh over when the poet will again visit the lovely spot. But Li Po, risen now into a higher zone, recoils from the thought of descending to this world again; we read the last line as a contented, almost defiant, exclamation of relief.

Li Po's other poem on T'ai-po, while sharing the same general theme as the preceding poem, is as we shall see a somewhat more involved composition. It is the fifth of his series of 59 **"Olden Airs"** and reads as follows:

> Grand White—so mottled misted-green!
> The starry chronograms in thickset ranks above it.
> Three hundred *li* away from heaven,

4 Aloof like this, it is sundered from the world.
In its midst there is a green-faxed gaffer;
Cloaked in clouds, he lounges with the pines and
snow.
He does not laugh, does not converse either;
8 His tenebrous roost is located in a rugged cave.
I have come—and happen on the Realized Person;
Kneeling long, I ask for his treasured acroama.
So resplendent—he suddenly smiles freely at me,
12 For conferral, takes up an exposition on refining
drugs,
I shall transmit those remarks, engraved on my bones;
Raising up his person, now he is gone in a lightning-
flash!
Lifting my gaze far away, I cannot catch up to him:
16 In hazy state, my five emotions are inflamed.
—But it is I in future who will devise cinnabar gran-
ules,
And forever be separated from the persons of this
world![49]

Li Po begins with a cry of appreciative joy at the mountain's sun- and cloud-speckled gray-green appearance. He then sees the peak in broader perspective, as an *axis astrorum,* with the patterned ranks of stars crowning its summit. The "heaven" of line 3 is Ch'ang-an, the terrestrial analogue of paradise, a long 300 *li* away. T'ai-po Shan hardly seems part of the same world to which the T'ang capital belongs—it occupies a different, more lofty sphere of existence (the sense here is phonetically stressed by the complete deflected-tone make-up of line 4). And its resident genius is, not surprisingly, an exceptional person, a "green-faxed gaffer" who wears the mountain clouds as his cape, is wholly at ease on T'ai-po's steep slopes, at home in a precipitous crevice, and craves no intercourse or dialogue with human representatives. The old fellow's "green" hair betrays the effects of his spiritual attainments. He is actually growing younger, his hair recapturing the patinous gloss of that of an adolescent.

Perceiving, when he comes upon him, that this is in fact a *chen-jen* or Realized Person, the poet humbly beseeches him to impart his arcane teachings. Quite unexpectedly, the transcendent one "smiles freely" at the poet (the more unexpected, because we have already been told—in an emphatic line, all in deflected tones again—that he *does not* smile or converse). As so often in Li Po's verses featuring encounters with higher beings, he is the lucky recipient of divine dispensation. Here his prize is an allocution "on refining drugs"; he is given esoteric instructions on concocting an elixir that will conduce to transcendent status. We should remark that the verb used in this line (line 8) is *zhou, the formally correct term for the transferral of valued lore from master to pupil, and also that the line is entirely in deflected tones—as though it were italicized: this is clearly, for the poet, a momentous occurrence.

The lesson finished, Li Po vows never to forget it; it has been "engraved on my bones." And then, suddenly, his immortal teacher speeds away like a bolt from the sky. The departure of these unearthly entities is always abrupt and

nebulous: their occasional visits to this world are, after all, supreme acts of grace and condescension, and are not to be prolonged. The poet strains to follow by sight the airborne path of his fleeting master, but it is impossible—the phenomenal cannot keep pace with the noumenal. (Here again, for the fourth time, we have a line completely in deflected-tone words. And we see the pattern now, if we have not before: all of these specially stressed lines highlight the subtle rarity—of aspect, action, cognition, or nature—of either the mountain or the Realized Person whom the poet discovered there.[50]) Forlornly gazing after this guest from the heavens, Li Po feels himself rather confused and agitated. The phrase *ts'ang-jan* is interesting here.[51] It appears that Li Po has taken the connotation of the color-word *ts'ang*—usually a kind of maculated graygreen—and applied it figuratively to his emotional condition; hence my rendering, "in hazy state."[52] The "five emotions" (*wu ch'ing*) are usually defined as joy, anger, lamentation, delight, and resentment. For the Taoist they are also explained as "the divine pneumas of the five receptacles [in the body] of *yin* and *yang*."[53] The expression "my five emotions are inflamed" cannot help but recall one of the couplets spoken by Shadow to Form, in a poem of T'ao Ch'ien (372-427): "When the body is gone, fame vanishes too;/ In mind of this, my five emotions are inflamed."[54]

But the poet's disappointment at being left behind is merely temporary—as, he realizes, is his remaining tenure in this world. For he now owns the technique for translating himself, by alchemical means, to empy-real haunts.[55] Soon he shall no longer need to consort with the inhabitants of this lower sphere, but will enjoy eternal bliss with the Perfected on high. The detached air of this expectant and hopeful conclusion is tellingly emphasized in its prosody. For the first time in the poem we have, in line 17, a verse made up entirely of level-tone words: it is the long-withheld phonetic counter to the repetitive deflected-tone line that occurs in each of the four preceding stanzas and adds a welcome sonant complement. The concluding verse (line 18) then resolves the poem's tonal pattern, returning to the established deflected-tone refrain but with a level tone for the penultimate word, to balance—and set off effectively—the definitive termination in *byet, a deflected-tone word whose meaning ("be set apart") likewise resolves definitively the semantic pattern of the poem. The poet has come to rest in the contemplation of his own eventual transcendence.

In terms of its diction and imagery, this poem is more immediately accessible than any of the others we have considered. It contains little in the way of recondite allusions or of abstruse hints of canonical literature. Yet it still quite clearly depends on an understanding of the spiritual—and linguistic—concerns of T'ang Taoism. The dazzling enchantments of the Taoist heavens and scriptures shine through Li Po's verses with apparent but varying intensity. Those who have eyes to see may still recover some of the light.

*Notes*

1. For an examination of the pervasive Taoist elements in Li Po's series of six poems on "Wandering on Mount T'ai," see Paul W. Kroll, "Verses From on High: The Ascent of T'ai Shan," *T'oung Pao* 69 (1983), 248-60.

2. *Li T'ai-po ch'üan-chi* [hereafter *LTPCC*] (Taipei, 1975), 22.499; *Li Po chi chiao-chu* [hereafter *LPCCC*] (Shanghai, 1980), 22.1290.

3. HY 292, p. 10a.

4. "Teng O-mei," *LTPCC,* 21.470; *LPCCC,* 21.1212.

5. "Ying-yang pieh Yüan Tan-ch'iu chih Huai-yang," *LTPCC,* 15.348; *LPCCC,* 15.915. "Acroama"—that is, "secret, privately communicated teachings transmitted only to elect disciples"—renders the word *chüeh,* an important item in the vocabulary of Taoism, usually translated too weakly as "instructions."

6. "Chih Ling-yang shan, teng T'ien-chu shih, ch'ou Han shih-yü chien chao-yin Huang shan," *LTPCC,* 19.441; *LPCCC,* 19.1140.

7. "Li Han-li chi hsü," *LTPCC,* 31.708; *LPCCC,* "fu-lu," 3.1790. The elegant priest-poet Wu Yün, who had been called to Ch'ang-an earlier in the year and who was acquainted with Li Po, is also traditionally regarded as having a hand in Li Po's summons to the imperial court. It is worth noting that it was not merely for his literary prowess, but at least as much for his supposed spiritual attainments, that Li Po was welcomed to court.

8. "Yü-chen hsien-jen tz'u," *LTPCC,* 8.219; *LPCCC,* 8.577.

9. Nine representing the number of "full *yang,*" in correspondence with the sun, the greatest symbol of *yang* energy (*t'ai yang*) in the sky.

10. "Po-hao Tzu ko," *LTPCC,* 7.189; *LPCCC,* 7.499. Earlier in the poem Master Pekoe is said to "sup at dawn on marrow from stone"—this a preparation of powdered calcite from stalactites in limestone grottoes, conceived as a rare emission flowing from within the rocks of sacred mountains.

11. "Pin ko hsing, shang Hsin-p'ing chang-shih hsiung Ts'an," *LTPCC,* 7.184; *LPCCC,* 7.486; and "Chiu jih," *LTPCC,* 20.468; *LPCCC,* 20.1206.

12. *Tung-chen shang-ch'ing ch'ing-yao tzu-shu chin-ken chung-ching* (HY 1304), 2.18b-23b.

13. See the following subsection for remarks about this celestial region.

14. The ultimate heaven of the triad known as the Three Clarities (viz., Greatest Clarity [T'ai ch'ing], Highest Clarity, and Jade Clarity), the divine inhabitants of which have never revealed themselves to our corruptible world.

15. HY 1304, 2.18b.

16. See my article "Spreading Open the Barrier of Heaven," forthcoming in *Asiatische Studien* (1985), for discussion and an annotated translation of the entire text.

17. "Teng T'ai-po feng," *LTPCC,* 21.473; *LPCCC,* 21.1219.

18. "Fei lung yin, esh shou," No. 2, *LTPCC,* 3.91; *LPCCC,* 3.232. For Huang Ti's transformation in medieval times from a mythical "culture hero" to a Taoist Transcendent, see *Lieh-hsien chuan,* 1.2b-3a and especially the more lengthy *Kuang Huang Ti pen-hsing chi* (HY 290; Extensive Records of the Basic Deeds of the Yellow Thearch) and also the "Hsüan-yüan pen-chi" (Basic Annals of Hsüan-yüan) preserved in *Yün-chi ch'i-ch'ien,* 100.2b-32a.

19. "Shang yün yüeh," *LTPCC,* 3.103; *LPCCC,* 3.259. "Purple Tenuity" (Tzu wei), a circumpolar constellation made up largely of the stars of our Draco, was the protecting wall of the residence of "Heaven's Illustrious Great Theocrat" (T'ien huang ta ti), high counterpart of the terrestrial god-king.

20. HY 1304, 2.16a.

21. "Ts'ao ch'uang ta-huan, tseng Liu Kuan-ti," *LTPCC,* 10.261; *LPCCC,* 10.691.

22. This elixir is also referred to in the fourth of Li Po's group of "Olden Airs," where he claims he is himself fabricating the "Purple River Carriage" (*tzu ho ch'e,* this being the esoteric name for one stage in the firing process).

23. "Lu shan yao, chi Lu shih-yü Hsü-chou," *LTPCC,* 14.328; *LPCCC,* 14.863. The possible Taoist implications of the name here are enhanced by the fact that the poem ends with references to "Transcendent Persons," "the Jade Capital" (for which, see next subsection), and the Heaven of "Greatest Clarity."

24. "Teng kao ch'iu erh wang yüan-hai," *LTPCC,* 4.110; *LPCCC,* 4.283.

25. "Lu chün Yao tz'u, sung Tou ming-fu Po-hua huan hsi-ching," *LTPCC,* 16.380; *LPCCC,* 16.986.

26. *Wu-shang pi-yao* (HY 1130), 4.8a, citing *Tung-hsüan yü-chüeh ching.* We are also informed a bit further on (4.8b-9a) of the ten different names by which the mountain is known to transcendent beings.

27. Ibid., 21.1a, citing *Tung-hsüan ching.*

28. "Feng chien Kao tsun-shih Ju-kuei tao-shih, ch'uan tao-lu pi, kuei Pei-hai," *LTPCC,* 17.399; *LPCCC,* 17.1032.

29. The four cardinal and four inter-cardinal directions, plus zenith and nadir.

30. "Lu shan yao, chi Lu shih-yü Hsü-chou," *LTPCC,* 14.328; *LPCCC,* 14.863.

31. "Feng sheng p'ien," *LTPCC,* 5.138; *LPCCC,* 5.359. The best of Li Po's editor-commentators Wang Ch'i

(1696-1774) thinks that "Jade Capital" is here merely a metaphor for the T'ang capital, Ch'ang-an. I cannot agree.

32. *Sui shu* (The Documents of Sui) (Peking, 1973), 35.1092, in the bibliographic essay on Taoist writings.

33. So says Li Yang-ping, a paternal kinsman of the poet and editor of his works, in whose household Li Po was apparently residing at the time of his death, and who presumably had this information from Li Po himself. "Ts'ao-t'ang chi hsü," *LTPCC*, 31.706; *LPCCC*, "fu-lu," 3.1789. The Palace of the Purple Culmen was one of many score of Taoist temples of that name, the establishment of which had been mandated throughout the nation by Hsüan Tsung in 741, to commemorate the wonderful revelations of the deified Lao Tzu that occurred in the final years of the K'ai-yüan period (and which also led to the change of era-name in 742 to T'ien-pao, "Heavenly Treasure"). The temples had originally been called "fanes" (*miao*), but in 743 this was changed to "palace."

34. "Fang tao An-ling, yü Kai Huan wei yü tsao chen-lu, lin-pieh liu-tseng," *LTPCC*, 10.254; *LPCCC*, 10.672-73.

35. *Chin shu* (The Documents of Chin) (Peking, 1974), 50.1396-97; also *Shih-shuo hsin-yü* (New Colloquies of Tales of the World), 2B.2b, *SPTK*. The same words were used by Chang Yüeh (667-731) in the early eighth century to commend the verbal fullness of Yang Chiung's (650-694?) writing.

36. The most important local officials in Han times were, at least in theory, paid a salary of 2,000 piculs of grain. The phrase "two thousand piculs" hence came to connote the highest of the provincial bureaucracy.

37. There are three "cinnabar fields." The other two, "upper" and "middle," are located in the head and in the heart.

38. Or more precisely, "Heaven's Jade-cog" (*t'ien-hsüan*) and "Heaven's Armil" (*t'ien-chi*).

39. One finds this usage particularly in the "weft" texts (*wei*) of the Han dynasty. The employment of the bowl of the Dipper as a stellated protective headgear for the adept is common in medieval Taoist scriptures.

40. *T'ai-shang Lao chün chung-ching* (HY 1160; Inner Scripture of Lord Lao the Most High), 1.9a; also quoted in *Yün-chi ch'i-ch'ien*, 18.9a. This text also states that the dwelling spot in the human body of Jade-cog and Armil is the navel.

41. The second and third stars are named, as usual, "Heaven's Jade-cog" and "Heaven's Armil."

42. "Occult Tenebrity" (*hsüan ming*) and "Heaven's Balance-weight" (*t'ien ch'üan*) are other names for star #4.

43. "Latency of the West" is *hsi k'un*, directionally the northwest, epitome of *yin*, housing the seed of *yang* within it.

44. HY 1355, pp. 4b-5a. The rotas of immortality are kept in the (casements of the) south, at the Gate of Life.

45. In the system of *wu-hsing* correspondences, the North correlates symbolically with water and with the color black. See *Chen kao* (HY 1010; Entitlements of the Realized Ones), 15.1a-4b, for more extensive comments about Lo-feng.

46. "Feng chien Kao tsun-shih Ju-kuei tao-shih, ch'uan taolu pi, kuei Pei-hai," *LTPCC*, 17.399; *LPCCC*, 17.1032.

47. Alluding to the statement in *Chuang tzu*: "The Way is not able to be seen; if seen, that is not it." *Chuang tzu chi-shih* (Taipei, 1971), 22.330. This first line of the poem is given added emphasis by all five syllables being in deflected tones—a consciously unusual effect in a *lü-shih*.

48. According to the tenth-century *T'ang chih-yen* (Picked-up Words of T'ang) (Shanghai, 1978), 7.81, it was Ho Chih-chang (659-744) who first pronounced this identification. Ho is also credited as being the one to dub Li Po an "ostracized Transcendent" (*che hsien*).

49. "Ku feng, wu-shih-chiu shou," No. 5, *LTPCC*, 2.46-47; *LPCCC*, 2.102.

50. We might remark also the carefully arranged disposition of these lines in the body of the poem: final line of stanza 1, penultimate line of stanza 2, final line of stanza 3, penultimate line of stanza 4. It is as though the poem has a phonetic refrain. I have noticed the same sort of design in several other of Li Po's poems; I hope to discuss the question more fully in a future study. Surely, though, conscious phonetic patterning and periodic punctuation of this type must have contributed greatly to the vaunted musicality of Li Po's verse. Notice, too, how in the first two stanzas of this poem Li Po establishes a prosodic pattern of (OOXOX) for rhyming lines (excepting only the stressed, deflected-tone line 4); he then begins to vary the pattern in the following two stanzas but reverts to it as a mark of closural return in line 16.

51. There is no support in any edition for an emendation to *ts'ang-jan*, "woeful, grief-laden," which might seem appealing at first glance.

52. In the three other poems in which he employs the phrase ("Teng Huang shan Ling-hsiao t'ai, sung tsu-ti Li-yang wei Chi ch'ung fan chou fu Hua-yin," *LTPCC*, 18.421; *LPCCC*, 18.1086; "Ta t'ing k'u," *LTPCC*, 21.470; *LPCCC*, 21.1213; "Ch'iu teng Pa-ling wang Tung-t'ing," *LTPCC*, 21.483; *LPCCC*, 21.1247) it seems to suggest either a wavering mist or fading vegetation.

53. *Yün-chi ch'i-ch'ien*, 87.13b. Cf. the comment at

13.14b that "The five pneumas being vitalized, forthwith the five emotions are instinctively euphoric."

54. "Ying ta hsing, i shou," *Ch'üan Chin shih*, 6.4a (p. 603).

55. Technically speaking, transcendence by alchemical means gave access only to the heaven of Greatest Clarity.


## David Young (essay date 1990)

SOURCE: "Li Po," in *Five T'ang Poets*, Oberlin College Press, 1990, pp. 45-52.

[*In the following introduction to the Li Po section in his translation of the works of five T'ang poets, Young remarks on Li Po's sense of intoxication, freedom, and adventure, and discusses the poet's distinctive treatment of traditional themes.*]

He seems half-man, half-myth. The personality that informs the poems and that is haloed by a long tradition of deep affection may once have been less than legendary, but it can never have been ordinary. The Chinese have valued Li Po for his gaiety, freedom, sympathy and energy for so long that he has become a sort of archetype of the bohemian artist and puckish wanderer. The story that he drowned when he drunkenly tried to embrace the moon in the river is doubtless apocryphal, but it is also delightfully apt to anyone who knows his work; and the scholar who protested that the poem addressed to Tu Fu could not be by Li Po because the latter would never address the former with such levity and disrespect was laboring under a misplaced notion of decorum. The stories that have come down to us, whether legend or fact, have an effective way of integrating the life of the man and the spirit of the work, perhaps the nicest kind of gift that posterity can bestow on a poet.

A number of these poems are about drinking and being drunk, and while that theme is not exclusive to Li Po, it is one he is obviously particularly comfortable with. That partly tells us how much Li Po enjoyed his wine, but since lots of poets like to drink without ever feeling moved to write about it, we also need to see how it serves him as a poetic metaphor. Life at its best, as Li Po envisions it, is a kind of intoxication, an elevation; poetry, like good wine, should help us get perspective on ourselves and put the cares of the world aside. Even nature, as Li Po likes to present it, has a kind of intoxicated quality, especially in spring. The poet's presentation of himself as drunkenly enjoying some natural setting is thus a cleverly unpretentious way of presenting transcendent states of mind and being. This idea isn't exclusive to Li Po, but he handles the metaphor of the bibulous poet in a tipsy world as well as anyone before or since.

We can get some notion of Li Po's distinctive voice and manner if we compare his "climbing" poem, **"High in the Mountains, I Fail to Find the Wise Man,"** with a comparable Wang Wei poem, "Passing the Temple of Accumulated Fragrance." Both poets present themselves as wandering around half-lost in the mountains, looking for someone or something sacred. Wang Wei's progression of images is sure and exciting, moving to the quiet closure with the speaker meditating next to a still pond or lake as the evening comes on. Whether he has also found the temple scarcely seems to matter, since he has found, in effect, the peace of mind he was presumably searching for. Li Po's poem begins more abruptly, moves forward more unpredictably, and ends more astonishingly. Its movements from image to image seem like slightly larger leaps, and each image or sensation—the sight of the deer, the sudden sky overhead, the breathtakingly beautiful sight of the waterfall—is charged with delight and magic. The ending (if my interpretation of it is correct) is a more striking version of Wang Wei's idea: after this set of experiences, any upset or "grief" about failing in his original purpose is almost comically irrelevant. Each poet has his own strengths: Wang Wei's sure sense of detail and ability to pull a poem together around its closing image are especially impressive, along with his subtle handling of tone. In Li Po's case, there is a greater willingness to be centrifugal, to let the poem scatter in several directions, a risky tendency that fits nicely with the metaphoric "intoxication" I have spoken of, and that is surely one source of the legend of Li Po as carefree wanderer and social misfit.

Another difference from Wang Wei can be found in Li Po's willingness to cast poems in the voices of people other than himself. The most famous example is the great poem Ezra Pound translated under the title **"The River Merchant's Wife: A Letter."** My own examples are the little poem titled **"She Thinks of Him"** and the poem spoken by soldiers, **"'We Fought South of the Ramparts.'"** The first example serves to demonstrate how convincingly Li Po could speak through the sensibility and experience of a woman; the second shows the social and political insights he was capable of. Both are part of a larger tendency to sympathize with the world and people he encountered, an ability to enter fully into the experiences of others. This ability also gave Li Po his keen appreciation of the value of friendship. Like Wang Wei, he has times of solitude in which he appreciates total isolation, and, again like Wang Wei, he likes to balance such moments with company and conviviality. But the appreciation of the company of others that is somewhat ceremonious and guarded in Wang Wei becomes a heartfelt enthusiasm for friends and a genuine distress at parting from them in Li Po. Moments of separation fascinate him because of the challenge they present to his pursuit of elation, and his solutions, or resolutions, are poignant and various. Again, we are talking about one poet's handling of what was already a tradition—poems of friendship and leave-taking were a standard type by Li Po's time—but the distinctiveness and authenticity of that handling are among the hallmarks of Li Po's work.

Most of the experts now date Li Po's birth as 701, which would make him the same age as Wang Wei, and some eleven years older than Tu Fu. He seems to have been born outside of China, perhaps in present-day Afghanistan, but in any case he grew up in the mountainous southwestern province of Szechwan. As a boy he showed what would become a lifelong interest in meditation and spiritual discipline by going off to study with a hermit known as the Master of the Eastern Cliff. He was also, as a young man, something of a swordsman. His gifts eventually took him to the capital and the service of the Emperor, but he was too unruly for court life, and soon resumed his routine of travel, study, drinking bouts, and writing. During the period of civil war he fell in with a rebellious prince of the royal family and was imprisoned for a time. He died in relative poverty, famous in his own lifetime as an unusually gifted poet in a nation of poets.

The man who emerges from the poems and from the scraps of contemporary accounts was certainly not without flaws of character. He was boastful, given to exaggeration and downright lying, and irresponsible as a father, husband, and citizen. His status as a social misfit equipped him for the life of a recluse or monk, but unfortunately he had expensive tastes and loved good company, expensive wine, and dancing girls. He never stood for the Civil Service exams, an extraordinary thing when we recall that success in them depended so much upon poetic ability. As Arthur Waley puts it:

> The poems, then, are those of a man who in the eyes of a society largely dominated by bureaucratic values had completely failed in his career or rather had failed to have a career at all. There were poets who had lost their jobs and poets who after a time had returned voluntarily to private life. But that a great poet should never have had a job at all was almost unprecedented. Some people no doubt thought that such a situation was highly discreditable to the Government. Others, like Wei Hao, believed that to have given him a job would only have been asking for trouble. Li Po himself, in a poem addressed to his wife, confesses that his drunkenness made him as good as no husband at all; but he never seems to have faced the fact that it also disqualified him for official service.

What is striking about all this is that admiration for the poet had already begun to overshadow reservations about the man in Li Po's own lifetime, as it has certainly continued to do since.

To a highly tradition-bound poetry, Li Po brought a sense of freedom and adventure. He showed an extraordinary ability to exploit the openness of the Chinese language, its gaps and implications, so that, reading his direct and simple poems, we find ourselves supplying their richness and exploring their implications. Arthur Cooper speaks of the way the line that translates literally as *"drunk rise stalk brook moon"* in the poem I have called **"Indulgence"** (**"Abandon"** is Cooper's title) fills out in our imaginations so that we know what kind of landscape it is set in and find ourselves acting it out and participating in its emotions to a surprising degree. One could multiply such examples endlessly. Li Po has an intuitive grasp of the ge-

nius of his language and its possibilities for poetry, and it is his exploitation of this understanding that allows us to return again and again to his apparently simple and unpretentious poems for refreshment, imaginative exhilaration, and a sense of their capacity to outlast the limitations of the life and circumstances that produced them.

**Paula M. Varsano (essay date 1992)**

SOURCE: "Immediacy and Allusion in the Poetry of Li Bo," in *Harvard Journal of Asiatic Studies,* Vol. 52, No. 1, June, 1992, pp. 225-61.

[*In the following essay, Varsano contends that Li Po's deliberate use and manipulation of traditional poetic conventions plays an important role in his success as the quintessentially "immediate" poet who seems to respond spontaneously to the world around him, apparently unconstrained by the dictates of tradition.*]

The ideal of spontaneous expression—poetic expression as the unmediated, untransformed verbal manifestation of emotion—has remained a constant in Chinese poetic discourse ever since its first declaration in the Great Preface of the *Shijing:* "Poetry is that to which intention goes. While in the heart, it is intention; set forth in words, it is poetry. One's feelings are moved within and then take form in words. When words do not suffice, one sighs; when sighing does not suffice, then one sings; when singing does not suffice, unconsciously, one's hands will flutter and one's feet will stamp."[1] In the Six Dynasties, this canon of naturalness in expression, which we shall call "immediacy," started to find a wide range of application in Chinese critical discourse, now justifying such apparently artificial innovations as tonal regulation,[2] now railing against the threat of overrefinement and preciousness.[3] Critics have always differed over the implications and applications of this theory of poetic creation, but among partisans and detractors alike there seems to be a universal consensus that the poetry of Li Bo is the incarnation of "immediacy."

Many of the poems by Li Bo that survive today easily conform to the most stringent requirements of "natural" expression. Although adept at producing the most finely executed regulated verse, Li Bo habitually prefers a startingly clear and straightforward language to that which is ornate and convoluted. His images, prompted by perceived elements of the world around him, glide without a hitch into the imagined vista of the world above him. These moments of liberation from the sensory world explain, in large part, the durability of Li Bo's reputation as the "banished immortal." But this sobriquet owes itself to something more than a panoply of celestial images and flowing syntax. Possibly because of a reluctance to mar the image of the poet who could compose ten thousand poems when fueled with a good bottle of wine, little has been said that might account for those aspects of his work that are undeniably—even pointedly—rationally crafted. It is the goal of this article to explore in some detail one surprising— not to say paradoxical—way in which Li Bo succeeds in "crafting" immediacy into his poetry: his peculiar application of poetic convention.

The term, "poetic convention," broad as it is, simply refers to those pre-existing poetic structures that, when selected and used by the poet, link him or her to a received tradition. Judicious use of these structures enhances the effectiveness of a poem by providing the targeted reader with access to the inner state of the poet via a shared pathway. Depending upon their accessibility and degree of adherence to convention, the use of such shared elements ensures a variable degree of universality. Among such categories of poetic convention are the notable examples of allusion and genre. It is also possible that a poet, regarding the literary past from a certain perspective, will detect elements of convention that exist but have not been recognized. Lacking an identifiable textual or historical origin, such elements do not qualify as allusions. Not large enough to encompass a poem in its entirety and lacking any evidence of self-conscious evolution, they may not be labeled as genres. They manifest themselves subtly but cumulatively, in the form of the repeated gesture, the cultural artifact, or even the special vocabulary of a particular school of thought. Li Bo not only possessed the perspective necessary to identify such elements within his own tradition; he reveled in that ability.

In this article, I shall argue that Li Bo's particular use of his literary heritage, in the form of the various elements of poetic convention mentioned above, plays an important role in his success as the quintessentially "immediate" poet, the poet who seemed to respond spontaneously to the world around him, little guided by the dictates of a highly evolved poetic tradition. By using poetic convention, not as a means to unite himself with the shared emotions of humanity, but as a means to draw attention to his subjectivity, Li Bo inscribes the outsider's viewpoint into his poems; in this way, he transforms the self-conscious act of creativity into a sign of immediacy. In brief, the apparent freedom that characterizes Li Bo's poetry results not from the masking of creative effort behind a screen of false spontaneity, but from exposing that effort to the reader.

The discussion proceeds in three stages, moving from the smallest (and most easily recognizable) structure, textual allusion, to the somewhat larger and more amorphous realm of topical allusion (the Double Nine Festival), and finally to the domain of conventionladen gesture itself: the pouring and drinking of wine.

### Allusion And Immediacy

There is a bit of playfulness inherent in Li Bo's use of allusion as a springboard to immediate expression. The object of some criticism among Six Dynasties partisans of the expressionist view of poetry, allusion seems hardly the material on which to base a poetics of immediacy. Its

tenuous position when judged in light of such a poetics may be understood in terms of the one element setting it apart from other poetic tropes: unlike metaphor, which speaks to the intuition and draws upon little more than the information given within the poem itself, allusion invokes an outside textual source, thus calling into play a reader's acquired knowledge.[4] Understandably, the rational reflection leading to the utilization, as well as the reception, of an allusion renders its use questionable, at least to some of these Six Dynasties champions of natural poetic expression.

Li Bo nullified the debate by countering it with a frank attitude to the "allusiveness" of allusion. As manifested in the poems themselves, this entailed redirecting the reader's attention away from simply understanding the meaning of an allusion to recognizing the difference (or, in some cases, the studied similarity) established between an allusion and its textual reference. This practice, which we will examine in detail, enabled Li Bo to recreate immediacy on two levels. On the first and most obvious level, he defamiliarized allusions by explicitly referring to their pastness and assumed universality, thus leading his readers to rethink the commonplace and feel the *effect* of liberation, spontaneity. The second level of immediacy is a direct consequence of the first, insofar as it draws one's attention to the artist's elevated point of view. In explicitly referring to allusions as something externally imposed, as part of a received tradition from which he may select some elements and reject others, Li raises his voice above the chorus of the past—deliberately establishing that he directs their songs rather than being directed by it. This has immediate bearing upon his reputation as the "banished immortal"; if we regard allusion as the poetic embodiment of cyclical time, Li Bo was able to pose as one who had stepped beyond the bounds of that cycle.

### Allusion As Illusion

This confrontational view to allusion is evident in a poem that explicitly depicts the paradoxical process of searching out vehicles of immediate, individual expression. Time and time again, the poetic past—in both the form of allusion and that of conventionally determined expression— unavoidably insinuates itself into the mind of the poet, not only threatening to overshadow original expression, but promising to usurp those original feelings that must always remain the basis of such expression:

> I laugh at myself, on the road for so long,
> When will I settle down from wandering?
> Already willow branches are ready to be plucked,
> I reach up to take the longest bough.
> It flutters as I finger its spring colors,
> Long have I waited to send it to the one I miss.
> But who declared that we should value this thing?
> My yearning, more precious than a jade flower.
> Yesterday I dreamed I saw Huilian,
> This morning I was chanting the poem of Master Xie.
> The east wind gives rise to emerald grasses,
> And unwittingly yields a flowering pond.

I glanced down to play with it—suddenly twilight is
announced,
The night cry of the cuckoo is mournful.
I miss you as this fragrant season passes,
As trees in the courtyard drop red nectar.⁵

### "In Which I Write My Feelings to be Sent to My Cousin Li Zhao of Binzhou"

As in many of his poems, Li Bo opens this one with the
first person pronoun, the directness of which primes us for
a poem of spontaneous, "immediate" reflection. In the next
couplet, he establishes his physical orientation with equal
spontaneity: he sees before him a willow. Here, the boundary between immediate and literary experience starts to
dissolve; upon seeing a willow in bloom, any Chinese
reader or writer of poetry, especially one far away from
his loved ones, will inevitably recognize it as a traditional
sign for desiring to "detain" (*liu*) the departing loved one.
This link, which finds its roots in the homophonic relation
of *liu* and *liu,* extends beyond the realm of poetry into the
widely practiced social gesture of giving a willow branch
to someone who is about to go away.

For a moment, Li Bo confounds the natural object before
his eyes and the literary sign of acquired knowledge. He
does not immediately recognize that the "readiness" of the
willow has little to do with the willow itself but is rather a
function of his framing the scene (with himself in it)
through the lens of previous literary expression. So, moved
by the sight of the blooming willow, he lifts his hand in a
gesture that is so familiar that we see it before it is executed—to pluck off a branch. But, just as his fumbling attempt to express his feelings disturbs the delicate new
green, he recoils in exasperation: "But who declared that
we should value this thing? / My yearning more precious
than a jade flower." Stopping himself from completing the
gesture, he asserts that conventional expression is molding
not only his utterances, but his initial reactions to his "immediate" surroundings. Yet even this assertion, an apparent attempt at proclaiming his autonomy and subjectivity,
is couched in words borrowed from Poem #9 of the Nineteen Old Poems.⁶ Does this borrowing from the past signal
a surrender, a recognition that words fail him, or a sense
that everything worth saying has already been said? Or
does he refresh these ancient words by using them as a
weapon against banality? We withhold our judgment as we
move on to the second part of the poem.

The poem resumes in line 9 with poet recounting the event
of a dream he had had the previous night, retreating one
step back from the shared exterior world in which he sees
the willow, into the most private realm of his dreams. Yet
what he sees in his dream is a figure, which (unlike the
willow) exists not at all in the realm of his personal experience and is known to him exclusively through the reading of texts—through the poems he left behind. He sees
Xie Huilian, a poet who lived over three hundred years
before him. The literature recounts that Huilian's mere
presence was known to inspire his uncle Xie Lingyun to
produce his most beautiful lines of poetry. Once, when

Xie Lingyun was having difficulty writing a poem, Huilian's appearance in a dream enabled him to write the well-
known line, "The pond bears spring grasses" for his poem,
"Climbing the Tower Over the Pond".

Li Bo's allusion seems at first glance to be a means of
paying respect to Li Zhao, crediting him with Huilian's
ability to facilitate "writing his feelings"—the stated object of this poem. But if this were the sole intent, a single
reference would have sufficed. One property of allusion is,
after all, economy of expression. In this case, however, Li
Bo chooses to reproduce all of the elements of the original
story, without modifying it at all to suit his personal situation, with the result that he dreams of a figure who does
not belong to his experience, and wakes up chanting words
that do not spring from his own invention but belong almost verbatim to Xie Lingyun (line 10). Clearly then, a
muse from the past can only inspire writing that is past.
As in the case of the willow in bloom, the allusion to Xie
Huilian, though recognized and understood by all, seems
somewhat restrictive and schematic when put to the test of
capturing the poet's contemporary, personal reality.

The parallel between the dream and the willow is reinforced in line 13. Just as the poet reaches out to touch this
vision of a pond conjured up by Xie Lingyun's words, it
disappears with the onset of night. And just as in the earlier event, this vision is replaced, not by any unique reality, but by a sound of the past, to which poets of the past
had often turned every lonely wanderer's ears: the night
cry of the cuckoo. With the insertion of this well-known
sign, the frontier between landscape and literature is again
completely obfuscated, but one thing is clear: having now
twice discovered that the lexicon of past poetry cannot
sufficiently correspond to his own immediate experience,
Li Bo must find a way to conclude the poem simply in
terms of what he feels and sees. And so he does: he states
simply that he misses his friend as he witnesses the falling
of the flower petals.

In this poem, which explicitly illustrates the process of the
search for words to express his feelings, Li Bo is indisput-
ably "immediate," for herein he acknowledges his activity
as a consciously creating poet. By first rejecting convention, and finally selecting it on his own terms—in other
words, by making manifest his conscious choice—he
leaves no doubt as to the appropriateness of otherwise
hackneyed images. He thereby revives those images and
gives a new meaning to the practice of "pouring new wine
into old bottles."

In his of a broad range of allusions extending from the
textual to the topical, Li Bo exhibits his awareness of convention. Because this awareness supports him in his pose
as "outsider," Li Bo toys with the conventional use of allusions to establish the subjectivity of his vision. As examples of his use of textual allusion, we will look at **"In
Response to 'Tongtang Tune' by Censor Lu"** and **"Composed on Jade Maiden Spring in Ying Cheng, Anzhou."**
As in **"Writing My Feelings,"** Li Bo demonstrates the

"allusiveness" of allusion by attempting, and repeatedly failing, to obliterate the boundary between literary and immediate experience.

> So you boast that Tongtang is great,
> That Tongtang is more lovely than Yexi.
> And where is Tongtang?
> Far off, west of Xunyang.
>
> There the green vines softly twine, hanging from misty trees,
> And white herons cluster here and there, all along the sandy banks.
> Through a break between stone cliffs emerges a placid lake,
> A golden pool one hundred *zhang,* reflecting cloud and sun.
> And where is the old Canglang fisherman?
> Beating his oars, singing his fishing song, many are his pleasures.
>
> Should we meet I'd know him not,
> Appearing, disappearing, circling round Tongtang. 12
> Through clear water at the shore gleam pearl-white feet,
> Here yet another silk-washing maid of Wu.
> Go the length of the green pool, the pool grows more secluded,
> I'd swear this is the emerald flowing of spring in Wuling.
> The chickens and dogs of the Qin amid peach blossoms,
> Compared to Tongtang, the place would be put to shame.
>
> Tongtang—one cannot bear to leave,
> Leave ten times and, in time, return nine.
>
> Come upon this fine scene, my heart's already drunk,
> Suddenly a single bird comes from the sky.
> The moon rises out of green mountains and accompanies this traveler,
> All around from "bitter bamboo" arise the sounds of autumn.
>
> For a while I chant "White Snow in Spring" and gaze at the River of Stars,
> Dangling together both my feet I kick up frothy waves.
> Liang Hong and De Yao's days in Kuaiji,
> How could even they have known so much happiness as this?[7] 28

> In Response to 'Tongtang Tune' by Censor Lu

To appreciate the degree to which Li Bo has succeeded in toying with the traditional uses of allusion, we must note the importance of his choice of Kuaiji. Yexi is located in Kuaiji Prefecture, the supposed site of both Xi Shi's silk-washing and Liang Hong and his wife's final home. This geographical location links the two legendary figures introduced by the poet: the legendary beauty, Xi Shi, and the couple, Liang Hong and De Yao, via the seemingly incidental comparison of Tongtang to Yexi in line 1. But if we recall that the subject of the poem is not Kuaiji, but Tongtang—a place Li Bo does not see but nevertheless compares to Kuaiji—we see that the dual allusion is linked with a location that is not once-, but twice-removed from the poet's immediate reality.

Xi Shi and De Yao are also juxtaposed because the contrast between their stories is instructive. Xi Shi was a woman whose beauty fated her to become the tool of political warfare and who was instrumental in the downfall of her husband; De Yao (also known as Meng Guang) was homely, but her moral rectitude, intelligence, and devotion to her husband enabled him to survive and, ultimately, to flourish in adverse political circumstances.

Stepping back, now, to read Li Bo's poem as a response to a poem by Censor Lu, we can infer that Lu's poem was inspired by the beauty of Lake Tongtang, even though it is no longer extant. On one level, Li Bo's response may be read as a hyperbolic—and slightly playful—rejoinder to an earnest, if conventional landscape poem. Insofar as this is true, his poem is a play on a traditional form. But on another level, through the witty use of allusion, Li Bo actively engages the past and establishes his "immediate" voice.

**"Tongtang Tune"** begins with an echo. An echo—a disembodied voice—is the past act that lingers on in the telling, ringing in the ears long after the speaker has disappeared. "So you boast that Tongtang is great," repeats Li Bo. This abrupt beginning, almost a challenge, also establishes the narrator as reader, perhaps allied more closely to the reader of this poem than to the writer whose feelings were first stirred by the landscape. Although the landscape is not seen by our poet, it is familiar to him—of course he knows where it is (lines 3-4)—and so, with hardly an effort, its distant image is summoned before his mind's eye. At first the image is indeed nothing more than that, an image, lyrical and carefully balanced, depicted in the poem's only parallel couplet: "There the green vines softly twine, hanging from misty trees, / And white herons cluster here and there, all along the sandy banks."

Picturesque, yet the work of impersonal craft, this couplet constitutes a literary convention set up only to be surpassed. Elsewhere, its technical perfection and simple beauty might indicate an acceptance of received form; here it is employed to demonstrate the very inadequacy of that form, freezing the poet's vision in an illustration that is well-composed but altogether inadequate to Li Bo's own perception of the past. Thus, the form is discarded right after it is created, as Li Bo impatiently breaks through this barrier of convention and brings to life the picture he has taken.

In lines 7 and 8, the reader finds himself peering through a different barrier, sighting, along with the poet, the distant waters of Tongtang through the gap between the heights of two juxtaposed palisades of stone (a "stone gate"). And so Li Bo transmits to us the same experience he had when reading Censor Lu's poem—the reader's experience in which words uttered by someone else reverberate in the mind, mingling with memory to produce a scene so vivid that it seems to be external, right before our eyes. It is only in the next line (line 9) that, layer by layer, Li Bo begins the process of stripping away the external trappings of a shared objective reality.

Gazing now upon the body of water that has been conjured up so clearly, Li repeats the rhetorical question of the second couplet, this time asking the whereabouts of the legendary Canglang fisherman. The reader will recognize him as the old fisherman in the "Yu fu pian" of the *Chu ci* who contentedly sang these lines: "When the water of the Canglang is clean, it will serve to wash my capstrings; when the water of the Canglang is murky, it will serve to wash my feet."

Li's question could be read rhetorically, as a way of expressing the secluded beauty of the place, the perfect setting for a paragon of righteousness who goes into reclusion to escape serving in a corrupt government. In this new realm of subjectivity, however, nothing can be purely rhetorical. As allusion borders on the edge of illusion, the stock question of *huaigu* poetry—"Where is he now?"—seems, surprisingly, to permit the possibility of an answer. But he catches himself at the last minute, confessing his inability to recognize the fisherman whom he seems to know so well.

Shifting his gaze in line 13, Li again faces the past, which is at once irretrievable and indelible. There, clearly gleaming at the side of the pool are the white feet of the beautiful Xi Shi of Wu—but again he undermines the reality of this allusion, with the simple insertion of one word: she is "yet another" and not the historical woman. The pattern continues without a break in lines 15 and 16; echoing Tao Yuanming, he discovers this body of water to be the irretrievable utopia Peach Blossom Spring—but this is his misapprehension. Straining against this state of intoxicated confusion, he finally tries to reclaim the division between his immediate experience and the literary landscape by drawing a direct comparison between the Tongtang of his imagination and the Peach Blossom Spring of literary history. Not surprisingly, he comes to the conclusion that, "Compared to Tongtang, the place would be put to shame."

He concludes this section in lines 19 and 20 by turning definitively towards the landscape of his own imagination, but in exclaiming how difficult it is to leave the place, he again slips into past literature, joining his own voice with the voice of Censor Lu and the countless other poets who had written on the beauty of famous places.

Lines 19 and 20 approach cliché and would signal the end of the poem, were they nothing more than a commemoration of a journey to Tongtang. But just as the parallel couplet, a form that gives the impression of immediacy and timelessness, was used earlier (in lines 5 and 6) in such a way as to suggest its inadequacy for that purpose, so this familiar "ending" is set up to betray its usual function. Under the circumstances already created by this poem, this couplet strikes the reader as an attempt to return to the well-defined realm of literature where things are assumed to have a basis in reality.

Li Bo opens the final section in line 21 with a shake of his head and a readjustment of his vision, excusing himself for having been carried away by the beauty of an intoxicating scene. The switch from allusion to concrete images of reality—a bird, the moon over the mountains—combined with the return to a sense of the linear progression of time, would seem to signal an awakening from reverie. But these concrete images are highly conventional and the narrator is still a "traveler" (line 23), so the imaginary journey still has a basis in reality.

Finally, chanting long and low, Li Bo echoes with his lips an ancient tune, and echoes with a gesture an image which is no more likely to vanish than that of the lake itself: "For a while I chant 'White Snow in Spring' and gaze at the River of Stars, / Dangling together both my feet I kick up frothy waves." Joining his feet with those of Xi Shi, Li Bo goes beyond being moved by echoes he hears and becomes one himself. The metonymical relationship between the Milky Way—the "River of Stars"—and the waters of Tongtang (a relationship highlighted by their corresponding positions in this pair of lines), permits us to imagine that we have left behind the earthly body of water for the "frothy waves" of the River of Stars. He dangles his feet, not in real water, which, in Chinese poetry of remembrance, has always been the physical embodiment of time itself, but in a celestial river of stars that does not flow and is eternal. With this gesture, Li Bo removes himself from the flow of time, and so relinquishes the temporal perspective that prevents him from seeing allusions as inherited images belonging only to the past.

At this point in the poem, allusion and illusion can now successfully blend to create a highly subjective and unquestionably immediate "reality" for our poet. But, as we have come to expect, at the last moment he undermines this transcendance of the limits of time and space, reestablishing in one phrase his place in real time: "Liang Hong and De Yao's days in Kuaiji, / How could even he have known such happiness as this?" Li Bo's joy at the prospect of escaping the flow of time and, with it, the tyranny of the literary tradition, finds its final expression in an allusion to a past example of great happiness.

We are once again led to a question that is familiar to us from our reading of lines 4-8 of the first poem: given that Li Bo has drawn so much attention to the distinction between convention and personal expression, does his apparent succumbing to the authority of the past signal a sudden and final concession? Or does Li Bo intend an inconsistency to underline his conviction that allusion is inadequate (not to say ludicrous) as a means for personal expression?

Perhaps the answer is that Li Bo neither succumbs to the authority of the past, nor rejects allusion. Just as in the poem dedicated to Li Zhao, Li Bo plays with the possibility of a distinction between convention and personal expression; but more decisively than in that poem, he concludes by having them coincide. It would seem that, by clearly *choosing* to make the comparison with Liang Hong and De Yao (which can only be done after having demonstrated that a choice does indeed exist), he insists upon its appropriateness to his situation. By first establishing his independence from the tradition, he leaves no doubt as to the authenticity of his decision to conclude his poem within its parameters. At the same time, he infuses an old story with renewed significance.

Thus, as demonstrated in these first two poems, Li Bo enjoys employing allusion in such a way as to point up its quality of "allusiveness." By revealing that allusion is an element of conventional expression—a foil to his authentic and subjective expression—Li Bo manifests his role as outsider and conscious creator. And it is here that we see the direct link between Li Bo's use of allusion and his immediacy: if immediacy is to be understood as the poet's non-rational and authentic lyrical response to the world, Li Bo includes allusion among the things of the world to which he responds freely, poet that he is. By documenting in his poetry the self-conscious deliberation behind the act of creation, Li Bo suggests that such deliberation need not be antithetical to immediacy; on the contrary, the recording of the creative process becomes the most essential component of immediacy.

As we have seen in **"Tongtang Tune,"** verbs of mental acts or perceptions serve as simple but potent tools in the transposition of literary allusion into personal imagination. In the following poem, **"Composed on Jade Maiden Spring in Ying Cheng, Anzhou,"** the poet's blend of allusion and illusion is expanded to encompass the poem as a whole, creating an integrated reality that transcends time.

### "Composed on Jade Maiden Spring in Ying City, Anzhou"[8]

A goddess died in this secluded realm,
Where hot springs flow into a great river.
Yin and Yang congealed in flaming coals,
Creation cleaved open the enchanted fountains.
Earth's foundation smolders with crimson fire,
While by the sands wafts silk-white smoke.
Roiling pearls leap within a shining moon,
The dazzling mirror encasing empty sky.
Vapor floats forth full of orchid's fragrance,
With color that swells in blossoms of burning peach.
Scan it all minutely, the myriad variations merging within,
Skim along the waters, the Seven Marshes converge.
In curing illness, it is surpassed by none,
Only when change reaches fullness is the Tao complete.
For washing capstrings, cupped hands raise its pure limpidity,
You can dry your hair while playing with the water's flow.
It wanders down through the King of Chu's state,

And splits off to sprinkle the fields of Song Yu.
It could serve as a site of an imperial tour,
Pity that it is so remote!
Alone I shall follow the reverent waters,
Casting tiny ripples into the sea.[9]

Unlike "Tongtang Tune," this poem was composed by Li Bo on the occasion of his having actually visited a specific location. The first two lines remind the reader of the legend associated with the hot springs of Anzhou, but at this point the reference remains allusive and hence incomplete. (This allusion will become central later on, as our poet elaborates it in consistent, but hardly classical, terms.) By placing the reference to this myth at the beginning of the poem Li Bo locates the landscape within the literary tradition and suggests that the act of writing about the place continues that tradition. The strange vapors emitted by the spring—clearly the source of inspiration for the myth of the goddess—also lead the poet into another realm of shared literature: the literature of the world's creation. Water, fire, and smoke frequently play a role in the depiction of the process of creation, and thus lines 3-6 appear to be a natural transition. They seem to fill in a gap by describing, not the hot spring itself, but the metaphysical process that created it and continues to create it.

The poet accomplishes this transition by invoking, if only indirectly, "The Owl" by Jia Yi ("Heaven and earth are a crucible, Creation is the smith; Yin and Yang are the charcoal, the myriad things are the bronze")[10]—a *fu* poem whose metaphorical links between flowing water and the Tao are particularly appropriate here. This echo of ancient descriptions of Creation is further reinforced by the evocation of an ancient anonymous poem ("Crimson fire burns in its depths, blue-gray smoke wafts in its midst").[11]

These metaphysical, yet highly visual images prepare the reader for a fresh and vivid view of the somewhat common conceit that follows: "Roiling pearls leap within the shining moon, / The dazzling mirror encasing empty sky." With this parallel couplet, Li Bo subtly moves from a recalled (or imagined) description of the hidden forces responsible for the hot spring, to the reality of that hot spring as it appears before his eyes. Still, his vision has been shaped by shared lore. Just as in **"Tongtang Tune,"** knowledge derived from a shared body of literature enables Li Bo to "see" a landscape that is both literary and metaphysical: "Scan it all minutely, the myriad variations merging within, / Skim along the waters, the Seven Marshes converge."

These last lines offer Li Bo's privileged view as though anyone whose vision has been similarly shaped would be able to see it as well. While the expression "myriad variations" (*wan shu*) returns us to the Taoist canon,[12] and thus to a scene that can only be recalled or imagined, the assertions of his vision in the verb "to scan" (*lan*), reinforced by its position directly after a parallel couplet of pure perception, constitutes Li Bo's first step, in this poem, toward the blending of common references (allusion) and personal subjectivity (illusion). His simple reference to the Seven

Marshes then adds a small but effective flourish; we learn that our poet has even exceeded Sima Xiangru's expansive vision in "Rhapsody of Sir Vacuous": "I have heard that Chu has Seven Marshes, but I have seen only one of them, and I have never seen the others."[13]

In offering his vision, Li is also inscribing his presence for the first time since the title. Here at the central point of the poem, this privileged witnessing of the confluence of all things, of the conjoining of disparate bodies, excludes the poet from that very confluence and identifies him as observer; and we, as observers, are present at his side. From that moment, any pretense to objective (observable) reality is lost, along with the particularity of Jade Maiden Spring. The fantastic, colorful imagery now dissolves in a recitation of the various moral and spiritual values of all waters, as gleaned from such ancient texts as the *Shui jing zhu,* the *Yi jing,* and the *Chu ci.* In an exhaustive cataloguing of qualities reminiscent of the style of Han dynasty *fu* poetry, Li Bo reminds the reader of water that is now the moral purifier of Confucian lore (lines 15-16), now an indifferent unifier serving king and exile alike (lines 17-18).

So water evolves, undergoing a transformation from a concrete object with legendary associations, to something highly imaginary, and finally, at the moment when the poet explicitly takes his place as observer, to the totally abstract—a symbol of the poet's aspiration to be able to overcome all barriers (i.e., the corrupt emperor) and eventually become one with the impartial, unwavering purity of one Ocean. In every case the agent of this transformation is the poet's selection of various literary traditions already associated with water. By the end of the second half of the poem, the spring before our eyes has disappeared and been replaced by a familiar sign, not unlike the willow branch of **"In Which I Write my Feelings."** Thus, in the final couplet, it is reduced to its most abstract form as purely linguistic signifier in the term *chaw zong shui,* roughly translated as "water that worships [the sea]." This stringing together of past usage has by now drained away all watery imagery, making this expression all but perfectly interchangeable with "loyal servant."

Once again we see how the explicitness with which Li Bo handles allusion is often his weapon against convention. Insofar as past literary expression constitutes a stimulus rather than a response, insofar as he recognizes it as an object belonging to the objective world rather than to his inner nature, Li Bo manages to assert that particular brand of subjectivity for which he is renowned, thereby signifying his presence as outside observer. In this case, by filling out allusions in ways that are comprehensible within the traditional lexicon—but which go beyond the usual associations—he turns schemata into triggers for the imagination. In doing so, he steps beyond the bounds of convention in order to master it, making explicit his role as artist, and creating the impression of immediacy.

### In Pursuit of Forgetfulness

Li Bo's assertion of subjectivity may be expressed in the transformation of the literary past into personal vision, as we have seen; but it is also likely to find expression in the pursuit of forgetfulness, of starting anew. Already familiar as one of the inspirations underlying *fu gu* poetry, the desire to clear one's literary memory (so as to attain the immediacy of the ancients) is also evident in certain themes that are, by their very nature, particularly tied to memory. One of these is the **"Double-Nine Festival."**[14]

The writing of a poem on this festival requires that one engage in an extended act of remembrance on several levels. This sub-genre, if it may be so called, evokes the past with a complexity rivaling that of *yuefu,* for it mingles the social conventions of the festival with the literary conventions of the poetic theme. Moreover, the writing of these poems is in itself one convention of the festival, and "climbing high"—which is a sub-generic theme with distinct, if overlapping, conventions of its own—is a convention of the "Double Nine" treatment in poetry as well as a ritual of the festival. These elements combine to form a unique poetics of remembrance in which literary tradition is not simply invoked, but remembered. The resulting multiplication of levels of memory and tradition can threaten to eclipse the individual expression of the rememberer, but for a poet such as Li Bo, who delights in posing as the outsider, there is perhaps no better juncture at which to shape an individual voice and carve out a particular subjectivity.

Discontinuity of elements, systematic denial of readerly expectations—these are some of the ways in which a poet might suggest an internal ordering of the universe that is uniquely his own. The elements are drawn from a common world, and expectations are shaped by a shared literature. Li Bo's **"Ascending the Mountain on Double Nine"** is one poem whose discontinuity has led readers to appeal to external information in an effort to find that elusive unifying thread.[15]

> Yuanming, "Returning Home,"
> Did not follow the ways of the world.
> When he was lacking the stuff of the goblet,
> He then befriended a local magistrate. 4
> And having hailed the man in white,
> With a smile they poured out some yellow chrysanthemum wine.
>
> I, in coming here, did not fulfill my desire,
> In vain I passed the time this "Double Nine."
> How exceptional, he for whom the carriage was designated![16]
> So let us keep our engagement south of the city wall![17]
> Building a hillock to connect with Mount Xiang,
> Looking down upon the banks of the Wan River.
> Northland barbarians call upon jaded flutes,
> Girls of Yue play their "frosted strings."
> To make of oneself the descendant of generals,
> In pleasures which none can spy.
> Crimson carp surge up under Qin Gao,[18]
> White tortoise leads forth Bing Yi.[19]
> If the immortals are like them,
> Pour a libation and they will know from afar.

All those who've "climbed high" since times of old,
How many are still there today?
If on Cang Isle old promises break,[20]
One can still await the days to come.
Chains of mountains look like startled waves,
Their folded layers emerge from a darkened sea.

Wave my sleeves at those seated around,
In drunkeness what do they know?
Singing songs of Qi, send goblets all around,
And all rise up in formless dance.
The guests depart with the scattering leaves,
A hat flies off with the autumn wind.[21]
After parting I climbed this tower,
Wanting to speak of "Longing for You."[22]

### "Ascending the Mountain on Double Nine"

Here Li Bo uses a technique we might call "naming." In contrast with allusion, "naming" occurs when the poet *directly* refers to a tradition by a key word or phrase, thus placing emphasis on the act of mentioning rather than on what is mentioned. In this poem Li Bo combines "naming" with close adherence to elements of the tradition in order to give the impression that he is staying within the mainstream of the tradition. The very first line is "naming" at its most essential: "Yuanming, 'Returning Home.'" It is composed of the name of an author and his most representative work,[23] and stands at the beginning of the poem as a hard and self-enclosed grammatical nugget that stops the reader momentarily before the flow of the sentence leads him deeper into the poem. The title of the poem, which is still fresh in the reader's mind, may now appear to the reader as a naming as well, for it is non-specific in place and time, evocative of nothing so much as a literary tradition in its entirety.

The linking of these "names" (the Double Nine Festival and Tao Yuanming) at the beginning of the poem, otherwise connected only by a traditional association that exists independently of this particular poem (and will be described below),[24] presents itself as the result of spontaneous recall. The isolated first line soon reveals itself as introducing an equally free-floating six-line set piece. Leaving little to the reader's imagination, the words recount a well-known story; yet the poet adds nothing of his personal imagination to account for the structural gaps.

In the first section, Li Bo blends together two stories associated with Tao Yuanming, one regarding his composition of the "Gui qu lai ci" and the other establishing his link with the Double Nine Festival. Tersely couching them in a series of well-known phrases, Li reinforces the initial impression that he is uninvolved but reactive in the face of tradition. Lines 1 and 2 contain the simplest possible reference to a story in the *Jin shu* explaining that, rather than accept an invitation by the prefect, Tao resigned from his low-level position as secretary of Pengzhe County and retired home, where he wrote his "Gui qu lai ci." Lines 3 and 4 comprise the barest essence of the story of Wang Hong, censor of Linzhou, who was determined to meet with Tao. After having been politely but firmly spurned

several times, Wang contrived to have a wine stand set up along a road, which, he was told, Tao would take on his way to Lushan. True to Wang's expectations, Tao could not resist this temptation and "forgot" to continue on his journey. Wang joined Tao at the wine stand and engaged him in a long and deep conversation. Were it not for Tao's weakness for that "stuff of the goblet," the censor might not have been able to meet with him. Lines 5 and 6 blend this story into the one in which this same Wang Hong, having heard that Tao was without wine on the Double Nine Festival, sent him some via a white-robed messenger.[25]

The isolation of lines 1 through 6 is emphasized by the presence of "empty" words, or grammatical particles, at the beginning of each of lines 2 through 5. These particles suggest a causal relationship between phrases and stress the integrity of the section as a complete narrative. The separate status of this section within the poem subtly suggests a difference with what is to follow (although we do not yet know the basis of the contrast).

Line 7, opening the second part of the poem, introduces the subject of comparison: the poet himself. Unlike Tao Yuanming, who was given wine by kind and admiring officials so that he might join them in the traditional celebration, Li Bo has no such opportunity to relinquish, even momentarily, his position of "outsider." He is condemned to pass the holiday "unfulfilled," unable to partake of the tradition, but also unable to forget its requirements and remain entirely detached.

The second part of the poem has led the commentators to believe that Li Bo addresses the poem to a certain official on the building of a tower south of Xuancheng. This would seem to explain lines 9 and 10, in which he implicitly compares this official to Censor Zhou Jing of the Latter Han Dynasty as well as to his appointed *bie jia*, Chen Fan (see note 16). Read in this light, this allusion would simultaneously praise the *bie jia* of Xuancheng for his lucidity and steadfastness in recognizing and welcoming Li Bo (who had left the capital in disgrace nine years earlier), and praise those talents that liken him to the famous *bie jia* of the Han.

If we are inclined to agree with this interpretation, the second part of this poem may be read, as it is by the contemporary critic Ono Jitsunosuke, as hyperbolic gratitude and praise for the party to which Li Bo was invited, and the first part may be retroactively interpreted as saying that, until he was invited by the official, he *had been* unfulfilled, but then the official acted as his "man in white," and thus fulfilled his desire to be recognized. The odd, dry opening still resonates, however, subtly undermining such flattery. It has already attuned the reader to a poet who is fulfilling his own obligations (the writing of this occasional poem being one such obligation), while remaining aware of his role as outsider—both in the reality of his exile, and in the composition of this poem on the festival of remembrance.

The lofty point of view is sustained in the links from one couplet to the next, all the way to line 20, as a hypothetical, gradual ascent—an imaginary extrapolation of the sub-generic term of "climbing high." Each couplet is gleaned from a different category of the tradition, arranged in graduated increments of height and pleasure, until the second section ends as abruptly as it begins, upon reaching the furthest extreme of height and imagination—the domain of the immortals. Significantly, the assumption of their existence is held as strongly hypothetical—"If the immortals are like them"—undermining ever so slightly the conviction of our poet.

But Li Bo has fulfilled the demands of the festival and of the sub-genre, and so can finally reassume the role he had hinted at but concealed ever since the beginning: his role as creator of a poem and as individual freely considering his literary inheritance. It is in this role that he begins the third part of the poem, line 21, with the rhetorical question directed to all readers: "All those who've climbed high since times of old, / How many are there today?"

Without changing Li Bo's point of view, the third part of the poem bespeaks an immediacy that, as he steps out from behind the constraints of convention, confirms the unease with those constraints that was intimated in the preceding lines. Numerous features combine to reveal a poet who, once having executed his bow to the past, tries to reveal himself more directly: the straightforward vernacular construction of the opening rhetorical question; the personal rationalization in lines 23 and 24; the frankness concerning the superiority of his knowledge to that of the other guests (lines 27 and 28); the absence of adornment when referring to these "guests" (*bin*) as they take their leave (line 31); and the account of his solitary climb up this actual tower—emphasized in the Chinese by the article "this" (*tzu*).

This immediacy does not exclude the poet's awareness of the past, again immanent in the form of allusion. But, unlike the allusions that preceded, these are true textual allusions as opposed to mere namings. Consider, for example: "Chains of mountains look like startled waves, / Their folded layers emerge from a darkened sea." This comparison of mountains to waves, a direct reversal of a simile from the "Rhymeprose on the Sea" ("Hai fu") by Mu Hua (Jin dynasty),[26] is probably a bit more vivid as a result of the transformation, and more immediately appropriate to what he actually sees (although Wang Qi may be going a bit far in his characterization of this reversed line as "strange").[27] It is, in short, more his own precisely because it has been transformed; and perhaps that personalization is the sole function of this allusion. While half of the lines of this final section echo the poetry of previous writers, the poet's presentation of self is as strong as ever, and wine is used as the pretext for this vision that others might find slightly askew (line 28); but the internal, subjective reality to which he lays claim is composed of the bits and pieces of a literary reality that had always been shared.

From a beginning in which Li Bo was alone and sober, to a climax where he is a drunken participant in a communal celebration, he never relinquishes his outsider's stance. Whether those "seated all around" consist of the real celebrants at the party, or the ghostly presence of those others who have "'climbed high' since times of old," they finally scatter, leaving our poet alone in both imagination and reality. No one, then, is present to witness the flying off of a hat (see note 21), and the poem that goes unwritten. Once again, the tradition is negated by reality, and the poet, alone again (still?) on Double Nine, climbs a bit higher and expresses the desire to express his feeling of missing someone. In communicating the desire, he resorts once more to the naming of a tradition: "Chang xiang si"; perhaps the name evokes as much, if not more, than the emotion itself. It is, after all, a feeling that was first stirred by the conventional climb up the tower on this holiday.

In the poet's solitude, the desire to speak goes unfulfilled, just as in the case of the poem that should have been inspired by the hat blown away by the wind; one is only uncertain as to the cause of that silence—is it the lack of an audience, that the poem has already been written (by himself and others), or the knowledge that he himself is destined to join the other rememberers who have "climbed high," only to be lost in oblivion? The poem before us is the one he has written instead, ending as it began: with the poet's doomed effort to forget what he must remember merely in order to write. No matter how lofty and distant his vision, he still begins and ends the poem with the naming of works already executed, and then closes with resigned silence.

This time Li Bo's response to past literature falls short of creating a new avenue of expression. He neither quietly revolts with the assertion of a highly personal, if simple, statement, nor does he embrace convention with the passion of a returned literary exile. The silence at the end of this poem corresponds to that no-man's land stretching between personal and universal expression—a terrain which Li Bo avows himself as being unable to cross, at least for the moment delineated by the poem. But, in that very moment of silence, he adheres to the ideal of immediacy.

Wine plus a view from on high combine easily to blur the lines separating perception, imagination, and memory; the added context of the Double Nine Festival grants wine-drinking the status of shared convention. This festival, then, is rich for a poet with the preoccupations of a Li Bo, as we see in **"On the Ninth"**:

> Today the sky is fine,
> The water green and autumn's mountains gleaming.
> I take the gourd and pour some "Rose-cloud nectar,"
> Pluck a chrysanthemum and float its cold petals thereon.
> The land extends far, pine and stone are ancient,
> The wind carries aloft the clarity of string and reed.
> A peek in the goblet, reflects a joyful face,
> Alone I smile and then drink myself.
> A fallen hat, drunk beneath mountain moon,
> In vain I sing of missing my friend.[28]

>            **"On the Ninth"**

Li Bo's portrayal of immediate emotion, the gesture of plucking a chrysanthemum without immediately being drawn into associations of either collective or personal memory, is slightly undermined by his insertion of the textual allusion of lines 7 and 8. The sheer presence of the allusion, even more than its meaning, suggests that the communication of even the most personal and self-sufficient emotion relies ultimately on reference to the past, if it is to be understood by others. "A peek in the goblet, reflects a joyful face, / Alone I smile and then drink myself," recalls these lines by Tao Yuanming:

> Although, with one goblet, one can but toast alone,
> When the cup is finished, I myself pour from the gourd.[29]

Neither Ono Jitsunosuke nor the editors of *Li Bo ji jiaozhu* saw fit to reproduce the comment in which Wang Qi notes the origin of Li Bo's couplet, although this information adds significantly to the understanding of the poem. Up until this moment, our poet seems to have successfully sustained his subjective and immediate vision; a "naming" title minimizes the conventional demands of the occasional poem, and the plucking of chrysanthemums, even while the action echoes that of Tao Yuanming,[30] remains, above all, an image of sensuality. Aware of the tradition associated with the holiday, Li Bo still seems able to experience it afresh.

But these are clearly the words of Tao Yuanming, a poet well known for his Double Nine imagery—and these are the words which form the basis of the heart of Li Bo's poem. For Tao, the wine both intensifies the solitude, which is felt more acutely during this festival, and gives him consolation; it is meant to be shared, but he tries valiantly to find comfort in the freedom of being able to drink it as he pleases. The force of his denial of this sadness is exposed in the prominently placed word "although".

For Li, denial of sadness is almost synonymous with denial of the weight of the past. Since the struggle against sadness has been the dominant emotion of his poem up to that point, it is particularly fitting that this is the element of Tao's poem that he chooses to recall. Although it is a joyful face he finds reflected in his wine-cup, the reflection is both the declaration and the denial of his solitude; thus, his wittiest moment is precisely the moment when the inescapability of the past (and its requirement of melancholy) overcomes him. In "drinking himself", he plays cleverly on Tao's words, stepping carefully out of direct lineage and underlining his immediate relation with the festival and literary convention. At the same time, he—perhaps with some bitterness—exercises his wit on the need for companionship suggested by the festival itself. The ironic melancholy of solitude during a holiday that in name and custom demands wholeness and unity has not gone unnoticed by generations of poets before and after Li Bo; but Li Bo's loneliness is here intensified, for the literary record of their melancholy has been added as an integral part of the landscape.

Having thus made his bow to the past, Li Bo allows himself to remain under the spell of shared memory until the end of the poem. He drinks down his reflection and is left alone. In the resulting intoxication, he sees himself as replicating the past personage of *yuefu* fame, the "master of the mountains," Shan Gong, familiarly indicated by mentioning his fallen hat (perhaps combined with the "fallen hat" allusion of **"Ascending a Mountain on Double Nine"**).[31] This penultimate line is the only one in the poem that cannot be comfortably reshaped into the grammar of the vernacular, and it seems that the poet's retreat into solitude partially excludes the reader from sharing his vision as well.

Temporal continuity, too, seems to have eluded the reader as he is suddenly, and incidentally, informed that it is night. But even while "drunkenness" frees him from the constraints of grammatical precision, it brings back the forced quality of his denial of sadness and shared memory. Whatever impression of the poet's subjective freedom remains is finally compromised by the reflex recall of Shan Gong, that traditional incarnation of total freedom.

At last, and quite simply, Li Bo concludes his poem with a summation of all Double Nine poetry: "In vain I sing of missing my friend." Like the title, each word in this line is as non-specific (almost generic) as possible. We do not know which friend he has in mind, and we do not know what he is singing; the immediate, personal perspective of "Today" dissolves, leaving us with the featureless silhouette of a Chinese poet adding his voice to the chorus of the past. At the same time, in the final line of this, as well as other poems we have read, the reunification of the personal and universal voice is also the ultimate personal validation of a universally understood emotion.

### WINE: AN ALLUSION TO IMMEDIACY

One would think that enough has been written about Li Bo's relationship to wine to make it difficult to add anything new. Whether obligingly offered as evidence of his "romantic" (*Langman*) spirit,[32] or sardonically applauded as the agent that succeeded in illuminating a poet previously benighted by Taoist superstition,[33] the presence of wine in Li Bo's poetry and in the apocryphal stories surrounding him has most often been treated as biographical fact. And while it would probably be inaccurate to deny that the poet enjoyed drinking, one is equally misled by attempts to gauge his actual dependence on the substance by statistical calculations of the occurrence of related words in his corpus.

Wine-drinking, as a practice as well as a poetic gesture, is closely related to the value of immediacy. At the same time, it is a gesture well-entrenched in the Chinese poetic tradition. Given our poet's particular way of using elements of tradition to establish immediacy, it is not hard to see how the "stuff of the goblet" became an integral part of the Li Bo legend. Indeed, few elements of poetic convention lend themselves so easily as a prop to bolster the role of the outsider.

Wine and wine-drinking, in a way similar to the Double Nine Festival, lead a double life: one within and another beyond the realm of poetry. Li Bo's understanding of this adds immeasurably to the aura of immediacy in the drinking poem. In this dual role, wine traditionally "surrounds" the poet, modifying both his perceptive and expressive faculties. Between the poet and his poem, it acts as creative catalyst; and between the poet and the world, it erodes the barrier between memory (or imagination) and perception. Thus, when poured in libation to a deity or historical personage, it is an agent of remembrance which spans many generations, and when the libation is poured in the context of a poem, memory then naturally extends to the poetic tradition of this gesture. In contrast, when wine is imbibed as an intoxicant, it is an agent of forgetfulness, giving respite from care during hard times and allowing one the brief luxury of living for the moment;[34] within the poetic context, the pose of intoxication permits a moment of freedom from the various forms of convention.

Li Bo, acutely aware of the allusive quality inherent in the gesture of drinking wine, treats this convention in much the same way he treated the allusions cited above. By exposing wine imagery as an imposing tradition in need of renewal, he adheres to his brand of immediacy. As we will see in the poems to be discussed, he underlines his stance of uninvolved outsider by wittily exploiting the potential inherent in the dual nature of wine. Straddling allusion and illusion, his wine-drinking often carries with it the pathos of unfulfilled desire; not only is he liable to slip into forgetful intoxication during a traditional ceremony, but while in the midst of a "carefree" drinking party, he is more than likely to be painfully aware of the long tradition of *carpe diem* poetry. We have seen hints of this in the poem discussed above, but we find a more complex and evocative example in his poem, **"Facing Wine"**:

> I urge you not to refuse a cup,
> For the spring wind has come to laugh at us.
> Peach and plum trees are like old friends,
> Tipping forth their blossoms to open towards me.
> Swirling swallows call from emerald trees,
> Bright moon peers into the golden wine-cup.
> The rose-cheeked lad of yesterday,
> Today the white hairs grow apace.
> Brambles grew beneath Shi Hu's halls,
> Deer wandered on Gu Su Pavilion.
> The dwellings of emperors since times of old,
> Their walls and gates shut in yellow dust.
> If you do not drink the wine,
> Then where are the men of yesteryear?[35]

**"Facing Wine"**

From line 1 through line 12, there is little that may be called original in this standard *carpe diem* poem. As the poet moves from the seductiveness of spring (lines 3-6) to the treachery of its inevitable passage (lines 7 and 8), we find that the familiar historical allusions of lines 9 and 10, illustrating the ephemerality of man's works, fit naturally into the poem and are strictly within the bounds of read-

erly expectations. In his skillful adherence to a well-worn tradition, Li Bo thus far is uncharacteristically effacing his presence as creator, renouncing his usual claim to immediacy—even in the announced subjectivity of his drunkenness.

But then, in the posing of one final question: "If you do not drink the wine, / Then where are the men of yesteryear?" Li Bo once again steps out of the tradition and looks in, pointing up the duality in the nature of wine, and giving the lie to all that preceded. Clearly, this direct appeal to the reader recalls the opening couplet. In the first line, he had urged his companion (and reader) to drink down his wine; after all, it is the only way to forget the cruel passage of time. (But, as we noted earlier, in using wine to forget, he is implicitly remembering the entire literary tradition of doing just that.) It is only at the close of the poem, when he again urges his companion (and reader) to drink—but this time in the acknowledgment that doing so is a kind of libation to past greatness—that he succeeds in "forgetting" the demands of tradition and imprinting the poem with his stamp of immediacy. The reader thereby understands that Li Bo, even while writing "drunk," still can cast his outsider's glance upon wine itself, and reveal it as a poetic convention with its own allusive quality.

In thus writing *about* wine as a way of sustaining the past, and in doing so in the startling terms of deliberate nonsequitur ("If you don't drink the wine, / Then where are the men of yesteryear?"), Li Bo reveals both the implied obligation and its intrinsic absurdity. One drinks and, guided in part by tradition, uses the desire to forget as a pretext, but, actually, one is obliged to drink and, in the very action, to acknowledge the tradition. Just as one climbs the tower and, in so doing, remembers the rememberers, one drinks wine with the same result (and, implicitly, for the same purpose).

Interestingly, Li Bo's brand of immediacy, with its explicit revelation of implicit convention, is far from reflecting a cynical vision. Quite to the contrary, while reminding the reader of his role as the creator of this poem, insisting on his role as an outsider looking in on the tradition, he both reclaims his own immediacy as poet and reawakens the original, authentic emotion that lay at the base of the tradition.

The convention of wine-drinking carries yet another dimension that lends itself to the establishment of the poet's immediacy: it functions as a traditional (albeit not exclusively literary) allusion to a particularly private state of mind. The playfulness we noted earlier in Li Bo's use of convention is inherent in the assumption of an intoxicated state of mind. Similar to textual allusion, wine thereby provides a common path, based on shared experience or knowledge, whereby the reader may accede to the poet's internal state. At the same time, it conveys that this inner state may be so subjective as to preclude any ground for a shared vision. In the ultimate literary paradox, wine-drinking is subjectivity communicated.

As we will see in this next and final example, Li Bo's use of wine catalyzes certain processes of immediacy that we have already witnessed: the dismantling of the boundaries between allusion and illusion, between what is remembered and what is seen, and between what is imagined and what is perceived. And, in a gesture that is as much a challenge as it is an invitation, he uses it to enjoin the reader to share in this vision.

> The spring grasses seem to have an intention,
> Growing into a weave in the shade of the jade pavil-
> ion.
> The east wind blows sadness here,
> And so, white hairs encroach.
> I pour alone, but urge my lonely shadow to join me,
> And idly sing as I face the fragrant woods.
> But, you, tall pines, what do you understand,
> For whom do you whistle and hum?
> My hand dances with the moon on the rock,
> Across my knees rests a zither among flowers.
> That which lies beyond this wine-goblet,
> Placid and deep, is not my heart.[36]

**"Drinking Alone"**

As is often the case, the title elucidates every line in the poem: Li Bo is alone—and drinking. He alludes to his own subjectivity, even while asking the reader to share in it. When the poem opens, the presence of wine is as yet unmentioned. It is there, however, intensifying his solitude in relation to human society, on the one hand, and creating a companion presence in the personification of the natural world, on the other. Nature personified, at first rather tentatively in the spring grasses, then desolately in the shadow, and finally—impatiently and even desperately—in the pines, recalls the wished-for companion that Li Bo once found reflected in his wine-cup: the presence imagined by the poet in an effort to deny—and therefore to declare—his isolation. With the addition of the *carpe diem* theme (made explicit only in line 4), the would-be companion is quickly revealed to be a traitorous one, as the obstinate indifference of nature becomes a personal affront. As the apparent cause and, more to the point, as a conventionally understood sign of the skewed rapport between the poet and his surroundings, wine simultaneously increases the poet's solitude within the context of the poem and enhances the subjectivity of his vision as creator of the poem (thus enhancing as well the impression of immediacy).

The poet's exasperation reaches a peak in line 8, when his pleading question to the tall pines is left unanswered. The implicit effect of the wine acts as an allusion to the poet's immediacy and, in this role, allows the reader to go along with the poet in this tirade. At the same time, though, comprehension of the poet's intoxication also prevents the reader from anticipating the conclusion. Then, for a hopeful moment, Li Bo engages peacefully with nature and time, dissolving both his solitude and his mortality: "My hand dances with the moon on the rock," he seems to be saying. And, thanks to the ambiguous syntax of this phrase, the reader also hears the poet say, "My hand dances in the moon (-light) on the rock," as well as, "My hand *causes* the moon (-light) on the rock to dance." This, the only ambiguous line in the poem, demands particular attention; for an intoxicated moment, the boundaries are blurred in the mingling of hand and moon.

Only for a moment, however. In the very next line, the poet shifts his vision and the mist clears. Solidly lying across his lap is a zither—and the possibility of responding to the impersonal "whistle and hum" of the pines, of mingling his human voice with that of the woods, as his fleshly hand mingled with the moonlight. But, instead of leading us back to the blissfully indeterminate world of line 9, the poet (smitten, perhaps, by the sight of new flowers around the zither) plunges abruptly into a declaration which is nothing if it is not a clarification; "That which lies beyond this wine-goblet, / Placid and deep, is not my heart." The run-over syntax of this final couplet, echoing that of the opening, is largely responsible for conveying a feeling of spontaneous and unchecked vehemence. The forceful denial conveyed in the modal word, *fei* ("is not") adds the finishing touch. The poet leaves little doubt that he means what he says, that this statement is an unmediated declaration from the heart. At the same time, however, he excludes the reader from his subjective response to the world; the strangeness of the statement prevents him, at first, from fully understanding what he means. This combined depiction of unbridled emotion and pure subjectivity incarnates the immediacy so closely associated with Li Bo's poetry.

Examination of the couplet in question reveals exactly wherein lies its strangeness. Looking carefully at the binomial descriptive, *you you,* the reader realizes that its object is unclear; does *you you* refer to "that which lies beyond this wine-goblet," or just simply the "wine-goblet" (and, thus, the poet's heart) itself? Hoping to solve this part of the puzzle, the reader may recall this line from "*Zi Jin,*" one of the Airs of Zheng in the *Shijing*: "Green, green, the front of your robe; *you you* my heart".[37] Read as an allusion to the *Shijing* poem, line 12 might be read as a direct contradiction of the original: "*you you* is *not* my heart." In that case, the poet's heart is emphatically different from whatever we are to understand as *you you*. Yet, when divided differently, the couplet may also be understood as a reaffirmation of the line in the *Shijing*: "Everything that is not within the bounds of this wine cup—and *you you*—is not my heart."

The exact definition of *you you* is, like all binomial descriptives in the *Shijing*, problematic and only reinforces the ambiguity. Returning to the line from the *Shijing* cited above, the obvious gloss for this term is the one given as the first definition in the *Ciyuan*: "profound longing". This is reinforced by its appearance in another poem, **"*Zhong feng*"**:

> The great wind raises the dust,
> Will he kindly come calling?
> He doesn't come, he doesn't call,
> *You you* is my longing![38]

This seemingly straightforward allusion again supports the reading that *you you* refers most appropriately to the poet's heart. However, there are at least two other occurrences of this binomial descriptive within the *Shijing*, which are glossed alternately as "distant and limitless" ("*You you* the azure sky, / Where does it end?"),[39] and "calm and tranquil" ("*You you* the banners fly").[40] More effectively than any grammatical analysis, these glosses, especially the former one, link the expression more closely to the great expanse of all that is *not* the poet's heart.

Commentators have remained silent on this somewhat humorous puzzle Li Bo has left us. It seems quite obvious, however, especially in light of this discussion, that Li Bo is standing back and smiling at the commonly held understanding that binomial descriptives in the *Shijing* convey the essence of whatever object is being described. The fact that we cannot determine what that object is becomes all the funnier when we take into account how emphatic this vague declaration is.

But this is not the essence of the line, although it is another instance of the use of allusion to underline the individuality of the creative poet. The immediacy of the line goes beyond this show of wit: it is encoded as an allusion. Insofar as wine is traditionally both the catalyst and the sign of pure immediacy, the act of equating the contents of the cup with one's heart is universally comprehensible. Thus, the force of the closing line does not primarily lie in the assertion that wine is a refuge; rather it lies in the suggestion that wine is universally recognized as having a vast range of properties going far beyond—and even betraying—its apparent "placidity." Li Bo refuses to pinpoint to which of these properties he is alluding; the reader's resulting confusion, however, is the poet's orchestrated tribute to the ultimate subjectivity of wine. For Li Bo, wine is a gesture with infinite links to the poetic past, incarnating the very paradox upon which his "immediate" poetry is built: the use of convention to establish individuality, and the application of artifice to clear new ground for immediacy.

*Notes*

1. *Maoshi zhengyi*, 6 vols. (Hong Kong: Zhonghua shuju, 1964), 1:37-38.

2. Shen Yue, credited as the best-known spokesman for tonal regulation, justifies such ornamentation as being a reflection of the natural world, saying that colors and tones " . . . are in accord with the things of this world." See Shen Yue, "Songshu Xie Lingyun zhuan lun", as cited in Guo Shaoyu, ed., *Zhongguo lidai wenxue lunzhu jingxuan*, 3 vols. (Taipei: Huazheng shuju, 1980), 1:171-72.

3. One example may be found in Chen Zi'ang's well-known "Yu Dongfang zuoshi Li Xiuzhu pian bing xu". See Sheng Zuyu, comp., *Quan Tang shi* (Taipei: Hongye shuju, 1977), 83.895-96.

4. Examples of such critical stances regarding the use of allusion are common in the writings of such

critics as Zhong Rong, Shen Yue, and even (although less categorically) Liu Xie. The same attitude was exemplified in the Tang dynasty by Wang Changling and Jiao Ran. Zhong Rong, for example, is quite explicit in his introduction to the *Shi pin* when he writes: "When striving to sing out one's emotive nature, what good are allusions?" Zhong follows this by a list of preferred verses that reflect the expression of immediate perception alone and concludes the section saying: "How could (such verses as these) have been drawn from the classics or the *Historical Records?* Looking at the finest writings from ancient times to the present, most have not borrowed (from earlier works), and all are born of direct investigation." In He Wenhuan, *Lidai shihua*, 2 vols., (Beijing: Zhonghua shuju, 1981), pp. 4-5.

5. Ju Tuiyuan and Zhu Jincheng, eds., *Li Bo ji jiaozhu* 2 vols. (Shanghai: Shanghai guji chubanshe, 1980) [hereafter *LBJJZ*], p. 868.

6. The poem concludes, "But what in this thing is worth the giving? I am moved only by time's passage since we parted". In Xiao Tong ed., *Wenxuan* (Beijing: Zhonghua shuju, 1977), 29.633.

7. *LBJJZ*, p. 591.

8. Qing commentator Wang Qi cites from the *Yiwen leiju*: "Sheng Hong's Notes from Jingzhou' says: 'In Huizhe of Xinyang County there is a hot spring. During the winter months, before you have come within several miles of it, in the distance you can see white steam wafting up like smoke, reflecting colors above and below, in a shape like filigree window frames. There is even the form of a pair of cartwheels, so people recount that in ancient times there was a fair (jade-like) maiden who rode a carriage into this spring. Nowadays people see a young girl, glowing and lovely in appearance, whose coming and goings are sudden and brief.'" Wang Qi also includes a note from the "Yi tong zhi" mentioning that the local people say that Jade Maiden Spring is where the "Jade Maiden" would go to smelt cinnabar to attain immortality. See Wang Qi, ed., *Li Taibai quanji* (Beijing: Zhonghua shuju, 1957) [hereafter *LTBQJ*], 22.1007.

9. *LBJJZ*, p. 1263.

10. Translation adapted from that of J. R. Hightower in Cyril Birch, ed., *Anthology of Chinese Literature*, 2 vols. (New York: Grove Press, Inc., 1965) 1:138-40.

11. Cited by Wang Qi in *LTBQJ* 22.1008.

12. See, for ex., the *Huainan zi* (SPPY edition), pian 8 "Ben jing," p. 8a: "[Yin and Yang] continue the harmony of heaven and earth, give form to the entities of the myriad variations" "Crimson flame" is also mentioned in the context of creation in *Han wudi neizhuan* (*Zhengtong daozang* edition, 60 vols., Taipei: Yiwen yinshuguan yinhang, 1977) 8:6086.

13. As translated by David Knechtges in his translation and annotation of Xiao Tong, *Wenxuan or Selections*

*of Refined Literature,* 2 vols. (Princeton: Princeton University Press, 1987), 2:55.

14. See A. R. Davis, "The Double Ninth Festival in Chinese Poetry: A Study of Variations Upon a Theme," in Chow Tse-tsung, ed., *Wen Lin* (Madison: University of Wisconsin Press, 1968) pp. 45-64, for origins of the festival and an interesting discussion on how the theme was transmitted and transformed from Tao Yuanming through Li Bo and on down. However, Davis neglects to mention one origin of the tradition, cited in the *Yiwen leiju,* which adds some background to the custom of large gatherings on that holiday: "'The Record of Looking Upon the Sea' says: 'Forty paces north of the prefecture, there is a lakeside mountain, very flat and even. There is room for several hundreds of people to sit on it. The common people valued it highly. Every "Ninth," on the morning of [the festival of] chrysanthemum wine, the attendants at the banquet on this mountain would number as many as three or four hundred people.'" See Ouyang Xun et al., comp., *Yiwen leiju,* 4 vols. (Hong Kong: Zhonghua shuju, 1973) 4:81.

15. One Jitsunosuke, *Ritaihaku shika zenkai,* (Waseda University Press, 1981) follows Wang Qi's lead in suggesting that the title is probably incomplete, that this is probably an occasional poem commemorating the construction of a viewing terrace south of Xuancheng by a *bie jia,* or "administrative aide." This may well be the case, but Ono seems to feel that understanding this point illuminates the poem completely. However, as in many of Li Bo's poems (such as "Chang xiang si" and "Du Lu Pian"), the apparent discontinuity characterizing this poem arises from an unexpected reshaping of conventional links. See my "Transformation and Imitation: The Poetry of Li Bo" (Ph.D. diss., Princeton University, 1988), Chapter 2.

16. This is a reference to Zhou Jing, a censor of Yuzhou in the Latter Han Dynasty who stood firm in his evaluation of one Chen Fan, naming him to the position of "administrative aide" (*bie jia*). When Chen did not take up his position, Zhou refused to change his nomination and inscribed Chen's name on the *bie jia*'s carriage seat anyway. When Chen Fan heard of this, he hurried to accept his appointment. Li Bo uses this allusion to flatter the local *bie jia* of Xuanzhou, where he probably composed this poem. Recorded in the *Taiping yulan ji,* as cited in *LTBQJ,* p. 962, and *LBJJZ,* p. 1205.

17. This is probably a personal allusion to a previously arranged meeting for the holiday.

18. Qin Gao is a figure from the *Lie xian zhuan* who lived at the end of the Zhou dynasty. Because of his extraordinary talent in playing the zither, he became resident musician in the court of Prince Kang of the Song. One day he told his disciples that he was going to go into the Zhu River to fetch the dragon's

egg, and he fixed the day of his return. When on the appointed day they waited for him at the river's edge, Qin Gao finally emerged on the back of a carp. He remained on shore for one month, and then plunged back into the water.

19. Bing Yi is identified in the *Shanhai jing* as an immortal who has a human face, rides a pair of dragons, and is the only creature that can inhabit the depths of the remotest springs (cited in *LTBQJ,* p. 962). The white tortoise is an unrelated figure, and Wang Qi proposes that it might be a variant of from the "He bo" chapter of the *Chu ci.*

20. The Cang Isle is an island where immortals dwell.

21. Citing "The Biography of Meng Jia" in the *Jin shu,* Wang Qi states: "Meng Jia was Huan Wen's aide-de-camp. He was gentle and upright, and Wen valued him highly. On the Double Ninth, Wen went for an outing on Longshan Mountain and gathered all of his cohorts. At that time, all of the attendants were wearing their military uniforms. A wind blew off Jia's hat, but Jia did not realize it. Wen indicated to all of the guests not to say anything, so that he might observe his reaction. Jia went to the privy and was gone for a long time. Wen commanded that the hat be returned to him, and ordered Sun Sheng to compose a piece of writing teasing Jia and put it where Jia had been sitting. When Jia returned, he saw it and [wrote a piece] in response. His composition was very beautiful, and all around sighed [in admiration]" (*LTBQJ,* p. 963).

22. *LBJJZ,* p. 1204.

23. It is not absolutely necessary to read "Returning Home" as an abbreviation of the title of Tao Yuanming's well-known work, "Gui qu lai ci" (*Wenxuan,* 45.636), and many punctuated editions are printed without indicating that one should. However, few readers would miss the association, even while the two lines still read smoothly as a grammatical sentence.

24. For the story of Tao and the Double Nine Festival, see "Xu Jin yang qiu" in the *Yiwen leiju* (cited in *LTBQJ,* p. 961).

25. For the story of Tao, Wang Hong and the composition of the "Gui qu lai ci," see the *Jin shu* (cited in *LTBQJ,* p. 961).

26. The original line is: "The waves are like chains of mountains". Cited by Wang Qi in *LTBQJ,* p. 962. "Rhymeprose of the Sea" in its entirety may be found in the *Wenxuan,* 12. 179-83.

27. *LTBQJ,* p. 962.

28. *LBJJZ,* pp. 1206-7.

29. As cited in *LTBQJ,* p. 963, from Tao's poem, "Drinking Wine, #5."

30. "Pluck chrysanthemums at the eastern hedge, / And behold, in the distance, the southern mountains".

See Tao's "Drinking Wine, #4" in Shen Deqian, comp. and annot., *Gushi yuan* (Beijing: Zhonghua shuju, 1963), 9.201.

31. "Shan Gong" refers to Shan Tao of the Jin dynasty, one of the "Seven Sages of the Bamboo Grove," and perhaps best known for getting drunk beside Gaoyang Lake. He appears in Li Bo's *yuefu* poems, "Xiangyang Tune #4," as well "#2": "Whenever Shan Gong gets drunk / Tipsy and reeling, he goes down to Gaoyang / On his head a cap of white / Replaced upside down, and he remounts his horse". See *LBJJZ*, 1:374-6. From the *Shishuo xinyu,* which records the popular song then circulating about him. Line 4 above is a direct citation. See Liu Yiqing, *Shishuo xinyu,* 2 vols. (Shanghai: Shanghai guji chubanshe, 1982), 1:385-86.

32. Several generations of critics have associated wine with Li Bo's "romantic" spirit, a position which is best summed up by Wang Yunxi in "Preface," Part 3, in *LBJJZ*, pp. 13-20.

33. Guo Moruo, "Li Bo de Daojiao mixin ji qi jiaoxing", in *Li Bo yu Du Fu* (Beijing: Renmin wenxue chubanshe, 1972), pp. 134-155.

34. In "Drinking Wine, #5," Tao Yuanming uses the expression, "the stuff that makes one forget sorrows" (*wangyou wu*).

35. *LBJJZ,* p. 1352.

36. Ibid., p. 1340.

37. *MSZY,* p. 434.

38. Ibid., p. 191.

39. Ibid., p. 547. From the Airs of Tang, *"Bao yu"*

40. Ibid., p. 889. From the Lesser Elegentiae, *"Ju gong."*

---

# FURTHER READING

## Criticism

Barricelli, Jean-Pierre. "Nature Images in Leopardi and Li Po." *Tamkang Review* XVIII, Nos. 1-4 (Autumn 1987-Summer 1988): 1-10.

Compares Li Po's sensitivity for the natural world with that of the Italian poet Giacomo Leopardi.

Huang, Kuo-pin. "Li Po and Tu Fu: A Comparative Study." In *A Brotherhood in Song: Chinese Poetry and Poetics,* edited by Stephen C. Soong. Hong Kong: Chinese University Press, 1985, 386 p.

Points out that many critics, in comparing Li Po and Tu Fu's works, overlook the fact that Tu Fu was influenced by his older contemporary.

Kroll, Paul W. "Li Po's Inscription for the Great Bell of the Hua-ch'eng Monastery." *T'ang Studies* 13 (1995): 33-50.

Analysis of the inscription and preface written by Li Po on the bell of the Buddhist Hua-ch'eng Monastery.

———. "Li Po's *Rhapsody on the Great P'eng Bird.*" *Journal of Chinese Religions* 11 (Fall 1983): 1-17.

Annotated translation and discussion of Li Po's rhapsody on the gigantic bird of Chinese mythology.

Mair, Victor H. "Li Po's Letters in Pursuit of Political Patronage." *Harvard Journal of Asiatic Studies* 44, No. 1 (June 1984): 123-53.

Examines letters that Li Po wrote in search of political patronage and compares them with similar letters by other well-known T'ang poets to understand Li Po's "peculiarly enchanting and, on the whole, unsuccessful approach to officialdom."

Waley, Arthur. *The Poetry and Career of Li Po.* London: George Allen and Unwin, 1950, 123 p.

Study of the social and moral conditions under which Li Po worked. Waley observes that Li Po's work shows him to have been "boastful, callous, dissipated, irresponsible, and untruthful" and well as a drunkard who had little mystical understanding of Taoism and Buddhism.

# Paradise Lost

## John Milton

The following entry presents criticism of Milton's epic poem *Paradise Lost*. For discussion of Milton's complete poetic works, see *PC*, Volume 19.

## INTRODUCTION

Milton's great blank-verse epic poem, which retells the Biblical story of Adam and Eve and their fall from paradise, has been hailed since its initial publication as one of the towering achievements of English literature. The poet John Dryden, writing in 1677, called *Paradise Lost* "one of the greatest, most noble, and most sublime poems, which either this Age or Nation has producd," and others from William Blake to W. H. Auden have used it as a source of inspiration for their own writing. The work has also provoked more negative criticism than any other acknowledged classic: Samuel Johnson called the language of the poem "harsh and barbarous," Sir Walter Raleigh declared the work consisted of "dead ideas," and T. S. Eliot claimed Milton's style in the epic would have a harmful influence on English poetry. Despite the controversy sparked by the poem, however, it continues to be one of the most widely read and discussed works of English literature, with a reputation for greatness surpassed only by Shakespeare's plays. Critics have found the narrative poem rich with meaning on its many levels: political allusions, cosmology, use of language, Biblical content, characterization, use of the traditional epic form, moral and spiritual meanings, and philosophical implications. And all commentators on the poem, including its detractors, have marvelled at the range of subjects it treats, which include the universe, human physiology and psychology, the forces of nature, God and other celestial beings, and human reason and freedom.

## PLOT AND MAJOR CHARACTERS

The poem begins by declaring its subject—"man's first disobedience" and the consequences that ensued from that act—and invokes a "Heav'nly Muse" to aid the poet that he may assert Eternal Providence and "justify the ways of God to men." The first action takes place in hell, where Satan and his followers have recently been defeated in their war against God. They decide to take a different course of revenge by entering a new world that is to be created. Satan alone undertakes the journey to find this place. He travels across chaos, which is the great gulf between hell and heaven, until he sees the new universe. God sees Satan flying towards this world and foretells the

temptation and Fall, clearing his own justice and wisdom from imputation by explaining that He has created man free and able enough to have withstood his tempter. Meanwhile, Satan enters the outer reaches of the new creation. He flies to the sun, where he disguises himself as a cherub and tricks the angel Uriel into showing him to man's home. He finds Adam and Eve in their happy state and becomes jealous of them. He overhears them speak of God's commandment that they should not eat the forbidden fruit of the Tree of Knowledge, and so plots to seduce them to transgress. Uriel warns Gabriel and his angels, who are guarding the gate of Paradise, that some evil spirit had escaped hell and entered here in the shape of a good angel. Gabriel appoints two strong angels to look over Adam and Eve, lest the evil spirit should do some harm to them as they sleep. They find Satan at the ear of Eve, tempting her in a dream. The next morning Eve tells Adam of her troubling dream. God sends Raphael to warn Adam and Eve about Satan, and to render them inexcusable by telling them of their free will and the enemy at hand. On Adam's request, Raphael recounts to them the story of how Satan came to be as he is; how this favored angel waged war against God in heaven, how the Son, Messiah, cast him into hell, and how Satan persuaded his legions to follow him. He describes the war in heaven and the triumphant return of the Son after battle. Raphael goes on to explain how the world was created so mankind could replace the fallen angels. Satan returns to earth, and enters as a sleeping serpent. The serpent finds Eve alone and speaks to her in flattering tones. He explains that he learned speech and reason, neither of which he knew before, by tasting of a certain tree in the garden. Eve asks him to bring her to that tree, and finds it to be the forbidden Tree of Knowledge. The Serpent uses his wiles and arguments to induce her to eat. Eve is pleased with the taste, and deliberates a while whether to take it to Adam or not. She brings him the fruit and tells him what persuaded her to eat it. Adam is at first amazed, but he resigns himself because of his love for her and eats also, thereby joining her in her fate. As a result, their innocence is lost, they become aware of their nakedness, and they begin to accuse each other. The guardian angels return to heaven, saddened by man's failure, and the Son of God descends to earth to judge the sinners, and sentences them accordingly. God instructs his angels what alterations must take place on earth and in heaven because of what has transpired. Adam laments his fate as he begins to understand his fallen state. He rejects Eve's consolation, but she persists and he forgives her. She proposes they commit suicide, but Adam reminds her of God's promise that her offspring will wreak vengeance on the serpent. God sends Michael and his cherubim to dispossess the pair from Paradise, but first reveals to Adam the future events until the Great Flood that will result from his sin. Michael says also that the Seed of woman shall be the Savior who it was promised shall redeem mankind. Adam takes comfort in these later revelations. He rejoins Eve, who in her gentle sleep has regained quietness of mind and a sense of submission. Adam and Eve are sent away from Paradise, and a flaming sword is placed to guard the gates behind them.

## MAJOR THEMES

*Paradise Lost* reflects, on its most transparent level, the poet's major concern to justify God's way to men, to assert God's mystery, and give dramatic voice to the events we read about in Genesis. But the poem goes much deeper, and it has been read in a number of ways by critics: as a political allegory that deals with the issues of freedom that Milton had concerned himself with during the Revolution; as an unorthodox depiction of the Christian God and his treatment of humankind; as a thesis on predestination; and as a study of the epic hero in a Christian context. Critics interested in the political dimension of the work have read the poem in many different ways. Some see it as Milton's commentary on the events during and after the English Revolution: Milton, the advocate of a righteous cause who saw that cause destroyed and corrupted by evil forces, mourns the loss and looks for redemption not in this world but the next. Other readers have viewed Satan, for example, as "an unsuccessful Cromwell," and have com-

pared Satan's failed rebellion to that of Oliver Cromwell. There are of course familiar Biblical themes in the poem, including downfall and regeneration, and the triumph of good over evil. Scholars have pointed out also that the theme of loss pervades the poem, and this is underscored by images of darkness; the hope of regeneration is emphasized by references to light. Some others of the myriad thematic concerns include the interaction of male and female aspects (the sun's rays against the earth are a model for the union of Adam and Eve); the interrelation of love and war (the Son leads the angels into battle and also shows the greatest love in his self-sacrifice); the boundlessness of God's power and capacity (depicted in the recurring references to and sense of vastness in the poem); pride (embodied in Satan); loss of innocence; the power of poetry (depicted in Eve); and the beauty of creation (often seen in the nature imagery).

## CRITICAL RECEPTION

No poem in the English language has earned such extremes of praise and censure as *Paradise Lost*. It was very well received upon publication of the first edition in 1667. By the end of the seventeenth century, the poem was thought of in England and Europe as one of the great epics and a major work of literature and was generally admired for its boldness and originality as well as its exalted theme and rousing language. Appreciation of the poem, particularly of its epic features, continued into the eighteenth century. Many critics noted also the defects in the work, including Milton's personal intrusions into the poem, the badly wrought allegorical characters, and the excessive display of learning. Samuel Johnson's in 1781, for example, asserted that the poem "lacked human interest" and that we read the poem for "duty rather than pleasure," but acknowledged the poem's loftiness and extraordinary imaginativeness. Blake admired Satan's energy and spirit of rebellion, remarking that Milton "was a true Poet and of the Devil's Party without knowing it," spawning a great deal of interest in the character of Satan. Some critics have suggested that Satan is the true hero of the epic: he is the one with the most memorable lines, whose character is most fully developed and interesting, and with whom we almost cannot avoid having sympathy. Many readers have admired the spirit energy of rebellion that pervades the character. Others, however, have taken pains to point out that for Milton to make Satan the hero of the epic would be to contradict his own theology, and that while he finds Satan interesting, he does not admire him. As a Biblical epic, it is pointed out, *Paradise Lost* is an interpretation of Scripture, and God is the central figure.

The Romantic critics of the nineteenth century turned to considerations about the relationship between Milton's life and mind and his art. They also admired Milton as a revolutionary, with some like Percy Shelley extending Blake's notion of Satan as a glorious rebel. Later nineteenth-century critics generally held the poem in high regard, remarking especially on what many considered to be Milton's flawless rhythm and diction.

Critical opinion of the poem in the twentieth century was extensive, with literally hundreds of books being produced about the poem's every nuance. Early twentieth-century commentators noted Milton's humanism and his intellectual heritage that informed the work; others admired his knowledge of physical nature reflected in the poem. In the 1930s, the poem was criticized by a number of prominent thinkers, including T. S. Eliot, Ezra Pound, and the critic F. R. Leavis, who argued that Milton's style was rigid and lacking in sensuousness. Others defended Milton, with some predicting that the tide of criticism against Milton's style would disappear with the disappearance of the "modernist" poetic movement that spawned it. This seems largely to have been the case, and critical appreciation of Milton in the latter half of the twentieth century tended to acknowledge the epic's inherent greatness while pointing out its weaknesses. In the late twentieth century scholarship on the poem moved in innumerable directions, with, for example, feminist scholars examining Milton's treatment of women, Freudian critics trying to understand it in terms of the Oedipal nature of Milton's art, and deconstructionists applying to it the theories of Jacques Derrida. That critics of every generation have found and continue to find in the poem so many subjects so worthy of debate is a testament to its mystery and complexity and a clear indication of its profound importance to world literature.

---

# PRINCIPAL WORKS

## Poetry

*A Maske* [*Comus*] 1637
*Lycidas* 1638
*Epitaphium Damonis* [*Damon*] 1640
*Poems of Mr. John Milton, Both English and Latin, Compos'd at Several Times* 1645
*Paradise Lost: A Poem Written in Ten Books* [also published as *Paradise Lost: A Poem in Twelve Books*] 1667
*Paradise Regain'd: A Poem in IV Books. To Which Is Added Samson Agonistes* 1671
*The Sonnets of John Milton* 1883

## Other Major Works

*The Reason of Church-Governement Urg'd against Prelaty* (essay) 1642
*The Doctrine and Discipline of Divorce: Restor'd to the Good of Both Sexes, From the Bondage of Canon Law* (essay) 1643
*Areopagitica: A Speech of Mr. John Milton for the Liberty of Unlicenc'd Printing, To the Parlament of England* (essay) 1644
*The Judgment of Martin Bucer, Concerning Divorce Written to Edward the Sixt, in His Second Book of the Kingdom of Christ, and Now English, Wherin a Late Book*

*Restoring the Doctrine and Discipline of Divorce Is Heer Confirm'd and Justify'd By the Authoritie of Martin Bucer* (essay) 1644
*Tetrachordon: Expositions upon the Foure Chief Places in Scripture, Which Treat of Mariage, or Nullities in Mariage* (essay) 1645
*The Tenure of Kings and Magistrates, Proving That It is Lawfull, and Hath Been Held So Through All Ages, for Any Who Have the Power, to Call to Account a Tyrant, or Wicked King* (essay) 1649
*Joannis Miltoni angli Pro populo anglicano defensio, contra Claudii Anonymi* [*A Defence of the People of England*] (essay) 1651
*Joannis Miltoni angli pro se defensio contra Alexandrum Morum ecclesiasten, libelli famosi, cui titulus, regii sanguinis clamor ad coelum adversus parricidas anglicanos, authoren recte dictum* [*Second Defence of the People of England*] (essay) 1654
*The Readie & Easie Way to Establish a Free Commonwealth* (essay) 1660
*Of True Religion, Haeresie, Schism, Toleration, and What Best Means May Be Us'd against the Growth of Popery* (essay) 1673
*The Works of John Milton*. 18 vols. (essays, history, and poetry) 1931-38

---

# CRITICISM

### Andrew Marvell (poem date 1674)

SOURCE: "On *Paradise Lost*," in *The Critical Response to John Milton's Paradise Lost*, edited by Timothy C. Miller, Greenwood Press, 1997, pp. 28-29.

[*In the following dedicatory poem, which first appeared in the second edition of* Paradise Lost, *the poet Andrew Marvell praises his contemporary's bold and original effort that has "not miss'd one thought that could be fit" and whose greatness is in no way diminished for being in blank and not rhyming verse.*]

> When I beheld the Poet blind, yet bold,
> In slender Book his vast Design unfold,
> *Messiah* Crown'd, God's Reconcil'd Decree,
> Rebelling Angels, the Forbidden Tree,
> Heav'n, Hell, Earth, Chaos, All; the Argument
> Held me a while misdoubting his Intent,
> That he would ruine (for I saw him strong)
> The sacred Truths to Fable and old Song
> (So *Sampson* groap'd the Temples Posts in spight)
> The World o'rewhelming to revenge his sight.
>     Yet as I read, soon growing less severe,
> I lik'd his Project, the success did fear;
> Through that wide Field he his way should find
> O'er which lame Faith leads Understanding blind;
> Lest he perplex'd the things he would explain,
> And what was easy he should render vain.
>     Or if a Work so infinite he spann'd,
> Jealous I was that some less skilful hand

(Such as disquiet always what is well,
And by ill imitating would excell)
Might hence presume the whole Creations day
To change in Scenes, and show it in a Play.
     Pardon me, Might Poet, nor despise
My causeless, yet not impious, surmise.
But I am now convinc'd, and none will dare
Within thy Labours to pretend a share.
Thou hast not miss'd one thought that could be fit,
And all that was improper dost omit:
So that no room is here for Writers left,
But to detect their Ignorance or Theft.
     That Majesty which through thy Work doth
Reign
Draws the Devout, deterring the Profane.
And things divine thou treatst of in such state
As them preserves, and thee, inviolate.
At once delight and horrour on us seise,
Thou singst with so much gravity and ease;
And above humane flight dost soar aloft
With Plume so strong, so equal, and so soft.
The Bird nam'd from that Paradise you sing
So never flaggs, but always keeps on Wing.
     Where couldst thou words of such a compass
find?
Whence furnish such a vast expence of mind?
Just Heav'n thee like *Tiresias* to requite
Rewards with Prophesie thy loss of sight.
     Well mightst thou scorn thy Readers to allure
With tinkling Rhime, of thy own sense secure;
While the *Town-Bayes* writes all the while and spells,
And like a Pack-horse tires without his Bells:
Their Fancies like our Bushy-points appear,
The Poets tag them, we for fashion wear.
I too transported by the Mode offend,
And while I meant to Praise thee must Commend.
Thy Verse created like thy Theme sublime,
In Number, Weight, and Measure, needs not Rhime.

## Samuel Johnson (essay date 1781)

SOURCE: "From *The Lives of the English Poets,*" in *The Critical Response to John Milton's Paradise Lost,* edited by Timothy C. Miller, Greenwood Press, 1997, pp. 103-13.

[*In the following excerpt, which originally appeared in his nine-volume work on the lives of the English Poets, Johnson examines the epic's defects—claiming that we do not readily identify with the human protagonists and noting that "none wished it longer than it is"—as well as its greatness, saying that "in reading* Paradise Lost *we read of universal knowledge."*]

I am now to examine **Paradise Lost,** a poem, which, considered with respect to design, may claim the first place, and with respect to performance the second, among the productions of the human mind.

By the general consent of criticks, the first praise of genius is due to the writer of an epick poem, as it requires an assemblage of all the powers which are singly sufficient for other compositions. Poetry is the art of uniting pleasure with truth, by calling imagination to the help of reason. Epick poetry undertakes to teach the most important truths by the most pleasing precepts, and therefore, relates some great event in the most affecting manner. History must supply the writer with the rudiments of narration, which he must improve and exalt by a nobler art, must animate by dramatick energy, and diversify by retrospection and anticipation; morality must teach him the exact bounds, and different shades, of vice and virtue; from policy and the practice of life, he has to learn the discriminations of character, and the tendency of the passions, either single or combined; and physiology must supply him with illustrations and images. To put these materials to poetical use, is required an imagination capable of painting nature, and realizing fiction. Nor is he yet a poet till he has attained the whole extension of his language, distinguished all the delicacies of phrase, and all the colours of words, and learned to adjust their different sound to all the varieties of metrical modulation.

Bossu is of the opinion, that the poet's first work is to find a moral, which his fable is afterwards to illustrate and establish. This seems to have been the process only of Milton; the moral of other poems is incidental and consequent; in Milton's only it is essential and instrinsick. His purpose was the most useful and the most arduous: "to vindicate the ways of God to man;" to shew the reasonableness of religion, and the necessity of obedience to the divine law.

To convey this moral, there must be a fable, a narration artfully constructed, so as to excite curiosity, and surprise expectation. In this part of his work, Milton must be confessed to have equalled very other poet. He has involved in his account of the fall of man, the events which preceded, and those that were to follow it; he has interwoven the whole system of theology with such propriety, that every part appears to be necessary; and scarcely any recital is wished shorter for the sake of quickening the progress of the main action.

The subject of an epick poem is naturally an event of great importance. That of Milton is not the destruction of a city, the conduct of a colony, or the foundation of an empire. His subject is the fate of worlds, the revolutions of heaven and earth; rebellion against the supreme king, raised by the highest order of created beings; the overthrow of their host, and the punishment of their crime; the creation of a new race of reasonable creatures; their original happiness and innocence, their forfeiture of immortality, and their restoration to hope and peace.

Great events can be hastened or retarded only by persons of elevated dignity. Before the greatness displayed in Milton's poem, all other greatness shrinks away. The weakest of his agents are the highest and noblest of human beings, the original parents of mankind; with whose actions the elements consented; on whose rectitude, or deviation of will, depended the state of terrestrial nature, and the condition of all the future inhabitants of the globe. Of the other agents in the poem, the chief are such as it is irreverence to name on slight occasions. The rest are lower powers [6.221-223]; powers, which only the control of omnipotence restrains from laying creation waste, and filling the vast expanse of space with ruin and confusion. To display the motives and actions of being thus superiour, so far as human reason can examine them, or human imagination represent them, is the task which this mighty poet has undertaken and performed.

In the examination of epick poems much speculation is commonly employed upon the characters. The characters in the *Paradise Lost,* which admit of examination, are those of angels and of man; of angels good and evil; of man in his innocent and sinful state.

Among the angels, the virtue of Raphael is mild and placid, of easy condescension and free communication; that of Michael is regal and lofty, and, as may seem, attentive to the dignity of his own nature. Abdiel and Gabriel appear occasionally, and act as every incident requires; the solitary fidelity of Abdiel is very amiably painted.

Of the evil angels the characters are more diversified. To Satan, as Addison observes, such sentiments are given as suit "the most exalted and most depraved being." Milton has been censured, by Clarke, for the impiety which, sometimes, breaks from Satan's mouth; for there are thoughts, as he justly remarks, which no observation of character can justify, because no good man would willingly permit them to pass, however transiently, through his own mind. To make Satan speak as a rebel, without any such expressions as might taint the reader's imagination, was, indeed, one of the great difficulties in Milton's undertaking; and I cannot but think that he has extricated himself with great happiness. There is in Satan's speeches little that can give pain to a pious ear. The language of rebellion cannot be the same with that of obedience. The malignity of Satan foams in haughtiness and obstinacy; but his expressions are commonly general, and no otherwise offensive than as they are wicked.

The other chiefs of the celestial rebellion are very judiciously discriminated in the first and second books; and the ferocious character of Moloch appears, both in the battle and the council, with exact consistency.

To Adam and to Eve are given, during their innocence, such sentiments as innocence can generate and utter. Their love is pure benevolence and mutual veneration; their repasts are without luxury, and their diligence without toil. Their addresses to their Maker have little more than the voice of admiration and gratitude. Fruition left them nothing to ask, and innocence left them nothing to fear.

But with guilt enter distrust and discord, mutual accusation, and stubborn self-defence; they regard each other with alienated minds, and dread their creator as the avenger of their transgression. At last they seek shelter in his mercy,

soften to repentance, and melt in supplication. Both before and after the Fall, the superiority of Adam is diligently sustained.

Of the probable and the marvellous, two parts of a vulgar epick poem, which immerge the critick in deep consideration, the *Paradise Lost* requires little to be said. It contains the history of a miracle, of creation and redemption; it displays the power and the mercy of the supreme being; the probable, therefore, is marvellous, and the marvellous is probable. The substance of the narrative is truth; and, as truth allows no choice, it is, like necessity, superiour to rule. To the accidental or adventitious parts, as to every thing human, some slight exceptions may be made; but the main fabrick is immovably supported.

It is justly remarked by Addison, that this poem has, by the nature of it subject, the advantage above all others, that it is universally and perpetually interesting. All mankind will, through all ages, bear the same relation to Adam and to Eve, and must partake of that good and evil which extend to themselves.

Of the machinery . . . by which is meant the occasional interposition of supernatural power, another fertile topic of critical remarks, here is no room to speak, because every thing is done under the immediate and visible direction of heaven; but the rule is so far observed, that no part of the action could have been accomplished by any other means.

Of episodes, I think, there are only two, contained in Raphael's relation of the war in heaven, and Michael's prophetick account of the changes to happen in this world. Both are closely connected with the great action; one was necessary to Adam, as a warning, the other as a consolation.

To the completeness or integrity of the design, nothing can be objected; it has, distinctly and clearly, what Aristotle requires, a beginning, a middle, and an end. There is, perhaps, no poem, of the same length, from which so little can be taken without apparent mutilation. Here are no funeral games, nor is there any long description of a shield. The short digressions at the beginning of the third, seventh, and ninth books, might, doubtless, be spared; but superfluities so beautiful, who would take away? or who does not wish that the author of the Iliad had gratified succeeding ages with a little knowledge of himself? Perhaps no passages are more frequently or more attentively read, than those extrinsick paragraphs; and, since the end of poetry is pleasure, that cannot be unpoetical with which all are pleased.

The questions, whether the action of the poem be strictly one, whether the poem can be properly termed heroick, and who is the hero, are raised by such readers as draw their principles of judgment rather from books than from reason. Milton, though he entitled *Paradise Lost* only a poem, yet calls it himself heroick song. Dryden petulantly and indecently, denies the heroism of Adam, because he was overcome; but there is no reason why the hero should not be unfortunate, except established practice, since success and virtue do not go necessarily together. Cato is the hero of Lucan; but Lucan's authority will not be suffered by Quintilian to decide. However, if success be necessary, Adam's deceiver was at last crushed; Adam was restored to his Maker's favour, and, therefore, may securely resume his human rank.

After the scheme and fabrick of the poem, must be considered its component parts, the sentiments and the diction.

The sentiments, as expressive of manners, or appropriated to characters, are, for the greater part unexceptionably just.

Splendid passages, containing lessons or morality, or precepts of prudence, occur seldom. Such is the original formation of this poem, that, as it admits no human manners, till the Fall, it can give little assistance to human conduct. Its end is to raise the thoughts above sublunary cares or pleasures. Yet the praise of that fortitude, without which Abdiel maintained his singularity of virtue against the scorn of multitudes, may be accommodated to all times; and Raphael's reproof of Adam's curiosity after the planetary motions, with the answer returned by Adam, may be confidently opposed to any rule of life which any poet has delivered.

The thoughts which are occasionally called forth in the progress, are such as could only be produced by an imagination in the highest degree fervid and active, to which materials were supplied by incessant study and unlimited curiosity. The heat of Milton's mind might be said to sublimate his learning, to throw off into his work the spirit of science, unmingled with its grosser parts.

He had considered creation, in its whole extent, and his descriptions are, therefore, learned. He had accustomed his imagination to unrestrained indulgence, and his conceptions, therefore, were extensive. The characteristick quality of his poem is sublimity. He sometimes descends to the elegant, but his element is the great. He can occasionally invest himself with grace; but his natural port is gigantick loftiness. He can please, when pleasure is required; but it is his peculiar power to astonish.

He seems to have been well acquainted with his own genius, and to know what it was that Nature had bestowed upon him more bountifully than upon others; the power of displaying the vast, illuminating the splendid, enforcing the awful, darkening the gloomy, and aggravating the dreadful; he, therefore, chose a subject on which too much could not be said, on which he might tire his fancy, without the censure of extravagance.

The appearances of nature, and the occurrences of life, did not satiate his appetite of greatness. To paint things as they are requires a minute attention, and employs the memory rather than the fancy. Milton's delight was to sport in the wide regions of possibility; reality was a scene too narrow for his mind. He sent his faculties out upon discovery, into worlds where only imagination can travel, and delighted to form new modes of existence, and furnish sentiment and action to superious beings, to trace the counsels of hell, or accompany the choirs of heaven.

But he could not be always in other worlds; he must sometimes revisit earth, and tell of things visible and known. When he cannot raise wonder by sublimity of his mind, he gives delight by its fertility.

Whatever be his subject, he never fails to fill the imagination. But his images and descriptions of the scenes, or operations of Nature do not seem to be always copied from original form, nor to have the freshness, raciness, and energy of immediate observation. He saw Nature, as Dryden expresses it, "through the spectacles of books;" and, on most occasions, calls learning to assistance. The garden of Eden brings to his mind the vale of Enna, where Proserpine was gathering flowers. Satan makes his way through fighting elements, like Argo between the Cyanean rocks, or Ulysses between the two Sicilian whirlpools, when he shunned Charbydis on the "larboard." The mythological allusions have been justly censured, as not being always used with notice of their vanity; but they contribute variety to the narration, and produce an alternate exercise of the memory and the fancy.

His similes are less numerous, and more various, than those of his predecessors. But he does not confine himself within the limits of rigorous comparison: his great excellence is amplitude; and he expands the adventitious image beyond the dimensions which the occasion required. Thus comparing the shield of Satan to the orb of the moon, he crowds the imagination with the discovery of the telescope, and all the wonders which the telescope discovers.

Of his moral sentiments it is hardly praise to affirm that they excel those of all other poets; for this superiority he was indebted to his acquaintance with the sacred writings. The ancient epick poets, wanting the light of Revelation, were very unskilful teachers of virtue: their principal characters may be great, but they are not amiable. The reader may rise from their works with a greater degree of active or passive fortitude, and sometimes of prudence; but he will be able to carry away few precepts of justice, and none of mercy.

From the Italian writers it appears, that the advantages of even christian knowledge may be possessed in vain. Ariosto's pravity is generally known; and, though the Deliverance of Jerusalem may be considered as a sacred subject, the poet has been very sparing of moral instruction.

In Milton every line breathes sanctity of thought, and purity of manners, except when the train of the narration requires the introduction of the rebellious spirits; and even they are compelled to acknowledge their subjection to God, in such a manner as excites reverence, and confirms piety.

Of human beings there are but two; but those two are the parents of mankind, venerable before their fall for dignity and innocence, and amiable after it for repentance and submission. In their first state their affection is tender without weakness, and their piety sublime without presumption. When they have sinned, they shew how discord begins in mutual frailty, and how it ought to cease in mutual forbearance; how confidence of the divine favour is forfeited by sin, and how hope of pardon may be obtained by penitence and prayer. A state of innocence we can only conceive, if, indeed, in our present misery, it be possible to conceive it; but the sentiments and worship proper to a fallen and offending being, we have all to learn, as we have all to practise.

The poet, whatever be done, is always great. Our progenitors, in their first state, conversed with angels; even when folly and sin had degraded them, they had not in their humiliation, "the port of mean suitors;" and they rise again to reverential regard, when we find that their prayers were heard.

As human passions did not enter the world, before the fall, there is, in the *Paradise Lost,* little opportunity for the pathetick; but what little there is has not been lost. That passion which is peculiar to rational nature, the anguish arising from the consciousness of transgression, and the horrours attending the sense of divine displeasure, are very justly described and forcibly impressed. But the passions are moved only on one occasion; sublimity is the general and prevailing quality of this poem; sublimity variously modified, sometimes descriptive, sometimes argumentative.

The defects and faults of *Paradise Lost,* for faults and defects every work of man must have, it is the business of impartial criticism to discover. As, in displaying the excellence of Milton, I have not made long quotations, because of selecting beauties there had been no end, I shall in the same general manner, mention that which seems to deserve censure; for what Englishman can take delight in transcribing passages, which, if they lessen the reputation of Milton, diminish, in some degree, the honour of our country?

The generality of my scheme does not admit the frequent notice of verbal inaccuracies; which Bentley, perhaps better skilled in grammar than poetry, has often found, though he sometimes made them, and which he imputed to the obtrusions of a reviser, whom the author's blindness obliged him to employ; a supposition rash and groundless, if he thought it true; and vile and pernicious, if, as is said, he, in private, allowed it to be false.

The plan of *Paradise Lost* has this inconvenience, that it comprises neither human actions nor human manners. The man and woman who act and suffer are in a state which no other man or woman can ever know. The reader finds no transaction in which he can be engaged; beholds no condition in which he can, by any effort of imagination place himself; he has, therefore, little natural curiosity or sympathy.

We all, indeed, feel the effects of Adam's disobedience; we all sin, like Adam, and, like him, must all bewail our offences; we have restless and insidious enemies in the fallen angels; and in the blessed spirits we have guardians and friends; in the Redemption of mankind we hope to be included; in the description of heaven and hell we are, surely, interested, as we are all to reside, hereafter, either in the regions of horrour or of bliss.

But these truths are too important to be new; they have been taught to our infancy; they have mingled with our solitary thoughts and familiar conversation, and are habitually interwoven with the whole texture of life. Being, therefore, not new, they raise no unaccustomed emotion in the mind; what we knew before, we cannot learn; what is not unexpected, cannot surprise.

Of the ideas suggested by these awful scenes, from some we recede with reverence, except when stated hours require their association; and from others we shrink with horrour, or admit them only as salutary inflictions, as counterpoizes to our interests and passions. Such images rather obstruct the career of fancy than incite it.

Pleasure and terrour are, indeed, the genuine sources of poetry; but poetical pleasure must be such as human imagination can, at least, conceive, and poetical terrour such as human strength and fortitude may combat. The good and evil of eternity are too ponderous for the wings of wit; the mind sinks under them, in passive helplessness, content with calm belief and humble adoration.

Known truths, however, may take a different appearance, and be conveyed to the mind by a new train of intermediate images. This Milton has undertaken, and performed with pregnancy and vigour of mind peculiar to himself. Whoever considers the few radical positions which the scriptures afforded him, will wonder by what energetick operation he expanded them to such extent, and ramified them to so much variety, restrained, as he was, by religious reverence from licentiousness of fiction.

Here is a full display of the united force of study and genius; of a great accumulation of materials, with judgment to digest, and fancy to combine them: Milton was able to select from nature or from story, from ancient fable or from modern science, whatever could illustrate or adorn his thoughts. An accumulation of knowledge impregnated his mind, fermented by study, and exalted by imagination.

It has been, therefore, said, without an indecent hyperbole, by one of his encomiasts, that in reading *Paradise Lost,* we read of universal knowledge.

But original deficience cannot be supplied. The want of human interest is always felt. *Paradise Lost* is one of the books which the reader admires and lays down, and forgets to take up again. None ever wished it longer than it is. Its perusal is a duty rather than a pleasure. We read

Milton for instruction, retire harassed and overburdened, and look elsewhere for recreation; we desert our master, and seek for companions.

Another inconvenience of Milton's design is, that it requires the description of what cannot be described, the agency of spirits. He saw that immateriality supplied no images, and that he could not show angels acting but by instrument of action; he, therefore, invested them with form and matter. This, being necessary, was, therefore, defensible; and he should have secured the consistency of his system, by keeping immateriality out of sight, and enticing his reader to drop it from his thoughts. But he has, unhappily, perplexed his poetry with his philosophy. His infernal and celestial powers are sometimes pure spirit, and sometimes animated body. When Satan walks with his lance upon the "burning marle," he has a body; when, in his passage between hell and the new world, he is in danger of sinking into vacuity, and is supported by a gust of rising vapours, he has a body; when he animates the toad, he seems to be mere spirit, that can penetrate matter at pleasure; when he starts "up in his own shape," he has, at least, a determined form; and, when he is brought before Gabriel, he has "a spear and a shield," which he had the power of hiding in the toad, though the arms of the contending angels are evidently material.

The vulgar inhabitants of Pandaemonium, being "incorporeal spirits," are "at large, though without number," in a limited space: yet in the battle, when they were overwhelmed by mountains, their armour hurt them, "crushed in upon their substance, now grown gross by sinning." This, likewise, happened to the uncorrupted angels, who were overthrown the "sooner for their arms, for unarmed they might easily, as spirits, have evaded by contraction or remove." Even as spirits they are hardly spiritual; for "contraction" and "remove" are images of matter; but if they could have escaped without their armour, they might have escaped from it, and left only the empty cover to be battered. Uriel, when he rides on a sun-beam, is material; Satan is material when he is afraid of the prowess of Adam.

The confusion of spirit and matter, which pervades the whole narration of the war in heaven, fills it with incongruity; and the book, in which it is related, is, I believe, the favorite of children, and gradually neglected as knowledge is increased.

After the operation of immaterial agents which cannot be explained, may be considered that of allegorical persons, which have no real existence. To exalt causes into agents, to invest abstract ideas with form, and animate them with activity, has always been the right of poetry. But such airy beings are, for the most part, suffered only to do their natural office, and retire. Thus fame tells a tale, and victory hovers over a general, or perhaps on a standard; but fame and victory can do no more. To give them any real employment, or ascribe to them any material agency, is to make them allegorical no longer, but to shock the mind by ascribing effects to nonentity. In the Prometheus of Aeschylus, we see violence and strength, and in the Alcestis of Euripides, we see death, brought upon the stage, all as active persons of the drama; but no precedents can justify absurdity.

Milton's allegory of Sin and Death is, undoubtedly, faulty. Sin is, indeed, the mother of death, and may be allowed to be the portress of hell; but when they stop the journey of Satan, a journey described as real, and when death offers him battle, the allegory is broken. That sin and death should have shown the way to hell, might have been allowed; but they cannot facilitate the passage by building a bridge, because the difficulty of Satan's passage is described as real and sensible, and the bridge ought to be figurative. The hell assigned to the rebellious spirits is described as not less local than the residence of man. It is placed in some distant part of space, separated from the regions of harmony and order by a chaotick waste and an unoccupied vacuity; but sin and death worked up "a mole of aggravated soil," cemented with "asphaltus;" a work too bulky for ideal architects.

This unskillful allegory appears to me one of the greatest faults of the poem; and to this there was no temptation but the author's opinion of its beauty.

To the conduct of the narrative some objections may be made. Satan is, with great expectation, brought before Gabriel in Paradise, and is suffered to go away unmolested. The creation of man is represented as the consequence of the vacuity left in heaven by the expulsion of the rebels; yet Satan mentions it as a report "rife in heaven" before his departure.

To find sentiments for the state of innocence was very difficult; and something of anticipation, perhaps, is now and then discovered. Adam's discourse of dreams seems not to be the speculation of new-created being. I know not whether his answer to the angels reproof for curiosity does not want something of propriety; it is the speech of a man acquainted with many other men. Some philosophical notions, especially when the philosophy is false, might have been omitted. The angel, in a comparison, speaks of "timorous deer," before deer were yet timorous, and before Adam could understand the comparison.

Dryden remarks, that Milton has some flats among his elevations. This is only to say, that all the parts are not equal. In every work, one part must be for the sake of others; a palace must have passages; a poem must have transitions. It is no more to be required that wit should always be blazing, than that the sun should always stand at noon. In a great work there is a vicissitude of luminous and opaque parts, as there is in the world a succession of day and night. Milton, when he has expatiated in the sky, may be allowed, sometimes, to revisit earth; for what other author ever soared so high, or sustained his flight so long?

Milton, being well versed in the Italian poets, appears to have borrowed often from them; and, as every man catches something from his companions, his desire of imitating Ariosto's levity has disgraced his work with the Paradise of fools; a fiction not in itself ill-imagined, but too ludicrous for its place.

His play on words, in which he delights too often; his equivocations, which Bentley endeavours to defend by the example of the ancients; his unnecessary and ungraceful use of terms of art; it is not necessary to mention, because they are easily remarked, and generally censured; and at last bear so little proportion to the whole, that they scarcely deserve the attention of a critick.

Such are the faults of that wonderful performance, *Paradise Lost;* which he who can put in balance with its beauties must be considered not as nice but as dull, as less to be censured for want of candour, than pitied for want of sensibility.

Through all his greater works there prevails an uniform peculiarity of diction, a mode and cast of expression which bears little resemblance to that of any former writer, and which is so far removed from common use, that an unlearned reader, when he first opens his book, finds himself surprised by a new language.

This novelty has been, by those who can find nothing wrong in Milton, imputed to his laborious endeavours after words suitable to the grandeur of his ideas. "Our language," says Addison, "sunk under him." But the truth is, that, both in prose and verse, he had formed his style by a perverse and pedantick principle. He was desirous to use English words with a foreign idiom. This in all his prose is discovered and condemned; for there judgment operates freely, neither softened by the beauty, nor awed by the dignity of his thoughts; but such is the power of his poetry, that his call is obeyed without resistance, the reader feels himself in captivity to a higher and a nobler mind, and criticism sinks in admiration.

Milton's style was not modified by his subject; what is shown with greater extent in *Paradise Lost* may be found in *Comus.* One source of his peculiarity was his familiarity with the Tuscan poets; the disposition of his words is, I think, frequently Italian; perhaps, sometimes, combined with other tongues.

Of him, at last, may be said what Jonson says of Spenser, that he "wrote no language," but has formed what Butler calls a "Babylonish Dialect," in itself harsh and barbarous, but made by exalted genius and extensive learning, the vehicle of so much instruction and so much pleasure, that, like other lovers, we find grace in its deformity.

Whatever be the faults of his diction, he cannot want the praise of copiousness and variety; he was master of his language in its full extent; and has selected the melodious words with such diligence, that from his book alone the Art of English Poetry might be learned.

After his diction, something must be said of his versification. "The measure," he says, "is the English heroick verse without rhyme." Of this mode he had many examples among the Italians, and some in his own country. The earl of Surrey is said to have translated one of Virgil's books without rhyme; and, besides our tragedies, a few short poems had appeared in blank verse, particularly one tending to reconcile the nation to Raleigh's wild attempt upon Guiana, and probably written by Raleigh himself. These petty performances cannot be supposed to have much influenced Milton, who, more probably took his hint from Trissino's Italia Liberata; and, finding blank verse easier than rhyme, was desirous of persuading himself that it is better.

"Rhyme," he says, and says truly, "is no necessary adjunct of true poetry." But, perhaps, of poetry as a mental operation, meter or musick is no necessary adjunct: it is, however, by the musick of metre that poetry has been discriminated in all languages; and, in languages melodiously constructed with a due proportion of long and short syllables, metre is sufficient. But one language cannot communicate its rules to another; where meter is scanty and imperfect, some help is necessary. The musick of the English heroick line strikes the ear so faintly, that it is easily lost, unless all the syllables of every line cooperate together; this co-operation can be only obtained by the preservation of every verse unmingled with another, as a distinct system of sounds; and this distinctness is obtained and preserved by the artifice of rhyme. The variety of pauses, so much boasted by the lovers of blank verse, changes the measures of an English poet to the periods of a declaimer; and there are only a few skilful and happy readers of Milton, who enable their audience to perceive where the lines end or begin. "Blank verse," said an ingenious critick, "seems to be verse only to the eye."

Poetry may subsist without rhyme, but English poetry will not often please; nor can rhyme ever be safely spared, but where the subject is able to support itself. Blank verse makes some approach to that which is called lapidary style; has neither the easiness of prose, nor the melody of numbers, and, therefore, tires by long continuance. Of the Italian writers without rhyme, whom Milton alleges as precedents, not one is popular; what reason could urge in its defence, has been confuted by the ear.

But, whatever be the advantage of rhyme, I cannot prevail on myself to wish that Milton had been a rhymer; for I cannot wish his work to be other than it is; yet, like other heroes, he is to be admired rather than imitated. He that thinks himself capable of astonishing may write blank verse; but those that hope only to please, must condescend to rhyme.

The highest praise of genius is original invention. Milton cannot be said to have contrived the structure of an epick poem, and, therefore, owes reverence to that vigour and amplitude of mind to which all generations must be indebted for the art of poetical narration, for the texture of the fable, the variation of incidents, the interposition of dialogue, and all the stratagems that surprise and enchain attention. But, of all the borrowers from Homer, Milton is, perhaps, the least indebted. He was naturally a thinker for himself, confident of his own abilities, and disdainful of help or hindrance: he did not refuse admission to the thoughts or images of his predecessors, but he did not seek them. From his contemporaries he neither courted nor received support; there is in his writings nothing by which the pride of other authors might be gratified, or favour grained; no exchange of praise, nor solicitation of support. His great works were performed under discountenance, and in blindness; but difficulties vanished at his touch; he was born for whatever is arduous; and his work is not the greatest of heroick poems, only because it is not the first. [Notes have been dropped.]

**William Vaughn Moody (essay date 1899)**

SOURCE: "From *The Complete Poetical Works of John Milton*," in *The Critical Response to John Milton's Paradise Lost,* edited by Timothy C. Miller, Greenwood Press, 1997, pp. 192-95.

[*In the following excerpt, which originally appeared in his edition of Milton's poetry, Moody praises* Paradise Lost *as one of the greatest poems and declares that it is the epic's style which is its surest claim to enduring admiration.*]

As for his poetry, Milton must be thought of first and last as a master stylist. Keats is more poignant, Shakespeare more various, Coleridge more magical; but nobody who has written in English has had at his command the same unfailing majesty of utterance. His is the organ voice of England. The figure suggests, too, the defect of his qualities. His voice is always his own; he has none of the ventriloquism of the dramatic poets, none of the thaumaturgy by which they obscure themselves in their subject. Milton is always Miltonic, always lofty and grave, whether the subject sinks or rises. Through him we come nearest to that union of measure and might which is peculiar to the master poets of antiquity, and it is through a study of him that the defects of taste incident upon our modern systems of education can be most surely made good.

*Paradise Lost* is the last great episode in the movement of imagination of which Ariosto and Tasso in Italy, Camoëns in Portugal, and Spenser in England, are exemplars. With one of these, indeed, Camoëns Milton stands in a peculiarly interesting relation. The *Lusiad* of Camoëns treats of the voyages of the famous Portuguese navigators; its theme, therefore, is taken from recent, almost contemporary, history. The theme, however, is treated, one may say, centrifugally, the imagination of the poet circling out in such a way as to invest it with all manner of religious and mythopoeic suggestion. Milton, on the other hand, starting with a great religious and mythic theme, impressed upon it, consciously or unconsciously, the traits of the Puritan revolution in England.

For not only are the theology of the poem and its doctrine of social relations entirely Puritan, but, as has often been remarked, its chief figure and real hero, Lucifer, is the embodiment of that very spirit of revolt against arbitrary authority which swept Charles I. from the throne. Roughly speaking, Satan is an unsuccessful Cromwell, refusing to bow before the tyranny of irresponsible might, and Jehovah is a triumphant Stuart, robed in the white light of omnipotence. The theology and the politics of the poet are at variance, and this fact introduces into much of the poem an unconscious insincerity. The words of the rebel angel have an intense eloquence, and the account of his doings and of his domain a persuasive vividness and majesty, which contrasts oddly with the pedantic woodenness of many of the passages consecrated to the Deity. It was largely in the attempt to overcome this paradox by which his villain insisted upon being his hero, that Milton lost himself in those long disquisitions that make some of later books of the poem rather dreary reading.

Perhaps another fact contributing to the same result was that the writing of *Paradise Lost* was, as Taine suggests, really a feat of anachronism. Milton was producing a cosmology in an age of psychology. The whole tendency of Puritanism had been to make men look within, to fix attention upon the individual spirit and its responsibilities; Bunyan's *Grace Abounding* was therefore the significant book for the times, significant at least, for one half the nation; the other half was drifting fast toward the spirit of pure criticism. It is not strange, under these conditions, that Milton felt a constant temptation to abandon the picture for the sermon. His solemnly avowed intention to "justify the ways of God to men" was in the end a serious drag upon him.

There lurked in the subject another difficulty. The title *Paradise Lost,* although it suggests the central point about which the action moves, does not adequately suggest that action itself. The fall of man from innocence is only the point of convergence for a cosmic drama, the theatre of which is all space, and the time of which extends far back into the abyss before Time was. In this unimaginable vastness the earth hangs a mere drop, and the little drama of the Garden of Paradise dwindles necessarily almost into insignificance. Milton was never able to overcome this fault of perspective; however much he lingers over the human pair he is never able to centre our interest there. It is as if our eyes, accustomed to the glooms of Hell and glories of Heaven, had lost their power to see the temperate small sights of earth with keenness.

When all deductions are made, however, *Paradise Lost* remains for us one of the greatest of poems. With the exception of *Beowulf,* which by its language and subject lies remote from every-day appreciation, it is the only English poem with sufficient largeness of theme and breadth of treatment to deserve the name of epic. It is of course not an epic of the Homeric type, springing spontaneously in an unlettered age from the imaginative life of a whole nation; but granted the age of sophistication in which it was produced, it did in a remarkable way seize and draw together the imaginative elements of English thought. The Bible was in Milton's day the centre and substance of that thought. It was for many years almost the only book accessible to the nation at large, and that too at a time when intellectual curiosity was profoundly stirred by the impulses of the Renaissance. The stories of the Bible, its cosmology, its chronology, its imagery, had sunk into the tissue of English thought like a rich and sombre dye. When Milton adopted the story of Genesis as his subject, he was seizing the true epic instinct upon material genuinely national,—much more national than the story of King Arthur or any of the historical British kings could have been, because not only the belief but the passion of the race was engaged by it.

Unfortunately for one part of Milton's appeal, the fabric upon which he wrought had in it elements of decay of which no one of his generation, and he least of all, had an inkling. As we have come to apprehend more clearly the essentials of religious truth as distinguished from its accidental outlines, one great hold which the poem had over the minds of readers has failed.

But in this case "less is more." Our fathers saw in *Paradise Lost* a system of irrefragable truth such as we cannot see, but as a consequence of this falling away of the veil of dogma, we see in it qualities of beauty which escaped their pious gaze. No crash of systems can drown its noble music, and the fading away of dogma leaves the splendor of its symbolism only the more essentially worthy of regard. Then, too, as we get farther away from the conditions which gave the poem birth, its human meaning takes on a pathos which the very sternness of their belief prevented our forefathers from seeing.

It is style, both in the broad and in the narrow sense, which gives *Paradise Lost* it surest claim to enduring admiration. Everywhere there is an indefinable distinction of thought and image; the imagination speaks with a divine largeness of idiom. Or if not quite everywhere,—if Christ's marking off of the creation with golden compasses, if the description of Sin and Death as guardians of the gates of Hell, if the cannonading of the celestial armies in Heaven, are instances of unplastic imagination,—these exceptions serve only to throw into relief a myraid other pictures of commanding vitality and splendor. It is questionable whether any other poem except the *Divine Comedy* affords so many unforgettable pictures. Milton's blindness which at first thought might be deemed crushingly against him here, really helped him. Cut off forever from the light of the sun, he turned his imagination passionately in upon the memories of color and form which he had carried with him into darkness, and took delight in giving to the obscure shades of hell and the vague glories of heaven a startling concreteness and actuality. And these pictures, almost without exception, possess a quality very rare in the history of imagination, a quality which can only be hinted at by the abused epithet "sublime." Even the pictures of Dante, placed beside them, have an everyday colloquial

look. Milton's all "dilated stand like Teneriffe or Atlas." De Quincey was right in declaring that the pervading presence of this quality gives *Paradise Lost* its unique worth, and makes of it a work which, if lost, could not be guessed at from the work of other minds. And to match this quality in the manner of thought there is everywhere present a corresponding quality of expression, a diction and a rhythm so large that they seem made for more than mortal lips to tell of more than earthly happenings, yet so harmoniously adjusted to their task that their largeness is felt less than their justice. William Blake, in one of his prophetical books, says that Milton's house in the Spiritual Kingdom is Palladian, not Gothic. Palladian it is, and in this century we have dwelt by preference in the Gothic house of mind, loving the wayward humor of its adornment, the mysticism and confusion of its design. But from time to time we must purify our vision with the more ample and august lines of the house which Milton has builded.

## C. S. Lewis (essay date 1942)

SOURCE: "From *A Preface to Paradise Lost*," in *Milton: Modern Essays in Criticism*, edited by Arthur E. Barker, Oxford University Press, 1965, pp. 92-100.

[*In the following essay, which originally appeared in his highly influential full-length treatment of* Paradise Lost, *Lewis calls Satan "the best drawn of Milton's characters" but insists that the poet did not admire his creation.*]

Before considering the character of Milton's Satan it may be desirable to remove an ambiguity by noticing that Jane Austen's Miss Bates could be described either as a very entertaining or a very tedious person. If we said the first, we should mean that the author's portrait of her entertains us while we read; if we said the second, we should mean that it does so by being the portrait of a person whom the other people in *Emma* find tedious and whose like we also should find tedious in real life. For it is a very old critical discovery that the imitation in art of unpleasing objects may be a pleasing imitation. In the same way, the proposition that Milton's Satan is a magnificent character may bear two senses. It may mean that Milton's presentation of him is a magnificent poetical achievement which engages the attention and excites the admiration of the reader. On the other hand, it may mean that the real being (if any) whom Milton is depicting, or any real being like Satan if there were one, or a real human being in so far as he resembles Milton's Satan, is or ought to be an object of admiration and sympathy, conscious or unconscious, on the part of the poet or his readers or both. The first, so far as I know, has never till modern times been denied; the second, never affirmed before the times of Blake and Shelley—for when Dryden said that Satan was Milton's "hero" he meant something quite different. It is, in my opinion, wholly erroneous. In saying this I have, however, trespassed beyond the bounds of purely literary criticism. In what follows, therefore, I shall not labour directly to convert those who admire Satan, but only to make a little clearer what it is they are admiring. That Milton could not have shared their admiration will then, I hope, need no argument.

The main difficulty is that any real exposition of the Satanic character and the Satanic predicament is likely to provoke the question "Do you, then, regard *Paradise Lost* as a comic poem?" To this I answer, No; but only those will fully understand it who see that it might have been a comic poem. Milton has chosen to treat the Satanic predicament in the epic form and has therefore subordinated the absurdity of Satan to the misery which he suffers and inflicts. Another author, Meredith, has treated it as comedy with consequent subordination of its tragic elements. But *The Egoist* remains, none the less, a pendant to *Paradise Lost,* and just as Meredith cannot exclude all pathos from Sir Willoughby, so Milton cannot exclude all absurdity from Satan, and does not even wish to do so. That is the explanation of the Divine laughter in *Paradise Lost* which has offended some readers. There is a real offence in it because Milton has imprudently made his Divine Persons so anthropomorphic that their laughter arouses legitimately hostile reactions in us—as though we were dealing with an ordinary conflict of wills in which the winner ought not to ridicule the loser. But it is a mistake to demand that Satan, any more than Sir Willoughby, should be able to rant and posture through the whole universe without, sooner or later, awaking the comic spirit. The whole nature of reality would have to be altered in order to give him such immunity, and it is not alterable. At that precise point where Satan or Sir Willoughby meets something real, laughter *must* arise, just as steam must when water meets fire. And no one was less likely than Milton to be ignorant of this necessity. We know from his prose works that he believed everything detestable to be, in the long run, also ridiculous; and mere Christianity commits every Christian to believing that "the Devil is (in the long run) an ass."

What the Satanic predicament consists in is made clear, as Mr. Williams points out, by Satan himself. On his own showing he is suffering from a "sense of injur'd merit" (I, 98). This is a well known state of mind which we can all study in domestic animals, children, film-stars, politicians, or minor poets; and perhaps nearer home. Many critics have a curious partiality for it in literature, but I do not know that any one admires it in life. When it appears, unable to hurt, in a jealous dog or a spoiled child, it is usually laughed at. When it appears armed with the force of millions on the political stage, it escapes ridicule only by being more mischievous. And the cause from which the Sense of Injured Merit arose in Satan's mind—once more I follow Mr. Williams—is also clear. "He thought himself impaired" (V, 662). He thought himself impaired because Messiah had been pronounced Head of the Angels. These are the "wrongs" which Shelley described as "beyond measure." A being superior to himself in kind, by whom he himself had been created—a being far above him in the natural hierarchy—had been preferred to him in honour by an authority whose right to do so was not disputable, and

in a fashion which, as Abdiel points out, constituted a compliment to the angels rather than a slight (V, 823-43). No one had in fact done anything to Satan; he was not hungry, nor over-tasked, nor removed from his place, nor shunned, nor hated—he only thought himself impaired. In the midst of a world of light and love, of song and feast and dance, he could find nothing to think of more interesting than his own prestige. And his own prestige, it must be noted, had and could have no other grounds than those which he refused to admit for the superior prestige of Messiah. Superiority in kind, or Divine appointment, or both—on what else could his own exalted position depend? Hence his revolt is entangled in contradictions from the very outset, and he cannot even raise the banner of liberty and equality without admitting in a tell-tale parenthesis that "Orders and Degrees Jarr not with liberty" (V, 789). He wants hierarchy and does not want hierarchy. Throughout the poem he is engaged in sawing off the branch he is sitting on, not only in the quasi-political sense already indicated, but in a deeper sense still, since a creature revolting against a creator is revolting against the source of his own powers—including even his power to revolt. Hence the strife is most accurately described as "Heav'n ruining from Heav'n" (VI, 868), for only in so far as he also is "Heaven"—diseased, perverted, twisted, but still a native of Heaven—does Satan exist at all. It is like the scent of a flower trying to destroy the flower. As a consequence the same rebellion which means misery for the feelings and corruption for the will, means Nonsense for the intellect.

Mr. Williams has reminded us in unforgettable words that "Hell is inaccurate," and has drawn attention to the fact that Satan lies about every subject he mentions in *Paradise Lost.* But I do not know whether we can distinguish his conscious lies from the blindness which he has almost willingly imposed on himself. When, at the very beginning of his insurrection, he tells Beelzebub that Messiah is going to make a tour "through all the Hierarchies . . . and give Laws" (V, 688-90) I suppose he may still know that he is lying; and similarly when he tells his followers that "all this haste of midnight march" (V, 774) had been ordered in honour of their new "Head." But when in Book I he claims that the "terror of his arm" had put God in doubt of "his empire," I am not quite certain. It is, of course, mere folly. There never had been any war between Satan and God, only between Satan and Michael; but it is possible that he now believes his own propaganda. When in Book X he makes to his peers the useless boast that Chaos had attempted to oppose his journey "protesting Fate supreame" (480) he may really, by then, have persuaded himself that this was true; for far earlier in his career he has become more a Lie than a Liar, a personified self-contradiction.

This doom of Nonsense—almost, in Pope's sense, of Dulness—is brought out in two scenes. The first is his debate with Abdiel in Book V. Here Satan attempts to maintain the heresy which is at the root of his whole predicament—the doctrine that he is a self-existent being, not a derived being, a creature. Now, of course, the property of a self-existent being is that it can understand its own existence; it is *causa sui.* The quality of a created being is that it just finds itself existing, it knows not how nor why. Yet at the same time, if a creature is silly enough to try to prove that it was not created, what is more natural than for it to say, "Well, I wasn't there to see it being done"? Yet what is more futile, since in thus admitting ignorance of its own beginnings it proves that those beginnings lay outside itself? Satan falls instantly into this trap (850 et seq.)—as indeed he cannot help doing—and produces as proof of his self-existence what is really its disproof. But even this is not Nonsense enough. Uneasily shifting on the bed of Nonsense which he has made for himself, he then throws out the happy idea that "fatal course" really produced him, and finally, with a triumphant air, the theory that he sprouted from the soil like a vegetable. Thus, in twenty lines, the being too proud to admit derivation from God, has come to rejoice in believing that he "just grew" like Topsy or a turnip. The second passage is his speech from the throne in Book II. The blindness here displayed reminds one of Napoleon's utterance after his fall, "I wonder what Wellington will do now?—he will never be content to become a private citizen again." Just as Napoleon was incapable of conceiving, I do not say the virtues, but even the temptations, of an ordinarily honest man in a tolerably stable commonwealth, so Satan in this speech shows complete inability to conceive any state of mind but the infernal. His argument assumes as axiomatic that in any world where there is any good to be envied, subjects will envy their sovereign. The only exception is Hell, for there, since there is no good to be had, the sovereign cannot have more of it, and therefore cannot be envied. Hence he concludes that the infernal monarchy has a stability which the celestial lacks. That the obedient angels might love to obey is an idea which cannot cross his mind even as a hypothesis. But even within this invincible ignorance contradiction breaks out; for Satan makes this ludicrous proposition a reason for hoping ultimate victory. He does not, apparently, notice that every approach to victory must take away the grounds on which victory is hoped. A stability based on perfect misery, and therefore diminishing with each alleviation of that misery, is held out as something likely to assist in removing the misery altogether (II, 11-43).

What we see in Satan is the horrible co-existence of a subtle and incessant intellectual activity with an incapacity to understand anything. This doom he has brought upon himself; in order to avoid seeing one thing he has, almost voluntarily, incapacitated himself from seeing at all. And thus, throughout the poem, all his torments come, in a sense, at his own bidding, and the Divine judgement might have been expressed in the words *"thy* will be done." He says "Evil be thou my good" (which includes "Nonsense be thou my sense") and his prayer is granted. It is by his own will that he revolts; but not by his own will that Revolt itself tears its way in agony out of his head and becomes a being separable from himself, capable of enchanting him (II, 749-66) and bearing him unexpected and

unwelcome progeny. By his own will he becomes a serpent in Book IX; in Book X he is a serpent whether he will or no. This progressive degradation, of which he himself is vividly aware, is carefully marked in the poem. He begins by fighting for "liberty," however misconceived; but almost at once sinks to fighting for "Honour, Dominion, glorie, and renoune" (VI, 422). Defeated in this, he sinks to that great design which makes the main subject of the poem—the design of ruining two creatures who had never done him any harm, no longer in the serious hope of victory, but only to annoy the Enemy whom he cannot directly attack. (The coward in Beaumont and Fletcher's play, not daring to fight a duel, decided to go home and beat his servants.) This brings him as a spy into the universe, and soon not even a political spy, but a mere peeping Tom leering and writhing in prurience as he overlooks the privacy of two lovers, and there described, almost for the first time in the poem, not as the fallen Archangel or Hell's dread Emperor, but simply as "the Devil" (IV, 502)—the salacious grotesque, half bogey and half buffoon, of popular tradition. From hero to general, from general to politician, from politician to secret service agent, and thence to a thing that peers in at bedroom or bathroom windows, and thence to a toad, and finally to a snake—such is the progress of Satan. This progress, misunderstood, has given rise to the belief that Milton began by making Satan more glorious than he intended and then, too late, attempted to rectify the error. But such an unerring picture of the "sense of injured merit" in its actual operations upon character cannot have come about by blundering and accident. We need not doubt that it was the poet's intention to be fair to evil, to give it a run for its money—to show it *first* at the height, with all its rants and melodrama and "Godlike imitated state" about it, and *then* to trace what actually becomes of such self-intoxication when it encounters reality. Fortunately we happen to know that the terrible soliloquy in Book IV (32-113) was conceived and in part composed before the first two books. It was from this conception that Milton started and when he put the most specious aspects of Satan at the very beginning of his poem he was relying on two predispositions in the minds of his readers, which in that age, would have guarded them from our later misunderstanding. Men still believed that there really was such a person as Satan, and that he was a liar. The poet did not foresee that his work would one day meet the disarming simplicity of critics who take for gospel things said by the father of falsehood in public speeches to his troops.

It remains, of course, true that Satan is the best drawn of Milton's characters. The reason is not hard to find. Of the major characters whom Milton attempted he is incomparably the easiest to draw. Set a hundred poets to tell the same story and in ninety of the resulting poems Satan will be the best character. In all but a few writers the "good" characters are the least successful, and every one who has ever tried to make even the humblest story ought to know why. To make a character worse than oneself it is only necessary to release imaginatively from control some of the bad passions which, in real life, are always straining at the leash; the Satan, the Iago, the Becky Sharp, within each of us, is always there and only too ready, the moment the leash is slipped, to come out and have in our books that holiday we try to deny them in our lives. But if you try to draw a character better than yourself, all you can do is to take the best moments you have had and to imagine them prolonged and more consistently embodied in action. But the real high virtues which we do not possess at all, we cannot depict except in a purely external fashion. We do not really know what it feels like to be a man much better than ourselves. His whole inner landscape is one we have never seen, and when we guess it we blunder. It is in their "good" characters that novelists make, unawares, the most shocking self-revelations. Heaven understands Hell and Hell does not understand Heaven, and all of us, in our measure, share the Satanic, or at least the Napoleonic, blindness. To project ourselves into a wicked character, we have only to stop doing something, and something that we are already tired of doing; to project ourselves into a good one we have to do what we cannot and become what we are not. Hence all that is said about Milton's "sympathy" with Satan, his expression in Satan of his own pride, malice, folly, misery, and lust, is true in a sense, but not in a sense peculiar to Milton. The Satan in Milton enables him to draw the character well just as the Satan in us enables us to receive it. Not as Milton, but as man, he has trodden the burning marl, pursued vain war with heaven, and turned aside with leer malign. A fallen man *is* very like a fallen angel. That, indeed, is one of the things which prevents the Satanic predicament from becoming comic. It is too near us; and doubtless Milton expected all readers to perceive that in the long run either the Satanic predicament or else the delighted obedience of Messiah, of Abdiel, of Adam, and of Eve, must be their own. It is therefore right to say that Milton has put much of himself into Satan; but it is unwarrantable to conclude that he was pleased with that part of himself or expected us to be pleased. Because he was, like the rest of us, damnable, it does not follow that he was, like Satan, damned.

Yet even the "good" characters in *Paradise Lost* are not so unsuccessful that a man who takes the poem seriously will doubt whether, in real life, Adam or Satan would be the better company. Observe their conversation. Adam talks about God, the Forbidden Tree, sleep, the difference between beast and man, his plans for the morrow, the stars, and the angels. He discusses dreams and clouds, the sun, the moon, and the planets, the winds, and the birds. He relates his own creation and celebrates the beauty and majesty of Eve. Now listen to Satan: in Book I at line 83 he starts to address Beelzebub; by line 94 he is stating his own position and telling Beelzebub about his "fixt mind" and "injured merit." At line 241 he starts off again, this time to give his impressions of Hell: by line 252 he is stating his own position and assuring us (untruly) that he is "still the same." At line 622 he begins to harangue his followers; by line 635 he is drawing attention to the excellence of his public conduct. Book II opens with his speech from the throne; before we have had eight lines he is lecturing the assembly on his right to leadership. He meets

Sin—and states his position. He sees the Sun; it makes him think of his own position. He spies on the human lovers; and states his position. In Book IX he journeys round the whole earth; it reminds him of his own position. The point need not be laboured. Adam, though locally confined to a small park on a small planet, has interests that embrace "all the choir of heaven and all the furniture of earth." Satan has been in the Heaven of Heavens and in the abyss of Hell, and surveyed all that lies between them, and in that whole immensity has found only one thing that interests Satan. It may be said that Adam's situation made it easier for him, than for Satan, to let his mind roam. But that is just the point. Satan's monomaniac concern with himself and his supposed rights and wrongs is a necessity of the Satanic predicament. Certainly, he has no choice. He has chosen to have no choice. He has wished to "be himself," and to be in himself and for himself, and his wish has been granted. The Hell he carries with him is, in one sense, a Hell of infinite boredom. Satan, like Miss Bates, is interesting to read about; but Milton makes plain the blank uninterestingness of *being* Satan.

To admire Satan, then, is to give one's vote not only for a world of misery, but also for a world of lies and propaganda, of wishful thinking, of incessant autobiography. Yet the choice is possible. Hardly a day passes without some slight movement towards it in each one of us. That is what makes *Paradise Lost* so serious a poem. The thing is possible, and the exposure of it is resented. Where *Paradise Lost* is not loved, it is deeply hated. As Keats said more rightly than he knew, "there is death" in Milton. We have all skirted the Satanic island closely enough to have motives for wishing to evade the full impact of the poem. For, I repeat, the thing is possible; and after a certain point it is prized. Sir Willoughby may be unhappy, but he *wants* to go on being Sir Willoughby. Satan *wants* to go on being Satan. That is the real meaning of his choice "Better to reign in Hell, than serve in Heav'n." Some, to the very end, will think this a fine thing to say; others will think that it fails to be roaring farce only because it spells agony. On the level of literary criticism the matter cannot be argued further. Each to his taste.

### Helen Gardner (essay date 1948)

SOURCE: "Milton's "Satan" and the Theme of Damnation in Elizabethan Tragedy," in *Milton: Modern Essays in Criticism*, edited by Arthur E. Barker, Oxford University Press, 1965, pp. 205-17.

[*In the following essay, originally published in* English Studies *in 1948, Gardner considers the character of Satan, responding to other critics' assessments of him and determining that Milton developed the figure dramatically throughout the poem and "expended his creative energies and his full imaginative powers in exploring the fact of perversity within a single heroic figure."*]

We are all familiar with the progeny of Milton's Satan and the effort of most recent criticism has been directed towards clearing the Satan of Milton's poem from his associations with the Promethean rebel of romantic tradition. But the question whether Satan had any ancestors has hardly been raised, or has been dismissed by reference to the devil of popular tradition, or by an allusion to the heroic figure of the Old English *Genesis B*. The late Mr. Charles Williams, in an essay on Milton which seems likely to become a classic, and Mr. C. S. Lewis, building, as he delighted to own, on Mr. Williams, destroyed, one hopes for ever, the notion that Satan had grounds for his rebellion.[1] But when we have agreed that Satan's "wrongs" which "exceed all measure" exist only in Shelley's generous imagination, and that it is easier to draw a bad character than a good, and have assented to the statement that Satan's career is a steady progress from bad to worse and ends with his complete deformity, we still have no explanation of why the Romantic critics stood **Paradise Lost** on its head, or why the "common reader" finds the imaginative impact of the first books so much more powerful than that of the last, or why, as one re-reads the poem, the exposure of Satan's malice and meanness seems curiously irrelevant. There remains always, untouched by the argument, the image of enormous pain and eternal loss. It is out of key with the close of the poem, which does not drive it from our memory, nor absorb it.

"From hero to general, from general to politician, from politician to secret service agent, and thence to a thing that peers in at bedroom or bathroom windows, and thence to a toad, and finally to a snake—such is the progress of Satan," writes Mr. Lewis, and he rightly declares that there is no question of Milton's beginning by making Satan too glorious and then, too late, attempting to rectify the error. "Such an unerring picture of 'the sense of injured merit' in its actual operations upon character cannot have come about by blundering and accident." We can parallel this account of the career of Satan, but not from Iago and Becky Sharp, whom Mr. Lewis cites as examples of bad characters who are more interesting than their virtuous opposites. From a brave and loyal general, to a treacherous murderer, to a hirer of assassins, to an employer of spies, to a butcher, to a coward, to a thing with no feeling for anything but itself, to a monster and a "hell-hound": that is a summary of the career of Macbeth. From a proud philosopher, master of all human knowledge, to a trickster, to a slave of phantoms, to a cowering wretch: that is a brief sketch of the progress of Dr. Faustus. With varying use of mythological machinery, this theme of the deforming of a creature in its origin bright and good, by its own willed persistence in acts against its own nature, is handled by Shakespeare and Marlowe, and with great power, but in a purely naturalistic setting, by Middleton and Rowley in *The Changeling*. It is on the tragic stage that we find the idea of damnation in English literature before **Paradise Lost**. "Satan," writes Mr. Williams, "is the Image of personal clamour for personal independence." He is in rebellion against "the essential fact of things." The same can be said of Faustus, of Macbeth, and of Beatrice-Joanna, and it is particularly interesting to notice that in *Macbeth* and

*The Changeling* the dramatists have altered their sources to bring out the full implications of the theme.

The devil was a comic character in the medieval drama; in the Elizabethan period he virtually disappears in his own person from the greater plays. But what Mr. Lewis calls "the Satanic predicament" is there, and it appears in the tragic, not the comic mode of vision. The terrible distinction between devils and men in popular theology lay in the irreversibility of the fall of the angels. Unlike men the fallen angels were incapable of repentance and so for them there was no pardon. As Donne puts it: "To those that fell, can appertaine no reconciliation; no more then to those that die in their sins; for *Quod homini mors, Angelis casus;* The fall of the Angels wrought upon them, as the death of a man does upon him; They are both equally incapable of change to better."[2] Donne recognizes that some of the Fathers thought that "the devill retaining still his faculty of free will, is therefore capable of repentance, and so of benefit by this comming of Christ";[3] but this is exactly the point which Aquinas denies and Donne assents to his view. Aquinas decides that the fallen angels cannot repent, since, though they know the beginnings of penitence in fear, their free-will is perverted: "Quid-quid in eis est naturale, totum est bonum et ad bonum inclinans, sed liberum arbitrium in eis est in malo obstinatum; et quia motus virtutis et vitii non sequitur inclinationem naturae, sed magis motum liberi arbitrii; ideo non oportet, quamvis naturaliter inclinentur ad bonum, quod motus virtutis in eis sit, vel esse possit."[4] In the tragic world of Faustus and Macbeth we find presented to us in human terms this incapacity for change to a better state. It never occurs to us that Macbeth will turn back, or indeed that he can; and though Marlowe, in this more merciful, as he is always more metaphysical, than Shakespeare, keeps before us the fact of Faustus's humanity by the urgings of the Good Angel, yet to the Good Angel's "Faustus, repent; yet God will pity thee," comes at once the Bad Angel's response: "Thou art a spirit;[5] God cannot pity thee"; and to Faustus's

> Who buzzeth in mine ears, I am a spirit?
> Be I a devil, yet God may pity me;
> Yea, God will pity me, if I repent.

comes the confident statement of the Bad Angel: "Ay, but Faustus never shall repent"; to which Faustus gives a despairing assent: "My heart is harden'd, I cannot repent."[6]

In the three plays mentioned, along with this incapacity for change to a better state, or repentance, go two other closely related ideas. The initial act is an act against nature, it is a primal sin, in that it contradicts the "essential fact of things," and its author knows that it does so. It is not an act committed by mistake; it is not an error of judgment, it is an error of will. [The act is unnatural] and so are its results; it deforms the nature which performs it. The second idea is the irony of retributive justice. The act is performed for an imagined good, which appears so infinitely desirable that the conditions for its supposed satisfaction are accepted; but a rigorous necessity reigns and sees to it that though the conditions are exacted literally, the desire is only granted ironically, and this is inevitable, since the desire is for something forbidden by the very nature of man. . . .[7]

It is not suggested that there is any direct relation between these three plays, in the sense that one was inspired by the others; nor is it suggested that when Milton drew his Satan he had these great tragic figures in mind. What is suggested is that Satan belongs to their company, and if we ask where the idea of damnation was handled with seriousness and intensity in English literature before Milton, we can only reply: on the tragic stage. Satan is, of course, a character in an epic, and he is in no sense the hero of the epic as a whole. But he is a figure of heroic magnitude and heroic energy, and he is developed by Milton with dramatic emphasis and dramatic intensity. He is shown, to begin with, engaged in heroic and stupendous enterprises, and again and again in moments of dramatic clash; rousing his supine followers, awaiting his moment in the great debate, confronted with Sin and Death and Chaos itself, flinging taunt for taunt at his angelic adversaries. But most strikingly he is presented to us by the means by which the great Elizabethan dramatists commended their tragic heroes to our hearts and imaginations: by soliloquy. Milton gives to Satan no less than five long soliloquies in Eden, three in the fourth book and two in the ninth.[8] In them he reveals to us "the hot Hell that always in him burnes," and recalls again and again

> the bitter memorie
> Of what he was, what is, and what must be
> Worse.

It is in them that the quality which makes Satan a tragic figure appears most strikingly, and it is the quality Mr. Lewis makes weightiest against him: his egoism.

"Satan's monomaniac concern with himself and his supposed rights and wrongs is a necessity of the Satanic predicament," says Mr. Lewis. The same is true of the great tragic heroes of Shakespeare, and this capacity of theirs to expose relentlessly the full horror of their situations is just what makes them the heroes of their plays.[9] The predicament of Claudius is direr than Hamlet's, but Shakespeare pays little attention to it; Malcolm is the righteous avenger of a horrible crime, but the sympathy we feel for him we take for granted. We are held enthralled instead by the voice of Hamlet, defining for us his "bad dreams" or that of Macbeth telling us of solitude. If we are to complain that wherever he goes, and whatever he sees, Satan finds nothing of interest but himself, and to compare him unfavourably with Adam, who can converse on topics of general interest such as the stars, what should we say of Lear, who finds in the majesty of the storm or the misery of the naked beggarman only fresh incentives to talk about the unkindness of his daughters? If we can say of a speech of Satan's that "it fails to be roaring farce only because it spells agony," we can say the same of Macbeth, complaining at the close of a career of murderous egoism that he

has no friends, or of Beatrice-Joanna, "a woman dipp'd in blood" talking of modesty. Satan is an egoist and Satan is a comic character in exactly the same way as Hamlet, Macbeth, Othello, and Lear are egoists and comic characters. "O gull! O dolt!" cries Emilia to Othello. We do not pity him the less because we assent.

The critical problem of *Paradise Lost* seems to me to lie here. We are concerned with Satan in a way that is quite different from the way we are concerned with Adam and Eve. In Mr. Lewis's treatment this is quite clear. He uses all his skill to make us regard Satan as a despicable human being, discussing him in terms of "children, filmstars, politicians, or minor poets"; but he uses equal skill to make us realize we must not regard Adam in this way. If he is right, as I think he is, in pressing a distinction between our attitudes to the two figures, he poses an acute problem for the reader of *Paradise Lost,* and appears to convict Milton of the artistic failure involved in a mixture of kinds.

The distinction I feel I would express in rather different terms. Adam and Even are representative figures, and the act they perform is a great symbolic act. The plucking of the apple is not in itself imaginatively powerful; its power over us springs from its very triviality; the meaning and the consequences are so much greater than the image of a hand stretched out to pluck the fruit. The temptation and fall of Eve is profound in its psychological analysis, but it lacks the shock of dramatic situation. As Mr. Lewis says: "The whole thing is so quick, each new element of folly, malice, and corruption enters so unobtrusively, so naturally, that it is hard to realize we have been watching the genesis of murder. We expect something more like Lady Macbeth's 'unsex me here.'" In other words the situation is not dramatically exploited, lingered on. The scenes between Adam and Eve are deeply human, but they lack the terror, and the dreadful exaggeration of tragedy. The quarrel is only too sadly life-like, but it does not appal us, as does the spectacle of Othello striking Desdemona. In the ninth book and the books that follow, Milton is tracing with insight, with humanity and with humility the process in man through sin to repentance. The progress is steady and ordered; what is said is fully adequate to the situation, appropriate but not astounding. But Satan's defiance of God is not expressed by a symbolic gesture; in his rebellion the act and its meaning are one. And in the earlier books, and indeed wherever Satan appears, what is said goes beyond the necessities of the narrative, because Milton was writing as a tragic artist obsessed by his imagination of a particular experience, and exploring it with the maximum intensity. The experience might be called "exclusion." Wherever he goes, whatever he looks at, Satan is perpetually conscious of this. His exclusion is self-willed, as is the exclusion of Faustus, Macbeth and Beatrice-Joanna. Like them he gazes on a heaven he cannot enter; like them he is in the end deformed; like them he remains in the memory with all the stubborn objectivity of the tragic.

If it can be accepted that Satan as he is conceived and presented to us is a tragic figure, it is possible to suggest another explanation for the Romantic misconception of the poem than a dislike of Milton's theology. The early nineteenth century was greatly concerned it would seem with tragic experience; its great poets wanted to be "miserable and mighty poets of the human heart." All of them attempted to write tragedy, but, with the possible exception of *The Cenci,* they produced nothing that is admitted to be fully tragic. It was also a period remarkable for penetrating and subtle Shakespearian criticism, but for a criticism which lost a sense of the play in its discussion of the psychology of the characters, and which tended to minimize in the tragic heroes the very thing that made them tragic and not pathetic, the evil in them. In the criticism of the period Hamlet is "a sweet prince," Lear "a man more sinned against than sinning." Hamlet's savagery and Lear's appalling rages are overlooked. Lamb turned from the stage because he could not bear the cruel comedy of *King Lear,* nor the sight of Desdemona in Othello's arms. Realized intensely in the mind, divorced from his action in the play, the tragic hero was reshaped. It is of the essence of tragedy that it forces us to look at what we normally do not care to look at, and have not invented for ourselves.[10] The failure either to write or to appreciate tragedy in the Romantic period springs from the same cause: the Romantic poets' pre-occupation with themselves, and their lack of capacity to submit themselves to the "mystery of things." The famous passage in which Keats defined Shakespeare's quality as "Negative Capability" goes to the root of the matter. But "Negative Capability" is as necessary to the spectator and critic of tragedy as to its creator. The tragic is destroyed when we identify the hero with ourselves. Just as the Romantic critics tended to see the heroes of Shakespeare's tragedies as more admirable, more tender, more purely pathetic than they are, so feeling Satan's kinship with the tragic hero they sentimentalized him and made him conform to their limited conception of tragedy. Because he was to be pitied, they minimized the evil in him, inventing wrongs to explain and excuse it.[11]

The present age is also not an age of great tragic writing, though there are some signs of a revival of the tragic spirit. Its best poetry is symbolic, and its criticism, in reviving for us the medieval tradition of allegory, tends towards an allegorical interpretation of all art. Mr. Lewis, in exposing Shelley's misconceptions, has inverted the Romantic attitude, for the effect of his chapter on Satan is to make us feel that because Satan is wicked, and wicked with no excuse, he is not to be pitied, but is to be hated and despised. Shelley saw in Satan the indomitable rebel against unjust tyranny, and while regretting the "taints" in his character excused them. Mr. Lewis, who thinks more harshly of himself and of human nature than Shelley did, exposes Satan with all the energy and argumentative zeal which we used to hear our European Service employing in denouncing the lies of Goebbels and revealing the true nature of the promises of Hitler. Both Shelley's passionate sympathy and Mr. Lewis's invective derive from the same fundamental attitude: "It is we who are Satan." As often

happens with plural statements, this is a merely verbal extension of the singular; that is to say it is infected by an egoism that distorts the proper function of the tragic. When we contemplate the lost Archangel, we should not be seeing ourselves in heroic postures defying tyrants, nor weighing up our chances of ending in Hell, any more than, while we watch the progress of Lear, we should be thinking how ungrateful other people are to us for our goodness to them, or resolving to think before we speak next time. Though Shelley and Mr. Lewis are on different sides, they agree in taking sides. Neither of them accepts the complexity of the emotion which Satan arouses.

The tragic is something outside ourselves which we contemplate with awe and pity. Aristotle began the perversion of tragic theory when he suggested that the terror we feel is a terror that the same fate may befall us. Aristotle was a philosopher and a moralist, and, like many of his kind since, wanted to make tragedy safe and useful. But tragedy does not exist to provide us with horrid warnings. "Pity," said Stephen Dedalus, expanding the cryptic Aristotelian formula, "is the feeling which arrests the mind in the presence of whatsoever is grave and constant in human sufferings and unites it with the human sufferer. Terror is the feeling which arrests the mind in the presence of whatsoever is grave and constant in human sufferings and unites it with the secret cause."[12] We accept the justice by which the tragic hero is destroyed. Indeed if it were not for the justice we should have no pity for him. The acceptance of the justice makes possible the pity, and the pity calls for the justice without which it would turn to loathing. But the cause must be secret in tragedy; it must be felt within the facts exposed; what is hateful in the tragic world is that Eternal Law should argue.

The unity of tragedy is destroyed if the critic makes himself either the champion of the hero or the advocate of Eternal Law. Tragedy "arrests the mind" as the sufferings of others do, but as our own do not. But in life the arrest is short, for we are involved in the necessity of action. As spectators of tragedy we are released from our perpetual burden of asking ourselves what we ought to do. To use tragedy either as a moral example or as a moral warning is to destroy the glory of tragedy, the power it has to release us from ourselves by arousing in us the sense of magnitude and the sense of awe. Wordsworth, the most untragic of great poets, saw something of the nature of tragedy when he wrote,

> Suffering is permanent, obscure and dark,
> And shares the nature of infinity.

Tragedy may present us with a "false infinite" but it has that nature. It is permanent "with such permanence as time has." Like the rock in Mr. Eliot's *The Dry Salvages,*

> Waves wash over it, fogs conceal it;
> On a halcyon day it is merely a monument,
> In navigable weather it is always a seamark
> To lay a sudden course by: but in the sombre season
> Or the sudden fury, is what it always was.

The figure of Satan has this imperishable significance. If he is not the heroic rebel of Shelley's imagination, neither is he merely an "unerring picture of the 'sense of injur'd merit' in its actual operations upon character."

But if Mr. Lewis's view seems like an inversion of Shelley's, Mr. Williams's is not very unlike Blake's. What Blake perceived in *Paradise Lost* was a radical dualism, which was perhaps the inevitable effect of treating the myth in epic form. Among the many difficulties inherent in the subject was the difficulty of knowing how much to include in the direct action and how much to put into relations. It was impossible for Milton to begin where his tragedy *Adam Unparadised* was to have begun, in Paradise; the direct action would have been insufficient to fill the epic form. Even as it is, *Paradise Lost* is overweighted with relations. Epic tradition forbade him to begin at the beginning with the exaltation of the Son. Possibly his decision to begin with the moment when Satan lifts his head from the burning waves was inevitable once he had decided against the dramatic form in which he first conceived the subject. But the effect of beginning there, and of the whole of the "Prologue in Hell" is to make the action of the poem seem to originate in Hell, and to make the acts of Heaven seem only the response called out by the energies of Hell. However much Milton contradicts this later and asserts the overriding Will, the structure and design of his poem contradict and fight against his intention. The parallel, so often praised, between the silence in Hell, and the silence in Heaven reinforces the feeling of dualism, since *contraria sunt aequalia,* and Satan and the Son seem balanced against each other, as Blake saw them to be, while the priority of the scene in Hell seems to make Heaven parody Hell rather than Hell Heaven. Mr. Williams's statement that "the Son is the Image of Derivation in Love, and Satan is the Image of personal clamour for personal independence" is not unlike Blake's assertion of "the contraries from which spring what the religious call good and evil." It suggests at least that Milton made Satan too important in the scheme of his poem.

Perhaps the problem which *Paradise Lost* presents to the critic has its origin in Milton's own change of mind over the form in which he was to write his masterpiece. He first chose the subject of the Fall of Man as suited to a tragedy, and we know that he not only planned the disposition of his material in dramatic form, but actually began the writing. His draft *Adam Unparadised* provides Lucifer with two soliloquies: in the first he was to "bemoan himself" and "seek revenge upon man"; in the second he was to appear "relating and consulting on what he had done to the destruction of man." The first soliloquy was therefore to have been mainly expository, and in the second Lucifer was to take over the duty of the classical messenger and relate the catastrophe. The strict concentration of classical tragedy would have prevented Lucifer from usurping on the main interest, and his predicament, however much he "bemoaned himself," would have been subordinated to the whole design. Why Milton changed his mind we do not know, and he set himself a problem of extraordinary diffi-

culty in choosing to treat this particular subject in epic form. He had somehow to fill the large epic structure, and it is difficult to see how else he could have done it than by expanding Satan's rôle. But it is possible that he turned away from tragedy because his interest had radiated out from the true centre of the action, the Fall itself, and his imagination demanded the larger freedom of the epic. Certainly the fact that Phillips remembered seeing the opening lines of Satan's first soliloquy as part of the projected tragedy suggests that Milton's conception of Satan began to form early, and it may have been that the writing of this first soliloquy showed Milton that the tragic form would not allow him to develop his conception as fully as he wished to. But whether the decision to begin his poem with Satan in Hell was simply the inevitable result of enlarging his action to make it sufficient for an epic, or whether it was Milton's interest in Satan that led him to abandon tragedy for epic, and he therefore naturally began with Satan, the figure of Satan, originally conceived dramatically, is developed dramatically throughout, and Milton expended his creative energies and his full imaginative power in exploring the fact of perversity within a single heroic figure. In this, as in much else, he is what we loosely call an Elizabethan, sacrificing simplicity of effect and strength of design to imaginative opportunity; creating the last great tragic figure in our literature and destroying the unity of his poem in doing so. The dualism which Blake found in the poem's thought, and which in Mr. Williams's analysis seems to dictate its design, is certainly there in its manner. The strong emotions of pity and terror do not mix well with the interest, sympathy and "admiration" which we feel for the heroes of what Mr. Lewis has called "the secondary epic," and, with the possible exception of Hazlitt, no critic of note has done justice to both Satan and Adam as artistic creations. The subject demanded an "infernal Serpent"; instead Milton has given us "a lost Archangel." There would be no difficulty if Satan were simply an Iago; the difficulty arises because he is a Macbeth.

*Notes*

1. See *The English Poems of Milton,* with a preface by Charles Williams, (World's Classics) 1940, and C. S. Lewis, *A Preface to Paradise Lost,* 1942.

2. *LXXX Sermons,* 1640, p. 9. A recent reading of Donne's *Sermons* for another purpose has impressed upon me how often Donne provides the comment of a theologian or a moralist upon the tragedies of his contemporaries.

3. *Ibid.,* p. 66.

4. *S.T.,* Supplement, Q. XVI, Art. 3.

5. *Spirit* here as elsewhere in the play means evil spirit, or devil.

6. All quotations from *Dr. Faustus* are from the edition of Dr. F. S. Boas, 1932. The point that Faustus is presented to us as incapable of real repentance, though like the devils he knows the beginnings of

penitence in fear and "believes and trembles," is obscured if we accept, as Dr. Boas does, the suggestion of Mr. H. T. Baker (*Modern Language Notes,* vol. XXI, pp. 86-7) and transfer to Faustus the close of the Old Man's speech in Act v, scene i (p. 161). In this most touching scene the Old Man makes a last appeal to Faustus to remember his humanity:

> Though thou hast now offended like a man,
> Do not persever in it like a devil;
> Yet, yet, thou hast an amiable soul,
> If sin by custom grow not into nature.

7. Donne supplies us with a comment on the "omnipotence" of Faustus, the "kingship" of Macbeth and the "marriage" of Beatrice-Joanna, when he says: "For small wages, and ill-paid pensions we serve him (Satan); and lest any man should flatter and delude himselfe, in saying, I have my wages, and my reward before hand, my pleasures in this life, the punishment, (if ever) not till the next, The Apostle destroyes that dreame, with that question of confusion, *What fruit had you then in those things, of which you are now ashamed?* Certainly sin is not a gainfull way; . . . fruitlesness, unprofitableness before, shame and dishoner after." *LXXX Sermons,* p. 65. [EDITOR'S NOTE. In the pages omitted here, Miss Gardner discusses Faustus, Macbeth, and Beatrice-Joanna, in the plays instanced above.]

8. In spite of the explanatory and anticipatory element in these soliloquies, their general effect, particularly in the two longest, IV, 32-113 and IX, 99-178, is quite different from the effect of the soliloquies of villains such as Richard III or Iago. In them we are conscious of activity of intellect and atrophy of feeling; here, as in the soliloquies of Hamlet or Macbeth, the plans announced are less important than the analysis of the hero's predicament.

9. Henry James puts this well in the preface to *The Princess Casamassima,* London, 1921, p. viii. "This in fact I have ever found rather terribly the point—that the figures in any picture, the agents in any drama, are interesting only in proportion as they feel their respective situations; since the consciousness, on their part, of the complication exhibited forms for us their link of connection with it. But there are degrees of feeling—the muffled, the faint, the just sufficient, the barely intelligent, as we may say; and the acute, the intense, the complete, in a word—the power to be finely aware and richly responsible. It is those moved in this latter fashion who "get most" out of all that happens to them and who in so doing enable us, as readers of their record, as participators by a fond attention, also to get most. Their being finely aware—as Hamlet and Lear, say, are finely aware—*makes* absolutely the intensity of their adventure, gives the maximum of sense to what befalls them."

10. It may be suggested that the success of *The Cenci,* compared with other tragedies of the period, is partly due to the fact that the story was not invented by Shelley. He plainly felt some of the "superstitious horror" which he tells us the story still aroused in Italy, and was fascinated by the portrait of Beatrice.

11. In the preface to *Prometheus Unbound,* Shelley compared Satan with Prometheus and declared that Prometheus is the "more poetical character" since he is "exempt from the taints of ambition, envy, revenge, and a desire for personal aggrandisement, which, in the Hero of *Paradise Lost,* interfere with the interest." He thought that the character of Satan "engenders in the mind a pernicious casuistry which leads us to weigh his faults with his wrongs, and to excuse the former because the latter exceed all measure." When he wrote the preface to *The Cenci,* Shelley had abandoned the notion that moral perfection made a character poetically interesting, and acknowledged that if Beatrice had been "wiser and better" she would not have been a tragic character, but he speaks again of the "casuistry" by which we try to justify what she does, while feeling that it needs justification. When he compared Milton's God and his Devil in *A Defence of Poetry,* Shelley declared Satan was morally superior on the grounds that his situation and his wrongs excused in him the revengefulness which is hateful in his triumphant Adversary. In all these passages one can see Shelley's feeling that the Hero is a person whose side we take. The theme of a nature warped by suffering injustice, and repaying crime with crime, is certainly tragic when handled with seriousness and moral integrity as in *The Cenci,* though it slides all too easily into the sentimental absurdities of the Byronic outcast, and it is always in danger of shallowness. It is the tragic formula of an age which does not believe in original sin, and thinks of evil as not bred in the heart, but caused by circumstances.

12. James Joyce, *A Portrait of the Artist as a Young Man,* chapter v.

[EDITOR'S NOTE. Miss Gardner's interpretation of *Paradise Lost* is further developed in her forthcoming volume in the series of Alexander Lectures, University of Toronto. See the items listed with the preceding essay; and on some other literary models see W. Blissett, *JHI,* XVIII (1957), 221-32; R. M. Bottwood, *CJ,* XLVII (1952), 183-6; E. E. Kellett, *London Quarterly and Holborn Review,* CLXIV (1939), 88-99.]

**Arthur E. Barker (essay date 1949)**

SOURCE: "Structural Pattern in *Paradise Lost,*" in *Milton: Modern Essays in Criticism,* edited by Arthur E. Barker, Oxford University Press, 1965, pp. 142-55.

[*In the following essay, originally published in* Philological Quarterly *in 1949, Barker discusses how in* Paradise Lost *Milton moved away from a Virgilian ten-book, five-act structure to a twelve-book form that ultimately serves to reduce Satan's power over the poem.*]

Milton, as Professor Thompson has said, "realized that form is determined not by rule or precedent but by the thought to be expressed. Hence he adapted the pattern of the epic to his own ends, and wrote as a creative artist."[1]

From its opening invocation *Paradise Lost* invites attention to this process of adaptation and transcendence. The initial statement of the threefold subject (disobedience and woe, till restoration) immediately suggests specific comparison with the opening statement of the *Aeneid* (Troy fall and wandering, till the new city be founded). This suggestion is reinforced periodically throughout; so also is the opening invocation's adventurous claim to no middle flight above the Aonian mount, no mere description of the loss and restoration of an earthly city. And one of the chief pleasures of the student of Milton has always been to watch, under the guidance of skilled commentators from Addison to Professor Thompson, how Milton expressively modifies the conventions and the pattern of epic to suit the meanings of his theme.

So guided, most of us readily agree with Addison's observation that *Paradise Lost* does not fall short "of the *Iliad* or *Aeneid* in the beauties which are essential to that kind of writing"; and it is to be hoped that the tradition so established may somehow be continued in spite of the difficulties of increasing unfamiliarity with Milton's classical models. The process of adaptation was in fact one of Milton's chief instruments of expression. Each of his important poems assumes as one of its points of departure a tradition of interpretation and a convention of form, and in each of them successful communication depends very largely on a recognition of likeness as the basis for expressive variation. Nor is this the case merely with conventional detail. It may be doubted whether the total force of *Paradise Lost* can ever be felt by a reader who does not recognize how its total pattern reproduces while modifying and modifies while reproducing the total pattern of the *Aeneid*.

It is not difficult to win from a modern reader half of this recognition. But when one has shown that the *Aeneid* has indeed a significant structural pattern—six Odyssean books of wandering balanced by six Achillean books of war and establishment, three distinct movements of four books each, six groups of two books apiece, with the structural weight so made to fall on a series of prophecies of glory to be won from apparent failure—when one has indicated by simple arithmetic the controlling structural pattern of Virgil's epic and has turned to Milton's awareness of it, one is almost certain to be met by the complaint that Milton does not imitate it adequately. Before long one is likely to find oneself dealing, like Professor Thompson on another occasion[2], with the implications of Addison's remark

that the tenth book of *Paradise Lost* "is like the last act of a well-constructed tragedy, in which all who had a part in it are drawn up before the audience, and represented under those circumstances in which the determination of the action has placed them." Are not the succeeding books, it is asked, superfluous, or at any rate (as Addison notes) "not generally reckoned among the most shining books of the poem"? And does not this mean, among other things, that Milton's imitation of the Virgilian pattern is inadequate?

It is difficult to convince a modern reader that Milton's intention was not merely to copy but to adapt the Virgilian pattern, to use the classical models as bases for variations which would assist in the expression of the Christian theme. The paradox of the Christian theme is itself difficult enough to express convincingly. Milton already found it so. But it is perhaps just here that the comparison and contrast with Virgil may be of most effect. We have at any rate a suggestive point of contrast in the attitudes of the two poets towards their work. The Roman poet on his death-bed, we are told, gave direction that his beautifully patterned epic should be burned; the blind Milton, in the year of his death, produced a "revised and augmented" edition of his poem, correcting errors in spelling and punctuation and even tinkering with its division into books in order to change what the title-page of 1667 had described as "a poem written in ten books" into "a poem in twelve books." This tinkering is Milton's last recorded comment on his poem.

II

At first sight this change in numeration seems of little moment. Editors usually draw our attention to the fact that, by the simple process of dividing roughly in half the two longest of his 1667 books, Milton accomplished a redivision ever since regarded as perfectly just. The change involved no shifting about of material whatsoever, and only the slightest of additions. Four lines were added at the beginning of the new book VIII to provide the appearance of a new departure; they indicate, it is said, no change in direction; our first parent is merely represented as guilty of a momentary lapse of attention in the middle of Raphael's lecture. Similarly, five lines were added for the beginning of the new book XII (and the Argument was slightly revised); Michael is merely made to pause for a moment in his partially illustrated address, "betwixt the world destroy'd and world restor'd." That is all. Milton has perceived that a poem which invites comparison with the ancient epics, and particularly with Virgil, ought to have twelve books, not ten.

It seems a strangely retarded perception. Someone should ask at least for once the eminently simple-minded question. "What cause . . . ?"

With almost any other poet, though blind, this question might well be left unasked. English Renaissance poetry is a major field of bibliographical activity because of infinitely numerous revisions of more extensive importance than this. Yet the meticulousness with which the blind Milton revised *Paradise Lost* for the 1674 edition, with the absence of any other major changes of any kind, suggests the desirability of contemplating even this shred of evidence as to the author's intention in a poem so vast and variously interpreted. And there are two characteristics of Milton's major poems which suggest that the question may not be unprofitable. One is his habit of using a conventional form as a point of departure; the other his architectonic skill. Both depend in considerable measure for their success on simple clarity in the initial massing and division of material.

The effect of balance more or less characteristic of any work of art frequently arrives in Milton at a mathematical plainness almost suggestive of the counting of lines. We need not suppose that his muse worked quite so mechanically or laid so lowly a burden on herself; but Milton's mind operated at ease only when he perceived in or imposed on his material a precise mathematical division of some sort. No doubt such precision gave him a much-needed sense of security and control. At any rate, it is certainly a fact (of which I once tried to make something . . .) that much of the force of the "Hymn" of the *Nativity Ode* and also of *Lycidas* is derived from the modulation of three equally and precisely balanced movements, similar in figurative (or structural) pattern, yet evolving a cumulative effect through variation. At the other end of Milton's career, *Samson Agonistes,* it is well known, consists of five perfectly regular and almost mathematically equal "acts," each reproducing and developing towards its completion the basic pattern of trial and triumph in defeat. Milton did not always reach such precision. The genre of *Comus* could perhaps hardly have sustained such rigorous definition as is possible in other forms, though its much revised structure deserves closer analysis from this point of view; implicit in *Paradise Regained* there is such a structural pattern, though handled in a way unusual with Milton. But it is obvious that this simple effect of balance was of importance to him, and one can sometimes watch him striving to impose a pattern of exact balance where none perhaps existed. A large example (upon which I have commented at length elsewhere) is to be seen in his attempt in *Defensio Secunda* in 1654 to see in his controversial activity a consistent threefold pattern; in the 1640's, he says, he perceived that there were three species of liberty; the chronological blocks of his prose deal with them in an orderly and (it is implied) predetermined sequence. It is curious that a mind so bent on well-balanced hinging should feel it desirable to change the book divisions of its major production after a seven-year interval.

The habit of taking as an expressive point of departure some traditionally fixed or even highly conventionalized form (sonnet, masque, elegy, epic, tragedy), and the instinctive habit of dealing with poetic material in clearly defined and precisely balanced blocks held together and given extension by their reproduction of some basic pattern, are not of course merely Miltonic habits. They are only more obvious in him than they are generally in the poetic art of the Renaissance—or of any highly conscious creative period. They contribute to one of the uses of poetry which was of the utmost importance to him. As Professor Woodhouse and Professor Tillyard among others have indicated, Milton's major poems seem to have performed a cathartic function for the poet himself: each seems in its creation a process whereby the poet resolves a paralysing tension. This is obvious in the cases of *Lycidas* and *Samson Agonistes;* and, properly handled, the obvious need not divert us for long from the poem to the poet. It would seem that in moments of tension Milton found a secure point of departure in the fixity of some traditional form (and, of course, though it is not in question here, some traditional complex of ideas), and that the precise balancing of blocks of poetic material afforded him a secure and regularized channel within which to resolve the tension by the working out of variations.

Does this generalization hold for *Paradise Lost* as well as for *Lycidas* and *Samson Agonistes?* If one's first (though not one's final) observation about "a true poem" is that it is "a composition and pattern," why did Milton in 1674 find himself dissatisfied with the composition and pattern implied by the division of the material of *Paradise Lost* into ten books? Is it possible that the simple redivision into twelve books ("differently disposed," as Edward Philips tells us, ". . . by his own hand, that is by his own appointment") indicates that the process of resolution had not quite clarified itself when Milton published the poem in 1667, that subsequently he saw in it a pattern which the ten-book division tended to obscure?

### III

The original ten-book division immediately suggests comparison with the drama. It inevitably recalls Davenant's projected structure for *Gondibert.* It also implies that the structure of *Paradise Lost* owes much to the neo-classical theory, formulated by the Italians and of great force among Milton's English predecessors, which closely associated the tragic and the epic forms and resulted in a long series of abortive five-act epic experiments.[3] The relation of Milton's theory to this tradition deserves closer attention; the redivision of *Paradise Lost* seems at first to suggest that he never quite made up his mind as to whether "the rules of Aristotle herein are strictly to be kept, or nature to be followed. . . ."

However that may be, the 1667 edition of *Paradise Lost* presents a firmly organized five-act epic, perfectly exemplifying what were thought to be the Aristotelian requirements for structure. It successfully achieves what Sidney had earlier attempted, and it certainly out-Gondiberts Davenant. Its plot is seen at a glance to consist of five "acts" (with appropriate "scenes"), and the cumulative effect of these acts is exactly what Davenant said it should be.

Act I presents Satan's revival in Hell, and the council's sketching out of the plot against man with Satan's voyage to the universe; books 1 and 2. (Throughout, in order to reduce the exposition to the very nadir of *simplesse,* Arabic numerals will be used to indicate the books of 1667, Roman for those of 1674.) Act II, having opened with a scene in Heaven firmly focussed on the curve of Satan's flight, carries him to earth and leads to his first attempt to put the plot in operation; books 3 and 4. Act III, with that freedom which is one of the recognized advantages of epic, returns us in actual time to events in the past, the war in Heaven and Satan's defeat; books 5 and 6. In terms of formal development—the subject of actual and apparent time is far too complex for attention here—it gives a decided turn to the plot's development: Satan is twice temporarily defeated. Act IV is the crucial act. It consists of books 7 and 8: book 7, Raphael's account of the Creation and the colloquy on astronomy and woman, now known to us as books VII and VIII; and book 8, the book of the Fall, known to us as book IX. This act decisively changes the direction of the action: Satan has at last succeeded; and this "counterturn" is confirmed by the final act, books 9 and 10. Act V presents the immediate consequences of the Fall (book 9, now known to us as X), and the scriptural vision of misery, Michael's prophecy, with the expulsion from Paradise (book 10, now known to us as XI and XII).

The ideal formal requirements for five-act epic set forth in the Preface to *Gondibert* could hardly be more adequately fulfilled. Says Davenant:

> The first *Act* is the general preparative, by rendring the chiefest characters of persons, and ending with something that looks like an obscure promise of design. [So in **Paradise Lost** Satan, and the first sketch of the design against man which provides the poem with its plot.] The second begins with an introducement of new persons [God, the Son, the angels], so finishes all the characters [Adam and Eve], and ends with some little performance of that design which was promis'd at the parting of the first *Act* [Satan inducing Eve's dream of evil]. The third makes a visible correspondence in the underwalks, or lesser intrigues, of persons [Satan's conflict with God], and ends with an ample turn of the main design and expectation of new [Satan's temporary defeat in Heaven, from which, as we know, he has already partially recovered]. The fourth, ever having occasion to be the longest [so indeed it certainly is in **Paradise Lost,** 1667] gives a notorious turn to all the underwalks [the Creation], and a counterturn to that main design which chang'd in the third [Satan's successful achievement of man's fall]. The fifth begins with an intire diversion of the main and dependent Plotts [the penitence of Adam and Eve, the Son's intercession, Satan's return to hell—though perhaps here alone Milton faults in his design], then makes the general correspondence of the persons more discernible [Michael's implied commentary on the action], and ends with an easy untying [in **Paradise Lost,** uneasy tying?], of those particular knots which made a contexture of the whole, leaving such satisfaction of probabilities with the Spectator as may perswade him that neither Fortune in the fate of Persons, nor the Writer in the Representment, have been unnatural or exorbitant.[4]

It seems a pity that the Satanic interpreters of **Paradise Lost** have not generally been familiar with the five-act epic theory, or with Davenant's preface, or with the 1667 edition, when such satisfaction of probabilities might have been theirs. For the implications of the ten-book division of the poem are too plain to need much comment. The five-act structural emphasis comes down heavily on the crucial fourth act: Satan's successful counterturning of God's creative design when man's fall is accomplished. The "main design," artfully left doubtful at the end of the first two acts, and given a "turn" at the end of the third, receives its definitive pattern through the counterturn at the end of the fourth (book 8, or IX). What follows in the final act, the vision of unending earthly misery and the expulsion from Paraside, serves only to make clear the pattern of woe which makes the contexture of the whole.

Was it Milton's aim in the redivision of the poem in 1674 to shift this weight of emphasis from the book of the Fall, and so to offset the not merely dramatic but tragic implications of the counterturn in what looked like Act IV? The redivision does not change the actual structure of his poem in any way. Does it, however, by suggesting a different structural pattern, bring out implications muted in the earlier division?

### IV

A poem is not, in spite of Davenant and neo-classicism, a "building"; it moves in time, it does not stand in space. Yet a poet may not unjustifiably say, with Davenant, "you may next please, having examined the substance, to take a view of the form, and observe if I have methodically and with discretion disposed of the materials.. . ." Under some circumstances he may even be justified in imitating some of the architectural tricks, so popular in the seventeenth century, whereby an appearance of considerable extension is given to an unavoidably narrow edifice.

If the term "baroque" is applicable to Milton, it can certainly be used to describe the most obvious effect he achieved by turning books 7 and 10 into books VII and VIII and books XI and XII. Did he remember at this point, one wonders, the baroque illusion which offsets the narrowness of the Laudian chapel at Peterhouse (where flowing curves along the short horizontal much extend the facade) or the great curve of the collonade of St. Peter's? However that may be, the effect of the redivision in this respect is no mere illusion. It gives to the material of his poem following the defeat of Satan in Heaven an appearance of extension equal to its actual original weight in number of lines. The total number of lines in the last four books of the original poem is some three hundred—but *only* some three hundred—less than that of the first six books. The division of this material into six books gives the poem the just balance demanded by the treatment its theme has received. It is the ten-book division which, in this respect, is an illusion. Is the five-act pattern an illusion also?

The division into twelve more than modifies the five-act scheme. By presenting an arrangement reminiscent of Virgil's it induces a pattern of emphasis very different from that examined in the preceding section. Obviously the twelve books of 1674 fall into six groups of two books each. The first three groups remain as they were, with the decision of the action left temporarily in the balance. But the fourth group now presents, not the Creation and Fall (7 and 8), but the Creation and Adam's progressive understanding of his situation through his colloquy with Raphael (old 7 become VII and VIII). The fifth group now presents in combination Adam's fall and penitence (the second half of old Act IV with the first half of old Act V; old 8 and 9, new IX and X). And the sixth the vision of human misery, and Michael's prophecy of the Messiah with the expulsion (old 10 become XI and XII).

The shift in grouping is so simple, involving as it does mere numbering, that the importance of the result may pass unrecognized. The mind of a responsive reader does rest, consciously or unconsciously, at the end of each book of a long poem, and at the end of each pair. The reader is induced so to rest in *Paradise Lost* by the invocations and the new departures in subject matter in the first three pairs of the poem. This rhythm will be continued to the end. In the 1667 arrangement the mind will come to rest on the Fall and the expulsion; looking backward, it will see its rests at the ends of the first three groups as premonitions of these events. In the 1674 version, it will come to rest on Adam's understanding of his situation (and of love), reached under Raphael's direction, on the contrition of Adam and Eve and their hope of mercy, and consequently on the Messianic prophecy of final victory as well as on the expulsion from Paradise.

As one looks back over a poem in which the rests have come as they do in the 1674 division, one sees that the structural stress has throughout fallen with increasing weight on the foreshadowings of the Son's ultimate triumph, on the operations of the divine mercy and love. It is here that *Paradise Lost* reproduces while modifying the large structural pattern of the *Aeneid,* with its steadily repeated prophecies of Roman glory. The correspondence is not exact. How could it be? But the expressive reminiscence is clear in 1674, as it was not in 1667. Indeed, whereas the prophecy sounded most clearly by Virgil at the end of books two (Creusa), four (Mercury), six (the Sibyl), and eight (Vulcan), dies away in the fury of the struggle with Turnus, the prophetic note of *Paradise Lost* swells from the ambiguity of Satan's view from the steps that link Heaven and Earth, and of the scales seen aloft, through the victory of the Son in Heaven to Michael's final prophecy. Moreover, in the new pattern, implications lost in the tragic structure of 1667, are underlined for the memory. One example must suffice. We are in error when we see the discourse on love at the end of book VIII and of the fourth group merely as prelude to and motivation for the Fall; it is also prelude to man's restoration and to the reconciliation of Adam and Eve at the end of book X and of group five. Adam in fact falls in imagination when he speaks wildly of Eve's beauty in book VIII; he is restored to sanity by the intervention of Raphael before the

book ends. When at the end of the next two-book group we come to rest on the reconciliation of Adam and Eve, we shall look back across the Fall, not so much to Adam's imaginative lapse as to the sanity Raphael taught. And we shall look forward to Adam's restoration to something more than mere sanity at the end of the two-book group to come.

Such is Milton's discretion in the new disposition of his materials. The purpose of the redivision is to reduce the structural emphasis on the Fall of man and to increase the emphasis on his restoration. And this shift in emphasis is underlined by other structural effects of the redivision which combine to shift onward the poem's centre of gravity.

V

The ten books of 1667 will divide in but two ways: into five "acts" and into two blocks of five. The twelve books of 1674 (such is the force of simple arithmetic) divide in three ways.

Like the *Aeneid,* the *Paradise Lost* of 1674 consists of three movements of four books apiece. As with the "Hymn" of the *Nativity Ode* and with *Lycidas,* the three movements develop variations on a basic pattern. Virgil's first movement of four books turns upon Dido (and Creusa); his second carries Aeneas from Carthage to the moment when Turnus is about to attack, by way of the Sibyl; his third describes the war with the Latins. No correspondence to this pattern of three large and equally balanced movements is suggested by the ten-book division of 1667. In 1674 the three movements are clearly defined: one turns upon Satan, one upon the Son, one upon Man. The curve of the first is defined by Satan, reviving and frustrated, of the second by the Son as avenging justice and as creative love, of the third by Adam's fall and restoration. The rests at the ends of the first two movements fall upon the scales seen in heaven and on the delicate balance of Adam's original perfection, of the third on the balance to be made up at the last.

Each of these movements pauses and turns, as do Virgil's, upon its centre. It is not merely the direction of Satan's actual flight which changes between books III and IV; the apparent revival which has brought him to the verge of heaven's light now becomes a clear process of degeneration marked by God's comments, Satan's soliloquy, and his discomfiture in the garden. So the second turns with the Son from avenging justice to creation. So the third turns from sin through penance towards regeneration.

However one looks at the structure of *Paradise Lost* in its new division, attention is focused firmly on one point, variously indicated from different angles. The ten-book division presents a five-act structure, and that structure is tragic. Its centre, if it has one, lies between books 5 and 6; that is to say, in the midst of the War in Heaven, with evil at its most arrogant height. But that centre is an illusion which obscures the halving of the poem by actual number of lines. The redivision of 1674 presents a poem which in structural pattern, however viewed, hangs self-balanced on its centre. That centre is between books VI and VII, with evil on the one hand frustrated, and on the other creation and recreation. Every structural subdivision in the poem is so aimed.

Is the new absent-mindedness of our first parent, one wonders, after all so insignificant, as he

> Thought him still speaking, still stood fixt to hear;
> Then as new wak't thus gratefully repli'd . . . ;

or Michael's medial pause? And is it wholly a flight of fancy to see the simple redivision as changing a tragic pattern into the three-fold pattern of a divine comedy, underlining the intention expressed in the opening invocation by throwing into clearer relief the adaptation and modification of the Virgilian pattern?

Yet it would not be true to say that by the simple act of redivision Milton has repudiated the theory of the five-act epic. Five acts can still be readily discerned in the 1674 poem, though they are not the same as those of 1667. Milton makes no sacrifices; to be "still closing up truth to truth" is for him the golden rule in epic structure as well as in theology and arithmetic. The first two "acts" remain unchanged: books I and II, Satan's revival and the sketching out of the plot; books III and IV, his arrival in Paradise and the failure of his first attempt. But Act III is no longer simply books V and VI, the war in heaven and Satan's defeat; it is now the whole of Raphael's reminiscential narrative, with the commentary, books V to VIII, in the actual time-scheme of the poem one day. Act IV is now books IX and X, the Fall and its consequences ending in penitence, in the actual time-scheme one more day, while Act V has become books XI and XII (old 10), man's misery and redemption or, in terms of Adam himself, the process of regeneration, the work of but another day.

In this dramatic scheme the new Act III provides a most "ample turn of the main design and expectation of new," but the turn is no longer in Satan's temporary defeat at the hands of avenging justice; it is in the operations of creative love as it acts purposefully, and in Adam's progressive recognition of its meaning. Act IV, still the crucial act, no longer gives "a counterturn to that main design which changed in the third," for its end is no longer Satan's success but man's penitence and reconciliation; it therefore underlines the turn of Act III and prepares for the final victory to be prophesied in Act V.

The dramatic and epic structural patterns are thus brought into exact alignment by the simple redivision of 1674. *Paradise Lost* is in fact the consummate example of five-act epic structure. Its author's final tinkering clarified its beautifully coherent epic pattern on the Virgilian model and adjusted its drama to leave with the reader a much deeper "satisfaction of probabilities."

## VI

Did Milton succeed through this redivision in changing "those notes" to epic? That is another question. It is with structural pattern that we have been directly concerned throughout, and with intention as it expresses itself in structural emphasis, not with execution. We have indeed been dealing with an imitation of an imitation several times removed, and with the shadow of a fictional skeleton. The substance (and indeed the actual shape) of the fiction remained quite unchanged in 1674. But the change does alter the light in which it appears, and may suggest that it is at once less questionable and more questionable than has sometimes been thought.

Milton, it is clear, was by no means unaware of what has been called "the unconscious meaning" of *Paradise Lost.* It may be that in 1667 he was not quite aware of it, or that for some reason or other he was then much inclined towards it; it is certainly emphasized by his having written in ten books. But the 1674 renumbering indicates his consciousness of Satan's power over the poem, and (if it was not simply a trivial toying) the new disposition was meant to strengthen Satan's chains. Its motive was to shift the poem's emphasis and its centre in a way that would point more clearly to its stated intention. *Paradise Lost* was always meant to be a poem whose beginning is disobedience, which middle is woe, and whose ultimate end is restoration. It may be that the intention was clouded in 1667, or that Milton's view of restoration was obscured. The 1674 revision is at any rate an effort to clarify the poem's ways.

It is also clear that Milton's control over his vast material never wavered, though he may not always have been clear as to what he was doing or had done with it. He renumbers his books; he does not change his argument. The masses have been set in their places, though they have not been properly identified. And yet one must pause. If the disposition of the masses was patient of a tragic pattern of structural interpretation in 1667, the unmoved masses remain patient of it after the tinkering of 1674. If they were patient of a Virgilian patterning in 1674, they were already so in 1667. No amount of arithmetical ingenuity can obscure this fact. One must read both poems and see both patterns, for the two patterns suspend the theme between the horns of a paradox. This is the chief function of its structure.

Among the Miltonic virtues we have lately been taught to question—from organ music and amplifying imagery to simple honesty—architectonic skill is not yet numbered. Every interpreter, of whatever colour, will allude to it, even if it be only of purpose to imply in passing that this is a virtue typical of rigid Puritan neoclassicism. Both the devoted enthusiast and the iconoclast underline his claims to consistency and therewith his claim to having raised his great argument to a solid architectural height. The enthusiast would see him as a noble Colossus, last of some titanic race of Renaissance poets, towering in splendidly integrated certainty above the New Atlantis and the mutable flood engulfing it. The iconoclast chooses to see him either as inflexibly imposing his rigorous and suffocating will on paradise, or as hypocritically pretending to an assurance which nevertheless only reveals the confusion of his motives. Milton has, to be sure, himself invited such interpretations; but it might be better if we ignored them and saw him more often (as Carlyle saw a lesser poet) as one "carrying a bit of chaos about him . . . which he is manufacturing into cosmos." He is not profitably to be identified with any of these monsters of our distraught imagination—or of his own.

Nor are his great poems, for all their regularity of structure, to be regarded as rigidly static compositions of the architectural order appropriate to Victorian tombs and monuments. They are works of poetic art, the pattern of their evolution in time beginning usually as a reminiscence of some pattern established in the past, and nearly always controlled by easily recognizable structural balance, but always in process of development through conflict and resolution towards a harmony which is dynamic because it is the result of tension released in a creative act. This harmony they by no means always perfectly achieve, less frequently than Milton himself wished to believe. Nor need they so achieve it. They do not represent or express or entomb an unutterable perfection; they indicate a direction in which perfection may be achieved. At their best they pause, like Michael, betwixt a world destroyed and world restored; and the creative act for poet and reader often comes afterwards, while the poem is "thought . . . still speaking," like Raphael.

*Paradise Lost* (Professor Bush has made one certain) is to be regarded as no mausoleum of decayed classicism. It is rather to be read as a metaphor of spiritual evolution. Its structural pattern is neither rigidly fixed nor shifted; it is shifting. The firmness with which Milton defines his structural blocks serves chiefly to sustain the Christian paradox on which the metaphor is hinged. It would seem that in the redivision of 1674 Milton underlines the direction of the shifting. Whatever the cause, it indicates what Professor Thompson himself has so well illustrated: he remained intent on the perfect adaptation of the pattern to the end.

### Notes

1. *Essays on Milton*, 1914, pp. 83-4.

2. "For *Paradise Lost, XI-XII*," *Philological Quarterly,* XXII (1943), 376-82.

3. On this theory before Milton, see R. H. Perkinson, "The Epic in Five Acts," *Studies in Philology,* XLIII (1946), 465-81.

4. *Critical Essays of the Seventeenth Century,* ed. Spingarn, II, 17-18.

   [EDITOR'S NOTE. For other comments on the structure and patterns of *Paradise Lost,* see E. E. Stoll, *UTQ,* III (1933-34), 3-16; B. Rajan, *"Paradise Lost" and the Seventeenth Century Reader,* 1947; A.

S. P. Woodhouse, *UTQ,* XXII (1952-53), 109-27; R. Colie, *JWCI,* XXIII (1960), 127-38; J. B. Stroup, *TSL,* VI (1961), 71-5; H. F. Robins, *JEGP,* LX (1961), 699-711; O. B. Hardison, Jr., *The Enduring Monument,* 1962; on classical models and principles, C. M. Bowra, *From Virgil to Milton,* 1945; D. Bush, *CJ,* XLVII (1952), 178-82, 203-4; J. Richardson, *CL,* XVI (1962), 321-31; K. Svendsen, *PQ,* XXVIII (1949), 185-206; J. M. Steadman, *SN,* XXXI (1959), 159-73; on the dramatic element, J. H. Hanford, *SP,* XIV (1917), 178-95; R. Durr, *JAAC,* XIII (1955), 520-26; D. Knight, *SAQ,* 63 (1964), 44-59.]

### Geoffrey Hartman (essay date 1958)

SOURCE: "Milton's Counterplot," in *Milton: A Collection of Critical Essays,* edited by Louis L. Martz, Prentice-Hall, Inc., 1968, pp. 100-108.

[*In the following essay, which was originally published in* ELH: A Journal of English Literary History *in 1958, Hartman claims that there are two plots in the epic that work to contrapuntal effect and which serve to emphasize God's remoteness and power.*]

Milton's description of the building of Pandemonium ends with a reference to the architect, Mammon, also known to the ancient world as Mulciber:

> and how he fell
> From Heav'n, they fabl'd, thrown by angry *Jove*
> Sheer o'er the Crystal Battlements: from Morn
> To Noon he fell, from Noon to dewy Eve,
> A Summer's day; and with the setting Sun
> Dropt from the Zenith like a falling Star,
> On *Lemnos* th' ægæan Isle
>
> (*Paradise Lost* I, 740-6).

These verses stand out from a brilliant text as still more brilliant; or emerge from this text, which repeats on several levels the theme of quick or erring or mock activity, marked by a strange mood of calm, as if the narrative's burning wheel had suddenly disclosed a jewelled bearing. Their subject is a Fall, and it has been suggested that Milton's imagination was caught by the anticipation in the Mulciber story of a myth which stands at the center of his epic. Why the "caught" imagination should respond with a pastoral image, evoking a fall gradual and cool like the dying of a summer's day, and the sudden, no less aesthetically distant, dropping down of the star, is not explained. One recalls, without difficulty, similar moments of relief or distancing, especially in the cosmic fret of the first books: the comparison of angel forms lying entranced on the inflamed sea with autumnal leaves on Vallombrosa's shady brooks, or the simile of springtime bees and of the dreaming peasant at the end of Book I, or the applause following Mammon's speech in Book II, likened to lulling if hoarse cadence of winds after a storm, or even the appearance to

Satan of the world, when he has crossed Chaos and arrives with torn tackle in full view of this golden-chained star of smallest magnitude.

The evident purpose of the Mulciber story is to help prick inflated Pandemonium, and together with the lines that follow, to emphasize that Mammon's building is as shaky as its architect. This fits in well with the plot of the first two books, a description of the satanic host's effort to build on hell. But the verses on Mulciber also disclose, through their almost decorative character, a second plot, simultaneously expressed with the first, and which may be called the counterplot. Its hidden presence is responsible for the contrapuntal effects of the inserted fable.

The reader will not fail to recognize in Milton's account of the progress of Mulciber's fall the parody of a biblical rhythm: "And the evening and the morning were the (first) day." The thought of creation is present to Milton, somehow associated with this fall. Moreover, the picture of *angry* Jove blends with and gives way to that of *crystal* battlements, and the imperturbability of the summer's day through which the angel drops:

> from Morn
> To Noon he fell, from Noon to dewy Eve,
> A Summer's day;

while in the last part of his descent an image of splendor and effortlessness outshines that of anger or ignominy:

> and with the setting Sun
> Dropt from the Zenith like a falling Star.

In context, of course, this depiction is condemned as mere fabling, and there is nothing splendid or aloof in the way Milton retells the story:

> thus they relate,
> Erring; for he with his rebellious rout
> Fell long before; nor aught avail'd him now
> To have built in Heav'n high Tow'rs; nor did he scape
> By all his Engines, but was headlong sent
> With his industrious crew to build in hell.

(746-51)

Yet for a moment, while moving in the charmed land of pagan fable, away from the more literal truth in which he seeks supremacy over all fable, Milton reveals the overwhelming, if not autonomous drive of his imagination. Mulciber draws to himself a rhythm reminiscent of the account of the world's creation, and his story suggests both God and the creation undisturbed (Crystal Battlements . . . dewy Eve) by a fall which is said to occur later than the creation, yet actually preceded it. Here, surely, is a primary instance of Milton's automatically involving the idea of creation with that of the Fall. But further, and more fundamental, is the feeling of the text that God's anger is not anger at all, rather calm prescience, which sees that no fall will ultimately disturb the creation, whether Mulciber's fabled or Satan's real or Adam's universal Fall.

Milton's feeling for this divine imperturbability, for God's omnipotent knowledge that the creation will outlive death and sin, when expressed in such an indirect manner, may be characterized as the counterplot. For it does not often work on the reader as independent theme or subplot, but lodges in the vital parts of the overt action, emerging from it like good from evil. The root-feeling (if feeling is the proper word) for imperturbable providence radiates from many levels of the text. It has been given numerous interpretations in the history of criticism, the best perhaps, though impressionistic, by Coleridge: "Milton is the deity of prescience: he stands *ab extra* and drives a fiery chariot and four, making the horses feel the iron curb which holds them in." Satan's fixed mind and high disdain are perverted reflectors of this same cold passion, but doomed to perish in the restlessness of hell, and its compulsive gospel of the community of damnation. So deep-working is this spirit of the "glassy, cool, translucent wave," already invoked in *Comus,* that other poets find hard to resist it, and, like Wordsworth, seek to attain similar virtuosity in expressing "central peace, subsisting at the heart Of endless agitation." Milton's control is such, that even in the first dramatic account of Satan's expulsion, he makes the steady flame of God's act predominate over the theme of effort, anger, and vengefulness: in the following verses "Ethereal Sky" corresponds to the "Crystal Battlements" of Mulciber's fall, and the image of a projectile powerfully but steadily thrust forth (evoked in part by the immediate duplication of stress, letter and rhythmic patterns) recreates the imperturbability of that other, summer space:

> Him the Almighty Power
> Hurl'd headlong flaming from th'Ethereal Sky
> With hideous ruin and combustion down
> To bottomless perdition, there to dwell
> In Adamantine Chains and penal Fire . . .

(44-8)

One of the major means of realizing the counterplot is the simile. Throughout *Paradise Lost,* and eminently in the first two books, Milton has to bring the terrible sublime home to the reader's imagination. It would appear that he can only do this by way of analogy. Yet Milton rarely uses straight analogy, in which the observer and observed remain, relative to each other, on the same plane. Indeed, his finest effects are to employ magnifying and diminishing similes. Satan's shield, for example, is described as hanging on his shoulder like the moon, viewed through Galileo's telescope from Fiesole or in Valdarno (I, 284-91). The rich, elaborate pattern of such similes has often been noted and variously explained. Certain details, however, may be reconsidered.

The similes, first of all, not only magnify or diminish the doings in hell, but invariably put them at a distance. Just as the "Tuscan Artist" sees the moon through his telescope, so the artist of *Paradise Lost* shows hell at considerable remove, through a medium which, while it clarifies, also intervenes between reader and object. Milton varies points-of-view shifting in space and time so skilfully, that our sense of the reality of hell, of its power vis-a-vis man or God, never remains secure. Spirits, we know, can assume any shape they please; and Milton, like Spenser, uses this imaginative axiom to destroy the idea of the simple location of good and evil in the spiritual combat. But despite the insecurity, the abyss momentarily glimpsed under simple event, Milton's main effort in the first books is to make us believe in Satan as a real and terrible agent, yet never as an irresistible power. No doubt at all of Satan's influence: his success is writ large in religious history: which may also be one reason for the epic enumeration of demonic names and place-names in Book I. Nevertheless, even as we are closest to Satan, presented with the hottest view of hell's present and future appeal, all suggestion of irresistible influence must be expunged, if Milton's two means of divine justification, man's free will and God's foreknowledge of the creation's triumph, are to win consent.

These two dominant concepts, expressed through the counterplot, shed a calm and often cold radiance over all of **Paradise Lost,** issuing equally from the heart of faith and the center of self-determination. The similes must persuade us that man was and is "sufficient to have stood, though free to fall" (III, 99), that his reason and will, however fiercely tempted and besieged, stand on a pinnacle as firm and precarious as that on which the Christ of *Paradise Regained* (IV, 541 ff) suffers his last, greatest, archetypal temptation. They must show the persistence, in the depth of danger, passion or evil, of imperturbable reason, of a power working *ab extra.*

This they accomplish in several ways. They are, for example, marked by an emphasis on place names. It is the *Tuscan* artist who views the moon (Satan's shield) from the top of *Fesole* or in *Valdarno* through his optic glass, while he searches for new Lands, Rivers, Mountains on the spotty globe. Do not the place names serve to anchor this observer, and set him off from the vastness and vagueness of hell, its unnamed and restless geography, as well as from his attempt to leave the earth and rise by science above the lunar world? A recital of names is, of course, not reassuring of itself: no comfort accrues in hearing Moloch associated with *Rabba, Argob, Basan, Arnon,* or sinful Solomon with *Hinnom, Tophet, Gehenna* (I, 397-405). The point is that these places were once neutral, innocent of bloody or holy associations; it is man who has made them what they are, made the proper name a fearful or a hopeful sign (cf. XI, 836-39). Will Valdarno and Fiesole become such by-words as Tophet and Gehenna? At the moment they are still hieroglyphs, words whose ultimate meaning is in the balance. They suggest the inviolate shelter of the created world rather than the incursions of a demonic world. Yet we sense that, if Galileo uses the shelter and Ark of this world to dream of other worlds, paying optical rites to the moon, Fiesole, Valdarno, even Vallombrosa may yield to the tug of a demonic interpretation and soon become a part of hell's unprotected marl.

Though the figure of the observer *ab extra* is striking in Milton's evocation of Galileo, it becomes more subtly

patent in a simile a few lines further on, which tells how the angel forms lay entranced on hell's inflamed sea

> Thick as Autumnal Leaves that strow the Brooks
> In *Vallombrosa,* where th'Etrurian shades
> High overarch't imbow'r; or scatter'd sedge
> Afloat, when with fierce winds *Orion* arm'd
> Hath vext the Red-Sea Coast, whose waves o'erthrew
> *Busiris* and his *Memphian* Chivalry,
> While with perfidious hatred they pursu'd
> The sojourners of *Goshen,* who beheld
> From the safe shore thir floating Carcasses
> And broken Chariot Wheels

(302-11)

A finer modulation of aesthetic distance can hardly be found: we start at the point of maximum contrast, with the angels prostrate on the lake, in a region "vaulted with fire" (298), viewed as leaves fallen seasonally on a sheltered brook vaulted by shade; go next to the image of sea-weed scattered by storm, and finally, without break of focus, to the Israelites watching "from the safe shore" the floating bodies and parts of their pursuers. And, as in music, where one theme fading, another emerges to its place, while the image of calm and natural death changes to that of violent and supernatural destruction, the figure of the observer *ab extra* becomes explicit, substituting for the original glimpse of inviolable peace.

Could the counterplot be clearer? A simile intended to sharpen our view of the innumerable stunned host of hell, just before it is roused by Satan, at the same time sharpens our sense of the imperturbable order of the creation, and of the coming storm, and of the survival of man through providence and his safe-shored will. Satan, standing clear of the rout, prepares to vex his legions to new evil:

> on the Beach
> Of that inflamed Sea, he stood and call'd
> His Legions, Angel Forms, who lay intrans't
> Thick as Autumnal Leaves . . .

but the scenes the poet himself calls up mimic hell's defeat before Satan's voice is fully heard, and whatever sought to destroy the calm of autumnal leaves lies lifeless as scattered sedge. The continuity of the similes hinges on the middle image of Orion, which sketches both Satan's power to rouse the fallen host and God's power to scatter and destroy it. In this "plot counterplot" the hand of Satan is not ultimately distinguishable from the will of God.

A further instance, more complex still, is found at the end of Book I. Milton compares the host gathered in the gates of Pandemonium to bees at springtime (768 ff). The wonder of this incongruity has been preserved by many explanations. It is clearly a simile which, like others we have adduced, diminishes hell while it magnifies creation. The bees are fruitful, and their existence in the teeth of Satan drowns out the sonorous *hiss* of hell. Their "straw-built Citadel" will survive "bossy" Pandemonium. As Dr. Johnson kicking the stone kicks all excessive idealism, so

Milton's bees rub their balm against all excessive demonism. But the irony may not end there. Are the devils not those bees who bring food out of the eater, sweetness out of the strong (Judges 15: 5-19)?

It may also be more than a coincidence that the most famous in this genre of similes describes the bustle of the Carthaginians as seen by storm-exiled Aeneas (*Aeneid* I, 430-40). Enveloped in a cloud by his divine mother, Aeneas looks down from the top of a hill onto a people busily building their city like a swarm of bees at summer's return, and is forced to cry: "O fortunati, quorum iam moenia surgunt!"—o fortunate people, whose walls are already rising! Then Vergil, as if to dispel any impression of despair, adds: *mirabile dictu,* a wonder! Aeneas walks among the Carthaginians made invisible by divine gift.

Here the counterplot thickens, and we behold one of Milton's amazing transpositions of classical texts. Aeneas strives to found Rome, which will outlast Carthage. The bees building in Vergil's text intimate a spirit of creativity seasonally renewed and independent of the particular civilization. The bees in Milton's text represent the same privilege and promise. Aeneas wrapped in the cloud is the observer *ab extra,* the person on the shore, and his impatient cry is of one who desires to build a civilization beyond decay, perhaps even beyond the wrath of the gods. An emergent, as yet invisible figure in Milton's text shares the hero's cry: he has seen Mammon and his troop build Pandemonium, Satan's band swarm triumphant about their citadel: despite this, can the walls of creation outlive Satan as Rome the ancient world?

All this would be putative or extrinsic if based solely on the simile of the bees. For this simile, like the middle image of Orion vexing the Red Sea, is indeterminate in its implications, a kind of visual pivot in a series of images which act in sequence and once more reveal the counterplot. Its indeterminacy is comparable to Milton's previously mentioned use of proper nouns, and his overall stylistic use of the *pivot,* by means of which images and words are made to refer both backwards and forwards, giving the verse period unusual balance and flexibility. The series in question begins with the trooping to Pandemonium, and we now give the entire modulation which moves through several similes:

>         all access was throng'd, the Gates
> And Porches wide, but chief the spacious Hall
> (Though like a cover'd field, where Champions bold
> Wont ride in arm'd, and at the Soldan's chair
> Defi'd the best of *Paynim* chivalry
> To mortal combat or career with Lance)
> Thick swarm'd, both on the ground and in the air,
> Brusht with the hiss of rustling wings. As Bees
> In spring time, when the Sun with *Taurus* rides,
> Pour forth thir populous youth about the Hive
> In clusters; they among fresh dews and flowers
> Fly to and fro, or on the smoothed Plank,
> The suburb of thir Straw-built Citadel,
> New rubb'd with Balm, expatiate and confer

> Thir State affairs. So thick the aery crowd
> Swarm'd and were strait'n'd; till the Signal giv'n,
> Behold a wonder! they but now who seem'd
> In bigness to surpass Earth's Giant Sons
> Now less than smallest Dwarfs, in narrow room
> Throng numberless, like that Pigmean Race
> Beyond the *Indian* Mount, or Faery Elves,
> Whose midnight Revels, by a Forest side
> Or Fountain some belated Peasant sees,
> Or dreams he sees, while over-head the Moon
> Sits Arbitress, and nearer to the Earth
> Wheels her pale course, they on thir mirth and dance
> Intent, with jocund Music charm his ear;
> At once with joy and fear his heart rebounds.

>                 (761-88)

The very images which marshall the legions of hell to our view reveal simultaneously that the issue of Satan's triumph or defeat, his real or mock power, is in the hand of a *secret arbiter,* whether God and divine prescience or man and free will. In the first simile the observer *ab extra* is the Soldan, who as a type of Satan overshadows the outcome of the combat between pagan and christian warriors in the "cover'd field." The second simile is indeterminate in tenor, except that it diminishes the satanic thousands, blending them and their war-like intents with a picture of natural, peaceful creativity, Sun and Taurus presiding in place of the Soldan. "Behold a wonder!" echoes the *mirabile dictu* of Vergil's story, and prepares the coming of a divine observer. The mighty host is seen to shrink to the size of Pigmies (the third simile), and we know that these, the "small infantry," as Milton had called them with a pun reflecting the double perspective of the first books, can be overshadowed by Cranes (575-6). The verse period then carries us still further from the main action as the diminished devils are also compared to Faery Elves glimpsed at their midnight revels by some belated Peasant. From the presence and pomp of hell we have slowly slipped into a pastoral.

Yet does not this static moment hide an inner combat more real than that for which hell is preparing? It is midnight, the pivot between day and day, and in the Peasant's mind a similar point of balance seems to obtain. He is not fully certain of the significance or even reality of the Fairy ring. Like Aeneas in Hades, who glimpses the shade of Dido (*Aeneid* VI, 450-5), he "sees, Or dreams he sees" something barely distinguishable from the pallid dark, obscure as the new moon through clouds. What an intensity of calm is here, reflecting a mind balanced on the critical pivot, as a point of stillness is reached at greatest remove from the threats and reverberations of hell! But even as the man stands uncertain, the image of the moon overhead becomes intense, it has sat there all the time as arbiter, now wheels closer to the earth, and the Peasant's heart rebounds with a secret intuition bringing at once joy and fear.

The moon, clearly, is a last transformation of the image of the observer *ab extra,* Soldan, Sun and Taurus, Peasant. What was a type of Satan overshadowing the outcome of the real or spiritual combat is converted into a presentment of the individual's naive and autonomous power of discrimination, his free reason, secretly linked with a superior influence, as the moon overhead. The figure of the firmly placed observer culminates in that of the secret arbiter. Yet this moon is not an unambiguous symbol of the secret arbiter. A feeling of the moon's uncertain, changeable nature—incorruptible yet spotty, waxing and waning (I, 284-291; II, 659-666; see also "mooned horns," IV, 978, quoted below)—is subtly present. It reflects this series of images in which the poet constantly suggests, destroys and recreates the idea of an imperturbably transcendent discrimination. The moon that "Sits Arbitress" seems to complete the counterplot, but is only the imperfect sign of a figure not revealed till Book IV. Thus the whole cycle of to and fro, big and small, Pigmies or Elves, seeing or dreaming, far and near, joy and fear, this uneasy flux of couplets, alternatives and reversals, is continued when we learn, in the final lines of Book I, that far within Pandemonium, perhaps as far from consciousness as hell is from the thoughts of the Peasant or demonic power from the jocund, if intent music of the fairy revelers, Satan and the greatest of his Lords sit in their own, unreduced dimensions.

We meet the Peasant once more in *Paradise Lost,* and in a simile which seems to want to outdo the apparent incongruity of all others. At the end of Book IV, Gabriel and his files confront Satan apprehended squatting in Paradise, a toad at the ear of Eve. A heroically contemptuous exchange follows, and Satan's taunts finally so incense the Angel Squaddron that they

> Turn'd fiery red, sharp'ning in mooned horns
> Thir Phalanx, and began to hem him round
> With ported Spears, as thick as when a field
> Of *Ceres* ripe for harvest waving bends
> Her bearded Grove of ears, which way the wind
> Sways them; the careful Plowman doubting stands
> Lest on the threshing floor his hopeful sheaves
> Prove chaff. On th'other side *Satan* alarm'd
> Collecting all his might dilated stood,
> Like *Teneriff* or *Atlas* unremov'd:
> His stature reacht the Sky, and on his Crest
> Sat horror Plum'd; nor wanted in his grasp
> What seem'd both Spear and Shield: now dreadful deeds
> Might have ensu'd, nor only Paradise
> In this commotion, but the Starry Cope
> Of Heav'n perhaps, or all the Elements
> At least had gone to rack, disturb'd and torn
> With violence of this conflict, had not soon
> Th'Eternal to prevent such horrid fray
> Hung forth in Heav'n his golden Scales, yet seen
> Betwixt *Astrea* and the *Scorpion* sign,
> Wherein all things created first he weigh'd,
> The pendulous round Earth with balanc'd Air
> In counterpoise, now ponders all events,
> Battles and Realms . . .

> (978-1002)

The question of Satan's power does not appear to be academic, at least not at first. The simile which, on previous

occasions, pretended to illustrate hell's greatness but actually diminished hell and magnified the creation, is used here just as effectively against heaven. Milton, by dilating Satan, and distancing the spears of the angel phalanx as ears ready for reaping, creates the impression of a balance of power between heaven and hell. Yet the image which remains in control is neither of Satan nor of the Angels but of the wheatfield, first as its bearded ears bend with the wind, then as contemplated by the Plowman. Here the counterplot achieves its most consummate form. *Paradise Lost* was written not for the sake of heaven or hell but for the sake of the creation. What is all the fuss about if not to preserve the "self-balanc't" earth? The center around which and to which all actions turn is whether man can stand though free to fall, whether man and the world can survive their autonomy. The issue may not therefore be determined on the supernatural level by the direct clash of heaven and hell, only by these two arbiters: man's free will, and God's foreknowledge. The ripe grain sways in the wind, so does the mind which has tended it. Between ripeness and ripeness gathered falls the wind, the threshing floor, the labour of ancient *ears,* the question of the relation of God's will to man's will. The ears appear to be at the mercy of the wind, what about the thoughts, the "hopeful sheaves" of the Plowman? The fate of the world lies between Gabriel and Satan, but also between the wind and the ripe ears, but also between man and his thoughts. Finally God, supreme arbiter, overbalances the balance with the same pair of golden scales (suspended yet between Virgin and Scorpion) in which the balanced earth weighed at its first creation.

## Frank Kermode (essay date 1960)

SOURCE: "Adam Unparadised," in *The Living Milton: Essays by Various Hands,* Routledge and Kegan Paul, 1960, pp. 122-42.

*[In the following essay, Kermode contends that the basic theme of* Paradise Lost *is the recognition of lost possibilities and says that to embody this theme Milton exhibits life in a "great symbolic attitude" and not through explanations of how and why.]*

Miss Rosemond Tuve, in her magnificent and too brief book, has persuasively expounded Milton's treatment in the minor poems of certain great central themes. They lie at the heart of each poem and govern its secondary characteristics of imagery and diction; given the theme, the poet thinks in the figures appropriate to it, and in every case the theme and the figures have a long and rich history. 'The subject of *L'Allegro* is every man's Mirth, our Mirth, the very Grace herself with all she can include';[1] the *Hymn on the Morning of Christ's Nativity* proliferates images of harmony because its theme is the Incarnation. I now take a step of which Miss Tuve would probably not approve, and add that beneath these figures and themes there is Milton's profound and personal devotion to an even more radical topic, potentially coextensive with all human experience: the loss of Eden. In the **Hymn** there is a moment of peace and harmony in history—the 'Augustan peace', which looks back to human wholeness and incorruption, as well as forward to a time when, after generations of human anguish, the original harmony will be restored. The same moment of stillness, poised between past and future, is there in 'At a Solemn Musick', for music remembers as well as prefigures. In **Comus** too there is presented that moment of harmony, of reunion and restitution, that prefigures the final end, and in **Comus** as in the others there is an emphasis on the long continuance of grief and suffering; for in the much misunderstood Epilogue Adonis is still not cured of his wound and Venus 'sadly sits'. Only in the future will Cupid be united with Psyche and the twins of Paradise, Youth and Joy, be born. **Lycidas** tells of disorder, corruption, false glory as incident to life here and now, with order, health, and the perfect witness of God to come. All of them speak of something that is gone.

**Paradise Lost** deals most directly with this basic theme, the recognition of lost possibilities of joy, order, health, the contrast between what we can imagine as human and what is so here and now; the sensuous import of the myth of the lost Eden. To embody this theme is the main business of **Paradise Lost;** thus will life be displayed in some great symbolic attitude and not by the poet's explanations of the how and the why. His first task is to get clear the human experience of the potency of delight, and its necessary frustration, and if he cannot do that the poem will fail no matter what is added of morality, theology or history.

My difficulty in establishing this point is that some will think it too obvious to be thus laboured, and others will think it in need of much more elaborate defence. What is rare is to find people who read **Paradise Lost** as if it were true that the power of joy and its loss is its theme; and though it is true that for certain well-known and important reasons Milton's poem is not accessible to the same methods of reading as Romantic literature, it is also true that this is the theme of *The Prelude* and that we can do some harm by insisting too strongly upon differences at the expense of profound similarities. Anyway, I think I can make my point in a somewhat different way by a reference to Bentley, and in particular to his observations on the last lines of **Paradise Lost,** stale as this subject may seem.

Adam, hearing Michael's promise of a time when 'Earth / Shall all be Paradise, far happier place / Than this of *Eden*' (xii. 463-5) is 'replete with joy and wonder' (468) and replies with the famous cry of *felix culpa:*

> full of doubt I stand,
> Whether I should repent me now of sin
> By mee done and occasiond, or rejoice
> Much more, that much more good thereof shall spring
>     . . .

> (473-6)

Michael says that the Comforter will watch over and arm the faithful; Adam, benefiting by Michael's foretelling of

the future (in which 'time stands fixt' as it does in the poem) has now all possible wisdom (575-6); and Eve is well content with her lot. And thus matters stand when Eden is closed, and Adam and Eve move away

> The World was all before them, where to choose
> Thir place of rest, and Providence thir guide:
> They hand in hand with wandring steps and slow,
> Through *Eden* took thir solitarie way.

> (xii. 646-9)

'Why' asks Bentley, 'does this distich dismiss our first parents in anguish, and the reader in melancholy? And how can the expression be justified, *with wandring steps and slow?* Why *wandring?*

Erratick steps? Very improper, when, in the line before, they were *guided by Providence*. And why slow? even when Eve has professed her readiness and alacrity for the journey:

>     but now lead on;
> In me is no delay.

And why their *solitarie way?* All words to represent a sorrowful parting? when even their former walks in Paradise were as solitary as their way now; there being nobody besides them two both here and there. Shall I therefore, after so many prior presumptions, presume at last to offer a distich, as close as may be to the author's words, and *entirely agreeable to his scheme?*

> Then hand in hand with *social* steps their way
> Through Eden took, *with heavenly comfort cheer'd.*'

Bentley assumes that he has exact knowledge of Milton's 'scheme', and quarrels with the text for not fitting it. He seems to be forgetting God's instructions to Michael—'so send them forth, though sorrowing, yet in peace' (xi. 117), and also Adam's knowledge of the events leading up to the happy consummation; yet it remains true that if Milton's 'scheme' was simply to show that everything would come out right in the end, and that this should keenly please both Adam and ourselves, Bentley is not at all silly here; or if he is, so are more modern commentators who, supported by all that is now known about the topic *felix culpa,* tend to read the poem in a rather similar way though without actually rewriting it, by concentrating on Milton's intention, somewhat neglected in the past, to present this belated joy of Adam's as central to the whole poem. There is, of course, such an intention or 'scheme'; the mistake is to suppose that it is paramount. It is in fact subsidiary, **Paradise Lost** being a poem, to the less explicable theme of joy and woe, which has to be expressed in terms of the myth, as a contrast between the original justice of Paradise and the mess of history: between Paradise and Paradise lost. The poem is tragic. If we regard it as a document in the history of ideas, ignoring what it does to our senses, we shall of course find ideas, as Bentley did, and conceivably the closing lines will seem out of true. But our disrespect for Bentley's Milton, and in this place particularly, is

proof that the poem itself will prevent our doing this unless we are very stubborn or not very susceptible to poetry. The last lines of the poem are, we *feel,* exactly right,
for all that Adam has cried out for pleasure; death de-
nounced, he has lost his Original Joy. The tragedy is a
matter of *fact,* of life as we feel it; the hope of restoration
is a matter of faith, and faith is 'the substance of things
hoped for, the evidence of things unseen'—a matter altogether less simple, sensuous, and passionate, altogether
less primitive. We are reminded that 'the conception that
man is mortal, by his nature and essence, seems to be entirely alien to mythical and primitive religious thought'.[2]
In the poem we deplore the accidental loss of native immortality more than we can applaud its gracious restoration.

One of the effects of mixing up Milton with the Authorized Version, and of intruding mistaken ideas of Puritanism into his verse, is that it can become very hard to see
what is made absolutely plain: that for Milton the joy of
Paradise is very much a matter of the senses. The Authorized Version says that 'the Lord God planted a garden'
(Gen. ii. 8) and that he 'took the man and put him into the
garden of Eden to dress it and keep it' (ii. 15). But even in
Gen. ii. 8 the Latin texts usually have *in paradisum vo-
luptatis* 'into a paradise of pleasure'—this is the reading
of the Vulgate currently in use. And the Latin version of ii.
15 gives *in paradiso deliciarum.* Milton's Paradise is that
of the Latin version; in it, humanity without guilt is 'to all
delight of human sense expos'd' (iv. 206), and he insists
on this throughout. Studying the exegetical tradition on
this point, Sister Mary Corcoran makes it plain that Milton
pushes this sensuous pleasure much harder than his
'scheme' as Bentley and others might conceive it, required.
For example, he rejected the strong tradition that the first
marriage was not consummated until after the Fall, choosing to ignore the difficulty about children conceived before
but born after it. For this there may be an historical explanation in the Puritan cult of married love; but it could not
account for what has been called Milton's 'almost Dionysiac treatment'[3] of sexuality before the Fall; Sister Corcoran is sorry that she can't even quite believe the assertion
that 'in those hearts / Love unlibidinous reignd (v. 449-
50).[4]

In fact Milton went to great trouble to get this point firmly
made; had he failed no amount of finesse in other places
could have held the poem together; and it is therefore just
as well that nothing in the poem is more beautifully
achieved.

Why was innocent sexuality so important to Milton's
poem? Why did he take on the task of presenting an Adam
and an Eve unimaginably privileged in the matter of sensual gratification 'to all delight of human sense expos'd'?
There is a hint of the answer in what I have written earlier
about his view of the function of poetry. Believing as he
did in the inseparability of matter and form, except by an
act of intellectual abstraction, Milton could not allow a
difference of kind between soul and body; God

> created all
> Such to perfection, one first matter all,
> Indu'd with various forms, various degrees
> Of substance, and in things that live, of life;
> But more refin'd, more spiritous and pure,
> As nearer to him plac't or nearer tending
> Each in thir several active Sphears assignd,
> Till body up to spirit work, in bounds
> Proportiond to each kind. So from the root
> Springs lighter the green stalk, from thence the leaves
> More aerie, last the bright consummat flowre
> Spirits odorous breathes: flowrs and thir fruit
> Mans nourishment, by gradual scale sublim'd
> To vital Spirits aspire, to animal,
> To intellectual, give both life and sense,
> Fancie and understanding, whence the Soule
> Reason receives, and reason is her being,
> Discursive or Intuitive; discourse
> Is oftest yours, the latter most is ours . . .

>                                                         (v. 471-89)

An acceptance of Raphael's position involves, given the
cosmic scale of the poem, a number of corollaries which
Milton does not shirk. Matter, the medium of the senses, is
continuous with spirit; or 'spirit, being the more excellent
substance, virtually and essentially contains within itself
the inferior one; as the spiritual and rational faculty contains the corporeal, that is, the sentient and vegetative
faculty' (*De Doctrina Christiana* I. vii). It follows that the
first matter is of God, and contains the potentiality of
form,[5] so the body is not to be thought of in disjunction
from the soul, of which 'rational', 'sensitive' and
'vegetative' are merely aspects. Raphael accordingly goes
out of his way to explain that the intuitive reason of the
angels differs only in degree from the discursive reason of
men; and Milton that there is materiality in angelic spirit.
It is a consequence of this that part of Satan's sufferings
lie in a deprivation of sensual pleasure. Milton's thought is
penetrated by this doctrine, which, among other things, accounts for his view of the potency of poetry for good or
ill; for poetry works through pleasure, by sensuous delight; it can help 'body up to spirit work' or it can create
dangerous physiological disturbance. Obviously there
could be no more extreme challenge to the power and virtue of his art than this: to require of it a representation of
ecstatic sensual pleasure, a *voluptas* here and only here not
associated with the possibility of evil: 'delight to Reason
join'd' (ix. 243). The loves of Paradise must be an unimaginable joy to the senses, yet remain 'unlibidinous'.

If we were speaking of Milton rather than of his poem we
might use this emphasis on materiality, on the dignity as
well as the danger of sense, to support a conclusion similar to that of De Quincey in his account of Wordsworth:
'his intellectual passions were fervent and strong; but they
rested upon a basis of preternatural animal sensibility dif-
fused through *all* the animal passions (or appetites); and
something of that will be found to hold of all poets who
have been great by original force and power . . .' (De
Quincey was thinking about Wordsworth's facial resemblance to Milton). And it would be consistent with such an
account that Milton also had, like Wordsworth, a constant

awareness of the dangers entailed by a powerful sensibility. This gives us the short reason why, when Milton is representing the enormous bliss of innocent sense, he does not do so by isolating it and presenting it straightforwardly. He sees that we must grasp it at best deviously; we understand joy as men partially deprived of it, with a strong sense of the woeful gap between the possible and the actual in physical pleasure. And Milton's prime device for ensuring that we should thus experience his Eden is a very sophisticated, perhaps a 'novelistic' one: we see all delight through the eyes of Satan.

I shall return to this, and to the other more or less distorting glasses that Milton inserts between us and the voluptuousness of Eden; but first it seems right to say a word in general on a neglected subject, Milton's varying of the point of view in this poem. He uses the epic poet's privilege of intervening in his own voice, and he does this to regulate the reader's reaction; but some of the effects he gets from this device are far more complicated than is sometimes supposed. The corrective comments inserted after Satan has been making out a good case for himself are not to be lightly attributed to a crude didacticism; naturally they are meant to keep the reader on the right track, but they also allow Milton to preserve the energy of the myth. While we are hearing Satan we are not hearing the comment; for the benefit of a fallen audience the moral correction is then applied, but its force is calculatedly lower; and the long-established custom of claiming that one understands Satan better than Milton did is strong testimony to the tact with which it is done. On this method the devil can have good tunes. Not only does his terrible appearance resemble an eclipse which 'with fear of change / Perplexes Monarchs' (i. 598-9), but his oratory can include sound republican arguments—God is 'upheld by old repute, / Consent or custom' (639-40). This sort of thing makes its point before the authorial intervention corrects it. Milton even takes the risk of refraining from constant intervention and Satan-baiting in the first book, where the need for magnificence and energy is greatest. It is the second that the intense persuasions of the angelic debaters are firmly qualified; the speech of Belial is a notable case, for it is poignantly and humanly reasonable, but hedged before and behind by sharp comments on its hollowness and lack of nobility. We may find this argument attractive, but we ought to know that it has a wider moral context, and this the comment provides. At the other extreme, when God is laying down the law or Raphael telling Adam what he needs to know, the presentation is bare and unambiguous not because there is nothing the author wants to draw one's attention to but because these are not the places to start on the difficult question of how the reader's senses enhance or distort the truth; it is when the fallen study the deviousness of the fallen that corrective comment is called for, but even there sense must be given its due.

Of all the feats of narrative sophistication in the poem the most impressive is the presentation of the delights of Paradise under the shadow of Satan. He approaches out of chaos and darkness; a warning voice cries 'Woe to th'inhabitants on Earth' (iv. 5); he is 'inflam'd with rage' (9) as he moves in on calm and joy; and the consequences of the coming encounter are prefigured in the terminal words of lines 10-12: *Mankind . . . loss . . . Hell.* Before him Eden lies 'pleasant' (28); but we are not to see the well-tempered joys of its inhabitants before we have studied, with Uriel in the sun, the passionate fact of Satan, marred by 'distempers foule' (118), a condition possible only to the fallen. He fares forward to Eden, 'delicious Paradise' (132); distemper and delight are about to meet. A good deal is made of the difficulty of access to Eden; not, I think, because Satan would find it difficult—he 'in contempt / At one slight bound high overleap'd all bound' (180-1)—but because *we* must find it so; we are stumbling, disorientated, with Satan into an unintelligible purity:

> And of pure now purer aire
> Meets his approach, and to the heart inspires
> Vernal delight and joy, able to drive
> All sadness but despair: now gentle gales
> Fanning thir odoriferous wings dispense
> Native perfumes, and whisper whence they stole
> Those baumie spoils. As when to them who sail
> Beyond the *Cape of Hope,* and now are past
> *Mozambic,* off at Sea North-East winds blow
> *Sabean* Odours from the spicie shore
> Of *Arabie* the blest, with such delay
> Well pleas'd they slack thir course, and many a League
> Cheerd with the grateful smell old Ocean smiles.
> So entertaind those odorous sweets the Fiend
> Who came thir bane, though with them better pleas'd
> Than *Asmodeus* with the fishie fume,
> That drove him, though enamourd, from the Spouse
> Of *Tobits* Son, and with a vengeance sent
> From *Media* post to *Egypt,* there fast bound.
>
> (152-71)

This passage is preceded by praises of the colours of Paradise, and of delights directed at the senses of hearing, touch and taste; here the sense of smell is predominant, and Milton provides a remarkable association of fallen and unfallen odours. What becomes of the scents of Eden? They decay, and another smell replaces them, as Death himself will describe:

> a scent I draw
> Of carnage, prey innumerable, and taste
> The savour of Death from all things there that live
> . . .
> So saying, with delight he snuffd the smell
> Of mortal change on Earth.
>
> (x. 267 ff.)

At first Milton uses a lot of force to establish a situation lacking entirely this evil smell. 'Of pure now purer aire'— we are moving into the very centre of purity, delight and joy, where no sadness could survive save irredeemable hopelessness (a hint that even this purity cannot repel Satan). The breezes carry scents which betray their paradisal origin: 'baumie' is a key-word in the life-asserting parts of the poem, being used in the sense in which Donne uses it in the 'Nocturnall', as referring to the whole principle of life and growth; compare 'virtue', meaning natural vitality, in the same parts. The simile of the perfumes drifting out to sea from Arabia Felix refers to this breeze-borne odour, but also, with a characteristic and brilliant syntactical turn, to its effect upon Satan, the next topic treated; 'as when' seems at first to refer back, then to refer forward. This effect is helped by the Miltonic habit of boxing off formal similes with fullstops before and after. Satan checks himself at this influx of sensual delight; but we are reminded, with maximum force, of the difference between Satan and the sailors, by the emphatic 'Who came thir bane'. And this dissonance prepares us for the fuller ambiguities introduced by the reference to Asmodeus, a lustful devil who was driven away from Sarah by the stink of burning fish-liver. Why does Milton go about to fetch Asmodeus into his verses? The point is not the one he explicitly makes, that Satan liked the smell of Eden better than Asmodeus the smell of fish-liver; anybody who believes that will believe all he is told about Milton's sacrificing sense to sound, and so forth. The point is partly that Satan is also going to be attracted by a woman; partly that he too will end by being, as a direct consequence of his attempt upon her, 'fast bound'; but the poet's principal intention is simply to get into the context a bad smell. The simile offers as an excuse for its existence a perfunctory logical connection with what is being said; but it is used to achieve a purely sensuous effect. As soon as we approach Eden there is a mingling of the good actual odour with a bad one, of Life with Death.

Another rather similar and equally rich effect is produced by another very long sentence, iv. 268-311. From the dance of 'Universal *Pan* / Knit with the *Graces*' (286-7) we pass on to negative comparisons between Eden and other gardens. All the negations work at an unimportant level of discourse; they are denials of similarity which would not be worth making if they did not imply powerful resemblances. Eden is not the vale of Enna, nor Eve Proserpina, nor Satan Dis, nor Ceres Christ. Though Daphne was saved from a devil by a divine act, her grove was not Eden, and though 'old *Cham*' protected in another garden the 'Florid Son' of Amalthea, this does not mean that the garden of Bacchus was the same paradise as that in which another lover of pleasure, almost divine, was, though inadequately, protected. In their unlikeness they all tell us more about the truth of Eden; yet it is upon their unlikeness that Milton is still, apparently, dwelling when his Satan breaks urgently in; they are all

> wide remote
> From this *Assyrian* Garden, where the Fiend
> Saw undelighted all delight . . .
>
> (285-6)

Whereupon, having included the undelighted Satan in the enormous, delighted scene, Milton goes on, still without a full period, to an elaborate account of Adam and Eve. . . .

Joy and Woe, the shadow of one over the other, the passage from one to the other, are the basic topic of the poem.

We turn now to Adam unparadised, to Joy permanently overshadowed by Woe, light by dark, nature by chaos, love by lust, fecundity by sterility. Death casts these shadows. It is not difficult to understand why a very intelligent Italian, reading **Paradise Lost** for the first time, should have complained to me that he had been curiously misled about its subject; for, he said, 'it is a poem about Death'.

> For who would lose
> Though full of pain, this intellectual being?
>
> (ii. 146-7)

Belial asks the question, as Claudio had done; it is a human reaction, and most of the time we do not relish the thought of being without 'sense and motion' (ii. 151); nor can we help it if this is to be called 'ignoble' (ii. 227). In the same book, Milton gives Death allegorical substance, if 'substance might be calld that shaddow seemd' (669); for it is all darkness and shapelessness, a 'Fantasm' (743), all lust and anger, its very name hideous (788). The only thing it resembles is Chaos, fully described in the same book; and it stands in relation to the order and delight of the human body as Chaos stands to Nature. So, when Satan moved out of Chaos into Nature, he not only 'into Nature brought / Miserie' (vi. 267), but into Life brought Death, and into Light (which is always associated with order and organic growth) darkness. At the end of Book ii he at last, 'in a cursed hour' (1055), approaches the pendant world, having moved towards it from Hell through Chaos; and the whole movement of what might be called the *sensuous* logic of the poem so far—the fall into darkness and disorder, the return to light and order—is triumphantly halted at the great invocation to Light which opens Book iii. But the return is of course made with destructive intent. We see the happiness of a man acquainted with the notion of Death but having no real knowledge of it—'So neer grows Death to Life, what e're Death is, / Som dreadful thing no doubt' (iv. 425-6); and then, after the long interruption of Books v-viii, which represent the everything which stretched between life and death, we witness the crucial act from which the real knowledge of Death will spring, when Eve took the fruit, 'and knew not eating Death' (ix. 792). The syntax, once again, is Greek; but we fill it with our different and complementary English senses: 'she knew not that she was eating death'; 'she knew not Death even as she ate it'; 'although she was so bold as to eat Death for the sake of knowledge, she still did not know—indeed she did not even know what she had known before, namely that this was a sin'. Above all she *eats* Death, makes it a part of her formerly incorruptible body, and so explains the human sense of the possibility of incorruption, so tragically belied by fact. The function of Death in the poem is simple enough; it is 'to destroy, or unimmortal make / All kinds' (x. 611-2). There is, of course, the theological explanation to be considered, that the success of Death in this attempt is permissive; but in terms of the poem this is really no more than a piece of dogmatic cheering-up, and Milton, as usual, allows God himself to do the explaining (x. 616 ff.). From the human point of view, the intimation of unimmortality takes priority over the intellectual comfort of God's own theodicy, simply because a man can feel, and can feel the possibility of immortality blighted.

Milton saw the chance, in Book ix, of presenting very concretely the impact of Death on Life; and it would be hard to think of a fiction more completely achieved. The moment is of Eve's return to Adam, enormously ignorant and foolishly cunning, 'with Countnance blithe. . . . But in her Cheek distemper flushing glowd' (ix. 886-7). This flush is a token of unimmortality; and then, since 'all kinds' are to be affected, the roses fade and droop in Adam's welcoming garland. He sees that Eve is lost, 'Defac't, deflowrd, and now to Death devote' (901). He retreats into Eve's self-deception; but all is lost.

The emphasis here is on *all;* from the moment of eating the fruit to that of the descent of 'prevenient grace' (end of Book x and beginning of xi) Adam and Eve have lost everything, and are, without mitigation, to death devote. If one bears this steadily in mind the tenth book is a lot easier to understand; it seems often to be misread. Adam, 'in a troubl'd Sea of passion tost' (718) cries out 'O miserable of happie!' (720) and laments the end of the 'new glorious World' (721). He feels particularly the corruption of love:

> O voice once heard
> Delightfully, *Encrease and multiply,*
> Now death to hear!
>
> (729-31)

and sums up in a couplet using the familiar pseudo-rhyme: 'O fleeting joyes / Of Paradise, deare bought with lasting woes!' (741-2). He has knowledge of the contrast between then and now, but of nothing else. Deprived of Original Justice, he is now merely natural; hence the importance of remembering that he is here simply a human being in a situation that is also simple, and capable of being felt naturally, upon our pulses. Deprived as he is, Adam finds life 'inexplicable' (754); knowing nothing of the great official plan by which good will come of all this, his speculations are by the mere light of nature. Rajan made something of this in his explanation of how Milton got his heterodox theology into the poem—mortalism, for example, is not very tendentious if proffered as the opinion of a totally corrupt man.[6] But, much more important, Adam is here for the first time true kindred to the reader. The primary appeal of poetry is to the natural man; that is why it is called simple, sensuous and passionate. When Eve proposes that they should practise a difficult abstinence in order not to produce more candidates for unimmortality, or Adam considers suicide (x. 966 ff.) we should be less conscious of their errors than of their typicality. Whatever the mind may make of it, the sensitive body continues to feel the threat of unimmortality as an outrage:

> Why is life giv'n
> To be thus wrested from us? rather why
> Obtruded on us thus? who, if we knew
> What we receive, would either not accept

> Life offerd, or soon beg to lay it down,
> Glad to be so dismisst in peace.
>
> (xi. 502-7)

Michael's treatment of the same topic that the Duke inflicts upon Claudio in *Measure for Measure* can only strengthen such sentiments:

> thou must outlive
> Thy youth, thy strength, thy beauty, which will change
> To witherd weak and gray; thy Senses then
> Obtuse, all taste of pleasure must forgo,
> To what thou hast, and for the Air of youth
> Hopeful and cheerful, in thy blood will reign
> A melancholly damp of cold and dry
> To weigh thy spirits down, and last consume
> The Baum of Life.
>
> (xi. 538-46)

Whatever the consolation offered by Death—no one would wish to 'eternize' a life so subject to distempers of every kind—it is not pretended that this makes up for the loss of the 'two fair gifts . . . Happiness / And Immortalitie' (xi. 56-8). Most criticism of the verse of Book x and xi amounts to a complaint that it is lacking in sensuousness; but this is founded on a misunderstanding of the poem. ***Paradise Lost*** must be seen as a whole; and whoever tries to do this will see the propriety of this change of tone, this diminution of *sense* in the texture of the verse.

A striking example of this propriety is the second of the formal salutations to Eve, Adam's in xi. 158 ff., which I have already discussed in connection with v. 385 ff. Here Adam sees that Eve is responsible not only for death but for the victory over it; as she herself says, 'I who first brought Death on all, am grac't / The source of life' (xi. 168-9). This paradox, considered as part of the whole complex in which Milton places it, seems to me much more central to the mood of the poem than the famous *felix culpa,* because it is rooted in nature, and related to our habit of rejoicing that life continues, in spite of death, from generation to generation. Yet Adam is still under the shadow of death, and his restatement of the theme Venus-Eve-Mary is very properly deprived of the sensuous context provided for Raphael's salutation; and since the second passage cannot but recall the first, we may be sure that this effect was intended.

There, is indeed, another passage which strongly supports this view of the centrality of the paradox of Eve as destroyer and giver of life, and it has the same muted quality, casts the same shadow over the power and delight of love. This is the curious vision of the union between the sons of Seth and the daughters of Cain (xi. 556-636). The Scriptural warrant for this passage is extremely slight, though there were precedents for Milton's version. Adam rejoices to see these godly men united in love with fair women:

> Such happy interview and fair event
> Of love and youth not lost, Songs, Garlands, Flowrs

And charming Symphonies attachd the heart
Of *Adam,* soon enclin'd to admit delight,
The bent of Nature . . .

(593-7)

And he thanks the angel, remarking that 'Here Nature seems fulfilld in all her ends' (602). He is at once coldly corrected; these women, against the evidence of Adam's own senses, are 'empty of all good' (616), and nothing but ill comes from the 'Sons of God' (622) yielding up all their virtue to them. Milton remembered how much of Pandora there was in Eve. From women Adam is taught to expect woe; but, more important, this change in the divine arrangements means that the evidence of the senses, the testimony of pleasure, is no longer a reliable guide:

Judge not what is best
By pleasure, though to Nature seeming meet . . .

(603-4)

*Paradise Lost* is a poem about death, and about pleasure and its impairment. It is not very surprising that generations of readers failed to see the importance to Milton's 'scheme' of Adam's exclamation upon a paradox which depends not upon the senses but upon revelation; I mean the assurance that out of all this evil good will come as testimony of a benevolent plan

more wonderful
Than that which by creation first brought forth
Light out of darkness.

(xii. 471-3)

The senses will not recognize that out of their own destruction will come forth 'Joy and eternal Bliss' (xii. 551). In that line Milton echoes the *Comus* Epilogue—Joy will come from the great wound the senses have suffered, but it is a joy measured by what we have had and lost. And the sense of loss is keener by far than the apprehension of things unseen, the remote promise of restoration. The old Eden we know, we can describe it, inlay it with a thousand known flowers and compare it with a hundred other paradises; throughout the whole history of loss and deprivation the poets have reconstructed it with love. The new one may be called 'happier farr', but poetry cannot say much more about it because the senses do not know it. The paradise of Milton's poem is the lost, the only true, paradise; we confuse ourselves, and with the same subtlety confuse the 'simple' poem, if we believe otherwise.

Shelley spoke of Milton's 'bold neglect of a direct moral purpose', and held this to be 'the most decisive proof of the supremacy of Milton's genius'. 'He mingled, as it were', Shelley added, 'the elements of human nature as colours upon a single pallet, and arranged them in the composition of his great picture according to the laws of epic truth; that is, according to the laws of that principle by which a series of actions of the external universe and of intelligent and ethical beings is calculated to excite the sympathy of succeeding generations of mankind.'[7] This

passage follows upon the famous observations on Satan, and is itself succeeded by and involved with a Shelleyan attack on Christianity; and perhaps in consequence of this it has not been thought worth much attention except by those specialized opponents who contend for and against Satan in the hero-ass controversy. Theirs is an interesting quarrel, but its ground ought to be shifted; and in any case this is not the occasion to reopen it. But the remarks of Shelley I have quoted seem to me substantially true; so, rightly understood, do the much-anathematized remarks of Blake. I say 'substantially' because Milton himself would perhaps have argued that he accepted what responsibility he could for the moral effect of his poem, and that in any case he specifically desiderated a 'fit' audience, capable of making its own distinctions between moral good and evil. Yet in so far as poetry works through the pleasure it provides—a point upon which Milton and Shelley would agree—it must neglect 'a direct moral purpose'; and in so far as it deals with the passions of fallen man it has to do with Blake's hellish energies. And however much one may feel that they exaggerated the truth in applying it to Milton, one ought to be clear that Shelley and Blake were not simply proposing naughty Romantic paradoxes because they did not know enough. Indeed they show us a truth about *Paradise Lost* which later commentary, however learned, has made less and less accessible.

With these thoughts in my mind, I sometimes feel that the shift of attention necessary to make friends out of some of Milton's most potent modern enemies is in reality a very small one. However this may be, I want to end by citing Mr. Robert Graves; not because I have any hope of persuading him from his evidently and irrationally powerful distaste for Milton, but to give myself the pleasure of quoting one of his poems. It is called 'Pure Death', and in it Mr. Graves speculates on a theme that he might have found, superbly extended, in Milton's epic:

We looked, we loved, and therewith instantly
Death became terrible to you and me.
By love we disenthralled our natural terror
From every comfortable philosopher
Or tall grey doctor of divinity:
Death stood at last in his true rank and order.[8]

Milton gives us this perception, but 'according to the laws of epic truth'; which is to say, he exhibits life in a great symbolic attitude.

*Notes*

1. *Images and Themes in Five Poems by Milton* (1957), p. 20.

2. E. Cassirer, *An Essay on Man* (1944), pp. 83-4.

3. Harris Fletcher, *Milton's Rabbinical Readings* (1930), p. 185.

4. *Paradise Lost with reference to the Hexameral Background* (1945), pp. 76 ff.

5. See W. B. Hunter, Jr., 'Milton's Power of Matter', *Journal of the History of Ideas,* xiii (1952), 551-62.

6. B. Rajan, *Paradise Lost and the Seventeenth Century Reader* (1947), Cap ii.

7. *A Defence of Poetry,* in *Shelley's Literary and Philosophical Criticism,* ed. J. Shawcross (1909), p. 146.

8. *Collected Poems* (1959), p. 71.

**Don Cameron Allen (essay date 1961)**

SOURCE: "The Descent to Light," in *The Harmonious Vision: Studies in Milton's Poetry*, The Johns Hopkins University Press, 1970, pp. 122-42.

[*In the following essay, which was originally published in* The Journal of English and Germanic Philology *in 1961, Allen suggests that* Paradise Lost *should be thought of as an allegory about allegory and sees the movement in the epic as similar to that in the myths of Orpheus and Hercules, as the characters descend into darkness before ascending to light.*]

Though the English Protestants of the seventeenth century were, to their ultimate spiritual distress, so devoted to the literal interpretation of the Bible that they considered it the primary and superior reading, their affection for the letter and the historical sense did not prevent them from searching the text for types and allegories. This practice, of course, bore the taint of popery and hindered the full powers of the *fides divina;* yet it often yielded excellent results and enabled one to skirt the marsh of a troublesome passage. Though not addicted to the allegorical method, Milton was no stranger to it. He might scorn Amaryllis and Neaera, but he could spend an occasional moment of leisure with what Luther called "these whores of allegory." The latter books of *Paradise Lost* and the tragedy of *Samson* proved that he was quite a talented typologist, who could find foreshadowings of the great Advocate of Grace in the biographical records of the advocates of the Law. More than this, Milton, unlike many of his contemporaries who were inclined to be universal in their analogical researches, made fine discriminations between types because he believed in what we might now call "typological evolution."

An example of Milton's interpretative discretion is his refusal to accept—although in this he was contrary to theological opinion—the patriarch Aaron as a full type of Christ. He contended that this first priest simply adumbrated the priestly offices of Jesus.[1] When he came to this conclusion, Milton was flatly correcting the assertions of the Anglican prelates; but on another similar occasion he was mentally flexible enough to correct himself.[2] Since he also believed in a dynamic typology that changed as the sacred history was unrolled, he was quick to admit that symbols valid before the Law[3] were afterwards worthless.[4] He could also insist on the gradual revelation of types and symbols because he believed that the thunder and trumpets' "clang" on Mt. Sinai proclaimed, among other things,

a new form of typology and established Moses, who was, in a guarded sense, "the Divine Mediator" and "the type of the Law,"[5] as a master typologist. This evaluation had more than human worth because it was Jehovah who instructed Moses so that he could teach this mode of interpretation to men.

> Ordaine them Lawes; part such as appertaine
> To civil Justice, part religious Rites
> Of sacrifice, informing them by types
> And shadowes, of that destind Seed to bruise
> The Serpent, by what meanes he shall achieve
> Mankinds deliverance
>
> (*PL,* XII. 230-35).

These words are placed in the mouth of the Archangel Michael, who at this moment is manipulating the magic lantern of holy shadows and who is also an experienced exegete skilled in all four senses. Shortly after speaking this gloss, he announces that the main purpose of the Old Testament is to prepare the sons of Adam for a "better Cov'nant, disciplin'd / From shadowie Types to Truth, from Flesh to Spirit" (XII. 302-303). The mighty angel thus suggests that man can ascend (as humbled Adam has ascended from the Vale of Despond to the Mount of the Visions of God) from the darkness of sin and ignorance into the light of truth, from the shadow of type and symbol into the white blaze of the eternal literal.

It must be confessed that typology, even at its finest, is little more than hindsight prophecy; it points surely to the Advent, but it is best understood when the Word is made Flesh. Allegory—a game that even Jehovah plays[6]—is, in Milton's somewhat reluctant opinion, a possible form of revealed knowledge. This knowledge may be useful in some instances and not in others. When, for example, Moses urges the Israelites not to plow with an ox and an ass, Milton, who has been searching Deuteronomy for divorce evidence, perceives that the Hebrew lawgiver has the Miltons in mind,[7] an interpretation that speaks better for a sense of mystery than for a sense of humor. In his poetry Milton uses allegory with somewhat better artistry than a modern reader might imagine. An illustration of this skill appears when he shows Satan, orbiting in space and viewing the margin of Heaven and the angelic ladder of which "Each stair mysteriously was meant" (III. 516). By reminding us that Jacob's ladder had allegorical force, Milton prepares us for Raphael's subsequent description of the *scala perfectionis,* "the common gloss of theologians." There is likewise poetic irony resident in the fact that Satan, who is totally without hope, is permitted to see what will be interpreted as Adam's way of assuming angelic nature.

In general Milton probably defined allegory as a downward descent of knowledge, a revealing of suprarational information that enabled the humble learner to ascend. Raphael's well known comment on his account of the celestial battles (V. 570-76; VI. 893-96) and Milton's open admission that he can only accept the six days of Creation allegorically (VII. 176-79) make the Miltonic conception of allegory plain. For the poet, allegory is the only means of communication between a superior mind aware of grand principles, such as the enduring war between Good and Evil, and a lesser mind incapable of higher mathematics. It is essentially a form of revelation, or, as Vaughan would put it, "a candle tin'd at the Sun."

To burnish this observation, I should like to point to events within the confines of the epic that could be called an allegory about allegory. This sacred fiction begins to be written in Book II when Satan, leaving Hell for Eden, retains, except for his momentary ventures into several forms of symbolic wildlife, the literalness of satanship, never putting on the ruddy complexion, the horns, hoof, and tail by which he was recognized in the allegorical world. The celestial messengers, however, are real creatures and stay feathered and decorous so that Adam, unlike his sons, does not "entertain angels unawares." It is otherwise with Satan's strange relative, Death. At first he "seems" to be crowned and to shake his ghastly dart; actually, he is a vast black shadow, formless, not "Distinguishable in member, joynt, or limb, / Or substance" (II. 668-69). He is by no means the symbolic person who writes the dreary colophon to all human stories or who is stonily portrayed in ecclesiastical monuments. Once he has crossed his bridge into our world, he is better known. Although he is "not mounted yet / On his pale horse," we are familiar with his "vaste unhide-bound Corps" and we understand his hearty hunger for whatever "the Sithe" of his companion Time "mowes down" (X. 588-606). The bridge between the two worlds is a convention of infernal histories; but in *Paradise Lost,* it could also be called the Bridge of Allegory.

There is no doubt that at times Milton read the Scriptures for meanings other than the literal one, but he also was aware, thanks to a long tradition, that the pagans had a glimmer of Christian truth. Their lamp was scantily fueled and the wick smoked, but with proper adjustments it could be made to give off a "pale religious light." It took almost four centuries to light this lamp in the Church; the pagan philosophers and their idolatrous legends had first to be suppressed. Then, taking over the methods of the same heathen brethren, the Christian scholars began searching the mythology for physical, moral, and spiritual notions that had been bequeathed to men by the sons of Noah. The moral commentaries of Bishops Fulgentius and Eustathius on pagan literature encouraged others to unshell these truths, and in Renaissance England Chapman, Bacon, Reynolds, Sandys, Ross, and Boys searched the pagans for what had been better revealed in the Bible or was narrated in the Books of Creation. All of them were infected to some degree with the current confidence in a universal philosophical system, a disease nourished by earlier mystagogues such as Ficino, Pico della Mirandola, and Agostino Steucho, and best known to us in the fine clinical case of Theophilus Gale. Given the virulence of the epidemic, we are, consequently, not surprised when the daemon from "the threshold of Jove's Court" touches on it.

> He tell ye, 'tis not vain or fabulous
> (Though so esteem'd by shallow ignorance)

What the sage Poets taught by th' heavenly Muse,
Storied of old in high immortal verse
Of dire *Chimaeras* and enchanted Isles,
And rifted Rocks whose entrance leads to Hell,
For such there be, but unbelief is blind

(***Comus,*** 512-18).

After reading this speech in ***Comus,*** we understand why the mythological remembrances in ***Paradise Lost*** are sometimes more than ornamental, why their submerged moral or spiritual meanings enable them to consort with and support the braver Christian myths. The multicolored phoenix, first underwritten by Clement of Rome as a Christ symbol, adorns Milton's own adventual allegory: the descent of Raphael through the air, "a *Phoenix,* gaz'd by all" (V. 272). Eden, expressed in vegetable grandeur, is quickly seared with evil foreboding when Milton likens it to the meadows of Enna, those sinister fields "where *Proserpin* gath'ring flow'rs / Herself a fairer Flow'r by gloomy *Dis* / Was gather'd" (IV. 269-71). When Milton compares Adam and Eve to Deucalion and Pyrrha (XI. 8-14), even we do not need a whole series of pious mythologizers to make the point; and foolish Pandora hardly needs the testimony of a Father as old as Tertullian[8] to inform us that she is the pagan half-memory of silly Eve (IV. 712-19). Milton is quite conventional in permitting pagan legend to lend its soft biceps to Christian power. His method of searching for metaphoric support in heathen culture also enables him to stand aside from the other characters of the epic and act as a commentator on the pre-Christian world from the vantage point of a postclassical man. Among the various pagan figures with whom Milton plants his poetry, two rise above the rest; they are the poet-theologian Orpheus and the demigod Hercules. Both are attractive to him because of their Christian meaning.

From the flats of the first ***Prolusion*** through the latter ranges of ***Paradise Lost,*** Milton accents the legend of Orpheus in a way that suggests self-identification. The Greek hero was praised in antiquity and by men of later ages for softening the human heart and turning it through his higher magic to the useful and the good.[9] Christian as these achievements were, Orpheus, as Milton knew, enlarged them by singing of Chaos and Old Night and by teaching Musaeus the reality of the one God. St. Augustine, a Father beloved by Milton when he agreed with him, complained that Orpheus' theology was very poor stuff;[10] but other primitive theologians from Athenagoras onward hailed the Greek as unique among the unelect in explaining divine matters as a Christian would.[11] There is, as I have said, little doubt that Milton thought of the murdered poet as one of his own grave predecessors, and this view was probably enhanced by that of the Christian mythologists who described Orpheus as a pagan type of Christ.[12]

Clement of Alexandria is the first to bring both harrowers of Hell together, although his comments are actually an angry rejection of pagan complaints about Christian imitativeness. He brands the Christian doctrines of Orpheus as spurious and mocks the alleged majesty of his songs; then he turns with a "not so my singer" to praise the new Orpheus, who tamed the lions of wrath, the swine of gluttony, the wolves of rapine.[13] Religious Eusebius makes a similar comparison in a more kindly fashion:

> The Saviour of men through the instrument of the human body which he united to his divinity shows himself all saving and blessing, as Greek Orpheus who by the skillful playing of his lyre tamed and subdued wild animals. The Greeks, I say, sang of his miracles and believed that the inspired accents of the divine poet not only affected animals but also trees who left their places at his singing to follow him. So is the voice of our Redeemer, a voice filled with divine wisdom which cures all evil received in the hearts of men.[14]

The history of Orpheus as a pagan type of Christ can be traced for many centuries;[15] by Milton's time it was such a part of the symbolic fabric of Christianity that one had only to think of "lyre" to say "cross." It is, for example, Orpheus who comes into John Donne's mind when he writes in "Goodfriday," "Could I behold those hands which span the Poles, / And tune all sphaeres at once, peirc'd with those holes?" This is the occasional image of Christ on the lyre, but the open comparison is conventionally stated for us by Giles Fletcher:

> Who doth not see drown'd in Deucalion's name
> (When earth his men, and sea had lost his shore)
> Old Noah; and in Nisus lock, the fame
> Of Sampson yet alive; and long before
> In Phaethon's, mine owne fall I deplore:
> But he that conquer'd hell, to fetch againe
> His virgin widowe, by a serpent slaine,
> Another Orpheus was the dreaming poets feigne.[16]

Thus Christians hallowed Orpheus for his half-success as a saviour of men and for his frustrated attempt to lead a soul out of Hell's darkness.

Tatian, in his *Oration Against the Greeks,* had argued that Orpheus and Hercules were the same person;[17] Milton would hardly say this, though he found in the demigod foreshadowings of both Samson and Christ. His admission of the Christian Hercules to his pantheon begins with the **"Nativity Ode,"** where we are shown the infant Jesus "in his swaddling bands" ready to control the snaky Typhon and the rest of "the damned crew." It is Hercules, too, who is praised in *The Tenure of Kings* for his suppression of tyrants,[18] a superb Miltonic exploit; and he is recalled in the twenty-third sonnet for his rescue of Alcestis from the dark floor of Hell. He was, of course, attractive to Christians for other reasons. Begotten by Jove of a mortal woman, he early chose the right path, eschewing "the broad way and the green"; and, according to the almost Christian Seneca, "Jove's great son" devoted his whole life, in the best Stoic manner, to the conquest of his passions and the suppression of vice.[19] His major exploits were against the forces of darkness. We first hear of him in the *Iliad* (V. 397) as he strikes Hades with his "swift arrow" to leave him in anguish among the dead. No wonder that he thrice descended into Hell with somewhat better fortunes than those of Orpheus.

When Milton read the Orphic poems, he read the one that praises Hercules as a human saviour, but the comparison between Christ and Hercules, like the comparison between Christ and Orpheus, had been made before Milton's birth. "Ipse Christus verus fuit Hercules, qui per vitam aerumnosam omnia monstra superavit et edomuit."[20] The analogy was firmly established across the Channel, where Hercules Gallus was a stern rival of Francus, by d'Aubigne's *L'Hercule Chrestien,*[21] a moral prose on the labors Christianly read. This book inspired the *Hercule Chrestien*[22] of Ronsard, who advises his reader to swim a little below his surface:

> Mais ou est l'oeil, tant soit-il aveugle,
> Ou est l'esprit, tant soit-il desreigle,
> S'il veut un peu mes paroles comprendre,
> Que par raison je ne luy face entendre,
> Que la plus-part des choses qu'on escrit
> De Hercule, est deve a un seul Jesuschrist.

Chaplain Ross, a good Scot, can put it bluntly: "Our blessed Saviour is the true Hercules."[23]

There is little question that these two pagan Christ-types were congenial to Milton not only for their Christian grace notes but for their reflection of Miltonic ideals. Both heroes were received in the "sweet Societies / That sing, and singing in their glory move," because, as Boethius made clear,[24] they early chose the proper ascent to Heaven. Their accomplishments and their exploits were the sort that Milton himself might read in his own book of hope. But there is more to it than this. Hercules and Orpheus were types— not so good as Moses or Enoch, of course—of the strong Son of God and the Singer of the New Song. The event in their story that tied the hard knot of analogy was their descent into the darkness, their triumphs or half-triumphs in Hell, and their return into the light and, eventually, to the holy summits. In this process of descent and ascent, of entering the dark to find the light, the two halves of the coin of allegory were united.

II

The visual imagery of *Paradise Lost* depends to some extent on verbs of rising and falling, of descent and ascent, and on contrasts between light and darkness. These modes of expression coil about the demands of the central theme as the serpent coils about the forbidden tree so that we may be urged to abandon the horizontal movement of human history for the vertical motion of the spiritual life, the dark nothingness of ignorance and evil for the light of ultimate truth and reality. The descent of Milton into the darkness of Hell before he rises to the great "Globe of circular light" is a sound Christian rescript. "Descend," says St. Augustine, "that you may ascend." "Descende ut ascendas, humiliare ut exalteris."[25] Christ's double descent— first into the flesh and then into the dark Saturday of Hell— furnished those who humbled themselves with a map of Christian progress. One goes down in humility into the dark so that one may ascend in triumph to the light. Satan and his squires know this course well enough to pervert it.

When the black tyrant, who has been "Hurl'd headlong" down, addresses his companions, he pretends, contrary to fact, that the descent was voluntary and a preparation for ascension. "From this descent / Celestial Virtues rising, will appear / More glorious and more dread than from no fall" (II. 14-16). Satan's prideful qualification is enough to make the word *rising* ironic; but his falsehood is not only believed but seconded by the deluded Moloch, who describes with desperate wit the millions that "longing wait / The Signal to ascend" and boastfully asserts "That in our proper motion we ascend / Up to our native seat: descent and fall / To us is adverse" (II. 55-77). Moloch's knowledge is no better than his grammar, for he, like his fellows, has gone about it the wrong way. He has already ascended in pride; been guilty of a "sursum cor contra Dominum,"[26] and so he has "frozen and fallen like a flake of snow."[27] The literature of the Church knows all these phrases for the fate of the prideful aspirant; it tells us that those who descend in humility arise to those heights. "Unde Satan elatus cecidit, fidelis homo sublevatus ascendat."[28] The humble ascend to the light; the proud enter the depths, the "caligo tenebrarum densissima."[29] For those in hope of seeing the light that Satan truly detests, the road is easily followed, because both roads, as Bernard of Clairvaux puts it, are the same:

> The same steps lead up to the throne and down; the same road leads to the city and from it; one door is the entrance of the house and the exit; Jacob saw the angels ascending and descending on the same ladder. What does all this mean? Simply that if you desire to return to truth, you do not have to seek a new way which you do not know, but the known way by which you descended. Retracing your steps, you may ascend in humility by the same path which you descended in pride.[30]

Augustine's descent in humility is paralleled by Bernard's descent in pride, because both are dark ways that lead upward to light. Had Milton's Adam been humble in obedience, he would have ascended, as Raphael, who had read the Church Fathers,[31] made plain (V. 490-505). But Adam sacrificed his prospects of angelic perfection for the immediate rewards of romantic love; even then, however, his subsequent humility guarantees his ascension. The demons also talk of ascending, but "self-tempted," they are secure in their fall. The bitter pride and the prideful unrepentance that governs them is embossed by Satan in his soul-revealing soliloquy:

> O foul descent! that I who erst contended
> With Gods to sit the highest, am now constrain'd
> Into a Beast, and mixt with bestial slime,
> This essence to incarnate and imbrute,
> That to the hight of Deitie aspir'd:
> But what will not Ambition and Revenge
> Descend to? who aspires must down as low
> As high he soar'd . . .
>
> (IX. 163-70).

Satan, in other words, knows the rules. In time his legions will rise far enough to occupy the middle air, but they will not advance into the "precincts of light." Depth and dark are really their "native seat." Their master is very honest about this, admitting, as he returns from the grand seduction, that he finds descent "through darkness" an easy road (X. 393-98).

It is darkness, as well as descent, even though it is "darkness visible" that plagues the newcomers to Hades. They sit in the gloom, as Gregory the Great tell us, "inwardly dark amidst the everlasting darkness of damnation."[32] Behind them are "the happy Realms of Light" (I. 85), which they have exchanged for a dreary plain, "void of light" (I. 180). Once they were famed as God's "Bright-harness'd Angels"; now they spend their time plotting how to "affront" God's holy light "with thir darkness" (I. 389-91), confounding "Heav'n's purest Light" "with blackest Insurrection" (II. 136-37). In alternate moments they console themselves with foolish or violent plans for an escape to light (II. 220, 376-78), but Satan, who has read the sixth book of the *Aeneid,* reminds them that "Long is the way / And hard, that out of Hell leads up to Light" (II. 432-33). In Satan's church—and theology informs us that he has one—this might be called the diabolique of darkness; the counter-Church opposes to this opaqueness the sublime metaphysic of light.

We need not scratch through the Bible or the smaller gravel of the theologians to find the moral interpretation of the blackness of Hell, of the mind of evil, or what Milton's Jehovah calls the "dark designs." The Christian conscience is fully aware of the dark symbols. Ignorance, sin and sinner, damnation, Hell and its provost are festooned with black against a midnight ground, and the speculations of Beatus Jung are seldom required to expound the Christian tradition. Opposed to this night of negation is what might be called the *tenebrae in bono* which is consonant with the descent in humility and is explained by the divine darkness that even Mammon knows.

> This deep world
> Of darkness do we dread? How oft amidst
> Thick clouds and dark doth Heav'n's all-ruling Sire
> Choose to reside, his Glory unobscur'd,
> And with the Majesty of darkness round
> Covers his Throne; from whence deep thunders roar
> Must'ring thir rage, and Heav'n resembles Hell?
> As he our Darkness, cannot we his Light
> Imitate when we please?
>
> (II. 262-70).

If these were not English devils, we would put this down to conscious humor; but the absence of jest is proclaimed when Pandaemonium is lighted with sputtering gas lamps that badly imitate Heaven's essential light. The dark with which God mantles himself is as different from Hell-dark as Hell-fire is from Heaven's blazing cressets. Moses, who ascended Mt. Sinai to enter the dark folds of God's light, could lecture the swart Mammon in hermeneutics.

Though Orpheus and Hercules enter the dark and arise to the light, the basic Christian idea of the dark god in the divine night is a totally different concept. For the ancients, light was the essence of existence and the sun shone in their temples, bathing the clear gods in bright gold. Death was the greatest of horrors, not because it deprived one of limb and motion but rather because it extinguished the mortal world of light. Dying Antigone weeps because never again will she see the holy light (879-80), and her lamentation is heard again and again in Greek tragedy.[33] Light was life, and it was also wisdom. For Plato φως is the means by which men who live in the realm of shadow almost place their hands on the unknown and unknowable.[34] The Roman stoics soothed themselves with the same consolation of light; hence Seneca can remind the suffering Helvia that "The gleams of night" enable one to commune with celestial beings and keep one's mind "always directed toward the sight of kindred things above."[35] The Christians, too, saw Jehovah as a bright God, the Father of Lights, and in his human manifestation, the *Lux Mundi,*[36] but they also knew him as a god in darkness,[37] assuming his cloak of clouds.[38] The figure of a darkened god visible only in the soul's night demanded an explanatory inscription on the entablature.

The Christian doctrine of the light in darkness begins when Philo Judaeus, the stepfather of exegesis, interpreted Exodus 20:21. The broad cloud on Mt. Sinai, he writes, is the allegory of Moses' attempt to understand the invisible and incorporeal nature of Jehovah;[39] it is also, in a more general sense, the symbolic exposition of the process by which the contemplative mind tries to comprehend the immaterial.[40] More than a century later, Roman Plotinus compared man's perception of common experience to wandering through the statues of the gods that crowd the outskirts of a temple.[41] The luminous soul has, truly enough, descended into darkness[42] when it has entered the flesh, but it still provides an inner light.[43] Once it has reached its limit this light is also changed into an obscurity;[44] but this limit does not blind the inner sight by which one may ascend to the light in the shadows (ελλαμψις η εις το σκοτος), the spiritual habitation which is the goal of the wise.[45] Philo, accounting for the experience of Moses, and Plotinus, elaborating on the light metaphysic of Plato, offered to western man an esoteric explanation of divine light: it hides itself in the dark and one must enter the cloud to find it.

Milton, who had only the rudimentary chronology of his age to guide him, would probably think of Plato as a contemporary of Moses. He would certainly accept the Pseudo-Dionysius, the great exponent of this philosophy, as the disciple of St. Paul and the coeval of Philo. He would, consequently, assign all these similar doctrines to the first Christian era. The facts, as we now know and as I intend to relate them, were otherwise, and it is Gregory of Nyssa, whom Milton was reading before he wrote *An Apology,* who was the precursor of the Areopagite and who brought this doctrine into the fold of the Church. Gregory invented the poignant oxymoron "bright darkness" (λαμπρςςγνςφς),[46] a trope that haunts the rhetoric of mystics ever afterward. In his *Life of Moses* he is troubled

by the god who first showed himself in light and then in a dark shroud. He sought and found a solution for this strangeness. The Logos is first seen as light, but as one ascends, it becomes dark because one realizes that it surpasses ordinary knowledge and is separated from mortal comprehension by the *tenebrae.*[47] This is why Moses first saw God as light. Becoming more perfect in understanding by putting aside false knowledge of the divine, he passed from the primary light of the Logos, which dissipates impiety, into the divine dark. In this night, his mind, rejecting "the simple aspects of things," was fixed in a stasis of contemplation so that here he saw the true light where God is.[48] In this way Gregory wrote out the Christian explanations of the dark experience which the person who called himself Dionysius would some centuries later make an intrinsic part of Christian knowledge.

The light metaphysic of the Pseudo-Dionysius also owes much to Origen's doctrine of the double vision obtained through the eyes of the sense and the eyes of the mind. In order that the external eyes of men may be blinded, Origen writes, and that the inner eyes may see, Christ endured the humility of incarnation. By this descent, he, who healed the blind by miracle, blinded our external eyes so that he could cure our inner sight.[49] The Pseudo-Dionysius begins his *Mystical Theology* with the request that he may be allowed to ascend to those oracles where the mysteries of theology are seen in a darkness brighter than light.[50] He yearns to enter the "divine darkness"[51] where the human handicap of seeing and being seen is removed and all forms of external perception are blinded in the sacred darkness that is inaccessible light.[52] For him . . . when the searcher has arrived at its limits, which are complete negation, he will see at last without veils.[53] The Pseudo-Dionysius supports this doctrine with the example of Moses, who penetrated into "the cloud of unknowing" by closing his human eyes to all the vanities of mortal knowledge.[54] Moses, it is true, did not see God's face but only the divine place;[55] nonetheless, his intellectual eyes, like those of the supercelestial Intelligences and Seraphim,[56] were cleansed of the "mass of obscurity."[57]

After the tenth century the vogue of the Pseudo-Dionysius and his doctrine was enormous. Hilduin, John Scot, Hincmar, Radebert, John of Salisbury, Sarrazin, Hugo of St. Victor, Albert the Great, and St. Thomas found spiritual fascination in his writings.[58] The excitement of the Middle Ages was shared by the members of the Florentine Academy, by Ficino, who translated the Areopagite and wrote his own *De Lumine,* and by Pico della Mirandola, who discovered in the Pseudo-Dionysius a fellow exotic. But the light metaphysic of this fifth-century Greek was particularly illuminating to those who followed the upward mystic road, to John of the Cross, Ruusbroec, Tauler, and Suso, all of whom walked the way marked out by Richard of St. Victor[59] and St. Bonaventura. The manuals of the latter saint are rubricated with the paradoxical notion that to see one must become blind: "Excaecatio est summa illuminatio." One must search, says Bonaventura, for the night of light, but only those who have found it know what it is.

Jacob's ladder is placed on these three levels, the top reaching Heaven and so is Solomon's throne where sits the king wise and in peace, lovable as the most precious husband and most desirable. Upon him the angels desire to look and the love of holy souls yearns for him just as the stag seeks fountains of water. Hither in the manner of fire, our spirit is made skillful by a most fervent desire for the ascent but is carried by a wise ignorance beyond itself into darkness and delight so that it not only says with the bride: "We will run after thee to the odor of thy ointments," but also sings with the prophet: "and night shall be my light in my pleasure." What this nocturnal and delightful illumination is no one knows unless he tries it, and unless grace is given divinely no one tries it; and no one is given it unless he trains himself for it.[60]

The same mode of expression is found in Dante, who like Virgil and Milton descended into Hell, who went into the dark in order to see the light. The poetic allegory comes at the beginning when Dante leaves the forest of this world and having endured the night with piety prepares to enter the dark downward path so that he may ascend to the triple circle of final illumination.

> Ma poi ch'io fui al piè d'un colle giunto,
> Là dove terminava quella valle
> Che m'avea di paura il cor compunto,
> Guardai in alto, e vidi le sue spalle
> Vestite già de' raggi del pianeta
> Che mena dritto altrui per ogni calle.
> Allor fu la paura un poco queta
> Che nel lago del cor m'era durata
> La notte ch' io passai con tanta pièta

(I. 13-21).

Milton's poetic realization of the themes of descent and ascent, of the necessity of entering the dark in order to see the light, of the descent of light itself so that men may see, and of the inner eye that knows only when the exterior sight is gone, is constantly before us as we read him. These themes were carried to exorbitant excess by the mystics, but we must remember that in spite of the emphasis given them by this nervous faith they have a simple Christian provenience. It is in the plain sense, which seems nowadays to be extravagant, that Milton puts them to use. The descent of humility comes before us as early as the **"Nativity Ode"** when we are told how the Son of God forsook the "Courts of everlasting Day" to choose "with us a darksome House of mortal Clay." The same theme comes forward again when Christ is assured that he will not degrade his nature "by descending" to assume that of man. "Therefore thy Humiliation shall exalt / With thee thy Manhood also to this Throne" (*PL,* III. 303-14). On the human level the poet seeking perfection rises from the day of **"L'Allegro"** and enters the night, "the high lonely Tow'r," of **"Il Penseroso."** Thus he, too, enters the dark, as Moses did, in order to reach the dawn and the "Prophetic strain." As Milton leaves the light of the first poem that reveals only the "aspects of things," Orpheus lifts his head, but in the night of the second he hears the singing of both Orpheus and his son Musaeus. It is in darkness, too,

that fallen Adam descends so that the day of fleshly surrender be followed by the night of remorse and humility; through this course, the father of men ascends to God, first, in prayer and, then, in vision.

The theme of the inner eyes, so comforting to the blind man, makes its appearance as early as the Second Defence,[61] where Milton compares his blindness with his opponent's spiritual dark: "mine keeps from my view only the colored surfaces of things, while it leaves me at liberty to contemplate the beauty and stability of virtue and truth." ***Samson Agonistes,*** if it is the last work, almost depends on this idea. At the bottom of despair Samson, "a moving grave," doubts that "light is in the Soul" (92) and sees only "double darkness nigh at hand" (593). But Samson's night becomes day when in the complete negation of himself he yields humbly to the "rousing motions in me" (1382); then the Semichorus can sing:

> But he though blind of sight,
> Despis'd and thought extinguish'd quite,
> With inward eyes illuminated
> His fiery virtue rous'd
> From under ashes into sudden flame

(1687-91).

We must turn, however, to ***Paradise Lost,*** and especially to two of its invocations, to find all of this in flower.

The epic opens with the great address recalling Moses' ascent from the low vale to the summit of Sinai to enter the clouded light that awaits him. The experience of "that Shepherd, who first taught the chosen Seed" reminds Milton of the brook of Siloa which flowed into Siloam's pool, "fast by the Oracle of God," where Christ healed the blind man, curing at once both the inward and the exterior eyes. The types of both Old and New Testament are then personally read as the poet prays for the ascent toward light. "What in me is dark / Illumine, what is low raise and support; / That to the highth of this great Argument.. . ." Prayer is itself the humble act, preface to Milton's descent into the dark underground of Satan's province.

It is possible that Milton begins in Hell because he who met Casella "in the milder shades of Purgatory" began there. There is, however, a difference between the two poets and their purposes. Dante enters Hell (although the allegorical process of conversion and Christian education is a reader's requirement) because the literal demanded it. Milton's descent is an artistic voluntary. In moral sense Dante descends that he may ascend; he enters the dark to find the light. In doing so he takes Milton by the hand, but the reason is doctrinal rather than poetic. Having explored the dark bottom of pride, Milton rises toward the light. The preface to Book III recounts this ascension:

> Thee I revisit now with bolder wing,
> Escap't the *Stygian* Pool, though long detained
> In that obscure sojourn, while in my flight
> Through utter and through middle darkness borne
> With other notes than to th'*Orphean* Lyre

I sung of *Chaos* and *Eternal Night*,
Taught by the heav'nly Muse to venture down
The dark descent, and up to reascend,
Though hard and rare

(III. 13-21).

Milton, like Moses, sees the "Holy Light," but like the great type of the Redeemer he must descend to his "Native Element." Light, however, is given the inner eye, and, like Vaughan's Nicodemus, he can "at mid-night speak with the Sun!" It is more than sixteen hundred years after the typified event; yet the English poet joins himself to the procession, heathen and Christian, of those who acted in the great allegory of faith, who descended to ascend, who entered the darkness to see the light.

*Notes*

1. *Church Government, Works* (New York, 1931-38), III, 202-205; hereafter I shall cite only volume and page.

2. *Hirelings*, VI, 55, 58; *Christian Doctrine*, XIV, 311.

3. *Christian Doctrine*, XVI, 191.

4. *Ibid.*, XVI, 197.

5. *Ibid.*, XVI, 111.

6. *Ibid.*, XV, 145.

7. *Doctrine and Discipline*, III, 419; *Colasterion*, IV, 265.

8. *Liber de Corona, Patrologia Latina*, II, 85.

9. J. Wirl, *Orpheus in der englischen Literatur* (Vienna and Leipzig, 1913). Milton's orphic imagery has been studied by Caroline Mayerson, "The Orpheus Image in Lycidas," *PMLA*, LXIV (1949), 189-207. The Columbia *Index* may be consulted for Milton's references to Orpheus.

10. *Contra Faustum, PL,* XLII, 282; *De Civitate*, XVIII. 14.

11. *Legatio pro Christianis, Patrologia Graeca*, VI, 928.

12. Fulgentius, *Philosophi Mythologiarum libri tres* (Basel, 1536), 77-79; Berchorius, *Metamorphosis Ovidiana Moraliter* (s.l., 1509), fol. lxxiii; Boccaccio, *Della Genealogia degli Dei,* [Illegible Text] Betussi (Venice, 1585), 87; dell'Anguillara and Horologgi, *Le Metamorphosi* (Venice, 1584), 357, 387; Comes, *Mythologiae* (Padua, 1616), 401-402, 548; Ross, *Mystagogus Poeticus* (London, 1648), 334-37.

13. *Cohortatio ad Gentes, PG,* VIII, 56-57.

14. *Panegyric to Constantine, PG,* XX, 1409.

15. Lampridius informs us in his life of Alexander Severus (a work cited by Milton in *Of Reformation*) that this Emperor erected shrines to Abraham, Christ, and Orpheus: see *Historiae Augustæ Scriptores* (Frankfurt, 1588), II, 214. Antonio Bosio has a chapter on why Christians compared Orpheus and Christ in *Roma Sotterano* (Rome, 1630). For an account of the Orpheus-Christ metaphor in Spanish literature see Pablo Cabanas, *El Mito de Orfeo en la literatura Española* (Madrid, 1948), 153-76.

16. *The Poetical Works,* ed. F. Boas (Cambridge, Eng., 1908), I, 59-60. One of the earliest English comparisons is found in Gavin Douglas: see *Poetical Works,* ed. Small (Edinburgh, 1874), II, 18. Wither objects to these comparisons in *A Preparation to the Psalter,* 1619 (Spenser Society, 1884), 77-78.

17. *PG,* VI, 885.

18. *Op. cit.,* V, 19; for other references to Hercules see the Columbia *Index*. The Samson-Hercules-Christ identification is explored by Krouse, *Milton's Samson and the Christian Tradition* (Princeton, 1949), 44-45.

19. *Dial.,* II. 2. 2; see also Apuleius, *Florida,* 14, and Servius on *Aeneid,* VI. 119-23. The moral mythologers who read Christ into Orpheus also found the same connections between Christ and Hercules: see Fulgentius, 32, 39-42; Boccaccio, 210-14; Gyraldus, *Hercules,* in *Opera* (Leyden, 1696), I, 571-98; Alciati, *Emblemata* (Leyden, 1593), 50-54, 505-508; Valeriano, *Hieroglyphica* (Basel, 1556), fols, 23ᵛ, 109ᵛ, 247ᵛ, 386; Comes, 272-74.

20. G. Budé, *De Asse et partibus* (Paris, 1532), p. lxix.

21. *Oeuvres,* ed. Reaume and de Caussade (Paris, 1877), II, 226-31. Annibal Caro writes the Duchess of Castro: "Sotto il misterio d'Ercole si dinota Cristo, il quale estrinse il vizio, come Ercole uccise Cacco" (*Lettere Familiari* [Padua, 1763], I, 253).

22. *Oeuvres,* ed. Vaganay (Paris, 1924), VI, 137-45.

23. *Op. cit.,* 169.

24. *Consolations,* III, met. 12; IV, met. 7.

25. *Sermo* CCXCVII, *PL,* XXXIX, 2313-14; *Confessiones,* IV. 12; *De Civitate,* VII. 33; *Enarratio in Psalmos PL,* XXXVII, 1596-1600, 1606.

26. *Sermo XXV, PL,* XXXVIII, 168.

27. *In Job, PL,* XXXIV, 875.

28. Cassiodorus, *Exposition in Psalter, PL,* LXX, 1036.

29. Anselm, *Liber de Similitudinibus, PL,* CLIX, 664-65.

30. *De Gradibus Humilitatis,* ed. Burch (Cambridge, Mass., 1940), 176.

31. For patristic comments on the perfectibility of an unfallen Adam, see Hugo of St. Victor, *De Vanitate Mundi, PL,* CLXXVI, 723; St. Thomas, *Summa,* I. 102. 4; Pico della Mirandola, *De Hominis Dignitate,* ed. Garin (Florence, 1942), 104, 106; J. Donne, *Sermons,* ed. Potter and Simpson (Berkeley, Calif., 1953-60), II, 123, VII, 108.

32. *In Ezechielem, PL,* LXXVI, 1290.

33. See also Sophocles, *Aias,* 854-65, *Oedipus Col.,* 1549-51, and Euripides, *Iph. Aul.,* 1281-82, 1506-1509.

34. *Republic,* VI. 508-509, VII. 518; *Phaedo,* 99; see J. Stenzel, "Der Begriff der Erleuchtung bei Platon," *Die Antike,* II (1926), 235-37.

35. *Ad Helviam,* VIII. 5-6; see also Plutarch, *De Genio Soc.,* 590 B.

36. Psalms 36:9, 104:2; Wisdom, 7:21-25; I Timothy 6:16; I John 1:5.

37. Exodus 20:21, II Chronicles 6:1, II Samuel 22:12, Psalms 18:11-12, 97:2, Job 22:14.

38. Ezekiel 1:4, Revelation 1:7.

39. *Vita Mosis,* I. 28.

40. *De Poster. Caini,* 5.

41. *Enneads,* VI. 9, 11, 8-22.

42. *Ibid.,* IV. 3, 9, 23-29.

43. *Ibid.,* V. 3, 17, 27-37.

44. *Ibid.,* IV. 3, 9, 23-26.

45. *Ibid.,* II. 9, 12, 31; I. 6, 9, 22-24; see M. de Corte, "Plotin et la nuit de l'esprit," *Etudes Carmélitaines,* II (1938), 102-15.

46. *In Cantica Canticorum, PG,* XLIV, 1000-1001. It should be noted that Tertullian prior to his polemic against Montanism describes an "obumbratio mentis" as a preface to divine knowledge; see *Ad Marcion, PL,* II, 413, and *De Anima,* ed. Waszink (Amsterdam, 1947), p. 62 and notes. Ambrose considers the *tenebrae* as a requirement of the prophetic state: *De Abraham, PL,* XIV, 484.

47. *Op. cit., PG,* XLIV, 376-77.

48. *In Cantica, ibid.,* 1001.

49. *Contra Celsum, PG,* XI, 1476.

50. *Op. cit., PG,* III, 997.

51. *Ibid.,* 1000.

52. *Epistolae, ibid.,* 1073.

53. *T.M., ibid.,* 1000-1001.

54. *Ibid.,* 1001.

55. *Ibid.,* 1000.

56. *De Coelesti Hierarchia, ibid.,* 205.

57. *De Divinis Nominibus, ibid.,* 700-701; see H. C. Peuch, "La Ténèbre mystique chez le Pseudo-Denys," *Etudes Carmélitaines,* II (1938), 33-53.

58. P. G. Théry, "Denys au moyen age," *Etudes Carmélitaines,* II (1938), 68-74.

59. *Benjamin Minor, PL,* CXCVI, 52.

60. *Breviloquium, Opera Omnia* (Florence, 1891), V, 260.

61. *Op. cit.,* VIII, 71.

**B. Rajan (essay date 1964)**

SOURCE: "The Language of *Paradise Lost,*" in *Milton: A Collection of Critical Essays,* edited by Louis L. Martz, Prentice-Hall, Inc., 1968, pp. 56-60.

[*In the following essay, which was originally published in 1964 as a introduction to his edition of the first two books of* Paradise Lost, *Rajan surveys other critics' responses to the style of the epic and claims that the work's diction, sound, and imagery contribute to the poetic result of a lucid surface whose depths are charged with meaning.*]

***Paradise Lost*** has not one style but several, as Pope was among the first to recognise. There is, at the simplest level of discrimination, an infernal style, a celestial style, and styles for Paradise before and after the fall. But the infernal style itself differs both mechanically and actually, in the heroic preparations of the first book, in the "great consult" in Pandemonium and in Satan's encounter with Sin and Death. The other styles reveal similar and substantial differences of application. In these circumstances it may seem irrelevant to talk of the poem's style at all, but the word, though deceptive, is not wholly beside the point. With all its variations, the language of the poem has a basic homogeneity and in fact one of the pleasures of reading ***Paradise Lost*** is to discover the wide differences the language can accommodate, without imperilling its unitive power. In this sense also the poem makes alive a basic quality of the reality which it celebrates.

Sublimity is a quality usually conceded to ***Paradise Lost,*** though it is argued that the sublimity is monolithic, that its price is petrification and that the style marches on irrespective of what is inside it. But perspicuity is not ordinarily associated with the poem, the general impression being that its syntax, its erudition and its latinised usages combine to invest it with a pervasive obscurity. Mr. Eliot is typical in observing that "the complication of a Miltonic sentence is an active complication, a complication deliberately introduced into what was a previously simplified and abstract thought." Although this is from the 1936 essay, we also find Mr. Eliot, in his 1947 recantation, still proclaiming that Milton's style is personal rather than classic, that its elevation is not the elevation of a common style, that in Milton "there is always the maximal, never the minimal, alteration of ordinary language" and that as a poet, Milton is "probably the greatest of all eccentrics." Similarly, Mr. Leavis observes: "So complete, and so mechanically habitual, is Milton's departure from the English order, structure and accentuation that he often produces passages that have to be read through several times before one can see how they go, though the Miltonic mind has nothing to offer that could justify obscurity—no obscurity was intended: it is merely that Milton has forgotten the English language." . . .

Fortunately all generalisations about ***Paradise Lost*** (including those that offer themselves as truisms) have to encounter and survive the text. The following lines from the ninth book are quoted not only because the syntax is uniformly unorthodox, but also because the unorthodoxy is maintained at a crisis in the action, in other words, under conditions of potentially maximum irrelevance:

> From his slack hand the Garland wreath'd for *Eve*
> Down dropd, and all the faded Roses shed:
> Speechless he stood and pale, till thus at length
> First to himself he inward silence broke.

It should not be necessary to point out how the first inversion sets in motion the succession of linked *a*'s that makes "slack" a reality in the sound and pace of the verse, or how the wreathing of the *e* sound in "wreath'd for *Eve*" is made more vivid by the placing of *"Eve"* at the climax of the line. The plummeting force of "Down dropd" is created both by the inversion and by its dramatic positioning (which the previous inversion has made possible). These departures from the normal word-order indicate how the syntax is being manoeuvred to create a pattern of impact rather than a logical or grammatical sequence. In this context "all the faded Roses shed" is surprising only in analysis. Within the poetry itself, it spreads out of the numbness of "Down dropd," so that Adam's paralysis seems to be measured by the manner in which it passes out into nature, withering the roses with the same shock that withers him. The image succeeds precisely by not calling attention to itself, by being shaped into the situation, into the inert downward movement. The next inversion places "Speechless" at the beginning of the line; both the stressed position and its anchoring by "stood" (the alliteration is, of course, purposive) charge the word with the surrounding sense of deadness. We are made aware that Adam's speechlessness is not ordinary consternation but the mental surface of his "inward silence." The separation of "speechless" and "pale" by "stood" (a favourite Miltonic device) is similarly functional; both in the syntax and in the reality being enacted, the inner condition is precedent and decisive. "Pale," we must also remember, was a stronger word to Milton's contemporaries than it is to us. The suggestion here is of the pallor of death. One recalls the "shuddring horror pale" of the fallen angels and the "pale and dreadful" light of their damnation. In this context, "till thus at length" is creatively ambiguous; the grammatical coupling with "he inward silence broke" is deliberately weakened by the inversion of the fourth line and this enables the emotional link with "Speechless he stood" to become active in the total movement. "First to himself" delays and defines the climax. Adam is not soliloquising. Rather, he is seeking to achieve a response out of the momentary paralysis of his being, to create out of inward silence a ground for interior debate. The movement and tension of the poetry, charged with meaning beneath the lucid surface, shape and intensify this reality. Diction, syntax, sound and imagery contribute purposefully to the poetic result.

This analysis has been pursued in some detail to indicate that the poetry of ***Paradise Lost*** can bear and will respond to a far greater pressure of interpretation than it normally receives. It also suggests that "the complication of a Miltonic sentence" is a creative rather than an "active complication" if indeed it is a complication at all; the true aim seems to be the playing of metrical against grammatical forces to form and embolden the emotional line. This conclusion is not limited to the "simpler" kind of writing that has been analysed; the following lines present a characteristically different surface but are modelled by essentially similar forces. The quotation is from one of those passages in the third book where God the Father turns a school divine, though according to some of our better scholars, he speaks more like a seventeenth century rhetorician, an ideal student of Puttenham and Peacham.

> Man disobeying
> Disloyal breaks his fealtie, and Sinns
> Against the high Supremacie of Heav'n
> Affecting God-head and so loosing all,
> To expiate his Treason hath naught left,
> But to destruction sacred and devote,
> He with his whole posteritie must die:
> Die hee or Justice must; unless for him
> Som other able, and as willing, pay
> The rigid satisfaction, death for death.
> Say Heav'nly Powers, where shall we find such love,
> Which of ye will be mortal to redeem
> Mans mortal crime, and just th' unjust to save?
> Dwels in all Heaven charitie so deare?

One is expected to note such touches as the manner in which "high supremacie" recalls I, 132, tying the human sin to the angelic. Less obvious, but equally part of the underlying network, is the exact premonition in "But to destruction sacred and devote" of the truth which breaks into Adam's inward silence (IX, 901) as he faces the finality of Eve's sin. The irony of "Affecting God-head and so loosing all" has a sardonic validity in itself but the punishment is also measured by the presumption and the legal matching of the two is part of the poem's concept of justice. Some may find the use of the images of kingship curious, but Milton's view that the only true monarchy is that of Heaven (XII, 67-71) is not only consistent but republican. In any case the imagery, with its legalistic undertone, makes possible the intensification of disobedience into disloyalty and finally into treason, thus dictating the measured and monolithic verdict: "He with his whole posteritie must die". One notes how the quasi-rhymes bind the judgment together and how the crucial words "He" and "die" stand dramatically at the beginning and end of the line. Then comes the concentration, the sudden swoop of emphasis, as these terminal words are driven and fused together, with both the inversion, the emphatic "hee" and the brief almost ferocious power of the movement, joining to assert the law in its angry finality. Everything is to the purpose now. The semicolon after "Die hee or Justice must" reinforces the compulsive strength of "must" and once again the inversion strengthens the impact. At the same time the strong medial pause coming after an auxiliary verb creates a sense of expectation, of basic incompleteness; the movement in its clenched decisiveness dictates the relaxation into the lines that follow. The body of the verse begins to react to the awareness of a law transformed by charity. Though the language of "Som other able, and as willing" remains legalistic, the fluent movement of the verse, the suggestion of infinite love in "willing" escapes from and redefines the merely legal. In the next line, the two tendencies are forced into creative collision. "Death for death" states the law in its sterile absoluteness, an absoluteness reflected fully in the conclusive, hammer-like movement. But in "rigid satisfaction" the organic word plays against and undermines the mechanical. The legal content of "satisfaction" engages with "rigid" and with "death for death", locking itself into the circle of crime and punishment. But the overtones of life and growth in the word point securely to a higher satisfaction, a reality beyond the exactions of the law. The line is a fortress which only love can enter but the language in erecting it has also breached it. The relaxation of the movement is now both logical and organic. One need only note the way in which the two uses of "mortal" preserve the legal equivalence while opening the way into the wider paradox of "just th' unjust to save". In terms of the "rigid satisfaction" the balance is inequitable but the poetry has established a higher reality. It has created a world in which charity becomes an imaginative fact as well as a theological principle. This is an achievement of peculiar difficulty since sensuous imagery is forbidden by the circumstances, and the animating forces must therefore be those of syntax, and of word-play precisely and imaginatively controlled. Given these limited resources the result is a triumph of considerably more than craftsmanship.

These two widely different passages suggest both the variety of Milton's style and the criteria to which the style is answerable. That the verse will bear considerable scrutiny is evident and in fact the most difficult temptation to reject in modern criticism is that which seeks to establish complexity, irony, ambiguity and paradox as controlling qualities of Milton's writing. It is not merely convenient but reassuring to suggest that there is one right way of using poetic language and that Milton's poetry like all poetry, can be found true to that way. To deny the complexity of **Paradise Lost** would of course, be perverse; but that does not mean that complexity should be regarded as a principle shaping the local life of the language. The complexity of Milton's epic is less one of surface than of reverberation. It arises not so much from the immediate context, as from the connection of that context to other contexts and eventually to the context of the whole poem and of the cosmic order drawn into and recreated within it. Svendsen is right in arguing that "the basic mode of **Paradise Lost** is ambivalence" and paradox and irony are equally vital in its total effect. But these qualities operate through the poem's structure rather than its texture. The surface is not characteristically complex, and the resources of diction, syntax and imagery cooperate to clarify and intensify, rather than to qualify the main thrust of the poetry. Coleridge understood this when he observed that "the connection of the sentences and the position of the words are exquisitely artificial; but the position is rather according to the logic of passion or universal logic than to the logic of grammar." A more recent critic, Professor Wright, describes Milton's style as "unusually clear and forceful" while MacCaffrey begins a perceptive discussion by stat-

ing: "elevation, not breadth is the principal dimension of epic. Unity and elevation demand that there should be a single—even, in a sense, a simple—effect produced in the reader, and this end is not to be accomplished by a style with a verbally complex surface."

All this is clearly as it should be. If the style is to develop its primary (and symbolic) qualities of sublimity, of propulsive power, of designed and inexorable movement, it can only do so through a deliberate simplicity of surface. The other qualities which matter are not sacrificed and indeed are realized to a far greater extent than in any other poem of this magnitude. They live, however, not so much on the surface, as in the weight of qualification, connection and commentary which the whole poem places behind every point on its surface. Milton's observation that poetry is more simple, sensuous, and passionate than rhetoric is surely not meant as an attempt to confuse us about the predominant qualities of his verse. The style is capable of "metaphysical" effects or more correctly, it can frequently draw the metaphysical into the heroic; but it remains heroic and not metaphysical. The distinction is important not only in terms of decorum, but as an indication of how to read the poem, of how to respond to its impact and its tactics. The present writer is frankly not appalled by the discovery that there is more than one way of using poetic language or that Milton is Milton because he is not Donne. The open society of poetry ought to have room for the excellences of both.

## Michael Fixler (essay date 1969)

SOURCE: "Milton's Passionate Epic," in *Milton Studies*, Vol. 1, 1969, pp. 167-92.

[*In the following essay, Fixler shows that Milton conceived* Paradise Lost *as a form of devotional celebration, a revelation and praise of God and his mysteries.*]

I grateful to the anonymous reviewer who recently in the *Times Literary Supplement* called for a study of **Paradise Lost** that would show it to be not only a logical epic and a deliberate epic, but a passionate epic as well. May I here offer a partial installment of an essay in this direction, covenanting with my audience for its later more complete fulfilment, though probably in a context where Milton's passion would be seen as an aspect of his whole sense of what poetry was for, how it worked, and how its energies originated. The immediate occasion for the reviewer's wish was a notice of Ernest Sirluck's excellent lecture in which at a crucial point Sirluck quoted from *The Doctrine and Discipline of Divorce* a sentence with some relevance for the problem of the justice of God's ways with men. "The hidden wayes of his providence we adore & search not; but the law is his reveled wil." Milton, Sirluck suggests, declined "to seek final refuge in mystery." In **Paradise Lost** he deliberately undertakes to justify God's ways by questioning them first, and in so doing I gather it is meant that he turned his back on the alternative option, to magnify and exalt the ways of God to men.[1]

I propose to disagree with what I take to be Sirluck's undeveloped suggestion, for the alternative he apparently thinks was excluded by Milton's intention to justify God is not in fact incompatible with that intention. It is only necessary to see Milton's purpose, as deliberately indicated as anything else we know about *Paradise Lost,* in larger terms than may be narrowly inferred from the stated argument. As Sirluck shows, the epic in every respect was deliberately conceived, but we have not exhausted the possibilities of what Milton meant to do when we can determine the full nature of the theological problems involved in justifying rationally or poetically God's Providence and Man's free will. The poem itself, and Milton knew it, was a symbolic action. The doing of it was part of its meaning, and the thrust of that part of the meaning was not in the direction of logic or dialectic, but in the direction of worship and adoration, much as a Christian devotionally affirms his faith in "the substance of things hoped for, the evidence of things not seen." The poem, in short, is indeed an argument, but no less a song of praise, a formal act of adoration celebrating the mystery of God's ways; and as such it is by the nature of its devotional energy more than an epic; it is a passionate epic. I do not hope to be able to demonstrate this fully now, only to begin.[2] For the time being, what I wish to show is that Milton conceived *Paradise Lost* as a form of devotional celebration that involved three separate assumptions. The first one concerned the relationship of poetry to worship; the second concerned the relationship of poetic inspiration and *energia* to that disciplined enthusiasm which Milton thought of as the fiery spirit of prayer which with prompt eloquence flowed from his own lips, as it did from the mouth of his creature Adam, "in Prose or numerous Verse"; and the third concerned the nature of that audience for whom the poem in its devotional character was intended.

The last assumption needs a moment's consideration now though it is most relevant to the end of my discussion. If the poem has a complex character the distinctiveness of its elements reaches into all sorts of consequences. What the argument of the poem justifies in a rational or dramatic sense wears another aspect than that which is adored, namely, the mystery of the hidden ways of God's Providence; and by a kind of mimetic principle the celebration of that mystery takes place at a level of symbolic action and meaning that is intentionally obscure, designed, as Bacon wrote of "Poesy Parabolical," or allusive poetry, to retire and obscure the mysteries of religion and policy. In Neoplatonic poetics much was made of the decorum of mystic obscurity, though the techniques of mystery were not essentially thought of as being occultly mystifying, being rather treated as an art of evoking specific things most people would not quite grasp except vaguely or as the commonplace images of mythology. The point of such techniques was to discriminate those unworthy to understand from those who were worthy. If we cannot hear, said Milton of the hidden harmony of the spheres, the fault is

in ourselves and not in the stars. The story Pythagoras told of that music, he went on, was an allegory, for neither the poets nor divine oracles ever "display before the eyes of the vulgar any holy or secret mystery unless it be in some way cloaked or veiled."[3]

Such language as the young Milton used here is implicitly or metaphorically sacramental, and reminds me of Robert Frost's revelation at the end of *Directive* that inasmuch as his poem concerned a mystery its comprehension was a kind of sacramental test, a chalice with which to drink from the waters of life, but hidden "Under a spell so the wrong ones can't find it, / So can't get saved, as Saint Mark says they mustn't." There is, in effect, I shall try to show, a similar revelation in *Paradise Lost,* and its point is to discriminate two kinds of audience. The manner of the revelation is proper to the poem's devotional character and specifically concerns the mystery which sacramentally the poem celebrates, a mystery ultimately reducible to the mystery of election, that arbitrary Will whereby God so created things as to save some and to damn others. But neither the revelation nor the implicitly devotional character exists within the poem as a layer of allegory, as we understand that term to mean a distinctive and alternative pattern of autonomous significance. Rather these meanings are a matter of the poem's depth, an extension toward the outermost ranges of evocative suggestiveness of the primary, essential significance of Milton's work.

In several places in *Paradise Lost* what is ordinarily implicit is made explicit, and in one passage in particular the effect is perceptibly odd enough to make readers sometimes wonder whether there might not be some textual error, an instance of oversight or confused reference on Milton's part. I want to use the passage as a clue, the end of a thread unravelling which may help us to see more plainly the whole implicit character of the poem, especially since it stands in some relationship to Milton's explicit intention, which as we know was to "assert Eternal Providence / And justify the ways of God to men." Both dramatically and by a kind of prolepsis this argument is amplified in the third book as Satan wings his way toward Eden, watched from above by God, who foretells the consequences, exculpates himself, and accepts the Son's offer to redeem mankind. At the conclusion of this divine exchange the angelic chorus is heard for the first time in the poem singing in adoration and praise of the Father and the Son. Then at the very end of the choral passage there is a startling shift in pronoun so that the worship is no longer described from an outside perspective, in terms such as "Thee Father first *they* sung," but from within as by a worshipper, moved by the Son's promised atonement.

> O unexampl'd love,
> Love nowhere to be found less than Divine!
> Hail Son of God, Savior of Men, thy Name
> Shall be the copious matter of *my* Song
> Henceforth, and never shall *my* Harp thy praise
> Forget, nor from thy Father's praise disjoin.[4]

Verity's note on these lines illustrates the trouble a reader has to take in order to digest the meaning. First he suggests that possibly Milton meant to represent the chorus of angels speaking as one individual. But this is not very convincing, so he reluctantly admits a possibility which evidently strikes him as a little puzzling, that Milton might himself be speaking, or rather, we should say, singing with the creatures of his own poetry.[5]

I think there is little reason to doubt this is Milton's voice in its own poetic identity, the same, for example, that imaginatively joined "the Angel choir" in the induction of the **Nativity Ode,** and that in the "high-raised phantasy" of **At A Solemn Music** both visualized and heard the angel's worship with which mankind had once been concordant, and with which it would be at last once more concordant when all would be restored, men and angels worshipping together, singing "in endless morns of light." To explain the passage in **Paradise Lost** it is only necessary to postulate that within the context of the poem Milton saw time telescoped into the instant of adoration, so that imagining that primordial moment when human destiny and divine love were fixed was like imagining that moment when in the restoration of all things he, John Milton, would find himself worshipping among the saints and angels, again singing in endless morns of light. Nor was the idea as remote from Milton's sense of possibilities as the antipodes of Alpha and Omega, the beginning and the end. There had been indeed a time when the imagination of that worship was so forcibly immediate, so wrapped up with his hopes for the Church's total reformation, that he could anticipate shortly the translation of his heavenly worship into the earthly form of his poetic calling or vocation, as he did in both **Of Reformation** and **Animadversions,** where in outbursts of euphoric and extemporary apocalyptic prayer he described the role he would play as a poet in the consummation of the purified Church. The first perspective in **Of Reformation** was visionary, beginning with an image of himself "amidst the *Hymns,* and *Halleluiahs* of *Saints* . . . offering at high *strains* in new and lofty *Measures* to sing and celebrate thy *divine mercies,* and *marvelous Judgements*"; and ending with the conceit that somehow the Millennium had come and with it the Marriage Supper of the Lamb wherein the saints would be rewarded by worshipping "in supereminence of *beatific Vision* progressing the *datelesse* and *irrevoluble* Circle of *Eternity,*" while the rest, the damned, would be separated from them and cast into Hell. The view was much the same in *Animadversions* where again he promised to "take up a Harp and sing" to God "an elaborate Song to Generations."[6]

Notwithstanding some abatement of enthusiasm, this assumption that *his* worship would be consummately an extraordinary kind of devotional poetry seems to have been very much a part of the picture in *The Reason of Church-Government,* when Milton surveyed the literary possibilities available to the sacred poet, concluding that all were means by which God might be served, whether with respect to Christian edification or with respect to devotion. By assimilating the latter to poetry he appeared to add an ingredient to Renaissance poetics not wholly novel, but certainly rarely realized as fully as it was to be later in

*Paradise Lost.* The poet, Milton wrote, was like the pulpited minister, his function being to teach and "to celebrate in glorious and lofty Hymns the throne and equipage of Gods Almightinesse, and what he works, and what he suffers to be wrought with high providence in his Church. . . ."[7] Clearly this is the theoretical context for the passage where Milton set himself singing among the angels, and in a broader sense it is also the justification for the view I take that *Paradise Lost* is as much a devotional poem as it is an epic. The poem itself, the copious matter of his song, as Milton referred to it in the angelic chorus, was to be a praise of God and of his name. And when he referred to his song I take it he meant not only his poem, but, with the word "henceforth," all of his poetry, as if in a ceremonial act of self-consecration he was rededicating himself to the purposes of divine worship, renouncing every literary ambition which would not serve *ad majorem Dei gloriam.*

Worship, to be sure, was in Puritan terms a very broad concept, being, in fact, as Milton described it, everything that as the love of God expressed faith, or the knowledge of God.[8] Consequently on a strictly literal basis the argument of *Paradise Lost,* as it relates to the knowledge of God and his ways, may be described as Milton's faith itself; but the expression of it, as something offered before both men and God, may be described as an act of worship. However, in an even more precise degree the poem is an act of worship in a way that any pious action indiscriminately is not, or even in a way other kinds of devotional poetry are not. Most devotional poetry is meditational and the forms of meditational poetry generally represent various kinds of self-absorbed communion with God. So far as such poetry acknowledges readers it allows itself to be overheard. But *Paradise Lost* as a publicly directed devotional work involves its readers, or possibly *intends* to involve *some* of its readers, as if they were implicitly participants in a common worship, or, in short, as participants in an extraordinary act of extemporary liturgical service. It is true that we do not think of liturgies as being either poetic or didactic in their primary significance, but certainly devotional orders of worship may be edifying even while they are most ceremonially sacramental.

In fact Puritan liturgies were both aggressively edifying and self-consciously experimental, the dislike of the formal, prescribed liturgy being the source of one of the most zealous of all Puritan causes. Milton early testified to his zeal in this respect, and apparently as he grew older he also found uncongenial even the small degree of liturgical formalism the Puritans were obliged to accept in order to sustain any regular kind of worship. At least this is how I interpret the conjunction of his vehement dislike of set prayers and his eventual withdrawal from participation in all real church services. Whether he would have abandoned congregational worship, the public profession and testimony to faith, if he had not an alternative public devotional channel peculiar to his own talent and calling, may be fairly asked. It seems to me that the intensity of Milton's self-consecration in the angelic chorus is some indication that he had indeed confronted the options and made a deliberate choice, as deliberate as the one he had made as a young man when he offered himself as a poet to the service of God, but this time it was in recognition that poetry was for all intents and purposes his whole worship, the most perfect public expression of his faith.[9]

The fact that the gesture was made within a chorus of angelic worship is, moreover, quite striking. It could, for example, have been made at the beginning in the invocation to the poem, as its predecessor had been made in the induction of the *Nativity Ode.* It was as if Milton chose the chorus to emphasize the nature of true worship as he most ideally conceived it in the words of *At A Solemn Music*— "Aye sung before the sapphire-color'd throne / To him that sits thereon." Worship, when it could at last be the worship of the glorified Saints, would be an eternal effluence "of sanctity and love," a happiness that "may orbe it selfe into a thousand vagancies of glory and delight, and with a kind of eccentricall equation be as it were an invariable Planet of joy and felicity." If the poets, as Sidney said, sang of a golden world, as against the brazen reality of the historians, why should not Milton as a liturgical poet take his pattern from the image of beatific and fully perfected worship presented in the Apocalypse? But in doing so he was guided by a distinction between visionary and real worship that I think would have been fully evident to him; namely, that the visionary worship of the Apocalypse celebrated a mystery whose nature was only shadowed forth in human experience, a mystery concerning the nature of the end, which like the beginning would be a separation of heavenly souls from the damned.[10]

> Then shall thy Saints unmixt, and from th' impure
> Far separate, circling thy holy Mount
> Unfeigned *Halleluiahs* to thee sing,
> Hymns of high praise.
>
> (VI, 742-45)

These are the words of the Son going off to triumph in the War in Heaven, casting his eye typologically past Armageddon. In this perspective he looks more immediately past the Fall, past his own Incarnation, past his human trial—of which again the War in Heaven is the type—past, in short, the whole mixed condition subsequent to the spontaneous generation of evil.

As Sirluck rightly observed, Milton's theology and poetry "divide mankind into *three* groups," rather than merely two, the saved and the damned. Between the pre-elected saints, and those who damned by God damn themselves, there is the bulk of mankind, each individually possessing in some degree a sufficient measure of prevenient grace to save himself from the consequences of original sin. For that large, indeterminably broad class of sinners who might be saints, worship as it might ideally be practiced on earth was also a means of evangelical edification, something doctrinal, something which might prove to be a call "To Prayer, repentance, and obedience due" (*PL* III, 191). But the apotheosis of worship, or visionary worship in its

Apocalyptic images, was conceived in terms of the ultimately absolute separation of saints and sinners, when there would be manifest the perfect circularity of the mystery that Paul preached to the Romans: "For whom he did foreknow he also did predestinate to be conformed to the image of his Son. . . . Moreover, whom he did predestinate, them he also called: and whom he called, them he also justified; and whom he justified, them he also glorified."[11] This arbitrary separation, this glorification, as well as damnation, would be part of the mystery of the hidden ways of God's Providence, which, Milton said, "we adore and search not." True, the mystery has a tragic, problematic aspect as the setting for the whole moral quest, but to suggest that the argument of the poem concerns only the moral quest, the justification that edifies at the expense of the adoration of the mystery, would, I think, only give us half of Milton's intention.

Sirluck believes that Milton declined "to seek final refuge in mystery," refused, in short, mainly to justify God by magnifying and exalting his ways. His decision "determined the nature of his poem—the substance, the form, the temper and the approach; a poem that should be doctrinal to a nation; a fully deliberate epic." I cannot really disagree with this, but it seems to me preferable to look at the work as an affirmation that went beyond God's unsatisfactory logic and the whole labyrinthine maze of theological problems concerning fate, foreknowledge and free will. I suggest that on a superior plane Milton saw God's ways as being ultimately justified in mystery, that is to say at a point beyond comprehension though not beyond apprehension. Indeed Milton makes this point in a passage in *Paradise Lost* that works at the level of cryptic allusiveness I referred to earlier, a level proper to the fact that what is being intimated or obscurely revealed as a mystery expresses the whole logic-defying paradox of the *felix culpa.* Being a symbolic rather than a discursive statement the passage also suggests the mimetic principle whereby the mystery of God's justice becomes incorporated into the mystery of harmony itself. For unless he thought he could tap "the hidden soul of harmony," as Milton called it in *L'Allegro,* I do not believe he would have imagined himself capable of writing *Paradise Lost.*[12]

I have touched on this passage lightly elsewhere, but since it concerns an act of mystic worship, it is more integral to my argument here, and I would like to go more deeply into it now. In a sense the action represents the real beginning of the matters in the poem. As Raphael relates the War in Heaven, he starts, without referring to it, with the occasion at which evil is conceived, for as soon as the Father has proclaimed the begetting of the Son, Sin also is engendered. It was then that the hosts of heaven were to confess the Son as Lord, being happy in obedience, "United as one individual Soul / For ever happy"; or damned without end if disobedient. "All seem'd well pleas'd, all seem'd, but were not all," Raphael says, in words which can only allusively remind the reader that Satan at this point would have conceived Sin, though he did not give birth to her until his open declaration of defiance at the first rebellious council. Whereupon there follows a concert of worship of the kind apparently customary during heaven's devotional hours. But now the chief worshipper, next to the Son himself, feigns adoration and in being false implicitly holds within him the whole train of evil and idolatry which was to follow. That a new element has entered the common devotions is hidden from all save God, and the worship thus has a distinct implicit meaning for him, as its movement seems in part to work counter to his will and yet within the divine purpose, resolved and reconciled in a pattern intended to be neither quite understood by others, nor yet to be quite altogether inapprehensible, if only as a harmonic design.

> That day, as other solemn days, they spent
> In song and dance about the sacred Hill,
> Mystical dance, which yonder starry Sphere
> Of Planets and of fixt in all her Wheels
> Resembles nearest, mazes intricate,
> Eccentric, intervolv'd, yet regular
> Then most, when most irregular they seem:
> And in thir motions harmony Divine
> So smooths her charming tones, that God's own ear
> Listens delighted.
>
> (V, 618-27)

What God is listening to is a choral service affirming, in a way he alone understands, the *felix culpa,* figured within the harmony of the *discordia concors.* The mystic dance of worship is at once an image of fully harmonic but indescribable celestial motions and a figure for the moral resolution of the problem of justice in the ineffable beauty of the music of God's hidden ways.[13]

This orbing into "a thousand vagancies of glory and delight . . . with a kind of eccentricall equation" was the worship to which Milton himself aspired when he looked forward to joining the heavenly chorus as "an invariable Planet of joy and felicity." But the type of such worship, as Milton saw it, was not only an image of beatitude, but even more significantly an image of divine justice. And indeed this is in a general way the origin of the image of the celestial choral dance in Plato—as a harmonic symbol of justice.[14] I would distinguish the difference between the symbolic intimations of this figure in **Paradise Lost** and God's explicit statement of the justice of his case in Book III as the difference between poetry and logic or rhetoric, even though when God explicitly justifies himself he speaks in Miltonic pentameters. Poetry, Milton said in *Of Education,* was the pre-eminent or crowning attainment in that course of learning whose object was "to repair the ruins of our first parents by regaining to know God aright, and out of that knowledge to love him, to imitate him, to be like him, as we may the neerest by possessing our souls of true vertue, which being united to the heavenly grace of faith makes up the highest perfection." Poetry was pre-eminent, being "more simple, sensuous and passionate"[15] than its nearly related colleagues rhetoric and logic. I take it that he meant poetry was direct, intuitive, and intense, with intensity or passion referring to the poetic rapture animating the whole poetic process in the direction of the

imaginative movement most natural for him, the soaring flight or the ascent to the heavens. Poetry, as the language of symbolic accommodation, Milton seems to imply, is the closest intellectual apprehension we may have of God and his ways, the highest intuitive point in the scale of human intelligence.

Consider for a moment Raphael's allegory of the earthly plant whose flower gives off a spiritual effluence.

> So from the root
> Springs lighter the green stalk, from thence the leaves
> More aery, last the bright consummate flow'r
> Spirits odorous breathes.
>
> (V, 479-82)

The spirituality at the furthermost reach is a quality of understanding or knowledge beyond the reach of discursive intelligence and within the pale of that intuitive apprehension of things peculiar to angelic minds. Adam, and presumably all men to the extent of their regeneracy or likeness to God, may aspire to sublime their understanding to this point, and such knowledge would ultimately be beatific, constituting both knowledge (faith) and ineffably joyful worship. The promise of the *felix culpa* is thus that Adam will in beatitude overgo even the original condition of his primal nature, the model on which God created him:

> a Creature who not prone
> And Brute as other Creatures, but endu'd
> With Sanctity of Reason, might erect
> His Stature, and upright with Front serene
> Govern the rest, self-knowing, and from thence
> Magnanimous to correspond with Heav'n,
> But grateful to acknowledge whence his good
> Descends, thither with heart and voice and eyes
> Directed, in Devotion, to adore
> And worship God Supreme.
>
> (VII, 506-15)

Man, who is created in the similitude of God and the angels, by virtue of that similitude or magnanimity, that knowledge of his correspondence with heaven, is enabled to correspond or commune with heaven; for in knowing himself he knows God, and in knowing God he worships him. Thus magnanimity, or the knowledge of one's spiritual grandeur in the *likeness* to God and his angels, was effectively the knowledge also of one's *communion* with God and the angels.[16]

As early as the third Prolusion Milton had affirmed that the road through self-knowledge was the way to know "those holy minds and intelligences whose company" the spirit "must hereafter join." And if he took the opportunity, as Northrop Frye once remarked, to practice poetic elegies on every fresh corpse that came his way, it seemed less a lugubrious morbidity than a feeling for occasions whereby he might project himself into the conceit of the blessed soul's destination. He found the way there, in fact, by every route imaginable, in poems and exercises as different as **Il Penseroso, At A Solemn Music,** the **Nativity**

*Ode,* Prolusion VII, *Ad Patrem, Lycidas, Epitaphium Damonis,* and *At A Vacation Exercise.* In the last, particularly, he identified his aspiration as being in effect a quest for his ideal poetic theme, "some graver subject,"

> Such where the deep transported mind may soar
> Above the wheeling poles, and at Heav'n's door
> Look in.

And here the mythological conceit of "what unshorn *Apollo* sings," like the choral dance of the Muses in *Il Penseroso,* was a figure for the highest poetic theme, the mystery of beatific worship.[17] Considering the frequency of his allusions to that theme, their preeminence in regard to all his aspirations, how deliberately ought Milton to have stated his devotional intentions with respect to his major work? If he was not likely to abandon his faith in the glorified reward of the saints as an inexpressible worship, a transcendence of poetry and music, would he be likely to forget that men were created to adore God, and that his calling as a poet was to a form of service that was in the very image of Man's first and last end, the glory of perfect worship?

Every aspiration led him on in that direction, even when worship meant a service to God on the level of that lowly race, "where that immortal garland is to be run for, not without dust and heat." Worship was the first of God's commandments, to love him with all one's heart and might, and to Milton this meant the exercise of that zeal which signified the sanctification of God's name, the consecration of what was called *energia,* poetic passion or forcibleness. Zeal, he wrote, begging "leave to soare a while as the Poets use," was a "substance . . . etherial, arming in compleat diamond," and ascending the heavens in a "fiery chariot drawn with two blazing Meteors figur'd like beasts . . . resembling two of those four which *Ezechiel* and S. *John* saw." Zeal, he proclaimed, was the very essence of his own proper humor, a fiery grace of temperament, God-given that he might become an incandescent instrument to arouse righteousness in others. And zeal, as it scourged the enemies of faith, was also itself the very energy of faith, arousing everywhere the spirit of prayer by whose motion the general worship of God was animated. From the same stock of apocalyptic imagery as the fiery chariot of zeal came the figure Milton evoked in his prose hymn in *Animadversions,* where the spirit of prayer mantling England was associated with the Son of Man in the midst of the golden candlesticks about to restore the pure service of his worship through the work of those of his servants who tended the holy oil and fed the ever-burning lamps of devotion.[18]

This spirit of prayer was the Puritan Pegasus, the personification of the holy spontaneity which animated the purest kind of worship, that of extemporary prayer. The practical worship to which radical Puritans especially aspired (as against the visionary worship that governed their ultimate aspirations) was above all extemporary, like that of Adam and Eve unfallen, whose orisons were

> each Morning duly paid
> In various style, for neither various style

> Nor holy rapture wanted they to praise
> Thir Maker, in fit strains pronounce or sung
> Unmeditated, such prompt eloquence
> Flow'd from thir lips.

> (V, 145-50)

Later, after the Fall and contrite in heart, Adam and Eve pray by virtue of prevenient grace, with devotion

> which the Spirit of prayer
> Inspir'd, and wing'd for Heav'n with speedier flight
> Than loudest Oratory.

> (XI, 6-8)

Their prayers arrive personified before the glowing golden altar of God, which more generally represents the fiery nature of the divine love that reciprocally kindles the fire of zeal in his worshippers. It was this fiery, elemental, almost quintessential quality in the spirit of prayer that probably suggested to Milton its relationship to poetic inspiration and poetic rapture, for the latter, like the spirit of prayer, was also an aspiration toward the love of God. In and beyond its fourth stage or degree, poetic rapture, the so-called *furor poeticus,* was identified in Neoplatonic poetics with a quintessential fire betokening the experience of the love of God, which correspondingly as the object of zeal was the fulfilment of the first commandment. Hence when Milton spoke of his ambition to create a work inspired "by devout prayer to that eternall Spirit who can enrich with all utterance and knowledge and sends out his Seraphim with the hallow'd fire of his Altar to touch and purify the lips,"[19] he was describing very concretely both the essence of the highest poetic rapture and the devotional gesture with which he opened the *Nativity Ode,* bidding his spirit join its "voice unto the Angel Choir, / From out his secret Altar toucht with hallow'd fire."

The nature of that fiery spirit may perhaps be illustrated by a passage in *Ad Patrem,* Milton's apologia justifying for his father's benefit his own choice of a poet's career. Underlying the poem was, of course, his need to identify his gifts with the Puritan idea of a spiritual vocation, and so his object was to insinuate the virtual identity of poetry and prayer. Yet so allusively was the matter framed that it has not been hitherto remarked that the mythological trappings of this part of the poem clothe what Milton chose to treat as a Christian mystery, namely the ascent to ultimate beatific vision.[20] The vision itself, merely touched on here, is of a kind with the powerful climax we find in *Lycidas,* and again described at the conclusion of the elegy for the dead Diodati, whom he imagined in his spirit enacting "the immortal marriage where hymns and the ecstatic sound of the lyre mingle with the choric dances of the blessed, and festal throngs revel under the thyrsus of Zion." In the poem to his father the same beatific climax is aproached through a sequence of poetic degrees, last in which is the vision of "that day when we return to our own native Olympus and the fixed ages of changeless eternity have begun." The progression to this point had been through four stages that strongly suggest each level in the hierarchy of the raptures of poetic inspiration, moving quickly through the first three: the kindling of the poetic power in its original afflatus as a heavenly seed in the human mind, mythologically associated both with the Muses and with Prometheus; the poetic power by which the higher gods bind the darker, chthonic forces in men and nature, associated with Orpheus and Dionysus; and the prophetic rapture of the Apollonian furor. Finally there is evoked the fourth rapture of heavenly Love, which often took on an Apocalyptic form and here appears as the Olympian worship of mythologized saints. Imagining their communion in that rapturous millennial apotheosis, Milton said to his father, "we too shall move with golden crowns through the spaces of heaven, blending sweet songs with the soft notes of the lyre, so that the sound shall ring through the starry vault from pole to pole."

The meaning of this ascent was, I think, supposed to be precisely fixed by a glancing reference to a conviction that in the poetic flight itself, as in the instantaneous heavenward winging of the spirit of prayer, beatitude is in some measure touched. Thus if Milton imagined the ascent by way of the poetic raptures to be in some sense a recapitulation of the imaginative stages in the contemplation of beatitude, he also apparently conceived the poetic ascent as a progressive intensification of the powers of spiritual insight, inspired by a motion which was at once an impulse to pray and an impulse to know. The origin of that impulse was metaphorically a celestial influence, an emanation like that from beyond the Empyrean, blending, as it were, the virtues of Urania and the Holy Spirit, but also investing it with the quality of what Puritans called the spirit of prayer. "Even now," Milton concluded the passage, "the fiery spirit who circles the swift spheres is himself singing in harmony with their celestial music, his immortal melody."[21]

In the elemental system of universal correspondences that all this development appears to presuppose, fire is the purest and highest element in the harmonic tetrachord of the basic elements, corresponding to the music of the spheres, which tonally is the fourth or top note in the tetrachord of universal musical essences: those of the harmonic well-tuned strings, the concordance of a harmonious body and soul, the harmony of a just state, and finally the fourth harmony of the celestial spheres. By the same token fire corresponds with the fourth and highest of the poetic raptures, the love of God, so that the fiery spirit of prayer circling the heavens like a Neoplatonic daemon of celestial influence is one and the same with the inspiration of visionary poetry. These "mystic" implications, it should be said, are compressed within an allusiveness that seems the vaguest mythological furniture, so that at first, in a casual reading, nothing more than the mythological enhancement of poetry's dignity seems intended. While we might well miss the point of it all, one wonders whether the elder Milton, as his son's quite real and specific reader, knew what the young Milton was talking about, or whether here, as in **Paradise Lost,** the possible expectations of actual

readers shaped poetic intention and poetic self-definition far less than an imagination of some other, more insubstantial audience.

So we return to the question of Milton's audience, and it should be seen that now this has become a matter of considerable significance. Other points at issue in determining the nature and intention of Milton's epic can possibly be resolved by referring to the poem's obvious formal comprehensiveness. The epic genre was encyclopaedic, encompassing in its scope of meaning the expression of all knowledge,[22] while Milton himself made the point that such comprehensive knowledge was preeminently crowned by two objects, the knowledge of God, i.e., of his nature and of his ways, and the knowledge of his true worship. On this basis one could readily proceed to reconcile the argument that **Paradise Lost** was conceived deliberately as justifying God in faith with the argument that just as deliberately it was conceived as an act of worship. There is a difficulty obstructing too simple an accommodation of these views, however, and it is nicely isolated by Sirluck's concluding judgment that Milton's intention in justifying God's ways was to write "a poem that should be found doctrinal to a nation." My view, on the contrary, leads me to reach for quite another proof-text, the one from the invocation to Book VII, when as a suppliant to the Muse Milton asks Urania to govern his song, "and fit audience find though few," topping off that specification with a request that she drive far off a motley crew, presumably representing a type of unworthy reader.

Since these gifts belong to Urania, the sister of Eternal Wisdom, the Muse whose influence emanates from the Empyrean, and whose sphere is the outermost boundary between earth and God's heaven, presumably those she was asked to exclude would represent readers of unsanctified understanding, possibly without enough grace to respond to Milton's own fervor. In biblical language, these would be the men of Belial (the least zealous of the fallen angels), whose demonic name in Hebrew signifies lewdness or little spiritual understanding. Years earlier, in the *Reason of Church-Government,* Milton digressed from his proper subject to divulge unusual things of himself, and became aware that he was after all writing "in the cool element of prose, a mortall thing among many readers of no *Empyreall* conceit."[23] Let me press this point for a moment, for if I read the early passage correctly, the readers who do possess a touch of Empyreal conceit are those he might with more propriety expect to find in the fiery Empyreal element of poetry, rather than in the cool element of prose.

And the invocation of Urania distinguishes readers into two classes, not those three which would separate mankind in terms of saints, sinners, and all in between who possess an indeterminable degree of prevenient grace. Whether we may regard as saints and sinners the two classes of readers Milton distinguishes in the poem should emerge, I think, from a close reading of the highly allusive texture of the passage. But at least in the context of visionary worship that Milton elsewhere describes there are only two imaginable divisions of mankind, and only one class of participants are imaginable in visionary worship, which takes place "from th' impure / Far separate." Even in the mortal condition, as Milton wrote in *Areopagitica,* where the wheat could not be separated from the tares, where worship was in fact mixed, a symbolic gesture was customary as in some form the fitness of each for sacramental participation was tested so that all might not be spiritually in jeopardy. What radical Puritans objected to in state-enforced conformity was that such conformity as much inhibited the right to exclude the unworthy from sacramental worship as it constrained the righteous to participate in the impurity of an indiscriminate communion. Hence exclusion as a sacramental necessity suggested even to Milton an imaginable occasion when the rigor of force might be required in religion. "We read not," Milton wrote, "that Christ ever exercised force but once, and that was to drive profane ones out of his temple."[24]

In *Paradise Lost* such a ritual gesture of exclusion is implicit in the request to Urania. But it occurs here and not elsewhere because of Urania's special relationship to the gift of "Empyreall conceit," or regenerate understanding. And Urania herself is made to preside over this section of the poem, the account of Creation, because Creation is a metaphor for spiritual procreation, wherein, as Milton once wrote, the minister begets "a number of faithfull men, making a creation like to God's, by infusing his spirit and likenesse into them, to their salvation, as God did into him." Moreover, the communication of this evangelical ardor, this zeal, was an act of a sacred, solemn, and sanctifying nature, expressing the very essence of worship, namely the implicit conviction that to sanctify life was to renew God's creation. As Mircea Eliade suggests, the meaning of the ceremony, ritual, or holy story which recreates the mythic origins of things is a sacramental repetition of the cosmogony, a symbolic way of affirming the identity of the here and now with the primordial mystery of holiness.[25] For Milton that primordial moment was of a piece with the eschatological moment, and hence the repetition of the cosmogony, as if by an exquisite mythic instinct, is in *Paradise Lost* placed halfway between the beginning and the end. "Half yet remains unsung," Milton noted in his invocation; and in that context he recalled as well the original mystery which preceded even Creation when, as he addressed Urania,

> Thou with Eternal Wisdom didst converse,
> Wisdom thy Sister, and with her didst play
> In presence of th' Almighty Father.
>
> (VII, 9-11)

Urania ("The meaning, not the Name") was to Milton an intellectual and spiritual force, perhaps a personification of that ethereal spirit encompassing the spiritual influence of all the other celestial spheres. She represented the boundary between the created universe and the immutable heavens, the region toward which regenerate human understanding invariably aspired, as if to sublime itself into the spirit of prayer and the spirit of wisdom; that is, as if to sublime itself into something wholly quintessential and angelically intuitive. Hence Urania was to be approached with fervor, and at the same time with an awareness of the spiritual danger attending the flight into her realm.

There is an aspect of devotion which is attended by terror, and indeed without this numinous dread it is perhaps unlikely that the passionate experience of the holy can be fully sustained.[26] For Milton such dread seems to have been identified with the possible desecration of his gift, "that one Talent which is death to hide," and in the figurative form of mythology he seems to have associated it, as in *Lycidas,* with the dismemberment of Orpheus, the sacred poet who had served Apollo's temple but was torn to pieces by demonic furies. The invocation to Urania stresses the elements of safety and danger in the experience of first having breathed "Empyreal air," and then of being with "safety guided down" by the Muse to his native element; though like Bellerophon, who had been punished for aspiring to see Heaven, he as a poet had probed divine mysteries. Now he went on

> Standing on Earth, not rapt above the Pole,
> More safe I Sing with mortal voice, unchang'd
> To hoarse or mute, though fall'n on evil days,
> On evil days though fall'n, and evil tongues;
> In darkness, and with dangers compast round,
> And solitude; yet not alone, while thou
> Visit'st my slumbers Nightly, or when Morn
> Purples the East: still govern thou my Song,
> *Urania,* and fit audience find, though few.
> But drive far off the barbarous dissonance
> Of *Bacchus* and his Revellers, the Race
> Of that wild Rout that tore the *Thracian* Bard
> In *Rhodope,* where Woods and Rocks had Ears
> To rapture, till the savage clamor drown'd
> Both Harp and Voice; nor could the Muse defend
> Her Son. So fail not thou, who thee implores:
> For thou art Heavn'ly, shee an empty dream.
>
> (VII, 23-39)

The passage recalls the invocation in Book III, when having reascended from the underworld where imaginatively "With other notes than to th' *Orphean* Lyre" he had consorted with devils, Milton then addressed Holy Light: "thee I revisit safe" (III, 21).

However easily we may read these lines in terms of an oblique personal allusion to his isolation in the England of Charles II, there seems to me no doubt that at a more profound level, what the Lady in *Comus* intimated was the true Orphic power, or the "flame of sacred vehemence,"[27] is responsible for their strange forcefulness in evoking both serenity and the terrifying murder of Orpheus. I suggest Milton's deeper meaning may be determined by the play in the thrice repeated use in the invocations of the word "safety," which in English translates what is expressed by the Latin *salus* and the Greek *soteria,* namely, salvation. This meaning would account for the fact that the passage expresses with such singular gravity a numinous dread centered not only on the flight into the Empyrean but aroused also by what is literally a holy terror of communion with the profane. For salvation is only within the Body of Christ, the true, or Mystical or Invisible Church. As Milton knew it to be dogmatically stated: *Nulla salus extra ecclesiam,* there is no salvation or spiritual safety outside of the Church; and hence only within a true communion of spiritual understanding may the heavenly mysteries be shared. "Good men," he once wrote years earlier, "dare not against Gods command hold communion . . . in holy things" with sinners. "And this will be accompanied with a religious dred of being outcast from the company of Saints, and from the fatherly protection of God in his Church, to consort with the devil and his angels."[28]

Thus while the poem as an offering of evangelical edification acknowledges the great middle ground of readers, to whom sufficient prevenient grace is accorded for them to rise or fall by their own understanding and will, at its most intense personal moments the poem for Milton was a devotional gesture of a sacramental character, implicitly welcoming the communion of the saints, but closing itself off from the spiritual participation of those who were not meant to be saved, and therefore were not meant to understand.[29] The element of implicit meaning suggested by the use of the word "safety" as salvation has the effect of postulating a relationship between Milton and his ideal audience which is somewhat like that of a liturgical celebrant and his congregation.

Indeed it would seem that this meaning was clearly recognized by Andrew Marvell who, in writing most of his commendation of *Paradise Lost* around the theme of the dangers the poem courted, congratulated Milton specifically on the technical accomplishment whereby he sustained the decorum of sublimity. Marvell's point was that in so doing Milton insured the spiritual safety of himself and his proper readers.

> That Majesty which through thy Work doth Reign
> Draws the Devout, deterring the Profane,
> And things divine thou treat'st of in such state
> As them preserves, and thee, inviolate.

It is interesting to note how elsewhere in his poem Marvell manages to suggest that Dryden, who tried to exploit *Paradise Lost* by turning it into a heroic play, was somehow the wrong kind of reader. Who might have been the right kind of reader? The answer is suggested in the contrast afforded by the story of how Thomas Ellwood read the manuscript of the poem, asking the one thoughtful pious question which was Ellwood's only recorded comment. "Thou hast said much here of Paradise Lost, but what hast thou to say of Paradise Found?" To which Milton did not directly reply, but took the matter sufficiently to heart and wrote *Paradise Regained.*[30] Clearly, if anyone was qualified to belong among the fit audience though few it was the Quaker Ellwood, whose cultural and aesthetic responses were probably not up to those of the common seventeenth-century reader of heroic poetry, to say nothing of John Dryden.

But as a Quaker Ellwood knew that faith was expressed by a spontaneous motion of the spirit, that its aspirations were visionary, and that worship was a wider concept than anything merely confined between church walls. Faith went out into the world where it encountered moral tragedy and doubt, the trial of despair, but armored with the intensity of zeal. Only when faith was triumphant and there was no further need to justify God's ways and magnify or adore his Providence might a man return to his peace, as the chorus says at the end of *Samson Agonistes,* with "calm of mind, all passion spent."

*Notes*

1. *Times Literary Supplement* review of Ernest Sirluck's *"Paradise Lost": A Deliberate Epic* (Cambridge, 1967), February 8, 1968, p. 134. (The reviewer alludes as well to Dennis Burden's book, *The Logical Epic* [Cambridge, Mass., 1967]). Sirluck, p. 28, was quoting a passage found in *The Complete Prose of John Milton* (henceforth designated as *CPW*), ed. Don M. Wolfe (New Haven, 1953-), II, 292. That Milton regarded the mystery of Providence as a subject proper to be considered and celebrated in a public context is suggested by his very first venture into polemical prose, *Of Reformation,* which opens with him reflecting on "these deep and retired thoughts . . . of God, and of his miraculous *ways,* and works, amongst men." The tract, which in one sense may be said to be about the revelation of the mystery of God's providential dealing with England, appropriately ends with a formal act of adoration. *CPW,* I, 519, 613-17.

2. In another study I undertake to show that as an act of worship Milton's epic is not an epic as anyone else had ever imagined the genre before, since it has an implicit "mystic" form identified with the Revelation of St. John, the scriptural work traditionally associated with the mystery of Providence. See "The Apocalypse Within *Paradise Lost,*" to appear in a volume of essays on the tercentenary of *Paradise Lost,* edited by Thomas Kranidas and to be published by the University of California Press.

3. Francis Bacon, *The Advancement of Learning,* II; *Works,* ed. J. Spedding (New York, 1870), VI, 204-05. On Neoplatonic poetics, see, for example, Leone Ebreo, *The Philosophy of Love,* trans. F. Friedeberg-Seeley and J. H. Barnes (London, 1937), pp. 110-14; and, closer to Milton's milieu, Henry Reynoldes, *Mythomystes* (1632). Relevant studies are those of Rhodes Dunlap, "The Allegorical Interpretation of Renaissance Literature," *PMLA,* LXXXII (March, 1967), 39-43; and Edgar Wind, *Pagan Mysteries in the Renaissance* (New Haven, 1958), particularly ch. 1. For Milton on Pythagoras, see Prolusion II, *CPW,* I, 235-36.

4. *PL* III, 410-15, my italics. All quotations from the

English poems are from *John Milton: Complete Poems and Major Prose,* ed. M. Y. Hughes (New York, 1957).

5. *Paradise Lost,* ed. A. W. Verity (Cambridge, 1936), II, 439.

6. *CPW,* I, 616, 706.

7. *Ibid.,* 816-17.

8. *The Christian Doctrine,* I, i; *Prose Works,* ed. J. A. St. John (London, 1848-1881), IV, 12-13.

9. On Puritan liturgies, see Horton Davies, *The Worship of the English Puritans* (London, 1948). Milton's withdrawal from public worship is recorded by John Toland in the *Life.* See the *Early Lives of Milton,* ed. Helen Darbishire (London, 1965), p. 195. See also Elegy VI to Charles Diodati, accompanying the *Nativity Ode;* and Milton's Letter VIII, (*CPW,* I, 326-27), also to Diodati, concerning the relationship of his spiritual destiny to his aesthetic quest. Finally, there is the sacramental significance of Milton's covenanting with his readers in the *Reason of Church-Government,* partially perceived by Ernest Sirluck in "Milton's Idle Right Hand," *JEGP,* LX (1961), 767-69. In the *Christian Doctrine* (II, iv; *Prose Works,* ed. St. John, V, 42-45), individual vows publicly undertaken for special reasons are classed as a form of worship and the non-performance of them as a kind of sacrilege. The word sacrament originally meant a religious vow. It was generally true that the Puritans regarded any solemn act of public dedication or commitment as a form of divine worship—witness the Solemn League and Covenant of the Puritan Revolution and the Mayflower Compact (cf. Horton Davies, p. 86). Both Milton's covenant in the prose and his affirmation in the chorus of *Paradise Lost* assume, therefore, the character of solemn acts of sacramental self-dedication and partake of the character of worship.

10. Seriatim: *Reason of Church-Government, CPW,* I, 752; and Sir Philip Sidney, *The Defense of Poesie,* in *Literary Criticism, Plato to Dryden,* ed. A. H. Gilbert (New York, 1940), pp. 412-13. On the visionary worship of the Apocalypse, see my study "The Apocalypse Within *Paradise Lost.*"

11. Sirluck, *A Deliberate Epic,* p. 20, and *PL,* III, 173-202; Romans 8:29-30.

12. Sirluck, *A Deliberate Epic,* p. 28; *L'Allegro,* l. 144.

13. I discuss this passage briefly in "The Apocalypse Within *Paradise Lost,*" in much the same sense as does Joseph Summers, as a kind of metaphor for Milton's poetry itself. Summers, I think rightly, intimates that the dance represents "what Milton perceived as most glorious in the ways of God as well as . . . what he intended and achieved within his own poem." *The Muse's Method* (Cambridge, Mass., 1962), p. 85.

14. For Plato music and dancing were mimetic, representing most directly the harmony discernible in the sight of the starry courses and inferentially known to govern the universe. The dance as well as the experience of music were means by which men participated in heavenly or divine harmony and came to know it. To be sure, harmony was a comprehensive term for Plato, but among the attributes of the divine perfection which it represented, and which were to be imitated, was divine justice. Hence in a state where there were just laws, there, correspondingly, dances would be taught that in a pure manner imitated the heavenly dances. See *Laws* II, (40-41) on pedagogic and religious dances, and the *Timaeus* (47), where the whole Creation is figured as a dance of intelligences who are identified with the stars. Knowledge or the experience of this celestial harmony of the heavenly intelligences, Plato wrote, was to be applied to "the causes of our own intelligence which are akin to them, the unperturbed to the perturbed." To this passage might be compared Milton's description of his epic plans, which, among other things, would serve "to allay the perturbations of the mind, and set the affections in right tune." Milton apparently proposed this object in terms of what immediately followed, or by means which celebrated "in glorious and lofty Hymns the throne and equipage of Gods Almightinesse, and what he works, and what he suffers to be wrought with high providence in his Church." This literary and devotional program, with its calculated effect on the reason and the emotions, is, of course, a synopsis of a kind of mimetic literary harmony that not only imitates God's hidden harmony (the harmony of his ways) but functions as worship. Hence as worship and in the confidence assumed by the act of imitation it serves to justify God's ways. The imagery of the program Milton described in the *Reason of Church-Government,* like the image of the mystic dance in *Paradise Lost,* assimilates the Platonic idea of the celestial harmonies to the image of the choral worship which in the Apocalypse gives the notion of heavenly harmony a totally different turn. Yet it was the Apocalyptic harmony which Milton quite early came to consider as the type or the abstract of all harmony, describing the heavenly worship as a disciplined but free concord of the kind "which with her musicall cords preserves and holds . . . together" all parts of all "sociable perfection in this life" (*The Reason of Church-Government, CPW,* I, 751-52). Compare also *PL* V, 175-78, where the seven planetary bodies in their spheres "move / In mystic Dance not without Song." In the history of the idea of the sacred choral dance Christ, or the Son with his angels, became the center of the dance, replacing Apollo as the leader of the Muses in the cosmic dance of worship. Patristic and later references are extensive. See Hugo Rahner, *Greek Myths and Christian Mystery,* trans. Brian Battershaw (London, 1963), pp. 67-68, 150, and C. A. Patrides, *Milton and the Christian Tradition*

(Oxford, 1966), p. 43. John Colet, for example, describes the communion service as "a chorus, and more radiant sacred dance" led by Christ, and calls this a figure of the type used in Scripture to express the heavenly mysteries. In *Two Treatises on the Hierarchies of Dionysius,* ed. J. H. Lupton (London, 1869), pp. 59-60.

15. *CPW,* II, 366-67, 403.

16. Concerning Milton's sense of magnanimity and its significance much more might be said by way of argument, since most critical discussions of what Milton meant by magnanimity generally refer it to the *Nicomachean Ethics* and assume it to be a secular virtue. Milton used the word frequently and almost invariably in the sense he defined in the *Christian Doctrine,* as the reflection of the measure of the regenerate soul's likeness to God. Thus the concept of magnanimity was the basis of Milton's thinking concerning self-knowledge as well as the basis for the variable degrees of regenerate understanding which he apparently believed distinguished even the saints. What he meant by magnanimity also related to the quality of his spiritual egotism, for the term describes his sense of possessing within himself a very large share of the divine intelligence. In addition to Scripture, which declared Man to be created in the divine image, a likely source for Milton's concept of magnanimity is the *Timaeus* (29-30), where God's goodness is described as moving him to create others who would "be so far as possible like himself." On magnanimity, see *Of Reformation* and the *Reason of Church-Government, CPW,* I, 571, 842; and the *Christian Doctrine,* I, iv; II, ix; ed. St. John, IV, 59; V, 94-95. In the last text magnanimity is also treated as the source of zeal, while its ultimate object is described as beatitude. Cf. Augustine, "For to teach a man how to love himself was this end appointed, whereunto he refers all his works for beatitude." *City of God,* X, iv; trans. J. Healy (London, 1945), I, 276.

17. Prolusion III, *CPW,* I, 247. Milton had a hierarchical view of significant poetic themes, just as he had a hierarchical view of poetic genres and of so many other things. The highest form of poetry was an expression of the highest reach of human knowledge, which was "to know anything distinctly of God, and of his true worship" (*Reason of Church-Government, CPW,* I, 801; and cf. Prolusion VII, *CPW,* I, 291). Ralph W. Condee, in "The Structure of Milton's 'Epitaphium Damonis'," *SP,* LXII (1965), 577-94, discusses Milton's hierarchical gradation of poetic themes and genres in relation to the structure of the elegy for Diodati.

18. On worship and the love of God as the first commandment, see Deut. v, 7 and the Mosaic gloss in Deut. vi, 4-5. See *Areopagitica, CPW,* II, 515, for the reference to the "immortal garland." On zeal and Milton's temperamental humor, and on zeal in

relation to the spirit of prayer, see *An Apology, CPW,* I, 900, 936-43; and *Animadversions, CPW,* I, 706-07.

19. *The Reason of Church-Government, CPW,* I, 821. On the *furor poeticus,* the seminal text is Plato's *Ion,* 543; its Renaissance treatment may be seen in Marsilio Ficino's *In Platonis Ionem, vel de furore poetico, Opera Omnia* (Bale, 1561), pp. 1281-84; *In Convivium,* pp. 1361-62; and *In Phaedum,* pp. 1257-59. A good general summary of the Neoplatonic concept of the poetic rapture is that of Frances Yates, in *The French Academies of the Sixteenth Century* (London, 1947), pp. 80-84. Miss Yates shows the poetic furor to have been figuratively conceived as a series of successive raptures mounting by stages under the guidance of the Muses who involve the soaring spirit in their dance. The association of the poetic rapture with the first commandment seems to have been what Peter Martyr had in mind when he suggested in his *Commonplaces* that poets ought to use their powers to celebrate and worship God "with all their mind, with all their heart and with all their strength." Peter Martyr is cited by Lily Campbell, "The Christian Muse," *The Huntington Library Bulletin,* 8 (1935), 32.

20. The fusion of apocalyptic and Platonic conceptions of the ascent to beatitude, which is incidental in this poem but constant in Milton's poetry, is more extensively illustrated in Robert Greville, Lord Brooke, *The Nature of Truth* (London, 1641), a short treatise at the heart of which is a discussion of the scale of ascent to beatitude. Lord Brooke's work was animated by the purest apocalyptic enthusiasm, and Lord Brooke himself was greatly admired by Milton, who eulogized him in the *Areopagitica* (*CPW,* II, 560). The translation of *Ad Patrem* (and also of *Epitaphium Damonis*) used here is that of Douglas Bush, in his edition of *The Complete Poetical Works of John Milton* (Boston, 1965).

21. Cf. the image in the *Timaeus* (37), where the *anima mundi* circling with the motion of the physical universe and drawing to itself the rational aspirations of human souls suggests what seems to be Milton's idea of the drawing together of rapturous inspiration and the circling spirit. The whole subject of the meaning of the Spirit for Milton should be studied, I believe, against the background of those Neoplatonic ideas analyzed with great skill by D. P. Walker in *Spiritual and Demonic Magic from Ficino to Campanella* (London, 1958). Walker's section on Telesio seems particularly relevant. But at the same time what must be taken into account in considering Milton's conception of the Spirit is the fact that in Milton's work Puritanism and Neoplatonism fused. Consider, for example, the following passage from the *Reason of Church-Government* (*CPW,* I, 841-42), which illustrates Milton's zeal, its relationship to his sense

of magnanimity, and its reliance on the elemental systems of correspondences peculiar to Neoplatonic theories of psychology and poetic *energia*. The passage does not mention the Spirit but obviously has great bearing on any consideration of it. "And if the love of God as a fire sent from Heaven to be ever kept alive upon the altar of our hearts, be the first principle of all godly and vertuous actions in men, this pious and just honouring of ourselves is the second, and may be thought as the radical moisture and fountain head, whence every laudable and worthy enterprize issues forth. And although I have giv'n it the name of a liquid thing yet is it not incontinent to bound it self, as humid things are, but hath in it a most restraining and powerfull abstinence to start back and glob it self upward from the mixture of any ungenerous and unbeseeming motion. . . . How shall a man know to do himselfe this right, how performe this honourable duty of estimation and respect towards his own soul and body? which way will leade him best to this hill top of sanctity and goodnesse above which there is no higher ascent but to the love of God which from this self-pious regard cannot be asunder?"

22. See Northrop Frye, *The Return of Eden* (Toronto, 1964), ch. 1.

23. *CPW,* I, 808. My italics.

24. *Areopagitica, CPW,* II, 564; *Of Civil Power,* in *The Student's Milton,* ed. F. A. Patterson (New York, 1957), p. 876.

25. *Animadversions, CPW,* I, 721; Eliade, "Cosmic and Eschatological Renewal," in *The Sacred and the Profane,* trans. W. R. Trask (New York, 1959); and "The Regeneration of Time," in *Cosmos and History,* trans. W. R. Trask (New York, 1959).

26. The term "numinous dread" was given currency by Rudolph Otto, *The Idea of the Holy,* trans. J. W. Harvey (London, 1957), who identified it as intimately associated with the psychic experience of sanctity. Cf. Milton's induction to his rapturous apocalyptic prayer in *Of Reformation,* "O Sir, I doe now feele my selfe in wrapt on the sodaine into those mazes and *Labyrinths* of dreadful and hideous thoughts.. . ." (*CPW,* I, 613).

27. Ll. 793-99. See also the concluding paragraph of Milton's passionate declamation at the end of the *Readie and Easie Way* where he invokes an Orphic religious power that might enable him to "raise of these stones . . . children of reviving liberty." *Student's Milton,* p. 914.

28. *Reason of Church-Government, CPW,* I, 841. The *O.E.D.* records a meaning for *safe* related to salvation, but not one for *safety.* Instances of the use of *safety* in the sense of salvation can be found in John Owen's treatise *Of Communion, Works,* ed. W. H. Goold (Edinburgh, 1862), II, 44-45, and in an

elaboration of a Scriptural text by Lancelot Andrewes, who spins out the multiple possibilities of the words *soter, salus,* and *safety.* The passage is quoted by T. S. Eliot in his essay on Andrewes, which is reprinted as an introduction to *The Private Devotions of Lancelot Andrewes,* ed. and trans. F. W. Brightman (New York, 1961), p. xvi. The Smectymnuan Stephen Marshall also punned on the word, but in a different sense. In a sermon preached before the House of Commons Marshall turned the political catch-phrase, *salus populi suprema lex* into *Salus Ecclesia suprema lex,* recovering for *safety* in the second context its original spiritual sense. See *Meroz Cursed* (London, 1641), p. 18. A similar play seems evident in two instances in *Samson Agonistes,* the first being the Chorus' phrase in its hymn to God, concerning men "such as thou hast solemnly elected, / With gifts and graces eminently adorn'd / To some great work, thy glory, / And people's safety" (ll. 678-81); and the second being Samson's words concerning Dalila, to whom he had betrayed his "most sacred trust / Of secrecy, my safety, and my life" (ll. 1001-02).

29. Milton's conception of the meaning of such a thing as regenerate understanding can only be lightly touched on here. But see the *Christian Doctrine,* II, ii: "The treasures of wisdom [i.e., knowing the will of God] are not to be rashly lavished on such as are incapable of appreciating them." *Prose Works,* ed. St. John, V, 11.

30. *The History of the Life of Thomas Ellwood* (1714), in *The Student's Milton,* p. xlviii.


## Barbara K. Lewalski (essay date 1974)

SOURCE: "Milton on Women—Yet Once More," in *Milton Studies,* Vol. VI, 1974, pp. 3-20.

[*In the following essay, Lewalski responds to a feminist study of* Paradise Lost *that looks at the work in terms of sociological role definitions and asserts that such analyses are limited in their ability to assess the true complexity of Milton's treatment of women and the universality of the poem's concerns.*]

It was bound to happen sooner or later—a feminist analysis of Milton on women. So bad, though, has been Milton's press on the "woman question" that the exercise might have seemed hardly worth the trouble, a merely ritual beating of a very dead horse. However, Marcia Landy's article, recently published in *Milton Studies,*[1] does not merely resurrect the stereotypes of Milton the misogynist importing his own domestic problems into his poems, or Milton the Puritan necessarily echoing and reaffirming the paternalistic ethos and values of the Judeo-Christian tradition. She recognizes at the outset that a great mythopoeic writer reworks and re-creates the myths he inherits, out of "his own consciousness and . . . the consciousness of his time."[2] Nevertheless, her analysis of familial roles and relationships in *Paradise Lost,* culminating in a description of Milton's Eve as a submissive and dependent wife relegated to domestic tasks and valued chiefly for her procreative role, seems to me to miss what is most important in Milton's presentation of the "two great Sexes [which] animate the World" (VII, 151).[3]

Professor Landy begins with a short list of distinguished women Miltonists—which could have been much extended—and then calls attention to the anomaly that none of them has yet attempted a feminist analysis of his work. Of course it may be true, as the article implies, that our consciousnesses have not been raised far enough to permit us to relax the posture of scholarly objectivity imposed by a male-dominated critical climate, so as to be able to treat the poem from the vantage point of female experience. I suspect, though, that it is not so much naiveté about the necessary limits of scholarly objectivity that has deterred us from this enterprise (Miltonists, men and women alike, have always been ready enough to create Milton in their own images) so much as a different set of theoretical and methodological assumptions about how we experience, and what we value in, poems and especially this poem.

My own reservations concerning feminist critiques generally and this article in particular emerge from the following presuppositions. (1) After assenting readily enough to the proposition that our perceptions of art are necessarily affected in important ways by race, class, or sex, I would yet affirm the capacity of great art to transcend these lesser categories of human experience and speak to our common humanity. Which of us, male or female, old or young, black or white, rich or poor, does not understand and respond to King Lear's agony on his heath? On this score, a feminist analysis of *Paradise Lost,* with its nearly exclusive emphasis upon the image and role of woman in the poem, may do real violence to a woman reader's imaginative experience of and response to everything else that the poem contains—Satan's rebellion, Adam's intellectual quest, the idyl of Edenic life, the heroism of Abdiel, the glorious vitality of the Creation scene, and much more. (2) Feminist criticism often seems prone to substitute sociological for literary analysis. Though the article in question incorporates considerable literary detail, still the categories imported from sociology and anthropology—the analysis of family roles—provide a very partial set of terms for approaching the portrayal of Adam and Eve in the poem. It will not surprise any of us, surely, to discover that Milton, like everyone else in his era, thought in terms of hierarchy and of the patriarchal family. But an analysis centered almost exclusively upon the language and postures of family relationship necessarily imposes a conventional and somewhat distorted framework for examining Milton's re-creation of the myth of the first man and woman. To see that re-creation clearly requires a sensitive literary analysis of speech, scene, and action in the poem. (3) Great poets of necessity mediate their visions of human experience through the categories available to them, but if we read perceptively we will not be tempted either to condemn them or to condescend to them on that account. We will not, because they are gloriously and supremely right about the most essential things, presenting us with a vision of the human condition which astonishes by its profundity even though the categories through which it is rendered may be outmoded. Homer of course presented the Trojan War against the backdrop of Olympus and all those now defunct gods, but no one has known or shown more fully the utter futility, the pointless brutality, the moral deterioration attendant upon protracted warfare. (The *Iliad* should perhaps be made required reading for presidents and Pentagon officials.) Dante of course perceived his universe in Ptolemaic and Thomistic categories, but no one of any age has shown more vividly or analyzed more trenchantly the modes, varieties, and postures of human evil—particularly those of the intellectual order. And Milton of course accepted the categories of hierarchy and the natural inferiority of woman, yet his reworking of the Adam and Eve myth has explored with remarkable incisiveness and profundity a basic human predicament. Each character is shown to bear full individual responsibility for his or her own choices, his or her own growth (or lack of it), his or her own contribution to the preservation and perfecting of the human environment; but at the same time, each experiences to the depths of his soul the need for the other, the inescapable bonds of human interdependence. And the truly surprising thing about Milton's portrayal of Eve is that he has examined this dilemma as carefully in regard to the woman as to the man. Indeed, I am tempted to say that few writers of any era—including our own—have taken women so seriously as Milton does, as multifaceted human beings with impressive intellectual and moral powers and responsibilities.

That apparently outrageous statement will take some proving, and I will begin with a few clarifications regarding Eve's role and activities in Eden. The point here is that, far from being relegated to an exclusively or primarily domestic role, Eve in the ideal (prelapsarian) human marriage is shown to participate fully in the entire range of human activities. That the division of labor along sexual lines is a concomitant of the Fall is more than hinted in Book IX, when Eve's proposal that they undertake separate gardening tasks as a means to greater efficiency is shown to lead directly to the Fall. The Edenic condition is a life of sharing and partnership in almost all activities: for Adam, Eve is "Sole partner and sole part of all these joys" (IV, 411). To be sure, Eve does prepare and serve the noonday meal when Raphael pays his visit (they didn't share the cooking—or rather, the selection, pressing, and setting forth of the fruits from the abundance Edenic Nature provides). But Eve is not off about these tasks while the gentlemen talk about higher things—the dilemma of the modern hostess. It is all accomplished in the moments from Adam's first view of the approaching angel to the time of his arrival in Eden. Nor does Eve withdraw for the washing-up while the gentlemen have their port and cigars: it is curious that many readers (including Professor Landy) seem not to notice that Eve is present throughout almost the whole of the series of lectures Raphael provides to satisfy the first couple's intellectual curiosity about their world. She is thus as fully instructed as Adam is about the substance of the universe—"one first matter all"—and the curiously fluid conception of hierarchy this monism sustains, according to which angels and men are seen to differ in degree only, not in kind, and human beings are encouraged to expect the gradual refinement of their own natures to virtually angelic condition (V, 470-505).[4] (How much more fluid, then, the hierarchical distinctions between man and woman?) Eve is present also for the epic account of the War in Heaven and all the vicarious insights that story provides about the nature of evil, of temptation, of obedience and fidelity. Again, she is present for the account of the Creation—graphically described, as Michael Lieb and others have shown,[5] in terms of the imagery of human sexuality—and therefore is led, as Adam is, to apprehend that sexuality as participation in God's divine creativity. She departs only when Adam poses his astronomical question—and then not because the men wish her gone (her grace "won who saw to wish her stay" [VIII, 43]), nor yet because of any incapacity: "Yet went she not, as not with such discourse / Delighted, or not capable her ear / Of what was high" (VIII, 48-50). In part she leaves for dramatic convenience so that Adam may discuss his marital problem with Raphael, and, as the poet insists, she will receive all the information later, from Adam's account. The prelapsarian educational curriculum, then, is precisely the same for the woman as for the man— ontology, cosmology, metaphysics, moral philosophy, history, epic poetry, divine revelation, physics, and astronomy. And the method is the same except in regard to the last-mentioned topic—though Adam does indeed take the initiative throughout by asking the lecturer leading questions. This identity of educational experiences for the sexes was hardly a conventional concept in the mid-seventeenth century, though it is entirely consonant with Milton's sense of marriage as, in its essence, human companionship and partnership.

Fully shared work in and responsibility for the human world is hardly a seventeenth-century (or even a twentieth-century) commonplace either, yet it is central to Milton's rendering of the Edenic life. As I have argued in more detail elsewhere,[6] both Adam and Eve are images of God "the sovran Planter" in that they must preserve, cultivate, sustain, and raise to higher levels of perfection the world which has been made for them. This labor, though not arduous, is absolutely essential since the highly cultivated garden, made as all things are from the materials of chaos, will revert to wilderness without constant creative ordering. Adam observes in Book IV (623-32) that the couple can barely cope on a day-to-day basis with the "wanton growth" of the garden, to maintain it in a condition of ordered beauty; indeed, at times it is marred by "overgrown" paths and "unsightly" blossoms strewn about. Later Eve makes the same point: the work is "Our pleasant task," yet "what we by day / Lop overgrown, or prune, or prop, or bind, / One night or two with wanton growth derides / Tending to wild" (IX, 207-12). The narrator also testifies to the truth of this description—"much thir work outgrew /

The hands' dispatch of two Gard'ning so wide" (IX, 212-13)—though both expect the task to be easier when they have progeny to share it. The point, however, is that Eve, far from being confined to her bower and her domestic concerns while Adam forges forth in the outside world, is imagined to share fully with her mate in the necessary work of that world.

She shares as well in all the other duties and pleasures, all the other kinds of human self-expression and creativity that the poem records. Not least among these is the delight of simple human conversation and dialogue, the constant, ongoing discussion with Adam about the flood of new observations and experiences that bursts in upon them day by day—whether the mystery of the stars shining at night, or the sudden challenge of hospitality for an angelic guest, or the untoward occurrence of a bad dream, or whatever. Eve participates with Adam also in "naming" the lesser orders of creation, thereby showing her comprehension of their natures, her rightful dominion over them, and her command of the human power of symbolization. That Adam named the animals and she the plants is indicated when she laments the leaving of her beloved flowers, "which I bred up with tender hand / From the first op'ning bud, and gave ye Names" (XI, 276-77). She names a lesser order of creation than Adam (hierarchy again), but she shares in the activity, a point unperceived by many critics, including Professor Landy, who take Adam's supposedly exclusive naming function as evidence that poetry and the arts of language are for Milton a masculine prerogative.[7] But Eve's command of the arts of language is evident throughout the poem. She is no mean rhetorician, as her graceful, ritualistic addresses to Adam demonstrate—as does, in another mode, her skillful argumentation in the marital dispute. She is a poet as well, composing each day with Adam those divine poems and praises of God which they both in "various style" and in "fit strains pronounct or sung / Unmeditated." As the narrator observes, "prompt eloquence / Flow'd from thir lips, in Prose or numerous Verse, / More tuneable than needed Lute or Harp" (V, 146-51). Eve is also a poet in her own right: nothing in Milton's epic is more artful, melodious, and graceful than the love lyric she addresses to Adam (IV, 641-56) which begins, "Sweet is the breath of morn." To be sure, it is not in the highest genre of poetry according to the common Renaissance scale or Milton's own, but of its kind it is superb.

Enough has perhaps been said to establish the point that Eve, though perceived as Adam's hierarchical inferior, is not relegated to the domestic sphere, nor her creativity confined to her maternal role; rather she—"accomplisht Eve" (IV, 660)—shares and participates in the full range of human activities and achievements. But Professor Landy's further point about Milton's emphasis upon Eve's maternity as that which is somehow necessary to validate her sexual relation to Adam[8] ought to be confronted directly. On this issue, two observations may be made. In the first place, it should be observed that Adam is as constantly and honorifically addressed in terms alluding to his paternity of the human race as Eve is in relation to her maternity: such language is not intended to limit either one to the confines of the familial role (the inadequacies of the sociological analysis become clearest here) but rather to insist upon the honor and dignity shared by both as progenitors of the entire human race. The narrator constantly refers to them in such terms, thereby relating himself and his readers to them as their descendants. They are "our Grand Parents" (I, 29); Eve is "our general Mother" (IV, 492); Adam is "our first Father" (IV, 495) or again "our great Progenitor" (V, 544). Similarly, in his epithalamion to them—"Hail Wedded Love" (IV, 751-75)—the narrator in his emphasis upon their progeny adopts again the perspective of one of their descendants, besides of course conforming to the norms of the genre. Raphael, who addresses Eve in the striking phrase foreshadowing the later *Ave* to the Virgin—"Hail Mother of Mankind" (V, 388)—addresses Adam in similar terms—"Sire of men" (VIII, 218). And while Eve recalls that when she was first presented to Adam she was promised that she would "bear / Multitudes like thyself, and thence be call'd / Mother of human Race," Adam similarly recalls that in his own first moments after creation a divine voice referred to his role as patriarch: "Adam, rise / First Man, of Men innumerable ordain'd / First Father" (IV, 296-98). These terms are not sociological or anthropological role definitions, but praises of the human participation in the superabundant divine creativity.

Second, the text of the poem does not sustain the assertion that the recognition of Eve as mother is prior to and sanction for her roles as lover and spouse. She is certainly not so presented to the reader, who first sees Eve as a young girl on her honeymoon, her hair disheveled in wanton ringlets, engaged in "youthful dalliance" and casual love play with her husband (IV, 304-40).[9] Nor is she so perceived by Adam, who in his long argument with God urges and demonstrates most forcefully his need for a mate—not for progeny but for companionship: "Of fellowship I speak / Such as I seek, fit to participate / All rational delight" (IV, 289-91). And when he claims her as his wife after she makes a move to turn from him back to her own "wat'ry image," he does so in terms of his desire for her as companion and lover: she was made of his flesh and bone that she might be "Henceforth an individual solace dear; / Part of my Soul . . . My other half" (IV, 486-88). God in establishing their marriage sets forth the same order of priorities: commending Adam for his sound argument and agreeing to his request, God observes, "I, ere thou spak'st, / Knew it not good for Man to be alone," and he promises to bring to Adam "Thy likeness, thy fit help, thy other self" (VIII, 444-50). Also, Eve records that when the divine voice wooed her from the contemplation of her own image in the pool it promised first that she would "enjoy him / Whose image thou art," and only then that she would bear "Multitudes like thyself" and be called "Mother of human Race" (IV, 472-75). And even that last reference, in context, is not so much an emphasis upon her maternity as

such as upon her opportunity now to exchange illusory images for true ones, which she can bring into substantial existence.

This emphasis upon marriage as human companionship is precisely what we should expect from the Milton of the divorce tracts, those remarkable documents which argued for divorce on grounds of incompatibility, precisely on the assumption that the prime end of marriage, as defined authoritatively in the Genesis story, is human companionship. The argument seemed both preposterous and scandalous to Milton's contemporaries, who had learned from the Church Fathers, the medieval scholastics, and most of the Protestant theologians that marriage was instituted primarily for progeny and the relief of lust (in recognition of which priorities the various Protestant countries permitted divorce or annulment for impotence, adultery, or desertion) and only secondarily for mutual help and assistance.[10] But Milton insists that the Genesis account bears out his own emphasis upon the companionship of the mind and spirit as the chief end of marriage:

> What his [God's] chiefe end was of creating woman to be joyned with man, his own instituting words declare, and are infallible to informe us what is mariage, and what is no mariage . . . "*It is not good,*" saith he, "*that man should be alone; I will make him a help meet for him.*" From which words so plain, lesse cannot be concluded . . . then that in God's intention a meet and happy conversation is the chiefest and the noblest end of mariage; for we find here no expression so necessarily implying carnall knowledg, as this prevention of lonelinesse to the mind and spirit of man. . . . And indeed it is a greater blessing from God, more worthy so excellent a creature as man is, and a higher end to honour and sanctifie the league of mariage, whenas the solace and satisfaction of the mind is regarded and provided for before the sensitive pleasing of the body. And with all generous persons maried thus it is, that where the minde and person pleases aptly, there some unaccomplishment of the bodies delight may be better borne with, then when the mind hangs off in an unclosing disproportion, though the body be as it ought; for there all corporall delight will soon become unsavoury and contemptible.[11]

It is true that Milton sets forth his argument for divorce almost entirely from the standpoint of the needs and rights of the husband. But it is also evident that despite Milton's acceptance of the commonplace of female subordination in the natural hierarchy, he did not make of women either sex objects or mother figures. Indeed, the passage quoted and the entire drift of the divorce tracts show him to be as convinced as even a modern feminist might wish that the dispelling of these particular stereotypes of woman is of the first importance to the happiness of the male sex.

To come now to what is of basic significance in Milton's reworking of the myth of Adam and Eve—his exploration, on the one hand, of each individual's personal responsibility for his own choices, for the direction of his own life; and on the other hand, of the powerful emotional, psychological, and spiritual bonds which make man and woman inextricably interdependent. In the course of this exploration, Milton's treatment of the archetypal woman achieves extraordinary depth and dimension.

Before and after the Fall, both Adam and Eve show some disposition to avoid or lessen the tensions involved in hard choices or the guilt attendant upon wrong choices by appealing to the fact of their interdependence to cast responsibility upon each other. But the poem permits this rationale to neither of them: each is "Sufficient to have stood, though free to fall" (IV, 99), and each must assume responsibility for his own choices. Adam is lightly satirized on several occasions as he pronounces the time-honored male complaints about women as the source of all difficulties and problems and then is roundly rebuked for his foolishness by whatever heavenly visitant is on the scene at the time. In his still unfallen state Adam complains to Raphael (who assumes for the moment the role of the first marriage counselor) that the passion he feels for Eve tends to unsettle his judgment of her qualities and her nature in relation to his own and concludes that the fault is somehow Eve's (or Nature's): she has been made too fair, or Nature has made him too weak by taking too much from his side in making her. But Raphael will have none of it: the angel does not assume that the tension and difficulty Adam is experiencing are out of place in Eden, but rather "with contracted brow" he places the responsibility for dealing with them squarely on Adam's shoulders: "Accuse not Nature, she hath done her part; / Do thou but thine" (VIII, 561-62). This tendency in Adam is strengthened after the Fall and is expressed in several tirades against Eve and all womankind. Nothing in Milton's treatment of the first human couple is more sharply perceived than the inevitable transformation—when the pressure of suffering and guilt make the heroic posture impossible to sustain—of the self-sacrificing romantic hero ready to die with his lady into a cad ready to denounce that same lady before the bar of God's judgment in an effort to excuse himself. Eve on that occasion was "not before her Judge / Bold or loquacious" and her simple confession—"The Serpent me beguil'd, and I did eat" (X, 160-62)—contrasts impressively with Adam's garrulous complaints against both the woman and the God who gave him to her:

> This Woman whom thou mad'st to be my help,
> And gav'st me as thy perfet gift, so good,
> So fit, so acceptable, so Divine,
> That from her hand I could suspect no ill,
> And what she did, whatever in itself,
> Her doing seem'd to justify the deed;
> She gave me of the Tree, and I did eat
>
> (X, 137-43)

But he is not indulged in this blame-shifting: the stern judge insists that he had no business making her his God, nor yet (given her general inferiority to him) his guide in this momentous matter. Later, in the exchange with Michael, Adam shows that he still has not learned his lesson, as he comments on the daughters of Cain, "But still I

see the tenor of Man's woe / Holds on the same, from Woman to begin" (XI, 632-33). Michael, however, gives such misogynist platitudes short shrift, retorting sharply, "From Man's effeminate slackness it begins" (XI, 634).

Eve just after the Fall is also ready to shift her guilt to Adam, observing that he should have forbidden her absolutely to go off to work by herself: "Being as I am, why didst not thou the Head / Command me absolutely not to go, / Going into such danger as thou said'st" (IX, 1156-58). Many critics who write about the marital dispute take the same tack, assuming that what was finally required of Adam should all else fail was a flat command. But this is to miss the point badly: as marriage is conceived in Eden, Adam is Eve's superior and appointed guide, but not her lord and master. Eve is no dependent child-wife: her choices are and must be freely her own, and she bears adult responsibility for them, even as Adam does for his.[12] Adam is accordingly indignant at Eve's words, as a flagrant misrepresentation of the terms of their relationship:

> I warn'd thee, I admonish'd thee, foretold
> The danger, and the lurking Enemy
> That lay in wait; beyond this had been force,
> And force upon free Will hath here no place
>
> (IX, 1171-74)

Indeed, what came to be required of Eve during the marital dispute was not at all childlike dependence but a level of maturity which she (like most of her progeny) could not quite manage in the heat of disputation—the ability to give over an erroneous position without seeking to save face, the grace to admit and be persuaded by the better arguments, and the willingness to eschew too hardy adolescent adventure-seeking in response to counsels of prudence. Adam also needed more maturity than he was master of in the dispute—notably, the capacity to stand up to prolonged emotional pressure without caving in before it.

We are given early on a model of how Adam's leadership should properly function, so as to preserve and enhance Eve's freedom of choice, personal growth, and adult responsibility. This is at the scene of Eve's presentation to Adam when she turns from him back to the fairer image of herself in the water, and Adam proceeds to urge his claim to her firmly and rationally, on the grounds of her origin and nature, and his love. The alternatives thus sharply posed permit Eve to make her choice—to advance from the sterile condition of self-admiration, "pin'd with vain desire" (IV, 466), to human relationship and love, and on the basis of her new experience to adjust her scale of values, recognizing the superiority of wisdom over beauty. In terms of this model we can see what went wrong in the marital dispute. Adam not only ceased to press his own case forcefully and rationally under the pressure of Eve's dismay, but at length he virtually sent her away, supplied with a rationale for going which she had not thought of for herself:

> But if thou think, trial unsought may find
> Us both securer than thus warn'd thou seem'st,

Go; for thy stay, not free, absents thee more;
Go in thy native innocence, rely
On what thou hast of virtue, summon all,
For God towards thee hath done his part, do thine

                                        (IX, 370-75)

This is a serious abnegation of Adam's proper leadership role: he ought not to command Eve, but neither ought he to argue her case for her. It is as if he had said on that earlier occasion, "If you really want to go back and stare at yourself in that pond, go ahead; it might turn out to be a useful experience." The result is that instead of enhancing Eve's freedom of choice Adam has restricted it, for in the charged emotional climate of their dispute—offered this new reason for going and hearing the reiterated emphatic directive, "Go"—Eve could hardly make another choice if she wanted to. She *is* still responsible for her choice for all that, though Adam has unintentionally made it much harder for her to choose rightly. Her uneasiness about the decision is reflected in the fact that she seeks at once to place responsibility for the decision upon Adam:

With thy permission then, and thus forewarn'd
Chiefly by what thy own last reasoning words
Touch'd only, that our trial. when least sought,
May find us both perhaps far less prepar'd,
The willinger I go—

                                        (IX, 378-82)

It must be emphasized, however, that Milton's Eve is not foredoomed to fall before Satan's wiles because her intellectual powers are comparatively weaker than Adam's. Abdiel apparently had no great reputation as an intellectual giant among the angels, but he did very well in his debate with Satan by holding fast to the main point. In Eve's case, Milton has taken some pains to devise the temptation sequence so as to demonstrate that she was intellectually "sufficient to have stood." We see evidence of this sufficiency in her wry comment upon Satan's fulsome flattery: "Serpent, thy overpraising leaves in doubt / The virtue of that Fruit, in thee first prov'd" (IX, 615-16). She is evidently enjoying the flattery, but she is perfectly aware that it *is* flattery, and that the element of falsehood might indeed call into question the "virtue of that Fruit." She does not take the warning from this that she should, but intellectually her perception is quite sound. Later, when she first discovers that the tree the serpent spoke of was indeed the forbidden tree, she shows that she understands clearly the basic principle needed to withstand Satan's subsequent argument—the fact that the tree lies under the special and direct prohibition of God (and hence outside the law of reason), whereas in all other matters Adam and Eve are guided by the law of reason:

But of this Tree we may not taste nor touch;
God so commanded, and left that Command
Sole Daughter of his voice; the rest, we live
Law to ourselves, our Reason is our Law.

                                        (IX, 651-54)

Satan's entire strategy from this point forward is to confuse the two categories of law which Eve here distinguishes so precisely—to develop, that is, a plethora of reasons and rational arguments demonstrating the probable harmlessness of the tree and the probable benefits to be gained from eating its fruit. But such rational considerations are in this single case quite beside the point, as Eve had perceived clearly enough in the speech cited. In testimony to her soundness at this point in the poem, the narrator uses the epithet "yet sinless" to describe her—for the last time. She is soon brought by Satan's magnificent rhetoric and her own unruly desires to lose her hold on this clear distinction, permitting herself to be bedazzled and deluded by those arguments. But my point is that among the many complex factors involved in Eve's fall, one which is specifically excluded is insufficient intellectual power. Milton has taken great care to present the first woman as having faculties "sufficient" to make free and responsible choices—always for Milton the precondition for any practice of or growth in virtue.

In another genre and in the setting of the fallen world Milton portrays a girl who successfully resists a highly intelligent tempter—and indeed overmatches him in intellectual argument. The Lady in *Comus* is no one's favorite Miltonic character, I suppose, but she certainly displays woman's sufficiency to meet the challenges of life and to make free and responsible choices. At the time of her temptation this Lady is also without her appointed male protectors, her brothers, though quite without her intention or fault. Moreover, this Miltonic Lady has a firmer intellectual grasp of the realities of life in the "blind mazes of this tangl'd Wood" (181) than have her brothers: the Platonizing Elder Brother, serenely confident of the power of Chastity, tends to confuse his sister with Diana the huntress, invulnerable to harm and able for all conquests (420-46); the fearful Younger Brother is convinced that she is helpless alone and certain to be ravished (393-407). The Lady, though, is quite aware that she is not invulnerable, but she knows also that she may rely with confidence upon her own virtue and the aid of heaven to withstand such trials as may present themselves. While lost, she decides her course of action by a rational appraisal of the options available to her: she follows the noises heard in the dark wood though she perceives them to be "the sound / of Riot and ill-manag'd Merriment" (171-72) because she must ask directions of someone; and she accepts the disguised Comus' offer of shelter because she has no grounds for distrusting the supposed shepherd, and because it seems that she could not be "In a Place / Less warranted than this or less secure" (326-27). But she is neither naive nor credulous: she knows that in the dark wood and in the human condition one cannot know all the circumstances bearing upon such decisions, and her prayer as she follows Comus indicates an awareness that there may be difficulties to come: "Eye me blest Providence, and square my trial / To my proportion'd strength" (329-30).

In her long debate with Comus, the Lady claims only to be able to preserve her mind inviolate: "Fool, do not boast, / Thou canst not touch the freedom of my mind / With all thy charms" (662-64). She is not proof against violence, nor against the forces of natural sensuality represented by Comus, which have power to "immancle" her body "while Heav'n sees good" (665). But to preserve the freedom of her mind in intellectual debate with Comus is no mean feat, especially since many critics of the poem have been so thoroughly bedazzled by his "dear Wit and gay Rhetoric" (790) as to suppose that he wins the debate, or at least finishes in a draw.[13] The Lady's debating strategies differ from those of her opponent, to be sure, but an examination of her speech and of Comus' response to it reveals clearly enough that the victory is hers. She meets the first point, the issue of the nature of Nature, by denouncing with keen logical incisiveness the "false rules prankt in reason's garb" (759) which Comus derives from his eloquent description of a Nature so lavish and excessively abundant in her productivity as to require man's incessant and prodigal rifling of her ever-burgeoning stores of goods and beauties. The Lady did not require the instruction of modern ecologists to perceive that this is an absurd description of the postlapsarian world, that Nature did not intend that "her children should be riotous / With her abundance" (763-64), and that indeed,

> If every just man that now pines with want
> Had but a moderate and beseeming share
> Of that which lewdly-pamper'd Luxury
> Now heaps upon some few with vast excess,
> Nature's full blessings would be well dispens't
> In unsuperfluous even proportion,
> And she no whit encumber'd with her store.
>
> (768-74)

I think we may agree that the Lady wins this point. The other issue, the value and power of Chastity and Virginity, she simply refuses to debate with Comus, for the same reason that Christ counseled against casting pearls before swine, or Socrates remarked the futility of describing to a sensual man the higher joys of the intellectual life[14]—the sheer incapacity of the hearer to understand the argument. But the Lady is stirred by her subject to display something of that "flame of sacred vehemence" (795) which, she asserts, would characterize her praise of "the sage / And serious doctrine of Virginity" (786-87), should she deign to undertake the topic. And however the reader might understand the specific import and the merit of her subject, she makes her point with Comus. He confesses his sense that "some superior power" sets off her words, bathing him in a "cold shudd'ring dew" (801-02), and, conscious of defeat, he gives over the debate and turns to force. Of the strength and sufficiency of this woman's intellect and character, I think we can have no doubt.

Milton does then examine at length the inescapable, individual challenge of responsible choice as it affects women as well as men, insisting that (whatever the mitigating personal or social circumstances) each is sufficient to meet whatever trials may come. But he examines also, with equal care, the strong bonds of human interdependence. Adam and Eve create problems for each other, even in Eden, yet each needs the other to achieve anything resem-

bling a human life, or to experience that life as worth living. Adam makes this point forcefully in his own case: although he is given Eden and all the earth as his domain, he yet finds himself unsatisfied and so pleads with God for a mate. Arguing that he is neither a beast able to find companionship with other beasts, nor yet a God sufficient unto himself, he articulates man's great need of human fellowship—"By conversation with his like to help, / Or solace his defects" (VIII, 418-19). Adam's fall, as we know, is chiefly motivated by his sudden, overwhelming consciousness of loneliness and misery in a world lacking his beloved companion:

> How can I live without thee, how forgo
> Thy sweet Converse and Love so dearly join'd,
> To live again in these wild Woods forlorn?
> Should God create another *Eve,* and I
> Another Rib afford, yet loss of thee
> Would never from my heart.
>
> (IX, 908-13)

Eve has a similar awareness of her need of Adam, for she knows she would still be staring at her image in the pool had not the divine voice brought her to him—"There I had fix't / Mine eyes till now, and pin'd with vain desire" (IV, 465-66). She expresses this awareness also in her beautiful love lyric, which catalogues all the sweet delights in Eden and then culminates in the statement that none of these "without thee is sweet" (IV, 656).

The Fall intensifies their need for companionship and mutual help. Eve, recoiling before Adam's fierce rage—"Out of my sight, thou Serpent" (X, 867)—gives expression to the desolation and aimlessness her life must have without him in these sad new conditions:

> bereave me not,
> Whereon I live, thy gentle looks, thy aid,
> Thy counsel in this uttermost distress,
> My only strength and stay: forlorn of thee,
> Whither should I betake me, where subsist?
>
> (X, 918-22)

Adam's necessity to her (and hers to him) is again evidenced after their reconciliation, as his reasoned critique of her recommendation of sterility or suicide as means for saving their progeny from woe clarifies for them both the divine plan for salvation—penitence, and reliance upon the redeemer to be born of Eve's seed. Indeed, despite Adam's harsh denunciations of Eve and of all womankind under the impetus of his terrible misery, Eve is, if anything, shown to be even more necessary to Adam than he to her. For although their reconciliation with each other and with God is in the final analysis made possible by the removal of the "stony" from their hearts by "prevenient Grace" (XI, 3-4), Eve is the human agent of Adam's salvation, bringing him from the utter hopelessness and immobility of despair to some capacity for thought and action. Without her, he must have remained groveling on the ground, helpless and hopeless, driven into an "Abyss of fears / And horrors . . . out of which / I find no way, from deep to deeper plung'd" (X, 842-44). It is Eve's persistent admissions of guilt, pleas for forgiveness, and expressions of love that revive in Adam those feelings and emotions which bind him to his kind and make life seem again endurable. Eve's behavior breaks through the syndrome of mutual recriminations into which they were heretofore locked, thus making reconciliation possible. Moreover, in her offer to plead with God to transfer upon her the entire sentence of punishment, she echoes the Son's offer to die for man—an inadequate human type of the divine heroism to be sure, but yet the immediate cause of the "redemption" of Adam from his self-destructive anger and despair.[15] Much as he valued intellect, Milton did not forget the superiority of love in the Christian scale of values, and in his reworking of the Adam and Eve myth it is the woman who is made a type of the Messiah's redemptive love.

In that unforgettable final scene, as Adam and Eve "hand in hand with wand'ring steps and slow, / Through *Eden* took thir solitary way" (XII, 648-49), we are again reminded of the depth of our need for each other on this "subjected Plain" as friends, lovers, husbands, and wives. And the verbal paradox of the last lines—"hand in hand," "solitary"—underscores again the basic human dilemma Milton has pointed up with such honesty and clarity in his re-creation of the myth of the first man and woman: on the one hand, the capacity and responsibility of both Adam and Eve for "solitary" choices defining the direction of their own lives, and on the other, their intense need of each other to give that life human shape and to make it endurable. The complexity and profundity of this view of the human condition is matched by few writers, even among those more enlightened about the matter of woman's equality. If our rightful contemporary concern with this equality prevents some readers from perceiving or responding to the Miltonic vision, that is surely unfortunate. Happily, though, great poets have a way of rising like phoenixes from whatever ashes are left in the wake of social and intellectual revolutions, so no doubt it will not be long before we can all again read Milton for what is of enduring importance rather than what is historically conditioned in his conception of man and woman.

### Notes

1. "Kinship and the Role of Women in *Paradise Lost,*" *Milton Studies,* IV, ed. James D. Simmonds (Pittsburgh, 1972), pp. 3-18.

2. Ibid., p. 5.

3. All quotations from Milton's poetry are from *John Milton: Complete Poems and Major Prose,* ed. Merritt Y. Hughes (New York, 1957).

4. For further development of this point, see Irene Samuel, *Dante and Milton* (Ithaca, N.Y., 1966), pp. 146-62.

5. *The Dialectics of Creation: Patterns of Birth and Regeneration in "Paradise Lost"* (Amherst, Mass., 1970), esp. pp. 56-78; Joseph Summers, *The Muse's Method* (London, 1962), pp. 112-46.

6. "Innocence and Experience in Milton's Eden," in *New Essays on "Paradise Lost,"* ed. Thomas Kranidas (Berkeley, 1969), pp. 86-117.

7. "Kinship and the Role of Women," p. 7.

8. Ibid., pp. 9-11.

9. Professor Landy's argument seems to invest the term "matron" as it appears in Milton's poem with a somewhat misleading sense: "The first human kiss recorded is placed on Eve's 'Matron lip,' and this identification as mother seems to precede that as spouse." Of course the Latin etymology is clear enough, and Milton often played on etymological meanings, but the *OED* indicates that from its first recorded use in English (1375) to Milton's own time the term "matron" meant simply "married woman."

10. See Ernest Sirluck, ed., "Introduction" to *Complete Prose Works of John Milton* (New Haven, 1959), II, 137-58. To be sure, Milton could and did cite notable Protestant Reformers—chiefly Bucer, Calvin, Fagius, Pareus, and Rivetus—as authorities for some parts of his argument, but the total view of marriage and divorce as set forth by Milton was far outside the mainstream of contemporary opinion.

11. *The Doctrine and Discipline of Divorce,* in *Complete Prose Works,* II, 245-46.

12. This point has been argued cogently and persuasively by Stella P. Revard, "Eve and the Doctrine of Responsibility in *Paradise Lost,*" *PMLA,* LXXXVIII (1973), 69-78.

13. See, e.g., Don C. Allen, *The Harmonious Vision* (Baltimore, Md., 1954), pp. 24-40; E. M. W. Tillyard, *Studies in Milton* (London, 1960), pp. 87-96; and Cleanth Brooks and J. W. Hardy, eds., *Poems of Mr. John Milton* (New York, 1968), pp. 215-23.

14. Matthew vii, 6; Plato, *Republic,* IX, 581-86.

15. This link between Eve's speech and the Redeemer's is noted by Summers, *Muse's Method,* pp. 176-85. Cf. *PL* III, 236-41 and X, 932-36.

### Louis L. Martz (essay date 1980)

SOURCE: "The Power of Choice," in *Poet of Exile: A Study of Milton's Poetry,* Yale University Press, 1980, pp. 3-19.

[*In the following excerpt from his full-length study of Milton's poetry, Martz discusses the importance of the notion of choice in the epic, pointing out that for Milton human dignity depends on the power of choice—which includes choosing to err as well as make amends for errors.*]

Adam and Eve, before the Fall, have all our basic psychological qualities: they are "frail" in the sense that their power of choice may wrongly choose; choice is difficult because "wandering thoughts" and passions and the wild work of fancy are all part of the broad field in which human choice must operate. Adam and Eve find it difficult to choose rightly because they are so "unexperienc't"; their descendants find it difficult to choose because they have so much experience, see so many possibilities, dangers, and advantages. Yet in Milton's universe the power of choice is essential to man's perfection and man's happiness, whether fallen or unfallen. That is why the words "choice" and "choose" ring throughout *Paradise Lost,* from the opening words of Satan, "and in my choyce / To reign is worth ambition though in Hell . . ." (1.261-62) through the words of God declaring "Reason also is choice," on to the famous closing lines where Adam and Eve must learn "where to choose / Thir place of rest" (12.646-47).[1]

As in these instances, so in book 8 these crucial words are placed in an emphatic position, at the end of a line, when Adam recalls the divine prohibition in the very phrase that Satan has used in book 1:

> Sternly he pronounc'd
> The rigid interdiction, which resounds
> Yet dreadful in mine eare, though in my choice
> Not to incur . . .

> [8.333-36]

The power of choice, then, is essential to Milton's view of the dynamic, progressive, eternal expansion of God's goodness; by warning and experience man must learn to manage the gift of freedom, and seek his happiness beyond the limitations of the flesh.

Nothing could stress the essential humanity of Adam and Eve more strongly than the scene that opens book 9, after Satan has uttered his Euripidean, or Senecan prologue to the tragedy of the Fall (99-178). Here Milton brings our grand parents closer to us than we have thus far seen them. This is not done suddenly: it has been a gradual process from their first appearance in book 4. The more we see of them and the more we hear them talk, the more they seem like us. In book 5, for example, Adam and Eve have already begun to drop the formal modes of address that marked their speeches in book 4. When Adam sees the angel approaching his door he calls to Eve, who is within "due at her hour" preparing dinner,

> Haste hither *Eve,* and worth thy sight behold
> Eastward among those Trees, what glorious shape
> Comes this way moving . . .
>         But goe with speed,
> And what thy stores contain, bring forth and poure
> Abundance, fit to honour and receive
> Our Heav'nly stranger . . .

> [5.308-10,313-16]

Eve is amused at Adam's abrupt and excited concern for her "stores" and she answers in a leisurely and stately way (one can imagine her quiet smile):

> *Adam,* earths hallowd mould,
> Of God inspir'd, small store will serve, where store,

All seasons, ripe for use hangs on the stalk;
> Save what by frugal storing firmness gains
> To nourish, and superfluous moist consumes:
> But I will haste and from each bough and break,
> Each Plant & juiciest Gourd will pluck such choice
> To entertain our Angel guest, as hee
> Beholding shall confess that here on Earth
> God hath dispenst his bounties as in Heav'n.
>     So saying, with dispatchful looks in haste
> She turns, on hospitable thoughts intent
> What choice to chuse for delicacie best . . .

> [5.321-33]

Thus Eve shows her command of the household affairs, using her reason wittily to pun before going forth to exercise her power of choice in the preparation of that elegant vegetarian meal.[2]

The sense of comedy here, enforced by Milton's own quiet wit in regarding this pastoral feast—"No fear lest Dinner coole"—is carried on in the early part of book 9, where, though Milton has said that he must now change his notes to tragic, the first act of his tragedy might well be described as a domestic comedy. Here at the outset the grand titles of address are completely dropped, and Adam and Eve are introduced simply as the "human pair." "And *Eve* first to her Husband thus began," without any of those words about "My Author and Disposer," "Unargu'd I obey," and so on, such as we heard in book 4. Eve opens her speech here in what might be called a normal wifely fashion: "*Adam,*" she says, quite informally—

> *Adam,* well may we labour still to dress
> This Garden, still to tend Plant, Herb and Flour.
> Our pleasant task enjoyn'd, but till more hands
> Aid us, the work under our labour grows,
> Luxurious by restraint; what we by day
> Lop overgrown, or prune, or prop, or bind,
> One night or two with wanton growth derides
> Tending to wilde.

> [9.205-212]

We must believe that Eve is truly concerned about her work here, and not simply fishing for a compliment, for Milton's whole account of life in Paradise has stressed the importance of this element of labor.[3] Milton is placing a special stress upon the words of Genesis where God says to Adam and Eve: "Be fruitful and multiply, and replenish the earth, and subdue it," along with the later statement that "the Lord God took the man, and put him into the garden of Eden to dress it and to keep it," with man's duties clarified by the statement that before this "there was not a man to till the ground" (Gen. 1:28; 2:5, 15). Eve's concern for the results of their "labour" of dressing and redressing is one of the problems raised by the whole Creation's "wanton" tendency to be fruitful and multiply, even to the extent of "tending to wilde." Nature's vitality, whether in vegetation or in man and woman, is not easy to "subdue" and keep in reasonable order.

The point has been clearly made in book 5 as Milton describes the angel's approach to Adam's door:

> through Groves of Myrrhe,
> And flouring Odours, Cassia, Nard, and Balme;
> A Wilderness of sweets; for Nature here
> Wantond as in her prime, and plaid at will
> Her Virgin Fancies, pouring forth more sweet,
> Wilde above rule or art; enormous bliss.
>
> [5.292-97]

Here again the words "wantond" and "wilde" give the clue to the inherent problem: things unconfined and unrestrained tend to become "luxurious", tend to run beyond the rule and art of reason. Man's duty is to bring these "Virgin Fancies" of nature under the control of reason, for fancy, we recall, can make "wilde work". Eve is therefore completely right to show concern over the way in which their labors seem ineffective. Adam himself has explained to Eve the importance of their labor in book 4, as they retire to their blissful bower:

> When *Adam* thus to *Eve:* Fair Consort, th' hour
> Of night, and all things now retir'd to rest
> Mind us of like repose, since God hath set
> Labour and rest, as day and night to men
> Successive, and the timely dew of sleep
> Now falling with soft slumbrous weight inclines
> Our eye-lids; other Creatures all day long
> Rove idle unimploid, and less need rest;
> Man hath his daily work of body or mind
> Appointed, which declares his Dignitie,
> And the regard of Heav'n on all his waies;
> While other Animals unactive range,
> And of thir doings God takes no account.
>
> [4.610-22]

The word "account" tells us to take the divine "regard" on all man's ways in two senses: God holds man's ways in high regard, with affection and respect—but also, the eye of God is watching all man's ways, and will take account of how he performs his appointed tasks. Therefore, Adam adds, at dawn "we must be ris'n / And at our pleasant labour," which he then proceeds to describe with exactly the conditions that are worrying Eve in book 9:

> to reform
> You flourie Arbors, yonder Allies green,
> Our walks at noon, with branches overgrown,
> That mock our scant manuring, and require
> More hands then ours to lop thir wanton growth . . .
>
> [4.624-29]

There again is the word "wanton", along with the witty play on the Latin base of *manuring*—working with the hands, for such work is surely needed: "Those Blossoms also, and those dropping Gumms, / That lie bestrowne unsightly and unsmooth, / Ask riddance, if we mean to tread with ease . . ." (4.630-32).

Thus Eve is right to be concerned over the results of their labor, and right to consider ways of improving its effect:

> Thou therefore now advise
> Or hear what to my mind first thoughts present,

> Let us divide our labours, thou where choice
> Leads thee, or where most needs, whether to wind
> The Woodbine round this Arbour, or direct
> The clasping Ivie where to climb, while I
> In yonder Spring of Roses intermixt
> With Myrtle, find what to redress till Noon . . .
>
> [9.212-19]

She suggests this division of labor because, she adds, when they are together they waste too much time in looking at each other and smiling and talking, and thus "th' hour of Supper comes unearn'd" (9.225).

"To whom mild answer *Adam* thus return'd," maintaining something of that earlier formality of address, along with some measure of masculine condescension:

> Sole *Eve,* Associate sole, to me beyond
> Compare above all living Creatures deare,
> Well hast thou motion'd, wel thy thoughts imployd
> How we might best fulfill the work which here
> God hath assign'd us, nor of me shalt pass
> Unprais'd: for nothing lovelier can be found
> In woman, then to studie houshold good,
> And good workes in her Husband to promote.
>
> [9.227-34]

Adam sounds here as though he had observed hundreds of women: clearly Adam is becoming Everyman. But, he adds, life in Eden is not supposed to be so arduous. It is quite all right for us to look and smile at each other while we work; and then he makes man's first strategic error, for he goes on to say:

> But other doubt possesses me, least harm
> Befall thee sever'd from me; for thou knowst
> What hath bin warn'd us, what malicious Foe
> Envying our happiness, and of his own
> Despairing, seeks to work us woe and shame
> By sly assault . . .
>
> [9.251-56]

Considering this danger, then, Adam advises,

> leave not the faithful side
> That gave thee being, stil shades thee and protects.
> The Wife, where danger or dishonour lurks,
> Safest and seemliest by her Husband staies,
> Who guards her, or with her the worst endures.
>
> [9.265-69]

Here again, Adam is speaking with the voice of Everyman in the daily world, foreshadowing his decision to eat the apple and with her the worst endure. Eve in her reply becomes Everywoman, too, as she withdraws to her earlier mode of formal address:

> To whom the Virgin Majestie of *Eve,*
> As one who loves, and some unkindness meets,
> With sweet austeer composure thus reply'd.
> Of spring of Heav'n and Earth, and all Earths
> Lord . . .
>
> [9.270-73]

She goes on to say that she knows all about this enemy, for Adam has told her about Satan, and she has overheard the warning of the departing angel. Thus she is shocked to think that Adam would mistrust her:

> But that thou shouldst my firmness therfore doubt
> To God or thee, because we have a foe
> May tempt it, I expected not to hear . . .
> Thoughts, which how found they harbour in thy brest,
> *Adam,* missthought of her to thee so dear?
>       To whom with healing words *Adam* reply'd.
> Daughter of God and Man, immortal *Eve* . . .

[9.279-81,288-91]

I do trust you, he says, I do, but—and then he flounders into a very unconvincing argument: I am only trying to prevent the dishonor that lies in the fact of being tempted. Then he tries a stronger point, which one wishes that he had tried first. I cannot get along without you, he says, I will be stronger in your presence: "I from the influence of thy looks receave / Access in every Vertue, in thy sight / More wise, more watchful, stronger . . ." (9.309-11). And now Milton tells us very plainly what he is about, for by his introductory phrasing he places the scene in our own world:

> So spake domestick *Adam* in his care
> And Matrimonial Love, but *Eve,* who thought
> Less attributed to her Faith sincere,
> Thus her reply with accent sweet renewd.
>       If this be our condition, thus to dwell
> In narrow circuit strait'nd by a Foe,
> Suttle or violent, we not endu'd
> Single with like defence, wherever met,
> How are we happie, still in fear of harm?
>       . . . . .
> Fraile is our happiness, if this be so,
> And *Eden* were no *Eden* thus expos'd.

[9.318-26,340-41]

This is not what Adam has been saying: they are not confined to a narrow circuit; they can go anywhere together. And this idea that they are made, or ought to be made, to meet temptation singly—this represents, as Milton's whole poem before this has made clear, a misunderstanding of the nature of the universe, where nothing stands alone, but everything lives best in the linked universe of love, with respect for those above and care for those below. This is why Adam at last replies "fervently," exclaiming:

> O Woman, best are all things as the will
> Of God ordaind them, his creating hand
> Nothing imperfet or deficient left
> Of all that he Created . . .

[9.343-46]

The meaning of Eden, he says, has nothing to do with this idea of complete personal independence. The freedom of the will, Adam goes on to explain, exercises its power of choice within a universe of interdependent and mutual responsibility: "Not then mistrust, but tender love enjoynes, / That I should mind thee oft, and mind thou me" (9.357-

58). "Mind" here does not mean simply "obey", but rather means "Pay attention to," "be mindful" of one another's best interests and advice. Then Adam goes on to make the choice very plain: "Wouldst thou approve thy constancie, approve / First thy obedience;" (9.367-68) that is, obedience to what is clearly Adam's wish and best advice. He leaves it up to her to choose, saying: "But if thou think" (and clearly he does not think so)

> trial unsought may finde
> Us both securer then thus warnd thou seemst,
> Go; for thy stay, not free, absents thee more . . .

[9.370-72]

Adam seems to be telling her that if she thinks that staying together, not seeking trial, may create a sense of false security, then it is better for her to go, since she will be staying with him against her will.

To some readers Adam has seemed weak here, but the question is highly debatable, for it may well seem that Adam is only carrying out here the view of the workings of free will that the poem has over and over again explained to us and to Adam. He has made it plain that he does not wish her to go; he has asked for her obedience to this wish. His respect for human reason makes it impossible for him to detain her by force and his love for Eve makes it impossible for him to speak more harshly. It is true that later on, after the Fall, in that unpleasant scene of domestic bickering, Eve snaps back at Adam with the bitter reproach:

> why didst not thou the Head
> Command me absolutely not to go,
> Going into such danger as thou saidst?
> Too facil then thou didst not much gainsay,
> Nay, didst permit, approve, and fair dismiss.
> Hadst thou bin firm and fixt in thy dissent,
> Neither had I transgress'd, nor thou with mee.

[9.1155-61]

But here she is angrily distorting the effect of Adam's earlier speech, where Adam seems to hope that by this evidence of his respect for her intelligence, she will come round to his point of view:

> Go in thy native innocence, relie
> On what thou hast of vertue, summon all,
> For God towards thee hath done his part, do thine.

[9.373-75]

With this meagre compliment, Adam reminds Eve that her part is to be mindful of Adam's best advice. And Adam still seems to hope that Eve will choose to take his advice.

"So spake the Patriarch of Mankinde," says Milton, but the Patriarch soon suffers the fate of his sons:

> but *Eve*
> Persisted, yet submiss, though last, repli'd.
> With thy permission then . . .

[9.376-78]

Has he really given her permission to go? It would be more accurate to say that he has given her permission to disobey his wishes if she chooses to do so, and this is exactly the permission that God himself allows the freedom of the will. God, to be sure, has laid down his commandment absolutely, but it is not, I think, valid to argue from this that Adam should have been equally absolute. Even in Milton's day, the relation between husband and wife could not have been regarded as precisely analogous to the relation between God and man. Of course we think of Milton's earlier statement in book 4:

> Hee for God only, shee for God in him:
> His fair large Front and Eye sublime declar'd
> Absolute rule . . .

> [4.299-301]

But this at once is followed by the passage where he adds that Eve's "subjection" must be "requir'd with gentle sway." It is this gentle sway that Adam is attempting to exert here, but Eve, insisting on her own right to choose, makes the wrong choice. That is, the consequences prove her wrong, but neither of them can possibly know that she will fall. And we notice that Milton does not, as she departs, subject Eve to any very strong condemnation. Instead, he describes her situation and her beauty in terms that draw our strong sympathies toward her unprotected state, her utterly innocent beauty, her earnest work, her good intentions. She means no harm, and she really does have the welfare of her garden at heart. Anyhow, she is not going far—only to that rose garden over there, yonder, as she says: they can see the spot from where they are standing.

Now, as she ominously withdraws her hand from her husband's hand, Milton surrounds her with a fragrant cloud of pagan myths—all of them concerned with attractive, beneficent spirits and deities of nature:

> and like a Wood-Nymph light
> *Oread* or *Dryad,* or of *Delia's* Traine,
> Betook her to the Groves, but *Delia's* self
> In gate surpass'd and Goddess-like deport,
> Though not as shee with Bow and Quiver armd,
> But with such Gardning Tools as Art yet rude,
> Guiltless of fire had formd, or Angels brought.
> To *Pales,* or *Pomona,* thus adornd,
> Likest she seemd, *Pomona* when she fled
> *Vertumnus,* or to *Ceres* in her Prime,
> Yet Virgin of *Proserpina* from *Jove.*

> [9.386-96]

Everyone has felt an ominous undercurrent here, as in the phrase "Guiltless of fire," the allusion to Pomona and her persistent wooer, Vertumnus, or the oblique reference to the sorrows of Ceres, through the loss of her daughter to the prince of Hades. But the dominant effect of all these myths is quite favorable to Eve: Delia is Diana, and by using twice the unusual name Delia, Milton reminds us of her birth, along with Apollo, on the pure and sacred island of Delos. Pales, ancient Roman goddess of flocks and

herds, was a beneficent deity, worshipped by rites of purification. As for the story of Pomona, Milton has given the allusion an ominous twist by referring to the time when, he says, she "fled Vertumnus." Yet in Ovid's *Metamorphoses* this is quite an amusing and harmless story, where Pomona provides a true original for Milton's Eve:

> Gardens and fruit were all her care; no other
> Was ever more skilled or diligent. Woods and rivers
> Were nothing to her, only the fields, the branches
> Bearing the prosperous fruits. She bore no javelin,
> But the curved pruning-hook, to trim the branches,
> Check too luxuriant growth, or make incision
> For the engrafted twig to thrive and grow in.
> She would not let them thirst: the flowing waters
> Poured down to the roots. This was her love, her passion.
> Venus was nothing to her . . .

But all the rustic gods try to win her, especially Vertumnus, who tries every possible disguise, every possible verbal manoeuvre, for over a hundred lines of Ovid, with no effect at all on the cool maiden. So at last, in desperation, he throws off his latest disguise

> and stood before her
> In the light of his own radiance, as the sun
> Breaks through the clouds against all opposition.
> Ready for force, he found no need; Pomona
> Was taken by his beauty, and her passion
> Answered his own.

> [*Met.* 14.624-34,767-71, trans. Humphries]

Such is the atmosphere of purity and harmlessness that Milton gives to Eve.

When the poet bursts out in his own voice with his commentary, he cannot bring himself quite to blame her, though it looks at first as though he is going to do so: "O much deceav'd, much failing, hapless *Eve,*" he cries, but then the sentence bends over the line, in Milton's metamorphic way and assumes a different meaning, for it appears that the poet is saying only that she is deceived in thinking that she will return to Adam by noon, in time to have Adam's lunch ready. Her failing, we see, is her failing to return to Adam as she now promises:

> And all things in best order to invite
> Noontide repast, or Afternoons repose.
> O much deceav'd, much failing, hapless *Eve,*
> Of thy presum'd return! event perverse!
> Thou never from that houre in Paradise
> Foundst either sweet repast, or sound repose . . .

> [9.402-07]

Notice that Milton does not say "perverse woman" but simply "perverse event," that is to say, outcome contrary to her and Adam's expectations. Thus the poet's sympathy and pitying admiration play over the figure of Eve as she works among her roses:

> them she upstaies
> Gently with Mirtle band, mindless the while,
> Her self,

(that is, not attentive to herself, with all her mind focused on the flowers)

> though fairest unsupported Flour
> From her best prop so farr, and storm so nigh.
>
> [9.430-33]

Then, as we watch the serpent crawling "Among thick-wov'n Arborets and Flours . . . the hand of *Eve,*" we realize that her gardening labors have already produced here an effect that, Milton says, surpasses the "feigned" gardens of Adonis, or the Gardens of King Alcinous in the *Odyssey,* or that true garden described in the Song of Solomon. Finally, to cap the climax of this mood of sympathy and admiration, Milton brings forward his greatest tribute to the beauty of the earth, as tended and inhabited now by fallen man and woman:

> As one who long in populous City pent,
> Where Houses thick and Sewers annoy the Aire,
> Forth issuing on a Summers Morn to breathe
> Among the pleasant Villages and Farmes
> Adjoynd, from each thing met conceaves delight,
> The smell of Grain, or tedded Grass, or Kine.
> Or Dairie, each rural sight, each rural sound;
> If chance with Nymphlike step fair Virgin pass,
> What pleasing seemd, for her now pleases more,
> She most, and in her looks summs all Delight.
> Such Pleasure took the Serpent to behold
> This Flourie Plat, the sweet recess of *Eve*
> Thus earlie, thus alone; her Heav'nly forme
> Angelic, but more soft, and Feminine,
> Her graceful Innocence, her every Aire
> Of gesture or lest action overawd
> His Malice, and with rapine sweet bereav'd
> His fierceness of the fierce intent it brought . . .
>
> [9.445-62]

The effects of this great pastoral moment seem to be double. First, it throws our sympathy overwhelmingly toward Eve: so beautiful, so talented, so innocent: how unfair it seems that she should be permitted to undergo temptation by such an adversary, whose hypocrisy we know that she can never penetrate. Even Uriel, the regent of the sun, we recall, could not penetrate the disguise of that youthful cherub in book 3. At the same time the comparison suggests that Satan's design will not be wholly successful. He has not utterly destroyed God's Paradise of Delight, since the poet here still delights in these man-made scenes of farm and village, and in feminine beauty, almost as much as he delights in this imagined garden and in Eve herself.

The same kind of sympathy is thrown toward Adam before his fall, and thus much argument has raged over whether or not Adam is justified in his anguished, intuitive, passionate decision to eat the fruit and die with Eve:

> How can I live without thee, how forgoe
> Thy sweet Converse and Love so dearly joyn'd . . .
>
> [9.908-09]

Yet the poet, in his abstract assertions after the Fall, and in his picture of the painful bickering of Adam and Eve, leaves no doubt that we are supposed to condemn them both. The trouble is that Milton's sympathetic presentation makes it difficult to condemn them very firmly. As Waldock sees the problem: "the poem asks from us, at one and the same time, two incompatible responses. It requires us . . . with the full weight of our minds to believe that Adam did right, and simultaneously requires us with the full weight of our minds to believe that he did wrong. The dilemma is as critical as that, and there is no way of escape." Exactly, this is the effect of book 9, but Waldock then goes on to see this as, in some sense, a failure in Milton's total design: "*Paradise Lost* cannot take the strain at its centre, it breaks there, the theme is too much for it. . . . if the net effect of all [Milton's] labour is to justify man's ways against God's ways: well, that was one of the risks, inherent in the venture, that he did not see."[4]

But it is hard to believe that Milton, long choosing and beginning late, after a lifetime of theological study and speculation, did not understand all the risks of his venture. It seems too easy a way out to say that Milton's unconscious sympathies have led him to give a more favorable portrait of Adam and Eve than he meant to give; or that his desire to write an interesting poem led him to undermine his theological purpose; or that Milton was not really interested in the Fall so much as in portraying human nature as he knew it.

The two incompatible responses that Waldock describes result from Milton's ultimate, climactic presentation of the problems inherent in the power of choice. With Eve, vanity, ambition, and the illusions fostered by Satan lead to her disastrous choice; but such tendencies to wild are part of her perfection: she must learn by experience, since warning has not sufficed, to manage herself better, to use her reason more wisely. With Adam, passion for Eve has overcome his reason; and he too must now learn from experience to use his reason with better effect. What Milton is stressing above all is his view that there is *not a break* between the unfallen and the fallen state; there is a *continuity* implicit in the irresistible diffusion of God's goodness. God's plan was to make us as we are. Thus Eve's unruly tendencies, Adam's commotion strange, and that domestic argument where Eve chooses to go off alone—such things do not represent a couple *fallen* before the Fall, but a couple *perfectly human* before the Fall, truly the "human pair." By its constant emphasis on man's "perfection" before the Fall, the poem asks us to revise and expand our easy notions of what constituted that original innocence and perfection.[5]

Strong emotions, Milton implies, are a part of man's perfection. The tug and pull of two reasoning minds, the disagreement between two individuals who both possess the freedom of the will—this too is part of man's perfection, for how could freedom otherwise exist and how could life be of the slightest interest without that freedom? All these qualities, Milton makes clear, must of course be kept under the gentle sway of reason—but then, as Milton insists in that remarkable parenthesis of book 3, "Reason also is choice." Strange as it may seem, the problem of making the right choice, the problem of the right exercise of freedom, is shown to be as difficult before the Fall as it is afterwards. We must remember the chief point of that heavenly dialogue in book 3: that the power of choice remains essentially the same in man, whether before or after the Fall. Before the Fall, Milton's God insists, man was made "sufficient to have stood"; after the Fall, Milton's God still insists, man has "what may suffice." Man's power of choice will be renewed by grace, and the universal link of love will be made evident to man through his knowledge that the Son of God became man and died to save mankind.

Milton's view of Adam and Eve, from the moment of their creation, emphasizes the growing, kinetic, dynamic quality of their awareness. They are born in a state of perfection which involves the ability to learn from experience and instruction. Thus Eve in book 4 is led by the divine voice to leave her "watry image" and to look upon Adam, and then, as she turns to flee, she is brought back by Adam's plea to her proper place as Adam's mate. Milton's view of man's "perfection" is never static or passive: man's dignity depends upon the power of choice, which inevitably includes the right to err as well as the right to make amends for error. To Milton man's "perfection" lies in man's ability to grow, however painfully, in wisdom and understanding.

*Notes*

1. Milton's theme of "choice" is the basis for the illuminating explorations by Leslie Brisman in *Milton's Poetry of Choice and Its Romantic Heirs* (Ithaca: Cornell University Press, 1973). For the importance of "choice" in the poem see the careful study by Jon Lawry in *The Shadow of Heaven,* chapter 4: "'Most Reason is that Reason Overcome': Choice in *Paradise Lost.*"

2. See the similar interpretation by Arnold Stein in *The Art of Presence: The Poet and Paradise Lost* (Berkeley: University of California Press, 1977), pp. 99-101: for his subtle interpretation of the following argument between Adam and Eve see pp. 112-21.

3. See the studies by Evans and Lewalski noted above (chapter 6, n. 7). For the idea that Eve is "not sincere" in her suggestion, see Tillyard, *Studies in Milton,* p. 17.

4. A. J. A. Waldock, *Paradise Lost and Its Critics* (Cambridge: Cambridge University Press, 1947), pp. 56-57.

5. See the studies of Evans and Lewalski noted above (chapter 6, n. 7).

## Joan Malory Webber (essay date 1980)

SOURCE: "The Politics of Poetry: Feminism and *Paradise Lost,*" in *Milton Studies,* Vol. XIV, 1980, pp. 3-24.

[*In the following essay, Webber claims that Milton, however awkwardly and imperfectly, breaks new ground when he raises issues concerning women's rights and importance.*]

In the highly delicate investigation of the relationship between politics and poetry, epic makes an obvious, though exhausting, field of inquiry. Traditionally, epic is described as a mingling of history with myth. Whatever this formula may actually mean, its effect is always that we are pulled in two ways, between a concern for the facts of the story (where was Troy? and when?) and a response to the universality of its symbols (Troy is any dying civilization). In epic we cannot have the one without the other: if Troy does not mean something, it does not matter where it was; if we do not know its actual history, we cannot be sure that our way of using the symbol is legitimate. Our uncertainty and ignorance in these matters are reflected in criticism's disarray.

One of the most blatant problems concerns the political orientation of the genre. We have a tendency to think of epic history (or politics), as well as myth, as conservative of a cultural past. Yet these materials may just as easily be instruments for social change. In fact, every major Western epic is revolutionary with respect to human consciousness.[1] Most significant poetry can make some analogous claim, but the epic purports to summarize its own culture, praise it, and at the same time subvert it, pointing the way to something higher.[2] Obviously an epic is not a tract, or a piece of socialist realism: even Milton, when he wrote **Paradise Lost,** had given up present hope for communal action, concluding that minds must change themselves before the world can change. The political poet's task is neither to man the barricades nor utterly to transcend his own time, but to speak through, challenge, and transform the political materials and symbols of his time so as ideally to facilitate communal fostering of human possibilities, or to enable the individual person to resist the moribund or tyrannical state.

In its deceptively Homeric simplicity,[3] its apparent Christian moralism, its obvious personal involvement, and its relative nearness to our own time, Milton's epic poetry is conducive to easy stereotyping that allows us to approach it with distorting preconceptions. The difficulty of suspending disbelief when entering Milton's world should give us pause. We think of him as a poet of the past, yet in the great division that we make between the medieval and the modern age, Milton has to be considered a modern. To read him is to confront the central realities of our own culture, and we tend to react against some of those realities without recognizing that Milton himself is doing the same thing.[4] Studying the story of Adam and Eve, one is led to Milton's divorce tracts or *Areopagitica,* and from there to more modern documents on divorce and free speech. Then we attack Milton with weapons which he himself gave us the power to create by being among the first to recognize these issues.[5] With regard to cultural context, Milton's poetry puts us in a particularly difficult position. Because he himself was among those who first saw and helped to define the problems of our age, it is hard to put his ideas into historical perspective or to establish an aesthetic threshold to allow disinterested enjoyment of his art. He does not represent an antiquated part of our culture, as many unwary readers suppose. He anticipates our whole culture, with all its self-defeating conflicts, and asks us to choose change. Yet he speaks from a time that was itself a most unclear, ungainly, and mutilated mixture of ancient and modern ways, when nothing that we have now, including our problems, could have been taken for granted.

Despite the three hundred years between then and now, Milton almost makes possible an understanding of what it would be like to read a modern epic. Nothing else in our literature prepares us for the naive intensity of many readers' involvement in this poem. Almost everyone is either for or against *Paradise Lost* (or both at once); many see their own causes reflected or distorted in it. Its wholeness defeats argument, a fact which in itself breeds discontent. And so, because his issues are so contemporary, we find an easier course in detaching them from the poem and from the historical literary contexts which may not justify Milton, but do explain him.

In this essay, I wish to examine the role of women in his epics, from the particular perspective of Sandra K. Gilbert's recent analysis of the charge that *Paradise Lost* is misogynistic and patriarchal.[6] I choose this topic because it is politically far-reaching. Milton did not select our myth of origins only because he was a Christian concerned with the problem of evil. He believed that successful marriages (which he called fit conversations) are crucial to individual happiness, to the well-being of the state, and, indeed, to the right understanding of the world. Furthermore, Western epic is a genre notable for its extensive, significant attention to women characters. Yet, as women consider the poem, disagreement increases as to its value for them, based on interpretations of Milton's attitude, or the attitude expressed in the poem, toward women's place in life, and the nature of the system of growth and meaning that defines "women's place."[7]

Gilbert's essay, typifying the opposition, argues that "because the myth of origins that Milton articulates in *Paradise Lost* summarizes a long misogynistic tradition, literary women from Mary Wollstonecraft to Virginia Woolf have recorded anxieties about his paradigmatic patriarchal poetry." She believes that the poem tells the story of woman's secondness and otherness, her consequent fall and exclusion from heaven and poetry, her alliance with Satan, Sin, and Death. Hence women readers have allayed anxieties by "rereading, misreading, and misinterpreting *Paradise Lost*."[8] In developing her argument, Gilbert lumps together women's reactions to Milton with their reactions to patriarchal poetry in general, and she implies that their responses are to ideas that really are in the poem.

*Paradise Lost* certainly is a story of otherness, and of alienation. In explaining the ways of God, or perhaps in coming to terms with them, Milton shows that in his mind alienation is a necessary risk, and perhaps even a necessary fact, of Creation. But to think of the story as featuring Eve's particular alliance with evil is surely to distort the myth, and to ignore the historical context (not of misogyny, but of revolution) from which the poem came. It may well be that in trying to adjust the perspective for a more accurate political reading, I will sometimes appear to be submitting the cause of women to that of humanity: that is a familiar and often justifiable charge against men who would rather consider any other rights than those of women. Yet the opposite risk is to let the literature of our common humanity be needlessly sacrificed. In this instance, it must be remembered that we are dealing with the seventeenth century, when almost no politically radical woman could or would have dissociated herself from men regarding the issues of religious and secular freedom which were then being fought out. Furthermore, Milton's sense of the direction in which humanity has to move is generally one which prepares the way for feminist thinking. When he did raise issues involving women's importance and women's rights, he was awkwardly and imperfectly breaking ground.

Gilbert does not acknowledge either the seventeenth-century or the epic context of *Paradise Lost,* or the context of Milton's own life and writings. As opposed to critics like Barbara Lewalski, whose findings she appears to think are "academic,"[9] she sets out to consider not only "Milton's own intentions and assertions" but also the "implications of Milton's ideas for women."[10] At best such a separation of language from effect indicates a deep distrust of, or lack of concern for, Milton's use of words. And because Gilbert limits her territory to *Paradise Lost,* together with familiar platitudes about Milton's domestic life, she cannot adequately examine what his ideas and their implications are. More perhaps than most, revolutionary poets have to be read as a whole. The context of Milton's life and works has everything to do with every part of his writing. The prose tells us how to read the poetry.[11] Most important of all, *Paradise Lost* precedes and is incomplete without *Paradise Regained.*

Margaret Fuller wrote in 1846 that Milton was one of the fathers of her own age, a true understander of liberty, justice, marriage, and education, a father whose achievement still far outdistanced that of America, his child.[12] No doubt revolutionary fathers are as hard to accept as any other kind, but at least their inclination is to force rejection of patriarchy and conservative patriarchal systems, not to espouse them. When he wrote *Paradise Lost,* Milton was a fifty-two-year-old ex-convict who had narrowly escaped execution for opposing the restoration of Charles II at a time when most of his compatriots were changing their politics or taking shelter. The poem Milton had once intended to write was the old story of King Arthur. In choosing to write *Paradise Lost* instead, he could not and did not merely shift from one sort of patriarchy to another. We do not, of course, have his own explanation for the change. But it is apparent that he was abandoning a story that features one-man rule, an aristocratic society, and sex roles so stereotyped that their validity had already been challenged in poetry that Milton knew well.[13] The form and content of biblical epic, in Milton's handling of them, are layered with complexities and implications that exploit and overturn their traditions, while using them to orient and enlighten the knowing reader.

As a rewriting of the Bible in the late seventeenth century, *Paradise Lost* had to satisfy orthodoxy or fall under censorship.[14] In a superficially convincing way it appears as a bulwark of conservatism. Yet, even to read the Bible in English had not long before been an uncertain right. The orthodox King James Bible owed everything to Tyndale's formidably influential translation, with its pugnacious marginalia emphasizing political interpretation and application. Milton's primary tenets, stressed over and over throughout his revolutionary prose, are self-control, self-knowledge, and internal freedom, in total opposition to what he calls external things. Since for him it was absolutely impossible that God could ordain any law contrary to human good, the external authority of the Bible always supports the inner promptings of the human spirit, even when, by our lights, he has to wrench the text to make this happen.[15] A double tension of this sort, between external control and inner conviction in Milton's own life, and between his inner convictions and some of the doctrines set forth in the Bible, informs all his involvement with the Bible, both in poetry and in prose.

The form of *Paradise Lost* is not only biblical; it is also epic. And, as previously indicated, Western epic traditionally undermines itself, providing criticism of the culture it is supposedly designed to admire. Just as Homer's poems implicitly criticize the Greek religious system, so do Milton's attack the Christianity of his peers. Moreover, in the Renaissance, the Bible itself was considered to be an epic: for translators like Tyndale it was the epic story of the chosen people, of whom the English nation was the contemporary realization. The fusion of Bible story with epic form very much increased the historical pertinence of Milton's poem, as at the same time the two elements radicalized each other. The Bible is famous for its denial of the decorum and aristocratic focus that epic had preserved,[16] and the history of biblical interpretation had long served as a tool for reinterpretation of epic. Epic, on the other hand, in its own history demonstrates cultural relativism; and in its character it shows how to undercut the reigning culture while seeming to praise it. *Paradise Lost* takes every advantage of its complex tradition's capacity to appear to be doing one thing while actually achieving something else.

At least one further significant element in this history ought to be mentioned. Foxe's *Book of Martyrs,* second only to the Bible as a best-seller of the age, had long promoted that idea that the Bible is the epic story of the chosen people of whom the English are the contemporary representatives.[17] Like the Bible, Foxe stressed the value of the lives of ordinary men and women, and, by recording

the tortuous changes of religion that took place throughout the sixteenth century, increased the Puritan sense that individual conscience is more trustworthy than any reigning monarch. The failure of the revolution necessitated one more shift in emphasis: the chosen people themselves had broken their commitment. In *Paradise Lost* Milton says that true heroism requires patience, martyrdom, and loneliness.[18] No reigning monarch, no one leader or party, can be trusted, only the just, self-knowing solitary being.[19] Such a belief has obvious appeal to all men and women who find themselves victimized, and at once suggests one reason why women, who have always had to work by indirection and in isolation, still find value in the poem.

Renaissance artists were very fond of "turning pictures," optical illusions which change foreground with background in a seemingly arbitrary way, to emphasize completely different scenes from different perspectives.[20] It is thus, I think, with the limited Old Testament God of Book III of *Paradise Lost,* a figure who may be ironically modeled after Homer's Zeus,[21] and who has appeared to many readers, including Gilbert, as the autocratic designer of the conservative politics of heaven.[22] Surrounding this figure, as background or foreground, is a much ampler idea or power, a force for life that is neither anthropomorphized nor sexed, and to which even the God of Book III defers by giving the scepter and the power to his Son, who is to bring all creation into this greater unity, when "God shall be all in all" (III, 317-41). This is the bright and fluent source imagined in terms of light and fountain at the beginning of Book III:

> Hail holy Light, offspring of Heav'n first-born,
> Or of th' eternal Coeternal beam
> May I express thee unblam'd? since God is Light,
> And never but in unapproached light
> Dwelt from Eternitie, dwelt then in thee,
> Bright effluence of bright essence increate.
>
> (III, 1-6)

All precedence and place here become mysterious. Between Satan's extensive maligning of his anthropomorphized God, and Milton's own portrayal of such a limited and inimical figure, is this luminous Being completely surpassing or encompassing the realm of ordinary human meaning. The syntax makes it possible to conceive of this Being as a God beyond God, certainly beyond rational expression. To the extent that any version of deity is anthropomorphic, one might say that he is not yet deity in this sense.

The God who is a character in Book III and elsewhere in *Paradise Lost,* self-justifying, dictatorial, and judgmental as well as splendid, roughly corresponds to the Christian idea of God in the Old Testament.[23] No doubt seventeenth-century readers accepted such a figure more easily than we do today. But Milton does not accept him, nor is this God satisfied with himself. He is in process toward full realization of the higher state imagined in the images of light. The only way to achieve that condition is by abnegation of title and rank. In illustration of that necessity, God gives the power and the scepter to his Son, but it is anticipated that at the end the scepter will simply become unnecessary: all life will be one with God. While the language, that "God shall be all in all," is biblical, and while the Bible is ordinarily understood to demonstrate that the more primitive Old Testament view of God yields to the New Testament sense of a God possessed of the more "feminine" qualities of love and mercy, this dramatic presentation of the change is Milton's own.

Although the words "Father" and "Son" refer to important concepts in the poem, the reality is very far from being simply a male patriarchal system, and not only because it is unusual for the patriarch to surrender his power voluntarily, foreseeing the end of all rule. The Son is begotten of the Father, out of time and out of any known sexual meaning. He then serves the Father as means of creation and separation, and also as a force for unity. Milton did not believe in the Holy Ghost as a distinct and equal part of a Trinity.[24] The Spirit, who seems interchangeable with God, the Son, and the Muse, is a symbolic, androgynous creative power. The extensive language of fertility and creativity everywhere in the poem prevents a conclusion that heaven is simply asexual. Nor is it the case, as Gilbert claims, that the female is excluded from heaven.[25] Wisdom and Understanding, for example, are female powers that existed in heaven before all Creation (VII, 1-12), although not necessarily named and bounded. Ordinarily, however, the descriptions of reproduction and creativity are so expressed as to prevent the sexes from falling into contraries. Both male and female muses are invoked. The angels "can either sex assume, or both; so soft / And uncompounded is thir Essence pure" (I, 424). When Adam questions Raphael about sex in heaven, Raphael blushes and declares, without reference to male or female characteristics, that sex is superior there because flesh presents no impediments (VIII, 618-29). Male and female are aspects of Creation, like light and dark, which grow more distinct the farther they are removed from heaven. And as heaven itself, in God's evolving process, moves closer to unity, its gradations may be expected to fall away with time.

In an interesting essay which Gilbert cites, Northrop Frye discusses the applicability to Milton's poetry "of the two great mythological structures" of our heritage—one, ruled by a male father-god, which dominates our culture from "the beginning of the Christian era down to the Romantic movement," and the other, centered on a mother-goddess, which has more frequently been influential in modern times. Frye traces in Milton a basic adherence to the father myth, the conception of a male creator superior to created nature, and the assumption that in all natural things male reason is superior to female imagination, even though that creative imagination is what the poet requires. Nature can be led upward toward the divine, or downward with the demonic: Eve, as representative of nature, has affinities both ways. But Frye also indicates, quite apart from Eve's partial association with the demonic, that she is given an unusual amount of independent power in the poem. "The

father-myth is an inherently conservative one; the other is more naturally revolutionary, and the revolutionary emphasis in Milton shows how near he is to the mythology of Romanticism."[26]

Frye's essay rightly indicates that, rather than merely contributing to a long tradition of Christian misogynism, as Gilbert believes, Milton drew upon a much deeper, more primitive set of oppositions which Western culture had for thousands of years colored in a way that now seems prejudicial to women. Milton is obviously not only reworking this tradition but preparing it for its demise in the anticipated final unification of all things in God. Yet it is important in his poetry; it represents to him the way in which life has chosen to work itself out, for good and for ill. It is also an essential part of the epic line within which he is working, and so something needs to be said of it and of the problems which it presents for women readers.

As a great deal of our literature and mythology shows, the human mind, conscious or unconscious, has a strong tendency to group all experience, all phenomena, into opposites: up-down, day-night, sun-moon, reason-imagination, strength-softness, creating-nurturing, heaven-earth, and male-female.[27] Although most people who discuss the subject are quick to point out that the terms *male* and *female* are intended symbolically rather than literally (Jung believed that each person contains both elements), still women through the ages have always been associated with these "female" characteristics. Further, since men have been the thinkers and the writers, the female characteristics have often acquired connotations both of otherness and of evil, as men have projected their fears and fantasies upon the other sex. These patterns are extremely clear in the treatment of women in epic poetry.[28] On the one hand, there are women who guide and inspire, although their roles are externally passive compared to those of men, who seek, wage war, conquer, and find. Such women are Penelope, Beatrice, and Gloriana. On the other hand, there are witch-women, who seek to beguile, seduce, distract, and corrupt, such as Circe, Armida, and Duessa. All other epic women, with a very few exceptions, belong somewhere on the spectrum between these extremes. In some very real sense, men are associated with process and women with goals: women can deceive because they know, and compel because they are. Some epic writers, particularly those who include warrior women in their stories, raise women to a position of greater equality of function, but men and women are almost always seen as fundamentally different from each other, as they are in Milton.[29]

Part of Milton's task in justifying the ways of God to men is to explain why these differences exist. One question we would ask now is whether they do, whether indeed men and women are dissimilar, but for Milton such separations are a necessary aspect of Creation itself. Creation is by contraries; things are defined only by their opposites; self requires other. As soon as there are opposites, there is the potentiality for conflict even though Creation's end is a higher unity. Milton's God, who contains all opposites, shows conflict within himself:[30] when these differences are externally realized, the possibility of problems is realized as well, and the problems themselves make possible growth and change. Everything in the epic portrays a universe in process: that is a large part of the explanation of God's ways. Even God, in Milton's view, could not make instant perfection. In addition, Milton is changing the terms of epic and the traditional ways of looking at reality. The extraordinary power of the poetry is its ability to celebrate simultaneously so many different ways of thought and being, both the God of Old Testament righteousness and the New Testament God of change, contraries and their dissolution, inequality and equality between men and women.

Eve reflects every female potentiality that could enter the mind of a Renaissance epic writer and Christian humanist. Placed in the chain of being in a position officially subordinate to Adam's, she combines the opposite epic functions of witch and inspiration, being both Adam's downfall and his means of recovery. As Northrop Frye shows, she contains and reflects all the values associated with the mother-goddess, as well as the demonic associations that the Renaissance made with that cult. And she is a strong, human woman. Since even—or especially—today, women are struggling with just this problem of the multiple roles and definitions that have been thrust upon them, and which, with varying attitudes and in varying combinations, they perceive in themselves, Milton's Eve does generate intense feelings of identification. The first acts of her life portray a familiar dilemma: she wants to reflect upon herself, to look at herself in a pool and gain self-knowledge, but in order to know herself she is required to turn her attention to Adam, an alien other. The whole relationship between Adam and Eve, in fact, is affected by this stress between self-sufficiency and mutual need. As I will show a little later on, either posture, overindulged, becomes destructive, and balance is hard to maintain.

Traditional epic poetry, like the Bible, is patriarchal. Superficially, at least, it has to do with battles, journeys, conquests, the founding of nations. Ordinarily no problem and no success in epic occurs independently of women. Yet despite the near equality of warrior women, as exemplified most outstandingly by Britomart in Spenser's *Faerie Queene*, *Paradise Lost* is the first epic in which the active heroic role is shared equally between the sexes. Despite Britomart's obvious worldly equality, her goal is to find Artegall and marry him. *Paradise Lost* is the first epic whose scene is, in effect, the home, woman's traditional sphere, rather than the world of warfare and quest outside. Adam is called "domestic Adam" (IX, 318); when he shows signs of interest in places far removed from home, Raphael chastises him. Eve, in turn, has no supernatural or witchlike powers with which to tempt Adam or initiate the subsequent process of restoration. Although their weaknesses and their strengths differ, they are equally fallible; their epic battle is in large part their struggle to recognize and support each other's humanity. Many critics have pointed out in contrast the satirical, mock-heroic tone of Milton's treatment of Satan's "heroic" journey to Eden

and of the epic warfare between the angels. It is one of the most remarkable things about the poem that seemingly insignificant domestic quarreling, set side by side with traditional epic endeavor, achieves such obvious, overwhelming importance. Human relationships are at the center of cosmic loss and gain.

Thus, while in most epics marriage or some analogous union is a symbol of the fulfillment for which the hero strives, in *Paradise Lost* marriage is a main subject and theme of the poem. Although the setting of Eden seems far removed from ordinary life, much that happens there is commonplace. The poem traces the lives of a man and woman from their first courtship through their first great disillusionment to their acceptance of life in the world that their descendants and Milton's readers know. Contrary to Gilbert's idea that Eve is a "divine afterthought,"[31] she is from the beginning an essential part of the whole design of growth and change achieved through opposition, which involves risk. The first test laid upon both Adam and Eve, when they are created, is to recognize that they need each other as they exemplify that large pattern of opposites without which nothing in the world, or even the world itself, could exist. Definition is in relation to something or someone else: to recognize one's incompleteness is an essential sign of self-knowledge. So God was pleased with Adam when Adam expressed a longing for a companion, although not when Adam allowed himself to be dominated by desire and need.

Milton had an obvious dislike for the courtly tradition that reifies woman (and man too) by making her an object of adoration. Adam's disposition to do this falsifies both Adam's and Eve's positions, and prepares her for the false adulation of the serpent. Romanticized married love, relatively new in the Renaissance, was the preferred Puritan model:[32] recognition of the woman as helpmeet released her both from the decorative, idealized courtly role and from her more common treatment as household drudge, and gave her an everyday value and importance that she would not have again for a long time.[33]

Adam and Eve are often spoken of in language that implies absolute equality. Adam asks God for an equal, one who can share "all rational delight," and is granted "thy likeness, thy fit help, thy other self" (VIII, 450), whom Adam sees as "Bone of my Bone, Flesh of my Flesh, my Self / Before me" (VIII, 494). Eve, upon her creation, is less sure of Adam's importance to her, and shows preference for her own image reflected in a pool before she is persuaded that she is part of Adam's soul, and, as he tells her, "My other half" (IV, 488). Both Adam and Eve are majestic, made in the image of God, and free.

At the same time, in this many-faceted scheme of things, the sexes are different: men are suited to "contemplation and valor," women to "softness" and "sweet attractive grace." This is a summarizing of traditional epic virtues, as they are personified in Odysseus and Penelope, or Prince Arthur and Gloriana. "Sweet attractive grace" is the equivalent of the powers that enable Beatrice to bring Dante out of hell. Sweetness is a capacity for love which Adam said was lacking in him before Eve was created; grace is the capacity for salvation; and attractiveness is the quality that attracts or draws, making it possible for two to become one. We see frequent signs of Adam's or Eve's particular qualities turning up in the other: just as Adam acquires sweetness, Eve demonstrates the power of contemplation.

In addition to all these complex reformations of biblical and epic material, the reader is required to see Adam and Eve as symbolic reflections of the great contraries of the universe—sun and moon, earth and sky, reason and imagination. The act of Creation results in such contraries, which, however, are to be restored to wholeness in God by being raised to a fuller unity than they originally enjoyed. Creation is essentially divisive: heaven and earth were made by what Milton calls God's "divorcing command"[34] that sorted out the warring but indistinguishable elements of chaos. That is, Milton here thinks of the word "divorcing" as expressive of a positive act: only divorce could create coherence. Yet inherent in that word also is the recognition that Creation began with imperfection, that it consisted in separating rather than in uniting, and that the Creation therefore remains unfinished, caught up in a progress toward a higher unity.

Adam and Eve, two parts of a theoretically inseparable whole, were in this sense divorced at the moment of Eve's creation, and, god-like as they are, their harmony is possible only because of disjunction. Milton's justification of God is that Creation is good, that inherent in creation is this divorcing process, which is in itself some sort of fortunate fall. Milton is quite clear that divorce in our modern sense was not invented for Adam and Eve.[35] They are above, or prior to, that, but they feel the strain of their twoness. Even Eve's words, "unargued I obey," by calling attention to the possibility of argument, both demonstrate and deny the strain.

Thus, although Milton says that his divorce tracts are not intended for this couple, we cannot help seeing in their marriage an illustration of what he means by both the best and the worst of wedded bliss. Marriage for him is a covenant, like that between man and God, and the covenant can be broken by spiritual or intellectual disagreement and incompatibility. When adultery is the only permissible reason for divorce, and the risks of adultery are so much greater for women than for men, it is easy for the man to control the marriage and his own freedom. Milton argues that the physical bond is much less important than the spiritual one, and that as soon as spiritual attunement is denied, the marriage is ended. Although he did not conceive of marriage without a dominant partner, he did suppose that this role might be taken by the wife, if she should exceed her husband in wisdom, and that either wife or husband could initiate divorce.[36]

In the divorce tracts, Milton asks that marriage be removed from control of any ruling hierarchy, religious or civil, and placed in the power of the partners themselves. In theory, at least, this action would give the woman a legal means to remove herself from the power of paternal authorities and to negotiate equally in the matter of her own destiny. Milton's poem also makes it obvious that the reality of divorce affects day-to-day marital relations. Since marriage is based on mutual consent, unchangeable disagreement constitutes divorce. When Eve decides that the pair should work separately for a few hours, Adam cannot force her to change her mind. Since she is determined to go, a refusal of permission would constitute at the very least an opening of the way to divorce. Later, Adam could divorce Eve on any number of grounds, but he chooses to abandon himself to her.[37] In the recriminations which follow, they see that they have broken covenant with God, themselves, and each other, but as Eve took the first step away from the marriage, she now is first to try to repair the damage, and Adam, while pretending opposition, follows her all the way.

It is no mere lip service (Gilbert's term)[38] that Milton offers to matrimony. For him it is the basic, central figure of the way the world is, and of the way it could be—sometimes in a pattern of higher and lower status, sometimes in a balance of equals, sometimes stressing the separateness of the partners and sometimes their unity. For him the epic goal was the wholeness that marriage offers, figured also in every part of the universe that grows through its many opposites, and figured ultimately in the visionary time when "God shall be all in all." The challenge that confronts us now is whether it is possible to retain that ideal, perhaps the only remaining idea that makes poetry out of life, while reaching beyond the particular poetry that seems to promote male dominance. While accepting this dominance, Milton himself searched beyond it as much as anyone in his age.

Eve and Adam were meant to move upward through the chain of being, free of death, until they reached the status of angels, and, eventually, without suffering death, to become one with God. Their destiny as free agents required them to be educated, and for this purpose God sent Raphael to teach them. Among the many remarkable attributes of *Paradise Lost* is its pervasive didacticism. The four central books of the poem are devoted to the education of the first man and woman. Both Eve and Adam listen to and absorb all that Raphael has to tell them, understanding with equal aptitude, as Milton tells us.[39] When Eve leaves before Raphael does, her departure serves several purposes, the most important of which is probably that it leaves Adam free to discuss her with the angel, in the section where he is told, but does not really admit, that he is an excessively doting husband.[40]

Adam and Eve are both gardeners in this poem, a conception not without precedent, although Milton did choose to avoid the familiar division of labor according to which Adam delves and Eve spins. In her additional responsibilities for the household, Eve may be a prototype for the modern woman who fulfills her profession and is expected to do the dishes as well, or, more pleasingly, a forerunner of the Renaissance lady who presided over the great house and its surrounding villages. In any case, Adam is out of place here, nervously asking her to bring out her best stores for Raphael, and having no idea how food is preserved in Paradise. Since Eve's work is more comprehensive than his, it is understandable that she is the one who becomes preoccupied with the problem of their labor; Milton himself appears to agree that she has some reason for her concern.

Eve's cosmic association is with physical nature, which legitimately concerns the couple in their immediate day-to-day obligations, as well as in their thoughts about their descendants. Adam's association is with sky, which is supposed to make him more aware of God, but which also gives him a penchant for abstract speculation and generalization, and often makes him seem abstracted and ill at ease with ordinary life. Although both attend to lectures, Eve is more responsive to dreams: the work of reeducating her after the Fall thus is much less laborious than that of teaching Adam, who has to have everything explained to him. These are aspects of the traditional opposition between the minds of men and those of women. But both the way in which they are educated together by a tutor and the way in which they set forth together as travelers into an unknown world emphasize the opportunities which were at least sometimes available to both men and women in the Renaissance, and perhaps never again with quite the same balance of excitement and fear.

I have saved the problem of Satan for last, because it involves the most crucial issues for *Paradise Lost* and *Paradise Regained* in our time. Gilbert sees him romantically, commenting on his enormous attractiveness, especially to women, because he expresses their own need to rebel. But as most readers have noticed, Satan loses almost all his attractions after the opening two books of the poem, nor is there ever justification for describing him either as "a handsome devil" or as a "curly-haired Byronic hero."[41] Gilbert also sees him, more correctly, as a lover of incest and an artist of death. Here, more than anywhere else, it is important to recognize that for Milton God represents life. Because Satan has rebelled against life, he can love only himself and death (two objects which finally amount to the same thing). Gilbert does see women as being caught in a trap if they turn from God to Satan, but the attractiveness that she ascribes to Satan is more imaginary than she, and some of her authors, realize.

Satan is a perfect example of a patriarchal, domineering figure. His reason for rebellion is that he is totally threatened by God's decision to hand over the scepter to the Son. Abdiel's argument that the Son's new role will enable all Creation to be more closely united in God expresses exactly what Satan fears, that his own status must be lost or shared. He prefers hierarchy in hell to unity in heaven, and he tries to convince Eve of the rightness of his own distorted perspective. Satan is that odd kind of rebel who reacts against change: consequently, any reader who, like some of the romantics, wants to use him as a model has to misread and misinterpret Milton in order to do it.

Another point of importance: in all of Milton's poems there are patterns of resemblances, and in seeing affinities between Eve and Satan, Gilbert has merely selected one thread of this pattern in *Paradise Lost.* Satan also resembles the poet and God;[42] Eve resembles Sin, Satan, Adam, the earth, Mary, and God. Milton, like everyone else in the Renaissance, is concerned with correspondences; they are a way of ordering experience. He is characteristic of his time also in believing that sin easily disguises itself as virtue, that evil and good so greatly resemble one another that it is difficult to choose the right path. In emphasizing likenesses between Eve, Adam, himself, and Satan, the poet wants to show that they do exist, that they are a constant danger, and that they can be overcome. Awareness of the danger may help us to avoid being surprised by sin.

Roland M. Frye's recent book, *Milton's Imagery and the Visual Arts,* provides valuable information not only about the traditional nature of these parallels, but also about the choices Milton made. In deciding how to portray Satan at the moment of the temptation of Eve, Milton rejected the possibility of "a serpent with the torso and head of a man," by means of which he could easily have created a "curly-haired Byronic hero." He also chose not to portray a woman-headed serpent, possibly with Eve's own face, a device extremely popular in the iconographic tradition. Such a figure would stress Eve's self-love, and give credence to Gilbert's argument for an incestuous undertone in the connection between woman and serpent. But, as Frye notes at this point, Milton "was not an antifeminist and could scarcely have put a 'lady visage' on his Tempter without seeming to some readers to invite an identification of the devil with woman."[43]

Imagination, allied with darkness and the muse, seems to Milton particularly vulnerable to invasion by Satanic elements. There is darkness in God also—Milton makes that very clear: from a cave near the throne of God both darkness and light proceed, and Satan himself, after all, is of God's creation. Just because the faculty of imagination is not always subject to reason, it is more suspect than reason, but it is not therefore *inferior*. Milton suspects his own poetic gift: possibly it is something of his own invention and not of God. He will not therefore deny or suppress it, but it may be that he stresses imagination excessively because he works in an irrational medium.

The most important and interesting element in this train of thought is the growth, in the Renaissance, of attention to subjectivity and to knowledge for its own sake. These are mirror images of each other: to be lost in oneself, Narcissus-like, may be to lose oneself; one may also become lost in the stars. Both activities are seen in the Renaissance as gifts which may be misused. Contemplation of self may lead to holiness or self-worship; contemplation of the stars may be a way of praising God's works or of trying to play God. As always, Adam's and Eve's vulnerabilities are opposite to one another. Eve's subjectivity makes her open to self-adulation; Adam's interest in the stars and his tendency toward idolatry make him forgetful of himself. Both lead to loss of accurate seeing of relationships. Satan exemplifies both extremes. The birth of Sin and his incest with her demonstrate his perverse self-love; his mastery of technology warns of the possible results of Adam's innocent speculations about outer space. Milton may have wished that these tendencies in human nature, both for good and for evil, could be shut off, but he knew better. They lead to alienation in our world, in any case.

Satan's alienation is absolute because he has carried to a perverse and absolute extreme the opposing tendencies manifested in Eve and Adam. Choosing self-love over love of life (an untenable paradox), his aim is to oppose God with himself, but God is the only standard to which he can apply. He argues that heaven and hell are both within, but has to choose God's standards (the norms of life) for definition. He wishes to make the world his empire, and does, by profaning it: everything is defined by its usefulness to him in his efforts to turn it against its true character in God's world. Thus he is unable to know either himself or the world, and becomes a totally alienated being.

The tendencies that destroy Satan are rejected by Eve and Adam as they choose each other and God (or life) over their own selfish and power-seeking propensities. Thus they have within them the possibility of paradise, even though it is apparent at the end of *Paradise Lost* that they must experience alienation henceforth as a way of life. Eve's unselfish recognition and acknowledgment of her need for Adam begins to save both of them from the negative tendencies in themselves. Previous scholars have observed the bold paralleling of Eve with the Son, at the end of Book X and the opening of Book XI, as both offer to accept all responsibility for human sin.[44] Frye too notes that Eve's compassionate and decisive role in the redemptive process has few precedents.[45] Yet sending Adam and Eve out alone, hand in hand (a detail apparently original in Milton) into the world,[46] Milton was not satisfied, and *Paradise Regained* is an attempt to deal with the central problem raised but not solved in *Paradise Lost:* what to do about subjectivity and alienation.

Subjectivity is seen in *Paradise Lost* as a female characteristic, and external knowing as a male one. Eve's first act is to contemplate herself, and Adam's to contemplate the heavens. Neither characteristic is in itself morally tarnished. In fact, both conventionally lead to knowledge of God. But they can also lead to individualism, another quality by which we now define the Renaissance and both praise and lament our own age. Modern readers often criticize the childlike natures of Adam and Eve. But Milton's first man and first woman are like that just because they have not yet fallen into self-consciousness and alienation, which are necessary to individualism as we know it. Renaissance thinkers clearly recognized that spiritual fragmentation and decay are allowed and even fostered by individualism. Milton had to consider this postlapsarian condition, which had become so evident in his time. The fear and fascination surrounding the problem are exemplified in Satan, who resembles numerous other Renaissance figures in the boundless energy with which he will address himself to any self-serving and ultimately self-destructive goal. He cannot be saved because he cannot submit himself to a larger whole.

If Sin is seen as female, so, obviously, is Mary in *Paradise Regained,* to whom Eve is often compared in *Paradise Lost,* and who traditionally is given the role of second Eve to Jesus' second Adam. She is the nurturing woman who helps Jesus to know himself, and helps to keep us from thinking of Jesus as either incomplete or aggressively masculine. In the poem he departs from and returns to his mother's house. His main activities in the poem (which, like *Paradise Lost,* rejects traditional epic action) are learning to know himself and rejecting the world that Satan has to offer. The poem says that he descended into himself (*PR* II, 111): it is the first epic in which subjectivity is made so explicit; and he names correctly the false worldly lures with which Satan would seduce him. Thus he repairs the damage done to self by Adam and Eve, and acknowledges the damage done to the world. Obviously, also, he combines the qualities of Adam and Eve which had been distinguished in their creation.

The sterility of both internal and external narcissism is well portrayed by Satan. Jesus' only recourse is to reject everything that Satan has to offer, as Satan had rejected everything of God. And one may read the poem as prophetic of the despair of the twentieth century, which has followed the Renaissance into a subjectivity now devoid both of God and of faith in anything. Satan and Jesus are two major aspects of modern consciousness, but one may conclude by feeling that there is nothing to choose between them. It is of course immensely important to recall that, as incarnation of the Son, Jesus is to represent and further the goal of reuniting all things in God. Satan has become devoted to holding in stasis the outward-moving, still hierarchical forms of Creation, turning them into grim parodies of themselves: thus an angel becomes a devil, and men and women become sex objects to one another. The Son's (and now Jesus') work is to carry all things beyond their separateness, into a fulfillment in perfect unity.

Jesus has rejected external things and power politics. Yet the "yes" that he says to life as symbolized by God, the "yes" that he says thereby to his own sense of wholeness, gives him the power to walk on water, stand on air, and be ministered to by angels. It also enables him to return to his mother's house instead of being dashed to pieces on the rocks. So a necessary connection between male and female may be restored here in a pattern of reciprocity that attempts to correct both the old patriarchal values and the medieval values of knight and lady. Standing on the pinnacle of his father's temple,[47] Jesus repeats the effort of

*Paradise Lost* to reject patriarchal symbol and hierarchy. Learning from and in turn enlightening his mother, he restores the original pattern from which courtly love was derived.

*Paradise Regained* appears to be a poem of worldly rejection that prepares the way for romanticism by teaching descent into the self and admitting the total corruption of the world. Milton believed that humanity's only hope was in the subjective faith of the lonely man or woman. But it must also be remembered that Jesus, in appearing to reject everything the world offers, rejects only Satan's secular world. Under that tarnished surface, Milton believed, could still be found the perfect Eden of Eve and Adam, and human relationships based in natural love. In the atmosphere of doubt, fear, and greed in which the poem takes place, the role of Jesus must to a large extent appear negative. Mary's faith in the nature behind appearances, and her ability to make a link between the physical and the spiritual, are easy to miss in the context of the duel between Satan and her Son. But, as Michael has already insisted to Adam, the duel involves no exercise of power. Jesus rejects all of the so-called masculine values. His return to his mother's house is an affirmation of the new Adam, the new man.

*Notes*

1. For documentation of this point, see Joan Webber, *Milton and His Epic Tradition* (Seattle, 1978).

2. If Homer's poems celebrate the prowess of Greece and detail the military culture, they also question (perhaps deny) the sanity of the Trojan War. The *Aeneid* describes both the founding of Rome and the huge price that had to be paid for it. Tasso tells of a city (Jerusalem) that had to be destroyed in order to be saved. Camoens describes the utter decadence that overwhelms new lands after they have been discovered and claimed for Portugal. Spenser, Milton's immediate predecessor, in his romance epic presents the profound inadequacies of courtly love. The epics do not describe a better way. In fact, they do not utterly reject the world that they have, but in seeing its limitations they prepare the way for advance.

3. By these words I mean to suggest the large-scale sculpturing and the spare story line that so totally distinguish Milton from most of his predecessors. This apparent clarity is deceiving, but its artistic provenance is quite legitimately Homeric.

4. It is commonplace to speak of the English Civil Wars as the watershed between the medieval and the modern world, and to recognize thinkers like Descartes as the fathers of modern consciousness. It obviously follows that a poet like Milton, who lived through the Civil Wars on the rebel side, might also be seen as having helped to shape our world. See Jackie Di Salvo, "Blake Encountering Milton: Politics and the Family in *Paradise Lost* and *The*

*Four Zoas,*" in *Milton and the Line of Vision,* ed. Joseph A. Wittreich, Jr. (Madison, Wis., 1975), pp. 143-84. On this point in general see also Christopher Hill, *Milton and the English Revolution* (New York, 1977).

5. Milton's genius for seeing the underlying issues in contemporary controversies, and for seeing issues of freedom where others had been unwilling to look, enabled him to pioneer the work of freedom on many different fronts. Rather than concern himself with the degree of liberty appropriate to Baptists, Levellers, or Quakers, as others were doing, he examined the validity (for him the necessity) of free expression. Rather than assume the divine sanctity of marriage, he examined it as a human institution entirely dependent for its success on the enduring compatibility of two fallible human beings. This almost unique ability to grasp the essentials of a problem makes us wonder why he could not trace out all the implications in the same way we ourselves would do it. Such an attitude not only shows a lack of appreciation for the magnitude of the achievement; it is also ahistorical.

6. "Patriarchal Poetry and Women Readers: Reflections on Milton's Bogey," *PMLA,* XCIII (1978), 368-82. Gilbert's focus is on the reactions to *Paradise Lost* of a number of (mostly nineteenth-century) women writers, but she indicates that they are reacting to a conservative, patriarchal, misogynistic poem. In other words, she is not just representing what she regards as their point of view: she believes them to be right. While her essay does summarize some very persistent complaints about Milton, it also badly misrepresents both Milton and many of her authors, and probably ought to be answered point by point on their behalf. However, such a direct attack would dilute concentration on the most essential issue of how to read Milton. In the present essay I have tried, in fairness to Milton's own style of argument, to speak to that underlying issue. In the course of this endeavor, I do not mean to argue that Milton was not in some sense a "patriarchal" poet: he lived in the seventeenth century, and it seems pointless to complain that he was of his age. It is much more worthwhile to celebrate the extent to which, by transcending his time, he enabled us to ask for freedoms that he himself could not yet imagine.

Some examples of Gilbert's misreadings of Milton are that in *Paradise Lost* a solitary Father-God is the only creator of all things, that Adam speaks for Milton (and for God), that the Fall is responsible for human generation, that Adam's fall is more fortunate than Eve's, that spirits are all masculine, that Satan is a handsome devil throughout much of *Paradise Lost,* that Satan "explores" his own secret depths, and that he is concerned with liberty and justice. Both in her reading of Milton, and in her analysis of women writers, Gilbert makes the mistake of assuming that a character's viewpoint can be identified with the author's. For example, although Charlotte Brontë's Shirley has a low opinion of Milton's characterization of Eve, Milton is first on the list of authors whom Charlotte recommended to her sister Emily, ahead of Shakespeare, about whose morality she has reservations, and far ahead of Pope, whom she says she does not admire; see Elizabeth Gaskell, *The Life of Charlotte Brontë* (London, 1908), p. 85. For more accurate readings of these writers, one should look at the works themselves, as well as at those of other critics, as, to take one example, Stuart Curran, "The Siege of Hateful Contraries: Shelley, Mary Shelley, Byron, and *Paradise Lost,*" in *Milton and the Line of Vision,* ed. Joseph A. Wittreich, Jr. (Madison, Wis., 1975), pp. 209-30.

7. Previous writing on this subject includes Marcia Landy, "Kinship and the Role of Women in *Paradise Lost,*" *Milton Studies,* IV, ed. James D. Simmonds (Pittsburgh, 1972), pp. 3-18; Barbara K. Lewalski, "Milton on Women—Yet Once More," *Milton Studies,* VI, ed. James D. Simmonds (Pittsburgh, 1974), pp. 3-20; Di Salvo, "Blake Encountering Milton."

8. Gilbert, Abstract, p. 357. Lewalski's fine essay, referred to in my previous note, anticipates much that I have to say here and obviates some of Gilbert's arguments, such as the idea that Eve's creativity is only in motherhood, while Adam is the poet and intellectual.

9. Gilbert, "Patriarchal Poetry," p. 369.

10. Ibid., p. 381, n. 8.

11. On this point, see Northrop Frye, *Five Essays on Milton's Epics* (London, 1966), pp. 94ff.

12. In "The Prose Works of Milton," *Papers on Literature and Art* (New York, 1846), pp. 38-39.

13. I am thinking especially of the mockery of the courtly codes in Ariosto's *Orlando Furioso* and, with more thoughtfully directed point, in Spenser's *Faerie Queene,* where the sexism of the Arthurian world is made apparent.

14. On the problem of censorship, see Hill, *Milton and the English Revolution,* chap. 29, "Paradise Lost."

15. For the most famous examples of Milton's practice, see his use of the biblical texts on divorce in the divorce tracts.

16. One might bear in mind this antithetical tradition in considering Sandra Gilbert's attack on Milton's "masculine" Latinity. The question of whether Milton was or was not a Latinate poet is still, oddly enough, very controversial; some of the scholarship is summarized in my book *The Eloquent "I": Style and Self in Seventeenth-Century Prose* (Madison, Wis., 1966), pp. 287-88. Northrop Frye argues that "simplicity of language is a deep moral principle to Milton," and that he was "the first great English

writer to fight for semantic sanity" (*Five Essays on Milton's Epics,* pp. 122-24). In fact, heroic language is subverted in *Paradise Lost,* just as heroic ideas are, until what finally emerges is the stripped style of *Paradise Regained.*

17. William Haller, *Foxe's Book of Martyrs and the Elect Nation* (London, 1963).

18. IX, 31-32, in *The Works of John Milton,* II (New York, 1931), hereafter cited as CM. Future references will be to this edition and will be given in the text.

19. Abdiel is the obvious model of the fully formed heroic individual. The acceptance of the isolated person as heroic model occurs in Milton from necessity of his age, not from conviction. The concept of individualism is new in the Renaissance, not even fully articulated, yet the dangers of individualism inherited by our age are already apparent to Milton, as they were to a long line of subsequent antidemocratic English thinkers, and this problem will be a central issue in my discussion. For Milton, individualism is a means to a communal end.

20. On this see, for example, Rosalie Colie, *"My Ecchoing Song": Andrew Marvell's Poetry of Criticism* (Princeton, 1970), "Visual Traditions," pp. 192-218.

21. I am extending a suggestion made by Northrop Frye, who suggests that God's self-justifying speech in Book III is modeled on the speech of Zeus at the opening of the *Odyssey;* see *Five Essays on Milton's Epics,* p. 105.

22. Gilbert, "Patriarchal Poetry," pp. 368, 375.

23. For discussion and bibliography, see my "Milton's God," *ELH,* XL (1973), 514-31.

24. *Christian Doctrine,* in *Complete Prose Works of John Milton,* VI (New Haven, 1973), ed. Maurice Kelley, I, VI, "Of the Holy Spirit," pp. 281-98. This edition is hereafter cited as YP.

25. "Patriarchal Poetry," p. 373. As so often, here Gilbert accepts the word of a character, in this case disgruntled Adam, who after the Fall imagines that heaven contains male spirits only.

26. Northrop Frye, "The Revelation to Eve," in *Paradise Lost: A Tercentenary Tribute,* ed. B. Rajan (Toronto, 1969), p. 46.

27. For discussion and bibliography, see Robert Ornstein, *The Psychology of Consciousness* (New York, 1972), p. 67.

28. Webber, *Milton and His Epic Tradition.*

29. For women now the question of how to make use of this extensive literature is extremely perplexing. Women are not in agreement as to the validity of these sexual distinctions. Nor can one be sure to what extent the literature creates or merely reflects

them. If the stereotypes ought not to be perpetuated, then how does one deal with the literature?

30. See Don Parry Norford, "'My other half': The Coincidence of Opposites in *Paradise Lost,*" *MLQ,* XXXVI (1975), 21-53.

31. "Patriarchal Poetry," p. 371.

32. See William Haller, "Hail Wedded Love," *ELH,* XIII (1946), 79-97; William and Malleville Haller, "The Puritan Art of Love," *Huntington Library Quarterly,* V (1942), 235-72; C. S. Lewis, *The Allegory of Love: A Study in Medieval Tradition* (London, 1953).

33. Hill, *Milton and the English Revolution,* p. 119. Research on this subject has yielded controversial evidence. For a somewhat different interpretation, see Lawrence Stone, *The Family, Sex and Marriage in England, 1500-1800* (New York, 1977), p. 202.

34. John Milton, *The Doctrine and Discipline of Divorce,* YP, II, 273.

35. *Tetrachordon,* YP, II, 665. Christopher Hill speculates interestingly on Milton's possible influence, and lack of influence, on Charlotte Brontë, who compares blind Rochester to Milton's Samson. Like Milton, Rochester lives long enough to gain a happy marriage. The divorce that Milton could envisage "still seemed impossible two centuries later"; see *Milton and the English Revolution,* p. 140.

36. *Tetrachordon,* p. 589: "then a superior and more natural law comes in, that the wiser should govern the less wise, whether male or female." It is apparent throughout the tracts that Milton addresses himself to both men and women; the title of his initial tract begins, *The Doctrine and Discipline of Divorce Restored to the good of both Sexes.*

37. Eve committed idolatry in worshiping the tree, and to Milton idolatry was a more serious offense than adultery. But Adam committed idolatry in worshiping Eve.

38. "Patriarchal Poetry," p. 374.

39. In allowing Eve an education equal to Adam's, Milton certainly departs very far from the usual practice of his day: only a few aristocratic women were ordinarily privileged to learn so much. Since this episode of the poem is central, it seems strange that critics continue to believe that Eve has been denied the benefit of Raphael's instruction. This is a different kind of misreading from that which Gilbert claims women have had to exercise.

40. It also shows us, as Arnold Stein points out, that when Adam has other things on his mind, he is not so concerned about Eve's spending time alone in the Garden (*The Art of Presence: The Poet and "Paradise Lost"* [Berkeley, 1977]).

41. Gilbert, "Patriarchal Poetry," p. 375. Gilbert ascribes this unlikely epithet to T. S. Eliot, on the authority of Harold Bloom in *The Anxiety of Influence* (New York, 1973). I have not found the source in Eliot.

42. On these intentional parallels, see William Riggs, *The Christian Poet in "Paradise Lost"* (Berkeley, 1972).

43. *Milton's Imagery and the Visual Arts* (Princeton, 1978), p. 168.

44. Lewalski, "Milton on Women—Yet Once More," p. 19. Joseph Summers, *The Muse's Method* (Cambridge, Mass., 1962), pp. 176-85.

45. *Milton's Imagery,* p. 294.

46. Ibid., pp. 314-15.

47. The act of standing on the pinnacle of the temple, which concludes the series of temptations in Book IV of *Paradise Regained,* is meant to recall the opening of *Paradise Lost,* in which Milton says that the Spirit prefers "Before all Temples th' upright heart and pure" (*PL* I, 17-18).

## Balachandra Rajan (essay date 1983)

SOURCE: "*Paradise Lost:* The Uncertain Epic," in *Milton Studies,* Vol. XVII, 1983, pp. 105-19.

[*In the following essay, Rajan argues that* Paradise Lost *is a mixed-genre poem whose primary genre of epic undergoes revisionary treatment in Milton's hands and holds that the work seeks its identity between possibilities of epic and tragedy, or loss and restoration.*]

The problem of the genre of ***Paradise Lost*** seems to have been a problem from the day the poem was published. Dryden may have said that "this man . . . cuts us all out and the ancients too,"[1] but it did not take long for the caution of the critic to make its inroads on the generosity of the poet. In the preface to *Sylvae* (1685) the objections are stylistic—to the "flats" among Milton's elevations, to his "antiquated words," and to the "perpetual harshness" of their sound. But eight years later, in the *Discourse Concerning the Original and Progress of Satire,* the qualifications become more substantial. The earlier objections are repeated, and Milton's lack of talent in rhyming is added to them. But we are also told that Milton's subject "is not that of an heroic poem properly so called. His design is the losing of our happiness: his event is not prosperous like that of all other epic works; his heavenly machines are many and his human persons are but two."[2] In the dedication to his translation of the *Aeneid* (1697) Dryden begins by saying that "a heroic poem, truly such, is undoubtedly the greatest work which the soul of man is capable to perform."[3] Homer and Virgil are sovereign in the genre. "The next, but the next with a long interval between was the *Jerusalem.*"[4] Spenser would have had a better case than some continental claimants to the succession "had his action been finished, or had been one." Milton's title would have been less suspect "if the devil had not been his hero, instead of Adam; if the giant had not failed the knight, and driven him out of his stronghold, to wander through the world with his lady errant; and if there had not been more machining persons than human in his poem."[5] Dryden, it will be observed, gives his objections force by both repeating and extending them. To earlier statements about the unfortunate outcome and the excess of heavenly machinery in *Paradise Lost* he now adds the suggestion that the action, the epic propriety of which may be dubious, is in any case centered on the wrong hero. The persistence of crucial objections and the adding of related ones thus come to constitute a platform from which the genre of the poem can be interrogated.

Much can be discerned from Dryden's platform. The unfortunate outcome exposes Milton's poem to consideration as tragic rather than epic. If Satan is the hero, he is the hero within an antiquest that invites us to view *Paradise Lost* as anti-epic or parodic epic. Addison's response to Dryden argues that no hero was intended but suggests Christ, if need be, as the hero. This defense of the poem converts it into a providential epic, but one which engages the human only at its periphery.[6] It thus undermines one of Dryden's objections but only at the cost of underlining another. The Romantic reinstatement of Satan as the hero is, of course, not an endorsement of Dryden. It attacks the question of what the poem is by suggesting that there is a poem other than the official poem in which the real nature of Milton's accomplishment is to be found. Generic uncertainty is compounded by viewing *Paradise Lost* as an act of creative subversion in which the true poem overthrows the establishment exercise.

The two-poem theory, in turn, has ramifications which continue into the present. We can simply reverse the Romantic valuation and regard the true poem as the official one. The true poem can then stand in relation to the false as icon does to idol, or as reality to parody within an antithetical universe.[7] We can regard the two poems as confronting each other creatively or as A. J. A. Waldock would have it, locked in destructive conflict.[8] It can be argued that the two poems only appear to be two and that it is the purpose of reader education to bring them into concurrence.[9] Finally, like A. S. P. Woodhouse, we can think of the two poems as engaged with each other through a double protagonist, each functioning within a different genre.[10]

It may be that the course of criticism after Dryden is misguided and that, as John M. Steadman proposes, Milton is writing an "illustrious" epic fully compatible with Italian Neo-Aristotelianism, while Dryden's criticisms are made from the vantage point of a Neo-Aristotelianism that is distinctly French.[11] Certainly neither Aristotle nor the Italians prescribe a fortunate outcome for the epic. But Milton published *Paradise Lost* in 1667, when Italian Neo-Aristotelianism was hardly representative of current critical trends. We are accustomed to these gestures of obsolescence in Milton, which include the imaginative adoption of a slightly antiquated model of the universe. The voice

of the outsider is also a voice from the past, a voice disowning if not excoriating the triviality of the present. Nevertheless, the history of reading *Paradise Lost* points to real difficulties which are not disposed of by a more accurate generic assignation. A poem which may be two poems initially or finally, in which there are three possible heroes and even the possibility of two heroes rather than one, is not a poem about which one can be certain.

Some of the problems of placing *Paradise Lost* are interestingly suggested by William Willkie in a preface (1757) to a heroic poem of his own. Willkie is writing about the difficulties of reconciling the untrue with the true, or historical, in an epic poem. Spenser accomplishes this reconciliation through the evasions of allegory. Willkie then notes (remembering Dryden) that in *Paradise Lost* "persons in machinery overshadow the human characters" and adds (remembering Addison) that "the heroes of the poem are all of them immortal." *Paradise Lost* escapes a requirement that looms over epic poetry by being "a work altogether irregular. . . . The subject of it is not epic, but tragic. . . . Adam and Eve are not designed to be objects of admiration, but of pity. . . . It is tragic in its plot but epic in its dress and machinery."[12]

Willkie may be the first critic to recognize that *Paradise Lost* is not only a mixed-genre poem but a mixed-genre poem with a different protagonist for each of its primary genres. It is true that given Aristotle's views of the importance of plot, the identification of the epic with "dress and machinery" relegates it to a status in *Paradise Lost* which is peripheral rather than central. It is also true that Willkie describes *Paradise Lost* as "altogether irregular," though he does so in an age which was beginning to admire irregularity; the observation does not mean that the poem is to be reproached for its generic lawlessness. Nevertheless, Willkie's remarks do broach the question of whether it is necessary or even desirable to locate *Paradise Lost* unambiguously within any single genre.

It may be argued that the difficulties surrounding the generic assignation of *Paradise Lost* are difficulties encountered by the reader rather than difficulties to which the author admits. That does not make the difficulties any less real, but it may be instructive to look at some of the ways in which the poem announces itself and at the related proposition that the poem always knows what kind of a poem it is. *Paradise Lost* treats itself as "adventurous Song" in the first book (13), as "sacred Song" in the third book (29), as "Song" of which the "copious matter" is the Son's name and arts (III, 412-13), as "Song" related to "celestial song" in the seventh book (12, 30), and as "Heroic Song" in the ninth book, but only after the audience has been advised that the forthcoming notes of the song will be "Tragic" (6, 25). These descriptions are not so divergent as to render reconciliation difficult, but they certainly do not suggest resolute consistency in the poem's classification of itself. They suggest rather the desire to have the best of several worlds, which is characteristic of a mixed-genre poet.

In the poems that precede *Paradise Lost,* Milton's attitude to inherited genres is powerfully revisionary. We console ourselves by describing it as a strong case of tradition and the individual talent or by saying, as John Reesing does, that Milton strains the mold but does not break it.[13] The *Ode on the Morning of Christ's Nativity,* in describing itself as both a hymn and an ode, may be initiating Milton's career with a mixed-genre announcement.[14] In *Comus* the poet makes use of the antithetical dispositions of a genre new enough to be open to experiment in order to construct a staging ground for issues and confrontations which we have come to call Miltonic. *Lycidas* directs the capacity of the pastoral for protest into a protest against the pastoral genre itself. In each case Milton identifies certain propensities of the genre as giving the genre its way of achieving understanding and then reorganizes the form around those propensities. In each case the ordering power of the genre is made to compass a higher degree of inclusiveness than the genre has hitherto accommodated. We can expect these creative habits to continue as Milton comes to his most inclusive undertaking.

A primary characteristic of the epic is inclusiveness. When Aristotle differentiates tragedy from epic, he does not do so on the basis of the outcome, the agent, or the emotion excited by the literary work. His concern is with the manner of presentation and the magnitude of the action.[15] The tragic action should confine itself as far as possible to a single circuit of the sun. The epic action can be longer, and a month is extended to a year by Italian critics. While the longer action can sustain itself by an adequate proliferation of incident, the epic, as it graduates from the tale of a tribe to the statement of a civilization, tends increasingly to sustain itself by cultural omnivorousness as much as by narrative complication. The epic and the encyclopedic are thus brought into convergence. In a late epic the encyclopedic interest will involve consideration of the uses of the past, including the past of the epic genre itself. When the generic inheritance is codified to the extent of seeming petrified, the consideration can be revisionary and can extend—as is arguable in Milton's case—into a revisionary treatment of the whole past. A genre can also be enlarged and thus freed from impending exhaustion of possibilities by incorporating into it the possibilities of another genre not hitherto digested. Mixed genres are thus a natural deliverance from the constraints of a genre which it is necessary to use and which has already been used too heavily. In an epic, such absorptiveness can be particularly felicitous since it is clearly the literary application of a principle on which the epic has increasingly been based. An encyclopedic epic should include a generic compendium.

Studies by Rosalie Colie and more recently by Barbara Lewalski have drawn attention tellingly to the generic inclusiveness of *Paradise Lost.*[16] Lewalski's suggestion that the various genres in the epic are means of accommodation to the reader, or of the narrator within the poem to the auditor, also responds to a problem that arises when we think of the epic as a generic compendium. The encyclo-

pedic substance of an epic is a matter of what it contains; the generic variety is a matter of how what is contained is conveyed. Multeity of genres is most convincingly called for when the area of exploration is sufficiently inclusive to require more than one style of mediation or access. God's creation, as a fully comprehensive poem, is also a poem that engages us in an adequate variety of relationships. Any mimesis of the perfect original should be similarly rich in means of accommodation or opportunities for engagement.[17]

Nevertheless, it should not be assumed that the purpose, or even the designed purpose, of generic multeity is always to contribute to the overall harmony, to show how many styles of discourse lead us to the one Word, or to the unifying capability that is the "one word" of the poem. Multiple genres can provide the ingredients for subversion as well as for synthesis. Their purpose may be to show not the overall concord but the fragmentation of any single style of understanding that unavoidably comes about when the fictive is brought into engagement with the actual. I am not suggesting that Milton's use of mixed genres was governed by this principle or that it proceeded to this point irrespective of the original principle by which it was governed. But on the other hand it is not easy to argue that his poem is the unperturbed implementation of a "great idea" or "fore-conceit," as the Creation is in the seventh book of *Paradise Lost.* A blueprint for the epic must have existed in the author's mind, particularly if, as Allan H. Gilbert long ago argued,[18] the poem was not written in the order in which it unfolds. But the blueprint cannot have been unaffected by the stresses and strains within the poem and by the poem's reconsideration of itself during the deeply frustrating decade of its formation.

If many genres are to be fitted together harmoniously in a poem, they must be subject to a primary genre which is unambiguously proclaimed and clearly dominant. When a primary genre is subject to revisionary treatment and when its status is further undermined by another genre asserting a claim to primacy, the subordinate genres are as likely to reflect this central confrontation as to soothe it.

In *The Reason of Church-Government* (1642), Milton was asking himself "whether those dramatic constitutions wherein Sophocles and Euripides raigne" were not "more doctrinal and exemplary to a nation" (YP, I, 812-15) than the epic undertaking by which he was fascinated.[19] We know from Edward Phillips that *Paradise Lost* began as a tragedy and that Milton showed Phillips the first ten lines of Satan's address to the sun as the planned beginning of the drama he intended to write.[20] The draft of "Adam unparadiz'd" in the Trinity manuscript shows us the dramatic nucleus in which *Paradise Lost* began. Even though the poem moved away from the nucleus it continued to remain engaged to its origins.

The ten books of the first edition of *Paradise Lost,* read as five acts of two books each, are tragic in several of their dispositons. In the fourth act the Creation is undone by the

Fall. The fifth act gives us the tragic aftermath of the fourth, the expansion of evil into space and its extension into history. The repentance of Adam and Eve, sandwiched between two huge movements of destructiveness, simply does not have the importance which the twelve-book version succeeds in winning from it. It is true that Christ's victory is the climax of the third act, but this matters less when Satan's victory is so effectively dominant in the fifth.

If this reading of the tragic weight of the ten-book structure is not erroneous, we can regard the twelve-book version as designed, among other things, to take corrective action. The creative forces are underlined slightly in the poems contest of energies. Christ's presence in the poem is strengthened by the division of the poem into three parts, each consisting of four books, with Christ the protagonist of the four central books. Two victories of light—the Battle in Heaven, and the Creation—are juxtaposed at the center of this central part. The repentance of Adam and Eve is given greater weight. Having said this much, it becomes important to add that the degree of corrective action is slight. It may be that no more could be done, since the poem had been in print for seven years. It may also be that Milton did not wish to do more.

Arthur E. Barker rightly observes that the twelve-book version does not supersede the ten-book one, that one must read both poems and be aware of both patterns, and that the poem is suspended "between the horns of a paradox."[21] For such a paradox to exist, the poem's primary genres must be in contest with, rather than concordant with, each other. The poem does not seek the assimilation of one genre by another or even, to quote Coleridge's famous phrase, "the balance or reconciliation of opposite or discordant qualities."[22] Rather it seeks to navigate between genres, remaining responsive to the current of each without surrendering to the pull of either.

Such a hypothesis seems natural when we remind ourselves of the poem's antithetical world, the embattled contraries between which the choosing center is suspended, as the poem itself is suspended creatively between competing claims on its identity. It is not simply a mixed-genre poem but a poem of which generic uncertainty may be a keynote. Critics may be understandably reluctant to admit uncertainty at the heart of a poem. A work of art thus divided is considered to be in a state of civil war. But creative indeterminacy can also be read as a sign of the authentic rather than the chaotic. Two powerful patterns of possibility contest with each other, as they do in reality. The outcome will shift from moment to moment. The poem's obligation is to draw the field of force and not to delineate the local and interim settlement.

Against this hypothesis it can be argued that Aristotle treats tragedy and epic as concordant genres.[23] The manner of presentation and the magnitude of the action are important but not fundamental differences and certainly not differences that might place either genre in potential conflict with the other. When Thomas Hobbes tells us that "the heroic poem, dramatic, is tragedy," he is carrying convergence a step further. He does so in proceeding to the masterfully sterile conclusion that "there can be no more or less than six kinds of poetry."[24] The Italian critics avoid Hobbes's overwhelming simplicity, but, as Steadman shows, they do not on the whole regard tragedy and epic as divergent.[25]

This objection has force. It can be partially countered by arguing that even though the Italian critics may not have seen tragedy and epic as divergent, they did recognize the creative potentiality of divergent genres. If God's creation is the perfect poem, its mimesis may consist not only of simulating its variety (which includes generic variety) but also of simulating the manner in which the first poem triumphed over its own divisiveness. Creation, we must not forget, was won out of chaos, from equal energies implacably opposed. The best poem may be that in which the center succeeds in holding against the maximum of centrifugal force. Like Milton's universe, such a poem is continually threatened by its contents. Tasso seems to be advocating a poetics of contrariety on this model when he argues that "the art of composing a poem resembles the plan of the Universe which is composed of contraries." He goes on to maintain that "such a variety will be so much the more marvellous as it brings with it a measure of difficulty and almost impossibility."[26] Guarini is less given to the tour de force than Tasso. In defending tragicomedy, Guarini considers it as a third genre arising from two genres which are divergent, but not so divergent that they cannot be creatively mingled. Each genre tempers the other so that the overall composition corresponds more fully "to the mixture of the human body which consists entirely in the tempering of the four humors."[27]

There is thus some sanction in Renaissance criticism for divergent genres curbing each other's excesses, or divergent genres being made to submit to the cohesive force of the poem. Milton's poem can be viewed from both prospects, but like any deeply creative achievement it has to go beyond the gestures towards it that are made by critical theory.

As has been indicated, Milton equivocates mildly about the kind of song he is singing when he links *Paradise Lost* to that particular word. The varying epithets are not difficult to bring together, but the variations remind us to be cautious in our classification of the poem. No more than a reminder is needed, since the poem at its very outset, in announcing the compass of its subject, is also conveying that announcement through a vivid drama of contesting genres. The opening lines of *Paradise Lost* have been commented on in great detail and from what may seem every possible perspective,[28] but their status as a generic manifesto still remains to be examined. In attempting the unattempted Milton may have been attempting an unattempted mixture.

Milton's virtuosity in stating the subject of the whole poem before the predicate of its initial sentence isolates the first five lines spectacularly from the narrative flow. The minidrama of these lines is therefore all the more effective in counselling us not only on what the poem is to be about but also on how it is to be experienced. From the beginning the tragic weight accumulates, reinforced by the alliterative joinings and by the alternative scansions of the first line. If the dominant stress falls on "Mans," we are reading a poem somberly homocentric in its allocation of destructiveness. If it falls on "First" we are reading a poem of the gestation of evil, with the alliterative movement through "First," "Fruit," and "Forbidden" compounding the inexorable growth.[29] "Tree," "tast," and "mortal" are the origin of this growth, though dramatically they are arrived at as its climax, the tragic center of the darkening song. "World" and "woe" sound the dimensions of a universe of tragedy. Nothing so far has restrained the onward movement, the accumulation of sorrow. The prospective genre of the poem—tragedy—has been uncomprisingly and, it would seem, irrevocably stated. Yet on the basis of a text from the Book of Romans (v, 19) a countermovement launches itself, generating itself from the previous movements by virtue of the coupling between man and "greater Man." There is even a counter-alliteration, responding to the massed alliterative linkages of destructiveness, affirming the victory of the light in "Restore" and "regain." This is what one might say on a superficial reading. A reading more open to the poem's reality would recognize that the relationship between human tragedy and providential epic is more complex than the simple overcoming of one genre by another. It is possible to say, by adjusting one's mind slightly to the impact of the opening, that the epic retrieval stands at the horizon of the poem, while the tragic gestation (to which the bulk of the first five lines are given) unavoidably dominates its stage. It is possible to reflect on the distancing force of "till" and ask if the deliverance at the horizon is more than potential. How far does the tragic actuality frustrate and even nullify the epic promise? It is certainly true, as the mind moves with the poem in its unfolding, that we cannot avoid passing through the tragic proliferation before arriving at the genre that might contain it. The two genres are, in fact, inexorably entangled by the powerfully staged drama of the poem's syntax. The poem does not choose between affiliations. It forms itself out of the contest between them.

*Paradise Lost* presents itself not only as a mixed-genre poem but as a mixed-genre poem of deep generic uncertainty. It has to be uncertain because the very history that it seeks to understand has, perhaps fortunately, not yet found its genre. The poem seeks its identity between contesting possibilities, as does that human community which is both the poem's subject and its audience.

Though the contest of primary genres in the opening lines of *Paradise Lost* has been examined, not every genre in those first five lines has been identified. Between the accumulating onslaught of the tragic, "Under her own weight groaning" as the twelfth book says of history (539), and the restorative encirclement of the providential, there is the muted phrase "With loss of *Eden.*" The residual allit-

eration with "World" and "woe" attaches this part of the line to the tragic momentum. The loss can be taken as the sum of our sadness, the distillation of everything that has gone before it in the sentence. But the half-line is also an entry into a possible triumphant future, that Ithaca which the highest of heroes may regain. The phrase stands between two worlds, distanced from itself by the poem's initial onslaught of destructiveness and distanced again from itself by the postponing force of "till." The curiously nondescript language suggests the absence, or rather the residual and unavoidably veiled presence, of what the phrase invokes. It can no longer be known in its own right but only through the genres of loss and seeking.

In the days when it was fashionable to distinguish between the real and the nominal subjects of *Paradise Lost,* Paul Elmer More observed that the real subject of the poem was Paradise.[30] The remark is neither naive nor tautological. The strong affinities of Eden with Arcadia, the Golden Age, and the pastoral strain in the Bible not only establish it in the landscape of memory, including literary memory, but also affiliate it to a third genre, the pastoral. The three genres, in turn, affiliate themselves to the three main locales of the poem, so that we can think with caution but without injustice of a tragic Hell (including human fallenness), an epic Heaven, and a pastoral Paradise. Since the forces in the universe of *Paradise Lost* converge so powerfully upon its choosing center, one can argue that the pastoral understanding plays a crucial part in the poem's declaration of itself.

John R. Knott, Jr., skillfully underlines the *otium* of Paradise, its "grateful vicissitude," the harmony of man with nature, and the harmony of nature with itself.[31] Cities in *Paradise Lost* are not statements of civilization. Babel and Pandemonium tell of their pride. The world is likened once to a metropolis "With glistering Spires and Pinnacles adornd" (III, 550), but it is viewed thus by Satan in the image of the desirable. Little is said of the metropolitan amenities of Heaven except that its shape is "undetermined," that it is adorned with opal towers and battlements of sapphire (II, 1047-50), and that the dust of its main road is gold (VII, 577). It is Satan, not God, who lives in what might metaphorically be called a palace, a superstructure built on a structure of pyramids and towers "From Diamond Quarries hew'n, and Rocks of Gold" (V, 754-61). Heaven is most frequently spoken of in pastoral language, possibly as an accommodation to Adam, who is unfamiliar with city life, but more probably to indicate the continuity between the celestial and the unfallen.

Yet though the ideal order of *Paradise Lost* has extensive pastoral elements and though the poem can be poignantly pastoral in its nostalgia, the "happy rural seat of various view" (IV, 247) does not always open out into pastoral prospects. The weeping trees that are spoken of in the next line suggest a place haunted by tragedy as well as by creative plenitude. There is much foreboding in the language of Paradise—in the wantonness of its energies, the "mazy error" of its brooks, and in its surpassing of that "fair field" where the "fairer flower," Proserpina, was gathered (V, 294-97; IV, 268-72; IV, 237-40). More important, Paradise is not a place of tranquility, of fragile but deep peace before the gathering storm. In its nature it is free from the burden of the past, but in its nature it is also singularly subject to the anxieties of the unprecedented. Nearly everything that happens in Paradise happens for the first time, so if one's response to life is not the result of a preexistent, celestially implanted program, it can only come together and manifest a pattern through a series of related improvisations. Baffling dreams, angelic visitations, and discussions with the author of one's being on the need of the self for an otherness seem part of the normalities of Paradise.

"Is there no change of death in Paradise?" Wallace Stevens asks. "Does ripe fruit never fall? Or do the boughs / Hang always heavy in that perfect sky."[32] In the stasis of perfection, all change is the death of perfection. Yet not to change is to perpetuate the permanence of lifelessness. Milton provides for change in Paradise that is quite other than the "change of death," thereby adroitly satisfying the second of Stevens's desiderata for a supreme fiction: "It must change."[33] In his repeated use of the figure of the dance in describing ideal order, he advises us of a perfection consummated in motion rather than memorialized in stillness.[34] Motion must include alteration in one's state of being as well as alteration in one's place, and this alteration takes place, as Raphael suggests, by the working of a body up to spirit, "in bounds / Proportioned to each kind" (V, 478-79). Such evolution cannot take place by standing still on an ontological escalator. In a world in which the perfection of the human species includes the power of free choice—a power the importance of which is underlined by the enormous cosmic price which the divine is prepared to pay to keep it in being—there must be a steady succession of opportunities for self-formative choosing. It is hard to believe that Adam and Eve, if they had not eaten of the apple, would have lived happily ever after as creative gardeners.[35] The Appleton estate in Marvell's poem subversively mimeticizes the world from which it withdraws. Milton's Garden, in its crises, makes itself continuous with that future which is to become its tragic legacy. It is no accident that the images Michael uses to characterize progress in history correspond to the images Raphael uses to characterize upward evolution on the ontological scale (V, 996-98; V, 575-77; XII, 300-304). In the first place, the equivalence makes evident the restoration of the *status quo ante*. By making himself eligible for the continuing intervention of "supernal grace," man is able to stand as he once did "On even ground against his mortal foe" (III, 179). In the second place, the statement of equivalence, made through figures of progress with which we are not unfamiliar, joins the prelapsarian and postlapsarian worlds. The status of man is radically different, and his commitment to destructiveness requires the steady application of a counterforce that no longer lies within his natural capacity. But if the conditions for that counterforce are brought into being, the two worlds can reflect each other in their opportunities and challenges. The pastoral idyll never quite existed. The Garden was fully itself only in creative dependence on a shaping principle beyond itself. It was not a place of withdrawal but of change and growth built on evolving interrelationships with the entire structure of reality which surrounded it. What was lost was not the Garden but that creative possibility which the Garden embodied and promised.

This excursion into the poem suggests how it responds to those stresses and balances which the first five lines urge so compellingly on our reading of what follows. The pastoral statement does not exist by itself. It is annexed in the first place to a tragic unfolding through which we are obliged to make our way in order to measure what is meant by "loss of *Eden*." It is attached in the second place to a providential counter-poem through which the lost possibilities can be recovered and fulfilled. In fact, its location and attachments are suggestive of the created world in *Paradise Lost,* suspended from Heaven by a golden chain and connected to Hell by a causeway. What the pastoral center comes to mean depends on how it is oriented. As a generic claim, it must yield to those more powerful claimants which seek possession of the structure of things.[36] The drama of genres which the first five lines enact is thus singularly accurate in prefiguring not only the generic character of the poem but the disposition of real forces which that character represents.

One of the unusual strengths of *Paradise Lost* is the poem's capacity to reconsider itself. It can indulge in "tedious havoc" and then excoriate it (IX, 27-33). It can describe the fall of Mulciber in language of limpid beauty and then pull us back from our involvement with a "Thus they relate / Erring" (I, 738-48), leaving us to wonder whether the event is being questioned or whether language itself is being rebuked as falsification. It propounds huge structures of elaboration and ornament to arrive at the "upright heart" in its unadorned authenticity. It uses the past with lavish erudition and overgoes it with competitive zest, largely to underline the obsolescence of what it invokes. It appoints Michael, the leader of the angelic battalions, to preach the politics of nonviolence and the primacy of the interior victory. Some of these dismissals are designed to educate the reader and to instruct him in discriminating truth from its cunning resemblance (see YP, II, 154). Others arise because the poem, in charting the progress from shadowy types to truth, endows itself with a history that to some degree mirrors the history it interprets. But we are also looking at a poem that is endeavoring to achieve its identity and which, as the opening lines have promised, will form itself among contesting generic possibilities. It must not only make itself but justify what it makes against the challenges of an era of deep change. Since its attitude to the inheritance is so powerfully revisionary, honesty demands that it also be self-revising.

In the fifth book of *Paradise Lost* Adam and Eve, after a troubled night, do not simply address the Almighty in prayer. Rather they participate in a prayer which the whole creation offers to its maker out of the way in which it moves and lives. The prayer is Vaughan's "great hymn / And Symphony of nature," the ardent music of "the world in tune." It is also Herbert's "something understood," a structure of relationships which the mind experiences as the ground of its being.[37] "Firm peace" and "wonted calm" are its consequences (V, 209-10). We are told that Adam and Eve have previously made their "unisons" in "various style" (145-46). The plentitude of innocence offers more than one way of access and relationship. The "unmediated" art of the person praying (148-49)[38] may even find the opportunity to invent a genre.

At the end of the tenth book, Adam and Eve pray again. The first prayer preceded the descent of Raphael. The second precedes the descent of Michael. The world has changed, and a lost structure of possibility, borne away as in the real world on the flood of history's disappointments, has also taken with it its proper language. The new desolation calls for the unadorned, the concentration on what is primary. Many poems have an energy of destitution within them, waving their leaves and flowers in the sun so that they may wither into the truth of themselves.[39] In *Paradise Lost* that destitutive energy is launched by an immense act of original destructiveness. From the moment that Adam and Eve eat the apple, much in the poem is rendered obsolete, including some of its literary genres. In these stern dismissals lies a great deal of the poem's authenticity as well as its weight of sadness. But the world remains before us and remains capable of yielding us its language. If *Paradise Lost* is an uncertain epic, it is uncertain not because it is confused or vacillating, but because it is clear about how it must form itself.

### Notes

1. *Early Lives of Milton,* ed. Helen Darbishire (London, 1932), p. 296.

2. *Of Dramatic Poetry and Other Critical Essays,* ed. George Watson (London, 1962), II, 32, 84-85.

3. Ibid., II, 223.

4. Ibid., II, 232. For further statements on the sovereignty of Virgil and Homer in the genre, see II, 167; II, 195. Spenser (II, 150; II, 83-84) is Virgilian. But Milton, though Spenser's "poetical son" (II, 270), is Homeric rather than Virgilian (II, 150).

5. Ibid., II, 233.

6. *Milton, The Critical Heritage,* ed. John T. Shawcross (London, 1970), p. 166.

7. John M. Steadman, *Milton and the Renaissance Hero* (Oxford, 1967); Balachandra Rajan, "The Cunning Resemblance," in *Milton Studies,* VII, ed. Albert C. Labriola and Michael Lieb (Pittsburgh, 1975), pp. 29-48.

8. *"Paradise Lost" and Its Critics* (Cambridge, 1947).

9. Stanley Fish, *Surprised by Sin* (Berkeley and Los Angeles, 1971).

10. *The Heavenly Muse,* ed. Hugh MacCallum (Toronto, 1972), pp. 176-94.

11. *Epic and Tragic Structure in "Paradise Lost"* (Chicago, 1976).

12. William Willkie, "Preface to the *Epigoniad,*" in *Milton 1732-1801, the Critical Heritage,* ed. John T. Shawcross (London, 1972), p. 240.

13. *Milton's Poetic Art* (Cambridge, Mass., 1969), p. 49. See also p. 135.

14. For the poem as a hymn see Philip Rollinson, "Milton's Nativity Poem and the Decorum of Genre," in *Milton Studies,* VII, pp. 165-88. For the poem as an ode, see David B. Morris, "Drama and Stasis in Milton's *Ode on the Morning of Christ's Nativity,*" SP, LVII (1971), 207-22. For the poem as both, see Hugh MacCallum, "The Narrator of Milton's *On the Morning of Christ's Nativity,*" in *Familiar Colloquy: Essays Presented to Arthur Edward Barker,* ed. Patricia Bruckmann (Salzburg, 1976), pp. 179-95. Milton's reference in *The Reason of Church-Government* to "magnifick Odes and Hymns" (YP, I, 815), suggests that he may have thought of the two genres as strongly related to each other. The relationship may well be in the manner envisaged by Nehemiah Rogers, who writes of hymns as "special songs of praise and thanksgiving" and of odes as containing "doctrine of the chiefe good, or mans eternall felicitie" and as being made "after a more majesticall forme, than ordinary" (*A Strange Vineyard in Palaestina: in an Exposition of Isaiahs Parabolical Song of the Beloved* [London, 1623], pp. 8-9).

15. *Poetics,* 1449b, 1459b.

16. Rosalie Colie, *The Resources of Kind: Genre Theory in the Renaissance,* ed. Barbara K. Lewalski (Berkeley and Los Angeles, 1973); Lewalski, "The Genres of *Paradise Lost,*" paper read at the Modern Language Association Meeting, San Francisco, Dec. 28, 1979; cf. Lewalski's essay in this volume.

17. Tasso describes the writing of a poem as "a work almost godlike that seems to imitate the First Maker" (*Discourses on the Heroic Poem,* trans. Mariella Cavalchini and Irene Samuel [Oxford, 1971], p. 97). For the creation as the perfect poem see also S. K. Heninger, Jr., *Touches of Sweet Harmony* (San Marino, Calif., 1976), pp. 290-94.

18. *On the Composition of "Paradise Lost"* (Chapel Hill, N.C., 1947).

19. "Milton's "whether" reflects the continuous controversy about the status of epic and tragedy relative to each other. The Renaissance and, more emphatically, Dryden found epic the higher of the two genres. But Aristotle (*Poetics,* 1402a) had declared in favor of tragedy.

20. "The Life of Mr. John Milton," in *Early Lives of Milton,* pp. 72-73.

21. "Structural Pattern in *Paradise Lost,*" rpt. in *Milton: Modern Essays in Criticism,* ed. Arthur E. Barker (New York, 1965), p. 154.

22. *Biographia Literaria,* XIV.

23. *Poetics,* loc. cit.

24. "The Answer of Mr. Hobbes to Sr. Will. D'Avenant's Preface before *Gondibert,*" in *Critical Essays of the Seventeenth Century,* ed. J. E. Spingarn, 3 vols. (Oxford, 1908), II, 54-55.

25. *Epic and Tragic Structure in "Paradise Lost."*

26. *Discourses on the Heroic Poem,* p. 78.

27. "The Compendium of Tragicomic Poetry," in *Literary Criticism: Plato to Dryden,* ed. Allan H. Gilbert (New York, 1940), p. 512.

28. Among the examinations are David Daiches, "The Opening of *Paradise Lost,*" in *The Living Milton,* ed. Frank Kermode (London, 1960), pp. 55-69, and Joseph Summers, *The Muse's Method* (London, 1962), pp. 11-31. Book-length studies of the invocations include Anne D. Ferry, *Milton's Epic Voice* (Cambridge, Mass., 1963), and William Riggs, *The Christian Poet in "Paradise Lost"* (Berkeley and Los Angeles, 1972).

29. In asking some seventy students to read this line, I have found that 45 percent put the dominant stress on "Mans" and 45 percent put it on "First." The remainder put it on the third syllable of "disobedience." Of those stressing "Mans," the great majority were men. Of those stressing "First" the great majority were women.

30. *Shelburne Essays,* quoted by E. M. W. Tillyard, *Milton* (London, 1930), p. 283.

31. *Milton's Pastoral Vision* (Chicago, 1971). The phrase from PL "grateful vicissitude" (VI, 8), describes the alternation of light and darkness issuing from a cave within the mount of God. It is used by Summers (*Muse's Method,* pp. 71-86) as emblematic of Paradise.

32. "Sunday Morning," in *Harmonium* (New York, 1923), p. 92.

33. *Notes Toward a Supreme Fiction* (Cummington, Mass., 1942), p. 21.

34. Summers, *Muse's Method,* pp. 85-86.

35. See, for example, Barbara K. Lewalski, "Innocence and Experience in Milton's Eden," in *New Essays on "Paradise Lost,"* ed. Thomas Kranidas (Berkeley and Los Angeles, 1969), pp. 86-117.

36. Knott observes (*Milton's Pastoral Vision,* p. xiv) that "the very conflict of modes, epic against pastoral, seems to doom Eden in advance."

37. Vaughan, "The Morning-watch," in *The Complete Poetry of Henry Vaughan,* ed. French Fogle (New York, 1964), pp. 176-77. Herbert, "Prayer" (1), in *The Works of George Herbert,* ed. F. E. Hutchinson (Oxford, 1941), p. 51.

38. Since the poet cannot attain a prelapsarian oneness with creation, his verse in *PL,* IX, 24 is "unpremeditated" rather than "unmeditated." The word has specific and intriguing echoes in the "unpremeditated art" of Shelley's skylark and in the "unpremeditated, joyous energy" which Yeats finds in the statues of Mausolus and Artemisia at the British Museum (*Autobiographies* [London, 1955], p. 150).

39. The thought is from Yeats, "The Coming of Wisdom with Times," in *Collected Poems* (London, 1950), p. 105.

## Diane McColley (essay date 1988)

SOURCE: "Eve and the Arts of Eden," in *Milton and the Idea of Woman,* edited by Julia M. Walker, University of Illinois Press, 1988, pp. 100-19.

[*In the following essay, McColley argues that for Milton, Eve is the embodiment of poetry, as "she personifies poesy in her work, in the imagery associated with her, and in the method of her vocation."*]

Near the end of Book 4 of *Paradise Lost,* we come upon a multilayered image. Innocent Adam and Eve, in the innermost, flower-decked, awe-encircled bower, sleep in one another's arms. Squatting by Eve, Lucifer turned Satan turned toad pours poison into her ear in the form of "Vain hopes, vain aims, inordinate desires / Blown up with high conceits engend'ring pride." Standing over Satan, the archangel Ithuriel, searcher-out of truth, touches him "lightly" with his spear, causing *him* literally to be "blown up"—as is fitting for the father of gunpowder—into his own shape, an inadvertent frog-prince or reverse Orgolio, for "no falsehood can endure / Touch of Celestial temper, but returns / Of force to its own likeness" (4.807-19).[1]

The literalness of Satan's exposure by the literalization of conceits; his explosion at the touch of truth; Milton's literal reading of Genesis; and his attention everywhere to the letter of language—etymology, metaphoric roots and branches, connotations spelled and dispelled, links of sense (as image) with sense (as significance)—beg us to reconsider the modern notion that the meaning of literature has little to do with the words. Ithuriel, with his more vocal companion Zephon, has been instructed to "Search through this Garden; leave unsearched no nook" (4.789). He is therefore a figura of the reader, and his searching and disclosing comments on the critic's calling, which is to search every nook of the poem and, using the tempered spear of interpretation "to [which] must be added industrious and select reading, steady observation, [and] insight into all seemly and generous arts and affairs,"[2] to free the text to do its work.

Ithuriel's spear contrasts to Satan's, also presumably of celestial temper, but misused to prop the "uneasy steps" of "unblest feet" (1.295, 238): a figure of limping prosody on unhallowed grounds; and Satan's spear contrasts also to

Moses' rod, which struck water out of rock, and Aaron's, which flowered. It becomes the wand he holds before his pseudo-decent steps while he is disguised as an inquisitive cherub, which like Comus's charming rod can only disable. It is a staff of unlife.

Satan throughout is a cautionary kinetic emblem for the act of interpretation. We can use the spear of criticism to free the text, or we can pour venom, distempers, phantasms, and high conceits into it. "Throughout," William Kerrigan comments, "Milton associates Satan with violence to inward parts."[3] And whenever there is a rape of the text, Eve gets the worst of it. Whenever we appropriate the poem for our own textual politics, we exploit Eve as text object. She is the receptacle of our inordinate desires, sexual frustrations, marital discontents; vain hopes, yearning dreams, unattained ideals; patronizing tolerance for her pretty, wifely officiousness, her feminine whims, her bustling household economy, or whatever we think we do well to put up with in those around us; matronizing resentment for the endowment of less dignity than Adam's and less power than God's; acclaim for poaching God's sole reminder that "it is he that hath made us and not we ourselves"; anger for millennia of hierarchic thinking; helplessness. It is part of the poem's work to elicit these feelings so that we can recognize them and take due action. But it is an even larger part to help us recognize and love goodness, of which unfallen Adam and Eve are both brimfull. How is it that we find so much fault with them and miss so much grace? If we let our modern habit of looking for base motives obscure their goodness, their "Truth shall retire / Bestuck with sland'rous darts, and works of Faith / Rarely be found" (12.535-37). The cure is to exercise a principle of interpretation Milton calls "*candor*: whereby we cheerfully acknowledge the gifts of God in our neighbor, and interpret all his [her] words and actions in a favorable sense"—unless he [she] attempts to "seduce or deter us from the love of God and true religion."[4] The antidote for "sland'rous darts" is the celestial temper of Ithuriel's spear.[5]

Those actions which enter into a woman, rather than issue out of her—let us hope Milton thought—defile not. The action that issues out of Eve in Book 9 and ushers in murder, war, cruelty, malice, fraud, disease, and death contrasts utterly to the acts that issue out of her before that choice is made. We see in her the ability to make it, but unless we see in her also the ability to choose joy we turn food to wind and lose the means Milton offers to repair the world we know and the selves we are as he says his and our aim is.[6]

There is a curious lack of faith in, and even desire for, undefiled joy in the modern world, a sense that a life of rampant blessedness would somehow be less interesting than one providing opportunity for, or tolerance of, or warfare against, every vice. For Milton sin was defect and inanition. People who think that perpetual paradise (or what may be regained of it) would be dull must not only be undelighted by sensuous and erotic pleasures, as Joseph Sum-

mers and Edward Le Comte and others have richly declared,[7] but must not much care for music, gardening, angels, children, ethically considered scientific inquiry, the glory of the Lord, the funniness of animals, good government, good care of the whole earth, or conversation of the most felicitous reciprocity, dense with poetic shoots. Adam and Eve have plenty to do and be, without "vain hopes, vain aims." Yet it seems to me that on the whole more attention has been paid to Satan than to Adam and Eve and more to what is wrong with Eve and Adam than to what is right with them. And one of the things that is right with them is that they are splendid artists, blithely engaged in acts that are pregnant with all the arts that do not hurt the earth, nor the community, nor the soul, but, contrariwise, enhance them all: poetic speech, music, the rudiments of dance and dramatic play, and, in the form of horticulture, all visual and fruitful beauty-making. God's sculpturing of Adam and Eve, and the jewel-tones of his Garden, wrought with the luminous detail of a van Eyck painting (4.236-66, for example) portray God as Artifex and his human images as artists, as all of these Edenic arts show them to be. In all of them, Eve takes at least equal part with Adam, and often she takes the lead. Does the fact that Eve's questing imagination is subsequent or rather precedent to Adam's tempered reasoning, both needs it and feeds it, make it any less vital to the poet who intends his song to soar above the Aonian mount?

I should like therefore to consider Eve's part in the arts of Eden, beginning with what I perceive as her role as the embodiment of Milton's defense—and, at her fall, his critique—of poesy.

While Eve in Book 8, attended by graces and amoretti, visits bud and bloom that "touched by her fair tendance" gladlier grow, Adam attempts to tell a not very sympathetic "Interpreter Spirit" how he feels about her. She is a handmade present from God, his "last, best gift," but God may have subducted "more than enough" from *him*. He is in charge of her, but he is "transported." He knows that her mind is "less exact," yet "Greatness of mind and nobleness their seat / Build in her loveliest," yet these things "subject not"; their union is "Harmony" (8.528-605). Their courting dance patterns forth similar transpositions: "she turned . . . I followed her . . . she . . . approved . . . I led her." Heaven and earth also join to approve: Heaven sheds "selectest influence," Earth gives "sign," airs fling rose, fling odors from the spicy shrub, "the amorous Bird of Night" sings spousal (8.507-19).

The pattern echoes an analogous equi-vocation and union in *Of Education*: "Logic" (which is also "well-couched") will "open her contracted palm into a graceful and ornate rhetoric . . . To which poetry would be made subsequent, or indeed rather precedent, as being less subtle and fine," ("less exact") "but more simple, sensuous, and passionate," and decorum will teach "what religious, what glorious and magnificent use might be made of poetry, both in divine and humane things." That equivocation in turn echoes Sidney: "For poesy must not be drawn by the ears; it must be gently led, or rather it must lead; which is partly the cause that made the ancient-learned affirm that it was a divine gift."[8]

Milton may have felt much as Adam did, as he couched his argument in the amazing beauty of his sensuous verse—or hers who brought it nightly to his ear. The relation between the "less winning soft" but "manly" grace and wisdom of his stern fable and the delight of verse "adorn'd / With what all Earth or Heaven could bestow" (4.479-90, 8.482-83) is a delicate marriage. The marriage of Adam and Eve tropes its reciprocities. As you can see, I find Milton's poesy and his *istoria* to be "one flesh."

Eve embodies and performs a great many properties and processes that Milton elsewhere attributes to poetry itself, or to himself as poet. These properties belong both to poesy, or the art and craft of making poems, and to poetics, or the *gnosis* and *praxis* of interpreting poems, since for Milton one Spirit "who can enrich with all utterance and knowledge" touches both. Milton did not write tracts called *Poetics* or *A Defense of Poesy*. But Eve, the special carrier of fancy, which is both subsequent and precedent to understanding, figures forth Milton's own art. The images associated with her and her work are conventional metaphors for poetry. Her accounts of her creation and of her dream manifest the function of imagination in discerning and choosing good. Her bucolic songs of praise are allied to the legendary Arcadian origins of poetry and to Milton's youthful intention to follow those "who never write but honor of them to whom they devote their verse, displaying sublime and pure thoughts, without transgression."[9] Her temptation and fall represent the abuse of poesy by a politic libertine and the divorce of verse from truth: Satan has replaced his limping feet with redundant coils, making intricate seem straight (9.504, 632), and by erecting his argument on a false base debases poetry to propaganda and devises reductive criticism. Eve's final going forth rejoined to Adam and refreshed by propitious dreams mimes the renovation of the imagination that art can provide and its reunion with reerected reason, so that humankind may carry seeds of goodness even into a world of woe.

In considering Eve as poesy I do not wish to allegorize her or her work, but to see her as a speaking portrait of the artist. One of the habits of mind that Milton revises in *Paradise Lost* is that allegorizing of Scripture that makes Adam reason, mind, or soul, Eve passion, sense, or flesh, and the Garden abstract moral virtue.[10] Adam and Eve are each whole human personages developing in all the ways humans do in relation to each other and to God, nature, angels, art, and experience; and the Garden burgeons and beckons as gardens do, needing and repaying real care.[11] However, in those manifold relations, Eve especially figures forth poetic graces and poetic imagination, the work of the faculty of fancy, which shapes the representations of the senses into significant forms (5.104-5), as poems do.

It is her work that most startlingly metaphors the poetic process: startlingly, because no one else had shown Adam and Eve working before the Fall, much less imagined Eve singularly engaged in acts of creative stewardship and design as a regular part of her life, producing—like illuminated texts—"thick-wov'n Arborets and Flow'rs / Imborder'd on each bank, the hand of *Eve*" (9.436-37).[12]

In the Renaissance, the art of poesy was habitually troped by the art of gardening. *Anthology* means either knowledge of flowers or flowers of knowledge. Titles of collections proliferate Arborets and Flowers: *Poetical Blossoms, The Garden of the Muses, A Hundredth Sundry Flowers, The Arbor of Amity, Underwoods, A Posy of Gilliflowers, Hesperides, A Paradise of Dainty Devices, A Bower of Delights, The Shepherd's Garland, Flosculum Poeticum,* to name a few. Puttenham and Shakespeare use the trope of gardening for the relation of art to nature; Spenser describes contrasting bowers that epitomize degenerative and regenerative art; Herbert, Donne, and Marvell wreathe poetical garlands.[13] Sidney says that "Christ vouchsafed to use the flowers" of poetry[14] and later Christopher Smart would say that "flowers are peculiarly the poetry of Christ."[15] Herbert writes "And so I came to Phansies Meadow strow'd / With many a flower" and, in "The Flower," "now in age I bud again . . . and relish versing."[16] Milton himself calls his yet-unwritten poems "no bud or blossom," joins other poets to strew the laureate hearse of Lycidas with flowers cast by the Sicilian muse, offers "some Flowers and some bays" of verse to the marchioness of Winchester, makes his Genius a keeper of Arcadian groves, and like Herbert compares the return of his poetic inspiration, in Elegy V, to the reviving earth in spring, who twines her hair with flowers powerful to charm.

Eve is specifically responsible for buds and blossoms in *Paradise Lost* (8.40-47, 9.424-33, 11.273-81). Even though Adam and Eve were joined and enjoined by God to dress as well as keep the Garden, it was unheard of before Milton to show them gardening, and especially to make Eve a gardener even more committed and original than Adam, and so a figura of the poet's own work; and equally unheard of to join her in naming the creatures by having her name the flowers (11.277): *naming,* until then, had been Adam's prerogative.[17] It implies knowing, and so being able to aid, the natures of God's creatures. And the natures of flowers are of some consequence in *Paradise Lost.* On "the bright consummate flow'r / [That] Spirits odorous breathes" depends all nurture: "flow'rs and their fruit, / Man's nourishment, by gradual scale sublim'd . . . give both life and sense, / Fancy and understanding, whence the soul / Reason receives, and reason is her being, / Discursive, or Intuitive" (5.481-88). Raphael is being quite literal. Flowers work up to fruit, fruit nourishes the bodily senses, those feed fancy and understanding, and these reason. The crossing over from body to spirit, if such a distinction may be made at all, occurs at the bridge of fancy. But flowers are consummate as well as prevenient, their "spirits odorous" a figure of prayer and they of poetry, which is both subsequent and precedent to reason, nourishing the soul and nourished by it.

Anyone who tries to write, or even read, may recognize in Eve's naming, nursing, propping, pruning, watering, selecting, supporting, and adorning the actions of this work that "under our labour grows" (9.208) and in her plea for freedom and a little solitude a condition she shares with Milton in his solitary lucubrations and independent-minded literary practice.

The analogy between Eve's art and the poet's own is like the sun: obvious to all eyes, and so sometimes not regarded. Almost everything she does or says before the Fall allies her to Milton's craft in some way. Her first speech is about looking into a mirror. When poetry is not a garden, it is often a mirror: a *Speculum Humanum,* a *Mirror for Magistrates,* a *Muses' Looking-Glass,* a "mirror held up to nature to show virtue her own feature, scorn her own image."[18] But Milton cautions us against using poetry only as a mirror. Eve, stretched on the flowery bank of Eden's mirror, at first sees only herself, as we too are prone to do, but when she knows that the reflection is her own image she (not unhesitatingly) joins her fanciful nature (but Milton has exalted fancy to conjunction with understanding) to Adam's wise one. Janet Knedlik has characterized Satan's mental state as an "utter inability to imagine . . . that he could be truly changed by anything external to himself."[19] The fallen angel is, indeed, unable to imagine freshly at all; he merely projects his present states or deconstructs what others imagine. His undelighted broodings frame Eve's tale of her mirror and of her choice to let herself be enlarged by someone outside herself. (This virtue of openness to enlargement is also the source of her vulnerability, and of the text's. She will later credulously allow herself to be reduced by someone outside herself, as interpreters may reduce the text in their commentaries.) In choosing to be enlarged, Eve does not "exist to, for, and from herself," as Christine Froula thinks she ought to do,[20] but she does not feel herself impaired or breached by her expansion until Satan fathers upon her a poetic of Eve for Eve's sake. Every character in the poem has the choice of being fostered or not by "God's uncontroulable intent,"[21] as does the poet; and the reader has the choice of being nourished or not by the incalculable enlargements the poem offers.

Eve personifies poesy in her work, in the imagery associated with her, and in the method of her vocation. She identifies the voice that calls her from her mirror simply as "a voice." Adam says she was "Led by her Heavenly Maker, though unseen, / And guided by his voice" (8.485-86). But the narrator speaks of the day "the genial Angel to our Sire / Brought her" (4.712-13). Did Milton nod? Or does the *equi* vocation echo Milton's *in* vocation of both the Holy Spirit and the Celestial Muse?

Led by God or his messenger, Eve is divinely wrought and brought, but not fixed and finished: God gave man, as Raleigh says, to be his own painter.[22] As a wife she is, like a Muse, or a poem a-making, incalculable, surprising, much beyond expectation, notable for having a will of her own. Adam learns that his image or other half is not *just* his im-

age, has much to give, can enlarge and change *him,* is not for him (though she becomes for Satan) a text object to be possessed and exploited but a nigh-overwhelming bliss, almost too beautiful to bear, like "amourous delight" or Monteverdi's music or Milton's poem. She needs, as Adam will say fancy does, Reason well erect if harmony, not only solo voice and audience, is to survive; but she is also an erector of reason; his, but not all his, as Milton says his poesy is not all his, but "Hers who brings it nightly to my Ear" (9.47).

Eve's divine origin and calling put her at the crux of present discourse about poetic authority and the nature of inspiration. In her exchange with Edward Pechter in *Critical Inquiry,* Christine Froula says with some asperity, "Mr. Pechter apparently imagines that I take the Holy Spirit to be an actual entity."[23] The exchange delineates a watershed in literary studies between those who treat poems strictly as historical artifacts and those who find that art and language can be numinous. If Milton's Holy Spirit—whom he asks to "raise and support" his poesy as Eve stoops to support her roses—is a fiction, it pretends to confer a preposterous authority. But if his invocations report experiences of God tested on his own pulses, they claim no poetical prelacy, but an access Milton insisted was equally available to all who seek it, however great or humble their tasks.

Milton again intimately links Eve to his own calling in a love song to Adam that echoes his invocations by its form and imagery: especially the image of the nightingale, whom in his first sonnet Milton had adopted as his poetic emblem. In his invocations, Milton wanders night and morn "where the Muses haunt / Clear Spring, or shady Grove, or Sunny Hill" (3.27-38)

> Then feed[s] on thoughts that voluntary move
> Harmonious numbers; as the wakeful bird
> Sings darkling, and, in shadiest Covert hid
> Tunes her nocturnal note.
>
> (3.37-40)

Eve sings her nocturn as she and Adam move hand in hand toward a bower collaboratively wrought by God and Eve, whose "thickest covert was inwoven shade" of those most poetical flowers, laurel and myrtle, and whose nuptial bed Eve has decked with flowers and garlands. Her song "with thee conversing I forget all time," lauds "All seasons and their change":

> Sweet is the breath of morn . . .
> . . . sweet the coming on
> Of grateful Ev'ning mild; then Silent Night,
> With this her Solemn Bird and this fair Moon,
> And these the Gems of Heav'n, her starry train:
> But neither breath of Morn, when she ascends
> Nor charm of earliest Birds, nor rising Sun
> On this delightful land, nor herb, fruit, flow'r
> Glist'ring with dew, nor fragrance after showers,
> Nor grateful Ev'ning mild, nor silent Night,
> With this her solemn Bird, nor walk by Moon,
> Or glittering Star-light, without thee is sweet.
>
> (4.640-56)

Eve's speech, with its gracious, dancelike measures,[24] repeats the rhythms and imagery of Milton's own state: less happy than hers, except when, like her, he is touched and enlightened from beyond himself.

> Thus with the Year
> Seasons return, but not to me returns
> Day, or the sweet approach of Ev'n or Morn,
> Or sight of vernal bloom, or Summer's Rose,
> Or flocks, or herds, or human face divine . . .
> So much the rather thou Celestial Light
> Shine inward . . .
>
> (3.40-44, 51-52)

Before they enter the bower, Eve and Adam say a prayer that begins "Thou also mad'st the Night." Those archetypal critics who see Eve and femaleness associated with darkness and the moon and think she must therefore inevitably fall must read that prayer differently than I do, and Milton's relation to the Muse who brings his poem "Nightly" to his ear. And Eve's question, just after her song, about the stars—"for whom / This glorious sight, when sleep hath shut all eyes?"—is, similarly, often alleged as egocentric questioning of the divine economy, and so a foreshadowing of her fall. But an interest in stars is the province of Urania, the Muse of astronomy and of Milton, who links "harmonious numbers" to cosmic harmony. And Eve's question elicits from Adam a brief defense of the arts as he celebrates "celestial voices" with "heavenly touch of instrumental sounds / In full harmonic number joined / [that] lift our thoughts to Heaven" (4.682-86).

Just as remarkable as Milton's giving Eve a part in naming is the fact that in their unfallen conversations he gives Eve and Adam almost an equal number of lines. He neither makes Adam the dominant proprietor of Edenic language, nor Eve either a figure of the female vice of loquacity—even in her conversation with the Serpent—or an emblem of the virtue so often exhorted to women, silence, except when she refrains from interrupting her husband's eager after-dinner inquiries of a communicative spacetraveler. In their unfallen conversations, she has almost an equal voice—217 lines to Adam's 230—a semitone, one might say, apart. Their verbal conversation is "meet" in innumerable interinanimating ways: hers more adventurous, playful, sweet, charming, questioning; his graver, explanatory, sequential and consequential upon hers. Each is sufficient in both reason and spontaneous grace, but in proportion due; together their words resonate like part music, to the enhancement of both.

When Raphael arrives and Adam requests a feast, Eve's reply (5.321-30) recapitulates Milton's claim of spontaneity in his art and his statements about decorum and "various style." She then considers "What choice [things] to choose for delicacy best, / What order, so contriv'd as not to mix / Tastes, not well join'd, inelegant, but bring / Taste after taste upheld with kindliest change" (5.333-36). The passage, thick with puns, calls attention to its own language. "Contrive" derives from *Tropos,* style or figure of speech; "inelegant" means, literally, not choice: from *eligere,* select; "kindliest" hints at "the kindly fruits of the earth"[25] and at the decorum of poetic kinds. Milton, also long choosing, also gathers, orders, tempers, changes, and disposes kinds in answerable style.

In her dream, Eve experiences in fancy the operations of evil without doing evil, as the poet must do to depict evil without being corrupted by it; and Adam's explanation of the relations of reason and fancy (5.100-121) makes fancy both subsequent (or subordinate) and precedent (or provident) to reason, which is but choosing. When she goes off to practice the art of gardening as usual, having persuaded Adam not to let the Foe destroy their artistic liberty, she is much like the poet who continues to sing though "with dangers compast round, / And solitude; yet not alone . . ." (7.27-28) as long as the Spirit whose Temple is the upright heart is with her, and like poetic imagination, whose stay not free absents it more.

But, as Sidney says, "that which being rightly used doth most good, being abused doth most harm. . . . For I will not deny that a man's wit [or a clever fallen angel's] may make poesy infect the fancy with unworthy objects."[26] Satan is nearly rapt from his evil by Eve in naked innocence figuring forth good things; instead he infects her fancy, and she Adam's, and "So is that honey-flowing matron eloquence apparelled, or rather disguised, in a courtesanlike painted affectation . . . with figures and flowers extremely winter-starved."[27] Satan divorces the signifier from the signified, makes words an autonomous language-game in which he feigns a trivial and tyrannical patriarch; and he psychologizes the inclination for forbidden fruit and its alleged power that he has projected into Eve as a "need." Language becomes an instrument for deception and exploitation, an implement of rape, rather than an instrument for the pleasure of discovering and nurturing goodness. Eve, thus abused, poisons Adam; Adam, thus diseased, whores Eve; the result is fratricide.

"But what, shall the abuse of a thing make the right use odious?"[28] It is not Eve's imaginative freedom that causes her wild work, but her corruption: a corruption made possible by the receptivity that is, like that of poetic language, a rich virtue when rightly used. As a part of the process of her regeneration, her fancy is the faculty that receives separate divine attention, in a healing dream that reconnects the fancy to the Word. As Adam and Eve set forth from the Garden with the task of erecting the infected will and taking goodness in hand, neither is subsequent or precedent. Like Sidney's art and nature, and like Milton's shaping intent and shapely text, Adam and Eve go forth hand in hand, bearing the seeds of an infinite progeny.

The metatext of Ithuriel's spear, wherein we are invited by kinetic mimesis to stand as angelic interpreters or squat as Aristophanic landfrogs, is surrounded by concentric scenes all of which also touch in some way on the nature and uses of imagination. Most of them also present to ours with great delicacy and intimacy the mutuality of paradisal marriage. In the nearest sphere, before Eve's dream, she and Adam make love festively, by connubial rites, and after it by honesty and solace. In the next, they pray. Before their evening prayer, Adam discourses on the nature of their work, and after their morning prayer they set out to do it. In the evening, Eve says or sings a love song to Adam, and in the morning Adam says or sings a love song to Eve. Before that, they entertain a fallen angel unawares, and after, they entertain an unfallen one awares. And, lest anyone in Milton's audience think any of the arts intrinsically irreligious, *both* angels indulge in feigning along the way. Satan sits like a cormorant—who are a dime a dozen and all sit the same way—and misreads the Garden without delight. Raphael arrives as a phoenix—of whom there is only one—feigning in play, for sheer pleasure, gaz'd on by all the fowls, and reads God's book of creatures with charity and candor. Raphael sails on steady wing, upheld by buxom air, in contrast to Satan's sudden sprawls: one artist hand in hand with nature, the other opposed and subject to fatuous falls (2.927-42, 4.194-204, 5.266-74).

These concentric passages contain every sort of imaginative exercise, with Eve's dream and Adam's explanation of what imagination was made for at their center. They demonstrate that no art or pleasure is forbidden that does not deceive, exploit, or enslave, and that imagination can be an antidote against evil as well as a means to apprehend goodness. Ithuriel's action discloses Satan, as the dream itself might have done, to free Eve; the poison Satan pours into her ear might have been a mithridate against further nocence. And that pattern recapitulates the poem. In it, Milton gives us innocent goodness in all its rich and various beauty; he shows it blighted; he shows it beginning to be restored; and he hands us the threads of continuance.

Framing the dream, Milton embodies creativity in the two most interesting and intimate of human mutual activities, sex and prayer. The fact that the prayer may be sung further links the two, for procreativity and creativity had in the Renaissance firm philosophical connections, especially with regard to music.

The question is still sometimes belabored whether unfallen Adam and Eve, in the vulgar phrase, "had sex" in *Paradise Lost.* The problem is that if Paradise is in good working order, everything including Adam and Eve is presumed fertile, so that every sexual union should produce issue: those "more hands" that Adam and Eve, artists and gardners, metonymically look forward to. But if conception had occurred before the Fall, Cain would have been born without original sin. There are several objections. According to Genesis, Cain was conceived after the expulsion. Even if we read Genesis 4:1 retrospectively, we are left with the difficulty that the murder of Abel is surely the archetypal effect of the archetypal sin. If it were not, Cain's sin would have stood "in the following of Adam," as the Ninth Article of Religion puts it, rather than "the fault and corruption of the Nature of every man, that naturally is en-

gendered of the offspring of Adam; whereby man is very far gone from original righteousness." Milton is quite clear about rejecting the Pelagian heresy that denies the corporate nature of sin.[29] Therefore, Cain was not conceived in the course of the nuptial embraces Milton's Adam and Eve enjoy in their flower-decked, nightingale-serenaded bower (4.736-75).

This either-or dilemma—that either Eve and Adam remained virgins and only embraced allegorically, as the Fathers thought, or Cain was conceived in Paradise—Milton apparently regarded as a false one. The idea that every divinely sanctioned sexual act produces offspring is classical, not scriptural. Every sacrosanct rape by a pagan god begets a hero, or a troublemaker, but the mothers of scriptural heroes—Isaac, Samson, John the Baptist—often had to wait through years of married barrenness to bear them. If Adam and Eve had not fallen, Eve would probably have been bloomingly pregnant most of the time, and each child a new burgeoning microcosm of tenderness, beauty, wit, talent, and unexpected views. But although she might produce a child every solar year, I see no reason to suppose that Eve was not connected to the cycles of the moon or that there might not have been a period of sheer amorous delight before the first conception, in aid of the other purposes of marriage Milton lists first[30] and in preparation for the beginning of new life.

Nevertheless, wedded love is the "true source of human offspring," a "perpetual Fountain of Domestic sweets" in that way as well as in the multifloriate pleasures of erotic mutuality; and in his apostrophe to it, Milton with his celestial spear dispels the vain imaginings of prurient hypocrisy. This passage is balanced, on the other side of the dream, by Adam's aubade and his discourse upon good and bad uses of imagination, concluded with a kiss of peace.

In the two scenes before and after the dream, Adam and Eve turn toward each other. In the two scenes before and after that, they turn together toward God to pray. Since in the act of prayer Adam and Eve become poets and singers, they are figurae of the unfallen artist and exempla of the regenerate one, inventing and performing the genre that Sidney calls "that lyrical kind of songs and sonnets: which, Lord, if He gave us good minds, how well it might be employed, and with how heavenly fruit, both private and public, in singing the praises of the immortal beauty, the immortal goodness of that God who giveth us hands to write and wits to conceive; of which we might well want words, but never matter; of which we could turn our eyes to nothing but we should ever have new budding occasions."[31]

Although I have argued lengthily that Eve was right to defend the exercise of creative freedom even if it meant being sometimes on her own and at risk,[32] I do not want to overstress her separate and singular talents. Eve as monody is a fresh and astonishing creature of her author, but Adam and Eve as harmony are the core of the world. The art form in which that harmony most fully resounds is their evening (4.724-35) and morning (5.153-208) prayers.

Milton's warm-toned drawing forth of Adam and Eve together in prayer before the Fall is almost without precedent; but glimmers of such a life appear in a few rare visual depictions. An engraving by Nicholaes de Bruyn, after Maerten de Vos, illustrates the Admonition; but Jan Theodor de Bry's version of the same original has as its inscription the first verse of Psalm 117: "O praise the Lord all ye peoples, praise him all ye nations," all nations being incipient within Adam and Eve.[33] And an illustration bound into English Bibles in the mid-seventeenth century identifies a similar image as the Institution of the Sabbath.[34] Original righteousness, though not as popular as original sin, is at least acknowledged in these unusual representations, which are part of the early seventeenth-century impulse that Milton's account of richly joyous Edenic activity brings to its fullest consummation.

Mutual spontaneous prayer—two people together visibly and audibly opening their souls to God—is perhaps the most intimate and risky of human activities. It almost inevitably increases love, and in baring themselves to the Spirit, the pray-ers bare themselves in "holy rapture" to obvious, vulnerable growth of soul. If you add music—and, echoing the Prayer Book rubrics, Milton tells us that the prayers of Adam and Eve are either "pronounced or sung"—the opportunity for heavenly interchange is redoubled. Milton's yoking together of the act of prayer and the act of love, "whatever Hypocrites austerely talk," is perfectly natural, and is supported in the case of sung prayer by Renaissance theories of music. For the eternal verities of pitch and measure link music mathematically to the mystic Dance of the cosmos and to the divine forms in the mind of God, and so set the affections in right tune. And, for Galileo and Kepler, the pleasure of music was akin to the pleasure of lovemaking. For they saw musical proportions as corresponding to the "proportion due" of male and female. In one of his letters, Kepler, explaining the geometry of music, says, "Non puto me posse clarius et palpabilius rem explicare, quam si dicam te videre imagines illic mentulae, hic vulvae." Galileo said that the interval of the fifth produces "such a tickling and stimulation of the cartilage of the eardrum that, tempering the sweetness with a dash of sharpness, it seems delightfully to kiss and bite at the same time," and Kepler that "the progeny of the pentagon, the major third and the minor third, move our souls, images of God, to emotions comparable to the business of generation."[35]

The mutuality of their love and the goodness of the whole creation form the theme of the evening prayer of Adam and Eve, when "both stood, / Both turn'd, and under op'n Sky"—which Raphael will call God's Book—"ador'd / The God that made both Sky, Air, Earth, and Heav'n / Which they beheld, the Moon's resplendent Globe / And starry Pole" (4.720-24). The exactness of "resplendent" images their own relation to God as Artifex and that of the creation for which they speak. The moment is the more

dramatic when we recall that in Vondel's version of the story, Adam *leaves* Eve in order to pray, "and in my solitude / Give thanks to [God] for thy companionship," thus allowing Satan to find Eve alone.[36]

The abrupt beginning, "Thou also mad'st the night," suggests a psalm-verse that could have begun their earlier unrecorded morning prayer, "This is the day that the Lord hath made; we will rejoice and be glad in it" (118:24): one appointed for Easter and so known to Milton in numerous jubilant settings. Here, Adam and Eve rejoice in each other and in their coming children.

Their morning prayer is both more liturgical and more explicitly connected with Milton's work as a poet. It is an "unmeditated" canticle based on the Song of the Three Children from the apocryphal portion of the Book of Daniel, which is the morning canticle in the Book of Common Prayer called the Benedicite, and on Psalm 148, said or sung at Evening Prayer on the thirtieth and thirty-first of every month. Both sources call upon all of nature, from angels to cattle to creeping things, to praise the Lord. They reappeared in the metrical psalters set to authorized church tunes, bound into sixteenth- and seventeenth-century prayer books; in numerous harmonized versions of these printed for home use; and in entirely different translations and settings such as George Wither's, set for two voices by Orlando Gibbons,[37] and George Sandys's, set by Henry Lawes "to new Tunes for private Devotion: and a thorow Base, for Voice, or Instrument" and published in 1637, shortly after Lawes's collaboration with Milton on the *Mask Presented at Ludlow-Castle*. Lawes also published selected psalm settings "for three voices and a thorow-Base" with an equal number by his brother William as a memorial to him, prefaced by commendatory poems including Milton's sonnet to "Harry . . . that with smooth air couldst humour best our tongue," in 1648: the same year that Milton contributed a series of metrical psalms in which he uncharacteristically confined his muse to the common meter needed for the common tunes. Lawes's two-part settings are singable by anyone and his viol, or wife, or child, or any two or more people; other settings provide a range of musical difficulty and interest reaching to the polychoral polyphony of the Chapel Royal.

Psalm-singing was a major national pastime in Milton's day.[38] Nearly all of his first readers would have some experience of it—not only in the hearing, but in the doing—to bring to their reading of the canticles of Adam and Eve. They, of course, are accomplished artists, but even the singing of simple harmonies available to the youngest or newest singer can give a taste of the pleasure and sense of communion that psalm-singing affords. Milton suggests that sung prayer, spontaneously embellished in various style, is one of the inexhaustible felicities of unfallen or regenerate life; and he illustrates its possibilities by incorporating the effects of music into words, as his admired Mazzoni observes in Dante,[39] a process that is the inverse of the Renaissance composer's practice of incorporating the effects of words into music.

Some of the musical treatment of words that informs Milton's verbal treatment of music may be found in Adrien Batten's setting of Psalm 117,[40] the psalm attributed to Adam and Eve by the inscription of de Bry's representation of them praying before the Fall. Batten's word-painting includes close weaving of four vocal lines (which would have required an amicable Cain and Abel for the inner parts), each voice having a comfortably small range, to achieve the serene harmonies suitable to the text; use of moderate polyphony on "all ye nations"; tender and beseeching harmonic changes on "merciful kindness"; strong unanimity on "for his truth endureth"; and melisma extending "forever and ever." As is usual in Renaissance music, one must ignore the bar lines and time signatures and attend to the ways the musical line is responsive to the words: within the steady pulse of "strictest measure even" the phrasing shifts back and forth between common or earthly time, in twos and fours, and triple or "perfect" time on words naming the attributes of God. "His merciful kindness" enters in triple time; "is ever more and more towards us" reverts to common time; "the truth of the Lord" is in triple time; but the two kinds of time, the earthly fours and the heavenly threes, flow together as fluidly as temporal and eternal activities may be supposed to do in Eden.

Milton's hymn is, we might say, the proposed archetype of the scriptural hymns it spontaneously elaborates. Adam and Eve are not, like the Three Hebrew Children, in a fiery furnace; but they have just had their first taste of evil, in Eve's dream, and we the readers have spent two books in hell and more in the hell of Satan's self. The three children in the fiery furnace, refreshed by a wind an angel brings, can still praise fire. And as we are refreshed by the wind of the Spirit that blows through these joyful lines, we are also aware of the misuse the fallen angel makes of the creatures they invoke. He has used the sun and a tree-top as spying posts, entered the Garden through mists and exhalations, and winged and walked the earth as a bird, a tiger, a lion, and a toad; he will become a snake that lowly creeps: all "not nocent yet." And like the Psalmist, Adam and Eve, in their closing petition, recognize the need for "God's merciful kindness."

The imagery of their song partakes of textural and prosodic as well as thematic musical interest. The recurrent figure denoted by the words "Circle," "Circlet," "crown," "Sphere," and "Perpetual Circle" links earth's creatures to the cosmic mystic dance and suggests the "perfect measure" that in Renaissance notation is denoted by a circle. But the measure varies, like Batten's, to suit the words: Within the steady pulse of decasyllabic lines, if you count only the major stresses, God is described in triple time, as

    Unspéakable, who sít'st above these Héavens.

"In these thy lowest works" shifts back to iambs. Angels have varied meters, then at line 164 we are back to earth decidedly in fours:

    On Éarth join áll ye Créatures to extól
    Hím first, hím last, hím midst, and without énd:

with three firm stresses concerning God within the line. The five wandering fires get more regular pentameter, and "His práise, who out of Dárkness call'd up Líght" gets three primary stresses. The four elements that in quaternion run get four-beat lines until the exhortation to ceaseless change, in which they vary. "Hail universal Lord" invites three accents; and the concluding lines move from earthly to heavenly time in a way that prosodically restores the tranquillity for which they plead.

Rather than rhyme, there is a closely woven harmony of similar sounds: dawn, morn, prime; praise, rise, sky, flies; frame, then, seem. Often this close weaving is onomatopoetic, providing verbal tone painting: "Ye Mists and Exhalations that now rise"; "wet the thirsty Earth with falling showers"; "Fountains and yee, that warble, as ye flow, / Melodious murmurs"; the swoop of "ye Birds / That singing up to Heaven Gate ascend" (and how pleasant to know that Adam and Eve knew their Shakespeare); the syncopation of syntax against line at "mix / And nourish all things, let your ceaseless change / Vary. . . ."

In the act of prayer, Adam and Eve become poets and singers, and so figurae of the poet and of the mutual spontaneous prayer Milton preferred to a fixed liturgy: both poet and worshipper should be freely responsive to the indwelling Spirit, though they may use established genres within whose structures spontaneous art can always find new budding occasions. As Milton's celestial patroness "inspires / Easy [his] unpremeditated verse" (9.23-24), so for Adam and Eve "neither various style / nor holy rapture wanted they to praise / Their Maker, in fit strains pronounced or sung / Unmeditated; such prompt eloquence / Flow'd from their lips, in prose or numerous Verse, / More tuneable than needed Lute or Harp / To add more sweetness" (5.146-52). Imagine doing that. Could anything be more engaging than the mutual, spontaneous production of poetry and song, made possible by shared rapture and established structure? Milton leaves it to our imaginations to figure out how two people linked in happy nuptial league can unanimously compose spontaneous songs, even when blessed with union of mind "or in [them] both one soul": whether by antiphonal verses or mutual infusion by the celestial muse;[41] but no doubt in Paradise, even more than in Sidney's Arcadia where improvised poetic exchanges often occur, such acts of spontaneous composition would be endlessly diverse and interesting. If the Fall had not interrupted their courses, Adam and Eve—prime artists with God's image and the Holy Ghost fresh within them—might have continued to compose in various style, increasing voice parts as their tribe increased to something like—on grand occasions—Michael Praetorius's setting of the Benedicite, which begins with two voice parts—Adam and Eve as it were—and increases to five hundred voices, human and instrumental, gathering in all the voices of creation with copious opportunities for word-painting, all these voices growing more delicately harmonious as they increase, while the refrains expand to cosmic resonance and the word "Domino" receives increasing tenderness.

In spite of its Venetian origin, I see no reason why Adam and Eve should not be imagined or we encouraged to make such music; Milton had no objection to letting "the pealing Organ blow / To the full voic'd quire below, / In Service high and Anthems cleer, / As may with sweetnes through mine ear, / Dissolve me into extacies / And bring all Heav'n before mine eyes."[42] Unfallen or regenerate, the whole human family might "join thir vocal Worship to the Choir of Creatures wanting voice" (9.198-99) as secretaries of God's praise. Surely to do so in the various style, the fluid responsiveness, and the exfoliation of the life of words characteristic of Renaissance music and of Milton's verse proliferates endless pleasures and by literally joining hearts to heaven nourishes *this* resplendent globe.[43]

### Notes

1. Quotations from *Paradise Lost* are from the edition of Merritt Y. Hughes (New York, 1962).

2. From *The Reason of Church Government Urged Against Prelaty,* in *The Student's Milton,* ed. Frank Allen Patterson (New York, 1930), p. 526. All quotations from Milton's prose are from this edition, hereafter cited as *SM.*

3. William Kerrigan, *The Sacred Complex* (Cambridge, Mass., 1983), p. 245.

4. John Milton, *De Doctrina Christiana,* in *SM,* pp. 1070 and 1066.

5. Perhaps I should mention that at the time of writing this section I had not read John Guillory's interesting (and puzzling) emblematic use of Ithuriel's spear as poetic principle in *Poetic Authority: Spenser, Milton, and Literary History* (New York, 1983), pp. 148-51.

6. John Milton, *Of Education,* in *SM,* p. 726.

7. Joseph Summers, *The Muse's Method* (London, 1962); Edward Le Comte, *Milton and Sex* (New York, 1978).

8. John Milton, *Of Education,* p. 729; Sir Philip Sidney, *An Apology for Poetry,* ed. Forrest G. Robinson (Indianapolis, 1970), p. 72.

9. John Milton, *An Apology for Smectymnuus,* in *SM,* p. 549.

10. J. M. Evans discusses allegorical readings in *"Paradise Lost" and the Genesis Tradition* (Oxford, 1968), pp. 69-99. Milton selectively retains many connotations from these readings, but discards implications that set nature against spirit or mythologize Adam and Eve. For a contemporary allegorizing treatment of the Genesis story see Troilo Lancetta's *Scena Tragica d'Adamo e d'Eua* (Venice, 1644).

11. On the abundant significance of literal gardens and gardening in relation to literature, philosophy, and religion in the English Renaissance, see Charlotte F. Otten, *Environ'd with Eternity: God, Poems, and Plants in Sixteenth and Seventeenth Century England* (Lawrence, 1985).

12. "Hand" as handwork may pun on "hand" as handwriting or "character."

13. George Puttenham, *The Arte of English Poesie* (London, 1589), pp. 308-13; Shakespeare, *The Winter's Tale* 4.4; Spenser, *The Faerie Queene* II.12 and III.6; Herbert, "A Wreath"; Donne, "La Corona"; Marvell, "The Coronet."

14. Sidney, p. 51.

15. Christopher Smart, *Jubilate Agno,* l. 506, in the edition by W. H. Bond (London, 1954), p. 106.

16. George Herbert, "The Pilgrimage" and "The Flower," in *The English Poems of George Herbert,* ed. C. A. Patrides (Totowa, 1975), pp. 151 and 172.

17. In the visual arts, however, Eve is sometimes present at the naming; see for example *A Thirteenth Century Breviary in the Library of Alnwick Castle,* intro. Eric George Millar (Oxford, 1958).

18. *Hamlet* 3.2.

19. Janet Knedlik, "Medieval Metaphysics and Temporal Process in Milton's *Paradise Lost,*" a paper presented at the Nineteenth International Congress on Medieval Studies, Kalamazoo, 1984.

20. Christine Froula, "When Eve Reads Milton: Undoing the Canonical Economy," *Critical Inquiry,* 10 (Dec., 1983), 328.

21. *Samson Agonistes* 1754.

22. Sir Walter Raleigh, *The History of the World* (1614), p. 35.

23. Christine Froula, "Pechter's Specter: Milton's Bogey Writ Small," *Critical Inquiry,* 11 (Sept., 1984), 173. Professor Froula's work is an extraordinarily honest exhibition of the intention to read *Paradise Lost* from the point of view of a feminist sociology of religion, asserting for example that "Adam fashions a god that is invisible *to Eve* in order to master her" (p. 173).

24. In a broad sense (not the technical, prosodic one) Eve's poem is a *rondeau,* which originates in dance; and it perhaps suggests the form of a round dance in which the partners circle in opposite directions, then return to join together.

25. From the Litany, prescribed to be used at least three times a week, in the Book of Common Prayer.

26. Sidney, p. 59. Milton echoes Sidney's words, with regard to marriage, in *Tetrachordon, SM,* p. 673: "what doth most harm in the abusing, used rightly doth most good."

27. Sidney, p. 81.

28. Sidney, p. 60.

29. Milton, *De Doctrina Christiana,* 1.11.

30. That is, "a mutual help to piety" and "to civil fellowship of love and amity; then, to generation . . . ," Milton, *Tetrachordon,* pp. 657-58.

31. Sidney, p. 80.

32. In *Milton's Eve* (Urbana, 1983), especially chap. 5.

33. The engraving by de Bruyn is part of a creation series available in the Print Room of the Reiksmuseum, Amsterdam (inv. no. A22380). The de Bry (with the inscription, backwards, in French) is in the Museum Plantin-Moretus, Antwerp, Cat. nr. I/B635, and is reproduced in F. W. H. Hollstein, *Dutch and Flemish Etchings, Engravings, and Woodcuts, ca.* 1450-1700 *(Amsterdam,* 1949-), 4:27.

34. William Slatyer (compiler) and Jacob Floris Van Langeren (engraver), STC 22634.5. Photograph reproduced by permission of the British Library.

35. Both Galileo and Kepler are quoted in D. P. Walker, *Studies in Musical Science in the Late Renaissance,* Studies of the Warburg Institute, 37 (London and Leiden, 1978), pp. 32 and 53-54.

36. Joost van den Vondel, *Adam in Ballingschap* (1664), trans. Watson Kirkconnell, in *The Celestial Cycle* (Toronto, 1952), p. 462.

37. George Wither, *The Hymnes and Songs of the Church* (London, 1623).

38. For an account of this movement see Nicholas Temperley, *Music of the English Parish Church* (Cambridge, 1979), chap. 3.

39. Giacopo Mazzoni, *On the Defense of the Comedy of Dante: Introduction and Summary,* trans. Robert L. Montgomery (Tallahassee, 1983), p. 58.

40. Batten (1591-1637?), "O Praise the Lord," from John Barnard's *First Book of Selected Church Musick* (1641), available in a modern edition by Anthony Greening in *The Oxford Book of Tudor Anthems,* compiled by Christopher Morris (Oxford, 1978).

41. Possible performances of this passage have been suggested by Joseph H. Summers, in *The Muse's Method: An Introduction to "Paradise Lost"* (Cambridge, Mass., 1962), pp. 75-83, and Louise Schleiner, *The Living Lyre in English Verse from Elizabeth through the Restoration* (Columbia, Mo., 1984), pp. 134-36.

42. *Il Penseroso* 161-66, in *SM,* p. 29.

43. This essay was written with the help of a grant from the Research Council of Rutgers, the State University of New Jersey. A portion of it is reprinted, with permission, from *Milton Quarterly.*

## Michael Wilding (essay date 1995)

SOURCE: "Thir Sex Not Equal Seem'd': Equality in *Paradise Lost,*" in *Of Poetry and Politics: New Essays on Milton and His World,* edited by P. G. Stanwood, Center for Medieval and Early Renaissance Studies, 1995, pp. 172-85.

[*In the following essay, Wilding argues that in* Paradise Lost *Milton is less concerned with the issue of sexual equality than with the revolutionary aim of achieving total human equality, "of restoring us to that still unregained blissful seat."*]

The first description of Adam and Eve is a crucial passage for our understanding of *Paradise Lost:*

> . . . but wide remote
> From this *Assyrian* Garden, where the Fiend
> Saw undelighted all delight, all kind
> Of living Creatures new to sight and strange:
> Two of far nobler shape erect and tall,
> Godlike erect, with native Honor clad
> In naked Majesty seem'd Lords of all,
> And worthy seem'd, for in their looks Divine
> The image of thir glorious Maker shone,
> Truth, Wisdome, Sanctitude severe and pure,
> Severe, but in true filial freedom plac't;
> Whence true autority in men; though both
> Not equal, as thir sex not equal seem'd;
> For contemplation hee and valor form'd,
> For softness shee and sweet attractive Grace,
> Hee for God only, shee for God in him:
> His fair large Front and Eye sublime declar'd
> Absolute rule; and Hyacinthine Locks
> Round from his parted forelock manly hung
> Clust'ring, but not beneath his shoulders broad:
> Shee as a veil down to the slender waist
> Her unadorned golden tresses wore
> Dishevell'd, but in wanton ringlets wav'd
> As the Vine curls her tendrils, which impli'd
> Subjection, but requir'd with gentle sway,
> And by her yielded, by him best receiv'd,
> Yielded with coy submission, modest pride,
> And sweet reluctant amorous delay.
> Nor those mysterious parts were then conceal'd,
> Then was not guilty shame: dishonest shame
> Of Nature's works, honor dishonorable,
> Sin-bred, how have ye troubl'd all mankind
> With shows instead, mere shows of seeming pure,
> And banisht from man's life his happiest life,
> Simplicity and spotless innocence.[1] (4.284-318)

Not surprisingly, this description is provocative, confrontational, argumentative, and fraught with ambiguity. How could it be otherwise? Twenty-five years ago Helen Gardner wrote of book 4, lines 296-99, "No lines have, I suppose, been more quoted and quoted against Milton than these. But all that is Milton's is the unequivocal firmness and clarity with which he states the orthodox view of his age."[2] Twenty years earlier, similarly troubled by the passage, Balachandra Rajan had resorted to a similar explanation: "It typified the deepest and most impersonal feelings of the time."[3]

Yet in so many of his beliefs Milton the revolutionary challenged "the orthodox view of his age" and "the deepest and most impersonal feelings of the time." Is it likely he so passively accepts them here? The male supremacist, anti-egalitarian, and absolutist sentiments are proclaimed with an extraordinary brusqueness, yet "the unequivocal firmness and clarity" ascribed to them by Helen Gardner are upon examination remarkably lacking. The passage is permeated with equivocation and uncertainty in its repetition of "seem'd" and "seeming":

> In naked Majesty seem'd Lords of all,
> And worthy seem'd . . .
>
>       . . . . .
>    . . . though both
> Not equal, as thir sex not equal seem'd.
>
>           (4.290-91, 295-96)

The sense of false appearance in "seem'd" is reinforced by Milton's use of "seeming" in the clearly unambiguous sense of deceit only twenty lines on: "With shows instead, mere shows of seeming pure" (4.315). At so crucial a passage, why does Milton offer "seem'd"? Why not "as thir sex not equal was," if that was what he meant? Why is the unambiguous avoided?[4]

If "thir sex not equal seem'd" and if "seeming" is false, does that mean that their sex *was* equal? The uncertainties of "seem'd" spread elsewhere. To find Adam and Eve described as "seem'd Lords of all" makes us wonder whether they were really lords of all, and ask what weight does "Lords" carry from a revolutionary who had supported the abolition of the House of Lords. Is "Lords of all" the same as "Lords of the World" (1.32), or is it a more excessive version? Even stranger is the terse proclamation of "Absolute rule" (4.301) from an intransigent opponent of absolutism.

This first description of Adam and Eve is problematical, of course, because, as commentators have recurrently pointed out,[5] it is presented through Satan's perceptions:

> . . . this *Assyrian* Garden, where the Fiend
> Saw undelighted all delight, all kind
> Of living Creatures new to sight and strange:
> Two of far nobler shape . . .
>
>           (4.284-88)

Marcia Landy's reading is hence questionable when she writes "we are told by the narrator, lest we misunderstand, that Adam and Eve are 'not equal, as thir sex not equal seem'd.'"[6] This is not something told us by the narrator, but something perceived by and mediated through Satan's prejudiced vision. His sight is darkened, "undelighted," and distortive; it "seem'd" that way to Satan. It would make sense that Adam and Eve "seem'd Lords of all" to Satan with his preoccupations about authority, that he should see their relationship as political and inegalitarian, that he should see Adam as absolutist, and that he should offer a political interpretation of the way Eve's hair

> . . . in wanton ringlets wav'd
> As the Vine curls her tendrils, which impli'd
> Subjection.
>
>           (4.306-8)

Again there is ambiguity. The image "implies," but does not clearly state. This is apt since the image of the vine and elm traditionally represents mutuality, reciprocity, and fertility, but not subjection, as Peter Demetz and Todd H. Sammons have scrupulously demonstrated.[7] If subjection is an implication it is a false one—one taken by Satan or the careless fallen reader. It is a suspect political authoritarian interpretation analogous to the way Adam's "fair large Front and Eye sublime declar'd / Absolute rule."[8]

If we take the description of Adam and Eve as recording Satan's interpretative vision, then we can suggest that Satan is projecting a political, hierarchical hell onto an Eden that is something other. At the beginning of book 4 we were told

> . . . for within him Hell
> He brings, and round about him, nor from Hell
> One step no more than from himself can fly
> By change of place.
>
>           (4.20-23)

At the end of his encounter with Adam and Eve, Satan's soliloquy suggests just such a habit of projection, demonstrated in the opening words in which he literally projects hell onto Eden: "O Hell! what do mine eyes with grief behold" (4.358), and he goes on to relate to Adam and Eve in a political, hierarchical way, offering them "League" and a reception in hell of "all her Kings" (4.375,383).[9] That Satan's thinking is absolutist, tyrannical, Milton spells out explicitly in a voice unambiguously narratorial:

> So spake the Fiend, and with necessity,
> The Tyrant's plea, excus'd his devilish deeds.
>
>           (4.393-94)

The vision of an inegalitarian, hierarchical, and absolutist paradise, then, we can interpret as a Satanic vision.[10] This is what Satan imports from hell, and this is what he turns paradise into. The perceived unequal relationships are not ideal but proleptic of the postlapsarian human condition. The seeming inequality, the seeming lordship, the declared absolutism, the implied subjection—these are all from hell and all to come on earth. But the true paradise is to be deduced from the opposite of Satan's vision, the paradise to come from the negation of the negation.[11] This reading can be supported both by significant absence and by explicit evidence in the poem.

The absences first—some already remarked by previous commentators. Aers and Hodge ask, "'Absolute rule' for instance: does Adam really have that? To the horror of the orthodox he does not claim it in the crucial exchange with Eve before the Fall."[12] And Marcia Landy remarks of Milton's treatment of Adam and Eve's postlapsarian quarrels that "in spite of his psychological insight into the ways in which mental conflict is acted out, he does not see their struggle as arising from the stringent boundaries of hierarchy, with male dominance and female subordination, which make conflict inevitable."[13] Significantly, the absolutism and hierarchy are not features of the dramatized dynamic of Adam and Eve's relationship.

We might have expected the alleged hierarchical relationship of Adam and Eve to be spelled out in the authoritative account of creation given by Raphael, but again it is most significantly absent:

> Let us make now Man in our image, Man
> In our similitude, and let them rule
> Over the Fish and Fowl of Sea and Air,
> Beast of the Field, and over all the Earth,
> And every creeping thing that creeps the ground.
> This said, he form'd thee, *Adam,* thee O Man
> Dust of the ground, and in thy nostrils breath'd
> The breath of Life; in his own Image hee
> Created thee, in the Image of God
> Express, and thou becam'st a living Soul.
> Male he created thee, but thy consort
> Female for Race; then bless'd Mankind, and said,
> Be fruitful, multiply, and fill the Earth,
> Subdue it, and throughout Dominion hold
> Over Fish of the Sea, and Fowl of the Air,
> And every living thing that moves on the Earth.
>
> (7.519-34)

Authority over fish, fowl, and beasts is spelled out here; but there is no mention of "Lords of all" and no mention of "rule" or "dominion" by mankind over mankind, or by one sex over another. Mary Nyquist remarks that the reference to Eve here is "meagre,"[14] as indeed it is. But it is importantly non-discriminatory, unlike the Satanic observations of book 4, and the meagerness, the very absence of comment, is in itself significant. As the Diggers declared in *The True Levellers Standard* (1649), "Man had domination given to him, over the beasts, birds and fishes; but not one word was spoken in the beginning, that one branch of mankind should rule over another. And the reason is this. Every single man, male and female, is a perfect creature of himself."[15] Domination is explicitly limited to "beasts, birds and fishes" here on the basis of absence in Genesis. Milton perpetuates that significant absence in Raphael's Genesis-based account, and reasserts the interpretation in Adam's comments on Nimrod:

> O execrable Son so to aspire
> Above his Brethren, to himself assuming
> Authority usurpt, from God not giv'n:
> He gave us only over Beast, Fish, Fowl
> Dominion absolute; that right we hold
> By his donation; but Man over men
> He made not Lord; such title to himself
> Reserving, human left from human free.
>
> (12.64-71)

The model for human society is "fair equality, fraternal state" (12.26) which Nimrod has rejected for "Dominion undeserv'd / Over his brethren" (12.27-28). How then could Adam's "fair large front" legitimately declare "Absolute rule"?[16]

Marcia Landy acknowledged that Adam's assessment of Nimrod "might seem to argue for egalitarianism. It cer-

tainly argues against externally imposed dominion by king or overlord. Yet the equality of fraternity is qualified throughout *Paradise Lost* by the idea of merit."[17] Certainly there is a hierarchy of merit in *Paradise Lost,* but this is something very different from a fixed hierarchy of birth, rank, caste, or class, and in in no way conflicts with egalitarianism. The confusion of these different sorts of hierarchy has caused considerable problems in interpreting *Paradise Lost,* especially in those feminist readings that have too readily accepted the Satanic rigid hierarchy.[18]

The hierarchy of birth, caste, rank, or class which rigidly fixes its components and allows little or no change, which is predetermined, is one that institutionalizes privilege, power, and inequality. Admiringly defined by C. S. Lewis, it is a system represented by Satan, a model for postlapsarian earthly dynasties, for monarchical, feudal, imperial, and class structures.[19]

The hierarchy of moral and spiritual development that Milton has Raphael describe in book 5 is entirely different. A "curiously fluid conception of hierarchy," as Barbara Lewalski characterizes it,[20] it is a dynamic model of alchemical circulation and continual refinement.[21] There is no fixed inequality. It is open to everything to ascend spiritually. This is the divine hierarchy, one of process and ascent, not rule and repression.

> To whom the winged Hierarchy repli'd.
> O *Adam,* one Almighty is, from whom
> All things proceed, and up to him return,
> If not deprav'd from good, created all
> Such to perfection, one first matter all,
> Indu'd with various forms various degrees
> Of substance, and in things that live, of life;
> But more refin'd, more spiritous, and pure,
> As neerer to him plac't or nearer tending
> Each in thir several active Spheres assign'd,
> Till body up to spirit work, in bounds
> Proportion'd to each kind. So from the root
> Springs lighter the green stalk, from thence the leaves
> More aery, last the bright consummate flow'r
> Spirits odorous breathes: flow'rs and thir fruit
> Man's nourishment, by gradual scale sublim'd
> To vital spirits aspire, to animal,
> To intellectual, give both life and sense.
> Fancy and understanding, whence the Soul
> Reason receives, and reason is her being,
> Discursive, or Intuitive; discourse
> Is oftest yours, the latter most is ours,
> Differing but in degree, of kind the same.
> Wonder not then, what God for you saw good
> If I refuse not, but convert, as you,
> To proper substance; time may come when men
> With Angels may participate, and find
> No inconvenient Diet, nor too light Fare:
> And from these corporal nutriments perhaps
> Your bodies may at last turn all to spirit,
> Improv'd by tract of time, and wing'd ascend
> Ethereal, as wee, or may at choice
> Here or in Heav'nly Paradises dwell.
>
> (5.468-500)

As Raphael makes clear, this is a dynamic, evolutionary process. It is a flowing scale of ascent, not a fixed hierarchy. It utterly subverts any fixed political or social or gender roles.[22]

Moreover, the unequivocal inapplicability of fixed gender roles is clear when we relate this passage to what we were told in book 1 about spirits:

> For Spirits when they please
> Can either Sex assume, or both.
>
>                                        (1.423-24)

Since Adam and Eve may "at last turn all to Spirit" and since "Spirits when they please / Can either Sex assume, or both," any assertion of gender hierarchy is ultimately unsustainable.

The concepts of sexual inequality and absolute rule are introduced so brusquely and indeed brutally into the portrayal of Paradise that the reader might expect they would be active concepts in the presented relationship of Adam and Eve in the events leading up to the Fall.[23] Strikingly, this is not so. Nor is equality an issue in Satan's temptation. His strategy is to flatter Eve, to suggest her unique superiority—"who shouldst be seen / A Goddess among Gods, ador'd and serv'd / By Angels numberless" (9.546-48), "no Fair to thine / Equivalent or second" (9.608-9). Only after Eve has eaten the apple does she raise the issue of equality, considering whether to share her knowledge with Adam

> . . . and give him to partake
> Full happiness with mee, or rather not,
> But keep the odds of Knowledge in my power
> Without Copartner? so to add what wants
> In Female Sex, the more to draw his Love,
> And render me more equal, and perhaps,
> A thing not undesirable, sometime
> Superior: for inferior who is free?
>
>                                        (9.818-25)

"She is feeling inferior for the first time," Dorothy Miller remarks of these lines.[24] Eve only expresses this sense of any inequality when she is fallen. This suggests that inequality is a part of the fallen world, projected by Eve when she herself has fallen.[25]

And now in the fallen world, confusions abound. Marcia Landy remarks, "The speech portrays the idea of equality as confused in Eve's mind with dominance. She errs, like Satan, in confusing hierarchy and equality of affection."[26] But Landy too readily accepts a pejorative account of Eve:

> By violating boundaries and moving to adopt more power through Satan's offers of equality, power, and authority, Eve identified herself as a deviant. In other words, her resistance to subordination is invalidated and stigmatized through its association with the archetypal subverter, Satan. Are we to consider Eve's rebellion and the rebellion of all women against subordination as evil?[27]

The issue is more tangled than that. Firstly, Eve undoubtedly errs in eating the apple. Secondly, equality is not an issue in her temptation: it is an explanation, a rationalization, that enters afterwards. Indeed, it can only enter later if, as I have suggested, inequality was not the reality of the paradisal relationship but rather something that "seem'd" the case in Satan's distorted and evil perception.

So although Eve in falling is stigmatized through her association with Satan, this in no way stigmatizes the egalitarian impulse. Once in the fallen, Satanic world the question "for inferior who is free?" is a valid one.

The complicating factor, of course, is that though Satan uses the rhetoric of egalitarianism in rousing supporters for his rebellion, his own motives are profoundly unegalitarian. As Joseph Wittreich puts it, "Satan's strategy is to employ a rhetoric of equality through which he would bring all creation under subjection."[28] Satan's handling of the issue of egalitarianism shows all his political and oratorical shiftiness:

> Will ye submit your necks, and choose to bend
> The supple knee? ye will not, if I trust
> To know ye right, or if ye know yourselves
> Natives and Sons of Heav'n possest before
> By none, and if not equal all, yet free,
> Equally free; for Orders and Degrees
> Jar not with liberty, but well consist.
> Who can in reason then or right assume
> Monarchy over such as live by right
> His equals, if in power and splendor less,
> In freedom equal? . . .
>
>                                        (5.787-97)

Equality is a part—and only a part—of Satan's rhetoric, but never of his social practice. His rhetoric is a serpentine display of confusion and contradiction. Orders and degrees certainly do jar with liberty.[29] That is why those observations of "thir sex not equal seem'd," "Absolute rule," and "implied subjection" conflict with a true vision of Paradise and alert us that there is a Satanic rhetoric intruding. Satan plays hypocritically with a rhetoric of egalitarianism but acts as an absolutist monarch and sets up a patriarchal dynasty with Sin and Death. About this there are no ambiguities. The narratorial voice denotes him firmly as "Monarch" (2.467) and "Tyrant" (4.394). It is essential to stress, however, that Satan's use of the language of equality in no way discredits the concept of equality. Indeed, his lack of egalitarian practice serves to confirm egalitarianism as a good: "fair equality" (12.26). To reply at last to Marcia Landy, No, we do not have to consider the rebellion of all women against subordination as evil. But Satan is a bad model. Satan's "rebellion" was an attempt to establish tyranny, authoritarian rule. Human rebellion for the good is a rebellion against the Satanic authoritarian, an attempt to "Restore us, and regain the blissful Seat" (1.5) by following the way of Christ:[30] a model, indeed, that Eve does follow, her "On mee, mee only" (10.832) echoing Christ's speech (3.236). Social subordination is a Satanic practice introduced by the Fall. But it was not present before the

Fall, nor does Milton present Eve as rebelling against it, for it is not shown as present.

The issues of equality and masculine rule are raised again in the judgment and punishment episode in book 10. Again, the passages are fraught with ambiguity. And it is this ambiguity I want to continue to stress. There is certainly a male supremacist, authoritarian, inegalitarian reading prominent in the poem, as numerous critical accounts testify; but at the same time the ambiguities and contradictions and cross-references serve to undermine and deconstruct this reading. They do not do so to the extent of utterly canceling it; but they certainly qualify and challenge it, demonstrating that there was a tension and a debate, which the poem embodies and expresses.

In the judgment there is a wavering between whether Adam treated Eve as his "superior, or but equal." Do we read these as alternatives, or as equally unacceptable parallels in God's view?

> To whom the sovran Presence thus repli'd.
> Was shee thy God, that her thou didst obey
> Before his voice, or was shee made thy guide,
> Superior, or but equal, that to her
> Thou didst resign thy Manhood, and the Place
> Wherein God set thee above her made of thee,
> And for thee, whose perfection farr excell'd
> Hers in all real dignity: Adorn'd
> She was indeed, and lovely to attract
> Thy Love, not thy Subjection, and her Gifts
> Were such as under Government well seem'd,
> Unseemly to bear rule, which was thy part
> And person, hadst thou known thyself aright.

(10.144-56)

The floating possibility is that seeing Eve as superior was wrong, as opposed to seeing her as "but equal." If Adam had seen her as "but equal" then his own inner rationality should have allowed him to make a better judgment of what she proposed.[31] Again there is the "seem'd," complicated further by a play on "unseemly": "her Gifts / Were such as under Government well seem'd, / Unseemly to bear rule, which was thy part."

And what might seem a firm resolution of the ambiguity here, that Eve was "Unseemly to bear rule, which was thy part" dissolves again when we come to Eve's punishment:

> . . . to thy Husband's will
> Thine shall submit, hee over thee shall rule.

(10.195-96)

How is this a punishment, if it was already the case before the Fall? Nowhere does Milton say the husband's rule over the woman was reiterated.[32] It is not presented as a reassertion, but as a punishment in parallel with "Children thou shalt bring / In sorrow forth" (10.194-95). And if submission to the husband's will is a punishment for eating the apple, then before the Fall such a submission of man to woman did not apply. In the paradisal state, man

and woman, then, lived in equality. But why is it all so ambiguous? In a legalistic episode of judgment and punishment, we might have expected clarity and scrupulous unambiguity. Yet ambiguity permeates the episode, as it does the whole expression of sexual equality.

The assertion of women's equality was contentious in the seventeenth century as it is today. The moves towards freedom and equality for women had scandalized the ruling classes: Clarendon expresses his horror at women and the lower orders preaching in church.[33] But Milton is not only writing about gender equality. He is writing about something that was much more revolutionary and subversive: equality, human equality. This was a truly subversive doctrine, and its developing expression in the late 1640s had provoked the full repression of the bourgeois revolutionary state. The levellers, the diggers and such like were extirpated with a fervor never applied to extirpating royalists.

As Christopher Hill continues to remind us, "Milton wrote under censorship, and was himself a marked man, lucky not to have been hanged, drawn and quartered in 1660. Two of his books were burnt. So he had to be very careful how he said things he wanted to say."[34] Assertions of egalitarianism could only be made carefully and obliquely. Like the assertion that Paradise was communist, that there was no private ownership, also in book 4, it can only be inserted glancingly, in passing, amidst other issues:

> Hail wedded Love, mysterious Law, true source
> Of human offspring, sole propriety
> In Paradise of all things common else.

(4.750-52)

The issue of common ownership emerges in a discussion of human sexuality. Similarly, the issues of sexual equality rapidly lead on to "sweet reluctant amorous delay" and "those mysterious parts" (4.311-12). Within one contentious issue, human sexuality, Milton involves another contentious issue, egalitarianism and common ownership.

This is not to undercut the issue of gender equality at all. It is not undercut in the poem. But it is firmly attached to that more inclusive and revolutionary aim of achieving total human equality, of restoring us to that still unregained blissful seat, of liberty without orders and degrees, without discrimination, with all things common.

*Notes*

1. All quotations from Milton's poetry follow Hughes.
2. Helen Gardner, *"A Reading of Paradise Lost"* (Oxford: Clarendon Press, 1965), 8.
3. Balachandra Rajan, *"Paradise Lost" and the Seventeenth-Century Reader* (London: Chatto and Windus, 1947), 66.
4. David Aers and Bob Hodge have noted the "seem'd"s but conclude "these doubts or equivocations are not dominant, and the passage

basically supports a male supremacist reading" ("'Rational Burning': Milton on Sex and Marriage," *MS* 13 [1979]: 23). Julia M. Walker, "'For each seem'd either': Free Will and Predestination in *Paradise Lost*," *MQ* 20 (1986), examining Milton's use of "seem'd" in relation to free will and predestination in *Paradise Lost*, suggests:

> Throughout the poem, Milton uses "seems" in three different ways: first and most simply, "seems" is used to mean a false appearance, a seeming not an actual reality; second, and more ambiguous, "seems" is used as "appears" but without a clear judgment about reality; . . . finally and most confusingly, "seems" is actually equated with some form of the verb "to be."

And she attributes "thir sex not equal seem'd" to his hypothetical "some form of the verb to be" (20). This is an unconvincing redefinition. Cf. also Stephen M. Fallon, "The Uses of 'Seems' and the Spectre of Predestination," *MS* 21 (1987): 99-101, and Julia M. Walker, "Free Will, Predestination, and Ghost-Busting," *MS* 21 (1987): 101-2.

5. See for example Diane Kelsey McColley, *Milton's Eve* (Urbana: Univ. of Illinois Press, 1983), 40, and Gardner, 81.

6. Marcia Landy, "'A Free and Open Encounter': Milton and the Modern Reader," *MS* 9 (1976): 17.

7. Peter Demetz, "The Elm and the Vine: Notes Toward the History of a Marriage Topos," *PMLA* 73 (1958): 521-32; Todd H. Sammons, "'As the Vine Curls Her Tendrils': Marriage Topos and Erotic Countertopos in *Paradise Lost*," *MQ* 20 (1986): 117-27.

8. Aers and Hodge, 22. "One might wonder whether 'declar'd' (4.300) undercuts the whole speech on male rule since these signs may only 'declare' absolute rule to the fallen Satan, who does not know what Raphael told Adam, 'that Great / Or Bright infers not Excellence'" (8.90-91). Nonetheless Aers and Hodge see "these doubts or equivocations" as "not dominant."

9. Michael Wilding, *Dragons Teeth: Literature in the English Revolution* (Oxford: Clarendon Press, 1987), 227.

10. Dennis H. Burden's model of "the Satanic poem" contained within *Paradise Lost* is useful here. See his *The Logical Epic: A Study of the Argument of* Paradise Lost (London: Routledge and Kegan Paul, 1967), 57ff.

11. "Milton's stridently masculinist 'Hee for God only, shee for God in him,'" as Mary Nyquist has categorized it, can perhaps now be resituated as *Satan's* stridently masculinist sentiment. It has worried readers as far back as Richard Bentley, who proposed emending it to "Hee for God only, shee for

God *and* him." See Mary Nyquist, "The Genesis of Gendered Subjectivity in the Divorce Tracts and in *Paradise Lost*," in *Re-membering Milton*, ed. Nyquist and Margaret W. Ferguson (New York and London: Methuen, 1987), 107; *Dr. Bentley's Emendations on the Twelve Books of Milton's* Paradise Lost (London, 1732), 15.

12. Aers and Hodge, 22.

13. Landy, 23.

14. Nyquist, 117.

15. See Christopher Hill, ed., *Winstanley: The Law of Freedom and Other Writings* (Harmondsworth: Penguin, 1973), 77.

16. Of course, when we turn back to book 4, "Absolute rule" is not explicitly applied to man ruling over woman: the context seems to imply it, but the expression is ambiguous and evasive. It is an appropriate Satanic suggestion, inexplicit, insinuating. It can always be plausibly denied and interpreted as applying only to "beast, fish, fowl"—though male supremacism is the prime Satanic implication.

17. Landy, 9.

18. Landy, passim; William Shullenberger, "Wrestling with the Angel: *Paradise Lost* and Feminist Criticism," *MQ* 20 (1986): 74: "The doctrine of woman's subordination is explicit in the text"; Virginia R. Mollenkott, "Milton and Women's Liberation," *MQ* 7 (1973): 101: "Milton treated the subject of female subordination in the most objective fashion possible, not with egotistical gratification but because his view of a hierarchical universe would allow no other concept"; Ricki Heller, "Opposites of Wifehood: Eve and Dalila," *MS* 24 (1988): 190. The hierarchical, gender-discriminatory model is, of course, endemic in non-feminist readings such as, for example, Joseph H. Summers, *The Muse's Method: An Introduction to "Paradise Lost"* (London: Chatto and Windus, 1962):

> The inequality of man and woman is imaged as clearly as is their perfection. It is not only modern ideas of the equality of the sexes which may make this passage difficult for us; the democratic assumption that ideally every individual *should* be self-sufficient and our tendency to define "perfection" as eternal self-sufficiency complicate our difficulties further (95).

19. C. S. Lewis, *A Preface to "Paradise Lost"* (London: Oxford Univ. Press, 1942), 72-80.

20. Barbara K. Lewalski, "Milton on Women—Yet Once More," *MS* 6 (1974): 6.

21. On the alchemical, see Alastair Fowler in *The Poems of John Milton*, ed. John Carey and Alastair Fowler (London: Longman, 1968), 704; and see also

Michael Lieb, *The Dialectics of Creation: Patterns of Birth and Regeneration in "Paradise Lost"* (Amherst: Univ. of Massachusetts Press, 1970), 229-44.

22. Cf. Marilyn R. Farwell, "Eve, the Separation Scene, and the Renaissance Idea of Androgyny," *MS* 16 (1982): 13: "Thus, anyone who at one point represents the natural and material world is not bound to remain at that level. Theoretically then, Eve has the potential to grow into more wisdom and spirituality."

23. The sheer blatancy of the inegalitarian and absolutist ideas expressed in the vision of Adam and Eve in book 4 has inevitably shocked readers. And this very brusqueness and brutality may well be interpreted as Milton's strategy for shocking readers into reassessing their attitudes. Stanley Fish's model for reading *Paradise Lost* could well be applied here: "Milton consciously wants to worry his reader, to force him to doubt the correctness of his responses and to bring him to the realization that his inability to read the poem with any confidence in his own perceptions is its focus" (*Surprised by Sin: The Reader in "Paradise Lost"* [Berkeley: Univ. of California Press, 1967], 4).

24. Dorothy Durkee Miller, "Eve," *JEGP* 61 (1962): 546.

25. Oddly, Diane K. McColley puts it the other way: "Equality in any case is a fallen concept—the legal recourse of a race not much given to rejoicing in the goodness, much less the superiority, of others—needed to rectify injustices that no one in a state of sinless blessedness would consider committing" ("Milton and the Sexes," in *The Cambridge Companion to Milton,* ed. Dennis Danielson [Cambridge: Cambridge Univ. Press, 1989], 159).

26. Landy, 21.

27. Landy, 19. The parallels between Eve and Satan are stressed in Sandra M. Gilbert, "Patriarchal Poetry and Women Readers: Reflections on Milton's Bogey," *PMLA* 93 (1978): 368-82, and King-Kok Cheung, "Beauty and the Beast: A Sinuous Reflection of Milton's Eve," *MS* 23 (1987): 197-214.

28. Joseph Wittreich, Jr., *Feminist Milton* (Ithaca: Cornell Univ. Press, 1987), 90-91. And see John M. Steadman, "Satan and the Argument from Equality," in his *Milton's Epic Characters: Image and Idol* (Chapel Hill: Univ. of North Carolina Press, 1959), 160-73.

29. Satan's argument is hampered by the fact that he particularly wants to avoid equality among his own faction, and therefore has to turn aside for a moment to explain (789ff.) that "Orders and Degrees Jarr not with liberty." He is not very explicit on the subject, *et pour cause.* The

passage is one of those where (rightly and inevitably) an element of grim comedy is permitted. (Lewis, 76)

Mollenkott, however, writes, "It is . . . generally true that 'Orders and Degrees jar not with liberty'" (101).

30. Wilding, 226; Fredric Jameson, "Religion and Ideology," in *Literature and Power in the Seventeenth Century,* ed. Francis Barker et al. (Colchester; Univ. of Essex Press, 1981), 329.

31. Cf. Dennis Danielson, "Through the Telescope of Typology: What Adam Should Have Done," *MQ* 23 (1989): 121-27.

32. Cf. Maureen Quilligan, *Milton's Spenser: The Politics of Reading* (Ithaca: Cornell Univ. Press, 1983), 237: "Her punishment is not merely to bear children in pain, but to (re)submit to her husband's will"; and see also James Grantham Turner, *One Flesh: Paradisal Marriage and Sexual Relations in the Age of Milton* (Oxford: Clarendon Press, 1987).

33. Edward Hyde, earl of Clarendon, *The History of the Rebellion and Civil Wars in England* (Oxford, 1704), 3:32.

34. Christopher Hill, "*Samson Agonistes* Again," *Literature and History,* 2d ser., 1 (1990): 24. For a full discussion of the topic, see "Censorship and English Literature," in *The Collected Essays of Christopher Hill: Writing and Revolution in Seventeenth-Century England* (Brighton: Harvester Press, 1985), 1:32-71.

---

# FURTHER READING

## Bibliographies

Klemp, P. J. *Paradise Lost: An Annotated Bibliography.* Magill Bibliographies. Lanham, Md.: The Scarecrow Press, 1996, 249 p.

Bibliography with descriptions of secondary sources organized by subject and individual book in the epic.

———ed. *The Essential Milton: An Annotated Bibliography of Major Modern Studies.* Boston: G. K. Hall, 1989, 474 p.

Bibliography of secondary criticism on Milton, with a section devoted to works on *Paradise Lost.*

## Criticism

Barker, A. E, ed. *Milton: Modern Essays in Criticism.* New York: Oxford University Press, 1965, 483 p.

Collection of essays by noted critics that provide stimulating introductions to the works or highlight significant issues in Milton scholarship; includes articles on *Paradise Lost* by Douglas Bush, A. B. Chambers, C. S. Lewis, and Irene Samuel.

Blamires, Harry. *Milton's Creation: A Guide through Paradise Lost.* London: Methuen & Co. Ltd., 1971, 308 p.
Escorts the reader through the text, providing general notes on the poem, clarifying difficult passages, and offering detailed analyses of crucial passages.

Broadbent, J. B. *Some Graver Subject: An Essay on Paradise Lost.* London: Chatto and Windus, 1960, 303 p.
Claims that, from a historical point of view, *Paradise Lost* is a reactionary work, and also that Milton presents his subject matter in an intellectual rather than a mystical manner.

Burden, Dennis. *The Logical Epic: A Study of the Argument of Paradise Lost.* Cambridge, Mass.: Harvard University Press, 1967, 117 p.
Examines how Milton treats his subject matter in light of the constraints presented in his source materials, and argues that in writing his poem Milton had to scrutinize the Bible with an eye to its rationality and logic.

Bush, Douglas. *Paradise Lost in Our Time.* Gloucester, Mass.: Peter Smith, 1957, 117 p.
Four essays originally delivered as lectures discussing the reaction against Milton in the mid-twentieth century, and exploring the work's religious and ethical themes, characters and drama, and poetical texture.

DiCesare, Mario A. "*Paradise Lost* and the Epic Tradition." *Milton Studies* I (1969): 31-50.
Examines some of the ways in which Milton, following Virgil, modified the epic tradition.

Empson, William. *Milton's God.* London: Chatto and Windus, 1961, 249 p.
Influential study that paints a grim portrait of God in *Paradise Lost.*

Fish, Stanley Eugene. *Surprised by Sin: The Reader in Paradise Lost.* Berkeley: University of California Press, 1967, 361 p.
Argues that "the uniqueness of the poem's theme—man's first disobedience and the fruit thereof—results in the reader's being simultaneously a participant in the action and a critic of his own performance."

Fixler, Michael. "The Apocalypse Within *Paradise Lost.* In *New Essays on Paradise Lost,* pp. 131-78. edited by Thomas Kranidas, Berkeley: University of California Press, 1969.
Suggests that Milton based *Paradise Lost* on an elaborate systematic transformation of the Apocalypse or Revelation of St. John.

Frye, Northrop. *The Return of Eden.* Toronto: University of Toronto Press, 1965, 151 p.
Essays discussing the epic structure, style, and themes of the poem.

Gardner, Helen. *A Reading of Paradise Lost.* Oxford: Clarendon Press, 1965, 131 p.
Detailed reading of the epic with discussions of Milton's creation of an intensely dramatic universe, the poem's extraordinary scope of space and time, and Satan as a tragic figure.

Kermode, Frank, ed. *The Living Milton: Essays by Various Hands.* London: Routledge and Kegan Paul, 1960, 179 p.
Collection of essays by distinguished scholars, many of which are frequently reprinted; includes essays on *Paradise Lost.*

Kranidas, Thomas, ed. *New Essays on Paradise Lost.* Berkeley: University of California Press, 1969. 180 p.
Important volume of essays with articles by Stanley Fish, John T. Shawcross, and A. B. Chambers.

Leonard, John. *Naming in Paradise: Milton and the Language of Adam and Eve.* Oxford: Clarendon Press, 1990, 304 p.
Study of the poem's language.

Lindenbaum, Peter. "Lovemaking in Milton's Paradise." *Milton Studies* VI (1975): 277-306.
Asserts that Milton's emphasis on Adam and Eve's lovemaking before the fall encourages readers to view sexual love as the "sum of prelapsarian bliss" and appreciate the complexities in Adam's decision to disobey God because of his love for Eve.

Lewis, C. S. *A Preface to Paradise Lost.* London: Oxford University Press, 1942, 143 p.
One of the most important and original works of Milton criticism that touches on various subjects, including the poem's solemn tone, Christian orthodoxy, Eve's pride, Adam's uxoriousness, and Milton's God;. Lewis claims also that the final two books form a "grave structural flaw."

MacCaffrey, Isabel Gamble. *Paradise Lost as "Myth."* Cambridge, Mass.: Harvard University Press, 1959, 229 p.
Argues that Milton uses the myth of the cyclic journey to portray humanity's movement from an original state of glory (creation) to exile (the fall) and back to God (redemption).

Martz, Louis L. "*Paradise Lost:* The Journey of the Mind." In *The Paradise Within: Studies in Vaughn, Traherne, and Milton.* New Haven, CONN: Yale University Press, 1964, pp. 103-67
Claims that *Paradise Lost* is concerned with "a renewal of human vision" and that the epic's narrator looks toward a recovery of paradise.

Rajan, Balachandra, ed. *Paradise Lost: A Tercentenary Tribute.* Toronto: University of Toronto Press, 1969, 140 p.
  Volume of critical essays including contributions by noted critics such as Northrop Frye, Arthur E. Barker, and Hugh MacCallum.

Raleigh, Sir Walter. "*Paradise Lost:* The Scheme." In *Milton.* pp. 77-125. London: Edward Arnold, 1900.
  Claims that Milton in the poem "serves Satan," and says that while the poem does not concern modern readers "it is not the less an eternal monument because it is a monument to dead ideas."

———"*Paradise Lost:* The Actors. The Later Poems." In *Milton.* pp. 126-174. London: Edward Arnold, 1900.
  Considers that the poem's epic value comes from Satan's character and achievement, argues that Milton bases his universe on political rather than religious principles, sees Milton's God as a "Whimsical Tyrant," and praises Milton's power of style despite his pedantic treatment of abstract thought.

Ricks, Christopher. *Milton's Grand Style.* Oxford: Clarendon Press, 1963, 154 p.
  Offers a detailed analysis of the style of *Paradise Lost,* and answers critics who have called the language of the work monotonous, ritualistic, and unsubtle.

Steadman, John. *Milton's Epic Characters: Image and Idol.* Chapel Hill: University of North Carolina Press, 1959, 343 p.
  Explores the intellectual background of *Paradise Lost* and *Paradise Regained* with particular emphasis on problems of characterization.

Steadman, John. *Epic and Tragic Structure in Paradise Lost.* Chicago: University of Chicago Press, 1976, 189 p.
  Asserts that Milton beautifully accommodates the temptation story to an ideal of the epic form, and that he invests the traditional heroic poem with Christian matter and meaning.

Stein, Arnold. *Answerable Style: Essays on Paradise Lost.* Minneapolis: University of Minnesota Press, 1953, 166 p.
  Important general study reprinted in numerous volumes of critical essays. Stein discusses, among other things, the character of Satan, the war in heaven, grotesque imagery, the archetype of the garden, and the cosmic and domestic drama of the epic.

———"Imagining Death: The Ways of Milton." *Milton Studies* XXIX (1992): 105-20.
  Examines Milton's thoughts on death as revealed in *Paradise Lost* and other works.

Summers, Joseph H. *The Muse's Method: An Introduction to Paradise Lost.* Cambridge, Mass.: Harvard University Press, 1962, 227 p.
  Introductory reading of *Paradise Lost* with each chapter offering a different method or approach toward the epic. Summers includes a textual analysis of the opening lines, an examination of the uses of grotesque parody and comedy, a discussion of the definition of "good" or "Perfection," and a discussion of the centrality of the "Two Great Sexes."

Tillyard, E. M. W. *Studies in Milton.* London: Chatto and Windus, 1950, 176 p.
  A frequently reprinted study that considers such themes as the Fall, Adam and Eve's disobedience, the couple's reconciliation, and the character of Satan.

# Marge Piercy
## 1936-

American novelist, poet, and essayist.

## INTRODUCTION

Piercy is a prominent feminist poet whose political commitment informs her work. Her verse often focuses on individuals struggling to escape oppressive social roles. Frankly polemical, Piercy's colloquial, free verse poetry passionately excoriates such phenomena as sexism, capitalism, and pollution, using exaggerated imagery and unabashed emotionalism in service of her social commentary.

## BIOGRAPHICAL INFORMATION

Piercy was born to a Jewish mother and a Welsh father in a working-class neighborhood in Detroit. After attending the University of Michigan as a scholarship student, she moved to Chicago and received a Masters degree from Northwestern University. Much of Piercy's work during the 1960s and 1970s emerged directly from her involvement in the radical youth organization Students for a Democratic Society. She has also been very supportive of feminist issues. As a poet, novelist, and commentator, she has a large international following, and her work has been translated into a number of languages. She lives in Massachusetts and continues to write novels and poetry.

## MAJOR WORKS

In her poetry, Piercy's political concerns are often expressed in an anguished or angry first-person narrative. Her first publication, *Breaking Camp*, is a volume of poetry that balances expressions of outrage at impoverished living conditions in Chicago with personal accounts of joy in love and being alive. In the 1970s, she shifted her emphasis from poverty, racism, and the Vietnam War to the struggle for women's rights. The poems collected in *To Be of Use*, *Living in the Open*, and *The Moon Is Always Female* reflect her commitment to exposing the damaging effects of patriarchy in contemporary American society and her condemnation of the roles ascribed to women by the male establishment. Piercy's works of the 1980s emphasize the politics of city-planning and the poet's sensual pleasure in such activities as gardening, making love, and cooking. In more recent works, such as *Available Light* and *The Art of Blessing the Day: Poems with a Jewish Theme*, Piercy celebrates her Jewish heritage.

## CRITICAL RECEPTION

Critical analyses of Piercy's verse often consider the essential role of political and social commentary, with re-

viewers perceiving her emphasis on such social problems as poverty, the destruction of the environment, gentrification of old neighborhoods, and civil and women's rights as commendable. Some critics have faulted her work for excessive, often violent imagery as well as a self-righteous tone. Yet she is praised for aspects of her personal poetry, particularly her sensuality, humor, and playfulness.

---

## PRINCIPAL WORKS

### Poetry

*Breaking Camp* 1968
*Hard Loving* 1969
*To Be of Use* 1973
*Living in the Open* 1976

*The Twelve-Spoked Wheel Flashing* 1978
*The Moon Is Always Female* 1980
*Circles on the Water: Selected Poems of Marge Piercy* 1982
*Stone, Paper, Knife* 1983
*My Mother's Body* 1985
*Available Light* 1988
*Mars and Her Children* 1992
*What are Big Girls Made of?* 1997
*The Art of Blessing the Day: Poems with a Jewish Theme* 1999
*Early Grrrl: The Poems of Marge Piercy* 1999

## Other Major Works

*Going Down Fast* (novel) 1969
*Dance the Eagle to Sleep* (novel) 1971
*Small Changes* (novel) 1973
*Woman on the Edge of Time* (novel) 1976
*The High Cost of Living* (novel) 1978
*Vida* (novel) 1980
*Braided Lives* (novel) 1982
*Parti-Colored Blocks for a Quilt: Poets on Poetry* (essays) 1982
*Fly Away Home* (novel) 1984
*Gone to Soldiers* (novel) 1987
*Summer People* (novel) 1989
*He, She, and It* (novel) 1991
*Body of Glass* (novel) 1992
*The Longings of Women* (novel) 1994
*City of Darkness, City of Light* (novel) 1996
*Storm Tide* [with Ira Wood] (novel) 1998

---

# CRITICISM

### Marge Piercy (essay date 1982)

SOURCE: "Inviting the Muse," in *Parti-Colored Blocks for a Quilt*, The University of Michigan Press, 1982, pp. 5-17.

[*In the following essay, Piercy describes the initial steps of her creative process—inspiration and concentration.*]

Here is Henry Thoreau from his journal for October 26, 1853, although he is talking about spring. "That afternoon the dream of the toads rang through the elms by Little River and affected the thoughts of men, though they were not conscious that they heard it. How watchful we must be to keep the crystal well that we are made, clear!"

Writing poems can be divided crudely into three kinds of labor: beginning and getting well and hard into it; pushing through inner barriers and finding the correct form; drawing back and judging what you have done and what is still to be done or redone. This essay is about the first stage, learning how to flow, how to push yourself, how to reach that cone of concentration I experience at its best as a tower of light, when all the voices in the head are one voice.

I do not know how to teach that, although concentration can be learned and worked on the same as flattening stomach muscles or swimming farther. You could perhaps set someone to studying a rock or a leaf or a bird—perhaps a warbler. Nothing requires more concentration than trying to observe a warbler up in the leafy maze of a summer tree. If I were really and truly teaching poetry, I would probably drive everybody crazy by sending them off to notice the shades of sand on a beach.

Of course observation isn't concentration, but learning to do one brings on the ability to do the other. My mother taught me to observe. A woman who had not been allowed to finish the tenth grade, she had some extraordinary ideas about how to raise very young children. Later when I was grown out of dependency and highly imperfect, she had trouble with me and could not endure my puberty. However, when I was little enough to fit comfortably into her arms and lap, we played unusual games. She had contempt for people who did not observe, who did not notice, and would require me to remember the houses we passed going to the store, or play mental hide-and-seek in other people's houses that we had visited. We would give each other three random objects or words to make stories around. We would try to guess the stories of people we saw on the bus and would argue to prove or disprove each other's theories.

I suppose such training might have produced what she wanted, a sharply observant person like herself, a reporter's mentality, a little Sherlock Holmes in Shirley Temple guise. What it created in me was observation suffused with imagination, since our life was on the whole skimpy, hard, surrounded by violence outdoors and containing familial violence within, a typical patriarchal working-class family in inner-city Detroit. Blacks and whites fought; the Polish and Blacks who lived across Tireman (a street) fought the Irish who went to parochial school. The neighborhood offered the kind of stable family life writers like Christopher Lasch, beating the dolly of the new narcissism, love to harken back to. Although husbands sometimes took off and not infrequently had girlfriends on the side, women almost never walked out of their homes. Wife beating was common, child beating just as common; drunkenness, drug abuse, rape, molestation of children occurred on every block but families went on from generation to generation. In such a neighborhood where the whites were comprised of Polish, Irish, a few Italian and German Catholics, of some remaining WASP and some newly arrived Appalachian families (I divide the Appalachian WASP from the others because they were often Celts, and because they were looked down on by everybody as hillbillies and provided some of my closest friends), being a Jew was walking around with a kick-me sign. I'd say the level of tolerance for lesbians was higher than that for Jews. You learn to observe street action and people's muscular tensions and involuntary tics rather closely.

Detroit sprawls there, willfully ugly mile after flat smoggy mile; yet what saves it are trees. Every abandoned vacant lot becomes a jungle in a couple of years. Our tiny backyard was rampant with tomatoes, beans, herbs, lettuce, onions, Swiss chard. One of the earliest poems I wrote and still like is subtly about sex and overtly about peonies. Pansies, iris, mock orange, wisteria, hollyhocks along the alley fence, black-eyed Susans, goldenglow whose stems were red with spider mites, bronze chrysanthemums, a lilac bush by the compost pile. Nothing to me will ever be more beautiful than the flowers in that yard, except my mother when I was young.

You learn to sink roots into your childhood and feed on it, twist it, wring it, use it again and again. Sometimes one daub of childhood mud can set a whole poem right or save a character. It's not always a matter of writing about your family, although at times we all do that. You use your childhood again and again in poems about totally other things. You learn how to use that rush of energy and how to make sure your use transcends the often trivial and ludicrous associations you are touching and drawing power from.

Some poets get going, get the flow by reading other poets. You learn whose writing moves you to your own, whether it's Whitman or the King James version of the Bible or Rukeyser or Neruda in Spanish or in translation. Actually I've never met anyone who got themselves going by reading poetry in any other language than the one they were working in, but I'm curious if anybody does. On the other hand I have met a number of poets who use work in translation to prime themselves. It is a priming act we're talking about. You set the words and rhythms going through you and you begin to align yourself. It has disadvantages, of course; if you are the least impressionable you may produce involuntary pastiche. You may find yourself churning out imagery that is bookishly exotic, imagery culled from others and bearing the imprint of being on loan like clothes that fit badly. Some poets use poetry of another time to prime themselves, to minimize the unintentional fertilization.

This priming can happen by accident. Oftentimes I am reading poetry and suddenly a poem starts, that change in the brain, maybe words, maybe an image, maybe an idea. It need not even be poetry. That quotation from Thoreau that begins this essay instigated a poem called **"Toad dreams."** I remember starting a poem in the middle of reading a *Natural History* magazine or the *Farmers Almanac.*

I think of that instigation as having a peculiar radiance; that is, the idea, the image, the rhythm, the phrase—radiates. I find myself wanting to attend to it. I may not know at once, often I may not find out for several drafts, what that meaning, that implication, that web of associations

and train of utterances will be or even in what direction I am being led. Sometimes the original moment radiates in many directions. Then my problem is sorting out the direction to pursue first or exclusively.

At that point if concentration is not forthcoming, the whole possibility may be blown. If you can lose a novel by talking it out, you can easily destroy a poem by not paying attention. I have lost many poems that way; I must lose one a week because I can't get to a typewriter or even to a piece of paper fast enough—sometimes can't break through to silence, to solitude, to a closed door. I am not good at working at cafe tables, as Sartre was supposed to do, although I have written on planes often enough. Even then I work only when I have a bit of space, never while wedged in the middle seat. I need at least a seat between me and any other person to work on a plane. At home, I need a closed door.

Poems can be aborted by answering the phone at the wrong moment. They can be aborted when an alien rhythm forces itself in, or the wrong other words are juxtaposed. I cannot work with a radio on loud enough to hear the words, or a television, or music with words playing. I have trouble working at all with music on, for the rhythms are much too insistent. I know other writers who work to music, but I cannot do so. Rhythm is extremely important to me in building the line and the poem, so any other insistent rhythm interferes. Irregular rhythms—hammering on a construction site nearby—have little effect.

I had a friend in Brooklyn who used to work with wax plunges in her ears, but I find that difficult. I talk my poems aloud and my voice roaring in my head gives me a headache. However, I pass on this method as it may do the trick for you. I know another writer who uses a white noise machine, the type usually purchased to help you sleep. I used to run an air conditioner to screen the noises from outside the apartment, when it seemed to me that every window opening onto the center of our block in Adelphi had a radio or a TV or both turned to top decibel.

Often I begin a poem simply by paying attention to myself, by finding what is stirring in there. I need a quiet moment. I try to use the routine of waking to bring me to work, whether into a novel I am working on or into poetry. I work best in the morning, although I started out believing myself to be a night person. I changed over during the sixties when the one quiet time I was assured of was before the rest of the antiwar movement in New York was awake. I learned to get out of bed and to use waking to move toward work.

Without the pressure on me now to work before friends are stirring, I need not rush to the typewriter but I preserve my attention. I always do some exercises in the morning and I take a morning bath. All of that routine I use to become thoroughly awake but retain some of the connectedness, some of the rich associativeness of dreaming sleep. I don't want to shed that dark energy of dreams, nor to lose that concentration and involvement in the clutter of the day. I don't think of it quite as self-involvement. I remember when a relationship that had been part of my life for seventeen years was breaking up, I would wake very early after three or four hours sleep and lie in anxiety and pain. Nonetheless by the time I rose through my morning schedule, when I came to the typewriter, I was clear of my immediate anguish and fussing and ready to turn them into work or to write about something entirely different.

I am not saying every writer should get up, eat a good breakfast, take a hot bath and do exercises without talking much to anyone, and then she will write richly. I am trying to say that you must learn how to prepare in a daily way for the combination of concentration and receptivity, a clearing that is also going down into yourself and also putting antennae out. One thing I cannot do and work well is worry about something in my life. If I sit at the typewriter fussing about where the money to pay the real estate taxes is coming from or whether my lover loves me more or less today, whether I am spending too much money on oil this winter, whether the decision taken at the MORAL meeting was correct, I will not find my concentration. I can carry emotions to my typewriter but I must be ready to use and transmute them. They must already be a little apart. It is not exactly emotion recollected in tranquility I mean, although for twenty-five years I have contemplated that phrase with increasing respect. I often feel the emotion but with less ego, less anxiety than in ordinary life. The emotion—the pain, the regret, the anger, the pleasure—is becoming energy. I suppose whenever I find my life too much more fascinating than work, I work less and write less well. I certainly write fiction poorly in these stretches. I produce some poems, often decent ones, but my output is down.

Such periods are not frequent because I love to write more than almost anything—not essays, to be honest, but poems and novels. I am still writing in letters to friends this week that I am immensely relieved that I have finally shipped off my novel *Braided Lives* to my publisher in its last draft. I do in fact feel as if an elephant had risen daintily from its perch on my chest and ambled away. Free, free at last, oh free! Of course it will return soon enough all penciled over with the comments of some copyeditor enamored of commas and semicolons ("Fuck all that shit; we're not going anyplace," is a typical copyeditor improvement). Comes back again as galleys. But essentially it is gone, finished.

Then yesterday afternoon Woody and I were chatting about the next novel I am planning to start as soon as I put this volume together and finish the next volume of poetry. Say, December? It is June now. He made a suggestion as I was mulling over something about the novel and I fell on it immediately and began chewing it, worrying it. It was just right. In the evening in the car on the way to see a movie two towns away, we began chatting again about my next novel until I shrieked that we must stop it, because I cannot get to it before December.

I try to put on with other writers how much I suffer at this excruciating martyrdom and all that posing we are expected to do, but the simple truth is I love to write and I think it an enormous con that I actually get paid for doing it. After all I did it for ten years without pay.

Find out when you work best and arrange the days that you have to write or the hours you have, to channel yourself into full concentration. If like Sylvia Plath you have only from 4:00 A.M. till the babies wake, if you have only from 6:00 A.M. till 9:00 A.M. as I did in New York, if you have only weekends or only Sundays or only afternoons from 3:30 to 5:30, you have to figure out the funnel that works for you: the set of habitual acts that shuts out distractions and ego noise, shuts out your household, your family, and brings you quickly to the state of prime concentration.

Whatever habits you develop as a writer, your ability to work cannot depend on them. I went from writing late afternoons and evenings to writing mornings because that was the only time I could be sure of. I used to smoke all the time I wrote. I imagined I could not write without the smoke of a cigarette curling around me. Then my lungs gave out. I had to die or learn to live without smoking. Given that choice I abandoned smoking rather fast. I can't say my productivity was amazing the couple of years afterwards, but that was mostly because I had chronic bronchitis and it was a while before I was not sick at least fifty percent of the time with too high a fever to work. I have had to give up alcohol at times and to give up coffee, my keenest addiction of all, for periods, and work goes on whatever I am giving up so long as I have enough strength to make it to the typewriter and sit there.

You may permit yourself any indulgence to get going, so long as you can have it: Cuban cigars, a toke of the best weed, Grandma Hogfat's Pismire Tea, a smelly old jacket: but you have to be able to figure out just what is ritual and what is necessity. I really need silence and to be let alone during the first draft. I like having a typewriter but can produce a first draft of poetry without it; I cannot write prose without a typewriter as I write too slowly by hand. My handwriting is barely legible to me. All the other props are ritual. I have my sacred socks, my window of tree, my edge-notched card memory annex, my bird fetish necklace hanging over the typewriter, my Olympia standard powered by hand, my reference works on nearby shelves, my cats coming and going, my good coffee downstairs where I am forced to go and straighten my back on the hour as I should. But I have written in vastly less comfort and doubtless will do so again. Don't talk yourself into needing a corklined room, although if someone gives it to you, fine. Do ask the price.

For many years I felt an intense and negotiable gratitude to my second husband because while I had supported myself from age eighteen and was doing part-time jobs, at a certain point he offered me five years without having to work at shit jobs to establish myself as a writer. I took the offer and by the end of five years was making a decent in-come—decent by my standards, compared to what I earned as part-time secretary, artist's model, telephone operator, store clerk and so on.

Not until I was putting this volume together and looking at my own output over the years since I began writing poetry seriously and began my first (dreadful) novel at fifteen, did I ever realize that I was less productive during those years of being supported than before or since. Women have to be very cautious with gift horses. We feel guilty. Traditional roles press us back and down. When I stayed home I was a writer in my eyes but a housewife in the world's and largely in my husband's view. Why wasn't the floor polished? What had I been doing all day?

I began to write at a decent clip again not during those two years of traditional wifehood in Brookline but in New York when I was passionately involved in the antiwar movement and working as an organizer at least six hours a day and sometimes twelve.

I am not saying we work best if we use up a lot of our lives doing other work. Some poets do; few prose writers do. It depends on the type of other work in part; I think the less that other work has to do with writing, with writers, with words, the better. I understand the temptation young writers have to take jobs associated with writing. That may be the only affirmation that you are a writer available in the often many years before publication certifies your occupation to the people around you. I don't think I could have resisted writer's residencies if they had been available when I was un- or underpublished. In an ideal world for writers we would be paid while apprenticing at some minimum wage and then encouraged to do something entirely different part-time, in work parties digging sewers or putting in gardens or taking care of the dying, at a reasonable wage.

What I am saying is that the choice may be offered to a woman to stay home (where it is much, much nicer than going out to a lousy job) and write because the amount she can earn as a part-time female worker is negligible from the viewpoint of a professional or skilled male wage earner. The offer can help but it also can hinder. You may find yourself doing a full-time job instead without pay and writing in the interstices—just as before except that you may have even less time that is really yours and you have lost your independent base of income.

Similarly a job teaching can be wonderful because it answers the questions, what do you do? If you get hired as a writer after you have published, say, five short stories, you have sudden legitimacy. If you started in workshops and got an MFA, you have more legitimacy. You have items to add to your resume. Of course once you have taken the teaching job, you may have little time to write, especially given the way the academic marketplace is a buyer's market and teaching loads are getting heavier. You're certified a writer, you deal professionally with literature and words,

you make better money and are more respectable in middle-class society, but you have less time and energy to put into your own writing than you would if you worked as a waiter or secretary.

Actually sitting and writing novel after novel before one gets accepted at last the way fiction writers usually must do, or actually working and working on poems till they're right when hardly anybody publishes them and when they do you're read by two librarians, three editors, and six other poets, gives you little to put in your resume. We all make it as we can, and I do a lot of gigs. Unless writers are of draftable age, we are seldom offered money to do something overtly bad like kill somebody or blow up hospitals or burn villages, seldom paid to invent nerve gases or program data bases for the CIA. The jobs available to us range from the therapeutic to the mildly helpful to the pure bullshit to the menial and tedious; all of them sometimes prevent us from writing and sometimes enable us to write. Jobs that have nothing to do with writing often provide more stimulation to the gnome inside who starts poems than jobs that involve teaching writing or writing copy.

When I am trying to get going and find myself empty, often the problem is that I desire to write a poem rather than one specific poem. That is the case sometimes when I have been working eight hours a day finishing up a novel and have not had the time to write poems or the mental space that allows them to begin forming. That is when the writer's notebook or whatever equivalent you use (my own memory annex is on edge-notched cards) can if it is well-organized disgorge those tidbits put in it. I think of those jottings as matches, the images, the poem ideas, the lines that wait resurrection. Often lines that were cut from other poems will in time serve as the instigation for their own proper home. For me the absolute best way to get going is to resort to my memory annex. That summons the Muse, my own muse for sure.

The notion of a muse is less archaic than a lot of vintage mythology because most poets have probably experienced being picked up by the nape of the neck, shaken, and dumped again miles from where your daily life or ordinary preoccupations could have been expected to bring you. *Duende,* Lorca called that possession. Poems that come down like Moses from the mountaintop, that bore their way through my mind, are not better or worse than poems I labor on for two days, two months, or fifteen years. Nonetheless I always remember which ones arrived that way. Sometimes in writing I experience myself as other. Not in the sense of the "I" as social artifact, the other that strangers or intimates see; the mask the camera catches off guard. When we see ourselves videotaped, often we experience a sense of nakedness and say, "so that is what I am really like," as if the exterior because we usually cannot see it is therefore the truth of our lives. Nor do I mean the artifact we construct, the "I" writers perhaps more than most people make up out of parts of ourselves and parts of our books, as camouflage and advertisement.

What I mean is simply that in writing the poet sometimes transcends the daily self into something clearer. I have often had the experience of looking up from the typewriter, the page, and feeling complete blankness about who I am—the minutia of my daily life, where I am, why. I have for a moment no sex, no history, no character. Past a certain point I will not hear the phone. I respect that self, that artisan who feels empty of personal concern even when dealing with the stuff of my intimate life. I guess the only time I am ever free of the buzz of self-concern and the sometimes interesting, often boring reflection of consciousness on itself, is during moments when I am writing and moments when I am making love. I overvalue both activities because of the refreshment of quieting the skull to pure attention.

That to me is ecstasy, rapture—being seized as if by a raptor, the eagle in **"The Rose and the Eagle"**—the loss of the buzz of ego in the intense and joyous contemplation of something, whether a lover, a sensation, the energy, the image, the artifact. The ability to move into the state I called concentration is a needful preliminary to, in the first and commonest case, the work that you gradually build, or in the second and rarer case, the visit from necessity, the poems that fall through you entire and burning like a meteorite.

In a society that values the ability to see visions, such as some of the Plains Indians did, many people will manage to crank out a few visions at least at critical moments in their lives; very few people will not manage a vision at least once. Some will become virtuosos of vision.

In a society where seeing visions is usually punished by imprisonment, torture with electroshock, heavy drugging that destroys coordination and shortens life expectancy, very few people will see visions. Some of those who do so occasionally will learn early on to keep their mouths shut, respect the visions, use them but keep quiet about seeing or hearing what other people say is not there. A few of my poems are founded in specific visions: "Curse of the earth magician on a metal land" which also was the seed of *Dance the Eagle to Sleep;* "The sun" from the Tarot card sequence "Laying down the tower," which was the seed of *Woman on the Edge of Time.*

That a poem is visionary in inception does not mean it comes entire. Actually writing a poem or any other artifact out of a vision is often a great deal of work. The hinge poem, for the month of Beth in **The Lunar Cycle,** called **"At the well"** was a case in point. I first wrote a version of that experience in 1959, when it happened. Here I am finally being able to bring off the poem that is faithful to it in 1979.

To me, no particular value attaches to the genesis of a poem. I am not embarrassed by the sense I have at times of being a conduit through which a poem forces itself and I am not embarrassed by working as long as it takes to build a poem—in the case I just mentioned, twenty years.

I write poems for specific occasions, viewing myself as a useful artisan. I have written poems for antiwar rallies, for women's day rallies, for rallies centering on the rights and abuses of mental institution inmates. I have written poems to raise money for the legal defense of political prisoners, for Inez Garcia, who shot the man who raped her, for Shoshana Rihm-Pat Swinton, for many years a political fugitive and finally acquitted of all charges. I wrote a poem for a poster to raise money for Transition House (a shelter for battered women) along with a beautiful graphic by Betsy Warrior, a warrior for women indeed. I wrote a poem to be presented to the Vietnamese, delegation at Montreal, during meetings with antiwar activists.

Some of those occasional poems (as some of the category that arrive like a fast train) are among my best poems; some are mediocre. Frequently I find the necessity to write a poem for a specific purpose or occasion focuses me; perhaps coalesces is a better verb. A charged rod enters the colloidal substance of my consciousness and particles begin to adhere. **"For Shoshana-Pat Swinton"** is a meditation on feeling oneself active in history that I consider a very strong poem, for instance. I was, of course, to deal with the figure of the political fugitive as a paradigm of certain women's experiences as well as a touchstone for our recent political history in *Vida*; that swirl of ideas and images was obiously rich for me. What doesn't touch you, you can't make poems of.

One last thing I have learned about starting a poem is that if you manage to write down a certain amount when you begin, and failing that, to memorize enough, you will not lose it. If you cannot memorize or scribble that essential sufficient fragment, the poem will dissolve. Sometimes a couple of lines are ample to preserve the impulse till you can give it your full attention. Often it is a started first draft, maybe what will become eventually the first third of the poem, that I carry to my typewriter. But if I can't memorize and record that seed, that match, the instigating factor, then I have lost that particular poem.

Good work habits are nothing more than habits that let you work, that encourage you to pay attention. Focus is most of it: to be fierce and pointed, so that everything else momentarily sloughs away.

## Marge Piercy (essay date 1982)

SOURCE: "Revision in Action: Chipping and Building," in *Parti-Colored Blocks for a Quilt*, The University of Michigan Press, 1982, pp. 79-98.

[*In the following essay, Piercy explicates the final stages of her creative process, in particular how she revises and finishes her poems.*]

I have put together three accounts of the process of writing through various drafts toward the finished poems. Each of these brief descriptions includes the various drafts of the poem I was working on. Each process offers a somewhat different route between onslaught and finished product, with differing problems to solve en route.

HOW "BECOMING NEW" BECAME

**"Becoming new"** started as a rambling love lyric of no particular distinction in first draft. Not atypically, however, for the type of poem revised by cutting as much as by rewriting, most of the imagery of which the later poem would be built was present in the wordy original. Some poems I work on from a stark beginning into more elaboration and development. Some poems, like this one, need pruning to reach a shape.

**"How it feels to be touching you"**

> An Io moth, orange
> and yellow as butter
> winging through the night
> miles to mate
> crumbling in the hand to dust
> hardly smearing the wall.
> It feels like a brick
> square and sturdy and pleasing
> to the eye and hand
> ready to be used
> to build something
> I can keep warm in
> keep tools in
> walk on.
> Hardy as an onion and layered.
> Going into the blood like garlic
> secretly antibiotic.
> Sour as rose hips.
> Gritty as whole grains.
> Sweet and fragrant as thyme honey.
> Scarce as love,
> my dear, what we have started.
> Its substance goes out between us
> like a hair
> that any weight could break,
> like a morning web shining.
> It flares into pockets of meeting,
> dark pools of touch.
> What does it mean to me?
> What does it mean to you?
> We are meaning together.
> We become new selves in private.
> When I am turning slowly
> in our woven hammocks of talk
> when I am melting like chocolate
> our bodies glued together
> I taste myself quite new
> I smell like a book
> just off the press
> You smell like hot bread.
> Though I seem to be standing still
> I am flying flying flying
> in the trees of your eyes.

By the next version, still with the same title, the poem begins to assume a little shape. It is in paragraphs now, centered each around the imagery. I cut some of the wordier

sections but I am still adrift, not yet focussed on what in the experience or the blob of the poem is interesting. The ending is the one that will stay through all versions of the poem. These first two versions were done in rapid succession.

**"How it feels to be touching you"**

> An Io moth, orange
> and yellow as butter
> wings through the night
> miles to mate,
> crumbles in the hand to dust
> hardly smearing the wall.
>
> We feel like a brick
> square and sturdy and pleasing
> to the eye and hand
> ready to be used
> to build something
> I can keep warm in
> keep tools in
> walk on.
>
> Hardy as an onion and layered.
> Going into the blood like garlic
> pungent and antibiotic.
> Sour as rose hips.
> Gritty as whole grains.
> Sweet and fragrant as thyme honey.
> Its substance goes out between us
> like a hair
> that any weight could break,
> like a morning web shining.
> It flares into pockets of meeting,
> dark pools of touch.
>
> We are meaning together.
> When I am turning slowly
> in the woven hammocks of our talk
> when I am melting like chocolate
> our bodies glued together
> I taste myself quite new
> I smell like a book
> just off the press
> You smell like hot bread.
> Though I seem to be standing still
> I am flying flying flying
> in the trees of your eyes.

At that point I put the poem aside for a while. When I took it out again, I decided that what is interesting is that the two people were friends who have become lovers while still being friends. The wonder of the friend developing the charisma and magic that a lover possesses while still being the same friend is the focus of the poem. The imagery that stresses the strength and dailiness in terms of bricks, buildings, tools disappears, as being irrelevant to the revelation of sensuous pleasure. I realized as I returned to the poem and began to shape it, to focus it, that the sensuality was important to the poem and equally important was leaving the sexes ambiguous. The poem had begun as one about a man with whom in the course of a long friendship, I had a three-week sexual involvement; but by the time I returned to work on it, the piece seemed to me more about friendships between women that become love relationships. Then I realized I wanted to make the poem truly and carefully androgynous (a word I am not fond of) because friendship is.

The hair imagery disappeared when I realized I was using the same metaphor in another poem of about the same vintage—**"Bridging,"** also contained in *To Be of Use*—where the imagery is far more relevant to a completely different theme. The associations of smelling like a book just off the press seemed inappropriate to the new focus, and the hot bread image seemed trite, so they were lopped off, replaced by a simple statement of the theme. The first stanza remained the same.

### "Something borrowed"

How it feels to be touching
you: an Io moth, orange
and yellow as butter
wings through the night
miles to mate,
crumbles in the hand
hardly smears the wall.

Yet our meaning together
is hardy as an onion
and layered.
Going into the blood like garlic,
pungent and antibiotic.
Sour as rose hips.
Gritty as whole grain.
Sweet and fragrant as thyme honey:
this substance goes out between us
a morning web shining.

When I am turning slowly
in the woven hammocks of our talk,
when I am melting like chocolate
our bodies glued together
I taste myself quite new
in your mouth.

You are not my old friend.
How did I used to sit
and look at you?
Though I seem to be standing still
I am flying flying flying
in the trees of your eyes.

In the next version, published in *To Be of Use* and anthologized, the title settled into **"We become new."** In fact there is an anthology named for this poem: *We Become New,* edited by Lucille Iverson and Kathryn Ruby (New York: Bantam Books, 1975). This title emphasized what I had fixed on as the core of the poem. There are many routes into poems. Sometimes when I launch into a poem, I know exactly where I'm going, although it may take me one or many drafts to fix that vision in words. Sometimes, as in this poem, the basic imagery is there but I don't know quite what I'm getting at for a while. I have to hack away at it until I perceive what it is I'm trying to say,

even in a case this simple. The discovery of the secret sensuality or the repressed sexuality in a friendship either between women or between a man and a woman is a common experience that makes this poem interesting to a number of people, who have mentioned it to me, or written me about it. We tend to see people with whom we make love as more luminous, more radiantly physical than those with whom we haven't been as intimate. In the case of someone we have known for a long time or perhaps even worked with, we had thought we knew her or him quite well. We feel dazzled with the change of perception love-making brings.

The morning web shining I liked, but somehow it didn't fit. It wasn't exactly a web I was dealing with—not a couple formation. Furthermore, I had noticed a strong oral component in the imagery, especially after the first stanza, and I like that and wished to concentrate on it. The moth smeared on the wall also disappeared. What does crushing a moth have to do with sensuality unless you're being a little weirder than I intended? I decided the image was peculiar and distracting.

The two changes I like best occur in the third stanza, where the chocolate image finally comes into its own, and where what is experienced new when the perimeters of the relationship change, is "everything" rather than "myself." In that small context, I like the large claim.

### "We become new"

How it feels to be touching
you: an Io moth, orange
and yellow as pollen,
wings through the night
miles to mate,
could crumble in the hand.

Yet our meaning together
is hardy as an onion
and layered.
Goes into the blood like garlic.
Sour as rose hips.
Gritty as whole grain.
Fragrant as thyme honey.

When I am turning slowly
in the woven hammocks of our talk,
when I am chocolate melting into you,
I taste everything new
in your mouth.

You are not my old friend.
How did I used to sit
and look at you? Now
though I seem to be standing still
I am flying flying flying
in the trees of your eyes.

When I included this poem, finally, in my selected poems (*Circles on the Water* [1982]), the only change I made was to move the last line of stanza two down to become the first line of stanza three. That brought the poem into regular six line stanzas. Although I talk a lot about the ear being primary, that is one of the occasional changes made primarily for the eyes. I liked the look on the page better.

### THE EVOLUTION OF "ROUGH TIMES"

**"Rough times"** is a poem that began with a rather prosy fragment:

> Those who speak of good and simple
> in the same mouthful
> who say good and innocent
> inhabit some other universe than I struggle through
>
> I find it hard to be good
> and the good hard: hard to know
> hard to choose when known
> and hard to accomplish when chosen:
> rocky, sprace and
>
> good makes my hands bleed,
> good keeps me awake with fear, lying on broken
> shards
> good pickles me in the vinegar of guilt
> good goads me with burrs in my underwear

I have no idea whatsoever about the meaning of "rocky, sprace and." However, this note was a sufficient fragment to launch the poem, not immediately I think. The above jottings were an idea for a poem which remained dormant for a while—in this case I think a matter of weeks. The fragment arose from my irritation with the presumption that good is simple or clear, that ethics and matters of right and wrong are as automatic to decide as calling up the time by dialing N-E-R-V-O-U-S on the telephone and resetting your watch for accuracy. If you do not accept the prevailing patriarchal standards of right and wrong, then you have to hammer out your own ethics at the same time that you try to change yourself to adhere to your values.

A short time—weeks—later, I wrote a true first draft. The first stanza is one that will remain through all subsequent drafts, but after that, I had a lot more trouble. This version remains fairly prosy although some of the imagery about two thirds of the way through is strong enough to stay the route. Finally this version simply trails off. I could find no completion to my complaint.

> Trying to live
> as if we were an experiment
> conducted by the future.
>
> Tearing down the walls of cells
> when nothing has been evolved
> to replace that protection.
>
> A prolonged vivisection
> of my own tissues, carried out
> under the barking muzzle of guns.
>
> Those who speak of good and simple
> in the same mouthful of tongue and teeth

> inhabit some other universe
> than I trundle my bag of bones through.
>
> . . .
>
> I find it hard to know what's good,
> hard to choose when known,
> hard to accomplish it when chosen,
> hard to repeat it when blundered through.
>
> . . .
>
> Good runs the locomotive of the night over my bed/
> chest
> good pickles me in the vinegar of guilt
> good robs the easy words as they rattle over my teeth
> and leave me naked as an egg.
>
> Some love comfort and some pleasure;
> perhaps of the good, the beautiful and the true
> each person can crave
>
> We are tools who carve ourselves

You can see here two of the stanzas evolving as I work. I was playing with crave/carve at the end but the playing came to nothing.

The next draft still has no title. The beginning three line stanzas are slowly taking shape. Finally, I have an ending; I see where the poem is going. Basically, the verb "evolve" in the second stanza had hidden inside it my ending.

Evolution is a concept with a marked place in my poetry, forming an important element in poems such as **"For Shoshana-Pat Swinton"** about taking an active role in history; **"Two higher mammals"** about trying to change from what I mistakenly believed then about human prehistory as predators, for I hadn't yet read Richard Leakey or Elizabeth Fisher; **"For Walter and Lilian Lowenfels"** about trying to grasp one's own time; **"The perpetual migration"** from *The Lunar Cycle,* that compares us to seabirds and views our whole prehistory and history in terms of social evolution; and the recent poem **"Let us gather at the river."**

The poem is still shapeless and wordy, but it begins to acquire a direction and a consciousness of its intent.

> We are trying to live
> as if we were an experiment
> conducted by the future,
>
> bulldozing / bombing / blasting
> Blasting the walls of the cells
> that nothing has yet
> been evolved to replace.
>
> A prolonged vivisection
> on my own tissues, carried out
> under the barking muzzle of guns.
>
> Those who speak of the good and simple
> in the same mouthful of tongue and teeth / in the same

    sandwich
inhabit some other universe
than I trundle my bag of bones through.

I find it hard to know what's good,
hard to choose when known,
hard to accomplish when chosen,
hard to repeat when blundered into.

Good draws blood from my scalp and the roots of my
nerves.
Good runs the locomotive of the night over my bed.
Good pickles me in the brown vinegar of guilt.
Good robs the easy words as they rattle off my teeth
and leaves me naked as an egg.

We are tools who carve ourselves,
blind hands righting each other,
usually wrong.

Remember that pregnancy is beautiful only
to those who don't look closely
at the distended belly, waterlogged legs, squashed
bladder
clumsily she lumbers and wades, who is about
to give birth.

No new idea is seldom borne on the halfshell
attended by graces.
More commonly it's modeled of baling wire and acne.
More commonly it wheezes and tips over.
Most mutants die; the minority refract
the race through the prisms of their genes.

How ugly were the first fish with air sacs
as they hauled up on the muddy flats
heaving and gasping. How clumsy we are in this huge
air
we reach with such effort
and can not yet breathe.

I think the association of Venus with the lungfishes is that they are both born from the ocean, with tremendous novelty. And like Lucretius, I associate Venus with the energy in nature. That's what the as yet unnamed reference to her is doing here.

Finally comes the version printed in *Living in the Open.* The poem now has a title taken from a periodical called *Rough Times,* where the poem was first published. *Rough Times* was the second incarnation of the collectively edited periodical known, in order, as *Journal of Radical Therapy, Rough Times, Radical Therapist,* and finally *State and Mind.* I named the poem for a magazine that made a genuine and prolonged effort to connect the personal and the political with fairness to both, that recognized the problems of attempting to live in new ways, that dealt with the bruises and abrasions of living in a brutal, racist, and deeply hierarchical society but also dealt consistently with the casualties of trying to change that society. The whole collective at *Rough Times* was extremely helpful when I was researching mental institutions, psychosurgery, and electrode implantation for *Woman on the Edge of Time.*

The poem in this final version has also acquired a dedication to Nancy Henley, now head of women's studies at UCLA. At that time Nancy was living in the Boston area and we saw each other frequently. We are friends equally fascinated through our different disciplines by the personal and the political dimensions of the psychology of every day life—how men and women and people with different positions in the social hierarchy and different amounts of power address each other, touch each other, question or confront each other. When I was writing *Small Changes* and Nancy was writing *He Says/She Says,* we often exchanged observations.

Nancy Henley is a rare dear person, a passionately committed feminist with a strong sense of economic issues, a woman who deals with the theory of social change and also with the practical consequences, who has always taken on far more than her share of the daily work of change— the unglamorous equivalent of taking out the garbage in committee work—as well as writing, speaking, and always thinking clearly and well. I know how hard her life and her choices have been at times, so I dedicated the poem to her.

I had by this version decided on a combination of three line and five line stanzas. The "yard engine" was a better metaphor than in earlier versions, for I remember in childhood watching yard engines shuttle back and forth, back and forth. The extended description of the ninth month of pregnancy has been reduced to one line. The reference to Botticelli's Venus is more explicit and reduced in length.

One of the technical aspects of the poem that picked up the most as the drafts went on is the matter of line breaks. Note the difference between the rather flat:

> Most mutants die; the minority refract
> the race through the prisms of their genes.

and the less obvious, far more potent setting off of the image:

> Most mutants die; only
> a minority refract the race
> through the prisms of their genes.

The tools who carve each other have dropped out entirely, as that image didn't belong to the rest of the poem once I had found my predominant biological metaphors. The vivisection image came early and I still like it, reflecting as it does the pain attendant upon trying to live as if you were changed while trying to change the society.

One of the reasons I worked on the poem after its rather unpromising beginning was a sense that such a subject is difficult to tackle in a lyric but also important. A great many people try to live ethically with a sense of wanting to move toward a better future; but I have seen little in the poetry of our time that alludes to that not uncommon activity. I changed the parallel sentence structure in the last stanza because I wanted to emphasize our clumsiness rather than to emphasize equally the ugliness of the lung-fish. I also had used the rhetorical device of initial repetitions earlier in the poem in two places: the four lines in the fifth stanza that begin with "Good" followed by a verb, and the last two lines of the sixth stanza, which both begin "More commonly it." I liked the first two instances of initial repetition much better than the third usage.

I think the final strength of the poem lies in the increasingly concrete language and images and the hard-working vivid verbs. Thus while the poem is about a fairly abstract idea, it is not an abstract poem.

### "Rough times"

*—for Nancy Henley*

We are trying to live
as if we were an experiment
conducted by the future,

blasting cell walls
that no protective seal or inhibition
has evolved to replace.

I am conducting a slow vivisection
on my own tissues, carried out
under the barking muzzle of guns.

Those who speak of good and simple
in the same sandwich of tongue and teeth
inhabit some other universe.

Good draws blood from my scalp and files my nerves.
Good runs the yard engine of the night over my bed.
Good pickles me in the brown vinegar of guilt.
Good robs the easy words as they rattle off my teeth,
leaving me naked as an egg.

Remember that pregnancy is beautiful only
at a distance from the distended belly.
A new idea rarely is born like Venus attended by
graces.
More commonly it's modeled of baling wire and acne.
More commonly it wheezes and tips over.

Must mutants die: only
a minority refract the race
through the prisms of their genes.

Those slimy fish with air sacs were ugly
as they hauled up on the mud flats
heaving and gasping. How clumsy we are
in this new air we reach with such effort
and cannot yet breathe.

### Genesis of "The Sun"

The scheme of the Tarot poems, the eleven cards of a Tarot reading, was worked out before I began the first of the poems. I no longer have any memory of in what order I first wrote the poems, but the earliest fragment of **"The Sun"** I have extant dates from the scheme of the whole. On a piece of paper I have listed the cards I planned to work with—not even the final list, for in the notes on that

piece of graph paper, three of the cards are different from those I actually wrote about. Next to the sun I have written:

> us into the new world
> concrete images of liberation
> from the garden outward
> naked on a horse that is not bridled
> androgynous child

The first draft of the poem I can find begins with the image on the deck I was using created by Pamela Colman Smith and Arthur Edward Waite, as do all subsequent versions of the poem. That description comprises about a third of this draft.

From that point on, in the last two-thirds of the poem, I was describing a particular vision, also the seed of *Woman on the Edge of Time,* which did emerge from meditation on this particular card when I was preparing to write the Tarot poems. Some of the cards I was able to penetrate immediately and got a fast fix on what in their imagery and their symbols I wanted to use and how I wanted to treat them; others of the cards resisted my comprehension (beyond the obvious, I mean). **"The Sun"** was a resistant one until it came blindingly.

Thus the structure of this particular poem was set a priori: beginning with the card and then proceeding to an attempt to embody what I had imagined. Even the image of the sunrise that ends the poem in all versions was a given, being obvious in the card and given in the vision. The struggle with the different versions is almost entirely a struggle of cleaner, stronger language and better rhythms. I was committed to a fairly long line in all the Tarot poems.

### "The Total Influence or Outcome: The Sun"

Androgynous child whose hair curls into flowers,
naked you ride the horse, without saddle or bridle,
naked too between your thighs, from the walled garden
　　outward.
Coarse sunflowers of desire, whose seeds the birds
and I eat
which they break on their beaks and I with my teeth,
nod upon your journey: child of the morning
whose sun can only be born red from us who strain to
give
　　birth.
Joy to the world, joy, and the daughters of the sun
will dance
Grow into your horse, child: let there be no more riders and
　　ridden.
Learn his strong thighs and teach him your good brain.
A horse running in a field yanks the throat open like a
bell
swinging with joy, you will run too and work and till
and
　　make good.
Child, where are you headed, with your arms spread

wide,
as a shore, have I been there, have I seen it shining
like oranges among their waxy leaves on a morning
tree?
I do not know your dances, I cannot translate your
tongue
into words of my own, your pleasures are strange to
me
as the rites of bees: yet you are the golden flowers
of a melon vine, that grows out of my belly
up where I cannot see any more in the full strong sun.
My eyes cannot make out those shapes of children
like burning clouds
who are not what we are: they go barefoot on the land
like
    savages,
they have computers as household pets, they are six or
seven
    sexes
and all one sex, they do not own or lease or control:
they are of one body and they are private as shamans
learning their magic at the teats of stones.
They are all magicians and do not any more forget
their
    birthright of self
dancing in and out through the gates of the body standing
    wide.
Like a bear lumbering and clumsy and speaking no
tongue
they know, I waddle into the fields of their play.
We are not the future, we are stunted slaves mumbling
over
the tales of dragons our masters tell us, but we will be
free
and you children will be free of us and uncomprehending
as we are of those shufflers in caves who scraped for
fire
and banded together at last to hunt the saber-toothed
tiger,
the mastodon with its tusks, the giant cave bear,
the predators that had penned them up in the dark,
cowering
    so long.
The sun is rising, look, it is the sun.
I cannot look on its face, the brightness blinds me,
but from my own shadow becoming distinct, I know
that now at last it is growing light.

In the next draft I have preserved, the poem has assumed verse paragraphs and has been cut somewhat. There are many small omissions and small developments, but not enough difference for me to feel it is worth quoting in its entirety. The image of the melon vine came out of an old woodcut I had seen, medieval I believe, where Abraham sees all his descendants growing up out of his prostrate body.

However, I do feel it's worth quoting the third draft.

### "The Total Influence or Outcome of the Matter: The Sun"

Androgynous child whose hair curls into flowers,

naked you ride the horse without saddle or bridle
easy between your thighs, from the walled garden outward.

Coarse sunflowers of desire whose seeds birds crack
open
nod upon your journey, child of the morning whose
sun
can only be born bloody from us who strain to give
birth

Joy to the world, joy, and the daughters of the sun
will dance
like motes of pollen in the summer air
Grow into your horse, child: let there be no more riders and
    ridden.

Child, where are you heading with arms spread wide
as a shore, have I been there, have I seen that land
shining
as oranges do among their waxy leaves on a morning
tree?
I do not know your dances, I cannot translate your
tongue
to words of my own, your pleasures are strange to me
as the rites of bees; yet you are the yellow flower
of a melon vine growing out of my belly
though it climbs up where I cannot see in the strong
sun.

My eyes cannot decipher those shapes of children like
burning clouds
who are not what we are: they go barefoot like sav-
ages,
they have computers as household pets; they are six
or seven
    sexes
and only one sex; they do not own or lease or control.
They are of one body and of tribes. They are private
as
    shamans
learning each her own magic at the teats of stones.
They are all magicians and technicians
and do not any more forget their birthright of self
dancing in and out through the gates of the body standing
    wide.

A bear lumbering I waddle into the fields of their
play.
We are stunted slaves mumbling over the tales
of dragons our masters tell us, but we will be free.
Our children will be free of us uncomprehending
as are we of those shufflers in caves who scraped for
fire
and banded together at last to hunt the saber-toothed
tiger,
the tusked mastodon, the giant cave bear,
predators that had penned them up, cowering so long.

The sun is rising, look: it is blooming new.
I cannot look in the sun's face, its brightness blinds
me
but from my own shadow becoming distinct I know
that now at last it is beginning to grow light.

Here the second paragraph has become quite short. The extended development of the horse has been lopped back to one line. In the fourth paragraph the children of the future have become not merely magicians but magicians and technicians, a not particularly felicitous phrase. The "gates of the body" I associate with Blake, some amalgam of his "The doors of perception" with "Twelve gates to the City," a song I recall from civil rights days.

I am still having trouble with the image and words of the last paragraph. I am aware as I write it of Plato's cave. I am still having trouble with the line breaks and the phrasing of the words themselves.

The final version of the poem makes many small changes: in the second line, "the horse" becomes "a horse" in keeping with its diminished importance while the second paragraph has been assimilated into the first. I have finally realized that it is not the future sun that ought to be bleeding but the mother giving birth, and fixed that.

In the second verse paragraph, the replacement of "to words of my own" with "to words I use" is a matter of rhythm. The image of the oranges among their leaves on that tree has finally gone—it never quite took or worked—and been replaced by a far more appropriate image "like sun spangles on clean water rippling," a line superior in its rhythm by far. The sun entering that line meant I had to change the last line of the stanza, where to avoid repetition "strong sun" became "strong light," a more accurate word in that context.

The children have stopped being "like" burning clouds and that has become an alternate way to see them. There are many small cuts there, "seven sexes" for "six or seven sexes"—I was thinking of paramecia. "The teats of stones" has become "the teats of stones and trees" because I wanted a longer line and because that seemed to me more evocative of the kind of earth reverence I was trying to bring to mind. Finally it is "technicians and peasants" they become. "Magic" has already appeared and what I wanted was the connection to the basic means of production, agriculture, the commitment to the land insisted on, along with the full use of science. Finally instead of only a "birthright of self" it is that plus "their mane of animal pride" they do not forget. I wanted to describe a people sensual, proudly physical, connected to other living beings and the earth, who were also highly civilized in the best sense.

"The fields of their play" has become "the fields of their work games" because I wanted to emphasize their productivity and did not want them to sound trivial or infantile.

I finally got the ending together. That changing smell of the air at dawn is something I have often noticed in the country. I also got the line breaks functional at last in the ending.

> The sun is rising, feel it: the air smells fresh.
> I cannot look in the sun's face, its brightness blinds

me,
but from my own shadow becoming distinct
I know that now at last
it is beginning to grow light.

When I put this poem in my selected poems (*Circles on the Water* [1982]) I made only one change. I took out the mastodon, as not properly a predator and because it was messing up the line breaks. I broke it as follows:

> and banded together at last to hunt the saber-toothed
> tiger,
> the giant cave bear, predators
> that had penned them up cowering so long.

**Eleanor Bender (essay date 1991)**

SOURCE: "Visions of a Better World: The Poetry of Marge Piercy," in *Ways of Knowing: Essays on Marge Piercy*, edited by Sue Walker and Eugenie Hamner, 1991, pp. 1-14.

[*In the following essay, Bender provides a thematic overview of Piercy's verse.*]

Perhaps more than any other poet of her generation, Marge Piercy is most explicit in confronting the political, social, and economic realities of her time. A poet of conscience, Piercy does not separate her politics from her life, or her life from her poetry. Like Muriel Rukeyser before her, Marge Piercy's poetry is not confessional. Her poems never apologize, suffer from guilt, or dwell on some abstract evil. Piercy is concerned with the work of words. Her images are bold and hard hitting, her language always direct and on target. Her poetry is the result of an examined life, and each new book mirrors her personal growth as she enlarges her vision and evolves as a poet.

While individual poems focus on specific experiences with men, women, and community, Piercy's overall intention is to show how her love of men, her love of women, her love of community are intertwined. Love is how we live in the world and all love is lived in a cultural context in the same way that food is grown, wars are fought, and money is spent. Read chronologically, her first six volumes document Piercy's understanding of what it means to love.

Her first book, *Breaking Camp* (1968), is an anthology of her best early poems. The works that follow are more thematically realized as books. *Breaking Camp* is a workshop collection, the strongest poems of which introduce the political acumen of her later work. **"Visiting a Deadman on a Summer Day"** points to the disparities between the urban rich and the urban poor, the role of capitalism in creating war, the senseless wasting of human potential. While the spirit of the Vietnam War protestors burns through this poem, Piercy also comes to terms with the fact that her own poetry must break through "past structures . . . hiding its iron frame in masonry." In **"Noon of the Sunbather,"** "a woman nude on a rooftop" confirms her right to survive midst an imagery of concrete oppression. The god's breath turns her to ashes "but the ashes dance. Each ashfleck leaps at the sun." The ashflecks represent Piercy's emerging feminism. **"Breaking Camp,"** the title poem that completes this volume, emphasizes the feminist construct that will take hold in succeeding books. In it Piercy declares: "I belong to nothing but my work carried like a prayer rug on my back." Her conviction is that her own work will not be dependent upon the judgment of others. She will be the architect of herself in order to allow her poetry greater freedom of her mind and body.

**"Walking into Love,"** the opening poem for *Hard Loving* (1969), was written when Piercy was around thirty. This poem is about the community she helped to create, first in the antiwar movement and Students for a Democratic Society, and later in the women's movement. In a letter dated June 4, 1980, Piercy writes: "It was a relationship that is not a monogamous relationship. It was a relationship that was political and personal and serious, although not monogamous" (Letter to Eleanor Bender). The poet admits to feeling disoriented and afraid. She realizes she must discard the heavy weight of her past, which consists of:

> a saw, a globe, a dictionary,
> a doll leaking stuffing,
> a bouquet of knitting needles,
> a basin of dried heads.
>
> (*Hard Loving* 11)

With her "saw," she will break open her past and reveal its true contents. The "globe" she carries is the world in need of change, and what Adrienne Rich has called *re-vision*.[1] The "dictionary" contains a language that has defined her. She will turn it into her most useful tool, that of the power of words to establish new definitions. The "doll leaking stuffing" is her childhood, her memory, and a reminder of her own mortality. The "bouquet of knitting needles" is a symbol of what the culture expects from a woman. The "basin of dried heads" holds the authority figures who have discouraged her from making her journey. She has managed to sever those relationships. She continues: "Withered and hard as a spider / I crawl among bones: awful charnel knowledge / of failure, of death, of decay." The poet is well aware that the history of creative women has long been shrouded in images of secrecy, darkness, and insanity. She will not be stopped. Piercy sees herself, and all women, as missing links between the past and the future. Like the web of a spider, her work, her politics, her art, will be spun from her *self*. She will weave this web carefully in order to sustain, nourish, and extend life for herself and others. For those who would "make soup" of her, she will "hide in webs / of mocking voices," allowing her poetry to speak the truth.

Section three of **"Walking into Love,"** which Piercy calls "Meditation in my favorite position," celebrates the fact that she is as much a sexual being as she is an intellectual being. While her mind explores the meaning of life, her body is life: "Words end, / and body goes on / and something / small and wet and real / is exchanged." Physical love reenacts creation. And for Piercy, sex is a way of experiencing being alive that is a source of energy. In section four, the poet voices her resentment of the prejudice that persists against sexual women in "the eyes of others" who "measure and condemn." She sees sexual needs as being as vital to her sense of well-being as nourishing food. But she insists that a woman's bodily appetites equal her responsibilities to the culture as a whole.

**"Walking into Love"** was published at a time when the women's movement was gaining momentum. Adrienne Rich had written of the arrival of the "new" women in her discursive poem "Snapshots of a Daughter-In-Law" (1958-1960). Other brilliant women were writing unsparingly about what it meant to be a woman in the Post-Modernist era. So when Marge Piercy writes in section five of **"Walking into Love"**: "There is a bird in my chest / with wings too broad / with beak that rips me / waiting to get out," she is giving form to her own powerful, creative, sexual self struggling to be born. When this happens, the iron weight of the 1950's—when all women were virgins, and all men heroes and saints—is lifted from her chest: "I open my mouth / to let you out / and your shining blinds me." The "shining" is that of spiritual release. It is blinding only in so far as the poet is new to her own power. When the intensity of this experience eases, the poet sees with a clearer light: "Sometimes, sometimes / I can ask for what I want: / I have begun to trust you." This trust is not arrived at easily. It comes out of a commitment to work through both the external and internal barriers that exist between men and women and between human beings and their culture.

In twenty-three lines, Piercy's poem **"Community"** outlines some of the realism of her experiences with political movements: "Loving feels lonely in a violent world." She lived too close to the failures: "Love is arthritic. Mistrust swells like a prune. / Perhaps we gather so they may dig one big cheap grave." The world is a community, and we must all love as if our lives depended on it because they do:

> We have to build our city, our camp
> from used razorblades and bumpers and aspirin boxes
> in the shadow of the nuclear plant that kills the fish
> with coke bottle lamps flickering
> on the chemical night.
>
> (*Hard Loving* 17)

In Piercy's view it is possible to build a new, stronger community out of the wreckage of the past. She does not advocate a revolution that serves to further destruction. She believes in turning used technology into useful instruments. "Used razorblades and bumpers and aspirin boxes" are the tools of survival for a dispossessed society.

**"The Friend"** is one in a series of poems about the kinds of destructive relationships that undermine the strengths of a community. The man in **"The Friend"** demands of the woman that she cut off her hands and burn her body because it is "not clean and smells like sex." He not only finds her sex threatening, but he sees love itself as a threat to this power. Piercy writes of this poem: "'**The Friend**' is part of a sequence about the friends that aren't friends, neighbors that aren't neighbors, relationships that aren't relationships, community that isn't community" (Letter to Eleanor Bender, 4 June 1980). The poet knows that people are deceived by their own need to be close to others. She addresses this point in **"Simple-Song"**:

> When we are going toward someone we say
> you are just like me
> your thoughts are my brothers and sisters
> word matches word
> how easy to be together.
>
> (*Hard Loving* 35)

Then, after a relationship has ended:

> When we are leaving someone we say
> how strange you are
> we cannot communicate
> we can never agree
> how hard, hard and weary to be together.
>
> (*Hard Loving* 35)

All of her needs cannot be met by one person. She remains open to her needs, and to the needs of others. This is loving: "an act / that cannot outlive / the open hand / the open eye / the door in the chest standing open."

The lovers in *Hard Loving* are experimenting with love, searching for the right partners. **"Becoming Strangers"** describes a state where a love is "There and not there . . . fading into your smoky flesh / to charge out butting." Then he acts as if he doesn't know her, "as if out of bed / if you recognized me / I might charge you something." Passions come more easily than the right partners. Piercy learns to set certain ground rules for love. Starting with **"Loving an Honest Man,"** Piercy insists her relationship with men must add, not subtract from her life:

> So we live with each other: not against
> not over or under or in tangent.
> Secretive in joy and touching, back to back
> sensual taproot feeding deep in the soil
> we face out with hands open and usually bruised,
> crafting messages of lightning in common brick.
>
> (*Hard Loving* 54)

The men she loves will be men who share fully her pleasures and her dreams. **"Loving an Honest Man"** is her way of accepting responsibility for future generations who will "grow out of us who love freedom and each other."

Marge Piercy dedicated her third book of poetry *To Be Of Use* (1973) to the women's movement. **"The Nuisance"** is written in the voice of a woman whose consciousness has been sufficiently raised for her to confront her lover with the totality of her presence in the world:

> I am an inconvenient woman.
> You might trade me in on a sheepdog or a llama.
> You might trade me in for a yak.
> They are faithful and demand only straw.
> They make good overcoats.
> They never call you on the telephone.
>
> (*To Be Of Use* 12)

This woman still finds it necessary to coach her lover's ego. She seems to be trying to take some of the edge off the power of her feelings. But more importantly, she no longer fears her own vulnerability. She recognizes that she has sex drives that cannot be disguised in any other form than what they are, which is to want her lover to want her "as directly and simply and variously / as a cup of hot coffee." Piercy, along with other women poets of her generation, learned to be a sexual challenger: "To want to, to have to, to miss what can't have room to happen. / I carry my love for you / around with me like my teeth / and I am starving." The woman in **"The Nuisance"** is learning to distinguish between what is love, and what is not love. This is a necessary step in discovering how to use love as a source for both individual and collective strength.

**"The Winning Argument"** offers a parable of a more or less traditional male and female relationship. The relationship is centered around the man. When the woman begins to sense that something is lacking in this arrangement, the man accuses her of being insane. In the second stanza, the man decides that sex is "bad for the health," so he throws her "out the door." Finally the woman realizes she is better off risking the dangers of the outside world rather than suffer the slow death of servitude. By the late 1960s, women were prime for this kind of decision because women were beginning to think of their domestic lives in political terms. Piercy understands the issues behind the need for women's equality and warns feminists against a too narrow vision: "If what we change does not change us / we are playing with blocks" (**"A Shadow Play for Guilt"**).

**"The Woman in the Ordinary"** offers this description of a sixties woman: "a yam of a woman of butter and brass, / compounded of acid and sweet like a pineapple, / like a handgrenade set to explode, / like a goldenrod ready to bloom." Piercy's repeated concern is that this "new" woman must come to terms with her responsibility to herself and her community. The title poem, **"To Be of Use,"** is written in praise of work, any productive work, required of these women.

> I want to be with people who submerge
> in the task, who go into the fields to harvest
> and work in a row and pass the bags along,
> who stand in the line and haul in their places,
> who are not parlor generals and field deserters
> but move in a common rhythm
> when the food must come in or the fire be put out.
>
> (*To Be Of Use* 12)

Several of the poems in Marge Piercy's fourth book of poetry, *Living in the Open* (1976), were written around the same time period as *To Be Of Use.* However, *Living in the Open,* published three years later, marks an important shift in the development of Piercy's poetry. Fourteen poems make up the first section, titled "A Particular Place To Be Healed." The "place" is Wellfleet, Massachusetts, on Cape Cod. The poems build a bridge between the hard, grinding toil of her city life and the softer, cleaner, more generous landscape of Wellfleet. The poems of "A Particular Place To Be Healed" also reflect the spiritual and physical renewal made possible through feminism and her success at earning a living as a writer.

The poet explores the relationship between her body and the world of birds, salt marsh, meadow grasses, fiddle crabs, samphire, and sea lavender. She applies the communal philosophy set forth in *To Be Of Use* to gardening and living and working with people she loves and trusts. The landscape becomes her teacher and respect for this teacher allows her ideas about love to take root and grow. Her poems take on a broader, more spiritual composition. The long, sequential poem "Sand Roads" describes her arrival in Wellfleet by car. Each of the first seven sections merges with the next, revealing the poet's awareness of the land's response to human history. The seventh section, "The Development," ends:

> Forgive us, grey fox, our stealing
> your home, our loving
> this land carved into lots
> over a shrinking watertable
> where the long sea wind that blows
> the sand whispers to developers
> money, money, money.

> (*Living in the Open* 28)

In section eight, "The Road Behind the Last Dune" the poet's life is renewed in the presence of the sea:

> Flow out to the ancient cold
> mothering embrace, cold
> and weightless yourself
> as a fish, over the buried
> wrecks. Then with respect
> let the breakers drive you
> up and out into
> the heavy air, your heart
> pounding. The warm scratchy sand
> like a receiving blanket
> holds you up gasping with life.

> (*Living in the Open* 31)

The sea's "mothering embrace" is her future seeking to release the ideas carried within the gravitational pull of her writing. The waves crest with the maturity of her perceptions restoring her to a physical understanding of the earth's history and its future.

Piercy's poetry never loses touch with her childhood in Detroit, Michigan, who she is, how she has chosen to live.

In this work, what will come to be known as the middle period of her poetry, we see her moving beyond the trap doors of past wounds toward a greater freedom of her capacities as a living woman. The title poem, **"Living in the Open,"** is about the possibilities that result from living in multiple relationships with people:

> Can you imagine not having to lie?
> To try to tell what you feel and want
> Till sometimes you can even see
> each other clear and strange
> as a photograph of your hand.

> (*Living in the Open* 46)

Her insistence on the truth is what makes such a private person a public writer. She does not play the part of a mercurial messenger. She is the tough street sister who comes directly to the point:

> We are all hustling and dealing
> as we broil on the iron gates of the city.
> Our minds charred, we collide and veer off.

> Hard and spiny, we taste of DDT.
> We trade each other in.
> Talk is a poker game,
> bed is a marketplace,
> love is a soggy trap.

> (*Living in the Open* 46-47)

Piercy understands that to live on her own terms, without apology, is to be something of an outsider. But to her, competition is fragmenting and uses up energy. If we really love, if we are political, if we are artists, there is no need for "trade-ins or betrayals, / only the slow accretion of community, / hand on hand."

The last stanza can be read as an open love letter to those whom she sees as her true audience, all those who have learned how to "move in common rhythm":

> Help me to be clear and useful.
> Help me to help you.
> You are not my insurance, not my vacation,
> not my romance, not my job, not my garden.
> You wear your own flags and colors and your own
> names.
> I will never have you.
> I am a friend who loves you.

> (*Living in the Open* 48)

Piercy has written a number of richly sensual love poems intrinsic to the structure of her work. While several poems appear to be moments of passion recollected in tranquility, there is usually a political message. **"Unclench Yourself"** expresses in sexual terms the same kind of ideas she articulates in political terms:

> You will find
> that in this river
> we can breathe
> we can breathe

and under water see
small gardens and bright fish
too tender
too tender
for the air.

(*Living in the Open* 59)

Sex allows for the magical world that is possible between women and men.

The poems of Piercy's fifth volume, *The Twelve-Spoked Wheel Flashing* (1978), are concerned with what it means to love and work together in day-to-day mature relationships. Her willingness to nurture patiently a relationship is implicit in **"The Summer We Almost Split."** She refers to how she almost "patented the M. Piercy Total Weight Loss / Through Total Relationship Loss Diet." She admits that she is not immune to breakdowns in communications with those she loves. She and her lover reconcile: "Well, we came back, didn't we, crawling / and clawing. We came to this place / under a hard clear light and this new / understanding." This "new understanding" is built upon a love that forgives, a love that doesn't unravel at every snag in the armor, a love that gathers in the feelings of a woman and feelings of a man and reaffirms their future together.

The poems of *The Twelve Spoked Wheel Flashing* are organized around commonplace events—eating, sleeping, writing letters, cooking, keeping warm, the shifts in weather, the blending of one day into another. Within the structure of the seasons and the span of one year, Piercy writes about her fear of failure, the fear of loss, of being alone, the fear of dying. The poet expresses her philosophy in **"If They Come in the Night"**:

> We all lose
> everything. We lose
> ourselves. We are lost.
>
> Only what we manage to do
> lasts, what love sculpts from us;
> but what I count, my rubies, my
> children, are those moments
> wide open when I know clearly
> who I am, who you are, what we
> do, a marigold, an oakleaf, a meteor,
> with all my senses hungry and filled
> at once like a pitcher with light.

(*The Twelve-Spoked Wheel Flashing* 114)

Marge Piercy has reached "Those moments / wide open" because she continued the journey that began "above the treeline" in **"Walking into Love."** Her creative integrity enabled her to go on to the prophetic visions of *The Moon Is Always Female* (1980). This book is divided into two sections: **"Hand Games"** are definitely not head games.[2] They are based on instinct and an optimism about the future. She writes in the opening poem, **"The Inside Dance"**: "Dance like a jackrabbit / in the dunegrass, dance / not for release . . . but for the promise." Here, at the age of forty-

three, Piercy works toward a more profound understanding of relationships between all cycles of life, past, present, and future.

**"Intruding"** concerns every animal's instinct to protect its nest, to leave its own mark, while living with the threat of instant destruction. To be human is to be an invader, to be always marching "on somebody's roof." While the poems of **"Hand Games"** respect the delicate balance of nature, the background is always that of a world where "Radiation is like oppression, / the average daily kind of subliminal toothache / you get almost used to" (**"The Long Death"**). Whereas in **"Community"** (*Hard Loving*, 1969), Piercy was a fugitive from "the shadow of the nuclear plant that kills the fish / with coke bottle lamps flickering / on the chemical night," she now takes a more public stance in reminding everyone that they are guilty of neglecting the needs of the future:

> We acquiesce at murder so long as it is slow,
> murder from asbestos dust, from tobacco,
> from lead in the water, from sulphur in the air,
> and fourteen years later statistics are printed
> on the rise in leukemia among children.
> We never see their faces.

(*The Moon Is Always Female* 35)

**"To Have Without Holding"** says that it "hurts" to love "without air, to love consciously, / conscientiously, concretely, constructively." But it is love that allows the human to feel human, to feel that the body is a significant medium for imposing its needs upon the world. Love is the context for survival. Piercy's definitions for love are summarized in the last stanza of **"The Name I Call You"**:[3]

> Love is work. Love is pleasure. Love
> is studying. Love is holding and
> letting go without going away.
> Love is returning and turning
> and rebuilding and building new.
> Love is words mating like falcons a mile
> high, love is work growing
> strong and blossoming like an apple tree,
> like two rivers that flow together,
> love is our minds stretching out webs
> of thought and wonder and argument slung
> across the flesh or the wires of distance,
> love is the name I call you.

(*Stone, Paper, Knife* 97)

**"The Lunar Cycle"** is inspired by *The Lunar Calendar,* published by the Luna Press. This calendar has thirteen months and is centered around the times that the moon rises and sets in all its phases. Piercy writes in her brief introduction to these poems: "Rediscovering the lunar calendar has been a part of rediscovering woman's past, but it has also meant for me a series of doorways to some of the nonrational aspects of being a living woman." The key words in the title poem, **"The Moon Is Always Female,"** are "priest," "doctor" and "teacher." The poet reaffirms the female as the original creator, the original doctor, and the original teacher of human life. It is a supreme irony that these original powers have been used in the destructive domestication of women throughout recorded history.

Piercy points to the horrible fact of female clitorectomy: "in a quarter / of the world girl children are so maimed." Technically, a clitorectomy assures that a woman can bear children, while being denied sexual fulfillment. In fearing a woman's sexual fulfillment, a culture fears original power and the mystery of creation itself. Yet, all religions, all cultures are founded upon this kind of a sexual power base. The equivalent for man would mean: "You are left / your testicles but they are sewed to your / crotch . . . so that your precious / semen can be siphoned out."

Piercy's proclamation is: "Never even at knife point have I wanted / or been willing to be or become a man. / I want only to be myself and free." Piercy, the woman, the poet, the teacher, is the moon, subject to changes and cycles of fullness. In this book her desire is to travel deeper into the body and all its senses, into a creative intelligence unbound by the conformities of time, place, and sex.

In **"Cutting the Grapes Free,"** the grapevine is used as a metaphor for energy-time. The fruit it bears is androgynous: "Now the grapes swell in the sun yellow / black and ruby mounds of breast / and testicle." From her blood there flows "fermented poetry," which the vine works to mature into song: "Vine, from my blood is fermented / poetry and from yours wine that tunes my sinews / and nerves till they sing instead of screeching." She admits to receiving a great deal of her energy needs from men: "I do not seek to leap free from the wheel / of change but to dance in that turning." She further develops the messages of her earlier poetry, that of the necessity of working together, working with the land, and with the forces of gravity that spin us all on the same axis.

*Notes*

1. "When We Dead Awaken: Writing as Re-Vision," *Adrienne Rich's Poetry*, ed. Barbara Charlesworth Gelpi and Albert Gelpi (New York: Norton, 1975) 90-98.

2. I am indebted to Kendra Moore for this insight concerning Marge Piercy's Hand Games.

3. "The name I call you" was included in the original manuscript for *The Moon Is Always Female*, mailed to me by Piercy on 10 September 1979. The poem was later deleted from the book for inclusion in her collection, *Stone, Paper, Knife.*

*Works Cited*

Piercy, Marge. *Breaking Camp*. Middletown: Wesleyan UP, 1968.

———. *Hard Loving*. Middletown: Wesleyan UP, 1969.

———. Letter to Eleanor M. Bender. 4 June 1980.

———. *Living in the Open*. New York: Knopf, 1976.

———. *The Moon Is Always Female*. New York: Knopf, 1980.

———. *The Twelve-Spoked Wheel Flashing*. New York: Knopf, 1978.

Rich, Adrienne. *Adrienne Rich's Poetry*. Ed. Barbara Charlesworth Gelpi and Albert Gelpi. New York: Norton, 1975.

**Jeanne Lebow (essay date 1991)**

SOURCE: "Bearing Hope Back into the World: Marge Piercy's *Stone, Paper, Knife*," in *Ways of Knowing: Essays on Marge Piercy*, edited by Sue Walker and Eugenie Hamner, 1991, pp. 60-71.

[*In the following essay, Lebow asserts that "the publication of* Stone, Paper, Knife *marks Piercy's full evolution into a doer, a user of tools, a woman who has created her own vision of the world on paper."*]

In "Through the Cracks: Growing Up in the Fifties," a 1974 essay in *Parti-Colored Blocks for a Quilt*, Marge Piercy felt that "Success was telling some truth, creating some vision on paper" (207); however, she did not have hope of altering the world around her: "For if you cannot conceive of doing anything to alter your world, you reserve your admiration for manipulating concepts about those who have done something, or even for those who manipulate concepts about others who have manipulated concepts" (205).

Now, however, the publication of ***Stone, Paper, Knife*** marks Piercy's full evolution into a doer, a user of tools, a woman who has created her own vision of the world on paper.

Stone, paper, knife—these symbols, which Piercy redefines, are both the ancient tools of primitive man and the creative tools of artists: painters, photographers, printmakers, sculptors, children, and writers. In the first two sections of the book, "Mrs. Frankenstein's Dairy" and "In the Marshes of the Blood River," stone, paper, and knife are negative forces of the old repressive order; however, in the last two sections, "Digging In" and "Elementary Odes," stone, paper, and knife are elements of nature as well as hopeful forces for change and wholeness. Thus, the tools represent the circularity of incorporating old values into a new vision. The book, ***Stone, Paper, Knife,*** therefore, not only represents an evolution in the symbolic use of the tools of a children's game and an evolution from negative to positive relationships, but also reflects the growth of the poet's world view from anger to hope, a hope that rings out more clearly here than in any of Piercy's other collections of poems.

Not only are stone, paper, and knife historical tools for mankind, but also they are appropriately old tools for

Piercy. While *Stone, Paper, Knife* reveals the full evolution of the tools and of Piercy's world view, these three symbols do appear in her earlier work. In fact, they dominate the poem **"Athena in the front lines,"** published five years earlier in *The Twelve-Spoked Wheel Flashing* and selected for inclusion in her collection *Circles on the Water*. In this poem, a woman who believes that making is "an attack too, on bronze, on air, on time," Piercy see words as beneficial stones, "pebbles / sucked from mouth to mouth since Chaucer" (206). Containing the metaphor of the artist as well as the three symbolic tools, this earlier poem is the forerunner of the new book of poetry. The tools appear as follows in **"Athena in the front lines"**:

The stone:

Wring the stones of the hillside
for the lost plays of Sophocles they heard.
Art is nonaccident. Like love, it is
a willed tension up through the mind
balancing thrust and inertia, energy
stored in a bulb. Then the golden
trumpet of the narcissus pokes up
willfully into the sun, focusing the world.

The knife:

The epigraphs stabbed the Song of Songs
through the smoking heart

. . . . .

Generations of women wrote poems and hid
them in drawers, because an able
woman is a bad woman.

The paper:

A woman scribbling for no one doodles,
dabbles in madness, dribbles shame.
Art requires a plaza in the mind, a space
lit by the sun of regard. That tension
between maker and audience, that feedback.

(206-207)

Because Piercy knows that destruction of the old order must occur before the world can be remade, "Mrs. Frankenstein's Diary," the first section of *Stone, Paper, Knife,* tells of the death of such an old order in the form of a long relationship. In her early essay "Through the Cracks," Piercy explains why the old order must die: "Mutually exclusive sex roles divided humanity into winners and losers, makers and made, doers and done, fuckers and fuckees, yin and yang, and who the hell wants to be passive, moist, cold, receptive, unmoving, inert: sort of the superbasement of humanity" (212). Of the two types of men that Piercy says women were trained to love in the fifties, the Sensitive Hood and Iceman, Dr. Frankenstein is Iceman: "the block of stone, destructive but not usually self-destructive"; without the ability to love, he is the "perfect tool of empire, whether in his study or his factory or his trenchcoat" (124-25). It is therefore no accident that readers of "Mrs. Frankenstein" see Dr. Frankenstein as stone:

An old howitzer, a sewing machine,
a Concorde engine, chrome bumpers,
a scientist trained never to feel,
a fucking machine, a stone face
without ears to hear others.

(3)

If stone is one of the major metaphors for Dr. Frankenstein himself, living under the weight of that stone describes Mrs. Frankenstein's role in the relationship, a situation Piercy examines at length in **"The weight"**: "All too long I have been carrying a weight / balanced on my head as I climb the stairs / up from the subway in rush hour jostle" (24). Not only has she been forced to carry around this weight, but the weight sits on her:

Wife was a box you kept pushing me down
into like a trunk crammed to overflowing
with off-season clothes, whose lid
you must push on to shut. You sat
on my head. You sat on my belly.

(26)

Dr. Frankenstein's heart of stone lies parallel to his arid personality, a temperament that resembles a desert of pulverized rock. At the beginning of **"The weight,"** Piercy's Mrs. Frankenstein says: "I lived in the winter drought of his anger, / cold and dry and bright. I could not breathe" (24). And at the poem's end, she states:

Your anger was a climate I inhabited
like a desert in dry frigid weather
of high thin air and ivory sun,
sand dunes the wind lifted into stinging
clouds that blinded and choked me
where the only ice was in the blood. (26)

At the same time that the poem **"Where nothing grows"** continues the drought imagery, it also emphasizes both Piercy's rejection of this desert and her rejection of the old order which it represents. She watches the old lover march off into the desert, but she does not follow him, nor does she choose "stones and arid / spikes of cactus" (29).

Rocks also represent the materialistic success which Dr. Frankenstein embraces. In **"A visit from the ex,"** Piercy states, "You showed me your new quartz / movement solar batteried gold / Cadillac mistress" (37). The emphasis of his lifestyle is emphasized by the gift packages at the end of the poem, packages that do not even contain quartz but are "all empty" (37).

In **"Ragged ending,"** the vulnerability of woman shreds like the gift wrap on these empty boxes, leaving only tattered remnants:

Every middle-aged woman abandoned
by her longest love blows
in the night wind like torn
newspapers, shredding.

(17)

Saying that a woman in the hands of a man can be a powerless tool—a powerless piece of torn paper—Piercy is showing the position of paper, the second symbol, within the old order of section one. Here, in **"It breaks,"** the poet talks of the unprotected trust and wallpaper of the relationship standing stripped:

> Suddenly we are naked,
> abandoned. The plaster of bedrooms
> hangs exposed to the street, wall
> paper, pink and beige skins of broken
> intimacy torn and flapping.
>
> (39)

Because Piercy fears that paper contracts and trusts will never be the same, the poem concludes with a restricted faith in love and partnership, a reservation symbolized by her refusal to "share a joint checking account" in the future (40).

The final poem of the section, **"Wind is the wall of the year,"** heightens the image of trusting women as fragile, as capable of being "brushed aside" by Iceman: "The strong broad wind of autumn brushes / before it torn bags, seared apple skins, / moth wings, scraps of party velvet" (41). Although trees and their paper products are often at the mercy of Iceman, in **"The deck that pouts,"** Piercy plans to resurrect herself from self-pity and from ashes: "I rise to rebuild my house / of cards, of paper, here / at the meeting place of winds" (9). When she does rise, she arms herself with the knife, the third image of the book, and says, in the same poem, "I must grasp / my decisions like swords" (8).

Extending her belief that a relationship is a living thing that can die at the hands of a cold scientist, Piercy shows in section two, **"In the Marshes of the Blood River,"** how scientists are killing not only women as individuals but the community of women, as well as the larger community of the earth. Both **"The disturbance"** and **"Jill in the box"** bring back the motif of the wife in the box that appears in section one, but this time the social implications are wider. On one level, **"The disturbance"** examines the need for fathers and mothers to share child care, while on another level, it calls for community-wide child care: "Should we really just cram mother / back in the broom closet with baby / and go on with our business" (57). Piercy continues the closet image with **"Jill in the box"**; however, this poem asserts that women are not merely pushed down like puppets with the weight of stones upon them, but also are mutilated if they try to peep "at sunlight through drawn curtains" or try "to push through hunger to knowledge" (61). Here Piercy sees swords and knives in the hands of the enemy: "The nation bristles still with busy people / who long to cut off women's hands and feet, / forbid us to bloom rampant and scarlet" (61).

Piercy believes that knives and papers also have been used as dual weapons aimed at the larger community. In **"Down at the bottom of things,"** the "long bills" of herons are seen both as knives that stab and as bureaucratic bills that kill:

> In the salty estuary of the blood river
> small intermittent truths dart
> in fear through the eel grass, and the nastier
> facts come striding, herons stabbing
> with long bills yet graceful when they rise in heavy
> flight. Here we deal with archaic base
>    of advertising slogans and bureaucratic
> orders that condemn babies to kwashiorkor,
> here on the mud flats of language.
>
> (62)

Writing in **"For the Furies,"** Piercy plots appropriate ends for each greedy exploiter who threatens the community with paper, stone, and knives. Here in the last poem of the section, she invokes the Furies, avenging feminine spirits of retributive justice in Greek mythology, spirits whose heads were wreathed with serpents. She curses all of the Icemen who treat people as pieces of paper or as rocks: the generals who play war games, the chemical company presidents who pollute the rivers, the man from the utility company who says radiation is harmless, cigarette advertisers, the men who make movies where women are raped and "enjoy" it "as you might enjoy an electric saw / taking off your thumb" (72), and slum landlords who bribe fire inspectors and who hide behind "paper corporations." She curses those who think that they are not guilty because they kill indirectly as though they were filling out an order blank: "For them, murder is ordering a pair of ski / boots from a catalog. The dead, the mangled / are faceless others removed like rock" from the bed of a highway (76). Society punishes crimes against the old paternal order, crimes against the government, banks, or wealthy landowners. But, as Piercy notes, "crimes against / the mother are honored, paid in gold" (76). The poet calls for people to join together to fight these crimes against women, these Mack-the-Knife crimes against Mother Earth.

But Piercy is not a poet filled with curses. The first two sections tell of the death of love and earth at the hands of Iceman, but the third and fourth sections deal with the hope of regenerating love and land. Here stone, paper, and knife become the tools for "Digging In" and become "elementary" forces, as the two section titles suggest. And here the phoenix rises as a new house in **"The Annealing,"** the first poem of "Digging In," a new house founded "without evasion, without denial / on the bedrock of death" (70). Through connotation and denotation, the compound word "bedrock" represents the loving foundation of a new relationship built on equality as well as the couple's foundation of the living earth around them. Piercy takes the bedrock image to another level in **"A private bestiary,"** a poem that pictures the lovers as dolphins, falcons, snakes, snails, "hot-blooded" dinosaurs, and finally as peaceful rocks, "braille" "bestiaries" curled together in bed: "stones / sleeping in our mountainside fossils / locked inside" (115).

Just as nature uses heat and pressure to create fossils, man can produce his own rocks—crockery and glass—by heating clay and silica. Using the image of household china, Piercy tells of a changing point of view when she describes in **"Mornings in various years"** how her mornings have evolved from a day with Dr. Frankenstein, a "day piled up / before me like dirty dishes" to a day alone where "I would trip / on ghostly shards of broken / domestic routines" (94) to a day with the new lover, an "unblemished day before us / like a clean white ironstone platter / waiting to be filled" (95). Piercy believes also in picking up the pieces and recycling them to make something new and beautiful from something broken. From "broken gutter bottles, / pain and jagged edges, loss and waste, / the refuse of city lives jangling," the poet and her lover piece together a stained glass window (**"The name I call you"** 96). In this new life, "the name I call you" is not Dr. Frankenstein but "love" (97). It is therefore no coincidence that Piercy returns to the image of "stained glass windows that shape / light into icons" as a unification of the world's "jagged edges" in her final poem of the book (**"Stone, paper, knife"** 143).

Again connecting love with the world of living things in this third section, Piercy shows that love, like the earth and the plants which grow in its crumbled rock, must be cultivated tenderly. She tells how her Hungarian hot pepper bush wilted during a lovers' quarrel. And in the final stanza of **"Death of the Hungarian hot pepper bush,"** Piercy, no longer passive or powerless, takes the initiative for "reseeding" the relationship. Continuing the fertility imagery in a later poem in the section, "In which she begs (like everybody else) that love may last," the poet prays for a hothouse love where she is a rose that blooms all year (116).

Paralleling this hothouse image is the incubation image which Piercy works throughout the first three sections in order to prepare for the final hatching of hope in the last section. Beginning as an infertile "stone" that "will never hatch into a chick / or even a beetle" (**"From something, nothing"** 27), the egg evolves into a poem that breaks "on the rim of the iron pan" and bleeds out (**"It weeps away"** 69). The second section of the book describes the interim period where Piercy has seen herself and the community of "the great world egg" cracked by the cold scientist (**"Very late July"** 71). Here Piercy fears that, in addition to cracking the egg, the scientists and others will cook and eat it:

> It's an araucana
> egg, all blue and green
> swaddled in filmy clouds.
> Don't let them cook and gobble it,
> azure and jungle green egg laid
> by the extinct phoenix of the universe.
>
> (**"Let us gather at the river"** 48)

Yet here in the third section, "real chickens lay real eggs" (**"The West Main Book Store chickens"** 98), and Piercy and her lover find "the as yet unbroken / blue egg of spring is [their] joy as [they] twist / and twine about each other in the bed" (**"Snow, snow"** 103).

Because the four elements—air, earth, fire, and water—represent Mother Nature's tools, as stone, paper, and knife

can be mankind's tools, the final section, "Elementary Odes," is the poet's integration of the relationships between man and woman, between mankind and planet. These four odes prepare readers for the different look at the game of stone, paper, knife that Piercy gives in her final poem.

In **"What goes up,"** the first ode, Piercy explains that the feathers or down of air is "our second skin"; "the intimate element, in / and out of our bodies all day, feeding / us quietly, stoking our little fires" and entering us "like a lover" (120). Although the wind can be gentle, here it can also be a knife that "kills" and "tears down" and "resculpts" (121).

The second poem of the section represents rock in its commonest form. Again Piercy returns to the image of bedrock:

> You are the bed we all sleep on.
> You are the food we eat, the food
> we ate, the food we will become.
> We are walking trees rooted in you.
>
> (**"The common living dirt"** 123)

Personifying the earth as a mortal goddess, Piercy chastises readers because they have lost primitive man's belief in the earth as living and therefore as vulnerable to death. The greed of the cold scientist thus endangers all eggs, all "jewels of the genes wrapped in seed" (125). Piercy again asserts, "Power warps because it involves joy / in domination; also because it means / forgetting how we too starve" (125). She continues:

> Because you can die of overwork, because
> you can die of the fire that melts
> rock, because you can die of the poison
> that kills the beetle and the slug,
> we must come again to worship you
> on our knees, the common living dirt.
>
> (**"The common living dirt"** 125)

In the third poem of the section, **"Ashes, ashes, all fall down,"** Piercy describes the paradox of fire, that warming element which has the power to dissolve rock: "Emblem of all we have seized upon / in nature, energy made property, / as what we use uses us" (126). Fire represents a force that we "depend on" that in turn "enslaves us," a force that we "live by" that eventually "kills us" (126). Fire is passion that "simplifies like surgery," a fire that burns "the friends who can't clear out / fast enough" (127). Yet as Piercy notes, life without fire is the "architecture / of airports, laundromats" (128). To avoid blandness and coldness, we must leap through fire "to bring the sun around" because it may not return "without risk" (128). Without passion, the world belongs to Iceman: "Glaciers slide down the mountains / choking the valleys" (129). Reintroducing the idea of the fragile self as paper, Piercy continues the paradox of fire by suggesting that not only is breathing "a little burning," but also life is burning where "what we burn / is all the others we eat and drink" and "what we burn / is ourselves" (129). However, Piercy affirms that, while the back may "bow like a paper match," we can rise from the ashes (129).

Water, the final element, receives its tribute in **"The pool that swims in us,"** the poem where Piercy shows mankind and nature united in "the whole world river" (135). Here the "ocean we carry inside" is "bottled to nourish us among alien rocks," to join us in "wet jokes and wet creams" (131). The poet contrasts the way dolphins cooperate with each other with the way that people "among rock and cement" fear and use each other (132). The poet's answer to her own question of "How can we feel part of one another?" is to "feel on our nerves the great pattern" (133). In this poem Piercy echoes the image of *Circles on the Water,* the title of her book of selected poems which she was putting together when she made a decision to rewrite the poem that became the beginning of "Elementary Odes"; "we are of one tide ebbing and flowing. / We are one circular pool. Ideas spread / in ripples" (134). The last two stanzas, however, offer a more hopeful resolution of man, woman, planet, and the four elements than does any of her previous work:

> We carry in the wet cuneiform of proteins
> the long history of working to be human.
> In this time we will fail into ashes,
> fail into twisted metal and dry bones,
> or break through into a sea of shared abundance
> where man must join woman and dolphin and whale
> in salty joy, in flowing trust.
>
> We must feel our floating on the whole world river,
> all people breathing the same thin skin of air,
> all people growing our food in the same worn
> dirt, all drinking water from the same
> vast cup of clay. We must be healed at last
> to our soft bodies and our hard planet
> to make fruitful conscious history in common.
>
> ("**The pool that swims in us**" 134-35)

When readers encounter the final poem, which is also the title poem, they realize that Piercy has molded the rest of the book as preparation. Here she asks "Who shall bear hope back into the world?" and explains how to use the elements of the children's game of stone, paper, knife in new ways to bring back spring into our world. Although "[p]aper covers stone, / knife cuts paper, stone breaks knife," Piercy states, "you learn each one's strength and weakness / are light and shadows thrown by one source" (**"Stone, paper, knife"** 136). In other words, all people and all tools are part of one earth and, therefore, are interrelated in the game of life.

In stanza two, games become "lighter rituals," and art becomes "game only if you play at it" (136). Piercy is here suggesting that we "play at it" instead of "Stubbing" our toes "on habit" (137). She asks, in stanza three, what we should "give over to habit like an old slipper / flung to the dog" and what we should "save and strip" (139). The answer, given in stanza four, is to celebrate good habits, rituals, and "holy days" that "give our passing dignity" (140). Stanza five warns to "let go" the old, destructive games played with stone, paper, and knife:

> We can be addicted to the stone
> of submission, of security, addicted
> to the paper of mobility, blowing
> lighter than dust and thin as water.
> We can be addicted to the cleaver
> of our will and go hacking through.
> Security, power, freedom contradict.
>
> ("**Stone, paper, knife**" 141)

This stanza also asks how to reorganize the game:

> How can we open our hands and let go
> the old dangerous toys we clutch
> hard, the mama dolls, the cowboy
> six-shooters, the Monopoly sets,
> the ray guns and rockets? How can we
> with only stone and paper and knife
> build with imagination a better game?
>
> (141-142)

Stanza six provides the answer in the form of a plea to replace apathetic games with mobilization and "the hard clear image of hope" (142). Even though evil tries to control both the elements and the tools by turning fire into bombs, by poisoning the waters, by selling children "like newspapers" on street corners, "we" must quit "sulking in corners" and bear hope: "Who shall bear hope, who else but us? / After us is the long wind blowing / off the ash pit of blasted genes" (143). And how does Piercy suggest bearing this hope? She says:

> We must begin with the stone of mass
> resistance, and pile stone on stone on stone,
> begin cranking out whirlwinds of paper,
> the word that embodies before any body
> can rise to dance on the wind, and the sword
> of action that cuts through. We must shine
> with hope, stained glass windows that shape
> light into icons, glow like lanterns
> borne before a procession.
>
> ("**Stone, paper, knife**" 143-44)

Piercy's final question of *Stone, Paper, Knife*—"Who shall bear hope back into the world?"—places her clearly in the midst of those politically active women writers who would like to see men, women, and the earth together in warm, interdependent relationships. She therefore echoes and answers the questions Toni Cade Bambara raised in "What It Is I Think I'm Doing Anyhow":

> And the questions that face the millions of us on the earth are—in whose name will the twenty-first century be claimed? Can the planet be rescued from the psychopaths? Where are the evolved, poised-for-light adepts who will assume the task of administering power in a human interest, of redefining power as being not the privilege or class right to define, deform, and dominate but as the human responsibility to define, transform and develop?
>
> (*The Writer on Her Work* 153)

Because **Stone, Paper, Knife** offers a redefinition of power, tools, and games, it reveals both Piercy's willingness to accept responsibility and her hope and faith that others will join her.

In "Thoughts on Writing: A Diary," Susan Griffin explains the difference between the old and the new literary orders:

> . . . the most interesting creative work is being done at the moment by those who are excluded and have departed from the dominant culture—women, people of color, homosexuals. And this work, unlike the decadent, and abstract, and dadaist, and concrete [almost scientific usage of words, as sound units without sense], and mechanistic work of the dominant culture, is not despairing. This work is radiant with will, with the desire to speak; it sings with the clear tones of long-suppressed utterance, is brilliant with light, with powerful and graceful forms, with forms that embody feeling and enlarge the capacity of the beholder, of the listener, to feel.
>
> *(The Writer on Her Work* 116)

These words well describe Piercy's use of the "powerful and graceful forms" of stone, paper, and knife as tools to create both a new world order and a new literary order in the four sections of her new book of poems. For **Stone, Paper, Knife** recognizes what Piercy has noted in her earlier poem, **"Athena in the front lines"**: "Making is an attack on dying, on chaos, / on blind inertia, on the second law / of thermodynamics, on indifference, on cold," and "writing implies faith in someone listening" (207).

**Stone, Paper, Knife** is both an attack on what Iceman has done to the world and a statement of faith in the rebirth of hope. Although Piercy used some of the symbols before and stated some of the themes in similar ways, the difference between **Stone, Paper, Knife** and her earlier collections of poems is the fact that now the poet herself is truly "in the front lines" yet does not despair. She believes in the hope of being heard.

*Works Cited*

Piercy, Marge. *Circles on the Water: Selected Poems of Marge Piercy.* New York: Knopf, 1982.

———. "Through the Cracks." *Partisan Review* 42(1974), 202-16. Rpt. as "Through the Cracks: Growing Up in the Fifties." *Parti-Colored Blocks for a Quilt.* Ann Arbor: U of Michigan P, 1982. 113-28.

———. *Stone, Paper, Knife.* New York: Knopf, 1983.

Sternberg, Janet, ed. *The Writer on Her Work.* New York: Norton, 1983.

**Ronald Nelson (essay date 1991)**

SOURCE: "The Renewal of the Self By Returning to the Elements," in *Ways of Knowing: Essays on Marge Piercy,* edited by Sue Walker and Eugenie Hamner, 1991, pp. 73-89.

[*In the following essay, Nelson considers the theme of healing in Piercy's verse.*]

Marge Piercy speaks of poetry as "utterance that heals on two levels." First, it heals the psyche because "it can fuse for the moment all the different kinds of knowing in its saying." Second, it can heal "as a communal activity. It can make us share briefly the community of feeling and hoping that we want to be. It can create a rite in which we experience each other with respect and draw energy" ("Mirror Images" 189-90). Healing is a timely metaphor. In *World in Collapse,* John Killinger describes "a universal situation in which man is buffeted, upended, and generally perplexed by a world not of his making and certainly beyond his control" (2). Martin Esslin, in his aptly titled book on Harold Pinter, *The Peopled Wound,* suggests that the worst wounds are those inflicted by people. In *No Exit,* Sartre goes so far as to define hell as other people. One frequent result of the complexities of modern life is a sense of "cosmic loneliness" (Killinger 148). Anguish is another. Piercy's healing metaphor acknowledges the physical and mental wounds that are an inevitable part of inhabiting the planet. It also acknowledges that these wounds, being deep enough to destroy the self, require careful treatment.

What comes through strongly in **Stone, Paper, Knife** (1983) is Piercy's attempt to treat these wounds, perhaps to heal them. She locates the sore, applies medication, and, without being didactic, suggests ways to avoid subsequent wounds. Her artistry, like that of other fine writers, provides subtle clues to understanding and dealing with oneself and others in a difficult world. Reflecting the role of the artist described by Joseph Conrad in his Preface to *"The Nigger of the "Narcissus,"* she probes "to reach the secret spring of responsive emotions" (13). Her appeal is, in Conrad's words:

> to our less obvious capacities: to that part of our nature which, because of the warlike conditions of existence, is necessarily kept out of sight within the more resisting and hard qualities—like the vulnerable body within a steel armour. . . . [She] speaks to our capacity for delight and wonder, to the sense of mystery surrounding our lives; to our sense of pity, and beauty, and pain; to the latent feeling of fellowship with all creation— and to the subtle but invincible conviction of solidarity that knits together the loneliness of innumerable hearts.
>
> (12)

In "Elementary Odes," the final section of **Stone, Paper, Knife,** Piercy explores the basics of life in terms of the four traditional elements: earth, air, fire, and water. By returning to the elements she enables readers to share in the renewal of self.

Five long poems constitute "Elementary Odes," the first four of which focus primarily on the four elements individually, while the final poem, the title poem, integrates them into a concluding statement of belief. They progress from air in **"What goes up,"** to earth in **"The common** living dirt," to fire in **"Ashes, ashes, all fall down,"** to water in **"The pool that swims in us,"** and finally to **"Stone, paper, knife."** While demonstrating both positive and negative aspects, these poems celebrate the elements because they make life possible. Piercy realizes that the interdependence of all things as part of "the great pattern" ("The pool that swims in us" 133) is a matter of survival and self-fulfillment.

The techniques that Piercy uses assure an appreciation of the elements and of life itself, in all its forms, and draw readers into these odes. The ancient belief that everything was once made of earth, water, fire, and air creates both an appreciation of the timelessness of these elements and a genuine concern for the future. The titles of the poems challenge readers to reflect on their possible implications. Piercy also engages readers by addressing each element in the second person and converses imaginatively with it. Her searching questions invite answers as she links the elements and juxtaposes them in phrases that force the mind to contemplate their beauty. Readers become convinced of the interrelatedness of all things, and this conviction—being a part of the world rather than apart from it—provides spiritual refreshment.

## WHAT GOES UP

In the first poem, **"What goes up,"** Piercy is concerned with air, its inhabitants, and its characteristics. Her title takes the reader imaginatively upward in mid-air while simultaneously tempting the completion of the cliche: "must come down." This subtle lifting and lowering anticipates the second poem in the section, "The common living dirt." **"What goes up"** shows the creatures that inhabit the airy realm, primarily birds, in flight or on foot. The air itself appears in a state of heightened tension at the peak of its savage fury or in a state of dissipated energy, of restful calm. The colors that the sky can assume are described in memorable hues. Piercy insures the very palpability of the air by its juxtaposition with the other elements. Knowledge of the world of the air—what its qualities are and what takes place in it—results from her penetrating description of things external and internal. This knowledge develops intimacy and unity with nature.

At the start of the poem, Piercy describes the experience of Jack Swedberg, a construction worker who, having seen a bald eagle, purchases a camera and returns to capture its majesty photographically. She immortalizes the moment in a word which, like the click of a camera, reflects Swedberg's new calling: "Conversion" (119). As a result of this "first encounter with the fierce queen of winds," he has become a different kind of construction worker, one who composes artistically, rather than in, or perhaps in addition to, a utilitarian way. The irreversibility of his new vocation is encompassed in Piercy's summation of the experience: "The raptor seized him into art, carried / off to his vocation like a rabbit." The artistic product of Swedberg's camera captures his new-found appreciation:

A photograph of an eagle just setting down

on the ice of Quabbin, pinions outspread:
look a winter storm in the eye.

(119)

This sequence provides a fresh perspective on a creature that alights on a stretch of ice with quiet dignity, "pinions outspread," and faces impending adversity. This initial image of gathered composure serves as a beacon of hope that carries through to the final lines of **"Stone, paper, knife."**

In the fourth stanza Piercy mentions that it does not take the rare and noble eagle to inspire an appreciation of wildlife:

The local hawks drag awe from me,
a giant reel of wire unwinding up the sky,
me, a fish on the bottom of my pond, hooked.

(119)

This passage metaphorically and dynamically affirms her connection with all life, from hawk to fish, as well as with art. Both she and Swedberg are in the grasp of art, as surely as the rabbit and the fish. The hook at the end of the wire is deeply embedded in her—"the bottom of my pond." Readers, too, become inescapably involved in the reassurance of belonging to the scheme of things.

Then, as if transported in the "ocean of air"—"a phrase that lacks / vividness till you fly"—readers are reminded of the fact that:

We are feathered with air, downed
with it. Air is our second skin.
It enters us like a lover, or we die.

(119-20)

The air envelops and penetrates as Piercy addresses it and says:

. . . you are the intimate element, in
and out of our bodies all day, feeding
us quietly, stoking our little fires.

(120)

As in the phrase "ocean of air," Piercy's description gains strength through interrelation with another element. The air, so essential to human beings, has also shaped the bodies of birds: "the hummingbird / who spins sunlight into jewels"; it is intimately related to other flying creatures as well: "The monarch rising among the milkweed" and "A cloud / of floating exclamation points: / fritillaries" (121). These reminders of the everyday interplay of air with the creatures that rely on it for their existence are arresting.

Piercy sees the sky not in its traditional blue, but in countless colors: "pigeon gray, / wet granite, pearl mist," "split pea soup," "sulphurous / brown gray," and "white." It is varied both in color and mood as it erupts into "banging brass / gongs," "slamming oaken / doors," "tearing on pines," storms that can be "vaster than imagination" (120, 122):

Here on this
sandbar we fear the storm but relish it.
It kills. It tears down. It resculpts

the shore . . .

(121)

In spite of a close call—"Death brushes dark wings /
against our shoulders but flies on"—"we venture out to
confront / an altered world," cleansed in the "washed air"
like the jaegers who "stand bemused in the marsh." Hope,
"banked low . . . flares up yellow / and hot and leaps, as
we live and breathe" (122). A feeling of guarded optimism
develops after confronting the whims of the air—now savage, now gentle.

### THE COMMON LIVING DIRT

Emerging into the "washed air" after the storm, Piercy
confronts the earth in the second poem, **"The common
living dirt."** She celebrates the lovely products of the
soil—woman, mother, abused victim, and goddess—and
urges a worshipful regard for the earth.

The first stanza describes delicate, lovely plants that
emerge from the soil: "The small ears prick on the bushes,
/ furry buds, shoots tender and pale." These plants elicit
respect because of their fragility and tiny defense mecha-
nisms. Like the colors in **"What goes up,"** these plants
are deep in hue: "delicate gold, chartreuse, crimson, /
mauve speckled, just dashed on" (123).

Piercy then describes the soil of spring just after winter:

The soil stretches naked. All winter
hidden under the down comforter of snow,
delicious now, rich in the hand
as chocolate cake: the fragrant busy
soil the worm passes through her gut
and the beetle swims in like a lake.

(123)

The soil is personified as a naked woman from whom not
the blanket but the "down comforter" of snow has been removed. Because of its gustatory and tactile richness, the
soil, which the snow has covered and then exposed, invites both worm and beetle to move within it, a penetra-
tion that is considered fulfilling. Again Piercy combines
more than one element to provide a whole greater than individual parts.

As she addresses the undressed soil—"You can live thousands of years / undressing in the spring"—Piercy acknowledges the intensity of her attachment:

As I kneel to put the seeds in
careful as stitching, I am in love.
You are the bed we all sleep on.
You are the food we eat, the food
we ate, the food we will become.
We are walking trees rooted in you. (123)

Her posture of reverence and care reflects her passionate
realization that the soil provides the essentials of life. She
finds fulfillment there, while deliberately and sensitively
working with the common living dirt, assisting it to realize
its potential. Appreciating the gifts of the soil, past,
present, and future, brings fulfillment. The line, "We are
walking trees rooted in you," suggests a phallic image that
reiterates the first lines of stanza two: "The soil stretches
naked." The description of fertility, which pictures the soil
after "undressing in the spring"—"your black /
body, your
red body, you brown body / penetrated by the rain. Here /
is the goddess unveiled, / the earth opening her strong
thighs"—reinforces the sexual image. The soil receives
and continues whatever is put into it with the dignity and
beauty of a "goddess unveiled."

Both women and the soil have been taken for granted,
have been tread upon unthinkingly for too long. Misuse
has created the faulty assumption that the soil would yield
its fruits forever:

We have contempt for what we spring
from. Dirt, we say, you're dirt
as if we were not all your children.

(124)

This arrogance suggests that a change of attitude—"the
simplest gratitude"—is needed:

We lack the knowledge we showed ten
thousand years past, that you live
a goddess but mortal, that what we take
must be returned; that the poison we drop
in you will stunt our children's growth.

(124)

This insistent use of parallel structure makes the poem potent. With each "that," "that," "that," Piercy urges readers to change their attitudes. Bound "to the seasons, / to the
will of the plants," to ready corn and ripe peaches, she
worships on her knees—"laying / the seeds in you, that
worship rooted / in need, in hunger, in kinship, / flesh of
the planet with my own flesh"—and experiences the joy of
seeing a garden as "a chapel" and "a meadow / gone wild
in grass and flower" as "a cathedral."

In the final two stanzas, Piercy considers the reasons that
power corrupts:

Power warps because it involves joy
in domination; also because it means
forgetting how we too starve, break
like a corn stalk in the wind, how we
die like the spinach of drought,
how what slays the vole slays us.

(125)

Forgetting their fragile mortality and attempting to be
dominant, people are out of harmony with the world; their
perspectives are distorted. They must humble themselves
by coming to their knees in recognition of their true rela-

tionship with the soil. With heightened awareness of their interdependence with it, they have some hope of survival.

### ASHES, ASHES, ALL FALL DOWN

Piercy's poem on fire—**"Ashes, ashes, all fall down"**—is an attempt to come to grips with the third of the elements and with her own life as part of the universal experience. The title of the poem suggests the children's game of "Ring-a-ring- o'roses," one version of which concludes, "We all fall down."[1] It also evokes thought of the phoenix legend, and that evocation brings the disturbing realization that consuming others is part of survival. To become more aware of what life is and how to survive is to become re-vitalized to the extent of partially dispelling the darkness of ignorance.

Addressing the element in Part One, Piercy notes that, un-like the other elements dealt with so far, fire "cannot enter us. No pain / is like your touch" (126). She reminds read-ers that once they lived without fire, but being dependent on it, they are now caught in a kind of mutual destruction:

> . . . what we use uses us; what
> we depend on enslaves us; what
> we live by kills us.
>
> (126)

Perhaps to escape that chilling thought,

> We stretch out our hands to the fire
> place watching the colors shift
> until the mind gives up buried images
> like the secret blue in the log
> the flame unlocks.
>
> (126)

But from the hearth she recalls burning scenes of horror—both physical and mental conflagrations—and emphasizes the depth of her involvement in memory. For example, in the last stanza of Part Two, she tells of her jealousy:

> Burning, burning, I huddled over the cauldron
> of my jealousy bubbling like hot lead.
> Under my hilly day a fire in a coal mine
> was smouldering, consuming invisibly
> the solid earth.
>
> (127)

She laments the waste of self, a valuable resource, as she smoulders within, unwittingly a phoenix.

Opening the third part with the line, "Passion simplifies like surgery," Piercy powerfully suggests that her passions have cut into her—an image that anticipates stanza three of the next poem: "A scalpel slits us open like a busted / bag of groceries, and out we ooze" (131). Using the word "burn" in two senses, she attempts to deal with her injury:

> We burn, and what we burn are the books,
> the couch, the rug, the bed, the houseplants,
> the friends who can't clear out
> fast enough.
>
> (127)

Considering alternately the passionate life and the passion-less life, she settles on neither:

> Burning, burning, we can't live
> in the fire. Nor can we in ice.
> Long ago we wandered from our homeland
> tropics following game to these harsh
> but fertile shores.
>
> (128)

To leave the security of home is to search for a richer se-curity, one that entails great risk but holds the elusive promise of fulfillment.

In the fourth part Piercy recalls ancestors who "leapt / through fire, to bring the sun around," an act that involved personal danger. She seems to urge risk-taking, for

> Without risk gradually the temperature
> drops, slowly, slowly. One day you notice
> the roses have all died. The next year
> no corn ripens.
>
> Then even the wheat rots where it stands.
> Glaciers slide down the mountains
> choking the valleys. The birds are gone.
> On the north side of the heart, the snow
> never melts.
>
> (128-29)

The consequences of life without risk are physical and spiritual death. Staring into fire and seeing figures, she re-members moments of bliss: "the memory / of times I have danced in ecstasy all night, / my hair on fire." Such Di-onysian moments are worth the risk.

In Part Five Piercy qualifies what she said about fire in the first of Part One—"you cannot enter us. No pain / is like your touch" (126). Refining her knowledge of the element, she realizes that, paradoxically, fire does enter, for "breath-ing is a little burning. . . . All the minute furnaces stoked inside / warm our skin" (129). In so doing, she perceives the destructiveness of fire, both literally and figuratively; to live is to destroy both self and others:

> Life is a burning, and what we burn
> is all the others we eat and drink.
> We burn the carrot, we burn the cow,
> we burn the calf, we burn the peach,
> we burn the wine.
>
> Life is a burning, and what we burn
> is ourselves . . . the dark hair powdering
> to grey ashes.
>
> (129-30)

By defining life in terms of fire, she is able to grasp an un-settling truth. This she articulates in an address to the fire: "You are all we cannot live with / or without."

### THE POOL THAT SWIMS IN US

> Noses drip. Armpits sweat. Eyes weep.
> We are born from a small salt pond

yet immersed in our own element we drown.
We have no natural habitat, we have
no home.

(131-32)

Unlike birds that inhabit the air and worms that live in the earth, "We have been making a home badly for millennia." Piercy's sense of homelessness is implied at the start of this poem, where she recounts her departure from her lover. She takes comfort "from the slack of my pleased flesh / and the salty damp of my thighs." Her anguished sense of waste, of loss, is graphic:

We are wet jokes and wet dreams.
A scalpel slits us open like a busted
bag of groceries, and out we ooze.

(131)

In Part Two Piercy notices how dolphins help one another though they have "no houses, / no coins, no tools or tolls, no warehouses, / no armies, classes or taxes" (132). They are "wise cousins" who have much to teach. People seem only to fear, use, or destroy each other. "[T]en thousand years of bad habits" must be corrected.

Part Three questions, "How can we feel part of one another?" (133), as Piercy seeks ways to correct the errors of humans. They must become aware of the unity of the world, the interrelatedness of all creatures and all phenomena:

The same water rises from the well, runs
through us and falls to rush through sewers.
We are of one tide ebbing and flowing.
We are one circular pool . . .
One river is gliding, spurting,
soaking through every living cell. The calm
that drinks the tide and the high-rise
dweller turning the faucet share that fluid.

(134)

Because everyone is influenced by what happens, "We must feel on our nerves the great pattern" (133). Such a feeling demands the kind of gut recognition that combines the rational with the irrational to grip the soul in a lasting way. Only by breaking "through into a sea of shared abundance / where man must join woman and dolphin and whale / in salty joy, in flowing trust" is it possible to survive, to be healed and "make fruitful conscious history in common" (134-35).

### STONE, PAPER, KNIFE

**"Stone, paper, knife,"** the title poem, is the last of the five "Elementary Odes." With its 197 lines stretching through six parts, it is the longest and most challenging poem. The title is adapted from the children's game, "Stone, Paper, Scissors," in which two or more participants count to three and show with one hand either stone (closed fist), paper (flat hand), or scissors (index and middle fingers in a V-shape).[2] The rules of the game are as follows: paper covers stone, scissors cut paper, stone breaks scissors.[3] This game of chance involves outguessing the others in the group and, if successful, either slapping (paper as winner), punching (stone as winner), or whanging with two fingers (scissors as winner) the others.[4] The version of the game that Piercy presents—substituting "knife" for "scissors"—may express the version familiar to her, or it may be a reshaping of the original to serve her artistic aim. In either case, the use of "knife" makes the game more serious and potentially deadly.

The front cover of ***Stone, Paper, Knife*** depicts three hands holding the respective objects: one covering a piece of paper, another grasping a jacknife, and a third closed around a primitive-looking fragment of stone pointed inward. The essence of the game is captured on the cover, where the three possibilities converge in timeless tableau. A unity is thereby suggested. Moreover, an extension toward a literal reality is intimated by the inclusion of actual implements in the picture. Indeed, these tools assume symbolic qualities, pointing the way toward significant action. Using these instruments as extensions of the hand, Piercy suggests how to go beyond the children's game by using these implements constructively.

The first part of the poem gives the rules of this age-old game, then the imponderables, such as guessing at what the others will show and plotting their intentions. The game teaches the players the "strength and weakness" of each other: that they are "light and shadows thrown by one source" (136).

Part Two extends the idea of games to art. Leading into the concept, Piercy says that she likes "plain pokers . . . not games where / every red odd card is wild." She prefers to work with the hand she has been dealt and suggests the necessity of overcoming obstacles in games in order to derive benefits: "Grace shines in precisely doing / what the structure makes difficult." By reworking ideas, people create art, which is "game only if you play at it, / a mirror that reflects from the inside out." Playing with and shaping the materials of the mind into art can satiate a universal longing: "We like knowing what is to happen / with small surprises" (136). People need certainty and unexpected moments of pleasure to make life interesting. However, when the stakes are higher than mere diversion, the artist is justified in leading readers to experience "gross shocks / that stretch us till we grow or break" (137). In these poems Piercy has provided moments of truth as well as shocks.

In Part Three, Piercy speaks of the habits that thwart attempts to find fulfillment. Whether it is the insistent and habitual demands of the baby, the cat, the dog, or the men she has lain with—"who required exactly muttered / obscene formulae, precise caresses"—the result is the same: a loss of vitality. People become victims of habit and lose touch with the world around them. "Repetition numbs," as Piercy notes:

How easily we turn off the fingertips
like lightbulbs to save energy,

pull in from the nerve endings
capped like the gleaming teeth,
then starve out impulse.

. . . . .

In repetition, a sense of identity
lulls, gathered into a tight ball
like socks in a drawer, mingled, woolly.

(138)

The task is to keep the senses alive and individuality intact, but "We cannot listen to every sound, / open as a
baby, as a microphone." It is a matter of deciding what to
"give over to habit" and what to "save and strip" (138-39).

The establishment of meaningful personal relationships
makes it possible to transcend the deadening influence of
habit, even to transform habits into important rituals, as
Piercy describes in Part Four. Here she celebrates meeting
Ira Wood:

I met my dear on Passover, so each seder
marks exit and entry, liberation
and a chosen bond.

(139)

Such rare relationships in which there is "commitment"
make life worthwhile; such celebrations refresh and en-
noble the spirit:

Feasts,
holy days give our passing dignity
as we shuffle round the circle dance
through seasons revolving stately as planets
from strong light slowly into the cold.

(140)

Like the eagle in **"What goes up,"** people gather composure as they realize they are an integral part of the cosmos,
and this thought provides a measure of reassurance as they
move toward the grave.

Posing a series of questions directly to readers in Part
Five, Piercy considers the value of security and power. To
be too dependent can be a destructive drug:

We can be addicted to the cleaver
of our will and go hacking through.
Security, power, freedom contradict.

(141)

The crucial questions are:

How can we open our hands and let go
the old dangerous toys we clutch
hard, the mama dolls, the cowboy
six-shooters, and Monopoly sets,
the ray guns and rockets? How can we
with only stone and paper and knife
build with imagination a better game?

(141-42)

Piercy gives the fitting climax to the book—a vision of
life so powerful that it forces a realization of how the
world has gone awry: how religious fanatics hypocritically
assume superiority, how people have developed bombs
that are capable of annihilating, how pollution spoils water, how disease wastes, how girls are used and women
cruelly abused, how the powerless elderly freeze, and how
government does little to rectify matters. Such a vision of
the human condition compels a compassionate understanding of the situation. To see as Piercy sees demands change,
but letting go of childish games becomes easier after seeing where the old ways have led.

Piercy ends the poem and the book by addressing the subject of hope. The human spirit needs to soar while feet implanted firmly on earth assume the burden of responsibility. Commitment translates into action as Piercy asks,
"Who shall bear hope, who else but us?" Those who are
willing to return to the earth and its inhabitants, cherishing
both, can find fulfillment by living whole and by working
toward improving conditions. Piercy's vision of what must
be done becomes clear:

We must begin with the stone of mass
resistance, and pile stone on stone on stone,
begin cranking out whirlwinds of paper,

the word that embodies before any body
can rise to dance on the wind, and the sword
of action that cuts through. We must shine
with hope, stained glass windows that shape
light into icons, glow like lanterns
borne before a procession.

(143-44)

**"Stone, paper, knife,"** the children's game, becomes
through transformation "a better game" with important
consequences. Based on construction rather than destruction, Piercy's visions suggest that deliberate collective action can move the modern world toward resolution of its
problems. Instead of scissors or knife, she offers "the
sword / of action that cuts through," a vision which culminates in a religious perspective grounded in reverence for
life and its perpetuation.

Piercy's political vision necessitates a careful and sensitive
observation of the world. She urges people to notice "Jaegers / stand[ing] bemused in the marsh" (122) and "A
cloud / of floating exclamation points: / fritillaries" (121),
or stoop to feel the texture of the soil. Such an approach
expands the consciousness by stretching it between extremes of calmness and violence, ugliness and beauty, fire
and ice, the external and the internal, the remote past and
the uncertain future, contempt and gratitude, the passionate and the passionless life, the using of others and the
helping of others.

Exercising the rational and irrational within establishes
contact with elementary matters that are forgotten or misunderstood. Whereas failure to value the physical world
allows people to fall prey to bad habits and stagnant per-

sonal relationships and to inflict wounds upon themselves and others, healing comes from a renewed appreciation of what is fundamental in life. Piercy's "Elementary Odes" leads to a state of grace.

*Notes*

1. As recorded in the *Oxford Dictionary of Nursery Rhymes,* the original rhyme reads:

Ring-a-ring o'roses,
A pocket full of posies,
   A-tishoo! A-tishoo!
We all fall down.

This version may have had its origin at the time of the Great Plague: "A rosy rash . . . was a symptom of the plague, posies of herbs were carried as protection, sneezing was a final fatal symptom, and *all fall down* was exactly what happened" (364-65). See also James Leasor, *The Plague and the Fire,* and William S. Baring-Gould and Cecil Baring-Gould, *The Annotated Mother Goose* (252-53).

2. This game seems to have had its origin in an ancient game called "hic, haec, hoc." See The Diagram Group, *The Way to Play* (270).

3. Other possibilities that have come to my attention are "stone bends scissors" and "stone crushes scissors."

4. As described in *The Way to Play,* early versions of the game were nonviolent, the participants simply winning or losing each round and playing "a predetermined number of rounds" (270).

*Works Cited*

Baring-Gould, William S., and Cecil Baring-Gould. *The Annotated Mother Goose.* New York: Potter, 1962.

Conrad, Joseph. Preface. *The Nigger of the "Narcissus".* 1987. Garden City: Doubleday, 1914. 11-16.

The Diagram Group. *The Way to Play.* New York: Paddington, 1975.

Esslin, Martin. *The Peopled Wound.* Garden City: Doubleday, 1970.

Killinger, John. *World in Collapse.* New York: Dell, 1971.

Leasor, James. *The Plague and the Fire.* New York: McGraw, 1961.

Opie, Iona, and Peter Opie, Eds. *The Oxford Dictionary of Nursery Rhymes.* Oxford: Clarendon, 1962.

Piercy, Marge. "Mirror Images." *Parti-Colored Blocks for a Quilt.* Ann Arbor: U of Michigan P, 1982. 208-18.

————. *Stone, Paper, Knife.* New York: Knopf, 1983.

## Eleanor Bender (essay date 1991)

SOURCE: "Marge Piercy's *Laying Down The Tower*: A Feminist Tarot Reading," in *Ways of Knowing: Essays on Marge Piercy*, edited by Sue Walker and Eugenie Hamner, 1991, pp. 101-10.

[*In the following essay, Bender explores Piercy's use of Tarot imagery and feminist perspective in* Laying Down The Tower.]

In the eleven poems of ***Laying Down the Tower,*** Marge Piercy takes a feminist perspective in interpreting the symbolism of the ancient Tarot. As the concluding section of ***To Be of Use,*** these poems show the development of the poet's feminist consciousness through the early 1970's. Over a decade later, they typify what historian Gerda Lerner noted when speaking on "The Rise of Feminist Consciousness" at Stephens College:

In discussing the rise of feminist consciousness, let us notice that it takes place historically in certain distinct stages: 1) the awareness of a wrong; 2) the development of a sense of sisterhood; 3) women begin autonomously to define their goals and strategies for change and 4) they develop an alternate vision of the future.

Marge Piercy reaches the fourth stage, the alternate vision, in ***Laying Down the Tower*** and by a process of self-examination, comes to a revelation. In her introduction to these poems the poet states: "Here I am reconciling myself to my own history and trying to bring my sense of that history to you" (***To Be of Use*** 72).

Piercy uses the Rider Deck designed by Pamela Colman Smith under the direction of Arthur Edward Waite. This deck is made up of seventy-eight cards and is divided into two major groups: twenty-two Major Arcana cards and fifty-six Lesser Arcana cards. Arcana is the Latin word for secrets, mysteries (Gray 12). She includes four Major Arcana cards: The Tower, The Emperor, The Judgment, and The Sun. These are all trump cards. The others are drawn from the Lesser Arcana which contain four suits including the court cards: King, Queen, Page, and Knight. These suits are called Swords, Wands, Cups, and Pentacles. Today's ordinary deck of playing cards descends from the Tarot deck.

Piercy begins her reading by choosing her Significator, the card that is placed on the table before a question can be asked of the Tarot. This is the Queen of Pentacles, the card designated for a mature woman of dark hair and eyes. This queen is Marge Piercy. Her throne is sculpted with ripe apples and pears, images common to her poetry. The top of her headrest is the shape of a crescent moon, a reminder of her birth described in a later poem about her mother, **"Crescent Moon Like a Canoe"** (***The Moon Is Always Female*** 1980). It is carved with the face of the androgyne who is set free in her final Sun card. Her armrest is decorated with the head of a domestic and friendly goat. The rabbit frolicking in the foreground is content with this environment. The distant mountains are bright blue, and the rivers that come from them suggest a continual flow of energy and renewal. The closer one examines this card, the closer one comes to understanding Marge Piercy the woman and the poet. In **"The Queen of pentacles"** she writes: "This is my deck I unwrap, and this is the card for me. / I will in any house find quickly like my sister the cat

/ the most comfortable chair, snug out of drafts" (73). She is learning to create her own space. She is sensual, she is productive, she is linked to the possibilities for growth. The soil in her garden nurtures a society of plurality and diversity:

> I am at home in that landscape of unkempt garden,
> mulch and manure, thorny blackberry and sunflower
> and grape
> 　　　coiling,
> tomato plants mad with fecundity bending their stakes,
> asparagus waving fronds in the wind.
>
> 　　　　　　　　　　　　　　　　　　(120)

Piercy's mother kept a "victory garden" in Detroit in the 1940's. In this regard, she is her mother's daughter: "Even in a New York apartment with dirt / brought in bags like chocolate candy, I raised herbs" (74). It is her deep-rooted respect for the land that motivates her to lay out her cards: "Too many have been murdered from the sky, / the soil has been tainted and blows away and the water stinks" (74). The golden pentacle she holds on her lap is life. Before she fully can share her vision of it, she must dig her "hands into the ground."

The first card Piercy draws from her deck is the card that covers the Significator and represents the general atmosphere surrounding the question asked, the influence at work around it. This is **"The Tower Struck by Lightning Reversed; The Overturning of the Tower."** The illustration shows a gray tower on fire. Smoke is spewing from all angles. A man and woman are falling to the rocks below. A larger-than-life crown captures the flames on the left, while lightning strikes on the right. (From the vantage point of the 1980's, these images are prophetic.) When this card is reversed it means its influences are weakened. Piercy's resentment is that "all my life I have been a prisoner under the Tower" (77). She goes on to recount the history of towers: The Tower of Babylon, the Tower of London, the Twin Towers of the "World Trade Center spewing asbestos, / tallest, biggest and menacing as fins on an automobile, / horns on a Minotaur programmed to kill" (78). The "weight of the tower" is in the poet. But the Tower cannot be brought down by her alone: "The Tower will fall if we pull together, / Then the Tower reversed, symbol of tyranny and oppression, / shall not be set upright" (79). By laying "the tower on its side," and turning it into "a communal longhouse," the structure of power changes from that of a hierarchy to a non-hierarchal vision of human connection.

Piercy continues with **"That Which Opposes the Overthrowing of the Tower: The Nine of Cups."** This card is laid sideways on top of the Tower reversed. Eden Gray calls this "the wish card, a key card on which the results of the seeker's question can depend" (63). This card represents, in Piercy's words, "the ultimate consumer, the overlord" (81). He sits triumphantly before nine golden cups filled with other people's money. He owns everything. He is the Man. He functions to keep the Tower standing be-

cause if it falls, he falls with it. He could be Leon's father in her novel *Going Down Fast* (1969). He is rich at the expense of the poor, and he is ruthless: "He is your landlord; he shuts off the heat and the light and the water, / he shuts off air, he shuts off growth, he shuts off your sex" (82). The nine of cups embodies the evils of capitalism; it is a negative rather than a positive influence. In her novel *Woman on the Edge of Time* (1976), there is no nine of cups. Piercy's "wish" is to overthrow his influence along with the Tower.

The next card is placed directly below the Tower reversed. This is **"The Influence Passing: The Knight of Swords."** A man on horseback is brandishing a sword as he rides into the wind. He is dressed in armor, and the plume on his helmet is flagging for victory. The storm clouds could be smoke from the burning tower. He rides with determination. This card relates to her experience with Students for a Democratic Society and the anti-war movement: "We rushed in waves at the Tower and were hurtled back" (85). This influence must not be allowed to pass:

> Run, keep running, don't look sideways.
> The blood is raining down all the time, how can we rest?'
> How can we pause to think, how can we argue with you,
> how can we pause to reason and win you over?
> Conscience is the sword we wield,
> conscience is the sword that runs us through.
>
> 　　　　　　　　　　　　　　　　　　(126)

The Knight of Swords is followed by **"That Which is Now Behind, Previous Condition: The Eight of Swords."** A bound and blindfolded woman stands on marshy ground below the rocky promontory at the base of the Tower. Eight swords form a fence behind her. They are the swords that remain from the battle led by the Knight of Swords: "Bound, blinded, stymied, with bared blades for walls / and alone, my eyes and mouth filled with dark" (87). She is faced with making a conscious decision to free herself and continue the fight. The swords are there for her to use. The puddles of water at her feet are what is left of the political activism of the 1960's: "We had grown used to / a Movement, that sense of thaw, / things breaking loose and opening and doors pushed by the wind" (87). Now it is time to regroup and examine what went wrong: "We clashed on each other, we chopped, we never hit harder than when we were axing a comrade two feet to the right. / Factions charred our energies. Repression ground us" (88).

The woman on this card will learn to work with others, not as a camp follower, but as a leader of struggle. She will no longer isolate herself in the service of the knights. Piercy documented the ways women were used by men in the sixties in her first novel, *Dance the Eagle to Sleep* (1970). This is a healing poem, because she is attempting to put anger behind her:

> There is finally a bone in the heart that does not break
> when we remember we are still part of each other,

the muscle of hope that goes on in the dark
pumping the blood that feeds us.

(127)

The next card, **"The Influence Coming into Play: The
Seven of Pentacles,"** forms the top of the outer circle.
The traditional meaning of this card is growth through effort and hard work (Gray 57). A farmer leans on his hoe
contemplating what appears to be a large beanstalk or a
grapevine. Six pentacles adorn the green, bushy leaves.
They represent the ideas in place in the first six cards. The
seventh pentacle lies between his left foot and the base of
the hoe. The farmer that wields this hoe is the female artist who is digging into the soil and turning over new possibilities for growth. She is coming to an understanding of
her own health and capacity for survival. Piercy advises
her:

> Live as if you liked yourself, and it may happen:
> reach out, keep reaching out, keep bringing in.
> This is how we are going to live for a long time: not
> always,
> for every gardener knows that after the digging, after
> the planting,
> after the long season of tending and growth, the har-
> vest comes.

(90)

The woman artist is the arbiter of harmonious growth. She
cannot afford to be "stymied" by inaction. Piercy tells her
to "Weave real connections, create real nodes, build real
houses" (90). This is how to win over the opposing influences of the Tower and the Nine of Cups.

**"The Aim, The Best that Can be Hoped For: The Ma-
gician,"** completes the outer circle. The number one card
in the Major Arcana, the Magician stands for creative
power. Before him there is a table arranged with the symbols of the four suit cards: pentacle, cup, sword, and wand.
The poet ignores the obvious mysticism of the card and
points to the table itself—perhaps it is a kitchen table,
symbol of women gathering, women working. In Piercy's
experience, the Magician does not provide for workable,
human equality:

> We had thought we were waiting our Messiah, our
> Lenin,
> our golden Organizer who would fuse us into one
> body
> but now we see when we grow heads they lop them
> off.
> We must be every one the connection between energy
> and mass,
> every one the lightning that strikes to topple the tower.

(92)

Her discouragement with the sexism of the political activism of the 1960's is her natural entree to the woman's
movement:

> Give birth to me, sisters, in struggle we transform
> ourselves, but how often, how often
> we need help to cut loose, to cry out, to breathe!
> . . . . .

This morning we must make each other strong.
Change is qualitative: we are
each other's miracle.

(130)

The next four cards are placed to the right of the outer
circle creating a step ladder to the final Sun card. The first
rung is the **"Querent's Attitude as It Bears Upon the
Matter: The Three of Cups."** This is Piercy's card for
the Women's Movement as it gathers momentum. Two
women face a third woman whose back is toward us. This
third woman is identified with the poet. She wears a cloak
the same color of burnt orange as the gown worn by the
Queen of Pentacles. She has left her garden to dance with
others. Her hair is mixed with the light of the sun. The
woman to her left wears a dress similar to the color of the
Tower. The woman on her right is wearing a light brown
tunic the color of the soil. She holds a bunch of grapes in
her free hand. All three women have braided flowers into
their hair: "A poem is dancing; it goes out of a mouth to
your ears / and for some moments aligns us, / so we wheel
and turn together" (95). The mold of traditional male and
female pairing is broken in the feminization of art and
work. The self comes in several ways to its knowing, and
negative energy is released through the dance: "When I
dance I forget myself, I am danced. / Music fills me to
overflowing and the power moves / up from my feet to my
fingers, making leaves as sap does" (96). Piercy does not
hoard her power; she warns us that the dance is always in
danger of being stopped by the Tower:

> Even after Altamont, even after we have discovered
> we are still death's darling children, born of the print-
> out,
> the laser, the war-game, the fragmentation weapons of
> education,
> still we must bear joy back into the world.

(131)

Feminism will not be realized through technology, education, or war. A true and lasting feminism will depend on
the work of understanding "That every thing is a part of
something else" (97).

Piercy's ninth poem card, **"The House, The Environment: The Emperor,"** reveals the figure of the Emperor.
His throne has none of the sensual imagery of the throne
of the Queen of Pentacles. The rams' heads are emblems
of War. The globe in his left palm is the symbol of dominion. Piercy writes, "He holds a globe like something he
might bite into" (99). He is seated against a background of
"sterile mountains," in contrast to the growth and renewal
flowing from the mountains of the Queen of Pentacles. He
wears so much protection, that if he stood up, he would
fall over from the weight. The weight is obviously not *in*
the Queen of Pentacles; it is *on* him materially. His un-
yielding crown keeps his head erect, incapable of swaying
to the music of the Three of Cups. While the women dance,
the Emperor is as still as the stone of his throne. So, while

the Queen of Pentacles is surrounded by creativity and the abundance of nature, the Emperor is an entity unto himself:

> The Man from Mars with sterile mountains at his back—
> perhaps strip-mined. Perhaps the site of weapons testing—
> if we opened that armor like a can, would we find a robot?
> quaking old flesh? the ghost of an inflated bond issue?
>
> (133)

His is "the house of power grown old." The male in "mail" armor. His enemies are woman, love, music, art, and community. His throne could become our grave; his landscape our burial ground. He sits for materialism, sexism, and racism.

This card follows the Three of Cups to tell us that if we don't work together in numbers, our dance is only a May Day romp. The significance of what we are up against is that:

> There is in the dance of all things together no profit
> for each feeds the next and all pass through each other,
> the serpent whose tail is in her mouth,
> our mother earth turning.
> Now the wheel of the seasons sticks and the circle is broken
> and life spills out in an oil slick to rot the seas.
>
> (101)

The next to the last poem, **"What is Most Hoped and / or Most Feared: The Judgment,"** is a card of not turning our energies back, and of knowing our history:

> I call on the dead, I call on the defeated, on the starved,
> the sold, the tortured, the executed, the robbed:
> Indian women bayoneted before their children at Sand Creek,
> miners who choked on the black lung,
> strikers shot down at Pullman and Republic Steel,
> women bled to death of abortions men made illegal,
> sold, penned in asylums, lobotomized, raped and torn open,
> every black killed by police, national guard, mobs and armies.
>
> (103)

These are the victims not revealed to us in our American history texts. The blast of the poet's trumpet calls back these dead: "Live in us: give us your strength, give us your counsel, / give us your rage and your will to come at last into the light" (103). She is putting her morality and our morality to the test: to stand up as the dead stand up in this card in order to open ourselves to an examined life. The dead are men, women, and children. Their coffins are floating in the water that runs off from the mountains. The symbolism here is that knowledge of these lives will replenish the living.

The question that begins the last stanza has a familiar ring: *"Why do you choose to be noisy, to fight, to make trouble?"* This is a question asked of women from childhood on by mothers, fathers, brothers, teachers, landlords and lovers. The question is deaf to the answer which is: "You ask me, not understanding I have been born raw and new" (104). Here she is at the third stage outlined by Gerda Lerner. She has begun autonomously to define her goals and strategies for change. These changes mean she will not "crawl back in the cavern / where I lay with my neck bowed. / I have grown. I am not myself. / I am too many" (104).

**"The Outcome of the Matter: The Sun"** completes her reading. Here a smiling, naked child rides a horse without bridle and saddle. Behind the child there is a wall lined with sunflowers, not swords. The dominant image is a large, bright sun sending out rays that command the sky. The rays alternate with curved shafts, which are female, and straight shafts which are male. The sun's expression is one of peace and harmony. The sun's face is androgynous like the child whose arms and legs are spread like the sun's rays. Everything on this card signifies an openness of mind, body and spirit. The banner the child holds aloft is much larger than the child. It is the same color as the Queen of Pentacle's gown, the woman's shawl in The Tower, the merchant's hat in the Nine of Cups, the woman's dress in the Eight of Swords, the plume in the helmet of the Knight of Swords, the lead dancer in the Three of Cups, and the cross on the flag of the angel's horn in Judgment. It is a deeper, more organic color than the Magician's robe and the farmer's tunic in the Seven of Pentacles. Here it flows victoriously. The horse could be the same horse ridden by the Knight of Swords, but now the horse is not charging into battle. Piercy writes: "androgynous child whose hair curls into flowers. . . . Grow into your horse, let there be / no more riders or ridden" (105). The orange color that dots the child's hair in a natural crown sprouts a distinctive feather. It is the color of blood mixed with earth, the same predominant color of the Queen's gown. This child bears the seal of nature and of art and signifies the restored world.

If the Sun card exists in the Tarot, does it mean such a period of peace and harmony ever existed in history? Or is this the artist's dream? If it happened, or could happen, the Tarot and its images of sexism, materialism and power would be obsolete:

> Child, where are you heading with arms spread wide
> as a shore, have I been there, have I seen that land shining
> like sun spangles or clean water rippling?
> I do not know your dances, I cannot translate your tongue
> to words I use, your pleasures are strange to me
> as the rites of bees; yet you are the yellow flower
> of a melon vine growing out of my belly
> though it climbs up where I cannot see in the strong light.
>
> (106)

Piercy is not naive about her vision of the future. She knows that the utopian model of the Sun card will not occur in her lifetime. Her faith in the future is implicit in the last stanza

> The sun is rising, feel it: the air smells fresh.
> I cannot look in the sun's face, its brightness blinds me,
> but from my own shadow becoming distinct
> I know that now at last
> it is beginning to grow light.

> (107)

Piercy's view of the future in **Laying Down The Tower** is still in the working stages. However, it is through these poems that she sets herself free to discover the path to the future.

*Works Cited*

Gray, Eden. *Mastering the Tarot.* New York: Signet, 1973.

Kaplan, Stuart R. *The Encyclopedia of Tarot.* U.S. Games Systems, Inc. 1978.

Lerner, Gerda. "The Rise of Feminist Consciousness." Symposium. Stephens College. Columbia, 16 Feb. 1983.

Piercy, Marge. *To Be of Use.* New York: Doubleday, 1973.

---

**Additional coverage of Piercy's life and career is contained in the following sources published by the Gale Group:** *Contemporary Authors*, Vols. 21-24R; *Contemporary Authors Autobiography Series*, Vol. 1; *Contemporary Authors New Revision Series*, Vols. 13, 43, 66; *Contemporary Literary Criticism*, Vols. 3, 6, 14, 18, 27, 62; *Dictionary of Literary Biography*, Vol. 120; and *Major 20th-Century Writers*.

# Lizette Woodworth Reese
## 1856–1935

American poet, prose writer, and short story writer.

## INTRODUCTION

Although relatively unknown today, Reese was a popular American poet during the late Victorian and Edwardian periods. Praised for her concise style, her emotional yet never sentimental voice, and her nostalgic subjects, Reese earned a devoted following among critics and the public throughout her life. However, with the advent of modern poetic styles and her death, Reese faded into relative obscurity. Today she is known primarily as a transitional writer, bridging the gap between the Victorian and modern poets. In addition to her poetry, Reese published three books of recollections of late nineteenth-century small town life.

## BIOGRAPHICAL INFORMATION

Reese was born in the small Maryland town of Waverly, then known as Huntingdon, on January 9, 1856. One of four sisters, Reese remained in the Baltimore area throughout her lifetime. After attending public schools, which Reese supplemented with a voracious appetite for classic English literature, she secured a position as a teacher at Saint John's Parish School in 1873. In June 1874, she published her first poem "The Deserted House," in *Southern Magazine*. Although the poem lacked the skill of her later work, Reese established the themes and style for which she would be known: a solemn tone, the theme of eternal nature juxtaposed against the decay of society, the personification of nature, the simple and efficient use of language, and a brevity of description. During the next thirteen years Reese continued to write and publish in magazines such as the *Atlantic Monthly*, *Harper's Monthly* and *Scribner's*. In 1887 Reese used her own funds to publish her first collection of poems, *A Branch of May*. She sent copies of the work to such noted critics as Thomas Wentworth Higginson, William Dean Howells, and Edmund Clarence Stedman, who would become an influential figure in her career. Critics responded enthusiastically to her short, straightforward poetry which differed from the heavy, grandiose verse of the Victorians. Reese was able to publish her second volume of poetry with Houghton Mifflin in 1891. Upon the publication of her third collection in 1896, Reese had established herself as a noteworthy poet in America and England. After teaching in the Baltimore public schools for forty-five years while concurrently pursuing a writing career, Reese retired in 1921 and devoted

more of her time to writing. Before her death in 1935 she published five more collections of poetry and wrote two works of childhood recollections. After her death a final volume of poetry, *The Old House in the Country*, was published in 1936.

## MAJOR WORKS

Reese published eleven works of poetry, spanning from her first self-published collection *A Branch of May* in 1887 to her posthumously published *The Old House in the Country* in 1936. Although she acquired greater skill throughout her career and experimented somewhat with form, her work is generally uniform in style, voice, tone, and content. Reese rejected social commentary and observations on modernity and industrialization, instead focusing on aspects of nature and life which she had witnessed in her quiet rural surroundings in Waverly. She chose such subjects as death, religion, and pastoral scenes. In 1909 she published *A Wayside Lute*, which contained her best known and most highly regarded poem, the sonnet "Tears."

Reese primarily wrote short, rhymed, metered verse, often employing the sonnet form. She was known and admired for her concise voice and unsentimental tone which differed from the earlier Victorian poets and gave her poetry a distinctly modern air. In 1927 she published *Little Henrietta*, a collection of thirty-nine short poems that narrate the story of her cousin Henrietta Matilda. This work constitutes her only unrhymed poetry.

## CRITICAL RECEPTION

During her lifetime Reese enjoyed popularity from critics and the public alike, encountering little difficulty publishing her poetry. Although critics agreed that she was among the minor poets of her age, the publication of each of her volumes was met with favorable reviews. However, Reese's popularity did not sustain past her death. Although her works are still included in anthologies and scholars, have conceded her role as a transitional figure in American poetry, little new critical scholarship has been written about Reese in the second half of the twentieth century. During her lifetime such reviewers as Genevieve Taggard, Louis Untermeyer, and Carlin T. Kindilien compared Reese's writing to Emily Dickinson's poetry, although each noted that Reese failed to achieve the sharpness and skill of Dickinson. Kindilien observed, "Like Emily Dickinson, Lizette Reese turned from the American scene and wrote a personal poetry that analyzed universals, but, unlike the Amherst poet, she was not to receive the critical attention that would have made known her achievement." Other critics have compared her writing with that of Robert Herrick and Edna St. Vincent Millay. Reviewers have praised her brevity, concision, phrasing, and restraint. Though her tone was nostalgic and her subject matter often somber, commentators have noted that through her sincerity and simplicity Reese's poetry never sounded sentimental. However, Mark Van Doren has argued that her poetry "lack[ed] original salt" and Louise Bogan has despaired the absence of intellectuality and range in Reese's work.

---

# PRINCIPAL WORKS

## Poetry

*A Branch of May: Poems* 1887
*A Handful of Lavender* 1891
*A Quiet Road* 1896
*A Wayside Lute* 1909
*Spicewood* 1920
*Wild Cherry* 1923
*The Selected Poems* 1926
*Little Henrietta* 1927
*White April, and Other Poems* 1930
*Pastures and Other Poems* 1933

*The Old House in the Country* 1936

## Other Major Works

*A Victorian Village: Reminiscences of Other Days* (reminiscences) 1929
*The York Road* (reminiscences and short stories) 1931
*Worleys* (fiction) 1936

---

# CRITICISM

### *The Nation* (review date 1896)

SOURCE: A Review of *A Quiet Road*, in *The Nation* (New York), Vol. 63, No. 1641, December 10, 1896, p. 443.

*[In the review below, the critic praises Reese's voice as calm.]*

*A Quiet Road,* by Lizette Woodworth Reese, has that calm, lily-scented atmosphere which always belongs to this lady's poems; she knows how to make the most of what we have that is colonial and picturesque; and this is done without straining or affectation. She even takes pains to explain in a footnote that the "Dorset levels" in the poem which follows are not transatlantic, but are only on the Eastern Shore of Maryland, and that she has therefore a full right to dwell on them and theirs (p. 57):

> **"The Lavender Woman—A Market Song."**
> Crooked, like the bough the March wind bends wall-ward across the sleet.
> Stands she at her blackened stall in the loud market street;
> All about her in the sun, full-topped, exceeding sweet,
> Lie bundles of gray lavender, a-shrivel in the heat.
> What the Vision that is mine, coming over and o'er?
> 'Tis the Dorset levels, aye, behind me and before:
> Creeks that slip without a sound from flaggy shore to shore:
> Orchards gnarled with springtimes and as gust-bound as of yore.
> Oh, the panes at sunset burning rich-red as the rose!
> Oh, colonial chimneys that the punctual swallow knows!
> Land where like a memory the salt scent stays or goes,
> Where wealthy is the reaper and right glad is he that sows
> Drips and drips the last June rain, but toward the even-fall
> Copper gleam the little pools behind the pear-trees tall:
> In a whirl of violet, and the fairest thing of all,
> The lavender, the lavender sways by the sagging wall.
>
> . . . . .
>
> Oh, my heart, why should you break at any thoughts like these?

So sooth are they of the old time that they should
bring you ease;
Of Hester in the lavender and out among the bees,
Clipping the long stalks one by one under the Dorset
trees.

## Mark Van Doren (review date 1921)

SOURCE: "Fashions," in *The Nation* (New York), Vol.
112, No. 2914, May 11, 1921, p. 693.

[*In the following review of* Spicewood, *Van Doren finds
Reese's work too ordered and lacking in force.*]

When Jessie B. Rittenhouse in 1904 wrote sketches of
eighteen "Younger American Poets" she put Miss Reese in
the second place as one who was mistress of a certain poignant primness, as one who was a feminine Robert Herrick. The quality implied in the comparison was debatable
then and is more debatable now. Miss Reese's sonnets and
quatrain-songs are impeccable in meter and phrasing, are
irreproachable in sentiment; but they lack original salt.
Their edges are frilled and lavendered, while their central
designs are woven of gentle archaisms—"nowhit," "of a
surety," "this many a year," "hushes where the lonely are,"
"all palely sweet," "candlelight," "wayfarer," "deem"—
which Herrick did not or would not now employ. A little
conscious archness in rhyme-words and endinglines will
not make up for a great monotony of neatness. Any poetical idea is new to the poet who makes it so; Miss Reese's
are laced and ivoried over with unvarying, respectable age.
Her book is not without charm, but it is without force.
. . .

## Louis Untermeyer (essay date 1923)

SOURCE: "Lizette Woodworth Reese," in *American Poetry Since 1900*, Henry Holt and Company, 1923, pp. 300-
02.

[*In the following excerpt, Untermeyer views Reese's poetry as lucid, surprising, and well-crafted.*]

Philosophies, fashions, innovations, movements, concern
[Lizette Woodworth Reese] not at all; her poetry is bare of
social interpretations, problems, almost of ideas. Song, unabashed, actually antiquated song is what she delights in.
And out of tunes with little novelty or *nuance,* she evokes
a personal grace that is as fragrant as an old-fashioned
flower garden. Miss Reese's realization of this quality
finds its fullest expression in the volumes which she has
significantly entitled *A Branch of May* (1887), *A Handful
of Lavender* (1891), *A Quiet Road* (1896), *A Wayside
Lute* (1909). These volumes, in the chaste reissues printed
by Thomas B. Mosher, show Miss Reese as the forerunner
of Sara Teasdale, Edna Millay and the new generation to
whom simplicity in song is a first essential. Miss Reese

thrives within her narrow borders. Her verse is at home
behind clipped hedges, among Belleek teacups and delicate Sèvres; I would not be surprised to learn that she
writes it in black lace mitts. But it is not only her reticence which gives her work its quality; it is its very excellence of definition. **"Spicewood," "Spinning Tops,"
"Bible Stories," "Driving Home the Cows"** are among a
score whose very craftsmanship is delightful. There is a
lucidity, almost a translucence, in such poems. One can
find this limpid color in the sonnets, of which the following is representative.

> The east is yellow as a daffodil.
> Three steeples—three stark swarthy arms—are thrust
> Up from the town. The gnarlèd poplars thrill
> Down the long street in some keen salty gust—
> Straight from the sea and all the sailing ships—
> Turn white, black, white again, with noises sweet
> And swift. Back to the night the last star slips.
> High up the air is motionless, a sheet
> Of light. The east grows yellower apace,
> And trembles: then, once more, and suddenly,
> The salt wind blows, and in that moment's space
> Flame roofs, and poplar-tops, and steeples three;
> From out the mist that wraps the river-ways,
> The little boats, like torches, start ablaze.
>
> **"Sunrise"**

Miss Reese's lines are full of happy surprises. She speaks
of "daffodils, lighting their candles in the April grass," in a
deserted garden walk, "the lean bush crouching hints old
royalty," she sees that, before the rain, "the poplar shows
its white teeth to the gust"; in **"Tears,"** which is possibly
Miss Reese's finest sonnet, she has this vividly suggestive
octave.

> When I consider Life and its few years—
> A wisp of fog betwixt us and the sun;
> A call to battle, and the battle done
> Ere the last echo dies within our ears;
> A rose choked in the grass; an hour of fears;
> The gusts that past a darkening shore do beat;
> The burst of music down an unlistening street—
> I wonder at the idleness of tears.

**"The Dust," "Witch Hazel," "Ellen Hanging Clothes,"
"After,"** are among many which reveal this poet's simple
illuminations. Frequently she suggests a milder Emily
Dickinson—her epigrams are less pointed, her epithets
less startling—and there is always, as in the following
poem, a living translation of the thing observed.

> Towns, lovers, quarrels, bloom—
>     All change from day to day,
> But not that steadfast room,
>     Far and far away.
> The stiff chairs ranged around;
>     The blue jar flowered wide;
> The quick, close racing sound
>     Of poplar trees outside—
> I daresay all are there;
>     There still two pictures keep—
> The girl so tall and fair;
>     Christ with His foolish sheep.
>
> **"The Room"**

## Harriet Monroe (review date 1924)

SOURCE: "Faint Perfume," in *Poetry*, Vol. 23, No. VI, March, 1924, pp. 341-42.

[*In the following review of* Wild Cherry, *Monroe argues that while Reese's poems are effective, she too often relies on Victorian mannerisms.*]

Soft scented poems are these, delicately frail and fine, sprung from a shy and isolated soul; an expression of wistfulness, of the ache of smothered emotions. They are carefully studied, they don't try to say or do anything original; but they sing, with musical taste and precision, a clear pure little minor tune all in the same key.

Mostly they are simply written, and in modern diction, but Miss Reese should discard *of yore* from her vocabulary—a convenient rhyme, in five places at least, for *door* or *floor,* but worn to shreds long since, and moreover inexactly used in such a present-tense line as

As one who comes back to a house of yore.

In a few other details also one finds this poet yielding to Victorian temptations.

Some of the portraits are delicately sketched. **"A Puritan Lady,"** for example, after the first two ineffectual stanzas, gives a real picture:

Humble and high in one,
    Cool, certain, different,
She lasts; scarce saint, yet half a child,
    As hard, as innocent.

What grave long afternoons,
    What caged airs round her blown,
Stripped her of humor, left her bare
    As cloud, or wayside stone?—

Made her as clear a thing,
    In this slack world as plain,
As a white flower on a grave
    Or sharp sleet at a pane?

**"Spring Ecstasy"**, **"To Love"**, **"Before the Look of You"**—these and other poems are faint whiffs of faded perfume—a bit trite, perhaps, like pressed flowers. Here is *To Love:*

Take me and break me, Love;
    Make me into a thing
More memorable than a star,
    Or a tall flower in spring.

If this you will not do,
    Down to oblivion thrust;
Into a sleek forgotten grave
    Crumble me to dust!

## David Morton (review date 1924)

SOURCE: A Review of *Wild Cherry*, in *The Outlook*, Vol. 136, No. 11, March 12, 1924, pp. 439-40.

[*In the review below, Morton praises the quality of Reese's work and laments that she has failed to garner critical attention.*]

Of late our ears have been filled with the noise of new names—to the extent of drowning out altogether the thin sound of names that are not noisy and that are no longer new. In the circumstances, it is not surprising that a new book of poems by Lizette Woodworth Reese should issue from the press and take its place upon the shelves with no loud heralding or hoarse huzzas. Miss Reese and her readers would not have it otherwise; yet from such a disparity in the degree of attention a confusion of values is apt to result.

Masters with his revealing epitaphs, Frost with his distinctive New England folk, and Amy Lowell with her gorgeous tapestries and delicate images—to mention only three who live in the mouth of publicity—each brought a new and peculiar contribution to poetry in English. Miss Reese—not just to-day, nor yesterday, but even the day before yesterday—with her exquisite refinement of thought and feeling, her delicate and perfect phrasing, and her sensitive and lyrical response to the frail and beautiful things of earth and of the spirit, also brought, and brings, a distinctive contribution. If it is less startling than these others, and no longer so new as theirs, these are considerations which impair not at all its genuine and lasting worth.

Some years ago, I remember, Padraic Colum had some sober and sound things to say on the subject of publicity and fame. The differences in origin, constituencies, and destiny between the two are so obvious that it would seem needless to dwell upon them. But it is serviceable to note, by way of preserving a responsible sense of values, that the two are seldom coextensive in proportions, and that the growth of the latter is quiet and gradual; that it is based upon human needs adequately served; that it proceeds without noise at a time when the blare of the day's trumpets is all of other things.

Something of this sort has gone on in the case of Miss Reese and her poetry. She has ceased to be of any great use to the heralds of publicity. Her accent was never a startling or revolutionary thing. And now even the delicate and sweet distinction that it had is no longer a novelty. How should one call the populace together to shout to them, for example, **"A Girl's Mood"**:

I love a prayer-book;
I love a thorn-tree
That blows in the grass
As white as can be.

I love an old house
Set down in the sun,
And the windy old roads
That thereabout run.

I love blue, thin frocks;
Green stones one and all;
A sky full of stars,
A rose at the fall.

> A lover I love;
> Oh, had I but one,
> I would give him all these,
> Myself, and the sun!

This is scarcely the right pitch or the proper matter for ear-splitting. But I suspect that it represents an old, old verity with fidelity—certainly with a delicate and trembling vividness, and a virginal music no less authentic for being thin.

Something of this same fresh and unspoiled quality inhabits most of the poetry in this latest book of a writer who began publishing when most of her better-known and wearily sophisticated colleagues in the art were yet in knee-breeches or pinafores. This virginal freshness—the innocent and ingenuous pleasure in the immediate joys and melancholies of existence—is the same delicate bloom in this volume that it was in *A Handful of Lavender,* published as long ago as 1892.

Above I have said something of Miss Reese's exquisite refinement of feeling and of her sensitive and lyrical, response to things frail and lovely. Both of these qualities might be enlarged upon to the profit and delight of those surfeited with disordered and self-conscious poetry, merging over into pathology as its proper field. But it were more serviceable and delightful to reprint, as an instance and a characteristic sonnet, **"Triumph"**:

> Heart's measure gave I. Is it all forgot?
> Winds cannot blow or beat it into dust.
> Or waters cover it, or moth or rust
> Corrupt it into aught that it was not.
> For what is more remembered than the spring?
> The scarlet tulips running through the grass
> By a wet wall, and gone with but Alas?
> (I know not how I know this old, old thing).
> How now, poor one, that loved me for a space?
> Mine is the triumph of the tulip flower;
> My ruined April will not let you by;
> To east my laughter, and to west my face,
> Housed with you ever down some
> poignant hour,
> There drifts the scrap of music that was I.

The poem is worth citing as an instance of certain outstanding qualities in Miss Reese's work as a whole—faultless technique, sensitive and delicate phrasing, and of passion restrained, yet glowing, and the element of repose which we associate with the finest art when it has fused jagged experience into a perfect and significant entity.

## Genevieve Taggard (review date 1926)

SOURCE: "The Horns of the Morning," in *The New York Herald Tribune*, July 11, 1926, p. 5.

[*In the following review of* The Selected Poems of Lizette Woodworth Reese, *Taggard states that the poems possess "deep feeling" and compares Reese's writing to that of Edna Millay and Emily Dickinson.*]

Miss reese has a slow and fragile gift, by means of which she has accomplished very high things. She has refused to be many things her gift might imply, and she has written the sonnet **"Tears,"** with its Miltonic beginning, which consoles us in the end for its lack of Miltonic grandeur and stern-ness by being the purest and tenderest of poems.

> When I consider Life and its few years—
> A wisp of fog betwixt us and the sun;
> A call to battle, and the battle done
> Ere the last echo dies within our ears;
> A rose choked in the grass; an hour of fears;
> The gusts that past a darkening shore do beat;
> A burst of music down an unlistening street—
> I wonder at the idleness of tears.
> Ye old, old dead and ye of yesternight,
> Chieftains and bards and keepers of sheep,
> By every cup of sorrow that you had,
> Loose me from tears, and make me see aright
> How each hath back what once he stayed to weep;
> Homer his sight, David his little lad.

This is Miss Reese's seventh book, and the poems that conclude it are less in the May, Lavender and Wild-Cherry mood than her earlier ones. The dead friend and the dead lover, wayside lanes, rain, holy days and praise of common things permeate everything she writes. Spiritual things are always unique and real to her soul's eyes. Perhaps that is why she seems to care so little for fresh and rugged sight of the world around her. She lives in a dream country, the world of Housman, and all gentle English-fond poets. Her slowness and quietness and lack of cleverness make her seem like a little petal from the tree of Miss Millay, which has burst into a large heaven-set cloud.

Indeed, a careful reading of Miss Reese shows a kinship to both Edna Millay and Emily Dickinson. Her total quality is remote from them, but certain units and symbols in both are observed and touched with the same feminine mind.

> But just now out in the lane
> Oh the scent of mint was plain!

has been cast in better form in **"My Heart, Being Hungry"**:

> Nor linger in the rain to mark
> The smell of tansy through the dark.

My guess is that Miss Reese influenced the early Miss Millay; and curiously enough the later Miss Reese writes clearly aware of her contemporary in such lines as:

> My dear, my dear, forgive me for the wrong.

and

> I dig amongst the roots of life.

I cannot prove at all my feeling that Miss Reese is close in kin to Emily Dickinson. But among the large number of her readers I think there will be some who will catch the likeness at odd moments. Emily Dickinson constructed poems like atoms, which when caught under a microscope prove to be as much universe as atom. Miss Reese is not so angular, so bold, so tremendous or so exquisite. But she speaks the same language, although the defeat and victory that exist side by side in Emily Dickinson are never in her. The undeniable metaphysical talent in her is softened by white beauty.

Her best poems are least resigned. Like **"The Dust"** and **"Immortality"** and **"Waiting"** and **"Love Came Back at Fall of Dew,"** this called **"Tragic Books"** from her new poems, has a brief, plain beauty:

> That I have lived I know; that I
> Have loved is quite as plain;
> Why read of Lear, a wild old king,
> Of Cæsar stabbed in vain?
>
> The bitter fool, the Dover heath,
> The stumbling in the grass
> I know. I know the windy crowd,
> And Rome as in a glass.
>
> Life taught them all. These later days
> Are full enough of rain;
> I will not weep unless I must,
> Or break my heart again.

**"Telling the Bees"** and **"Lydia Is Gone This Many a Year"** are poems with a sad delicacy, too fragile and unhurried to be sentimental. Miss Reese's lyric gift lies not in what she says, nor the manner of her saying it, neither of which is unusual, but in a very deep and quiet permanency of feeling, as difficult to describe as the opening of a million small buds on a tree. In **"To a Town Poet"** she instructs a younger generation:

> Let trick of words be past;
> Strict with the thought, unfearful of the form,
> So shall you find the way and hold it fast,
> The world hear, at last,
> The horns of morning sound above the storm.

**Padraic Colum (review date 1926)**

SOURCE: "In the Line of Herrick," in *The Saturday Review of Literature*, Vol. III, No. 1, July 31, 1926, p. 7.

[*In the following review of* The Selected Poems of Lizette Woodworth Reese, *Colum praises Reese as innovative and remarks on her handling of traditional poetic forms, particularly the sonnet.*]

Frank Harris, as he has recorded, judged H. L. Mencken to be a whimsical critic of poetry because of his praise of Lizette Woodworth Reese's poems. "She has written more sound poetry, more genuinely eloquent and beautiful poetry, than all the new poets put together." Mencken certainly underrated the work of the new poets. Frank Harris, on the other hand, was wildly wrong when he drew from that statement the conclusion, "Mencken simply doesn't care for poetry at all." It happens that he was right when he said that Lizette Woodworth Reese wrote beautiful poetry, and because of this righteous judgment a multitude of arbitrary judgments may in the end be forgiven H. L. M.

Lizette Woodworth Reese's poetry has for its characteristic quality an emotion that has been schooled and that finds its interpretation in things that, traditionally, have been found lovable—simple and natural things. There may be readers who, on looking into her book and finding that it offers no innovations in form and that it has much about cherry trees and country lanes, will make up their minds that it is all conventional. If they do it will be because they are not able to distinguish between originality and novelty. Lizette Woodworth Reese has an emotional being that is strong enough to fill out the convention; she is sufficiently well instructed in, and sufficiently sympathetic with, the body of traditional English poetry to be able to use the conventional forms readily and spontaneously. Indeed, the use of these forms is part of a virtue that she possesses—a virtue rare enough in these days, the virtue of not being self-regarding, of not insisting upon one's own inventiveness.

All her poems give the effect of rarities and this is because she writes for one reason only—to give release to an emotion that has been experienced and dwelt upon. Her emotion is always basically a human one, and it is always expressed in terms of things ordinarily seen and known—

> Lovely, secure, unhastening things,
> Fast-kept for this, grip as of yore;—
> The drowsy traffic of the bees;
> The scarlet haws beyond a door.

Hers is a poetry we want to read over and over again; it is a poetry we can live with; it is like bread, like a bowl, like a faggot in a fire, like a blossoming tree down a laneway. It is a poetry that deals with loss and reconciliation, and that is able to invest these themes with dignity and with fairness. Her most famous poem is the sonnet **"Tears."** Reading it in this selection, I find it memorable indeed—I find that I know it by heart and that I had failed to notice before that it is imperfect as a sonnet seeing that it introduces into the octave a couplet that differs from the rhyme-scheme that had been provided for. A sonnet near it, **"Tell Me Some Way,"** is as fine as **"Tears,"** and a comparison of the two suggests a thought on the sonnet-form. **"Tears"** enters and stays in our memory because of a rhetorical element that is in it—an element that is not in the other sonnet. The word "rhetoric" is of bad import when used in connection with a poem. But does not a sonnet, to some extent, appeal to what is reflective in us, and is there not a kind of rhetoric that is addressed to what is reflective as distinct from what is emotional in us?

It is one of the mysteries of American literature how Lizette Woodworth Reese writes poetry that is so completely in the tradition of English poetry. She is not of New England. Her ancestry, I think, is Welsh, German, and Irish. Yet she writes as if there had been nothing between her and an English that had come from Herrick, and nothing to break a melody that had been known to all the poets of the English countryside. It is true that in one of her poems she has peach-trees blossoming where peach-trees could never grow—in Dorset or Devon—but although she may be mistaken about a detail here and there in the landscape, her poetry is in and of the English tradition. Perhaps I have made too much use of the words "tradition," and "convention." Lizette Woodworth Reese's poetry is individual and personal. And this volume of **Selected Poems** will make wide and secure the franchise that the half dozen books of verse already published have won for her.

## Lawrence S. Morris (review date 1926)

SOURCE: "Some Flowers Down a Lane," in *The New Republic: A Journal of Opinion*, Vol. 48, No. 612, August 25, 1926, pp. 23-4.

[*In the following review of* Selected Poems, *Morris comments on Reese's tone and sense of nostalgia.*]

Miss Reese has been singing quietly for many years. Now, with a sense that the day is waning, she has just as quietly issued her **Selected Poems.** We can read over in these few pages what she hopes we will keep of her gentle song, spun in an old-time garden by a firm heart heavy with nostalgia. Some of these poems are already familiar. The new ones have the same simplicity of speech and the same motifs: separation, loneliness, remembrance of lost love and the beauty of familiar things. Amid the box hedges and colonial chimneys of the old East Shore of Maryland these poems have taken refuge from the "brawling days" of our American life. The fragile sturdiness of hollyhocks is in their pages. She is living now before the War, and her voice comes bravely from behind a soft gray veil.

It is inevitable that her poems should have something of the deliberation of box hedges. In her lonely days she has learned to love the bordered paths, the bees in lavender, the poplar trees across the road. These things are fragrant with the sweet earth, but they are also tamed. They do not grow carelessly where the sun invites them. Miss Reese is close enough to the earth to have its healthy sweetness, but her poetry, like her garden, has been set out and trimmed. It never opens effortlessly in the grass like spring hepathicas, nor flares, like sumac, unexpectedly upon a hill. It is the view from the front window:

> There is no loveliness so plain
> As a tall poplar in the rain.
>
> But oh, the hundred things and more
> That come in at the door!

> The smack of mint, old joy, old pain,
> Caught in the gray and tender rain.

The praise of "common things" runs through all the volume and is full of murmured affection; it never attains the sudden breathlessness which makes Edna Millay's poems of familiar things flutter so poignantly in the imagination, and escape in the same moment they are grasped.

The remembrance of past losses lingers for Miss Reese in the scent of intimate flowers. In lyrics and sonnets she sings all the moods of sad memories staunchly borne—for within her garden she is a stoic. She has traced the diminuendo of grief through its gradual subsiding, until it becomes the infrequent stab brought we no longer know just why, by an encounter of odor or gleaming briar. It is always the echo of grief we find in her pages; she has nowhere impaled on stripped and vibrant words, as a freer poet would have, the agony of grief itself. Even grief speaks behind the soft gray veil.

As if she were aware that as a poet she had been denied the unashamed nakedness she feels the need of, she has made an appeal to Life:

> Unpetal the flower of me,
> And cast it to the gust;
> Betray me if you will;
> Trample me to dust.
>
> But that I should go bare,
> But that I should go free
> Of any hurt at all—
> Do not this thing to me!

The words are themselves a confession that in spite of her stoic willingness the appeal had already been rejected. To realize their limitation one has only to place them beside another poem by Edna Millay: those twelve ultimate lines entitled Feast.

> I drank at every vine.
>   The last was like the first.
> I came upon no wine
>   So wonderful as thirst.

Miss Millay's poem rises to an assertion of ecstasy, Miss Reese's remains a prayer. She writes with feeling, with clear intelligence, with sensitiveness to every gentle beauty. The wilder beauties lie, of course, outside her garden. And even within her garden, in spite of her stoic love of loveliness, and her patient searching for clean simple words, the piercing phrase which trembles in revealment has never blinded her page.

Time will make an even more rigorous selection of her works than she has made. It will discard her sonnets to dead poets and the other short poems whose inspiration is literary. But it will keep a handful of her songs of the "gray and tender rain," and two or three sonnets, including certainly **"The Look of the Hedge"** and that splendid one with its Shakespearean first line, "When I consider Life and its few years." To have compelled this much of a nod from Time is an accomplishment.

### Virginia R. McCormick (review date 1926)

SOURCE: A Review of *The Selected Poems of Lizette Woodworth Reese*, in *Catholic World*, Vol. 124, No. 739, October, 1926, pp. 133-34.

[*In the review below, McCormick commends Reese's poetry for its tone and restraint.*]

Here is a volume reflecting credit upon both publisher and poet; the binding is dignified and durable, a combination rare in these days. The paper is of a rich and creamy loveliness and the print clear and definite, free from all typographical errors. So much for the mechanical technique!

The spirit of the book is the poetry between the covers, and since the spirit is Miss Reese it is triumphant, fearless, and sometimes militant! Miss Reese's poetic gift is the lyrical one, the highest in poetry; she sings of all things true, and fresh, and strong. She does not believe in the impressionistic school; she chisels her outlines with infinite pains and fearless daring. Her English has none of the sloppiness of the modern cults; she is Anglo-Saxon both in thought and language: "If I derive from anyone," she laughingly says, "it is Herrick." Like Herrick she sees beauty in all nature about her, but she is more of an artist than a preacher, and always resists the desire to point a moral through her poetry, a weakness all too evident in the gentle divine.

This collection shows a fine sense of selectivity, in sharp contrast with the cumbersome volumes of collected verse conspicuous on all sides. Only Robert Frost, with his high sense of values, has shown such restraint in our day. With Miss Reese artistic restraint is a predominating characteristic, and one often feels the effect of the unsaid word as keenly as the polished phrase upon the printed page.

The book has, according to the index, twenty new poems, but there are ten more scattered among the pages, that are for the first time included in a book. In the group of new poems at the end of the volume, such lyrics as **"Apples,"** **"To One Who Died Young," "Sanctuary," "Romance,"** **"Tragic Books,"** and **"Reparation"** would stamp any collection as distinguished. Perhaps the eight-line lyric, **"Fortune,"** in this division, does as much as any of her poems to give us Miss Reese, as young after seven books of poems, dating from 1887 to 1926, as when she received her first check from Scribner's for the immortal sonnet, **"Tears"**:

> "I have so little, yet am rich;
> I pay my bread with gold
> Filched from wild mustard by the road,
> As much as I can hold.

> "I have such plenty, yet am poor;
> I pay my roof with tears
> Shed for the time when I was young
> And unaware of years."

### William Rose Benet (review date 1927)

SOURCE: "Poets in Collected Editions," in *The Yale Review*, Vol. XVII, No. 1, October, 1927, pp. 367-74.

[*In the following review of* Selected Poems, *Benet states that although Reese is limited in her subjects, she writes her style of poetry well.*]

Over twenty years ago a critic of poetry said of Miss Lizette Woodworth Reese, "To be rare and quaint without being fantastic, to have swift-conceiving fancy that turns into poetry the near-by thing that many overlook—this is Miss Reese's gift." That remains true. Her *Selected Poems* are gathered together from small former volumes the titles of which are so indicative that I shall quote them, *A Branch of May*, *A Handful of Lavender*, *A Quiet Road*, *A Wayside Lute*, *Spicewood*, *Wild Cherry*. Herbs and simples occur and recur in her limpid stanzas. Her phrasing is all of "the pear-tree's flakes of snow," "the smack of mint," "gust to gust in shrubberies tall," the "strict scent of box," "the quick, close, racing sound of poplar trees outside." These phrases illustrate the keen observation of her senses and also the fact that her poems are drawn from the life of her own place and the comparative quietude immediately encompassing her.

Distinctly, though we think of Miss Reese as a feminine rural Herrick, she also displays the intuitive power of vision that the delicate Herrick sometimes displayed. Her lyrics are, in general, better than her sonnets, though perhaps her finest poem is a sonnet. Yet, all in all, she has cultivated her strict garden admirably.

### Jean Starr Untermeyer (review date 1930)

SOURCE: "Lyric Veteran," in *The Saturday Review of Literature*, Vol. VII, No. 15, November 1, 1930, pp. 283-84.

[*In the following review of* White April, *Untermeyer argues that the collection as a whole fails to indicate the importance and skill of Reese as a poet, although her stature is more apparent in select individual poems.*]

It would be an ill thing for Lizette Woodworth Reese as well as for themselves if most of her readers should know her only by her latest book of poems, **White April,** embodying though it does many of her excellencies. Reading this book as a purely contemporaneous work, one could see at a glance its perfections and its limitations. And yet one would not know this woman as a pioneer—one who, in a lesser but no less consistent way than Emily Dickinson, released woman's poetry from a stilted and sentimental pattern into an arresting and highly personal expression. Here is a woman in her mid-seventies writing with the verve and tenderness of a young girl; and so long and so consistently has she influenced more than a generation of women poets, that, read casually today, she seems one only slightly more gifted among a score of talented writers.

It is a curious exercise to track down this influence, to seize upon the salient features that her imitators, conscious or unconscious, have incorporated into their own verses. It is not form. Miss Reese's forms are the traditional forms of our lyric verse, with a preponderance of short quatrains and occasional sonnets. What makes her poems so effective, aside from their intrinsic beauty, is the habit of seeing common things romantically and bringing into sudden and almost violent juxtaposition the heroic and the humble, the minute and the momentous. Nowhere does she do this more characteristically than in:

> Love not a loveliness too much,
> For it may turn and clutch you so,
> That you be less than any serf,
> And at its bidding go.
>
> Be master; otherwise you grow
> Too small, too humble, like to one
> Long dispossessed, who stares through tears
> At his lost house across the sun.
>
> Wild carrot in an old field here,
> A steeple choked with music there,
> Possess, as part of what is yours;
> Thus prove yourself the heir.
>
> Your barony is sky and land,
> From morning's start to the night's close;
> Bend to your need Orion's hounds,
> Or the thin fagot of a rose.
>
> "Ownership"

Again and again she employs this method and where the contrasts are not directly stated, they are implied.

A few repeated themes run through her work: love and betrayal; the suffering and solace of spring; the eternal lure of nature, and the veriest little of philosophy. The titles of her books (*White April*, *A Branch of May*, *A Handful of Layender*, *A Quiet Road*, *Wild Cherry*) like her poems, have a distressing if rustic similarity. The note is personal and unmistakably feminine. Her vocabulary, while it lacks the outstanding singularity of Emily Dickinson's, has a certain aromatic pertness and clipped grace, that with a few notable exceptions, has been taken over by a body of younger women writers. So much so that one might read aloud anonymously a dozen pieces from **"White April"**—such sharply different poems as **"Words," "Heat," "Afar," "Things," "Succory"**—and ascribe them to at least a half-dozen assorted authors.

This is not to belittle Miss Reese. She made this field hers and has impressed her pattern on a generation. It is only to say that it needs an historical memory to be able to read these poems without a sense of echo. This is the dissatisfaction of reading the book as a book (a method disastrous and unfair to all except epic or dramatic poetry). The rewards come with individual poems in which Miss Reese breaks through her self-imposed mannerisms into a larger utterance.

## Eda Lou Walton (review date 1933)

SOURCE: "The Stripped but Permanent Few," in *The Nation* (New York), Vol. 137, November 15, 1933, p. 571.

[*In the following review of* Pastures and Other Poems, *Walton argues that while Reese's voice is not modern, her writing has such genius that she will appeal to the modern reader.*]

Miss Reese is a "stripped" romantic, I suppose, if we must define her philosophy. But she is very like this, her own stanza:

> A rich fragility was theirs,
> Warm poverty of hue,
> The little that is more than much,
> The stripped, but permanent few.

***Pastures and Other Poems*** is going to throw its modern readers into a deep nostalgia for the simple, the just, the rightly beautiful. They will turn temporarily from the intricate poets of the city, the rhetoricians, to these old verities which Miss Reese so beautifully expresses. In a world where truth is temporal these verities seem terribly poignant, almost lost to us save for their shadow on our memory.

One of the finest of our minor poets—and most poets today are minor—Miss Reese has been too little appreciated. Over and over again with exquisite simplicity and sincerity she achieves the perfect brief lyric. With a single image drawn from nature closely observed, she says more about human life than many a more ornate or difficult poet may say. Her art is so precise, so quiet, so unpretentious that it is difficult to discuss. The critic blurs her work by trying to define it.

Humble words, the simplest in our vocabulary, simple images of objects familiar to every country dweller, the restrained quatrain form, or the fine sonnet—these are the elements of Miss Reese's poetry. Her faith is personal, unorthodox, the certainty that God is to be found if we seek him. But her mind takes into account without flinching all the conflicting facts in life. She accepts the impermanence of beauty as beauty's real significance. She accepts sorrow and death. She is never sentimental or blind. Miss Reese looks steadily and long at whatever she sees as beautiful and she sets down exactly what is there but in the pattern of art. She interprets humble things as eternal. The lad driving home his father's cows at dusk becomes, for the housewives seeing him while they set the supper tables, a lasting picture:

> Long as they lived they saw
> A picture old and fine;
> They saw the golden lad;
> They saw the golden kine.

The asters "clumped in gapings of a fence" mean:

> Yet not from Apriling are these;
> Wars know they, grate of spears;
> Their settled looks are raised upon
> A dynasty of tears.

There are very few poets today who have kept so acute an awareness of nature along with so accurate a knowledge of the humble heart. Nature with no sensual or romantic embroiderings is understood by Miss Reese to epitomize the perfection toward which man aspires. Nothing man himself invents seems so sure a symbol of beauty and permanence as does the thorn tree or the rose. The choosing of the simplest image described by the simplest adjective is a kind of genius with this poet. The reader is left marveling that such ordinary words can become so magical. Miss Reese has something of the early romantic poets' skill in keeping a perfect realism fused with a gentle romanticism and humanitarianism. Here is the intensity of the quiet, thoughtful mind. And her art is entirely her own. Never once in all the years she has been writing has she been influenced away from doing the type of poem she could do best. With a long life behind her and the wisdom of that life behind her words she sets down very directly what she knows and feels. Her communication is so perfect, because of the homely language beautifully employed, that there is no barrier between her and even her most modern reader. Such a modern reader might be under the influence of Eliot or the new English communist-intellectual school and still feel deeply the message that Miss Reese conveys.

## Louise Bogan (review date 1936)

SOURCE: "Out of Memory," in *Poetry*, Vol. XLIX, No. II, November, 1936, pp. 97-8.

[*In the following review of* The Old House in the Country, *Bogan argues that despite the limited and repetitive subject matter, Reese's poetry is appealing because of its simplicity and poignance.*]

Lizette Woodworth Reese's first book of poems, *A Branch of May,* was printed privately and parochially in Baltimore in 1887. Her beautiful long poem, *Little Henrietta,* appeared forty years later, in 1927. *The Old House in the Country* was written in 1913, and is given to us, according to Hervey Allen who writes a preface for it, in a more or less unrevised form. Miss Reese's later lyrics appeared a

few years ago in the volume, *Pastures,* and this older and not particularly distinguished longer effort will, no doubt, be the only volume of her posthumously published poetry.

The ingredients of Miss Reese's poetry never varied. Throughout her long career they continued to be memories of her childhood and girlhood, spent in the countryside near Baltimore. No lyric poet ever worked more strictly within a limited range. There is a monotonous classic air, the air of the *Greek Anthology,* enclosing her repeated concern with the season of spring, the distinct fruit and blossom of every season, the look of light and shadow upon familiar ground, the scent of box; grief and death and joy and youth which all pass into time and are forgotten. Her distinction was based on the sincerity which backed up her delicate range—an untiring and flawless sincerity that brought her quality through the deadest decades in American history, still pure and fresh to our own day.

*The Old House in the Country* is written in the same stanza form as *Little Henrietta:* five five-beat lines, a three-beat line, four five-beat lines. This stanza is a perfect carrier for the simplicity of the material and the resignation and nostalgia of the material's tone. Like the stripped and naked quatrains of the later lyrics it makes firm, without chilling, the difficult poignancy of the emotion expressed, which might easily have slipped over into sentimentality of the most appalling kind. The break within the stanza halts the feeling, brings it up short, and weights it with a kind of silence.

> By a spent tree in a great solemn field
> A half-wind stirs the falling leaves, and makes
> A swirl of grizzled gold. Black overhead
> A crow caws once, no more.

In the present volume this stanza is rhymed, an effect Miss Reese did not repeat in *Little Henrietta,* which must be later work.

It is so rare for a lyric talent to deepen rather than to spread wider and more thinly, that we do not protest against the limitation of subject, the emotional recession, the lack of intellectual range in this poetry. Miss Reese wrote always out of memory, and in memory everything is diminished and clarified. All is lightly, brightly colored and gently regretted; loss and love and change are again and again absolved of their magnitude, their rage, and their power of destruction. Even now, with trumped-up and insincere poetic frenzies all about us, there is something for us in the true report of senses keen as a child's, keyed to a delicate poetic imagination. We can still answer, when we hear them in poetry, a good heart and a good ear.

## *American Literature* (review date 1937)

SOURCE: Review of *The Old House in the Country*, in *American Literature*, Vol. 8, January, 1937, pp. 350-51.

[*In the review below, the critic praises* The Old House in the Country *as among Reese's best writing.*]

Unfinished though they are, these two posthumous works of Miss Reese, who died last December, are two of the best things she ever wrote. ***The Old House in the Country*** is a group of fifty-two poems written in a ten-line stanza resembling the sonnet. Written apparently in 1913, they contain vivid memories of Miss Reese's early life. For the most part, the poems read like finished work, although, as Mr. Allen points out, there is "a blurred place here and there and a certain discursiveness at times; effects which one can be certain Miss Reese would herself have eliminated and welded into a whole had further time been permitted her." *Worleys* is probably part of an unfinished longer story, although the episode with which it deals is practically complete in itself. In it we see through the eyes of an eight-year-old Maryland girl the end of the Civil War, the homecoming and death of her father, a Confederate soldier, the scattering of the slaves on the plantation leaving only Mam Rachel to look after Adelaide and her mother. The material seems conventional enough, but in the author's treatment it never lapses into sentimentality.

## Carlin T. Kindilien (essay date 1957)

SOURCE: "The Village World of Lizette Woodworth Reese," in *The South Atlantic Quarterly,* Vol. LVI, 1957, pp. 91-104.

[*In the following essay, Kindilien provides in-depth analysis of Reese's literary devices and important themes in her poetry.*]

The first volume of poetry written by Lizette Woodworth Reese appeared unheralded and without explanation in 1887, the year following the death of Emily Dickinson. Cutting through the ruling pattern in the direction selected by a later school of lyrists, she entered a literary scene in which she was to have a secure and merited place for the next half century. Paul Hamilton Hayne, Sidney Lanier, Walt Whitman, Henry Wadsworth Longfellow, John Greenleaf Whittier, and James Russell Lowell were alive and writing when Lizette Reese was a young girl, but she seems to have been little affected by any of these poets. Nor did the New Poetry of the central years of her life turn her in any way from the direction in which she had set out. Her habit of well-doing persisted through the years along with the fine effects of her earliest verse. Never startling the American audience—hers was not the type of work that attracts wide attention—she was well received, and her poetry was rightly appraised by several critics during her lifetime.

Had she read widely in the critical reviews she would have found herself compared with Sappho, Elizabeth Browning, Poe, Dante, Milton, and Shakespeare; she would also have seen her poetry dismissed as "Victorian,"

"sweet but insignificant," and even "a bit trite." Unfortunately, the critical balance between these views was not established before most Americans relegated the name of Lizette Reese to their literary recognition vocabulary. Most of the four hundred and some odd poems composed by this "lovely little lady" who spent her life teaching English in the Baltimore school system were lost sight of after her death in 1935. Like Emily Dickinson, Lizette Reese turned from the American scene and wrote a personal poetry that analyzed universals, but, unlike the Amherst poet, she was not to receive the critical attention that would have made known her achievement. Preoccupied with eternal values, she found them in a world which she re-created in her dozen volumes of verse, a world out of time and place, a Victorian village on the outskirts of modern America. The simplicity and artlessness of her poetry are surface characteristics; its sense of atmosphere and transient emotions, its quick sensory appeals, its immediacy and its intensity are qualities of a technique that is rare in the poetry of any nation. Avoiding sentimentality and personal griefs, cutting her images sharply and fitting them cleanly to various forms, she treated the single, subjective experience that was her life in the objective world of her poetry. The poetry that depicts the individual in relation to the universal cannot be simple: necessarily, hers was the complex expression of one who sensed the briefness of man's stay in a world that mingled beauty and sorrow.

At the heart of the experience recorded in this poetry is Lizette Reese's memory of her childhood in the suburbs of Baltimore in what was then a village called Huntingdon, later renamed Waverly. In this little village, set in pastoral country, the young girl found imaginative stimulants in Waverly's two stores and its Episcopal church, among her neighbors, and especially in the orchards and fields which were cut by the historic York Road. Her father, a stern and silent Welshman, did not provide much money for the family, but there was a mother who was more companion than disciplinarian and "there were traditions, and books, and plain thinking, and direct speech, and dignity of life and work, and liberty to move about, and grow up in." With her three sisters, she gaped at the impressive funerals that moved along the Road, pinned a Confederate flag to her undergarment when Waverly became occupied territory, laughed and ran to meet the organ-grinder, the lamplighter, and the chimney sweep, joined the crowd of children on a blackberrying party, and frequently turned to her orchard sanctuary to explore the world of books that was opening to her.

Educated chiefly in the private schools of the neighborhood, Lizette Reese was thought ready at seventeen to begin the life of a teacher. For several years she taught the small children of Waverly in the parish school of St. John's Episcopal Church. Her first published poem, **"The Deserted House,"** appeared in the *Southern Magazine* in 1874, a year after she began teaching. Thus was the pattern of her life established early. She was subsequently employed in the public schools of Baltimore, first in one of the English-German schools then in vogue, next as a teacher of English literature at the Colored High School, where she spent four of the happiest years of her life, and finally as a member of the staff of Western High School, where she remained until her retirement in 1925 after forty-five years of continuous teaching.

Poetic composition was always a difficult labor for this woman, but after the reception of her first poem, she kept on writing for various weekly and monthly publications and in 1887 she brought out as a subscription work from the press of Cushing and Bailey of Baltimore her first book of poems, *A Branch of May.* In 1891 these verses and additional ones made up a second book, *A Handful of Lavender,* published by Houghton-Mifflin. *A Quiet Road* in 1896 marked the end of her first period of creative activity; nothing new was to be offered until 1909, when Thomas Bird Mosher, who had acquired the rights to her earlier works and had issued them in limited editions, published a book of new poems entitled *A Wayside Lute.* During the next decade—the period of the dominance of free verse—she wrote little and explained the long reticence with characteristic simplicity: "I had nothing to say." The four collections which came out during the 1920's: *Spice-wood, Wild Cherry, Selected Poems,* and *Little Henrietta* (her only book of unrhymed verse), and the three volumes of the following decade: *White April, Pastures,* and *The Old House in the Country* completed the body of poetry which Lizette Reese prepared for an audience. Interspersed with this poetry were several volumes of prose, two books of reminiscent essays, *A Victorian Village* and *The York Road,* and an unfinished autobiographical novel, *Worleys,* which was published shortly after her death in 1935.

The matter of "influence" and "school" is a dangerous assignment for the critic of Lizette Reese's poetry. The modern reader may be too disposed to sense familiar overtones, too quick to place these verses in their literary cubbyhole, and too reluctant to recognize in this schoolteacher's poetry the qualities that have marked the genius of Sidney Lanier, Emily Dickinson, and Robert Frost. A cursory reading of the several volumes brings out the evidence of the genteel poet: here again are the lovers' laments, the romantic ballads, the hymns to lost youth and lost loveliness, and the long chain of sonnet generalities that would gladden the hearts of such poetic idealists as Edmund Stedman, Richard Gilder, and Thomas Bailey Aldrich. There was even the dissociation from the American scene that seemed a prerequisite for the lovers of the genteel: were not the tributes to Herrick, Keats, and Lamb perfectly reconcilable with the atmosphere of the English countryside that so clearly identified each of her volumes? The admirers of the genteel would have nodded approvingly at Lizette Reese's own analysis of her literary favorites and have found ample evidence for claiming her as their own. During her formative period she had loved Dickens with all his faults (*Vanity Fair* and *The Scarlet Letter* were cruel experiences); she ran with the crowd to read *Sartor Resartus* ("a crabbed, wise book"); she was fond of Wordsworth (but the *Excursion* was wearisome); she thought Elizabeth a better poet than Robert Browning

(she had no use for the analytical studies of the Browning Clubs: "It was like taking literature by the throat"), and "Tennyson was master." "Genteel" would seem to be the word for this poetry written by a Baltimore spinster; it has been the word for readers who have marked only the anthology selections and have skimmed her own recollections of her literary antecedents.

Along with this Victorian reading list there were references to works which most of the genteel poets would not have troubled to read: *Pilgrim's Progress* was more than a childhood experience to this poet (it was "a real, almost too real a book to me. . . . Even now, when I read it, I feel that same sense of poignant exaltation which I felt at first"); she knew the writings of Richard Baxter, Jeremy Taylor, Thomas à Kempis, and Cardinal Newman; Herbert and Vaughan and Waller filled out the world that Herrick had sketched for her; the admirer of Keats and Lamb saved some of her devotion for Stevenson, Henley, and Emily Dickinson; and when she looked for a quotation to cap one selection for her poems she found it not in the verses of "master" Tennyson but in the pages of William Blake. And what of this English atmosphere? "The setting," Lizette Reese wrote in reviewing her own poetry, "is pure Maryland, nothing more." The Victorian village which centered her universe was the Maryland village in which she had grown up: it was a locale that was as authentic and as subtle as the garden of Emily Dickinson or the hill pasture of Robert Frost. An occasional poem captured the memory of one of her visits to England, but almost inevitably it was an American scene that gave fiber to her poetry. The trees and the bushes and the flowers, the marshes and the orchards and the roads, the fog and the dust and the rain were all part of a native experience.

And, finally, the form which she selected to record this experience called up a body of images and symbols which would have left a genteel critic shaking his head if he read with any feeling. Beginning to write poetry in the day when the sentimental and the banal were the rule in figures of speech, Lizette Reese ignored the conventions in her finest poems to describe a genuine world with a penetrating imagery. The genteel poets wrote of the natural world about them in terms of the pattern set out in Tennyson's rose garden; Lizette Reese saw and heard and felt a living world that was unknown to them. She objectified and intensified with a rare fidelity the sounds of this world, whether the heavy silence of an autumn afternoon:

> I never knew a house so still
> As this: Not anywhere,
> But a cloud's sound is here,
> A flip of air.

or the tearing cry of a crow overhead:

> The crying of the crows about us thrust!
> Scraped carefully to the bone, as dry, as bare,
> Ready to snap, that sound deep in the air.

The fog that clung to the Waverly fields and lanes was as personal as death:

What grave has cracked and let this frail thing out,
To press its poor face to the window-pane;
Or, head hidden in frayed cloak, to drift about
The mallow bush, then out to the wet lane?

The death of a season prompted a paradoxical imagery:

Frost is the fire
That burns up the rose;
Stem, petal and leaf,
At the last it goes.

The language of the genteel gave way to an imagery of the violent: the worshipper of spring was dragged off to satisfy the will of "the white fury"; the earth was "raw" after its making of a song; the wild asters sprang from war and "a dynasty of tears"; the old house was strangled to force its secrets; and pain ("the ancient whip of God") promised a fulfilment in another world. While a modern reader may recognize at many turns the conventional qualities of the poetry of Lizette Reese, he must finally acknowledge that in her background, her interests, her form—in short, in the world which she portrayed for herself and her readers—this poet left behind her an intensely perceptive record of one who saw in the commonplace all the material she needed for her expression and her life. The simplicity with which she expressed this world is the simplicity that is second nature to all great lyrists; the depth of the experience that is her poetry is one that American readers can no longer neglect without great loss.

The life which Lizette Reese came to know in Waverly was unhurried and secure. The toll gate on the York Road shut out the world and left intact a village microcosm in which a poet might find an artistic haven. Neither the round of the seasons nor the changing landmarks disturbed the stability of this world, for the objective qualities of this locale were only means to the poet's real aim: an expression of the serenity, the wonder, and the ecstasy which her native village prompted. In the commonness of life—in its stones and grass and trees and walls and roofs—she found her correlatives. The garden retreats, the heavily vined deserted houses, the hush of village roads, and the stretch of marsh land away to the sea were all taken over from the region of her birth. The seasonal changes that transformed Waverly before her eyes—the "blackberry rain" of midsummer, the ice coated garden walls, the dust blown streets, and the white madness of spring—were beautifully evoked in her poetry. The color and precision of the sensory impressions in these poems were responsible for the sense of immediacy which she was able to convey.

The directness, lucidity, and economy of her images—trademarks of her style—frequently joined with a feeling for metaphor:

The days go out with shouting; nights are loud;
Wild, warring shapes the wood lifts in the cold;
The moon's a sword of keen, barbaric gold,
Plunged to the hilt into a pitch black cloud.

The promise of permanence that breathed through so much of the Waverly scene conditioned the quiet mood of most of Lizette Reese's poetry, but usually connected with this awareness of calmness and peacefulness was one of wonder. The garden was a retreat from the noise of the world of fact; it was also "a spiritual market" in which one might sense "the continuity of life, the keeping on of affairs . . . the certain security of the incomings and outwanderings of nature." The orchard was a playground and a sanctuary that called up the same mood, but the central image of her wonder-filled verse was a lovely old hawthorn-bush that stood in one corner of her yard. The symbol of the soul-searing mutability of life was this white flowering bush that blossomed before her eyes in a burning, white loveliness. "I think," she was to write near the end of her life, "this bush took the measure of all the poetry that was in me. More than anything else did it hold for me the essence and the substance of all loveliness." Here was the symbol—the pattern for the world she was reporting in poetry—of loveliness, of changelessness, and of spiritual romance. The strange and extraordinary romance which concerned itself with the secret matters of the spirit was the most legitimate interest of the poet. Sensing the beauty in life and in death, she could perpetuate this beauty in word and phrase and help man to readjust "the changes and chances, the confusions and the rancors of life."

The search for permanence in the seemingly impermanent natural world led the poet to an always complex, frequently ambiguous, and occasionally obscure expression of her attitude toward nature. Like William Wordsworth, she found the restorative quality:

Along the pastoral ways I go,
To get the healing of the trees;
The ghostly news the hedges know;
To hive me honey like the bees,

Against the time of snow.

Like Emily Dickinson she felt the sympathy of the world at her feet:

I heard the spouts begin to cry
    As I came over the hill;
How could they know the poignant thing
    That I had kept so still?

Like Henry Thoreau she cryptically imaged the rising **"Smoke"**:

To this the stars and Arthur. This the end
Even of a song;
To be a wealth for nothingness to spend,
A splendor, and become a wrong.

Like Robert Frost she discovered the beauty of a deserted hill pasture:

Perpetual beauty here of line and form,
Surfeit nor scarceness, and it fills my cup

> With sustenance enough for me to keep
> My heart from bitterness, my spirit warm.

The common denominator of these various attitudes is an uninhibited pursuit of the manifold offerings of the natural world. Ever receptive to the shapes and the colors and sounds of this world, she recorded them with the earnest attachment of Thoreau. Her lyrics were full of the color of orchards, meadows, forests, and gardens; yet white was her favorite color and one that she used for a manifold suggestiveness. Her ecstatic reaction to the whiteness of the returning spring reflects the intensity of her feeling of sympathy with nature:

> Oh, let me run and hide,
>     Let me run straight to God;
> The weather is so mad with white
>     From sky down to the clod!
>
> If but one thing were so,
>     Lilac, or thorn out there,
> It would not be, indeed,
>         So hard to bear.
>
> The weather has gone mad with white;
>         The cloud, the highway touch;
> White lilac is enough;
>         White thou too much!

No less representative of the poetic mind of Lizette Reese than this devotion to the natural world was her concern with death. One of the dominant moods of these poems was based on her concept of death and its control of life. Born into a society that looked upon death as "a solemn fact, not to be run away from, but to be faced, a cup that must be drunk down to the dregs," she came to believe that an acceptance of death was a recognition of the importance of the individual. This personal, never morbid, preoccupation with death led her to observe on every hand its manifestations and its relation to a moral perspective. Guided by an aesthetic that affirmed poetry's hold on the spiritual side of life and its key to things "eternal in the heavens," Lizette Reese came to look upon death as the only possible fulfilment of the promise of beauty which surrounded her in this world:

> I shall stand at my door,
> Cross a field in a gust,
> In a gust that will whip
> My mouth full of dust.
>
> Immortal loveliness
> Will fall on me;
> Shake, break me into tears—
> Road, water, golden tree!

Only the poems of Emily Dickinson afford a suitable parallel to Lizette Reese's utilization of death as a core theme of an aesthetic. In her ballads, her lyrics, and her sonnets, the constant recourse was to a study of the meaning of death. Death was not frightening to the young girl who contemplated "the Dead Folk in the grass" and "the lovely, greedy Dead" who met her on the threshold of her father's house. With no verbal tricks and without a trace of banality, Lizette Reese expressed a personal comprehension of death. Critics have unwisely minimized the moral purport of her verse; her understanding went beyond the beauty of familiar things. For example, while there was much of the traditional and the orthodox in her religious precepts, she did not blindly accept the conventional views: she could write that "Creeds grow so thick along the way / Their boughs hide God; I cannot pray." Like Stephen Crane and Emily Dickinson, who were not satisfied with "the God of many men," Lizette Reese sought a personal God, a God who explained her joy in this world and her expectation of an even greater happiness after death.

The age of faith had not passed by the village of Waverly. As sure of God as they were of the morning sun, her people played and worked in a religious atmosphere that the poet described as "a survival of an exaggerated Puritanism." The emphasis on individual responsibility to God made the idea of duty paramount. Only the naïve and sentimental doubted the existence of sin; only the irrational questioned the way of the Lord. A reader senses time and again the God of Edward Taylor in these lines by a woman who wrote two centuries after him:

> Lord, oft some gift of Thee I pray;
>     Thou givest bread of finest wheat;
> Empty I turn upon my way,
>     Counting a stone more sweet.
>
> Thou bid'st me speed; then sit I still;
>     Thou bid'st me stay; then do I go;
> Lord, make me Thine in deed and will,
>     And ever keep me so!

But the God of Lizette Reese was not a copy of the Puritans'; she met the mysterious God of her insight on a familiar ground. Requiring neither a biblical revelation nor a doctrinal contract, she "knew" instinctively that He was responsible for the blessings of this world that surrounded her; she relished the "deliberate strangeness" of her God: "Tree-top, though far, is nearer than a clod; / God being strange, eternally is new." This was an incomprehensible Godhead, but one that man could know and worship in his heart—a protective Father who provided for his children and awaited their return. This concept of death and a personal God enabled Lizette Reese to look forward—with the Puritans and with Emily Dickinson —to a harvest and a fulfilment. The silence of death struck her at first "like a whip / One held too tightly in a too hard hand," and death appeared once as a strangler who "claps a cold hand upon [one's]lips"; but the silence passed, and Death itself was throttled, and man started "on a new race from earth to sun":

> I am Thy grass, O Lord!
>     I grow up sweet and tall
> But for a day; beneath Thy sword
>     To lie at evenfall.

Yet have I not enough
   In that brief day of mine?
The wind, the bees, the wholesome stuff
   The sun pours out like wine.
Behold, this is my crown;

   Love will not let me be;
Love holds me here; Love cuts me down;
   And it is well with me.

Lord, Love, keep it but so;
   Thy purpose is full plain;
I die that after I may grow
   As tall, as sweet again.

She painted no detailed pictures of a reunion with the divine, and there was not the slightest accent of a mystic. Entirely natural and unaffected, Lizette Reese affirmed her belief in the immortality of the human soul on the basis of the love and beauty which made mortal life intensely meaningful to her. The universal emotional values which she beheld in every part of her village world gave her a faith that "Old Age holds more than I shall need, / Death more than I can spend." Such an attitude is the framework in which Lizette Reese's poetry should be studied. Emily Dickinson built her aesthetic around a similar attitude, but with a different emphasis. Now unconventional and again orthodox, Emily Dickinson never succeeded in presenting a final system of thought. Uniquely and courageously exploring every corridor that presented itself, she spent a lifetime probing a personal faith that centered in her theory of death. Lizette Reese found a similar faith; she accepted it and was able to write a poetry of great thematic and stylistic variety.

The influence of Emily Dickinson on the later poetry of Lizette Reese deserves some attention, if only for their community of interests. Her most important themes took their form too early to have been guided by the New England poet, but in several poems she left evidence of her awareness of Emily Dickinson. Looking upon poetry as a personal thing, both poets set out to transform the terms of the natural world into human experience. Utilizing a wide selection of images drawn from nature, village life, the elements, the firmament, literature, and even the household, Lizette Reese, like her counterpart, was able to communicate the effect of sudden revelation:

I had a house; I had a yard
Crammed with marigolds, so high,
So deep in fire, that it was hard
Not to believe, if I went by,
I would be blistered to the bone.

     * * *

Who is in love with loveliness,
   Need not shake with cold;
For he may tear a star in two,
   And frock himself in gold.

Lizette Reese was undoubtedly more confined to the local scene than was Emily Dickinson, but she was no less aware of the contrast of fact and appearance:

Two things I did on Hallows Night:—
Made my house April-clear;
Left open wide my door
To the ghosts of the year.

Then one came in. Across the room
It stood up long and fair—
The ghost that was myself—
And gave me stare for stare.

Holding her images in tight control by means of simile and metaphor, just as Emily Dickinson relied frequently on personification and paradox, Lizette Reese suggested a vagueness and an exoticism by a choice of place names, colors, and literary allusions. A wood-thrush called to her mind visions of Rome and Camelot; a Puritan lady was visualized in one poem against the background of Salem, Oxford, Sidon, "towered Antwerp" and "wild Carthage"; and throughout her poetry apple trees, cooking crocks, and Waverly jostled with "the gold of Tarshish," "the mad quays of Babylon," and Tyre, Nineveh, and Avalon. Similar also to the technique of Emily Dickinson was her resort to a tone of whimsy to avoid sentimentality in dealing with serious subjects. In the following poem, the condensation, the colloquial quality, the homely imagery—the central thought of life, death, immortality—remind one of the poetry of Emily Dickinson and her New England ancestor, Anne Bradstreet:

A loaf may be enough
To keep you from the clod;
You need a ghostlier stuff
To company with God.

The crops grow in a field,
Beneath the ripening sun;
And of the flesh one yield,
And of the spirit one.

The far things get between,
When you stoop down to reap;
Their harvest falls unseen
Under the sickle's sweep.

You stack it long and sweet,
Unknowing, with pant of breath;
And you, if this you eat,
Shall never taste of death.

In a late poem, Lizette Reese addressed an "Emily" who "bragged her stock was Puritan" although "her usual mood was Cavalier." It was no more than right that one who joined in her own work the two moods should have been cognizant of her famous predecessor. The question of influence *per se* is secondary to the example that both women have left American literature in their records of the impact of experience on a poetic mind.

Lizette Woodworth Reese was more than a follower of Emily Dickinson, more than a pastoral poet, and more than a lyrist of the commonplace: she was a woman of poetic power who re-created a village world of nineteenth century America in which to describe the transient moods and emotions of the life she loved. Her "strange hunger" for the loveliness of the seen and the unseen world could be satisfied only by a supreme exertion of her mind and art. The "rich fragility" of many of her lines covers a tough core of experience. She was ready to pay the price that all artists must render who would give form to an ideal:

> What must you pay for each,
> Else loveliness fare amiss?
> Yourself nailed to a Tree—
> This.

In one of her finest sonnets, she wondered at "the idleness of tears" before the fact of man's brief sojourn in this world, but most of her verse expresses the magnificent curiosity that discovered in the framework of a Victorian village a sustaining and vigorous faith in beauty. This village provided the atoms of her poetry; Lizette Reese proved through theme and image that these atoms held a universe.

## Robert J. Jones (essay date 1992)

SOURCE: "Introduction," in *In Praise of Common Things: Lizette Woodworth Reese Revisited*, edited by Robert J. Jones, Greenwood Press, 1992, pp. 1-18.

[*In the following essay, Jones provides an overview of Reese's life and career.*]

In 1921, Lizette Woodworth Reese sent to the *Saturday Review of Literature*, along with **Spicewood** her small volume of poems, a short note. In it she wrote, "I am small, fair, grey, and good-humored. Also quick tempered. I love Life, and Beauty, and People."[1] It was a succinct summary of her personality, but did little to indicate her powers of observation and recall, her sensitivity, or the exquisite simplicity of her writing.

She published, in a life of 80 years, ten slim books of poetry, a short book of selected poems, stories and poems in various periodicals, two books of prose reminiscences, and a fragment of a novel. The revolution in poetic styles and tastes which came about in the first quarter of the 20th century quickly relegated her work to the background, though perceptive critics of the 1920's, notably H. L. Mencken, Edmund Wilson, Louis Untermeyer, Padraic Colum, and William Rose Benet, realized that even though she was thoroughly a 19th century woman she had broken literary trail by cutting through the fluffiness and sentimentality characteristic of many of her contemporary poets, both men and women.

Louis Untermeyer, including her in his anthologies, felt that she was a generation ahead of her time and that she influenced a generation of women poets.[2]

The sculptor Grace Turnbull, half seriously, thought it possible that Lizette Reese was a medium, transmitting to the world the poetic lines of "someone out there."[3] Reese's longtime amanuensis Effie Smither Hunley was puzzled by the blend of genius and the ordinary in the poet. She mentioned it to Reese, who replied, "Yes, I know. I talk one way and write another." Hunley's puzzlement was based on her observations of Reese's ability, despite the genius which set her apart, "to fit in with all phases of life. She made the adjustment so well that more than once she was called 'unimpressing.'"[4]

Turnbull, who knew the poet for fifty years and sculpted a Baltimore monument memorializing her, found it difficult to believe that this plain and outwardly passionless person could write such lovely, passionate poetry. Lizette Woodworth Reese simply did not look or act as many people thought a poet would look and act. This "normality" was what made her such good copy for newspaper and magazine feature writers who wrote stories about her regularly, stories which emphasized the incongruity of the little spinster schoolteacher writing poetry (especially love poetry) admired by the greats of the international literary scene and read by thousands.

Harriet Monroe, who founded *Poetry: A Magazine of Verse* in 1912 and was the great nurturer of "modern" poetry, could always recognize the virtues of the past. When Lizette Reese died, Monroe commented on her poetry's "rare unity and harmony . . . a clear pure minor tone, all in the same key."[5]

But that was then, in the first third of the 20th century. Since her death in 1935, the name and works of Lizette Woodworth Reese have faded despite the respect of famous writers and responsible critics of her time, despite the wide reading given her works in her lifetime, and despite the great press she got for years. She was, indeed, not without honor in her own country, and in many other countries. There has been in the past fifty years much lamentation and gnashing of teeth about her literary fate by many who knew her and many more who loved her poems. Those who lament and gnash are also fading in time. Along with their complaints, however, has been the unified wish for a collected edition of her writings so that future generations can read her when all the schools and movements and fads of her time have settled into their proper places in the continuum, and when it will be seen (it is hoped) that Lizette Woodworth Reese was one of the world's true poets, that her poetry was a turning point in the rejection of the archaisms of the 19th century and an influence on the poetry revolutionaries of the early 20th.

"Miss Reese's writing has the finish of true art and a fine maturity of spirit," said Edgar Lee Masters. "She has always, I think, lived a life apart. The things that last in poetry are not like those that journalistically report life, but seek for truth which lies rather in an inner life."[6]

The simplicity of her lines and the freshness of her images have connected her with the poetry of Emily Dickinson, although she published two of her volumes before she ever heard of Dickinson. A critical study in the 1980's described her as among the best poets of her time "whose lapidary lyrics contain quick flashes of insight reminiscent of Emily Dickinson's."[7] The work of both poets paved the way for the Imagists twenty years later, although they most certainly were not concerned about paving ways. They wrote what they saw and felt in language and images that were sharp and real. Reese was the more traditional in form, yet inspired and free within those forms. "The use of these forms," Padraic Colum noted, "is the virtue of not being self-regarding, of not insisting on one's own inventiveness." Her poems, he continued, were expressed "in terms of things ordinarily seen and known."[8]

*In terms of things ordinarily seen and known*—one of the basic tenets of the Amy Lowell-Ezra Pound concept of Imagism: sharply carved images in colloquial language. Surely they had read and were influenced by the Baltimore schoolmarm, as they had read and were influenced by Emily Dickinson. Robert Frost, Vachel Lindsay, and Edward Arlington Robinson were her admirers. Naturally, women poets admired her even more for the advance work she had done for them. R. P. Harriss, Baltimore newspaperman and noted critic of the arts, wrote in an appreciation of her in 1930:

> She has influenced American lyric poetry as no other woman has done; far more than Emily Ball Dickinson, whose genius remained hidden from the public until comparatively recent years. Edna St. Vincent Millay, who along with Sara Teasdale, may be considered among the prominent contemporary women lyrists who are deeply indebted to Miss Reese, has yet to surpass her in technical skill and in the realm of pure lyricism.[9]

Harriss, her long-time friend and advocate, wrote not as just a hometown booster. A North Carolinian, he had been recruited to the *Baltimore Evening Sun* by H. L. Mencken in the late 1920's. He said later that Reese, Mencken, and Gerald Johnson[10] were three reasons he came to Baltimore. He became acquainted with Reese's poetry while he was a student at Duke University and made her acquaintance shortly after he arrived in Baltimore.

Albert Warner Dowling, a Baltimore teacher-poet and Reese devotee, was one of those who urged a single complete edition of her works shortly after her death. "But who will read Miss Reese?" he asked rhetorically, ". . . generations coming of age, sick of the chaotic minds of many of the present day greats should come upon her prose and poetry as an antidote. Perhaps in the peaceful dignity and inherent beauty of her life they will find not only the mental solace they need, but some hope for their own lives and the lives of their generation."[11] He wrote that over a generation ago. Her work remains scattered in library copies of defunct periodicals and in little books that most libraries do not have.

Dowling wrote several newspaper articles in Baltimore in the decade after Reese's death deploring the fact that she was out-of-print and likely to remain so if a one-volume collection of her work was not forthcoming. He acknowledged that she was adequately commemorated in monuments—a bust at Johns Hopkins University, plaques at the Enoch Pratt Free Library and Western High School, and Grace Turnbull's monument on the campus of Eastern High School—but that was not his point. "In Baltimore," he wrote, "the danger is in keeping alive the memory of the poet while neglecting her works. Until such times as the poems themselves are accessible, any local celebrations can be but half sincere."[12]

Her last books, **The Old House in the Country** and *Worleys,* were published posthumously in a boxed set in 1936. Rarely does one of her books appear in the used-book market which could imply that they have been cherished by their owners and the owners' descendants. In its 150th anniversary issue in 1987 *Baltimore Sun* wrote, "Lizette Reese was hailed during her lifetime as one of the most distinguished poets in the country. Why, then, is she so little read today? Before long someone will suggest perhaps rescuing her poetry from undeserved oblivion."

Her townsman H. L. Mencken sounded the same note even earlier. In 1920 he wrote, "She seems to be almost unknown to Baltimoreans in general. And yet the plain fact remains that she is an artist of the very first dignity, as artists go in America, and that, save for the single exception of Poe, she is undoubtedly the greatest that has ever lived south of the Mason and Dixon line."[13]

He loved her poetry—and he didn't even *like* much poetry. "Miss Reese's poetry," he wrote, "invariably reminds me of Haydn's music. There is the same dependence upon the obvious—and the same sly discovery that the obvious is really full of strange and beautiful significances."[14]

The "obvious" she wrote about were common things:

> For stock and stone
> For grass, and pool' for quince tree blown
> A virginal white in spring;
> And for the wall beside,
> Gray, gentle, wide;
> For roof, loaf, everything,
> I praise Thee, Lord;
> For toil, and ache, and strife,
> And all the commonness of life.[15]

She loved the *commonness* of life, distinguishing it always from the *commonplace.* Things common to her were the basic ingredients of life, always around us, *common* to everyone. The commonplace, in contrast, was the trite and ordinary, common things that had been badly used. All her life she observed such commonness as the beauty of the earth, and all her life she tried to describe it and praise it in her poetry. The earth's rebirth in spring was miraculous to her. It kept her young, as it does the earth. In her prose reminiscence *A Victorian Village* she wrote of a "widespreading lovely old hawthorn bush [which] took the measure of all the poetry which was in me. More than anything else did it hold for me the essence and the substance of all loveliness."[16]

Her continual themes were of nature and its bounty of beauty, of death and rebirth as symbolized by nature's cycle, of joy, love, pain, suffering—even despair—and death, all gifts from the God whom she and the people in her Victorian village were as sure of "as we were of the sun."[17]

Lizette Woodworth Reese was born in that rural village, two miles from Baltimore, in 1856. It was then called Huntingdon but the name had to be changed in 1865 when the villagers petitioned for a post office and were told that there was another Huntingdon in Maryland with a post office so a different name had to be used. The name *Waverly* was chosen. The church the Reeses attended was then and still is St. John's of Huntingdon.

It was at that church—in the parish school—that she received her early formal education. After graduation from Baltimore's Eastern High School in 1873, she was hired to teach in St. John's school. "I was seventeen years of age," she wrote, "my frocks just lengthened, my blonde hair just put up, raw, dreamy, fond of young people, and with the gift of authority . . . of the theory of teaching, I knew nothing at all."[18]

The gift of authority came through her mother, Louisa Gabler Reese. "My father," she wrote, "died many years before my mother, so long ago that he is now scarcely more than a misty figure, and from the day of his death, and little by little, she became the single and assured autocrat of the neighborhood. A lively tyranny, if that at all, which expended itself in an extraordinary straightforwardness of speech, which sometimes set us to trembling, but at others rocked us with bubbling and unholy glee."[19]

The father was David Reese. He had been brought as a boy to the United States from his native Wales. The mother came as a child from Germany. Lizette and her twin Sophia were the first two of five Reese children—four girls and a boy. Mrs. Reese and her children lived with her parents in Waverly while David Reese fought with Confederate forces in the Civil War. The children learned German as well as English, and being bilingual helped Lizette in her teaching career. After two years at St. John's, she was given a position at an English-German school in downtown Baltimore. She taught half the day in German, the other half in English—for 21 years. In 1897 she went as a teacher of literature to Baltimore's Colored High School. Four years later, when the school board decided that black students should have black teachers, she was transferred to Western High School, an all-girl school which was the city's western counterpart of her own Eastern High School. She taught at Western until she retired in 1921. "I taught forty-five years in the public schools of Baltimore," she wrote, "and the requirements of the profession left me little time in which to sit down at a desk with pencil and paper and fall to the business of composition. I learned to compose both poetry and prose in my mind, stanza by stanza, paragraph by paragraph, before I put it down in writing."[20]

She wrote her first poem in 1874 ("in contradistinction to some scribblings I had done before")[21] about an old de-serted house she passed on her way to and from St. John's school. Accompanied by one of her high school teachers,[22] she took it to William Hand Browne, editor of the *Southern Magazine* in Baltimore. Browne, later a professor of English at Johns Hopkins University, was impressed and wrote to her accepting her poem. He did not conceal his suprise at receiving such a mature poem from one so young. He told her he saw many verses—too many, he implied—which were not poetry at all, so that when he received writings in the mail his expectations were not very high; thus, he was greatly pleased to find a real poem whose author could feel emotions and had the talent to express them.[23] He suggested minor changes, and published **"The Deserted House"** in his June, 1874 edition. Her by-line was her only remuneration, but she knew then she *was* a writer. She wrote and wrote—mostly poems—and three years later had a subscription edition published. *A Branch of May* contained 33 poems. A Baltimore printing firm charged her $92 for 300 copies, about a hundred of them subscribed to by friends. Twenty-five copies were sent to critics and prominent literary figures; the rest were sold to the public. "After paying all the bills," she wrote, "I had a few dollars left over."[24]

She sent one of the review copies to Edmund C. Stedman, a New York newspaper critic and anthologist. He responded enthusiastically, and a friendship began. At gatherings in his home, she met many of the literary celebrities of the period, one of whom was William Dean Howells, dean indeed of American letters in the last part of the 19th century and the early part of the 20th. He wrote of her book, "In these [poems] we fancy properties distinctly Southern . . . the tendency to a close, loving, and vivid picture of nature in which the attitude of the poet mainly supplies the human interest."[25]

In 1891, the Houghton Mifflin Company of Boston published her second book of verse, *A Handful of Lavender,* which included the 33 poems of *A Branch of May* plus 42 new ones. Forty-three poems appeared in 1896 in a volume entitled *A Quiet Road,* also published by Houghton Mifflin and dedicated to "the sweet memory of Sidney Lanier." Lanier, the Georgia born musician and poet, lived most of his life in Baltimore and died there in 1881 when Lizette Reese was a 25-year-old schoolteacher with hope of becoming a poet. She never met him.

A 13 year gap then occurred in her output of poetry. "I had nothing to say, except at long intervals," she wrote later, "and therefore did not try to say it."[26] The explanation doesn't satisfy. She was not the kind of poet who has *new* things to say. She tried to say *old* things in fresh ways. Her poetry was about common things, universal emotions, and she worked to find different ways and words to express them. The gap began just as she completed 21 years of teaching at the English-German School and began teaching at the Colored High School. The change of jobs, followed by another change four years later, could have had an effect on her writing. Albert Dowling felt that Reese's need to make a living (which she did not make from her writing—ever) affected her output: "One cannot deny the evidence," he wrote, "that after her retirement, she produced nine of her fourteen books. Had she been freed from part of her teaching duties during her early years, she might have produced more and risen to greater heights."[27] Whatever the reason for the hiatus, it ended in 1908 when Thomas Bird Mosher of Portland, Maine came on the scene.

Mosher operated a small publishing house, printing small, exquisite volumes. William Marion Reedy, editor of the influential literary paper, *The Mirror,* in St. Louis, expressed the general feeling about Mosher's publications, "Everything that comes from Mosher is exquisitely printed. The exquisitry is that of simplicity—no folderol, gimcrackery or didoes in decoration, no tawdriness of binding."[28] He was the perfect publisher for Lizette Reese. Her simple and exquisite poems benefited by his simple "exquisitry."

He first corresponded with her in 1908, asking permission to reprint her poem **"Robert Louis Stevenson"** in his annual catalogue, and mentioning by the way that if she had a book of verse in mind he would feel privileged to publish it. He also told her that her first book, *A Branch of May,* should be reprinted,[29] which he did in 1909. He also published *A Wayside Lute* that year. It contained 51 poems including her best-known work, **"Tears."** (p. 38) That sonnet was the essence of Lizette Woodworth Reese to the majority of her devotees for the rest of her life and beyond. It juxtaposes despair and hope. Its octet characterizes life as "a wisp of fog betwixt us and the sun" and a "burst of music down an unlistening street." Considering life's meaninglessness, the poet wonders at the "idleness of tears." Why cry over the meaningless? Then the switch. She calls upon the ancient dead, with their store of faith and wisdom, to "loose me from tears, and make me see aright/ How each hath back what once he stayed to weep." It is the standard elegy. The poet asks the seemingly unanswerable question and then answers it with an article of faith. But rarely has it been so well expressed. It touched the public nerve, and stayed in the public mind for four decades.

Rarely was a feature story written about her in newspaper or magazine that **"Tears"** was not quoted in full. In 1923, alumnae of her Western High School commissioned the sculptor Hans Schuler to produce a bronze tablet inscribed with the poem. It has been displayed at the school's various locations ever since. Publications all over the world reprinted **"Tears"** in her obituaries in 1935. It was variously called one of the best, one of the five best, one of the ten best, one of the select—a-number best in the English language. A *Baltimore News* writer, Robert Garland, in an article about Reese in 1920 quoted but didn't identify "a world-famous poet whose sonnets are particularly fine" whom he asked to name the six best sonnets in the English language. Said the poet, "any six of Shakespeare," which pretty well took care of sonnet categorization to Garland's way of thinking.[30]

Mencken apparently honestly loved **"Tears"** and he was wryly amused by his feelings about the poem:

> Nothing could do more violence to my conscious beliefs. Put into prose, the doctrine in the poem would make me laugh. There is no man in Christendom who is less Christian than I am. But here the dead hand grabs me by the ear. My barbarian ancestors were converted to Christianity in the year 535, and remained of that faith until near the middle of the 18th Century, and perhaps a thousand years (maybe even two or three thousand) of worship of heathen gods before that—at least thirteen hundred years of uninterrupted belief in the immortality of the soul. Is it any wonder that, betrayed by the music of Miss Reese's Anglo-Saxon monosyllables, my conscious faith is lulled to sleep, thus giving my subconscious a chance to wallow in its immemorial superstition?[31]

Mencken had long been familiar with **"Tears"** before it was printed in *A Wayside Lute.* After she sent him a copy of the book, he wrote to her, "I wish I could thank you enough for that perfect book. If you knew how boundless is my admiration for Tears you would know how glad I am to have it in such a setting. In all honesty, I am almost afraid to mention that sonnet in print for when I do I cease to be a critic and become a rhapsodist! But I shall face the risk before long—whatever its dreads."[32] He faced it many times in the succeeding years—in the *Evening Sun, Smart Set, American Mercury,* and *Nation.* The sonnet was first published in *Scribner's Magazine* in November, 1899. The check in payment arrived the day in July when her family hung crepe at the door to signify the death of her father, yet she didn't remember writing it with her father in mind. In her letter to Thomas Mosher accepting his offer to bring out a volume of her poems, she wrote that **"Tears"** had been reprinted so many times that she felt it was worn out and that she did not consider it her best. Rather, she felt "Today" (p. 117), the lead poem in *A Wayside Lute,* was her high-water mark.[33]

On May 2, 1943, some three hundred admirers of the person and the art of Lizette Woodworth Reese gathered at the Enoch Pratt Free Library in Baltimore for the unveiling of a bronze tablet commemorating the poet. It was sculpted by Beatrice Fenton on commission from the Reese Memorial Society. The tablet, eight feet high, features the Graeco-Roman figure of a young woman strewing petals, symbolizing, said the sculptor, lyric poetry. In relief below the figure is the eighth stanza of **"Today."**

> What go into the making of a song?
> A thousand years agone,
> And more that are to dawn,
> And this one moment pulsing strange and
>     strong;
> And every moment, be it near or far,
> Joy-lit, or drab with woe,
> And every great and low,
> The rose, the worm, the tempest and the
>     star.

*A Wayside Lute* was the only original Reese book that Mosher published. In 1915 he reprinted *A Handful of Lavender* and the following year, *A Quiet Road.*

From 1909 until 1920, Reese devotees had to be satisfied with the Mosher reissues and the occasional appearance of one of her poems in a newspaper or magazine. She was then persuaded by the Norman, Remington Publishing Company of Baltimore to gather enough for a new volume.

That volume of 51 poems, *Spicewood,* came out in 1920, dedicated to her mother who died in 1917. *"You were too exquisite a thing to hold,"* she wrote in the first of two sonnets to her, *"Because I weep, my head bowed to the dust, / Is not that with your own you walk at last, / But that I am so poor, so poor a thing!"*

In 1921 she was 65 years old, eligible and ready for retirement, although there was not much pension for retired schoolteachers in Baltimore. She had taught for 48 years, 46 of them in the Baltimore City schools. Her retirement was effective in June and she sailed on a trip to England with Bessie Kleibacker, a fellow teacher at the Western High School.[34] This was the poet's second trip to England. The first one was in 1903. She went again in 1926, this time visiting poet-novelist Walter De La Mare with whom she had corresponded since 1922 when he wrote to her asking permission to use **"Lydia Is Gone This Many A Year"** (p. 39) in a collection of poetry for young people. The *Baltimore Sun* lamented that "the gentle woman who has spent her life not only in improving and broadening the minds of those who have come under her tutelage, but in strengthening their souls, finding time besides to write verse that has brought her fame but no monetary return of consequence, now is spending her declining years without definite occupation."[35] The Baltimore teachers pension was $40 a month. She was eligible for a Maryland State teachers pension of $200 a year but there were many applicants ahead of her and not enough money to pay them all, so she was on the waiting list.

She was busy in retirement, placing poems in many national magazines and making a little money lecturing and reading her poetry. Honors came her way. In 1924 the founding chapter of *Phi Beta Kappa* at The College of William and Mary elected her an honorary member. She was appointed honorary president of Baltimore's Edgar Allan Poe Society. The Western High School commissioned the **"Tears"** plaque. The Tudor and Stuart Club, a literary group at Johns Hopkins, elected her an honorary member and she was so notified in an October 1925 letter from the club's secretary Alger Hiss.[36]

Norman, Remington published **Wild Cherry** in 1923. The novelist Hervey Allen wrote to her to tell her he thought it was her best book but he was concerned about the publisher feeling that Norman, Remington had not produced a product that the poems deserved. He recommended that when she put out an edition of collected works that she deal with a better publisher. He felt that a collected edition was the book that succeeding generations would know her by and should be one which wouldn't fall apart after a few years usage.[37]

Lizette Woodworth Reese approaching 70 was a hotter property than she had ever been. Alfred Harcourt of Harcourt & Brace, at the suggestion of Louis Untermeyer, wrote her about publishing her work.[38] Thanking her for sending him a copy of **Spicewood** Mencken added, "I wish I could induce you to come into *The Smart Set* oftener."[39] John Hall Wheelock, the poet-editor, wrote to tell her that he loved **Wild Cherry** and commented on her lean style which nonethless was musical and serene. He assured her that she was a sincere and genuine artist in contrast to the many writers of the day whose work, though praised, was actually undisciplined and insincere.[40]

Various publishers felt it was time to bring out a collection of her work. That's what Harcourt had in mind in his letter. Mencken mentioned it in his note about **Wild Cherry.** Apparently she too had been thinking about it for some time, and was ready when John Farrar of The George H. Doran Company made her an offer sometime in early 1925. She wrote to Flora Lamb, who had become manager of the Mosher Company after Thomas Mosher's death in 1923, telling her that Doran had offered her a contract for a collected edition, adding that she was getting on in years and would like to have a collected volume while she lived. She felt such a book would increase Mosher's sales of her little books.[41]

Lamb was not convinced. She replied that she was glad about Reese's opportunity but had to consider the interest of her company and that a collected volume would probably kill Mosher's sales. At that time, the company had about 1000 Reese books on hand. Would Doran be amenable to buying them? If so, she would have no objection to a collected edition.[42] The day after Reese wrote to Flora Lamb she received a letter from Farrar outlining a potential agreement. Some kind of deal was made with Lamb apparently; *The Selected Poems of Lizette Woodworth Reese* was published in 1926.

On the evening of December 16, 1926, a dinner was given in her honor at the Hotel Brevoort in New York City. Newspaper stories gave the impression that it was a spontaneous gesture by noted writers when actually it was a device of John Farrar to promote *The Selected Poems.* He invited just about every well-known writer, editor, and critic in the country, many of whom apparently wanted to attend but couldn't. An illustrious group did attend, however: Robert Frost, Elinor Wylie and her husband William Rose Benet, Hervey Allen, Sara Teasdale, Margaret Widdemer, Dubose Heyward, Henry Seidel Teasdale, Canby, Marguerite Wilkinson, Burton Rascoe, Laurence Stallings, Anna Hempstead Branch, and Edwin Markham (who traveled from San Francisco for the occasion). Benet had written her two months earlier sending a clip of Padraic Colum's review of **The Selected Poems** which had appeared in the *Saturday Review of Literature.* He was the magazine's associate editor (to Canby) and he wrote to tell her he looked forward to printing some of her work in the future.[43] Mencken also wrote her about her collection, "Reading it is a great pleasure. I wish you'd give me a chance at some of your new poems for the American Mercury."[44] Vachel Lindsay wrote to John Farrar, regretting his inability to attend the dinner and declaring, in his usual enthusiastic and overblow style that Lizette Woodworth Reese deserve a banquet served by the Gods.[45] Katherine Lee Bates was under a doctor's care. She wrote to Reese to tell her that she would be at the banquet in spirit.[46] Regrets were sent by Edgar Lee Masters, Edward Arlington Robinson, Christopher Morley, Percy MacKaye, Babette Deutsch, and Jessie Rittenhouse, among others. Louis Untermeyer telegraphed his regrets because he was not well enough to attend. His message congratulated the poet referring to her as the spiritual godmother of such poets as Edna St. Vincent Millay, Sara Teasdale, and Elinor Wylie, and he wondered how many who delighted in incisive poetry realized how much she was owed.[47]

She was 70 years old in the year of the testimonial dinner and was looked upon as the grand old lady of American poetry. Her reviews generally were glowing. There seemed to be continual surprise that she could still write at all, much less turn out the fresh lines she did in **Wild Cherry** and **Spicewood.** Edmund Wilson commented that year, "Miss Lizette Woodworth Reese astonishes one by continuing to write, not only the same fine quality, but almost with the same freshness as forty years ago.[48] Christopher Morley, one of her townsmen (Pennsylvania-born, Baltimore-reared), admired her but was not above chiding her. He wrote her a note praising **Spicewood** but criticized a line in **"Ellen Hanging Clothes"** that described the girl as *cut out some old book.* He pointed out that the phrase is incomplete in meaning without *out of or from,* and that this bothered him particularly because the sonnet was one of her best.[49] Apparently she didn't like the sonnet as well as he did because she did not include it in her book of selected poems.

In 1927 Doran published her **Little Henrietta,** an elegy for a child who was not only the poet's cousin who died at age six but "the universal child, the one who had died, or who was dying every hour in all parts of the world."[50] Increasing years did not dull the sharpness of her mind.

John Farrar left the Doran company in 1929 to join two sons of the mystery writer Mary Roberts Rinehart in establishing the firm of Farrar and Rinehart which was to publish the remaining works of Lizette Reese. In 1929 *A Victorian Village,* the first of two prose memoirs, was published, followed in 1931 by *The York Road.* In 1930 **White April,** a book of poems, appeared. Most of what is known about Reese's childhood and teaching career, her likes and dislikes in literature, and her association with fellow writers is found in *A Victorian Village. The York Road* is a series of sketches of life and customs in her village in the last half of the 19th century. Another book of poems, **Pastures,** came out in 1933.

In July, 1936, seven months after Lizette Reese's death, Farrar and Rinehart published two additional works in a boxed set: **The Old House in the Country** and *Worleys.*

**The Old House in the Country** is a 52 stanza nominally narrative poem, but consisting of scattered and mostly unconnected reflections on the Victorian village. She started it in 1913, worked on it periodically, and borrowed from it frequently for other poems. It was found in her papers after her death. In his introduction to it, Hervey Allen admitted that it is inferior Reese. The reader, he wrote, "must be prepared for a blurred place here and there and a certain discursiveness at times, effects which one can be certain Miss Reese would herself have eliminated and welded into a whole had further time been permitted her.[51]

*Worleys* is a four-chapter fragment of a novel set in the period immediately after the end of the Civil War. Its central figure is an eight-year-old girl on a plantation outside a southern village (Worleys) waiting for her father to return after Lee's surrender. It is obviously autobiographical writing by the woman who was terrified as a child by Union soldiers camping on the York Road and who watched Lincoln's funeral cortege as it moved from one Baltimore train station to another on the trip to Springfield. Lizette Reese's prose is stilted Victorian, where her poetry is not. In *Worleys,* the steady dwindling of food at the plantation is an "inexorable diminution"—a black mammy's deft lifting of a kettle from a stove is "hierarchic." The fragment is interesting only because she wrote it.

In 1931, she was given the honorary degree of Doctor of Literature by Goucher College. R. P. Harriss felt that she "secretly hoped that Johns Hopkins would award her an honorary degree. By so doing, the Hopkins would have honored itself more than the poet, but apparently no one then [at Hopkins] thought so.[52] Also in 1931, she was named poet laureate of General Federation of Women's Clubs.

She was 75 that year. The Poetry Society of Maryland held a special reception to honor her and asked Mencken to be master-of-ceremonies. Robert Frost was present having come to visit his daughter, a nurse, who was at that time a patient in a Baltimore hospital. Mencken had never met Lizette Reese despite having lived less than five miles from her all his life. They corresponded regularly over the years. Seeing her for the first time, he was surprised. "I had expected a rather bulky person, very schoolteacherish in manner," he wrote in his diary, "[but] she turned out to be a small, brisk body, with little shyness and no apparent conventionality.[53] Though he described the evening as flat, Mencken was in good form in his remarks. "One hears from the mathematicians that she is 75 years old, but the figures are quite meaningless," he said,

> She is really the youngest among us and she will never grow old. All the rages and follies, the postures and artificialities of her time have left her unmoved and her work unmarred. She has never forsaken true poetry to write metaphysical treatises, or catalogues, or college yells. She writes always like the true poet that she is, without guile and out of the heart. If Mozart were alive today he would be setting her lines. And if Herrick were alive, he would be with us tonight.[54]

These were golden years for her despite the pains of the financial depression of the 1930's. She lectured and read her poems as often as she could to help out the household where the four sisters had been together since the death of their mother. Lizette even wrote out handbills to advertise an upcoming reading or lecture at her home, listing a $1 admission charge. She was interviewed yearly by the Baltimore papers on her birthday and she willingly commented on the literary scene. Her natural conservatism became stronger in old age, which should be no surprise to anyone who has gotten old or closely watched others grow old. She had always worked in traditional modes and never approved of writers sacrificing beauty for realism. "Self-expression in itself," she told a reporter on her 75th birthday, "is no credible performance. The savage can express himself in howls and crude dances. Beasts are capable of expressing themselves in their cries. It may be stark and primitive, but it has no place in poetry."[55]

Louis Untermeyer visited her in Baltimore on her birthday in 1935, the last birthday she would see. From their conversation he concluded that she had little regard for any literary tradition except her own. She proceeded to lecture him, charging that Pound and Eliot were charlatans who had devised an elaborate hoax, and were not the *avant garde* of a new poetry as they claimed or was claimed for them. It was one thing to be open-minded, she said, but another to be taken in by such fakers.[56] This reference, of course, was to most of the modernists in American poetry. Yet, as early as 1920 in a *Baltimore News* interview with Robert Garland, she said she looked for great things from Edna St. Vincent Millay. "Her Renascence," she said, "contains some strikingly beautiful work, sincere, worthy and appealing." She said she considered Sara Teasdale the best of American lyric writers. "I don't understand free verse," she continued,

> To me it seems to have no law and less order. As a rule these versifiers have no sense of humor and no imagination, but, nonetheless, they have succeeded in bringing some writers back to reality. But they take themselves entirely too seriously, making no distinction between the common and the common place. The common may have the essence of beauty, while the commonplace never has.[57]

She admitted, however, that Walt Whitman and his followers had destroyed much of the affectation of Victorian poetic diction and cleared the air of artificiality, much as she had herself done with more traditional verse forms. "Imagism," she said, "when it had spent its initial force, had succeeded in shaking up and revigorating [sic] the traditionalists; this was worth every blow struck in the battle."[58]

As might be expected of a child of the 19th century, she was offended by the sexual liberties taken in literature. Her last published poem was addressed *To an Indecent Novelist,*

> You measure by a ditch, and not a height,
> Make life no deeper than a country bin

> One keeps for apples on a winter's night,
> Thence prate the immaturities of sin.
> You weigh by littles, by some cracked emprise.
> Why not by that one thing a man has done
> In some vast hour, beneath hot, hating eyes,
> When hard against a wall, he fought and won?
> The spirit still outwits the lagging flesh:
> Cross but one lane, and you shall find again
> That righteousness is older still than lust;
> Strict loveliness of living find afresh,
> Sound women, too, and reasonable men,
> That not yet all the gentlefolk are dust.[59]

She took sick with a kidney infection in the middle of November, 1935, while in Norfolk, Virginia for a poetry reading. She was rushed to her Baltimore home and when she didn't respond to treatment there she was taken to Church Home and Infirmary, the same hospital in which, 86 years before, Edgar Allan Poe died. The *Baltimore Sun* reported on December 2nd, "For the first time in nearly fourscore years, Lizette Woodworth Reese, poet and author, is taking a rest cure. As she lay in bed today, she smiled and said that she 'was getting along slowly.' She is having no callers, receiving no mail except cards and good wishes from her many friends, is transacting no business, writing no verse or prose—not even reading, just resting."

At 4:30 on the morning of December 17th, she died.

She was buried in the churchyard of St. John's of Huntingdon beside her parents. Her brother David, dead at 29, was already there. Three other Reese sisters were buried in the plot later: Mary in 1939, Lizette's twin Sophia in 1948, and Margaretta Reese Dietrich in 1955.

At her request a paraphrase of *Isaiah 42:10* was carved on the face of her gravestone,

> I will sing a new song unto the Lord.

Her sisters chose **"In Memoriam,"** the concluding lines from *A Wayside Lute* for the inscription on the back of the stone,

> The day long sped;
> A roof; a bed;
> No years;
> No tears.

*Notes*

1. Referred to by Christopher Morley in his "Bowling Green" column in *SRL*, December 28, 1935, eleven days after the poet's death.

2. Modern American Poetry, Harcourt, Brace & Co., New York, 1942.

3. In conversation with the editor in the fall of 1962.

4. *Gardens, Houses and People,* Baltimore, Maryland, June 1947.

5. *Poetry*, February, 1936, pp.277-278.

6. In an interview in the *Baltimore News Post,* January 24, 1925. Masters (1869-1950), a Kansas lawyer most famous for his *Spoon River Anthology,* also wrote biographies of Abraham Lincoln, Walt Whitman, Vachel Lindsay, and Mark Twain.

7. *Modern American Poetry—1865-1950,* Alan Shucard, Fred Moramarco, William Sullivan; G.K. Hall & Co., Boston, 1989.

8. In his review of *Selected Poems of Lizette Woodworth Reese* in *SRL,* September 24, 1926.

9. "April Weather: The Poetry of Lizette Woodworth Reese," *The South Atlantic Quarterly,* Volume XXIX, Number 2, April, 1930.

10. Gerald White Johnson (1890-1980), editorial and feature writer for the Baltimore Evening Sun and author of numerous books of political analysis. He was a graduate of Wake Forest and was writing for the Greensboro, North Carolina *Daily News* and teaching journalism at the University of North Carolina when Mencken spotted him and recruited him for the *Sunpapers.* He, too, became a Reese devotee.

11. "Lizette Woodworth Reese: An Appreciation", *The Southern Literary Messenger,* Volume II, Number 2, p. 102 February, 1940.

12. "The Fame of a Poet", *Baltimore Evening Sun,* January 27, 1947.

13. "Literary Note", *Baltimore Evening Sun,* February 23, 1920.

14. *Baltimore Evening Sun,* October 24, 1915.

15. "In Praise of Common Things" from *AWL.*

16. *VV,* p. 101.

17. Ibid, p. 5.

18. Ibid, p. 214.

19. Ibid, p. 284-285.

20. Ibid, p. 267.

21. Ibid, p. 242.

22. Laura V. De Valin, a teacher of English literature at the Eastern High School. In 1926, Reese dedicated her *Selected Poems* to the memory of De Valin and another teacher, Anne Cullington.

23. William Hand Browne to LWR, March 31, 1874; in the collection of Sallie Dietrich Brown and Lizette Dietrich Hannegan.

24. *VV,* p. 244.

25. "Editor's Study", *Harper's New Monthly Magazine,* September, 1888.

26. *VV,* p. 249.

27. Dowling, "Lizette Woodworth Reese: An appreciation" op.cit., p. 102.

28. *The Mirror,* St. Louis, December 2, 1909.

29. Thomas B. Mosher to LWR, September 10, 1908; CWBL.

30. *Baltimore News,* April 1, 1920.

31. "The Poet and His Art," *The Smart Set,* June, 1920, pp. 138-143.

32. HLM to LWR, October 14, 1909; BCHS.

33. LWR to Mosher, October 23, 1908; CWBL

34. It was Miss Kleibacker who later stated that Lizette Reese should have been relieved of tedious administrative duties so that she could concentrate on her creative work.

35. "State Pension For Miss Reese Is Facing Delay" *The Baltimore Sun,* September 17, 1921.

36. Hiss (1904-) a Baltimorean, was a graduate of Johns Hopkins and Harvard Law School. He served as one of Oliver Wendell Holmes, Jr.'s law clerks before entering and rising high in the U.S. State Department. In a 1948 *cause celebre* he was accused by ex-communist spy Whittaker Chambers of complicity in a spy ring. Hiss denied the charge before a Senate committee and was eventually tried in a civil court on a perjury charge. He was found guilty and sent to prison for four years in the early 1950's.

37. Hervey Allen to LWR, November 8, 1923; CWBL. [Editor's note: My copies of *Wild Cherry* and its Norman, Remington predecessor *Spicewood,* were bought in the used book market in the early 1960's. At this writing (1991) both are in excellent condition after 68 and 71 years respectively——R.J.J.]

38. Alfred Harcourt to LWR, April 15, 1925; CWBL.

39. HLM to LWR, December 10, 1920; CWBL.

40. John Hall Wheelock to LWR, October 28, 1923; CWBL.

41. LWR to Flora Lamb, February 6, 1925; CWBL.

42. Flora Lamb to LWR, February 12, 1925; CWBL.

43. William Rose Benet to LWR, October 8, 1926; CWBL.

44. HLM to LWR, October 11, 1926; CWBL.

45. Vachel Lindsay to John Farrar, December 11, 1926; CWBL.

46. Katherine Lee Bates to LWR, December 13, 1926; CWBL. Miss Bates (1859-1929) was Professor of English at Wellesley College from 1891 to 1925. She wrote various volumes of poetry. Her most famous poem is "America The Beautiful" which was set to the melody "Materna" by Samuel Ward.

47. Louis Untermeyer (telegram) to LWR, December 15, 1926; CWBL.

48. "The All-Star Literary Vaudeville" *The New Republic,* June 30, 1926.

49. Christopher Morley to LWR, January 6, 1921; CWBL.

50. *VV*, p. 252.

51. Introduction to *OHIC*, p. vii.

52. "Memo on an Immortal" *Gardens, Houses And People*, Baltimore, June, 1947.

53. *The Diary of H. L. Mencken,* edited by Charles A. Fecher, Alfred A. Knopf, New York, 1989; pp. 9-10; entry of January 14, 1931.

54. "Poetess Praised By Mencken On Seventy-fifth Birthday" *Baltimore Sun,* January 13, 1931.

55. "Self-Expression Derided By Baltimore Poetess" *Baltimore Sun,* January 9, 1931.

56. Described in a letter from Untermeyer to Sally Bruce Kinsolving (1876-1962, February 24, 1936 (EPFL). Mrs. Kinsolving, herself a poet, was a longtime friend of Miss Reese. She was the wife of the famous Arthur Barksdale Kinsolving (1861-1952), rector of Old Saint Paul's in Baltimore.

57. Robert Garland, Baltimore News, April 1, 1930.

58. *VV*, p. 263.

59. Printed in *Gardens, Houses And People,* Baltimore, January 1936.

## Robert J. Jones (essay date 1992)

SOURCE: *In Praise of Common Things: Lizette Woodworth Reese Revisited*, edited by Robert J. Jones, Greenwood Press, 1992, pp. 184.

[*In the following excerpt, Jones provides in-depth analysis of Reese's critical reception, use of language, and subject matter.*]

It is easy to love spring, difficult to find someone who dislikes it. Spring was Lizette Reese's lifelong passion; April was its focal point of ecstasy and hope. It was an extravagant but understandable use of her poetic license which permitted her to write in the title sonnet of **White April,** *"The orchard is a pool, wherein I drown"*, whence *"Dripping with April, April to the heart, / I run back to the house and bolt the door!"* If, indeed, she bolted the door against April, you can be sure she went right to a window to look some more. Everyone feels the impact of spring, but few can describe it well. She was able to put into her nature poetry—as Alexander Pope described true poetic style—"what oft was thought, but ne'er so well expressed."[1]

Such expression was not easy for her to write. "My thought was quick, the picture in my mind clear," she wrote,

> but the expression slow in coming; it was always a hard process to make my words as vital and distinct as

my thoughts and my pictures were. I have never understood the expression in the Bible—"the pen of a ready writer."

*[Psalms, XLV:1]*[2]

Each spring she saw again the obvious and felt compelled to describe it again, but, as Mencken noted, she found strange and beautiful significances in the obvious. The major significance of nature to her was its manifestation of the Christian faith: the cycle of birth-life-death-rebirth.

In the second of her two books of prose reminiscences, *The York Road,* she wrote,

> Every garden is a spiritual market at which we deal. Here are those wares which no thief can break into and carry away. The fixity, the sureness of things is one of the greatest of those wares. A snowdrop is always white, and forever holds that green tip on the edge; a jonquil always cupped in gold. This is the law of the place. You are struck a hard blow; perhaps it is the breaking into pieces of an old dream, or the death of a friend, or the treachery of one whom you trusted as you trusted yourself. At first the world staggers under you; numb and dumb you try to settle yourself into the hard and bitter new order of things. And yet everything in the garden goes on as before. Even the dry sound of a seedpod cracking open—as tiny a business as that— remains the same. This changelessness at first is one of the most bewildering of human experiences. If all, or but one, were different, a little, only a little, you might—you think—the more easily bear and forget. But—after a while it is this very changelessness which works your cure. To look out and see that unquenched blaze of scarlet geraniums in a corner of your garden is to see a candle to light you on your way. A sense of the continuity of life, the keeping on of affairs, of the certain security of the incomings and outwanderings of nature comes to you. Here is a staff to lean upon, a crook to clutch. Here are the everlasting arms.[3]

Half her books of poetry have spring titles: **A Branch of May**, **A Handful of Lavender**, **Spicewood**, **Wild Cherry**, and **White April**. Her author-friend Hervey Allen wrote of her, "The sweet sorrow of all vanished springtimes forever renewed themselves for her in the poignant mutability of each returning April. The symbol of it in her poetry is a white flowering bush suddenly breaking into blossom; the burning loveliness of it, the white flowering thorn! There was no prosey mortar in the walls of her verse; she cut her images sharply and they fitted clean."[4]

She was devoted to the poetry of Robert Herrick, the English divine of the seventeenth century, about whom it is written, "Scarcely any poet has used short lines so exquisitely."[5] The same applies to Lizette Reese. Most of her verse is distilled of excess words, but not of the beauty of meaning. Mencken, a skillful distiller of words and student of meaning, wrote of her, "Her ear is phenomenally acute. She senses the finer music in the unadorned phrase; she leans to a Haydn-like clarity; she knows that there is a true sonorousness in monosyllables.[6]"

Yet, it is fruitless to try in prose to describe poetic condensation and imagery. Jessie B. Rittenhouse, herself a poet, tried to do this briefly in her introduction to the reissue of *A Branch Of May,* and as quickly gave up. "But when the final word is said," she wrote, "the charm of Miss Reese's work eludes one; to analyze it is to capture a white butterfly, which escapes leaving the dust of its wing in one's hand." . . .

"From the outset," wrote Jessie Rittenhouse, "Miss Reese has been the poet of yesterday, the poet of life acted upon by the alchemy of time. Even her earliest, her youngest work . . . is not young; the age-old pain is in it and stirs with all unrest."[7] Does this contradict the description of her as the poet of spring, the April poet? "Yet ever is the old at root of new," she wrote in her second book of poetry.[8] Nature's cycle is always at the core of her thinking and feeling. She continually summons the bittersweet of mournful remembrance only to lift herself to joy in the hope of salvation.

The sonnet **"Tears"** which begins this section on remembrance is her finest expression of hope in the face of despair. It was first published in *Scribner's Magazine* in November, 1899, and was included in her book *A Wayside Lute* ten years later. It was reprinted many times during her life. Friends and associates throughout the years prevailed upon her to write it out for them and sign it, a chore for her because unlike most schoolteachers of her era she had a pinched, nearly illegible handwriting—to such an extent that Hervey Allen admitted in his introduction to the posthumous *Old House In The Country* that producing the book required guesswork about some words in the manuscript that she had worked on intermittently for 22 years.

She may even have gotten weary of **"Tears."** As noted in this book's introduction, she did not consider it her best poem. Most everyone else who read her work did, however. "I have been questioned so often in regard to this fourteen line poem," she wrote,

> that I feel here is the place in which to answer every inquiry at once. I wrote the sonnet, as I remember, the early part of 1899, and mailed it, with another, to Mr. Bridges, editor of Scribner's Magazine, where it became public in November of the same year. It immediately received commendation.

> What was the reason for my writing this sonnet? I have no explicit answer ready. It is true that my father, long an invalid, may have been in my mind, but I was never conscious of this, for people, continually in ill health, are in a sense the last ones whom you connect with dying. My father, however, died very suddenly in July, 1899, and the check for **"Tears"** arrived the day on which the crepe was hung at the door, a few hours after his death. This is all I can tell about the matter.[9]

The Irish critic, Padraic Colum, reviewing Lizette's *Selected Poems* in 1926 for the *Saturday Review* wrote, somewhat surprised, that he realized he knew **"Tears"** by

heart, and also "that I had failed to notice that it is imperfect as a sonnet seeing that it introduces into the octave a couplet that differs from the rhyme scheme that has been provided for it." His reference is to lines six and seven in which the end words *beat* and *street* do not match the *sun* and *done* of lines two and three as puristically they should in the classical Petrarchan sonnet whose format **"Tears"** generally follows.

Colum's criticism probably didn't bother her at all, coming as it did a quarter of a century after the sonnet's initial and great success. The first record of criticism of her poetry is in a letter from William Hand Browne, the editor who first published **"The Deserted House"** in Baltimore's *Southern Magazine.* She accepted some of his criticism but not all of his suggestions, changing phrases he objected to but not changing them to the phrases he suggested.

One of the successful turn-of-the-century writers Lizette met at an Edmund Stedman literary gathering in New York was Edith Thomas[10] who had written her a letter in 1888 commenting on *A Branch Of May* which she liked; however, she had various criticisms of the Reese style, particularly in such usages as *ablow, aflow, abrim,* criticisms which Lizette mentioned in *A Victorian Village* forty years later. She never completely rid herself of the archaic usages. After submitting some poems to the *Atlantic Monthly* in the spring of 1888, she received a note from its editor Thomas Bailey Aldrich[11], a snippy note, rejecting the poems despite the fact that he liked their freshness, perception, and literary quality. He offered some advice on style, noting that she most often ended her sonnets with a couplet, something that just wouldn't do. It was his opinion that such usage destroyed the flow of the sonnet and turned what should have been a musical effect into nothing more than an epigram.[12]

Rarely after that did she close her sonnets with a couplet, despite the precedent of Shakespeare. Her sonnets are invariably constructed in the Petrarchan form, although she continued to use in lines six and seven different rhymes from those in lines two and three.

Christopher Morley, not averse to correcting her as we have seen, commented on her sonnets in a brief obituary in the *Saturday Review.* "By that one sonnet [**"Tears"**]," he wrote,

> she will live long, though she wrote much other excellent verse. Several other of her sonnets seem, until you examine them closely, almost as good as **"Tears"**; then you see that there is some slip in transmission; they haven't the absolute inevitability that the sonnet requires; the wheel of thought has slipped and the rail had to be sanded. A sonnet is like a ski-jump: it's either perfect or it's nothing. The initial momentum must carry all the way through; you can't stop in the middle and think it out again.[13]

Mencken genuinely loved **"Tears"** but was puzzled by his feeling for it since it is based on a religious belief he totally rejected. Eventually he came to the conclusion that the "overpowering impressiveness of certain lofty poetry depends largely, if not entirely, upon the very fact that it is incredible. Look for this gorgeous unveracity" [he continued]

> and you will find it often. Suppose the *Odyssey,* for example were reduced to straightforward prose, what would be the result? Simply a long string of tedious impossibilities. So, too, with the *Iliad,* the *Divine Comedy,* and the *Psalms.* And so, too, with that greatest of poems in prose [*The Sermon on the Mount*] . . . the meek, as we all learn by bitter experience, do not inherit the earth, and everyone that asketh does not receive, and it is not safe to take no thought for raiment. Thus with all the works of the bards and bishops. It is overpoweringly beautiful, but it is also untrue, and its very potency and beauty lie in its bold untruth.[14]

Mencken admired **"Tears"** for its effective simplicity of language. "I cannot refrain from calling attention to its direct and appealing simplicity—to the archaic purity of its language," he wrote,

> In all its words there is scarcely one not of purely Anglo-Saxon origin. And it is Old English, too, in its simple faith, its serenity, its freedom from Latin extravagance. Where, outside of the King James Bible will you find a more naif and beautiful presentation of the great race idea of the fatherhood of God? . . . there is plainly visible in the sonnet that naked grandeur of word and phrase, that ingenuous homeliness, that avoidance of striving which made English so rugged and straightforward a tongue in the days before learning cursed its masters with self-consciousness and Latin embellishments crept in to bedizen and obfuscate it.[15]

Lizette Woodworth Reese, like most everyone else, cherished what was good about the past, and though she often saw the past enveloped in a rosy haze, much of her poetry of remembrance deals with life's often-painful realities. She had, as Hervey Allen put it, "an almost Biblical sense of the briefness of man's sojourn in a world whose mingled beauty and sorrow continued for many decades to wring occasional exclamations of poetry from her brave lips. This poetry was not simple. It was the music of life."[16]

"Death was a solemn fact, not to be run away from, but to be faced, a cup which must be drunk down to the dregs," she wrote in *A Victorian Village.* The first of her two long narrative poems, **Little Henrietta,** tells one of the most affecting stories possible—the death of a beloved child. She saw in the past beauty and sadness, pleasure and pain ("the ancient whip of God")[17], remembering in her poems such disparate things as a neighborhood woman's foolish penchant for fans, and the terrors the girl Lizette felt when Union soldiers camped outside her house during the Civil War.

She continually sought, as she advises a young poet, to "snatch the departed mood."[18] . . .

Harriet Monroe, the editor of *Poetry,* felt that Lizette Reese wrote beautiful but minor poetry, and other critics thought the same. Mary Colum wrote, "This poetry of hers will persist not because the author was cleverer or more original than other writers, but because in some way her nerves were more subtle in response to the kinds of life and experiences that came her way."[19] Poets are generally categorized as minor if original thinking is not detected in their work or if they do not espouse causes. Lizette Reese's effectiveness was not in original thought but in her sensitive observation of life and nature and her beautifully concise description of it. She was not a poet of causes nor did she propound new ideas. Hervey Allen observed, "Almost alone among the several generations and the many tribes of poetesses whose careers her own life spanned [she] nobly refrained from elaborating upon the general dolors of being a female or from harping upon some peculiarly sensitive difficulty of her own personality."[20] Her artistic purpose was to give meaningful expression to life's beauties and verities.

"Reese was not indifferent to the issues of her time," one critic wrote, "but she did not consider her lyrics as a forum for any causes except those of emotion and beauty."

> Her subjects may vary from love to death to nature, but the theme almost always comes back to the belief that an appreciation of experience depends on isolating the "mood" associated with it and then crystallizing it through sensory appeal, especially the tactile, auditory, and olfactory imagery which further distinguishes her poetry.[21]

She told her publisher Thomas Mosher she thought **"Today"** (p.117) from *A Wayside Lute* her best poem. She was probably right. In it she expressed in beautiful, trenchant, controlled lines—all of her lines were controlled—her philosophy of life and devotion to the family of man:

> To every age some mystery all its own,
> That makes its dullest air,
> A something hushed and fair;
> Down every age some breath of Beauty blown;
> Each day is but a pool within the grass,
> A haunted gusty thing,
> Of ancient fashioning,
> Where earth and heaven do meet as in a glass.

"Poetry I learned first of all in Mother Goose," she wrote, "Here were quackery and philosophy, laughing and crying, the crooked and the straight business of life."

> Into the musical jangle and jingle I plunged headlong, to emerge with a lyric deposit which has stuck to me all my days. "Over the hills and far away." This was April, and dusk, and an endless procession of cloudy people going by and never coming back any more. "A misty, moisty morning." This was November weather in a word or two. I fastened upon every scrap of poetry which came my way [she continued]. Shakespeare, of course. I was familiar with the sound of him long before I understood his meaning. There is often a sense for sound without a corresponding sense for sense. Milton's Paradise Lost was parsed away from me. I have said that I was never taught literature, but there

was this one exception in the case of the impoverished teacher who put grammar above poetry. I could never finish Wordsworth's Excursion because it wearied me too much, but this poet grew on me. And Browning? He was a perfect godsend to those people who loved to read what they did not quite understand.[22]

She called herself a Victorian (called Mencken one, too) but, apparently, didn't really think she was. "The Victorians had a full cup," she wrote, "and it spilled over. I think this is the reason that their faults, worst amongst which were their over-elaboration and sentimentality, are so apparent."[23]

Her verbal cup never spilled over. When she began writing, her art was so individual, "It defied classification," R. P. Harriss wrote,

> American versifiers, with few exceptions, were content to write bookish imitations, academic translations from the classics . . . their diction was as hackneyed and mushy as their conceits. *'Tis, 'twere, 'e'en,* and *prithee,* and all the other poetic gimcracks from which all freshness had long been wrung, were regularly employed.[24]

As locked in as she was to traditional meters and rhymes, she rarely used the traditional classical images. Even though she deplored most free verse, she recognized the value of the "modern" poetry in throwing off archaic bonds. From her earliest work, creating simple, sharp, sensory images in colloquial language, she was a forerunner of the Imagists. She liked the poems of Amy Lowell, Sara Teasdale, Elinor Wylie, and Edna St. Vincent Millay. She thought Robert Frost was real "but bald", and that Vachel Lindsay was "touched."[25] All of them, at least publicly,[26] appreciated her work, though she was well into her middle years by the time those poets had reached their ascendancy and their testimonials could have been the perfunctory devotion accorded an ancient of their craft.

Once again, in considering the art of Lizette Woodworth Reese, it is instructive to turn to Mencken who noted in her sonnet **"To Art,"** "honest endeavor, high purpose, undaunted courage."

> What are the ends of art? "to idle at the door, while the wharves call and the ships go by? To sail and drift under an April sky?" The poet answers no. Art must do more than merely reflect; it must also inspire. Reacting upon man, it must awaken in him a passion for effort— "cry through the dark and drive the world to light"— "strike at the heart of time, and rouse the years.[27]

She went no further than that in discussing or justifying her art. The justification was the impulse and need to do it. "Beauty is a constant thing," she wrote; "one loveliness goes, another comes. Wherever there is beauty—no matter what the century—there also is the poet.[28]"

*Notes*

1. *Essay On Criticism,* 1711, Line 97

2. *VV,* pp. 243.

3. *YR,* pp. 255-256.

4. From the introduction to *OHIC,* p. vi.

5. From *The Concise Cambridge History of English Literature,* The MacMillan Company, New York, 1946, pp. 344-345.

6. *The Baltimore Evening Sun,* January 3, 1911.

7. From the introduction to *ABOM.*

8. "Autumn To Spring", line 21, from *AQR.*

9. *VV,* pp. 249-250.

10. Edith Matilda Thomas (1854-1925), American poet, author of *A New Year's Masque* (1885), *Lyrics And Sonnets* (1887), *The Inverted Torch* (1890), *The Dancers* (1903), and *The Flower From The Ashes* (1915).

11. Thomas Bailey Aldrich (1836-1907), American author and editor. Editor *Atlantic Monthly* (1881-90), author of *The Story Of A Bad Boy* (1870), *Marjorie Daw* (1873), and several volumes of poetry.

12. Letter from Thomas Bailey Aldrich, June 18, 1888, from the collection of Sallie Dietrich Brown and Lizette Dietrich Hannegan.

13. "Bowling Green", *SRL,* December 28, 1935.

14. "In Praise Of A Poet", *The Smart Set,* May, 1910.

15. "Lizette Reese", *The Baltimore Evening Sun,* Part II, by H. L.M., January 3, 1911. It should be noted that Mencken was not in his time, nor since, considered an informed judge of poetry. In his 1977 book *H. L. Mencken,* W.H.A. Williams of Arizona State University commented, "In poetry Mencken's competence ran only to the more traditional forms and styles. His admiration for the works of Sara Teasdale and Lizette Woodworth Reese was certainly not misplaced. Yet, he remained largely unmoved by the work of practically all of those men and women now regarded as the major American poets of his day."

16. From introduction to *OHIC.*

17. From "Pain", *WA.*

18. In "To A Town Poet" from *AQR.*

19. quoted by Louis Untermeyer in *Modern American Poetry,* Harcourt Brace and Company, New York, 1942. Mary Gunning Colum (1887-1957), Irish-American literary critic, wife of Padraic Colum, wrote *From These Roots* (1937), a history of modern literary criticism. *Life and the Dream* (1947) is her autobiography.

20. from the introduction to *OHIC* p.vi.

21. Ronald K. Giles, "Lizette Woodworth Reese" from *A Critical Survey of Poetry, English Language Series,* edited by Frank N. Magill Salem Press, Englewood, New Jersey, Vol. 6, 1982.

22. *VV,* p. 185.

23. *VV,* p. 208.

24. R. P. Harriss, "April Weather: The Poetry of Lizette Woodworth Reese", *The South Atlantic Quarterly,* Volume XXIX, Number 2, April, 1930.

25. R. P. Harriss, "The Ribs of Spring", *The Baltimore Evening Sun,* December 20, 1935.

26. Elinor Wylie and Robert Frost spoke at the testimonial dinner in New York in 1926.

27. HLM, "Lizette Reese", *The Baltimore Sun,* January 4, 1911.

28. *VV,* p. 267.

## FURTHER READING

Wirth, Alexander C. "Introduction." In *Complete Bibliography of Lizette Woodworth Reese,* pp. 5-6. Baltimore: The Proof Press, 1937.

Praises Reese's writing and predicts the future popularity of her poems.

# Angelos Sikelianos
## 1884-1951

Greek poet and dramatist.

## INTRODUCTION

A leading figure in twentieth-century Greek literature, Sikelianos is remembered chiefly for his poetry and dramas written in celebration of the intellectual, spiritual, and esthetic ideals of Hellenism. Rich in imagery and symbolism, which are often drawn from the traditions of both Christianity and Greek mythology, his works convey their author's strong identification with nature and his desire to express universal human experiences.

## BIOGRAPHICAL INFORMATION

The youngest of seven children, Sikelianos was born on the island of Levkas. He studied law in Athens for two years, but abandoned his studies to join a theater group in 1902. After publishing some early poems in literary periodicals, he established himself as one of the most important new poets in Greece with *Alafroiskiotos*, which has been described as the "spiritual autobiography" of his youth. A tour of the monasteries on Mount Athos and other historic sites with the novelist Nikos Kazantzakis in 1914 and 1915 instilled in Sikelianos an admiration for Greek history and culture that would eventually dominate his writings. During World War II, the occupation of Greece by Italian and German forces aroused his patriotic spirit, and he responded by giving public readings of his nationalistic works denouncing tyranny. Following the war, he was elected president of the Society of Greek Writers. After suffering a debilitating stroke, he died in 1951.

## MAJOR WORKS

Sikelianos's poetry has been praised for its rich lyricism and its sophisticated allusions to various philosophies and religious traditions of ancient Greece. In *Alafroiskiotos*, which symbolically presents the reawakening of the Hellenic spirit, Sikelianos celebrates the natural world and recasts Greek myth in personal terms. The five-volume *Prologhos sti zoi* is regarded as his most ambitious poetic work and the most complete expression of his philosophy. Dedicated to what he perceived as the five components of experience—nature, race, love, religion, and the will to create—*Prologhos sti zoi* explores his conception of the universal religious myth. The death of Sikelianos's sister inspired another important work, *Mitir Theou*, in which the central figure symbolizes both the Virgin Mary and the Greek goddess Demeter, and blending of sources that critics consider typical of his approach to poetry.

## CRITICAL RECEPTION

Critics have noted similarities between Sikelianos's works and those of other Greek poets of the twentieth century, particularly George Seferis and Kostes Palamas. While Sikelianos shared an affinity for Greek mythology with Seferis and a sympathy for the Greek people with Palamas, his own poetry is distinguished by its incorporation of Christian themes. Additional analyses have focused on his patriotism, manifest in his use of Greek mythology and history and his advocacy of Greek political liberation.

---

## PRINCIPAL WORKS

### Poetry

*Alafroiskiotos* 1909
*Prologhos sti zoi* 5 vols. 1915-47
*Mitir Theou* 1917
*To Pascha ton Ellinon* 1919
*Dhelfikos loghos* [*The Delphic Word*] 1927
*Akritika* [*Akritan Songs*] 1942
*Lyrikos vios* 3 vols. 1946-47
*Apanta* 14 vols. (poetry and dramas) 1965-80
*Selected Poems* 1979

### Other Major Works

*O dhithyramvos tou rodhou* [*The Dithyramb of the Rose*] (drama) 1932
*O Dhedhalos stin Kriti* (drama) 1943
*Sivilla* (drama) 1944
*O Hristos sti Romi* (drama) 1946
*O thanatos tou Dhiyieni* (drama) 1947
*Asklipios* (drama) 1954

---

## CRITICISM

### Edmund Keeley and Philip Sherrard (essay date 1961)

SOURCE: An introduction to *Six Poets of Modern Greece*, translated by Edmund Keeley and Philip Sherrard, Alfred A. Knopf, 1961, pp. 3-27.

[*In the following essay, Keeley and Sherrard discuss six contemporary Greek poets, including Sikelanianos.*]

When the Greek War of Independence broke out in 1821, two poets, Dionysios Solomos and Andreas Kalvos, had already begun to give expression to the re-awakening consciousness of the Greek people. Throughout the nineteenth century other poets followed these pioneers, all working in a tradition whose roots, set in the age-old demotic Greek heritage, were native and local in the best sense. The prolific master Kostis Palamas, writing his major work round the end of the century, was perhaps the most influential of these. In a way, his work marks a turning point. The strongly romantic and optimistic temper of the nineteenth century, which Palamas fully expresses, now gives place to new attitudes. On the one hand, Anghelos Sikelianos, while remaining essentially faithful to the local Greek tradition, seeks to give it new depth by incorporating into his poetry the intellectual vision of ancient religious traditions. On the other hand, the Alexandrian poet Constantine Cavafy introduces an element of matter-of-fact irony which, gently but effectively, confronts the reader with a human situation that, whatever else it may be, is neither romantic nor optimistic.

From the point of view of the native Greek tradition in which Solomos, Kalvos, and Palamas all wrote, the poetry of Constantine Cavafy (1863-1933), a selection from which opens this anthology, might scarcely seem to be Greek at all. Its background is very different from that of these other poets. Indeed, to begin with, it scarcely appears to have any real background of its own, and the early poems in the main do little more than reflect the fashionable literary attitudes of the last decades of the nineteenth century. Behind them one can discern the compound but somewhat etiolated shadow of such figures as Gautier, Henri Murger, Huysmans, Wilde and Pater: aesthetic, feminine, haunted by a sense of corruption, indifferent to if not scornful of nature, fastidious, devoted to art as the expression and stimulant of fine sensations, and looking upon works of art as little more than a superior and sophisticated form of aphrodisiac:

I do not want real narcissi—nor lilies
do I like, nor real roses:
the banal, the common gardens they adorn,
their flesh gives me bitterness, fatigue, and pain—
I am bored with their perishable charms.
Give me artificial flowers—the glories of metal and glass—
which neither wither nor rot, with shapes that do not age.
Flowers from the splendid gardens of another country
where Theories, and Rhythms, and Knowledge live.

Flowers I love kneaded of glass and gold
of faithful Art the faithful gifts;
with colours more beautifully tinted than those of nature,
and wrought with mother-of-pearl and enamel,
with leaves and stems ideal.
They draw their grace from wise and purest Aestheti-cism;
they do not sprout in the filth of earth and mud.

If they have no aroma we shall douse them with fragrance,
we shall burn before them oils of perfume.

Some of the early poems have a certain elegance and polish, but they all share, as we have noted, one central weakness: Cavafy wrote them without possessing any real personal background, without having made his own a "landscape" of figures, of visibilia, with wider terms of reference than those provided by the rootless *fin de siècle* aestheticism whose moods and attitudes he sought to express. It is always one of the major tasks of a poet to provide himself with such a "landscape," and when society possesses a tradition, the images and symbols of which are common to the great majority of the people, this task is relatively simple; when there is no such tradition, it is considerably more difficult. Collective myths, collective terms of reference, lose their hold, the poet no longer shares any recognized background of imagery with the rest of society, and, whether he likes it or not, he is forced more and more into isolation. If at the same time, as is often the case, he is unable to discover for himself any purpose that transcends his individuality, and has therefore nothing left to value but what concerns the life of the senses only, his poetry is in danger of becoming the mere indulgence of private sentiment and emotion.

It was in a situation such as this that Cavafy found himself. Condemned—whether by choice or by fate is not the question—to that kind of aesthetic life which had been the interest of those figures under whose influence he wrote his first poems, how, in giving expression to this life, could he yet avoid falling back on the already debased language and imagery of an effete romanticism? Where could he find the landscape of figures, the visibilia, adequate to his purpose? As we have suggested, Cavafy had no relationship with the Greek demotic tradition on which poets like Solomos and Sikelianos, for instance, could draw with such fruitfulness; to pretend that he had would merely have meant substituting one alien background for another. In any case, the Greek demotic tradition was fundamentally heroic and patriotic, and as such was hardly likely to appeal to Cavafy, who, a colonial Greek, was little concerned with the political destiny of a new Greece; his pessimistic vision foresaw a future of conquest, decay, and death from which relief could be found only in present aesthetic pleasure, in a stoic reserve, and in the recollection of a past already long since perished.

Just how Cavafy lighted on the "landscape" through which he could speak with greater point and freedom, it is difficult to say. But it may have been that in the modern Alexandria in which he lived there were enough visible reminders of and associations with an older Alexandria to stimulate his curiosity and to suggest that *recherche du temps perdu* which his poetry was increasingly to become. It may have been that in the mixed races and the confusion of tongues, in the Christian churches and the pagan ruins, in the bustle of the port and in the bargaining of merchants in bazaar and market of his contemporary environment, there was enough to lead Cavafy to discover, largely through reading, a whole vanished world in which he could see, as in a mirror, the faithful reflection of that human condition which it was his desire to portray. At all events, behind the mercantilism of present-day Alexandria, Cavafy began to discern the lineaments of the great hellenistic Alexandria, the capital of the Ptolemies, centre of a flourishing kingdom and a rich terrain, peopled by Greek, Jew, Egyptians, by all the races of the Middle East. The Alexandria which Cavafy "discovered" was in fact the crown and focus of that extraordinary hellenistic world which included also such famed cities as Antioch and Jerusalem, Seleukeia and Ephesus, and numbered kingdoms like those of Syria, of Media, of Commagene, and of Macedonia itself, from which, with the conquests of Alexander the Great, all had begun. It was a curious, chequered world, knit mainly by the common Greek language. "Then he was that best of things," Cavafy was to write, "a Hellene: mankind has no quality more precious." And in a mock-serious poem he celebrates the expedition which gave the word Hellene the status it had in the world of which Alexandria was the centre:

> And from that amazing all-Greek expedition,
> the victorious, the brilliant,
> the much talked of, the glorified
> as no other has ever been glorified,
> the incomparable, we ourselves emerged:
> the great new hellenic world.
>
> We: the Alexandrians, the Antiochians,
> the Seleukeians, and the countless
> other Greeks of Egypt and of Syria,
> and those of Media, and of Persia, and all the rest.
> With the far-reaching domination,
> with the many-sided activity of prudent assimilation,
> and the Common Greek Tongue
> which we carried into Bactria, to the Indians.

It was in this hellenistic Alexandrian world, then, that Cavafy found the "landscape" through which he could express himself with pertinence and urbanity. Out of it he was to build his "myth" of a personal and at the same time perennial human condition, that of the tired, rapacious, over-refined man who is the generic hero of his poems, *homo Europaeus,* as we might call him, of our not so late humanist period. For that after all is the principal figure that emerges from behind the many masks which Cavafy gives him: the sick guest of an aesthetic city, of a Greco-Roman asylum, full of selfish desires and absurd vanities, ageing into impotence and ugliness, purified by every longing, sapped by every depravity, all sentiment and all fatigue, devoted to fate and pain as the morphinist to his drug, lonely, hollowed out, old as the ages, all nostalgia, animal and sage, all bare, with no ambitions, gnawed by the dread of death, by the relentless dance of time that sweeps all that he loves into oblivion, and finding relief only in his art where he can watch with something approaching a detached irony the spectacle of a life of pleasure, folly, misfortune, vice, and sybaritic elegance which

he now can never again enjoy. The poems included here, all in Cavafy's mature voice, express different aspects of his aesthetic city and the life of which it was the centre.

. . . . .

We have suggested that Cavafy, in creating his own landscape and his own tradition, remained isolated from both the contemporary Greek scene and the main currents of the Greek tradition; in contrast, Anghelos Sikelianos (1884-1951), turned to exactly those sources that Cavafy had ignored.

There are two main aspects to the poetry of Sikelianos. On the one hand, there is the lyric assertion of the natural world and of the human body as part of it. On the other hand, there is the austere vision of the seer who knows that the natural world is full of tragedy and suffering and that the true centre of man's life is elsewhere. There is a refusal to deny the senses, a suspicion of all renunciation and asceticism; and there is the lifting up, as it were, into an intensity of contemplation in which all earth-life is forgotten. There is the celebration of, and the insistence on, the holiness of life's spontaneous manifestations and energies; and there is the formal and hieratic awareness of a divine order, a conviction that man's failure to realise and to conform his life to this order leads to ultimate calamity. Both aspects belong to the total experience of the poetry, and the poems that follow have been selected with this in mind.

The first group in this selection are from among Sikelianos's earlier poems, and for the most part are representative of the first aspect of his poetry: the lyrical assertion of the natural world and its beauty. They are simple, direct, unaffected. Things are seen with a clear eye, with clear senses, with feelings undulled by custom and fixed routine. There is an immediate and reciprocal relationship between the poet and the world he describes, the lands and seas of Greece. Nature and natural events are felt as part of the poet's own subjective experience; the poet's life and the life of nature mingle:

> The lightning I encountered
> before it left the cloud. At the sound
> of the thunder-bolt echoed
> the first heart-beat of my joy;
> at light awakenings,
> at the sudden rustle of leaves,
> at the full peal of bells,
> at the night quietness of crickets,
> at the first talk in the road
> at morning, at the first windows
> of the fishermen opening, at the rising
> deep from the trees of many birds,
> at dawn scents,
> and at the sudden
> ring of the breeze which sounds
> in space, at the spring's gush
> which fills
> the golden pitcher of my love!

These early poems represent a phase in the poet's growth to maturity. This growth is not that of the mind alone; it is much more organic than that. It is the growth of the whole person, body and soul together, instinct and mind together, an awakening and overflowing of an integral sense of life. At the same time there is implicit even in this early poetry what one might call a "mythological" attitude towards life, a sense that there are certain more than natural forces at work in the universe, giving meaning and reality to the world perceived through the senses. There is a supernatural world as well as a natural world, there is the invisible as well as the visible. Not that these two worlds are opposed to, or radically separated from, one another. Rather, the natural world is penetrated by the forces of the supernatural world; it is in some sense an expression of these forces. Man's life is seen as incomplete and thwarted if he fails to realize this, if he persists in living as if the natural world, that which he can observe through his senses and with his mind, is the only world. His real fulfilment and purpose can only be achieved through a growing awareness of supernatural realities, through the growth of spiritual insight. Here the other aspect of Sikelianos's poetry comes into its own, that which expresses the poet's search for and perception of a divine order. But the impulse for this search, for this act of creative understanding, comes from experience of the natural world. From direct, sensual contact with living things man draws in the vital nourishment for his own life. This is the sap that feeds his growth, that stimulates new organs of perception. Intense physical delight turns into an illumination of the mind.

Sikelianos derived what we have called the "mythological" attitude towards life, implicit even in his early poetry, from the people of Greece and their immediate tradition. The lives of the people—harsh, poor, cruel as they often were—still possessed, in the time of Sikelianos's youth, a poetry, a vitality, a feeling of reverence and wonder before creation which had been largely lost in the West (and which have since been largely lost in Greece). Above all, the people of Sikelianos's youth had preserved through the centuries a wealth of song, legend, and dance in which were enshrined the perceptions and understandings, the qualities of thought and feeling, of a way of life whose roots went far back into the past.

Participation in a tradition such as that of the Greek people is of the utmost value for the poet. Even if he is unaware of the true nature of the wisdom it preserves, his attitude towards, and his sense of, life will nevertheless be permeated by it; his poetry, although unconsciously, will reflect it. This would seem to be what happened in Sikelianos's case. He had the good fortune to be born into a Greece where the traditional memory was still alive, where the traditional pattern of life still flourished, and where he found an ancient soul and an ancient aura. Instinctively he turned towards it. He mixed his life with its life, his roots with the roots which nourished the lives of the people:

> And to the people I descended;
> and the doors of the houses
> opened so quietly
> as if the doors of a tomb.
> And it was as if they embraced me

> returning from the grave—
> thus
> the fates the thread had woven—
> or as if for me the dead
> had come alive again:
> so deep in the ground did our roots mingle,
> so were our branches raised
> into the heavens.

Some of Sikelianos's most beautiful poems are those in which he draws upon and expresses aspects of the lives and customs of the Greek people as he knew them: the extract from the long poem, **"The Village Wedding,"** in the following selection bears witness to this.

But it is one thing to write poetry which expresses—as Sikelianos's early poetry does express—a mythological attitude towards life, and another to have full and conscious understanding of the principles upon which such an attitude depends. Or, to put this another way: Sikelianos had found in the Greece into which he was born a living tradition of ideas, images, and symbols which had been preserved, even though in a confused fashion, in the memory of the people, in their legend, poetry, and dance. He had been nourished by this tradition and this memory; they had become part of him, and his responses and attitudes had to a large extent been determined by them. Since the process had in a way been an unconscious one, his task now was to make it conscious, to discover the true nature of those ideas, images, and symbols still implicit in the people's tradition. For this tradition itself was preserving in an incomplete and fragmentary way a knowledge which on a higher level had been lost. What was this knowledge and where could it be found in its more complete form? "The problem was then for me," Sikelianos writes of this stage in his development. "By what way and with what means could I achieve essential contact with and understanding of this tradition?"

His search for this contact and understanding led him to pre-Socratic Greece. It seemed to him that in this period the true nature of that mythological attitude towards life implicit in his early poems—as in the art, beliefs and customs of the Greek people—had been consciously formulated and enshrined. Orphism, the teaching of Pythagoras, the Mysteries of Eleusis, all bore witness to this, as did the poetry of Pindar and Aeschylus. In all these, Sikelianos saw expressed what was essentially the same understanding of life, an understanding which transcended blood-groups and clans, upheld the brotherhood of man, and preserved a sense of unity embracing not only mankind but all living things. It was an understanding which Sikelianos determined to restore through his poetry to the modern world. For now it was no longer only a question of the poet giving expression to his own lyrical experience of life. It was also a question of bringing back to contemporary man some consciousness of those supernatural realities without which, according to the poet, his life would be thwarted and incomplete. All Sikelianos's later poetry springs from his awareness of these realities and his desire to awaken once more in others something of the insight and the fulfilment they brought him. Using for the most part images and symbols of the Orphic and Pythagorean tradition, though in later life more and more completing these with the images and symbols of Christianity, Sikelianos developed a poetry that is both visionary and tragic, rhapsodic and sombre, joyous and full of sorrow. But its last word is not one of despair; for beyond the desolation of time and place, of death itself, is always the reality of peace and reconciliation, the "mystical first glory" of life, whose presence, the poet believed, man could ignore only at the price of his own defeat. The second group of poems in the following selection are representative of the poetry Sikelianos wrote under the influence of this vision.

The "mythological" attitude of Sikelianos was essentially a matter of intellectual and spiritual conviction; that of George Seferis (b. 1900) is more a matter of sensibility, of intense, poetic response to the history of his race. In Seferis's poetry myth is used not so much to transmit spiritual insight as to dramatize a universal mood and state of mind; nor is myth used as a self-conscious method by which shape and order are given to the confusion and anarchy of the modern world, as it is by certain other contemporary poets. In contrast to these latter, we find in Seferis a poet who turns to myth more from a sense of personal identity with his mythology than a sense of its convenience as a means, as a method of ordering the disorder of an alien vision.

This personal sense of myth pervades the selection from his work offered here. Throughout the selection one may discern a central figure, a central *persona,* who "relates" the poetry. The persona might best be seen as a sea-captain, the ghost of Odysseus, "father" of the poet. He is the voice in the two long poems, *Mythical Story* and *"Thrush,"* and he serves as the poet's mask in many of the shorter lyrics. Seferis first describes him in "On a Foreign Verse" (1931); the sense of kinship between Odysseus and the poet, between the mythical hero and the mariners of Seferis's childhood in Smyrna, is apparent in the following excerpt:

> It is the great Odysseus; he who had them build the wooden
> horse and so the Achaeans conquered Troy.
> I imagine he is coming to explain how I too may build a wooden
> horse to conquer my Troy.
> Because he speaks humbly and peacefully, without effort, one
> might say he knows me like a father
> or like certain aged mariners, who, leaning against their nets, at
> a time when the wind began to rage with the fury of winter,
> recited to me, in my childhood, the song of Erotocritos with
> tears in their eyes . . .

The captain tells the poet about "the torment you feel when the sails of your ship are inflated by memory"; about "the bitterness of seeing your companions submerged by

the elements, scattered; one by one"; about "how strangely your courage returns in talking to the dead, when the living who are left to you no longer suffice." These three themes, suggested by the Odyssey myth, are among the most insistent in Seferis's poetry. They are sentiments that no doubt became particularly familiar to this poet after the loss of his childhood home in the Asia Minor disaster of 1922 and during his years away from Greece both in the diplomatic service and as an official of the exiled war-time Government; but the important thing is that they are sentiments shared by the wandering exile of all ages, and it is through the mythical background that this universal, historical extension is dramatized.

The longing of Odysseus for the return voyage to Ithaca and his memories of a distant home haunt the "I" of *Mythical Story* and *"Thrush."* Friends and relatives lost or changed, weak companions submerged or dying, are ever on the mind of Seferis's persona. As late as "Stratis the Mariner on the Dead Sea," written eleven years after the poem quoted above, we find:

> In the Dead Sea
> enemies and friends
> wife and children
> other relations
> go and find them.

Again, in "Stratis the Mariner among the Agapanthi" (1942), our modern Odysseus bemoans the fate of his "poor, idiotic" companion Elpenor, who broke his neck in a drunken fall from the roof on Circe's palace. The persona here echoes the sea captain of "On a Foreign Verse" when he cries:

> It is painful and difficult, the living are not enough for me
> first because they do not speak, and then
> because I have to ask the dead
> in order to advance.

But the dead know "the language of flowers only," the flowers of Homer's asphodel plain, where Odysseus had gone in order to seek guidance from the shades concerning his return home to Ithaca. Seferis's hero, trying to reach his home, finds himself exiled in Transvaal where there are no asphodels—only agapanthi (African lilies) whose "language" he does not understand. The agapanthi hold the dead speechless so that they cannot offer him the guidance that will make his homeward journey possible.

A similar nostalgia and sense of alienation, illuminated by different symbols and dramatized in a somewhat different context, inform what many critics consider to be Seferis's finest poem, "The King of Asine." Here the mythological source is the *Iliad:* a single phrase identifying the King of Asine as one of the heroes who sailed with the expedition to Troy. The setting of the poem is his ruined acropolis, on a bluff near Nauplia. The phrase, now forgotten, and the king's citadel, now no more than a graveyard of stones, come to represent all that remains of the lost paradise which the nostalgia of the modern Odysseus constantly evokes and which he perennially seeks. Behind these symbols there is only the void of the past, the void of experience which has now become simply memory, of emotion which time has turned to stone—the void, finally, of the poet himself:

> And the poet lingers, looking at the stones, and asks himself
> does there really exist
> among these ruined lines, edges, points, hollows, and curves
> does there really exist
> here where one meets the path of rain, wind, and ruin
> does there exist the movement of the face, shape of the tenderness
> of those who diminished so strangely in our lives,
> those who remained the shadow of waves and thoughts boundless as the sea
> or perhaps, no, nothing is left but the weight
> the nostalgia of the weight of a living being
> there where we now remain unsubstantial, bending
> like the branches of an awful willow-tree heaped in the permanence of despair
> while the yellow current slowly carries down rushes uprooted in the mud
> image of a form turned to marble by the decision of an eternal bitterness:
> the poet a void.

This poem illustrates what is perhaps the most exciting attribute of Seferis's genius: his ability to capture the mood of a current historical moment through images that evoke the history of his race, his ability to express a contemporary state of mind in terms of the enduring qualities that define his nation: its landscape, its literature, its tangible and legendary past. The image of the past haunts the persona even when he becomes most intimate and lyrical, even when the setting and occasion that arouse him are most immediate:

> And the bird that flew away last winter
> with a broken wing
> the shelter of life,
> and the young woman who left to play
> with the dogteeth of summer
> and the soul which screeching sought the lower world
> and the country like a large plane-leaf swept along by the torrent of the sun
> with the ancient monuments and the contemporary sorrow.

A constant source, really a symbol, of the persona's nostalgia is the figure of a woman, as the passage above suggests. This figure first appears in "Song of Love" (1930) as an apparition out of the past that comes to haunt the poem's hero with memories of an intensely sensual experience, a union, achieved at the height of fate's rising cycle and then suddenly destroyed with the downward cycle, "the cycle which brings the sorrows." The intensity of the experience is lost in "the rocking of a foreign embrace," but the memory of it persists as a heavy, recurrent rhythm—at the end of this poem and throughout the trav-

els of the modern Odysseus. In "Stratis the Mariner Describes a Man," the man described reports: "you know, I love a woman who left for the underworld," and a bit later, "I loved a girl . . . I think they called her Vaso, Froso, or Bilio; so I forgot the sea." The apparition appears again in "15" of *Mythical Story;* it has become even less tangible than it was in "Song of Love": the fractured form of silence which the poet cannot touch and which returns, as quickly as it came, to the shadows of another world:

> Beneath the plane-tree, near the water, amidst the laurel
> sleep removed you and scattered you
> around me, near me, without my being able to touch the whole of you
> one as you were with your silence;
> seeing your shadow grow and diminish
> lose itself in the other shadows, in the other world
> which released you yet held you back.

One of Seferis's latest poems, "Engomi" (1955), concludes with an apotheosis of the woman figure. She rises out of the level plain at Engomi in Cyprus "with the unripe breasts of the Virgin, a dance motionless," to vanish in the womb of the sky like an Assumption; the poet's memory is stirred by a vision of "breasts among leaves, lips moist." This fusion of the sensual and the spiritual, of the tangible and the intangible, characterizes the figure whenever she appears. To the modern Odysseus she is an image of love's highest ecstasy, an image of "the other world," the lost paradise, where love cuts time in two and where the heart has not been turned to marble by insensitivity or frustration, a world which our hero longs for and seeks during his exile but which he reaches only in memory.

This brief account of Seferis's persona might seem to substantiate the poet's own view of himself expressed in an essay on *"Thrush":* "I am a monotonous and obstinate man who for twenty years . . . have not ceased to say the same things again and again." A more just and accurate view is that Seferis's poems, at least those offered in this selection, constitute one long work, a modern *Odyssey,* of a different and, it would seem to us, more significant nature than that of another modern Greek writer, Nikos Kazanzakis, examples of whose work we have not included in this anthology. In Seferis's Odyssey, unity and coherence are achieved by the repetition of related motifs and the presence, always, of the same central intelligence or sensibility. This central intelligence or sensibility is sometimes called Stratis the Mariner, but normally remains an anonymous "I." As heir to the ancient wandering hero, he serves as an eloquent voice for all men of our age who are tormented by a sense of alienation and who long to return to a lost paradise, that is, for all men who share the perennial experience of Odysseus.

The three poets who conclude this anthology—Antoniou, Elytis, and Gatsos—belong to the generation that flowered between the mid-thirties and the mid-forties, a rich period in Greek letters, one which has not been equalled since. It was during this period that Seferis arrived at maturity with the publication of *Mythical Story, Gymnopaidia,* his excellent translation of Eliot, his *Book of Exercises,* and his two volumes called *Log Book I* and *Log Book II;* it was also the last occasion for any sort of unity or group vitality in the Greek literary world.

There was, surprisingly, considerable activity during the occupation, but the civil war and long period of recovery which followed proved to be disruptive. Good poets went on writing as individual poets will during periods of crisis—one is reminded of Cavafy's Phernazis in the poem "Darius"—but there was nothing to give the world of letters shape, no cause or movement or organ that might serve to define the established and recognize the young: if Phernazis was still alive and singing, his critics were either dead or deaf. In the late thirties, criticism was abundant, and there were several lively reviews. The most influential of these was *Ta Nea Grammata,* under George Katsimbalis and Andreas Karantonis; here Sikelianos published some of his finest work, here Seferis's new voice found its most responsive audience—the voice that was to dominate Greek letters for the following twenty-five years—and here some of the best new poets, including Antoniou and Elytis, received their earliest encouragement.

There is something of Seferis's nostalgia in the work of D. I. Antoniou (b. 1906). Antoniou has spent most of his life at sea as an officer in the merchant marine; the context of his poetry is that of the seaman's experience: voyages to exotic harbours, the memory of distant places, the loneliness of exile, the joy and agony of the return:

> We brought you no more than stories
> of distant places, memories
> of precious things, of perfumes.
>
> Do not seek their weight upon your hands;
> your hands should be less human
> for all we held in exile;
> the experience of touch, the struggle of weight,
> exotic colours
> you should feel in our words only
> this night of our return.

Another poem begins: "Should we turn back? / —sorrow waits for us in the past: / what you failed to exhaust on journeys, / baring your heart"; and a third: "Tonight you remembered the beginning / the evening of rain when you decided / to make experience of the nostalgia for distant places / that left us useless / for life."

The context is familiar: the long journey and the torment of exile are motifs which Seferis exploited thoroughly and eloquently. But the nostalgia here is more subjective: the poet's voice is not masked by that of a persona, nor is the nostalgia transformed, through the agency of myth, into an historical emotion, into a sense of the eternally tragic in life, as it is in Seferis. What Antoniou gives us is a lyrical statement of a mood—a mood that grows out of immedi-

ate experience—repeated, qualified, elaborated until it becomes a metaphor, finally a representative state of mind. He conveys in his own terms (terms that remain more personal and ultimately less profound than those of Seferis) the feeling of loss in the wanderer who longs for the distant homeland—his "landscape beneath the southern sky"—and the commitment to remembrance that his wandering compels. It is, in one sense, a national state of mind, as the literature of the period amply indicates: the experience of exile is among the more typical for the contemporary Greek. This is what gives Antoniou's personal metaphor a broader dimension, a larger significance; his mood becomes to an extent generic, his statement of it a contemporary definition.

Odysseus Elytis (b. 1911) appeared (in *Ta Nea Grammata*) for the first time in 1935. His earliest poetry demonstrated an enthusiasm for the manner of the French Surrealists as profound as the enthusiasm for the technique of the French post-Symbolists which Seferis had revealed in his first poems at the beginning of the decade. What Elytis offered in *Ta Nea Grammata* and his volume *Orientations* (1940) was a surrealism which had a highly personal tone and a specific local habitation; the tone was lyrical, humorous, fanciful—everything that is young; the habitation was the landscape and climate of Greece, particularly the landscape of the Aegean islands. The quality of his lyricism and the surrealist influence are seen characteristically in "The Mad Pomegranate Tree," a lovely poem, full of song and laughter and sunlight, a celebration of the lyric spirit itself:

> In these all-white courtyards where the south wind
> blows
> Whistling through vaulted arcades, tell me, is it the
> mad pomegrante tree
> That leaps in the light, scattering its fruitful laughter
> With windy wilfulness and whispering, tell me, is it
> the mad
> pomegranate tree
> That quivers with foliage newly born at dawn
> Raising high its colours in a shiver of triumph?
>
>               · · · · ·
>
> In petticoats of April first and cicadas of the feast of
> mid-August
> Tell me, that which plays, that which rages, that which
> can entrice
> Shaking out of the threats their evil black darkness
> Spilling in the sun's embrace intoxicating birds
> Tell me, that which opens its wings on the breast of
> things
> On the breast of our deepest dreams, is that the mad
> pomegrante

The central image here—the pomegranate tree as a playful sprite who occasions all that is hopeful and gay, that is, as the embodiment of a mood—typifies what the poet himself has called the "personal mythology" of his verse: "Repeated metamorphoses—a girl that becomes fruit, a morning disposition that becomes a tree, an idea that becomes incarnate in a human form—create a personal mythology which, without divorcing itself from feeling, finds its correlation in the world of the poet's metaphysical experience." The mystery of change, the transformation of the inanimate into the human and the human into something stranger, is hardly a new theme in poetry; what surrealism did for Elytis was to give him a means of exploiting this ancient theme in terms of his contemporary landscape and his personal sensibility, a sensibility thoroughly responsive to the beauty of Greece.

The evocation of landscape and climate through surrealist images is everywhere apparent in Elytis's early verse. In this poem we have "the saffron ruffle of day / Richly embroidered with scattered songs" and the tree "Fluttering a handkerchief of leaves of cool flame, / A sea near birth with a thousand ships and more," or "adorn[ing] itself in jealousy with seven kinds of feathers, / Girding the eternal sun with a thousand blinding prisms." The sea and the sun are so consistently celebrated as to suggest a kind of pagan mysticism, a pantheism, a worship of the gods of water and light. The poet himself has said that his vision is "essentially that of the marine world of the Aegean, with a certain mystical extension that has its centre in the midday and the light." In his poems, this vision is never, of course, reduced to a theology or even a statement of faith; it is always represented by specific images or observed settings, most palpably in the volume with the significant title of *The First Sun* (1943), from which the large part of our selection comes.

The poems in this volume offer a landscape which is both typical and personal; it is the landscape of Greece highlighted by the poet's almost religious adoration:

> Drinking the sun of Corinth
> Reading the marble ruins
> Striding across vineyards and seas
> Sighting along the harpoon
> A votive fish that slips away
> I found the leaves that the psalm of the sun memorizes
> The living land that desire opens joyously.
> I drink water, cut fruit,
> Thrust my hand into the wind's foliage
> The lemon trees irrigate the pollen of summer
> The green birds tear my dreams
> I leave with a glance
> A wide glance in which the world is recreated
> Beautiful from the beginning to the dimensions of the heart!

The familiar ruins, the vineyards, the lemon trees, the sea and the sun, are all here, and so is the voice of the poet offering up a hymn in worship of what he sees. The climate too is immediately recognizable, yet even when the poet describes it in his simplest style, his description seems an act of praise:

> A long time has passed since the last rain was heard
> Above the ants and lizards
> Now the sun burns endlessly
> The fruit paints its mouth

> The pores in the earth open slowly
> And beside the water that drips in syllables
> A huge plant gazes into the eye of the sun.

In another passage, an abrupt change in rhythm, a repeated phrase, suddenly turns the description of a familiar setting into a cry of ecstasy:

> The images of the Resurrection
> On walls that the pine-trees scratched with their fingers
> This whitewash that carries the noonday on its back
> And the cicadas, the cicadas in the ears of the trees.

*The First Sun* appeared during the occupation and for some time now has been out of print. Elytis published one more poem at the conclusion of the war, a long and substantial elegy on a hero of the Albanian campaign, then remained silent for thirteen years, that is, until the publication in 1958 of excerpts from a work called "Worthy is it" (the complete text appeared in a volume with that title published in 1959), and in 1960 of a short volume entitled *Six and One Regrets for the Sky,* from which we have chosen "The Autopsy" and "Beauty and the Illiterate." This long silence, now fortunately broken, was symptomatic of the general lethargy in Greek letters following the occupation. Another extremely talented contemporary, Nikos Gatsos (b. 1912) suffered the same fate, without any reprieve so far. Along with Seferis and Elytis, Gatsos belonged to the group that made *Ta Nea Grammata* prosper in the late thirties. He published a single volume of verse in 1943, *Amorgos,* then became silent (except for a number of translations, including a highly praised version of Lorca's *Blood Wedding*). But his single volume of verse was a startling contribution to contemporary Greek poetry: it was more impressive in quality than any first volume of poems since Seferis's *Turning Point,* published twelve years earlier. Especially exciting was the toughness of the poet's sensibility and the vitality of his diction, which was a fusion of the traditional and the colloquial. Lines such as the following (only a vague approximation in translation) offered not only a new voice but a new possibility for extending the permissible language of poetry:

> In the griever's courtyard no sun rises
> Only worms appear to mock the stars
> Only horses sprout upon the ant hills
> And bats eat birds and cast off sperm.

> In the griever's courtyard night never sets
> Only the foliage vomits forth a river of tears
> When the devil passes by to mount the dogs
> And the crows swim in a well of blood.

> In the griever's courtyard the eye has gone dry
> The brain has frozen and the heart turned to stone
> Frog-flesh hangs from the spider's teeth
> Hungry locusts scream at the vampire's feet.

This violence of language is ultimately tempered by a lyricism reminiscent of Elytis: "It was the face of May, the moon's whiteness / A step light as a tremor on the meadow

/ A kiss of the foam-trimmed sea." And the fanciful image, engendered once again by French surrealism, is offered occasionally as a counterpoint to harsher matter: we find, for example, "the snow-covered meadows of the moon," and "the kerchief of some evening" and "the ready embrace of the wounded sea." In fact, the defining characteristic of this verse—the characteristic that establishes its originality—is an ever-present tension between the violent and the lyrical, the harsh and the tender, the crude and the beautiful: in specific images, in the juxtaposition of lines, in the structure of whole poems. The passage quoted above, for example, gives us worms mocking stars, bats eating birds, foliage vomiting forth tears, a heart turned to stone; and all of this is juxtaposed with a quiet ending. The second poem in this selection, "They Say the Mountains Tremble," offers a similar series of oppositions: two small cyclamens kissing in the mud, and eagle building its nest "within your eyes," a penguin's tear falling in the frozen wilderness, the knife of some sorrow penetrating the cheek of hope, brigands singing in aromatic groves. The opening of the poem is typically violent:

> They say the mountains tremble and the fir-trees rage
> When night gnaws the tile-pins to let in the kalli-
> kantzari
> When hell gulps down the torrents' foaming toil
> Or when the hair of the pepper tree becomes the north-
> wind's plaything

In contrast, the ending is again quiet, almost reverential (a mood reinforced by the allusion to the Eucharist):

> Enough to find a sharp sickle and a plough in a joyful
> hand
> Enough if a little wheat flowers for the feasts,
> A little wine for remembrance, a little water for the
> dust.

The tension between contraries carries over into the poet's attitude towards experience. In this poem it is that between despair and hope, cynicism and expectation (especially plausible tensions when one remembers that the poem was written during the Occupation):

> But here on this damp bank there is one way only
> One deceptive way and you must take it
> You must plunge into blood before time forestalls
> you,
> Cross over opposite to find your companions again
> Flowers birds deer
> To find another sea, another tenderness,
> To take Achilles' horses by the reins
> Instead of sitting dumb scolding the river
> Stoning the river like the mother of Kitso
> Because you too will be lost and your beauty will
> have aged.

The speaker's bravado hides a bitterness, a bitterness against decay and dying youth (the earlier allusion to Heraclitus is to the point). His hope of crossing to "another sea, another tenderness" is undercut by this bitterness: the way over is deceptive, and the need to take it is made im-

perative by the certainty of old age and death. The attitude here recalls the longing for a lost paradise in Seferis's poetry—the references to companions, to another sea, to the classical figure reinforce this—but in Gatsos the tone is more stark, and the longing is reduced to its barest elements, the little most necessary to sustain body and soul: wheat, wine, and water.

. . . . .

These, then, are the six poets who have spoken most forcefully in contemporary Greek verse. Since each has his individuality and his specific interest, any generalization that includes all of them, that attempts to define the group as a whole, must be regarded with some suspicion. It can be safely said, however, that the one thing which most clearly distinguishes modern Greek poetry from that of other Western countries and which gives the contemporary movement a certain unity is the ardent consciousness that these poets share of being Greek; each projects his personal vision in terms of what that word most clearly designates for him: a mythology, a history, a landscape, a state of mind—sometimes all four of these. There is no contemporary verse more intensely local in the broadest meaning of the term, no verse that gives a more precise sense of a nation's present experience. There is also no verse more conscious of its heritage. The expression of the personal in terms of the historical, the translation of the subjective into the more objective, always characteristic of these poets, is very much in keeping with the method and spirit of their ancient Greek and Byzantine ancestors. Both in its individual representatives and as a whole the poetry of modern Greece is thus the latest expression of a long and noble tradition, a tradition in which it is sufficiently accomplished to sing without embarrassment and without presumption.

## Edmund Keeley and Philip Sherrard (essay date 1979)

SOURCE: An introduction to *Angelos Sikelianos: Selected Poems*, translated by Edmund Keeley and Philip Sherrard, Princeton University Press, 1979, pp. xiii-xx.

[*In the following essay, Keeley and Sherrard underscore Sikelianos's affirmation of the natural world and his conception of the poet as prophet.*]

Angelos Sikelianos (1884-1951) is a traditional poet in both the craft and thought that he gave to his art, more so perhaps than Cavafy, who was twenty years his senior, and Seferis, who was by fewer years his junior. Broadly speaking, there are two main aspects to his poetry: on the one hand, the lyrical affirmation of the natural world and of the human body as part of it, and on the other, the vision of the seer who knows that the natural world is doomed to tragic suffering and who aspires "to rise above this flesh-consuming rhythm" in order to find fulfillment in another order of reality. There is the celebration of all life's forms and sensual energies, and there is that contemplative, sometimes almost mystical intensity which transcends the merely temporal and fugitive. Both these aspects belong to the total experience of the poetry, and we have kept them in mind in making our choices for this volume, as we did for our earlier, more limited selection in *Six Poets of Modern Greece* (1960). The versions which appeared in that selection have now been completely revised.

Sikelianos's early work for the most part expresses the lyrical affirmation of the natural world and its beauty. The vision is in one sense simple, direct, unaffected, yet it is also highly metaphoric and syntactically complicated. One is reminded of some of the "nature" poetry of Dylan Thomas. In both poets there is an intimate and dynamic relationship between the poet and his "local habitation," in Sikelianos's case, the land and seas of Greece. Nature and natural forms are felt to share in the poet's own subjective experience; the force that feeds the one feeds the other:

> The sea's sound floods my veins,
> above me the sun
> grinds like a millstone,
> the wind beats its full wings,
> the world's axle throbs heavily.
> I cannot hear my deepest breath,
> and the sea grows calm to the sand's edge
> and spreads deep inside me.

or again:

> As in a glass hive my soul moved inside me,
>     a joyful bee-swarm
> that, secretly increasing, seeks to release into the trees
>     its grapelike cluster.
> And I felt the earth was crystal beneath my feet,
>     the soil transparent,
> for the strong and peaceful bodies of tall plane trees
>     rose up around me.

Yet this world—this physical configuration of the earth, the seas and sky of Greece—is not simply natural. It is also full of divinities. The horse on which the poet rides at sunset to the top of the red rock of Acrocorinth—

> Was it the hour? The rich odors?
> Was it the sea's deep saltiness?
> The forest's breathing far away?

—is also, "had the meltemi held strong / a little longer," the mythic Pegasus. And the he-goat that in the burning midday heat moves away from the herd to stand on the edge of the shore opposite Salamis, "upper lip pulled back so that his teeth shone . . . / huge, erect, smelling the white-crested sea / until sunset," captures in the majesty of his goatish form the vitality of Pan.

In other words, implicit even in these early poems is what one might call a mythological or metaphysical attitude toward life. There is a supernatural world as well as a natural world, there is the invisible as well as the visible. According to Sikelianos, everything in the natural and visible world when rightly perceived can be seen as the expression of the supernatural and the invisible. All is a manifestation of an original divine life and is therefore holy. At the same time, when man's vision is unpurified or "uninitiated," man usually regards everything as existing in its own right and apart from the divine, a perspective that implies disunity, a disintegration or dismemberment of the original wholeness of things. The task of the man with true knowledge and insight—the task of the prophet, the sage, or the visionary poet—is to restore this lost unity and to reconcile natural with supernatural, visible with invisible, first in his own life and then by making others aware of their divided state. As the poet phrases it in **"Daedalus,"** for the prophet, sage, and visionary poet

> . . . the earth and the heavens are one
> and our own thought is the world's hearth and center,
> since we also say that earth may mingle with the stars
> as a field's subsoil with its topsoil, so that the heavens too
> may bring forth wheat . . .

In these symbolic terms Sikelianos expresses both the existential fact of man's living in a kind of sundered reality—time separated from eternity, flesh from spirit—and also the possibility of this dichotomy being healed through an act of creative understanding and mediation.

The source of this view of life appears to have been two-fold, or at least to have a dual character. In the first instance, Sikelianos derived it from the Greek people and their traditions, from the village pattern of life that still flourished in the poet's childhood. There he found an ancient soul and an ancient aura. And there he found a vital reality to sustain his art. How richly Sikelianos was able to draw on images and rituals enshrined in the lives of the Greek people is evident from his long poem **"The Village Wedding,"** which is but one of his many poems that spring from the same source.

But Sikelianos did not regard the Greek people as the originators of the beliefs and practices to which they still adhered. On the contrary, he saw their traditions as the rapidly disappearing reflection of a far more universal and ancient form of wisdom, the oral library, so to speak, of Greece's most profound culture. Their beliefs were a relic of a former knowledge. Their collective memory was a repository of images and symbols whose source lay in a fully articulated metaphysical tradition. Sikelianos increasingly came to see this tradition, in its Greek form, as most adequately embodied in the pre-Socratic world. The vision of the pre-Socratics, he felt, was free from those dichotomies that to a greater or lesser extent have fragmented later systems. Then, the metaphysician did not stifle the poet or the poet the human being. Nature and the supernatural were linked together inseparably, aspects of life's organic wholeness in which such divisions were surpassed. Sikelianos regarded Orphism and the cult of Dionysus, the teachings of Pythagoras, the Mysteries of Eleusis, and the mantic center at Delphi as four of the main expressions of this tradition. In these he found a shared vision that proclaimed not only the brotherhood of all men but of all living creatures and that placed man as the channel of communication between higher and lower states of existence, between the visible and the invisible. And he believed this tradition was not incompatible with that of Christianity, the actual religion of the Greek people for most of the past two thousand years. Sikelianos saw both traditions as enshrining what is essentially the same wisdom. Two of his finest long poems, **"Easter of the Greeks"** and **"Mother of God,"** move authoritatively within a completely Christian ethos, while the poem with which we conclude the present selection, **"Agraphon,"** is based on an unrecorded episode in the life of the Christian Savior. Indeed, Sikelianos felt no embarrassment in invoking "my Christ and my Dionysus" in a single breath. Yet it is the pre-Socratic tradition that remains archetypal for him.

Of particular importance for Sikelianos was the role of poetry and of the poet in the ancient tradition that influenced him most. It was something of the same role that he himself aspired to fill in modern Greece: the poet standing at the center of his world as inspired prophet and seer, teacher and mystagogue. Sikelianos considered Pindar and Aeschylus to be the two poets of ancient Greece who best fulfilled this definition of the poet's role. And they fulfilled it through their use of myth, myth understood not as a rhetorical or metaphorical device but as a spontaneous creation of the human soul directed toward the revelation of a hidden spiritual life. In this context, Sikelianos quoted Schelling with approval: "Mythology contains within it all religious truth. Religion is not mythology, as modern scholars imagine. On the contrary, mythology is religion. All myths are true. They are not fabrications about what does not exist, but revelations of what always exists. Persephone of the Mysteries of Eleusis does not merely symbolize, but is truly, for those who can understand her, a living being. The same can be said where all the gods are concerned." The same can also be said for all those divine or semidivine figures whom Sikelianos invokes in his poetry, for his use of myth is essentially in keeping with the significance that Schelling attributes to it.

Given Sikelianos's conception of the poet as seer, as agent for bringing into close communion the mortal and the divine, it is not surprising to find that his persona—the first-person voice that is the dominant one in his poems—often seems larger than life, almost a force in nature that transcends humanity, the voice for rhetoric that is divinely inspired:

> And there, from my being's depths, from the depths
> where a god lay hidden in my mind's shadow,
> the holy delirium was now set free,
> and from the obscurity of my silences
> powerful verses suddenly engulfed
> my brain . . .

The persona often assumes the manner and dress of a priest, an ascetic who has been initiated into the mysteries and who can address the gods and even their grand earthly habitations directly:

> O Taygetus,

> bronze mountain,
> at last you receive me as an ascetic!

> what new impulses
> nourished my untamable and silent strength,
> veil of the tumult on your five peaks
> where the snow was slowly thawing,

> aerial cataracts
> of the flowering oleander
> on the escarpments,

> dawning of the Doric Apollo
> before my eyes,
> O harsh sculptured form
> on the red unsoftened bronze!

This hierophantic, rhapsodic voice is possibly the one least accessible to a contemporary Western sensibility, not only because that sensibility has been trained in our time to question rhetoric of almost any kind, but because the voice depends for credibility and vitality on the character of the language it offers, on the resonances and surprises that Sikelianos's quite magnificent use of demotic brings to the Greek reader—all of which is lost in translation. When the voice succeeds in the original (and it does not always), it is likely to fail in English to some degree.

There is evidence in Sikelianos's later poems that during the latter part of his life the poet went through a personal crisis marked by suffering and that the subsequent catharsis brought both a new humility and a renewed sense of his mission. There is also evidence that the poet's growth in the years immediately before the Second World War prepared him to understand and confront his country's cruel fate during the war years with a kind of prophetic wisdom more profound than anything in his previous poetry. At all events, during this period the rhapsodic voice surrenders to a voice in which the poet, combining the subjective and the narrative, speaks with a solemn, tragic dignity. This voice is represented in our selection by the poems **"Daedalus," "The Sacred Way"** and, above all perhaps, **"Agraphon,"** the latter written during the devastating Athenian autumn of 1941 under the German occupation of Greece. In these poems the poet is no longer the hierophant transmitting a godly message through priestly rhetoric. He allows the myth at the poem's center to have its own life through narrative exposition, then brings himself into the myth by analogy, sharing its significance, joining his own experience of suffering and commitment to its revelation, but holding his focus on what the myth has already established. In this way the personal dimension does not overwhelm the metaphorical, and the subjective rhetoric in the poem becomes transformed into the universal and sublime.

Sikelianos was a prolific writer by comparison with Cavafy and Seferis. Along with the three volumes of collected poems that he published under the title *Lyrical Life,* he wrote several plays in verse and a considerable number of essays on various themes. And in contrast to both Cavafy and

Seferis, a substantial number of his poems are over ten pages long ("**The Village Wedding**" and "**Artemis Orthia**" in our selection are among these). Three of the longest poems, "**Mother of God,**" "**Easter of the Greeks,**" and "**Delphic Song,**" are considered to be among his major poems; but since two of them are written in decapentasyllabic couplets (the traditional meter of modern Greek folk poetry) and the third in equally formal quatrains, it proved impossible for us to offer a just representation of these in English. Sikelianos was a formal poet in the sense that he never wrote in free verse, and he often turned to the sonnet form (our selection includes six sonnets) or other strict forms of his own devising. We have not attempted to duplicate any of his forms literally, but we have tried to offer a metrical equivalent in each instance, with a loose blank verse the prevailing form in the rendering of his later poems. Our selection has been dictated more than anything else by a sense of justice both to the original and to the English language: we have not included any work that seems to us to treat the original harshly, and we have tried to limit our choice to those translations that have some life of their own in English. The selection has been severe, and for this reason it may not give the image of the poet that Sikelianos himself would have preferred: that of the sleepless artificer (his own term) with a lifelong commitment to the role of poet-prophet in the tradition of Pindar and Aeschylus or, in more recent times, of Hölderlin, Yeats, and St. John Perse. But we hope that what we offer here is sufficient to exemplify the sensibility, aspiration, and achievement that make Sikelianos one of the major Greek poets of his century.

**John Simon (review date 1981)**

SOURCE: A review of *Selected Poems*, in *Poetry*, Vol. CXXXVII, No. 4, January, 1981, pp. 220-42.

[*In the following essay, Simon provides an unfavorable assessment of Sikelianos's poetry.*]

We come now to two modern Greek poets. First, Angelos Sikelianos (1884—1951), whose *Selected Poems* were translated (and, in some instances, retranslated) by Edmund Keeley and Philip Sherrard. Sikelianos was a mixture of neo-romanticism and symbolism from the West (mostly French) which intense, home-grown nationalism, which in his case was more cultural and mystical than political—he and his American first wife tried, with much effort and expense, to revive the Delphic Games. A friend of the first Greek modernist, Kostis Palamas, and, off and on, of Nikos Kazantzakis, Sikelianos was also influenced by his brother-in-law, Raymond Duncan, Isadora's brother. He was active in reviving Greek tragedy both at home and abroad, and himself wrote a number of tragedies. He also fought in the Balkan War and endured hardship during the German occupation in World War II. Most extraordinary was his death: paralyzed by a stroke, and perhaps dejected when the Greek Academy failed to make him a member,

he died from drinking Lysol, which his maid had mistakenly given him instead of Nujol.

Sikelianos's vision, as the translators expound in their Introduction, combines elements of Orphism, Pythagoreanism, the mysteries of Eleusis (which the poet studied extensively), and the cult of Delphi as a religious-cultural-athletic center. His world view combined that of the Pre-Socratics with Christianity, Dionysus rubbing shoulders with Jesus. The poet is a seer mediating between the visible and invisible worlds, between the mortal and the divine. If this sounds both somewhat vague and a trifle commonplace, so, I fear, is much of the poetry—although, of course, I cannot appreciate "the resonances and surprises that Sikelianos's quite magnificent use of demotic brings to the Greek reader." Perhaps Sikelianos has indeed "produced some of the most striking lyrical poetry written in the twentieth century," as Constantine Trypanis has argued, but on the evidence of these translations I cannot see it. In fact, the poetry strikes me as so old-fashioned even for its time that I am surprised that it was written in *Demotiki,* the spoken language, rather than in the archaizing, stilted *Katharevousa.* This is particularly true of the early poems, e.g., the sonnets here unfortunately translated into rhymeless verse, and a poem such as "**Aphrodite Rising,**" which ends: "Nymphs of the breeze, hurry; Cymothoe, Glauce, come grip me / under my arms. / I did not think I'd find myself so suddenly caught up / in the sun's embrace." In the Greek, the short lines rhyme; but neither rhyme nor magnificent use of demotic can mitigate such triviality.

Or consider the ending of "**The First Rain**":

I could not, as I breathed,
choose among the scents,
but culled them all, and drank them
as one drinks joy and sorrow
suddenly sent by fate;
I drank them all,
and when I touched your waist,
my blood became a nightingale,
became like the running waters.

The sound, even I can tell, is better in the Greek, but there is something hopelessly commonplace about drinking joy or sorrow suddenly sent by fate—even if it is mixed with rain water (wouldn't Perrier be better?); and though the blood becoming a nightingale gives off a baroque trill, it is undercut by that mundane comparison (on a rainy day, remember!) to the running waters. The images tend to be somewhat predictable in this poetry: the poet's horse turns into Pegasus, the lead goat in a herd is metamorphosed into the god Pan, a dying man's bed is "the mystical trireme of Dionysus," and so on in almost formulaic cross references between ancient and modern Greece. Take this image from "**The Village Wedding**": "His body drinks the sun, / drinks as a hot beach of fine sand / the ever-renewing foam." (Note, incidentally, the lapse in the English here: either "like a hot beach" or "as a hot beach does" is required.) I am disturbed by the contrary nature of the things compared, though this is doubtless intentional; still, I cannot equate a body's drinking the sun, and thus parching, with a sandy beach being flooded by foam.

Look now at the conclusion of the longish poem in the late manner, **"Daedalus"**:

> . . . father, at those times
> when life's bitterness weighs with its full burden
> on our hearts, and our strength can be roused no more
> by youth
> but only by the Will that stands watchful
> even over the grave, because to It the sea
> which hugs the drowned remorselessly is itself shallow,
> and shallow too the earth where the dead sleep;
>
> in the dawn hours, as still we struggle on,
> while the living and the dead both lie in the same
> dreamless or dream-laden slumber, do not stop
> ascending in front of us, but climb always
> with slow even wings the heavens of our Thought,
> eternal Daedalus, Dawnstar of the Beyond.

This strikes me as decent minor poetry (shouldn't the twentieth-century poet let the sleeping dead lie?), very competently translated. Everything works here: cadence, imagery, sentiment, and thought harmonize skillfully, but without great originality or depth. Yet there are no awkwardnesses, as in this image from the long, earlier poem, **"A Village Wedding,"** where the bridegroom is exhorted by the poet: "Let him now reap the deepest field / of creative fragrance." Not only does the abstract "creative" (even if taken in the humbler sense of "procreative") clash with the very specific "fragrance," but also the reduction of sexual fulfillment to a mere olfactory experience, however pleasant, strikes me as, if I may put it so, anticlimactic. Nor does the translators', presumably unintentional, jingle—*reap deepest*—prove helpful.

In the main, though, the translators have done a respectably less than brilliant job, and I am a trifle disturbed by their steady bypassing of subjunctives (e.g., "as though a whole world is coming apart," "as if the world had disappeared and nature alone was left," etc.) and consistent misspelling of "anointed" as "annointed" (pp. 59 and 144). They are careless at times: in **"Dionysus Encradled,"** for instance, an "infant" would be more suitable than a "baby"; "in vain I strain" (twice in the same poem) jars with its uncalled-for rhyme. Occasionally they even lapse into translatorese, as in **"Because I Deeply Praised,"** where we find "here life starts, here ends" and "for secret is earth's live creative pulse." Still, they have done well enough to convince me that Sikelianos is a repetitious poet with a few, constantly reiterated, conceits. There is the notion of the past contained in the present: "I'd taken this same road centuries before" (**"The Sacred Way"**), "And the rhythm of our horses now / . . . still lives / under obscure hoofprints of ancient horses / left in the same holy ground" (**"Attic"**); and there is the related concept of two worlds in one: "the living and the dead both lie in the same / dreamless or dream-laden slumber" (**"Daedalus"**).

"Everything, visible and invisible, we and the heroes and the gods too, / move forward inside the same eternal sphere!" (**"Attic"**). All the sesamenesses have a way of becoming all the same to the reader, whether the rhetoric waxes too rhapsodic or the rhapsode turns into a mere rhetorician.

### Edmund Keeley (essay date 1981)

SOURCE: "Ancient Greek Myth in Angelos Sikelianos," in *Byzantine and Modern Greek Studies*, Vol. 7, 1981, pp. 105-17.

[*In the following essay, Keeley considers the role of Greek mythology in Sikelianos's verse.*]

In the introduction to **Angelos Sikelianos: Selected Poems,**[1] the translators speak of Sikelianos's 'mythological attitude . . . toward life' and of his conception of myth not so much 'as a rhetorical or metaphorical device but as a spontaneous creation of the human soul directed toward the revelation of a hidden spiritual life', in short, of mythology as a kind of religion closely related to Schelling's perception of the function of myth. These remarks, written originally some years ago, may have their just proportion of truth, but in keeping with most introductory remarks, they strike me as rather too general, rather too undiscriminating when one brings them face to face with Sikelianos's practice at different moments of his career. I want to try to be more discriminating by considering the role of myth—specifically ancient Greek myth—in the poet's work both early and late in his career. I think it is a changing role, perhaps not in his fundamental association of gods with a contemporary landscape and his revelation of those mysteries that lie hidden in our everyday lives, but in the mode of this association and this revelation, and in the depth of their poetic significance.

The first of the early poems most relevant to our theme is **'The Horses of Achilles'** (1909) [English translation]:

> Field of asphodels, beside you
> two horses neighed
> as they went by at a gallop.
> Their backs gleamed like a wave;
> they came up out of the sea,
> tore over the deserted sand,
> necks straining high, towering,
> white foam at the mouth, stallion-strong.
> In their eyes
> lightning smoldered;
> and, waves themselves, they plunged again
> into the waves,
> foam into the sea's foam,
> and vanished. I recognized
> those stallions: one of them
> took on a human voice to prophesy.
> The hero held the reins;
> he spurred, hurling
> his godlike youth forward . . .

Sacred stallions, fate
has kept you indestructible,
fixing on your pure black foreheads,
charm against the profane eye,
a large and pure white talisman.

There is a wonderful innocence in the poet's handling of the mythology in this poem. The horses are described in the first instance as one might describe any gallant horses in the field next door, except for a certain metaphoric heightening—'their back gleamed like a wave'—and a touch of heroic diction such as 'towering' and 'stallion-strong', all preparing for the stated mystery of the lightning smoldering in their eyes and their supernatural union with the natural world: 'waves themselves, they plunged again / into the waves, foam into the sea's foam, / and vanished'. But the poet doesn't leave it at that; he goes on to tell us, charmingly, that he recognized those stallions named in the title of his poem, one of them known to be a prophet, and he even has the hero to whom they belong suddenly spur them on in his godlike way. And he concludes the movement from objective description to subjective accommodation by actually addressing the stallions in order to underline their immortality and their spiritual incorruptibility.

It is an uncomplicated evocation of the myth, perhaps too limited in its nuances when one compares it to Cavafy's relatively early poem of the same title. Cavafy's handling of the myth underlines not the rather obvious mystery of the horses' immortality and incorruptibility but their almost human compassion as they weep over the 'eternal disaster of death' which they come to recognize as the lot of even heroic mortals when they find Patroklos dead. But if we accept Sikelianos's poem on its own terms, which are neither pretentious nor profound, it does serve through its rhetoric to bring some new life into the myth.

A more subtle example of the same early mode is found in the poem **'Aphrodite Rising'** (1915) [translated], where the poet again restricts himself to an evocation of a well-known myth with no fundamental reinterpretation and only a limited extension of the myth's significance, but with the difference that in this instance he assumes a fully dramatic stance, and instead of bringing himself directly into the mythical context as commentator—not to say as master of ceremonies in the occasion of mystery—allows the myth to speak for itself, almost literally, since the poem is a dramatic monologue with the goddess of love herself as speaker:

In the blessed rose light of dawn, look how I rise,
my arms held high.
The sea's godlike calm bids me to ascend
into the blue air.
O but the sudden breaths of earth, filling my breasts,
rousing me
from head to foot.
O Zeus, the sea is heavy, and my loosened hair drags me
down like a stone.

Nymphs of the breeze, hurry; Cymothoe, Glauce, come grip me
under the arms.
I did not think I'd find myself so suddenly caught up
in the sun's embrace.

This poem is more in the late Cavafian mode than either of the two poems called **'The Horses of Achilles'**, partly because it is a dramatic monologue, more importantly because the significance of the poet's mythic evocation comes to us not by way of his subjective commentary but directly out of the particular manner and substance of the evocation itself, namely the wonderful tension in Sikelianos's goddess between the impulse toward divine ascension and earthly habitation, or to put it another way, the paradox of her emerging godliness so overwhelmed by those sudden breaths of earth that rouse her from head to foot and by the passion of her being caught up in the sun's embrace beyond even divine expectation.

Another early poem, **'Pan'** (1914) [translated], takes a middle ground between the two modes we have explored so far. In this instance the mythical context is established overtly by the title alone. The opening stanzas of the poem could pass—in fact, do pass—for a characteristic lyrical rendering of the contemporary Greek landscape and seascape in the manner of those poems in Sikelianos that celebrate the natural world, especially as heightened by the poet's ecstatic response to what his eye sees and his gut feels:

Over rocks on the deserted shore, over the burning heat
of harsh pebbles,
beside the emerald waves, noon, like a fountain,
rose shimmering.
Salamis a blue trireme deep in the sea,
in spring's spindrift;
the pines and mastic trees of Kineta a deep breath
I drew inside me.
The sea burst into foam and, beaten by the wind,
shattered white,
and a flock of goats, countless, iron-gray, plummeted headlong
down the hill.

But in the best early poems of Sikelianos, the natural world subtly serves as a mask for the supernatural world; the poet's heightened response derives in part from his premonition, then his conviction, that divinities are hiding behind the façade of earthly presences. In this instance, the flock of goats plummeting down the hillside soon becomes an occasion for that kind of mystery, namely the metamorphosis of the herd's lord and master into the god Pan, rising to face the sea as though some secret sun ritual has called him up out of the slumber of the ages:

[translation]

They gathered in close, crowding the brush
and wild thyme,
and as they gathered, a drowsiness seized

both goats and man.
And then, over the shore's stones and the goats' swel-
　ter,
dead silence;
and between their horns, as from a tripod, the sun's
　quick heat
shimmered upward.
Then we saw the herd's lord and master, the he-goat,
　rise alone
and move off, his tread slow and heavy,
toward a rock
wedged into the sea to shape a perfect lookout point;
there he stopped,
on the very edge where spray dissolves,
and leaning motionless,
upper lip pulled back so that his teeth shone,
he stood
huge, erect, smelling the white-crested sea
until sunset.

In this poem Sikelianos is no longer a subjective respon-
dent; he is an objective narrator. Again there is no overt
commentary on the mythical context that emerges; the un-
stated mystery of Pan's apparition in the noon-day heat on
the shore between Eleusis and Corinth is sufficient for his
purpose because it works dramatically, without need for
underlining, to present his case for our believing that the
ancient pastoral gods are still very much with us—or at
least still were as recently as the 1920s, when Kineta was
open country for goats and their attendant herdsmen rather
than tourists and their attendant entrepreneurs.

I turn now to Sikelianos's later work, in particular to the
poems **'Daedalus'** and **'The Sacred Way'**, both published
during the period immediately preceding World War II and
after the poet had apparently suffered a personal crisis that
was resolved, at least as far as his work is concerned, by
the emergence of a new and powerful tragic vision. Anyway these two poems and several others of his late years
reveal a depth of perception that clearly transcends the
personal lyricism and even the access to mystery that established his strong reputation in earlier years. And it is in
some measure Sikelianos's new approach to myth—ancient Greek myth in particular—that allowed his broad-
ened vision to find an effective voice. The new approach
can be described as the total assimilation of the myth by
the poet's point of view. The subjective element here is
not that of a poet addressing his mythic material so as to
highlight it or to comment on its vitality or even to personalize the mystery in it in order to give it new life and
make it dramatically contemporary, though aspects of these
earlier modes are still in evidence, are still brought into
play by the poet when they are needed to further his purpose. The subjective element has now become, more than
anything else, the essential definition that the poet brings
to the myth, his unembarrassed if sometimes complex
statement of the wisdom he finds in it. And he also doesn't
hesitate to impose whatever rhetorical pressure he feels his
material should bear so as to make his interpretation of the
myth, his insight into the meaning he finds there, a persuasive poetic act. In short, the approach is that of the seer,
the inspired didact, presenting his mythological lesson in a

manner intended to capture our hearts as well as our minds.
The dominant tone—and it is a tone characteristic of much
of the best of Sikelianos's late work—sounds clearly at
the start of the poem entitled **'Daedalus'** [translated]:

> The fate of Icarus could have been no other
> than to fly and to perish . . . Because when he put on
> freedom's awe-inspiring wings, their equipoise the art
> of his great father, it was youth alone
> that flung his body into danger, even if
> he also failed, perhaps, to find their secret balance.

That, in so many words, is the meaning of Icarus's fate:
given his youth, he could not have done other than he did;
the necessary impulse of his young blood is what took him
too close to the sun. And with this quick view of the mythical figure who has so often moved the poetic imagination
and even here occasions the lamentation of men 'untried
by suffering', Sikelianos settles that aspect of his myth's
mystery and turns to the aspect that really interests him,
namely the meaning of the 'great father's' fate, that of the
sleepless artificer, Daedalus. Sikelianos's focus becomes
what one might call the reverse side of the coin that Auden examines in his famous poem, 'Musée des Beaux-
Arts'. Auden's message is that the masters who best depicted moments of mystery—'the miraculous birth', 'the
dreadful martyrdom'—always juxtaposed the mystery with
moments of ordinary unmysterious life, the doggy life that
has the torturer's horse 'scratching its innocent behind on
a tree', or, in the case of Breughel's *Icarus,* has everything
turning away leisurely from the disaster, including the 'expensive delicate ship' that sails calmly on despite the
amazing thing it has seen: a boy falling out of the sky. In
short, Auden emphasizes how well the Old Masters understood the *human* position of suffering. Sikelianos on the
other hand emphasizes the superhuman position of suffering and the danger of misapprehension that lies in too
much concern for the merely human. As we have seen,
those who give way to an excess of lamentation over
Icarus's necessary fate are called 'untried by suffering', as
are those, along with their feeble women, who call the father Daedalus harsh, or self-serving, or a man in pursuit of
the impossible, presumably for having devised wings
which would lead to his son's death at the same time as a
second set brought Daedalus his own freedom. Contrary to
the lamenters, the feeble of heart and the undiscerning,
Sikelianos sees in Daedalus not only the supremely dedicated artist who carries his grand work forward even when
those around him consider it 'the mere bauble of an idle
mind', but a figure Christlike in his mission to rise above
'this flesh-consuming rhythm', above the crowd, the
waves, even the frontiers of lament in order to 'save with
his own soul the soul of the world'. It is a difficult message to transmit, but in one of those mysterious ways that
poetry sometimes moves, Sikelianos brings it off, perhaps
first of all because he manages successfully to personalize
the myth's teaching without banality, and, more important,
because he courageously allows his voice to assume a
grand style appropriate to the grandeur of his conviction:

[translation]

father,
since for us too the earth and the heavens are one
and our own thought is the world's hearth and center,
since we also say that earth may mingle with the stars
as a field's subsoil with its topsoil, so that the heavens
too
may bring forth wheat:
　　　　　　　father, at those times
when life's bitterness weighs with its full burden
on our hearts, and our strength can be roused no more
by youth
but only by the Will that stands watchful
even over the grave, because to It the sea
which hugs the drowned remorselessly is itself shallow,
and shallow too the earth where the dead sleep;

in the dawn hours, as still we struggle on,
while the living and the dead both lie in the same
dreamless or dream-laden slumber, do not stop
ascending in front of us, but climb always
with slow even wings the heavens of our Thought,
eternal Daedalus, Dawnstar of the Beyond.

Since **'The Sacred Way'** is among Sikelianos's best known and most discussed poems (that is, within the small circle that discusses Sikelianos at all), only a few remarks are called for here. In terms of our theme, the poem should be identified as the most original manifestation of the progress we have been outlining. What happens in this poem is another version of the kind of assimilation and personalization of ancient sources that we saw in **'Daedalus'**, and even beyond that, an attempt on the poet's part to create his own myth in the image of his ancient ancestors. The poet begins his spiritual journey in this poem by setting out from Athens on the road that leads to the home of the Eleusinian Mysteries—an avenue that he tells us he has always looked upon as 'the Soul's road'. And the roadside rock he chooses to rest on in his journey seems to him 'like a throne / long predestined for me', so that when he settles on it he forgets if 'it was to-day that I'd set out or if / I'd taken this road centuries before'. The ground is thus fully prepared for the mythical dimension that the poet brings to the tale that follows, the little mystery play involving a passing gypsy and his two dancing bears, mother and child, the mother bear enormous enough to seem, in the poet's words, the Great Goddess, the Eternal Mother. And when we are shown her rising up in her immense weariness to dance vigorously because she sees the gypsy tug cruelly at the wound in her child's nostril, this touchingly human gesture on her part can become—given the mythical context that the poet has cunningly established—something of a ritual act that transforms the mother bear into a 'huge testifying symbol / of all primaeval suffering for which, / throughout the human centuries, the soul's / tax has still not been paid. Because the soul / has been and still is in Hell'.

[original Greek omitted]

And our assent to this gesture and the meaning given it permits us to accept the poet's own sudden humility, even

the whispered conviction, the affirmation, that ends the poem as the poet's question 'Will the time, the moment ever come when the bear's soul / and the gypsy's and my own, that I call initiated, / will feast together?' finds an answer from the voice of mystery: 'It will come'.

[original Greek omitted]

The poem is one of Sikelianos's very finest, and so is **'Daedalus'**. That is what permits me to speak of a progress in the poet's use of ancient Greek sources. It is always convenient for the structure of a critic's argument to see a poet getting better as he moves from youth to maturity to old age, but of course this is hardly always the case; one thinks of great poets who couldn't carry us the whole distance without ending up boring us beyond reasonable expectation: Wordsworth and Browning, for example. But like Yeats in our tradition and Cavafy in the Greek tradition, Sikelianos did produce some of his finest work in his later years, and his growth to the status of major poet is demonstrated, I think, in at least some measure by the progress in his use of myth that I have tried to illustrate here.

*Notes*

1. Translated and introduced by Edmund Keeley and Philip Sherrard (Princeton, 1979).

### Edmund Keeley (essay date 1983)

SOURCE: "Sikelianos: The Sublime Voice," in *Modern Greek Poetry: Voice and Myth*, Princeton University Press, 1983, pp. 31-52.

*[In the following essay, Keeley places Sikelianos's later poetry within its historical and social context.]*

Readers of contemporary Western poetry in the English-speaking world are usually familiar with the work of C. P. Cavafy and George Seferis to some degree and of Odysseus Elytis and Yannis Ritsos to a lesser degree, but very few have read Angelos Sikelianos (1884-1951), the poet who was next in importance to Cavafy in establishing the demotic tradition during the first half of this century and who was considered by Seferis to be equivalent in stature within that tradition to Yeats within ours. My principal concern here is with Sikelianos's late and, to my mind, his best poems, but given the general lack of access to him in the original outside Greece and the strictly selected character of English translations,[1] the English-speaking reader can have little sense of the range of his career. It may be useful, therefore, for me to set his late poems against the background out of which they emerged, that is, the sources that shaped him and the several early voices that were eventually transformed into the major voice that we hear at moments during the last two decades of his life.

Sikelianos is a traditional poet in both the craft and thought that he gave his art, even more so perhaps than Cavafy, who was twenty years his senior, and Seferis, who was fewer years his junior. And that aspect of the Greek tradition that nourished Sikelianos is rather different from what English-speaking readers of Cavafy and Seferis are likely to expect. Sikelianos's work is rooted neither in the Hellenistic world of the diaspora that provided the principal historical context for Cavafy's poetic myth, nor in the Homeric and Platonic worlds that sustained Seferis's imagination, among other sources. Sikelianos drew his inspiration primarily from the pre-Socratic tradition, with Orphism and the cult of Dionysus, the teaching of Pythagoras, the Mysteries of Eleusis, and the mantic center at Delphi four of the main influences from this tradition. As Philip Sherrard has pointed out,[2] in these sources Sikelianos found a shared perspective that proclaimed not only the brotherhood of all men but of all living creatures and that placed man as the channel of communication between higher and lower states of existence, between the visible and the invisible. The pre-Socratic tradition also gave the poet his highest calling, that of inspired prophet and seer, of teacher and mystagogue, a calling that Sikelianos himself aspired to in modern Greece, as he believed Pindar and Aeschylus had in the classical period and as perhaps Wallace Stevens, in our day, would have understood with the largest sympathy since he gave poets the title "priests of the invisible."

Sikelianos saw the poet exercising the role of priest and seer largely through the agency of myth, in the sense that Schelling defined the term, that is, myth not as a fabrication but as a revelation of divine truth, a revelation of what is universal and timeless, with gods seen not merely as symbols but as living beings. We have ample evidence of Sikelianos's preoccupation with myth in this sense from his earliest work through the late period that most interests us here; yet, however much he may have been concerned with the representation of eternal mysteries, of a universe where the ancient gods still survived palpably, his starting point in the best of his early poems was the natural world around him and the life of the senses that nourished his humanity. The natural world was for him inevitably a Greek world, both in its physical configuration and in its embodiment of traditional folk elements. And the poet who brings the gods to life in this natural world is a man of flesh and blood with the rhetoric characteristic of his people when touched by that passionate, sublime sense of something deeply interfused that rolls through all things (as Wordsworth put it):[3]

> The sun set over Acrocorinth
> burning the rock red. From the sea
> a fragrant smell of seaweed now began
> to intoxicate my slender stallion.
>
> Foam on the bit, the white of his eye
> bared fully, he struggled to break
> my grip, tight on the reins,
> to leap free into open space.
>
> Was it the hour? The rich odors?
> Was it the sea's deep saltiness?
> The forest's breathing far away?

> O had the meltemi held strong
> a little longer, I would have gripped
> the reins and flanks of mythic Pegasus!

> **("On Acrocorinth")**[4]

When Pan, in the early poem of that title, suddenly rises up over the burning heat of harsh pebbles on the shore opposite contemporary Salamis, the poet, in his easy passing between the world of flesh and the world of divinities, captures the god's vitality by focusing on the majesty of his goatish form:

> Then we saw the herd's lord and master, the he-goat
> rise alone
> and move off, hoof-beats slow and heavy,
> toward a rock
> wedged into the sea to shape a perfect lookout point;
> there he stopped,
> on the very edge where spray dissolves,
> and leaning motionless,
> upper lip pulled back so that his teeth shone,
> he stood
> huge, erect, smelling the white-crested sea
> until sunset.

Given Sikelianos's conception of the poet as seer, as agent for bringing into close communion the mortal and the divine, it is not surprising to find that his persona, the first-person voice which is the dominant one in his earlier poems, often seem larger than life, almost a force in nature that transcends humanity, anyway the voice for rhetoric that seems both inspired and on occasion, grandiloquent. The persona sometimes actually assumes the identity and style of a self-ordained hierophant, an ascetic who has been initiated into the mysteries of both Dionysus and Christ, a voice that can directly address the gods and even their grand earthly habitations, as in the following excerpts from **"Hymn to Artemis Orthia"**:

> O Taygetus,
> bronze mountain,
> at last you receive me as an ascetic! . . .
>
> what new impulses
> nourished my untamable and silent strength,
>
> veil of the tumult on your five peaks
> where the snow was slowly thawing,
>
> aerial cataracts
> of the flowering oleander
> on the escarpments,
> dawning of the Doric Apollo
> before my eyes,
> O harsh sculptured form
> on the red unsoftened bronze!

This hierophantic, rhapsodic voice is the one least accessible to a contemporary Western sensibility, not only because that sensibility has been trained in our time to question rhetoric of almost any kind, but because the voice depends for credibility and vitality on the character of the language it offers, on the resonances and surprises that Sikelianos's creative—one could even say prototypical—use of demotic brings to the Greek reader. When the voice succeeds in the original (and it does not always), it is likely to fail in translation to some degree. The early voices of Sikelianos that are more accessible to the English-speaking reader, that better survive the dangerous crossing from one language to another, are those of the first person, sometimes overtly subjective persona celebrating the natural world around him and his union with it (as in **"The Return," "The First Rain,"** and **"Thalero"**) or the rituals of peasant life that still evoke a rich—if dying—folk tradition (as in **"The Village Wedding"**) and the poet's narrative voice telling the miracle of Dante's birth or of a Doric virgin's first embrace.[5] But the greatest voice of all, to my mind, appears during the mid-thirties to mid-forties, beginning some fifteen years after the latest of the poems I have been quoting, a voice that brilliantly combines the subjective and the narrative in those late poems that reveal Sikelianos's sublime tragic vision.

There is evidence in the poems themselves that this vision of the immediately pre-World War II years was influenced by a personal crisis of some kind, one perhaps having to do in part with the death of Sikelianos's attempt to revive Delphi as a cultural and educational center and his increasing sense of alienation from his contemporaries, perhaps in part with his separation from his first wife (Eva Palmer) and eventually from his only son. It was in any case a crisis marked by suffering, and the subsequent catharsis seems to have brought the poet both a new humility and a renewed sense of mission. There is also implicit evidence that this personal catharsis in the years immediately before the war prepared Sikelianos to understand and to dramatize his country's cruel fate early in the German Occupation—dramatize it with the kind of prophetic wisdom that makes **"Agraphon"** one of the major Greek poems of this century. But **"Daedalus"** is the poem that first gives us a clear insight into the poet's late tragic sense of life, and it is in this poem that we discover the particular voice he fashioned to express what he had come to understand. The narrative focuses on Daedalus—the great artificer, model for the poet—and Daedalus's persistence in the pursuit of a dream, that is, the creation of wings that will raise him "above the crowd, / above the waves that swallowed up his child, / above even the frontiers of lament, to save / with his own soul the soul of the world." It is a dream of creation that he holds to despite the misrepresentation, the condemnation, of "men untried by suffering" and "feeble and embittered women" who call him a "harsh father" for keeping to his fearful course in order to save his own pathetic life, though "his sun was near its setting." The narrative voice shifts to the subjective in the last stanza as the poet establishes his kinship with the tireless artificer and his noble search for the impossible, for that "awe-inspiring Art" which "the dull crowd" considers to be "the mere bauble of an idle mind.":

> But you, great father, father of all of us
> who from our earliest years have seen that everything
> lies in the grave's shadow and who, with words

or chisel, have struggled with all our spirit
to rise above this flesh-consuming rhythm:
> father,
since for us too the earth and the heavens are one
and our own thought is the world's hearth and center,
since we also say that earth may mingle with the stars
as a field's subsoil with its topsoil, so that the heavens too
may bring forth wheat:
> father, at those times
when life's bitterness weighs with its full burden
on our hearts, and our strength can be roused no more by
> youth
but only by the Will, that stands watchful
even over the grave, because to It the sea
which hugs the drowned remorselessly is itself shallow,
and shallow too the earth where the dead sleep;
in the dawn hours, as still we struggle on,
while the living and the dead both lie in the same
dreamless or dream-laden slumber, do not stop
ascending in front of us, but climb always
with slow even wings the heavens of our Thought,
eternal Daedalus, Dawnstar of the Beyond.

The voice here, though essentially personal, is rather different from that of the rhapsodic first-person seer who inhabits much of Sikelianos's earlier verse. The poet is no longer the hierophant transmitting a godly message through priestly rhetoric; he allows the myth at the poem's center to have its own life through narrative exposition, then brings himself into the myth by analogy, sharing its significance, joining his own experience of suffering and commitment to its revelation, but holding his focus on what the myth has already established, so that the personal dimension does not overwhelm the metaphorical. As a result, the voice in this poem is both convincing and sublime, and it carries a new implication of humility.

A similar voice speaks in **"The Sacred Way,"** among the very best of the prewar poems. The subjective element is there from the start as the poet alludes rather more directly to the personal crisis that was only implicit in the previous poem: "Through the new wound that fate had opened in me . . ." and "like one long sick when he first ventures forth / to milk life from the outside world, I walked / alone at dusk. . . ." But he quickly establishes a mythological framework for this personal journey of the spirit by describing the sacred road to Eleusis that is its setting, a road he sees as a river bearing ox-drawn carts that are loaded with people who seem shades of the dead. And in this setting his journey merges with that of others taken centuries ago along the same road. Before the metaphor becomes uncomfortably labored, the poet moves on to his narrative about a gypsy and two dancing bears, and though there are further allusions to Demeter, Alcmene, and the Holy Virgin in support of the mythological framework, the tragic sense of life at the heart of the poem emerges most powerfully from the story that the poet tells of a mother bear rising up in pain out of an ill-fated tenderness to dance vigorously so that her innocent child will be spared a premature knowledge of the suffering that is his inevitable destiny:

> And then, as they drew near to me, the gypsy,
> before I'd really noticed him, saw me,
> took his tambourine down from his shoulder,
> struck it with one hand, and with the other tugged
> fiercely at the chains. And the two bears
> rose on their hind legs heavily. One of them,
> the larger—clearly she was the mother—
> her head adorned with tassels of blue beads
> crowned by a white amulet, towered up
> suddenly enormous, as if she were
> the primordial image of the Great Goddess,
> the Eternal Mother, sacred in her affliction,
> who, in human form, was called Demeter
> here at Eleusis, where she mourned her daughter,
> and elsewhere, where she mourned her son,
> was called Alcmene or the Holy Virgin.
> And the small bear at her side, like a big toy,
> like an innocent child, also rose up, submissive,
> not sensing yet the years of pain ahead
> or the bitterness of slavery mirrored
> in the burning eyes his mother turned on him.
>
> But because she, dead tired, was slow to dance,
> the gypsy, with a single dexterous jerk
> of the chain hanging from the young bear's nostril—
> bloody still from the ring that had pierced it
> perhaps a few days before—made the mother,
> groaning with pain, abruptly straighten up
> and then, her head turning toward her child,
> dance vigorously.

It is through this convincingly narrated action that the poet earns our assent to the mother bear's mythic role as "huge testifying symbol / of all primaeval suffering for which, / throughout the human centuries, the soul's / tax has still not been paid. Because the soul / has been and still is in Hell." And it is through the carefully plotted merging of the narrative and personal elements, of the mythical figure as eternal sufferer and the persona as "slave to this world," that the poet persuades us to accept both the tragic implications of the poem and the tentative resolution that concludes it:

> Then, as the gypsy
> at last went on his way, again dragging
> the slow-footed bears behind him, and vanished
> in the dusk, my heart prompted me once more
> to take the road that terminates among
> the ruins of the Soul's temple, at Eleusis.
> And as I walked my heart asked in anguish:
> "Will the time, the moment ever come when the bear's soul
> and the gypsy's and my own, that I call initiated,
> will feast together?"
>             And as I moved on, night fell,
> and again through the wound that fate had opened in me
> I felt the darkness flood my heart as water
> pours through a hole in a sinking ship.
> Yet when—as though it has been thirsting for that

> flood—
> my heart sank down completely into the darkness,
> sank completely as though to drown in the darkness,
> a murmur spread through all the air above me,
> a murmur,
>             and it seemed to say:
>             "It will come."

The poem **"Agraphon,"** written during the devastating Athenian autumn of 1941 under the German Occupation, is the purest example of Sikelianos's late mode. Two-thirds of the poem consists of a narrated parable that is offered without introduction, except that which is implied by the title: a saying or tradition about Christ not recorded in the Gospels or capable of being traced to its original source. The parable tells a story of corruption outside the walls of Zion that Jesus, walking with his disciples, sees as a metaphor for corruption inside the city; but more important, He finds within the corruption, represented literally by a dog's stinking carcass, the glitter of white teeth "like hailstones, like a lily, beyond decay, / a great pledge, mirror of the Eternal, but also / the harsh lightning-flash, the hope of Justice." The parable is presented as straight narrative, then the personal voice is heard for the last third of the poem, not as a commentary on what has been presented but as an assimilation of it into the poet's immediate world, where the Zion of his time has become analogous to that corrupt city which Christ knew, and where the tragic circumstances enveloping the poet have brought him to that final knowledge and humility which the ancient poets tell us can come from intense suffering alone. The poet prays:

> And now, Lord, I,
> the very least of men, ponder your words,
> and filled with one thought, I stand before you:
> grant me, as now I walk outside this Zion,
> and the world from end to end is all ruins, garbage,
> all unburied corpses choking the sacred
> springs of breath, inside and outside the city:
> grant me, Lord, as I walk through this terrible stench,
> one single moment of Your holy calm,
> so that I, dispassionate, may also pause
> among this carrion and with my own eyes
> somewhere see a token, white as hailstones,
> as the lily—something glittering suddenly
> deep inside me, above the putrefaction,
> beyond the world's decay, like the dog's teeth
> at which that sunset You gazed, Lord, in wonder:
> a great pledge, mirror of the Eternal, but also
> the harsh lightning-flash, the hope of Justice!

The voice in this poem moves us perhaps as no other in Sikelianos's verse not so much because the reality of that bitter 1941 season gives substance to his rhetoric, but because the poet's prayer comes to us after he has narrated a story, a myth in Schelling's sense, that provides both an objective and a generalized context for his personal, his national, predicament. Again, what there is of subjective rhetoric in the poem becomes tranferred into the universal and the sublime.

During the period of the German Occupation, Sikelianos wrote a number of poems that were a direct, uncomplicated, unsubtle expression of his passionate concern for his country's fate, poems meant to rouse the spirit of resistance and to celebrate the heroic stance of his people. Overt rhetoric returned in the nation's service. Every Greek schoolchild of the period (including those of the Greek diaspora) still remembers the opening lines of the famous poem Sikelianos recited over the coffin of Kostis Palamas, his eminent predecessor, on February 28, 1943:

> Blow, bugles . . . Thundering bells,
> shake the whole country, from end to end . . .[6]

The recitation itself was an act of resistance, followed as it was by Sikelianos's booming voice rendering the forbidden Greek national anthem for the entertainment of the plain-clothed German occupiers who had come to mix, rather bewildered, with the huge crowd of mourners at Palamas's funeral. Now, so many years after the fact, one perhaps sees those lines on Palamas's death and other patriotic poems of the time as the least satisfactory manifestation of Sikelianos's late voice—that is, viewed from a strictly literary perspective. But what I want to emphasize in conclusion is that Sikelianos did in fact write one poem that successfully projected, through the agency of myth, both his passionate feeling for his country's fate—that harsh lightning-flash hope of Justice—and his more universal tragic sense of life. There are lines in **"Agraphon"** that I believe will long survive as poetry both in and beyond the context of their historical occasion and specifi-

cally national impulse. That accomplishment by itself demonstrates why Sikelianos is one of the truly great masters in the modern Greek tradition.

*Notes*

1. *Six Poets of Modern Greece,* trans. Edmund Keeley and Philip Sherrard (London, 1960 and New York, 1961) offered an early selection now out of print. More recent selections include those in *Modern Greek Poetry,* trans. Kimon Friar (New York, 1973); *Angelos Sikelianos: Selected Poems,* trans. Edmund Keeley and Philip Sherrard (Princeton and London, 1979); and *The Dark Crystal,* trans. Edmund Keeley and Philip Sherrard (Athens, 1981), published in the United States as *Voices of Modern Greece* (Princeton, 1981).

2. *Review of National Literatures* (Fall, 1974), p. 100.

3. In "Lines Composed a Few Miles above Tintern Abbey."

4. Translations of Sikelianos in this essay are from *Sikelianos: Selected Poems.* See that volume for relevant notes, e.g., on "meltemi."

5. *See Sikelianos: Selected Poems,* "The Mother of Dante" and "Doric."

6. From "Palamas" in Sikelianos's *Lyrical Life,* 5.

---

**Additional coverage of Sikelianos's life and career is contained in the following sources published by the Gale Group:** *Twentieth-Century Literary Criticism*, **Vol. 39.**

# How to Use This Index

The main references

Calvino, Italo
1923-1985 ....... CLC 5, 8, 11, 22, 33, 39,
73; SSC 3

**list all author entries in the following Gale Literary Criticism series:**

*BLC* = *Black Literature Criticism*
*CLC* = *Contemporary Literary Criticism*
*CLR* = *Children's Literature Review*
*CMLC* = *Classical and Medieval Literature Criticism*
*DA* = *DISCovering Authors*
*DAB* = *DISCovering Authors: British*
*DAC* = *DISCovering Authors: Canadian*
*DAM* = *DISCovering Authors: Modules*
  *DRAM:* *Dramatists Module;* *MST:* *Most-Studied Authors Module;*
  *MULT:* *Multicultural Authors Module;* *NOV:* *Novelists Module;*
  *POET:* *Poets Module;* *POP:* *Popular Fiction and Genre Authors Module*
*DC* = *Drama Criticism*
*HLC* = *Hispanic Literature Criticism*
*LC* = *Literature Criticism from 1400 to 1800*
*NCLC* = *Nineteenth-Century Literature Criticism*
*NNAL* = *Native North American Literature*
*PC* = *Poetry Criticism*
*SSC* = *Short Story Criticism*
*TCLC* = *Twentieth-Century Literary Criticism*
*WLC* = *World Literature Criticism, 1500 to the Present*

The cross-references

See also CANR 23; CA 85-88;
obituary CA116

**list all author entries in the following Gale biographical and literary sources:**

*AAYA* = *Authors & Artists for Young Adults*
*AITN* = *Authors in the News*
*BEST* = *Bestsellers*
*BW* = *Black Writers*
*CA* = *Contemporary Authors*
*CAAS* = *Contemporary Authors Autobiography Series*
*CABS* = *Contemporary Authors Bibliographical Series*
*CANR* = *Contemporary Authors New Revision Series*
*CAP* = *Contemporary Authors Permanent Series*
*CDALB* = *Concise Dictionary of American Literary Biography*
*CDBLB* = *Concise Dictionary of British Literary Biography*
*DLB* = *Dictionary of Literary Biography*
*DLBD* = *Dictionary of Literary Biography Documentary Series*
*DLBY* = *Dictionary of Literary Biography Yearbook*
*HW* = *Hispanic Writers*
*JRDA* = *Junior DISCovering Authors*
*MAICYA* = *Major Authors and Illustrators for Children and Young Adults*
*MTCW* = *Major 20th-Century Writers*
*SAAS* = *Something about the Author Autobiography Series*
*SATA* = *Something about the Author*
*YABC* = *Yesterday's Authors of Books for Children*

# Literary Criticism Series
# Cumulative Author Index

**20/1631**
See Upward, Allen

**A/C Cross**
See Lawrence, T(homas) E(dward)

**Abasiyanik, Sait Faik** 1906-1954
See Sait Faik
See also CA 123

**Abbey, Edward** 1927-1989 .......... **CLC 36, 59**
See also CA 45-48; 128; CANR 2, 41; DA3;
MTCW 2

**Abbott, Lee K(ittredge)** 1947- .......... **CLC 48**
See also CA 124; CANR 51; DLB 130

**Abe, Kobo** 1924-1993 ...... **CLC 8, 22, 53, 81;
DAM NOV**
See also CA 65-68; 140; CANR 24, 60;
DLB 182; MTCW 1, 2

**Abelard, Peter** c. 1079-c. 1142 ...... **CMLC 11**
See also DLB 115, 208

**Abell, Kjeld** 1901-1961 ..................... **CLC 15**
See also CA 111

**Abish, Walter** 1931- ........................... **CLC 22**
See also CA 101; CANR 37; DLB 130

**Abrahams, Peter (Henry)** 1919- ......... **CLC 4**
See also BW 1; CA 57-60; CANR 26; DLB
117; MTCW 1, 2

**Abrams, M(eyer) H(oward)** 1912- ... **CLC 24**
See also CA 57-60; CANR 13, 33; DLB 67

**Abse, Dannie** 1923- .......... **CLC 7, 29; DAB;
DAM POET**
See also CA 53-56; CAAS 1; CANR 4, 46,
74; DLB 27; MTCW 1

**Achebe, (Albert) Chinua(lumogu)**
1930- ...... **CLC 1, 3, 5, 7, 11, 26, 51, 75,
127; BLC 1; DA; DAB; DAC; DAM
MST, MULT, NOV; WLC**
See also AAYA 15; BW 2, 3; CA 1-4R;
CANR 6, 26, 47; CLR 20; DA3; DLB
117; MAICYA; MTCW 1, 2; SATA 38,
40; SATA-Brief 38

**Acker, Kathy** 1948-1997 ............ **CLC 45, 111**
See also CA 117; 122; 162; CANR 55

**Ackroyd, Peter** 1949- ................... **CLC 34, 52**
See also CA 123; 127; CANR 51, 74; DLB
155; INT 127; MTCW 1

**Acorn, Milton** 1923- .............. **CLC 15; DAC**
See also CA 103; DLB 53; INT 103

**Adamov, Arthur** 1908-1970 ......... **CLC 4, 25;
DAM DRAM**
See also CA 17-18; 25-28R; CAP 2; MTCW
1

**Adams, Alice (Boyd)** 1926-1999 .. **CLC 6, 13,
46; SSC 24**
See also CA 81-84; 179; CANR 26, 53, 75,
88; DLBY 86; INT CANR-26; MTCW 1,
2

**Adams, Andy** 1859-1935 ................. **TCLC 56**
See also YABC 1

**Adams, Brooks** 1848-1927 .............. **TCLC 80**
See also CA 123; DLB 47

**Adams, Douglas (Noel)** 1952- .... **CLC 27, 60;
DAM POP**
See also AAYA 4; BEST 89:3; CA 106;
CANR 34, 64; DA3; DLBY 83; JRDA;
MTCW 1

**Adams, Francis** 1862-1893 ............. **NCLC 33**

**Adams, Henry (Brooks)**
1838-1918 ........ **TCLC 4, 52; DA; DAB;
DAC; DAM MST**
See also CA 104; 133; CANR 77; DLB 12,
47, 189; MTCW 1

**Adams, Richard (George)** 1920- ... **CLC 4, 5,
18; DAM NOV**
See also AAYA 16; AITN 1, 2; CA 49-52;
CANR 3, 35; CLR 20; JRDA; MAICYA;
MTCW 1, 2; SATA 7, 69

**Adamson, Joy(-Friederike Victoria)**
1910-1980 .................................. **CLC 17**
See also CA 69-72; 93-96; CANR 22;
MTCW 1; SATA 11; SATA-Obit 22

**Adcock, Fleur** 1934- ........................... **CLC 41**
See also CA 25-28R, 182; CAAE 182;
CAAS 23; CANR 11, 34, 69; DLB 40

**Addams, Charles (Samuel)**
1912-1988 ................................... **CLC 30**
See also CA 61-64; 126; CANR 12, 79

**Addams, Jane** 1860-1945 ................. **TCLC 76**

**Addison, Joseph** 1672-1719 ................. **LC 18**
See also CDBLB 1660-1789; DLB 101

**Adler, Alfred (F.)** 1870-1937 .......... **TCLC 61**
See also CA 119; 159

**Adler, C(arole) S(chwerdtfeger)**
1932- ...................................... **CLC 35**
See also AAYA 4; CA 89-92; CANR 19,
40; JRDA; MAICYA; SAAS 15; SATA
26, 63, 102

**Adler, Renata** 1938- ...................... **CLC 8, 31**
See also CA 49-52; CANR 5, 22, 52;
MTCW 1

**Ady, Endre** 1877-1919 .................... **TCLC 11**
See also CA 107

**A.E.** 1867-1935 ........................... **TCLC 3, 10**
See also Russell, George William

**Aeschylus** 525B.C.-456B.C. .. **CMLC 11; DA;
DAB; DAC; DAM DRAM, MST; DC
8; WLCS**
See also DLB 176

**Aesop** 620(?)B.C.-564(?)B.C. ......... **CMLC 24**
See also CLR 14; MAICYA; SATA 64

**Affable Hawk**
See MacCarthy, Sir(Charles Otto) Desmond

**Africa, Ben**
See Bosman, Herman Charles

**Afton, Effie**
See Harper, Frances Ellen Watkins

**Agapida, Fray Antonio**
See Irving, Washington

**Agee, James (Rufus)** 1909-1955 ...... **TCLC 1,
19; DAM NOV**
See also AITN 1; CA 108; 148; CDALB
1941-1968; DLB 2, 26, 152; MTCW 1

**Aghill, Gordon**
See Silverberg, Robert

**Agnon, S(hmuel) Y(osef Halevi)** 1888-1970
**CLC 4, 8, 14; SSC 30**
See also CA 17-18; 25-28R; CANR 60;
CAP 2; MTCW 1, 2

**Agrippa von Nettesheim, Henry Cornelius**
1486-1535 ............................... **LC 27**

**Aguilera Malta, Demetrio** 1909-1981
See also CA 111; 124; CANR 87; DAM
MULT, NOV; DLB 145; HLCS 1; HW 1

**Agustini, Delmira** 1886-1914
See also CA 166; HLCS 1; HW 1, 2

**Aherne, Owen**
See Cassill, R(onald) V(erlin)

**Ai** 1947- ................................... **CLC 4, 14, 69**
See also CA 85-88; CAAS 13; CANR 70;
DLB 120

**Aickman, Robert (Fordyce)**
1914-1981 ................................. **CLC 57**
See also CA 5-8R; CANR 3, 72

**Aiken, Conrad (Potter)** 1889-1973 .... **CLC 1,
3, 5, 10, 52; DAM NOV, POET; PC 26;
SSC 9**
See also CA 5-8R; 45-48; CANR 4, 60;
CDALB 1929-1941; DLB 9, 45, 102;
MTCW 1, 2; SATA 3, 30

**Aiken, Joan (Delano)** 1924- .............. **CLC 35**
See also AAYA 1, 25; CA 9-12R, 182;
CAAE 182; CANR 4, 23, 34, 64; CLR 1,
19; DLB 161; JRDA; MAICYA; MTCW
1; SAAS 1; SATA 2, 30, 73; SATA-Essay
109

**Ainsworth, William Harrison** 1805-1882
**NCLC 13**
See also DLB 21; SATA 24

**Aitmatov, Chingiz (Torekulovich)**
1928- ......................................... **CLC 71**
See also CA 103; CANR 38; MTCW 1;
SATA 56

**Akers, Floyd**
See Baum, L(yman) Frank

**Akhmadulina, Bella Akhatovna**
1937- ................... **CLC 53; DAM POET**
See also CA 65-68

**Akhmatova, Anna** 1888-1966 ..... **CLC 11, 25,
64, 126; DAM POET; PC 2**
See also CA 19-20; 25-28R; CANR 35;
CAP 1; DA3; MTCW 1, 2

**Aksakov, Sergei Timofeyvich** 1791-1859
**NCLC 2**
See also DLB 198

**Aksenov, Vassily**
See Aksyonov, Vassily (Pavlovich)

**Akst, Daniel** 1956- ............................ **CLC 109**
See also CA 161

**Aksyonov, Vassily (Pavlovich)**
1932- ............................ **CLC 22, 37, 101**
See also CA 53-56; CANR 12, 48, 77

**Akutagawa, Ryunosuke**
1892-1927 ............................ **TCLC 16**
See also CA 117; 154

**Alain** 1868-1951 ............................ **TCLC 41**
See also CA 163

**Alain-Fournier** ................................. **TCLC 6**
See also Fournier, Henri Alban DLB 65

**Alarcon, Pedro Antonio de**
1833-1891 .................................. **NCLC 1**

**Alas (y Urena), Leopoldo (Enrique Garcia)**
1852-1901 ............................ **TCLC 29**
See also CA 113; 131; HW 1

**Albee, Edward (Franklin III)** 1928- . **CLC 1,
2, 3, 5, 9, 11, 13, 25, 53, 86, 113; DA;
DAB; DAC; DAM DRAM, MST; DC
11; WLC**
See also AITN 1; CA 5-8R; CABS 3;
CANR 8, 54, 74; CDALB 1941-1968;
DA3; DLB 7; INT CANR-8; MTCW 1, 2

**Alberti, Rafael** 1902- ............................ **CLC 7**
See also CA 85-88; CANR 81; DLB 108;
HW 2

**Albert the Great** 1200(?)-1280 ...... **CMLC 16**
See also DLB 115

**Alcala-Galiano, Juan Valera y**
See Valera y Alcala-Galiano, Juan

**Alcott, Amos Bronson** 1799-1888 .... **NCLC 1**
See also DLB 1

**Alcott, Louisa May** 1832-1888 . **NCLC 6, 58,
83; DA; DAB; DAC; DAM MST, NOV;
SSC 27; WLC**
See also AAYA 20; CDALB 1865-1917;
CLR 1, 38; DA3; DLB 1, 42, 79; DLBD
14; JRDA; MAICYA; SATA 100; YABC
1

**Aldanov, M. A.**
See Aldanov, Mark (Alexandrovich)

**Aldanov, Mark (Alexandrovich)**
1886(?)-1957 ............................ **TCLC 23**
See also CA 118; 181

**Aldington, Richard** 1892-1962 .......... **CLC 49**
See also CA 85-88; CANR 45; DLB 20, 36,
100, 149

**Aldiss, Brian W(ilson)** 1925- . **CLC 5, 14, 40;
DAM NOV; SSC 36**
See also CA 5-8R; CAAS 2; CANR 5, 28,
64; DLB 14; MTCW 1, 2; SATA 34

**Alegria, Claribel** 1924- .......... **CLC 75; DAM
MULT; HLCS 1; PC 26**
See also CA 131; CAAS 15; CANR 66;
DLB 145; HW 1; MTCW 1

**Alegria, Fernando** 1918- .................. **CLC 57**
See also CA 9-12R; CANR 5, 32, 72; HW
1, 2

**Aleichem, Sholom** ........ **TCLC 1, 35; SSC 33**
See also Rabinovitch, Sholem

**Aleixandre, Vicente** 1898-1984
See also CANR 81; HLCS 1; HW 2

**Alepoudelis, Odysseus**
See Elytis, Odysseus

**Aleshkovsky, Joseph** 1929-
See Aleshkovsky, Yuz
See also CA 121; 128

**Aleshkovsky, Yuz** ............................ **CLC 44**
See also Aleshkovsky, Joseph

**Alexander, Lloyd (Chudley)** 1924- ... **CLC 35**
See also AAYA 1, 27; CA 1-4R; CANR 1,
24, 38, 55; CLR 1, 5, 48; DLB 52; JRDA;
MAICYA; MTCW 1; SAAS 19; SATA 3,
49, 81

**Alexander, Meena** 1951- .................. **CLC 121**
See also CA 115; CANR 38, 70

**Alexander, Samuel** 1859-1938 ........ **TCLC 77**

**Alexie, Sherman (Joseph, Jr.)**
1966- .................. **CLC 96; DAM MULT**
See also AAYA 28; CA 138; CANR 65;
DA3; DLB 175, 206; MTCW 1; NNAL

**Alfau, Felipe** 1902- ............................ **CLC 66**
See also CA 137

**Alfred, Jean Gaston**
See Ponge, Francis

**Alger, Horatio Jr., Jr.** 1832-1899 .... **NCLC 8,
83**
See also DLB 42; SATA 16

**Algren, Nelson** 1909-1981 ..... **CLC 4, 10, 33;
SSC 33**
See also CA 13-16R; 103; CANR 20, 61;
CDALB 1941-1968; DLB 9; DLBY 81,
82; MTCW 1, 2

**Ali, Ahmed** 1910- ............................ **CLC 69**
See also CA 25-28R; CANR 15, 34

**Alighieri, Dante**
See Dante

**Allan, John B.**
See Westlake, Donald E(dwin)

**Allan, Sidney**
See Hartmann, Sadakichi

**Allan, Sydney**
See Hartmann, Sadakichi

**Allen, Edward** 1948- ........................ **CLC 59**

**Allen, Fred** 1894-1956 .................... **TCLC 87**

**Allen, Paula Gunn** 1939- ....... **CLC 84; DAM
MULT**
See also CA 112; 143; CANR 63; DA3;
DLB 175; MTCW 1; NNAL

**Allen, Roland**
See Ayckbourn, Alan

**Allen, Sarah A.**
See Hopkins, Pauline Elizabeth

**Allen, Sidney H.**
See Hartmann, Sadakichi

**Allen, Woody** 1935- ......... **CLC 16, 52; DAM
POP**
See also AAYA 10; CA 33-36R; CANR 27,
38, 63; DLB 44; MTCW 1

**Allende, Isabel** 1942- . **CLC 39, 57, 97; DAM
MULT, NOV; HLC 1; WLCS**
See also AAYA 18; CA 125; 130; CANR
51, 74; DA3; DLB 145; HW 1, 2; INT
130; MTCW 1, 2

**Alleyn, Ellen**
See Rossetti, Christina (Georgina)

**Allingham, Margery (Louise)**
1904-1966 ............................ **CLC 19**
See also CA 5-8R; 25-28R; CANR 4, 58;
DLB 77; MTCW 1, 2

**Allingham, William** 1824-1889 ...... **NCLC 25**
See also DLB 35

**Allison, Dorothy E.** 1949- .................. **CLC 78**
See also CA 140; CANR 66; DA3; MTCW
1

**Allston, Washington** 1779-1843 ....... **NCLC 2**
See also DLB 1

**Almedingen, E. M.** ............................ **CLC 12**
See also Almedingen, Martha Edith von
SATA 3

**Almedingen, Martha Edith von** 1898-1971
See Almedingen, E. M.
See also CA 1-4R; CANR 1

**Almodovar, Pedro** 1949(?)- ........... **CLC 114;
HLCS 1**
See also CA 133; CANR 72; HW 2

**Almqvist, Carl Jonas Love**
1793-1866 ................................ **NCLC 42**

**Alonso, Damaso** 1898-1990 .............. **CLC 14**
See also CA 110; 131; 130; CANR 72; DLB
108; HW 1, 2

**Alov**
See Gogol, Nikolai (Vasilyevich)

**Alta** 1942- ...................................... **CLC 19**
See also CA 57-60

**Alter, Robert B(ernard)** 1935- ......... **CLC 34**
See also CA 49-52; CANR 1, 47

**Alther, Lisa** 1944- ........................ **CLC 7, 41**
See also CA 65-68; CAAS 30; CANR 12,
30, 51; MTCW 1

**Althusser, L.**
See Althusser, Louis

**Althusser, Louis** 1918-1990 ............ **CLC 106**
See also CA 131; 132

**Altman, Robert** 1925- ............... **CLC 16, 116**
See also CA 73-76; CANR 43

**Alurista** 1949-
See Urista, Alberto H.
See also DLB 82; HLCS 1

**Alvarez, A(lfred)** 1929- ................. **CLC 5, 13**
See also CA 1-4R; CANR 3, 33, 63; DLB
14, 40

**Alvarez, Alejandro Rodriguez** 1903-1965
See Casona, Alejandro
See also CA 131; 93-96; HW 1

**Alvarez, Julia** 1950- .......... **CLC 93; HLCS 1**
See also AAYA 25; CA 147; CANR 69;
DA3; MTCW 1

**Alvaro, Corrado** 1896-1956 ........... **TCLC 60**
See also CA 163

**Amado, Jorge** 1912- .......... **CLC 13, 40, 106;
DAM MULT, NOV; HLC 1**
See also CA 77-80; CANR 35, 74; DLB
113; HW 2; MTCW 1, 2

**Ambler, Eric** 1909-1998 .............. **CLC 4, 6, 9**
See also CA 9-12R; 171; CANR 7, 38, 74;
DLB 77; MTCW 1, 2

**Amichai, Yehuda** 1924- ... **CLC 9, 22, 57, 116**
See also CA 85-88; CANR 46, 60; MTCW
1

**Amichai, Yehudah**
See Amichai, Yehuda

**Amiel, Henri Frederic** 1821-1881 .... **NCLC 4**

**Amis, Kingsley (William)**
1922-1995 ...... **CLC 1, 2, 3, 5, 8, 13, 40,
44, 129; DA; DAB; DAC; DAM MST,
NOV**
See also AITN 2; CA 9-12R; 150; CANR 8,
28, 54; CDBLB 1945-1960; DA3; DLB
15, 27, 100, 139; DLBY 96; INT
CANR-8; MTCW 1, 2

**Amis, Martin (Louis)** 1949- .... **CLC 4, 9, 38,
62, 101**
See also BEST 90:3; CA 65-68; CANR 8,
27, 54, 73; DA3; DLB 14, 194; INT
CANR-27; MTCW 1

**Ammons, A(rchie) R(andolph)**
1926- ...... **CLC 2, 3, 5, 8, 9, 25, 57, 108;
DAM POET; PC 16**
See also AITN 1; CA 9-12R; CANR 6, 36,
51, 73; DLB 5, 165; MTCW 1, 2

**Amo, Tauraatua i**
See Adams, Henry (Brooks)

**Amory, Thomas** 1691(?)-1788 ............. **LC 48**

**Anand, Mulk Raj** 1905- .. **CLC 23, 93; DAM
NOV**
See also CA 65-68; CANR 32, 64; MTCW
1, 2

**Anatol**
See Schnitzler, Arthur

**Anaximander** c. 610B.C.-c.
546B.C. ............................ **CMLC 22**

**Anaya, Rudolfo A(lfonso)** 1937- ...... **CLC 23;
DAM MULT, NOV; HLC 1**
See also AAYA 20; CA 45-48; CAAS 4;
CANR 1, 32, 51; DLB 82, 206; HW 1;
MTCW 1, 2

**Andersen, Hans Christian**
1805-1875 ....... **NCLC 7, 79; DA; DAB;
DAC; DAM MST, POP; SSC 6; WLC**
See also CLR 6; DA3; MAICYA; SATA
100; YABC 1

**Anderson, C. Farley**
  See Mencken, H(enry) L(ouis); Nathan, George Jean
**Anderson, Jessica (Margaret) Queale** 1916- **CLC 37**
  See also CA 9-12R; CANR 4, 62
**Anderson, Jon (Victor)** 1940- . **CLC 9; DAM POET**
  See also CA 25-28R; CANR 20
**Anderson, Lindsay (Gordon)**
  1923-1994 ................ **CLC 20**
  See also CA 125; 128; 146; CANR 77
**Anderson, Maxwell** 1888-1959 ....... **TCLC 2; DAM DRAM**
  See also CA 105; 152; DLB 7; MTCW 2
**Anderson, Poul (William)** 1926- ....... **CLC 15**
  See also AAYA 5; CA 1-4R, 181; CAAE 181; CAAS 2; CANR 2, 15, 34, 64; CLR 58; DLB 8; INT CANR-15; MTCW 1, 2; SATA 90; SATA-Brief 39; SATA-Essay 106
**Anderson, Robert (Woodruff)**
  1917- ................ **CLC 23; DAM DRAM**
  See also AITN 1; CA 21-24R; CANR 32; DLB 7
**Anderson, Sherwood** 1876-1941 ..... **TCLC 1, 10, 24; DA; DAB; DAC; DAM MST, NOV; SSC 1; WLC**
  See also AAYA 30; CA 104; 121; CANR 61; CDALB 1917-1929; DA3; DLB 4, 9, 86; DLBD 1; MTCW 1, 2
**Andier, Pierre**
  See Desnos, Robert
**Andouard**
  See Giraudoux, (Hippolyte) Jean
**Andrade, Carlos Drummond de** ...... **CLC 18**
  See also Drummond de Andrade, Carlos
**Andrade, Mario de** 1893-1945 ....... **TCLC 43**
**Andreae, Johann V(alentin)**
  1586-1654 ................ **LC 32**
  See also DLB 164
**Andreas-Salome, Lou** 1861-1937 ... **TCLC 56**
  See also CA 178; DLB 66
**Andress, Lesley**
  See Sanders, Lawrence
**Andrewes, Lancelot** 1555-1626 ............. **LC 5**
  See also DLB 151, 172
**Andrews, Cicily Fairfield**
  See West, Rebecca
**Andrews, Elton V.**
  See Pohl, Frederik
**Andreyev, Leonid (Nikolaevich)** 1871-1919
  **TCLC 3**
  See also CA 104
**Andric, Ivo** 1892-1975 .......... **CLC 8; SSC 36**
  See also CA 81-84; 57-60; CANR 43, 60; DLB 147; MTCW 1
**Androvar**
  See Prado (Calvo), Pedro
**Angelique, Pierre**
  See Bataille, Georges
**Angell, Roger** 1920- ........................ **CLC 26**
  See also CA 57-60; CANR 13, 44, 70; DLB 171, 185
**Angelou, Maya** 1928- .... **CLC 12, 35, 64, 77; BLC 1; DA; DAB; DAC; DAM MST, MULT, POET, POP; WLCS**
  See also AAYA 7, 20; BW 2, 3; CA 65-68; CANR 19, 42, 65; CDALBS; CLR 53; DA3; DLB 38; MTCW 1, 2; SATA 49
**Anna Comnena** 1083-1153 ........... **CMLC 25**
**Annensky, Innokenty (Fyodorovich)**
  1856-1909 ............................... **TCLC 14**
  See also CA 110; 155
**Annunzio, Gabriele d'**
  See D'Annunzio, Gabriele
**Anodos**
  See Coleridge, Mary E(lizabeth)

**Anon, Charles Robert**
  See Pessoa, Fernando (Antonio Nogueira)
**Anouilh, Jean (Marie Lucien Pierre)**
  1910-1987 ....... **CLC 1, 3, 8, 13, 40, 50; DAM DRAM; DC 8**
  See also CA 17-20R; 123; CANR 32; MTCW 1, 2
**Anthony, Florence**
  See Ai
**Anthony, John**
  See Ciardi, John (Anthony)
**Anthony, Peter**
  See Shaffer, Anthony (Joshua); Shaffer, Peter (Levin)
**Anthony, Piers** 1934- .... **CLC 35; DAM POP**
  See also AAYA 11; CA 21-24R; CANR 28, 56, 73; DLB 8; MTCW 1, 2; SAAS 22; SATA 84
**Anthony, Susan B(rownell)**
  1916-1991 ........................ **TCLC 84**
  See also CA 89-92; 134
**Antoine, Marc**
  See Proust, (Valentin-Louis-George-Eugene-) Marcel
**Antoninus, Brother**
  See Everson, William (Oliver)
**Antonioni, Michelangelo** 1912- ......... **CLC 20**
  See also CA 73-76; CANR 45, 77
**Antschel, Paul** 1920-1970
  See Celan, Paul
  See also CA 85-88; CANR 33, 61; MTCW 1
**Anwar, Chairil** 1922-1949 ............. **TCLC 22**
  See also CA 121
**Anzaldua, Gloria** 1942-
  See also CA 175; DLB 122; HLCS 1
**Apess, William** 1798-1839(?) ........ **NCLC 73; DAM MULT**
  See also DLB 175; NNAL
**Apollinaire, Guillaume** 1880-1918 .. **TCLC 3, 8, 51; DAM POET; PC 7**
  See also Kostrowitzki, Wilhelm Apollinaris de CA 152; MTCW 1
**Appelfeld, Aharon** 1932- ............ **CLC 23, 47**
  See also CA 112; 133; CANR 86
**Apple, Max (Isaac)** 1941- .............. **CLC 9, 33**
  See also CA 81-84; CANR 19, 54; DLB 130
**Appleman, Philip (Dean)** 1926- ........ **CLC 51**
  See also CA 13-16R; CAAS 18; CANR 6, 29, 56
**Appleton, Lawrence**
  See Lovecraft, H(oward) P(hillips)
**Apteryx**
  See Eliot, T(homas) S(tearns)
**Apuleius, (Lucius Madaurensis)**
  125(?)-175(?) ............................ **CMLC 1**
  See also DLB 211
**Aquin, Hubert** 1929-1977 ................ **CLC 15**
  See also CA 105; DLB 53
**Aquinas, Thomas** 1224(?)-1274 ..... **CMLC 33**
  See also DLB 115
**Aragon, Louis** 1897-1982 .. **CLC 3, 22; DAM NOV, POET**
  See also CA 69-72; 108; CANR 28, 71; DLB 72; MTCW 1, 2
**Arany, Janos** 1817-1882 ................. **NCLC 34**
**Aranyos, Kakay**
  See Mikszath, Kalman
**Arbuthnot, John** 1667-1735 .................. **LC 1**
  See also DLB 101
**Archer, Herbert Winslow**
  See Mencken, H(enry) L(ouis)
**Archer, Jeffrey (Howard)** 1940- ...... **CLC 28; DAM POP**
  See also AAYA 16; BEST 89:3; CA 77-80; CANR 22, 52; DA3; INT CANR-22

**Archer, Jules** 1915- ........................... **CLC 12**
  See also CA 9-12R; CANR 6, 69; SAAS 5; SATA 4, 85
**Archer, Lee**
  See Ellison, Harlan (Jay)
**Arden, John** 1930- ....... **CLC 6, 13, 15; DAM DRAM**
  See also CA 13-16R; CAAS 4; CANR 31, 65, 67; DLB 13; MTCW 1
**Arenas, Reinaldo** 1943-1990 . **CLC 41; DAM MULT; HLC 1**
  See also CA 124; 128; 133; CANR 73; DLB 145; HW 1; MTCW 1
**Arendt, Hannah** 1906-1975 ........ **CLC 66, 98**
  See also CA 17-20R; 61-64; CANR 26, 60; MTCW 1, 2
**Aretino, Pietro** 1492-1556 ................... **LC 12**
**Arghezi, Tudor** 1880-1967 ................. **CLC 80**
  See also Theodorescu, Ion N. CA 167
**Arguedas, Jose Maria** 1911-1969 .... **CLC 10, 18; HLCS 1**
  See also CA 89-92; CANR 73; DLB 113; HW 1
**Argueta, Manlio** 1936- ...................... **CLC 31**
  See also CA 131; CANR 73; DLB 145; HW 1
**Arias, Ron(ald Francis)** 1941-
  See also CA 131; CANR 81; DAM MULT; DLB 82; HLC 1; HW 1, 2; MTCW 2
**Ariosto, Ludovico** 1474-1533 ................. **LC 6**
**Aristides**
  See Epstein, Joseph
**Aristophanes** 450B.C.-385B.C. ....... **CMLC 4; DA; DAB; DAC; DAM DRAM, MST; DC 2; WLCS**
  See also DA3; DLB 176
**Aristotle** 384B.C.-322B.C. .... **CMLC 31; DA; DAB; DAC; DAM MST; WLCS**
  See also DA3; DLB 176
**Arlt, Roberto (Godofredo Christophersen)**
  1900-1942 ....... **TCLC 29; DAM MULT; HLC 1**
  See also CA 123; 131; CANR 67; HW 1, 2
**Armah, Ayi Kwei** 1939- . **CLC 5, 33; BLC 1; DAM MULT, POET**
  See also BW 1; CA 61-64; CANR 21, 64; DLB 117; MTCW 1
**Armatrading, Joan** 1950- ................. **CLC 17**
  See also CA 114
**Arnette, Robert**
  See Silverberg, Robert
**Arnim, Achim von (Ludwig Joachim von Arnim)** 1781-1831 ..... **NCLC 5; SSC 29**
  See also DLB 90
**Arnim, Bettina von** 1785-1859 ....... **NCLC 38**
  See also DLB 90
**Arnold, Matthew** 1822-1888 ..... **NCLC 6, 29; DA; DAB; DAC; DAM MST, POET; PC 5; WLC**
  See also CDBLB 1832-1890; DLB 32, 57
**Arnold, Thomas** 1795-1842 ........... **NCLC 18**
  See also DLB 55
**Arnow, Harriette (Louisa) Simpson**
  1908-1986 ....................... **CLC 2, 7, 18**
  See also CA 9-12R; 118; CANR 14; DLB 6; MTCW 1, 2; SATA 42; SATA-Obit 47
**Arouet, Francois-Marie**
  See Voltaire
**Arp, Hans**
  See Arp, Jean
**Arp, Jean** 1887-1966 ......................... **CLC 5**
  See also CA 81-84; 25-28R; CANR 42, 77
**Arrabal**
  See Arrabal, Fernando
**Arrabal, Fernando** 1932- ... **CLC 2, 9, 18, 58**
  See also CA 9-12R; CANR 15

**Arreola, Juan Jose** 1918- ....... **SSC 38; DAM MULT; HLC 1**
See also CA 113; 131; CANR 81; DLB 113; HW 1, 2

**Arrick, Fran** ...................................... **CLC 30**
See also Gaberman, Judie Angell

**Artaud, Antonin (Marie Joseph)** 1896-1948 **TCLC 3, 36; DAM DRAM**
See also CA 104; 149; DA3; MTCW 1

**Arthur, Ruth M(abel)** 1905-1979 ..... **CLC 12**
See also CA 9-12R; 85-88; CANR 4; SATA 7, 26

**Artsybashev, Mikhail (Petrovich)** 1878-1927 **TCLC 31**
See also CA 170

**Arundel, Honor (Morfydd)**
1919-1973 ................................. **CLC 17**
See also CA 21-22; 41-44R; CAP 2; CLR 35; SATA 4; SATA-Obit 24

**Arzner, Dorothy** 1897-1979 .............. **CLC 98**

**Asch, Sholem** 1880-1957 ................... **TCLC 3**
See also CA 105

**Ash, Shalom**
See Asch, Sholem

**Ashbery, John (Lawrence)** 1927- .. **CLC 2, 3, 4, 6, 9, 13, 15, 25, 41, 77, 125; DAM POET; PC 26**
See also CA 5-8R; CANR 9, 37, 66; DA3; DLB 5, 165; DLBY 81; INT CANR-9; MTCW 1, 2

**Ashdown, Clifford**
See Freeman, R(ichard) Austin

**Ashe, Gordon**
See Creasey, John

**Ashton-Warner, Sylvia (Constance)**
1908-1984 ................................. **CLC 19**
See also CA 69-72; 112; CANR 29; MTCW 1, 2

**Asimov, Isaac** 1920-1992 ..... **CLC 1, 3, 9, 19, 26, 76, 92; DAM POP**
See also AAYA 13; BEST 90:2; CA 1-4R; 137; CANR 2, 19, 36, 60; CLR 12; DA3; DLB 8; DLBY 92; INT CANR-19; JRDA; MAICYA; MTCW 1, 2; SATA 1, 26, 74

**Assis, Joaquim Maria Machado de**
See Machado de Assis, Joaquim Maria

**Astley, Thea (Beatrice May)** 1925- .. **CLC 41**
See also CA 65-68; CANR 11, 43, 78

**Aston, James**
See White, T(erence) H(anbury)

**Asturias, Miguel Angel** 1899-1974 .... **CLC 3, 8, 13; DAM MULT, NOV; HLC 1**
See also CA 25-28; 49-52; CANR 32; CAP 2; DA3; DLB 113; HW 1; MTCW 1, 2

**Atares, Carlos Saura**
See Saura (Atares), Carlos

**Atheling, William**
See Pound, Ezra (Weston Loomis)

**Atheling, William, Jr.**
See Blish, James (Benjamin)

**Atherton, Gertrude (Franklin Horn)**
1857-1948 ................................. **TCLC 2**
See also CA 104; 155; DLB 9, 78, 186

**Atherton, Lucius**
See Masters, Edgar Lee

**Atkins, Jack**
See Harris, Mark

**Atkinson, Kate** ................................... **CLC 99**
See also CA 166

**Attaway, William (Alexander)** 1911-1986 **CLC 92; BLC 1; DAM MULT**
See also BW 2, 3; CA 143; CANR 82; DLB 76

**Atticus**
See Fleming, Ian (Lancaster); Wilson, (Thomas) Woodrow

**Atwood, Margaret (Eleanor)** 1939- ... **CLC 2, 3, 4, 8, 13, 15, 25, 44, 84; DA; DAB; DAC; DAM MST, NOV, POET; PC 8; SSC 2; WLC**
See also AAYA 12; BEST 89:2; CA 49-52; CANR 3, 24, 33, 59; DA3; DLB 53; INT CANR-24; MTCW 1, 2; SATA 50

**Aubigny, Pierre d'**
See Mencken, H(enry) L(ouis)

**Aubin, Penelope** 1685-1731(?) ............... **LC 9**
See also DLB 39

**Auchincloss, Louis (Stanton)** 1917- .. **CLC 4, 6, 9, 18, 45; DAM NOV; SSC 22**
See also CA 1-4R; CANR 6, 29, 55, 87; DLB 2; DLBY 80; INT CANR-29; MTCW 1

**Auden, W(ystan) H(ugh)** 1907-1973 . **CLC 1, 2, 3, 4, 6, 9, 11, 14, 43; DA; DAB; DAC; DAM DRAM, MST, POET; PC 1; WLC**
See also AAYA 18; CA 9-12R; 45-48; CANR 5, 61; CDBLB 1914-1945; DA3; DLB 10, 20; MTCW 1, 2

**Audiberti, Jacques** 1900-1965 ......... **CLC 38; DAM DRAM**
See also CA 25-28R

**Audubon, John James** 1785-1851 . **NCLC 47**

**Auel, Jean M(arie)** 1936- ......... **CLC 31, 107; DAM POP**
See also AAYA 7; BEST 90:4; CA 103; CANR 21, 64; DA3; INT CANR-21; SATA 91

**Auerbach, Erich** 1892-1957 ........... **TCLC 43**
See also CA 118; 155

**Augier, Emile** 1820-1889 ................ **NCLC 31**
See also DLB 192

**August, John**
See De Voto, Bernard (Augustine)

**Augustine** 354-430 ....... **CMLC 6; DA; DAB; DAC; DAM MST; WLCS**
See also DA3; DLB 115

**Aurelius**
See Bourne, Randolph S(illiman)

**Aurobindo, Sri**
See Ghose, Aurabinda

**Austen, Jane** 1775-1817 ...... **NCLC 1, 13, 19, 33, 51, 81; DA; DAB; DAC; DAM MST, NOV; WLC**
See also AAYA 19; CDBLB 1789-1832; DA3; DLB 116

**Auster, Paul** 1947- ............................ **CLC 47**
See also CA 69-72; CANR 23, 52, 75; DA3; MTCW 1

**Austin, Frank**
See Faust, Frederick (Schiller)

**Austin, Mary (Hunter)** 1868-1934 . **TCLC 25**
See also CA 109; 178; DLB 9, 78, 206

**Averroes** 1126-1198 ......................... **CMLC 7**
See also DLB 115

**Avicenna** 980-1037 ......................... **CMLC 16**
See also DLB 115

**Avison, Margaret** 1918- ........... **CLC 2, 4, 97; DAC; DAM POET**
See also CA 17-20R; DLB 53; MTCW 1

**Axton, David**
See Koontz, Dean R(ay)

**Ayckbourn, Alan** 1939- ...... **CLC 5, 8, 18, 33, 74; DAB; DAM DRAM**
See also CA 21-24R; CANR 31, 59; DLB 13; MTCW 1, 2

**Aydy, Catherine**
See Tennant, Emma (Christina)

**Ayme, Marcel (Andre)** 1902-1967 .... **CLC 11**
See also CA 89-92; CANR 67; CLR 25; DLB 72; SATA 91

**Ayrton, Michael** 1921-1975 ................ **CLC 7**
See also CA 5-8R; 61-64; CANR 9, 21

**Azorin** ................................................. **CLC 11**
See also Martinez Ruiz, Jose

**Azuela, Mariano** 1873-1952 . **TCLC 3; DAM MULT; HLC 1**
See also CA 104; 131; CANR 81; HW 1, 2; MTCW 1, 2

**Baastad, Babbis Friis**
See Friis-Baastad, Babbis Ellinor

**Bab**
See Gilbert, W(illiam) S(chwenck)

**Babbis, Eleanor**
See Friis-Baastad, Babbis Ellinor

**Babel, Isaac**
See Babel, Isaak (Emmanuilovich)

**Babel, Isaak (Emmanuilovich)** 1894-1941(?) **TCLC 2, 13; SSC 16**
See also CA 104; 155; MTCW 1

**Babits, Mihaly** 1883-1941 ............... **TCLC 14**
See also CA 114

**Babur** 1483-1530 ................................. **LC 18**

**Baca, Jimmy Santiago** 1952-
See also CA 131; CANR 81; DAM MULT; DLB 122; HLC 1; HW 1, 2

**Bacchelli, Riccardo** 1891-1985 .......... **CLC 19**
See also CA 29-32R; 117

**Bach, Richard (David)** 1936- .......... **CLC 14; DAM NOV, POP**
See also AITN 1; BEST 89:2; CA 9-12R; CANR 18; MTCW 1; SATA 13

**Bachman, Richard**
See King, Stephen (Edwin)

**Bachmann, Ingeborg** 1926-1973 ....... **CLC 69**
See also CA 93-96; 45-48; CANR 69; DLB 85

**Bacon, Francis** 1561-1626 .............. **LC 18, 32**
See also CDBLB Before 1660; DLB 151

**Bacon, Roger** 1214(?)-1292 ........... **CMLC 14**
See also DLB 115

**Bacovia, George** ................................ **TCLC 24**
See also Vasiliu, Gheorghe DLB 220

**Badanes, Jerome** 1937- ...................... **CLC 59**

**Bagehot, Walter** 1826-1877 ........... **NCLC 10**
See also DLB 55

**Bagnold, Enid** 1889-1981 ...... **CLC 25; DAM DRAM**
See also CA 5-8R; 103; CANR 5, 40; DLB 13, 160, 191; MAICYA; SATA 1, 25

**Bagritsky, Eduard** 1895-1934 ......... **TCLC 60**

**Bagrjana, Elisaveta**
See Belcheva, Elisaveta

**Bagryana, Elisaveta** 1893-1991 ......... **CLC 10**
See also Belcheva, Elisaveta CA 178; DLB 147

**Bailey, Paul** 1937- ............................ **CLC 45**
See also CA 21-24R; CANR 16, 62; DLB 14

**Baillie, Joanna** 1762-1851 ............... **NCLC 71**
See also DLB 93

**Bainbridge, Beryl (Margaret)** 1934- . **CLC 4, 5, 8, 10, 14, 18, 22, 62; DAM NOV**
See also CA 21-24R; CANR 24, 55, 75, 88; DLB 14; MTCW 1, 2

**Baker, Elliott** 1922- ............................ **CLC 8**
See also CA 45-48; CANR 2, 63

**Baker, Jean H.** ............................ **TCLC 3, 10**
See also Russell, George William

**Baker, Nicholson** 1957- .......... **CLC 61; DAM POP**
See also CA 135; CANR 63; DA3

**Baker, Ray Stannard** 1870-1946 .... **TCLC 47**
See also CA 118

**Baker, Russell (Wayne)** 1925- .......... **CLC 31**
See also BEST 89:4; CA 57-60; CANR 11, 41, 59; MTCW 1, 2

**Bakhtin, M.**
See Bakhtin, Mikhail Mikhailovich

**Bakhtin, M. M.**
See Bakhtin, Mikhail Mikhailovich

**Bakhtin, Mikhail**
See Bakhtin, Mikhail Mikhailovich

**Bakhtin, Mikhail Mikhailovich** 1895-1975
　**CLC 83**
　See also CA 128; 113
**Bakshi, Ralph** 1938(?)- ..................... **CLC 26**
　See also CA 112; 138
**Bakunin, Mikhail (Alexandrovich)**
　1814-1876 ......................... **NCLC 25, 58**
**Baldwin, James (Arthur)** 1924-1987 . **CLC 1,**
　**2, 3, 4, 5, 8, 13, 15, 17, 42, 50, 67, 90,**
　**127; BLC 1; DA; DAB; DAC; DAM**
　**MST, MULT, NOV, POP; DC 1; SSC**
　**10, 33; WLC**
　See also AAYA 4; BW 1; CA 1-4R; 124;
　CABS 1; CANR 3, 24; CDALB 1941-
　1968; DA3; DLB 2, 7, 33; DLBY 87;
　MTCW 1, 2; SATA 9; SATA-Obit 54
**Ballard, J(ames) G(raham)** 1930- . **CLC 3, 6,**
　**14, 36; DAM NOV, POP; SSC 1**
　See also AAYA 3; CA 5-8R; CANR 15, 39,
　65; DA3; DLB 14, 207; MTCW 1, 2;
　SATA 93
**Balmont, Konstantin (Dmitriyevich)**
　1867-1943 ................................ **TCLC 11**
　See also CA 109; 155
**Baltausis, Vincas**
　See Mikszath, Kalman
**Balzac, Honore de** 1799-1850 ... **NCLC 5, 35,**
　**53; DA; DAB; DAC; DAM MST, NOV;**
　**SSC 5; WLC**
　See also DA3; DLB 119
**Bambara, Toni Cade** 1939-1995 ...... **CLC 19,**
　**88; BLC 1; DA; DAC; DAM MST,**
　**MULT; SSC 35; WLCS**
　See also AAYA 5; BW 2, 3; CA 29-32R;
　150; CANR 24, 49, 81; CDALBS; DA3;
　DLB 38; MTCW 1, 2; SATA 112
**Bamdad, A.**
　See Shamlu, Ahmad
**Banat, D. R.**
　See Bradbury, Ray (Douglas)
**Bancroft, Laura**
　See Baum, L(yman) Frank
**Banim, John** 1798-1842 .................. **NCLC 13**
　See also DLB 116, 158, 159
**Banim, Michael** 1796-1874 ............. **NCLC 13**
　See also DLB 158, 159
**Banjo, The**
　See Paterson, A(ndrew) B(arton)
**Banks, Iain**
　See Banks, Iain M(enzies)
**Banks, Iain M(enzies)** 1954- ............. **CLC 34**
　See also CA 123; 128; CANR 61; DLB 194;
　INT 128
**Banks, Lynne Reid** ........................... **CLC 23**
　See also Reid Banks, Lynne AAYA 6
**Banks, Russell** 1940- .................... **CLC 37, 72**
　See also CA 65-68; CAAS 15; CANR 19,
　52, 73; DLB 130
**Banville, John** 1945- .................. **CLC 46, 118**
　See also CA 117; 128; DLB 14; INT 128
**Banville, Theodore (Faullain) de** 1832-1891
　**NCLC 9**
**Baraka, Amiri** 1934- . **CLC 1, 2, 3, 5, 10, 14,**
　**33, 115; BLC 1; DA; DAC; DAM MST,**
　**MULT, POET, POP; DC 6; PC 4;**
　**WLCS**
　See also Jones, LeRoi BW 2, 3; CA 21-24R;
　CABS 3; CANR 27, 38, 61; CDALB
　1941-1968; DA3; DLB 5, 7, 16, 38;
　DLBD 8; MTCW 1, 2
**Barbauld, Anna Laetitia**
　1743-1825 ................................ **NCLC 50**
　See also DLB 107, 109, 142, 158
**Barbellion, W. N. P.** ........................ **TCLC 24**
　See also Cummings, Bruce F(rederick)
**Barbera, Jack (Vincent)** 1945- ......... **CLC 44**
　See also CA 110; CANR 45
**Barbey d'Aurevilly, Jules Amedee** 1808-1889
　**NCLC 1; SSC 17**

See also DLB 119
**Barbour, John** c. 1316-1395 .......... **CMLC 33**
　See also DLB 146
**Barbusse, Henri** 1873-1935 .............. **TCLC 5**
　See also CA 105; 154; DLB 65
**Barclay, Bill**
　See Moorcock, Michael (John)
**Barclay, William Ewert**
　See Moorcock, Michael (John)
**Barea, Arturo** 1897-1957 ................ **TCLC 14**
　See also CA 111
**Barfoot, Joan** 1946- .......................... **CLC 18**
　See also CA 105
**Barham, Richard Harris**
　1788-1845 ................................ **NCLC 77**
　See also DLB 159
**Baring, Maurice** 1874-1945 .............. **TCLC 8**
　See also CA 105; 168; DLB 34
**Baring-Gould, Sabine** 1834-1924 ... **TCLC 88**
　See also DLB 156, 190
**Barker, Clive** 1952- ...... **CLC 52; DAM POP**
　See also AAYA 10; BEST 90:3; CA 121;
　129; CANR 71; DA3; INT 129; MTCW
　1, 2
**Barker, George Granville**
　1913-1991 ....... **CLC 8, 48; DAM POET**
　See also CA 9-12R; 135; CANR 7, 38; DLB
　20; MTCW 1
**Barker, Harley Granville**
　See Granville-Barker, Harley
　See also DLB 10
**Barker, Howard** 1946- ...................... **CLC 37**
　See also CA 102; DLB 13
**Barker, Jane** 1652-1732 ....................... **LC 42**
**Barker, Pat(ricia)** 1943- ............. **CLC 32, 94**
　See also CA 117; 122; CANR 50; INT 122
**Barlach, Ernst (Heinrich)**
　1870-1938 ................................ **TCLC 84**
　See also CA 178; DLB 56, 118
**Barlow, Joel** 1754-1812 .................. **NCLC 23**
　See also DLB 37
**Barnard, Mary (Ethel)** 1909- .......... **CLC 48**
　See also CA 21-22; CAP 2
**Barnes, Djuna** 1892-1982 .... **CLC 3, 4, 8, 11,**
　**29, 127; SSC 3**
　See also CA 9-12R; 107; CANR 16, 55;
　DLB 4, 9, 45; MTCW 1, 2
**Barnes, Julian (Patrick)** 1946- ........ **CLC 42;**
　**DAB**
　See also CA 102; CANR 19, 54; DLB 194;
　DLBY 93; MTCW 1
**Barnes, Peter** 1931- ...................... **CLC 5, 56**
　See also CA 65-68; CAAS 12; CANR 33,
　34, 64; DLB 13; MTCW 1
**Barnes, William** 1801-1886 ............ **NCLC 75**
　See also DLB 32
**Baroja (y Nessi), Pio** 1872-1956 ..... **TCLC 8;**
　**HLC 1**
　See also CA 104
**Baron, David**
　See Pinter, Harold
**Baron Corvo**
　See Rolfe, Frederick (William Serafino Aus-
　tin Lewis Mary)
**Barondess, Sue K(aufman)**
　1926-1977 ..................................... **CLC 8**
　See also Kaufman, Sue CA 1-4R; 69-72;
　CANR 1
**Baron de Teive**
　See Pessoa, Fernando (Antonio Nogueira)
**Baroness Von S.**
　See Zangwill, Israel
**Barres, (Auguste-) Maurice**
　1862-1923 ................................ **TCLC 47**
　See also CA 164; DLB 123
**Barreto, Afonso Henrique de Lima**
　See Lima Barreto, Afonso Henrique de

**Barrett, (Roger) Syd** 1946- ............... **CLC 35**
**Barrett, William (Christopher)** 1913-1992
　**CLC 27**
　See also CA 13-16R; 139; CANR 11, 67;
　INT CANR-11
**Barrie, J(ames) M(atthew)**
　1860-1937 .......... **TCLC 2; DAB; DAM**
　**DRAM**
　See also CA 104; 136; CANR 77; CDBLB
　1890-1914; CLR 16; DA3; DLB 10, 141,
　156; MAICYA; MTCW 1; SATA 100;
　YABC 1
**Barrington, Michael**
　See Moorcock, Michael (John)
**Barrol, Grady**
　See Bograd, Larry
**Barry, Mike**
　See Malzberg, Barry N(athaniel)
**Barry, Philip** 1896-1949 .................. **TCLC 11**
　See also CA 109; DLB 7
**Bart, Andre Schwarz**
　See Schwarz-Bart, Andre
**Barth, John (Simmons)** 1930- ... **CLC 1, 2, 3,**
　**5, 7, 9, 10, 14, 27, 51, 89; DAM NOV;**
　**SSC 10**
　See also AITN 1, 2; CA 1-4R; CABS 1;
　CANR 5, 23, 49, 64; DLB 2; MTCW 1
**Barthelme, Donald** 1931-1989 ... **CLC 1, 2, 3,**
　**5, 6, 8, 13, 23, 46, 59, 115; DAM NOV;**
　**SSC 2**
　See also CA 21-24R; 129; CANR 20, 58;
　DA3; DLB 2; DLBY 80, 89; MTCW 1, 2;
　SATA 7; SATA-Obit 62
**Barthelme, Frederick** 1943- ...... **CLC 36, 117**
　See also CA 114; 122; CANR 77; DLBY
　85; INT 122
**Barthes, Roland (Gerard)**
　1915-1980 ............................. **CLC 24, 83**
　See also CA 130; 97-100; CANR 66;
　MTCW 1, 2
**Barzun, Jacques (Martin)** 1907- ...... **CLC 51**
　See also CA 61-64; CANR 22
**Bashevis, Isaac**
　See Singer, Isaac Bashevis
**Bashkirtseff, Marie** 1859-1884 ....... **NCLC 27**
**Basho**
　See Matsuo Basho
**Basil of Caesaria** c. 330-379 ......... **CMLC 35**
**Bass, Kingsley B., Jr.**
　See Bullins, Ed
**Bass, Rick** 1958- ................................ **CLC 79**
　See also CA 126; CANR 53; DLB 212
**Bassani, Giorgio** 1916- ........................ **CLC 9**
　See also CA 65-68; CANR 33; DLB 128,
　177; MTCW 1
**Bastos, Augusto (Antonio) Roa**
　See Roa Bastos, Augusto (Antonio)
**Bataille, Georges** 1897-1962 ............. **CLC 29**
　See also CA 101; 89-92
**Bates, H(erbert) E(rnest)**
　1905-1974 . **CLC 46; DAB; DAM POP;**
　**SSC 10**
　See also CA 93-96; 45-48; CANR 34; DA3;
　DLB 162, 191; MTCW 1, 2
**Bauchart**
　See Camus, Albert
**Baudelaire, Charles** 1821-1867 . **NCLC 6, 29,**
　**55; DA; DAB; DAC; DAM MST,**
　**POET; PC 1; SSC 18; WLC**
　See also DA3
**Baudrillard, Jean** 1929- .................... **CLC 60**
**Baum, L(yman) Frank** 1856-1919 ... **TCLC 7**
　See also CA 108; 133; CLR 15; DLB 22;
　JRDA; MAICYA; MTCW 1, 2; SATA 18,
　100
**Baum, Louis F.**
　See Baum, L(yman) Frank

**Baumbach, Jonathan** 1933- .......... **CLC 6, 23**
See also CA 13-16R; CAAS 5; CANR 12, 66; DLBY 80; INT CANR-12; MTCW 1

**Bausch, Richard (Carl)** 1945- .......... **CLC 51**
See also CA 101; CAAS 14; CANR 43, 61, 87; DLB 130

**Baxter, Charles (Morley)** 1947- ....... **CLC 45, 78; DAM POP**
See also CA 57-60; CANR 40, 64; DLB 130; MTCW 2

**Baxter, George Owen**
See Faust, Frederick (Schiller)

**Baxter, James K(eir)** 1926-1972 ....... **CLC 14**
See also CA 77-80

**Baxter, John**
See Hunt, E(verette) Howard, (Jr.)

**Bayer, Sylvia**
See Glassco, John

**Baynton, Barbara** 1857-1929 ......... **TCLC 57**

**Beagle, Peter S(oyer)** 1939- ........ **CLC 7, 104**
See also CA 9-12R; CANR 4, 51, 73; DA3; DLBY 80; INT CANR-4; MTCW 1; SATA 60

**Bean, Normal**
See Burroughs, Edgar Rice

**Beard, Charles A(ustin)** 1874-1948 ............................ **TCLC 15**
See also CA 115; DLB 17; SATA 18

**Beardsley, Aubrey** 1872-1898 ........... **NCLC 6**

**Beattie, Ann** 1947- ..... **CLC 8, 13, 18, 40, 63; DAM NOV, POP; SSC 11**
See also BEST 90:2; CA 81-84; CANR 53, 73; DA3; DLBY 82; MTCW 1, 2

**Beattie, James** 1735-1803 ............... **NCLC 25**
See also DLB 109

**Beauchamp, Kathleen Mansfield** 1888-1923
See Mansfield, Katherine
See also CA 104; 134; DA; DAC; DAM MST; DA3; MTCW 2

**Beaumarchais, Pierre-Augustin Caron de**
1732-1799 ....................................... **DC 4**
See also DAM DRAM

**Beaumont, Francis** 1584(?)-1616 ....... **LC 33; DC 6**
See also CDBLB Before 1660; DLB 58, 121

**Beauvoir, Simone (Lucie Ernestine Marie Bertrand) de** 1908-1986 .... **CLC 1, 2, 4, 8, 14, 31, 44, 50, 71, 124; DA; DAB; DAC; DAM MST, NOV; SSC 35; WLC**
See also CA 9-12R; 118; CANR 28, 61; DA3; DLB 72; DLBY 86; MTCW 1, 2

**Becker, Carl (Lotus)** 1873-1945 ..... **TCLC 63**
See also CA 157; DLB 17

**Becker, Jurek** 1937-1997 ............... **CLC 7, 19**
See also CA 85-88; 157; CANR 60; DLB 75

**Becker, Walter** 1950- ......................... **CLC 26**

**Beckett, Samuel (Barclay)**
1906-1989 .. **CLC 1, 2, 3, 4, 6, 9, 10, 11, 14, 18, 29, 57, 59, 83; DA; DAB; DAC; DAM DRAM, MST, NOV; SSC 16; WLC**
See also CA 5-8R; 130; CANR 33, 61; CD-BLB 1945-1960; DA3; DLB 13, 15; DLBY 90; MTCW 1, 2

**Beckford, William** 1760-1844 ........ **NCLC 16**
See also DLB 39

**Beckman, Gunnel** 1910- ................... **CLC 26**
See also CA 33-36R; CANR 15; CLR 25; MAICYA; SAAS 9; SATA 6

**Becque, Henri** 1837-1899 ................. **NCLC 3**
See also DLB 192

**Becquer, Gustavo Adolfo** 1836-1870
See also DAM MULT; HLCS 1

**Beddoes, Thomas Lovell**
1803-1849 ................................ **NCLC 3**
See also DLB 96

**Bede** c. 673-735 .............................. **CMLC 20**
See also DLB 146

**Bedford, Donald F.**
See Fearing, Kenneth (Flexner)

**Beecher, Catharine Esther**
1800-1878 ............................... **NCLC 30**
See also DLB 1

**Beecher, John** 1904-1980 .................... **CLC 6**
See also AITN 1; CA 5-8R; 105; CANR 8

**Beer, Johann** 1655-1700 ........................ **LC 5**
See also DLB 168

**Beer, Patricia** 1924-1999 ................... **CLC 58**
See also CA 61-64; 183; CANR 13, 46; DLB 40

**Beerbohm, Max**
See Beerbohm, (Henry) Max(imilian)

**Beerbohm, (Henry) Max(imilian)** 1872-1956
**TCLC 1, 24**
See also CA 104; 154; CANR 79; DLB 34, 100

**Beer-Hofmann, Richard**
1866-1945 ................................ **TCLC 60**
See also CA 160; DLB 81

**Begiebing, Robert J(ohn)** 1946- ....... **CLC 70**
See also CA 122; CANR 40, 88

**Behan, Brendan** 1923-1964 ...... **CLC 1, 8, 11, 15, 79; DAM DRAM**
See also CA 73-76; CANR 33; CDBLB 1945-1960; DLB 13; MTCW 1, 2

**Behn, Aphra** 1640(?)-1689 ....... **LC 1, 30, 42; DA; DAB; DAC; DAM DRAM, MST, NOV, POET; DC 4; PC 13; WLC**
See also DA3; DLB 39, 80, 131

**Behrman, S(amuel) N(athaniel)** 1893-1973
**CLC 40**
See also CA 13-16; 45-48; CAP 1; DLB 7, 44

**Belasco, David** 1853-1931 ................. **TCLC 3**
See also CA 104; 168; DLB 7

**Belcheva, Elisaveta** 1893- .................. **CLC 10**
See also Bagryana, Elisaveta

**Beldone, Phil "Cheech"**
See Ellison, Harlan (Jay)

**Beleno**
See Azuela, Mariano

**Belinski, Vissarion Grigoryevich** 1811-1848
**NCLC 5**
See also DLB 198

**Belitt, Ben** 1911- ............................... **CLC 22**
See also CA 13-16R; CAAS 4; CANR 7, 77; DLB 5

**Bell, Gertrude (Margaret Lowthian)**
1868-1926 ............................... **TCLC 67**
See also CA 167; DLB 174

**Bell, J. Freeman**
See Zangwill, Israel

**Bell, James Madison** 1826-1902 ... **TCLC 43; BLC 1; DAM MULT**
See also BW 1; CA 122; 124; DLB 50

**Bell, Madison Smartt** 1957- ...... **CLC 41, 102**
See also CA 111; 183; CAAE 183; CANR 28, 54, 73; MTCW 1

**Bell, Marvin (Hartley)** 1937- ....... **CLC 8, 31; DAM POET**
See also CA 21-24R; CAAS 14; CANR 59; DLB 5; MTCW 1

**Bell, W. L. D.**
See Mencken, H(enry) L(ouis)

**Bellamy, Atwood C.**
See Mencken, H(enry) L(ouis)

**Bellamy, Edward** 1850-1898 ........... **NCLC 4**
See also DLB 12

**Belli, Gioconda** 1949-
See also CA 152; HLCS 1

**Bellin, Edward J.**
See Kuttner, Henry

**Belloc, (Joseph) Hilaire (Pierre Sebastien Rene Swanton)** 1870- ........ **TCLC 7, 18; DAM POET; PC 24**
See also CA 106; 152; DLB 19, 100, 141, 174; MTCW 1; SATA 112; YABC 1

**Belloc, Joseph Peter Rene Hilaire**
See Belloc, (Joseph) Hilaire (Pierre Sebastien Rene Swanton)

**Belloc, Joseph Pierre Hilaire**
See Belloc, (Joseph) Hilaire (Pierre Sebastien Rene Swanton)

**Belloc, M. A.**
See Lowndes, Marie Adelaide (Belloc)

**Bellow, Saul** 1915- . **CLC 1, 2, 3, 6, 8, 10, 13, 15, 25, 33, 34, 63, 79; DA; DAB; DAC; DAM MST, NOV, POP; SSC 14; WLC**
See also AITN 2; BEST 89:3; CA 5-8R; CABS 1; CANR 29, 53; CDALB 1941-1968; DA3; DLB 2, 28; DLBD 3; DLBY 82; MTCW 1, 2

**Belser, Reimond Karel Maria de** 1929-
See Ruyslinck, Ward
See also CA 152

**Bely, Andrey** .......................... **TCLC 7; PC 11**
See also Bugayev, Boris Nikolayevich
MTCW 1

**Belyi, Andrei**
See Bugayev, Boris Nikolayevich

**Benary, Margot**
See Benary-Isbert, Margot

**Benary-Isbert, Margot** 1889-1979 .... **CLC 12**
See also CA 5-8R; 89-92; CANR 4, 72; CLR 12; MAICYA; SATA 2; SATA-Obit 21

**Benavente (y Martinez), Jacinto** 1866-1954
**TCLC 3; DAM DRAM, MULT; HLCS 1**
See also CA 106; 131; CANR 81; HW 1; MTCW 1, 2

**Benchley, Peter (Bradford)** 1940- . **CLC 4, 8; DAM NOV, POP**
See also AAYA 14; AITN 2; CA 17-20R; CANR 12, 35, 66; MTCW 1, 2; SATA 3, 89

**Benchley, Robert (Charles)**
1889-1945 ........................... **TCLC 1, 55**
See also CA 105; 153; DLB 11

**Benda, Julien** 1867-1956 ................ **TCLC 60**
See also CA 120; 154

**Benedict, Ruth (Fulton)**
1887-1948 ................................ **TCLC 60**
See also CA 158

**Benedict, Saint** c. 480-c. 547 ......... **CMLC 29**

**Benedikt, Michael** 1935- .............. **CLC 4, 14**
See also CA 13-16R; CANR 7; DLB 5

**Benet, Juan** 1927- ............................. **CLC 28**
See also CA 143

**Benet, Stephen Vincent** 1898-1943 . **TCLC 7; DAM POET; SSC 10**
See also CA 104; 152; DA3; DLB 4, 48, 102; DLBY 97; MTCW 1; YABC 1

**Benet, William Rose** 1886-1950 .... **TCLC 28; DAM POET**
See also CA 118; 152; DLB 45

**Benford, Gregory (Albert)** 1941- ..... **CLC 52**
See also CA 69-72, 175; CAAE 175; CAAS 27; CANR 12, 24, 49; DLBY 82

**Bengtsson, Frans (Gunnar)**
1894-1954 ................................ **TCLC 48**
See also CA 170

**Benjamin, David**
See Slavitt, David R(ytman)

**Benjamin, Lois**
See Gould, Lois

**Benjamin, Walter** 1892-1940 ......... **TCLC 39**
See also CA 164

**Benn, Gottfried** 1886-1956 .............. **TCLC 3**
See also CA 106; 153; DLB 56

**Bennett, Alan** 1934- ........ **CLC 45, 77; DAB; DAM MST**
See also CA 103; CANR 35, 55; MTCW 1, 2

**Bennett, (Enoch) Arnold**
1867-1931 ............................ **TCLC 5, 20**
See also CA 106; 155; CDBLB 1890-1914;
DLB 10, 34, 98, 135; MTCW 2
**Bennett, Elizabeth**
See Mitchell, Margaret (Munnerlyn)
**Bennett, George Harold** 1930-
See Bennett, Hal
See also BW 1; CA 97-100; CANR 87
**Bennett, Hal** ................................. **CLC 5**
See also Bennett, George Harold DLB 33
**Bennett, Jay** 1912- .......................... **CLC 35**
See also AAYA 10; CA 69-72; CANR 11,
42, 79; JRDA; SAAS 4; SATA 41, 87;
SATA-Brief 27
**Bennett, Louise (Simone)** 1919- ...... **CLC 28;
BLC 1; DAM MULT**
See also BW 2, 3; CA 151; DLB 117
**Benson, E(dward) F(rederic)** 1867-1940
**TCLC 27**
See also CA 114; 157; DLB 135, 153
**Benson, Jackson J.** 1930- ................. **CLC 34**
See also CA 25-28R; DLB 111
**Benson, Sally** 1900-1972 ................... **CLC 17**
See also CA 19-20; 37-40R; CAP 1; SATA
1, 35; SATA-Obit 27
**Benson, Stella** 1892-1933 ................ **TCLC 17**
See also CA 117; 155; DLB 36, 162
**Bentham, Jeremy** 1748-1832 .......... **NCLC 38**
See also DLB 107, 158
**Bentley, E(dmund) C(lerihew)** 1875-1956
**TCLC 12**
See also CA 108; DLB 70
**Bentley, Eric (Russell)** 1916- ........... **CLC 24**
See also CA 5-8R; CANR 6, 67; INT
CANR-6
**Beranger, Pierre Jean de**
1780-1857 ................................ **NCLC 34**
**Berdyaev, Nicolas**
See Berdyaev, Nikolai (Aleksandrovich)
**Berdyaev, Nikolai (Aleksandrovich)**
1874-1948 ................................ **TCLC 67**
See also CA 120; 157
**Berdyayev, Nikolai (Aleksandrovich)**
See Berdyaev, Nikolai (Aleksandrovich)
**Berendt, John (Lawrence)** 1939- ...... **CLC 86**
See also CA 146; CANR 75; DA3; MTCW
1
**Beresford, J(ohn) D(avys)**
1873-1947 ................................ **TCLC 81**
See also CA 112; 155; DLB 162, 178, 197
**Bergelson, David** 1884-1952 .......... **TCLC 81**
**Berger, Colonel**
See Malraux, (Georges-)Andre
**Berger, John (Peter)** 1926- ........... **CLC 2, 19**
See also CA 81-84; CANR 51, 78; DLB 14,
207
**Berger, Melvin H.** 1927- .................... **CLC 12**
See also CA 5-8R; CANR 4; CLR 32;
SAAS 2; SATA 5, 88
**Berger, Thomas (Louis)** 1924- .. **CLC 3, 5, 8,
11, 18, 38; DAM NOV**
See also CA 1-4R; CANR 5, 28, 51; DLB
2; DLBY 80; INT CANR-28; MTCW 1, 2
**Bergman, (Ernst) Ingmar** 1918- ...... **CLC 16,
72**
See also CA 81-84; CANR 33, 70; MTCW
2
**Bergson, Henri(-Louis)** 1859-1941 . **TCLC 32**
See also CA 164
**Bergstein, Eleanor** 1938- .................... **CLC 4**
See also CA 53-56; CANR 5
**Berkoff, Steven** 1937- ........................ **CLC 56**
See also CA 104; CANR 72
**Bermant, Chaim (Icyk)** 1929- .......... **CLC 40**
See also CA 57-60; CANR 6, 31, 57
**Bern, Victoria**
See Fisher, M(ary) F(rances) K(ennedy)

**Bernanos, (Paul Louis) Georges** 1888-1948
**TCLC 3**
See also CA 104; 130; DLB 72
**Bernard, April** 1956- ......................... **CLC 59**
See also CA 131
**Berne, Victoria**
See Fisher, M(ary) F(rances) K(ennedy)
**Bernhard, Thomas** 1931-1989 ..... **CLC 3, 32,
61**
See also CA 85-88; 127; CANR 32, 57;
DLB 85, 124; MTCW 1
**Bernhardt, Sarah (Henriette Rosine)**
1844-1923 ................................ **TCLC 75**
See also CA 157
**Berriault, Gina** 1926- . **CLC 54, 109; SSC 30**
See also CA 116; 129; CANR 66; DLB 130
**Berrigan, Daniel** 1921- ........................ **CLC 4**
See also CA 33-36R; CAAS 1; CANR 11,
43, 78; DLB 5
**Berrigan, Edmund Joseph Michael, Jr.**
1934-1983
See Berrigan, Ted
See also CA 61-64; 110; CANR 14
**Berrigan, Ted** .................................... **CLC 37**
See also Berrigan, Edmund Joseph Michael,
Jr. DLB 5, 169
**Berry, Charles Edward Anderson** 1931-
See Berry, Chuck
See also CA 115
**Berry, Chuck** ................................... **CLC 17**
See also Berry, Charles Edward Anderson
**Berry, Jonas**
See Ashbery, John (Lawrence)
**Berry, Wendell (Erdman)** 1934- ... **CLC 4, 6,
8, 27, 46; DAM POET; PC 28**
See also AITN 1; CA 73-76; CANR 50, 73;
DLB 5, 6; MTCW 1
**Berryman, John** 1914-1972 ... **CLC 1, 2, 3, 4,
6, 8, 10, 13, 25, 62; DAM POET**
See also CA 13-16; 33-36R; CABS 2;
CANR 35; CAP 1; CDALB 1941-1968;
DLB 48; MTCW 1, 2
**Bertolucci, Bernardo** 1940- ............... **CLC 16**
See also CA 106
**Berton, Pierre (Francis Demarigny)** 1920-
**CLC 104**
See also CA 1-4R; CANR 2, 56; DLB 68;
SATA 99
**Bertrand, Aloysius** 1807-1841 ........ **NCLC 31**
**Bertran de Born** c. 1140-1215 ........ **CMLC 5**
**Besant, Annie (Wood)** 1847-1933 ..... **TCLC 9**
See also CA 105
**Bessie, Alvah** 1904-1985 ................... **CLC 23**
See also CA 5-8R; 116; CANR 2, 80; DLB
26
**Bethlen, T. D.**
See Silverberg, Robert
**Beti, Mongo** . **CLC 27; BLC 1; DAM MULT**
See also Biyidi, Alexandre CANR 79
**Betjeman, John** 1906-1984 ...... **CLC 2, 6, 10,
34, 43; DAB; DAM MST, POET**
See also CA 9-12R; 112; CANR 33, 56;
CDBLB 1945-1960; DA3; DLB 20;
DLBY 84; MTCW 1, 2
**Bettelheim, Bruno** 1903-1990 .......... **CLC 79**
See also CA 81-84; 131; CANR 23, 61;
DA3; MTCW 1, 2
**Betti, Ugo** 1892-1953 ......................... **TCLC 5**
See also CA 104; 155
**Betts, Doris (Waugh)** 1932- ...... **CLC 3, 6, 28**
See also CA 13-16R; CANR 9, 66, 77;
DLBY 82; INT CANR-9
**Bevan, Alistair**
See Roberts, Keith (John Kingston)
**Bey, Pilaff**
See Douglas, (George) Norman
**Bialik, Chaim Nachman**
1873-1934 ................................ **TCLC 25**
See also CA 170

**Bickerstaff, Isaac**
See Swift, Jonathan
**Bidart, Frank** 1939- ......................... **CLC 33**
See also CA 140
**Bienek, Horst** 1930- ....................... **CLC 7, 11**
See also CA 73-76; DLB 75
**Bierce, Ambrose (Gwinett)** 1842-1914(?)
**TCLC 1, 7, 44; DA; DAC; DAM MST;
SSC 9; WLC**
See also CA 104; 139; CANR 78; CDALB
1865-1917; DA3; DLB 11, 12, 23, 71, 74,
186
**Biggers, Earl Derr** 1884-1933 ........ **TCLC 65**
See also CA 108; 153
**Billings, Josh**
See Shaw, Henry Wheeler
**Billington, (Lady) Rachel (Mary)**
1942- ........................................... **CLC 43**
See also AITN 2; CA 33-36R; CANR 44
**Binyon, T(imothy) J(ohn)** 1936- ....... **CLC 34**
See also CA 111; CANR 28
**Bioy Casares, Adolfo** 1914-1999 ... **CLC 4, 8,
13, 88; DAM MULT; HLC 1; SSC 17**
See also CA 29-32R; 177; CANR 19, 43,
66; DLB 113; HW 1, 2; MTCW 1, 2
**Bird, Cordwainer**
See Ellison, Harlan (Jay)
**Bird, Robert Montgomery**
1806-1854 .................................. **NCLC 1**
See also DLB 202
**Birkerts, Sven** 1951- ....................... **CLC 116**
See also CA 128; 133; 176; CAAE 176;
CAAS 29; INT 133
**Birney, (Alfred) Earle** 1904-1995 .. **CLC 1, 4,
6, 11; DAC; DAM MST, POET**
See also CA 1-4R; CANR 5, 20; DLB 88;
MTCW 1
**Biruni, al** 973-1048(?) .................... **CMLC 28**
**Bishop, Elizabeth** 1911-1979 ..... **CLC 1, 4, 9,
13, 15, 32; DA; DAC; DAM MST,
POET; PC 3**
See also CA 5-8R; 89-92; CABS 2; CANR
26, 61; CDALB 1968-1988; DA3; DLB
5, 169; MTCW 1, 2; SATA-Obit 24
**Bishop, John** 1935- ........................... **CLC 10**
See also CA 105
**Bissett, Bill** 1939- ................. **CLC 18; PC 14**
See also CA 69-72; CAAS 19; CANR 15;
DLB 53; MTCW 1
**Bissoondath, Neil (Devindra)**
1955- .............................. **CLC 120; DAC**
See also CA 136
**Bitov, Andrei (Georgievich)** 1937- ... **CLC 57**
See also CA 142
**Biyidi, Alexandre** 1932-
See Beti, Mongo
See also BW 1, 3; CA 114; 124; CANR 81;
DA3; MTCW 1, 2
**Bjarme, Brynjolf**
See Ibsen, Henrik (Johan)
**Bjoernson, Bjoernstjerne (Martinius)**
1832-1910 ............................... **TCLC 7, 37**
See also CA 104
**Black, Robert**
See Holdstock, Robert P.
**Blackburn, Paul** 1926-1971 .......... **CLC 9, 43**
See also CA 81-84; 33-36R; CANR 34;
DLB 16; DLBY 81
**Black Elk** 1863-1950 ........... **TCLC 33; DAM
MULT**
See also CA 144; MTCW 1; NNAL
**Black Hobart**
See Sanders, (James) Ed(ward)
**Blacklin, Malcolm**
See Chambers, Aidan
**Blackmore, R(ichard) D(oddridge)**
1825-1900 ................................ **TCLC 27**
See also CA 120; DLB 18

**Blackmur, R(ichard) P(almer) 1904-1965**
**CLC 2, 24**
See also CA 11-12; 25-28R; CANR 71;
CAP 1; DLB 63

**Black Tarantula**
See Acker, Kathy

**Blackwood, Algernon (Henry) 1869-1951**
**TCLC 5**
See also CA 105; 150; DLB 153, 156, 178

**Blackwood, Caroline 1931-1996 .... CLC 6, 9,**
**100**
See also CA 85-88; 151; CANR 32, 61, 65;
DLB 14, 207; MTCW 1

**Blade, Alexander**
See Hamilton, Edmond; Silverberg, Robert

**Blaga, Lucian 1895-1961 ................... CLC 75**
See also CA 157

**Blair, Eric (Arthur) 1903-1950**
See Orwell, George
See also CA 104; 132; DA; DAB; DAC;
DAM MST, NOV; DA3; MTCW 1, 2;
SATA 29

**Blair, Hugh 1718-1800 ................... NCLC 75**

**Blais, Marie-Claire 1939- .... CLC 2, 4, 6, 13,**
**22; DAC; DAM MST**
See also CA 21-24R; CAAS 4; CANR 38,
75; DLB 53; MTCW 1, 2

**Blaise, Clark 1940- ........................... CLC 29**
See also AITN 2; CA 53-56; CAAS 3;
CANR 5, 66; DLB 53

**Blake, Fairley**
See De Voto, Bernard (Augustine)

**Blake, Nicholas**
See Day Lewis, C(ecil)
See also DLB 77

**Blake, William 1757-1827 ....... NCLC 13, 37,**
**57; DA; DAB; DAC; DAM MST,**
**POET; PC 12; WLC**
See also CDBLB 1789-1832; CLR 52;
DA3; DLB 93, 163; MAICYA; SATA 30

**Blasco Ibanez, Vicente**
**1867-1928 .......... TCLC 12; DAM NOV**
See also CA 110; 131; CANR 81; DA3; HW
1, 2; MTCW 1

**Blatty, William Peter 1928- .... CLC 2; DAM**
**POP**
See also CA 5-8R; CANR 9

**Bleeck, Oliver**
See Thomas, Ross (Elmore)

**Blessing, Lee 1949- ........................... CLC 54**

**Blish, James (Benjamin) 1921-1975 . CLC 14**
See also CA 1-4R; 57-60; CANR 3; DLB
8; MTCW 1; SATA 66

**Bliss, Reginald**
See Wells, H(erbert) G(eorge)

**Blixen, Karen (Christentze Dinesen)**
**1885-1962**
See Dinesen, Isak
See also CA 25-28; CANR 22, 50; CAP 2;
DA3; MTCW 1, 2; SATA 44

**Bloch, Robert (Albert) 1917-1994 .... CLC 33**
See also AAYA 29; CA 5-8R, 179; 146;
CAAE 179; CAAS 20; CANR 5, 78;
DA3; DLB 44; INT CANR-5; MTCW 1;
SATA 12; SATA-Obit 82

**Blok, Alexander (Alexandrovich) 1880-1921**
**TCLC 5; PC 21**
See also CA 104; 183

**Blom, Jan**
See Breytenbach, Breyten

**Bloom, Harold 1930- ................. CLC 24, 103**
See also CA 13-16R; CANR 39, 75; DLB
67; MTCW 1

**Bloomfield, Aurelius**
See Bourne, Randolph S(illiman)

**Blount, Roy (Alton), Jr. 1941- .......... CLC 38**
See also CA 53-56; CANR 10, 28, 61; INT
CANR-28; MTCW 1, 2

**Bloy, Leon 1846-1917 .................... TCLC 22**
See also CA 121; 183; DLB 123

**Blume, Judy (Sussman) 1938- .. CLC 12, 30;**
**DAM NOV, POP**
See also AAYA 3, 26; CA 29-32R; CANR
13, 37, 66; CLR 2, 15; DA3; DLB 52;
JRDA; MAICYA; MTCW 1, 2; SATA 2,
31, 79

**Blunden, Edmund (Charles)**
**1896-1974 ............................. CLC 2, 56**
See also CA 17-18; 45-48; CANR 54; CAP
2; DLB 20, 100, 155; MTCW 1

**Bly, Robert (Elwood) 1926- ....... CLC 1, 2, 5,**
**10, 15, 38, 128; DAM POET**
See also CA 5-8R; CANR 41, 73; DA3;
DLB 5; MTCW 1, 2

**Boas, Franz 1858-1942 ................... TCLC 56**
See also CA 115; 181

**Bobette**
See Simenon, Georges (Jacques Christian)

**Boccaccio, Giovanni 1313-1375 ... CMLC 13;**
**SSC 10**

**Bochco, Steven 1943- ....................... CLC 35**
See also AAYA 11; CA 124; 138

**Bodel, Jean 1167(?)-1210 .............. CMLC 28**

**Bodenheim, Maxwell 1892-1954 .... TCLC 44**
See also CA 110; DLB 9, 45

**Bodker, Cecil 1927- ......................... CLC 21**
See also CA 73-76; CANR 13, 44; CLR 23;
MAICYA; SATA 14

**Boell, Heinrich (Theodor)**
**1917-1985 ..... CLC 2, 3, 6, 9, 11, 15, 27,**
**32, 72; DA; DAB; DAC; DAM MST,**
**NOV; SSC 23; WLC**
See also CA 21-24R; 116; CANR 24; DA3;
DLB 69; DLBY 85; MTCW 1, 2

**Boerne, Alfred**
See Doeblin, Alfred

**Boethius 480(?)-524(?) .................... CMLC 15**
See also DLB 115

**Boff, Leonardo (Genezio Darci) 1938-**
See also CA 150; DAM MULT; HLC 1;
HW 2

**Bogan, Louise 1897-1970 ....... CLC 4, 39, 46,**
**93; DAM POET; PC 12**
See also CA 73-76; 25-28R; CANR 33, 82;
DLB 45, 169; MTCW 1, 2

**Bogarde, Dirk 1921-1999**
See Van Den Bogarde, Derek Jules Gaspard
Ulric Niven

**Bogosian, Eric 1953- ........................ CLC 45**
See also CA 138

**Bograd, Larry 1953- ........................ CLC 35**
See also CA 93-96; CANR 57; SAAS 21;
SATA 33, 89

**Boiardo, Matteo Maria 1441-1494 ........ LC 6**

**Boileau-Despreaux, Nicolas 1636-1711 . LC 3**

**Bojer, Johan 1872-1959 ................... TCLC 64**

**Boland, Eavan (Aisling) 1944- .. CLC 40, 67,**
**113; DAM POET**
See also CA 143; CANR 61; DLB 40;
MTCW 2

**Boll, Heinrich**
See Boell, Heinrich (Theodor)

**Bolt, Lee**
See Faust, Frederick (Schiller)

**Bolt, Robert (Oxton) 1924-1995 ...... CLC 14;**
**DAM DRAM**
See also CA 17-20R; 147; CANR 35, 67;
DLB 13; MTCW 1

**Bombal, Maria Luisa 1910-1980 ...... SSC 37;**
**HLCS 1**
See also CA 127; CANR 72; HW 1

**Bombet, Louis-Alexandre-Cesar**
See Stendhal

**Bomkauf**
See Kaufman, Bob (Garnell)

**Bonaventura ................................... NCLC 35**
See also DLB 90

**Bond, Edward 1934- ......... CLC 4, 6, 13, 23;**
**DAM DRAM**
See also CA 25-28R; CANR 38, 67; DLB
13; MTCW 1

**Bonham, Frank 1914-1989 ............... CLC 12**
See also AAYA 1; CA 9-12R; CANR 4, 36;
JRDA; MAICYA; SAAS 3; SATA 1, 49;
SATA-Obit 62

**Bonnefoy, Yves 1923- .. CLC 9, 15, 58; DAM**
**MST, POET**
See also CA 85-88; CANR 33, 75; MTCW
1, 2

**Bontemps, Arna(ud Wendell)**
**1902-1973 ..... CLC 1, 18; BLC 1; DAM**
**MULT, NOV, POET**
See also BW 1; CA 1-4R; 41-44R; CANR
4, 35; CLR 6; DA3; DLB 48, 51; JRDA;
MAICYA; MTCW 1, 2; SATA 2, 44;
SATA-Obit 24

**Booth, Martin 1944- ........................ CLC 13**
See also CA 93-96; CAAS 2

**Booth, Philip 1925- .......................... CLC 23**
See also CA 5-8R; CANR 5, 88; DLBY 82

**Booth, Wayne C(layson) 1921- ......... CLC 24**
See also CA 1-4R; CAAS 5; CANR 3, 43;
DLB 67

**Borchert, Wolfgang 1921-1947 ........ TCLC 5**
See also CA 104; DLB 69, 124

**Borel, Petrus 1809-1859 ................. NCLC 41**

**Borges, Jorge Luis 1899-1986 ... CLC 1, 2, 3,**
**4, 6, 8, 9, 10, 13, 19, 44, 48, 83; DA;**
**DAB; DAC; DAM MST, MULT; HLC**
**1; PC 22; SSC 4; WLC**
See also AAYA 26; CA 21-24R; CANR 19,
33, 75; DA3; DLB 113; DLBY 86; HW 1,
2; MTCW 1, 2

**Borowski, Tadeusz 1922-1951 .......... TCLC 9**
See also CA 106; 154

**Borrow, George (Henry)**
**1803-1881 ................................ NCLC 9**
See also DLB 21, 55, 166

**Bosch (Gavino), Juan 1909-**
See also CA 151; DAM MST, MULT; DLB
145; HLCS 1; HW 1, 2

**Bosman, Herman Charles**
**1905-1951 ................................ TCLC 49**
See also Malan, Herman CA 160

**Bosschere, Jean de 1878(?)-1953 ... TCLC 19**
See also CA 115

**Boswell, James 1740-1795 ...... LC 4, 50; DA;**
**DAB; DAC; DAM MST; WLC**
See also CDBLB 1660-1789; DLB 104, 142

**Bottoms, David 1949- ...................... CLC 53**
See also CA 105; CANR 22; DLB 120;
DLBY 83

**Boucicault, Dion 1820-1890 ........... NCLC 41**

**Boucolon, Maryse 1937(?)-**
See Conde, Maryse
See also BW 3; CA 110; CANR 30, 53, 76

**Bourget, Paul (Charles Joseph) 1852-1935**
**TCLC 12**
See also CA 107; DLB 123

**Bourjaily, Vance (Nye) 1922- ........ CLC 8, 62**
See also CA 1-4R; CAAS 1; CANR 2, 72;
DLB 2, 143

**Bourne, Randolph S(illiman) 1886-1918**
**TCLC 16**
See also CA 117; 155; DLB 63

**Bova, Ben(jamin William) 1932- ...... CLC 45**
See also AAYA 16; CA 5-8R; CAAS 18;
CANR 11, 56; CLR 3; DLBY 81; INT
CANR-11; MAICYA; MTCW 1; SATA 6,
68

**Bowen, Elizabeth (Dorothea Cole) 1899-1973**
**CLC 1, 3, 6, 11, 15, 22, 118; DAM NOV;**
**SSC 3, 28**

See also CA 17-18; 41-44R; CANR 35; CAP 2; CDBLB 1945-1960; DA3; DLB 15, 162; MTCW 1, 2

**Bowering, George** 1935- ............. **CLC 15, 47**
See also CA 21-24R; CAAS 16; CANR 10; DLB 53

**Bowering, Marilyn R(uthe)** 1949- .... **CLC 32**
See also CA 101; CANR 49

**Bowers, Edgar** 1924- ........................... **CLC 9**
See also CA 5-8R; CANR 24; DLB 5

**Bowie, David** ............................... **CLC 17**
See also Jones, David Robert

**Bowles, Jane (Sydney)** 1917-1973 ..... **CLC 3, 68**
See also CA 19-20; 41-44R; CAP 2

**Bowles, Paul (Frederick)** 1910- ..... **CLC 1, 2, 19, 53; SSC 3**
See also CA 1-4R; CAAS 1; CANR 1, 19, 50, 75; DA3; DLB 5, 6; MTCW 1, 2

**Box, Edgar**
See Vidal, Gore

**Boyd, Nancy**
See Millay, Edna St. Vincent

**Boyd, William** 1952- ............. **CLC 28, 53, 70**
See also CA 114; 120; CANR 51, 71

**Boyle, Kay** 1902-1992 ........ **CLC 1, 5, 19, 58, 121; SSC 5**
See also CA 13-16R; 140; CAAS 1; CANR 29, 61; DLB 4, 9, 48, 86; DLBY 93; MTCW 1, 2

**Boyle, Mark**
See Kienzle, William X(avier)

**Boyle, Patrick** 1905-1982 ................... **CLC 19**
See also CA 127

**Boyle, T. C.** 1948-
See Boyle, T(homas) Coraghessan

**Boyle, T(homas) Coraghessan** 1948- ........ **CLC 36, 55, 90; DAM POP; SSC 16**
See also BEST 90:4; CA 120; CANR 44, 76; DA3; DLBY 86; MTCW 2

**Boz**
See Dickens, Charles (John Huffam)

**Brackenridge, Hugh Henry** 1748-1816 ......................... **NCLC 7**
See also DLB 11, 37

**Bradbury, Edward P.**
See Moorcock, Michael (John)
See also MTCW 2

**Bradbury, Malcolm (Stanley)** 1932- ............... **CLC 32, 61; DAM NOV**
See also CA 1-4R; CANR 1, 33; DA3; DLB 14, 207; MTCW 1, 2

**Bradbury, Ray (Douglas)** 1920- .... **CLC 1, 3, 10, 15, 42, 98; DA; DAB; DAC; DAM MST, NOV, POP; SSC 29; WLC**
See also AAYA 15; AITN 1, 2; CA 1-4R; CANR 2, 30, 75; CDALB 1968-1988; DA3; DLB 2, 8; MTCW 1, 2; SATA 11, 64

**Bradford, Gamaliel** 1863-1932 ....... **TCLC 36**
See also CA 160; DLB 17

**Bradley, David (Henry), Jr.** 1950- ... **CLC 23, 118; BLC 1; DAM MULT**
See also BW 1, 3; CA 104; CANR 26, 81; DLB 33

**Bradley, John Ed(mund, Jr.)** 1958- . **CLC 55**
See also CA 139

**Bradley, Marion Zimmer** 1930- ...... **CLC 30; DAM POP**
See also AAYA 9; CA 57-60; CAAS 10; CANR 7, 31, 51, 75; DA3; DLB 8; MTCW 1, 2; SATA 90

**Bradstreet, Anne** 1612(?)-1672 ...... **LC 4, 30; DA; DAC; DAM MST, POET; PC 10**
See also CDALB 1640-1865; DA3; DLB 24

**Brady, Joan** 1939- ......................... **CLC 86**
See also CA 141

**Bragg, Melvyn** 1939- ......................... **CLC 10**
See also BEST 89:3; CA 57-60; CANR 10, 48; DLB 14

**Brahe, Tycho** 1546-1601 ....................... **LC 45**

**Braine, John (Gerard)** 1922-1986 . **CLC 1, 3, 41**
See also CA 1-4R; 120; CANR 1, 33; CD-BLB 1945-1960; DLB 15; DLBY 86; MTCW 1

**Bramah, Ernest** 1868-1942 ............. **TCLC 72**
See also CA 156; DLB 70

**Brammer, William** 1930(?)-1978 ...... **CLC 31**
See also CA 77-80

**Brancati, Vitaliano** 1907-1954 ........ **TCLC 12**
See also CA 109

**Brancato, Robin F(idler)** 1936- ........ **CLC 35**
See also AAYA 9; CA 69-72; CANR 11, 45; CLR 32; JRDA; SAAS 9; SATA 97

**Brand, Max**
See Faust, Frederick (Schiller)

**Brand, Millen** 1906-1980 .................... **CLC 7**
See also CA 21-24R; 97-100; CANR 72

**Branden, Barbara** ........................... **CLC 44**
See also CA 148

**Brandes, Georg (Morris Cohen)** 1842-1927 **TCLC 10**
See also CA 105

**Brandys, Kazimierz** 1916- ................. **CLC 62**

**Branley, Franklyn M(ansfield)** 1915- ....................................... **CLC 21**
See also CA 33-36R; CANR 14, 39; CLR 13; MAICYA; SAAS 16; SATA 4, 68

**Brathwaite, Edward (Kamau)** 1930- ...... **CLC 11; BLCS; DAM POET**
See also BW 2, 3; CA 25-28R; CANR 11, 26, 47; DLB 125

**Brautigan, Richard (Gary)** 1935-1984 .... **CLC 1, 3, 5, 9, 12, 34, 42; DAM NOV**
See also CA 53-56; 113; CANR 34; DA3; DLB 2, 5, 206; DLBY 80, 84; MTCW 1; SATA 56

**Brave Bird, Mary** 1953-
See Crow Dog, Mary (Ellen)
See also NNAL

**Braverman, Kate** 1950- .................... **CLC 67**
See also CA 89-92

**Brecht, (Eugen) Bertolt (Friedrich)** 1898-1956 ........ **TCLC 1, 6, 13, 35; DA; DAB; DAC; DAM DRAM, MST; DC 3; WLC**
See also CA 104; 133; CANR 62; DA3; DLB 56, 124; MTCW 1, 2

**Brecht, Eugen Berthold Friedrich**
See Brecht, (Eugen) Bertolt (Friedrich)

**Bremer, Fredrika** 1801-1865 .......... **NCLC 11**

**Brennan, Christopher John** 1870-1932 ........................... **TCLC 17**
See also CA 117

**Brennan, Maeve** 1917-1993 ................. **CLC 5**
See also CA 81-84; CANR 72

**Brent, Linda**
See Jacobs, Harriet A(nn)

**Brentano, Clemens (Maria)** 1778-1842 ................................. **NCLC 1**
See also DLB 90

**Brent of Bin Bin**
See Franklin, (Stella Maria Sarah) Miles (Lampe)

**Brenton, Howard** 1942- .................... **CLC 31**
See also CA 69-72; CANR 33, 67; DLB 13; MTCW 1

**Breslin, James** 1930-1996
See Breslin, Jimmy
See also CA 73-76; CANR 31, 75; DAM NOV; MTCW 1, 2

**Breslin, Jimmy** ............................. **CLC 4, 43**
See also Breslin, James AITN 1; DLB 185; MTCW 2

**Bresson, Robert** 1901- ..................... **CLC 16**
See also CA 110; CANR 49

**Breton, Andre** 1896-1966 .. **CLC 2, 9, 15, 54; PC 15**
See also CA 19-20; 25-28R; CANR 40, 60; CAP 2; DLB 65; MTCW 1, 2

**Breytenbach, Breyten** 1939(?)- .. **CLC 23, 37, 126; DAM POET**
See also CA 113; 129; CANR 61

**Bridgers, Sue Ellen** 1942- ................ **CLC 26**
See also AAYA 8; CA 65-68; CANR 11, 36; CLR 18; DLB 52; JRDA; MAICYA; SAAS 1; SATA 22, 90; SATA-Essay 109

**Bridges, Robert (Seymour)** 1844-1930 ... **TCLC 1; DAM POET; PC 28**
See also CA 104; 152; CDBLB 1890-1914; DLB 19, 98

**Bridie, James** .............................. **TCLC 3**
See also Mavor, Osborne Henry DLB 10

**Brin, David** 1950- .......................... **CLC 34**
See also AAYA 21; CA 102; CANR 24, 70; INT CANR-24; SATA 65

**Brink, Andre (Philippus)** 1935- . **CLC 18, 36, 106**
See also CA 104; CANR 39, 62; INT 103; MTCW 1, 2

**Brinsmead, H(esba) F(ay)** 1922- ...... **CLC 21**
See also CA 21-24R; CANR 10; CLR 47; MAICYA; SAAS 5; SATA 18, 78

**Brittain, Vera (Mary)** 1893(?)-1970 . **CLC 23**
See also CA 13-16; 25-28R; CANR 58; CAP 1; DLB 191; MTCW 1, 2

**Broch, Hermann** 1886-1951 ........... **TCLC 20**
See also CA 117; DLB 85, 124

**Brock, Rose**
See Hansen, Joseph

**Brodkey, Harold (Roy)** 1930-1996 ... **CLC 56**
See also CA 111; 151; CANR 71; DLB 130

**Brodskii, Iosif**
See Brodsky, Joseph

**Brodsky, Iosif Alexandrovich** 1940-1996
See Brodsky, Joseph
See also AITN 1; CA 41-44R; 151; CANR 37; DAM POET; DA3; MTCW 1, 2

**Brodsky, Joseph** 1940-1996 ..... **CLC 4, 6, 13, 36, 100; PC 9**
See also Brodskii, Iosif; Brodsky, Iosif Alexandrovich MTCW 1

**Brodsky, Michael (Mark)** 1948- ....... **CLC 19**
See also CA 102; CANR 18, 41, 58

**Bromell, Henry** 1947- ....................... **CLC 5**
See also CA 53-56; CANR 9

**Bromfield, Louis (Brucker)** 1896-1956 ................ **TCLC 11**
See also CA 107; 155; DLB 4, 9, 86

**Broner, E(sther) M(asserman)** 1930- ....................................... **CLC 19**
See also CA 17-20R; CANR 8, 25, 72; DLB 28

**Bronk, William (M.)** 1918-1999 ........ **CLC 10**
See also CA 89-92; 177; CANR 23; DLB 165

**Bronstein, Lev Davidovich**
See Trotsky, Leon

**Bronte, Anne** 1820-1849 ............. **NCLC 4, 71**
See also DA3; DLB 21, 199

**Bronte, Charlotte** 1816-1855 ....... **NCLC 3, 8, 33, 58; DA; DAB; DAC; DAM MST, NOV; WLC**
See also AAYA 17; CDBLB 1832-1890; DA3; DLB 21, 159, 199

**Bronte, Emily (Jane)** 1818-1848 ... **NCLC 16, 35; DA; DAB; DAC; DAM MST, NOV, POET; PC 8; WLC**
See also AAYA 17; CDBLB 1832-1890; DA3; DLB 21, 32, 199

**Brooke, Frances** 1724-1789 ............ **LC 6, 48**
See also DLB 39, 99

**Brooke, Henry** 1703(?)-1783 ................. **LC 1**
See also DLB 39

**Brooke, Rupert (Chawner)**
1887-1915 ......... **TCLC 2, 7; DA; DAB;**
**DAC; DAM MST, POET; PC 24; WLC**
See also CA 104; 132; CANR 61; CDBLB
1914-1945; DLB 19; MTCW 1, 2

**Brooke-Haven, P.**
See Wodehouse, P(elham) G(renville)

**Brooke-Rose, Christine** 1926(?)- ...... **CLC 40**
See also CA 13-16R; CANR 58; DLB 14

**Brookner, Anita** 1928- ........ **CLC 32, 34, 51;**
**DAB; DAM POP**
See also CA 114; 120; CANR 37, 56, 87;
DA3; DLB 194; DLBY 87; MTCW 1, 2

**Brooks, Cleanth** 1906-1994 . **CLC 24, 86, 110**
See also CA 17-20R; 145; CANR 33, 35;
DLB 63; DLBY 94; INT CANR-35;
MTCW 1, 2

**Brooks, George**
See Baum, L(yman) Frank

**Brooks, Gwendolyn** 1917- ..... **CLC 1, 2, 4, 5,**
**15, 49, 125; BLC 1; DA; DAC; DAM**
**MST, MULT, POET; PC 7; WLC**
See also AAYA 20; AITN 1; BW 2, 3; CA
1-4R; CANR 1, 27, 52, 75; CDALB 1941-
1968; CLR 27; DA3; DLB 5, 76, 165;
MTCW 1, 2; SATA 6

**Brooks, Mel** ............................... **CLC 12**
See also Kaminsky, Melvin AAYA 13; DLB
26

**Brooks, Peter** 1938- ......................... **CLC 34**
See also CA 45-48; CANR 1

**Brooks, Van Wyck** 1886-1963 ........... **CLC 29**
See also CA 1-4R; CANR 6; DLB 45, 63,
103

**Brophy, Brigid (Antonia)**
1929-1995 ................. **CLC 6, 11, 29, 105**
See also CA 5-8R; 149; CAAS 4; CANR
25, 53; DA3; DLB 14; MTCW 1, 2

**Brosman, Catharine Savage** 1934- ..... **CLC 9**
See also CA 61-64; CANR 21, 46

**Brossard, Nicole** 1943- ..................... **CLC 115**
See also CA 122; CAAS 16; DLB 53

**Brother Antoninus**
See Everson, William (Oliver)

**The Brothers Quay**
See Quay, Stephen; Quay, Timothy

**Broughton, T(homas) Alan** 1936- ..... **CLC 19**
See also CA 45-48; CANR 2, 23, 48

**Broumas, Olga** 1949- ................. **CLC 10, 73**
See also CA 85-88; CANR 20, 69

**Brown, Alan** 1950- ........................... **CLC 99**
See also CA 156

**Brown, Charles Brockden**
1771-1810 ....................... **NCLC 22, 74**
See also CDALB 1640-1865; DLB 37, 59,
73

**Brown, Christy** 1932-1981 ............... **CLC 63**
See also CA 105; 104; CANR 72; DLB 14

**Brown, Claude** 1937- ........ **CLC 30; BLC 1;**
**DAM MULT**
See also AAYA 7; BW 1, 3; CA 73-76;
CANR 81

**Brown, Dee (Alexander)** 1908- . **CLC 18, 47;**
**DAM POP**
See also AAYA 30; CA 13-16R; CAAS 6;
CANR 11, 45, 60; DA3; DLBY 80;
MTCW 1, 2; SATA 5, 110

**Brown, George**
See Wertmueller, Lina

**Brown, George Douglas**
1869-1902 ............................... **TCLC 28**
See also CA 162

**Brown, George Mackay** 1921-1996 ... **CLC 5,**
**48, 100**
See also CA 21-24R; 151; CAAS 6; CANR
12, 37, 67; DLB 14, 27, 139; MTCW 1;
SATA 35

**Brown, (William) Larry** 1951- ......... **CLC 73**
See also CA 130; 134; INT 133

**Brown, Moses**
See Barrett, William (Christopher)

**Brown, Rita Mae** 1944- ....... **CLC 18, 43, 79;**
**DAM NOV, POP**
See also CA 45-48; CANR 2, 11, 35, 62;
DA3; INT CANR-11; MTCW 1, 2

**Brown, Roderick (Langmere) Haig-**
See Haig-Brown, Roderick (Langmere)

**Brown, Rosellen** 1939- ..................... **CLC 32**
See also CA 77-80; CAAS 10; CANR 14,
44

**Brown, Sterling Allen** 1901-1989 ...... **CLC 1,**
**23, 59; BLC 1; DAM MULT, POET**
See also BW 1, 3; CA 85-88; 127; CANR
26; DA3; DLB 48, 51, 63; MTCW 1, 2

**Brown, Will**
See Ainsworth, William Harrison

**Brown, William Wells** 1813-1884 ... **NCLC 2;**
**BLC 1; DAM MULT; DC 1**
See also DLB 3, 50

**Browne, (Clyde) Jackson** 1948(?)- ... **CLC 21**
See also CA 120

**Browning, Elizabeth Barrett** 1806-1861
**NCLC 1, 16, 61, 66; DA; DAB; DAC;**
**DAM MST, POET; PC 6; WLC**
See also CDBLB 1832-1890; DA3; DLB
32, 199

**Browning, Robert** 1812-1889 . **NCLC 19, 79;**
**DA; DAB; DAC; DAM MST, POET;**
**PC 2; WLCS**
See also CDBLB 1832-1890; DA3; DLB
32, 163; YABC 1

**Browning, Tod** 1882-1962 ................. **CLC 16**
See also CA 141; 117

**Brownson, Orestes Augustus** 1803-1876
**NCLC 50**
See also DLB 1, 59, 73

**Bruccoli, Matthew J(oseph)** 1931- ... **CLC 34**
See also CA 9-12R; CANR 7, 87; DLB 103

**Bruce, Lenny** ..................................... **CLC 21**
See also Schneider, Leonard Alfred

**Bruin, John**
See Brutus, Dennis

**Brulard, Henri**
See Stendhal

**Brulls, Christian**
See Simenon, Georges (Jacques Christian)

**Brunner, John (Kilian Houston)** 1934-1995
**CLC 8, 10; DAM POP**
See also CA 1-4R; 149; CAAS 8; CANR 2,
37; MTCW 1, 2

**Bruno, Giordano** 1548-1600 ................. **LC 27**

**Brutus, Dennis** 1924- ......... **CLC 43; BLC 1;**
**DAM MULT, POET; PC 24**
See also BW 2, 3; CA 49-52; CAAS 14;
CANR 2, 27, 42, 81; DLB 117

**Bryan, C(ourtlandt) D(ixon) B(arnes)** 1936-
**CLC 29**
See also CA 73-76; CANR 13, 68; DLB
185; INT CANR-13

**Bryan, Michael**
See Moore, Brian

**Bryan, William Jennings**
1860-1925 ................................ **TCLC 99**

**Bryant, William Cullen** 1794-1878 . **NCLC 6,**
**46; DA; DAB; DAC; DAM MST,**
**POET; PC 20**
See also CDALB 1640-1865; DLB 3, 43,
59, 189

**Bryusov, Valery Yakovlevich** 1873-1924
**TCLC 10**
See also CA 107; 155

**Buchan, John** 1875-1940 .... **TCLC 41; DAB;**
**DAM POP**
See also CA 108; 145; DLB 34, 70, 156;
MTCW 1; YABC 2

**Buchanan, George** 1506-1582 ............... **LC 4**
See also DLB 152

**Buchheim, Lothar-Guenther** 1918- .... **CLC 6**
See also CA 85-88

**Buchner, (Karl) Georg** 1813-1837 . **NCLC 26**

**Buchwald, Art(hur)** 1925- ................. **CLC 33**
See also AITN 1; CA 5-8R; CANR 21, 67;
MTCW 1, 2; SATA 10

**Buck, Pearl S(ydenstricker)**
1892-1973 ....... **CLC 7, 11, 18, 127; DA;**
**DAB; DAC; DAM MST, NOV**
See also AITN 1; CA 1-4R; 41-44R; CANR
1, 34; CDALBS; DA3; DLB 9, 102;
MTCW 1, 2; SATA 1, 25

**Buckler, Ernest** 1908-1984 .... **CLC 13; DAC;**
**DAM MST**
See also CA 11-12; 114; CAP 1; DLB 68;
SATA 47

**Buckley, Vincent (Thomas)**
1925-1988 ................................. **CLC 57**
See also CA 101

**Buckley, William F(rank), Jr.** 1925- . **CLC 7,**
**18, 37; DAM POP**
See also AITN 1; CA 1-4R; CANR 1, 24,
53; DA3; DLB 137; DLBY 80; INT
CANR-24; MTCW 1, 2

**Buechner, (Carl) Frederick** 1926- . **CLC 2, 4,**
**6, 9; DAM NOV**
See also CA 13-16R; CANR 11, 39, 64;
DLBY 80; INT CANR-11; MTCW 1, 2

**Buell, John (Edward)** 1927- ............. **CLC 10**
See also CA 1-4R; CANR 71; DLB 53

**Buero Vallejo, Antonio** 1916- ..... **CLC 15, 46**
See also CA 106; CANR 24, 49, 75; HW 1;
MTCW 1, 2

**Bufalino, Gesualdo** 1920(?)- ............. **CLC 74**
See also DLB 196

**Bugayev, Boris Nikolayevich** 1880-1934
**TCLC 7; PC 11**
See also Bely, Andrey CA 104; 165; MTCW
1

**Bukowski, Charles** 1920-1994 ... **CLC 2, 5, 9,**
**41, 82, 108; DAM NOV, POET; PC 18**
See also CA 17-20R; 144; CANR 40, 62;
DA3; DLB 5, 130, 169; MTCW 1, 2

**Bulgakov, Mikhail (Afanas'evich)** 1891-1940
**TCLC 2, 16; DAM DRAM, NOV; SSC**
**18**
See also CA 105; 152

**Bulgya, Alexander Alexandrovich** 1901-1956
**TCLC 53**
See also Fadeyev, Alexander CA 117; 181

**Bullins, Ed** 1935- ......... **CLC 1, 5, 7; BLC 1;**
**DAM DRAM, MULT; DC 6**
See also BW 2, 3; CA 49-52; CAAS 16;
CANR 24, 46, 73; DLB 7, 38; MTCW 1,
2

**Bulwer-Lytton, Edward (George Earle**
**Lytton)** 1803-1873 .............. **NCLC 1, 45**
See also DLB 21

**Bunin, Ivan Alexeyevich**
1870-1953 ..................... **TCLC 6; SSC 5**
See also CA 104

**Bunting, Basil** 1900-1985 ..... **CLC 10, 39, 47;**
**DAM POET**
See also CA 53-56; 115; CANR 7; DLB 20

**Bunuel, Luis** 1900-1983 .. **CLC 16, 80; DAM**
**MULT; HLC 1**
See also CA 101; 110; CANR 32, 77; HW
1

**Bunyan, John** 1628-1688 ... **LC 4; DA; DAB;**
**DAC; DAM MST; WLC**
See also CDBLB 1660-1789; DLB 39

**Burckhardt, Jacob (Christoph)** 1818-1897
**NCLC 49**

**Burford, Eleanor**
See Hibbert, Eleanor Alice Burford

**Burgess, Anthony** .. **CLC 1, 2, 4, 5, 8, 10, 13, 15, 22, 40, 62, 81, 94; DAB**
See also Wilson, John (Anthony) Burgess AAYA 25; AITN 1; CDBLB 1960 to Present; DLB 14, 194; DLBY 98; MTCW 1

**Burke, Edmund** 1729(?)-1797 ........ **LC 7, 36; DA; DAB; DAC; DAM MST; WLC**
See also DA3; DLB 104

**Burke, Kenneth (Duva)** 1897-1993 ... **CLC 2, 24**
See also CA 5-8R; 143; CANR 39, 74; DLB 45, 63; MTCW 1, 2

**Burke, Leda**
See Garnett, David

**Burke, Ralph**
See Silverberg, Robert

**Burke, Thomas** 1886-1945 ............. **TCLC 63**
See also CA 113; 155; DLB 197

**Burney, Fanny** 1752-1840 .. **NCLC 12, 54, 81**
See also DLB 39

**Burns, Robert** 1759-1796 . **LC 3, 29, 40; DA; DAB; DAC; DAM MST, POET; PC 6; WLC**
See also CDBLB 1789-1832; DA3; DLB 109

**Burns, Tex**
See L'Amour, Louis (Dearborn)

**Burnshaw, Stanley** 1906- ........ **CLC 3, 13, 44**
See also CA 9-12R; DLB 48; DLBY 97

**Burr, Anne** 1937- ................................. **CLC 6**
See also CA 25-28R

**Burroughs, Edgar Rice** 1875-1950 . **TCLC 2, 32; DAM NOV**
See also AAYA 11; CA 104; 132; DA3; DLB 8; MTCW 1, 2; SATA 41

**Burroughs, William S(eward)** 1914-1997 **CLC 1, 2, 5, 15, 22, 42, 75, 109; DA; DAB; DAC; DAM MST, NOV, POP; WLC**
See also AITN 2; CA 9-12R; 160; CANR 20, 52; DA3; DLB 2, 8, 16, 152; DLBY 81, 97; MTCW 1, 2

**Burton, Sir Richard F(rancis)** 1821-1890 **NCLC 42**
See also DLB 55, 166, 184

**Busch, Frederick** 1941- .... **CLC 7, 10, 18, 47**
See also CA 33-36R; CAAS 1; CANR 45, 73; DLB 6

**Bush, Ronald** 1946- ............................ **CLC 34**
See also CA 136

**Bustos, F(rancisco)**
See Borges, Jorge Luis

**Bustos Domecq, H(onorio)**
See Bioy Casares, Adolfo; Borges, Jorge Luis

**Butler, Octavia E(stelle)** 1947- ......... **CLC 38, 121; BLCS; DAM MULT, POP**
See also AAYA 18; BW 2, 3; CA 73-76; CANR 12, 24, 38, 73; DA3; DLB 33; MTCW 1, 2; SATA 84

**Butler, Robert Olen (Jr.)** 1945- ....... **CLC 81; DAM POP**
See also CA 112; CANR 66; DLB 173; INT 112; MTCW 1

**Butler, Samuel** 1612-1680 ............. **LC 16, 43**
See also DLB 101, 126

**Butler, Samuel** 1835-1902 . **TCLC 1, 33; DA; DAB; DAC; DAM MST, NOV; WLC**
See also CA 143; CDBLB 1890-1914; DA3; DLB 18, 57, 174

**Butler, Walter C.**
See Faust, Frederick (Schiller)

**Butor, Michel (Marie Francois)**
1926- ........................ **CLC 1, 3, 8, 11, 15**
See also CA 9-12R; CANR 33, 66; DLB 83; MTCW 1, 2

**Butts, Mary** 1892(?)-1937 ............... **TCLC 77**
See also CA 148

**Buzo, Alexander (John)** 1944- .......... **CLC 61**
See also CA 97-100; CANR 17, 39, 69

**Buzzati, Dino** 1906-1972 .................... **CLC 36**
See also CA 160; 33-36R; DLB 177

**Byars, Betsy (Cromer)** 1928- ............ **CLC 35**
See also AAYA 19; CA 33-36R, 183; CAAE 183; CANR 18, 36, 57; CLR 1, 16; DLB 52; INT CANR-18; JRDA; MAICYA; MTCW 1; SAAS 1; SATA 4, 46, 80; SATA-Essay 108

**Byatt, A(ntonia) S(usan Drabble)**
1936- ..... **CLC 19, 65; DAM NOV, POP**
See also CA 13-16R; CANR 13, 33, 50, 75; DA3; DLB 14, 194; MTCW 1, 2

**Byrne, David** 1952- ........................... **CLC 26**
See also CA 127

**Byrne, John Keyes** 1926-
See Leonard, Hugh
See also CA 102; CANR 78; INT 102

**Byron, George Gordon (Noel)** 1788-1824 **NCLC 2, 12; DA; DAB; DAC; DAM MST, POET; PC 16; WLC**
See also CDBLB 1789-1832; DA3; DLB 96, 110

**Byron, Robert** 1905-1941 ............... **TCLC 67**
See also CA 160; DLB 195

**C. 3. 3.**
See Wilde, Oscar

**Caballero, Fernan** 1796-1877 ......... **NCLC 10**

**Cabell, Branch**
See Cabell, James Branch

**Cabell, James Branch** 1879-1958 .... **TCLC 6**
See also CA 105; 152; DLB 9, 78; MTCW 1

**Cable, George Washington**
1844-1925 .................... **TCLC 4; SSC 4**
See also CA 104; 155; DLB 12, 74; DLBD 13

**Cabral de Melo Neto, Joao** 1920- ... **CLC 76; DAM MULT**
See also CA 151

**Cabrera Infante, G(uillermo)** 1929- . **CLC 5, 25, 45, 120; DAM MULT; HLC 1**
See also CA 85-88; CANR 29, 65; DA3; DLB 113; HW 1, 2; MTCW 1, 2

**Cade, Toni**
See Bambara, Toni Cade

**Cadmus and Harmonia**
See Buchan, John

**Caedmon** fl. 658-680 ......................... **CMLC 7**
See also DLB 146

**Caeiro, Alberto**
See Pessoa, Fernando (Antonio Nogueira)

**Cage, John (Milton, Jr.)** 1912-1992 . **CLC 41**
See also CA 13-16R; 169; CANR 9, 78; DLB 193; INT CANR-9

**Cahan, Abraham** 1860-1951 .......... **TCLC 71**
See also CA 108; 154; DLB 9, 25, 28

**Cain, G.**
See Cabrera Infante, G(uillermo)

**Cain, Guillermo**
See Cabrera Infante, G(uillermo)

**Cain, James M(allahan)** 1892-1977 .. **CLC 3, 11, 28**
See also AITN 1; CA 17-20R; 73-76; CANR 8, 34, 61; MTCW 1

**Caine, Hall** 1853-1931 .................... **TCLC 99**

**Caine, Mark**
See Raphael, Frederic (Michael)

**Calasso, Roberto** 1941- ..................... **CLC 81**
See also CA 143

**Calderon de la Barca, Pedro**
1600-1681 .......... **LC 23; DC 3; HLCS 1**

**Caldwell, Erskine (Preston)**
1903-1987 .. **CLC 1, 8, 14, 50, 60; DAM NOV; SSC 19**
See also AITN 1; CA 1-4R; 121; CAAS 1; CANR 2, 33; DA3; DLB 9, 86; MTCW 1, 2

**Caldwell, (Janet Miriam) Taylor (Holland)**
1900-1985 .. **CLC 2, 28, 39; DAM NOV, POP**
See also CA 5-8R; 116; CANR 5; DA3; DLBD 17

**Calhoun, John Caldwell**
1782-1850 ................................. **NCLC 15**
See also DLB 3

**Calisher, Hortense** 1911- ..... **CLC 2, 4, 8, 38; DAM NOV; SSC 15**
See also CA 1-4R; CANR 1, 22, 67; DA3; DLB 2; INT CANR-22; MTCW 1, 2

**Callaghan, Morley Edward**
1903-1990 ...... **CLC 3, 14, 41, 65; DAC; DAM MST**
See also CA 9-12R; 132; CANR 33, 73; DLB 68; MTCW 1, 2

**Callimachus** c. 305B.C.-c.
240B.C. .................................. **CMLC 18**
See also DLB 176

**Calvin, John** 1509-1564 ...................... **LC 37**

**Calvino, Italo** 1923-1985 .... **CLC 5, 8, 11, 22, 33, 39, 73; DAM NOV; SSC 3**
See also CA 85-88; 116; CANR 23, 61; DLB 196; MTCW 1, 2

**Cameron, Carey** 1952- ...................... **CLC 59**
See also CA 135

**Cameron, Peter** 1959- ....................... **CLC 44**
See also CA 125; CANR 50

**Camoens, Luis Vaz de** 1524(?)-1580
See also HLCS 1

**Camoes, Luis de** 1524(?)-1580
See also HLCS 1

**Campana, Dino** 1885-1932 ............. **TCLC 20**
See also CA 117; DLB 114

**Campanella, Tommaso** 1568-1639 ....... **LC 32**

**Campbell, John W(ood, Jr.)**
1910-1971 ................................. **CLC 32**
See also CA 21-22; 29-32R; CANR 34; CAP 2; DLB 8; MTCW 1

**Campbell, Joseph** 1904-1987 ............ **CLC 69**
See also AAYA 3; BEST 89:2; CA 1-4R; 124; CANR 3, 28, 61; DA3; MTCW 1, 2

**Campbell, Maria** 1940- .......... **CLC 85; DAC**
See also CA 102; CANR 54; NNAL

**Campbell, (John) Ramsey** 1946- ..... **CLC 42; SSC 19**
See also CA 57-60; CANR 7; INT CANR-7

**Campbell, (Ignatius) Roy (Dunnachie)**
1901-1957 ................................. **TCLC 5**
See also CA 104; 155; DLB 20; MTCW 2

**Campbell, Thomas** 1777-1844 ....... **NCLC 19**
See also DLB 93; 144

**Campbell, Wilfred** ............................ **TCLC 9**
See also Campbell, William

**Campbell, William** 1858(?)-1918
See Campbell, Wilfred
See also CA 106; DLB 92

**Campion, Jane** .................................. **CLC 95**
See also CA 138; CANR 87

**Camus, Albert** 1913-1960 ...... **CLC 1, 2, 4, 9, 11, 14, 32, 63, 69, 124; DA; DAB; DAC; DAM DRAM, MST, NOV; DC 2; SSC 9; WLC**
See also CA 89-92; DA3; DLB 72; MTCW 1, 2

**Canby, Vincent** 1924- ....................... **CLC 13**
See also CA 81-84

**Cancale**
See Desnos, Robert

**Canetti, Elias** 1905-1994 .. **CLC 3, 14, 25, 75, 86**
See also CA 21-24R; 146; CANR 23, 61, 79; DA3; DLB 85, 124; MTCW 1, 2

**Canfield, Dorothea F.**
See Fisher, Dorothy (Frances) Canfield

**Canfield, Dorothea Frances**
See Fisher, Dorothy (Frances) Canfield

**Canfield, Dorothy**
See Fisher, Dorothy (Frances) Canfield
**Canin, Ethan** 1960- ............................... CLC 55
See also CA 131; 135
**Cannon, Curt**
See Hunter, Evan
**Cao, Lan** 1961- ...................................... CLC 109
See also CA 165
**Cape, Judith**
See Page, P(atricia) K(athleen)
**Capek, Karel** 1890-1938 ... TCLC 6, 37; DA;
DAB; DAC; DAM DRAM, MST, NOV;
DC 1; SSC 36; WLC
See also CA 104; 140; DA3; MTCW 1
**Capote, Truman** 1924-1984 . CLC 1, 3, 8, 13,
19, 34, 38, 58; DA; DAB; DAC; DAM
MST, NOV, POP; SSC 2; WLC
See also CA 5-8R; 113; CANR 18, 62;
CDALB 1941-1968; DA3; DLB 2, 185;
DLBY 80, 84; MTCW 1, 2; SATA 91
**Capra, Frank** 1897-1991 ................... CLC 16
See also CA 61-64; 135
**Caputo, Philip** 1941- .......................... CLC 32
See also CA 73-76; CANR 40
**Caragiale, Ion Luca** 1852-1912 ...... TCLC 76
See also CA 157
**Card, Orson Scott** 1951- ..... CLC 44, 47, 50;
DAM POP
See also AAYA 11; CA 102; CANR 27, 47,
73; DA3; INT CANR-27; MTCW 1, 2;
SATA 83
**Cardenal, Ernesto** 1925- ....... CLC 31; DAM
MULT, POET; HLC 1; PC 22
See also CA 49-52; CANR 2, 32, 66; HW
1, 2; MTCW 1, 2
**Cardozo, Benjamin N(athan)** 1870-1938
TCLC 65
See also CA 117; 164
**Carducci, Giosue (Alessandro Giuseppe)**
1835-1907 ................................. TCLC 32
See also CA 163
**Carew, Thomas** 1595(?)-1640 . LC 13; PC 29
See also DLB 126
**Carey, Ernestine Gilbreth** 1908- ...... CLC 17
See also CA 5-8R; CANR 71; SATA 2
**Carey, Peter** 1943- ................. CLC 40, 55, 96
See also CA 123; 127; CANR 53, 76; INT
127; MTCW 1, 2; SATA 94
**Carleton, William** 1794-1869 .......... NCLC 3
See also DLB 159
**Carlisle, Henry (Coffin)** 1926- .......... CLC 33
See also CA 13-16R; CANR 15, 85
**Carlsen, Chris**
See Holdstock, Robert P.
**Carlson, Ron(ald F.)** 1947- ................ CLC 54
See also CA 105; CANR 27
**Carlyle, Thomas** 1795-1881 .. NCLC 70; DA;
DAB; DAC; DAM MST
See also CDBLB 1789-1832; DLB 55; 144
**Carman, (William) Bliss**
1861-1929 ...................... TCLC 7; DAC
See also CA 104; 152; DLB 92
**Carnegie, Dale** 1888-1955 .............. TCLC 53
**Carossa, Hans** 1878-1956 .............. TCLC 48
See also CA 170; DLB 66
**Carpenter, Don(ald Richard)**
1931-1995 ................................. CLC 41
See also CA 45-48; 149; CANR 1, 71
**Carpenter, Edward** 1844-1929 ....... TCLC 88
See also CA 163
**Carpentier (y Valmont), Alejo** 1904-1980
CLC 8, 11, 38, 110; DAM MULT; HLC
1; SSC 35
See also CA 65-68; 97-100; CANR 11, 70;
DLB 113; HW 1, 2
**Carr, Caleb** 1955(?)- ......................... CLC 86
See also CA 147; CANR 73; DA3

**Carr, Emily** 1871-1945 ................... TCLC 32
See also CA 159; DLB 68
**Carr, John Dickson** 1906-1977 .......... CLC 3
See also Fairbairn, Roger CA 49-52; 69-72;
CANR 3, 33, 60; MTCW 1, 2
**Carr, Philippa**
See Hibbert, Eleanor Alice Burford
**Carr, Virginia Spencer** 1929- ........... CLC 34
See also CA 61-64; DLB 111
**Carrere, Emmanuel** 1957- ............... CLC 89
**Carrier, Roch** 1937- ........ CLC 13, 78; DAC;
DAM MST
See also CA 130; CANR 61; DLB 53;
SATA 105
**Carroll, James P.** 1943(?)- ................ CLC 38
See also CA 81-84; CANR 73; MTCW 1
**Carroll, Jim** 1951- ............................ CLC 35
See also AAYA 17; CA 45-48; CANR 42
**Carroll, Lewis** .... NCLC 2, 53; PC 18; WLC
See also Dodgson, Charles Lutwidge CD-
BLB 1832-1890; CLR 2, 18; DLB 18,
163, 178; DLBY 98; JRDA
**Carroll, Paul Vincent** 1900-1968 ...... CLC 10
See also CA 9-12R; 25-28R; DLB 10
**Carruth, Hayden** 1921- ..... CLC 4, 7, 10, 18,
84; PC 10
See also CA 9-12R; CANR 4, 38, 59; DLB
5, 165; INT CANR-4; MTCW 1, 2; SATA
47
**Carson, Rachel Louise** 1907-1964 ... CLC 71;
DAM POP
See also CA 77-80; CANR 35; DA3;
MTCW 1, 2; SATA 23
**Carter, Angela (Olive)** 1940-1992 ...... CLC 5,
41, 76; SSC 13
See also CA 53-56; 136; CANR 12, 36, 61;
DA3; DLB 14, 207; MTCW 1, 2; SATA
66; SATA-Obit 70
**Carter, Nick**
See Smith, Martin Cruz
**Carver, Raymond** 1938-1988 ..... CLC 22, 36,
53, 55, 126; DAM NOV; SSC 8
See also CA 33-36R; 126; CANR 17, 34,
61; DA3; DLB 130; DLBY 84, 88;
MTCW 1, 2
**Cary, Elizabeth, Lady Falkland** 1585-1639
LC 30
**Cary, (Arthur) Joyce (Lunel)** 1888-1957
TCLC 1, 29
See also CA 104; 164; CDBLB 1914-1945;
DLB 15, 100; MTCW 2
**Casanova de Seingalt, Giovanni Jacopo**
1725-1798 ................................... LC 13
**Casares, Adolfo Bioy**
See Bioy Casares, Adolfo
**Casely-Hayford, J(oseph) E(phraim)**
1866-1930 ...... TCLC 24; BLC 1; DAM
MULT
See also BW 2; CA 123; 152
**Casey, John (Dudley)** 1939- .............. CLC 59
See also BEST 90:2; CA 69-72; CANR 23
**Casey, Michael** 1947- .......................... CLC 2
See also CA 65-68; DLB 5
**Casey, Patrick**
See Thurman, Wallace (Henry)
**Casey, Warren (Peter)** 1935-1988 .... CLC 12
See also CA 101; 127; INT 101
**Casona, Alejandro** ............................ CLC 49
See also Alvarez, Alejandro Rodriguez
**Cassavetes, John** 1929-1989 .............. CLC 20
See also CA 85-88; 127; CANR 82
**Cassian, Nina** 1924- ........................... PC 17
**Cassill, R(onald) V(erlin)** 1919- ... CLC 4, 23
See also CA 9-12R; CAAS 1; CANR 7, 45;
DLB 6
**Cassirer, Ernst** 1874-1945 ............... TCLC 61
See also CA 157

**Cassity, (Allen) Turner** 1929- ....... CLC 6, 42
See also CA 17-20R; CAAS 8; CANR 11;
DLB 105
**Castaneda, Carlos (Cesar Aranha)**
1931(?)-1998 ...................... CLC 12, 119
See also CA 25-28R; CANR 32, 66; HW 1;
MTCW 1
**Castedo, Elena** 1937- ........................ CLC 65
See also CA 132
**Castedo-Ellerman, Elena**
See Castedo, Elena
**Castellanos, Rosario** 1925-1974 ....... CLC 66;
DAM MULT; HLC 1
See also CA 131; 53-56; CANR 58; DLB
113; HW 1; MTCW 1
**Castelvetro, Lodovico** 1505-1571 ........ LC 12
**Castiglione, Baldassare** 1478-1529 ...... LC 12
**Castle, Robert**
See Hamilton, Edmond
**Castro (Ruz), Fidel** 1926(?)-
See also CA 110; 129; CANR 81; DAM
MULT; HLC 1; HW 2
**Castro, Guillen de** 1569-1631 ............. LC 19
**Castro, Rosalia de** 1837-1885 ... NCLC 3, 78;
DAM MULT
**Cather, Willa**
See Cather, Willa Sibert
**Cather, Willa Sibert** 1873-1947 ...... TCLC 1,
11, 31, 99; DA; DAB; DAC; DAM
MST, NOV; SSC 2; WLC
See also AAYA 24; CA 104; 128; CDALB
1865-1917; DA3; DLB 9, 54, 78; DLBD
1; MTCW 1, 2; SATA 30
**Catherine, Saint** 1347-1380 ........... CMLC 27
**Cato, Marcus Porcius** 234B.C.-149B.C.
CMLC 21
See also DLB 211
**Catton, (Charles) Bruce** 1899-1978 . CLC 35
See also AITN 1; CA 5-8R; 81-84; CANR
7, 74; DLB 17; SATA 2; SATA-Obit 24
**Catullus** c. 84B.C.-c. 54B.C. .......... CMLC 18
See also DLB 211
**Cauldwell, Frank**
See King, Francis (Henry)
**Caunitz, William J.** 1933-1996 ......... CLC 34
See also BEST 89:3; CA 125; 130; 152;
CANR 73; INT 130
**Causley, Charles (Stanley)** 1917- ....... CLC 7
See also CA 9-12R; CANR 5, 35; CLR 30;
DLB 27; MTCW 1; SATA 3, 66
**Caute, (John) David** 1936- .... CLC 29; DAM
NOV
See also CA 1-4R; CAAS 4; CANR 1, 33,
64; DLB 14
**Cavafy, C(onstantine) P(eter)** 1863-1933
TCLC 2, 7; DAM POET
See also Kavafis, Konstantinos Petrou CA
148; DA3; MTCW 1
**Cavallo, Evelyn**
See Spark, Muriel (Sarah)
**Cavanna, Betty** ................................ CLC 12
See also Harrison, Elizabeth Cavanna
JRDA; MAICYA; SAAS 4; SATA 1, 30
**Cavendish, Margaret Lucas**
1623-1673 ................................... LC 30
See also DLB 131
**Caxton, William** 1421(?)-1491(?) ........ LC 17
See also DLB 170
**Cayer, D. M.**
See Duffy, Maureen
**Cayrol, Jean** 1911- ............................ CLC 11
See also CA 89-92; DLB 83
**Cela, Camilo Jose** 1916- ........ CLC 4, 13, 59,
122; DAM MULT; HLC 1
See also BEST 90:2; CA 21-24R; CAAS
10; CANR 21, 32, 76; DLBY 89; HW 1;
MTCW 1, 2

**Celan, Paul** ......... **CLC 10, 19, 53, 82; PC 10**
See also Antschel, Paul DLB 69

**Celine, Louis-Ferdinand** ... **CLC 1, 3, 4, 7, 9, 15, 47, 124**
See also Destouches, Louis-Ferdinand DLB 72

**Cellini, Benvenuto** 1500-1571 ............... **LC 7**

**Cendrars, Blaise** 1887-1961 ...... **CLC 18, 106**
See also Sauser-Hall, Frederic

**Cernuda (y Bidon), Luis**
1902-1963 ........... **CLC 54; DAM POET**
See also CA 131; 89-92; DLB 134; HW 1

**Cervantes, Lorna Dee** 1954-
See also CA 131; CANR 80; DLB 82;
HLCS 1; HW 1

**Cervantes (Saavedra), Miguel de** 1547-1616
**LC 6, 23; DA; DAB; DAC; DAM MST, NOV; SSC 12; WLC**

**Cesaire, Aime (Fernand)** 1913- . **CLC 19, 32, 112; BLC 1; DAM MULT, POET; PC 25**
See also BW 2, 3; CA 65-68; CANR 24, 43, 81; DA3; MTCW 1, 2

**Chabon, Michael** 1963- .................... **CLC 55**
See also CA 139; CANR 57

**Chabrol, Claude** 1930- ...................... **CLC 16**
See also CA 110

**Challans, Mary** 1905-1983
See Renault, Mary
See also CA 81-84; 111; CANR 74; DA3;
MTCW 2; SATA 23; SATA-Obit 36

**Challis, George**
See Faust, Frederick (Schiller)

**Chambers, Aidan** 1934- .................... **CLC 35**
See also AAYA 27; CA 25-28R; CANR 12, 31, 58; JRDA; MAICYA; SAAS 12;
SATA 1, 69, 108

**Chambers, James** 1948-
See Cliff, Jimmy
See also CA 124

**Chambers, Jessie**
See Lawrence, D(avid) H(erbert Richards)

**Chambers, Robert W(illiam)** 1865-1933
**TCLC 41**
See also CA 165; DLB 202; SATA 107

**Chamisso, Adelbert von**
1781-1838 ............................... **NCLC 82**
See also DLB 90

**Chandler, Raymond (Thornton)** 1888-1959
**TCLC 1, 7; SSC 23**
See also AAYA 25; CA 104; 129; CANR 60; CDALB 1929-1941; DA3; DLBD 6;
MTCW 1, 2

**Chang, Eileen** 1920-1995 .................... **SSC 28**
See also CA 166

**Chang, Jung** 1952- ............................ **CLC 71**
See also CA 142

**Chang Ai-Ling**
See Chang, Eileen

**Channing, William Ellery**
1780-1842 ................................. **NCLC 17**
See also DLB 1, 59

**Chao, Patricia** 1955- ...................... **CLC 119**
See also CA 163

**Chaplin, Charles Spencer**
1889-1977 ................................. **CLC 16**
See also Chaplin, Charlie CA 81-84; 73-76

**Chaplin, Charlie**
See Chaplin, Charles Spencer
See also DLB 44

**Chapman, George** 1559(?)-1634 ......... **LC 22;**
**DAM DRAM**
See also DLB 62, 121

**Chapman, Graham** 1941-1989 ......... **CLC 21**
See also Monty Python CA 116; 129;
CANR 35

**Chapman, John Jay** 1862-1933 ....... **TCLC 7**
See also CA 104

**Chapman, Lee**
See Bradley, Marion Zimmer

**Chapman, Walker**
See Silverberg, Robert

**Chappell, Fred (Davis)** 1936- ..... **CLC 40, 78**
See also CA 5-8R; CAAS 4; CANR 8, 33, 67; DLB 6, 105

**Char, Rene(-Emile)** 1907-1988 .... **CLC 9, 11, 14, 55; DAM POET**
See also CA 13-16R; 124; CANR 32;
MTCW 1, 2

**Charby, Jay**
See Ellison, Harlan (Jay)

**Chardin, Pierre Teilhard de**
See Teilhard de Chardin, (Marie Joseph)
Pierre

**Charlemagne** 742-814 .................... **CMLC 37**

**Charles I** 1600-1649 ........................... **LC 13**

**Charriere, Isabelle de** 1740-1805 .. **NCLC 66**

**Charyn, Jerome** 1937- .............. **CLC 5, 8, 18**
See also CA 5-8R; CAAS 1; CANR 7, 61;
DLBY 83; MTCW 1

**Chase, Mary (Coyle)** 1907-1981 ........... **DC 1**
See also CA 77-80; 105; SATA 17; SATA-Obit 29

**Chase, Mary Ellen** 1887-1973 ............. **CLC 2**
See also CA 13-16; 41-44R; CAP 1; SATA 10

**Chase, Nicholas**
See Hyde, Anthony

**Chateaubriand, Francois Rene de** 1768-1848
**NCLC 3**
See also DLB 119

**Chatterje, Sarat Chandra** 1876-1936(?)
See Chatterji, Saratchandra
See also CA 109

**Chatterji, Bankim Chandra** 1838-1894
**NCLC 19**

**Chatterji, Saratchandra** ................. **TCLC 13**
See also Chatterje, Sarat Chandra

**Chatterton, Thomas** 1752-1770 ..... **LC 3, 54;**
**DAM POET**
See also DLB 109

**Chatwin, (Charles) Bruce**
1940-1989 . **CLC 28, 57, 59; DAM POP**
See also AAYA 4; BEST 90:1; CA 85-88;
127; DLB 194, 204

**Chaucer, Daniel**
See Ford, Ford Madox

**Chaucer, Geoffrey** 1340(?)-1400 .. **LC 17, 56;**
**DA; DAB; DAC; DAM MST, POET;**
**PC 19; WLCS**
See also CDBLB Before 1660; DA3; DLB 146

**Chavez, Denise (Elia)** 1948-
See also CA 131; CANR 56, 81; DAM MULT; DLB 122; HLC 1; HW 1, 2;
MTCW 2

**Chaviaras, Strates** 1935-
See Haviaras, Stratis
See also CA 105

**Chayefsky, Paddy** ............................ **CLC 23**
See also Chayefsky, Sidney DLB 7, 44;
DLBY 81

**Chayefsky, Sidney** 1923-1981
See Chayefsky, Paddy
See also CA 9-12R; 104; CANR 18; DAM DRAM

**Chedid, Andree** 1920- ...................... **CLC 47**
See also CA 145

**Cheever, John** 1912-1982 ..... **CLC 3, 7, 8, 11, 15, 25, 64; DA; DAB; DAC; DAM MST, NOV, POP; SSC 1, 38; WLC**
See also CA 5-8R; 106; CABS 1; CANR 5, 27, 76; CDALB 1941-1968; DA3; DLB 2, 102; DLBY 80, 82; INT CANR-5;
MTCW 1, 2

**Cheever, Susan** 1943- .................. **CLC 18, 48**
See also CA 103; CANR 27, 51; DLBY 82;
INT CANR-27

**Chekhonte, Antosha**
See Chekhov, Anton (Pavlovich)

**Chekhov, Anton (Pavlovich)** 1860-1904
**TCLC 3, 10, 31, 55, 96; DA; DAB; DAC; DAM DRAM, MST; DC 9; SSC 2, 28; WLC**
See also CA 104; 124; DA3; SATA 90

**Chernyshevsky, Nikolay Gavrilovich**
1828-1889 ................................. **NCLC 1**

**Cherry, Carolyn Janice** 1942-
See Cherryh, C. J.
See also CA 65-68; CANR 10

**Cherryh, C. J.** ................................ **CLC 35**
See also Cherry, Carolyn Janice AAYA 24;
DLBY 80; SATA 93

**Chesnutt, Charles W(addell)** 1858-1932
**TCLC 5, 39; BLC 1; DAM MULT; SSC 7**
See also BW 1, 3; CA 106; 125; CANR 76;
DLB 12, 50, 78; MTCW 1, 2

**Chester, Alfred** 1929(?)-1971 ............. **CLC 49**
See also CA 33-36R; DLB 130

**Chesterton, G(ilbert) K(eith)** 1874-1936
**TCLC 1, 6, 64; DAM NOV, POET; PC 28; SSC 1**
See also CA 104; 132; CANR 73; CDBLB 1914-1945; DLB 10, 19, 34, 70, 98, 149, 178; MTCW 1, 2; SATA 27

**Chiang, Pin-chin** 1904-1986
See Ding Ling
See also CA 118

**Ch'ien Chung-shu** 1910- .................... **CLC 22**
See also CA 130; CANR 73; MTCW 1, 2

**Child, L. Maria**
See Child, Lydia Maria

**Child, Lydia Maria** 1802-1880 .. **NCLC 6, 73**
See also DLB 1, 74; SATA 67

**Child, Mrs.**
See Child, Lydia Maria

**Child, Philip** 1898-1978 ............... **CLC 19, 68**
See also CA 13-14; CAP 1; SATA 47

**Childers, (Robert) Erskine**
1870-1922 ................................. **TCLC 65**
See also CA 113; 153; DLB 70

**Childress, Alice** 1920-1994 .. **CLC 12, 15, 86, 96; BLC 1; DAM DRAM, MULT, NOV; DC 4**
See also AAYA 8; BW 2, 3; CA 45-48; 146;
CANR 3, 27, 50, 74; CLR 14; DA3; DLB 7, 38; JRDA; MAICYA; MTCW 1, 2;
SATA 7, 48, 81

**Chin, Frank (Chew, Jr.)** 1940- ............. **DC 7**
See also CA 33-36R; CANR 71; DAM MULT; DLB 206

**Chislett, (Margaret) Anne** 1943- ...... **CLC 34**
See also CA 151

**Chitty, Thomas Willes** 1926- ............ **CLC 11**
See also Hinde, Thomas CA 5-8R

**Chivers, Thomas Holley**
1809-1858 ................................. **NCLC 49**
See also DLB 3

**Choi, Susan** ................................... **CLC 119**

**Chomette, Rene Lucien** 1898-1981
See Clair, Rene
See also CA 103

**Chopin, Kate** .. **TCLC 5, 14; DA; DAB; SSC 8; WLCS**
See also Chopin, Katherine CDALB 1865-1917; DLB 12, 78

**Chopin, Katherine** 1851-1904
See Chopin, Kate
See also CA 104; 122; DAC; DAM MST, NOV; DA3

**Chretien de Troyes** c. 12th cent. - . **CMLC 10**
See also DLB 208

Christie
  See Ichikawa, Kon
Christie, Agatha (Mary Clarissa) 1890-1976
    CLC 1, 6, 8, 12, 39, 48, 110; DAB; DAC;
    DAM NOV
  See also AAYA 9; AITN 1, 2; CA 17-20R;
    61-64; CANR 10, 37; CDBLB 1914-1945;
    DA3; DLB 13, 77; MTCW 1, 2; SATA 36
Christie, (Ann) Philippa
  See Pearce, Philippa
  See also CA 5-8R; CANR 4
Christine de Pizan 1365(?)-1431(?) ....... LC 9
  See also DLB 208
Chubb, Elmer
  See Masters, Edgar Lee
Chulkov, Mikhail Dmitrievich
    1743-1792 ..................................... LC 2
  See also DLB 150
Churchill, Caryl 1938- .... CLC 31, 55; DC 5
  See also CA 102; CANR 22, 46; DLB 13;
    MTCW 1
Churchill, Charles 1731-1764 ................ LC 3
  See also DLB 109
Chute, Carolyn 1947- ....................... CLC 39
  See also CA 123
Ciardi, John (Anthony) 1916-1986 . CLC 10,
    40, 44, 129; DAM POET
  See also CA 5-8R; 118; CAAS 2; CANR 5,
    33; CLR 19; DLB 5; DLBY 86; INT
    CANR-5; MAICYA; MTCW 1, 2; SAAS
    26; SATA 1, 65; SATA-Obit 46
Cicero, Marcus Tullius 106B.C.-43B.C.
    CMLC 3
  See also DLB 211
Cimino, Michael 1943- ..................... CLC 16
  See also CA 105
Cioran, E(mil) M. 1911-1995 ........... CLC 64
  See also CA 25-28R; 149
Cisneros, Sandra 1954- . CLC 69, 118; DAM
    MULT; HLC 1; SSC 32
  See also AAYA 9; CA 131; CANR 64; DA3;
    DLB 122, 152; HW 1, 2; MTCW 2
Cixous, Helene 1937- ........................ CLC 92
  See also CA 126; CANR 55; DLB 83;
    MTCW 1, 2
Clair, Rene ..................................... CLC 20
  See also Chomette, Rene Lucien
Clampitt, Amy 1920-1994 .... CLC 32; PC 19
  See also CA 110; 146; CANR 29, 79; DLB
    105
Clancy, Thomas L., Jr. 1947-
  See Clancy, Tom
  See also CA 125; 131; CANR 62; DA3;
    INT 131; MTCW 1, 2
Clancy, Tom ......... CLC 45, 112; DAM NOV,
    POP
  See also Clancy, Thomas L., Jr. AAYA 9;
    BEST 89:1, 90:1; MTCW 2
Clare, John 1793-1864 ......... NCLC 9; DAB;
    DAM POET; PC 23
  See also DLB 55, 96
Clarin
  See Alas (y Urena), Leopoldo (Enrique
    Garcia)
Clark, Al C.
  See Goines, Donald
Clark, (Robert) Brian 1932- ............. CLC 29
  See also CA 41-44R; CANR 67
Clark, Curt
  See Westlake, Donald E(dwin)
Clark, Eleanor 1913-1996 ............. CLC 5, 19
  See also CA 9-12R; 151; CANR 41; DLB 6
Clark, J. P.
  See Clark, John Pepper
  See also DLB 117
Clark, John Pepper 1935- . CLC 38; BLC 1;
    DAM DRAM, MULT; DC 5
  See also Clark, J. P. BW 1; CA 65-68;
    CANR 16, 72; MTCW 1

Clark, M. R.
  See Clark, Mavis Thorpe
Clark, Mavis Thorpe 1909- ............. CLC 12
  See also CA 57-60; CANR 8, 37; CLR 30;
    MAICYA; SAAS 5; SATA 8, 74
Clark, Walter Van Tilburg
    1909-1971 ..................................... CLC 28
  See also CA 9-12R; 33-36R; CANR 63;
    DLB 9, 206; SATA 8
Clark Bekederemo, J(ohnson) P(epper)
  See Clark, John Pepper
Clarke, Arthur C(harles) 1917- .... CLC 1, 4,
    13, 18, 35; DAM POP; SSC 3
  See also AAYA 4; CA 1-4R; CANR 2, 28,
    55, 74; DA3; JRDA; MAICYA; MTCW
    1, 2; SATA 13, 70
Clarke, Austin 1896-1974 ... CLC 6, 9; DAM
    POET
  See also CA 29-32; 49-52; CAP 2; DLB 10,
    20
Clarke, Austin C(hesterfield) 1934- .. CLC 8,
    53; BLC 1; DAC; DAM MULT
  See also BW 1; CA 25-28R; CAAS 16;
    CANR 14, 32, 68; DLB 53, 125
Clarke, Gillian 1937- ....................... CLC 61
  See also CA 106; DLB 40
Clarke, Marcus (Andrew Hislop) 1846-1881
    NCLC 19
Clarke, Shirley 1925- ....................... CLC 16
Clash, The
  See Headon, (Nicky) Topper; Jones, Mick;
    Simonon, Paul; Strummer, Joe
Claudel, Paul (Louis Charles Marie)
    1868-1955 ............................. TCLC 2, 10
  See also CA 104; 165; DLB 192
Claudius, Matthias 1740-1815 ....... NCLC 75
  See also DLB 97
Clavell, James (duMaresq)
    1925-1994 .. CLC 6, 25, 87; DAM NOV,
    POP
  See also CA 25-28R; 146; CANR 26, 48;
    DA3; MTCW 1, 2
Cleaver, (Leroy) Eldridge
    1935-1998 . CLC 30, 119; BLC 1; DAM
    MULT
  See also BW 1, 3; CA 21-24R; 167; CANR
    16, 75; DA3; MTCW 2
Cleese, John (Marwood) 1939- ......... CLC 21
  See also Monty Python CA 112; 116;
    CANR 35; MTCW 1
Cleishbotham, Jebediah
  See Scott, Walter
Cleland, John 1710-1789 ................. LC 2, 48
  See also DLB 39
Clemens, Samuel Langhorne 1835-1910
  See Twain, Mark
  See also CA 104; 135; CDALB 1865-1917;
    DA; DAB; DAC; DAM MST, NOV; DA3;
    DLB 11, 12, 23, 64, 74, 186, 189; JRDA;
    MAICYA; SATA 100; YABC 2
Cleophil
  See Congreve, William
Clerihew, E.
  See Bentley, E(dmund) C(lerihew)
Clerk, N. W.
  See Lewis, C(live) S(taples)
Cliff, Jimmy ................................... CLC 21
  See also Chambers, James
Cliff, Michelle 1946- ........... CLC 120; BLCS
  See also BW 2; CA 116; CANR 39, 72;
    DLB 157
Clifton, (Thelma) Lucille 1936- ....... CLC 19,
    66; BLC 1; DAM MULT, POET; PC
    17
  See also BW 2, 3; CA 49-52; CANR 2, 24,
    42, 76; CLR 5; DA3; DLB 5, 41; MAI-
    CYA; MTCW 1, 2; SATA 20, 69
Clinton, Dirk
  See Silverberg, Robert

Clough, Arthur Hugh 1819-1861 ... NCLC 27
  See also DLB 32
Clutha, Janet Paterson Frame 1924-
  See Frame, Janet
  See also CA 1-4R; CANR 2, 36, 76; MTCW
    1, 2
Clyne, Terence
  See Blatty, William Peter
Cobalt, Martin
  See Mayne, William (James Carter)
Cobb, Irvin S(hrewsbury)
    1876-1944 ..................................... TCLC 77
  See also CA 175; DLB 11, 25, 86
Cobbett, William 1763-1835 .......... NCLC 49
  See also DLB 43, 107, 158
Coburn, D(onald) L(ee) 1938- ......... CLC 10
  See also CA 89-92
Cocteau, Jean (Maurice Eugene Clement)
    1889-1963 .... CLC 1, 8, 15, 16, 43; DA;
    DAB; DAC; DAM DRAM, MST, NOV;
    WLC
  See also CA 25-28; CANR 40; CAP 2;
    DA3; DLB 65; MTCW 1, 2
Codrescu, Andrei 1946- .......... CLC 46, 121;
    DAM POET
  See also CA 33-36R; CAAS 19; CANR 13,
    34, 53, 76; DA3; MTCW 2
Coe, Max
  See Bourne, Randolph S(illiman)
Coe, Tucker
  See Westlake, Donald E(dwin)
Coen, Ethan 1958- ......................... CLC 108
  See also CA 126; CANR 85
Coen, Joel 1955- ........................... CLC 108
  See also CA 126
The Coen Brothers
  See Coen, Ethan; Coen, Joel
Coetzee, J(ohn) M(ichael) 1940- ...... CLC 23,
    33, 66, 117; DAM NOV
  See also CA 77-80; CANR 41, 54, 74; DA3;
    MTCW 1, 2
Coffey, Brian
  See Koontz, Dean R(ay)
Coffin, Robert P(eter) Tristram 1892-1955
    TCLC 95
  See also CA 123; 169; DLB 45
Cohan, George M(ichael)
    1878-1942 ..................................... TCLC 60
  See also CA 157
Cohen, Arthur A(llen) 1928-1986 ...... CLC 7,
    31
  See also CA 1-4R; 120; CANR 1, 17, 42;
    DLB 28
Cohen, Leonard (Norman) 1934- ...... CLC 3,
    38; DAC; DAM MST
  See also CA 21-24R; CANR 14, 69; DLB
    53; MTCW 1
Cohen, Matt 1942- ................. CLC 19; DAC
  See also CA 61-64; CAAS 18; CANR 40;
    DLB 53
Cohen-Solal, Annie 19(?)- ............... CLC 50
Colegate, Isabel 1931- ..................... CLC 36
  See also CA 17-20R; CANR 8, 22, 74; DLB
    14; INT CANR-22; MTCW 1
Coleman, Emmett
  See Reed, Ishmael
Coleridge, M. E.
  See Coleridge, Mary E(lizabeth)
Coleridge, Mary E(lizabeth) 1861-1907
    TCLC 73
  See also CA 116; 166; DLB 19, 98
Coleridge, Samuel Taylor
    1772-1834 ....... NCLC 9, 54; DA; DAB;
    DAC; DAM MST, POET; PC 11; WLC
  See also CDBLB 1789-1832; DA3; DLB
    93, 107
Coleridge, Sara 1802-1852 ............. NCLC 31
  See also DLB 199

Coles, Don 1928- ................................. **CLC 46**
See also CA 115; CANR 38

Coles, Robert (Martin) 1929- ......... **CLC 108**
See also CA 45-48; CANR 3, 32, 66, 70;
INT CANR-32; SATA 23

Colette, (Sidonie-Gabrielle)
1873-1954 . **TCLC 1, 5, 16; DAM NOV;
SSC 10**
See also CA 104; 131; DA3; DLB 65;
MTCW 1, 2

Collett, (Jacobine) Camilla (Wergeland)
1813-1895 ................................. **NCLC 22**

Collier, Christopher 1930- ................ **CLC 30**
See also AAYA 13; CA 33-36R; CANR 13,
33; JRDA; MAICYA; SATA 16, 70

Collier, James L(incoln) 1928- ........ **CLC 30;
DAM POP**
See also AAYA 13; CA 9-12R; CANR 4,
33, 60; CLR 3; JRDA; MAICYA; SAAS
21; SATA 8, 70

Collier, Jeremy 1650-1726 ..................... **LC 6**

Collier, John 1901-1980 ..................... **SSC 19**
See also CA 65-68; 97-100; CANR 10;
DLB 77

Collingwood, R(obin) G(eorge) 1889(?)-1943
**TCLC 67**
See also CA 117; 155

Collins, Hunt
See Hunter, Evan

Collins, Linda 1931- ........................... **CLC 44**
See also CA 125

Collins, (William) Wilkie
1824-1889 ............................ **NCLC 1, 18**
See also CDBLB 1832-1890; DLB 18, 70,
159

Collins, William 1721-1759 . **LC 4, 40; DAM
POET**
See also DLB 109

Collodi, Carlo 1826-1890 ............... **NCLC 54**
See also Lorenzini, Carlo CLR 5

Colman, George 1732-1794
See Glassco, John

Colt, Winchester Remington
See Hubbard, L(afayette) Ron(ald)

Colter, Cyrus 1910- ........................... **CLC 58**
See also BW 1; CA 65-68; CANR 10, 66;
DLB 33

Colton, James
See Hansen, Joseph

Colum, Padraic 1881-1972 ............... **CLC 28**
See also CA 73-76; 33-36R; CANR 35;
CLR 36; MAICYA; MTCW 1; SATA 15

Colvin, James
See Moorcock, Michael (John)

Colwin, Laurie (E.) 1944-1992 .... **CLC 5, 13,
23, 84**
See also CA 89-92; 139; CANR 20, 46;
DLBY 80; MTCW 1

Comfort, Alex(ander) 1920- .... **CLC 7; DAM
POP**
See also CA 1-4R; CANR 1, 45; MTCW 1

Comfort, Montgomery
See Campbell, (John) Ramsey

Compton-Burnett, I(vy)
1884(?)-1969 ........ **CLC 1, 3, 10, 15, 34;
DAM NOV**
See also CA 1-4R; 25-28R; CANR 4; DLB
36; MTCW 1

Comstock, Anthony 1844-1915 ...... **TCLC 13**
See also CA 110; 169

Comte, Auguste 1798-1857 ............. **NCLC 54**

Conan Doyle, Arthur
See Doyle, Arthur Conan

Conde (Abellan), Carmen 1901-
See also CA 177; DLB 108; HLCS 1; HW
2

Conde, Maryse 1937- .... **CLC 52, 92; BLCS;
DAM MULT**
See also Boucolon, Maryse BW 2; MTCW
1

Condillac, Etienne Bonnot de
1714-1780 ..................................... **LC 26**

Condon, Richard (Thomas)
1915-1996 ...... **CLC 4, 6, 8, 10, 45, 100;
DAM NOV**
See also BEST 90:3; CA 1-4R; 151; CAAS
1; CANR 2, 23; INT CANR-23; MTCW
1, 2

Confucius 551B.C.-479B.C. .. **CMLC 19; DA;
DAB; DAC; DAM MST; WLCS**
See also DA3

Congreve, William 1670-1729 ........ **LC 5, 21;
DA; DAB; DAC; DAM DRAM, MST,
POET; DC 2; WLC**
See also CDBLB 1660-1789; DLB 39, 84

Connell, Evan S(helby), Jr. 1924- . **CLC 4, 6,
45; DAM NOV**
See also AAYA 7; CA 1-4R; CAAS 2;
CANR 2, 39, 76; DLB 2; DLBY 81;
MTCW 1, 2

Connelly, Marc(us Cook) 1890-1980 . **CLC 7**
See also CA 85-88; 102; CANR 30; DLB
7; DLBY 80; SATA-Obit 25

Connor, Ralph ........................................ **TCLC 31**
See also Gordon, Charles William DLB 92

Conrad, Joseph 1857-1924 .... **TCLC 1, 6, 13,
25, 43, 57; DA; DAB; DAC; DAM
MST, NOV; SSC 9; WLC**
See also AAYA 26; CA 104; 131; CANR
60; CDBLB 1890-1914; DA3; DLB 10,
34, 98, 156; MTCW 1, 2; SATA 27

Conrad, Robert Arnold
See Hart, Moss

Conroy, Pat
See Conroy, (Donald) Pat(rick)
See also MTCW 2

Conroy, (Donald) Pat(rick) 1945- ... **CLC 30,
74; DAM NOV, POP**
See also Conroy, Pat AAYA 8; AITN 1; CA
85-88; CANR 24, 53; DA3; DLB 6;
MTCW 1

Constant (de Rebecque), (Henri) Benjamin
1767-1830 ..................................... **NCLC 6**
See also DLB 119

Conybeare, Charles Augustus
See Eliot, T(homas) S(tearns)

Cook, Michael 1933- ......................... **CLC 58**
See also CA 93-96; CANR 68; DLB 53

Cook, Robin 1940- ........ **CLC 14; DAM POP**
See also AAYA 32; BEST 90:2; CA 108;
111; CANR 41; DA3; INT 111

Cook, Roy
See Silverberg, Robert

Cooke, Elizabeth 1948- ..................... **CLC 55**
See also CA 129

Cooke, John Esten 1830-1886 ......... **NCLC 5**
See also DLB 3

Cooke, John Estes
See Baum, L(yman) Frank

Cooke, M. E.
See Creasey, John

Cooke, Margaret
See Creasey, John

Cook-Lynn, Elizabeth 1930- . **CLC 93; DAM
MULT**
See also CA 133; DLB 175; NNAL

Cooney, Ray ......................................... **CLC 62**

Cooper, Douglas 1960- ..................... **CLC 86**

Cooper, Henry St. John
See Creasey, John

Cooper, J(oan) California (?)- ......... **CLC 56;
DAM MULT**
See also AAYA 12; BW 1; CA 125; CANR
55; DLB 212

Cooper, James Fenimore
1789-1851 ...................... **NCLC 1, 27, 54**
See also AAYA 22; CDALB 1640-1865;
DA3; DLB 3; SATA 19

Coover, Robert (Lowell) 1932- ...... **CLC 3, 7,
15, 32, 46, 87; DAM NOV; SSC 15**
See also CA 45-48; CANR 3, 37, 58; DLB
2; DLBY 81; MTCW 1, 2

Copeland, Stewart (Armstrong)
1952- ........................................... **CLC 26**

Copernicus, Nicolaus 1473-1543 ......... **LC 45**

Coppard, A(lfred) E(dgar)
1878-1957 ................... **TCLC 5; SSC 21**
See also CA 114; 167; DLB 162; YABC 1

Coppee, Francois 1842-1908 .......... **TCLC 25**
See also CA 170

Coppola, Francis Ford 1939- ... **CLC 16, 126**
See also CA 77-80; CANR 40, 78; DLB 44

Corbiere, Tristan 1845-1875 .......... **NCLC 43**

Corcoran, Barbara 1911- .................. **CLC 17**
See also AAYA 14; CA 21-24R; CAAS 2;
CANR 11, 28, 48; CLR 50; DLB 52;
JRDA; SAAS 20; SATA 3, 77

Cordelier, Maurice
See Giraudoux, (Hippolyte) Jean

Corelli, Marie 1855-1924 ................ **TCLC 51**
See also Mackay, Mary DLB 34, 156

Corman, Cid 1924- ............................... **CLC 9**
See also Corman, Sidney CAAS 2; DLB 5,
193

Corman, Sidney 1924-
See Corman, Cid
See also CA 85-88; CANR 44; DAM POET

Cormier, Robert (Edmund) 1925- ... **CLC 12,
30; DA; DAB; DAC; DAM MST, NOV**
See also AAYA 3, 19; CA 1-4R; CANR 5,
23, 76; CDALB 1968-1988; CLR 12, 55;
DLB 52; INT CANR-23; JRDA; MAI-
CYA; MTCW 1, 2; SATA 10, 45, 83

Corn, Alfred (DeWitt III) 1943- ....... **CLC 33**
See also CA 179; CAAE 179; CAAS 25;
CANR 44; DLB 120; DLBY 80

Corneille, Pierre 1606-1684 ..... **LC 28; DAB;
DAM MST**

Cornwell, David (John Moore)
1931- ................. **CLC 9, 15; DAM POP**
See also le Carre, John CA 5-8R; CANR
13, 33, 59; DA3; MTCW 1, 2

Corso, (Nunzio) Gregory 1930- .... **CLC 1, 11**
See also CA 5-8R; CANR 41, 76; DA3;
DLB 5, 16; MTCW 1, 2

Cortazar, Julio 1914-1984 ... **CLC 2, 3, 5, 10,
13, 15, 33, 34, 92; DAM MULT, NOV;
HLC 1; SSC 7**
See also CA 21-24R; CANR 12, 32, 81;
DA3; DLB 113; HW 1, 2; MTCW 1, 2

CORTES, HERNAN 1484-1547 ......... **LC 31**

Corvinus, Jakob
See Raabe, Wilhelm (Karl)

Corwin, Cecil
See Kornbluth, C(yril) M.

Cosic, Dobrica 1921- ......................... **CLC 14**
See also CA 122; 138; DLB 181

Costain, Thomas B(ertram)
1885-1965 ................................... **CLC 30**
See also CA 5-8R; 25-28R; DLB 9

Costantini, Humberto 1924(?)-1987 . **CLC 49**
See also CA 131; 122; HW 1

Costello, Elvis 1955- ........................... **CLC 21**

Costenoble, Philostene
See Ghelderode, Michel de

Cotes, Cecil V.
See Duncan, Sara Jeannette

Cotter, Joseph Seamon Sr.
1861-1949 ...... **TCLC 28; BLC 1; DAM
MULT**
See also BW 1; CA 124; DLB 50

**Couch, Arthur Thomas Quiller**
See Quiller-Couch, Sir Arthur (Thomas)
**Coulton, James**
See Hansen, Joseph
**Couperus, Louis (Marie Anne)** 1863-1923
**TCLC 15**
See also CA 115
**Coupland, Douglas** 1961- ..... **CLC 85; DAC;**
**DAM POP**
See also CA 142; CANR 57
**Court, Wesli**
See Turco, Lewis (Putnam)
**Courtenay, Bryce** 1933- ..................... **CLC 59**
See also CA 138
**Courtney, Robert**
See Ellison, Harlan (Jay)
**Cousteau, Jacques-Yves** 1910-1997 .. **CLC 30**
See also CA 65-68; 159; CANR 15, 67;
MTCW 1; SATA 38, 98
**Coventry, Francis** 1725-1754 ............... **LC 46**
**Cowan, Peter (Walkinshaw)** 1914- .... **SSC 28**
See also CA 21-24R; CANR 9, 25, 50, 83
**Coward, Noel (Peirce)** 1899-1973 . **CLC 1, 9,**
**29, 51; DAM DRAM**
See also AITN 1; CA 17-18; 41-44R;
CANR 35; CAP 2; CDBLB 1914-1945;
DA3; DLB 10; MTCW 1, 2
**Cowley, Abraham** 1618-1667 ............... **LC 43**
See also DLB 131, 151
**Cowley, Malcolm** 1898-1989 ............. **CLC 39**
See also CA 5-8R; 128; CANR 3, 55; DLB
4, 48; DLBY 81, 89; MTCW 1, 2
**Cowper, William** 1731-1800 . **NCLC 8; DAM**
**POET**
See also DA3; DLB 104, 109
**Cox, William Trevor** 1928- ... **CLC 9, 14, 71;**
**DAM NOV**
See also Trevor, William CA 9-12R; CANR
4, 37, 55, 76; DLB 14; INT CANR-37;
MTCW 1, 2
**Coyne, P. J.**
See Masters, Hilary
**Cozzens, James Gould** 1903-1978 . **CLC 1, 4,**
**11, 92**
See also CA 9-12R; 81-84; CANR 19;
CDALB 1941-1968; DLB 9; DLBD 2;
DLBY 84, 97; MTCW 1, 2
**Crabbe, George** 1754-1832 ............. **NCLC 26**
See also DLB 93
**Craddock, Charles Egbert**
See Murfree, Mary Noailles
**Craig, A. A.**
See Anderson, Poul (William)
**Craik, Dinah Maria (Mulock)** 1826-1887
**NCLC 38**
See also DLB 35, 163; MAICYA; SATA 34
**Cram, Ralph Adams** 1863-1942 ..... **TCLC 45**
See also CA 160
**Crane, (Harold) Hart** 1899-1932 .... **TCLC 2,**
**5, 80; DA; DAB; DAC; DAM MST,**
**POET; PC 3; WLC**
See also CA 104; 127; CDALB 1917-1929;
DA3; DLB 4, 48; MTCW 1, 2
**Crane, R(onald) S(almon)**
1886-1967 ................................. **CLC 27**
See also CA 85-88; DLB 63
**Crane, Stephen (Townley)**
1871-1900 .......... **TCLC 11, 17, 32; DA;**
**DAB; DAC; DAM MST, NOV, POET;**
**SSC 7; WLC**
See also AAYA 21; CA 109; 140; CANR
84; CDALB 1865-1917; DA3; DLB 12,
54, 78; YABC 2
**Cranshaw, Stanley**
See Fisher, Dorothy (Frances) Canfield
**Crase, Douglas** 1944- ......................... **CLC 58**
See also CA 106
**Crashaw, Richard** 1612(?)-1649 ......... **LC 24**
See also DLB 126

**Craven, Margaret** 1901-1980 .......... **CLC 17;**
**DAC**
See also CA 103
**Crawford, F(rancis) Marion** 1854-1909
**TCLC 10**
See also CA 107; 168; DLB 71
**Crawford, Isabella Valancy**
1850-1887 ................................. **NCLC 12**
See also DLB 92
**Crayon, Geoffrey**
See Irving, Washington
**Creasey, John** 1908-1973 ................... **CLC 11**
See also CA 5-8R; 41-44R; CANR 8, 59;
DLB 77; MTCW 1
**Crebillon, Claude Prosper Jolyot de (fils)**
1707-1777 ................................. **LC 1, 28**
**Credo**
See Creasey, John
**Credo, Alvaro J. de**
See Prado (Calvo), Pedro
**Creeley, Robert (White)** 1926- .. **CLC 1, 2, 4,**
**8, 11, 15, 36, 78; DAM POET**
See also CA 1-4R; CAAS 10; CANR 23,
43; DA3; DLB 5, 16, 169; DLBD 17;
MTCW 1, 2
**Crews, Harry (Eugene)** 1935- ..... **CLC 6, 23,**
**49**
See also AITN 1; CA 25-28R; CANR 20,
57; DA3; DLB 6, 143, 185; MTCW 1, 2
**Crichton, (John) Michael** 1942- .... **CLC 2, 6,**
**54, 90; DAM NOV, POP**
See also AAYA 10; AITN 2; CA 25-28R;
CANR 13, 40, 54, 76; DA3; DLBY 81;
INT CANR-13; JRDA; MTCW 1, 2;
SATA 9, 88
**Crispin, Edmund** ............................... **CLC 22**
See also Montgomery, (Robert) Bruce DLB
87
**Cristofer, Michael** 1945(?)- ... **CLC 28; DAM**
**DRAM**
See also CA 110; 152; DLB 7
**Croce, Benedetto** 1866-1952 .......... **TCLC 37**
See also CA 120; 155
**Crockett, David** 1786-1836 ............... **NCLC 8**
See also DLB 3, 11
**Crockett, Davy**
See Crockett, David
**Crofts, Freeman Wills** 1879-1957 .. **TCLC 55**
See also CA 115; DLB 77
**Croker, John Wilson** 1780-1857 .... **NCLC 10**
See also DLB 110
**Crommelynck, Fernand** 1885-1970 .. **CLC 75**
See also CA 89-92
**Cromwell, Oliver** 1599-1658 ................. **LC 43**
**Cronin, A(rchibald) J(oseph)**
1896-1981 ................................. **CLC 32**
See also CA 1-4R; 102; CANR 5; DLB 191;
SATA 47; SATA-Obit 25
**Cross, Amanda**
See Heilbrun, Carolyn G(old)
**Crothers, Rachel** 1878(?)-1958 ....... **TCLC 19**
See also CA 113; DLB 7
**Croves, Hal**
See Traven, B.
**Crow Dog, Mary (Ellen)** (?)- ........... **CLC 93**
See also Brave Bird, Mary CA 154
**Crowfield, Christopher**
See Stowe, Harriet (Elizabeth) Beecher
**Crowley, Aleister** ............................... **TCLC 7**
See also Crowley, Edward Alexander
**Crowley, Edward Alexander** 1875-1947
See Crowley, Aleister
See also CA 104
**Crowley, John** 1942- ......................... **CLC 57**
See also CA 61-64; CANR 43; DLBY 82;
SATA 65
**Crud**
See Crumb, R(obert)

**Crumarums**
See Crumb, R(obert)
**Crumb, R(obert)** 1943- ..................... **CLC 17**
See also CA 106
**Crumbum**
See Crumb, R(obert)
**Crumski**
See Crumb, R(obert)
**Crum the Bum**
See Crumb, R(obert)
**Crunk**
See Crumb, R(obert)
**Crustt**
See Crumb, R(obert)
**Cruz, Victor Hernandez** 1949-
See also BW 2; CA 65-68; CAAS 17;
CANR 14, 32, 74; DAM MULT, POET;
DLB 41; HLC 1; HW 1, 2; MTCW 1
**Cryer, Gretchen (Kiger)** 1935- ......... **CLC 21**
See also CA 114; 123
**Csath, Geza** 1887-1919 .................. **TCLC 13**
See also CA 111
**Cudlip, David R(ockwell)** 1933- ....... **CLC 34**
See also CA 177
**Cullen, Countee** 1903-1946 ....... **TCLC 4, 37;**
**BLC 1; DA; DAC; DAM MST, MULT,**
**POET; PC 20; WLCS**
See also BW 1; CA 108; 124; CDALB
1917-1929; DA3; DLB 4, 48, 51; MTCW
1, 2; SATA 18
**Cum, R.**
See Crumb, R(obert)
**Cummings, Bruce F(rederick)** 1889-1919
See Barbellion, W. N. P.
See also CA 123
**Cummings, E(dward) E(stlin)** 1894-1962
**CLC 1, 3, 8, 12, 15, 68; DA; DAB;**
**DAC; DAM MST, POET; PC 5; WLC**
See also CA 73-76; CANR 31; CDALB
1929-1941; DA3; DLB 4, 48; MTCW 1,
2
**Cunha, Euclides (Rodrigues Pimenta) da**
1866-1909 ................................. **TCLC 24**
See also CA 123
**Cunningham, E. V.**
See Fast, Howard (Melvin)
**Cunningham, J(ames) V(incent)** 1911-1985
**CLC 3, 31**
See also CA 1-4R; 115; CANR 1, 72; DLB
5
**Cunningham, Julia (Woolfolk)**
1916- ..................................... **CLC 12**
See also CA 9-12R; CANR 4, 19, 36;
JRDA; MAICYA; SAAS 2; SATA 1, 26
**Cunningham, Michael** 1952- ............ **CLC 34**
See also CA 136
**Cunninghame Graham, R. B.**
See Cunninghame Graham, Robert
(Gallnigad) Bontine
**Cunninghame Graham, Robert (Gallnigad)**
**Bontine** 1852-1936 .................. **TCLC 19**
See also Graham, R(obert) B(ontine) Cun-
ninghame CA 119; 184; DLB 98
**Currie, Ellen** 19(?)- ............................ **CLC 44**
**Curtin, Philip**
See Lowndes, Marie Adelaide (Belloc)
**Curtis, Price**
See Ellison, Harlan (Jay)
**Cutrate, Joe**
See Spiegelman, Art
**Cynewulf** c. 770-c. 840 ................... **CMLC 23**
**Czaczkes, Shmuel Yosef**
See Agnon, S(hmuel) Y(osef Halevi)
**Dabrowska, Maria (Szumska)** 1889-1965
**CLC 15**
See also CA 106
**Dabydeen, David** 1955- ..................... **CLC 34**
See also BW 1; CA 125; CANR 56

**Dacey, Philip** 1939- ........................... **CLC 51**
See also CA 37-40R; CAAS 17; CANR 14, 32, 64; DLB 105

**Dagerman, Stig (Halvard)**
1923-1954 ............................................ **TCLC 17**
See also CA 117; 155

**Dahl, Roald** 1916-1990 ...... **CLC 1, 6, 18, 79; DAB; DAC; DAM MST, NOV, POP**
See also AAYA 15; CA 1-4R; 133; CANR 6, 32, 37, 62; CLR 1, 7, 41; DA3; DLB 139; JRDA; MAICYA; MTCW 1, 2; SATA 1, 26, 73; SATA-Obit 65

**Dahlberg, Edward** 1900-1977 .. **CLC 1, 7, 14**
See also CA 9-12R; 69-72; CANR 31, 62; DLB 48; MTCW 1

**Daitch, Susan** 1954- ......................... **CLC 103**
See also CA 161

**Dale, Colin** ....................................... **TCLC 18**
See also Lawrence, T(homas) E(dward)

**Dale, George E.**
See Asimov, Isaac

**Dalton, Roque** 1935-1975
See also HLCS 1; HW 2

**Daly, Elizabeth** 1878-1967 ................. **CLC 52**
See also CA 23-24; 25-28R; CANR 60; CAP 2

**Daly, Maureen** 1921- ......................... **CLC 17**
See also AAYA 5; CANR 37, 83; JRDA; MAICYA; SAAS 1; SATA 2

**Damas, Leon-Gontran** 1912-1978 .... **CLC 84**
See also BW 1; CA 125; 73-76

**Dana, Richard Henry Sr.**
1787-1879 ........................................ **NCLC 53**

**Daniel, Samuel** 1562(?)-1619 .............. **LC 24**
See also DLB 62

**Daniels, Brett**
See Adler, Renata

**Dannay, Frederic** 1905-1982 . **CLC 11; DAM POP**
See also Queen, Ellery CA 1-4R; 107; CANR 1, 39; DLB 137; MTCW 1

**D'Annunzio, Gabriele** 1863-1938 ... **TCLC 6, 40**
See also CA 104; 155

**Danois, N. le**
See Gourmont, Remy (-Marie-Charles) de

**Dante** 1265-1321 .... **CMLC 3, 18; DA; DAB; DAC; DAM MST, POET; PC 21; WLCS**
See also DA3

**d'Antibes, Germain**
See Simenon, Georges (Jacques Christian)

**Danticat, Edwidge** 1969- .................. **CLC 94**
See also AAYA 29; CA 152; CANR 73; MTCW 1

**Danvers, Dennis** 1947- ...................... **CLC 70**

**Danziger, Paula** 1944- ....................... **CLC 21**
See also AAYA 4; CA 112; 115; CANR 37; CLR 20; JRDA; MAICYA; SATA 36, 63, 102; SATA-Brief 30

**Da Ponte, Lorenzo** 1749-1838 ........ **NCLC 50**

**Dario, Ruben** 1867-1916 ....... **TCLC 4; DAM MULT; HLC 1; PC 15**
See also CA 131; CANR 81; HW 1, 2; MTCW 1, 2

**Darley, George** 1795-1846 ............... **NCLC 2**
See also DLB 96

**Darrow, Clarence (Seward)**
1857-1938 ........................................ **TCLC 81**
See also CA 164

**Darwin, Charles** 1809-1882 ........... **NCLC 57**
See also DLB 57, 166

**Daryush, Elizabeth** 1887-1977 ...... **CLC 6, 19**
See also CA 49-52; CANR 3, 81; DLB 20

**Dasgupta, Surendranath**
1887-1952 ........................................ **TCLC 81**
See also CA 157

**Dashwood, Edmee Elizabeth Monica de la Pasture** 1890-1943
See Delafield, E. M.
See also CA 119; 154

**Daudet, (Louis Marie) Alphonse** 1840-1897 **NCLC 1**
See also DLB 123

**Daumal, Rene** 1908-1944 ............... **TCLC 14**
See also CA 114

**Davenant, William** 1606-1668 ............. **LC 13**
See also DLB 58, 126

**Davenport, Guy (Mattison, Jr.)**
1927- ................. **CLC 6, 14, 38; SSC 16**
See also CA 33-36R; CANR 23, 73; DLB 130

**Davidson, Avram (James)** 1923-1993
See Queen, Ellery
See also CA 101; 171; CANR 26; DLB 8

**Davidson, Donald (Grady)**
1893-1968 ........................ **CLC 2, 13, 19**
See also CA 5-8R; 25-28R; CANR 4, 84; DLB 45

**Davidson, Hugh**
See Hamilton, Edmond

**Davidson, John** 1857-1909 ............. **TCLC 24**
See also CA 118; DLB 19

**Davidson, Sara** 1943- ......................... **CLC 9**
See also CA 81-84; CANR 44, 68; DLB 185

**Davie, Donald (Alfred)** 1922-1995 .... **CLC 5, 8, 10, 31; PC 29**
See also CA 1-4R; 149; CAAS 3; CANR 1, 44; DLB 27; MTCW 1

**Davies, Ray(mond Douglas)** 1944- ... **CLC 21**
See also CA 116; 146

**Davies, Rhys** 1901-1978 .................... **CLC 23**
See also CA 9-12R; 81-84; CANR 4; DLB 139, 191

**Davies, (William) Robertson**
1913-1995 ....... **CLC 2, 7, 13, 25, 42, 75, 91; DA; DAB; DAC; DAM MST, NOV, POP; WLC**
See also BEST 89:2; CA 33-36R; 150; CANR 17, 42; DA3; DLB 68; INT CANR-17; MTCW 1, 2

**Davies, Walter C.**
See Kornbluth, C(yril) M.

**Davies, William Henry** 1871-1940 ... **TCLC 5**
See also CA 104; 179; DLB 19, 174

**Davis, Angela (Yvonne)** 1944- ......... **CLC 77; DAM MULT**
See also BW 2, 3; CA 57-60; CANR 10, 81; DA3

**Davis, B. Lynch**
See Bioy Casares, Adolfo; Borges, Jorge Luis

**Davis, B. Lynch**
See Bioy Casares, Adolfo

**Davis, H(arold) L(enoir)** 1894-1960 . **CLC 49**
See also CA 178; 89-92; DLB 9, 206

**Davis, Rebecca (Blaine) Harding** 1831-1910 **TCLC 6; SSC 38**
See also CA 104; 179; DLB 74

**Davis, Richard Harding**
1864-1916 ........................................ **TCLC 24**
See also CA 114; 179; DLB 12, 23, 78, 79, 189; DLBD 13

**Davison, Frank Dalby** 1893-1970 ..... **CLC 15**
See also CA 116

**Davison, Lawrence H.**
See Lawrence, D(avid) H(erbert Richards)

**Davison, Peter (Hubert)** 1928- ......... **CLC 28**
See also CA 9-12R; CAAS 4; CANR 3, 43, 84; DLB 5

**Davys, Mary** 1674-1732 .................. **LC 1, 46**
See also DLB 39

**Dawson, Fielding** 1930- ...................... **CLC 6**
See also CA 85-88; DLB 130

**Dawson, Peter**
See Faust, Frederick (Schiller)

**Day, Clarence (Shepard, Jr.)** 1874-1935 **TCLC 25**
See also CA 108; DLB 11

**Day, Thomas** 1748-1789 ........................ **LC 1**
See also DLB 39; YABC 1

**Day Lewis, C(ecil)** 1904-1972 . **CLC 1, 6, 10; DAM POET; PC 11**
See also Blake, Nicholas CA 13-16; 33-36R; CANR 34; CAP 1; DLB 15, 20; MTCW 1, 2

**Dazai Osamu** 1909-1948 ................. **TCLC 11**
See also Tsushima, Shuji CA 164; DLB 182

**de Andrade, Carlos Drummond** 1892-1945
See Drummond de Andrade, Carlos

**Deane, Norman**
See Creasey, John

**Deane, Seamus (Francis)** 1940- ...... **CLC 122**
See also CA 118; CANR 42

**de Beauvoir, Simone (Lucie Ernestine Marie Bertrand)**
See Beauvoir, Simone (Lucie Ernestine Marie Bertrand) de

**de Beer, P.**
See Bosman, Herman Charles

**de Brissac, Malcolm**
See Dickinson, Peter (Malcolm)

**de Campos, Alvaro**
See Pessoa, Fernando (Antonio Nogueira)

**de Chardin, Pierre Teilhard**
See Teilhard de Chardin, (Marie Joseph) Pierre

**Dee, John** 1527-1608 ........................... **LC 20**

**Deer, Sandra** 1940- ............................ **CLC 45**

**De Ferrari, Gabriella** 1941- ............. **CLC 65**
See also CA 146

**Defoe, Daniel** 1660(?)-1731 .... **LC 1, 42; DA; DAB; DAC; DAM MST, NOV; WLC**
See also AAYA 27; CDBLB 1660-1789; CLR 61; DA3; DLB 39, 95, 101; JRDA; MAICYA; SATA 22

**de Gourmont, Remy(-Marie-Charles)**
See Gourmont, Remy (-Marie-Charles) de

**de Hartog, Jan** 1914- ......................... **CLC 19**
See also CA 1-4R; CANR 1

**de Hostos, E. M.**
See Hostos (y Bonilla), Eugenio Maria de

**de Hostos, Eugenio M.**
See Hostos (y Bonilla), Eugenio Maria de

**Deighton, Len** ..................... **CLC 4, 7, 22, 46**
See also Deighton, Leonard Cyril AAYA 6; BEST 89:2; CDBLB 1960 to Present; DLB 87

**Deighton, Leonard Cyril** 1929-
See Deighton, Len
See also CA 9-12R; CANR 19, 33, 68; DAM NOV, POP; DA3; MTCW 1, 2

**Dekker, Thomas** 1572(?)-1632 . **LC 22; DAM DRAM; DC 12**
See also CDBLB Before 1660; DLB 62, 172

**Delafield, E. M.** 1890-1943 ............. **TCLC 61**
See also Dashwood, Edmee Elizabeth Monica de la Pasture DLB 34

**de la Mare, Walter (John)**
1873-1956 ..... **TCLC 4, 53; DAB; DAC; DAM MST, POET; SSC 14; WLC**
See also CA 163; CDBLB 1914-1945; CLR 23; DA3; DLB 162; MTCW 1; SATA 16

**Delaney, Franey**
See O'Hara, John (Henry)

**Delaney, Shelagh** 1939- ......... **CLC 29; DAM DRAM**
See also CA 17-20R; CANR 30, 67; CDBLB 1960 to Present; DLB 13; MTCW 1

**Delany, Mary (Granville Pendarves)**
1700-1788 ...................................... LC 12
**Delany, Samuel R(ay, Jr.)** 1942- .. CLC 8, 14,
   38; BLC 1; DAM MULT
   See also AAYA 24; BW 2, 3; CA 81-84;
   CANR 27, 43; DLB 8, 33; MTCW 1, 2
**De La Ramee, (Marie) Louise** 1839-1908
   See Ouida
   See also SATA 20
**de la Roche, Mazo** 1879-1961 .......... CLC 14
   See also CA 85-88; CANR 30; DLB 68;
   SATA 64
**De La Salle, Innocent**
   See Hartmann, Sadakichi
**Delbanco, Nicholas (Franklin)**
   1942- ................................... CLC 6, 13
   See also CA 17-20R; CAAS 2; CANR 29,
   55; DLB 6
**del Castillo, Michel** 1933- ................ CLC 38
   See also CA 109; CANR 77
**Deledda, Grazia (Cosima)** 1875(?)-1936
   TCLC 23
   See also CA 123
**Delgado, Abelardo B(arrientos)** 1931-
   See also CA 131; CAAS 15; DAM MST,
   MULT; DLB 82; HLC 1; HW 1, 2
**Delibes, Miguel** ............................. CLC 8, 18
   See also Delibes Setien, Miguel
**Delibes Setien, Miguel** 1920-
   See Delibes, Miguel
   See also CA 45-48; CANR 1, 32; HW 1;
   MTCW 1
**DeLillo, Don** 1936- ..... CLC 8, 10, 13, 27, 39,
   54, 76; DAM NOV, POP
   See also BEST 89:1; CA 81-84; CANR 21,
   76; DA3; DLB 6, 173; MTCW 1, 2
**de Lisser, H. G.**
   See De Lisser, H(erbert) G(eorge)
   See also DLB 117
**De Lisser, H(erbert) G(eorge)** 1878-1944
   TCLC 12
   See also de Lisser, H. G. BW 2; CA 109;
   152
**Deloney, Thomas** 1560(?)-1600 ............ LC 41
   See also DLB 167
**Deloria, Vine (Victor), Jr.** 1933- ...... CLC 21,
   122; DAM MULT
   See also CA 53-56; CANR 5, 20, 48; DLB
   175; MTCW 1; NNAL; SATA 21
**Del Vecchio, John M(ichael)** 1947- .. CLC 29
   See also CA 110; DLBD 9
**de Man, Paul (Adolph Michel)** 1919-1983
   CLC 55
   See also CA 128; 111; CANR 61; DLB 67;
   MTCW 1, 2
**DeMarinis, Rick** 1934- ...................... CLC 54
   See also CA 57-60, 184; CAAE 184; CAAS
   24; CANR 9, 25, 50
**Dembry, R. Emmet**
   See Murfree, Mary Noailles
**Demby, William** 1922- ........ CLC 53; BLC 1;
   DAM MULT
   See also BW 1, 3; CA 81-84; CANR 81;
   DLB 33
**de Menton, Francisco**
   See Chin, Frank (Chew, Jr.)
**Demetrius of Phalerum** c.
   307B.C.- ................................. CMLC 34
**Demijohn, Thom**
   See Disch, Thomas M(ichael)
**de Molina, Tirso** 1580-1648
   See also HLCS 2
**de Montherlant, Henry (Milon)**
   See Montherlant, Henry (Milon) de
**Demosthenes** 384B.C.-322B.C. ...... CMLC 13
   See also DLB 176
**de Natale, Francine**
   See Malzberg, Barry N(athaniel)

**Denby, Edwin (Orr)** 1903-1983 ........ CLC 48
   See also CA 138; 110
**Denis, Julio**
   See Cortazar, Julio
**Denmark, Harrison**
   See Zelazny, Roger (Joseph)
**Dennis, John** 1658-1734 ....................... LC 11
   See also DLB 101
**Dennis, Nigel (Forbes)** 1912-1989 ...... CLC 8
   See also CA 25-28R; 129; DLB 13, 15;
   MTCW 1
**Dent, Lester** 1904(?)-1959 .............. TCLC 72
   See also CA 112; 161
**De Palma, Brian (Russell)** 1940- ...... CLC 20
   See also CA 109
**De Quincey, Thomas** 1785-1859 ...... NCLC 4
   See also CDBLB 1789-1832; DLB 110; 144
**Deren, Eleanora** 1908(?)-1961
   See Deren, Maya
   See also CA 111
**Deren, Maya** 1917-1961 ........... CLC 16, 102
   See also Deren, Eleanora
**Derleth, August (William)**
   1909-1971 ............................... CLC 31
   See also CA 1-4R; 29-32R; CANR 4; DLB
   9; DLBD 17; SATA 5
**Der Nister** 1884-1950 ..................... TCLC 56
**de Routisie, Albert**
   See Aragon, Louis
**Derrida, Jacques** 1930- .............. CLC 24, 87
   See also CA 124; 127; CANR 76; MTCW 1
**Derry Down Derry**
   See Lear, Edward
**Dersonnes, Jacques**
   See Simenon, Georges (Jacques Christian)
**Desai, Anita** 1937- ..... CLC 19, 37, 97; DAB;
   DAM NOV
   See also CA 81-84; CANR 33, 53; DA3;
   MTCW 1, 2; SATA 63
**Desai, Kiran** 1971- .......................... CLC 119
   See also CA 171
**de Saint-Luc, Jean**
   See Glassco, John
**de Saint Roman, Arnaud**
   See Aragon, Louis
**Descartes, Rene** 1596-1650 ............ LC 20, 35
**De Sica, Vittorio** 1901(?)-1974 ......... CLC 20
   See also CA 117
**Desnos, Robert** 1900-1945 .............. TCLC 22
   See also CA 121; 151
**Destouches, Louis-Ferdinand**
   1894-1961 ............................... CLC 9, 15
   See also Celine, Louis-Ferdinand CA 85-
   88; CANR 28; MTCW 1
**de Tolignac, Gaston**
   See Griffith, D(avid Lewelyn) W(ark)
**Deutsch, Babette** 1895-1982 .............. CLC 18
   See also CA 1-4R; 108; CANR 4, 79; DLB
   45; SATA 1; SATA-Obit 33
**Devenant, William** 1606-1649 ............. LC 13
**Devkota, Laxmiprasad** 1909-1959 . TCLC 23
   See also CA 123
**De Voto, Bernard (Augustine)** 1897-1955
   TCLC 29
   See also CA 113; 160; DLB 9
**De Vries, Peter** 1910-1993 ..... CLC 1, 2, 3, 7,
   10, 28, 46; DAM NOV
   See also CA 17-20R; 142; CANR 41; DLB
   6; DLBY 82; MTCW 1, 2
**Dewey, John** 1859-1952 ................. TCLC 95
   See also CA 114; 170
**Dexter, John**
   See Bradley, Marion Zimmer
**Dexter, Martin**
   See Faust, Frederick (Schiller)
**Dexter, Pete** 1943- .. CLC 34, 55; DAM POP
   See also BEST 89:2; CA 127; 131; INT 131;
   MTCW 1

**Diamano, Silmang**
   See Senghor, Leopold Sedar
**Diamond, Neil** 1941- ......................... CLC 30
   See also CA 108
**Diaz del Castillo, Bernal** 1496-1584 .. LC 31;
   HLCS 1
**di Bassetto, Corno**
   See Shaw, George Bernard
**Dick, Philip K(indred)** 1928-1982 ... CLC 10,
   30, 72; DAM NOV, POP
   See also AAYA 24; CA 49-52; 106; CANR
   2, 16; DA3; DLB 8; MTCW 1, 2
**Dickens, Charles (John Huffam)** 1812-1870
   NCLC 3, 8, 18, 26, 37, 50; DA; DAB;
   DAC; DAM MST, NOV; SSC 17; WLC
   See also AAYA 23; CDBLB 1832-1890;
   DA3; DLB 21, 55, 70, 159, 166; JRDA;
   MAICYA; SATA 15
**Dickey, James (Lafayette)**
   1923-1997 .... CLC 1, 2, 4, 7, 10, 15, 47,
   109; DAM NOV, POET, POP
   See also AITN 1, 2; CA 9-12R; 156; CABS
   2; CANR 10, 48, 61; CDALB 1968-1988;
   DA3; DLB 5, 193; DLBD 7; DLBY 82,
   93, 96, 97, 98; INT CANR-10; MTCW 1,
   2
**Dickey, William** 1928-1994 .......... CLC 3, 28
   See also CA 9-12R; 145; CANR 24, 79;
   DLB 5
**Dickinson, Charles** 1951- ................. CLC 49
   See also CA 128
**Dickinson, Emily (Elizabeth)** 1830-1886
   NCLC 21, 77; DA; DAB; DAC; DAM
   MST, POET; PC 1; WLC
   See also AAYA 22; CDALB 1865-1917;
   DA3; DLB 1; SATA 29
**Dickinson, Peter (Malcolm)** 1927- .. CLC 12,
   35
   See also AAYA 9; CA 41-44R; CANR 31,
   58, 88; CLR 29; DLB 87, 161; JRDA;
   MAICYA; SATA 5, 62, 95
**Dickson, Carr**
   See Carr, John Dickson
**Dickson, Carter**
   See Carr, John Dickson
**Diderot, Denis** 1713-1784 ................... LC 26
**Didion, Joan** 1934- ......... CLC 1, 3, 8, 14, 32,
   129; DAM NOV
   See also AITN 1; CA 5-8R; CANR 14, 52,
   76; CDALB 1968-1988; DA3; DLB 2,
   173, 185; DLBY 81, 86; MTCW 1, 2
**Dietrich, Robert**
   See Hunt, E(verette) Howard, (Jr.)
**Difusa, Pati**
   See Almodovar, Pedro
**Dillard, Annie** 1945- .. CLC 9, 60, 115; DAM
   NOV
   See also AAYA 6; CA 49-52; CANR 3, 43,
   62; DA3; DLBY 80; MTCW 1, 2; SATA
   10
**Dillard, R(ichard) H(enry) W(ilde)** 1937-
   CLC 5
   See also CA 21-24R; CAAS 7; CANR 10;
   DLB 5
**Dillon, Eilis** 1920-1994 ..................... CLC 17
   See also CA 9-12R, 182; 147; CAAE 182;
   CAAS 3; CANR 4, 38, 78; CLR 26; MAI-
   CYA; SATA 2, 74; SATA-Essay 105;
   SATA-Obit 83
**Dimont, Penelope**
   See Mortimer, Penelope (Ruth)
**Dinesen, Isak** ............ CLC 10, 29, 95; SSC 7
   See also Blixen, Karen (Christentze
   Dinesen) MTCW 1
**Ding Ling** .......................................... CLC 68
   See also Chiang, Pin-chin
**Diphusa, Patty**
   See Almodovar, Pedro

**Disch, Thomas M(ichael)** 1940- ... **CLC 7, 36**
    See also AAYA 17; CA 21-24R; CAAS 4;
    CANR 17, 36, 54; CLR 18; DA3; DLB 8;
    MAICYA; MTCW 1, 2; SAAS 15; SATA
    92
**Disch, Tom**
    See Disch, Thomas M(ichael)
**d'Isly, Georges**
    See Simenon, Georges (Jacques Christian)
**Disraeli, Benjamin** 1804-1881 ... **NCLC 2, 39,**
    **79**
    See also DLB 21, 55
**Ditcum, Steve**
    See Crumb, R(obert)
**Dixon, Paige**
    See Corcoran, Barbara
**Dixon, Stephen** 1936- ......... **CLC 52; SSC 16**
    See also CA 89-92; CANR 17, 40, 54; DLB
    130
**Doak, Annie**
    See Dillard, Annie
**Dobell, Sydney Thompson**
    1824-1874 ................................ **NCLC 43**
    See also DLB 32
**Doblin, Alfred** ................................ **TCLC 13**
    See also Doeblin, Alfred
**Dobrolyubov, Nikolai Alexandrovich**
    1836-1861 ................................... **NCLC 5**
**Dobson, Austin** 1840-1921 .............. **TCLC 79**
    See also DLB 35; 144
**Dobyns, Stephen** 1941- ...................... **CLC 37**
    See also CA 45-48; CANR 2, 18
**Doctorow, E(dgar) L(aurence)**
    1931- ....... **CLC 6, 11, 15, 18, 37, 44, 65,**
    **113; DAM NOV, POP**
    See also AAYA 22; AITN 2; BEST 89:3;
    CA 45-48; CANR 2, 33, 51, 76; CDALB
    1968-1988; DA3; DLB 2, 28, 173; DLBY
    80; MTCW 1, 2
**Dodgson, Charles Lutwidge** 1832-1898
    See Carroll, Lewis
    See also CLR 2; DA; DAB; DAC; DAM
    MST, NOV, POET; DA3; MAICYA;
    SATA 100; YABC 2
**Dodson, Owen (Vincent)**
    1914-1983 ......... **CLC 79; BLC 1; DAM**
    **MULT**
    See also BW 1; CA 65-68; 110; CANR 24;
    DLB 76
**Doeblin, Alfred** 1878-1957 .............. **TCLC 13**
    See also Doblin, Alfred CA 110; 141; DLB
    66
**Doerr, Harriet** 1910- ........................... **CLC 34**
    See also CA 117; 122; CANR 47; INT 122
**Domecq, H(onorio Bustos)**
    See Bioy Casares, Adolfo
**Domecq, H(onorio) Bustos**
    See Bioy Casares, Adolfo; Borges, Jorge
    Luis
**Domini, Rey**
    See Lorde, Audre (Geraldine)
**Dominique**
    See Proust, (Valentin-Louis-George-
    Eugene-) Marcel
**Don, A**
    See Stephen, SirLeslie
**Donaldson, Stephen R.** 1947- ......... **CLC 46;**
    **DAM POP**
    See also CA 89-92; CANR 13, 55; INT
    CANR-13
**Donleavy, J(ames) P(atrick)** 1926- .... **CLC 1,**
    **4, 6, 10, 45**
    See also AITN 2; CA 9-12R; CANR 24, 49,
    62, 80; DLB 6, 173; INT CANR-24;
    MTCW 1, 2

**Donne, John** 1572-1631 ........ **LC 10, 24; DA;**
    **DAB; DAC; DAM MST, POET; PC 1;**
    **WLC**
    See also CDBLB Before 1660; DLB 121,
    151
**Donnell, David** 1939(?)- ...................... **CLC 34**
**Donoghue, P. S.**
    See Hunt, E(verette) Howard, (Jr.)
**Donoso (Yanez), Jose** 1924-1996 ... **CLC 4, 8,**
    **11, 32, 99; DAM MULT; HLC 1; SSC**
    **34**
    See also CA 81-84; 155; CANR 32, 73;
    DLB 113; HW 1, 2; MTCW 1, 2
**Donovan, John** 1928-1992 ................. **CLC 35**
    See also AAYA 20; CA 97-100; 137; CLR
    3; MAICYA; SATA 72; SATA-Brief 29
**Don Roberto**
    See Cunninghame Graham, Robert
    (Gallnigad) Bontine
**Doolittle, Hilda** 1886-1961 . **CLC 3, 8, 14, 31,**
    **34, 73; DA; DAC; DAM MST, POET;**
    **PC 5; WLC**
    See also H. D. CA 97-100; CANR 35; DLB
    4, 45; MTCW 1, 2
**Dorfman, Ariel** 1942- ...... **CLC 48, 77; DAM**
    **MULT; HLC 1**
    See also CA 124; 130; CANR 67, 70; HW
    1, 2; INT 130
**Dorn, Edward (Merton)** 1929- ... **CLC 10, 18**
    See also CA 93-96; CANR 42, 79; DLB 5;
    INT 93-96
**Dorris, Michael (Anthony)**
    1945-1997 ........ **CLC 109; DAM MULT,**
    **NOV**
    See also AAYA 20; BEST 90:1; CA 102;
    157; CANR 19, 46, 75; CLR 58; DA3;
    DLB 175; MTCW 2; NNAL; SATA 75;
    SATA-Obit 94
**Dorris, Michael A.**
    See Dorris, Michael (Anthony)
**Dorsan, Luc**
    See Simenon, Georges (Jacques Christian)
**Dorsange, Jean**
    See Simenon, Georges (Jacques Christian)
**Dos Passos, John (Roderigo)**
    1896-1970 ... **CLC 1, 4, 8, 11, 15, 25, 34,**
    **82; DA; DAB; DAC; DAM MST, NOV;**
    **WLC**
    See also CA 1-4R; 29-32R; CANR 3;
    CDALB 1929-1941; DA3; DLB 4, 9;
    DLBD 1, 15; DLBY 96; MTCW 1, 2
**Dossage, Jean**
    See Simenon, Georges (Jacques Christian)
**Dostoevsky, Fedor Mikhailovich** 1821-1881
    **NCLC 2, 7, 21, 33, 43; DA; DAB; DAC;**
    **DAM MST, NOV; SSC 2, 33; WLC**
    See also DA3
**Doughty, Charles M(ontagu)** 1843-1926
    **TCLC 27**
    See also CA 115; 178; DLB 19, 57, 174
**Douglas, Ellen** .................................. **CLC 73**
    See also Haxton, Josephine Ayres; William-
    son, Ellen Douglas
**Douglas, Gavin** 1475(?)-1522 .............. **LC 20**
    See also DLB 132
**Douglas, George**
    See Brown, George Douglas
**Douglas, Keith (Castellain)**
    1920-1944 ................................ **TCLC 40**
    See also CA 160; DLB 27
**Douglas, Leonard**
    See Bradbury, Ray (Douglas)
**Douglas, Michael**
    See Crichton, (John) Michael
**Douglas, (George) Norman**
    1868-1952 ................................ **TCLC 68**
    See also CA 119; 157; DLB 34, 195
**Douglas, William**
    See Brown, George Douglas

**Douglass, Frederick** 1817(?)-1895 .. **NCLC 7,**
    **55; BLC 1; DA; DAC; DAM MST,**
    **MULT; WLC**
    See also CDALB 1640-1865; DA3; DLB 1,
    43, 50, 79; SATA 29
**Dourado, (Waldomiro Freitas) Autran** 1926-
    **CLC 23, 60**
    See also CA 25-28R; 179; CANR 34, 81;
    DLB 145; HW 2
**Dourado, Waldomiro Autran** 1926-
    See Dourado, (Waldomiro Freitas) Autran
    See also CA 179
**Dove, Rita (Frances)** 1952- ........ **CLC 50, 81;**
    **BLCS; DAM MULT, POET; PC 6**
    See also BW 2; CA 109; CAAS 19; CANR
    27, 42, 68, 76; CDALBS; DA3; DLB 120;
    MTCW 1
**Doveglion**
    See Villa, Jose Garcia
**Dowell, Coleman** 1925-1985 .............. **CLC 60**
    See also CA 25-28R; 117; CANR 10; DLB
    130
**Dowson, Ernest (Christopher)** 1867-1900
    **TCLC 4**
    See also CA 105; 150; DLB 19, 135
**Doyle, A. Conan**
    See Doyle, Arthur Conan
**Doyle, Arthur Conan** 1859-1930 .... **TCLC 7;**
    **DA; DAB; DAC; DAM MST, NOV;**
    **SSC 12; WLC**
    See also AAYA 14; CA 104; 122; CDBLB
    1890-1914; DA3; DLB 18, 70, 156, 178;
    MTCW 1, 2; SATA 24
**Doyle, Conan**
    See Doyle, Arthur Conan
**Doyle, John**
    See Graves, Robert (von Ranke)
**Doyle, Roddy** 1958(?)- ...................... **CLC 81**
    See also AAYA 14; CA 143; CANR 73;
    DA3; DLB 194
**Doyle, Sir A. Conan**
    See Doyle, Arthur Conan
**Doyle, Sir Arthur Conan**
    See Doyle, Arthur Conan
**Dr. A**
    See Asimov, Isaac; Silverstein, Alvin
**Drabble, Margaret** 1939- ...... **CLC 2, 3, 5, 8,**
    **10, 22, 53, 129; DAB; DAC; DAM**
    **MST, NOV, POP**
    See also CA 13-16R; CANR 18, 35, 63;
    CDBLB 1960 to Present; DA3; DLB 14,
    155; MTCW 1, 2; SATA 48
**Drapier, M. B.**
    See Swift, Jonathan
**Drayham, James**
    See Mencken, H(enry) L(ouis)
**Drayton, Michael** 1563-1631 ..... **LC 8; DAM**
    **POET**
    See also DLB 121
**Dreadstone, Carl**
    See Campbell, (John) Ramsey
**Dreiser, Theodore (Herman Albert)**
    1871-1945 .... **TCLC 10, 18, 35, 83; DA;**
    **DAC; DAM MST, NOV; SSC 30; WLC**
    See also CA 106; 132; CDALB 1865-1917;
    DA3; DLB 9, 12, 102, 137; DLBD 1;
    MTCW 1, 2
**Drexler, Rosalyn** 1926- .................... **CLC 2, 6**
    See also CA 81-84; CANR 68
**Dreyer, Carl Theodor** 1889-1968 ...... **CLC 16**
    See also CA 116
**Drieu la Rochelle, Pierre(-Eugene)**
    1893-1945 ................................ **TCLC 21**
    See also CA 117; DLB 72
**Drinkwater, John** 1882-1937 ......... **TCLC 57**
    See also CA 109; 149; DLB 10, 19, 149
**Drop Shot**
    See Cable, George Washington

**Droste-Hulshoff, Annette Freiin von**
1797-1848 ........................ NCLC 3
See also DLB 133

**Drummond, Walter**
See Silverberg, Robert

**Drummond, William Henry**
1854-1907 ............................ TCLC 25
See also CA 160; DLB 92

**Drummond de Andrade, Carlos** 1902-1987
**CLC 18**
See also Andrade, Carlos Drummond de CA
132; 123

**Drury, Allen (Stuart)** 1918-1998 ....... CLC 37
See also CA 57-60; 170; CANR 18, 52; INT
CANR-18

**Dryden, John** 1631-1700 ........ LC 3, 21; DA;
**DAB; DAC; DAM DRAM, MST,**
**POET; DC 3; PC 25; WLC**
See also CDBLB 1660-1789; DLB 80, 101,
131

**Duberman, Martin (Bauml)** 1930- ..... CLC 8
See also CA 1-4R; CANR 2, 63

**Dubie, Norman (Evans)** 1945- .......... CLC 36
See also CA 69-72; CANR 12; DLB 120

**Du Bois, W(illiam) E(dward) B(urghardt)**
1868-1963 ... CLC 1, 2, 13, 64, 96; BLC
1; DA; DAC; DAM MST, MULT,
NOV; WLC
See also BW 1, 3; CA 85-88; CANR 34,
82; CDALB 1865-1917; DA3; DLB 47,
50, 91; MTCW 1, 2; SATA 42

**Dubus, Andre** 1936-1999 ..... CLC 13, 36, 97;
**SSC 15**
See also CA 21-24R; 177; CANR 17; DLB
130; INT CANR-17

**Duca Minimo**
See D'Annunzio, Gabriele

**Ducharme, Rejean** 1941- .................... CLC 74
See also CA 165; DLB 60

**Duclos, Charles Pinot** 1704-1772 .......... LC 1

**Dudek, Louis** 1918- ...................... CLC 11, 19
See also CA 45-48; CAAS 14; CANR 1;
DLB 88

**Duerrenmatt, Friedrich** 1921-1990 ... CLC 1,
4, 8, 11, 15, 43, 102; DAM DRAM
See also CA 17-20R; CANR 33; DLB 69,
124; MTCW 1, 2

**Duffy, Bruce** 1953(?)- ......................... CLC 50
See also CA 172

**Duffy, Maureen** 1933- ........................ CLC 37
See also CA 25-28R; CANR 33, 68; DLB
14; MTCW 1

**Dugan, Alan** 1923- ........................... CLC 2, 6
See also CA 81-84; DLB 5

**du Gard, Roger Martin**
See Martin du Gard, Roger

**Duhamel, Georges** 1884-1966 ............. CLC 8
See also CA 81-84; 25-28R; CANR 35;
DLB 65; MTCW 1

**Dujardin, Edouard (Emile Louis)** 1861-1949
TCLC 13
See also CA 109; DLB 123

**Dulles, John Foster** 1888-1959 ....... TCLC 72
See also CA 115; 149

**Dumas, Alexandre (pere)**
See Dumas, Alexandre (Davy de la
Pailleterie)

**Dumas, Alexandre (Davy de la Pailleterie)**
1802-1870 ...... NCLC 11, 71; DA; DAB;
DAC; DAM MST, NOV; WLC
See also DA3; DLB 119, 192; SATA 18

**Dumas, Alexandre (fils)**
1824-1895 ...................... NCLC 71; DC 1
See also AAYA 22; DLB 192

**Dumas, Claudine**
See Malzberg, Barry N(athaniel)

**Dumas, Henry L.** 1934-1968 ........ CLC 6, 62
See also BW 1; CA 85-88; DLB 41

**du Maurier, Daphne** 1907-1989 .. CLC 6, 11,
59; DAB; DAC; DAM MST, POP; SSC
18
See also CA 5-8R; 128; CANR 6, 55; DA3;
DLB 191; MTCW 1, 2; SATA 27; SATA-
Obit 60

**Dunbar, Paul Laurence** 1872-1906 . TCLC 2,
12; BLC 1; DA; DAC; DAM MST,
MULT, POET; PC 5; SSC 8; WLC
See also BW 1, 3; CA 104; 124; CANR 79;
CDALB 1865-1917; DA3; DLB 50, 54,
78; SATA 34

**Dunbar, William** 1460(?)-1530(?) ........ LC 20
See also DLB 132, 146

**Duncan, Dora Angela**
See Duncan, Isadora

**Duncan, Isadora** 1877(?)-1927 ....... TCLC 68
See also CA 118; 149

**Duncan, Lois** 1934- ............................ CLC 26
See also AAYA 4; CA 1-4R; CANR 2, 23,
36; CLR 29; JRDA; MAICYA; SAAS 2;
SATA 1, 36, 75

**Duncan, Robert (Edward)**
1919-1988 .... CLC 1, 2, 4, 7, 15, 41, 55;
DAM POET; PC 2
See also CA 9-12R; 124; CANR 28, 62;
DLB 5, 16, 193; MTCW 1, 2

**Duncan, Sara Jeannette**
1861-1922 ............................ TCLC 60
See also CA 157; DLB 92

**Dunlap, William** 1766-1839 ............. NCLC 2
See also DLB 30, 37, 59

**Dunn, Douglas (Eaglesham)** 1942- .... CLC 6,
40
See also CA 45-48; CANR 2, 33; DLB 40;
MTCW 1

**Dunn, Katherine (Karen)** 1945- ....... CLC 71
See also CA 33-36R; CANR 72; MTCW 1

**Dunn, Stephen** 1939- ......................... CLC 36
See also CA 33-36R; CANR 12, 48, 53;
DLB 105

**Dunne, Finley Peter** 1867-1936 ...... TCLC 28
See also CA 108; 178; DLB 11, 23

**Dunne, John Gregory** 1932- ............. CLC 28
See also CA 25-28R; CANR 14, 50; DLBY
80

**Dunsany, Edward John Moreton Drax**
**Plunkett** 1878-1957
See Dunsany, Lord
See also CA 104; 148; DLB 10; MTCW 1

**Dunsany, Lord** ............................. TCLC 2, 59
See also Dunsany, Edward John Moreton
Drax Plunkett DLB 77, 153, 156

**du Perry, Jean**
See Simenon, Georges (Jacques Christian)

**Durang, Christopher (Ferdinand)**
1949- ................................... CLC 27, 38
See also CA 105; CANR 50, 76; MTCW 1

**Duras, Marguerite** 1914-1996 . CLC 3, 6, 11,
20, 34, 40, 68, 100
See also CA 25-28R; 151; CANR 50; DLB
83; MTCW 1, 2

**Durban, (Rosa) Pam** 1947- .............. CLC 39
See also CA 123

**Durcan, Paul** 1944- ......... CLC 43, 70; DAM
**POET**
See also CA 134

**Durkheim, Emile** 1858-1917 .......... TCLC 55

**Durrell, Lawrence (George)**
1912-1990 .... CLC 1, 4, 6, 8, 13, 27, 41;
DAM NOV
See also CA 9-12R; 132; CANR 40, 77;
CDBLB 1945-1960; DLB 15, 27, 204;
DLBY 90; MTCW 1, 2

**Durrenmatt, Friedrich**
See Duerrenmatt, Friedrich

**Dutt, Toru** 1856-1877 ...................... NCLC 29

**Dwight, Timothy** 1752-1817 .......... NCLC 13
See also DLB 37

**Dworkin, Andrea** 1946- ..................... CLC 43
See also CA 77-80; CAAS 21; CANR 16,
39, 76; INT CANR-16; MTCW 1, 2

**Dwyer, Deanna**
See Koontz, Dean R(ay)

**Dwyer, K. R.**
See Koontz, Dean R(ay)

**Dwyer, Thomas A.** 1923- ................. CLC 114
See also CA 115

**Dye, Richard**
See De Voto, Bernard (Augustine)

**Dylan, Bob** 1941- ........... CLC 3, 4, 6, 12, 77
See also CA 41-44R; DLB 16

**E. V. L.**
See Lucas, E(dward) V(errall)

**Eagleton, Terence (Francis)** 1943-
See Eagleton, Terry
See also CA 57-60; CANR 7, 23, 68;
MTCW 1, 2

**Eagleton, Terry** ................................... CLC 63
See also Eagleton, Terence (Francis) MTCW
1

**Early, Jack**
See Scoppettone, Sandra

**East, Michael**
See West, Morris L(anglo)

**Eastaway, Edward**
See Thomas, (Philip) Edward

**Eastlake, William (Derry)**
1917-1997 ................................. CLC 8
See also CA 5-8R; 158; CAAS 1; CANR 5,
63; DLB 6, 206; INT CANR-5

**Eastman, Charles A(lexander)** 1858-1939
TCLC 55; DAM MULT
See also CA 179; DLB 175; NNAL; YABC
1

**Eberhart, Richard (Ghormley)**
1904- .. CLC 3, 11, 19, 56; DAM POET
See also CA 1-4R; CANR 2; CDALB 1941-
1968; DLB 48; MTCW 1

**Eberstadt, Fernanda** 1960- .............. CLC 39
See also CA 136; CANR 69

**Echegaray (y Eizaguirre), Jose (Maria**
**Waldo)** 1832-1916 .... TCLC 4; HLCS 1
See also CA 104; CANR 32; HW 1; MTCW
1

**Echeverria, (Jose) Esteban (Antonino)**
1805-1851 ................................. NCLC 18

**Echo**
See Proust, (Valentin-Louis-George-
Eugene-) Marcel

**Eckert, Allan W.** 1931- ..................... CLC 17
See also AAYA 18; CA 13-16R; CANR 14,
45; INT CANR-14; SAAS 21; SATA 29,
91; SATA-Brief 27

**Eckhart, Meister** 1260(?)-1328(?) ... CMLC 9
See also DLB 115

**Eckmar, F. R.**
See de Hartog, Jan

**Eco, Umberto** 1932- ........ CLC 28, 60; DAM
**NOV, POP**
See also BEST 90:1; CA 77-80; CANR 12,
33, 55; DA3; DLB 196; MTCW 1, 2

**Eddison, E(ric) R(ucker)**
1882-1945 ............................ TCLC 15
See also CA 109; 156

**Eddy, Mary (Ann Morse) Baker** 1821-1910
TCLC 71
See also CA 113; 174

**Edel, (Joseph) Leon** 1907-1997 .. CLC 29, 34
See also CA 1-4R; 161; CANR 1, 22; DLB
103; INT CANR-22

**Eden, Emily** 1797-1869 .................. NCLC 10

**Edgar, David** 1948- .. CLC 42; DAM DRAM
See also CA 57-60; CANR 12, 61; DLB 13;
MTCW 1

**Edgerton, Clyde (Carlyle)** 1944- ...... CLC 39
See also AAYA 17; CA 118; 134; CANR
64; INT 134

**Edgeworth, Maria** 1768-1849 .... **NCLC 1, 51**
　See also DLB 116, 159, 163; SATA 21
**Edison, Thomas** 1847-1931 ............. **TCLC 96**
**Edmonds, Paul**
　See Kuttner, Henry
**Edmonds, Walter D(umaux)**
　1903-1998 ................................. **CLC 35**
　See also CA 5-8R; CANR 2; DLB 9; MAI-
　CYA; SAAS 4; SATA 1, 27; SATA-Obit
　99
**Edmondson, Wallace**
　See Ellison, Harlan (Jay)
**Edson, Russell** ............................ **CLC 13**
　See also CA 33-36R
**Edwards, Bronwen Elizabeth**
　See Rose, Wendy
**Edwards, G(erald) B(asil)**
　1899-1976 .................................. **CLC 25**
　See also CA 110
**Edwards, Gus** 1939- ..................... **CLC 43**
　See also CA 108; INT 108
**Edwards, Jonathan** 1703-1758 ....... **LC 7, 54;**
　**DA; DAC; DAM MST**
　See also DLB 24
**Efron, Marina Ivanovna Tsvetaeva**
　See Tsvetaeva (Efron), Marina (Ivanovna)
**Ehle, John (Marsden, Jr.)** 1925- ...... **CLC 27**
　See also CA 9-12R
**Ehrenbourg, Ilya (Grigoryevich)**
　See Ehrenburg, Ilya (Grigoryevich)
**Ehrenburg, Ilya (Grigoryevich)** 1891-1967
　**CLC 18, 34, 62**
　See also CA 102; 25-28R
**Ehrenburg, Ilyo (Grigoryevich)**
　See Ehrenburg, Ilya (Grigoryevich)
**Ehrenreich, Barbara** 1941- ............. **CLC 110**
　See also BEST 90:4; CA 73-76; CANR 16,
　37, 62; MTCW 1, 2
**Eich, Guenter** 1907-1972 ................. **CLC 15**
　See also CA 111; 93-96; DLB 69, 124
**Eichendorff, Joseph Freiherr von** 1788-1857
　**NCLC 8**
　See also DLB 90
**Eigner, Larry** ........................................ **CLC 9**
　See also Eigner, Laurence (Joel) CAAS 23;
　DLB 5
**Eigner, Laurence (Joel)** 1927-1996
　See Eigner, Larry
　See also CA 9-12R; 151; CANR 6, 84; DLB
　193
**Einstein, Albert** 1879-1955 ............. **TCLC 65**
　See also CA 121; 133; MTCW 1, 2
**Eiseley, Loren Corey** 1907-1977 ........ **CLC 7**
　See also AAYA 5; CA 1-4R; 73-76; CANR
　6; DLBD 17
**Eisenstadt, Jill** 1963- ........................ **CLC 50**
　See also CA 140
**Eisenstein, Sergei (Mikhailovich)** 1898-1948
　**TCLC 57**
　See also CA 114; 149
**Eisner, Simon**
　See Kornbluth, C(yril) M.
**Ekeloef, (Bengt) Gunnar**
　1907-1968 ... **CLC 27; DAM POET; PC
　23**
　See also CA 123; 25-28R
**Ekelof, (Bengt) Gunnar**
　See Ekeloef, (Bengt) Gunnar
**Ekelund, Vilhelm** 1880-1949 .......... **TCLC 75**
**Ekwensi, C. O. D.**
　See Ekwensi, Cyprian (Odiatu Duaka)
**Ekwensi, Cyprian (Odiatu Duaka)** 1921-
　**CLC 4; BLC 1; DAM MULT**
　See also BW 2, 3; CA 29-32R; CANR 18,
　42, 74; DLB 117; MTCW 1, 2; SATA 66
**Elaine** ................................................. **TCLC 18**
　See also Leverson, Ada

**El Crummo**
　See Crumb, R(obert)
**Elder, Lonne III** 1931-1996 .................. **DC 8**
　See also BLC 1; BW 1, 3; CA 81-84; 152;
　CANR 25; DAM MULT; DLB 7, 38, 44
**Elia**
　See Lamb, Charles
**Eliade, Mircea** 1907-1986 .................. **CLC 19**
　See also CA 65-68; 119; CANR 30, 62;
　MTCW 1
**Eliot, A. D.**
　See Jewett, (Theodora) Sarah Orne
**Eliot, Alice**
　See Jewett, (Theodora) Sarah Orne
**Eliot, Dan**
　See Silverberg, Robert
**Eliot, George** 1819-1880 ...... **NCLC 4, 13, 23,
　41, 49; DA; DAB; DAC; DAM MST,
　NOV; PC 20; WLC**
　See also CDBLB 1832-1890; DA3; DLB
　21, 35, 55
**Eliot, John** 1604-1690 ............................ **LC 5**
　See also DLB 24
**Eliot, T(homas) S(tearns)**
　1888-1965 ...... **CLC 1, 2, 3, 6, 9, 10, 13,
　15, 24, 34, 41, 55, 57, 113; DA; DAB;
　DAC; DAM DRAM, MST, POET; PC
　5; WLC**
　See also AAYA 28; CA 5-8R; 25-28R;
　CANR 41; CDALB 1929-1941; DA3;
　DLB 7, 10, 45, 63; DLBY 88; MTCW 1,
　2
**Elizabeth** 1866-1941 ....................... **TCLC 41**
**Elkin, Stanley L(awrence)**
　1930-1995 .. **CLC 4, 6, 9, 14, 27, 51, 91;
　DAM NOV, POP; SSC 12**
　See also CA 9-12R; 148; CANR 8, 46; DLB
　2, 28; DLBY 80; INT CANR-8; MTCW
　1, 2
**Elledge, Scott** ..................................... **CLC 34**
**Elliot, Don**
　See Silverberg, Robert
**Elliott, Don**
　See Silverberg, Robert
**Elliott, George P(aul)** 1918-1980 ........ **CLC 2**
　See also CA 1-4R; 97-100; CANR 2
**Elliott, Janice** 1931- ........................... **CLC 47**
　See also CA 13-16R; CANR 8, 29, 84; DLB
　14
**Elliott, Sumner Locke** 1917-1991 ..... **CLC 38**
　See also CA 5-8R; 134; CANR 2, 21
**Elliott, William**
　See Bradbury, Ray (Douglas)
**Ellis, A. E.** ........................................... **CLC 7**
**Ellis, Alice Thomas** .......................... **CLC 40**
　See also Haycraft, Anna DLB 194; MTCW
　1
**Ellis, Bret Easton** 1964- ..... **CLC 39, 71, 117;
　DAM POP**
　See also AAYA 2; CA 118; 123; CANR 51,
　74; DA3; INT 123; MTCW 1
**Ellis, (Henry) Havelock**
　1859-1939 .................................... **TCLC 14**
　See also CA 109; 169; DLB 190
**Ellis, Landon**
　See Ellison, Harlan (Jay)
**Ellis, Trey** 1962- ................................. **CLC 55**
　See also CA 146
**Ellison, Harlan (Jay)** 1934- ... **CLC 1, 13, 42;
　DAM POP; SSC 14**
　See also AAYA 29; CA 5-8R; CANR 5, 46;
　DLB 8; INT CANR-5; MTCW 1, 2
**Ellison, Ralph (Waldo)** 1914-1994 .... **CLC 1,
　3, 11, 54, 86, 114; BLC 1; DA; DAB;
　DAC; DAM MST, MULT, NOV; SSC
　26; WLC**
　See also AAYA 19; BW 1, 3; CA 9-12R;
　145; CANR 24, 53; CDALB 1941-1968;
　DA3; DLB 2, 76; DLBY 94; MTCW 1, 2

**Ellmann, Lucy (Elizabeth)** 1956- ..... **CLC 61**
　See also CA 128
**Ellmann, Richard (David)**
　1918-1987 ................................. **CLC 50**
　See also BEST 89:2; CA 1-4R; 122; CANR
　2, 28, 61; DLB 103; DLBY 87; MTCW
　1, 2
**Elman, Richard (Martin)**
　1934-1997 ................................. **CLC 19**
　See also CA 17-20R; 163; CAAS 3; CANR
　47
**Elron**
　See Hubbard, L(afayette) Ron(ald)
**Eluard, Paul** ................................. **TCLC 7, 41**
　See also Grindel, Eugene
**Elyot, Sir Thomas** 1490(?)-1546 ......... **LC 11**
**Elytis, Odysseus** 1911-1996 ........ **CLC 15, 49,
　100; DAM POET; PC 21**
　See also CA 102; 151; MTCW 1, 2
**Emecheta, (Florence Onye) Buchi**
　1944- .. **CLC 14, 48, 128; BLC 2; DAM
　MULT**
　See also BW 2, 3; CA 81-84; CANR 27,
　81; DA3; DLB 117; MTCW 1, 2; SATA
　66
**Emerson, Mary Moody**
　1774-1863 ................................ **NCLC 66**
**Emerson, Ralph Waldo** 1803-1882 . **NCLC 1,
　38; DA; DAB; DAC; DAM MST,
　POET; PC 18; WLC**
　See also CDALB 1640-1865; DA3; DLB 1,
　59, 73
**Eminescu, Mihail** 1850-1889 .......... **NCLC 33**
**Empson, William** 1906-1984 ... **CLC 3, 8, 19,
　33, 34**
　See also CA 17-20R; 112; CANR 31, 61;
　DLB 20; MTCW 1, 2
**Enchi, Fumiko (Ueda)** 1905-1986 ..... **CLC 31**
　See also CA 129; 121; DLB 182
**Ende, Michael (Andreas Helmuth)**
　1929-1995 ................................. **CLC 31**
　See also CA 118; 124; 149; CANR 36; CLR
　14; DLB 75; MAICYA; SATA 61; SATA-
　Brief 42; SATA-Obit 86
**Endo, Shusaku** 1923-1996 ..... **CLC 7, 14, 19,
　54, 99; DAM NOV**
　See also CA 29-32R; 153; CANR 21, 54;
　DA3; DLB 182; MTCW 1, 2
**Engel, Marian** 1933-1985 ................. **CLC 36**
　See also CA 25-28R; CANR 12; DLB 53;
　INT CANR-12
**Engelhardt, Frederick**
　See Hubbard, L(afayette) Ron(ald)
**Engels, Friedrich** 1820-1895 .......... **NCLC 85**
　See also DLB 129
**Enright, D(ennis) J(oseph)** 1920- .. **CLC 4, 8,
　31**
　See also CA 1-4R; CANR 1, 42, 83; DLB
　27; SATA 25
**Enzensberger, Hans Magnus**
　1929- ............................. **CLC 43; PC 28**
　See also CA 116; 119
**Ephron, Nora** 1941- ..................... **CLC 17, 31**
　See also AITN 2; CA 65-68; CANR 12, 39,
　83
**Epicurus** 341B.C.-270B.C. ............. **CMLC 21**
　See also DLB 176
**Epsilon**
　See Betjeman, John
**Epstein, Daniel Mark** 1948- ................ **CLC 7**
　See also CA 49-52; CANR 2, 53
**Epstein, Jacob** 1956- ......................... **CLC 19**
　See also CA 114
**Epstein, Jean** 1897-1953 ................ **TCLC 92**
**Epstein, Joseph** 1937- ....................... **CLC 39**
　See also CA 112; 119; CANR 50, 65
**Epstein, Leslie** 1938- ......................... **CLC 27**
　See also CA 73-76; CAAS 12; CANR 23,
　69

**Equiano, Olaudah** 1745(?)-1797 ......... **LC 16; BLC 2; DAM MULT**
See also DLB 37, 50

**ER** ...................................... **TCLC 33**
See also CA 160; DLB 85

**Erasmus, Desiderius** 1469(?)-1536 ...... **LC 16**

**Erdman, Paul E(mil)** 1932- ............... **CLC 25**
See also AITN 1; CA 61-64; CANR 13, 43, 84

**Erdrich, Louise** 1954- ........ **CLC 39, 54, 120; DAM MULT, NOV, POP**
See also AAYA 10; BEST 89:1; CA 114; CANR 41, 62; CDALBS; DA3; DLB 152, 175, 206; MTCW 1; NNAL; SATA 94

**Erenburg, Ilya (Grigoryevich)**
See Ehrenburg, Ilya (Grigoryevich)

**Erickson, Stephen Michael** 1950-
See Erickson, Steve
See also CA 129

**Erickson, Steve** 1950- ........................ **CLC 64**
See also Erickson, Stephen Michael CANR 60, 68

**Ericson, Walter**
See Fast, Howard (Melvin)

**Eriksson, Buntel**
See Bergman, (Ernst) Ingmar

**Ernaux, Annie** 1940- .......................... **CLC 88**
See also CA 147

**Erskine, John** 1879-1951 ................ **TCLC 84**
See also CA 112; 159; DLB 9, 102

**Eschenbach, Wolfram von**
See Wolfram von Eschenbach

**Eseki, Bruno**
See Mphahlele, Ezekiel

**Esenin, Sergei (Alexandrovich)** 1895-1925
**TCLC 4**
See also CA 104

**Eshleman, Clayton** 1935- ................... **CLC 7**
See also CA 33-36R; CAAS 6; DLB 5

**Espriella, Don Manuel Alvarez**
See Southey, Robert

**Espriu, Salvador** 1913-1985 ............... **CLC 9**
See also CA 154; 115; DLB 134

**Espronceda, Jose de** 1808-1842 ..... **NCLC 39**

**Esquivel, Laura** 1951(?)-
See also AAYA 29; CA 143; CANR 68; DA3; HLCS 1; MTCW 1

**Esse, James**
See Stephens, James

**Esterbrook, Tom**
See Hubbard, L(afayette) Ron(ald)

**Estleman, Loren D.** 1952- ..... **CLC 48; DAM NOV, POP**
See also AAYA 27; CA 85-88; CANR 27, 74; DA3; INT CANR-27; MTCW 1, 2

**Euclid** 306B.C.-283B.C. .................. **CMLC 25**

**Eugenides, Jeffrey** 1960(?)- .............. **CLC 81**
See also CA 144

**Euripides** c. 485B.C.-406B.C. ....... **CMLC 23; DA; DAB; DAC; DAM DRAM, MST; DC 4; WLCS**
See also DA3; DLB 176

**Evan, Evin**
See Faust, Frederick (Schiller)

**Evans, Caradoc** 1878-1945 ............. **TCLC 85**

**Evans, Evan**
See Faust, Frederick (Schiller)

**Evans, Marian**
See Eliot, George

**Evans, Mary Ann**
See Eliot, George

**Evarts, Esther**
See Benson, Sally

**Everett, Percival L.** 1956- ................ **CLC 57**
See also BW 2; CA 129

**Everson, R(onald) G(ilmour)** 1903- . **CLC 27**
See also CA 17-20R; DLB 88

**Everson, William (Oliver)**
1912-1994 ......................... **CLC 1, 5, 14**
See also CA 9-12R; 145; CANR 20; DLB 212; MTCW 1

**Evtushenko, Evgenii Aleksandrovich**
See Yevtushenko, Yevgeny (Alexandrovich)

**Ewart, Gavin (Buchanan)**
1916-1995 ........................... **CLC 13, 46**
See also CA 89-92; 150; CANR 17, 46; DLB 40; MTCW 1

**Ewers, Hanns Heinz** 1871-1943 ..... **TCLC 12**
See also CA 109; 149

**Ewing, Frederick R.**
See Sturgeon, Theodore (Hamilton)

**Exley, Frederick (Earl)** 1929-1992 .... **CLC 6, 11**
See also AITN 2; CA 81-84; 138; DLB 143; DLBY 81

**Eynhardt, Guillermo**
See Quiroga, Horacio (Sylvestre)

**Ezekiel, Nissim** 1924- ....................... **CLC 61**
See also CA 61-64

**Ezekiel, Tish O'Dowd** 1943- ............. **CLC 34**
See also CA 129

**Fadeyev, A.**
See Bulgya, Alexander Alexandrovich

**Fadeyev, Alexander** ........................ **TCLC 53**
See also Bulgya, Alexander Alexandrovich

**Fagen, Donald** 1948- .......................... **CLC 26**

**Fainzilberg, Ilya Arnoldovich** 1897-1937
See Ilf, Ilya
See also CA 120; 165

**Fair, Ronald L.** 1932- ........................ **CLC 18**
See also BW 1; CA 69-72; CANR 25; DLB 33

**Fairbairn, Roger**
See Carr, John Dickson

**Fairbairns, Zoe (Ann)** 1948- ............. **CLC 32**
See also CA 103; CANR 21, 85

**Falco, Gian**
See Papini, Giovanni

**Falconer, James**
See Kirkup, James

**Falconer, Kenneth**
See Kornbluth, C(yril) M.

**Falkland, Samuel**
See Heijermans, Herman

**Fallaci, Oriana** 1930- ................. **CLC 11, 110**
See also CA 77-80; CANR 15, 58; MTCW 1

**Faludy, George** 1913- .......................... **CLC 42**
See also CA 21-24R

**Faludy, Gyoergy**
See Faludy, George

**Fanon, Frantz** 1925-1961 ... **CLC 74; BLC 2; DAM MULT**
See also BW 1; CA 116; 89-92

**Fanshawe, Ann** 1625-1680 .................. **LC 11**

**Fante, John (Thomas)** 1911-1983 ..... **CLC 60**
See also CA 69-72; 109; CANR 23; DLB 130; DLBY 83

**Farah, Nuruddin** 1945- ...... **CLC 53; BLC 2; DAM MULT**
See also BW 2, 3; CA 106; CANR 81; DLB 125

**Fargue, Leon-Paul** 1876(?)-1947 .... **TCLC 11**
See also CA 109

**Farigoule, Louis**
See Romains, Jules

**Farina, Richard** 1936(?)-1966 ............. **CLC 9**
See also CA 81-84; 25-28R

**Farley, Walter (Lorimer)**
1915-1989 ............................ **CLC 17**
See also CA 17-20R; CANR 8, 29, 84; DLB 22; JRDA; MAICYA; SATA 2, 43

**Farmer, Philip Jose** 1918- ............ **CLC 1, 19**
See also AAYA 28; CA 1-4R; CANR 4, 35; DLB 8; MTCW 1; SATA 93

**Farquhar, George** 1677-1707 ... **LC 21; DAM DRAM**
See also DLB 84

**Farrell, J(ames) G(ordon)**
1935-1979 .................................. **CLC 6**
See also CA 73-76; 89-92; CANR 36; DLB 14; MTCW 1

**Farrell, James T(homas)** 1904-1979 . **CLC 1, 4, 8, 11, 66; SSC 28**
See also CA 5-8R; 89-92; CANR 9, 61; DLB 4, 9, 86; DLBD 2; MTCW 1, 2

**Farren, Richard J.**
See Betjeman, John

**Farren, Richard M.**
See Betjeman, John

**Fassbinder, Rainer Werner**
1946-1982 ................................ **CLC 20**
See also CA 93-96; 106; CANR 31

**Fast, Howard (Melvin)** 1914- .......... **CLC 23; DAM NOV**
See also AAYA 16; CA 1-4R, 181; CAAE 181; CAAS 18; CANR 1, 33, 54, 75; DLB 9; INT CANR-33; MTCW 1; SATA 7; SATA-Essay 107

**Faulcon, Robert**
See Holdstock, Robert P.

**Faulkner, William (Cuthbert)** 1897-1962
**CLC 1, 3, 6, 8, 9, 11, 14, 18, 28, 52, 68; DA; DAB; DAC; DAM MST, NOV; SSC 1, 35; WLC**
See also AAYA 7; CA 81-84; CANR 33; CDALB 1929-1941; DA3; DLB 9, 11, 44, 102; DLBD 2; DLBY 86, 97; MTCW 1, 2

**Fauset, Jessie Redmon**
1884(?)-1961 ......... **CLC 19, 54; BLC 2; DAM MULT**
See also BW 1; CA 109; CANR 83; DLB 51

**Faust, Frederick (Schiller)** 1892-1944(?)
**TCLC 49; DAM POP**
See also CA 108; 152

**Faust, Irvin** 1924- ................................ **CLC 8**
See also CA 33-36R; CANR 28, 67; DLB 2, 28; DLBY 80

**Fawkes, Guy**
See Benchley, Robert (Charles)

**Fearing, Kenneth (Flexner)**
1902-1961 ................................. **CLC 51**
See also CA 93-96; CANR 59; DLB 9

**Fecamps, Elise**
See Creasey, John

**Federman, Raymond** 1928- .......... **CLC 6, 47**
See also CA 17-20R; CAAS 8; CANR 10, 43, 83; DLBY 80

**Federspiel, J(uerg) F.** 1931- ............. **CLC 42**
See also CA 146

**Feiffer, Jules (Ralph)** 1929- ..... **CLC 2, 8, 64; DAM DRAM**
See also AAYA 3; CA 17-20R; CANR 30, 59; DLB 7, 44; INT CANR-30; MTCW 1; SATA 8, 61, 111

**Feige, Hermann Albert Otto Maximilian**
See Traven, B.

**Feinberg, David B.** 1956-1994 .......... **CLC 59**
See also CA 135; 147

**Feinstein, Elaine** 1930- ...................... **CLC 36**
See also CA 69-72; CAAS 1; CANR 31, 68; DLB 14, 40; MTCW 1

**Feldman, Irving (Mordecai)** 1928- ..... **CLC 7**
See also CA 1-4R; CANR 1; DLB 169

**Felix-Tchicaya, Gerald**
See Tchicaya, Gerald Felix

**Fellini, Federico** 1920-1993 ......... **CLC 16, 85**
See also CA 65-68; 143; CANR 33

**Felsen, Henry Gregor** 1916-1995 ..... **CLC 17**
See also CA 1-4R; 180; CANR 1; SAAS 2; SATA 1

**Fenno, Jack**
See Calisher, Hortense

**Fenollosa, Ernest (Francisco)** 1853-1908
**TCLC 91**
**Fenton, James Martin** 1949- ............. **CLC 32**
See also CA 102; DLB 40
**Ferber, Edna** 1887-1968 ............... **CLC 18, 93**
See also AITN 1; CA 5-8R; 25-28R; CANR
68; DLB 9, 28, 86; MTCW 1, 2; SATA 7
**Ferguson, Helen**
See Kavan, Anna
**Ferguson, Samuel** 1810-1886 ......... **NCLC 33**
See also DLB 32
**Fergusson, Robert** 1750-1774 ............. **LC 29**
See also DLB 109
**Ferling, Lawrence**
See Ferlinghetti, Lawrence (Monsanto)
**Ferlinghetti, Lawrence (Monsanto)** 1919(?)-
**CLC 2, 6, 10, 27, 111; DAM POET; PC
1**
See also CA 5-8R; CANR 3, 41, 73;
CDALB 1941-1968; DA3; DLB 5, 16;
MTCW 1, 2
**Fernandez, Vicente Garcia Huidobro**
See Huidobro Fernandez, Vicente Garcia
**Ferre, Rosario** 1942- ......... **SSC 36; HLCS 1**
See also CA 131; CANR 55, 81; DLB 145;
HW 1, 2; MTCW 1
**Ferrer, Gabriel (Francisco Victor) Miro**
See Miro (Ferrer), Gabriel (Francisco
Victor)
**Ferrier, Susan (Edmonstone)** 1782-1854
**NCLC 8**
See also DLB 116
**Ferrigno, Robert** 1948(?)- ................ **CLC 65**
See also CA 140
**Ferron, Jacques** 1921-1985 .... **CLC 94; DAC**
See also CA 117; 129; DLB 60
**Feuchtwanger, Lion** 1884-1958 ........ **TCLC 3**
See also CA 104; DLB 66
**Feuillet, Octave** 1821-1890 ............. **NCLC 45**
See also DLB 192
**Feydeau, Georges (Leon Jules Marie)**
1862-1921 ....... **TCLC 22; DAM DRAM**
See also CA 113; 152; CANR 84; DLB 192
**Fichte, Johann Gottlieb**
1762-1814 ........................... **NCLC 62**
See also DLB 90
**Ficino, Marsilio** 1433-1499 ................. **LC 12**
**Fiedeler, Hans**
See Doeblin, Alfred
**Fiedler, Leslie A(aron)** 1917- .. **CLC 4, 13, 24**
See also CA 9-12R; CANR 7, 63; DLB 28,
67; MTCW 1, 2
**Field, Andrew** 1938- ........................ **CLC 44**
See also CA 97-100; CANR 25
**Field, Eugene** 1850-1895 .................. **NCLC 3**
See also DLB 23, 42, 140; DLBD 13; MAI-
CYA; SATA 16
**Field, Gans T.**
See Wellman, Manly Wade
**Field, Michael** 1915-1971 ............... **TCLC 43**
See also CA 29-32R
**Field, Peter**
See Hobson, Laura Z(ametkin)
**Fielding, Henry** 1707-1754 ..... **LC 1, 46; DA;
DAB; DAC; DAM DRAM, MST, NOV;
WLC**
See also CDBLB 1660-1789; DA3; DLB
39, 84, 101
**Fielding, Sarah** 1710-1768 ............. **LC 1, 44**
See also DLB 39
**Fields, W. C.** 1880-1946 ................. **TCLC 80**
See also DLB 44
**Fierstein, Harvey (Forbes)** 1954- .... **CLC 33;
DAM DRAM, POP**
See also CA 123; 129; DA3
**Figes, Eva** 1932- ............................. **CLC 31**
See also CA 53-56; CANR 4, 44, 83; DLB
14

**Finch, Anne** 1661-1720 ............. **LC 3; PC 21**
See also DLB 95
**Finch, Robert (Duer Claydon)**
1900- ......................................... **CLC 18**
See also CA 57-60; CANR 9, 24, 49; DLB
88
**Findley, Timothy** 1930- . **CLC 27, 102; DAC;
DAM MST**
See also CA 25-28R; CANR 12, 42, 69;
DLB 53
**Fink, William**
See Mencken, H(enry) L(ouis)
**Firbank, Louis** 1942-
See Reed, Lou
See also CA 117
**Firbank, (Arthur Annesley) Ronald**
1886-1926 .................................. **TCLC 1**
See also CA 104; 177; DLB 36
**Fisher, Dorothy (Frances) Canfield**
1879-1958 ................................ **TCLC 87**
See also CA 114; 136; CANR 80; DLB 9,
102; MAICYA; YABC 1
**Fisher, M(ary) F(rances) K(ennedy)**
1908-1992 ........................... **CLC 76, 87**
See also CA 77-80; 138; CANR 44; MTCW
1
**Fisher, Roy** 1930- ............................. **CLC 25**
See also CA 81-84; CAAS 10; CANR 16;
DLB 40
**Fisher, Rudolph** 1897-1934 .. **TCLC 11; BLC
2; DAM MULT; SSC 25**
See also BW 1, 3; CA 107; 124; CANR 80;
DLB 51, 102
**Fisher, Vardis (Alvero)** 1895-1968 ...... **CLC 7**
See also CA 5-8R; 25-28R; CANR 68; DLB
9, 206
**Fiske, Tarleton**
See Bloch, Robert (Albert)
**Fitch, Clarke**
See Sinclair, Upton (Beall)
**Fitch, John IV**
See Cormier, Robert (Edmund)
**Fitzgerald, Captain Hugh**
See Baum, L(yman) Frank
**FitzGerald, Edward** 1809-1883 ....... **NCLC 9**
See also DLB 32
**Fitzgerald, F(rancis) Scott (Key)** 1896-1940
**TCLC 1, 6, 14, 28, 55; DA; DAB; DAC;
DAM MST, NOV; SSC 6, 31; WLC**
See also AAYA 24; AITN 1; CA 110; 123;
CDALB 1917-1929; DA3; DLB 4, 9, 86;
DLBD 1, 15, 16; DLBY 81, 96; MTCW
1, 2
**Fitzgerald, Penelope** 1916- ... **CLC 19, 51, 61**
See also CA 85-88; CAAS 10; CANR 56,
86; DLB 14, 194; MTCW 2
**Fitzgerald, Robert (Stuart)**
1910-1985 ................................ **CLC 39**
See also CA 1-4R; 114; CANR 1; DLBY
80
**FitzGerald, Robert D(avid)**
1902-1987 ................................ **CLC 19**
See also CA 17-20R
**Fitzgerald, Zelda (Sayre)**
1900-1948 ................................ **TCLC 52**
See also CA 117; 126; DLBY 84
**Flanagan, Thomas (James Bonner)** 1923-
**CLC 25, 52**
See also CA 108; CANR 55; DLBY 80; INT
108; MTCW 1
**Flaubert, Gustave** 1821-1880 .... **NCLC 2, 10,
19, 62, 66; DA; DAB; DAC; DAM
MST, NOV; SSC 11; WLC**
See also DA3; DLB 119
**Flecker, Herman Elroy**
See Flecker, (Herman) James Elroy
**Flecker, (Herman) James Elroy** 1884-1915
**TCLC 43**
See also CA 109; 150; DLB 10, 19

**Fleming, Ian (Lancaster)** 1908-1964 . **CLC 3,
30; DAM POP**
See also AAYA 26; CA 5-8R; CANR 59;
CDBLB 1945-1960; DA3; DLB 87, 201;
MTCW 1, 2; SATA 9
**Fleming, Thomas (James)** 1927- ...... **CLC 37**
See also CA 5-8R; CANR 10; INT CANR-
10; SATA 8
**Fletcher, John** 1579-1625 .......... **LC 33; DC 6**
See also CDBLB Before 1660; DLB 58
**Fletcher, John Gould** 1886-1950 .... **TCLC 35**
See also CA 107; 167; DLB 4, 45
**Fleur, Paul**
See Pohl, Frederik
**Flooglebuckle, Al**
See Spiegelman, Art
**Flying Officer X**
See Bates, H(erbert) E(rnest)
**Fo, Dario** 1926- ............. **CLC 32, 109; DAM
DRAM; DC 10**
See also CA 116; 128; CANR 68; DA3;
DLBY 97; MTCW 1, 2
**Fogarty, Jonathan Titulescu Esq.**
See Farrell, James T(homas)
**Follett, Ken(neth Martin)** 1949- ..... **CLC 18;
DAM NOV, POP**
See also AAYA 6; BEST 89:4; CA 81-84;
CANR 13, 33, 54; DA3; DLB 87; DLBY
81; INT CANR-33; MTCW 1
**Fontane, Theodor** 1819-1898 ......... **NCLC 26**
See also DLB 129
**Foote, Horton** 1916- ........ **CLC 51, 91; DAM
DRAM**
See also CA 73-76; CANR 34, 51; DA3;
DLB 26; INT CANR-34
**Foote, Shelby** 1916- ..... **CLC 75; DAM NOV,
POP**
See also CA 5-8R; CANR 3, 45, 74; DA3;
DLB 2, 17; MTCW 2
**Forbes, Esther** 1891-1967 ................. **CLC 12**
See also AAYA 17; CA 13-14; 25-28R; CAP
1; CLR 27; DLB 22; JRDA; MAICYA;
SATA 2, 100
**Forche, Carolyn (Louise)** 1950- ....... **CLC 25,
83, 86; DAM POET; PC 10**
See also CA 109; 117; CANR 50, 74; DA3;
DLB 5, 193; INT 117; MTCW 1
**Ford, Elbur**
See Hibbert, Eleanor Alice Burford
**Ford, Ford Madox** 1873-1939 ... **TCLC 1, 15,
39, 57; DAM NOV**
See also CA 104; 132; CANR 74; CDBLB
1914-1945; DA3; DLB 162; MTCW 1, 2
**Ford, Henry** 1863-1947 .................... **TCLC 73**
See also CA 115; 148
**Ford, John** 1586-(?) .......................... **DC 8**
See also CDBLB Before 1660; DAM
DRAM; DA3; DLB 58
**Ford, John** 1895-1973 ........................ **CLC 16**
See also CA 45-48
**Ford, Richard** 1944- ................... **CLC 46, 99**
See also CA 69-72; CANR 11, 47, 86;
MTCW 1
**Ford, Webster**
See Masters, Edgar Lee
**Foreman, Richard** 1937- ................... **CLC 50**
See also CA 65-68; CANR 32, 63
**Forester, C(ecil) S(cott)** 1899-1966 ... **CLC 35**
See also CA 73-76; 25-28R; CANR 83;
DLB 191; SATA 13
**Forez**
See Mauriac, Francois (Charles)
**Forman, James Douglas** 1932- ......... **CLC 21**
See also AAYA 17; CA 9-12R; CANR 4,
19, 42; JRDA; MAICYA; SATA 8, 70
**Fornes, Maria Irene** 1930- . **CLC 39, 61; DC
10; HLCS 1**
See also CA 25-28R; CANR 28, 81; DLB
7; HW 1, 2; INT CANR-28; MTCW 1

**Forrest, Leon (Richard)** 1937-1997 .. **CLC 4; BLCS**
See also BW 2; CA 89-92; 162; CAAS 7; CANR 25, 52, 87; DLB 33

**Forster, E(dward) M(organ)**
1879-1970 ...... **CLC 1, 2, 3, 4, 9, 10, 13, 15, 22, 45, 77; DA; DAB; DAC; DAM MST, NOV; SSC 27; WLC**
See also AAYA 2; CA 13-14; 25-28R; CANR 45; CAP 1; CDBLB 1914-1945; DA3; DLB 34, 98, 162, 178, 195; DLBD 10; MTCW 1, 2; SATA 57

**Forster, John** 1812-1876 ................. **NCLC 11**
See also DLB 144, 184

**Forsyth, Frederick** 1938- ........ **CLC 2, 5, 36; DAM NOV, POP**
See also BEST 89:4; CA 85-88; CANR 38, 62; DLB 87; MTCW 1, 2

**Forten, Charlotte L.** .......... **TCLC 16; BLC 2**
See also Grimke, Charlotte L(ottie) Forten
DLB 50

**Foscolo, Ugo** 1778-1827 .................... **NCLC 8**

**Fosse, Bob** ................................ **CLC 20**
See also Fosse, Robert Louis

**Fosse, Robert Louis** 1927-1987
See Fosse, Bob
See also CA 110; 123

**Foster, Stephen Collins**
1826-1864 .................................. **NCLC 26**

**Foucault, Michel** 1926-1984 . **CLC 31, 34, 69**
See also CA 105; 113; CANR 34; MTCW 1, 2

**Fouque, Friedrich (Heinrich Karl) de la Motte** 1777-1843 ...................... **NCLC 2**
See also DLB 90

**Fourier, Charles** 1772-1837 ........... **NCLC 51**

**Fournier, Pierre** 1916- ..................... **CLC 11**
See also Gascar, Pierre CA 89-92; CANR 16, 40

**Fowles, John (Philip)** 1926- .. **CLC 1, 2, 3, 4, 6, 9, 10, 15, 33, 87; DAB; DAC; DAM MST; SSC 33**
See also CA 5-8R; CANR 25, 71; CDBLB 1960 to Present; DA3; DLB 14, 139, 207; MTCW 1, 2; SATA 22

**Fox, Paula** 1923- ..................... **CLC 2, 8, 121**
See also AAYA 3; CA 73-76; CANR 20, 36, 62; CLR 1, 44; DLB 52; JRDA; MAICYA; MTCW 1; SATA 17, 60

**Fox, William Price (Jr.)** 1926- .......... **CLC 22**
See also CA 17-20R; CAAS 19; CANR 11; DLB 2; DLBY 81

**Foxe, John** 1516(?)-1587 ...................... **LC 14**
See also DLB 132

**Frame, Janet** 1924- . **CLC 2, 3, 6, 22, 66, 96; SSC 29**
See also Clutha, Janet Paterson Frame

**France, Anatole** ................................ **TCLC 9**
See also Thibault, Jacques Anatole Francois
DLB 123; MTCW 1

**Francis, Claude** 19(?)- ...................... **CLC 50**

**Francis, Dick** 1920- ........ **CLC 2, 22, 42, 102; DAM POP**
See also AAYA 5, 21; BEST 89:3; CA 5-8R; CANR 9, 42, 68; CDBLB 1960 to Present; DA3; DLB 87; INT CANR-9; MTCW 1, 2

**Francis, Robert (Churchill)**
1901-1987 .................................. **CLC 15**
See also CA 1-4R; 123; CANR 1

**Frank, Anne(lies Marie)**
1929-1945 . **TCLC 17; DA; DAB; DAC; DAM MST; WLC**
See also AAYA 12; CA 113; 133; CANR 68; DA3; MTCW 1, 2; SATA 87; SATA-Brief 42

**Frank, Bruno** 1887-1945 ................. **TCLC 81**
See also DLB 118

**Frank, Elizabeth** 1945- ..................... **CLC 39**
See also CA 121; 126; CANR 78; INT 126

**Frankl, Viktor E(mil)** 1905-1997 ...... **CLC 93**
See also CA 65-68; 161

**Franklin, Benjamin**
See Hasek, Jaroslav (Matej Frantisek)

**Franklin, Benjamin** 1706-1790 .. **LC 25; DA; DAB; DAC; DAM MST; WLCS**
See also CDALB 1640-1865; DA3; DLB 24, 43, 73

**Franklin, (Stella Maria Sarah) Miles (Lampe)** 1879-1954 ................... **TCLC 7**
See also CA 104; 164

**Fraser, (Lady) Antonia (Pakenham)** 1932-
**CLC 32, 107**
See also CA 85-88; CANR 44, 65; MTCW 1, 2; SATA-Brief 32

**Fraser, George MacDonald** 1925- ...... **CLC 7**
See also CA 45-48, 180; CAAE 180; CANR 2, 48, 74; MTCW 1

**Fraser, Sylvia** 1935- ......................... **CLC 64**
See also CA 45-48; CANR 1, 16, 60

**Frayn, Michael** 1933- ........ **CLC 3, 7, 31, 47; DAM DRAM, NOV**
See also CA 5-8R; CANR 30, 69; DLB 13, 14, 194; MTCW 1, 2

**Fraze, Candida (Merrill)** 1945- ........ **CLC 50**
See also CA 126

**Frazer, J(ames) G(eorge)**
1854-1941 ................................. **TCLC 32**
See also CA 118

**Frazer, Robert Caine**
See Creasey, John

**Frazer, Sir James George**
See Frazer, J(ames) G(eorge)

**Frazier, Charles** 1950- ..................... **CLC 109**
See also CA 161

**Frazier, Ian** 1951- ............................. **CLC 46**
See also CA 130; CANR 54

**Frederic, Harold** 1856-1898 .......... **NCLC 10**
See also DLB 12, 23; DLBD 13

**Frederick, John**
See Faust, Frederick (Schiller)

**Frederick the Great** 1712-1786 .......... **LC 14**

**Fredro, Aleksander** 1793-1876 ......... **NCLC 8**

**Freeling, Nicolas** 1927- ..................... **CLC 38**
See also CA 49-52; CAAS 12; CANR 1, 17, 50, 84; DLB 87

**Freeman, Douglas Southall**
1886-1953 ................................. **TCLC 11**
See also CA 109; DLB 17; DLBD 17

**Freeman, Judith** 1946- ..................... **CLC 55**
See also CA 148

**Freeman, Mary E(leanor) Wilkins** 1852-1930
**TCLC 9; SSC 1**
See also CA 106; 177; DLB 12, 78

**Freeman, R(ichard) Austin**
1862-1943 ................................. **TCLC 21**
See also CA 113; CANR 84; DLB 70

**French, Albert** 1943- ........................ **CLC 86**
See also BW 3; CA 167

**French, Marilyn** 1929- ......... **CLC 10, 18, 60; DAM DRAM, NOV, POP**
See also CA 69-72; CANR 3, 31; INT CANR-31; MTCW 1, 2

**French, Paul**
See Asimov, Isaac

**Freneau, Philip Morin** 1752-1832 ... **NCLC 1**
See also DLB 37, 43

**Freud, Sigmund** 1856-1939 ............ **TCLC 52**
See also CA 115; 133; CANR 69; MTCW 1, 2

**Friedan, Betty (Naomi)** 1921- .......... **CLC 74**
See also CA 65-68; CANR 18, 45, 74; MTCW 1, 2

**Friedlander, Saul** 1932- ..................... **CLC 90**
See also CA 117; 130; CANR 72

**Friedman, B(ernard) H(arper)**
1926- .................................. **CLC 7**
See also CA 1-4R; CANR 3, 48

**Friedman, Bruce Jay** 1930- ...... **CLC 3, 5, 56**
See also CA 9-12R; CANR 25, 52; DLB 2, 28; INT CANR-25

**Friel, Brian** 1929- .... **CLC 5, 42, 59, 115; DC 8**
See also CA 21-24R; CANR 33, 69; DLB 13; MTCW 1

**Friis-Baastad, Babbis Ellinor**
1921-1970 .................................. **CLC 12**
See also CA 17-20R; 134; SATA 7

**Frisch, Max (Rudolf)** 1911-1991 ... **CLC 3, 9, 14, 18, 32, 44; DAM DRAM, NOV**
See also CA 85-88; 134; CANR 32, 74; DLB 69, 124; MTCW 1, 2

**Fromentin, Eugene (Samuel Auguste)**
1820-1876 ................................. **NCLC 10**
See also DLB 123

**Frost, Frederick**
See Faust, Frederick (Schiller)

**Frost, Robert (Lee)** 1874-1963 ... **CLC 1, 3, 4, 9, 10, 13, 15, 26, 34, 44; DA; DAB; DAC; DAM MST, POET; PC 1; WLC**
See also AAYA 21; CA 89-92; CANR 33; CDALB 1917-1929; DA3; DLB 54; DLBD 7; MTCW 1, 2; SATA 14

**Froude, James Anthony**
1818-1894 ................................. **NCLC 43**
See also DLB 18, 57, 144

**Froy, Herald**
See Waterhouse, Keith (Spencer)

**Fry, Christopher** 1907- ......... **CLC 2, 10, 14; DAM DRAM**
See also CA 17-20R; CAAS 23; CANR 9, 30, 74; DLB 13; MTCW 1, 2; SATA 66

**Frye, (Herman) Northrop**
1912-1991 ............................... **CLC 24, 70**
See also CA 5-8R; 133; CANR 8, 37; DLB 67, 68; MTCW 1, 2

**Fuchs, Daniel** 1909-1993 ............... **CLC 8, 22**
See also CA 81-84; 142; CAAS 5; CANR 40; DLB 9, 26, 28; DLBY 93

**Fuchs, Daniel** 1934- ......................... **CLC 34**
See also CA 37-40R; CANR 14, 48

**Fuentes, Carlos** 1928- .. **CLC 3, 8, 10, 13, 22, 41, 60, 113; DA; DAB; DAC; DAM MST, MULT, NOV; HLC 1; SSC 24; WLC**
See also AAYA 4; AITN 2; CA 69-72; CANR 10, 32, 68; DA3; DLB 113; HW 1, 2; MTCW 1, 2

**Fuentes, Gregorio Lopez y**
See Lopez y Fuentes, Gregorio

**Fuertes, Gloria** 1918- ......................... **PC 27**
See also CA 178, 180; DLB 108; HW 2

**Fugard, (Harold) Athol** 1932- . **CLC 5, 9, 14, 25, 40, 80; DAM DRAM; DC 3**
See also AAYA 17; CA 85-88; CANR 32, 54; MTCW 1

**Fugard, Sheila** 1932- ......................... **CLC 48**
See also CA 125

**Fuller, Charles (H., Jr.)** 1939- ......... **CLC 25; BLC 2; DAM DRAM, MULT; DC 1**
See also BW 2; CA 108; 112; CANR 87; DLB 38; INT 112; MTCW 1

**Fuller, John (Leopold)** 1937- ........... **CLC 62**
See also CA 21-24R; CANR 9, 44; DLB 40

**Fuller, Margaret** ........................ **NCLC 5, 50**
See also Fuller, Sarah Margaret

**Fuller, Roy (Broadbent)** 1912-1991 ... **CLC 4, 28**
See also CA 5-8R; 135; CAAS 10; CANR 53, 83; DLB 15, 20; SATA 87

**Fuller, Sarah Margaret** 1810-1850
See Fuller, Margaret
See also CDALB 1640-1865; DLB 1, 59, 73, 83

**Fulton, Alice** 1952- ............................ **CLC 52**
See also CA 116; CANR 57, 88; DLB 193

**Furphy, Joseph** 1843-1912 .............. **TCLC 25**
See also CA 163

**Fussell, Paul** 1924- ........................... **CLC 74**
See also BEST 90:1; CA 17-20R; CANR 8,
21, 35, 69; INT CANR-21; MTCW 1, 2

**Futabatei, Shimei** 1864-1909 ......... **TCLC 44**
See also CA 162; DLB 180

**Futrelle, Jacques** 1875-1912 .......... **TCLC 19**
See also CA 113; 155

**Gaboriau, Emile** 1835-1873 ........... **NCLC 14**

**Gadda, Carlo Emilio** 1893-1973 ....... **CLC 11**
See also CA 89-92; DLB 177

**Gaddis, William** 1922-1998 ... **CLC 1, 3, 6, 8,**
**10, 19, 43, 86**
See also CA 17-20R; 172; CANR 21, 48;
DLB 2; MTCW 1, 2

**Gage, Walter**
See Inge, William (Motter)

**Gaines, Ernest J(ames)** 1933- ...... **CLC 3, 11,**
**18, 86; BLC 2; DAM MULT**
See also AAYA 18; AITN 1; BW 2, 3; CA
9-12R; CANR 6, 24, 42, 75; CDALB
1968-1988; CLR 62; DA3; DLB 2, 33,
152; DLBY 80; MTCW 1, 2; SATA 86

**Gaitskill, Mary** 1954- ........................ **CLC 69**
See also CA 128; CANR 61

**Galdos, Benito Perez**
See Perez Galdos, Benito

**Gale, Zona** 1874-1938 ........... **TCLC 7; DAM**
**DRAM**
See also CA 105; 153; CANR 84; DLB 9,
78

**Galeano, Eduardo (Hughes)** 1940- . **CLC 72;**
**HLCS 1**
See also CA 29-32R; CANR 13, 32; HW 1

**Galiano, Juan Valera y Alcala**
See Valera y Alcala-Galiano, Juan

**Galilei, Galileo** 1546-1642 .................... **LC 45**

**Gallagher, Tess** 1943- ...... **CLC 18, 63; DAM**
**POET; PC 9**
See also CA 106; DLB 212

**Gallant, Mavis** 1922- .. **CLC 7, 18, 38; DAC;**
**DAM MST; SSC 5**
See also CA 69-72; CANR 29, 69; DLB 53;
MTCW 1, 2

**Gallant, Roy A(rthur)** 1924- ............. **CLC 17**
See also CA 5-8R; CANR 4, 29, 54; CLR
30; MAICYA; SATA 4, 68, 110

**Gallico, Paul (William)** 1897-1976 ..... **CLC 2**
See also AITN 1; CA 5-8R; 69-72; CANR
23; CANR 9, 171; MAICYA; SATA 13

**Gallo, Max Louis** 1932- .................... **CLC 95**
See also CA 85-88

**Gallois, Lucien**
See Desnos, Robert

**Gallup, Ralph**
See Whitemore, Hugh (John)

**Galsworthy, John** 1867-1933 .... **TCLC 1, 45;**
**DA; DAB; DAC; DAM DRAM, MST,**
**NOV; SSC 22; WLC**
See also CA 104; 141; CANR 75; CDBLB
1890-1914; DA3; DLB 10, 34, 98, 162;
DLBD 16; MTCW 1

**Galt, John** 1779-1839 ........................ **NCLC 1**
See also DLB 99, 116, 159

**Galvin, James** 1951- ......................... **CLC 38**
See also CA 108; CANR 26

**Gamboa, Federico** 1864-1939 ........ **TCLC 36**
See also CA 167; HW 2

**Gandhi, M. K.**
See Gandhi, Mohandas Karamchand

**Gandhi, Mahatma**
See Gandhi, Mohandas Karamchand

**Gandhi, Mohandas Karamchand** 1869-1948
**TCLC 59; DAM MULT**
See also CA 121; 132; DA3; MTCW 1, 2

**Gann, Ernest Kellogg** 1910-1991 ..... **CLC 23**
See also AITN 1; CA 1-4R; 136; CANR 1,
83

**Garber, Eric** 1943(?)-
See Holleran, Andrew

**Garcia, Cristina** 1958- ...................... **CLC 76**
See also CA 141; CANR 73; HW 2

**Garcia Lorca, Federico** 1898-1936 . **TCLC 1,**
**7, 49; DA; DAB; DAC; DAM DRAM,**
**MST, MULT, POET; DC 2; HLC 2;**
**PC 3; WLC**
See also CA 104; 131; CANR 81; DA3;
DLB 108; HW 1, 2; MTCW 1, 2

**Garcia Marquez, Gabriel (Jose)**
1928- .... **CLC 2, 3, 8, 10, 15, 27, 47, 55,**
**68; DA; DAB; DAC; DAM MST,**
**MULT, NOV, POP; HLC 1; SSC 8;**
**WLC**
See also AAYA 3; BEST 89:1, 90:4; CA 33-
36R; CANR 10, 28, 50, 75, 82; DA3;
DLB 113; HW 1, 2; MTCW 1, 2

**Garcilaso de la Vega, El Inca** 1503-1536
See also HLCS 1

**Gard, Janice**
See Latham, Jean Lee

**Gard, Roger Martin du**
See Martin du Gard, Roger

**Gardam, Jane** 1928- ......................... **CLC 43**
See also CA 49-52; CANR 2, 18, 33, 54;
CLR 12; DLB 14, 161; MAICYA; MTCW
1; SAAS 9; SATA 39, 76; SATA-Brief 28

**Gardner, Herb(ert)** 1934- ................. **CLC 44**
See also CA 149

**Gardner, John (Champlin), Jr.** 1933-1982
**CLC 2, 3, 5, 7, 8, 10, 18, 28, 34; DAM**
**NOV, POP; SSC 7**
See also AITN 1; CA 65-68; 107; CANR
33, 73; CDALBS; DA3; DLB 2; DLBY
82; MTCW 1; SATA 40; SATA-Obit 31

**Gardner, John (Edmund)** 1926- ...... **CLC 30;**
**DAM POP**
See also CA 103; CANR 15, 69; MTCW 1

**Gardner, Miriam**
See Bradley, Marion Zimmer

**Gardner, Noel**
See Kuttner, Henry

**Gardons, S. S.**
See Snodgrass, W(illiam) D(e Witt)

**Garfield, Leon** 1921-1996 .................. **CLC 12**
See also AAYA 8; CA 17-20R; 152; CANR
38, 41, 78; CLR 21; DLB 161; JRDA;
MAICYA; SATA 1, 32, 76; SATA-Obit 90

**Garland, (Hannibal) Hamlin** 1860-1940
**TCLC 3; SSC 18**
See also CA 104; DLB 12, 71, 78, 186

**Garneau, (Hector de) Saint-Denys** 1912-1943
**TCLC 13**
See also CA 111; DLB 88

**Garner, Alan** 1934- ..... **CLC 17; DAB; DAM**
**POP**
See also AAYA 18; CA 73-76, 178; CAAE
178; CANR 15, 64; CLR 20; DLB 161;
MAICYA; MTCW 1, 2; SATA 18, 69;
SATA-Essay 108

**Garner, Hugh** 1913-1979 ................... **CLC 13**
See also CA 69-72; CANR 31; DLB 68

**Garnett, David** 1892-1981 ................... **CLC 3**
See also CA 5-8R; 103; CANR 17, 79; DLB
34; MTCW 2

**Garos, Stephanie**
See Katz, Steve

**Garrett, George (Palmer)** 1929- .. **CLC 3, 11,**
**51; SSC 30**
See also CA 1-4R; CAAS 5; CANR 1, 42,
67; DLB 2, 5, 130, 152; DLBY 83

**Garrick, David** 1717-1779 ....... **LC 15; DAM**
**DRAM**
See also DLB 84

**Garrigue, Jean** 1914-1972 ............... **CLC 2, 8**
See also CA 5-8R; 37-40R; CANR 20

**Garrison, Frederick**
See Sinclair, Upton (Beall)

**Garro, Elena** 1920(?)-1998
See also CA 131; 169; DLB 145; HLCS 1;
HW 1

**Garth, Will**
See Hamilton, Edmond; Kuttner, Henry

**Garvey, Marcus (Moziah, Jr.)** 1887-1940
**TCLC 41; BLC 2; DAM MULT**
See also BW 1; CA 120; 124; CANR 79

**Gary, Romain** .................................. **CLC 25**
See also Kacew, Romain DLB 83

**Gascar, Pierre** ................................ **CLC 11**
See also Fournier, Pierre

**Gascoyne, David (Emery)** 1916- ....... **CLC 45**
See also CA 65-68; CANR 10, 28, 54; DLB
20; MTCW 1

**Gaskell, Elizabeth Cleghorn** 1810-1865
**NCLC 70; DAB; DAM MST; SSC 25**
See also CDBLB 1832-1890; DLB 21, 144,
159

**Gass, William H(oward)** 1924- . **CLC 1, 2, 8,**
**11, 15, 39; SSC 12**
See also CA 17-20R; CANR 30, 71; DLB
2; MTCW 1, 2

**Gassendi, Pierre** 1592-1655 ............... **LC 54**

**Gasset, Jose Ortega y**
See Ortega y Gasset, Jose

**Gates, Henry Louis, Jr.** 1950- ......... **CLC 65;**
**BLCS; DAM MULT**
See also BW 2, 3; CA 109; CANR 25, 53,
75; DA3; DLB 67; MTCW 1

**Gautier, Theophile** 1811-1872 .. **NCLC 1, 59;**
**DAM POET; PC 18; SSC 20**
See also DLB 119

**Gawsworth, John**
See Bates, H(erbert) E(rnest)

**Gay, John** 1685-1732 .. **LC 49; DAM DRAM**
See also DLB 84, 95

**Gay, Oliver**
See Gogarty, Oliver St. John

**Gaye, Marvin (Penze)** 1939-1984 ..... **CLC 26**
See also CA 112

**Gebler, Carlo (Ernest)** 1954- ........... **CLC 39**
See also CA 119; 133

**Gee, Maggie (Mary)** 1948- ............... **CLC 57**
See also CA 130; DLB 207

**Gee, Maurice (Gough)** 1931- ........... **CLC 29**
See also CA 97-100; CANR 67; CLR 56;
SATA 46, 101

**Gelbart, Larry (Simon)** 1923- .... **CLC 21, 61**
See also CA 73-76; CANR 45

**Gelber, Jack** 1932- ............. **CLC 1, 6, 14, 79**
See also CA 1-4R; CANR 2; DLB 7

**Gellhorn, Martha (Ellis)**
1908-1998 ............................. **CLC 14, 60**
See also CA 77-80; 164; CANR 44; DLBY
82, 98

**Genet, Jean** 1910-1986 .. **CLC 1, 2, 5, 10, 14,**
**44, 46; DAM DRAM**
See also CA 13-16R; CANR 18; DA3; DLB
72; DLBY 86; MTCW 1, 2

**Gent, Peter** 1942- ............................. **CLC 29**
See also AITN 1; CA 89-92; DLBY 82

**Gentile, Giovanni** 1875-1944 .......... **TCLC 96**
See also CA 119

**Gentlewoman in New England, A**
See Bradstreet, Anne

**Gentlewoman in Those Parts, A**
See Bradstreet, Anne

**George, Jean Craighead** 1919- ......... **CLC 35**
See also AAYA 8; CA 5-8R; CANR 25;
CLR 1; DLB 52; JRDA; MAICYA; SATA
2, 68

George, Stefan (Anton) 1868-1933 . TCLC 2, 14
    See also CA 104
Georges, Georges Martin
    See Simenon, Georges (Jacques Christian)
Gerhardi, William Alexander
    See Gerhardie, William Alexander
Gerhardie, William Alexander 1895-1977
    CLC 5
    See also CA 25-28R; 73-76; CANR 18; DLB 36
Gerstler, Amy 1956- .......................... CLC 70
    See also CA 146
Gertler, T. ........................................ CLC 34
    See also CA 116; 121; INT 121
Ghalib ........................................ NCLC 39, 78
    See also Ghalib, Hsadullah Khan
Ghalib, Hsadullah Khan 1797-1869
    See Ghalib
    See also DAM POET
Ghelderode, Michel de 1898-1962 ..... CLC 6, 11; DAM DRAM
    See also CA 85-88; CANR 40, 77
Ghiselin, Brewster 1903- ................... CLC 23
    See also CA 13-16R; CAAS 10; CANR 13
Ghose, Aurabinda 1872-1950 ......... TCLC 63
    See also CA 163
Ghose, Zulfikar 1935- ........................ CLC 42
    See also CA 65-68; CANR 67
Ghosh, Amitav 1956- ......................... CLC 44
    See also CA 147; CANR 80
Giacosa, Giuseppe 1847-1906 ........... TCLC 7
    See also CA 104
Gibb, Lee
    See Waterhouse, Keith (Spencer)
Gibbon, Lewis Grassic ...................... TCLC 4
    See also Mitchell, James Leslie
Gibbons, Kaye 1960- ....... CLC 50, 88; DAM POP
    See also CA 151; CANR 75; DA3; MTCW 1
Gibran, Kahlil 1883-1931 ........... TCLC 1, 9; DAM POET, POP; PC 9
    See also CA 104; 150; DA3; MTCW 2
Gibran, Khalil
    See Gibran, Kahlil
Gibson, William 1914- .. CLC 23; DA; DAB; DAC; DAM DRAM, MST
    See also CA 9-12R; CANR 9, 42, 75; DLB 7; MTCW 1; SATA 66
Gibson, William (Ford) 1948- ... CLC 39, 63; DAM POP
    See also AAYA 12; CA 126; 133; CANR 52; DA3; MTCW 1
Gide, Andre (Paul Guillaume) 1869-1951
    TCLC 5, 12, 36; DA; DAB; DAC; DAM MST, NOV; SSC 13; WLC
    See also CA 104; 124; DA3; DLB 65; MTCW 1, 2
Gifford, Barry (Colby) 1946- ........... CLC 34
    See also CA 65-68; CANR 9, 30, 40
Gilbert, Frank
    See De Voto, Bernard (Augustine)
Gilbert, W(illiam) S(chwenck) 1836-1911
    TCLC 3; DAM DRAM, POET
    See also CA 104; 173; SATA 36
Gilbreth, Frank B., Jr. 1911- ........... CLC 17
    See also CA 9-12R; SATA 2
Gilchrist, Ellen 1935- ...... CLC 34, 48; DAM POP; SSC 14
    See also CA 113; 116; CANR 41, 61; DLB 130; MTCW 1, 2
Giles, Molly 1942- ............................. CLC 39
    See also CA 126
Gill, Eric 1882-1940 ......................... TCLC 85
Gill, Patrick
    See Creasey, John

Gilliam, Terry (Vance) 1940- ............. CLC 21
    See also Monty Python AAYA 19; CA 108; 113; CANR 35; INT 113
Gillian, Jerry
    See Gilliam, Terry (Vance)
Gilliatt, Penelope (Ann Douglass) 1932-1993
    CLC 2, 10, 13, 53
    See also AITN 2; CA 13-16R; 141; CANR 49; DLB 14
Gilman, Charlotte (Anna) Perkins (Stetson) 1860-1935 ....... TCLC 9, 37; SSC 13
    See also CA 106; 150; MTCW 1
Gilmour, David 1949- ........................ CLC 35
    See also CA 138, 147
Gilpin, William 1724-1804 ............. NCLC 30
Gilray, J. D.
    See Mencken, H(enry) L(ouis)
Gilroy, Frank D(aniel) 1925- .............. CLC 2
    See also CA 81-84; CANR 32, 64, 86; DLB 7
Gilstrap, John 1957(?)- ..................... CLC 99
    See also CA 160
Ginsberg, Allen 1926-1997 .... CLC 1, 2, 3, 4, 6, 13, 36, 69, 109; DA; DAB; DAC; DAM MST, POET; PC 4; WLC
    See also AITN 1; CA 1-4R; 157; CANR 2, 41, 63; CDALB 1941-1968; DA3; DLB 5, 16, 169; MTCW 1, 2
Ginzburg, Natalia 1916-1991 ....... CLC 5, 11, 54, 70
    See also CA 85-88; 135; CANR 33; DLB 177; MTCW 1, 2
Giono, Jean 1895-1970 .................. CLC 4, 11
    See also CA 45-48; 29-32R; CANR 2, 35; DLB 72; MTCW 1
Giovanni, Nikki 1943- ....... CLC 2, 4, 19, 64, 117; BLC 2; DA; DAB; DAC; DAM MST, MULT, POET; PC 19; WLCS
    See also AAYA 22; AITN 1; BW 2, 3; CA 29-32R; CAAS 6; CANR 18, 41, 60; CDALBS; CLR 6; DA3; DLB 5, 41; INT CANR-18; MAICYA; MTCW 1, 2; SATA 24, 107
Giovene, Andrea 1904- ....................... CLC 7
    See also CA 85-88
Gippius, Zinaida (Nikolayevna) 1869-1945
    See Hippius, Zinaida
    See also CA 106
Giraudoux, (Hippolyte) Jean 1882-1944
    TCLC 2, 7; DAM DRAM
    See also CA 104; DLB 65
Gironella, Jose Maria 1917- ............. CLC 11
    See also CA 101
Gissing, George (Robert) 1857-1903 ....... TCLC 3, 24, 47; SSC 37
    See also CA 105; 167; DLB 18, 135, 184
Giurlani, Aldo
    See Palazzeschi, Aldo
Gladkov, Fyodor (Vasilyevich) 1883-1958
    TCLC 27
    See also CA 170
Glanville, Brian (Lester) 1931- ........... CLC 6
    See also CA 5-8R; CAAS 9; CANR 3, 70; DLB 15, 139; SATA 42
Glasgow, Ellen (Anderson Gholson) 1873-1945 ............... TCLC 2, 7; SSC 34
    See also CA 104; 164; DLB 9, 12; MTCW 2
Glaspell, Susan 1882(?)-1948 . TCLC 55; DC 10
    See also CA 110; 154; DLB 7, 9, 78; YABC 2
Glassco, John 1909-1981 ................... CLC 9
    See also CA 13-16R; 102; CANR 15; DLB 68
Glasscock, Amnesia
    See Steinbeck, John (Ernst)

Glasser, Ronald J. 1940(?)- ............... CLC 37
Glassman, Joyce
    See Johnson, Joyce
Glendinning, Victoria 1937- ............. CLC 50
    See also CA 120; 127; CANR 59; DLB 155
Glissant, Edouard 1928- . CLC 10, 68; DAM MULT
    See also CA 153
Gloag, Julian 1930- .......................... CLC 40
    See also AITN 1; CA 65-68; CANR 10, 70
Glowacki, Aleksander
    See Prus, Boleslaw
Gluck, Louise (Elisabeth) 1943- .. CLC 7, 22, 44, 81; DAM POET; PC 16
    See also CA 33-36R; CANR 40, 69; DA3; DLB 5; MTCW 2
Glyn, Elinor 1864-1943 ................... TCLC 72
    See also DLB 153
Gobineau, Joseph Arthur (Comte) de 1816-1882 ................................ NCLC 17
    See also DLB 123
Godard, Jean-Luc 1930- .................. CLC 20
    See also CA 93-96
Godden, (Margaret) Rumer 1907-1998 ............................. CLC 53
    See also AAYA 6; CA 5-8R; 172; CANR 4, 27, 36, 55, 80; CLR 20; DLB 161; MAI-CYA; SAAS 12; SATA 3, 36; SATA-Obit 109
Godoy Alcayaga, Lucila 1889-1957
    See Mistral, Gabriela
    See also BW 2; CA 104; 131; CANR 81; DAM MULT; HW 1, 2; MTCW 1, 2
Godwin, Gail (Kathleen) 1937- ..... CLC 5, 8, 22, 31, 69, 125; DAM POP
    See also CA 29-32R; CANR 15, 43, 69; DA3; DLB 6; INT CANR-15; MTCW 1, 2
Godwin, William 1756-1836 .......... NCLC 14
    See also CDBLB 1789-1832; DLB 39, 104, 142, 158, 163
Goebbels, Josef
    See Goebbels, (Paul) Joseph
Goebbels, (Paul) Joseph 1897-1945 ............................. TCLC 68
    See also CA 115; 148
Goebbels, Joseph Paul
    See Goebbels, (Paul) Joseph
Goethe, Johann Wolfgang von 1749-1832
    NCLC 4, 22, 34; DA; DAB; DAC; DAM DRAM, MST, POET; PC 5; SSC 38; WLC
    See also DA3; DLB 94
Gogarty, Oliver St. John 1878-1957 ................................ TCLC 15
    See also CA 109; 150; DLB 15, 19
Gogol, Nikolai (Vasilyevich) 1809-1852
    NCLC 5, 15, 31; DA; DAB; DAC; DAM DRAM, MST; DC 1; SSC 4, 29; WLC
    See also DLB 198
Goines, Donald 1937(?)-1974 . CLC 80; BLC 2; DAM MULT, POP
    See also AITN 1; BW 1, 3; CA 124; 114; CANR 82; DA3; DLB 33
Gold, Herbert 1924- ........... CLC 4, 7, 14, 42
    See also CA 9-12R; CANR 17, 45; DLB 2; DLBY 81
Goldbarth, Albert 1948- ................ CLC 5, 38
    See also CA 53-56; CANR 6, 40; DLB 120
Goldberg, Anatol 1910-1982 ............. CLC 34
    See also CA 131; 117
Goldemberg, Isaac 1945- ................... CLC 52
    See also CA 69-72; CAAS 12; CANR 11, 32; HW 1

**Golding, William (Gerald)**
1911-1993 ..... **CLC 1, 2, 3, 8, 10, 17, 27, 58, 81; DA; DAB; DAC; DAM MST, NOV; WLC**
See also AAYA 5; CA 5-8R; 141; CANR 13, 33, 54; CDBLB 1945-1960; DA3; DLB 15, 100; MTCW 1, 2

**Goldman, Emma** 1869-1940 .......... **TCLC 13**
See also CA 110; 150

**Goldman, Francisco** 1954- ................ **CLC 76**
See also CA 162

**Goldman, William (W.)** 1931- ...... **CLC 1, 48**
See also CA 9-12R; CANR 29, 69; DLB 44

**Goldmann, Lucien** 1913-1970 .......... **CLC 24**
See also CA 25-28; CAP 2

**Goldoni, Carlo** 1707-1793 .......... **LC 4; DAM DRAM**

**Goldsberry, Steven** 1949- ................ **CLC 34**
See also CA 131

**Goldsmith, Oliver** 1728-1774 . **LC 2, 48; DA; DAB; DAC; DAM DRAM, MST, NOV, POET; DC 8; WLC**
See also CDBLB 1660-1789; DLB 39, 89, 104, 109, 142; SATA 26

**Goldsmith, Peter**
See Priestley, J(ohn) B(oynton)

**Gombrowicz, Witold** 1904-1969 .... **CLC 4, 7, 11, 49; DAM DRAM**
See also CA 19-20; 25-28R; CAP 2

**Gomez de la Serna, Ramon**
1888-1963 ............................ **CLC 9**
See also CA 153; 116; CANR 79; HW 1, 2

**Goncharov, Ivan Alexandrovich** 1812-1891
**NCLC 1, 63**

**Goncourt, Edmond (Louis Antoine Huot) de**
1822-1896 ........................ **NCLC 7**
See also DLB 123

**Goncourt, Jules (Alfred Huot) de** 1830-1870
**NCLC 7**
See also DLB 123

**Gontier, Fernande** 19(?)- .................. **CLC 50**

**Gonzalez Martinez, Enrique** 1871-1952
**TCLC 72**
See also CA 166; CANR 81; HW 1, 2

**Goodman, Paul** 1911-1972 ..... **CLC 1, 2, 4, 7**
See also CA 19-20; 37-40R; CANR 34; CAP 2; DLB 130; MTCW 1

**Gordimer, Nadine** 1923- ...... **CLC 3, 5, 7, 10, 18, 33, 51, 70; DA; DAB; DAC; DAM MST, NOV; SSC 17; WLCS**
See also CA 5-8R; CANR 3, 28, 56, 88; DA3; INT CANR-28; MTCW 1, 2

**Gordon, Adam Lindsay**
1833-1870 ............................ **NCLC 21**

**Gordon, Caroline** 1895-1981 . **CLC 6, 13, 29, 83; SSC 15**
See also CA 11-12; 103; CANR 36; CAP 1; DLB 4, 9, 102; DLBD 17; DLBY 81; MTCW 1, 2

**Gordon, Charles William** 1860-1937
See Connor, Ralph
See also CA 109

**Gordon, Mary (Catherine)** 1949- .... **CLC 13, 22, 128**
See also CA 102; CANR 44; DLB 6; DLBY 81; INT 102; MTCW 1

**Gordon, N. J.**
See Bosman, Herman Charles

**Gordon, Sol** 1923- ............................ **CLC 26**
See also CA 53-56; CANR 4; SATA 11

**Gordone, Charles** 1925-1995 ........ **CLC 1, 4; DAM DRAM; DC 8**
See also BW 1, 3; CA 93-96, 180; 150; CAAE 180; CANR 55; DLB 7; INT 93-96; MTCW 1

**Gore, Catherine** 1800-1861 ........... **NCLC 65**
See also DLB 116

**Gorenko, Anna Andreevna**
See Akhmatova, Anna

**Gorky, Maxim** 1868-1936 ..... **TCLC 8; DAB; SSC 28; WLC**
See also Peshkov, Alexei Maximovich
MTCW 2

**Goryan, Sirak**
See Saroyan, William

**Gosse, Edmund (William)**
1849-1928 ............................... **TCLC 28**
See also CA 117; DLB 57, 144, 184

**Gotlieb, Phyllis Fay (Bloom)** 1926- .. **CLC 18**
See also CA 13-16R; CANR 7; DLB 88

**Gottesman, S. D.**
See Kornbluth, C(yril) M.; Pohl, Frederik

**Gottfried von Strassburg** fl. c.
1210- ............................... **CMLC 10**
See also DLB 138

**Gould, Lois** ..................................... **CLC 4, 10**
See also CA 77-80; CANR 29; MTCW 1

**Gourmont, Remy (-Marie-Charles) de**
1858-1915 ......................... **TCLC 17**
See also CA 109; 150; MTCW 2

**Govier, Katherine** 1948- .................. **CLC 51**
See also CA 101; CANR 18, 40

**Goyen, (Charles) William**
1915-1983 ................... **CLC 5, 8, 14, 40**
See also AITN 2; CA 5-8R; 110; CANR 6, 71; DLB 2; DLBY 83; INT CANR-6

**Goytisolo, Juan** 1931- . **CLC 5, 10, 23; DAM MULT; HLC 1**
See also CA 85-88; CANR 32, 61; HW 1, 2; MTCW 1, 2

**Gozzano, Guido** 1883-1916 ................. **PC 10**
See also CA 154; DLB 114

**Gozzi, (Conte) Carlo** 1720-1806 .... **NCLC 23**

**Grabbe, Christian Dietrich**
1801-1836 ........................... **NCLC 2**
See also DLB 133

**Grace, Patricia Frances** 1937- .......... **CLC 56**
See also CA 176

**Gracian y Morales, Baltasar**
1601-1658 ............................... **LC 15**

**Gracq, Julien** ............................. **CLC 11, 48**
See also Poirier, Louis DLB 83

**Grade, Chaim** 1910-1982 ................. **CLC 10**
See also CA 93-96; 107

**Graduate of Oxford, A**
See Ruskin, John

**Grafton, Garth**
See Duncan, Sara Jeannette

**Graham, John**
See Phillips, David Graham

**Graham, Jorie** 1951- .................. **CLC 48, 118**
See also CA 111; CANR 63; DLB 120

**Graham, R(obert) B(ontine) Cunninghame**
See Cunninghame Graham, Robert (Gallnigad) Bontine
See also DLB 98, 135, 174

**Graham, Robert**
See Haldeman, Joe (William)

**Graham, Tom**
See Lewis, (Harry) Sinclair

**Graham, W(illiam) S(ydney)**
1918-1986 ............................... **CLC 29**
See also CA 73-76; 118; DLB 20

**Graham, Winston (Mawdsley)**
1910- ........................................ **CLC 23**
See also CA 49-52; CANR 2, 22, 45, 66; DLB 77

**Grahame, Kenneth** 1859-1932 ...... **TCLC 64; DAB**
See also CA 108; 136; CANR 80; CLR 5; DA3; DLB 34, 141, 178; MAICYA; MTCW 2; SATA 100; YABC 1

**Granovsky, Timofei Nikolaevich** 1813-1855
**NCLC 75**
See also DLB 198

**Grant, Skeeter**
See Spiegelman, Art

**Granville-Barker, Harley**
1877-1946 ......... **TCLC 2; DAM DRAM**
See also Barker, Harley Granville CA 104

**Grass, Guenter (Wilhelm)** 1927- ... **CLC 1, 2, 4, 6, 11, 15, 22, 32, 49, 88; DA; DAB; DAC; DAM MST, NOV; WLC**
See also CA 13-16R; CANR 20, 75; DA3; DLB 75, 124; MTCW 1, 2

**Gratton, Thomas**
See Hulme, T(homas) E(rnest)

**Grau, Shirley Ann** 1929- . **CLC 4, 9; SSC 15**
See also CA 89-92; CANR 22, 69; DLB 2; INT CANR-22; MTCW 1

**Gravel, Fern**
See Hall, James Norman

**Graver, Elizabeth** 1964- .................... **CLC 70**
See also CA 135; CANR 71

**Graves, Richard Perceval** 1945- ....... **CLC 44**
See also CA 65-68; CANR 9, 26, 51

**Graves, Robert (von Ranke)**
1895-1985 .. **CLC 1, 2, 6, 11, 39, 44, 45; DAB; DAC; DAM MST, POET; PC 6**
See also CA 5-8R; 117; CANR 5, 36; CDBLB 1914-1945; DA3; DLB 20, 100, 191; DLBD 18; DLBY 85; MTCW 1, 2; SATA 45

**Graves, Valerie**
See Bradley, Marion Zimmer

**Gray, Alasdair (James)** 1934- .......... **CLC 41**
See also CA 126; CANR 47, 69; DLB 194; INT 126; MTCW 1, 2

**Gray, Amlin** 1946- .......................... **CLC 29**
See also CA 138

**Gray, Francine du Plessix** 1930- ..... **CLC 22; DAM NOV**
See also BEST 90:3; CA 61-64; CAAS 2; CANR 11, 33, 75, 81; INT CANR-11; MTCW 1, 2

**Gray, John (Henry)** 1866-1934 ...... **TCLC 19**
See also CA 119; 162

**Gray, Simon (James Holliday)**
1936- ................................. **CLC 9, 14, 36**
See also AITN 1; CA 21-24R; CAAS 3; CANR 32, 69; DLB 13; MTCW 1

**Gray, Spalding** 1941- ..... **CLC 49, 112; DAM POP; DC 7**
See also CA 128; CANR 74; MTCW 2

**Gray, Thomas** 1716-1771 ....... **LC 4, 40; DA; DAB; DAC; DAM MST; PC 2; WLC**
See also CDBLB 1660-1789; DA3; DLB 109

**Grayson, David**
See Baker, Ray Stannard

**Grayson, Richard (A.)** 1951- ........... **CLC 38**
See also CA 85-88; CANR 14, 31, 57

**Greeley, Andrew M(oran)** 1928- ..... **CLC 28; DAM POP**
See also CA 5-8R; CAAS 7; CANR 7, 43, 69; DA3; MTCW 1, 2

**Green, Anna Katharine**
1846-1935 ............................... **TCLC 63**
See also CA 112; 159; DLB 202

**Green, Brian**
See Card, Orson Scott

**Green, Hannah**
See Greenberg, Joanne (Goldenberg)

**Green, Hannah** 1927(?)-1996 ............. **CLC 3**
See also CA 73-76; CANR 59

**Green, Henry** 1905-1973 ......... **CLC 2, 13, 97**
See also Yorke, Henry Vincent CA 175; DLB 15

**Green, Julian (Hartridge)** 1900-1998
See Green, Julien
See also CA 21-24R; 169; CANR 33, 87; DLB 4, 72; MTCW 1

**Green, Julien** ........................... **CLC 3, 11, 77**
See also Green, Julian (Hartridge) MTCW 2

**Green, Paul (Eliot)** 1894-1981 ......... **CLC 25; DAM DRAM**
See also AITN 1; CA 5-8R; 103; CANR 3; DLB 7, 9; DLBY 81

**Greenberg, Ivan** 1908-1973
See Rahv, Philip
See also CA 85-88

**Greenberg, Joanne (Goldenberg)** 1932- ...................................... **CLC 7, 30**
See also AAYA 12; CA 5-8R; CANR 14, 32, 69; SATA 25

**Greenberg, Richard** 1959(?)- ........... **CLC 57**
See also CA 138

**Greene, Bette** 1934- .......................... **CLC 30**
See also AAYA 7; CA 53-56; CANR 4; CLR 2; JRDA; MAICYA; SAAS 16; SATA 8, 102

**Greene, Gael** ...................................... **CLC 8**
See also CA 13-16R; CANR 10

**Greene, Graham (Henry)** 1904-1991 .... **CLC 1, 3, 6, 9, 14, 18, 27, 37, 70, 72, 125; DA; DAB; DAC; DAM MST, NOV; SSC 29; WLC**
See also AITN 2; CA 13-16R; 133; CANR 35, 61; CDBLB 1945-1960; DA3; DLB 13, 15, 77, 100, 162, 201, 204; DLBY 91; MTCW 1, 2; SATA 20

**Greene, Robert** 1558-1592 .................. **LC 41**
See also DLB 62, 167

**Greer, Richard**
See Silverberg, Robert

**Gregor, Arthur** 1923- .......................... **CLC 9**
See also CA 25-28R; CAAS 10; CANR 11; SATA 36

**Gregor, Lee**
See Pohl, Frederik

**Gregory, Isabella Augusta (Persse)** 1852-1932 .................................. **TCLC 1**
See also CA 104; 184; DLB 10

**Gregory, J. Dennis**
See Williams, John A(lfred)

**Grendon, Stephen**
See Derleth, August (William)

**Grenville, Kate** 1950- ........................ **CLC 61**
See also CA 118; CANR 53

**Grenville, Pelham**
See Wodehouse, P(elham) G(renville)

**Greve, Felix Paul (Berthold Friedrich)** 1879-1948
See Grove, Frederick Philip
See also CA 104; 141; 175; CANR 79; DAC; DAM MST

**Grey, Zane** 1872-1939 . **TCLC 6; DAM POP**
See also CA 104; 132; DA3; DLB 212; MTCW 1, 2

**Grieg, (Johan) Nordahl (Brun)** 1902-1943 **TCLC 10**
See also CA 107

**Grieve, C(hristopher) M(urray)** 1892-1978 **CLC 11, 19; DAM POET**
See also MacDiarmid, Hugh; Pteleon CA 5-8R; 85-88; CANR 33; MTCW 1

**Griffin, Gerald** 1803-1840 ............... **NCLC 7**
See also DLB 159

**Griffin, John Howard** 1920-1980 ..... **CLC 68**
See also AITN 1; CA 1-4R; 101; CANR 2

**Griffin, Peter** 1942- .......................... **CLC 39**
See also CA 136

**Griffith, D(avid Lewelyn) W(ark)** 1875(?)-1948 ................ **TCLC 68**
See also CA 119; 150; CANR 80

**Griffith, Lawrence**
See Griffith, D(avid Lewelyn) W(ark)

**Griffiths, Trevor** 1935- ............... **CLC 13, 52**
See also CA 97-100; CANR 45; DLB 13

**Griggs, Sutton Elbert** 1872-1930(?) .......................... **TCLC 77**
See also CA 123; DLB 50

**Grigson, Geoffrey (Edward Harvey)** 1905-1985 .............................. **CLC 7, 39**
See also CA 25-28R; 118; CANR 20, 33; DLB 27; MTCW 1, 2

**Grillparzer, Franz** 1791-1872 ......... **NCLC 1; SSC 37**
See also DLB 133

**Grimble, Reverend Charles James**
See Eliot, T(homas) S(tearns)

**Grimke, Charlotte L(ottie) Forten** 1837(?)-1914
See Forten, Charlotte L.
See also BW 1; CA 117; 124; DAM MULT, POET

**Grimm, Jacob Ludwig Karl** 1785-1863 **NCLC 3, 77; SSC 36**
See also DLB 90; MAICYA; SATA 22

**Grimm, Wilhelm Karl** 1786-1859 .. **NCLC 3, 77; SSC 36**
See also DLB 90; MAICYA; SATA 22

**Grimmelshausen, Johann Jakob Christoffel von** 1621-1676 ................ **LC 6**
See also DLB 168

**Grindel, Eugene** 1895-1952
See Eluard, Paul
See also CA 104

**Grisham, John** 1955- .... **CLC 84; DAM POP**
See also AAYA 14; CA 138; CANR 47, 69; DA3; MTCW 2

**Grossman, David** 1954- .................... **CLC 67**
See also CA 138

**Grossman, Vasily (Semenovich)** 1905-1964 **CLC 41**
See also CA 124; 130; MTCW 1

**Grove, Frederick Philip** ................... **TCLC 4**
See also Greve, Felix Paul (Berthold Friedrich) DLB 92

**Grubb**
See Crumb, R(obert)

**Grumbach, Doris (Isaac)** 1918- . **CLC 13, 22, 64**
See also CA 5-8R; CAAS 2; CANR 9, 42, 70; INT CANR-9; MTCW 2

**Grundtvig, Nicolai Frederik Severin** 1783-1872 ................................. **NCLC 1**

**Grunge**
See Crumb, R(obert)

**Grunwald, Lisa** 1959- ....................... **CLC 44**
See also CA 120

**Guare, John** 1938- ........... **CLC 8, 14, 29, 67; DAM DRAM**
See also CA 73-76; CANR 21, 69; DLB 7; MTCW 1, 2

**Gudjonsson, Halldor Kiljan** 1902-1998
See Laxness, Halldor
See also CA 103; 164

**Guenter, Erich**
See Eich, Guenter

**Guest, Barbara** 1920- ....................... **CLC 34**
See also CA 25-28R; CANR 11, 44, 84; DLB 5, 193

**Guest, Edgar A(lbert)** 1881-1959 ... **TCLC 95**
See also CA 112; 168

**Guest, Judith (Ann)** 1936- .......... **CLC 8, 30; DAM NOV, POP**
See also AAYA 7; CA 77-80; CANR 15, 75; DA3; INT CANR-15; MTCW 1, 2

**Guevara, Che** ...................... **CLC 87; HLC 1**
See also Guevara (Serna), Ernesto

**Guevara (Serna), Ernesto** 1928-1967 ......... **CLC 87; DAM MULT; HLC 1**
See also Guevara, Che CA 127; 111; CANR 56; HW 1

**Guicciardini, Francesco** 1483-1540 ..... **LC 49**

**Guild, Nicholas M.** 1944- .................. **CLC 33**
See also CA 93-96

**Guillemin, Jacques**
See Sartre, Jean-Paul

**Guillen, Jorge** 1893-1984 ....... **CLC 11; DAM MULT, POET; HLCS 1**
See also CA 89-92; 112; DLB 108; HW 1

**Guillen, Nicolas (Cristobal)** 1902-1989 ... **CLC 48, 79; BLC 2; DAM MST, MULT, POET; HLC 1; PC 23**
See also BW 2; CA 116; 125; 129; CANR 84; HW 1

**Guillevic, (Eugene)** 1907- ................. **CLC 33**
See also CA 93-96

**Guillois**
See Desnos, Robert

**Guillois, Valentin**
See Desnos, Robert

**Guimaraes Rosa, Joao** 1908-1967
See also CA 175; HLCS 2

**Guiney, Louise Imogen** 1861-1920 ................................. **TCLC 41**
See also CA 160; DLB 54

**Guiraldes, Ricardo (Guillermo)** 1886-1927 **TCLC 39**
See also CA 131; HW 1; MTCW 1

**Gumilev, Nikolai (Stepanovich)** 1886-1921 **TCLC 60**
See also CA 165

**Gunesekera, Romesh** 1954- .............. **CLC 91**
See also CA 159

**Gunn, Bill** ........................................ **CLC 5**
See also Gunn, William Harrison DLB 38

**Gunn, Thom(son William)** 1929- .. **CLC 3, 6, 18, 32, 81; DAM POET; PC 26**
See also CA 17-20R; CANR 9, 33; CDBLB 1960 to Present; DLB 27; INT CANR-33; MTCW 1

**Gunn, William Harrison** 1934(?)-1989
See Gunn, Bill
See also AITN 1; BW 1, 3; CA 13-16R; 128; CANR 12, 25, 76

**Gunnars, Kristjana** 1948- ................. **CLC 69**
See also CA 113; DLB 60

**Gurdjieff, G(eorgei) I(vanovich)** 1877(?)-1949 ............................ **TCLC 71**
See also CA 157

**Gurganus, Allan** 1947- . **CLC 70; DAM POP**
See also BEST 90:1; CA 135

**Gurney, A(lbert) R(amsdell), Jr.** 1930- ..... **CLC 32, 50, 54; DAM DRAM**
See also CA 77-80; CANR 32, 64

**Gurney, Ivor (Bertie)** 1890-1937 ... **TCLC 33**
See also CA 167

**Gurney, Peter**
See Gurney, A(lbert) R(amsdell), Jr.

**Guro, Elena** 1877-1913 ................... **TCLC 56**

**Gustafson, James M(oody)** 1925- ... **CLC 100**
See also CA 25-28R; CANR 37

**Gustafson, Ralph (Barker)** 1909- ..... **CLC 36**
See also CA 21-24R; CANR 8, 45, 84; DLB 88

**Gut, Gom**
See Simenon, Georges (Jacques Christian)

**Guterson, David** 1956- ...................... **CLC 91**
See also CA 132; CANR 73; MTCW 2

**Guthrie, A(lfred) B(ertram), Jr.** 1901-1991 **CLC 23**
See also CA 57-60; 134; CANR 24; DLB 212; SATA 62; SATA-Obit 67

**Guthrie, Isobel**
See Grieve, C(hristopher) M(urray)

**Guthrie, Woodrow Wilson** 1912-1967
See Guthrie, Woody
See also CA 113; 93-96

**Guthrie, Woody** ................................. **CLC 35**
See also Guthrie, Woodrow Wilson

**Gutierrez Najera, Manuel** 1859-1895
See also HLCS 2

**Guy, Rosa (Cuthbert)** 1928- ............. **CLC 26**
See also AAYA 4; BW 2; CA 17-20R;
CANR 14, 34, 83; CLR 13; DLB 33;
JRDA; MAICYA; SATA 14, 62

**Gwendolyn**
See Bennett, (Enoch) Arnold

**H. D.** ............. **CLC 3, 8, 14, 31, 34, 73; PC 5**
See also Doolittle, Hilda

**H. de V.**
See Buchan, John

**Haavikko, Paavo Juhani** 1931- .. **CLC 18, 34**
See also CA 106

**Habbema, Koos**
See Heijermans, Herman

**Habermas, Juergen** 1929- ............... **CLC 104**
See also CA 109; CANR 85

**Habermas, Jurgen**
See Habermas, Juergen

**Hacker, Marilyn** 1942- ...... **CLC 5, 9, 23, 72,
91; DAM POET**
See also CA 77-80; CANR 68; DLB 120

**Haeckel, Ernst Heinrich (Philipp August)**
1834-1919 ............................... **TCLC 83**
See also CA 157

**Hafiz** c. 1326-1389 ...................... **CMLC 34**

**Hafiz** c. 1326-1389(?) ...................... **CMLC 34**

**Haggard, H(enry) Rider**
1856-1925 ................................. **TCLC 11**
See also CA 108; 148; DLB 70, 156, 174,
178; MTCW 2; SATA 16

**Hagiosy, L.**
See Larbaud, Valery (Nicolas)

**Hagiwara Sakutaro** 1886-1942 ..... **TCLC 60;
PC 18**

**Haig, Fenil**
See Ford, Ford Madox

**Haig-Brown, Roderick (Langmere)**
1908-1976 ................................... **CLC 21**
See also CA 5-8R; 69-72; CANR 4, 38, 83;
CLR 31; DLB 88; MAICYA; SATA 12

**Hailey, Arthur** 1920- ..... **CLC 5; DAM NOV,
POP**
See also AITN 2; BEST 90:3; CA 1-4R;
CANR 2, 36, 75; DLB 88; DLBY 82;
MTCW 1, 2

**Hailey, Elizabeth Forsythe** 1938- ..... **CLC 40**
See also CA 93-96; CAAS 1; CANR 15,
48; INT CANR-15

**Haines, John (Meade)** 1924- ............. **CLC 58**
See also CA 17-20R; CANR 13, 34; DLB
212

**Hakluyt, Richard** 1552-1616 ............... **LC 31**

**Haldeman, Joe (William)** 1943- ....... **CLC 61**
See also Graham, Robert CA 53-56, 179;
CAAE 179; CAAS 25; CANR 6, 70, 72;
DLB 8; INT CANR-6

**Hale, Sarah Josepha (Buell)** 1788-1879
**NCLC 75**
See also DLB 1, 42, 73

**Haley, Alex(ander Murray Palmer)**
1921-1992 . **CLC 8, 12, 76; BLC 2; DA;
DAB; DAC; DAM MST, MULT, POP**
See also AAYA 26; BW 2, 3; CA 77-80;
136; CANR 61; CDALBS; DA3; DLB 38;
MTCW 1, 2

**Haliburton, Thomas Chandler** 1796-1865
**NCLC 15**
See also DLB 11, 99

**Hall, Donald (Andrew, Jr.)** 1928- ...... **CLC 1,
13, 37, 59; DAM POET**
See also CA 5-8R; CAAS 7; CANR 2, 44,
64; DLB 5; MTCW 1; SATA 23, 97

**Hall, Frederic Sauser**
See Sauser-Hall, Frederic

**Hall, James**
See Kuttner, Henry

**Hall, James Norman** 1887-1951 ..... **TCLC 23**
See also CA 123; 173; SATA 21

**Hall, Radclyffe**
See Hall, (Marguerite) Radclyffe
See also MTCW 2

**Hall, (Marguerite) Radclyffe** 1886-1943
**TCLC 12**
See also CA 110; 150; CANR 83; DLB 191

**Hall, Rodney** 1935- ......................... **CLC 51**
See also CA 109; CANR 69

**Halleck, Fitz-Greene** 1790-1867 .... **NCLC 47**
See also DLB 3

**Halliday, Michael**
See Creasey, John

**Halpern, Daniel** 1945- ...................... **CLC 14**
See also CA 33-36R

**Hamburger, Michael (Peter Leopold)** 1924-
**CLC 5, 14**
See also CA 5-8R; CAAS 4; CANR 2, 47;
DLB 27

**Hamill, Pete** 1935- ........................... **CLC 10**
See also CA 25-28R; CANR 18, 71

**Hamilton, Alexander**
1755(?)-1804 ......................... **NCLC 49**
See also DLB 37

**Hamilton, Clive**
See Lewis, C(live) S(taples)

**Hamilton, Edmond** 1904-1977 ........... **CLC 1**
See also CA 1-4R; CANR 3, 84; DLB 8

**Hamilton, Eugene (Jacob) Lee**
See Lee-Hamilton, Eugene (Jacob)

**Hamilton, Franklin**
See Silverberg, Robert

**Hamilton, Gail**
See Corcoran, Barbara

**Hamilton, Mollie**
See Kaye, M(ary) M(argaret)

**Hamilton, (Anthony Walter) Patrick**
1904-1962 ................................. **CLC 51**
See also CA 176; 113; DLB 191

**Hamilton, Virginia** 1936- ...... **CLC 26; DAM
MULT**
See also AAYA 2, 21; BW 2, 3; CA 25-28R;
CANR 20, 37, 73; CLR 1, 11, 40; DLB
33, 52; INT CANR-20; JRDA; MAICYA;
MTCW 1, 2; SATA 4, 56, 79

**Hammett, (Samuel) Dashiell**
1894-1961 .... **CLC 3, 5, 10, 19, 47; SSC
17**
See also AITN 1; CA 81-84; CANR 42;
CDALB 1929-1941; DA3; DLBD 6;
DLBY 96; MTCW 1, 2

**Hammon, Jupiter** 1711(?)-1800(?) . **NCLC 5;
BLC 2; DAM MULT, POET; PC 16**
See also DLB 31, 50

**Hammond, Keith**
See Kuttner, Henry

**Hamner, Earl (Henry), Jr.** 1923- ...... **CLC 12**
See also AITN 2; CA 73-76; DLB 6

**Hampton, Christopher (James)**
1946- ........................................ **CLC 4**
See also CA 25-28R; DLB 13; MTCW 1

**Hamsun, Knut** ...................... **TCLC 2, 14, 49**
See also Pedersen, Knut

**Handke, Peter** 1942- ... **CLC 5, 8, 10, 15, 38;
DAM DRAM, NOV**
See also CA 77-80; CANR 33, 75; DLB 85,
124; MTCW 1, 2

**Handy, W(illiam) C(hristopher)** 1873-1958
**TCLC 97**
See also BW 3; CA 121; 167

**Hanley, James** 1901-1985 ..... **CLC 3, 5, 8, 13**
See also CA 73-76; 117; CANR 36; DLB
191; MTCW 1

**Hannah, Barry** 1942- ............ **CLC 23, 38, 90**
See also CA 108; 110; CANR 43, 68; DLB
6; INT 110; MTCW 1

**Hannon, Ezra**
See Hunter, Evan

**Hansberry, Lorraine (Vivian)** 1930-1965
**CLC 17, 62; BLC 2; DA; DAB; DAC;
DAM DRAM, MST, MULT; DC 2**
See also AAYA 25; BW 1, 3; CA 109; 25-
28R; CABS 3; CANR 58; CDALB 1941-
1968; DA3; DLB 7, 38; MTCW 1, 2

**Hansen, Joseph** 1923- ....................... **CLC 38**
See also CA 29-32R; CAAS 17; CANR 16,
44, 66; INT CANR-16

**Hansen, Martin A(lfred)**
1909-1955 ............................... **TCLC 32**
See also CA 167

**Hanson, Kenneth O(stlin)** 1922- ....... **CLC 13**
See also CA 53-56; CANR 7

**Hardwick, Elizabeth (Bruce)**
1916- ................... **CLC 13; DAM NOV**
See also CA 5-8R; CANR 3, 32, 70; DA3;
DLB 6; MTCW 1, 2

**Hardy, Thomas** 1840-1928 .. **TCLC 4, 10, 18,
32, 48, 53, 72; DA; DAB; DAC; DAM
MST, NOV, POET; PC 8; SSC 2; WLC**
See also CA 104; 123; CDBLB 1890-1914;
DA3; DLB 18, 19, 135; MTCW 1, 2

**Hare, David** 1947- ........................ **CLC 29, 58**
See also CA 97-100; CANR 39; DLB 13;
MTCW 1

**Harewood, John**
See Van Druten, John (William)

**Harford, Henry**
See Hudson, W(illiam) H(enry)

**Hargrave, Leonie**
See Disch, Thomas M(ichael)

**Harjo, Joy** 1951- ...... **CLC 83; DAM MULT;
PC 27**
See also CA 114; CANR 35, 67; DLB 120,
175; MTCW 2; NNAL

**Harlan, Louis R(udolph)** 1922- ........ **CLC 34**
See also CA 21-24R; CANR 25, 55, 80

**Harling, Robert** 1951(?)- .................. **CLC 53**
See also CA 147

**Harmon, William (Ruth)** 1938- ........ **CLC 38**
See also CA 33-36R; CANR 14, 32, 35;
SATA 65

**Harper, F. E. W.**
See Harper, Frances Ellen Watkins

**Harper, Frances E. W.**
See Harper, Frances Ellen Watkins

**Harper, Frances E. Watkins**
See Harper, Frances Ellen Watkins

**Harper, Frances Ellen**
See Harper, Frances Ellen Watkins

**Harper, Frances Ellen Watkins** 1825-1911
**TCLC 14; BLC 2; DAM MULT, POET;
PC 21**
See also BW 1, 3; CA 111; 125; CANR 79;
DLB 50

**Harper, Michael S(teven)** 1938- ... **CLC 7, 22**
See also BW 1; CA 33-36R; CANR 24;
DLB 41

**Harper, Mrs. F. E. W.**
See Harper, Frances Ellen Watkins

**Harris, Christie (Lucy) Irwin**
1907- ...................................... **CLC 12**
See also CA 5-8R; CANR 6, 83; CLR 47;
DLB 88; JRDA; MAICYA; SAAS 10;
SATA 6, 74

**Harris, Frank** 1856-1931 ................ **TCLC 24**
See also CA 109; 150; CANR 80; DLB 156,
197

**Harris, George Washington**
1814-1869 ............................... **NCLC 23**
See also DLB 3, 11

**Harris, Joel Chandler** 1848-1908 ... **TCLC 2;
SSC 19**
See also CA 104; 137; CANR 80; CLR 49;
DLB 11, 23, 42, 78, 91; MAICYA; SATA
100; YABC 1

**Harris, John (Wyndham Parkes Lucas)**
Beynon 1903-1969
See Wyndham, John
See also CA 102; 89-92; CANR 84

Harris, MacDonald .......................... CLC 9
See also Heiney, Donald (William)
Harris, Mark 1922- ........................... CLC 19
See also CA 5-8R; CAAS 3; CANR 2, 55,
83; DLB 2; DLBY 80
Harris, (Theodore) Wilson 1921- ..... CLC 25
See also BW 2, 3; CA 65-68; CAAS 16;
CANR 11, 27, 69; DLB 117; MTCW 1
Harrison, Elizabeth Cavanna 1909-
See Cavanna, Betty
See also CA 9-12R; CANR 6, 27, 85
Harrison, Harry (Max) 1925- .......... CLC 42
See also CA 1-4R; CANR 5, 21, 84; DLB
8; SATA 4
Harrison, James (Thomas) 1937- ...... CLC 6,
14, 33, 66; SSC 19
See also CA 13-16R; CANR 8, 51, 79;
DLBY 82; INT CANR-8
Harrison, Jim
See Harrison, James (Thomas)
Harrison, Kathryn 1961- .................... CLC 70
See also CA 144; CANR 68
Harrison, Tony 1937- ................. CLC 43, 129
See also CA 65-68; CANR 44; DLB 40;
MTCW 1
Harriss, Will(ard Irvin) 1922- .......... CLC 34
See also CA 111
Harson, Sley
See Ellison, Harlan (Jay)
Hart, Ellis
See Ellison, Harlan (Jay)
Hart, Josephine 1942(?)- ....... CLC 70; DAM
POP
See also CA 138; CANR 70
Hart, Moss 1904-1961 .......... CLC 66; DAM
DRAM
See also CA 109; 89-92; CANR 84; DLB 7
Harte, (Francis) Bret(t)
1836(?)-1902 ... TCLC 1, 25; DA; DAC;
DAM MST; SSC 8; WLC
See also CA 104; 140; CANR 80; CDALB
1865-1917; DA3; DLB 12, 64, 74, 79,
186; SATA 26
Hartley, L(eslie) P(oles) 1895-1972 ... CLC 2,
22
See also CA 45-48; 37-40R; CANR 33;
DLB 15, 139; MTCW 1, 2
Hartman, Geoffrey H. 1929- ............. CLC 27
See also CA 117; 125; CANR 79; DLB 67
Hartmann, Eduard von
1842-1906 ............................... TCLC 97
Hartmann, Sadakichi 1867-1944 ... TCLC 73
See also CA 157; DLB 54
Hartmann von Aue c. 1160-c.
1205 ........................................ CMLC 15
See also DLB 138
Hartmann von Aue 1170-1210 ...... CMLC 15
Haruf, Kent 1943- ............................. CLC 34
See also CA 149
Harwood, Ronald 1934- ........ CLC 32; DAM
DRAM, MST
See also CA 1-4R; CANR 4, 55; DLB 13
Hasegawa Tatsunosuke
See Futabatei, Shimei
Hasek, Jaroslav (Matej Frantisek)
1883-1923 .................................. TCLC 4
See also CA 104; 129; MTCW 1, 2
Hass, Robert 1941- ... CLC 18, 39, 99; PC 16
See also CA 111; CANR 30, 50, 71; DLB
105, 206; SATA 94
Hastings, Hudson
See Kuttner, Henry
Hastings, Selina ............................... CLC 44
Hathorne, John 1641-1717 ................. LC 38
Hatteras, Amelia
See Mencken, H(enry) L(ouis)

Hatteras, Owen ................................. TCLC 18
See also Mencken, H(enry) L(ouis); Nathan,
George Jean
Hauptmann, Gerhart (Johann Robert)
1862-1946 ....... TCLC 4; DAM DRAM;
SSC 37
See also CA 104; 153; DLB 66, 118
Havel, Vaclav 1936- ... CLC 25, 58, 65; DAM
DRAM; DC 6
See also CA 104; CANR 36, 63; DA3;
MTCW 1, 2
Haviaras, Stratis ............................... CLC 33
See also Chaviaras, Strates
Hawes, Stephen 1475(?)-1523(?) ......... LC 17
See also DLB 132
Hawkes, John (Clendennin Burne, Jr.)
1925-1998 .. CLC 1, 2, 3, 4, 7, 9, 14, 15,
27, 49
See also CA 1-4R; 167; CANR 2, 47, 64;
DLB 2, 7; DLBY 80, 98; MTCW 1, 2
Hawking, S. W.
See Hawking, Stephen W(illiam)
Hawking, Stephen W(illiam) 1942- . CLC 63,
105
See also AAYA 13; BEST 89:1; CA 126;
129; CANR 48; DA3; MTCW 2
Hawkins, Anthony Hope
See Hope, Anthony
Hawthorne, Julian 1846-1934 ........ TCLC 25
See also CA 165
Hawthorne, Nathaniel 1804-1864 . NCLC 39;
DA; DAB; DAC; DAM MST, NOV;
SSC 3, 29; WLC
See also AAYA 18; CDALB 1640-1865;
DA3; DLB 1, 74; YABC 2
Haxton, Josephine Ayres 1921-
See Douglas, Ellen
See also CA 115; CANR 41, 83
Hayaseca y Eizaguirre, Jorge
See Echegaray (y Eizaguirre), Jose (Maria
Waldo)
Hayashi, Fumiko 1904-1951 .......... TCLC 27
See also CA 161; DLB 180
Haycraft, Anna 1932-
See Ellis, Alice Thomas
See also CA 122; CANR 85; MTCW 2
Hayden, Robert E(arl) 1913-1980 . CLC 5, 9,
14, 37; BLC 2; DA; DAC; DAM MST,
MULT, POET; PC 6
See also BW 1, 3; CA 69-72; 97-100; CABS
2; CANR 24, 75, 82; CDALB 1941-1968;
DLB 5, 76; MTCW 1, 2; SATA 19; SATA-
Obit 26
Hayford, J(oseph) E(phraim) Casely
See Casely-Hayford, J(oseph) E(phraim)
Hayman, Ronald 1932- ...................... CLC 44
See also CA 25-28R; CANR 18, 50, 88;
DLB 155
Haywood, Eliza (Fowler)
1693(?)-1756 ............................. LC 1, 44
See also DLB 39
Hazlitt, William 1778-1830 ...... NCLC 29, 82
See also DLB 110, 158
Hazzard, Shirley 1931- ...................... CLC 18
See also CA 9-12R; CANR 4, 70; DLBY
82; MTCW 1
Head, Bessie 1937-1986 .... CLC 25, 67; BLC
2; DAM MULT
See also BW 2, 3; CA 29-32R; 119; CANR
25, 82; DA3; DLB 117; MTCW 1, 2
Headon, (Nicky) Topper 1956(?)- ..... CLC 30
Heaney, Seamus (Justin) 1939- ..... CLC 5, 7,
14, 25, 37, 74, 91; DAB; DAM POET;
PC 18; WLCS
See also CA 85-88; CANR 25, 48, 75; CD-
BLB 1960 to Present; DA3; DLB 40;
DLBY 95; MTCW 1, 2

Hearn, (Patricio) Lafcadio (Tessima Carlos)
1850-1904 ................................... TCLC 9
See also CA 105; 166; DLB 12, 78, 189
Hearne, Vicki 1946- .......................... CLC 56
See also CA 139
Hearon, Shelby 1931- ........................ CLC 63
See also AITN 2; CA 25-28R; CANR 18,
48
Heat-Moon, William Least ............... CLC 29
See also Trogdon, William (Lewis) AAYA 9
Hebbel, Friedrich 1813-1863 ........ NCLC 43;
DAM DRAM
See also DLB 129
Hebert, Anne 1916- ..... CLC 4, 13, 29; DAC;
DAM MST, POET
See also CA 85-88; CANR 69; DA3; DLB
68; MTCW 1, 2
Hecht, Anthony (Evan) 1923- ...... CLC 8, 13,
19; DAM POET
See also CA 9-12R; CANR 6; DLB 5, 169
Hecht, Ben 1894-1964 .......................... CLC 8
See also CA 85-88; DLB 7, 9, 25, 26, 28,
86
Hedayat, Sadeq 1903-1951 ............. TCLC 21
See also CA 120
Hegel, Georg Wilhelm Friedrich 1770-1831
NCLC 46
See also DLB 90
Heidegger, Martin 1889-1976 .......... CLC 24
See also CA 81-84; 65-68; CANR 34;
MTCW 1, 2
Heidenstam, (Carl Gustaf) Verner von
1859-1940 .................................... TCLC 5
See also CA 104
Heifner, Jack 1946- ........................... CLC 11
See also CA 105; CANR 47
Heijermans, Herman 1864-1924 .... TCLC 24
See also CA 123
Heilbrun, Carolyn G(old) 1926- ....... CLC 25
See also CA 45-48; CANR 1, 28, 58
Heine, Heinrich 1797-1856 ....... NCLC 4, 54;
PC 25
See also DLB 90
Heinemann, Larry (Curtiss) 1944- ... CLC 50
See also CA 110; CAAS 21; CANR 31, 81;
DLBD 9; INT CANR-31
Heiney, Donald (William) 1921-1993
See Harris, MacDonald
See also CA 1-4R; 142; CANR 3, 58
Heinlein, Robert A(nson) 1907-1988 . CLC 1,
3, 8, 14, 26, 55; DAM POP
See also AAYA 17; CA 1-4R; 125; CANR
1, 20, 53; DA3; DLB 8; JRDA; MAICYA;
MTCW 1, 2; SATA 9, 69; SATA-Obit 56
Helforth, John
See Doolittle, Hilda
Hellenhofferu, Vojtech Kapristian z
See Hasek, Jaroslav (Matej Frantisek)
Heller, Joseph 1923- .. CLC 1, 3, 5, 8, 11, 36,
63; DA; DAB; DAC; DAM MST, NOV,
POP; WLC
See also AAYA 24; AITN 1; CA 5-8R;
CABS 1; CANR 8, 42, 66; DA3; DLB 2,
28; DLBY 80; INT CANR-8; MTCW 1, 2
Hellman, Lillian (Florence)
1906-1984 .. CLC 2, 4, 8, 14, 18, 34, 44,
52; DAM DRAM; DC 1
See also AITN 1, 2; CA 13-16R; 112;
CANR 33; DA3; DLB 7; DLBY 84;
MTCW 1, 2
Helprin, Mark 1947- ....... CLC 7, 10, 22, 32;
DAM NOV, POP
See also CA 81-84; CANR 47, 64;
CDALBS; DA3; DLBY 85; MTCW 1, 2
Helvetius, Claude-Adrien 1715-1771 .. LC 26
Helyar, Jane Penelope Josephine 1933-
See Poole, Josephine
See also CA 21-24R; CANR 10, 26; SATA
82

**Hemans, Felicia** 1793-1835 ............. **NCLC 71**
   See also DLB 96
**Hemingway, Ernest (Miller)**
   1899-1961 .... **CLC 1, 3, 6, 8, 10, 13, 19,**
   **30, 34, 39, 41, 44, 50, 61, 80; DA;**
   **DAB; DAC; DAM MST, NOV; SSC 1,**
   **25, 36; WLC**
   See also AAYA 19; CA 77-80; CANR 34;
   CDALB 1917-1929; DA3; DLB 4, 9, 102,
   210; DLBD 1, 15, 16; DLBY 81, 87, 96,
   98; MTCW 1, 2
**Hempel, Amy** 1951- ........................... **CLC 39**
   See also CA 118; 137; CANR 70; DA3;
   MTCW 2
**Henderson, F. C.**
   See Mencken, H(enry) L(ouis)
**Henderson, Sylvia**
   See Ashton-Warner, Sylvia (Constance)
**Henderson, Zenna (Chlarson)**
   1917-1983 ................................. **SSC 29**
   See also CA 1-4R; 133; CANR 1, 84; DLB
   8; SATA 5
**Henkin, Joshua** ................................ **CLC 119**
   See also CA 161
**Henley, Beth** ..................... **CLC 23; DC 6**
   See also Henley, Elizabeth Becker CABS 3;
   DLBY 86
**Henley, Elizabeth Becker** 1952-
   See Henley, Beth
   See also CA 107; CANR 32, 73; DAM
   DRAM, MST; DA3; MTCW 1, 2
**Henley, William Ernest** 1849-1903 .. **TCLC 8**
   See also CA 105; DLB 19
**Hennissart, Martha**
   See Lathen, Emma
   See also CA 85-88; CANR 64
**Henry, O.** ............ **TCLC 1, 19; SSC 5; WLC**
   See also Porter, William Sydney
**Henry, Patrick** 1736-1799 .................... **LC 25**
**Henryson, Robert** 1430(?)-1506(?) ...... **LC 20**
   See also DLB 146
**Henry VIII** 1491-1547 ........................ **LC 10**
   See also DLB 132
**Henschke, Alfred**
   See Klabund
**Hentoff, Nat(han Irving)** 1925- ........ **CLC 26**
   See also AAYA 4; CA 1-4R; CAAS 6;
   CANR 5, 25, 77; CLR 1, 52; INT CANR-
   25; JRDA; MAICYA; SATA 42, 69;
   SATA-Brief 27
**Heppenstall, (John) Rayner**
   1911-1981 ................................... **CLC 10**
   See also CA 1-4R; 103; CANR 29
**Heraclitus** c. 540B.C.-c. 450B.C. ... **CMLC 22**
   See also DLB 176
**Herbert, Frank (Patrick)**
   1920-1986 ......... **CLC 12, 23, 35, 44, 85;**
   **DAM POP**
   See also AAYA 21; CA 53-56; 118; CANR
   5, 43; CDALBS; DLB 8; INT CANR-5;
   MTCW 1, 2; SATA 9, 37; SATA-Obit 47
**Herbert, George** 1593-1633 ..... **LC 24; DAB;**
   **DAM POET; PC 4**
   See also CDBLB Before 1660; DLB 126
**Herbert, Zbigniew** 1924-1998 ..... **CLC 9, 43;**
   **DAM POET**
   See also CA 89-92; 169; CANR 36, 74;
   MTCW 1
**Herbst, Josephine (Frey)**
   1897-1969 ................................. **CLC 34**
   See also CA 5-8R; 25-28R; DLB 9
**Heredia, Jose Maria** 1803-1839
   See also HLCS 2
**Hergesheimer, Joseph** 1880-1954 ... **TCLC 11**
   See also CA 109; DLB 102, 9
**Herlihy, James Leo** 1927-1993 ........... **CLC 6**
   See also CA 1-4R; 143; CANR 2

**Hermogenes** fl. c. 175- .................... **CMLC 6**
**Hernandez, Jose** 1834-1886 ........... **NCLC 17**
**Herodotus** c. 484B.C.-429B.C. ....... **CMLC 17**
   See also DLB 176
**Herrick, Robert** 1591-1674 ........ **LC 13; DA;**
   **DAB; DAC; DAM MST, POP; PC 9**
   See also DLB 126
**Herring, Guilles**
   See Somerville, Edith
**Herriot, James** 1916-1995 ..... **CLC 12; DAM**
   **POP**
   See also Wight, James Alfred AAYA 1; CA
   148; CANR 40; MTCW 2; SATA 86
**Herris, Violet**
   See Hunt, Violet
**Herrmann, Dorothy** 1941- ................ **CLC 44**
   See also CA 107
**Herrmann, Taffy**
   See Herrmann, Dorothy
**Hersey, John (Richard)** 1914-1993 .... **CLC 1,**
   **2, 7, 9, 40, 81, 97; DAM POP**
   See also AAYA 29; CA 17-20R; 140; CANR
   33; CDALBS; DLB 6, 185; MTCW 1, 2;
   SATA 25; SATA-Obit 76
**Herzen, Aleksandr Ivanovich** 1812-1870
   **NCLC 10, 61**
**Herzl, Theodor** 1860-1904 .............. **TCLC 36**
   See also CA 168
**Herzog, Werner** 1942- ...................... **CLC 16**
   See also CA 89-92
**Hesiod** c. 8th cent. B.C.- .................. **CMLC 5**
   See also DLB 176
**Hesse, Hermann** 1877-1962 ... **CLC 1, 2, 3, 6,**
   **11, 17, 25, 69; DA; DAB; DAC; DAM**
   **MST, NOV; SSC 9; WLC**
   See also CA 17-18; CAP 2; DA3; DLB 66;
   MTCW 1, 2; SATA 50
**Hewes, Cady**
   See De Voto, Bernard (Augustine)
**Heyen, William** 1940- .................. **CLC 13, 18**
   See also CA 33-36R; CAAS 9; DLB 5
**Heyerdahl, Thor** 1914- ...................... **CLC 26**
   See also CA 5-8R; CANR 5, 22, 66, 73;
   MTCW 1, 2; SATA 2, 52
**Heym, Georg (Theodor Franz Arthur)**
   1887-1912 ................................... **TCLC 9**
   See also CA 106; 181
**Heym, Stefan** 1913- .......................... **CLC 41**
   See also CA 9-12R; CANR 4; DLB 69
**Heyse, Paul (Johann Ludwig von)** 1830-1914
   **TCLC 8**
   See also CA 104; DLB 129
**Heyward, (Edwin) DuBose**
   1885-1940 ................................ **TCLC 59**
   See also CA 108; 157; DLB 7, 9, 45; SATA
   21
**Hibbert, Eleanor Alice Burford** 1906-1993
   **CLC 7; DAM POP**
   See also BEST 90:4; CA 17-20R; 140;
   CANR 9, 28, 59; MTCW 2; SATA 2;
   SATA-Obit 74
**Hichens, Robert (Smythe)**
   1864-1950 ................................ **TCLC 64**
   See also CA 162; DLB 153
**Higgins, George V(incent)** 1939- ... **CLC 4, 7,**
   **10, 18**
   See also CA 77-80; CAAS 5; CANR 17,
   51; DLB 2; DLBY 81, 98; INT CANR-
   17; MTCW 1
**Higginson, Thomas Wentworth** 1823-1911
   **TCLC 36**
   See also CA 162; DLB 1, 64
**Highet, Helen**
   See MacInnes, Helen (Clark)
**Highsmith, (Mary) Patricia**
   1921-1995 .......... **CLC 2, 4, 14, 42, 102;**
   **DAM NOV, POP**
   See also CA 1-4R; 147; CANR 1, 20, 48,
   62; DA3; MTCW 1, 2

**Highwater, Jamake (Mamake)**
   1942(?)- ...................................... **CLC 12**
   See also AAYA 7; CA 65-68; CAAS 7;
   CANR 10, 34, 84; CLR 17; DLB 52;
   DLBY 85; JRDA; MAICYA; SATA 32,
   69; SATA-Brief 30
**Highway, Tomson** 1951- ........ **CLC 92; DAC;**
   **DAM MULT**
   See also CA 151; CANR 75; MTCW 2;
   NNAL
**Higuchi, Ichiyo** 1872-1896 ............. **NCLC 49**
**Hijuelos, Oscar** 1951- ........... **CLC 65; DAM**
   **MULT, POP; HLC 1**
   See also AAYA 25; BEST 90:1; CA 123;
   CANR 50, 75; DA3; DLB 145; HW 1, 2;
   MTCW 2
**Hikmet, Nazim** 1902(?)-1963 ........... **CLC 40**
   See also CA 141; 93-96
**Hildegard von Bingen** 1098-1179 . **CMLC 20**
   See also DLB 148
**Hildesheimer, Wolfgang** 1916-1991 .. **CLC 49**
   See also CA 101; 135; DLB 69, 124
**Hill, Geoffrey (William)** 1932- ...... **CLC 5, 8,**
   **18, 45; DAM POET**
   See also CA 81-84; CANR 21; CDBLB
   1960 to Present; DLB 40; MTCW 1
**Hill, George Roy** 1921- ...................... **CLC 26**
   See also CA 110; 122
**Hill, John**
   See Koontz, Dean R(ay)
**Hill, Susan (Elizabeth)** 1942- .... **CLC 4, 113;**
   **DAB; DAM MST, NOV**
   See also CA 33-36R; CANR 29, 69; DLB
   14, 139; MTCW 1
**Hillerman, Tony** 1925- . **CLC 62; DAM POP**
   See also AAYA 6; BEST 89:1; CA 29-32R;
   CANR 21, 42, 65; DA3; DLB 206; SATA
   6
**Hillesum, Etty** 1914-1943 .............. **TCLC 49**
   See also CA 137
**Hilliard, Noel (Harvey)** 1929- .......... **CLC 15**
   See also CA 9-12R; CANR 7, 69
**Hillis, Rick** 1956- ............................... **CLC 66**
   See also CA 134
**Hilton, James** 1900-1954 ................ **TCLC 21**
   See also CA 108; 169; DLB 34, 77; SATA
   34
**Himes, Chester (Bomar)** 1909-1984 .. **CLC 2,**
   **4, 7, 18, 58, 108; BLC 2; DAM MULT**
   See also BW 2; CA 25-28R; 114; CANR
   22; DLB 2, 76, 143; MTCW 1, 2
**Hinde, Thomas** ............................ **CLC 6, 11**
   See also Chitty, Thomas Willes
**Hine, (William) Daryl** 1936- ............. **CLC 15**
   See also CA 1-4R; CAAS 15; CANR 1, 20;
   DLB 60
**Hinkson, Katharine Tynan**
   See Tynan, Katharine
**Hinojosa(-Smith), Rolando (R.)** 1929-
   See Hinojosa-Smith, Rolando
   See also CA 131; CAAS 16; CANR 62;
   DAM MULT; DLB 82; HLC 1; HW 1, 2;
   MTCW 2
**Hinojosa-Smith, Rolando** 1929-
   See Hinojosa(-Smith), Rolando (R.)
   See also CAAS 16; HLC 1; MTCW 2
**Hinton, S(usan) E(loise)** 1950- ......... **CLC 30,**
   **111; DA; DAB; DAC; DAM MST,**
   **NOV**
   See also AAYA 2; CA 81-84; CANR 32,
   62; CDALBS; CLR 3, 23; DA3; JRDA;
   MAICYA; MTCW 1, 2; SATA 19, 58
**Hippius, Zinaida** ............................... **TCLC 9**
   See also Gippius, Zinaida (Nikolayevna)
**Hiraoka, Kimitake** 1925-1970
   See Mishima, Yukio
   See also CA 97-100; 29-32R; DAM DRAM;
   DA3; MTCW 1, 2

**Hirsch, E(ric) D(onald), Jr.** 1928- .... **CLC 79**
See also CA 25-28R; CANR 27, 51; DLB 67; INT CANR-27; MTCW 1

**Hirsch, Edward** 1950- ................ **CLC 31, 50**
See also CA 104; CANR 20, 42; DLB 120

**Hitchcock, Alfred (Joseph)**
1899-1980 .................................... **CLC 16**
See also AAYA 22; CA 159; 97-100; SATA 27; SATA-Obit 24

**Hitler, Adolf** 1889-1945 .................. **TCLC 53**
See also CA 117; 147

**Hoagland, Edward** 1932- ................ **CLC 28**
See also CA 1-4R; CANR 2, 31, 57; DLB 6; SATA 51

**Hoban, Russell (Conwell)** 1925- . **CLC 7, 25; DAM NOV**
See also CA 5-8R; CANR 23, 37, 66; CLR 3; DLB 52; MAICYA; MTCW 1, 2; SATA 1, 40, 78

**Hobbes, Thomas** 1588-1679 ................ **LC 36**
See also DLB 151

**Hobbs, Perry**
See Blackmur, R(ichard) P(almer)

**Hobson, Laura Z(ametkin)**
1900-1986 ............................ **CLC 7, 25**
See also CA 17-20R; 118; CANR 55; DLB 28; SATA 52

**Hochhuth, Rolf** 1931- .. **CLC 4, 11, 18; DAM DRAM**
See also CA 5-8R; CANR 33, 75; DLB 124; MTCW 1, 2

**Hochman, Sandra** 1936- ................ **CLC 3, 8**
See also CA 5-8R; DLB 5

**Hochwaelder, Fritz** 1911-1986 ........ **CLC 36; DAM DRAM**
See also CA 29-32R; 120; CANR 42; MTCW 1

**Hochwalder, Fritz**
See Hochwaelder, Fritz

**Hocking, Mary (Eunice)** 1921- ........ **CLC 13**
See also CA 101; CANR 18, 40

**Hodgins, Jack** 1938- ...................... **CLC 23**
See also CA 93-96; DLB 60

**Hodgson, William Hope**
1877(?)-1918 .......................... **TCLC 13**
See also CA 111; 164; DLB 70, 153, 156, 178; MTCW 2

**Hoeg, Peter** 1957- ............................ **CLC 95**
See also CA 151; CANR 75; DA3; MTCW 2

**Hoffman, Alice** 1952- ... **CLC 51; DAM NOV**
See also CA 77-80; CANR 34, 66; MTCW 1, 2

**Hoffman, Daniel (Gerard)** 1923- . **CLC 6, 13, 23**
See also CA 1-4R; CANR 4; DLB 5

**Hoffman, Stanley** 1944- ...................... **CLC 5**
See also CA 77-80

**Hoffman, William M(oses)** 1939- ..... **CLC 40**
See also CA 57-60; CANR 11, 71

**Hoffmann, E(rnst) T(heodor) A(madeus)**
1776-1822 .................. **NCLC 2; SSC 13**
See also DLB 90; SATA 27

**Hofmann, Gert** 1931- ...................... **CLC 54**
See also CA 128

**Hofmannsthal, Hugo von**
1874-1929 ...... **TCLC 11; DAM DRAM; DC 4**
See also CA 106; 153; DLB 81, 118

**Hogan, Linda** 1947- .. **CLC 73; DAM MULT**
See also CA 120; CANR 45, 73; DLB 175; NNAL

**Hogarth, Charles**
See Creasey, John

**Hogarth, Emmett**
See Polonsky, Abraham (Lincoln)

**Hogg, James** 1770-1835 .................. **NCLC 4**
See also DLB 93, 116, 159

**Holbach, Paul Henri Thiry Baron** 1723-1789 **LC 14**

**Holberg, Ludvig** 1684-1754 .................. **LC 6**

**Holcroft, Thomas** 1745-1809 ......... **NCLC 85**
See also DLB 39, 89, 158

**Holden, Ursula** 1921- ...................... **CLC 18**
See also CA 101; CAAS 8; CANR 22

**Holderlin, (Johann Christian) Friedrich**
1770-1843 .................... **NCLC 16; PC 4**

**Holdstock, Robert**
See Holdstock, Robert P.

**Holdstock, Robert P.** 1948- ............... **CLC 39**
See also CA 131; CANR 81

**Holland, Isabelle** 1920- ...................... **CLC 21**
See also AAYA 11; CA 21-24R, 181; CAAE 181; CANR 10, 25, 47; CLR 57; JRDA; MAICYA; SATA 8, 70; SATA-Essay 103

**Holland, Marcus**
See Caldwell, (Janet Miriam) Taylor (Holland)

**Hollander, John** 1929- .......... **CLC 2, 5, 8, 14**
See also CA 1-4R; CANR 1, 52; DLB 5; SATA 13

**Hollander, Paul**
See Silverberg, Robert

**Holleran, Andrew** 1943(?)- ............... **CLC 38**
See also Garber, Eric CA 144

**Holley, Marietta** 1836(?)-1926 ...... **TCLC 100**
See also CA 118; DLB 11

**Hollinghurst, Alan** 1954- ............. **CLC 55, 91**
See also CA 114; DLB 207

**Hollis, Jim**
See Summers, Hollis (Spurgeon, Jr.)

**Holly, Buddy** 1936-1959 .................. **TCLC 65**

**Holmes, Gordon**
See Shiel, M(atthew) P(hipps)

**Holmes, John**
See Souster, (Holmes) Raymond

**Holmes, John Clellon** 1926-1988 ...... **CLC 56**
See also CA 9-12R; 125; CANR 4; DLB 16

**Holmes, Oliver Wendell, Jr.**
1841-1935 ................................ **TCLC 77**
See also CA 114

**Holmes, Oliver Wendell**
1809-1894 ........................ **NCLC 14, 81**
See also CDALB 1640-1865; DLB 1, 189; SATA 34

**Holmes, Raymond**
See Souster, (Holmes) Raymond

**Holt, Victoria**
See Hibbert, Eleanor Alice Burford

**Holub, Miroslav** 1923-1998 ................ **CLC 4**
See also CA 21-24R; 169; CANR 10

**Homer** c. 8th cent. B.C.- .. **CMLC 1, 16; DA; DAB; DAC; DAM MST, POET; PC 23; WLCS**
See also DA3; DLB 176

**Hongo, Garrett Kaoru** 1951- ............... **PC 23**
See also CA 133; CAAS 22; DLB 120

**Honig, Edwin** 1919- .......................... **CLC 33**
See also CA 5-8R; CAAS 8; CANR 4, 45; DLB 5

**Hood, Hugh (John Blagdon)** 1928- . **CLC 15, 28**
See also CA 49-52; CAAS 17; CANR 1, 33, 87; DLB 53

**Hood, Thomas** 1799-1845 ............... **NCLC 16**
See also DLB 96

**Hooker, (Peter) Jeremy** 1941- .......... **CLC 43**
See also CA 77-80; CANR 22; DLB 40

**hooks, bell** ............................. **CLC 94; BLCS**
See also Watkins, Gloria Jean MTCW 2

**Hope, A(lec) D(erwent)** 1907- ....... **CLC 3, 51**
See also CA 21-24R; CANR 33, 74; MTCW 1, 2

**Hope, Anthony** 1863-1933 ............. **TCLC 83**
See also CA 157; DLB 153, 156

**Hope, Brian**
See Creasey, John

**Hope, Christopher (David Tully)**
1944- .......................................... **CLC 52**
See also CA 106; CANR 47; SATA 62

**Hopkins, Gerard Manley**
1844-1889 ............ **NCLC 17; DA; DAB; DAC; DAM MST, POET; PC 15; WLC**
See also CDBLB 1890-1914; DA3; DLB 35, 57

**Hopkins, John (Richard)** 1931-1998 .. **CLC 4**
See also CA 85-88; 169

**Hopkins, Pauline Elizabeth**
1859-1930 ...... **TCLC 28; BLC 2; DAM MULT**
See also BW 2, 3; CA 141; CANR 82; DLB 50

**Hopkinson, Francis** 1737-1791 ........... **LC 25**
See also DLB 31

**Hopley-Woolrich, Cornell George** 1903-1968
See Woolrich, Cornell
See also CA 13-14; CANR 58; CAP 1; MTCW 2

**Horatio**
See Proust, (Valentin-Louis-George-Eugene-) Marcel

**Horgan, Paul (George Vincent O'Shaughnessy)** 1903-1995 . **CLC 9, 53; DAM NOV**
See also CA 13-16R; 147; CANR 9, 35; DLB 212; DLBY 85; INT CANR-9; MTCW 1, 2; SATA 13; SATA-Obit 84

**Horn, Peter**
See Kuttner, Henry

**Hornem, Horace Esq.**
See Byron, George Gordon (Noel)

**Horney, Karen (Clementine Theodore Danielsen)** 1885-1952 ............ **TCLC 71**
See also CA 114; 165

**Hornung, E(rnest) W(illiam)** 1866-1921 **TCLC 59**
See also CA 108; 160; DLB 70

**Horovitz, Israel (Arthur)** 1939- ...... **CLC 56; DAM DRAM**
See also CA 33-36R; CANR 46, 59; DLB 7

**Horvath, Odon von**
See Horvath, Oedoen von
See also DLB 85, 124

**Horvath, Oedoen von** 1901-1938 ... **TCLC 45**
See also Horvath, Odon von; von Horvath, Oedoen CA 118

**Horwitz, Julius** 1920-1986 ................ **CLC 14**
See also CA 9-12R; 119; CANR 12

**Hospital, Janette Turner** 1942- ......... **CLC 42**
See also CA 108; CANR 48

**Hostos, E. M. de**
See Hostos (y Bonilla), Eugenio Maria de

**Hostos, Eugenio M. de**
See Hostos (y Bonilla), Eugenio Maria de

**Hostos, Eugenio Maria**
See Hostos (y Bonilla), Eugenio Maria de

**Hostos (y Bonilla), Eugenio Maria de**
1839-1903 ................................ **TCLC 24**
See also CA 123; 131; HW 1

**Houdini**
See Lovecraft, H(oward) P(hillips)

**Hougan, Carolyn** 1943- .................... **CLC 34**
See also CA 139

**Household, Geoffrey (Edward West)**
1900-1988 .................................... **CLC 11**
See also CA 77-80; 126; CANR 58; DLB 87; SATA 14; SATA-Obit 59

**Housman, A(lfred) E(dward)** 1859-1936 **TCLC 1, 10; DA; DAB; DAC; DAM MST, POET; PC 2; WLCS**
See also CA 104; 125; DA3; DLB 19; MTCW 1, 2

**Housman, Laurence** 1865-1959 ....... **TCLC 7**
See also CA 106; 155; DLB 10; SATA 25

**Howard, Elizabeth Jane** 1923- ..... **CLC 7, 29**
See also CA 5-8R; CANR 8, 62

**Howard, Maureen** 1930- ......... **CLC 5, 14, 46**
See also CA 53-56; CANR 31, 75; DLBY
83; INT CANR-31; MTCW 1, 2

**Howard, Richard** 1929- .......... **CLC 7, 10, 47**
See also AITN 1; CA 85-88; CANR 25, 80;
DLB 5; INT CANR-25

**Howard, Robert E(rvin)**
1906-1936 ................................... **TCLC 8**
See also CA 105; 157

**Howard, Warren F.**
See Pohl, Frederik

**Howe, Fanny (Quincy)** 1940- ........... **CLC 47**
See also CA 117; CAAS 27; CANR 70;
SATA-Brief 52

**Howe, Irving** 1920-1993 ................... **CLC 85**
See also CA 9-12R; 141; CANR 21, 50;
DLB 67; MTCW 1, 2

**Howe, Julia Ward** 1819-1910 ........ **TCLC 21**
See also CA 117; DLB 1, 189

**Howe, Susan** 1937- ......................... **CLC 72**
See also CA 160; DLB 120

**Howe, Tina** 1937- ........................... **CLC 48**
See also CA 109

**Howell, James** 1594(?)-1666 ................. **LC 13**
See also DLB 151

**Howells, W. D.**
See Howells, William Dean

**Howells, William D.**
See Howells, William Dean

**Howells, William Dean** 1837-1920 .. **TCLC 7,
17, 41; SSC 36**
See also CA 104; 134; CDALB 1865-1917;
DLB 12, 64, 74, 79, 189; MTCW 2

**Howes, Barbara** 1914-1996 .............. **CLC 15**
See also CA 9-12R; 151; CAAS 3; CANR
53; SATA 5

**Hrabal, Bohumil** 1914-1997 ........ **CLC 13, 67**
See also CA 106; 156; CAAS 12; CANR
57

**Hroswitha of Gandersheim** c. 935-c. 1002
**CMLC 29**
See also DLB 148

**Hsun, Lu**
See Lu Hsun

**Hubbard, L(afayette) Ron(ald)** 1911-1986
**CLC 43; DAM POP**
See also CA 77-80; 118; CANR 52; DA3;
MTCW 2

**Huch, Ricarda (Octavia)**
1864-1947 ................................. **TCLC 13**
See also CA 111; DLB 66

**Huddle, David** 1942- ....................... **CLC 49**
See also CA 57-60; CAAS 20; DLB 130

**Hudson, Jeffrey**
See Crichton, (John) Michael

**Hudson, W(illiam) H(enry)**
1841-1922 ................................. **TCLC 29**
See also CA 115; DLB 98, 153, 174; SATA
35

**Hueffer, Ford Madox**
See Ford, Ford Madox

**Hughart, Barry** 1934- ....................... **CLC 39**
See also CA 137

**Hughes, Colin**
See Creasey, John

**Hughes, David (John)** 1930- ............. **CLC 48**
See also CA 116; 129; DLB 14

**Hughes, Edward James**
See Hughes, Ted
See also DAM MST, POET; DA3

**Hughes, (James) Langston**
1902-1967 ....... **CLC 1, 5, 10, 15, 35, 44,
108; BLC 2; DA; DAB; DAC; DAM
DRAM, MST, MULT, POET; DC 3;
PC 1; SSC 6; WLC**
See also AAYA 12; BW 1, 3; CA 1-4R; 25-
28R; CANR 1, 34, 82; CDALB 1929-

1941; CLR 17; DA3; DLB 4, 7, 48, 51,
86; JRDA; MAICYA; MTCW 1, 2; SATA
4, 33

**Hughes, Richard (Arthur Warren)**
1900-1976 ......... **CLC 1, 11; DAM NOV**
See also CA 5-8R; 65-68; CANR 4; DLB
15, 161; MTCW 1; SATA 8; SATA-Obit
25

**Hughes, Ted** 1930-1998 . **CLC 2, 4, 9, 14, 37,
119; DAB; DAC; PC 7**
See also Hughes, Edward James CA 1-4R;
171; CANR 1, 33, 66; CLR 3; DLB 40,
161; MAICYA; MTCW 1, 2; SATA 49;
SATA-Brief 27; SATA-Obit 107

**Hugo, Richard F(ranklin)**
1923-1982 ............. **CLC 6, 18, 32; DAM
POET**
See also CA 49-52; 108; CANR 3; DLB 5,
206

**Hugo, Victor (Marie)** 1802-1885 .... **NCLC 3,
10, 21; DA; DAB; DAC; DAM DRAM,
MST, NOV, POET; PC 17; WLC**
See also AAYA 28; DA3; DLB 119, 192;
SATA 47

**Huidobro, Vicente**
See Huidobro Fernandez, Vicente Garcia

**Huidobro Fernandez, Vicente Garcia**
1893-1948 ................................. **TCLC 31**
See also CA 131; HW 1

**Hulme, Keri** 1947- .......................... **CLC 39**
See also CA 125; CANR 69; INT 125

**Hulme, T(homas) E(rnest)**
1883-1917 ................................. **TCLC 21**
See also CA 117; DLB 19

**Hume, David** 1711-1776 .................. **LC 7, 56**
See also DLB 104

**Humphrey, William** 1924-1997 ......... **CLC 45**
See also CA 77-80; 160; CANR 68; DLB
212

**Humphreys, Emyr Owen** 1919- ........ **CLC 47**
See also CA 5-8R; CANR 3, 24; DLB 15

**Humphreys, Josephine** 1945- ..... **CLC 34, 57**
See also CA 121; 127; INT 127

**Huneker, James Gibbons**
1857-1921 ................................. **TCLC 65**
See also DLB 71

**Hungerford, Pixie**
See Brinsmead, H(esba) F(ay)

**Hunt, E(verette) Howard, (Jr.)**
1918- ......................................... **CLC 3**
See also AITN 1; CA 45-48; CANR 2, 47

**Hunt, Francesca**
See Holland, Isabelle

**Hunt, Kyle**
See Creasey, John

**Hunt, (James Henry) Leigh**
1784-1859 .... **NCLC 1, 70; DAM POET**
See also DLB 96, 110, 144

**Hunt, Marsha** 1946- ......................... **CLC 70**
See also BW 2, 3; CA 143; CANR 79

**Hunt, Violet** 1866(?)-1942 .............. **TCLC 53**
See also CA 184; DLB 162, 197

**Hunter, E. Waldo**
See Sturgeon, Theodore (Hamilton)

**Hunter, Evan** 1926- ........ **CLC 11, 31; DAM
POP**
See also CA 5-8R; CANR 5, 38, 62; DLBY
82; INT CANR-5; MTCW 1; SATA 25

**Hunter, Kristin (Eggleston)** 1931- .... **CLC 35**
See also AITN 1; BW 1; CA 13-16R;
CANR 13; CLR 3; DLB 33; INT CANR-
13; MAICYA; SAAS 10; SATA 12

**Hunter, Mary**
See Austin, Mary (Hunter)

**Hunter, Mollie** 1922- ....................... **CLC 21**
See also McIlwraith, Maureen Mollie
Hunter AAYA 13; CANR 37, 78; CLR 25;
DLB 161; JRDA; MAICYA; SAAS 7;
SATA 54, 106

**Hunter, Robert** (?)-1734 ...................... **LC 7**

**Hurston, Zora Neale** 1903-1960 .. **CLC 7, 30,
61; BLC 2; DA; DAC; DAM MST,
MULT, NOV; DC 12; SSC 4; WLCS**
See also AAYA 15; BW 1, 3; CA 85-88;
CANR 61; CDALBS; DA3; DLB 51, 86;
MTCW 1, 2

**Husserl, E. G.**
See Husserl, Edmund (Gustav Albrecht)

**Husserl, Edmund (Gustav Albrecht)**
1859-1938 ................................ **TCLC 100**
See also CA 116; 133

**Huston, John (Marcellus)**
1906-1987 ............................... **CLC 20**
See also CA 73-76; 123; CANR 34; DLB
26

**Hustvedt, Siri** 1955- ........................ **CLC 76**
See also CA 137

**Hutten, Ulrich von** 1488-1523 ............. **LC 16**
See also DLB 179

**Huxley, Aldous (Leonard)**
1894-1963 ....... **CLC 1, 3, 4, 5, 8, 11, 18,
35, 79; DA; DAB; DAC; DAM MST,
NOV; WLC**
See also AAYA 11; CA 85-88; CANR 44;
CDBLB 1914-1945; DA3; DLB 36, 100,
162, 195; MTCW 1, 2; SATA 63

**Huxley, T(homas) H(enry)**
1825-1895 ................................ **NCLC 67**
See also DLB 57

**Huysmans, Joris-Karl** 1848-1907 ... **TCLC 7,
69**
See also CA 104; 165; DLB 123

**Hwang, David Henry** 1957- .. **CLC 55; DAM
DRAM; DC 4**
See also CA 127; 132; CANR 76; DA3;
DLB 212; INT 132; MTCW 2

**Hyde, Anthony** 1946- ....................... **CLC 42**
See also CA 136

**Hyde, Margaret O(ldroyd)** 1917- ..... **CLC 21**
See also CA 1-4R; CANR 1, 36; CLR 23;
JRDA; MAICYA; SAAS 8; SATA 1, 42,
76

**Hynes, James** 1956(?)- ..................... **CLC 65**
See also CA 164

**Hypatia** c. 370-415 ........................ **CMLC 35**

**Ian, Janis** 1951- ............................... **CLC 21**
See also CA 105

**Ibanez, Vicente Blasco**
See Blasco Ibanez, Vicente

**Ibarbourou, Juana de** 1895-1979
See also HLCS 2; HW 1

**Ibarguengoitia, Jorge** 1928-1983 ...... **CLC 37**
See also CA 124; 113; HW 1

**Ibsen, Henrik (Johan)** 1828-1906 ... **TCLC 2,
8, 16, 37, 52; DA; DAB; DAC; DAM
DRAM, MST; DC 2; WLC**
See also CA 104; 141; DA3

**Ibuse, Masuji** 1898-1993 ................. **CLC 22**
See also CA 127; 141; DLB 180

**Ichikawa, Kon** 1915- ....................... **CLC 20**
See also CA 121

**Idle, Eric** 1943- ............................... **CLC 21**
See also Monty Python CA 116; CANR 35

**Ignatow, David** 1914-1997 .. **CLC 4, 7, 14, 40**
See also CA 9-12R; 162; CAAS 3; CANR
31, 57; DLB 5

**Ignotus**
See Strachey, (Giles) Lytton

**Ihimaera, Witi** 1944- ....................... **CLC 46**
See also CA 77-80

**Ilf, Ilya** .......................................... **TCLC 21**
See also Fainzilberg, Ilya Arnoldovich

**Illyes, Gyula** 1902-1983 ..................... **PC 16**
See also CA 114; 109

**Immermann, Karl (Lebrecht)** 1796-1840
**NCLC 4, 49**
See also DLB 133

**Ince, Thomas H.** 1882-1924 ............ **TCLC 89**

**Inchbald, Elizabeth** 1753-1821 ...... **NCLC 62**
See also DLB 39, 89

**Inclan, Ramon (Maria) del Valle**
See Valle-Inclan, Ramon (Maria) del

**Infante, G(uillermo) Cabrera**
See Cabrera Infante, G(uillermo)

**Ingalls, Rachel (Holmes)** 1940- ......... **CLC 42**
See also CA 123; 127

**Ingamells, Reginald Charles**
See Ingamells, Rex

**Ingamells, Rex** 1913-1955 .............. **TCLC 35**
See also CA 167

**Inge, William (Motter)** 1913-1973 ..... **CLC 1,
8, 19; DAM DRAM**
See also CA 9-12R; CDALB 1941-1968;
DA3; DLB 7; MTCW 1, 2

**Ingelow, Jean** 1820-1897 ................. **NCLC 39**
See also DLB 35, 163; SATA 33

**Ingram, Willis J.**
See Harris, Mark

**Innaurato, Albert (F.)** 1948(?)- ... **CLC 21, 60**
See also CA 115; 122; CANR 78; INT 122

**Innes, Michael**
See Stewart, J(ohn) I(nnes) M(ackintosh)

**Innis, Harold Adams** 1894-1952 .... **TCLC 77**
See also CA 181; DLB 88

**Ionesco, Eugene** 1909-1994 ... **CLC 1, 4, 6, 9,
11, 15, 41, 86; DA; DAB; DAC; DAM
DRAM, MST; DC 12; WLC**
See also CA 9-12R; 144; CANR 55; DA3;
MTCW 1, 2; SATA 7; SATA-Obit 79

**Iqbal, Muhammad** 1873-1938 ........ **TCLC 28**

**Ireland, Patrick**
See O'Doherty, Brian

**Iron, Ralph**
See Schreiner, Olive (Emilie Albertina)

**Irving, John (Winslow)** 1942- ... **CLC 13, 23,
38, 112; DAM NOV, POP**
See also AAYA 8; BEST 89:3; CA 25-28R;
CANR 28, 73; DA3; DLB 6; DLBY 82;
MTCW 1, 2

**Irving, Washington** 1783-1859 . **NCLC 2, 19;
DA; DAB; DAC; DAM MST; SSC 2,
37; WLC**
See also CDALB 1640-1865; DA3; DLB 3,
11, 30, 59, 73, 74, 186; YABC 2

**Irwin, P. K.**
See Page, P(atricia) K(athleen)

**Isaacs, Jorge Ricardo** 1837-1895 ... **NCLC 70**

**Isaacs, Susan** 1943- ....... **CLC 32; DAM POP**
See also BEST 89:1; CA 89-92; CANR 20,
41, 65; DA3; INT CANR-20; MTCW 1, 2

**Isherwood, Christopher (William Bradshaw)**
1904-1986 .. **CLC 1, 9, 11, 14, 44; DAM
DRAM, NOV**
See also CA 13-16R; 117; CANR 35; DA3;
DLB 15, 195; DLBY 86; MTCW 1, 2

**Ishiguro, Kazuo** 1954- . **CLC 27, 56, 59, 110;
DAM NOV**
See also BEST 90:2; CA 120; CANR 49;
DA3; DLB 194; MTCW 1, 2

**Ishikawa, Hakuhin**
See Ishikawa, Takuboku

**Ishikawa, Takuboku**
1886(?)-1912 ... **TCLC 15; DAM POET;
PC 10**
See also CA 113; 153

**Iskander, Fazil** 1929- ....................... **CLC 47**
See also CA 102

**Isler, Alan (David)** 1934- .................. **CLC 91**
See also CA 156

**Ivan IV** 1530-1584 ............................... **LC 17**

**Ivanov, Vyacheslav Ivanovich** 1866-1949
**TCLC 33**
See also CA 122

**Ivask, Ivar Vidrik** 1927-1992 ........... **CLC 14**
See also CA 37-40R; 139; CANR 24

**Ives, Morgan**
See Bradley, Marion Zimmer

**Izumi Shikibu** c. 973-c. 1034 ........ **CMLC 33**

**J. R. S.**
See Gogarty, Oliver St. John

**Jabran, Kahlil**
See Gibran, Kahlil

**Jabran, Khalil**
See Gibran, Kahlil

**Jackson, Daniel**
See Wingrove, David (John)

**Jackson, Jesse** 1908-1983 ................. **CLC 12**
See also BW 1; CA 25-28R; 109; CANR
27; CLR 28; MAICYA; SATA 2, 29;
SATA-Obit 48

**Jackson, Laura (Riding)** 1901-1991
See Riding, Laura
See also CA 65-68; 135; CANR 28; DLB
48

**Jackson, Sam**
See Trumbo, Dalton

**Jackson, Sara**
See Wingrove, David (John)

**Jackson, Shirley** 1919-1965 . **CLC 11, 60, 87;
DA; DAC; DAM MST; SSC 9; WLC**
See also AAYA 9; CA 1-4R; 25-28R; CANR
4, 52; CDALB 1941-1968; DLB 6;
MTCW 2; SATA 2

**Jacob, (Cyprien-)Max** 1876-1944 .... **TCLC 6**
See also CA 104

**Jacobs, Harriet A(nn)**
1813(?)-1897 ........................... **NCLC 67**

**Jacobs, Jim** 1942- ............................... **CLC 12**
See also CA 97-100; INT 97-100

**Jacobs, W(illiam) W(ymark)** 1863-1943
**TCLC 22**
See also CA 121; 167; DLB 135

**Jacobsen, Jens Peter** 1847-1885 .... **NCLC 34**

**Jacobsen, Josephine** 1908- ........ **CLC 48, 102**
See also CA 33-36R; CAAS 18; CANR 23,
48

**Jacobson, Dan** 1929- ..................... **CLC 4, 14**
See also CA 1-4R; CANR 2, 25, 66; DLB
14, 207; MTCW 1

**Jacqueline**
See Carpentier (y Valmont), Alejo

**Jagger, Mick** 1944- ............................ **CLC 17**

**Jahiz, al-** c. 780-c. 869 ................... **CMLC 25**

**Jakes, John (William)** 1932- . **CLC 29; DAM
NOV, POP**
See also AAYA 32; BEST 89:4; CA 57-60;
CANR 10, 43, 66; DA3; DLBY 83; INT
CANR-10; MTCW 1, 2; SATA 62

**James, Andrew**
See Kirkup, James

**James, C(yril) L(ionel) R(obert)** 1901-1989
**CLC 33; BLCS**
See also BW 2; CA 117; 125; 128; CANR
62; DLB 125; MTCW 1

**James, Daniel (Lewis)** 1911-1988
See Santiago, Danny
See also CA 174; 125

**James, Dynely**
See Mayne, William (James Carter)

**James, Henry Sr.** 1811-1882 .......... **NCLC 53**

**James, Henry** 1843-1916 ... **TCLC 2, 11, 24,
40, 47, 64; DA; DAB; DAC; DAM
MST, NOV; SSC 8, 32; WLC**
See also CA 104; 132; CDALB 1865-1917;
DA3; DLB 12, 71, 74, 189; DLBD 13;
MTCW 1, 2

**James, M. R.**
See James, Montague (Rhodes)
See also DLB 156

**James, Montague (Rhodes)**
1862-1936 .................. **TCLC 6; SSC 16**
See also CA 104; DLB 201

**James, P. D.** 1920- ............... **CLC 18, 46, 122**
See also White, Phyllis Dorothy James
BEST 90:2; CDBLB 1960 to Present;
DLB 87; DLBD 17

**James, Philip**
See Moorcock, Michael (John)

**James, William** 1842-1910 ....... **TCLC 15, 32**
See also CA 109

**James I** 1394-1437 .............................. **LC 20**

**Jameson, Anna** 1794-1860 .............. **NCLC 43**
See also DLB 99, 166

**Jami, Nur al-Din 'Abd al-Rahman**
1414-1492 .................................... **LC 9**

**Jammes, Francis** 1868-1938 .......... **TCLC 75**

**Jandl, Ernst** 1925- ............................ **CLC 34**

**Janowitz, Tama** 1957- ... **CLC 43; DAM POP**
See also CA 106; CANR 52

**Japrisot, Sebastien** 1931- .................. **CLC 90**

**Jarrell, Randall** 1914-1965 .... **CLC 1, 2, 6, 9,
13, 49; DAM POET**
See also CA 5-8R; 25-28R; CABS 2; CANR
6, 34; CDALB 1941-1968; CLR 6; DLB
48, 52; MAICYA; MTCW 1, 2; SATA 7

**Jarry, Alfred** 1873-1907 . **TCLC 2, 14; DAM
DRAM; SSC 20**
See also CA 104; 153; DA3; DLB 192

**Jawien, Andrzej**
See John Paul II, Pope

**Jaynes, Roderick**
See Coen, Ethan

**Jeake, Samuel, Jr.**
See Aiken, Conrad (Potter)

**Jean Paul** 1763-1825 ........................ **NCLC 7**

**Jefferies, (John) Richard**
1848-1887 ................................ **NCLC 47**
See also DLB 98, 141; SATA 16

**Jeffers, (John) Robinson** 1887-1962 .. **CLC 2,
3, 11, 15, 54; DA; DAC; DAM MST,
POET; PC 17; WLC**
See also CA 85-88; CANR 35; CDALB
1917-1929; DLB 45, 212; MTCW 1, 2

**Jefferson, Janet**
See Mencken, H(enry) L(ouis)

**Jefferson, Thomas** 1743-1826 ......... **NCLC 11**
See also CDALB 1640-1865; DA3; DLB
31

**Jeffrey, Francis** 1773-1850 ............. **NCLC 33**
See also DLB 107

**Jelakowitch, Ivan**
See Heijermans, Herman

**Jellicoe, (Patricia) Ann** 1927- .......... **CLC 27**
See also CA 85-88; DLB 13

**Jemyma**
See Holley, Marietta

**Jen, Gish** ................................................ **CLC 70**
See also Jen, Lillian

**Jen, Lillian** 1956(?)-
See Jen, Gish
See also CA 135

**Jenkins, (John) Robin** 1912- ............ **CLC 52**
See also CA 1-4R; CANR 1; DLB 14

**Jennings, Elizabeth (Joan)** 1926- . **CLC 5, 14**
See also CA 61-64; CAAS 5; CANR 8, 39,
66; DLB 27; MTCW 1; SATA 66

**Jennings, Waylon** 1937- ..................... **CLC 21**

**Jensen, Johannes V.** 1873-1950 ...... **TCLC 41**
See also CA 170

**Jensen, Laura (Linnea)** 1948- .......... **CLC 37**
See also CA 103

**Jerome, Jerome K(lapka)**
1859-1927 ................................... **TCLC 23**
See also CA 119; 177; DLB 10, 34, 135

**Jerrold, Douglas William**
1803-1857 ................................... **NCLC 2**
See also DLB 158, 159

**Jewett, (Theodora) Sarah Orne** 1849-1909
**TCLC 1, 22; SSC 6**

See also CA 108; 127; CANR 71; DLB 12, 74; SATA 15

**Jewsbury, Geraldine (Endsor)** 1812-1880 **NCLC 22**
See also DLB 21

**Jhabvala, Ruth Prawer** 1927- . **CLC 4, 8, 29, 94; DAB; DAM NOV**
See also CA 1-4R; CANR 2, 29, 51, 74; DLB 139, 194; INT CANR-29; MTCW 1, 2

**Jibran, Kahlil**
See Gibran, Kahlil

**Jibran, Khalil**
See Gibran, Kahlil

**Jiles, Paulette** 1943- ..................... **CLC 13, 58**
See also CA 101; CANR 70

**Jimenez (Mantecon), Juan Ramon**
1881-1958 ........ **TCLC 4; DAM MULT, POET; HLC 1; PC 7**
See also CA 104; 131; CANR 74; DLB 134; HW 1; MTCW 1, 2

**Jimenez, Ramon**
See Jimenez (Mantecon), Juan Ramon

**Jimenez Mantecon, Juan**
See Jimenez (Mantecon), Juan Ramon

**Jin, Ha** 1956- .................................. **CLC 109**
See also CA 152

**Joel, Billy** ........................................... **CLC 26**
See also Joel, William Martin

**Joel, William Martin** 1949-
See Joel, Billy
See also CA 108

**John, Saint** 7th cent. - .................... **CMLC 27**

**John of the Cross, St.** 1542-1591 ........ **LC 18**

**John Paul II, Pope** 1920- ................ **CLC 128**
See also CA 106; 133

**Johnson, B(ryan) S(tanley William)**
1933-1973 ............................... **CLC 6, 9**
See also CA 9-12R; 53-56; CANR 9; DLB 14, 40

**Johnson, Benj. F. of Boo**
See Riley, James Whitcomb

**Johnson, Benjamin F. of Boo**
See Riley, James Whitcomb

**Johnson, Charles (Richard)** 1948- .... **CLC 7, 51, 65; BLC 2; DAM MULT**
See also BW 2, 3; CA 116; CAAS 18; CANR 42, 66, 82; DLB 33; MTCW 2

**Johnson, Denis** 1949- ........................ **CLC 52**
See also CA 117; 121; CANR 71; DLB 120

**Johnson, Diane** 1934- ............... **CLC 5, 13, 48**
See also CA 41-44R; CANR 17, 40, 62; DLBY 80; INT CANR-17; MTCW 1

**Johnson, Eyvind (Olof Verner)** 1900-1976 **CLC 14**
See also CA 73-76; 69-72; CANR 34

**Johnson, J. R.**
See James, C(yril) L(ionel) R(obert)

**Johnson, James Weldon**
1871-1938 .. **TCLC 3, 19; BLC 2; DAM MULT, POET; PC 24**
See also BW 1, 3; CA 104; 125; CANR 82; CDALB 1917-1929; CLR 32; DA3; DLB 51; MTCW 1, 2; SATA 31

**Johnson, Joyce** 1935- ........................ **CLC 58**
See also CA 125; 129

**Johnson, Judith (Emlyn)** 1936- .... **CLC 7, 15**
See also Sherwin, Judith Johnson CA 25-28R; 153; CANR 34

**Johnson, Lionel (Pigot)**
1867-1902 ............................... **TCLC 19**
See also CA 117; DLB 19

**Johnson, Marguerite (Annie)**
See Angelou, Maya

**Johnson, Mel**
See Malzberg, Barry N(athaniel)

**Johnson, Pamela Hansford**
1912-1981 ......................... **CLC 1, 7, 27**
See also CA 1-4R; 104; CANR 2, 28; DLB 15; MTCW 1, 2

**Johnson, Robert** 1911(?)-1938 ........ **TCLC 69**
See also BW 3; CA 174

**Johnson, Samuel** 1709-1784 . **LC 15, 52; DA; DAB; DAC; DAM MST; WLC**
See also CDBLB 1660-1789; DLB 39, 95, 104, 142

**Johnson, Uwe** 1934-1984 .. **CLC 5, 10, 15, 40**
See also CA 1-4R; 112; CANR 1, 39; DLB 75; MTCW 1

**Johnston, George (Benson)** 1913- .... **CLC 51**
See also CA 1-4R; CANR 5, 20; DLB 88

**Johnston, Jennifer** 1930- ................... **CLC 7**
See also CA 85-88; DLB 14

**Joinville, Jean de** 1224(?)-1317 ..... **CMLC 38**

**Jolley, (Monica) Elizabeth** 1923- ..... **CLC 46; SSC 19**
See also CA 127; CAAS 13; CANR 59

**Jones, Arthur Llewellyn** 1863-1947
See Machen, Arthur
See also CA 104; 179

**Jones, D(ouglas) G(ordon)** 1929- ..... **CLC 10**
See also CA 29-32R; CANR 13; DLB 53

**Jones, David (Michael)** 1895-1974 .... **CLC 2, 4, 7, 13, 42**
See also CA 9-12R; 53-56; CANR 28; CDBLB 1945-1960; DLB 20, 100; MTCW 1

**Jones, David Robert** 1947-
See Bowie, David
See also CA 103

**Jones, Diana Wynne** 1934- ................ **CLC 26**
See also AAYA 12; CA 49-52; CANR 4, 26, 56; CLR 23; DLB 161; JRDA; MAICYA; SAAS 7; SATA 9, 70, 108

**Jones, Edward P.** 1950- ..................... **CLC 76**
See also BW 2, 3; CA 142; CANR 79

**Jones, Gayl** 1949- .. **CLC 6, 9; BLC 2; DAM MULT**
See also BW 2, 3; CA 77-80; CANR 27, 66; DA3; DLB 33; MTCW 1, 2

**Jones, James** 1921-1977 ...... **CLC 1, 3, 10, 39**
See also AITN 1, 2; CA 1-4R; 69-72; CANR 6; DLB 2, 143; DLBD 17; DLBY 98; MTCW 1

**Jones, John J.**
See Lovecraft, H(oward) P(hillips)

**Jones, LeRoi** ............... **CLC 1, 2, 3, 5, 10, 14**
See also Baraka, Amiri MTCW 2

**Jones, Louis B.** 1953- ......................... **CLC 65**
See also CA 141; CANR 73

**Jones, Madison (Percy, Jr.)** 1925- ...... **CLC 4**
See also CA 13-16R; CAAS 11; CANR 7, 54, 83; DLB 152

**Jones, Mervyn** 1922- ................... **CLC 10, 52**
See also CA 45-48; CAAS 5; CANR 1; MTCW 1

**Jones, Mick** 1956(?)- ......................... **CLC 30**

**Jones, Nettie (Pearl)** 1941- ............... **CLC 34**
See also BW 2; CA 137; CAAS 20; CANR 88

**Jones, Preston** 1936-1979 ................. **CLC 10**
See also CA 73-76; 89-92; DLB 7

**Jones, Robert F(rancis)** 1934- ........... **CLC 7**
See also CA 49-52; CANR 2, 61

**Jones, Rod** 1953- .............................. **CLC 50**
See also CA 128

**Jones, Terence Graham Parry**
1942- ................................... **CLC 21**
See also Jones, Terry; Monty Python CA 112; 116; CANR 35; INT 116

**Jones, Terry**
See Jones, Terence Graham Parry
See also SATA 67; SATA-Brief 51

**Jones, Thom (Douglas)** 1945(?)- ....... **CLC 81**
See also CA 157; CANR 88

**Jong, Erica** 1942- .......... **CLC 4, 6, 8, 18, 83; DAM NOV, POP**
See also AITN 1; BEST 90:2; CA 73-76; CANR 26, 52, 75; DA3; DLB 2, 5, 28, 152; INT CANR-26; MTCW 1, 2

**Jonson, Ben(jamin)** 1572(?)-1637 .. **LC 6, 33; DA; DAB; DAC; DAM DRAM, MST, POET; DC 4; PC 17; WLC**
See also CDBLB Before 1660; DLB 62, 121

**Jordan, June** 1936- ........ **CLC 5, 11, 23, 114; BLCS; DAM MULT, POET**
See also AAYA 2; BW 2, 3; CA 33-36R; CANR 25, 70; CLR 10; DLB 38; MAICYA; MTCW 1; SATA 4

**Jordan, Neil (Patrick)** 1950- ........... **CLC 110**
See also CA 124; 130; CANR 54; INT 130

**Jordan, Pat(rick M.)** 1941- .............. **CLC 37**
See also CA 33-36R

**Jorgensen, Ivar**
See Ellison, Harlan (Jay)

**Jorgenson, Ivar**
See Silverberg, Robert

**Josephus, Flavius** c. 37-100 .......... **CMLC 13**

**Josiah Allen's Wife**
See Holley, Marietta

**Josipovici, Gabriel (David)** 1940- ...... **CLC 6, 43**
See also CA 37-40R; CAAS 8; CANR 47, 84; DLB 14

**Joubert, Joseph** 1754-1824 .............. **NCLC 9**

**Jouve, Pierre Jean** 1887-1976 .......... **CLC 47**
See also CA 65-68

**Jovine, Francesco** 1902-1950 .......... **TCLC 79**

**Joyce, James (Augustine Aloysius)**
1882-1941 .. **TCLC 3, 8, 16, 35, 52; DA; DAB; DAC; DAM MST, NOV, POET; PC 22; SSC 3, 26; WLC**
See also CA 104; 126; CDBLB 1914-1945; DA3; DLB 10, 19, 36, 162; MTCW 1, 2

**Jozsef, Attila** 1905-1937 ................. **TCLC 22**
See also CA 116

**Juana Ines de la Cruz** 1651(?)-1695 .... **LC 5; HLCS 1; PC 24**

**Judd, Cyril**
See Kornbluth, C(yril) M.; Pohl, Frederik

**Juenger, Ernst** 1895-1998 ................ **CLC 125**
See also CA 101; 167; CANR 21, 47; DLB 56

**Julian of Norwich** 1342(?)-1416(?) . **LC 6, 52**
See also DLB 146

**Junger, Ernst**
See Juenger, Ernst

**Junger, Sebastian** 1962- .................. **CLC 109**
See also AAYA 28; CA 165

**Juniper, Alex**
See Hospital, Janette Turner

**Junius**
See Luxemburg, Rosa

**Just, Ward (Swift)** 1935- .............. **CLC 4, 27**
See also CA 25-28R; CANR 32, 87; INT CANR-32

**Justice, Donald (Rodney)** 1925- .. **CLC 6, 19, 102; DAM POET**
See also CA 5-8R; CANR 26, 54, 74; DLBY 83; INT CANR-26; MTCW 2

**Juvenal** c. 60-c. 13 .......................... **CMLC 8**
See also Juvenalis, Decimus Junius DLB 211

**Juvenalis, Decimus Junius** 55(?)-c. 127(?)
See Juvenal

**Juvenis**
See Bourne, Randolph S(illiman)

**Kacew, Romain** 1914-1980
See Gary, Romain
See also CA 108; 102

**Kadare, Ismail** 1936- ........................ **CLC 52**
See also CA 161

**Kadohata, Cynthia** ................... **CLC 59, 122**
  See also CA 140
**Kafka, Franz** 1883-1924 . **TCLC 2, 6, 13, 29,**
  **47, 53; DA; DAB; DAC; DAM MST,**
  **NOV; SSC 5, 29, 35; WLC**
  See also AAYA 31; CA 105; 126; DA3;
  DLB 81; MTCW 1, 2
**Kahanovitsch, Pinkhes**
  See Der Nister
**Kahn, Roger** 1927- ............................ **CLC 30**
  See also CA 25-28R; CANR 44, 69; DLB
  171; SATA 37
**Kain, Saul**
  See Sassoon, Siegfried (Lorraine)
**Kaiser, Georg** 1878-1945 ................. **TCLC 9**
  See also CA 106; DLB 124
**Kaletski, Alexander** 1946- ................. **CLC 39**
  See also CA 118; 143
**Kalidasa** fl. c. 400- ............. **CMLC 9; PC 22**
**Kallman, Chester (Simon)**
  1921-1975 ....................................... **CLC 2**
  See also CA 45-48; 53-56; CANR 3
**Kaminsky, Melvin** 1926-
  See Brooks, Mel
  See also CA 65-68; CANR 16
**Kaminsky, Stuart M(elvin)** 1934- ..... **CLC 59**
  See also CA 73-76; CANR 29, 53
**Kandinsky, Wassily** 1866-1944 ....... **TCLC 92**
  See also CA 118; 155
**Kane, Francis**
  See Robbins, Harold
**Kane, Paul**
  See Simon, Paul (Frederick)
**Kanin, Garson** 1912-1999 ................. **CLC 22**
  See also AITN 1; CA 5-8R; 177; CANR 7,
  78; DLB 7
**Kaniuk, Yoram** 1930- ........................ **CLC 19**
  See also CA 134
**Kant, Immanuel** 1724-1804 ..... **NCLC 27, 67**
  See also DLB 94
**Kantor, MacKinlay** 1904-1977 ............ **CLC 7**
  See also CA 61-64; 73-76; CANR 60, 63;
  DLB 9, 102; MTCW 2
**Kaplan, David Michael** 1946- ........... **CLC 50**
**Kaplan, James** 1951- ......................... **CLC 59**
  See also CA 135
**Karageorge, Michael**
  See Anderson, Poul (William)
**Karamzin, Nikolai Mikhailovich** 1766-1826
  **NCLC 3**
  See also DLB 150
**Karapanou, Margarita** 1946- ........... **CLC 13**
  See also CA 101
**Karinthy, Frigyes** 1887-1938 .......... **TCLC 47**
  See also CA 170
**Karl, Frederick R(obert)** 1927- ........ **CLC 34**
  See also CA 5-8R; CANR 3, 44
**Kastel, Warren**
  See Silverberg, Robert
**Kataev, Evgeny Petrovich** 1903-1942
  See Petrov, Evgeny
  See also CA 120
**Kataphusin**
  See Ruskin, John
**Katz, Steve** 1935- ............................. **CLC 47**
  See also CA 25-28R; CAAS 14, 64; CANR
  12; DLBY 83
**Kauffman, Janet** 1945- ..................... **CLC 42**
  See also CA 117; CANR 43, 84; DLBY 86
**Kaufman, Bob (Garnell)** 1925-1986 . **CLC 49**
  See also BW 1; CA 41-44R; 118; CANR
  22; DLB 16, 41
**Kaufman, George S.** 1889-1961 ...... **CLC 38;**
  **DAM DRAM**
  See also CA 108; 93-96; DLB 7; INT 108;
  MTCW 2
**Kaufman, Sue** ................................... **CLC 3, 8**
  See also Barondess, Sue K(aufman)

**Kavafis, Konstantinos Petrou** 1863-1933
  See Cavafy, C(onstantine) P(eter)
  See also CA 104
**Kavan, Anna** 1901-1968 ......... **CLC 5, 13, 82**
  See also CA 5-8R; CANR 6, 57; MTCW 1
**Kavanagh, Dan**
  See Barnes, Julian (Patrick)
**Kavanagh, Julie** 1952- ..................... **CLC 119**
  See also CA 163
**Kavanagh, Patrick (Joseph)**
  1904-1967 ..................................... **CLC 22**
  See also CA 123; 25-28R; DLB 15, 20;
  MTCW 1
**Kawabata, Yasunari** 1899-1972 ..... **CLC 2, 5,**
  **9, 18, 107; DAM MULT; SSC 17**
  See also CA 93-96; 33-36R; CANR 88;
  DLB 180; MTCW 2
**Kaye, M(ary) M(argaret)** 1909- ....... **CLC 28**
  See also CA 89-92; CANR 24, 60; MTCW
  1, 2; SATA 62
**Kaye, Mollie**
  See Kaye, M(ary) M(argaret)
**Kaye-Smith, Sheila** 1887-1956 ....... **TCLC 20**
  See also CA 118; DLB 36
**Kaymor, Patrice Maguilene**
  See Senghor, Leopold Sedar
**Kazan, Elia** 1909- .................... **CLC 6, 16, 63**
  See also CA 21-24R; CANR 32, 78
**Kazantzakis, Nikos** 1883(?)-1957 .... **TCLC 2,**
  **5, 33**
  See also CA 105; 132; DA3; MTCW 1, 2
**Kazin, Alfred** 1915-1998 ..... **CLC 34, 38, 119**
  See also CA 1-4R; CAAS 7; CANR 1, 45,
  79; DLB 67
**Keane, Mary Nesta (Skrine)** 1904-1996
  See Keane, Molly
  See also CA 108; 114; 151
**Keane, Molly** ..................................... **CLC 31**
  See also Keane, Mary Nesta (Skrine) INT
  114
**Keates, Jonathan** 1946(?)- ................. **CLC 34**
  See also CA 163
**Keaton, Buster** 1895-1966 ................. **CLC 20**
**Keats, John** 1795-1821 ...... **NCLC 8, 73; DA;**
  **DAB; DAC; DAM MST, POET; PC 1;**
  **WLC**
  See also CDBLB 1789-1832; DA3; DLB
  96, 110
**Keene, Donald** 1922- .......................... **CLC 34**
  See also CA 1-4R; CANR 5
**Keillor, Garrison** ........................ **CLC 40, 115**
  See also Keillor, Gary (Edward) AAYA 2;
  BEST 89:3; DLBY 87; SATA 58
**Keillor, Gary (Edward)** 1942-
  See Keillor, Garrison
  See also CA 111; 117; CANR 36, 59; DAM
  POP; DA3; MTCW 1, 2
**Keith, Michael**
  See Hubbard, L(afayette) Ron(ald)
**Keller, Gottfried** 1819-1890 .... **NCLC 2; SSC**
  **26**
  See also DLB 129
**Keller, Nora Okja** ........................... **CLC 109**
**Kellerman, Jonathan** 1949- .. **CLC 44; DAM**
  **POP**
  See also BEST 90:1; CA 106; CANR 29,
  51; DA3; INT CANR-29
**Kelley, William Melvin** 1937- .......... **CLC 22**
  See also BW 1; CA 77-80; CANR 27, 83;
  DLB 33
**Kellogg, Marjorie** 1922- ..................... **CLC 2**
  See also CA 81-84
**Kellow, Kathleen**
  See Hibbert, Eleanor Alice Burford
**Kelly, M(ilton) T(errence)** 1947- ...... **CLC 55**
  See also CA 97-100; CAAS 22; CANR 19,
  43, 84

**Kelman, James** 1946- .................. **CLC 58, 86**
  See also CA 148; CANR 85; DLB 194
**Kemal, Yashar** 1923- ................... **CLC 14, 29**
  See also CA 89-92; CANR 44
**Kemble, Fanny** 1809-1893 ............. **NCLC 18**
  See also DLB 32
**Kemelman, Harry** 1908-1996 ............ **CLC 2**
  See also AITN 1; CA 9-12R; 155; CANR 6,
  71; DLB 28
**Kempe, Margery** 1373(?)-1440(?) ... **LC 6, 56**
  See also DLB 146
**Kempis, Thomas a** 1380-1471 ............. **LC 11**
**Kendall, Henry** 1839-1882 ............. **NCLC 12**
**Keneally, Thomas (Michael)** 1935- ... **CLC 5,**
  **8, 10, 14, 19, 27, 43, 117; DAM NOV**
  See also CA 85-88; CANR 10, 50, 74; DA3;
  MTCW 1, 2
**Kennedy, Adrienne (Lita)** 1931- ..... **CLC 66;**
  **BLC 2; DAM MULT; DC 5**
  See also BW 2, 3; CA 103; CAAS 20;
  CABS 3; CANR 26, 53, 82; DLB 38
**Kennedy, John Pendleton**
  1795-1870 ................................... **NCLC 2**
  See also DLB 3
**Kennedy, Joseph Charles** 1929-
  See Kennedy, X. J.
  See also CA 1-4R; CANR 4, 30, 40; SATA
  14, 86
**Kennedy, William** 1928- .. **CLC 6, 28, 34, 53;**
  **DAM NOV**
  See also AAYA 1; CA 85-88; CANR 14,
  31, 76; DA3; DLB 143; DLBY 85; INT
  CANR-31; MTCW 1, 2; SATA 57
**Kennedy, X. J.** ............................... **CLC 8, 42**
  See also Kennedy, Joseph Charles CAAS 9;
  CLR 27; DLB 5; SAAS 22
**Kenny, Maurice (Francis)** 1929- ..... **CLC 87;**
  **DAM MULT**
  See also CA 144; CAAS 22; DLB 175;
  NNAL
**Kent, Kelvin**
  See Kuttner, Henry
**Kenton, Maxwell**
  See Southern, Terry
**Kenyon, Robert O.**
  See Kuttner, Henry
**Kepler, Johannes** 1571-1630 ................ **LC 45**
**Kerouac, Jack** ....... **CLC 1, 2, 3, 5, 14, 29, 61**
  See also Kerouac, Jean-Louis Lebris de
  AAYA 25; CDALB 1941-1968; DLB 2,
  16; DLBD 3; DLBY 95; MTCW 2
**Kerouac, Jean-Louis Lebris de** 1922-1969
  See Kerouac, Jack
  See also AITN 1; CA 5-8R; 25-28R; CANR
  26, 54; DA; DAB; DAC; DAM MST,
  NOV, POET, POP; DA3; MTCW 1, 2;
  WLC
**Kerr, Jean** 1923- ............................... **CLC 22**
  See also CA 5-8R; CANR 7; INT CANR-7
**Kerr, M. E.** ............................... **CLC 12, 35**
  See also Meaker, Marijane (Agnes) AAYA
  2, 23; CLR 29; SAAS 1
**Kerr, Robert** ...................................... **CLC 55**
**Kerrigan, (Thomas) Anthony** 1918- .. **CLC 4,**
  **6**
  See also CA 49-52; CAAS 11; CANR 4
**Kerry, Lois**
  See Duncan, Lois
**Kesey, Ken (Elton)** 1935- ..... **CLC 1, 3, 6, 11,**
  **46, 64; DA; DAB; DAC; DAM MST,**
  **NOV, POP; WLC**
  See also AAYA 25; CA 1-4R; CANR 22,
  38, 66; CDALB 1968-1988; DA3; DLB
  2, 16, 206; MTCW 1, 2; SATA 66
**Kesselring, Joseph (Otto)**
  1902-1967 ........ **CLC 45; DAM DRAM,**
  **MST**
  See also CA 150

**Kessler, Jascha (Frederick)** 1929- ...... **CLC 4**
See also CA 17-20R; CANR 8, 48

**Kettelkamp, Larry (Dale)** 1933- ....... **CLC 12**
See also CA 29-32R; CANR 16; SAAS 3;
SATA 2

**Key, Ellen** 1849-1926 ..................... **TCLC 65**

**Keyber, Conny**
See Fielding, Henry

**Keyes, Daniel** 1927- ...... **CLC 80; DA; DAC;
DAM MST, NOV**
See also AAYA 23; CA 17-20R, 181; CAAE
181; CANR 10, 26, 54, 74; DA3; MTCW
2; SATA 37

**Keynes, John Maynard**
1883-1946 ............................... **TCLC 64**
See also CA 114; 162, 163; DLBD 10;
MTCW 2

**Khanshendel, Chiron**
See Rose, Wendy

**Khayyam, Omar** 1048-1131 ......... **CMLC 11;
DAM POET; PC 8**
See also DA3

**Kherdian, David** 1931- .................. **CLC 6, 9**
See also CA 21-24R; CAAS 2; CANR 39,
78; CLR 24; JRDA; MAICYA; SATA 16,
74

**Khlebnikov, Velimir** ....................... **TCLC 20**
See also Khlebnikov, Viktor Vladimirovich

**Khlebnikov, Viktor Vladimirovich** 1885-1922
See Khlebnikov, Velimir
See also CA 117

**Khodasevich, Vladislav (Felitsianovich)**
1886-1939 ............................... **TCLC 15**
See also CA 115

**Kielland, Alexander Lange**
1849-1906 ................................. **TCLC 5**
See also CA 104

**Kiely, Benedict** 1919- .................. **CLC 23, 43**
See also CA 1-4R; CANR 2, 84; DLB 15

**Kienzle, William X(avier)** 1928- ..... **CLC 25;
DAM POP**
See also CA 93-96; CAAS 1; CANR 9, 31,
59; DA3; INT CANR-31; MTCW 1, 2

**Kierkegaard, Soren** 1813-1855 ..... **NCLC 34,
78**

**Kieslowski, Krzysztof** 1941-1996 .... **CLC 120**
See also CA 147; 151

**Killens, John Oliver** 1916-1987 ........ **CLC 10**
See also BW 2; CA 77-80; 123; CAAS 2;
CANR 26; DLB 33

**Killigrew, Anne** 1660-1685 ..................... **LC 4**
See also DLB 131

**Kim**
See Simenon, Georges (Jacques Christian)

**Kincaid, Jamaica** 1949- .... **CLC 43, 68; BLC
2; DAM MULT, NOV**
See also AAYA 13; BW 2, 3; CA 125;
CANR 47, 59; CDALBS; CLR 63; DA3;
DLB 157; MTCW 2

**King, Francis (Henry)** 1923- ....... **CLC 8, 53;
DAM NOV**
See also CA 1-4R; CANR 1, 33, 86; DLB
15, 139; MTCW 1

**King, Kennedy**
See Brown, George Douglas

**King, Martin Luther, Jr.**
1929-1968 .......... **CLC 83; BLC 2; DA;
DAB; DAC; DAM MST, MULT;
WLCS**
See also BW 2, 3; CA 25-28; CANR 27,
44; CAP 2; DA3; MTCW 1, 2; SATA 14

**King, Stephen (Edwin)** 1947- .... **CLC 12, 26,
37, 61, 113; DAM NOV, POP; SSC 17**
See also AAYA 1, 17; BEST 90:1; CA 61-
64; CANR 1, 30, 52, 76; DA3; DLB 143;
DLBY 80; JRDA; MTCW 1, 2; SATA 9,
55

**King, Steve**
See King, Stephen (Edwin)

**King, Thomas** 1943- ... **CLC 89; DAC; DAM
MULT**
See also CA 144; DLB 175; NNAL; SATA
96

**Kingman, Lee** ..................................... **CLC 17**
See also Natti, (Mary) Lee SAAS 3; SATA
1, 67

**Kingsley, Charles** 1819-1875 ......... **NCLC 35**
See also DLB 21, 32, 163, 190; YABC 2

**Kingsley, Sidney** 1906-1995 ............... **CLC 44**
See also CA 85-88; 147; DLB 7

**Kingsolver, Barbara** 1955- ........ **CLC 55, 81;
DAM POP**
See also AAYA 15; CA 129; 134; CANR
60; CDALBS; DA3; DLB 206; INT 134;
MTCW 2

**Kingston, Maxine (Ting Ting) Hong** 1940-
**CLC 12, 19, 58, 121; DAM MULT,
NOV; WLCS**
See also AAYA 8; CA 69-72; CANR 13,
38, 74, 87; CDALBS; DA3; DLB 173,
212; DLBY 80; INT CANR-13; MTCW
1, 2; SATA 53

**Kinnell, Galway** 1927- ..... **CLC 1, 2, 3, 5, 13,
29, 129; PC 26**
See also CA 9-12R; CANR 10, 34, 66; DLB
5; DLBY 87; INT CANR-34; MTCW 1, 2

**Kinsella, Thomas** 1928- ................. **CLC 4, 19**
See also CA 17-20R; CANR 15; DLB 27;
MTCW 1, 2

**Kinsella, W(illiam) P(atrick)** 1935- . **CLC 27,
43; DAC; DAM NOV, POP**
See also AAYA 7; CA 97-100; CAAS 7;
CANR 21, 35, 66, 75; INT CANR-21;
MTCW 1, 2

**Kinsey, Alfred C(harles)**
1894-1956 ............................... **TCLC 91**
See also CA 115; 170; MTCW 2

**Kipling, (Joseph) Rudyard**
1865-1936 ........ **TCLC 8, 17; DA; DAB;
DAC; DAM MST, POET; PC 3; SSC
5; WLC**
See also AAYA 32; CA 105; 120; CANR
33; CDBLB 1890-1914; CLR 39; DA3;
DLB 19, 34, 141, 156; MAICYA; MTCW
1, 2; SATA 100; YABC 2

**Kirkland, Caroline M.** 1801-1864 . **NCLC 85**
See also DLB 3, 73, 74; DLBD 13

**Kirkup, James** 1918- .......................... **CLC 1**
See also CA 1-4R; CAAS 4; CANR 2; DLB
27; SATA 12

**Kirkwood, James** 1930(?)-1989 .......... **CLC 9**
See also AITN 2; CA 1-4R; 128; CANR 6,
40

**Kirshner, Sidney**
See Kingsley, Sidney

**Kis, Danilo** 1935-1989 ....................... **CLC 57**
See also CA 109; 118; 129; CANR 61; DLB
181; MTCW 1

**Kivi, Aleksis** 1834-1872 ................... **NCLC 30**

**Kizer, Carolyn (Ashley)** 1925- ... **CLC 15, 39,
80; DAM POET**
See also CA 65-68; CAAS 5; CANR 24,
70; DLB 5, 169; MTCW 2

**Klabund** 1890-1928 ....................... **TCLC 44**
See also CA 162; DLB 66

**Klappert, Peter** 1942- ....................... **CLC 57**
See also CA 33-36R; DLB 5

**Klein, A(braham) M(oses)**
1909-1972 . **CLC 19; DAB; DAC; DAM
MST**
See also CA 101; 37-40R; DLB 68

**Klein, Norma** 1938-1989 ................. **CLC 30**
See also AAYA 2; CA 41-44R; 128; CANR
15, 37; CLR 2, 19; INT CANR-15; JRDA;
MAICYA; SAAS 1; SATA 7, 57

**Klein, T(heodore) E(ibon) D(onald)** 1947-
**CLC 34**
See also CA 119; CANR 44, 75

**Kleist, Heinrich von** 1777-1811 ...... **NCLC 2,
37; DAM DRAM; SSC 22**
See also DLB 90

**Klima, Ivan** 1931- ........ **CLC 56; DAM NOV**
See also CA 25-28R; CANR 17, 50

**Klimentov, Andrei Platonovich** 1899-1951
See Platonov, Andrei
See also CA 108

**Klinger, Friedrich Maximilian von**
1752-1831 .................................. **NCLC 1**
See also DLB 94

**Klingsor the Magician**
See Hartmann, Sadakichi

**Klopstock, Friedrich Gottlieb** 1724-1803
**NCLC 11**
See also DLB 97

**Knapp, Caroline** 1959- ..................... **CLC 99**
See also CA 154

**Knebel, Fletcher** 1911-1993 ............... **CLC 14**
See also AITN 1; CA 1-4R; 140; CAAS 3;
CANR 1, 36; SATA 36; SATA-Obit 75

**Knickerbocker, Diedrich**
See Irving, Washington

**Knight, Etheridge** 1931-1991 . **CLC 40; BLC
2; DAM POET; PC 14**
See also BW 1, 3; CA 21-24R; 133; CANR
23, 82; DLB 41; MTCW 2

**Knight, Sarah Kemble** 1666-1727 ......... **LC 7**
See also DLB 24, 200

**Knister, Raymond** 1899-1932 ......... **TCLC 56**
See also DLB 68

**Knowles, John** 1926- . **CLC 1, 4, 10, 26; DA;
DAC; DAM MST, NOV**
See also AAYA 10; CA 17-20R; CANR 40,
74, 76; CDALB 1968-1988; DLB 6;
MTCW 1, 2; SATA 8, 89

**Knox, Calvin M.**
See Silverberg, Robert

**Knox, John** c. 1505-1572 ..................... **LC 37**
See also DLB 132

**Knye, Cassandra**
See Disch, Thomas M(ichael)

**Koch, C(hristopher) J(ohn)** 1932- .... **CLC 42**
See also CA 127; CANR 84

**Koch, Christopher**
See Koch, C(hristopher) J(ohn)

**Koch, Kenneth** 1925- .... **CLC 5, 8, 44; DAM
POET**
See also CA 1-4R; CANR 6, 36, 57; DLB
5; INT CANR-36; MTCW 2; SATA 65

**Kochanowski, Jan** 1530-1584 ............. **LC 10**

**Kock, Charles Paul de** 1794-1871 . **NCLC 16**

**Koda Rohan** 1867-
See Koda Shigeyuki

**Koda Shigeyuki** 1867-1947 ............. **TCLC 22**
See also CA 121; 183; DLB 180

**Koestler, Arthur** 1905-1983 ... **CLC 1, 3, 6, 8,
15, 33**
See also CA 1-4R; 109; CANR 1, 33; CD-
BLB 1945-1960; DLBY 83; MTCW 1, 2

**Kogawa, Joy Nozomi** 1935- ..... **CLC 78, 129;
DAC; DAM MST, MULT**
See also CA 101; CANR 19, 62; MTCW 2;
SATA 99

**Kohout, Pavel** 1928- .......................... **CLC 13**
See also CA 45-48; CANR 3

**Koizumi, Yakumo**
See Hearn, (Patricio) Lafcadio (Tessima
Carlos)

**Kolmar, Gertrud** 1894-1943 ........... **TCLC 40**
See also CA 167

**Komunyakaa, Yusef** 1947- ......... **CLC 86, 94;
BLCS**
See also CA 147; CANR 83; DLB 120

**Konrad, George**
See Konrad, Gyoergy

**Konrad, Gyoergy** 1933- .......... **CLC 4, 10, 73**
See also CA 85-88

**Konwicki, Tadeusz** 1926- ....... **CLC 8, 28, 54, 117**
See also CA 101; CAAS 9; CANR 39, 59; MTCW 1

**Koontz, Dean R(ay)** 1945- .... **CLC 78; DAM NOV, POP**
See also AAYA 9, 31; BEST 89:3, 90:2; CA 108; CANR 19, 36, 52; DA3; MTCW 1; SATA 92

**Kopernik, Mikolaj**
See Copernicus, Nicolaus

**Kopit, Arthur (Lee)** 1937- ..... **CLC 1, 18, 33; DAM DRAM**
See also AITN 1; CA 81-84; CABS 3; DLB 7; MTCW 1

**Kops, Bernard** 1926- ......................... **CLC 4**
See also CA 5-8R; CANR 84; DLB 13

**Kornbluth, C(yril) M.** 1923-1958 .... **TCLC 8**
See also CA 105; 160; DLB 8

**Korolenko, V. G.**
See Korolenko, Vladimir Galaktionovich

**Korolenko, Vladimir**
See Korolenko, Vladimir Galaktionovich

**Korolenko, Vladimir G.**
See Korolenko, Vladimir Galaktionovich

**Korolenko, Vladimir Galaktionovich**
1853-1921 ............................. **TCLC 22**
See also CA 121

**Korzybski, Alfred (Habdank Skarbek)**
1879-1950 ............................... **TCLC 61**
See also CA 123; 160

**Kosinski, Jerzy (Nikodem)**
1933-1991 .... **CLC 1, 2, 3, 6, 10, 15, 53, 70; DAM NOV**
See also CA 17-20R; 134; CANR 9, 46; DA3; DLB 2; DLBY 82; MTCW 1, 2

**Kostelanetz, Richard (Cory)** 1940- .. **CLC 28**
See also CA 13-16R; CAAS 8; CANR 38, 77

**Kostrowitzki, Wilhelm Apollinaris de**
1880-1918
See Apollinaire, Guillaume
See also CA 104

**Kotlowitz, Robert** 1924- ...................... **CLC 4**
See also CA 33-36R; CANR 36

**Kotzebue, August (Friedrich Ferdinand) von**
1761-1819 ............................... **NCLC 25**
See also DLB 94

**Kotzwinkle, William** 1938- ..... **CLC 5, 14, 35**
See also CA 45-48; CANR 3, 44, 84; CLR 6; DLB 173; MAICYA; SATA 24, 70

**Kowna, Stancy**
See Szymborska, Wislawa

**Kozol, Jonathan** 1936- ...................... **CLC 17**
See also CA 61-64; CANR 16, 45

**Kozoll, Michael** 1940(?)- ................... **CLC 35**

**Kramer, Kathryn** 19(?)- ..................... **CLC 34**

**Kramer, Larry** 1935- .. **CLC 42; DAM POP; DC 8**
See also CA 124; 126; CANR 60

**Krasicki, Ignacy** 1735-1801 .............. **NCLC 8**

**Krasinski, Zygmunt** 1812-1859 ....... **NCLC 4**

**Kraus, Karl** 1874-1936 ..................... **TCLC 5**
See also CA 104; DLB 118

**Kreve (Mickevicius), Vincas** 1882-1954
**TCLC 27**
See also CA 170

**Kristeva, Julia** 1941- ........................ **CLC 77**
See also CA 154

**Kristofferson, Kris** 1936- ................... **CLC 26**
See also CA 104

**Krizanc, John** 1956- .......................... **CLC 57**

**Krleza, Miroslav** 1893-1981 ....... **CLC 8, 114**
See also CA 97-100; 105; CANR 50; DLB 147

**Kroetsch, Robert** 1927- ......... **CLC 5, 23, 57; DAC; DAM POET**
See also CA 17-20R; CANR 8, 38; DLB 53; MTCW 1

**Kroetz, Franz**
See Kroetz, Franz Xaver

**Kroetz, Franz Xaver** 1946- .............. **CLC 41**
See also CA 130

**Kroker, Arthur (W.)** 1945- ................ **CLC 77**
See also CA 161

**Kropotkin, Peter (Aleksieevich)** 1842-1921
**TCLC 36**
See also CA 119

**Krotkov, Yuri** 1917- ........................... **CLC 19**
See also CA 102

**Krumb**
See Crumb, R(obert)

**Krumgold, Joseph (Quincy)**
1908-1980 ............................... **CLC 12**
See also CA 9-12R; 101; CANR 7; MAICYA; SATA 1, 48; SATA-Obit 23

**Krumwitz**
See Crumb, R(obert)

**Krutch, Joseph Wood** 1893-1970 ..... **CLC 24**
See also CA 1-4R; 25-28R; CANR 4; DLB 63, 206

**Krutzch, Gus**
See Eliot, T(homas) S(tearns)

**Krylov, Ivan Andreevich**
1768(?)-1844 ............................. **NCLC 1**
See also DLB 150

**Kubin, Alfred (Leopold Isidor)** 1877-1959
**TCLC 23**
See also CA 112; 149; DLB 81

**Kubrick, Stanley** 1928-1999 ............. **CLC 16**
See also AAYA 30; CA 81-84; 177; CANR 33; DLB 26

**Kumin, Maxine (Winokur)** 1925- ..... **CLC 5, 13, 28; DAM POET; PC 15**
See also AITN 2; CA 1-4R; CAAS 8; CANR 1, 21, 69; DA3; DLB 5; MTCW 1, 2; SATA 12

**Kundera, Milan** 1929- . **CLC 4, 9, 19, 32, 68, 115; DAM NOV; SSC 24**
See also AAYA 2; CA 85-88; CANR 19, 52, 74; DA3; MTCW 1, 2

**Kunene, Mazisi (Raymond)** 1930- ... **CLC 85**
See also BW 1, 3; CA 125; CANR 81; DLB 117

**Kunikida Doppo** 1871-1908 ......... **TCLC 100**

**Kunitz, Stanley (Jasspon)** 1905- .. **CLC 6, 11, 14; PC 19**
See also CA 41-44R; CANR 26, 57; DA3; DLB 48; INT CANR-26; MTCW 1, 2

**Kunze, Reiner** 1933- ........................ **CLC 10**
See also CA 93-96; DLB 75

**Kuprin, Aleksander Ivanovich** 1870-1938
**TCLC 5**
See also CA 104; 182

**Kureishi, Hanif** 1954(?)- ................... **CLC 64**
See also CA 139; DLB 194

**Kurosawa, Akira** 1910-1998 .... **CLC 16, 119; DAM MULT**
See also AAYA 11; CA 101; 170; CANR 46

**Kushner, Tony** 1957(?)- ......... **CLC 81; DAM DRAM; DC 10**
See also CA 144; CANR 74; DA3; MTCW 2

**Kuttner, Henry** 1915-1958 .............. **TCLC 10**
See also CA 107; 157; DLB 8

**Kuzma, Greg** 1944- ............................ **CLC 7**
See also CA 33-36R; CANR 70

**Kuzmin, Mikhail** 1872(?)-1936 ...... **TCLC 40**
See also CA 170

**Kyd, Thomas** 1558-1594 ......... **LC 22; DAM DRAM; DC 3**
See also DLB 62

**Kyprianos, Iossif**
See Samarakis, Antonis

**La Bruyere, Jean de** 1645-1696 ......... **LC 17**

**Lacan, Jacques (Marie Emile)** 1901-1981
**CLC 75**
See also CA 121; 104

**Laclos, Pierre Ambroise Francois Choderlos de** 1741-1803 ........................... **NCLC 4**

**Lacolere, Francois**
See Aragon, Louis

**La Colere, Francois**
See Aragon, Louis

**La Deshabilleuse**
See Simenon, Georges (Jacques Christian)

**Lady Gregory**
See Gregory, Isabella Augusta (Persse)

**Lady of Quality, A**
See Bagnold, Enid

**La Fayette, Marie (Madelaine Pioche de la Vergne Comtes** 1634-1693 ............. **LC 2**

**Lafayette, Rene**
See Hubbard, L(afayette) Ron(ald)

**La Fontaine, Jean de** 1621-1695 ........ **LC 50**
See also MAICYA; SATA 18

**Laforgue, Jules** 1860-1887 . **NCLC 5, 53; PC 14; SSC 20**

**Lagerkvist, Paer (Fabian)**
1891-1974 ...... **CLC 7, 10, 13, 54; DAM DRAM, NOV**
See also Lagerkvist, Par CA 85-88; 49-52; DA3; MTCW 1, 2

**Lagerkvist, Par** ............................... **SSC 12**
See also Lagerkvist, Paer (Fabian) MTCW 2

**Lagerloef, Selma (Ottiliana Lovisa)**
1858-1940 ......................... **TCLC 4, 36**
See also Lagerlof, Selma (Ottiliana Lovisa) CA 108; MTCW 2; SATA 15

**Lagerlof, Selma (Ottiliana Lovisa)**
See Lagerloef, Selma (Ottiliana Lovisa)
See also CLR 7; SATA 15

**La Guma, (Justin) Alex(ander)** 1925-1985
**CLC 19; BLCS; DAM NOV**
See also BW 1, 3; CA 49-52; 118; CANR 25, 81; DLB 117; MTCW 1, 2

**Laidlaw, A. K.**
See Grieve, C(hristopher) M(urray)

**Lainez, Manuel Mujica**
See Mujica Lainez, Manuel
See also HW 1

**Laing, R(onald) D(avid)** 1927-1989 . **CLC 95**
See also CA 107; 129; CANR 34; MTCW 1

**Lamartine, Alphonse (Marie Louis Prat) de**
1790-1869 . **NCLC 11; DAM POET; PC 16**

**Lamb, Charles** 1775-1834 ..... **NCLC 10; DA; DAB; DAC; DAM MST; WLC**
See also CDBLB 1789-1832; DLB 93, 107, 163; SATA 17

**Lamb, Lady Caroline** 1785-1828 ... **NCLC 38**
See also DLB 116

**Lamming, George (William)** 1927- ... **CLC 2, 4, 66; BLC 2; DAM MULT**
See also BW 2, 3; CA 85-88; CANR 26, 76; DLB 125; MTCW 1, 2

**L'Amour, Louis (Dearborn)**
1908-1988 ...... **CLC 25, 55; DAM NOV, POP**
See also AAYA 16; AITN 2; BEST 89:2; CA 1-4R; 125; CANR 3, 25, 40; DA3; DLB 206; DLBY 80; MTCW 1, 2

**Lampedusa, Giuseppe (Tomasi) di** 1896-1957
**TCLC 13**
See also Tomasi di Lampedusa, Giuseppe CA 164; DLB 177; MTCW 2

**Lampman, Archibald** 1861-1899 ... **NCLC 25**
See also DLB 92

**Lancaster, Bruce** 1896-1963 ............. **CLC 36**
See also CA 9-10; CANR 70; CAP 1; SATA 9

**Lanchester, John** ............... **CLC 99**

**Landau, Mark Alexandrovich**
    See Aldanov, Mark (Alexandrovich)

**Landau-Aldanov, Mark Alexandrovich**
    See Aldanov, Mark (Alexandrovich)

**Landis, Jerry**
    See Simon, Paul (Frederick)

**Landis, John** 1950- .......................... **CLC 26**
    See also CA 112; 122

**Landolfi, Tommaso** 1908-1979 .... **CLC 11, 49**
    See also CA 127; 117; DLB 177

**Landon, Letitia Elizabeth**
    1802-1838 ............................... **NCLC 15**
    See also DLB 96

**Landor, Walter Savage**
    1775-1864 ............................... **NCLC 14**
    See also DLB 93, 107

**Landwirth, Heinz** 1927-
    See Lind, Jakov
    See also CA 9-12R; CANR 7

**Lane, Patrick** 1939- ... **CLC 25; DAM POET**
    See also CA 97-100; CANR 54; DLB 53;
    INT 97-100

**Lang, Andrew** 1844-1912 ............... **TCLC 16**
    See also CA 114; 137; CANR 85; DLB 98,
    141, 184; MAICYA; SATA 16

**Lang, Fritz** 1890-1976 .............. **CLC 20, 103**
    See also CA 77-80; 69-72; CANR 30

**Lange, John**
    See Crichton, (John) Michael

**Langer, Elinor** 1939- ......................... **CLC 34**
    See also CA 121

**Langland, William** 1330(?)-1400(?) ... **LC 19;
    DA; DAB; DAC; DAM MST, POET**
    See also DLB 146

**Langstaff, Launcelot**
    See Irving, Washington

**Lanier, Sidney** 1842-1881 ..... **NCLC 6; DAM
    POET**
    See also DLB 64; DLBD 13; MAICYA;
    SATA 18

**Lanyer, Aemilia** 1569-1645 ........... **LC 10, 30**
    See also DLB 121

**Lao-Tzu**
    See Lao Tzu

**Lao Tzu** fl. 6th cent. B.C.- ............... **CMLC 7**

**Lapine, James (Elliot)** 1949- ............ **CLC 39**
    See also CA 123; 130; CANR 54; INT 130

**Larbaud, Valery (Nicolas)**
    1881-1957 ............................... **TCLC 9**
    See also CA 106; 152

**Lardner, Ring**
    See Lardner, Ring(gold) W(ilmer)

**Lardner, Ring W., Jr.**
    See Lardner, Ring(gold) W(ilmer)

**Lardner, Ring(gold) W(ilmer)** 1885-1933
    **TCLC 2, 14; SSC 32**
    See also CA 104; 131; CDALB 1917-1929;
    DLB 11, 25, 86; DLBD 16; MTCW 1, 2

**Laredo, Betty**
    See Codrescu, Andrei

**Larkin, Maia**
    See Wojciechowska, Maia (Teresa)

**Larkin, Philip (Arthur)** 1922-1985 ... **CLC 3,
    5, 8, 9, 13, 18, 33, 39, 64; DAB; DAM
    MST, POET; PC 21**
    See also CA 5-8R; 117; CANR 24, 62; CD-
    BLB 1960 to Present; DA3; DLB 27;
    MTCW 1, 2

**Larra (y Sanchez de Castro), Mariano Jose
    de** 1809-1837 ......................... **NCLC 17**

**Larsen, Eric** 1941- ........................... **CLC 55**
    See also CA 132

**Larsen, Nella** 1891-1964 .... **CLC 37; BLC 2;
    DAM MULT**
    See also BW 1; CA 125; CANR 83; DLB
    51

**Larson, Charles R(aymond)** 1938- ... **CLC 31**
    See also CA 53-56; CANR 4

**Larson, Jonathan** 1961-1996 ............ **CLC 99**
    See also AAYA 28; CA 156

**Las Casas, Bartolome de** 1474-1566 ... **LC 31**

**Lasch, Christopher** 1932-1994 ....... **CLC 102**
    See also CA 73-76; 144; CANR 25; MTCW
    1, 2

**Lasker-Schueler, Else** 1869-1945 ... **TCLC 57**
    See also CA 183; DLB 66, 124

**Laski, Harold** 1893-1950 ............... **TCLC 79**

**Latham, Jean Lee** 1902-1995 ........... **CLC 12**
    See also AITN 1; CA 5-8R; CANR 7, 84;
    CLR 50; MAICYA; SATA 2, 68

**Latham, Mavis**
    See Clark, Mavis Thorpe

**Lathen, Emma** ...................................... **CLC 2**
    See also Hennissart, Martha; Latsis, Mary
    J(ane)

**Lathrop, Francis**
    See Leiber, Fritz (Reuter, Jr.)

**Latsis, Mary J(ane)** 1927(?)-1997
    See Lathen, Emma
    See also CA 85-88; 162

**Lattimore, Richmond (Alexander)** 1906-1984
    **CLC 3**
    See also CA 1-4R; 112; CANR 1

**Laughlin, James** 1914-1997 .............. **CLC 49**
    See also CA 21-24R; 162; CAAS 22; CANR
    9, 47; DLB 48; DLBY 96, 97

**Laurence, (Jean) Margaret (Wemyss)**
    1926-1987 . **CLC 3, 6, 13, 50, 62; DAC;
    DAM MST; SSC 7**
    See also CA 5-8R; 121; CANR 33; DLB
    53; MTCW 1, 2; SATA-Obit 50

**Laurent, Antoine** 1952- ..................... **CLC 50**

**Lauscher, Hermann**
    See Hesse, Hermann

**Lautreamont, Comte de**
    1846-1870 ................. **NCLC 12; SSC 14**

**Laverty, Donald**
    See Blish, James (Benjamin)

**Lavin, Mary** 1912-1996 . **CLC 4, 18, 99; SSC
    4**
    See also CA 9-12R; 151; CANR 33; DLB
    15; MTCW 1

**Lavond, Paul Dennis**
    See Kornbluth, C(yril) M.; Pohl, Frederik

**Lawler, Raymond Evenor** 1922- ....... **CLC 58**
    See also CA 103

**Lawrence, D(avid) H(erbert Richards)**
    1885-1930 .... **TCLC 2, 9, 16, 33, 48, 61,
    93; DA; DAB; DAC; DAM MST, NOV,
    POET; SSC 4, 19; WLC**
    See also CA 104; 121; CDBLB 1914-1945;
    DA3; DLB 10, 19, 36, 98, 162, 195;
    MTCW 1, 2

**Lawrence, T(homas) E(dward)** 1888-1935
    **TCLC 18**
    See also Dale, Colin CA 115; 167; DLB
    195

**Lawrence of Arabia**
    See Lawrence, T(homas) E(dward)

**Lawson, Henry (Archibald Hertzberg)**
    1867-1922 ................. **TCLC 27; SSC 18**
    See also CA 120; 181

**Lawton, Dennis**
    See Faust, Frederick (Schiller)

**Laxness, Halldor** ............................... **CLC 25**
    See also Gudjonsson, Halldor Kiljan

**Layamon** fl. c. 1200- ..................... **CMLC 10**
    See also DLB 146

**Laye, Camara** 1928-1980 ... **CLC 4, 38; BLC
    2; DAM MULT**
    See also BW 1; CA 85-88; 97-100; CANR
    25; MTCW 1, 2

**Layton, Irving (Peter)** 1912- ....... **CLC 2, 15;
    DAC; DAM MST, POET**
    See also CA 1-4R; CANR 2, 33, 43, 66;
    DLB 88; MTCW 1, 2

**Lazarus, Emma** 1849-1887 ............... **NCLC 8**

**Lazarus, Felix**
    See Cable, George Washington

**Lazarus, Henry**
    See Slavitt, David R(ytman)

**Lea, Joan**
    See Neufeld, John (Arthur)

**Leacock, Stephen (Butler)**
    1869-1944 . **TCLC 2; DAC; DAM MST**
    See also CA 104; 141; CANR 80; DLB 92;
    MTCW 2

**Lear, Edward** 1812-1888 ................. **NCLC 3**
    See also CLR 1; DLB 32, 163, 166; MAI-
    CYA; SATA 18, 100

**Lear, Norman (Milton)** 1922- .......... **CLC 12**
    See also CA 73-76

**Leautaud, Paul** 1872-1956 ............. **TCLC 83**
    See also DLB 65

**Leavis, F(rank) R(aymond)**
    1895-1978 ............................... **CLC 24**
    See also CA 21-24R; 77-80; CANR 44;
    MTCW 1, 2

**Leavitt, David** 1961- ..... **CLC 34; DAM POP**
    See also CA 116; 122; CANR 50, 62; DA3;
    DLB 130; INT 122; MTCW 2

**Leblanc, Maurice (Marie Emile)** 1864-1941
    **TCLC 49**
    See also CA 110

**Lebowitz, Fran(ces Ann)** 1951(?)- ... **CLC 11,
    36**
    See also CA 81-84; CANR 14, 60, 70; INT
    CANR-14; MTCW 1

**Lebrecht, Peter**
    See Tieck, (Johann) Ludwig

**le Carre, John** ................ **CLC 3, 5, 9, 15, 28**
    See also Cornwell, David (John Moore)
    BEST 89:4; CDBLB 1960 to Present;
    DLB 87; MTCW 2

**Le Clezio, J(ean) M(arie) G(ustave)** 1940-
    **CLC 31**
    See also CA 116; 128; DLB 83

**Leconte de Lisle, Charles-Marie-Rene**
    1818-1894 ............................... **NCLC 29**

**Le Coq, Monsieur**
    See Simenon, Georges (Jacques Christian)

**Leduc, Violette** 1907-1972 .............. **CLC 22**
    See also CA 13-14; 33-36R; CANR 69;
    CAP 1

**Ledwidge, Francis** 1887(?)-1917 .... **TCLC 23**
    See also CA 123; DLB 20

**Lee, Andrea** 1953- ... **CLC 36; BLC 2; DAM
    MULT**
    See also BW 1, 3; CA 125; CANR 82

**Lee, Andrew**
    See Auchincloss, Louis (Stanton)

**Lee, Chang-rae** 1965- ....................... **CLC 91**
    See also CA 148

**Lee, Don L.** ......................................... **CLC 2**
    See also Madhubuti, Haki R.

**Lee, George W(ashington)**
    1894-1976 ......... **CLC 52; BLC 2; DAM
    MULT**
    See also BW 1; CA 125; CANR 83; DLB
    51

**Lee, (Nelle) Harper** 1926- . **CLC 12, 60; DA;
    DAB; DAC; DAM MST, NOV; WLC**
    See also AAYA 13; CA 13-16R; CANR 51;
    CDALB 1941-1968; DA3; DLB 6;
    MTCW 1, 2; SATA 11

**Lee, Helen Elaine** 1959(?)- ............... **CLC 86**
    See also CA 148

**Lee, Julian**
    See Latham, Jean Lee

**Lee, Larry**
    See Lee, Lawrence

Lee, Laurie 1914-1997 .......... **CLC 90; DAB; DAM POP**
See also CA 77-80; 158; CANR 33, 73; DLB 27; MTCW 1

Lee, Lawrence 1941-1990 ................. **CLC 34**
See also CA 131; CANR 43

Lee, Li-Young 1957- ........................ **PC 24**
See also CA 153; DLB 165

Lee, Manfred B(ennington) 1905-1971 ................................... **CLC 11**
See also Queen, Ellery CA 1-4R; 29-32R; CANR 2; DLB 137

Lee, Shelton Jackson 1957(?)- ....... **CLC 105; BLCS; DAM MULT**
See also Lee, Spike BW 2, 3; CA 125; CANR 42

Lee, Spike
See Lee, Shelton Jackson
See also AAYA 4, 29

Lee, Stan 1922- ................................... **CLC 17**
See also AAYA 5; CA 108; 111; INT 111

Lee, Tanith 1947- ................................ **CLC 46**
See also AAYA 15; CA 37-40R; CANR 53; SATA 8, 88

Lee, Vernon ........................ **TCLC 5; SSC 33**
See also Paget, Violet DLB 57, 153, 156, 174, 178

Lee, William
See Burroughs, William S(eward)

Lee, Willy
See Burroughs, William S(eward)

Lee-Hamilton, Eugene (Jacob) 1845-1907 **TCLC 22**
See also CA 117

Leet, Judith 1935- ............................. **CLC 11**

Le Fanu, Joseph Sheridan 1814-1873 ..... **NCLC 9, 58; DAM POP; SSC 14**
See also DA3; DLB 21, 70, 159, 178

Leffland, Ella 1931- ........................... **CLC 19**
See also CA 29-32R; CANR 35, 78, 82; DLBY 84; INT CANR-35; SATA 65

Leger, Alexis
See Leger, (Marie-Rene Auguste) Alexis Saint-Leger

Leger, (Marie-Rene Auguste) Alexis Saint-Leger 1887-1975 .. **CLC 4, 11, 46; DAM POET; PC 23**
See also CA 13-16R; 61-64; CANR 43; MTCW 1

Leger, Saintleger
See Leger, (Marie-Rene Auguste) Alexis Saint-Leger

Le Guin, Ursula K(roeber) 1929- ..... **CLC 8, 13, 22, 45, 71; DAB; DAC; DAM MST, POP; SSC 12**
See also AAYA 9, 27; AITN 1; CA 21-24R; CANR 9, 32, 52, 74; CDALB 1968-1988; CLR 3, 28; DA3; DLB 8, 52; INT CANR-32; JRDA; MAICYA; MTCW 1, 2; SATA 4, 52, 99

Lehmann, Rosamond (Nina) 1901-1990 ................................. **CLC 5**
See also CA 77-80; 131; CANR 8, 73; DLB 15; MTCW 2

Leiber, Fritz (Reuter, Jr.) 1910-1992 ................................. **CLC 25**
See also CA 45-48; 139; CANR 2, 40, 86; DLB 8; MTCW 1, 2; SATA 45; SATA-Obit 73

Leibniz, Gottfried Wilhelm von 1646-1716 **LC 35**
See also DLB 168

Leimbach, Martha 1963-
See Leimbach, Marti
See also CA 130

Leimbach, Marti ............................... **CLC 65**
See also Leimbach, Martha

Leino, Eino ........................................ **TCLC 24**
See also Loennbohm, Armas Eino Leopold

Leiris, Michel (Julien) 1901-1990 ..... **CLC 61**
See also CA 119; 128; 132

Leithauser, Brad 1953- ...................... **CLC 27**
See also CA 107; CANR 27, 81; DLB 120

Lelchuk, Alan 1938- ............................ **CLC 5**
See also CA 45-48; CANR 20; CANR 1, 70

Lem, Stanislaw 1921- ............. **CLC 8, 15, 40**
See also CA 105; CAAS 1; CANR 32; MTCW 1

Lemann, Nancy 1956- ...................... **CLC 39**
See also CA 118; 136

Lemonnier, (Antoine Louis) Camille 1844-1913 ............................... **TCLC 22**
See also CA 121

Lenau, Nikolaus 1802-1850 ........... **NCLC 16**

L'Engle, Madeleine (Camp Franklin) 1918- **CLC 12; DAM POP**
See also AAYA 28; AITN 2; CA 1-4R; CANR 3, 21, 39, 66; CLR 1, 14, 57; DA3; DLB 52; JRDA; MAICYA; MTCW 1, 2; SAAS 15; SATA 1, 27, 75

Lengyel, Jozsef 1896-1975 ................. **CLC 7**
See also CA 85-88; 57-60; CANR 71

Lenin 1870-1924
See Lenin, V. I.
See also CA 121; 168

Lenin, V. I. ....................................... **TCLC 67**
See also Lenin

Lennon, John (Ono) 1940-1980 .. **CLC 12, 35**
See also CA 102

Lennox, Charlotte Ramsay 1729(?)-1804 **NCLC 23**
See also DLB 39

Lentricchia, Frank (Jr.) 1940- .......... **CLC 34**
See also CA 25-28R; CANR 19

Lenz, Siegfried 1926- .......... **CLC 27; SSC 33**
See also CA 89-92; CANR 80; DLB 75

Leonard, Elmore (John, Jr.) 1925- . **CLC 28, 34, 71, 120; DAM POP**
See also AAYA 22; AITN 1; BEST 89:1, 90:4; CA 81-84; CANR 12, 28, 53, 76; DA3; DLB 173; INT CANR-28; MTCW 1, 2

Leonard, Hugh ................................... **CLC 19**
See also Byrne, John Keyes DLB 13

Leonov, Leonid (Maximovich) 1899-1994 **CLC 92; DAM NOV**
See also CA 129; CANR 74, 76; MTCW 1, 2

Leopardi, (Conte) Giacomo 1798-1837 ............................... **NCLC 22**

Le Reveler
See Artaud, Antonin (Marie Joseph)

Lerman, Eleanor 1952- ...................... **CLC 9**
See also CA 85-88; CANR 69

Lerman, Rhoda 1936- ...................... **CLC 56**
See also CA 49-52; CANR 70

Lermontov, Mikhail Yuryevich 1814-1841 **NCLC 47; PC 18**
See also DLB 205

Leroux, Gaston 1868-1927 ............. **TCLC 25**
See also CA 108; 136; CANR 69; SATA 65

Lesage, Alain-Rene 1668-1747 ....... **LC 2, 28**

Leskov, Nikolai (Semyonovich) 1831-1895 **NCLC 25; SSC 34**

Lessing, Doris (May) 1919- ... **CLC 1, 2, 3, 6, 10, 15, 22, 40, 94; DA; DAB; DAC; DAM MST, NOV; SSC 6; WLCS**
See also CA 9-12R; CAAS 14; CANR 33, 54, 76; CDBLB 1960 to Present; DA3; DLB 15, 139; DLBY 85; MTCW 1, 2

Lessing, Gotthold Ephraim 1729-1781 . **LC 8**
See also DLB 97

Lester, Richard 1932- ........................ **CLC 20**

Lever, Charles (James) 1806-1872 ............................... **NCLC 23**
See also DLB 21

Leverson, Ada 1865(?)-1936(?) ....... **TCLC 18**
See also Elaine CA 117; DLB 153

Levertov, Denise 1923-1997 .. **CLC 1, 2, 3, 5, 8, 15, 28, 66; DAM POET; PC 11**
See also CA 1-4R, 178; 163; CAAE 178; CAAS 19; CANR 3, 29, 50; CDALBS; DLB 5, 165; INT CANR-29; MTCW 1, 2

Levi, Jonathan ............................... **CLC 76**

Levi, Peter (Chad Tigar) 1931- ........ **CLC 41**
See also CA 5-8R; CANR 34, 80; DLB 40

Levi, Primo 1919-1987 . **CLC 37, 50; SSC 12**
See also CA 13-16R; 122; CANR 12, 33, 61, 70; DLB 177; MTCW 1, 2

Levin, Ira 1929- .......... **CLC 3, 6; DAM POP**
See also CA 21-24R; CANR 17, 44, 74; DA3; MTCW 1, 2; SATA 66

Levin, Meyer 1905-1981 .......... **CLC 7; DAM POP**
See also AITN 1; CA 9-12R; 104; CANR 15; DLB 9, 28; DLBY 81; SATA 21; SATA-Obit 27

Levine, Norman 1924- ...................... **CLC 54**
See also CA 73-76; CAAS 23; CANR 14, 70; DLB 88

Levine, Philip 1928- .. **CLC 2, 4, 5, 9, 14, 33, 118; DAM POET; PC 22**
See also CA 9-12R; CANR 9, 37, 52; DLB 5

Levinson, Deirdre 1931- .................... **CLC 49**
See also CA 73-76; CANR 70

Levi-Strauss, Claude 1908- ................ **CLC 38**
See also CA 1-4R; CANR 6, 32, 57; MTCW 1, 2

Levitin, Sonia (Wolff) 1934- ............. **CLC 17**
See also AAYA 13; CA 29-32R; CANR 14, 32, 79; CLR 53; JRDA; MAICYA; SAAS 2; SATA 4, 68

Levon, O. U.
See Kesey, Ken (Elton)

Levy, Amy 1861-1889 ..................... **NCLC 59**
See also DLB 156

Lewes, George Henry 1817-1878 ... **NCLC 25**
See also DLB 55, 144

Lewis, Alun 1915-1944 ..................... **TCLC 3**
See also CA 104; DLB 20, 162

Lewis, C. Day
See Day Lewis, C(ecil)

Lewis, C(live) S(taples) 1898-1963 .... **CLC 1, 3, 6, 14, 27, 124; DA; DAB; DAC; DAM MST, NOV, POP; WLC**
See also AAYA 3; CA 81-84; CANR 33, 71; CDBLB 1945-1960; CLR 3, 27; DA3; DLB 15, 100, 160; JRDA; MAICYA; MTCW 1, 2; SATA 13, 100

Lewis, Janet 1899-1998 .................... **CLC 41**
See also Winters, Janet Lewis CA 9-12R; 172; CANR 29, 63; CAP 1; DLBY 87

Lewis, Matthew Gregory 1775-1818 ......................... **NCLC 11, 62**
See also DLB 39, 158, 178

Lewis, (Harry) Sinclair 1885-1951 . **TCLC 4, 13, 23, 39; DA; DAB; DAC; DAM MST, NOV; WLC**
See also CA 104; 133; CDALB 1917-1929; DA3; DLB 9, 102; DLBD 1; MTCW 1, 2

Lewis, (Percy) Wyndham 1882(?)-1957 **TCLC 2, 9; SSC 34**
See also CA 104; 157; DLB 15; MTCW 2

Lewisohn, Ludwig 1883-1955 ......... **TCLC 19**
See also CA 107; DLB 4, 9, 28, 102

Lewton, Val 1904-1951 ................... **TCLC 76**

Leyner, Mark 1956- ......................... **CLC 92**
See also CA 110; CANR 28, 53; DA3; MTCW 2

**Lezama Lima, Jose** 1910-1976 .... **CLC 4, 10, 101; DAM MULT; HLCS 2**
See also CA 77-80; CANR 71; DLB 113; HW 1, 2

**L'Heureux, John (Clarke)** 1934- ...... **CLC 52**
See also CA 13-16R; CANR 23, 45, 88

**Liddell, C. H.**
See Kuttner, Henry

**Lie, Jonas (Lauritz Idemil)** 1833-1908(?) **TCLC 5**
See also CA 115

**Lieber, Joel** 1937-1971 ........................ **CLC 6**
See also CA 73-76; 29-32R

**Lieber, Stanley Martin**
See Lee, Stan

**Lieberman, Laurence (James)**
1935- ...................................... **CLC 4, 36**
See also CA 17-20R; CANR 8, 36

**Lieh Tzu** fl. 7th cent. B.C.-5th cent. B.C.
**CMLC 27**

**Lieksman, Anders**
See Haavikko, Paavo Juhani

**Li Fei-kan** 1904-
See Pa Chin
See also CA 105

**Lifton, Robert Jay** 1926- .................. **CLC 67**
See also CA 17-20R; CANR 27, 78; INT CANR-27; SATA 66

**Lightfoot, Gordon** 1938- .................. **CLC 26**
See also CA 109

**Lightman, Alan P(aige)** 1948- .......... **CLC 81**
See also CA 141; CANR 63

**Ligotti, Thomas (Robert)** 1953- ...... **CLC 44; SSC 16**
See also CA 123; CANR 49

**Li Ho** 791-817 .................................. **PC 13**

**Liliencron, (Friedrich Adolf Axel) Detlev von** 1844-1909 ........................ **TCLC 18**
See also CA 117

**Lilly, William** 1602-1681 ..................... **LC 27**

**Lima, Jose Lezama**
See Lezama Lima, Jose

**Lima Barreto, Afonso Henrique de**
1881-1922 .............................. **TCLC 23**
See also CA 117; 181

**Limonov, Edward** 1944- .................... **CLC 67**
See also CA 137

**Lin, Frank**
See Atherton, Gertrude (Franklin Horn)

**Lincoln, Abraham** 1809-1865 ......... **NCLC 18**

**Lind, Jakov** ..................... **CLC 1, 2, 4, 27, 82**
See also Landwirth, Heinz CAAS 4

**Lindbergh, Anne (Spencer) Morrow** 1906-
**CLC 82; DAM NOV**
See also CA 17-20R; CANR 16, 73; MTCW 1, 2; SATA 33

**Lindsay, David** 1878-1945 .............. **TCLC 15**
See also CA 113

**Lindsay, (Nicholas) Vachel**
1879-1931 . **TCLC 17; DA; DAC; DAM MST, POET; PC 23; WLC**
See also CA 114; 135; CANR 79; CDALB 1865-1917; DA3; DLB 54; SATA 40

**Linke-Poot**
See Doeblin, Alfred

**Linney, Romulus** 1930- ..................... **CLC 51**
See also CA 1-4R; CANR 40, 44, 79

**Linton, Eliza Lynn** 1822-1898 ....... **NCLC 41**
See also DLB 18

**Li Po** 701-763 ..................... **CMLC 2; PC 29**

**Lipsius, Justus** 1547-1606 ................... **LC 16**

**Lipsyte, Robert (Michael)** 1938- ..... **CLC 21; DA; DAC; DAM MST, NOV**
See also AAYA 7; CA 17-20R; CANR 8, 57; CLR 23; JRDA; MAICYA; SATA 5, 68, 113

**Lish, Gordon (Jay)** 1934- ... **CLC 45; SSC 18**
See also CA 113; 117; CANR 79; DLB 130; INT 117

**Lispector, Clarice** 1925(?)-1977 ....... **CLC 43; HLCS 2; SSC 34**
See also CA 139; 116; CANR 71; DLB 113; HW 2

**Littell, Robert** 1935(?)- ..................... **CLC 42**
See also CA 109; 112; CANR 64

**Little, Malcolm** 1925-1965
See Malcolm X
See also BW 1, 3; CA 125; 111; CANR 82; DA; DAB; DAC; DAM MST, MULT; DA3; MTCW 1, 2

**Littlewit, Humphrey Gent.**
See Lovecraft, H(oward) P(hillips)

**Litwos**
See Sienkiewicz, Henryk (Adam Alexander Pius)

**Liu, E** 1857-1909 ............................ **TCLC 15**
See also CA 115

**Lively, Penelope (Margaret)** 1933- .. **CLC 32, 50; DAM NOV**
See also CA 41-44R; CANR 29, 67, 79; CLR 7; DLB 14, 161, 207; JRDA; MAICYA; MTCW 1, 2; SATA 7, 60, 101

**Livesay, Dorothy (Kathleen)** 1909- ... **CLC 4, 15, 79; DAC; DAM MST, POET**
See also AITN 2; CA 25-28R; CAAS 8; CANR 36, 67; DLB 68; MTCW 1

**Livy** c. 59B.C.-c. 17 ....................... **CMLC 11**
See also DLB 211

**Lizardi, Jose Joaquin Fernandez de**
1776-1827 ............................... **NCLC 30**

**Llewellyn, Richard**
See Llewellyn Lloyd, Richard Dafydd Vivian
See also DLB 15

**Llewellyn Lloyd, Richard Dafydd Vivian**
1906-1983 .............................. **CLC 7, 80**
See also Llewellyn, Richard CA 53-56; 111; CANR 7, 71; SATA 11; SATA-Obit 37

**Llosa, (Jorge) Mario (Pedro) Vargas**
See Vargas Llosa, (Jorge) Mario (Pedro)

**Lloyd, Manda**
See Mander, (Mary) Jane

**Lloyd Webber, Andrew** 1948-
See Webber, Andrew Lloyd
See also AAYA 1; CA 116; 149; DAM DRAM; SATA 56

**Llull, Ramon** c. 1235-c. 1316 ........ **CMLC 12**

**Lobb, Ebenezer**
See Upward, Allen

**Locke, Alain (Le Roy)** 1886-1954 . **TCLC 43; BLCS**
See also BW 1, 3; CA 106; 124; CANR 79; DLB 51

**Locke, John** 1632-1704 .................... **LC 7, 35**
See also DLB 101

**Locke-Elliott, Sumner**
See Elliott, Sumner Locke

**Lockhart, John Gibson** 1794-1854 .. **NCLC 6**
See also DLB 110, 116, 144

**Lodge, David (John)** 1935- ... **CLC 36; DAM POP**
See also BEST 90:1; CA 17-20R; CANR 19, 53; DLB 14, 194; INT CANR-19; MTCW 1, 2

**Lodge, Thomas** 1558-1625 ................. **LC 41**

**Lodge, Thomas** 1558-1625 ................. **LC 41**
See also DLB 172

**Loennbohm, Armas Eino Leopold** 1878-1926
See Leino, Eino
See also CA 123

**Loewinsohn, Ron(ald William)**
1937- ..................................... **CLC 52**
See also CA 25-28R; CANR 71

**Logan, Jake**
See Smith, Martin Cruz

**Logan, John (Burton)** 1923-1987 ....... **CLC 5**
See also CA 77-80; 124; CANR 45; DLB 5

**Lo Kuan-chung** 1330(?)-1400(?) .......... **LC 12**

**Lombard, Nap**
See Johnson, Pamela Hansford

**London, Jack** .......... **TCLC 9, 15, 39; SSC 4; WLC**
See also London, John Griffith AAYA 13; AITN 2; CDALB 1865-1917; DLB 8, 12, 78, 212; SATA 18

**London, John Griffith** 1876-1916
See London, Jack
See also CA 110; 119; CANR 73; DA; DAB; DAC; DAM MST, NOV; DA3; JRDA; MAICYA; MTCW 1, 2

**Long, Emmett**
See Leonard, Elmore (John, Jr.)

**Longbaugh, Harry**
See Goldman, William (W.)

**Longfellow, Henry Wadsworth** 1807-1882
**NCLC 2, 45; DA; DAB; DAC; DAM MST, POET; WLCS**
See also CDALB 1640-1865; DA3; DLB 1, 59; SATA 19

**Longinus** c. 1st cent. - .................... **CMLC 27**
See also DLB 176

**Longley, Michael** 1939- ...................... **CLC 29**
See also CA 102; DLB 40

**Longus** fl. c. 2nd cent. - .................... **CMLC 7**

**Longway, A. Hugh**
See Lang, Andrew

**Lonnrot, Elias** 1802-1884 ............... **NCLC 53**

**Lopate, Phillip** 1943- ......................... **CLC 29**
See also CA 97-100; CANR 88; DLBY 80; INT 97-100

**Lopez Portillo (y Pacheco), Jose**
1920- ..................................... **CLC 46**
See also CA 129; HW 1

**Lopez y Fuentes, Gregorio**
1897(?)-1966 ............................. **CLC 32**
See also CA 131; HW 1

**Lorca, Federico Garcia**
See Garcia Lorca, Federico

**Lord, Bette Bao** 1938- ....................... **CLC 23**
See also BEST 90:3; CA 107; CANR 41, 79; INT 107; SATA 58

**Lord Auch**
See Bataille, Georges

**Lord Byron**
See Byron, George Gordon (Noel)

**Lorde, Audre (Geraldine)**
1934-1992 ... **CLC 18, 71; BLC 2; DAM MULT, POET; PC 12**
See also BW 1, 3; CA 25-28R; 142; CANR 16, 26, 46, 82; DA3; DLB 41; MTCW 1, 2

**Lord Houghton**
See Milnes, Richard Monckton

**Lord Jeffrey**
See Jeffrey, Francis

**Lorenzini, Carlo** 1826-1890
See Collodi, Carlo
See also MAICYA; SATA 29, 100

**Lorenzo, Heberto Padilla**
See Padilla (Lorenzo), Heberto

**Loris**
See Hofmannsthal, Hugo von

**Loti, Pierre** ....................................... **TCLC 11**
See also Viaud, (Louis Marie) Julien DLB 123

**Lou, Henri**
See Andreas-Salome, Lou

**Louie, David Wong** 1954- ................. **CLC 70**
See also CA 139

**Louis, Father M.**
See Merton, Thomas

**Lovecraft, H(oward) P(hillips)** 1890-1937
**TCLC 4, 22; DAM POP; SSC 3**

See also AAYA 14; CA 104; 133; DA3; MTCW 1, 2

**Lovelace, Earl** 1935- ......................... **CLC 51**
See also BW 2; CA 77-80; CANR 41, 72; DLB 125; MTCW 1

**Lovelace, Richard** 1618-1657 .............. **LC 24**
See also DLB 131

**Lowell, Amy** 1874-1925 .... **TCLC 1, 8; DAM POET; PC 13**
See also CA 104; 151; DLB 54, 140; MTCW 2

**Lowell, James Russell** 1819-1891 .... **NCLC 2**
See also CDALB 1640-1865; DLB 1, 11, 64, 79, 189

**Lowell, Robert (Traill Spence, Jr.)** 1917-1977 .... **CLC 1, 2, 3, 4, 5, 8, 9, 11, 15, 37, 124; DA; DAB; DAC; DAM MST, NOV; PC 3; WLC**
See also CA 9-12R; 73-76; CABS 2; CANR 26, 60; CDALBS; DA3; DLB 5, 169; MTCW 1, 2

**Lowenthal, Michael (Francis)** 1969- ......................................... **CLC 119**
See also CA 150

**Lowndes, Marie Adelaide (Belloc)** 1868-1947 **TCLC 12**
See also CA 107; DLB 70

**Lowry, (Clarence) Malcolm** 1909-1957 ............. **TCLC 6, 40; SSC 31**
See also CA 105; 131; CANR 62; CDBLB 1945-1960; DLB 15; MTCW 1, 2

**Lowry, Mina Gertrude** 1882-1966
See Loy, Mina
See also CA 113

**Loxsmith, John**
See Brunner, John (Kilian Houston)

**Loy, Mina** ...... **CLC 28; DAM POET; PC 16**
See also Lowry, Mina Gertrude DLB 4, 54

**Loyson-Bridet**
See Schwob, Marcel (Mayer Andre)

**Lucan** 39-65 ...................................... **CMLC 33**
See also DLB 211

**Lucas, Craig** 1951- ........................... **CLC 64**
See also CA 137; CANR 71

**Lucas, E(dward) V(errall)** 1868-1938 ....................................... **TCLC 73**
See also CA 176; DLB 98, 149, 153; SATA 20

**Lucas, George** 1944- .......................... **CLC 16**
See also AAYA 1, 23; CA 77-80; CANR 30; SATA 56

**Lucas, Hans**
See Godard, Jean-Luc

**Lucas, Victoria**
See Plath, Sylvia

**Lucian** c. 120-c. 180 ...................... **CMLC 32**
See also DLB 176

**Ludlam, Charles** 1943-1987 ........ **CLC 46, 50**
See also CA 85-88; 122; CANR 72, 86

**Ludlum, Robert** 1927- .... **CLC 22, 43; DAM NOV, POP**
See also AAYA 10; BEST 89:1, 90:3; CA 33-36R; CANR 25, 41, 68; DA3; DLBY 82; MTCW 1, 2

**Ludwig, Ken** ..................................... **CLC 60**

**Ludwig, Otto** 1813-1865 .................. **NCLC 4**
See also DLB 129

**Lugones, Leopoldo** 1874-1938 ...... **TCLC 15; HLCS 1**
See also CA 116; 131; HW 1

**Lu Hsun** 1881-1936 ........... **TCLC 3; SSC 20**
See also Shu-Jen, Chou

**Lukacs, George** ................................. **CLC 24**
See also Lukacs, Gyorgy (Szegeny von)

**Lukacs, Gyorgy (Szegeny von)** 1885-1971
See Lukacs, George
See also CA 101; 29-32R; CANR 62; MTCW 2

**Luke, Peter (Ambrose Cyprian)** 1919-1995 **CLC 38**
See also CA 81-84; 147; CANR 72; DLB 13

**Lunar, Dennis**
See Mungo, Raymond

**Lurie, Alison** 1926- .............. **CLC 4, 5, 18, 39**
See also CA 1-4R; CANR 2, 17, 50, 88; DLB 2; MTCW 1; SATA 46, 112

**Lustig, Arnost** 1926- .......................... **CLC 56**
See also AAYA 3; CA 69-72; CANR 47; SATA 56

**Luther, Martin** 1483-1546 ............... **LC 9, 37**
See also DLB 179

**Luxemburg, Rosa** 1870(?)-1919 ..... **TCLC 63**
See also CA 118

**Luzi, Mario** 1914- .............................. **CLC 13**
See also CA 61-64; CANR 9, 70; DLB 128

**Lyly, John** 1554(?)-1606 ........... **LC 41; DAM DRAM; DC 7**
See also DLB 62, 167

**L'Ymagier**
See Gourmont, Remy (-Marie-Charles) de

**Lynch, B. Suarez**
See Bioy Casares, Adolfo; Borges, Jorge Luis

**Lynch, B. Suarez**
See Bioy Casares, Adolfo

**Lynch, David (K.)** 1946- .................... **CLC 66**
See also CA 124; 129

**Lynch, James**
See Andreyev, Leonid (Nikolaevich)

**Lynch Davis, B.**
See Bioy Casares, Adolfo; Borges, Jorge Luis

**Lyndsay, Sir David** 1490-1555 ............. **LC 20**

**Lynn, Kenneth S(chuyler)** 1923- ...... **CLC 50**
See also CA 1-4R; CANR 3, 27, 65

**Lynx**
See West, Rebecca

**Lyons, Marcus**
See Blish, James (Benjamin)

**Lyre, Pinchbeck**
See Sassoon, Siegfried (Lorraine)

**Lytle, Andrew (Nelson)** 1902-1995 ... **CLC 22**
See also CA 9-12R; 150; CANR 70; DLB 6; DLBY 95

**Lyttelton, George** 1709-1773 ............... **LC 10**

**Maas, Peter** 1929- .............................. **CLC 29**
See also CA 93-96; INT 93-96; MTCW 2

**Macaulay, Rose** 1881-1958 ......... **TCLC 7, 44**
See also CA 104; DLB 36

**Macaulay, Thomas Babington** 1800-1859 **NCLC 42**
See also CDBLB 1832-1890; DLB 32, 55

**MacBeth, George (Mann)** 1932-1992 ............................ **CLC 2, 5, 9**
See also CA 25-28R; 136; CANR 61, 66; DLB 40; MTCW 1; SATA 4; SATA-Obit 70

**MacCaig, Norman (Alexander)** 1910- ........ **CLC 36; DAB; DAM POET**
See also CA 9-12R; CANR 3, 34; DLB 27

**MacCarthy, Sir(Charles Otto) Desmond** 1877-1952 ................................. **TCLC 36**
See also CA 167

**MacDiarmid, Hugh** ..... **CLC 2, 4, 11, 19, 63; PC 9**
See also Grieve, C(hristopher) M(urray) CDBLB 1945-1960; DLB 20

**MacDonald, Anson**
See Heinlein, Robert A(nson)

**Macdonald, Cynthia** 1928- ......... **CLC 13, 19**
See also CA 49-52; CANR 4, 44; DLB 105

**MacDonald, George** 1824-1905 ........ **TCLC 9**
See also CA 106; 137; CANR 80; DLB 18, 163, 178; MAICYA; SATA 33, 100

**Macdonald, John**
See Millar, Kenneth

**MacDonald, John D(ann)** 1916-1986 .. **CLC 3, 27, 44; DAM NOV, POP**
See also CA 1-4R; 121; CANR 1, 19, 60; DLB 8; DLBY 86; MTCW 1, 2

**Macdonald, John Ross**
See Millar, Kenneth

**Macdonald, Ross** ...... **CLC 1, 2, 3, 14, 34, 41**
See also Millar, Kenneth DLBD 6

**MacDougal, John**
See Blish, James (Benjamin)

**MacEwen, Gwendolyn (Margaret)** 1941-1987 ............................. **CLC 13, 55**
See also CA 9-12R; 124; CANR 7, 22; DLB 53; SATA 50; SATA-Obit 55

**Macha, Karel Hynek** 1810-1846 .... **NCLC 46**

**Machado (y Ruiz), Antonio** 1875-1939 ................................. **TCLC 3**
See also CA 104; 174; DLB 108; HW 2

**Machado de Assis, Joaquim Maria** 1839-1908 ..... **TCLC 10; BLC 2; HLCS 2; SSC 24**
See also CA 107; 153

**Machen, Arthur** ................. **TCLC 4; SSC 20**
See also Jones, Arthur Llewellyn CA 179; DLB 36, 156, 178

**Machiavelli, Niccolo** 1469-1527 ..... **LC 8, 36; DA; DAB; DAC; DAM MST; WLCS**

**MacInnes, Colin** 1914-1976 .......... **CLC 4, 23**
See also CA 69-72; 65-68; CANR 21; DLB 14; MTCW 1, 2

**MacInnes, Helen (Clark)** 1907-1985 ........ **CLC 27, 39; DAM POP**
See also CA 1-4R; 117; CANR 1, 28, 58; DLB 87; MTCW 1, 2; SATA 22; SATA-Obit 44

**Mackenzie, Compton (Edward Montague)** 1883-1972 ................................. **CLC 18**
See also CA 21-22; 37-40R; CAP 2; DLB 34, 100

**Mackenzie, Henry** 1745-1831 ........ **NCLC 41**
See also DLB 39

**Mackintosh, Elizabeth** 1896(?)-1952
See Tey, Josephine
See also CA 110

**MacLaren, James**
See Grieve, C(hristopher) M(urray)

**Mac Laverty, Bernard** 1942- ............ **CLC 31**
See also CA 116; 118; CANR 43, 88; INT 118

**MacLean, Alistair (Stuart)** 1922(?)-1987 .. **CLC 3, 13, 50, 63; DAM POP**
See also CA 57-60; 121; CANR 28, 61; MTCW 1; SATA 23; SATA-Obit 50

**Maclean, Norman (Fitzroy)** 1902-1990 .... **CLC 78; DAM POP; SSC 13**
See also CA 102; 132; CANR 49; DLB 206

**MacLeish, Archibald** 1892-1982 ... **CLC 3, 8, 14, 68; DAM POET**
See also CA 9-12R; 106; CANR 33, 63; CDALBS; DLB 4, 7, 45; DLBY 82; MTCW 1, 2

**MacLennan, (John) Hugh** 1907-1990 . **CLC 2, 14, 92; DAC; DAM MST**
See also CA 5-8R; 142; CANR 33; DLB 68; MTCW 1, 2

**MacLeod, Alistair** 1936- ....... **CLC 56; DAC; DAM MST**
See also CA 123; DLB 60; MTCW 2

**Macleod, Fiona**
See Sharp, William

**MacNeice, (Frederick) Louis**
1907-1963 ........ **CLC 1, 4, 10, 53; DAB; DAM POET**
See also CA 85-88; CANR 61; DLB 10, 20; MTCW 1, 2

**MacNeill, Dand**
See Fraser, George MacDonald

**Macpherson, James** 1736-1796 ........... **LC 29**
See also Ossian DLB 109

**Macpherson, (Jean) Jay** 1931- ........ **CLC 14**
See also CA 5-8R; DLB 53

**MacShane, Frank** 1927- ................. **CLC 39**
See also CA 9-12R; CANR 3, 33; DLB 111

**Macumber, Mari**
See Sandoz, Mari(e Susette)

**Madach, Imre** 1823-1864 ............... **NCLC 19**

**Madden, (Jerry) David** 1933- ....... **CLC 5, 15**
See also CA 1-4R; CAAS 3; CANR 4, 45; DLB 6; MTCW 1

**Maddern, Al(an)**
See Ellison, Harlan (Jay)

**Madhubuti, Haki R.** 1942- . **CLC 6, 73; BLC 2; DAM MULT, POET; PC 5**
See also Lee, Don L. BW 2, 3; CA 73-76; CANR 24, 51, 73; DLB 5, 41; DLBD 8; MTCW 2

**Maepenn, Hugh**
See Kuttner, Henry

**Maepenn, K. H.**
See Kuttner, Henry

**Maeterlinck, Maurice** 1862-1949 ... **TCLC 3; DAM DRAM**
See also CA 104; 136; CANR 80; DLB 192; SATA 66

**Maginn, William** 1794-1842 ............ **NCLC 8**
See also DLB 110, 159

**Mahapatra, Jayanta** 1928- .... **CLC 33; DAM MULT**
See also CA 73-76; CAAS 9; CANR 15, 33, 66, 87

**Mahfouz, Naguib (Abdel Aziz Al-Sabilgi)**
1911(?)-
See Mahfuz, Najib
See also BEST 89:2; CA 128; CANR 55; DAM NOV; DA3; MTCW 1, 2

**Mahfuz, Najib** ....................... **CLC 52, 55**
See also Mahfouz, Naguib (Abdel Aziz Al-Sabilgi) DLBY 88

**Mahon, Derek** 1941- .................. **CLC 27**
See also CA 113; 128; DLB 40

**Mailer, Norman** 1923- ... **CLC 1, 2, 3, 4, 5, 8, 11, 14, 28, 39, 74, 111; DA; DAB; DAC; DAM MST, NOV, POP**
See also AAYA 31; AITN 2; CA 9-12R; CABS 1; CANR 28, 74, 77; CDALB 1968-1988; DA3; DLB 2, 16, 28, 185; DLBD 3; DLBY 80, 83; MTCW 1, 2

**Maillet, Antonine** 1929- .. **CLC 54, 118; DAC**
See also CA 115; 120; CANR 46, 74, 77; DLB 60; INT 120; MTCW 2

**Mais, Roger** 1905-1955 ................... **TCLC 8**
See also BW 1, 3; CA 105; 124; CANR 82; DLB 125; MTCW 1

**Maistre, Joseph de** 1753-1821 ....... **NCLC 37**

**Maitland, Frederic** 1850-1906 ........ **TCLC 65**

**Maitland, Sara (Louise)** 1950- ........ **CLC 49**
See also CA 69-72; CANR 13, 59

**Major, Clarence** 1936- . **CLC 3, 19, 48; BLC 2; DAM MULT**
See also BW 2, 3; CA 21-24R; CAAS 6; CANR 13, 25, 53, 82; DLB 33

**Major, Kevin (Gerald)** 1949- . **CLC 26; DAC**
See also AAYA 16; CA 97-100; CANR 21, 38; CLR 11; DLB 60; INT CANR-21; JRDA; MAICYA; SATA 32, 82

**Maki, James**
See Ozu, Yasujiro

**Malabaila, Damiano**
See Levi, Primo

**Malamud, Bernard** 1914-1986 .. **CLC 1, 2, 3, 5, 8, 9, 11, 18, 27, 44, 78, 85; DA; DAB; DAC; DAM MST, NOV, POP; SSC 15; WLC**
See also AAYA 16; CA 5-8R; 118; CABS 1; CANR 28, 62; CDALB 1941-1968; DA3; DLB 2, 28, 152; DLBY 80, 86; MTCW 1, 2

**Malan, Herman**
See Bosman, Herman Charles; Bosman, Herman Charles

**Malaparte, Curzio** 1898-1957 ........ **TCLC 52**

**Malcolm, Dan**
See Silverberg, Robert

**Malcolm X** ...... **CLC 82, 117; BLC 2; WLCS**
See also Little, Malcolm

**Malherbe, Francois de** 1555-1628 ......... **LC 5**

**Mallarme, Stephane** 1842-1898 ...... **NCLC 4, 41; DAM POET; PC 4**

**Mallet-Joris, Francoise** 1930- .......... **CLC 11**
See also CA 65-68; CANR 17; DLB 83

**Malley, Ern**
See McAuley, James Phillip

**Mallowan, Agatha Christie**
See Christie, Agatha (Mary Clarissa)

**Maloff, Saul** 1922- ..................... **CLC 5**
See also CA 33-36R

**Malone, Louis**
See MacNeice, (Frederick) Louis

**Malone, Michael (Christopher)**
1942- ........................... **CLC 43**
See also CA 77-80; CANR 14, 32, 57

**Malory, (Sir) Thomas**
1410(?)-1471(?) ......... **LC 11; DA; DAB; DAC; DAM MST; WLCS**
See also CDBLB Before 1660; DLB 146; SATA 59; SATA-Brief 33

**Malouf, (George Joseph) David**
1934- .................................. **CLC 28, 86**
See also CA 124; CANR 50, 76; MTCW 2

**Malraux, (Georges-)Andre**
1901-1976 ........ **CLC 1, 4, 9, 13, 15, 57; DAM NOV**
See also CA 21-22; 69-72; CANR 34, 58; CAP 2; DA3; DLB 72; MTCW 1, 2

**Malzberg, Barry N(athaniel)** 1939- ... **CLC 7**
See also CA 61-64; CAAS 4; CANR 16; DLB 8

**Mamet, David (Alan)** 1947- .. **CLC 9, 15, 34, 46, 91; DAM DRAM; DC 4**
See also AAYA 3; CA 81-84; CABS 3; CANR 15, 41, 67, 72; DA3; DLB 7; MTCW 1, 2

**Mamoulian, Rouben (Zachary)** 1897-1987 **CLC 16**
See also CA 25-28R; 124; CANR 85

**Mandelstam, Osip (Emilievich)**
1891(?)-1938(?) ........ **TCLC 2, 6; PC 14**
See also CA 104; 150; MTCW 2

**Mander, (Mary) Jane** 1877-1949 ... **TCLC 31**
See also CA 162

**Mandeville, John** fl. 1350- ............. **CMLC 19**
See also DLB 146

**Mandiargues, Andre Pieyre de** ........ **CLC 41**
See also Pieyre de Mandiargues, Andre DLB 83

**Mandrake, Ethel Belle**
See Thurman, Wallace (Henry)

**Mangan, James Clarence**
1803-1849 ................ **NCLC 27**

**Maniere, J.-E.**
See Giraudoux, (Hippolyte) Jean

**Mankiewicz, Herman (Jacob)** 1897-1953 **TCLC 85**
See also CA 120; 169; DLB 26

**Manley, (Mary) Delariviere**
1672(?)-1724 ............................ **LC 1, 42**
See also DLB 39, 80

**Mann, Abel**
See Creasey, John

**Mann, Emily** 1952- ............................. **DC 7**
See also CA 130; CANR 55

**Mann, (Luiz) Heinrich** 1871-1950 ... **TCLC 9**
See also CA 106; 164; 181; DLB 66, 118

**Mann, (Paul) Thomas** 1875-1955 ... **TCLC 2, 8, 14, 21, 35, 44, 60; DA; DAB; DAC; DAM MST, NOV; SSC 5; WLC**
See also CA 104; 128; DA3; DLB 66; MTCW 1, 2

**Mannheim, Karl** 1893-1947 .......... **TCLC 65**

**Manning, David**
See Faust, Frederick (Schiller)

**Manning, Frederic** 1887(?)-1935 ... **TCLC 25**
See also CA 124

**Manning, Olivia** 1915-1980 .......... **CLC 5, 19**
See also CA 5-8R; 101; CANR 29; MTCW 1

**Mano, D. Keith** 1942- .................... **CLC 2, 10**
See also CA 25-28R; CAAS 6; CANR 26, 57; DLB 6

**Mansfield, Katherine** . **TCLC 2, 8, 39; DAB; SSC 9, 23, 38; WLC**
See also Beauchamp, Kathleen Mansfield DLB 162

**Manso, Peter** 1940- ...................... **CLC 39**
See also CA 29-32R; CANR 44

**Mantecon, Juan Jimenez**
See Jimenez (Mantecon), Juan Ramon

**Manton, Peter**
See Creasey, John

**Man Without a Spleen, A**
See Chekhov, Anton (Pavlovich)

**Manzoni, Alessandro** 1785-1873 .... **NCLC 29**

**Map, Walter** 1140-1209 ................. **CMLC 32**

**Mapu, Abraham (ben Jekutiel)** 1808-1867 **NCLC 18**

**Mara, Sally**
See Queneau, Raymond

**Marat, Jean Paul** 1743-1793 ............... **LC 10**

**Marcel, Gabriel Honore** 1889-1973 . **CLC 15**
See also CA 102; 45-48; MTCW 1, 2

**March, William** 1893-1954 ............ **TCLC 96**

**Marchbanks, Samuel**
See Davies, (William) Robertson

**Marchi, Giacomo**
See Bassani, Giorgio

**Margulies, Donald** ............................ **CLC 76**

**Marie de France** c. 12th cent. - ..... **CMLC 8; PC 22**
See also DLB 208

**Marie de l'Incarnation** 1599-1672 ...... **LC 10**

**Marier, Captain Victor**
See Griffith, D(avid Lewelyn) W(ark)

**Mariner, Scott**
See Pohl, Frederik

**Marinetti, Filippo Tommaso** 1876-1944 **TCLC 10**
See also CA 107; DLB 114

**Marivaux, Pierre Carlet de Chamblain de**
1688-1763 ........................... **LC 4; DC 7**

**Markandaya, Kamala** .................. **CLC 8, 38**
See also Taylor, Kamala (Purnaiya)

**Markfield, Wallace** 1926- ................... **CLC 8**
See also CA 69-72; CAAS 3; DLB 2, 28

**Markham, Edwin** 1852-1940 ......... **TCLC 47**
See also CA 160; DLB 54, 186

**Markham, Robert**
See Amis, Kingsley (William)

**Marks, J**
See Highwater, Jamake (Mamake)

**Marks-Highwater, J**
See Highwater, Jamake (Mamake)

**Markson, David M(errill)** 1927- ....... **CLC 67**
See also CA 49-52; CANR 1

**Marley, Bob** ....................... **CLC 17**
See also Marley, Robert Nesta

**Marley, Robert Nesta** 1945-1981
See Marley, Bob
See also CA 107; 103

**Marlowe, Christopher** 1564-1593 ...... **LC 22, 47; DA; DAB; DAC; DAM DRAM, MST; DC 1; WLC**
See also CDBLB Before 1660; DA3; DLB 62

**Marlowe, Stephen** 1928-
See Queen, Ellery
See also CA 13-16R; CANR 6, 55

**Marmontel, Jean-Francois** 1723-1799 .. **LC 2**

**Marquand, John P(hillips)**
1893-1960 ............................ **CLC 2, 10**
See also CA 85-88; CANR 73; DLB 9, 102; MTCW 2

**Marques, Rene** 1919-1979 ..... **CLC 96; DAM MULT; HLC 2**
See also CA 97-100; 85-88; CANR 78; DLB 113; HW 1, 2

**Marquez, Gabriel (Jose) Garcia**
See Garcia Marquez, Gabriel (Jose)

**Marquis, Don(ald Robert Perry)** 1878-1937
**TCLC 7**
See also CA 104; 166; DLB 11, 25

**Marric, J. J.**
See Creasey, John

**Marryat, Frederick** 1792-1848 ........ **NCLC 3**
See also DLB 21, 163

**Marsden, James**
See Creasey, John

**Marsh, Edward** 1872-1953 ............. **TCLC 99**

**Marsh, (Edith) Ngaio** 1899-1982 ....... **CLC 7, 53; DAM POP**
See also CA 9-12R; CANR 6, 58; DLB 77; MTCW 1, 2

**Marshall, Garry** 1934- ..................... **CLC 17**
See also AAYA 3; CA 111; SATA 60

**Marshall, Paule** 1929- .. **CLC 27, 72; BLC 3; DAM MULT; SSC 3**
See also BW 2, 3; CA 77-80; CANR 25, 73; DA3; DLB 157; MTCW 1, 2

**Marshallik**
See Zangwill, Israel

**Marsten, Richard**
See Hunter, Evan

**Marston, John** 1576-1634 ........ **LC 33; DAM DRAM**
See also DLB 58, 172

**Martha, Henry**
See Harris, Mark

**Marti (y Perez), Jose (Julian)** 1853-1895
**NCLC 63; DAM MULT; HLC 2**
See also HW 2

**Martial** c. 40-c. 104 .......... **CMLC 35; PC 10**
See also DLB 211

**Martin, Ken**
See Hubbard, L(afayette) Ron(ald)

**Martin, Richard**
See Creasey, John

**Martin, Steve** 1945- ......................... **CLC 30**
See also CA 97-100; CANR 30; MTCW 1

**Martin, Valerie** 1948- ......................... **CLC 89**
See also BEST 90:2; CA 85-88; CANR 49

**Martin, Violet Florence**
1862-1915 ............................... **TCLC 51**

**Martin, Webber**
See Silverberg, Robert

**Martindale, Patrick Victor**
See White, Patrick (Victor Martindale)

**Martin du Gard, Roger**
1881-1958 ............................... **TCLC 24**
See also CA 118; DLB 65

**Martineau, Harriet** 1802-1876 ....... **NCLC 26**
See also DLB 21, 55, 159, 163, 166, 190; YABC 2

**Martines, Julia**
See O'Faolain, Julia

**Martinez, Enrique Gonzalez**
See Gonzalez Martinez, Enrique

**Martinez, Jacinto Benavente y**
See Benavente (y Martinez), Jacinto

**Martinez Ruiz, Jose** 1873-1967
See Azorin; Ruiz, Jose Martinez
See also CA 93-96; HW 1

**Martinez Sierra, Gregorio**
1881-1947 ............................... **TCLC 6**
See also CA 115

**Martinez Sierra, Maria (de la O'LeJarraga)**
1874-1974 ............................... **TCLC 6**
See also CA 115

**Martinsen, Martin**
See Follett, Ken(neth Martin)

**Martinson, Harry (Edmund)**
1904-1978 ............................... **CLC 14**
See also CA 77-80; CANR 34

**Marut, Ret**
See Traven, B.

**Marut, Robert**
See Traven, B.

**Marvell, Andrew** 1621-1678 .. **LC 4, 43; DA; DAB; DAC; DAM MST, POET; PC 10; WLC**
See also CDBLB 1660-1789; DLB 131

**Marx, Karl (Heinrich)** 1818-1883 . **NCLC 17**
See also DLB 129

**Masaoka Shiki** ........................... **TCLC 18**
See also Masaoka Tsunenori

**Masaoka Tsunenori** 1867-1902
See Masaoka Shiki
See also CA 117

**Masefield, John (Edward)**
1878-1967 ..... **CLC 11, 47; DAM POET**
See also CA 19-20; 25-28R; CANR 33; CAP 2; CDBLB 1890-1914; DLB 10, 19, 153, 160; MTCW 1, 2; SATA 19

**Maso, Carole** 19(?)- ......................... **CLC 44**
See also CA 170

**Mason, Bobbie Ann** 1940- ... **CLC 28, 43, 82; SSC 4**
See also AAYA 5; CA 53-56; CANR 11, 31, 58, 83; CDALBS; DA3; DLB 173; DLBY 87; INT CANR-31; MTCW 1, 2

**Mason, Ernst**
See Pohl, Frederik

**Mason, Lee W.**
See Malzberg, Barry N(athaniel)

**Mason, Nick** 1945- ........................... **CLC 35**

**Mason, Tally**
See Derleth, August (William)

**Mass, William**
See Gibson, William

**Master Lao**
See Lao Tzu

**Masters, Edgar Lee** 1868-1950 ....... **TCLC 2, 25; DA; DAC; DAM MST, POET; PC 1; WLCS**
See also CA 104; 133; CDALB 1865-1917; DLB 54; MTCW 1, 2

**Masters, Hilary** 1928- ..................... **CLC 48**
See also CA 25-28R; CANR 13, 47

**Mastrosimone, William** 19(?)- .......... **CLC 36**

**Mathe, Albert**
See Camus, Albert

**Mather, Cotton** 1663-1728 ................. **LC 38**
See also CDALB 1640-1865; DLB 24, 30, 140

**Mather, Increase** 1639-1723 ................. **LC 38**
See also DLB 24

**Matheson, Richard Burton** 1926- .... **CLC 37**
See also AAYA 31; CA 97-100; CANR 88; DLB 8, 44; INT 97-100

**Mathews, Harry** 1930- ................. **CLC 6, 52**
See also CA 21-24R; CAAS 6; CANR 18, 40

**Mathews, John Joseph** 1894-1979 .. **CLC 84; DAM MULT**
See also CA 19-20; 142; CANR 45; CAP 2; DLB 175; NNAL

**Mathias, Roland (Glyn)** 1915- ......... **CLC 45**
See also CA 97-100; CANR 19, 41; DLB 27

**Matsuo Basho** 1644-1694 ...................... **PC 3**
See also DAM POET

**Mattheson, Rodney**
See Creasey, John

**Matthews, (James) Brander**
1852-1929 ............................... **TCLC 95**
See also DLB 71, 78; DLBD 13

**Matthews, Greg** 1949- ...................... **CLC 45**
See also CA 135

**Matthews, William (Procter, III)** 1942-1997
**CLC 40**
See also CA 29-32R; 162; CAAS 18; CANR 12, 57; DLB 5

**Matthias, John (Edward)** 1941- ......... **CLC 9**
See also CA 33-36R; CANR 56

**Matthiessen, F. O.** 1902-1950 ....... **TCLC 100**
See also DLB 63

**Matthiessen, Peter** 1927- ... **CLC 5, 7, 11, 32, 64; DAM NOV**
See also AAYA 6; BEST 90:4; CA 9-12R; CANR 21, 50, 73; DA3; DLB 6, 173; MTCW 1, 2; SATA 27

**Maturin, Charles Robert**
1780(?)-1824 ............................ **NCLC 6**
See also DLB 178

**Matute (Ausejo), Ana Maria** 1925- .. **CLC 11**
See also CA 89-92; MTCW 1

**Maugham, W. S.**
See Maugham, W(illiam) Somerset

**Maugham, W(illiam) Somerset** 1874-1965
**CLC 1, 11, 15, 67, 93; DA; DAB; DAC; DAM DRAM, MST, NOV; SSC 8; WLC**
See also CA 5-8R; 25-28R; CANR 40; CDBLB 1914-1945; DA3; DLB 10, 36, 77, 100, 162, 195; MTCW 1, 2; SATA 54

**Maugham, William Somerset**
See Maugham, W(illiam) Somerset

**Maupassant, (Henri Rene Albert) Guy de**
1850-1893 . **NCLC 1, 42, 83; DA; DAB; DAC; DAM MST, SSC 1; WLC**
See also DA3; DLB 123

**Maupin, Armistead** 1944- ..... **CLC 95; DAM POP**
See also CA 125; 130; CANR 58; DA3; INT 130; MTCW 2

**Maurhut, Richard**
See Traven, B.

**Mauriac, Claude** 1914-1996 ............... **CLC 9**
See also CA 89-92; 152; DLB 83

**Mauriac, Francois (Charles)**
1885-1970 .......... **CLC 4, 9, 56; SSC 24**
See also CA 25-28; CAP 2; DLB 65; MTCW 1, 2

**Mavor, Osborne Henry** 1888-1951
See Bridie, James
See also CA 104

**Maxwell, William (Keepers, Jr.)**
1908- .................................... **CLC 19**
See also CA 93-96; CANR 54; DLBY 80; INT 93-96

**May, Elaine** 1932- ........................... **CLC 16**
See also CA 124; 142; DLB 44

**Mayakovski, Vladimir (Vladimirovich)**
1893-1930 ......................... **TCLC 4, 18**
See also CA 104; 158; MTCW 2

**Mayhew, Henry** 1812-1887 ............. **NCLC 31**
See also DLB 18, 55, 190

**Mayle, Peter** 1939(?)- ......................... **CLC 89**
See also CA 139; CANR 64

**Maynard, Joyce** 1953- .................... **CLC 23**
  See also CA 111; 129; CANR 64
**Mayne, William (James Carter)**
  1928- ......................................... **CLC 12**
  See also AAYA 20; CA 9-12R; CANR 37,
    80; CLR 25; JRDA; MAICYA; SAAS 11;
    SATA 6, 68
**Mayo, Jim**
  See L'Amour, Louis (Dearborn)
**Maysles, Albert** 1926- .................... **CLC 16**
  See also CA 29-32R
**Maysles, David** 1932- .................... **CLC 16**
**Mazer, Norma Fox** 1931- ................ **CLC 26**
  See also AAYA 5; CA 69-72; CANR 12,
    32, 66; CLR 23; JRDA; MAICYA; SAAS
    1; SATA 24, 67, 105
**Mazzini, Guiseppe** 1805-1872 ........ **NCLC 34**
**McAlmon, Robert (Menzies)** 1895-1956
  **TCLC 97**
  See also CA 107; 168; DLB 4, 45; DLBD
    15
**McAuley, James Phillip** 1917-1976 .. **CLC 45**
  See also CA 97-100
**McBain, Ed**
  See Hunter, Evan
**McBrien, William Augustine** 1930- .. **CLC 44**
  See also CA 107
**McCaffrey, Anne (Inez)** 1926- ........ **CLC 17;**
  **DAM NOV, POP**
  See also AAYA 6; AITN 2; BEST 89:2; CA
    25-28R; CANR 15, 35, 55; CLR 49; DA3;
    DLB 8; JRDA; MAICYA; MTCW 1, 2;
    SAAS 11; SATA 8, 70
**McCall, Nathan** 1955(?)- .................. **CLC 86**
  See also BW 3; CA 146; CANR 88
**McCann, Arthur**
  See Campbell, John W(ood, Jr.)
**McCann, Edson**
  See Pohl, Frederik
**McCarthy, Charles, Jr.** 1933-
  See McCarthy, Cormac
  See also CANR 42, 69; DAM POP; DA3;
    MTCW 2
**McCarthy, Cormac** 1933- ...... **CLC 4, 57, 59,**
  **101**
  See also McCarthy, Charles, Jr. DLB 6, 143;
    MTCW 2
**McCarthy, Mary (Therese)**
  1912-1989 .. **CLC 1, 3, 5, 14, 24, 39, 59;**
  **SSC 24**
  See also CA 5-8R; 129; CANR 16, 50, 64;
    DA3; DLB 2; DLBY 81; INT CANR-16;
    MTCW 1, 2
**McCartney, (James) Paul** 1942- . **CLC 12, 35**
  See also CA 146
**McCauley, Stephen (D.)** 1955- ......... **CLC 50**
  See also CA 141
**McClure, Michael (Thomas)** 1932- ... **CLC 6,**
  **10**
  See also CA 21-24R; CANR 17, 46, 77;
    DLB 16
**McCorkle, Jill (Collins)** 1958- ......... **CLC 51**
  See also CA 121; DLBY 87
**McCourt, Frank** 1930- .................. **CLC 109**
  See also CA 157
**McCourt, James** 1941- ...................... **CLC 5**
  See also CA 57-60
**McCourt, Malachy** 1932- ............... **CLC 119**
**McCoy, Horace (Stanley)**
  1897-1955 .............................. **TCLC 28**
  See also CA 108; 155; DLB 9
**McCrae, John** 1872-1918 ............... **TCLC 12**
  See also CA 109; DLB 92
**McCreigh, James**
  See Pohl, Frederik
**McCullers, (Lula) Carson (Smith)** 1917-1967
  **CLC 1, 4, 10, 12, 48, 100; DA; DAB;**
  **DAC; DAM MST, NOV; SSC 9, 24;**
  **WLC**

  See also AAYA 21; CA 5-8R; 25-28R;
    CABS 1, 3; CANR 18; CDALB 1941-
    1968; DA3; DLB 2, 7, 173; MTCW 1, 2;
    SATA 27
**McCulloch, John Tyler**
  See Burroughs, Edgar Rice
**McCullough, Colleen** 1938(?)- ......... **CLC 27,**
  **107; DAM NOV, POP**
  See also CA 81-84; CANR 17, 46, 67; DA3;
    MTCW 1, 2
**McDermott, Alice** 1953- ................... **CLC 90**
  See also CA 109; CANR 40
**McElroy, Joseph** 1930- ................ **CLC 5, 47**
  See also CA 17-20R
**McEwan, Ian (Russell)** 1948- .... **CLC 13, 66;**
  **DAM NOV**
  See also BEST 90:4; CA 61-64; CANR 14,
    41, 69, 87; DLB 14, 194; MTCW 1, 2
**McFadden, David** 1940- ................... **CLC 48**
  See also CA 104; DLB 60; INT 104
**McFarland, Dennis** 1950- ................ **CLC 65**
  See also CA 165
**McGahern, John** 1934- ... **CLC 5, 9, 48; SSC**
  **17**
  See also CA 17-20R; CANR 29, 68; DLB
    14; MTCW 1
**McGinley, Patrick (Anthony)** 1937- . **CLC 41**
  See also CA 120; 127; CANR 56; INT 127
**McGinley, Phyllis** 1905-1978 ............. **CLC 14**
  See also CA 9-12R; 77-80; CANR 19; DLB
    11, 48; SATA 2, 44; SATA-Obit 24
**McGinniss, Joe** 1942- ...................... **CLC 32**
  See also AITN 2; BEST 89:2; CA 25-28R;
    CANR 26, 70; DLB 185; INT CANR-26
**McGivern, Maureen Daly**
  See Daly, Maureen
**McGrath, Patrick** 1950- ................... **CLC 55**
  See also CA 136; CANR 65
**McGrath, Thomas (Matthew)** 1916-1990
  **CLC 28, 59; DAM POET**
  See also CA 9-12R; 132; CANR 6, 33;
    MTCW 1; SATA 41; SATA-Obit 66
**McGuane, Thomas (Francis III)**
  1939- ................... **CLC 3, 7, 18, 45, 127**
  See also AITN 2; CA 49-52; CANR 5, 24,
    49; DLB 2, 212; DLBY 80; INT CANR-
    24; MTCW 1
**McGuckian, Medbh** 1950- .... **CLC 48; DAM**
  **POET; PC 27**
  See also CA 143; DLB 40
**McHale, Tom** 1942(?)-1982 ............. **CLC 3, 5**
  See also AITN 1; CA 77-80; 106
**McIlvanney, William** 1936- .............. **CLC 42**
  See also CA 25-28R; CANR 61; DLB 14,
    207
**McIlwraith, Maureen Mollie Hunter**
  See Hunter, Mollie
  See also SATA 2
**McInerney, Jay** 1955- .... **CLC 34, 112; DAM**
  **POP**
  See also AAYA 18; CA 116; 123; CANR
    45, 68; DA3; INT 123; MTCW 2
**McIntyre, Vonda N(eel)** 1948- .......... **CLC 18**
  See also CA 81-84; CANR 17, 34, 69;
    MTCW 1
**McKay, Claude** . **TCLC 7, 41; BLC 3; DAB;**
  **PC 2**
  See also McKay, Festus Claudius DLB 4,
    45, 51, 117
**McKay, Festus Claudius** 1889-1948
  See McKay, Claude
  See also BW 1, 3; CA 104; 124; CANR 73;
    DA; DAC; DAM MST, MULT, NOV,
    POET; MTCW 1, 2; WLC
**McKuen, Rod** 1933- ...................... **CLC 1, 3**
  See also AITN 1; CA 41-44R; CANR 40
**McLoughlin, R. B.**
  See Mencken, H(enry) L(ouis)

**McLuhan, (Herbert) Marshall** 1911-1980
  **CLC 37, 83**
  See also CA 9-12R; 102; CANR 12, 34, 61;
    DLB 88; INT CANR-12; MTCW 1, 2
**McMillan, Terry (L.)** 1951- ....... **CLC 50, 61,**
  **112; BLCS; DAM MULT, NOV, POP**
  See also AAYA 21; BW 2, 3; CA 140;
    CANR 60; DA3; MTCW 2
**McMurtry, Larry (Jeff)** 1936- .. **CLC 2, 3, 7,**
  **11, 27, 44, 127; DAM NOV, POP**
  See also AAYA 15; AITN 2; BEST 89:2;
    CA 5-8R; CANR 19, 43, 64; CDALB
    1968-1988; DA3; DLB 2, 143; DLBY 80,
    87; MTCW 1, 2
**McNally, T. M.** 1961- ...................... **CLC 82**
**McNally, Terrence** 1939- ... **CLC 4, 7, 41, 91;**
  **DAM DRAM**
  See also CA 45-48; CANR 2, 56; DA3;
    DLB 7; MTCW 2
**McNamer, Deirdre** 1950- .................. **CLC 70**
**McNeal, Tom** ...................................... **CLC 119**
**McNeile, Herman Cyril** 1888-1937
  See Sapper
  See also CA 184; DLB 77
**McNickle, (William) D'Arcy**
  1904-1977 ......... **CLC 89; DAM MULT**
  See also CA 9-12R; 85-88; CANR 5, 45;
    DLB 175, 212; NNAL; SATA-Obit 22
**McPhee, John (Angus)** 1931- ........... **CLC 36**
  See also BEST 90:1; CA 65-68; CANR 20,
    46, 64, 69; DLB 185; MTCW 1, 2
**McPherson, James Alan** 1943- .. **CLC 19, 77;**
  **BLCS**
  See also BW 1, 3; CA 25-28R; CAAS 17;
    CANR 24, 74; DLB 38; MTCW 1, 2
**McPherson, William (Alexander)**
  1933- ......................................... **CLC 34**
  See also CA 69-72; CANR 28; INT
    CANR-28
**Mead, George Herbert** 1873-1958 . **TCLC 89**
**Mead, Margaret** 1901-1978 ............... **CLC 37**
  See also AITN 1; CA 1-4R; 81-84; CANR
    4; DA3; MTCW 1, 2; SATA-Obit 20
**Meaker, Marijane (Agnes)** 1927-
  See Kerr, M. E.
  See also CA 107; CANR 37, 63; INT 107;
    JRDA; MAICYA; MTCW 1; SATA 20,
    61, 99; SATA-Essay 111
**Medoff, Mark (Howard)** 1940- ... **CLC 6, 23;**
  **DAM DRAM**
  See also AITN 1; CA 53-56; CANR 5; DLB
    7; INT CANR-5
**Medvedev, P. N.**
  See Bakhtin, Mikhail Mikhailovich
**Meged, Aharon**
  See Megged, Aharon
**Meged, Aron**
  See Megged, Aharon
**Megged, Aharon** 1920- ........................ **CLC 9**
  See also CA 49-52; CAAS 13; CANR 1
**Mehta, Ved (Parkash)** 1934- ............. **CLC 37**
  See also CA 1-4R; CANR 2, 23, 69; MTCW
    1
**Melanter**
  See Blackmore, R(ichard) D(oddridge)
**Melies, Georges** 1861-1938 ............. **TCLC 81**
**Melikow, Loris**
  See Hofmannsthal, Hugo von
**Melmoth, Sebastian**
  See Wilde, Oscar
**Meltzer, Milton** 1915- ...................... **CLC 26**
  See also AAYA 8; CA 13-16R; CANR 38;
    CLR 13; DLB 61; JRDA; MAICYA;
    SAAS 1; SATA 1, 50, 80
**Melville, Herman** 1819-1891 ... **NCLC 3, 12,**
  **29, 45, 49; DA; DAB; DAC; DAM**
  **MST, NOV; SSC 1, 17; WLC**
  See also AAYA 25; CDALB 1640-1865;
    DA3; DLB 3, 74; SATA 59

**Menander** c. 342B.C.-c. 292B.C. ... **CMLC 9;
DAM DRAM; DC 3**
See also DLB 176

**Menchu, Rigoberta** 1959-
See also HLCS 2

**Menchu, Rigoberta** 1959-
See also CA 175; HLCS 2

**Mencken, H(enry) L(ouis)**
1880-1956 ...................... **TCLC 13**
See also CA 105; 125; CDALB 1917-1929;
DLB 11, 29, 63, 137; MTCW 1, 2

**Mendelsohn, Jane** 1965(?)- ............. **CLC 99**
See also CA 154

**Mercer, David** 1928-1980 ........ **CLC 5; DAM
DRAM**
See also CA 9-12R; 102; CANR 23; DLB
13; MTCW 1

**Merchant, Paul**
See Ellison, Harlan (Jay)

**Meredith, George** 1828-1909 .. **TCLC 17, 43;
DAM POET**
See also CA 117; 153; CANR 80; CDBLB
1832-1890; DLB 18, 35, 57, 159

**Meredith, William (Morris)** 1919- .... **CLC 4,
13, 22, 55; DAM POET; PC 28**
See also CA 9-12R; CAAS 14; CANR 6,
40; DLB 5

**Merezhkovsky, Dmitry Sergeyevich**
1865-1941 ................................. **TCLC 29**
See also CA 169

**Merimee, Prosper** 1803-1870 ... **NCLC 6, 65;
SSC 7**
See also DLB 119, 192

**Merkin, Daphne** 1954- ...................... **CLC 44**
See also CA 123

**Merlin, Arthur**
See Blish, James (Benjamin)

**Merrill, James (Ingram)** 1926-1995 .. **CLC 2,
3, 6, 8, 13, 18, 34, 91; DAM POET; PC
28**
See also CA 13-16R; 147; CANR 10, 49,
63; DA3; DLB 5, 165; DLBY 85; INT
CANR-10; MTCW 1, 2

**Merriman, Alex**
See Silverberg, Robert

**Merriman, Brian** 1747-1805 .......... **NCLC 70**

**Merritt, E. B.**
See Waddington, Miriam

**Merton, Thomas** 1915-1968 ..... **CLC 1, 3, 11,
34, 83; PC 10**
See also CA 5-8R; 25-28R; CANR 22, 53;
DA3; DLB 48; DLBY 81; MTCW 1, 2

**Merwin, W(illiam) S(tanley)** 1927- ... **CLC 1,
2, 3, 5, 8, 13, 18, 45, 88; DAM POET**
See also CA 13-16R; CANR 15, 51; DA3;
DLB 5, 169; INT CANR-15; MTCW 1, 2

**Metcalf, John** 1938- ........................... **CLC 37**
See also CA 113; DLB 60

**Metcalf, Suzanne**
See Baum, L(yman) Frank

**Mew, Charlotte (Mary)** 1870-1928 .. **TCLC 8**
See also CA 105; DLB 19, 135

**Mewshaw, Michael** 1943- ................... **CLC 9**
See also CA 53-56; CANR 7, 47; DLBY 80

**Meyer, Conrad Ferdinand**
1825-1905 ................................. **NCLC 81**
See also DLB 129

**Meyer, June**
See Jordan, June

**Meyer, Lynn**
See Slavitt, David R(ytman)

**Meyer-Meyrink, Gustav** 1868-1932
See Meyrink, Gustav
See also CA 117

**Meyers, Jeffrey** 1939- ...................... **CLC 39**
See also CA 73-76; CANR 54; DLB 111

**Meynell, Alice (Christina Gertrude
Thompson)** 1847-1922 ............. **TCLC 6**
See also CA 104; 177; DLB 19, 98

**Meyrink, Gustav** .............................. **TCLC 21**
See also Meyer-Meyrink, Gustav DLB 81

**Michaels, Leonard** 1933- .... **CLC 6, 25; SSC
16**
See also CA 61-64; CANR 21, 62; DLB
130; MTCW 1

**Michaux, Henri** 1899-1984 .......... **CLC 8, 19**
See also CA 85-88; 114

**Micheaux, Oscar (Devereaux)** 1884-1951
**TCLC 76**
See also BW 3; CA 174; DLB 50

**Michelangelo** 1475-1564 ...................... **LC 12**

**Michelet, Jules** 1798-1874 ............. **NCLC 31**

**Michels, Robert** 1876-1936 ............ **TCLC 88**

**Michener, James A(lbert)**
1907(?)-1997 ........ **CLC 1, 5, 11, 29, 60,
109; DAM NOV, POP**
See also AAYA 27; AITN 1; BEST 90:1;
CA 5-8R; 161; CANR 21, 45, 68; DA3;
DLB 6; MTCW 1, 2

**Mickiewicz, Adam** 1798-1855 .......... **NCLC 3**

**Middleton, Christopher** 1926- .......... **CLC 13**
See also CA 13-16R; CANR 29, 54; DLB
40

**Middleton, Richard (Barham)** 1882-1911
**TCLC 56**
See also DLB 156

**Middleton, Stanley** 1919- .............. **CLC 7, 38**
See also CA 25-28R; CAAS 23; CANR 21,
46, 81; DLB 14

**Middleton, Thomas** 1580-1627 .......... **LC 33;
DAM DRAM, MST; DC 5**
See also DLB 58

**Migueis, Jose Rodrigues** 1901- ......... **CLC 10**

**Mikszath, Kalman** 1847-1910 ........ **TCLC 31**
See also CA 170

**Miles, Jack** ...................................... **CLC 100**

**Miles, Josephine (Louise)**
1911-1985 .. **CLC 1, 2, 14, 34, 39; DAM
POET**
See also CA 1-4R; 116; CANR 2, 55; DLB
48

**Militant**
See Sandburg, Carl (August)

**Mill, John Stuart** 1806-1873 .... **NCLC 11, 58**
See also CDBLB 1832-1890; DLB 55, 190

**Millar, Kenneth** 1915-1983 ... **CLC 14; DAM
POP**
See also Macdonald, Ross CA 9-12R; 110;
CANR 16, 63; DA3; DLB 2; DLBD 6;
DLBY 83; MTCW 1, 2

**Millay, E. Vincent**
See Millay, Edna St. Vincent

**Millay, Edna St. Vincent**
1892-1950 .......... **TCLC 4, 49; DA; DAB;
DAC; DAM MST, POET; PC 6;
WLCS**
See also CA 104; 130; CDALB 1917-1929;
DA3; DLB 45; MTCW 1, 2

**Miller, Arthur** 1915- ...... **CLC 1, 2, 6, 10, 15,
26, 47, 78; DA; DAB; DAC; DAM
DRAM, MST; DC 1; WLC**
See also AAYA 15; AITN 1; CA 1-4R;
CABS 3; CANR 2, 30, 54, 76; CDALB
1941-1968; DA3; DLB 7; MTCW 1, 2

**Miller, Henry (Valentine)**
1891-1980 .... **CLC 1, 2, 4, 9, 14, 43, 84;
DA; DAB; DAC; DAM MST, NOV;
WLC**
See also CA 9-12R; 97-100; CANR 33, 64;
CDALB 1929-1941; DA3; DLB 4, 9;
DLBY 80; MTCW 1, 2

**Miller, Jason** 1939(?)- ......................... **CLC 2**
See also CA 73-76; DLB 7

**Miller, Sue** 1943- .......... **CLC 44; DAM POP**
See also BEST 90:3; CA 139; CANR 59;
DA3; DLB 143

**Miller, Walter M(ichael, Jr.)** 1923- ... **CLC 4,
30**
See also CA 85-88; DLB 8

**Millett, Kate** 1934- ........................... **CLC 67**
See also AITN 1; CA 73-76; CANR 32, 53,
76; DA3; MTCW 1, 2

**Millhauser, Steven (Lewis)** 1943- .... **CLC 21,
54, 109**
See also CA 110; 111; CANR 63; DA3;
DLB 2; INT 111; MTCW 2

**Millin, Sarah Gertrude** 1889-1968 ... **CLC 49**
See also CA 102; 93-96

**Milne, A(lan) A(lexander)**
1882-1956 ..... **TCLC 6, 88; DAB; DAC;
DAM MST**
See also CA 104; 133; CLR 1, 26; DA3;
DLB 10, 77, 100, 160; MAICYA; MTCW
1, 2; SATA 100; YABC 1

**Milner, Ron(ald)** 1938- ....... **CLC 56; BLC 3;
DAM MULT**
See also AITN 1; BW 1; CA 73-76; CANR
24, 81; DLB 38; MTCW 1

**Milnes, Richard Monckton**
1809-1885 .............................. **NCLC 61**
See also DLB 32, 184

**Milosz, Czeslaw** 1911- ...... **CLC 5, 11, 22, 31,
56, 82; DAM MST, POET; PC 8;
WLCS**
See also CA 81-84; CANR 23, 51; DA3;
MTCW 1, 2

**Milton, John** 1608-1674 ......... **LC 9, 43; DA;
DAB; DAC; DAM MST, POET; PC 19,
29; WLC**
See also CDBLB 1660-1789; DA3; DLB
131, 151

**Min, Anchee** 1957- ........................... **CLC 86**
See also CA 146

**Minehaha, Cornelius**
See Wedekind, (Benjamin) Frank(lin)

**Miner, Valerie** 1947- ......................... **CLC 40**
See also CA 97-100; CANR 59

**Minimo, Duca**
See D'Annunzio, Gabriele

**Minot, Susan** 1956- ........................... **CLC 44**
See also CA 134

**Minus, Ed** 1938- ............................... **CLC 39**

**Miranda, Javier**
See Bioy Casares, Adolfo

**Miranda, Javier**
See Bioy Casares, Adolfo

**Mirbeau, Octave** 1848-1917 .......... **TCLC 55**
See also DLB 123, 192

**Miro (Ferrer), Gabriel (Francisco Victor)**
1879-1930 ................................. **TCLC 5**
See also CA 104

**Mishima, Yukio** 1925-1970 .... **CLC 2, 4, 6, 9,
27; DC 1; SSC 4**
See also Hiraoka, Kimitake DLB 182;
MTCW 2

**Mistral, Frederic** 1830-1914 .......... **TCLC 51**
See also CA 122

**Mistral, Gabriela** ................ **TCLC 2; HLC 2**
See also Godoy Alcayaga, Lucila MTCW 2

**Mistry, Rohinton** 1952- ......... **CLC 71; DAC**
See also CA 141; CANR 86

**Mitchell, Clyde**
See Ellison, Harlan (Jay); Silverberg, Robert

**Mitchell, James Leslie** 1901-1935
See Gibbon, Lewis Grassic
See also CA 104; DLB 15

**Mitchell, Joni** 1943- .......................... **CLC 12**
See also CA 112

**Mitchell, Joseph (Quincy)**
1908-1996 ................................. **CLC 98**
See also CA 77-80; 152; CANR 69; DLB
185; DLBY 96

**Mitchell, Margaret (Munnerlyn)** 1900-1949
**TCLC 11; DAM NOV, POP**

See also AAYA 23; CA 109; 125; CANR 55; CDALBS; DA3; DLB 9; MTCW 1, 2

**Mitchell, Peggy**
See Mitchell, Margaret (Munnerlyn)

**Mitchell, S(ilas) Weir** 1829-1914 .... **TCLC 36**
See also CA 165; DLB 202

**Mitchell, W(illiam) O(rmond)** 1914-1998 **CLC 25; DAC; DAM MST**
See also CA 77-80; 165; CANR 15, 43; DLB 88

**Mitchell, William** 1879-1936 ......... **TCLC 81**

**Mitford, Mary Russell** 1787-1855 ... **NCLC 4**
See also DLB 110, 116

**Mitford, Nancy** 1904-1973 ................ **CLC 44**
See also CA 9-12R; DLB 191

**Miyamoto, (Chujo) Yuriko** 1899-1951 .............................. **TCLC 37**
See also CA 170, 174; DLB 180

**Miyazawa, Kenji** 1896-1933 ........... **TCLC 76**
See also CA 157

**Mizoguchi, Kenji** 1898-1956 .......... **TCLC 72**
See also CA 167

**Mo, Timothy (Peter)** 1950(?)- ........... **CLC 46**
See also CA 117; DLB 194; MTCW 1

**Modarressi, Taghi (M.)** 1931- .......... **CLC 44**
See also CA 121; 134; INT 134

**Modiano, Patrick (Jean)** 1945- ......... **CLC 18**
See also CA 85-88; CANR 17, 40; DLB 83

**Moerck, Paal**
See Roelvaag, O(le) E(dvart)

**Mofolo, Thomas (Mokopu)** 1875(?)-1948 **TCLC 22; BLC 3; DAM MULT**
See also CA 121; 153; CANR 83; MTCW 2

**Mohr, Nicholasa** 1938- ......... **CLC 12; DAM MULT; HLC 2**
See also AAYA 8; CA 49-52; CANR 1, 32, 64; CLR 22; DLB 145; HW 1, 2; JRDA; SAAS 8; SATA 8, 97; SATA-Essay 113

**Mojtabai, A(nn) G(race)** 1938- ..... **CLC 5, 9, 15, 29**
See also CA 85-88; CANR 88

**Moliere** 1622-1673 ..... **LC 10, 28; DA; DAB; DAC; DAM DRAM, MST; WLC**
See also DA3

**Molin, Charles**
See Mayne, William (James Carter)

**Molnar, Ferenc** 1878-1952 .. **TCLC 20; DAM DRAM**
See also CA 109; 153; CANR 83

**Momaday, N(avarre) Scott** 1934- ...... **CLC 2, 19, 85, 95; DA; DAB; DAC; DAM MST, MULT, NOV, POP; PC 25; WLCS**
See also AAYA 11; CA 25-28R; CANR 14, 34, 68; CDALBS; DA3; DLB 143, 175; INT CANR-14; MTCW 1, 2; NNAL; SATA 48; SATA-Brief 30

**Monette, Paul** 1945-1995 .................. **CLC 82**
See also CA 139; 147

**Monroe, Harriet** 1860-1936 ........... **TCLC 12**
See also CA 109; DLB 54, 91

**Monroe, Lyle**
See Heinlein, Robert A(nson)

**Montagu, Elizabeth** 1720-1800 ........ **NCLC 7**

**Montagu, Elizabeth** 1917- ................ **NCLC 7**
See also CA 9-12R

**Montagu, Mary (Pierrepont) Wortley** 1689-1762 ........................... **LC 9; PC 16**
See also DLB 95, 101

**Montagu, W. H.**
See Coleridge, Samuel Taylor

**Montague, John (Patrick)** 1929- ..... **CLC 13, 46**
See also CA 9-12R; CANR 9, 69; DLB 40; MTCW 1

**Montaigne, Michel (Eyquem) de** 1533-1592 **LC 8; DA; DAB; DAC; DAM MST; WLC**

**Montale, Eugenio** 1896-1981 ... **CLC 7, 9, 18; PC 13**
See also CA 17-20R; 104; CANR 30; DLB 114; MTCW 1

**Montesquieu, Charles-Louis de Secondat** 1689-1755 ........................................ **LC 7**

**Montgomery, (Robert) Bruce** 1921(?)-1978
See Crispin, Edmund
See also CA 179; 104

**Montgomery, L(ucy) M(aud)** 1874-1942 **TCLC 51; DAM MST**
See also AAYA 12; CA 108; 137; CLR 8; DA3; DLB 92; DLBD 14; JRDA; MAICYA; MTCW 2; SATA 100; YABC 1

**Montgomery, Marion H., Jr.** 1925- .... **CLC 7**
See also AITN 1; CA 1-4R; CANR 3, 48; DLB 6

**Montgomery, Max**
See Davenport, Guy (Mattison, Jr.)

**Montherlant, Henry (Milon) de** 1896-1972 **CLC 8, 19; DAM DRAM**
See also CA 85-88; 37-40R; DLB 72; MTCW 1

**Monty Python**
See Chapman, Graham; Cleese, John (Marwood); Gilliam, Terry (Vance); Idle, Eric; Jones, Terence Graham Parry; Palin, Michael (Edward)
See also AAYA 7

**Moodie, Susanna (Strickland)** 1803-1885 **NCLC 14**
See also DLB 99

**Mooney, Edward** 1951-
See Mooney, Ted
See also CA 130

**Mooney, Ted** ........................................ **CLC 25**
See also Mooney, Edward

**Moorcock, Michael (John)** 1939- ...... **CLC 5, 27, 58**
See also Bradbury, Edward P. AAYA 26; CA 45-48; CAAS 5; CANR 2, 17, 38, 64; DLB 14; MTCW 1, 2; SATA 93

**Moore, Brian** 1921-1999 ... **CLC 1, 3, 5, 7, 8, 19, 32, 90; DAB; DAC; DAM MST**
See also CA 1-4R; 174; CANR 1, 25, 42, 63; MTCW 1, 2

**Moore, Edward**
See Muir, Edwin

**Moore, G. E.** 1873-1958 ................. **TCLC 89**

**Moore, George Augustus** 1852-1933 ................... **TCLC 7; SSC 19**
See also CA 104; 177; DLB 10, 18, 57, 135

**Moore, Lorrie** ........................ **CLC 39, 45, 68**
See also Moore, Marie Lorena

**Moore, Marianne (Craig)** 1887-1972 .... **CLC 1, 2, 4, 8, 10, 13, 19, 47; DA; DAB; DAC; DAM MST, POET; PC 4; WLCS**
See also CA 1-4R; 33-36R; CANR 3, 61; CDALB 1929-1941; DA3; DLB 45; DLBD 7; MTCW 1, 2; SATA 20

**Moore, Marie Lorena** 1957-
See Moore, Lorrie
See also CA 116; CANR 39, 83

**Moore, Thomas** 1779-1852 .............. **NCLC 6**
See also DLB 96, 144

**Mora, Pat(ricia)** 1942-
See also CA 129; CANR 57, 81; CLR 58; DAM MULT; DLB 209; HLC 2; HW 1, 2; SATA 92

**Moraga, Cherrie** 1952- ........ **CLC 126; DAM MULT**
See also CA 131; CANR 66; DLB 82; HW 1, 2

**Morand, Paul** 1888-1976 .... **CLC 41; SSC 22**
See also CA 184; 69-72; DLB 65

**Morante, Elsa** 1918-1985 ............. **CLC 8, 47**
See also CA 85-88; 117; CANR 35; DLB 177; MTCW 1, 2

**Moravia, Alberto** 1907-1990 .... **CLC 2, 7, 11, 27, 46; SSC 26**
See also Pincherle, Alberto DLB 177; MTCW 2

**More, Hannah** 1745-1833 ............... **NCLC 27**
See also DLB 107, 109, 116, 158

**More, Henry** 1614-1687 ........................ **LC 9**
See also DLB 126

**More, Sir Thomas** 1478-1535 ........ **LC 10, 32**

**Moreas, Jean** .................................... **TCLC 18**
See also Papadiamantopoulos, Johannes

**Morgan, Berry** 1919- ........................... **CLC 6**
See also CA 49-52; DLB 6

**Morgan, Claire**
See Highsmith, (Mary) Patricia

**Morgan, Edwin (George)** 1920- ....... **CLC 31**
See also CA 5-8R; CANR 3, 43; DLB 27

**Morgan, (George) Frederick** 1922- .. **CLC 23**
See also CA 17-20R; CANR 21

**Morgan, Harriet**
See Mencken, H(enry) L(ouis)

**Morgan, Jane**
See Cooper, James Fenimore

**Morgan, Janet** 1945- ......................... **CLC 39**
See also CA 65-68

**Morgan, Lady** 1776(?)-1859 ........... **NCLC 29**
See also DLB 116, 158

**Morgan, Robin (Evonne)** 1941- ......... **CLC 2**
See also CA 69-72; CANR 29, 68; MTCW 1; SATA 80

**Morgan, Scott**
See Kuttner, Henry

**Morgan, Seth** 1949(?)-1990 .............. **CLC 65**
See also CA 132

**Morgenstern, Christian** 1871-1914 .. **TCLC 8**
See also CA 105

**Morgenstern, S.**
See Goldman, William (W.)

**Moricz, Zsigmond** 1879-1942 ......... **TCLC 33**
See also CA 165

**Morike, Eduard (Friedrich)** 1804-1875 **NCLC 10**
See also DLB 133

**Moritz, Karl Philipp** 1756-1793 ........... **LC 2**
See also DLB 94

**Morland, Peter Henry**
See Faust, Frederick (Schiller)

**Morley, Christopher (Darlington)** 1890-1957 **TCLC 87**
See also CA 112; DLB 9

**Morren, Theophil**
See Hofmannsthal, Hugo von

**Morris, Bill** 1952- ............................. **CLC 76**

**Morris, Julian**
See West, Morris L(anglo)

**Morris, Steveland Judkins** 1950(?)-
See Wonder, Stevie
See also CA 111

**Morris, William** 1834-1896 .............. **NCLC 4**
See also CDBLB 1832-1890; DLB 18, 35, 57, 156, 178, 184

**Morris, Wright** 1910-1998 .. **CLC 1, 3, 7, 18, 37**
See also CA 9-12R; 167; CANR 21, 81; DLB 2, 206; DLBY 81; MTCW 1, 2

**Morrison, Arthur** 1863-1945 ......... **TCLC 72**
See also CA 120; 157; DLB 70, 135, 197

**Morrison, Chloe Anthony Wofford**
See Morrison, Toni

**Morrison, James Douglas** 1943-1971
See Morrison, Jim
See also CA 73-76; CANR 40

**Morrison, Jim** ................................... **CLC 17**
See also Morrison, James Douglas

**Morrison, Toni** 1931- . **CLC 4, 10, 22, 55, 81, 87; BLC 3; DA; DAB; DAC; DAM MST, MULT, NOV, POP**
See also AAYA 1, 22; BW 2, 3; CA 29-32R; CANR 27, 42, 67; CDALB 1968-1988; DA3; DLB 6, 33, 143; DLBY 81; MTCW 1, 2; SATA 57

**Morrison, Van** 1945- ......................... **CLC 21**
See also CA 116; 168

**Morrissy, Mary** 1958- ......................... **CLC 99**

**Mortimer, John (Clifford)** 1923- ..... **CLC 28, 43; DAM DRAM, POP**
See also CA 13-16R; CANR 21, 69; CD-BLB 1960 to Present; DA3; DLB 13; INT CANR-21; MTCW 1, 2

**Mortimer, Penelope (Ruth)** 1918- ...... **CLC 5**
See also CA 57-60; CANR 45, 88

**Morton, Anthony**
See Creasey, John

**Mosca, Gaetano** 1858-1941 ............. **TCLC 75**

**Mosher, Howard Frank** 1943- .......... **CLC 62**
See also CA 139; CANR 65

**Mosley, Nicholas** 1923- ................. **CLC 43, 70**
See also CA 69-72; CANR 41, 60; DLB 14, 207

**Mosley, Walter** 1952- ........... **CLC 97; BLCS; DAM MULT, POP**
See also AAYA 17; BW 2; CA 142; CANR 57; DA3; MTCW 2

**Moss, Howard** 1922-1987 ...... **CLC 7, 14, 45, 50; DAM POET**
See also CA 1-4R; 123; CANR 1, 44; DLB 5

**Mossgiel, Rab**
See Burns, Robert

**Motion, Andrew (Peter)** 1952- .......... **CLC 47**
See also CA 146; DLB 40

**Motley, Willard (Francis)** 1909-1965 ................................. **CLC 18**
See also BW 1; CA 117; 106; CANR 88; DLB 76, 143

**Motoori, Norinaga** 1730-1801 ........ **NCLC 45**

**Mott, Michael (Charles Alston)** 1930- ................................. **CLC 15, 34**
See also CA 5-8R; CAAS 7; CANR 7, 29

**Mountain Wolf Woman** 1884-1960 .. **CLC 92**
See also CA 144; NNAL

**Moure, Erin** 1955- ........................... **CLC 88**
See also CA 113; DLB 60

**Mowat, Farley (McGill)** 1921- ........ **CLC 26; DAC; DAM MST**
See also AAYA 1; CA 1-4R; CANR 4, 24, 42, 68; CLR 20; DLB 68; INT CANR-24; JRDA; MAICYA; MTCW 1, 2; SATA 3, 55

**Mowatt, Anna Cora** 1819-1870 ...... **NCLC 74**

**Moyers, Bill** 1934- ........................... **CLC 74**
See also AITN 2; CA 61-64; CANR 31, 52

**Mphahlele, Es'kia**
See Mphahlele, Ezekiel
See also DLB 125

**Mphahlele, Ezekiel** 1919- ... **CLC 25; BLC 3; DAM MULT**
See also Mphahlele, Es'kia BW 2, 3; CA 81-84; CANR 26, 76; DA3; MTCW 2

**Mqhayi, S(amuel) E(dward) K(rune Loliwe)** 1875-1945 ...... **TCLC 25; BLC 3; DAM MULT**
See also CA 153; CANR 87

**Mrozek, Slawomir** 1930- ............... **CLC 3, 13**
See also CA 13-16R; CAAS 10; CANR 29; MTCW 1

**Mrs. Belloc-Lowndes**
See Lowndes, Marie Adelaide (Belloc)

**Mtwa, Percy** (?)- ................................ **CLC 47**

**Mueller, Lisel** 1924- ................... **CLC 13, 51**
See also CA 93-96; DLB 105

**Muir, Edwin** 1887-1959 ............. **TCLC 2, 87**
See also CA 104; DLB 20, 100, 191

**Muir, John** 1838-1914 .................... **TCLC 28**
See also CA 165; DLB 186

**Mujica Lainez, Manuel** 1910-1984 ... **CLC 31**
See also Lainez, Manuel Mujica CA 81-84; 112; CANR 32; HW 1

**Mukherjee, Bharati** 1940- ....... **CLC 53, 115; DAM NOV; SSC 38**
See also BEST 89:2; CA 107; CANR 45, 72; DLB 60; MTCW 1, 2

**Muldoon, Paul** 1951- ....... **CLC 32, 72; DAM POET**
See also CA 113; 129; CANR 52; DLB 40; INT 129

**Mulisch, Harry** 1927- ........................ **CLC 42**
See also CA 9-12R; CANR 6, 26, 56

**Mull, Martin** 1943- ........................... **CLC 17**
See also CA 105

**Muller, Wilhelm** ........................ **NCLC 73**

**Mulock, Dinah Maria**
See Craik, Dinah Maria (Mulock)

**Munford, Robert** 1737(?)-1783 ............. **LC 5**
See also DLB 31

**Mungo, Raymond** 1946- ................... **CLC 72**
See also CA 49-52; CANR 2

**Munro, Alice** 1931- .... **CLC 6, 10, 19, 50, 95; DAC; DAM MST, NOV; SSC 3; WLCS**
See also AITN 2; CA 33-36R; CANR 33, 53, 75; DA3; DLB 53; MTCW 1, 2; SATA 29

**Munro, H(ector) H(ugh)** 1870-1916
See Saki
See also CA 104; 130; CDBLB 1890-1914; DA; DAB; DAC; DAM MST, NOV; DA3; DLB 34, 162; MTCW 1, 2; WLC

**Murdoch, (Jean) Iris** 1919-1999 ... **CLC 1, 2, 3, 4, 6, 8, 11, 15, 22, 31, 51; DAB; DAC; DAM MST, NOV**
See also CA 13-16R; 179; CANR 8, 43, 68; CDBLB 1960 to Present; DA3; DLB 14, 194; INT CANR-8; MTCW 1, 2

**Murfree, Mary Noailles** 1850-1922 ... **SSC 22**
See also CA 122; 176; DLB 12, 74

**Murnau, Friedrich Wilhelm**
See Plumpe, Friedrich Wilhelm

**Murphy, Richard** 1927- ..................... **CLC 41**
See also CA 29-32R; DLB 40

**Murphy, Sylvia** 1937- ...................... **CLC 34**
See also CA 121

**Murphy, Thomas (Bernard)** 1935- ... **CLC 51**
See also CA 101

**Murray, Albert L.** 1916- ................... **CLC 73**
See also BW 2; CA 49-52; CANR 26, 52, 78; DLB 38

**Murray, Judith Sargent** 1751-1820 ........................... **NCLC 63**
See also DLB 37, 200

**Murray, Les(lie) A(llan)** 1938- ........ **CLC 40; DAM POET**
See also CA 21-24R; CANR 11, 27, 56

**Murry, J. Middleton**
See Murry, John Middleton

**Murry, John Middleton** 1889-1957 ................................. **TCLC 16**
See also CA 118; DLB 149

**Musgrave, Susan** 1951- ................... **CLC 13, 54**
See also CA 69-72; CANR 45, 84

**Musil, Robert (Edler von)** 1880-1942 ........... **TCLC 12, 68; SSC 18**
See also CA 109; CANR 55, 84; DLB 81, 124; MTCW 2

**Muske, Carol** 1945- ........................ **CLC 90**
See also Muske-Dukes, Carol (Anne)

**Muske-Dukes, Carol (Anne)** 1945-
See Muske, Carol
See also CA 65-68; CANR 32, 70

**Musset, (Louis Charles) Alfred de** 1810-1857 **NCLC 7**
See also DLB 192

**Mussolini, Benito (Amilcare Andrea)** 1883-1945 ................................ **TCLC 96**
See also CA 116

**My Brother's Brother**
See Chekhov, Anton (Pavlovich)

**Myers, L(eopold) H(amilton)** 1881-1944 **TCLC 59**
See also CA 157; DLB 15

**Myers, Walter Dean** 1937- ..... **CLC 35; BLC 3; DAM MULT, NOV**
See also AAYA 4, 23; BW 2; CA 33-36R; CANR 20, 42, 67; CLR 4, 16, 35; DLB 33; INT CANR-20; JRDA; MAICYA; MTCW 2; SAAS 2; SATA 41, 71, 109; SATA-Brief 27

**Myers, Walter M.**
See Myers, Walter Dean

**Myles, Symon**
See Follett, Ken(neth Martin)

**Nabokov, Vladimir (Vladimirovich)** 1899-1977 ....... **CLC 1, 2, 3, 6, 8, 11, 15, 23, 44, 46, 64; DA; DAB; DAC; DAM MST, NOV; SSC 11; WLC**
See also CA 5-8R; 69-72; CANR 20; CDALB 1941-1968; DA3; DLB 2; DLBD 3; DLBY 80, 91; MTCW 1, 2

**Naevius** c. 265B.C.-201B.C. ........... **CMLC 37**
See also DLB 211

**Nagai Kafu** 1879-1959 .................... **TCLC 51**
See also Nagai Sokichi DLB 180

**Nagai Sokichi** 1879-1959
See Nagai Kafu
See also CA 117

**Nagy, Laszlo** 1925-1978 ...................... **CLC 7**
See also CA 129; 112

**Naidu, Sarojini** 1879-1943 ............. **TCLC 80**

**Naipaul, Shiva(dhar Srinivasa)** 1945-1985 **CLC 32, 39; DAM NOV**
See also CA 110; 112; 116; CANR 33; DA3; DLB 157; DLBY 85; MTCW 1, 2

**Naipaul, V(idiadhar) S(urajprasad)** 1932- **CLC 4, 7, 9, 13, 18, 37, 105; DAB; DAC; DAM MST, NOV; SSC 38**
See also CA 1-4R; CANR 1, 33, 51; CD-BLB 1960 to Present; DA3; DLB 125, 204, 206; DLBY 85; MTCW 1, 2

**Nakos, Lilika** 1899(?)- ...................... **CLC 29**

**Narayan, R(asipuram) K(rishnaswami)** 1906- . **CLC 7, 28, 47, 121; DAM NOV; SSC 25**
See also CA 81-84; CANR 33, 61; DA3; MTCW 1, 2; SATA 62

**Nash, (Frediric) Ogden** 1902-1971 . **CLC 23; DAM POET; PC 21**
See also CA 13-14; 29-32R; CANR 34, 61; CAP 1; DLB 11; MAICYA; MTCW 1, 2; SATA 2, 46

**Nashe, Thomas** 1567-1601(?) .............. **LC 41**
See also DLB 167

**Nashe, Thomas** 1567-1601 ................... **LC 41**

**Nathan, Daniel**
See Dannay, Frederic

**Nathan, George Jean** 1882-1958 .... **TCLC 18**
See also Hatteras, Owen CA 114; 169; DLB 137

**Natsume, Kinnosuke** 1867-1916
See Natsume, Soseki
See also CA 104

**Natsume, Soseki** 1867-1916 ........ **TCLC 2, 10**
See also Natsume, Kinnosuke DLB 180

**Natti, (Mary) Lee** 1919-
See Kingman, Lee
See also CA 5-8R; CANR 2

**Naylor, Gloria** 1950- .... **CLC 28, 52; BLC 3; DA; DAC; DAM MST, MULT, NOV, POP; WLCS**
See also AAYA 6; BW 2, 3; CA 107; CANR 27, 51, 74; DA3; DLB 173; MTCW 1, 2

**Neihardt, John Gneisenau**
1881-1973 .................................. **CLC 32**
See also CA 13-14; CANR 65; CAP 1; DLB
9, 54

**Nekrasov, Nikolai Alekseevich** 1821-1878
**NCLC 11**

**Nelligan, Emile** 1879-1941 .............. **TCLC 14**
See also CA 114; DLB 92

**Nelson, Willie** 1933- .......................... **CLC 17**
See also CA 107

**Nemerov, Howard (Stanley)**
1920-1991 .......... **CLC 2, 6, 9, 36; DAM
POET; PC 24**
See also CA 1-4R; 134; CABS 2; CANR 1,
27, 53; DLB 5, 6; DLBY 83; INT CANR-
27; MTCW 1, 2

**Neruda, Pablo** 1904-1973 .. **CLC 1, 2, 5, 7, 9,
28, 62; DA; DAB; DAC; DAM MST,
MULT, POET; HLC 2; PC 4; WLC**
See also CA 19-20; 45-48; CAP 2; DA3;
HW 1; MTCW 1, 2

**Nerval, Gerard de** 1808-1855 ... **NCLC 1, 67;
PC 13; SSC 18**

**Nervo, (Jose) Amado (Ruiz de)** 1870-1919
**TCLC 11; HLCS 2**
See also CA 109; 131; HW 1

**Nessi, Pio Baroja y**
See Baroja (y Nessi), Pio

**Nestroy, Johann** 1801-1862 ............ **NCLC 42**
See also DLB 133

**Netterville, Luke**
See O'Grady, Standish (James)

**Neufeld, John (Arthur)** 1938- ........... **CLC 17**
See also AAYA 11; CA 25-28R; CANR 11,
37, 56; CLR 52; MAICYA; SAAS 3;
SATA 6, 81

**Neumann, Alfred** 1895-1952 ......... **TCLC 100**
See also CA 183; DLB 56

**Neville, Emily Cheney** 1919- ............. **CLC 12**
See also CA 5-8R; CANR 3, 37, 85; JRDA;
MAICYA; SAAS 2; SATA 1

**Newbound, Bernard Slade** 1930-
See Slade, Bernard
See also CA 81-84; CANR 49; DAM
DRAM

**Newby, P(ercy) H(oward)**
1918-1997 ........ **CLC 2, 13; DAM NOV**
See also CA 5-8R; 161; CANR 32, 67; DLB
15; MTCW 1

**Newlove, Donald** 1928- ........................ **CLC 6**
See also CA 29-32R; CANR 25

**Newlove, John (Herbert)** 1938- ........ **CLC 14**
See also CA 21-24R; CANR 9, 25

**Newman, Charles** 1938- ................. **CLC 2, 8**
See also CA 21-24R; CANR 84

**Newman, Edwin (Harold)** 1919- ...... **CLC 14**
See also AITN 1; CA 69-72; CANR 5

**Newman, John Henry** 1801-1890 .. **NCLC 38**
See also DLB 18, 32, 55

**Newton, (Sir)Isaac** 1642-1727 ........ **LC 35, 52**

**Newton, Suzanne** 1936- .................... **CLC 35**
See also CA 41-44R; CANR 14; JRDA;
SATA 5, 77

**Nexo, Martin Andersen**
1869-1954 ................................. **TCLC 43**

**Nezval, Vitezslav** 1900-1958 .......... **TCLC 44**
See also CA 123

**Ng, Fae Myenne** 1957(?)- .................. **CLC 81**
See also CA 146

**Ngema, Mbongeni** 1955- .................. **CLC 57**
See also BW 2; CA 143; CANR 84

**Ngugi, James T(hiong'o)** .......... **CLC 3, 7, 13**
See also Ngugi wa Thiong'o

**Ngugi wa Thiong'o** 1938- .. **CLC 36; BLC 3;
DAM MULT, NOV**
See also Ngugi, James T(hiong'o) BW 2;
CA 81-84; CANR 27, 58; DLB 125;
MTCW 1, 2

**Nichol, B(arrie) P(hillip)** 1944-1988 . **CLC 18**
See also CA 53-56; DLB 53; SATA 66

**Nichols, John (Treadwell)** 1940- ....... **CLC 38**
See also CA 9-12R; CAAS 2; CANR 6, 70;
DLBY 82

**Nichols, Leigh**
See Koontz, Dean R(ay)

**Nichols, Peter (Richard)** 1927- .... **CLC 5, 36,
65**
See also CA 104; CANR 33, 86; DLB 13;
MTCW 1

**Nicolas, F. R. E.**
See Freeling, Nicolas

**Niedecker, Lorine** 1903-1970 ..... **CLC 10, 42;
DAM POET**
See also CA 25-28; CAP 2; DLB 48

**Nietzsche, Friedrich (Wilhelm)** 1844-1900
**TCLC 10, 18, 55**
See also CA 107; 121; DLB 129

**Nievo, Ippolito** 1831-1861 ............... **NCLC 22**

**Nightingale, Anne Redmon** 1943-
See Redmon, Anne
See also CA 103

**Nightingale, Florence** 1820-1910 ... **TCLC 85**
See also DLB 166

**Nik. T. O.**
See Annensky, Innokenty (Fyodorovich)

**Nin, Anais** 1903-1977 ..... **CLC 1, 4, 8, 11, 14,
60, 127; DAM NOV, POP; SSC 10**
See also AITN 2; CA 13-16R; 69-72;
CANR 22, 53; DLB 2, 4, 152; MTCW 1,
2

**Nishida, Kitaro** 1870-1945 .............. **TCLC 83**

**Nishiwaki, Junzaburo** 1894-1982 ........ **PC 15**
See also CA 107

**Nissenson, Hugh** 1933- ................... **CLC 4, 9**
See also CA 17-20R; CANR 27; DLB 28

**Niven, Larry** ........................................ **CLC 8**
See also Niven, Laurence Van Cott AAYA
27; DLB 8

**Niven, Laurence Van Cott** 1938-
See Niven, Larry
See also CA 21-24R; CAAS 12; CANR 14,
44, 66; DAM POP; MTCW 1, 2; SATA
95

**Nixon, Agnes Eckhardt** 1927- ........... **CLC 21**
See also CA 110

**Nizan, Paul** 1905-1940 .................... **TCLC 40**
See also CA 161; DLB 72

**Nkosi, Lewis** 1936- ... **CLC 45; BLC 3; DAM
MULT**
See also BW 1, 3; CA 65-68; CANR 27,
81; DLB 157

**Nodier, (Jean) Charles (Emmanuel)**
1780-1844 ................................. **NCLC 19**
See also DLB 119

**Noguchi, Yone** 1875-1947 ............... **TCLC 80**

**Nolan, Christopher** 1965- .................. **CLC 58**
See also CA 111; CANR 88

**Noon, Jeff** 1957- ............................. **CLC 91**
See also CA 148; CANR 83

**Norden, Charles**
See Durrell, Lawrence (George)

**Nordhoff, Charles (Bernard)** 1887-1947
**TCLC 23**
See also CA 108; DLB 9; SATA 23

**Norfolk, Lawrence** 1963- ................... **CLC 76**
See also CA 144; CANR 85

**Norman, Marsha** 1947- ........ **CLC 28; DAM
DRAM; DC 8**
See also CA 105; CABS 3; CANR 41;
DLBY 84

**Normyx**
See Douglas, (George) Norman

**Norris, Frank** 1870-1902 .................... **SSC 28**
See also Norris, (Benjamin) Frank(lin, Jr.)
CDALB 1865-1917; DLB 12, 71, 186

**Norris, (Benjamin) Frank(lin, Jr.)** 1870-1902
**TCLC 24**
See also Norris, Frank CA 110; 160

**Norris, Leslie** 1921- .......................... **CLC 14**
See also CA 11-12; CANR 14; CAP 1; DLB
27

**North, Andrew**
See Norton, Andre

**North, Anthony**
See Koontz, Dean R(ay)

**North, Captain George**
See Stevenson, Robert Louis (Balfour)

**North, Milou**
See Erdrich, Louise

**Northrup, B. A.**
See Hubbard, L(afayette) Ron(ald)

**North Staffs**
See Hulme, T(homas) E(rnest)

**Norton, Alice Mary**
See Norton, Andre
See also MAICYA; SATA 1, 43

**Norton, Andre** 1912- ........................ **CLC 12**
See also Norton, Alice Mary AAYA 14; CA
1-4R; CANR 68; CLR 50; DLB 8, 52;
JRDA; MTCW 1; SATA 91

**Norton, Caroline** 1808-1877 ........... **NCLC 47**
See also DLB 21, 159, 199

**Norway, Nevil Shute** 1899-1960
See Shute, Nevil
See also CA 102; 93-96; CANR 85; MTCW
2

**Norwid, Cyprian Kamil**
1821-1883 ................................ **NCLC 17**

**Nosille, Nabrah**
See Ellison, Harlan (Jay)

**Nossack, Hans Erich** 1901-1978 ......... **CLC 6**
See also CA 93-96; 85-88; DLB 69

**Nostradamus** 1503-1566 ...................... **LC 27**

**Nosu, Chuji**
See Ozu, Yasujiro

**Notenburg, Eleanora (Genrikhovna) von**
See Guro, Elena

**Nova, Craig** 1945- .......................... **CLC 7, 31**
See also CA 45-48; CANR 2, 53

**Novak, Joseph**
See Kosinski, Jerzy (Nikodem)

**Novalis** 1772-1801 ........................... **NCLC 13**
See also DLB 90

**Novis, Emile**
See Weil, Simone (Adolphine)

**Nowlan, Alden (Albert)** 1933-1983 . **CLC 15;
DAC; DAM MST**
See also CA 9-12R; CANR 5; DLB 53

**Noyes, Alfred** 1880-1958 ...... **TCLC 7; PC 27**
See also CA 104; DLB 20

**Nunn, Kem** ........................................ **CLC 34**
See also CA 159

**Nye, Robert** 1939- . **CLC 13, 42; DAM NOV**
See also CA 33-36R; CANR 29, 67; DLB
14; MTCW 1; SATA 6

**Nyro, Laura** 1947- ........................... **CLC 17**

**Oates, Joyce Carol** 1938- .. **CLC 1, 2, 3, 6, 9,
11, 15, 19, 33, 52, 108; DA; DAB;
DAC; DAM MST, NOV, POP; SSC 6;
WLC**
See also AAYA 15; AITN 1; BEST 89:2;
CA 5-8R; CANR 25, 45, 74; CDALB
1968-1988; DA3; DLB 2, 5, 130; DLBY
81; INT CANR-25; MTCW 1, 2

**O'Brien, Darcy** 1939-1998 ............... **CLC 11**
See also CA 21-24R; 167; CANR 8, 59

**O'Brien, E. G.**
See Clarke, Arthur C(harles)

**O'Brien, Edna** 1936- ..... **CLC 3, 5, 8, 13, 36,
65, 116; DAM NOV; SSC 10**
See also CA 1-4R; CANR 6, 41, 65; CD-
BLB 1960 to Present; DA3; DLB 14;
MTCW 1, 2

**O'Brien, Fitz-James** 1828-1862 ..... **NCLC 21**
See also DLB 74

**O'Brien, Flann** ........... **CLC 1, 4, 5, 7, 10, 47**
See also O Nuallain, Brian

**O'Brien, Richard** 1942- ..................... **CLC 17**
See also CA 124

**O'Brien, (William) Tim(othy)** 1946- . **CLC 7, 19, 40, 103; DAM POP**
See also AAYA 16; CA 85-88; CANR 40, 58; CDALBS; DA3; DLB 152; DLBD 9; DLBY 80; MTCW 2

**Obstfelder, Sigbjoern** 1866-1900 .... **TCLC 23**
See also CA 123

**O'Casey, Sean** 1880-1964 .... **CLC 1, 5, 9, 11, 15, 88; DAB; DAC; DAM DRAM, MST; DC 12; WLCS**
See also CA 89-92; CANR 62; CDBLB 1914-1945; DA3; DLB 10; MTCW 1, 2

**O'Cathasaigh, Sean**
See O'Casey, Sean

**Ochs, Phil** 1940-1976 ......................... **CLC 17**
See also CA 65-68

**O'Connor, Edwin (Greene)**
1918-1968 ................................. **CLC 14**
See also CA 93-96; 25-28R

**O'Connor, (Mary) Flannery**
1925-1964 .... **CLC 1, 2, 3, 6, 10, 13, 15, 21, 66, 104; DA; DAB; DAC; DAM MST, NOV; SSC 1, 23; WLC**
See also AAYA 7; CA 1-4R; CANR 3, 41; CDALB 1941-1968; DA3; DLB 2, 152; DLBD 12; DLBY 80; MTCW 1, 2

**O'Connor, Frank** ........... **CLC 23; SSC 5**
See also O'Donovan, Michael John DLB 162

**O'Dell, Scott** 1898-1989 ..................... **CLC 30**
See also AAYA 3; CA 61-64; 129; CANR 12, 30; CLR 1, 16; DLB 52; JRDA; MAICYA; SATA 12, 60

**Odets, Clifford** 1906-1963 ..... **CLC 2, 28, 98; DAM DRAM; DC 6**
See also CA 85-88; CANR 62; DLB 7, 26; MTCW 1, 2

**O'Doherty, Brian** 1934- ..................... **CLC 76**
See also CA 105

**O'Donnell, K. M.**
See Malzberg, Barry N(athaniel)

**O'Donnell, Lawrence**
See Kuttner, Henry

**O'Donovan, Michael John**
1903-1966 ................................. **CLC 14**
See also O'Connor, Frank CA 93-96; CANR 84

**Oe, Kenzaburo** 1935- ........... **CLC 10, 36, 86; DAM NOV; SSC 20**
See also CA 97-100; CANR 36, 50, 74; DA3; DLB 182; DLBY 94; MTCW 1, 2

**O'Faolain, Julia** 1932- .... **CLC 6, 19, 47, 108**
See also CA 81-84; CAAS 2; CANR 12, 61; DLB 14; MTCW 1

**O'Faolain, Sean** 1900-1991 ...... **CLC 1, 7, 14, 32, 70; SSC 13**
See also CA 61-64; 134; CANR 12, 66; DLB 15, 162; MTCW 1, 2

**O'Flaherty, Liam** 1896-1984 ....... **CLC 5, 34; SSC 6**
See also CA 101; 113; CANR 35; DLB 36, 162; DLBY 84; MTCW 1, 2

**Ogilvy, Gavin**
See Barrie, J(ames) M(atthew)

**O'Grady, Standish (James)**
1846-1928 ................................. **TCLC 5**
See also CA 104; 157

**O'Grady, Timothy** 1951- ................... **CLC 59**
See also CA 138

**O'Hara, Frank** 1926-1966 ....... **CLC 2, 5, 13, 78; DAM POET**
See also CA 9-12R; 25-28R; CANR 33; DA3; DLB 5, 16, 193; MTCW 1, 2

**O'Hara, John (Henry)** 1905-1970 . **CLC 1, 2, 3, 6, 11, 42; DAM NOV; SSC 15**
See also CA 5-8R; 25-28R; CANR 31, 60; CDALB 1929-1941; DLB 9, 86; DLBD 2; MTCW 1, 2

**O Hehir, Diana** 1922- ........................ **CLC 41**
See also CA 93-96

**Ohiyesa**
See Eastman, Charles A(lexander)

**Okigbo, Christopher (Ifenayichukwu)**
1932-1967 ... **CLC 25, 84; BLC 3; DAM MULT, POET; PC 7**
See also BW 1, 3; CA 77-80; CANR 74; DLB 125; MTCW 1, 2

**Okri, Ben** 1959- ................................... **CLC 87**
See also BW 2, 3; CA 130; 138; CANR 65; DLB 157; INT 138; MTCW 2

**Olds, Sharon** 1942- .... **CLC 32, 39, 85; DAM POET; PC 22**
See also CA 101; CANR 18, 41, 66; DLB 120; MTCW 2

**Oldstyle, Jonathan**
See Irving, Washington

**Olesha, Yuri (Karlovich)** 1899-1960 .. **CLC 8**
See also CA 85-88

**Oliphant, Laurence** 1829(?)-1888 .. **NCLC 47**
See also DLB 18, 166

**Oliphant, Margaret (Oliphant Wilson)**
1828-1897 .......... **NCLC 11, 61; SSC 25**
See also DLB 18, 159, 190

**Oliver, Mary** 1935- ................ **CLC 19, 34, 98**
See also CA 21-24R; CANR 9, 43, 84; DLB 5, 193

**Olivier, Laurence (Kerr)** 1907-1989 . **CLC 20**
See also CA 111; 150; 129

**Olsen, Tillie** 1912- ........ **CLC 4, 13, 114; DA; DAB; DAC; DAM MST; SSC 11**
See also CA 1-4R; CANR 1, 43, 74; CDALBS; DA3; DLB 28, 206; DLBY 80; MTCW 1, 2

**Olson, Charles (John)** 1910-1970 .. **CLC 1, 2, 5, 6, 9, 11, 29; DAM POET; PC 19**
See also CA 13-16; 25-28R; CABS 2; CANR 35, 61; CAP 1; DLB 5, 16, 193; MTCW 1, 2

**Olson, Toby** 1937- ............................. **CLC 28**
See also CA 65-68; CANR 9, 31, 84

**Olyesha, Yuri**
See Olesha, Yuri (Karlovich)

**Ondaatje, (Philip) Michael** 1943- .... **CLC 14, 29, 51, 76; DAB; DAC; DAM MST; PC 28**
See also CA 77-80; CANR 42, 74; DA3; DLB 60; MTCW 2

**Oneal, Elizabeth** 1934-
See Oneal, Zibby
See also CA 106; CANR 28, 84; MAICYA; SATA 30, 82

**Oneal, Zibby** ................................... **CLC 30**
See also Oneal, Elizabeth AAYA 5; CLR 13; JRDA

**O'Neill, Eugene (Gladstone)** 1888-1953 **TCLC 1, 6, 27, 49; DA; DAB; DAC; DAM DRAM, MST; WLC**
See also AITN 1; CA 110; 132; CDALB 1929-1941; DA3; DLB 7; MTCW 1, 2

**Onetti, Juan Carlos** 1909-1994 ... **CLC 7, 10; DAM MULT, NOV; HLCS 2; SSC 23**
See also CA 85-88; 145; CANR 32, 63; DLB 113; HW 1, 2; MTCW 1, 2

**O Nuallain, Brian** 1911-1966
See O'Brien, Flann
See also CA 21-22; 25-28R; CAP 2

**Ophuls, Max** 1902-1957 ................ **TCLC 79**
See also CA 113

**Opie, Amelia** 1769-1853 ................. **NCLC 65**
See also DLB 116, 159

**Oppen, George** 1908-1984 ...... **CLC 7, 13, 34**
See also CA 13-16R; 113; CANR 8, 82; DLB 5, 165

**Oppenheim, E(dward) Phillips** 1866-1946
**TCLC 45**
See also CA 111; DLB 70

**Opuls, Max**
See Ophuls, Max

**Origen** c. 185-c. 254 ....................... **CMLC 19**

**Orlovitz, Gil** 1918-1973 ................... **CLC 22**
See also CA 77-80; 45-48; DLB 2, 5

**Orris**
See Ingelow, Jean

**Ortega y Gasset, Jose** 1883-1955 ... **TCLC 9; DAM MULT; HLC 2**
See also CA 106; 130; HW 1, 2; MTCW 1, 2

**Ortese, Anna Maria** 1914- ............... **CLC 89**
See also DLB 177

**Ortiz, Simon J(oseph)** 1941- . **CLC 45; DAM MULT, POET; PC 17**
See also CA 134; CANR 69; DLB 120, 175; NNAL

**Orton, Joe** ..................... **CLC 4, 13, 43; DC 3**
See also Orton, John Kingsley CDBLB 1960 to Present; DLB 13; MTCW 2

**Orton, John Kingsley** 1933-1967
See Orton, Joe
See also CA 85-88; CANR 35, 66; DAM DRAM; MTCW 1, 2

**Orwell, George** ......... **TCLC 2, 6, 15, 31, 51; DAB; WLC**
See also Blair, Eric (Arthur) CDBLB 1945-1960; DLB 15, 98, 195

**Osborne, David**
See Silverberg, Robert

**Osborne, George**
See Silverberg, Robert

**Osborne, John (James)** 1929-1994 .... **CLC 1, 2, 5, 11, 45; DA; DAB; DAC; DAM DRAM, MST; WLC**
See also CA 13-16R; 147; CANR 21, 56; CDBLB 1945-1960; DLB 13; MTCW 1, 2

**Osborne, Lawrence** 1958- ................ **CLC 50**

**Osbourne, Lloyd** 1868-1947 .......... **TCLC 93**

**Oshima, Nagisa** 1932- ...................... **CLC 20**
See also CA 116; 121; CANR 78

**Oskison, John Milton** 1874-1947 .. **TCLC 35; DAM MULT**
See also CA 144; CANR 84; DLB 175; NNAL

**Ossian** c. 3rd cent. - ....................... **CMLC 28**
See also Macpherson, James

**Ostrovsky, Alexander** 1823-1886 .. **NCLC 30, 57**

**Otero, Blas de** 1916-1979 ................. **CLC 11**
See also CA 89-92; DLB 134

**Otto, Rudolf** 1869-1937 .................... **TCLC 85**

**Otto, Whitney** 1955- ......................... **CLC 70**
See also CA 140

**Ouida** ............................................... **TCLC 43**
See also De La Ramee, (Marie) Louise DLB 18, 156

**Ousmane, Sembene** 1923- ... **CLC 66; BLC 3**
See also BW 1, 3; CA 117; 125; CANR 81; MTCW 1

**Ovid** 43B.C.-17 . **CMLC 7; DAM POET; PC 2**
See also DA3; DLB 211

**Owen, Hugh**
See Faust, Frederick (Schiller)

**Owen, Wilfred (Edward Salter)** 1893-1918
**TCLC 5, 27; DA; DAB; DAC; DAM MST, POET; PC 19; WLC**
See also CA 104; 141; CDBLB 1914-1945; DLB 20; MTCW 2

Owens, Rochelle 1936- .......................... **CLC 8**
See also CA 17-20R; CAAS 2; CANR 39

Oz, Amos 1939- ...... **CLC 5, 8, 11, 27, 33, 54;**
**DAM NOV**
See also CA 53-56; CANR 27, 47, 65;
MTCW 1, 2

Ozick, Cynthia 1928- ......... **CLC 3, 7, 28, 62;**
**DAM NOV, POP; SSC 15**
See also BEST 90:1; CA 17-20R; CANR
23, 58; DA3; DLB 28, 152; DLBY 82;
INT CANR-23; MTCW 1, 2

Ozu, Yasujiro 1903-1963 ................... **CLC 16**
See also CA 112

Pacheco, C.
See Pessoa, Fernando (Antonio Nogueira)

Pacheco, Jose Emilio 1939-
See also CA 111; 131; CANR 65; DAM
MULT; HLC 2; HW 1, 2

Pa Chin ............................................ **CLC 18**
See also Li Fei-kan

Pack, Robert 1929- ........................... **CLC 13**
See also CA 1-4R; CANR 3, 44, 82; DLB 5

Padgett, Lewis
See Kuttner, Henry

Padilla (Lorenzo), Heberto 1932- ..... **CLC 38**
See also AITN 1; CA 123; 131; HW 1

Page, Jimmy 1944- ............................. **CLC 12**

Page, Louise 1955- ............................ **CLC 40**
See also CA 140; CANR 76

Page, P(atricia) K(athleen) 1916- ...... **CLC 7,**
**18; DAC; DAM MST; PC 12**
See also CA 53-56; CANR 4, 22, 65; DLB
68; MTCW 1

Page, Thomas Nelson 1853-1922 ....... **SSC 23**
See also CA 118; 177; DLB 12, 78; DLBD
13

Pagels, Elaine Hiesey 1943- ............ **CLC 104**
See also CA 45-48; CANR 2, 24, 51

Paget, Violet 1856-1935
See Lee, Vernon
See also CA 104; 166

Paget-Lowe, Henry
See Lovecraft, H(oward) P(hillips)

Paglia, Camille (Anna) 1947- .......... **CLC 68**
See also CA 140; CANR 72; MTCW 2

Paige, Richard
See Koontz, Dean R(ay)

Paine, Thomas 1737-1809 ............... **NCLC 62**
See also CDALB 1640-1865; DLB 31, 43,
73, 158

Pakenham, Antonia
See Fraser, (Lady) Antonia (Pakenham)

Palamas, Kostes 1859-1943 ............. **TCLC 5**
See also CA 105

Palazzeschi, Aldo 1885-1974 ............ **CLC 11**
See also CA 89-92; 53-56; DLB 114

Pales Matos, Luis 1898-1959
See also HLCS 2; HW 1

Paley, Grace 1922- ........ **CLC 4, 6, 37; DAM**
**POP; SSC 8**
See also CA 25-28R; CANR 13, 46, 74;
DA3; DLB 28; INT CANR-13; MTCW 1,
2

Palin, Michael (Edward) 1943- ........ **CLC 21**
See also Monty Python CA 107; CANR 35;
SATA 67

Palliser, Charles 1947- ...................... **CLC 65**
See also CA 136; CANR 76

Palma, Ricardo 1833-1919 ............. **TCLC 29**
See also CA 168

Pancake, Breece Dexter 1952-1979
See Pancake, Breece D'J
See also CA 123; 109

Pancake, Breece D'J .......................... **CLC 29**
See also Pancake, Breece Dexter DLB 130

Panko, Rudy
See Gogol, Nikolai (Vasilyevich)

Papadiamantis, Alexandros
1851-1911 ................................ **TCLC 29**
See also CA 168

Papadiamantopoulos, Johannes 1856-1910
See Moreas, Jean
See also CA 117

Papini, Giovanni 1881-1956 ........... **TCLC 22**
See also CA 121; 180

Paracelsus 1493-1541 ........................ **LC 14**
See also DLB 179

Parasol, Peter
See Stevens, Wallace

Pardo Bazan, Emilia 1851-1921 ........ **SSC 30**

Pareto, Vilfredo 1848-1923 ............. **TCLC 69**
See also CA 175

Parfenie, Maria
See Codrescu, Andrei

Parini, Jay (Lee) 1948- ..................... **CLC 54**
See also CA 97-100; CAAS 16; CANR 32,
87

Park, Jordan
See Kornbluth, C(yril) M.; Pohl, Frederik

Park, Robert E(zra) 1864-1944 ..... **TCLC 73**
See also CA 122; 165

Parker, Bert
See Ellison, Harlan (Jay)

Parker, Dorothy (Rothschild)
1893-1967 .... **CLC 15, 68; DAM POET;**
**PC 28; SSC 2**
See also CA 19-20; 25-28R; CAP 2; DA3;
DLB 11, 45, 86; MTCW 1, 2

Parker, Robert B(rown) 1932- ........ **CLC 27;**
**DAM NOV, POP**
See also AAYA 28; BEST 89:4; CA 49-52;
CANR 1, 26, 52; INT CANR-26; MTCW
1

Parkin, Frank 1940- ......................... **CLC 43**
See also CA 147

Parkman, Francis Jr., Jr.
1823-1893 ................................. **NCLC 12**
See also DLB 1, 30, 186

Parks, Gordon (Alexander Buchanan) 1912-
**CLC 1, 16; BLC 3; DAM MULT**
See also AITN 2; BW 2, 3; CA 41-44R;
CANR 26, 66; DA3; DLB 33; MTCW 2;
SATA 8, 108

Parmenides c. 515B.C.-c.
450B.C. ..................................... **CMLC 22**
See also DLB 176

Parnell, Thomas 1679-1718 ................. **LC 3**
See also DLB 94

Parra, Nicanor 1914- ...... **CLC 2, 102; DAM**
**MULT; HLC 2**
See also CA 85-88; CANR 32; HW 1;
MTCW 1

Parra Sanojo, Ana Teresa de la 1890-1936
See also HLCS 2

Parrish, Mary Frances
See Fisher, M(ary) F(rances) K(ennedy)

Parson
See Coleridge, Samuel Taylor

Parson Lot
See Kingsley, Charles

Partridge, Anthony
See Oppenheim, E(dward) Phillips

Pascal, Blaise 1623-1662 ..................... **LC 35**

Pascoli, Giovanni 1855-1912 ........... **TCLC 45**
See also CA 170

Pasolini, Pier Paolo 1922-1975 .. **CLC 20, 37,**
**106; PC 17**
See also CA 93-96; 61-64; CANR 63; DLB
128, 177; MTCW 1

Pasquini
See Silone, Ignazio

Pastan, Linda (Olenik) 1932- ......... **CLC 27;**
**DAM POET**
See also CA 61-64; CANR 18, 40, 61; DLB
5

Pasternak, Boris (Leonidovich) 1890-1960
**CLC 7, 10, 18, 63; DA; DAB; DAC;**
**DAM MST, NOV, POET; PC 6; SSC 31;**
**WLC**
See also CA 127; 116; DA3; MTCW 1, 2

Patchen, Kenneth 1911-1972 .. **CLC 1, 2, 18;**
**DAM POET**
See also CA 1-4R; 33-36R; CANR 3, 35;
DLB 16, 48; MTCW 1

Pater, Walter (Horatio) 1839-1894 .. **NCLC 7**
See also CDBLB 1832-1890; DLB 57, 156

Paterson, A(ndrew) B(arton) 1864-1941
**TCLC 32**
See also CA 155; SATA 97

Paterson, Katherine (Womeldorf)
1932- .................................. **CLC 12, 30**
See also AAYA 1, 31; CA 21-24R; CANR
28, 59; CLR 7, 50; DLB 52; JRDA; MAI-
CYA; MTCW 1; SATA 13, 53, 92

Patmore, Coventry Kersey Dighton
1823-1896 ................................... **NCLC 9**
See also DLB 35, 98

Paton, Alan (Stewart) 1903-1988 ...... **CLC 4,**
**10, 25, 55, 106; DA; DAB; DAC; DAM**
**MST, NOV; WLC**
See also AAYA 26; CA 13-16; 125; CANR
22; CAP 1; DA3; DLBD 17; MTCW 1, 2;
SATA 11; SATA-Obit 56

Paton Walsh, Gillian 1937-
See Walsh, Jill Paton
See also AAYA 11; CANR 38, 83; DLB
161; JRDA; MAICYA; SAAS 3; SATA 4,
72, 109

Patton, George S. 1885-1945 .......... **TCLC 79**

Paulding, James Kirke 1778-1860 ... **NCLC 2**
See also DLB 3, 59, 74

Paulin, Thomas Neilson 1949-
See Paulin, Tom
See also CA 123; 128

Paulin, Tom ..................................... **CLC 37**
See also Paulin, Thomas Neilson DLB 40

Pausanias c. 1st cent. - ................... **CMLC 36**

Paustovsky, Konstantin (Georgievich)
1892-1968 ................................... **CLC 40**
See also CA 93-96; 25-28R

Pavese, Cesare 1908-1950 .. **TCLC 3; PC 13;**
**SSC 19**
See also CA 104; 169; DLB 128, 177

Pavic, Milorad 1929- ....................... **CLC 60**
See also CA 136; DLB 181

Pavlov, Ivan Petrovich 1849-1936 . **TCLC 91**
See also CA 118; 180

Payne, Alan
See Jakes, John (William)

Paz, Gil
See Lugones, Leopoldo

Paz, Octavio 1914-1998 . **CLC 3, 4, 6, 10, 19,**
**51, 65, 119; DA; DAB; DAC; DAM**
**MST, MULT, POET; HLC 2; PC 1;**
**WLC**
See also CA 73-76; 165; CANR 32, 65;
DA3; DLBY 90, 98; HW 1, 2; MTCW 1,
2

p'Bitek, Okot 1931-1982 .... **CLC 96; BLC 3;**
**DAM MULT**
See also BW 2, 3; CA 124; 107; CANR 82;
DLB 125; MTCW 1, 2

Peacock, Molly 1947- ....................... **CLC 60**
See also CA 103; CAAS 21; CANR 52, 84;
DLB 120

Peacock, Thomas Love
1785-1866 ................................. **NCLC 22**
See also DLB 96, 116

Peake, Mervyn 1911-1968 ............. **CLC 7, 54**
See also CA 5-8R; 25-28R; CANR 3; DLB
15, 160; MTCW 1; SATA 23

Pearce, Philippa ................................ **CLC 21**
See also Christie, (Ann) Philippa CLR 9;
DLB 161; MAICYA; SATA 1, 67

**Pearl, Eric**
See Elman, Richard (Martin)
**Pearson, T(homas) R(eid)** 1956- ....... **CLC 39**
See also CA 120; 130; INT 130
**Peck, Dale** 1967- ................................ **CLC 81**
See also CA 146; CANR 72
**Peck, John** 1941- ................................ **CLC 3**
See also CA 49-52; CANR 3
**Peck, Richard (Wayne)** 1934- ......... **CLC 21**
See also AAYA 1, 24; CA 85-88; CANR
19, 38; CLR 15; INT CANR-19; JRDA;
MAICYA; SAAS 2; SATA 18, 55, 97;
SATA-Essay 110
**Peck, Robert Newton** 1928- .... **CLC 17; DA;**
**DAC; DAM MST**
See also AAYA 3; CA 81-84, 182; CAAE
182; CANR 31, 63; CLR 45; JRDA; MAI-
CYA; SAAS 1; SATA 21, 62, 111; SATA-
Essay 108
**Peckinpah, (David) Sam(uel)**
1925-1984 ................................ **CLC 20**
See also CA 109; 114; CANR 82
**Pedersen, Knut** 1859-1952
See Hamsun, Knut
See also CA 104; 119; CANR 63; MTCW
1, 2
**Peeslake, Gaffer**
See Durrell, Lawrence (George)
**Peguy, Charles Pierre** 1873-1914 ... **TCLC 10**
See also CA 107
**Peirce, Charles Sanders**
1839-1914 ................................ **TCLC 81**
**Pellicer, Carlos** 1900(?)-1977
See also CA 153; 69-72; HLCS 2; HW 1
**Pena, Ramon del Valle y**
See Valle-Inclan, Ramon (Maria) del
**Pendennis, Arthur Esquir**
See Thackeray, William Makepeace
**Penn, William** 1644-1718 .................... **LC 25**
See also DLB 24
**PEPECE**
See Prado (Calvo), Pedro
**Pepys, Samuel** 1633-1703 .......... **LC 11; DA;**
**DAB; DAC; DAM MST; WLC**
See also CDBLB 1660-1789; DA3; DLB
101
**Percy, Walker** 1916-1990 ....... **CLC 2, 3, 6, 8,**
**14, 18, 47, 65; DAM NOV, POP**
See also CA 1-4R; 131; CANR 1, 23, 64;
DA3; DLB 2; DLBY 80, 90; MTCW 1, 2
**Percy, William Alexander**
1885-1942 ................................ **TCLC 84**
See also CA 163; MTCW 2
**Perec, Georges** 1936-1982 ......... **CLC 56, 116**
See also CA 141; DLB 83
**Pereda (y Sanchez de Porrua), Jose Maria**
**de** 1833-1906 ......................... **TCLC 16**
See also CA 117
**Pereda y Porrua, Jose Maria de**
See Pereda (y Sanchez de Porrua), Jose
Maria de
**Peregoy, George Weems**
See Mencken, H(enry) L(ouis)
**Perelman, S(idney) J(oseph)**
1904-1979 .. **CLC 3, 5, 9, 15, 23, 44, 49;**
**DAM DRAM; SSC 32**
See also AITN 1, 2; CA 73-76; 89-92;
CANR 18; DLB 11, 44; MTCW 1, 2
**Peret, Benjamin** 1899-1959 ........... **TCLC 20**
See also CA 117
**Peretz, Isaac Loeb** 1851(?)-1915 ... **TCLC 16;**
**SSC 26**
See also CA 109
**Peretz, Yitzkhok Leibush**
See Peretz, Isaac Loeb
**Perez Galdos, Benito** 1843-1920 ... **TCLC 27;**
**HLCS 2**
See also CA 125; 153; HW 1

**Peri Rossi, Cristina** 1941-
See also CA 131; CANR 59, 81; DLB 145;
HLCS 2; HW 1, 2
**Perrault, Charles** 1628-1703 ..... **LC 3, 52, 56**
See also MAICYA; SATA 25
**Perry, Anne** 1938- ......................... **CLC 126**
See also CA 101; CANR 22, 50, 84
**Perry, Brighton**
See Sherwood, Robert E(mmet)
**Perse, St.-John**
See Leger, (Marie-Rene Auguste) Alexis
Saint-Leger
**Perutz, Leo(pold)** 1882-1957 ......... **TCLC 60**
See also CA 147; DLB 81
**Peseenz, Tulio F.**
See Lopez y Fuentes, Gregorio
**Pesetsky, Bette** 1932- ...................... **CLC 28**
See also CA 133; DLB 130
**Peshkov, Alexei Maximovich** 1868-1936
See Gorky, Maxim
See also CA 105; 141; CANR 83; DA;
DAC; DAM DRAM, MST, NOV; MTCW
2
**Pessoa, Fernando (Antonio Nogueira)**
1888-1935 ....... **TCLC 27; DAM MULT;**
**HLC 2; PC 20**
See also CA 125; 183
**Peterkin, Julia Mood** 1880-1961 ...... **CLC 31**
See also CA 102; DLB 9
**Peters, Joan K(aren)** 1945- .............. **CLC 39**
See also CA 158
**Peters, Robert L(ouis)** 1924- ............ **CLC 7**
See also CA 13-16R; CAAS 8; DLB 105
**Petofi, Sandor** 1823-1849 ............... **NCLC 21**
**Petrakis, Harry Mark** 1923- ............... **CLC 3**
See also CA 9-12R; CANR 4, 30, 85
**Petrarch** 1304-1374 ............ **CMLC 20; DAM**
**POET; PC 8**
See also DA3
**Petronius** c. 20-66 ......................... **CMLC 34**
See also DLB 211
**Petrov, Evgeny** ................................. **TCLC 21**
See also Kataev, Evgeny Petrovich
**Petry, Ann (Lane)** 1908-1997 ..... **CLC 1, 7, 18**
See also BW 1, 3; CA 5-8R; 157; CAAS 6;
CANR 4, 46; CLR 12; DLB 76; JRDA;
MAICYA; MTCW 1; SATA 5; SATA-Obit
94
**Petursson, Halligrimur** 1614-1674 ........ **LC 8**
**Peychinovich**
See Vazov, Ivan (Minchov)
**Phaedrus** c. 18B.C.-c. 50 ............... **CMLC 25**
See also DLB 211
**Philips, Katherine** 1632-1664 ............... **LC 30**
See also DLB 131
**Philipson, Morris H.** 1926- ............... **CLC 53**
See also CA 1-4R; CANR 4
**Phillips, Caryl** 1958- . **CLC 96; BLCS; DAM**
**MULT**
See also BW 2; CA 141; CANR 63; DA3;
DLB 157; MTCW 2
**Phillips, David Graham**
1867-1911 ................................ **TCLC 44**
See also CA 108; 176; DLB 9, 12
**Phillips, Jack**
See Sandburg, Carl (August)
**Phillips, Jayne Anne** 1952- ........ **CLC 15, 33;**
**SSC 16**
See also CA 101; CANR 24, 50; DLBY 80;
INT CANR-24; MTCW 1, 2
**Phillips, Richard**
See Dick, Philip K(indred)
**Phillips, Robert (Schaeffer)** 1938- .... **CLC 28**
See also CA 17-20R; CAAS 13; CANR 8;
DLB 105
**Phillips, Ward**
See Lovecraft, H(oward) P(hillips)

**Piccolo, Lucio** 1901-1969 .................. **CLC 13**
See also CA 97-100; DLB 114
**Pickthall, Marjorie L(owry) C(hristie)**
1883-1922 ................................ **TCLC 21**
See also CA 107; DLB 92
**Pico della Mirandola, Giovanni** 1463-1494
**LC 15**
**Piercy, Marge** 1936- .... **CLC 3, 6, 14, 18, 27,**
**62, 128; PC 29**
See also CA 21-24R; CAAS 1; CANR 13,
43, 66; DLB 120; MTCW 1, 2
**Piers, Robert**
See Anthony, Piers
**Pieyre de Mandiargues, Andre** 1909-1991
See Mandiargues, Andre Pieyre de
See also CA 103; 136; CANR 22, 82
**Pilnyak, Boris** .................................. **TCLC 23**
See also Vogau, Boris Andreyevich
**Pincherle, Alberto** 1907-1990 .... **CLC 11, 18;**
**DAM NOV**
See also Moravia, Alberto CA 25-28R; 132;
CANR 33, 63; MTCW 1
**Pinckney, Darryl** 1953- ..................... **CLC 76**
See also BW 2, 3; CA 143; CANR 79
**Pindar** 518B.C.-446B.C. .... **CMLC 12; PC 19**
See also DLB 176
**Pineda, Cecile** 1942- ......................... **CLC 39**
See also CA 118
**Pinero, Arthur Wing** 1855-1934 ... **TCLC 32;**
**DAM DRAM**
See also CA 110; 153; DLB 10
**Pinero, Miguel (Antonio Gomez)** 1946-1988
**CLC 4, 55**
See also CA 61-64; 125; CANR 29; HW 1
**Pinget, Robert** 1919-1997 ....... **CLC 7, 13, 37**
See also CA 85-88; 160; DLB 83
**Pink Floyd**
See Barrett, (Roger) Syd; Gilmour, David;
Mason, Nick; Waters, Roger; Wright, Rick
**Pinkney, Edward** 1802-1828 .......... **NCLC 31**
**Pinkwater, Daniel Manus** 1941- ....... **CLC 35**
See also Pinkwater, Manus AAYA 1; CA
29-32R; CANR 12, 38; CLR 4; JRDA;
MAICYA; SAAS 3; SATA 46, 76
**Pinkwater, Manus**
See Pinkwater, Daniel Manus
See also SATA 8
**Pinsky, Robert** 1940- ....... **CLC 9, 19, 38, 94,**
**121; DAM POET; PC 27**
See also CA 29-32R; CAAS 4; CANR 58;
DA3; DLBY 82, 98; MTCW 2
**Pinta, Harold**
See Pinter, Harold
**Pinter, Harold** 1930- .. **CLC 1, 3, 6, 9, 11, 15,**
**27, 58, 73; DA; DAB; DAC; DAM**
**DRAM, MST; WLC**
See also CA 5-8R; CANR 33, 65; CDBLB
1960 to Present; DA3; DLB 13; MTCW
1, 2
**Piozzi, Hester Lynch (Thrale)** 1741-1821
**NCLC 57**
See also DLB 104, 142
**Pirandello, Luigi** 1867-1936 ...... **TCLC 4, 29;**
**DA; DAB; DAC; DAM DRAM, MST;**
**DC 5; SSC 22; WLC**
See also CA 104; 153; DA3; MTCW 2
**Pirsig, Robert M(aynard)** 1928- ... **CLC 4, 6,**
**73; DAM POP**
See also CA 53-56; CANR 42, 74; DA3;
MTCW 1, 2; SATA 39
**Pisarev, Dmitry Ivanovich**
1840-1868 ................................ **NCLC 25**
**Pix, Mary (Griffith)** 1666-1709 ............. **LC 8**
See also DLB 80
**Pixerecourt, (Rene Charles) Guilbert de**
1773-1844 ................................ **NCLC 39**
See also DLB 192
**Plaatje, Sol(omon) T(shekisho)** 1876-1932
**TCLC 73; BLCS**

See also BW 2, 3; CA 141; CANR 79

**Plaidy, Jean**
See Hibbert, Eleanor Alice Burford

**Planche, James Robinson**
1796-1880 ............................... **NCLC 42**

**Plant, Robert** 1948- ........................... **CLC 12**

**Plante, David (Robert)** 1940- ..... **CLC 7, 23, 38; DAM NOV**
See also CA 37-40R; CANR 12, 36, 58, 82; DLBY 83; INT CANR-12; MTCW 1

**Plath, Sylvia** 1932-1963 ..... **CLC 1, 2, 3, 5, 9, 11, 14, 17, 50, 51, 62, 111; DA; DAB; DAC; DAM MST, POET; PC 1; WLC**
See also AAYA 13; CA 19-20; CANR 34; CAP 2; CDALB 1941-1968; DA3; DLB 5, 6, 152; MTCW 1, 2; SATA 96

**Plato** 428(?)B.C.-348(?)B.C. ... **CMLC 8; DA; DAB; DAC; DAM MST; WLCS**
See also DA3; DLB 176

**Platonov, Andrei** ............................. **TCLC 14**
See also Klimentov, Andrei Platonovich

**Platt, Kin** 1911- ............................... **CLC 26**
See also AAYA 11; CA 17-20R; CANR 11; JRDA; SAAS 17; SATA 21, 86

**Plautus** c. 251B.C.-184B.C. ... **CMLC 24; DC 6**
See also DLB 211

**Plick et Plock**
See Simenon, Georges (Jacques Christian)

**Plimpton, George (Ames)** 1927- ....... **CLC 36**
See also AITN 1; CA 21-24R; CANR 32, 70; DLB 185; MTCW 1, 2; SATA 10

**Pliny the Elder** c. 23-79 ................. **CMLC 23**
See also DLB 211

**Plomer, William Charles Franklin** 1903-1973
**CLC 4, 8**
See also CA 21-22; CANR 34; CAP 2; DLB 20, 162, 191; MTCW 1; SATA 24

**Plowman, Piers**
See Kavanagh, Patrick (Joseph)

**Plum, J.**
See Wodehouse, P(elham) G(renville)

**Plumly, Stanley (Ross)** 1939- ........... **CLC 33**
See also CA 108; 110; DLB 5, 193; INT 110

**Plumpe, Friedrich Wilhelm**
1888-1931 ............................... **TCLC 53**
See also CA 112

**Po Chu-i** 772-846 ........................... **CMLC 24**

**Poe, Edgar Allan** 1809-1849 ..... **NCLC 1, 16, 55, 78; DA; DAB; DAC; DAM MST, POET; PC 1; SSC 34; WLC**
See also AAYA 14; CDALB 1640-1865; DA3; DLB 3, 59, 73, 74; SATA 23

**Poet of Titchfield Street, The**
See Pound, Ezra (Weston Loomis)

**Pohl, Frederik** 1919- ........... **CLC 18; SSC 25**
See also AAYA 24; CA 61-64; CAAS 1; CANR 11, 37, 81; DLB 8; INT CANR-11; MTCW 1, 2; SATA 24

**Poirier, Louis** 1910-
See Gracq, Julien
See also CA 122; 126

**Poitier, Sidney** 1927- ........................... **CLC 26**
See also BW 1; CA 117

**Polanski, Roman** 1933- ..................... **CLC 16**
See also CA 77-80

**Poliakoff, Stephen** 1952- ................... **CLC 38**
See also CA 106; DLB 13

**Police, The**
See Copeland, Stewart (Armstrong); Summers, Andrew James; Sumner, Gordon Matthew

**Polidori, John William** 1795-1821 . **NCLC 51**
See also DLB 116

**Pollitt, Katha** 1949- ................... **CLC 28, 122**
See also CA 120; 122; CANR 66; MTCW 1, 2

**Pollock, (Mary) Sharon** 1936- ......... **CLC 50; DAC; DAM DRAM, MST**
See also CA 141; DLB 60

**Polo, Marco** 1254-1324 ................. **CMLC 15**

**Polonsky, Abraham (Lincoln)**
1910- ....................................... **CLC 92**
See also CA 104; DLB 26; INT 104

**Polybius** c. 200B.C.-c. 118B.C. ...... **CMLC 17**
See also DLB 176

**Pomerance, Bernard** 1940- ... **CLC 13; DAM DRAM**
See also CA 101; CANR 49

**Ponge, Francis** 1899-1988 . **CLC 6, 18; DAM POET**
See also CA 85-88; 126; CANR 40, 86

**Poniatowska, Elena** 1933-
See also CA 101; CANR 32, 66; DAM MULT; DLB 113; HLC 2; HW 1, 2

**Pontoppidan, Henrik** 1857-1943 .... **TCLC 29**
See also CA 170

**Poole, Josephine** ............................... **CLC 17**
See also Helyar, Jane Penelope Josephine
SAAS 2; SATA 5

**Popa, Vasko** 1922-1991 ..................... **CLC 19**
See also CA 112; 148; DLB 181

**Pope, Alexander** 1688-1744 .......... **LC 3; DA; DAB; DAC; DAM MST, POET; PC 26; WLC**
See also CDBLB 1660-1789; DA3; DLB 95, 101

**Porter, Connie (Rose)** 1959(?)- ....... **CLC 70**
See also BW 2, 3; CA 142; SATA 81

**Porter, Gene(va Grace) Stratton**
1863(?)-1924 ........................... **TCLC 21**
See also CA 112

**Porter, Katherine Anne** 1890-1980 ... **CLC 1, 3, 7, 10, 13, 15, 27, 101; DA; DAB; DAC; DAM MST, NOV; SSC 4, 31**
See also AITN 2; CA 1-4R; 101; CANR 1, 65; CDALBS; DA3; DLB 4, 9, 102; DLBD 12; DLBY 80; MTCW 1, 2; SATA 39; SATA-Obit 23

**Porter, Peter (Neville Frederick)**
1929- ................................... **CLC 5, 13, 33**
See also CA 85-88; DLB 40

**Porter, William Sydney** 1862-1910
See Henry, O.
See also CA 104; 131; CDALB 1865-1917; DA; DAB; DAC; DAM MST; DA3; DLB 12, 78, 79; MTCW 1, 2; YABC 2

**Portillo (y Pacheco), Jose Lopez**
See Lopez Portillo (y Pacheco), Jose

**Portillo Trambley, Estela** 1927-1998
See also CANR 32; DAM MULT; DLB 209; HLC 2; HW 1

**Post, Melville Davisson**
1869-1930 ............................... **TCLC 39**
See also CA 110

**Potok, Chaim** 1929- ... **CLC 2, 7, 14, 26, 112; DAM NOV**
See also AAYA 15; AITN 1, 2; CA 17-20R; CANR 19, 35, 64; DA3; DLB 28, 152; INT CANR-19; MTCW 1, 2; SATA 33, 106

**Potter, Dennis (Christopher George)**
1935-1994 ............................... **CLC 58, 86**
See also CA 107; 145; CANR 33, 61; MTCW 1

**Pound, Ezra (Weston Loomis)** 1885-1972
**CLC 1, 2, 3, 4, 5, 7, 10, 13, 18, 34, 48, 50, 112; DA; DAB; DAC; DAM MST, POET; PC 4; WLC**
See also CA 5-8R; 37-40R; CANR 40; CDALB 1917-1929; DA3; DLB 4, 45, 63; DLBD 15; MTCW 1, 2

**Povod, Reinaldo** 1959-1994 ............. **CLC 44**
See also CA 136; 146; CANR 83

**Powell, Adam Clayton, Jr.**
1908-1972 ......... **CLC 89; BLC 3; DAM MULT**
See also BW 1, 3; CA 102; 33-36R; CANR 86

**Powell, Anthony (Dymoke)** 1905- . **CLC 1, 3, 7, 9, 10, 31**
See also CA 1-4R; CANR 1, 32, 62; CDBLB 1945-1960; DLB 15; MTCW 1, 2

**Powell, Dawn** 1897-1965 ................... **CLC 66**
See also CA 5-8R; DLBY 97

**Powell, Padgett** 1952- ....................... **CLC 34**
See also CA 126; CANR 63

**Power, Susan** 1961- ........................... **CLC 91**

**Powers, J(ames) F(arl)** 1917-1999 ..... **CLC 1, 4, 8, 57; SSC 4**
See also CA 1-4R; 181; CANR 2, 61; DLB 130; MTCW 1

**Powers, John J(ames)** 1945-
See Powers, John R.
See also CA 69-72

**Powers, John R.** ................................. **CLC 66**
See also Powers, John J(ames)

**Powers, Richard (S.)** 1957- .............. **CLC 93**
See also CA 148; CANR 80

**Pownall, David** 1938- ....................... **CLC 10**
See also CA 89-92; 180; CAAS 18; CANR 49; DLB 14

**Powys, John Cowper** 1872-1963 ... **CLC 7, 9, 15, 46, 125**
See also CA 85-88; DLB 15; MTCW 1, 2

**Powys, T(heodore) F(rancis)** 1875-1953
**TCLC 9**
See also CA 106; DLB 36, 162

**Prado (Calvo), Pedro** 1886-1952 ... **TCLC 75**
See also CA 131; HW 1

**Prager, Emily** 1952- ......................... **CLC 56**

**Pratt, E(dwin) J(ohn)**
1883(?)-1964 ....... **CLC 19; DAC; DAM POET**
See also CA 141; 93-96; CANR 77; DLB 92

**Premchand** ....................................... **TCLC 21**
See also Srivastava, Dhanpat Rai

**Preussler, Otfried** 1923- ................... **CLC 17**
See also CA 77-80; SATA 24

**Prevert, Jacques (Henri Marie)** 1900-1977
**CLC 15**
See also CA 77-80; 69-72; CANR 29, 61; MTCW 1; SATA-Obit 30

**Prevost, Abbe (Antoine Francois)** 1697-1763
**LC 1**

**Price, (Edward) Reynolds** 1933- ... **CLC 3, 6, 13, 43, 50, 63; DAM NOV; SSC 22**
See also CA 1-4R; CANR 1, 37, 57, 87; DLB 2; INT CANR-37

**Price, Richard** 1949- ..................... **CLC 6, 12**
See also CA 49-52; CANR 3; DLBY 81

**Prichard, Katharine Susannah** 1883-1969
**CLC 46**
See also CA 11-12; CANR 33; CAP 1; MTCW 1; SATA 66

**Priestley, J(ohn) B(oynton)**
1894-1984 ......... **CLC 2, 5, 9, 34; DAM DRAM, NOV**
See also CA 9-12R; 113; CANR 33; CDBLB 1914-1945; DA3; DLB 10, 34, 77, 100, 139; DLBY 84; MTCW 1, 2

**Prince** 1958(?)- ................................. **CLC 35**

**Prince, F(rank) T(empleton)** 1912- .. **CLC 22**
See also CA 101; CANR 43, 79; DLB 20

**Prince Kropotkin**
See Kropotkin, Peter (Aleksieevich)

**Prior, Matthew** 1664-1721 ..................... **LC 4**
See also DLB 95

**Prishvin, Mikhail** 1873-1954 .......... **TCLC 75**

**Pritchard, William H(arrison)**
1932- ....................................... **CLC 34**
See also CA 65-68; CANR 23; DLB 111

**Pritchett, V(ictor) S(awdon)**
1900-1997 ...... **CLC 5, 13, 15, 41; DAM
NOV; SSC 14**
See also CA 61-64; 157; CANR 31, 63;
DA3; DLB 15, 139; MTCW 1, 2

**Private 19022**
See Manning, Frederic

**Probst, Mark** 1925- ........................... **CLC 59**
See also CA 130

**Prokosch, Frederic** 1908-1989 ...... **CLC 4, 48**
See also CA 73-76; 128; CANR 82; DLB
48; MTCW 2

**Propertius, Sextus** c. 50B.C.-c.
16B.C. ........................ **CMLC 32**
See also DLB 211

**Prophet, The**
See Dreiser, Theodore (Herman Albert)

**Prose, Francine** 1947- ........................ **CLC 45**
See also CA 109; 112; CANR 46; SATA
101

**Proudhon**
See Cunha, Euclides (Rodrigues Pimenta)
da

**Proulx, Annie**
See Proulx, E(dna) Annie

**Proulx, E(dna) Annie** 1935- .. **CLC 81; DAM
POP**
See also CA 145; CANR 65; DA3; MTCW
2

**Proust, (Valentin-Louis-George-Eugene-)
Marcel** 1871-1922 ....... **TCLC 7, 13, 33;
DA; DAB; DAC; DAM MST, NOV;
WLC**
See also CA 104; 120; DA3; DLB 65;
MTCW 1, 2

**Prowler, Harley**
See Masters, Edgar Lee

**Prus, Boleslaw** 1845-1912 ............... **TCLC 48**

**Pryor, Richard (Franklin Lenox Thomas)**
1940- ........................................... **CLC 26**
See also CA 122; 152

**Przybyszewski, Stanislaw**
1868-1927 ............................... **TCLC 36**
See also CA 160; DLB 66

**Pteleon**
See Grieve, C(hristopher) M(urray)
See also DAM POET

**Puckett, Lute**
See Masters, Edgar Lee

**Puig, Manuel** 1932-1990 .... **CLC 3, 5, 10, 28,
65; DAM MULT; HLC 2**
See also CA 45-48; CANR 2, 32, 63; DA3;
DLB 113; HW 1, 2; MTCW 1, 2

**Pulitzer, Joseph** 1847-1911 ............. **TCLC 76**
See also CA 114; DLB 23

**Purdy, A(lfred) W(ellington)** 1918- ... **CLC 3,
6, 14, 50; DAC; DAM MST, POET**
See also CA 81-84; CAAS 17; CANR 42,
66; DLB 88

**Purdy, James (Amos)** 1923- .... **CLC 2, 4, 10,
28, 52**
See also CA 33-36R; CAAS 1; CANR 19,
51; DLB 2; INT CANR-19; MTCW 1

**Pure, Simon**
See Swinnerton, Frank Arthur

**Pushkin, Alexander (Sergeyevich)** 1799-1837
**NCLC 3, 27, 83; DA; DAB; DAC; DAM
DRAM, MST, POET; PC 10; SSC 27;
WLC**
See also DA3; DLB 205; SATA 61

**P'u Sung-ling** 1640-1715 ....... **LC 49; SSC 31**

**Putnam, Arthur Lee**
See Alger, Horatio Jr., Jr.

**Puzo, Mario** 1920-1999 ........ **CLC 1, 2, 6, 36,
107; DAM NOV, POP**
See also CA 65-68; CANR 4, 42, 65; DA3;
DLB 6; MTCW 1, 2

**Pygge, Edward**
See Barnes, Julian (Patrick)

**Pyle, Ernest Taylor** 1900-1945
See Pyle, Ernie
See also CA 115; 160

**Pyle, Ernie** 1900-1945 ..................... **TCLC 75**
See also Pyle, Ernest Taylor DLB 29;
MTCW 2

**Pyle, Howard** 1853-1911 ................. **TCLC 81**
See also CA 109; 137; CLR 22; DLB 42,
188; DLBD 13; MAICYA; SATA 16, 100

**Pym, Barbara (Mary Crampton)** 1913-1980
**CLC 13, 19, 37, 111**
See also CA 13-14; 97-100; CANR 13, 34;
CAP 1; DLB 14, 207; DLBY 87; MTCW
1, 2

**Pynchon, Thomas (Ruggles, Jr.)**
1937- ...... **CLC 2, 3, 6, 9, 11, 18, 33, 62,
72; DA; DAB; DAC; DAM MST, NOV,
POP; SSC 14; WLC**
See also BEST 90:2; CA 17-20R; CANR
22, 46, 73; DA3; DLB 2, 173; MTCW 1,
2

**Pythagoras** c. 570B.C.-c. 500B.C. . **CMLC 22**
See also DLB 176

**Q**
See Quiller-Couch, SirArthur (Thomas)

**Qian Zhongshu**
See Ch'ien Chung-shu

**Qroll**
See Dagerman, Stig (Halvard)

**Quarrington, Paul (Lewis)** 1953- ..... **CLC 65**
See also CA 129; CANR 62

**Quasimodo, Salvatore** 1901-1968 ..... **CLC 10**
See also CA 13-16; 25-28R; CAP 1; DLB
114; MTCW 1

**Quay, Stephen** 1947- ......................... **CLC 95**

**Quay, Timothy** 1947- ......................... **CLC 95**

**Queen, Ellery** .............................. **CLC 3, 11**
See also Dannay, Frederic; Davidson,
Avram (James); Lee, Manfred
B(ennington); Marlowe, Stephen; Stur-
geon, Theodore (Hamilton); Vance, John
Holbrook

**Queen, Ellery, Jr.**
See Dannay, Frederic; Lee, Manfred
B(ennington)

**Queneau, Raymond** 1903-1976 ..... **CLC 2, 5,
10, 42**
See also CA 77-80; 69-72; CANR 32; DLB
72; MTCW 1, 2

**Quevedo, Francisco de** 1580-1645 ....... **LC 23**

**Quiller-Couch, SirArthur (Thomas)**
1863-1944 ............................... **TCLC 53**
See also CA 118; 166; DLB 135, 153, 190

**Quin, Ann (Marie)** 1936-1973 ............ **CLC 6**
See also CA 9-12R; 45-48; DLB 14

**Quinn, Martin**
See Smith, Martin Cruz

**Quinn, Peter** 1947- ........................... **CLC 91**

**Quinn, Simon**
See Smith, Martin Cruz

**Quintana, Leroy V.** 1944-
See also CA 131; CANR 65; DAM MULT;
DLB 82; HLC 2; HW 1, 2

**Quiroga, Horacio (Sylvestre)** 1878-1937
**TCLC 20; DAM MULT; HLC 2**
See also CA 117; 131; HW 1; MTCW 1

**Quoirez, Francoise** 1935- ................... **CLC 9**
See also Sagan, Francoise CA 49-52; CANR
6, 39, 73; MTCW 1, 2

**Raabe, Wilhelm (Karl)** 1831-1910 . **TCLC 45**
See also CA 167; DLB 129

**Rabe, David (William)** 1940- .. **CLC 4, 8, 33;
DAM DRAM**
See also CA 85-88; CABS 3; CANR 59;
DLB 7

**Rabelais, Francois** 1483-1553 ...... **LC 5; DA;
DAB; DAC; DAM MST; WLC**

**Rabinovitch, Sholem** 1859-1916
See Aleichem, Sholom
See also CA 104

**Rabinyan, Dorit** 1972- .................... **CLC 119**
See also CA 170

**Rachilde**
See Vallette, Marguerite Eymery

**Racine, Jean** 1639-1699 . **LC 28; DAB; DAM
MST**
See also DA3

**Radcliffe, Ann (Ward)** 1764-1823 ... **NCLC 6,
55**
See also DLB 39, 178

**Radiguet, Raymond** 1903-1923 ...... **TCLC 29**
See also CA 162; DLB 65

**Radnoti, Miklos** 1909-1944 ............. **TCLC 16**
See also CA 118

**Rado, James** 1939- ............................. **CLC 17**
See also CA 105

**Radvanyi, Netty** 1900-1983
See Seghers, Anna
See also CA 85-88; 110; CANR 82

**Rae, Ben**
See Griffiths, Trevor

**Raeburn, John (Hay)** 1941- ............. **CLC 34**
See also CA 57-60

**Ragni, Gerome** 1942-1991 ................. **CLC 17**
See also CA 105; 134

**Rahv, Philip** 1908-1973 ..................... **CLC 24**
See also Greenberg, Ivan DLB 137

**Raimund, Ferdinand Jakob** 1790-1836
**NCLC 69**
See also DLB 90

**Raine, Craig** 1944- ..................... **CLC 32, 103**
See also CA 108; CANR 29, 51; DLB 40

**Raine, Kathleen (Jessie)** 1908- ..... **CLC 7, 45**
See also CA 85-88; CANR 46; DLB 20;
MTCW 1

**Rainis, Janis** 1865-1929 ................. **TCLC 29**
See also CA 170

**Rakosi, Carl** 1903- ........................... **CLC 47**
See also Rawley, Callman CAAS 5; DLB
193

**Raleigh, Richard**
See Lovecraft, H(oward) P(hillips)

**Raleigh, Sir Walter** 1554(?)-1618 .. **LC 31, 39**
See also CDBLB Before 1660; DLB 172

**Rallentando, H. P.**
See Sayers, Dorothy L(eigh)

**Ramal, Walter**
See de la Mare, Walter (John)

**Ramana Maharshi** 1879-1950 ........ **TCLC 84**

**Ramoacn y Cajal, Santiago**
1852-1934 ............................... **TCLC 93**

**Ramon, Juan**
See Jimenez (Mantecon), Juan Ramon

**Ramos, Graciliano** 1892-1953 ........ **TCLC 32**
See also CA 167; HW 2

**Rampersad, Arnold** 1941- ............... **CLC 44**
See also BW 2, 3; CA 127; 133; CANR 81;
DLB 111; INT 133

**Rampling, Anne**
See Rice, Anne

**Ramsay, Allan** 1684(?)-1758 ................. **LC 29**
See also DLB 95

**Ramuz, Charles-Ferdinand**
1878-1947 ............................... **TCLC 33**
See also CA 165

**Rand, Ayn** 1905-1982 ...... **CLC 3, 30, 44, 79;
DA; DAC; DAM MST, NOV, POP;
WLC**
See also AAYA 10; CA 13-16R; 105; CANR
27, 73; CDALBS; DA3; MTCW 1, 2

**Randall, Dudley (Felker)** 1914- ......... **CLC 1; BLC 3; DAM MULT**
See also BW 1, 3; CA 25-28R; CANR 23, 82; DLB 41

**Randall, Robert**
See Silverberg, Robert

**Ranger, Ken**
See Creasey, John

**Ransom, John Crowe** 1888-1974 .. **CLC 2, 4, 5, 11, 24; DAM POET**
See also CA 5-8R; 49-52; CANR 6, 34; CDALBS; DA3; DLB 45, 63; MTCW 1, 2

**Rao, Raja** 1909- ..... **CLC 25, 56; DAM NOV**
See also CA 73-76; CANR 51; MTCW 1, 2

**Raphael, Frederic (Michael)** 1931- ... **CLC 2, 14**
See also CA 1-4R; CANR 1, 86; DLB 14

**Ratcliffe, James P.**
See Mencken, H(enry) L(ouis)

**Rathbone, Julian** 1935- ..................... **CLC 41**
See also CA 101; CANR 34, 73

**Rattigan, Terence (Mervyn)** 1911-1977 ............. **CLC 7; DAM DRAM**
See also CA 85-88; 73-76; CDBLB 1945-1960; DLB 13; MTCW 1, 2

**Ratushinskaya, Irina** 1954- ............... **CLC 54**
See also CA 129; CANR 68

**Raven, Simon (Arthur Noel)** 1927- .. **CLC 14**
See also CA 81-84; CANR 86

**Ravenna, Michael**
See Welty, Eudora

**Rawley, Callman** 1903-
See Rakosi, Carl
See also CA 21-24R; CANR 12, 32

**Rawlings, Marjorie Kinnan** 1896-1953 ........................ **TCLC 4**
See also AAYA 20; CA 104; 137; CANR 74; CLR 63; DLB 9, 22, 102; DLBD 17; JRDA; MAICYA; MTCW 2; SATA 100; YABC 1

**Ray, Satyajit** 1921-1992 .. **CLC 16, 76; DAM MULT**
See also CA 114; 137

**Read, Herbert Edward** 1893-1968 ..... **CLC 4**
See also CA 85-88; 25-28R; DLB 20, 149

**Read, Piers Paul** 1941- ........... **CLC 4, 10, 25**
See also CA 21-24R; CANR 38, 86; DLB 14; SATA 21

**Reade, Charles** 1814-1884 ......... **NCLC 2, 74**
See also DLB 21

**Reade, Hamish**
See Gray, Simon (James Holliday)

**Reading, Peter** 1946- ......................... **CLC 47**
See also CA 103; CANR 46; DLB 40

**Reaney, James** 1926- .. **CLC 13; DAC; DAM MST**
See also CA 41-44R; CAAS 15; CANR 42; DLB 68; SATA 43

**Rebreanu, Liviu** 1885-1944 ........... **TCLC 28**
See also CA 165

**Rechy, John (Francisco)** 1934- ...... **CLC 1, 7, 14, 18, 107; DAM MULT; HLC 2**
See also CA 5-8R; CAAS 4; CANR 6, 32, 64; DLB 122; DLBY 82; HW 1, 2; INT CANR-6

**Redcam, Tom** 1870-1933 ................. **TCLC 25**

**Reddin, Keith** ..................................... **CLC 67**

**Redgrove, Peter (William)** 1932- . **CLC 6, 41**
See also CA 1-4R; CANR 3, 39, 77; DLB 40

**Redmon, Anne** ................................... **CLC 22**
See also Nightingale, Anne Redmon DLBY 86

**Reed, Eliot**
See Ambler, Eric

**Reed, Ishmael** 1938- .. **CLC 2, 3, 5, 6, 13, 32, 60; BLC 3; DAM MULT**
See also BW 2, 3; CA 21-24R; CANR 25, 48, 74; DA3; DLB 2, 5, 33, 169; DLBD 8; MTCW 1, 2

**Reed, John (Silas)** 1887-1920 ........... **TCLC 9**
See also CA 106

**Reed, Lou** ............................................. **CLC 21**
See also Firbank, Louis

**Reese, Lizette Woodworth** 1856-1935 . **PC 29**
See also CA 180; DLB 54

**Reeve, Clara** 1729-1807 ................... **NCLC 19**
See also DLB 39

**Reich, Wilhelm** 1897-1957 ............. **TCLC 57**

**Reid, Christopher (John)** 1949- ....... **CLC 33**
See also CA 140; DLB 40

**Reid, Desmond**
See Moorcock, Michael (John)

**Reid Banks, Lynne** 1929-
See Banks, Lynne Reid
See also CA 1-4R; CANR 6, 22, 38, 87; CLR 24; JRDA; MAICYA; SATA 22, 75, 111

**Reilly, William K.**
See Creasey, John

**Reiner, Max**
See Caldwell, (Janet Miriam) Taylor (Holland)

**Reis, Ricardo**
See Pessoa, Fernando (Antonio Nogueira)

**Remarque, Erich Maria** 1898-1970 ... **CLC 21; DA; DAB; DAC; DAM MST, NOV**
See also AAYA 27; CA 77-80; 29-32R; DA3; DLB 56; MTCW 1, 2

**Remington, Frederic** 1861-1909 ..... **TCLC 89**
See also CA 108; 169; DLB 12, 186, 188; SATA 41

**Remizov, A.**
See Remizov, Aleksei (Mikhailovich)

**Remizov, A. M.**
See Remizov, Aleksei (Mikhailovich)

**Remizov, Aleksei (Mikhailovich)** 1877-1957 **TCLC 27**
See also CA 125; 133

**Renan, Joseph Ernest** 1823-1892 .. **NCLC 26**

**Renard, Jules** 1864-1910 ................. **TCLC 17**
See also CA 117

**Renault, Mary** ........................ **CLC 3, 11, 17**
See also Challans, Mary DLBY 83; MTCW 2

**Rendell, Ruth (Barbara)** 1930- . **CLC 28, 48; DAM POP**
See also Vine, Barbara CA 109; CANR 32, 52, 74; DLB 87; INT CANR-32; MTCW 1, 2

**Renoir, Jean** 1894-1979 ..................... **CLC 20**
See also CA 129; 85-88

**Resnais, Alain** 1922- ......................... **CLC 16**

**Reverdy, Pierre** 1889-1960 ............... **CLC 53**
See also CA 97-100; 89-92

**Rexroth, Kenneth** 1905-1982 .... **CLC 1, 2, 6, 11, 22, 49, 112; DAM POET; PC 20**
See also CA 5-8R; 107; CANR 14, 34, 63; CDALB 1941-1968; DLB 16, 48, 165, 212; DLBY 82; INT CANR-14; MTCW 1, 2

**Reyes, Alfonso** 1889-1959 .. **TCLC 33; HLCS 2**
See also CA 131; HW 1

**Reyes y Basoalto, Ricardo Eliecer Neftali**
See Neruda, Pablo

**Reymont, Wladyslaw (Stanislaw)** 1868(?)-1925 ............................ **TCLC 5**
See also CA 104

**Reynolds, Jonathan** 1942- ............. **CLC 6, 38**
See also CA 65-68; CANR 28

**Reynolds, Joshua** 1723-1792 ................. **LC 15**
See also DLB 104

**Reynolds, Michael Shane** 1937- ....... **CLC 44**
See also CA 65-68; CANR 9

**Reznikoff, Charles** 1894-1976 ............ **CLC 9**
See also CA 33-36; 61-64; CAP 2; DLB 28, 45

**Rezzori (d'Arezzo), Gregor von** 1914-1998 **CLC 25**
See also CA 122; 136; 167

**Rhine, Richard**
See Silverstein, Alvin

**Rhodes, Eugene Manlove** 1869-1934 ................................ **TCLC 53**

**Rhodius, Apollonius** c. 3rd cent. B.C.- ....................................... **CMLC 28**
See also DLB 176

**R'hoone**
See Balzac, Honore de

**Rhys, Jean** 1890(?)-1979 ...... **CLC 2, 4, 6, 14, 19, 51, 124; DAM NOV; SSC 21**
See also CA 25-28R; 85-88; CANR 35, 62; CDBLB 1945-1960; DA3; DLB 36, 117, 162; MTCW 1, 2

**Ribeiro, Darcy** 1922-1997 ................. **CLC 34**
See also CA 33-36R; 156

**Ribeiro, Joao Ubaldo (Osorio Pimentel)** 1941- ................................ **CLC 10, 67**
See also CA 81-84

**Ribman, Ronald (Burt)** 1932- ............. **CLC 7**
See also CA 21-24R; CANR 46, 80

**Ricci, Nino** 1959- .............................. **CLC 70**
See also CA 137

**Rice, Anne** 1941- .. **CLC 41, 128; DAM POP**
See also AAYA 9; BEST 89:2; CA 65-68; CANR 12, 36, 53, 74; DA3; MTCW 2

**Rice, Elmer (Leopold)** 1892-1967 ...... **CLC 7, 49; DAM DRAM**
See also CA 21-22; 25-28R; CAP 2; DLB 4, 7; MTCW 1, 2

**Rice, Tim(othy Miles Bindon)** 1944- .................................. **CLC 21**
See also CA 103; CANR 46

**Rich, Adrienne (Cecile)** 1929- ... **CLC 3, 6, 7, 11, 18, 36, 73, 76, 125; DAM POET; PC 5**
See also CA 9-12R; CANR 20, 53, 74; CDALBS; DA3; DLB 5, 67; MTCW 1, 2

**Rich, Barbara**
See Graves, Robert (von Ranke)

**Rich, Robert**
See Trumbo, Dalton

**Richard, Keith** ................................... **CLC 17**
See also Richards, Keith

**Richards, David Adams** 1950- ......... **CLC 59; DAC**
See also CA 93-96; CANR 60; DLB 53

**Richards, I(vor) A(rmstrong)** 1893-1979 ............................ **CLC 14, 24**
See also CA 41-44R; 89-92; CANR 34, 74; DLB 27; MTCW 2

**Richards, Keith** 1943-
See Richard, Keith
See also CA 107; CANR 77

**Richardson, Anne**
See Roiphe, Anne (Richardson)

**Richardson, Dorothy Miller** 1873-1957 ................................ **TCLC 3**
See also CA 104; DLB 36

**Richardson, Ethel Florence (Lindesay)** 1870-1946
See Richardson, Henry Handel
See also CA 105

**Richardson, Henry Handel** ............. **TCLC 4**
See also Richardson, Ethel Florence (Lindesay) DLB 197

**Richardson, John** 1796-1852 ........ **NCLC 55; DAC**
See also DLB 99

**Richardson, Samuel** 1689-1761 ...... **LC 1, 44;**
**DA; DAB; DAC; DAM MST, NOV;**
**WLC**
See also CDBLB 1660-1789; DLB 39

**Richler, Mordecai** 1931- ...... **CLC 3, 5, 9, 13,**
**18, 46, 70; DAC; DAM MST, NOV**
See also AITN 1; CA 65-68; CANR 31, 62;
CLR 17; DLB 53; MAICYA; MTCW 1,
2; SATA 44, 98; SATA-Brief 27

**Richter, Conrad (Michael)**
1890-1968 ..................................... **CLC 30**
See also AAYA 21; CA 5-8R; 25-28R;
CANR 23; DLB 9, 212; MTCW 1, 2;
SATA 3

**Ricostranza, Tom**
See Ellis, Trey

**Riddell, Charlotte** 1832-1906 ......... **TCLC 40**
See also CA 165; DLB 156

**Ridge, John Rollin** 1827-1867 ...... **NCLC 82;**
**DAM MULT**
See also CA 144; DLB 175; NNAL

**Ridgway, Keith** 1965- ...................... **CLC 119**
See also CA 172

**Riding, Laura** .................................. **CLC 3, 7**
See also Jackson, Laura (Riding)

**Riefenstahl, Berta Helene Amalia** 1902-
See Riefenstahl, Leni
See also CA 108

**Riefenstahl, Leni** ............................... **CLC 16**
See also Riefenstahl, Berta Helene Amalia

**Riffe, Ernest**
See Bergman, (Ernst) Ingmar

**Riggs, (Rolla) Lynn** 1899-1954 ..... **TCLC 56;**
**DAM MULT**
See also CA 144; DLB 175; NNAL

**Riis, Jacob A(ugust)** 1849-1914 ..... **TCLC 80**
See also CA 113; 168; DLB 23

**Riley, James Whitcomb**
1849-1916 ........ **TCLC 51; DAM POET**
See also CA 118; 137; MAICYA; SATA 17

**Riley, Tex**
See Creasey, John

**Rilke, Rainer Maria** 1875-1926 .. **TCLC 1, 6,**
**19; DAM POET; PC 2**
See also CA 104; 132; CANR 62; DA3;
DLB 81; MTCW 1, 2

**Rimbaud, (Jean Nicolas) Arthur** 1854-1891
**NCLC 4, 35, 82; DA; DAB; DAC; DAM**
**MST, POET; PC 3; WLC**
See also DA3

**Rinehart, Mary Roberts**
1876-1958 ................................. **TCLC 52**
See also CA 108; 166

**Ringmaster, The**
See Mencken, H(enry) L(ouis)

**Ringwood, Gwen(dolyn Margaret) Pharis**
1910-1984 ................................... **CLC 48**
See also CA 148; 112; DLB 88

**Rio, Michel** 19(?)- .............................. **CLC 43**

**Ritsos, Giannes**
See Ritsos, Yannis

**Ritsos, Yannis** 1909-1990 ........ **CLC 6, 13, 31**
See also CA 77-80; 133; CANR 39, 61;
MTCW 1

**Ritter, Erika** 1948(?)- ........................ **CLC 52**

**Rivera, Jose Eustasio** 1889-1928 ... **TCLC 35**
See also CA 162; HW 1, 2

**Rivera, Tomas** 1935-1984
See also CA 49-52; CANR 32; DLB 82;
HLCS 2; HW 1

**Rivers, Conrad Kent** 1933-1968 ........ **CLC 1**
See also BW 1; CA 85-88; DLB 41

**Rivers, Elfrida**
See Bradley, Marion Zimmer

**Riverside, John**
See Heinlein, Robert A(nson)

**Rizal, Jose** 1861-1896 ...................... **NCLC 27**

**Roa Bastos, Augusto (Antonio)**
1917- .... **CLC 45; DAM MULT; HLC 2**
See also CA 131; DLB 113; HW 1

**Robbe-Grillet, Alain** 1922- .... **CLC 1, 2, 4, 6,**
**8, 10, 14, 43, 128**
See also CA 9-12R; CANR 33, 65; DLB
83; MTCW 1, 2

**Robbins, Harold** 1916-1997 .... **CLC 5; DAM**
**NOV**
See also CA 73-76; 162; CANR 26, 54;
DA3; MTCW 1, 2

**Robbins, Thomas Eugene** 1936-
See Robbins, Tom
See also CA 81-84; CANR 29, 59; DAM
NOV, POP; DA3; MTCW 1, 2

**Robbins, Tom** ........................ **CLC 9, 32, 64**
See also Robbins, Thomas Eugene AAYA
32; BEST 90:3; DLBY 80; MTCW 2

**Robbins, Trina** 1938- ........................ **CLC 21**
See also CA 128

**Roberts, Charles G(eorge) D(ouglas)**
1860-1943 ................................... **TCLC 8**
See also CA 105; CLR 33; DLB 92; SATA
88; SATA-Brief 29

**Roberts, Elizabeth Madox**
1886-1941 ................................... **TCLC 68**
See also CA 111; 166; DLB 9, 54, 102;
SATA 33; SATA-Brief 27

**Roberts, Kate** 1891-1985 .................. **CLC 15**
See also CA 107; 116

**Roberts, Keith (John Kingston)**
1935- ......................................... **CLC 14**
See also CA 25-28R; CANR 46

**Roberts, Kenneth (Lewis)**
1885-1957 ................................... **TCLC 23**
See also CA 109; DLB 9

**Roberts, Michele (B.)** 1949- .............. **CLC 48**
See also CA 115; CANR 58

**Robertson, Ellis**
See Ellison, Harlan (Jay); Silverberg, Robert

**Robertson, Thomas William** 1829-1871
**NCLC 35; DAM DRAM**

**Robeson, Kenneth**
See Dent, Lester

**Robinson, Edwin Arlington**
1869-1935 ... **TCLC 5; DA; DAC; DAM**
**MST, POET; PC 1**
See also CA 104; 133; CDALB 1865-1917;
DLB 54; MTCW 1, 2

**Robinson, Henry Crabb**
1775-1867 ................................... **NCLC 15**
See also DLB 107

**Robinson, Jill** 1936- .......................... **CLC 10**
See also CA 102; INT 102

**Robinson, Kim Stanley** 1952- ........... **CLC 34**
See also AAYA 26; CA 126; SATA 109

**Robinson, Lloyd**
See Silverberg, Robert

**Robinson, Marilynne** 1944- .............. **CLC 25**
See also CA 116; CANR 80; DLB 206

**Robinson, Smokey** ............................ **CLC 21**
See also Robinson, William, Jr.

**Robinson, William, Jr.** 1940-
See Robinson, Smokey
See also CA 116

**Robison, Mary** 1949- .................. **CLC 42, 98**
See also CA 113; 116; CANR 87; DLB 130;
INT 116

**Rod, Edouard** 1857-1910 ............... **TCLC 52**

**Roddenberry, Eugene Wesley** 1921-1991
See Roddenberry, Gene
See also CA 110; 135; CANR 37; SATA 45;
SATA-Obit 69

**Roddenberry, Gene** ........................... **CLC 17**
See also Roddenberry, Eugene Wesley
AAYA 5; SATA-Obit 69

**Rodgers, Mary** 1931- ........................ **CLC 12**
See also CA 49-52; CANR 8, 55; CLR 20;
INT CANR-8; JRDA; MAICYA; SATA 8

**Rodgers, W(illiam) R(obert)**
1909-1969 .................................... **CLC 7**
See also CA 85-88; DLB 20

**Rodman, Eric**
See Silverberg, Robert

**Rodman, Howard** 1920(?)-1985 ........ **CLC 65**
See also CA 118

**Rodman, Maia**
See Wojciechowska, Maia (Teresa)

**Rodo, Jose Enrique** 1872(?)-1917
See also CA 178; HLCS 2; HW 2

**Rodriguez, Claudio** 1934- ................ **CLC 10**
See also DLB 134

**Rodriguez, Richard** 1944-
See also CA 110; CANR 66; DAM MULT;
DLB 82; HLC 2; HW 1, 2

**Roelvaag, O(le) E(dvart)**
1876-1931 .................................. **TCLC 17**
See also CA 117; 171; DLB 9

**Roethke, Theodore (Huebner)** 1908-1963
**CLC 1, 3, 8, 11, 19, 46, 101; DAM**
**POET; PC 15**
See also CA 81-84; CABS 2; CDALB 1941-
1968; DA3; DLB 5, 206; MTCW 1, 2

**Rogers, Samuel** 1763-1855 ............. **NCLC 69**
See also DLB 93

**Rogers, Thomas Hunton** 1927- ......... **CLC 57**
See also CA 89-92; INT 89-92

**Rogers, Will(iam Penn Adair)** 1879-1935
**TCLC 8, 71; DAM MULT**
See also CA 105; 144; DA3; DLB 11;
MTCW 2; NNAL

**Rogin, Gilbert** 1929- ........................ **CLC 18**
See also CA 65-68; CANR 15

**Rohan, Koda**
See Koda Shigeyuki

**Rohlfs, Anna Katharine Green**
See Green, Anna Katharine

**Rohmer, Eric** ................................... **CLC 16**
See also Scherer, Jean-Marie Maurice

**Rohmer, Sax** .................................. **TCLC 28**
See also Ward, Arthur Henry Sarsfield DLB
70

**Roiphe, Anne (Richardson)** 1935- .. **CLC 3, 9**
See also CA 89-92; CANR 45, 73; DLBY
80; INT 89-92

**Rojas, Fernando de** 1465-1541 .......... **LC 23;**
**HLCS 1**

**Rojas, Gonzalo** 1917-
See also HLCS 2; HW 2

**Rojas, Gonzalo** 1917-
See also CA 178; HLCS 2

**Rolfe, Frederick (William Serafino Austin**
**Lewis Mary)** 1860-1913 ........ **TCLC 12**
See also CA 107; DLB 34, 156

**Rolland, Romain** 1866-1944 ........... **TCLC 23**
See also CA 118; DLB 65

**Rolle, Richard** c. 1300-c. 1349 ...... **CMLC 21**
See also DLB 146

**Rolvaag, O(le) E(dvart)**
See Roelvaag, O(le) E(dvart)

**Romain Arnaud, Saint**
See Aragon, Louis

**Romains, Jules** 1885-1972 .................. **CLC 7**
See also CA 85-88; CANR 34; DLB 65;
MTCW 1

**Romero, Jose Ruben** 1890-1952 .... **TCLC 14**
See also CA 114; 131; HW 1

**Ronsard, Pierre de** 1524-1585 . **LC 6, 54; PC**
**11**

**Rooke, Leon** 1934- . **CLC 25, 34; DAM POP**
See also CA 25-28R; CANR 23, 53

**Roosevelt, Franklin Delano**
1882-1945 ................................. **TCLC 93**
See also CA 116; 173

Roosevelt, Theodore 1858-1919 ..... **TCLC 69**
See also CA 115; 170; DLB 47, 186
Roper, William 1498-1578 .................... **LC 10**
Roquelaure, A. N.
See Rice, Anne
Rosa, Joao Guimaraes 1908-1967 ... **CLC 23;
HLCS 1**
See also CA 89-92; DLB 113
Rose, Wendy 1948- .. **CLC 85; DAM MULT;
PC 13**
See also CA 53-56; CANR 5, 51; DLB 175;
NNAL; SATA 12
Rosen, R. D.
See Rosen, Richard (Dean)
Rosen, Richard (Dean) 1949- .......... **CLC 39**
See also CA 77-80; CANR 62; INT
CANR-30
Rosenberg, Isaac 1890-1918 .......... **TCLC 12**
See also CA 107; DLB 20
Rosenblatt, Joe ................................. **CLC 15**
See also Rosenblatt, Joseph
Rosenblatt, Joseph 1933-
See Rosenblatt, Joe
See also CA 89-92; INT 89-92
Rosenfeld, Samuel
See Tzara, Tristan
Rosenstock, Sami
See Tzara, Tristan
Rosenstock, Samuel
See Tzara, Tristan
Rosenthal, M(acha) L(ouis)
1917-1996 ........................... **CLC 28**
See also CA 1-4R; 152; CAAS 6; CANR 4,
51; DLB 5; SATA 59
Ross, Barnaby
See Dannay, Frederic
Ross, Bernard L.
See Follett, Ken(neth Martin)
Ross, J. H.
See Lawrence, T(homas) E(dward)
Ross, John Hume
See Lawrence, T(homas) E(dward)
Ross, Martin
See Martin, Violet Florence
See also DLB 135
Ross, (James) Sinclair 1908-1996 ... **CLC 13;
DAC; DAM MST; SSC 24**
See also CA 73-76; CANR 81; DLB 88
Rossetti, Christina (Georgina) 1830-1894
**NCLC 2, 50, 66; DA; DAB; DAC; DAM
MST, POET; PC 7; WLC**
See also DA3; DLB 35, 163; MAICYA;
SATA 20
Rossetti, Dante Gabriel 1828-1882 . **NCLC 4,
77; DA; DAB; DAC; DAM MST,
POET; WLC**
See also CDBLB 1832-1890; DLB 35
Rossner, Judith (Perelman) 1935- . **CLC 6, 9,
29**
See also AITN 2; BEST 90:3; CA 17-20R;
CANR 18, 51, 73; DLB 6; INT CANR-
18; MTCW 1, 2
Rostand, Edmond (Eugene Alexis)
1868-1918 ........ **TCLC 6, 37; DA; DAB;
DAC; DAM DRAM, MST; DC 10**
See also CA 104; 126; DA3; DLB 192;
MTCW 1
Roth, Henry 1906-1995 ..... **CLC 2, 6, 11, 104**
See also CA 11-12; 149; CANR 38, 63;
CAP 1; DA3; DLB 28; MTCW 1, 2
Roth, Philip (Milton) 1933- ... **CLC 1, 2, 3, 4,
6, 9, 15, 22, 31, 47, 66, 86, 119; DA;
DAB; DAC; DAM MST, NOV, POP;
SSC 26; WLC**
See also BEST 90:3; CA 1-4R; CANR 1,
22, 36, 55; CDALB 1968-1988; DA3;
DLB 2, 28, 173; DLBY 82; MTCW 1, 2
Rothenberg, Jerome 1931- .......... **CLC 6, 57**
See also CA 45-48; CANR 1; DLB 5, 193

Roumain, Jacques (Jean Baptiste) 1907-1944
**TCLC 19; BLC 3; DAM MULT**
See also BW 1; CA 117; 125
Rourke, Constance (Mayfield) 1885-1941
**TCLC 12**
See also CA 107; YABC 1
Rousseau, Jean-Baptiste 1671-1741 ...... **LC 9**
Rousseau, Jean-Jacques 1712-1778 .... **LC 14,
36; DA; DAB; DAC; DAM MST; WLC**
See also DA3
Roussel, Raymond 1877-1933 ........ **TCLC 20**
See also CA 117
Rovit, Earl (Herbert) 1927- ................ **CLC 7**
See also CA 5-8R; CANR 12
Rowe, Elizabeth Singer 1674-1737 ..... **LC 44**
See also DLB 39, 95
Rowe, Nicholas 1674-1718 .................... **LC 8**
See also DLB 84
Rowley, Ames Dorrance
See Lovecraft, H(oward) P(hillips)
Rowson, Susanna Haswell 1762(?)-1824
**NCLC 5, 69**
See also DLB 37, 200
Roy, Arundhati 1960(?)- .................. **CLC 109**
See also CA 163; DLBY 97
Roy, Gabrielle 1909-1983 .......... **CLC 10, 14;
DAB; DAC; DAM MST**
See also CA 53-56; 110; CANR 5, 61; DLB
68; MTCW 1; SATA 104
Royko, Mike 1932-1997 ................... **CLC 109**
See also CA 89-92; 157; CANR 26
Rozewicz, Tadeusz 1921- .. **CLC 9, 23; DAM
POET**
See also CA 108; CANR 36, 66; DA3;
MTCW 1, 2
Ruark, Gibbons 1941- ......................... **CLC 3**
See also CA 33-36R; CAAS 23; CANR 14,
31, 57; DLB 120
Rubens, Bernice (Ruth) 1923- .... **CLC 19, 31**
See also CA 25-28R; CANR 33, 65; DLB
14, 207; MTCW 1
Rubin, Harold
See Robbins, Harold
Rudkin, (James) David 1936- .......... **CLC 14**
See also CA 89-92; DLB 13
Rudnik, Raphael 1933- ....................... **CLC 7**
See also CA 29-32R
Ruffian, M.
See Hasek, Jaroslav (Matej Frantisek)
Ruiz, Jose Martinez ......................... **CLC 11**
See also Martinez Ruiz, Jose
Rukeyser, Muriel 1913-1980 . **CLC 6, 10, 15,
27; DAM POET; PC 12**
See also CA 5-8R; 93-96; CANR 26, 60;
DA3; DLB 48; MTCW 1, 2; SATA-Obit
22
Rule, Jane (Vance) 1931- .................. **CLC 27**
See also CA 25-28R; CAAS 18; CANR 12,
87; DLB 60
Rulfo, Juan 1918-1986 ...... **CLC 8, 80; DAM
MULT; HLC 2; SSC 25**
See also CA 85-88; 118; CANR 26; DLB
113; HW 1, 2; MTCW 1, 2
Rumi, Jalal al-Din 1297-1373 ....... **CMLC 20**
Runeberg, Johan 1804-1877 .......... **NCLC 41**
Runyon, (Alfred) Damon
1884(?)-1946 ........................... **TCLC 10**
See also CA 107; 165; DLB 11, 86, 171;
MTCW 2
Rush, Norman 1933- ......................... **CLC 44**
See also CA 121; 126; INT 126
Rushdie, (Ahmed) Salman 1947- .... **CLC 23,
31, 55, 100; DAB; DAC; DAM MST,
NOV, POP; WLCS**
See also BEST 89:3; CA 108; 111; CANR
33, 56; DA3; DLB 194; INT 111; MTCW
1, 2

Rushforth, Peter (Scott) 1945- .......... **CLC 19**
See also CA 101
Ruskin, John 1819-1900 ................. **TCLC 63**
See also CA 114; 129; CDBLB 1832-1890;
DLB 55, 163, 190; SATA 24
Russ, Joanna 1937- ........................... **CLC 15**
See also CANR 11, 31, 65; DLB 8; MTCW
1
Russell, George William 1867-1935
See Baker, Jean H.
See also CA 104; 153; CDBLB 1890-1914;
DAM POET
Russell, (Henry) Ken(neth Alfred)
1927- ........................................ **CLC 16**
See also CA 105
Russell, William Martin 1947- ........ **CLC 60**
See also CA 164
Rutherford, Mark .......................... **TCLC 25**
See also White, William Hale DLB 18
Ruyslinck, Ward 1929- ...................... **CLC 14**
See also Belser, Reimond Karel Maria de
Ryan, Cornelius (John) 1920-1974 ...... **CLC 7**
See also CA 69-72; 53-56; CANR 38
Ryan, Michael 1946- ......................... **CLC 65**
See also CA 49-52; DLBY 82
Ryan, Tim
See Dent, Lester
Rybakov, Anatoli (Naumovich) 1911-1998
**CLC 23, 53**
See also CA 126; 135; 172; SATA 79;
SATA-Obit 108
Ryder, Jonathan
See Ludlum, Robert
Ryga, George 1932-1987 ....... **CLC 14; DAC;
DAM MST**
See also CA 101; 124; CANR 43; DLB 60
S. H.
See Hartmann, Sadakichi
S. S.
See Sassoon, Siegfried (Lorraine)
Saba, Umberto 1883-1957 ............. **TCLC 33**
See also CA 144; CANR 79; DLB 114
Sabatini, Rafael 1875-1950 ............ **TCLC 47**
See also CA 162
Sabato, Ernesto (R.) 1911- ........ **CLC 10, 23;
DAM MULT; HLC 2**
See also CA 97-100; CANR 32, 65; DLB
145; HW 1, 2; MTCW 1, 2
Sa-Carneiro, Mario de 1890-1916 . **TCLC 83**
Sacastru, Martin
See Bioy Casares, Adolfo
Sacastru, Martin
See Bioy Casares, Adolfo
Sacher-Masoch, Leopold von 1836(?)-1895
**NCLC 31**
Sachs, Marilyn (Stickle) 1927- ......... **CLC 35**
See also AAYA 2; CA 17-20R; CANR 13,
47; CLR 2; JRDA; MAICYA; SAAS 2;
SATA 3, 68; SATA-Essay 110
Sachs, Nelly 1891-1970 ............... **CLC 14, 98**
See also CA 17-18; 25-28R; CANR 87;
CAP 2; MTCW 2
Sackler, Howard (Oliver)
1929-1982 ................................. **CLC 14**
See also CA 61-64; 108; CANR 30; DLB 7
Sacks, Oliver (Wolf) 1933- ............... **CLC 67**
See also CA 53-56; CANR 28, 50, 76; DA3;
INT CANR-28; MTCW 1, 2
Sadakichi
See Hartmann, Sadakichi
Sade, Donatien Alphonse Francois, Comte
de 1740-1814 .......................... **NCLC 47**
Sadoff, Ira 1945- ................................. **CLC 9**
See also CA 53-56; CANR 5, 21; DLB 120
Saetone
See Camus, Albert
Safire, William 1929- ........................ **CLC 10**
See also CA 17-20R; CANR 31, 54

**Sagan, Carl (Edward)** 1934-1996 .... **CLC 30, 112**
See also AAYA 2; CA 25-28R; 155; CANR 11, 36, 74; DA3; MTCW 1, 2; SATA 58; SATA-Obit 94

**Sagan, Francoise** ............. **CLC 3, 6, 9, 17, 36**
See also Quoirez, Francoise DLB 83; MTCW 2

**Sahgal, Nayantara (Pandit)** 1927- .... **CLC 41**
See also CA 9-12R; CANR 11, 88

**Saint, H(arry) F.** 1941- ..................... **CLC 50**
See also CA 127

**St. Aubin de Teran, Lisa** 1953-
See Teran, Lisa St. Aubin de
See also CA 118; 126; INT 126

**Saint Birgitta of Sweden** c.
1303-1373 .............................. **CMLC 24**

**Sainte-Beuve, Charles Augustin** 1804-1869
**NCLC 5**

**Saint-Exupery, Antoine (Jean Baptiste
Marie Roger) de** 1900-1944 .... **TCLC 2, 56; DAM NOV; WLC**
See also CA 108; 132; CLR 10; DA3; DLB 72; MAICYA; MTCW 1, 2; SATA 20

**St. John, David**
See Hunt, E(verette) Howard, (Jr.)

**Saint-John Perse**
See Leger, (Marie-Rene Auguste) Alexis Saint-Leger

**Saintsbury, George (Edward Bateman)**
1845-1933 ................................ **TCLC 31**
See also CA 160; DLB 57, 149

**Sait Faik** .................................... **TCLC 23**
See also Abasiyanik, Sait Faik

**Saki** .................................... **TCLC 3; SSC 12**
See also Munro, H(ector) H(ugh) MTCW 2

**Sala, George Augustus** .................... **NCLC 46**

**Saladin** 1138-1193 ......................... **CMLC 38**

**Salama, Hannu** 1936- .................... **CLC 18**

**Salamanca, J(ack) R(ichard)** 1922- .. **CLC 4, 15**
See also CA 25-28R

**Salas, Floyd Francis** 1931-
See also CA 119; CAAS 27; CANR 44, 75; DAM MULT; DLB 82; HLC 2; HW 1, 2; MTCW 2

**Sale, J. Kirkpatrick**
See Sale, Kirkpatrick

**Sale, Kirkpatrick** 1937- .................... **CLC 68**
See also CA 13-16R; CANR 10

**Salinas, Luis Omar** 1937- ..... **CLC 90; DAM MULT; HLC 2**
See also CA 131; CANR 81; DLB 82; HW 1, 2

**Salinas (y Serrano), Pedro** 1891(?)-1951
**TCLC 17**
See also CA 117; DLB 134

**Salinger, J(erome) D(avid)** 1919- .. **CLC 1, 3, 8, 12, 55, 56; DA; DAB; DAC; DAM MST, NOV, POP; SSC 2, 28; WLC**
See also AAYA 2; CA 5-8R; CANR 39; CDALB 1941-1968; CLR 18; DA3; DLB 2, 102, 173; MAICYA; MTCW 1, 2; SATA 67

**Salisbury, John**
See Caute, (John) David

**Salter, James** 1925- ................. **CLC 7, 52, 59**
See also CA 73-76; DLB 130

**Saltus, Edgar (Everton)** 1855-1921 . **TCLC 8**
See also CA 105; DLB 202

**Saltykov, Mikhail Evgrafovich** 1826-1889
**NCLC 16**

**Samarakis, Antonis** 1919- .................. **CLC 5**
See also CA 25-28R; CAAS 16; CANR 36

**Sanchez, Florencio** 1875-1910 ........ **TCLC 37**
See also CA 153; HW 1

**Sanchez, Luis Rafael** 1936- .............. **CLC 23**
See also CA 128; DLB 145; HW 1

**Sanchez, Sonia** 1934- .... **CLC 5, 116; BLC 3; DAM MULT; PC 9**
See also BW 2, 3; CA 33-36R; CANR 24, 49, 74; CLR 18; DA3; DLB 41; DLBD 8; MAICYA; MTCW 1, 2; SATA 22

**Sand, George** 1804-1876 ..... **NCLC 2, 42, 57; DA; DAB; DAC; DAM MST, NOV; WLC**
See also DA3; DLB 119, 192

**Sandburg, Carl (August)** 1878-1967 . **CLC 1, 4, 10, 15, 35; DA; DAB; DAC; DAM MST, POET; PC 2; WLC**
See also AAYA 24; CA 5-8R; 25-28R; CANR 35; CDALB 1865-1917; DA3; DLB 17, 54; MAICYA; MTCW 1, 2; SATA 8

**Sandburg, Charles**
See Sandburg, Carl (August)

**Sandburg, Charles A.**
See Sandburg, Carl (August)

**Sanders, (James) Ed(ward)** 1939- ... **CLC 53; DAM POET**
See also CA 13-16R; CAAS 21; CANR 13, 44, 78; DLB 16

**Sanders, Lawrence** 1920-1998 ......... **CLC 41; DAM POP**
See also BEST 89:4; CA 81-84; 165; CANR 33, 62; DA3; MTCW 1

**Sanders, Noah**
See Blount, Roy (Alton), Jr.

**Sanders, Winston P.**
See Anderson, Poul (William)

**Sandoz, Mari(e Susette)** 1896-1966 .. **CLC 28**
See also CA 1-4R; 25-28R; CANR 17, 64; DLB 9, 212; MTCW 1, 2; SATA 5

**Saner, Reg(inald Anthony)** 1931- ....... **CLC 9**
See also CA 65-68

**Sankara** 788-820 ......................... **CMLC 32**

**Sannazaro, Jacopo** 1456(?)-1530 .......... **LC 8**

**Sansom, William** 1912-1976 .......... **CLC 2, 6; DAM NOV; SSC 21**
See also CA 5-8R; 65-68; CANR 42; DLB 139; MTCW 1

**Santayana, George** 1863-1952 ........ **TCLC 40**
See also CA 115; DLB 54, 71; DLBD 13

**Santiago, Danny** ................................ **CLC 33**
See also James, Daniel (Lewis) DLB 122

**Santmyer, Helen Hoover** 1895-1986 . **CLC 33**
See also CA 1-4R; 118; CANR 15, 33; DLBY 84; MTCW 1

**Santoka, Taneda** 1882-1940 ........... **TCLC 72**

**Santos, Bienvenido N(uqui)**
1911-1996 .......... **CLC 22; DAM MULT**
See also CA 101; 151; CANR 19, 46

**Sapper** ................................ **TCLC 44**
See also McNeile, Herman Cyril

**Sapphire**
See Sapphire, Brenda

**Sapphire, Brenda** 1950- ..................... **CLC 99**

**Sappho** fl. 6th cent. B.C.- ..... **CMLC 3; DAM POET; PC 5**
See also DA3; DLB 176

**Saramago, Jose** 1922- ..... **CLC 119; HLCS 1**
See also CA 153

**Sarduy, Severo** 1937-1993 .......... **CLC 6, 97; HLCS 1**
See also CA 89-92; 142; CANR 58, 81; DLB 113; HW 1, 2

**Sargeson, Frank** 1903-1982 ............... **CLC 31**
See also CA 25-28R; 106; CANR 38, 79

**Sarmiento, Domingo Faustino** 1811-1888
See also HLCS 2

**Sarmiento, Felix Ruben Garcia**
See Dario, Ruben

**Saro-Wiwa, Ken(ule Beeson)**
1941-1995 ................................ **CLC 114**
See also BW 2; CA 142; 150; CANR 60; DLB 157

**Saroyan, William** 1908-1981 ... **CLC 1, 8, 10, 29, 34, 56; DA; DAB; DAC; DAM DRAM, MST, NOV; SSC 21; WLC**
See also CA 5-8R; 103; CANR 30; CDALBS; DA3; DLB 7, 9, 86; DLBY 81; MTCW 1, 2; SATA 23; SATA-Obit 24

**Sarraute, Nathalie** 1900- . **CLC 1, 2, 4, 8, 10, 31, 80**
See also CA 9-12R; CANR 23, 66; DLB 83; MTCW 1, 2

**Sarton, (Eleanor) May** 1912-1995 ..... **CLC 4, 14, 49, 91; DAM POET**
See also CA 1-4R; 149; CANR 1, 34, 55; DLB 48; DLBY 81; INT CANR-34; MTCW 1, 2; SATA 36; SATA-Obit 86

**Sartre, Jean-Paul** 1905-1980 . **CLC 1, 4, 7, 9, 13, 18, 24, 44, 50, 52; DA; DAB; DAC; DAM DRAM, MST, NOV; DC 3; SSC 32; WLC**
See also CA 9-12R; 97-100; CANR 21; DA3; DLB 72; MTCW 1, 2

**Sassoon, Siegfried (Lorraine)**
1886-1967 . **CLC 36; DAB; DAM MST, NOV, POET; PC 12**
See also CA 104; 25-28R; CANR 36; DLB 20, 191; DLBD 18; MTCW 1, 2

**Satterfield, Charles**
See Pohl, Frederik

**Saul, John (W. III)** 1942- ...... **CLC 46; DAM NOV, POP**
See also AAYA 10; BEST 90:4; CA 81-84; CANR 16, 40, 81; SATA 98

**Saunders, Caleb**
See Heinlein, Robert A(nson)

**Saura (Atares), Carlos** 1932- ........... **CLC 20**
See also CA 114; 131; CANR 79; HW 1

**Sauser-Hall, Frederic** 1887-1961 ...... **CLC 18**
See also Cendrars, Blaise CA 102; 93-96; CANR 36, 62; MTCW 1

**Saussure, Ferdinand de**
1857-1913 ................................ **TCLC 49**

**Savage, Catharine**
See Brosman, Catharine Savage

**Savage, Thomas** 1915- ..................... **CLC 40**
See also CA 126; 132; CAAS 15; INT 132

**Savan, Glenn** 19(?)- ......................... **CLC 50**

**Sayers, Dorothy L(eigh)**
1893-1957 ....... **TCLC 2, 15; DAM POP**
See also CA 104; 119; CANR 60; CDBLB 1914-1945; DLB 10, 36, 77, 100; MTCW 1, 2

**Sayers, Valerie** 1952- ................ **CLC 50, 122**
See also CA 134; CANR 61

**Sayles, John (Thomas)** 1950- . **CLC 7, 10, 14**
See also CA 57-60; CANR 41, 84; DLB 44

**Scammell, Michael** 1935- .................. **CLC 34**
See also CA 156

**Scannell, Vernon** 1922- ..................... **CLC 49**
See also CA 5-8R; CANR 8, 24, 57; DLB 27; SATA 59

**Scarlett, Susan**
See Streatfeild, (Mary) Noel

**Scarron**
See Mikszath, Kalman

**Schaeffer, Susan Fromberg** 1941- ..... **CLC 6, 11, 22**
See also CA 49-52; CANR 18, 65; DLB 28; MTCW 1, 2; SATA 22

**Schary, Jill**
See Robinson, Jill

**Schell, Jonathan** 1943- ..................... **CLC 35**
See also CA 73-76; CANR 12

**Schelling, Friedrich Wilhelm Joseph von**
1775-1854 ................................ **NCLC 30**
See also DLB 90

**Schendel, Arthur van** 1874-1946 ... **TCLC 56**

**Scherer, Jean-Marie Maurice** 1920-
See Rohmer, Eric
See also CA 110

**Schevill, James (Erwin)** 1920- ............ **CLC 7**
See also CA 5-8R; CAAS 12

**Schiller, Friedrich** 1759-1805 . **NCLC 39, 69;
DAM DRAM; DC 12**
See also DLB 94

**Schisgal, Murray (Joseph)** 1926- ....... **CLC 6**
See also CA 21-24R; CANR 48, 86

**Schlee, Ann** 1934- .............................. **CLC 35**
See also CA 101; CANR 29, 88; SATA 44;
SATA-Brief 36

**Schlegel, August Wilhelm von** 1767-1845
**NCLC 15**
See also DLB 94

**Schlegel, Friedrich** 1772-1829 ........ **NCLC 45**
See also DLB 90

**Schlegel, Johann Elias (von)** 1719(?)-1749
**LC 5**

**Schlesinger, Arthur M(eier), Jr.**
1917- ......................................... **CLC 84**
See also AITN 1; CA 1-4R; CANR 1, 28,
58; DLB 17; INT CANR-28; MTCW 1,
2; SATA 61

**Schmidt, Arno (Otto)** 1914-1979 ...... **CLC 56**
See also CA 128; 109; DLB 69

**Schmitz, Aron Hector** 1861-1928
See Svevo, Italo
See also CA 104; 122; MTCW 1

**Schnackenberg, Gjertrud** 1953- ....... **CLC 40**
See also CA 116; DLB 120

**Schneider, Leonard Alfred** 1925-1966
See Bruce, Lenny
See also CA 89-92

**Schnitzler, Arthur** 1862-1931 . **TCLC 4; SSC
15**
See also CA 104; DLB 81, 118

**Schoenberg, Arnold** 1874-1951 ...... **TCLC 75**
See also CA 109

**Schonberg, Arnold**
See Schoenberg, Arnold

**Schopenhauer, Arthur** 1788-1860 .. **NCLC 51**
See also DLB 90

**Schor, Sandra (M.)** 1932(?)-1990 ..... **CLC 65**
See also CA 132

**Schorer, Mark** 1908-1977 .................... **CLC 9**
See also CA 5-8R; 73-76; CANR 7; DLB
103

**Schrader, Paul (Joseph)** 1946- ......... **CLC 26**
See also CA 37-40R; CANR 41; DLB 44

**Schreiner, Olive (Emilie Albertina)**
1855-1920 ................................ **TCLC 9**
See also CA 105; 154; DLB 18, 156, 190

**Schulberg, Budd (Wilson)** 1914- .. **CLC 7, 48**
See also CA 25-28R; CANR 19, 87; DLB
6, 26, 28; DLBY 81

**Schulz, Bruno** 1892-1942 .. **TCLC 5, 51; SSC
13**
See also CA 115; 123; CANR 86; MTCW 2

**Schulz, Charles M(onroe)** 1922- ....... **CLC 12**
See also CA 9-12R; CANR 6; INT
CANR-6; SATA 10

**Schumacher, E(rnst) F(riedrich)** 1911-1977
**CLC 80**
See also CA 81-84; 73-76; CANR 34, 85

**Schuyler, James Marcus** 1923-1991 .. **CLC 5,
23; DAM POET**
See also CA 101; 134; DLB 5, 169; INT
101

**Schwartz, Delmore (David)**
1913-1966 ... **CLC 2, 4, 10, 45, 87; PC 8**
See also CA 17-18; 25-28R; CANR 35;
CAP 2; DLB 28, 48; MTCW 1, 2

**Schwartz, Ernst**
See Ozu, Yasujiro

**Schwartz, John Burnham** 1965- ....... **CLC 59**
See also CA 132

**Schwartz, Lynne Sharon** 1939- ........ **CLC 31**
See also CA 103; CANR 44; MTCW 2

**Schwartz, Muriel A.**
See Eliot, T(homas) S(tearns)

**Schwarz-Bart, Andre** 1928- ............ **CLC 2, 4**
See also CA 89-92

**Schwarz-Bart, Simone** 1938- . **CLC 7; BLCS**
See also BW 2; CA 97-100

**Schwitters, Kurt (Hermann Edward Karl
Julius)** 1887-1948 ..................... **TCLC 95**
See also CA 158

**Schwob, Marcel (Mayer Andre)** 1867-1905
**TCLC 20**
See also CA 117; 168; DLB 123

**Sciascia, Leonardo** 1921-1989 .. **CLC 8, 9, 41**
See also CA 85-88; 130; CANR 35; DLB
177; MTCW 1

**Scoppettone, Sandra** 1936- .............. **CLC 26**
See also AAYA 11; CA 5-8R; CANR 41,
73; SATA 9, 92

**Scorsese, Martin** 1942- ................ **CLC 20, 89**
See also CA 110; 114; CANR 46, 85

**Scotland, Jay**
See Jakes, John (William)

**Scott, Duncan Campbell**
1862-1947 ...................... **TCLC 6; DAC**
See also CA 104; 153; DLB 92

**Scott, Evelyn** 1893-1963 .................... **CLC 43**
See also CA 104; 112; CANR 64; DLB 9,
48

**Scott, F(rancis) R(eginald)**
1899-1985 ................................ **CLC 22**
See also CA 101; 114; CANR 87; DLB 88;
INT 101

**Scott, Frank**
See Scott, F(rancis) R(eginald)

**Scott, Joanna** 1960- ............................ **CLC 50**
See also CA 126; CANR 53

**Scott, Paul (Mark)** 1920-1978 ...... **CLC 9, 60**
See also CA 81-84; 77-80; CANR 33; DLB
14, 207; MTCW 1

**Scott, Sarah** 1723-1795 ........................ **LC 44**
See also DLB 39

**Scott, Walter** 1771-1832 . **NCLC 15, 69; DA;
DAB; DAC; DAM MST, NOV, POET;
PC 13; SSC 32; WLC**
See also AAYA 22; CDBLB 1789-1832;
DLB 93, 107, 116, 144, 159; YABC 2

**Scribe, (Augustin) Eugene**
1791-1861 ..... **NCLC 16; DAM DRAM;
DC 5**
See also DLB 192

**Scrum, R.**
See Crumb, R(obert)

**Scudery, Madeleine de** 1607-1701 ........ **LC 2**

**Scum**
See Crumb, R(obert)

**Scumbag, Little Bobby**
See Crumb, R(obert)

**Seabrook, John**
See Hubbard, L(afayette) Ron(ald)

**Sealy, I. Allan** 1951- .......................... **CLC 55**

**Search, Alexander**
See Pessoa, Fernando (Antonio Nogueira)

**Sebastian, Lee**
See Silverberg, Robert

**Sebastian Owl**
See Thompson, Hunter S(tockton)

**Sebestyen, Ouida** 1924- ..................... **CLC 30**
See also AAYA 8; CA 107; CANR 40; CLR
17; JRDA; MAICYA; SAAS 10; SATA
39

**Secundus, H. Scriblerus**
See Fielding, Henry

**Sedges, John**
See Buck, Pearl S(ydenstricker)

**Sedgwick, Catharine Maria**
1789-1867 ................................ **NCLC 19**
See also DLB 1, 74

**Seelye, John (Douglas)** 1931- .............. **CLC 7**
See also CA 97-100; CANR 70; INT 97-
100

**Seferiades, Giorgos Stylianou** 1900-1971
See Seferis, George
See also CA 5-8R; 33-36R; CANR 5, 36;
MTCW 1

**Seferis, George** ............................ **CLC 5, 11**
See also Seferiades, Giorgos Stylianou

**Segal, Erich (Wolf)** 1937- . **CLC 3, 10; DAM
POP**
See also BEST 89:1; CA 25-28R; CANR
20, 36, 65; DLBY 86; INT CANR-20;
MTCW 1

**Seger, Bob** 1945- ................................ **CLC 35**

**Seghers, Anna** ........................................ **CLC 7**
See also Radvanyi, Netty DLB 69

**Seidel, Frederick (Lewis)** 1936- ........ **CLC 18**
See also CA 13-16R; CANR 8; DLBY 84

**Seifert, Jaroslav** 1901-1986 .. **CLC 34, 44, 93**
See also CA 127; MTCW 1, 2

**Sei Shonagon** c. 966-1017(?) .......... **CMLC 6**

**Séjour, Victor** 1817-1874 ..................... **DC 10**
See also DLB 50

**Sejour Marcou et Ferrand, Juan Victor**
See S

**Selby, Hubert, Jr.** 1928- ........ **CLC 1, 2, 4, 8;
SSC 20**
See also CA 13-16R; CANR 33, 85; DLB 2

**Selzer, Richard** 1928- ......................... **CLC 74**
See also CA 65-68; CANR 14

**Sembene, Ousmane**
See Ousmane, Sembene

**Senancour, Etienne Pivert de** 1770-1846
**NCLC 16**
See also DLB 119

**Sender, Ramon (Jose)** 1902-1982 ...... **CLC 8;
DAM MULT; HLC 2**
See also CA 5-8R; 105; CANR 8; HW 1;
MTCW 1

**Seneca, Lucius Annaeus** c. 1-c.
65 ......... **CMLC 6; DAM DRAM; DC 5**
See also DLB 211

**Senghor, Leopold Sedar** 1906- ........ **CLC 54;
BLC 3; DAM MULT, POET; PC 25**
See also BW 2; CA 116; 125; CANR 47,
74; MTCW 1, 2

**Senna, Danzy** 1970- .......................... **CLC 119**
See also CA 169

**Serling, (Edward) Rod(man)**
1924-1975 ................................ **CLC 30**
See also AAYA 14; AITN 1; CA 162; 57-
60; DLB 26

**Serna, Ramon Gomez de la**
See Gomez de la Serna, Ramon

**Serpieres**
See Guillevic, (Eugene)

**Service, Robert**
See Service, Robert W(illiam)
See also DAB; DLB 92

**Service, Robert W(illiam)** 1874(?)-1958
**TCLC 15; DA; DAC; DAM MST,
POET; WLC**
See also Service, Robert CA 115; 140;
CANR 84; SATA 20

**Seth, Vikram** 1952- .......... **CLC 43, 90; DAM
MULT**
See also CA 121; 127; CANR 50, 74; DA3;
DLB 120; INT 127; MTCW 2

**Seton, Cynthia Propper** 1926-1982 .. **CLC 27**
See also CA 5-8R; 108; CANR 7

**Seton, Ernest (Evan) Thompson** 1860-1946
**TCLC 31**
See also CA 109; CLR 59; DLB 92; DLBD
13; JRDA; SATA 18

**Seton-Thompson, Ernest**
See Seton, Ernest (Evan) Thompson

**Settle, Mary Lee** 1918- ............... **CLC 19, 61**
See also CA 89-92; CAAS 1; CANR 44, 87; DLB 6; INT 89-92

**Seuphor, Michel**
See Arp, Jean

**Sevigne, Marie (de Rabutin-Chantal)**
Marquise de 1626-1696 .............. **LC 11**

**Sewall, Samuel** 1652-1730 .................. **LC 38**
See also DLB 24

**Sexton, Anne (Harvey)** 1928-1974 ..... **CLC 2, 4, 6, 8, 10, 15, 53; DA; DAB; DAC; DAM MST, POET; PC 2; WLC**
See also CA 1-4R; 53-56; CABS 2; CANR 3, 36; CDALB 1941-1968; DA3; DLB 5, 169; MTCW 1, 2; SATA 10

**Shaara, Jeff** 1952- ............................ **CLC 119**
See also CA 163

**Shaara, Michael (Joseph, Jr.)**
1929-1988 .............. **CLC 15; DAM POP**
See also AITN 1; CA 102; 125; CANR 52, 85; DLBY 83

**Shackleton, C. C.**
See Aldiss, Brian W(ilson)

**Shacochis, Bob** .................................. **CLC 39**
See also Shacochis, Robert G.

**Shacochis, Robert G.** 1951-
See Shacochis, Bob
See also CA 119; 124; INT 124

**Shaffer, Anthony (Joshua)** 1926- ..... **CLC 19; DAM DRAM**
See also CA 110; 116; DLB 13

**Shaffer, Peter (Levin)** 1926- .. **CLC 5, 14, 18, 37, 60; DAB; DAM DRAM, MST; DC 7**
See also CA 25-28R; CANR 25, 47, 74; CDBLB 1960 to Present; DA3; DLB 13; MTCW 1, 2

**Shakey, Bernard**
See Young, Neil

**Shalamov, Varlam (Tikhonovich)**
1907(?)-1982 ............................ **CLC 18**
See also CA 129; 105

**Shamlu, Ahmad** 1925- ...................... **CLC 10**

**Shammas, Anton** 1951- ..................... **CLC 55**

**Shange, Ntozake** 1948- .... **CLC 8, 25, 38, 74, 126; BLC 3; DAM DRAM, MULT; DC 3**
See also AAYA 9; BW 2; CA 85-88; CABS 3; CANR 27, 48, 74; DA3; DLB 38; MTCW 1, 2

**Shanley, John Patrick** 1950- ............. **CLC 75**
See also CA 128; 133; CANR 83

**Shapcott, Thomas W(illiam)** 1935- .. **CLC 38**
See also CA 69-72; CANR 49, 83

**Shapiro, Jane** .................................... **CLC 76**

**Shapiro, Karl (Jay)** 1913- . **CLC 4, 8, 15, 53; PC 25**
See also CA 1-4R; CAAS 6; CANR 1, 36, 66; DLB 48; MTCW 1, 2

**Sharp, William** 1855-1905 .............. **TCLC 39**
See also CA 160; DLB 156

**Sharpe, Thomas Ridley** 1928-
See Sharpe, Tom
See also CA 114; 122; CANR 85; INT 122

**Sharpe, Tom** ........................................ **CLC 36**
See also Sharpe, Thomas Ridley DLB 14

**Shaw, Bernard** ................................... **TCLC 45**
See also Shaw, George Bernard BW 1; MTCW 2

**Shaw, G. Bernard**
See Shaw, George Bernard

**Shaw, George Bernard** 1856-1950 .. **TCLC 3, 9, 21; DA; DAB; DAC; DAM DRAM, MST; WLC**
See also Shaw, Bernard CA 104; 128; CDBLB 1914-1945; DA3; DLB 10, 57, 190; MTCW 1, 2

**Shaw, Henry Wheeler** 1818-1885 .. **NCLC 15**
See also DLB 11

**Shaw, Irwin** 1913-1984 .......... **CLC 7, 23, 34; DAM DRAM, POP**
See also AITN 1; CA 13-16R; 112; CANR 21; CDALB 1941-1968; DLB 6, 102; DLBY 84; MTCW 1, 21

**Shaw, Robert** 1927-1978 ..................... **CLC 5**
See also AITN 1; CA 1-4R; 81-84; CANR 4; DLB 13, 14

**Shaw, T. E.**
See Lawrence, T(homas) E(dward)

**Shawn, Wallace** 1943- ........................ **CLC 41**
See also CA 112

**Shea, Lisa** 1953- ................................. **CLC 86**
See also CA 147

**Sheed, Wilfrid (John Joseph)** 1930- . **CLC 2, 4, 10, 53**
See also CA 65-68; CANR 30, 66; DLB 6; MTCW 1, 2

**Sheldon, Alice Hastings Bradley**
1915(?)-1987
See Tiptree, James, Jr.
See also CA 108; 122; CANR 34; INT 108; MTCW 1

**Sheldon, John**
See Bloch, Robert (Albert)

**Shelley, Mary Wollstonecraft (Godwin)**
1797-1851 ..... **NCLC 14, 59; DA; DAB; DAC; DAM MST, NOV; WLC**
See also AAYA 20; CDBLB 1789-1832; DA3; DLB 110, 116, 159, 178; SATA 29

**Shelley, Percy Bysshe** 1792-1822 .. **NCLC 18; DA; DAB; DAC; DAM MST, POET; PC 14; WLC**
See also CDBLB 1789-1832; DA3; DLB 96, 110, 158

**Shepard, Jim** 1956- ........................... **CLC 36**
See also CA 137; CANR 59; SATA 90

**Shepard, Lucius** 1947- ....................... **CLC 34**
See also CA 128; 141; CANR 81

**Shepard, Sam** 1943- .... **CLC 4, 6, 17, 34, 41, 44; DAM DRAM; DC 5**
See also AAYA 1; CA 69-72; CABS 3; CANR 22; DA3; DLB 7, 212; MTCW 1, 2

**Shepherd, Michael**
See Ludlum, Robert

**Sherburne, Zoa (Lillian Morin)** 1912-1995
**CLC 30**
See also AAYA 13; CA 1-4R; 176; CANR 3, 37; MAICYA; SAAS 18; SATA 3

**Sheridan, Frances** 1724-1766 ................ **LC 7**
See also DLB 39, 84

**Sheridan, Richard Brinsley**
1751-1816 .. **NCLC 5; DA; DAB; DAC; DAM DRAM, MST; DC 1; WLC**
See also CDBLB 1660-1789; DLB 89

**Sherman, Jonathan Marc** ................. **CLC 55**

**Sherman, Martin** 1941(?)- ................ **CLC 19**
See also CA 116; 123; CANR 86

**Sherwin, Judith Johnson** 1936-
See Johnson, Judith (Emlyn)
See also CANR 85

**Sherwood, Frances** 1940- .................. **CLC 81**
See also CA 146

**Sherwood, Robert E(mmet)**
1896-1955 ......... **TCLC 3; DAM DRAM**
See also CA 104; 153; CANR 86; DLB 7, 26

**Shestov, Lev** 1866-1938 ................... **TCLC 56**

**Shevchenko, Taras** 1814-1861 ........ **NCLC 54**

**Shiel, M(atthew) P(hipps)**
1865-1947 ................................... **TCLC 8**
See also Holmes, Gordon CA 106; 160; DLB 153; MTCW 2

**Shields, Carol** 1935- ....... **CLC 91, 113; DAC**
See also CA 81-84; CANR 51, 74; DA3; MTCW 2

**Shields, David** 1956- ......................... **CLC 97**
See also CA 124; CANR 48

**Shiga, Naoya** 1883-1971 ..... **CLC 33; SSC 23**
See also CA 101; 33-36R; DLB 180

**Shikibu, Murasaki** c. 978-c. 1014 ... **CMLC 1**

**Shilts, Randy** 1951-1994 ................... **CLC 85**
See also AAYA 19; CA 115; 127; 144; CANR 45; DA3; INT 127; MTCW 2

**Shimazaki, Haruki** 1872-1943
See Shimazaki Toson
See also CA 105; 134; CANR 84

**Shimazaki Toson** 1872-1943 ............ **TCLC 5**
See also Shimazaki, Haruki DLB 180

**Sholokhov, Mikhail (Aleksandrovich)**
1905-1984 ............................... **CLC 7, 15**
See also CA 101; 112; MTCW 1, 2; SATA-Obit 36

**Shone, Patric**
See Hanley, James

**Shreve, Susan Richards** 1939- .......... **CLC 23**
See also CA 49-52; CAAS 5; CANR 5, 38, 69; MAICYA; SATA 46, 95; SATA-Brief 41

**Shue, Larry** 1946-1985 .......... **CLC 52; DAM DRAM**
See also CA 145; 117

**Shu-Jen, Chou** 1881-1936
See Lu Hsun
See also CA 104

**Shulman, Alix Kates** 1932- ........... **CLC 2, 10**
See also CA 29-32R; CANR 43; SATA 7

**Shuster, Joe** 1914- ............................ **CLC 21**

**Shute, Nevil** ........................................ **CLC 30**
See also Norway, Nevil Shute MTCW 2

**Shuttle, Penelope (Diane)** 1947- ......... **CLC 7**
See also CA 93-96; CANR 39, 84; DLB 14, 40

**Sidney, Mary** 1561-1621 ................ **LC 19, 39**

**Sidney, Sir Philip** 1554-1586 ........ **LC 19, 39; DA; DAB; DAC; DAM MST, POET**
See also CDBLB Before 1660; DA3; DLB 167

**Siegel, Jerome** 1914-1996 ................. **CLC 21**
See also CA 116; 169; 151

**Siegel, Jerry**
See Siegel, Jerome

**Sienkiewicz, Henryk (Adam Alexander Pius)**
1846-1916 ............................... **TCLC 3**
See also CA 104; 134; CANR 84

**Sierra, Gregorio Martinez**
See Martinez Sierra, Gregorio

**Sierra, Maria (de la O'LeJarraga) Martinez**
See Martinez Sierra, Maria (de la O'LeJarraga)

**Sigal, Clancy** 1926- ............................. **CLC 7**
See also CA 1-4R; CANR 85

**Sigourney, Lydia Howard (Huntley)**
1791-1865 ............................... **NCLC 21**
See also DLB 1, 42, 73

**Siguenza y Gongora, Carlos de** 1645-1700
**LC 8; HLCS 2**

**Sigurjonsson, Johann** 1880-1919 ... **TCLC 27**
See also CA 170

**Sikelianos, Angelos** 1884-1951 ...... **TCLC 39; PC 29**

**Silkin, Jon** 1930- ...................... **CLC 2, 6, 43**
See also CA 5-8R; CAAS 5; DLB 27

**Silko, Leslie (Marmon)** 1948- .... **CLC 23, 74, 114; DA; DAC; DAM MST, MULT, POP; SSC 37; WLCS**
See also AAYA 14; CA 115; 122; CANR 45, 65; DA3; DLB 143, 175; MTCW 2; NNAL

**Sillanpaa, Frans Eemil** 1888-1964 ... **CLC 19**
See also CA 129; 93-96; MTCW 1

**Sillitoe, Alan** 1928- ... **CLC 1, 3, 6, 10, 19, 57**
See also AITN 1; CA 9-12R; CAAS 2; CANR 8, 26, 55; CDBLB 1960 to Present; DLB 14, 139; MTCW 1, 2; SATA 61

Silone, Ignazio 1900-1978 ............... **CLC 4**
See also CA 25-28; 81-84; CANR 34; CAP 2; MTCW 1

Silver, Joan Micklin 1935- ............. **CLC 20**
See also CA 114; 121; INT 121

Silver, Nicholas
See Faust, Frederick (Schiller)

Silverberg, Robert 1935- ......... **CLC 7; DAM POP**
See also AAYA 24; CA 1-4R; CAAS 3; CANR 1, 20, 36, 85; CLR 59; DLB 8; INT CANR-20; MAICYA; MTCW 1, 2; SATA 13, 91; SATA-Essay 104

Silverstein, Alvin 1933- ..................... **CLC 17**
See also CA 49-52; CANR 2; CLR 25; JRDA; MAICYA; SATA 8, 69

Silverstein, Virginia B(arbara Opshelor) 1937- ........................................ **CLC 17**
See also CA 49-52; CANR 2; CLR 25; JRDA; MAICYA; SATA 8, 69

Sim, Georges
See Simenon, Georges (Jacques Christian)

Simak, Clifford D(onald) 1904-1988 . **CLC 1, 55**
See also CA 1-4R; 125; CANR 1, 35; DLB 8; MTCW 1; SATA-Obit 56

Simenon, Georges (Jacques Christian) 1903-1989 .......... **CLC 1, 2, 3, 8, 18, 47; DAM POP**
See also CA 85-88; 129; CANR 35; DA3; DLB 72; DLBY 89; MTCW 1, 2

Simic, Charles 1938- ... **CLC 6, 9, 22, 49, 68; DAM POET**
See also CA 29-32R; CAAS 4; CANR 12, 33, 52, 61; DA3; DLB 105; MTCW 2

Simmel, Georg 1858-1918 .............. **TCLC 64**
See also CA 157

Simmons, Charles (Paul) 1924- ........ **CLC 57**
See also CA 89-92; INT 89-92

Simmons, Dan 1948- .... **CLC 44; DAM POP**
See also AAYA 16; CA 138; CANR 53, 81

Simmons, James (Stewart Alexander) 1933- **CLC 43**
See also CA 105; CAAS 21; DLB 40

Simms, William Gilmore 1806-1870 .............................. **NCLC 3**
See also DLB 3, 30, 59, 73

Simon, Carly 1945- ........................... **CLC 26**
See also CA 105

Simon, Claude 1913-1984 . **CLC 4, 9, 15, 39; DAM NOV**
See also CA 89-92; CANR 33; DLB 83; MTCW 1

Simon, (Marvin) Neil 1927- ... **CLC 6, 11, 31, 39, 70; DAM DRAM**
See also AAYA 32; AITN 1; CA 21-24R; CANR 26, 54, 87; DA3; DLB 7; MTCW 1, 2

Simon, Paul (Frederick) 1941(?)- ..... **CLC 17**
See also CA 116; 153

Simonon, Paul 1956(?)- ..................... **CLC 30**

Simpson, Harriette
See Arnow, Harriette (Louisa) Simpson

Simpson, Louis (Aston Marantz) 1923- ...... **CLC 4, 7, 9, 32; DAM POET**
See also CA 1-4R; CAAS 4; CANR 1, 61; DLB 5; MTCW 1, 2

Simpson, Mona (Elizabeth) 1957- .... **CLC 44**
See also CA 122; 135; CANR 68

Simpson, N(orman) F(rederick) 1919- ........................................... **CLC 29**
See also CA 13-16R; DLB 13

Sinclair, Andrew (Annandale) 1935- . **CLC 2, 14**
See also CA 9-12R; CAAS 5; CANR 14, 38; DLB 14; MTCW 1

Sinclair, Emil
See Hesse, Hermann

Sinclair, Iain 1943- ............................ **CLC 76**
See also CA 132; CANR 81

Sinclair, Iain MacGregor
See Sinclair, Iain

Sinclair, Irene
See Griffith, D(avid Lewelyn) W(ark)

Sinclair, Mary Amelia St. Clair 1865(?)-1946
See Sinclair, May
See also CA 104

Sinclair, May 1863-1946 ............. **TCLC 3, 11**
See also Sinclair, Mary Amelia St. Clair CA 166; DLB 36, 135

Sinclair, Roy
See Griffith, D(avid Lewelyn) W(ark)

Sinclair, Upton (Beall) 1878-1968 ..... **CLC 1, 11, 15, 63; DA; DAB; DAC; DAM MST, NOV; WLC**
See also CA 5-8R; 25-28R; CANR 7; CDALB 1929-1941; DA3; DLB 9; INT CANR-7; MTCW 1, 2; SATA 9

Singer, Isaac
See Singer, Isaac Bashevis

Singer, Isaac Bashevis 1904-1991 .. **CLC 1, 3, 6, 9, 11, 15, 23, 38, 69, 111; DA; DAB; DAC; DAM MST, NOV; SSC 3; WLC**
See also AAYA 32; AITN 1, 2; CA 1-4R; 134; CANR 1, 39; CDALB 1941-1968; CLR 1; DA3; DLB 6, 28, 52; DLBY 91; JRDA; MAICYA; MTCW 1, 2; SATA 3, 27; SATA-Obit 68

Singer, Israel Joshua 1893-1944 .... **TCLC 33**
See also CA 169

Singh, Khushwant 1915- .................. **CLC 11**
See also CA 9-12R; CAAS 9; CANR 6, 84

Singleton, Ann
See Benedict, Ruth (Fulton)

Sinjohn, John
See Galsworthy, John

Sinyavsky, Andrei (Donatevich) 1925-1997 **CLC 8**
See also CA 85-88; 159

Sirin, V.
See Nabokov, Vladimir (Vladimirovich)

Sissman, L(ouis) E(dward) 1928-1976 ............................. **CLC 9, 18**
See also CA 21-24R; 65-68; CANR 13; DLB 5

Sisson, C(harles) H(ubert) 1914- ........ **CLC 8**
See also CA 1-4R; CAAS 3; CANR 3, 48, 84; DLB 27

Sitwell, Dame Edith 1887-1964 ..... **CLC 2, 9, 67; DAM POET; PC 3**
See also CA 9-12R; CANR 35; CDBLB 1945-1960; DLB 20; MTCW 1, 2

Siwaarmill, H. P.
See Sharp, William

Sjoewall, Maj 1935- ........................... **CLC 7**
See also CA 65-68; CANR 73

Sjowall, Maj
See Sjoewall, Maj

Skelton, John 1463-1529 ..................... **PC 25**

Skelton, Robin 1925-1997 ................. **CLC 13**
See also AITN 2; CA 5-8R; 160; CAAS 5; CANR 28; DLB 27, 53

Skolimowski, Jerzy 1938- ................. **CLC 20**
See also CA 128

Skram, Amalie (Bertha) 1847-1905 .......................... **TCLC 25**
See also CA 165

Skvorecky, Josef (Vaclav) 1924- ...... **CLC 15, 39, 69; DAC; DAM NOV**
See also CA 61-64; CAAS 1; CANR 10, 34, 63; DA3; MTCW 1, 2

Slade, Bernard ............................ **CLC 11, 46**
See also Newbound, Bernard Slade CAAS 9; DLB 53

Slaughter, Carolyn 1946- .................. **CLC 56**
See also CA 85-88; CANR 85

Slaughter, Frank G(ill) 1908- .......... **CLC 29**
See also AITN 2; CA 5-8R; CANR 5, 85; INT CANR-5

Slavitt, David R(ytman) 1935- ..... **CLC 5, 14**
See also CA 21-24R; CAAS 3; CANR 41, 83; DLB 5, 6

Slesinger, Tess 1905-1945 ............... **TCLC 10**
See also CA 107; DLB 102

Slessor, Kenneth 1901-1971 .............. **CLC 14**
See also CA 102; 89-92

Slowacki, Juliusz 1809-1849 .......... **NCLC 15**

Smart, Christopher 1722-1771 .. **LC 3; DAM POET; PC 13**
See also DLB 109

Smart, Elizabeth 1913-1986 ............. **CLC 54**
See also CA 81-84; 118; DLB 88

Smiley, Jane (Graves) 1949- ...... **CLC 53, 76; DAM POP**
See also CA 104; CANR 30, 50, 74; DA3; INT CANR-30

Smith, A(rthur) J(ames) M(arshall) 1902-1980 ...................... **CLC 15; DAC**
See also CA 1-4R; 102; CANR 4; DLB 88

Smith, Adam 1723-1790 ..................... **LC 36**
See also DLB 104

Smith, Alexander 1829-1867 ......... **NCLC 59**
See also DLB 32, 55

Smith, Anna Deavere 1950- ............. **CLC 86**
See also CA 133

Smith, Betty (Wehner) 1896-1972 .... **CLC 19**
See also CA 5-8R; 33-36R; DLBY 82; SATA 6

Smith, Charlotte (Turner) 1749-1806 ............................. **NCLC 23**
See also DLB 39, 109

Smith, Clark Ashton 1893-1961 ....... **CLC 43**
See also CA 143; CANR 81; MTCW 2

Smith, Dave ............................... **CLC 22, 42**
See also Smith, David (Jeddie) CAAS 7; DLB 5

Smith, David (Jeddie) 1942-
See Smith, Dave
See also CA 49-52; CANR 1, 59; DAM POET

Smith, Florence Margaret 1902-1971
See Smith, Stevie
See also CA 17-18; 29-32R; CANR 35; CAP 2; DAM POET; MTCW 1, 2

Smith, Iain Crichton 1928-1998 ....... **CLC 64**
See also CA 21-24R; 171; DLB 40, 139

Smith, John 1580(?)-1631 ..................... **LC 9**
See also DLB 24, 30

Smith, Johnston
See Crane, Stephen (Townley)

Smith, Joseph, Jr. 1805-1844 ........ **NCLC 53**

Smith, Lee 1944- ......................... **CLC 25, 73**
See also CA 114; 119; CANR 46; DLB 143; DLBY 83; INT 119

Smith, Martin
See Smith, Martin Cruz

Smith, Martin Cruz 1942- .... **CLC 25; DAM MULT, POP**
See also BEST 89:4; CA 85-88; CANR 6, 23, 43, 65; INT CANR-23; MTCW 2; NNAL

Smith, Mary-Ann Tirone 1944- ........ **CLC 39**
See also CA 118; 136

Smith, Patti 1946- .......................... **CLC 12**
See also CA 93-96; CANR 63

Smith, Pauline (Urmson) 1882-1959 ............................. **TCLC 25**

Smith, Rosamond
See Oates, Joyce Carol

Smith, Sheila Kaye
See Kaye-Smith, Sheila

Smith, Stevie .......... **CLC 3, 8, 25, 44; PC 12**
See also Smith, Florence Margaret DLB 20; MTCW 2

**Smith, Wilbur (Addison)** 1933- ........ **CLC 33**
See also CA 13-16R; CANR 7, 46, 66;
MTCW 1, 2

**Smith, William Jay** 1918- .................. **CLC 6**
See also CA 5-8R; CANR 44; DLB 5; MAI-
CYA; SAAS 22; SATA 2, 68

**Smith, Woodrow Wilson**
See Kuttner, Henry

**Smolenskin, Peretz** 1842-1885 ....... **NCLC 30**

**Smollett, Tobias (George)** 1721-1771 ... **LC 2,
46**
See also CDBLB 1660-1789; DLB 39, 104

**Snodgrass, W(illiam) D(e Witt)**
1926- .......... **CLC 2, 6, 10, 18, 68; DAM
POET**
See also CA 1-4R; CANR 6, 36, 65, 85;
DLB 5; MTCW 1, 2

**Snow, C(harles) P(ercy)** 1905-1980 ... **CLC 1,
4, 6, 9, 13, 19; DAM NOV**
See also CA 5-8R; 101; CANR 28; CDBLB
1945-1960; DLB 15, 77; DLBD 17;
MTCW 1, 2

**Snow, Frances Compton**
See Adams, Henry (Brooks)

**Snyder, Gary (Sherman)** 1930- . **CLC 1, 2, 5,
9, 32, 120; DAM POET; PC 21**
See also CA 17-20R; CANR 30, 60; DA3;
DLB 5, 16, 165, 212; MTCW 2

**Snyder, Zilpha Keatley** 1927- .......... **CLC 17**
See also AAYA 15; CA 9-12R; CANR 38;
CLR 31; JRDA; MAICYA; SAAS 2;
SATA 1, 28, 75, 110; SATA-Essay 112

**Soares, Bernardo**
See Pessoa, Fernando (Antonio Nogueira)

**Sobh, A.**
See Shamlu, Ahmad

**Sobol, Joshua** .................................. **CLC 60**

**Socrates** 469B.C.-399B.C. .............. **CMLC 27**

**Soderberg, Hjalmar** 1869-1941 ...... **TCLC 39**

**Sodergran, Edith (Irene)**
See Soedergran, Edith (Irene)

**Soedergran, Edith (Irene)**
1892-1923 ................................ **TCLC 31**

**Softly, Edgar**
See Lovecraft, H(oward) P(hillips)

**Softly, Edward**
See Lovecraft, H(oward) P(hillips)

**Sokolov, Raymond** 1941- ..................... **CLC 7**
See also CA 85-88

**Solo, Jay**
See Ellison, Harlan (Jay)

**Sologub, Fyodor** ................................ **TCLC 9**
See also Teternikov, Fyodor Kuzmich

**Solomons, Ikey Esquir**
See Thackeray, William Makepeace

**Solomos, Dionysios** 1798-1857 ....... **NCLC 15**

**Solwoska, Mara**
See French, Marilyn

**Solzhenitsyn, Aleksandr I(sayevich)** 1918-
**CLC 1, 2, 4, 7, 9, 10, 18, 26, 34, 78; DA;
DAB; DAC; DAM MST, NOV; SSC 32;
WLC**
See also AITN 1; CA 69-72; CANR 40, 65;
DA3; MTCW 1, 2

**Somers, Jane**
See Lessing, Doris (May)

**Somerville, Edith** 1858-1949 ......... **TCLC 51**
See also DLB 135

**Somerville & Ross**
See Martin, Violet Florence; Somerville,
Edith

**Sommer, Scott** 1951- ......................... **CLC 25**
See also CA 106

**Sondheim, Stephen (Joshua)** 1930- . **CLC 30,
39; DAM DRAM**
See also AAYA 11; CA 103; CANR 47, 68

**Song, Cathy** 1955- ............................... **PC 21**
See also CA 154; DLB 169

**Sontag, Susan** 1933- .... **CLC 1, 2, 10, 13, 31,
105; DAM POP**
See also CA 17-20R; CANR 25, 51, 74;
DA3; DLB 2, 67; MTCW 1, 2

**Sophocles** 496(?)B.C.-406(?)B.C. .... **CMLC 2;
DA; DAB; DAC; DAM DRAM, MST;
DC 1; WLCS**
See also DA3; DLB 176

**Sordello** 1189-1269 .......................... **CMLC 15**

**Sorel, Georges** 1847-1922 ............... **TCLC 91**
See also CA 118

**Sorel, Julia**
See Drexler, Rosalyn

**Sorrentino, Gilbert** 1929- .. **CLC 3, 7, 14, 22,
40**
See also CA 77-80; CANR 14, 33; DLB 5,
173; DLBY 80; INT CANR-14

**Soto, Gary** 1952- ............. **CLC 32, 80; DAM
MULT; HLC 2; PC 28**
See also AAYA 10; CA 119; 125; CANR
50, 74; CLR 38; DLB 82; HW 1, 2; INT
125; JRDA; MTCW 2; SATA 80

**Soupault, Philippe** 1897-1990 .......... **CLC 68**
See also CA 116; 147; 131

**Souster, (Holmes) Raymond** 1921- .... **CLC 5,
14; DAC; DAM POET**
See also CA 13-16R; CAAS 14; CANR 13,
29, 53; DA3; DLB 88; SATA 63

**Southern, Terry** 1924(?)-1995 ............. **CLC 7**
See also CA 1-4R; 150; CANR 1, 55; DLB
2

**Southey, Robert** 1774-1843 .............. **NCLC 8**
See also DLB 93, 107, 142; SATA 54

**Southworth, Emma Dorothy Eliza Nevitte**
1819-1899 ................................ **NCLC 26**

**Souza, Ernest**
See Scott, Evelyn

**Soyinka, Wole** 1934- .... **CLC 3, 5, 14, 36, 44;
BLC 3; DA; DAB; DAC; DAM
DRAM, MST, MULT; DC 2; WLC**
See also BW 2, 3; CA 13-16R; CANR 27,
39, 82; DA3; DLB 125; MTCW 1, 2

**Spackman, W(illiam) M(ode)**
1905-1990 ................................... **CLC 46**
See also CA 81-84; 132

**Spacks, Barry (Bernard)** 1931- ........ **CLC 14**
See also CA 154; CANR 33; DLB 105

**Spanidou, Irini** 1946- ........................ **CLC 44**

**Spark, Muriel (Sarah)** 1918- ..... **CLC 2, 3, 5,
8, 13, 18, 40, 94; DAB; DAC; DAM
MST, NOV; SSC 10**
See also CA 5-8R; CANR 12, 36, 76; CD-
BLB 1945-1960; DA3; DLB 15, 139; INT
CANR-12; MTCW 1, 2

**Spaulding, Douglas**
See Bradbury, Ray (Douglas)

**Spaulding, Leonard**
See Bradbury, Ray (Douglas)

**Spence, J. A. D.**
See Eliot, T(homas) S(tearns)

**Spencer, Elizabeth** 1921- .................. **CLC 22**
See also CA 13-16R; CANR 32, 65, 87;
DLB 6; MTCW 1; SATA 14

**Spencer, Leonard G.**
See Silverberg, Robert

**Spencer, Scott** 1945- ......................... **CLC 30**
See also CA 113; CANR 51; DLBY 86

**Spender, Stephen (Harold)**
1909-1995 ........ **CLC 1, 2, 5, 10, 41, 91;
DAM POET**
See also CA 9-12R; 149; CANR 31, 54;
CDBLB 1945-1960; DA3; DLB 20;
MTCW 1, 2

**Spengler, Oswald (Arnold Gottfried)**
1880-1936 ............................... **TCLC 25**
See also CA 118

**Spenser, Edmund** 1552(?)-1599 ..... **LC 5, 39;
DA; DAB; DAC; DAM MST, POET;
PC 8; WLC**
See also CDBLB Before 1660; DA3; DLB
167

**Spicer, Jack** 1925-1965 .......... **CLC 8, 18, 72;
DAM POET**
See also CA 85-88; DLB 5, 16, 193

**Spiegelman, Art** 1948- ...................... **CLC 76**
See also AAYA 10; CA 125; CANR 41, 55,
74; MTCW 2; SATA 109

**Spielberg, Peter** 1929- ........................ **CLC 6**
See also CA 5-8R; CANR 4, 48; DLBY 81

**Spielberg, Steven** 1947- .................... **CLC 20**
See also AAYA 8, 24; CA 77-80; CANR
32; SATA 32

**Spillane, Frank Morrison** 1918-
See Spillane, Mickey
See also CA 25-28R; CANR 28, 63; DA3;
MTCW 1, 2; SATA 66

**Spillane, Mickey** ............................ **CLC 3, 13**
See also Spillane, Frank Morrison MTCW
2

**Spinoza, Benedictus de** 1632-1677 ........ **LC 9**

**Spinrad, Norman (Richard)** 1940- ... **CLC 46**
See also CA 37-40R; CAAS 19; CANR 20;
DLB 8; INT CANR-20

**Spitteler, Carl (Friedrich Georg)** 1845-1924
**TCLC 12**
See also CA 109; DLB 129

**Spivack, Kathleen (Romola Drucker)** 1938-
**CLC 6**
See also CA 49-52

**Spoto, Donald** 1941- .......................... **CLC 39**
See also CA 65-68; CANR 11, 57

**Springsteen, Bruce (F.)** 1949- .......... **CLC 17**
See also CA 111

**Spurling, Hilary** 1940- ...................... **CLC 34**
See also CA 104; CANR 25, 52

**Spyker, John Howland**
See Elman, Richard (Martin)

**Squires, (James) Radcliffe**
1917-1993 ................................. **CLC 51**
See also CA 1-4R; 140; CANR 6, 21

**Srivastava, Dhanpat Rai** 1880(?)-1936
See Premchand
See also CA 118

**Stacy, Donald**
See Pohl, Frederik

**Stael, Germaine de** 1766-1817
See Stael-Holstein, Anne Louise Germaine
Necker Baronn
See also DLB 119

**Stael-Holstein, Anne Louise Germaine
Necker Baronn** 1766-1817 ....... **NCLC 3**
See also Stael, Germaine de DLB 192

**Stafford, Jean** 1915-1979 .. **CLC 4, 7, 19, 68;
SSC 26**
See also CA 1-4R; 85-88; CANR 3, 65;
DLB 2, 173; MTCW 1, 2; SATA-Obit 22

**Stafford, William (Edgar)**
1914-1993 .. **CLC 4, 7, 29; DAM POET**
See also CA 5-8R; 142; CAAS 3; CANR 5,
22; DLB 5, 206; INT CANR-22

**Stagnelius, Eric Johan** 1793-1823 . **NCLC 61**

**Staines, Trevor**
See Brunner, John (Kilian Houston)

**Stairs, Gordon**
See Austin, Mary (Hunter)

**Stairs, Gordon**
See Austin, Mary (Hunter)

**Stalin, Joseph** 1879-1953 ................ **TCLC 92**

**Stannard, Martin** 1947- .................... **CLC 44**
See also CA 142; DLB 155

**Stanton, Elizabeth Cady**
1815-1902 ................................ **TCLC 73**
See also CA 171; DLB 79

Stanton, Maura 1946- ......................... CLC 9
See also CA 89-92; CANR 15; DLB 120

Stanton, Schuyler
See Baum, L(yman) Frank

Stapledon, (William) Olaf
1886-1950 ......................... TCLC 22
See also CA 111; 162; DLB 15

Starbuck, George (Edwin)
1931-1996 .......... CLC 53; DAM POET
See also CA 21-24R; 153; CANR 23

Stark, Richard
See Westlake, Donald E(dwin)

Staunton, Schuyler
See Baum, L(yman) Frank

Stead, Christina (Ellen) 1902-1983 ... CLC 2,
5, 8, 32, 80
See also CA 13-16R; 109; CANR 33, 40;
MTCW 1, 2

Stead, William Thomas
1849-1912 ................................. TCLC 48
See also CA 167

Steele, Richard 1672-1729 .................... LC 18
See also CDBLB 1660-1789; DLB 84, 101

Steele, Timothy (Reid) 1948- ............ CLC 45
See also CA 93-96; CANR 16, 50; DLB
120

Steffens, (Joseph) Lincoln
1866-1936 ................................. TCLC 20
See also CA 117

Stegner, Wallace (Earle) 1909-1993 .. CLC 9,
49, 81; DAM NOV; SSC 27
See also AITN 1; BEST 90:3; CA 1-4R;
141; CAAS 9; CANR 1, 21, 46; DLB 9,
206; DLBY 93; MTCW 1, 2

Stein, Gertrude 1874-1946 .... TCLC 1, 6, 28,
48; DA; DAB; DAC; DAM MST, NOV,
POET; PC 18; WLC
See also CA 104; 132; CDALB 1917-1929;
DA3; DLB 4, 54, 86; DLBD 15; MTCW
1, 2

Steinbeck, John (Ernst) 1902-1968 ... CLC 1,
5, 9, 13, 21, 34, 45, 75, 124; DA; DAB;
DAC; DAM DRAM, MST, NOV; SSC
11, 37; WLC
See also AAYA 12; CA 1-4R; 25-28R;
CANR 1, 35; CDALB 1929-1941; DA3;
DLB 7, 9, 212; DLBD 2; MTCW 1, 2;
SATA 9

Steinem, Gloria 1934- ......................... CLC 63
See also CA 53-56; CANR 28, 51; MTCW
1, 2

Steiner, George 1929- .. CLC 24; DAM NOV
See also CA 73-76; CANR 31, 67; DLB 67;
MTCW 1, 2; SATA 62

Steiner, K. Leslie
See Delany, Samuel R(ay, Jr.)

Steiner, Rudolf 1861-1925 ............. TCLC 13
See also CA 107

Stendhal 1783-1842 ........ NCLC 23, 46; DA;
DAB; DAC; DAM MST, NOV; SSC
27; WLC
See also DA3; DLB 119

Stephen, Adeline Virginia
See Woolf, (Adeline) Virginia

Stephen, Sir Leslie 1832-1904 ......... TCLC 23
See also CA 123; DLB 57, 144, 190

Stephen, Sir Leslie
See Stephen, Sir Leslie

Stephen, Virginia
See Woolf, (Adeline) Virginia

Stephens, James 1882(?)-1950 .......... TCLC 4
See also CA 104; DLB 19, 153, 162

Stephens, Reed
See Donaldson, Stephen R.

Steptoe, Lydia
See Barnes, Djuna

Sterchi, Beat 1949- ......................... CLC 65

Sterling, Brett
See Bradbury, Ray (Douglas); Hamilton,
Edmond

Sterling, Bruce 1954- ......................... CLC 72
See also CA 119; CANR 44

Sterling, George 1869-1926 ............. TCLC 20
See also CA 117; 165; DLB 54

Stern, Gerald 1925- .................... CLC 40, 100
See also CA 81-84; CANR 28; DLB 105

Stern, Richard (Gustave) 1928- ... CLC 4, 39
See also CA 1-4R; CANR 1, 25, 52; DLBY
87; INT CANR-25

Sternberg, Josef von 1894-1969 ....... CLC 20
See also CA 81-84

Sterne, Laurence 1713-1768 .. LC 2, 48; DA;
DAB; DAC; DAM MST, NOV; WLC
See also CDBLB 1660-1789; DLB 39

Sternheim, (William Adolf) Carl 1878-1942
TCLC 8
See also CA 105; DLB 56, 118

Stevens, Mark 1951- ......................... CLC 34
See also CA 122

Stevens, Wallace 1879-1955 ...... TCLC 3, 12,
45; DA; DAB; DAC; DAM MST,
POET; PC 6; WLC
See also CA 104; 124; CDALB 1929-1941;
DA3; DLB 54; MTCW 1, 2

Stevenson, Anne (Katharine) 1933- .. CLC 7,
33
See also CA 17-20R; CAAS 9; CANR 9,
33; DLB 40; MTCW 1

Stevenson, Robert Louis (Balfour)
1850-1894 . NCLC 5, 14, 63; DA; DAB;
DAC; DAM MST, NOV; WLC
See also AAYA 24; CDBLB 1890-1914;
CLR 10, 11; DA3; DLB 18, 57, 141, 156,
174; DLBD 13; JRDA; MAICYA; SATA
100; YABC 2

Stewart, J(ohn) I(nnes) M(ackintosh)
1906-1994 ......................... CLC 7, 14, 32
See also CA 85-88; 147; CAAS 3; CANR
47; MTCW 1, 2

Stewart, Mary (Florence Elinor)
1916- ...................... CLC 7, 35, 117; DAB
See also AAYA 29; CA 1-4R; CANR 1, 59;
SATA 12

Stewart, Mary Rainbow
See Stewart, Mary (Florence Elinor)

Stifle, June
See Campbell, Maria

Stifter, Adalbert 1805-1868 .. NCLC 41; SSC
28
See also DLB 133

Still, James 1906- ......................... CLC 49
See also CA 65-68; CAAS 17; CANR 10,
26; DLB 9; SATA 29

Sting 1951-
See Sumner, Gordon Matthew
See also CA 167

Stirling, Arthur
See Sinclair, Upton (Beall)

Stitt, Milan 1941- ......................... CLC 29
See also CA 69-72

Stockton, Francis Richard 1834-1902
See Stockton, Frank R.
See also CA 108; 137; MAICYA; SATA 44

Stockton, Frank R. ......................... TCLC 47
See also Stockton, Francis Richard DLB
42, 74; DLBD 13; SATA-Brief 32

Stoddard, Charles
See Kuttner, Henry

Stoker, Abraham 1847-1912
See Stoker, Bram
See also CA 105; 150; DA; DAC; DAM
MST, NOV; DA3; SATA 29

Stoker, Bram 1847-1912 ....... TCLC 8; DAB;
WLC
See also Stoker, Abraham AAYA 23; CD-
BLB 1890-1914; DLB 36, 70, 178

Stolz, Mary (Slattery) 1920- ............ CLC 12
See also AAYA 8; AITN 1; CA 5-8R;
CANR 13, 41; JRDA; MAICYA; SAAS
3; SATA 10, 71

Stone, Irving 1903-1989 . CLC 7; DAM POP
See also AITN 1; CA 1-4R; 129; CAAS 3;
CANR 1, 23; DA3; INT CANR-23;
MTCW 1, 2; SATA 3; SATA-Obit 64

Stone, Oliver (William) 1946- ........... CLC 73
See also AAYA 15; CA 110; CANR 55

Stone, Robert (Anthony) 1937- ... CLC 5, 23,
42
See also CA 85-88; CANR 23, 66; DLB
152; INT CANR-23; MTCW 1

Stone, Zachary
See Follett, Ken(neth Martin)

Stoppard, Tom 1937- ... CLC 1, 3, 4, 5, 8, 15,
29, 34, 63, 91; DA; DAB; DAC; DAM
DRAM, MST; DC 6; WLC
See also CA 81-84; CANR 39, 67; CDBLB
1960 to Present; DA3; DLB 13; DLBY
85; MTCW 1, 2

Storey, David (Malcolm) 1933- . CLC 2, 4, 5,
8; DAM DRAM
See also CA 81-84; CANR 36; DLB 13, 14,
207; MTCW 1

Storm, Hyemeyohsts 1935- ..... CLC 3; DAM
MULT
See also CA 81-84; CANR 45; NNAL

Storm, Theodor 1817-1888 ................. SSC 27

Storm, (Hans) Theodor (Woldsen) 1817-1888
NCLC 1; SSC 27
See also DLB 129

Storni, Alfonsina 1892-1938 . TCLC 5; DAM
MULT; HLC 2
See also CA 104; 131; HW 1

Stoughton, William 1631-1701 ........... LC 38
See also DLB 24

Stout, Rex (Todhunter) 1886-1975 ..... CLC 3
See also AITN 2; CA 61-64; CANR 71

Stow, (Julian) Randolph 1935- ... CLC 23, 48
See also CA 13-16R; CANR 33; MTCW 1

Stowe, Harriet (Elizabeth) Beecher
1811-1896 ....... NCLC 3, 50; DA; DAB;
DAC; DAM MST, NOV; WLC
See also CDALB 1865-1917; DA3; DLB 1,
12, 42, 74, 189; JRDA; MAICYA; YABC
1

Strabo c. 64B.C.-c. 25 .................... CMLC 37
See also DLB 176

Strachey, (Giles) Lytton
1880-1932 ................................. TCLC 12
See also CA 110; 178; DLB 149; DLBD
10; MTCW 2

Strand, Mark 1934- ......... CLC 6, 18, 41, 71;
DAM POET
See also CA 21-24R; CANR 40, 65; DLB
5; SATA 41

Straub, Peter (Francis) 1943- . CLC 28, 107;
DAM POP
See also BEST 89:1; CA 85-88; CANR 28,
65; DLBY 84; MTCW 1, 2

Strauss, Botho 1944- ......................... CLC 22
See also CA 157; DLB 124

Streatfeild, (Mary) Noel
1895(?)-1986 ......................... CLC 21
See also CA 81-84; 120; CANR 31; CLR
17; DLB 160; MAICYA; SATA 20; SATA-
Obit 48

Stribling, T(homas) S(igismund) 1881-1965
CLC 23
See also CA 107; DLB 9

**Strindberg, (Johan) August**
1849-1912 ........ **TCLC 1, 8, 21, 47; DA;
DAB; DAC; DAM DRAM, MST; WLC**
See also CA 104; 135; DA3; MTCW 2

**Stringer, Arthur** 1874-1950 ........... **TCLC 37**
See also CA 161; DLB 92

**Stringer, David**
See Roberts, Keith (John Kingston)

**Stroheim, Erich von** 1885-1957 ..... **TCLC 71**

**Strugatskii, Arkadii (Natanovich)** 1925-1991
**CLC 27**
See also CA 106; 135

**Strugatskii, Boris (Natanovich)**
1933- .......................................... **CLC 27**
See also CA 106

**Strummer, Joe** 1953(?)- ..................... **CLC 30**

**Strunk, William, Jr.** 1869-1946 ...... **TCLC 92**
See also CA 118; 164

**Stryk, Lucien** 1924- ............................. **PC 27**
See also CA 13-16R; CANR 10, 28, 55

**Stuart, Don A.**
See Campbell, John W(ood, Jr.)

**Stuart, Ian**
See MacLean, Alistair (Stuart)

**Stuart, Jesse (Hilton)** 1906-1984 ... **CLC 1, 8,
11, 14, 34; SSC 31**
See also CA 5-8R; 112; CANR 31; DLB 9,
48, 102; DLBY 84; SATA 2; SATA-Obit
36

**Sturgeon, Theodore (Hamilton)** 1918-1985
**CLC 22, 39**
See also Queen, Ellery CA 81-84; 116;
CANR 32; DLB 8; DLBY 85; MTCW 1,
2

**Sturges, Preston** 1898-1959 ............ **TCLC 48**
See also CA 114; 149; DLB 26

**Styron, William** 1925- .... **CLC 1, 3, 5, 11, 15,
60; DAM NOV, POP; SSC 25**
See also BEST 90:4; CA 5-8R; CANR 6,
33, 74; CDALB 1968-1988; DA3; DLB
2, 143; DLBY 80; INT CANR-6; MTCW
1, 2

**Su, Chien** 1884-1918
See Su Man-shu
See also CA 123

**Suarez Lynch, B.**
See Bioy Casares, Adolfo; Borges, Jorge
Luis

**Suassuna, Ariano Vilar** 1927-
See also CA 178; HLCS 1; HW 2

**Suckow, Ruth** 1892-1960 ................... **SSC 18**
See also CA 113; DLB 9, 102

**Sudermann, Hermann** 1857-1928 .. **TCLC 15**
See also CA 107; DLB 118

**Sue, Eugene** 1804-1857 .................... **NCLC 1**
See also DLB 119

**Sueskind, Patrick** 1949- .................... **CLC 44**
See also Suskind, Patrick

**Sukenick, Ronald** 1932- ........ **CLC 3, 4, 6, 48**
See also CA 25-28R; CAAS 8; CANR 32;
DLB 173; DLBY 81

**Suknaski, Andrew** 1942- .................. **CLC 19**
See also CA 101; DLB 53

**Sullivan, Vernon**
See Vian, Boris

**Sully Prudhomme** 1839-1907 ........ **TCLC 31**

**Su Man-shu** ...................................... **TCLC 24**
See also Su, Chien

**Summerforest, Ivy B.**
See Kirkup, James

**Summers, Andrew James** 1942- ....... **CLC 26**

**Summers, Andy**
See Summers, Andrew James

**Summers, Hollis (Spurgeon, Jr.)**
1916- .......................................... **CLC 10**
See also CA 5-8R; CANR 3; DLB 6

**Summers, (Alphonsus Joseph-Mary
Augustus) Montague**
1880-1948 ................................ **TCLC 16**
See also CA 118; 163

**Sumner, Gordon Matthew** ............... **CLC 26**
See also Sting

**Surtees, Robert Smith** 1803-1864 .. **NCLC 14**
See also DLB 21

**Susann, Jacqueline** 1921-1974 ........... **CLC 3**
See also AITN 1; CA 65-68; 53-56; MTCW
1, 2

**Su Shih** 1036-1101 ........................ **CMLC 15**

**Suskind, Patrick**
See Sueskind, Patrick
See also CA 145

**Sutcliff, Rosemary** 1920-1992 ......... **CLC 26;
DAB; DAC; DAM MST, POP**
See also AAYA 10; CA 5-8R; 139; CANR
37; CLR 1, 37; JRDA; MAICYA; SATA
6, 44, 78; SATA-Obit 73

**Sutro, Alfred** 1863-1933 .................... **TCLC 6**
See also CA 105; DLB 10

**Sutton, Henry**
See Slavitt, David R(ytman)

**Svevo, Italo** 1861-1928 ...... **TCLC 2, 35; SSC
25**
See also Schmitz, Aron Hector

**Swados, Elizabeth (A.)** 1951- ........... **CLC 12**
See also CA 97-100; CANR 49; INT 97-
100

**Swados, Harvey** 1920-1972 ................. **CLC 5**
See also CA 5-8R; 37-40R; CANR 6; DLB
2

**Swan, Gladys** 1934- .......................... **CLC 69**
See also CA 101; CANR 17, 39

**Swanson, Logan**
See Matheson, Richard Burton

**Swarthout, Glendon (Fred)**
1918-1992 ................................. **CLC 35**
See also CA 1-4R; 139; CANR 1, 47; SATA
26

**Sweet, Sarah C.**
See Jewett, (Theodora) Sarah Orne

**Swenson, May** 1919-1989 ...... **CLC 4, 14, 61,
106; DA; DAB; DAC; DAM MST,
POET; PC 14**
See also CA 5-8R; 130; CANR 36, 61; DLB
5; MTCW 1, 2; SATA 15

**Swift, Augustus**
See Lovecraft, H(oward) P(hillips)

**Swift, Graham (Colin)** 1949- ...... **CLC 41, 88**
See also CA 117; 122; CANR 46, 71; DLB
194; MTCW 2

**Swift, Jonathan** 1667-1745 ..... **LC 1, 42; DA;
DAB; DAC; DAM MST, NOV, POET;
PC 9; WLC**
See also CDBLB 1660-1789; CLR 53;
DA3; DLB 39, 95, 101; SATA 19

**Swinburne, Algernon Charles** 1837-1909
**TCLC 8, 36; DA; DAB; DAC; DAM
MST, POET; PC 24; WLC**
See also CA 105; 140; CDBLB 1832-1890;
DA3; DLB 35, 57

**Swinfen, Ann** ...................................... **CLC 34**

**Swinnerton, Frank Arthur**
1884-1982 ................................. **CLC 31**
See also CA 108; DLB 34

**Swithen, John**
See King, Stephen (Edwin)

**Sylvia**
See Ashton-Warner, Sylvia (Constance)

**Symmes, Robert Edward**
See Duncan, Robert (Edward)

**Symonds, John Addington**
1840-1893 ............................... **NCLC 34**
See also DLB 57, 144

**Symons, Arthur** 1865-1945 ............. **TCLC 11**
See also CA 107; DLB 19, 57, 149

**Symons, Julian (Gustave)**
1912-1994 ...................... **CLC 2, 14, 32**
See also CA 49-52; 147; CAAS 3; CANR
3, 33, 59; DLB 87, 155; DLBY 92;
MTCW 1

**Synge, (Edmund) J(ohn) M(illington)**
1871-1909 . **TCLC 6, 37; DAM DRAM;
DC 2**
See also CA 104; 141; CDBLB 1890-1914;
DLB 10, 19

**Syruc, J.**
See Milosz, Czeslaw

**Szirtes, George** 1948- ........................ **CLC 46**
See also CA 109; CANR 27, 61

**Szymborska, Wislawa** 1923- ............. **CLC 99**
See also CA 154; DA3; DLBY 96; MTCW
2

**T. O., Nik**
See Annensky, Innokenty (Fyodorovich)

**Tabori, George** 1914- ........................ **CLC 19**
See also CA 49-52; CANR 4, 69

**Tagore, Rabindranath** 1861-1941 ... **TCLC 3,
53; DAM DRAM, POET; PC 8**
See also CA 104; 120; DA3; MTCW 1, 2

**Taine, Hippolyte Adolphe**
1828-1893 ............................... **NCLC 15**

**Talese, Gay** 1932- ............................. **CLC 37**
See also AITN 1; CA 1-4R; CANR 9, 58;
DLB 185; INT CANR-9; MTCW 1, 2

**Tallent, Elizabeth (Ann)** 1954- ......... **CLC 45**
See also CA 117; CANR 72; DLB 130

**Tally, Ted** 1952- .............................. **CLC 42**
See also CA 120; 124; INT 124

**Talvik, Heiti** 1904-1947 .................. **TCLC 87**

**Tamayo y Baus, Manuel**
1829-1898 ................................. **NCLC 1**

**Tammsaare, A(nton) H(ansen)** 1878-1940
**TCLC 27**
See also CA 164

**Tam'si, Tchicaya U**
See Tchicaya, Gerald Felix

**Tan, Amy (Ruth)** 1952- . **CLC 59, 120; DAM
MULT, NOV, POP**
See also AAYA 9; BEST 89:3; CA 136;
CANR 54; CDALBS; DA3; DLB 173;
MTCW 2; SATA 75

**Tandem, Felix**
See Spitteler, Carl (Friedrich Georg)

**Tanizaki, Jun'ichiro** 1886-1965 ... **CLC 8, 14,
28; SSC 21**
See also CA 93-96; 25-28R; DLB 180;
MTCW 2

**Tanner, William**
See Amis, Kingsley (William)

**Tao Lao**
See Storni, Alfonsina

**Tarantino, Quentin (Jerome)**
1963- ...................................... **CLC 125**
See also CA 171

**Tarassoff, Lev**
See Troyat, Henri

**Tarbell, Ida M(inerva)** 1857-1944 . **TCLC 40**
See also CA 122; 181; DLB 47

**Tarkington, (Newton) Booth** 1869-1946
**TCLC 9**
See also CA 110; 143; DLB 9, 102; MTCW
2; SATA 17

**Tarkovsky, Andrei (Arsenyevich)** 1932-1986
**CLC 75**
See also CA 127

**Tartt, Donna** 1964(?)- ....................... **CLC 76**
See also CA 142

**Tasso, Torquato** 1544-1595 ................. **LC 5**

**Tate, (John Orley) Allen** 1899-1979 .. **CLC 2,
4, 6, 9, 11, 14, 24**
See also CA 5-8R; 85-88; CANR 32; DLB
4, 45, 63; DLBD 17; MTCW 1, 2

**Tate, Ellalice**
See Hibbert, Eleanor Alice Burford
**Tate, James (Vincent)** 1943- ..... **CLC 2, 6, 25**
See also CA 21-24R; CANR 29, 57; DLB 5, 169
**Tauler, Johannes** c. 1300-1361 ...... **CMLC 37**
See also DLB 179
**Tavel, Ronald** 1940- ........................... **CLC 6**
See also CA 21-24R; CANR 33
**Taylor, C(ecil) P(hilip)** 1929-1981 .... **CLC 27**
See also CA 25-28R; 105; CANR 47
**Taylor, Edward** 1642(?)-1729 ... **LC 11; DA; DAB; DAC; DAM MST, POET**
See also DLB 24
**Taylor, Eleanor Ross** 1920- ................ **CLC 5**
See also CA 81-84; CANR 70
**Taylor, Elizabeth** 1912-1975 ..... **CLC 2, 4, 29**
See also CA 13-16R; CANR 9, 70; DLB 139; MTCW 1; SATA 13
**Taylor, Frederick Winslow**
1856-1915 ................................ **TCLC 76**
**Taylor, Henry (Splawn)** 1942- ......... **CLC 44**
See also CA 33-36R; CAAS 7; CANR 31; DLB 5
**Taylor, Kamala (Purnaiya)** 1924-
See Markandaya, Kamala
See also CA 77-80
**Taylor, Mildred D.** ........................... **CLC 21**
See also AAYA 10; BW 1; CA 85-88; CANR 25; CLR 9, 59; DLB 52; JRDA; MAICYA; SAAS 5; SATA 15, 70
**Taylor, Peter (Hillsman)** 1917-1994 .. **CLC 1, 4, 18, 37, 44, 50, 71; SSC 10**
See also CA 13-16R; 147; CANR 9, 50; DLBY 81, 94; INT CANR-9; MTCW 1, 2
**Taylor, Robert Lewis** 1912-1998 ....... **CLC 14**
See also CA 1-4R; 170; CANR 3, 64; SATA 10
**Tchekhov, Anton**
See Chekhov, Anton (Pavlovich)
**Tchicaya, Gerald Felix** 1931-1988 .. **CLC 101**
See also CA 129; 125; CANR 81
**Tchicaya U Tam'si**
See Tchicaya, Gerald Felix
**Teasdale, Sara** 1884-1933 ................. **TCLC 4**
See also CA 104; 163; DLB 45; SATA 32
**Tegner, Esaias** 1782-1846 ................. **NCLC 2**
**Teilhard de Chardin, (Marie Joseph) Pierre**
1881-1955 ................................ **TCLC 9**
See also CA 105
**Temple, Ann**
See Mortimer, Penelope (Ruth)
**Tennant, Emma (Christina)** 1937- .. **CLC 13, 52**
See also CA 65-68; CAAS 9; CANR 10, 38, 59, 88; DLB 14
**Tenneshaw, S. M.**
See Silverberg, Robert
**Tennyson, Alfred** 1809-1892 ... **NCLC 30, 65; DA; DAB; DAC; DAM MST, POET; PC 6; WLC**
See also CDBLB 1832-1890; DA3; DLB 32
**Teran, Lisa St. Aubin de** ................... **CLC 36**
See also St. Aubin de Teran, Lisa
**Terence** c. 184B.C.-c. 159B.C. ...... **CMLC 14; DC 7**
See also DLB 211
**Teresa de Jesus, St.** 1515-1582 ........... **LC 18**
**Terkel, Louis** 1912-
See Terkel, Studs
See also CA 57-60; CANR 18, 45, 67; DA3; MTCW 1, 2
**Terkel, Studs** ..................................... **CLC 38**
See also Terkel, Louis AAYA 32; AITN 1; MTCW 2
**Terry, C. V.**
See Slaughter, Frank G(ill)

**Terry, Megan** 1932- .......................... **CLC 19**
See also CA 77-80; CABS 3; CANR 43; DLB 7
**Tertullian** c. 155-c. 245 .................. **CMLC 29**
**Tertz, Abram**
See Sinyavsky, Andrei (Donatevich)
**Tesich, Steve** 1943(?)-1996 .......... **CLC 40, 69**
See also CA 105; 152; DLBY 83
**Tesla, Nikola** 1856-1943 .................. **TCLC 88**
**Teternikov, Fyodor Kuzmich** 1863-1927
See Sologub, Fyodor
See also CA 104
**Tevis, Walter** 1928-1984 .................... **CLC 42**
See also CA 113
**Tey, Josephine** ................................. **TCLC 14**
See also Mackintosh, Elizabeth DLB 77
**Thackeray, William Makepeace** 1811-1863
**NCLC 5, 14, 22, 43; DA; DAB; DAC; DAM MST, NOV; WLC**
See also CDBLB 1832-1890; DA3; DLB 21, 55, 159, 163; SATA 23
**Thakura, Ravindranatha**
See Tagore, Rabindranath
**Tharoor, Shashi** 1956- ...................... **CLC 70**
See also CA 141
**Thelwell, Michael Miles** 1939- ......... **CLC 22**
See also BW 2; CA 101
**Theobald, Lewis, Jr.**
See Lovecraft, H(oward) P(hillips)
**Theodorescu, Ion N.** 1880-1967
See Arghezi, Tudor
See also CA 116
**Theriault, Yves** 1915-1983 .... **CLC 79; DAC; DAM MST**
See also CA 102; DLB 88
**Theroux, Alexander (Louis)** 1939- .... **CLC 2, 25**
See also CA 85-88; CANR 20, 63
**Theroux, Paul (Edward)** 1941- ..... **CLC 5, 8, 11, 15, 28, 46; DAM POP**
See also AAYA 28; BEST 89:4; CA 33-36R; CANR 20, 45, 74; CDALBS; DA3; DLB 2; MTCW 1, 2; SATA 44, 109
**Thesen, Sharon** 1946- ...................... **CLC 56**
See also CA 163
**Thevenin, Denis**
See Duhamel, Georges
**Thibault, Jacques Anatole Francois**
1844-1924
See France, Anatole
See also CA 106; 127; DAM NOV; DA3; MTCW 1, 2
**Thiele, Colin (Milton)** 1920- ............. **CLC 17**
See also CA 29-32R; CANR 12, 28, 53; CLR 27; MAICYA; SAAS 2; SATA 14, 72
**Thomas, Audrey (Callahan)** 1935- .... **CLC 7, 13, 37, 107; SSC 20**
See also AITN 2; CA 21-24R; CAAS 19; CANR 36, 58; DLB 60; MTCW 1
**Thomas, Augustus** 1857-1934 ........ **TCLC 97**
**Thomas, D(onald) M(ichael)** 1935- . **CLC 13, 22, 31**
See also CA 61-64; CAAS 11; CANR 17, 45, 75; CDBLB 1960 to Present; DA3; DLB 40, 207; INT CANR-17; MTCW 1, 2
**Thomas, Dylan (Marlais)**
1914-1953 ... **TCLC 1, 8, 45; DA; DAB; DAC; DAM DRAM, MST, POET; PC 2; SSC 3; WLC**
See also CA 104; 120; CANR 65; CDBLB 1945-1960; DA3; DLB 13, 20, 139; MTCW 1, 2; SATA 60
**Thomas, (Philip) Edward**
1878-1917 ....... **TCLC 10; DAM POET**
See also CA 106; 153; DLB 98

**Thomas, Joyce Carol** 1938- .............. **CLC 35**
See also AAYA 12; BW 2, 3; CA 113; 116; CANR 48; CLR 19; DLB 33; INT 116; JRDA; MAICYA; MTCW 1, 2; SAAS 7; SATA 40, 78
**Thomas, Lewis** 1913-1993 ............... **CLC 35**
See also CA 85-88; 143; CANR 38, 60; MTCW 1, 2
**Thomas, M. Carey** 1857-1935 ....... **TCLC 89**
**Thomas, Paul**
See Mann, (Paul) Thomas
**Thomas, Piri** 1928- ............ **CLC 17; HLCS 2**
See also CA 73-76; HW 1
**Thomas, R(onald) S(tuart)** 1913- ...... **CLC 6, 13, 48; DAB; DAM POET**
See also CA 89-92; CAAS 4; CANR 30; CDBLB 1960 to Present; DLB 27; MTCW 1
**Thomas, Ross (Elmore)** 1926-1995 .. **CLC 39**
See also CA 33-36R; 150; CANR 22, 63
**Thompson, Francis Clegg**
See Mencken, H(enry) L(ouis)
**Thompson, Francis Joseph**
1859-1907 ................................ **TCLC 4**
See also CA 104; CDBLB 1890-1914; DLB 19
**Thompson, Hunter S(tockton)**
1939- ... **CLC 9, 17, 40, 104; DAM POP**
See also BEST 89:1; CA 17-20R; CANR 23, 46, 74, 77; DA3; DLB 185; MTCW 1, 2
**Thompson, James Myers**
See Thompson, Jim (Myers)
**Thompson, Jim (Myers)**
1906-1977(?) .............................. **CLC 69**
See also CA 140
**Thompson, Judith** ............................ **CLC 39**
**Thomson, James** 1700-1748 ... **LC 16, 29, 40; DAM POET**
See also DLB 95
**Thomson, James** 1834-1882 ......... **NCLC 18; DAM POET**
See also DLB 35
**Thoreau, Henry David** 1817-1862 .. **NCLC 7, 21, 61; DA; DAB; DAC; DAM MST; WLC**
See also CDALB 1640-1865; DA3; DLB 1
**Thornton, Hall**
See Silverberg, Robert
**Thucydides** c. 455B.C.-399B.C. ..... **CMLC 17**
See also DLB 176
**Thurber, James (Grover)**
1894-1961 ....... **CLC 5, 11, 25, 125; DA; DAB; DAC; DAM DRAM, MST, NOV; SSC 1**
See also CA 73-76; CANR 17, 39; CDALB 1929-1941; DA3; DLB 4, 11, 22, 102; MAICYA; MTCW 1, 2; SATA 13
**Thurman, Wallace (Henry)**
1902-1934 ........ **TCLC 6; BLC 3; DAM MULT**
See also BW 1, 3; CA 104; 124; CANR 81; DLB 51
**Tibullus, Albius** c. 54B.C.-c.
19B.C. ...................................... **CMLC 36**
See also DLB 211
**Ticheburn, Cheviot**
See Ainsworth, William Harrison
**Tieck, (Johann) Ludwig**
1773-1853 ............. **NCLC 5, 46; SSC 31**
See also DLB 90
**Tiger, Derry**
See Ellison, Harlan (Jay)
**Tilghman, Christopher** 1948(?)- ....... **CLC 65**
See also CA 159
**Tillinghast, Richard (Williford)**
1940- ........................................ **CLC 29**
See also CA 29-32R; CAAS 23; CANR 26, 51

**Timrod, Henry** 1828-1867 .............. **NCLC 25**
    See also DLB 3
**Tindall, Gillian (Elizabeth)** 1938- ...... **CLC 7**
    See also CA 21-24R; CANR 11, 65
**Tiptree, James, Jr.** ...................... **CLC 48, 50**
    See also Sheldon, Alice Hastings Bradley
    DLB 8
**Titmarsh, Michael Angelo**
    See Thackeray, William Makepeace
**Tocqueville, Alexis (Charles Henri Maurice
    Clerel, Comte) de** 1805-1859 . **NCLC 7,
    63**
**Tolkien, J(ohn) R(onald) R(euel)** 1892-1973
    **CLC 1, 2, 3, 8, 12, 38; DA; DAB; DAC;
    DAM MST, NOV, POP; WLC**
    See also AAYA 10; AITN 1; CA 17-18; 45-
    48; CANR 36; CAP 2; CDBLB 1914-
    1945; CLR 56; DA3; DLB 15, 160;
    JRDA; MAICYA; MTCW 1, 2; SATA 2,
    32, 100; SATA-Obit 24
**Toller, Ernst** 1893-1939 ................. **TCLC 10**
    See also CA 107; DLB 124
**Tolson, M. B.**
    See Tolson, Melvin B(eaunorus)
**Tolson, Melvin B(eaunorus)** 1898(?)-1966
    **CLC 36, 105; BLC 3; DAM MULT,
    POET**
    See also BW 1, 3; CA 124; 89-92; CANR
    80; DLB 48, 76
**Tolstoi, Aleksei Nikolaevich**
    See Tolstoy, Alexey Nikolaevich
**Tolstoy, Alexey Nikolaevich**
    1882-1945 ................................ **TCLC 18**
    See also CA 107; 158
**Tolstoy, Count Leo**
    See Tolstoy, Leo (Nikolaevich)
**Tolstoy, Leo (Nikolaevich)**
    1828-1910 .. **TCLC 4, 11, 17, 28, 44, 79;
    DA; DAB; DAC; DAM MST, NOV;
    SSC 9, 30; WLC**
    See also CA 104; 123; DA3; SATA 26
**Tomasi di Lampedusa, Giuseppe** 1896-1957
    See Lampedusa, Giuseppe (Tomasi) di
    See also CA 111
**Tomlin, Lily** ............................... **CLC 17**
    See also Tomlin, Mary Jean
**Tomlin, Mary Jean** 1939(?)-
    See Tomlin, Lily
    See also CA 117
**Tomlinson, (Alfred) Charles** 1927- .... **CLC 2,
    4, 6, 13, 45; DAM POET; PC 17**
    See also CA 5-8R; CANR 33; DLB 40
**Tomlinson, H(enry) M(ajor)** 1873-1958
    **TCLC 71**
    See also CA 118; 161; DLB 36, 100, 195
**Tonson, Jacob**
    See Bennett, (Enoch) Arnold
**Toole, John Kennedy** 1937-1969 ..... **CLC 19,
    64**
    See also CA 104; DLBY 81; MTCW 2
**Toomer, Jean** 1894-1967 .... **CLC 1, 4, 13, 22;
    BLC 3; DAM MULT; PC 7; SSC 1;
    WLCS**
    See also BW 1; CA 85-88; CDALB 1917-
    1929; DA3; DLB 45, 51; MTCW 1, 2
**Torley, Luke**
    See Blish, James (Benjamin)
**Tornimparte, Alessandra**
    See Ginzburg, Natalia
**Torre, Raoul della**
    See Mencken, H(enry) L(ouis)
**Torrence, Ridgely** 1874-1950 .......... **TCLC 97**
    See also DLB 54
**Torrey, E(dwin) Fuller** 1937- ........... **CLC 34**
    See also CA 119; CANR 71
**Torsvan, Ben Traven**
    See Traven, B.
**Torsvan, Benno Traven**
    See Traven, B.

**Torsvan, Berick Traven**
    See Traven, B.
**Torsvan, Berwick Traven**
    See Traven, B.
**Torsvan, Bruno Traven**
    See Traven, B.
**Torsvan, Traven**
    See Traven, B.
**Tournier, Michel (Edouard)** 1924- .... **CLC 6,
    23, 36, 95**
    See also CA 49-52; CANR 3, 36, 74; DLB
    83; MTCW 1, 2; SATA 23
**Tournimparte, Alessandra**
    See Ginzburg, Natalia
**Towers, Ivar**
    See Kornbluth, C(yril) M.
**Towne, Robert (Burton)** 1936(?)- ..... **CLC 87**
    See also CA 108; DLB 44
**Townsend, Sue** ................................... **CLC 61**
    See also Townsend, Susan Elaine AAYA 28;
    SATA 55, 93; SATA-Brief 48
**Townsend, Susan Elaine** 1946-
    See Townsend, Sue
    See also CA 119; 127; CANR 65; DAB;
    DAC; DAM MST
**Townshend, Peter (Dennis Blandford)** 1945-
    **CLC 17, 42**
    See also CA 107
**Tozzi, Federigo** 1883-1920 .............. **TCLC 31**
    See also CA 160
**Traill, Catharine Parr** 1802-1899 .. **NCLC 31**
    See also DLB 99
**Trakl, Georg** 1887-1914 ....... **TCLC 5; PC 20**
    See also CA 104; 165; MTCW 2
**Transtroemer, Tomas (Goesta)**
    1931- ............. **CLC 52, 65; DAM POET**
    See also CA 117; 129; CAAS 17
**Transtromer, Tomas Gosta**
    See Transtroemer, Tomas (Goesta)
**Traven, B.** (?)-1969 ....................... **CLC 8, 11**
    See also CA 19-20; 25-28R; CAP 2; DLB
    9, 56; MTCW 1
**Treitel, Jonathan** 1959- ..................... **CLC 70**
**Trelawny, Edward John**
    1792-1881 ................................ **NCLC 85**
    See also DLB 110, 116, 144
**Tremain, Rose** 1943- ......................... **CLC 42**
    See also CA 97-100; CANR 44; DLB 14
**Tremblay, Michel** 1942- .......... **CLC 29, 102;
    DAC; DAM MST**
    See also CA 116; 128; DLB 60; MTCW 1,
    2
**Trevanian** ........................................ **CLC 29**
    See also Whitaker, Rod(ney)
**Trevor, Glen**
    See Hilton, James
**Trevor, William** 1928- .. **CLC 7, 9, 14, 25, 71,
    116; SSC 21**
    See also Cox, William Trevor DLB 14, 139;
    MTCW 2
**Trifonov, Yuri (Valentinovich)** 1925-1981
    **CLC 45**
    See also CA 126; 103; MTCW 1
**Trilling, Diana (Rubin)** 1905-1996 . **CLC 129**
    See also CA 5-8R; 154; CANR 10, 46; INT
    CANR-10; MTCW 1, 2
**Trilling, Lionel** 1905-1975 ....... **CLC 9, 11, 24**
    See also CA 9-12R; 61-64; CANR 10; DLB
    28, 63; INT CANR-10; MTCW 1, 2
**Trimball, W. H.**
    See Mencken, H(enry) L(ouis)
**Tristan**
    See Gomez de la Serna, Ramon
**Tristram**
    See Housman, A(lfred) E(dward)
**Trogdon, William (Lewis)** 1939-
    See Heat-Moon, William Least
    See also CA 115; 119; CANR 47; INT 119

**Trollope, Anthony** 1815-1882 ... **NCLC 6, 33;
    DA; DAB; DAC; DAM MST, NOV;
    SSC 28; WLC**
    See also CDBLB 1832-1890; DA3; DLB
    21, 57, 159; SATA 22
**Trollope, Frances** 1779-1863 ......... **NCLC 30**
    See also DLB 21, 166
**Trotsky, Leon** 1879-1940 ................ **TCLC 22**
    See also CA 118; 167
**Trotter (Cockburn), Catharine**
    1679-1749 ................................... **LC 8**
    See also DLB 84
**Trotter, Wilfred** 1872-1939 ............ **TCLC 99**
**Trout, Kilgore**
    See Farmer, Philip Jose
**Trow, George W. S.** 1943- ................ **CLC 52**
    See also CA 126
**Troyat, Henri** 1911- ......................... **CLC 23**
    See also CA 45-48; CANR 2, 33, 67;
    MTCW 1
**Trudeau, G(arretson) B(eekman)** 1948-
    See Trudeau, Garry B.
    See also CA 81-84; CANR 31; SATA 35
**Trudeau, Garry B.** ........................... **CLC 12**
    See also Trudeau, G(arretson) B(eekman)
    AAYA 10; AITN 2
**Truffaut, Francois** 1932-1984 ... **CLC 20, 101**
    See also CA 81-84; 113; CANR 34
**Trumbo, Dalton** 1905-1976 .............. **CLC 19**
    See also CA 21-24R; 69-72; CANR 10;
    DLB 26
**Trumbull, John** 1750-1831 ............. **NCLC 30**
    See also DLB 31
**Trundlett, Helen B.**
    See Eliot, T(homas) S(tearns)
**Tryon, Thomas** 1926-1991 .......... **CLC 3, 11;
    DAM POP**
    See also AITN 1; CA 29-32R; 135; CANR
    32, 77; DA3; MTCW 1
**Tryon, Tom**
    See Tryon, Thomas
**Ts'ao Hsueh-ch'in** 1715(?)-1763 ........... **LC 1**
**Tsushima, Shuji** 1909-1948
    See Dazai Osamu
    See also CA 107
**Tsvetaeva (Efron), Marina (Ivanovna)**
    1892-1941 ............. **TCLC 7, 35; PC 14**
    See also CA 104; 128; CANR 73; MTCW
    1, 2
**Tuck, Lily** 1938- ................................ **CLC 70**
    See also CA 139
**Tu Fu** 712-770 ........................................ **PC 9**
    See also DAM MULT
**Tunis, John R(oberts)** 1889-1975 ..... **CLC 12**
    See also CA 61-64; CANR 62; DLB 22,
    171; JRDA; MAICYA; SATA 37; SATA-
    Brief 30
**Tuohy, Frank** ....................................... **CLC 37**
    See also Tuohy, John Francis DLB 14, 139
**Tuohy, John Francis** 1925-1999
    See Tuohy, Frank
    See also CA 5-8R; 178; CANR 3, 47
**Turco, Lewis (Putnam)** 1934- ..... **CLC 11, 63**
    See also CA 13-16R; CAAS 22; CANR 24,
    51; DLBY 84
**Turgenev, Ivan** 1818-1883 .... **NCLC 21; DA;
    DAB; DAC; DAM MST, NOV; DC 7;
    SSC 7; WLC**
**Turgot, Anne-Robert-Jacques**
    1727-1781 ................................... **LC 26**
**Turner, Frederick** 1943- ................... **CLC 48**
    See also CA 73-76; CAAS 10; CANR 12,
    30, 56; DLB 40
**Tutu, Desmond M(pilo)** 1931- ........ **CLC 80;
    BLC 3; DAM MULT**
    See also BW 1, 3; CA 125; CANR 67, 81

**Tutuola, Amos** 1920-1997 ...... **CLC 5, 14, 29; BLC 3; DAM MULT**
See also BW 2, 3; CA 9-12R; 159; CANR 27, 66; DA3; DLB 125; MTCW 1, 2

**Twain, Mark** ..... **TCLC 6, 12, 19, 36, 48, 59; SSC 34; WLC**
See also Clemens, Samuel Langhorne
AAYA 20; CLR 58, 60; DLB 11, 12, 23, 64, 74

**Tyler, Anne** 1941- . **CLC 7, 11, 18, 28, 44, 59, 103; DAM NOV, POP**
See also AAYA 18; BEST 89:1; CA 9-12R; CANR 11, 33, 53; CDALBS; DLB 6, 143; DLBY 82; MTCW 1, 2; SATA 7, 90

**Tyler, Royall** 1757-1826 .................... **NCLC 3**
See also DLB 37

**Tynan, Katharine** 1861-1931 ........... **TCLC 3**
See also CA 104; 167; DLB 153

**Tyutchev, Fyodor** 1803-1873 ......... **NCLC 34**

**Tzara, Tristan** 1896-1963 ...... **CLC 47; DAM POET; PC 27**
See also CA 153; 89-92; MTCW 2

**Uhry, Alfred** 1936- .. **CLC 55; DAM DRAM, POP**
See also CA 127; 133; DA3; INT 133

**Ulf, Haerved**
See Strindberg, (Johan) August

**Ulf, Harved**
See Strindberg, (Johan) August

**Ulibarri, Sabine R(eyes)** 1919- ........ **CLC 83; DAM MULT; HLCS 2**
See also CA 131; CANR 81; DLB 82; HW 1, 2

**Unamuno (y Jugo), Miguel de** 1864-1936
**TCLC 2, 9; DAM MULT, NOV; HLC 2; SSC 11**
See also CA 104; 131; CANR 81; DLB 108; HW 1, 2; MTCW 1, 2

**Undercliffe, Errol**
See Campbell, (John) Ramsey

**Underwood, Miles**
See Glassco, John

**Undset, Sigrid** 1882-1949 ........ **TCLC 3; DA; DAB; DAC; DAM MST, NOV; WLC**
See also CA 104; 129; DA3; MTCW 1, 2

**Ungaretti, Giuseppe** 1888-1970 ... **CLC 7, 11, 15**
See also CA 19-20; 25-28R; CAP 2; DLB 114

**Unger, Douglas** 1952- ........................ **CLC 34**
See also CA 130

**Unsworth, Barry (Forster)** 1930- .... **CLC 76, 127**
See also CA 25-28R; CANR 30, 54; DLB 194

**Updike, John (Hoyer)** 1932- . **CLC 1, 2, 3, 5, 7, 9, 13, 15, 23, 34, 43, 70; DA; DAB; DAC; DAM MST, NOV, POET, POP; SSC 13, 27; WLC**
See also CA 1-4R; CABS 1; CANR 4, 33, 51; CDALB 1968-1988; DA3; DLB 2, 5, 143; DLBD 3; DLBY 80, 82, 97; MTCW 1, 2

**Upshaw, Margaret Mitchell**
See Mitchell, Margaret (Munnerlyn)

**Upton, Mark**
See Sanders, Lawrence

**Upward, Allen** 1863-1926 ............... **TCLC 85**
See also CA 117; DLB 36

**Urdang, Constance (Henriette)** 1922- .......................................... **CLC 47**
See also CA 21-24R; CANR 9, 24

**Uriel, Henry**
See Faust, Frederick (Schiller)

**Uris, Leon (Marcus)** 1924- ......... **CLC 7, 32; DAM NOV, POP**
See also AITN 1, 2; BEST 89:2; CA 1-4R; CANR 1, 40, 65; DA3; MTCW 1, 2; SATA 49

**Urista, Alberto H.** 1947-
See Alurista
See also CA 45-48, 182; CANR 2, 32; HLCS 1; HW 1

**Urmuz**
See Codrescu, Andrei

**Urquhart, Guy**
See McAlmon, Robert (Menzies)

**Urquhart, Jane** 1949- ............. **CLC 90; DAC**
See also CA 113; CANR 32, 68

**Usigli, Rodolfo** 1905-1979
See also CA 131; HLCS 1; HW 1

**Ustinov, Peter (Alexander)** 1921- ....... **CLC 1**
See also AITN 1; CA 13-16R; CANR 25, 51; DLB 13; MTCW 2

**U Tam'si, Gerald Felix Tchicaya**
See Tchicaya, Gerald Felix

**U Tam'si, Tchicaya**
See Tchicaya, Gerald Felix

**Vachss, Andrew (Henry)** 1942- ....... **CLC 106**
See also CA 118; CANR 44

**Vachss, Andrew H.**
See Vachss, Andrew (Henry)

**Vaculik, Ludvik** 1926- ........................ **CLC 7**
See also CA 53-56; CANR 72

**Vaihinger, Hans** 1852-1933 ............. **TCLC 71**
See also CA 116; 166

**Valdez, Luis (Miguel)** 1940- .. **CLC 84; DAM MULT; DC 10; HLC 2**
See also CA 101; CANR 32, 81; DLB 122; HW 1

**Valenzuela, Luisa** 1938- ........... **CLC 31, 104; DAM MULT; HLCS 2; SSC 14**
See also CA 101; CANR 32, 65; DLB 113; HW 1, 2

**Valera y Alcala-Galiano, Juan** 1824-1905
**TCLC 10**
See also CA 106

**Valery, (Ambroise) Paul (Toussaint Jules)** 1871-1945 ... **TCLC 4, 15; DAM POET; PC 9**
See also CA 104; 122; DA3; MTCW 1, 2

**Valle-Inclan, Ramon (Maria) del** 1866-1936
**TCLC 5; DAM MULT; HLC 2**
See also CA 106; 153; CANR 80; DLB 134; HW 2

**Vallejo, Antonio Buero**
See Buero Vallejo, Antonio

**Vallejo, Cesar (Abraham)** 1892-1938 .. **TCLC 3, 56; DAM MULT; HLC 2**
See also CA 105; 153; HW 1

**Valles, Jules** 1832-1885 ................... **NCLC 71**
See also DLB 123

**Vallette, Marguerite Eymery** 1860-1953
**TCLC 67**
See also CA 182; DLB 123, 192

**Valle Y Pena, Ramon del**
See Valle-Inclan, Ramon (Maria) del

**Van Ash, Cay** 1918- ........................... **CLC 34**

**Vanbrugh, Sir John** 1664-1726 ......... **LC 21; DAM DRAM**
See also DLB 80

**Van Campen, Karl**
See Campbell, John W(ood, Jr.)

**Vance, Gerald**
See Silverberg, Robert

**Vance, Jack** ......................................... **CLC 35**
See also Vance, John Holbrook DLB 8

**Vance, John Holbrook** 1916-
See Queen, Ellery; Vance, Jack
See also CA 29-32R; CANR 17, 65; MTCW 1

**Van Den Bogarde, Derek Jules Gaspard Ulric Niven** 1921-1999 ............. **CLC 14**
See also CA 77-80; 179; DLB 19

**Vandenburgh, Jane** .......................... **CLC 59**
See also CA 168

**Vanderhaeghe, Guy** 1951- ................. **CLC 41**
See also CA 113; CANR 72

**van der Post, Laurens (Jan)** 1906-1996 ..................................... **CLC 5**
See also CA 5-8R; 155; CANR 35; DLB 204

**van de Wetering, Janwillem** 1931- ... **CLC 47**
See also CA 49-52; CANR 4, 62

**Van Dine, S. S.** .............................. **TCLC 23**
See also Wright, Willard Huntington

**Van Doren, Carl (Clinton)** 1885-1950 ..................................... **TCLC 18**
See also CA 111; 168

**Van Doren, Mark** 1894-1972 ........ **CLC 6, 10**
See also CA 1-4R; 37-40R; CANR 3; DLB 45; MTCW 1, 2

**Van Druten, John (William)** 1901-1957
**TCLC 2**
See also CA 104; 161; DLB 10

**Van Duyn, Mona (Jane)** 1921- ...... **CLC 3, 7, 63, 116; DAM POET**
See also CA 9-12R; CANR 7, 38, 60; DLB 5

**Van Dyne, Edith**
See Baum, L(yman) Frank

**van Itallie, Jean-Claude** 1936- ............ **CLC 3**
See also CA 45-48; CAAS 2; CANR 1, 48; DLB 7

**van Ostaijen, Paul** 1896-1928 ........ **TCLC 33**
See also CA 163

**Van Peebles, Melvin** 1932- .......... **CLC 2, 20; DAM MULT**
See also BW 2, 3; CA 85-88; CANR 27, 67, 82

**Vansittart, Peter** 1920- ...................... **CLC 42**
See also CA 1-4R; CANR 3, 49

**Van Vechten, Carl** 1880-1964 ........... **CLC 33**
See also CA 183; 89-92; DLB 4, 9, 51

**Van Vogt, A(lfred) E(lton)** 1912- ........ **CLC 1**
See also CA 21-24R; CANR 28; DLB 8; SATA 14

**Varda, Agnes** 1928- ........................... **CLC 16**
See also CA 116; 122

**Vargas Llosa, (Jorge) Mario (Pedro)** 1936-
**CLC 3, 6, 9, 10, 15, 31, 42, 85; DA; DAB; DAC; DAM MST, MULT, NOV; HLC 2**
See also CA 73-76; CANR 18, 32, 42, 67; DA3; DLB 145; HW 1, 2; MTCW 1, 2

**Vasiliu, Gheorghe** 1881-1957
See Bacovia, George
See also CA 123

**Vassa, Gustavus**
See Equiano, Olaudah

**Vassilikos, Vassilis** 1933- ................. **CLC 4, 8**
See also CA 81-84; CANR 75

**Vaughan, Henry** 1621-1695 ................. **LC 27**
See also DLB 131

**Vaughn, Stephanie** ........................... **CLC 62**

**Vazov, Ivan (Minchov)** 1850-1921 . **TCLC 25**
See also CA 121; 167; DLB 147

**Veblen, Thorstein B(unde)** 1857-1929 ............................... **TCLC 31**
See also CA 115; 165

**Vega, Lope de** 1562-1635 .... **LC 23; HLCS 2**

**Venison, Alfred**
See Pound, Ezra (Weston Loomis)

**Verdi, Marie de**
See Mencken, H(enry) L(ouis)

**Verdu, Matilde**
See Cela, Camilo Jose

**Verga, Giovanni (Carmelo)** 1840-1922 ................. **TCLC 3; SSC 21**
See also CA 104; 123

**Vergil** 70B.C.-19B.C. ... **CMLC 9; DA; DAB; DAC; DAM MST, POET; PC 12; WLCS**
See also Virgil DA3

**Verhaeren, Emile (Adolphe Gustave)**
   1855-1916 ................. **TCLC 12**
   See also CA 109
**Verlaine, Paul (Marie)** 1844-1896 .. **NCLC 2,
   51; DAM POET; PC 2**
**Verne, Jules (Gabriel)** 1828-1905 ... **TCLC 6,
   52**
   See also AAYA 16; CA 110; 131; DA3;
   DLB 123; JRDA; MAICYA; SATA 21
**Very, Jones** 1813-1880 ..................... **NCLC 9**
   See also DLB 1
**Vesaas, Tarjei** 1897-1970 .................. **CLC 48**
   See also CA 29-32R
**Vialis, Gaston**
   See Simenon, Georges (Jacques Christian)
**Vian, Boris** 1920-1959 ...................... **TCLC 9**
   See also CA 106; 164; DLB 72; MTCW 2
**Viaud, (Louis Marie) Julien** 1850-1923
   See Loti, Pierre
   See also CA 107
**Vicar, Henry**
   See Felsen, Henry Gregor
**Vicker, Angus**
   See Felsen, Henry Gregor
**Vidal, Gore** 1925- ...... **CLC 2, 4, 6, 8, 10, 22,
   33, 72; DAM NOV, POP**
   See also AITN 1; BEST 90:2; CA 5-8R;
   CANR 13, 45, 65; CDALBS; DA3; DLB
   6, 152; INT CANR-13; MTCW 1, 2
**Viereck, Peter (Robert Edwin)**
   1916- .............................. **CLC 4; PC 27**
   See also CA 1-4R; CANR 1, 47; DLB 5
**Vigny, Alfred (Victor) de**
   1797-1863 .. **NCLC 7; DAM POET; PC
   26**
   See also DLB 119, 192
**Vilakazi, Benedict Wallet**
   1906-1947 ......................... **TCLC 37**
   See also CA 168
**Villa, Jose Garcia** 1904-1997 .............. **PC 22**
   See also CA 25-28R; CANR 12
**Villarreal, Jose Antonio** 1924-
   See also CA 133; DAM MULT; DLB 82;
   HLC 2; HW 1
**Villaurrutia, Xavier** 1903-1950 ...... **TCLC 80**
   See also HW 1
**Villehardouin** 1150(?)-1218(?) ....... **CMLC 38**
**Villiers de l'Isle Adam, Jean Marie Mathias
   Philippe Auguste, Comte de** 1838-1889
   **NCLC 3; SSC 14**
   See also DLB 123
**Villon, Francois** 1431-1463(?) ............. **PC 13**
   See also DLB 208
**Vinci, Leonardo da** 1452-1519 ........... **LC 12**
**Vine, Barbara** ................................. **CLC 50**
   See Rendell, Ruth (Barbara) BEST 90:4
**Vinge, Joan (Carol) D(ennison)**
   1948- ........................... **CLC 30; SSC 24**
   See also AAYA 32; CA 93-96; CANR 72;
   SATA 36, 113
**Violis, G.**
   See Simenon, Georges (Jacques Christian)
**Viramontes, Helena Maria** 1954-
   See also CA 159; DLB 122; HLCS 2; HW
   2
**Virgil** 70B.C.-19B.C.
   See Vergil
   See also DLB 211
**Visconti, Luchino** 1906-1976 ............ **CLC 16**
   See also CA 81-84; 65-68; CANR 39
**Vittorini, Elio** 1908-1966 ......... **CLC 6, 9, 14**
   See also CA 133; 25-28R
**Vivekananda, Swami** 1863-1902 .... **TCLC 88**
**Vizenor, Gerald Robert** 1934- ....... **CLC 103;
   DAM MULT**
   See also CA 13-16R; CAAS 22; CANR 5,
   21, 44, 67; DLB 175; MTCW 2; NNAL

**Vizinczey, Stephen** 1933- .................. **CLC 40**
   See also CA 128; INT 128
**Vliet, R(ussell) G(ordon)**
   1929-1984 ........................ **CLC 22**
   See also CA 37-40R; 112; CANR 18
**Vogau, Boris Andreyevich** 1894-1937(?)
   See Pilnyak, Boris
   See also CA 123
**Vogel, Paula A(nne)** 1951- ................ **CLC 76**
   See also CA 108
**Voigt, Cynthia** 1942- ......................... **CLC 30**
   See also AAYA 3, 30; CA 106; CANR 18,
   37, 40; CLR 13, 48; INT CANR-18;
   JRDA; MAICYA; SATA 48, 79; SATA-
   Brief 33
**Voigt, Ellen Bryant** 1943- ................. **CLC 54**
   See also CA 69-72; CANR 11, 29, 55; DLB
   120
**Voinovich, Vladimir (Nikolaevich)** 1932-
   **CLC 10, 49**
   See also CA 81-84; CAAS 12; CANR 33,
   67; MTCW 1
**Vollmann, William T.** 1959- .. **CLC 89; DAM
   NOV, POP**
   See also CA 134; CANR 67; DA3; MTCW
   2
**Voloshinov, V. N.**
   See Bakhtin, Mikhail Mikhailovich
**Voltaire** 1694-1778 ........... **LC 14; DA; DAB;
   DAC; DAM DRAM, MST; SSC 12;
   WLC**
   See also DA3
**von Aschendrof, BaronIgnatz**
   See Ford, Ford Madox
**von Daeniken, Erich** 1935- ............... **CLC 30**
   See also AITN 1; CA 37-40R; CANR 17,
   44
**von Daniken, Erich**
   See von Daeniken, Erich
**von Heidenstam, (Carl Gustaf) Verner**
   See Heidenstam, (Carl Gustaf) Verner von
**von Heyse, Paul (Johann Ludwig)**
   See Heyse, Paul (Johann Ludwig von)
**von Hofmannsthal, Hugo**
   See Hofmannsthal, Hugo von
**von Horvath, Odon**
   See Horvath, Oedoen von
**von Horvath, Oedoen** -1938
   See Horvath, Oedoen von
   See also CA 184
**von Liliencron, (Friedrich Adolf Axel)
   Detlev**
   See Liliencron, (Friedrich Adolf Axel) De-
   tlev von
**Vonnegut, Kurt, Jr.** 1922- . **CLC 1, 2, 3, 4, 5,
   8, 12, 22, 40, 60, 111; DA; DAB; DAC;
   DAM MST, NOV, POP; SSC 8; WLC**
   See also AAYA 6; AITN 1; BEST 90:4; CA
   1-4R; CANR 1, 25, 49, 75; CDALB 1968-
   1988; DA3; DLB 2, 8, 152; DLBD 3;
   DLBY 80; MTCW 1, 2
**Von Rachen, Kurt**
   See Hubbard, L(afayette) Ron(ald)
**von Rezzori (d'Arezzo), Gregor**
   See Rezzori (d'Arezzo), Gregor von
**von Sternberg, Josef**
   See Sternberg, Josef von
**Vorster, Gordon** 1924- ...................... **CLC 34**
   See also CA 133
**Vosce, Trudie**
   See Ozick, Cynthia
**Voznesensky, Andrei (Andreievich)** 1933-
   **CLC 1, 15, 57; DAM POET**
   See also CA 89-92; CANR 37; MTCW 1
**Waddington, Miriam** 1917- .............. **CLC 28**
   See also CA 21-24R; CANR 12, 30; DLB
   68
**Wagman, Fredrica** 1937- ................... **CLC 7**
   See also CA 97-100; INT 97-100

**Wagner, Linda W.**
   See Wagner-Martin, Linda (C.)
**Wagner, Linda Welshimer**
   See Wagner-Martin, Linda (C.)
**Wagner, Richard** 1813-1883 ............. **NCLC 9**
   See also DLB 129
**Wagner-Martin, Linda (C.)** 1936- .... **CLC 50**
   See also CA 159
**Wagoner, David (Russell)** 1926- .... **CLC 3, 5,
   15**
   See also CA 1-4R; CAAS 3; CANR 2, 71;
   DLB 5; SATA 14
**Wah, Fred(erick James)** 1939- ......... **CLC 44**
   See also CA 107; 141; DLB 60
**Wahloo, Per** 1926-1975 ...................... **CLC 7**
   See also CA 61-64; CANR 73
**Wahloo, Peter**
   See Wahloo, Per
**Wain, John (Barrington)** 1925-1994 . **CLC 2,
   11, 15, 46**
   See also CA 5-8R; 145; CAAS 4; CANR
   23, 54; CDBLB 1960 to Present; DLB 15,
   27, 139, 155; MTCW 1, 2
**Wajda, Andrzej** 1926- ....................... **CLC 16**
   See also CA 102
**Wakefield, Dan** 1932- ......................... **CLC 7**
   See also CA 21-24R; CAAS 7
**Wakoski, Diane** 1937- .... **CLC 2, 4, 7, 9, 11,
   40; DAM POET; PC 15**
   See also CA 13-16R; CAAS 1; CANR 9,
   60; DLB 5; INT CANR-9; MTCW 2
**Wakoski-Sherbell, Diane**
   See Wakoski, Diane
**Walcott, Derek (Alton)** 1930- .... **CLC 2, 4, 9,
   14, 25, 42, 67, 76; BLC 3; DAB; DAC;
   DAM MST, MULT, POET; DC 7**
   See also BW 2; CA 89-92; CANR 26, 47,
   75, 80; DA3; DLB 117; DLBY 81;
   MTCW 1, 2
**Waldman, Anne (Lesley)** 1945- ......... **CLC 7**
   See also CA 37-40R; CAAS 17; CANR 34,
   69; DLB 16
**Waldo, E. Hunter**
   See Sturgeon, Theodore (Hamilton)
**Waldo, Edward Hamilton**
   See Sturgeon, Theodore (Hamilton)
**Walker, Alice (Malsenior)** 1944- ... **CLC 5, 6,
   9, 19, 27, 46, 58, 103; BLC 3; DA;
   DAB; DAC; DAM MST, MULT, NOV,
   POET, POP; SSC 5; WLCS**
   See also AAYA 3; BEST 89:4; BW 2, 3;
   CA 37-40R; CANR 9, 27, 49, 66, 82;
   CDALB 1968-1988; DA3; DLB 6, 33,
   143; INT CANR-27; MTCW 1, 2; SATA
   31
**Walker, David Harry** 1911-1992 ...... **CLC 14**
   See also CA 1-4R; 137; CANR 1; SATA 8;
   SATA-Obit 71
**Walker, Edward Joseph** 1934-
   See Walker, Ted
   See also CA 21-24R; CANR 12, 28, 53
**Walker, George F.** 1947- . **CLC 44, 61; DAB;
   DAC; DAM MST**
   See also CA 103; CANR 21, 43, 59; DLB
   60
**Walker, Joseph A.** 1935- ....... **CLC 19; DAM
   DRAM, MST**
   See also BW 1, 3; CA 89-92; CANR 26;
   DLB 38
**Walker, Margaret (Abigail)**
   1915-1998 .......... **CLC 1, 6; BLC; DAM
   MULT; PC 20**
   See also BW 2, 3; CA 73-76; 172; CANR
   26, 54, 76; DLB 76, 152; MTCW 1, 2
**Walker, Ted** ................................... **CLC 13**
   See also Walker, Edward Joseph DLB 40
**Wallace, David Foster** 1962- ..... **CLC 50, 114**
   See also CA 132; CANR 59; DA3; MTCW
   2

**Wallace, Dexter**
See Masters, Edgar Lee
**Wallace, (Richard Horatio) Edgar** 1875-1932
**TCLC 57**
See also CA 115; DLB 70
**Wallace, Irving** 1916-1990 .......... **CLC 7, 13;**
**DAM NOV, POP**
See also AITN 1; CA 1-4R; 132; CAAS 1;
CANR 1, 27; INT CANR-27; MTCW 1,
2
**Wallant, Edward Lewis** 1926-1962 ... **CLC 5,**
**10**
See also CA 1-4R; CANR 22; DLB 2, 28,
143; MTCW 1, 2
**Wallas, Graham** 1858-1932 ........... **TCLC 91**
**Walley, Byron**
See Card, Orson Scott
**Walpole, Horace** 1717-1797 ................ **LC 49**
See also DLB 39, 104
**Walpole, Hugh (Seymour)**
1884-1941 ................................... **TCLC 5**
See also CA 104; 165; DLB 34; MTCW 2
**Walser, Martin** 1927- ........................ **CLC 27**
See also CA 57-60; CANR 8, 46; DLB 75,
124
**Walser, Robert** 1878-1956 .... **TCLC 18; SSC**
**20**
See also CA 118; 165; DLB 66
**Walsh, Jill Paton** ............................... **CLC 35**
See also Paton Walsh, Gillian CLR 2
**Walter, Villiam Christian**
See Andersen, Hans Christian
**Wambaugh, Joseph (Aloysius, Jr.)**
1937- ....... **CLC 3, 18; DAM NOV, POP**
See also AITN 1; BEST 89:3; CA 33-36R;
CANR 42, 65; DA3; DLB 6; DLBY 83;
MTCW 1, 2
**Wang Wei** 699(?)-761(?) ....................... **PC 18**
**Ward, Arthur Henry Sarsfield** 1883-1959
See Rohmer, Sax
See also CA 108; 173
**Ward, Douglas Turner** 1930- ........... **CLC 19**
See also BW 1; CA 81-84; CANR 27; DLB
7, 38
**Ward, E. D.**
See Lucas, E(dward) V(errall)
**Ward, Mary Augusta**
See Ward, Mrs. Humphry
**Ward, Mrs. Humphry** 1851-1920 .. **TCLC 55**
See also DLB 18
**Ward, Peter**
See Faust, Frederick (Schiller)
**Warhol, Andy** 1928(?)-1987 ............. **CLC 20**
See also AAYA 12; BEST 89:4; CA 89-92;
121; CANR 34
**Warner, Francis (Robert le Plastrier)** 1937-
**CLC 14**
See also CA 53-56; CANR 11
**Warner, Marina** 1946- ...................... **CLC 59**
See also CA 65-68; CANR 21, 55; DLB
194
**Warner, Rex (Ernest)** 1905-1986 ...... **CLC 45**
See also CA 89-92; 119; DLB 15
**Warner, Susan (Bogert)**
1819-1885 ................................. **NCLC 31**
See also DLB 3, 42
**Warner, Sylvia (Constance) Ashton**
See Ashton-Warner, Sylvia (Constance)
**Warner, Sylvia Townsend**
1893-1978 ............... **CLC 7, 19; SSC 23**
See also CA 61-64; 77-80; CANR 16, 60;
DLB 34, 139; MTCW 1, 2
**Warren, Mercy Otis** 1728-1814 ..... **NCLC 13**
See also DLB 31, 200

**Warren, Robert Penn** 1905-1989 .. **CLC 1, 4,**
**6, 8, 10, 13, 18, 39, 53, 59; DA; DAB;**
**DAC; DAM MST, NOV, POET; SSC 4;**
**WLC**
See also AITN 1; CA 13-16R; 129; CANR
10, 47; CDALB 1968-1988; DA3; DLB
2, 48, 152; DLBY 80, 89; INT CANR-10;
MTCW 1, 2; SATA 46; SATA-Obit 63
**Warshofsky, Isaac**
See Singer, Isaac Bashevis
**Warton, Thomas** 1728-1790 ..... **LC 15; DAM**
**POET**
See also DLB 104, 109
**Waruk, Kona**
See Harris, (Theodore) Wilson
**Warung, Price** 1855-1911 .............. **TCLC 45**
**Warwick, Jarvis**
See Garner, Hugh
**Washington, Alex**
See Harris, Mark
**Washington, Booker T(aliaferro)** 1856-1915
**TCLC 10; BLC 3; DAM MULT**
See also BW 1; CA 114; 125; DA3; SATA
28
**Washington, George** 1732-1799 .......... **LC 25**
See also DLB 31
**Wassermann, (Karl) Jakob**
1873-1934 ................................... **TCLC 6**
See also CA 104; 163; DLB 66
**Wasserstein, Wendy** 1950- .. **CLC 32, 59, 90;**
**DAM DRAM; DC 4**
See also CA 121; 129; CABS 3; CANR 53,
75; DA3; INT 129; MTCW 2; SATA 94
**Waterhouse, Keith (Spencer)** 1929- . **CLC 47**
See also CA 5-8R; CANR 38, 67; DLB 13,
15; MTCW 1, 2
**Waters, Frank (Joseph)** 1902-1995 .. **CLC 88**
See also CA 5-8R; 149; CAAS 13; CANR
3, 18, 63; DLB 212; DLBY 86
**Waters, Roger** 1944- ......................... **CLC 35**
**Watkins, Frances Ellen**
See Harper, Frances Ellen Watkins
**Watkins, Gerrold**
See Malzberg, Barry N(athaniel)
**Watkins, Gloria Jean** 1952(?)-
See hooks, bell
See also BW 2; CA 143; CANR 87; MTCW
2
**Watkins, Paul** 1964- ........................... **CLC 55**
See also CA 132; CANR 62
**Watkins, Vernon Phillips**
1906-1967 ................................... **CLC 43**
See also CA 9-10; 25-28R; CAP 1; DLB 20
**Watson, Irving S.**
See Mencken, H(enry) L(ouis)
**Watson, John H.**
See Farmer, Philip Jose
**Watson, Richard F.**
See Silverberg, Robert
**Waugh, Auberon (Alexander)** 1939- .. **CLC 7**
See also CA 45-48; CANR 6, 22; DLB 14,
194
**Waugh, Evelyn (Arthur St. John)** 1903-1966
**CLC 1, 3, 8, 13, 19, 27, 44, 107; DA;**
**DAB; DAC; DAM MST, NOV, POP;**
**WLC**
See also CA 85-88; 25-28R; CANR 22; CD-
BLB 1914-1945; DA3; DLB 15, 162, 195;
MTCW 1, 2
**Waugh, Harriet** 1944- ......................... **CLC 6**
See also CA 85-88; CANR 22
**Ways, C. R.**
See Blount, Roy (Alton), Jr.
**Waystaff, Simon**
See Swift, Jonathan
**Webb, Beatrice (Martha Potter)** 1858-1943
**TCLC 22**
See also CA 117; 162; DLB 190

**Webb, Charles (Richard)** 1939- ......... **CLC 7**
See also CA 25-28R
**Webb, James H(enry), Jr.** 1946- ...... **CLC 22**
See also CA 81-84
**Webb, Mary Gladys (Meredith)** 1881-1927
**TCLC 24**
See also CA 182; 123; DLB 34
**Webb, Mrs. Sidney**
See Webb, Beatrice (Martha Potter)
**Webb, Phyllis** 1927- ........................... **CLC 18**
See also CA 104; CANR 23; DLB 53
**Webb, Sidney (James)** 1859-1947 .. **TCLC 22**
See also CA 117; 163; DLB 190
**Webber, Andrew Lloyd** .................... **CLC 21**
See also Lloyd Webber, Andrew
**Weber, Lenora Mattingly**
1895-1971 ................................... **CLC 12**
See also CA 19-20; 29-32R; CAP 1; SATA
2; SATA-Obit 26
**Weber, Max** 1864-1920 .................. **TCLC 69**
See also CA 109
**Webster, John** 1579(?)-1634(?) ... **LC 33; DA;**
**DAB; DAC; DAM DRAM, MST; DC**
**2; WLC**
See also CDBLB Before 1660; DLB 58
**Webster, Noah** 1758-1843 .............. **NCLC 30**
See also DLB 1, 37, 42, 43, 73
**Wedekind, (Benjamin) Frank(lin)** 1864-1918
**TCLC 7; DAM DRAM**
See also CA 104; 153; DLB 118
**Weidman, Jerome** 1913-1998 ............. **CLC 7**
See also AITN 2; CA 1-4R; 171; CANR 1;
DLB 28
**Weil, Simone (Adolphine)**
1909-1943 ................................. **TCLC 23**
See also CA 117; 159; MTCW 2
**Weininger, Otto** 1880-1903 ............ **TCLC 84**
**Weinstein, Nathan**
See West, Nathanael
**Weinstein, Nathan von Wallenstein**
See West, Nathanael
**Weir, Peter (Lindsay)** 1944- ............. **CLC 20**
See also CA 113; 123
**Weiss, Peter (Ulrich)** 1916-1982 .. **CLC 3, 15,**
**51; DAM DRAM**
See also CA 45-48; 106; CANR 3; DLB 69,
124
**Weiss, Theodore (Russell)** 1916- ... **CLC 3, 8,**
**14**
See also CA 9-12R; CAAS 2; CANR 46;
DLB 5
**Welch, (Maurice) Denton**
1915-1948 ................................. **TCLC 22**
See also CA 121; 148
**Welch, James** 1940- ..... **CLC 6, 14, 52; DAM**
**MULT, POP**
See also CA 85-88; CANR 42, 66; DLB
175; NNAL
**Weldon, Fay** 1931- . **CLC 6, 9, 11, 19, 36, 59,**
**122; DAM POP**
See also CA 21-24R; CANR 16, 46, 63;
CDBLB 1960 to Present; DLB 14, 194;
INT CANR-16; MTCW 1, 2
**Wellek, Rene** 1903-1995 ................... **CLC 28**
See also CA 5-8R; 150; CAAS 7; CANR 8;
DLB 63; INT CANR-8
**Weller, Michael** 1942- ................... **CLC 10, 53**
See also CA 85-88
**Weller, Paul** 1958- ............................. **CLC 26**
**Wellershoff, Dieter** 1925- .................. **CLC 46**
See also CA 89-92; CANR 16, 37
**Welles, (George) Orson** 1915-1985 .. **CLC 20,**
**80**
See also CA 93-96; 117
**Wellman, John McDowell** 1945-
See Wellman, Mac
See also CA 166

**Wellman, Mac** 1945- .......................... **CLC 65**
  See also Wellman, John McDowell; Wellman, John McDowell

**Wellman, Manly Wade** 1903-1986 ... **CLC 49**
  See also CA 1-4R; 118; CANR 6, 16, 44; SATA 6; SATA-Obit 47

**Wells, Carolyn** 1869(?)-1942 .......... **TCLC 35**
  See also CA 113; DLB 11

**Wells, H(erbert) G(eorge)**
  1866-1946 . **TCLC 6, 12, 19; DA; DAB; DAC; DAM MST, NOV; SSC 6; WLC**
  See also AAYA 18; CA 110; 121; CDBLB 1914-1945; DA3; DLB 34, 70, 156, 178; MTCW 1, 2; SATA 20

**Wells, Rosemary** 1943- ..................... **CLC 12**
  See also AAYA 13; CA 85-88; CANR 48; CLR 16; MAICYA; SAAS 1; SATA 18, 69

**Welty, Eudora** 1909- ...... **CLC 1, 2, 5, 14, 22, 33, 105; DA; DAB; DAC; DAM MST, NOV; SSC 1, 27; WLC**
  See also CA 9-12R; CABS 1; CANR 32, 65; CDALB 1941-1968; DA3; DLB 2, 102, 143; DLBD 12; DLBY 87; MTCW 1, 2

**Wen I-to** 1899-1946 ........................ **TCLC 28**

**Wentworth, Robert**
  See Hamilton, Edmond

**Werfel, Franz (Viktor)** 1890-1945 ... **TCLC 8**
  See also CA 104; 161; DLB 81, 124

**Wergeland, Henrik Arnold**
  1808-1845 ................................. **NCLC 5**

**Wersba, Barbara** 1932- .................... **CLC 30**
  See also AAYA 2, 30; CA 29-32R, 182; CAAE 182; CANR 16, 38; CLR 3; DLB 52; JRDA; MAICYA; SAAS 2; SATA 1, 58; SATA-Essay 103

**Wertmueller, Lina** 1928- .................. **CLC 16**
  See also CA 97-100; CANR 39, 78

**Wescott, Glenway** 1901-1987 .. **CLC 13; SSC 35**
  See also CA 13-16R; 121; CANR 23, 70; DLB 4, 9, 102

**Wesker, Arnold** 1932- ... **CLC 3, 5, 42; DAB; DAM DRAM**
  See also CA 1-4R; CAAS 7; CANR 1, 33; CDBLB 1960 to Present; DLB 13; MTCW 1

**Wesley, Richard (Errol)** 1945- ........... **CLC 7**
  See also BW 1; CA 57-60; CANR 27; DLB 38

**Wessel, Johan Herman** 1742-1785 ........ **LC 7**

**West, Anthony (Panther)**
  1914-1987 ................................. **CLC 50**
  See also CA 45-48; 124; CANR 3, 19; DLB 15

**West, C. P.**
  See Wodehouse, P(elham) G(renville)

**West, (Mary) Jessamyn** 1902-1984 ... **CLC 7, 17**
  See also CA 9-12R; 112; CANR 27; DLB 6; DLBY 84; MTCW 1, 2; SATA-Obit 37

**West, Morris L(anglo)** 1916- ........ **CLC 6, 33**
  See also CA 5-8R; CANR 24, 49, 64; MTCW 1, 2

**West, Nathanael** 1903-1940 ....... **TCLC 1, 14, 44; SSC 16**
  See also CA 104; 125; CDALB 1929-1941; DA3; DLB 4, 9, 28; MTCW 1, 2

**West, Owen**
  See Koontz, Dean R(ay)

**West, Paul** 1930- ..................... **CLC 7, 14, 96**
  See also CA 13-16R; CAAS 7; CANR 22, 53, 76; DLB 14; INT CANR-22; MTCW 2

**West, Rebecca** 1892-1983 ... **CLC 7, 9, 31, 50**
  See also CA 5-8R; 109; CANR 19; DLB 36; DLBY 83; MTCW 1, 2

**Westall, Robert (Atkinson)**
  1929-1993 ........................... **CLC 17**
  See also AAYA 12; CA 69-72; 141; CANR 18, 68; CLR 13; JRDA; MAICYA; SAAS 2; SATA 23, 69; SATA-Obit 75

**Westermarck, Edward** 1862-1939 . **TCLC 87**

**Westlake, Donald E(dwin)** 1933- ....... **CLC 7, 33; DAM POP**
  See also CA 17-20R; CAAS 13; CANR 16, 44, 65; INT CANR-16; MTCW 2

**Westmacott, Mary**
  See Christie, Agatha (Mary Clarissa)

**Weston, Allen**
  See Norton, Andre

**Wetcheek, J. L.**
  See Feuchtwanger, Lion

**Wetering, Janwillem van de**
  See van de Wetering, Janwillem

**Wetherald, Agnes Ethelwyn**
  1857-1940 ................................. **TCLC 81**
  See also DLB 99

**Wetherell, Elizabeth**
  See Warner, Susan (Bogert)

**Whale, James** 1889-1957 ................ **TCLC 63**

**Whalen, Philip** 1923- ..................... **CLC 6, 29**
  See also CA 9-12R; CANR 5, 39; DLB 16

**Wharton, Edith (Newbold Jones)** 1862-1937 **TCLC 3, 9, 27, 53; DA; DAB; DAC; DAM MST, NOV; SSC 6; WLC**
  See also AAYA 25; CA 104; 132; CDALB 1865-1917; DA3; DLB 4, 9, 12, 78, 189; DLBD 13; MTCW 1, 2

**Wharton, James**
  See Mencken, H(enry) L(ouis)

**Wharton, William (a pseudonym)** .. **CLC 18, 37**
  See also CA 93-96; DLBY 80; INT 93-96

**Wheatley (Peters), Phillis**
  1754(?)-1784 ...... **LC 3, 50; BLC 3; DA; DAC; DAM MST, MULT, POET; PC 3; WLC**
  See also CDALB 1640-1865; DA3; DLB 31, 50

**Wheelock, John Hall** 1886-1978 ....... **CLC 14**
  See also CA 13-16R; 77-80; CANR 14; DLB 45

**White, E(lwyn) B(rooks)**
  1899-1985 . **CLC 10, 34, 39; DAM POP**
  See also AITN 2; CA 13-16R; 116; CANR 16, 37; CDALBS; CLR 1, 21; DA3; DLB 11, 22; MAICYA; MTCW 1, 2; SATA 2, 29, 100; SATA-Obit 44

**White, Edmund (Valentine III)**
  1940- ............. **CLC 27, 110; DAM POP**
  See also AAYA 7; CA 45-48; CANR 3, 19, 36, 62; DA3; MTCW 1, 2

**White, Patrick (Victor Martindale)**
  1912-1990 . **CLC 3, 4, 5, 7, 9, 18, 65, 69**
  See also CA 81-84; 132; CANR 43; MTCW 1

**White, Phyllis Dorothy James** 1920-
  See James, P. D.
  See also CA 21-24R; CANR 17, 43, 65; DAM POP; DA3; MTCW 1, 2

**White, T(erence) H(anbury)**
  1906-1964 ................................. **CLC 30**
  See also AAYA 22; CA 73-76; CANR 37; DLB 160; JRDA; MAICYA; SATA 12

**White, Terence de Vere** 1912-1994 ... **CLC 49**
  See also CA 49-52; 145; CANR 3

**White, Walter**
  See White, Walter F(rancis)
  See also BLC; DAM MULT

**White, Walter F(rancis)**
  1893-1955 ................................. **TCLC 15**
  See also White, Walter BW 1; CA 115; 124; DLB 51

**White, William Hale** 1831-1913
  See Rutherford, Mark
  See also CA 121

**Whitehead, Alfred North**
  1861-1947 ................................. **TCLC 97**
  See also CA 117; 165; DLB 100

**Whitehead, E(dward) A(nthony)**
  1933- ...................................... **CLC 5**
  See also CA 65-68; CANR 58

**Whitemore, Hugh (John)** 1936- ....... **CLC 37**
  See also CA 132; CANR 77; INT 132

**Whitman, Sarah Helen (Power)** 1803-1878 **NCLC 19**
  See also DLB 1

**Whitman, Walt(er)** 1819-1892 .. **NCLC 4, 31, 81; DA; DAB; DAC; DAM MST, POET; PC 3; WLC**
  See also CDALB 1640-1865; DA3; DLB 3, 64; SATA 20

**Whitney, Phyllis A(yame)** 1903- ..... **CLC 42; DAM POP**
  See also AITN 2; BEST 90:3; CA 1-4R; CANR 3, 25, 38, 60; CLR 59; DA3; JRDA; MAICYA; MTCW 2; SATA 1, 30

**Whittemore, (Edward) Reed (Jr.)**
  1919- ...................................... **CLC 4**
  See also CA 9-12R; CAAS 8; CANR 4; DLB 5

**Whittier, John Greenleaf**
  1807-1892 ........................... **NCLC 8, 59**
  See also DLB 1

**Whittlebot, Hernia**
  See Coward, Noel (Peirce)

**Wicker, Thomas Grey** 1926-
  See Wicker, Tom
  See also CA 65-68; CANR 21, 46

**Wicker, Tom** ...................................... **CLC 7**
  See also Wicker, Thomas Grey

**Wideman, John Edgar** 1941- ...... **CLC 5, 34, 36, 67, 122; BLC 3; DAM MULT**
  See also BW 2, 3; CA 85-88; CANR 14, 42, 67; DLB 33, 143; MTCW 2

**Wiebe, Rudy (Henry)** 1934- .. **CLC 6, 11, 14; DAC; DAM MST**
  See also CA 37-40R; CANR 42, 67; DLB 60

**Wieland, Christoph Martin**
  1733-1813 ................................. **NCLC 17**
  See also DLB 97

**Wiene, Robert** 1881-1938 .............. **TCLC 56**

**Wieners, John** 1934- .......................... **CLC 7**
  See also CA 13-16R; DLB 16

**Wiesel, Elie(zer)** 1928- ....... **CLC 3, 5, 11, 37; DA; DAB; DAC; DAM MST, NOV; WLCS**
  See also AAYA 7; AITN 1; CA 5-8R; CAAS 4; CANR 8, 40, 65; CDALBS; DA3; DLB 83; DLBY 87; INT CANR-8; MTCW 1, 2; SATA 56

**Wiggins, Marianne** 1947- ................. **CLC 57**
  See also BEST 89:3; CA 130; CANR 60

**Wight, James Alfred** 1916-1995
  See Herriot, James
  See also CA 77-80; SATA 55; SATA-Brief 44

**Wilbur, Richard (Purdy)** 1921- ..... **CLC 3, 6, 9, 14, 53, 110; DA; DAB; DAC; DAM MST, POET**
  See also CA 1-4R; CABS 2; CANR 2, 29, 76; CDALBS; DLB 5, 169; INT CANR-29; MTCW 1, 2; SATA 9, 108

**Wild, Peter** 1940- .............................. **CLC 14**
  See also CA 37-40R; DLB 5

**Wilde, Oscar** 1854(?)-1900 .... **TCLC 1, 8, 23, 41; DA; DAB; DAC; DAM DRAM, MST, NOV; SSC 11; WLC**
  See also CA 104; 119; CDBLB 1890-1914; DA3; DLB 10, 19, 34, 57, 141, 156, 190; SATA 24

Wilder, Billy ............................ **CLC 20**
  See also Wilder, Samuel DLB 26
Wilder, Samuel 1906-
  See Wilder, Billy
  See also CA 89-92
Wilder, Thornton (Niven)
  1897-1975 .. **CLC 1, 5, 6, 10, 15, 35, 82;**
  **DA; DAB; DAC; DAM DRAM, MST,**
  **NOV; DC 1; WLC**
  See also AAYA 29; AITN 2; CA 13-16R;
  61-64; CANR 40; CDALBS; DA3; DLB
  4, 7, 9; DLBY 97; MTCW 1, 2
Wilding, Michael 1942- ..................... **CLC 73**
  See also CA 104; CANR 24, 49
Wiley, Richard 1944- ....................... **CLC 44**
  See also CA 121; 129; CANR 71
Wilhelm, Kate ............................... **CLC 7**
  See also Wilhelm, Katie Gertrude AAYA
  20; CAAS 5; DLB 8; INT CANR-17
Wilhelm, Katie Gertrude 1928-
  See Wilhelm, Kate
  See also CA 37-40R; CANR 17, 36, 60;
  MTCW 1
Wilkins, Mary
  See Freeman, Mary E(leanor) Wilkins
Willard, Nancy 1936- .................... **CLC 7, 37**
  See also CA 89-92; CANR 10, 39, 68; CLR
  5; DLB 5, 52; MAICYA; MTCW 1; SATA
  37, 71; SATA-Brief 30
William of Ockham 1285-1347 ..... **CMLC 32**
Williams, Ben Ames 1889-1953 ..... **TCLC 89**
  See also CA 183; DLB 102
Williams, C(harles) K(enneth)
  1936- ............ **CLC 33, 56; DAM POET**
  See also CA 37-40R; CAAS 26; CANR 57;
  DLB 5
Williams, Charles
  See Collier, James L(incoln)
Williams, Charles (Walter Stansby)
  1886-1945 ......................... **TCLC 1, 11**
  See also CA 104; 163; DLB 100, 153
Williams, (George) Emlyn
  1905-1987 ......... **CLC 15; DAM DRAM**
  See also CA 104; 123; CANR 36; DLB 10,
  77; MTCW 1
Williams, Hank 1923-1953 ............ **TCLC 81**
Williams, Hugo 1942- ...................... **CLC 42**
  See also CA 17-20R; CANR 45; DLB 40
Williams, J. Walker
  See Wodehouse, P(elham) G(renville)
Williams, John A(lfred) 1925- ..... **CLC 5, 13;**
  **BLC 3; DAM MULT**
  See also BW 2, 3; CA 53-56; CAAS 3;
  CANR 6, 26, 51; DLB 2, 33; INT
  CANR-6
Williams, Jonathan (Chamberlain) 1929-
  **CLC 13**
  See also CA 9-12R; CAAS 12; CANR 8;
  DLB 5
Williams, Joy 1944- ........................ **CLC 31**
  See also CA 41-44R; CANR 22, 48
Williams, Norman 1952- ................... **CLC 39**
  See also CA 118
Williams, Sherley Anne 1944- ......... **CLC 89;**
  **BLC 3; DAM MULT, POET**
  See also BW 2, 3; CA 73-76; CANR 25,
  82; DLB 41; INT CANR-25; SATA 78
Williams, Shirley
  See Williams, Sherley Anne
Williams, Tennessee 1911-1983 . **CLC 1, 2, 5,**
  **7, 8, 11, 15, 19, 30, 39, 45, 71, 111; DA;**
  **DAB; DAC; DAM DRAM, MST; DC**
  **4; WLC**
  See also AAYA 31; AITN 1, 2; CA 5-8R;
  108; CABS 3; CANR 31; CDALB 1941-
  1968; DA3; DLB 7; DLBD 4; DLBY 83;
  MTCW 1, 2

Williams, Thomas (Alonzo)
  1926-1990 ........................... **CLC 14**
  See also CA 1-4R; 132; CANR 2
Williams, William C.
  See Williams, William Carlos
Williams, William Carlos
  1883-1963 .... **CLC 1, 2, 5, 9, 13, 22, 42,**
  **67; DA; DAB; DAC; DAM MST,**
  **POET; PC 7; SSC 31**
  See also CA 89-92; CANR 34; CDALB
  1917-1929; DA3; DLB 4, 16, 54, 86;
  MTCW 1, 2
Williamson, David (Keith) 1942- ..... **CLC 56**
  See also CA 103; CANR 41
Williamson, Ellen Douglas 1905-1984
  See Douglas, Ellen
  See also CA 17-20R; 114; CANR 39
Williamson, Jack ............................ **CLC 29**
  See also Williamson, John Stewart CAAS
  8; DLB 8
Williamson, John Stewart 1908-
  See Williamson, Jack
  See also CA 17-20R; CANR 23, 70
Willie, Frederick
  See Lovecraft, H(oward) P(hillips)
Willingham, Calder (Baynard, Jr.)
  1922-1995 ......................... **CLC 5, 51**
  See also CA 5-8R; 147; CANR 3; DLB 2,
  44; MTCW 1
Willis, Charles
  See Clarke, Arthur C(harles)
Willis, Fingal O'Flahertie
  See Wilde, Oscar
Willy
  See Colette, (Sidonie-Gabrielle)
Willy, Colette
  See Colette, (Sidonie-Gabrielle)
Wilson, A(ndrew) N(orman) 1950- .. **CLC 33**
  See also CA 112; 122; DLB 14, 155, 194;
  MTCW 2
Wilson, Angus (Frank Johnstone) 1913-1991
  **CLC 2, 3, 5, 25, 34; SSC 21**
  See also CA 5-8R; 134; CANR 21; DLB
  15, 139, 155; MTCW 1, 2
Wilson, August 1945- ... **CLC 39, 50, 63, 118;**
  **BLC 3; DA; DAB; DAC; DAM**
  **DRAM, MST, MULT; DC 2; WLCS**
  See also AAYA 16; BW 2, 3; CA 115; 122;
  CANR 42, 54, 76; DA3; MTCW 1, 2
Wilson, Brian 1942- ........................ **CLC 12**
Wilson, Colin 1931- ..................... **CLC 3, 14**
  See also CA 1-4R; CAAS 5; CANR 1, 22,
  33, 77; DLB 14, 194; MTCW 1
Wilson, Dirk
  See Pohl, Frederik
Wilson, Edmund 1895-1972 .. **CLC 1, 2, 3, 8,**
  **24**
  See also CA 1-4R; 37-40R; CANR 1, 46;
  DLB 63; MTCW 1, 2
Wilson, Ethel Davis (Bryant) 1888(?)-1980
  **CLC 13; DAC; DAM POET**
  See also CA 102; DLB 68; MTCW 1
Wilson, John 1785-1854 ................... **NCLC 5**
Wilson, John (Anthony) Burgess 1917-1993
  See Burgess, Anthony
  See also CA 1-4R; 143; CANR 2, 46; DAC;
  DAM NOV; DA3; MTCW 1, 2
Wilson, Lanford 1937- .......... **CLC 7, 14, 36;**
  **DAM DRAM**
  See also CA 17-20R; CABS 3; CANR 45;
  DLB 7
Wilson, Robert M. 1944- ............... **CLC 7, 9**
  See also CA 49-52; CANR 2, 41; MTCW 1
Wilson, Robert McLiam 1964- ......... **CLC 59**
  See also CA 132
Wilson, Sloan 1920- ....................... **CLC 32**
  See also CA 1-4R; CANR 1, 44
Wilson, Snoo 1948- ......................... **CLC 33**
  See also CA 69-72

Wilson, William S(mith) 1932- ......... **CLC 49**
  See also CA 81-84
Wilson, (Thomas) Woodrow 1856-1924
  **TCLC 79**
  See also CA 166; DLB 47
Winchilsea, Anne (Kingsmill) Finch Counte
  1661-1720
  See Finch, Anne
Windham, Basil
  See Wodehouse, P(elham) G(renville)
Wingrove, David (John) 1954- ......... **CLC 68**
  See also CA 133
Winnemucca, Sarah 1844-1891 ..... **NCLC 79**
Winstanley, Gerrard 1609-1676 ......... **LC 52**
Wintergreen, Jane
  See Duncan, Sara Jeannette
Winters, Janet Lewis ...................... **CLC 41**
  See also Lewis, Janet DLBY 87
Winters, (Arthur) Yvor 1900-1968 .... **CLC 4,**
  **8, 32**
  See also CA 11-12; 25-28R; CAP 1; DLB
  48; MTCW 1
Winterson, Jeanette 1959- .... **CLC 64; DAM**
  **POP**
  See also CA 136; CANR 58; DA3; DLB
  207; MTCW 2
Winthrop, John 1588-1649 ................ **LC 31**
  See also DLB 24, 30
Wirth, Louis 1897-1952 ................. **TCLC 92**
Wiseman, Frederick 1930- ............... **CLC 20**
  See also CA 159
Wister, Owen 1860-1938 ................ **TCLC 21**
  See also CA 108; 162; DLB 9, 78, 186;
  SATA 62
Witkacy
  See Witkiewicz, Stanislaw Ignacy
Witkiewicz, Stanislaw Ignacy 1885-1939
  **TCLC 8**
  See also CA 105; 162
Wittgenstein, Ludwig (Josef Johann)
  1889-1951 ............................. **TCLC 59**
  See also CA 113; 164; MTCW 2
Wittig, Monique 1935(?)- ................. **CLC 22**
  See also CA 116; 135; DLB 83
Wittlin, Jozef 1896-1976 ................... **CLC 25**
  See also CA 49-52; 65-68; CANR 3
Wodehouse, P(elham) G(renville) 1881-1975
  **CLC 1, 2, 5, 10, 22; DAB; DAC; DAM**
  **NOV; SSC 2**
  See also AITN 2; CA 45-48; 57-60; CANR
  3, 33; CDBLB 1914-1945; DA3; DLB 34,
  162; MTCW 1, 2; SATA 22
Woiwode, L.
  See Woiwode, Larry (Alfred)
Woiwode, Larry (Alfred) 1941- ... **CLC 6, 10**
  See also CA 73-76; CANR 16; DLB 6; INT
  CANR-16
Wojciechowska, Maia (Teresa)
  1927- ........................................ **CLC 26**
  See also AAYA 8; CA 9-12R, 183; CAAE
  183; CANR 4, 41; CLR 1; JRDA; MAI-
  CYA; SAAS 1; SATA 1, 28, 83; SATA-
  Essay 104
Wojtyla, Karol
  See John Paul II, Pope
Wolf, Christa 1929- ............... **CLC 14, 29, 58**
  See also CA 85-88; CANR 45; DLB 75;
  MTCW 1
Wolfe, Gene (Rodman) 1931- ......... **CLC 25;**
  **DAM POP**
  See also CA 57-60; CAAS 9; CANR 6, 32,
  60; DLB 8; MTCW 2
Wolfe, George C. 1954- ........ **CLC 49; BLCS**
  See also CA 149

**Wolfe, Thomas (Clayton)**
1900-1938 ...... **TCLC 4, 13, 29, 61; DA; DAB; DAC; DAM MST, NOV; SSC 33; WLC**
See also CA 104; 132; CDALB 1929-1941; DA3; DLB 9, 102; DLBD 2, 16; DLBY 85, 97; MTCW 1, 2

**Wolfe, Thomas Kennerly, Jr.** 1930-
See Wolfe, Tom
See also CA 13-16R; CANR 9, 33, 70; DAM POP; DA3; DLB 185; INT CANR-9; MTCW 1, 2

**Wolfe, Tom** ................ **CLC 1, 2, 9, 15, 35, 51**
See also Wolfe, Thomas Kennerly, Jr. AAYA 8; AITN 2; BEST 89:1; DLB 152

**Wolff, Geoffrey (Ansell)** 1937- .......... **CLC 41**
See also CA 29-32R; CANR 29, 43, 78

**Wolff, Sonia**
See Levitin, Sonia (Wolff)

**Wolff, Tobias (Jonathan Ansell)**
1945- .................................... **CLC 39, 64**
See also AAYA 16; BEST 90:2; CA 114; 117; CAAS 22; CANR 54, 76; DA3; DLB 130; INT 117; MTCW 2

**Wolfram von Eschenbach** c. 1170-c. 1220 **CMLC 5**
See also DLB 138

**Wolitzer, Hilma** 1930- ........................ **CLC 17**
See also CA 65-68; CANR 18, 40; INT CANR-18; SATA 31

**Wollstonecraft, Mary** 1759-1797 ..... **LC 5, 50**
See also CDBLB 1789-1832; DLB 39, 104, 158

**Wonder, Stevie** .................................... **CLC 12**
See also Morris, Steveland Judkins

**Wong, Jade Snow** 1922- .................... **CLC 17**
See also CA 109; SATA 112

**Woodberry, George Edward** 1855-1930 **TCLC 73**
See also CA 165; DLB 71, 103

**Woodcott, Keith**
See Brunner, John (Kilian Houston)

**Woodruff, Robert W.**
See Mencken, H(enry) L(ouis)

**Woolf, (Adeline) Virginia**
1882-1941 .. **TCLC 1, 5, 20, 43, 56; DA; DAB; DAC; DAM MST, NOV; SSC 7; WLC**
See also Woolf, Virginia Adeline CA 104; 130; CANR 64; CDBLB 1914-1945; DA3; DLB 36, 100, 162; DLBD 10; MTCW 1

**Woolf, Virginia Adeline**
See Woolf, (Adeline) Virginia
See also MTCW 2

**Woollcott, Alexander (Humphreys)**
1887-1943 ................................... **TCLC 5**
See also CA 105; 161; DLB 29

**Woolrich, Cornell** 1903-1968 ........... **CLC 77**
See also Hopley-Woolrich, Cornell George

**Woolson, Constance Fenimore** 1840-1894 **NCLC 82**
See also DLB 12, 74, 189

**Wordsworth, Dorothy** 1771-1855 .. **NCLC 25**
See also DLB 107

**Wordsworth, William** 1770-1850 .. **NCLC 12, 38; DA; DAB; DAC; DAM MST, POET; PC 4; WLC**
See also CDBLB 1789-1832; DA3; DLB 93, 107

**Wouk, Herman** 1915- ... **CLC 1, 9, 38; DAM NOV, POP**
See also CA 5-8R; CANR 6, 33, 67; CDALBS; DA3; DLBY 82; INT CANR-6; MTCW 1, 2

**Wright, Charles (Penzel, Jr.)** 1935- .. **CLC 6, 13, 28, 119**
See also CA 29-32R; CAAS 7; CANR 23, 36, 62, 88; DLB 165; DLBY 82; MTCW 1, 2

**Wright, Charles Stevenson** 1932- ... **CLC 49; BLC 3; DAM MULT, POET**
See also BW 1; CA 9-12R; CANR 26; DLB 33

**Wright, Frances** 1795-1852 ........... **NCLC 74**
See also DLB 73

**Wright, Frank Lloyd** 1867-1959 .... **TCLC 95**
See also CA 174

**Wright, Jack R.**
See Harris, Mark

**Wright, James (Arlington)**
1927-1980 ........ **CLC 3, 5, 10, 28; DAM POET**
See also AITN 2; CA 49-52; 97-100; CANR 4, 34, 64; CDALBS; DLB 5, 169; MTCW 1, 2

**Wright, Judith (Arandell)** 1915- ..... **CLC 11, 53; PC 14**
See also CA 13-16R; CANR 31, 76; MTCW 1, 2; SATA 14

**Wright, L(aurali) R.** 1939- ............... **CLC 44**
See also CA 138

**Wright, Richard (Nathaniel)**
1908-1960 .... **CLC 1, 3, 4, 9, 14, 21, 48, 74; BLC 3; DA; DAB; DAC; DAM MST, MULT, NOV; SSC 2; WLC**
See also AAYA 5; BW 1; CA 108; CANR 64; CDALB 1929-1941; DA3; DLB 76, 102; DLBD 2; MTCW 1, 2

**Wright, Richard B(ruce)** 1937- .......... **CLC 6**
See also CA 85-88; DLB 53

**Wright, Rick** 1945- ............................. **CLC 35**

**Wright, Rowland**
See Wells, Carolyn

**Wright, Stephen** 1946- ...................... **CLC 33**

**Wright, Willard Huntington** 1888-1939
See Van Dine, S. S.
See also CA 115; DLBD 16

**Wright, William** 1930- ...................... **CLC 44**
See also CA 53-56; CANR 7, 23

**Wroth, LadyMary** 1587-1653(?) .......... **LC 30**
See also DLB 121

**Wu Ch'eng-en** 1500(?)-1582(?) ............. **LC 7**

**Wu Ching-tzu** 1701-1754 ...................... **LC 2**

**Wurlitzer, Rudolph** 1938(?)- .... **CLC 2, 4, 15**
See also CA 85-88; DLB 173

**Wyatt, Thomas** c. 1503-1542 ............... **PC 27**
See also DLB 132

**Wycherley, William** 1641-1715 ...... **LC 8, 21; DAM DRAM**
See also CDBLB 1660-1789; DLB 80

**Wylie, Elinor (Morton Hoyt)** 1885-1928 **TCLC 8; PC 23**
See also CA 105; 162; DLB 9, 45

**Wylie, Philip (Gordon)** 1902-1971 ... **CLC 43**
See also CA 21-22; 33-36R; CAP 2; DLB 9

**Wyndham, John** ................................. **CLC 19**
See also Harris, John (Wyndham Parkes Lucas) Beynon

**Wyss, Johann David Von**
1743-1818 ................................. **NCLC 10**
See also JRDA; MAICYA; SATA 29; SATA-Brief 27

**Xenophon** c. 430B.C.-c. 354B.C. ... **CMLC 17**
See also DLB 176

**Yakumo Koizumi**
See Hearn, (Patricio) Lafcadio (Tessima Carlos)

**Yamamoto, Hisaye** 1921- ........ **SSC 34; DAM MULT**

**Yanez, Jose Donoso**
See Donoso (Yanez), Jose

**Yanovsky, Basile S.**
See Yanovsky, V(assily) S(emenovich)

**Yanovsky, V(assily) S(emenovich)** 1906-1989 **CLC 2, 18**
See also CA 97-100; 129

**Yates, Richard** 1926-1992 ......... **CLC 7, 8, 23**
See also CA 5-8R; 139; CANR 10, 43; DLB 2; DLBY 81, 92; INT CANR-10

**Yeats, W. B.**
See Yeats, William Butler

**Yeats, William Butler** 1865-1939 .... **TCLC 1, 11, 18, 31, 93; DA; DAB; DAC; DAM DRAM, MST, POET; PC 20; WLC**
See also CA 104; 127; CANR 45; CDBLB 1890-1914; DA3; DLB 10, 19, 98, 156; MTCW 1, 2

**Yehoshua, A(braham) B.** 1936- .. **CLC 13, 31**
See also CA 33-36R; CANR 43

**Yellow Bird**
See Ridge, John Rollin

**Yep, Laurence Michael** 1948- ........... **CLC 35**
See also AAYA 5, 31; CA 49-52; CANR 1, 46; CLR 3, 17, 54; DLB 52; JRDA; MAICYA; SATA 7, 69

**Yerby, Frank G(arvin)** 1916-1991 . **CLC 1, 7, 22; BLC 3; DAM MULT**
See also BW 1, 3; CA 9-12R; 136; CANR 16, 52; DLB 76; INT CANR-16; MTCW 1

**Yesenin, Sergei Alexandrovich**
See Esenin, Sergei (Alexandrovich)

**Yevtushenko, Yevgeny (Alexandrovich)** 1933- **CLC 1, 3, 13, 26, 51, 126; DAM POET**
See also CA 81-84; CANR 33, 54; MTCW 1

**Yezierska, Anzia** 1885(?)-1970 ......... **CLC 46**
See also CA 126; 89-92; DLB 28; MTCW 1

**Yglesias, Helen** 1915- .................... **CLC 7, 22**
See also CA 37-40R; CAAS 20; CANR 15, 65; INT CANR-15; MTCW 1

**Yokomitsu Riichi** 1898-1947 .......... **TCLC 47**
See also CA 170

**Yonge, Charlotte (Mary)**
1823-1901 ................................. **TCLC 48**
See also CA 109; 163; DLB 18, 163; SATA 17

**York, Jeremy**
See Creasey, John

**York, Simon**
See Heinlein, Robert A(nson)

**Yorke, Henry Vincent** 1905-1974 ..... **CLC 13**
See also Green, Henry CA 85-88; 49-52

**Yosano Akiko** 1878-1942 .... **TCLC 59; PC 11**
See also CA 161

**Yoshimoto, Banana** ......................... **CLC 84**
See also Yoshimoto, Mahoko

**Yoshimoto, Mahoko** 1964-
See Yoshimoto, Banana
See also CA 144

**Young, Al(bert James)** 1939- . **CLC 19; BLC 3; DAM MULT**
See also BW 2, 3; CA 29-32R; CANR 26, 65; DLB 33

**Young, Andrew (John)** 1885-1971 ...... **CLC 5**
See also CA 5-8R; CANR 7, 29

**Young, Collier**
See Bloch, Robert (Albert)

**Young, Edward** 1683-1765 ............... **LC 3, 40**
See also DLB 95

**Young, Marguerite (Vivian)**
1909-1995 ................................. **CLC 82**
See also CA 13-16; 150; CAP 1

**Young, Neil** 1945- ............................. **CLC 17**
See also CA 110

**Young Bear, Ray A.** 1950- ..... **CLC 94; DAM MULT**
See also CA 146; DLB 175; NNAL

**Yourcenar, Marguerite** 1903-1987 ... **CLC 19, 38, 50, 87; DAM NOV**
  See also CA 69-72; CANR 23, 60; DLB 72; DLBY 88; MTCW 1, 2
**Yuan, Chu** 340(?)B.C.-278(?)B.C. . **CMLC 36**
**Yurick, Sol** 1925- ................................. **CLC 6**
  See also CA 13-16R; CANR 25
**Zabolotsky, Nikolai Alekseevich** 1903-1958 **TCLC 52**
  See also CA 116; 164
**Zagajewski, Adam** ............................... **PC 27**
**Zamiatin, Yevgenii**
  See Zamyatin, Evgeny Ivanovich
**Zamora, Bernice (B. Ortiz)** 1938- .. **CLC 89; DAM MULT; HLC 2**
  See also CA 151; CANR 80; DLB 82; HW 1, 2
**Zamyatin, Evgeny Ivanovich** 1884-1937 **TCLC 8, 37**
  See also CA 105; 166
**Zangwill, Israel** 1864-1926 ............. **TCLC 16**
  See also CA 109; 167; DLB 10, 135, 197
**Zappa, Francis Vincent, Jr.** 1940-1993
  See Zappa, Frank
  See also CA 108; 143; CANR 57
**Zappa, Frank** ...................................... **CLC 17**
  See also Zappa, Francis Vincent, Jr.
**Zaturenska, Marya** 1902-1982 ..... **CLC 6, 11**
  See also CA 13-16R; 105; CANR 22

**Zeami** 1363-1443 .................................... **DC 7**
**Zelazny, Roger (Joseph)** 1937-1995 . **CLC 21**
  See also AAYA 7; CA 21-24R; 148; CANR 26, 60; DLB 8; MTCW 1, 2; SATA 57; SATA-Brief 39
**Zhdanov, Andrei Alexandrovich** 1896-1948 **TCLC 18**
  See also CA 117; 167
**Zhukovsky, Vasily (Andreevich)** 1783-1852 **NCLC 35**
  See also DLB 205
**Ziegenhagen, Eric** ........................... **CLC 55**
**Zimmer, Jill Schary**
  See Robinson, Jill
**Zimmerman, Robert**
  See Dylan, Bob
**Zindel, Paul** 1936- ..... **CLC 6, 26; DA; DAB; DAC; DAM DRAM, MST, NOV; DC 5**
  See also AAYA 2; CA 73-76; CANR 31, 65; CDALBS; CLR 3, 45; DA3; DLB 7, 52; JRDA; MAICYA; MTCW 1, 2; SATA 16, 58, 102
**Zinov'Ev, A. A.**
  See Zinoviev, Alexander (Aleksandrovich)
**Zinoviev, Alexander (Aleksandrovich)** 1922- **CLC 19**
  See also CA 116; 133; CAAS 10

**Zoilus**
  See Lovecraft, H(oward) P(hillips)
**Zola, Emile (Edouard Charles Antoine)** 1840-1902 ........ **TCLC 1, 6, 21, 41; DA; DAB; DAC; DAM MST, NOV; WLC**
  See also CA 104; 138; DA3; DLB 123
**Zoline, Pamela** 1941- ........................ **CLC 62**
  See also CA 161
**Zorrilla y Moral, Jose** 1817-1893 .... **NCLC 6**
**Zoshchenko, Mikhail (Mikhailovich)** 1895-1958 ................. **TCLC 15; SSC 15**
  See also CA 115; 160
**Zuckmayer, Carl** 1896-1977 ............. **CLC 18**
  See also CA 69-72; DLB 56, 124
**Zuk, Georges**
  See Skelton, Robin
**Zukofsky, Louis** 1904-1978 ... **CLC 1, 2, 4, 7, 11, 18; DAM POET; PC 11**
  See also CA 9-12R; 77-80; CANR 39; DLB 5, 165; MTCW 1
**Zweig, Paul** 1935-1984 ................ **CLC 34, 42**
  See also CA 85-88; 113
**Zweig, Stefan** 1881-1942 ................ **TCLC 17**
  See also CA 112; 170; DLB 81, 118
**Zwingli, Huldreich** 1484-1531 ............. **LC 37**
  See also DLB 179

# *PC* Cumulative Nationality Index

## AMERICAN

Aiken, Conrad (Potter)  **26**
Ammons, A(rchie) R(andolph)  **16**
Ashbery, John (Lawrence)  **26**
Auden, W(ystan) H(ugh)  **1**
Baraka, Amiri  **4**
Berry, Wendell (Erdman)  **28**
Bishop, Elizabeth  **3**
Bogan, Louise  **12**
Bradstreet, Anne  **10**
Brodsky, Joseph  **9**
Brooks, Gwendolyn  **7**
Bryant, William Cullen  **20**
Bukowski, Charles  **18**
Carruth, Hayden  **10**
Clampitt, Amy  **19**
Clifton, (Thelma) Lucille  **17**
Crane, (Harold) Hart  **3**
Cullen, Countee  **20**
Cummings, E(dward) E(stlin)  **5**
Dickinson, Emily (Elizabeth)  **1**
Doolittle, Hilda  **5**
Dove, Rita (Frances)  **6**
Dunbar, Paul Laurence  **5**
Duncan, Robert (Edward)  **2**
Eliot, T(homas) S(tearns)  **5**
Emerson, Ralph Waldo  **18**
Ferlinghetti, Lawrence (Monsanto)  **1**
Forche, Carolyn (Louise)  **10**
Frost, Robert (Lee)  **1**
Gallagher, Tess  **9**
Ginsberg, Allen  **4**
Giovanni, Nikki  **19**
Gluck, Louise (Elisabeth)  **16**
Hammon, Jupiter  **16**
Harjo, Joy  **27**
Harper, Frances Ellen Watkins  **21**
Hass, Robert  **16**
Hayden, Robert E(arl)  **6**
H. D.  **5**
Hongo, Garrett Kaoru  **23**
Hughes, (James) Langston  **1**
Jeffers, (John) Robinson  **17**
Johnson, James Weldon  **24**
Kinnell, Galway  **26**
Knight, Etheridge  **14**
Kumin, Maxine (Winokur)  **15**
Kunitz, Stanley (Jasspon)  **19**
Levertov, Denise  **11**
Levine, Philip  **22**
Lindsay, (Nicholas) Vachel  **23**
Lorde, Audre (Geraldine)  **12**
Lowell, Amy  **13**

Lowell, Robert (Traill Spence Jr.)  **3**
Loy, Mina  **16**
Madhubuti, Haki R.  **5**
Masters, Edgar Lee  **1**
McKay, Claude  **2**
Meredith, William (Morris)  **28**
Merrill, James (Ingram)  **28**
Merton, Thomas  **10**
Millay, Edna St. Vincent  **6**
Momaday, N(avarre) Scott  **25**
Moore, Marianne (Craig)  **4**
Nash, (Frediric) Ogden  **21**
Nemerov, Howard (Stanley)  **24**
Olds, Sharon  **22**
Olson, Charles (John)  **19**
Ortiz, Simon J(oseph)  **17**
Parker, Dorothy (Rothschild)  **28**
Piercy, Marge  **29**
Pinsky, Robert  **27**
Plath, Sylvia  **1**
Poe, Edgar Allan  **1**
Pound, Ezra (Weston Loomis)  **4**
Reese, Lizette Woodworth  **29**
Rexroth, Kenneth  **20**
Rich, Adrienne (Cecile)  **5**
Robinson, Edwin Arlington  **1**
Roethke, Theodore (Huebner)  **15**
Rose, Wendy  **13**
Rukeyser, Muriel  **12**
Sanchez, Sonia  **9**
Sandburg, Carl (August)  **2**
Schwartz, Delmore (David)  **8**
Sexton, Anne (Harvey)  **2**
Shapiro, Karl (Jay)  **25**
Snyder, Gary (Sherman)  **21**
Song, Cathy  **21**
Soto, Gary  **28**
Stein, Gertrude  **18**
Stevens, Wallace  **6**
Stryk, Lucien  **27**
Swenson, May  **14**
Toomer, Jean  **7**
Viereck, Peter (Robert Edwin)  **27**
Wakoski, Diane  **15**
Walker, Margaret (Abigail)  **20**
Wheatley (Peters), Phillis  **3**
Whitman, Walt(er)  **3**
Williams, William Carlos  **7**
Wylie, Elinor (Morton Hoyt)  **23**
Zukofsky, Louis  **11**

## ARGENTINIAN

Borges, Jorge Luis  **22**

## AUSTRALIAN

Wright, Judith (Arandell)  **14**

## AUSTRIAN

Trakl, Georg  **20**

## CANADIAN

Atwood, Margaret (Eleanor)  **8**
Bissett, Bill  **14**
Ondaatje, (Philip) Michael  **28**
Page, P(atricia) K(athleen)  **12**

## CHILEAN

Neruda, Pablo  **4**

## CHINESE

Li Ho  **13**
Li Po  **29**
Tu Fu  **9**
Wang Wei  **18**

## CUBAN

Guillen, Nicolas (Cristobal)  **23**

## ENGLISH

Arnold, Matthew  **5**
Auden, W(ystan) H(ugh)  **1**
Behn, Aphra  **13**
Belloc, (Joseph) Hilaire (Pierre Sebastien
  Rene Swanton)  **24**
Blake, William  **12**
Bradstreet, Anne  **10**
Bridges, Robert (Seymour)  **28**
Bronte, Emily (Jane)  **8**
Brooke, Rupert (Chawner)  **24**
Browning, Elizabeth Barrett  **6**
Browning, Robert  **2**
Byron, George Gordon (Noel)  **16**
Carew, Thomas  **29**
Carroll, Lewis  **18**
Chaucer, Geoffrey  **19**
Chesterton, G(ilbert) K(eith)  **28**
Clare, John  **23**
Coleridge, Samuel Taylor  **11**
Davie, Donald (Alfred)  **29**
Day Lewis, C(ecil)  **11**
Donne, John  **1**
Dryden, John  **25**
Eliot, George  **20**
Eliot, T(homas) S(tearns)  **5**
Graves, Robert (von Ranke)  **6**
Gray, Thomas  **2**
Gunn, Thom(son William)  **26**

451

Hardy, Thomas **8**
Herbert, George **4**
Herrick, Robert **9**
Hopkins, Gerard Manley **15**
Housman, A(lfred) E(dward) **2**
Hughes, Ted **7**
Jonson, Ben(jamin) **17**
Keats, John **1**
Kipling, (Joseph) Rudyard **3**
Larkin, Philip (Arthur) **21**
Levertov, Denise **11**
Loy, Mina **16**
Marvell, Andrew **10**
Milton, John **19, 29**
Montagu, Mary (Pierrepont) Wortley **16**
Noyes, Alfred **27**
Owen, Wilfred (Edward Salter) **19**
Page, P(atricia) K(athleen) **12**
Pope, Alexander **26**
Rossetti, Christina (Georgina) **7**
Sassoon, Siegfried (Lorraine) **12**
Shelley, Percy Bysshe **14**
Sitwell, Dame Edith **3**
Smart, Christopher **13**
Smith, Stevie **12**
Spenser, Edmund **8**
Swift, Jonathan **9**
Swinburne, Algernon Charles **24**
Tennyson, Alfred **6**
Tomlinson, (Alfred) Charles **17**
Wordsworth, William **4**
Wyatt, Thomas **27**

## FILIPINO

Villa, Jose Garcia **22**

## FRENCH

Apollinaire, Guillaume **7**
Baudelaire, Charles **1**
Breton, Andre **15**
Gautier, Theophile **18**
Hugo, Victor (Marie) **17**
Laforgue, Jules **14**
Lamartine, Alphonse (Marie Louis Prat) de **16**
Leger, (Marie-Rene Auguste) Alexis Saint-Leger **23**
Mallarme, Stephane **4**
Marie de France **22**
Merton, Thomas **10**
Nerval, Gerard de **13**
Rimbaud, (Jean Nicolas) Arthur **3**
Ronsard, Pierre de **11**
Tzara, Tristan **27**
Valery, (Ambroise) Paul (Toussaint Jules) **9**
Verlaine, Paul (Marie) **2**
Vigny, Alfred (Victor) de **26**
Villon, Francois **13**

## GERMAN

Bukowski, Charles **18**
Enzensberger, Hans Magnus **28**

Goethe, Johann Wolfgang von **5**
Heine, Heinrich **25**
Holderlin, (Johann Christian) Friedrich **4**
Rilke, Rainer Maria **2**

## GREEK

Elytis, Odysseus **21**
Homer **23**
Pindar **19**
Sappho **5**
Sikelianos, Angelos **29**

## HUNGARIAN

Illyes, Gyula **16**

## INDIAN

Kalidasa **22**
Tagore, Rabindranath **8**

## IRISH

Day Lewis, C(ecil) **11**
Heaney, Seamus (Justin) **18**
Joyce, James (Augustine Aloysius) **22**
McGuckian, Medbh **27**
Swift, Jonathan **9**
Yeats, William Butler **20**

## ITALIAN

Dante **21**
Gozzano, Guido **10**
Martial **10**
Montale, Eugenio **13**
Pasolini, Pier Paolo **17**
Pavese, Cesare **13**
Petrarch **8**

## JAMAICAN

McKay, Claude **2**

## JAPANESE

Hagiwara Sakutaro **18**
Ishikawa, Takuboku **10**
Matsuo Basho **3**
Nishiwaki, Junzaburo **15**
Yosano Akiko **11**

## LEBANESE

Gibran, Kahlil **9**

## MARTINICAN

Cesaire, Aime (Fernand) **25**

## MEXICAN

Juana Ines de la Cruz **24**
Paz, Octavio **1**

## NICARAGUAN

Alegria, Claribel **26**
Cardenal, Ernesto **22**
Dario, Ruben **15**

## NIGERIAN

Okigbo, Christopher (Ifenayichukwu) **7**

## PERSIAN

Khayyam, Omar **8**

## POLISH

Milosz, Czeslaw **8**
Zagajewski, Adam **27**

## PORTUGUESE

Pessoa, Fernando (Antonio Nogueira) **20**

## ROMAN

Ovid **2**
Vergil **12**

## ROMANIAN

Cassian, Nina **17**
Celan, Paul **10**
Tzara, Tristan **27**

## RUSSIAN

Akhmatova, Anna **2**
Bely, Andrey **11**
Blok, Alexander (Alexandrovich) **21**
Brodsky, Joseph **9**
Lermontov, Mikhail Yuryevich **18**
Mandelstam, Osip (Emilievich) **14**
Pasternak, Boris (Leonidovich) **6**
Pushkin, Alexander (Sergeyevich) **10**
Tsvetaeva (Efron), Marina (Ivanovna) **14**

## SALVADORAN

Alegria, Claribel **26**

## SCOTTISH

Burns, Robert **6**
MacDiarmid, Hugh **9**
Scott, Walter **13**

## SENEGALESE

Senghor, Leopold Sedar **25**

## SOUTH AFRICAN

Brutus, Dennis **24**

## SPANISH

Fuertes, Gloria **27**
Garcia Lorca, Federico **3**
Jimenez (Mantecon), Juan Ramon **7**

## SWEDISH

Ekeloef, (Bengt) Gunnar **23**

## SYRIAN

Gibran, Kahlil **9**

## WELSH

Thomas, Dylan (Marlais) **2**

# *PC* Cumulative Title Index

"0015 hours Mayday CQ Position 41 46'
    North 50 14' West" (Enzensberger) **28**:155
"16.ix.65" (Merrill) **28**:220
"52 Oswald Street" (Kinnell) **26**:258
"The 151st Psalm" (Shapiro) **25**:285
"164 East 72nd Street" (Merrill) **28**:285
"1969, Ireland of the Bombers" (Davie) **29**:105-
    06, 108, 120
"1977, Near Mullingar" (Davie) **29**:105, 108
"1912-1952 Full Cycle" (Viereck) **27**:264
"A" (Zukofsky) **11**:337-40, 345-46, 351, 356-
    58, 361-67, 369-73, 383, 385-93, 395-99
"A" 1-9 (Zukofsky) **11**:380
"A" 1-12 (Zukofsky) **11**:343-44, 367-68
"Agave in the West" (Davie) **29**:110
"A celle qui est trop gaie" (Baudelaire) **1**:44,
    60-2
"A Colón" (Dario) **15**:84, 115
"A Félix Guiliemardet" (Lamartine) **16**:284
"A Francisca" (Dario) **15**:107, 111
"A Jenn de la Peruse, poète dramatique"
    (Ronsard) **11**:246
"A la Forest de Gastine" (Ronsard) **11**:228
"A la musique" (Rimbaud) **3**:258, 276, 283
"A la santé" (Apollinaire) **7**:44, 46-7
"A l'Italie" (Apollinaire) **7**:22
"A lo lejos" (Jimenez) **7**:199
"A los poetas risueños" (Dario) **15**:95
"A mi alma" (Jimenez) **7**:194
"A Philippes des-Portes Chartrain" (Ronsard)
    **11**:269-70
"A Roosevelt" (Dario) **15**:77, 81, 90, 106, 115
"A son ame" (Ronsard) **11**:244
"A ti" (Dario) **15**:99
"A une heure du matin" (Baudelaire) **1**:59, 72
"A une Malabaraise" (Baudelaire) **1**:49
"A une passante" (Baudelaire) **1**:45, 73
"A une raison" (Rimbaud) **3**:260
"A Verlaine" (Dario) **15**:93
"Aaron" (Herbert) **4**:102, 114, 130
"Aaron Stark" (Robinson) **1**:460, 467
"Abandon" (Li Po) **29**:177
"The Abandoned Newborn" (Olds) **22**:329
*ABC of Economics* (Pound) **4**:328
"ABCs" (Olson) **19**:267, 271, 316
"The Abduction" (Kunitz) **19**:181-82
"L'abeille" (Valery) **9**:353, 387-88, 393-94
"Abel" (Stein) **18**:316
"Abel and Cain" (Baudelaire)
    See "Abel et Caïn"
"Abel et Caïn" (Baudelaire) **1**:68
"Abel's Bride" (Levertov) **11**:175
"Der Abend" (Trakl) **20**:237-38, 244, 251, 258
"Abendland" (Trakl) **20**:231-32, 235, 240-44,
    251, 269
"Abendländisches Lied" (Trakl) **20**:231, 236,
    248-49, 251, 258, 269
"Abendlied" (Trakl) **20**:239, 269
"Abendmahl, Venezianisch, 16. Jahrhundert"
    (Enzensberger) **28**:165
"abgelegenes haus" (Enzensberger) **28**:140
"Abishag" (Gluck) **16**:126, 141
"Abnegation" (Rich) **5**:365

"Aboard the Santa Maria" (Illyes) **16**:248
"Abode" (Milosz) **8**:215
"The Abominable Lake" (Smith) **12**:353
"The Abortion" (Sexton) **2**:349
"About Opera" (Meredith) **28**:195, 206
"About Poetry" (Meredith) **28**:193-94
"About the House" (Auden) **1**:21, 24
"About the Phoenix" (Merrill) **28**:239
"About These Verses" (Pasternak) **6**:251
*Above the Barriers* (Pasternak)
    See *Poverkh barierov*
"Above These Cares" (Millay) **6**:235
"Abraham and Orpheus" (Schwartz) **8**:306,
    308-09
"Abraham Lincoln Walks at Midnight"
    (Lindsay) **23**:275, 280, 284, 288, 294-95
"Abril sus flores abría" (Guillen) **23**:125
*Abrojos* (Dario) **15**:94
*Absalom and Achitophel* (Dryden) **25**:82-3, 88,
    106-08, 113-14
"abschied von einem mittwoch"
    (Enzensberger) **28**:136
"Absence" (Gozzano) **10**:178
"L'absence, ny l'oubly, ny la course du jour"
    (Ronsard) **11**:246
"Absences" (Larkin) **21**:249-51
"Absences" (Shapiro) **25**:
"L'Absente" (Senghor) **25**:255, 258
"Absentia animi" (Ekeloef) **23**:59-60, 63, 76,
    86
"Absent-Minded Professor" (Nemerov) **24**:266
"Absolute Clearance" (Ashbery) **26**:
"Absolute Clearance" (Ashbery) **26**:124
"Absolute Retreat" (Finch)
    See "The Petition for an Absolute Retreat"
"Absolution" (Brooke) **24**:52
"Absolution" (Sassoon) **12**:241, 250, 252, 261,
    276, 278, 280
"Abstract Old Woman in a Room" (Momaday)
    **25**:
"Abt Vogler" (Browning) **2**:37, 75, 80, 88, 95
"El abuelo" (Guillen) **23**:134-37
"Abur Don Pepe" (Guillen) **23**:126
"The Abyss" (Roethke) **15**:270
"The Abyss of War" (Owen) **19**:343
"Abzählreime" (Celan) **10**:124-25
"Academic" (Roethke) **15**:246
*Academic Squaw: Reports to the World from
    the Ivory Tower* (Rose) **13**:233, 238
"Acceptance" (Sassoon) **12**:259
"Accès" (Tzara) **27**:229-31
"Accidentally on Purpose" (Frost) **1**:213
"Accomplishment" (Gallagher) **9**:59
"An Account of a Visit to Hawaii" (Meredith)
    **28**:171, 189
*An Account of a Weatherbeaten Journey*
    (Matsuo Basho)
    See *Nozarashi kikō*
"Accountability" (Dunbar) **5**:133, 146
"Les accroupissements" (Rimbaud) **3**:284
"The Accuser" (Milosz) **8**:204
"Ach, um deine feuchten Schwingen" (Goethe)
    **5**:247

"The Ache of Marriage" (Levertov) **11**:169
"Achieving a Poem while Drinking Alone" (Tu
    Fu) **9**:327
"Achille's Song" (Duncan) **2**:115
"Acon" (H. D.) **5**:273
*Aconsejo beber hilo* (Fuertes) **27**:10-12
"Acquainted with the Night" (Frost) **1**:197, 205-
    06, 208
"Across Lamarck Col" (Snyder) **21**:288
"Across the Bay" (Davie) **29**:110
"An Acrostic" (Poe) **1**:446
"Act of Union" (Heaney) **18**:196
"Acuario" (Alegria) **26**:
"Ad Castitatem" (Bogan) **12**:117
"Ad Libitum" (Elytis) **21**:132-33
"Ad Mariam" (Hopkins) **15**:159, 164, 166
*Ad Patrem* (Milton) **29**:241
"Adam" (Tomlinson) **17**:316, 342
"Adam" (Williams) **7**:350, 354
"Adam and Eve" (Shapiro) **25**:284-85, 287,
    290-91, 301, 320
*Adam & Eve & the City* (Williams) **7**:350, 402
"adam thinking" (Clifton) **17**:30, 36
"The Adamant" (Roethke) **15**:272, 291
"Adam's Curse" (Yeats) **20**:338
"Adam's Way" (Duncan) **2**:103
"The Addict" (Sexton) **2**:364
*Additional Poems* (Housman) **2**:176-77, 190
"Address for a Prize-Day" (Auden) **1**:8, 37
"Address of Beelzebub" (Burns) **6**:83-4, 88-9
"Address to a Lark" (Clare) **23**:39
"Address to a Louse" (Burns)
    See "To a Louse, on Seeing One on a
    Lady's Bonnet at Church"
"Address to Imagination" (Wheatley) **3**:335
*An Address to Miss Phillis Wheatly* (Hammon)
    **16**:179, 187-89
"Address to My Soul" (Wylie) **23**:303, 305,
    310, 313, 322, 333
"Address to Saxham" (Carew) **29**:7-8, 41-43
"Address to the Angels" (Kumin) **15**:204
"Address to the De'il" (Burns) **6**:49, 78, 83-4,
    87
"Adelaide Abner" (Smith) **12**:310, 326
"L'adieu" (Apollinaire) **7**:48
"L'adieu" (Lamartine) **16**:277, 299
"Adieu" (Rimbaud) **3**:273
"Adieu á Charlot" (Ferlinghetti) **1**:181-82, 188
"Adieu, Mlle. Veronique" (Brodsky) **9**:2, 5
"Adieux a la poesie" (Lamartine) **16**:273
"Adieux à Marie Stuart" (Swinburne) **24**:313
"The Adirondacs" (Emerson) **18**:76-77, 111,
    113
"Adivinanzas" (Guillen) **23**:106
"The Admiral's Ghost" (Noyes) **27**:121, 134
"admonitions" (Clifton) **17**:31
"Adolescence" (Dove) **6**:106
"Adolescence—III" (Dove) **6**:109
"Adolescencia" (Jimenez) **7**:183, 209
"The Adolescent" (Jimenez)
    See "Adolescencia"
"Adolescent" (Tsvetaeva)
    See "Otrok"

"Adonais" (Arnold) **5**:7
"Adonais" (Wylie) **23**:323
*Adonais: An Elegy on the Death of John Keats*
    (Shelley) **14**:164, 171, 174, 178, 183, 186-
    89, 197, 211, 218, 233-34, 236-37, 239-40
"Adonis" (H. D.) **5**:269, 304, 308
"Adonis" (Ronsard) **11**:251
*Adrastea* (Herder) **14**:171, 173, 178, 192, 211-
    12, 217, 221-24, 233-37, 239
"Adult Bookstore" (Shapiro) **25**:306-307, 322
"Adulthood" (Giovanni) **19**:110, 139
"Adulto? Mai" (Pasolini) **17**:261
"An Advancement of Learning" (Heaney)
    **18**:187, 190, 200
"Advent" (Merton) **10**:340
"Advent" (Rossetti) **7**:290, 297
*Advent* (Rilke) **2**:280
"Advent, 1966" (Levertov) **11**:176
"Adventures" (Pavese) **13**:205
"Adventures of Isabel" (Nash) **21**:265
*Adventures While Preaching the Gospel of
    Beauty* (Lindsay) **23**:278, 295
"Adventures While Singing These Songs"
    (Lindsay) **23**:282
"Adversity" (Gray)
    See "Ode to Adversity"
"Advertencia" (Fuertes) **27**:26
"The Advice" (Roethke) **15**:274
"Advice about Roses" (Stein) **18**:313
"Advice to the Girls" (Harper) **21**:207, 216
"Advocates" (Graves) **6**:144
"Ae Fond Kiss" (Burns) **6**:97
"Aedh Hears the Cry ofthe Sedge" (Yeats)
    **20**:347
*Aeginetan Odes* (Pindar) **19**:406
"Aeneas and Dido" (Brodsky) **9**:7
*The Aeneid* (Vergil) **12**:358, 361, 364-68, 371-
    73, 375-78, 380-99, 401-08
"The Aeolian Harp" (Coleridge) **11**:51, 63,
    73-4, 81-2, 88, 91, 97, 106-07, 109
"Aesthetic" (Tomlinson) **17**:327, 344
"The Aesthetic Point of View" (Auden) **1**:12,
    15
"Aesthetics of the Shah" (Olds) **22**:314
"Aether" (Ginsberg) **4**:81
"Afar" (Reese) **29**:336
"Affliction" (Herbert) **4**:118, 131
"Affliction I" (Herbert) **4**:111-12, 128, 131-32
"Affliction IV" (Herbert) **4**:112, 120
"The Affliction of Margaret----of----"
    (Wordsworth) **4**:402
"The Affliction of Richard" (Bridges) **28**:88
"Afin qu'àtout jamais" (Ronsard) **11**:242
"Africa" (Giovanni) **19**:141
"Africa" (McKay) **2**:221
*Africa* (Blake) **12**:13
*Africa* (Petrarch) **8**:239-42, 246, 258, 260, 266-
    68, 278
"Africa and My New York" (Viereck) **27**:278,
    282
"The African Chief" (Bryant) **20**:4
"An African Elegy" (Duncan) **2**:103
"After" (Reese) **29**:330
"After a Death" (Tomlinson) **17**:336
"After a Flight" (Montale) **13**:158
"After a Flight" (Montefiore)
    See "Dopa una fuga"
"After a Journey" (Hardy) **8**:88, 93, 118, 135
"After a Long Illness" (Duncan) **2**:119
"After a Rain" (Pasternak) **6**:271
"After a Tempest" (Bryant) **20**:37-8
"After a Visit" (At Padraic Colum's Where
    There Were Irish PoetsCullen) **20**:60, 69
"After an Accident" (Davie) **29**:129
*After and Before the Lightning* (Ortiz) **17**:245
"After Apple-Picking" (Frost) **1**:193, 221-22
"After Dark" (Rich) **5**:364
"After Death" (Rossetti) **7**:269, 280, 287
"After Grace" (Merrill) **28**:234, 250
"After great stormes the cawme retornes"
    (Wyatt) **27**:311
"After Hearing a Waltz by Bartok" (Lowell)

    **13**:84
"After Keats" (Levine)
    See "Having Been Asked 'What Is a Man?'
    I Answer"
"after Kent State" (Clifton) **17**:17, 35
"After Long Silence" (Yeats) **20**:328-29
"After Making Love We Hear Footsteps"
    (Kinnell) **26**:259, 292
"After Many Days" (Dunbar) **5**:137
"After Mecca" (Brooks) **7**:63, 81
"After Paradise" (Milosz) **8**:209
*After Parting* (Bely)
    See *Posle razluki*
"After Rain" (Page) **12**:168, 178, 190
"After Reading Mickey in the Night Kitchen
    for the Third Time before Bed" (Dove)
    **6**:121
"After Reading Sylvia Plath" (Clampitt) **19**:99
*After Russia* (Tsvetaeva)
    See *Posle Rossii*
"After the Agony" (Atwood) **8**:6
"After the Ball" (Merrill) **28**:270
"After the Cleansing of Bosnia" (Kumin)
    **15**:224
"After the Cries of the Birds" (Ferlinghetti)
    **1**:173-74, 176
"After the Deluge" (Rimbaud)
    See "Après le déluge"
"After the Fire" (Merrill) **28**:221-22, 225, 258,
    263-64
"After the Flood, We" (Atwood) **8**:12
"After the Funeral: In Memory of Anne Jones"
    (Thomas) **2**:390
"After the Gentle Poet Kobayashi Issa" (Hass)
    **16**:196
"After the Last Dynasty" (Kunitz) **19**:179
"After the Persian" (Bogan) **12**:107, 118, 124-
    25, 129
"After the Sentence" (Brutus) **24**:106
"After the Storm" (Stryk) **27**:203
"After the stubbornly cheerful day" (Brutus)
    **24**:118
"After the Surprising Conversions" (Lowell)
    **3**:202-03
"After the Winter" (McKay) **2**:228
"After Troy" (H. D.) **5**:268
"After Twenty Years" (Rich) **5**:384
"After wards" (Stein) **18**:313
"After Work" (Snyder) **21**:288
"Afterimages" (Lorde) **12**:155
"Aftermath" (Plath) **1**:389
"Aftermath" (Sassoon) **12**:269, 289
"Afternoon" (Parker) **28**:362
*Afternoon of a Faun* (Mallarme)
    See *L'après-midi d'un faune*
"Afternoon on a Hill" (Millay) **6**:235-36
"Afternoon Rain in State Street" (Lowell) **13**:79
"The After-thought" (Smith) **12**:329-32
"An Afterward" (Heaney) **18**:243
"Afterwards" (Hardy) **8**:101, 131
"Afterword" (Atwood) **8**:11
"Afterword" (Brodsky) **9**:25
"Afterword" (Carruth) **10**:71
"An Afterword: For Gwen Brooks"
    (Madhubuti) **5**:346
"Afton Water" (Burns)
    See "Sweet Afton"
"Again" (Nemerov) **24**:291
"Again Again" (Viereck) **27**:265
"Again and Again and Again" (Sexton) **2**:353
"Again I Visited" (Pushkin)
    See "Vnov' Ya Posetil"
"Against a comely Coistroun" (Skelton) **25**:339
"Against Botticelli" (Hass) **16**:198
"Against System Builders" (Goethe) **5**:229
"Agape" (Kinnell) **26**:287
"Agatha" (Eliot) **20**:101, 123
"Agatha" (Valery)
    See "Agathe; ou, La sainte du sommeil"
"The Agatha Christie Books by the Window"
    (Ondaatje) **28**:335

"Agathe; ou, La sainte du sommeil" (Valery)
    **9**:357, 400-01
"Age" (Larkin) **21**:227, 236, 248
"The Age" (Mandelstam) **14**:121
"The Age Demanded" (Pound) **4**:320
*The Age of Anxiety: A Baroque Eclogue*
    (Auden) **1**:14, 23, 33-4, 39
"The Ages" (Bryant) **20**:4, 35
"The Ages of Man" (Bradstreet)
    See "The Four Ages of Man"
*The Ages of the Year* (Cassian) **17**:6
"Aging Refugee from the Old Country"
    (Viereck) **27**:280
"An Agnostic" (Smith) **12**:352
"The Agony" (Herbert) **4**:100
"An Agony. As Now" (Baraka) **4**:16, 24
"Agora que conmigo" (Juana Ines de la Cruz)
    **24**:187
"Agosta the Winged Man and Rasha the Black
    Dove" (Dove) **6**:109
"Agraphon" (Sikelianos) **29**:366, 374-75
"Agrippina in the Golden House of Nero"
    (Lowell) **3**:222
"Agua sexual" (Neruda) **4**:306
"Ah, Are You Digging on My Grave?" (Hardy)
    **8**:131
"Ah! Sun-Flower" (Blake) **12**:34
"Ahasuerus" (Nemerov) **24**:257, 295
"Ahora habla Dios" (Fuertes) **27**:28
"Ahvan" (Tagore) **8**:415
"Ai critici cattolici" (Pasolini) **17**:258
"Aigeltinger" (Williams) **7**:370
"L'aigle du casque" (Hugo) **17**:56
*Aika* (Nishiwaki) **15**:238
"The Aim, The Best that Can be Hoped For:
    The Magician" (Piercy) **29**:325
"The Aim Was Song" (Frost) **1**:194
"Aimless Journey" (Tagore)
    See "Niruddesh yatra"
"Air" (Toomer) **7**:333
"Air and Fire" (Berry) **28**:11
*L'air de l'eau* (Breton) **15**:51-2
"Air de sémiramis" (Valery) **9**:365, 391-92
"Air Liner" (Shapiro) **25**:296
"Aire and Angels" (Donne) **1**:130, 149
"Airen" (Hagiwara Sakutaro) **18**:167, 180
"Airman's Virtue" (Meredith) **28**:182-83
*Airs & Tributes* (Brutus) **24**:110-11, 117
"The Airy Christ" (Smith) **12**:295, 330-31, 333
"Aix-en-Provence" (Rexroth) **20**:209
"Ajanta" (Rukeyser) **12**:204, 214, 219, 224
"Ajedrez I" (Borges) **22**:83-5
"Ajedrez II" (Borges) **22**:84-5
"Akatsuki no kane" (Ishikawa) **10**:214
*Akogare* (Ishikawa) **10**:194, 212-16
"Al Aaraaf" (Poe) **1**:437, 449
"Al amor cualquier curioso" (Juana Ines de la
    Cruz) **24**:184, 234
"Al iniciar el estudio de la gramática
    anglosajona" (Borges) **22**:99
"Al lector" (Dario) **15**:105
"Al maragen de mis libros de estudios"
    (Guillen) **23**:97
"Al mio grillo" (Montale) **13**:138
"Al mismo individuo" (Guillen) **23**:126
"Al pintor Swaminathan" (Paz) **1**:354
"Al poeta español Rafael Alberti, entregándole
    un jamón" (Guillen) **23**:134
"Al que ingrato me deja, busco ama" (Juana
    Ines de la Cruz) **24**:183
*Al que quiere!* (Williams) **7**:344-45, 348-49,
    377-79, 387-88, 398, 405-10
"Al soneto con mi alma" (Jimenez) **7**:192
"Ala bāb al-haykal" (Gibran) **9**:78
"Alaba los ojos negros de Julia" (Dario) **15**:114
"Alabama Poem" (Giovanni) **19**:140
"Alabaster" (Merrill) **28**:283
"Al-ajnihah" (Gibran) **9**:78
"Alas, a Prince" (Tu Fu) **9**:317
"Alas the While" (Wyatt) **27**:318
"Alaska" (Snyder) **21**:300

"Alastor; or, The Spirit of Solitude" (Shelley) **14**:171, 173, 178, 192, 211-12, 217, 221-24, 233-37, 239
*Al-'awāsif* (Gibran) **9**:79-81
"Al-bahr" (Gibran) **9**:80
"Albaniad" (Elytis) **21**:115
"L'albatros" (Baudelaire) **1**:65
"A Albert Durer" (Hugo) **17**:94-95
*Albertine Disparue* (Enzensberger) **28**:156
"Albertus" (Gautier) **18**:142-43, 151-54, 160-64
*Albertus, ou l'âme et le péché: légende théologique* (Gautier) **18**:147, 149-51, 154
*Album de vers anciens, 1890-1900* (Valery) **9**:363, 365, 386-87, 390-91, 395
"The Alchemist" (Bogan) **12**:98, 103, 114
"The Alchemist" (Meredith) **28**:187
"Alchemy of the Word" (Rimbaud)
　　See "Alchimie du verbe"
"Alchimie du verbe" (Rimbaud) **3**:261, 267, 274
"An Alcoholic's Death" (Hagiwara Sakutaro)
　　See "Death of an Alcoholic"
*Alcools* (Apollinaire) **7**:6, 9-10, 12, 14-15, 38-46, 48-9
"Alejamiento" (Borges) **22**:92
"Aleksandru" (Pushkin) **10**:421
"Aleluja" (Pasolini) **17**:256
"Alewives Pool" (Kinnell) **26**:238
"Alexander's Feast; or, The Power of Musique. An Ode, in Honour of St. Cecilia's Day" (Dryden)
"Alexandria" (Shapiro) **25**:295
*Alexis und Dora* (Goethe) **5**:240
"Alfansa" (Forche) **10**:134, 169-70
"Alfonso" (McKay) **2**:205
"Alfred the Great" (Smith) **12**:296, 316
"Algernon, Who Played with a Loaded Gun, and, on Missing His Sister, Was Reprimanded by His Father" (Belloc) **24**:26
*Algiers in Wartime* (Viereck) **27**:265
"Al-hurūf al-nāriyah" (Gibran) **9**:78
*Alí dagli occhi azzurri* (Pasolini) **17**:264-65
"Alice" (Graves) **6**:139
"Alice Du Clos" (Coleridge) **11**:106
"Alice Fell" (Wordsworth) **4**:404, 415
"Alive" (Harjo) **27**:56
*Alive: Poems, 1971-1972* (Wright) **14**:372, 375
"Al-jamāl" (Gibran) **9**:81
"All, All Are Gone the Old Familiar Quotations" (Nash) **21**:273
"All and Some" (Ashbery) **26**:
"All and Some" (Ashbery) **26**:124, 127, 135
"All Clowns Are Masked and All Personae" (Schwartz) **8**:305
"All Guilt and Innocence Turned Upside Down" (Schwartz) **8**:285
"All Hallows" (Gluck) **16**:126-27, 132, 140-43, 148-49
"All I Gotta Do" (Giovanni) **19**:108, 112
"All in Green Went My Love Riding" (Cummings) **5**:87
"All Is Mine" (Guillen)
　　See "Tengo"
*All Is Mine* (Guillen)
　　See *Tengo*
"All Kinds of Caresses" (Ashbery) **26**:139
"All kings and all their favourites" (Donne)
　　See "The Anniversarie"
"All Life in a Life" (Masters) **1**:326, 328, 335-36, 342
"All Morning" (Roethke) **15**:271
"All Mountain" (H. D.) **5**:305
*All My Pretty Ones* (Sexton) **2**:346-47, 349-50, 353, 355, 360-61, 370
"All Nearness Pauses, While a Star Can Grow" (Cummings) **5**:109
"All of Us Always Turning Away for Solace" (Schwartz) **8**:305
"All Souls' Day" (Sassoon) **12**:258
"All Sounds Have been as Music" (Owen) **19**:336

*All: The Collected Short Poems, 1923-1958* (Zukofsky) **11**:348-49, 351, 354-56, 393-94
*All: The Collected Shorter Poems, 1956-64* (Zukofsky) **11**:349, 353, 356, 383, 390
"All the Dead Dears" (Plath) **1**:388, 407
"All the Earth, All the Air" (Roethke) **15**:286
"All the Fancy Things" (Williams) **7**:394
"All the Spirit Powers Went to Their Dancing Place" (Snyder) **21**:291
"All Things Conspire" (Wright) **14**:338
"All Worlds Have Halfsight, Seeing Either With" (Cummings) **5**:111
"Alla Francia" (Pasolini) **17**:295
"Allá lejos" (Dario) **15**:93
"Allá lejos" (Guillen) **23**:126
"All-destroyer" (Tagore)
　　See "Sarvaneshe"
"an alle fernsprechteilenhmer" (Enzensberger) **28**:134, 136, 140
"Allégorie" (Baudelaire) **1**:56
"The Allegory of the Wolf Boy" (Gunn) **26**:
"L'Allegro" (Milton) **19**:201-02, 226, 228-34, 249, 254-56; **29**:220, 232, 239
*L'Allegro* (Milton) **29**:220, 239
"Alley Rats" (Sandburg) **2**:304
"Alliance of Education and Government" (Gray)
　　See "Essay on the Alliance of Education and Government"
"Allie" (Graves) **6**:141
"The Allies" (Lowell) **13**:76, 78
"Allons adieu messieurs tachez de revenir" (Apollinaire) **7**:22
"Alloy" (Rukeyser) **12**:210
"Almanac" (Swenson) **14**:268
"Almansor" (Heine) **25**:145, 160
"Almas de Duralex" (Fuertes) **27**:23
*Almas de violeta* (Jimenez) **7**:199
*Al-mawakib* (Gibran) **9**:79-81
"Almond" (McGuckian) **27**:92-93, 105
"The Almond of the World" (Elytis) **21**:132
"Almost a Fantasy" (Montale) **13**:151
"Alone" (Joyce) **22**:
"Alone" (Poe) **1**:442-44
"Alone I Go along the Road" (Lermontov) **18**:281, 298, 303
"Alone in a Shower" (Hongo) **23**:197
"Along History" (Rukeyser) **12**:228
"Along the Field as We Came By" (Housman) **2**:183
"The Alphabet" (Shapiro) **25**:283, 291, 298-99
"Alphabets" (Heaney) **18**:230-31, 237
"Alphonso of Castile" (Emerson) **18**:71
"Alquimia" (Borges) **22**:94
"Al-shā'ir" (Gibran) **9**:79
"The Altar" (Herbert) **4**:114, 120, 130
"The Altar of Righteousness" (Swinburne) **24**:350-54
*The Altar of the Past* (Gozzano)
　　See *L'altare del Passato*
*L'altare del Passato* (Gozzano) **10**:177
"Altarwise by Owl-light" (Thomas) **2**:388-89, 403, 406
"Einem alten Architekten in Rom" (Brodsky) **9**:2, 4
"Alternate Thoughts from Underground" (Atwood) **8**:40
"Altitude: 15,000" (Meredith) **28**:173
*Alturas de Macchu Picchu* (Neruda) **4**:282, 284-85, 292-93
"Al-umm wa wahīduha" (Gibran) **9**:78
"Always a Rose" (Lee) **24**:247-48, 251
"Always and always the amaranth astir" (Villa) **22**:346
"Always I did want more God" (Villa) **22**:352
"Always the Mob" (Sandburg) **2**:302
"Always to Love You America" (Viereck) **27**:279-80
"The Alyscamps at Arles" (Swenson) **14**:255
"Alysoun" (Snyder) **21**:288
"am or" (Bissett) **14**:14

"Am Rand Eines alten Brunes" (Trakl) **20**:265
"Am/Trak" (Baraka) **4**:39
"Am Was. Are Leaves Few This. Is This a or" (Cummings) **5**:107
"Ama tu ritmo..." (Dario) **15**:101
"Amado dueño mío" (Juana Ines de la Cruz) **24**:181
"Amām 'arsh al-jamāl" (Gibran) **9**:79
"Amante dulce del alma" (Juana Ines de la Cruz) **24**:189
"Los amantes viejos" (Aleixandre) **15**:5-7
"Les Amants de Montmorency" (Vigny) **26**:391, 411-12
"Amaranth" (H. D.) **5**:305
*Amaranth* (Robinson) **1**:477-78, 482-83
"Ambarvalia" (Nishiwaki) **15**:238
*Ambarvalia* (Nishiwaki) **15**:228-29, 232-41
"The Ambassador" (Smith) **12**:330, 339
"Ambassadors of Grief" (Sandburg) **2**:308
*Ambit* (Aleixandre)
　　See *Ambito*
*Ambito* (Aleixandre) **15**:9, 16, 27, 29-32
"Ambitus" (Cassian) **17**:6
"Ambulances" (Larkin) **21**:229-30, 234
"Ame" (Nishiwaki) **15**:228
"Amen!" (Rossetti) **7**:268
"Amen" (Trakl) **20**:248
"El amenazado" (Borges) **22**:80-1
"America" (McKay) **2**:212
"America" (Merrill) **28**:267
"America" (Wheatley) **3**:363
*America: A Prophecy, 1793* (Blake) **12**:13, 25-7, 63
"America, I Do Not Invoke Your Name in Vain" (Neruda)
　　See "América, no invoco tu nombre en vano"
"América, no invoco tu nombre en vano" (Neruda) **4**:292
"The American" (Kipling) **3**:161
"American Change" (Ginsberg) **4**:53, 84
"American Journal" (Hayden) **6**:188-89, 191-92, 195
*American Journal* (Hayden) **6**:194-96
"American Miscellany" (H. D.) **5**:268
*American Scenes and Other Poems* (Tomlinson) **17**:309, 317-18, 325-26, 333, 335, 337, 341-42, 348, 352
*Americana* (Viereck) **27**:263
*Amers* (Perse) **23**:217, 221, 223, 233, 237-47, 249-56
"Ametas and Thestylis Making Hay-Ropes" (Marvell) **10**:269, 271, 294, 304
"L'amica di nonna speranza" (Gozzano) **10**:177, 181-82
"L'amico che dorme" (Pavese) **13**:229
*Les amies* (Verlaine) **2**:432
*L' Amitié du Prince* (Perse) **23**:217, 246
*Amitié d'un Prince* (Perse) **23**:211, 221, 230, 249-50
"Among Ourselves" (Meredith) **28**:216
"Among School Children" (Yeats) **20**:316, 326, 328, 330, 332, 336-38, 340-42
"Among the Gods" (Kunitz) **19**:149, 173
"Among the Tombs" (Kinnell) **26**:256
"Among the Trees" (Bryant) **20**:14, 47
"Among Those Killed in the Dawn Raid Was a Man Aged a Hundred" (Thomas) **2**:388
"Amor e'l cor gentil" (Dante) **21**:73
"Amor mundi" (Rossetti) **7**:282
*Amores* (Ovid) **2**:234-35, 237-38, 242-43, 245, 251, 253-54, 258-59, 261
*Amoretti* (Spenser) **8**:329, 388-89
*Amoretti and Epithalamion* (Spenser) **8**:388
"Amos" (Postscript 1968Walker) **20**:278-79
"Amos-1963" (Walker) **20**:278-79
"Amour" (Verlaine) **2**:416-17, 425
"L'amour et le crâne" (Baudelaire) **1**:45
"Amour parcheminé" (Breton) **15**:52
"Les amours" (Laforgue) **14**:74
*Amours* (Ronsard) **11**:220-21, 246, 250, 254, 256, 258, 275, 277-78, 293

*Amours de Cassandre* (Ronsard) **11**:247-48
"Amours d'Eurymedon et de Calliree"
    (Ronsard) **11**:241
*Amours diverses* (Ronsard) **11**:270
"Amphibian" (Browning) **2**:80
*Amplitude: New and Selected Poems*
    (Gallagher) **9**:57-62
"Amravan" (Tagore) **8**:416
"Amsterdam" (Merrill) **28**:223
*Amubaruwaria* (Nishiwaki) **15**:232, 240
"Amy's Cruelty" (Browning) **6**:23, 28, 32
"An den Knaben Elis" (Trakl) **20**:226, 234-35,
    246
"An den Wassern Babels" (Celan) **10**:127-28
"An einen Frühverstorbenen" (Trakl) **20**:230
"Ana María" (Guillen) **23**:102
*Anabase* (Perse) **23**:209-14, 216-18, 221-23,
    225-28, 230-31, 233-34, 241-43, 246, 248,
    250, 253, 256-59, 261
*Anabasis* (Perse)
    See *Anabase*
"Anactoria" (Swinburne) **24**:308, 310-11, 322,
    325-26, 343, 360-61
"Anahorish" (Heaney) **18**:201-2, 241, 251
"Ananta jivan" (Tagore) **8**:406
"Ananta maran" (Tagore) **8**:406
"Anaphora" (Bishop) **3**:37, 56
"Anasazi" (Snyder) **21**:295-96
"Anashuya and Vijaya" (Yeats) **20**:343
*An Anatomie of the World* (Donne)
    See *The First Anniversarie. An Anatomie of
    the World. Wherein By Occasion of the
    untimely death of Mistris Elizabeth
    Drury, the frailtie and decay of this
    whole World is represented*
"An Anatomy of Migraine" (Clampitt) **19**:92
"Ancestors" (Pavese) **13**:204
"The Ancestors" (Wright) **14**:353
"Ancestral Houses" (Yeats) **20**:349
"Ancestral Photograph" (Heaney) **18**:200
"Anchar" (Pushkin) **10**:373
"Anchorage" (Harjo) **27**:55, 58, 63, 65-66
"The Anchored Angel" (Villa) **22**:348-49
*The Ancient Acquaintance* (Skelton) **25**:345,
    351
"The Ancient Briton Lay Ynder His Rock"
    (Hughes) **7**:147
"Ancient discipline" (Pavese)
    See "Disciplina antica"
"An Ancient Gesture" (Millay) **6**:232, 240
"The Ancient Heroes and the Bomber Pilot"
    (Hughes) **7**:132
"Ancient History" (Sassoon) **12**:258
"the ancient lord laydee un th univers"
    (Bissett) **14**:27
*The Ancient Mariner* (Coleridge)
    See *The Rime of the Ancient Mariner: A
    Poet's Reverie*
"Ancient One" (Montale)
    See "Antico, sono ubriacato della tua voce"
"The Ancient Sage" (Tennyson) **6**:407
"An Ancient to Ancients" (Hardy) **8**:121
"Ancient Wisdom Speaks" (H. D.) **5**:307
"Ancora ad Annecy" (Montale) **13**:138
*And* (Cummings)
    See *&*
*& (Cummings)* **5**:75, 92-3, 95, 104-05
"And a Few Negroes Too" (Madhubuti)
    See "A Message All Blackpeople Can Dig
    (& A Few Negroes Too)"
"And a Wisdom as Such" (Duncan) **2**:115
"And Another Thing" (Giovanni) **19**:118
"& Co." (Shapiro) **25**:295
"And Death Shall Have No Dominion"
    (Thomas) **2**:379, 385, 389-90, 397
"And Did Those Feet in Ancient Time Walk
    upon England's Mountains Green?"
    (Blake) **12**:45
"And I Dreamt I Was a Tree" (Alegria) **26**:
"And if an eye may save or slay" (Wyatt)
    **27**:354
"And in the Hanging Gardens" (Aiken) **26**:24

"And in the Human Heart" (Aiken) **26**:22
"And One for My Dame" (Sexton) **2**:363
"And Pass" (Toomer) **7**:332
"And So Goodbye to Cities" (Merton) **10**:334,
    344
"And So Today" (Sandburg) **2**:307-08
"And Socializing" (Ashbery) **26**:163
"And the Children of Birmingham" (Merton)
    **10**:334, 341
". . .And the Clouds Return after the Rain"
    (Smith) **12**:331
"and the green wind is mooving thru the
    summr trees" (Bissett) **14**:33
"And The Land Is Just As Dry" (Ortiz) **17**:227
"And the Stars Were Shining" (Ashbery)
    **26**:164-166
*And the Stars Were Shining* (Ashbery) **26**:164-
    166
"And the Trains Go On" (Levine) **22**:224
"And There Was a Great Calm" (Hardy) **8**:119
"And They Call This Living!" (Stryk) **27**:203
"And Ut Pictura Poesis Is Her Name"
    (Ashbery) **26**:118, 123, 135
"And What About the Children" (Lorde) **12**:139
"And with What Bodies Do They Come?"
    (Dickinson) **1**:102
"And You as Well Must Die" (Millay) **6**:211
"El andaluz universal" (Jimenez) **7**:205
"Andenken" (Holderlin) **4**:172, 178
"der andere" (Enzensberger) **28**:139
"Andrea del Sarto" (Browning) **2**:37, 86, 88, 95
"Andrée Rexroth" (Rexroth) **20**:206-07
"Andromeda" (Hopkins) **15**:134, 148
"Andromeda Chained to Her Rock the Great
    Nebula in her Heart" (Rexroth) **20**:196
"Anecdote" (Parker) **28**:360
"Anecdote for Fathers" (Wordsworth) **4**:425-28
*Anecdote of Rain* (Zagajewski) **27**:389, 399
"Anecdote of the Jar" (Stevens) **6**:309, 326-27
"Anecdote of the Prince of Peacocks"
    (Stevens) **6**:309
"Anelida and Arcite" (Chaucer) **19**:10, 74
*Anew* (Zukofsky) **11**:342, 347, 382-83
"L'ange du méridien" (Rilke) **2**:275
"L'ange, fragment épique" (Lamartine) **16**:266
"Das angebrochene Jahr" (Celan) **10**:124
"Angel" (Lermontov) **18**:274, 276, 279
"Angel" (Merrill) **28**:248
"Angel Boley" (Smith) **12**:352
"Angel Butcher" (Levine) **22**:222-23
*The Angel of History* (Forche) **10**:160, 169
"Angel smerti" (Lermontov) **18**:300
"The Angel Sons" (Lindsay) **23**:281
"Angel Surrounded by Paysans" (Stevens)
    **6**:304
"Los Angeles Poems" (Davie) **29**:99
"L'angelo nero" (Montale) **13**:134
*Angelos Sikelianos: Selected Poems*
    (Sikelianos) **29**:368
*Angels and Earthly Creatures* (Wylie) **23**:303-
    304, 307, 309, 313-14
*Angels of the Love Affair* (Sexton) **2**:365,
    367
"Angelus" (Fuertes) **27**:39
"The Anger of the Sea" (Ishikawa)
    See "Umi no ikari"
"Anger's Freeing Power" (Smith) **12**:295, 311,
    330
"Anglais Mort à Florence" (Stevens) **6**:311
*Angle of Ascent* (Hayden) **6**:188, 190, 194
*Angle of Geese, and Other Poems* (Momaday)
    **25**:187, 188-89, 193
"An Anglican Lady: in memoriam Margaret
    Hine" (Davie) **29**:116
"Angling A Day" (Kinnell) **26**:260
"Anglo-Mongrels and the Rose" (Loy) **16**:316,
    322
"The Angry God" (Ferlinghetti) **1**:183
"Angry Love" (Aleixandre) **15**:19
"Angry Samson" (Graves) **6**:151
"The Anguish" (Millay) **6**:217
"Anima" (Carruth) **10**:85

"De Anima" (Nemerov) **24**:289
"Anima hominis" (Yeats) **20**:327
*Animadversions upon the Remonstrants
    Defence* (Milton) **29**:238
*Animal de fondo* (Jimenez) **7**:183-84, 203, 211,
    214
"Animal de luz" (Neruda) **4**:289
*Animal of Depth* (Jimenez)
    See *Animal de fondo*
*Animal of Inner Depths* (Jimenez)
    See *Animal de fondo*
"Animal of Light" (Neruda)
    See "Animal de luz"
"Animal, Vegetable, and Mineral" (Bogan)
    **12**:92, 99, 107, 125
"Animals Are Passing from Our Lives"
    (Levine) **22**:213
*The Animals in That Country* (Atwood) **8**:3-4,
    12, 15-16, 23
*Animula* (Eliot) **5**:194, 197-98, 203
"Anklage" (Goethe) **5**:248
"Ankor Wat" (Ginsberg) **4**:61
"Anna" (Wyatt) **27**:345
"anna speaks of the childhood of mary her
    daughter" (Clifton) **17**:37
"Annabel Lee" (Poe) **1**:425, 429, 434, 438, 441,
    444, 447-48
"Annandale Again" (Robinson) **1**:476
"Anne" (Valery) **9**:374, 392
"Anne Boleyn's Song" (Sitwell) **3**:315
"Anne Hay" (Carew)
    See "Obsequies to the Lady Anne Hay"
"Anne Rutledge" (Masters) **1**:334, 348
"The Annealing" (Piercy) **29**:314
*L'année terrible* (Hugo) **17**:55-56, 65, 97-99,
    101
*Les Années funestes* (Hugo) **17**:65
"Annetta" (Montale) **13**:138
"The Anniad" (Brooks) **7**:53, 58, 61, 80, 102,
    104
*Annie Allen* (Brooks) **7**:53-4, 56-8, 60-2, 68,
    75, 78, 80-1, 85, 91, 96, 102, 104-05
"Annie Hill's Grave" (Merrill) **28**:248
"Annie's Arctic Snake" (Wakoski) **15**:334
"Annihilation" (Aiken) **26**:24
"The Anniversarie" (Donne) **1**:130
*The Anniversaries* (Donne) **1**:145-48, 155-56,
    158
"Anniversario" (Montale) **13**:110
"An Anniversary" (Berry) **28**:12-13
"Anniversary" (Elytis) **21**:118-19, 134
"The Anniversary" (Lowell) **13**:66, 97
"Anniversary" (Marvell)
    See "The First Anniversary of the
    Government under O. C."
"Anniversary" (Montale)
    See "Anniversario"
"The Anniversary" (Stryk) **27**:204
*Anno Domini MCMXXI* (Akhmatova) **2**:3, 13-
    14, 18
"Annual" (Swenson) **14**:284
"The Annunciation" (Merton) **10**:339
"Annunciation Eve" (Tsvetaeva)
    See "Kanun Blagoveshchen'ia"
*Annunciations* (Tomlinson) **17**:359-60
"Annus Mirabilis" (Larkin) **21**:237
"Annus Mirabilis: The Year of Wonders, 1666"
    (Dryden) **25**:90-1, 93, 95, 99, 115-16
"El año lírico" (Dario) **15**:95, 117
"anodetodalevy" (Bissett) **14**:31
"Another Animal" (Swenson) **14**:284
*Another Animal* (Swenson) **14**:246, 251-52,
    260, 264, 267, 274, 277, 282-83
"Another August" (Merrill) **28**:221
"Another Letter to My Husband" (Bradstreet)
    **10**:28
"Another New-yeeres Gift; or song for the
    Circumcision" (Herrick) **9**:118, 120
"Another Poem for Me—After Recovering
    from an O.D." (Knight) **14**:39, 43, 53
"Another Son" (McGuckian) **27**:100
"Another Space" (Page) **12**:180, 190, 197-98

"Another Spring" (Levertov) **11**:169-70
"Another Spring" (Rexroth) **20**:207
"Another Time" (Auden) **1**:18-19, 30, 34
"Another Time" (Soto) **28**:402
"Another Word on the Scientific Aspiration"
  (Lindsay) **23**:269
"Another Year" (Williams) **7**:370
"anrufung des fisches" (Enzensberger) **28**:136
"Answer" (Finch)
  See "Ardelia's Answer to Ephelia"
"Answer!" (Guillen)
  See "Responde tú"
"The Answer" (Herbert) **4**:130
"The Answer" (Jeffers) **17**:129, 131
*The Answer* (Montagu) **16**:340-41, 346
"An Answer to the Rebus" (Wheatley) **3**:363
"Answering a Layman's Question" (Li Po)
  **29**:142
"Answering a Question in the Mountains"
  (Ashbery) **26**:129
"Answering Magistrate Chang" (Wang Wei)
  **18**:364-65
"Antaeus" (Heaney) **18**:203, 207-9
"Antaeus: A Fragment" (Owen) **19**:354
"Antaryami" (Tagore) **8**:408
"Ante Aram" (Brooke) **24**:62
"Ante Lucem" (Blok) **21**:2, 23
"Ante Mortem" (Jeffers) **17**:117, 141
"An Antebellum Sermon" (Dunbar) **5**:120, 123,
  133, 147
"Antecedents" (Tomlinson) **17**:302-04, 306,
  311, 323, 338
"Antenati" (Pavese) **13**:217, 220, 225-26
"Antéros" (Nerval) **13**:181, 191-92, 194, 198
"Anthem for Doomed Youth" (Owen) **19**:326,
  332, 336, 346, 360-63, 365-67, 369-70
*Anthology* (Jimenez)
  See *Antolojía poética (1898-1953)*
"Antico, sono ubriacato della tua voce"
  (Montale) **13**:115, 141
"Anti-Desperation" (Arnold) **5**:7
"Antigone" (Arnold) **5**:8
"Antigua casa madrileña" (Aleixandre) **15**:34,
  36
"Antinous" (Pessoa) **20**:165, 169
"Antiphon" (Herbert) **4**:103
"The Antiphon" (Levertov) **11**:198
"Anti-poem" (Shapiro) **25**:316, 321
"Antipoema?" (Fuertes) **27**:48
"The Antiquity of Freedom" (Bryant) **20**:43, 47
*L'Antitête* (Tzara) **27**:234-37
"Anti-Vietnam War Peace Mobilization"
  (Ginsberg) **4**:76
*Antología mayor* (Guillen) **23**:142
*Antología total* (Aleixandre) **15**:32
*Antología y poemas* (Fuertes) **27**:10-1
*Antología y poemas del suburbio* (Fuertes)
  **27**:10, 18
*Antologia y poemas del suburbio Aconsejo
  beber hilo* (Fuertes)
*Antolojía poética* (1898-1953Jimenez) **7**:183-84
"Antrim" (Jeffers) **17**:117
"Any Human to Another" (Cullen) **20**:60
"Any Porch" (Parker) **28**:353-54
"anyone lived in a pretty how town"
  (Cummings) **5**:81
"Anywhere is a Street into the Night"
  (Momaday) **25**:202, 212
*Aoneko* (Hagiwara Sakutaro) **18**:170, 172-73,
  175-77, 181-83
"Apache Love" (Ortiz) **17**:224
"Apache Red" (Ortiz) **17**:228
"The Apartment Is as Silent as Paper"
  (Mandelstam) **14**:149
"The Apennines" (Bryant) **20**:16-17
"Apes and Ivory" (Noyes) **27**:114
"Aphorisms, I" (Villa) **22**:355
"Aphorisms, II" (Villa) **22**:353, 355
"Aphorisms, III" (Villa) **22**:355
"Aphorisms on Futurism" (Loy) **16**:311-13,
  316, 322, 324
"Aphrodite" (Gluck) **16**:150

"Aphrodite Ode" (Sappho)
  See "Ode to Aphrodite"
"Aphrodite Rising" (Sikelianos) **29**:367, 369
"Apocalipsis" (Cardenal) **22**:112, 125, 129
"Apocalypse"
  See "Apocalipsis"
"Apocalypse"
  See "Apocalipsis"
"Apocalypse: Umbrian Master, about 1490"
  (Enzensberger) **28**:151
"Apogee of Celery" (Neruda)
  See "Apogeo del apio"
"Apogeo del apio" (Neruda) **4**:277
"Apollo at Pheræ" (Masters) **1**:329
"Apollo in New York" (Viereck) **27**:278
"Apollo of the Physiologists" (Graves) **6**:152-53
"An Apollonian Elegy" (Duncan) **2**:105
*Apollonius of Tyana* (Olson) **19**:282, 298
"Apollo's Edict" (Swift) **9**:252
"Apologia pro poemate meo" (Owen) **19**:329,
  334-35, 344, 348, 353-55, 370
"Apologies to the Federal Bureau of
  Investigation" (Giovanni) **19**:108
"Apology for Bad Dreams" (Jeffers) **17**:129-30,
  142, 147
"The Apology of Demetrius" (Masters) **1**:343
"Apology of Genius" (Loy) **16**:308, 321
"An Apology to the Lady Cartaret" (Swift)
  **9**:296
*Apophoreta* (Martial) **10**:230, 241
"Apostrophe to a Dead Friend" (Kumin)
  **15**:218-20
"The Apostrophe to Vincentine" (Stevens) **6**:309
"apoteos" (Ekeloef) **23**:75
"Apparent Failure" (Browning) **2**:68
"The Apparition" (Donne) **1**:130, 152
"The Apparition of His Mistress Calling Him
  to Elizium" (Herrick) **9**:93, 103, 133,
  138-39
"The Apparitions" (Yeats) **20**:351
"An Appeal to the American People" (Harper)
  **21**:190
"Appearances" (Gluck) **16**:157, 161
*Appendice* (Pasolini) **17**:279
"Appendix Form in Poetry" (Viereck) **27**:287
"Appendix to the Anniad Leaves from a
  Loose-Leaf War Diary" (Brooks) **7**:61
"L'Appennino" (Pasolini) **17**:270
"Appetite" (Smith) **12**:310
"The Apple" (Kinnell) **26**:261
"The Apple" (Page) **12**:168, 170
"Apple" (Soto) **28**:398
"The Apple Blossom Snow Blues" (Lindsay)
  **23**:264
"An Apple Gathering" (Rossetti) **7**:260-1, 280
"Apple Tragedy" (Hughes) **7**:143, 159
"The Apple Tree" (Berry) **28**:5
"The Apple Tree" (Parker) **28**:364
"The Apple Trees" (Gluck) **16**:126-27, 132,
  140, 142
"The Apple Woman's Complaint" (McKay)
  **2**:210
"Apples and Water" (Graves) **6**:141
"Appleton House" (Marvell)
  See "Upon Appleton House"
*The Applewood Cycles* (Viereck) **27**:286, 289
"The Applicant" (Plath) **1**:394, 400-01
"Applies" (Reese) **29**:335
"The Appology" (Finch) **21**:140, 159, 162, 167,
  178
"Apprehensions" (Duncan) **2**:110, 112
"An Apprentice Angel" (MacDiarmid) **9**:155
"Approach to Thebes" (Kunitz) **19**:156, 161,
  168, 173-74
"Approaches" (Nemerov) **24**:
"The Approaching Silence" (Illyes) **16**:248
*Approximate Man* (Tzara)
  See *L'Homme approximatif*
"Appuldurcombe Park" (Lowell) **13**:84
"Après le déluge" (Rimbaud) **3**:261
"Après une lecture de Dante" (Hugo) **17**:96-97

*L'après-midi d'un faune* (Mallarme) **4**:186, 188,
  190, 197, 207-08
"April" (Gluck) **16**:171
"April 1885" (Bridges) **28**:83
"April Fables" (Nishiwaki) **15**:231
*April Galleons* (Ashbery)
"April Is the Saddest Month" (Williams) **7**:351,
  354, 400
"April was Opening its Flowers" (Guillen)
  See "April was Opening its Flowers"
"Aquarelles" (Verlaine) **2**:415
"L'aquarium" (Laforgue) **14**:72
"The Aquarium" (Lowell) **13**:79
"Aquatre heures du matin" (Rimbaud) **3**:274
"Aquí estoy expuesta como todos" (Fuertes)
  **27**:25
"Arabel" (Masters) **1**:328
*Arap Petra Velikogo* (Pushkin) **10**:394
*Ararat* (Gluck) **16**:157-64, 168, 170
*Arbre des voyageurs* (Tzara) **27**:234
*Arbuthnot* (Pope)
  See *An Epistle to Dr. Arbuthnot*
"L'Arc" (Perse) **23**:228
"The Arc Inside and Out" (Ammons) **16**:12, 61
"L'arca" (Montale) **13**:113
"La Arcadia perdida" (Cardenal) **22**:132
"Arcady Unheeding" (Sassoon) **12**:240, 275
*Archaeologist of Morning* (Olson) **19**:268, 282,
  306, 308
"Archaic Figure" (Clampitt) **19**:92
*Archaic Figure* (Clampitt) **19**:91-3
*The Archeology of Movies and Books*
  (Wakoski) **15**:372-73
*Archer* (Viereck) **27**:285, 288-89, 291-92
*Archer in the Marrow* (Viereck) **27**:287-88, 292
*Archer in the Marrow The Applewood Cycles
  1967-1987* (Viereck) **27**:285-86
"Archibald Higbie" (Masters) **1**:333
"The Archipelago" (Holderlin)
  See "Der Archipelagus"
"Der Archipelagus" (Holderlin) **4**:147-48, 164
"An Architecture" (Berry) **28**:4, 7
"Architecture" (Stevens) **6**:293
"The Architecture: Passages 9" (Duncan) **2**:107
"Ardelia to Melancholy" (Finch) **21**:146, 150,
  152, 157, 165, 168, 177-80
"Ardelia's Answer to Ephelia" (Finch) **21**:148,
  154-55, 163, 165
*The Ardent Slingsman* (Neruda)
  See *El hondero entusiasta, 1923-1924*
"Ardilla de los tunes de un katu" (Cardenal)
  **22**:131
"La arena traicionada" (Neruda) **4**:292-93
"Arethusa" (Shelley) **14**:167
"The Argument" (Aiken) **26**:24
"The Argument of His Book" (Herrick) **9**:85,
  95, 97, 101, 105, 107-10, 116, 132-34, 138-
  39, 141
"Ariadne" (H. D.) **5**:304
*Arias tristes* (Jimenez) **7**:199, 209
"Ariel" (Plath) **1**:381, 409, 413
*Ariel* (Plath) **1**:379-80, 383-84, 387, 389-91,
  393-96, 405-07, 410-11
"Ariettes oubliées" (Verlaine) **2**:431
"Arion" (Eliot) **20**:123, 125, 134-35, 145
"Arioso" (Mandelstam) **14**:144
"Ariosto and the Arabs" (Borges) **22**:92
"Ariso" (Ishikawa) **10**:215
*Aristophanes' Apology* (Browning) **2**:96
"Arizona Desert" (Tomlinson) **17**:331, 341
"The Ark" (Montale)
  See "L'arca"
"The Armada" (Swinburne) **24**:312
"Armageddon" (Tennyson) **6**:407-08, 413,
  415-19
"Armed with the vision of narrow wasps"
  (Mandelstam)
  See "Vooruzhennyi zren'em uzkikh os"
"Armenia" (Mandelstam) **14**:118
"Les armes miraculeuses" (Cesaire) **25**:8, 29
*Les Armes Miraculeuses* (Cesaire) **25**:15, 18,
  21, 29-30, 44

"Armgart" (Eliot) **20**:101, 116, 124, 131, 133-36, 144
"Armor's Undermining Modesty" (Moore) **4**:267
"Arms" (Tagore)
See "Bahu"
"Arms and the Boy" (Owen) **19**:336, 354, 358
"Army Song" (Wang Wei) **18**:367
*Ārogya* (Tagore) **8**:424, 426
"Around Pastor Bonhoeffer" (Kunitz) **19**:158
"Arras" (Page) **12**:168, 170, 178, 180, 189-90, 197
"Arremba sulla strinata proda" (Montale) **13**:116
"Arrest of Antoñito the Camborio" (Garcia Lorca)
See "Prendimiento de Antoñito el Camborio"
"Arrival" (Guillen) **23**:105
"Arrival at Santos" (Bishop) **3**:44
"The Arrival of the Bee Box" (Plath) **1**:410-13
"Arrivals, Departures" (Larkin) **21**:236
"Arriving at the Frontier on a Mission" (Wang Wei) **18**:367, 389
"Arrow" (Dove) **6**:123
"Arrows of Flowers" (Bissett) **14**:7
*Ars Amandi* (Ovid)
See *Ars amatoria*
*Ars amatoria* (Ovid) **2**:233-34, 238-39, 241-47, 253-55, 261
"Ars poetica" (Dove) **6**:121-22
"Ars poetica?" (Milosz) **8**:197, 201
"Ars Poetica: A Found Poem" (Kumin) **15**:216
"Arsenio" (Montale) **13**:107, 120, 124-25, 147, 164
"Arsinoë" (Ekeloef) **23**:59, 61
"Art" (Emerson) **18**:98
"L'art" (Gautier) **18**:128, 156-57, 164
"An Art Called Gothonic" (Olson) **19**:305
*L'Art d'être grand-père* (Hugo) **17**:65, 86
*Art of Love* (Ovid)
See *Ars amatoria*
"Art of Poetry" (Verlaine)
See "L'Art poètique"
"The Art of Response" (Lorde) **12**:140
*The Art of Worldly Wisdom* (Rexroth) **20**:179, 181-83, 192, 198, 203, 211, 213
"L'Art poètique" (Verlaine) **2**:416-18, 428, 430-34
*Art the Herald* (Noyes) **27**:140
"Arte poética" (Guillen) **23**:128
"L'arte povera" (Montale) **13**:138
"Artémis" (Nerval) **13**:173, 179, 181, 184-87, 195-96, 198
"Artemis Orthia" (Sikelianos) **29**:367
"Artemis Prologuises" (Browning) **2**:26
"Artificer" (Milosz) **8**:191
"Artillerie" (Herbert) **4**:101, 129
"Artillery" (Herbert)
See "Artillerie"
"The Artist" (Blok) **21**:16
"An Artist" (Heaney) **18**:215
"An Artist" (Jeffers) **17**:141
"The Artist" (Kunitz) **19**:161, 168, 173-75
"The Artists' and Models' Ball" (Brooks) **7**:107
"An Arundel Tomb" (Larkin) **21**:229-30, 234, 238-39, 258
"As a Possible Lover" (Baraka) **4**:16
"As a World Would Have It" (Robinson) **1**:460
"As Any" (Men's Hells Having Wrestled withCummings) **5**:108
"As Bad as a Mile" (Larkin) **21**:233-34
"As Children Together" (Forche) **10**:144, 156-57, 168-69
"As Eagles Soar" (Toomer) **7**:340
"As Envoy to the Barbarian Pass" (Wang Wei) **18**:362
"As Expected" (Gunn) **26**:
*As Fine As Melanctha* (Stein) **18**:327
"As Flowers Are" (Kunitz) **19**:155, 162
"As for Fame I've Had It" (Ammons) **16**:44
"As Hermes Once" (Keats) **1**:279

"As I Ebb'd with the Ocean of Life" (Whitman) **3**:396-97, 421
"As I Grow Older" (Hughes) **1**:251
"As I Lay with My Head on Your Lap Camarado" (Whitman) **3**:379
"As I Sat Alone by Blue Ontario's Shore" (Whitman) **3**:377, 387
"As I Went Down to Havre de Grace" (Wylie) **23**:305, 310, 324
"As in a rose the true fire moves" (Villa) **22**:351
"As Is the Sea Marvelous" (Cummings) **5**:104
"As kingfishers catch fire" (Hopkins) **15**:169
"As Lovers Do" (MacDiarmid) **9**:156
"As Loving Hind" (Bradstreet) **10**:35-6
"As My Blood Was Drawn" (Hayden) **6**:194
"As One Does Sickness Over" (Dickinson) **1**:94
"As One Put Drunk into the Packet Boat" (Ashbery) **26**:120
"As one who hath sent forth on bold emprise" (Belloc) **24**:10
"As Seen by Disciples" (Brooks) **7**:63
*As Ten, as Twenty* (Page) **12**:163-64, 167, 173, 193
"As the Dead Prey upon Us" (Olson) **19**:321, 323
"As virtuous men pass mildly away" (Donne)
See "A Valediction: forbidding mourning"
"As We Desired" (Guillen)
See "Como quisimos"
"As We Know" (Ashbery) **26**:136-138, 141, 156, 172
*As We Know* (Ashbery) **26**:131-132, 135-137, 140
"As Weary Pilgrim" (Bradstreet) **10**:8, 15, 28, 34, 36-7
"As You Came from the Holy Land" (Ashbery) **26**:
"As You Leave Me" (Knight) **14**:41, 43, 52
"Asahya bhalobasa" (Tagore) **8**:405
"Ascending the Mountain on Double Nine" (Li Po) **29**:183-84, 186
"Ascensão de Vasco da Gama" (Pessoa) **20**:155
"aschermittwoch" (Enzensberger) **28**:134
"Ash Snow or Moonlight" (Lee) **24**:240
"The Ash Tree" (Marie de France)
See "Le Fraisne"
"Ashar nairashya" (Tagore) **8**:405
*Ashes* (Bely)
See *Pepel'*
"Ashes, ashes, all fall down" (Piercy) **29**:315, 318, 320
"The Ashes of Gramsci" (Pasolini) **17**:258, 284, 288-89
*The Ashes of Gramsci* (Pasolini)
See *Le ceneri di Gramscí*
*The Ashes of Gramsci* (Pasolini) **17**:286-87
"Ashes of Life" (Millay) **6**:206
*Ashes: Poems New and Old* (Levine) **22**:218-19, 223-24
"Ashurnatsirpal III" (Sandburg) **2**:323
*Ash-Wednesday* (Eliot) **5**:162-64, 170, 174, 186, 192, 194, 197-206, 209-10
"Asian Birds" (Bridges) **28**:51, 85
"Aside" (Shapiro) **25**:295
"Ask Me No More" (Tennyson) **6**:366
"Ask me no more where Jove bestows" (Carew) **29**:5
"Ask the Roses" (Levine) **22**:224
*Ask Your Mama: 12 Moods for Jazz* (Hughes) **1**:249, 251-53, 261, 268, 270
"The Asking" (Soto) **28**:400-01
"Asleep" (Owen) **19**:336, 354, 359, 368
*Asolando* (Browning) **2**:96
*Asolando: Fancies and Facts* (Browning) **2**:66-7, 88
"An Aspect of Love, Alive in the Fire and Ice" (Brooks) **7**:82, 88, 91, 94
"Aspen Tree" (Celan) **10**:112-13
*Asphalt Georgics* (Carruth) **10**:77, 91
"Asphodel, That Greeny Flower" (Williams) **7**:371, 375, 390-92, 402-03
"The Ass" (Smith) **12**:302-6, 319

"Assassin" (Hass) **16**:195
"The Assassin" (Sexton) **2**:365 .
"Assassin" (Tomlinson) **17**:318, 322, 325-27, 341, 345-46
"Assassination Raga" (Ferlinghetti) **1**:173
"Assault" (Millay) **6**:236, 238
"Assay of the Infinite Man" (Neruda)
See *Tentativa del hombre infinto*
"An Assent to Wildflowers" (Meredith) **28**:192
"The Assertion" (Day Lewis) **11**:146
"Assommons les pauvres" (Baudelaire) **1**:59
"The Assumption" (Noyes) **27**:136
"Astigmatism" (Lowell) **13**:84
"Astrea Redux. A Poem on the Happy Restoration and Return of His Sacred Majesty Charles the Second" (Dryden)
"the astrologer predicts at mary's birth" (Clifton) **17**:37
"Astronauts" (Hayden) **6**:194
"The Astronomer Poems" (Wakoski) **15**:348, 365
"Astrophel" (Swinburne) **24**:313
"Astrophel: A Pastoral Elegy" (Spenser) **8**:365, 367, 387
"The Asylum" (Carruth) **10**:71, 82-4
"At a Bach Concert" (Rich) **5**:352, 387, 393
"At a Calvary near the Ancre" (Owen) **19**:334, 341, 362-63
"At a Concert of Music" (Aiken) **26**:24, 72
"At a Country Funeral" (Berry) **28**:16, 29
"At a Country Hotel" (Nemerov) **24**:260
"At a Glance" (Tomlinson) **17**:333
"At a Hasty Wedding" (Hardy) **8**:85
"At a Lunar Eclipse" (Hardy) **8**:89
"At a Party" (Bogan) **12**:106
"At a Potato Digging" (Heaney) **18**:200
"At a Solemn Music" (Milton)
See "At a Solemn Music"
*At A Solemn Music* (Milton) **29**:238-40
"At a Solemn Musick" (Schwartz) **8**:289
*At A Vacation Exercise* (Milton) **29**:241
"At a Wayside Shrine" (Owen) **19**:362
"At a Window" (Sandburg) **2**:300
"At Algeciras--A Meditation upon Death" (Yeats) **20**:342
"At Auden's Grave" (Shapiro) **25**:322
"At Baia" (H. D.) **5**:267
"At Barstow" (Tomlinson) **17**:353, 355
"At Candle-Lightin' Time" (Dunbar) **5**:122
"At Castle Boterel" (Hardy) **8**:118
"At Cedar Creek" (Wright) **14**:375
"At Cooloolah" (Wright) **14**:344, 371
"At Dawn" (Milosz) **8**:210
"At Daybreak" (Sassoon) **12**:247
"At Daybreak" (Zagajewski) **27**:389
"At Dusk" (Cummings) **5**:93, 106
"At Easterly" (Clampitt) **19**:100
"At First, at Last" (Swenson) **14**:262, 288
"At Grass" (Larkin) **21**:229, 238-39, 244, 251, 257
"At Hanratty's" (Tomlinson) **17**:361
"At Holwell Farm" (Tomlinson) **17**:326, 341, 349, 352, 354
"At Ithaca" (H. D.) **5**:268
"At Melville's Tomb" (Crane) **3**:90, 103
"At My Father's Grave" (MacDiarmid) **9**:156
"At My Hospital Window" (Viereck) **27**:294, 296
"At Night" (Ekeloef) **23**:85
"At North Farm" (Ashbery) **26**:
"At North Farm" (Ashbery) **26**:159-160
"At Odd Moments" (Brutus) **24**:116
"At One O'Clock in the Morning" (Baudelaire)
See "A une heure du matin"
"At School" (Smith) **12**:330, 333
"At Sea" (Toomer) **7**:336
"At Su Terrace Viewing the Past" (Li Po) **29**:145
*At Terror Street and Agony Way* (Bukowski) **18**:23
"At That Hour" (Joyce)
See "III"

"At the Back of the North Wind" (Gunn) **26**:
"At the Ball Game" (Williams) **7**:368, 385
"At the Beach" (Alegria) **26**:
"At the Birth of an Age" (Jeffers) **17**:111, 130,141-42, 144
"At the Caberet-Vert" (Rimbaud)
  See "Au caberet-vert"
"at the cemetary walnut grove plantation south carolina 1989" (Clifton) **17**:30
"At the Centre" (Gunn) **26**:226
"At the Edge" (Tomlinson) **17**:343, 345
"At the Fall of an Age" (Jeffers) **17**:141, 144
"At the Faucet of June" (Williams) **7**:382-83, 387-89, 410
"At the feet of others I did not forget" (Lermontov)
  See "At the feet of others I did not forget"
"At the Ferocious phenomenon of 5 O'clock I find Myself" (Cummings) **5**:93
"At the Fillmore" (Levine) **22**:224
"At the Fishhouses" (Bishop) **3**:42, 46, 48
"At the Gare Bruxelles-Midi" (Ferlinghetti) **1**:183
"At the Gates of the Tombs" (Sandburg) **2**:307
"At the German Writers Conference in Munich" (Dove) **6**:109
"At the Grave of Henry Vaughan" (Sassoon) **12**:246-47
"At the Hairdresser's" (Brooks) **7**:58, 68, 86, 102
"At the Head of This Street a Gasping Organ is Waving Moth-" (Cummings) **5**:93
"At the Indian Killer's Grave" (Lowell) **3**:202
"At the Lincoln Monument in Washington, August 28, 1963" (Walker) **20**:277-78
"At the Loom: Passages 2" (Duncan) **2**:107
"At the Museum of Modern Art" (Swenson) **14**:265
"At the National Black Assembly" (Baraka) **4**:28, 38
"At the Piano" (Hardy) **8**:93
"At the River Charles" (Viereck) **27**:282
"At the Tourist Centre in Boston" (Atwood) **8**:5, 23
*At the Very Edge of the Sea* (Akhmatova)
  See *U samovo morya*
"At the Well" (Piercy) **29**:300
"At The-Place-of-Sadness" (Gallagher) **9**:64
"At This Point" (Montale)
  See "A questo punto"
"At Waking" (Hardy) **8**:104
"At Welsh's Tomb" (Wakoski) **15**:353
*Atalanta in Calydon* (Swinburne) **24**:340
*Atarashiki yokujō* (Hagiwara Sakutaro) **18**:175
"Atavism" (Wylie) **23**:301, 307
"Atavismo" (Pavese) **13**:209, 214
*Atemwende* (Celan) **10**:96-7, 105, 110
"AThe Miracle" (Bukowski) **18**:5
"Athena in the front lines" (Piercy) **29**:313, 317
"Atherton's Gambit" (Robinson) **1**:466
"Atlanta in Camden Town" (Carroll) **18**:46
*Atlanta Offering Poems* (Harper) **21**:189
"The Atlantic" (Tomlinson) **17**:333
"Atlantic City Waiter" (Cullen) **20**:52, 64
"Atlantic Oil" (Pavese) **13**:223
"Atlantis" (Crane) **3**:90, 97, 106, 110-11
"An Atlas of the Difficult World" (Rich) **5**:398
*An Atlas of the Difficult World: Poems, 1988-1991* (Rich) **5**:398-99
*Atta Troll: Ein Sommernachtstraum* (Heine) **25**:132-34, 137-38, 164
"Attack" (Sassoon) **12**:266, 283-84, 286
"An Attempt at a Room" (Tsvetaeva)
  See "Popytka komnaty"
"An Attempt at Jealousy" (Tsvetaeva)
  See "Popytka revnosti"
"Attention, Attention" (Baraka) **4**:24
"Attic" (Sikelianos) **29**:368
"The Attic Which Is Desire" (Williams) **7**:351, 399
"Attis" (Tennyson) **6**:363

"Atys, the Land of Biscay" (Housman) **2**:179, 181
"Au caberet-vert" (Rimbaud) **3**:283
"Au Clair de la lune" (MacDiarmid) **9**:191
"Au Comte d'Orsay" (Lamartine) **16**:267
"Au lecteur" (Baudelaire) **1**:46, 57, 67, 70
"Au platane" (Valery) **9**:365, 394-96
"Au Rossignol" (Lamartine) **16**:280
"Au Roy" (Ronsard)
  See "Discours au Roy"
"Au Salon" (Pound) **4**:364
"Aubade" (Gluck) **16**:133
"Aubade" (Larkin) **21**:259
"Aubade" (Lowell) **13**:93
"Aubade" (Sitwell) **3**:297
"Aubade" (Smith) **12**:331
"Aubade: Harlem" (Merton) **10**:340
"Aubade: Lake Erie" (Merton) **10**:333, 340, 350
"Aubade—The Annunciation" (Merton) **10**:339
"Aube" (Rimbaud) **3**:261-62, 264
"L'aube spirituelle" (Baudelaire) **1**:56, 63
"The Auction" (Kinnell) **26**:286
"Audley Court" (Tennyson) **6**:365
"Auf dem See" (Goethe) **5**:255
"Auguries of Innocence" (Blake) **12**:35-6
"Augurios" (Paz) **1**:361
"August" (Belloc) **24**:29
"August" (Rich) **5**:371
"August" (Wylie) **23**:319, 322, 332
"August 22, 1939" (Rexroth) **20**:195
"August First" (Carruth) **10**:91
"An August Midnight" (Hardy) **8**:112
"August Night" (Swenson) **14**:266, 284
"August on Sourdough, A Visit from Dick Brewer" (Snyder) **21**:288
"August Was Foggy" (Snyder) **21**:288
*Aujourd'hui* (Hugo) **17**:80
"Aul Bastundzi" (Lermontov) **18**:300
"The Auld Farmer's New Year Morning Salutation" (Burns)
  See "The Auld Farmer's New Year Morning Salutation"
"The Auld Farmer's New Year's Day Address to His Auld Mare Maggie" (Burns) **6**:78
"Auld Lang Syne" (Burns) **6**:59, 75, 98-9
"AÚN" (Dario) **15**:98
*Aún* (Neruda) **4**:289
"Aunque cegué de mirarte" (Juana Ines de la Cruz) **24**:187
"Aunt Chloe's Politics" (Harper) **21**:200, 202, 213
"Aunt Filiberta and her Cretonnes" (Alegria) **26**:
"Aunts" (McGuckian) **27**:95
"La aurora" (Garcia Lorca) **3**:141
"Aurora Borealis" (Dove) **6**:110
*Aurora Leigh* (Browning) **6**:2, 6-7, 10-13, 21-3, 25-6, 31-2, 34-8, 40, 44, 46
"The Auroras of Autumn" (Roethke) **15**:280
"The Auroras of Autumn" (Stevens) **6**:338
*Auroras of Autumn* (Stevens) **6**:303, 335
"Aurore" (Valery) **9**:356, 363, 365, 367-68, 371, 394, 396
"Aus der Harzreise" (Heine) **25**:139
"Aus einer Sturmnacht" (Rilke) **2**:277
"Ausencia" (Borges) **22**:94
*Ausgewahlte gedichte* (Celan) **10**:102
"Aussi bien que les cigales" (Apollinaire) **7**:18, 22
"Aussöhnung" (Goethe) **5**:250-51
"The Author to her Book" (Bradstreet) **10**:7, 18, 27, 34
"The Author upon Himself" (Swift) **9**:295-96, 304, 306, 308-09
"The Author's Earnest Cry and Prayer" (Burns) **6**:78-9
"The Author's Manner of Living" (Swift) **9**:295
"Author's Note on Marabouts and Planted Poets" (Viereck) **27**:259, 262
"Auto Wreck" (Shapiro) **25**:279, 288, 297, 312, 319, 325

"Autobiografía" (Fuertes) **27**:49
"Autobiography" (Ferlinghetti) **1**:177-80, 183-84, 187
"Autobiography" (Gunn) **26**:205, 208
"Autobiography" (Harjo) **27**:71
*Autobiography* (Zukofsky) **11**:365
"Autochthon" (Masters) **1**:333
"Automatism of Taste" (Tzara) **27**:235
"Automne" (Apollinaire) **7**:42
"L'automne" (Lamartine) **16**:277, 290, 298, 301
"Automne malade" (Apollinaire) **7**:39, 42-3
"Autoprólogo" (Fuertes) **27**:23
"Autopsicografia" (Pessoa) **20**:172
"The Autopsy" (Elytis) **21**:123
"Autopsychography" (Pessoa)
  See "Autopsicografia"
"Autre complainte de Lord Pierrot" (Laforgue) **14**:81, 97
*Autre complainte de Lord Pierrot* (Laforgue) **14**:62, 88
"Autre complainte de l'orgue de barbarie" (Laforgue) **14**:81, 98
*Autrefois* (Hugo) **17**:80
"The Autumn" (Lamartine)
  See "L'automne"
"Autumn" (Lowell) **13**:97
"Autumn" (Neruda)
  See "Otoño"
"Autumn" (Pasternak) **6**:266
"Autumn" (Smith) **12**:345
"Autumn" (Tomlinson) **17**:339
"Autumn Bonfire" (Alegria) **26**:
"An Autumn Burning" (Berry) **28**:9
"Autumn Cellars" (Montale) **13**:149-50
"Autumn Chapter in a Novel" (Gunn) **26**:
"Autumn Cove Song #5" (Li Po) **29**:145
"Autumn Equinox" (Rich) **5**:351-52, 393
"Autumn Forest" (Pasternak) **6**:267
"Autumn Gold: New England Fall" (Ginsberg) **4**:54
"Autumn in California" (Rexroth) **20**:194, 214
"Autumn Lament" (Mallarme)
  See "Plainte d'automne"
"Autumn Meditation" (Wang Wei) **18**:343
"Autumn Sequence" (Rich) **5**:363, 382
"Autumn Song" (Dario)
  See "Canción otoñal"
"Autumn Valentine" (Parker) **28**:365
"Autumnal" (Dario) **15**:117
*Autumnal Leaves* (Hugo) **17**:44
"Auvergnat" (Belloc) **24**:34
"Aux Chrétiens" (Lamartine) **16**:280
"Aux Ecluses du vide" (Cesaire) **25**:12
"Aux ruines de Montfort-L'Amaury" (Hugo) **17**:89
"Avant-dernier mot" (Laforgue) **14**:95
"Avarice" (Herbert) **4**:102, 130
"Ave atque Vale" (Swinburne) **24**:321, 330-35, 337
"Ave Imperatrix!" (Kipling) **3**:190
"Ave Maria" (Crane) **3**:84, 86
"Avenel Gray" (Robinson)
  See "Mortmain"
"Avenue" (Pinsky) **27**:175
"The Avenue Bearing the Initial of Christ into the New World" (Kinnell) **26**:
"The Avenue Bearing the Initial of Christ into the New World" (Kinnell) **26**:236-37, 239, 241, 257, 262, 264, 289
"Avenue of Limes" (Pasternak) **6**:267
"The Avenue of Poplars" (Williams) **7**:382
"Aviary" (McGuckian) **27**:81, 98
"Avis de tirs" (Cesaire) **25**:29
"Aviso a los gobernantes del mundo" (Fuertes) **27**:2
"Avisos" (Pessoa) **20**:162
"Avocado Lake" (Soto) **28**:375, 379
"Avondale" (Smith) **12**:352
"Avondall" (Smith) **12**:352
*Avon's Harvest* (Robinson) **1**:465-66, 468-69
"Avtobus" (Tsvetaeva) **14**:325, 327

*Awake in th Red Desert* (Bissett) **14**:12, 14, 18-19
"Awake, my heart, to be loved: awake, awake" (Bridges) **28**:53, 63, 87
"Awakening" (Stryk) **27**:184, 186-87, 189, 206, 213
*Awakening* (Stryk) **27**:181, 195-98, 202-3, 213-16
"Awakening of the Waterfall" (Tagore)
  See "Nirjharer svapnabhanga"
"Away, Melancholy" (Smith) **12**:333
"Awe and Devastation of Solomos" (Elytis) **21**:135
"Awful Music" (Merton) **10**:337
*The Awful Rowing Toward God* (Sexton) **2**:360, 367-68, 371-73
"The Awthorn" (Clare) **23**:46-7
"Axe Handles" (Snyder) **21**:308
*Axe Handles* (Snyder) **21**:299-302, 307-10, 320
"The Ax-Helve" (Frost) **1**:215
*The Axion Esti* (Elytis) **21**:118, 120-30, 133
"Ay qué tristeza que tengo!" (Guillen) **23**:119-20, 127
"Ayer me dijeron negro" (Guillen) **23**:142
"Ayíasma" (Ekeloef) **23**:64
"Aylmer's Field" (Tennyson) **6**:362
"Aymerillot" (Hugo) **17**:58
*Ázma iroikó ke pénthimo yia ton haméno anthipolohaghó tis Álvanías* (Elytis) **21**:115, 120, 124, 127-29
"Azrail" (Lermontov) **18**:300
*Azul* (Dario) **15**:78, 86-7, 91-2, 94-6, 102-03, 105-07, 115, 117-18, 120
"L'azur" (Mallarme) **4**:199-200, 208, 213
"The Azure" (Mallarme)
  See "L'azur"
"Azure and Gold" (Lowell) **13**:60
"Babbitry" (Stryk) **27**:211
"The Babe" (Olson) **19**:319-20
"Babočka" (Brodsky) **9**:29
"The Baby" (Nash) **21**:278
"Baby" (Sexton) **2**:367
"Baby Picture" (Sexton) **2**:370
"Baby song" (Gunn) **26**:210
"Baby V" (Levine)
  See "Baby Villon"
"Baby Villon" (Levine) **22**:213
"Babyhood" (Swinburne) **24**:323
"Babylon Revisited" (Baraka) **4**:18
"The Bacchae" (H. D.) **5**:305
"Bacchanales" (Ronsard) **11**:230-32, 234
"Bacchanalia" (Pasternak) **6**:267
"Bacchus" (Emerson) **18**:85, 99, 103, 106
"Bacchus and the Pirates" (Noyes) **27**:121, 124-25, 133
"Bachelor" (Meredith) **28**:189
"Bachelor Uncle" (Wright) **14**:348
"Back Again, Home" (Madhubuti) **5**:324, 329, 338
*The Back Country* (Snyder) **21**:288, 291-92, 296, 300
"Back from a Walk" (Garcia Lorca)
  See "Vuelta de paseo"
"back in th city" (Bissett) **14**:30
"The Back o' Beyond" (MacDiarmid) **9**:196
"Back to Life" (Gunn)
"Backdrop Addresses Cowboy" (Atwood) **8**:4, 16, 41
"The Backlash Blues" (Hughes) **1**:251, 257
"The Backside of the Academy" (Rukeyser) **12**:236
"The Backward Look" (Nemerov) **24**:287, 301
"Backyard" (Wright) **14**:377
"The Bacterial War" (Nemerov) **24**:298
*The Bad Child's Book of Beasts* (Belloc) **24**:12, 23-6, 35
"Bad Dreams" (Browning) **2**:59
"Bad Dreams" (Pinsky) **27**:145
"The Bad Glazier" (Baudelaire)
  See "Le mauvais vitrier"
"Bad Man" (Hughes) **1**:270
"Bad Morning" (Hughes) **1**:241

"Bad Ol' Stagolee" (Walker) **20**:287
"The Bad Old Days" (Rexroth) **20**:218
*The Bad Parents' Garden of Verse* (Nash) **21**:264-65
"Bad Penny" (Levine) **22**:218
"The Bad Season Makes the Poet Sad" (Herrick) **9**:89, 103, 109, 115
"Badger" (Clare) **23**:7
"The Badgers" (Heaney) **18**:219, 244
"Baha'u'llah in the Garden of Ridwan" (Hayden) **6**:185-86, 196, 198
"Bahnhofstrasse" (Joyce) **22**:137
"Bahu" (Tagore) **8**:407
"Baignée" (Valery) **9**:392
"La bailerina de los pies desnudos" (Dario) **15**:80
"Le baiser" (Char) **15**:138, 144, 171
*The Bak-Chesarian fountain: A Tale of the Tauride* (Pushkin)
  See *Bakhchisaraiski Fontan*
*The Bakhchisarai Fontan* (Pushkin)
  See *Bakhchisaraiski Fontan*
*Bakhchisaraiski Fontan* (Pushkin) **10**:358, 365, 386-88, 411, 417, 419, 421
"Le Bal" (Vigny) **26**:410-11
"Bal des pendus" (Rimbaud) **3**:281, 283
"La balada azul" (Guillen) **23**:100, 140
"Balada de los dos abuelos" (Guillen) **23**:103, 132, 138
*Baladas de primavera* (Jimenez) **7**:184
*Balākā* (Tagore) **8**:413-15, 418, 427
"Balakhana" (McGuckian) **27**:82, 93
"Balanchine's" (Merrill) **28**:254
"Le balcon" (Baudelaire) **1**:45, 63
"The Balcony" (Baudelaire)
  See "Le balcon"
"Balcony Scene" (Shapiro) **25**:316
"Balder Dead" (Arnold) **5**:35, 37, 58-9, 62
"Balin and Balan" (Tennyson) **6**:376-77
"Ballad" (Ammons) **16**:25
"Ballad" (Pasternak) **6**:270
"Ballad Fourth: The Trogger" (Burns) **6**:78
"Ballad of Army Wagons" (Tu Fu) **9**:330
"The Ballad of Ballymote" (Gallagher) **9**:42
"The Ballad of Beautiful Words" (Nash) **21**:273
"A Ballad of Boding" (Rossetti) **7**:271
"The Ballad of Chocolate Mabbie" (Brooks) **7**:57, 68, 102, 104
"The Ballad of East and West" (Kipling) **3**:157, 182-83, 188
"Ballad of Faith" (Williams) **7**:363
"The Ballad of Father O'Hart" (Yeats) **20**:349
"A Ballad of François Villon" (Swinburne) **24**:324
"The Ballad of Jakko Hill" (Kipling) **3**:187
"The Ballad of Late Annie" (Brooks) **7**:102-04
"The Ballad of Launcelot and Elaine" (Masters) **1**:328
"The Ballad of Margie Polite" (Hughes) **1**:241, 243, 247
"Ballad of Missing Lines" (Rukeyser) **12**:228
"The Ballad of Moll Magee" (Yeats) **20**:337
"The Ballad of Nat Turner" (Hayden) **6**:176, 178-80, 186-87, 194-95, 198
"Ballad of Pearl May Lee" (Brooks) **7**:57, 68, 86, 103-04
"A Ballad of Remembrance" (Hayden) **6**:200
*A Ballad of Remembrance* (Hayden) **6**:183, 188, 194-95
"The Ballad of Rudolph Reed" (Brooks) **7**:62, 96
"A Ballad of Sark" (Swinburne) **24**:313
"Ballad of Simón Caraballo" (Guillen) **23**:106
*The Ballad of St. Barbara and Other Verses* (Chesterton) **28**:96-97
"The Ballad of Sue Ellen Westerfield" (Hayden) **6**:196
"Ballad of the Black Sorrow" (Garcia Lorca)
  See "Romance de la pena negra"
"The Ballad of the Bolivar" (Kipling) **3**:164
"The Ballad of the Brown Girl" (Cullen) **20**:55, 64, 85-86

*The Ballad of the Brown Girl: An Old Ballad Retold* (Cullen) **20**:61, 77, 79, 86
"The Ballad of the Children of the Czar" (Schwartz) **8**:302, 305, 309
"Ballad of the Dark Trouble" (Garcia Lorca)
  See "Romance de la pena negra"
"Ballad of the Five Senses" (MacDiarmid) **9**:157, 193
"Ballad of the Free" (Walker) **20**:276, 284, 292
"The Ballad of the Harp-Weaver" (Millay) **6**:211, 225, 233
"Ballad of the Hoppy Toad" (Walker) **20**:290-92
"Ballad of the Jollie Gleeman" (Viereck) **27**:259
"The Ballad of the King's Jest" (Kipling) **3**:182
"Ballad of The Ladies of Past Times" (Villon)
  See "Ballade des Dames du Temps Jadis"
"Ballad of the Landlord" (Hughes) **1**:258, 267
"Ballad of the Little Square" (Garcia Lorca)
  See "Ballada de la Placeta"
"The Ballad of the Lonely Masturbator" (Sexton) **2**:352, 370
"The Ballad of the Long-Legged Bait" (Thomas) **2**:382, 393, 402
"Ballad of the Moon, the Moon" (Garcia Lorca)
  See "Romance de la luna, luna"
"The Ballad of the Red Earl" (Kipling) **3**:181-82
"Ballad of the Spanish Civil Guard" (Garcia Lorca)
  See "Romance de la Guardia Civil Española"
"Ballad of the Summoned Man" (Garcia Lorca) **3**:147
"The Ballad of the True Beast" (Hayden) **6**:196-97
"Ballad of the Two Grandfathers" (Guillen)
  See "Balada de los dos abuelos"
*The Ballad of the White Horse* (Chesterton) **28**:93, 100, 105-08, 119-28
"Ballad of the World Extinct" (Celan)
  See "Ballade von der erloschenen Welt"
"The Ballad of Valès-Dunes" (Belloc) **24**:11
"Ballad Written in a Clinic" (Montale)
  See "Ballata scritta in una clinica"
"Ballada de la Placeta" (Garcia Lorca) **3**:125
"Ballade" (Dunbar) **5**:139-40
"Ballade" (Gautier) **18**:348-51
"Ballade" (Stryk) **27**:191
"Ballade de bon conseil" (Villon) **13**:394-95
"Ballade de bonne doctrine" (Villon) **13**:394-95, 404-05
"Ballade de conclusion" (Villon) **13**:417
"Ballade de la Grosse Margot" (Villon) **13**:389-90, 393
"Ballade de mercy" (Villon) **13**:399, 413
"Ballade des contre verites" (Villon) **13**:414
"Ballade des Dames du Temps Jadis" (Villon) **13**:374, 405, 409-10
"Ballade des femmes de Paris" (Villon) **13**:380, 390, 413
"Ballade des Langues Envieuses" (Villon) **13**:404
"Ballade des menus propos" (Villon) **13**:409
"Ballade des Pendus" (Villon)
  See "Epitaphe Villon"
"Ballade des proverbes" (Villon) **13**:404, 414
"Ballade des seigneurs du temps jadis" (Villon) **13**:410
"Ballade du concours de Blois" (Villon) **13**:392, 414
"La ballade du Mal Aimé" (Apollinaire)
  See "La chanson du mal-aimé"
"Ballade d'une grande dame" (Chesterton) **28**:117
"Ballade of a Talked-off Ear" (Parker) **28**:363
"Ballade of Big Plans" (Parker) **28**:354
"Ballade of Dead Ladies" (Villon) **13**:387, 390-91
"Ballade of Fat Margot" (Villon)
  See "Ballade de la Grosse Margot"
"Ballade of Hell and Mrs Roebeck" (Belloc) **24**:49

"A Ballade of Interesting News" (Belloc) **24**:42
"A Ballade of Suicide" (Chesterton) **28**:99
"Ballade of the Critic" (Shapiro) **25**:281
"Ballade of the Hanged" (Villon)
  See "Epitaphe Villon"
"Ballade of the Women of Paris" (Villon)
  See "Ballade des femmes de Paris"
"Ballade of Unfortunate Mammals" (Parker)
  **28**:351, 363
"Ballade pour prier Nostre Dame" (Villon)
  **13**:403, 405, 413
"Ballade pour Robert d'Estouteville" (Villon)
  **13**:395, 415
"Ballade to Our Lady" (Villon) **13**:390-91
"Ballade vom Auszug der drei" (Celan) **10**:126
"Ballade von der erloschenen Welt" (Celan)
  **10**:125
*Ballades en Jargon* (Villon) **13**:404, 406
*Ballads for Sale* (Lowell) **13**:76, 84-5
*Ballads of Spring* (Jimenez)
  See *Baladas de primavera*
"Ballata scritta in una clinica" (Montale)
  **13**:108, 131, 167
"The Ballet" (Meredith) **28**:193, 215
"Ballet" (Pavese)
  See "Balletto"
"Balletto" (Pavese) **13**:205, 226
"Balloons" (Plath) **1**:391
"The Ballroom at Sandover" (Merrill) **28**:235
*Bally* (Gunn) **26**:
*Balustion's Adventure* (Browning) **2**:85-6, 95
"Bamboo" (Hagiwara Sakutaro)
  See "Take"
"Bamboo Lodge" (Wang Wei) **18**:382
*Banabani* (Tagore) **8**:416
"Banaphul" (Tagore) **8**:405
"La Bande Noire" (Hugo) **17**:87-88
"Bandi" (Tagore) **8**:407, 412
"Bandot" (Stryk) **27**:204-5
"The Bands and the Beautiful Children" (Page)
  **12**:169, 177
"Banga bir" (Tagore) **8**:407
"The Bangkok Gong" (Kumin) **15**:213
"The Bangs" (Montale)
  See "La frangia dei capelli"
"Banishment" (Sassoon) **12**:267, 288
"A Banjo Song" (Dunbar) **5**:146
"A Banjo Song" (Johnson) **24**:136, 141
"The Banker's Daughter" (Lowell) **3**:218, 221
"Banking Coal" (Toomer) **7**:333
"The bankrupt Peace Maker" (Lindsay) **23**:269
"Banks of a Stream Where Creatures Bathe"
  (Merrill) **28**:223, 255
"Banneker" (Dove) **6**:105, 109
"The Banner Bearer" (Williams) **7**:389-90
"The Banners" (Duncan) **2**:102
"Banquet" (Gozzano) **10**:183
"The Banquet" (Herbert) **4**:134
*The Banquet* (Dante)
  See *Convivio*
"Bantams in Pine-Woods" (Stevens) **6**:293, 303,
  327
"Banyan" (Swenson) **14**:273
"Baptism" (Herbert) **4**:100
"Baptism" (McKay) **2**:211
"A Baptist Childhood" (Davie) **29**:101, 112
"Barbare" (Cesaire) **25**:23-25, 28, 31, 37
"Barbare" (Rimbaud) **3**:261
*Barbare* (Cesaire) **25**:10
"Barbecue" (Stryk) **27**:208
"The Bard" (Gray) **2**:134-35, 139, 143-44, 146,
  148, 151-54
"The Bards" (Graves) **6**:140, 144
"Bards of Passion and of Mirth" (Keats) **1**:312
"Barefoot" (Sexton) **2**:352
"The Barefoot Dancer" (Dario)
  See "La bailerina de los pies desnudos"
*Barely and Widely, 1956-1958* (Zukofsky)
  **11**:348
*Barking at the Moon* (Hagiwara Sakutaro)
  See *Tsuki ni hoeru*

"Barking Hall: A Year After" (Swinburne)
  **24**:318-19
"Barmaids Are Diviner than Mermaids" (Nash)
  **21**:265
"The Barn" (Heaney) **18**:194, 200
"Barnsley, 1966" (Davie) **29**:102
"Barnsley and District" (Davie) **29**:111
"Baroque Comment" (Bogan) **12**:90, 92, 97,
  101
"A Baroque Sunburst" (Clampitt) **19**:90
"Barrabas. Eine Phantasie" (Trakl) **20**:239
*Barrack Room Ballads and Other Verses*
  (Kipling) **3**:155-56, 159-60, 163, 165,
  167-69, 177, 182, 187-89
"The Barrel Organ" (Noyes) **27**:115-16, 133,
  136-38
"The Barrier" (McKay) **2**:212
"Bartok" (Illyes) **16**:231
"Base Details" (Sassoon) **12**:268, 277, 280
"Baseball and Writing" (Moore) **4**:242, 256,
  259-60
"Baseball Canto" (Ferlinghetti) **1**:183
"Basement Apartment" (Shapiro) **25**:316
"A Basin of Eggs" (Swenson) **14**:250
"The Basket" (Lowell) **13**:84, 95-6
"Baskets" (Gluck) **16**:152
"A Bastard Peace" (Williams) **7**:369
"The Bastille" (Brooke) **24**:66, 80, 84, 89
"Bateau ivre" (Hugo) **17**:65
*Le bateau ivre* (Rimbaud) **3**:249, 257-58, 268-
  70, 272-74, 282, 286
"The Bath" (Snyder) **21**:292, 297
"A Bather" (Lowell) **13**:93-6
"The Bathers" (Shapiro) **25**:304
"Bathos" (Pope) **26**:357
"Batjushkov" (Mandelstam) **14**:118
"Batouque" (Cesaire) **25**:29
"Battalion-Relief" (Sassoon) **12**:269
"The Battle" (Brooks) **7**:67
"The Battle of Brunanburh" (Tennyson) **6**:363,
  369
*The Battle of Marathon: A Poem* (Browning)
  **6**:19
"The Battle of Osfrontalis" (Hughes) **7**:123,
  142, 160-61
"Battle Problem" (Meredith) **28**:172, 189
"The Battlefield" (Bryant) **20**:5
"Battlewagon" (Meredith) **28**:174
"Baudelaire" (Schwartz) **8**:311, 319
"Bayn al-kharā'ib" (Gibran) **9**:79
"Bayonne Turnpike to Tuscarora" (Ginsberg)
  **4**:54
"Bayou Afternoon" (Clampitt) **19**:102
*Be Angry at the Sun and Other Poems* (Jeffers)
  **17**:123, 135
"Be Still, My Soul, Be Still" (Housman) **2**:184,
  192
"Beach at Versilia" (Montale)
  See "Proda di Versilia"
"Beach Glass" (Clampitt) **19**:88
"The Beach Head" (Gunn) **26**:218
*"The Beach Head"* (Gunn) **26**:
"The Beach Women" (Pinsky) **27**:162
"The Beachcomber" (Stryk) **27**:185-86
"Beachy" (Sandburg) **2**:300
"The Beaks of Eagles" (Jeffers) **17**:145
"Beale Street Love" (Hughes) **1**:269
"The Bean Eaters" (Brooks) **7**:55-6, 62, 69, 100
*The Bean Eaters* (Brooks) **7**:56-8, 62-3, 67, 81,
  86, 95-6, 98-9, 101-02, 105, 107
"Beans with Garlic" (Bukowski) **18**:23
"The Bean-Stalk" (Millay) **6**:237, 239
"The Bear" (Frost) **1**:203-04
"The Bear" (Kinnell) **26**:241-42, 244, 252, 257,
  262-63, 273, 291
"The Bear" (Momaday) **25**:185-86, 188, 191,
  193-95, 201-202, 209-10, 220
"The Bear and the Garden-Lover" (Moore)
  **4**:261
"The Bearer of Evil Tidings" (Frost) **1**:202
*Beast in View* (Rukeyser) **12**:231-32
"The Beast's Confession to the Priest" (Swift)

  **9**:281, 295
"The Beaters" (Gunn) **26**:198, 201, 220
"Le beau navire" (Baudelaire) **1**:60
"Beau sang giclé" (Cesaire) **25**:44-5
"La beauté" (Baudelaire) **1**:61, 65
"Beauté de femmes, leur faiblesse, et ces
  mains pâles" (Verlaine) **2**:416
"The Beautiful American Word, Sure"
  (Schwartz) **8**:302, 315
"Beautiful Black Men" (with compliments and
  apologies to all not mentioned by
  nameGiovanni) **19**:106-7, 112
"Beautiful Lofty Things" (Yeats) **20**:307
"A Beautiful Young Nymph Going to Bed.
  Written for the Honour of the Fair Sex"
  (Swift) **9**:257, 262, 267-69, 279, 281, 283-
  84, 286, 291, 295, 298, 301-03
"A beautifull Mistris" (Carew) **29**:9
"The Beauty" (Pushkin) **10**:371
"Beauty" (Wylie) **23**:300, 313, 327, 333
*Beauty* (Jimenez)
  See *Belleza*
"Beauty and Beauty" (Brooke) **24**:56, 62
"Beauty and Sadness" (Song) **21**:341, 347
"Beauty and the Beast" (Dove) **6**:108
"Beauty and the Beast" (Tomlinson) **17**:323
"Beauty and the Illiterate" (Elytis) **21**:123
"The Beauty of the Head" (Swenson) **14**:281
"Beauty Shoppe" (Brooks) **7**:59, 102
"Beauty Who Took Snuff" (Pushkin) **10**:407
"Bebop Boys" (Hughes) **1**:267
"Because I Deeply Praised" (Sikelianos) **29**:368
"Because I Love You" (Last NightCummings)
  **5**:105
"Because I Was Not Able to Restrain Your
  Hands" (Mandelstam) **14**:114, 118
"Because One Is Always Forgotten" (Forche)
  **10**:138, 142, 144, 153, 155
"Because,thy,smile,is,primavera" (Villa) **22**:356,
  358
*Beckonings* (Brooks) **7**:84, 94
"Becoming new" (Piercy) **29**:301
"Becoming Strangers" (Piercy) **29**:309
"The Bed by the Window" (Jeffers) **17**:131
"The Bed in the Sky" (Snyder) **21**:289
"Bed Time" (Hughes) **1**:255
"Bedfordshire" (Davie) **29**:116
"The Bedpost" (Graves) **6**:141
"A Bedtime Story" (Hughes) **7**:159
"The Bee Meeting" (Plath) **1**:394, 410-13
*Bee Time Vine* (Stein) **18**:316-34, 336, 341-42,
  344, 349-54
"Beech" (Frost) **1**:197
"Beech, Pine, and Sunlight" (Lowell) **13**:64
*Beechen Vigil and Other Poems* (Day Lewis)
  **11**:148
"Beehive" (Toomer) **7**:311, 320, 334
"Bee-Keeper" (Nemerov) **24**:
"The Beekeeper Speaks" (Nemerov) **24**:262,
  274
"The Beekeeper's Daughter" (Plath) **1**:389,
  410-12
"Beeny Cliff" (Hardy) **8**:136
"Bees Stopped" (Ammons) **16**:46
"Beethoven Attends the C Minor Seminar"
  (Tomlinson) **17**:320
"Beethoven Opus 111" (Clampitt) **19**:82, 85, 89
"Before a Blue Light" (Kumin) **15**:211
"Before a Midnight Breaks in Storm" (Kipling)
  **3**:183
"Before an Old Painting of the Crucifixion"
  (Momaday)
"Before I Knocked and Flesh Let Enter"
  (Thomas) **2**:383, 402
"Before Knowledge" (Hardy) **8**:89
"Before the Altar" (Lowell) **13**:69, 83
"Before the Battle" (Sassoon) **12**:262
"Before the Birth of one of her Children"
  (Bradstreet) **10**:12, 18
"Before the Dance" (Tomlinson) **17**:319, 328,
  330
"Before the Judgment" (Duncan) **2**:116

"Before the Look of You" (Reese) **29**:331
"Before the Storm" (Lowell) **13**:60-1
"Before the Trip" (Montale)
    See "Prima del viaggio"
"Before We Mothernaked Fell" (Thomas) **2**:402
"Before We Sinned" (Incarnate DevilThomas) **2**:402
"Begat" (Sexton) **2**:366
"The Beggar to Mab, the Fairies' Queen" (Herrick) **9**:86
"The Beggars" (Wordsworth) **4**:377
"The Beggar's Valentine" (Lindsay) **23**:286
"The Beginner" (Kipling) **3**:183
"Beginner's Guide" (Nemerov) **24**:285
"The Beginning" (Brooke) **24**:56, 82
"The Beginning" (Gluck) **16**:164, 167
"Beginning a Poem of These States" (Ginsberg) **4**:81
"The Beginning and the End" (Jeffers) **17**:128, 132, 141
*The Beginning and the End and Other Poems* (Jeffers) **17**:114-15, 123, 128, 136
"The Beginning of September" (Hass) **16**:199, 210
"The Beginning of the End of the World" (Clifton) **17**:29
"Beginnings" (Hayden) **6**:190
"The Beginnings" (Kipling) **3**:192
"Behind the Arras" (Dunbar) **5**:133
"Behind the Mirror" (Gunn) **26**:210-213
"Beiname" (Goethe) **5**:248
"Being" (Gunn) **26**:
"The Being as Memory" (Carruth) **10**:71
"The Being as Moment" (Carruth) **10**:71
"The Being as Prevision" (Carruth) **10**:71
"Being Beauteous" (Rimbaud) **3**:261, 263-64
"Being of Beauty" (Rimbaud) **3**:263
"Being Young and Green" (Millay) **6**:236
"Le Bel oiseau déchiffrant l'inconnu au couple d'amoureux" (Breton) **15**:49
*Belaia staia* (Akhmatova)
    See *Belaya staya*
*Belaia staja* (Akhmatova)
    See *Belaya staya*
*Belaya staya* (Akhmatova) **2**:3, 6, 11-12, 18
"Belderg" (Heaney) **18**:203
"Belfast on a Sunday Afternoon" (Davie) **29**:106-08
"Belfast on a Sunday Morning" (Davie) **29**:119
"Belfast Tune" (Brodsky) **9**:28
"Believe History" (Jeffers) **17**:141
"La bell au bois dormant" (Valery) **9**:392
"La belle dame sans merci" (Keats) **1**:279, 282, 304-05
"La belle Dorothée" (Baudelaire) **1**:49
"La belle époque" (Milosz) **8**:211
"La Belle Hequmière aux filles de joie" (Villon) **13**:389
"Belle lecon aux enfants perdus" (Villon) **13**:394-95
*Belleza* (Jimenez) **7**:202
"The Bells" (Poe) **1**:430-31, 439, 441
"The Bells" (Sexton) **2**:359
*Bells and Pomegrantes* (Browning) **2**:27, 70
"Bells in the Rain" (Wylie) **23**:328-29
"Bells in Winter" (Milosz) **8**:189, 205
*Bells in Winter* (Milosz) **8**:174
*Bells of Lombardy* (Stryk) **27**:214-15, 218
"Bells of Winter" (Milosz)
    See "Bells in Winter"
"The Bells that Signed" (Day Lewis) **11**:144
"Belly Song" (Knight) **14**:46, 48
*Belly Song and Other Poems* (Knight) **14**:41-2, 48, 52
"Below" (Celan) **10**:118
"Below Tintern" (Tomlinson) **17**:334, 336
"Belsazar" (Heine) **25**:140
"Belsen, Day of Liberation" (Hayden) **6**:194
"Belts" (Kipling) **3**:162
"Ben Jonson Entertains a Man from Stratford" (Robinson) **1**:462, 468, 487
"Benares" (Borges) **22**:72

"Bending the Bow" (Duncan) **2**:107
*Bending the Bow* (Duncan) **2**:104, 107, 113-116, 119, 125, 127
"Beneath a Cool Shade" (Behn) **13**:15
"Beneath My Hand and Eye the Distant Hills, Your Body" (Snyder) **21**:288
*Beneath the Fortinaria* (Bukowski) **18**:21
"Bénédiction" (Baudelaire) **1**:54, 70
"Benediction" (Kunitz) **19**:148
"Bengali Heroes" (Tagore)
    See "Banga bir"
"Benjamin Pantier" (Masters) **1**:347
"Bennie's Departure" (McKay) **2**:225
"Ben's Last Fight" (Merton) **10**:345
*Beowulf* **22**:1-65
*Beppo: A Venetian Story* (Byron) **16**:83, 115-20
"Berck-Plage" (Plath) **1**:390
"Bereavement" (Smith) **12**:351
"Bereft" (Hardy) **8**:131
"Bergidylle" (Heine) **25**:145
"Berkeley Eclogue" (Hass) **16**:217
"Berlin" (Ferlinghetti) **1**:167
"Berlin in ruins" (Gunn) **26**:211-212
"Berlin Is Hard on Colored Girls" (Lorde) **12**:142
*The Berlin Songbook* (Bely)
    See *Berlinsky pesennik*
*Berlinsky pesennik* (Bely) **11**:7
"Bermudas" (Marvell) **10**:268-69, 271, 275, 289, 311, 313-14
"Berry Holden" (Masters) **1**:324
"Bertha in the Lane" (Browning) **6**:17
"Los besos" (Aleixandre) **15**:38
"Bessey of the Glen" (Clare) **23**:25
"The Best of It" (Sassoon) **12**:248, 260
"Best Year's" (Soto) **28**:398-99
*Le bestiaire; ou, Cortège d'Orphée* (Apollinaire) **7**:48
*Bestiary/Bestiario* (Neruda) **4**:286-87
"A Bestiary for My Daughters Mary and Katharine" (Rexroth) **20**:187, 190, 195, 218
"Bestiary U.S.A." (Sexton) **2**:367
"Besuch bei Ingres" (Enzensberger) **28**:150
"Besy" (Pushkin) **10**:413
"Betancourt" (Baraka) **4**:15
"Betraktelse" (Ekeloef) **23**:76
"Betrayal" (Pavese)
    See "Tradimento"
"The Betrothal" (Apollinaire)
    See "Les fiançailles"
"The Betrothal" (Millay) **6**:211
"Betrothed" (Bogan) **12**:127-28
"A Better Resurrection" (Rossetti) **7**:290
"Between Our Selves" (Lorde) **12**:139
*Between Our Selves* (Lorde) **12**:137, 156
"Between the Porch and the Altar" (Lowell) **3**:200, 203-04, 206
"Between Us" (Merrill) **28**:252
"Between Walls" (Williams) **7**:399, 402
"Beucolicks" (Herrick) **9**:89
"Beverly Hills, Chicago" (Brooks) **7**:81
"Beware!" (Wylie) **23**:322
"Beware, Madam!" (Graves) **6**:163
"Bewick Finzer" (Robinson) **1**:467
"Beyond Even Faithful Legends" (Bissett) **14**:6, 24, 31
*Beyond Even Faithful Legends* (Bissett)
    See *Selected Poems: Beyond Even Faithful Legends*
"Beyond Harm" (Olds) **22**:325, 341
"Beyond Sharp Control" (Brutus) **24**:116
"Beyond the Alps" (Lowell) **3**:205, 211, 218, 221
*Beyond the Mountains* (Rexroth) **20**:185-86
"Beyond the Last Lamp" (Hardy) **8**:125
"Beyond the Pleasure Principle" (Nemerov) **24**:260
"Bez nazvaniya" (Pasternak) **6**:288
"Bezverie" (Pushkin) **10**:409, 411
"Bhagna mandir" (Tagore) **8**:415
"Bhairavi gan" (Tagore) **8**:407

*Bhānu singha* (Tagore) **8**:403
*Bhanusingh Thakurer padavali* (Tagore) **8**:405
"Bhar" (Tagore) **8**:412
"Biafra" (Levertov) **11**:176, 194
"Bianca among the Nightingales" (Browning) **6**:23-4, 28, 32, 38, 40
"The Bible Defense of Slavery" (Harper) **21**:190, 208, 217
"Bible Stories" (Reese) **29**:330
"bibliographie" (Enzensberger) **28**:137
"Bickford's Buddha" (Ferlinghetti) **1**:186-87
"Bien loin d'ici" (Baudelaire) **1**:49
"Bien que le trait de vostre belle face" (Ronsard) **11**:250
"Bifurcation" (Tzara) **27**:229-31
"The Big Baboon" (Belloc) **24**:24
"Big Bastard with a Sword" (Bukowski) **18**:13
"Big Bessie Throws Her Son into the Street" (Brooks) **7**:63, 81
"Big Elegy" (Brodsky)
    See "The Great Elegy for John Donne"
"Big Fat Hairy Vision of Evil" (Ferlinghetti) **1**:167
"The Big Graveyard" (Viereck) **27**:262
"The Big Heart" (Sexton) **2**:368
"Big John Henry" (Walker) **20**:287
"Big Momma" (Madhubuti) **5**:326, 344
"Big Wind" (Roethke) **15**:276, 279
"The Bight" (Bishop) **3**:50, 52-4
"Les bijoux" (Baudelaire) **1**:61
"Bill of Fare" (Enzensberger) **28**:142
"The Billboard Painters" (Ferlinghetti) **1**:183
"Billboards" (Ondaatje) **28**:328, 331
"Billboards and Galleons" (Lindsay) **23**:287
*Billy the Kid* (Ondaatje) **28**:293-94, 296-97
"Bimini" (Heine) **25**:167
"The Biographer's Mandate" (Nemerov) **24**:289
"Il Biondomoro" (Pasolini) **17**:264
"Birches" (Frost) **1**:196, 221, 225, 227-28, 230
"Birches" (Wylie) **23**:326
"Bird" (Harjo) **27**:72
"The Bird and the Arras" (Finch) **21**:157, 160, 172
"The Bird Auction" (McGuckian) **27**:94
"Bird Call Valley" (Wang Wei) **18**:381-82, 391
"The Bird Frau" (Dove) **6**:108
"Bird of Air" (H. D.) **5**:287
"The Bird with the Coppery, Keen Claws" (Stevens) **6**:293, 304
"Birdbrain!" (Ginsberg) **4**:62, 76
"Birdcage Walk" (Merton) **10**:351
"Birdcries Stream" (Wang Wei)
    See "Birdcries Stream"
"The Birds" (Belloc) **24**:5, 8
"Birds" (Cesaire) **25**:46
"Birds" (Jeffers) **17**:147
"Birds" (Wright) **14**:347, 349, 353, 366
*Birds* (Perse)
    See *Oiseaux*
*Birds* (Wright) **14**:348-49, 354
"Birds for Janet" (Ondaatje) **28**:318, 332
"Birds in the Night" (Verlaine) **2**:415
"Birds of Prey" (McKay) **2**:212
"The birds that sing on Autumn eves" (Bridges) **28**:84
"Birds without Descent" (Aleixandre) **15**:19-21
"Bird-Singing Stream" (Wang Wei) **18**:360, 376, 380-81, 386, 390
"The Biretta" (Heaney) **18**:256
"Birmingham" (Walker) **20**:283, 287
"Birmingham Sunday" (Hughes) **1**:252
"Birth and Death" (Jeffers) **17**:141
"Birth and Death" (Swinburne) **24**:324
"The Birth in a Narrow Room" (Brooks) **7**:54, 80
"Birth of a Fascist" (Viereck) **27**:280
"Birth of a Genius among Men" (MacDiarmid) **9**:153
"Birth of a Smile" (Mandelstam)
    See "Rozhdenie ulybki"
"The Birth of Christ" (Garcia Lorca)
    See "Nacimiento de Cristo"

*The Birth of Kumara* (Kalidasa)
See *Kumārasambhava*
*The Birth of the Prince* (Kalidasa)
See *Kumārasambhava*
"Birth of the Virgin" (Swenson) **14**:285
*The Birth of the War-God* (Kalidasa)
See *Kumārasambhava*
"Birthday" (Aleixandre) **15**:16
"Birthday" (Jeffers) **17**:141
"A Birthday" (Rossetti) **7**:276, 278, 280
*The Birthday* (Merrill) **28**:270
*The Birthday* (Merrill) **28**:
"A Birthday Cake for Lionel" (Wylie)
**23**:321-22
"A Birthday Kid Poem" (Ortiz) **17**:228
"Birthday on the Beach" (Nash) **21**:270
"Birthday Poem" (Shapiro) **25**:263
"Birthday Sonnet" (Wylie) **23**:315
"Birthmarks" (Song) **21**:341
"The Birthplace" (Heaney) **18**:214
"Bisclavret" (Marie de France) **22**:258, 260,
268, 272, 282-84, 286, 298-99
"Bishop Blougram" (Browning) **2**:37
"Bishop Blougram's Apology" (Browning)
**2**:43, 73
"The Bishop Orders His Tomb at St. Praxed's"
(Browning) **2**:37, 48, 82, 94
"The Biting Insects" (Kinnell) **26**:288
"The Bitter River" (Hughes) **1**:251
*Bixby Canyon to Jessore Road* (Ginsberg) **4**:89
"Black and Unknown Bards" (Johnson) **24**:137,
142
"The Black Angel" (Montale)
See "L'angelo nero"
*Black Armour* (Wylie) **23**:301-302, 307, 309-
10, 324, 332
"Black Art" (Baraka) **4**:10, 19, 25, 40
"The Black Art" (Sexton) **2**:373
*Black Arts* (Baraka) **4**:18
"Black Bill's Honeymoon" (Noyes) **27**:123, 134
"Black Blood" (Blok) **21**:5
"Black Buttercups" (Clampitt) **19**:83, 86, 91
"The Black Christ" (Madhubuti) **5**:339-40
*The Black Christ and Other Poems* (Cullen)
**20**:59, 62, 64, 68
"The Black Christ" (Hopefully Dedicated to
White AmericaCullen) **20**:59, 64-66, 68,
71, 73-75, 87
"Black Cock" (Montale)
See "Gallo cedrone"
"The Black Cottage" (Frost) **1**:193, 198
"BLACK DADA NIHILISMUS" (Baraka) **4**:9,
14
"Black Dancer in the Little Savoy" (Hughes)
**1**:246
"Black Eagle Returns to St. Joe" (Masters)
**1**:344
"Black Earth" (Mandelstam)
See "Chernozem"
"Black Earth" (Moore) **4**:251
*Black Feeling, Black Talk* (Giovanni) **19**:133,
135, 139
*Black Feeling, Black Talk, Black Judgement*
(Giovanni) **19**:107-8, 110-11, 114, 118,
120-22, 124, 128, 136
"The Black Goddess" (Graves) **6**:154
"Black Hair" (Soto) **28**:379-80
"Black Harmonium" (Hagiwara Sakutaro)
See "Kuroi fūkin"
*Black Hosts* (Senghor)
See *Hosties noires*
"Black Jackets" (Gunn) **26**:201
*Black Judgement* (Giovanni) **19**:135, 139, 143
"Black Leather Because Bumblebees Look
Like It" (Wakoski) **15**:326
"Black Love" (Madhubuti) **5**:342
"Black Magdalens" (Cullen) **20**:56, 62, 64
"Black Magic" (Sanchez) **9**:223, 234
*Black Magic: Sabotage, Target Study, Black
Art; Collected Poetry, 1961-1967*
(Baraka) **4**:6, 8, 16-18, 24, 26
"Black Majesty" (Cullen) **20**:64

"The Black Mammy" (Johnson) **24**:142
"The Black Man Is Making New Gods"
(Baraka) **4**:19
"Black March" (Smith) **12**:300-01, 308, 319,
326
"The Black Mesa" (Merrill) **28**:223, 255
"Black Money" (Gallagher) **9**:36, 53
"Black Mother Woman" (Lorde) **12**:154, 156-57
"Black Nude" (Tomlinson) **17**:311
"Black Panther" (Hughes) **1**:251-52
"Black People!" (Baraka) **4**:19, 25-6
"The Black Pit" (Hayden) **6**:187
"Black Power Chant" (Baraka) **4**:19
*Black Pride* (Madhubuti) **5**:321, 336, 338-41,
346
"Black Pudding" (Gallagher) **9**:64
"Black Sampson of Brandywine" (Dunbar)
**5**:129, 131, 138
"Black Shroud" (Ginsberg) **4**:90
"Black Silk" (Gallagher) **9**:50, 59, 62
"Black Sketches" (Madhubuti) **5**:337
"Black Song" (Guillen)
See "Canto negro"
"Black Tambourine" (Crane) **3**:98
*The Black Unicorn* (Lorde) **12**:137-38, 141-42,
144, 148, 151, 153-55, 157-58, 160
"The Black Virginity" (Loy) **16**:322
"Black/White" (Wright) **14**:366
*Black white* (Illyes)
See *Fekete feher*
"The Black Winds" (Williams) **7**:383-85,
388-89
"Black Woman" (Senghor) **25**:224-30
"Blackberrying" (Plath) **1**:407-09
"Blackberry-Picking" (Heaney) **18**:192
*The Blackbird* (Zagajewski) **27**:396
"Blackgirl Learning" (Madhubuti) **5**:344
"Blackman/An Unfinished History"
(Madhubuti) **5**:326, 343, 345
*Blacks* (Brooks) **7**:105
"Black-Shouldered Kite" (Wright) **14**:344
"The Blacksmith's Serenade" (Lindsay) **23**:264
"The Blackstone Rangers" (Brooks) **7**:88, 90-1
"Blackstudies" (Lorde) **12**:147, 158
"Blake" (Borges) **22**:97
"Blame not my lute" (Wyatt) **27**:315, 324
"Blanc" (Valery) **9**:392
"Blanco" (Soto) **28**:375
*Blanco* (Paz) **1**:355-56, 358, 363, 368-69, 372,
374, 376-77
"Blasting from Heaven" (Levine) **22**:223
"Blaubeuren" (Tomlinson) **17**:360
"Bleeding" (Swenson) **14**:269-70, 285
"Blessed are They that Mourn" (Bryant) **20**:6
"Blessed Sleep" (Johnson) **24**:159
"The Blessed Virgin, Compared to the Air We
Breathe" (Hopkins) **15**:166
"The Blessed Virgin Mary Compared to a
Window" (Merton) **10**:330, 338
"A Blessing in Disguise" (Ashbery) **26**:
"A Blessing in Disguise" (Ashbery) **26**:129,
143
*Blew Ointment* (Bissett) **14**:5
*blew trewz* (Bissett) **14**:7-8
"Blighters" (Sassoon) **12**:263, 277, 282
"Blind Curse" (Ortiz) **17**:246
"The Blind Doge at 83" (Viereck) **27**:280
"The Blind Man" (Wright) **14**:337, 369
"Blind Panorama of New York" (Garcia Lorca)
See "Panorama ceigo de Nueva York"
"Der blinde junge" (Loy) **16**:309, 316
"Der blinde Sänger" (Holderlin) **4**:147
"The Blinded Bird" (Hardy) **8**:98
*Blindenschrift* (Enzensberger) **28**:133-35, 138-
40, 143, 150
"Bliss" (Pushkin) **10**:407
*Bliznets v tuchakh* (Pasternak) **6**:263, 275
"blk/chant" (Sanchez) **9**:204, 225, 234
"blk / wooooomen / chant" (Sanchez) **9**:225
"Blödigkeit" (Holderlin) **4**:148
"Blood and the Moon" (Yeats) **20**:313
"Blood Feud" (Wylie) **23**:301

"Bloodbirth" (Lorde) **12**:157
"Bloodsmiles" (Madhubuti) **5**:337
"The Bloody Sire" (Jeffers) **17**:139
*The Bloomingdale Papers* (Carruth) **10**:78-84
"The Blossom" (Blake) **12**:7, 23, 33
"The Blossome" (Donne) **1**:126, 130, 147
"The Blow" (Hardy) **8**:94
"The Blow" (Neruda)
See "El golpe"
"Blow and Counterblow" (Montale)
See "Botta e riposta"
"The Blow-Fly" (Graves) **6**:163
"Blowing Boy" (Page) **12**:177
*Blue* (Dario)
See *Azul*
"Blue and White Lines after O'Keeffe" (Song)
**21**:331, 334, 336, 340-41
"The Blue Cat" (Hagiwara Sakutaro) **18**:181
*Blue Cat* (Hagiwara Sakutaro)
See *Aoneko*
*The Blue Estuaries: Poems, 1923-1968*
(Bogan) **12**:96-7, 100-03, 107, 112,
120-21
"Blue Evening" (Brooke) **24**:57-8, 76
"Blue Farm" (McGuckian) **27**:95
"The Blue from Heaven" (Smith) **12**:302, 304,
319, 331, 333
"Blue Gem Creeper" (Tagore)
See "Nilamanilata"
"Blue Lantern" (Song) **21**:331, 338-40, 343
"The Blue Meridian" (Toomer) **7**:309, 311-12,
324-26, 328-29, 336,-37, 340
"Blue Moles" (Plath) **1**:389
"Blue Monday" (Wakoski) **15**:325, 348
"A Blue Ribbon at Amesbury" (Frost) **1**:196
*The Blue Shadows* (Nemerov) **24**:
"The Blue She Brings with Her" (McGuckian)
**27**:81-82
"Blue Sky Rain" (McGuckian) **27**:82, 93
"The Blue Swallows" (Nemerov) **24**:300
*The Blue Swallows* (Nemerov) **24**:260-63, 274,
277, 281, 289, 291
"The Blue Theatre" (Alegria) **26**:
"The Blue Tower" (Stryk) **27**:214
"A Blue Woman with Sticking out Breasts
Hanging" (Cummings) **5**:99, 103
"Bluebeard" (Millay) **6**:205
"Blueberries" (Frost) **1**:225
"The Blue-Flag in the Bog" (Millay) **6**:233
"Blues" (Meredith) **28**:187
"Blues at Dawn" (Hughes) **1**:266
*A Blues Book for Blue Black Magical Women*
(Sanchez) **9**:207, 211-16, 218-20, 228-29,
234, 238-41, 243
"Blues for Ruby Matrix" (Aiken) **26**:29
*Blues for Ruby Matrix* (Aiken) **26**:24
"Boädicea" (Tennyson) **6**:360, 363
"The Boat" (Sexton) **2**:365
"The Boat of Life" (Ishikawa)
See "Inochi no fune"
"The Boat of the White Feather Bird"
(Ishikawa)
See "Shiraha no toribune"
"Boat Ride" (Gallagher) **9**:50-1, 58-60
"Boats on the Marne" (Montale) **13**:146
"The Bobby to the Sneering Lady" (McKay)
**2**:226
"Bobo's Metamorphosis" (Milosz) **8**:187
*Le Bocage* (Ronsard) **11**:246
"Boccaccio: The Plague Years" (Dove) **6**:109
"THE BODY" (Bissett) **14**:9, 34
"Body" (Tagore)
See "Tanu"
"Body and Soul: A Mediation" (Kumin) **15**:206
"Body of Summer" (Elytis) **21**:115
*Body of This Death* (Bogan) **12**:85-7, 103-04,
116, 119-20, 126-28
"Body of Waking" (Rukeyser) **12**:217, 220
*Body of Waking* (Rukeyser) **12**:217, 219-21,
224
*Body Rags* (Kinnell) **26**:240-42, 244, 246, 257,
261, 290-91, 293

"Bog Oak" (Heaney) **18**:201
"Bog Queen" (Heaney) **18**:188, 195, 211
"Bogland" (Heaney) **18**:188, 195, 201, 205, 209, 211
"Bohemia" (Parker) **28**:363
"The Bohemian" (Dunbar) **5**:125
"Le bois amical" (Valery) **9**:391
*Bojarin Orsha* (Lermontov) **18**:300
"Bokardo" (Robinson) **1**:468
"Bomba" (Fuertes) **27**:39, 45
"Bomba atómica" (Guillen) **23**:124
"Bombardment" (Lowell) **13**:78
"Une bombe aux Feuillantines" (Hugo) **17**:100
"Bombinations of a Chimera" (MacDiarmid) **9**:193
"Bonaparte" (Lamartine) **16**:277, 291
"Bone Dreams" (Heaney) **18**:188, 204
"The Bones of My Father" (Knight) **14**:43,52
*Bones of the Cuttlefish* (Montale)
    See *Ossi di seppia*
"The Bones Speak" (Wright) **14**:337, 339
"Bonfire" (Gallagher) **9**:61-2
"Bongo Song" (Guillen)
    See "La canción del bongo"
*Bonheur* (Verlaine) **2**:417
*La bonne chanson* (Verlaine) **2**:413-14, 419, 431-32
"The Bonnie Broukit Bairn" (MacDiarmid) **9**:156, 160. 187
"Les bons chiens" (Baudelaire) **1**:58-9
"Bonsal" (Guillen) **23**:126
"The Book" (Dario)
    See "El libro"
"A Book" (Stein) **18**:325, 348
"Book Buying in the Tenderloin" (Hass) **16**:195
*The Book of Ahania* (Blake) **12**:13
"Book of Ancestors" (Atwood) **8**:28-9, 42
"The Book of Annandale" (Robinson) **1**:460-61
*The Book of Earth* (Noyes) **27**:130, 132-133, 135
"The Book of Ephraim" (Merrill) **28**:224-25, 227-31, 235-37, 243, 245, 260-61, 263, 266, 271-75, 278
*Book of Fame* (Chaucer)
    See *House of Fame*
*The Book of Folly* (Sexton) **2**:355-56, 360, 365, 368
*Book of Gypsy Ballads* (Garcia Lorca)
    See *Primer romancero gitano*
"The Book of Hours of Sister Clotilde" (Lowell) **13**:84
*The Book of Light* (Clifton) **17**:31
*The Book of Los* (Blake) **12**:62-4
"The Book of Myths" (Harjo) **27**:66-67
*The Book of Nightmares* (Kinnell) **26**:241-45, 247-49, 252-58, 261, 264-67, 271-75, 283, 291-93
*Book of Pictures* (Rilke)
    See *Buch der Bilder*
*The Book of Purgatory* (Marie de France)
    See *L'Espurgatoire Saint Patrice*
*Book of Questions* (Neruda)
    See *Libro de las preguntas*
*Book of Saint Valentines Day of the Parlement of Briddes* (Chaucer)
    See *Parlement of Foules*
*Book of Songs* (Garcia Lorca)
    See *Canciones*
*Book of Songs* (Heine) **25**:153-54
"The Book of the Dead" (Rukeyser) **12**:203, 207, 213
*The Book of the Dead* (Rukeyser) **12**:210
*Book of the Duchess* (Chaucer) **19**:6, 10, 13, 21, 23, 38, 64-9, 71-4, 76
*Book of the Duchesse* (Chaucer)
    See *Book of the Duchess*
*Book of the Five and Twenty Ladies* (Chaucer)
    See *Legend of Good Women*
*The Book of Thel* (Blake) **12**:19, 33-5, 37, 51
*Book of Troilus* (Chaucer)
    See *Troilus and Criseyde*

*The Book of Urizen* (Blake) **12**:15, 19, 35, 38, 60, 62
*Book of Vagaries* (Neruda)
    See *Extravagario*
*A Book of Verses* (Masters) **1**:332, 342
"Booker T. Washington" (Dunbar) **5**:131
"Boom!" (Nemerov) **24**:266, 278
"A Boon" (Meredith) **28**:174
"Boone" (Berry) **28**:28, 38
"Boop-Boop-Adieup Little Group!" (Nash) **21**:265
"A Boor" (Bukowski) **18**:15
"Boot Hill" (Ondaatje) **28**:304
"Boots" (Kipling) **3**:192
"Booz endormi" (Hugo) **17**:65, 85
"Bora Ring" (Wright) **14**:335, 340, 374
*The Borderers* (Wordsworth) **4**:416
*Borderland* (Tagore)
    See *Prāntik*
*The Borderland* (Tagore)
    See *Prāntik*
"Born in December" (Rukeyser) **12**:224
*Born of a Woman: New and Selected Poems* (Knight) **14**:37-9, 41-2, 46, 49, 51-2
"Borodinó" (Lermontov) **18**:278, 283, 290, 297, 304
"Boston" (Stryk) **27**:203
"A Boston Ballad" (Whitman)
    See "Poem of Apparitions in Boston in the 73rd Year of These States"
"The Boston Evening Transcript" (Eliot) **5**:153
"The Boston Hymn" (Emerson) **18**:77, 113, 119-20
"The Botanic Garden" (Noyes) **27**:129
"Botanical Gardens" (Masters) **1**:330
"Botanical Gardens" (Wright) **14**:341
"A Botanical Trope" (Meredith) **28**:190
"Botta e riposta" (Montale) **13**:129, 131, 134, 147, 165
"Bottle Green" (Smith) **12**:333
"The Bottle in the Sea" (Vigny)
    See "La bouteille à la mer"
"Boudaries" (Wright) **14**:374
*Bouge of Court* (Skelton) **25**:329, 336-37, 340, 343, 349-50, 352, 361-62, 364-65, 367
"Bound No'th Blues" (Hughes) **1**:254
"A Boundless Moment" (Frost) **1**:218
"Bouquet" (Dario) **15**:113
*The Bourgeois Poet* (Shapiro) **25**:287-90, 292-94, 297, 299, 301-302, 308-11, 314-17, 321-22, 325
"Bournemouth" (Verlaine) **2**:416
"La bouteille à la mer" (Vigny) **26**:367, 371, 380-83, 391-92, 397, 402-404
"Bova" (Pushkin) **10**:407
"The Bowl and the Rim" (Graves) **6**:128
"The Bowl of Blood" (Jeffers) **17**:123, 144
"Bowls" (Moore) **4**:265
"A Box" (Stein) **18**:320-31, 349-50, 353
"A Box and Its Contents" (Ashbery) **26**:133
"The Boy" (Tagore) **8**:417
"Boy Driving his Father to Confession" (Heaney) **18**:243
"Boy with a Sea Dream" (Page) **12**:168, 170
"Boy with Book of Knowledge" (Nemerov) **24**:287
"Boy with His Hair Cut Short" (Rukeyser) **12**:223
*The Boyar Orsha* (Lermontov) **18**:279
"Boy-Man" (Shapiro) **25**:279, 297, 319
"Boys. Black." (Brooks) **7**:84
"A Boy's Summer Song" (Dunbar) **5**:138
*A Boy's Will* (Frost) **1**:192, 195, 197, 207, 213-14, 223-24
"Bracken Hills in Autumn" (MacDiarmid) **9**:197
"Brahma" (Emerson) **18**:83, 85, 88
"Braid Scots: An Inventory and Appraisement" (MacDiarmid)
    See "Gairmscoile"
"Braiding" (Lee) **24**:247
"Brainstorm" (Nemerov) **24**:257, 268
"Braly Street" (Soto) **28**:375, 378-79, 384-85

"A Branch from Palestine" (Lermontov) **18**:298
*A Branch of May* (Reese) **29**:330, 335-37, 339, 345-46, 351-52
"La branche d'amandier" (Lamartine) **16**:278
"Branches" (McGuckian) **27**:105
"Brancusi's Golden Bird" (Loy) **16**:321
"A Brand" (Johnson) **24**:160
"Brandons Both" (Rossetti) **7**:271
"Le brasier" (Apollinaire) **7**:47
"Brass Keys" (Sandburg) **2**:329
"Brass Spittoons" (Hughes) **1**:241, 263, 265
*Bratya Razboiniki* (Pushkin) **10**:358, 365, 386
"Bravery" (Gunn) **26**:
*Braving the Elements* (Merrill) **28**:220-23, 228-29, 244, 254, 256, 258-59, 281
"Brawl" (Garcia Lorca)
    See "Reyerta"
"The Brazier" (Apollinaire)
    See "Le brasier"
"Brazil, January 1, 1502" (Bishop) **3**:56
"Brazil-Copacabana" (Guillen) **23**:117
"Brazilian Fazenda" (Page) **12**:178, 183, 190
"Brazzaville 22 Feb 72" (Brutus) **24**:123
"Bread" (Olds) **22**:328
"Bread" (Pasternak) **6**:267
"Bread Alone" (Wylie) **23**:311, 324
"Bread and Music" (Aiken) **26**:24, 72
"Bread and Wine" (Cullen) **20**:62
"Bread and Wine" (Holderlin)
    See "Brot und Wein"
*Bread in the Wilderness* (Merton) **10**:352
*The Bread of Time* (Levine) **22**:231
"The Break" (Pasternak) **6**:280-82
"The Break" (Sexton) **2**:352-53
"Break, Break, Break" (Tennyson) **6**:358
"Break of Day" (Sassoon) **12**:244, 277
"Breake of Day" (Donne) **1**:152
"Breakfast" (Stauffer) **18**:322-23
"Breaking Camp" (Piercy) **29**:308
*Breaking Camp* (Piercy) **29**:307
"Breaking Green" (Ondaatje) **28**:331
"The Breaking of the Rainbows" (Nemerov) **24**:288
"Breaking Open" (Rukeyser) **12**:221, 224, 230
*Breaking Open* (Rukeyser) **12**:220, 224-25, 230
"Breaking Out" (Ammons) **16**:45, 63
"Breaklight" (Clifton) **17**:35
"The Breast" (Sexton) **2**:352, 364
"Breasts" (Tagore)
    See "Stan"
"the breath" (Bissett) **14**:19, 24, 29, 34
"The Breathing" (Levertov) **11**:171
"Breathing Landscape" (Rukeyser) **12**:209
"The Breathing, the Endless News" (Dove) **6**:122
*Breathing the Water* (Levertov) **11**:200, 202-05, 209-10
*Breath-Turning* (Celan)
    See *Atemwende*
"Bredon Hill" (Housman) **2**:160, 182-83, 185
"Brennan" (Wright) **14**:375
"Brennende liebe, 1904" (Gluck) **16**:128
"Brer Rabbit, You's de Cutes' of 'Em All" (Johnson) **24**:142, 163
"Brevity" (Wright) **14**:375-76
"Brian the Still-Hunter" (Atwood) **8**:19
"Briar Rose (Sleeping Beauty)" (Sexton) **2**:354, 365, 368
"The Bridal Ballad" (Poe) **1**:428, 432, 445, 447
*The Bridal of Triermain* (Scott) **13**:297, 301-02, 311-12, 314, 317, 320
"Bridal Piece" (Gluck) **16**:127
"Bride and Groom Lie Hidden for Three Days" (Hughes) **7**:165, 168
"The Bride in the Country" (Montagu) **16**:338
"The Bride of Abydos: A Turkish Tale" (Byron) **16**:91, 109
"Bride Song" (Rossetti) **7**:264
"The Bridegroom" (Kipling) **3**:183
"The Bride-Night Fire" (Hardy) **8**:99
*Brides of Reason* (Davie) **29**:92-95, 107, 111, 116-17

"Bridge" (Ammons) **16**:40-1,54
*The Bridge* (Crane) **3**:84-5, 87-90, 93-8, 100-01, 105-10
"The Bridge of Estador" (Crane) **3**:100
"Bridging" (Piercy) **29**:302
"Briefings" (Ammons) **16**:31
*Briefings: Poems Small and Easy* (Ammons) **16**:10, 21-23, 28, 45-6
*The Brigand Brothers* (Pushkin)
   See *Bratya Razboiniki*
"Bright Star" (Keats) **1**:279
"Bright Sunlight" (Lowell) **13**:64
"The Brigs of Ayr" (Burns) **6**:78
"Brilliant Sad Sun" (Williams) **7**:396, 409
"Brindis cotidiano" (Fuertes) **27**:39
"Bring Down the Beams" (Bukowski) **18**:4
"Bring the Day" (Roethke) **15**:252, 273-74, 301-02
"Bring the Wine" (Li Po) **29**:145
*The Bringer of Water* (Berry) **28**:35
"Bringers" (Sandburg) **2**:316-17, 324
"bringing home th bacon" (Bissett) **14**:34
"Bringing in New Couples" (Hughes) **7**:166
"Bringnal Banks are Wild and Fair For a' That" (Scott) **13**:278
"Brise marine" (Mallarme) **4**:208
"The British Church" (Herbert) **4**:100
"Brittle Beauty" (Wyatt) **27**:302
"Broadcast" (Larkin) **21**:237
"The Broadstone" (Jeffers) **17**:117
"Broagh" (Heaney) **18**:202, 241
"Brod und Wein" (Holderlin)
   See "Brot und Wein"
"A Broken Appointment" (Hardy) **8**:88, 110
"The Broken Balance" (Jeffers) **17**:144
"The Broken Dark" (Hayden) **6**:181, 193-95
"Broken Dreams" (Yeats) **20**:328
*The Broken Ground* (Berry) **28**:2-5, 14, 31
"The Broken Home" (Merrill) **28**:221, 227, 230, 253
"Broken Jar" (Paz)
   See "El cántaro roto"
"The Broken Man" (Wylie) **23**:321
"The Broken Pitcher" (Paz)
   See "El cántaro roto"
"The Broken Tower" (Crane) **3**:90, 103, 111
"The Broken Wings" (Gibran) **9**:75
"The Bronco That Would Not Be Broken" (Lindsay) **23**:269, 273, 286
"Bronz Trumpets and Sea Water" (Wylie) **23**:301, 315
*Bronze* (Merrill) **28**:247-68, 272
"A Bronze Head" (Yeats) **20**:332
*The Bronze Horseman* (Pushkin)
   See *Medny Vsadnik*
"The Bronze Horses" (Lowell) **13**:60, 62, 64, 73, 80, 82
"Bronze Tablets" (Lowell) **13**:76, 78
"Bronzeville Man with a Belt in the Back" (Brooks) **7**:106
"A Bronzeville Mother Loiters in Mississippi. Meanwhile a Mississippi Mother Burns Bacon" (Brooks) **7**:56, 62, 81, 86, 96, 98-9
"Bronzeville Woman in a Red Hat" (Brooks) **7**:58, 62
"The Brook" (Tennyson) **6**:357, 359
"Brook Farm" (Toomer) **7**:323
"Brooklyn Bridge Nocturne" (Garcia Lorca)
   See "Ciudad sin sueño"
"Brot und Wein" (Holderlin) **4**:146-51, 161, 166, 169, 171, 176
"Brother and Sister" (Eliot) **20**:102, 124
"Brother and Sisters" (Wright) **14**:336, 340, 351
"Brother, Do Not Give Your Life" (Yosano Akiko)
   See "Kimi Shinitamô koto nakare"
"Brothers" (Johnson) **24**:130-31, 138, 142, 161, 170
"The Brothers" (Wordsworth) **4**:374, 380, 381, 393, 402, 414

*The Brothers Highwaymen* (Pushkin)
   See *Bratya Razboiniki*
*Brothers, I Loved You All: Poems, 1969-1977* (Carruth) **10**:69-70, 72-3, 91
"Brought from Beyond" (Clampitt) **19**:102
"A Brown" (Stein) **18**:3312
"Brown Boy to Brown Girl" (Cullen) **20**:64
"A Brown Girl Dead" (Cullen) **20**:55, 62
"The Brown Menace or Poem to the Survival of Roaches" (Lorde) **12**:154-55, 158
"Brown River, Smile" (Toomer) **7**:324
"Browning resuelve ser poeta" (Borges) **22**:98
"Brown's Descent" (Frost) **1**:195
"A Bruised Reed Shall He Not Break" (Rossetti) **7**:290; **50**:314
"Bryan, Bryan, Bryan, Bryan" (Lindsay) **23**:265, 270, 273-74, 279, 287-88, 294-95
"Bubba" (Sanchez) **9**:240
*Buch der Bilder* (Rilke) **2**:266-67
"Buch der Lieder" (Bridges) **28**:88
*Buch der Lieder* (Heine) **25**:129-131, 139-41, 143, 145-46, 157-58, 161, 164
"The Buck in the Snow" (Millay) **6**:238
*The Buck in the Snow, and Other Poems* (Millay) **6**:213-14
"Buck Lake Store Auction" (Ondaatje) **28**:335
*Buckthorn* (Akhmatova)
   See *Podorozhnik*
*Bucolic Comedies* (Sitwell) **3**:293, 302-04, 307-08, 319, 322
"Bucolics" (Auden) **1**:23
*Bucolics* (Vergil)
   See *Georgics*
"The Buddhist Painter Prepares to Paint" (Carruth) **10**:89
"The Buds Now Stretch" (Roethke) **15**:288
"Buenos Aires" (Lowell) **3**:214
"La bufera" (Montale) **13**:113, 131
*La bufera e altro* (Montale) **13**:103-04, 107, 113-14, 117-18, 122, 125, 131-33, 141, 148-49, 156, 160, 165-67
"Buffalo Bill's Defunct" (Cummings) **5**:93
"Le buffet" (Rimbaud) **3**:271, 283
"The Bugler-Boy" (Hopkins) **15**:138
"The Bugler's First Communion" (Hopkins) **15**:136, 144
"Buick" (Shapiro) **25**:288, 295, 297, 319, 322, 325
"Build Soil: A Political Pastoral" (Frost) **1**:196, 199, 203, 217
"Builder Kachina" (Rose) **13**:236-37
"The Building" (Larkin) **21**:255
"The Building of the Trophy" (Rose) **13**:235
"The Bull" (Wright) **14**:333, 359
"The Bull Moses" (Hughes) **7**:131, 140, 158
"Bull Song" (Atwood) **8**:25
"Bullfrog" (Hughes) **7**:165
"Bullocky" (Wright) **14**:336, 340, 345, 349, 351, 357, 360, 368
"Bumming" (McKay) **2**:226
"The Bunch of Grapes" (Herbert) **4**:123, 125
"The Burden" (Kipling) **3**:183
"A Burden" (Rossetti) **7**:286
"Burden" (Tagore)
   See "Bhar"
"The Burghers" (Hardy) **8**:99
"The Burglar of Babylon" (Bishop) **3**:48, 56
"The Burial-place" (Bryant) **20**:3
"The Buried City" (Chesterton) **28**:101
"The Buried Life" (Arnold) **5**:37-8, 41-5, 47, 49-50, 59, 64
"The Burly Fading One" (Hayden) **6**:196
"The Burn" (Kinnell) **26**:290
"Burn and burn and burn" (Bukowski) **18**:24
"Burned" (Levine) **22**:220-21, 227-28, 232
"The Burning" (Momaday) **25**:200-201
"The Burning Child" (Clampitt) **19**:83
"Burning Hills" (Ondaatje) **28**:327, 332-33
*Burning in Water Drowning in Flame: Selected Poems 1955-1973* (Bukowski) **18**:21

"The Burning of Paper Instead of Children" (Rich) **5**:371, 393-95
"Burning Oneself Out" (Rich) **5**:360
"The Burning Passion" (MacDiarmid) **9**:153
"Burning River" (Ortiz) **17**:233
"Burning the Christmas Greens" (Williams) **7**:360
"Burning the Tomato Worms" (Forche) **10**:132, 134, 142
"Burnt Lands" (Pavese) **13**:205
"Burnt Norton" (Eliot) **5**:164, 166-68, 171, 174, 177-85, 201, 210
"The Burnt-Out Spa" (Plath) **1**:389
"Bury Me In a Free Land" (Harper) **21**:185, 187, 190, 192
"A Bus along St. Clair: December" (Atwood) **8**:40
"Búscate plata" (Guillen) **23**:142
"The Buses Headed for Scranton" (Nash) **21**:271
"The Bush Garden" (Atwood) **8**:38-9
"Busie old foole" (Donne)
   See "The Sunne Rising"
"The Business Man of Alicante" (Levine) **22**:213
"Busker" (Stryk) **27**:208
"But Born" (Aleixandre) **15**:5
"But He Was Cool; or, He Even Stopped for Green Lights" (Madhubuti) **5**:329, 341
"But Not Forgotten" (Parker) **28**:362
"But We've the May" (Cummings)
   See "Song"
"'Butch' Weldy" (Masters) **1**:324
"Buteo Regalis" (Momaday) **25**:186, 188, 193, 195, 199, 210, 220
*Butterflies* (Gozzano)
   See *Le farfalle*
"The Butterfly" (Brodsky)
   See "Babočka"
"The Butterfly" (Giovanni) **19**:112
"Butterfly Piece" (Hayden) **6**:194, 198
"Butterflyweed" (Ammons) **16**:4
"Buying the Dog" (Ondaatje) **28**:335
"by 3/6/51" (Olson) **19**:316
"By a Reactionary" (Chesterton) **28**:114
*By Avon River* (H. D.) **5**:302
"By God I Want above Fourteenth" (Cummings) **5**:94
"By Lamplight" (Kunitz) **19**:171
"By Night When Others Soundly Slept" (Bradstreet) **10**:62
"By Rugged Ways" (Dunbar) **5**:131
*By the Earth's Corpse* (Hardy) **8**:121
"By the Fireside" (Browning) **2**:76, 78-9, 88
"By the Hoof of the Wild Goat" (Kipling) **3**:186
"By the Lake" (Sitwell) **3**:325
"By the North Sea" (Swinburne) **24**:313-17, 319, 327, 329, 343
"By the Road" (Williams) **7**:382-83
*By the Seashore* (Akhmatova)
   See *U samovo morya*
"By The Stream" (Dunbar) **5**:127
"By the Waters of Babylon" (Celan)
   See "An den Wassern Babels"
"By Twilight" (Swinburne) **24**:317
"By Wauchopeside" (MacDiarmid) **9**:197, 199
"By-pass" (Wright) **14**:373
"Bypassing Rue Descartes" (Milosz) **8**:200
"The Byrnies" (Gunn) **26**:186
"Byzantium" (Yeats) **20**:308, 310, 316, 327, 334-35
"a C." (Montale) **13**:138
"Ça le creux" (Cesaire) **25**:33
"Ca' the Yowes to the Knowes" (Burns) **6**:76
"Cabala" (Swenson) **14**:288
"Cabaret" (Hughes) **1**:237
"Cabaret Girl Dies on Welfare Island" (Hughes) **1**:247
"A Cabin in the Clearing" (Frost) **1**:212
"A Cabin Tale" (Dunbar) **5**:120
*Cables to Rage* (Lorde) **12**:140

"Cables to Rage, or I've Been Talking on This Street Corner a Hell of a Long Time" (Lorde) **12**:155
"Cables to the Ace" (Merton) **10**:337
*Cables to the Ace; or, Familiar Liturgies of Misunderstanding* (Merton) **10**:338, 345, 348, 351, 354
"Caboose Thoughts" (Sandburg) **2**:302
"Cabra" (Joyce) **22**:149
"Le cacot" (Lamartine) **16**:284
*Cadastre* (Cesaire) **25**:12, 15, 17, 30-2, 35-6, 38-9
"Cadenus and Vanessa" (Swift) **9**:253-55, 296
"A Cadenza" (Clampitt) **19**:102
"Cadenza" (Hughes) **7**:159
"Caerulei Oculi" (Gautier) **18**:125
"Caesar when that the traytour of Egipt" (Wyatt) **27**:339
*Caesar's Gate* (Duncan) **2**:101
"Café" (Milosz) **8**:175
"Café at Rapallo" (Montale) **13**:148
"Cafe du neant" (Loy) **16**:312-13, 328
"Café Tableau" (Swenson) **14**:275
*A Cage of Spines* (Swenson) **14**:247-48, 252, 260, 277, 284
*Cahier d'un retour au pays natal* (Cesaire) **25**:2-3, 5-7, 10-11, 13-16, 18-19, 29-33, 41-4, 47-9, 51-6, 58-61, 63, 65
"Cain" (Nemerov) **24**:261
*Cain* (Byron) **16**:86, 88, 90, 103-05, 108, 111
"Cake" (Stein) **18**:322
"A Calder" (Shapiro) **25**:291
*The Calender* (Spenser)
   See *The Shepheardes Calender: Conteyning Twelve Æglogues Proportionable to the Twelve Monethes*
"Calendrier lagunaire" (Cesaire) **25**:33, 45
"Caliban upon Setebos" (Browning) **2**:58-9, 88, 95
"The Calico Cat" (Lindsay) **23**:281
"The California Water Plan" (Snyder) **21**:291
*Californians* (Jeffers) **17**:134-35, 138
"The Call" (Brooke) **24**:57, 82
"The Call" (Herbert) **4**:130
"Call" (Lorde) **12**:139, 141
"The Call Across the Valley of Not-Knowing" (Kinnell) **26**:251, 269, 273-75
"Call It Fear" (Harjo) **27**:54, 61
"Call it love" (Enzensberger) **28**:139
"Call Me Back Again" (Tagore)
   See "Ebar phirao more"
"The Call of the Wild" (Snyder) **21**:292-93, 297
*Call Yourself Alive?* (Cassian) **17**:4, 6, 13
"Las Calles" (Borges) **22**:68
"Callie Ford" (Brooks) **7**:62, 69
*Calligrammes* (Apollinaire) **7**:3, 9-10, 12, 35-6, 42, 44, 46, 48-9
"A Calling" (Kumin) **15**:210
"Calliope" (H. D.) **5**:304
"Callow Captain" (Graves) **6**:133
"The Calls" (Owen) **19**:336
"The Calm" (Donne) **1**:122
"The Calm" (Gallagher) **9**:58
"Calming Kali" (Clifton) **17**:24
"Calmly We Walk Through This April's Day" (Schwartz) **8**:305-06
"Calverley's" (Robinson) **1**:466
"Calypso" (H. D.) **5**:306
"The Cambridge Ladies Who Live in Furnished Souls" (Cummings) **5**:94
"Cambridge, Spring 1937" (Schwartz) **8**:301
"The Camel" (Nash) **21**:278
"Camelia" (Tagore) **8**:417
"El camello" (auto de los Reyes MagosFuertes) **27**:8, 15, 31
"Camilo" (Guillen) **23**:128
"Caminos" (Dario) **15**:82
"Camp" (Fuertes) **27**:23
"Camp 1940" (Senghor) **25**:235
"Camp and Cloister" (Browning) **2**:26
"Camping at Split Rock" (Wright) **14**:366

"Camps of Green" (Whitman) **3**:378
"Can Grande's Castle" (Lowell) **13**:60
*Can Grande's Castle* (Lowell) **13**:60, 62-3, 65-6, 72-4, 79-83, 93
"Caña" (Guillen) **23**:98
"canada" (Bissett) **14**:25, 34
*Canada Gees Mate for Life* (Bissett) **14**:26
"The Canadian" (Bissett) **14**:10, 25
"Canal" (Tomlinson) **17**:313, 343
"The Canal's Drowning Black" (Hughes) **7**:148
"Canción de otoño en primavera" (Dario) **15**:96, 107, 109-11
"La canción del bongo" (Guillen) **23**:106, 111-14, 132, 136, 139
"Canción otoñal" (Dario) **15**:82
"Canción tonta" (Garcia Lorca) **3**:136
*Canciones* (Garcia Lorca) **3**:118-19, 148-49
"candide" (Enzensberger) **28**:134, 136
"The Candle in the Cabin" (Lindsay) **23**:286
"Candle, Lamp, and Firefly" (Gallagher) **9**:59
"Candle-Lightin' Time" (Dunbar) **5**:122
"Candles at 330" (McGuckian) **27**:91
*Candles in Babylon* (Levertov) **11**:198-201, 209
"The Candlestick" (Brodsky) **9**:3
*Cane* (Toomer) **7**:309-11, 319, 323-24, 326, 330, 332-33, 335, 339-41
"El cangrejo" (Guillen) **23**:124
"The Cannery" (Stryk) **27**:211
"canoe" (Bissett) **14**:23
"The Canonization" (Bridges) **28**:73
"The Canonization" (Donne) **1**:126, 130, 132-34
"Canon's Yeoman's Prologue" (Chaucer) **19**:26
"Canon's Yeoman's Tale" (Chaucer) **19**:13, 19
"Canta el sinsonte en el Turquino" (Guillen) **23**:124
*Cantares Mexicanos I* (Cardenal) **22**:127-28, 129, 132
*Cantares Mexicanos II* (Cardenal) **22**:127-28, 129, 132
"Cantares mexicanos" (IICardenal) **22**:128, 130
"Cantares mexicanos" (ICardenal) **22**:127, 130
"El cántaro roto" (Paz) **1**:361
*Canterburie-Tales* (Chaucer)
   See *Canterbury Tales*
*Canterbury Tales* (Chaucer) **19**:3, 6, 13, 16, 18, 20, 22, 24, 26-7, 34, 37, 43-50, 52-4, 60, 64
"Canthara" (Williams) **7**:367
"Canti Romani" (Ferlinghetti) **1**:183
"Canticle" (Berry) **28**:3-4
"Cantique des colonnes" (Valery) **9**:366, 394
"Canto I" (Pound) **4**:334, 357
"Canto VIII" (Pound) **4**:353
"Canto XIV" (Pound) **4**:328, 358
"Canto XV" (Pound) **4**:358
"Canto XVI" (Pound) **4**:328
"Canto XXVI" (Pound) **4**:324
"Canto XXVII" (Pound) **4**:325, 345
"Canto XLI" (Pound) **4**:357
"Canto XLVII" (Pound) **4**:346-47, 349
"Canto L" (Pound) **4**:360, 362
"Canto LI" (Pound) **4**:326
"Canto LXXIV" (Pound) **4**:345-49, 352, 354
"Canto LXXV" (Pound) **4**:347, 349
"Canto LXXVI" (Pound) **4**:352-53
"Canto LXXVIII" (Pound) **4**:349
"Canto LXXIX" (Pound) **4**:349
"Canto LXXX" (Pound) **4**:345, 349
"Canto LXXXI" (Pound) **4**:349, 352
"Canto LXXXII" (Pound) **4**:349, 352
"Canto LXXXIII" (Pound) **4**:345, 348
"Canto LXXXIV" (Pound) **4**:345, 348
"Canto LXXXVI" (Pound) **4**:347
"Canto XCI" (Pound) **4**:354
"Canto C" (Pound) **4**:360-62
"Canto CI" (Pound) **4**:353
"Canto CIV" (Pound) **4**:357
"Canto CX" (Pound) **4**:353
"Canto CXIII" (Pound) **4**:353-54
"Canto CXV" (Pound) **4**:354
"Canto CXVI" (Pound) **4**:353-54
"Canto CXVIII" (Pound) **4**:353

"Canto CXX" (Pound) **4**:354
"Canto a Bolivar" (Neruda) **4**:279-80
"Canto à la Argentina" (Dario) **15**:82, 115
"Canto a las madres de los milicianos muertos" (Neruda) **4**:278
"Canto a Stalingrado" (Neruda) **4**:279
"Canto de la sangre" (Dario) **15**:91-2, 96, 105
*Canto general de Chile* (Neruda) **4**:279-82, 291-96
"Canto nacional" (Cardenal) **22**:103
"Canto negro" (Guillen) **23**:134
"Canto notturno di un pastore errante nell'Asia" (Montale) **13**:109
"Canto popolare" (Pasolini) **17**:294
"Canto sobre unas ruinas" (Neruda) **4**:309
"Canto82" (Viereck) **27**:283
*Cantos* (Pound) **4**:332, 343-45, 350-54
*Cantos de vida y esperanza* (Dario) **15**:78, 80, 87, 89, 91-2, 96, 103-05, 107, 109, 115, 117, 120
"Cantos of Mutabilitie" (Spenser) **8**:344, 346, 375, 396
*Cantos para soldados y sones para turistas* (Guillen) **23**:99, 101, 131, 133, 140
"Canvas" (Zagajewski) **27**:387-88, 393, 395
*Canvas* (Zagajewski) **27**:389, 393, 399
"Canyon de Chelly" (Ortiz) **17**:225
"Canzone" (Mandelstam) **14**:138
"Canzone on an Old Proverb" (Stryk) **27**:198
"Canzones" (Okigbo)
   See "Four Canzones (1957-1961)"
*Canzoni* (Pound) **4**:317
*Canzoniere* (Petrarch) **8**:218, 220, 224-40, 242-45, 247-49, 251-65, 268-73, 276-78
"Cape Breton" (Bishop) **3**:39, 58-9
"Cape Cod" (Brodsky)
   See "A Cape Cod Lullaby"
"A Cape Cod Lullaby" (Brodsky) **9**:7, 19
"A Cape Cod Lullaby" (Brodsky)
   See "A Cape Cod Lullaby"
"Cape Hatteras" (Crane) **3**:86-7, 90, 96, 106-10
"Cape Mootch" (Pasternak) **6**:251
"Capitol Air" (Ginsberg) **4**:62, 76, 83
"Cappadocian Song" (Carruth) **10**:89
"Caprice" (Cullen) **20**:55
"Captain Craig" (Robinson) **1**:460, 467, 483, 486
*Captain Craig* (Robinson) **1**:462-63, 470-72, 474, 490
"Captain in Time of Peace" (Gunn) **26**:
*Captain Lavender* (McGuckian) **27**:104-106
*Captains* (Gunn) **26**:
*The Captive of the Caucasus* (Pushkin)
   See *Kavkazsky plennik*
"A Captive of the Khan" (Tsvetaeva)
   See "Khansky polon"
"Captured by the Khan" (Tsvetaeva)
   See "Khansky polon"
"Car Wreck" (Shapiro) **25**:205
"A Carafe That Is a Blind Glass" (Stein) **18**:318, 334
"The Card Players" (Larkin) **21**:237
"Careless Water" (Stein) **18**:334
"Caribbean Sunset" (Hughes) **1**:236
"Caritas" (Cummings) **5**:94
"Carlos among the Candles" (Stevens) **6**:295
"Carmen" (Blok) **21**:26
"Carnal Knowledge" (Gunn) **26**:182, 188, 199-200, 207, 210, 218
"Carnaval" (Gautier) **18**:125
"Carnegie Hall: Rescued" (Moore) **4**:242
"Carnegie, Oklahoma, 1919" (Momaday) **25**:221
"Carnevale di Gerti" (Montale) **13**:117
"Carol" (Merton) **10**:340
"Carol" (Nemerov) **24**:258
"A Carol for Children" (Nash) **21**:275
*Carolina Said Song* (Ammons) **16**:19
"Carousing Students" (Pushkin) **10**:407
"The Carpenter's Son" (Housman) **2**:192
"A Carpet Not Bought" (Merrill) **28**:253
"Carrefour" (Lowell) **13**:85

"La carretera" (Cardenal) **22**:
"Carrier" (Meredith) **28**:174, 186
"Carriers of the Dream Wheel" (Momaday)
　**25**:199, 217
"A Carrion" (Baudelaire)
　See "Une charogne"
"Carrion Comfort" (Hopkins) **15**:144
"Carrying Mission to the Frontier" (Wang Wei)
　See "Carrying Mission to the Frontier"
"The Carrying Ring" (McGuckian) **27**:105
"Carta a Miguel Otero Silva, en Caracas,
　1948" (Neruda) **4**:293
"Carta de creencia" (Paz) **1**:376
"Carta de la eme" (Fuertes) **27**:37
"Carta de la Habana" (Guillen) **23**:127
"Carta explicatoria de Gloria" (Fuertes) **27**:17,
　48-9
"Cartographies of Silence" (Rich) **5**:378-79,
　394-95
"The Cartography of Memory" (Alegria) **26**:
"Cartoons of Coming Shows Unseen Before"
　(Schwartz) **8**:291
"The Cartridges" (Levine) **22**:213
"La cartuja" (Dario) **15**:102
"The Caruso Poem" (Bissett) **14**:4, 19
"La casa dei doganieri" (Montale) **13**:114
*La casa dei doganieri* (Montale) **13**:106, 138
"Casa Elena" (Borges) **22**:92
*Casa Guidi Windows: A Poem* (Browning) **6**:2,
　6-9, 16, 36, 38, 41, 46
"Casa in costruzione" (Pavese) **13**:226
"Casa sul mare" (Montale) **13**:137, 147, 164
"Casabianca" (Bishop) **3**:37, 56, 67
"La casada infiel" (Garcia Lorca) **3**:119, 132,
　134
*Case d'armons* (Apollinaire) **7**:21-2
"A Case of Murder" (Hagiwara Sakutaro)
　See "Satsujin jiken"
**** Casements" (Ashbery) **26**:
"Case-moth" (Wright) **14**:374
"Caspar Hauser Song" (Trakl) **20**:226, 259-60,
　267, 269
"Cassandra" (Bogan) **12**:110
"Cassandra" (Jeffers) **17**:139
"Cassandra" (Robinson) **1**:487
"Cassinus and Peter, a Tragic Elegy" (Swift)
　**9**:262, 270, 274, 279, 286, 288, 298, 302-03
"Cast rěci" (Brodsky) **9**:7, 19
*Cast rěci* (Brodsky) **9**:6-8, 13-15, 26-7, 29-31
"Castástrofe en Sewell" (Neruda) **4**:294
"The Castaways" (McKay) **2**:221
"Castilian" (Wylie) **23**:310, 312
"Casting and Gathering" (Heaney) **18**:257
"The Castle" (Graves) **6**:131, 135, 142, 144
"The Castle" (Tomlinson) **17**:308, 311
"Casualty" (Heaney) **18**:198, 211, 240, 246
"The Casualty" (Hughes) **7**:114
"The Cat" (Kinnell) **26**:287
"The Cat" (Kinnell) **26**:286
"The Cat and the Moon" (Yeats) **20**:304
"The Cat and the Saxophone" (Hughes) **1**:236
"The Catalpa Tree" (Bogan) **12**:129, 131
"Catarina to Camoens" (Browning) **6**:16-17, 38
"Catastrophe at Sewell" (Neruda)
　See "Castástrofe en Sewell"
"the catch" (Bukowski) **18**:25
"A Catch of Shy Fish" (Brooks) **7**:105
"Catchment" (Kumin) **15**:209, 211, 223
"Catedral" (Borges) **22**:92
"Categories" (Giovanni) **19**:110-12, 116
*Cathay* (Pound) **4**:317, 364, 366
"Catherine of Alexandria" (Dove) **6**:107, 109
"Catherine of Siena" (Dove) **6**:107, 109
"Cato Braden" (Masters) **1**:33, 343
"Cats" (Hagiwara Sakutaro)
　See "Neko"
"Cats and a Cock" (Rukeyser) **12**:209
*Cats and Bats and Things with Wings* (Aiken)
　**26**:24, 30
"Catterskill Falls" (Bryant) **20**:14-16, 43
"Cattle Gredo" (Milosz) **8**:207
"Cattle Show" (MacDiarmid) **9**:160, 176

"Catullus" (Nishiwaki) **15**:238
*The Caucasian Captive* (Pushkin)
　See *Kavkazsky plennik*
"Cauchemar" (Gautier) **18**:142, 164
"Caupolicán" (Dario) **15**:95
"Cause & Effect" (Swenson) **14**:264
"Causerie" (Baudelaire) **1**:45, 66
*Cautionary Tales for Children* (Belloc) **24**:21,
　26, 49
*Cautionary Verses* (Belloc) **24**:13-15, 17-18,
　23, 27
"Le Cavalier poursuivi" (Gautier) **18**:142-43
"Cavalier Tunes" (Browning) **2**:26, 36
*Cave Birds: An Alchemical Cave Drama*
　(Hughes) **7**:153-58, 162-65, 171
"Cave Canem" (Millay) **6**:233
*Cavender's House* (Robinson) **1**:471-72, 475,
　479, 483
"Caves" (Wakoski) **15**:363
"Cawdor" (Jeffers) **17**:107-08, 110
*Cawdor, and Other Poems* (Jeffers) **17**:110,135
"Ce que dit la bouche d'ombre" (Hugo) **17**:66,
　83-84, 90
"Ce qui est à moi" (Cesaire) **25**:43
"Ce qu'on entend sur la montagne" (Hugo)
　**17**:91
"Ce siècle est grand et fort" (Hugo) **17**:94
"Cease, Cease, Aminta to Complain" (Behn)
　**13**:7
"The Cedars" (Wright) **14**:339, 346
"The Ceiba" (Alegria) **26**:
"The Ceiba" (Alegria) **26**:
"La ceinture" (Valery) **9**:372, 374, 387, 396
"A Celebration" (Williams) **7**:345
*A Celebration of Charis in Ten Lyric Pieces*
　(Jonson) **17**:169-70, 180, 194-96, 207, 214
"Celestial Freedom" (Aleixandre) **15**:19
"Celestial Globe" (Nemerov) **24**:263, 274
*Celestial Hoyden* (Lowell) **3**:199
"Celestial Music" (Gluck) **16**:158
"The Celestial Poets" (Neruda)
　See "Los poetas celestes"
"Celestials at the Board of Projects" (Milosz)
　**8**:214
"Celia singing" (Carew) **29**:25
"Celia's Birthday Poem" (Zukofsky) **11**:342
"Celibacy at Twenty" (Olds) **22**:338
"Célibat, célibat, tout n'est que célibat"
　(Laforgue) **14**:76
"Cell Song" (Knight) **14**:40, 52-3
"The Cellar" (Soto) **28**:371
"Cellar Hole in Joppa" (Kumin) **15**:190
"The Cellar of Memory" (Akhmatova) **2**:20
"Celle qui sort de l'onde" (Valery) **9**:392
"Cells" (Kipling) **3**:163
"The Celtic Fringe" (Smith) **12**:339
"Cemetery, Stratford Connecticut" (Rose)
　**13**:239
"La cena triste" (Pavese) **13**:205, 208
*The Cenci* (Shelley) **14**:165, 171-75, 182-83,
　196, 202-03, 205, 208-10, 213
*Ceneri* (Pasolini) **17**:294-95
"Le ceneri di Gramscí" (Pasolini) **17**:263, 265,
　271, 284-85, 289-92, 294-95
*Le ceneri di Gramscí* (Pasolini) **17**:255, 263-
　67, 269-70, 272, 286-87, 293
"The Census-Taker" (Frost) **1**:194
"The Centaur" (Swenson) **14**:248, 252, 255,
　262-63, 281-82, 288
"El centinela" (Borges) **22**:79
"Centipede Sonnet" (Villa) **22**:351
"Central Europe" (Zagajewski) **27**:398
"Central Park" (Lowell) **3**:226
*A Century of Roundels* (Swinburne) **24**:313,
　322-27
*Cerebro y corazon* (Guillen) **23**:104, 133-34
"Ceremonies for Candlemasse Eve" (Herrick)
　**9**:99
"Ceremonies for Christmasse" (Herrick) **9**:99,
　104
"Ceremony after a Fire Raid" (Thomas) **2**:382,
　388

"Certain Mercies" (Graves) **6**:152
"A Certain Morning Is" (Villa) **22**:350
"Certainty" (Paz) **1**:355
"César" (Valery) **9**:391
"Ceux qui luttent" (Smith) **12**:333
"Cezanne at Aix" (Tomlinson) **17**:304, 306, 335
"Chaadayevu" (Pushkin) **10**:408
"Chacun sa chimère" (Baudelaire) **1**:58
"La chaine a mille anneaux" (Lamartine) **16**:284
"Chains" (Apollinaire)
　See "Liens"
"A Chair" (Stein) **18**:319, 349
*Chaitāli* (Tagore) **8**:403, 409-10
"Le Chaitivel" (Marie de France) **22**:248-49,
　255, 258, 260, 267-73, 295
"Chaka" (Senghor) **25**:241, 255
"The Challenge" (Graves) **6**:137
*Chamber Music* (Joyce) **22**:
"La chambre double" (Baudelaire) **1**:54, 58
"Chameli-vitan" (Tagore) **8**:416
*The Champion* (Tsvetaeva)
　See *Molodets*
*Les Champs Magnétiques* (Breton) **15**:58, 68,
　73
"Chance" (H. D.) **5**:304
"Chance Meeting" (H. D.) **5**:304
"Chance Topic" (Tu Fu) **9**:324, 327
"The Chances" (Owen) **19**:334, 344, 347
"The Chances of Rhyme" (Tomlinson) **17**:333,
　340
"Chanchal" (Tagore) **8**:415
"The Change" (Finch) **21**:175
"The Change" (Hardy) **8**:93
"Change" (Kunitz) **19**:147
"Change" (Pasternak)
　See "Peremena"
"Change" (Wright) **14**:379
"Change Is Not Always Progress" (Madhubuti)
　**5**:344
"The Change: Kyoto-Tokyo Express"
　(Ginsberg) **4**:50, 63, 81
"Change of Season" (Lorde) **12**:154, 157
*A Change of World* (Rich) **5**:352-53, 358, 360,
　362, 369, 375, 387-88, 392
"Change upon Change" (Browning) **6**:32
"The Changed Woman" (Bogan) **12**:94, 103
"The Changeful World" (MacDiarmid) **9**:183
*The Changing Light at Sandover* (Merrill)
　**28**:259-60, 262-63, 265-79, 281
"Changing Mind" (Aiken) **26**:14
"Changing Diapers" (Snyder) **21**:300
"Changing the Children" (Kumin) **15**:215
*Ch'ang-ku* (Li Ho) **13**:44
"Channel 13" (Merrill) **28**:267
"Channel Firing" (Hardy) **8**:119-21
"A Channel Passage" (Brooke) **24**:53-4, 63, 83
"A Channel Passage" (Swinburne) **24**:313,
　317-18
"Chanon's Yeoman's Tale" (Chaucer)
　See "Canon's Yeoman's Tale"
"Chanson" (Hugo) **17**:80
"La chanson des ingénues" (Verlaine) **2**:431
"La chanson du mal-aimé" (Apollinaire) **7**:3,
　7-9, 11, 15, 22, 44, 46-9
"Chanson du petit hypertrophique" (Laforgue)
　**14**:66, 93
"Chanson du Présomptif" (Perse) **23**:230
"Chanson Juive" (Celan) **10**:127-28
"Chanson of a Lady in the Shade" (Celan)
　**10**:112
"Chanson un peu naïve" (Bogan) **12**:86, 90, 92,
　101, 103
*Chansons des rues et des bois* (Hugo) **17**:55,
　65, 67, 72
*Chansons pour elle* (Verlaine) **2**:417
"Chant d'amour" (Lamartine) **16**:291-92
"Chant d'automne" (Baudelaire) **1**:60, 62-3
"Chant de guerre parisien" (Rimbaud) **3**:255,
　284
"Chant de l'horizon en champagne"
　(Apollinaire) **7**:22
"Chant de Printemps" (Senghor) **25**:258

*Le chant du sacre* (Lamartine) **16**:279

"Chant for Dark Hours" (Parker) **28**:352, 360

"A Chant for Young/Brothas and Sistuhs" (Sanchez) **9**:218, 225

"Chant to Be Used in Processions around a Site with Furnaces" (Merton) **10**:334, 337

"Chantre" (Apollinaire) **7**:48

*Les chants de Crépuscule* (Hugo) **17**:43, 45, 52, 63, 91-94

*Chants d'ombre* (Senghor) **25**:224, 227, 230-33, 236, 238, 241, 243-44, 255

"Les chants lyriques de Saül" (Lamartine) **16**:277, 290

*Chants pour Naëtt* (Senghor) **25**:225, 227, 232, 238-40

*Chants pour signare* (Senghor)
    See *Chants pour Naëtt*

"Chaos in Motion and Not in Motion" (Stevens) **6**:307-10, 313

"Chaos Poem" (Atwood) **8**:24

"Chaos Staggered" (Ammons) **16**:46

"The Chapel-Organist" (Hardy) **8**:100, 124

"Chaplinesque" (Crane) **3**:98-100

"A Character" (Montagu) **16**:338

"The Character of Holland" (Marvell) **10**:271

"The Character of the Happy Warrior" (Wordsworth) **4**:377

*Characters of Women* (Pope) **26**:239

"The Charge of the Light Brigade" (Tennyson) **6**:359

"The Chariot" (Dickinson) **1**:84, 86

"Charioteer" (H. D.) **5**:268

"The Charioteer of Delphi" (Merrill) **28**:241

"La charite" (Ronsard) **11**:236, 243, 263-64

"Charivari" (Atwood) **8**:38

"Charles Augustus Fortescue, Who always Did what was Right, and so accumulated an Immense Fortune" (Belloc) **24**:26

"Charles on Fire" (Merrill) **28**:253

"Charleston in the 1860s" (Rich) **5**:383

"Charlotte Corday" (Tomlinson) **17**:345-46, 350

"Charlotte's Delivery" (McGuckian) **27**:105

"A Charm" (Dickinson) **1**:112

*Charmes; ou, Poèmes* (Valery) **9**:355, 358, 365-67, 371, 374, 386-88, 390-96

"Charms" (Snyder) **21**:294, 297

"The Charnel Rose" (Aiken) **26**:11, 15, 37

*The Charnel Rose* (Aiken) **26**:6, 22, 70, 72

"Une charogne" (Baudelaire) **1**:48

"The Chase" (Toomer) **7**:338, 340

"Chase Henry" (Masters) **1**:324

"Chasing the Paper-Shaman" (Rose) **13**:238

*Chast' rechi* (Brodsky)
    See *Cast rĕci*

"Le chat" (Ronsard) **11**:280, 282

"Chateau de Muzot" (Tomlinson) **17**:315, 324

"Le Château du souvenir" (Gautier) **18**:125, 129, 157

"Le châtiment de Tartuff" (Rimbaud) **3**:283

*Les Châtiments* (Hugo) **17**:45, 53-54, 65, 74, 78-80, 91

"Les chats blancs" (Valery) **9**:391

"The Chaunty of the Nona" (Belloc) **24**:6, 31

"Che Guevara" (Guillen) **23**:127

"Cheddar Pinks" (Bridges) **28**:80-1, 85

"The Cheer" (Meredith) **28**:205, 217

*The Cheer* (Meredith) **28**:177, 179-82, 197-200, 202, 205-09, 215

*Cheerleader for the Funeral* (Cassian) **17**:13

"Chekhov in Nice" (Stryk) **27**:187

"Chekhov on Sakhalin" (Heaney) **18**:214

"Chelyuskintsy" (Tsvetaeva) **14**:328

"Le chêne" (Lamartine) **16**:293

"Les chercheuses de poux" (Rimbaud) **3**:271, 276

"Les chères, mains qui furent miennes" (Verlaine) **2**:416

"Cherish You Then the Hope I Shall Forget" (Millay) **6**:211

"Cherkesy" (Lermontov) **18**:278, 299

"Chernozem" (Mandelstam) **14**:150-51, 154

"Cherry Blossoms" (Gallagher) **9**:65

"The Cherry Tree" (Gunn) **26**:205

"The Chestnut Casts His Flambeaux" (Housman) **2**:199

"Un cheval de race" (Baudelaire) **1**:59

"The Cheval-Glass" (Hardy) **8**:100

*Les chevaliers* (Lamartine) **16**:269

"La chevelure" (Baudelaire) **1**:45, 66-7, 69

"Chevelure" (Cesaire) **25**:10, 17

"Chevrefoil" (Marie de France) **22**:248, 255, 257-58, 262-64, 266-67, 269, 272, 274, 301

"Chhabi" (Tagore) **8**:414

"Chi vuol veder" (Petrarch) **8**:256

"Chiare fresche e dolci acque" (Petrarch) **8**:221, 230, 232-33, 235-36

"Chicago" (Sandburg) **2**:317, 322-23, 333, 335, 339

"The Chicago Defender Sends a Man to Little Rock" (Brooks) **7**:62

"The Chicago Picasso" (Brooks) **7**:82

*Chicago Poems* (Sandburg) **2**:300-02, 307-08, 312, 314, 316-18, 321, 333, 335-36, 338-39

"Chicago Poet" (Sandburg) **2**:339

"The Chicago Train" (Gluck) **16**:149, 153

"Chicken" (Stein) **18**:313

"Chicory and Daisies" (Williams) **7**:373, 407

"Chief Standing Water" (Tomlinson) **17**:309

"Chievrefueil" (Marie de France)
    See "Chevrefoil"

"Chiffres et constellations amoureux d'une femme" (Breton) **15**:49

"The Child" (Carruth) **10**:71

"Child" (Sandburg) **2**:329

"The Child" (Wright) **14**:352

"Child and Wattle Tree" (Wright) **14**:352

"Child Harold" (Clare) **23**:46

"Child Harold" (Clare) **23**:25-6

"Child of Europe" (Milosz) **8**:191-92

"Child of the Sixtieth Century" (Viereck) **27**:259, 280

"Child Poems" (H. D.) **5**:305

"The Child Who Is Silent" (Shapiro) **25**:303

"The Child Who Saw Midas" (Sitwell) **3**:308

*Childe Harold's Pilgrimage: A Romaunt* (Byron) **16**:69, 72-7, 81-90, 107, 111

"Childe Roland to the Dark Tower Came" (Browning) **2**:64, 85-6, 88

"Childe Rolandine" (Smith) **12**:302, 350, 354

"Childhood" (Trakl) **20**:226

"Childhood" (Walker) **20**:276-77

"Childhood among the Ferns" (Hardy) **8**:125-26

"The Childhood of Jesus" (Pinsky) **27**:157

"A Childish Prank" (Hughes) **7**:123, 143, 161

"Childless Father" (Wordsworth) **4**:374, 428

"Childlessness" (Merrill) **28**:221, 244, 249

"Children Coming Home from School" (Gluck) **16**:159

"Children of Darkness" (Graves) **6**:137

"The Children of the Night" (Robinson) **1**:459, 467, 486

*The Children of the Night* (Robinson) **1**:459, 462-63, 466, 474

"The Children of the Poor" (Brooks) **7**:55, 62, 75, 78

"The Children's Song" (Kipling) **3**:171

"A Child's Grave at Florence" (Browning) **6**:6

"Child's Talk in April" (Rossetti) **7**:274

"chile" (Bissett) **14**:24

"A Chile" (Guillen) **23**:127

"Chilterns" (Brooke) **24**:56, 67

"Chimaera Sleeping" (Wylie) **23**:311, 314, 322

*The Chimeras* (Nerval)
    See *Les Chimères*

"La Chimère" (Gautier) **18**:141-42

*Les Chimères* (Nerval) **13**:172, 174, 176, 179-80, 182, 184, 187, 191-92, 194-95

"Chimes for Yahya" (Merrill) **28**:260, 263

"The Chimney Sweeper" (Blake) **12**:7, 9, 34-5

*China Poems* (Brutus) **24**:117

"Chinatown" (Song) **21**:349

"The Chinese Banyan" (Meredith) **28**:171, 175, 189

*Chinese Dynasty Cantos* (Pound) **4**:352

"The Chinese Nightingale" (Lindsay) **23**:269, 272-73, 275-76, 278, 281-82, 286-87, 291-94

*The Chinese Nightingale, and Other Poems* (Lindsay) **23**:292

*Chinesisch-deutsche Jahres-und Tageszeiten* (Goethe) **5**:251

"Chiron" (Holderlin) **4**:148, 166

"Chitateli gazet" (Tsvetaeva) **14**:315

*Chitra* (Tagore) **8**:408-09, 415, 418

*Chō o yumemu* (Hagiwara Sakutaro) **18**:176

"Chocorua to Its Neighbour" (Stevens) **6**:335

*A Choice of Kipling's Verse Made by T. S. Eliot with an Essay on Rudyard Kipling* (Kipling) **3**:175

"A Choice of Weapons" (Kunitz) **19**:148

"Choir" (Hongo) **23**:199

"The Choir" (Kinnell) **26**:261

"The Choir Invisible" (Eliot)
    See "O May I Join the Choir Invisible"

"Choix entre deux pations" (Hugo) **17**:101

"Cholera" (Dove) **6**:108

"Choorka" (McGuckian) **27**:110

"The Choosers" (Smith) **12**:327

"The Choral Union" (Sassoon) **12**:242

"Choriambics" (Brooke) **24**:62

"Choriambiscs II" (Brooke) **24**:57, 60

"Choros Sequence from Morpheus" (H. D.) **5**:304

"Chorus" (Lorde) **12**:159

"A Chorus of Ghosts" (Bryant) **20**:16

*Chosen Defects* (Neruda)
    See *Defectos escogidos: 2000*

*Chosen Poems: Old and New* (Lorde) **12**:142, 146, 148, 154, 157

"Le Chretien Mourant" (Lamartine) **16**:277

"Chrismus on the Plantation" (Dunbar) **5**:133-34

"Le Christ aux Oliviers" (Nerval) **13**:173, 177, 181, 198

"Christ for Sale" (Lowell) **3**:203

"Christ Has Arisen" (Pushkin)
    See "Khristos Voskres"

"Christ in Alabama" (Hughes) **1**:264

"Christ in Flanders" (Lowell) **3**:203

*Christ is Arisen* (Bely)
    See *Hristos voskres*

*Christ is Risen* (Bely)
    See *Hristos voskres*

"Christ of Pershing Square" (Stryk) **27**:190, 203

"Christ Recrucified" (Cullen) **20**:72

*Christabel* (Coleridge) **11**:41-2, 51-3, 84-5, 90-1, 104, 110

"The Christian Statesman" (Masters) **1**:344

"Christiane R." (Goethe) **5**:246

"Le Christianisme" (Owen) **19**:336, 341

"Christmas at Black Rock" (Lowell) **3**:201

"A Christmas Ballad" (Brodsky) **9**:2, 4

"The Christmas Cactus" (Clampitt) **19**:87

"A Christmas Card" (Merton) **10**:340

"A Christmas Card of Halley's Comet" (Nemerov) **24**:289

"Christmas Eve" (Ammons) **16**:58, 60, 65

"Christmas Eve" (Sexton) **2**:363

"Christmas Eve: Australia" (Shapiro) **25**:279, 286, 296, 300

"Christmas Eve under Hooker's Statue" (Lowell) **3**:200, 203

"Christmas Eve--Market Square" (Page) **12**:169

"Christmas in India" (Kipling) **3**:186

"Christmas in Simla" (Kipling) **3**:182

"Christmas on the Hudson" (Garcia Lorca)
    See "Navidad en el Hudson"

"Christmas on the Plantation" (Dunbar)
    See "Chrismus on the Plantation"

"Christmas Poem, 1965" (Ondaatje) **28**:292

"Christmas Poem for Nancy" (Schwartz) **8**:316

"A Christmas Song for the Three Gaids" (Chesterton) **28**:125

"Christmas Tree" (Shapiro) **25**:269, 286

"Christmas Tree--Market Square" (Page) **12**:169

*Christmas-Eve* (Browning) **2**:31-2, 44, 70-1
*Christmas-Eve and Easter Day* (Browning) **2**:33, 36, 70, 95
"Christs Incarnation" (Herrick) **9**:119
*Chronophagia* (Cassian) **17**:6, 13
"Chrysallis" (Montale) **13**:151
"Chu Ming-How" (Stryk) **27**:198
"Chüeh-chü" (Tu Fu) **9**:323
"El Chulo" (Guillen) **23**:101
"Chumban" (Tagore) **8**:407
"The Church" (Herbert) **4**:103, 113
"The Church and the Hotel" (Masters) **1**:343
"Church Building" (Harper) **21**:198, 200, 213
"The Church Floore" (Herbert) **4**:109, 119
"Church Going" (Larkin) **21**:228, 230, 236-37, 247, 255, 259
"The Church Militant" (Herbert) **4**:100, 130
"Church Monuments" (Herbert) **4**:100, 119
"Church Music" (Herbert) **4**:100, 131
"The Church of Brou" (Arnold) **5**:6, 9, 12, 50
"The Church Porch" (Herbert) **4**:100-01, 103, 107, 126
"The Church-Bell" (Wylie) **23**:328
"Church-Going" (Heaney) **18**:223
"Church-lock and Key" (Herbert) **4**:127
"Churchyard" (Gray)
  See "Elegy Written in a Country Churchyard"
"Churning Day" (Heaney) **18**:186
"The Chute" (Olds) **22**:319-22
*La chute d'un ange* (Lamartine) **16**:263, 265, 269-70, 285-87, 293-94, 296-97
"Chuva Oblíqua" (Pessoa) **20**:151, 165
"Chuy" (Soto) **28**:372, 382
"Ciant da li ciampanis" (Pasolini) **17**:256, 265
"Ciants di muart" (Pasolini) **17**:256
"The Cicadas" (Wright) **14**:346
"Cicadas" (Zagajewski) **27**:397
"Ciel brouillé" (Baudelaire) **1**:61, 66
"Cielo de tercera" (Fuertes) **27**:31
*La cifra* (Borges) **22**:95, 97, 99
"Un cigare allume que Fume" (Apollinaire)
  See "Paysage"
"Cigola la carrucola del pozzo" (Montale) **13**:164
"Le cimetière marin" (Bishop) **3**:46
"Le cimetière marin" (Valery) **9**:348, 351-52, 355, 358, 361, 363-80, 382, 384, 387, 389-93, 395-96, 398
*The Circassian* (Lermontov)
  See *The Circassian*
*The Circassian Boy* (Lermontov)
  See *The Novice*
"Circe's Power" (Gluck) **16**:171
*The Circle Game* (Atwood) **8**:3, 12, 15, 18, 26-8
"Circles in th Sun" (Bissett) **14**:8, 19, 33
*Circles on the Water* (Piercy) **29**:302, 307, 313
"The Circuit of Apollo" (Finch) **21**:162, 168
"Circuit total par la lune et par la couleur" (Tzara) **27**:224
"A Circular Play" (Stein) **18**:347
"Circulation of the Song" (Duncan) **2**:127
"Circumjack Cencrastus" (MacDiarmid) **9**:157
"Circumstance" (Lowell) **13**:94
"The Circus Animals' Desertion" (Yeats) **20**:307, 311, 313, 327, 332, 336
"Cirque d'hiver" (Bishop) **3**:37
"El cisne" (Dario) **15**:113
"Los cisnes" (Dario) **15**:115
"The Cited" (Garcia Lorca)
  See "Romance del emplazado"
"Cities and Thrones and Powers" (Kipling) **3**:183
"Citizen Cain" (Baraka) **4**:17, 24
"Citronia" (Heine) **25**:160, 171-80
"Città in campagna" (Pavese) **13**:227
"The City" (Blok) **21**:24
"The City" (Nash) **21**:272
"The City" (Pasternak)
  See "Gorod"
"The City: A Cycle" (Stryk) **27**:216
"The City Asleep" (Wright) **14**:362

"A City Dead House" (Whitman) **3**:379
"City in the Country" (Pavese)
  See "Città in campagna"
"The City in the Sea" (Poe) **1**:426, 431, 434, 438, 443-45
"The City in Which I Love You" (Lee) **24**:241
*The City in Which I Love You* (Lee) **24**:240, 242-44
"The City Limits" (Ammons) **16**:11, 23, 37, 46
"City Midnight Junk Strains for Frank O'Hara" (Ginsberg) **4**:47
"City of Monuments" (Rukeyser) **12**:230
"The City of the Dead" (Gibran) **9**:73
"City of the Wind" (Stryk) **27**:191
"The City Planners" (Atwood) **8**:13
"City Psalm" (Rukeyser) **12**:221
"City Trees" (Millay) **6**:207
"City Walk-Up, Winter 1969" (Forche) **10**:141, 144, 147, 157-58
"City without a Name" (Milosz) **8**:194-95
"City without Walls" (Auden) **1**:20
"The City-Mouse and the Country-Mouse" (Wyatt) **27**:331
"The City's Love" (McKay) **2**:211
"Ciudad" (Borges) **22**:94
"Ciudad sin sueño" (Garcia Lorca) **3**:139-40
"Ciudad viva, ciudad muerta" (Aleixandre) **15**:35
"Ciudades" (Cardenal)
  See "Las ciudades perdidas"
"Las ciudades perdidas" (Cardenal) **22**:126-28, 132
"Civil Rights Poem" (Baraka) **4**:11, 19
"Civilization and Its Discontents" (Ashbery) **26**:108, 113
"Clad All in Brown" (Swift) **9**:256-57
"The Claim" (Browning) **6**:14
"Clair de lune" (Apollinaire) **7**:45-6
"Clair de lune" (Verlaine) **2**:413, 420, 429
"Claire de terre" (Breton) **15**:51-2
"Claribel" (Tennyson) **6**:358-60, 365
"Claribel A Melody" (McGuckian) **27**:83
"Clasping of Hands" (Herbert) **4**:130
"Class" (Tomlinson) **17**:320
"Class Struggle" (Baraka) **4**:30, 38
"Class Struggle in Music" (Baraka) **4**:40
"The Class Will Come to Order" (Kunitz) **19**:150
"Claud Antle" (Masters) **1**:334
"Claude Glass" (Ondaatje) **28**:314
"Claus von Stuffenberg 1944" (Gunn) **26**:197
"El clavicordio de la abuela" (Dario) **15**:80
"Clay" (Baraka) **4**:30
"clay and morning star" (Clifton) **17**:29
"Cleaning Day" (Wright) **14**:356
"Cleaning the Candelabrum" (Sassoon) **12**:248, 259
"Clean,like,iodoform,between,the,tall" (Villa) **22**:356-57
"Clear and gentle stream" (Bridges) **28**:83
"Clear Autumn" (Rexroth) **20**:209
"Clear, with Light Variable Winds" (Lowell) **13**:94
"Clearances" (Heaney) **18**:228-29, 232, 238
"Cleared" (Kipling) **3**:167
"The Clearing" (Baraka) **4**:5, 15
"The Clearing" (Berry) **28**:38
*Clearing* (Berry) **28**:7-9
"Clearing the Title" (Merrill) **28**:267, 269-70
"The Cleaving" (Lee) **24**:241, 244, 248-49, 251-52
"Cleon" (Browning) **2**:36, 82, 95
"Cleopomop y Heliodemo" (Dario) **15**:81
"Clepsydra" (Ashbery) **26**:126, 157, 166
"The Clepsydras of the Unknown" (Elytis) **21**:119
"The Clerk's Journal" (Aiken) **26**:25
*The Clerk's Journal: Being the Diary of a Queer Man* (Aiken) **26**:46-8, 50
"Clerk's Tale" (Chaucer) **19**:13, 29, 54-60
"The Cliff" (Lermontov) **18**:297
"Cliff Klingenhagen" (Robinson) **1**:467, 486

"Clifford Ridell" (Masters) **1**:344-46
"The Cliff-Top" (Bridges) **28**:67
"The Climate of Thought" (Graves) **6**:139, 143
"Climbing a Mountain" (Hagiwara Sakutaro) **18**:178
"Climbing Alone All Day" (Rexroth) **20**:193
"Climbing Milestone Mountain" (Rexroth) **20**:203
"Climbing Pien-chüeh Temple" (Wang Wei) **18**:371
"Climbing T'ai-po's Peak" (Li Po) **29**:188
"Climbing the Streets of Worcester, Mass." (Harjo) **27**:66
"Climbing to the Monastery of Perception" (Wang Wei) **18**:384
"The Clinging Vine" (Robinson) **1**:468
"The Clipped Stater" (Graves) **6**:128, 137
"A Cloak" (Levertov) **11**:176, 194
"La cloche fêlée" (Baudelaire) **1**:65
"A Clock in the Square" (Rich) **5**:352
"The Clock of Tomorrow" (Apollinaire)
  See "L'lorloge de demain"
"The Clock Stopped" (Dickinson) **1**:108
"The Clod and the Pebble" (Blake) **12**:7
"Clorinda and Damon" (Marvell) **10**:268, 271
"Closed for Good" (Frost) **1**:213
"Close-Up" (Ammons) **16**:24
"Clothes" (Sexton) **2**:367
"The Cloud" (Shelley) **14**:167, 171, 196, 207, 212
"Cloud" (Toomer) **7**:338
"Cloud-Catch" (Hongo) **23**:204
*The Cloud-Messenger* (Kalidasa)
  See *Meghadūta*
"Clouds" (Ashbery) **26**:124
"Clouds" (Brooke) **24**:57-8, 73, 85
"Clouds" (Levine) **22**:214, 219, 222
"Clouds" (Tomlinson) **17**:312
*The Clouds* (Williams) **7**:370
"Clover" (Dario)
  See "Trébol"
"The Clown Chastized" (Mallarme)
  See "Le pitre châtié"
*Clown's Houses* (Sitwell) **3**:290, 294, 301-02
*The Club of Queer Trades* (Chesterton) **28**:97
*Cluster of Songs* (Tagore)
  See *Gitāli*
*Cluster of Songs* (Tagore)
  See *Gitāli*
"Coal" (Lorde) **12**:153
*Coal* (Lorde) **12**:142, 148
"The Coal Picker" (Lowell) **13**:84
"The Coast" (Meynell) **16**:196
"The Coast Guard's Cottage" (Wylie) **23**:324
"Coast of Trees" (Ammons) **16**:45, 62
*A Coast of Trees* (Ammons) **16**:31, 45, 62
"The Coastwise Lights" (Kipling) **3**:162
"A Coat" (Yeats) **20**:320
"The Coats" (Gallagher) **9**:60
"Cobwebs" (Rossetti) **7**:278
"The Cock and the Fox" (Chaucer)
  See "Nun's Priest's Tale"
"The Cocked Hat" (Masters) **1**:325-26, 328-29, 342
"Cockerel" (Hagiwara Sakutaro) **18**:173
"The Cocks" (Pasternak) **6**:253
"Coconut Palm" (Tagore)
  See "Narikel"
"Cocotte" (Gozzano) **10**:178
"Coda" (Ekeloef) **23**:76, 86
"The Code" (Frost) **1**:195, 208, 226
"A Code of Morals" (Kipling) **3**:190
"Coeur, couronne et miroir" (Apollinaire) **7**:32-6
"La coeur volé" (Rimbaud) **3**:270
"Cogióme sin prevención" (Juana Ines de la Cruz) **24**:234
"Cohorte" (Perse) **23**:254-57
*Coins and Coffins* (Wakoski) **15**:338, 344, 356, 369
"Cold" (Cassian) **17**:12, 15
"Cold in the Earth" (Bronte)
  See "Remembrance"

"Cold Iron" (Kipling) **3**:171
"Cold-Blooded Creatures" (Wylie) **23**:314
"La colère de Samson" (Vigny) **26**:366, 368, 371, 380-81, 391, 401, 412, 416
"Coleridge" (McGuckian) **27**:101
"Colesberg" (Brutus) **24**:105
"Colin Clout" (Spenser)
    See *Colin Clouts Come Home Againe*
*Colin Clouts Come Home Againe* (Spenser) **8**:336, 367, 387, 396
"The Coliseum" (Poe) **1**:439
"The Collar" (Gunn) **26**:185
"The Collar" (Herbert) **4**:102-03, 112-13, 130-31
"The Collar" (Herrick) **9**:141
*Collected Earlier Poems* (Williams) **7**:367-69, 374-75, 378, 382, 387-88, 392-94, 406-07, 409
*Collected Early Poems* (Pound) **4**:355
*The Collected Greed, Parts 1-13* (Wakoski) **15**:356
*Collected Later Poems* (Williams) **7**:370, 375
*The Collected Longer Poems of Kenneth Rexroth* (Rexroth) **20**:197, 202, 204, 209-10, 214
*Collected Lyrics* (Millay) **6**:227
*Collected Poems* (Aiken) **26**:21, 24, 43-5
*Collected Poems* (Bridges) **28**:74, 77-8
*The Collected Poems* (Chesterton) **28**:99, 109
*Collected Poems* (Cummings) **5**:82-4, 87, 107, 111
*Collected Poems* (Frost) **1**:203
*Collected Poems* (Graves) **6**:153, 165, 171
*Collected Poems* (Hardy) **8**:89, 95-6, 98, 101, 118, 124
*Collected Poems* (Larkin) **21**:256, 258
*Collected Poems* (Lindsay) **23**:265, 280-82, 285-86, 288, 292, 294
*Collected Poems* (MacDiarmid)
*Collected Poems* (Millay) **6**:227
*Collected Poems* (Milosz)
    See *Czeslaw Milosz: The Collected Poems, 1931-1987*
*Collected Poems* (Moore) **4**:235-36, 238, 247, 254, 271
*Collected Poems* (Olson) **19**:316
*Collected Poems* (Pinsky) **27**:168
*The Collected Poems* (Plath) **1**:406
*Collected Poems* (Robinson) **1**:467, 469, 480
*Collected Poems* (Rossetti)
    See *The Poetical Works of Christina Georgina Rossetti*
*Collected Poems* (Sassoon) **12**:246-47
*Collected Poems* (Sitwell) **3**:299, 301, 303-05, 308, 318-21, 325
*Collected Poems* (Stevens) **6**:306
*Collected Poems* (Stryk) **27**:207, 209-10, 212-16
*Collected Poems* (Tomlinson) **17**:342, 351, 355, 361
*Collected Poems* (Yeats) **20**:307, 336-37
*Collected Poems 1934* (Williams) **7**:360, 372, 402
*Collected Poems, 1938* (Graves) **6**:166
*Collected Poems, 1955* (Graves) **6**:138, 140-43, 145
*Collected Poems, 1909-1935* (Eliot) **5**:173, 176, 179, 211
*Collected Poems, 1912-1944* (H. D.) **5**:297, 305
*Collected Poems, 1923-1953* (Bogan) **12**:93, 95-6, 120, 125
*Collected Poems, 1929-1933* (Day Lewis) **11**:123
*Collected Poems, 1940-1978* (Shapiro) **25**:313, 315
*Collected Poems, 1947-1980* (Ginsberg) **4**:71-2, 76-9, 83-4, 86, 89
*Collected Poems, 1950-1970* (Davie) **29**:101, 111, 122
*Collected Poems, 1951-1971* (Ammons) **16**:10, 20, 27, 40, 46, 54, 61

*Collected Poems, 1957-1982* (Berry) **28**:25-29, 32, 37-39, 43-4
*The Collected Poems of A. E. Housman* (Housman) **2**:175-76, 180
*The Collected Poems of Christopher Smart* (Smart) **13**:347
*Collected Poems of Elinor Wylie* (Wylie) **23**:304, 306, 312, 314, 330-31
*Collected Poems of H. D.* (H. D.) **5**:268, 270, 276
*The Collected Poems of Hart Crane* (Crane) **3**:89-90
*The Collected Poems of Howard Nemerov* (Nemerov) **24**:298-99, 301
*The Collected Poems of Jean Toomer* (Toomer) **7**:340-41
*The Collected Poems of Muriel Rukeyser* (Rukeyser) **12**:224, 226, 235
*The Collected Poems of Octavio Paz, 1957-1987* (Paz) **1**:374-76
*The Collected Poems of Rupert Brooke* (Brooke) **24**:52, 54, 61, 71
*The Collected Poems of Stevie Smith* (Smith) **12**:307, 309, 313-17, 320, 327, 346-47, 350, 352
*The Collected Poems of Theodore Roethke* (Roethke) **15**:281, 283-84, 288
*The Collected Poems of Thomas Merton* (Merton) **10**:336-337, 345, 348, 351
*The Collected Poems of Wallace Stevens* (Stevens) **6**:304
*The Collected Poems of Wilfred Owen* (Owen) **19**:351
*Collected Poetry Notebook* (Cesaire) **25**:48-9
*Collected Shorter Poems, 1927-1957* (Auden) **1**:30
*Collected Shorter Poems, 1930-1950* (Auden) **1**:30
*Collected Shorter Poems, 1946-1991* (Carruth) **10**:89, 91
*The Collected Shorter Poems of Kenneth Rexroth* (Rexroth) **20**:197-98, 202, 204-05
*Collected Sonnets* (Millay) **6**:227
*Collected Works* (Akhmatova) **2**:19
*Collected Works* (Rossetti)
    See *The Poetical Works of Christina Georgina Rossetti*
*The Collected Works of Billy the Kid* (Ondaatje) **28**:298, 304, 314-16, 327, 338-39
*A Collection of Celebrated Love Poems* (Hagiwara Sakutaro)
    See *A Collection of Celebrated Love Poems*
*Collection of Short Songs on Innocent Love* (Hagiwara Sakutaro)
    See *Collection of Short Songs on Innocent Love*
"Collective Dawns" (Ashbery) **26**:144, 153
"College Breakfast Party" (Eliot) **20**:125
"The College Garden" (Bridges) **28**:79-80
"Les collines" (Apollinaire) **7**:12
"The Colloquies" (Gozzano) **10**:175, 180
*The Colloquies* (Gozzano)
    See *I Colloqui*
"Colloquy in Black Rock" (Lowell) **3**:201, 216-17, 227
"Colloquy of the Centaurs" (Dario)
    See "Coloquio de los centauros"
"Collos. 3.3" (Herbert) **4**:130
*Collyn Clout* (Skelton) **25**:329-30, 336, 337, 341-42, 348, 356, 374
"La colombe poisnardée et le jet d'eau" (Apollinaire) **7**:18, 20-2
"A Colombia" (Guillen) **23**:127
"The Colonel" (Forche) **10**:136, 138, 140, 145, 153, 167, 169
"Colonel Fantock" (Sitwell) **3**:293, 301, 325
"Coloquio de los centauros" (Dario) **15**:88, 92, 96, 112, 114
*Color* (Cullen) **20**:52-54, 56-58, 62, 66-67, 72, 77, 79, 81-83, 85-86
"The Color Sergeant" (Johnson) **24**:142

"The Colored Band" (Dunbar) **5**:134, 147
"The Colored Soldiers" (Dunbar) **5**:129-31, 133-34, 140
"Colors" (Cullen) **20**:65
"The Colors of Night" (Momaday) **25**:199, 202-203, 217-18
*The Colossus, and Other Poems* (Plath) **1**:380-81, 84, 388-89, 391, 394, 396, 404, 407, 410, 414
"The Colour Machine" (Gunn) **26**:
"The Colour Shop" (McGuckian) **27**:106
"A Coloured Print by Shokei" (Lowell) **13**:61
"A Coltrane Poem" (Sanchez) **9**:225
"Columbian Ode" (Dunbar) **5**:128
"Combat Cultural" (Moore) **4**:259
"Come" (Smith) **12**:316
"Come Break with Time" (Bogan) **12**:87, 101, 105-06, 122
"Come, Come Now" (Aleixandre) **15**:15
"Come Death" (Smith) **12**:315
"Come Death" (2Smith) **12**:314, 317, 319
"Come In" (Frost) **1**:197, 213, 230
"Come on, Come back" (Smith) **12**:295
"Come Republic" (Masters) **1**:329, 343
"Come se Quando" (Bridges) **28**:76-9
"Come Thunder" (Okigbo) **7**:235
"Come to the Bower" (Heaney) **18**:197
"The Comedian as the Letter C" (Stevens) **6**:293, 295-96, 304, 306, 310, 330, 335
*La Comédie de la Mort* (Gautier) **18**:143-46, 155, 159, 163
*La comédie de la mort* (Gautier) **18**:131-32, 134-35, 141, 155
*Comedy* (Dante)
    See *La divina commedia*
"The Comet" (Aleixandre) **15**:5
"The Comet at Yell'ham" (Hardy) **8**:89
"Comfort" (Browning) **6**:21
"Coming" (Larkin) **21**:238, 244
"Coming Close" (Levine) **22**:220
"Coming Down through Somerset" (Hughes) **7**:166
"The Coming Fall" (Levertov) **11**:185
*The Coming Forth by Day of Osiris Jones* (Aiken) **26**:8, 11, 57
"Coming Home" (Gallagher) **9**:36
"Coming Home from the Post Office" (Levine) **22**:221, 228
"Coming of Age in Michigan" (Levine) **22**:220, 228
"The Coming of Arthur" (Tennyson) **6**:408
"The Coming of Kali" (Clifton) **17**:24
"The Coming of the End" (Moments of VisionHardy) **8**:92
"The Coming of Wisdom with Time" (Yeats) **20**:338
*Coming through Slaughter* (Ondaatje) **28**:298
"Commander Lowell 1887-1950" (Lowell) **3**:219, 235
"Comme Dieu Dispense de Graces" (Stevens) **6**:294
"Comme on voit sur la branche" (Ronsard) **11**:218, 234, 236, 240
"Comme un beau pré despouillè de ses fleurs" (Ronsard) **11**:250
*Commedia* (Dante)
    See *La divina commedia*
"The Commemorative Mound of the Decorated Tree" (Ishikawa)
    See "Nishikigizuka"
"Comment against the Lamp" (Hughes) **1**:266
"Commentary" (Milosz) **8**:212-13
"Commodore Barry" (Davie) **29**:106, 109-10
"A Common Ground" (Levertov) **11**:169
"The common living dirt" (Piercy) **29**:315, 317-19
"The Commonweal" (Swinburne) **24**:312
"Communication in White" (Madhubuti) **5**:340
"Communion" (Herbert) **4**:100
"A Communist to Others" (Auden) **1**:15
"Community" (Piercy) **29**:308, 311
"The Commuted Sentence" (Smith) **12**:327

*Cómo atar* (Fuertes) **27**:27, 30
*Cómo atar los bigotes al tigre* (Fuertes) **27**:17-8, 25-7, 31, 49
"Como del cielo llovido" (Guillen) **23**:126
"Como quisimos" (Guillen) **23**:126
"The Compact: At Volterra" (Tomlinson) **17**:350
"The Companion of a Mile" (Noyes) **27**:134
"The Companions" (Nemerov) **24**:263
"Company" (Dove) **6**:111, 119
"Company" (Smith) **12**:325
"The Company of Lovers" (Wright) **14**:336, 340, 351, 371
"A Comparative Peace" (Brutus) **24**:116
"Comparatives" (Momaday) **25**:191, 193-194
"Comparison" (Dunbar) **5**:125
"Compass" (Borges) **22**:74
"Compensation" (Dunbar) **5**:121
"The Complaint" (Wordsworth)
See "The Complaint of the Forsaken Indian Woman"
"The Complaint of the Forsaken Indian Woman" (Wordsworth) **4**:347, 427-28
"Complaint of the Poor Knight Errant" (Laforgue) **14**:64
"Complaint of the Poor Knight Errant" (Laforgue)
See "Complainte du pauvre chevalier-errant"
"Complainte à Notre-Dame des soirs" (Laforgue) **14**:94
"Complainte de cette bonne lune" (Laforgue) **14**:93
*Complainte de la bonne défunte* (Laforgue) **14**:81, 98
"Complainte de la fin des journées" (Laforgue) **14**:98
"Complainte de la lune en province" (Laforgue) **14**:98
"Complainte de l'ange incurable" (Laforgue) **14**:85, 89-90, 98
"Complainte de l'automne monotone" (Laforgue) **14**:80
"Complainte de l'époux outragé" (Laforgue) **14**:81, 93
"Complainte de Lord Pierrot" (Laforgue) **14**:81, 93, 98
"Complainte de l'organiste de Nice" (Laforgue) **14**:93
"Complainte de l'orgue de barbarie" (Laforgue) **14**:95
"Complainte des blackboulés" (Laforgue) **14**:81, 96
"Complainte des complaintes" (Laforgue) **14**:95
"Complainte des consolations" (Laforgue) **14**:81
"Complainte des débats mélancoliques et littéraires" (Laforgue) **14**:64, 97
"Complainte des formalités nuptiales" (Laforgue) **14**:81, 96
"Complainte des grands pins dans une ville abandonée" (Laforgue) **14**:81, 96
"Complainte des pianos qu'on entend dans les quartiersaisés" (Laforgue) **14**:81, 93-5
"Complainte des printemps" (Laforgue) **14**:81, 98
"Complainte des voix sous le figuier bouddhique" (Laforgue) **14**:96
"Complainte du fœtus de Poète" (Laforgue) **14**:93, 96, 98
"Complainte du pauvre chevalier-errant" (Laforgue) **14**:98
"Complainte du pauvre corps humain" (Laforgue) **14**:81
"Complainte du pauvre jeune homme" (Laforgue) **14**:81, 93
"Complainte du Roi de Thulé" (Laforgue) **14**:81, 86, 89, 93, 98
"Complainte du sage de Paris" (Laforgue) **14**:95
"Complainte d'un certain dimanche" (Laforgue) **14**:96-8
"Complainte d'une convalescence en mai" (Laforgue) **14**:96, 98

"Complainte propitiatoire à l'inconscient" (Laforgue) **14**:66, 94-5
"Complainte sous le figuier boudhique" (Laforgue) **14**:81
"Complainte sur certains ennuis" (Laforgue) **14**:94, 97
"Complainte sur certains temps déplacés" (Laforgue) **14**:94
"Complainte-épitaphe" (Laforgue) **14**:95
"Complainte-Placet de Faust fils" (Laforgue) **14**:95, 98
*Les complaintes* (Laforgue) **14**:57, 64, 66, 68-9, 70-2, 80-1, 92, 94-5, 97-8
"Complaintes des pubertés difficiles" (Laforgue) **14**:80, 98
*Complaints: Containing Sundrie Small Poemes of the Worlds Vanitie* (Spenser) **8**:366
"The Complement" (Carew) **29**:32
*The Complete Collected Poems of William Carlos Williams, 1906-1938* (Williams) **7**:348, 355
*The Complete Poems* (Dickinson) **1**:102
*Complete Poems* (Sandburg) **2**:322-24, 328-29, 331, 333, 340
*The Complete Poems, 1927-1979* (Bishop) **3**:50, 66
*The Complete Poems of Frances Ellen Watkins Harper* (Harper) **21**:197
*The Complete Poems of Marianne Moore* (Moore) **4**:251, 254, 256, 270
*The Complete Poem's of Paul Laurence Dunbar* (Dunbar) **5**:120, 136
*The Complete Poetical Works* (Lowell) **13**:95
*Complete Poetical Works of Samuel Taylor Coleridge* (Coleridge) **11**:44, 71
*Complete Verse* (Belloc) **24**:23, 36, 39
*Complete Works* (Aleixandre)
See *Obras completas*
*Complete Works* (Jeffers) **17**:125
*Complete Works* (Mandelstam) **14**:106
"The Complete Works of Francois Villon" (Villon) **13**:413
"Complicate" (Kunitz) **19**:156
"Complicity" (Gallagher) **9**:37
"Composed on Jade Maiden Spring in Ying Cheng, Anzhou" (Li Po) **29**:179, 182
"Composed on the Cold Food Day" (Wang Wei) **18**:362
"Composition in Bhairavi" (Tagore)
See "Bhairavi gan"
"Comprehending" (Ortiz) **17**:246
"Comptine" (Cesaire) **25**:31
"Comrades Four" (McKay) **2**:225
*Comus: A Maske* (Milton) **29**:200, 212, 221, 226, 228, 243, 252, 272
"Con la Carta de la Habana" (Guillen) **23**:126
"Conceit of Master Gysbrecht" (Browning) **2**:38
"Conceive a Man, Should He Have Anything" (Cummings) **5**:106
"The Concert" (Millay) **6**:215
"Concert at the Railroad Station" (Mandelstam)
See "Koncert na vokzale"
"The Concert of Hyacinths" (Elytis) **21**:119
"Concerto to a Runaway" (Bissett) **14**:9
"Conch-Shell" (Wright) **14**:364
*Le concile féerique* (Laforgue) **14**:72, 81, 96
"Conciliator, Who Had Never Believed" (Holderlin) **4**:178
"Conclusion" (Sassoon) **12**:258
"Concord" (Swinburne) **24**:324, 326
"Concord Hymn" (Emerson) **18**:111
"Concord Ode" (Emerson) **18**:84, 88
"Concord River" (Rich) **5**:354
"The Condemned" (Page) **12**:174-75
*A Coney Island of the Mind* (Ferlinghetti) **1**:164-65, 167-77, 184, 187
"A Conference of the Powers" (Kipling) **3**:160
"Confession" (Baudelaire) **1**:61
"confession" (Clifton) **17**:37
"Confession" (Gluck) **16**:160
"Confession" (Heaney) **18**:243

"The Confession" (Lermontov) **18**:300
"A Confession" (Milosz) **8**:197
"The Confessional" (Browning) **2**:30
"Confessional" (Chesterton) **28**:95
"Confessions" (Browning) **6**:32
"Confessions of a Second-Rate, Sensitive Mind" (Tennyson) **6**:347
"The Confessions of Count Mowgli de Sade" (Nash) **21**:267
"Confessions of the Life Artist" (Gunn) **26**:207, 211, 226
"The Confidantes" (Kumin) **15**:215
"Confidential Instructions" (Kunitz) **19**:148
"Configurations" (Ammons) **16**:23
*Configurations* (Paz) **1**:355
"Confinement" (McGuckian) **27**:101
"The Confirmation" (Shapiro) **25**:286, 300
"Confiteor" (Trakl) **20**:263-64, 269
"The Conflict" (Day Lewis) **11**:126, 150
"Confusion of the Senses" (Rexroth) **20**:221
"Congo" (Lindsay) **23**:264, 266, 268, 270, 272-73, 275-76, 278, 282-84, 286-87, 289, 294, 297
*The Congo and Other Poems* (Lindsay) **23**:267-68, 295
"The Congo Love Song" (Johnson) **24**:151
"A Congratulatory Poem to Her Most Sacred Majesty on the Universal Hopes of All Loyal Persons for a Prince of Wales" (Behn) **13**:32
*A Congratulatory Poem to . . . Queen Mary upon Her Arrival in England* (Behn) **13**:9
*Los conjurados* (Borges) **22**:95, 99
"Conjuring in Heaven" (Hughes) **7**:159
*Connecting the Dots* (Kumin) **15**:224
"Connections" (Wright) **14**:376-77
"The Connoisseuse of Slugs" (Olds) **22**:312
"Connubii Flores, or the Well-Wishes at Weddings" (Herrick) **9**:86, 112
"The Conquererors" (Dunbar) **5**:131
"The Conqueror Worm" (Poe) **1**:437, 443
"Conquête de l'aube" (Cesaire) **25**:10
"A Conrado Benítez" (Guillen) **23**:128
"The Cons cientious Objector" (Shapiro) **25**:297
"Conscience" (Herbert) **4**:109, 129
"La Conscience" (Hugo) **17**:65, 85
"Conscience and Remorse" (Dunbar) **5**:115, 125
"Les Consciences atténuantes" (Tzara) **27**:235
"Conscious" (Owen) **19**:347, 361-63
"Consciousness" (Milosz)
See "Świadomość"
"Conscript" (Larkin) **21**:225
"Conscription Camp" (Shapiro) **25**:313, 324-25
"Conscripts" (Sassoon) **12**:242, 280
"The Consecrating Mother" (Sexton) **2**:374
"Conseil d'ami" (Valery) **9**:391
"Consequences" (Meredith) **28**:213
"Conserving the Magnitude of Uselessness" (Ammons) **16**:54
"Considering the Snail" (Gunn) **26**:201, 207-208, 210, 213
"Consolation" (McKay) **2**:225
"Consorting with Angels" (Sexton) **2**:363
*The Conspirators* (Borges)
See *Los conjurados*
*Constab Ballads* (McKay) **2**:208, 210, 216, 221-22, 225-27
"Constancie" (Herbert) **4**:109
"The Constant" (Ammons) **16**:6
"Constantly Risking Absurdity" (Ferlinghetti) **1**:182
"Constellation" (Stryk) **27**:208, 212
*Constellations* (Breton) **15**:48-9, 55, 59-60, 62
"Construction" (Shapiro) **25**:295
"Constructions" (Loy) **16**:316
"Conte" (Rimbaud) **3**:261-63
"Conte Colibri" (Cesaire) **25**:44-5
"Contemplations" (Bradstreet) **10**:7-8, 19-21, 27-30, 35, 42, 65
*Les contemplations* (Hugo) **17**:50, 53-54, 64, 66-67, 74, 78, 80-84, 86-87, 89-92, 95
"The Contender" (Hughes) **7**:155

"The Contention" (Sassoon) **12**:259
"Contest of the Bards" (Ginsberg) **4**:58-9
"The Continent" (Duncan) **2**:109-13
"Continent's End" (Jeffers) **17**:131
"Contingency" (Ammons) **16**:6
*Continuation des amours* (Ronsard) **11**:220, 230
"Continuum" (Levertov) **11**:207-09
"Contra mortem" (Carruth) **10**:83
*Contra Mortem* (Carruth) **10**:71
"A Contract" (Lermontov) **18**:303-4
"Contralto" (Gautier) **18**:157
"The Contraption" (Swenson) **14**:250
"The Contrariness of the Mad Farmer" (Berry) **28**:20
"The Contrast" (Harper) **21**:207, 216
"Contre les bûcherons de la forêt de Gastine" (Ronsard) **11**:236-37, 242
"Le Contrediz de Franc Gontier" (Villon) **13**:415
"Control Burn" (Snyder) **21**:292
"Contusion" (Plath) **1**:391, 394
"The Conundrum of the Workshop" (Kipling) **3**:167
"The Convalescent" (Gozzano) **10**:177
"The Convent Threshold" (Rossetti) **7**:267, 281-2, 291, 295-6, 298
"Conventionality" (Kipling) **3**:190
"The Convergence of the Twain" (Hardy) **8**:116
"Conversacíon" (Cardenal) **22**:117
"Conversation" (Giovanni) **19**:118
"The Conversation" (Masters) **1**:326
*Conversation at Midnight* (Millay) **6**:220, 223, 244
"Conversation in Moscow" (Levertov) **11**:197
"The Conversation of Prayer" (Thomas) **2**:390
"Conversation with a Fireman from Brooklyn" (Gallagher) **9**:44, 60
"Conversation with my Inspiration" (Tsvetaeva)
See "Razgovor s geniem"
"Conversations with Jeanne" (Milosz) **8**:213
"Conversing with Paradise" (Nemerov) **24**:285
"Conversion" (Toomer) **7**:320, 334
"The Convert" (Shapiro) **25**:286, 296, 298
"Convict" (Wordsworth) **4**:373
"Convivio!" (Williams) **7**:361
*Convivio* (Dante) **21**:48-53, 66, 73-4, 83, 87-92
"Cooking" (Stein) **18**:322-326
"A Cooking Egg" (Eliot) **5**:184
"Cook's Mountains" (Page) **12**:183, 190
"The Cool Web" (Graves) **6**:172
"Coole Park, 1929" (Yeats) **20**:322
"Coon Song" (Ammons) **16**:19, 41, 44, 46
"Coopérants du contingent" (Senghor) **25**:255
"Coplas americans" (Guillen) **23**:126
"Cop-Out Session" (Knight) **14**:46, 52
"Copper Red and the Seven Dachsies" (Cassian) **17**:3
*Copper Sun* (Cullen) **20**:56-59, 61-62, 64-65, 75, 77, 85-86
"cops" (Baraka) **4**:12
"A Coquette Conquered" (Dunbar) **5**:122
"Coquetterie posthume" (Gautier) **18**:125, 157-60, 163
"Le cor" (Vigny) **26**:369, 402-403, 410
"Cor Mio" (Rossetti) **7**:278
*El corazón amarillo* (Neruda) **4**:287, 289
*El corazón con que vivo* (Guillen) **23**:133
"El corazón de Pedro de Valdivia" (Neruda) **4**:293
"El corazón magellanico" (Neruda) **4**:281
"Corinna, Pride of Drury-Lane" (Swift) **9**:283-84
"Corinna's Going a-Maying" (Herrick) **9**:99-101, 104-05, 116, 120, 122-23, 125, 132, 137, 142, 145
"Coriolanus and His Mother" (Schwartz) **8**:282-83, 290-91, 297-98, 301, 308-09, 312
"The Corner of Night and Morning" (Lowell) **13**:64
"Cornet Solo" (Day Lewis) **11**:145
*Cornhuskers* (Sandburg) **2**:302, 304, 307, 309, 313-14, 316, 323, 338-39
"Cornish Heroic Song for Valda Trevlyn" (MacDiarmid) **9**:180, 183
"Corno Inglese" (Montale) **13**:105
"A Corn-Song" (Dunbar) **5**:122
*La Corona* (Donne) **1**:136-39, 145, 147
"A Coronal" (Williams) **7**:345, 362
"The Coronet" (Marvell) **10**:267, 271, 274, 277, 293, 313-14
"The Corporal" (Gunn) **26**:224
"Corps perdu" (Cesaire) **25**:30
*Corps perdu* (Cesaire) **25**:30-2, 35, 44
"The Corpse of a Cat" (Hagiwara Sakutaro)
See "Neko no shigai"
"Corpse Song" (Atwood) **8**:23, 25
"Correction: Eve Delved and Adam Span" (Nash) **21**:273
"Correspondances" (Baudelaire) **1**:55, 65, 69-70
"Correspondences" (Rukeyser) **12**:226, 233
"La Corrida" (Hayden) **6**:194
"The Corridor" (Gunn) **26**:193
"Cors de chasse" (Apollinaire) **7**:42
*The Corsair* (Byron) **16**:91-5, 109
*The Corsair* (Lermontov) **18**:299
"Corson's Inlet" (Ammons) **16**:21, 23, 29, 35-7, 54
*Corson's Inlet* (Ammons) **16**:4-5, 20, 28
"The Cortege" (Gibran) **9**:73
"Cortège for Rosenbloom" (Stevens) **6**:293
*Cortege of Orpheus* (Apollinaire)
See *Le bestiaire; ou, Cortège d'Orphée*
"Cosmic Comics" (Nemerov) **24**:301
"The Cossack" (Pushkin) **10**:407
"Cossack Cradlesong" (Lermontov) **18**:268, 278, 281, 304
"The Cost of Pleasure" (Bryant) **20**:46
"Costa Magic" (Loy) **16**:313
"The Costa San Giorgio" (Loy) **16**:313, 318-20, 322, 327
"The Cottage Dweller" (Tagore)
See "Kutir-vasi"
"The Cottar's Saturday Night" (Burns) **6**:50, 57, 74, 79, 96
*Cotton Candy on a Rainy Day* (Giovanni) **19**:114, 116-18, 123, 125, 128, 130, 134, 137, 142-43
"Cotton Song" (Toomer) **7**:319, 321
"Cottonmouth Country" (Gluck) **16**:139
"Cougar Meat" (Gallagher) **9**:59, 62
"Could Man Be Drunk for Ever" (Housman) **2**:195
*Count Nulin* (Pushkin)
See *Graf Nulin*
"Counter Serenade" (Viereck) **27**:263
"Counter-Attack" (Sassoon) **12**:256-57, 264-65, 277-78
*Counter-Attack and Other Poems* (Sassoon) **12**:242, 250, 253, 257-58, 260, 263-64, 266-69, 272, 276-77
"A Counterpoint" (Aiken) **26**:4
"Counter-Walk, Reversals" (Viereck) **27**:277
*The Countess Cathleen* (Yeats) **20**:298, 302-3, 353
*Counting Backward* (Cassian) **17**:6
"Counting the Beats" (Graves) **6**:136-37, 155
*The Country between Us* (Forche) **10**:136-38, 140, 143-46, 148, 150-53, 155, 157-59, 161, 165-66, 169
"A Country Burial" (Dickinson) **1**:79
"A Country Girl" (McKay) **2**:224
"A Country Life: To His Brother, Master Thomas Herrick" (Herrick) **9**:86, 110-13, 115
"The Country Life, to the Honoured Master Endimion Porter, Groome of the Bed-Chamber to His Majesty" (Herrick) **9**:101, 139, 144
*The Country of a Thousand Years of Peace and Other Poems* (Merrill) **28**:220, 225, 228-29, 231, 234, 238-42, 244, 246-47, 259
"Country of Marriage" (Berry) **28**:11-13, 44
*The Country of Marriage* (Berry) **28**:7, 13
*Country Sentiment* (Graves) **6**:127, 129, 132
"The Country Squire and the Mandrake" (Smart) **13**:348
"Country Stars" (Meredith) **28**:180, 192
"Country Town" (Wright) **14**:350
"The Country Whore" (Pavese)
See "La puttana contadina"
"The Countryside" (Pushkin)
See "Derevnya"
"County Ward" (Soto) **28**:370, 376-77
"Le Coup de couteau du soleil dans le dos des villes surprises" (Cesaire) **25**:30
*Un coup de dés jamais n'abolira le hasard* (Mallarme) **4**:192, 199, 202-03, 208-09, 217-18
"Coup d'evential..." (Apollinaire) **7**:34-5
"The Couple" (Cassian) **17**:11
"Courage" (Akhmatova)
See "Muzhestvo"
*Court Poems* (Montagu) **16**:338
"The Court Revolt" (Gunn) **26**:
"A Courtesy" (Wylie) **23**:322
"Courtship" (Dove) **6**:112
"Cousin Kate" (Rossetti) **7**:270, 276, 280, 289, 291
"Couteaux midi" (Cesaire) **25**:37
"The Cove" (Clampitt) **19**:83
"Coversation" (Tagore)
See "Sambhashan"
"The Cow" (Nash) **21**:278
"The Cow in Apple-Time" (Frost) **1**:195, 197
"Cowley Rider" (Masters) **1**:334
"Cowper's Grave" (Browning) **6**:6, 21
"Cows: A Vision" (Gallagher) **9**:36
"The Cows at Night" (Carruth) **10**:85
"The Coy Mistress" (Marvell)
See "To His Coy Mistress"
"Crab-Angel" (Loy) **16**:307
"The Crack" (Levertov) **11**:159
"The Cracked Bell" (Baudelaire)
See "La cloche fêlée"
"The Crack-up of American Optimism" (Viereck) **27**:284
"A Cradle Song" (Blake) **12**:7, 10, 33
"A Cradle Song" (Yeats) **20**:337
*Craft* (Tsvetaeva)
See *Remeslo*
*Craftsmanship* (Tsvetaeva)
See *Remeslo*
"Crag Jack's Apostasy" (Hughes) **7**:147
"Cramped in That Funnelled Hole" (Owen) **19**:336
"Crass Times" (Viereck) **27**:278, 281
"Crass Times Redeemed by Dignity of Souls" (Viereck) **27**:258-60, 273
"La cravate et la montre" (Apollinaire) **7**:32, 34-5
"Crazy Horse names his daughter" (Clifton) **17**:25
"Crazy Jane" (Day Lewis) **11**:151
"Crazy Jane and Jack the Journeyman" (Yeats) **20**:328
"Crazy Jane Talks with the Bishop" (Yeats) **20**:327-28
"A Crazy Spiritual" (Ginsberg) **4**:79
"Crazy Weather" (Ashbery) **26**:153
"Creating the World" (Milosz) **8**:214
"creation" (Clifton) **17**:37
"The Creation" (Gibran) **9**:73
"The Creation" (Johnson) **24**:128-29, 133, 139, 143-44, 149, 152-53, 156, 164, 166-69
*Creation* (Noyes) **27**:138
"The Creation, according to Coyote" (Ortiz) **17**:231
"Creation Myth" (Berry) **28**:9
"Creation of Anguish" (Nemerov) **24**:261, 285
"Creation-Annihilation" (Wright) **14**:375
"creative writing class" (Bukowski) **18**:19
"Creatures" (Kumin) **15**:182

"Creatures in the Dawn" (Aleixandre) **15**:6, 15, 38
"Crecen altas las flores" (Guillen) **23**:126
"Credat Judaeus" (Kipling) **3**:194
"Credences of Summer" (Ashbery) **26**:153
"Credences of Summer" (Stevens) **6**:306, 335, 338
"Credo" (Jeffers) **17**:117,129
"Credo" (Kumin) **15**:213, 215-16, 224
"Credo" (Robinson) **1**:485-86
"Credo" (Stryk) **27**:198
"The Cremona Violin" (Lowell) **13**:60, 77, 96
"Crepuscolo di sabbiatori" (Pavese) **13**:226
*Crepúsculario* (Neruda) **4**:276, 278
"Crépuscule" (Apollinaire) **7**:40
"Crépuscule" (Hugo) **17**:67, 81-82
"Le crépuscule du soir" (Baudelaire) **1**:58-9
"Crescent Moon like a Canoe" (Piercy) **29**:323
"The Crevasse" (Tsvetaeva)
    See "Rasshchelina"
"Crevasses" (Cesaire) **25**:33
"The Crew of the Chelyuskin" (Tsvetaeva)
    See "Chelyuskintsy"
"Le cri de l'âme" (Lamartine) **16**:266
*The Criminal* (Lermontov) **18**:299
"The Crimson Cyclamen" (Williams) **7**:350, 354
"Cripples and Other Stories" (Sexton) **2**:363, 365
"Le Cristal automatique" (Cesaire) **25**:20
"The Critic and the Writer of Fables" (Finch) **21**:163
*A Critical Fable* (Lowell) **13**:65, 74-6
"Critics and Connoisseurs" (Moore) **4**:232, 257, 270
"De Critters' Dance" (Dunbar) **5**:145
"La Crocifissione" (Pasolini) **17**:265
"Croft" (Smith) **12**:333
"A la croix" (Lamartine) **16**:284
"The Crooked Stick" (Wylie) **23**:301
"Cross" (Hughes) **1**:235, 243, 263-64
"The Cross Spider" (Swenson) **14**:273
"The Crosse" (Donne) **1**:136
"The Crosse" (Herbert) **4**:111
"The Crossed Apple" (Bogan) **12**:101, 110-11
"Crossing Aguadilla" (Tomlinson) **17**:361
"Crossing Brooklyn Ferry" (Sexton) **2**:361
"Crossing Brooklyn Ferry" (Tomlinson) **17**:337
"Crossing Brooklyn Ferry" (Whitman) **3**:377, 379, 391-93, 399-400, 410, 415
"Crossing Over" (Meredith) **28**:200
"Crossing the Atlantic" (Sexton) **2**:363
"Crossing the Bar" (Tennyson) **6**:359
*Crossing the Water: Transitional Poems* (Plath) **1**:391, 394, 396, 404
"Crossing the Yellow River to Ch'ing-ho" (Wang Wei) **18**:362, 366-68, 373
"Crossroads" (Gunn) **26**:214
"The Cross-Roads" (Lowell) **13**:60, 76-7
"Crotchets" (Nemerov) **24**:290
"Crow Alights" (Hughes) **7**:130
"Crow and Mama" (Hughes) **7**:132
"Crow and the Birds" (Hughes) **7**:159
*The Crow and the Heart* (Carruth) **10**:70, 78, 89
"Crow and the Sea" (Hughes) **7**:144
"Crow Blacker Than Ever" (Hughes) **7**:138
"Crow Communes" (Hughes) **7**:143
*Crow: From the Life and Songs of the Crow* (Hughes) **7**:129-30, 133, 137-39, 141-43, 145, 152-53, 155-61, 163, 168-71
"Crow Frowns" (Hughes) **7**:159
"Crow Goes Hunting" (Hughes) **7**:142, 160-61
"Crow Hill" (Hughes) **7**:131, 150
"Crow Jane in High Society" (Baraka) **4**:16
"Crow on a Withered Branch" (Matsuo Basho) **3**:32
"Crow on the Beach" (Hughes) **7**:138, 144
"Crow Sickened" (Hughes) **7**:138
"Crow Song" (Atwood) **8**:25
"The Crowded Street" (Bryant) **20**:5, 36

"A Crowded Trolley Car" (Wylie) **23**:309, 328, 332
"Crowdieknowe" (MacDiarmid) **9**:156
"Crowds" (Baudelaire)
    See "Les foules"
"Crowing-Hen Blues" (Hughes) **1**:256
"The Crown of Bays" (Smith) **12**:319
"The Crown of Gold" (Smith) **12**:295, 315
"Crown of Thorns" (Celan)
    See "Dornenkranz"
"Crowned Out" (Celan) **10**:113
*Crowned with Dreams* (Rilke) **2**:280
"Crowns and Garlands" (Hughes) **1**:252
"Crow's Account of St. George" (Hughes) **7**:161, 171
"Crow's Account of the Battle" (Hughes) **7**:133, 144, 152
"Crow's Account of the Battle" (Hughes) **7**:133, 144, 152
"Crow's Battle Fury" (Hughes) **7**:143
"Crow's Elephant Totem Song" (Hughes) **7**:138, 144
"Crow's Last Stand" (Hughes) **7**:123, 144
"Crow's Nerve Fails" (Hughes) **7**:144
"Crow's Playmates" (Hughes) **7**:144
"Crow's Theology" (Hughes) **7**:159, 161
"Crow's Undersong" (Hughes) **7**:167
"Crow's Vanity" (Hughes) **7**:144
"Crucibles of Love" (Graves) **6**:172
"Le crucifix" (Lamartine) **16**:278
*Crucifix in a Deathhand: New Poems, 1963-1965* (Bukowski)
"The Crucifix in the Filing Cabinet" (Shapiro) **25**:286, 290, 300
"The Crucifixion" (Akhmatova) **2**:15
"Crucifixión" (Garcia Lorca) **3**:140
"Crucifixion" (Garcia Lorca)
    See "Crucifixión"
"The Crucifixion" (Johnson) **24**:128, 144, 156, 165, 169
"The Cruel Falcon" (Jeffers) **17**:117, 120
"The Cruell Maid" (Herrick) **9**:101
"The Cruise" (Merrill) **28**:239, 241
"Cruising 99" (Hongo) **23**:196-98
"Crumbs or the Loaf" (Jeffers) **17**:130
"Crusades of Silence" (Cesaire) **25**:18
*Crusoé* (Perse) **23**:231
"Crusoe in England" (Bishop) **3**:48, 63-4, 66-7, 70
"The Cry" (Levertov) **11**:198
"The Cry" (Masters) **1**:326
"Cry Ararat!" (Page) **12**:168, 190, 198
*Cry Ararat!* (Page) **12**:167, 179, 184, 190, 197
"Cry Faugh" (Graves) **6**:135
"The Cry of the Children" (Browning) **6**:6, 17, 21, 27, 30, 42
"The Cry of the Human" (Browning) **6**:7, 21
"Cry to Rome: From the Chrysler Building Tower" (Garcia Lorca) **3**:141
"Crying" (Kinnell) **26**:260
"The Crystal" (Aiken) **26**:
"The Crystal" (Aiken) **26**:29-30, 45
"The Crystal Cabinet" (Blake) **12**:36
"Crystals Like Blood" (MacDiarmid) **9**:187
*Cuaderno San Martín* (Borges) **22**:71, 73, 93-4
"Cualquier tiempo pasado fue peor" (Guillen) **23**:126
"Cuchualain" (Day Lewis) **11**:151
"Cuckoo Song" (H. D.) **5**:267
"Cudjoe Fresh from de Lecture" (McKay) **2**:224, 226
"Cuento de dos jardines" (Paz) **1**:361, 363
"The Cuirassiers of the Frontier" (Graves) **6**:133
"The Culprit" (Housman) **2**:162, 164, 169, 179, 186
"Cultural Exchange" (Hughes) **1**:250, 252
"Culture and Anarchy" (Rich) **5**:386
"The Culture-Hug Blues" (Viereck) **27**:279
"cum cum cum cumly witchcraft i know you care" (Bissett) **14**:34
"The Cup" (Wright) **14**:347

*Cup of Blizzards* (Bely)
    See *Kubok metelej: Chetviortiia simfoniia*
"The Cup of Paint" (Lindsay) **23**:286
*The Cup of Snowstorms* (Bely)
    See *Kubok metelej: Chetviortiia simfoniia*
"Cupid and Psyche" (Elytis) **21**:135
"The Cure" (Graves) **6**:155
"A Cure at Porlock" (Clampitt) **19**:87
"A Cure of Souls" (Levertov) **11**:171
"A Curfew" (Clampitt) **19**:91
"A Curious Man's Dream" (Baudelaire)
    See "Le rêve d'un curieux"
"Curl Up and Diet" (Nash) **21**:265
"The Current" (Berry) **28**:14-15
"The Curse" (Millay) **6**:211
"A Curse against Elegies" (Sexton) **2**:351
"A Curse for a Nation" (Browning) **6**:27
"The Curse of Cromwell" (Yeats) **20**:326
"Curtain" (Dunbar) **5**:119
"The Curtain" (Wright) **14**:355
"The Curve" (Levertov) **11**:176
"Custodian" (Kumin) **15**:223
"The Customs-Officer's House" (Montale)
    See "La casa dei doganieri"
"Cut" (Plath) **1**:385, 392
"A Cutlet" (Stein) **18**:349
"The Cutting Edge" (Levine) **22**:215
"Cutting the Grapes Free" (Piercy) **29**:312
"Cuttings" (Roethke) **15**:291, 296-98, 312
"Cuttings" (LaterRoethke) **15**:260, 297-98, 302, 312, 314
*Cuttlefish Bones* (Montale)
    See *Ossi di seppia*
"Cutty Sark" (Crane) **3**:84, 90, 106
"Cybernetics" (Nemerov) **24**:261, 282-83, 301
"The Cycads" (Wright) **14**:346
"The Cyclads" (Aiken) **26**:36
"The Cycle" (Jeffers) **17**:141
"The Cycle" (Roethke) **15**:265
"The Cyclical Night" (Borges) **22**:73
"Cyclops" (Shelley) **14**:227
"Le cygne" (Baudelaire) **1**:45, 66, 71
"Cyparissus" (Duncan) **2**:103
"Cypress Avenue" (Davie) **29**:110
"Cyrano en España" (Dario) **15**:80
"Cyrano in Spain" (Dario)
    See "Cyrano en España"
*Czeslaw Milosz: The Collected Poems, 1931-1987* (Milosz) **8**:190-91, 197-98, 202, 206-07, 213-15
"D. R." (Zukofsky) **11**:351, 396
"Da, ia lezhu v zemle . . ." (Mandelstam) **14**:151
"Da una torre" (Montale) **13**:113
"Daddy" (Plath) **1**:382-83, 386-87, 392-93, 395-97, 400-02, 406-07, 414
"Daedalus" (Sikelianos) **29**:365-66, 368, 370-71
"The Daemon" (Bogan) **12**:100, 110
"The Daemon of the World" (Shelley) **14**:185
*The Daffodil Murderer* (Sassoon) **12**:252, 270, 274-77
"Daffodildo" (Swenson) **14**:277, 287
"Daffy Duck in Hollywood" (Ashbery) **26**:153
"Daguerreotype Taken in Old Age" (Atwood) **8**:39
"Un dahlia" (Verlaine) **2**:431
"The Dahlia Gardens" (Clampitt) **19**:82, 90-1
"Dahomey" (Lorde) **12**:160
"The Daily Globe" (Nemerov) **24**:278
*The Daily Holidays* (Cassian) **17**:6
"Les daimons" (Ronsard) **11**:225, 279, 281-82
"The Dainty Monsters" (Ondaatje) **28**:292-93
*The Dainty Monsters* (Ondaatje) **28**:291-92, 294, 298-99, 318, 327, 331-32, 335
"Daisies Are Broken" (Williams) **7**:406
"The Daisy" (Tennyson) **6**:357, 360
"Daisy Frazer" (Masters) **1**:334
"Daisy-Cutter" (McGuckian) **27**:76, 103
"Daisy's Song" (Keats) **1**:311
"Dakar Doldrums" (Ginsberg) **4**:72
"The Dale" (Lamartine)
    See "Le vallon"
"Dalhousie Farm" (Meredith) **28**:181

"The Dalliance of the Eagles" (Whitman) **3**:397

"The Dam" (Rukeyser) **12**:210

*Dam 'ah wabitisāmah* (Gibran) **9**:73, 75, 77-8, 81

"Dämmerung" (Celan) **10**:124-25

"Damned Women" (Baudelaire)
See "Femmes damnées"

"Damon Being Asked a Reason for Loveing" (Behn) **13**:18

"Damon the Mower" (Marvell) **10**:266, 293, 295-97, 315

"The Dampe" (Donne) **1**:130

"The Dance" (Baraka) **4**:16

"Dance" (Cassian) **17**:13

"The Dance" (Crane) **3**:84, 86, 88, 90

"The Dance" (Larkin) **21**:259

"Dance" (Pavese)
See "Balletto"

"The Dance" (Roethke) **15**:266-67, 269, 273, 279

"The Dance at the Phoenix" (Hardy) **8**:99

"The Dance of Death" (Blok)
See "Danse macabre"

"Dance of Death" (Garcia Lorca)
See "Danza de la muerte"

*The Dance of Death* (Auden) **1**:8

"Dance of the Macabre Mice" (Stevens) **6**:296

"Dance the Orange" (Hayden) **6**:196

"The Dancer" (H. D.) **5**:305

"Dances of Death" (Blok)
See "Danse macabre"

"Dancing on the Grave of a Son of a Bitch" (Wakoski) **15**:346

*Dancing on the Grave of a Son of a Bitch* (Wakoski) **15**:336, 348, 365

"The Danger of Writing Defiant Verse" (Parker) **28**:350, 363

*Dangling in the Tournefortia* (Bukowski) **18**:15

"Daniel Bartoli" (Browning) **2**:84

"Daniel Jazz" (Lindsay) **23**:264, 270, 286

"Danny Deever" (Kipling) **3**:170-71, 179, 188-89, 191

"Dans le restaurant" (Eliot) **5**:185

"Dansa di Narcís" (Pasolini) **17**:281

"Danse macabre" (Blok) **21**:6, 14, 20

"Danse russe" (Williams) **7**:353, 367, 408

"Dante Études, Book Two" (Duncan) **2**:114-16, 127

"Danza de la muerte" (Garcia Lorca) **3**:121

"La danza del espiritu" (Cardenal) **22**:131

"Daphnaida" (Spenser) **8**:365, 367

"Daphnis and Chloe" (Marvell) **10**:265, 271, 291-92, 301

"Darest Thou Now O Soul" (Whitman) **3**:378

"Darien" (Graves) **6**:137, 144, 168

"The Dark and the Fair" (Kunitz) **19**:162, 169

"Dark Blood" (Walker) **20**:273, 282

"Dark Eye in September" (Celan) **10**:112

"Dark Gift" (Wright) **14**:338, 353, 356

"Dark Girl's Rhyme" (Parker) **28**:356

"The Dark Hills" (Robinson) **1**:468

*The Dark One* (Tagore)
See *Shyamali*

"The Dark Ones" (Wright) **14**:373

"Dark Prophecy: I Sing of Shine" (Knight) **14**:39

"Dark Song" (Ammons) **16**:4

"Dark Song" (Sitwell) **3**:291

*Dark Summer* (Bogan) **12**:87, 89, 105-06, 120-23

"Dark Waters of the Beginning" (Okigbo) **7**:231

"Dark Wild Honey" (Swenson) **14**:276

*Dark World* (Carruth) **10**:71, 91

"Darkling Summer, Ominous Dusk, Rumorous Rain" (Schwartz) **8**:319

"The Darkling Thrush" (Hardy) **8**:98, 105-06, 121, 131

"Darkness" (Aleixandre) **15**:5

"Darkness" (Byron) **16**:86, 89

"Darkness Chex George Whitman" (Ferlinghetti) **1**:183

"Darkness of Death" (Pasternak) **6**:253

"Darling! Because My Blood Can Sing" (Cummings) **5**:108

"Darling Daughters" (Smith) **12**:326

"Darling, It's Frightening! When a Poet Loves ..." (Pasternak) **6**:251

"Darling Room" (Tennyson) **6**:353

"Dary Tereka" (Lermontov) **18**:268, 281, 290, 295

"Dat Dirty Rum" (McKay) **2**:222

"Dat ol' Mare o' Mine" (Dunbar) **5**:134

"Date Lilia" (Hugo) **17**:94

"Dates" (Ondaatje) **28**:327, 331

"Dates: Penkhull New Road" (Tomlinson) **17**:347, 352

"Dative Haruspices" (Rexroth) **20**:215

"A Daughter I" (Levertov) **11**:209

"A Daughter II" (Levertov) **11**:209

"Daughter Moon" (Wakoski) **15**:366

"The Daughter of the Forest" (Gibran)
See "Amām 'arsh al-jamāl"

*Daughters of Fire* (Nerval)
See *Les filles du feu*

"Daughters with Curls" (Stevens) **6**:292

"David" (Pasolini) **17**:252, 281

"David and Bathsheba in the Public Garden" (Lowell) **3**:205-06, 215

"David's Lamentation for Saul and Jonathan" (Bradstreet) **10**:6

"David's Night at Veliès" (Merrill) **28**:220

"Davy Jones' Door-Bell" (Lindsay) **23**:264

"Dawlish Fair" (Keats) **1**:311

"Dawn" (Brooke) **24**:53, 64, 82

"Dawn" (Dunbar) **5**:125, 128

"Dawn" (Garcia Lorca)
See "La aurora"

"Dawn Adventure" (Lowell) **13**:63

"Dawn after Storm" (Zukofsky) **11**:368

"Dawn Bombardment" (Graves) **6**:144

"Dawn Bombardment" (Graves) **6**:144

"The Dawn Wind" (Kipling) **3**:183

"Dawnbreaker" (Hayden) **6**:198

"The Dawning" (Herbert) **4**:102

"Dawn's Rose" (Hughes) **7**:138, 144, 159

"Day" (Ammons) **16**:12

"The Day After" (Soto) **28**:302

"Day and Night" (Montale)
See "Giorno e notte"

"The Day Before the Trial" (Swinburne) **24**:355

*Day by Day* (Lowell) **3**:231-32

"The Day Dream" (Coleridge) **11**:91, 106

"The Day Is a Poem" (Jeffers) **17**:141

"The Day is Done" (Dunbar) **5**:126

"The Day Is Gone" (Keats) **1**:279

"TH DAY MAY CUM" (Bissett) **14**:34

"The Day of Battle" (Housman) **2**:160

"The Day of Judgement" (Swift) **9**:259, 265, 281, 295

"Day of Kings" (Hugo) **17**:58

"The Day of the Eclipse" (Merrill) **28**:239, 243

"A Day on the Big Branch" (Nemerov) **24**:257, 261

"Day or Night" (Rossetti) **7**:276

"Day Six O'Hare Telephone" (Merton) **10**:336

"Day That I Have Loved" (Brooke) **24**:58, 62, 76

"The Day the Mountains Move" (Yosano Akiko)
See "Yama no ugoku hi"

"The Day They Eulogized Mahalia" (Lorde) **12**:156

"The day was five-headed" (Mandelstam)
See "Den' stoial na piati golovakh"

"A Day With Her" (McGuckian) **27**:76, 102

"The Day You Were Born" (Song) **21**:344

"Daybreak" (Hagiwara Sakutaro) **18**:178

"Daybreak" (Hughes) **1**:255

"Daybreak" (Kinnell) **26**:260-61

"Daybreak" (Soto) **28**:377-78

"A Daydream in Summer" (Clare) **23**:25

"Daylight Savings" (Parker) **28**:362

"Days" (Emerson) **18**:76, 82, 84, 88-91, 96, 102

"Days" (Larkin) **21**:235, 246

"Days of 1935" (Merrill) **28**:235, 256

"Days of 1941 and '44" (Merrill) **28**:270

"Days of 1964" (Merrill) **28**:220-21, 250-51

"Days of 1971" (Merrill) **28**:230, 235, 258

"The Day's Ration" (Emerson) **18**:88

*The Days Run Away Like Wild Horses over the Hills* (Bukowski) **18**:14, 19

"Daystar" (Dove) **6**:111

"dDionysus in Old Age" (Viereck) **27**:295

"Las de l'amer repos" (Mallarme) **4**:203

"Dea Roma" (Lowell) **3**:199-200

"Deacon Taylor" (Masters) **1**:323

"The Dead" (Brooke) **24**:63, 74

"The Dead" (Day Lewis) **11**:147

"The Dead" (Montale)
See "I morti"

*The Dead and the Living* (Olds) **22**:309-10, 314-16, 318-19, 321-22, 324, 326, 328, 338-39

"Dead Are My People" (Gibran) **9**:73

"The Dead Beat" (Owen) **19**:347

"Dead before Death" (Rossetti) **7**:288

"The Dead by the Side of the Road" (Snyder) **21**:292-93

"The Dead Fox Hunter" (Graves) **6**:166

"The Dead King" (Kipling) **3**:182

*The Dead Lecturer* (Baraka) **4**:5-6, 16-17, 23, 31, 37

"Dead Men's Love" (Brooke) **24**:53, 56

"Dead Musicians" (Sassoon) **12**:267

"The Dead Pan" (Browning) **6**:7, 19

*The Dead Priestess Speaks* (H. D.) **5**:305

"The Dead Princess and the Seven Heroes" (Pushkin)
See "Skazka o Mertvoy Tsarevne"

"The Dead Shall Be Raised Incorruptible" (Kinnell) **26**:245, 251, 254, 267

"The Dead II" (Brooke) **24**:59, 88

"Deaf Poem" (Gallagher) **9**:62

"Dean Dixon, Welcome Home" (Stryk) **27**:204

"The Dean of St. Patrick's to Thomas Sheridan" (Swift) **9**:295

"The Dean to Himself on St. Cecilia's Day" (Swift) **9**:295

*The Dean's Provocation for Writing the "Lady's Dressing Room"* (Montagu) **16**:345

"The Dean's Reasons" (Swift) **9**:295

"Dear Child of God" (Smith) **12**:335

"Dear Female Heart" (Smith) **12**:295

"Dear Judas" (Jeffers) **17**:109-10, 144

*Dear Judas and Other Poems* (Jeffers) **17**:109, 124, 135

"Dear Little Sirmio" (Smith) **12**:331

"Dear Muse" (Smith) **12**:335

"Dear Patron of My Virgin Muse" (Burns) **6**:84

"Dear Strager Extant in Memory by the Blue Juaniata" (Kinnell) **26**:250, 267

"Dear Toni..." (Lorde) **12**:157

"Death" (Herbert) **4**:113

"Death" (Lermontov)
See "Death"

"Death" (Olds) **22**:325

"Death" (Shelley) **14**:166

"Death and Birth" (Swinburne) **24**:324

"Death and Co." (Plath) **1**:397

"Death and Daphne" (Swift) **9**:260

"Death and Doctor Hornbook" (Burns) **6**:56, 88

"The Death and Dying Words of Poor Mailie" (Burns) **6**:52, 61, 63-4

"The Death and Last Confession of Wandering Peter" (Belloc) **24**:5

"Death and Love" (Browning) **6**:16

"Death and Morality" (Olds) **22**:323, 342

"Death and Murder" (Olds) **22**:326

*Death and Taxes* (Parker) **28**:349-51, 363-65

"Death and the Maiden" (Nemerov) **24**:259, 268, 270-71

"Death and the Maiden" (Wylie) **23**:317

"The Death Baby" (Sexton) **2**:373

"Death Carol" (Whitman) **3**:378

"Death, corollary to Life" (Villa) **22**:354
"The Death Dance" (Madhubuti) **5**:339
"Death Fugue" (Celan)
  See "Todesfuge"
"Death, Great Smoothener" (Swenson) **14**:250,
  286
"Death in Mexico" (Levertov) **11**:205-06, 209
"Death in Moonlight" (Kunitz) **19**:155
"A Death in the Desert" (Browning) **2**:36, 45,
  72-73, 95
"A Death in the Desert" (Tolson) **17**:328
*Death in This Garden* (Bunuel)
  See *La mort en ce jardin*
"Death Invited" (Swenson) **14**:266, 286
"Death Is a Woman" (Harjo) **27**:68, 70, 72-3
*The Death Notebooks* (Sexton) **2**:360-61, 367-
  68, 370-72
"Death of a Ceiling" (McGuckian) **27**:90
"Death of a Favorite Cat" (Gray)
  See "Ode on the Death of a Favourite Cat,
    Drowned in a Tub of Gold Fishes"
"Death of a Frog" (Hagiwara Sakutaro)
  See "Kaeru no shi"
"The Death of A. G. A." (Bronte) **8**:65, 74
"Death of a Naturalist" (Heaney) **18**:200, 207,
  247-48, 252
*Death of a Naturalist* (Heaney) **18**:186, 189-90,
  192, 194, 199-201, 205-8, 215, 220, 238,
  247, 255
"Death of a Student" (Shapiro) **25**:309, 316
"Death of a Young Son by Drowning"
  (Atwood) **8**:38-9
"Death of an Alcoholic" (Hagiwara Sakutaro)
  **18**:167, 178
"Death of Antoñito the Camborio" (Garcia
  Lorca)
  See "Muerte de Antoñito el Camborio"
"The Death of Artists" (Baudelaire)
  See "The Death of Artists"
"Death of Autumn" (Millay) **6**:236
*The Death of Blanche the Duchess* (Chaucer)
  See *Book of the Duchess*
"The Death of Channing" (Bryant) **20**:46
"The Death of Crazy Horse" (Clifton) **17**:25
"Death of Emma Goldman" (Shapiro) **25**:311,
  324
"The Death of Fred Clifton" (Clifton) **17**:25, 27
"The Death of God" (Montale)
  See "La morte di Dio"
"The Death of Lovers" (Baudelaire)
  See "La mort des amants"
"The Death of Mr. Mounsel" (Smith) **12**:323
"The Death of Oenone" (Tennyson) **6**:360
"The Death of Richard Wagner" (Swinburne)
  **24**:323, 329
"The Death of Smet-Smet" (Brooke) **24**:56, 66
"Death of Socrates" (Lamartine)
  See *La morte de Socrate*
"The Death of the Beloved" (Rilke) **2**:272-73
"The Death of the Fathers" (Sexton) **2**:356,
  365-67
"The Death of the Firstborn" (Dunbar) **5**:140
"The Death of the Flowers" (Bryant) **20**:9, 12
"The Death of the Hired Man" (Frost) **1**:195,
  197, 209, 216, 221, 226, 228-29
"Death of the Hungarian hot pepper bush"
  (Piercy) **29**:315
"Death of the Lord Protector" (Marvell)
  See "Poem upon the Death of O. C."
"The Death of the Other Children" (Atwood)
  **8**:39
"Death of the Poet" (Lermontov) **18**:277, 281
"Death of the Poet" (Pasternak) **6**:268
"The Death of the Princess" (Senghor) **25**:232
"The Death of the Sheriff" (Lowell) **3**:200, 206
"The Death of the Wolf" (Vigny)
  See "La mort du loup"
"A Death on Easter Day" (Swinburne) **24**:319
"Death Piece" (Roethke) **15**:272
"The Death Room" (Graves) **6**:142, 144
"Death Shall Have No Dominion" (Thomas)
  See "And Death Shall Have No Dominion"

"Death, That Struck when I Was Most
  Confiding" (Bronte) **8**:65
"Death the Barber" (Williams) **7**:388
"Death to Van Gogh's Ear!" (Ginsberg) **4**:63,
  74-5
"A Death-Day Recalled" (Hardy) **8**:136
"Deaths" (Swenson) **14**:286
"Deaths and Entrances" (Thomas) **2**:380-82,
  388, 390
"The Deaths of Uncles" (Kumin) **15**:202
"Debat du cuer et du corps de Villon" (Villon)
  **13**:394, 396
"The Debate" (Lermontov) **18**:295, 297
"Debate with the Rabbi" (Nemerov) **24**:277
"Débauche" (Gautier) **18**:164
"Débris" (Cesaire)
"The Debt" (Dunbar) **5**:120, 125
"A Decade" (Lowell) **13**:97
"Decay" (Herbert) **4**:102
"The Decay of Vanity" (Hughes) **7**:113
"December" (Belloc) **24**:29
"December 1" (Milosz) **8**:215
"December 4th" (Sexton) **2**:372
"December 9th" (Sexton) **2**:352-53
"December 10th" (Sexton) **2**:364
"December 12th" (Sexton) **2**:352-53
"December 14th" (Sexton) **2**:353
"December 16th" (Sexton) **2**:352-53
"December 18th" (Sexton) **2**:352
"Deceptions" (Larkin) **21**:237
"Deciduous Branch" (Kunitz) **19**:147
"The Deciduous Trees" (Meredith) **28**:190
"The deck that pouts" (Piercy) **29**:314
*Declaration* (Wyatt) **27**:369
"Decline" (Trakl)
  See "Untergang"
"The Deconstruction of Emily Dickinson"
  (Kinnell) **26**:294
"Decorum and Terror Homage to Goethe and
  Hart Crane" (Viereck) **27**:279
"Dedica" (Pasolini) **17**:281
"The Dedication" (Herbert) **4**:125
"A Dedication" (Merrill) **28**:240
"Dedication" (Milosz) **8**:193
"Dedication" (Wylie) **23**:303
*Dedication* (Ekeloef) **23**:75-6
"Dedication for a Plot of Ground" (Williams)
  **7**:362, 394
"Dedication in Time" (Schwartz)
  See "Time's Dedication"
"A Dedication of Three Hats" (Gray) **6**:166
"Dedication to Hunger" (Gluck) **16**:151, 154-55
"Dedication: To William Morris" (Swinburne)
  **24**:313
"Dedications" (Rich) **5**:401
"Dedicatory Epistle" (Swinburne) **24**:351
"Dedicatory Ode" (Belloc) **24**:3, 6, 8, 11
"Dedicatory Poem" (Meredith) **28**:187
"Deem as ye list upon good cause" (Wyatt)
  **27**:354
"The Deep Sea Cables" (Kipling) **3**:162
*Deep Song* (Garcia Lorca)
  See *Poema del cante jondo*
"Deep Woods" (Nemerov) **24**:288
"Deeply Morbid" (Smith) **12**:329, 346
"Deep-sea Fishing" (MacDiarmid) **9**:167
"Deer Dancer" (Harjo) **27**:71
"Deer Enclosure" (Wang Wei)
  See "Deer Enclosure"
"Deer Park" (Wang Wei) **18**:383, 385-86, 391,
  393
"Deer Walled" (Wang Wei)
  See "Deer Walled"
*Defectos escogidos: 2000* (Neruda) **4**:287
*Defence* (Wyatt) **27**:369-70
"Defending My Tongue" (Clifton) **17**:28
"definition for blk / children" (Sanchez) **9**:224,
  232
"Definition in the Face of Unnamed Fury"
  (Dove) **6**:111
"Definition of Blue" (Ashbery) **26**:119, 123
"Definition of Creativity" (Pasternak) **6**:271

"The Definition of Love" (Marvell) **10**:264,
  266, 271, 274, 277, 291, 294, 299-303, 312,
  316, 319
"The Definition of Poetry" (Pasternak)
  See "Opredelenyie poezii"
"The Definition of the Creative Power"
  (Pasternak) **6**:254
"Deher milan" (Tagore) **8**:407
"Dehorning" (Hughes) **7**:166
"Dein Schimmer" (Celan) **10**:124-25
"Dejaneira" (Arnold) **5**:8
"Dejection" (Shelley) **14**:168
"Dejection: An Ode" (Coleridge) **11**:41, 52-3,
  58, 69-73, 90-2, 105-09
"Delfica" (Nerval) **13**:181, 194
"Delgusa Gardens" (Stryk) **27**:192
"Delicate Criss-Crossing Beetle Trails Left in
  the Sand" (Snyder) **21**:300
"The Delight Song of Tsoai-talee" (Momaday)
  **25**:189, 196, 204, 213, 220
"The Delinquent" (Dunbar) **5**:119
"Deliverance" (Graves) **6**:157
"The Deliverance" (Harper) **21**:192, 199-201,
  211
"Deliverance From a Fit of Fainting"
  (Bradstreet) **10**:26, 61-2
"Della primavera trasportata al morale"
  (Williams) **7**:408
"Delphi" (H. D.) **5**:305
"The Delphic Oracle upon Plotinus" (Yeats)
  **20**:312, 329, 334
"Delphic Song" (Sikelianos) **29**:367
"Delphine et Hippolyte" (Baudelaire)
  See "Femmes damnées"
"Delta" (Montale) **13**:134, 164
"Delta" (Walker) **20**:272-73, 275, 278, 281-83
"La déluge" (Vigny) **26**:367, 380-81, 391, 398,
  401-402, 411
"The Deluge" (Vigny)
  See "La déluge"
"Dem aufgehenden Vollmonde" (Goethe) **5**:249
"Demain dès l'aube" (Hugo) **17**:64
"Démarrage" (Tzara) **27**:229-31
*The Demesne of the Swans* (Tsvetaeva)
  See *Lebediny stan*
"Demi-Exile. Howth" (Davie) **29**:107, 109, 119
"The Demiurge's Laugh" (Frost) **1**:213
"Demobilization" (Shapiro) **25**:273, 296
"Democracy" (Hughes) **1**:241, 252, 258
"The Demon" (Pushkin) **10**:406, 412-13, 418
*The Demon* (Lermontov) **18**:271-72, 274, 279,
  282-83, 297-98, 302
"The Demon Lover" (Rich) **5**:392
"Demonology" (Ronsard)
  See "Les daimons"
"Demos and Dionysus" (Robinson) **1**:470, 487
"An den Mond" (Goethe) **5**:246-47
"Den' stoial na piati golovakh" (Mandelstam)
  **14**:152
"Denial" (Herbert) **4**:114, 119-20
"Denver Doldrum" (Ginsberg) **4**:74
"Deola Thinking" (Pavese) **13**:205
"Deola's Return" (Pavese)
  See "Ritorno di Deola"
"Départ" (Gautier) **18**:155
*Departmental Ditties* (Kipling) **3**:155-56, 159,
  165, 182, 190-91
"Departure" (Forche) **10**:137, 144, 156, 169
"Departure" (Gluck) **16**:142, 149-50, 172
"Departure" (Millay) **6**:211
"The Departure" (Olds) **22**:310, 312, 321-22
"Departure" (Plath) **1**:388, 407-08
"Departure" (Tomlinson) **17**:336, 346
"Departure in the Dark" (Day Lewis) **11**:145
"The Departure Song of the Divine Strings"
  (Li Ho) **13**:52
*Depends: A Poet's Notebook* (Montale)
  See *Quaderno de quattro anni*
"Deposition from love" (Carew) **29**:3-4, 46
"Depression Before Spring" (Stevens) **6**:313

"Dept. of Philosophy" (Enzensberger) **28**:151
"Depth of Love" (Graves) **6**:172
"The Depths" (Apollinaire)
See "Loin du pigeonnier"
"The Derelict" (Kipling) **3**:183
"Derevnya" (Pushkin) **10**:421
"Derev'ya" (Tsvetaeva) **14**:317
*Derivations: Selected Poems, 1950-1956*
(Duncan) **2**:105-06
"Le dernier chant de pèlerinage de Childe
Harold" (Lamartine) **16**:268, 279, 292
"Dernier jour du monde" (Hugo) **17**:87, 89
"Dernière Levée" (Breton) **15**:50
*Dernières Poésies* (Gautier) **18**:143
"Derniers vers" (Rimbaud) **3**:285
*Les derniers vers de Jules Laforgue* (Laforgue)
**14**:56-7, 59-62, 68-77, 80-3, 88, 93, 95-7
*Les derniers vers de Pierre de Ronsard,
gentilhomme vandomois* (Ronsard) **11**:244,
269, 274
"Des Beautés qui'il voudroit en s'amie"
(Ronsard) **11**:247
"Des Faux" (Apollinaire) **7**:46
"Des imagistes" (Williams) **7**:345
"Desajuste en el desgaste" (Fuertes) **27**:27
"Descartes and the Stove" (Tomlinson) **17**:319
"Descending Figure" (Gluck) **16**:151
*Descending Figure* (Gluck) **16**:130-34, 144,
147, 150-51, 153-56, 159, 170
"The Descent" (Brooke) **24**:77
"The Descent" (Kinnell) **26**:236, 252, 280
"The Descent" (Williams) **7**:403
"The Descent from the Cross" (Rossetti) **7**:264,
285
"The Descent of Odin, an Ode" (Gray) **2**:146,
148-49, 152
*The Descent of Winter* (Williams) **7**:349, 352-
53, 368, 400, 402
"A Descent through the Carpet" (Atwood) **8**:12,
19
"Description of a City Shower" (Swift) **9**:252,
265, 275-79
"Description of a Masque" (Ashbery) **26**:170
"A Description of the Fifteenth of November:
A Portrait of T. S. Eliot" (Stein) **18**:341
"Description of the Morning" (Swift) **9**:265
"Description without Place" (Stevens) **6**:338
*Descriptive Sketches* (Wordsworth) **4**:372
"El Desdichado" (Nerval) **13**:174-75, 178-80,
184-87, 195
"Desecration of the Gravestone of Rose P"
(Pinsky) **27**:175
*Le desert* (Lamartine) **16**:276, 282, 284, 286
"The Desert Music" (Williams) **7**:374
*The Desert Music, and Other Poems*
(Williams) **7**:371, 402-03
"Desert Places" (Frost) **1**:213, 229
"The Deserted House" (Reese) **29**:338, 345,
352
"The Deserted House" (Tennyson) **6**:358
"The Deserted Plantation" (Dunbar) **5**:117, 123
"The Deserter" (Smith) **12**:300, 330-31, 333
"Desertion" (Brooke) **24**:57, 63
"Le Désespéranto" (Tzara) **27**:234
"Le désespoir" (Lamartine) **16**:279, 282-83,
290-91, 293
"Design" (Frost) **1**:227-28
"Désir" (Apollinaire) **7**:3
"Desir" (Lamartine) **16**:281
"Le Désir de la Gloire" (Hugo) **17**:88
"Desire" (Hughes) **1**:240
"Desire" (Toomer) **7**:338
"Desk" (Tsvetaeva)
See "Stol"
"A Desoignated National Park" (Ortiz) **17**:227
*Desolation Is a Delicate Thing* (Wylie) **23**:322
"Despair" (Lamartine)
See "Le désespoir"
"Despedida" (Borges) **22**:94
"A Desperate Vitality" (Pasolini)
See "Una Disperata Vitalita"
"Despite and Still" (Graves) **6**:154

"Despondency, an Ode" (Burns) **6**:71
*Les Destinees* (Vigny) **26**:366-69, 371, 391-92,
394, 397, 401-404, 412-13
"Destino de la carne" (Aleixandre) **15**:38
"Destino del poeta" (Paz) **1**:358
"Destiny" (Arnold) **5**:43, 50
*Destiny* (Hagiwara Sakutaro)
See *Destiny*
"The Destiny of Nations" (Coleridge) **11**:49,
63-4, 80
"The Destroyer" (Graves) **6**:166
"Destroyers" (Kipling) **3**:183
*La destrucción o el amor* (Aleixandre) **15**:14-
16, 18, 21-6, 31-4, 39-40, 42
"La destruction" (Baudelaire) **1**:63, 71
"The Destruction of Long Branch" (Pinsky)
**27**:161, 163-65
*Destruction or Love* (Aleixandre)
See *La destrucción o el amor*
"Detail" (Williams) **7**:369
"Detente, sombra de mi bien esquivo" (Juana
Ines de la Cruz) **24**:180, 184, 187, 238
"Detroit Conference of Unity and Art"
(Giovanni) **19**:115
"Deus Amanz" (Marie de France)
See "Les Dous Amanz"
"Der Deutsche dankt" (Goethe) **5**:248
*Deutschland: Ein Wintermärchen* (Heine)
**25**:132-38, 152, 179
*Deuxième édition du cinquiesme livre des odes*
(Ronsard) **11**:246
"Developers at Crystal River" (Merrill) **28**:261
"Development" (Browning) **2**:96
"The Deviation" (Gluck) **16**:135-36
"The Devil and the Lady" (Tennyson) **6**:372,
408-09
"The Devil at Berry Pomery" (Graves) **6**:142,
144
"Devil on Ice" (Davie) **29**:114-15
"The Devils" (Pushkin)
See "Besy"
"The Devil's Advice to Story Tellers" (Graves)
**6**:143
"The Devon Maid" (Keats) **1**:311
"A Devonshire Folk Song" (Noyes) **27**:136
"Devotion: That It Flow; That There Be
Concentration" (Gallagher) **9**:45, 59
"Devotion to Duty" (Sassoon) **12**:257-58
"Devyatsat pyaty god" (Pasternak) **6**:265, 272
"Dezember" (Trakl) **20**:265
"Dharma prachar" (Tagore) **8**:407
"A Diagram of Life" (Swenson) **14**:262
"Diagrams" (Gunn) **26**:195-196, 198
"The Dial Tone" (Nemerov) **24**:262
"Dialectic" (Cassian) **17**:13
*Diálogos del conocimiento* (Aleixandre) **15**:6-7,
12-13, 16-17, 39
"A Dialogu" (Swinburne) **24**:323
"A Dialogue" (Herbert) **4**:130
"Dialogue" (Wright) **14**:343
"A Dialogue between Old England and New"
(Bradstreet) **10**:5, 17, 21, 33
"A Dialogue between the Resolved Soul, and
Created Pleasure" (Marvell) **10**:265, 271,
274, 277, 290-91, 294, 314
"A Dialogue between the Soul and Body"
(Marvell) **10**:265, 271, 274, 290, 313, 316
"A Dialogue between the Two Horses"
(Marvell) **10**:276
"A Dialogue between Thyrsis and Dorinda"
(Marvell) **10**:271, 314
"A Dialogue of Self and Soul" (Yeats) **20**:313,
315-16, 327, 333, 337
"A Dialogue of Watching" (Rexroth) **20**:218
"Dialogue on Women's Rights" (Harper) **21**:198
*Dialogues of Knowledge* (Aleixandre)
See *Diálogos del conocimiento*
"Dialogues of the Dogs" (Burns)
See "The Twa Dogs"
"Diamant du coeur" (Gautier) **18**:130, 157
"Diamantina" (Montale) **13**:138

*The Diamond Cutters, and Other Poems* (Rich)
**5**:350, 352-54, 358, 362-63, 368-69, 388,
392
"The Diamond Merchant" (Wakoski) **15**:348
*The Diamond Merchant* (Wakoski) **15**:325
*Diario del '71* (Montale) **13**:138, 144, 158
*Diario del '71 e del '72* (Montale) **13**:138-39,
152, 160, 168
*Diario del '72* (Montale) **13**:138, 144
*El diario que a diario* (Guillen) **23**:111, 133
*Diaro de un poeta recien casado* (Jimenez)
**7**:197, 201-02, 208, 212, 214
*Diary of '71 and '72* (Montale)
See *Diario del '71 e del '72*
"Diary of a Change" (Rukeyser) **12**:218
"Diary of a Naturalist" (Milosz) **8**:206
*Diary of a Newly-Wed Poet* (Jimenez)
See *Diaro de un poeta recien casado*
"Diaspora" (Lorde) **12**:138, 140
"Il diaul cu la mari" (Pasolini) **17**:253
"Dice mía" (Dario) **15**:113
"Dices que no te acuerdas, Clori, y mientes"
(Juana Ines de la Cruz) **24**:234
"La dicha" (Borges) **22**:95, 99
"Dichterberuf" (Holderlin) **4**:169
"Dichtung" (Baraka) **4**:17
"Dick, a Maggot" (Swift) **9**:296
"The Dictators" (Neruda) **4**:282
"The Dictatorship of the Proletariat" (Baraka)
**4**:38-9
"Dictée en présence du glacier du Rhône"
(Hugo) **17**:91
"The Dictionaries" (Soto) **28**:399
"Didactic Piece" (Bogan) **12**:122
"Dido's Farewell to Aeneas" (Smith) **12**:331
"An die Hofnung" (Holderlin) **4**:148
"An die Jungen Dichter" (Holderlin) **4**:165
"An die Natur" (Holderlin) **4**:142
"An die Verstummten" (Trakl) **20**:236
"An die Vertummten" (Trakl) **20**:232
"Died of Starvation" (Harper) **21**:191, 203, 210,
216
"Died of Wounds" (Sassoon) **12**:262
"Dieu" (Lamartine) **16**:265-66, 272, 274, 277,
285, 290-91
*Dieu* (Hugo) **17**:65-66, 73-74, 81, 84, 86, 91
"The Differences" (Gunn) **26**:224
"Diffugere Nives" (Noyes) **27**:136
"Digging" (Heaney) **18**:200, 206-8, 216, 243
"Dignity of Soul" (Viereck) **27**:281
"Digo que yo no soy un hombre puro"
(Guillen) **23**:123-24
"Diktaren om dikten" (Ekeloef) **23**:90
"Dilemma" (Parker) **28**:362
"Dili" (Pasolini) **17**:251
"El dilitada guerra" (Neruda) **4**:295
"Dimanches" (Laforgue) **14**:72-3, 76, 78
"Dime vencedor rapaz" (Juana Ines de la Cruz)
**24**:234
*Dining* (Nash) **21**:269
"Dining-Room Tea" (Brooke) **24**:77-8, 82, 88
"Dinner Guest: Me" (Hughes) **1**:252
"The Dinner Party" (Lowell) **13**:79
"Il Dio-Caprone" (Pavese) **13**:204, 207
"Dionysus" (Elytis) **21**:119
"Dionysus Encradled" (Sikelianos) **29**:368
"Dionysus in Doubt" (Robinson) **1**:470
*Dionysus in Doubt* (Robinson) **1**:470
*Dios deseado y deseante: Animal de fondo con
numerosos poemas iñeditos* (Jimenez)
**7**:197, 207
"Dios llama al fontanero" (Fuertes) **27**:28
"Diptych with Votive Tablet" (Paz)
See "Preparatory Exercise (Dyptych with
Votive Tablet)"
*Directionscore: Selected and New Poems*
(Madhubuti) **5**:330, 336, 346
"Directive" (Frost) **1**:213, 227
"Director of Alienation" (Ferlinghetti) **1**:187
"Dirge" (Emerson) **18**:69, 102
"Dirge" (Smith) **12**:292, 344
"A Dirge" (Tennyson) **6**:359

"Dirge for a Righteous Kitten" (Lindsay) **23**:281
"Dirge for a Town in France" (Merton) **10**:350
"Dirge for the New Sunrise" (August 6, 1945Sitwell) **3**:327
"A Dirge upon the Death of the Right Valiant Lord, Bernard Stuart" (Herrick) **9**:131
"Dirt and Not Copper" (Stein) **18**:319, 328
"The Dirty Word" (Shapiro) **25**:299
"Dis Aliter Visum" (Browning) **2**:68
"Disabled" (Owen) **19**:336, 354, 357
"The Disappearing Island" (Heaney) **18**:232
"Disappointed" (Enzensberger) **28**:167
"The Disappointment" (Behn) **13**:7, 10-11, 13-14, 16, 25-6, 28
"A Disaster" (Hughes) **7**:142, 160-61
"Disaster" (Valery)
    See "Sinistre"
"The Discharge" (Herbert) **4**:109, 113, 120, 129
"Disciplina antica" (Pavese) **13**:226
"Discipline" (Herbert) **4**:121
"Discipline" (Herbert)
    See "Throw Away Thy Rod"
*The Discipline of the Harp* (Cassian) **17**:6
"The Disclosure" (Levertov) **11**:169
"Discontents in Devon" (Herrick) **9**:108
"Discord" (Swinburne) **24**:324
"Discotheque" (Merrill) **28**:254
*Discours* (Ronsard)
    See *Discours des misères de ce temps*
"Discours à Pierre Lescot" (Ronsard) **11**:266
"Discours au Roy" (Ronsard) **11**:244, 284, 291
"Discours de misères de ce temps" (Ronsard) **11**:248
*Discours des misères de ce temps* (Ronsard) **11**:224, 250
"Discours en forme d'élégie" (Ronsard) **11**:248
"Discovering Michael as the King of Spain" (Wakoski) **15**:329
"The Discovery" (Hardy) **8**:101
"The Discovery of the Madeiras" (Frost) **1**:196, 206
"The Discovery of the Pacific" (Gunn) **26**:207-208
*Discrepancies and Apparitions* (Wakoski) **15**:323-24
"Discretions of Alcibiades" (Pinsky) **27**:162
"Disdaine Returned" (Carew) **29**:32-34
"Disembarking at Quebec" (Atwood) **8**:36, 40
"Disenchantment a Tone Poem" (Aiken) **26**:7, 29
"Disillusionment" (Hughes) **1**:246
"The Disinherited" (Nerval)
    See "El Desdichado"
"The Dismal Chimes of Bells" (Lermontov) **18**:302
"The Dismissal of Tyng" (Harper) **21**:190, 218
"The Disoblig'd Love" (Behn) **13**:20
"Disorder Overtakes Us All Day Long" (Schwartz) **8**:285
"Una Disperata Vitalita" (Pasolini) **17**:257-58, 286, 288-89
"Dispersal" (Sassoon) **12**:259
"Displaced People" (Pavese) **13**:218
"Disputation" (Heine) **25**:170
"The Disquieted Muses" (Plath)
    See "The Disquieting Muses"
"The Disquieting Muses" (Plath) **1**:388, 407
"Dissect This Silence" (Kunitz) **19**:148
"Dissentient Voice" (Davie) **29**:93, 112-15
"The Dissolution" (Donne) **1**:154
"Distance" (Kumin) **15**:223-24
"Distance" (Milosz)
    See "Odlegtose"
"Distance" (Parker) **28**:364
*Distances* (Okigbo) **7**:228, 234-35, 240-41, 243-47, 251, 253, 255
"Distancia" (Borges) **22**:92
"The Distant Winter" (Levine) **22**:212, 216
"Distinctions" (Tomlinson) **17**:314, 328
"The Distressed Damsel" (Smart) **13**:348
"The disturbance" (Piercy) **29**:314
"Dit d'errance" (Cesaire) **25**:31, 38, 44

"Dithyrambes" (Ronsard) **11**:230-32
"Ditty" (Hardy) **8**:90
"Diuturna enfermedad de la Esperanza" (Juana Ines de la Cruz) **24**:225
"La Diva" (Gautier) **18**:135-140
"Divagación" (Dario) **15**:96, 103-05, 119-20
*Divagations* (Mallarme) **4**:202, 210
"The Diver" (Hayden) **6**:187, 193, 198
"The Diverse Causes" (Ondaatje) **28**:292
*Diversifications* (Ammons) **16**:24, 61
*La divina commedia"* (Dante) **21**:48-57, 59, 63, 65-6, 69, 73-7, 80-5, 87-8, 90-3, 95, 97-9, 102, 104-05, 108-11
"Divina psiquis" (Dario) **15**:101
*Divine Comedies: Poems* (Merrill) **28**:220-21, 224-25, 227-32, 246, 260, 263, 272, 281
*Divine Comedy* (Dante)
    See *La divina commedia"*
"The Divine Image" (Blake) **12**:5, 7, 33
"A Divine Mistris" (Carew) **29**:9
*The Divine Pilgrim* (Aiken) **26**:10, 22, 47, 53
*Divine Poems* (Donne) **1**:158
"Divine Psyche" (Dario)
    See "Divina psiquis"
"The Diviner" (Heaney) **18**:200
"Diving into the Wreck" (Rich) **5**:371, 374, 376, 394-95
*Diving into the Wreck: Poems, 1971-1972* (Rich) **5**:360, 362, 365, 367-68, 370-72, 384, 388-90, 393
"Divinità in incognito" (Montale) **13**:133
"Divinitie" (Herbert) **4**:108, 130
"Divinity" (Kinnell) **26**:286
"Division" (Bogan) **12**:98, 106, 121
"The Division" (Hardy) **8**:93
"The Division of Parts" (Sexton) **2**:351, 359-60, 367
"The Divorce Papers" (Sexton) **2**:356, 367
"Divorce, Thy Name Is Woman" (Sexton) **2**:359
"Divorcing" (Levertov) **11**:197
*Dīwān* (Ekeloef)
    See *Dīwān över fursten av Emigón*
*Dīwān över fursten av Emigón* (Ekeloef) **23**:63-5, 67-71, 77-8, 85
"Les djinns" (Hugo) **17**:63, 70, 76
"Do." (Cummings) **5**:106
"Do Józefa Sadzika" (Milosz) **8**:190
"Do not compare: the living are incomparable" (Mandelstam)
    See "Ne sravnivai: zhivushchii nesravnim"
"Do Not Embrace Your Mind's New Negro Friend" (Meredith) **28**:187
"Do Not Touch" (Pasternak) **6**:260
"Do Take Muriel Out" (Smith) **12**:331, 337
"Do the Others Speak of Me Mockingly, Maliciously?" (Schwartz) **8**:306
"Doc Hill" (Masters) **1**:327
"Dock Rats" (Moore) **4**:251
"Docker" (Heaney) **18**:200
"Dockery and Son" (Larkin) **21**:228-31, 233, 236-37, 241
"The Doctor" (Smith) **12**:330
"Doctor Mohawk" (Lindsay) **23**:285, 287
"The Doctor of the Heart" (Sexton) **2**:365
"A Document" (Wright) **14**:356, 362
"Documentary" (Alegria) **26**:
"Dodger Point Lookout" (Snyder) **21**:300
"Does It Matter?" (Sassoon) **12**:267-68, 285
"Does the Road Wind Up-hill all the Way?" (Rossetti) **7**:293
"Dog" (Ferlinghetti) **1**:184
"A Dog Named Ego, the Snowflakes as Kisses" (Schwartz) **8**:307, 314
"De Dog Rose" (McKay) **2**:223
"Dog-Days" (Lowell) **13**:64
"Dogovor" (Lermontov) **18**:303-4
"Dogs Are Shakespearean, Children Are Strangers" (Schwartz) **8**:306, 312
"A Dog's Best Friend Is His Illiteracy" (Nash) **21**:273
"A Dog's Life" (MacDiarmid) **9**:155
"Dolce Ossessione" (Viereck) **27**:259

"Le dolci rime d'amor ch'io solia" (Dante) **21**:88
"The Doll" (Lowell) **13**:84-5
"The Doll" (Wylie) **23**:321
"The Dolls" (Yeats) **20**:336, 340
"A Doll's 'Arabian Nights'" (Lindsay) **23**:264, 277
"Dolly's Mistake" (Clare) **23**:40
"Dolores" (Swinburne) **24**:308-09, 360, 362-63
"Dolorida" (Vigny) **26**:401, 411
*The Dolphin* (Lowell) **3**:224, 229-30, 232-33, 239-41
*A Dome of Many-Coloured Glass* (Lowell) **13**:60, 69
"Dome of Sunday" (Shapiro) **25**:279-80, 283, 286, 295, 305, 308, 310, 315-17, 324-25
"La Domenica Uliva" (Pasolini) **17**:256
*Domesday Book* (Masters) **1**:330-33, 335-36, 339
"Domestic Poem for a Summer Afternoon" (Page) **12**:181
*Domik v Kolomne* (Pushkin) **10**:366, 381-86, 391, 400
"Domiki staroi Moskvy" (Tsvetaeva) **14**:318
"Domination of Black" (Stevens) **6**:293-94
"Le Dompteur de lions se souvient" (Tzara) **27**:224
"Don du poème" (Mallarme) **4**:196
"Don Juan" (Clare) **23**:26
*Don Juan* (Byron) **16**:77-88, 90-2, 95-102, 106-08, 110-13, 115-17, 120
"Don Juan aux enfers" (Baudelaire) **1**:47
"Don Juan in Hades" (Baudelaire)
    See "Don Juan aux enfers"
"Done Into Verse" (Belloc) **24**:43-4
"The Donkey" (Chesterton) **28**:101
"The Donkey" (Smith) **12**:318
"Donna Clara" (Heine) **25**:145
"Donne che avete intelletto d'amore" (Dante) **21**:73, 86
"Donne perdute" (Pavese) **13**:225
"Donneycarney" (Joyce)
    See "XXXI"
"Don't Be Cross Amanda" (Nash) **21**:271
*Don't Cry, Scream* (Madhubuti) **5**:324-25, 328, 336, 338, 340-46
*Don't Go Out of the Door* (Li Ho) **13**:42
"Don't Grow Old" (Ginsberg) **4**:84
"Don't Laugh at my Prophetic Anguish" (Lermontov) **18**:281
"Don't Look Now But Mary Is Everbody" (Viereck) **27**:258, 274, 278
"Don't Trust Yourself" (Lermontov) **18**:281
"Don't Wanna Be" (Sanchez) **9**:229
"Doom" (Dario)
    See "Lo fatal"
"Doom Is the House without the Door" (Dickinson) **1**:111
"Dooms-day" (Herbert) **4**:131
*The Door in the Wall* (Tomlinson) **17**:360-61
*Door into the Dark* (Heaney) **18**:191, 194-95, 199-201, 203, 205-6, 209, 215, 220, 225-26, 228
"Doors, Doors, Doors" (Sexton) **2**:349
"Dopa una fuga" (Montale) **13**:134
"Dope" (Baraka) **4**:40
"Dora" (Tennyson) **6**:360
"Dora Markus" (Montale) **13**:106, 113-14, 119
"Dora Williams" (Masters) **1**:347
"La dormeuse" (Valery) **9**:365-66, 374, 387, 392-93, 396
"Dornenkranz" (Celan) **10**:128-30
"Dorothée" (Baudelaire)
    See "La belle Dorothée"
"Las dos cartas" (Guillen) **23**:126
"Dos niños" (Guillen) **23**:139
"Dos vidas" (Aleixandre) **15**:7
"Dotage" (Herbert) **4**:130
"Dotterel" (Wright) **14**:348
*The Double Axe and Other Poems* (Jeffers) **17**:123-24, 130, 136, 146-47

Title Index

"The Double Chamber" (Baudelaire)
    See "La chambre double"
"The Double Dream of Spring" (Ashbery)
    **26**:115
*The Double Dream of Spring* (Ashbery) **26**:115,
    118-119, 124-125, 128, 130, 138, 144, 148-
    149, 153-154, 169
"Double Feature" (Hayden) **6**:194-95
"The Double Image" (Sexton) **2**:350, 355-56,
    359, 361-63, 372
"Double Image" (Wright) **14**:348
*The Double Image* (Levertov) **11**:163-64
"Double Monologue" (Rich) **5**:374
"Double Negative" (Nemerov) **24**:289
"Double Ode" (Rukeyser) **12**:225
*Double Persephone* (Atwood) **8**:21
"The Double Standard" (Harper) **21**:187, 191,
    207
*The Double Tree: Selected Poems, 1942-1976*
    (Wright) **14**:366
"The Double Voices" (Atwood) **8**:16, 32
"Doubled Mirrors" (Rexroth) **20**:217
"Double-Nine Festival" (Li Po) **29**:183
"The Doubtful Passage" (Cardenal)
    See "El estrecho dudoso"
"Doubts" (Brooke) **24**:57, 85
"The Dougtful Passage"
    See "El estrecho dudoso"
"Les Dous Amanz" (Marie de France) **22**:258,
    269, 271-73, 275
"The Dove Breeder" (Hughes) **7**:116
"The Dove in Spring" (Stevens) **6**:313
*The Dove of Popular Flight—Elegies* (Guillen)
    See *La paloma de vuelo popular: Elegiás*
"Dover" (Auden) **1**:16
"Dover Beach" (Arnold) **5**:8, 13, 16-18, 35, 38,
    47, 49, 53, 58, 64-5
"Dov'era il tennis" (Montale) **13**:160
"Down" (Graves) **6**:142, 144
"Down at the bottom of things" (Piercy) **29**:314
"Down, Wanton, Down!" (Graves) **6**:151, 153,
    165
"The Downs" (Bridges) **28**:83
"The Downs" (Bridges) **28**:67
*dq1Indentured"* (Wylie) **23**:305
"Words of Comfort to the Scratched on a
    Mirror#dq2 (Parker) **28**:361
"Dr. Swift to Mr. Pope while He Was Writing
    the Dunciad" (Swift) **9**:295
"The Draft Horse" (Frost) **1**:213
*A Draft of Eleven New Cantos*
    (XXXI-XLIPound) **4**:321-22, 353, 357-58
*A Draft of Shadows* (Paz)
    See *Pasado en claro*
*Drafts and Fragments of Cantos CX to CXVII*
    (Pound) **4**:352-54
"Dragon" (Ondaatje) **28**:298
"The Dragon and the Undying" (Sassoon)
    **12**:278
"The Dragon and the Unicorn" (Rexroth)
    **20**:204, 221
*The Dragon and the Unicorn* (Rexroth) **20**:181-
    82, 184, 192, 205, 208, 210, 212-14
"Dragonfly" (Bogan) **12**:107-08
*Drake* (Noyes) **27**:114-15, 119, 123, 125, 127,
    134
"A Drama of Exile" (Browning) **6**:6, 20-1, 26,
    31, 34, 46
*Dramatic Lyrics* (Browning) **2**:26, 35, 66, 94
"Dramatic Poem: Voice of Silence" (Ishikawa)
    See "Gekishi: Chimmoku no koe"
*Dramatic Romances and Lyrics* (Browning)
    **2**:94
*Dramatis Personae* (Browning) **2**:34, 45, 94-5
*Dramatis Personae* (Yeats) **20**:328
"Drawing Lessons" (Nemerov) **24**:302-03
"The Drawn-Out War" (Neruda)
    See "El dilitada guerra"
"The Dream" (Berry) **28**:38
"A Dream" (Blake) **12**:7, 33-4
"The Dream" (Bogan) **12**:111
"The Dream" (Browning) **6**:19

"A Dream" (Bryant) **20**:15
"A Dream" (Burns) **6**:89
"The Dream" (Byron) **16**:73, 76
"Dream" (Heaney) **18**:201
"Dream" (Juana Ines de la Cruz)
    See "Primero sueño"
"The Dream" (Roethke) **8**:
"The Dream" (Sassoon) **12**:267
"The Dream" (Stryk) **27**:204
"A Dream" (Swenson) **14**:288
"Dream" (Tagore)
    See "Svapna"
"Dream" (Wright) **14**:367, 373
"The Dream, 1863" (Hayden) **6**:180, 188
"Dream and Madness" (Trakl)
    See "Traum und Umnachtung"
"Dream Boogie" (Hughes) **1**:266
"A Dream Deferred" (Hughes) **1**:266
"Dream Drumming" (Rukeyser) **12**:222
"A Dream in Three Colors" (McGuckian) **27**:90
"The Dream Language of Fergus"
    (McGuckian) **27**:83, 88-90
"A Dream Lies Dead" (Parker) **28**:363
*The Dream of a Common Language: Poems,
    1974-1977* (Rich) **5**:373-76, 378, 384, 389
"The Dream of Angling the Dream of Cool
    Rain" (Wakoski) **15**:365
"A Dream of Comparison" (Smith) **12**:330,
    332-33, 345, 352
"A Dream of Fair Women" (Tennyson) **6**:353,
    359-60
"The Dream of Knowledge" (Schwartz) **8**:297,
    311
"A Dream of Nourishment" (Smith) **12**:326
"A Dream of Small Children" (Song) **21**:341,
    343
"Dream of the Future" (Jeffers) **17**:141
"A Dream of Whitman Paraphrased,
    Recognized, and Made More Vivid by
    Renoir" (Schwartz) **8**:318
"Dream of Youth" (Tagore)
    See "Yauvan-svapna"
"A Dream or No" (Hardy) **8**:135
"A Dream" (RealEkeloef) **23**:80
"Dream Variations" (Hughes) **1**:248
"A Dream within a Dream" (Poe) **1**:434
"Dreamdust" (Hughes) **1**:241
"The Dreame" (Donne) **1**:147, 152
"The Dreame" (Herrick) **9**:109
"The Dreamer" (Pushkin) **10**:407
"The Dreamer" (Tennyson) **6**:372
"Dreamers" (Sassoon) **12**:284, 286
"The Dreamer's Song" (Ortiz) **17**:245
"The Dream-Follower" (Hardy) **8**:108
*Dreaming of Butterflies* (Hagiwara Sakutaro)
    See *Dreaming of Butterflies*
"Dreaming of Hair" (Lee) **24**:242, 247
"Dream-Land" (Poe) **1**:433-34, 436, 438
"Dreams" (Giovanni) **19**:110
"Dreams" (Poe) **1**:436
"Dreams about Clothes" (Merrill) **28**:254
"Dreams in War Time" (Lowell) **13**:84
"Dreams of Suicide," (Meredith) **28**:199, 205
*Dreamtigers* (Borges)
    See *El hacedor*
"Drei Blicke in einen Opal" (Trakl) **20**:261-62
"Dressing to Wait a Table" (McKay) **2**:205
"Dried Marjoram" (Lowell) **13**:61
"The Drifter off Tarentum" (Kipling) **3**:183
*Drifting into War* (Bissett) **14**:10, 33
"A Driftwood Altar" (Ashbery) **26**:163
"Drink to Me Only with Thine Eyes" (Jonson)
    **17**:170, 180
"The Drinker" (Lowell) **3**:212
"Drinking Alone by Moonlight" (Li Po) **29**:188
"Driving Gloves" (Wakoski) **15**:347
"Driving Home the Cows" (Reese) **29**:330
"Dropping Eyelids Among the Aerial Ash"
    (Ammons) **16**:39
"Drought" (Wright) **14**:353
"Drought Year" (Wright) **14**:366
"The Drowned Child" (Gluck) **16**:129-30, 150

"The Drowning Poet" (Merrill) **28**:225
"Drozhzhi mira dorogie" (Mandelstam) **14**:153
"Drug Store" (Shapiro) **25**:268, 295, 319, 322
"Druidic Rimes" (Nemerov) **24**:301
"A Drumlin Woodchuck" (Frost) **1**:213
"Drummer Hodge" (Hardy) **8**:121
"Drums" (Okigbo) **7**:234
*Drum-Taps* (Whitman) **3**:389, 414, 418
*A Drunk Man Looks at the Thistle*
    (MacDiarmid) **9**:151-52, 158, 167-70,
    173, 175, 181, 186, 189-93
"The Drunkard" (Sitwell) **3**:299
"The Drunkard's Child" (Harper) **21**:191, 210,
    216
"The Drunkard's Funeral" (Lindsay) **23**:269,
    283-84
"The Drunkards in the Streetn" (Lindsay)
    **23**:284
"Drunken Americans" (Ashbery) **26**:167
*The Drunken Boat* (Rimbaud)
    See *Le bateau ivre*
"The Drunken Fisherman" (Lowell) **3**:199-200,
    202, 204, 212
"The Dry Salvages" (Eliot) **5**:164-65, 167-69,
    180-81, 183, 186, 210
"Dryads" (Sassoon) **12**:240, 275
"Du coton dans les oreilles" (Apollinaire) **7**:22
"Du haut de la muraille de Paris" (Hugo) **17**:100
"Du liegst" (Celan) **10**:98
"Du sei wei du" (Celan) **10**:100-01
"Dublin Georgian" (Davie) **29**:110, 120
"Dublin Georgian (2)" (Davie) **29**:121
"Dublinesque" (Larkin) **21**:237, 244
"Dubrovnik October 14, 1980, 10:45 p. m."
    (Ginsberg) **4**:62
"The Duchess Potatoes" (Wakoski) **15**:330
"Duck Blind" (Hass) **16**:217
"A Duck for Dinner" (Stevens) **6**:322
"The Duckpond" (Stryk) **27**:188, 195-97, 202-
    03, 206
"Due donne in cima de la mente mia" (Dante)
    **21**:74
"Due nel crepuscolo" (Montale) **13**:107, 150
"Due sigarette" (Pavese) **13**:225-28
"Duel" (Hagiwara Sakutaro) **18**:167
"The Dug-Out" (Sassoon) **12**:281, 283
*Duineser Elegien* (Rilke) **2**:268-69, 279-82,
    285-87, 294-95
*Duino Elegies/Elegies* (Rilke)
    See *Duineser Elegien*
*Duke of Albany* (Skelton) **25**:330
"Dulce Et Decorum Est" (Owen) **19**:347, 353,
    357, 359-61, 364-65, 370-71
"Dulcia Linquimus Arva" (Borges) **22**:79
"Dully Gumption's Addendum" (Hughes) **7**:120
"Dulnesse" (Herbert) **4**:112
"La dulzura del ángelus" (Dario) **15**:81, 96
"Duma" (Lermontov) **18**:268-69, 279, 281, 283,
    297, 304
"Duncan" (Gunn) **26**:228
"Duncan Gray" (Burns) **6**:57, 59, 100
*Dunciad* (Pope) **26**:304-305, 314-17, 319, 321-
    22, 326-27, 334, 338-40, 357-61
*Dunciad in Four Books* (Pope) **26**:358-59
"Dunciad Variorum" (Pope) **26**:356-61
"Duncton Hill" (Belloc) **24**:10, 49
"The Dungeon" (Wordsworth) **4**:373
"Duns Scotus" (Lowell) **3**:201
"Duns Scotus's Oxford" (Hopkins) **15**:144
"Duranta asha" (Tagore) **8**:407
"Duration" (Paz) **1**:355
"Durham in March" (Tomlinson) **17**:361
"During a Solar Eclipse" (Nemerov) **24**:288
"During a Transatlantic Call" (Lowell) **3**:241
"During Fever" (Lowell) **3**:206, 220, 243, 245
"During the Eichmann Trial" (Levertov) **11**:169,
    193
"During the Passaic Strike of 1926"
    (Zukofsky) **11**:351, 396
"During Wind and Rain" (Hardy) **8**:88, 113
"Dusha" (Pasternak) **6**:267, 285
"Dusha moja mrachna" (Lermontov) **18**:302

"Dust" (Brooke) **24**:57
"The Dust" (Reese) **29**:330, 333
"Dust" (Wright) **14**:379
"Dust Bowl" (Hughes) **1**:240
"Dust in the Eyes" (Frost) **1**:195
"Dust of Snow" (Frost) **1**:195, 218
"Dusting" (Dove) **6**:111, 113
"Dusty Braces" (Snyder) **21**:293
"Dutch Graves in Bucks County" (Stevens) **6**:302
"Dutch Painters" (Zagajewski) **27**:403
"Duty is my Lobster" (Smith) **12**:340
"Dva brata" (Lermontov) **18**:299
"Dva sokola" (Lermontov) **18**:288
*Dvenadsat* (Blok) **21**:8-12, 16-17, 21-2, 26-9, 31, 33-9, 41-3
"Dvukh stanov ne beots, a— esli gost sluchainyi" (Tsvetaeva) **14**:325
"Dyâli" (Cesaire) **25**:40
"Dying Away" (Meredith) **28**:200
"The Dying Bondman" (Harper) **21**:187, 207
"The Dying Christian" (Harper) **21**:208, 215-16
"The Dying Mother" (Harper) **21**:197
"The Dying Queen" (Harper) **21**:198
"The Dying Swan" (Tennyson) **6**:359, 389-91
"The Dykes" (Kipling) **3**:182
*The Dynasts: A Drama of the Napoleonic Wars* (Hardy) **8**:79-81, 85-7, 95-6, 104, 108, 111, 121-22
*The Dynasty of Raghu* (Kalidasa)
    See *Raghuvaṃśa*
"Dytiscus" (MacDiarmid) **9**:157, 183
"Dyvers Dothe Use" (Wyatt) **27**:316
"Dzhulio" (Lermontov) **18**:300
"E. P. Ode Pour L'Election de son Sepulchre" (Pound) **4**:319
"Each and All" (Emerson) **18**:84, 94-96, 98-101, 107
"Each Bird Walking" (Gallagher) **9**:44
"Each Day of Summer" (Swenson) **14**:276
"Each of You" (Lorde) **12**:154
"Eagle" (Kunitz) **19**:147
"The Eagle and the Mole" (Wylie) **23**:301, 309, 322, 327, 334
"Eagle Confin'd in a College Court" (Smart) **13**:341
*Eagle or Sun?* (Paz) **1**:354, 359
"Eagle Poem" (Harjo) **27**:67
"The Eagle That Is Forgotten" (Lindsay) **23**:277, 288, 294, 296
"The Eagle-Feather Fan" (Momaday) **25**:217
"Early Chronology" (Sassoon) **12**:245
"Early Evening Quarrel" (Hughes) **1**:247
"Early Lynching" (Sandburg) **2**:330
"Early March" (Sassoon) **12**:254, 259
"An Early Martyr" (Williams) **7**:353, 368
*An Early Martyr, and Other Poems* (Williams) **7**:350, 399, 402
"The Early Morning" (Belloc) **24**:5, 34
"Early Morning: Cape Cod" (Swenson) **14**:276
"The Early Morning Light" (Schwartz) **8**:294
"Early Poems" (Noyes) **27**:138
*Early Poems* (Crane) **3**:90-1
*Early Poems, 1935-1955* (Paz) **1**:373, 375
*Early Verse of Rudyard Kipling, 1877-99: Unpublished, Uncollected, and Rarely Collected Poems* (Kipling) **3**:193
"The Earrings" (Montale)
    See "Gli orecchini"
"Ears in the Turrets Hear" (Thomas) **2**:379
"Earth" (Bryant) **20**:4, 17, 19, 35, 47
"The Earth" (Noyes) **27**:129
"The Earth" (Sexton) **2**:372, 374
"Earth" (Toomer) **7**:333
"Earth Again" (Milosz) **8**:209
"Earth and Fire" (Berry) **28**:11
"Earth and I Give You Turquoise" (Momaday) **25**:188, 193, 207
*The Earth Gods* (Gibran) **9**:71, 75, 80
"The Earth in Snow" (Blok) **21**:4-5
"The Earth is Called Juan" (Neruda)
    See "La tierra se llama Juan"

"the Earth Lantern" (Bissett) **14**:7
"Earth Psalm" (Levertov) **11**:170
"Earth Triumphant" (Aiken) **26**:7
*Earth Triumphant* (Aiken) **26**:21, 50
"Earth Walk" (Meredith) **28**:214
*Earth Walk: New and Selected Poems* (Meredith) **28**:178, 180-81, 194-95, 207, 210, 213-15
"Earth Your Dancing Place" (Swenson) **14**:283
*Earthlight* (Breton) **15**:73-4
"Earthly Creatures" (Wylie) **23**:311
*The Earth-Owl and Other Moon-People* (Hughes) **7**:120
"Earth's Answer" (Blake) **12**:7, 35, 44
"Earth's Bubbles" (Blok) **21**:14, 24, 31
"Earth's Children Cleave to Earth" (Bryant) **20**:16
"Earth-Song" (Emerson) **18**:79, 88
"Earthy Anecdote" (Stevens) **6**:294
"East Coker" (Eliot) **5**:164, 167-69, 171, 179-82, 198, 210
"East Coker" (Roethke) **15**:279
"East of Suez" (Kipling) **3**:179
"East of the Sun West of the Moon" (Wakoski) **15**:348
"East River" (Swenson) **14**:254
*East Slope* (Paz)
    See *Ladera este*
"The East that is Now Pale, the East that is Now Silent" (Bely)
    See "Vostok  pobledneuskii,  vostok onemesvshii"
"East, West, North, and South of a Man" (Lowell) **13**:87
*East Wind* (Lowell) **13**:76, 84-5
"Eastbourne" (Montale) **13**:106, 109, 120-21, 128-29, 148, 152
*An East-End Coffee-Stall* (Noyes) **27**:140
"An East-End Curate" (Hardy) **8**:101
"Easter" (Herbert) **4**:100, 120
"Easter" (Kinnell) **26**:238, 279
"Easter" (Studwell)
    See "Easter: Wahiawa, 1959"
"Easter 1916" (Yeats) **20**:311, 313-14, 323, 325, 327, 349
*Easter Day* (Browning) **2**:32, 45, 71-2, 75
"Easter Eve 1945" (Rukeyser) **12**:225
"Easter Hymn" (Housman) **2**:184
"Easter Moon and Owl" (Wright) **14**:373, 375
"Easter Morning" (Ammons) **16**:30-2, 46, 63-4
"Easter of the Greeks" (Sikelianos) **29**:366-67
"Easter: Wahiawa, 1959" (Song) **21**:331, 335, 338, 340, 342-43, 350
"Easter Wings" (Herbert) **4**:114, 120, 130
*Eastern Lyrics* (Hugo)
    See *Les orientales*
*Eastern Slope* (Paz)
    See *Ladera este*
"Eastern War Time" (Rich) **5**:398
"Eastport to Block Island" (Rich) **5**:352
"Eating Fire" (Atwood) **8**:27-8
"Ebar phirao more" (Tagore) **8**:409
"Ébauche d'un serpent" (Valery) **9**:352-53, 365-67, 371, 374, 384, 387, 390, 394-99
*Ebb and Flow* (Ishikawa) **10**:212-13, 215
"éboulis" (Cesaire) **25**:45
"Ecce Puer" (Joyce) **22**:140-41, 147-48, 151-52
"The Ecclesiast" (Ashbery) **26**:114
*Ecclesiastical Sketches* (Wordsworth) **4**:399
*Ecclesiastical Sonnets* (Wordsworth)
    See *Ecclesiastical Sketches*
"Echo" (Lorde) **12**:155
"Echo" (Rossetti) **7**:280-81
"Echo" (Tagore)
    See "Pratidhyani"
"Echoes" (Carroll) **18**:46
"The Echoing Green" (Blake) **12**:7
"L'eclatante victoire de Saarebrück" (Rimbaud) **3**:283
"L'eclatante victorie de Sarrebruck" (Rimbaud) **3**:283
"El eclipse" (Jimenez) **7**:200

"Eclogue" (Ronsard) **11**:262
"Eclogue" (Stevens) **6**:333
"Eclogue 4" (Vergil) **12**:363, 370, 372, 382-85, 392
"Eclogue 6" (Vergil) **12**:365, 371
"Eclogue 10" (Vergil) **12**:370-71
"Eclogue I: The Months" (Bridges) **28**:67, 84
"Eclogue II" (Bridges) **28**:87-8
"Eclogue IV: Winter" (Brodsky) **9**:22, 28-9
"An Eclogue, or Pastorall between Endymion Porter and Lycidas Herrick" (Herrick) **9**:86
"Eclogue V: Summer" (Brodsky) **9**:21, 28
"Eclogues" (Herrick) **9**:89
*Eclogues* (Petrarch) **8**:246
*Eclogues* (Vergil) **12**:365, 370-72, 375, 383, 388
"Ecologue" (Ginsberg) **4**:54, 82, 85, 89
"Economia de Tahuantinsuyo" (Cardenal) **22**:127-28, 132
"Economic Man" (Nemerov) **24**:289
"The Economy of Tahuantinsuyo"
    See "Economia de Tahuantinsuyo"
"Ecoutez la chanson bien douce" (Verlaine) **2**:416
"Écrit sur la Porte" (Perse) **23**:231
"Les Écrits s'en vont" (Breton) **15**:51
"The Ecstasy" (Carruth) **10**:71
"The Ecstasy" (Donne)
    See "The Exstasie"
"Eddi's Service" (Kipling) **3**:183
"An Eddy" (Carew) **29**:10, 48
"Eden" (Tomlinson) **17**:342, 354
"Eden" (Wright) **14**:336, 341
"Eden Retold" (Shapiro) **25**:290
"The Edge" (Gluck) **16**:125, 153
"Edge" (Plath) **1**:391, 393, 397
"The Edge" (Stryk) **27**:198, 203
"Edge of Love" (Aleixandre) **15**:19, 23
"Edgehill Fight" (Kipling) **3**:183
"Edina, Scotia's Darling Seat!" (Burns) **6**:74
"Edinstvennye dni" (Pasternak) **6**:286
"Editorial Impressions" (Sassoon) **12**:268
"Edmonton, thy cemetery . . ." (Smith) **12**:293, 300
"Education" (Madhubuti) **5**:338
"Education a Failure" (Williams) **7**:370
"Education and Government" (Gray)
    See "Essay on the Alliance of Education and Government"
"Edward Gray" (Tennyson) **6**:358
"Edward III" (Blake)
    See "King Edward the Third"
"The Eel" (Montale)
    See "L'anguilla"
"Eel" (Rukeyser) **12**:211
"The Eemis Stane" (MacDiarmid) **9**:158, 187
"eet me alive" (Bissett) **14**:34
"The Effect" (Sassoon) **12**:285
"The Effectual Marriage" (Loy) **16**:333
"Effort at Speech" (Meredith) **28**:214
*Effort at Speech* (Meredith) **28**:216-17
*Efterlämnade dikter* (Ekeloef) **23**:78
*The Egerton Ms* (Wyatt) **27**:360
"The Egg" (Gluck) **16**:125, 138-39
"The Egg and the Machine" (Frost) **1**:203
"Egg-Head" (Hughes) **7**:116, 118, 135, 140, 161
"Eggs" (Hagiwara Sakutaro) **18**:168
"Eggs" (Olds) **22**:311, 338
"Eggs and Nestlings" (Wright) **14**:348
"Ego" (Shapiro) **25**:320
"Ego Tripping" (Giovanni) **19**:118, 123, 141
"The Egoist" (Neruda)
    See "El egoísta"
"El egoísta" (Neruda) **4**:290
*Egorushka* (Tsvetaeva) **14**:326-27
*Ego-Tripping and Other Poems for Young People* (Giovanni) **19**:123, 136
"Egy ev" (Illyes) **16**:239
"Ehcu Fugaces" (Belloc) **24**:10
"ehre sei der sellerie" (Enzensberger) **28**:140

"The Eichmann Trial" (Levertov)
  See "During the Eichmann Trial"
"VIII" (Joyce) **22**:144-45, 153, 167, 170, 173
"8 Ahau" (Cardenal)
  See "Katun 8 Ahau"
"Eight Drinking Immortals" (Tu Fu) **9**:330
"Eight Laments" (Tu Fu) **9**:333-38, 341-42
"Eight Observations on the Nature of Eternity"
  (Tomlinson) **17**:328
"Eight O'Clock" (Housman) **2**:162, 164, 169,
  182
"Eight Years After" (Davie) **29**:108
"XVIII" (Joyce) **22**:145, 165, 167, 169
"18 Nov 71" (Brutus) **24**:123
*18 Poems* (Thomas) **2**:378, 382, 384
"Eighteen West Eleventh Street" (Merrill)
  **28**:222, 244, 258
"1887" (Housman) **2**:192, 194
"1805" (Graves) **6**:152
"The Eighth Crusade" (Masters) **1**:330
"Eighth Duino Elegy" (Rilke) **2**:291, 293
*Eighth Isthmian* (Pindar)
  See *Isthmian 8*
*Eighth Olympian* (Pindar)
  See *Olympian 8*
*Eighth Pythian* (Pindar)
  See *Pythian 8*
*80 Flowers* (Zukofsky) **11**:392
"84th Street, Edmonton" (Atwood) **8**:9
"Einstein Freud & Jack" (Nemerov) **24**:302
"Der Einzige" (Holderlin) **4**:150, 156, 166
"Ekloga 4-aya: Zimnyaya" (Brodsky)
  See "Eclogue IV: Winter"
"Eldorado" (Poe) **1**:433, 439
"Eleanore" (Tennyson) **6**:350
"Elected Silence" (Sassoon) **12**:258
"Electra on Azalea Path" (Plath) **1**:410-11
"Electra-Orestes" (H. D.) **5**:305
"Electric Elegy" (Zagajewski) **27**:389
"The Electric Tram" (Noyes) **27**:122
"Electrical Storm" (Hayden) **6**:186, 194-95
"Elegía" (Borges) **22**:95
*Elegía* (Neruda) **4**:287
*Elegía a Jacques Roumain* (Guillen) **23**:133
"Elegía a Jesús Menéndez" (Guillen) **23**:100-
  101, 125
"Elegía moderna del motivo cursi" (Guillen)
  **23**:109-10, 128
"An Elegiac Fragment" (Duncan) **2**:101
"An Elegiac Poem on the Death of George
  Whitefield" (Wheatley) **3**:336, 340, 343,
  348
"Elegiac Stanzas" (Wordsworth) **4**:406-07
"Elegiacs" (Tennyson) **6**:385
"Elégie" (Gautier) **18**:135
"Elegie" (Goethe) **5**:248, 251
"Elegie IV: The Perfume" (Donne) **1**:130
"Elegie VIII: The Comparison" (Donne) **1**:124
"Elegie XI: The Bracelet" (Donne) **1**:122
"Elegie XII: His parting from her" (Donne)
  **1**:130
"Elegie XVI: On his mistris" (Donne) **1**:130
"Elegie à Cassandre" (Ronsard) **11**:246, 248
"L'Elégie à Guillaume des Autels sur le
  Tumulte d'Amboise" (Ronsard) **11**:248
"Elegie à Hélène" (Ronsard) **11**:229
"l'elegie à J. Hurault, sieur de la pitardière"
  (Ronsard) **11**:249
"Elegie á Janet, peintre du Roi" (Ronsard)
  **11**:243, 247
"L'elégie à Lovs de Masures" (Ronsard) **11**:248
"Elégie à Marie Stuart" (Ronsard) **11**:224, 237
"Elegie A M. A. De Muret" (Ronsard) **11**:246,
  248
"Elegie à son livre" (Ronsard) **11**:248
"Elegie au Seigneur Baillon, trésorier de
  l'Epargne du Roi" (Ronsard) **11**:249
"Elegie au Seigneur L'Huillier" (Ronsard)
  **11**:242
"Elégie de minuit" (Senghor) **25**:255
"Elégie des circoncis" (Senghor) **25**:255
"Elégie des eaux" (Senghor) **25**:255, 258

"Elégie des Saudades" (Senghor) **25**:233
"Elegie du printemps" (Ronsard) **11**:242, 250
"Elegie du Verre à Jan Brinon" (Ronsard)
  **11**:247
"Elegie en forme d'épitaphe d'Antoine
  Chateignier" (Ronsard) **11**:246, 248
"An Elegie on the La: Pen: sent to my
  Mistresse out of France" (Carew) **29**:61-
  62, 71-73
"Elegie on the Lady Jane Pawlet, Marchion: of
  Winton" (Jonson) **17**:206
"Elégie pour Georges Pompidou" (Senghor)
  **25**:254-55, 257-59
"Elégie pour Jean-Marie" (Senghor) **25**:255-56,
  259
"elégie pour Martin Luther King" (Senghor)
  **25**:258
"An Elegie upon that Honourable and
  renowned Knight Sir Philip Sidney, who
  was untimely slaine at the Seige of
  Zutphon, Annol586" (Bradstreet) **10**:31,
  48, 54
"An Elegie upon the Death of the Deane of
  Pauls, Dr. John Donne" (Carew) **29**:17,
  22, 63, 75
"Elegie upon the untimely death of the
  incomparable Prince Henry" (Donne)
  **1**:122
"Elegier I" (Ekeloef) **23**:76
*Elegies* (Donne) **1**:129-30, 147
*Elegies* (Jimenez)
  See *Elejías*
*Elegies* (Ovid)
  See *Tristia*
*Elegies* (Rilke) **2**:280-82, 285-87, 294
*Elegies* (Rukeyser) **12**:207, 211-13
"Elegies And Epistles" (Wylie) **23**:311
"Elegies for Paradise Valley" (Hayden) **6**:191-
  92, 194-95
*Elégies majeures* (Senghor) **25**:254-56, 258
*Elegies of Gloom* (Ovid)
  See *Tristia*
*The Elegies of Jutting Rock* (Elytis)
  See *Ta eleýa tis Oxópetras*
"Elegija" (Pushkin) **10**:413-14
"Elegy" (Berry) **28**:14-17, 19, 31
"Elegy" (Bridges) **28**:67, 87
"Elegy" (Ekeloef)
  See *En Mölna-elegi*
"Elegy" (Heaney) **18**:241-43
"Elegy" (Jonson) **17**:175
"Elegy" (Marvell)
  See "Poem upon the Death of O. C."
"Elegy" (Pushkin)
  See "Elegija"
"Elegy" (Roethke) **15**:267
"Elegy" (Walker) **20**:278-79
"Elegy" (Zagajewski) **27**:396
*Elegy* (Neruda)
  See *Elegía*
"Elegy before Death: At Settignano" (Day
  Lewis) **11**:151
"Elegy for a Dead Soldier" (Shapiro) **25**:263,
  269, 277, 279-80, 288-89, 295, 310, 316
"Elegy for a friend killed in the civil war"
  (Paz) **1**:352
"Elegy for a Long-haired Student" (Stryk)
  **27**:203
"Elegy for a Nature Poet" (Nemerov) **24**:293
"Elegy for Alto" (Okigbo) **7**:231, 235, 244
"An Elegy for D. H. Lawrence" (Williams)
  **7**:350, 354-55
"Elegy for Father Stephen" (Merton) **10**:344
"An Elegy for Five Old Ladies" (Merton)
  **10**:333, 343
"Elegy for Jane" (Roethke) **15**:309
"Elegy for John Donne" (Brodsky)
  See "The Great Elegy for John Donne"
"Elegy for N. N." (Milosz) **8**:186, 207
"Elegy: For Robert Lowell" (Brodsky) **9**:7, 8
"Elegy for Slit-Drum" (Okigbo) **7**:233, 235,
  244

"Elegy for the Monastery Barn" (Merton)
  **10**:331, 342, 349
"Elegy for Y. Z." (Milosz) **8**:174, 198, 203
*Elegy in April and September* (Owen) **19**:366
"Elegy of the Wind" (Okigbo) **7**:235
"Elegy: On a Lady Whom Grief for the Death
  of Her Betrothed Killed" (Bridges) **28**:87
*Elegy on Dead Fashion* (Sitwell) **3**:295, 300,
  304
"Elegy on Poor Mailie" (Burns)
  See "The Death and Dying Words of Poor
  Mailie"
"Elegy on the Death of King James" (Finch)
  **21**:169
"Elegy on the Death of Robert Ruisseaux"
  (Burns) **6**:67
"Elegy on the Dust" (Gunn) **26**:190-191, 193,
  203
"Elegy on the Ruins of Pickworth Rutlandshire
  Hastily composed and written with a
  Pencil on the Spot'" (Clare) **23**:12
"Elegy: The Summer-House on the Mound"
  (Bridges) **28**:80, 84
"Elegy to the Memory of an Unfortunate
  Lady" (Jonson) **17**:206
"Elegy to the Memory of an Unfortunate
  Lady" (Pope) **26**:314, 319, 324
"Elegy Written in a Country Churchyard"
  (Gray) **2**:134-37, 139-43, 145, 148, 151-
  52, 155
"Elegy Written on a Frontporch" (Shapiro)
  **25**:295
"Elegy XLII" (Jonson)
  See "Elegy XLII"
*Elejías* (Jimenez) **7**:184
"Element" (Page) **12**:168, 170
"Elemental Metamorphosis" (Kunitz) **19**:155
*The Elemental Odes* (Neruda)
  See *Odas elementales*
*Elementary Odes* (Neruda)
  See *Odas elementales*
"The Elements" (Bradstreet)
  See "The Four Elements"
"The Elements" (Emerson) **18**:77
"Elements And Angels" (Wylie) **23**:311
*The Elements of San Joaquin* (Soto) **28**:369,
  371, 373, 376, 383-85
"Eleonora Duse" (Lowell) **13**:91
"Elephants" (Moore) **4**:235, 260
"Elévation" (Baudelaire) **1**:46, 70
"Elevator Boy" (Hughes) **1**:263
"XI" (Joyce) **22**:136, 138, 145, 164, 169-70
"11/8" (Williams) **7**:368
"Eleventh Century Doors" (Kumin) **15**:180
"11th Floor, West 4th Street" (Swenson) **14**:261
*Eleventh Nemean* (Pindar)
  See *Nemean 11*
*Eleventh Olympian* (Pindar)
  See *Olympian 11*
*Eleventh Pythian* (Pindar)
  See *Pythian 11*
"El-Hajj Malik El-Shabazz" (Hayden) **6**:176,
  180-81, 187, 196
"Eliduc" (Marie de France) **22**:239, 245, 248,
  258, 265, 268-75, 278, 281-82, 294
"The Elixir" (Herbert) **4**:134
"Eliza Harris" (Harper) **21**:190, 192, 194, 201,
  204-05, 215
"Elizabeth" (Ondaatje) **28**:292
"Elizabeth" (Poe) **1**:446
"Elizabeth Gone" (Sexton) **2**:359
"Ellen Hanging Clothes" (Reese) **29**:330, 348
"Elm" (Plath) **1**:390, 394
"Elm" (Stryk) **27**:212
"Elms" (Gluck) **16**:152
"Eloa" (Vigny) **26**:391, 398, 411
*Éloges* (Perse) **23**:209-11, 217, 222, 229-32,
  234, 237, 241-43, 254
"Elogio de la seguidilla" (Dario) **15**:114
*Elogio de la sombra* (Borges) **22**:71, 75-6
"Eloisa to Abelard" (Pope) **26**:318-19, 326, 339
*Eloisa to Abelard* (Pope) **26**:304

"Elsewhere" (Sassoon) **12**:252
"A Elvire" (Lamartine) **16**:290
"Elvis Presley" (Gunn) **26**:219
*Emaux et camées* (Gautier) **18**:127-28, 130, 138, 146, 154, 156, 158-59, 161, 164
*Emblems of a Season of Fury* (Merton) **10**:334, 343, 349-51
"Emblems of Conduct" (Crane) **3**:82
"The Embrace" (Gluck) **16**:156
"The Emerald" (Merrill) **28**:222, 244, 257
*Emerald Ice: Selected Poems 1962-1987* (Wakoski) **15**:370, 372
"Emergency Haying" (Carruth) **10**:91
"TH EMERGENCY WARD" (Bissett) **14**:10-11, 17, 34
"l'emigrant de Landor Road" (Apollinaire) **7**:42, 47
"Emigranten" (Ekeloef) **23**:61
"Emilie vor ihrem Brauttag" (Holderlin) **4**:141
"Emily Before Her Wedding" (Holderlin)
    See "Emilie vor ihrem Brauttag"
"Emily Brontë" (Bridges) **28**:88
"Emily Brosseau" (Masters) **1**:333
"Emily Sparks" (Masters) **1**:327, 347
*Empedocles* (Holderlin)
    See *Empedokles*
"Empedocles on Etna" (Arnold) **5**:5, 9-10, 12, 23, 35-6, 42-3, 45, 50-1, 56-7
*Empedocles on Etna, and Other Poems* (Arnold) **5**:2, 25, 30, 35, 42, 50, 55, 57
*Empedokles* (Holderlin) **4**:146
"Empeoro y mejoro" (Fuertes) **27**:15
"The Emperor of Ice-Cream" (Stevens) **6**:293, 296
"The Emperor's New Sonnet" (Villa) **22**:351
"Employment I" (Herbert) **4**:100, 111
"Employment II" (Herbert) **4**:111, 131
"Employments" (Herbert) **4**:100
"Emporium" (Shapiro) **25**:295
*Empty Chestnuts* (Matsuo Basho)
    See *Minashiguri*
*Empty Mirror* (Ginsberg) **4**:48, 73, 80, 91
"En bateau" (Verlaine) **2**:431
"En dröm" (Ekeloef) **23**:57, 76
"En la Ausencia" (Fuertes) **27**:44
"En las constelaciones" (Dario) **15**:99, 101
*En natt i Otocac* (Ekeloef) **23**:63, 69, 76
*En natt på horisonten* (Ekeloef) **23**:77
*En natt vid horisonten* (Ekeloef) **23**:62, 89
"En pocas palabras" (Fuertes) **27**:49
"En que describe racionalmente los efectos irracionales del amor" (Juana Ines de la Cruz) **24**:186
*En självbiografi* (Ekeloef) **23**:90
"En Trinacria" (Dario) **15**:107-09
*En un vasto dominio* (Aleixandre) **15**:4, 7, 11-12, 17, 34, 41
"En vano tu canto suena" (Juana Ines de la Cruz) **24**:225
"En värld är varje människa" (Ekeloef) **23**:57
"En verklighet" (Ekeloef) **23**:76
*Enamels and Cameos* (Gautier)
    See *Emaux et camées*
"El enamorado" (Borges) **22**:95
"The Enchanted Island" (Noyes) **27**:121-23
"Enchanter's Handmaiden" (Wylie) **23**:324
"Enchantment through Fire" (Blok) **21**:20
"The Encounter" (Gluck) **16**:167
"Encounter" (Pavese) **13**:202
"Encounter" (Wright) **14**:374
"Encounter in August" (Kumin) **15**:209
*Encounters* (Aleixandre) **15**:4
"Encores au Lecteur" (Ronsard) **11**:249
"End" (Hughes) **1**:240
"The End" (Owen) **19**:334
"The End" (Pasternak) **6**:268
"An End" (Rossetti) **7**:280
"The End" (Tomlinson) **17**:340
"The End of 1968" (Montale)
    See "Fine del '68"
*The End of a Fine Epoch* (Brodsky)
    See *Konets prekrasnoy epokhi*

"End of a Year" (Lowell) **3**:228
"The End of March" (Bishop) **3**:48-9, 72
"End of Play" (Graves) **6**:137
"End of Summer" (Kunitz) **19**:186
"The End of the Episode" (Hardy) **8**:91
"The End of the Owls" (Enzensberger) **28**:142, 147
"The End of the Search" (Masters) **1**:344
"The End of the World" (Gluck) **16**:152
"End of the World" (Jeffers) **17**:141
"End of the World: Weekend, near Toronto" (Atwood) **8**:13
"End of the Year" (Tagore)
    See "Varshashesh"
"End of the Year 1912" (Hardy) **8**:124
"The End of Your Life" (Levine) **22**:214
*Endeavors of Infinite Man* (Neruda)
    See *Tentativa del hombre infinito*
"An Ending" (Kipling) **3**:194
"Endless Life" (Ferlinghetti) **1**:180, 182-83, 185
*Endless Life: Selected Poems* (Ferlinghetti) **1**:180, 182, 184-85
"Endor" (Nemerov) **24**:261
"Ends" (Frost) **1**:213
"Endurance" (Forche) **10**:141-42, 144, 147, 156
"Endymion" (Nemerov) **24**:259
*Endymion* (Keats)
    See *Endymion: A Poetic Romance*
*Endymion: A Poetic Romance* (Keats) **1**:275-79, 282, 288, 290-91, 308-09, 311, 313-14
"Enemies" (Sassoon) **12**:242
"Enfance" (Rimbaud) **3**:262, 265
"L'Enfant grect" (Hugo) **17**:75
"Enfermera de pulpos" (Fuertes) **27**:8, 26
"The Engagement" (Swenson) **14**:265
"Engführung" (Celan) **10**:96, 99, 117
"The Engine Drain" (Smith) **12**:327
"England" (Davie) **29**:98-99, 103
"England" (Moore) **4**:251
"England 1830" (Clare) **23**:37
"England: An Ode" (Swinburne) **24**:312
"England in 1819" (Shelley) **14**:210
*English Bards and Scotch Reviewers* (Byron) **16**:77, 82
"The English Bull Dog, Dutch Mastiff, and Quail" (Smart) **13**:348
"The English Flag" (Kipling) **3**:157, 161
"The English Graves" (Chesterton) **28**:99
"English Horn" (Montale)
    See "Corno Inglese"
"English Idylls" (Tennyson) **6**:409
"English Lessons" (Pasternak) **6**:251
"An English Revenant" (Davie) **29**:108
"An English Wood" (Graves) **6**:144, 166
*The English Works of George Herbert* (Herbert) **4**:103
"The Englishman in Italy" (Browning) **2**:62
"The Englishman in Sorrento" (Browning) **2**:38
"An Enigma" (Poe) **1**:446
"Enigma for an Angel" (Brodsky) **9**:2
"Enivrez-vous" (Baudelaire) **1**:58
"Ennui" (Viereck) **27**:263
*Enoch Arden* (Tennyson) **6**:360, 365
"Enough" (Moore) **4**:260
*Enough Rope* (Parker) **28**:345-48, 351, 353, 356-57, 359-61
"Enriching the Earth" (Berry) **28**:11, 43
"Enter No" (Silence Is the Blood Whose FleshCummings) **5**:111
"L'enterrement" (Verlaine) **2**:431
"L'enthousiasme" (Lamartine) **16**:276, 290
*The Enthusiastic Slinger* (Neruda)
    See *El hondero entusiasta, 1923-1924*
*The Entire Son* (Guillen)
    See *El son entero*
"Entrada a la madera" (Neruda) **4**:277, 306-07
"Entrance into Wood" (Neruda)
    See "Entrada a la madera"
*Entre la piedra y la flor* (Paz) **1**:369
*Entries* (Berry) **28**:30-1
"Entry in an Album" (Lermontov) **18**:302

"Entwurf einer Hymne an die Madonna" (Holderlin) **4**:150
"The Envelope" (Kumin) **15**:203, 207, 221-22
"Envoi" (Meredith) **28**:174, 187
"Envoy" (Johnson) **24**:145
"The Envoys" (Merrill) **28**:220
"Envy" (H. D.) **5**:305
"The Eolian Harp" (Coleridge)
    See "The Aeolian Harp"
"Ephemera" (Lowell) **13**:74
"Ephemera" (Yeats) **20**:337
"Ephemerid" (Loy) **16**:316
"Ephyphatha" (MacDiarmid) **9**:156
"Epidermal Macabre" (Roethke) **15**:272
"Epigram I" (Rexroth) **20**:180
"Epigram CI" (Jonson) **17**:158, 167, 173, 175, 182, 189-90, 208
"Epigram CII" (Jonson) **17**:157, 197
"Epigram CIII" (Jonson) **17**:197-98, 202
"Epigram CIV" (Jonson) **17**:202
"Epigram CVII" (Jonson) **17**:166
"Epigram CVIII" (Jonson) **17**:166
"Epigram CXVI" (Jonson) **17**:164
"Epigram CXXIV" (Jonson) **17**:193
"Epigram CXXXIII" (Jonson) **17**:189
"Epigram IV" (Jonson) **17**:156
"Epigram LIX" (Jonson) **17**:164
"Epigram LXV" (Jonson) **17**:157, 197
"Epigram LXXVI" (Jonson) **17**:159, 174, 192, 198, 200, 205, 214
"Epigram on Lady Elizabeth" (Jonson)
    See "Epigram on Lady Elizabeth"
"Epigram: To a Friend, and Sonne" (Jonson)
    See "Epigram: To a Friend, and Sonne"
"Epigram X" (Jonson) **17**:157
"Epigram XCI" (Jonson) **17**:201
"Epigram XCIV" (Jonson) **17**:159, 202
"Epigram XIV" (Jonson) **17**:166, 174
"Epigram XLIII" (Jonson) **17**:199
"Epigram XLV" (Jonson) **17**:193
"Epigram XVIII" (Jonson) **17**:179
"Epigram XXIII" (Jonson) **17**:197
"Epigram XXXV" (Jonson) **17**:156
"Epigramas" (Guillen) **23**:121
*Epigramas* (Cardenal) **22**:104, 117, 124-25, 131
*Epigrammata* (Martial) **10**:243
*Epigrammaton libri* (Martial)
    See *Epigrammata*
*Epigrams* (Cardenal)
    See *Epigramas*
*Epigrams* (Jonson) **17**:156-58, 169, 179, 196-97, 201-02, 206
*Epigrams* (Martial)
    See *Epigrammata*
"Epilog" (Heine) **25**:162, 178
"Epilogue" (Cullen) **20**:57
"Epilogue" (Verlaine) **2**:432
"Epilogue to the Drama Founded on 'stSt. Roman's Welle'" (Scott) **13**:293
*Epilogue to the Satires* (Pope) **26**:319-20, 340
"Epilogue to the Tragedy of Jane Shore" (Finch) **21**:154
*Epinicia* (Pindar) **19**:378
*Epipsychidion* (Shelley) **14**:163, 171, 173-75, 178, 187, 189, 192-93, 196-97, 208, 233-37, 239-40
"Episode" (Valery) **9**:391
"Epistle" (Dario)
    See "Epístola"
"Epistle" (Lee) **24**:242
"An Epistle answering one that asked to be Sealed of the Tribe of Ben" (Jonson)
    See "An Epistle answering one that asked to be Sealed of the Tribe of Ben"
"Epistle Containing the Strange Medical Experiences of Karshish the Arab Physician" (Browning) **2**:36
"An Epistle from Ardelia to Mrs. Randolph in answer to her Poem upon Her Verses" (Finch) **21**:167
"Epistle from Mrs. Yonge to Her Husband" (Montagu) **16**:346

*Epistle III* (Pope) **26**:325-26
"An Epistle, Inviting a Friend to Supper"
  (Jonson)
  See "An Epistle, Inviting a Friend to
  Supper"
*Epistle IV* (Pope) **26**:325
"Epistle John Hamilton to Reynolds" (Keats)
  **1**:289, 305
"An Epistle Mendicant" (Jonson)
  See "An Epistle Mendicant"
"Epistle to a Friend" (Jonson)
  See "Epistle to a Friend"
"Epistle to a Friend, to perswade him to the
  Warres" (Jonson)
  See "Epistle to a Friend, to perswade him
  to the Warres"
"An Epistle to a Lady, Who Desired the
  Author to Make Verses on Her, in the
  Heroick Style" (Swift) **9**:256, 259-60, 281
"Epistle to a Young Friend" (Burns) **6**:71, 96
"Epistle to Augusta" (Byron) **16**:86
"Epistle to Augustus" (Pope) **26**:320-21
*Epistle to Burlington* (Pope) **26**:353, 359
"Epistle to Dr. Arbuthnot" (Pope) **26**:318, 338,
  361
*An Epistle to Dr. Arbuthnot* (Pope) **26**:311, 320,
  339-46
"Epistle to Elizabeth Countesse of Rutland"
  (Jonson)
  See "Epistle to Elizabeth Countesse of
  Rutland"
"Epistle to John Rankine, Enclosing Some
  Poems" (Burns) **6**:65, 83
"Epistle to J.R*******" (Burns)
  See "Epistle to John Rankine, Enclosing
  Some Poems"
"Epistle: To Katherine, Lady Aubigny"
  (Jonson)
  See "Epistle: To Katherine, Lady Aubigny"
"An Epistle to Master John Selden" (Jonson)
  See "An Epistle to Master John Selden"
"Epistle to Sir Edward Sacvile, now Earl of
  Dorset" (Jonson)
  See "Epistle to Sir Edward Sacvile, now
  Earl of Dorset"
"Epistle to the Olympians" (Nash) **21**:279-80
"Epistle to William Simpson of Ochiltree, May
  1785" (Burns) **6**:69
"The Epistles" (Burns) **6**:49, 66-71, 79, 81
*Epistles* (Ovid)
  See *Heroides*
*Epistolæ Heroidum* (Ovid)
  See *Heroides*
"Epístola" (Dario) **15**:89-90
"Epistola a monsenor Casaldaliga" (Cardenal)
  **22**:103
"Epistre a ses amis" (Villon) **13**:395
"Epitáfio de B Dias" (Pessoa) **20**:155
"Epitaph" (Alegria) **26**:
"Epitaph" (Tsvetaeva)
  See "Nadgrobie"
"Epitaph" (Williams) **7**:345
"Epitaph" (Wylie) **23**:322-23
"Epitaph for a Darling Lady" (Parker) **28**:346
"Epitaph for a Poet" (Cullen) **20**:60
"Epitaph for Anton Schmidt" (Gunn) **26**:203
"Epitaph for My Father" (Walker) **20**:289, 293
"Epitaph for the Race of Man" (Millay) **6**:217,
  230
"Epitaph: Hubert Hastings, Parry" (Bridges)
  **28**:77
"Epitaph on an Army of Mercenaries"
  (Housman) **2**:177
"Epitaph on Salathiel Pavy" (Jonson)
  See "Epitaph on Salomon Pavy"
"Epitaph on Salomon Pavy" (Jonson) **17**:179
"Epitaph on the Lady S. Wife to Sir W.S."
  (Carew) **29**:62
"Epitaph on the Politician Himself" (Belloc)
  **24**:31, 40
"Epitaph to Master Vincent Corbet" (Jonson)
  **17**:174

"An Epitaph upon a Child" (Herrick) **9**:129
"An Epitaph upon a Virgin" (Herrick) **9**:131
"Epitaphe Villon" (Villon) **13**:390, 394, 408,
  410-11, 417-18
*Epitaphium Damonis* (Milton) **29**:241
"Epitaphs of the War" (Kipling) **3**:171, 192
"Epithalamie on Sir Clipseby Crew and His
  Lady" (Herrick)
  See "A Nuptiall Song, or Epithalamie on
  Sir Clipseby Crew and His Lady"
"An Epithalamie to Sir Thomas Southwell and
  His Ladie" (Herrick) **9**:86
"Epithalamion" (Herrick)
  See "A Nuptiall Song, or Epithalamie on
  Sir Clipseby Crew and His Lady"
"Epithalamion" (Hopkins) **15**:124
"Epithalamion" (Spenser) **8**:336, 389
"An Epithalamion, or mariage song on the
  Lady Elizabeth, and Count Palatine being
  married on St. Valentines day" (Donne)
  **1**:124
"The Epithalamium" (Housman) **2**:199
"Epithalamium" (Pessoa) **20**:165, 169
"An Epitome" (Sassoon) **12**:260
"Epitre a M. de Sainte-Beuve" (Lamartine)
  **16**:267
"Épître à Marie d'Orléans" (Villon) **13**:399,
  413
"Epîtres à la Princesse" (Senghor) **25**:258
"Epîtres à la Princesse" (Senghor) **25**:255
*Epode* (Jonson)
  See *Epode*
"Equal Opportunity" (Lorde) **12**:140
"Equilibrist" (Swenson) **14**:274, 283
"Equinox" (Lorde) **12**:157
"Equitan" (Marie de France) **22**:239-41, 258,
  265, 269, 271, 278, 296-98
"Era un aire suave" (Dario) **15**:79, 95, 107,
  109, 118-19
"Eramos Tres" (Alegria) **26**:
"Ere Sleep Comes Down to Soothe the Weary
  Eyes" (Dunbar) **5**:121, 124
"The Eremites" (Graves) **6**:140
"Erige Cor Tuum ad Me in Coelum" (H. D.)
  **5**:307
"Erikönig" (Goethe) **5**:239, 254
*Eril* (Perse) **23**:246
"Erinna" (Eliot) **20**:137
"Erinnerung an Frankreich" (Celan) **10**:121
"eriuuerung un die schrecken der jugend"
  (Enzensberger) **28**:136
*Erklärung* (Heine) **25**:162
"Erl-King" (Goethe)
  See "Erikönig"
*Erlkönig* (Goethe) **5**:257
"L'ermite" (Apollinaire) **7**:46-7
"Ermunterung" (Holderlin) **4**:148
"Eroded Hills" (Wright) **14**:353, 378
"Eroica" (Ginsberg) **4**:62
"L'eroismo" (Montale) **13**:156
"Eros" (Bridges) **28**:74-5, 86-7
*Eros and Psyche* (Bridges) **28**:47, 59, 68, 86
"Eros at Temple Stream" (Levertov) **11**:169
"Eros turannos" (Robinson) **1**:468, 490, 493-
  94, 497
"Erosion: Transkei" (Brutus) **24**:113
*Erotic Adventures* (Ovid)
  See *Amores*
"Erwache, Friederike" (Goethe) **5**:246
"Es así" (Neruda) **4**:311
"Es obligatorio" (Fuertes) **27**:12
"Es War Einmal" (Smith) **12**:312
"Escaparate" (Borges) **22**:92
"The Escape" (Levine) **22**:233
"Escape" (Wylie) **23**:301, 309, 329
"Escolares" (Guillen) **23**:127
"Escrito" (Fuertes) **27**:48
*Esope* (Marie de France)
  See *The Fables*
*Espacia* (Jimenez) **7**:203, 213-14
*Espadas como labios* (Aleixandre) **15**:6, 18, 21,
  30-1, 39-41

*España* (Gautier) **18**:155
*España en el corazón: himno a las glorias del
  pueblo en la guerra* (1936-1937 Neruda)
  **4**:278, 283, 287, 307-09, 311
"Especially When the October Wind"
  (Thomas) **2**:384
"L'espoir luit comme un brin de paille dans
  l'étable" (Verlaine) **2**:416
"L'Esprit Pur" (Vigny) **26**:371, 374, 392, 402-
  404, 413
"L'esprit saint" (Lamartine) **16**:264, 277
*Espurgatoire* (Marie de France)
  See *L'Espurgatoire Saint Patrice*
*L'Espurgatoire Saint Patrice* (Marie de France)
  **22**:287-89, 291, 293, 300
*An Essay on Criticism* (Pope) **26**:300, 302-303,
  314-15, 318, 320-22, 340
*An Essay on Man* (Pope) **26**:304, 307-308, 314,
  318, 326, 328-33, 335, 338-40, 351-56, 359
"Essay on Mind" (Browning) **6**:27
*An Essay on Mind, with other Poems*
  (Browning) **6**:19-20, 26
"Essay on Poetics" (Ammons) **16**:10-11, 23,
  28, 47-9
"Essay on Psychiatrists" (Pinsky) **27**:144-45,
  160, 162, 173, 175-76
*Essay on Rime* (Shapiro) **25**:264-65, 267-68,
  270, 274-79, 285, 288, 290-91, 296, 310,
  319, 322-23
"Essay on Stone" (Carruth) **10**:83
"Essay on the Alliance of Education and
  Government" (Gray) **2**:136
"An Essay on War" (Duncan) **2**:105
"Esse" (Milosz) **8**:182, 187
"Essential Beauty" (Larkin) **21**:229
*The Essential Etheridge Knight* (Knight)
  **14**:52-3
*Essex Poems, 1963-1967* (Davie) **29**:113,
  122-23
"Está bien" (Guillen) **23**:127
"Está el bisonte imperial" (Guillen) **23**:125
"Esta tarde, mi bien, cuando te hablaba"
  (Juana Ines de la Cruz) **24**:180
*La estación violenta* (Paz) **1**:353, 359-60, 362
"Estar del cuerpo" (Aleixandre) **15**:35
"Estate di San Martino" (Pavese) **13**:244
"Una estatua en el silencio" (Neruda) **4**:289
"Estatura del vino" (Neruda) **4**:277, 301
"Este libro" (Fuertes) **27**:17, 38
"Este que ves engaño colorido" (Juana Ines de
  la Cruz) **24**:225
*Esthétique du Mal* (Stevens) **6**:300, 302
"Estimable Mable" (Brooks) **7**:94
*Estío* (Jimenez) **7**:212
"Estival" (Dario) **15**:117
"El estrecho dudoso" (Cardenal) **22**:119-23,
  125-27
*El estrecho dudoso* (Cardenal) **22**:
"Estudio preliminar" (Dario) **15**:80
"Et Le Sursaut Soudain" (Senghor) **25**:248
*Et moi aussi je suis peintre* (Apollinaire) **7**:34
*Les états-généraux* (Breton) **15**:50, 52, 62
"Etched Away" (Celan) **10**:97
"Été" (Valery) **9**:351, 373, 392
"Eternal Death" (Tagore)
  See "Ananta maran"
"Eternal Life" (Tagore)
  See "Ananta jivan"
*Eternidades* (Jimenez) **7**:187, 208, 212-13
"Eternite de la nature, brievete de l'homme"
  (Lamartine) **16**:283
"Eternity" (Crane) **3**:90
"An Eternity" (Williams) **7**:394
*Eternity* (Smart)
  See *On the Eternity of the Supreme Being*
"The Eternity of Nature" (Clare) **23**:3-4, 26
"Ethelinda" (Smart)
  See "To Ethelinda"
"Ethiopia" (Harper) **21**:189, 202, 208, 215, 217
*Éthiopiques* (Senghor) **25**:231-32, 238, 241, 255
"Ethnobotany" (Snyder) **21**:297
"Les étoiles" (Lamartine) **16**:291

"Eton" (Gray)
    See "Ode on a Distant Prospect of Eton
        College"
"Eton College Ode" (Gray)
    See "Ode on a Distant Prospect of Eton
        College"
*Etroits sont les vaisseaux* (Perse) **23**:244-45
"Etude" (Stryk) **27**:183, 189
"Etude de mains" (Gautier) **18**:129, 158
"The Eucalypt and the National Character"
    (Wright) **14**:374
"Euclid" (Millay) **6**:211
"Eufori" (Ekelof) **23**:
"Eugene Carman" (Masters) **1**:324
*Eugene Onegin* (Pushkin)
    See *Yevgeny Onegin*
"Eulalie" (Poe) **1**:441
"Eulenspiegelei" (Smith) **12**:327, 342
"Eulogy for Slick" (Knight) **14**:49
"Eunice Aviles" (Alegria) **26**:
"Eupheme" (Jonson) **17**:213
"Euphoria" (Ekeloef) **23**:76
"Euphrosyne" (Arnold) **5**:43
*Eureka: A Prose Poem* (Poe) **1**:422-24, 430-31,
    437-38, 442-43, 450
"Europe" (Ashbery) **26**:113, 118, 138, 151
*Europe: A Prophecy, 1794* (Blake) **12**:13, 26,
    35, 57, 61
"The European Gentleman" (Belloc) **24**:
"Eurydice" (H. D.) **5**:298, 304
"Evadne" (H. D.) **5**:267
"Evangelist" (Davie) **29**:93-94, 108, 111-12,
    114-15
"Evanston 4 June 72" (Brutus) **24**:123
"Eva's Farewell" (Harper) **21**:201, 208, 218
"Evasion" (Tzara) **27**:230-31
"Eve" (Rossetti) **7**:264, 291
"Eve" (Williams) **7**:350, 354, 394-95
"Eve in Heaven" (Wylie) **23**:326
"The Eve of All Souls" (Clampitt) **19**:87
"The Eve of St. Agnes" (Keats) **1**:279, 282,
    285-6, 288, 296, 298, 307-10
"The Eve of St. John" (Scott) **13**:269
"Eve of St. Mark" (Keats)
    See "The Eve of St. Mark"
"The Eve of St. Mark" (Keats) **1**:279, 304
"Eve Scolds" (Wright) **14**:373, 375
"Eve Sings" (Wright) **14**:373
"Eve to her Daughter" (Wright) **14**:356
"Evelyn" (Stryk) **27**:208
"Evelyn Hope" (Browning) **2**:38
"Evelyn Ray" (Lowell) **13**:66, 91
"Even" (Burns) **6**:50
"Even If All Desires Things Moments Be"
    (Cummings) **5**:95
"The Even Sea" (Swenson) **14**:249, 263
"Even Song" (Herbert) **4**:133
"Evening" (Merton) **10**:340
"Evening" (Trakl)
    See "Der Abend"
"Evening" (Wheatley)
    See "An Hymn to the Evening"
*Evening* (Akhmatova)
    See *Vecher*
*Evening Album* (Tsvetaeva)
    See *Vecherny albom*
"The Evening Bell" (Ishikawa)
    See "Yube no kane"
"Evening Dance of the Grey Flies" (Page)
    **12**:190
*Evening Dance of the Grey Flies* (Page) **12**:181,
    198-99
"The evening darkens over" (Bridges) **28**:87
"Evening Fantasy" (Holderlin) **4**:140
"Evening in the Country" (Ashbery) **26**:124,
    159
"Evening in the Sanitarium" (Bogan) **12**:92,
    99-101, 107, 121
"The Evening of Ants" (Soto) **28**:378-79
"Evening of the Visitation" (Merton) **10**:339
"Evening on the Broads" (Swinburne) **24**:313,
    322, 329, 343

"The Evening Primrose" (Parker) **28**:349, 351,
    363
"The Evening Sea" (Ishikawa)
    See "Yube no umi"
"Evening Song" (Toomer) **7**:320
*Evening Songs* (Tagore)
    See *Sandhya sangit*
"Evening Star" (Bogan) **12**:98, 100
"Evening Star" (Poe) **1**:448
"The Evening That Love Enticed You Down
    into the Ballroom" (Ronsard)
    See "Le soir qu'amour vous fist en la salle
        descendre"
*An Evening Thought: Salvation by Christ with
    Penetential Cries* (Hammon) **16**:176-79,
    183-87
"Evening Twilight" (Baudelaire)
    See "Le crepuscule du soir"
"An Evening Under Newly Cleared Skies"
    (Wang Wei) **18**:369
"Evening Voluntary" (Wordsworth) **4**:408
"Evensong" (Aiken) **26**:5
"The Event" (Dove) **6**:110, 112, 114
*Events and Wisdoms: Poems, 1957-1963*
    (Davie) **29**:110-11, 123, 129
"Ever mine hap is slack" (Wyatt) **27**:357
"The Everlasting Gospel" (Blake) **12**:31
"The Everlasting Voices" (Yeats) **20**:309
"Everness" (Borges) **22**:89
"Every Blessed Day" (Levine) **22**:221
"Every Lovely Limb's a Desolation" (Smith)
    **12**:314
"Every Soul Is a Circus" (Lindsay) **23**:274, 280
"Every Traveler Has One Vermont Poem"
    (Lorde) **12**:138
*Everyone Sang* (Sassoon) **12**:280, 284, 289
"Everything Came True" (Pasternak) **6**:266
"eve's version" (Clifton) **17**:29, 36
*Evgeni Onegin* (Pushkin)
    See *Yevgeny Onegin*
"Evidence" (Harjo) **27**:64
"The Evil" (Rimbaud)
    See "Le mal"
"Eviradnus" (Hugo) **17**:59, 61
"Evolution" (Swenson) **14**:247, 251, 255, 275,
    283-84, 286
"Evolutionary Poem No. 1" (Knight) **14**:42
"Evolutionary Poem No. 2" (Knight) **14**:42
"Evolution-Sustenance-Dissolution" (Tagore)
    See "Srishti-sthiti-pralaya"
"The Evolver" (Baraka) **4**:24
"evry whun at 2 oclock" (Bissett) **14**:33
"Ex ponto" (Ekeloef) **23**:76
"Ex vermibus" (MacDiarmid) **9**:190
"Exactly what is unexact" (Villa) **22**:354
"Exageraciones divinas" (Fuertes) **27**:30
"The Exam" (Olds) **22**:324
"Examination at the Womb-Door" (Hughes)
    **7**:159
"Examination of the Hero in a Time of War"
    (Stevens) **6**:318
"The Example" (Belloc) **24**:27
"Examples of Created Systems" (Meredith)
    **28**:200
"An Excellent New Ballad; or, The True
    English Dean to Be Hang'd for a Rape"
    (Swift) **9**:267
"The Excesses of God" (Jeffers) **17**:132
"The Exchange" (Swenson) **14**:255, 288
"Exchanging Hats" (Bishop) **3**:64
*Exclamations: Music of the Soul* (Nishiwaki)
    **15**:237
"The Excrement Poem" (Kumin) **15**:207
"La excursion" (Fuertes) **27**:17
*The Excursion, Being a Portion of "The
    Recluse"* (Wordsworth) **4**:377-78, 383,
    392, 397-99, 402-03, 405-09
"Excuse" (Arnold)
    See "Urania"
"Execration upon Vulcan" (Jonson)
    See "Execration upon Vulcan"
"Exhortation" (Bogan) **12**:122

*Exil* (Perse) **23**:209, 211, 213-14, 216-18, 221-
    22, 231, 234, 240-42, 246, 248-50, 252,
    254, 256
*Exile and Other Poems* (Perse)
    See *Exil*
*Exile's Letter* (Li Po) **29**:141
"The Exile's Return" (Lowell) **3**:200, 202, 234
"The Exit" (Elytis) **21**:134
"Exit, Pursued by a Bear" (Nash) **21**:271
"Exmoor" (Clampitt) **19**:81, 88
"The Exorcism" (Roethke)
"Exordium" (Noyes) **27**:127
"The Expatriate" (Forche) **10**:138, 141, 144,
    156
"The Expatriates" (Sexton) **2**:359
"An Expedient-Leonardo da Vinci's-and a
    Query" (Moore) **4**:242
"Experience Is the Angled Road" (Dickinson)
    **1**:111
"L'Expiation" (Hugo) **17**:79-80
"The Expiration" (Donne) **1**:130
"Explaining a Few Things" (Neruda)
    See "Explico algunas cosas"
"The Explanation" (Kipling) **3**:183
"Explanation" (Pasternak) **6**:266
"Explanation and Apology, Twenty Years
    After" (Carruth) **10**:78
*An Explanation of America* (Pinsky) **27**:143-
    46,153, 155-56, 162-63, 173, 176
"Explico algunas cosas" (Neruda) **4**:297, 310-11
"The Explorers" (Atwood) **8**:13
"The Explorers" (Rich) **5**:362
"Explosion" (Harjo) **27**:56
"Expostulation and Reply" (Wordsworth) **4**:419
"An Expostulation with Inigo Jones" (Jonson)
    **17**:181-82
"Exposure" (Heaney) **18**:194, 205
"Exposure" (Owen) **19**:327, 332, 334
"Express" (Sandburg) **2**:340
"Expression" (Clare) **23**:44
"Expression" (Gunn) **26**:217
"Expressions of Sea Level" (Ammons) **16**:29,
    42, 46; **108**:22
*Expressions of Sea Level* (Ammons) **16**:4-5, 20,
    27, 53
"The Exstasie" (Donne) **1**:126, 128, 130, 135,
    147, 152
"Extase" (Hugo) **17**:91
"Extempore Effusion upon the Death of James
    Hogg" (Wordsworth) **4**:402
"Extracts from Addresses to the Academy of
    Fine Ideas" (Stevens) **6**:314
*Extracts from an Opera* (Keats) **1**:311
"Un extrano" (Gallagher) **9**:66
"Extrano accidente" (Fuertes) **27**:14, 27
*Extravagario* (Neruda) **4**:290
"Extremes and Moderations" (Ammons) **16**:10-
    11, 18, 23, 28, 47-9
*Exultations* (Pound) **4**:317
"Exvoto pour un naufrage" (Cesaire) **25**:32
"Eyasion" (Tzara) **27**:230
"Eye and Tooth" (Lowell) **3**:215
"The Eyeglasses" (Williams) **7**:381-83
"The Eye-Mote" (Plath) **1**:389
"Eyes and Tears" (Marvell) **10**:270-71
*Eyes at the Back of Our Heads* (Levertov)
    See *With Eyes at the Back of Our Heads*
"The Eyes of the Poor" (Baudelaire)
    See "Les yeux des pauvres"
"Ezekiel Saw the Wheel" (Montale) **13**:109,
    129, 165
"Ezerskij" (Pushkin) **10**:391, 394
"F O Matthiessen An Anniversary" (Shapiro)
    **25**:320, 322, 324
"Fable" (Cassian) **17**:13
"Fable" (Emerson) **18**:103-4
"A Fable" (Gluck) **16**:161
"Fable" (Wylie) **23**:310, 316, 319
"Fable of the Cock and the Fox" (Chaucer)
    See "Nun's Priest's Tale"
"The Fable of the Fragile Butterfly" (Wakoski)
    **15**:333

*The Fables* (Marie de France) **22**:287-88
*Fables* (Smart) **13**:341
"Fables about Error" (Meredith) **28**:175, 194, 213, 215
"Fables of the Moscow Subway" (Nemerov) **24**:268
"The Fabulists, 1914-1918" (Kipling) **3**:172
"Fabulous Ballard" (Wylie) **23**:321
*Façade* (Sitwell) **3**:294, 303, 306, 319, 322, 325, 328
"The Face" (Levine) **22**:224
"Face" (Toomer) **7**:310, 333
"Face and Image" (Tomlinson) **17**:348
"Face behind the Pane" (An Old Man's GazeAleixandre)
    See "Rostro tras el cristal (Mirada del viejo)"
"Face Lift" (Plath) **1**:394
"The Faces" (Stryk) **27**:202
"Faces" (Whitman) **3**:397
"Facing" (Swenson) **14**:284, 286
"Facing the Oxford" (Guillen)
    See "Frente al Oxford"
"Facing Wine with Memories of Lord Ho; Introduction and Two Poems" (Li Po) **29**:146, 187
"Fackelzug" (Celan) **10**:127
*The Fact of a Doorframe: Poems Selected and New, 1950-1984* (Rich) **5**:388-89
"Facteur Cheval" (Breton) **15**:50
"Factory Windows Are Always Broken" (Lindsay) **23**:268, 273, 276
"Facts" (Levine) **22**:221
"Facts" (Snyder) **21**:295-97
"Faded Leaves" (Arnold) **5**:13
*Fadensonnen* (Celan) **10**:96, 98
*The Faerie Queene, Disposed into Twelve Bookes Fashioning XII Morall Vertues* (Spenser) **8**:323-25, 327-28, 330, 332-34, 337, 339, 341-47, 349-50, 354, 360-61, 363, 365, 369, 371-72, 374-78, 380-82, 384-85, 388-93, 395-97
"Fafaia" (Brooke) **24**:62
"Fafnir and the Knights" (Smith) **12**:302, 329
"The Failed Spirit" (Smith) **12**:333
"Failure" (Brooke) **24**:75
"A Failure" (Day Lewis) **11**:147
"The Failure of Buffalo to Levitate" (Hass) **16**:195
"Faim" (Rimbaud) **3**:271, 282
"Faina" (Blok) **21**:20
*Faina* (Blok) **21**:24
"Fair Choice" (Hughes) **7**:135
"Fair Daffodils" (Herrick)
    See "To Daffadills"
"Fair Elenor" (Blake) **12**:31
"The Fair in the Woods" (Gunn) **26**:219
"The Fair One in My Mind" (Tagore)
    See "Manas-sundari"
"Fair Recluse" (Smart) **13**:341
"The Fair Singer" (Marvell) **10**:270-71, 294, 300
"Fair Weather" (Parker) **28**:348
"A Fairer Hope, A Brighter Morn" (Harper) **21**:190
"The Fairest One of All" (Kumin) **15**:201, 222
"The Fairie Temple: or, Oberons Chappell. Dedicated to Mr. John Merrifield, Counsellor at Law" (Herrick) **9**:86
*Fairies and Fusiliers* (Graves) **6**:165
"The Fairy" (Blake) **12**:34
"The Fairy Goldsmith" (Wylie) **23**:301, 318-21, 325-26, 329-30, 332
"Fairy Land" (Poe) **1**:440
"A Fairy Tale" (Lowell) **13**:96
"Fairy Tales" (Pushkin)
    See "Skazki"
*Fairy Tales* (Pushkin)
    See *Skazki*
"Fairytale" (Wright) **14**:338
*A Fairy-Tale for Children* (Lermontov) **18**:282, 303

"Faith" (Herbert) **4**:100, 119
"Faith" (Lamartine)
    See "La foi"
"The Faith" (Nemerov) **24**:287
"Faith Healing" (Larkin) **21**:229-30, 258
"Faithfully Tinyig at Twilight Voice" (Cummings) **5**:110
"The Faithless Bride" (Garcia Lorca)
    See "La casada infiel"
"The Faithless Wife" (Garcia Lorca)
    See "La casada infiel"
"Fakes" (Apollinaire)
    See "Des Faux"
"The Falcon" (Wylie) **23**:328
"Falcon City" (Tsvetaeva)
    See "Sokolinya slobodka"
"The Falcon Woman" (Graves) **6**:156, 172
"The Fall" (Ammons) **16**:42
"Fall" (Dario)
    See "Autumnal"
"Fall" (Neruda)
    See "Otoño"
"Fall 1961" (Lowell) **3**:215
"Fall and Spring" (Soto) **28**:399, 403
"Fall Festival" (Holderlin) **4**:141
"Fall, Leaves, Fall" (Bronte) **8**:68-9
*The Fall of America: Poems of These States 1965-1971* (Ginsberg) **4**:53-7, 59, 63-4, 66-7, 81
*The Fall of an Angel* (Lamartine)
    See *La chute d'un ange*
"The Fall of Night" (Merton) **10**:340
"The Fall of Rome" (Auden) **1**:23
"The Fall of Zalona" (Bronte) **8**:59
"Fall, Sierra Nevada" (Rexroth) **20**:205-06
"Fall Time" (Sandburg) **2**:316
"The Fallen Angels" (Sexton) **2**:373
"Fallen Leaves" (Illyes) **16**:243
"Fallen Majesty" (Yeats) **20**:330
"Fallen Moon" (Aleixandre) **15**:18, 20, 22
"The Fallen Tower of Siloam" (Graves) **6**:137, 143
"Fallen Women" (Pavese)
    See "Donne perdute"
"Falling Asleep by Firelight" (Meredith) **28**:171
"Falling Asleep over the 'Aeneid'" (Lowell) **3**:205
"Falling Leaves and Early Snow" (Rexroth) **20**:207
"The Falling of the Leaves" (Yeats) **20**:344
*The Falling Star's Path* (Yosano Akiko) **11**:301
"The Fallow Deer at the Lonely House" (Hardy) **8**:124
"The Falls" (Kinnell) **26**:257
"Falls Country" (Wright) **14**:378
"The Falls of Love" (Moss) **28**:137, 140, 144
"The False Heart" (Belloc) **24**:31
*False Justice* (Hagiwara Sakutaro)
    See *Kyomō no seigi*
"False Prophet" (Wylie) **23**:310, 324
"A False Step" (Browning) **6**:23
"Falsetto" (Montale) **13**:115-16
*Fama y obras pósthumas* (Juana Ines de la Cruz) **24**:227-29, 231
"Familiar Letter to Siegfried Sassoon" (Graves) **6**:131
"Family" (Brooks) **7**:93
"The Family in Spring" (Soto) **28**:400
*Family Pictures* (Brooks) **7**:63-4, 66, 83, 91, 94-5
*Family Reunion* (Nash) **21**:267-68
"Famous Poet" (Hughes) **7**:114, 139
*The Famous Tragedy of the Queen of Cornwall* (Hardy) **8**:95
"The Fan" (Montale)
    See "Il ventaglio"
"A Fancy" (Carew) **29**:70-72, 74-76
"Fancy Etchings" (Harper) **21**:193, 197
"Fanfara" (Montale) **13**:134
"Fanfare, Coda and Finale" (Walker) **20**:294
"Fanscombe Barn" (Finch) **21**:143
"Fantaisies d'hiver" (Gautier) **18**:129

"Fantasia on 'The Nut-Brown Maid'" (Ashbery) **26**:134, 140, 156, 162
"A Fantasy" (Gluck) **16**:158, 163
"Fantoches" (Verlaine) **2**:430
"Un fantôme" (Baudelaire) **1**:64
"Fantômes" (Cesaire) **25**:10
"Far Away" (Guillen)
    See "Far Away"
"Far Away and Long Ago" (Stevens) **6**:293
"The Far Field" (Roethke) **15**:280, 310, 317
*The Far Field* (Roethke) **15**:271, 282-83, 303, 309, 311
"Far in a Western Brookland" (Housman) **2**:180
"Far Known to Sea and Shore" (Housman) **2**:179
"Far Niente" (Gautier) **18**:172
"Far Off" (Jimenez)
    See "A lo lejos"
"Far Rockaway" (Schwartz) **8**:291, 302-03, 305
"Far West" (Snyder) **21**:300
"Farabundo Marti" (Alegria) **26**:
"La farandola dei fanciulli" (Montale) **13**:116
"Farewel Love and all thy lawes for ever" (Wyatt) **27**:304, 318, 340-41
"Farewell" (Kinnell) **26**:287
"Farewell" (Kipling) **3**:189
"The Farewell" (Lamartine)
    See "L'adieu"
"Farewell" (Lermontov) **18**:301
"A Farewell" (Owen) **19**:336
"Farewell" (Smith) **12**:301, 339
"Farewell" (Tagore)
    See "Viday"
"Farewell" (Wang Wei) **18**:387
"Farewell in the Mountains" (Wang Wei) **18**:387
"Farewell Love" (Wyatt) **27**:317
"Farewell Sweet Dust" (Wylie) **23**:322
"A Farewell to Alexandria" (Bronte) **8**:73
"A Farewell to America" (Wheatley) **3**:341
"Farewell to Arcady" (Dunbar) **5**:140
"Farewell to Barn and Stack and Tree" (Housman) **2**:161
"A Farewell to Celadon, on His Going to Ireland" (Behn) **13**:8
"Farewell to Florida" (Stevens) **6**:297, 305
"Farewell to Heaven" (Tagore)
    See "Svarga ha'ite biday"
"Farewell to love" (Donne) **1**:147
"Farewell to Nancy" (Burns) **6**:58
"Farewell to Poetry" (Herrick) **9**:95, 102, 136
"Farewell to Spring" (Wang Wei) **18**:
"Farewell to the Vertuous Gentle-woman" (Jonson)
    See "To the World. A Farwell for a Gentlewoman, Vertuous and Nobel"
"Farewell to Van Gogh" (Tomlinson) **17**:301, 314
"Farewells" (Alegria) **26**:
*La farfalla di Dinard* (Montale) **13**:161
*Le farfalle* (Gozzano) **10**:177-78, 184
"The Faring" (Tomlinson) **17**:349
"Farish Street" (Walker) **20**:294
*Färjesång* (Ekeloef) **23**:57, 62, 76
"The Farm Child's Lullaby" (Dunbar) **5**:138
"Farmer" (Stryk) **27**:203, 210
"The Farmer" (Williams) **7**:384
"Farmer's Death" (MacDiarmid) **9**:187, 191
"The Farmer's Wife" (Sexton) **2**:350
"The Farmer's Wife" (Tomlinson) **17**:311, 349, 358
*Farming: A Handbook* (Berry) **28**:5-7, 11-12, 35-6, 43
*Farmstead of Time* (Celan)
    See *Zeitgehöft*
"Farre off" (Ondaatje) **28**:336
"Farwell Frost, or Welcome the Spring" (Herrick) **9**:109
"Fast-Anchor'd Eternal O Love!" (Whitman) **3**:396
*Fasti* (Ovid) **2**:238, 241, 243-45, 253-55, 260-61

*De Fastis* (Ovid)
　See *Fasti*
"Fat Lip" (Guillen)
　See "Negro bembón"
"The Fat Man in the Mirror" (Lowell) **3**:205
"Fat William and the Trains" (Sitwell) **3**:301
"Fata Morgana" (Rossetti) **7**:280
*Fata Morgana* (Breton) **15**:51-2, 55, 62
"Fatal Interview" (Wylie) **23**:305
*Fatal Interview* (Millay) **6**:213, 215-16, 218,
　224, 230, 235, 239, 241, 243
"Fatal Sisters" (Gray) **2**:135
"Fate" (Olds) **22**:311, 322
"The Fates" (Owen) **19**:342
*The Father* (Olds) **22**:319-21, 323-24, 326, 330,
　332-34, 338, 340-42
"Father and Daughter" (Sanchez) **9**:220-21, 229
"Father and Daughter" (Song) **21**:337
"Father and Son" (Kunitz) **19**:152, 154, 165,
　175, 177-79
"Father and Son" (Schwartz) **8**:301-03, 305,
　314
"Father Ch., Many Years Later" (Milosz) **8**:181,
　202, 205
"Father Explains" (Milosz) **8**:207
"Father Father Abraham" (Johnson) **24**:160
"A Father for a Fool" (Smith) **12**:333
"The Father of My Country" (Wakoski) **15**:324,
　345, 354, 358
"Father, on His Unsonment" (Villa) **22**:349
"A Father out Walking on the Lawn" (Dove)
　**6**:109
"Fatherhood" (Pavese) **13**:203
"The Fathers" (Sassoon) **12**:168, 282
"Father's Bedroom" (Lowell) **3**:219-20
"Father's Song" (Kumin) **15**:201
"Fatigue" (Belloc) **24**:49
"Fatigue" (Lowell) **13**:60
"The Faun" (Plath) **1**:388
"The Faun Sees" (Zukofsky) **11**:368
"La fausse morte" (Valery) **9**:393, 396
"Faust" (Ashbery) **26**:118
"Faustina; or, Rock Roses" (Bishop) **3**:60
"Faustus and Helen" (IICrane) **3**:79, 80, 96, 98,
　100
"Faustus and I" (Sexton) **2**:367, 373
"The Fawn" (Millay) **6**:214
"Faynting I folowe" (Wyatt) **27**:343
"Fe Me Sal" (McKay) **2**:225
"Fear and Fame" (Levine) **22**:228
"The Fear of Beasts" (Meredith) **28**:171
"The Fear of Bo-talee" (Momaday) **25**:189,
　212-13
"The Fear of Death Disturbs Me" (Meredith)
　**28**:181
"Fearless" (Tagore)
　See "Nirbhay"
"Fears and Scruples" (Browning) **2**:59
"Fears in Solitude" (Coleridge) **11**:92, 94, 97-
　104
*Fears in Solitude* (Coleridge) **11**:100
*The Feast of the Assumption 1676* (Juana Ines
　de la Cruz) **24**:177
"A Feaver" (Donne) **1**:126, 130, 153
"February" (Hughes) **7**:147
"February" (Kumin) **15**:222
"february 11, 1990" (Clifton) **17**:30
"February Evening in New York" (Levertov)
　**11**:167
"February Seventeenth" (Hughes) **7**:162, 165
"The Fed" (Blok) **21**:11
"feed th prisoners now baby" (Bissett) **14**:32
"The Feeders" (Davie) **29**:110
"Feeding Out Wintery Cattle at Twilight"
　(Hughes) **7**:166
"Feel Me" (Swenson) **14**:267, 270, 288
"Feeling and Precision" (Moore) **4**:251
"Feeling Fucked Up" (Knight) **14**:43, 46
"The Feelings" (Olds) **22**:326
*Fekete feher* (Illyes) **16**:232
"Feliciano me adora y le aborrezco" (Juana
　Ines de la Cruz) **24**:183

"Felix" (Alegria) **26**:
"Felix Randal" (Hopkins) **15**:170
"The Felloe'd Year" (Graves) **6**:137
"Fellow Creatures" (Nash) **21**:265
"Feminist Manifesto" (Loy) **16**:329, 332, 334
"Femme a la blonde aisselle coiffant sa
　chevelure a la lueur des etioles" (Breton)
　**15**:48
"La Femme adultere" (Vigny) **26**:381, 410-11
"Femme dans la nuit" (Breton) **15**:48
"Femme et chatte" (Verlaine) **2**:431
"Femme et oiseau" (Breton) **15**:48, 55-6, 58-60
"Femme noire" (Senghor) **25**:224, 239
"Femmes au bord d'un lac a la surface irisee
　par le passage d'un cygne" (Breton) **15**:49
"Femmes damnées" (Baudelaire) **1**:62
"Femmes sur la plage" (Breton) **15**:48
"Fence Posts" (Snyder) **21**:307
"Les fenêtres" (Apollinaire) **7**:18, 36, 44
"Les fenêtres" (Baudelaire) **1**:59
"Les fenêtres" (Mallarme) **4**:208
"Feodosija" (Mandelstam) **14**:113
*Ferishtah's Fancies* (Browning) **2**:59
"Fern" (Hughes) **7**:121
"Fern Hill" (Thomas) **2**:382, 385, 392, 396-99,
　405
"Fernão de Magalhães" (Pessoa) **20**:155
*Ferrements* (Cesaire) **25**:13, 23, 32, 44
*Ferrying Across* (Tagore)
　See *Kheya*
*Fervor de Buenos Aires* (Borges) **22**:68-9, 71-2,
　79, 93-4
*Fervor of Buenos Aires* (Borges)
　See *Fervor de Buenos Aires*
"Festival of Spring" (Tagore)
　See "Vasanter Kusumer mela"
*Festus* (Aiken) **26**:7, 29
"Fetchin' Water" (McKay) **2**:216, 223
"Fêtes de la faim" (Rimbaud) **3**:259
*Fêtes galantes* (Verlaine) **2**:413-15, 424-25,
　430-32
"Feuer-Nacht" (Bogan) **12**:94, 121
*Les feuilles d'automne* (Hugo) **17**:42-45, 52,
　63, 66, 68, 90-93
"A Fever" (Donne)
　See "A Feaver"
"Fever" (Gunn) **26**:220
"A Fever" (Merrill) **28**:221
"Fever 103°" (Plath) **1**:382, 386, 393
"A Few Coins" (Soto) **28**:371
"A Few Figs from Thistles" (Millay) **6**:208,
　211, 234
*A Few Figs from Thistles* (Millay) **6**:207, 211-
　12, 227, 230, 233-35, 237, 239
"Fiammetta Breaks Her Peace" (Dove) **6**:109
"Les fiançailles" (Apollinaire) **7**:43-4, 46, 48
"Ficha Ingreso Hospital General" (Fuertes) **27**:3
"Fiddler Jones" (Masters) **1**:333
"Fidelity" (Wordsworth) **4**:383
"Field" (Soto) **28**:375, 377-78, 384-85
*Field Guide* (Hass) **16**:194-95, 197, 199-201,
　209, 212, 214, 216, 222, 228
"A Field of Light" (Roethke)
"The Field Pansy" (Clampitt) **19**:94, 96
"Field Work" (Heaney) **18**:245
*Field Work* (Heaney) **18**:197-99, 211-12, 215,
　238-40, 242, 245-47, 255-57
*Fields of Wonder* (Hughes) **1**:240-44, 247, 268
"Fiend, Dragon, Mermaid" (Graves) **6**:142, 145
"Fierce Hope" (Tagore)
　See "Duranta asha"
"Fiesta" (Pasolini) **17**:253
*Fifine at the Fair* (Browning) **2**:42-4, 50, 72,
　75, 80, 82, 96
"XV" (Joyce) **22**:138, 145, 170
"The Fifteenth Amendment" (Harper) **21**:197
"Fifteenth Farewell" (Bogan) **12**:86
*Fifth Decad of Cantos* (Pound) **4**:324
"Fifth Grade Autobiography" (Dove) **6**:120
*Fifth Nemean* (Pindar)
　See *Nemean 5*
*Fifty Poems* (Cummings) **5**:84, 107-08

"Fifty Years" (Johnson) **24**:127, 131, 143, 145-
　47, 154, 157-60
*Fifty Years, and Other Poems* (Johnson) **24**:127,
　131, 141-49, 152-55, 157, 159, 162, 166
"50-50" (Hughes) **1**:247
*55 Poems* (Zukofsky) **11**:341
"Fight" (Bukowski) **18**:15
*Fight Back: For the Sake of the People, for
　the Sake of the Land* (Ortiz) **17**:222-223,
　233, 239, 244
"Fight Him Fair Nigger" (Knight) **14**:49
"Fight to a Finish" (Sassoon) **12**:267
"Fighting South of the Ramparts" (Li Po)
　**29**:139
*Fighting Terms: A Selection* (Gunn) **26**:181,
　183, 188, 197, 199-200, 205-206, 210-12,
　215-19, 229
"La figlia che piange" (Eliot) **5**:153, 184
"La figue l'oeillet et la pipe a opium"
　(Apollinaire) **7**:32
"Figure from Politics" (Meredith) **28**:187
"The Figure in the Scene" (Hardy) **8**:137
"The Figured Wheel" (Pinsky) **27**:163, 165,
　173-76
*The Figured Wheel* (Pinsky) **27**:175
"The Figurehead" (Shapiro) **25**:316, 325
"Figures" (Hayden) **6**:196
*Figures of Thought: Speculations on the
　Meaning of Poetry and Other Essays*
　(Nemerov) **24**:299, 303
"Figurine" (Hughes) **1**:245
"La fileuse" (Valery) **9**:391
"Los filibusteros" (Cardenal) **22**:110
"La Fille de Jephte" (Vigny) **26**:401, 410
*Les filles du feu* (Nerval) **13**:176-78, 192, 195
"Filling the Boxes of Joseph Cornell"
　(Wakoski) **15**:324
"La fin de la journée" (Baudelaire) **1**:54
*La fin de Satan* (Hugo) **17**:65, 74, 81, 84, 88,
　91
"Final Act" (Alegria) **26**:
"Final Call" (Hughes) **1**:252
"Final Face" (Aleixandre) **15**:4
"Final Fire" (Aleixandre) **15**:18-19
"Final Shadow" (Aleixandre) **15**:16
"The Final Slope" (Stryk) **27**:203
"the final solution" (Sanchez) **9**:224
"Finding" (Brooke) **24**:57-8
"The Finding of the Moon" (Wright) **14**:356
"Finding the One Brief Note" (Kumin) **15**:215
*Findings* (Berry) **28**:5
*Fine Clothes to the Jew* (Hughes) **1**:237-38,
　244, 246, 254-55, 258, 260, 262-63, 268-71
"Fine del '68" (Montale) **13**:134
"La fine dell'infanzia" (Montale) **13**:115-16
"Finis" (Montale) **13**:139
"Finisterne" (Montale) **13**:156, 165-66
*Finisterre* (Montale) **13**:103, 106, 127-30
"Fins" (Sandburg) **2**:307
"The Fire" (Atwood) **8**:39
"The Fire" (Belloc) **24**:32
"The Fire" (Brodsky) **9**:2
"The Fire" (Gluck) **16**:127
"Fire" (Toomer) **7**:333
"Fire" (Zagajewski) **27**:380
"Fire and Ice" (Frost) **1**:194, 197
"Fire and Sleet and Candlelight" (Wylie)
　**23**:301, 307
"Fire at Murdering Hut" (Wright) **14**:339
"Fire Island" (Swenson) **14**:271, 285-86
"Fire on the Hills" (Jeffers) **17**:117, 127
"Fire Poem" (Merrill) **28**:241-42
"Fire Practice" (McKay) **2**:225
*The Fire Screen* (Merrill) **28**:220-21, 228, 230-
　31, 258, 264, 281
*The Fire Screen* (Merrill) **28**:
"Fire Song" (Ekeloef) **23**:51
"Fire Station" (Bukowski) **18**:16
"'Fire Stop Thief Help Murder Save the
　World'" (Cummings) **5**:107
"The Firebombers" (Sexton) **2**:365
"Fired" (Hughes) **1**:247

"Fireflies" (Swenson) **14**:250
"The Firemen's Ball" (Lindsay) **23**:265, 268, 281
"Firenze" (Ferlinghetti) **1**:183
"Fireworks" (Shapiro) **25**:269
*Fir-Flower Tablets* (Lowell) **13**:64, 74, 93
"The 1st" (Clifton) **17**:17
"First" (Kipling) **3**:160
"First, a poem must be magical" (Villa) **22**:352
"The First American" (Toomer) **7**:337
"The First and Last Night of Love" (Cassian) **17**:4, 6
*The First and Second Anniversaries* (Donne)
    See *The Anniversaries*
*The First Anniversarie. An Anatomie of the World. Wherein By Occasion of the untimely death of Mistris Elizabeth Drury, the frailtie and decay of this whole World is represented* (Donne) **1**:122, 145-50, 152, 155-57
"The First Anniversary of the Government Under His Highness the Lord Protector" (Marvell)
    See "The First Anniversary of the Government under O. C."
"The First Anniversary of the Government under O. C." (Marvell) **10**:270-71, 290, 294, 305, 312, 318
*First Book* (Blok) **21**:2
*The First Book of Urizen* (Blake)
    See *The Book of Urizen*
"First Calf" (Heaney) **18**:203
"First Carolina Said Song" (Ammons) **16**:5
"The First Celestial Adventure of M Antipyrine" (Tzara) **27**:249
*The First Cities* (Lorde) **12**:137
"First Communion" (Alegria) **26**:
"First Communion" (Kinnell) **26**:
"First Communion" (Kinnell) **26**:239
"First Day of the Future" (Kinnell) **26**:277
*The First Decade: Selected Poems* (Duncan) **2**:105-06
*First Dream* (Juana Ines de la Cruz) **24**:207
"First Early Mornings Together" (Pinsky) **27**:144
"First Elegy" (Rilke) **2**:281, 286
"First Elegy" (Rukeyser) **12**:219
*The First Encounter* (Bely)
    See *Pervoe svidanie*
"First Epistle of the First Book of Horace" (Pope)
    See *Satires and Epistles of Horace, Imitated*
"First Fig" (Millay) **6**:227
"First Fight. Then Fiddle" (Brooks) **7**:75
"First Georgic" (Vergil) **12**:364
"The First Gloss" (Heaney) **18**:216
"First Goodbye" (Gluck) **16**:165-67
*The First Half of "A"-9* (Zukofsky) **11**:339, 396-97
"First Hymn to Lenin" (MacDiarmid) **9**:177-78, 182
*First Hymn to Lenin, and Other Poems* (MacDiarmid) **9**:158, 162, 171, 177, 196
"First Inclined to Take What It Is Told" (Brooks) **7**:74
"First Lesson about Man" (Merton) **10**:344-45
"First Letters from a Steamer" (McGuckian) **27**:82
"The First Man" (Gunn) **26**:191
"First Meditation" (Roethke) **15**:272, 274, 279
*The First Meetings* (Bely)
    See *Pervoe svidanie*
"First Memory" (Gluck) **16**:157
"First, Mills" (Hughes) **7**:149
*The First Morning* (Viereck) **27**:264-65
*First Morning* (Viereck) **27**:280-81, 283
*First Nemean* (Pindar)
    See *Nemean 1*
"First News from Villafranca" (Browning) **6**:23-4
"First Night" (Olds) **22**:309

"The First Noni Daylight" (Harjo) **27**:64
"First Objectives" (MacDiarmid) **9**:154
"The First of All My Dreams Was of" (Cummings) **5**:109
"The First of January" (Lermontov) **18**:201
*First Olympian* (Pindar)
    See *Olympian 1*
"First Page" (Stein) **18**:313
"The First Part" (Page) **12**:190
*First Poems* (Merrill) **28**:
*First Poems* (Merrill) **28**:224, 228-9, 233-4, 238-40, 243-4, 262, 281
*First Poems, 1946-1954* (Kinnell) **26**:279
"First Praise" (Williams) **7**:405
*First Pythian* (Pindar)
    See *Pythian 1*
"The First Rain" (Sikelianos) **29**:367, 373
"First Song" (Akhmatova)
    See "Pervaya pesenka"
"First Song" (Kinnell) **26**:253, 257
*First Song* (Kinnell) **26**:236-38, 253, 262
*the first sufi line* (Bissett) **14**:17
"The First Sunday in Lent" (Lowell) **3**:206
*The First Symphony* (Bely)
    See *Severnaia simfoniia: Pervia geroicheskaia*
"The First Time" (Shapiro) **25**:283, 300, 302, 320
*First Voronezh Notebook* (Mandelstam) **14**:149, 152, 154
*Firstborn* (Gluck) **16**:124-25, 127, 130-32, 134, 138-40, 143-44, 147-49, 151, 153
"Der Fischer" (Goethe) **5**:239
"The Fish" (Bishop) **3**:37, 39, 42-3, 50-2, 54, 60, 66, 69, 75
"The Fish" (Brooke) **24**:58, 63, 65, 87
"The Fish" (Moore) **4**:236, 243, 252, 257
"Fish" (Stryk) **27**:209
"Fish Crier" (Sandburg) **2**:332, 338
"The Fish that Walked" (Sexton) **2**:370, 373
"Fisherman" (Kinnell) **26**:260
"The Fisherman" (Yeats) **20**:324-25
"The Fisherman and the Fish" (Pushkin)
    See "Skazka o Rybake i Rybke"
*The Fisherman's Art* (Ovid)
    See *Halieutica*
"Fishing at Dawn" (Hughes) **7**:120
"Fishing for Eel Totems" (Atwood) **8**:12
"Fishing the White Water" (Lorde) **12**:137
"Fishing with My Daughter in Miller's Meadow" (Stryk) **27**:204, 208, 214
"Fishnet" (Lowell) **3**:229
"Fist" (Levine) **22**:214, 223, 227
"Fit of Fainting" (Bradstreet)
    See "Deliverance From a Fit of Fainting"
"A Fit of Rime Against Rime" (Jonson)
    See "A Fit of Rime Against Rime"
"The Fitting" (Millay) **6**:230, 239
"The Fitting of the Mask" (Kunitz) **19**:154
"V" (Joyce) **22**:138, 162, 167
"Five Accounts of a Monogamous Man" (Meredith) **28**:171, 175, 193-94, 213
"Five Aspects of Fear" (Levertov) **11**:164
"The Five Day Rain" (Levertov) **11**:169
"Five Flights Up" (Bishop) **3**:48-9, 72
"5 Jan 72" (Brutus) **24**:124
*The Five Nations* (Kipling) **3**:192
"Five Senses" (Wright) **14**:348, 363
*Five Senses: Selected Poems* (Wright) **14**:348, 354, 361, 371
"Five Songs" (Rilke) **2**:273
"Five Things" (Goethe) **5**:228
*Five Variations on a Theme* (Sitwell) **3**:304
"Five Vignettes" (Toomer) **7**:332
"Five Walks on the Edge" (Viereck) **27**:277
"Five-Finger Exercises" (Eliot) **5**:185
"Le flacon" (Baudelaire) **1**:45
*Flagons and Apples* (Jeffers) **17**:133, 138
"Le flambeau vivant" (Baudelaire) **1**:56, 61
"The Flame Tree" (Wright) **14**:347
"Flame-Heart" (McKay) **2**:216, 228
"Flammonde" (Robinson) **1**:462, 468, 476

"Flashes and Dedications" (Montale)
    See "Flashes e dediche"
"Flashes e dediche" (Montale) **13**:106, 166-67
"Flat-Foot Drill" (McKay) **2**:225
"Flatted Fifth" (Hughes) **1**:267
"The Flaw" (Lowell) **3**:226-28
"The Flaw in Paganism" (Parker) **28**:351, 363
"A Flayed Crow in the Hall of Judgement" (Hughes) **7**:165
"The Flea" (Donne) **1**:134, 152
"Flèche D'or" (Merrill) **28**:254
"Fleckno" (Marvell) **10**:271, 294
"Flee on Your Donkey" (Sexton) **2**:351, 363-64
*Fleeting Moments* (Tagore)
    See *Kshanikā*
*Fleeting Moments* (Tagore)
    See *Kshanikā*
*Fleeting Thoughts* (Tagore)
    See *Kshanikā*
*Fleeting Thoughts* (Tagore)
    See *Kshanikā*
"Fleming Helphenstine" (Robinson) **1**:466
"Flesh" (Wright) **14**:347
"The Flesh and the Spirit" (Bradstreet) **10**:7-8, 13, 21, 29-30, 38
"Fletcher McGee" (Masters) **1**:345
"La Fleur qui fait le printemps" (Gautier) **18**:128-29
*Les fleurs du mal* (Baudelaire) **1**:44-51, 53-8, 60, 62-5, 67-71
"Flies Enter through a Closed Mouth" (Neruda)
    See "Por boca cerrada entran moscas"
"Flight" (Brooke) **24**:56
"The Flight" (Roethke) **15**:302
"Flight" (Sexton) **2**:347, 361
"Flight into Egypt" (Auden) **1**:38
"The Flight into Egypt" (Merton) **10**:330
*A Flight of Cranes* (Tagore)
    See *Balākā*
*A Flight of Swans* (Tagore)
    See *Balākā*
*A Flight of Swans* (Tagore)
    See *Balākā*
"Flight to the City" (Williams) **7**:385, 387-88
"The Flitting" (McGuckian) **27**:78, 97
"Floating" (Rexroth) **20**:216
"Floating of the River of Han" (Wang Wei) **18**:362
"The Flood" (Tomlinson) **17**:333
"The Flood" (Wright) **14**:337-38
*The Flood* (Tomlinson) **17**:332, 336, 349, 354
"The Flood of Years" (Bryant) **20**:10, 16-18
"Flooded Meadows" (Gunn) **26**:219
"Flooding" (Celan) **10**:105
"Florence" (Lowell) **3**:213, 236
"Florida" (Bishop) **3**:37
"Flow Chart" (Ashbery) **26**:
*Flow Chart* (Ashbery) **26**:164
"Flow Gently Sweet Afton" (Burns)
    See "Sweet Afton"
"The Flower" (Herbert) **4**:104, 109, 113, 118, 127, 131-32
"The Flower and the Rock" (Page) **12**:178
*Flower, Fist, and Bestial Wail* (Bukowski) **18**:3, 5
*Flower Herding on Mount Monadnock* (Kinnell) **26**:236, 257, 290
"Flower in the Crannied Wall" (Tennyson) **6**:358
"The Flower Master" (McGuckian) **27**:78
*The Flower Master* (McGuckian) **27**:77-80, 84-85, 95-97, 101, 104
"Flower of Five Blossoms" (Kinnell) **26**:286
"The Flower of Old Japan" (Noyes) **27**:116-17, 139
*The Flower of Old Japan* (Noyes) **27**:116, 139
"Flowered Sitting Room" (McGuckian) **27**:105
"The Flower-Fed Buffaloes" (Lindsay) **23**:279
"The Flowering of the Rod" (H. D.) **5**:271-72, 274-75, 293, 296, 306, 309, 314-16
"Flowering Plum" (Gluck) **16**:128, 154

"The Flowering Tree" (Bridges) **28**:77, 80
"The Flowers" (Kipling) **3**:161, 167
"Flowers from the Volcano" (Alegria) **26**:
*Flowers from the Volcano* (Alegria) **26**:
*The Flowers of Evil* (Baudelaire)
   See *Les fleurs du mal*
"The Flume" (Bogan) **12**:95, 121
"La flûte" (Vigny) **26**:367, 392, 403, 413
"La Flute" (Vigny) **26**:367
"Flute Notes from a Reedy Pond" (Plath) **1**:389
"A Flute Overheard" (Rexroth) **20**:195
"Flute-Maker, with an Accompaniment"
   (Browning) **2**:88
"Flutender" (Celan) **10**:105
"FLux et reflux" (Hugo) **17**:100
"The Fly" (Blake) **12**:7, 34
"The Fly" (Brodsky) **9**:29
"The Fly" (Kinnell) **26**:255
"The Fly" (Shapiro) **25**:269, 324, 326
"A Fly that flew into my Mistress her Eye"
   (Carew) **29**:87
"Flying Above California" (Gunn) **26**:201, 219
"Flying Crooked" (Graves) **6**:149, 151
"Flying Home" (Kinnell) **26**:259, 261
"Flying Home from Utah" (Swenson) **14**:261
"Flying out of It" (Ferlinghetti) **1**:175
"Flying to Byzantium" (Merrill) **11**:189
"Flying Underground" (Giovanni) **19**:143
"Foam" (Enzensberger) **28**:146-48, 156
"Fog" (Cassian) **17**:6
"Fog" (Sandburg) **2**:301, 303
"Fog" (Soto) **28**:377, 384
"The Foggy, Foggy Blue" (Schwartz) **8**:317
"La foi" (Lamartine) **16**:277, 291
"Folie de Minuit" (Lowell) **13**:90-1
"Folk Song" (Parker) **28**:355
"Follies" (Sandburg) **2**:303
"Follow that Stagecoach" (Wakoski) **15**:323
"Follower" (Heaney) **18**:200
"Folly" (MacDiarmid) **9**:153
"The Folly of Being Comforted" (Yeats)
"Fonction du poète" (Hugo) **17**:77, 97
"Fontana di aga del me pais" (Pasolini) **17**:259
"The Food Chain" (Kumin) **15**:208
"Food for Fire, Food for Thought" (Duncan)
   **2**:120-21
"Fool Errant" (Lowell) **13**:83
"Fool o' the Moon" (Lowell) **13**:67, 83, 86
"The Foolish Heart" (Cullen) **20**:59
"Foolish Men" (Juana Ines de la Cruz)
   See "Hombres necios que acusáis"
"Footfalls" (Ashbery) **26**:
"Footnote to Howl" (Ginsberg) **4**:65, 68, 70
*Footprints* (Levertov) **11**:189
"The Foot-Washing" (Ammons) **16**:58
"For" (Zukofsky) **11**:349
"For a Birthday" (Gunn) **26**:206
"For a Dead Lady" (Robinson) **1**:461, 490,
   492-93
"For a Dead Vole" (Smith) **12**:317
"For a Fatherless Son" (Plath) **1**:397
"For a few Hopi Ancestors" (Rose) **13**:233
"For a Good Dog" (Nash) **21**:268
"For a Lady Who Must Write Verse" (Parker)
   **28**:363
"For a Lovely Lady" (Cullen) **20**:52, 55
"For a Marriage" (Bogan) **12**:94
"For a Muse Meant" (Duncan) **2**:105
"For a Pastoral Family" (Wright) **14**:375, 378
"For a Picture of St. Dorothea" (Hopkins)
   **15**:144, 159-62
"For a Poet" (Cullen) **20**:85
"For a Russian Poet" (Rich) **5**:383
"For a Sad Lady" (Parker) **28**:360
"For a' that" (Scott) **13**:293
"For A' That and A' That" (Burns)
   See "Is There for Honest Poverty"
"For a Young Artist" (Hayden) **6**:187, 189-90,
   196, 198
"For All Who Ever sent Lace Valentines"
   (Lindsay) **23**:265

"For Alva Benson and For Those Who Have
   Learned to Speak" (Harjo) **27**:55, 64
"For an Assyrian Frieze" (Viereck) **27**:260, 280
"For Andy Goodman, Michael Schwerner, and
   James Chaney" (Walker) **20**:277-78, 287
"For Anna Mae Pictou Aquash, Whose Spirit
   Is Present Here and in the Dappled Stars"
   (For We Remember the Story and Tell It
   Again So that We May All LiveHarjo)
   **27**:71
"For Anne at Passover" (Kumin) **15**:180
"For Annie" (Poe) **1**:425, 434, 437, 444-45,
   447
"For Black People" (Madhubuti) **5**:327, 345
"For Black Poets Who Think of Suicide"
   (Knight) **14**:42
"For Chekhov" (Hass) **16**:199, 214
"For Clarice" (Brooks) **7**:56
"For Danton" (Tomlinson) **17**:345-46, 350
"For Deliverance from a Fever" (Bradstreet)
   **10**:36, 60
"For Each of You" (Lorde) **12**:157
"For Eleanor and Bill Monahan" (Williams)
   **7**:392-93
"For Eleanor Boylan Talking with God"
   (Sexton) **2**:371
"For Eli Jacobsen" (Rexroth) **20**:181
"For Eric Dolphy" (Knight) **14**:39
"For Freckle-Faced Gerald" (Knight) **14**:41-2
"For George Santayana" (Lowell) **3**:219
"For God While Sleeping" (Sexton) **2**:351, 360-
   61, 371
"For Godsake hold your tongue, and let me
   love" (Donne)
   See "The Canonization"
"For Guillaume Apollinaire" (Meredith) **28**:194,
   208
"For Gwendolyn Brooks" (Giovanni) **19**:113
"For Helen" (Stryk) **27**:203
"For Hettie in Her Fifth Month" (Baraka) **4**:15
"For His Father" (Meredith) **28**:180, 191, 194
"For Jane Myers" (Gluck) **16**:128
"For John Clare" (Ashbery) **26**:125
"For John, Who Begs Me Not to Enquire
   Further" (Sexton) **2**:347, 350, 357
"For Johnny Pole on the Forgotten Beach"
   (Sexton) **2**:349-50, 353
"For Julia in Nebraska" (Rich) **5**:385
"For Koras and Balafons" (Senghor) **25**:231
*For Lizzie and Harriet* (Lowell) **3**:224, 226
"For M." (Zagajewski) **27**:396
"For Malcolm, a Year After" (Knight) **14**:38
"For marilyn m" (Bukowski) **18**:22
"For Memory" (Rich) **5**:395
"For Miriam" (Tomlinson) **17**:336-37, 349
"For Mr. Death Who Stands with His Door
   Open" (Sexton) **2**:367, 372
"For My Brother" (Song) **21**:331, 341
"For My Brother Reported Missing in Action,
   1943" (Merton) **10**:331-32, 342, 349
"For My Daughter" (Wright) **14**:348, 355, 362
"For My Lady" (Sanchez) **9**:209, 225
"For My Lover, Returning to His Wife"
   (Sexton) **2**:353, 372
"For My Mothers" (Gluck) **16**:132, 138, 149
"For My People" (Walker) **20**:272, 274, 280-
   81, 283, 285, 289, 294
*For My People* (Walker) **20**:274-76, 281-83,
   285-86, 289, 292-93
"For My Son on the Highways of His Mind"
   (Kumin) **15**:192, 201
"For New England" (Wright) **14**:340, 362
"For Precision" (Wright) **14**:342-43, 347
"For Proserpine" (Kunitz) **19**:175
"For Proust" (Merrill) **28**:248
"For R. C. B." (Parker) **28**:362
"For Rhoda" (Schwartz) **8**:282
"For Robert Frost" (Kinnell) **26**:
"For Robert Frost" (Kinnell) **26**:284
"For Sale" (Lowell) **3**:219-20
"For Saundra" (Giovanni) **19**:114-15, 139

"For Shoshana-Pat Swinton" (Piercy) **29**:300,
   303
"For Sidney Bechet" (Larkin) **21**:227
"For Signs" (Gunn) **26**:204, 214
"For the Better" (Finch) **21**:181
"for the blind" (Clifton) **17**:26
"For the Boy Who Was Dodger Point Lookout
   Fifteen Years Ago" (Snyder) **21**:288
"For the Children" (Snyder) **21**:298
"For the Commander of The Eliza" (Heaney)
   **18**:186-87, 200, 207
"For the Conjunction of Two Planets" (Rich)
   **5**:360
"For the Felling of a Tree in Harvard Yard"
   (Rich) **5**:359
"For the Furies" (Piercy) **29**:314
*For the Guitar* (Borges)
   See *Para las seis cuerdas*
"For the Kent State Martyrs" (Brutus) **24**:119
"For the Marriage of Faustus and Helen"
   (Crane) **3**:81, 83, 90, 92, 95, 97
"For the One Who Would Not Take His Life
   in His Hands" (Schwartz) **8**:313
"For the One Who Would Not Take Man's
   Life In His Hands" (Schwartz) **8**:301, 313
"For the Prisoners in South Africa" (Brutus)
   **24**:111
"For the Quaternary Age" (Wright) **14**:373
"For the Record" (Lorde) **12**:140
"For the Restoration of My Dear Husband
   from a Burning Ague" (Bradstreet) **10**:26,
   62
"For the Revolutionary Outburst by Black
   People" (Baraka) **4**:39
"For the Stranger" (Forche) **10**:144, 157, 168
*For the Time Being* (Auden) **1**:17, 23, 34, 36-7
"For the Union Dead" (Lowell) **3**:211-14, 223-
   24, 226, 232
*For the Union Dead* (Lowell) **3**:211-14, 223-
   24, 226, 232
"For the Word is Flesh" (Kunitz) **19**:147, 152
"For the Year of the Insane" (Sexton) **2**:363
"For Those Sisters & Brothers in Gallup"
   (Ortiz) **17**:232
"For Tom Postell, Dead Black Poet" (Baraka)
   **4**:10-11, 19
"For Two Girls Setting Out in Life" (Viereck)
   **27**:262
"For Two Lovers in the Year 2075 in the
   Canadian Woods" (Meredith) **28**:199
"For Unborn Malcolms" (Sanchez) **9**:218-19,
   224, 233
"For Walter and Lilian Lowenfels" (Piercy)
   **29**:303
*For You: Poems* (Carruth) **10**:83
*Force of Light* (Celan)
   See *Lichtzwang*
"The Force That through the Green Fuse
   Drives the Flower" (Thomas) **2**:384-84
"Forcing House" (Roethke) **15**:295
"Ford Madox Ford" (Lowell) **3**:219
"Forebears" (Pavese)
   See "Antenati"
"Foreign Flower" (Tagore)
   See "Videshi phul"
"Foreigner" (Page) **12**:170
*The Forerunner* (Gibran) **9**:69, 71, 75, 79
"Forerunners" (Emerson) **18**:79, 84
"Forest" (Swenson) **14**:268
"The Forest" (Wright) **14**:348, 361
*The Forest* (Jonson) **17**:158-59, 169, 180, 194
"The Forest Hymn" (Bryant) **20**:3, 14, 18, 23,
   29, 33
*The Forest I* (Jonson) **17**:180, 194
*The Forest II* (Jonson) **17**:158-59, 161, 165,
   169, 182, 189, 202-06, 209, 214
*The Forest II* (Jonson) **17**:163
*The Forest III* (Jonson) **17**:158-59, 161, 163,
   192, 210
*Forest Leaves* (Harper) **21**:185
*Forest Moon* (Paz)
   See *Luna silvestre*

"The Forest of Wild Thyme" (Noyes) **27**:116
*The Forest of Wild Thyme* (Noyes) **27**:139
"Forest Path" (Ishikawa)
   See "Mori no michi"
"The Forest Path" (Wright) **14**:339
*The Forest VII* (Jonson) **17**:176
*The Forest XI* (Jonson) **17**:159, 172
*The Forest XII* (Jonson) **17**:158, 160, 214, 217
*The Forest XIII* (Jonson) **17**:158, 160, 163, 192
*The Forest XV* (Jonson) **17**:162, 171-72
*The Forests of Lithuania* (Davie) **29**:95-96, 109
"Forêt dans la Hache" (Breton) **15**:52
"La foret merveilleuse ou je vis donne un bal"
   (Apollinaire) **7**:3
"The Forge" (Heaney) **18**:200, 221, 223
"Le forgeron" (Rimbaud) **3**:277, 283, 285
"Forget not Yet" (Wyatt) **27**:315, 324, 357
"For-Get-Me-Not" (Stein) **18**:313
"The Forging" (Borges)
   See "Forjadura"
"forgiving my father" (Clifton) **17**:18
"Forgotten Arietta" (Verlaine)
   See "Ariettes oubliées"
"A Forgotten Miniature" (Hardy) **8**:137-38
"Forgotten Song" (Ashbery) **26**:162
"Forjadura" (Borges) **22**:72
"The Forlorn Sea" (Smith) **12**:326
"Form without Love" (Aleixandre) **15**:18-19,
   22-3
"Forming Child" (Ortiz) **17**:225, 231
"Forms of the Earth at Abiquiu" (Momaday)
   **25**:201-203
"The Forsaken" (Lowell) **13**:62
"A Forsaken Garden" (Swinburne) **24**:324, 338,
   344
"The Forsaken Merman" (Arnold) **5**:5-8, 12-13,
   17-18, 34-5, 38-9, 42, 49
*Forslin* (Aiken) **26**:6-7, 27
"Forties Flick" (Ashbery) **26**:149
"The Fortress" (Sexton) **2**:362
"Fortunatus Nimium" (Bridges) **28**:73, 75,
   89-90
"Fortune..." (Ferlinghetti) **1**:183
"Fortune-Telling" (Tsvetaeva)
   See "Gadan'e"
"Forty Singing Seamen" (Noyes) **27**:133
*Forty Singing Seamen and Other Poems*
   (Noyes) **27**:133
*45 Mercy Street* (Sexton) **2**:356, 359, 367, 374
*XLI Poems* (Cummings) **5**:104
"Forward Observers" (Stryk) **27**:203
"Fosterling" (Heaney) **18**:259
"Les foules" (Baudelaire) **1**:59
*Found Objects* (Zukofsky) **11**:346
"Founders Day. A Secular Ode on the Ninth
   Jubilee of Eton College" (Bridges) **28**:67,
   71
"The Fountain" (Bryant) **20**:4, 43, 47
"The Fountain" (Wordsworth) **4**:374, 399
"A Fountain, a Bottle, a Donkey's Ear and
   Some Books" (Frost) **1**:194
"The Fountain of Ammannati" (Stryk) **27**:183-
   84, 192
"Fountain Piece" (Swenson) **14**:263-64
"The Fountains of Aix" (Swenson) **14**:250, 255,
   285-86
"IV" (Joyce) **22**:145, 163, 166, 168, 173
"The Four Ages" (Nemerov) **24**:293-24, 297
"The Four Ages of Man" (Bradstreet) **10**:4, 17,
   30, 45
"Four Auguries" (Atwood) **8**:27-8
"The Four Brothers" (Sandburg) **2**:302
"Four Canzones" (1957-1961Okigbo) **7**:247-48
"Four Dancers at an Irish Wedding"
   (Gallagher) **9**:37
"4 daughters" (Clifton) **17**:25
"Four Dheetziyama Poems" (Ortiz) **17**:225
"The Four Elements" (Bradstreet) **10**:11, 17, 41
"Four Evasions" (Atwood) **8**:24, 27-8
"Four Eyes" (Ondaatje) **28**:292, 329, 331
"Four for Sir John Davies" (Roethke) **15**:263,
   273-74, 286

"The Four Gospels" (Goethe) **5**:229
"Four in a Family" (Rukeyser) **12**:223
"Four Kantian Lyrics" (Tomlinson) **17**:311, 342
*The Four Men* (Brooke) **24**:89
"The Four Monarchies" (Bradstreet) **10**:4-5,
   17-18, 20-1, 27, 31, 33-4, 40, 46-7
"Four Notions of Love and Marriage"
   (Momaday) **25**:189
"Four O'Clock Summer Street" (McGuckian)
   **27**:82, 90
"4 Other Countries" (Zukofsky) **11**:348
"Four Poems from New Zealand" (Wright)
   **14**:377
"Four Preludes on Playthings of the Wind"
   (Sandburg) **2**:316, 340
*The Four Quartets* (Eliot) **5**:162-65, 174, 178-
   80, 182, 186, 196, 198, 200, 205-06, 208,
   210-11
"The Four Seasons of the Year" (Bradstreet)
   **10**:17, 44
"Four Sides to a House" (Lowell) **13**:61
"Four Sonnets" (Nemerov) **24**:256
"The Four Sorrows" (Marie de France)
   See "Le Chaitivel"
"4/25/89 late" (Clifton) **17**:30
*The Four Years' Notebook* (Montale)
   See *Quaderno de quattro anni*
*The Four Zoas: The Torments of Love and
   Jealousy in the Death and Judgement of
   Albion the Ancient Man* (Blake) **12**:13-21,
   25-9, 32, 35-8, 41, 47, 49-50, 60-4, 73
"XIV" (Joyce) **22**:138, 145, 160, 163-66,
   168-70
"14 Dec." (Ammons) **16**:22
*Fourteenth Olympian* (Pindar)
   See *Olympian 14*
"Fourth Georgic" (Vergil) **12**:365, 371
"Fourth Meditation" (Roethke) **15**:272, 278
"The Fourth Month of the Landscape
   Architect" (Rich) **5**:384
*Fourth Nemean* (Pindar)
   See *Nemean 4*
"Fourth of July" (Hughes) **7**:119
"Fourth of July in Maine" (Lowell) **3**:226
*Fourth Pythian* (Pindar)
   See *Pythian 4*
*Fourth Quarter and Other Poems* (Wright)
   **14**:372-75
*The Fourth Symphony* (Bely)
   See *Kubok metelej: Chetviortiia simfoniia*
*Fowre Hymnes* (Spenser) **8**:332, 334, 337, 390
"The Fox" (Tomlinson) **17**:327
"Fox" (Wright) **14**:376
"Fox Trot" (Sitwell) **3**:297, 303
"Foxes' Moon" (Tomlinson) **17**:343
"Foxhunt" (Hughes) **7**:166
"Fra Lippo Lippi" (Browning) **2**:37, 88, 95
*Fra Rupert* (Landor) **5**:95
"Fragment" (Ashbery) **26**:118, 125, 135, 144,
   156-157
"A Fragment" (Bryant)
   See "Inscription for the Entrance into a
   Wood"
"Fragment" (Finch) **21**:140, 172
"Fragment" (Johnson) **24**:142, 148
"Fragment: As Bronze may be much
   Beautified" (Owen) **19**:352
"Fragment from Correspondence" (Nemerov)
   **24**:298
"Fragment: I saw his Round Mouth's
   Crimson" (Owen) **19**:352
"Fragment of an 'Antigone'" (Arnold) **5**:48-9
"Fragment Thirty-Six" (H. D.) **5**:268, 270
"Fragments du narcisse" (Valery) **9**:348, 365-
   66, 372, 393, 395-96
"Fragments from a Poem to be entitled 'The
   Sentimental Exile'" (Brooke) **24**:68, 80,
   89
"Fragments from the Deluge" (Okigbo) **7**:231,
   246, 255
"Fragoletta" (Swinburne) **24**:361-62
"Frailty" (Herbert) **4**:135

"Le Fraisne" (Marie de France) **22**:241, 248,
   258, 269, 271-72, 275, 277-78, 282
"Frame" (Rich) **5**:396
*Frameless Windows, Squares of Light* (Song)
   **21**:334, 344, 345-46
"Frammento alla morte" (Pasolini) **17**:295
"France" (Sassoon) **12**:276, 278
"France: An Ode" (Coleridge)
   See "Ode to France"
*La Franciade* (Ronsard)
   See *Les quatre premiers livres de la
   Franciade*
"Francie's Fingers" (Wylie) **23**:324
"Francis Furini" (Browning) **2**:72, 75, 84-5
"Francisco, I'll Bring You Red Carnations"
   (Levine) **22**:225
"La frangia dei capelli" (Montale) **13**:111, 128
"Franklin's Tale" (Chaucer) **19**:11-13, 15, 17,
   27, 33, 47, 53, 61
"Franz Schubert A Press Conference"
   (Zagajewski) **27**:382, 385, 401
"Fraud" (Blok) **21**:37
"Fraulein Reads Instructive Rhymes" (Kumin)
   **15**:180
"Frederick Douglass" (Dunbar) **5**:131, 134, 143
"Frederick Douglass" (Hayden) **6**:176, 183,
   188, 196, 199
"Free" (McKay) **2**:225
"Free Fantasia: Tiger Flowers" (Hayden)
   **6**:194-95
"Free Labor" (Harper) **21**:217-18
"Free Thoughts" (Blok) **21**:31
"The Freebooters" (Cardenal)
   See "Los filibusteros"
"Freedman" (Heaney) **18**:205
"Freedom" (Hughes) **1**:252
"Freedom New Hampshire" (Kinnell) **26**:236,
   238, 242, 284, 289
*Freedom under Parole* (Paz)
   See *Libertad bajo palabra*
"Freedom's Plow" (Hughes) **1**:250, 258
*The Freeing of the Dust* (Levertov) **11**:197-98,
   213
"Freeing the Boat" (Tu Fu) **9**:320
"Freezing" (Meredith) **28**:177
"La frégate 'La Sérieuse'" (Vigny) **26**:411
"A French Poem" (Merton) **10**:337
"French Poems" (Ashbery) **26**:118
*The French Revolution* (Blake) **12**:13, 25, 63
"A French Rooster" (Stein) **18**:313
"Frente al Oxford" (Guillen) **23**:126
"Frenzy" (Sexton) **2**:368
"Fresh Stain" (Gallagher) **9**:62, 64
*Fresko-Sonett* (Heine) **25**:160
"Fresne" (Marie de France)
   See "Le Fraisne"
"Friar's Tale" (Chaucer) **19**:11, 13-14
"Friday the Thirteenth" (Ginsberg) **4**:75
"Friday: The Toilette: Lydia" (Montagu) **16**:338,
   347-49
"The Friend" (Piercy) **29**:308-09
"The Friend" (Smith) **12**:318
"The Friend of Grandmother Speranza"
   (Gozzano)
   See "L'amica di nonna speranza"
"The Friend of the Fourth Decade" (Merrill)
   **28**:220-21, 269
"Friend Who Has Been Reading Jacques
   Lacan" (Hass) **16**:199
"The Friend Who Is Sleeping" (Pavese)
   See "Adventures"
"Friends" (Ashbery) **26**:145
"Friends" (Sexton) **2**:365
"Friendship" (Stryk) **27**:204, 208
"Friendship Between Ephelia and Ardelia"
   (Finch) **21**:164
"The Frightened Man" (Bogan) **12**:86
*The Frightening World* (Blok) **21**:25
"Frimaire" (Lowell) **13**:97
"Friso" (Dario) **15**:112
"Frisson" (Gautier) **18**:164

"A Frivolous Conversation" (Milosz) **8**:194
"Frog Autumn" (Plath) **1**:388
"The Frog Prince" (Smith) **12**:305, 323, 341
"Froid jaune" (Tzara) **27**:227
"A Frolick" (Herrick) **9**:103
"From a Daybook" (Swenson) **14**:273
"From a Notebook" (Merrill) **28**:248
"From a Notebook, October '68—May '69"
    (Levertov) **11**:176, 180, 195
"From a Survivor" (Rich) **5**:360
"From a Tower" (Montale)
    See "Da una torre"
"From a Train Window" (Millay) **6**:214
"From an Old House in America" (Rich) **5**:373-
    74, 394
"From Ancient Fangs" (Viereck) **27**:263
"From Another Sore Fit" (Bradstreet) **10**:61-2
*From Feathers to Iron* (Day Lewis) **11**:123-24,
    128-30, 135, 138-39, 142, 148-52
"From Grants to Gallup, New Mexico" (Ortiz)
    **17**:233
"From House to Home" (Rossetti) **7**:260-1, 276,
    282, 284, 290
"From Memory" (Forche) **10**:135
"From Memory" (Zagajewski) **27**:396
"From Morpheus" (H. D.) **5**:270
"From My Diary, July, 1914" (Owen) **19**:338,
    343, 346
"From My Notes for a Series of Lectures on
    Murder" (Smith) **12**:343
*From Sand Creek: Rising in This Heart Which
    Is Our America* (Ortiz) **17**:222, 230, 234,
    239-240
*From Snow and Rock, from Chaos: Poems,
    1965-1972* (Carruth) **10**:71, 91
"From something, nothing" (Piercy) **29**:315
"From Superstition" (Pasternak) **6**:260
"From the Bridge" (Alegria) **26**:
"From the Cave" (Lorde) **12**:143
"From the Childhood of Jesus" (Pinsky) **27**:164,
    175
"From the Coptic" (Smith) **12**:313-14
"From the Corpse Woodpiles, from the Ashes"
    (Hayden) **6**:194-95, 198
"From the Crest" (Berry) **28**:43
"From the Cupola" (Merrill) **28**:222-3, 226,
    228, 234-5, 250, 257, 270
*From the Cutting Room Floor* (Merrill) **28**:269
"From the Dark Tower" (Cullen) **20**:57-58, 63,
    70, 76
"From the Dressing-Room" (McGuckian) **27**:98
"From the Eleventh Finger" (Wakoski) **15**:350
*From the First Nine* (Merrill) **28**:263
"From the First Underworld" (McGuckian)
    **27**:105
"From the Frontier of Writing" (Heaney)
    **18**:231-32
"From the Garden" (Sexton) **2**:351
"From the Highest Camp" (Gunn) **26**:
"From the House of Yemanjá" (Lorde) **12**:151
"From the Lives of Things" (Zagajewski)
    **27**:389
"From the Motorway" (Tomlinson) **17**:354-55
"From the Rising of the Sun" (Milosz)
    See "From Where the Sun Rises"
*From the Rising of the Sun* (Milosz)
    See *Gdziewschodzi stònce i kedy zapada*
"From the Same" (Belloc) **24**:32
"From The School Anthology: Albert Frolov"
    (Brodsky) **9**:4
"From the Seacoast" (Tsvetaeva)
    See "S morya"
*From the Sick-Bed* (Tagore)
    See *Rogsajyae*
"From 'The Snow Lamp'" (Hayden) **6**:194-95
"From the Surface" (Pinsky) **27**:145
"From the Top of the Stairs" (Zagajewski)
    **27**:382
"From the Wave" (Gunn) **26**:196-197, 204, 215
"From the Wellington Museum" (Wright)
    **14**:377
"From the White Place" (Song) **21**:331, 340

*From Threshold to Threshold* (Celan)
    See *Von Schwelle zu Schwelle*
"From Where the Sun Rises" (Milosz) **8**:203-05
*From Where the Sun Rises to Where It Sets*
    (Milosz)
    See *Gdziewschodzi stònce i kedy zapada*
"Frondes Agrestes" (Tomlinson) **17**:315, 359
"Front Door Soliloquy" (Graves) **6**:143
"Front Lines" (Snyder) **21**:297, 319
"Front the Ages with a Smile" (Masters) **1**:335
"Frontispiece" (Swenson) **14**:249, 253
"Die Frösche von Bikini" (Enzensberger)
    **28**:150
"Frost at Midnight" (Coleridge) **11**:51, 53, 57-8,
    84, 89, 97, 100, 102-04
"The Frost of Death Was on the Pane"
    (Dickinson) **1**:104
"Frost-Bamboo Ranges" (Wang Wei) **18**:362
"Frosty Night" (Graves) **6**:141
"The Frozen City" (Nemerov) **24**:255
"The Frozen Greenhouse" (Hardy) **8**:92
*Das Frühwerk* (Celan) **10**:121
"Fruit" (Zagajewski) **27**:394
"Fruit of the Flower" (Cullen) **20**:52-53, 86
"The Fruit Shop" (Lowell) **13**:78
"Fruitlands" (Toomer) **7**:323
"Frustration" (Parker) **28**:362
"Fuga" (Pasolini) **17**:264
"The Fugitive" (Lermontov) **18**:282
"The Fugitive" (Stryk) **27**:198
*Fugitive* (Tagore)
    See *Palātakā*
"The Fugitive's Wife" (Harper) **21**:206
"El fugitivo" (Neruda) **4**:292
"Fuite d'Enfance" (Smith) **12**:325, 344
"Fulfilment" (Pasternak) **6**:267
"Full Circle" (Viereck) **27**:267-68
"Full Fathom Five" (Plath) **1**:388-89
"Full Moon" (Graves) **6**:136, 151
"Full Moon" (Hayden) **6**:187, 194-95
"Full Moon" (Wylie) **23**:322
"Full Moon and Little Frieda" (Hughes) **7**:137,
    142, 168
"Full Moon New Guinea" (Shapiro) **25**:325
"Full Well Yt Maye be Sene" (Wyatt) **27**:316
"Fullness of Time" (Tomlinson) **17**:321
"Fumatori di carta" (Pavese) **13**:225, 227
"Fundamental Disagreement with Two
    Contemporaries" (Rexroth) **20**:196
"The Funeral" (Brooks) **7**:53, 87
"The Funeral of Bobo" (Brodsky) **9**:8
"The Funeral of Youth" (Brooke) **24**:53, 78
"Funeral Rites" (Heaney) **18**:203-4, 210-11
"The Funerall" (Donne) **1**:130
"A Funerall Elegie" (Donne) **1**:146-47, 154-58;
    **24**:151, 184-85, 188
"The Funerall Rites of the Rose" (Herrick)
    **9**:126
"Fünf Gesänge" (Rilke) **2**:265-69
"Funnel" (Sexton) **2**:345, 350
"Für die Mouche" (Heine) **25**:148
*Die Furie des Verschwindens* (Enzensberger)
    **28**:150, 159, 161, 163
"The Furies" (Masters) **1**:329, 343
"The Furies" (Sexton) **2**:367
"Furious Versions" (Lee) **24**:240, 243, 248, 251
"The Furious Voyage" (Graves) **6**:130, 143
"The Furniture of a Woman's Mind" (Swift)
    **9**:295
"Fürstin" (Goethe) **5**:249
"Further Arrivals" (Atwood) **8**:36, 39
*A Further Range* (Frost) **1**:195-97, 202
"Fury Of Rain" (Harjo) **27**:66
"The Fury of Sundays" (Sexton) **2**:367, 373
"The Fury of the Cocks" (Sexton) **2**:371
"Fuscello teso" (Montale) **13**:134
"Les fusillés" (Hugo) **17**:101
"Futility" (Owen) **19**:330, 342, 347, 359,
    365-68
"The Future" (Arnold) **5**:18, 43-5
"Future and Past" (Browning) **6**:16
"The Future Life" (Bryant) **20**:4, 9

"Future Present" (Shapiro) **25**:324
"Futuro" (Guillen) **23**:99
"Fuzzy-Wuzzy" (Kipling) **3**:156, 158, 167,
    186-87
"Gadan'e" (Tsvetaeva) **14**:312-14
"Gaiety" (Sitwell) **3**:294
"Gairmscoile" (MacDiarmid) **9**:188-89, 193
"Gakusei" (Ishikawa) **10**:215
"Galatea Encore" (Brodsky) **9**:25, 27
"Galerías Preciadas" (Fuertes) **27**:13-4
"Galla Placidia" (Ekeloef) **23**:60
"The Gallery" (Marvell) **10**:271, 300
"The Galley" (Kipling) **3**:182
"The Galley-Slave" (Kipling) **3**:157
"Gallo cedrone" (Montale) **13**:108, 111
"The Galloping Cat" (Smith) **12**:311
"The Game" (Gluck) **16**:124
"Game after Supper" (Atwood) **8**:3
"Game Mistress" (Cassian) **17**:11
"A Game of Monopoly in Chavannes"
    (Kumin) **15**:211
"Gangrene" (Levine) **22**:212
"Ganymed" (Goethe) **5**:247, 254
"Ganymede" (Holderlin) **4**:148, 166
"The Gap" (Tomlinson) **17**:347
"Garage Sale" (Shapiro) **25**:322
"Garbo at the Gaumont" (McGuckian) **27**:107,
    109-111
"The Garden" (Gluck) **16**:130, 150-51, 168
"Garden" (H. D.) **5**:275, 303
"The Garden" (Marvell) **10**:266, 268, 271-73,
    277, 283-85, 287-92, 294, 297, 311, 313-
    14, 318
"The Garden" (Montale)
    See "L'orto"
*The Garden* (Gluck) **16**:129
"Garden Abstract" (Crane) **3**:81
"Garden by Moonlight" (Lowell) **13**:64, 98
"The Garden in September" (Bridges) **28**:67
"The Garden in September" (Bridges) **28**:83
"The Garden of Boccaccio's" (Coleridge)
    **11**:104-09
"the garden of delight" (Clifton) **17**:36
"The Garden of Earthly Delights" (Milosz)
    **8**:181, 209
"The Garden of Gethsemane" (Pasternak) **6**:285
"Garden of Love" (Blake) **12**:7, 33
"Garden of Nightingales" (Blok)
    See "The Nightingale Garden"
"The Garden of Proserpine" (Swinburne)
    **24**:345
*The Garden of the Prophet* (Gibran) **9**:75
"The Garden Party" (Belloc) **24**:27
"The Garden Party" (Davie) **29**:93
"The Garden Seat" (Hardy) **8**:100
"The Garden Sees" (Elytis) **21**:132
"The Garden Wall" (Levertov) **11**:169
"Gardener" (Graves) **6**:151
*Gardeners and Astronomers* (Sitwell) **3**:321
"The Gardener's Daughter" (Tennyson) **6**:354
"Gare" (Tzara) **27**:223-24
"Gare au bord de la mer" (Laforgue) **14**:76
"Gareth and Lynette" (Tennyson) **6**:373, 376
*The Garland of Laurel* (Skelton) **25**:350-51,
    353, 356, 369-75
*Garland of Songs* (Tagore)
    See *Gitimālya*
"The Gate at the Center" (Olson) **19**:283
"The Gate in His Head" (Ondaatje) **28**:294,
    296, 322, 327, 334
"The Gates" (Rukeyser) **12**:224
*The Gates* (Rukeyser) **12**:220, 222, 225
*The Gates of Paradise* (Blake) **12**:46
"The Gates of the Arsenal" (Milosz) **8**:191
*The Gates of Wrath: Rhymed Poems,
    1948-1952* (Ginsberg) **4**:55-7, 63, 79, 91
"The Gateway" (Wright) **14**:338, 346
*The Gateway* (Wright) **14**:334, 336-38, 341,
    345-46, 349, 354, 374
"Gather Ye Rosebuds while Ye May" (Herrick)
    See "To the Virgins, to Make Much of
    Time"

"A Gathered Church" (Davie) **29**:101, 112-13
"Gathering Apricots" (Milosz) **8**:212, 215
"Gathering Leaves" (Frost) **1**:218
*Gathering the Tribes* (Forche) **10**:132-35, 137, 141-43, 145, 148, 152, 156, 158, 165-66, 168-69
"GATSBY'S THEORY OF AESTHETICS" (Baraka) **4**:19, 24
*Gaudete* (Hughes) **7**:154-58, 161-65, 171
*Gavriiliada* (Pushkin) **10**:364, 410-12
*The Gavriiliada* (Pushkin)
  See *Gavriiliada*
"Gay Chaps at the Bar" (Brooks) **7**:70, 73, 89
"Gazing on the Great Peak" (Tu Fu) **9**:329
"Gazing on the Peak" (Tu Fu) **9**:328
"Gde, vysokaya, tvoy tsyganyonok" (Akhmatova) **2**:12
*Gdziewschodzi stônce i kedy zapada* (Milosz) **8**:174-75, 178, 186, 188, 195-97, 206-07
"Le géant blanc lépreux du paysage" (Tzara) **27**:226-28
"geburtsanzeige" (Enzensberger) **28**:135
"Geddondillo" (Nash) **21**:269
*Gedichte* (Trakl) **20**:245, 250
*Gedichte, 1853 und 1854* (Heine) **25**:146, 161, 178
*Gedichte 1938-1944* (Celan) **10**:121-24, 129
*Gedichte: 1955-1970* (Enzensberger) **28**:159
"Geese Gone Beyond" (Snyder) **21**:308
"gegen die lämmer" (Enzensberger) **28**:135
"Gegen-Strophen" (Rilke) **2**:295
"Gehazi" (Kipling) **3**:171, 182
"Gekishi: Chimmoku no koe" (Ishikawa) **10**:213
"The Genealogy of My Hero" (Pushkin)
  See "Rodoslovnaya Moego Geroya"
"The General" (Sassoon) **12**:268
"General Bloodstock's Lament for England" (Graves) **6**:143
"The General Elliot" (Graves) **6**:150
"General Prologue" (Chaucer) **19**:13, 15, 23-5, 34-6, 43-5, 50-2, 54, 60
"General Prologue" (Marie de France) **22**:
*General Song* (Neruda)
  See *Canto general de Chile*
"General William Booth Enters into Heaven" (Lindsay) **23**:267, 276-78, 289, 294, 297
*General William Booth Enters into Heaven, and Other Poems* (Lindsay) **23**:264, 278, 282-83, 292
"The Generals" (Ferlinghetti) **1**:183
"Generation" (Clifton) **17**:26
"Generation" (Page) **12**:177
"Generation III" (Lorde) **12**:143
*Generations: A Memoir* (Clifton) **17**:23, 25-27, 32
"The Generations of Men" (Frost) **1**:193
"Una generazione" (Pavese) **13**:213
"Genesis" (Knight) **14**:52
"Genesis" (Roethke) **15**:291-96
"Genesis" (Shapiro) **25**:284
*Genesis: Book One* (Schwartz) **8**:283-84, 301, 304, 308-10
"Genesis of After the Cries of the Birds" (Ferlinghetti) **1**:186
"Genetic Expedition" (Dove) **6**:122
"Geneva Restored" (Tomlinson) **17**:311, 359
"Genevieve" (Lorde) **12**:140
"Genevieve and Alexandra" (Robinson) **1**:470
"Génie" (Rimbaud) **3**:261-62
"Le génie dans l'obsurité" (Lamartine) **16**:290
"Genie's Prayer under the Kitchen Sink" (Dove) **6**:123
"Gente che non capisce" (Pavese) **13**:218, 227
"Gentle Lady" (Joyce)
  See "XXVIII"
"The Gentleman from Shallot" (Bishop) **3**:37
"The Gentleman of Shallot" (Bishop)
  See "The Gentleman from Shallot"
"Gentleman-Rankers" (Kipling) **3**:161
"Gentlemen, I Address You Publicly" (Rexroth) **20**:184

"The Gentlest Lady" (Parker) **28**:362
"Geographers" (Shapiro) **25**:270
"The Geographic Center" (Kumin) **15**:215-16
*Geography III* (Bishop) **3**:48-9, 63, 66, 69, 73, 75
*The Geography of Lograire* (Merton) **10**:334-35, 338, 348, 351
"George Washington and the Invention of Dynamite" (Wakoski) **15**:358
"George Washington and the Loss of His Teeth" (Wakoski) **15**:357
*The George Washington Poems* (Wakoski) **15**:324, 357-58
"George Washington: the Whole Man" (Wakoski) **15**:359
"Georgeline" (Rose) **13**:236
"Georgia Dusk" (Toomer) **7**:310, 319-20, 334
*Georgics* (Vergil) **12**:358-61, 364-66, 370-71, 373-77, 383, 385-86, 391-92
"Geraldine" (Bronte) **8**:67, 73-4
"Germanien" (Holderlin) **4**:149
*Germany: A Winter's Tale* (Heine)
  See *Deutschland: Ein Wintermärchen*
"Gerontion" (Day Lewis) **11**:151
"Gerontion" (Eliot) **5**:160-62, 165, 171, 173, 183-85, 189, 195-97, 204, 209
*Gesammelte Werke* (Celan) **10**:100-01, 124
"Gesang der Geister über den Wassern" (Goethe) **5**:239
"Gesang des Abgeschiedenen" (Trakl) **20**:240-41
"Gesta maximalista" (Borges) **22**:92
"Gethsemane" (Kipling) **3**:171
"Gethsemani" (Lamartine) **16**:297
*Gethsemani, Ky.* (Cardenal) **22**:103, 125-26
"Getting in the Wood" (Snyder) **21**:300, 302
"Getting There" (Plath) **1**:412
"Getting Throught" (Merrill) **28**:248
"gewimmer und firmanment" (Enzensberger) **28**:136
"Das Gewitter" (Trakl) **20**:237-38, 251, 257
"The Geysers" (Gunn) **26**:198, 204, 208, 220
"A Ghost" (Baudelaire)
  See "Un fantôme"
"Ghost" (Lowell) **3**:203
"Ghost Crabs" (Hughes) **7**:137, 158-59
"The Ghost Hammer" (Pinsky) **27**:158
"A Ghost May Come" (Ginsberg) **4**:74
"Ghost of a Chance" (Rich) **5**:363, 370
"Ghosts" (Sexton) **2**:350
"Ghosts as Cocoons" (Stevens) **6**:297
"The Ghost's Leave-taking" (Plath) **1**:381, 388
"The Ghosts of James and Peirce in Harvard Yard" (Schwartz) **8**:302
"The Ghosts of the Buffaloes" (Lindsay) **23**:275, 279, 287
"The Ghost's Petition" (Rossetti) **7**:273
"Giant Toad" (Bishop) **3**:65
*The Giaour: A Fragment of a Turkish Tale* (Byron) **16**:91-2
"The Gibber" (Roethke) **15**:262
"Gibson" (Baraka) **4**:30
"Gic to Har" (Rexroth) **20**:193
"Gidget Agonistes" (Reed) **26**:137
"The Gift" (Bukowski) **18**:5
"The Gift" (Gluck) **16**:151
"The Gift" (H. D.) **5**:266, 270, 303
"The Gift" (Lee) **24**:240
"Gift" (Milosz) **8**:209
"Gift" (Tagore)
  See "Upahar"
"The Gift" (Williams) **7**:371
"Gift for a Believer" (Levine) **22**:223, 225
"The Gift of a Satin Brocade" (Tu Fu) **9**:318
"The Gift of God" (Robinson) **1**:462, 467-68
"The Gift of Harun Al-Rashid" (Yeats) **20**:319
"The Gift of the Sea" (Kipling) **3**:183
"The Gift Outright" (Frost) **1**:212-13, 224
"Gift Poem" (Rukeyser) **12**:231
*Gifts at Meeting* (Wylie) **23**:320
"Gifts of Rain" (Heaney) **18**:201, 210

"The Gifts of the Terek" (Lermontov)
  See "Dary Tereka"
"Gigot Sleeves" (McGuckian) **27**:107-109
"Gin" (Levine) **22**:220
"Ginga no jo" (Matsuo Basho) **3**:13
"Ginza Samba" (Pinsky) **27**:175
"Giorno e notte" (Montale) **13**:111
"Giovanni and the Indians" (Page) **12**:168
"Giovanni Franchi" (Loy) **16**:333
*Gipsies* (Pushkin)
  See *Tsygany*
*Gipsy Ballads* (Lorca)
  See *Primer romancero gitano*
"Girl Drowned in a Well" (Garcia Lorca) **3**:139
*A Girl in Winter* (Larkin) **21**:225, 232
"The girl of live marble" (Gunn) **26**:212
"Girl Powdering Her Neck" (Song) **21**:347
"The Girl the North Wind Brought" (Elytis) **21**:123
"The Girl Who Loves to Shoot" (Smith) **12**:326
"Girls Bathing, Galway, 1965" (Heaney) **18**:224
"Girls in the Plural" (McGuckian) **27**:92-94
"A Girl's Mood" (Reese) **29**:331
"Girl's Song" (Bogan) **12**:90, 100
"Girls Working in Banks" (Shapiro) **25**:306, 322
"Git Dough" (Guillen)
  See "Búscate plata"
*Gitāli* (Tagore) **8**:413, 427
*Gitanjali* (Tagore) **8**:402, 412-14, 416, 418
*Gitimālya* (Tagore) **8**:413
"Giuseppe Caponsacchi" (Browning) **2**:41
"Give All to Love" (Emerson) **18**:85, 88, 113
"Give and Take" (Meredith) **28**:199
"Give Way, Ye Gates" (Roethke) **15**:252, 261, 298-99, 301-02
*Give Your Heart to the Hawks and Other Poems* (Jeffers) **17**:135, 142-43, 147
"A Given Grace" (Tomlinson) **17**:309, 316, 335
"Given to Li Po" (Tu Fu) **9**:330
"Givings" (Ammons) **16**:63
*Gladiolus* (McGuckian) **27**:96
"Gladly Still" (Borges)
  See "Jactancia de quietud"
"The Gladness of Nature" (Bryant) **20**:40
"Gladstone Street" (Tomlinson) **17**:319
"The Glance" (Herbert) **4**:132
"Glanmore Sonnets" (Heaney) **18**:198
"Glanmore Sonnets IV" (Heaney) **18**:238
"The Glass" (Olds) **22**:323, 332
"Glass" (Wakoski) **15**:325
"The Glass Air" (Page) **12**:178
*The Glass Air* (Page) **12**:189-90
"Glazed Glitter" (Stein) **18**:322
"Gleneden's Dream" (Bronte) **8**:67
"Glimpse" (Hughes) **7**:153
"The Global Lobal Blues" (Viereck) **27**:279
"Le gloire" (Lamartine) **16**:276, 298
"The Glory Is fallen Out of" (Cummings) **5**:105
"The Glory of the Day Was in Her Face" (Johnson) **24**:154
*The Glory of the Nightingales* (Robinson) **1**:472-73, 475, 479, 483
"Glory of Women" (Sassoon) **12**:267
*Glossolalia Poéma o zvuke* (Bely) **11**:9, 11
"The Glove" (Browning) **2**:29, 38
"Glück der Entfernung" (Goethe) **5**:246
"The Glutton" (Graves) **6**:150
"Gnat-Psalm" (Hughes) **7**:136-37, 159
*Gnomes and Occasions* (Nemerov) **24**:284-86, 288
"Gnothi Seauton" (Emerson) **18**:97
"Go and Look for Bread" (Guillen)
  See "Búscate plata"
"Go burning sighs" (Wyatt) **27**:352
"Go Down Death" (Johnson) **24**:128-29, 139, 144, 156, 164-65, 167, 169
"Go, Fetch to Me a Pint o' Wine" (Burns) **6**:76
"Go Get Money" (Guillen)
  See "Búscate plata"
"Goat Ode in Mid-Dive" (Viereck) **27**:295

"Goat's Leaf" (Marie de France)
See "Chevrefoil"
"Gobernador" (Guillen) **23**:127
*The Goblet of Blizzards* (Bely)
See *Kubok metelej: Chetviortiia simfoniia*
"Goblin Market" (Rossetti) **7**:259, 261, 266, 268, 272-3, 279-80, 282, 288-94, 298-304
*Goblin Market, and Other Poems* (Rossetti) **7**:259, 261, 279, 296-7
"Goblin Revel" (Sassoon) **12**:240
"God" (Swenson) **14**:281, 281, 286
*The God* (H. D.) **5**:303
"God and Devil" (Smith) **12**:331
*God Desired and Desiring* (Jimenez)
See *Dios deseado y deseante: Animal de fondo con numerosos poemas inéditos*
"God Is a Distant, Stately Lover" (Dickinson) **1**:93
"The God of Flowers" (Levertov) **11**:198
"The God of Youth" (Holderlin)
See "Der Gott der Jugend"
"God Speaks" (Smith) **12**:335
"God the Drinker" (Smith) **12**:326-27
"God the Eater" (Smith) **12**:326, 333
"God Works in a Mysterious Way" (Brooks) **7**:74
*Godbey* (Masters) **1**:339
"The Goddess" (Levertov) **11**:159, 168
"Goddess in the Wood" (Brooke) **24**:57
*Godel's Proof, New Poems 1965* (Rexroth) **20**:196
"God-Forgotten" (Hardy) **8**:104, 121
"Godolphin Horne Who Was Cursed with the Sin of Pride and Became a Boot-Black" (Belloc) **24**:26
"Gods" (Cullen) **20**:53
"Gods" (Sexton) **2**:373
"The Gods Are Here" (Toomer) **7**:336
"God's Education" (Hardy) **8**:121
"God's Funeral" (Hardy) **8**:131
"God's Providence" (Herrick) **9**:91
*God's Trombones: Seven Negro Sermons in Verse* (Johnson) **24**:128-29, 132-33, 141, 143-44, 149, 152-56, 159, 161, 164-70
"God's World" (Millay) **6**:205, 215
"God's World" (Pasternak) **6**:268-69
*Goethe's Works* (Goethe) **5**:223
"Gog" (Hughes) **7**:126, 139
"The Go-goat" (Pavese)
See "Il Dio-Caprone"
"The Going" (Hardy) **8**:91, 113, 118, 133-35
"Going" (Larkin) **21**:227, 242
"Going Away" (Hagiwara Sakutaro)
See "Ryojo"
*Going for the Rain* (Ortiz) **17**:222, 226-227, 231-232, 238, 244
"Going from the Capital to Feng-hsien, Singing My Feelings" (Tu Fu) **9**:332
"Going To and Fro" (Lowell) **3**:215
"Going to Horse Flats" (Jeffers) **17**:141
"Going to School" (Shapiro) **25**:291, 320, 326
*Going to War with All My Relations: New and Selected Poems* (Rose) **13**:242
"Gold and Black" (Ondaatje) **28**:328
*The Gold Cell* (Olds) **22**:314-16, 318-21, 324, 326, 328
"Gold Coast Customs" (Sitwell) **3**:300, 305-06, 308-09, 314, 316, 319-20, 325-26
"Gold Hair" (Browning) **2**:95
*Gold in Azure* (Bely)
See *Zoloto v lazuri*
"The Gold Key" (Sexton) **2**:364
"The Gold Lily" (Gluck) **16**:170
*The Gold of the Tigers: Selected Later Poems* (Borges)
See *El oro de los tigres*
"The Golden Age" (Behn) **13**:8, 22, 26, 32-4, 39
"The Golden Boat" (Tagore)
See "Sonar tari"
"Golden Bough" (Wylie) **23**:314

"The Golden Cockerel" (Reisman)
See "Skazka o Zolotom Petushke"
"TH GOLDEN DAWN" (Bissett) **14**:24, 32
"The Golden Echo" (Hopkins) **15**:125, 152
"The golden gates of sleep unbar" (Shelley) **14**:177
"Golden Hair" (Owen) **19**:338
*The Golden Hynde and Other Poems* (Noyes) **27**:117
"The Golden Net" (Blake) **12**:36
"Golden Silences" (Rossetti) **7**:271
"The Golden Supper" (Tennyson) **6**:374
"The Golden Tortoise" (Dario)
See "La tortuga de oro..."
"Golden Venetian Light" (Olson) **19**:305
"The Golden Whales of California" (Lindsay) **23**:264, 269, 274, 288
"Goldfish" (Bukowski) **18**:5
"goldner schnittmusterbogen zur poetischen wiederaufrüstung" (Enzensberger) **28**:136-37, 141
"The Goldsmith" (Sassoon) **12**:257
"Le golfe de Baïa" (Lamartine) **16**:277, 290, 302
"Le golfe de Genes" (Lamartine) **16**:266
"Golgotha" (Sassoon) **12**:261-62
"Goliath of Gath. 1 Sam. Chap. XVII" (Wheatley) **3**:354-55, 357-61
"Golos proshlogo" (Bely) **11**:24
"El golpe" (Neruda) **4**:288
"Gone" (Heaney) **18**:201
"Gone" (Sandburg) **2**:303, 316
"Good Frend" (H. D.) **5**:297, 302
"Good Friday" (Clampitt) **19**:81, 88
"Good Friday" (Donne)
See "Goodfriday 1613: Riding Westward"
"Good Friday" (Herbert) **4**:120
"Good Friday" (Rossetti) **7**:268, 283
"Good Friday and Easter Morning" (Ammons) **16**:63
"Good Friday: Rex Tragicus, or Christ Going to His Crosse" (Herrick) **9**:109, 121
*Good Intentions* (Nash) **21**:266
*A Good Journey* (Ortiz) **17**:224-27, 229-30, 232-33, 240, 244
"The Good Life" (Hughes) **7**:119
"Good Morning, America" (Sandburg) **2**:330
*Good Morning America* (Sandburg) **2**:318-19, 321, 323
"Good Morning Revolution" (Hughes) **1**:268
*Good News About the Earth* (Clifton) **17**:16, 22-24, 26, 35
"Good Night" (Williams) **7**:348
*A Good Time Was Had by All* (Smith) **12**:292, 314-15, 317, 325
*Good Times: Poems* (Clifton) **17**:16-17, 20-21, 23-24, 26, 31, 35
*Good Woman: Poems and a Memoir, 1969-1980* (Clifton) **17**:25-26, 38
"Goodbye!" (Baraka) **4**:11
"Good-bye" (Emerson) **18**:74
"Goodbye" (Kinnell) **26**:292
"Goodbye Christ" (Hughes) **1**:268
"Good-bye to the Mezzogiorno" (Auden) **1**:17
"Goodbye, Unwashed Russia" (Lermontov) **18**:281
"Goodfriday 1613: Riding Westward" (Donne) **1**:139, 158-59
"Goo-dmore-ning (en" (Cummings) **5**:107
"The good-morrow" (Donne) **1**:125, 130-34, 147, 152-54
"Goodnight" (Lee) **24**:241
"The Goodnight" (Ondaatje) **28**:318
"Goody Blake and Harry Gill" (Wordsworth) **4**:381, 414
"The Goose" (Stryk) **27**:203
"The Goose Fish" (Nemerov) **24**:261, 289-90
"Goose Pond" (Kunitz) **19**:178
"Gooseberry Fool" (Clampitt) **19**:86
"Gorbunov and Gorchakov" (Brodsky) **9**:4-6, 10-12, 26-7
"The Gorge" (Stryk) **27**:189, 203

"Gorod" (Pasternak) **6**:264
"Gorodok" (Pushkin) **10**:410
"Gospel" (Dove) **6**:117
"The Gossamers" (Tomlinson) **17**:310, 312
"Gost" (Lermontov) **18**:288
"Gothic Letter on a Hot Night" (Atwood) **8**:24
"Der Gott der Jugend" (Holderlin) **4**:142
"Gott im Mittelalter" (Rilke) **2**:275
"Die Götter Griechenlands" (Heine) **25**:145
*Götterdämmerung* (Heine) **25**:145
"Das Göttliche" (Goethe) **5**:239
"The Gourd Dancer" (Momaday) **25**:198-99, 214-16, 221
*The Gourd Dancer* (Momaday) **25**:193-97, 200-202, 205, 212, 216, 219-20
"Le goût du néant" (Baudelaire) **1**:68
"Gow's Watch" (Kipling) **3**:181
"Grabaciones" (Cardenal) **22**:131-32
"Grace" (Emerson) **18**:98
"Grace" (Herbert) **4**:111, 129
*Grace Abounding* (Ammons) **16**:63
*Grace Notes* (Dove) **6**:120-22
"Grace's House" (Merton) **10**:340-41, 350, 353
*Gracias Haus* (Merton) **10**:341
*Graf Nulin* (Pushkin) **10**:366, 386, 390, 400-01
"La Graine" (Perse) **23**:228
"Grainne's Sleep Song" (McGuckian) **27**:82
*Grains et issues* (Tzara) **27**:241-42, 251-52
"The Grammarian's Funeral" (Browning) **2**:37, 51
*El gran zoo* (Guillen) **23**:100
"The Grand Canyon" (Merrill) **28**:247, 272
"Grand complainte de la ville de Paris" (Laforgue) **14**:97
"Grand Galop" (Ashbery) **26**:126, 143
"Grand Marshal Kao's Dapple" (Tu Fu) **9**:330
"Le Grand Midi" (Cesaire) **25**:29-30
"The Grand Question Debated" (Swift) **9**:260
"Grand River Marshes" (Masters) **1**:330, 333
*Le Grand Testament* (Villon)
See *Le Testament*
"Une grande dame" (Verlaine) **2**:430-31
"The Grandfather" (Guillen)
See "El abuelo"
"Grandfather Arthur Winslow" (Lowell) **3**:200
"Grandma We Are Poets" (Clifton) **17**:29-30
"Grandmother in the Garden" (Gluck) **16**:124
"Grandmother Speranza's Friend" (Gozzano)
See "L'amica di nonna speranza"
"Grandmother's Clavichord" (Dario)
See "El clavicordio de la abuela"
"Grandparents" (Lowell) **3**:217-20
"Granite and Steel" (Moore) **4**:259, 261
"Granny and the Golden Bridge" (Alegria) **26**:
"Grant's Tomb Revisited" (Shapiro) **25**:322
"Grape Sherbet" (Dove) **6**:106, 109
"Graph for Action" (Williams) **7**:369
"Grappa in September" (Pavese) **13**:218
"Grappling in the Central Blue" (Kumin) **15**:209-10
"Grasses" (Gunn) **26**:219
"Gratitude" (Lermontov) **18**:281
"Gratitude" (Smart) **13**:361
"The Grauballe Man" (Heaney) **18**:210-11
"A Grave" (Moore) **4**:243, 251
"A Grave Illness" (Page) **12**:199
"Gravelly Run" (Ammons) **16**:29
"Graves" (Sandburg) **2**:303
"Graves Are Made to Waltz On" (Viereck) **27**:258
"Graveyard at Bolinas" (Hass) **16**:196, 209
"The Graveyard by the Sea" (Valery)
See "Le cimetière marin"
"Gray Eyes" (Gallagher) **9**:51
"The Gray Heron" (Kinnell) **26**:259
"The Great Adventure of Max Breuck" (Lowell) **13**:60, 96
"Great American Waterfront Poem" (Ferlinghetti) **1**:188
"Great Canzon" (Rexroth) **20**:190
"The Great Chinese Dragon" (Ferlinghetti) **1**:176

"The Great Elegy for John Donne" (Brodsky)
   **9**:2, 4, 10, 26
"The Great Explosion" (Jeffers) **17**:130
"The Great Figure" (Williams) **7**:399, 401, 410
"The Great Fillmore Street Buffalo Drive"
   (Momaday) **25**:221
"The Great Homecoming" (Sikelianos) **29**:373
"The Great Hunt" (Sandburg) **2**:300, 316
"The Great Lament of My Obscurity One"
   (Tzara) **27**:249
"The Great Lover" (Brooke) **24**:53, 56-7, 59,
   65, 78, 87-8
"The Great Mother" (Snyder) **21**:297
"The Great Nebula of Andromeda" (Rexroth)
   **20**:190
"The Great Palace of Versailles" (Dove) **6**:111
"Great Snoring and Norwich" (Sitwell) **3**:301
"The Great Society, Mark X" (Nemerov) **24**:280
"The Great Sunset" (Jeffers) **17**:130
"Great Things" (Hardy) **8**:112
"Great Unaffected Vampires and the Moon"
   (Smith) **12**:330-31
*The Great Valley* (Masters) **1**:329, 332, 342-43
"Greater Love" (Owen) **19**:327, 332, 335, 337,
   344, 347, 353-54, 358-59
*Greater Testament* (Villon)
   See *Le Testament*
"The Greater Whiteness" (Swenson) **14**:264
"Greed" (Wakoski) **15**:325, 331, 351-52
*Greed* (Wakoski) **15**:325, 355-56, 372
*Greed, Parts 1 & 2* (Wakoski) **15**:324
*Greed, Parts 8, 9, 11* (Wakoski) **15**:345-46
*Greed, Parts 5-7* (Wakoski) **15**:347
"The Greed to Be Fulfilled" (Wakoski) **15**:357
"The Greek Women" (Merton) **10**:349
"Green" (Verlaine) **2**:415
"Green Flows the River of Lethe-O" (Sitwell)
   **3**:309
"Green Grow the Rashes O" (Burns) **6**:67, 74
*The Green Helmet* (Yeats) **20**:328
"Green Lantern's Solo" (Baraka) **4**:16
"Green Linnaeus" (Zagajewski) **27**:394
"The Green Man" (Olson) **19**:283
"The Green Man: For the Boston Strangler"
   (Atwood) **8**:7
"Green Memory" (Hughes) **1**:267
"The Green Menagerie" (Viereck) **27**:296
"The Green Parrakeet" (Lowell) **13**:88
"Green Red Brown and White" (Swenson)
   **14**:261
"Green River" (Bryant) **20**:14, 16, 19, 34, 42
"Green Song" (Sitwell) **3**:312, 317
*Green Song* (Sitwell) **3**:308, 320
"Green Stream" (Wang Wei) **18**:378
*The Green Wave* (Rukeyser) **12**:204-05, 209,
   213
"Green Ways" (Kunitz) **19**:162
"The Green Well" (Kumin) **15**:215
"Green Wood" (Pavese) **13**:218
"The Greenest Continent" (Stevens) **6**:317-19
"The Greenhouse" (Merrill) **28**:243-44
"The Greeting" (Tomlinson) **17**:354
"Greetings to the Eagle" (Dario)
   See "Salutación al águila"
"Greetings to the Optimist" (Dario)
   See "Salutación del optimista"
"Les grenades" (Valery) **9**:387-90, 394, 396
"Grenades Are Not Free" (Sanchez) **9**:235
"Die Grenadiere" (Heine) **25**:140
"Grenouille" (Guillen) **23**:111
"Grenzen der Menschheit" (Goethe) **5**:239
"Los Grernios en el frente" (Neruda) **4**:309
"Gretel in Darkness" (Gluck) **16**:125, 140, 143-
   44, 149
"The Grey Monk" (Blake) **12**:35-7, 70
"Grey Sparrow" (Levertov) **11**:160
*The Grid of Language* (Celan)
   See *Sprachgitter*
"Grief" (Browning) **6**:41
"A Grief Ago" (Thomas) **2**:405
"Grief for Dead Soldiers" (Hughes) **7**:114-15
"Grief Thief of Time" (Thomas) **2**:405

"Grifel' naja oda" (Mandelstam) **14**:121-22,
   129, 148
"Griffin of the Night" (Ondaatje) **28**:329
"The Grindstone" (Frost) **1**:197
"The grocer Hudson Kearley, he" (Belloc) **24**:41
"Grodek" (Trakl) **20**:226, 229, 236-38, 244,
   250-51, 253, 255-58, 260
"La Grosse Margot" (Villon)
   See "Ballade de la Grosse Margot"
"Grosses Geburtstagsblaublau mit Reimzeug
   und Assonanz" (Celan) **10**:124
"Grotesques" (Graves) **6**:142, 144
"Grotesques" (Lowell) **13**:77
"The Ground Mist" (Levertov) **11**:160
*Ground Work: Before the War* (Duncan) **2**:114-
   17, 119, 125
*Ground Work II: In the Dark* (Duncan) **2**:119,
   127
"Growing Old" (Arnold) **5**:13, 19, 23
"Grown-up" (Millay) **6**:234-35
"Growth" (Levine) **22**:220, 228
"The Growth of Lorraine" (Robinson) **1**:461
*The Growth of Love* (Bridges) **28**:49, 68, 71,
   86-8
"Grub First, Then Ethics" (Auden) **1**:24
"Guadeloupe, W.I." (Guillen) **23**:99
"The Guardian Angel" (Browning) **2**:73
*The Guardian of the Flock* (Pessoa) **20**:167-68
"A Guerilla Handbook" (Baraka) **4**:16
"Guerre" (Breton) **15**:62
"Guerre" (Rimbaud) **3**:264
"A Guest Arrives" (Tu Fu) **9**:323
"Guía comercial" (Fuertes) **27**:12
"El guía de la abadía" (Fuertes) **27**:30
"A guichard" (Lamartine) **16**:286
"Guide" (Ammons) **16**:20, 34, 57
*Guide to Kulchur* (Pound) **4**:354, 359
*Guide to the Ruins* (Nemerov) **24**:255, 260, 264
*Guide to the Underworld* (Ekeloef) **23**:85
"Guigemar" (Marie de France)
   See "Lay of Guigemar"
"Guildeluec and Gualadun" (Marie de France)
   See "Eliduc"
*Guillén Man-making Words* (Guillen) **23**:102,
   104, 123
"The Guilty Man" (Kunitz) **19**:160
"Guinness" (Hughes) **7**:123
"Guitar or Moon" (Aleixandre) **15**:20
"Guitare" (Laforgue) **14**:80
"The Gulf" (Levertov) **11**:194
"Gulls" (Hayden) **6**:185, 193-94
"Gulls" (Williams) **7**:378
"Gum" (Toomer) **7**:333
"Gumber" (Belloc) **24**:10
"Gum-Trees Stripping" (Wright) **14**:341-42,
   347
"The Gun" (Shapiro) **25**:269, 295, 297, 312
"Gunga Din" (Kipling) **3**:157-58, 179, 187-89,
   191
"The Gunman and the Debutante" (Parker)
   **28**:354
"Guns as Keys: And the Great Gate Swings"
   (Lowell) **13**:60, 64, 72, 81-2
"The Guttural Muse" (Heaney) **18**:198, 217
"Guy" (Emerson) **18**:111
"Gwin, King of Norway" (Blake) **12**:60
"The Gymnosophist" (Ekeloef) **23**:63, 86
"Gypsies" (Clare) **23**:15
*The Gypsies* (Pushkin)
   See *Tsygany*
*Gypsy Balladeer* (Garcia Lorca)
   See *Primer romancero gitano*
*Gypsy Ballads* (Garcia Lorca)
   See *Primer romancero gitano*
"Gypsy Man" (Hughes) **1**:270
"The Gypsy Nun" (Garcia Lorca)
   See "La monja gitana"
"The Gyres" (Yeats) **20**:314, 333
"H" (Rimbaud) **3**:261
"H. O." (Borges) **22**:80-1, 95
"Ha chi je na I Am Coming" (Forche) **10**:134
"The Habit of Perfection" (Hopkins) **15**:136

*El habitante y su esperanza* (Neruda) **4**:276,
   281
"Habits" (Giovanni) **19**:118
"El hacedor" (Borges) **22**:76, 95
*El hacedor* (Borges) **22**:71
"Hacia la esclava Quisqueya" (Guillen) **23**:125
"Had I not this life decreed" (Villa) **22**:354
"Hafen" (Celan) **10**:105
"Haffär al-qubür" (Gibran) **9**:79
"The Hag Is Astride" (Herrick) **9**:86
"Hagia Sophia" (Merton) **10**:334
"Hago versos, señores" (Fuertes) **27**:49
"Haiku" (Sanchez) **9**:230
"Hailstones" (Heaney) **18**:237
"Haircut" (Shapiro) **25**:288, 318, 322
"Hairy" (Swenson) **14**:253
"Halahal" (Tagore) **8**:405
"Halcyon" (H. D.) **5**:304
"Half of Life" (Holderlin)
   See "Hälfte des Lebens"
*Half Sun Half Sleep* (Swenson) **14**:260, 285
*The Halfbreed Chronicles and Other Poems*
   (Rose) **13**:235-36, 239-40
"Half-Caste Girl" (Wright) **14**:351
"Half-dream" (Wright) **14**:373
"The Half-moon Westers Low, My Love"
   (Housman) **2**:183
"Hälfte des Lebens" (Holderlin) **4**:143, 148,
   167
"Halfway" (Ammons) **16**:6
*Halfway* (Kumin) **15**:179, 192, 198
*Halieticon/On Fishing* (Ovid)
   See *Halieutica*
*Halieutica* (Ovid) **2**:232, 242, 253
"Hallowe'en" (Aiken) **26**:30, 41, 45, 53
"Hallowe'en" (Aiken) **26**:
"Hallowe'en" (Burns) **6**:50, 55, 57, 77, 91
"A Halt in the Desert" (Brodsky)
   See "Ostanovka v pustyne"
"Hamatreya" (Emerson) **18**:79, 102-4, 111
"The Hambone and the Heart" (Sitwell) **3**:295
"The Ham-Bone of a Saint" (Shapiro) **25**:300
"El hambre" (Guillen) **23**:116
"Hame" (MacDiarmid) **9**:192
"The Hammers" (Lowell) **13**:60, 78
"Ha'nacker Mill" (Belloc) **24**:8, 22
"HAND" (Bissett) **14**:32
"The Hand at Callow Hill Farm" (Tomlinson)
   **17**:311
"Hand Games" (Piercy) **29**:311
"The Hand That Signed the Paper" (Thomas)
   **2**:388
"Handed Down" (Clampitt) **19**:102
*A Handful of Lavender* (Reese) **29**:330, 332,
   335-36, 339, 345-46, 351
*A Handful of Sand* (Ishikawa)
   See *Ichiaku no suna*
"The Handicapped at Risen Hotel" (Wakoski)
   **15**:369
"The Handing Down" (Berry) **28**:38
"Handprints" (Rose) **13**:238
"Hands" (Levertov) **11**:159
*The Hands of Day* (Neruda)
   See *Las manos del día*
"Hands, on a Trip to Wisconsin" (Meredith)
   **28**:175
*Handshakes* (Illyes)
   See *Kezfogasok*
"Hanging in Heaven" (Hagiwara Sakutaro)
   See "Hanging in Heaven"
"Hangman's Oak" (Millay) **6**:217
"Hansel and Gretel" (Sexton) **2**:364, 368
"Hapax" (Rexroth) **20**:217, 220
"Happier Dead" (Baudelaire)
   See "Le mort joyeux"
"The Happiest Day..." (Poe) **1**:432
"Happiness" (Borges)
   See "La dicha"
"Happiness" (Gluck) **16**:131, 144, 151
"Happiness" (Owen) **19**:355
"Happiness" (Sandburg) **2**:308, 332, 334
"Happiness in Herat" (Paz) **1**:361

"The Happy Journalist" (Belloc) **24**:29
"Happy Warrior" (Wordsworth) **4**:391
"Harbor" (Celan) **10**:105
"The Harbor at Seattle" (Hass) **16**:217, 226
"Harbor Dawn" (Crane) **3**:88-9
"The Harbour" (Belloc) **24**:29
"Hard Daddy" (Hughes) **1**:270
*Hard Facts: Excerpts* (Baraka) **4**:29, 36-9
"Hard Fist" (Ammons) **16**:44
*Hard Labor* (Pavese)
    See *Lavorare stanca*
*A Hard Land* (Illyes)
    See *Nehez fold*
"Hard Lard" (Ammons) **16**:43
"Hard Lines" (Zukofsky) **11**:351
*Hard Lines* (Nash) **21**:263
*Hard Loving* (Piercy) **29**:308-09, 311
"Hard Luck" (Hughes) **1**:255, 269
"Hard Roads in Shu" (Li Po) **29**:144
"Hard Rock Returns to Prison" (Knight) **14**:42, 52
"Hard Times" (Ashbery) **26**:154
"Hard Times" (McKay) **2**:209
"Hard Times Redeemed by Soft Discarded Values" (Viereck) **27**:258-59
"Hardcastle Crags" (Hughes) **7**:149
"Hardcastle Crags" (Plath) **1**:388
"Hardships of Travel" (Li Po) **29**:141
"The Harem at Erechtheion" (Ekeloef) **23**:66
"Harem Trousers" (McGuckian) **27**:90
"Harlem Dance Hall" (Hughes) **1**:247
"The Harlem Dancer" (McKay) **2**:213-14
"Harlem Shadows" (McKay) **2**:213
*Harlem Shadows* (McKay) **2**:213-14, 227
"Harlem Sweeties" (Hughes) **1**:247
"Harlem Wine" (Cullen) **20**:63
"The Harm of Living" (Montale)
    See "Il male di vivere"
"Harmonie du soir" (Baudelaire) **1**:46, 68-9, 71
*Les harmonies* (Lamartine) **16**:262-67
*Harmonies poétiques et religieuses* (Lamartine) **16**:279-82, 285-86, 292-93
*Harmonies religieuses* (Lamartine) **16**:257-62
*Harmonium* (Stevens) **6**:292, 294-95, 297-98, 300-01, 305, 309-11, 313-15, 329-30, 332-33, 336-37
*Harold the Dauntles* (Scott) **13**:269, 281, 312
*Harold's Leap* (Smith) **12**:335
"Harom oreg" (Illyes) **16**:239
"The Harp and the King" (Wright) **14**:343, 347
"The Harp Song of the Dane Women" (Kipling) **3**:171, 183
*Harps and Violins* (Blok) **21**:25-6
"The Harp-Weaver" (Millay)
    See "The Ballad of the Harp-Weaver"
*The Harp-Weaver, and Other Poems* (Millay) **6**:211, 214-15, 224-25, 228, 230-31, 242
"Harriet Beecher Stowe" (Dunbar) **5**:128
"Harriet Tubman" (Walker) **20**:289
"Harriet's Donkey" (Lowell) **3**:241
"The Harrowing of Hell" (Rilke) **2**:275
"Harry Gill" (Wordsworth)
    See "Goody Blake and Harry Gill"
"Harry Ploughman" (Hopkins) **15**:134, 160
"Harry Semen" (MacDiarmid) **9**:180, 196-97
"Hartleap Well" (Wordsworth) **4**:404, 414, 427-28
"Harvest" (Levine) **22**:218
"Harvest" (McGuckian) **27**:100
"Harvest" (Sitwell) **3**:311
"Harvest" (Soto) **28**:377
"The Harvest Bow" (Heaney) **18**:243
"Harvest Festival" (Tomlinson) **17**:328
"The Harvest Knot" (Heaney)
    See "The Harvest Bow"
"Harvest Song" (Toomer) **7**:311, 317, 320, 333, 335
"Harzreise im Winter" (Goethe) **5**:247
"Has Your Soul Sipped" (Owen) **19**:346, 352
"Hassan's Journey into the World" (Thomas) **2**:402

"Hate Blows a Bubble of Despair into" (Cummings) **5**:107
"Hate whome ye list" (Wyatt) **27**:325
"Hatem--, i.e. Goethe" (Goethe) **5**:228
"Haunted" (Sassoon) **12**:240
"Haunted Country" (Jeffers) **17**:117
"Haunted House" (Graves) **6**:142
"A Haunted House" (Swenson) **14**:248
"Haunted in Old Japan" (Noyes) **27**:127
"The Haunted Oak" (Dunbar) **5**:131
"The Haunted Palace" (Poe) **1**:424, 437-38, 443
"The Haunter" (Hardy) **8**:93, 118, 135, 138
"Hauntings" (Brooke) **24**:57, 85
"Havana Rose" (Crane) **3**:90
*Have Come, Am Here* (Villa) **22**:346-47, 351
"Have Mercy upon Me My Soul" (Gibran) **9**:73
"Having Been Asked 'What Is a Man?' I Answer" (Levine) **22**:220
"Having No Ear" (Davie) **29**:114-15
"The Haw Lantern" (Heaney) **18**:230, 233
*The Haw Lantern* (Heaney) **18**:226-28, 230, 232-33, 237
"The Hawk in the Rain" (Hughes) **7**:117-18, 121, 129, 165
*The Hawk in the Rain* (Hughes) **7**:112-13, 115-20, 123, 131, 135-36, 139-41, 150, 162-63, 165-66
"Hawk Roosting" (Hughes) **7**:113, 125, 140-41, 151, 164, 169
"Hawkshead and Dachau in a Christmas Glass" (Davie) **29**:108
"The Hawks" (Montale) **13**:149
"Hawks" (Tomlinson) **17**:347
"The Hawk's Cry in Autumn" (Brodsky) **9**:27
"The Hawthorn Hedge" (Wright) **14**:336, 340
"Hawthorn Tide" (Swinburne) **24**:313, 317-18
"The Hawthorn Tree" (Gluck) **16**:171
"Hawthorne" (Lowell) **3**:212, 216
"Hay" (Tomlinson) **17**:347, 354
"Hayāt al-hubb" (Gibran) **9**:78
"The Hayswater Boat" (Arnold) **5**:50
*Hazard, the Painter* (Meredith) **28**:179, 195-99, 206-07, 214, 216
"Hazard's Optimism" (Meredith) **28**:202, 215
"The Hazel Grove" (Pasternak) **6**:252
"He" (Ferlinghetti) **1**:174-76
"He Abjures Love" (Hardy) **8**:90
"He Acts" (Zagajewski) **27**:385
"He Doesn't Know It" (Aleixandre) **15**:4
"He Has a Good Time There" (Duncan) **2**:101
"He hath put all things under his feet" (Bryant) **20**:7
"He Heard the Newsboy Shouting 'Europe! Europe!'" (Schwartz) **8**:293
"He Held Radical Light" (Ammons) **16**:34
"He Is Last Seen" (Atwood) **8**:10
"He is not ded that sometyme hath a fall" (Wyatt) **27**:337-338, 340, 343
"He Revisits His First School" (Hardy) **8**:102
"He Sees Through Stone" (Knight) **14**:43
"He that loves a rosy cheek" (Carew)
    See "Disdaine Returned"
"He who finds a horseshoe" (Mandelstam)
    See "Nashedshij podkovu"
"He who found a Horseshoe" (Mandelstam)
    See "Nashedshij podkovu"
"The Head above the Fog" (Hardy) **8**:97
"Head against White" (Atwood) **8**:27
*Head and Heart* (Guillen)
    See *Cerebro y corazón*
"Head of a Woman" (McGuckian) **27**:101
"Headwaters" (Momaday) **25**:197
"Healing Animal" (Harjo) **27**:70
"Hear Me" (Levine) **22**:223
"Hearn in Matsue" (Stryk) **27**:187, 208
"The Heart" (Trakl)
    See "Das Herz"
"Heart and Mind" (Sitwell) **3**:312, 323
"The Heart and the Lyre" (Bogan) **12**:126
"Heart, Crown and Mirror" (Apollinaire)
    See "Coeur, couronne et miroir"

"The Heart of a Constab" (McKay) **2**:216, 225-26
"The Heart of Pedro de Valdivia" (Neruda)
    See "El corazón de Pedro de Valdivia"
"Heart Stirrings" (McKay) **2**:223
"Heartbeat" (Harjo) **27**:56
"Heartless Rhoda" (McKay) **2**:221
"The Hearts" (Pinsky) **27**:157-58, 161, 164-65, 170
*The Heart's Garden/The Garden's Heart* (Rexroth) **20**:204, 209-10, 213-14
*The Heart's Journey* (Sassoon) **12**:258, 271, 289
"Heat" (H. D.)
    See "Garden"
"Heat" (Reese) **29**:336
"HEAt MAkes TH HEARt's wINDOw" (Bissett) **14**:32
"Heatwave" (Hughes) **7**:120
"L'héautontimorouménos" (Baudelaire) **1**:63
"Heaven" (Brooke) **24**:56, 64, 73, 78
"Heaven" (Herbert) **4**:102, 114, 130
"Heaven" (Tagore)
    See "Svarga"
"Heaven Alive" (Garcia Lorca) **3**:141
*Heaven and Earth* (Byron) **16**:88-9, 102-06, 109
"Heaven Is but the Hour" (Masters) **1**:344
"Heavenly City, Earthly City" (Duncan) **2**:105
*Heavenly City, Earthly City* (Duncan) **2**:100, 126
"Heavensgate" (Okigbo) **7**:250-51
*Heavensgate* (Okigbo) **7**:221-25, 228, 231-32, 236, 240, 242, 245, 247-48
"The Heavy Bear That Goes with Me" (Schwartz) **8**:290-91, 297, 306-09, 311, 313-14
"die hebammen" (Enzensberger) **28**:140
"Heber" (Smith) **12**:327, 336
"Hebräische Melodien" (Heine) **25**:170, 175
"Hebrew Melodies" (Heine)
    See "Hebräische Melodien"
"Hector in the Garden" (Browning) **6**:16
"Hector Kane" (Robinson) **1**:476
"Hedge Island, a Retrospect and a Prophecy" (Lowell) **13**:72, 82
"A Hedge of Rubber Trees" (Clampitt) **19**:98
"The Hedgehog" (Clare) **23**:7
"Hedgerows" (Tomlinson) **17**:354
"He-goat God" (Pavese)
    See "Il Dio-Caprone"
"Heidenröslein" (Goethe) **5**:254
"Height" (Ammons) **16**:6
*The Heights of Macchu Picchu* (Neruda)
    See *Alturas de Macchu Picchu*
"Heil Heilige Nacht!" (Nash) **21**:266
"The Heiligenstadt Testament" (Shapiro) **25**:307
"Heimkehr" (Heine) **25**:130-37, 139, 141-42, 144-45, 158, 161, 163-64
*Die Heimkehr* (Heine) **25**:161
"Die Heimkehr No 20" (Heine) **25**:144
"Die Heimkehr No 25" (Heine) **25**:144
"Heimkunft" (Holderlin) **4**:141, 146
"Heine La Salle" (Masters) **1**:334
"Heine's Grave" (Arnold) **5**:34, 52, 63-4
*Heinrich Heine's Book of Songs* (Heine)
    See *Buch der Lieder*
"Helen" (Elytis) **21**:131
"Helen" (H. D.) **5**:268, 300
"Helen" (Parker) **28**:362
*Helen in Egypt* (H. D.) **5**:276-84, 292-93, 297-301
"Helen of Troy" (Masters) **1**:325, 328, 342
*Helena* (Vigny) **26**:367
"Hélène" (Valery) **9**:380
"Hélène, la reine triste" (Valery) **9**:380, 391
"Helen's Rape" (Gunn) **26**:182-183
"Helian" (Trakl) **20**:239-40, 253, 259
"Helicon" (Heaney) **18**:207
"Heliodora" (H. D.) **5**:270
*Heliodora, and Other Poems* (H. D.) **5**:267-68, 304-05

"Helios and Athene" (H. D.) **5**:290-92, 305
"Hell" (Graves) **6**:151
*Hell* (Dante)
   See *Inferno*
"The Hell Cantos" (Pound) **4**:328, 357, 360
"Hell Gate" (Housman) **2**:162, 165, 167, 199
*Hellas* (Shelley) **14**:171, 175, 188-9, 195, 197,
   241
"Hellenistics" (Jeffers) **17**:117
"The Helmet" (Levine) **22**:223
"Helpstone" (Clare) **23**:11, 39
"Helter Skelter; or, The Hue and Cry after the
   Attorneys Going to Ride the Circuit"
   (Swift) **9**:271
"Hemmed-in Males" (Williams) **7**:369
"The Hen Flower" (Kinnell) **26**:243, 249-50,
   252, 266, 274
"Henceforth, from the Mind" (Bogan) **12**:105,
   113
"Hendecasyllabics" (Swinburne) **24**:320
"Henri Rousseau and Friends" (Ondaatje)
   **28**:298
"Henry and Mary" (Graves) **6**:141
"The Henry Manley Blues" (Kumin) **15**:208
"Henry Manley Living Alone Keeps Time"
   (Kumin) **15**:208
"Henry Purcell" (Hopkins) **15**:144, 168
"Her Becoming" (Roethke) **15**:269, 272-74
"Her Dead Brother" (Lowell) **3**:205-06
"Her Death and After" (Hardy) **8**:99
"Her Early Work" (Swenson) **14**:276-77
"Her Eyes" (Robinson) **1**:459
"Her/Flesh" (Cummings) **5**:95
"Her Garden" (Belloc) **24**:38-9
"Her Immortality" (Hardy) **8**:131
"Her Kind" (Sexton) **2**:359
"Her Lips Are Copper Wire" (Toomer) **7**:320,
   332, 340
"Her Management" (Swenson) **14**:248
"Her Music" (Belloc) **24**:29
"Her Triumph" (Jonson) **17**:180
"Hera of Samos" (Clampitt) **19**:87
"Heraldos" (Dario) **15**:96
"Herbseele" (Trakl) **20**:265
*Hercule Chrestien* (Ronsard) **11**:273
"Hercules and Antaeus" (Heaney) **18**:203, 207-
   210
"The Herd of Does" (MacDiarmid) **9**:156
"Here" (Larkin) **21**:238-39, 253-55
"Here and Now" (Stryk) **27**:211
*Here and Now* (Levertov) **11**:159, 163, 188
"Here Come the Saints" (Gunn) **26**:206-207
"Here she lies, a pretty bud" (Herrick)
   See "Upon a Child That Died"
"Heredity" (Hardy) **8**:129
"La herencia" (Guillen) **23**:118-19
"Here's to Opening and upward, to Leaf and
   to Sap" (Cummings) **5**:106
"Here's to the Mice" (Lindsay) **23**:269
"The Heretic's Tragedy" (Browning) **2**:37, 59,
   88
"Heriot's Ford" (Kipling) **3**:181
"Heritage" (Cullen) **20**:52-54, 57, 64-65, 72,
   82, 87
"Herman and Dorothea" (Goethe)
   See *Hermann und Dorothea*
*Hermann und Dorothea* (Goethe) **5**:223, 225-
   26, 236, 239, 257-59, 261
"Hermaphroditus" (Swinburne) **24**:308-11, 317,
   361-63
"Hermes" (H. D.) **5**:273
"Hermes of The Ways" (H. D.) **5**:303
"Hermetic Definition" (H. D.) **5**:281, 283, 285,
   289, 297, 299
"Hermetic Poem" (Kunitz) **19**:172
"The Hermit" (Apollinaire)
   See "L'ermite"
"The Hermit" (McKay) **2**:222
"The Hermit at Outermost House" (Plath) **1**:389
"The Hermit Goes Up Attic" (Kumin) **15**:190
*The Herne's Egg* (Yeats) **20**:335
"Hero" (Madhubuti) **5**:342

"The Hero" (Moore) **4**:265
"The Hero" (Sassoon) **12**:242, 263, 277, 280,
   283, 285
*Hérodiade* (Mallarme) **4**:188, 190, 196-97, 199-
   203, 208, 213, 218-25
*Herodias* (Mallarme)
   See *Hérodiade*
"Heroes Are Gang Leaders" (Baraka) **4**:10
*Heroic and Elegiac Song for the Lost Second
   Lieutenant of the Alb nian Campaign*
   (Elytis)
   See *Ázma iroikó ke pénthimo yia ton
      haméno anthipolohaghó tis Alvanías*
"Heroic Poem in Praise of Wine" (Belloc)
   **24**:13, 20, 22, 33, 39
"Heroic Simile" (Hass) **16**:198
"Heroics" (Wylie) **23**:324
*Heroides* (Ovid) **2**:234, 238-39, 243-46, 253-54
*Heroines* (Ovid)
   See *Heroides*
"Heroique Stanzas to the Glorious Memory of
   Cromwell" (Dryden) **25**:101
"Heroism" (Montale)
   See "L'eroismo"
"Heron Rex" (Ondaatje) **28**:332, 334
"Herrin" (Goethe) **5**:249
"Hertha" (Swinburne) **24**:308, 312, 343
"Das Herz" (Trakl) **20**:235-36
"das herz von gröuland" (Enzensberger) **28**:138
"Her-zie" (Smith) **12**:339
"Hesperia" (Swinburne) **24**:313, 316, 318, 323
"The Hesperides" (Tennyson) **6**:351
*Hesperides: or, The Works Both Humane &
   Divine of Robert Herrick, Esq.* (Herrick)
   **9**:85, 87, 89, 90, 92-6, 100, 102, 104-06,
   108-10, 116-17, 122, 125, 127-29, 132-35,
   138, 140, 143-46
"Hevyn and erth" (Wyatt) **27**:349-50
"He-Who-Came-Forth" (Levertov) **11**:177
"Hey Yu" (Bissett) **14**:7
"Hey-Hey Blues" (Hughes) **1**:240
*Hi no tori* (Yosano Akiko) **11**:308
"Hiawatha's Photographing" (Carroll) **18**:46
"Hibernaculum" (Ammons) **16**:10, 12, 20, 23,
   29, 47-9, 60
"Hibiscus on the Sleeping Shores" (Stevens)
   **6**:294-95, 305
"Hidden Door" (Ferlinghetti) **1**:166
*Hiding the Universe: Poems by Wang Wei*
   (Wang Wei) **18**:382, 390
"Hieroglyphic" (Harjo) **27**:66
"th high green hill" (Bissett) **14**:20
*Th High Green Hill* (Bissett) **14**:14, 16, 18-21
"High in the Mountains, I Fail to Find the
   Wise Man" (Li Po) **29**:176
"The High Malady" (Pasternak)
   See "Vysokaya bolesn"
"High Noon" (Clampitt) **19**:97
"The High Oaks Barking Hall July 19th 1896"
   (Swinburne) **24**:318-20
"High Quality Information" (Snyder) **21**:326
"High Talk" (Yeats) **20**:336
"High to Low" (Hughes) **1**:258, 267
"High Windows" (Larkin) **21**:238, 259
*High Windows* (Larkin) **21**:250, 259
*The Higher Mathamatics* (Chesterton) **28**:99
"The Higher Patheism in a Nutshell"
   (Swinburne) **24**:320
"The Higher Unity" (Chesterton) **28**:94
"Highway: Michigan" (Roethke) **15**:246, 294
"Highway Patrol" (Ferlinghetti) **1**:187
"The Highwayman" (Noyes) **27**:133, 136
"Hiking on the Coast Range" (Rexroth) **20**:215
"The Hill" (Brooke) **24**:72, 77
"The Hill" (Masters) **1**:345
"The Hill" (Tomlinson) **17**:314, 316, 337
"The Hill and Grove at Bill-Borrow" (Marvell)
   See "Upon the Hill and Grove at
   Billborow"
"Hill at Parramatta" (Shapiro) **25**:269
"The Hill Wife" (Frost) **1**:195, 202, 229
*The Hilliad* (Smart) **13**:333

"Hill-Stone Was Content" (Hughes) **7**:149
"Himno del mar" (Borges) **22**:92
"Himno entre ruinas" (Paz) **1**:353, 360-61, 363
*The Hind and the Panther* (Dryden) **25**:81-2
"L'hinne de Bacus" (Ronsard) **11**:230, 232-33
"The Hinterland" (Clampitt) **19**:90
"Hippocrene" (Clampitt) **19**:92
"Hippolytus" (H. D.) **5**:267
"The Hippopotamus" (Carroll) **18**:31
"The Hippopotamus" (Eliot) **5**:187
"The Hippopotamus" (Nash) **21**:280
"Hippy Mo" (Smith) **12**:314, 327, 339
"Hiroshima, Watts, My Lai" (Hayden) **6**:190
"His Age, Dedicated to His Peculiar Friend,
   M. John Wickes, under the Name
   Posthumus" (Herrick) **9**:103, 107, 114-15
"His Anthem, to Christ on the Crosse"
   (Herrick) **9**:121
"His Bargain" (Yeats) **20**:332
"His Blindness" (Browning) **6**:16
"His Confession" (Herrick) **9**:109, 117
"His Confidence" (Yeats) **20**:314, 332-33
"His Creed" (Herrick) **9**:104
"His Death" (Browning) **6**:16
"His Embalming to Julia" (Herrick) **9**:127, 129
"His farwell unto Poetrie" (Herrick)
   See "Farewell to Poetry"
"His Grange, or Private Wealth" (Herrick) **9**:89
"His Lachrimae, or Mirth, Turn'd to
   Mourning" (Herrick) **9**:108
"His Meditation upon Death" (Herrick) **9**:109
*His Noble Numbers: or, His Pious Pieces,
   Wherein He Sings the Birth of His
   Christ: and Sighes for His Saviours
   Suffering on the Crosse* (amongst Other
   ThingsHerrick) **9**:85, 87, 90-2, 94-5, 100-
   01, 104, 106, 109-10, 117-18, 122, 140-41
"His Own Epitaph" (Herrick) **9**:131
"His Phoenix" (Yeats) **20**:329
"His Poetry His Pillar" (Herrick) **9**:89, 106
"His Prayer for Absolution" (Herrick) **9**:94,
   109, 117, 141
"His Prayer to Ben Jonson" (Herrick)
   See "Prayer to Ben Jonson"
"His Returne to London" (Herrick) **9**:89, 98,
   108
"His Shield" (Moore) **4**:247-48, 261
"His Shining Helmet: Its Horsehair Crest"
   (Gallagher) **9**:62
"His Smell" (Olds) **22**:326
"His Stillness" (Olds) **22**:321, 340
"His Tears to Thamasis" (Herrick) **9**:108
"His Terror" (Olds) **22**:324
"His Winding-Sheet" (Herrick) **9**:109
"His Words to Christ, Going to the Crosse"
   (Herrick) **9**:121
"Hispaniola" (Clampitt) **19**:102
*Histoire du Régent* (Perse) **23**:230
*Historia de Gloria* (Fuertes) **27**:20-5, 34-42,
   44-7
*Historia de la noche* (Borges) **22**:95-6
*Historia del corazón* (Aleixandre) **15**:3-4, 7,
   11, 15-16, 22, 41
"Histories" (Tomlinson) **17**:326, 344, 350
"History" (Berry) **28**:8
"History" (Soto) **28**:378
*History* (Lowell) **3**:224, 226, 228-29, 231-32
"History: 13" (Olds) **22**:319
"History is the Memory of Time" (Olson)
   **19**:271
"History Lesson" (Kumin) **15**:194, 202
"History of a Literary Movement" (Nemerov)
   **24**:258
"The History of Karate" (Soto) **28**:400
"History of My Heart" (Pinsky) **27**:176
*History of My Heart* (Pinsky) **27**:163-64, 173,
   176
*History of Peter I* (Pushkin)
   See *The History of Peter the Great*
*The History of Peter the Great* (Pushkin) **10**:394
*The History of the Heart* (Aleixandre)
   See *Historia del corazón*

A *History of the Night* (Borges)
See *Historia de la noche*
"History of the Poet as a Whore" (Madhubuti)
**5**:329
"The History of the Twentieth Century"
(Brodsky) **9**:19
"The History of the World: A T.V.
Docu-Drama" (Ferlinghetti) **1**:184
"History on Wheels" (Baraka) **4**:29
"Hitherto Uncollected" (Moore) **4**:259
"The Hitlerian Spring" (Montale)
See "La primavera Hitleriana"
"Hitoyo enishi" (Hagiwara Sakutaro) **18**:168-69
"Hits and Runs" (Sandburg) **2**:316
"L'Hiver qui vient" (Laforgue) **14**:72-4, 78, 90
"Hochbeglückt in deiner Liebe" (Goethe) **5**:247
"The Hock-Cart, or Harvest Home" (Herrick)
**9**:141-42
"Hod Putt" (Masters) **1**:345
"Hoeing" (Soto) **28**:378
"Hold Me" (Levine) **22**:217
"Hölderlin" (Schwartz) **8**:316
"The Holdfast" (Herbert) **4**:123
"Holding On" (Levine) **22**:214
"Holding Out" (Rich) **5**:357
"Holding the Mirror up to Nature" (Nemerov)
**24**:291
"Holiday" (Sitwell) **3**:311-12, 326
"Holiday Inn Blues" (Ferlinghetti) **1**:187
*The Hollow Men* (Eliot) **5**:163, 171, 174, 180,
185, 191, 193, 198, 206, 209
"Hollywood" (Shapiro) **25**:295
"Holy Baptisme I" (Herbert) **4**:120
"The Holy Child's Song" (Merton) **10**:330, 340
"Holy City of Song" (Noyes) **27**:127
"Holy Cross Day" (Browning) **2**:38, 63
"The Holy Fair" (Burns) **6**:49, 53, 57, 83-4,
86-8, 91, 94
"The Holy Grail" (Tennyson) **6**:407
"holy night" (Clifton) **17**:18, 24, 38
"Holy Satyr" (H. D.) **5**:268
"Holy Scriptures I" (Herbert) **4**:126
"Holy Scriptures 2" (Herbert) **4**:133
"Holy Sonnet XIV: Batter my heart,
three-person'd God" (Donne) **1**:138
*Holy Sonnets* (Donne) **1**:128, 136, 138-40
"Holy Spring" (Thomas) **2**:382, 390
"Holy Thursday" (Blake) **12**:5, 7, 23-4, 34-5
"Holy Willie's Prayer" (Burns) **6**:53, 65, 83,
85-6, 88-9, 96
"Homage" (Viereck) **27**:284
"Homage and Valediction" (Tomlinson) **17**:338
*Homage to Clio* (Auden) **1**:17
"A Homage to John Keats" (Clampitt) **19**:91
"Homage to Literature" (Rukeyser) **12**:211
"homage to mine" (Clifton) **17**:24
"Homage to Paul Mellon, I.M. Pei, Their
Gallery, and Washington City" (Meredith)
**28**:198
"Homage to Paul Robeson" (Hayden) **6**:192,
195
"Homage to Rimbaud" (Montale)
See "Omaggio a Rimbaud"
"Homage to Sextus Propertius" (Pound) **4**:317-
18, 333, 363-66
"Homage to the Empress of the Blues"
(Hayden) **6**:188, 196
"Homage to the Tree" (Tagore)
See "Vriksha-vandana"
"Homage to William Cowper" (Davie) **29**:104
"Homage to Yalta" (Brodsky) **9**:7
"Hombres necios que acusáis" (Juana Ines de
la Cruz) **24**:220
"Home" (Brooke) **24**:57
"Home" (Herbert) **4**:102, 130-31
"Home" (Lorde) **12**:138-39
"Home after Three Months Away" (Lowell)
**3**:206, 209, 216, 221
"Home After Three Months Away" (Sexton)
**2**:350
"Home at Grasmere" (Wordsworth) **4**:414
"Home Burial" (Frost) **1**:193, 195, 229

*Home Course in Religion* (Soto) **28**:394, 396,
398-400, 403
"Home for the Holidays" (Nemerov) **24**:295
"Home Home Home" (Ferlinghetti) **1**:180
"Home Is So Sad" (Larkin) **21**:242
"Home, James" (Viereck) **27**:264
"Home Thoughts" (Sandburg) **2**:309
*Homeage to the American Indians*
See *Homenaje a los indios americanos*
"The Homecoming" (Hardy) **8**:99
"The Homecoming" (Holderlin)
See "Heimkunft"
"Homecoming" (Sanchez) **9**:207, 209, 223
"Homecoming" (Shapiro) **25**:273
"Homecoming" (Viereck) **27**:265, 280
*Homecoming* (Heine)
See *Die Heimkehr*
*Homecoming* (Sanchez) **9**:204, 206-07, 210-13,
215-16, 218-19, 222, 224, 229, 231-34, 237-
38, 242
"Homecomings" (Heaney) **18**:244
*Homegirls and Hand Grenades* (Sanchez)
**9**:228, 230-31, 234-36, 238, 244
"Homeland" (Bely)
See "Rodine"
"Homeland" (Clampitt) **19**:100, 102
*Homenaje a los indios americanos* (Cardenal)
**22**:103, 124-26, 128, 131-32
*Homenaje a Pablo Neruda de los poetas
espanoles: Tres cantos materiales*
(Neruda) **4**:277, 306
"Homenaje y profanaciones" (Paz) **1**:356-57
"Homeric Simile" (Meredith) **28**:174, 182, 187
*The Homestead Called Damascus* (Rexroth)
**20**:182, 209-12, 214
"Home-Thoughts" (McKay) **2**:228
"Hometown Piece for Messers Alston and
Reese" (Moore) **4**:256, 259
"Homily" (Viereck) **27**:280
"Homily on the Piety of All Herd Animals"
(Viereck) **27**:280
"Homily on the Piety of All Herd Animals" (A
Mammoth IdyllViereck) **27**:280
"L'homme" (Lamartine) **16**:275, 285, 290-91,
297-98
*L'Homme approximatif* (Tzara) **27**:234, 237-38,
240-42, 249
"Homuneulue Artifex" (Merrill) **28**:248
*El hondero entusiasta, 1923-1924* (Neruda)
**4**:276
*Honey and Salt* (Sandburg) **2**:336, 339
"Honey Bud" (Tagore)
See "Madhumanjari"
"The Honeysuckle" (Marie de France)
See "Chevrefoil"
"The Hooks of a Corset" (Milosz) **8**:182, 197,
210
"Hop o' My Thumb" (Ashbery) **26**:127, 160
"Hope" (Clare) **23**:44
"Hope" (Milosz) **8**:187-88, 192
"Hope Is a Subtle Glutton" (Dickinson) **1**:111
*Hopes and Impediments: Selected Essays*
(Achebe) **6**:1015
"Hope's Despari" (Tagore)
See "Ashar nairashya"
"The Hop-Garden" (Smart) **13**:330-31, 333, 342
"Hopi Overlay" (Rose) **13**:233
"The Hopsital" (Lermontov) **18**:284-85
"La hora cero" (Cardenal)
See "La hora O"
"La hora O" (Cardenal) **22**:111
*la hora 0* (Cardenal) **22**:103-4, 124-25, 131
*Horace* (Smart)
See *The Works of Horace, Translated into
Verse*
"Horace, Lib. 2 Sat. 6. Part of It Imitated"
(Swift) **9**:297
"Horace to Leuconoë" (Robinson) **1**:459
"Horae Canonicae" (Auden) **1**:17
"An Horatian Ode upon Cromwell's Return
from Ireland" (Marvell) **10**:259, 261-62,

264, 267-71, 275, 277, 289, 292, 294-95,
305-09, 311, 317-18
"Horatio Alger Uses Scag" (Baraka) **4**:30
"Horizons and Rains" (Ortiz) **17**:227
"Horizons Home" (Ortiz) **17**:226
"Horizonte" (Pessoa) **20**:155
"The Horn" (Vigny)
See "Le cor"
"The Horn of Egremont Castle" (Wordsworth)
**4**:377
"Horned Purple" (Williams) **7**:368
"The Horned Rampion" (Clampitt) **19**:102
"Hornpipe" (Sitwell) **3**:297, 303
"L'horreur sympathique" (Baudelaire) **1**:55
"A Horrible Religious Error" (Hughes) **7**:144
"Hors des jours étrangers" (Cesaire) **25**:31
"Horse" (Gluck) **16**:164
"Horse" (Hughes) **7**:143
"Horse" (Hugo) **17**:67
"Horse and Swan Feeding" (Swenson) **14**:246,
262, 277
"The Horse Show" (Williams) **7**:391, 394
"The Horse That Died of Shame" (Momaday)
**25**:189, 213
"Horseman in Rain" (Neruda) **4**:282
"Horses" (Berry) **28**:9
"Horses" (Hughes) **7**:118
"Horses" (Sandburg) **2**:324
*Horses Don't Bet on People and Neither Do I*
(Bukowski) **18**:15
"The Horses of Achilles" (Sikelianos)
**29**:160
"The Horsewoman" (Kumin) **15**:194
"Hortus" (Marvell) **10**:284, 286, 288
"Horus" (Nerval) **13**:180-81, 187-91
"Hosea" (Walker) **20**:278-79
"Hospes Comesque Corporis" (Wylie) **23**:310
"Hospital Barge at Cérisy" (Owen) **19**:342
"A Hospital named 'Hotel Universe'"
(Viereck) **27**:263
"Hospital / poem" (for etheridge
9/26/69Sanchez) **9**:225
"The Hostage" (Smith) **12**:329-30, 333
"Hostel" (McGuckian) **27**:76, 100
*Hosties noires* (Senghor) **25**:231, 233, 235, 238,
248, 254-55
"The Hosting of the Sidhe" (Yeats) **20**:344, 346
"Hot" (Bukowski) **18**:24
"Hotblood on Friday" (Gunn) **26**:
"Hôtel" (Apollinaire) **7**:48
"Hotel" (McGuckian)
See "Hostel"
"Hotel Bed" (Graves) **6**:143-44
"Hotel de l'Univers et Portugal" (Merrill)
**28**:234
"Hotel Genève" (Song) **21**:335-36, 338-41
*Hotel Lautreamont* (Ashbery) **26**:161-164, 166
"The Hotel of Lost Light" (Kinnell) **26**:273
"Hotel Steinplatz" (Olson) **19**:305
"The Hour and the Ghost" (Rossetti) **7**:280
"The Hour of Cowdust" (Ondaatje) **28**:337
"The Hour of Fate" (Lindsay) **23**:281
*Hours of Idleness* (Byron) **16**:86
*Hous of Fame* (Chaucer)
See *House of Fame*
"House" (Browning) **2**:59, 66
"The House" (Merrill) **28**:273
"The House" (Sexton) **2**:361-62
"The House and the Vineyard" (Lamartine)
See "La vigne et la maison"
*House, Bridge, Fountain, Gate* (Kumin) **15**:192,
194, 202, 208
"House by the Sea" (Montale)
See "Casa sul mare"
"A House Divided" (Ondaatje) **28**:293
"The House Fly" (Merrill) **28**:282-83, 285-87
"House Guest" (Bishop) **3**:56
"The House in Main St." (Lowell) **13**:84
*The House of Dust* (Aiken) **26**:4, 6, 8, 13, 22,
27, 31, 36, 50, 72
*House of Fame* (Chaucer) **19**:5, 10, 14, 17-18,
20-3, 73

"A House of Mercy" (Smith) **12**:326, 334-35
"The House of Over-Dew" (Smith) **12**:330, 332-33
*House of the Customs Men* (Montale)
    See *La casa dei doganieri*
"The House of the Dead" (Apollinaire)
    See "La maison des mortes"
"The House of the Heart" (Wakoski) **15**:348, 354
"The House on Bishop Street" (Dove) **6**:113
*The House on Marshland* (Gluck) **16**:125-30, 132-33, 136, 139-44, 147-49, 151, 153-54, 157
*House on the Corner* (Dove)
    See *The Yellow House on the Corner*
"The House on the Hill" (Robinson) **1**:459
"The House, The Environment: The Emperor" (Piercy) **29**:325
"House Under Construction" (Pavese)
    See "Casa in costruzione"
*Houseboat Days* (Ashbery) **26**:140, 144-145, 153, 155, 162, 172
"Housecleaning" (Giovanni) **19**:140
"The Householder" (Browning) **2**:59
"The Housekeeper" (Frost) **1**:193
"The Houses of Old Moscow" (Tsvetaeva)
    See "Domiki staroi Moskvy"
"Housewife" (Sexton) **2**:346, 370
"Houston 6 PM" (Zagajewski) **27**:402
"How" (Atwood) **8**:24
"The How and the Why" (Tennyson) **6**:347
"How Annandale Went Out" (Robinson) **1**:461
"How Cruel is the Story of Eve" (Smith) **12**:309
"How Do You See?" (Smith) **12**:325, 332-33, 352
"How Do You Tell a Story?" (Wakoski) **15**:372
"How Everything Happens" (Based on a Study of the WaveSwenson) **14**:271
"How Few, of All the Hearts That Loved" (Bronte) **8**:50, 74
"How I Came to Be a Graduate Student" (Rose) **13**:232
"How it feels to be touching you" (Piercy) **29**:301
"How It Goes On" (Kumin) **15**:207
"How It Is" (Kumin) **15**:204, 218-20
"How It Strikes a Contemporary" (Browning) **2**:80
"How Lilies Came White" (Herrick) **9**:143
"How Lisa Loved the King" (Eliot) **20**:124
"How Lucy Backslid" (Dunbar) **5**:122, 146
"How Many Bards" (Keats) **1**:313
"How Many Heavens" (Sitwell) **3**:312
"How Many Nights" (Kinnell) **26**:257
"How Marigolds Came Yellow" (Herrick) **9**:102
"How Much Can It Hurt" (Levine) **22**:215
"How Much Earth" (Levine) **22**:219
"How Naked, How without a Wall" (Millay) **6**:238
"How Roses Came Red" (Herrick) **9**:143
"How Samson Bore Away the Gates of Gaza" (Lindsay) **23**:276
"How Shall I Woo Thee" (Dunbar) **5**:126
"How Sweet I roam'd" (Blake) **12**:32, 36
"How the Wallflower Came First" (Herrick) **9**:102
"How to Be Old" (Swenson) **14**:250, 288
"How to Die" (Sassoon) **12**:267, 285
"How to Enter a Big City" (Merton) **10**:337, 344
"How to Make a Good Chili Stew" (Ortiz) **17**:228, 233
"How Very Often at a Fashionable Ball" (Lermontov) **18**:297
"how we avoid prayr" (Bissett) **14**:32
"How We Danced" (Sexton) **2**:366
"How Yesterday Looked" (Sandburg) **2**:305
"Howard Lamson" (Masters) **1**:338
"Howarth Churchyard" (Arnold) **5**:33-4, 52
"Howl" (Ginsberg) **4**:44-9, 51, 57-61, 63-5, 67-70, 73-5, 79
*Howl, and Other Poems* (Ginsberg) **4**:73, 87

*Howling at the Moon* (Hagiwara Sakutaro)
    See *Tsuki ni hoeru*
"The Howling of Wolves" (Hughes) **7**:137, 142, 159
*Hristos voskres* (Bely) **11**:7, 24, 28, 31, 33
"Hsiang Consort" (Li Ho) **13**:51-2
"Hsin-i Village" (Wang Wei) **18**:362
"The Hudsonian Curlew" (Snyder) **21**:292, 297, 308
"Hue, carcan!" (Laforgue) **14**:93
*Hugh Selwyn Mauberley* (Pound) **4**:318-21, 330, 338-39, 341-42, 348
"Hughie At The Inn" (Wylie) **23**:311
"Hugo at Théophile Gautier's Grave" (Lowell) **3**:224
"Huhediblu" (Celan) **10**:124
"L'Huillier, si nous perdons ceste belle Princess" (Ronsard) **11**:250
"8e vision" (Lamartine) **16**:265
"The Human Abstract" (Blake) **12**:10, 34
"Human Affection" (Smith) **12**:310
"Human Applause" (Holderlin)
    See "Menschenbeifall"
"Human Burning" (Aleixandre) **15**:19, 21
"Human Condition" (Gunn) **26**:185
"Human Cylinders" (Loy) **16**:322
"Human Grief" (Trakl)
    See "Menschliche Trauer"
*Human Shows, Far Phantasies, Songs, and Trifles* (Hardy) **8**:89
*Human Wishes* (Hass) **16**:215-17, 221-22
"Humanly Speaking" (Davie) **29**:110
"A Humane Materialist . . ." (Smith) **12**:331
"L'humanitè" (Lamartine) **16**:266, 281, 293
"The Humanities Building" (Shapiro) **25**:322
"Humanity I Love You" (Cummings) **5**:90
"Humble Jar" (Song) **21**:344-48
"The Humble Petition of Frances Harris" (Swift) **9**:251, 296
"The humble Petition of poore Ben: To . . . King Charles" (Jonson)
    See "The humble Petition of poore Ben: To . . . King Charles"
"The Humble-Bee" (Emerson) **18**:79, 84-85, 93, 99
"Humiliation" (Blok) **21**:5, 15
"The Humming-Bird" (Dickinson) **1**:79
"The Humours" (Bradstreet)
    See "Of the Four Humours in Man's Constitution"
*The Humours of the Court* (Bridges)
"Hunchback Girl: She Thinks of Heaven" (Brooks) **7**:53, 69, 80
"The Hunchback in the Park" (Thomas) **2**:394
"A Hundred Collars" (Frost) **1**:215
"Hunger" (Cullen) **20**:63, 76
"Hunger" (Rich) **5**:374
"Hunger in the South" (Neruda) **4**:282
"Hungerfield" (Jeffers) **17**:129, 136
*Hungerfield and Other Poems* (Jeffers) **17**:123, 136
"The Hunter" (Williams) **7**:360
"The Hunter of the Prairies" (Bryant) **20**:23
"The Hunter's Serenade" (Bryant) **20**:15
*The Hunting of the Snark: An Agony in Eight Fits* (Carroll) **18**:30-33, 40-49
"Hunting Watch" (Wang Wei) **18**:389
"Huntress" (H. D.) **5**:269
"The Huntress and Her Dogs" (MacDiarmid) **9**:191
*Huntsman, What Quarry?* (Millay) **6**:230-31, 233-34, 242
"Hurrah for Karamazov!" (Viereck) **27**:279
"Hurrah for Positive Science" (Whitman) **3**:384
"Hurrah for Thunder" (Okigbo) **7**:235, 247
"The Hurricane" (Bryant) **20**:15
"The Hurricane" (Finch)
    See "A Pindarick Poem upon the Hurricane"
"Hurry Up Please It's Time" (Sexton) **2**:367-68
"Hurt Hawks" (Jeffers) **17**:117, 129
"Hurt Hawks II" (Jeffers) **17**:110

"Hush'd Be the Camps To-day" (Whitman) **3**:418
"The Hyacinth Symphony" (Elytis) **21**:131
"L'hydre Univers tordant son corps écaillé d'astres" (Hugo) **17**:90
"L'hylas" (Ronsard) **11**:235
"Hyme" (Donne)
    See "Hymne to God my God, in my sicknesse"
*Hymen* (H. D.) **5**:266-70
"Hymme to God My God, in My Sicknesse" (Donne)
    See "Hymne to God my God, in my sicknesse"
"Hymn" (Ammons) **16**:27, 40, 57-8, 60, 63-5
"Hymn" (Dunbar) **5**:137
"Hymn" (Poe) **1**:446
"Hymn among the Ruins" (Paz)
    See "Himno entre ruinas"
"Hymn before Sunrise in the Vale of Chamouni" (Coleridge) **11**:48-9, 53, 55-8, 92
"Hymn from a Watermelon Pavilion" (Stevens) **6**:292
"Hymn IV" (Ammons) **16**:22
"Hymn of Apollo" (Shelley) **14**:167, 170
"Hymn of Death" (Lamartine)
    See "Hymne de la mort"
"Hymn of Not Much Praise for New York City" (Merton) **10**:344
"Hymn of Pan" (Shelley) **14**:167, 177
"Hymn of the Morning" (Lamartine)
    See "L'hymne du matin"
"A Hymn of the Sea" (Bryant) **20**:3, 13
"Hymn of the Waldenses" (Bryant) **20**:5
*Hymn on the Morning of Christ's Nativity* (Milton) **29**:220-21
"Hymn to Adversity" (Gray)
    See "Ode to Adversity"
"Hymn to Aphrodite" (Sappho)
    See "Ode to Aphrodite"
"Hymn to Artemis Orthia" (Sikelianos) **29**:372
"Hymn to Beauty" (Baudelaire)
    See "Hymne à la beauté"
"Hymn to Beauty" (Spenser)
    See "An Hymne in Honour of Beautie"
"Hymn to Death" (Bryant) **20**:4, 10, 13, 16, 18
"An Hymn to Diana" (Jonson) **17**:171, 182, 207
"Hymn to Earth" (Wylie) **23**:304-306, 308, 311, 323
"An Hymn to God the Father" (Jonson) **17**:172
"An Hymn to Humanity" (Wheatley) **3**:338, 340-41, 348, 361, 363
"Hymn to Ignorance" (Gray) **2**:143, 155
"Hymn to Intellectual Beauty" (Shelley) **14**:166, 169, 177-8, 187, 217, 234, 237-8
"Hymn to Lanie Poo" (Baraka) **4**:15
"Hymn to Physical Pain" (Kipling) **3**:192
"Hymn to Proserpine" (Swinburne) **24**:316, 320, 338, 345-48
"An Hymn to the Evening" (Wheatley) **3**:361, 363
"An Hymn to the Morning" (Wheatley) **3**:361
"Hymn to the Seal" (Smith) **12**:295
"Hymn to the Supreme Being, on Recovery from a Dangerous Fit of Illness" (Smart) **13**:346
"Hymne" (Baudelaire) **1**:63
"Hymne à la beauté" (Baudelaire) **1**:71
"Hymne au Christ" (Lamartine) **16**:280, 293
"L'hymne au soleil" (Lamartine) **16**:277
"Hymne de Calaïs et de Zetes" (Ronsard) **11**:287
"Hymne de la mort" (Lamartine) **16**:283
"Hymne de la Mort" (Ronsard) **11**:226-27, 244, 269, 272-74
"L'hymne de la nuit" (Lamartine) **16**:262, 266, 292
"Hymne de l'ange de la terre apres la destruction de globe" (Lamartine) **16**:265, 281, 287

"Hymne de l'autonne" (Ronsard) **11**:230, 232-34, 267, 279

"L'Hymne de l'hiver" (Ronsard) **11**:266

"Hymne de Pollux et de Castor" (Ronsard) **11**:284, 287

"L'hymne du matin" (Lamartine) **16**:267, 279, 292

"Hymne du printemps" (Ronsard) **11**:242

"An Hymne in Honour of Beautie" (Spenser) **8**:331, 337

"An Hymne in Honour of Love" (Spenser) **8**:337

"Hymne of Beauty" (Spenser)
　See "An Hymne in Honour of Beautie"

"An Hymne of Heavenly Beautie" (Spenser) **8**:332, 336-37, 345

"An Hymne of Heavenly Love" (Spenser) **8**:329, 332, 336-37, 345

"Hymne of Love" (Spenser)
　See "An Hymne in Honour of Love"

"A Hymne to Christ, at the authors last going into Germany" (Donne) **1**:139

"Hymne to God my God, in my sicknesse" (Donne) **1**:140, 158

"A Hymne to God the Father" (Donne) **1**:138-39

"Hymnes" (Spenser) **8**:331

*Hymnes* (Ronsard) **11**:248

*Hymnes* (Spenser)
　See *Fowre Hymnes*

"Hymnes in Honor of Love and Beauty" (Spenser) **8**:331

*Hymns* (Ronsard)
　See *Hymnes*

*Hymns and Spiritual Songs for the Fasts and Festivals of the Church of England* (Smart) **13**:332, 340-42, 368

*Hymns for Children* (Smart)
　See *Hymns for the Amusement of Children*

*Hymns for the Amusement of Children* (Smart) **13**:340, 349, 361

*Hymns for the Fasts and Festivals* (Smart)
　See *Hymns and Spiritual Songs for the Fasts and Festivals of the Church of England*

"Hymns to Death" (Ginsberg) **4**:58

"Hyōhakusha no uta" (Hagiwara Sakutaro) **18**:183

*Hyōtō* (Hagiwara Sakutaro) **18**:176, 181, 183-84

*Hyperion* (Keats) **1**:278-79, 281-82, 284, 287-91, 305, 309

*Hyperions Schiksalslied* (Holderlin) **4**:151

"Hypocrite lecteur" (Baudelaire)
　See "Au lecteur"

"Hypocrite Swift" (Bogan) **12**:95, 101, 125

*I. 3* (Pindar)
　See *Isthmian 3*

*I. 4* (Pindar)
　See *Isthmian 4*

"I abide and abide" (Wyatt) **27**:302

"I Am" (Clare) **23**:22

"I Am" (Smith) **12**:314

"I Am a Beggar Always" (Cummings) **5**:100

"I Am a Victim of Telephone" (Ginsberg) **4**:85

"I Am an Old Town Square" (Viereck) **27**:280

"I Am as I Am" (Wyatt) **27**:317

"'I Am Cherry Alive,' the Little Girl Sang" (Schwartz) **8**:318

*I Am in the Unstable Hour* (Paz)
　See *Vrindaban*

"I Am of Ireland" (Yeats) **20**:328

"I Am She" (Giovanni) **19**:143

"I Am to My Own Heart Merely a Serf" (Schwartz) **8**:306

"I am writing to you" (Lermontov) **18**:303

"I and Your Eyes" (Knight) **14**:39-40, 46

"I Ask My Mother to Sing" (Lee) **24**:245

"I at creation" (Clifton) **17**:35

"i belong with th wind" (Bissett) **14**:34

"I Cannot Forget the High Spell" (Bryant) **20**:29

"I Cannot Stand Tears" (Bukowski) **18**:4

"I climb the mossy bank of the glade" (Bridges) **28**:86

"I Climbed into the Tousled Hayloft" (Mandelstam) **14**:118, 122

*I Colloqui* (Gozzano) **10**:173, 176-81, 183-86

"I come and go" (Brutus) **24**:116

"i come from halifax" (Bissett) **14**:31

"I Could Believe" (Levine) **22**:234

"I Cry, Love! Love!" (Roethke) **15**:248, 284, 298-301

"I Did Not Know the Spoils of Joy" (Schwartz) **8**:299

"I Do Confess Thou Art Sae Fair" (Burns) **6**:81

"I Don't Know Why You Think" (Guillen)
　See "No sé por qué piensas tú"

"I don't love you" (Baraka) **4**:19

"I Dream a World" (Hughes) **1**:259

"I dut chaoy i dhi i gody" (Blok) **21**:17

"I Dwell in Possibility" (Dickinson) **1**:102

"I Dwelled in Hell on Earth to Write This Rhyme" (Ginsberg) **4**:79

"I Explain a Few Things" (Neruda)
　See "Explico algunas cosas"

"I Found Her Out There" (Hardy) **8**:134

"I Found the Words to Every Thought" (Dickinson) **1**:102

"I from my window where the meuse is wide" (Belloc) **24**:11

"I fynde no peace" (Wyatt) **27**:342, 358

"I Give You Back" (Harjo) **27**:57, 61

"I Go Back to May 1937" (Olds) **22**:318

"I Had a Dream . . ." (Smith) **12**:295, 305-06, 318, 345

"I Had No Human Fears" (Wordsworth) **4**:420

"I Hate America" (Ginsberg) **4**:74

"I Have" (Guillen)
　See "Tengo"

*I Have* (Guillen)
　See *Tengo*

"I Have Believed That I Prefer to Live" (Wylie) **23**:314

"i have evn herd uv thee" (Bissett) **14**:33

"I Have Forgotten the Word I Wanted to Say" (Mandelstam) **14**:116, 155

"I Have Had to Learn to Live With My Face" (Wakoski) **15**:326, 330

"I Have Lived in England" (Bukowski) **18**:5

"I Have Longed to Move Away" (Thomas) **2**:379, 389

"I Have Outlived My Desires" (Pushkin)
　See "Ia Perezhil Svoi Zhelan'ia"

"I Hear an Army" (Joyce)
　See "XXXVI"

"I Heard Immanuel Singing" (Lindsay) **23**:284, 288

"I Heard Wild Geese" (Ekeloef) **23**:87

"i herd ya laffin in th water" (Bissett) **14**:33

"I Hoed and Trenched and Weeded" (Housman) **2**:192

*I kalosíni stis likoporiés* (Elytis) **21**:128

"I Keep repeating the first line" (Tsvetaeva)
　See "Vse Povtoryayv pervyi stikh"

"I Knew a Woman" (Roethke) **15**:275, 286, 289

"I Knew Not 'Twas So Dire a Crime" (Bronte) **8**:72

"I Know" (Bely)
　See "Znayu"

"I Know All This When Gipsy Fiddles Cry" (Lindsay) **23**:275, 280, 287

"I Know I Am but Summer" (Millay) **6**:225

"I Know This Vicious Minute's Hour" (Thomas) **2**:405

*I, Laminarian* (Cesaire)
　See *moi, Laminaire*

"I Lay Next to You All Night Trying Awake to Understand the Watering Places of the Moon" (Wakoski) **15**:364

"I Like Stroking Leaves" (Alegria) **26**:

"I live in a proper kitchen garden" (Mandelstam)
　See "Ia zhivu na vazhnykh ogorodakh"

"I Look at My Hand" (Swenson) **14**:281

"I Look at the Future With Fear" (Lermontov) **18**:281

"I Look into My Glass" (Hardy) **8**:90

"I love all beauteous things" (Bridges) **28**:84

"I love frosty breath . . . and reality is reality" (Mandelstam)
　See "Liubliu moroznoe dykhan'e"

"I Lovve Loyyd" (Wyatt) **27**:371

"I, Maximus of Glouster, to You" (Olson) **19**:276, 280-81

"I May, I Might, I Must" (Moore) **4**:256

"I Might Have Seen It" (Ashbery) **26**:133

"I must live, though I've already died twice" (Mandelstam)
　See "Ia dolzhen zhit', khotia ia dvazhdy umer"

"I Need, I Need" (Roethke) **15**:252, 272-73, 277, 298

"I Never Hear That One Is Dead" (Dickinson) **1**:94

"I Never Saw a Moor" (Dickinson) **1**:101

"I Only Am Escaped Alone to Tell Thee" (Nemerov) **24**:261

"I Plant in Your Favor This Tree of Cybele" (Ronsard)
　See "Je plante en la faveur cest arbre de Cybelle"

"I Pressed My Hands Together..." (Akhmatova) **2**:11

"I Pursue a Form" (Dario)
　See "Yo persigo una forma"

"I Reckon—When I Count at All—/First—Poets" (Dickinson) **1**:96

"I Remember" (Smith) **12**:314, 320

"I Remember, I Remember" (Larkin) **21**:228, 231, 246

"I Rode with My Darling" (Smith) **12**:327

"I Said" (H. D.) **5**:305

"I Said It" (Baraka) **4**:13

"I Save Your Coat, but You Lose It Later" (Gallagher) **9**:44, 60

"I Saw Eternity" (Bogan) **12**:89, 100, 121

"I Saw in Louisiana a Live-Oak Growing" (Whitman) **3**:402

"I Saw Thee on Thy Bridal Day" (Poe)
　See "Song"

"I See around Me Tombstones Grey" (Bronte) **8**:74

"I See the Boys of Summer" (Thomas) **2**:384

"I Shall Never See You Again" (Masters) **1**:333, 338

"I Sing of Olaf Glad and Big" (Cummings) **5**:88

"I Sing the Body Electric" (Whitman) **3**:385, 396

"I sing when my throat is moist . . ." (Mandelstam)
　See "Poiu kngda gortan' syra . . ."

"I Sit by the Window" (Brodsky) **9**:8, 13

"I Sit in My Room" (Toomer) **7**:337

"I sonetti del ritorno" (Gozzano) **10**:188

"I Stop Writing the Poem" (Gallagher) **9**:65

"I Struck a Diminished Seventh" (Ammons) **16**:39

"I Swore to Stab the Sonnet" (Shapiro) **25**:322

"I Take Care of You: A Lantern Dashes by in the Glass" (Gallagher) **9**:50

"I Taste a Liquor Never Brewed" (Dickinson) **1**:80

"I Taste the Ashes of Your Death" (Bukowski) **18**:7

"I Tell You for Several Years of My Madness I Heard the Voice of Lilith Singing in the Trees of Chicago" (Carruth) **10**:85

"I think, yes, a leopard in Duty blue would" (Villa) **22**:355

"I Thirst" (Harper) **21**:198

"I to My Perils" (Housman) **2**:180

*I Too Am a Painter* (Apollinaire)
　See *Et moi aussi je suis peintre*

"I, Too, Sing America" (Hughes) **1**:241, 258-59

"I Travel as a Phantom Now" (Hardy) **8**:89

"I Vecchi" (Pound) **4**:317

"I' vo pensando" (Petrarch) **8**:227

"I Wandered Lonely as a Cloud" (Wordsworth) **4**:388, 400
"I Want New York" (Nash) **21**:263
"I Wanted to be There When My Father Died" (Olds) **22**:325-26, 341-42
"I wanted to stay in September" (Cassian) **17**:5
"I Was Born in Lucerne" (Levine) **22**:226
"i was just cummin" (Bissett) **14**:34
"I was not young long; I met the soul early" (Villa) **22**:351
"I Was Reading a Scientific Article" (Atwood) **8**:13
"I Was Washing Outside in the Darkness" (Mandelstam) **14**:122
"I Went into the Maverick Bar" (Snyder) **21**:293, 296-97
"I wept for my youth" (Kunitz) **19**:175
"I Will Be" (Cummings) **5**:93
"I will break God's seamless skull" (Villa) **22**:352
"I Will Lie Down" (Swenson) **14**:286
"I Will Put Chaos into Fourteen Lines" (Millay) **6**:243, 246
"I Will Sing You One-O" (Frost) **1**:195
"I Will Wade Out" (Cummings) **5**:91
"I Wish I Had Great Knowledge or Great Art" (Schwartz) **8**:294
"I wonder by my troth" (Donne)
   See "The good-morrow"
"I Would Have Been a Trumpet Player If I Hadn't Gone to College" (Baraka) **4**:36
"I Would I Were a Careless Child" (Byron) **16**:73, 86-8
"I would not be thought less than a man" (Brutus) **24**:116
"I Would Not Paint—a Picture" (Dickinson) **1**:102
"I Would Return South" (Neruda)
   See "Quiero volver a sur"
*I Wouldn't Have Missed It* (Nash) **21**:277
"Ia dolzhen zhit', khotia ia dvazhdy umer" (Mandelstam) **14**:151
"Ia Perezhil Svoi Zhelan'ia" (Pushkin) **10**:412
"Ia zhivu na vazhnykh ogorodakh" (Mandelstam) **14**:152
"Ibadan Lagos Kano London 5 Jan 72" (Brutus) **24**:123
*Ibis* (Ovid) **2**:238, 242, 244
*IBM* (Bissett) **14**:15
"Ibo" (Hugo) **17**:83, 89
"Icarian Wings" (Cullen) **20**:67
"Ice Cream at Blaunberg" (Tomlinson) **17**:353
"The Ice Eagle" (Wakoski) **15**:324, 363
*The Ice Land* (Hagiwara Sakutaro)
   See *Hyōtō*
"Ice Storm" (Hayden) **6**:194
"Ice Storm" (Hayden) **6**:193
"The Ice-Cream Wars" (Ashbery) **26**:136
"The Ice-Storm" (Pinsky) **27**:174
*Ichiaku no suna* (Ishikawa) **10**:193, 200-02, 204-05, 210-11, 216
"Ichigatsu" (Nishiwaki) **15**:231-32
"Icicles" (Pinsky) **27**:158
*Ici-haut. Pamyati Maksimilian Voloshin* (Tsvetaeva) **14**:324
*Iconographs* (Swenson) **14**:268-72, 274, 281, 285-86
"Idaho" (Ashbery) **26**:137
"The Idea of Ancestry" (Knight) **14**:39, 41, 43-4, 52-3
"The Idea of Order at Key West" (Stevens) **6**:305, 307, 325, 327
"The Idea of Trust" (Gunn) **26**:207, 220
"The Ideal Father" (Olds) **22**:322
"Ideal Landscape" (Rich) **5**:393
"Ideas" (Merrill) **28**:267
"L'idee de Dieu" (Lamartine) **16**:265-66, 293
"Identity" (Ammons) **16**:27, 29
"Identity: A Poem" (Stein) **18**:334
"The Idiot Boy" (Wordsworth) **4**:372, 374, 381, 416-18, 426-27
"Idoto" (Okigbo) **7**:223, 225

"Idyl" (Parker) **28**:355
"Idyll" (Roethke) **15**:246
*Idylls of the Bible* (Harper) **21**:185
*Idylls of the Hearth* (Tennyson) **6**:360
*Idylls of the King* (Tennyson) **6**:358, 360, 369, 374, 376, 379, 406-08
"If" (Kipling) **3**:176, 183-84, 188
"If Anyone Had Told Me" (Aleixandre)
   See "If Someone Could Have Told Me"
"If Anything Will Level with You Water Will" (Ammons) **16**:54
"If Blood Were Not as Powerful as It Is" (Gallagher) **9**:59
"If Fun Is Fun Isn't That Enough?" (Nash) **21**:274
"If I Am Too Brown or Too White for You" (Rose) **13**:241
"If I Had Children" (Swenson) **14**:279
"if i have made, my lady, intricate" (Cummings) **5**:87
"If I Think About You Again It Will Be the Fifty-Third Monday of Next Year" (Harjo) **27**:70
"If I were Paris" (Johnson) **24**:144
"If I Were Tickled by the Rub of Love" (Thomas) **2**:384, 386, 401
"If in Beginning Twilight of Winter Will Stand" (Cummings) **5**:109-10
"If It Chance Your Eye Offend You" (Housman) **2**:184
"If It Were You" (Page) **12**:179
"If, My Darling" (Larkin) **21**:236, 248
"If My Head Hurt a Hair's Foot" (Thomas) **2**:386, 407
"If Only" (Rossetti) **7**:280
"If Someone Could Have Told Me" (Aleixandre) **15**:4
"If There are Any Heavens My Mother Will Have" (All by HerselfCummings) **5**:88
"If They Come in the Night" (Piercy) **29**:311
"If waker care if sudden pale colour" (Wyatt) **27**:368
"If We Must Die" (McKay) **2**:206-07, 211, 217, 220, 229
"If We Take All Gold" (Bogan) **12**:122
"If yet I have not all thy love" (Donne)
   See "Lovers infinitenesse"
*If You Call This Cry a Song* (Carruth) **10**:77
"IFF" (Nemerov) **24**:289
*Igitur* (Mallarme) **4**:199, 201-03, 208
"Ignorance" (Larkin) **21**:227, 246
"I,it,was,that,saw" (Villa) **22**:355
"Ike" (Dove) **6**:109
"Ikey's Worth I'm" (GoldbergCummings) **5**:82
"Il nini muart" (Pasolini) **17**:251, 256, 281, 284
"Il penseroso" (Gray) **2**:141
*Il Penseroso* (Milton) **29**:240-41
"Il Penseroso" (Milton) **19**:193, 201-02, 226, 229-33, 249, 255; **29**:232
"Il pleut" (Apollinaire) **7**:20, 34
"Il reduce" (Gozzano) **10**:184-85, 190
"Il y a" (Apollinaire) **7**:22
*Iliad* (Homer) **23**:149, 151-53, 155-57, 159-63, 165-72, 175-89, 191
*Iliads* (Homer)
   See *Iliad*
*Ilias* (Homer)
   See *Iliad*
*Ílios o prótos* (Elytis) **21**:119-20, 124, 127
"I'll Run Wild in the Dark Streets Gypsy Camp" (Mandelstam) **14**:119
"I'll tell thee now what thou shalt doe" (dear loveDonne)
   See "A Valediction: of the booke"
"Illic Jacet" (Housman) **2**:184
"Illinois Farmer" (Sandburg) **2**:316
"The Illiterate" (Meredith) **28**:188
"The Illumination" (Kunitz) **19**:174-75, 178
"Illuminations" (Gluck) **16**:151
*Illuminations* (Rimbaud)
   See *Les illuminations*

*Les illuminations* (Rimbaud) **3**:249, 254, 259-65, 279
*The Illustrated Wilfred Funk* (Ferlinghetti) **1**:186
"Illustration" (Ashbery) **26**:123, 137
"The Illustration" (Levertov) **11**:168
"Ilu, the Talking Drum" (Knight) **14**:39, 41, 44-6
*I'm a Stranger Here Myself* (Nash) **21**:264
"I'm a Whore Are You Satisfied?" (Alegria) **26**:
"Im Hafen" (Heine) **25**:157-58, 160, 163-64
"I'm Here" (Roethke) **15**:270, 272, 279
"Im Osten" (Trakl) **20**:225-26, 250, 255-56
"I'm Still Not Patriarch" (Mandelstam) **14**:122
"I'm Unwilling" (Ammons) **16**:44
"I'm Wife....I'm Woman Now" (Dickinson) **1**:93
"The Image" (Day Lewis) **11**:146
*The Image and the Law* (Nemerov) **24**:255, 260, 264, 285, 288-89, 298
"An Image from a Past Life" (Yeats) **20**:328
*The Image Maker* (Merrill) **28**:
*The Image Marker* (Merrill) **28**:270
"The Image of God" (Browning) **6**:20
"The Images" (Rich) **5**:385, 396
*Images à Crusoé* (Perse) **23**:210, 217, 228, 230, 234-35, 247, 254, 256-57
"Images for Godard" (Rich) **5**:366, 391
"Images of Angels" (Page) **12**:168-69, 177, 190
"Images of Perfection" (Tomlinson) **17**:349
"Imagination" (Wheatley)
   See "On Imagination"
"Imago" (Clampitt) **19**:82
*L'imitation de Notre-Dame la lune* (Laforgue) **14**:57, 61, 70-1, 80, 97
"Imitation of Byron" (Lermontov) **18**:302
"An Imitation of Spenser" (Blake) **12**:31
*Imitations* (Lowell) **3**:213, 223, 228, 232
"Imitations of Drowning" (Sexton) **2**:363
"Imitations of Horace" (Swift) **9**:265
*Imitations of Horace* (Pope)
   See *Satires and Epistles of Horace, Imitated*
"Immature Pebbles" (Zukofsky) **11**:355
"The Immigrants" (Atwood) **8**:38
"The Immigration Department" (Cassian) **17**:5-6
*The Immortal Husband* (Merrill) **28**:227
*The Immortal Husband* (Merrill) **28**:
"The Immortal Part" (Housman) **2**:179, 192
"L'immortalité" (Lamartine) **16**:275, 279, 291, 300, 302
"Immortality" (Lamartine)
   See "L'immortalité"
"Immortality" (Reese) **29**:333
"Immortality Ode" (Wordsworth)
   See "Ode: Intimations of Immortality from Recollections of Early Childhood"
"The Immortals" (Parker) **28**:360
"The Impalpabilities" (Tomlinson) **17**:327, 357
"Impasse" (Hughes) **1**:260
"L'impenitent" (Verlaine) **2**:417
"The Impercipient" (Hardy) **8**:107-08, 112
"Imperia" (Gautier) **18**:125
"The Imperial Bison is" (Guillen)
   See "The Imperial Bison is"
"The Impossible Indispensibility of the Ars Poetica" (Carruth) **10**:86
"Impossible to Tell" (Pinsky) **27**:174-76
"The Impossible Woman/Ideal" (Jimenez)
   See "Quimérica"
"The Imprefect Lover" (Sassoon) **12**:258
"Impressionism" (Mandelstam) **14**:118
"Impressionist Picture of a Garden" (Lowell) **13**:95
"Imprint for Rio Grande" (Toomer) **7**:337
"Impromptu on Lord Holland's House" (Gray)
   See "On Lord Holland's Seat near Margate, Kent"
"An Improvisation for the Stately Dwelling" (Ammons) **16**:32, 63

"Improvisations: Lights and Snow" (Aiken)
    **26**:50
"The Improvisatore" (Coleridge) **11**:105
"In a Boat" (Ashbery) **26**:
"In a Boat" (Belloc) **24**:5
"In a Buggy at Dusk" (Milosz) **8**:205
"In a Caledonian Forest" (MacDiarmid) **9**:176
"In a Castle" (Lowell) **13**:70
"In a Cemetery" (Aleixandre) **15**:18
"In a Dark Time" (Roethke) **15**:268, 276, 278,
    281, 306, 313
"In a Gondola" (Browning) **2**:26
"In a Rosary" (Swinburne) **24**:322, 324
"In a Ship Recently Raised from the Sea"
    (Page) **12**:168, 184
"In a Spanish Garden" (Stryk) **27**:187
"In a Station of the Metro" (Pound) **4**:355
"In a Strange House" (Kunitz) **19**:148
"In a Time of Dearth" (Lowell) **13**:83
"In a Time of Revolution for Instance"
    (Ferlinghetti) **1**:188
"In a Troubled Key" (Hughes) **1**:254-55
*In a Vast Dominion* (Aleixandre)
    See *En un vasto dominio*
"In a Waiting-Room" (Hardy) **8**:107
"In a Whispering Gallery" (Hardy) **8**:108
"In an Artist's Studio" (Rossetti) **7**:284-85
"In Another Fashion" (Ondaatje) **28**:298, 318
"In Answer of an Elegiacal Letter, upon the
    Death of the King of Sweden, from
    Aurelian Townsend, inviting me to write
    on that subject" (Carew) **29**:13, 50, 74
"In Arden" (Tomlinson) **17**:326, 343, 346-48,
    353
"In August" (Soto) **28**:380
*In Autumn* (Ekeloef) **23**:71
"In Blood's Domaine" (Duncan) **2**:120
"In Broken Images" (Graves) **6**:134-35, 137,
    151, 153
"In casa del sopravissuto" (Gozzano) **10**:180,
    183, 185, 189
"In Celebration of My Uterus" (Sexton)
    **2**:352-53
"In Chopin's Garden" (Davie) **29**:110
*In Cold Hell, in Thicket* (Olson) **19**:284
"In Country Heaven" (Thomas) **2**:395
"In Country Sleep" (Thomas) **2**:395
"In court to serve" (Wyatt) **27**:367
"In Defense of Metaphysics" (Tomlinson)
    **17**:315
*In Defense of the Earth* (Rexroth) **20**:181, 186,
    188, 190, 192, 194, 209
"In der Fremde" (Bridges) **28**:77, 81
"In deserto" (Gautier) **18**:156
"In Distrust of Merits" (Moore) **4**:236, 238,
    240, 249, 261, 267-69
*In Dreams Begin Responsibilities, and Other
    Stories* (Schwartz) **8**:281-82, 291, 294,
    300-01, 305-07, 319
"In England" (Brodsky) **9**:8
"In Eternum I was ons Determed" (Wyatt)
    **27**:318, 324
"In Evening Air" (Roethke) **15**:275, 281
"In Examination" (Brooke) **24**:57
"In Excelsis" (Lowell) **13**:91, 97
"In Explanation of Our Times" (Hughes) **1**:258
"In Extremis: Poems about My Father" (Berry)
    **28**:30
"In Florida" (Swenson) **14**:272
"In Freiburg Station" (Brooke) **24**:62, 66
"In Gallarus Oratory" (Heaney) **18**:201, 223
*In Gemäldegalerien* (Heine) **25**:131
"In Golden Gate Park That Day" (Ferlinghetti)
    **1**:183
"In Gratitude to Beethoven" (Wakoski) **15**:345
"In Guernsey" (Swinburne) **24**:325-26
"In Harmony with Nature" (Arnold) **5**:31, 38,
    49
"In Her Praise" (Graves) **6**:171-72
"In Honor of David Anderson Brooks, My
    Father" (Brooks) **7**:62

"In Honour of Du Bartas" (Bradstreet) **10**:2, 6,
    52
"In Honour of that High and Mighty Princess,
    Queen Elizabeth, of Happy Memory"
    (Bradstreet) **10**:37, 56
"In Hospital" (Pasternak)
    See "V bol'nitse"
"In Italy" (Brodsky) **9**:23
"In January" (Brooke) **24**:61, 82
"In Just-" (Cummings) **5**:88, 104
"In Laughter" (Hughes) **7**:159
"In Lieu of the Lyre" (Moore) **4**:259
"In limine" (Montale) **13**:114-15, 165
"In Love Made Visible" (Swenson) **14**:274, 284
"In Loving Memory of the Late Author of
    Dream Songs" (Meredith) **28**:180, 199,
    202, 205, 216-17
*In Mad Love and War* (Harjo) **27**:66-67
"In Meath in May" (Davie) **29**:120
"In Memoriam" (Brodsky) **9**:23
"In Memoriam" (Bryant) **20**:45
"In Memoriam" (Carruth) **10**:85
"In Memoriam" (Reese) **29**:349
"In Memoriam" (Roethke) **15**:279
*In Memoriam* (Tennyson) **6**:354, 359-60, 362-
    64, 367-71, 379, 388, 392-94, 398-99, 403,
    405-08, 412, 416
*In Memoriam James Joyce* (MacDiarmid)
    **9**:163-66, 173, 180, 182-84, 186
"In Memoriam Mae Noblitt" (Ammons) **16**:62
"In Memoriam N. K. M."
    (1889-1947Meredith) **28**:190
"In Memoriam PW Jr 1921-1980" (Kumin)
    **15**:221
"In Memoriam Stratton Christensen"
    (Meredith) **28**:185, 209
"In Memoriam: Wallace Stevens" (Duncan)
    **2**:114
"In Memory: After a Friend's Sudden Death"
    (Levertov) **11**:206
"In Memory of A. I. Odoevsky" (Lermontov)
    **18**:268, 298
"In Memory of Ann Jones" (Thomas)
    See "After the Funeral: In Memory of
    Anne Jones"
"In Memory of Arthur Winslow" (Lowell) **3**:218
"In Memory of Elena" (Forche)
    See "The Memory of Elena"
"In Memory of Eva Gore-Booth and Con
    Markiewicz" (Yeats) **20**:349
"In Memory of Major Robert Gregory"
    (Tomlinson) **17**:307
"In Memory of Major Robert Gregory" (Yeats)
    **20**:321, 327
"In Memory of My Dear Grandchild Elizabeth
    Bradstreet" (Bradstreet) **10**:27, 45
"In Memory of Radio" (Baraka) **4**:14
"In Memory of Robert Frost" (Meredith)
    **28**:195, 202, 216
"In Memory of W. B. Yeats" (Auden) **1**:14
"In Memory of Walter Savage Landor"
    (Swinburne) **24**:335
"In Michigan" (Masters) **1**:329
"In Mind" (Levertov) **11**:211-13
"In Montgomery" (Brooks) **7**:82
"In Monument Valley" (Merrill) **28**:255
"In morte del realismo" (Pasolini) **17**:259
"In My Craft or Sullen Art" (Thomas) **2**:383
"In My Day We Used to Call It
    Pussy-Whipped" (Bukowski) **18**:15
"In My Dreams" (Smith) **12**:343
*In My Honor* (Rilke) **2**:280
"In My Solitary Hours" (Bradstreet) **10**:62-3
"In Neglect" (Frost) **1**:192
"In Nine Sleep Valley" (Merrill) **28**:223
"in nova scotia th peopul" (Bissett) **14**:32
*In Other Words* (Swenson) **14**:272-74, 277, 279-
    80, 283, 287
*In Our Terribleness* (Some Elements and
    Meaning in Black StyleBaraka) **4**:19-21
"In Our Time" (Rukeyser) **12**:216

*In Parallel* (Verlaine)
    See *Parallèlement*
"In Paris in a Loud Dark Winter" (Ferlinghetti)
    **1**:165
"In Plaster, with a Bronze Wash" (Meredith)
    See "Thoughts on One's Head"
"In Praise of Cities" (Gunn) **26**:186, 231
"In Praise of Darkness" (Borges)
    See *Elogio de la sombra*
*In Praise of Darkness*
    See *Elogio de la sombra*
*In Praise of Darkness* (Borges)
    See *Elogio de la sombra*
"In Praise of Johnny Appleseed" (Lindsay)
    **23**:280, 288
*In Praise of Krishna* (Levertov) **11**:181
"In Praise of Limestone" (Auden) **1**:17, 20
"In Praise of Marriages" (Wright) **14**:342, 365
"In Praise of the Fool" (Olson) **19**:283
"In Procession" (Graves) **6**:138
"In Quest of the Tao in An-Ling, I Met Kai
    Huan Who Fashioned for Me a Register
    of the Realized Ones; Left Behind As a
    Present When About to Depart" (Li Po)
    **29**:169
"In Rain" (Berry) **28**:16
*In Reckless Ecstasy* (Sandburg) **2**:334
"In reference to her children" (Bradstreet)
    **10**:13, 26-7, 34-5, 43, 59
"In Reply When Lesser Officials of Chung-tu
    Brought a Pot of Wine and Two Fish to
    My Inn as Gifts" (Li Po) **29**:146
"In Response to 'Tongtang Tune' by Censor
    Lu" (Li Po) **29**:179-80, 182
"In Santa Maria del Popolo" (Gunn) **26**:186,
    201, 219
"In Shadow" (Crane) **3**:98-9
"In Sickness" (Swift) **9**:295
"In Silence" (Merton) **10**:347, 349
"In Sleep" (Montale)
    See "Nel sonno"
"In Society" (Ginsberg) **4**:71
"In Strange Cities" (Zagajewski) **27**:394
"In Strasbourg in 1349" (Ammons) **16**:39
"In Summer" (Dunbar) **5**:139
"In Tall Grass" (Sandburg) **2**:324
"In Tenebris" (IHardy) **8**:94, 110
"In Thankful Remembrance for My Dear
    Husband's Safe Arrival" (Bradstreet)
    **10**:60-1, 64
"In That Time when It Was Not the Fashion"
    (Gallagher) **9**:60
"In the Bahamas" (Hass) **16**:217
"In the Balance" (Tomlinson) **17**:346
"In the Bamboo Hut" (Kinnell) **26**:260
"In the Beach House" (Sexton) **2**:363
"In the Beauty Created by Others"
    (Zagajewski) **27**:381, 383
"In the Beginning" (Sanchez) **9**:228-29
"In the Beginning" (Thomas) **2**:403
"In the Bodies of Words" (Swenson) **14**:287
*In the Clearing* (Frost) **1**:212-13, 224
"In the Constellations" (Dario)
    See "En las constelaciones"
"In the Courtroom" (Sanchez) **9**:225
"In the Dark and Cloudy Day" (Housman)
    **2**:193
"In the Days of Prismatic Color" (Moore)
    **4**:251-52, 257-58
"In the Deep Museum" (Sexton) **2**:346, 348,
    351, 360-61
"In the East" (Trakl)
    See "Im Osten"
"In the Forest" (Pasternak)
    See "V lesu"
"In the friendly dark" (Brutus) **24**:122
"In the Fullness of Time" (Tomlinson) **17**:312,
    321, 341
"In the Glass of Fashion" (Nemerov) **24**:289,
    291
"In the Greenhouse" (Montale)
    See "Nella serra"

"In the Hall of Mirrors" (Merrill) **28**:242, 244
"In the Hands of a Blindman" (Gallagher) **9**:60
"In the Heart of Contemplation" (Day Lewis) **11**:144
"In the Hills" (Bely) **11**:5
"In the Hotel of Lost Night" (Kinnell) **26**:251, 267
"In the M5 Restaurant" (Hughes) **7**:162
"In the Market-Place" (Nemerov) **24**:291
"In the Marshes of the Blood River" (Piercy) **29**:314
"In the Mecca" (Brooks) **7**:78, 81-2, 88-91
*In the Mecca* (Brooks) **7**:62-3, 66, 81-3, 88, 90-1, 94, 105, 107
"In the Month of March" (Viereck) **27**:278
"In the Moonlight" (Hardy) **8**:124
"In the mountains" (Wang Wei) **18**:376, 380, 383
"In the Naked Bed, in Plato's Cave" (Schwartz) **8**:291, 297, 301-02, 308-09, 311, 316
"In the Neolithic Age" (Kipling) **3**:167
"In the Night" (Smith) **12**:345
"In the Park" (Kumin) **15**:209-11, 211
"In the Park" (Montale) **13**:151
"In the Park" (Smith) **12**:345, 352-54
"In the Past" (Zagajewski) **27**:383
"In the Pink" (Sassoon) **12**:242, 262
"In The Plaza" (Aleixandre) **15**:6, 11-12, 17
*In the Presence of the Sun: A Gathering of Shields* (Momaday) **25**:220-22
"In the Public Garden" (Moore) **4**:259
"In the Rain" (H. D.) **5**:304
"In the Restaurant" (Blok) **21**:3
"In the Restaurant" (Hardy) **8**:124
"In the Ruins of New York City" (Merton) **10**:344, 349
"In the Same Boat" (Kipling) **3**:183
"In the Sconset Bus" (Williams) **7**:409
"In the Secret Room" (Wakoski) **15**:348
"In the Shelter" (Day Lewis) **11**:151
"In the Square" (Aleixandre)
  See "In The Plaza"
"In the Stopping Train" (Davie) **29**:115, 124, 126, 129
"In the Survivor's Home" (Gozzano)
  See "In casa del sopravissuto"
"In the Tank" (Gunn) **26**:203
"In the Tents of Akbar" (Dunbar) **5**:138
"In the Tradition" (Baraka) **4**:40
"In the Underworld" (Rukeyser) **12**:220
"In the Waiting Room" (Bishop) **3**:59, 69-70
"In the Waxworks" (Shapiro) **25**:273
"In the White Giant's Thigh" (Thomas) **2**:395, 404
"In the Wilderness" (Graves) **6**:128-29
"In the winter in Paris" (Guillen) **23**:103
"In the Wood" (Pasternak) **6**:252-53, 259
"In This Age of Hard Trying, Nonchalance Is Good and ..." (Moore) **4**:229, 270
"In those days you were like a moter to me" (Tsvetaeva)
  See "V ony dni, ty mne byla kak mat'"
"in ths forest" (Bissett) **14**:27
"In Time of Mourning" (Swinburne) **24**:319
"In Time of Plague" (Gunn) **26**:231
"In Time of 'The Breaking of Nations'" (Hardy) **8**:115, 121
"In Time of War" (Auden) **1**:18
"In vain with eye a with a nail" (Tsvetaeva)
  See "Naprasno glazom kak gvozdem"
"In Valleys Green and Still" (Housman) **2**:180
"In Warm Rooms Before a Blue Light" (Kumin) **15**:211
"In Warsaw" (Milosz) **8**:192
"In Weather" (Hass) **16**:196, 200, 202-03
*In What Hour* (Rexroth) **20**:177, 183, 192-93, 198, 214-15, 217
"In what torne ship" (Donne)
  See "A Hymne to Christ, at the authors last going into Germany"

"In Which I Write My Feelings to be Sent to My Cousin Li Zhao of Binzhou" (Li Po) **29**:179, 183
"In Yüeh Viewing the Past" (Li Po) **29**:145
"Inauguration Day: January 1953" (Lowell) **3**:214, 218, 222
"Incantation" (Milosz) **8**:202
"Incantation" (Pinsky) **27**:166
"Incantation at Assisi" (Viereck) **27**:267
"Incantesimo" (Montale) **13**:110
"Incarnation" (Rexroth) **20**:206, 216
"Incense of the Lucky Virgin" (Hayden) **6**:195
"Incespicare" (Montale) **13**:134
"Incident" (Cullen) **20**:61
"Incident on a Journey" (Gunn) **26**:218
*Incidental Numbers* (Wylie) **23**:311, 321, 325-26, 331
"Inclusions" (Browning) **6**:5-6, 15
"Incompatibilities" (Hughes) **7**:113
"Incontro" (Montale) **13**:165
"Incontro" (Pavese) **13**:217
"The Incorrigible Dirigible" (Carruth) **10**:88
"Independence Day" (Bukowski) **18**:15
"The Independent Man" (Brooks) **7**:53
"An Indian at the Burial-Ground of His Father" (Bryant) **20**:36
"Indian Bread" (Kinnell) **26**:238
"The Indian Girl's Lament" (Bryant) **20**:10, 17
*Indian Journals, March 1962-May 1963* (Ginsberg) **4**:53, 56, 60
"Indian Serenade" (Montale)
  See "Serenata indiana"
"Indian Summer" (Parker) **28**:347
"Indian Summer" (Pavese)
  See "Estate di San Martino"
"The Indian to His Love" (Yeats) **20**:343
"Indiana" (Crane) **3**:88, 106-07
"THE INDIANS WERE WELCOMED AS BRIDGEBUILDERS" (Bissett) **14**:33
*L'Indicateur des chemins de coeur* (Tzara) **27**:229, 231, 234
"Indictment of Senior Officers" (Olds) **22**:307
"Indifference" (Arnold)
  See "Euphrosyne"
"The Indifferent" (Donne) **1**:125
"The Indigo Glass in the Grass" (Stevens) **6**:324
"Indisciplina" (Pavese) **13**:214, 226
"Indispensability of Eyes" (Olds) **22**:307
"The Individual Man" (Duncan) **2**:118
"The Indivisible Incompatibles" (Swenson) **14**:284
"Indolence" (Bridges) **28**:48, 83
"The Indolent Monk" (Baudelaire)
  See "Le mauvais moine"
"Indulgence" (Li Po) **29**:177
"The Indweller" (Tagore)
  See "Antaryami"
"Infant" (Smith) **12**:310, 326
"Infant Joy" (Blake) **12**:7, 9, 33-4
"Infant Sorrow" (Blake) **12**:7, 31, 34
"Infanta Marina" (Stevens) **6**:311
"An Inference of Mexico" (Hayden) **6**:194, 198
*Inferno* (Dante) **21**:53, 56, 59-67, 69-72, 75-7, 81-5, 89, 95-6, 98-9, 101, 103-08
"L'infini dans les cieux" (Lamartine) **16**:266, 280, 284-85
"Inflation Blues" (Walker) **20**:294
"The Influence Coming into Play: The Seven of Pentacles" (Piercy) **29**:325
"The Influence Passing: The Knight of Swords" (Piercy) **29**:324
"El ingenuo" (Borges) **22**:97, 99
"Ingoldsby Legends" (Browning) **2**:36
"Ingrateful Beauty Threatened" (Carew) **29**:3, 9, 18, 32, 34, 71
*The Inhabitant and His Hope* (Neruda)
  See *El habitante y su esperanza*
"Inheritor" (Wright)
  See "Eroded Hills"
"Inhuman World" (Aleixandre) **15**:20
"The Inhumanist" (Jeffers) **17**:136

"The Iniquity of the Fathers upon the Children" (Rossetti) **7**:289-90
"Initial, Daemonic, and Celestial Love" (Emerson) **18**:93
"Initiations" (Okigbo) **7**:224-25, 232, 237
"Injudicious Gardening" (Moore) **4**:266
"The Injury" (Williams) **7**:360
"The Inlet" (Gluck) **16**:125
*The Inn Album* (Browning) **2**:68, 96
"The Inner Kingdom" (Dario)
  See "El reino interior"
*The Inner Room* (Merrill) **28**:281
"Innocence" (Gunn) **26**:197, 201
"Innocence" (Levine) **22**:228
"Innocent Landscape" (Wylie) **23**:305-306, 333-34
"The Innocents" (Wylie) **23**:302-303, 310
"Inochi no fune" (Ishikawa) **10**:213, 215
"ins lesebuch für die oberstufe" (Enzensberger) **28**:135
"Inscription for the Entrance into a Wood" (Bryant) **20**:4, 17, 19, 35, 40, 47
"Insensibility" (Owen) **19**:327, 337, 340, 347-48, 355, 357, 369-70
"Inside a mountain idles an idol" (Mandelstam)
  See "Vnutri gory bezdeistvuet kumir"
"The Inside Dance" (Piercy) **29**:311
*Inside the Blood Factory* (Wakoski) **15**:324-25, 341, 348, 350-51, 362-63, 365
"The Insidious Dr. Fu Man Chu" (Baraka) **4**:15
"L'insinuant" (Valery) **9**:395
*Insomnia* (Tsvetaeva) **14**:299, 301
"Insomnia. Homer. Tautly Swelling Sails. . ." (Mandelstam) **14**:141
"Insomniac" (Plath) **1**:399
"Insomnio" (Borges) **22**:92
"Inspection" (Owen) **19**:335, 354, 356
"Inspiration" (Lowell) **3**:245
"Installation of the Duke of Grafton as Chancellor of Cambridge" (Gray) **2**:143
"The Instant" (Levertov) **11**:166, 168
"Instead of Camargue" (Swenson) **14**:249
"Instinct" (Pavese)
  See "L'istinto"
"The Instruction Manual" (Ashbery) **26**:111, 129, 159, 164
"Instructions to the Double" (Gallagher) **9**:58, 60
*Instructions to the Double* (Gallagher) **9**:35-7, 43, 53-4, 58
"Instructions to the Orphic Adept" (Graves) **6**:133
"Insufficiency" (Browning) **6**:15
"Insularum Ocelle" (Swinburne) **24**:326
"The Insulted and Injured" (Viereck) **27**:279
*Intact Wind* (Paz)
  See *Viento entero*
*Intellectual Things* (Kunitz) **19**:147-48, 153, 155, 159-61, 163, 185
"The Intellectuals" (Shapiro) **25**:270, 312
*Inter mezzo* (Heine) **25**:131
"Intercettazione telefonica" (Montale) **13**:133
"Interface" (Wright) **14**:373
"Interference" (Ammons) **16**:6
"Intérieur" (Valery) **9**:365, 396
"Interim" (Levertov) **11**:176, 195-96
"Interim" (Millay) **6**:205-07, 214
"The Interlude" (Shapiro) **25**:303, 326
"Intermezzo" (Montale) **13**:106
"Intermezzo No 1" (Heine) **25**:141
"Intermission 3" (Brooks) **7**:58, 62, 91, 104
"Interplay" (Wright) **14**:348
"Interrogaciones" (Dario) **15**:100
"The Interrogation of the Man of Many Hearts" (Sexton) **2**:352
"Interruption" (Graves) **6**:137, 143-44
"Interview" (Ekeloef) **23**:86-7
"Interview" (Parker) **28**:361
"Interview with a Tourist" (Atwood) **8**:14
"Intimation of Immortality" (Smith) **12**:313
"Intimations of Immorality" (Sappho) **5**:418

"Intimations of Immortality" (Thomas) **2**:392
"Intimations of Immortality" (Wordsworth)
    See "Ode: Intimations of Immortality from
        Recollections of Early Childhood"
*Intimité marine* (Cesaire) **25**:22
"Into My Heart and Air That Kills" (Housman)
    **2**:192
"Into My Own" (Frost) **1**:213
"Into the Golden Vessel of Great Song"
    (Millay) **6**:211
"Into the Shandy Westerness" (Rexroth) **20**:196
"Into the Tree" (Milosz) **8**:198
"Into the Twilight" (Yeats) **20**:346
"Introduction" (Blake) **12**:7, 32, 34-5, 43-7
"The Introduction" (Finch) **21**:155-57, 159,
    161, 181
"Intruding" (Piercy) **29**:311
"The Intrusion" (Graves) **6**:156
"Les Invalides" (Kinnell) **26**:260
"Invasions" (Kunitz) **19**:148
"Invective Against Swans" (Stevens) **6**:294
*Invectives* (Verlaine) **2**:419
"Invernal" (Dario) **15**:117
"Invictus" (Parker) **28**:355
"De invierno" (Dario) **15**:107-08, 110
"INVISIBLE" (Villa) **22**:356
"invisible presence" (Ekeloef)
    See "osynlig närvaro"
*Invisible Reality* (Jimenez)
    See *La realidad invisible*
"The Invitation" (Clare) **23**:23
"L'invitation au voyage" (Baudelaire) **1**:69
"The Invitation to Daphnis" (Finch) **21**:139,
    153-54, 161
"Invitation to Miss Marianne Moore" (Bishop)
    **3**:44
"Invitation to the Country" (Bridges) **28**:66, 69
"Invite to Eternity" (Clare) **23**:22-4, 26
"L'invocation" (Lamartine) **16**:277, 279, 290
"Invocation" (Lamartine)
    See "L'invocation"
"Invocation" (Levertov) **11**:177
"Invocation" (Sitwell) **3**:312
"An Invocation to Sleep" (Finch) **21**:143, 146,
    179-80
"Io poeta delle Ceneri" (Pasolini) **17**:292
"Iola, Kansas" (Clampitt) **19**:95-6
"Ione" (Dunbar)
"Iork" (Brodsky)
    See "York: In Memoriam W. H. Auden"
"The Ireland of the Bombers" (Davie)
    See "1969, Ireland of the Bombers"
"Iride" (Montale) **13**:109, 111, 121-22, 130-31,
    152, 166
"Iris" (Montale)
    See "Iride"
"Irises" (Lee) **24**:240
"An Irish Airman Foresees His Death" (Yeats)
    **20**:304
"The Irish Cliffs of Moher" (Stevens) **6**:304
"Iron" (Zagajewski) **27**:381, 387
"the Iron Characters" (Nemerov) **24**:262, 279
"Iron Hans" (Sexton) **2**:365-68
"Iron Landscapes" (Gunn) **26**:197-198, 206,
    214
"Iron Train" (Zagajewski) **27**:402
"L'irrémédiable" (Baudelaire) **1**:55
"L'Irréparable" (Baudelaire) **1**:68
*is 5* (Cummings) **5**:77, 92, 95, 104
"Is Her Name" (Ashbery) **26**:
"Is it possible?" (Wyatt) **27**:353
"Is It True?" (Sexton) **2**:368, 374
"Is It Wise" (Smith) **12**:343
"Is My Team Ploughing" (Housman) **2**:180,
    193, 196
*I's* (Pronounced EyesZukofsky) **11**:357
"Is There for Honest Poverty" (Burns) **6**:58, 83
"Is There No Way Out?" (Paz)
    See "¿No hay salida?"
"Isaac and Archibald" (Robinson) **1**:467, 486-
    87, 496
"Isabel" (Tennyson) **6**:387

"Isabella" (Keats) **1**:279, 282, 288-89, 296
"Isabella; or, The Pot of Basil" (Keats)
    See "Isabella"
"Isaiah" (Walker) **20**:278
"Isaiah LXII: 1-8" (Wheatley) **3**:357
"Isba Song" (McGuckian) **27**:103
"Ischia" (Lamartine) **16**:287, 291
"Ishtar" (Wright) **14**:363
*Isla ignorada* (Fuertes) **27**:10, 19, 21
"Isla ignorado" (Fuertes) **27**:43
"The Island" (Forche) **10**:138, 152, 161, 166
"Island" (Hughes) **1**:244, 248
"An Island" (Robinson) **1**:465, 467
*The Island* (Allard) **24**:116
*The Island* (Byron) **16**:86, 88, 90, 109
"The Island Hawk" (Noyes) **27**:122
"Island in the Works" (Merrill) **28**:268, 270-71
"Island of Night" (Kinnell) **26**:257
"The Island of Statues" (Yeats) **20**:343, 346,
    353
"The Islanders" (Kipling) **3**:179, 192
"The Islands" (H. D.) **5**:268
"The Islands" (Hayden) **6**:191, 193, 200
"Islands and Towers" (Zagajewski) **27**:389
"Ismaïl Bey" (Lermontov) **18**:278, 300
"Isolation: To Marguerite" (Arnold) **5**:13, 18
"Isolationist" (Page) **12**:170
"L'isolement" (Lamartine) **16**:265, 274-77, 290,
    298-301
"Ispoved" (Lermontov) **18**:300
"Israel" (Shapiro) **25**:283, 285, 297-98, 307,
    320, 325
"Israfel" (Poe) **1**:438, 447-48
"The Issues" (Olds) **22**:313
*Isthm. VII* (Pindar)
    See *Isthmian 7*
*Isthmian 3* (Pindar) **19**:426
*Isthmian 4* (Pindar) **19**:426
*Isthmian 6* (Pindar) **19**:398, 414, 421-22
*Isthmian 7* (Pindar) **19**:425
*Isthmian 8* (Pindar) **19**:398, 424
"L'istinto" (Pavese) **13**:205, 213
"Isto" (Pessoa) **20**:172
"It breaks" (Piercy) **29**:314
*It Catches My Heart in Its Hands: New and
    Selected Poems, 1955-1963* (Bukowski)
    **18**:5, 21
"It Is a Living Coral" (Williams) **7**:369
"It Is a Spring Afternoon" (Sexton) **2**:352
"It Is Everywhere" (Toomer) **7**:337, 340
"It Is My Thoughts That Color My Soul"
    (Wylie) **23**:322
"It Is No Longer Possible" (Aleixandre) **15**:20
"It is over" (Guillen)
    See "It is over"
"It Is So" (Neruda)
    See "Es así"
"It Is the First Mild Day of March"
    (Wordsworth)
    See "Lines on the First Mild Day of
        March"
"It Is Well" (Brooke) **24**:71-2
"It may be good" (Wyatt) **27**:316, 329, 341
"It Must Be Sophisticated" (Ashbery) **26**:161
"It Must Be the Milk" (Nash) **21**:278-79
"It Must Give Pleasure" (Stevens) **6**:329
"It Nods and Curtseys and Recovers"
    (Housman) **2**:192-93
"It Was a Face Which Darkness Could Kill"
    (Ferlinghetti) **1**:183
"It Was a' for Our Rightfu' King" (Burns) **6**:99
"It Was a Funky Deal" (Knight) **14**:46
"It Was a Gentle Breeze" (Dario)
    See "Era un aire suave"
"It Was a Soft Air" (Dario)
    See "Era un aire suave"
"It Was All Very Tidy" (Graves) **6**:142, 144
"It Was Black Black Took" (Stein) **18**:328
"It Was That Indian" (Ortiz) **17**:234
*It Was When* (Snyder) **21**:289
"It Was Winter" (Milosz) **8**:194
"It weeps away" (Piercy) **29**:315

"L'Italia" (Pasolini) **17**:270, 272
"Italia mia" (Petrarch) **8**:267, 270
"Italian Morning" (Bogan) **12**:106
"An Italian Visit" (Day Lewis) **11**:150
"Italy and France" (Browning) **2**:26
"Itching Heels" (Dunbar) **5**:146
"Ite, missa est" (Dario) **15**:113
"Ithaca" (Gluck) **16**:172
"Itinerary" (Kumin) **15**:220
"Itinerary of an Obession" (Kumin) **15**:220
"It's a New Day" (Sanchez) **9**:229
*It's a New Day: Poems for Young Brothas and
    Sistuhs* (Sanchez) **9**:207, 211-12, 215, 229,
    237
"It's both boring and sad" (Lermontov)
    **18**:268-69
"It's Dull and Dreary" (Lermontov) **18**:281
"Its Everlasting Possibility" (Pinsky) **27**:153
"Its Great Emptiness" (Pinsky) **27**:154
"Its Great Emptiness" (Pinsky) **27**:153
"It's Half an Hour Later Before" (Ammons)
    **16**:25
"Its Many Fragments" (Pinsky) **27**:153
"It's Nation Time" (Baraka) **4**:19, 26, 40
*It's Nation Time* (Baraka) **4**:19, 20, 26
"It's Not Going to Happen Again" (Brooke)
    **24**:84-5, 93
"It's over a (See Just" (Cummings) **5**:108
"It's Raining" (Apollinaire)
    See "Il pleut"
"It's Time, My Friend, It's Time" (Pushkin)
    See "Pora, Moi Drug, Pora"
"It's Unbecoming" (Pasternak) **6**:265
*I've Been a Woman* (Sanchez) **9**:207, 211-12,
    215-16, 218-22, 227, 229, 232, 238, 242
"I've Been Asleep" (Levine) **22**:218
"The Ivory Statuette" (Wylie) **23**:321
*Iz shesti knig* (Akhmatova) **2**:18
"Izalco roars" (Alegria) **26**:
"Izalco roars" (Alegria) **26**:
"Ja k vam pishu" (Lermontov) **18**:303
"Jabberwocky" (Carroll) **18**:36, 38-40, 48-50,
    52, 59-60
*Jack Kelso: A Dramatic Poem* (Masters) **1**:339
"Jack Straw's Castle" (Gunn) **26**:205
"Jack's Straw Castle" (Gunn) **26**:213, 228
*Jack's Straw Castle, and Other Poems* (Gunn)
    **26**:194-197, 204-206, 208, 210, 213, 219-
    220, 229
"Jackson, Mississippi" (Walker) **20**:283
"The Jacob's Ladder" (Gluck) **16**:171
*The Jacob's Ladder* (Levertov) **11**:168, 193,
    206
"Jactancia de quietud" (Borges) **22**:72
*Jadis et naguère* (Verlaine) **2**:416
"The Jaguar" (Hughes) **7**:118, 151, 163
"J'ai plus de souvenirs" (Baudelaire) **1**:67
"The Jain Bird Hospital in Delhi" (Meredith)
    **28**:215
"Jam Session" (Hughes) **1**:245
"The Jam Trap" (Tomlinson) **17**:314
"Jamāl al-mawt" (Gibran) **9**:78
"James Wetherell" (Robinson) **1**:467
"The Jam-Pot" (Kipling) **3**:190
"January" (Belloc) **24**:29
"January" (Hass) **16**:216
"January" (Nishiwaki)
    See "Ichigatsu"
"January" (Song) **21**:341
"January 1918" (Pasternak) **6**:261
"January 1919" (Pasternak) **6**:252
"January and May" (Chaucer)
    See "Miller's Tale"
"A January Night" (Hardy) **8**:110
"Jardín de invierno" (Neruda) **4**:287, 289-90
"El jardín triste se pierde" (Jimenez) **7**:199
*Jardines lejanos* (Jimenez) **7**:209
"Jarrama" (Ekeloef) **23**:76
"Jasmine Arbour" (Tagore)
    See "Chameli-vitan"
"Jaws" (Sandburg) **2**:330
"Jaybird" (Dunbar) **5**:144
"Jazzonia" (Hughes) **1**:246, 261

Title Index

"Je plaings le temps de ma jeunesse" (Villon) **13**:388-89
"Je plante en la faveur cest arbre de Cybelle" (Ronsard) **11**:277
"Je suis bruslé, Le Gast, d'une double chaleur" (Ronsard) **11**:250
"Je suis l'empire à la fin de la décadence" (Verlaine) **2**:416
"The Jealous Man" (Graves) **6**:142, 144
"Jealousy" (Brooke) **24**:56
"Jealousy--A Confessional" (Wakoski) **15**:356
"Jeanne d'Arc" (Gluck) **16**:140
"jed bi kor benkst trik" (Bissett) **14**:34
"Jefferson" (Shapiro) **25**:270
"Jehova" (Lamartine) **16**:280, 293
"Jehuda ben Halevy" (Heine) **25**:149
"Jemez" (Tomlinson) **17**:355
"The Jerboa" (Moore) **4**:233, 236, 243
"Jeremiah" (Walker) **20**:278
"Jeronimo's House" (Bishop) **3**:37, 47
"Jerusalem" (Blake) **12**:37
"Jerusalem" (Rich) **5**:383
*Jerusalem: The Emanation of the Giant Albion* (Blake) **12**:13, 20, 27, 29-32, 34-40, 43-4, 51-9, 61-75, 80
"Jessie Cameron" (Rossetti) **7**:280
"Jessie Mitchell's Mother" (Brooks) **7**:58, 62, 68, 96, 99-100, 102
"The Jester" (Hughes) **1**:235
"The Jester, A Ballad" (Bely)
    See "Shut, Bellada"
"Jester above It" (Bely)
    See "Shut Nad ney"
"Jesu" (Herbert) **4**:100
"Jesus and Isolt" (Pinsky) **27**:157, 175
"The Jesus Papers" (Sexton) **2**:360
"Jesus Walking" (Sexton) **2**:360-61, 373
"Le jet d'eau" (Baudelaire) **1**:61
*La jeune parque* (Valery) **9**:346-48, 351-58, 361, 363-67, 369-74, 379-85, 387, 390-96, 401-03
"La jeune prêtre" (Valery) **9**:391
"Jeunesse" (Rimbaud) **3**:261, 263
"Jew" (Shapiro) **25**:296-97
"The Jew at Christmas Eve" (Shapiro) **25**:283, 286, 300
"The Jeweled Stairs' Grievance" (Li Po) **29**:144
"Jewelled Bindings" (Wylie) **23**:320
*The Jewess of Toleldo* (Grillparzer)
    See *The Jewess of Toleldo*
"The Jewish Problem" (Shapiro) **25**:323
*The Jig of Forslin* (Aiken) **26**:5-7. 35
*The Jig of Forslin: A Symphony* (Aiken) **26**:16, 21-2
*Jill* (Larkin) **21**:225, 232
"Jill in the box" (Piercy) **29**:314
"Jim and Arabel's Sister" (Masters) **1**:328
"Jim at Sixteen" (McKay) **2**:223
"Jim Brown on the Screen" (Baraka) **4**:19
*Jim Crow's Last Stand* (Hughes) **1**:250, 253
*Th Jinx Ship nd Othr Trips* (Bissett) **14**:14
"Jitterbugs" (Baraka) **4**:12, 18
"Jivan devata" (Tagore) **8**:408
"Jivan madhyahna" (Tagore) **8**:407
"Jiving" (Dove) **6**:114, 117
"The Joachim Quartet" (Bridges) **28**:88
"Joal" (Senghor) **25**:241, 243-44, 246
"Joan and Darby" (Graves) **6**:156
"Joan of Arc" (Coleridge) **11**:80, 83, 97
"Joasaph and Fatumeh" (Ekeloef) **23**:67
"Job" (Blake) **12**:38
*Jocelyn: Épisode; Journal trouvé chez un curé de village* (Lamartine) **16**:257-61, 263-64, 269-70, 273-74, 286-87, 293, 297
"Jochanan Hakkadosh" (Browning) **2**:75
"Joel" (Walker) **20**:278-79
"Joggin' Erlong" (Dunbar) **5**:145
"A Johannes Brahms" (Borges) **22**:
"John and Anne" (Meredith) **28**:199, 205
"John Anderson, My Jo" (Burns) **6**:78, 98
"John Barleycorn" (Burns) **6**:52
"John Brown" (Hayden) **6**:192, 195

"John Brown" (Lindsay) **23**:264-65, 275, 279, 286
"John Brown" (Robinson) **1**:468
"John Burke" (Olson) **19**:305
"John Cowper Powys" (Masters) **1**:343
*John Deth: A Metaphysical Legend* (Aiken) **26**:12, 53
"John Donne in California" (Clampitt) **19**:92
"John Dryden" (Carruth) **10**:74
"John Gorham" (Robinson) **1**:462, 468, 478
"John I, 14" (Borges)
    See "Juan I, 14"
"John L. Sullivan, the Strong Boy of Boston" (Lindsay) **23**:265, 270, 273, 276
"John Maydew; or, The Allotment" (Tomlinson) **17**:326, 341
"John McLean" (1879-1923MacDiarmid) **9**:179
"Johnny Appleseed" (Masters) **1**:330
"Johnny Spain's White Heifer" (Carruth) **10**:74
"Joilet" (Sandburg) **2**:324
"Joke" (Bely)
    See "Shutka"
"A Joker" (Baudelaire)
    See "Un plaisant"
"La jolie rousse" (Apollinaire) **7**:3, 9, 49
"Jollie Gleeman" (Viereck) **27**:282
"The Jolly Beggars" (Burns) **6**:55-6, 58, 78, 90-6
"The Jolly Company" (Brooke) **24**:58
"Jonathan Edwards" (Lowell) **3**:212
"Jonathan Edwards in Western Massachusettes" (Lowell) **3**:216
"Jordan" (Herbert) **4**:102, 107, 113
"Jordan I" (Herbert) **4**:114, 129
"Jordan II" (Herbert) **4**:100, 114
*Jorge Luis Borges: Selected Poems 1923-1969* (Borges) **22**:71
"Joseph" (Forche) **10**:144, 156-57
"Joseph's Coat" (Herbert) **4**:130
"Joshua Tree" (Ammons) **16**:5
"Le joujou du pauvre" (Baudelaire) **1**:58
"Jour et nuit" (Cesaire) **25**:30
"Journal for my Daughter" (Kunitz) **19**:
"Journal Night Thoughts" (Ginsberg) **4**:52, 69
"Journal of an Airman" (Auden) **1**:5
"The Journalist Reader and Writer" (Lermontov) **18**:268-69, 281
*Journals: Early Fifties, Early Sixties* (Ginsberg) **4**:60, 69
*The Journals of Susanna Moodie* (Atwood) **8**:10-12, 15, 21, 29, 31, 33, 35-6, 40
"The Journey" (Kumin) **15**:198, 203
"Journey" (Millay) **6**:206
"Journey" (Olds) **22**:322
"The Journey Back" (Heaney) **18**:256
"Journey Home" (Page) **12**:178
"Journey North" (Tu Fu) **9**:332
"The Journey of Life" (Bryant) **20**:10
"Journey of the Magi" (Eliot) **5**:171, 177, 194, 197, 203, 205, 209
*Journey to a Known Place* (Carruth) **10**:70
*Journey to Love* (Williams) **7**:371, 403
"The Journey to the Interior" (Atwood) **8**:36
"Journey to the Interior" (Roethke) **15**:279, 310, 314
"Joy" (Enzensberger) **28**:142
"Joy" (Jeffers) **17**:106
"Joy" (Levertov) **11**:192
"The Joy and Agony of Improvisation" (Carruth) **10**:73
"Joy in Russia" (Bely) **11**:6
"Joy sweetest lifeborn joy" (Bridges) **28**:89
"Joyce Carol Oates Plays the Saturn Piano" (Wakoski) **15**:368
"Joyeuse Garde" (Swinburne) **24**:355
"The Joyful Black Demon of Sister Clara Flies through the Midnight Woods on Her Snowmobile" (Wakoski) **15**:332
"Joys Faces Friends" (Cummings) **5**:110
"Juan Figueroa, Casa del Yodo 'Maria Elena,' Antofagasta" (Neruda) **4**:294

"Juan Figueroa, Iodine Factory 'Maria Elena,' Antofagasta" (Neruda)
    See "Juan Figueroa, Casa del Yodo 'Maria Elena,' Antofagasta"
"Juan I, 14" (Borges) **22**:75, 96
"Juan's Song" (Bogan) **12**:90, 92, 100
"Jubal" (Eliot) **20**:101, 117, 119-20, 124, 134-37, 144
"Jubilate Agno" (Smart) **13**:339-40, 342-44, 346-48, 350-52, 355, 357-58, 360-69
*Jubilation* (Tomlinson) **17**:361
"Judas Iscariot" (Cullen) **20**:55-56, 67, 86
"Judas Kiss" (Kinnell) **26**:286-87
*Judgement Day* (Johnson) **24**:128-29, 164-65, 169
*Judges* (Vigny) **26**:368
"The Judgment" (Akhmatova) **2**:15
"Judgment" (Herbert) **4**:129
"The Judgment of Midas" (Smart) **13**:348
"Juice Joint: Northern City" (Hughes) **1**:243
"Julia" (Wordsworth) **4**:399
"Julian and Maddalo" (Shelley) **14**:173, 175, 182, 240
"Julian M. and A. G. Rochelle" (Bronte) **8**:52
"Julia's Petticoat" (Herrick) **9**:143
"Julio" (Lermontov)
    See "Julio"
"July" (Belloc) **24**:29
"July 8, 1656" (Bradstreet) **10**:60
"July, 1773" (Berry) **28**:38
"July, 1964" (Davie) **29**:124
"July 1968" (Levertov) **11**:194
"July, Against Hunger" (Kumin) **15**:207
"July in Vallombrosa" (Loy) **16**:313
"July in Washington" (Lowell) **3**:214
"July Midnight" (Lowell) **13**:64
"A July Night" (Ekeloef) **23**:58
"June" (Bryant) **20**:9, 14, 16, 18
"June: Dutch Harbor" (Meredith) **28**:170, 172, 185, 187
"Junge Leiden" (Heine) **25**:139
"The Jungle and the Sea" (Aleixandre) **15**:3, 14
*The Jungle Book* (Kipling) **3**:162, 185, 188-89
"Jungle Knot" (Ammons) **16**:4
"Das jüngste Gericht" (Rilke) **2**:277
*Junjo shokyoku shu* (Hagiwara Sakutaro) **18**:176, 182
"Junkman's Obbligato" (Ferlinghetti) **1**:165-66, 173
"Just Don't Never Give Up on Love" (Sanchez) **9**:234, 238, 244
"Just For Starters" (Ashbery) **26**:165
"Just Lost, When I Was Saved!" (Dickinson) **1**:97
"Just Wednesday" (Ashbery) **26**:
"Just Whistle a Bit" (Dunbar) **5**:137
"Justice" (Herbert) **4**:102
"Justice" (Hughes) **1**:252
"Justice II" (Herbert) **4**:131
"Justice Denied in Massachusetts" (Millay) **6**:223
"Justice Is Reason Enough" (Wakoski) **15**:336
"The Justice of the Peace" (Belloc) **24**:28
"Juvat ire jugis" (Arnold) **5**:36
"K Liciniju" (Pushkin) **10**:408
"K Likomedu, na Skiros" (Brodsky) **9**:5
"K moriu" (Pushkin) **10**:413
"K Muze" (Blok) **21**:6, 40
"K*** Ne dumaj chtob ja byl dostoin sozhalen'ja" (Lermontov) **18**:301, 304
"K pustoi zemle nevol'no pripadaia" (Mandelstam) **14**:155-56
*K Uranii* (Brodsky)
    See *To Urania: Selected Poems 1965-1985*
"Ka 'Ba" (Baraka) **4**:18
"Kabi kahini" (Tagore) **8**:405
"Kaddish" (Ginsberg) **4**:49-50, 53, 59, 61, 64-5, 72, 74, 81, 83-6, 91
*Kaddish, and Other Poems* (Ginsberg) **4**:47
"Kaeru no shi" (Hagiwara Sakutaro) **18**:168, 179
"Kaeru yo" (Hagiwara Sakutaro) **18**:180

*Kahini* (Tagore) **8**:410
*Kai oi* (Matsuo Basho) **3**:24
"Kai, Today" (Snyder) **21**:289
"Kak svetoteni muchenik Rembrandt"
    (Mandelstam) **14**:154
"Kalaloch" (Forche) **10**:133-35, 168
"Kalamzoo" (Lindsay) **23**:270
"Kaleidoscopes: Baroque" (Atwood) **8**:11
"Kali" (Clifton) **17**:23
"Kalimpong" (Tagore) **8**:426
"Kally" (Lermontov) **18**:300
"The Kallyope Yell" (Lindsay) **23**:266, 272,
    274-76, 280, 284, 289, 296
*Kalpana* (Tagore) **8**:410-11, 415
*Kamen'* (Mandelstam) **14**:106, 108, 112-15,
    117-18, 122, 135, 142
*Kamennyi gost'* (Pushkin) **10**:394
"Kanashi Tsukio" (Hagiwara Sakutaro) **18**:168
*Kanashiki gangu* (Ishikawa) **10**:195-97, 200-01,
    205, 210-11, 217
"Kansas" (Lindsay) **23**:273, 286
"Kansas City" (Harjo) **27**:55, 65, 72
"Kansas City to St. Louis" (Ginsberg) **4**:54, 57
"Kantian Lyrics I" (Tomlinson) **17**:346
"Kanun Blagoveshchen'ia" (Tsvetaeva) **14**:319-
    20, 322
"Das kapital" (Baraka) **4**:30, 38
"Das Kapitäl" (Rilke) **2**:275
"Kapuzinerberg" (SaltzbergBogan) **12**:100
*Kari o komal* (Tagore) **8**:406-07, 415
*Kashima kikō* (Matsuo Basho) **3**:27
*Katha* (Tagore) **8**:4'10
"Katharinal" (Heine) **25**:135
"Käthe Kollwitz" (Rukeyser) **12**:228-30
"Die Kathedrale" (Rilke) **2**:275
"Katherine's Dream" (Lowell) **3**:201
"Katun 8 Ahau" (Cardenal) **22**:129, 131
"Katun 11 Ahau" (Cardenal) **22**:128-29
*Kavkazsky plennik* (Pushkin) **10**:357-58, 364-
    65, 371, 386-88, 395, 415-21
"Kay Rutledge" (Masters) **1**:334
"Kayanerenhkowa" (Cardenal) **22**:128-29, 131
"Kazach'ja kolybel'naja pesnja" (Lermontov)
    **18**:304
"Keats House" (Stryk) **27**:203
"Keen" (Millay) **6**:225
"Keep a Pluggin' Away" (Dunbar) **5**:119
"keep on th grass" (Bissett) **14**:33
"Keeper of the Flocks" (Pessoa)
    See "O Guardador de Rebanhos"
"Keeping Informed in D.C." (Nemerov) **24**:262
"Keeping Their World Large" (Moore) **4**:236,
    268
"Keller Gegen Dom" (Williams) **7**:378
"Kellyburn Braes" (Burns) **6**:78
"Kent and Christendome" (Wyatt) **27**:331
"Kenyon Review, After the Sandstorm"
    (Bukowski) **18**:15
"Kept" (Bogan) **12**:105, 122
"The Key to Everything" (Swenson) **14**:247
"Key West: An Island Sheaf" (Crane) **3**:90
*Kezfogasok* (Illyes) **16**:231, 235
"Khadji Abrek" (Lermontov) **18**:285, 300
"Khalil al-kāfir" (Gibran) **9**:78
"Khansky polon" (Tsvetaeva) **14**:314-15
*Kheya* (Tagore) **8**:412-13, 415
"Khristos Voskres" (Pushkin) **10**:411-12
"The Kid" (Aiken) **26**:16, 41-2
"Kid" (Hayden) **6**:196
*The Kid* (Aiken) **26**:24, 30, 45
"The Kids Who Die" (Hughes) **1**:243
"Kierkegaard on Hegel" (Zagajewski) **27**:383,
    385
"A Kike is the Most Dangerous" (Cummings)
    **5**:82, 84
"Killala" (Davie) **29**:110
"Killauea" (Kinnell) **26**:286
"The Killer and the Dove" (Viereck) **27**:282
"KILLER WHALE" (Bissett) **14**:10-11, 17-18,
    34
"Killiecrankie" (Burns) **6**:78
"Killing the Spring" (Sexton) **2**:365

"Kilroy" (Viereck) **27**:263
"Kilroy's Carnival" (Schwartz) **8**:311
"Kimi Shinitamô koto nakare" (Yosano Akiko)
    **11**:320-26, 328-29
"Kin to Sorrow" (Millay) **6**:205
"The Kind Ghosts" (Owen) **19**:343
"The Kind Master and Dutiful Servant"
    (Hammon) **16**:177-78, 180-82, 190
"Kind of an Ode to Duty" (Nash) **21**:272
"A Kind of Ethics" (Gunn) **26**:206
*The Kind of Poetry I Want* (MacDiarmid) **9**:180,
    182, 184, 185-86
"Kind Sir: These Woods" (Sexton) **2**:358
*Kindai no Guwa* (Nishiwaki) **15**:231
"Kindliness" (Brooke) **24**:56, 77
"Kindness" (Plath) **1**:391, 393
*Kindness in the Wolfpasses* (Elytis)
    See *I kalosíni stis likoporiés*
"The King" (Kipling) **3**:161, 166
"King Arthur's Men Have Come Again"
    (Lindsay) **23**:283
"King Arthur's Tomb" (Swinburne) **24**:355
"King Ban" (Swinburne) **24**:355
*King Bolo* (Eliot) **5**:174
"King Edward the Third" (Blake) **12**:11, 61
"King Hamlet's Ghost" (Smith) **12**:311, 353
"A King in Funeral Procession" (Smith) **12**:315
*King Jasper* (Robinson) **1**:479, 483
"King Kong Meets Wallace Stevens"
    (Ondaatje) **28**:327, 333
*The King Maiden* (Tsvetaeva)
    See *Tsar-devitsa*
"King of Carrion" (Hughes) **7**:153
"The King of Harlem" (Garcia Lorca) **3**:139
"The King of the Ditchbacks" (Heaney) **18**:213
*The King of the Great Clock Tower* (Yeats)
    **20**:348
"King of the River" (Kunitz) **19**:157-59, 163,
    168, 172-73, 175, 180
"The King of Yellow Butterflies" (Lindsay)
    **23**:281
"King Solomon and the Queen of Sheba"
    (Lindsay) **23**:264, 280
"The Kingdom of Poetry" (Schwartz) **8**:289,
    308-09
"The Kingfisher" (Clampitt) **19**:82, 84
"King-fisher" (Montale) **13**:139
*The Kingfisher* (Clampitt) **19**:82-3, 85-91, 93
"The Kingfishers" (Olson) **19**:286, 308
"The Kings are Gone" (Bukowski) **18**:5
*The King's Daughter* (Bely) **11**:32
"King's Ransom" (Wylie) **23**:320
"The King's Task" (Kipling) **3**:183
"Kinship" (Heaney) **18**:195-96, 204, 210
"Kinship" (Wright) **14**:379
*Kiosk* (Enzensberger) **28**:166
"The Kirk's Alarm" (Burns) **6**:78
"The Kiss" (Sassoon) **12**:262
"The Kiss" (Sexton) **2**:353
"The Kiss" (Tagore)
    See "Chumban"
"The kiss at Bayreuth" (Gunn) **26**:212
"Kissee Lee" (Walker) **20**:286
"Kisses" (Cassian) **17**:12-13
*A Kist of Whistles: New Poems* (MacDiarmid)
    **9**:182
"Kita no umi" (Ishikawa) **10**:213
"Kitchenette Building" (Brooks) **7**:79
"The Kite" (Elytis) **21**:131
"Kite Flying" (McKay) **2**:223
"Kitty Hawk" (Frost) **1**:213
"KKK" (Guillen) **23**:121
"Klage" (Trakl) **20**:229, 236-37, 244, 250, 255-
    56, 258
"Klage II" (Trakl) **20**:250-51, 253
"Klarisu yunosha lyubil" (Lermontov) **18**:288
"Kleenex" (Shapiro) **25**:324
"Kleiner herbst dämon" (Enzensberger) **28**:140
"The Kneeling One" (Gallagher) **9**:57
"The Knight" (Hughes) **7**:126
"The Knight" (Rich) **5**:370

"The Knight Fallen on Evil Days" (Wylie)
    **23**:326
"Knight's" (Chaucer)
    See "Knight's Tale"
"Knight's Tale" (Chaucer) **19**:13, 56, 60, 70, 75
"The Knight's to the Mountain" (Scott) **13**:305
"Knocking Around" (Ashbery) **26**:133
"Knocking Donkey Fleas off a Poet from the
    Southside of Chi" (Madhubuti) **5**:323, 344
"The Knot" (Kumin) **15**:202
"The Knot" (Kunitz) **19**:176
"Knotted Letter" (Gallagher) **9**:63
"The Knowing Heart" (Roethke) **15**:293
"Knowing Rubén Darío" (Aleixandre) **15**:6
"Knowledge" (Bogan) **12**:101, 103, 120
*Knowledge, Acquaintance, Resort, Favour with
    Grace* (Skelton) **25**:344-45
"Knox" (Parker) **28**:362
"Knoxville, Tennessee" (Giovanni) **19**:139-41
"Knucks" (Sandburg) **2**:308, 324
"Kodachromes of the Island" (Hayden) **6**:183,
    193, 196, 198
"Kôgao no shi" (Yosano Akiko) **11**:324-26, 328
"Kogda b v pokornosti neznan'ja" (Lermontov)
    **18**:302
*Kogda razglyaetsya* (Pasternak) **6**:266-69,
    284-85
"Kogda v mrachneyshey iz stolits"
    (Akhmatova) **2**:12
"Koi wo koi suru hito" (Hagiwara Sakutaro)
    **18**:168, 180
"Koide shidō" (Hagiwara Sakutaro) **18**:183
*Koigoromo* (Yosano Akiko) **11**:306-07
"Kolbel'naya treskovogo mysa" (Brodsky)
    See "A Cape Cod Lullaby"
*Komboloi* (Merrill) **28**:256
"Koncert na vokzale" (Mandelstam) **14**:115,
    129
*Konec prekrasnoj èpox* (Brodsky)
    See *Konets prekrasnoy epokhi*
*Konets prekrasnoy epokhi* (Brodsky) **9**:7
"the konkreet pome is on its hed" (Bissett)
    **14**:32
"konkreet vizual" (Bissett) **14**:33-4
*Köp den blindes sång* (Ekeloef) **23**:76
*Kora in Hell: Improvisations* (Williams) **7**:344,
    349, 374-75, 377, 379-81, 383-84, 394, 400,
    405, 410
"A Korean Woman Seated by a Wall"
    (Meredith) **28**:177-78, 190
*Körper des Sommers* (Elytis) **21**:116
"Korsar" (Lermontov) **18**:299
"The Kraken" (Tennyson) **6**:360, 389, 391,
    406-10
"Kral Majales" (Ginsberg) **4**:82, 85
"Krasnopresnenskaya Station" (Momaday)
    **25**:202
"Krasnyi bychok" (Tsvetaeva) **14**:325
"Kronos; To Coachman Kronos" (Goethe)
    See "An Schwager Kronos"
"Krysolov" (Tsvetaeva) **14**:325-26
*Kshanikā* (Tagore) **8**:411
"Kubla Khan" (Coleridge) **11**:41-7, 51, 59, 73,
    75-9, 84-8, 90, 104, 107, 110
*Kubok metelej: Chetviortiia simfoniia* (Bely)
    **11**:3, 6-7, 14-17, 22
"Kubota" (Hongo) **23**:197
"küchenzettel" (Enzensberger) **28**:135, 140
"Kuda mne det'sia v etom Ianvare?"
    (Mandelstam) **14**:154
*Kumārasambhava* (Kalidasa) **22**:178, 180, 182,
    185, 188, 191-93, 196-206
"Kung Canto" (Pound) **4**:325
"Kure no kane" (Ishikawa) **10**:214
"Kuroi fūkin" (Hagiwara Sakutaro) **18**:178,
    182-83
"The Kursaal at Interlaken" (Rich) **5**:359
"Kutir-vasi" (Tagore) **8**:416
"Kutoa Umoja" (Baraka) **4**:26
"Kwa Mamu Zetu Waliotuzaa" (for our
    mothers who gave us birthSanchez) **9**:215-
    16, 221, 227, 229, 243

"Kyoko" (Ishikawa) **10**:213
*Kyomō no seigi* (Hagiwara Sakutaro) **18**:176, 182
*Le La* (Breton) **15**:54
"A la Ausencia" (Fuertes) **27**:44
"A la Colonne de la Place Vendôme" (Hugo) **17**:88-89
"A la muerte" (Fuertes) **27**:39, 45
"La: Pen" (Carew)
    See "An Elegie on the La: Pen: sent to my Mistresse out of France"
"A la Petra Camara" (Gautier) **18**:125
"L.A. to Wichita" (Ginsberg) **4**:54
*Laberinto* (Jimenez) **7**:200-01, 211
"Labor and Management" (Baraka) **4**:13
"The Laboratory" (Browning) **2**:60
"Laboratory Poem" (Merrill) **28**:241, 243
"The Laboring Skeleton" (Baudelaire)
    See "Le squelette laboureur"
*Labyrinth* (Jimenez)
    See *Laberinto*
"The Labyrinth of Life" (Walker) **20**:294
*Labyrinths, with Path of Thunder* (Okigbo) **7**:231, 233-35, 241-43, 248-49, 251-52, 254-56
"Le lac" (Lamartine) **16**:265, 268, 271, 276-77, 283, 290, 298, 301-02
"Lachin Y Gair" (Byron) **16**:86
"Lachrymae Christi" (Crane) **3**:82, 96-7, 102
"Lack of Discipline" (Pavese)
    See "Indisciplina"
"Lack of Faith" (Pushkin)
    See "Bezverie"
"Lackawanna" (Kinnell) **26**:294
"Laconic" (Elytis) **21**:116
"Lacrime" (Pasolini) **17**:265
*Ladera este* (Paz) **1**:354, 346, 361-63, 374, 376
"The Ladies" (Kipling) **3**:164, 166, 174
*Ladies and Gentlemen* (Belloc) **24**:27
"The Lads in Their Hundreds" (Housman) **2**:192
"The Lads of the Village" (Smith) **12**:330, 333
"Lady" (Carruth) **10**:74
"Lady Acheson Weary of the Dean" (Swift) **9**:295-96
"Lady Bank Dick" (Wakoski) **15**:363
"Lady Geraldine's Courtship" (Browning) **6**:10, 17-18, 26, 38-9, 42
"Lady Hsi" (Wang Wei) **18**:388-89
"The Lady in the Shingle" (Gluck) **16**:139
"Lady Lazarus" (Plath) **1**:382, 386, 391, 395-97, 400-01, 406-07, 410, 413-14
"Lady of Cowrie Palace" (Li Ho) **13**:51-4
*Lady of Miracles* (Cassian) **17**:13
"The Lady of Shalott" (Swinburne) **24**:357
"The Lady of Shalott" (Tennyson) **6**:350, 358-59, 378, 380, 395, 409-10
"The Lady of the Highest Prime" (Li Po) **29**:164
*The Lady of the Lake* (Scott) **13**:257-58, 261, 267-68, 270-71, 273, 276-79, 281, 283, 285, 289, 291, 293, 304, 310-11, 319-20
"The Lady of the Well-Spring" (Smith) **12**:304, 306, 329, 341
"A Lady Thinks She Is Thirty" (Nash) **21**:274
"The Lady Who Drove Me to the Airport" (Wakoski) **15**:369
"Lady's Boogie" (Hughes) **1**:266
"The Lady's Dressing Room" (Swift) **9**:257, 262, 268, 270, 273, 279, 281, 286-89, 291-92, 295, 298-99, 302-03
"Laeti et Errabundi" (Verlaine) **2**:417
"A l'Afrique" (Cesaire) **25**:5, 30, 32
"The Lag" (Rich) **5**:363
"Il lago di Annecy" (Montale) **13**:138
"Lai de Lanval" (Marie de France) **22**:
"Lai des Deuz Amanz" (Marie de France)
    See "Les Dous Amanz"
"Lair" (Pinsky) **27**:153
"Lais" (H. D.) **5**:268
*Lais* (Marie de France) **22**:246, 254-55, 260-62, 264-65, 268-75, 278, 281, 283-84, 287-88, 300-303
*Les Lais* (Villon) **13**:374-75, 377, 387, 396-99, 402, 404-05, 408-10, 412-13
"The Lake" (Lamartine)
    See "Le lac"
"The Lake" (Wright) **14**:348, 379
"Lake Boats" (Masters) **1**:330, 333
*Lake Effect Country* (Ammons) **16**:63
"The Lake Isle of Innisfree" (Yeats) **20**:310
"The Lake of Gaube" (Swinburne) **24**:312-20, 322, 341, 348
"A Lake Scene" (Swenson) **14**:262
"Lake Yi" (Wang Wei) **18**:379
"Lamarck" (Mandelstam) **14**:129
"The Lamb" (Blake) **12**:7, 9, 32, 62
"The Lambs of Grasmere" (Rossetti) **7**:266
"The Lame Boy and the Fairy" (Lindsay) **23**:281
"The Lament" (Burns) **6**:53
"Lament" (Gunn) **26**:
"Lament" (Hardy) **8**:135
"Lament" (Millay) **6**:211
"Lament" (Plath) **1**:410
"Lament" (Sexton) **2**:350
"Lament" (Trakl)
    See "Klage"
"Lament for Damon" (Milton) **19**:212
"Lament For Glasgerion" (Wylie) **23**:310
*Lament for Ignacio Sánchez Mejías* (Garcia Lorca)
    See *Llanto por Ignacio Sánchez Mejías*
"Lament for Pasiphaé" (Graves) **6**:144
*Lament for the Death of a Bullfighter* (Garcia Lorca)
    See *Llanto por Ignacio Sánchez Mejías*
"Lament for the Makers" (Pinsky) **27**:164
"Lament for the Poles of Buffalo" (Hass) **16**:195, 197
"Lament for Weldon Kees" (Stryk) **27**:204
"Lament for Yin Yao" (Wang Wei) **18**:379
"Lament of Mary Queen of Scots" (Burns) **6**:78
*The Lament of Tasso* (Byron) **16**:76
"Lament of the Belle Heaulmiere" (Villon) **13**:389-90
"Lament of the Drums" (Okigbo) **7**:224, 229-30, 244, 247, 254
"Lament of the Lavender Mist" (Okigbo) **7**:229, 248
"The Lament of the Masks: For W. B. Yeats: 1865-1939" (Okigbo) **7**:230, 245
"Lament of the Silent Sisters" (Okigbo)
    See "Silences: Lament of the Silent Sisters"
"Lamentationen" (Heine) **25**:131
"Lamentations" (Gluck) **16**:151, 154
"Lamentations" (Sassoon) **12**:267, 286
*Lamentations* (Gluck) **16**:129
"The Lamentations of Jeremy, for the most part according to Tremelius" (Donne) **1**:139
*Lamia, Isabella, The Eve of St. Agnes, and Other Poems* (Keats) **1**:276, 279, 281, 296, 307-09, 311
"Lamium" (Gluck) **16**:132, 171
"La lampe du temple" (Lamartine) **16**:292
"Lancelot" (Swinburne) **24**:355
*Lancelot* (Robinson) **1**:465, 468-70, 489, 491
"Lancer" (Housman) **2**:162
"Land" (Heaney) **18**:201
"The Land" (Kipling) **3**:171
"The Land Betrayed" (Neruda)
    See "La arena traicionada"
"The Land of Dreams" (Blake) **12**:35
*Land of Unlikeness* (Lowell) **3**:199, 202, 213, 216-17, 232
"The Land Where All Is Gained" (Tagore)
    See "Sab-peyechhir desh"
"Landcrab II" (Atwood) **8**:43
*Landesprcahe* (Enzensberger) **28**:133-35, 141, 143, 165
"The Landing" (Tomlinson) **17**:353
"Landing on the Moon" (Swenson) **14**:257
"Landlady, Count the Lawin" (Burns) **6**:81
*Landor's Poetry* (Pinsky) **27**:153
"The Landscape" (Masters) **1**:333, 344
"Landscape" (Merton) **10**:349
"Landscape" (Parker) **28**:362
"Landscape after a Battle" (Neruda)
    See "Paisaje después de una batalla"
"Landscape I" (Pavese)
    See "Paesaggio I"
"Landscape in Spring" (Soto) **28**:382
"Landscape of the Heart" (Jimenez)
    See "Paisaje del corazon"
"Landscape of the Star" (Rich) **5**:362
"Landscape of the Urinating Multitudes" (Battery Place NocturneGarcia Lorca)
    See "Paisaje de la multitud que orina"
"Landscape of the Vomiting Multitudes" (Coney Island DuskGarcia Lorca)
    See "Paisaje de la multitud que vomita"
"Landscape VI" (Pavese)
    See "Paesaggio VI"
"Landscape VII" (Pavese)
    See "Paesaggio VII"
*Landscape West of Eden* (Aiken) **26**:24, 29-30
"Landscape with Figures" (Ammons) **16**:6
"Landscape with Serifs" (Page) **12**:183
"Landscapes" (Eliot) **5**:166, 183
"Landscapes" (Wright) **14**:339, 342-43
*Landscapes of Living and Dying* (Ferlinghetti) **1**:180-81, 187
"The Lane of the Sky-Blue Waters" (Meredith) **28**:196
"The Lang Coortin" (Carroll) **18**:46
"Language" (Ortiz) **17**:231
*Language Lattice* (Celan)
    See *Sprachgitter*
"The Language of the Brag" (Olds) **22**:328
*language of the land* (Enzensberger)
    See *Landesprcahe*
"Language-Mesh" (Celan)
    See "Sprachgitter"
"L'anguilla" (Montale) **13**:111
"The Lantern Out of Doors" (Hopkins) **15**:145, 156
"Lanval" (Marie de France) **22**:241-45, 250-51, 254-55, 258, 260, 267-69, 271-72, 275, 282, 294, 29 7, 300-303
"Lanval Graelent Sir Landevall" (Marie de France) **22**:
"Laocoön Dream Recorded in Diary Dated 1943" (Swenson) **14**:288
"Laodamia" (Wordsworth) **4**:394, 399, 406-07
*Laon and Cythna* (Shelley) **14**:162, 169-73, 177, 181, 186-87, 189, 191-93, 213, 216-17, 233-38
"Laostic" (Marie de France)
    See "Laüstic"
"Lapis Lazuli" (Yeats) **20**:314, 333
"Lapraik II" (Burns)
    See "Second Epistle to John Lapraik"
"Lapse" (Dunbar) **5**:126
*Lara* (Byron) **16**:92, 109
"La larga busca" (Borges) **22**:95
"A Large Bad Picture" (Bishop) **3**:37, 70-1
*Large Testament* (Villon)
    See *Le Testament*
"Larks" (Bridges) **28**:85
"Larme" (Rimbaud) **3**:271
"Lasalle" (Davie) **29**:96
"Last" (Kipling) **3**:160
"Last Acts" (Olds) **22**:318, 323, 326, 337
*Last and Lost Poems of Delmore Schwartz* (Schwartz) **8**:311, 319
"Last Canto of Childe Harold" (Lamartine)
    See "Le dernier chant de pèlerinage de Childe Harold"
"The Last Chantey" (Kipling) **3**:161
"The Last Day" (Olds) **22**:33-37
"The Last Duchess" (Browning) **2**:30
*The Last Epiphany* (Aleixandre)
    See *Nacimiento último*
*The Last Harvest* (Tagore)
    See *Chaitāli*
"The Last Hiding Places of Snow" (Kinnell) **26**:259, 271-72

"Last Hill in a Vista" (Bogan) **12**:104
"The Last Instructions to a Painter" (Marvell) **10**:275
"The Last Invocation" (Whitman) **3**:378
"Last Kiss" (Olds) **22**:321
"The Last Laugh" (Owen) **19**:366
"Last Letter" (Gluck) **16**:164-65
"Last Lines" (Bronte) **8**:59
"Last Load" (Hughes) **7**:166
"Last Looks at the Lilacs" (Stevens) **6**:292
*The Last Lunar Baedeker* (Loy) **16**:330, 333
"The Last Man" (Gunn) **26**:203
"The Last Meeting" (Sassoon) **12**:262
"The Last Mowing" (Frost) **1**:206
"The Last Mummer" (Heaney) **18**:201
*The Last Night of the Earth Poems* (Bukowski) **18**:16, 19
*Last Octave* (Tagore)
    See *Shesh saptak*
"The Last of Saturdays" (Elytis) **21**:135
"The Last of the Flock" (Wordsworth) **4**:373, 415, 418
"The Last Oracle" (Swinburne) **24**:320, 347
"Last Poems" (Tagore)
    See "Śesh lekhā"
*Last Poems* (Browning) **6**:23-4, 38, 40
*Last Poems* (Celan) **10**:120
*Last Poems* (Housman) **2**:161-67, 173-76, 180-81, 186, 191, 196, 199-201
*Last Poems* (Yeats) **20**:307, 311, 314, 332
"Last Poems: XX—The Night Is Freezing Fast" (Housman) **2**:196
*The Last Poems of Elinor Wylie* (Wylie) **23**:321
"The Last Quatrain of the Ballad of Emmett Till" (Brooks) **7**:62
"The Last Question" (Parker) **28**:362
"The Last Rhyme of True Thomas" (Kipling) **3**:181-82
"The Last Ride Together" (Browning) **2**:75
"The Last River" (Kinnell) **26**:255, 257, 262, 290, 293
"The Last Signal" (Hardy) **8**:131
*Last Song* (Harjo) **27**:59, 64
"The Last Song of Lucifer" (Lindsay) **23**:284
"Last Supper" (Wylie) **23**:303, 308, 310
"The Last Suttee" (Kipling) **3**:183
"The Last Tournament" (Tennyson) **6**:376
"The Last Turn of the Screw" (Smith) **12**:295
*Last Volume* (Swift) **9**:255
*The Last Voyage* (Noyes) **27**:133
"The Last Word" (Tagore)
    See "Shesh katha"
"Last Words" (Olds) **22**:324
"Last Words" (Plath) **1**:396, 407
"Last Words of the Dying Recruit" (McKay) **2**:226
"Lastness" (Kinnell) **26**:252, 274-75
"Late" (Bogan) **12**:122
"Late" (Olds) **22**:318
*Late Arrival on Earth* (Ekeloef) **23**:66, 85, 88-90
"Late August" (Atwood) **8**:28-9, 42
"Late Beethoven" (Zagajewski) **27**:384-85
"Late Echo" (Ashbery) **26**:140
"Late Feast" (Zagajewski) **27**:395
"Late Last Night" (Hughes) **1**:243
*Late Lyrics and Earlier with Many Other Verses* (Hardy) **8**:89, 123
"Late Movies With Skyler" (Ondaatje) **28**:338
"Late Poem to My Father" (Olds) **22**:324
*Late Settings* (Merrill) **28**:266-68, 281
"The Late Snow & Lumber Strike of the Summer of Fifty-four" (Snyder) **21**:322
"Late Spring" (Hass) **16**:216, 222
"Late Spring Evening" (Bridges) **28**:85
"Lately, at Night" (Kumin) **15**:200
"Later Life" (Rossetti) **7**:278
*Later Poems* (Bridges) **28**:65
*The Later Poems of John Clare 1837-1864* (Clare) **23**:46
"Latest Face" (Larkin) **21**:236
"Lauda" (Milosz) **8**:201

"Lauda" (Paz) **1**:361
"The Laugh" (Graves) **6**:156
"Laughing Corn" (Sandburg) **2**:316
"Laughing Gas" (Ginsberg) **4**:74, 81
*Laughing Lost in the Mountains: Poems of Wang Wei* (Wang Wei) **18**:391
"The Laughing Song" (Blake) **12**:4, 7, 23
"Laughters" (Hughes)
    See "My People"
"The Laureate" (Graves) **6**:142, 144
"Laus Veneris" (Swinburne) **24**:308, 360-61
*Laus Veneris, and Other Poems and Ballads* (Swinburne)
    See *Poems and Ballads*
"Laüstic" (Marie de France) **22**:237, 258, 260, 264-66, 269-72, 301
"Lava" (Kinnell) **26**:260
"Lava" (Zagajewski) **27**:387
"The Lavender Woman-A Market Song" (Reese) **29**:329
"Lavorare stanca" (Pavese) **13**:203, 213, 225-27
*Lavorare stanca* (Pavese) **13**:201-02, 204-05, 210-14, 216-19, 222, 224-26, 228
"Law" (Lowell) **3**:214
"The Law I Love Is Major Mover" (Duncan) **2**:124
"The Laws of God, the Laws of Man" (Housman) **2**:162, 179
"Lay le Freyne" (Marie de France)
    See "Le Fraisne"
"Lay of Guigemar" (Marie de France) **22**:239-45, 258, 263-66, 268-76, 278, 293-94, 301
*The Lay of the Last Minstrel* (Scott) **13**:246, 248-51, 256, 258, 266, 269, 271, 273, 274-76, 279-83, 285, 303, 311-12, 315, 317-18
"The Layers" (Kunitz) **19**:180-81
*Laying Down the Tower* (Piercy) **29**:323, 327
"Laying the Dust" (Levertov) **11**:165
*Lays* (Marie de France)
    See *Lais*
*Lays of Twilight* (Hugo) **17**:44
"Lazarillo and the Beggar" (Aleixandre) **15**:4, 6
"Lazarus" (Robinson) **1**:468
"Lead Soldiers" (Lowell) **13**:78
"The Leaden Echo and the Golden Echo" (Hopkins) **15**:130-31, 143-44, 161
"The Leaden-Eyed" (Lindsay) **23**:268, 276, 281, 296
"The Leader" (Belloc) **24**:11
"The Leaders" (Brooks) **7**:63, 90
"Leaflets" (Rich) **5**:396
*Leaflets: Poems, 1965-1968* (Rich) **5**:357, 365, 370-72, 383, 388-89, 396, 399
"A Lean and Hungry Look" (Nemerov) **24**:291
"Leaping Falls" (Kinnell) **26**:238
"Lear Is Gay" (Hayden) **6**:187
"The Lea-Rig" (Burns) **6**:82
"Learning By Doing" (Nemerov) **24**:270
"Learning the Trees" (Nemerov) **24**:285
"Learning to Read" (Harper) **21**:192, 198, 200, 213
"Learning to Write" (Lorde) **12**:136
"Leather Jacket" (Page) **12**:172
"Leather Leggings" (Sandburg) **2**:302
*Leaves of Grass* (Whitman) **3**:370, 378-79, 382, 384, 386-87, 389, 397-99, 401, 404-08, 410-14, 416-17
"Leave-taking Near Shoku" (Pound) **4**:331
"Leaving" (Song) **21**:333, 335, 342-43
"Leaving L'Atelier-Aix-en-Provence" (Rexroth) **20**:196
"Leaving the Atocha Station" (Ashbery) **26**:113
"LEBANON VOICES" (Bissett) **14**:32
*lebanon voices* (Bissett) **14**:2
*Lebediny stan* (Tsvetaeva) **14**:313-14
"lebenslanf" (Enzensberger) **28**:135
"Lebenslauf" (Holderlin) **4**:147
"Lecture" (Milosz) **8**:200
"Lecture I" (Milosz) **8**:202
"Lecture IV" (Milosz) **8**:203
"Lecture VI" (Milosz) **8**:199
"Lecture VII" (Milosz) **8**:202

"Lecture on Mystery" (Zagajewski) **27**:400
"A Lecture upon the Shadow" (Donne) **1**:135, 145, 147
"Leda and the Swan" (Montale) **13**:150
"Leda and the Swan" (Yeats) **20**:315, 319
*Lee: A Dramatic Poem* (Masters) **1**:339
"Leech Gatherer" (Wordsworth) **4**:390, 394
"Leffingwell" (Robinson) **1**:466
"Left Behind" (Lowell) **13**:97
"The Leg" (Shapiro) **25**:268, 288, 297, 300-301
"Legacies" (Browning) **6**:16
"Legacies" (Giovanni) **19**:111
"Legacy" (Harjo) **27**:71
"Legend" (Crane) **3**:101
"Legend" (Wright) **14**:338
*Legend* (Chaucer)
    See *Legend of Good Women*
*Legend of Good Women* (Chaucer) **19**:7, 10, 21, 23-4, 34, 60, 64, 74
*The Legend of Jubal, and Other Poems* (Eliot) **20**:116, 123, 125, 131-32
"A Legend of Porcelain" (Lowell) **13**:61, 65
*The Legend of the Centuries* (Hugo)
    See *La légende des siècles*
"Legende" (Celan) **10**:126
"Lègende" (Laforgue) **14**:74
*La légende des siècles* (Hugo) **17**:49, 54-57, 60-61, 65, 68, 78, 80, 83-86, 89, 91
*Legende of Good Women* (Chaucer)
    See *Legend of Good Women*
"Légende théologique" (Gautier) **18**:162
"Legender" (Ekeloef) **23**:69, 71
*Legends* (Lowell) **13**:60-3, 65, 74, 83, 93
"Legends and Dirges" (Ekeloef) **23**:69
"The Legion Club" (Swift) **9**:281
"The Legs" (Graves) **6**:151
"The Lemons" (Montale) **13**:149
"Lengas dai frus di sera" (Pasolini) **17**:256
"Lenore" (Poe) **1**:434, 438, 445
"Lenox Avenue: Midnight" (Hughes) **1**:265
"Lent" (Herbert) **4**:100
"The Lent Lily" (Housman) **2**:184, 192
"Leon" (Cardenal) **22**:110
"A Leone Traverso" (Montale) **13**:139
"Leonine Elegiacs" (Tennyson) **6**:385-86
"Lepanto" (Chesterton) **28**:94, 99-100, 108, 125, 128-30
"The Leper" (Swinburne) **24**:307, 337
"Lerici" (Gunn) **26**:218
"leroy" (Baraka) **4**:19, 23
*The Lesbians* (Baudelaire)
    See *Les fleurs du mal*
*Les Lesbiennes* (Baudelaire)
    See *Les fleurs du mal*
"Lesbos" (Plath) **1**:394
"The Less Deceived" (Larkin) **21**:222
*The Less Deceived* (Larkin) **21**:224, 226-27, 230, 233, 235, 251-52, 255, 256, 259
*Lesser Testament* (Villon)
    See *Les Lais*
"The Lesson" (Levertov) **11**:167
"The Lesson" (Lowell) **3**:211
"A Lesson in Geography" (Rexroth) **20**:215
"Lestnitsa" (Tsvetaeva)
    See "Poèma lestnitsy"
"Let America Be America Again" (Hughes) **1**:250, 253
"Let Koras and Balafong Accompany Me" (Senghor)
    See "Que m'accompagnent Kôras et Balafong"
"Let Me Begin Again" (Levine) **22**:219, 225
"Let Me Enjoy" (Hardy) **8**:98
"Let me go, Voronezh . . ." (Mandelstam)
    See "Pusti menia, Voronezh . . ."
"let me tell yu a story of how they met" (Bissett) **14**:17
"Let My People Go" (Johnson) **24**:128-29, 139, 144, 166, 169
"Let No Charitable Hope" (Wylie) **23**:314, 323-24, 333-34
"Let not Love go to" (Noyes) **27**:134

"Let the Light Enter! The Dying Words of Goethe" (Harper) **21**:210
"Let the Rail Splitter Awake" (Alegria) **26**:
"Let us gather at the river" (Piercy) **29**:303, 315
"Let Us Prepare" (Swenson) **14**:268
"Letanía de los montes de la vida" (Fuertes) **27**:39
"Letanía de nuestro Señor Don Quijote" (Dario) **15**:96
"Leter 20: not a pastoral letter" (Olson) **19**:274
"Le lethe" (Baudelaire)
   See "Léthé"
"Léthé" (Baudelaire) **1**:72
"Lethe" (H. D.) **5**:287, 304
"Let's Beat Down the Poor" (Baudelaire)
   See "Assommons les pauvres"
"Let's, from Some Loud Unworld's Most Rightful Wrong" (Cummings) **5**:109
"A Letter" (Berry) **28**:6
"A Letter" (Bogan) **12**:95, 127
"Letter" (Hass) **16**:196
"Letter" (Montale)
   See "Lettera"
"The Letter" (Owen) **19**:347, 363-65
"Letter 2" (Olson) **19**:277, 281-82
"Letter 3" (Olson) **19**:273, 280, 282, 284
*Letter 3* (Brutus) **24**:106, 115
"Letter 4" (Olson) **19**:283
"Letter 5" (Brutus) **24**:101, 106
"Letter 5" (Olson) **19**:266, 271, 282-83
"Letter 6" (Olson) **19**:280, 282-83
*Letter 6* (Brutus) **24**:115
*Letter 7* (Brutus) **24**:115
"Letter 8" (Olson)
"Letter 9" (Olson) **19**:267, 281, 283-84
*Letter 9* (Brutus) **24**:115
"Letter 10" (Brutus) **24**:115
"Letter 10" (Olson) **19**:267, 281, 283-84
"Letter 11" (Olson) **19**:296
*Letter 13* (Brutus) **24**:99, 106, 115
"Letter 14" (Brutus) **24**:100
"Letter 14" (Olson) **19**:273
"Letter 15" (Olson) **19**:277
"Letter 16" (Brutus) **24**:101
*Letter 17* (Brutus) **24**:106, 115
"Letter for Jan" (Lorde) **12**:152
"Letter for Melville" (Olson) **19**:297
"Letter from Costa Brava" (Tomlinson) **17**:315
"A Letter from Li Po" (Aiken) **26**:45, 56-7
*A Letter from Li Po, and Other Poems* (Aiken) **26**:24, 29-30
"Letter from Our Man in Blossomtime" (Gluck) **16**:124
"A Letter from Phillis Wheatley" (Hayden) **6**:189, 192, 195
"Letter from Prague, 1968-78" (Forche) **10**:144, 156, 168-69
"Letter from the North" (Bukowski) **18**:4
"A Letter Home" (Sassoon) **12**:262
"Letter I" (Olson) **19**:282, 284
"A Letter in a Bottle" (Brodsky) **9**:3, 4
"Letter, May 2, 1959" (Olson) **19**:306
"Letter Number Forty-One" (Olson) **19**:306
"Letter of Advice to a Young Poet" (Swift) **9**:272
"Letter to a Bourgeois Friend Whom Once I Loved" (and Maybe Still Do If Love Is Valid) (Giovanni) **19**:115
"A Letter to a Brother of the Pen in Tribulation" (Behn) **13**:7, 30
"Letter to a Friend" (Wright) **14**:
"Letter to a Friend" (Wright) **14**:336, 338
"Letter to a Wound" (Auden) **1**:22
"Letter to Ann Landers" (Ondaatje) **28**:328
"A Letter to Basil" (Brutus) **24**:106, 108
"A Letter to Dafnis April: 2nd 1685" (Finch) **21**:165
"A Letter to Dr. Martin Luther King" (Sanchez) **9**:244
"Letter to G.N. from Wrest" (Carew) **29**:7-8, 11, 41-43, 46-48

"A Letter to Her Husband, Absent upon Public Employment" (Bradstreet) **10**:8, 28, 30, 34, 40, 65
"Letter to Jean-Paul Baudot, at Christmas" (Stryk) **27**:182, 196, 200, 202, 204-5, 215, 218
*Letter to Lord Byron* (Auden) **1**:22, 34
*A Letter to Lucian and Other Poems* (Noyes) **27**:135
"A Letter to Lucian the Sceptic Dated from the Island of Cos in the year AD 165" (Noyes) **27**:136
"Letter to Maxine Sullivan" (Carruth) **10**:87
"Letter to Miguel Otero Silva, in Caracas, 1948" (Neruda)
   See "Carta a Miguel Otero Silva, en Caracas, 1948"
"Letter to My Father from 40,000 Feet" (Olds) **22**:324-25
"A Letter to My Friends" (Merton) **10**:346-47
"A Letter to Sara Hutchinson" (Coleridge) **11**:69-72, 91
"Letter to the Countesse of Huntingdon" (Donne) **1**:130
"Letter to the Front" (Rukeyser) **12**:228, 231-34
"A Letter to the Same Person" (Finch) **21**:160, 164
"Letter to V-" (Wylie) **23**:324
"A Letter to William Carlos Williams" (Rexroth) **20**:193
"Letter Written during a January Northeaster" (Sexton) **2**:351
"Letter Written on a Ferry Crossing Long Island Sound" (Sexton) **2**:351, 361
"Lettera" (Montale) **13**:161
"Letters" (Cassian) **17**:5
*Letters* (Duncan) **2**:106
*Letters* (Ovid)
   See *Heroides*
"Letters and Other Worlds" (Ondaatje) **28**:315-16, 327, 329, 331
"Letters for the Dead" (Levine) **22**:220, 223
"Letters from a Land of Sinners" (Rich) **5**:354
*Letters from a Traveller's Pannier* (Matsuo Basho)
   See *Oi no obumi*
*Letters from Iceland* (Auden) **1**:9, 13
"Letters from the Ming Dynasty" (Brodsky) **9**:29
*Letters of the Heroines* (Ovid)
   See *Heroides*
*Letters to Martha and Other Poems from a South African Prison* (Brutus) **24**:99-100, 102, 104-09, 112, 114-15, 118-20
*Letters to Martha II* (Brutus) **24**:100
"Lettre à une femme" (Hugo) **17**:100
"Lettre-Océan" (Apollinaire) **7**:18, 25-9, 32, 34-7
"Lettres de l'Hivernage" (Senghor) **25**:232-33, 235, 247-51
"lettrs" (for a passing comet) (Bissett) **14**:20
*Letzte Gedichte und Gedanken* (Heine) **25**:172
"Letzter Abend" (Rilke) **2**:267
"Levedad" (Jimenez) **7**:201
"The Level at Which Sky Began" (Soto) **28**:370, 378
"Le Lever du soleil" (Breton) **15**:48
"Leviathan" (Neruda) **4**:282
"Lews estoilles envoyées à Monsieur de Pibrac en Polonne" (Ronsard) **11**:236-37, 239
"lExpression" (Gunn) **26**:
"Li occi dolenti" (Dante) **21**:73
"The Liar" (Baraka) **4**:17
"The Liars" (Sandburg) **2**:304
"Libation" (Ammons) **16**:4
"Libation" (Levertov) **11**:197
*Liber Spectaculorum* (Martial) **10**:230
*liberating skies* (Bissett) **14**:7-8, 16
"Liberation" (Gluck) **16**:156
"Liberation Poem" (Sanchez) **9**:209
"The Liberators" (Neruda)
   See "Los libertadores"

*Libertad bajo palabra* (Paz) **1**:353
"Los libertadores" (Neruda) **4**:292
"La liberte, ou une nuit a Rome" (Lamartine) **16**:278, 291
"The Libertine" (Behn) **13**:4
"Liberty" (Pushkin)
   See "Vol'nost': Oda"
"Liberty. An Ode" (Pushkin)
   See "Vol'nost': Oda"
"Liberty and Peace" (Wheatley) **3**:337, 341, 363
*Liberty behind the Words* (Paz)
   See *Libertad bajo palabra*
"Liberty's Twilight" (Mandelstam)
   See "The Twilight of Freedom"
"Libido" (Brooke) **24**:53
"The Librarian" (Olson) **19**:280
"El libro" (Dario) **15**:99, 101-02
*Libro de las preguntas* (Neruda) **4**:287, 290
*Libro de poemas* (Garcia Lorca) **3**:117-18, 147-49
*Libros inéditos de poesía* (Jimenez) **7**:201
"Licentiousness" (Cassian) **17**:5
*Lichee Nuts* (Masters) **1**:338
*Lichtzwang* (Celan) **10**:96, 98, 121
"Liddy's Orange" (Olds) **22**:315
"Lidice" (Day Lewis) **11**:146
"" (Liebeslied.Celan) **10**:123-24
"Liebestod" (Parker) **28**:362
"Liebhaber in allen Gestalten" (Goethe) **5**:246, 251
"Lieder" (Pasolini) **17**:256
*Lieder* (Heine) **25**:155
"Liens" (Apollinaire) **7**:28, 49
*Lieutenant Schmidt* (Pasternak) **6**:265, 272
"Life" (Bryant) **20**:16
"Life" (Dunbar) **5**:121, 124-26, 130
"Life" (Herbert) **4**:100, 113
"Life and Death at Sunrise" (Hardy) **8**:124
"The Life and Genuine Character of Dr. Swift" (Swift) **9**:280, 295
"Life and Letters" (Rich) **5**:352
"Life at War" (Levertov) **11**:176, 194
"The Life Beyond" (Brooke) **24**:57
"Life Cycle of Common Man" (Nemerov) **24**:283
*Life in the Forest* (Levertov) **11**:205, 207-10
"Life is More True than Reason Will Decieve" (Cummings) **5**:108
"Life Is Motion" (Stevens) **6**:333
"The life of Borodin" (Bukowski) **18**:22
"Life of Life" (Shelley) **14**:181
"The Life of Lincoln West" (Brooks) **7**:85, 91-2
"The Life of My Friend" (Blok) **21**:6, 20
*Life Sentence* (Cassian) **17**:10-13
*Life Studies* (Lowell) **3**:205-09, 211-14, 216-19, 221, 223, 227, 230, 232-33, 242-43
*Life Studies: Secular Love* (Ondaatje) **28**:316
"The Life That Is" (Bryant) **20**:8
"Life's Noonday" (Tagore)
   See "Jivan madhyahna"
"Life's Rendezvous" (Cullen) **20**:77
"Life's Work" (Kumin) **15**:202
"A Lifetime" (Bryant) **20**:8, 12, 46
"A Lifetime Later" (Ferlinghetti) **1**:183
"Lift Every Voice and Sing" (Johnson) **24**:136, 130-31, 143-44, 146, 154, 159-60, 166, 170
"The Lifting" (Olds) **22**:318, 325, 334-36, 340
"Lifting Belly" (Stein) **18**:327, 341-42
"th lifting hands" (Bissett) **14**:34
"Lifting my forehead and lowering my eyes" (Tsvetaeva)
   See "Zakinuv golovu i opustiv glaza"
"The Light" (Ferlinghetti) **1**:183
"Light" (Ondaatje) **28**:339-40
"Light" (Wakoski) **15**:369
"Light against Darkness" (Williams) **7**:385
"Light Becomes Darkness" (Williams) **7**:384, 388
"Light Becomes Where No Sun Shines" (Thomas)
   See "Light Breaks Where No Sun Shines"

*Light Beyond the Darkness* (Harper) **21**:189
"Light Breaks Where No Sun Shines" (Thomas) **2**:304
"A Light Breather" (Roethke) **15**:268, 309
*Light Compulsion* (Celan)
See *Lichtzwang*
"Light in Darkness" (Harper) **21**:197
"Light Love" (Rossetti) **7**:289
"The Light on the Pewter Dish" (Rexroth) **20**:196
"Light Sleeping" (Gunn) **26**:218
"A Light Snow-Fall after Frost" (Hardy) **8**:124
"The Light Tree" (Elytis) **21**:123
*The Light Tree and the Fourteenth Beauty* (Elytis) **21**:123, 133
"Light Verse on a Rock" (Wang Wei) **18**:358-59
"A Lighted Cigar That Is Smoking" (Apollinaire)
See "Paysage"
"The Lighted House" (Day Lewis) **11**:145-46
"Lightenings" (Heaney) **18**:259
"Lighthouse with Dead Leaves" (McGuckian) **27**:104
"Lightness" (Jimenez)
See "Levedad"
"Lightnin' Blues" (Dove) **6**:117
"The Lightning" (Swenson) **14**:285
"Lightning Storm on Fuji" (Nemerov) **24**:295
"Lights among Redwood" (Gunn) **26**:
*Like a Bulwark* (Moore) **4**:257
"Like a Sentence" (Ashbery) **26**:
"Like a Sitting Breeze" (Viereck) **27**:267-68, 283
"Like Ankle-rings" (Ekeloef) **23**:87
"Like Decorations in a Nigger Cemetery" (Stevens) **6**:308, 318
"Like Rembrandt, martyr of chiaroscuro" (Mandelstam)
See "Kak svetoteni muchenik Rembrandt"
"Like Snow" (Graves) **6**:144, 172
"Like the Thistledown" (Aleixandre) **15**:15
"Like, This Is What I Meant" (Baraka) **4**:38
"Like This Together" (Rich) **5**:364, 382
"Like Three Fair Branches from One Root Deriv'd" (Hass) **16**:199
"Lilacs" (Lowell) **13**:64, 67, 84-5, 98-9
"Lilian" (Tennyson) **6**:359
"Lilis Park" (Goethe) **5**:246
"The Lilly" (Blake) **12**:34-5
"The Lilly in a Christal" (Herrick) **9**:112-13, 115, 137-38, 144
*Les Limbes* (Baudelaire)
See *Les fleurs du mal*
"Limbo" (Coleridge) **11**:52, 85
"Limbo" (Graves) **6**:166
"Lime Trees in Winter Retouched" (McGuckian) **27**:102-104
"The Limit" (Aleixandre) **15**:6
"Limitation of Perfection" (Tagore)
See "Purner abhav"
"Limitations" (Sassoon) **12**:245
"Limited" (Sandburg) **2**:312
"Límites y espejo" (Aleixandre) **15**:42-3
"Limits" (Okigbo) **7**:241-42
*Limits* (Okigbo) **7**:223-28, 233-34, 246-48, 250-51
"Limits and mirror" (Aleixandre)
See "Límites y espejo"
"I limoni" (Montale) **13**:114, 119, 122
"The Lincoln Relics" (Kunitz) **19**:175, 178-80
"Lindau" (Montale) **13**:146
"Lineage" (Hughes) **7**:159
"Lineage" (Walker) **20**:281
"Linen Town" (Heaney) **18**:202
"The Liner She's a Lady" (Kipling) **3**:161
"Lines" (Harper) **21**:190, 218
"Lines" (Williams) **7**:351-52
"Lines about the Unknown Soldier" (Mandelstam)
See "Stikhi o neizvestnom soldate"

"Lines Above Tintern Abbey" (Wordsworth)
See "Lines Composed a Few Miles Above Tintern Abbey"
"Lines & Circularities" (Nemerov) **24**:288, 301
"Lines Composed a Few Miles Above Tintern Abbey" (Wordsworth) **4**:373, 387, 391, 409-12, 418-19, 425-26, 428
"Lines Composed While Climbing the Left Ascent of Brockley Coomb, Somersetshire, May 1795" (Coleridge) **11**:82
"Lines for a Book" (Gunn) **26**:185, 189
"Lines for a Picture of St. Dorothea" (Hopkins) **15**:144
"Lines for an Album" (Montale)
See "Per album"
"Lines for an Ode-Threnody on England" (Brooke) **24**:89
"Lines for an Old Man" (Eliot) **5**:170
"Lines in a Country Churchyard" (Shelley) **14**:166
"Lines Left upon a Seat in a Yew-Tree, Which Stands near the Lake of Esthwaite, on a Desolate Part of the Shore, Commanding a Beautiful Prospect" (Wordsworth) **4**:373, 418
"Lines on a Young Lady's Photograph Album" (Larkin) **21**:236
"Lines on an Autumnal Evening" (Coleridge) **11**:106
"Lines on Revisiting the Country" (Bryant) **20**:37-8
"Lines on the First Mild Day of March" (Wordsworth) **4**:418
"Lines to a Don" (Belloc) **24**:11, 29, 38
"Lines to a Movement in Mozart's E-Flat Symphony" (Hardy) **8**:114
"Lines to Miles O'Reilly" (Harper) **21**:197
"Lines to Myself" (Heaney) **18**:191
"Lines to Sour-Faced Gila" (Juana Ines de la Cruz) **24**:176
"Lines Written after Detecting in Myself a Yearning toward the Large, Wise, Calm, Richly Resigned, Benignant Act Put on by a Great Many People after Having Passed the Age of Thirty Five" (Bogan) **12**:115
"Lines Written among the Euganean Hills" (Shelley) **14**:171, 177, 235
"Lines Written at a Small Distance from My House, and Sent by My Little Boy to the Person to Whom They Are Addressed" (Wordsworth) **4**:418
"Lines Written in an Asylum" (Carruth) **10**:84, 89
"Lines Written in Anticipation of a London Paper Attaining a Guaranteed Circulation of Ten Million Daily" (Sassoon) **12**:251-52
"Lines Written in Early Spring" (Wordsworth) **4**:418
"Lines Written in Kensington Gardens" (Arnold) **5**:19, 35, 49
"Lines Written in the Library of Congress after the Cleanth Brooks Lecture" (Kumin) **15**:222
"Lines Written on My Nineteenth Birthday" (Owen) **19**:371
"Lingard and the Stars" (Robinson) **1**:464
"Lingua" (Pasolini) **17**:272
"Links" (Apollinaire)
See "Liens"
"The Linnet in the Rocky Dells" (Bronte) **8**:68-9
"Linoleum" (Gallagher) **9**:44, 56, 60
"The Lion" (Belloc) **24**:24
"Lion" (Wright) **14**:346
"Lion & Honeycomb" (Nemerov) **24**:262
"The Lion and the Lamb" (Wylie) **23**:309, 324
"The Lion in Love" (Moore) **4**:261
"The Lions" (Hayden) **6**:194, 197

"Liquid Metal Fast Breeder Reactor" (Snyder) **21**:293
"Lis" (Cummings) **5**:100
"Lisa" (Eliot) **20**:102
"Lisa May" (Dunbar) **5**:137
"Lisbon Revisited, 1923" (Pessoa) **20**:158, 169
"Listen" (Nash) **21**:274
"Listen Carefully" (Levine) **22**:234
"listen children" (Clifton) **17**:26
"Listen Here Blues" (Hughes) **1**:270
"Listen, Lord" (Johnson) **24**:144, 164
"Listenen to Big Black at S.F. State" (Sanchez) **9**:225
"The Litanie" (Donne) **1**:136-39, 147, 150
"Litanies" (Alegria) **26**:
"Les litanies de satan" (Baudelaire) **1**:45, 71
"The Litanies of Satan" (Baudelaire)
See "Les litanies de satan"
"Litany" (Ashbery) **26**:131-135, 140-143, 145, 156, 169-170, 172
"The Litany for Survival" (Lorde) **12**:137
"The Litany of the Dark People" (Cullen) **20**:57, 75
"The Litany of the Heroes" (Lindsay) **23**:266, 272, 285, 295
"Literary Statement On Struggle!" (Baraka) **4**:30
"The Literate Farmer and the Planet Venus" (Frost) **1**:210
"The Lithuanian" (Lermontov)
See "The Lithuanian"
"Lithuanian Dance Band" (Ashbery) **26**:145
"Lithuanian Nocturne" (Brodsky) **9**:22-4, 27
"Litovskii noktyurn" (Brodsky)
See "Lithuanian Nocturne"
"The Little Beauty That I Was Allowed" (Wylie) **23**:314
"A Little Bit of a Tumbler" (Stein) **18**:321, 334, 353
"The Little Black Boy" (Blake) **12**:7-8
"The Little Boy Found" (Blake) **12**:7
"A Little Boy Lost" (Blake) **12**:7, 23, 33-5
"Little Boy Lost" (Smith) **12**:321, 325, 332
"Little Boy Sick" (Smith) **12**:318
"Little Boy Stanton" (Garcia Lorca) **3**:143
"Little Brown Baby" (Dunbar) **5**:142
"A Little Called Pauline" (Stein) **18**:331
"A Little Child Shall Lead Them" (Harper) **21**:187
*The Little Children of the Snow* (Bryant)
See "The Little People of the Snow"
"A little demon in wet fur crept in" (Mandelstam)
See "Vlez besenok v mokroi sherstke"
"The Little Dog's Day" (Brooke) **24**:59
"Little Elegy" (Wylie) **23**:314-15
"Little Exercise" (Bishop) **3**:49
"Little Fanfare for Felix MacGowan" (Merrill) **28**:253
"The Little Friend" (Browning) **6**:14
"Little Fugue" (Plath) **1**:390
"The Little Ghost" (Millay) **6**:206
"Little Gidding" (Eliot) **5**:165-67, 169-70, 181-83, 185, 193, 204-05, 208, 210-11
"The Little Girl Found" (Blake) **12**:7, 33-4, 61
"A Little Girl Lost" (Blake) **12**:7, 33-4, 61
"Little Girl, My String Bean, My Lovely Woman" (Sexton) **2**:363
"Little Girls" (Page) **12**:176-77
"Little Green Sea" (Elytis) **21**:123
"Little Green Tree" (Hughes) **1**:243
*Little Henrietta* (Reese) **29**:337, 339, 348, 353
"The Little Hill" (Millay) **6**:214, 233
*The Little House of Kolomna* (Pushkin)
See *Domik v Kolomne*
"Little Jim" (McKay) **2**:216, 222
"The Little June Book" (Stevens) **6**:332-33
"The Little Larousse" (Zagajewski) **27**:401
"Little Lion Face" (Swenson) **14**:280
"Little Lobeila's Song" (Bogan) **12**:100-01, 111
"A Little Love of Life" (Stein) **18**:313
"Little Lyric" (Hughes) **1**:240

*The Little Mariner* (Elytis) **21**:134-35
"Little Mattie" (Browning) **6**:24
"Little Miss Muffet Sat on a Prophet" (Nash)
    **21**:265
"Little Old Letter" (Hughes) **1**:243
"The Little Old Women" (Baudelaire)
    See "Les petites vielles"
"The Little Ones" (Soto) **28**:371
"The Little Peasant" (Sexton) **2**:364, 368
"The Little People of the Snow" (Bryant)
    **20**:15-16
"De Little Pikaninny's Gone to Sleep"
    (Johnson) **24**:162
*Little Poems in Prose* (Baudelaire)
    See *Petits poèmes en prose: Le spleen de
    Paris*
"The Little Rapids" (Swenson) **14**:262
*The Little Sailor* (Elytis)
    See *The Little Mariner*
"A Little Scraping" (Jeffers) **17**:117
*The Little Seafarer* (Elytis)
    See *The Little Mariner*
"The Little Serving Maid" (Belloc) **24**:5
"Little Sleep's-Head Sprouting Hair in the
    Moonlight" (Kinnell) **26**:251, 283, 291
"Little Songs for Gaia" (Snyder) **21**:301
"Little Sonnet" (Wylie) **23**:332
"Little T. C." (Marvell)
    See "The Picture of Little T. C. in a
    Prospect of Flowers"
"A Little Testament" (Montale)
    See "Piccolo testamento"
"Little Tree" (Cummings) **5**:93
"A Little Uncomplicated Hymn" (Sexton) **2**:363
"The Little Vagabond" (Blake) **12**:7
"The Little White Rose" (MacDiarmid) **9**:154,
    176, 186
"Little Words" (Parker) **28**:363
"Littleblood" (Hughes) **7**:153, 168-69
*Liturgies intimes* (Verlaine) **2**:417-18
"Litvinka" (Lermontov) **18**:300
"Liubliu moroznoe dykhan'e" (Mandelstam)
    **14**:154
"Live" (Sexton) **2**:351, 364
"Live Niggers--Stop Bullshitting" (Baraka) **4**:18
*Live or Die* (Sexton) **2**:349, 351, 356, 362-65
"The lively sparks that issue from those eyes"
    (Wyatt) **27**:357
"Lives" (Rukeyser) **12**:207, 217, 228
"Living" (Levertov) **11**:186
"Living Earth" (Toomer) **7**:336-37
"Living in Sin" (Rich) **5**:351, 369
"Living in the Mountain on an Autumn Night"
    (Wang Wei) **18**:391
"Living in the Open" (Piercy) **29**:310
*Living in the Open* (Piercy) **29**:304, 310-11
"Living Near the Water" (Song) **21**:345-46
"A Living Pearl" (Rexroth) **20**:186-87, 216, 218
"LIVING WITH TH VISHYUN" (Bissett)
    **14**:34
*living with th vishyun* (Bissett) **14**:16-17
"Livingshayes" (Davie) **29**:115
*Le Livre de l'Espurgatorie* (Marie de France)
    See *L'Espurgatoire Saint Patrice*
*Llanto por Ignacio Sánchez Mejías* (Garcia
    Lorca) **3**:121-22, 124, 126, 128
"Llegada" (Guillen) **23**:99, 105-106
"Llewellyn and the Tree" (Robinson) **1**:462,
    468
"Lo! A Child Is Born" (MacDiarmid) **9**:178-79
"Lo fatal" (Dario) **15**:96
"Lo lo lógico" (Fuertes) **27**:22
"El lo sabe" (Fuertes) **27**:15
"The Load of Sugar-Cane" (Stevens) **6**:293
"Loch Torridon" (Swinburne) **24**:313
"lock lied" (Enzensberger) **28**:138-39
"The Lockless Door" (Frost) **1**:218
"Locks" (Bukowski) **18**:15
"Locksley Hall" (Tennyson) **6**:354, 357, 359-
    60, 363
"Locus" (Hayden) **6**:189, 194, 196
"The Locust Tree in Flower" (Williams) **7**:363

"The Locusts" (Merrill) **28**:231, 243
"Locutions des Pierrots, I" (Laforgue) **14**:81
"Locutions des Pierrots XIV" (Laforgue) **14**:89
"Lofty in the Palais de Danse" (Gunn) **26**:220
"Log" (Merrill) **28**:221-2, 256
"Logging 2" (Larkin) **21**:322
"Logos" (Hughes) **7**:120, 159
"Loi de formation du progrès" (Hugo) **17**:100
"Loin Cloth" (Sandburg) **2**:329
"Loin des oiseaux" (Rimbaud) **3**:274
"Loin du pigeonnier" (Apollinaire) **7**:18, 21, 23
"Loitering with a Vacant Eye" (Housman) **2**:193
"Lollocks" (Graves) **6**:137, 142, 144
"London" (Blake) **12**:7, 25, 34
"London" (Pinsky) **27**:150
"London Bridge" (Robinson) **1**:466, 468
"London Snow" (Bridges) **28**:51, 61, 70, 83
*Loneliness* (Paz)
    See *Soledad*
"A Lonely Character" (Hagiwara Sakutaro)
    See "Sabishii jinkaku"
"The Lonely Street" (Williams) **7**:362
"Lonesome" (Dunbar) **5**:119
"Long Afternoons" (Zagajewski) **27**:395
"Long Ages Past" (Owen) **19**:351
*Long Ago and Not So Long Ago* (Verlaine)
    See *Jadis et naguère*
"The Long Alley" (Roethke) **15**:248, 254
*The Long Approach* (Kumin) **15**:214, 221
"The Long Death" (Piercy) **29**:311
*Long Division: A Tribal History* (Rose) **13**:232
"A Long Dress" (Stein) **18**:349
"The Long Hunter" (Berry) **28**:38
"Long John Brown & Little Mary Bell"
    (Blake) **12**:35
"Long John Nelson and Sweetie Pie" (Walker)
    **20**:286
"The long love" (Wyatt) **27**:340, 355
"The long love that in my thought doth
    harbour" (Wyatt) **27**:358
"Long Past Moncada" (Rukeyser) **12**:231-32
"Long Screams" (Hughes) **7**:150
"Long Shadow at Dulce" (Momaday) **25**:219
"The Long Shadow of Lincoln: A Litany"
    (Sandburg) **2**:334
"A Long Story" (Gray) **2**:143, 152-53
"Long To'ds Night" (Dunbar) **5**:147
"The Long Tunnel Ceiling" (Hughes) **7**:148
"The Long Waters" (Roethke) **15**:310, 316-17
"Longing" (Arnold) **5**:42-3
"Longing" (Brutus) **24**:114
"The Longing" (Roethke) **15**:272, 274, 310,
    312-15
*Longing* (Ishikawa)
    See *Akogare*
"Longing for Heaven" (Bradstreet) **10**:27, 30,
    42
*A Longing for the Light: Selected Poems of
    Vicente Aleixandre* (Aleixandre) **15**:24
"Longing Is Like the Seed" (Dickinson) **1**:111
"Long-Legged Fly" (Yeats) **20**:315
*Longshot Peoms for Broke Players* (Bukowski)
    **18**:3-4
*Longshot Pomes for Brave Players* (Bukowski)
    **18**:5
"the lonliness of literacy" (Bissett) **14**:34
"The Look" (Olds) **22**:342
"Look!" (Smith) **12**:342
"Look Back" (Snyder) **21**:300
"Look Down from the High Terrace Seeing
    Off Reminder Li" (Wang Wei) **18**:370
"Look for You Yesterday, Here You Come
    Today" (Baraka) **4**:14-15
"Look Hart That Horse You Ride Is Wood"
    (Viereck) **27**:284
"Look on This Picture and on This" (Rossetti)
    **7**:277
"Look, Stranger, on This Island Now" (Auden)
    **1**:7-8, 12, 22, 30
"Look What You Did, Christopher!" (Nash)
    **21**:275
"Look You I'll Go Pray" (Lindsay) **23**:281

"Looking at a Picture on an Anniversary"
    (Hardy) **8**:137-38
"Looking at My Father" (Olds) **22**:321
"Looking at Pictures to be Put Away" (Snyder)
    **21**:287
*Looking for Luck* (Kumin) **15**:213, 216, 221,
    223-24
"Looking for Luck in Bangkok" (Kumin)
    **15**:214
"Looking for Nothing" (Snyder) **21**:310
"Looking for th Lammas" (Bissett) **14**:7
"Looking Forward" (Rossetti) **7**:277
"Looking Glass" (Gunn) **26**:206, 218
"Looking in a Mirror" (Atwood) **8**:32, 38
"Looking Up at the Top of a Blue Tree"
    (Hagiwara Sakutaro) **18**:177
"The Look of the Hedge" (Reese) **29**:334
"The Loom" (Masters) **1**:333
"The Loon's Cry" (Nemerov) **24**:295
"The Loon's Cry" (Nemerov) **24**:257, 292-93,
    295, 299-300
"The Loop" (Masters) **1**:329
"Loop" (Ondaatje) **28**:331
"Loot" (Kipling) **3**:160, 163, 174, 187
"Lord Lundy" (Belloc) **24**:18
"Lord of Elbë, on Elbë Hill" (Bronte) **8**:73
*The Lord of the Isles* (Scott) **13**:277, 281, 288,
    294, 296, 304, 311-12, 318, 321
*Lord Weary's Castle* (Lowell) **3**:200, 202-03,
    206-07, 211-12, 216-18, 224, 230-33
"Lorelei" (Plath) **1**:388-89
"L'lorloge de demain" (Apollinaire) **7**:32
"The Los Cities" (Cardenal)
    See "Las ciudades perdidas"
"De los periódicos" (Fuertes) **27**:12
"The Loser" (Stryk) **27**:201
"Losing Track" (Levertov) **11**:160, 169
"Loss" (H. D.) **5**:303
"The Loss of the Eurydice" (Hopkins) **15**:147,
    162
"The Loss of The Nabara" (Day Lewis)
    See "The Nabara"
"The Losse" (Finch) **21**:146, 179
"Lost" (Bukowski) **18**:24
"Lost" (Sandburg) **2**:303
"Lost and Found" (Levine) **22**:224
"The Lost Angel" (Levine) **22**:213
*lost angel mining company* (Bissett) **14**:6-7, 9,
    17, 19
"The Lost Bower" (Browning) **6**:7
"Lost Child" (Wright) **14**:349, 352
"Lost Commagene" (Elytis) **21**:135
*Lost Copper* (Rose) **13**:235, 237-38, 240
"The Lost Dancer" (Toomer) **7**:336
"Lost Horizon" (Ashbery) **26**:127
"Lost in Translation" (Merrill) **28**:227, 232,
    242, 260, 269
"The Lost Ingredient" (Sexton) **2**:350, 359
"The Lost Lilies" (Brooke) **24**:81
"Lost Love" (Graves) **6**:129
"The Lost Man" (Wright) **14**:339, 346
"The Lost Mistress" (Browning) **2**:38
"Lost Sister" (Song) **21**:331-32, 343, 350
"The Lost Son" (Roethke) **15**:248, 250, 255,
    262-63, 267-68, 270, 272, 275-76, 278, 284,
    298-99, 301-02
*The Lost Son, and Other Poems* (Roethke)
    **15**:246-50, 260, 282-83, 290-91, 296-97,
    304, 308-09
"The Lost Wine" (Valery)
    See "Le vin perdu"
"The Lotos-Eaters" (Tennyson) **6**:352, 358-60,
    409-12
"Lot's Wife" (Nemerov) **24**:255
"Lot's Wife 1988" (Clifton) **17**:29
*Lotto-Poems* (Cassian) **17**:6
"The Lotus and the Rose" (Lindsay) **23**:292
"Louenge a la court" (Villon) **13**:394-95
"A Lough Neagh Sequence" (Heaney) **18**:201
"Love" (Brooke) **24**:85
"Love" (Hagiwara Sakutaro)
    See "Airen"

"Love" (Herbert) :100, 114
"Love III" (Herbert) **4**:121
"Love Again" (Larkin) **21**:259
"Love among the Ruins" (Browning) **2**:88
"Love & Fame & Death" (Bukowski) **18**:5
"Love and Friendship" (Bronte) **8**:51
"Love and Harmony Combine" (Blake) **12**:32
"Love and Honour" (Belloc) **24**:29
"The Love and the Hate" (Jeffers) **17**:136
"Love and the Times" (Davie) **29**:110
*Love and War, Art and God* (Shapiro) **25**:318, 322
"Love Arm'd" (Behn) **13**:4, 7, 15, 23-5
"Love Came Back at Fall of Dew" (Reese) **29**:333
"Love Despoiled" (Dunbar) **5**:125
*Love Elegies* (Donne)
    See *Elegies*
"Love Fossil" (Olds) **22**:310, 317
"Love from the North" (Rossetti) **7**:260, 278, 280, 289
"Love in Barrenness" (Graves) **6**:172
"Love in Blood Time" (Olds) **22**:316
"Love in Fantastic Triumph Sat" (Behn)
    See "Love Arm'd"
"Love in Moonlight" (Gluck) **16**:169
"Love in the Museum" (Rich) **5**:393
"Love Is" (Swenson) **14**:283
*Love Is a Dog From Hell* (Bukowski) **18**:19
"Love Is a Piece of Paper Torn to Bits"
    (Bukowski) **18**:6
"Love is More Thicker than Forget"
    (Cummings) **5**:108
"Love is the Only God" (Cummings) **5**:107
"Love Joy" (Herbert) **4**:122-23, 125
"A Love Letter" (Dunbar) **5**:147
"Love Letter" (Meredith) **28**:170-71, 185
*Love Letter from an Impossible Land*
    (Meredith) **28**:170, 172, 177, 182-87, 194, 209-10, 216
"Love Letter From an Impossible Lane"
    (Meredith) **28**:190
"Love Letter Postmarked Van Beethoven"
    (Wakoski) **15**:326, 331
"Love Me!" (Smith) **12**:346
"The Love Nut" (Ferlinghetti) **1**:187
"The Love of Christ which Passeth
    Knowledge" (Rossetti) **7**:268, 290
"A Love of Death" (Pinsky) **27**:154
"LOVE OF LIFE, the 49th parallel" (Bissett)
    **14**:7, 10, 18
"Love on my hear from heaven fell" (Bridges)
    **28**:59
"Love Passes Beyond the Incredible Hawk of
    Innocence" (Wakoski) **15**:351
"Love Poem" (Gluck) **16**:150
"Love Poem" (Lorde) **12**:158
"Love Poem" (Page) **12**:177
"Love Poem" (Stryk) **27**:197, 203
"Love Poem For Real" (Giovanni) **19**:126
*Love Poems* (Sanchez) **9**:207, 212, 216, 218-
    21, 227, 229, 234, 237, 242
*Love Poems* (Sexton) **2**:349, 351-53, 355, 364-65
*The Love Poems of Marichiko* (Rexroth) **20**:203, 218
*The Love Poems of May Swenson* (Swenson)
    **14**:274-75, 280, 283-84
*Love Respelt* (Graves) **6**:154, 156
"Love Sex and Romance" (Wakoski) **15**:357
"Love Song" (Levertov) **11**:159, 171
"Love Song" (Sexton) **2**:363
"Love Song" (Williams) **7**:345, 406-07
"Love Song" (Wylie) **23**:314
"Love Song from the Gaelic" (Yeats) **20**:345-46
"A Love Song in the Modern Taste" (Swift)
    **9**:252, 268
"The Love Song of J. Alfred Prufrock" (Eliot)
    **5**:153-54, 157, 160, 206
"Love Song of Prufrock Junior" (Viereck)
    **27**:264
"Love Song to Eohippus" (Viereck) **27**:280

*Love Songs* (Loy) **16**:310, 314-15, 320-21, 323, 325-26, 328
"Love Songs I" (Loy) **16**:306
"Love Songs in Age" (Larkin) **21**:229, 258
*Love Songs to Joannes* (Loy) **16**:316, 332
"Love Songs VI" (Loy) **16**:307
"A Love Story" (Graves) **6**:129, 133, 136-37, 144, 163, 172
"The Love Tree" (Cullen) **20**:85
"Love Unknown" (Herbert) **4**:109, 112, 123, 129
"Love Winter When the Plant Says Nothing"
    (Merton) **10**:334
"Love without Hope" (Graves) **6**:141, 144, 149-50
"Love You Right Back" (Brooks) **7**:94
"Loveliest of Trees" (Housman) **2**:184-85, 192, 194-95
"Lovely Ladies" (Tu Fu) **9**:330
"The Lovely Lady" (Tu Fu) **9**:322
"A Lovely Love" (Brooks) **7**:81, 96, 100-01
*Love-Poems* (Ovid)
    See *Amores*
"The Lover" (Borges)
    See "El enamorado"
"The Lover" (Montagu) **16**:337
"The Lover hopeth of better chance" (Wyatt)
    **27**:338
"The lover lamentes the death of his love"
    (Wyatt) **27**:340
"The Lover of Love" (Hagiwara Sakutaro)
    See "Koi wo koi suru hito"
"The Lover Pleads with His Friend for Old
    Friends" (Yeats) **20**:330
"The Lover Seweth how He is Forsaken of
    Fortune who Sometime Favoured Him"
    (Wyatt) **27**:309
"A Lover since Childhood" (Graves) **6**:129
"The Lover Tells of the Rose in His Heart"
    (Yeats) **20**:338
"The Lovers" (Merrill) **28**:239, 243
"Lovers' Death" (Baudelaire)
    See "La mort des amants"
"Lovers infinitenesse" (Donne) **1**:130, 153
"Lovers of the Poor" (Brooks) **7**:86, 88, 96
"The Lover's Song" (Yeats) **20**:308
"The Lover's Tale" (Tennyson) **6**:358, 373-74, 379-80
*The Lovers Watch* (Behn)
    See *La Montre; or, The Lover's Watch*
"Loves Alchymie" (Donne) **1**:147, 159
"Love's Causes" (Browning) **6**:17
"Love's Diet" (Donne) **1**:127
"Love's Draft" (Dunbar) **5**:126
"Love's Expression" (Browning) **6**:17
"Love's Farewell" (Bronte) **8**:57
"Loves Growth" (Donne) **1**:153
"Love's Loneliness" (Yeats) **20**:333
"Love's New Creation" (Browning) **6**:17
"Love's Obstacles" (Browning) **6**:16
"The Loves of the Plants" (Noyes) **27**:129
"Love's Philosophy" (Shelley) **14**:167
"Love's Progress" (Roethke) **15**:289
"Love's Refuge" (Browning) **6**:17
"Love's Repetitions" (Browning) **6**:17
"Loves Riddles" (Donne) **1**:153
"Love's Sacrifice" (Browning) **6**:17
"Love's Trappist" (Chesterton) **28**:95
"" (Lovesong.Celan)
    See "(Liebeslied.)"
"The Love-Song of a Leprechaun" (Noyes)
    **27**:136
"Loving an Honest Man" (Piercy) **29**:309
"The Loving Shepherdess" (Jeffers) **17**:110, 131
"Loving the Killer" (Sexton) **2**:352-53
"Low Barometer" (Bridges) **28**:77
"The Low Sky" (Jeffers) **17**:117
"Low Tide" (Millay) **6**:236
"Low Tide at Schoodic" (Clampitt) **19**:86, 90
"Low to High" (Hughes) **1**:258, 267
"Lower Field—Enniscorthy" (Olson) **19**:293
"The Lowest Place" (Rossetti) **7**:274, 291

"The Lowest Room" (Rossetti)
    See "The Lowest Place"
"The Lowestoft Boat" (Kipling) **3**:183
"A Lu Mountain Song for the Palace Censor
    Empty-Boat Lu" (Li Po) **29**:156
"Lub O' Mine" (McKay) **2**:221
"Lucien Létinois" (Verlaine) **2**:416
"Lucifer in the Train" (Rich) **5**:354, 362, 393
"lucifer speaks in his own voice" (Clifton)
    **17**:37
"lucifer understanding at last" (Clifton) **17**:30
"Lucifer's Feast" (Noyes) **27**:122
"Lucks my fair falcon and your fellows all"
    (Wyatt) **27**:367
*The Lucky Bag* (MacDiarmid) **9**:158
"Lucretius" (Tennyson) **6**:358, 360, 378, 380
"lucy and her girls" (Clifton) **17**:13
"Lucy Gray" (Coleridge) **11**:73-4
"Lucy Gray" (Wordsworth) **4**:398, 404, 428
*Lueurs des tirs* (Apollinaire) **7**:22
*Luisa in Realityland* (Alegria) **26**:
"Luke Havergal" (Robinson) **1**:467, 475, 490-94
"Lull" (Roethke) **15**:246-50, 282
"Lull" (November, 1939Roethke) **15**:250
"Lullaby" (Dunbar) **5**:122
"Lullaby" (Gluck) **16**:170
"Lullaby" (Sexton) **2**:359
"Lullaby" (Sitwell) **3**:309, 311, 326
"Lullaby" (Yeats) **20**:328
"Lullaby" (Zagajewski) **27**:389
"Lullaby for Jumbo" (Sitwell) **3**:303
*Lullay Lullay like a Child* (Skelton) **25**:345
"The Lumens" (Olds) **22**:340
"La luna" (Borges) **22**:100
*Luna de enfrente* (Borges) **22**:71-2, 93-4
"Luna Habitabilis" (Gray) **2**:155
*Luna silvestre* (Paz) **1**:367
"Lunar Baedecker" (Loy) **16**:306-08, 321
*Lunar Baedecker* (Loy) **16**:306, 310, 316, 321-22, 330
*Lunar Baedecker and Time-tables* (Loy) **16**:306, 316
"The Lunar Cycle" (Piercy) **29**:311
*The Lunar Cycle* (Piercy) **29**:300, 303
"The Lunar Probe" (Kumin) **15**:180
"Lunch" (Stein) **18**:328
"Lundi rue Christine" (Apollinaire) **7**:18, 36
"Lune de miel" (Eliot) **5**:185, 191
"La lune est sterile" (Laforgue) **14**:61
*Lupercal* (Hughes) **7**:115, 118-20, 123, 135-38, 140-41, 150, 158, 162-63, 165, 169
"Lust" (Brooke) **24**:53, 56, 85
"Lustra" (Okigbo) **7**:221, 225, 232, 239, 250
*Lustra* (Pound) **4**:320, 365
"Lusts" (Verlaine)
    See "Luxures"
"Lux" (Hugo) **17**:54
"Luxures" (Verlaine) **2**:416
"Lyceia" (Graves) **6**:156
"Lycidas" (Arnold) **5**:7
"Lycidas" (Milton) **19**:193, 202, 211-13, 217, 219-26, 242, 250-53; **24**:320
*Lycidas* (Milton) **29**:212, 214, 241, 243, 272
"Lydia Is Gone This Many a Year" (Reese)
    **29**:333, 347
"Lyell's Hypothesis Again" (Rexroth) **20**:216, 218
"Lynch I" (Cesaire) **25**:30
"The Lynching" (McKay) **2**:205-06, 212, 217
"Lynching Song" (Hughes) **1**:241
"La Lyre" (Ronsard) **11**:266
"Lyric Intermezzo"
    See *Lyrisches Intermezzo*
"The Lyric Year" (Dario)
    See "El año lírico"
*Lyrical Ballads* (Coleridge) **11**:37, 59-60, 68, 91
*Lyrical Ballads, with a Few Other Poems*
    (Wordsworth) **4**:372-73, 375, 378, 380, 400, 412, 415-19, 425-29
"A Lyrick to Mirth" (Herrick) **9**:94, 103

*Lyrics of Love and Laughter* (Dunbar) **5**:119, 139
*Lyrics of Lowly Life* (Dunbar) **5**:117-18, 132, 136, 140
*Lyrisches Intermezzo* (Heine) **25**:130-31, 139, 141, 143, 161
"Lyrisches Intermezzo 26" (Heine) **25**:
"Lyrisches Intermezzo No 10" (Heine) **25**:142
"Lyrisches Intermezzo No 39" (Heine) **25**:144
"Lyrisches Intermezzo No.33" (Heine) **25**:142
"Lysergic Acid" (Ginsberg) **4**:74, 81
"Lyubil i ya v bylye gody" (Lermontov) **18**:293
"Lyubka" (Pasternak) **6**:253-54
"M AA l'anti-philosophe" (Tzara) **27**:235
"A M Alphonse de Lamartine" (Hugo) **17**:75, 90
"M Anti-psychologue" (Tzara) **27**:235
"M Antipyrine" (Tzara) **27**:235
"M Antitête" (Tzara) **27**:235
"A M de Chateaubriand" (Hugo) **17**:90
"Ma bohème" (Rimbaud) **3**:271, 276, 283
"Ma Man" (Hughes) **1**:270
"Macarius and the Pony" (Merton) **10**:351
"Macaw" (Bogan) **12**:86
*Macchu Picchu* (Neruda)
    See *Alturas de Macchu Picchu*
*MacFlecknoe; or, A Satire upon the Trew-Blew-Protestant Poet, T. S.* (Dryden) **25**:70, 114-16, 118, 120-23
"Mackinnon's Boat" (Tomlinson) **17**:344
"Macpherson's Farewell" (Burns) **6**:55
"MacStatesman and Co." (MacDiarmid) **9**:176
"Mad As the Mist and the Snow" (Yeats) **20**:328-29
"The Mad Farmer Manifesto: The First Amendment" (Berry) **28**:13
"Mad Judy" (Hardy) **8**:102
"The Mad Maid's Song" (Herrick) **9**:87
"The Mad Monk" (Coleridge) **11**:69
"The Mad Mother" (Wordsworth) **4**:374, 380
"A Mad Negro Soldier Confined at Munich" (Lowell) **3**:205, 218, 222
"The Mad Scene" (Merrill) **28**:254
"Mad Song" (Blake) **12**:31-2
"The Mad Woman of the GRand Armee" (Alegria) **26**:
"Madam and Her Might-Have Been" (Hughes) **1**:243
"Madam and the Wrong Visitor" (Hughes) **1**:243
"Madame de Soubise" (Vigny) **26**:410-11
"Madame Decrepitude" (Cassian) **17**:13
"A Madame Sand" (Nerval) **13**:178
"Madame Withouten Many Wordes" (Wyatt) **27**:316, 328, 330
"Das Mädchen spricht" (Goethe) **5**:249
"Madeleine" (Apollinaire) **7**:32
"Mademoiselle Bistouri" (Baudelaire) **1**:58
"A Mademoiselle Louise B" (Hugo) **17**:93
"Mademoiselle Veronique" (Brodsky) **9**:10
"Madhouse Bells" (Browning) **2**:30
"Madhouse Cells" (Browning) **2**:26
"Madhumanjari" (Tagore) **8**:416
*The Madman, His Parables and Poems* (Gibran) **9**:69, 71, 75, 77-80, 82
"Madman's Song" (Wylie) **23**:301, 309, 326, 328
"Madness" (Baraka) **4**:27
"The Madness of King Goll" (Yeats) **20**:344, 354
"The Madonna" (Tennyson) **6**:353
"Madonna of the Evening Flowers" (Lowell) **13**:60, 64, 67, 96
"Madrid 1937" (Neruda) **4**:310
"Madrigal" (Nemerov) **24**:256
"Madrigal triste" (Baudelaire) **1**:61
"Madrigali privati" (Montale) **13**:106, 167
"Madrugada" (Fuertes) **27**:7
"Madurai" (Paz) **1**:361
"The Madwoman's Miracle" (Wylie) **23**:321
"Le maestrine" (Pavese) **13**:221
"Magadalena" (Gautier) **18**:163-64

"Magasins du Louvre" (Loy) **16**:312, 328
"The Magellanic Clouds" (Wakoski) **15**:325, 363
*The Magellanic Clouds* (Wakoski) **15**:350-51, 363, 365-66
"The Magellanic Heart" (Neruda)
    See "El corazón magellanico"
"Les mages" (Hugo) **17**:83, 87
"Maggie, a Lady" (Rossetti) **7**:291
"The Magi" (Gluck) **16**:125, 140, 149
"Magic" (Dove) **6**:113
"Magic" (Levertov) **11**:209
"Magic Island" (Song) **21**:344
*The Magic Lantern* (Tsvetaeva)
    See *Volshebny fonar*
"TH MAGIC LURE OF SEA SHELLS" (Bissett) **14**:34
"The Magic Morning" (Smith) **12**:331
"Magician" (Shapiro) **25**:309
*The Magician's Feastletters* (Wakoski) **15**:356
*Magique* (Cesaire) **25**:36
"Magna est Veritas" (Smith) **12**:333
*The Magnetic Fields* (Breton)
    See *Les Champs Magnétiques*
*The Magnetic Mountain* (Day Lewis) **11**:123-26, 128-30, 135, 138-39, 143-45, 148, 151-52
"Magnets" (Cullen) **20**:60
"Magnitudo parvi" (Hugo) **17**:89
"Magnolia Flower" (Hughes) **1**:237
"The Magnolia Shadow" (Montale)
    See "L'ombra della magnolia"
"Magnolias in Snow" (Hayden) **6**:194, 196
"Magpie's Song" (Snyder) **21**:297
"Magpiety" (Milosz)
    See "Sroczość"
"Mahomets Gesang" (Goethe) **5**:247
*Mahua* (Tagore) **8**:415-16
"The Maid Servant at the Inn" (Parker) **28**:353
"The Maiden Marriage" (Swinburne) **24**:357
"Maiden May" (Rossetti) **7**:277
"Maiden Song" (Rossetti) **7**:264, 274-6, 289
"The Maiden without Hands" (Sexton) **2**:365
"A Maiden's Pledge" (Hardy) **8**:98
"Maiden's Sorrow" (Bryant) **20**:15
"The Maid's Thought" (Jeffers) **17**:117
"Maifest" (Goethe) **5**:251
"Mailied" (Goethe) **5**:245
"Mailie's Dying Words and Elegy" (Burns)
    See "The Death and Dying Words of Poor Mailie"
"Maillol" (Tomlinson) **17**:311, 314, 335
"Maisie" (Merrill) **28**:228, 254
"La maison des mortes" (Apollinaire) **7**:47
"La maison du Berger" (Vigny) **26**:370, 377, 386-87, 391-94, 396, 402, 404, 406, 409, 413
"La Maison d'Yves" (Breton) **15**:63-7
"Maison Flake" (Tzara) **27**:233
"Maithuna" (Paz) **1**:361, 368
"The Maja and the Old Woman" (Aleixandre) **15**:5-6
"Le Majeur Ydow" (Smith) **12**:331
"Major Macroo" (Smith) **12**:309, 317
"A Major Work" (Meredith) **28**:201
*Majors and Minors* (Dunbar) **5**:115, 117-18, 128, 132, 135-36, 142
"Make Big Money at Home! Write Poems in Spare Time!!" (Nemerov) **24**:267
"The Maker" (Borges)
    See "El hacedor"
"The Maker" (Illyes)
    See "Teremteni"
*The Maker* (Borges)
    See *El hacedor*
"The Makers" (Nemerov) **24**:289-90
"Making a Living" (Sexton) **2**:367
"Making a Sacher Torte" (Wakoski) **15**:355, 372
"the making of poems" (Clifton) **17**:27
"Making the Connection" (Kumin) **15**:208
"Le mal" (Rimbaud) **3**:283

"Malabaress" (Baudelaire)
    See "A une Malabaraise"
"Malachy Deagan" (Masters) **1**:343
"Malcolm" (Sanchez) **9**:224, 231
"Malcolm" (Walker) **20**:277
"Malcolm Spoke/Who listened?" (This Poem Is for My Consciousness TooMadhubuti) **5**:328, 341
"Il male di vivere" (Montale) **13**:105
"Malediction Upon Myself" (Wylie) **23**:303, 310
"Malinche" (Alegria) **26**:
"Le maline" (Rimbaud) **3**:283
"The Malingerer" (McKay) **2**:226
"'Mallorca,' un poema en el olvido" (Borges) **22**:92
"Malmaison" (Lowell) **13**:71, 78, 84
"Malourène" (Apollinaire) **7**:48
"Mammy Hums" (Sandburg) **2**:324
"Man" (Brooke) **24**:71, 75
"Man" (Herbert) **4**:100-01, 103
"Man" (Lamartine)
    See "L'homme"
"The Man against the Sky" (Robinson) **1**:462, 471, 490, 492-94
*The Man against the Sky* (Robinson) **1**:462-63, 467-68, 474
"Man and Dog" (Sassoon) **12**:255
"The Man and the Echo" (Yeats) **20**:314, 335
"Man and Wife" (Lowell) **3**:206, 209, 221, 245
"Man and Wife" (Sexton) **2**:363
"The Man beneath the Tree" (Wright) **14**:343, 345, 347
"Man Bites Dog-Days" (Nash) **21**:265
"The Man Born to Farming" (Berry) **28**:26
*Man Does, Woman Is* (Graves) **6**:154
"Man Doesn't Exist" (Aleixandre) **15**:20, 22
"The Man He Killed" (Hardy) **8**:102-03
"A Man I Am" (Smith) **12**:295
"Man in Black" (Plath) **1**:389
*A Man in the Divided Sea* (Merton) **10**:338, 346-47, 350
"Man into Men" (Hughes) **1**:241, 243
"Man is a Spirit" (Smith) **12**:297, 316
"Man of Lawe's Tale" (Chaucer)
    See "Man of Law's Tale"
"Man of Law's Tale" (Chaucer) **19**:13, 15, 24, 26, 45, 54-6, 59-60, 62
"A Man of the Middle Class" (Brooks) **7**:62
"Man of Words" (Ashbery) **26**:126
"The Man on His Death Bed" (Aleixandre) **15**:8
"The Man on the Dump" (Ashbery) **26**:153
"The Man on the Hotel Room Bed" (Kinnell) **26**:286
"The Man Seeking Experience Enquires His Way of a Drop of Water" (Hughes) **7**:116, 118
"Man Splitting Wood in the Daybreak" (Kinnell) **26**:293
"Man Spricht Deutsch" (Enzensberger) **28**:142
"The Man that are Falling" (Stevens) **6**:310
"Man, the Man-Hunter" (Sandburg) **2**:308
"Man the Master" (Merton) **10**:345
"A Man Walking and Singing" (Berry) **28**:3-4, 7, 18
"Man Was Made to Mourn" (Burns) **6**:68
*The Man Who Died Twice* (Robinson) **1**:469, 472, 475, 477, 483, 489-90
"The Man Who Dreamed of Fairyland" (Yeats) **20**:343, 354
"A Man Who Loves Love" (Hagiwara Sakutaro)
    See "Koi wo koi suru hito"
*The Man Who Shook Hands* (Wakoski) **15**:366
"The Man Whose Pharynx Was Bad" (Stevens) **6**:294
"The Man with a Past" (Hardy) **8**:93
*Man with a Sling* (Neruda)
    See *El hondero entusiasta, 1923-1924*
*The Man with Night Sweats* (Gunn) **26**:224, 228, 230-231
"Man with One Small Hand" (Page) **12**:170

*The Man with Seven Toes* (Ondaatje) **28**:298-302, 318, 322, 326-27

"The Man with the Blue Guitar" (Stevens) **6**:298, 323-24, 326, 337, 339

*The Man with the Blue Guitar, and Other Poems* (Stevens) **6**:304

"A Man Young and Old" (Yeats) **20**:328

"Manas-sundari" (Tagore) **8**:408

"Manciple's Tale" (Chaucer) **19**:11, 13, 48

"Mandalay" (Kipling) **3**:158, 160, 162, 167, 188-89, 192

"The Mandolin, the Carnation and the Bamboo" (Apollinaire)
 See "La mandoline, l'oeillet et le bambou"

"La mandoline, l'oeillet et le bambou" (Apollinaire) **7**:18, 20-2, 34, 36

*Manfred* (Byron) **16**:68-72, 82-4, 86-90, 108, 111

"Mango Grove" (Tagore)
 See "Amravan"

"Manhattan: Grace Church" (Clampitt) **19**:100

"Manhattan May Day Midnight" (Ginsberg) **4**:84

"Mania di solitudine" (Pavese) **13**:225

"Mania for solitude" (Pavese)
 See "Mania di solitudine"

"Manicure" (Brooks) **7**:53

"Mankind" (Trakl)
 See "Menschheit"

"The Man-Moth" (Bishop) **3**:37, 65

"The Manner of the World Nowadays" (Skelton) **25**:337

*Mannerly Margery Milk and Ale* (Skelton) **25**:345

"The Manor Garden" (Plath) **1**:389

*Las manos del día* (Neruda) **4**:288

"A Man's a Man for a' That" (Burns) **6**:60

"Man's Medley" (Herbert) **4**:101, 127

"Manscape" (Tomlinson) **17**:351-52

"Mansion" (Ammons) **16**:16, 20

"Mantis" (Zukofsky) **11**:341, 347, 356, 392-99

"'Mantis,' an Interpretation" (Zukofsky) **11**:341, 356, 394

"Manual System" (Sandburg) **2**:304

"Manuelzinho" (Bishop) **3**:59-60

"Many Farms Notes" (Ortiz) **17**:231

*Many Inventions* (Kipling) **3**:160

*Many Long Years Ago* (Nash) **21**:266

"The Many Mansions" (Levertov) **11**:201

"Many Swans" (Lowell) **13**:61, 64-5, 83

"Manyone Flying" (Swenson) **14**:283

"Manzanita" (Snyder) **21**:297

"The Map" (Bishop) **3**:37, 50-2

"The Map" (Stryk) **27**:203

*The Map of Love* (Thomas) **2**:381, 390

"A Map of the City" (Gunn) **26**:219

"A Map of the City" (Gunn) **26**:

"Maple and Sumach" (Day Lewis) **11**:144

"El mar" (Borges) **22**:99

"Mar Portugues" (Pessoa) **20**:170

*El mar y las campanas* (Neruda) **4**:287-88

"Mar y noche" (Aleixandre) **15**:16

"Mara" (Jeffers) **17**:146

"Marathon" (Gluck) **16**:152, 164, 166-67

"Marburg" (Pasternak) **6**:270-71, 281

"March" (Bryant) **20**:12

"March 21 1987" (Brutus) **24**:110

"The March of the Cameron Men" (Robinson) **1**:476

"March Twilight" (Bogan) **12**:111

*Marcha triunfal* (Dario) **15**:79-80, 85, 111

"Marchas pawnees" (Cardenal) **22**:131

"Marche de funèbre pour la mort de la terre" (Laforgue) **14**:95

"La marche impériale" (Valery) **9**:391

"Marchenbilder" (Ashbery) **26**:127, 150

"Marching Song" (Wang Wei) **18**:389

"Marcia funebre" (Pasolini) **17**:264

*Marconi's Cottage* (McGuckian) **27**:84, 91-92, 94-95, 99, 104-105, 110

"Margaret" (Sandburg) **2**:303

"Margaret" (Wordsworth) **4**:399

"Margarita Debayle" (Dario) **15**:80, 95

"Marginal Employment" (Clampitt) **19**:81, 88

"Margite, Marguerite and Margherita" (Stein) **18**:325, 334

"Margrave" (Jeffers) **17**:142

"I mari del sud" (Pavese) **13**:210, 212, 216, 220-26, 228

"Maria" (Gautier) **18**:126

*Maria Neféli* (Elytis) **21**:130-31

*Maria Nephele* (Elytis)
 See *Maria Neféli*

"Maria Stuart" (Pasternak) **6**:267

"Maria Wentworth" (Carew) **29**:59

"Maria Who Made Faces and a Deplorable Marriage" (Belloc) **24**:24

"The Mariachis--A Glimpse" (Wakoski) **15**:332

"Mariana" (Tennyson) **6**:359, 364, 387, 389, 391, 406-09, 411

"Mariana in the South" (Tennyson) **6**:350

"Marianne, My Mother, and Me" (Kumin) **15**:210-12

"Marichika" (Tagore) **8**:407

*Marilyn Monroe and Other Poems*
 See *Oracion por Marilyn Monroe y otros poemas*

"Marina" (Brooke) **24**:58

"Marina" (Eliot) **5**:164, 195, 205-06, 210

"Marine" (Rimbaud) **3**:261

*Mariner* (Coleridge)
 See *The Rime of the Ancient Mariner: A Poet's Reverie*

"Marines USA" (Guillen) **23**:126

*Marino Faliero: Doge of Venice* (Byron) **16**:103

"Mariposa de obsidiana" (Paz) **1**:364

"Maritime Ode" (Pessoa)
 See "Ode Marítima"

"The Mark" (Bogan) **12**:87-8, 98, 106, 121

"Market" (Hayden) **6**:194, 196

"Market at Turk" (Gunn) **26**:186, 219

*Marmion* (Scott) **13**:249-51, 256, 258, 261, 264, 266-68, 270-71, 273, 275-76, 279, 281-85, 287-90, 304, 311-12, 317-18

"The Marmozet" (Belloc) **24**:24

"Marriage" (Moore) **4**:230-31, 233, 243, 249, 251-52, 254-55, 258, 260-61

"Le marriage d'André Salmon" (Apollinaire)
 See "Poème lu au mariage d'André Salmon"

"The Marriage II" (Levertov) **11**:167

"A Marriage in the Sixties" (Rich) **5**:363

*The Marriage of Heaven and Hell* (Blake) **12**:12, 28, 36, 39-41, 47-51, 60-1, 64

"The Marriage of Hector and Andromache" (Sappho) **5**:414, 418

"The Marriage of Lord Fauconberg and Lady Mary Cromwell" (Marvell) **10**:270

"The Marriage Ring" (Blake) **12**:34

"The Married Man" (Kipling) **3**:192

"The Marrow" (Roethke) **15**:277, 281

"Marshall Washer" (Carruth) **10**:74

"Marsyas" (Masters) **1**:329

"The Marten" (Clare) **23**:7

"Martha" (Lorde) **12**:140, 157

"A Martial Law Carol" (Brodsky) **9**:26-7

"Martirio de Santa Olalla" (Garcia Lorca) **3**:132, 146

"The Martyr of Alabama" (Harper) **21**:190

*The Martyr of Alabama, and Other Poems* (Harper) **21**:189

"The Martyr Poets Did Not Tell" (Dickinson) **1**:96

"A Martyr: The Vigil of the Feast" (Rossetti) **7**:285

"The Martyrdom of Bishop Farrar" (Hughes) **7**:112

"Martyrdom of Saint Eulalia" (Garcia Lorca)
 See "Martirio de Santa Olalla"

"Une martyre" (Baudelaire) **1**:45, 48, 62

*The Marvelous Arithmetics of Distance* (Lorde) **12**:153

"Mary" (Blake) **12**:35, 43

"Mary and Gabriel" (Brooke) **24**:59, 78, 84

"Mary and the Seasons" (Rexroth) **20**:209

"Mary at the Feet of Christ" (Harper) **21**:191

"The 'Mary Gloster'" (Kipling) **3**:161, 167, 181

"Mary Morison" (Burns)
 See "Ye Are Na Mary Morison"

"Mary, Pity Women" (Kipling) **3**:161, 192

"Mary Winslow" (Lowell) **3**:206, 217-18

"mary's dream" (Clifton) **17**:19

"Marz has Ruined Nature, for the Moment" (Stevens) **6**:297

"The Mask" (Baudelaire)
 See "Le masque"

"Mask" (Illyes) **16**:245, 250

*Mask of Comus* (Milton)
 See *Comus: A Maske*

"The Masked Face" (Hardy) **8**:119

"Masked Woman's Song" (Bogan) **12**:100-01

"Masks" (Stryk) **27**:191, 197

"Masks of Dawn" (Paz) **1**:359

"Le masque" (Baudelaire) **1**:45, 65, 72

"Masque nègre" (Senghor) **25**:224

*The Masque of Anarchy* (Shelley) **14**:171, 175, 210

*A Masque of Mercy* (Frost) **1**:211

"The Masque of Plenty" (Kipling) **3**:181

*A Masque of Reason* (Frost) **1**:203-04, 206, 217

*The Masque of Snow* (Blok)
 See *Snezhnye maski*

"Masque of Tsars" (Viereck) **27**:280

"Masquerade in the Park" (Akhmatova) **2**:6

"Masqueraders" (Page) **12**:178

"Mass for the Day of St. Thomas Didymus" (Levertov) **11**:198, 200-01

"The Massage" (Kinnell) **26**:286

"The Master" (H. D.) **5**:306

"The Master" (Robinson) **1**:461, 465, 467

"Master and Mistress" (Kunitz) **19**:148

"Master Herrick's Farewell unto Poetry" (Herrick)
 See "Farewell to Poetry"

"Master Hugues of Saxe-Gotha" (Browning) **2**:37, 61, 88

"The Masters of the Heart Touched the Unknown" (Schwartz) **8**:292

"The Matachines" (Tomlinson) **17**:328-29

"The Match" (Marvell) **10**:271, 300

"Mater Potens" (Alegria) **26**:

"Materia humana" (Aleixandre) **15**:34

"Maternità" (Pavese) **13**:213

"Mathilde in Normady" (Rich) **5**:352, 359

"Matinée d'ivresse" (Rimbaud) **3**:261, 263, 271-73, 281-82

"Matinees" (Merrill) **28**:285-87

"Matins" (Gluck) **16**:170-71

"Matins" (Levertov) **11**:166

"Matoaka" (Clampitt) **19**:101-02

"Matrix" (Clampitt) **19**:102

"Matros v Moskve" (Pasternak) **6**:283

"Mattens" (Herbert) **4**:119

"Mattens, or Morning Prayer" (Herrick) **9**:118

"Matthew XXV: 30" (Borges) **22**:73-5

*Matthias at the Door* (Robinson) **1**:473-74, 479

"Mattino" (Pavese) **13**:230

"Maturity" (Ginsberg) **4**:87

*Maud, and Other Poems* (Tennyson) **6**:354, 356-57, 360, 363, 366, 373, 379-80, 383, 385, 387, 407

"Maude Clare" (Rossetti) **7**:260, 280, 291

"Maundy Thursday" (Owen) **19**:352, 358

"Mausfallen-Sprüchlein" (Morike) **1**:114

*Mausoleum* (Enzensberger) **28**:148-50, 154-55, 158, 165

"Le mauvais moine" (Baudelaire) **1**:59

"Le mauvais vitrier" (Baudelaire) **1**:67

"Mawu" (Lorde) **12**:143

"Maximus at the Harbor" (Olson) **19**:312-13

"Maximus From Dogtown--IV" (Olson) **19**:306

"Maximus of Gloucester" (Olson) **19**:294, 304

*The Maximus Poems* (Olson) **19**:266-67, 270-71, 273-75, 277, 279-83, 285-87, 294, 296-98, 304-7, 316

"Maximus, to Himself" (Olson) **19**:269
*Maximus, Vol. II* (Olson) **19**:306
*Maximus, Vol. III* (Olson) **19**:285, 287-88, 295, 305-7
"May" (Rossetti) **7**:265
"May 20, 1928" (Borges) **22**:76
"May 24, 1980" (Brodsky) **9**:24
"May 1943" (H. D.) **5**:307
"May 1968" (Olds) **22**:339
"may all thes blessings" (Bissett) **14**:30
"May Festival" (Goethe)
    See "Maifest"
"May It Be" (Pasternak) **6**:261
"The May Magnificat" (Hopkins) **15**:124-25, 165
*The May Queen* (Tennyson) **6**:359
"Mayapán" (Cardenal) **22**:128, 131
"Mayavada" (Tagore) **8**:408
"Maybe this is a sign of madness" (Mandelstam) **14**:155
"Maybe this is the beginning of madness" (Mandelstam)
    See "Mozhet byt' eto tochka bezumiia"
"May-Day" (Emerson) **18**:76, 88, 111
*May-Day and Other Pieces* (Emerson) **18**:75, 113
"Mayflower" (Aiken) **26**:
"Mayflower" (Aiken) **26**:41-2, 45
"The Mayor of Gary" (Sandburg) **2**:304, 308
"The Maypole Is Up" (Herrick) **9**:102, 145
"May's Love" (Browning) **6**:24
"A Maze of Sparks of Gold" (Rexroth) **20**:190
"Mazeppa" (Hugo) **17**:75
*Mazeppa* (Byron) **16**:83
"Mazurka" (McGuckian) **27**:101
"M.B." (Brodsky) **9**:10
"McAndrew's Hymn" (Kipling) **3**:161, 167, 170, 186, 192
"Me Again" (Rexroth) **20**:218
*Me Again: Uncollected Writings of Stevie Smith* (Smith) **12**:314, 333-34, 340, 343-44, 346-47
"Me centuplant Persée" (Cesaire) **25**:31
"Me crucé con un entierro" (Fuertes) **27**:11
"Me from Myself to Banish" (Dickinson) **1**:94
"Me Whoppin' Big-Tree Boy" (McKay) **2**:226
"Meadow Milk" (Bogan) **12**:110
*Meadowlands* (Gluck) **16**:171-73
"Meadowlands 3" (Gluck) **16**:171
"Meaning" (Milosz) **8**:215
"The Measure of Poetry" (Nemerov) **24**:303
"Meat without Mirth" (Herrick) **9**:98
"Mechanism" (Ammons) **16**:40
"Le médaillon toujours ferme" (Apollinaire) **7**:22
*The Medall. A Satire Against Sedition* (Dryden) **25**:74
*The Medea, and Some Poems* (Cullen) **20**:60-62, 66
*Medea the Sorceress* (Wakoski) **15**:372-73
*Le médecin malgré lui* (Williams) **7**:349
*Medicamina Faciei* (Ovid) **2**:238-39, 243, 251, 253, 258
"MEDICINE" (Bissett) **14**:20
*MEDICINE my mouths on fire* (Bissett) **14**:16, 19, 27
*Medieval Scenes* (Duncan) **2**:109
"Médiocriteé" (Laforgue) **14**:88
"Mediocritie in love rejected" (Carew) **29**:25, 32
"Meditation" (Baudelaire)
    See "Recueillement"
"Meditation" (Lermontov)
    See "Duma"
"Meditation at Lagunitas" (Hass) **16**:200, 209, 211, 219
"Meditation at Oyster River" (Roethke) **15**:265, 276, 310, 313, 316
"A Meditation for His Mistresse" (Herrick) **9**:101
"Meditation in the Spring Rain" (Berry) **28**:6
"A Meditation in Time of War" (Yeats) **20**:314

"A Meditation in Tuscany" (Browning) **6**:16
"The Meditation of the Old Fisherman" (Yeats) **20**:337
"Meditation on a June Evening" (Aiken) **26**:7, 50
"A Meditation on John Constable" (Tomlinson) **17**:341-42
"Meditation on Saviors" (Jeffers) **17**:142, 144-45
*Les meditations* (Lamartine) **16**:256-62, 265, 268-69
"Meditations in Time of Civil War" (Yeats) **20**:314, 342, 349
"Meditations of an Old Woman" (Roethke) **15**:262, 264-65, 273
*Méditations poétiques* (Lamartine) **16**:270, 272-82, 284-85, 287, 289-93, 302
"Mediterraneo" (Montale) **13**:115
*Medny Vsadnik* (Pushkin) **10**:367-68, 373-74, 385, 390-400, 414
"Medusa" (Bogan) **12**:85, 104-06, 111-12, 115, 117
"Medusa" (Cullen) **20**:69
"Medusa" (Dove) **6**:123
"Medusa" (Merrill) **28**:229
"Meeting" (Arnold) **5**:42
"Meeting" (Montale)
    See "Incontro"
"A Meeting" (Pasternak)
    See "Vstrecha"
"The Meeting" (Rukeyser) **12**:231
"A Meeting of Minds" (Lorde) **12**:135
"Meeting-House Hill" (Lowell) **13**:67
*Meghadūta* (Kalidasa) **22**:177-78, 182, 185, 188-89, 192, 194-95, 204-05, 207-08
*La meglio gioventù* (Pasolini) **17**:250-51, 254, 262, 264-67, 275, 279, 281-83, 293
"A Mehinaku Girl in Seclusion" (Song) **21**:344
"mehrere elstern" (Enzensberger) **28**:139
"Mein Karren knarrt nicht mehr" (Celan) **10**:124
"A Mei-p'i Lake Song" (Tu Fu) **9**:330-31, 333
"Melancholia" (Gautier) **18**:135
"Melancholia en Orizba" (Neruda) **4**:281
"Melancholy" (Bely) **11**:6
"Melancholy" (Bridges) **28**:76
"Melancholy in Orizaba" (Neruda)
    See "Melancholia en Orizba"
"A Melancholy Moon" (Baudelaire)
    See "Les tristesses de la lune"
*Melancolía* (Jimenez) **7**:211
"Melancthon" (Moore) **4**:254
"Mélange adultère de tout" (Eliot) **5**:185
"Melbourne" (Shapiro) **25**:269
"Melibee" (Chaucer)
    See "Tale of Melibee"
"Melinda on an Insippid Beauty in imitation of a fragment of Sapho's" (Finch) **21**:167
"Melody" (Tomlinson) **17**:341
"Memo from the Cave" (Gluck) **16**:147-48
"Memoir" (Pinsky) **27**:157
"Mémoire" (Rimbaud) **3**:262, 268
"Memoirs" (Meredith) **28**:199
"Memoirs of the World" (Gunn) **26**:203
"Memorabilia" (Masters) **1**:343
"Memorandum Confided by a Yucca to a Passion-Vine" (Lowell) **13**:61, 64
"À Memória do President Rei Sidónio" (Pessoa) **20**:154
"Memorial" (Pinsky) **27**:153
"Memorial" (Sanchez) **9**:224
"Memorial II" (Lorde) **12**:140, 157
"Memorial for the City" (Auden) **1**:23
"Memorial Tablet" (Sassoon) **12**:269
"Memories..." (Jimenez)
    See "Recuerdos..."
"Memories of My Father" (Kinnell) **26**:286
"Memories of the Forest" (Ishikawa)
    See "Mori no omoide"
"Memories of West Street and Lepke" (Lowell) **3**:206, 208, 220, 223, 237
"Memory" (Bogan) **12**:101, 120, 122
"A Memory" (Brooke) **24**:85-6

"A Memory" (Pavese) **13**:203
"Memory" (Roethke) **15**:275
"Memory" (Sassoon) **12**:269
"Memory" (Walker) **20**:283
"Memory" (Wright) **14**:376
"Memory I" (Rossetti) **7**:277
"The Memory of Elena" (Forche) **10**:136, 139, 152-53, 166, 169
"A Memory of the Players in a Mirror at Midnight" (Joyce) **22**:
"Memory of V. I. Ulianov" (Zukofsky) **11**:396
"A Memory Picture" (Arnold) **5**:49
"Men" (Parker) **28**:347, 354
"Men" (Toomer) **7**:336
*Men and Women* (Browning) **2**:66, 77, 94
"Men Improve with the Years" (Yeats) **20**:314
"Men Loved Wholly beyond Wisdom" (Bogan) **12**:104, 126
"Men of the North" (Harper) **21**:190
*Men, Women, and Ghosts* (Lowell) **13**:63, 71, 73, 76, 79, 85, 93
"The Menace" (Gunn) **26**:228
"El mendigo que entregaba un papel" (Fuertes) **27**:30
"Mending Wall" (Frost) **1**:225, 227, 229
"Mendocino Rose" (Hongo) **23**:199
"Menelaus and Helen" (Brooke) **24**:56, 65, 76, 79, 82
"Menons Klagen um Diotima" (Holderlin) **4**:141-42
"Menon's Lament for Diotime" (Holderlin)
    See "Menons Klagen um Diotima"
"Mens Creatrix" (Kunitz) **19**:159
*Mensagem* (Pessoa) **20**:154-57, 159-63, 165, 168, 170
"Mensaje" (Aleixandre) **15**:6, 10
"Menschenbeitfall" (Holderlin) **4**:165
"Menschheit" (Trakl) **20**:250, 253-55
"Menschliche Trauer" (Trakl) **20**:253
"Menschliches Elend" (Trakl) **20**:253
"Menses" (Millay) **6**:233
"Menstruation at Forty" (Sexton) **2**:363 .
"Mental Cases" (Owen) **19**:330, 336, 340-41, 343, 347, 353, 355, 359, 365, 368, 370-71
"The Mental Traveller" (Blake) **12**:36, 46, 48
"The Merchantmen" (Kipling) **3**:161
"Merchant's Tale" (Chaucer) **19**:13, 15, 28, 33, 62-3
"Mercury and the Elephant" (Finch) **21**:159, 161
"Merely Statement" (Lowell) **13**:86
"Mericano" (Ortiz) **17**:228
"Meridian" (Clampitt) **19**:83
"Meriggiare pallido e assorto" (Montale) **13**:105
"Merlin" (Emerson) **18**:81-82, 88, 99, 104, 106
*Merlin: A Poem* (Robinson) **1**:462-63, 465, 468-71, 482-83, 488-89, 491
"Merlin and the Gleam" (Tennyson) **6**:389, 407
"Merlin in the Cave He Speculates Without a Book" (Gunn) **26**:
"The Mermaid's Children" (Lowell) **3**:241
"The Mermen" (Crane) **3**:90
*Merope* (Arnold) **5**:8, 12, 35, 37, 45, 47, 58-60, 62-3
"The Merry Guide" (Housman) **2**:180, 192
"Merry Margaret" (Skelton) **25**:336
"The Merry Muses" (Burns) **6**:96
"Meru" (Yeats) **20**:326
"Merveilles de la guerre" (Apollinaire) **7**:3, 22
"Mes bouguins refemés" (Mallarme) **4**:199
"Mes deux Filles" (Hugo) **17**:82
"De Mes Haras" (Cesaire) **25**:10
"Mes petites amoureuses" (Rimbaud) **3**:262, 284
"Mescaline" (Ginsberg) **4**:74, 81
"Un mese fra i bambini" (Montale) **13**:134
*Les meslanges* (Ronsard) **11**:247, 266
"Message" (Aleixandre)
    See "Mensaje"
"Message" (Forche) **10**:139, 144, 154-55
"The Message" (Levertov) **11**:171
"The Message" (Sassoon) **12**:248

*Message* (Pessoa)
See *Mensagem*
"A Message All Blackpeople Can Dig" (& A
Few Negroes TooMadhubuti) **5**:329, 341
"Message for the Sinecurist" (Gallagher) **9**:62
"Message from the NAACP" (Baraka) **4**:11
"the message of crazy horse" (Clifton) **17**:25
"Message to a Black Soldier" (Madhubuti)
**5**:339
"Messages" (Senghor) **25**:255
"The Messenger" (Atwood) **8**:18
"The Messenger" (Gunn) **26**:
"The Messenger" (Gunn) **26**:219, 226
"The Messenger" (Merton) **10**:339
"The Messenger" (Sassoon) **12**:259
"A Messenger from the Horizon" (Merton)
**10**:334
"Messengers" (Gluck) **16**:127, 133, 142
"The Messiah" (Pope) **26**:314, 319, 322
"Messianic Eclogue" (Vergil)
See "Eclogue 4"
"Messias" (Shapiro) **25**:284, 317
"The Metal and the Flower" (Page) **12**:168, 178
*The Metal and the Flower* (Page) **12**:167, 171,
193
*Die Metamorphose der Pflanzen* (Goethe)
**5**:239-40
*Metamorphoses* (Ovid) **2**:233, 238-241, 244-45,
260
"Les métamorphoses du vampire" (Baudelaire)
**1**:48, 71
"The Metamorphoses of the Vampire"
(Baudelaire)
See "Les métamorphoses du vampire"
"Metamorphosis" (Gluck) **16**:163
"Metamorphosis" (Sitwell) **3**:304
*Metamorphosis* (Ovid)
See *Metamorphoses*
"Metaphors of a Magnifico" (Stevens) **6**:311-12
"The Metaphysical Automobile" (Nemerov)
**24**:284
"Metempsicosis" (Dario) **15**:101
"Metho Drinker" (Wright) **14**:333, 341
"The Metropolis" (Clampitt) **19**:90
"Métropolitain" (Rimbaud) **3**:265
"Mexican Divertimento" (Brodsky) **9**:12
"Mexican Divertissement" (Brodsky)
See "Mexican Divertimento"
"Mexicans Begin Jogging" (Soto) **28**:387
"Mezzo Forte" (Williams) **7**:405
"Mi chiquita" (Guillen) **23**:142
"Mi suerte" (Fuertes) **27**:14, 27
"Mi vida entera" (Borges) **22**:93
"Mi voz" (Aleixandre) **15**:40
"Mía" (Dario) **15**:107, 113
"La mia musa" (Montale) **13**:139
"Mia vita a te non chiedo lineamenti"
(Montale) **13**:139
"Miami You Are About to be Surprised"
(Merton) **10**:351
"MIA's" (Missing in Action and Other
AtlantasSanchez) **9**:230, 235, 244
"Micah" (Walker) **20**:278
"Michael" (Wordsworth) **4**:380-81, 394, 399,
402, 412, 414, 425, 428
*Michael Robartes and the Dancer* (Yeats)
**20**:310, 314
"Michel et Christine" (Rimbaud) **3**:264, 281
"The Microbe" (Belloc) **24**:15, 25
"Midas Among Goldenrod" (Merrill) **28**:239
"Mid-August at Sourdough Mountain Lookout"
(Snyder) **21**:286
"Middle Flight" (Meredith) **28**:174, 186
"Middle of a Long Poem on 'These States'"
(Ginsberg) **4**:47
"The Middle of Life" (Holderlin)
See "Hälfte des Lebens"
"Middle Passage" (Hayden) **6**:176-81, 183, 187-
88, 194, 196-200
"The Middle-Aged" (Rich) **5**:362-63, 367, 369
"The Midget" (Levine) **22**:
"Midnight" (Heaney) **18**:192

"Midnight" (Parker) **28**:351, 364
"Midnight" (Wright) **14**:337
"Midnight Chippie's Lament" (Hughes) **1**:255
"Midnight in Moscow" (Mandelstam) **14**:122
"A Midnight Interior" (Sassoon) **12**:246
"Midnight Nan at Leroy's" (Hughes) **1**:246
"Midnight on the Great Western" (Hardy) **8**:107
"Midnight Show" (Shapiro) **25**:295
"Midnight Snack" (Merrill) **28**:249
"Midnight Verses" (Akhmatova) **2**:16
"A Midnight Woman to the Bobby" (McKay)
**2**:224
*The Midsummer Cushion* (Clare) **23**:45
"A Midsummer Holiday" (Swinburne) **24**:313,
329
"Mid-Term Break" (Heaney) **18**:189
"Midway" (Graves) **6**:143
"Midwinter, Presolstice" (Atwood) **8**:2
"The Midwives" (Enzensberger) **28**:142
"La miej zoventút" (Pasolini) **17**:281
"Mientras dura vida, sobra el tiempo" (Forche)
**10**:135
"Mientras la Gracia me excita" (Juana Ines de
la Cruz) **24**:188
"Might These be Thrushes Climbing through
Almost (Do They" (Cummings) **5**:108
"The Mighty Flight" (Baraka) **4**:26
"Mignonne, allons voir si la rose" (Ronsard)
See "Ode à Cassandre: 'Mignonne, allon
voir'"
"Mildred's Thoughts" (Stein) **18**:346
"Mildred's Umbrella" (Stein) **18**:334
"A Mild-Spoken Citizen Finally Writes to the
White House" (Meredith) **28**:206
*Mileposts I* (Tsvetaeva)
See *Vyorsty I*
*Mileposts II* (Tsvetaeva)
See *Vyorsty II*
"Milk" (Stein) **18**:323, 330
"The Milk Factory" (Heaney) **18**:237
"Milk-Wort and Bog Cotton" (MacDiarmid)
**9**:160, 176, 199
"The Mill" (Robinson) **1**:468, 475, 478
"Mill Song" (Ekeloef) **23**:54
"Miller's" (Chaucer)
See "Miller's Tale"
"The Miller's Daughter" (Tennyson) **6**:350
"Miller's Tale" (Chaucer) **19**:11, 13-14, 40, 44,
54, 61
"Millibars of the Storm" (Cesaire) **25**:17
"Millibars of the Storn" (Cesaire) **25**:17
"The Millionaire" (Bukowski) **18**:13
"The Mills of the Kavanaughs" (Lowell) **3**:204,
206-07, 215, 217, 224, 226, 231
*The Mills of the Kavanaughs* (Lowell) **3**:204,
206-07, 215, 217, 224, 226, 231
"Milly; ou, La terre natale" (Lamartine) **16**:280,
286, 293
"Milpa" (Cardenal) **22**:131
*Milton* (Blake) **12**:13, 27, 30, 36-8, 42, 44-5,
50, 62-5, 73, 75-80
"Milun" (Marie de France) **22**:258, 264, 266,
268, 270-75, 295-96
"Mima: Elegía pagana" (Dario) **15**:110-11
*Minashiguri* (Matsuo Basho) **3**:11
*Mind Breaths: Poems, 1972-1977* (Ginsberg)
**4**:61, 82
"The Mind Hesitant" (Williams) **7**:390
"The Mind, Intractable Thing" (Moore) **4**:243
"The Mind is an Enchanted Thing" (Moore)
**4**:261
"The Mind of the Frontispiece to a Book"
(Jonson)
See "The Mind of the Frontispiece to a
Book"
*Mindwheel* (Pinsky) **27**:157, 171
"Mine own John Poyntz" (Wyatt) **27**:333-337,
341
*Mine the Harvest* (Millay) **6**:226, 231-33, 237,
242
"The Mine: Yamaguchi" (Stryk) **27**:185-86,
191, 202, 214

"Mineral" (Page) **12**:170
"Miners" (Owen) **19**:342-43, 346, 348, 365,
370
"Minesweepers" (Kipling) **3**:183
"Miniature" (Meredith) **28**:171
"Minicursi" (Fuertes) **27**:23
"Miniver Cheevy" (Robinson) **1**:462, 467, 478,
487, 496
"Minnesbilder" (Ekeloef) **23**:69
"Minnie and Mattie" (Rossetti) **7**:274
"A Minor Prophet" (Eliot) **20**:123, 140-41
"Minotaur" (Wylie) **23**:302-303, 306, 323
*Minstrels* (Sitwell) **3**:290
"Minstrel's Song, on the Restoration of Lord
Clifford the Shepherd" (Wordsworth)
**4**:377
*The Minstrelsy of the Scottish Border* (Scott)
**13**:249, 269, 278, 281, 306
"Minus 18 Street" (McGuckian) **27**:80
"The Minute" (Shapiro) **25**:306
"The Minute before Meeting" (Hardy) **8**:90
"Mirabeau Bridge" (Apollinaire)
See "Le pont Mirabeau"
*Mirabell: Books of Numbers* (Merrill) **28**:233,
235-38, 240, 251, 260-64, 275-77, 279, 281
"The Miracle" (Gunn) **26**:220
"A Miracle for Breakfast" (Bishop) **3**:46, 57
"Miracles" (Whitman) **3**:381
"Miraculous Weapons" (Cesaire)
See "Les armes miraculeuses"
"Mirage" (Tagore)
See "Marichika"
"Mirage of the Desert" (Masters) **1**:344
"The Mirages" (Hayden) **6**:193, 197
"Miranda Dies in the Fog, 1816" (Neruda)
See "Miranda muere en la niebla, 1816"
"Miranda muere en la niebla, 1816" (Neruda)
**4**:295
"Miranda's Supper" (Wylie) **23**:302, 307, 314-
15, 321
"Miriam's Song" (Harper) **21**:194-95
"Miró Celi una rosa que en el prado" (Juana
Ines de la Cruz) **24**:225
"Mirror" (Merrill) **28**:225, 242, 245-47
"A Mirror for Poets" (Gunn) **26**:
"Mirror Image" (Gluck) **16**:162-63
"The Mirror in the Roadway" (Tomlinson)
**17**:334
"The Mirror in the Woods" (Rexroth) **20**:181
"The Mirror in Which Two Are Seen as One"
(Rich) **5**:368
"The Mirror Of Madmen" (Chesterton) **28**:108
"Mirror Sermon" (Brutus) **24**:99
"The Mirrors" (Williams) **7**:370
"Mirrors & Windows" (Nemerov) **24**:292
*Mirrors and Windows* (Nemerov) **24**:256, 261,
264, 295-96
"Mis Adioses" (Alegria) **26**:
"Mis queridos difuntos" (Fuertes) **27**:12
"Misanthropos" (Gunn) **26**:188-190, 192-193,
214, 223, 225-226
*Misanthropos* (Gunn) **26**:203
*Miscellaneous Poems* (Harper) **21**:185
*Miscellaneous Poems* (Marvell) **10**:257, 277,
311
*Miscellanies* (Swift) **9**:251, 253, 255, 275
*A Miscellany of New Poems* (Behn) **13**:7
*Miscellany Poems on Several Occasions,
Written by a Lady, 1713* (Finch) **21**:140,
148, 161, 163-64, 172-73
"Mise en Scene" (Lowell) **13**:96
"Miserie" (Herbert) **4**:108, 121
"Misery" (Hughes) **1**:328
"The Misfit" (Day Lewis) **11**:147
"Misgiving" (Frost) **1**:195
"Miss B--"2 (Clare) **23**:25
"Miss Drake Proceeds to Supper" (Plath)
**1**:398-99
"Miss Gee" (Auden) **1**:30
"Miss Rosie" (Clifton) **17**:32-33
"The Missing" (Gunn) **26**:224
"Mississippi Levee" (Hughes) **1**:256

"Mississippi Mother" (Brooks) **7**:96
"the missyun" (Bissett) **14**:24, 34
"Mist in the Valley" (Noyes) **27**:134
"Míster no!" (Guillen) **23**:126
"Mithridates" (Emerson) **18**:71
"Mito" (Pavese) **13**:210, 228-29
"Mixed Feelings" (Ashbery) **26**:124, 127
"Mnemonic" (Lee) **24**:243
"The Mob" (Brutus) **24**:108
*Mock Beggar Hall* (Graves) **6**:127-28
"Mock Confessional" (Ferlinghetti) **1**:187
"Mock Orange" (Gluck) **16**:145, 164
*Mockingbird, Wish Me Luck* (Bukowski) **18**:19
"Models" (Clampitt) **19**:99
"Models" (Nemerov) **24**:290
"Modern Elegy of the Motif of Affectation" (Guillen)
    See "Modern Elegy of the Motif of Affectation"
*Modern Fable Poems* (Nishiwaki)
    See *Kindai no Guwa*
"Modern Love" (Keats) **1**:311
"Modern Poetry Is Prose (But It Is Saying PlentyFerlinghetti) **1**:182-83
"A Modern Sappho" (Arnold) **5**:12
*The Modern Traveller* (Belloc) **24**:25-7, 35
"A Modernist Ballade" (Belloc) **24**:39
"Modes of Being" (Levertov) **11**:197-98
"Modes of Pleasure" (Gunn) **26**:186, 219
"Modest Proposal" (Enzensberger) **28**:158, 161
"A Modest Proposal" (Hughes) **7**:118
"Modulations for a Solo Voice" (Levertov) **11**:209
*A Moelna Elegy* (Ekelof)
    See *En Mölna-elegi*
"Moesta et Errabunda" (Baudelaire) **1**:70
"Mogollon Morning" (Momaday) **25**:221
"Moharram" (Stryk) **27**:214
*Mohn und Gedächtnes* (Celan) **10**:95
*moi, Laminaire* (Cesaire) **25**:33, 41, 45
"Moïse" (Vigny) **26**:369, 380-81, 384, 391, 398, 401, 410-11
"Mole" (Stryk) **27**:199-200
"Molitva" (Tsvetaeva) **14**:312
"Molitvy" (Lermontov) **18**:303
"Molly Means" (Walker) **20**:291-92
*En Mölna-elegi* (Ekeloef) **23**:50-8, 62-3, 77-87
*Molodets* (Tsvetaeva) **14**:313, 325-26
"Moly" (Gunn) **26**:
*Moly* (Gunn) **26**:192, 196-197, 203-204, 206-207, 209, 212, 214-215, 219, 221, 226, 228-229
"Moment" (Nemerov) **24**:264
"Moment" (Zagajewski) **27**:381, 396
"The Moment Cleary" (Kursh) **15**:179
"Moment of Eternity" (MacDiarmid) **9**:193
"Moments of Glory" (Jeffers) **17**:141
"Mon Dieu m'a dit" (Verlaine) **2**:415
"Mon Enfance" (Hugo) **17**:75
"Mon héroïsme, quelle farce" (Cesaire) **25**:56
"Monadnoc" (Emerson) **18**:71, 74, 102-3, 111
"Monarchs" (Olds) **22**:307
"Monax" (Pushkin) **10**:407
"Monday: Roxana; or The Drawing-room" (Montagu) **16**:338, 348
*La moneda de hierro* (Borges) **22**:96-7
"Monet's 'Waterlilies'" (Hayden) **6**:183, 195
"Money" (Nemerov) **24**:262, 281
"Money Goes Upstream" (Snyder) **21**:300
"Money, Honey, Money" (Walker) **20**:294
"Mongo" (Lermontov) **18**:281
"Mongolian Idiot" (Shapiro) **25**:300, 325
"La monja gitana" (Garcia Lorca) **3**:132
"La monja y el ruiseñor" (Dario) **15**:107-08
"The Monk" (Pushkin)
    See "Monax"
"The Monkeys" (Moore) **4**:270
*The Monkey's Cloak* (Matsuo Basho)
    See *Sarumino*
*The Monkey's Raincoat* (Matsuo Basho)
    See *Sarumino*
"Monk's Tale" (Chaucer) **19**:13, 42, 45, 56, 63

"The Monk's Walk" (Dunbar) **5**:121, 137-38, 141
"Monna Innominata" (Rossetti) **7**:271, 275, 280-1
"Le monocle de mon oncle" (Stevens) **6**:292, 295, 303, 327
"Monody" (Zukofsky) **11**:368
"Monody on the Death of Chatterton" (Coleridge) **11**:49, 52
*The Monogram* (Elytis) **21**:123
"The Monoliths" (Momaday) **25**:219
"Monologo de Domingo" (Alegria) **26**:
"Monotone" (Sandburg) **2**:303
"Mont Blanc" (Shelley) **14**:206, 211-12, 217, 241
"Le mont des Oliviers" (Vigny) **26**:367-68, 370, 380, 383, 385, 391, 401, 412
*Montage of a Dream Deferred* (Hughes) **1**:244-45, 247-48, 251, 253, 258, 261, 263, 265-68, 270
"The Montain Village of Bastundzhi" (Lermontov)
    See "The Montain Village of Bastundzhi"
"Montcalm" (Davie) **29**:96
"A Month among Children" (Montale)
    See "Un mese fra i bambini"
"The Months: A Pageant" (Rossetti) **7**:280
"Montparnasse" (Apollinaire) **7**:34
*La Montre; or, The Lover's Watch* (Behn) **13**:3
*Une montre sentimentale* (Nishiwaki) **15**:237
"The Monument" (Bishop) **3**:37, 41-3, 48-9, 72
"Monument" (Pushkin)
    See "Pamjatnik"
"Monument Mountain" (Bryant) **20**:14, 29, 47
"Monument of Love" (Jimenez) **7**:184
"Mood" (Cullen) **20**:63, 75
"The moon" (Borges)
    See "La luna"
"The Moon" (Carruth) **10**:71
*Moon Across The Way*
    See *Luna de enfrente*
*Moon across the Way* (Borges)
    See *Luna de enfrente*
"Moon and Insect Panorama: Love Poem" (Garcia Lorca) **3**:141
"The Moon and the Yew Tree" (Plath) **1**:390, 409
"The Moon Being the Number 19" (Wakoski) **15**:364
*Moon Crossing Bridge* (Gallagher) **9**:62-5
"The Moon Explodes in Autumn as a Milkweed Pod" (Wakoski) **15**:364
"The Moon Has a Complicated Geography" (Wakoski) **15**:364
"The Moon in Your Hands" (H. D.) **5**:275
"The Moon is Always Female" (Piercy) **29**:311
*The Moon Is Always Female* (Piercy) **29**:311, 323
"The Moon Is the Number Eighteen" (Olson) **19**:293-94, 321
"Moon Lines, after Jiminez" (Ondaatje) **28**:335
"Moon Poems" (Lindsay) **23**:281
"Moon Tiger" (Levertov) **11**:177
"Moonlight" (Apollinaire)
    See "Clair de lune"
"Moonlight" (Harjo) **27**:56
"Moonlight" (Verlaine)
    See "Clair de lune"
"Moonlight and Jellyfish" (Hagiwara Sakutaro) **18**:168
"Moonlight Night" (Tu Fu) **9**:321
"Moonlight Night: Carmel" (Hughes) **1**:240
"Moonrise" (Plath) **1**:406
"Moonrise" (Sappho) **5**:416
"The Moon's Funeral" (Belloc) **24**:49
"Moon-Set" (Carruth) **10**:85
"Moonset Glouster" (Olson) **19**:322-23
"Moonstruck" (MacDiarmid) **9**:160
*The Moor of Peter the Great* (Pushkin)
    See *Arap Petra Velikogo*
"Moortown" (Hughes) **7**:162
*Moortown* (Hughes) **7**:157-58, 162-63, 165, 171

"The Moose" (Bishop) **3**:58-60, 73, 75
"The Moose Wallow" (Hayden) **6**:194-95
*A Moral Alphabet* (Belloc) **24**:16-18, 26
*Moral Essays* (Pope) **26**:320, 340
*Moral Tales* (Laforgue)
    See *Moralités légendaires*
"Morale" (Gautier) **18**:158
*Moralités légendaires* (Laforgue) **14**:70
"Morality" (Arnold) **5**:42
"Un morceau en forme de poire" (Wakoski) **15**:372
*Morceaux choisis* (Tzara) **27**:223-4
"More" (Stein) **18**:319, 330
*More Beasts—For Worse Children* (Belloc) **24**:24-6, 35
"More Clues" (Rukeyser) **12**:225
"More Foreign Cities" (Tomlinson) **17**:318
*More Peers* (Belloc) **24**:26-7, 41, 43, 49
*More Poems* (Housman) **2**:167, 171-74, 176, 182-83, 188
*More Poems, 1961* (Graves) **6**:154-56
*More Poems to Solve* (Swenson) **14**:276
"More Than a Fool's Song" (Cullen) **20**:57
"Mori no michi" (Ishikawa) **10**:213
"Mori no omoide" (Ishikawa) **10**:212-13
"Moriturus" (Millay) **6**:236
"Morning" (Gluck) **16**:152
"Morning" (Wheatley)
    See "An Hymn to the Morning"
"Morning" (Williams) **7**:352
"Morning After" (Hughes) **1**:256
"The Morning Baking" (Forche) **10**:142
"The Morning Bell" (Ishikawa)
    See "Akatsuki no kane"
"Morning Exercises" (Cassian) **17**:11
"Morning Express" (Sassoon) **12**:275
"A Morning Imagination of Russia" (Williams) **7**:350
"The Morning News" (Berry) **28**:11
"Morning, Noon, and Night" (Page) **12**:173
"A Morning Ride" (Kipling) **3**:194
"Morning Song" (Plath) **1**:390
"The Morning Song of Lord Zero" (Aiken) **26**:15, 24
*Morning Songs* (Tagore)
    See *Prabhat sangit*
"The Morning Star" (Pavese)
    See "Lo steddazzu"
"Morning, the Horizon" (Ortiz) **17**:245
"The Morning They Shot Tony Lopez" (Soto) **28**:375
"A Morning Wake among Dead" (Kinnell) **26**:256-57
"Morning-Land" (Sassoon) **12**:240
"Mornings in a New House" (Merrill) **28**:221
"Mornings in various years" (Piercy) **29**:315
"Mors" (Hugo) **17**:83
"Morskaya tsarevna" (Lermontov) **18**:292
"La Mort dans la vie" (Gautier) **18**:131, 155
"La Mort de Narcisse" (Ronsard) **11**:251
"La mort des amants" (Baudelaire) **1**:54, 73
"La mort des artistes" (Baudelaire) **1**:45
"Mort du duc de Berry" (Hugo) **17**:75
"La mort du loup" (Vigny) **26**:367, 369-70, 380-81, 401-402, 412-15
"La Mort du Soldat est près des choses naturelles" (5 MarsStevens) **6**:294
*La mort en ce jardin* (Bunuel) **15**:207, 218
"Le mort joyeux" (Baudelaire) **1**:45
"La mort rose" (Breton) **15**:52
*Mortal Acts, Mortal Words* (Kinnell) **26**:257, 260-61, 271, 280, 292
"Mortal Enemy" (Parker) **28**:362
"Mortal Girl" (Rukeyser) **12**:231
"Morte d'Arthur" (Tennyson) **6**:354, 358-59, 409
*La morte de Socrate* (Lamartine) **16**:263, 266, 273, 278-79, 291
"La morte di Dio" (Montale) **13**:133
"I morti" (Montale) **13**:105, 112
"Mortification" (Herbert) **4**:100-01, 120, 127, 133

"Mortmain" (Robinson) **1**:470
"Morts de quatre-vingt-douze et de quatre-vingt-treize" (Rimbaud) **3**:283
*Moscow Notebooks* (Mandelstam) **14**:150
"Moses" (Nemerov) **24**:295
"Moses" (Shapiro) **25**:296
*Moses: A Story of the Nile* (Harper) **21**:185, 187-89, 191-98, 201
"Mossbawn: Sunlight" (Heaney) **18**:197, 232
"The Most of It" (Frost) **1**:205-06, 230-31
"Most Things at Second Hand through Gloves We Touch" (Schwartz) **8**:293
"Most wretched heart" (Wyatt) **27**:353
"Mostly Hospital and Old Age" (Viereck) **27**:294
"Mostru o pavea" (Pasolini) **17**:253
"Mot" (Cesaire) **25**:31
*Mot* (Cesaire) **25**:38
"The Motel" (Olds) **22**:341
"Motet" No. 1 (Montale) **13**:120-22
"Motet" No. 2 (Montale) **13**:120, 122
"Motet" No. 3 (Montale) **13**:118-20
"Motet" No. 4 (Montale) **13**:120
"Motet" No. 5 (Montale) **13**:118, 121-22, 125, 127
"Motet" No. 6 (Montale) **13**:121-22, 150
"Motet" No. 7 (Montale) **13**:119, 122
"Motet" No. 8 (Montale)
    See "Mottetto" No. 8
"Motet" No. 9 (Montale) **13**:119, 122-24
"Motet" No. 10 (Montale) **13**:123
"Motet" No. 11 (Montale) **13**:124-25
"Motet" No. 12 (Montale) **13**:124
"Motet" No. 13 (Montale) **13**:124
"Motet" No. 14 (Montale) **13**:124
"Motet" No. 15 (Montale) **13**:125
"Motet" No. 17 (Montale) **13**:125-26
"Motet" No. 18 (Montale) **13**:125, 127
"Motet" No. 19 (Montale) **13**:126
"Motet" No. 20 (Montale) **13**:126
"Motet XX" (Montale) **13**:136
"The Mother" (Brooks) **7**:67
"The Mother" (Olds) **22**:309
"Mother" (Smith) **12**:326
*The Mother* (Sitwell) **3**:299
"Mother, among the Dustbins" (Smith) **12**:352
"Mother and Daughter" (Sexton) **2**:365
"Mother and Poet" (Browning) **6**:30-1
"Mother Dear" (McKay) **2**:222
"Mother Earth: Her Whales" (Snyder) **21**:293, 297
"Mother Farewell!" (Johnson) **24**:145
"Mother Goose" (Rexroth) **20**:195, 218
"Mother Hubberd's Tale" (Spenser)
    See "Prosopopoia; or, Mother Hubberds Tale"
"mother i am mad" (Clifton) **17**:19
"Mother in Wartime" (Hughes) **1**:252
"Mother Marie Therese" (Lowell) **3**:205
"Mother Night" (Johnson) **24**:127, 137, 159, 166
"Mother of God I Shall Pray in Humility" (Lermontov) **18**:296
"Mother Rosarine" (Kumin) **15**:191
"Mother to Son" (Hughes) **1**:241, 248-49, 262
*Mother, What is Man?* (Smith) **12**:326
"Motherland" (Lermontov) **18**:281
"Mother of God" (Sikelianos) **29**:366
"Mother-Right" (Rich) **5**:384
"Mothers" (Giovanni) **19**:140
"The Mother's Blessing" (Harper) **21**:197
"A Mother's Heroism" (Harper) **21**:194, 206, 217
"The Mother's Story" (Clifton) **17**:29
"The Moth-Signal" (Hardy) **8**:99
"Motion and Rest" (Toomer) **7**:338
"Motion of wish" (Kunitz) **19**:160
"The Motions" (Ammons) **16**:5
"The Motive for Metaphor" (Stevens) **6**:312-13, 340
*Motivos de son* (Guillen) **23**:97-98, 104-108, 110, 133, 141-45

"Motor Lights on a Hill Road" (Lowell) **13**:60
"A Motorbike" (Hughes) **7**:162
*The Motorcycle Betrayal Poems* (Wakoski) **15**:325-26, 331-32, 345, 350, 363, 366, 369-70
"Motoring" (Brooke) **24**:68
"Motteti" (Montale) **13**:105
"Mottetto" No. 8 (Montale) **13**:105, 113, 122, 127
"Motto" (Hughes) **1**:267
"The Motto on the Sundial" (Rexroth) **20**:192
"Motto to the Songs of Innocence and of Experience" (Blake) **12**:10
"The Mound Builders" (Kunitz) **19**:158
"Mount Chungnan" (Wang Wei) **18**:362-63
"Mount Mary" (Wright) **14**:343
"The Mount of Olives" (Vigny)
    See "Le mont des Oliviers"
"Mount Zion" (Hughes) **7**:147
"th mountain" (Bissett) **14**:20
"The Mountain" (Frost) **1**:226
*Mountain Interval* (Frost) **1**:197, 202, 207, 215
"The Mountain Spirit" (Wang Wei) **18**:382
*Mountain Talk* (Ammons) **16**:14
"The Mountaineer's Ballard" (Wylie) **23**:311
"Mountains" (Auden) **1**:17
"Mountains" (Hayden) **6**:194, 196
"Mountains" (Hughes) **7**:137
*Mountains and Rivers without End* (Snyder) **21**:299
"A Mounted Umbrella" (Stein) **18**:334, 349
"The Mourner's Bench" (Masters) **1**:339, 343
"Mournin' for Religion" (Masters) **1**:344
"Mourning" (Marvell) **10**:271, 301, 314
"A Mourning Forbidding Valediction" (Ashbery) **26**:161
"The Mouse's Nest" (Clare) **23**:7
"The Mouth of the Hudson" (Lowell) **3**:215
"The Mouth of Truth" (Ferlinghetti) **1**:183
"Mouvement" (Tzara) **27**:227
"Move Un-noticed to be Noticed: A Nationhood Poem" (Madhubuti) **5**:345
"Movement to Establish My Identity" (Wakoski) **15**:350
"Movements" (Tomlinson) **17**:327
"Movements II" (Tomlinson) **17**:343
"Movements IV" (Tomlinson) **17**:326, 341
"Movies" (Hughes) **1**:266
"Moving Fred's Outhouse/Geriatrics of Pine" (Ondaatje) **28**:335
"The Moving Image" (Wright) **14**:337, 362
*The Moving Image* (Wright) **14**:334-35, 338-41, 345-51, 353, 357, 368
"Moving South" (Wright) **14**:373
"The Moving to Griffin" (Ondaatje) **28**:291
"The Mower against gardens" (Marvell) **10**:266, 293, 297
"The Mower to the Glo-Worms" (Marvell) **10**:266, 296-97, 315
"The Mower's Song" (Marvell) **10**:266, 296-97
*Moya Rodoslovnaya* (Pushkin) **10**:391
"Mozart, 1935" (Stevens) **6**:296
"Mozhet byt' eto tochka bezumiia" (Mandelstam) **14**:152
"Mr. Bleaney" (Larkin) **21**:228-29, 241, 247-48
"Mr. Brodsky" (Tomlinson) **17**:311, 353
"Mr. Burnshaw and the Statue" (Stevens) **6**:297, 321
"Mr. Edwards and the Spider" (Lowell) **3**:215
"Mr. Eliot's Sunday Morning Service" (Eliot) **5**:184
"Mr. Flood's Party" (Robinson) **1**:478
"Mr. Mine" (Sexton) **2**:352
"Mr. Nixon" (Pound) **4**:320
"Mr. Over" (Smith) **12**:297, 339
"Mr. Seurat's Sunday Afternoon" (Schwartz)
    See "Seurat's Sunday Afternoon along the Seine"
"Mr. Sludge, 'The Medium'" (Browning) **2**:72, 82
"Mr. Styrax" (Pound) **4**:317
"Mrs. Alfred Uruguay" (Stevens) **6**:304

"Mrs Arbuthnot" (Smith) **12**:314
"Mrs. Benjamin Pantier" (Masters) **1**:347
"Mrs. Mandrill" (Nemerov) **24**:259, 268
"Mrs Simpkins" (Smith) **12**:344
"Mrs. Small" (Brooks) **7**:62, 69, 96-8
"Mrs. Walpurga" (Rukeyser) **12**:204
"Mrs. Williams" (Masters) **1**:347
"Mtsiri" (Lermontov) **18**:282-83, 298, 302
"Muchacha recién crecida" (Guillen) **23**:126
"Mud" (Cassian) **17**:4
"Mud" (Kumin) **15**:182
"The Mud Turtle" (Nemerov) **24**:274
"The Mud Vision" (Heaney) **18**:227-28, 230, 237
"Muerte de Antoñito el Camborio" (Garcia Lorca) **3**:131
"Los Muertos" (Fuertes) **27**:12
"Mugging" (Ginsberg) **4**:85
"Mugitusque Boum" (Hugo) **17**:83
"Muiopotmos; or, the Fate of the Butterflie" (Spenser) **8**:365, 367-68, 371
"La mujer desnuda" (Jimenez) **7**:213-14
*La mujer desnuda* (1918-1923Jimenez) **7**:213
"Mujer nueva" (Guillen) **23**:105
"Mulata" (Guillen) **23**:110, 142
"Mulatto" (Hughes) **1**:238, 263-64, 270
"The Mulch" (Kunitz) **19**:159
"Mulholland's Contract" (Kipling) **3**:161
*Multitudes, Multitudes* (Clampitt) **19**:87-8
"Mummia" (Brooke) **24**:77
*Mundo a solas* (Aleixandre) **15**:3, 18-24, 32-3
"The Munich Mannequins" (Plath) **1**:384, 391
"The Municipal Gallery Revisited" (Yeats) **20**:322, 324
"The Murder" (Brooks) **7**:68
"The Murder" (Page) **12**:178
*The Murder of Lidice* (Millay) **6**:220
"The Murder of William Remington" (Nemerov) **24**:258, 280
"Murder Poem No. 74321" (Rexroth) **20**:187
"The Murdered Traveller" (Bryant) **20**:40
"The Murderess" (Gluck) **16**:126
*A Muriel Rukeyser Reader* (Rukeyser) **12**:234
*Museum* (Dove) **6**:104-07, 109, 115-16, 118, 121
"Museum Guards" (LondonStryk) **27**:214
"The Mushroom Gatherers" (Davie) **29**:95
"Mushrooms" (Atwood) **8**:43
"Mushrooms" (Plath) **1**:389, 404, 406, 408
"Mushrooms" (Tomlinson) **17**:334, 347, 354
"A Music" (Berry) **28**:4
"Music" (Herbert) **4**:100
"Music" (Pasternak)
    See "Muzyka"
"The Music of Poetry" (Kinnell) **26**:288
"The Music of Time" (Larkin) **21**:227
"Music Swims Back to Me" (Sexton) **2**:359
"A Musical Comedy Thought" (Parker) **28**:354
"A Musical Instrument" (Browning) **6**:23
"The Musical Voice" (Ishikawa)
    See "Gakusei"
"Musician" (Bogan) **12**:124
"Musicks Empire" (Marvell) **10**:313
"Musketaquid" (Emerson) **18**:88, 91, 111
"Mussel Hunter at Rock Harbour" (Plath) **1**:388, 407
"Mutabilitie Cantos" (Spenser)
    See "Cantos of Mutabilitie"
"Mutability" (Brooke) **24**:56-7, 72, 85
"Mutability" (Shelley) **14**:166
"Mutation" (Bryant) **20**:34, 44
"Mutra" (Paz) **1**:369
"Mutton" (Stein) **18**:323-24
"Mutual Trust" (Merrill) **28**:257
"Muzhestvo" (Akhmatova) **2**:19
"Muzyka" (Pasternak) **6**:288
"Mwilu/or Poem for the Living" (Madhubuti) **5**:346
"My Autumn Walk" (Bryant) **20**:5, 46
*My Best Poems* (Aleixandre) **15**:18
"My Bohemian Life" (Rimbaud)
    See "Ma bohème"

"My Cats" (Smith) **12**:339

"My City" (Johnson) **24**:144, 154

"My Comforter" (Burroughs) **8**:51

"My Corn-cob Pipe" (Dunbar) **5**:133

"My Cousin in April" (Gluck) **16**:154

"My Cousin Muriel" (Clampitt) **19**:97

"My Daughter the Junkie on a Train" (Lorde)
    See "To My Daughter the Junkie on a Train"

"My Daughter's Aquarium" (Stryk) **27**:204

"My Dear and Loving Husband" (Bradstreet)
    See "To My Dear and Loving Husband His Goeing into England"

"My delight and thy delight" (Bridges) **28**:70

"My Dove, My Beautiful One" (Joyce)
    See "XIV"

"My Doves" (Browning) **6**:21

"my dream about being white" (Clifton) **17**:36

"My Dreams Are a Field Afar" (Housman) **2**:182

"My Dreams, My Work, Must Wait till after Hell" (Brooks) **7**:74

"My Erotic Double" (Ashbery) **26**:133

"My Fairy Godmother" (Hyde) **7**:147

"My Father Moved through Dooms of Feel" (Cummings)
    See "My Father Moved through Dooms of Love"

"My Father Moved through Dooms of Love" (Cummings) **5**:81, 89

"My Father Speaks to Me from the Dead" (Olds) **22**:323, 325, 338

"My Father's Breasts" (Olds) **22**:328

"My Fathers Came from Kentucky" (Lindsay) **23**:265

"My Father's Eyes" (Olds) **22**:332

"My Father's Funeral" (Shapiro) **25**:305

"My Father's Irish Setters" (Merrill) **28**:284

"My First Weeks" (Olds) **22**:338

"My Friend" (Gibran) **9**:77

"My galley charged with forgetfulness" (Wyatt) **27**:323-324, 357-358

"My Garden" (Emerson) **18**:76, 88

*My Geneology* (Pushkin)
    See *Moya Rodoslovnaya*

"My Gentlest Song" (Viereck) **27**:263, 278, 281

"My Good-byes" (Alegria) **26**:

"My Grandmother's Love Letters" (Crane) **3**:98

"My Granny's Hieland Hame" (Burns) **6**:98

"My Grave" (Levine) **22**:228

"My Hat" (Smith) **12**:331

"My Heart and I" (Browning) **6**:23

"My Heart, Being Hungry" (Reese) **29**:332

"My Heart Goes Out" (Smith) **12**:318, 325

"My Heart Was Full" (Smith) **12**:333

"My Hermitage in the Bamboo Grove" (Wang Wei) **18**:358

"My Hero's Genealogy" (Pushkin)
    See "Rodoslovnaya Moego Geroya"

"My Honey" (Guillen)
    See "Mi chiquita"

"My House" (Giovanni) **19**:112-13, 116, 140, 142-43

*My House* (Giovanni) **19**:107, 110-14, 116, 118, 121-25, 136-37, 140-41, 144

"My Indigo" (Lee) **24**:240, 244

"My Kate" (Browning) **6**:23

"My Lady of the Castle Grand" (Dunbar) **5**:134, 138

"My Lady's Lamentation and Complaint against the Dean" (Swift) **9**:295-96

"My Lady's Lips Are Like de Honey" (Johnson) **24**:141

"My Last Afternoon with Uncle Devereux Winslow" (Lowell) **3**:219, 222

"My Last Duchess" (Browning) **2**:37, 94

"My Life with the Wave" (Paz) **1**:354

"My Light with Yours" (Masters) **1**:333

"My Little Lovers" (Rimbaud)
    See "Mes petites amoureuses"

"My Loved Subject" (Jeffers) **17**:131

"My lute awake" (Wyatt) **27**:328, 339, 349, 357, 362

"My Luve Is Like a Red, Red Rose" (Burns) **6**:75, 77, 99

"My most. My most. O my lost!" (Villa) **22**:349

"My Mother" (McGuckian) **27**:96

"My Mother Remembers That She Was Beautiful" (Gallagher) **9**:58

"My Mother Would Be a Falconress" (Duncan) **2**:127

"My Mother's Life" (Meredith) **28**:182

*My mothers maydes* (Wyatt) **27**:304, 371

"My Mountain Home" (McKay) **2**:222

"My Muse" (Montale)
    See "La mia musa"

"My Muse" (Smith) **12**:312, 324, 336

"My Native Land" (Lermontov) **18**:297

"My Native Land, My Home" (McKay) **2**:216, 224

"My New-Cut Ashlar" (Kipling) **3**:183

"My Own" (Parker) **28**:350-51

"My Own Sweet Good" (Brooks) **7**:55

"My Paradise in Mallorca" (Alegria) **26**:

"My pen take payn" (Wyatt) **27**:339, 341

"My People" (Hughes) **1**:270

"My Poem" (Giovanni) **19**:111

"My Poets" (Levine) **22**:212

"My Portrait" (Pushkin) **10**:407

"My Pretty Dan" (McKay) **2**:221

"My Pretty Rose Tree" (Blake) **12**:34

"My Sad Captains" (Gunn) **26**:186, 197

"My Sad Captains" (Gunn) **26**:

*My Sad Captains, and Other Poems* (Gunn) **26**:181, 186, 189, 194-195, 197, 201-202, 207, 209, 211, 216, 218-219, 221, 223, 225-226

*My Sad Captains Touch* (Gunn) **26**:

"My Shy Hand" (Owen) **19**:336

"My Silks in Fine Array" (Blake) **12**:31

*My Sister, Life* (Pasternak)
    See *Sestra moia zhizn*

"My Soldier Lad" (McKay) **2**:223

"My Song" (Brooke) **24**:62, 72, 76

"My Songs" (Yosano Akiko)
    See "Waga Uta"

"My Sort of Man" (Dunbar) **5**:131

"My Soul" (Bradstreet) **10**:60-1

"My Soul Accused Me" (Dickinson) **1**:94

"My soul is dark" (Lermontov) **18**:202

"My Spectre around Me" (Blake) **12**:13

"My spirit kisseth thine" (Bridges) **28**:85

"My Spirit Will Not Haunt the Mound" (Hardy) **8**:118

"My Star" (Browning) **2**:59

"My sweet Ann Foot my bonny Ann" (Clare) **23**:25

"My Sweet Brown Gal" (Dunbar) **5**:119

"My Trip in a Dream to the Lady of Heaven Mountain: A Farewell to Several Gentlemen of Eastern Lu" (Li Po) **29**:153

"My Vegetarian Friend" (Eliot) **20**:123

"My Voice Not Being Proud" (Bogan) **12**:101, 120

"Mycerinus" (Arnold) **5**:13, 33-4, 37, 39, 48

"Mye Love toke Skorne" (Wyatt) **27**:316

"My-ness" (Milosz) **8**:179

"Myopia: A Night" (Lowell) **3**:215

"Myrtho" (Nerval) **13**:180

"Myself Was Formed—a Carpenter" (Dickinson) **1**:96

"Le mystère des trois cors" (Laforgue) **14**:73

"The Mysteries" (H. D.) **5**:305

"'Mystery Boy' Looks for Kin in Nashville" (Hayden) **6**:196

"The Mystic" (Noyes) **27**:138

*Mysticism for Beginners* (Zagajewski) **27**:396, 398-401

*Mystics and Zen Masters* (Merton) **10**:352

"Mystique" (Rimbaud) **3**:260

"Myth" (Pavese)
    See "Mito"

"Myth" (Rukeyser) **12**:228

*The Myth-Making Uncles* (Alegria) **26**:

"A Mythology Reflects its Region" (Stevens) **6**:306

*Myths and Texts* (Snyder) **21**:290-92, 297, 299, 322

*N. 4* (Pindar)
    See *Nemean 4*

*N. 7* (Pindar)
    See *Nemean 7*

*N. 9* (Pindar)
    See *Nemean 9*

"A na fruta" (Pasolini) **17**:274-77

"Na krasnom kone" (Tsvetaeva) **14**:315

*Na rannikh poezdakh* (Pasternak) **6**:282

"The Nabara" (Day Lewis) **11**:127, 130-31, 144

"Nachlied" (Trakl) **20**:259

*Nachtgesänge* (Holderlin) **4**:142, 146, 148, 166

"nachts wird kälter" (Enzensberger) **28**:140

"Nachwort" (Heine) **25**:172-75, 177, 179

"Naci en una buhardilla" (Fuertes) **27**:49

"Nací para poeta o para muerto" (Fuertes) **27**:49

"Nacimiento de Cristo" (Garcia Lorca) **3**:141

*Nacimiento último* (Aleixandre) **15**:9, 16

"Nada" (Jimenez) **7**:202

"Nadezhdoi Sladostnoi" (Pushkin) **10**:412

"Nadgrobie" (Tsvetaeva) **14**:325, 327

"Nadie" (Guillen) **23**:125

"Nafsī muthqa ah bi athmāriha" (Gibran) **9**:82

"Nah, im Aortenbogen" (Celan) **10**:101

"Nähe des Todes" (Trakl) **20**:248

"La naîade" (Gautier) **18**:141

"The Nail" (Hughes) **7**:143

"Naissance du duc de Bordeaux" (Hugo) **17**:75

"The naïve person" (Borges)
    See "El ingenuo"

"A Naive Poem" (Milosz)
    See "The World"

*Naivedya* (Tagore) **8**:411-13

"Naked and Essential" (Montale) **13**:141

"Naked Girl and Mirror" (Wright) **14**:356, 362

"A Name for All" (Crane) **3**:90, 104

"The Name I Call You" (Piercy) **29**:311, 315

"Nameless" (Pasternak)
    See "Bez nazvaniya"

"Nameless Flower" (Wright) **14**:347, 379

"Names" (Hayden) **6**:194

*The Names of the Lost* (Levine) **22**:223-24

"The Nana-Hex" (Sexton) **2**:365

"Nancy" (Wylie) **23**:301, 318-19, 324

"The Nape of the Neck" (Graves) **6**:166

"Napoleon na El'be" (Pushkin) **10**:409, 421

"Napoleon on the Elba" (Pushkin)
    See "Napoleon na El'be"

"Naprasno glazom kak gvozdem" (Tsvetaeva) **14**:325

"När man kommit så långt" (Ekeloef) **23**:76

"Narcisse parle" (Valery) **9**:350, 356, 363, 365, 385, 392, 395

"Narcissus Speaks" (Valery)
    See "Narcisse parle"

"Narikel" (Tagore) **8**:416

*Narraciones* (Garcia Lorca) **3**:148

"Narrative" (Stein) **18**:313

"A Narrow Escape" (Merrill) **28**:239, 243

*The Narrow Pond* (Matsuo Basho)
    See *Oku no hosomichi*

*The Narrow Road to the Deep North* (Matsuo Basho)
    See *Oku no hosomichi*

"I nascondigli" (Montale) **13**:138

"Nashedshij podkovu" (Mandelstam) **14**:121, 125, 130

"Nasturtium" (Gunn) **26**:

"The Nation Is Like Ourselves" (Baraka) **4**:19

"Nationality in Drinks" (Browning) **2**:59

"The Native Born" (Kipling) **3**:161-62

"A Native Hill" (Berry) **28**:39

*Native Land* (Blok) **21**:16

*Native Land* (Rich)
    See *Your Native Land, Your Life*

"A Nativity" (Yeats) **20**:319

"A Nativity" (1914-18 Kipling) **3**:183, 189

"Nativity Ode" (Milton)
   See "On the Morning of Christ's Nativity"
"Nativity Poem" (Gluck) **16**:125, 141
"Natrabach i na cytrze" (Milosz) **8**:186, 214
"Natural Music" (Jeffers) **17**:134-35
*Natural Numbers: New and Selected Poems*
   (Rexroth) **20**:209
"Natural Resources" (Rich) **5**:374, 380, 384-85
"Naturally" (Gallagher) **9**:43
"Naturally the Foundation Will Bear Your
   Expenses" (Larkin) **21**:223
"Nature" (Masters) **1**:336
"Nature II" (Emerson) **18**:102
"Nature and Free Animals" (Smith) **12**:323
"Nature morte" (Brodsky) **9**:4, 12
"The Nature of an Action" (Gunn) **26**:185
"Nature Poem" (Tomlinson) **17**:345, 348
*Nature: Poems Old and New* (Swenson) **14**:283,
   287-88
"Nature that gave the bee so feet a grace"
   (Wyatt) **27**:346-47
"Nature's Lineaments" (Graves) **6**:150-51
"Nature's Questioning" (Hardy) **8**:96
"Navidad en el Hudson" (Garcia Lorca) **3**:141
"Ne muchnistoi babochkoiu beloi"
   (Mandelstam) **14**:152, 156
"Ne Plus Ultra" (Coleridge) **11**:52
"Ne sravnivai: zhivushchii nesravnim"
   (Mandelstam) **14**:154
"Neap-tide" (Swinburne) **24**:313, 341, 343
"Near, as All That Is Lost" (Gallagher) **9**:64
"Near Keokuk" (Sandburg) **2**:332
"Near Lanivet, 1872" (Hardy) **8**:97, 125-26
"Near Mullingar" (Davie)
   See "1977, Near Mullingar"
"Near the Ocean" (Lowell) **3**:226-28, 233
*Near the Ocean* (Lowell) **3**:232
"Nearness of Death" (Trakl)
   See "Nähe des Todes"
"Nebraska" (Shapiro) **25**:313
*Necessities of Life: Poems, 1962-1965* (Rich)
   **5**:356, 363-64, 370-71, 382, 388-89, 397
"The Neckan" (Arnold) **5**:12
*The Necklace* (Tomlinson) **17**:299, 302-04, 317-
   18, 320-22, 327, 334-35, 341
"The Necktie and the Watch" (Apollinaire)
   See "La cravate et la montre"
"Necropolis" (Shapiro) **25**:279, 297, 318
"Need: A Chorale for Black Women's Voices"
   (Lorde) **12**:144, 154, 156, 158
"The Need of Being Versed in Country
   Things" (Frost) **1**:229, 231
"A Needed Poem for My Salvation" (Sanchez)
   **9**:208-09
"Negro bembón" (Guillen) **23**:98, 142
"Un negro canta en Nueva York" (Guillen)
   **23**:127
"A Negro Cemetery Next to a White One"
   (Nemerov) **24**:281
"Negro Dancers" (Hughes) **1**:236
"The Negro Hero" (Brooks) **7**:86
"A Negro Love Song" (Dunbar) **5**:132, 142
"Negro Mask" (Senghor) **25**:227-30
*The Negro of Peter the Great* (Pushkin)
   See *Arap Petra Velikogo*
"Negro Servant" (Hughes) **1**:247
"Negro Song" (Guillen) **23**:131
"A Negro Speaks of Rivers" (Hughes) **1**:241-
   42, 248, 258-59, 263, 268
"Negro Spiritual" (McKay) **2**:214
*Nehez fold* (Illyes) **16**:233, 238-39, 245
"La neige" (Vigny) **26**:401-402, 410-11
"Neige sur Paris" (Senghor) **25**:239
"Neiges" (Perse) **23**:213, 216-18, 220-21, 232,
   234, 250, 253, 256-57
"Neither Out Far nor in Deep" (Frost) **1**:197,
   218, 227-28
"Neither Sweet Pity, nor Lamentable Weeping"
   (Ronsard)
   See "Ny la douce pitie, ny le pleur
   lamentable"
"Neither Wanting More" (Swenson) **14**:284

"Neko" (Hagiwara Sakutaro) **18**:181
"Neko no shigai" (Hagiwara Sakutaro) **18**:182
"Nel Mezzo del Commin di Nostra Vita"
   (Duncan) **2**:103
"Nel parco di Caserta" (Montague) **13**:
"Nel parco di Caserta" (Montale) **13**:127
"Nel sonno" (Montale) **13**:107, 128, 150
"Nele de Kantule" (Cardenal) **22**:127, 132
"Nella serra" (Montale) **13**:110
"Nelly Meyers" (Ammons) **16**:5, 19
*Nem. IV* (Pindar)
   See *Nemean 4*
*Nem. VIII* (Pindar)
   See *Nemean 8*
*Nemean 1* (Pindar) **19**:398, 412
*Nemean 2* (Pindar) **19**:425
*Nemean 3* (Pindar) **19**:425
*Nemean 4* (Pindar) **19**:387, 391
*Nemean V* (Pindar)
   See *Nemean 5*
*Nemean 5* (Pindar) **19**:388, 420, 424
*Nemean 7* (Pindar) **19**:388, 413, 425
*Nemean 8* (Pindar) **19**:388, 413, 420, 425
*Nemean 9* (Pindar) **19**:405, 425
*Nemean 10* (Pindar) **19**:398, 405, 412
*Nemean 11* (Pindar) **19**:405
"Les Néréides" (Gautier) **18**:129, 141
"The Nereids of Seriphos" (Clampitt) **19**:92
"Nerve Gas part II" (Bissett) **14**:7
"Nestor's Bathtub" (Dove) **6**:109
*Nets to Catch the Wind* (Wylie) **23**:300-301,
   306, 309, 311, 324-34
*Netzahualcóyotl* (Cardenal) **22**:128, 130-31
*Neue Gedichte* (Heine) **25**:129-132
*Neue Gedichte* (Rilke) **2**:266-68, 275
*Der neue Pausias und sein Blumenmädchen*
   (Goethe) **5**:239-40
*Neuer Frühling* (Heine)
"The Neurotic" (Day Lewis) **11**:147
"Neutral Tones" (Hardy) **8**:88, 126, 130
"Never Again Would Birds' Song Be the
   Same" (Frost) **1**:231
"Never Such Love" (Graves) **6**:137
"Never to Dream of Spiders" (Lorde) **12**:143
"The New Age" (Smith) **12**:313, 316
"The New America" (Blok) **21**:8, 26, 29
*New and Collected Poems* (Soto) **28**:404
*New and Selected* (Viereck) **27**:275, 279, 280-
   82, 284
*New and Selected Poems* (Meredith) **28**:210,
   215
*New and Selected Poems* (Nemerov) **24**:258,
   260, 262, 264, 266, 268, 284, 286
*New and Selected Poems, 1940-1986* (Shapiro)
   **25**:318-22
*New and Selected Things Taking Place*
   (Swenson) **14**:274, 277, 280-81, 287
*New Cautionary Tales* (Belloc) **24**:27
*New Collected Poems* (Graves) **6**:166
"A New Day" (Levine) **22**:223-24
*New Desire* (Hagiwara Sakutaro)
   See *New Desire*
"New Grown Girl" (Guillen)
   See "New Grown Girl"
"New Hampshire" (Eliot) **5**:166, 169
*New Hampshire* (Frost) **1**:215, 224
"New Heavens for Old" (Lowell) **13**:85, 88
"The New Islands" (Bombal)
   See "The New Islands"
"New Koide Road" (Hagiwara Sakutaro)
   See "Koide shidō"
"New Legends" (Graves) **6**:149
*New Life* (Dante)
   See *La vita nuova*
"The New Little Larousse" (Zagajewski) **27**:401
"The New Love" (Parker) **28**:356
*A New Lovesong for Stalingrad* (Neruda)
   See *Nuevo canto de amor a Stalingrado*
"New Morality" (Coleridge) **11**:102-03
"New Mother" (Olds) **22**:312
"New Objectives, New Cadres" (Rexroth)
   **20**:215

"New Orleans" (Harjo) **27**:65
"New Orleans 30 Oct 71" (Brutus) **24**:124
*New Poems* (Arnold) **5**:12, 43, 50
*New Poems* (Bridges) **28**:51, 67, 69
*New Poems* (Heine)
   See *Neue Gedichte*
*New Poems* (Montale) **13**:143-46
*New Poems* (Rexroth) **20**:197, 204
*New Poems* (Rilke)
   See *Neue Gedichte*
*New Poems* (Rilke) **2**:280-81
*New Poems, 1962* (Graves) **6**:154
"A New Psalm for the Chapel of Kilmarnock"
   (Burns) **6**:89
"A New Reality Is Better Than a New Movie!"
   (Baraka) **4**:30
"A New Record" (Duncan) **2**:103
"The New Saddhus" (Pinsky) **27**:176
"New Season" (Levine) **22**:223
*New Selected Poems* (Levine) **22**:220-221, 223-
   24, 226, 228
"The New Sheriff" (Baraka) **4**:10, 15
"The New Sirens" (Arnold) **5**:5, 39
"A New Song" (Heaney) **18**:202, 241
*A New Song* (Hughes) **1**:242, 250, 253-54, 268
"The New Spirit" (Ashbery) **26**:108, 130, 169-
   170
*The New Spoon River* (Masters) **1**:333-34,
   344-45
"New Stanzas" (Montale)
   See "Nuove stanze"
"New Stanzas to Augusta" (Brodsky)
   See "Novye stansy k Avguste"
"A New Story" (Ortiz) **17**:234
"New Thoughts on Old Subjects" (Coleridge)
   **11**:105
"The New Woman" (Guillen)
   See "Mujer nueva"
"New World" (Momaday) **25**:199, 216
*The New World* (Masters) **1**:339
*New Year Letter* (Auden) **1**:16, 21, 23-24, 34
"The New Yeares Gift, or Circumcision Song"
   (Herrick)
   See "Another New-yeeres Gift; or song for
   the Circumcision"
"New Year's Dawn, 1947" (Jeffers) **17**:141
"New Year's Eve" (Hardy) **8**:104, 119
"New Year's Eve 1959" (Kursh) **15**:224
"New Year's Gift" (Herrick)
   See "A New-Yeares Gift Sent to Sir
   Simeon Steward"
"New Year's Greetings" (Tsvetaeva)
   See "Novogodnee"
"New York" (Gunn) **26**:209, 220
"New York" (Senghor) **25**:255
"New York" (Viereck) **27**:274
"New York 1962: Fragment" (Lowell) **3**:215
"New York at Night" (Lowell) **13**:79
"New York City 1970" (Lorde) **12**:146, 158
*The New York Head Shop and Museum*
   (Lorde) **12**:146-47, 154
"New York in August" (Davie) **29**:97, 110
"New York: Office and Denunciation" (Garcia
   Lorca)
   See "Nueva York: Oficina y denuncia"
"The New York Times" (Kumin) **15**:200
"The New Yorkers" (Giovanni) **19**:142
*The New Youth* (Pasolini)
   See *La nuova gioventù*
"New Zealand Poems" (Wright) **14**:377
"Newborn Girl-Child" (Guillen) **23**:132
"Newcomer" (Okigbo) **7**:233, 240
"News for the Delphic Oracle" (Yeats) **20**:312-
   13, 316, 334-35
"News from Mount Amiata" (Montale)
   See "Notizie dall'Amiata"
"News from the Cabin" (Swenson) **14**:253-54
"News Item" (Parker) **28**:347, 359
"Newspaper Readers" (Tsvetaeva)
   See "Chitateli gazet"
"Newsreel: Man and Firing Squad" (Atwood)
   **8**:23

"A New-Yeares Gift Sent to Sir Simeon Steward" (Herrick) **9**:102, 145
"A New-yeares gift. To the King" (Carew) **29**:52
"Next!" (Nash) **21**:270
*Next: New Poems* (Clifton) **17**:24, 26-28, 35-36
"Next, Please" (Larkin) **21**:226-27, 230, 235, 242, 246
*The Next Room of the Dream* (Nemerov) **24**:259, 262, 264, 266, 289
"Next to of Course God America I" (Cummings) **5**:89
*Next-to-Last Things: New Poems and Essays* (Kunitz) **19**:186
"Nezabudka" (Lermontov) **18**:188-89
"Nezdeshnii vecher" (Tsvetaeva) **14**:
*Ni tiro* (Fuertes) **27**:17
*Ni tiro ni veneno* (Fuertes) **27**:16
"Niagara" (Lindsay) **23**:275
"Nicaraguan canto" (Cardenal)
    See "Canto nacional"
"A nice day" (Bukowski) **18**:23
"A Nice Shady Home" (Stevens) **6**:292
"Nick and the Candlestick" (Plath) **1**:390
"Nicodemus" (Robinson) **1**:476, 485
*Die Niemandsrose* (Celan) **10**:95, 98-99, 113, 117, 121
"Nieve" (Guillen) **23**:109
"Nigerian Unity/or Little Niggers Killing Little Niggers" (Madhubuti) **5**:329, 341-42
"Nigger" (Sanchez) **9**:223, 232
"Nigger" (Shapiro) **25**:270
*The Nigger of Peter the Great* (Pushkin)
    See *Arap Petra Velikogo*
"Nigger Song: An Odyssey" (Dove) **6**:105;
"Nigger's Leap: New England" (Wright) **14**:335-36, 338, 340, 349-50, 368, 374
"Niggy the Ho" (Baraka) **4**:29, 38
"Night" (Blake) **12**:7-8, 23, 33, 61
"Night" (Bogan) **12**:96, 104
"Night" (Celan) **10**:112
"Night" (Giovanni) **19**:141
"Night" (Jeffers) **17**:107, 131, 145
"Night" (Pasternak)
    See "Noch'"
"Night" (Pavese)
    See "La notte"
"Night" (Rilke) **2**:275
"Night, a street, a lamp, a chemist's" (Blok)
    See "Noch' ulitsa fonar' apteka'"
"Night and the Child" (Wright) **14**:352
"Night Bear Which Frightened Cattle" (Atwood) **8**:39
"The Night Before" (Robinson) **1**:460
"The Night before Great Babylon" (Sitwell) **3**:310
"The Night Dances" (Plath) **1**:388, 390
"Night, Death, Mississippi" (Hayden) **6**:194, 196
"Night, Four Songs" (Hughes) **1**:240
"The Night Game" (Pinsky) **27**:159, 176
"Night Hours" (Blok) **21**:5
"Night in Maine" (Lowell) **3**:226
"Night in the Forest" (Kinnell) **26**:240
"Night in the Old Home" (Hardy) **8**:105
"The Night Is Freezing Fast" (Housman)
    See "Last Poems: XX—The Night Is Freezing Fast"
"The Night Journey" (Brooke) **24**:60
"Night Journey" (Roethke) **15**:246
"Night Launch" (Kumin) **15**:209
"Night Letter" (Kunitz) **19**:154, 157, 161, 169
"The Night My Father Got Me" (Housman) **2**:191
"Night of Sine" (Senghor)
    See "Nuit de Sine"
"Night Operations Coastal Command RAF" (Nemerov) **24**:287
"Night Out" (Harjo) **27**:55
"Night Piece" (Heaney) **18**:201, 217
"A Night Piece" (Smart) **13**:341, 347

"Night Pleasures" (Pavese)
    See "Piaceri notturni"
"Night Practice" (Swenson) **14**:266
"Night Shift" (Plath) **1**:388
"Night Song" (Gluck) **16**:145-47
"Night Song of an Asiatic Wandering Shepherd" (Montale)
    See "Canto notturno di un pastore errante nell'Asia"
"Night Taxi" (Gunn) **26**:231
"Night Thoughts" (Smith) **12**:337
"Night Train" (Hagiwara Sakutaro)
    See "Yogisha"
"Night Transfigured" (Tomlinson) **17**:319, 342
"Night Visits with the Family" (Swenson) **14**:281
"A Night with a Friend" (Li Po) **29**:146
"The Night-Blooming Cereus" (Hayden) **6**:194-95, 198
*The Night-Blooming Cereus* (Hayden) **6**:182, 184, 187, 190, 194
"Nightbreak" (Rich) **5**:358
"Night-Flowering Cactus" (Merton) **10**:334
"The Nightingale" (Coleridge) **11**:85, 106
"The Nightingale" (Finch)
    See "To the Nightingale"
"Nightingale" (Keats)
    See "Ode to a Nightingale"
"The Nightingale" (Marie de France)
    See "Laüstic"
"The Nightingale Garden" (Blok) **21**:20
*The Nightingale of the Catholic Church* (Pasolini)
    See *L'usignuolo della Chiesa Cattolica*
"Nightingales" (Bridges) **28**:64, 66, 70, 75-6
"The Nightingales" (Williams) **7**:345
"The Nightingales Nest" (Clare) **23**:4-5
"Nightmare" (Kumin) **15**:198
"Nightmare" (Lowell) **13**:78
"Nightmare" (Page) **12**:168
*The Nightmare Factory* (Kumin) **15**:190, 200, 208
"Nightmare in Chinandega" (Alegria) **26**:
"Night-Music" (Rukeyser) **12**:209, 211
"Nightpiece" (Joyce) **22**:
"Night-Piece" (Kunitz) **19**:148, 153
"Night-Piece" (Sassoon) **12**:240
"The Night-Piece to Julia" (Herrick) **9**:94, 132
"Nights and Days" (Rich) **5**:375
*Nights and Days* (Merrill) **28**:220, 225-28, 230-32, 234, 240, 250, 252-54, 281
"Nightsong: City" (Brutus) **24**:113
*Nightsongs* (Holderlin)
    See *Nachtgesänge*
"Night-Time in the Cemetery" (Smith) **12**:316
"The Nihilist as Hero" (Lowell) **3**:229
"Nikki-Rosa" (Giovanni) **19**:139
"Nilamanilata" (Tagore) **8**:416
"Nimmo" (Robinson) **1**:468
"Nimrod in September" (Sassoon) **12**:278
"Nina Replies" (Rimbaud)
    See "Les reparties de Nina"
"IX" (Joyce) **22**:160, 167
"Nine Lives" (Merrill) **28**:283
"Nine Poems for the Unborn Child" (Rukeyser) **12**:228
"Nine Sleep Valley" (Merrill) **28**:254-55
"Nine Variations in a Chinese Winter Setting" (Tomlinson) **17**:299, 331
"Nine Verses of the Same Song" (Berry) **28**:5
"XIX" (Joyce) **22**:145, 169, 171
"MCMXIV" (Larkin) **21**:229, 234
"1914" (Owen) **19**:352
*1914, and Other Poems* (Brooke) **24**:61, 63, 80, 85, 87-8
*1921-1925* (Mandelstam) **14**:151, 155
"Nineteen Hundred and Nineteen" (Yeats) **20**:314, 325, 350-51
"1909" (Apollinaire) **7**:46-7
"1963" (Dove) **6**:106
"The Nineteenth Century and After" (Yeats) **20**:314

*1933* (Levine) **22**:217-18, 223
*95 Poems* (Cummings) **5**:109-10
"96 Tears" (Hongo) **23**:199
*Ninfeas* (Jimenez) **7**:197, 199
"Ninth Elegy" (Rilke) **2**:281, 286-87
"Ninth Elegy: The Antagonists" (Rukeyser) **12**:223
*Ninth Nemean* (Pindar)
    See *Nemean 9*
"Ninth Psalm" (Sexton) **2**:367
*Ninth Pythian* (Pindar)
    See *Pythian 9*
"The Ninth Symphony of Beethoven Understood at Last as a Sexual Message" (Rich) **5**:360, 370
"Niobe in Distress for Her Children Slain by Apollo" (Wheatley) **3**:338, 355, 357-60
*Niobjeta ziemia* (Milosz) **8**:179, 211
"Nipping Pussy's Feet in Fun" (Smith) **12**:339
"Nirbhay" (Tagore) **8**:415
"Nirjharer svapnabhanga" (Tagore) **8**:406
"Niruddesh yatra" (Tagore) **8**:408
"Nishikigizuka" (Ishikawa) **10**:213
"Nitrate" (Levine) **22**:224
"Niwatori" (Hagiwara Sakutaro) **18**:174, 180
"Nixon's the One" (Meredith) **28**:176, 206
"No" (Stein) **18**:327
"No Believers in the Resurrection" (Mandelstam) **14**:120
"No Buyers: A Street Scene" (Hardy) **8**:101
"No Coward Soul Is Mine" (Bronte) **8**:51, 60, 69-70
"No dejan escribir" (Fuertes) **27**:49
"¿No hay salida?" (Paz) **1**:364
"No Hearing" (DiscoveringLowell) **3**:228
"No Man's Land" (Heaney) **18**:202
"No Matter, Never Mind" (Snyder) **21**:297
"No more" (Milosz) **8**:190, 193
"No More Ghosts" (Graves) **6**:132
"No More Marching" (Madhubuti) **5**:339
"No More Sacrifices" (Ortiz) **17**:223, 234
*No Nature: New and Selected Poems* (Snyder) **21**:324-25
"No One Remembers" (Levine) **22**:223
"No One Sentence" (Stein) **18**:313
*The No One's Rose* (Celan)
    See *Die Niemandsrose*
"No Possum, No Sop, No Taters" (Stevens) **6**:302
"No Resurrection" (Jeffers) **17**:141
"No Road" (Larkin) **21**:230, 235
"No Sanctuary" (Heaney) **18**:202
"No sé por qué piensas tú" (Guillen) **23**:140
"No Speech from the Scaffold" (Gunn) **26**:202
"No, Thank You, John!" (Rossetti) **7**:267, 281, 291
*No Thanks* (Cummings) **5**:106-07
"No Way of Knowing" (Ashbery) **26**:124, 144
"No Way of Knowing When This Song Began" (Mandelstam) **14**:118
"No Word" (Kunitz) **19**:170, 186
"No Worst, There Is None" (Hopkins) **15**:175
*Noah and the Waters* (Day Lewis) **11**:127-28, 144, 152-53
"Noah Built the Ark" (Johnson) **24**:128-29, 144, 155, 164-65, 169
"The Nobel Prize" (Pasternak)
    See "Nobelevskaya premiya"
"Nobelevskaya premiya" (Pasternak) **6**:268, 284
"The Noble Lady's Tale" (Hardy) **8**:99
"The Noble Lord" (Belloc) **24**:41
*Noble Numbers, or Pious Pieces* (Herrick)
    See *His Noble Numbers: or, His Pious Pieces, Wherein (amongst Other Things) He Sings the Birth of His Christ: and Sighes for His Saviours Suffering on the Crosse*
"Noble Sisters" (Rossetti) **7**:272, 274, 276, 280
"The Nobleman Orsha" (Lermontov) **18**:300
"Nobody" (Aleixandre) **15**:20, 22
"Nobody" (Guillen)
    See "Nobody"

"Nobody Comes" (Hardy) **8**:101, 125
"Nobody Owns th Earth" (Bissett) **14**:10
*Nobody Owns th Earth* (Bissett) **14**:10-12, 18
"Nobody's Lookin' but de Owl and de Moon" (Johnson) **24**:141
*The Nobody's Rose* (Celan)
    See *Die Niemandsrose*
*Les Noces d'Hérodiade* (Mallarme)
    See *Hérodiade*
"Noch'" (Pasternak) **6**:285
"Noch' ulitsa fonar' apteka'" (Blok) **21**:44
"Noch'I" (Lermontov) **18**:302
"Noch'II" (Lermontov) **18**:302
"Nocturnal Pleasures" (Pavese)
    See "Piaceri notturni"
"A Nocturnal Reverie" (Finch) **21**:140-41, 143, 146, 157, 160, 173-75
"A Nocturnal upon S. Lucies day, Being the shortest day" (Donne) **1**:130, 134, 149-50, 154
"Nocturne" (Pavese)
    See "Notturno"
"Nocturne in a Deserted Brickyard" (Sandburg) **2**:301, 303
*Nocturne of Remembered Spring and Other Poems* (Aiken) **26**:50, 72
"Nocturne of the Void" (Garcia Lorca)
    See "Nocturno del hueco"
"Nocturne vulgaire" (Rimbaud) **3**:264
*Nocturnes* (Senghor) **25**:231-33, 238-40, 255
"Nocturno de San Ildefonso" (Paz) **1**:370-72, 375
"Nocturno del hueco" (Garcia Lorca) **3**:139
"Nocturno en los muelles" (Guillen) **23**:106
"Nodier raconte" (Pound) **4**:317
"Noel: Christmas Eve" (Bridges) **28**:77, 81
"A Noiseless Patient Spider" (Whitman) **3**:390
"Un nom" (Lamartine) **16**:287
"Nomad Exquisite" (Stevens) **6**:293
*No-man's Rose* (Celan)
    See *Die Niemandsrose*
"Le non godute" (Gozzano) **10**:184
*Non Serviam* (Ekeloef) **23**:51, 58-9, 63, 76
"The Nonconformist" (Davie) **29**:102
"None with Him" (Rossetti) **7**:276, 284
*Nones* (Auden) **1**:23
"Nonne Preestes Tale" (Chaucer)
    See "Nun's Priest's Tale"
"Nonsense Rhyme" (Wylie) **23**:305
"Nonsun Blob a" (Cummings) **5**:109
"Noon" (Levine) **22**:214, 219, 222
"Noon of the Sunbather" (Piercy) **29**:308
"Noon Walk on the Asylum Lawn" (Sexton) **2**:359
"Noone' Autumnal This Great Lady's Gaze" (Cummings) **5**:107
"A Noon-Piece" (Smart) **13**:347
"Nor We of Her to Him" (Smith) **12**:326, 330
"Nora" (Toomer) **7**:317
"Die Nordsee" (Heine) **25**:139, 145, 158, 160, 162, 163
"Noria" (Cesaire) **25**:33
"Norma" (Sanchez) **9**:234
"Norma y paraíso de los negros" (Garcia Lorca) **3**:150
"North" (Heaney) **18**:203
*North* (Heaney) **18**:194-95, 197-99, 203, 205, 208-11, 215, 230, 238-39, 241, 246, 255
"th north aint easy to grow food in" (Bissett) **14**:25, 33
"North American Sequence" (Roethke) **15**:309-10, 312
"North American Time" (Rich) **5**:395
"North and South" (McKay) **2**:207
*North & South* (Bishop) **3**:37, 39, 50
"North Dakota North Light" (Momaday) **25**:219
"North Dublin" (Davie) **29**:95, 108, 120
"North Labrador" (Crane) **3**:83
*North of Boston* (Frost) **1**:193-95, 202, 207, 214, 217, 223-26
"The North Sea" (Davie) **29**:113

"The North Sea Undertaker's Complaint" (Lowell) **3**:216
*The North Ship* (Larkin) **21**:224-26, 230, 232-33, 235, 241, 251, 257, 259
"North Wind" (Montale)
    See "Tramontana"
"North Wind in October" (Bridges) **28**:67
*North Winter* (Carruth) **10**:70-71
*Northern Birds in Color* (Bissett) **14**:25
"Northern Door" (Ortiz) **17**:234
"Northern Elegies" (Akhmatova) **2**:4, 18
"The Northern Farmer" (Tennyson) **6**:358, 360
"The Northern Farmer--Old Style" (Tennyson) **6**:406
*Northern Heroic* (Bely)
    See *Severnaia    simfoniia:    Pervia geroicheskaia*
"A Northern Hoard" (Heaney) **18**:202-3
"Northern Liberal" (Hughes) **1**:252
"Northern River" (Wright) **14**:340
"The Northern Sea" (Ishikawa)
    See "Kita no umi"
*Northern Symphony* (Bely)
    See *Severnaia    simfoniia:    Pervia geroicheskaia*
*Northfield Poems* (Ammons) **16**:4-5, 28
"Northumberland House" (Smith) **12**:296
*Northwest Ecolog* (Ferlinghetti) **1**:187
"Northwood Path" (Gluck) **16**:126
*De nos oìseaux* (Tzara) **27**:233
"Nossis" (H. D.) **5**:268
"Nostalgia" (Jimenez)
    See "Nostaljia"
"Nostalgia" (Shapiro) **25**:269, 288, 325
"Nostalgic Catalogue" (Hongo) **23**:198-99
"Nostalgies d'obélisques" (Gautier) **18**:158, 163
"Nostaljia" (Jimenez) **7**:201
"Not a fighter for two positions, but— if I'm a casual guest" (Tsvetaeva)
    See "Dvukh stanov ne beots, a— esli gost sluchainyi"
"Not Both" (Meredith) **28**:208
"La not di maj" (Pasolini) **17**:252
"Not Every Day Fit for Verse" (Herrick) **9**:114
"Not Going to New York: A Letter" (Hass) **16**:198-99
"The Not Impossible Him" (Millay)
    See "To the Not Impossible Him"
"Not Leaving the House" (Snyder) **21**:289
"Not like a floury white butterfly" (Mandelstam)
    See "Ne muchnistoi babochkoiu beloi"
"Not Like Dante" (Ferlinghetti) **1**:182
"Not Planning a Trip Back" (Ashbery) **26**:165
*Not So Deep as a Well* (Parker) **28**:365
"Not So Far as the Forest" (Millay) **6**:238
"Not So, Not So" (Sexton) **2**:373
"Not That From Life, and All Its Woes" (Bryant) **20**:16
"Not There" (Gallagher) **9**:59
*Not This Pig* (Levine) **22**:212-13, 215-17, 220, 223, 226
"Not Waving but Drowning" (Smith) **12**:293, 300, 307, 319-21, 324, 328, 331, 333, 337, 347, 349, 354
*Not Waving but Drowning* (Smith) **12**:292-93
"Not with libations, but with Shouts and Laughter" (Millay) **6**:211, 244-46
"Not Yet" (Alegria) **26**:
"Nota biográfica" (Fuertes) **27**:18, 48-9
"note to myself" (Clifton) **17**:30
*Notebook* (Levertov)
    See "From a Notebook, October '68—May '69"
*Notebook 1967-68* (Lowell) **3**:223-26, 231-32, 239-40
"The Notebook in the Gate-legged Table" (Lowell) **13**:84
"Notebook of a Return to the Native Land" (Cesaire)
    See *Cahier d'un retour au pays natal*

*The Note-Book of William Blake* (Blake) **12**:11, 34-5
"Noted in the New York Times" (Kumin) **15**:209
"Notes at Edge" (Wright) **14**:375, 377
*Notes for a Guidebook* (Stryk) **27**:181, 183, 191-94, 197, 210, 214, 216, 218
"Notes for a Guidebook" (Stryk) **27**:186, 195
"Notes for a Little Play" (Hughes) **7**:130, 152
"Notes for a Speech" (Baraka) **4**:5
"Notes for an Elegy" (Meredith) **28**:170, 173, 181, 184-85, 187, 210
"Notes for the Legend of Salad Woman" (Ondaatje) **28**:329
*Notes from New York, and Other Poems* (Tomlinson) **17**:333-34, 336, 353-54
"Notes From Robin Hill Cottage" (Carruth) **10**:85
"Notes From the Air" (Ashbery) **26**:163
"Notes Made in the Piazzo San Marco" (Swenson) **14**:261
"Notes on a Conspiracy" (Rose) **13**:241
"Notes toward a Poem That Can Never Be Written" (Atwood) **8**:18, 43
"Notes Toward a Supreme Fiction" (Ashbery) **26**:
*Notes toward a Supreme Fiction* (Stevens) **6**:310, 314, 324, 326-37, 329, 335, 337
"Nothing and Something" (Harper) **21**:187, 191
"Nothing Down" (Dove) **6**:110, 112
"Nothing Endures" (Cullen) **20**:59
*Nothing for Tigers: Poems, 1959-1964* (Carruth) **10**:70
"Nothing Gold Can Stay" (Frost) **1**:194
"Nothing Makes Sense" (Giovanni) **19**:112
"Nothing Significant Was Really Said" (Larkin) **21**:259
"Nothing Stays Put" (Clampitt) **19**:94
"Nothing to Be Said" (Larkin) **21**:227
" (Nothing Whichful About" (Cummings) **5**:108
"Nothing will yield" (Nemerov) **24**:262
"Nothingness" (Jimenez)
    See "La mujer desnuda"
"Notizie dall'Amiata" (Montale) **13**:106, 121, 127
"Notre Dame de Chartres" (Meredith) **28**:171, 188-89
"Notre-Dame" (Gautier) **18**:144-46
"La notte" (Pavese) **13**:230
"Notturno" (Pavese) **13**:230
"Noubousse" (Apollinaire) **7**:48
"Noun" (Shapiro) **25**:276
"nouvelle bonte" (Cesaire) **25**:45
*Nouvelle confidences* (Lamartine) **16**:293
*Nouvelles méditations poétiques* (Lamartine) **16**:266, 271, 273-74, 277-79, 287, 290-09
*Nouvelles Odes* (Hugo) **17**:88
"Nova" (Jeffers) **17**:130
"A Novel" (Gluck) **16**:158, 161
"November" (Belloc) **24**:34
"November" (Bryant) **20**:37, 44
"November" (Hughes) **7**:119, 132-33, 136
"November Cotton Flower" (Toomer) **7**:319, 333-34
"November Surf" (Jeffers) **17**:117, 120, 132
*The Novice* (Lermontov) **18**:279
"The Novices" (Levertov) **11**:169
"Novissima verba" (Lamartine) **16**:268, 280, 283, 292-93, 297
"Novogodnee" (Tsvetaeva) **14**:325
"Novye stansy k Avguste" (Brodsky) **9**:4
"Now" (Sexton) **2**:352
"Now" (Walker) **20**:276
"Now Air Is Air and Thing Is Thing: No Bliss" (Cummings) **5**:110
"Now Close the Windows" (Frost) **1**:197
"Now Does Our World Descend" (Cummings) **5**:111
"Now He Knows All There Is to Know: Now He Is Acquainted with the Day and Night" (Schwartz) **8**:319
"Now Hollow Fires" (Housman) **2**:189

*Now in Wintry Delights* (Bridges) **28**:76-7
"Now It Is You I Praise, Banner" (Rilke) **2**:273
"Now Pine-Needles" (Smith) **12**:318
"Now Returned Home" (Jeffers) **17**:141
"Now that Holocaust and Crucifixion are
    Coffee-Table Books" (Viereck) **27**:293-94,
    296
"Now That I Am Never Alone" (Gallagher) **9**:62
"Now the Record Now Record" (Duncan) **2**:103
"Now This Cold Man" (Page) **12**:168, 170, 178,
    184
"Nox" (Hugo) **17**:54
*Nozarashi Diary* (Matsuo Basho) **3**:6
*Nozarashi kikō* (Matsuo Basho) **3**:11, 28
"NUCLEAR CICULAR" (Bissett) **14**:6, 24, 32
"Nude" (Cassian) **17**:4
"Nude Photograph" (Clifton) **17**:29
"The Nude Swim" (Sexton) **2**:352
"Nude Young Dancer" (Hughes) **1**:246
"La Nue" (Gautier) **18**:125, 129
"Nueva York: Oficina y denuncia" (Garcia
    Lorca) **3**:141, 151
*Nuevo canto de amor a Stalingrado* (Neruda)
    **4**:279-80
"The Nuisance" (Piercy) **29**:309
"La nuit blanche" (Kipling) **3**:172
"Nuit blanche" (Lowell) **13**:89-90
"La nuit d'Avril, 1915" (Apollinaire) **7**:3
"Nuit de Sine" (Senghor) **25**:224, 227, 255
"Nuits de juin" (Hugo) **17**:64
"Nullo" (Toomer) **7**:320, 330-31, 334
"Number 57" (Villa) **22**:346
"Number Man" (Sandburg) **2**:322
"Number 68 (Villa) **22**:347
"Number Three on the Docket" (Lowell) **13**:79,
    84-5
"The Numbers" (Ammons) **16**:5
"Numbers" (Hughes) **1**:267
"Numbers" (Smith) **12**:317
"Numbers, Letters" (Baraka) **4**:19
"The Numerous Blood" (Guillen)
    See "La sangre numerosa"
"Numpholeptos" (Browning) **2**:86, 88
"Nunc dimittis" (Brodsky) **9**:5
"Nunca se sabe" (Fuertes) **27**:17
"A Nun's Complaint" (Rilke) **2**:270
"Nuns Fret Not" (Millay) **6**:242
"Nuns in the Wind" (Rukeyser) **12**:211
"Nun's Priest's Tale" (Chaucer) **19**:6, 13-15,
    26, 31-2, 48, 52, 57, 75
*La nuova gioventù* (Pasolini) **17**:282-83, 287
"Nuova poesia in forma di rose" (Pasolini)
    **17**:274, 278
"Nuove stanze" (Montale) **13**:106, 120-21
"A Nuptiall Song, or Epithalamie on Sir
    Clipseby Crew and His Lady" (Herrick)
    **9**:86, 102, 139
"Nürnberge Rede" (Enzensberger) **28**:164
"Nurse Whitman" (Olds) **22**:322, 328
"A Nursery Rhyme" (Brooke) **24**:66
"Nursery Rhyme for a Seventh Son" (Wright)
    **14**:338
"Nursery Rhymes for Little Anglo-Indians"
    (Kipling) **3**:190
"Nurse's Song" (Blake) **12**:7, 21-2, 34
"Nurse's Song" (Gluck) **16**:148
"Nursing Home" (Page) **12**:176
"Nurture" (Kumin) **15**:209, 211
*Nurture* (Kumin) **15**:209-14, 221, 223
*Nux* (Ovid) **2**:244
"Ny la douce pitie, ny le pleur lamentable"
    (Ronsard) **11**:278
"The Nymph and the Faun" (Marvell)
    See "The Nymph Complaining for the
    Death of Her Faun"
"The Nymph Complaining for the Death of
    Her Faun" (Marvell) **10**:260-62, 266-67,
    271, 274, 277, 290, 294, 297, 301-02, 309-
    10, 315-16, 319, 325
"A Nympholept" (Swinburne) **24**:312-319, 322,
    326, 341, 348

*O. 1* (Pindar)
    See *Olympian 1*
*O. 7* (Pindar)
    See *Olympian 7*
*O. 8* (Pindar)
    See *Olympian 8*
*O. 9* (Pindar)
    See *Olympian 9*
*O. 14* (Pindar)
    See *Olympian 14*
"O Black and Unknown Bards" (Johnson)
    **24**:127, 146, 152, 160, 166
"O Captain! My Captain!" (Whitman) **3**:404,
    418, 422
"O Carib Isle!" (Crane) **3**:90
"O City, City" (Schwartz) **8**:302, 316
"O Daedalus, Fly Away Home" (Hayden) **6**:176,
    179, 189
"O das Quinas" (Pessoa) **20**:155
"O Desejado" (Pessoa) **20**:156
"O Didn't He Ramble" (Johnson) **24**:151, 170
"O dos Castelos" (Pessoa) **20**:155
"O Dreams, O Destinations" (Day Lewis)
    **11**:145
"O Florida, Venereal Soil" (Stevens) **6**:305, 339
"O Glorious France" (Masters) **1**:342
"O Guardador de Rebanhos" (Pessoa)
    **20**:151-52
"O Happy Dogs of England" (Smith) **12**:318,
    330
"O Hell" (Loy) **16**:316
"O Infante" (Pessoa) **20**:155
"O Lady, when the Tipped Cup of the Moon
    Blessed You" (Hughes) **7**:113
"O Lay Thy Loof in Mine, Lass" (Burns) **6**:76
"O, Let Me in This Ae Night" (Burns) **6**:81
"O Love, my muse" (Bridges) **28**:59
"O Love, Sweet Animal" (Schwartz) **8**:313
"O Love, the Interest Itself in Thoughtless
    Heaven..." (Auden) **1**:22
"O Lull Me, Lull Me" (Roethke) **15**:261, 273,
    299, 302
"O May I Join the Choir Invisible" (Eliot)
    **20**:123, 131, 136, 139, 143
"O me donzel" (Pasolini) **17**:252
"O Mon Dieu, vous m'avez blessé d'amour"
    (Verlaine) **2**:416
"O Mostrengo" (Pessoa) **20**:155
"O muse contiens-toi! muse aux hymnes
    d'airain" (Hugo) **17**:97
"O my companions, O my sister Sleep"
    (Belloc) **24**:38
"O my joy" (Bridges) **28**:63
"O my vague desires" (Bridges) **28**:59
"O Pastor Amoroso" (Pessoa) **20**:152
"O Pug!" (Smith) **12**:301
"O saisons, ô châteaux!" (Rimbaud) **3**:275
"O Sion of my heart" (Kunitz) **19**:175
"O Southland!" (Johnson) **24**:137, 142, 147,
    160
"O Sweet Spontaneous" (Cummings) **5**:105
"O Taste and See" (Levertov) **11**:169
*O Taste and See* (Levertov) **11**:159, 169, 171,
    211
"O, Tempora! O Mores!" (Poe) **1**:449
"O, Thou Opening, O" (Roethke) **15**:284, 300,
    302-03
"O to Be a Dragon" (Moore) **4**:249
"O Virtuous Light" (Wylie) **23**:311, 315
"O Wander Not So Far Away!" (Burroughs)
    **8**:73
"O Wha's Been Here afore Me, Lass"
    (MacDiarmid) **9**:155, 160
"O Word I Love to Sing" (McKay) **2**:217, 219
"O World of many Worlds" (Owen) **19**:352
"O Ye Tongues" (Sexton) **2**:367, 372-73
*Oak and Ivy* (Dunbar) **5**:128, 132
"The Oak Leaf" (Lermontov) **18**:281
"Oasis" (Stryk) **27**:187
"Oatmeal" (Kinnell) **26**:286
"Obedience" (Herbert) **4**:119, 125-26
"Obermann Once More" (Arnold) **5**:19, 63-4

"Oberon's Chappell" (Herrick)
    See "The Fairie Temple: or, Oberons
    Chappell. Dedicated to Mr. John
    Merrifield, Counsellor at Law"
"Oberon's Feast" (Herrick) **9**:90
"Oberon's Palace" (Herrick) **9**:86, 90, 137
"Obituary for a Living Lady" (Brooks) **7**:66-7,
    69
"The Objection to Being Stepped On" (Frost)
    **1**:215
"Objet d'Art" (Stryk) **27**:204
"Oblique Prayers" (Levertov) **11**:198, 201
*Oblique Prayers* (Levertov) **11**:198, 200-02,
    209
"Oblivion" (Smith) **12**:317, 354
"O-Bon: Dance for The Dead" (Hongo) **23**:199
"Oboroniaet son moiu donskuiu son"
    (Mandelstam) **14**:154
*Obra poética* (Borges) **22**:95
*Obra poética 1923-1967* (Borges) **22**:72, 96
*Obras completas* (Aleixandre) **15**:7, 18, 34
*Obras completas* (Juana Ines de la Cruz)
    **24**:202, 233
*Obras incompletas* (Fuertes) **27**:3-5, 19-21,
    23-5, 33-47
"Obsequies to the Lady Anne Hay" (Carew)
    **29**:6, 36, 38, 59-60, 66, 74
"Observation" (Larkin) **21**:259
"Observation of Facts" (Tomlinson) **17**:299,
    315, 335
*Observations* (Moore) **4**:229-30, 244, 249-52
"The Observatory" (Noyes) **27**:128
"The Observer" (Rich) **5**:370
"Obsessed by Her Beauty" (Viereck) **27**:263
"Obsidian Butterfly" (Paz)
    See "Mariposa de obsidiana"
*Obus couleur de lune* (Apollinaire) **7**:22
"Occasioned by Sir William Temple's Late
    Illness and Recovery" (Swift) **9**:250
*Le occasioni* (Montale) **13**:103-05, 108-09, 113-
    14, 117-21, 126-28, 131-32, 136, 141, 160,
    165-66
*The Occasions* (Montale)
    See *Le occasioni*
"L'occident" (Lamartine) **16**:266
"Ocean Waves" (Tagore)
    See "Sindhu-taranga"
"Ocean-Letter" (Apollinaire)
    See "Lettre-Océan"
"Oceano Nox" (Hugo) **17**:64
"Ocean's Love to Ireland" (Heaney)
*Octavie: L'illusion* (Nerval) **13**:177
"The Octets" (Mandelstam) **14**:152
"October" (Frost) **1**:225
"October" (Hayden) **6**:193, 195
"October" (Lorde) **12**:154
"October" (Sassoon) **12**:240
*October, and Other Poems* (Bridges)
"October Dawn" (Hughes) **7**:115
"October Journey" (Walker) **20**:284, 289
*October Journey* (Walker) **20**:284, 287, 289
"October Thought" (Heaney) **18**:191
"October Trees" (Sassoon) **12**:248, 254
"The Octopus" (Merrill) **28**:239, 242
"An Octopus" (Moore) **4**:233, 252, 254-55, 264
"Oda a Salvador Dali" (Garcia Lorca) **3**:136,
    138, 143
"Oda a Walt Whitman" (Garcia Lorca) **3**:121,
    127, 150
"Oda al edificio" (Neruda) **4**:285
"Oda al santísimo sacramento del altar:
    exposición y mundo" (Garcia Lorca)
    **3**:136, 138, 143
"Oda k nuzhniku" (Lermontov) **18**:284-85
"Oda solar al ejérito del pueblo" (Neruda) **4**:309
*Odas elementales* (Neruda) **4**:285, 287
*Odas Mínimas* (Guillen) **23**:100
"Ode" (Lamartine) **16**:291
"Ode" (Marvell)
    See "An Horatian Ode upon Cromwell's
    Return from Ireland"

"Ode" (Marvell)
See "An Horatian Ode upon Cromwell's Return from Ireland"
"Ode" (Tennyson) **6**:357
"Ode" (Wordsworth) **4**:377, 399, 403-04, 407
"Ode à Cassandre: 'Mignonne, allon voir'" (Ronsard) **11**:218-21, 234, 240
*Ode à Charles Fourier* (Breton) **15**:52, 61
"Ode á Joachim du Bellay" (Ronsard) **11**:280
"Ode à l'Amitié" (Hugo) **17**:87-88
"Ode à Michel de l'Hospital" (Ronsard) **11**:258, 287-91
"Ode à Victor Hugo" (Gautier) **18**:144
"Ode de la Paix" (Ronsard) **11**:283, 286, 289-91
"An Ode (Dedicated to the Under-Secretary for India in expectation of his immediate promotion to Cabinet rank through the Postmaster-GeneralBelloc) **24**:41
"Ode for All Rebels" (MacDiarmid) **9**:171, 176
"An Ode for Him" (Herrick) **9**:86
"Ode for Music" (Gray) **2**:153, 155
"Ode for St. Cecilia's Day" (Pope) **26**:315
"Ode Inscribed to W. H. Channing" (Emerson) **18**:88, 111
"Ode: Intimations of Immortality from Recollections of Early Childhood" (Wordsworth) **4**:387-88, 390, 395, 401, 403, 411
"Ode Marítima" (Pessoa) **20**:166, 169
"Ode: My Twenty-Fourth Year" (Ginsberg) **4**:73
"Ode: O Bosky Brook" (Tennyson) **6**:388-89
"Ode on a Distant Prospect of Eton College" (Gray) **2**:133-34, 137, 149-50, 153
"Ode on a Drop of Dew" (Marvell) **10**:269, 271, 277, 296, 313-14
"Ode on Indolence" (Keats) **1**:302-04, 307-08, 314
"Ode on Melancholy" (Keats) **1**:298-300, 306-07, 309, 312
"Ode on Spring" (Gray) **2**:133, 135, 143, 145, 152
"Ode on the Death of a Favourite Cat, Drowned in a Tub of Gold Fishes" (Gray) **2**:133, 146, 148, 152
*Ode on the Morning of Christ's Nativity* (Milton) **29**:212, 214, 238-41, 272
"Ode on the Pleasure Arising from Vicissitude" (Gray) **2**:143, 152-53
"Ode on the Progress of Poesy" (Gray)
See "The Progress of Poesy"
"Ode on the Spring" (Gray)
See "Ode on Spring"
"Ode on Vicissitude" (Gray)
See "Ode on the Pleasure Arising from Vicissitude"
"Ode on Vicissitude" (Gray) **2**:143, 152-53
"Ode secrète" (Valery) **9**:394-96
"Ode sur la naissance du duc de Bordeaux" (Lamartine) **16**:291
"Ode to a Beloved Woman" (Sappho)
See "Ode to Anactoria"
"The Ode to a Girl" (Sappho) **5**:408
"Ode to a Grecian Urn" (Keats) **1**:281-82, 290-98, 300, 303-04, 307, 313-15
"Ode to a Nightingale" (Keats) **1**:281-83, 295-98, 301, 303, 305, 307-09, 314-15
"Ode to Adversity" (Gray) **2**:133, 135, 138-39, 141, 152
"Ode to Anactoria" (Sappho) **5**:407, 411, 413
"Ode to Aphrodite" (Sappho) **5**:408, 411, 413, 431
"Ode to Apollo" (Keats) **1**:313
"Ode to Arnold Schoenberg" (Tomlinson) **17**:308, 317, 328, 337
"Ode to Atthis" (Sappho) **5**:416
"Ode to Autumn" (Keats) **1**:282-83, 298-302, 314-15
"Ode to Beauty" (Emerson) **18**:81
"Ode to Bill" (Ashbery) **26**:135, 159
"Ode to Dr. William Sancroft" (Swift) **9**:250
"Ode to Duty" (Wordsworth) **4**:401, 406-07

"Ode to Ethiopia" (Dunbar) **5**:124, 129, 131-34, 143
"Ode to Fame" (Masters) **1**:332
"Ode to Fear" (Day Lewis) **11**:147
"Ode to France" (Coleridge) **11**:92, 94, 99-101
"ode to frank silvera" (Bissett) **14**:34
"Ode to Freedom" (Pushkin)
See "Vol'nost': Oda"
"Ode to General Draper" (Smart) **13**:342
"The Ode to Hesperus" (Sappho) **5**:418
"Ode to Himself" (Jonson) **17**:166, 174
"Ode to Liberty" (Pushkin)
See "Vol'nost': Oda"
"Ode to Liberty" (Shelley) **14**:178
"An Ode to Love" (Behn) **13**:30
"Ode to Mæcenas" (Wheatley) **3**:333, 340-41, 344-45, 348, 354, 356-57, 361-62
"Ode to Memory" (Tennyson) **6**:347, 359-60
"Ode to Neptune" (Wheatley) **3**:354, 357, 361
"Ode to Plurality" (Zagajewski) **27**:381, 383, 385, 395-96
"Ode to Psyche" (Keats) **1**:295, 301, 305, 308-09, 314
"Ode to Salvador Dali" (Garcia Lorca)
See "Oda a Salvador Dali"
"Ode to San Francisco" (Tomlinson) **17**:361
"An Ode to Sir Clipsebie Crew" (Herrick) **9**:103
"Ode: To Sir William Sydney, on his Birth-day" (Jonson) **17**:158-59
"Ode to Sir William Temple" (Swift) **9**:250
*Ode to Stalin* (Mandelstam) **14**:133, 148-49, 153-55
"Ode to the Athenian Society" (Swift) **9**:250
"An Ode to the Birth of Our Saviour" (Herrick) **9**:119-20
"Ode to the Departing Year" (Coleridge) **11**:49, 54, 93-4
"Ode to the Latrine" (Lermontov)
See "Ode to the Latrine"
"Ode to the Most Blessed Sacrament" (Garcia Lorca)
See "Oda al santísimo sacramento del altar: exposición y mundo"
"Ode to the Most Holy Eucharist: Exposition and World" (Garcia Lorca)
See "Oda al santísimo sacramento del altar: exposición y mundo"
"Ode to the Nightingale" (Keats)
See "Ode to a Nightingale"
"Ode to the Sacrament" (Garcia Lorca)
See "Oda al santísimo sacramento del altar: exposición y mundo"
"Ode to the Sky Lark" (Shelley) **14**:167, 171, 175, 196, 198, 207, 212
"Ode to the Spleen" (Finch) **21**:140-41, 145-46, 150, 152, 156-57, 159, 163, 165-66, 168, 172, 180-81
"Ode to the Spring" (Gray)
See "Ode on Spring"
"Ode to the West Wind" (Shelley) **14**:167-9, 171, 177, 196, 205-06, 208, 211-12, 234, 236-37, 239-40
"Ode to Venus" (Sappho)
See "Ode to Aphrodite"
"The Ode To Venus" (Sappho) **5**:408
"Ode to Walt Whitman" (Garcia Lorca)
See "Oda a Walt Whitman"
"Ode Triunfal" (Pessoa) **20**:169
*Odes* (Gray) **2**:135
*Odes* (Hugo) **17**:55, 70, 87-90
*Odes* (Pindar) **19**:380
*Odes* (Ronsard) **11**:230, 234, 280, 287, 289, 291-92
*Odes* (Valery) **9**:365
*Odes et ballades* (Hugo) **17**:45, 62, 74-75, 90-91
*Odes et poésies diverses* (Hugo) **17**:62
*Odes to Simple Things* (Neruda)
See *Odas elementales*
"Ode-Thrnenody on England" (Brooke) **24**:70
"Odious Scenery" (Hagiwara Sakutaro) **18**:177
"Odlegtose" (Milosz) **8**:189

"The Odour" (Herbert) **4**:102, 134
*Odysseis* (Homer)
See *Odyssey*
*Odysses* (Homer)
See *Odyssey*
"Odysseus to Telemachus" (Brodsky) **9**:4
*Odyssey* (Homer) **23**:151-53, 155-58, 161, 165-66, 176-79, 186, 188-91
"Oeconomic divina" (Milosz) **8**:186-87
"Oedipus Crow" (Hughes) **7**:138
"The Oedipus Within" (Wakoski) **15**:324
"Oenone" (Tennyson) **6**:359, 410-12
"Oeuvre" (Stryk) **27**:193, 195, 201
*Oeuvres* (Ronsard) **11**:247, 254, 269, 272, 276
*Oeuvres complètes* (Cesaire) **25**:33
*Oeuvres complètes* (Mallarme) **4**:198
*Oeuvres completes* (Perse) **23**:254
*Oeuvres completes* (Tzara) **27**:232
*Les Oeuvres de Francois Villon* (Villon) **13**:373, 394
*Oeuvres poétiques* (Apollinaire) **7**:36
*Oeuvres poetiques completes* (Lamartine) **16**:268
"Of Beginning Light" (Tomlinson) **17**:333
"Of Being" (Levertov) **11**:199, 202
"Of De Witt Williams on His Way to Lincoln Cemetery" (Brooks) **7**:85
"Of Distress Being Humiliated by the Classical Chinese Poets" (Carruth) **10**:87-88
"Of Dying Beauty" (Zukofsky) **11**:368
"Of his love called Anna" (Wyatt) **27**:342
"Of Liberation" (Giovanni) **19**:108
"Of Modern Poetry" (Stevens) **6**:324
"Of others fained sorrow and the lovers fained mirth" (Wyatt) **27**:340
*Of Pen and Ink and Paper Scraps* (Stryk) **27**:214
*Of Reformation Touching Church-Discipline in England* (Milton) **29**:238
"OF TH LAND DIVINE SERVICE" (Bissett) **14**:30
*OF TH LAND DIVINE SERVICE* (Bissett) **14**:2, 10
"Of the Four Humours in Man's Constitution" (Bradstreet) **10**:17, 41
*Of the Progres of the Soule* (Donne)
See *The Second Anniversarie. Of the Progres of the Soule. Wherein, By Occasion Of the Religious death of Mistris Elizabeth Drury, the incommodities of the Soule in this life, and her exaltation in the next, are Contemplated*
"Of the Vanity of All Worldly Creatures" (Bradstreet)
See "The Vanity of All Worldly Things"
*Of the War* (Duncan) **2**:104
"Of the West" (Jeffers) **17**:130
"Off from swing shift" (Hongo) **23**:196-97, 203
"Off Point Lotus" (Kunitz) **19**:171
"Off Shore" (Swinburne) **24**:313
"Off the Campus Wits" (Brutus) **24**:106, 114
"Off the Turnpike" (Lowell) **13**:78, 85
"Offering" (Tagore)
See "Utsarga"
*An Offering to the Lares* (Rilke) **2**:280
"Offhand Compositions" (Wang Wei) **18**:370, 374
"Offices" (Page) **12**:173
"Often I Am Permitted to Return to a Meadow" (Duncan) **2**:120, 127
"Often Rebuked, yet Always Back Returning" (Bronte) **8**:50
"The Ogre" (Williams) **7**:349, 378, 393
"Ogres and Pygmies" (Graves) **6**:139, 142, 144, 151
"Oh" (Sexton) **2**:365
"Oh Christianity, Christianity" (Smith) **12**:325, 352
"Oh, Dear! Oh Dear! A Sonnet" (Brooke) **24**:52
"Oh death shall find me" (Brooke) **24**:52, 72, 76

Title Index

"Oh do not die" (Donne)
   See "A Feaver"
"Oh Fair Enough Are Sky and Plain"
   (Housman) **2**:193
"Oh Fairest of the Rural Maids" (Bryant) **20**:35
"Oh general en tu Pentágono!" (Guillen) **23**:126
"Oh General in Your Pentagon!" (Guillen)
   See "Oh General in Your Pentagon!"
"Oh, Look - I can Do It, Too" (Parker) **28**:354
"Oh n'insultez jamais une femme qui tombe!"
   (Hugo) **17**:66
"Oh, See How Thick the Gold Cup Flowers"
   (Housman) **2**:183, 185, 196
"Oh Think Not I Am Faithful to a Vow"
   (Millay) **6**:211
"Oh You Sabbatarians!" (Masters) **1**:344
*Oi no kobumi* (Matsuo Basho) **3**:6
*Oi no obumi* (Matsuo Basho) **3**:12
*Oiseaux* (Perse) **23**:239-41, 247-48, 253-54,
   256-57
*Oku no hosomichi* (Matsuo Basho) **3**:13, 27-30
*Ol. IX* (Pindar)
   See *Olympian 9*
*Ol. XI* (Pindar)
   See *Olympian 11*
"The Ol' Tunes" (Dunbar) **5**:122, 145
"The Old Adam" (Levertov) **11**:170
*Old and Modern Poems* (Vigny)
   See *Poèmes antiques et modernes*
"Old Countryside" (Bogan) **12**:87, 94, 113
"An Old Cracked Tune" (Kunitz) **19**:158
"The Old Cumberland Beggar" (Wordsworth)
   **4**:411-12, 428
"Old Dogs" (Smith) **12**:331-32
"Old Dominion" (Hass) **16**:198
"Old Dwarf Heart" (Sexton) **2**:361
"Old England" (McKay) **2**:225
"An Old Field Mowed for Appearances' Sake"
   (Meredith) **28**:194
"Old Flame" (Lowell) **3**:212, 215
"Old Florist" (Roethke) **15**:295
"Old Folks Home" (Stryk) **27**:210
"Old Folk's Home, Jerusalem" (Dove) **6**:123
"The Old Front Gate" (Dunbar) **5**:122
"Old Furniture" (Hardy) **8**:105
"Old Hills" (Ortiz) **17**:231
"The Old Horsefly" (Shapiro) **25**:324
*The Old Horsefly* (Shapiro) **25**:323
"Old House" (Wright) **14**:348-49, 353
*The Old House in the Country* (Reese) **29**:337-
   39, 348, 352
"The Old Huntsman" (Sassoon) **12**:240, 242,
   250, 252-53, 275-76
*The Old Huntsman and Other Poems*
   (Sassoon) **12**:249, 252, 256-57, 260, 263-
   64, 269, 272, 277
"The Old Italians Dying" (Ferlinghetti) **1**:182
"Old King Cole" (Robinson) **1**:468
"The Old King's New Jester" (Robinson) **1**:487
"An Old Lady's Winter Words" (Roethke)
   **15**:272, 278
"Old Laughter" (Brooks) **7**:61
"The Old Life" (Kinnell) **26**:277
"Old Lines" (Montale)
   See "Vecchi versi"
"The Old Lovers" (Aleixandre)
   See "Los amantes viejos"
"The Old Man Is Like Moses" (Aleixandre)
   **15**:4, 24
"The Old Man Travelling" (Wordsworth) **4**:374,
   416
"The Old Man's Counsel" (Bryant) **20**:35, 41
"The Old Man's Funeral" (Bryant) **20**:10
"Old Marrieds" (Brooks) **7**:53, 69, 79
"Old Mary" (Brooks) **7**:106
"Old Medium" (Enzensberger) **28**:167
"An Old Memory" (Dunbar) **5**:140
"Old Men" (Nash) **21**:263, 274
"The Old Neighbour and the New" (Hardy)
   **8**:104
"Old Oak of Summer Chace" (Tennyson) **6**:356

"Old, Old, Old Andrew Jackson" (Lindsay)
   **23**:280, 288
"Old Paint, Old Partner" (Kumin) **15**:220
"Old Park" (Jimenez) **7**:183
"An old Photograph" (Nemerov) **24**:255
"An Old Photograph of strangers" (Meredith)
   **28**:193
"Old Pictures in Florence" (Browning) **2**:37
"Old poet" (Bukowski) **18**:22
"The Old Poet" (Shapiro) **25**:304
"The Old Poet Moves to a New Apartment 14
   Times" (Zukofsky) **11**:353
"The Old Pond" (Matsuo Basho) **3**:32
*Old Possum's Book of Practical Cats* (Eliot)
   **6**:174
"The Old Prison" (Wright) **14**:359
"Old Revolution" (Enzensberger) **28**:166
"The Old Sceptic" (Noyes) **27**:139
*The Old sceptic* (Noyes) **27**:139
"Old Song" (Crane) **3**:90
"The Old Stoic" (Bronte) **8**:60
"An Old Story" (Robinson) **1**:459
" Old Timers" (Sandburg) **2**:302
"Old Trails" (Robinson) **1**:462
"The Old Vicarage, Grantchester" (Brooke)
   **24**:54, 58, 63-5, 68, 78, 86, 93
"Old Walt" (Hughes) **1**:257
"Old Woman" (Pinsky) **27**:160-61
"An Old Woman" (Sitwell) **3**:312, 326
"The Old Woman and the Statue" (Stevens)
   **6**:297
"Old Words" (Sanchez) **9**:221
"An Old World Thicket" (Rossetti) **7**:277
*The Oldest Killed Lake in North America*
   (Carruth) **10**:91
"Olive Grove" (Merrill) **28**:228
"The Olive in Its Orchard" (Housman) **2**:189-90
"The Olive Wood Fire" (Kinnell) **26**:278
*Olympian 1* (Pindar) **19**:380-81, 388-89, 396,
   398, 400, 402, 407, 413-17, 420, 422
*Olympian 2* (Pindar) **19**:381, 423
*Olympian 3* (Pindar) **19**:425
*Olympian 6* (Pindar) **19**:381, 389-90, 398, 414,
   420
*Olympian VII* (Pindar)
   See *Olympian 7*
*Olympian 7* (Pindar) **19**:396, 401, 406, 414
*Olympian 8* (Pindar) **19**:422-23
*Olympian 9* (Pindar) **19**:390
*Olympian 10* (Pindar) **19**:387-88
*Olympian 11* (Pindar) **19**:389, 412
*Olympian 13* (Pindar) **19**:387, 391, 398
*Olympian 14* (Pindar) **19**:421-23
*Olympian Odes 1* (Pindar)
   See *Olympian 1*
"A Olympio" (Hugo) **17**:76
*Om hösten* (Ekeloef) **23**:76
"Omaggio a Rimbaud" (Montale) **13**:111, 157
"L'ombra della magnolia" (Montale) **13**:109-
   10, 118, 126
"Ombre Chinoise" (Lowell) **13**:94
*Ommateum with Doxology* (Ammons) **16**:4-5,
   20, 24, 27, 39-44, 52-3
"Omnibus" (Tsvetaeva)
   See "Avtobus"
*Omniscience* (Smart)
   See *On the Omniscience of the Supreme
   Being*
"Omoide" (Ishikawa) **10**:213
"On a Bust" (Masters) **1**:342
"On a Certain Engagement South of Seoul"
   (Carruth) **10**:84, 89
"On a Child's Death" (Blok) **21**:15
"On a Clean Book" (Dunbar) **5**:125
"On a Conventicle" (Behn) **13**:7
"On a Copy of Verses Made in a Dream, and
   Sent to Me in a Morning before I Was
   Awake" (Behn) **13**:31
"On a Discovered Curl of Hair" (Hardy) **8**:137

"On a Distant Prospect of Eton College"
   (Gray)
   See "Ode on a Distant Prospect of Eton
   College"
"On a Drawing by Flavio" (Levine) **22**:223
"On a Drop of Dew" (Marvell)
   See "Ode on a Drop of Dew"
"On a Fine Morning" (Hardy) **8**:108
"On a Heath" (Hardy) **8**:93
"On a Juniper Tree, Cut Down to Make
   Busks" (Behn) **13**:7, 27-8
"On a Political Prisoner" (Yeats) **20**:314, 349
"On a Raised Beach" (MacDiarmid) **9**:157, 172,
   176, 180
"On a Red Steed" (Tsvetaeva)
   See "Na krasnom kone"
"On a Rocky Spur of Peoria" (Mandelstam)
   **14**:117
"On a Sentence by Pascal" (Schwartz) **8**:285,
   292
"On a Side Street" (Zagajewski) **27**:389
"On a Singing Girl" (Wylie) **23**:324
"On a Sledge, Overlaid with Straw"
   (Mandelstam) **14**:119
"On a Sleeping Friend" (Belloc) **24**:9
"On a Solemn Music" (Milton) **19**:211, 253
"On a Starry Night" (Dunbar) **5**:125-27
"On a Tree Fallen Across the Road" (Frost)
   **1**:213
"On a winter's night long time ago" (Belloc)
   **24**:34
"On Acrocorinth" (Sikelianos) **29**:372
"On Affliction" (Finch) **21**:144, 146
"On an Anthology of Chinese Poems" (Jeffers)
   **17**:140
"On an Old Roundel" (Swinburne) **24**:324-25,
   328-29
"On Anactoria" (Sappho)
   See "Ode to Anactoria"
"On Angels" (Milosz) **8**:201
"On Annunciation Day" (Tsvetaeva)
   See "V den' Blagoveshchen'ia"
"On Another Politician" (Belloc) **24**:36-7
"On Another's Sorrow" (Blake) **12**:7, 33
*On Ballycastle Beach* (McGuckian) **27**:80, 83-
   85, 90, 92-95, 99-102, 104
"On Barbara's Shore" (Wakoski) **15**:333
"On Beginning the Study of Anglo-Saxon
   Grammar" (Borges)
   See "Al iniciar el estudio de la gramática
   anglosajona"
"On Being Asked to Write a Poem Against the
   War in Vietnam" (Carruth) **10**:77
"On Being Brought from Africa to America"
   (Wheatley) **3**:338, 340, 346, 349, 353,
   362-63
"On Being Yanked from a Favorite Anthology"
   (Shapiro) **25**:323
"On Blake's Victory over the Spaniards"
   (Marvell)
   See "On the Victory Obtained by Blake
   over the Spaniards"
"On byl v krayu svyatom" (Lermontov) **18**:289
"On Cheating the Fiddler" (Parker) **28**:362
"On Childhood" (Bradstreet) **10**:38
"On Christmas Eve" (Lowell) **13**:85
"On Court-worme" (Jonson) **17**:197
"On Death" (Clare) **23**:44
"On Desire. A Pindarick" (Behn) **13**:8, 10, 14
"On Don Surly" (Jonson) **17**:197
"On Duelling" (Graves) **6**:144
*On Early Trains* (Pasternak)
   See *Na rannikh poezdakh*
"On Elgin Marbles" (Keats) **1**:279
"On Falling Asleep by Firelight" (Meredith)
   **28**:189-90, 213
"On Falling Asleep to Bird Song" (Meredith)
   **28**:192, 213
"On Flower Wreath Hill" (Rexroth) **20**:220-21
"On Food" (Belloc) **24**:17
"On Friendship" (Wheatley) **3**:363

"On Going Back to the Street after Viewing and Art Show" (Bukowski) **18**:5
"On Going Unnoticed" (Frost) **1**:205
"On Gut" (Jonson) **17**:174
"On Handling Some Small Shells from the Windward Islands" (Swenson) **14**:287
"On Himselfe" (Herrick) **9**:87, 89, 131
"On his being arrived at the age of twenty-three" (Milton)
  See "On his being arrived at the age of twenty-three"
"On His Books" (Belloc) **24**:31
"On His Mistris" (Donne)
  See "Elegie XVI: On his mistris"
"On Imagination" (Wheatley) **3**:336, 338, 353-55
"On Installing an American Kitchen in Lower Austria" (Auden) **1**:24
"On Jenkins' Hill" (Meredith) **28**:206
"On Julia's Clothes" (Herrick)
  See "Upon Julia's Clothes"
"On Leaving Some Friends" (Keats) **1**:313; **73**:311
"On Lieutenant Shift" (Jonson) **17**:197
"On Looking at a Copy of Alice Meynell's Poems Given to Me Years Ago by a Friend" (Lowell) **13**:85, 89-90, 99-100
"On Lookout Mountain" (Hayden) **6**:180, 194
"On Lord Holland's Seat near Margate, Kent" (Gray) **2**:143
"On Lucy Countesse of Bedford" (Jonson)
  See "On Lucy Countesse of Bedford"
"On Madison" (Tomlinson) **17**:353
"On Major General Lee" (Wheatley)
  See "Thoughts on His Excellency Major General Lee"
"On Mr. J. H. in a Fit of Sickness" (Behn) **13**:8
"On My First Daughter" (Jonson) **17**:172, 197
"On My First Son" (Jonson) **17**:172, 177, 197
"On My Own" (Levine) **22**:226
"On My Picture Left in Scotland" (Jonson)
  See "On My Picture Left in Scotland"
"On My Son's Return out of England" (Bradstreet) **10**:36, 60
"On My Way Out I Passed over You and the Verrazano Bridge" (Lorde) **12**:138-39
"On Myselfe" (Finch) **21**:146, 155, 165
"On Neal's Ashes" (Ginsberg) **4**:74
"On Not Being Listened To" (McGuckian) **27**:90
"On Obedience" (Duncan) **2**:114
"On Parting with My Wife, Jamina" (Milosz) **8**:211
"On Passing the New Menin Gate" (Sassoon) **12**:246
"On Poetry: A Rhapsody" (Swift) **9**:249
"On Police Brutality" (Walker) **20**:294
"On Portents" (Graves) **6**:149, 172-73
"On Prime Ministers" (Belloc) **24**:37
"On Reading an Old Baedeker in Schloss Leopoldskron" (Kumin) **15**:209, 212
"On Reading John Cage" (Paz) **1**:355, 363, 374
"On Reading Omar Khayyam" (Lindsay) **23**:283
"On Reading William Blake's 'The Sick Rose'" (Ginsberg) **4**:55
"On Recollection" (Wheatley) **3**:332, 340, 361
"On Returning to Detroit" (Forche) **10**:144, 156
"On Righteous Indignation" (Chesterton) **28**:114
"On Righteous Indignation" (Chesterton) **28**:114
"On San Gabriel Ridges" (Snyder) **21**:291
"On Scratchbury Camp" (Sassoon) **12**:259
"On Seeing Diana go Maddddddddd" (Madhubuti) **5**:344
"On Sir Voluptuous Beast" (Jonson) **17**:174, 212
"On Spies" (Jonson)
  See "On Spies"
"On Squaw Peak" (Hass) **16**:217
"On Swimming" (Zagajewski) **27**:396

"On the Alliance of Education and Government" (Gray)
  See "Essay on the Alliance of Education and Government"
"On the Author of . . . The Way to Health . . ." (Behn) **13**:8
"On the Battle of Kulikovo Field" (Blok) **21**:8, 26, 29
"On the Beach" (Alegria) **26**:
"On the Beach at Fontana" (Joyce) **22**:136
"On the Beach at Night" (Whitman) **3**:401
"On the Beach at Ostia" (Ferlinghetti) **1**:184
"On the Birth of a Black/Baby/Boy" (Knight) **14**:43
*On the Boiler* (Yeats) **20**:311
"On the Building of Springfield" (Lindsay) **23**:277, 281, 296
"On the Cliffs" (Swinburne) **24**:313, 315, 317, 319-20, 343
"On the Coming Victory" (Brutus) **24**:117
"On the Death of Mr. Grinhill, the Famous Painter" (Behn) **13**:8
*On the Death of Pushkin* (Lermontov) **18**:285
"On the Death of the Late Earl of Rochester" (Behn) **13**:8
"On the Death of the Noble Prince King Edward the Fourth" (Skelton) **25**:339
"On the Death of the Queen" (Finch) **21**:171-72
"On the Death of the Rev. Mr. George Whitefield" (Wheatley)
  See "An Elegiac Poem on the Death of George Whitefield"
"On the Death of the Reverend Dr. Sewall" (Wheatley) **3**:342
"On The Dedication of Dorothy Hall" (Dunbar) **5**:131, 134
"On the Departure Platform" (Hardy) **8**:90
"On the Double Ninth Remembering My Brothers" (Wang Wei) **18**:365, 386
"On the Downs" (Chesterton) **28**:98
"On the Duke of Buckingham" (Carew) **29**:61
"On the Eastern Front" (Trakl)
  See "Im Osten"
"On the Edge" (Levine) **22**:212
"On the Edge" (Lorde) **12**:137
*On the Edge* (Levine) **22**:211-12, 216
"On the Escalator" (Zagajewski) **27**:381
*On the Eternity of God* (Smart)
  See *On the Eternity of the Supreme Being*
*On the Eternity of the Supreme Being* (Smart) **13**:328, 343
"On the Extinction of the Venetian Republic" (Wordsworth) **4**:377
"On the Famous Voyage" (Jonson)
  See "On the Famous Voyage"
"On the Field of Kulikovo" (Blok)
  See "On the Battle of Kulikovo Field"
"On the First Discovery of Falseness in Amintas. By Mrs. B." (Behn) **13**:20-1
*On the Goodness of the Supreme Being* (Smart) **13**:340, 359-60
"On the Hall at Stowey" (Tomlinson) **17**:341, 344
"On the Happ Life" (Martial)
  See "Vitam quae faciunt beatiorem"
"On the Highest Pillar" (Montale)
  See "Sulla colonna più alta"
"On the Hill and Grove at Billborow" (Marvell)
  See "Upon the Hill and Grove at Billborow"
"On the Honourable Sir Francis Fane . . ." (Behn) **13**:8
"On the Idle Hill of Summer" (Housman) **2**:185
*On the Immensity of the Supreme Being* (Smart) **13**:343
"On the Island" (Brutus) **24**:115
"On the Lake" (Goethe)
  See "Auf dem See"
"On the Last Performance of" (Hongo) **23**:197
"On the Mantelpiece" (Lowell) **13**:83

"On the Morning of Christ's Nativity" (Milton) **19**:209, 251-54; **29**:229, 232
"On the Move" (Gunn) **26**:184-185, 200, 202, 207, 209
"On the Move" (Gunn) **26**:188-189, 196, 206-208
"On the Murder of Lieutenant José Del Castillo by the Falangist Bravo Martinez, July 12, 1936" (Levine) **22**:223, 225
"On the Ninth" (Li Po) **29**:185
"On the Occasion of National Mourning" (Nemerov) **24**:289
"On the Ocean Floor" (MacDiarmid) **9**:191
*On the Omniscience of the Supreme Being* (Smart) **13**:344
"On the Platform" (Nemerov) **24**:262
*On the Power of the Supreme Being* (Smart) **13**:344
"On the Republic" (Elytis) **21**:123
"On the Rhine" (Arnold) **5**:19, 43
"On the River" (Levine) **22**:228
"On the River Encountering Waters Like the Sea, I Wrote a Short Poem on the Spot" (Tu Fu) **9**:326
"On the Road" (Heaney) **18**:214
"On the Road" (McKay) **2**:205, 220
"On the Road Home" (Stevens) **6**:311-12
"On the Road to Woodlawn" (Roethke) **15**:291, 293-95
*On the Scale of One to One* (Cassian) **17**:6, 9
*On the Sick-Bed* (Tagore)
  See *Rogsajyae*
"On the South Coast" (Swinburne) **24**:313, 329
"On the Spring" (Gray)
  See "Ode on Spring"
"On the Spur of the Moment" (Tu Fu) **9**:323
"On the Square" (Aleixandre)
  See "In The Plaza"
"On the Stage of Ghosts a Pale Gleaming" (Mandelstam) **14**:120
"On the Subway" (Olds) **22**:314
"On the Tennis Court at Night" (Kinnell) **26**:260
"On the Threshold" (Gozzano) **10**:174
"On the Threshold of His Greatness, the Poet Comes Down with a Sore Throat" (Nemerov) **24**:267
"On the Victory Obtained by Blake over the Spaniards" (Marvell) **10**:270-71
"On the Way" (Robinson) **1**:468
"On the Way to Lycomedes of Scyrus" (Brodsky)
  See "K Likomedu, na Skiros"
"On the Way to School" (Aleixandre) **15**:24
"On the Wide Heath" (Millay) **6**:215, 232, 238
"On the Works of Providence" (Wheatley)
  See "Thoughts on the Works of Providence"
*On These I Stand: An Anthology of the Best Poems of Countee Cullen* (Cullen) **20**:75-76, 79, 82-83
*On This Island* (Auden)
  See "Look, Stranger, on This Island Now"
"On Those That Hated 'The Playboy of the Western World'" (Yeats) **20**:320
"On Torture, a Public Singer" (Belloc) **24**:34
"On Two Ministers of State" (Belloc) **24**:33, 41
"On Universalism" (Knight) **14**:37-8
"On Virtue" (Wheatley) **3**:361
"On Visiting the Tomb of Burns" (Keats) **1**:314
"On Walking Slowly After an Accident" (Smith) **12**:314, 316
"On Watching a World Series Game" (Sanchez) **9**:210, 225
"On Wenlock Edge" (Housman) **2**:180
"Once" (Celan) **10**:97
*Once Again* (Tagore)
  See *Punascha*
"Once and Again" (Carruth) **10**:91
"the once and future dead" (Clifton) **17**:19
"Once by the Pacific" (Frost) **1**:221
"Once in May" (Levine) **22**:217-18
"Once More, the Round" (Roethke) **15**:302

"L'Ondine et le pêcheur" (Gautier) **18**:141
"I" (Joyce) **22**:138, 144, 158, 162, 164, 166, 168
"One Art" (Bishop) **3**:62-3, 66-8
"One at One with his Desire" (Ammons) **16**:50
"One by One" (Levine) **22**:218
"One Day" (Brooke) **24**:86
"One Day in Spring" (Sitwell) **3**:311
"One Day We Play a Game" (Cullen) **20**:67
*One for the Rose* (Levine) **22**:220, 226
"The One Girl at the Boys' Party" (Olds) **22**:311
"One grief of thine" (Bridges) **28**:86
*One Handful of Sand* (Ishikawa)
   See *Ichiaku no suna*
*One Hundred Poems from the Chinese*
   (Rexroth) **20**:188, 204
*100 Selected Poems* (Cummings) **5**:86
"125th Street and Abomey" (Lorde) **12**:155, 160
"1 Jan." (Ammons) **16**:21
"1 January 1924" (Mandelstam) **14**:121, 134
"One: Many" (Ammons) **16**:6
"One More Brevity" (Frost) **1**:213
"One Morning in New Hampshire" (Swenson)
   **14**:249, 275
"One Need Not Be a Chamber to Be Haunted"
   (Dickinson) **1**:94
"One Night Stand" (Baraka) **4**:6
"One Night's Bond" (Hagiwara Sakutaro)
   **18**:168-69
"One O'Clock at Night" (Loy) **16**:312, 327
"One of Many" (Smith) **12**:314, 331, 333
"1.1.87" (Heaney) **18**:258
"One or Two I've Finished" (Stein) **18**:342
"One Person" (Wylie) **23**:304-305, 311, 314, 317-18, 321-24
"One Ralph Blossom Soliloquizes" (Hardy)
   **8**:124
"The One Remains" (Owen) **19**:368
"One Should Not Talk to a Skilled Hunter
   about What is Forbidden by the Buddha"
   (Snyder) **21**:292
"One Sided Shoot-Out" (Madhubuti) **5**:321, 345
"One Soldier" (Rukeyser) **12**:231
"The One Thing That Can Save America"
   (Ashbery) **26**:127, 148
"One Thousand Fearful Words for Fidel
   Castro" (Ferlinghetti) **1**:187
*1x1* (Cummings) **5**:83, 107-08
"One Viceroy Resigns" (Kipling) **3**:181, 186
"One View of the Question" (Kipling) **3**:184
"One Volume Missing" (Dove) **6**:114
*One Way Ticket* (Hughes) **1**:241, 243, 247, 252, 260-61, 268
"One We Knew" (Hardy) **8**:99, 132
"One Who Used To Beat His Way" (Kinnell)
   **26**:240
"The One Who Was" (Aleixandre) **15**:4
"One Word More" (Browning) **2**:66, 71, 95
"One World" (Tomlinson) **17**:333
"One year" (Illyes)
   See "Egy ev"
"One Year" (Olds) **22**:341
"One-Eye, Two-Eyes, Three-Eyes" (Sexton)
   **2**:365
"The One-Eyed King" (Levine) **22**:213
*Onegin's Journey* (Pushkin) **10**:400-01
"One-Legged Man" (Sassoon) **12**:242, 263
"One's-Self I Sing" (Whitman)
   See "Song of Myself"
"Onirocritique" (Apollinaire) **7**:12
"Only a Curl" (Browning) **6**:24, 30
"Only a Few Left" (Madhubuti) **5**:340
"Only a Little Sleep, a Little Slumber"
   (Hughes) **7**:154
"Only Child" (Page) **12**:170, 175-76
"The Only One" (Holderlin)
   See "Der Einzige"
"Ons As Me Thought" (Wyatt) **27**:316
"The Onset" (Frost) **1**:222

"Ontological Episode of the Asylum" (Carruth)
   **10**:89
"The Oon Olympian" (MacDiarmid) **9**:197
"Oonts" (Kipling) **3**:158
"The Open Boat" (Levine) **22**:223
*Open Eye, Open Heart* (Ferlinghetti) **1**:186-88
"Open House" (Roethke) **15**:291, 293, 302
*Open House* (Roethke) **15**:245-46, 248, 250, 256, 259, 282, 287, 290-91, 293-95, 298, 304
"Open It, Write" (Ekeloef) **23**:62, 64
"Open Rose" (McGuckian) **27**:105
"The Open Sea" (Meredith) **28**:182, 190, 212
"Open Sea" (Neruda) **4**:282
*The Open Sea* (Masters) **1**:333, 335
*The Open Sea* (Meredith) **28**:171, 174-75, 177, 181, 187-92, 194, 200-01, 210-11, 213, 215
"Open the Door to Me, O" (Burns) **6**:75
"Open the Gates" (Kunitz) **19**:155, 162, 173-74, 176-77, 186
*The Opening of the Field* (Duncan) **2**:103-04, 106, 113-14, 120, 122, 124-25, 127-28
*Openings* (Berry) **28**:5, 15-16
"An Opera House" (Lowell) **13**:79
"The Operation" (Sexton) **2**:348, 350, 353, 361, 365
"The Operation" (Tomlinson) **17**:360
"Operation Herod" (Alegria) **26**:
"Operation Herod" (Alegria) **26**:
"Ophélie" (Rimbaud) **3**:283
"Opiário" (Pessoa) **20**:166
"Oppositions" (Wright) **14**:379
"Oppositions debate with Mallarmé"
   (Tomlinson) **17**:338-39
"Opredelenyie poezii" (Pasternak) **6**:272, 285
"The Optimist's Salutation" (Dario)
   See "Salutación del optimista"
*Opus incertum* (Ekeloef) **23**:63, 76
*Opus incertum II* (Ekeloef) **23**:77
*Opus Posthumous* (Stevens) **6**:306, 339
"Opyt análiza chetyryokhstópnogo yàmba"
   (Bely) **11**:18
"Or, Solitude" (Davie) **29**:122-24
"Or When Your Sister Sleeps Around for
   Money" (Knight)
   See "The Violent Space (or when your
   sister sleeps around for money)"
"Oración" (Fuertes) **27**:5, 11, 30
"Oracion" (Neruda) **4**:278
"Oración para altas horas de la madrugada"
   (Fuertes) **27**:39
*Oracion por Marilyn Monroe y otros poemas*
   (Cardenal) **22**:125
"Oracle" (Heaney) **18**:201, 203
"The Oracle" (Merton) **10**:339
"Oracle over Managua" (Cardenal)
   See "Oráculo sobre Managua"
"The Oracles" (Housman) **2**:164
"Les oracles" (Vigny) **26**:369, 403, 405
"Oráculo sobre Managua" (Cardenal) **22**:103-06
"Oraculos" (Cardenal) **22**:131
*Oral Tradition* (Sikelianos)
   See "Agraphon"
"Orange In" (Stein) **18**:318, 328
"Orange of Midsummer" (Lowell) **13**:97
"The Orange Tree" (Levertov) **11**:169
"Orange-Tree" (Wright) **14**:341
"Oration on Death" (Bryant) **20**:13
*The Orators* (Auden) **1**:4-5, 8-11, 16, 22, 25, 30-1, 37
"Orbits" (Cassian) **17**:11
"Orchard" (H. D.)
   See "Priapus"
"The Orchid House" (McGuckian) **27**:97
*The Order of Nature* (Bryant) **20**:5
"Orders" (Duncan) **2**:125
"The Ordinary" (Stryk) **27**:208, 214
"An Ordinary Evening in New Haven"
   (Stevens) **6**:338
"An Ordinary Girl" (Sirkis) **8**:417
"An Ordinary Morning" (Levine) **22**:224

*An Ordinary Woman* (Clifton) **17**:21, 23-24, 26, 34, 37
"Ordinary Women" (Stevens) **6**:295
"The Ordination" (Burns) **6**:83, 88
*L'Ordre des Oiseaux* (Perse) **23**:254, 256
"Oread" (H. D.) **5**:268, 275, 304
"Gli orecchini" (Montale) **13**:108, 128
"Orestes-Theme" (H. D.) **5**:305
"Organelle" (Swenson) **14**:247
"Organic Bloom" (Kunitz) **19**:148
"Organs" (Swenson) **14**:276
"L'orgie Parisienne; ou, Paris se Repeuple"
   (Rimbaud) **3**:281
"Oriana" (Tennyson) **6**:359
"The Oriental Ballerina" (Dove) **6**:113
*Les orientales* (Hugo) **17**:45, 50-52, 55, 62-63, 70, 74-76, 87, 90-91
*Orientations* (Elytis)
   See *Prosanatolizmí*
"Origin" (Harjo) **27**:64
"The Origin of Cities" (Hass) **16**:199
"Original Child Bomb" (Merton) **10**:337
"Original Memory" (Harjo) **27**:68
"Original Sin" (Jeffers) **17**:132
"The Originators" (Merton) **10**:345
"Origins and History of Consciousness" (Rich)
   **5**:374
"Orion" (Elytis) **21**:118
"Orlovu" (Pushkin) **10**:409
"Ornières" (Rimbaud) **3**:264
*El oro de los tigres* (Borges) **22**:79-81, 93, 95
*The Orphan Angel* (Wylie) **23**:329
"The Orphan Reformed" (Smith) **12**:326
"L'Orphée" (Ronsard) **11**:251
"Orphée" (Valery) **9**:351
"L'orphelin" (Mallarme) **4**:202
"Orpheus" (Meredith) **28**:191-92
*Orpheus* (Rukeyser) **12**:207, 213-14, 220
"Orpheus and Eurydice" (Noyes) **27**:118, 134
"Orpheus. Eurydike. Hermes." (Rilke) **2**:295
"Orphic Scenario" (Nemerov) **24**:257, 294-97
"L'orto" (Montale) **13**:109-10, 113, 121-22, 133, 151
"Osgar" (Pushkin) **10**:407
"Osiris and Set" (Duncan) **2**:103
"Osiris, Come to Iris" (Thomas) **2**:402
*Osiris Jones* (Aiken) **26**:12, 29
"Osobny zeszyt" (Milosz) **8**:186-87, 199, 204
*Osorio* (Coleridge)
   See *Remorse*
*Ossi di seppia* (Montale) **13**:103, 105-07, 109, 112-17, 119, 122, 126-27, 131, 133-34, 139, 141, 143, 160, 162-66
"Ossian's Grave" (Jeffers) **17**:117
"Ostanovka v pustyne" (Brodsky) **9**:3, 5, 7
"Ostriches & Grandmothers" (Baraka) **4**:15
"osynlig närvaro" (Ekeloef) **23**:88-92
"The Other" (Borges)
   See "El otro"
"The Other" (Sexton) **2**:365
*The Other Half* (Wright) **14**:349, 355-56, 362, 366
"The Other Noah" (Elytis) **21**:123
"The Other One" (Borges)
   See "El otro"
"The Other Side" (Heaney) **18**:205
"The Other Tiger" (Borges)
   See "El otro tigre"
"Others I Am Not the First" (Housman) **2**:179, 195
"An Otherworldly Evening" (Tsvetaeva)
   See "Nezdeshnii vecher"
*Otho the Great* (Keats) **1**:279
"Otoño" (Neruda) **4**:290
"El otro" (Borges) **22**:74
*El otro, el mismo* (Borges) **22**:71, 73-4, 95-6, 98, 100
"El otro tigre" (Borges) **22**:73, 96-7
"Otrok" (Tsvetaeva) **14**:315-16
"Otryvok-A Fragment" (Lermontov) **18**:302
"The Otter" (Heaney) **18**:217, 239, 245
"An Otter" (Hughes) **7**:136, 140

"Our Bodies" (Levertov) **11**:169
"Our Bog Is Dood" (Smith) **12**:331, 333
"Our Cabal" (Behn) **13**:7, 20
*Our Dead Behind Us* (Lorde) **12**:137-39, 141-43, 148, 154-55, 157-58
"Our English Friends" (Harper) **21**:198
"Our Forward Shadows" (Swenson) **14**:276
"Our Friends in Jail" (Bissett) **14**:7
*Our Ground Time Here Will Be Brief* (Kumin) **15**:214, 217, 221
"Our Lady of the Sackcloth" (Kipling) **3**:183
"Our Lord and Our Lady" (Belloc) **24**:5
"Our Mother Pocahontas" (Lindsay) **23**:288
"Our Mothers" (Rossetti) **7**:286
"Our Names" (Ortiz) **17**:245
"Our Need" (Walker) **20**:283
"Our Prayer of Thanks" (Sandburg) **2**:316
"Our Storm" (Pasternak) **6**:271
"Our Whole Life" (Rich) **5**:391
"Ourselves or Nothing" (Forche) **10**:137, 143-44, 148, 154, 158-59, 161, 168
"Ourselves We Do Inter with Sweet Derision" (Dickinson) **1**:102
"Out" (Hughes) **7**:123, 149
"Out Is Out" (Nash) **21**:268
"Out of Debt" (McKay) **2**:222
"Out of My Head" (Swenson) **14**:255, 266, 282
"Out of Superstition" (Pasternak)
    See "From Superstition"
"Out of the Aegean" (Elytis) **21**:118
"Out of the Cradle Endlessly Rocking" (Whitman) **3**:378, 382, 391-92, 397, 401
"Out of the Sea, Early" (Swenson) **14**:264
"Out of the Watercolored Window, When You Look" (Schwartz) **8**:301
"Out on the Lawn I Lie in Bed..." (Auden) **1**:22
"OUT ON THE TOWN JOY RIDIN" (Bissett) **14**:31
"Out, Out—" (Frost) **1**:227
"Out to the Hard Road" (Lorde) **12**:138
"Out Walking" (Zagajewski) **27**:396
"Outcast" (McKay) **2**:213, 217, 221
*The Outcasts* (Sitwell) **3**:321
"The Outcome of Mr. Buck's Superstition" (Nash) **21**:267
"The Outcome of the Matter: The Sun" (Piercy) **29**:326
"The Outdoor Concert" (Gunn) **26**:195, 208
*Outdoor Show* (Cassian) **17**:6
"The Outer Banks" (Rukeyser) **12**:224
"The Outlaw" (Heaney) **18**:200
"Outlines" (Lorde) **12**:137
"Outside a Gate" (Lowell) **13**:94
"Outside my window" (Viereck) **27**:278
"Outside the Diner" (Gunn) **26**:214
"Outside the Operating Room of the Sex-Change Doctor" (Olds) **22**:316
"The Oven Bird" (Frost) **1**:222
"Ovenstone" (Guillen) **23**:102
"Over 2,000 Illustrations" (Bishop) **3**:67
*Over All the Obscene Boundaries: European Poems & Transitions* (Ferlinghetti) **1**:183-85
"Over Brooklyn Bridge" (Tomlinson) **17**:359
"Over Cities" (Milosz) **8**:186
"Over Denver Again" (Ginsberg) **4**:57
"Over Sir John's Hill" (Thomas) **2**:395, 404
"Over St. John's Hill" (Thomas)
    See "Over Sir John's Hill"
"Over Us If (as what Was Dusk Becomes" (Cummings) **5**:109
"The Overgrown Pasture" (Lowell) **13**:60, 78, 85
"Overheard" (Kipling) **3**:193
"Overheard" (Levertov) **11**:160
"Overland to the Islands" (Levertov) **11**:188, 192, 196
*Overland to the Islands* (Levertov) **11**:166, 188, 202
"Overlooking the River Stour" (Hardy) **8**:116-17
"Overpopulation" (Ferlinghetti) **1**:167, 175, 187

"Overture to a Dance of Locomotives" (Williams) **7**:345, 410
"Overtures to Death" (Day Lewis) **11**:144
*Overtures to Death and Other Poems* (Day Lewis) **11**:127-30, 144
"Ovid in Exile" (Graves) **6**:164
"Ovid, Old Buddy, I Would Discourse with You a While" (Carruth) **10**:88
*Ovnis'* (Cardenal)
    See *Los ovnis de oro*
*Los ovnis de oro* (Cardenal) **22**:126, 132
"Owatari Bridge" (Hagiwara Sakutaro)
    See "Ōwatari-bashi"
"Ōwatari-bashi" (Hagiwara Sakutaro) **18**:183
"Owen Ahern and His Dancers" (Yeats) **20**:328
"The Owl in the Sarcophagus" (Stevens) **6**:304
"Owl Song" (Atwood) **8**:25
*Owl's Clover* (Stevens) **6**:297-98, 317-20
"Owl's Song" (Hughes) **7**:160-61
"Ownership" (Reese) **29**:336, 344
"The Ox Tamer" (Whitman) **3**:377
"The Oxen" (Hardy) **8**:112, 121
"Oxen: Ploughing at Fiesole" (Tomlinson) **17**:311
"Oxford" (Auden) **1**:30
"Oysters" (Heaney) **18**:217, 239, 241
"Oysters" (Sexton) **2**:365
"Oysters" (Snyder) **21**:292
"Ozone" (Dove) **6**:121-23
*P. 1* (Pindar)
    See *Pythian 1*
*P. 2* (Pindar)
    See *Pythian 2*
*P. 3* (Pindar)
    See *Pythian 3*
*P. 4* (Pindar)
    See *Pythian 4*
*P. 5* (Pindar)
    See *Pythian 5*
*P. 6* (Pindar)
    See *Pythian 6*
*P. 8* (Pindar)
    See *Pythian 8*
*Pacchiarotto* (Browning) **2**:71
"Pacific Letter" (Ondaatje) **28**:316
"A Pacific State" (Milosz) **8**:205
"A Packet of Letters" (Bogan) **12**:94
*Paean 8* (Pindar) **19**:396
"Paesaggio I" (Pavese) **13**:204, 212, 220, 225-26
"Paesaggio II" (Pavese) **13**:212
"Paesaggio III" (Pavese) **13**:212
"Paesaggio V" (Pavese) **13**:212
"Paesaggio VI" (Pavese) **13**:228
"Paesaggio VII" (Pavese) **13**:204, 212
"Paesaggio VIII" (Pavese) **13**:212, 230
"The Pagan Isms" (McKay) **2**:219-20
"Pagan Prayer" (Cullen) **20**:65, 72
*A Pageant, and Other Poems* (Rossetti) **7**:270
*The Pageant of Seasons*
    See *Rtusamhāra*
"Pagett, M. P." (Kipling) **3**:190
"La página blanca" (Dario) **15**:103-04
*Paginas* (Jimenez) **7**:208, 212
"The Pahty" (Dunbar) **5**:116, 119, 122-23, 146
*Paid on Both Sides* (Auden) **1**:5, 8, 20, 30, 34
"Pain for a Daughter" (Sexton) **2**:363
"Pain Tells You Want to Wear" (McGuckian) **27**:103
"The Pains of Sleep" (Coleridge) **11**:41, 44
"The Painted Cup" (Bryant) **20**:23
*Painted Lace and Other Pieces (1914-1937* Stein) **18**:341
"Painted Steps" (Gallagher) **9**:45
"The Painter" (Ashbery) **26**:112, 167
"The Painter Dreaming in the Scholar's House" (Nemerov) **24**:285, 300
"The Painting" (Williams) **7**:394
"Painting the North San Juan School" (Snyder) **21**:300
"Paisaje de la multitud que orina" (Garcia Lorca) **3**:140

"Paisaje de la multitud que vomita" (Garcia Lorca) **3**:140
"Paisaje del corozon" (Jimenez) **7**:199
"Paisaje después de una batalla" (Neruda) **4**:309
"Los Pájaros Anidan" (Fuertes) **27**:51
"Palabras" (Aleixandre) **15**:39
"Las palabras" (Paz) **1**:358
"Las palabras del poeta" (Aleixandre) **15**:41
"Palabras en el trópico" (Guillen) **23**:106
"Palace" (Apollinaire)
    See "Palais"
"The Palace" (Ondaatje) **28**:337
"The Palace of Art" (Tennyson) **6**:353, 359-60, 370, 375, 378-80, 382, 409, 412
"The Palace of Pan" (Swinburne) **24**:313
"The Palace of the Babies" (Stevens) **6**:293
"Palais" (Apollinaire) **7**:45-6, 48
"Palais des Arts" (Gluck) **16**:130, 150
"Palamon and Arcite" (Chaucer)
    See "Knight's Tale"
*Palātakā* (Tagore) **8**:415
"A Pale Arrangement of Hands" (Song) **21**:334, 341-42
"Pale Horse" (Hagiwara Sakutaro) **18**:176-77
"Pale, Intent Noontide" (Montale)
    See "Meriggiare pallido e assorto"
"Pâline" (Apollinaire) **7**:48
"Palladium" (Arnold) **5**:8
"Pallas Athene" (Masters) **1**:344
"Palm" (Valery)
    See "Palme"
"Palm and Pine" (Kipling) **3**:179
"Palme" (Valery) **9**:363, 365, 367, 393-94
"Palo Alto: The Marshes" (Hass) **16**:218
*La paloma de vuelo popular: Elegiás* (Guillen) **23**:100, 124, 128, 133
"Pals" (Sandburg) **2**:303
"Paltry Nude" (Stevens) **6**:295
"The Paltry Nude Starts on a Spring Voyage" (Stevens) **6**:295
"Pamiatnik" (Pushkin)
    See "Pamjatnik"
"Pamjatnik" (Pushkin) **10**:408, 412, 415
"Pan" (Hugo) **17**:91
"Pan" (Sikelianos) **29**:369
"Pan and Luna" (Browning) **2**:88-9
"Pan and Thalassius" (Swinburne) **24**:315
"Pan and Thalassius" (Swinburne) **24**:315
"Panamá" (Guillen) **23**:126
"Panchishe vaisakh" (Tagore) **8**:415
"A Panegerick to Sir Lewis Pemberton" (Herrick) **9**:102
"A Panegyrick on the Dean in the Person of a Lady in the North" (Swift) **9**:262, 274, 295
"Panegyrique de la Renommée" (Ronsard) **11**:243
"The Pangolin" (Moore) **4**:235
"Panorama ceigo de Nueva York" (Garcia Lorca) **3**:141
*The Panther and the Lash: Poems of Our Times* (Hughes) **1**:251-52, 257-58, 260, 262, 268
"Pantomime" (Verlaine) **2**:430
"Paolo e Virginia" (Pavese) **13**:221
"The Papa and Mama Dance" (Sexton) **2**:349, 352-53
"Papà beve sempre" (Pavese) **13**:214
"Papa Love Baby" (Smith) **12**:315, 322, 325-26, 343
"The Paper Nautilus" (Moore) **4**:255
"The Paper on the Floor" (Bukowski) **18**:3
"The Paper Wind Mill" (Lowell) **13**:78
"Le papillon" (Lamartine) **16**:278
*Para las seis cuerdas* (Borges) **22**:71
"Parable of the Hostages" (Gluck) **16**:171
"The Parable of the Old Man and the Young" (Owen) **19**:335, 354, 356, 359, 370
*Paracelsus* (Browning) **2**:26-31, 34, 42-3, 48, 65-6, 73, 82, 91-3, 96
"Parade of Painters" (Swenson) **14**:253
"Paradis Perdu" (Nishiwaki) **15**:237

"Paradise" (Gallagher) **9**:64
"Paradise" (Gluck) **16**:161
"Paradise" (Herbert) **4**:114, 130
*Paradise Lost* (Milton) **19**:193-200, 203-12,
    219, 224, 234-36, 238, 240-49, 252, 254,
    258; **29**:194-292
"Paradise of Tears" (Bryant) **20**:10
"Paradise on the Roofs" (Pavese) **13**:204
*Paradise Regained* (Milton) **19**:204-06, 208,
    214-16, 219; **29**:212, 218, 244, 261, 266-68
*Paradiso* (Dante) **21**:49-50, 53-5, 57-8, 67, 69,
    72, 75-7, 81-2, 92, 94, 96, 103-06, 109-11
"Paradox" (Lowell) **13**:85
*The Paradox* (Noyes) **27**:138
"Paragraphs" (Carruth) **10**:74-5, 83, 85
"Parajaya saṅgīt" (Tagore) **8**:405
*Parallel Destinies* (Cassian) **17**:6
*Parallèlement* (Verlaine) **2**:414, 416-17, 419,
    425-26
"Paralysis" (Brooke) **24**:56, 77
"Paralytic" (Plath) **1**:391
"Paranoid" (Page) **12**:175
"Paraphrase" (Crane) **3**:102
"The Parasceve, or Preparation" (Herrick)
    **9**:117, 119
"Paratile of a Certain Virgin" (Parker) **28**:348
"Parchiarotto" (Browning) **2**:63, 71, 75
"Pardoner's Prologue" (Chaucer) **19**:26, 46
"Pardoner's Tale" (Chaucer) **19**:13, 30, 46, 49,
    51-2, 68
"Paréntesis pasional" (Borges) **22**:92
"Parents" (Meredith) **28**:180, 208
"The Parents: People Like Our Marriage,
    Maxie and Andrew" (Brooks) **7**:80
"Parfum exotique" (Baudelaire) **1**:45
"Paring the Apple" (Tomlinson) **17**:331
"Paris" (Ondaatje) **28**:298-99
"Paris" (Stryk) **27**:214
"Paris" (Vigny) **26**:402, 411-12
"Paris and Helen" (Schwartz) **8**:311
"Paris at Nightfall" (Baudelaire)
    See "Le crépuscule du soir"
"Paris in the Snow" (Senghor) **25**:241
*Paris Spleen* (Baudelaire)
    See *Petits poèmes en prose: Le spleen de
        Paris*
"A Parisian Dream" (Baudelaire)
    See "Rêve parisien"
*The Parisian Prowler* (Baudelaire)
    See *Petits poèmes en prose: Le spleen de
        Paris*
"Parisina" (Byron) **16**:109
"The Park" (Stryk) **27**:211
"Park Bench" (Hughes) **1**:242
"The Parklands" (Smith) **12**:317
*Parlement* (Chaucer)
    See *Parlement of Foules*
*Parlement of Foules* (Chaucer) **19**:10, 12, 20-3,
    38, 74
"Parleying with Charles Avison" (Browning)
    **2**:83
"Parleying with Gerard de Lairesse"
    (Browning) **2**:81, 83, 86
*Parleyings with Certain People of Importance
    in Their Day* (Browning) **2**:64, 85, 95-6
"Parlez-vous français" (Schwartz) **8**:302-03
"Parliament Hill Fields" (Plath) **1**:391
*Parliament of Fowls* (Chaucer)
    See *Parlement of Foules*
"Parlour-Piece" (Hughes) **7**:140
"Parnell's Funeral" (Yeats) **20**:326, 348
"Parodos" (Gluck) **16**:159-62
"Le parole" (Montale) **13**:134
"La Parole aux Oricous" (Cesaire) **25**:12
"Paroles sur la dune" (Hugo) **17**:64
"Parrots" (Wright) **14**:348
"Parsley" (Dove) **6**:105, 110
"The Parson's Daughter and the Seminarist"
    (Bely) **11**:3
"Parson's Tale" (Chaucer) **19**:37, 45, 47
*A Part* (Berry) **28**:4, 9-10
"Part of a Bird" (Cassian) **17**:4, 12-13

"A Part of Speech" (Brodsky)
    See "Cast řeči"
*A Part of Speech* (Brodsky)
    See *Cast řeči*
"Part of the Doctrine" (Baraka) **4**:18
"Part of the Seventh Epistle of the First Book
    of Horace Imitated and Addressed to the
    Earl of Oxford" (Swift) **9**:296
"Part of the Vigil" (Merrill) **28**:221, 224
"Parted" (Dunbar) **5**:125, 140
"Partial Accounts" (Meredith) **28**:205, 215
*Partial Accounts: New and Selected Poems*
    (Meredith) **28**:211-16
"Partial Comfort" (Parker) **28**:362
"Parting" (Ammons) **16**:63
"Parting" (Arnold) **5**:43, 55
"The Parting" (Harper) **21**:194
"The Parting" (Li Po) **29**:140
"Parting Gift" (Wylie) **23**:321
*Partitur* (Ekeloef) **23**:68-9, 78
"Partly from the Greek" (Belloc) **24**:32
"The Partner" (Roethke) **15**:256
"The Partner's Desk" (McGuckian) **27**:105
*Parts of a World* (Stevens) **6**:299, 311, 318
"A Part-Sequence for Change" (Duncan) **2**:103
"Parturition" (Loy) **16**:313-14, 318, 320, 325,
    329, 333
"The Party" (Dunbar)
    See "The Pahty"
"Les pas" (Valery) **9**:366, 374, 396
*Pasado en claro* (Paz) **1**:369, 371-72, 374
"Pascuas sangrientas de 1956" (Guillen) **23**:128
*Pasión de la tierra* (Aleixandre) **15**:3, 10, 18,
    29-32, 34, 40
"Pass on by" (Guillen)
    See "Sigue"
*Pass th Food Release th Spirit Book* (Bissett)
    **14**:15-16, 24
"Passage" (Ammons) **16**:6
"Passage" (Crane) **3**:82
"Passage" (Levertov) **11**:202
"Passage" (Okigbo) **7**:223-24, 231, 236-39,
    248-49, 251, 255
"Passage de l'oiseau divin" (Breton) **15**:49
"Passage to India" (Whitman) **3**:378, 394-98
"Passages 13" (Duncan) **2**:116
"Passages 21" (Duncan) **2**:116
"Passages 25" (Duncan) **2**:25
"Passages 26" (Duncan) **2**:116
"Passages 27" (Duncan) **2**:116
"Passages 29" (Duncan) **2**:116
"Passages 31" (Duncan) **2**:117
"Passages 35" (TribunalsDuncan) **2**:116, 118
"Passages 36" (Duncan) **2**:115-17
*The Passages of Joy* (Gunn) **26**:208-209, 211-
    212, 214, 216-217, 220, 230-231
"Le Passe" (Hugo) **17**:64
"Passe forth my wonted cryes" (Wyatt) **27**:362
"Passer mortuus est" (Millay) **6**:228
"A Passer-By" (Bridges) **28**:67, 70
"Passing Chao-ling Again" (Tu Fu) **9**:322
"The Passing Cloud" (Smith) **12**:339
"Passing Losses On" (Frost) **1**:200
"The Passing of Arthur" (Tennyson)
    See "Morte d'Arthur"
"The Passing of the Hawthorn" (Swinburne)
    **24**:313, 317
"Passing Through" (Kunitz) **19**:187
"Passing Through Little Rock" (Ortiz) **17**:227
*Passing Through: The Later Poems New and
    Selected* (Kunitz) **19**:186
"Passion" (Trakl) **20**:269
*The Passion of Claude McKay: Selected
    Poetry and Prose, 1912-1948* (McKay)
    **2**:218
*Passion of the Earth* (Aleixandre)
    See *Pasión de la tierra*
"La passione" (Pasolini) **17**:288
*Passione e ideologia* (Pasolini) **17**:250, 252,
    263-64, 291, 295
*Passport to the War* (Kunitz) **19**:148, 154,
    160-62

"The Past" (Bryant) **20**:9
"The Past" (Emerson) **18**:76
"Past" (Sanchez) **9**:219
*The Past* (Kinnell) **26**:277-78, 292-93
"Past and Future" (Browning) **6**:16, 41
"Past and Present" (Masters) **1**:343
"Past Days" (Swinburne) **24**:327, 329
"The Past Is the Present" (Moore) **4**:237
"Pastor hacia el puerto" (Aleixandre) **15**:35
"Pastoral" (Dove) **6**:120-21
"The Pastoral" (Soto) **28**:370
"Pastoral" (Viereck) **27**:271
"Pastoral" (Williams) **7**:367, 378
*Pastoral* (Williams) **7**:349
"Pastoral Dialogue" (Swift) **9**:261
"A Pastoral Pindaric . . ." (Behn) **13**:8
*Pastoral Poesy* (Clare) **23**:4
"A Pastoral to Mr. Stafford" (Behn) **13**:8, 32
"Pastorale" (Crane) **3**:98-9
*Pastorales* (Jimenez) **7**:184
"A Pastorall Song to the King" (Herrick) **9**:86
*Pastorals* (Pope) **26**:319, 321
*Pastorals* (Vergil)
    See *Georgics*
"Pastorela di Narcis" (Pasolini) **17**:253, 282
"The Pasture" (Frost) **1**:197, 212, 225
*Pastures and Other Poems* (Reese) **29**:336-37,
    339, 348
"Patent Leather" (Brooks) **7**:58, 68, 79
"Pater Filio" (Bridges) **28**:89
"Paternità" (Pavese) **13**:213, 229
"Paternity" (Pavese)
    See "Paternità"
"Paterson" (Ginsberg) **4**:73-5
*Paterson* (Williams) **7**:350, 354-60, 362, 364-
    65, 370-75, 377, 379, 392-95, 402-03,
    408-10
*Paterson I* (Williams) **7**:354, 357-58, 360, 365
*Paterson II* (Williams) **7**:363, 391-92
*Paterson IV* (Williams) **7**:363, 392
*Paterson V* (Williams) **7**:364-65, 370-71, 393
"Paterson: Episode 17" (Williams) **7**:360
"The Path" (Dunbar) **5**:125
"The Path Among the Stones" (Kinnell) **26**:252,
    269, 273, 275-76
"Path of the Chameleon" (Wylie) **23**:330
"Path of Thunder" (Okigbo) **7**:228, 246-47, 255
*Path of Thunder* (Okigbo)
    See *Labyrinths, with Path of Thunder*
"Paths and Thingscape" (Atwood) **8**:36
"Patience" (Graves) **6**:154
"Patience" (Lowell) **13**:60
"Patmos" (Holderlin) **4**:148, 150-51, 153, 155-
    57, 159, 166, 172
*Patria o muerte! The Great Zoo, and Other
    Poems by Nicolás Guillén* (Guillen)
    See *El gran zoo*
"Patriotic Poem" (Wakoski) **15**:358
"The Patroit" (Browning) **2**:60
"Patterns" (Lowell) **13**:60, 71, 76-7, 84-5, 89,
    96
"Patterns" (Wright) **14**:376
"Paul and Virginia" (Gozzano) **10**:176, 178,
    180-84
*Paul Celan: Poems* (Celan) **10**:95-6, 107-08,
    114
"Paul Robeson" (Brooks) **7**:92-3
"Paula Becker To Clara Westhoff" (Rich) **5**:379
*Pauline: A Fragment of a Confession*
    (Browning) **2**:25-6, 42-3, 48, 66, 90-2, 94
"Paul's Wife" (Frost) **1**:194
"Paumanok" (Clampitt) **19**:102
"A Pause for Thought" (Rossetti) **7**:280, 297
"Pauvre Lélian" (Verlaine) **2**:416
"Les pauvres à l'église" (Rimbaud) **3**:255
"Les pauvres gens" (Hugo) **17**:61
"Pavitra prem" (Tagore) **8**:407
"The Pawnbroker" (Kumin) **15**:180, 192, 200
"Pax" (Dario) **15**:82, 115
"Pay Day" (Hughes) **1**:255
"Pay Day" (McKay) **2**:226
"Paying Calls" (Hardy) **8**:105

"Paysage" (Apollinaire) **7**:32, 34-5
"Paysage Moralisé" (Auden) **1**:23
"Paysages belges" (Verlaine) **2**:415
"Peace" (Brooke) **24**:59, 74, 79-80, 87-9
"Peace" (Clare) **23**:44
"Peace" (Dario)
　　See "Pax"
"Peace" (Herbert) **4**:101, 134
"Peace" (Hopkins) **15**:127
"Peace" (Levine) **22**:219
"Peace" (Yeats) **20**:329
"The Peace-Offering" (Hardy) **8**:93
"Peach Blossom Spring" (Wang Wei) **18**:374
"Peacock" (Merrill) **28**:234
"The Peacock Room" (Hayden) **6**:193-95, 198
"Pear Tree" (H. D.) **5**:275
"The Pearch" (Kinney) **26**:
"The Pearl" (Herbert) **4**:100, 128
"The Pearl Diver" (Wylie) **23**:321
"Pearl Horizons" (Sandburg) **2**:307
"The Peasant Whore" (Pavese)
　　See "La puttana contadina"
"The Peasant's Confession" (Hardy) **8**:124
"Pedantic Literalist" (Moore) **4**:229
"Pedro as el cuando..." (Neruda) **4**:288
"Peekaboo, I Almost See You" (Nash) **21**:269-70
"Peele Castle" (Wordsworth)
　　See "Stanzas on Peele Castle"
"Peers" (Toomer) **7**:336-37
*Peers* (Belloc) **24**:49
"Pelleas and Ettarre" (Tennyson) **6**:376
"The Pen" (Kinnell) **26**:293
"A Pencil" (Hass) **16**:196
"Penelope" (Parker) **28**:362
"Penelope's Song" (Gluck) **16**:172
"The Peninsula" (Heaney) **18**:200, 222-23
"The Penitent" (Millay) **6**:211
*Penny Wheep* (MacDiarmid) **9**:151, 158, 166, 179, 188
"The Pennycandystore beyond the El" (Ferlinghetti) **1**:187
"Pensar, dudar" (Hugo) **17**:92, 96-97
"Pensées des morts" (Lamartine) **16**:280
"Pensieri di Deola" (Pavese) **13**:214
"Pente" (Tzara) **27**:229-31
"La pente de la rêverie" (Hugo) **17**:48, 91, 93
"Penthesilea" (Noyes) **27**:115
"Penúltima canción de Don Simón" (Fuertes) **27**:40
"Penumbra" (Lowell) **13**:64
"People" (Toomer) **7**:336-37
"The People" (Yeats) **20**:328
"THE PEOPLE BURNING" (Baraka) **4**:12
"People Getting Divorced" (Ferlinghetti) **1**:183
"People of Unrest" (Walker) **20**:282
"People Who Don't Understand" (Pavese)
　　See "Gente che non capisce"
"People Who Have No Children" (Brooks) **7**:75
"People Who've Been There" (Pavese) **13**:218
*The People, Yes* (Sandburg) **2**:317-18, 320-23, 325-26, 328, 330, 333, 335-39, 341
*A Peopled Landscape* (Tomlinson) **17**:305, 309, 317-18, 327, 333, 335, 337, 341
*Pepel'* (Bely) **11**:3-4, 6-7, 24, 30-2
"La pequeña oda a un negro boxeador cubano" (Guillen) **23**:98
"Pequeña oda a un negro boxeador cubano" (Guillen) **23**:99, 103, 105-107
"Per album" (Montale) **13**:130
"Per quella via che la bellezza corre" (Dante) **21**:74
"Per un ritorna al paese" (Pasolini) **17**:266
"The Perch" (Kinnell) **26**:287
"Lo perdido" (Borges) **22**:80
"Perdition" (Cesaire) **25**:29
"Perdition" (Chadwick) **25**:
"Perdón si por mis ojos..." (Neruda) **4**:288
"Peregrinaciones" (Dario) **15**:82
"Peregrinations" (Dario)
　　See "Peregrinaciones"
"Peregrine" (Wylie) **23**:307, 310, 324

"Perekop" (Tsvetaeva) **14**:326-27
"Peremena" (Pasternak) **6**:285
"The Perennial Answer" (Rich) **5**:351-52
"Perennials" (Levine) **22**:228
*Pereulochki* (Tsvetaeva) **14**:325-26
"Perfect" (MacDiarmid) **9**:177
"The Perfect Husband" (Nash) **21**:278
"The Perfect Sky" (Gallagher) **9**:59
"Perforation, Concerning Genius" (Pinsky) **27**:144
"The Performers" (Hayden) **6**:195
"Perhaps No Poem But All I Can Say and I Cannot Be Silent" (Levertov) **11**:198
"Perhaps the Best Time" (Meredith) **28**:174
"The Permanent Tourists" (Page) **12**:178, 181-89
"The perpetual migration" (Piercy) **29**:303
"Perpetuum Mobile: The City" (Williams) **7**:350
"Le Perroquet" (Perse) **23**:228, 254-56
"Persée et Andromède" (Laforgue) **14**:93
"Persephone" (Smith) **12**:331-32
"The Persian" (Smith) **12**:330
"A Persian Suite" (Stryk) **27**:186-87
"The Persian Version" (Graves) **6**:143, 152
*Persimmon* (Viereck) **27**:282, 284
*The Persimmon Tree* (Viereck) **27**:271
"Persimmons" (Lee) **24**:243, 246
*Person, Place, and Thing* (Shapiro) **25**:261-64, 267-69, 276, 285, 288, 295, 308, 318-19, 322, 324
*Personae* (Pound) **4**:317
"Personae separatae" (Montale) **13**:
"Personae Separatae" (Montale) **13**:106, 126
"Personal" (Hughes) **1**:241, 259
"Personal Creed" (Alegria) **26**:
"Personal Helicon" (Heaney) **18**:200, 217
"Personal Landscape" (Page) **12**:178, 190
"Personal Letter No. 2" (Sanchez) **9**:224, 232-33
"Personal Letter No. 3" (Sanchez) **9**:225
"Persuasions to Love" (Carew)
　　See "To A.L. Perswasions to Love"
"Perswasions to Enjoy" (Carew) **29**:36
"La perte de l'anio" (Lamartine) **16**:292
*Pervaja simfonija* (Bely) **11**:17
"Pervaya pesenka" (Akhmatova) **2**:9
*Pervoe svidanie* (Bely) **11**:3, 7-11, 17-21, 28-9, 31-3
"Pesnia poslednei vstrechi" (Akhmatova) **2**:11
"Peter" (Moore) **4**:257
"Peter" (Ondaatje) **28**:292-93, 298-99, 318, 321
"Peter and John" (Wylie) **23**:324
*Peter Bell* (Wordsworth) **4**:399, 420
*Peter Bell the Third* (Shelley) **14**:175
"Peter Goole" (Belloc) **24**:18
"Peter Quince at the Clavier" (Stevens) **6**:293, 295, 300-01
"Peterhot Holiday" (Lermontov) **18**:285
"Petit Paul" (Hugo) **17**:56
"Le Petit Roi de Galicie" (Hugo) **17**:61
*Le Petit Testament* (Villon)
　　See *Les Lais*
*Petite prière sans prétentions* (Laforgue) **14**:63
"Petite Ville" (Tzara) **27**:223
"Petite Ville en Sibérie" (Tzara) **27**:223
"Les petites vielles" (Baudelaire) **1**:45, 64
"Pétition" (Laforgue) **14**:73
"The Petition for an Absolute Retreat" (Finch) **21**:142-43, 145-48, 156-57, 164, 170, 172, 175
*Petits poèmes en prose: Le spleen de Paris* (Baudelaire) **1**:48-9, 58-9
"Petrificada petrificante" (Paz) **1**:367
"Pettichap's Nest" (Clare) **23**:5
"A Petticoat" (Stein) **18**:330, 341
"Pevitsa" (Tsvetaeva) **14**:325, 327
"Phaedra" (H. D.) **5**:267
"Phaius Orchid" (Wright) **14**:346, 361
*Phantasmagoria* (Carroll) **18**:46, 48
*Phantom Dwelling* (Wright) **14**:374-75, 379
"The Phantom Horsewoman" (Hardy) **8**:91, 136

"Phèdre" (Smith) **12**:331-32
"Phenomenal Survivals of Death in Nantucket" (Gluck) **16**:131, 135, 139
"The Phenomenology of Anger" (Rich) **5**:371-72, 384, 394
"Philemon and Baucis" (Gunn) **26**:214
*Philip Sparrow* (Skelton) **25**:330, 332-33, 335, 343-44, 346, 348, 353-54, 356-60, 367, 369, 374, 380-82, 384, 393-94, 396-400
"Phillis; or, The Progress of Love, 1716" (Swift) **9**:253
"Philomela" (Arnold) **5**:37-8, 41, 46-7
"The Philosopher and His Mistress" (Bridges) **28**:87
"The Philosopher to His Mistress" (Bridges) **28**:87
"The Philosophers" (Merton) **10**:337
"Philosophy" (Dunbar) **5**:144
"Philosophy" (Pasternak) **28**:361
"The Phoenix and the Tortoise" (Rexroth) **20**:178
*The Phoenix and the Tortoise* (Rexroth) **20**:180, 182-84, 192-94, 198-202, 210, 212-13, 217
"Phone Call from Mexico" (Page) **12**:198
"The Photograph" (Smith) **12**:308, 346
"Photograph of My Room" (Forche) **10**:144, 156
"Photograph of the Girl" (Olds) **22**:313
"The Photograph of the Unmade Bed" (Rich) **5**:366
"Photographs Courtesy of the Fall River Historical Society" (Olds) **22**:307
"Photomontage of the Urban Parks" (Viereck) **27**:280
"Photos of a Salt Mine" (Page) **12**:167-68, 189
"Phrases" (Rimbaud) **3**:263
"Physcial Union" (Tagore)
　　See "Deher milan"
"Physician's Tale" (Chaucer) **19**:15, 62
"Piaceri notturni" (Pavese) **13**:205, 226
"Piano" (Shapiro) **25**:269
"A Piano" (Stein) **18**:318, 350
"Piano after War" (Brooks) **7**:73
"The Piano Tuner's Wife" (Shapiro) **25**:303
"La pica" (Fuertes) **27**:30
"Picasso" (Pasolini) **17**:295
"Piccolo testamento" (Montale) **13**:104, 113, 165-66, 168
*Pickering MS* (Blake) **12**:35-7, 43
"Pickthorn Manor" (Lowell) **13**:60, 77, 84
"Pictor Ignatus" (Browning) **2**:30
"A Picture" (Nemerov) **24**:281
"The Picture" (Tagore)
　　See "Chhabi"
"Picture Bride" (Song) **21**:334-36, 347-48, 350
*Picture Bride* (Song) **21**:331-38, 340-41, 343-44, 346-50
"Picture of a Black Child with a White Doll" (Merton) **10**:341, 345
"The Picture of J. T. in a Prospect of Stone" (Tomlinson) **17**:326
"A Picture of Lee Ying" (Merton) **10**:341
"The Picture of Little J A" (Ashbery) **26**:172
"The Picture of Little T. C. in a Prospect of Flowers" (Marvell) **10**:271, 274, 277, 289, 294, 303-04
*Picture Show* (Sassoon) **12**:257-58, 269
"Pictures By Vuillard" (Rich) **5**:350
*Pictures from Brueghel, and Other Poems* (Williams) **7**:371-72, 374, 377, 392-93, 403, 408
"Pictures in Smoke" (Parker) **28**:361
*Pictures of the Floating World* (Lowell) **13**:73-4, 93-4, 96
*Pictures of the Gone World* (Ferlinghetti) **1**:167-69, 171-75, 186
"A Piece of Coffee" (Stein) **18**:333, 349
"Pied Beauty" (Hopkins) **15**:133, 158
"The Pied Piper" (Tsvetaeva)
　　See "Krysolov"
"Pied Piper of Hamelin" (Browning) **2**:36, 63
"Piedra" (Soto) **28**:378, 383

"Piedra de sol" (Paz) **1**:353
*Piedra de sol* (Paz) **1**:355-56, 358-59, 368-69, 371, 373, 375-77
"The Pier" (Hongo) **23**:201
"The Pier" (Merrill) **28**:267
"Pierce Street" (Gunn) **26**:231
"The Pier-Glass" (Graves) **6**:137, 142, 172
*The Pier-Glass* (Graves) **6**:128, 147, 150
*Pierrot fumiste* (Laforgue) **14**:81
"Pietà" (Gluck) **16**:130
"Pig Cupid" (Loy) **16**:314-15, 326
"Pig Glass, 1973-1978" (Ondaatje) **28**:327, 335, 337, 339-40
"Le pigeon" (Hugo) **17**:100
"Pigeon Woman" (Swenson) **14**:265
"Pigeons, Sussex Avenue" (Ondaatje) **28**:292
"Piggy to Joey" (Smith) **12**:321
"Pig's Eye View of Literature" (Parker) **28**:348, 353, 362
"Pike" (Hughes) **7**:136, 158
"The Pike" (Lowell) **13**:69
"A Pilgrim" (Bradstreet)
  See "As Weary Pilgrim"
"A Pilgrim Dreaming" (Levertov) **11**:209
"The Pilgrimage" (Herbert) **4**:109
"Pilgrimage" (Olds) **22**:309
"Pilgrimage" (Pinsky) **27**:158
*The Pilgrimage of Festus* (Aiken) **26**:13, 22
*Pili's Wall* (Levine) **22**:226
"The Pillar of Fame" (Herrick) **9**:106
"The pillar perished is" (Wyatt) **27**:357-58
"Le pin" (Ronsard) **11**:277
*A Pindaric on the Death of Our Late Sovereign* (Behn) **13**:8
*A Pindaric Poem on the Happy Coronation of . . . James II* (Behn) **13**:8
"Pindaric Poem to the Reverend Doctor Burnet" (Behn) **13**:32
"A Pindaric to Mr. P. Who Sings Finely" (Behn) **13**:8
"A Pindarick Poem upon the Hurricane" (Finch) **21**:163, 180
"The Pine" (Ronsard)
  See "Le pin"
"The Pine Planters" (Marty South's Reverie**Hardy**) **8**:101
"The Pine Trees and the Sky" (Brooke) **24**:76
*The Pink Church* (Williams) **7**:370
"Pink Dog" (Bishop) **3**:65
"The Pink Dress" (Wakoski) **15**:345, 374-75
"Pink Hands" (Soto) **28**:398-99
"Pink Melon Joy" (Stein) **18**:346
"The pinks along my garden walks" (Bridges) **28**:85
"Pinoy at The Coming World" (Hongo) **23**:198
"Pioggia d'agosto" (Gozzano) **10**:184-85
"The Piper" (Blake) **12**:9
*Pippa Passes* (Browning) **2**:28, 30, 35, 37, 67
"Il Pirla" (Montale) **13**:138
*The Pisan Cantos* (Pound) **4**:320, 337, 344-48, 352, 357-58, 360
"The Pit" (Roethke) **15**:302
"The Pit" (Stryk) **27**:195, 202
*The Pit and Other Poems* (Stryk) **27**:181, 183, 190, 193-94, 198, 214, 216
"Pit Viper" (Momaday) **25**:188, 193-94, 199
"The Pitchfork" (Heaney) **18**:256
*La Pitié suprême* (Hugo) **17**:65
"Le pitre châtié" (Mallarme) **4**:202
"Pity Me" (Wylie) **23**:321, 324
"Pity Me Not" (Millay) **6**:225
"Pity the Deep in Love" (Cullen) **20**:57
"Pity 'Tis, 'Tis True" (Lowell) **13**:84
"Place; & Names" (Olson) **19**:296
"Place for a Third" (Frost) **1**:194, 221
*The Place of Love* (Shapiro) **25**:267, 269, 309, 311, 315
"The Place of Value" (Nemerov) **24**:255
"The Place That Is Feared I Inhabit" (Forche) **10**:143
"Place We Have Been" (Ortiz) **17**:228
"A Placeless Heaven" (Heaney) **18**:233

"Places" (Hardy) **8**:91, 104, 135-36
"Places, Loved Ones" (Larkin) **21**:246
"A Plague of Starlings" (Hayden) **6**:185, 195
"The Plaid Dress" (Millay) **6**:234
"Plainte d'automne" (Mallarme) **4**:187
"Plainview: 1" (Momaday) **25**:195, 203, 207, 213
"Plainview: 2" (Momaday) **25**:189, 195-96, 200, 213
"Plainview: 3" (Momaday) **25**:196, 213-14
"Plainview: 4" (Momaday) **25**:196, 213-14
"Un plaisant" (Baudelaire) **1**:59
"Plan for the Young English King" (Pound) **4**:364
"Plan of Future Works" (Pasolini) **17**:257
*Planet News: 1961-1967* (Ginsberg) **4**:51-2, 65-6
"Planetarium" (Rich) **5**:366, 370
"Planh for the Young English King" (Pound) **4**:364
"Planning the Garden" (Lowell) **13**:64
"Planning the Perfect Evening" (Dove) **6**:106
*Plantain* (Akhmatova)
  See *Podorozhnik*
"The Plantation" (Heaney) **18**:201, 225
"A Plantation Bacchanal" (Johnson) **24**:153
"A Plantation Portrait" (Dunbar) **5**:147
"The Planted Skull" (Viereck) **27**:265
"The Planters" (Atwood) **8**:36
"Planting Trees" (Berry) **28**:37
*Platero and I* (Jimenez)
  See *Platero y Yo*
*Platero and I: An Andalusion Elegy* (Jimenez)
  See *Platero y Yo*
*Platero y Yo* (Jimenez) **7**:185-89, 191, 199-201, 203
"Plato Elaborated" (Brodsky) **9**:19, 20
"Platypus" (Wright) **14**:372
"THe Play Way" (Heaney) **18**:187
*The Player Queen* (Yeats) **20**:353
"Playing Cards" (Atwood) **8**:5, 7
"Playing the Inventions" (Nemerov) **24**:285-87
"Playing the Machine" (Nemerov) **24**:301
"Pleading" (McKay) **2**:223
"Please, Master" (Ginsberg) **4**:54, 90
"Pleasure Bay" (Pinsky) **27**:157-58, 161, 164-65, 169, 174, 176
"Pleasures" (Levertov) **11**:159, 164, 189
"Pleasure's Lament" (Tagore)
  See "Sukher vilap"
"Pleasures of Spring" (Clare) **23**:14
"Pledge" (Merrill) **28**:284
"Plegaria" (Jimenez) **7**:198
"Plein Ciel" (Hugo) **17**:62, 87
"Pleine Mer" (Hugo) **17**:62, 89
"Plennyi rytsar" (Lermontov) **18**:291
"Plessy vs. Ferguson: Theme and Variations" (Merton) **10**:345
"Pleurs dans la nuit" (Hugo) **17**:89
"Ploja four di dut" (Pasolini) **17**:287
"Ploja tai cunfins" (Pasolini) **17**:250-52, 265, 287
"Ploughing" (Pasternak) **6**:267
"Ploughing on Sunday" (Stevens) **6**:297, 333
*Pluies* (Perse) **23**:211, 213-14, 221, 232, 233-34, 247, 249-51, 253
"The Plumet Basilisk" (Moore) **4**:243
"The Plum's Heart" (Soto) **28**:381
"Plus Intra" (Swinburne) **24**:324
"Plus Ultra" (Swinburne) **24**:324
*Plusieurs sonnets* (Mallarme) **4**:214-15
"Pluto Incognito" (Viereck) **27**:296
"Plutonian Ode" (Ginsberg) **4**:61-2
*Plutonian Ode: Poems, 1977-1980* (Ginsberg) **4**:61-2
"Po' Boy Blues" (Hughes) **1**:254, 270
"Poderoso Quienseas" (Fuertes) **27**:38
"Podolie" (Apollinaire) **7**:48
*Podorozhnik* (Akhmatova) **2**:3, 13, 18
"Podrazhanije Bajronu" (Lermontov) **18**:302
"Poem" (Bishop) **3**:54-5, 70
"Poem" (Enzensberger) **28**:151

"Poem" (Gluck) **16**:142
"The Poem" (Kinnell) **26**:240-41
"Poem" (Kunitz) **19**:147
"The Poem" (Lowell) **13**:83
"Poem" (Meredith) **28**:199
"Poem" (Merton) **10**:349
"Poem" (Rukeyser) **12**:233
"Poem" (Sanchez) **9**:232
"A Poem" (Stein) **18**:313
"Poem" (Tomlinson) **17**:315, 323, 328, 332, 339, 342, 345
"The Poem" (Williams) **7**:399
"Poem 1" (Ferlinghetti) **1**:167
"Poem 2" (Ferlinghetti) **1**:173
"Poem 3" (Ferlinghetti) **1**:174
"Poem IV" (Auden) **1**:10
"Poem 4" (Ferlinghetti) **1**:174
"Poem 5" (Ferlinghetti) **1**:168, 172
"Poem V" (Rich) **5**:378
"Poem 6" (Ferlinghetti) **1**:168, 173-74
"Poem 7" (Ferlinghetti) **1**:187
"Poem VII" (Rich) **5**:378-79
"Poem 8" (Ferlinghetti) **1**:174
"Poem IX" (Auden) **1**:10
"Poem 10" (Ferlinghetti) **1**:172-73
"Poem 11" (Ferlinghetti) **1**:174-75
"Poem 13" (Ferlinghetti) **1**:169, 174
"Poem XIII" (Rich) **5**:379
"Poem 14" (Ferlinghetti) **1**:168, 170
"Poem 15" (Ferlinghetti) **1**:175
"Poem 16" (Ferlinghetti) **1**:175
"Poem 17" (Ferlinghetti) **1**:176
"Poem 18" (Ferlinghetti) **1**:174
"Poem 19" (Ferlinghetti) **1**:173, 175
"Poem 20" (Ferlinghetti) **1**:174, 176
"Poem XX" (Rich) **5**:379
"Poem 21" (Ferlinghetti) **1**:175
"Poem 22" (Ferlinghetti) **1**:169, 176
"Poem 23" (Ferlinghetti) **1**:172, 174
"Poem 24" (Ferlinghetti) **1**:168, 171, 175
"Poem XXV" (Auden) **1**:10
"Poem 25" (Ferlinghetti) **1**:169, 174-75
"Poem 26" (Ferlinghetti) **1**:174-75
"Poem 27" (Ferlinghetti) **1**:174
"Poem 143: The Festival Aspect" (Olson) **19**:306
"Poem about Morning" (Meredith) **28**:214
"Poem About People" (Pinsky) **27**:161-62, 173-74, 176
"Poem about the Future" (Enzensberger) **28**:142
"Poem about the Imperial Family" (Tsvetaeva)
  See "Poema o tsarskoi sem'e"
"The Poem as Mask: Orpheus" (Rukeyser) **12**:228
"Poem at Thirty" (Sanchez) **9**:224, 232-33, 240
"poem beginning in no and ending in yes" (Clifton) **17**:30
"Poem Beginning 'The'" (Zukofsky) **11**:366-69, 373-74, 381, 383-86, 390, 395
"A Poem Beginning with a Line by Pindar" (Duncan) **2**:121-22, 127
"A Poem Catching Up with an Idea" (Carruth) **10**:88
"A Poem for 3rd World Brothers" (Knight) **14**:42
"Poem for a Birthday" (Plath) **1**:381, 390
"A Poem for a Poet" (Madhubuti) **5**:327, 344
"A Poem for Anna Russ and Fanny Jones" (Baraka) **4**:39
"Poem for Aretha" (Giovanni) **19**:110
"A Poem for Black Hearts" (Baraka) **4**:18-19
"A Poem for Black Relocation Centers" (Knight) **14**:39, 52
"Poem" (For BMC No. 2**Giovanni**) **19**:139
"A Poem for Children, with Thoughts on Death" (Hammon) **16**:177-78, 180, 183, 187-89
"Poem" (for DCS 8th Graders—1966-67**Sanchez**) **9**:224
"Poem for Etheridge" (Sanchez) **9**:225, 242
"A Poem for Max 'Nordau" (Robinson) **1**:459
"Poem for Maya" (Forche) **10**:142, 157

"A Poem for My Father" (Sanchez) **9**:220, 225, 240
"Poem for My Son" (Kumin) **15**:199, 201
"A Poem for Myself" (Knight) **14**:39
"A Poem for Negro Intellectuals" (If There Bes Such a ThingMadhubuti) **5**:329
"Poem" (For No Name No. 2Giovanni) **19**:108
"Poem for Personnel Managers" (Bukowski) **18**:4, 6
"A Poem for Sterling Brown" (Sanchez) **9**:229
"A Poem for the Birth-day of the Right HonBLE the Lady Catherine Tufton" (Finch) **21**:164
"A Poem for the End of the Century" (Milosz) **8**:213
"A Poem for Willie Best" (Baraka) **4**:10-11
*A Poem Humbly Dedicated to the Great Pattern of Piety and Virtue Catherine Queen Dowager* (Behn) **13**:8
"Poem" (I lived in the first century of world wars. . . .Rukeyser) **12**:222
"Poem in C" (Toomer) **7**:333
"Poem in October" (Thomas) **2**:382, 392, 404
"poem in praise of menstruation" (Clifton) **17**:29-30, 36
"Poem in Prose" (Bogan) **12**:100, 107, 112
"Poem in Which I Refuse Contemplation" (Dove) **6**:120
"A Poem Looking for a Reader" (Madhubuti) **5**:323
"Poem No. 2" (Sanchez) **9**:220
"Poem No. 8" (Sanchez) **9**:242
"Poem No. 13" (Sanchez) **9**:213
"Poem of Apparitions in Boston in the 73rd Year of These States" (Whitman) **3**:386
"Poem of Autumn" (Dario)
　See "Poema de otoño"
*Poem of Autumn, and Other Poems* (Dario)
　See *Poema del otoño y otros poemas*
"The Poem of Flight" (Levine) **22**:225
"Poem of Memory" (Akhmatova) **2**:16
"A Poem of Praise" (Sanchez) **9**:242
"Poem of the Air" (Tsvetaeva)
　See "Poema vozdukha"
"Poem of the Body" (Whitman) **3**:385
*Poem of the Cante Jondo* (Garcia Lorca)
　See *Poema del cante jondo*
"Poem of the Daily Work of the Workmen and Workwomen of These States" (Whitman) **3**:385
*The Poem of the Deep Song* (Garcia Lorca)
　See *Poema del cante jondo*
"Poem of the End" (Tsvetaeva)
　See "Poèma kontsa"
"Poem of the Fourth Element" (Borges)
　See "Poema del cuarto elemento"
"Poem of the Hill" (Tsvetaeva)
　See "Poèma gory"
"Poem of the Mountain" (Tsvetaeva)
　See "Poèma gory"
"Poem of the Poet" (Whitman) **3**:386
"Poem of the Singers and of the Works of Poems" (Whitman) **3**:386
"Poem of the Staircase" (Tsvetaeva)
　See "Poèma lestnitsy"
"Poem of These States" (Ginsberg) **4**:66
"A Poem of Walt Whitman, an American" (Whitman) **3**:384, 414
"A Poem Off Center" (Giovanni) **19**:116
"Poem #19 in the Old Manner" (Li Po) **29**:146
"Poem on His Birthday" (Thomas) **2**:391
"A Poem Once Significant Now Happily Not" (Cullen) **20**:85
"Poem, or Beauty Hurts Mr. Vinal" (Cummings) **5**:96
"Poem out of Childhood" (Rukeyser) **12**:231, 235
"A POEM SOME PEOPLE WILL HAVE TO UNDERSTAND" (Baraka) **4**:16
"A Poem to Complement Other Poems" (Madhubuti) **5**:329, 342
"A Poem to Galway Kinnell" (Knight) **14**:38

"A Poem to My Daughter" (Pinsky) **27**:153
"Poem to My Husband from My Father's Daughter" (Olds) **22**:322
"A Poem to Peanut" (Brooks) **7**:90
"A Poem Upon the Death of His Late Highness the Lord Protector" (Marvell)
　See "Poem upon the Death of O. C."
"Poem upon the Death of O. C." (Marvell) **10**:270-71, 305, 312
"A Poem with Children" (Guillen)
　See "Poema con niños"
"A Poem with No Ending" (Levine) **22**:221, 224
"Poem With Refrains" (Pinsky) **27**:175
*Poem without a Hero: Triptych* (Akhmatova)
　See *Poema bez geroya: Triptykh*
"Poema a la eñe" (Fuertes) **27**:37
*Poema bez geroya: Triptykh* (Akhmatova) **2**:4, 6-8, 16, 18-21
"Poema con niños" (Guillen) **23**:139
"Poema de otoño" (Dario) **15**:81-2, 91, 96
*Poema del cante jondo* (Garcia Lorca) **3**:118, 123, 127, 129, 135, 137
"Poema del cuarto elemento" (Borges) **22**:74
*Poema del otoño y otros poemas* (Dario) **15**:86
"Poema en ón" (Fuertes) **27**:37
"Poèma gory" (Tsvetaeva) **14**:325
"Poema komnaty" (Tsvetaeva) **14**:325
"Poèma kontsa" (Tsvetaeva) **14**:301-02, 306, 316, 325
"Poèma lestnitsy" (Tsvetaeva) **14**:325
"Poema o tsarskoi sem'e" (Tsvetaeva) **14**:326-27
"Poema vozdukha" (Tsvetaeva) **14**:325
*Poemas de amor* (Guillen) **23**:100, 133
*Poemas de la consumación* (Aleixandre) **15**:4, 6-7, 12, 16-17, 25, 39, 41-4
*Poemas de transición* (Guillen) **23**:108
"Poeme à l'étranèr" (Perse) **23**:211-13, 217, 232, 234, 250, 256-57
"Poème de la femme" (Gautier) **18**:125, 129-30, 139, 157
"Le poème de la mer" (Rimbaud) **3**:272
"Poème liminaire" (Senghor) **25**:247
"Poème lu au mariage d'André Salmon" (Apollinaire) **7**:48
"Poème pour M Valery Larbaud" (Perse) **23**:223-24
*Poémes* (Breton) **15**:53
*Poèmes* (Ronsard) **11**:249
*Poèmes* (Senghor) **25**:232
*Poëmes* (Vigny) **26**:401, 410
*Poèmes antiques et modernes* (Vigny) **26**:367, 372, 374, 398-99, 401-402, 404, 410-12
*Poemes bibliques et modernes* (Vigny) **26**:391
*Poemes Philosophiques* (Vigny) **26**:368, 372, 412
*Poèmes saturniens* (Verlaine) **2**:413-15, 430-32
"Poemo" (Fuertes) **27**:49
"Poems" (Cooke) **6**:348, 394, 416
"Poems" (Shapiro) **25**:294, 320
"Poems" (Stein) **18**:313
*Poems* (Arnold) **5**:12, 43, 50
*Poems* (Auden) **1**:4, 8, 10
*Poems* (Berry) **28**:14-15
*Poems* (Brooke) **24**:55, 83
*Poems* (Browning) **6**:14, 16-17, 19, 21, 25-7, 32, 36-8, 41-2
*Poems* (Clare)
　See *The Poems of John Clare*
*Poems* (Emerson) **18**:82, 84, 100
*Poems* (Garcia Lorca)
　See *Libro de poemas*
*Poems* (Harper) **21**:185, 189, 193, 196-97, 209
*Poems* (Mandelstam) **14**:106, 135
*Poems* (Milton) **19**:221, 249-50
*Poems* (Moore) **4**:228, 239, 250-51, 264
*Poems* (Owen) **19**:325
*Poems* (Poe) **1**:428, 437, 441
*Poems* (Ronsard)
　See *Poèmes*
*Poems* (Rossetti) **7**:265

*Poems* (Williams) **7**:367, 374, 395, 398
*Poems* (Wordsworth) **4**:375, 401, 415
*Poems* (Yeats) **20**:347
*Poems 1911* (Brooke) **24**:52-4, 61, 80
*Poems, 1953* (Graves) **6**:154-55
*Poems, 1914-1926* (Graves) **6**:132
*Poems, 1923-1954* (Cummings) **5**:85, 89
*Poems, 1926-1930* (Graves) **6**:132
*Poems, 1938-1945* (Graves) **6**:129
*Poems, 1940-1953* (Shapiro) **25**:285, 297, 313, 317
*Poems, 1943-1947* (Day Lewis) **11**:147
*Poems, 1965-1975* (Heaney) **18**:206, 211
"Poems 1978-1980" (Wright) **14**:377-78
*Poems about Moscow* (Tsvetaeva) **14**:299
"Poems about St. Petersburg, II" (Akhmatova) **2**:12
*Poems and Ballads* (Swinburne) **24**:309, 314, 321, 324, 334, 337, 345, 347, 358, 362-63
*Poems and Ballads, second series* (Swinburne) **24**:319
*Poems and Drawings* (Bukowski) **18**:5
*Poems and Fragments* (Holderlin) **4**:171
*The Poems and Letters of Andrew Marvell* (Marvell) **10**:277
*Poems and New Poems* (Bogan) **12**:89, 91, 107, 120, 124-26
*Poems and Satires* (Graves) **6**:135
*Poems Barbarous* (Nishiwaki) **15**:237
*Poems before Congress* (Browning) **6**:6, 23, 27, 36
*Poems by Currer, Ellis, and Acton Bell* (Bronte) **8**:46
*Poems by Thomas Carew, Esquire* (Carew) **29**:64, 87
*Poems by Two Brothers* (Tennyson) **6**:358
*Poems, Chiefly in the Scottish Dialect* (Burns) **6**:49
*Poems, Chiefly Lyrical* (Tennyson) **6**:347, 385, 406-09
*Poems Descriptive of Rural Life and Scenery* (Clare) **23**:38-44
*Poems for People Who Don't Read Poems* (Enzensberger) **28**:141, 143-44, 156
*Poems for the Times* (Heine)
　See *Zeitgedichte*
*Poems from Algiers* (Brutus) **24**:112, 115, 117
*Poems from Prison* (Knight) **14**:38, 41, 46, 48, 52-3
"Poems from the Margins of Thom Gunn's 'Moly'" (Duncan) **2**:127
"The Poems I Have Lost" (Ortiz) **17**:227
"Poems in Classical Prosody" (Bridges) **28**:65
"Poems in Imitation of the Fugue" (Schwartz) **8**:289, 305
*Poems in Prose from Charles Baudelaire* (Baudelaire)
　See *Petits poèmes en prose: Le spleen de Paris*
*Poems in the Shape of a Rose* (Pasolini) **17**:286
*Poems in Wartime* (Day Lewis) **11**:145
"Poems of 1912-13" (Hardy) **8**:91-4, 132, 137-8
*Poems of a Jew* (Shapiro) **25**:282, 285, 287, 290, 297-302, 320
*Poems of Akhmatova* (Akhmatova) **2**:16
*Poems of André Breton: A Bilingual Anthology* (Breton) **15**:54
*Poems of Consummation* (Aleixandre)
　See *Poemas de la consumación*
*Poems of Ferdinand Pessoa* (Pessoa) **20**:168
*The Poems of Francois Villon* (Villon) **13**:412
*Poems of Gerard Manley Hopkins* (Bridges) **28**:
*Poems of Gerard Manley Hopkins* (Hopkins) **15**:129, 133
*The Poems of John Clare* (Clare) **23**:3, 9, 11-14
"Poems of Night" (Kinnell) **26**:257
"The Poems of Our Climate" (Stevens) **6**:299
*Poems of Paul Celan* (Celan)
　See *Paul Celan: Poems*
*The Poems of Samuel Taylor Coleridge* (Coleridge) **11**:70, 81, 83, 104

*Poems of Shadow* (Jimenez) **7**:183
*The Poems of Stanley Kunitz, 1928-1978* (Kunitz) **19**:175-76, 186
"Poems of the Past and Present" (Hardy) **8**:121
*Poems of the Past and Present* (Hardy) **8**:123, 125
*Poems on Affairs of State* (Marvell) **10**:311
*Poems on Miscellaneous Subjects* (Harper) **21**:184-86, 188, 193, 196-97, 203, 206, 208-09, 215, 217-18
"poems on my fortieth birthday" (Clifton) **17**:18
*Poems on Various Subjects, Religious and Moral, by Phillis Wheatley, Negro Servant to Mr. John Wheatley of Boston, in New England, 1773* (Wheatley) **3**:332-34, 336, 338, 345, 349-52, 356
*Poems Selected and New* (Page) **12**:180
*Poems: Selected and New, 1950-1974* (Rich) **5**:384, 387
"Poems Speaking of Buddha" (Lindsay) **23**:283
*Poems to Akhmatova* (Tsvetaeva)
    See "Stikhi K Akhmatovoi"
*Poems to Blok* (Tsvetaeva)
    See *Stikhi K Blok*
"Poems to Bohemia" (Tsvetaeva)
    See "Stikhi k Chekhii"
"Poems to my Son" (Tsvetaeva)
    See "Stikhi k synu"
"Poems to Pushkin" (Tsvetaeva)
    See "Stikhi k Pushkinu"
*Poems to Solve* (Swenson) **14**:276
*Poems upon Several Occasions, with a Voyage to the Island of Love* (Behn) **13**:3, 7-8, 16, 18
*Poems written before jumping out of an 8 story window* (Bukowski) **18**:13
"Poesi i sak" (Ekeloef) **23**:77
"Poesía" (Jimenez) **7**:183
"La poesía" (Paz) **1**:353
*Poesía* (Jimenez) **7**:202
"La poesía castellana" (Dario) **15**:95
"Poesia in forma di rosa" (Pasolini) **17**:274, 276-77
*Poesia in forma di rosa* (Pasolini) **17**:249, 273-74, 276
*La poesía juvenil* (Borges) **22**:92-3
*Poesía, moral, público* (Aleixandre) **15**:9
*Poesía superrealista* (Aleixandre) **15**:3, 22, 24
*Poesías completas* (Dario) **15**:93, 107
*Poesías últimas escojidas* (1918-1958Jimenez) **7**:214
"Poésie" (Valery) **9**:366, 394
*Poesie* (Pavese) **13**:207, 210, 215, 220-21, 223-30
"Poesie a Casarsa" (Pasolini) **17**:281
*Poesie a Casarsa* (Pasolini) **17**:252, 254, 257, 262, 264-67, 279-82
*Poesie e prose* (Gozzano) **10**:184-85
*Poesie edite e inedite* (Pavese) **13**:208, 219, 230
"Poesie incivili" (Pasolini) **17**:273
"Poésie; ou, Le paysage dans le Golfe de Glafenes" (Lamartine) **16**:262
"Poesie, ou Paysage dans le Golfe de Genes" (Lamartine) **16**:292
"Poésie sacrée" (Lamartine) **16**:274, 290
*Poèsies* (Gautier) **18**:126
*Poésies* (Valery) **9**:399
*Poésies complètes* (Gautier) **18**:147
*Poésies complètes* (Laforgue) **14**:72
*Poésies complétes* (Mallarme) **4**:206
*Poésies diverses* (Villon) **13**:394-95, 397, 402-03, 407, 411
"The Poet" (Aleixandre)
    See "El poeta"
"The Poet" (Bryant) **20**:11, 33
"The Poet" (Carruth) **10**:84
"The Poet" (Cullen) **20**:85
"The Poet" (Dario)
    See "El poeta"
"The Poet" (Day Lewis) **11**:146
"The Poet" (Dunbar) **5**:121, 136

"The Poet" (Emerson) **18**:88-89
"The Poet" (H. D.) **5**:306
"A Poet" (Hardy) **8**:90
"The Poet" (Lermontov) **18**:281, 298
"The Poet" (Rilke) **2**:280
"Poet" (Shapiro) **25**:283, 286, 311
"The Poet" (Tennyson) **6**:369
"Poet" (Viereck) **27**:259, 263, 272, 282
"The Poet acquires speech from afar. . ." (Tsvetaeva)
    See "Poèt—izdaleka zovodit rech'. . ."
"The Poet and His Book" (Millay) **6**:220
"The Poet and His Song" (Dunbar) **5**:118, 121, 134
"The Poet at Forty" (Nemerov) **24**:267
"Poet at Seventy" (Milosz) **8**:180, 197, 209
*Poet in New York* (Garcia Lorca)
    See *Poeta en Nueva York*
*Poet in Our Time* (Montale) **13**:146
"The Poet in the Machine Age" (Viereck) **27**:284
"The Poet in the World" (Levertov) **11**:172-74
"The Poet Laments the Coming of Old Age" (Sitwell) **3**:317
"The Poet of Ignorance" (Sexton) **2**:368
"A Poet Recognizing the Echo of the Voice" (Wakoski) **15**:350
"A Poet to His Baby Son" (Johnson) **24**:144
"The Poet, to His Book" (Merton) **10**:337
"Poet to Tiger" (Swenson) **14**:280
"El poeta" (Aleixandre) **15**:3, 15, 38, 40
"El poeta" (Dario) **15**:99
*Poeta de guardia* (Fuertes) **27**:13, 15-8, 21, 25, 27-31, 50
*Poeta en Nueva York* (Garcia Lorca) **3**:120-21, 125, 136-38, 140, 143, 148-51
"El poeta pregunta por Stella" (Dario) **15**:113
"Los poetas celestes" (Neruda) **4**:293
"Le Poète" (Hugo) **17**:91
"La poéte Mourant" (Lamartine) **16**:271, 273-74, 278
"Les poètes de sept ans" (Rimbaud) **3**:258
*Poetic Contemplations* (Lamartine)
    See *Les recueillements poétiques*
"Poetica" (Pavese) **13**:228
*The Poetical Meditations of M. Alphonse de La Martine* (Lamartine)
    See *Méditations poétiques*
*Poetical Sketches* (Blake) **12**:31-2, 36, 43, 60-1
*Poetical Works* (Montagu) **16**:338, 341
*The Poetical Works of Christina Georgina Rossetti* (Rossetti) **7**:282-83
*The Poetical Works of Rupert Brooke* (Brooke) **24**:61, 75-6, 80-1, 89
*The Poetical Works of S. T. Coleridge* (Coleridge) **11**:75
"Poetics" (Ammons) **16**:21-2, 28
"Poetics" (Pavese)
    See "Poetica"
"The Poetics of the Physical World" (Kinnell) **26**:289
"Poetik" (Ekeloef) **23**:77
"Poèt—izdaleka zovodit rech'. . ." (Tsvetaeva) **14**:323
"Poetry" (Arnold) **5**:41
"Poetry" (Goethe) **5**:227
"Poetry" (Moore) **4**:232, 235, 249, 251, 254, 270-71
"Poetry" (Pasternak) **6**:252, 262, 272, 279, 282
"Poetry" (Paz)
    See "La poesía"
*Poetry* (Pavese)
    See *Poesie*
"Poetry and Pleasure" (Pinsky) **27**:165
"Poetry and the World" (Pinsky) **27**:158
*Poetry and the World* (Pinsky) **27**:156-58, 160-61, 176
"Poetry dusint have to be" (Bissett) **14**:13, 27
"Poetry Festival" (Enzensberger) **28**:162
"Poetry for the Advanced" (Baraka) **4**:39
*Poetry Is* (Hughes) **7**:158
"Poetry is Not a Luxury" (Lorde) **12**:143

"Poetry is the Smallest" (Ammons) **16**:43
"Poetry of Departures" (Larkin) **21**:229
"Poetry Perpetuates the Poet" (Herrick) **9**:146
"Poets" (Herrick) **9**:91, 106
"The Poets are Silent" (Smith) **12**:354
"The Poet's Death Is His Life" (Gibran) **9**:73
"The Poets of Seven Years" (Rimbaud)
    See "Les poètes de sept ans"
"The Poet's Story" (Tagore)
    See "Kabi kahini"
"The Poet's Vow" (Browning) **6**:38-9
"The poet's words" (Aleixandre)
    See "Las palabras del poeta"
"The Point" (Hayden) **6**:193
"The Point" (Soto) **28**:371
"Point Joe" (Jeffers) **17**:130, 136
"Point Shirley" (Plath) **1**:389
"Le poison" (Baudelaire) **1**:45, 61
"Poison" (Tagore)
    See "Halahal"
"A Poison Tree" (Blake) **12**:7
*Poisson soluble* (Breton) **15**:48, 63, 68, 70
"Poiu kngda gortan' syra . . ." (Mandelstam) **14**:150, 154
*Polar Bear Hunt* (Bissett) **14**:16-17, 19
"Polder" (Heaney) **18**:245
"Policía" (Guillen) **23**:101
"A Polish Dictionary" (Zagajewski) **27**:381
"Political Poem" (Baraka) **4**:10
"Political Relations" (Lorde) **12**:141
"Politics" (Meredith) **28**:206, 214
"Polonius Passing Through a Stage" (Nemerov) **24**:294-95
*Poltava* (Pushkin) **10**:366-69, 371, 373, 390-91, 394, 409, 411
"Pomade" (Dove) **6**:111, 113
"Pomegranate" (Gluck) **16**:126, 140-41
"Pomegranates" (Valery)
    See "Les grenades"
*Pomes for Yoshi* (Bissett) **14**:11, 17-18
*Pomes Penyeach* (Joyce) **22**:
"Pompilia" (Browning) **2**:41
"The Pond" (Gluck) **16**:134
"The Pond" (Nemerov) **24**:261
"Le pont Mirabeau" (Apollinaire) **7**:11, 21
"Ponte Veneziano" (Tomlinson) **17**:342, 347, 349
"Les ponts" (Rimbaud) **3**:264
"The Poodler" (Merrill) **28**:234, 242
"The Pool and the Star" (Wright) **14**:346
"The pool that swims in us" (Piercy) **29**:316, 318
"Poor" (Brooke) **24**:59
"Poor Art" (Montale)
    See "L'arte povera"
"The Poor Child's Toy" (Baudelaire)
    See "Le joujou du pauvre"
"A Poor Christian Looks at the Ghetto" (Milosz) **8**:191-92, 214
"The Poor in Church" (Rimbaud)
    See "Les pauvres à l'église"
"Poor Mailie's Elegy" (Burns)
    See "The Death and Dying Words of Poor Mailie"
"The Poor of London" (Belloc) **24**:28
"Poor Pierrot" (Masters) **1**:330, 333
"Poor Poll" (Bridges) **28**:77-9
"Poor Susan" (Wordsworth) **4**:374
"Poor Woman in a City Church" (Heaney) **18**:200
"The Pope" (Browning) **2**:41, 72
"Pope to Bolingbroke" (Montagu) **16**:342
"The Pope's Penis" (Olds) **22**:316
"Poppa Chicken" (Walker) **20**:273, 276, 286
"Poppies" (Sandburg) **2**:303
"Poppies in July" (Plath) **1**:381, 388
"Poppies in October" (Plath) **1**:384
"A Poppy" (Bridges) **28**:67
*Poppy and Memory* (Celan)
    See *Mohn und Gedächtnes*
"Poppy Flower" (Hughes) **1**:240
"Popular Demand" (Merrill) **28**:284-85

"Popular Songs" (Ashbery) **26**:162
"Populist Manifesto" (Ferlinghetti) **1**:176, 182, 188
"Popytka komnaty" (Tsvetaeva) **14**:308, 325
"Popytka revnosti" (Tsvetaeva) **14**:306, 308
"Por boca cerrada entran moscas" (Neruda) **4**:290
"Pora, Moi Drug, Pora" (Pushkin) **10**:410
"Porcelain Bowl" (Gluck) **16**:150
"Porch Swing" (Kumin) **15**:215
"The Porcupine" (Kinnell) **26**:240-42, 244, 257, 262, 291
"Pornographer" (Hass) **16**:195
"Portail" (Gautier) **18**:143-45, 155-56
"Porter" (Hughes) **1**:242
"Pórtico" (Dario) **15**:113
"Portland, 1968" (Gluck) **16**:129, 150, 154
"Portovenere" (Montale) **13**:151
"Portrait" (Bogan) **12**:87, 101, 103
"A Portrait" (Browning) **2**:59
"The Portrait" (Graves) **6**:144
"The Portrait" (Kunitz) **19**:176-77, 179
"A Portrait" (Parker) **28**:360
"A Portrait" (Rossetti) **7**:296-7
"Portrait" (Wright) **14**:356, 362
"Portrait by a Neighbor" (Millay) **6**:233
"A Portrait in Greys" (Williams) **7**:409
"Portrait of a Girl" (Aiken) **26**:24, 72
"Portrait of a Lady" (Eliot) **5**:153, 161, 183, 185-86
"A Portrait of a Modern Lady" (Swift) **9**:259
"Portrait of a Women in Bed" (Williams) **7**:348, 367
"Portrait of an Old Woman on the College Tavern Wall" (Sexton) **2**:358
"Portrait of Georgia" (Toomer) **7**:310, 320, 334
"Portrait of Marina" (Page) **12**:168, 176, 189-90
"Portrait of Mrs Spaxton" (Tomlinson) **17**:311
"Portrait of the Artist" (Parker) **28**:351, 361
"Portrait of the Artist" (Tomlinson) **17**:320
"Portrait of the Artist as a Prematurely Old Man" (Nash) **21**:279
"Portrait of the Author" (Pavese) **13**:205
"Portrait of the Author as a Young Anarchist" (Rexroth) **20**:187
"Portrait of Three Conspirators" (Nemerov) **24**:292
"Portraits" (Cummings) **5**:94
*Portraits with a Name* (Aleixandre)
See *Retratos con nombre*
"The Portuguese Sea" (Pessoa)
See "Mar Portuguese"
"Die posaunenstelle" (Celan) **10**:98, 111
"Posesión del ayer" (Borges) **22**:95
"The Posie" (Burns) **6**:76
*Positives* (Gunn) **26**:202, 208. 219, 226
"Positives: For Sterling Plumpp" (Madhubuti) **5**:346
"Posle grozy" (Pasternak) **6**:267-68, 285
*Posle razluki* (Bely) **11**:3, 25, 32-3
*Posle Rossii* (Tsvetaeva) **14**:298, 306, 310-11, 315, 317, 324-25, 327
"Possessions" (Crane) **3**:83
"Possessive Case" (Stein) **18**:327
"Possom Trot" (Dunbar) **5**:133
"Possum Song" (Johnson) **24**:163
"Post aetatem nostram" (Brodsky) **9**:4
"Post mortem" (Jeffers) **17**:117, 141
"POST RESSURECTION CITY BLUES" (Bissett) **14**:31-2
"Postcard from Picadilly Street" (Ondaatje) **28**:329
"A Postcard from the Volcano" (Stevens) **6**:297
"Postcards for Bert Meyers" (Hongo) **23**:197
"Post-Graduate" (Parker) **28**:362
"A Post-Impressionist Susurration for the First of November, 1983" (Carruth) **10**:88
"Postlude" (Williams) **7**:345
"Postman Cheval" (Breton)
See "Facteur Cheval"
"Postmeridian" (Cassian) **17**:12
"A Post-Mortem" (Sassoon) **12**:248

"Postscript" (Kunitz) **19**:147
*Postscripts* (Tagore)
See *Punascha*
"The Posy" (Herbert) **4**:129
"The Pot of Flowers" (Williams) **7**:388
"Potato" (Viereck) **27**:279
"Potato Blossom Songs and Jigs" (Sandburg) **2**:316
"The Potatoes' Dance" (Lindsay) **23**:281
"Potter" (Ondaatje) **28**:318
"Pouir fêter des oiseaux" (Perse) **23**:254
*Pour feter une enfance* (3Perse) **23**:217, 221, 257
"Pour le livre d'amour" (Laforgue) **14**:80
"Pour Prende Congé" (Parker) **28**:362
"Pour saluer le tiers monde" (Cesaire) **25**:13
"Pouring the Milk Away" (Rukeyser) **12**:224
"Pourquoi mon âme est-elle triste?" (Lamartine) **16**:280
*Poverkh barierov* (Pasternak) **6**:263, 268-69
"Poverty" (Ammons) **16**:32
"Power" (Lorde) **12**:155
"Power" (Rich) **5**:377
"Power" (Rukeyser) **12**:210
"Power" (Wright) **14**:356, 362
"The Power and the Glory" (Sassoon) **12**:246
*Power Play* (Gunn) **26**:
*Power Politics* (Atwood) **8**:9, 12, 14-16, 21-4, 26, 31, 44
"Power to the People" (Walker) **20**:294
"Powers" (Milosz) **8**:202, 211
"Powhatan's Daughter" (Crane) **3**:86, 88, 105
*Prabhat sangit* (Tagore) **8**:405-06
"Practical People" (Jeffers) **17**:117
"A Practical Program for Monks" (Merton) **10**:334
"The Prairie" (Clampitt) **19**:93, 96-7
"Prairie" (Sandburg) **2**:303, 304, 307, 314, 316, 339
"Prairie Waters by Night" (Sandburg) **2**:316
"The Prairies" (Bryant) **20**:14, 19, 23-4, 29, 34, 40-1, 47
*Praise* (Hass) **16**:197-201, 210, 212, 215-16, 222, 226
"Praise II" (Herbert) **4**:121
"Praise III" (Herbert) **4**:125
"Praise Be" (Kumin) **15**:214
"Praise for an Urn" (Crane) **3**:90, 100
"Praise for Sick Women" (Snyder) **21**:325
"Praise to the End!" (Roethke) **15**:254, 272, 274, 284, 298-99, 301-02, 304, 307
*Praise to the End!* (Roethke) **15**:248-51, 256, 282-84, 298-99, 301-03, 309
*Prāntik* (Tagore) **8**:422-24
"Pratidhyani" (Tagore) **8**:406
"Pravahini" (Tagore) **8**:415
"The Prayer" (Browning) **6**:19
"The Prayer" (Herbert) **4**:102, 130
"Prayer" (Hughes) **1**:240
"Prayer" (Jimenez)
See "Plegaria"
"A Prayer" (Joyce) **22**:
"A Prayer" (Lermontov) **18**:303
"Prayer" (Olds) **22**:316, 328
"Prayer" (Roethke) **15**:260
"Prayer" (Toomer) **7**:320-22, 334-35
"A Prayer" (Tsvetaeva)
See "Molitva"
"Prayer" (Wright) **14**:356, 366
"Prayer I" (Herbert) **4**:115
"Prayer at Sunrise" (Johnson) **24**:145, 153
"Prayer for a Prayer" (Parker) **28**:351, 364
"Prayer for a Second Flood" (MacDiarmid) **9**:155-56, 197-98
*A Prayer for Marilyn Monroe and other poems* (Cardenal)
See *Oracion por Marilyn Monroe y otros poemas*
"A Prayer for my Daughter" (Tomlinson) **17**:307
"A Prayer for My Daughter" (Yeats) **20**:320, 328, 336, 338-39, 342

"A Prayer for My Son" (Yeats) **20**:336, 339-40
"Prayer for Peace" (Senghor)
See "Prière de paix"
"Prayer for the Great Family" (Snyder) **21**:297
"A Prayer of Columbus" (Whitman) **3**:379, 384, 395
"The Prayer of Nature" (Byron) **16**:87
"Prayer to Ben Jonson" (Herrick) **9**:86, 96
"Prayer to Masks" (Senghor) **25**:227, 229-30
"Prayer to My Mother" (Pasolini) **17**:289
"Prayer to the Father of Heaven" (Skelton) **25**:337, 339
"Prayers of Steel" (Sandburg) **2**:302, 311
"Praying on a 707" (Sexton) **2**:373
"Prayrs for th One Habitation" (Bissett) **14**:20
"The Preacher: Ruminates behind the Sermon" (Brooks) **7**:53, 87, 94
"Preamble" (Rukeyser) **12**:209
"Prece" (Pessoa) **20**:155-56
"Precedent" (Dunbar) **5**:133
"Precession of the Equinoxes" (Rexroth) **20**:193, 196
"The Precinct. Rochester" (Lowell) **13**:83
"Preciosa and the Wind" (Garcia Lorca)
See "Preciosa y el aire"
"Preciosa y el aire" (Garcia Lorca) **3**:146
"Precious Moments" (Sandburg) **2**:331
"Precious Yeast of the World" (Mandelstam)
See "Drozhzhi mira dorogie"
"The Precipice" (Wright) **14**:354
"Préface" (Gautier) **18**:154, 156
"La préface" (Olson) **19**:318-21, 323
"Preface of the Galaxy" (Matsuo Basho)
See "Ginga no jo"
*Preface to a Twenty Volume Suicide Note* (Baraka) **4**:5-6, 14-17, 27, 31, 37
"The Preferred Voice" (Baudelaire)
See "La Voix"
"Preguntas Frente al lago" (Cardenal) **22**:111
"Prelenstnitse" (Lermontov) **18**:303
"Prélude" (Hugo) **17**:91-93
"Prelude" (Swinburne) **24**:313, 355, 357
"A Prelude" (Tomlinson) **17**:327, 333
"Prelude" (Tomlinson) **17**:328
*The Prelude* (Wordsworth)
See *The Prelude; or, Growth of a Poets Mind: Autobiographical Poem*
*The Prelude; or, Growth of a Poets Mind: Autobiographical Poem* (Wordsworth) **4**:397, 402-09, 412, 414, 421-27
"Prelude: The Troops" (Sassoon) **12**:264
"Prelude to a Fairy Tale" (Sitwell) **3**:295, 300, 304
"Preludes" (Eliot) **5**:153
"Les préludes" (Lamartine) **16**:278
*Preludes* (Aiken) **26**:23, 29-30
"Préludes autobiographiques" (Laforgue) **14**:66, 95
*Preludes for Memnon; or, Preludes to Attitude* (Aiken) **26**:23, 29-30, 33, 38, 52-3, 57-69, 72
*Preludes to Attitude* (Aiken) **26**:38-39
*Preludes to Definition* (Aiken) **26**:38-9
*Premier livre des amours* (Ronsard) **11**:246
*Le premier livre des poemes* (Ronsard) **11**:280
"Le premier regret" (Lamartine) **16**:293
"Premier sourire du printemps" (Gautier) **18**:128
*La Première Aventure céleste de Mr Antipyrine* (Tzara) **27**:227
"Première soirèe" (Rimbaud) **3**:258, 283
"Les premières communions" (Rimbaud) **3**:260
"The Premonition" (Roethke) **15**:293
"Prendimiento de Antoñito el Camborio" (Garcia Lorca) **3**:131
"Preparatory Exercise" (Dyptych with Votive TabletPaz) **1**:374
"Prepare Thy Self" (Roethke) **15**:293
"The Prepositions" (Olds) **22**:320
"Pres Spoke in a Language" (Baraka) **4**:39
"Prescription of Painful Ends" (Jeffers) **17**:141-144-45

"The Prescriptive Stalls As" (Ammons) 16:25, 44
"The Presence" (Graves) 6:137
"The Presence" (Kumin) 15:181
"Presence" (Zagajewski) 27:389, 393
"Présense (Cesaire) 25:10
"The Presense" (Elytis) 21:130
"Present" (Sanchez) 9:219
"Present, Afterwards" (Aleixandre) 15:6
"The Present Age" (Harper) 21:190
Presented to Ch'en Shang (Li Ho) 13:44
"Presented to Wang Lun" (Li Po) 29:146
"Presented to Wei Pa, Gentleman in Retirement" (Tu Fu) 9:322
"President Lincoln's Proclamation of Freedom" (Harper) 21:197
"The President's Sheet" (Alegria) 26:
"Prèsomptif" (Perse) 23:230
"Press Release" (Merriman) 28:284-85
"Pressure to Grow" (Baraka) 4:30
"Pressures" (Wright) 14:375
"Prestupnik" (Lermontov) 18:289
"Pretty" (Smith) 12:301, 318, 321, 328
"The Pretty Bar-Keeper of the Mitre" (Smart) 13:341, 347
"The Pretty Barmaid" (Smart)
   See "The Pretty Bar-Keeper of the Mitre"
"The Pretty Redhead" (Apollinaire)
   See "La jolie rousse"
"Pretty Words" (Wylie) 23:314, 324
"Priapus" (H. D.) 5:275, 303
Priapus and the Pool and Other Poems (Aiken) 26:46
"La prière" (Lamartine) 16:276-77, 291, 299-301
"Prière aux Masques" (Senghor) 25:224,241
"Prière de paix" (Senghor) 25:231,254
"Prière du matin" (Verlaine) 2:416
"La prière pour tous" (Hugo) 17:45
"The Priest" (H. D.) 5:306
"The Priest and the Matador" (Bukowski) 18:4
"Prigovor" (Akhmatova) 2:8-9
"Prima del viaggio" (Montale) 13:134
"Primary Colors" (Song) 21:333-34, 343, 350
"A Primary Ground" (Rich) 5:361
"La primavera" (Jimenez) 7:193-94
"La primavera Hitleriana" (Montale) 13:104, 109, 145, 148, 165-66
"Primaveral" (Dario) 15:117
"Prime" (Lowell) 13:64, 67
Primer for Blacks (Brooks) 7:83, 86
"A Primer of the Daily Round" (Nemerov) 24:257, 283
Primer romancero gitano (Garcia Lorca) 3:119-21, 127, 130, 133-34, 136-38, 145-49
Primeras poesias (Jimenez) 7:209
"Primero sueño" (Juana Ines de la Cruz) 24:182-83, 189, 191-94, 198, 209, 211, 217, 220
"The Primitive" (Madhubuti) 5:322
"Primitive" (Olds) 22:307
"The Primitive" (Swenson) 14:264
"A Primitive Like an Orb" (Stevens) 6:314, 335
"'Primitivism' Exhibit" (Kumin) 15:209
"The Primrose" (Donne) 1:126, 130
"Primrose" (Herrick) 9:125
"Primrose" (Williams) 7:345
The Primrose Path (Nash) 21:263
"Prince Athanase" (Shelley) 14:189, 192, 202, 234-35
Prince Hohenstiel-Schwangau (Browning) 2:43, 47, 82, 95
"Prince Meow" (Cassian) 17:3
"The Prince of Darkness Passing through this House" (Wakoski) 15:363
"Prince Tank" (Viereck) 27:260, 280
"The Prince's Progress" (Rossetti) 7:262-4, 279-80, 287, 289, 293-4, 296-8
The Prince's Progress, and Other Poems (Rossetti) 7:261, 263, 266, 296
The Princess: A Medley (Tennyson) 6:354, 360, 364-65, 371, 409

The Princess and the Knights (Bely) 11:24
De principiis (Gray)
   See De principiis cogitandi
De principiis cogitandi (Gray) 2:154
"Prinkin' Leddie" (Wylie) 23:301
"Printemps" (Tzara) 27:223
"Prioress's Tale" (Chaucer) 19:13, 15, 54-6
"The Priory of St. Saviour, Glendalough" (Davie) 29:108-09
"La Prison" (Vigny) 26:380, 401-403, 410
"The Prisoner" (Bronte)
   See "Julian M. and A. G. Rochelle"
"The Prisoner" (Browning) 6:26
"The Prisoner" (Paz)
   See "El prisonero"
"The Prisoner" (Tagore)
   See "Bandi"
The Prisoner of Chillon, and Other Poems (Byron) 16:87
"The Prisoner of the Caucasus" (Lermontov) 18:278
The Prisoner of the Caucasus (Pushkin)
   See Kavkazsky plennik
"El prisonero" (Paz) 1:364-65
"The Prisoners" (Hayden) 6:194-95
"The Prisoner's Complaint" (Scott) 13:292
"The Prisoner's Dream" (Montale)
   See "Il Sogno del prigioniero"
"Privacy" (Rexroth) 20:221
"A private bestiary" (Piercy) 29:314
The Private Dining Room (Nash) 21:270-71
"Private Madrigals" (Montale)
   See "Madrigali privati"
"Private Means is Dead" (Smith) 12:309, 333
The Privilege (Kumin) 15:180-81, 200, 208
"A Prize Poem submitted by Mr. Lambkin of Burford to the Examiners of the University of Oxford on the Prescribed Poetic Theme Set by Them in 1893, 'The Benefits of the Electric Light'" (Belloc) 24:4
"The Probationer" (Page) 12:176
"The Problem" (Emerson) 18:74, 79, 84, 100-2
"Problemas del subdesarrollo" (Guillen) 23:121
"Problems of Underdevelopment" (Guillen)
   See "Problems of Underdevelopment"
"Procedures for Underground" (Atwood) 8:13, 19
Procedures for Underground (Atwood) 8:2-3, 12, 15-16, 21
"Le Procès à la Révolution" (Hugo) 17:102
"A Process" (Tomlinson) 17:323, 331, 339
"Processe of tyme worketh suche wounder" (Wyatt) 27:317, 320
"Processes" (Tomlinson) 17:322,327, 337-40
"A Procession at Candlemas" (Clampitt) 19:82-3, 89, 98
"Procession Poem" (Wakoski) 15:324
"Processionals, II" (Duncan) 2:101
"Proda di Versilia" (Montale) 13:112, 148
"The Prodigal Son" (Johnson) 24:128-29, 133, 156, 164, 169
"The Prodigal's Return" (Harper) 21:208
"The Produce District" (Gunn) 26:203, 231
"Proem: To Brooklyn Bridge" (Crane) 3:85, 88, 90, 107, 109
Profane Proses (Dario)
   See Prosas profanas, y otros poemas
"Profezie" (Pasolini) 17:277
"Proffitt and Batten" (Smith) 12:339
"Les profondeurs" (Apollinaire) 7:32, 34
"De profundis" (Browning) 6:5, 23
"De profundis" (MacDiarmid) 9:153
"De Profundis" (Trakl) 20:261-62
"Profusion du soir" (Valery) 9:391
"Progress" (Kumin) 15:214
"The Progress of Beauty, 1720" (Swift) 9:253, 257, 298-99
"The Progress of Faust" (Shapiro) 25:296
"The Progress of Poesy" (Gray) 2:133, 135, 137, 139, 143-44, 146, 148-49, 151-55

"The Progress of Poetry" (Gray)
   See "The Progress of Poesy"
"The Progress of Poetry" (Swift) 9:249
"Progress Report" (Ammons) 16:45
"Progress Report" (Kumin) 15:204, 208, 219
"Progression" (Smith) 12:316
"Progressive Insanities of a Pioneer" (Atwood) 8:4
"The Prohibition" (Donne) 1:130
"Projected Slide of an Unknown Soldier" (Atwood) 8:7
"Projection" (Nemerov) 24:268
A Prolegomenon to a Theodicy (Rexroth) 20:179, 183, 210-11
"Prolija memoria" (Juana Ines de la Cruz) 24:180
"Prolog" (Heine) 25:131
"Prólogo" (Borges) 22:95
"Prólogo" (Guillen) 23:127
"The Prologue" (Bradstreet) 10:2, 6, 11, 52
"Prologue" (Chaucer)
   See "General Prologue"
"Prologue" (Hughes) 7:154
"Prologue" (Hugo) 17:97
"Prologue" (Lorde) 12:156
"Prologue" (Marie de France) 22:246-48, 260, 264-66, 283-85, 293, 298
"Prologue" (Noyes) 27:119, 128
"Prologue" (Verlaine) 2:432
"Prologue: An Interim" (Levertov)
   See "Interim"
"Prologue at Sixty" (Auden) 1:20
"Prologue to a Saga" (Parker) 28:363-64
"Prologue to King John" (Blake) 12:31
"Prologue to the Wife of Bath's Tale" (Chaucer) 19:26
Prolusion (Milton) 29:228
"Promenade on Any Street" (Kunitz) 19:147-48
"Prometheus" (Dunbar) 5:146
"Prometheus" (Goethe) 5:247, 254
"Prometheus" (Graves) 6:137
"Prometheus" (Tomlinson) 17:315, 319, 322, 325-27, 341
Prometheus Bound, and Miscellaneous Poems (Browning) 6:16, 18
Prometheus on His Crag (Hughes) 7:155-56
Prometheus the Firegiver (Bridges)
"Prometheus Unbound" (Yeats) 20:333, 336
Prometheus Unbound (Shelley) 14:166-67, 171-75, 177, 183, 186-91, 193, 196-97, 202, 206, 212-13, 215-16, 218-21, 224-28, 232, 240-41
"The Promise" (Toomer) 7:338
"Promise and Fulfillment" (Dunbar) 5:121
"Promise Me" (Kunitz) 19:147
"The Promise of the Hawthorn" (Swinburne) 24:313, 317
"The Promised One" (Wright) 14:337
"The Promisers" (Owen) 19:336, 343
"Promontoire" (Rimbaud) 3:264
"Prooimion" (Viereck) 27:259
"Property" (Shapiro) 25:295
"Prophecy" (Wylie) 23:310, 323
"Prophecy on Lethe" (Kunitz) 19:162, 173-75
"Prophesy" (Cesaire) 25:
"The Prophet" (Lermontov) 18:281
"The Prophet" (Pushkin)
   See "Prorok"
The Prophet (Gibran) 9:69-75, 80-2
"The Prophet Lost in the Hills at Evening" (Belloc) 24:30
"Prophetic Soul" (Parker) 28:357, 360
"Prophetie" (Cesaire) 25:9, 19, 30
"Prophets for a New Day" (Walker) 20:278, 288
Prophets for a New Day (Walker) 20:275, 278-79, 283, 287-89, 292
"Propogation House" (Roethke) 15:296
"A propos d'Horace" (Hugo) 17:64
"Prorok" (Pushkin) 10:409, 414
Prosanatolizmí (Elytis) 21:118-19, 124, 127, 134

*Prosas profanas, y otros poemas* (Dario) **15**:78, 80, 82-4, 87-9, 91-2, 94-5, 97, 103-05, 109, 112-14, 117-20
*Prosas profanos, and Other Poems* (Dario)
　See *Prosas profanas, y otros poemas*
"Prose Poem" (Tomlinson) **17**:338, 340
*Prose Poems* (Baudelaire)
　See *Petits poèmes en prose: Le spleen de Paris*
"Prosopopoia; or, Mother Hubberds Tale" (Spenser) **8**:335, 365, 368-71, 390
"Prospective Immigrants Please Note" (Rich) **5**:370
*Prospectus to the Excursion* (Wordsworth)
　See *The Excursion, Being a Portion of "The Recluse"*
"Prospice" (Browning) **2**:51, 66
"Protest" (Cullen) **20**:57
*Protest Against Apartheid* (Brutus) **24**:100
"Protestant Easter" (Sexton) **2**:363
"Prothalamion" (Kumin) **15**:180
"Prothalamion" (Schwartz) **8**:290-91, 299, 301-02, 304-05
*Prothalamion; or, A Spousall Verse* (Spenser) **8**:336, 390
"The Proud Farmer" (Lindsay) **23**:287
"A Proud Lady" (Wylie) **23**:309, 321, 332
"Proud Maisie" (Scott) **13**:272, 278, 280
"Proverbs of Hell" (Blake) **12**:36, 49-50
"Provide, Provide" (Frost) **1**:227-28, 231
"Providence" (Herbert) **4**:102, 134
"La providence à l'homme" (Lamartine) **16**:276, 283, 291, 293
*Provinces* (Milosz) **8**:212, 214-15
"Provincia deserta" (Pound) **4**:366
"Provisional Conclusions" (Montale) **13**:131
*Provisional Conclusions* (Montale) **13**:135
"Provoda" (Tsvetaeva) **14**:309, 311, 315
"prozession" (Enzensberger) **28**:135-36
*Prufrock and Other Observations* (Eliot) **5**:152, 173, 184-85, 195, 204, 206
"The Psalm" (Bridges) **28**:80
"Psalm" (Celan) **10**:98, 101, 118, 120
"A Psalm" (Merton) **10**:332
"Psalm II" (Ginsberg) **4**:81
"Psalm 2" (Smart) **13**:330
"Psalm 94" (Smart) **13**:362
"Psalm 104" (Smart) **13**:332
"Psalm 105" (Smart) **13**:362
"Psalm 120" (Smart) **13**:363
"Psalm Concerning the Castle" (Levertov) **11**:177
"Psalm Praising the Hair of Man's Body" (Levertov) **11**:171
"Psalms" (Smart)
　See *A Translation of the Psalms of David, Attempted in the Spirit of Christianity, and Adapted to the Divine Service*
*Psalms of David* (Smart)
　See *A Translation of the Psalms of David, Attempted in the Spirit of Christianity, and Adapted to the Divine Service*
"The Psychiatrist's Song" (Bogan) **12**:101, 115
"Public Bar TV" (Hughes) **7**:120, 122
"Public Garden" (Lowell) **3**:199-200, 215
*Published and Unpublished Poems* (Pavese)
　See *Poesie edite e inedite*
"Puck of Pook's Hill" (Kipling) **3**:192
"Puck's Song" (Kipling) **3**:183, 192
"Pueblo Pot" (Millay) **6**:215
"Puedes?" (Guillen) **23**:116, 124, 127
"Puella Mea" (Cummings) **5**:104
"Puesto del Rastro" (Fuertes) **27**:22, 45-6
"the pull" (Bissett) **14**:22
"The Pulley" (Herbert) **4**:102
"The Pulling" (Olds) **22**:318, 323, 326, 340
*Punascha* (Tagore) **8**:417
*Punch: The Immortal Liar* (Aiken) **26**:22
"Punishment" (Heaney) **18**:196, 204, 210-11, 238
"The Puppets" (Page) **12**:184
*Purabi* (Tagore) **8**:415

"Pure Death" (Graves) **6**:137, 151
"The Pure Fury" (Roethke) **15**:258, 272, 277, 290
"Pure Love" (Tagore)
　See "Pavitra prem"
"The Pure Ones" (Hass) **16**:198
"Purely" (Villa) **22**:353
"Purely Local" (Rich) **5**:352
*Purgatorio* (Dante) **21**:49, 52-4, 58, 62-3, 69-82, 84-6, 91, 95-6, 104-05, 107-09
"Purgatory" (Lowell) **3**:241
*Purgatory* (Dante)
　See *Purgatorio*
*Purgatory* (Marie de France)
　See *L'Espurgatoire Saint Patrice*
*The Purgatory of St. Patrick* (Marie de France)
　See *L'Espurgatoire Saint Patrice*
"The Puritan" (Shapiro) **25**:270, 286
"A Puritan Lady" (Reese) **29**:331
"The Puritan's Ballard" (Wylie) **23**:310
"Purner abhav" (Tagore) **8**:414
"Purple Grackles" (Lowell) **13**:64, 67, 87, 98-9
"Les Pur-Sang" (Cesaire) **25**:8-9, 18
"The Purse of Aholibah" (Huneker) **27**:165
"The Purse Seine" (Jeffers) **17**:117
"Pursuit" (H. D.) **5**:287-88
"Pushkinskomu domu" (Blok) **21**:44
"Pusti menia, Voronezh . . ." (Mandelstam) **14**:152
"La puttana contadina" (Pavese) **13**:210, 219
"Putting to Sea" (Bogan) **12**:123
"Pygmalion" (H. D.) **5**:270, 304
"Pygmies Are Pygmies Still, Though Percht on Alps" (Brooks) **7**:55
"The Pyramids" (Brooke) **24**:66, 80
"Pyrotechnics" (Bogan) **12**:117
"Pyrotechnics" (Lowell) **13**:83
*Pyth. III* (Pindar)
　See *Pythian 3*
*Pyth. X* (Pindar)
　See *Pythian 10*
*Pyth XI* (Pindar)
　See *Pythian 11*
*Pythian 1* (Pindar) **19**:381, 389, 392-93, 400, 411-12, 424-25
*Pythian 2* (Pindar) **19**:402, 410, 420
*Pythian 3* (Pindar) **19**:390, 398, 402, 410, 412
*Pythian 4* (Pindar) **19**:381, 390, 396, 398-99, 405, 413, 420, 425
*Pythian 5* (Pindar) **19**:396, 408-11, 422-23, 425
*Pythian 6* (Pindar) **19**:400, 406
*Pythian 7* (Pindar) **19**:412
*Pythian 8* (Pindar) **19**:381, 391, 400, 406-07, 413, 426
*Pythian 9* (Pindar) **19**:391, 398, 400, 412-13
*Pythian 10* (Pindar) **19**:411-12, 425-26
*Pythian 11* (Pindar) **19**:413
*Pythian Odes 10* (Pindar)
　See *Pythian 10*
"La pythie" (Valery) **9**:353, 365-66, 369, 373, 379, 393
*Quaderno de quattro anni* (Montale) **13**:128, 153, 156, 160, 168
"Quaerendo Invenietis" (Nemerov) **24**:288
"Quai D'Orleans" (Bishop) **3**:37
"The Quake" (Stryk) **27**:203, 211
"Quake Theory" (Olds) **22**:309
"The Quaker Graveyard at Nantucket" (for Warren Winslow, Dead at SeaLowell) **3**:200-02, 204, 212, 217, 223, 233, 235-38
"Quaker Hill" (Crane) **3**:86, 90, 106
"Qualm" (Ashbery) **26**:152
"Quand vous serez bien vieille" (Ronsard) **11**:218-21
"Quando il soave mio fido conforto" (Petrarch) **8**:235
"The Quarrel" (Aiken) **26**:24
"The Quarrel" (Kunitz) **19**:175
"Quarrel in Old Age" (Yeats) **20**:328-31
"The Quarry" (Clampitt) **19**:82, 89
"Quarry Pigeon Cove" (Kumin) **15**:181
"Quashie to Buccra" (McKay) **2**:215, 223

"Quatrains" (Emerson) **18**:77
*Quatre de P. de Ronsard aux injures et calomnies* (Ronsard) **11**:291
"Quatre Dols" (Marie de France)
　See "Le Chaitivel"
*Les quatre premiers livres de la Franciade* (Ronsard) **11**:226, 234, 246, 271, 283, 286-87, 290
*Les quatre vents de l'esprit* (Hugo) **17**:65
"4e epoque" (Lamartine) **16**:264
*Que estás en la tierra* (Fuertes) **27**:44
"Que m'accompagnent Kôras et Balafong" (Senghor) **25**:255
"Que no me quiera Fabio, al verse amado" (Juana Ines de la Cruz) **24**:183
"Que nous avons le doute en nous" (Hugo) **17**:92-93
"quebec bombers" (Bissett) **14**:21-2
"The Queen and the Young Princess" (Smith) **12**:326, 352
*Queen Mab* (Shelley) **14**:170, 173, 178, 185-86, 212-17, 219, 222
"Queen of Bubbles" (Lindsay) **23**:277
"The Queen of Hearts" (Rossetti) **7**:272, 274
"The Queen of pentacles" (Piercy) **29**:323
"The Queen of the Night Walks Her Thin Dog" (Wakoski) **15**:363
"Queen Worship" (Browning) **2**:26
"Queen Yseult" (Swinburne) **24**:355
"Queen-Anne's Lace" (Williams) **7**:374
"Quelques Complaintes de la vie" (Laforgue) **14**:95
"Querent's Attitude as It Bears Upon the Matter: The Three of Cups" (Piercy) **29**:325
"The Quest" (Noyes) **27**:130
"The Quest of the Purple-Fringed" (Frost) **1**:218
"A Question" (Arnold) **5**:38
"The Question" (Rukeyser) **12**:225
"Question" (Swenson) **14**:250, 252, 282, 286
"Question and Answer" (Browning) **6**:5
"Question au clerc du quichet" (Villon) **13**:394
"A Question of Climate" (Lorde) **12**:136
"A Question of Essence" (Lorde) **12**:140
"Questions Beside the Lake" (Cardenal)
　See "Preguntas Frente al lago"
"Questions of Travel" (Bishop) **3**:55, 67
*Questions of Travel* (Bishop) **3**:48, 53, 59
"A questo punto" (Montale) **13**:158
"A qui la faute?" (Hugo) **17**:101
*Quia pawper amavi* (Pound) **4**:317
"Quick I the Death of Thing" (Cummings) **5**:108
"A Quickening: A Song for the Visitation" (Merton) **10**:339
"The Quickening of St. John Baptist" (Merton) **10**:339
"Quickly Delia" (Finch) **21**:178
"A quien leyere" (Borges) **22**:94
"Quiero saber" (Aleixandre) **15**:31
"Quiero volver a sur" (Neruda) **4**:281
"Quiet Evening" (Gluck) **16**:172
*A Quiet Road* (Reese) **29**:329-330, 335-36, 339, 345-46
"Quiet Work" (Arnold) **5**:12, 36, 38, 49
"Quietness" (Williams) **7**:382
"Quilted Spreads" (Ammons) **16**:44
*Quilting: Poems 1987-1990* (Clifton) **17**:28-29, 36
"Quimérica" (Jimenez) **7**:197
"Quinnapoxet" (Kunitz) **19**:175, 178-79
"The Quip" (Herbert) **4**:100, 102, 108, 119, 130
"R. A. F." (H. D.) **5**:307
"The Rabbi" (Hayden) **6**:195, 198
"Rabbi Ben Ezra" (Browning) **2**:51, 75, 95
"The Rabbi's Song" (Kipling) **3**:183
"The Rabbit" (Millay) **6**:238
"Race" (Dario)
　See "Raza"
"The Race" (Olds) **22**:319, 323, 326
"The Racer's Widow" (Gluck) **16**:139
"Rack" (Ammons) **16**:39

"A radio made of seawater" (Villa) **22**:356-57
"Radiometer" (Merrill) **28**:267
"Raft" (Ammons) **16**:20, 27
"The Raft" (Lindsay) **23**:273
"The Rag Man" (Hayden) **6**:195
"Raga Malkos" (Ekeloef) **23**:87
"Rages de césars" (Rimbaud) **3**:283
"Ragged ending" (Piercy) **29**:313
"The Ragged Schools of London" (Browning)
     See "A Song for the Ragged Schools of
     London"
"The Ragged Stocking" (Harper) **21**:191
*Raghuvamśa* (Kalidasa) **22**:180, 182, 185, 188-
     90, 198, 204-07
*Raices* (Alegria) **26**:
"Railroad Avenue" (Hughes) **1**:237
*The Railway Timetable of the Heart* (Tzara)
     **27**:250
"Rain" (Giovanni) **19**:109
"The Rain" (Levertov) **11**:176
"Rain" (Soto) **28**:370, 377
"Rain" (Stryk) **27**:201
"Rain" (Williams) **7**:349
"Rain at Bellagio" (Clampitt) **19**:87
"Rain Charm for the Duchy, a Blessed, Devout
     Drench for the Christening of a Prince
     Harry" (Hughes) **7**:171
"Rain Downriver" (Levine) **22**:224-25
"Rain Festival" (Tagore)
     See "Varsha-mangal"
"The Rain, It Streams on Stone and Hillock"
     (Housman) **2**:162
"Rain on a Grave" (Hardy) **8**:134
"Rain on the Borders" (Pasolini) **17**:287
"Rain or Hail" (Cummings) **5**:88
"Rain Outside of Everything" (Pasolini) **17**:287
"The Rainbow" (Kinnell) **26**:259-60
"rainbow music" (Bissett) **14**:24
"Rainforest" (Wright) **14**:375, 377
"The Rainmaker" (Cassian) **17**:4
"Rain-Song" (Dunbar) **5**:125
"Rainy Mountain Cemetery" (Momaday)
     **25**:190, 197
"The Rainy Season" (Meredith) **28**:187
"Raise the Shade" (Cummings) **5**:89
"Raleigh" (Cardenal) **22**:107, 110
"Raleigh Was Right" (Williams) **7**:360
"La rameur" (Valery) **9**:367, 395-96
"Rank and File" (Noyes) **27**:122
"Rano Raraku" (Breton) **15**:53-4
"Rap of a Fan..." (Apollinaire)
     See "Coup d'evential..."
"Rape" (Rich) **5**:361
"Rape of the Leaf" (Kunitz) **19**:147
*The Rape of the Lock* (Pope) **26**:303, 307-309,
     314-19, 322-23, 326-27, 340, 346-51
"The Raper from Passenack" (Williams) **7**:353,
     368, 399
"Rapids" (Ammons) **16**:63
"Rapids by the Luan Trees" (Wang Wei) **18**:370
"A Rapture" (Carew) **29**:10, 18, 27-28, 32, 34,
     36-38, 48, 71-72, 75-76, 87-88
"Rapunzel" (Sexton) **2**:368
"Rapunzel, Rapunzel" (Smith) **12**:341
"Rasshchelina" (Tsvetaeva) **14**:306-08
*Rat Jelly* (Ondaatje) **28**:294, 327-35
"Ratbert" (Hugo) **17**:59
"The Ratcatcher" (Tsvetaeva)
     See "Krysolov"
"Rational Man" (Rukeyser) **12**:220, 230
"The Rats" (Levine) **22**:213
"ratschlag auf höchster ebene" (Enzensberger)
     **28**:136
"rattle poem" (Bissett) **14**:21
"The Raven" (Poe) **1**:419-20, 424, 427, 429-34,
     436, 439-40, 443-44, 447, 452-53
"The Raven: A Christmas Tale" (Coleridge)
     **11**:109-17
*The Raven, and Other Poems* (Poe) **1**:437, 449
"The Ravine" (Carruth) **10**:85, 90
"Raving Mad" (Cesaire) **25**:15
*Les rayons et les ombres* (Hugo) **17**:45, 50-53,
     63-64, 67, 76-77, 87, 91-92, 97
"Raza" (Dario) **15**:115
"Razgovor s geniem" (Tsvetaeva) **14**:325
*Rbaiyyat* (Khayyam)
     See *Rubáiyát*
*Re:Creation* (Giovanni) **19**:108-11, 114, 118,
     122, 128, 136-37, 140-41
"The reaching out of warmth is never done"
     (Viereck) **27**:278
"Reaching Out with the Hands of the Sun"
     (Wakoski) **15**:363
"Re-Act for Action" (Madhubuti) **5**:338
"The Reader over My Shoulder" (Graves)
     **6**:143, 151
"Reading Aloud" (Gallagher) **9**:60
"Reading Apollinaire by the Rouge River"
     (Ferlinghetti) **1**:181, 187
"Reading Holderlin on the Patio with the Aid
     of a Dictionary" (Dove) **6**:109
"Reading my poems from World War II"
     (Meredith) **28**:180, 195
"Reading Myself" (Lowell) **3**:229
"Reading the Japanese Poet Issa" (Milosz)
     **8**:189
"Reading the Will" (Kipling) **3**:190
"Reading Time: 1 Minute 26 Seconds"
     (Rukeyser) **12**:206
"Readings of History" (Rich) **5**:355
"Ready for Goodbye" (Cassian) **17**:3
"The Real Estate Agents Tale" (Lowell) **13**:84
"Real Life" (Baraka) **4**:30
"Real Life" (Enzensberger) **28**:159
"The Real Revolution Is Love" (Harjo) **27**:70
"The Real Work" (Snyder) **21**:324-25
*The Real World* (Snyder) **21**:291
*La realidad invisible* (Jimenez) **7**:207
"Reality" (Pasolini) **17**:258
*Reality Sandwiches* (Ginsberg) **4**:67, 81
"Reapers" (Toomer) **7**:319, 333-34
"Reaping" (Lowell) **13**:60
"Reaping in Heat" (Heaney) **18**:191
"The Rear-Guard" (Sassoon) **12**:266
"Rearmament" (Jeffers) **17**:117, 121-22
"Reason and Imagination" (Smart) **13**:341, 347
*The Reason of Church Government* (Milton)
     **29**:272
"Reasons for Attendance" (Larkin) **21**:223, 229,
     244, 247
"Reawakening" (Pavese)
     See "Risveglio"
"The Rebel" (Belloc) **24**:12, 30, 38
"Le rebelle" (Baudelaire) **1**:55
"Rebellion" (Lowell) **3**:318
"The Rebels" (Ferlinghetti) **1**:184
"Rebirth" (Pushkin) **10**:408
"A Rebus by I. B." (Wheatley) **3**:338
"Recalling War" (Graves) **6**:137, 142, 144, 165
"The Recantation: An Ode. By S. T.
     Coleridge" (Coleridge) **11**:94, 99
"Recapitulations" (Shapiro) **25**:272-73, 285,
     296-97, 319-20, 324
"Receive Thy Sight" (Bryant) **20**:6
"The Recent Past" (Ashbery) **26**:143
"Recent Poems" (Davie) **29**:99
"Recessional" (Masters) **1**:333
"Recipe for Happiness in Khaboronsky"
     (Ferlinghetti) **1**:183
"The Recital" (Ashbery) **26**:130, 149
"Rècitation à l 'Éloge d'une Reine" (Perse)
     **23**:230
"Recitative" (Crane) **3**:81, 83
*Recklings* (Hughes) **7**:120, 122-23
"The Recluse" (Smith) **12**:299, 331, 333
*The Recluse; or Views on Man, Nature, and on
     Human Life* (Wordsworth) **4**:406-07, 409
"Recollection" (Wheatley)
     See "On Recollection"
"Recollections" (Swinburne) **24**:329
"Recollections of Bellagio" (Meredith) **28**:198,
     215
"Recollections of Solitude" (Bridges) **28**:60
"Recollections of the Arabian Nights"
     (Tennyson) **6**:347, 359, 389, 406, 408-09
*Recollections of Tsarskoe-Selo* (Pushkin)
     See "Vospominanie v Tsarskom Sele"
"The Recompense" (Tomlinson) **17**:349
"Reconciliation" (Day Lewis) **11**:147
"Reconciliation" (Milosz) **8**:213
"Reconciliation" (Sassoon) **12**:289
"Reconciliation" (Whitman) **3**:378
"The Record" (Berry) **28**:30
*Records of a Weather Exposed Skeleton*
     (Matsuo Basho)
     See *Nozarashi kiko*
"Recovering" (Rukeyser) **12**:225
"Recovery" (Ammons) **16**:6
"The Recovery" (Pushkin) **10**:408
*Recovery* (Tagore)
     See *Ārogya*
*Recovery* (Tagore)
     See *Ārogya*
"Recreaciones arqueológicas" (Dario) **15**:96
"The Recruit" (Housman) **2**:196
"A Recruit on the Corpy" (McKay) **2**:226
"Recueillement" (Baudelaire) **1**:65
*Les recueillements poétiques* (Lamartine)
     **16**:263, 268, 284-85
"Recuerdo" (Millay) **6**:215
"Recuerdos..." (Jimenez) **7**:199
"Red Armchair" (McGuckian) **27**:105
"A Red Carpet for Shelley" (Wylie) **23**:322,
     333
*Red Dust* (Levine) **22**:211, 213-15, 217-18, 222-
     23, 227-28
"The Red Knight" (Lowell) **13**:84
"The Red Lacquer Music Stand" (Lowell) **13**:78
"Red Maple Leaves" (Rexroth) **20**:221
"Red Poppy" (Gallagher) **9**:64
"A Red, Red Rose" (Burns)
     See "My Luve Is Like a Red, Red Rose"
"Red Riding Hood" (Sexton) **2**:354, 364
*Red Roses for Bronze* (H. D.) **5**:270-71, 304
"Red Silk Stockings" (Hughes) **1**:269
"Red Slippers" (Lowell) **13**:79
"The Red Steer" (Tsvetaeva)
     See "Krasnyi bychok"
"The Red Wheelbarrow" (Williams) **7**:378, 401-
     02, 409-10
"The Redbreast and the Butterfly"
     (Wordsworth) **4**:376
"Red-Cotton Nightcap Country" (Browning)
     **2**:96
"A Redeemer" (Jeffers) **17**:131, 141
"The Redeemer" (Sassoon) **12**:242, 249-51,
     261-62, 276, 278, 287
"Redemption" (Herbert) **4**:119, 130
"Redeployment" (Nemerov) **24**:287, 290
"Rediscovering America" (Alegria) **26**:
"Redwing" (Gallagher) **9**:62
"The Reed" (Lermontov) **18**:304
"The Reedbeds of the Hackensack" (Clampitt)
     **19**:87
"The Reefy Coast" (Ishikawa)
     See "Ariso"
"Reeve's Tale" (Chaucer) **19**:10, 13-14, 61
"Reference Back" (Larkin) **21**:228
"The Refiner's Gold" (Harper) **21**:189
"The Refinery" (Pinsky) **27**:158, 171-72, 176
"The Reflection: A Song" (Behn) **13**:18, 20-1
"Reflection in a Forest" (Auden) **1**:17
"Reflection in an Ironworks" (MacDiarmid)
     **9**:155
"Reflection on Ice-Breaking" (Nash) **21**:279
"Reflections" (Tomlinson) **17**:316, 324
"Reflections at Lake Louise" (Ginsberg) **4**:84
"Reflections by a Mailbox" (Kunitz) **19**:154
"Reflections on a Scottish Slum"
     (MacDiarmid) **9**:181
"Reflections on Having Left a Place of
     Retirement" (Coleridge) **11**:81
"Reflective" (Ammons) **16**:6
"Reflexion" (Lamartine) **16**:266, 285
"Reformation" (Finch) **21**:166

"Refrain" (Dove) **6**:117
"Refugees" (Zagajewski) **27**:402
"A Refusal to Mourn the Death, by Fire, of a
　　Child in London" (Thomas) **2**:382-83,
　　386, 388, 390, 398, 400
"Regarding Wave" (Snyder) **21**:297, 304-06
*Regarding Wave* (Snyder) **21**:285, 288-92, 300,
　　304-08, 310, 317, 322
"Règle" (Tzara) **27**:230-31
"Régles de l'Ode" (Hugo) **17**:90
"Regrets of the Belle Heaumiere" (Villon)
　　See "Lament of the Belle Heaulmiere"
"Rehabilitation & Treatment in the Prisons of
　　America" (Knight) **14**:53
"The Rehearsal" (Smith) **12**:330
"El reino interior" (Dario) **15**:79-80, 92, 96,
　　114
"Rejoice in the Lamb" (Smart)
　　See "Jubilate Agno"
*Rekviem: Tsikl stikhotvorenii* (Akhmatova) **2**:4,
　　7, 9, 15-16, 19-20
*Relations and Contraries* (Tomlinson) **17**:317,
　　342
"Relearning the Alphabet" (Levertov) **11**:195-98
*Relearning the Alphabet* (Levertov) **11**:176-78,
　　180, 193-94
"Religio" (Hugo) **17**:66
*Religio Laici; or, A Layman's Faith* (Dryden)
"Religion" (Dunbar) **5**:125
"The Religion of My Time" (Pasolini)
　　**17**:257-59
*The Religion of My Time* (Pasolini) **17**:285
*La religione del mio tempo* (Pasolini) **17**:264-
　　66, 270, 272-73, 295
"Religious Isolation" (Arnold) **5**:42
"A Religious Man" (Smith) **12**:352
"Religious Musings" (Coleridge) **11**:49-51, 53,
　　80-2, 93-6
"Religious Propaganda" (Tagore)
　　See "Dharma prachar"
"The Relique" (Donne) **1**:126, 130
"Relocation" (Ortiz) **17**:231
*Remains of Elmet* (Hughes) **7**:146, 149, 162
"Rembrandt to Rembrandt" (Robinson) **1**:487
"Remember" (Harjo) **27**:59
"Remember" (Rossetti) **7**:269, 280
"Rememberance" (Holderlin)
　　See "Andenken"
"Remembering Pearl Harbor at the
　　Tutankhamen Exhibit" (Kumin) **15**:196,
　　206, 208
"Remembering Robert Lowell" (Meredith)
　　**28**:177, 180
"Remembering the Thirties" (Davie) **29**:98
"Remembrance" (Bronte) **8**:52, 56, 60, 65, 68,
　　74-5
"Remembrance Has a Rear and Front"
　　(Dickinson) **1**:94
"Remembrance in Tsarskoe Selo" (Pushkin)
　　See "Vospominanie v Tsarskom Sele"
*Remeslo* (Tsvetaeva) **14**:315, 318, 324-25
"Reminiscence" (Ishikawa)
　　See "Omoide"
"Réminiscence" (Mallarme)
　　See "L'orphelin"
"Reminiscences at Tsarskoe Selo" (Pushkin)
　　See "Vospominanie v Tsarskom Sele"
"Remittance Man" (Wright) **14**:340, 348, 368
"Remords posthume" (Baudelaire) **1**:45
"Remorse" (Sassoon) **12**:282
*Remorse* (Coleridge) **11**:58
"Remorse for Intemperate Speech" (Yeats)
　　**20**:328, 333
"Remorse Is Memory Awake" (Dickinson)
　　**1**:111
"Removing the Plate of the Pump on the
　　Hydraulic System of the Backhoe"
　　(Snyder) **21**:307
*Ren'aimeikashū* (Hagiwara Sakutaro) **18**:170,
　　172
"Renaming the Kings" (Levine) **22**:215
"Renascence" (Millay)

*Renascence, and Other Poems* (Millay) **6**:204-
　　06, 225, 240
"Rendezvous" (Kumin) **15**:213, 224
"The Renewal" (Roethke) **15**:275
"Renewal of Strength" (Harper) **21**:189
"Renka" (Nishiwaki) **15**:238
"Renunciation" (Parker) **28**:360
"Reparation" (Reese) **29**:335
"Les reparties de Nina" (Rimbaud) **3**:271
"Repas" (Valery) **9**:391
"Repent" (Kumin) **15**:209, 211
"Repentance" (Herbert) **4**:120
"The Repetitive Heart" (Schwartz) **8**:292-93,
　　302
"Repining" (Rossetti) **7**:287
"Reply" (Bridges) **28**:66, 69
"Reply to Censure" (Roethke) **15**:291
"A Replycacion" (Skelton) **25**:374, 385
"Reponse aux adieux de Sir Walter Scott"
　　(Lamartine) **16**:283
"Report" (Harper) **21**:207, 216
"Report" (Illyes) **16**:243
"Report to the Mother" (Knight) **14**:52
"Repose of Rivers" (Crane) **3**:83, 90, 96
"Repression of War Experience" (Sassoon)
　　**12**:264, 267, 288
"The Reproach" (Gluck) **16**:152, 156, 164
"Reproach" (Graves) **6**:140, 144
"A Reproof of Gluttony" (Belloc) **24**:17
"The Republic" (Ondaatje) **28**:298
"Republican Living Rooms" (Olds) **22**:307
"Request for Requiems" (Hughes) **1**:243
"Request to a Year" (Wright) **14**:375
"A Request to the Graces" (Herrick) **9**:88
"Requeste à Monseigneur de Bourbon"
　　(Villon) **13**:413
"Requiem" (Berry) **28**:16-17
"Requiem" (Nash) **21**:273
*Requiem* (Rilke) **2**:267, 279
*Requiem: A Cycle of Poems* (Akhmatova)
　　See *Rekviem: Tsikl stikhotvorenii*
"Requiem for the Death of a Boy" (Rilke) **2**:279
"Requiem for the Spanish Dead" (Rexroth)
　　**20**:192
"Requiescat" (Arnold) **5**:12
*Rerum vulgarium fragmenta* (Petrarch)
　　See *Canzoniere*
"Rescue Poem" (Wakoski) **15**:324, 361
"Rescue with Yul Brynner" (Moore) **4**:242, 256,
　　259
*Residence on Earth* (Neruda)
　　See *Residencia en la tierra*
*Residence on Earth and Other Poems* (Neruda)
　　See *Residencia en la tierra*
*Residencia en la tierra* (Neruda) **4**:277, 2809,
　　282-83, 285, 293, 295, 300-01, 304, 306
*Residencia en la tierra, Vol. 1, 1925-31*
　　(Neruda)
　　See *Residencia en la tierra*
*Residencia en la tierra, Vol. 2, 1931-35*
　　(Neruda)
　　See *Residencia en la tierra*
*Residencia I* (Neruda)
　　See *Residencia en la tierra*
*Residencia II* (Neruda)
　　See *Residencia en la tierra*
*Residencia III* (Neruda)
　　See *Residencia en la tierra*
"Resignation" (Arnold) **5**:6, 18, 32, 34, 37-41,
　　43, 47, 49-51, 54
"Resignation" (Dunbar) **5**:133
"Resolution and Independence" (Wordsworth)
　　**4**:399, 404, 406, 411-12, 426
"The Resolve" (Levertov) **11**:170
"Resolve" (Plath) **1**:406
"Respectability" (Browning) **2**:95
"The Respectable Burgher on 'The Higher
　　Criticism'" (Hardy) **8**:124
*Responce aux injures* (Ronsard) **11**:234
"Responde tú" (Guillen) **23**:117, 127
"Respondez!" (Whitman) **3**:405
"Response" (Dunbar) **5**:139

"Résponse à une acte d'accusation" (Hugo)
　　**17**:64, 82
*Responsibilities, and Other Poems* (Yeats)
　　**20**:311, 320, 323, 342
"Responsibilities of the Poet" (Pinsky) **27**:160,
　　170
"Responso a Verlaine" (Dario) **15**:98
"A Responsory, 1948" (Merton) **10**:333
"Ressouvenir du lac Leman" (Lamartine)
　　**16**:286
"Ressurection, Imperfect" (Donne) **1**:147
"Rest" (Rossetti) **7**:277, 280
"Restless" (Tagore)
　　See "Chanchal"
"Restless Night" (Tu Fu) **9**:319, 323
"Résumé" (Parker) **28**:347, 363
"Resurrection" (Atwood) **8**:40
"Resurrection" (Jeffers) **17**:141
"The Resurrection of Jesus" (Harper) **21**:189
"Resurrection of the Right Side" (Rukeyser)
　　**12**:225
"Le Rétablissement de la Statue de Henri IV"
　　(Hugo) **17**:88
*Retaliation* (Blok)
　　See *Vozmezdie*
"Retired Ballerina, Central Park West"
　　(Ferlinghetti) **1**:183
"The Retired Colonel" (Hughes) **7**:140
"Retort" (Dunbar) **5**:125, 127
"Le retour" (Lamartine) **16**:286
*Retour au pays natal* (Cesaire)
　　See *Cahier d'un retour au pays natal*
*Retratos con nombre* (Aleixandre) **15**:4, 12, 16
"Retribution" (Blok) **21**:31
"Retribution" (Harper) **21**:190
*Retribution* (Blok)
　　See *Vozmezdie*
*The Retrieval System* (Kumin) **15**:203-09, 217,
　　221
"Retrospect" (Brooke) **24**:62, 64, 86
"The Return" (Alegria) **26**:
"The Return" (Brooke) **24**:61
"Return" (Forche) **10**:136-41, 144-45, 152, 154-
　　56, 162, 167
"The Return" (Hayden) **6**:194
"Return" (Heaney) **18**:201
"Return" (Jeffers) **17**:117, 119, 131, 141, 147
"Return" (Paz)
　　See "Vuelta"
"The Return" (Pound) **4**:355-56, 365
"The Return" (Roethke) **15**:274
"Return" (Wright) **14**:342
*The Return* (Bely)
　　See *Vozvrat: Tretiia simfoniia*
*Return* (Paz)
　　See *Vuelta*
"Return in Hinton" (Tomlinson) **17**:311, 327-28
"The Return of Helen" (McGuckian) **27**:77, 100
"The Return of Robinson Jeffers" (Hass)
　　**16**:195, 203, 228
"The Return of the Birds" (Bryant) **20**:46
"The Return of the Goddess" (Graves) **6**:137,
　　144
"Return to DeKalb" (Stryk) **27**:214
"Return to Hiroshima" (Stryk) **27**:187, 202, 216
"Return to Kraków in 1880" (Milosz) **8**:204
"A Return to Me" (Neruda)
　　See "Se vuelve a yo"
*Return to My Native Land* (Cesaire)
　　See *Cahier d'un retour au pays natal*
"Return to Oneself" (Neruda)
　　See "Se vuelve a yo"
"Return to Wang River" (Wang Wei) **18**:392
"The Return to Work" (Williams) **7**:369
"The Return Trip" (Ekeloef) **23**:54
"Returning" (Lowell) **3**:226
"Returning a Lost Child" (Gluck) **16**:124
"Returning North of Vortex" (Ginsberg) **4**:76
"Returning to Mount Sung" (Wang Wei) **18**:371
"Returning to the Rhetoric of an Early Mode"
　　(Duncan) **2**:109, 113
"Reuben Bright" (Robinson) **1**:467, 496

"Reuben Pantier" (Masters) **1**:347
"Reunion" (Forche) **10**:137, 142-44, 147, 157, 168
"The Reunion" (Harper) **21**:200, 214
"Le rêve d'un curieux" (Baudelaire) **1**:54
"Rêve Expérimental" (Tzara) **27**:242
"Rêve parisien" (Baudelaire) **1**:47, 54
"Reveillé" (Housman) **2**:164
"Reveille" (Hughes) **7**:123, 159
"The Reveillon" (Belloc) **24**:11
"The Revenant" (Meredith) **28**:181
"Revenge Fable" (Hughes) **7**:132, 143
"Reverdure" (Berry) **28**:8-9
"Reverie" (Browning) **2**:96
"Reversibilité" (Baudelaire) **1**:56, 67
"Reversionary" (Smith) **12**:314
"Revisiting the MacDowell Colony" (Kumin) **15**:222
*The Revolt of Islam* (Shelley)
  See *Laon and Cythna*
"The Revolution at Market Hill" (Swift) **9**:260
"Revolution in the Revolution in the Revolution" (Snyder) **21**:306
"The Revolutionary" (Stryk) **27**:208
"Revolutionary Dreams" (Giovanni) **19**:111
"Revolutionary Music" (Giovanni) **19**:110
"Revolutions" (Arnold) **5**:51
"Les revolutions" (Lamartine) **16**:280-81, 293
*Le revolver á cheveux blancs* (Breton) **15**:50-2
"Revolving Meditation" (Kunitz) **19**:174, 178
"Revulsion" (Hardy) **8**:91
*Rewards and Fairies* (Kipling) **3**:184
"Reyerta" (Garcia Lorca) **3**:131
"The Rhapsody of Life's Progress" (Browning) **6**:6
"Rhapsody on a Windy Night" (Eliot) **5**:153, 155, 171
"A Rhapsody on Poetry" (Swift) **9**:281
"Der Rhein" (Holderlin) **4**:143, 148, 153, 155, 173-74
"Rhénane d'automne" (Apollinaire) **7**:42
"The Rhine" (Holderlin)
  See "Der Rhein"
"Rhododendrons" (Gallagher) **9**:60
"The Rhodora" (Emerson) **18**:74, 82, 94, 96, 98-100, 102
"A Rhyme about an Electrical Advertising Sign" (Lindsay) **23**:296
"A Rhyme for All Zionists" (Lindsay) **23**:283
"The Rhyme of Reb Nachman" (Pinsky) **27**:175
"The Rhyme of the Duchess May" (Browning) **6**:28
"The Rhyme of the Three Captains" (Kipling) **3**:181-82
"The Rhyme of the Three Sealers" (Kipling) **3**:182
"Rhymed Address to All Renegade Campbellites Exhorting Them to Return" (Lindsay) **23**:265
*Rhymed Ruminations* (Sassoon) **12**:252
*Rhymes* (Jimenez)
  See *Rimas*
"Rhythm & Blues 1" (Baraka) **4**:16
"Rhythm of Autumn" (Garcia Lorca)
  See "Ritmo de otoño"
"La ricchezza" (Pasolini) **17**:270, 273, 295
"Richard Bone" (Masters) **1**:324
"Richard Cory" (Robinson) **1**:467, 475, 486
"Richard Hunt's 'Arachne'" (Hayden) **6**:186
"Richard Roe and John Doe" (Graves) **6**:141
"The Riddle" (Auden) **1**:34
"The Riddle" (Heaney) **18**:229, 232, 237
"Riddles" (Guillen) **23**:131
"The Ride" (Smith) **12**:315
"Ride to Aix" (Browning) **2**:35
"The Ridge Farm" (Ammons) **16**:46-7, 50-1
"Riding the Elevator into the Sky" (Sexton) **2**:373
"Rigamarole" (Williams) **7**:383, 389
"Right in the Trail" (Snyder) **21**:327
"The Right of Way" (Williams) **7**:387, 409, 411
"The Right Possessor" (Gunn) **26**:

"The Right Thing Happens to the Happy Man" (Roethke) **15**:270
"Right Wing Opinions" (Davie) **29**:97
"Right's Security" (Dunbar) **5**:127
*Rimas* (Jimenez) **7**:197, 199
*Rime* (Petrarch)
  See *Canzoniere*
*The Rime of the Ancient Mariner: A Poet's Reverie* (Coleridge) **11**:37-42, 44, 51, 53, 55, 58-69, 81, 84, 88-9, 92-7, 104, 106, 110, 117
*The Rime of the Ancyent Marinere* (Coleridge)
  See *The Rime of the Ancient Mariner: A Poet's Reverie*
*Rime sparse* (Petrarch)
  See *Canzoniere*
"Un rimorso" (Gozzano) **10**:188
*The Ring and the Book* (Browning) **2**:39-40, 42-4, 46-7, 53, 56, 63, 66-7, 73, 76-7, 82-3, 85, 88, 95
"The Ring and the Castle" (Lowell) **13**:60-1
"The Ring Cycle" (Merrill) **28**:285-87
"Ringing the Bells" (Sexton) **2**:350, 353
"Ringless" (Wakoski) **15**:324
*The Rings of Saturn* (Wakoski) **15**:368-69
"Los ríos del canto" (Neruda) **4**:293
"Riot" (Brooks) **7**:82, 88-9, 91
*Riot* (Brooks) **7**:63-4, 66, 82, 88, 91, 94
*Ripostes* (Pound) **4**:317, 355
"The Ripple" (Levertov) **11**:171
"A Ripple Song" (Kipling) **3**:183
"Riprap" (Snyder) **21**:284, 299, 302
*Riprap* (Snyder) **21**:286-87, 290-91, 297, 300, 322
"The Risen One" (Rilke) **2**:271 .
"Rising" (Berry) **28**:16, 18-19
"The Rising of the Sun" (Milosz)
  See "From Where the Sun Rises"
"The Rising Out" (McGuckian) **27**:102-104
"Risks and Possibilities" (Ammons) **16**:3, 29, 40
"Risveglio" (Pavese) **13**:229
"Rite of Passage" (Olds) **22**:312
"The Rites for Cousin Vit" (Brooks) **7**:66, 78, 81
"Rites for the Extrusion of a Leper" (Merton) **10**:345
"Rites of Passage" (Gunn) **26**:204
"Rites of Passage" (Stryk) **27**:204, 210
"Ritmo de otoño" (Garcia Lorca) **3**:125
"Ritorno di Deola" (Pavese) **13**:229
"Ritratto" (Pound) **4**:317
"Ritratto d'autore" (Pavese) **13**:213
"Ritter" (Rilke) **2**:266-67
"The Ritual of Memories" (Gallagher) **9**:60
"The Ritual of Memories" (Gallagher) **9**:60
"The Rival" (Plath) **1**:390
"The Rivals" (Dunbar) **5**:122
"The Rivals" (Johnson) **24**:141
"The River" (Arnold) **5**:19, 43
"The River" (Crane) **3**:84-6, 88-90, 95
"The River" (Emerson) **18**:97
"The River" (Tagore)
  See "Pravahini"
"River" (Viereck) **27**:277
*The River* (Hughes) **7**:163, 171
"The River, By Night" (Bryant) **20**:17
"The River God" (Smith) **12**:331, 337
*The River of Heaven* (Hongo) **23**:198-99, 201, 204
"River Roads" (Sandburg) **2**:316
"River Stop" (Tu Fu) **9**:319
"River Village" (Tu Fu) **9**:319
"The River-Merchant's Wife: A Letter" (Li Po) **29**:144, 176
"The Rivers" (Alegria) **26**:
*Rivers and Mountains* (Ashbery) **26**:107-108, 113-114, 116, 129, 142-143, 148, 154-155, 167, 173-174
"The Rivers of Song" (Neruda)
  See "Los ríos del canto"

"The River's Story" (Tagore)
  See "Tatinir katha"
"Riviere" (Montale) **13**:162
"The Rivulet" (Bryant) **20**:12, 14-15
"Rizpah" (Tennyson) **6**:372-73, 377, 379, 381, 411
"Rizpah, the Daughter of Ai" (Harper) **21**:191, 209, 218
"The Road" (Aiken) **26**:24, 46
"The Road" (Pinsky) **27**:168
"The Road" (Sassoon) **12**:242
"The Road and the End" (Sandburg) **2**:300
"The Road Between Here and There" (Kinnell) **26**:292
"The Road from Delphi" (Stryk) **27**:214
"The Road Not Taken" (Frost) **1**:202, 205, 213, 221, 230
"Road to Mandalay" (Kipling) **3**:179
*The Road to Ruin* (Sassoon) **12**:252, 270
"The Road to Shelter" (Gozzano) **10**:177
*The Road to Shelter* (Gozzano)
  See *La via del refugio*
"Road Up" (Smith) **12**:317
"Roads" (Dario)
  See "Caminos"
"The Roads Also" (Owen) **19**:343
"Roan Stallion" (Jeffers) **17**:107, 111, 113, 116, 127, 130, 135, 146
*Roan Stallion, Tamar, and Other Poems* (Jeffers) **17**:106, 122, 132, 135-37
"Roarers in a Ring" (Hughes) **7**:123
"Roast Opossum" (Dove) **6**:111
"Roastbeef" (Stein) **18**:327
"Robben Island" (Brutus) **24**:120
"The Robber" (MacDiarmid) **9**:155
*The Robber Brothers* (Pushkin)
  See *Bratya Razboiniki*
"Robbery" (Shapiro) **25**:312
"Robe of Love" (Yosano Akiko)
  See *Koigoromo*
"Robert Frost at Bread Loaf His Hand against a Tree" (Swenson) **14**:247, 253
"Robert G. Ingersoll" (Masters) **1**:343
"Robert Gould Shaw" (Dunbar) **5**:121
"Robert Louis Stevenson" (Reese) **29**:346
"Robert Lowell" (Shapiro) **25**:323
"Robert Schumann, Or: Musical Genius Begins with Affliction" (Dove) **6**:108
"Robin Hood's Heart" (Wylie) **23**:311
"Robin Song" (Hughes) **7**:134
"A Robyn Joly Robyn" (Wyatt) **27**:315
"Rocaille" (Gautier) **18**:141
"The Rock" (Stevens) **6**:303, 313
*Rock and Hawk* (Jeffers) **17**:137
"The Rock Below" (Graves) **6**:128-29
"The Rock of Rubies and the Quarry of Pearls" (Herrick) **9**:146
"Rockefeller is yo vice president, & yo mamma don't wear no drawers" (Baraka) **4**:30
"Rockpool" (Wright) **14**:376
"Rocky Acres" (Graves) **6**:151
"Rodine" (Bely) **11**:24
"Rodoslovnaya Moego Geroya" (Pushkin) **10**:391, 394
"Rodrigo" (Heine) **25**:159, 161
"The Roe Deer" (Tomlinson) **17**:335, 343
"Roger Clay's Proposal" (Merrill) **28**:234, 250
*Rogsajyae* (Tagore) **8**:424-26
*Rokeby* (Scott) **13**:265, 267-68, 277-78, 281, 285, 304, 307, 311, 318
"Roland Hayes Beaten" (Hughes) **1**:241, 243, 252
"The Roll of the Ages" (Noyes) **27**:136
"Rolling in at Twilight" (Snyder) **21**:288
"Rolling, Rolling" (Toomer) **7**:337
*Roma 1950 diario* (Pasolini) **17**:260
"Roman" (Rimbaud) **3**:271, 276
*Roman Bartholow* (Robinson) **1**:483, 489
"Roman Cadences" (Viereck) **27**:278
*The Roman Calendar* (Ovid)
  See *Fasti*

*Roman Elegies* (Goethe)
See *Römische Elegien*
*Roman Elegies II* (Brodsky) **9**:21
"Roman Fountain" (Bogan) **12**:99
"The Roman Road" (Smith) **12**:346
"Romance" (Cassian) **17**:4
"Romance" (Reese) **29**:335
"Romance" (Robinson) **1**:495
*Romance 48* (Juana Ines de la Cruz) **24**:215,
   217-18
"Romance de la Guardia Civil Española"
   (Garcia Lorca) **3**:131, 148
"Romance de la luna, luna" (Garcia Lorca)
   **3**:133
"Romance de la pena negra" (Garcia Lorca)
   **3**:133
"Romance del emplazado" (Garcia Lorca) **3**:133
"Romance moderne" (Williams) **7**:345
"A Romance of the Age" (Browning)
   See "Lady Geraldine's Courtship"
"Romance of the Spanish Civil Guard" (Garcia
   Lorca)
   See "Romance de la Guardia Civil
   Española"
"The Romance of the Swan's Nest"
   (Browning) **6**:32
"Romance sonámbulo" (Garcia Lorca) **3**:131,
   133, 147
*Romancero* (Heine)
   See *Romanzero*
*Romancero* (Pasolini) **17**:253-54, 279, 281
*Romancero gitano* (Garcia Lorca)
   See *Primer romancero gitano*
*Romances sans paroles* (Verlaine) **2**:414-15,
   418-19, 424, 431-32
"The Romantic" (Bogan) **12**:87, 100-01, 103
"The Romany Girl" (Emerson) **18**:77
*Romanzen* (Heine) **25**:131, 158-59
*Romanzero* (Heine) **25**:167
"The Romaunt of Margret" (Browning) **6**:32
"The Romaunt of the Page" (Browning) **6**:30,
   37-8, 42-3, 45
*Rome 1950 A Diary* (Pasolini) **17**:260-61
"Rome-Sickness" (Arnold) **5**:19
*Römische Elegien* (Goethe) **5**:239-40, 249, 255,
   257
"Römische Sarkophage" (Rilke) **2**:278
"Rondalla" (Gautier) **18**:125
"Roofers" (Hass) **16**:248
"The Roofwalker" (Rich) **5**:363, 392-93, 395
"The Room" (Aiken) **26**:24
"The Room" (Reese) **29**:330
"The Room of Mirrors" (Masters) **1**:344
"The Room of My Life" (Sexton) **2**:373
"The Room with the Tapestry Rug" (Giovanni)
   **19**:143
"Rooming-house, Winter" (Atwood) **8**:14
"Rooms" (Stryk) **27**:215, 218
"Roosevelt" (Lindsay) **23**:288
"Rooster" (Hagiwara Sakutaro)
   See "Rooster"
"Roosters" (Bishop) **3**:37, 46-8, 56-7, 60, 66
"Root Cellar" (Roethke) **15**:260, 295
"Roots" (Heaney) **18**:202
"Roots" (Hongo) **23**:198
"Roots" (Meredith) **28**:171, 175, 192, 194
"Roots and Branches" (Duncan) **2**:103, 110
*Roots and Branches* (Duncan) **2**:102, 105-06,
   109, 113-14, 119, 125
"Rosa divina que en gentil cultura"" (Juana
   Ines de la Cruz) **24**:225
"Rosa Mystica" (Hopkins) **15**:148, 159, 165
*La rosa profunda* (Borges) **22**:97
*La rosa separada: obra póstuma* (Neruda)
   **4**:287
*Rosalind and Helen* (Shelley) **14**:173, 175, 192,
   234
"Rosary Songs" (Trakl)
   See "Rosenkranzlieder"
"Rosas de elegía" (Guillen) **23**:100
"Le Rose" (Gautier) **18**:125
"The Rose" (Roethke) **15**:310-11

"The Rose" (Williams) **7**:386, 410
"The Rose" (Yeats) **20**:310
*Rose* (Lee) **24**:239-44
*The Rose* (Yeats) **20**:326, 328, 343, 347
"The Rose and the Cross" (Blok) **21**:31
"The Rose and the Eagle" (Bergin) **29**:
"The Rose and the Eagle" (Piercy) **29**:300
"La rose de l'infant" (Hugo) **17**:60-61, 65
"The Rose of the World" (Yeats) **20**:329
"Rose on the Heath" (Goethe)
   See "Heidenröslein"
"Rose, Rose" (Bukowski) **18**:5
"rose th night nd th green flowr" (Bissett) **14**:28,
   33
"The Rose Trellis" (McGuckian) **27**:94
"Roseamond" (Apollinaire)
   See "Rosemonde"
"Rosemonde" (Apollinaire) **7**:45, 47-8
"Rosenkranzlieder" (Trakl) **20**:233, 248
"Rosenschimmer" (Celan) **10**:122
"Roses" (Dove) **6**:109
"Roses" (Sandburg) **2**:324
"Le rossignol" (Lamartine) **16**:293
"Röster under jorden" (Ekeloef) **23**:76
"Rostro tras el cristal" (Mirada del
   viejoAleixandre) **15**:43
"Rosy" (Gluck) **16**:138
"Rosy-Checked Death" (Yosano Akiko)
   See "Kôgao no shi"
"Rotting Clam" (Hagiwara Sakutaro) **18**:167,
   177
"A Rotting Corpse" (Baudelaire)
   See "Une charogne"
"Rough times" (Piercy) **29**:303, 305
"A Round & A Canon" (Olson) **19**:281
"Round Dance Somewhere Around Oklahoma
   City/November Night" (Harjo) **27**:69
"Round the Turning" (Pasternak) **6**:267
"Round Trip" (Page) **12**:163
"The Roundel" (Swinburne) **24**:319, 322-23
*A Roundhead's Rallying Song* (Noyes) **27**:138
"De Route March" (McKay) **2**:225
"Route Marchin'" (Kipling) **3**:160
"A Route of Evanescence" (Dickinson) **1**:104
"Route Six" (Kunitz) **19**:175
"Rover" (Kunitz) **19**:175
"Rowing" (McGuckian) **27**:104
"Rowing" (Sexton) **2**:373
"The Rowing Endeth" (Sexton) **2**:371
"A Roxbury Garden" (Lowell) **13**:77-8, 96
"A Royal Princess" (Rossetti) **7**:272, 291
"Royauté" (Rimbaud) **3**:261-63
"Rozhdenie ulybki" (Mandelstam) **14**:152-53
*Rtusamhāra* (Kalidasa) **22**:177, 182, 184-85,
   208
*Rubáiyát* (Khayyam) **8**:143-45, 151-53, 157-70
*Ruba'iyat* (Khayyam)
   See *Rubáiyát*
"Rubies" (Emerson) **18**:77
"Ruby Brown" (Hughes) **1**:249
*La rueda dentada* (Guillen) **23**:109, 127, 133
"Rugby Chapel" (Arnold) **5**:33
"Ruin" (Garcia Lorca)
   See "Ruina"
"The Ruin" (Tomlinson) **17**:325-26, 335
"Ruina" (Garcia Lorca) **3**:139
"The Ruined Cottage" (Wordsworth) **4**:416, 418
"The Ruined Temple" (Tagore)
   See "Bhagna mandir"
"The Ruines of Time" (Spenser) **8**:366-67, 371
"Ruminants" (Joyce) **22**:149
"Rumour" (Tomlinson) **17**:317
"Rumpelstiltskin" (Sexton) **2**:364
"run tonight" (Bissett) **14**:16-17
*Run with the Hunted* (Bukowski) **18**:4-5
"Runagate, Runagate" (Hayden) **6**:176, 178-80,
   183, 185, 188, 194, 197-98
"The Runaway" (Frost) **1**:194
*The Runaway, and Other Stories* (Tagore)
   See *Palātakā*
"The Runaway Slave at Pilgrim's Point"
   (Browning) **6**:30, 37-8, 42-3, 45

"Runes" (Nemerov) **24**:262, 265, 268, 291
"Runes on Weland's Island" (Kipling) **3**:171
"Running on the Shore" (Swenson) **14**:288
"Running Water Music" (Snyder) **21**:306
"Rupture" (Pasternak) **6**:260
*The Rural Muse* (Clare) **23**:44
"Rural Objects" (Ashbery) **26**:124
"Rus in Urbe" (Meredith) **28**:171, 190
*Rusalka* (Lermontov) **18**:289-90, 292
*Rush/What Fuckan Theory* (Bissett) **14**:13
"Rusia en 1931" (Hass) **16**:224
*Ruslan and Lyudmila* (Pushkin)
   See *Ruslan i Lyudmila*
*Ruslan i Lyudmila* (Pushkin) **10**:357-58, 363-
   64, 375, 381-82, 386-88, 398, 404-09
"Russia" (Williams) **7**:370
"Russia comes into Poland" (Zagajewski)
   **27**:389, 394
"Russian Sonia" (Masters) **1**:327
*Rustic Elegies* (Sitwell) **3**:294-95, 319
"Rusty Crimson" (Christmas Day,
   1917Sandburg) **2**:331
"Ruth" (Wordsworth) **4**:380, 402
"Ruth and Naomi" (Harper) **21**:191, 194, 209,
   218
"Ru'ya'" (Gibran) **9**:79
"Ryght True It is" (Wyatt) **27**:318
"Ryojō" (Hagiwara Sakutaro) **18**:178
"S morya" (Tsvetaeva) **14**:325
*s th story i to* (Bissett) **14**:3, 5, 7-8
"Saadi" (Emerson) **18**:81, 87-88, 98, 104, 107
"Sábados" (Borges) **22**:93
"Sabala" (Tagore) **8**:415
"Sabás" (Guillen) **23**:103
"A Sabbath Morning at Sea" (Browning) **6**:14
"Sabbath Park" (McGuckian) **27**:101
*Sabbaths* (Berry) **28**:34, 39, 43-4
*Sabbaths: 1987-1990* (Berry) **28**:38, 43
"Sabishii jinkaku" (Hagiwara Sakutaro) **18**:177,
   181
*Sabotage* (Baraka) **4**:38
"Sab-peyechhir desh" (Tagore) **8**:412
"El sacamuelas" (Fuertes) **27**:35
"Sacrament" (Cullen) **20**:85
"Sacred Chant for the Return of Black Spirit
   and Power" (Baraka) **4**:27
"The Sacred Way" (Sikelianos) **29**:366, 368,
   370-71, 373
"The Sacrifice" (Herbert) **4**:107, 117, 120
"The Sacrifice of Er-Heb" (Kipling) **3**:181
"The Sacrilege" (Hardy) **8**:99
*Sad Airs* (Jimenez)
   See *Arias tristes*
"A Sad Distant View" (Hagiwara Sakutaro)
   **18**:176
*The sad field-hand* (Illyes)
   See *Szomoru beres*
"The Sad Garden Dissolves" (Jimenez)
   See "El jardín triste se pierde"
"Sad Moments" (Gallagher) **9**:64
"Sad Moonlit Night" (Hagiwara Sakutaro)
   See "Sad Moonlit Night"
"The Sad Shepherd" (Yeats) **20**:354
"Sad Song" (Kunitz) **19**:147, 155
"Sad Steps" (Larkin) **21**:229-30
"Sad Strains of a Gay Waltz" (Stevens)
   **6**:296-97
"The Sad Supper" (Pavese)
   See "La cena triste"
*Sad Toys* (Ishikawa)
   See *Kanashiki gangu*
"Sad Wine" (Pavese)
   See "Il vino triste"
"Sadako" (Soto) **28**:385
"Sadie and Maude" (Brooks) **7**:67, 69
*Sadness and Happiness: Poems* (Pinsky)
   **27**:143-44, 153, 156, 160-62, 173, 175-76
"The Sadness of Brothers" (Kinnell) **26**:260
"The Sadness of Lemons" (Levine) **22**:211
"Safety" (Brooke) **24**:59, 80, 88
"Saffron" (Smith) **12**:295
"Saga" (Viereck) **27**:265

Title Index

*Saga Diary* (Matsuo Basho)
See *Saga nikki*
*Saga nikki* (Matsuo Basho) **3**:29
*Sagan om Fatumeh* (Ekeloef) **23**:60, 65, 68-9, 77-8
"Sagesse" (H. D.) **5**:275
"Sagesse" (Hugo) **17**:77-78, 97
*Sagesse* (H. D.) **5**:282, 285
*Sagesse* (Verlaine) **2**:413, 415-19, 425-26, 430
"Said Song" (Ammons) **16**:19
"Said the Poet to the Analyst" (Sexton) **2**:358-59
"The Sail" (Lermontov) **18**:297
"The Sail of Ulysses" (Stevens) **6**:326, 328
"Sailing after Lunch" (Stevens) **6**:297, 338
"Sailing Home from Rapallo" (Lowell) **3**:205, 220, 245
"Sailing of the Swallow" (Swinburne) **24**:356-57
"The Sailing of the Swan" (Swinburne) **24**:313, 349, 357
"Sailing to Byzantium" (Yeats) **20**:308, 310, 316, 329, 333, 335, 346, 349
"A Sailor in Africa" (Dove) **6**:110
"Sailor in Moscow" (Pasternak)
See "Matros v Moskve"
"The Sailor's Mother" (Wordsworth) **4**:398, 402
"Saint" (Graves) **6**:141, 144, 151
"Saint" (Merrill) **28**:240-41
"The Saint" (Shapiro) **25**:268, 286
"A Saint about to Fall" (Thomas) **2**:408-09
"Saint Anthony and the Rose of Life" (Smith) **12**:308
"St. Augustine-by-the-Sea" (Swenson) **14**:288
"Saint Francis and Lady Clare" (Masters) **1**:325, 333
"Saint Francis and the Sow" (Kinnell) **26**:259-60, 292
"Sainte" (Mallarme) **4**:201
"Sainte-Nitouche" (Robinson) **1**:460
"Saints and Singing" (Stein) **18**:346
*La Saisiaz* (Browning) **2**:66, 68, 71-2, 74
*Une saison en enfer* (Rimbaud) **3**:249, 252-53, 260-66, 268, 270, 279, 286
"Un sajón" (Borges) **22**:98
"Sakyamuni Coming Out from the Mountain" (Ginsberg) **4**:49
"Sal" (Tagore) **8**:416
"La Salade" (Ronsard) **11**:240
*The Salamander* (Paz)
See *Salamandra*
*Salamandra* (Paz) **1**:353, 357, 360-62, 369
"Saliences" (Ammons) **16**:6, 23
*Salisbury Plain* (Wordsworth) **4**:429
"Sallie Chisum/Last Words on Billy the Kid. 4 a.m." (Ondaatje) **28**:338-39
"The Sallow Bird" (Smith) **12**:326
"El salmo de la pluma" (Dario) **15**:93
"The Salmon Fisher to the Salmon" (Heaney) **18**:225
"The Salmon Leap" (MacDiarmid) **9**:153
"Salmon-Fishing" (Jeffers) **17**:131
*Salmos* (Cardenal) **22**:103, 117-19, 125, 129-31
*Salmos Psalms of Struggle and Liberation* (Cardenal) **22**:118
"Salomé" (Laforgue) **14**:69, 72
"Salome';s Dancing-lesson," (Parker) **28**:351, 363
"The Salt Garden" (Nemerov) **24**:261
*The Salt Garden* (Nemerov) **24**:260-61, 264, 288-89
"Saltimbanque Elegie" (Rilke)
See "Saltimbanques"
"Saltimbanques" (Rilke) **2**:278, 295
"Les Saltimbanques" (Tzara) **27**:224
"Salts and Oils" (Levine) **22**:224
"Salutación al águila" (Dario) **15**:77, 90, 107, 115
"Salutación del optimista" (Dario) **15**:81, 115
"Salutation to the Eagle" (Dario)
See "Salutación al águila"
"Salute to Guinea" (Cesaire) **25**:32

"Salute to Our Allies" (Brutus) **24**:119
*Salutes and Censures* (Brutus) **24**:118-20
"Salvador Díaz Mirón" (Dario) **15**:118
"Sambhashan" (Tagore) **8**:417
"Samos" (Merrill) **28**:233
"Samothrake" (Ekeloef) **23**:76
"Samson" (Blake) **12**:31
*Samson Agonistes* (Milton) **29**:212, 227, 232, 244
*Samson's Anger* (Vigny)
See "La colère de Samson"
*Sämtliche Werke* (Heine) **25**:172
"The Samuel Pie" (Belloc) **24**:42
"San Diego Poem" (Ortiz) **17**:226, 233
"San Fernando Road" (Soto) **28**:369, 377, 384-85
"San Fruttuoso: The Divers" (Tomlinson) **17**:349
"San Ildefonso Nocturne" (Paz)
See "Nocturno de San Ildefonso"
"A San Juan de la Cruz" (Fuertes) **27**:14
*San Martín Copybook* (Borges)
See *Cuaderno San Martín*
"San Onofre, California" (Forche) **10**:141, 152-53, 155, 158
"Sanctuary" (Reese) **29**:335
"Sanctuary" (Wright) **14**:343
"Sanctuary" (Wylie) **23**:323, 329
"The Sand Altar" (Lowell) **13**:95
*Der Sand aus den Urnen* (Celan) **10**:95, 121
"Sand Dunes" (Frost) **1**:203, 218
*Sand from the Urns* (Celan)
See *Der Sand aus den Urnen*
"Sand Martin" (Clare) **23**:5
"The Sand-Diggrers' Twilight" (Pavese)
See "Crepuscolo di sabbiatori"
*Sandhya sangit* (Tagore) **8**:405-06
"Sandpiper" (Bishop) **3**:53-4
"Sands" (Cassian) **17**:11
*Le sanglot de la terre* (Laforgue) **14**:57, 64, 68-71, 74, 80-1, 95
"Sanglot perdu" (Laforgue) **14**:86, 88
"La sangre numerosa" (Guillen) **23**:128-29
*Sangschaw* (MacDiarmid) **9**:151, 158, 166, 187, 190-91, 196
"Santa" (Sexton) **2**:365
"Santa Ana a Oscuras" (Alegria) **26**:
"Santa Ana in the Dark" (Alegria) **26**:
"Santa Barbara Road" (Hass) **16**:217
"Santa Claus" (Nemerov) **24**:267
"Santa Cruz Propostions" (Duncan) **2**:116
"The Santa Fé Trail" (Lindsay) **23**:264, 268, 273, 278, 286-87, 294
"Santa Lucia" (Hass) **16**:211
"Santarém" (Bishop) **3**:64-5
"Santorini: Stopping the Leak" (Merrill) **28**:267-69
*Saōgi* (Yosano Akiko) **11**:310
"The Sap is Gone Out of the Trees" (Ammons) **16**:39
"Sapho" (Lamartine) **16**:277
"Sapphics" (Swinburne) **24**:320
"Sara" (Nishiwaki) **15**:241
"Sarajevo" (Nemerov) **24**:291
*Sarashina kikō* (Matsuo Basho) **3**:26
"Sarcophagi I" (Montale) **13**:116
*Sardanapalus* (Byron) **16**:91, 103, 109-10
*Sarumino* (Matsuo Basho) **3**:3, 4, 29
"Sarvaneshe" (Tagore) **8**:414
"Sashes and bearskins in the afternoon" (Davie) **29**:107
"Sashka" (Lermontov) **18**:278
"Satan Says" (Olds) **22**:319
*Satan Says* (Olds) **22**:307, 310, 312, 315, 317, 319-20, 322, 327-28
"Satanic Form" (Swenson) **14**:252
*Satin-Legs Smith* (Brooks)
See "The Sundays of Satin-Legs Smith"
"Satire III" (Wyatt) **27**:342
*Satires and Epistles of Horace, Imitated* (Pope) **26**:321
"Satires of Circumstance" (Hardy) **8**:124

*Satires of Circumstance* (Hardy) **8**:91, 97
*Satires of Dr. Donne Versified* (Pope) **26**:324-25
*Satires of Horace* (Pope) **26**:359
"A Satirical Elegy on the Death of a Late Famous General" (Swift) **9**:256, 294, 307
*Satirical Poems* (Sassoon) **12**:258
"The Satisfactions of the Mad Farmer" (Berry) **28**:43
"Satsujin jiken" (Hagiwara Sakutaro) **18**:177, 180
"Satturday: The Small Pox: Flavia" (Montagu) **16**:349
*Satura* (Montale) **13**:131-34, 138, 143, 148, 152, 161, 167
"Saturn's Rings" (Wakoski) **15**:369
"A Satyr" (Montagu) **16**:338
"The Satyr in the Periwig" (Sitwell) **3**:294
"Le satyre" (Hugo) **17**:62, 65, 85, 87, 89
"Satyre II" (Donne) **1**:144
"Satyre III" (Donne) **1**:125, 143, 147
*Satyres* (Donne) **1**:140-42, 145
"Saul" (Browning) **2**:36, 67-8, 72, 75
"Sausages" (Stein) **18**:353
"La sauvage" (Vigny) **26**:368-70, 372, 382, 402, 412
"Saved by Faith" (Harper) **21**:189, 208
"The Saving" (Pinsky) **27**:159
"A Saxon" (Borges)
See "Un sajón"
"Say, Lad, Have You Things to Do" (Housman) **2**:179, 192
"Saying It to Keep It from Happening" (Ashbery) **26**:136
"The Scales of the Eyes" (Nemerov) **24**:261-62
"Scapegoats and Rabies" (Hughes) **7**:137
"Scar" (Lorde) **12**:139
"Scarab" (Brutus) **24**:111
"Scarecrow" (Stryk) **27**:197
*A Scattering of Salts* (Merrill) **28**:281-82, 284-87
"A Scene on the Banks of the Hudson" (Bryant) **20**:14, 46
"Scenes of Childhood" (Merrill) **28**:248
"Schattenbild" (Enzensberger) **28**:139
"schaum" (Enzensberger) **28**:136
"Scheherazade" (Ashbery) **26**:127, 150
"Der Scheidende" (Heine) **25**:178-80
"Die Schildkröte" (Enzensberger) **28**:165
"schläferung" (Enzensberger) **28**:139
"Schneebett" (Celan) **10**:114
*Schneepart* (Celan) **10**:96, 98
"The Scholar" (Baraka) **4**:23
"The Scholar-Gipsy" (Arnold) **5**:7, 13, 18-24, 33-5, 37, 47, 51, 53, 53, 59
"The School Children" (Gluck) **16**:128, 132, 149
"School Days" (Ashbery) **26**:137
*School Figures* (Song) **21**:341, 347
"School Nights" (Soto) **28**:399
"The School of Desire" (Swenson) **14**:276, 284
"A School of Prayer" (Baraka) **4**:10, 18
"The School-Boy" (Blake) **12**:7, 34
*Schoolboy Lyrics* (Kipling) **3**:190, 193
"Schoolmaster" (Larkin) **21**:234, 241
"The Schoolmistresses" (Pavese)
See "Le maestrine"
"Schopenhauer's Crying" (Zagajewski) **27**:384
"An Schwager Kronos" (Goethe) **5**:245, 247, 251
"Science" (Jeffers) **17**:113
"Science has looked" (Owen) **19**:371
"The Science of the Night" (Kunitz) **19**:153, 170, 182
"Scilla" (Gluck) **16**:169
"Scirocco" (Montale) **13**:105, 125
"Scorpion" (Smith) **12**:301, 319, 333
*Scorpion and Other Poems* (Smith) **12**:299, 315
*Scots Unbound* (MacDiarmid) **9**:158, 175-76, 196
"Scots Wha Hae wi' Wallace Bled" (Burns) **6**:78
"Scouting" (Levine) **22**:220-21, 228, 231-32

"Screaming Tarn" (Bridges) **28**:68
"Screvo meu livro à beira-mágoa" (Pessoa) **20**:155-56
"Screw: A Technical Love Poem" (Wakoski) **15**:332
"Screw Guns" (Kipling) **3**:158
"Scripts for the Pageant" (Merrill) **28**:233-38, 243, 260-64, 276-78, 281
"Scroll" (Noyes) **27**:130
"Scrub" (Millay) **6**:235
"The Sculptor" (Plath) **1**:388-89
"Scurry" (Swenson) **14**:254
"Scyros" (Shapiro) **25**:268, 279
*The Scythians* (Blok)
    See *Skify*
"Se acabó" (Guillen) **23**:117, 125
"Se vuelve a yo" (Neruda) **4**:287
"The Sea" (Borges)
    See "El mar"
"The Sea" (Parker) **28**:351
"The Sea" (Swenson) **14**:288
"The Sea" (Williams) **7**:385, 387
"Sea and Night" (Aleixandre)
    See "Mar y noche"
*The Sea and the Bells* (Neruda)
    See *El mar y las campanas*
"The Sea and the Mirror: A Commentary on Shakespeare's Tempest" (Auden) **1**:22, 34
"Sea Calm" (Hughes) **1**:236
"Sea Change" (Tomlinson) **17**:321
"Sea Dirge" (Carroll) **18**:46
"Sea Dreams" (Tennyson) **6**:360
*Sea Garden* (H. D.) **5**:266-67, 288-90, 303
"The Sea Horse" (Graves) **6**:154
"Sea Iris" (H. D.) **5**:289
"Sea Lily" (H. D.) **5**:288
"Sea Lullaby" (Wylie) **23**:332
"Sea Poppies" (H. D.) **5**:288
"Sea Surface Full of Clouds" (Stevens) **6**:304, 332
"Sea Unicorns and Land Unicorns" (Moore) **4**:233
"Sea Violet" (H. D.) **5**:289
"The Sea Was Asleep" (Zagajewski) **27**:394
"Sea-Blue and Blood-Red" (Lowell) **13**:60, 64, 66, 72, 81, 83
"The Sea-Elephant" (Williams) **7**:360
"The Sea-Fairies" (Tennyson) **6**:348, 359
"The Seafarer" (Pound) **4**:317, 331, 364
*Seamarks* (Perse)
    See *Amers*
"The Seamless Garment" (MacDiarmid) **9**:177
"The Seamstress" (Song) **21**:331, 333-34, 336, 341, 350
"Sea-Nymph's Prayer to Okeanos" (Zukofsky) **11**:368
"The Search" (Herbert) **4**:101
"The Search" (Masters) **1**:343-44
"Searching for the Canto Fermo" (Wakoski) **15**:362
"Searching, Not Searching" (Rukeyser) **12**:224
"Searchlight Practice" (Wright) **14**:354
"Sea-Rose" (H. D.) **5**:288, 303
"Seascape" (Bishop) **3**:37
"Sea-Serpent" (MacDiarmid) **9**:193
*The Seashell Game* (Matsuo Basho)
    See *Kai oi*
"The Seashore" (Emerson) **18**:76, 80, 89, 91
"Seaside" (Brooke) **24**:58, 76, 84, 86, 88
"A Sea-Side Meditation" (Browning) **6**:20
*A Season in Hell* (Rimbaud)
    See *Une saison en enfer*
*The Season of Violence* (Paz)
    See *La estación violenta*
*Season Songs* (Hughes) **7**:157, 162, 171
"Seasonal" (Ashbery) **26**:166
"Seasons" (Bradstreet)
    See "The Four Seasons of the Year"
"Seasons" (Tomlinson) **17**:326
*The Seasons* (Kalidasa)
    See *Rtusamhāra*
"Seated Figure" (Gluck) **16**:153

*Seaton Prize Odes* (Smart) **13**:329
"Seattle 7 May 72" (Brutus) **24**:123
"Sea-Wind" (Mallarme) **4**:187
*Sebastian im Traum* (Trakl) **20**:236, 241, 244, 250
"Sebastian in Traum" (Trakl) **20**:228, 230-31
"Sécheresse" (Perse) **23**:255, 257
"The Second Angel" (Levine) **22**:213
*The Second Anniversarie. Of the Progres of the Soule. Wherein, By Occasion Of the Religious death of Mistris Elizabeth Drury, the incommodities of the Soule in this life, and her exaltation in the next, are Contemplated* (Donne) **1**:122, 145-51, 155-57
"Second April" (Millay) **6**:206
*Second April* (Millay) **6**:211-12, 214-15, 233, 242-44
"The Second Best" (Arnold) **5**:42
"Second Best" (Brooke) **24**:76, 84
"Second Best" (Brooke) **24**:59, 60
"Second Best Bed" (Shapiro) **25**:316
*The Second Birth* (Pasternak) **6**:253-54, 268, 281
*A Second Book* (Mandelstam)
    See *Vtoraya kniga*
"The Second Chambermaid's Song" (Yeats) **20**:332
"Second Chance" (Wakoski) **15**:347
"The Second Coming" (Yeats) **20**:308, 312-13, 319-20, 349
"Second Elegy" (Rilke)
    See "Second Song"
"Second Epistle to John Lapraik" (Burns) **6**:68-70, 78
"Second Fig" (Millay) **6**:227
"Second Georgic" (Vergil) **12**:359, 365
"Second Glance at a Jaguar" (Hughes) **7**:136-37
"Second Hymn to Lenin" (MacDiarmid) **9**:158, 177, 180-81, 197
*Second Hymn to Lenin, and Other Poems* (MacDiarmid) **9**:156, 179, 196
*The Second Jungle Book* (Kipling) **3**:162, 185, 188-89
"Second Language" (Gallagher) **9**:60
*Second livre des poemes* (Ronsard) **11**:282
"Second Nun's Tale" (Chaucer) **19**:13, 15
"Second Oldest Story" (Parker) **28**:362
*Second Olympian* (Pindar)
    See *Olympian 2*
"Second Populist Manifesto" (Ferlinghetti)
    See "Adieu á Charlot"
*Second Pythian* (Pindar)
    See *Pythian 2*
"The Second Rapture" (Carew) **29**:10
"The Second Sermon on the Warpland" (Brooks) **7**:63
"Second Song" (Bogan) **12**:90, 129
"Second Song" (Rilke) **2**:273-74, 286
"Second Song for the Worship of the Goddess at Yü Mountain: 'Bidding the Godeess Farewell'" (Wang Wei) **18**:369
*The Second Symphony* (Bely)
    See *Vtoraia simfoniia: Dramaticheskaia*
*Second Voronezh Notebook* (Mandelstam) **14**:133-34, 149, 152-53
*Second Year of Chang-ho* (Li Ho) **13**:42
"The Second-Best Bed" (Nemerov) **24**:291
"Second-Class Constable Alston" (McKay) **2**:205
"The Secret" (Merton) **10**:348
"Secret Festival; September Moon" (Levertov) **11**:177
*The Secret Meaning of Things* (Ferlinghetti) **1**:173-74, 176, 186-87
"Secret Music" (Sassoon) **12**:247
"The Secret of Machu Pichhu"
    See "El Secreto de Machu-Picchu"
"The Secret Sharer" (Gunn) **26**:
"Secretary" (Hughes) **7**:140
"El Secreto de Machu-Picchu" (Cardenal) **22**:132

*Secrets from the Center of the World* (Harjo) **27**:65, 68
*The Secrets of the Heart* (Gibran) **9**:72
"Secrets of the Trade" (Akhmatova) **2**:5
*Section: Rock-Drill, 85-95 de los cantares* (Pound) **4**:352, 357
*Secular Love* (Ondaatje) **28**:314-17, 340
"Sed de Correr" (Clampitt) **19**:100
"Seduction" (Giovanni) **19**:111, 113, 117
"Seed and Bran" (Tzara) **27**:242
"The Seed Cutters" (Heaney) **18**:203
"Seed Pods" (Snyder) **21**:305
"The Seed-Picture" (McGuckian) **27**:79, 97
*Seeds and Bran* (Tzara)
    See *Grains et issues*
*Seeds for a Hymn* (Paz)
    See *Semillas para un himno*
"Seeds of Liberty" (Alegria) **26**:
"Seeds of Liberty" (Alegria) **26**:
"Seeing a Friend Off" (Li Po) **29**:146
*Seeing Is Believing* (Tomlinson) **17**:302, 306, 317-18, 321, 323-24, 332-33, 335, 338, 341-42, 346, 352, 359
"Seeing the Bones" (Kumin) **15**:207, 209
"Seeing Things" (Nemerov) **24**:302
*Seeing Things* (Heaney) **18**:254-61
"The Seekonk Woods" (Kinnell) **26**:278, 293
"Seen by the Waits" (Hardy) **8**:130
*Segund antolojía poética* (Jimenez) **7**:178, 201
"Le Seigneur habite en toi" (Gautier) **18**:144
"Seizure" (Sappho)
    See "Ode to Anactoria"
*A Seizure of Limericks* (Aiken) **26**:24
"Seldom yet Now" (Graves) **6**:156
*Selected Failings* (Neruda)
    See *Defectos escogidos: 2000*
*Selected letters* (Williams) **7**:374
*Selected Poems* (Aiken) **26**:
*Selected Poems* (Ashbery) **26**:158
*Selected Poems* (Breton) **15**:57
*Selected Poems* (Brooks) **7**:81, 102
*Selected Poems* (Davie) **29**:127
*Selected Poems* (Duncan) **2**:102
*Selected Poems* (Frost) **1**:195
*Selected Poems* (H. D.) **5**:274
*Selected Poems* (Hayden) **6**:176, 178-79
*Selected Poems* (Kinnell) **26**:261-62, 288
*Selected Poems* (Levine) **22**:220
*Selected Poems* (Lowell) **3**:226-27
*Selected Poems* (McKay) **2**:207, 228
*Selected Poems* (Meredith) **28**:207
*Selected Poems* (Milosz) **8**:174
*Selected Poems* (Montale) **13**:135
*Selected Poems* (Moore) **4**:240, 242, 253
*Selected Poems* (Pasolini) **17**:289
*Selected Poems* (Rukeyser) **12**:210
*Selected Poems* (Senghor) **25**:238, 241, 245
*Selected Poems* (Sexton) **2**:347-48
*Selected Poems* (Shapiro) **25**:315
*Selected Poems* (Sitwell) **3**:320
*Selected Poems* (Smith) **12**:293, 309, 350
*Selected Poems* (Stryk) **27**:185, 187-89, 191, 197-98, 201-3
*Selected Poems* (Tomlinson) **17**:327, 345
*Selected Poems, 1928-1958* (Kunitz) **19**:148, 155, 157, 159, 161-63, 168-70, 173-76
*Selected Poems: Summer Knowledge (1938-1958* Schwartz)
    See *Summer Knowledge: New and Selected Poems, 1938-1958*
*Selected Poems, 1950-1975* (Gunn) **26**:206
*Selected Poems, 1951-1974* (Tomlinson) **17**:325
*Selected Poems, 1957-1967* (Hughes) **7**:163
*Selected Poems 1965-1975* (Atwood) **8**:23
*Selected Poems and New* (Villa) **22**:349, 351, 353-54
*Selected Poems and Prose of John Clare* (Clare) **23**:3-8, 11, 13-14
*Selected Poems: Beyond Even Faithful Legends* (Bissett) **14**:27-30, 34-5
*Selected Poems: German-English Bilingual Edition* (Enzensberger) **28**:166

*Selected Poems, Joseph Brodsky* (Brodsky) **9**:8
*The Selected Poems of Langston Hughes*
   (Hughes) **1**:248, 258
*The selected poems of Lizette Woodworth*
   *Reese* (Reese) **29**:334-35, 339, 347, 352
*Selected Poetry of Amiri Baraka/LeRoi Jones*
   (Baraka) **4**:31
*The Selected Poetry of Hayden Carruth*
   (Carruth) **10**:84
*The Selected Poetry of Robinson Jeffers*
   (Jeffers) **17**:111, 123, 130, 133, 136-37,
   141
*Selected Writings* (Olson) **19**:268, 276-77, 305,
   316-17
*Selected Writings of Juan Ramon Jimenez*
   (Jimenez)
      See *Antolojía poética (1898-1953)*
"Selective Service" (Forche) **10**:137, 144, 146,
   157, 165
"Self and Life" (Eliot) **20**:136
*The Self and the Other* (Borges)
      See *El otro, el mismo*
"Self in 1958" (Sexton) **2**:351
"Self Portrait" (Wylie) **23**:321
"The Self Unsatisfied Runs Everywhere"
   (Schwartz) **8**:285
"The Self-Abuser and the Suicide" (Viereck)
   **27**:279
"The Self-Betrayal Which Is Nothing New"
   (Schwartz) **8**:294
"Self-Criticism and Answer" (Day Lewis)
   **11**:128, 144
"Self-Criticism in February" (Jeffers) **17**:123,
   132
"Self-Dependence" (Arnold) **5**:19, 42-3, 49
"The Self-Hatred of Don L. Lee" (Madhubuti)
   **5**:337
"The Selfish One" (Neruda)
      See "El egoísta"
"Self-Portrait" (Cassian) **17**:7
"A Self-Portrait: David" (Tomlinson) **17**:346,
   348
"Self-Portrait in a Convex Mirror" (Ashbery)
   **26**:109, 119-21, 123-24, 126, 134, 140, 142-
   43, 147-50, 159, 171-72, 174
*Self-Portrait in a Convex Mirror* (Ashbery)
   **26**:115-16, 118, 124, 126-27, 130, 145, 148-
   50, 160, 169, 171, 174
"Self-Portrait in Tyvek Windbreaker"
   (tmMerrill) **28**:287
"Self-Praise" (Graves) **6**:139
"The Self-Unseeing" (Hardy) **8**:88, 129
"Selige Sehnsucht" (Goethe) **5**:248
"Selina, Countess of Huntingdon" (Davie)
   **29**:115-16
"Selinda and Cloris" (Behn) **13**:30
"Sella" (Bryant) **20**:15
"A Seltzer Bottle" (Stein) **18**:334
"The Selves" (Page) **12**:198
"La semaine Sainte" (Lamartine) **16**:277, 299
"The Semblables" (Williams) **7**:360
*Semillas para un himno* (Paz) **1**:353, 366
"Semper eadem" (Baudelaire) **1**:61, 72
"Semplicità" (Pavese) **13**:229
"The Sence of a Letter Sent Me, Made into
   Verse; to a New Tune" (Behn) **13**:31
"Sence You Went Away" (Johnson) **24**:132, 141,
   151, 154, 162
"Send No Money" (Larkin) **21**:234, 242, 248
"The Send-Off" (Owen) **19**:347
*Senlin: A Biography* (Aiken) **26**:4, 6, 12, 22,
   29, 70-2
*Senlin A Biography* (Aiken) **26**:
"Señor Diego Valverde" (Juana Ines de la
   Cruz) **24**:186
"Señor, para responderos" (Juana Ines de la
   Cruz) **24**:187
"Señora doña Ros" (Juana Ines de la Cruz)
   **24**:211
"Sensation" (Rimbaud) **3**:275, 283
"Sensation Time at the Home" (Merton)
      See "A Song: Sensation Time at the Home"

"Sense and Conscience" (Tennyson) **6**:372-73
*The Sense of Movement* (Gunn) **26**:181, 184-
   185, 188-189, 200-201, 206-207, 210, 212,
   218-220, 230
"Sensemayá" (Guillen) **23**:131-32, 134
"Sensibility! O La!" (Roethke) **15**:257, 278,
   299, 301
*The Sensitive Plant* (Shelley) **14**:167, 171, 175,
   193, 196, 198
"The Sensualists" (Roethke) **15**:275
*sent på jorden* (Ekeloef) **23**:62, 75, 77, 88
"Sent to My Two Little Children in the East of
   Lu" (Li Po) **29**:146
"The Sentence" (Akhmatova)
      See "Prigovor"
"The Sentence" (Graves) **6**:157
"A Sentence for Tyranny" (Hass) **16**:248
"Sentences" (Milosz) **8**:189
*Sentences* (Nemerov) **24**:288
*Sentences* (Nemerov) **24**:'
"The Sententious Man" (Roethke) **15**:272, 278
"The Sentimental Surgeon" (Page) **12**:176
"The Separate Notebooks" (Milosz)
      See "Osobny zeszyt"
*The Separate Notebooks* (Milosz) **8**:182, 195-97
*The Separate Rose* (Neruda)
      See *La rosa separada: obra póstuma*
"The Separation" (Gunn) **26**:
"Les sept epees" (Apollinaire) **7**:46
"Les sept vieillards" (Baudelaire) **1**:45, 65, 70
"September" (Belloc) **24**:29
"September" (Hughes) **7**:113, 118
"September" (Zagajewski) **27**:396
"September 1, 1939" (Auden) **1**:14, 25
"September 22nd" (Kumin) **15**:190
"September 1913" (Yeats) **20**:324-25
"September Afternoon in the Abandoned
   Barracks" (Zagajewski) **27**:391
"September on Jessore Road" (Ginsberg) **4**:59
"September Shooting" (Nemerov) **24**:288
"September Twilight" (Gluck) **16**:170
"Le Septiesme livre des poemes" (Ronsard)
   **11**:246
"Sepulchre" (Herbert) **4**:120
*Sequel to Drum-Taps* (Whitman) **3**:418, 422
"Sequence" (Wylie) **23**:310, 315, 322
*A Sequence for Francis Parkman* (Davie) **29**:96,
   98, 109
"Sequence, Sometimes Metaphysical"
   (Roethke) **15**:311
*Sequences* (Sassoon) **12**:247-48, 255, 257-60,
   271
"The Seraphim" (Browning) **6**:6, 20, 22, 26-7
*The Seraphim, and Other Poems* (Browning)
   **6**:14-15, 19, 26, 29, 31-2
"Serata romana" (Pasolini) **17**:265
"Serenade" (Viereck) **27**:263
"Serenade: Any Man to Any Woman" (Sitwell)
   **3**:309, 311, 314
"Serenata indiana" (Montale) **13**:107, 128
"The Sergeant's Weddin'" (Kipling) **3**:164, 192
"A Serious Step Lightly Taken" (Frost) **1**:203
"Sermon for Our Maturity" (Baraka) **4**:19
"A Sermon on the Warpland" (Brooks) **7**:63
"Le serpent" (Valery)
      See "Ébauche d'un serpent"
"Le serpent qui danse" (Baudelaire) **1**:62
*The Serrated Wheel* (Guillen)
      See *La rueda dentada*
*The Serrated Wheel* (Guillen)
      See *La rueda dentada*
"A Servant to Servants" (Frost) **1**:193, 228
"La servante au grand coeur" (Baudelaire)
   **1**:67-68
"Ses purs ongles très haut dèdiant leur onyx"
   (Mallarme)
      See "Sonnet en -yx"
"Sesenheimer Lyrik" (Goethe) **5**:245
"Śesh lekhā" (Tagore) **8**:424, 426-27
*Sestina* (Rukeyser) **12**:232
"Sestina: Altaforte" (Pound) **4**:356

"Sestina from the Home Gardener" (Wakoski)
   **15**:360
"Sestina of the Tramp Royal" (Kipling) **3**:160
*Sestra moia zhizn* (Pasternak) **6**:250-51, 254-
   55, 260, 263-65, 268-69, 271-72, 278-80,
   282, 285
"Set of Country Songs" (Hardy) **8**:127
"A Set of Romantic Hymns" (Duncan) **2**:103
"The Setting Sun" (Clare) **23**:40
"The Settle Bed" (Heaney) **18**:259
"The Settlers" (Atwood) **8**:12
"Le seul savant, c'est encore Moïse" (Verlaine)
   **2**:416
"Seurat's Sunday Afternoon along the Seine"
   (Schwartz) **8**:289-99, 317-18
"VII" (Joyce) **22**:136, 144, 167
"The Seven Ages" (Auden) **1**:39
"Seven Days for Eternity" (Elytis) **21**:123
"7.IV.64" (Snyder) **21**:287
"Les 7 500 000 oui (Publie (Hugo) **17**:98
"The Seven Old Men" (Baudelaire)
      See "Les sept vieillards"
"Seven Poems for Marthe, My Wife"
   (Rexroth) **20**:181
*The Seven Seas* (Kipling) **3**:159-62, 164, 167,
   192-93
"Seven Songs for a Journey" (Wright) **14**:369
"Seven Songs Written during the Ch'ien-yüan
   Era while Staying at T'ung-ku-hsien" (Tu
   Fu) **9**:322
*The Seven Storey Mountain* (Merton) **10**:
"Seven Strophes" (Brodsky) **9**:22
"The Seven Swords" (Apollinaire)
      See "Les sept epees"
"Seven Years from Somewhere" (Levine)
   **22**:219
*Seven Years from Somewhere* (Levine) **22**:218-
   19, 234
"XVII" (Joyce) **22**:136, 144, 164, 167
"Seventeen" (Zagajewski) **27**:389
"A Seventeen Morning" (Ammons) **16**:44
"1777" (Lowell) **13**:78, 84
"Seventeen Years" (Berry) **28**:9
"A Seventeenth Century Suite" (Duncan) **2**:115-
   16, 127
"Seventh Birthday of the First Child" (Olds)
   **22**:318
"Seventh Elegy" (Rilke) **2**:281, 286
*Seventh Isthmian* (Pindar)
      See *Isthmian 7*
*Seventh Nemean* (Pindar)
      See *Nemean 7*
"Seventh Psalm" (Sexton) **2**:367
"The Seventh Summer" (Levine) **22**:220
*73 Poems* (Cummings) **5**:109-11
*Several Poems Compiled with Great Variety of
   Wit and Learning, Full of Delight*
   (Bradstreet) **10**:43-5, 51
"Several Voices Out of a Cloud" (Bogan)
   **12**:100, 107, 124
*Severnaia simfoniia: Pervia geroicheskaia*
   (Bely) **11**:3, 12-15, 21
"A Sewerplant Grows in Harlem or I'm a
   Stranger Here Myself When Does the
   Next Swan Leave?" (Lorde) **12**:158
"Sex without Love" (Olds) **22**:328-29, 339
"El sexo" (Aleixandre) **15**:34
"Sext" (Auden) **1**:23
"Sextet" (Brodsky) **9**:19, 22
"Sexual Water" (Neruda)
      See "Agua sexual"
*Shackles* (Cesaire)
      See *Ferrements*
"The Shad-Blow Tree" (Gluck) **16**:126-27, 142
"Shade of Fonvizin" (Pushkin) **10**:408
"The Shadow" (Lowell) **13**:60-1, 83
"Shadow" (Stryk) **27**:201
"Shadow: 1970" (Wright) **14**:371
*The Shadow of Cain* (Sitwell) **3**:320, 327
"The Shadow of Fire" (Wright) **14**:376
*Shadow of Paradise* (Aleixandre)
      See *Sombra del paraíso*

"A Shadow Play for Guilt" (Piercy) 29:309
*Shadow Train: Fifty Lyrics* (Ashbery) 26:151-152, 154, 166-167
"Shadow-Maker" (Swenson) 14:261
"Shadows of Taste" (Clare) 23:14
"Shadows on the Wall" (Blok) 21:14
*The Shadowy Waters* (Yeats) 20:303, 353
"The Shaft" (Tomlinson) 17:342
*The Shaft* (Tomlinson) 17:325-27, 334-36, 338, 342-43, 347, 350, 353-54
"Shakespeare" (Arnold) 5:49
"Shakespeare" (Pasternak) 6:252
"Shakespeare in Harlem" (Hughes) 1:239, 242, 246-47, 254-56, 268, 270
"Shakespeare Say" (Dove) 6:109
"A Shakespearean Sonnet: To a Woman Liberationist" (Knight) 14:46
"Shalom" (Levertov) 11:170
"Shaman Mountain is High" (Li Ho) 13:51
"Shantung" (Lindsay) 23:265
"Shantung Or the Empire of China Is Crumbling Down" (Lindsay) 23:280
"Shape of Boeotia" (Elytis) 21:116
"The Shape of Death" (Swenson) 14:286
"The Shape of the Fire" (Roethke) 15:248, 254, 272, 274, 277, 282, 284-85, 287, 298
"Sharing Eve's Apple" (Keats) 1:311
"Shark Meat" (Snyder) 21:292, 308
"The Shark: Parents and Children" (Wakoski) 15:356
"The Sharp Ridge" (Graves) 6:156
"Sharpeville" (Brutus) 24:117
*Sharps and Flats* (Tagore)
    See *Kari o komal*
"Shatabdir surya" (Tagore) 8:412
"Shatter Me, Music" (Rilke) 2:275
"A Shawl" (Stein) 18:328, 348
"She" (Roethke) 15:275
"She Being Brand-New" (Cummings) 5:95
"SHE CALLS ME ADONIS" (Bissett) 14:32
"She Carries a 'Fat Gold Watch'" (Ondaatje) 28:292
"She Had Some Horses" (Harjo) 27:64-65
*She Had Some Horses* (Harjo) 27:56-8, 60, 64-65
"She of the Dancing Feet Sings" (Cullen) 20:63
"She Remembers the Future" (Harjo) 27:56
"She Said . . ." (Smith) 12:326
*She Steals My Heart* (Li Ho) 13:44
"She Tells Her Love while Half Asleep" (Graves) 6:144
"She Thinks of Him" (Li Po) 29:176
"She, to Him" (Hardy) 8:90
"She Weeps over Rahoon" (Joyce) 22:137
"She Wept, She Railed" (Kunitz) 19:151
"she won't ever forgive me" (Clifton) 17:25
"A Sheaf for Chicago" (Stryk) 27:187, 195, 210, 214
"The Sheaves" (Robinson) 1:478
"A Sheep Fair" (Hardy) 8:101
"Sheep in a Fog" (Plath) 1:408-09
"The Sheep Went On Being Dead" (Hughes) 7:149
*Sheepfold Hill: Fifteen Poems* (Aiken) 26:24
"Shell" (Zagajewski) 27:403
"Shells" (Nemerov) 24:299
"Sheltered Garden" (H. D.) 5:269, 303
"Shenendoah" (Shapiro) 25:284-85
*The Shepheardes Calender: Conteyning Twelve Æglogues Proportioned to the Twelve Monethes* (Spenser) 8:326-28, 335, 385-87
"The Shepherd" (Blake) 12:7, 32
"The Shepherd" (H. D.) 5:305
"The Shepherd" (Soto) 28:371
"Shepherd Bound for Mountain Pass" (Aleixandre) 15:12, 18
"The Shepherd's Brow, Fronting Forked Lightning" (Hopkins) 15:168
*The Shepherd's Calendar, with Village Stories, and Other Poems* (Clare) 23:10, 16-21, 37-8, 40, 44
*Shepherd's Home* (Vigny) 26:371

*Sherwood* (Noyes) 27:123
"She's Free" (Harper) 21:204
"Shesh katha" (Tagore) 8:407
*Shesh saptak* (Tagore) 8:417
"Shiberia no uta" (Ishikawa) 10:213
"The Shield of Achilles" (Auden) 1:23
"The Shih-men Monastery in the Lan-t'ien Mountains" (Wang Wei) 18:378
"Shillin' a Day" (Kipling) 3:191
"The Shimmer of Evil" (Roethke) 15:278
"Shine" (Knight) 14:49
"Shine, Perishing Republic" (Jeffers) 17:107, 117-19, 132
"Shipbuilding Office" (Page) 12:173, 176
"Shipman's" (Chaucer)
    See "Shipman's Tale"
"Shipman's Tale" (Chaucer) 19:13, 26
*Shipovnik tsvetyot* (Akhmatova) 2:9
*Ships and Other Figures* (Meredith) 28:171, 173, 186-87, 189, 210, 217
"Ships That Pass in the Night" (Dunbar) 5:121
"Shiraha no toribune" (Ishikawa) 10:214
*The Shires* (Davie) 29:116
"The Shirt" (Pinsky) 27:158, 164-65, 176
"Shitsurakuen" (Nishiwaki) 15:237, 239
"Shitsurakuen" (Nishiwaki) 15:
"Shiv and the Grasshopper" (Kipling) 3:183
"Shizumeru kane" (Ishikawa) 10:214
"The Shoes of Wandering" (Kinnell) 26:243, 249, 266, 272-73
"Shoot It Jimmy" (Williams) 7:383
"Shoot the Buffalo" (Momaday) 25:214
"A Shooting Incident" (Smith) 12:318, 346
"Shooting Script" (Rich) 5:366-67, 378, 383, 396-97
"Shootings of the Third of May" (Heaney) 18:205
"Shop" (Browning) 2:59
"The Shore" (Clampitt) 19:90
"Shoreline" (Heaney) 18:201, 203
"Shores" (Montale)
    See "Riviere"
"The Shorewatchers' House" (Montale) 13:150
"Short Poem" (Sanchez) 9:212, 223
*Short Prose Poems* (Baudelaire)
    See *Petits poèmes en prose: Le spleen de Paris*
"A Short Recess" (Milosz) 8:183, 186
*Short Songs of Pure Feelings* (Hagiwara Sakutaro)
    See *Junjo shokyoku shu*
"Short Summary" (Bogan) 12:101
*Shorter Poems* (Bridges) 28:52-3, 67, 69, 82-3
"The Shot" (Graves) 6:143-44
"The Shot" (Pushkin)
    See "Vystrel"
"The Shovel Man" (Sandburg) 2:332
"The Show" (Owen) 19:327, 336-37, 341, 343-44, 347, 353, 355, 359
"Shower" (Swift)
    See "Description of a City Shower"
"The Showings; Lady Julian of Norwich, 1342-1416" (Levertov) 11:210
"The Shrine" (H. D.) 5:270
*A Shropshire Lad* (Housman) 2:159-67, 171-78, 180-81, 183-84, 186-88, 191-95, 197, 199-200
*A Shropshire Land* (Belloc) 24:
"The Shroud" (Millay) 6:205
"The Shroud of Color" (Cullen) 20:52, 54-55, 57, 62, 64, 67, 69, 73, 84
"Shūchō" (Ishikawa) 10:212
*Shukumei* (Hagiwara Sakutaro) 18:176
*Shundeishū* (Yosano Akiko) 11:305
"Shun'ya" (Hagiwara Sakutaro) 18:181
"Shut, Bellada" (Bely) 11:24
"Shut Nad ney" (Bely) 11:24
"Shut Out" (Rossetti) 7:280
"Shut: Plamen" (Bely) 11:24
"Shutka" (Bely) 11:24
"Shuttles" (Swenson) 14:273
*Shyamali* (Tagore) 8:417

"Shylock" (Shapiro) 25:283
"Si acaso, Fabio mío" (Juana Ines de la Cruz) 24:180, 184, 187
"Si daros los buenos años" (Juana Ines de la Cruz) 24:180
"Si el desamor o el enojo" (Juana Ines de la Cruz) 24:186, 234
"Si es amor causa productiva" (Juana Ines de la Cruz) 24:189
"Si los riesgos del mar cpmsoderara" (Juana Ines de la Cruz) 24:225
"Sibir" (Tsvetaeva) 14:326
"Sibling Mysteries" (Rich) 5:373, 384
"Sibrandus Schafnaburgensis" (Browning) 2:59
"A Sibyl" (Atwood) 8:25
*Sibylline Leaves* (Coleridge) 11:57, 60, 97, 115
"Sic Transit" (Lowell) 3:213
"The Sick" (Page) 12:176
"A Sick Bed" (Bryant) 20:17, 46
"The Sick Child" (Gluck) 16:132, 136, 138
"The Sick King in Bokhara" (Arnold) 5:6, 39, 49
"Sick Leave" (Sassoon) 12:267, 288
"Sick Love" (Graves) 6:136-37, 142, 144, 151, 169
"The Sick Rose" (Blake) 12:7
"Sickly Face at the Bottom of the Ground" (Hagiwara Sakutaro) 18:175
"The Sickness unto Death" (Sexton) 2:372
*Sidestreets* (Tsvetaeva)
    See *Pereulochki*
"Sie erlischt" (Heine) 25:178
"Sie haben wegen der Trunkenheit" (Heine) 25:162
"Siena mi fe'; disfecemi Maremma" (Pound) 4:319
"Sierra Nevada" (Cardenal) 22:125, 131
"A Sigh" (Finch) 21:141
"The Sigh" (Hardy) 8:104
"Sigh" (Mallarme)
    See "Soupir"
"The Sigh That Heaves the Grasses" (Housman) 2:183, 191
"Sighs and Groans" (Herbert)
    See "Sighs and Grones"
"Sighs and Grones" (Herbert) 4:120, 133-34,
"Sighs are my food drink are my tears" (Wyatt) 27:369
"Sight" (Parker) 28:365
"Sightseeing on a Winter Day" (Wang Wei) 18:373
"The Sign" (Masters) 1:333, 337
"The Sign of Saturn" (Olds) 22:324
"The Sign of the Golden Shoe" (Noyes) 27:124
"Signal" (Tzara) 27:229-31
"The Signal from the House" (Kunitz) 19:172-73
"The Signature of All Things" (Rexroth) 20:196, 217
*The Signature of All Things: Poems, Songs, Elegies, Translations, and Epigrams* (Rexroth) 20:181, 183-84, 192-94, 203
"The Significance of Veteran's Day" (Ortiz) 17:226, 232
"The Signifying Monkey" (Knight) 14:49
"Signing the Pledge" (Harper) 21:191
"A Signature. A Herold. A Span" (Brooks) 7:90
"La Signorina Felicita" (Gozzano) 10:176-77, 180-83
"Signpost" (Jeffers) 17:129, 131, 145
"Signs and Tokens" (Hardy) 8:111
"Signs of Winter" (Clare) 23:28
"Sigue" (Guillen) 23:142
"Die silbe schmerz" (Celan) 10:102, 105
"The Silence" (Berry) 28:5, 7, 43
"Silence" (Eliot) 5:217
"Silence" (Masters) 1:325, 333, 342
"Silence" (Wright) 14:342
"Silence and Tears" (Smith) 12:341
"The Silence Answered Him Accusingly" (Schwartz) 8:293
*A Silence Opens* (Clampitt) 19:100-01

"Silences: Lament of the Silent Sisters"
(Okigbo) **7**:225, 228, 234, 244-47, 251
"Silent Faces at Crossroads" (Okigbo) **7**:255
"Silent in America" (Levine) **22**:212, 222
"Silent Service" (Sassoon) **12**:252
"Silent Sisters" (Okigbo)
See "Silences: Lament of the Silent Sisters"
"Silhouette of a Serpent" (Valery)
See "Ébauche d'un serpent"
"The Silken Tent" (Frost) **1**:196, 214
"Silly Song" (Garcia Lorca)
See "Canción tonta"
"Silos" (Dove) **6**:120
"Silver" (Ammons) **16**:5
"Silver Filigree" (Wylie) **23**:314, 322, 332
"The Silver Lily" (Gluck) **16**:170
"The Silver Swan" (Rexroth) **20**:221
"The Silver Tassie" (Burns) **6**:97
"Simaetha" (H. D.) **5**:266
*Simfonija* (1-agaBely)
See *Severnaia simfoniia: Pervia
geroicheskaia*
*Simfonija* (2-ajaBely)
See *Vtoraia simfoniia: Dramaticheskaia*
"Simon Lee" (Wordsworth) **4**:374, 416-17, 425-
26, 428
"Simon Legree" (Lindsay) **23**:264, 269, 273,
287
"Simon Surnamed Peter" (Masters) **1**:325, 342
"Simon the Cyrenian Speaks" (Cullen) **20**:56,
65
"Simple agonie" (Laforgue) **14**:73
"Simple Autumnal" (Bogan) **12**:87-8, 106, 121
*A Simple Lust: Selected Poems Including
Sirens, Knuckles, Boots; Letters to
Martha; Poems from Algiers, Thoughts
Abroad* (Brutus) **24**:113-16, 118
"Simple Sonatina" (Gallagher) **9**:60
*The Simple Truth* (Levine) **22**:228, 232-33
"Simples" (Joyce) **22**:
"Simple-Song" (Piercy) **29**:309
"Simplicity" (Pavese)
See "Semplicità"
"Sin" (Herbert) **4**:100
"Sin I" (Herbert) **4**:130
"Since 1619" (Walker) **20**:275, 283
"Since I am comming" (Donne)
See "Hymne to God my God, in my
sicknesse"
"Since we loved" (Bridges) **28**:86
"Since ye delight to know" (Wyatt) **27**:353
"Sindhu-taranga" (Tagore) **8**:407
"Sinfonía en gris mayor" (Dario) **15**:93, 96
"The Singer" (Levertov) **11**:183
"The Singer" (Tsvetaeva)
See "Pevitsa"
"A Singer Asleep" (Hardy) **8**:125
"Singers" (Hughes) **7**:123
"Singing Nigger" (Sandburg) **2**:316
"Singing School" (Heaney) **18**:205
"Single Sonnet" (Bogan) **12**:90, 107
"Single Vision" (Kunitz) **19**:154
"Singling & Doubling Together" (Ammons)
**16**:63-4
*Sing-Song: A Nursery Rhyme-Book* (Rossetti)
**7**:291
"Sinistre" (Valery) **9**:359, 381, 399-401
*The Sinking of the Titanic* (Enzensberger)
See "Der Untergand der Titanic"
"The Sinking Ship" (Rimbaud)
See "L'eclatante victoire de Saarebrück"
"Sinners in the Hands of an Angry God"
(Lowell) **3**:203
"The Sins of Kalamazoo" (Sandburg) **2**:308
"Sin's Round" (Herbert) **4**:114
"Sion" (Herbert) **4**:100
"Sir Galahad" (Masters) **1**:330, 333
"Sir Galahad" (Tennyson) **6**:359
"Sir John Herschel Remembers" (Noyes)
**27**:129
"Sir Thopas" (Chaucer) **19**:25, 33-4, 37, 47,
50-1

"Siren Limits" (Okigbo) **7**:240-46
"Siren Song" (Atwood) **8**:23, 25-6, 41
"Sirens, Knuckles, Boots" (Brutus) **24**:98-9,
112-13, 119
"The Sirens' Welcome to Cronos" (Graves)
**6**:144, 146
"Sirocco" (Montale)
See "Scirocco"
"Sister Maude" (Rossetti) **7**:260, 270, 272-3,
276, 280
"The Sisters" (Lowell) **13**:67
*The Sisters: A Tragedy* (Swinburne) **24**:348-50,
352
"Sisters in Arms" (Lorde) **12**:141, 151-53
"Sit-Ins" (Walker) **20**:276
"The Sitting" (Day Lewis) **11**:147
"The Sitting" (McGuckian) **27**:101
"Sitting Alone on an Autumn Night" (Wang
Wei) **18**:388
"The Situation in the West Followed by a Holy
Proposal" (Ferlinghetti) **1**:172
*The Situation of Poetry: Contemporary Poetry
and Its Traditions* (Pinsky) **27**:143, 153,
160, 164, 173
"S.I.W." (Owen) **19**:354, 357, 369, 371
"VI" (Joyce) **22**:136, 138, 145, 160, 167, 173
*Six and One Remorses for the Sky* (Elytis)
**21**:118, 122, 124, 133
"Six Casually Written Poems" (Wang Wei)
**18**:388
*Six Epistles to Eva Hesse* (Davie) **29**:99-100,
102, 104, 109
"Six Lectures in Verse" (Milosz) **8**:199-200,
202-03, 211
*Six Moral Tales from Jules Laforgue*
(Laforgue)
See *Moralités légendaires*
"Six O'Clock in Princes Street" (Owen) **19**:342
*Six Odes* (Auden) **1**:8
*Six Quatrains Composed in Jest* (Tu Fu) **9**:327
"Six Religious Lyrics" (Shapiro) **25**:320
"Six Variations" (Levertov) **11**:183
"Six Years Later" (Brodsky) **9**:7, 8, 19, 26
"Six Young Men" (Hughes) **7**:113
"Six-Bit Blues" (Hughes) **1**:256
"XVI" (Joyce) **22**:145, 162, 170
"The Sixteenth Floor" (Lowell) **13**:97
"Sixth Elegy" (Rilke) **2**:273
"Sixth Elegy. River Elegy" (Rukeyser)
**12**:231-32
*Sixth Isthmian* (Pindar)
See *Isthmian 6*
*Sixth Olympian* (Pindar)
See *Olympian 6*
*Sixth Pythian* (Pindar)
See *Pythian 6*
*65 Poems* (Celan) **10**:120
"The Size" (Herbert) **4**:100, 108
"Size and Tears" (Carroll) **18**:46
"Skateboard" (Gunn) **26**:215
"The Skaters" (Ashbery) **26**:107, 114, 129, 143,
151, 154-156
"Skazka o Mertvoy Tsarevne" (Pushkin) **10**:382
"Skazka o Pope i o Rabotnike Yego Balde"
(Pushkin) **10**:382
"Skazka o Rybake i Rybke" (Pushkin) **10**:382
"Skazka o Tsare Sultane" (Pushkin) **10**:381-83
"Skazka o Zolotom Petushke" (Pushkin)
**10**:382-83
"Skazki" (Pushkin) **10**:408
*Skazki* (Pushkin) **10**:381-86
"The Skeleton of the Future" (MacDiarmid)
**9**:176, 179
"Sketch" (Sandburg) **2**:303, 335
"Sketch for a Landscape" (Swenson) **14**:246,
262
"Sketches for a Portrait" (Day Lewis) **11**:148
*Sketches of Southern Life* (Harper) **21**:185, 187,
189, 191-93, 197-98, 200-01, 211, 213-14
"The Skies" (Aleixandre) **15**:19-20
*Skify* (Blok) **21**:9, 17, 21-2, 26, 28-9, 31, 35, 41
"Skin" (Larkin) **21**:229

"Skin Canoe" (Forche) **10**:134
"the skinny voice" (Cummings) **5**:99
"Skizze zu einem Sankt Georg" (Rilke) **2**:267
"Skullshapes" (Tomlinson) **17**:340, 357
"The Skunk" (Heaney) **18**:244
"Skunk Hour" (Lowell) **3**:209-11, 213-14, 221,
223, 227, 235, 243-46
"Skunk Hour" (Sexton) **2**:350
"The Sky Falling" (Soto) **28**:370
"The Sky Lark" (Clare) **23**:6
"Sky-House" (McGuckian) **27**:78
"Skylarks" (Hughes) **7**:121-22, 136-37
"The Skylarks of Mykonos" (Clampitt) **19**:87
*Skylight One: Fifteen Poems* (Aiken) **26**:24
"Skylights" (Gallagher) **9**:45
"Slabs of the Sunburnt West" (Sandburg) **2**:306,
308, 310-11, 314, 323, 330
*Slabs of the Sunburnt West* (Sandburg) **2**:306,
308, 311, 314, 323
"The Slacker Apologizes" (Viereck) **27**:273
"The Slacker Need Not Apologize" (Viereck)
**27**:263
"The Slanting Rain" (Pessoa)
See "Chuva Oblíqua"
"The Slate Ode" (Mandelstam)
See "Grifel' naja oda"
"The Slave Auction" (Harper) **21**:190, 194, 205-
06, 216-17
"slave cabin sotterly plantation maryland
1989" (Clifton) **17**:30
"The Slave Mother" (Harper) **21**:192, 194, 197,
203-04, 216
"The Slave Mother, A Tale of Ohio" (Harper)
**21**:197, 204-05, 210, 218
"The Sleep" (Browning) **6**:21
"Sleep" (Hughes) **1**:240
"Sleep" (Johnson) **24**:145, 159
"Sleep" (Pushkin) **10**:407
"Sleep and Poetry" (Keats) **1**:280, 289, 291-92,
313
"Sleep at Sea" (Rossetti) **7**:293, 296-7
"Sleep Brings No Joy to Me" (Bronte) **8**:74
"Sleep defends my Don drowsiness"
(Mandelstam)
See "Oboroniaet son moiu donskuiu son"
"Sleep of the Valiant" (Elytis) **21**:123
"The Sleep of the Valiant" (VariationElytis)
**21**:116
"The Sleep Worker" (Hardy) **8**:129
"The Sleeper" (Poe) **1**:434, 443-44
"The Sleepers" (Whitman) **3**:391, 396-97, 401
"Sleeping at Last" (Rossetti) **7**:287
"Sleeping Beauty" (Clifton) **17**:29
"The Sleeping Beauty" (Owen) **19**:358
"Sleeping Beauty" (Wylie) **23**:321
*The Sleeping Beauty* (Carruth) **10**:75-8, 83-4,
86, 91
*The Sleeping Beauty* (Sitwell) **3**:292-94, 298,
300-01, 303, 307-08, 310, 316-17, 320,
324-25
"The Sleeping Fury" (Bogan) **12**:100, 104
*The Sleeping Fury* (Bogan) **12**:88-90, 105, 109,
111, 120, 122-25, 131
"Sleeping on the Ceiling" (Bishop) **3**:37
"Sleeping Out Full Moon" (Brooke) **24**:57
"Sleeping with Animals" (Kumin) **15**:209, 211,
215, 223
"A Sleepless Night" (Levine) **22**:214
"Sleepwalker Ballad" (Garcia Lorca)
See "Romance sonámbulo"
"The slender wire above the sea of oats"
(Tsvetaeva)
See "U tonkoi pnovoloki nad volnoi ovsov"
"The Slippers of the Goddess of Beauty"
(Lowell) **13**:67
"Slips" (McGuckian) **27**:97
"Slip-Shoe Lovey" (Masters) **1**:333, 336
"Slow through the Dark" (Dunbar) **5**:131
"Slow Waker" (Gunn) **26**:
"Slug" (Roethke) **15**:274
"Sluicegates of Thought" (Tzara) **27**:235

"A Slumber Did My Spirit Steal"
　　(Wordsworth) **4**:420
"Small Action Poem" (Tomlinson) **17**:325
"Small Comment" (Sanchez) **9**:224
"Small Garden near a Field" (Gallagher) **9**:62
"The Small Hours" (Parker) **28**:359
"Small Hours" (Plath) **1**:391
"The Small Lady" (Smith) **12**:295
"A Small Light" (Song) **21**:344
"Small Moment (Nemerov) **24**:293
"Small Ode to a Black Cuban Boxer" (Guillen)
　　See "Pequeña oda a un negro boxeador
　　　cubano"
"A Small Peice of Wood" (McGuckian) **27**:107,
　　110-111
"Small Perfect Manhattan" (Viereck) **27**:263,
　　278
"Small Poems for the Winter Solstice"
　　(Atwood) **8**:44
"Small Song for Crossing a Big River"
　　(Cesaire) **25**:32
*Small Testament* (Villon)
　　See *Les Lais*
"A Small Will" (Montale)
　　See "Piccolo testamento"
"Smalltown Dance" (Wright) **14**:378-79
"Smelt Fishing" (Hayden) **6**:196
"Smert" (Lermontov) **18**:302
"The Smile" (Blake) **12**:35, 43
"The Smile" (Merrill) **28**:248
"Smile, Smile, Smile" (Owen) **19**:354, 357, 359
"Smoke" (McGuckian) **27**:97
"Smoke" (Reese) **29**:340
"Smoke and Earth" (Aleixandre) **15**:18-19
"Smoke and Steel" (Sandburg) **2**:304, 316
*Smoke and Steel* (Sandburg) **2**:304-08, 313-14,
　　316, 321, 323, 338
"The Smokers" (Shapiro) **25**:323
"Smokers of Cheap Cigarettes" (Pavese)
　　See "Fumatori di carta"
"Smokey the Bear Sutra" (Snyder) **21**:291
"Smudging" (Wakoski) **15**:331, 364
*Smudging* (Wakoski) **15**:332, 345, 364
"Snail" (Hughes) **1**:241
"The Snake" (Berry) **28**:25
"Snake" (Hughes) **1**:241
"Snake" (Roethke) **15**:272
"Snake Hymn" (Hughes) **7**:159
"Snake River" (McKay) **2**:216
"Snakecharmer" (Plath) **1**:388-89
"Snakeskin on a Gate" (Wright) **14**:356
"Snapshots of a Daughter-in-Law" (Rich)
　　**5**:370-72, 396
*Snapshots of a Daughter-in-Law: Poems,*
　　*1954-1962* (Rich) **5**:354, 358, 363, 369-
　　72, 374, 382, 388, 392
"Snarley-Yow" (Kipling) **3**:158
*Snezhnye maski* (Blok) **21**:20, 24
"The Snob" (Shapiro) **25**:295
"Snow" (Frost) **1**:195, 215
"Snow" (Hayden) **6**:193, 196
"Snow" (Hughes) **7**:155
"Snow" (Levine) **22**:225
"Snow" (Rich) **5**:366
"snow cummin" (Bissett) **14**:20
"The Snow Fairy" (McKay) **2**:228
"The Snow Fences" (Tomlinson) **17**:341
"Snow Jobs" (Merrill) **28**:284-85
"The Snow King" (Dove) **6**:108
"Snow King Chair Lift" (Merrill) **28**:222, 257
"The Snow Lamp" (Hayden) **6**:189, 192
"The Snow lies sprinkled on the beach"
　　(Bridges) **28**:89
"Snow Maiden" (Blok) **21**:9
*The Snow Mask* (Blok)
　　See *Snezhnye maski*
*The Snow Poems* (Ammons) **16**:23-6, 42-7, 49-
　　51, 54, 61-2, 65
"Snow) Says! Says" (Cummings) **5**:106
"Snow Shower" (Bryant) **20**:15-16
"Snow Signs" (Tomlinson) **17**:342, 345
"Snow, snow" (Piercy) **29**:315

"The Snow Storm" (Emerson) **18**:79-80, 88,
　　98, 107
"Snow Upon Paris" (Senghor) **25**:227
"Snow White" (Sexton) **2**:368
"Snowbed" (Celan)
　　See "Schneebett"
"Snowdrop" (Hughes) **7**:169
"Snowfall" (Gunn) **26**:203
"Snowfall" (Vigny)
　　See "La neige"
"Snowflakes as Kisses" (Schwarzweller) **8**:314
"The Snowman" (Page) **12**:167-68, 183
"Snows" (Perse)
　　See "Neiges"
"Snows" (Stryk) **27**:202-3
"So I Said I Am Ezra" (Ammons) **16**:39
"So Intricately Is This World Resolved"
　　(Kunitz) **19**:170
"So Much Depends" (Williams) **7**:362
"So Old" (Snyder) **21**:307
"So, so breake off this last lamenting kisse"
　　(Donne)
　　See "The Expiration"
"So sweet love seemed that April morn"
　　(Bridges) **28**:86
"So To Fatness Come" (Smith) **12**:326
"So We Grew Together" (Masters) **1**:326-26,
　　328
*Sobranie sochinenij* (Mandelstam) **14**:113, 117,
　　123
*Social Credit, An Impact* (Pound) **4**:328
"Sociedad de amigos y protectores" (Fuertes)
　　**27**:16
"Socrates' Ghost Must Haunt Me Now"
　　(Schwartz) **8**:302, 315
"The Sofa" (McGuckian) **27**:98
"Soft Wood" (Lowell) **3**:211
"Softer-Mother's Tale" (Wordsworth) **4**:373
"Il Sogno del prigioniero" (Montale) **13**:104
"Soho Cinema" (Lorde) **12**:140
"Sohrab and Rustum" (Arnold) **5**:9, 12-13, 33,
　　35, 37, 45, 52, 62
"The Soil-Map" (McGuckian) **27**:97
"Un soir" (Apollinaire) **7**:46
"Le soir" (Lamartine) **16**:275-76, 298-99, 302
"Soir de carnaval" (Laforgue) **14**:92
"Le soir qu'amour vous fist en la salle
　　descendre" (Ronsard) **11**:264-66
"Une soirée perdue" (Gautier) **18**:136-37
"Sokolinya slobodka" (Tsvetaeva) **14**:326
"El sol" (Aleixandre) **15**:25
"Sola con esperanza" (Fuertes) **27**:8, 29
*Sola en la sala* (Fuertes) **27**:17-8, 21, 38
"SOLACE IN WORDS" (Bissett) **14**:33
"Solar" (Larkin) **21**:250-51
"Solar Ode to the People's Army" (Neruda)
　　See "Oda solar al ejérito del pueblo"
"Solde" (Rimbaud) **3**:261, 264
"The Soldier" (Brooke) **24**:54, 59, 63-4, 71, 74,
　　80, 86-7, 89
"The Soldier" (Hopkins) **15**:144
*The Soldier* (Aiken) **26**:24
"Soldier, Soldier" (Kipling) **3**:163, 188-89
"The Soldiers" (Duncan) **2**:104
"Soldier's Dream" (Owen) **19**:341, 356
"Soldier's Farm" (Wright) **14**:340
"Soldier's Song" (Burns) **6**:78
"De Sole" (Tomlinson) **17**:336
"Soledad" (Hayden) **6**:194, 196
*Soledad* (Paz) **1**:366
*Soleil Cou-Coupé* (Cesaire) **25**:15, 23, 30-2, 35,
　　44
"Soleil et chair" (Rimbaud) **3**:251, 280, 283,
　　285
"Soliloquy" (Jeffers) **17**:132
"Soliloquy of a Misanthrope" (Hughes) **7**:116
"Soliloquy of the Spanish Cloister" (Browning)
　　**2**:37
"Le solitaire" (Lamartine) **16**:281
"The Solitary Reaper" (Wordsworth) **4**:399, 404
"Solitude" (Ishikawa)
　　See "Kyoko"

"La solitude" (Lamartine) **16**:277
"A Solitude" (Swinburne) **24**:327
"Solitudes at Sixty" (Sassoon) **12**:259
"Solo de lune" (Laforgue) **14**:74-6
"Solo de escalina" (Eliot) **5**:201
*Sombra del paraíso* (Aleixandre) **15**:6, 8, 10-
　　11, 15-16, 18, 21, 22-5, 33-4, 37-8, 40-1
"Sombre Figuration" (Stevens) **6**:298, 318, 320
*Some* (Ashbery) **26**:167, 172
"Some Answers Are Cold Comfort to the
　　Dead" (Schwartz) **8**:293
"Some Are Born" (Smith) **12**:316
"Some Brilliant Sky" (Wakoski) **15**:336
"Some Foreign Letters" (Sexton) **2**:350, 361,
　　363
"Some Foreign Wife" (Sexton) **2**:359
"Some Friends from Pascagoula" (Stevens)
　　**6**:337
"Some Lines" (Viereck) **27**:280
"Some Lines in Three Parts" (Viereck) **27**:263,
　　278, 280, 282
"Some Negatives: X at the Chateu" (Merrill)
　　**28**:242
"Some Notes on Organic Form" (Levertov)
　　**11**:160-62
"Some Quadrangles" (Swenson) **14**:273
*Some Time* (Zukofsky) **11**:343
"Some Trees" (Ashbery) **26**:118
*Some Trees* (Ashbery) **26**:111, 113, 118, 129,
　　135, 137, 143, 162, 164
*Some Trees* (Ashbery) **26**:
"Some Verses Upon the Burning of Our
　　House, July 10th, 1666" (Bradstreet) **10**:8,
　　19, 21, 27, 29-30, 34, 36-7, 42
"Somebody's Song" (Parker) **28**:351
"Someone Is Harshly Coughing as Before"
　　(Schwartz) **8**:301
"Something A Direction" (Tomlinson) **17**:312
"Something Borrowed" (Piercy) **29**:302
"Something for Hope" (Frost) **1**:200
"Something to Wear" (Levertov) **11**:165-66, 168
"Something Was Happening" (Hughes) **7**:154
"Sometimes Even Now" (Brooke) **24**:62
"Sometimes I fled the fire that me brent"
　　(Wyatt) **27**:368
"Somewhat Delayed Spring Song" (Parker)
　　**28**:355
"Somewhere" (Nemerov) **24**:262
"Somewhere East o' Suez" (Kipling) **3**:189
"Somewhere I Have Never Travelled, Gladly
　　Beyond" (Cummings) **5**:88
"Somewhere in Africa" (Sexton) **2**:364, 371
"Sommarnatten" (Ekeloef) **23**:76
"Sommation" (Hugo) **17**:98, 100
"Le Sommet de la tour" (Gautier) **18**:143, 146
"Somnambulent Ballad" (Garcia Lorca)
　　See "Romance sonámbulo"
"Somnambulist Ballad" (Garcia Lorca)
　　See "Romance sonámbulo"
"Son and Mother" (Blok) **21**:14
"Son del bloqueo" (Guillen) **23**:126
*El son entero* (Guillen) **23**:100, 108, 131, 139,
　　142
"Son más en una mazorca" (Guillen) **23**:125
*Son Motifs* (Guillen)
　　See *Motivos de son*
"Son number 6" (Guillen)
　　See "Son numero 6"
"Son numero 6" (Guillen) **23**:127, 130, 132,
　　139
"Sonar tari" (Tagore) **8**:408
*Sonar tari* (Tagore) **8**:409, 418, 427
"Sonata for Methylated Prose" (Ekeloef) **23**:85
"sonatform denaturerad prosa" (Ekeloef) **23**:75

"Sonatina" (Dario) **15**:79-80, 95, 107-08, 110, 119-20
*Sonetos espirituales* (Jimenez) **7**:191-92, 194-96, 202, 211
*Sonette* (Goethe) **5**:248, 250
*Sonette an Orpheus* (Rilke) **2**:267-68, 277, 280-81, 283, 290, 293, 295
*Die Sonette an Orpheus/Sonnets to Orpheus* (Rilke)
    See *Sonette an Orpheus*
"Song" (Behn)
    See "Love Arm'd"
"Song" (Berry) **28**:7-8
"Song" (Blake) **12**:6
"Song" (Bogan) **12**:86, 90, 103
"Song" (Bronte) **8**:62
"A Song" (Carew) **29**:19
"Song" (Cummings) **5**:109
"Song" (Donne) **1**:125
"Song" (H. D.) **5**:304
"Song" (Nemerov) **24**:256
"Song" (Poe) **1**:432
"The Song" (Roethke) **15**:269
"Song" (Rossetti) **7**:273, 276, 289
"Song" (Sitwell) **3**:313
"Song" (Williams) **7**:408
"Song" (Wright) **14**:338, 342, 347
"The Song and Dance of" (Olson) **19**:273
"Song: Aske me no more" (Carew) **29**:73
"Song Before Drinking" (Li Po) **29**:142
"Song Coming toward Us" (Forche) **10**:132
"Song for a Colored Singer" (Bishop) **3**:37
"Song for a Dark Girl" (Hughes) **1**:238, 243
"Song for a Lady" (Sexton) **2**:352
"Song for a Lyre" (Bogan) **12**:90, 92
"Song for a Phallus" (Hughes) **7**:132, 159, 171
"Song for a Red Night Gown" (Sexton) **2**:352-53
"Song for a Slight Voice" (Bogan) **12**:90, 92
"Song for a Viola d'Amore" (Lowell) **13**:88, 97
"A Song for J. H." (Behn) **13**:19
"A Song for New-Ark" (Giovanni) **19**:143
"Song for Nobody" (Merton) **10**:349
"A Song for Occupations" (Whitman) **3**:385, 401-02
"SONG FOR OOLJAH" (Bissett) **14**:33
"Song for Our Lady of Cobre" (Merton) **10**:
"A Song for Rosemarie" (Villa) **22**:354
"A Song for Simeon" (Eliot) **5**:194, 196-97, 203, 205, 209
*Song for St Cecilia's Day* (Dryden) **25**:75-8
"Song for the Death of Averroës" (Merton) **10**:343
"Song for the Last Act" (Bogan) **12**:124
"Song for the Mothers of Dead Militiamen" (Neruda)
    See "Canto a las madres de los milicianos muertos"
"Song for the Next River" (Gallagher) **9**:35
"Song for the Pockets" (Soto) **28**:375
"A Song for the Ragged Schools of London" (Browning) **6**:7, 23
"Song for the Rainy Season" (Bishop) **3**:67
"Song for the Saddest Ides" (Nash) **21**:263
"Song for the Squeeze Box" (Roethke) **15**:256
"A Song for the Year's End" (Zukofsky) **11**:349
"A Song from the Structures of Rime Ringing as the Poet Paul Celan Sings" (Duncan) **2**:117
"Song I" (Rilke) **2**:273
"Song in a Wine-Bar" (Wright) **14**:333
"Song in a year of Catastrophe" (Berry) **28**:43
"A Song in the Front Yard" (Brooks) **7**:69
"Song: Lift-Boy" (Graves) **6**:142, 144
"Song of a camera" (Gunn) **26**:212
"Song of a Dream Visit to T'ien-mu: Farewell to Those I Leave Behind" (Li Po) **29**:147
"The Song of a Rat" (Hughes) **7**:142, 155-56, 159
"Song of Another Tribe" (Rukeyser) **12**:217
"Song of Autumn in Spring" (Dario)
    See "Canción de otoño en primavera"

"Song of Defeat" (Tagore)
    See "Parajaya sangīt"
"Song of Despair" (Neruda) **4**:301
"The Song of Diego Valdez" (Kipling) **3**:182
"The Song of God's Child" (Li Ho) **13**:52
"Song of Invisible Boundaries" (Gluck) **16**:166
"A Song of Joys" (Whitman) **3**:402
"Song of Li Ling" (Wang Wei) **18**:389
"A Song of Liberty" (Blake) **12**:33
"Song of Love" (Lamartine)
    See "Chant d'amour"
"A Song of my heart" (Bridges) **28**:69
"Song of Myself" (Whitman) **3**:370, 394, 396-97, 399, 401-03, 405, 411-12, 414-17
"The Song of Nature" (Emerson) **18**:88
"Song of Opposites" (Keats) **1**:312
"Song of P'eng-ya" (Tu Fu) **9**:321, 332
"Song of Praise" (Cullen) **20**:52, 63
"A Song of Praise" (Sanchez) **9**:243
"A Song of Sherwood" (Noyes) **27**:136-137
"Song of Siberia" (Ishikawa)
    See "Shiberia no uta"
"Song of the Answerer" (Whitman) **3**:386, 390
"Song of the Banjo" (Kipling) **3**:160-61
"Song of the Beasts" (Brooke) **24**:59, 82
"Song of the Beautiful Ladies" (Tu Fu) **9**:320
"Song of the Bird" (Tagore)
    See "Vihanger gan"
"The Song of the Bongo" (Guillen)
    See "La canción del bongo"
"The Song of the Children" (Chesterton) **28**:100
"Song of the Children in Heaven" (Brooke) **24**:76
"The Song of the Cities" (Kipling) **3**:162
*The Song of the Cold* (Sitwell) **3**:320, 326
"Song of the Columns" (Valery)
    See "Cantique des colonnes"
"Song of the Crows roosting at night" (Li Po) **29**:143
"Song of the Dead" (Kipling) **3**:160, 162
"A Song of the Dust" (Sitwell) **3**:327
"A Song of the English" (Kipling) **3**:160-62, 164
"The Song of the Exiles" (Kipling) **3**:194
"The Song of the Final Meeting/Song of the Last Meeting" (Akhmatova)
    See "Pesnia poslednei vstrechi"
"The Song of the Galley Slaves" (Kipling) **3**:170
"The Song of the Happy Shepherd" (Yeats) **20**:354
"Song of the Heavenly Horse" (Li Po) **29**:159, 161
"Song of the Highest Tower" (Rimbaud) **3**:259
"The Song of the Ill-beloved" (Apollinaire)
    See "La chanson du mal-aimé"
"Song of the Little Square" (Garcia Lorca)
    See "Ballada de la Placeta"
*The Song of the Merchant Kaláshnikov* (Lermontov)
    See *The Song of Tzar Ivan Vasiljevich, His Young Life-Guardsman, and the Valiant Merchant Kaláshnikov*
"Song of the Open Road" (Whitman) **3**:387
"Song of the Peach Fountainhead" (Wang Wei) **18**:389
"The Song of the Pilgrims" (Brooke) **24**:76
"The Song of the Poorly Beloved" (Apollinaire)
    See "La chanson du mal-aimé"
"The Song of the Red War-Boat" (Kipling) **3**:183
"The Song of the Son" (Toomer) **7**:310, 317, 319, 334
"The Song of the Sons" (Kipling) **3**:162
"A Song of the Soul of Central" (Hughes) **1**:268
"Song of the Sower" (Bryant) **20**:14
"Song of the Stars" (Bryant) **20**:4
"Song of the Taste" (Snyder) **21**:297
"Song of the Worms" (Atwood) **8**:19, 25
*The Song of Tzar Ivan Vasiljevich, His Young Life-Guardsman, and the Valiant*

*Merchant Kaláshnikov* (Lermontov) **18**:278, 281-82, 304
"Song of Wandering" (Cesaire) **25**:
"Song of Women" (Masters) **1**:330, 333
*Song Offerings* (Tagore)
    See *Gitanjali*
"A Song on Gazing at Chung-nan Mountain For Hsü of the Secretariat" (Wang Wei) **18**:369
"A Song on Greife" (Finch) **21**:150, 152, 179
"Song over Some Ruins" (Neruda)
    See "Canto sobre unas ruinas"
"A Song: Sensation Time at the Home" (Merton) **10**:345
"A Song Sparrow Singing in the Fall" (Berry) **28**:7
"Song. 'Sweetest love, I do not goe'" (Donne) **1**:130
"Song: The Rev. MuBngwu Dickenson Ruminates behind the Sermon" (Brooks) **7**:94
"A Song to a Scotish Tune" (Come My Phillis Let Us ImproveBehn) **13**:18
"Song to a Scotish Tune" (When Jemmy First Began to LoveBehn) **13**:4, 7, 18, 32
"Song to Alfred Hitchcock and Wilkinson" (Ondaatje) **28**:291
"Song to Awaken a Little Black Child" (Guillen) **23**:132
*A Song to David* (Smart) **13**:328-34, 336-46, 352-54, 358, 360-65, 367-69
"Song to Ishtar" (Levertov) **11**:169
"A Song to No Music" (Brodsky) **9**:4, 9, 12
"A Song Untitled" (Hagiwara Sakutaro) **18**:173
"Song without Music" (Brodsky)
    See "A Song to No Music"
"Songe D'Athalie" (Smith) **12**:331
"Songin Black Armor" (Wylie) **23**:308, 310, 332
*Sóngoro cosongo: Poemas mulatos* (Guillen) **23**:98-100, 105-106, 111, 114, 131, 139, 142-44
"Songs" (Hughes) **1**:241
*Songs* (Garcia Lorca)
    See *Canciones*
"Songs:65o N" (Larkin) **21**:226
*Songs and Satires* (Masters) **1**:328, 335, 342
*Songs and Sonets* (Donne) **1**:130, 139, 145
*Songs and Sonnets, second series* (Masters) **1**:321, 325, 332
*Songs before Sunrise* (Swinburne) **24**:312
"Songs for a Colored Singer" (Bishop) **3**:37, 46-7
*Songs for Naëtt* (Senghor)
    See *Chants pour Naëtt*
*Songs for Soldiers and Tunes for Tourists* (Guillen)
    See *Cantos para soldados y sones para turistas*
"Songs for the People" (Harper) **21**:189
*Songs for the Republic* (Cassian) **17**:6
"Songs from Cyprus" (H. D.) **5**:304
"Songs in a Cornfield" (Rossetti) **7**:275
*Songs of Bhanusigh Thakur* (Tagore)
    See *Bhanusingh Thakurer padavali*
*Songs of Crow* (Hughes) **7**:140
"Songs of Education" (Chesterton) **28**:99
*Songs of Experience* (Blake) **12**:9-10, 23-5, 31, 33-5, 42-7, 61-2
*Songs of Innocence* (Blake) **12**:8-9, 19, 21-4, 32-4, 42, 61
*Songs of Innocence and of Experience: Shewing the Two Contrary States of the Human Soul* (Blake) **12**:8-11, 33-4, 42-3, 51
*Songs of Jamaica* (McKay) **2**:208, 210, 216, 221, 223-27
*Songs of Life and Hope* (Dario)
    See *Cantos de vida y esperanza*
"The Songs of Maximus" (Olson) **19**:282-83
"Songs of the Hen's Head" (Atwood) **8**:41

"Songs of the Ingenues" (Verlaine)
    See "La chanson des ingénues"
"Songs of the Runaway Bride" (Gallagher) **9**:37
"Songs of the Shade" (Senghor)
    See *Chants d'ombre*
*Songs of the Springtides* (Swinburne) **24**:322
"Songs of the Transformed" (Atwood) **8**:23,
    25-6
*Songs of Victory* (Pindar)
    See *Songs of Victory*
"Songs to Survive the Summer" (Hass) **16**:199,
    201, 210-16
"sonik prayr" (Bissett) **14**:27
"The Sonne" (Herbert) **4**:109
"Sonnet" (Bogan) **12**:98, 110
"Sonnet II" (Thomas) **2**:388
"Sonnet III" (Thomas) **2**:388
"Sonnet 7" (Milton) **19**:214, 256
"Sonnet VIII" (Thomas) **2**:388
"Sonnet X" (Thomas) **2**:388
"Sonnet XVI" (Browning) **6**:17
"Sonnet 16" (On his blindnessMilton) **19**:214
"Sonnet en -yx" (Mallarme) **4**:214-15, 218
"Sonnet Entitled How to Run the World)"
    (Cummings) **5**:106
"Sonnet for the Seventh of August" (Belloc)
    **24**:43-4
"Sonnet héroïque" (Verlaine) **2**:416
"Sonnet in Polka Dots" (Villa) **22**:351
"Sonnet in time of Revolt" (Brooke) **24**:62, 82
"Sonnet on an Alpine Night" (Parker) **28**:351
"Sonnet on Rare Animals" (Meredith) **28**:172,
    188
"Sonnet On Seeing a Piece of Our Artillery
    Brought Into Action" (Owen) **19**:336
"Sonnet Reversed" (Brooke) **24**:56, 64
"Sonnet (Suggested by some of the
    Proceedings of the Society for Physical
    ResearchBrooke) **24**:58, 73
"Sonnet: To a Child" (Owen) **19**:343
"Sonnet— to My Mother" (Poe) **1**:439, 445-46
"Sonnet V" (Wylie) **23**:304
"Sonnet with the Compliments of the Season"
    (Chesterton)
*Sonnets* (Carruth) **10**:91
*Sonnets* (Rilke) **2**:280-82
*Sonnets and Verse* (Belloc) **24**:11, 31-3, 36, 38,
    40
*Sonnets et madrigals pour astrée* (Ronsard)
    **11**:250
*Sonnets for Hélène* (Ronsard)
    See *Sonnets pour Hélène*
"Sonnets from an Ungrafted Tree" (Millay)
    **6**:224-25, 228, 230-32, 235, 239
*Sonnets from the Portuguese* (Browning) **6**:4-6,
    15-8, 22, 32, 36-9, 41-2, 46
"Sonnets of the Twelve Months" (Belloc) **24**:29
*Sonnets pour Hélène* (Ronsard) **11**:218, 220-22,
    239, 242, 250, 254, 275-76, 278, 283
"Sonnets That Please" (Stein) **18**:341
"Sono pronto ripeto, ma pronto a che?"
    (Montale) **13**:139
"sonora desert poem" (Clifton) **17**:27
"Soonest Mended" (Ashbery) **26**:125-126, 134,
    138, 141, 149
"Sorapis, 40 anni fa" (Montale) **13**:138
*Sordello* (Browning) **2**:26-30, 34, 42, 50, 65-6,
    73-6, 82, 92-6
"Sore Fit" (Bradstreet)
    See "From Another Sore Fit"
*Sorgen och stjärnan* (Ekeloef) **23**:76
"Sorrow" (Alegria) **26**:
*The Sorrow Dance* (Levertov) **11**:175-77,
    191-94
"Sorrow Home" (Walker) **20**:281-83
"Sorrowful Moonlit Night" (Hagiwara
    Sakutaro)
    See "Sorrowful Moonlit Night"
*Sortes Vergilianae* (Ashbery) **26**:149
"SOS" (Baraka) **4**:20
"Sosedka" (Lermontov) **18**:291
"Sotto la pioggia" (Montale) **13**:122

"The Soul" (Pasternak)
    See "Dusha"
"Soul, Be Calm" (Ishikawa)
    See "Tama yo shizume"
"A Soul, Geologically" (Atwood) **8**:3, 8, 19
"The Soul Has Bandaged Moments"
    (Dickinson) **1**:94
"Soul in Space" (Rilke) **2**:275
"Soul's Adventure" (Kunitz) **19**:148
"Soul's Desire" (Masters) **1**:342
"The Soul's Expression" (Browning) **6**:20, 26,
    30
"The Souls of the Slain" (Hardy) **8**:120-21
*Souls of Violet* (Jimenez)
    See *Almas de violeta*
"A Soul's Tragedy" (Browning) **2**:30, 37
"The Sound of the Trees" (Frost) **1**:197, 202
"Sound of War" (Aleixandre) **15**:4-6
"Sound Poem I" (Toomer) **7**:333
"Sound Poem II" (Toomer) **7**:333
"Sound Sleep" (Rossetti) **7**:267, 280
"Sounds" (Browning) **6**:20
"The sounds begin again" (Brutus) **24**:114, 116
"Sounds of Rain" (Heaney) **18**:260
"Sounds Out of Sorrow" (Masters) **1**:333
"Soup of the evening beautiful Soup" (Carroll)
    **18**:49
"Soupir" (Mallarme) **4**:187
*Sour Grapes* (Williams) **7**:344, 349, 367, 377,
    381, 399-400, 409-10
"The Source" (Olds) **22**:338
"La source dans les bois" (Lamartine) **16**:292
"Sources" (Levine) **22**:224
*Sources* (Rich) **5**:389-90, 397
"South" (Stryk) **27**:181, 200
"South Cottage" (Wang Wei) **18**:367
"The South Country" (Belloc) **24**:8, 10, 30
"South of My Days" (Wright) **14**:340, 349, 351,
    360, 378
"The South Wind" (Bridges) **28**:66
"Southeast Corner" (Brooks) **7**:58, 69, 80
"Souther Pacific" (Sandburg) **2**:302
"A Southern Night" (Arnold) **5**:8
"Southern Song" (Walker) **20**:272, 281-83
"The Southerner" (Shapiro) **25**:283, 296, 313
"Souvenir de Monsieur Poop" (Smith) **12**:313
"Le souvenir d'enfance; ou, La vie cachée"
    (Lamartine) **16**:276, 300, 302
"Souvent sur la montagne" (Lamartine) **16**:302
*The Sovereign Sun: Selected Poems* (Elytis)
    **21**:118-19
"Soviet Union" (Guillen)
    See "Unión Soviética"
"Sow" (Plath) **1**:388, 404
"The Sowing of Meaning" (Merton) **10**:332
"Soy como un árbol florido" (Guillen) **23**:125
"Soy Sauce" (Snyder) **21**:300
"Soy sólo una mujer" (Fuertes) **27**:7
*Space* (Aleixandre)
    See *Ambito*
*Space* (Jimenez)
    See *Espacia*
*space travl* (Bissett) **14**:34
"The Space We Live" (Levine) **22**:215
"Spaces We Leave Empty" (Song) **21**:343
*Spain* (Auden) **1**:22
*Spain* (Gautier)
    See *España*
*Spain at Heart* (Neruda)
    See *España en el corazón: himno a las
    glorias del pueblo en la guerra
    (1936-1937)*
*Spain in My Heart* (Neruda)
    See *España en el corazón: himno a las
    glorias del pueblo en la guerra
    (1936-1937)*
*Spain in the Heart* (Neruda)
    See *España en el corazón: himno a las
    glorias del pueblo en la guerra
    (1936-1937)*
*The Spanish Gypsy* (Eliot) **20**:90-100, 104-6,

111-15, 122-23, 126, 128-31, 137-39,
    141-48
"The Spanish Needle" (McKay) **2**:228
"Spanish School" (Smith) **12**:316
"Spare Us from Loveliness" (H. D.) **5**:273
"spark" (Bukowski) **18**:20
"The Spark" (Cullen) **20**:58
"A Spark in the Tinder of Knowing" (Rexroth)
    **20**:221
"A Sparkler" (Ashbery) **26**:137
"Sparrow Hills" (Pasternak) **6**:258
"Sparrow Song" (Li Po) **29**:140
"The Sparrow's Fall" (Harper) **21**:189
*The Sparrow's Fall and Other Poems* (Harper)
    **21**:187, 189
"Spasskoye" (Pasternak) **6**:252, 259
"Spätherbst in Venedig" (Rilke) **2**:267, 277,
    282, 288-90
"Speak, You Also" (Celan) **10**:99
"La Speakerine de Putney" (Smith) **12**:354
*Speaking for Scotland* (MacDiarmid) **9**:159
"Speaking of Love (of)" (Cummings) **5**:105
"speaking speaking" (Bissett) **14**:31
"Special Starlight" (Sandburg) **2**:331
"Specimen of an Induction to a Poem" (Keats)
    **1**:313
*Spectacula* (Martial)
    See *Liber Spectaculorum*
*Spectaculorum Liber* (Martial)
    See *Liber Spectaculorum*
*Spectrum* (Nishiwaki) **15**:228, 237
"Speech to the Young. Speech to the
    Progress-Toward" (Brooks) **7**:91, 94
"Speeches for Doctor Frankenstein" (Atwood)
    **8**:11
"Speech-Grille" (Celan)
    See "Sprachgitter"
*Speech-Grille, and Selected Poems* (Celan)
    See *Sprachgitter*
*The Speed of Darkness* (Rukeyser) **12**:216, 222,
    228, 230
*Speke Parott* (Skelton) **25**:329-31, 336, 341,
    348, 351-52, 360, 374, 377-78, 380-85
*Spektorsky* (Pasternak) **6**:253, 265, 283, 285
"Spel Against Demons" (Snyder) **21**:291-92,
    297
"The Spell" (Kumin) **15**:192
"Spell" (Montale)
    See "Incantesimo"
"The Spell of the Rose" (Hardy) **8**:93, 136
"Spelling" (Duncan) **2**:104
"Spelt from Sibyl's Leaves" (Hopkins) **15**:128,
    132-33, 138, 144
"A spending hand that alway poureth out"
    (Wyatt) **27**:371
"Spenser's Ireland" (Moore) **4**:258
"Sperm" (Kumin) **15**:202
"Sphere" (Ammons) **16**:31, 53
*Sphere: The Form of a Motion* (Ammons)
    **16**:23, 25, 27-30, 33, 46-7, 54, 60-1
"The Sphinx" (Emerson) **18**:71, 84, 88, 93, 102,
    110
"Le Sphinx" (Gautier) **18**:141
"The Sphinx" (Hayden) **6**:186
*Sphinx: A Poem Ascrib'd to Certain
    Anonymous Authors: By the Revd. S—t*
    (Swift)
    See "Ode to the Athenian Society"
"Le Sphynx vertébral" (Breton) **15**:51
"The Spice Tree" (Lindsay) **23**:268
"Spicewood" (Reese) **29**:330
*Spicewood* (Reese) **29**:335, 339, 347-48, 351
"Spider Blues" (Ondaatje) **28**:320, 327, 333
"Spider's Song" (Zagajewski) **27**:389
*Spielmann* (Grillparzer)
    See *Spielmann*
"Spight hathe no Powre" (Wyatt) **27**:315
"Spilt Milk" (Yeats) **20**:314
*Spin a Soft Black Song: Poems for Children*
    (Giovanni) **19**:136
"Spindrift" (Kinnell) **26**:257

Title Index

"The Spinner" (Valery)
    See "La fileuse"
"Spinning Tops" (Reese) **29**:330
"Spinster" (Plath) **1**:388
"The Spire Cranes" (Thomas) **2**:408
"Spirit" (Soto) **28**:370
"The Spirit Medium" (Yeats) **20**:314
"Spirit of History" (Milosz) **8**:204
"The Spirit of Place" (Rich) **5**:386
*The Spirit of Romance* (Pound) **4**:352
*Spirit Reach* (Baraka) **4**:19-20, 26
"Spirit's Song" (Bogan) **12**:90, 92, 100, 124
"A Spiritual" (Dunbar) **5**:123
"Spiritual" (Pasolini) **17**:253
"Spiritual Laws" (Emerson) **18**:94
*Spiritual Sonnets* (Jimenez)
    See *Sonetos espirituales*
"Spite" (Bukowski) **18**:5
"Spleen" (Baudelaire)
    See "Le spleen"
"Le spleen" (Baudelaire) **1**:55
"The Spleen" (Finch)
    See "Ode to the Spleen"
"Spleen" (Laforgue) **14**:84-5, 89
"Spleen" (Verlaine) **2**:415
*Le spleen de Paris* (Baudelaire)
    See *Petits poèmes en prose: Le spleen de Paris*
"Splitting Wood at Six Above" (Kumin) **15**:206, 219
"Spoke Joe to Jack" (Cummings) **5**:88
"Spontaneous Me" (Whitman) **3**:387
*Spoon River Anthology* (Masters) **1**:321-42, 344-49
"The Spooniad" (Masters) **1**:327
"Spor" (Lermontov) **18**:291
"Sport" (Hughes) **1**:270
"Sports Field" (Wright) **14**:362
"Sprachgitter" (Celan) **10**:112, 115, 129-30
*Sprachgitter* (Celan) **10**:95-6, 121
"A Sprig of Rosemary" (Lowell) **13**:64
"Spring" (Blake) **12**:7, 32
"The Spring" (Carew) **29**:8-9, 19
"Spring" (Dario)
    See "Primaveral"
"Spring" (Gray)
    See "Ode on Spring"
"Spring" (Hass) **16**:209
"Spring" (Hopkins) **15**:152
"Spring" (McGuckian) **27**:96
"Spring" (Millay) **6**:236
"Spring" (Pasternak) **6**:251
"Spring" (Rexroth) **20**:209
"Spring" (Sitwell) **3**:311
"Spring" (Williams) **7**:345, 399
*Spring and All* (Williams) **7**:349, 351, 353, 355, 373-78, 381-83, 387-88, 400-02, 405-06, 409-11
"Spring and Fall" (Hopkins) **15**:144
"The Spring and the Fall" (Millay) **6**:225
"Spring Comes to Murray Hill" (Nash) **21**:266
"Spring Day" (Ashbery) **26**:124
"Spring Day" (Lowell) **13**:79
"Spring Drawing" (Hass) **16**:215, 221
"Spring Drawing 2" (Hass) **16**:216
"Spring Ecstasy" (Reese) **29**:331
"Spring Flood" (Pasternak) **6**:266
"Spring goeth all in white" (Bridges) **28**:66-7
"Spring in New Hampshire" (McKay) **2**:228
*Spring in New Hampshire, and Other Poems* (McKay) **2**:213, 228
"Spring in the Garden" (Millay) **6**:215
"Spring Lake" (Masters) **1**:343
"Spring Night" (Hagiwara Sakutaro)
    See "Shun'ya"
"Spring Night in Lo-yang-Hearing a Flute" (Li Po) **29**:145
"Spring Oak" (Kinnell) **26**:237-38, 257
"Spring Ode I" (Bridges) **28**:84
"Spring Ode II" (Bridges) **28**:84
"Spring Offensive" (Owen) **19**:334, 337, 341-42, 344, 347, 353-55

"Spring Pastoral" (Wylie) **23**:321-22
"Spring Poem" (Atwood) **8**:24
"Spring Pools" (Frost) **1**:206
"Spring Prospect" (Tu Fu) **9**:322
"Spring Rain" (Hass) **16**:221-22
"Spring Rain" (Pasternak) **6**:251
"Spring Season of Muddy Roads" (Brodsky) **9**:2
"Spring Song" (Baraka) **4**:39
"Spring Song" (Clifton) **17**:16
*Spring Thaw* (Yosano Akiko)
    See *Shundeishū*
"Spring Thunder" (Rich) **5**:383
"Spring Uncovered" (Swenson) **14**:247, 250, 268
"Spring Warning" (Larkin) **21**:259
"A Spring Wooing" (Dunbar) **5**:145
"Springfield Magical" (Lindsay) **23**:284
"Spruce Woods" (Ammons) **16**:45
"Sprüche" (Goethe) **5**:248
"The Spur of Love" (MacDiarmid) **9**:189-90
"Squarings" (Heaney) **18**:254, 257-58
"Le squelette laboureur" (Baudelaire) **1**:45
"Squieres Tale" (Chaucer)
    See "Squire's Tale"
"Squire's Tale" (Chaucer) **19**:13
"The Squirrel" (Stryk) **27**:189, 203
"Srishti-sthiti-pralaya" (Tagore) **8**:406
"Śroczość" (Milosz) **8**:187
"St. Brandan" (Arnold) **5**:12
"St. Launce's Revisited" (Hardy) **8**:136
"St. Lucies Day" (Donne)
    See "A Nocturnal upon S. Lucies day, Being the shortest day"
*St. Patrick's Purgatory* (Marie de France)
    See *L'Espurgatoire Saint Patrice*
"St. Peter Relates an Incident of the Resurrection Day" (Johnson) **24**:133, 141, 144, 153, 161, 170
*St. Peter Relates an Incident: Selected Poems* (Johnson) **24**:130, 159, 162
"St. Praxed's Church" (Browning) **2**:30
"St. Simeon Stylites" (Tennyson) **6**:411
"Stages" (Meredith) **28**:180
"Stagirius" (Arnold) **5**:38
"Staircase" (Tsvetaeva)
    See "Poèma lestnitsy"
"Stalin" (Lowell) **3**:223
"Stalin Epigram" (Mandelstam) **14**:149, 153
"The Stalker" (Momaday)
"Stan" (Tagore) **8**:407
"Stances" (Gautier) **18**:163
"Stances de la fontaine de'Helene" (Ronsard) **11**:241
"La Standard Oil Co." (Neruda) **4**:296
"The Standard Oil Co." (Neruda)
    See "La Standard Oil Co."
"Standards and Paradise of the Blacks" (Garcia Lorca)
    See "Norma y paraíso de los negros"
"A Standing Ground" (Berry) **28**:43
"Standomi un giorno solo a la fenestra" (Petrarch) **8**:253-57
"The standstillness of unthought" (Villa) **22**:354
"The Stand-To" (Day Lewis) **11**:146
"Stand-to: Good Friday Morning" (Sassoon) **12**:241, 251, 262, 280
"Stanza" (Bogan) **12**:103
"Stanzas" (Brodsky) **9**:4
"Stanzas" (Mandelstam) **14**:151
"Stanzas from the Grande Chartreuse" (Arnold) **5**:18, 24, 33, 35, 52-3, 58
*Stanzas in Love with Life and August Again Again* (Viereck) **27**:265
"Stanzas in Meditation" (Stein) **18**:309-316, 335-37, 339-41, 343, 345-48
*Stanzas in Meditation* (Stein) **18**:309-316, 335-37, 339-41, 343, 345-48
"Stanzas in Memory of Edward Quillinan" (Arnold) **5**:52
"Stanzas in Memory of the Author of 'Obermann'" (Arnold) **5**:42, 50, 52

"Stanzas on Peele Castle" (Wordsworth) **4**:394, 410-11
"Stanzas to Bettine" (Browning) **6**:15
"Stanzas to Tolstoi" (Pushkin) **10**:409
"Stanzas Written at Night in Radio City" (Ginsberg) **4**:55
"Stanzas Written on Battersea Bridge during a South-Westerly Gale" (Belloc) **24**:30-1, 36
"The Star" (Masters) **1**:326, 333, 337, 342
*The Star* (Bely)
    See *Zvezda*
"A Star in a Stone-Boat" (Frost) **1**:194, 221
*stardust* (Bissett) **14**:30
"The Stare of the Man from the Provinces" (Nemerov) **24**:268
"Staring at the Sea on the Day of the Death of Another" (Swenson) **14**:288
"Starlight" (Meredith) **28**:171
"Starlight like Intuition Pierced the Twelve" (Schwartz) **8**:290-91
"The Starlight Night" (Hopkins) **15**:144, 152, 160, 162
"The Starling" (Lowell) **13**:61
"The Starling" (Smith) **12**:326
"The Starling" (Soto) **28**:375
"The Starred Coverlet" (Graves) **6**:156
"The Starry Night" (Sexton) **2**:350, 371-72
"Starry Night" (Sexton) **2**:350, 371-72
"Stars" (Hayden) **6**:184-85, 190, 194, 196
"The Star-Song: A Carroll to the King; Sung at White Hall" (Herrick) **9**:118, 119
"The Star-Splitter" (Frost) **1**:194
"Start Again Somewhere" (Gallagher) **9**:58
"Star-Talk" (Graves) **6**:166
"Starting from San Francisco" (Ferlinghetti) **1**:187
*Starting from San Francisco* (Ferlinghetti) **1**:166, 172-76, 187
*Starting Point* (Day Lewis) **11**:129
*Starved Rock* (Masters) **1**:332, 335, 338, 342-44
"The State of World Affairs from a Third Floor Window" (Bukowski) **18**:3
"Statement on Poetics" (Hayden) **6**:198
*Statements After an Arrest Under the Immorality Act* (Brutus) **24**:119
"The Staten Island Ferry" (Clampitt) **19**:100
"The State's Claim" (Ortiz) **17**:233
"Station" (Olds) **22**:307, 328
"Station Island" (Heaney) **18**:220, 240
*Station Island* (Heaney) **18**:211-12, 214-16, 218, 226, 228, 232, 237
"Stations" (Hughes) **7**:137
"Stations" (Lorde) **12**:140
"The Statue" (Belloc) **24**:9
"La Statue" (Hugo) **17**:64
"Statue and Birds" (Bogan) **12**:94, 101, 127
"The Statue at the World's End" (Stevens)
    See "Mr. Burnshaw and the Statue"
"Statue at Tsarskoye Selo" (Akhmatova) **2**:12
*The Statue Guest* (Pushkin)
    See *Kamennyi gost'*
"The Statue in Stocks-Market" (Marvell) **10**:276
"The Statue in the Garden" (Lowell) **13**:61
"A Statue in the Silence" (Neruda)
    See "Una estatua en el silencio"
"The Statue of Liberty" (Hardy) **8**:99
"The Statues" (Yeats) **20**:324, 334
"A Statute of Wine" (Neruda)
    See "Estatura del vino"
"Stay With Me" (Hongo) **23**:203
"Staying Alive" (Levertov) **11**:178-79, 195-96
"Steak" (Snyder) **21**:292-93
"Steal Away to Jesus" (Johnson) **24**:170
"Stealing Trout on a May Morning" (Hughes) **7**:120, 170
"Steam Shovel Cut" (Masters) **1**:343
"Lo steddazzu" (Pavese) **13**:229
"Steelhead" (Jeffers) **17**:141
"Steely Silence" (Wakoski) **15**:332
*Steeple Bush* (Frost) **1**:200, 205-06, 217
"The Steeple-Jack" (Moore) **4**:256

"Stella's Birthday, March 13, 1718-19" (Swift) **9**:255, 297
"Stellenbosch" (Kipling) **3**:176
"The Stenographers" (Page) **12**:163, 173
"Stepchild" (Hongo) **23**:197
"Stephen A. Douglas" (Masters) **1**:334
"Stepping Backward" (Rich) **5**:352
"Stepping Outside" (Gallagher) **9**:35
*Stepping Outside* (Gallagher) **9**:35
"Stepping Westward" (Wordsworth) **4**:395
"The Steps of the Commander" (Blok) **21**:6
*Stevie Smith: A Selection* (Smith) **12**:331, 348
*Stikhi K Akhmatovoi* (Tsvetaeva) **14**:321
*Stikhi K Blok* (Tsvetaeva) **14**:299, 311-12
*Stikhi k Chekhii* (Tsvetaeva) **14**:325, 327
*Stikhi k Pushkinu* (Tsvetaeva) **14**:324-25
*Stikhi k synu* (Tsvetaeva) **14**:328
"Stikhi o neizvestnom soldate" (Mandelstam) **14**:145, 148-49, 152, 155
*Stikhi o prekrasnoi dame* (Blok) **21**:13, 18, 24, 30
*Stikhotvoreniya* (Bely) **11**:29
"Still at Annecy" (Montale)
  See "Ancora ad Annecy"
"Still Do I Keep My Look, My Identity" (Brooks) **7**:71
"Still Falls the Rain" (Sitwell) **3**:310, 323, 326
"Still Life" (Gluck) **16**:128, 136, 139, 142
"Still Life" (Hughes) **7**:121, 137
"Still Night" (Smith) **12**:317
"Still Night Thoughts" (Li Po) **29**:145
"Still on Water" (Rexroth) **20**:206, 216
"The Still Time" (Kinnell) **26**:260, 281
"Stillborn" (Plath) **1**:391, 405
"Stillness" (Pasternak)
  See "Tishina"
"Stimme des Volks" (Holderlin) **4**:166
"Stinging" (Cummings)
  See "Sunset"
"Stings" (Plath) **1**:394, 410, 412-14
"Stixi na smert T. S. Èliota" (Brodsky) **9**:2, 4
"Stol" (Tsvetaeva) **14**:318
"The Stolen Child" (Yeats) **20**:337, 346
"Stond who so list" (Wyatt) **27**:331, 362, 367
"The Stone" (Carruth) **10**:71
"The Stone" (Soto)
  See "Piedra"
*Stone* (Mandelstam)
  See *Kamen'*
"A Stone Church Damaged by a Bomb" (Larkin) **21**:259
"The Stone from the Sea" (Celan) **10**:112
*The Stone Guest* (Pushkin)
  See *Kamennyi gost'*
"Stone, paper, knife" (Piercy) **29**:315-16, 318-19, 321-22
*Stone, Paper, Knife* (Piercy) **29**:312-13, 316-17, 321
"The Stone Verdict" (Heaney) **18**:229, 233
"The Stonecarver's Poem" (Levertov) **11**:169
"The Stones" (Plath) **1**:389-90
"Stones" (Zagajewski) **27**:389
"Stony Limits" (MacDiarmid) **9**:156, 176
*Stony Limits* (MacDiarmid) **9**:156, 158, 172-73, 175-76, 179-80, 182-84, 196, 200
"Stopping by Woods on a Snowy Evening" (Frost) **1**:194, 197, 208, 213-14, 221, 225
"Stop-Short" (Belloc) **24**:39
"La storia" (Montale) **13**:134
"Stories of Snow" (Page) **12**:164, 167-69, 172, 190, 197
*Stories of the Sioux* (Chief Standing Bear) **10**:333, 341-42
"The Storm" (Montale)
  See "La bufera"
"Storm" (Owen) **19**:353-54
"Storm" (Stryk) **27**:195, 212
"Storm" (Wright) **14**:342
*The Storm and Other Things* (Montale)
  See *La bufera e altro*
*The Storm and Other Things* (Montale)
  See *La bufera e altro*

"The Storm Came" (Kipling) **3**:171, 183
"Storm Ending" (Toomer) **7**:317, 330-32
"The storm is over" (Bridges) **28**:83
"Storm of Love" (Aleixandre) **15**:19
"Storm Warnings" (Rich) **5**:392, 396
"Storm Windows" (Nemerov) **24**:264-67, 270-71
"Story" (Wakoski) **15**:365
"Story Between Two Notes" (McGuckian) **27**:91
"The Story of a Citizen" (Gallagher) **9**:60, 62
"A Story of a Cock and a Bull" (Smart) **13**:348
"The Story of a Well-Made Shield" (Momaday) **25**:189, 213
"A Story of Courage" (Ortiz) **17**:246
"A Story of How a Wall Stands" (Ortiz) **17**:225
"The Story of Richard Maxfield" (Wakoski) **15**:346, 355, 361
*The Story of the Heart* (Aleixandre)
  See *Historia del corazón*
"The Story of Tommy" (Kipling) **3**:194
"Story of Two Gardens" (Paz)
  See "Cuento de dos jardines"
"La strada" (Pasolini) **17**:253
"Stradivarius" (Eliot) **20**:123, 125
"Straight Talk" (Giovanni) **19**:112
"Straight-Creek—Great Burn" (Snyder) **21**:297
*The Straightening* (Celan)
  See *Sprachgitter*
*Strains* (Brutus) **24**:121-22, 124
"The Strait" (Ammons) **16**:4
"The Straitening" (Celan)
  See "Engführung"
"The Strange and True Story of My Life with Billy the Kid" (Momaday) **25**:221
"The Strange Case" (Ondaatje) **28**:329
"Strange Fits of Passion" (Wordsworth) **4**:420
"Strange Fruit" (Harjo) **27**:71
"Strange Fruit" (Heaney) **18**:196
*The Strange Islands* (Merton) **10**:331, 342, 347, 349, 351
"Strange Meeting" (Owen) **19**:325-27, 329, 332, 335-37, 341-45, 347, 353, 355, 359, 370-71
"A Strange Song" (Wylie) **23**:324
"A Strange Story" (Wylie) **23**:307, 310
"Strangeness of Heart" (Sassoon) **12**:254
"The Stranger" (Blok) **21**:4, 24
"Stranger" (Merton) **10**:349
"The Stranger" (Rich) **5**:384
"The Strangers" (Berry) **28**:7
"Strategy" (Gallagher) **9**:59
"Stratford on Avon" (Davie) **29**:102
"Strato in Plaster" (Merrill) **28**:258
"Straw Hat" (Dove) **6**:110, 114
"Strawberry Hill" (Hughes) **7**:119, 148
"Strawberrying" (Swenson) **14**:273
"Stray Animals" (Song) **21**:332
"The Strayed Reveller" (Arnold) **5**:5, 12, 39, 50
*The Strayed Reveller, and Other Poems* (Arnold) **5**:8, 31, 38-9, 42, 48
"Stream and Sun at Glendalough" (Yeats) **20**:328
"The Stream of the Golden Honey was Pouring So Slow . . ." (Mandelstam) **14**:141
"The Street" (Soto) **28**:378, 383, 386
*A Street in Bronzeville* (Brooks) **7**:52-4, 56-8, 60-1, 67, 70, 75, 79-80, 85-7, 95, 102, 105
"Street Song" (Gunn) **26**:
"Street Song" (Sitwell) **3**:311
*Street Songs* (Sitwell) **3**:308, 320
"Street Window" (Sandburg) **2**:309
"Streets" (Verlaine) **2**:415
"Strephon and Chloe" (Swift) **9**:257-58, 262, 270, 274, 286, 288, 294, 298, 301
"Strephon's Song" (Belloc) **24**:6
"Stretcher Case" (Sassoon) **12**:242, 262
*Strike* (Viereck) **27**:280-82, 284
*Strike Through the Mask!* (Viereck) **27**:262-63, 278

"Stripping the vista to its depth" (Tomlinson) **17**:342
"Striptease-Tänzerinnen" (Enzensberger) **28**:165
"The Stroke" (Dove) **6**:111
"The Stroke" (Smith) **12**:314
"Strong Men, Riding Horses" (Brooks) **7**:106
"A Strong New Voice Pointing the Way" (Madhubuti) **5**:346
*Strountes* (Ekeloef) **23**:59-61, 63, 76-8
"The Structure of Rime" (Duncan) **2**:126
*The Structure of Rime* (Duncan) **2**:126
"The Structure of Rime II" (Duncan) **2**:125
"The Structure of Rime XXVIII" (Duncan) **2**:114
"The Structure of the Plane" (Rukeyser) **12**:202
"Struggle" (Hughes) **7**:165-66
"The Struggle Staggers Us" (Walker) **20**:289, 294
"Strumpet Song" (Plath) **1**:388
"Stubborn Hope" (Brutus) **24**:112
*Stubborn Hope: New Poems and Selections from "China Poems" and "Strains"* (Brutus) **24**:112, 116, 118, 122
"The Student" (Moore) **4**:260
*Studies in Song* (Swinburne) **24**:322
"The Studies of Narcissus" (Schwartz) **8**:311
"A Study" (Masters) **1**:342
"The Study of History" (Rich) **5**:365
"Study to Deserve Death" (Smith) **12**:318
"Stumbling" (Montale)
  See "Incespicare"
"Stump" (Heaney) **18**:202
*Stunden-Buch* (Rilke) **2**:277, 282, 288-90
*Stundenbuch/Das Stundenbuch/A Book for the Hours of Prayer* (Rilke)
  See *Stunden-Buch*
"Stupid Piety" (Goethe) **5**:229
"Stutgard" (Holderlin) **4**:147
"Style" (Baraka) **4**:9
"Style" (Moore) **4**:259
"Styx" (Duncan) **2**:119
"La suave agonie" (Valery) **9**:391-92
"Sub Contra" (Bogan) **12**:120
*Sub Specie Aeternitatis* (Hayden) **6**:194
"Sub Terra" (Williams) **7**:377
"A Subaltern" (Sassoon) **12**:242
"The Subalterns" (Hardy) **8**:111, 119
"A Substance In A Cushion" (Stein) **18**:321, 328, 349
"Suburb" (Smith) **12**:317
"The Subverted Flower" (Frost) **1**:198
"Success" (Brooke) **24**:56-7
"Succory" (Reese) **29**:336
"The Succubus" (Graves) **6**:163
*Such Counsels You Gave to Me and Other Poems* (Jeffers) **17**:135
"Suche Happe as I ame Happed in" (Wyatt) **27**:317, 352
"Sudden Journey" (Gallagher) **9**:50
"The Sudder Bazaar" (Kipling) **3**:190, 194
*El Sueño* (Juana Ines de la Cruz) **24**:212-15, 224-27, 235
"Suffer the Children" (Lorde) **12**:157
"Suffering" (Page) **12**:190
*Suffised not, Madam* (Wyatt) **27**:317
"Suffryng in sorow in hope to attayn" (Wyatt) **27**:310
"Sugar" (Stein) **18**:320, 322-23, 328, 334
"Sugar Loaf" (Hughes) **7**:121
"Suicide" (Bukowski) **18**:5
"Suicide" (Hughes) **1**:255
"The Suicide" (Millay) **6**:206
"Suicide Blues" (Rukeyser) **12**:228
"The Suicide in the Copse" (Graves) **6**:142, 144
"Suicide in the Trenches" (Sassoon) **12**:267, 285
"Suicide off Egg Rock" (Plath) **1**:389
"Suicide's Note" (Hughes) **1**:236
"Suis-je" (Laforgue) **14**:85
"The Suit" (Levine) **22**:225

"A Suite for Augustus" (Dove) **6**:106
"Suite furlana" (Pasolini) **17**:281-82
*Suite furlana* (Pasolini) **17**:252, 256, 279, 281
"Sukher vilap" (Tagore) **8**:405
"Sulla colonna più alta" (Montale) **13**:109, 111
"Sulla Greve" (Montale) **13**:152
"Sultry" (Lowell) **13**:95-6
"Sultry Rain" (Pasternak) **6**:257
*Summa poética 1929-1946* (Guillen) **23**:104
"Summary" (Sanchez) **9**:224, 232
"Summer" (Ashbery) **26**:124-125
"Summer" (Bryant) **20**:12
"Summer" (Dario)
    See "Estival"
"Summer" (Gluck) **16**:156, 166
"Summer" (Rossetti) **7**:280
"Summer" (Stryk) **27**:196, 208
"The Summer" (Trakl) **20**:226
"Summer" (Wright) **14**:377, 379
"Summer 1961" (Levertov) **11**:165
"Summer 1969" (Heaney) **18**:205
"Summer between Terms I" (Lowell) **3**:241
"Summer Day in the Mountains" (Li Po) **29**:145
"Summer Holiday" (Jeffers) **17**:132
"Summer Home" (Heaney) **18**:203
"'Summer Is Over" (Cummings) **5**:108-09
"Summer Knowledge" (Schwartz) **8**:297-98, 312-19
*Summer Knowledge: New and Selected Poems, 1938-1958* (Schwartz) **8**:289-91, 296, 301-02, 305, 309, 311
"A Summer Night" (Arnold) **5**:36, 42, 49, 50
"Summer Night Piece" (Lowell) **13**:64, 67
"The Summer People" (Merrill) **28**:224-25, 230-31, 235
"Summer Place" (Ammons) **16**:23, 47
"Summer Poem" (Enzensberger) **28**:141, 147-48
"A Summer Ramble" (Bryant) **20**:37, 39
"Summer Resort" (Page) **12**:173
"Summer Session" (Ammons) **16**:50
"Summer time T. V." (is witer than everSanchez) **9**:210-11, 213, 225
"The Summer We Almost Split" (Piercy) **29**:311
"Summer Wind" (Bryant) **20**:40
"Summer Wish" (Bogan) **12**:94-5, 98, 100, 106, 121-22
"Summer Words of a Sistuh Addict" (Sanchez) **9**:225
"A Summer's Dream" (Bishop) **3**:47
"Summer's Elegy" (Nemerov) **24**:291
"Summertime and the Living..." (Hayden) **6**:194, 196
"Summit Beach, 1921" (Dove) **6**:121
"Summoner's Tale" (Chaucer) **19**:13
"The Summons" (Auden) **1**:38
*Summonses of the Times* (Bely)
    See *Zovy vremen*
"The Sun" (Milosz) **8**:192, 207
"Sun" (Moore) **4**:243
"The Sun" (Nishiwaki)
    See "Taiyo"
"The Sun" (Noyes) **27**:129
"The Sun" (Piercy) **29**:305
"The Sun" (Sexton) **2**:351, 372
"The Sun" (Trakl) **20**:226
"The Sun Does Not Move" (Bissett) **14**:5
"The Sun Is near Meridan Height" (Bronte) **8**:73
"The Sun on the Letter" (Hardy) **8**:97
"The Sun Rising" (Donne)
    See "The Sunne Rising"
"The Sun Says His Prayers" (Lindsay) **23**:281
"Sun Stone" (Paz)
    See "Piedra de sol"
*Sun Stone* (Paz)
    See *Piedra de sol*
"Sun the First" (Elytis) **21**:131
*Sun the First* (Elytis)
    See *Ílios o prótos*
"Sunbathing on a Rooftop in Berkeley" (Kumin) **15**:203
"Sunday" (Herbert) **4**:100

"Sunday" (Hughes) **1**:255
"Sunday" (Nemerov) **24**:277
"A Sunday" (Soto) **28**:397-98, 400
"Sunday" (Williams) **7**:351
"Sunday in the Country" (Swenson) **14**:247, 250, 264
"Sunday Morning" (Stevens) **6**:292, 301, 304, 306, 327, 336
"Sunday Morning" (Whitman) **3**:391
"Sunday Morning Apples" (Crane) **3**:83, 90, 100
"A Sunday Morning Tragedy" (Hardy) **8**:99
"Sunday New Guinea" (Shapiro) **25**:269, 286, 295
"A Sunday with Shepherds and Herdboys" (Clare) **23**:13
*sunday work* (?Bissett) **14**:5, 16
"Sundays before noon" (Bukowski) **18**:23
"Sundays Kill More Men than Bombs" (Bukowski) **18**:4
"The Sundays of Satin-Legs Smith" (Brooks) **7**:69, 79-80, 85
"Sunderland" (Nemerov) **24**:295
"Sunderland" (Nemiroff) **24**:
"Sundew" (Atwood) **8**:13
*Sundry Phansies* (Kipling) **3**:193
"Sunflower" (Breton)
    See "Tournesol"
"The Sunflower" (Montale) **13**:138, 141, 149
"Sunflower Sutra" (Ginsberg) **4**:48, 50, 92
"Sung beneath the Alps" (Holderlin) **4**:142
"The Sunken Bell" (Ishikawa)
    See "Shizumeru kane"
"Sunlight" (Gunn) **26**:204, 214, 219
"Sunlight" (Heaney) **18**:203
"Sunlight and Flesh" (Rimbaud)
    See "Soleil et chair"
"The Sunne Rising" (Donne) **1**:125, 134, 145, 147, 152, 154
"Sunny Prestatyn" (Larkin) **21**:229
"Sunrise" (Reese) **29**:330
"Sunset" (Cummings) **5**:70, 94
"Sunset" (Dunbar) **5**:138-39
"Sunset" (Gluck) **16**:170
*Sunset Gun* (Parker) **28**:347-48, 351, 353, 362-63
"Sunset of the Century" (Tagore)
    See "Shatabdir surya"
"A Sunset of the City" (Brooks) **7**:68-9, 96
"Sunset on the Spire" (Wylie) **23**:324, 328
"Sunset Piece: After Reaching Rémy De Gourmont" (Cummings) **5**:71
*Sunstone* (Paz)
    See *Piedra de sol*
"Superfluous Advice" (Parker) **28**:362
"The Supper after the Last" (Kinnell) **26**:238, 257, 279
"Supper Time" (Hughes) **1**:255
"A Supplication for Love" (Browning) **6**:31
"Supposed Confessions of a Second-Rate Sensitive Mind" (Tennyson) **6**:406, 409
"Supreme Fiction" (Ammons) **16**:23
"Supuesto, discurso mío" (Juana Ines de la Cruz) **24**:180, 184
"Sur l'eau" (Valery) **9**:391-92
"Sur les lagunes" (Gautier) **18**:125
"Sur l'herbe" (Verlaine) **2**:430
"The Surface" (Swenson) **14**:261, 282
"The Surfer" (Wright) **14**:345
"The Surgeons" (Kunitz) **19**:151
"Surprise" (Parker) **28**:362
"Surprises" (Kumin) **15**:210, 223
*Surrealist Poetry* (Aleixandre)
    See *Poesía superrealista*
"Surrounded by Wild Turkeys" (Snyder) **21**:326
"Survival as Tao, Beginning at 5:00 a.m." (Carruth) **10**:88
"Survival of the Fittest" (Gozzano) **10**:183
"The Survivor" (Graves) **6**:137, 142, 144
"Survivors" (Sassoon) **12**:267-68, 285
"Suspension" (Lorde) **12**:158
"Sussex" (Kipling) **3**:167, 192

"Svapna" (Tagore) **8**:410-11
"Svarga" (Tagore) **8**:414
"Svarga ha'ite biday" (Tagore) **8**:409
"Swamp Plant" (Wright) **14**:374
"The Swan" (Baudelaire)
    See "Le cygne"
"The Swan" (Roethke) **15**:275, 288
"The Swans" (Dario)
    See "Los cisnes"
"The Swans" (Lowell) **13**:86
*The Swans' Encampment* (Tsvetaeva)
    See *Lebediny stan*
"The Swarm" (Plath) **1**:410, 412
"Swaziland" (Giovanni) **19**:141
"Sweeney among the Nightingales" (Eliot) **5**:184
*Sweeney Astray* (Heaney) **18**:215-18, 235
"Sweeney Redivivus" (Heaney) **18**:215, 228, 233
"The Sweeper of Ways" (Nemerov) **24**:282
"Sweet Afton" (Burns) **6**:77
"Sweet Boy, Give me Yr Ass" (Ginsberg) **4**:90
"A Sweet Flying Dream" (Ferlinghetti) **1**:183, 188
"Sweet Hopes" (Pushkin)
    See "Nadezhdoi Sladostnoi"
"Sweet like a Crow" (Ondaatje) **28**:338
"Sweet Mary Dove" (Clare) **23**:25
"Sweet Michel" (Browning) **2**:30
"The Sweet o' the Year" (Noyes) **27**:114
"The Sweet Primroses" (Hardy) **8**:130
"Sweet Susan" (Clare) **23**:25
"Sweet Things" (Gunn) **26**:209, 211
"Sweet Violets" (Parker) **28**:351
*Sweet Will* (Levine) **22**:221, 224, 226
"Sweetened Change" (Ammons) **16**:63
"Sweetest love, I do not goe" (Donne)
    See "Song. 'Sweetest love, I do not goe'"
*Swellfoot the Tyrant* (Shelley) **14**:175, 202
"Swells" (Ammons) **16**:32, 63
"Świadomość" (Milosz) **8**:209
"Swiftly walk over the western wave" (Shelley) **14**:177
"The Swimmer" (Olds) **22**:323, 325
"Swimmers" (Swenson) **14**:265, 276, 287
"A Swimmer's Dream" (Swinburne) **24**:313, 325
"Swimming Chenango Lake" (Tomlinson) **17**:316, 319, 321, 328
"The Swimming Race" (Noyes) **27**:116
"Switzerland" (Arnold) **5**:12-13
*Sword Blades and Poppy Seed* (Lowell) **13**:69-70, 76, 93
"A Sword in a Cloud of Light" (Rexroth) **20**:190
*Swords Like Lips* (Aleixandre)
    See *Espadas como labios*
"The Sycamore" (Berry) **28**:25
"Sydney Bridge" (Shapiro) **25**:269
"Sygil" (H. D.) **5**:306
"The Syllable Pain" (Celan) **10**:102
"Le sylphe" (Valery) **9**:387, 391, 393
*Sylvae* (Dryden) **25**:80
"Sylvia's Death" (Sexton) **2**:364, 370
"Symbolism in Painting" (Yeats) **20**:299
*The Symbolism of Poetry* (Yeats) **20**:336
"Symmetrical Companion" (Swenson) **14**:274, 284
"Sympathetic Portrait of a Child" (Williams) **7**:349
"Sympathy" (Dunbar) **5**:134
"Symphonie en blanc majeur" (Gautier) **18**:124-27, 129-30
"Symptoms of Love" (Graves) **6**:155
"The Synagogue" (Shapiro) **25**:263, 269, 283, 296, 299-300
"Syrinx" (Merrill) **28**:223, 256
"The Syrophenician Woman" (Harper) **21**:208, 215-16
"The System" (Ashbery) **26**:108, 130
"The Szechwan Road" (Li Po) **29**:140
*Szomoru beres* (Illyes) **16**:238, 247
*T. V. Baby Poems* (Ginsberg) **4**:47

*Ta eleýa tis Oxópetras* (Elytis) **21**:134-35
"Ta Lettre sur le Drap" (Senghor) **25**:233-34, 249
"Tabacaria" (Pessoa) **20**:166, 169
"Tabibito" (Nishiwaki) **15**:229
*Tabibito Kaerazu* (Nishiwaki) **15**:229-36
"A Table" (Stein) **18**:320-22, 324, 328, 330, 350
"Table I" (Milosz) **8**:210
"Table II" (Milosz) **8**:210
"Tableau" (Cullen) **20**:64
"Tag och skriv" (Ekeloef) **23**:51, 76, 78
"Tagore's Last Poems" (Tagore)
See "Śesh lekhā"
"Tahirassawichi en Washington" (Cardenal) **22**:131
"Tahirassawichi in Washington"
See "Tahirassawichi en Washington"
"Taiyo" (Nishiwaki) **15**:240-41
"Take" (Hagiwara Sakutaro) **18**:179
"Take a whole holiday in honour of this" (Day Lewis) **11**:130
"Take from My Palms" (Mandelstam) **14**:117
"Take heed of loving mee" (Donne)
See "The Prohibition"
"Take Wine" (Li Po) **29**:161
"Taken Aback" (McKay) **2**:221
"Taking" (Ondaatje) **28**:327, 332
"Taking In Wash" (Dove) **6**:111
"Taking Off My Clothes" (Forche) **10**:133, 135
"Taking the Lambs to Market" (Kumin) **15**:216
"Taking the Vows" (Alegria) **26**:
"Talbot Road" (Gunn) **26**:220, 229
"A Tale" (Bogan) **12**:85, 111, 127
"A Tale" (Coleridge) **11**:101
"A Tale" (Finch) **21**:166
*The Tale of Balen* (Swinburne) **24**:348, 350-54, 357
"The Tale of Custard the Dragon" (Nash) **21**:265
"Tale of Melibee" (Chaucer) **19**:26, 33, 47
"A Tale of Starvation" (Lowell) **13**:60, 84
*The Tale of Sunlight* (Soto) **28**:371, 384, 386
"The Tale of the Dead Princess and the Seven Heroes" (Pushkin)
See "Skazka o Mertvoy Tsarevne"
"The Tale of the Female Vagrant" (Wordsworth) **4**:373, 419
"The Tale of the Fisherman and the Fish" (Pushkin)
See "Skazka o Rybake i Rybke"
*The Tale of the Golden Cockerel* (Pushkin)
See "Skazka o Zolotom Petushke"
"The Tale of the Parson and His Man Balda" (Pushkin)
See "Skazka o Pope i o Rabotnike Yego Balde"
"A Tale of the Thirteenth Floor" (Nash) **21**:270-71
"The Tale of the Tsar Sultan" (Pushkin)
See "Skazka o Tsare Sultane"
"A Tale of Two Gardens" (Paz)
See "Cuento de dos jardines"
*Tales* (Chaucer)
See *Canterbury Tales*
"Tales of a Wayside Inn" (Noyes) **27**:129
*Tales of Canterbury* (Chaucer)
See *Canterbury Tales*
*Tales of the Mermaid Tavern* (Noyes) **27**:123-24, 126, 129, 134, 137
*Talifer* (Robinson) **1**:475, 477, 479, 483
"A Talisman" (Moore) **4**:232
"A Talk with Friedrich Nietzsche" (Zagajewski) **27**:389, 392
"Talking Back" (to W. H. AudenMeredith) **28**:216
"Talking in the Woods with Karl Amorelli" (Knight) **14**:43
"Talking Late with the Governor about the Budget" (Snyder) **21**:300, 326
"Talking Oak" (Tennyson) **6**:356
"Tam Glen" (Burns) **6**:59

"Tam o' Shanter" (Burns) **6**:55-8, 73-4, 76, 78, 81, 89, 96
"Tama yo shizume" (Ishikawa) **10**:213
"Tamar" (Jeffers) **17**:106-07, 111, 116, 130-32, 135, 138, 141, 146
*Tamar and Other Poems* (Jeffers) **17**:122, 124, 128, 135, 138, 146
"Tamara" (Lermontov) **18**:291-92, 298
"Tamarlane" (Poe) **1**:428, 436-38, 442, 444-45, 448
*Tamarlane, and Other Poems, By a Bostonian* (Poe) **1**:428, 432, 437, 449
*The Tambov Treasurer's Wife* (Lermontov) **18**:278, 282
"Tamer and Hawk" (Gunn) **26**:200, 221
"Tanghi-Garu Pass" (Paz) **1**:361
"Tangible Disaster" (Cesaire) **25**:18
"Tango" (Gluck) **16**:151, 154
"Tankas" (Borges) **22**:78
"Tanto e Amara" (Olson) **19**:320
"Tanu" (Tagore) **8**:407
"Die Tänzerin" (D.H.Sachs) **18**:162
"Tape for the Turn of the Year" (Ammons) **16**:31
*Tape for the Turn of the Year* (Ammons) **16**:3-4, 6, 21-4, 28, 35, 42-3, 47-50, 59-61, 64-5
"Tapestry" (Ashbery) **26**:
"The Tapestry" (Bridges) **28**:79
"Tapestry" (Cassian) **17**:5
*The Tapestry* (Bridges) **28**:76, 80-1
"Taproot" (Forche) **10**:142
*Taproot* (Stryk) **27**:191, 197-98, 215, 218
"Tarakar atmahatya" (Tagore) **8**:405
"Tarantella" (Belloc) **24**:7, 22, 31
*Target Study* (Baraka) **4**:38
"Tarkington Thou Should'st Be Living in This Hour" (Nash) **21**:273
"th tarot match covr uv th lovrs" (Bissett) **14**:33
"Tarrant Moss" (Kipling) **3**:183
"Tartuffe's Punishment" (Rimbaud)
See "Le châtiment de Tartuff"
"A Task" (Milosz) **8**:206
*The Tasking* (Sassoon) **12**:271
"Tatinir katha" (Tagore) **8**:406
"The Tattooed Man" (Hayden) **6**:195
"Tavern" (Millay) **6**:205
"The Taxi" (Lowell) **13**:93
"Taylor Street" (Gunn) **26**:213, 231
"T-Bar" (Page) **12**:177, 183, 188
"TCB" (Sanchez) **9**:225
"Tea at the Palaz of Hoon" (Stevens) **6**:304
"Teacher" (Walker) **20**:273, 286
"Teaching a Dumb Calf" (Hughes) **7**:166
"The Teamster" (Pavese) **13**:218
"Teamsters Union" (Shapiro) **25**:316
"The Tear" (Pushkin) **10**:407
*A Tear and a Smile* (Gibran)
See *Dam 'ah wabitisāmah*
"A Tear for Cressid" (Wylie) **23**:314
"Tear Gas" (Rich) **5**:393, 396
"Tears" (Reese) **29**:330, 332-33, 335, 346-47, 352-53
"Tears" (Sitwell) **3**:326
"Tears" (Whitman) **3**:379
"Tears and Laughter" (Gibran)
See *Dam 'ah wabitisāmah*
"Tears of an Excavator" (Pasolini) **17**:258, 289
*The Tears of the Blind Lions* (Merton) **10**:339
"Teasing the Nuns" (Shapiro) **25**:286, 300
"Teatro Bambino" (Lowell) **13**:94
"The Technique of Perfection" (Graves) **6**:128
"Teddungal" (Senghor) **25**:255
"Teddy Bears" (Swenson) **14**:273
"Tehran 3 May 68" (Brutus) **24**:123
"Telegramas de urgencia escribo" (Fuertes) **27**:16
"Telephoning God" (Soto) **28**:375
"Television Is a Baby Crawling Toward That Death Chamber" (Ginsberg) **4**:51, 76
"Television Poem" (Sanchez) **9**:210
"Tell Me" (Hughes) **1**:244

"Tell Me" (Toomer) **7**:335
*Tell Me Again How the White Heron Rises and Flies Across the Nacreous River at Twilight Toward the Distant Islands* (Carruth) **10**:86-7
"Tell Me Some Way" (Reese) **29**:333
*Tell Me, Tell Me: Granite, Steel, and Other Topics* (Moore) **4**:242, 259
"tell me what attackd yu" (Bissett) **14**:32
"Telling the Bees" (Reese) **29**:333
"Temas candentes Agricultura" (Fuertes) **27**:28
"The Temper" (Herbert) **4**:100, 118
"The Temper I" (Herbert) **4**:101, 111
*The Tempers* (Williams) **7**:344, 348, 367, 378, 395, 398, 405
"Tempest and Music" (Viereck) **27**:278, 280
"Tempid: Bellosguardo" (Montale) **13**:126
"The Temple" (Herrick)
See "The Fairie Temple: or, Oberons Chappell. Dedicated to Mr. John Merrifield, Counsellor at Law"
"Le temple" (Lamartine) **16**:277
"The Temple of Fame" (Pope) **26**:318-19, 331
*The Temple of Fame* (Pope) **26**:
*The Temple: Sacred Poems and Private Ejaculations* (Herbert) **4**:99-102, 106, 110, 114-18, 120-21, 123, 126, 129, 132-33
"Il tempo passa" (Pavese) **13**:209, 226
"Le Temps et les Cités" (Hugo) **17**:88
"Temps Perdu" (Parker) **28**:365
"Temptation" (Cassian) **17**:4
"The Temptation of St. Joseph" (Auden) **1**:38-39
*Temy i variatsi* (Pasternak) **6**:252, 255, 261, 264-65, 269, 271, 275, 277-81, 283
*Temy i var'iatsii* (Pasternak)
See *Temy i variatsi*
"X" (Joyce) **22**:136, 138, 145, 153, 160, 162, 168
"10 April 67" (Brutus) **24**:122
"A Tenancy" (Merrill) **28**:249-50, 268
"The Tenant" (Brodsky) **9**:2
"Ten-Day Leave" (Meredith) **28**:180, 186
*Tender Buttons: Objects, Food, Rooms* (Stein) **18**:316-34, 336, 341-42, 344, 349-54
*Tender only To One* (Smith) **12**:292, 326, 340, 343, 349
"Tenderness toward Existence" (Kinnell) **26**:251
"Tenebrae" (Celan) **10**:101-02, 118
"Tenebrae" (Levertov) **11**:176
"Tengo" (Guillen) **23**:106, 115
*Tengo* (Guillen) **23**:124-25, 127, 130-31, 133
"Tengo que deciros" (Fuertes) **27**:4
"Tenjō Ishi" (Hagiwara Sakutaro) **18**:178-79
"Tenki" (Nishiwaki) **15**:228
"The Tennessee Hero" (Harper) **21**:206, 218
"Tennis" (Pinsky) **27**:144, 162
"The Tennis Court Oath" (Ashbery) **26**:113
*The Tennis Court Oath* (Ashbery) **26**:108, 112-113, 118, 129, 137-138, 143, 163
"Tenor" (Guillen) **23**:122, 124
*Tentativa del hombre infinito* (Neruda) **4**:276
"Tentative Description of a Dinner to Promote the Impeachment of President Eisenhower" (Ferlinghetti) **1**:167
"Tenth Elegy" (Rilke) **2**:273, 286-87
"Tenth Muse" (Lowell) **3**:213
*The Tenth Muse Lately sprung up in America* (Bradstreet) **10**:2-3, 6-8, 12, 18, 20-1, 25-7, 29-31, 34, 37, 40-1, 43, 46, 51-2, 59
*Tenth Nemean* (Pindar)
See *Nemean 10*
*Tenth Olympian* (Pindar)
See *Olympian 10*
"Tenth Psalm" (Sexton) **2**:372
*Tenth Pythian* (Pindar)
See *Pythian 10*
"Tenuous and Precarious" (Smith) **12**:312, 337
*Tercera residencia, 1935-1945* (Neruda) **4**:291, 306
"Tercero antolojía poética" (Jimenez) **7**:195
"Teremteni" (Illyes) **16**:235, 249

"Terence, This Is Stupid Stuff" (Housman) **2**:193
"A Term" (Aleixandre) **15**:4
"Terminal" (Shapiro) **25**:324
"Terminal Day at Beverly Farms" (Lowell) **3**:219
"Terminal Resemblance" (Gluck) **16**:158
"Terminus" (Emerson) **18**:75-77, 113
"Terminus" (Heaney) **18**:227
"The Terrace at Berne" (Arnold) **5**:12, 19, 49
"The Terraced Valley" (Graves) **6**:135, 139, 143-44, 172
"A Terre" (Owen) **19**:327, 331, 336, 339-40, 357, 359, 368
"Territory" (Kumin) **15**:207
"Terror" (Levertov) **11**:169
"Terror and Decorum" (Viereck) **27**:267, 271
*Terror and Decorum* (Viereck) **27**:258-63, 277-84
"The Terror of Existing" (Montale)
    See "Il terrore di esistere"
"Il terrore di esistere" (Montale) **13**:139
"Tess's Lament" (Hardy) **8**:85
"The Test" (Emerson) **18**:77
"A Testament" (Lermontov) **18**:278
"Testament" (Stryk) **27**:215
*Le Testament* (Villon) **13**:374-75, 377, 379, 387-90, 393-418
"Testament Coran" (Pasolini) **17**:262, 279
*The Testament of Beauty* (Bridges)
"The Testament of Love" (Bridges) **28**:65
*Testament of Love* (Chaucer)
    See *Legend of Good Women*
"Testament of the Thief" (Kinnell) **26**:240
"The Testing Tree" (Kunitz) **19**:175, 178, 180, 183
*The Testing-Tree* (Kunitz) **19**:157, 161, 163, 168, 172-74, 176, 185-86
"Tête de faune" (Rimbaud) **3**:271
"Têtes du serail" (Hugo) **17**:75
"Teurer Freund" (Heine) **25**:161
"Texas" (Lowell) **13**:86
"texte symptome" (Marie de France) **22**:
"Thalamus" (MacDiarmid) **9**:168, 176-77
"Thalero" (Sikelianos) **29**:373
"Thamár y Amnón" (Garcia Lorca) **3**:120, 131-32, 134, 146
"Thanatopsis" (Bryant) **20**:10, 12, 14, 16-19, 21-3, 26-30, 32, 34, 41, 43, 47
"Thank God for Little Children" (Harper) **21**:197
"Thank You, Fog" (Auden) **1**:31
"Thanking My Mother for Piano Lessons" (Wakoski) **15**:325, 347
"A Thanksgiving" (Auden) **1**:31
"Thanksgiving" (Gluck) **16**:124, 129, 150
"Thanksgiving for a Habitat" (Auden) **1**:24
"Thanksgiving Ode" (Wordsworth) **4**:399
"Thanksgiving's Over" (Lowell) **3**:206
"That April night's menu" (Enzensberger) **28**:155
"That Blessed Hope" (Harper) **21**:189, 208, 217
"That Bright Chimeric Beast" (Cullen) **20**:67
"That Day" (Sexton) **2**:353
"That Day That Was That Day" (Lowell) **12**:85
"That Force" (Zagajewski) **27**:385
"That Kind of Thing" (Gallagher) **9**:61
"That Moment" (Hardy) **8**:94
"That Swan's Way" (Aleixandre) **15**:5
"That the Night Come" (Yeats) **20**:351
"That Which is Now Behind, Previous Condition: The Eight of Swords" (Piercy) **29**:324
"That which is one they shear and make it twain" (Belloc) **24**:37-8
"That Which Opposes the Overthrowing of the Tower: The Nine of Cups" (Piercy) **29**:324
"That Woman There" (Stryk) **27**:203
"That women are but men's shadows" (Jonson)
    See "That women are but men's shadows"
"That Year" (Olds) **22**:308, 320, 322
"The Thatcher" (Heaney) **18**:200

"That's the Place Indians Talk About" (Ortiz) **17**:228, 230-31, 234
"The" (Zukofsky)
    See "Poem Beginning 'The'"
"The Annihilation of Nothing" (Gunn) **26**:
"The Collar" (Gunn) **26**:
"The Discovery of the Pacific" (Gunn) **26**:
"The Fair in the Woods" (Gunn) **26**:
"Thébaide" (Gautier) **18**:146
*Theban Dithyramb* (Pindar) **19**:423
"The,bright,Centipede" (Villa) **22**:350
"The,caprice,of,canteloupe,is,to,be" (Villa) **22**:356-57
*Thee* (Aiken) **26**:24, 29
"Their Behaviour" (Brutus) **24**:99
"Their Frailty" (Sassoon) **12**:267
"Thekla's Answer" (Arnold) **5**:50
"thel" (Clifton) **17**:30
"Thelassius" (Swinburne) **24**:312-315
"Theme and Variation" (Hayden) **6**:186, 197
"Theme and Variations" (Pasternak) **6**:251
*Themes and Variations* (Pasternak)
    See *Temy i variatsi*
"Then I Saw What the Calling Was" (Rukeyser) **12**:223
"Theodore Dreiser" (Masters) **1**:343
"Theodore the Poet" (Masters) **1**:345
"Theological Cradle Songs" (Viereck) **27**:262
"Theology" (Dunbar) **5**:120, 125, 127
"Theology" (Hughes) **7**:123, 159
"Theory of Art" (Baraka) **4**:9
"Theory of Evil" (Hayden) **6**:194, 196
"Theory of Flight" (Rukeyser) **12**:207, 218, 225
*Theory of Flight* (Rukeyser) **12**:202-03, 206, 209-10, 226-27, 235-36
"Theory of Maya" (Tagore)
    See "Mayavada"
"A Theory of Prosody" (Levine) **22**:227
"Theory of Truth" (Jeffers) **17**:131, 142, 144
"ther may have been a tunnel thru which my train rolld" (Bissett) **14**:34
"There" (Verlaine) **2**:416
"There Are Birds" (Shapiro) **25**:294
"There Are Blk/Puritans" (Sanchez) **9**:218
"There Are Orioles in Woods and Lasting Length of Vowels" (Mandelstam) **14**:141
"There Are So Many Houses and Dark Streets without Help" (Bukowski) **18**:15
"There Are Things I Tell to No One" (Kinnell) **26**:258, 260-61, 280, 292
"There Has to Be a Jail for Ladies" (Merton) **10**:341
"There is a hill beside the silver Thames" (Bridges) **28**:66-7, 83
"There Is Only One of Everything" (Atwood) **8**:23, 28
"There Once Lived a Poor Knight" (Pushkin)
    See "Zhil Na Svete Rytsar' Bednyi"
"There Shines the Moon, at Noon of Night" (Bronte) **8**:75
"There Should be No Despair" (Bronte) **8**:68-9
"There Was a Child Went Forth" (Whitman) **3**:392, 396, 415
"There Was A Dance Sweetheart" (Harjo) **27**:69
"There Was a Lad Was Born in Kyle" (Burns) **6**:76
"There Was a Poor Knight" (Pushkin)
    See "Zhil Na Svete Rytsar' Bednyi"
"There Was a Saviour" (Thomas) **2**:390
"There was Never Nothing" (Wyatt) **27**:318
"There Was One" (Parker) **28**:362
*Therefore* (Mallarme)
    See *Igitur*
*There's a Trick with a Knife I'm Learning to Do: Poems, 1963-1978* (Ondaatje) **28**:327-40
"These" (Williams) **7**:360, 362-63
"These Are the Young" (Lindsay) **23**:281
"These States: To Miami Presidential Convention" (Ginsberg) **4**:82
"These Streets" (Levine) **22**:224

"Theseus and Ariadne" (Graves) **6**:136-37, 144, 146
"Thetis" (H. D.) **5**:267-68
"They" (Sassoon) **12**:241, 249, 263, 275, 277-78, 286
"They Are More on a Corncob" (Guillen)
    See "They Are More on a Corncob"
"They Are Not Missed" (Toomer) **7**:338-39
"They Are Not Ready" (Madhubuti) **5**:338
"They Clapped" (Giovanni) **19**:141
"They Eat Out" (Atwood) **8**:6
"They Feed They Lion" (Levine) **22**:216, 221, 227
*They Feed They Lion* (Levine) **22**:211, 213, 215, 217, 223
"They fle from me" (Wyatt) **27**:300, 302, 309, 314, 316, 329-31, 338, 343, 347-48, 355, 357, 362
"They Have Put Us on Hold" (Walker) **20**:294
"They Say it Snowed" (Ammons) **16**:44
"They Say This Isn't a Poem" (Rexroth) **20**:195-96
"They'd Never Know Me Now" (Masters) **1**:344
"Thick-Lipped Nigger" (Guillen)
    See "Negro bembón"
"The Thief" (Kunitz) **19**:150-51, 172, 175
"Thin Air" (Hass) **16**:215, 217
"The Thin People" (Plath) **1**:388, 406
"Things" (Reese) **29**:336
"Things of August" (Stevens) **6**:313
*Things Taking Place* (Swenson)
    See *New and Selected Things Taking Place*
"Things That Are Worse Than Death" (Olds) **22**:313
"Think No More, Lad: Laugh, Be Jolly" (Housman) **2**:179, 183, 185
"Think of It" (Celan) **10**:98
"Think Tank" (Merrill) **28**:267
"The Thinker" (Williams) **7**:353
"Thinking about El Salvador" (Levertov) **11**:198
"Thinking of Old Tu Fu" (Matsuo Basho) **3**:10
"Third Degree" (Hughes) **1**:248
"The Third Dimension" (Levertov) **11**:159
"Third Elegy" (Rilke) **2**:271
"Third Georgic" (Vergil) **12**:361
"Third Hymn to Lenin" (MacDiarmid) **9**:180-81, 197
*Third Nemean* (Pindar)
    See *Nemean 3*
*Third Olympian* (Pindar)
    See *Olympian 3*
"Third Psalm" (Sexton) **2**:367
*Third Pythian* (Pindar)
    See *Pythian 3*
*The Third Residence* (Neruda)
    See *Tercera residencia, 1935-1945*
*Third Residence* (Neruda)
    See *Tercera residencia, 1935-1945*
"The Third Sermon of the Warpland" (Brooks) **7**:88-9
"Third Song" (Rilke) **2**:273
*The Third Symphony* (Bely)
    See *Vozvrat: Tretiia simfoniia*
*Third Voronezh Notebook* (Mandelstam) **14**:149, 152, 155
"The Third World" (Ferlinghetti) **1**:186
"Third World Calling" (Ferlinghetti) **1**:183
"XIII" (Joyce) **22**:145, 168
"Thirteen Ways of Looking at a Blackbird" (Stevens) **6**:293, 326-27
*Thirteenth Olympian* (Pindar)
    See *Olympian 13*
"The Thirties Revisited" (Kumin) **15**:202
*Thirty Poems* (Merton) **10**:338-39, 350-51
"Thirty Rhymes to Hermit Chang Piao" (Tu Fu) **9**:326
"XXXV" (Joyce) **22**:138-39, 144, 154, 157, 161, 164
"XXXIV" (Joyce) **22**:139, 145, 157, 161-62, 164-65, 170
"XXXI" (Joyce) **22**:152, 164, 170

"XXXVI" (Joyce) **22**:136, 138, 144-45, 157, 161, 163-64
"XXXIII" (Joyce) **22**:145, 164, 166, 168, 173
"XXXII" (Joyce) **22**:145, 164, 167, 173
"XXXII" (Larkin) **21**:242
"This Black Rich Country" (Ammons) **16**:40
"This Bread I Break" (Thomas) **2**:379, 389
"This Cold Man" (Page)
   See "Now This Cold Man"
"This Compost" (Whitman) **3**:410
"This Configuration" (Ashbery) **26**:141
"This Corruptible" (Wylie) **23**:304-305, 308, 311, 316
"This Day" (Levertov) **11**:198-99, 201
"This Do, in Remembrance of Me" (Bryant) **20**:45
"This Florida: 1924" (Williams) **7**:369
"This Frieze of Birds" (Page) **12**:168
"This Is" (Ammons) **16**:54
"This Is a Photograph of Me" (Atwood) **8**:12, 23
"This is Disgraceful and Abominable" (Smith) **12**:293, 309
"This Is Just to Say" (Williams) **7**:363, 399, 401
*This Is My Century* (Walker) **20**:293
"This Is Noon" (Graves) **6**:166
"This Is Not For John Lennon" (And This Is Not a PoemGiovanni) **19**:142
"this is the tale" (Clifton) **17**:25, 27
"This Is the Track" (Owen) **19**:342
"This Is Their Fault" (Forche) **10**:142
"This day Died Again and" (Let's RememberCummings) **5**:107
"This Life" (Dove) **6**:108
"This Lime-Tree Bower My Prison" (Coleridge) **11**:51, 53, 72, 83, 88-9, 97, 104, 107
"This My Song is Made for Kerensky" (Lindsay) **23**:269
"This Near-At-Hand" (Rossetti) **7**:276
"This Occurs To Me" (Ortiz) **17**:225
"This Place Rumord to Have Been Sodom" (Duncan) **2**:127
"This Praying Fool" (Kumin) **15**:180
"This Room and Everything in It" (Lee) **24**:243
"This Side of Truth" (Thomas) **2**:390
"This sun on this rubble after rain" (Brutus) **24**:113
"This, That, and the Other" (Nemerov) **24**:298, 303
"This Urn Contains Earth from German Concentration Camps" (Lorde) **12**:136
"This Was a Poet" (Dickinson) **1**:96, 102
"This Way Is Not a Way" (Snyder) **21**:310
"Thistledown" (Merrill) **28**:228
"Thistles" (Hughes) **7**:121, 137
"Tho I cannot your crueltie constrain" (Wyatt) **27**:321
*Thomas and Beulah* (Dove) **6**:104, 107, 110-20, 122
"Thomas at the Wheel" (Dove) **6**:111
"Thomas Bewick" (Gunn) **26**:
"Thompson's Lunch Room" (Lowell) **13**:79
"Thorkild's Song" (Kipling) **3**:183
"The Thorn" (Wordsworth) **4**:381, 402, 412, 416-17, 426, 428
"A Thorn Forever in the Breast" (Cullen) **20**:63
"Thorn Piece" (Lowell) **13**:85
"Those Dancing Days Are Gone" (Yeats) **20**:328
"Those Times" (Sexton) **2**:362-63, 370
"Those Various Scalpels" (Moore) **4**:263-64, 270
*Those Who Ride the Night Winds* (Giovanni) **19**:126-27, 137-38, 142-43
"Those Winter Sundays" (Hayden) **6**:194-95
"The Thou" (Montale)
   See "Il tu"
"Thou Art Indeed Just, Lord" (Hopkins) **15**:171
"Thou didst delight my eyes" (Bridges) **28**:85
"Thou Famished Grave, I Will Not Fill Thee Yet" (Millay) **6**:242

"Thou Shalt Not Kill" (Rexroth) **20**:181, 187, 193, 205, 218
"Thou Unbelieving Heart" (Kunitz) **19**:155
"Though It Only Lasts a Moment" (Alegria) **26**:
"Thought for a Sunshiny morning" (Parker) **28**:362
"A Thought of Columbus" (Whitman)
   See "A Prayer of Columbus"
"The Thought-Fox" (Hughes) **7**:120, 158, 166, 168-69
"Thoughts about the Christian Doctrine of Eternal Hell" (Smith) **12**:301, 325, 333
"Thoughts about the Person from Porlock" (Smith) **12**:293, 330, 350
"Thoughts in 1932" (Sassoon) **12**:252
"Thoughts on a Breath" (Ginsberg) **4**:76
"Thoughts on His Excellency Major General Lee" (Wheatley) **3**:337
"Thoughts on One's Head" (Meredith) **28**:174, 211
"Thoughts on Saving the Manatee" (Kumin) **15**:211
"Thoughts on the Shape of the Human Body" (Brooke) **24**:56-7
"Thoughts on the Works of Providence" (Wheatley) **3**:332, 339, 358, 361, 363
"The Thousand and Second Night" (Merrill) **28**:222, 225-26, 228, 230-32, 234, 250, 252-53
"Thousand League Pool" (Tu Fu) **9**:333
"A Thousand Thousand Times" (Breton) **15**:73
*Thread-Suns* (Celan)
   See *Fadensonnen*
"Three" (Gunn) **26**:208
"III" (Joyce) **22**:144, 160, 162, 164, 166
"3 A.M. Kitchen: My Father Talking" (Gallagher) **9**:53
"Three Bushes" (Yeats) **20**:332
"The Three Captains" (Kipling) **3**:157
"The Three Conspirators" (Nemerov) **24**:293
"The Three Decker" (Kipling) **3**:161
"Three Desk Objects" (Atwood) **8**:2, 13
"Three Elegiac Poems" (Berry) **28**:15
"Three Faces" (Swinburne) **24**:329
"Three Floors" (Kunitz) **19**:178
"Three Ghosts" (Sandburg) **23**:309
"The Three Grayes" (Coleridge) **11**:117
"Three Green Windows" (Sexton) **2**:363
*Three Hundred and Sixty Degrees of Blackness Comin at You* (Sanchez) **9**:222
"Three Italian Pictures" (Loy) **16**:313
"The Three Kings" (Zagajewski) **27**:396
*Three Material Cantos* (Neruda)
   See *Homenaje a Pablo Neruda de los poetas espanoles: Tres cantos materiales*
*Three Material Songs* (Neruda)
   See *Homenaje a Pablo Neruda de los poetas espanoles: Tres cantos materiales*
"Three Meditations" (Levertov) **11**:169
"Three Modes of History and Culture" (Baraka) **4**:16
"Three Moments in Paris" (Loy) **16**:312, 327-28
"Three Movements and a Coda" (Baraka) **4**:9, 19, 24
"Three Nuns" (Rossetti) **7**:277
"3 of Swords--for dark men under the white moon" (Wakoski) **15**:362, 367
"Three old men" (Illyes)
   See "Harom oreg"
"Three Palm-Trees" (Lermontov)
   See "Tri palmy"
*Three Poems* (Ashbery) **26**:108-109, 114-116, 118, 123, 126, 130, 135, 143, 149, 167, 169-171, 173-174
*Three Poems under a Flag of Convenience* (Elytis) **21**:131
"Three Postcards from the Monastery" (Merton) **10**:332
"Three Songs" (Crane) **3**:106
*The Three Taverns* (Robinson) **1**:465-66, 468

"Three Things" (Yeats) **20**:328
"Three Times in Love" (Graves) **6**:172
"Three Times the Truth" (Elytis) **21**:123
"Three Travellers Watch a Sunrise" (Stevens) **6**:295
"Three United States Sonnets" (Cummings) **5**:94
"Three White Vases" (Swenson) **14**:273
"Threes" (Atwood) **8**:21
"Three-year-old" (Tagore)
   See "Tritiya"
*Threnodia Augustalis* (Dryden) **25**:88-9
"Threnody" (Emerson) **18**:69, 81, 84, 86, 90, 102-3, 112-3
"Threnody" (Parker) **28**:360
"Threnody for a Brown Girl" (Cullen) **20**:57-58, 62, 66
*Thrones, 96-109 de los cantares* (Pound) **4**:337-38, 352, 353, 357
"Through Corralitos under Rolls of Cloud" (Rich) **5**:401
"Through Nightmare" (Graves) **6**:137, 173
"Through the Looking Glass" (Ferlinghetti) **1**:173
"Through the Round Window" (McGuckian) **27**:83
"Through the Smoke Hole" (Snyder) **21**:292
"Throughout Our Lands" (Milosz) **8**:187, 194, 214
"Throw Away Thy Rod" (Herbert) **4**:103, 121
*A Throw of the Dice Never Will Abolish Chance* (Mallarme)
   See *Un coup de dés jamais n'abolira le hasard*
*A Throw of the Dice Will Never Abolish Chance* (Mallarme)
   See *Un coup de dés jamais n'abolira le hasard*
"Thrushes" (Hughes) **7**:119, 169
"Thrushes" (Sassoon) **12**:253
"Thrust and Riposte" (Montale)
   See "Botta e riposta"
"Thunder Can Break" (Okigbo)
   See "Come Thunder"
"Thunder in Tuscany" (Tomlinson) **17**:349-50
"Thunder, Momentarily Instantaneous" (Pasternak) **6**:251
"A Thunder-Storm" (Dickinson) **1**:79
"The Thunderstorm" (Trakl)
   See "Das Gewitter"
"Thursday" (Millay) **6**:208, 211
"Thursday: The Bassette Table: Smilinda, Cardelia" (Montagu) **16**:338, 349
"Thurso's Landing" (Jeffers) **17**:141-42
*Thurso's Landing, and Other Poems* (Jeffers) **17**:122, 124-25, 135, 142
"Thyestes" (Davie) **29**:107
"Thyrsis" (Arnold) **5**:7-8, 18-19, 21, 23-4, 33, 36, 45, 47, 52, 55-6
"Tiare Tahiti" (Brooke) **24**:53, 64, 66, 73-4, 78, 86
*Tide and Continuities* (Viereck) **27**:292, 294-96
*Tide and Continuities Last and First Poems 1995-1938* (Viereck) **27**:295
"The Tide at Long Point" (Swenson) **14**:247, 249
"Tierra de azules montañas" (Guillen) **23**:125
"Tierra del Fuego" (Zagajewski) **27**:396, 400
"Tierra en la sierra" (Guillen) **23**:127
"Tierra en la sierra y en el llano" (Guillen) **23**:127
"La tierra se llama Juan" (Neruda) **4**:294
"The Tiger" (Belloc) **24**:24
"The Tiger" (Blake)
   See "The Tyger"
"Till de folkhemske" (Ekeloef) **23**:76
"Tilly" (Joyce) **22**:
"Tilting Sail" (Hass) **16**:251
"Timbuctoo" (Tennyson) **6**:358, 389, 407-08, 413, 415-18
"Time and Life" (Swinburne) **24**:323
"The Time before You" (McGuckian) **27**:82

"Time Does Not Bring Relief" (Millay) **6**:205
"Time Goes By" (Pavese)
      See "Il tempo passa"
"Time in the Rock" (Aiken) **26**:19, 57
*Time in the Rock* (Aiken) **26**:6, 12, 23, 29, 52
"Time Is the Mercy of Eternity" (Rexroth)
      **20**:181, 208-09, 216-18
"Time Lapse with Tulips" (Gallagher) **9**:37
"Time of Disturbance" (Jeffers) **17**:141
"Time Passing, Beloved" (Davie) **29**:94, 100,
      108
"Time Spirals" (Rexroth) **20**:195, 217-18
"A Time to Dance" (Day Lewis) **11**:126
*A Time to Dance and Other Poems* (Day
      Lewis) **11**:126-27, 129
"Time to Kill in Gallup" (Ortiz) **17**:240
"A Timepiece" (Merrill) **28**:225, 234
"Times at Bellosguardo" (Montale) **13**:147, 152
"Time's Dedication" (Schwartz) **8**:305, 307,
      314
*Time's Laughingstocks and Other Verses*
      (Hardy) **8**:93, 123
"Times Passes" (Pavese)
      See "Il tempo passa"
"Time's Revenges" (Browning) **2**:33
"Times Square Water Music" (Clampitt) **19**:81,
      88
"The Times Table" (Frost) **1**:205
"Time-Travel" (Olds) **22**:322
"Tin Roof" (Ondaatje) **28**:314
"Tin Wedding Whistle" (Nash) **21**:268
"Tinder" (Heaney) **18**:202
"The Tingling Back" (Shapiro) **25**:317, 320
"Tintern Abbey" (Nemerov) **24**:
"Tintern Abbey" (Wordsworth)
      See "Lines Composed a Few Miles Above
      Tintern Abbey"
"Tiresias" (Tennyson) **6**:361
*Tiriel* (Blake) **12**:61
"Tirzey Potter" (Masters) **1**:338
"Tis April and the morning love" (Clare) **23**:23
"Tishina" (Pasternak) **6**:286
"Tithonus" (Tennyson) **6**:366, 411
"Title Divine Is Mine the Wife without the
      Sign" (Dickinson) **1**:93
"Titmouse" (Emerson) **18**:79, 103-4, 113
"To--" (Owen) **19**:352
"To--- -- -----" (Poe) **1**:436, 445
"To a Babe Smiling in Her Sleep" (Harper)
      **21**:197
"To a Book" (Wylie) **23**:303
"To a Brother in the Mystery" (Davie) **29**:96,
      102
"To a Brown Boy" (Cullen) **20**:52, 62
"To a Brown Girl" (Cullen) **20**:52, 62
"To A Butterfly" (Merrill) **28**:247
"To a Captious Critic" (Dunbar) **5**:125, 127,
      135
"To a Child Dancing in the Wind" (Yeats)
      **20**:338
"To a Child Running with Outstretched Arms
      in Canyon de Chelly" (Momaday) **25**:219
"To a Clergyman on the Death of His Lady"
      (Wheatley) **3**:357
"To a Common Prostitute" (Whitman) **3**:416
"To a Contemporary Bunkshooter" (Sandburg)
      **2**:317, 330
"To a Contemporary Bunk-Shooter"
      (Sandburg) **2**:317, 330
"To a Cuckoo at Coolanlough" (McGuckian)
      **27**:103
"to a dark moses" (Clifton) **17**:34
"To a Dead Child" (Bridges) **28**:57
"To a Dreamer" (Pushkin) **10**:407
"To a Fellow Scribbler" (Finch) **21**:168
"To a Fish Head Found on the Beach Near
      Malaga" (Levine) **22**:215
"To a Friend" (Arnold) **5**:12, 49
"To a Friend" (Herrick) **9**:90
"To a Friend" (Yeats) **20**:321
"To a Friend and Fellow-Poet" (MacDiarmid)
      **9**:183-84

"To a Friend in Time of Trouble" (Gunn) **26**:215
"To a Friend Whose Work Has Come to
      Triumph" (Sexton) **2**:370
"To a Fringed Gentian" (Bryant) **20**:12, 45
"To a Gentleman on His Voyage to Great
      Britain for the Recovery of His Health"
      (Wheatley) **3**:358
"To a Gipsy Child by the Sea-shore" (Arnold)
      **5**:38, 49-50
"To a Giraffe" (Moore) **4**:242-43
"To a Guinea Pig" (Shapiro) **25**:269
"To a Highland Girl" (Wordsworth) **4**:404
"To a Husband" (Lowell) **13**:74
"To a Japanese Poet" (Stryk) **27**:203-4
"To a Jealous Cat" (Sanchez) **9**:223, 232
"To a Lady and Her Children, On the Death of
      Her Son and Their Brother" (Wheatley)
      **3**:363
"To a Lady on Her Remarkable Preservation in
      an Hurricane in North Carolina"
      (Wheatley) **3**:354
"To a Lady on the Death of Three Relations"
      (Wheatley) **3**:343, 348
"To a Lady that desired I would love her"
      (Carew) **29**:3-4
"To a Lady's Countenance" (Wylie) **23**:321
"To a Louse, on Seeing One on a Lady's
      Bonnet at Church" (Burns) **6**:65, 79
"To a lovely woman" (Lermontov) **18**:303
"To a Mountain Daisy, on Turning One Down
      with the Plough in April, 1786" (Burns)
      **6**:50, 74
"To a Mouse, on Turning Her Up in Her Nest
      with the Plough, November, 1785"
      (Burns) **6**:50, 65, 74, 80, 96
"To a Passing Woman" (Baudelaire)
      See "A une passante"
"To a Poet" (Jimenez) **7**:183
"To a Poet" (McKay) **2**:206
"To a Poor Old Woman" (Williams) **7**:390, 399
"To a Portrait" (Lermontov) **18**:297
"To a Portrait in a Gallery" (Page) **12**:168
"To a Republican Friend" (Arnold) **5**:49
"To a Sad Daughter" (Ondaatje) **28**:316
"To a Seamew" (Swinburne) **24**:313, 328
"To a Shade" (Yeats) **20**:348
"to a Sinister Potato" (Viereck) **27**:259, 262,
      279
"To a Solitary Disciple" (Williams) **7**:357, 378
"To a Strategist" (Moore) **4**:266
"To a Town Poet" (Reese) **29**:333
"To a Waterfowl" (Bryant) **20**:5-6, 14, 18, 35,
      42
"To a Western Bard Still a Whoop and a
      Holler Away from English Poetry"
      (Meredith) **28**:174, 187, 207
"To a Winter Squirrel" (Brooks) **7**:82
"To a Wreath of Snow" (Bronte) **8**:67, 73
"To a Young Actress" (Pushkin) **10**:407
"To A Young Friend" (Burns)
      See "Epistle to a Young Friend"
"To a Young Girl" (Millay) **6**:217
"To a Young Girl" (Yeats) **20**:330
"To A.D., unreasonable distrustfull of her
      owne beauty" (Carew) **29**:29
"To Adversity" (Gray)
      See "Ode to Adversity"
"To A.L. Perswasions to Love" (Carew) **29**:10,
      23-24, 66-68
"To Alchymists" (Jonson) **17**:197
"To Alexander" (Pushkin)
      See "Aleksandru"
"To Alexis, in Answer to His Poem against
      Fruition" (Behn) **13**:26
"To All Brothers" (Sanchez) **9**:224, 232
"To All Brothers: From All Sisters" (Sanchez)
      **9**:221
"To All Gentleness" (Williams) **7**:354
"To All Sisters" (Sanchez) **9**:224, 231-32
"To America" (Johnson) **24**:131, 142, 148, 158,
      160

"To Amintas, upon Reading the Lives of Some
      of the Romans" (Behn) **13**:32
"To an Ancient" (Frost) **1**:200
"To an Athlete Dying Young" (Housman) **2**:180,
      183, 185, 191-94, 198, 201
"To an Old Philosopher in Rome" (Stevens)
      **6**:304, 324, 328
"To Another Housewife" (Wright) **14**:356
"To Anthea" (Herrick) **9**:145
"To Anthea Lying in Bed" (Herrick) **9**:137
"To Anthea, Who May Command Him Any
      Thing" (Herrick) **9**:102
"To Any Dead Officer Who Left School for the
      Army in l914" (Sassoon) **12**:268, 277
"To Aphrodite, with a Talisman" (Wylie)
      **23**:320, 324
"To Art" (Reese) **29**:354
"To Autumn" (Ashbery) **26**:160
"To Autumn" (Gluck) **16**:142, 149
"To Autumn" (Keats)
      See "Ode to Autumn"
"To Bargain Toboggan To-Woo!" (Nash) **21**:265
*To Bathurst* (Pope) **26**:340
"To Be a Jew in the Twentieth Century"
      (Rukeyser) **12**:234
"To Be Carved on a Stone at Thoor Ballylee"
      (Yeats) **20**:346, 348
"To Be in Love" (Brooks) **7**:81-2
"To Be Liked by You Would Be a Calamity"
      (Moore) **4**:250
"to Be of Use" (Piercy) **29**:309
*To Be of Use* (Piercy) **29**:302, 309-10, 323
"To Be Quicker for Black Political Prisoners"
      (Madhubuti) **5**:330, 346
"To be Sung" (Viereck) **27**:265
"To Be Sung on the Water" (Bogan) **12**:90, 124
*To Bedlam and Part Way Back* (Sexton) **2**:345-
      47, 349-50, 353, 355, 357-58, 360, 363, 367
"To Ben Jonson Upon occasion of his Ode of
      defiance annext to his play of the new
      Inne" (Carew) **29**:7, 32, 82
"To Bennie" (McKay) **2**:221
"To Blk/Record/Buyers" (Sanchez) **9**:209, 217
"To Blossoms" (Herrick) **9**:145
"To Bring the Dead to Life" (Graves) **6**:143
*To Burlington* (Pope) **26**:340
"To Camden" (Jonson)
      See "To Camden"
"To Carl Sandburg" (Lowell) **13**:67
"To Carry the Child" (Smith) **12**:320
"To Cedars" (Herrick) **9**:91
"To Celia" (Jonson) **17**:170, 196
"To Certain Critics" (Cullen) **20**:66, 83
"To Chaadaev" (Pushkin)
      See "Chaadayevu"
"To Change in a Good Way" (Ortiz) **17**:234
"To Charis" (Jonson)
      See "To Charis"
"To Christ Our Lord" (Kinnell) **26**:239
*To . . . Christopher Duke of Albemarle* (Behn)
      **13**:8
"To Chuck" (Sanchez) **9**:224, 233
"To Cipriano, in the Wind" (Levine) **22**:225
*To Circumjack Cencrastus* (MacDiarmid) **9**:151-
      53, 158, 171, 175-77, 197
"To Clarendon Hills and H.A.H." (McKay)
      **2**:222
"To Claudia Homonoea" (Wylie) **23**:324
"To Clio Muse of History" (Nemerov) **24**:262
"To Cole, the Painter, Departing For Europe"
      (Bryant) **20**:34, 44-5
"To Columbus" (Dario)
      See "A Colón"
"To Conclude" (Montale) **13**:146
"To Confirm a Thing" (Swenson) **14**:247, 252,
      278
"To Constantia Singing" (Shelley) **14**:177
"To Countess Rostopchina" (Lermontov) **18**:297
"To Daddy" (Lowell) **3**:226
"To Daffadills" (Herrick) **9**:101
"To Damon. To Inquire of Him If He Cou'd
      Tell Me by the Style, Who Writ Me a

Copy of Verses That Came to Me in an Unknown Hand" (Behn) **13**:30-1
"To Daphnie and Virginia" (Williams) **7**:360, 363, 392
"To Dean Swift" (Swift) **9**:295
"To Death" (Finch) **21**:179-80
"To Deism" (Wheatley) **3**:354
"To Delmore Schwartz" (Lowell) **3**:219, 222
"To Desire" (Behn) **13**:24
"To Dianeme" (Herrick) **9**:145
*To Disembark* (Brooks) **7**:84, 93
"To Dispel My Grief" (Tu Fu) **9**:326
"To *** Do not think I deserve regret" (Lermontov) **18**:301, 304
"To Doctor Alabaster" (Herrick) **9**:142
"To Don at Salaam" (Brooks) **7**:84, 92
*To Dream of A Butterfly* (Hagiwara Sakutaro)
　　See *To Dream of A Butterfly*
"To Earthward" (Frost) **1**:197
"To Electra" (Herrick) **9**:94
"To Elizabeth Ward Perkins" (Lowell) **13**:90
"To Elsie" (Williams) **7**:382, 384, 411
"To E.M.E." (McKay) **2**:223
"To Endymion" (Cullen) **20**:67, 86
"To Enemies" (Bely) **11**:24
"To Enter That Rhythm Where the Self is Lost" (Rukeyser) **12**:227
"To Eros" (Owen) **19**:352
"To Ethelinda" (Smart) **13**:331, 347
"To Evalyn for Christmas" (Shapiro) **25**:286
"To Eve Man's Dream of Wifehood As Described by Milton" (Lindsay) **23**:281
"To Evoke Posterity" (Graves) **6**:143, 152
"To Fausta" (Arnold) **5**:49
"To F.C. in Memoriam Palestine" (Chesterton) **28**:97
"To Find God" (Herrick) **9**:109
"To Fine Lady Would-bee" (Jonson) **17**:197
"To Flowers" (Herrick) **9**:102
"To Flush My Dog" (Browning) **6**:6-7
"To Ford Madox Ford in Heaven" (Williams) **7**:370
"To France" (Cullen) **20**:66
"To Francis Jammes" (Bridges) **28**:76
"To Galich" (Pushkin) **10**:407
"To George Sand: A Recognition" (Browning) **6**:26
"To Gerhardt" (Olson) **19**:307
"To Go By Singing" (Berry) **28**:3-4
"To Go to Lvov" (Zagajewski) **27**:381-82, 383-85, 387
"To God" (Herrick) **9**:94-5, 109, 118
"To God, His Good Will" (Herrick) **9**:118
"To God, on His Sicknesse" (Herrick) **9**:144
"To Gurdjieff Dying" (Toomer) **7**:338
"To Hafiz of Shiraz" (Wright) **14**:356, 366
"To Have Done Nothing" (Williams) **7**:383, 389, 410
"To Have Without Holding" (Piercy) **29**:311
"To Heaven" (Jonson)
　　See "To Heaven"
"To Helen" (Poe) **1**:420, 424, 426, 428, 431, 438-39, 441, 443-45, 447
"To Helen" (Stryk) **27**:204
"To Helen" (of Troy NY Viereck) **27**:294
"To Help" (Stein) **18**:313
"To Her" (Pushkin) **10**:408-09
"To Her Father with Some Verses" (Bradstreet) **10**:27, 35
"To Her Most Honoured Father Thomas Dudley" (Bradstreet) **10**:2
"To His Book" (Herrick) **9**:106, 109
"To His Closet-Gods" (Herrick) **9**:88
"To His Coy Mistress" (Marvell) **10**:259, 265, 269, 271, 273-74, 277-79, 281-82, 290-94, 297, 304, 310-11, 313
"To His Cynical Mistress" (Gunn) **26**:
"To His Excellency General George Washington" (Wheatley) **3**:337, 341
"To His Father" (Jeffers) **17**:131
"To His Friend on the Untuneable Times" (Herrick) **9**:89

"To His Girles" (Herrick) **9**:107
"To His Girles Who Would Have Him Sportfull" (Herrick) **9**:107
"To His Honor the Lieutenant Governor on the Death of His Lady" (Wheatley) **3**:340
"To His Mistresses" (Herrick) **9**:128, 146
"To His Paternall Countrey" (Herrick) **9**:108
"To His Savior, a Child; a Present, by a Child" (Herrick) **9**:120, 143
"To His Saviour, the New Yeers Gift" (Herrick) **9**:95
"To His Saviours Sepulcher: His Devotion" (Herrick) **9**:122
"To His Watch" (Hopkins) **15**:167
"To Homer" (Keats) **1**:279, 314
"To Imagination" (Bronte) **8**:54
"To Imagination" (Wheatley)
　　See "On Imagination"
"To Indianapolis 17 Nov 71" (Brutus) **24**:123
"To Insure Survival" (Ortiz) **17**:225
"To Ireland in the Coming Times" (Yeats) **20**:324, 347, 353
"To Ivor Gurney" (Tomlinson) **17**:354-55
"to joan" (Clifton) **17**:18
"To John Goldie, August 1785" (Burns) **6**:70, 78
"To John Keats, Poet: At Spring Time" (Cullen) **20**:62, 66, 86
"To Jos: Lo: Bishop of Exeter" (Herrick) **9**:146
"To Joseph Joachim" (Bridges) **28**:88
"To Joseph Sadzik" (Milosz)
　　See "Do Józefa Sadzika"
"To Juan at the Winter Solstice" (Graves) **6**:137, 144, 146, 168, 171-72
"To Julia" (Herrick) **9**:128, 143
"To Julia, in Her Dawne, or Day-breake" (Herrick) **9**:143
"To Julia, the Flaminica Dialis, or Queen-Priest" (Herrick) **9**:143
"To . . . K. Charles" (Jonson)
　　See "To . . . K. Charles"
"To K. Charles . . . 1629" (Jonson)
　　See "To K. Charles . . . 1629"
"To Keorapetse Kgositsile" (Willie Brooks) **7**:83, 92, 105
"To Kevin O'Leary Wherever He Is" (Levertov) **11**:189
"To King James"
　　See "To King James"
"To Lady Crew, upon the Death of Her Child" (Herrick)
　　See "To the Lady Crew, upon the Death of Her Child"
"To Laurels" (Herrick) **9**:127
"To Licinius" (Pushkin)
　　See "K Liciniju"
"To Live Merrily, and to Trust to Good Verses" (Herrick) **9**:96, 103-05, 107, 114
"To Lord Byron" (Keats) **1**:313
"To Lord Harley, on His Marriage" (Swift) **9**:254
"To Lose the Earth" (Sexton) **2**:363
"To Louise" (Dunbar) **5**:121
"To Love" (Aleixandre) **15**:19, 21
"To Love" (Reese) **29**:331
"To Lu Chi" (Nemerov) **24**:257
"To Lucia at Birth" (Graves) **6**:137
"To Lucy, Countesse of Bedford, with Mr. Donnes Satyres" (Jonson)
　　See "To Lucy, Countesse of Bedford, with Mr. Donnes Satyres"
"To Lyce" (Smart) **13**:348
"To Lycomedes on Scyros" (Brodsky)
　　See "K Likomedu, na Skiros"
"To Lysander at the Musick-Meeting" (Behn) **13**:30
"To Lysander, on Some Verses He Writ, and Asking More for His Heart than 'Twas Worth" (Behn) **13**:30
"To Make a Poem in Prison" (Knight) **14**:48
"To Marguerite" (Arnold) **5**:19, 64

"To Marguerite—Continued" (Arnold) **5**:13, 42-5, 49, 64
"To Mark Anthony in Heaven" (Williams) **7**:367
"To Mary" (Shelley) **14**:234-36
"To Mary Lady Wroth" (Jonson)
　　See "To Mary Lady Wroth"
"To Matilda Betham" (Coleridge) **11**:58
"To Mæcenas" (Wheatley)
　　See "Ode to Mæcenas"
"to merle" (Clifton) **17**:18
"To Mistress Isabel Pennell" (Skelton) **25**:336
"To Mistress Margaret Hussey" (Skelton) **25**:345
*To Mix with Time: New and Selected Poems* (Swenson) **14**:249-50, 254-55, 257, 260, 266, 268, 274, 278, 281-82, 285
"To Mr. Congreve" (Swift) **9**:250
"To Mr. Creech on His Excellent Translation of Lucretius" (under the Name of DaphnisBehn) **13**:8, 31
"To Mr. Delany, Nov. 10, 1718" (Swift) **9**:255
"To Mr. F. Now Earl of W." (Finch) **21**:153, 164
"To Mr R. W. 'If as mine is'" (Donne) **1**:124
"To Mrs. Harriet Beecher Stowe" (Harper) **21**:201, 205
"To Mrs. W. on Her Excellent Verses" (Writ in Praise of Some I Had Made on the Earl of RochesterBehn) **13**:8, 31
"To My Brother" (Bogan) **12**:117
"To My Brother" (Sassoon) **12**:261, 278
"To My Daughter the Junkie on a Train" (Lorde) **12**:146-47, 154
"To My Dear and Loving Husband His Goeing into England" (Bradstreet) **10**:13, 36, 40, 63
"To My Fairer Brethren" (Cullen) **20**:52
"To My Father" (Olds) **22**:325
"To my friend G.N. from Wrest" (Carew)
　　See "Letter to G.N. from Wrest"
"To My Friend Jerina" (Clifton) **17**:29
"To My Friend with an Identity Disk" (Owen) **19**:334, 358
"To My Greek" (Merrill) **28**:220, 262-63
"To My Honored Friend, Dr. Charleton" (Dryden) **25**:95
"To my Honoured friend, Master Thomas May, upon his Comedie, The Heire" (Carew) **29**:53
"To My Ill Reader" (Herrick) **9**:89
"To my Inconstant Mistress" (Carew) **29**:3-4, 9, 18, 32-34
"To My Lady Moreland at Tunbridge" (Behn) **13**:8, 29-30
"to my last period" (Clifton) **17**:29, 36
"To my lord Ignorant" (Jonson)
　　See "To my lord Ignorant"
"To My Mother" (Montale) **13**:112, 149, 152
"To my much honoured Friend, Henry Lord Carey of Lepington, upon his translation of Malvezzi" (Carew) **29**:65, 81
"To My Muse" (Jonson)
　　See "To My Muse"
"To My Playmate" (Viereck) **27**:263, 278, 281
"To My Prince's Command" (Wang Wei) **18**:366
"To My Rivall" (Carew) **29**:72
"To My Sister" (Roethke) **15**:275
"To my worthy Friend, M. D'Avenant, Upon his Excellent Play, The Just Italian" (Carew) **29**:83
"To my worthy friend Mr. George Sandys" (Carew) **29**:7, 17-18
"To Myself in an Album" (Zagajewski) **27**:389
"To Natal'ia" (Pushkin) **10**:404
"To Nature" (Holderlin)
　　See "An die Natur"
"To Night" (Shelley) **14**:171, 177
"To One in Paradise" (Poe) **1**:432-33, 437, 444, 446
"To One Who Died Young" (Reese) **29**:335

"To One Who Died Young" (Trakl)
    See "An einen Frühverstorbenen"
"To One Who Was With Me in the War"
    (Sassoon) **12**:246
"To Orlov" (Pushkin)
    See "Orlovu"
"To Paolo and Francesca in Purgatory" (Wylie)
    **23**:326
"To P'ei Ti" (Wang Wei) **18**:362-63, 373-74
"To Penshurst" (Jonson)
    See "To Penshurst"
"To Perenna" (Herrick) **9**:136-37
"To Perilla" (Herrick) **9**:127-28
"To Pile Like Thunder to Its Close"
    (Dickinson) **1**:102
"To Pliuskova" (Pushkin) **10**:409
"To R. B." (Hopkins) **15**:157
"To Raja Rao" (Milosz) **8**:195, 200
"To Remember" (Ekeloef) **23**:87
"To Rhea" (Emerson) **18**:102
"To Robert Burns" (Bridges) **28**:65
"To Robert Earle of Salisburie" (Jonson)
    See "To Robert Earle of Salisburie"
"To Robert Southey" (Coleridge) **11**:106
"To Robinson Jeffers" (Milosz) **8**:184, 199, 208
"To Roger Blin" (Stryk) **27**:203, 213
"To Roosevelt" (Dario)
    See "A Roosevelt"
"To S. M., A Young African Painter, on Seeing
    His Works" (Wheatley) **3**:336, 338, 344,
    362
"To Saxham" (Carew)
    See "Address to Saxham"
"To Science" (Poe) **1**:437
"To Secretary Ling-hu" (Wang Wei) **18**:373
"To Secretary Ling-hu" (Wang Wei) **18**:373
"To See a World in a Grain of Sand" (Blake)
    **12**:36
"To See the Heron" (Tomlinson) **17**:348
"To See the Heron" (Jonson)
    See "To Sir Horace Vere"
"To Sir Horace Vere" (Jonson)
    See "To Sir Horace Vere"
"To Sir Robert Wroth" (Jonson)
    See "To Sir Robert Wroth"
"To Sleep" (Graves) **6**:137
"To Some Winter Is Arrack" (Mandelstam)
    **14**:155
"To Speak of Woe That Is in Marriage"
    (Lowell) **3**:221, 245
"To Stand in Some" (AloneCummings) **5**:110
*To Stay Alive* (Levertov) **11**:178-80, 195
"To Stella, Visiting Me in My Sickness"
    (Swift) **9**:297
"To Stella, Who Collected and Transcribed His
    Poems, 1720" (Swift) **9**:255
"To Susan Countesse of Montgomerie"
    (Jonson)
    See "To Susan Countesse of Montgomerie"
"To Sylvia" (Herrick) **9**:97
"To T. A." (Kipling) **3**:191
"To The Airport" (Rich) **5**:382
"To the American Negro Troops" (Senghor)
    **25**:238
"To the Balloil Men Still in Africa" (Belloc)
    **24**:3, 11
"To the Bitter Sweet-Heart: A Dream" (Owen)
    **19**:352
"To the Boy Elis" (Trakl)
    See "An den Knaben Elis"
"To the Countess of Anglesie upon the
    immoderately-by-her lamented death of
    her Husband" (Carew) **29**:60-61
"To the Countesse of Bedford. 'Madame,
    reason is'" (Donne) **1**:123
"To the Countesse of Bedford. 'This twilight
    of'" (Donne) **1**:124
"To the Cuckoo" (Wordsworth) **4**:403
"To the Daisy" (Wordsworth) **4**:376
"To the Dean, when in England, in 1726"
    (Swift) **9**:255
"To the De'il" (Burns)
    See "Address to the De'il"
"To the Diaspora" (Brooks) **7**:84

"To the Dog Belvoir" (Smith) **12**:317
"To the Duke of Wellington" (Arnold) **5**:49
"To the Evening Star" (Blake) **12**:31
"To the Fair Clarinda Who Made Love to Me,
    Imagin'd More than Woman" (Behn)
    **13**:10, 13-14, 20, 22-3, 29
"To The Fringed Gentian" (Bryant) **20**:10, 35,
    45
"To the German Language" (Mandelstam)
    **14**:109
"To the Girl Who Lives in a Tree" (Lorde)
    **12**:154
"To the Governor and Legislature of
    Massachusetts" (Nemerov) **24**:262, 279
"To the Holy Ghost" (Skelton) **25**:339
"To the Honorable Edward Howard" (Behn)
    **13**:8
"To the Honorable the Lady Worsley at
    Longleat" (Finch) **21**:167, 176
"To the House" (Jeffers) **17**:131
"To the Immaculate Virgin, on a Winter Night"
    (Merton) **10**:339
"To the King" (Smart) **13**:342
"TO THE KING, upon His Comming with His
    Army into the West" (Herrick) **9**:109
"TO THE KING, upon His Welcome to
    Hampton-Court" (Herrick) **9**:109
"To the Lady Crew, upon the Death of Her
    Child" (Herrick) **9**:104, 131, 143
"To the Lark" (Herrick) **9**:98
*To the Memory of . . . George Duke of
    Buckingham* (Behn) **13**:9
"To the Memory of My Dear Daughter in Law,
    Mrs. Mercy Bradstreet" (Bradstreet) **10**:31
"To the Most Illustrious and Most Hopeful
    Prince, Charles" (Herrick) **9**:133
"To the Mothers of the Dead Militia" (Neruda)
    See "Canto a las madres de los milicianos
    muertos"
"To the Muse" (Blok)
    See "K Muze"
"To the Muses" (Blake) **12**:31
"To the Nightingale" (Finch) **21**:141, 144, 157-
    61, 175
"To the Not Impossible Him" (Millay) **6**:211,
    235
"To the Painter of an Ill-Drawn Picture of
    Cleone, the Honorable Mrs. Thynne"
    (Finch) **21**:164
"To the Peacock of France" (Moore) **4**:261
"To the Pious Memory of the Accomplisht
    Young Lady Mrs. Anne Killigrew"
    (Dryden) **25**:69
"To the Poet Who Happens to Be Black and
    the Black Poet Who Happens to Be a
    Woman" (Lorde) **12**:136
"To the Pushkin House" (Blok)
    See "Pushkinskomu domu"
"To the Queene" (Herrick) **9**:116
"To the Reader" (Baudelaire)
    See "Au lecteur"
"To the Reader" (Merrill) **28**:283
"To the Reader of Master William Davenant's
    Play" (Carew) **29**:84
"To the Right Honorable William, Earl of
    Dartmouth, His Majesty's Principal
    Secretary of State for North America"
    (Wheatley) **3**:337, 341, 343, 347, 350, 352
"To the Right Person" (Frost) **1**:200
"To the Road" (Dunbar) **5**:139
"To the Rose upon the Rood of Time" (Yeats)
    **20**:343
"To the Same" (Montagu) **16**:338
"To the Sea" (Larkin) **21**:238, 240
"To the Sea" (Pushkin)
    See "To the Sea"
"To the Second Person" (Skelton) **25**:339
"To the Shore" (Swenson) **14**:263
"To the Sister" (Trakl) **20**:248
"To the Snake" (Levertov) **11**:205
"To the South: On Its New Slavery" (Dunbar)
    **5**:131

"To the Statue" (Swenson) **14**:264
"To the Stone-Cutters" (Jeffers) **17**:117
"To the Tune of the Coventry Carol" (Smith)
    **12**:316, 330
"to the unborn and waiting children" (Clifton)
    **17**:19
"To the Union Savers of Cleveland" (Harper)
    **21**:190
"To the University of Cambridge, in New
    England" (Wheatley) **3**:337, 340-41, 344-
    45, 353
"To the Unknown God" (Hardy) **8**:121
"To the Unseeable Animal" (Berry) **28**:26
"To the Virgins, to Make Much of Time"
    (Herrick) **9**:100, 145
"To the Vision Seekers, Remember This"
    (Rose) **13**:241
"To the Water Nymphs Drinking at the
    Fountain" (Herrick) **9**:97
"To the White Fiends" (McKay) **2**:212, 216,
    218, 229
"To the Wife of a Sick Friend" (Millay) **6**:217
"To the World. A Farwell for a Gentlewoman,
    Vertuous and Nobel" (Jonson) **17**:172, 212
"To the Young Poets" (Holderlin)
    See "An die Jungen Dichter"
"To Thee" (Dario)
    See "A ti"
"To Thos. Floyd" (Bridges) **28**:88
"To Those Grown Mute" (Trakl) **20**:258
"To Those of My Sisters Who Kept Their
    Naturals" (Brooks) **7**:86
"To Time" (Clare) **23**:44
"To Tirzah" (Blake) **12**:7, 34-5
"To Tizengauzen" (Lermontov) **18**:284-85
*To Transfigure, To Organize* (Pasolini)
    See *Trasumanar e organizzar*
"To Urania" (Brodsky) **9**:25, 27
*To Urania: Selected Poems 1965-1985*
    (Brodsky) **9**:20, 23-4, 26, 29, 30
"To V. L. Davydovu" (Pushkin)
    See "V. L. Davydovu"
"To Victor Hugo of My Crow Pluto" (Moore)
    **4**:255, 259
"To Victory" (Sassoon) **12**:261, 263, 276
"To Virgil" (Tennyson) **6**:370
"To Waken an Old Lady" (Williams) **7**:345,
    353, 360, 363
"To Walk on Hills" (Graves) **6**:143
"To W.G.G." (McKay) **2**:226
"To What Listens" (Berry) **28**:9
"To What Serves Mortal Beauty" (Hopkins)
    **15**:144
"To William Simpson of Ochiltree, May 1785"
    (Burns)
    See "Epistle to William Simpson of
    Ochiltree, May 1785"
"To William Wordsworth Composed on the
    Night after His Recitation of a Poem on
    the Growth of the Individual Mind"
    (Coleridge) **11**:52-3, 58, 92, 106
"To Winkey" (Lowell) **13**:64
"To Winter" (Blake) **12**:32
"To Wisshe and Want" (Wyatt) **27**:316-317, 319
"To You" (Whitman) **3**:381
"To You Who Read My Book" (Cullen) **20**:55
"Toad dreams" (Piercy) **29**:297
"Toads" (Larkin) **21**:229, 234, 238
"Toads Revisited" (Larkin) **21**:229, 234, 237-
    38, 244
"Tobacco Shop" (Pessoa)
    See "Tabacaria"
"The Tobacconist's" (Pessoa)
    See "Tabacaria"
"A Toccata of Galuppi's" (Browning) **2**:37, 88
"Todas les efes tenía la novia que yo quería"
    (Fuertes) **27**:37
"Today" (Baraka) **4**:30
"Today" (Reese) **29**:346, 353
"Today and Tomorrow" (Rossetti) **7**:275, 277
"Todesfuge" (Celan) **10**:96, 102, 115-17,
    120-21

*Todo asusta* (Fuertes) **27**:10, 12
"Todtnauberg" (Celan) **10**:98
"Token Drunk" (Bukowski) **18**:15
"Told" (Levine) **22**:214, 224
"Tolerance" (Hardy) **8**:93
"Tolerance" (Pavese) **13**:205
"The Tollund Man" (Heaney) **18**:195, 202, 204, 210-11
"Tom May's Death" (Marvell) **10**:276
"Tom Merritt" (Masters) **1**:324
"Tom Snooks the Pundit" (Smith) **12**:333
"th tomato conspiracy aint worth a whol pome" (Bissett) **14**:23, 34
"The Tomb of Edgar Poe" (Mallarme)
　　See "Le tombeau d'Edgar Poe"
"The Tomb of Stuart Merrill" (Ashbery) **26**:145
"Tombeau de Charles IX" (Ronsard) **11**:243-44
"Le Tombeau de tres illustre Marguerite de France, duchesse de Savoye" (Ronsard) **11**:243-44
"Le tombeau d'Edgar Poe" (Mallarme) **4**:203, 209
"Le tombeau d'Edgard Poe" (Mallarme)
　　See "Le tombeau d'Edgar Poe"
"Le tombeau d'une mère" (Lamartine) **16**:264, 293
"The Tombstone-Maker" (Sassoon) **12**:242, 263
"Tom-Dobbin" (Gunn)
"Tomlinson" (Kipling) **3**:167, 182
"Tommy" (Kipling) **3**:187
"Tomorrow's Song" (Snyder) **21**:298
"Tom's Garland" (Hopkins) **15**:134, 138, 171
"Ton portrait" (Cesaire) **25**:31
"Ton Soir Mon Soir" (Senghor) **25**:249
"A Tone Poem" (Ashbery) **26**:132
"Tonique" (Tzara) **27**:230-31
"Too Blue" (Hughes) **1**:243
"Too Late" (Arnold) **5**:43, 56
"Toome" (Heaney) **18**:202, 204, 210, 241
"The Toome Road" (Heaney) **18**:246
"To--One word is too often profaned" (Shelley) **14**:233
*Topoemas* (Paz) **1**:363
*The Torch Bearers* (Noyes) **27**:128, 130, 133, 137-38
"Torch Procession" (Celan)
　　See "Fackelzug"
"The Torch-bearer's Race" (Jeffers) **17**:107
"Torero" (Stryk) **27**:187, 203, 214
"Torero nuestro de cada día" (Fuertes) **27**:38
"Tornado Warning" (Shapiro) **25**:306
"Tornant al pais" (Pasolini) **17**:252, 265
"La torre" (Olson) **19**:268, 293, 309-10
*The Torrent and the Night Before* (Robinson) **1**:459, 474, 484-85
"Torso" (Brodsky) **9**:8
"The Tortoise in Eternity" (Wylie) **23**:301, 309
"La tortuga de oro..." (Dario) **15**:99
"The Tortured Heart" (Rimbaud)
　　See "La coeur volé"
"The Total Influence or Outcome: The Sun" (Piercy) **29**:305-06
"Totem" (Cesaire) **25**:21-2
"Totem" (Plath) **1**:391, 393, 399, 412
"Totem" (Senghor) **25**:224, 230
"The Totem" (Swenson) **14**:249-50
"Totò Merùmeni" (Gozzano) **10**:184-88, 190
"Tou Wan Speaks to Her Husband, Liu Sheng" (Dove) **6**:107, 109
"Touch" (Gunn) **26**:195, 202, 207, 217, 219
"The Touch" (Sexton) **2**:352
*Touch* (Gunn) **26**:192, 196-197, 202-203, 207-209, 211-214, 219, 223, 225-226, 231
"Touch Me" (Kunitz) **19**:187
"Toujours Miroirs" (Senghor) **25**:251
"The Tour" (Plath) **1**:399-401
"Tour" (Wakoski) **15**:359
"Tour 5" (Hayden) **6**:189, 194
"Touring for Trujillo" (Guillen) **23**:126
"The Tourist and the Town" (Rich) **5**:353, 362
"Tournesol" (Breton) **15**:61-2

"Tout Entouré de Mon Regard" (Tomlinson) **17**:321, 339
*Toute la lyre* (Hugo) **17**:65, 86
"Toward an Organic Philosophy" (Rexroth) **20**:215, 217, 221
"Toward Siena" (Montale)
　　See "Verso Siena"
*Toward the Cradle of the World* (Gozzano)
　　See *Verso la cuna del mondo*
"Toward the Empty Earth" (Mandelstam)
　　See "K pustoi zemle nevol'no pripadaia"
*Toward the Gulf* (Masters) **1**:330, 332, 335, 342-44
"Toward the Piraeus" (H. D.) **5**:268, 304
"Toward the Solstice" (Rich) **5**:374
*Towards a New Poetry* (Wakoski) **15**:359
"Towards a New Scotland" (MacDiarmid) **9**:176
"Towards the Slave Quisqueya" (Guillen)
　　See "Towards the Slave Quisqueya"
"The Tower" (Yeats) **20**:310, 318, 320, 329, 334, 342
*The Tower* (Yeats) **20**:307, 311, 333, 335
"The Tower beyond Tragedy" (Jeffers) **17**:106, 108, 110, 112, 135, 144-46
*The Tower of Babel* (Merton) **10**:344, 349
"The Tower of Pisa" (Song) **21**:344
"The Tower of Siloam" (Graves) **6**:133
"The Tower Struck by Lightning Reversed; The Overturning of the Tower" (Piercy) **29**:324
"The Town" (Pushkin)
　　See "Gorodok"
"Town" (Soto) **28**:378, 385
"Town and Country" (Brooke) **24**:56
*The Town down the River* (Robinson) **1**:462-63, 467, 474, 478, 490
"The Town Dump" (Nemerov) **24**:257, 261, 291-92
"A Town Eclogue" (Swift) **9**:278
*Town Eclogues* (Montagu)
　　See *Court Poems*
"Towns in Colour" (Lowell) **13**:79
"Tract" (Williams) **7**:348, 362, 378
*Tractatus* (Marie de France) **22**:
"Tractor" (Hughes) **7**:166
"The Trade of an Irish Poet" (Heaney) **18**:201
"Tradimento" (Pavese) **13**:202, 226
"Traditions" (Heaney) **18**:252
"Tragedy of Teeth" (Kipling) **3**:194
"The Tragedy of the Leaves" (Bukowski) **18**:6, 21
"Tragic Books" (Reese) **29**:333, 335
"Tragic Destiny" (Aleixandre) **15**:10
"Traigo conmigo un cuidado" (Juana Ines de la Cruz) **24**:188
"Train Time" (Bogan) **12**:107
"Training" (Owen) **19**:336
"Trainor the Druggist" (Masters) **1**:347
"Trakat poetycki" (Milosz) **8**:198-99, 204
"Tramontana" (Montale) **13**:105, 126
"Tramontana at Lerici" (Tomlinson) **17**:342
"The Tramp Transfigured" (Noyes) **27**:121, 134
"Las Trampas USA" (Tomlinson) **17**:353
"A Trampwoman's Tragedy" (Hardy) **8**:99
"Trams" (Sitwell) **3**:301
"Transaction" (Ammons) **16**:22
"Transcedental Etude" (Rich) **5**:381
*The Transformation/Transformations* (Ovid)
　　See *Metamorphoses*
"Transformations" (Hardy) **8**:113
"Transformations" (Wright) **14**:339
*Transformations* (Sexton) **2**:349, 354-55, 362, 364-65, 368
"The Transformed One" (Olds) **22**:326
"Transgressing the Real" (Duncan) **2**:104
"Transients and Residents" (Gunn) **26**:220
"Transitional" (Williams) **7**:392
*Transitional Poem* (Day Lewis) **11**:123-25, 128-31, 133-35, 137, 143-45, 148, 151
"Translating the Birds" (Tomlinson) **17**:348, 350

*A Translation of the Psalms of David, Attempted in the Spirit of Christianity, and Adapted to the Divine Service* (Smart) **13**:330-32, 341-42, 362
"Translations" (Rich) **5**:397
*Translations, 1915-1920* (H. D.) **5**:304
*The Translations of Ezra Pound* (Pound) **4**:331
"Translations of the Psalms" (Wyatt) **27**:359
"Transparent Garments" (Hass) **16**:199, 210
"Transplanting" (Roethke) **15**:295
"Transport" (Meredith) **28**:174
"The Transport of Slaves from Maryland to Mississippi" (Dove) **6**:108
*Transport to Summer* (Stevens) **6**:301-03
"The Trap" (Wright) **14**:356
"Trapped Dingo" (Wright) **14**:345
"Le Trappist" (Vigny) **26**:401-402, 404
"The Trappist Abbey: Matins" (Merton) **10**:332
"The Trappist Cemetery, Gethsemani" (Merton) **10**:332-33, 342
"Trappists, Working" (Merton) **10**:332-33
*Trasumanar e organizzar* (Pasolini) **17**:273, 286
"Traum und Umnachtung" (Trakl) **20**:239, 268
"Träumerei am Abend" (Trakl) **20**:239
"Travel" (Brooke) **24**:66
"The Traveler" (Apollinaire)
　　See "Le voyageur"
"A Traveler at Night Writes His Thoughts" (Tu Fu) **9**:324
*The Traveler Does Not Return* (Nishiwaki)
　　See *Tabibito Kaerazu*
"Traveling on an Amtrack Train Could Humanize You" (Sanchez) **9**:234
"Traveling through Fog" (Hayden) **6**:194
"The Traveller and the Angel" (Wright) **14**:339, 346
"Traveller's Curse after Misdirection" (Graves) **6**:137
"Traveller's Palm" (Page) **12**:181
"Travelogue for Exiles" (Shapiro) **25**:269, 279, 290
"Travels in the South" (Ortiz) **17**:227, 231
"Tre donne intorno al cor mi son venute" (Dante) **21**:87
"The Treasure" (Brooke) **24**:87-9
"The Treasure" (Jeffers) **17**:117
"Treatise on Poetry" (Milosz)
　　See "Trakat poetycki"
"Trébol" (Dario) **15**:89
"The Tree" (Aleixandre) **15**:22
"The Tree" (Finch) **21**:149
"Tree" (Rukeyser) **12**:224
"Tree at My Window" (Frost) **1**:197, 205
"Tree Burial" (Bryant) **20**:14, 17
"Tree Disease" (Hughes) **7**:120
"Tree Planting" (Tagore)
　　See "Vriksha-ropan"
"A Tree Telling of Orpheus" (Levertov) **11**:177
*The Tree Witch* (Viereck) **27**:275-76, 278-80, 282
"The Trees" (Carruth) **10**:71
"Trees" (Hughes) **7**:120
"Trees" (Nemerov) **24**:266-67
"Trees" (Tsvetaeva)
　　See "Derev'ya"
"Trees" (Williams) **7**:351
"Trees in a Grove" (Meredith) **28**:170
"treez" (Bissett) **14**:24, 33
"La Treizieme" (Nerval) **13**:196; **67**:360
"Trelawnys Dream" (Meredith) **28**:215
"A Trellis for R." (Swenson) **14**:267, 280
*The Trembling of the Veil* (Yeats) **20**:330
"Tremor" (Zagajewski) **27**:395
*Tremor* (Zagajewski) **27**:380-81, 383-84, 389, 395, 397, 399
"Trench Poems" (Owen) **19**:350
"Trespass Into Spirit" (Baraka) **4**:24
*The Trespasser* (Stryk) **27**:191, 194, 197-98, 215-16, 218
"Trevenen" (Davie) **29**:103, 109
"Tri palmy" (Lermontov) **18**:268, 290-91, 293
"A Triad" (Rossetti) **7**:272-3, 275, 291

"The Trial" (Sassoon) **12**:260
"Trial of a Poet" (Shapiro) **25**:277-79
*Trial of a Poet* (Shapiro) **25**:273-74, 285, 290, 296, 319, 322, 324
"The Trial of Dead Cleopatra" (Lindsay) **23**:280, 286
"Trial-Pieces" (Heaney) **18**:246
"Tribal Scenes" (Song) **21**:345
"Tribe" (Song) **21**:336, 343
*Tribunals* (Duncan) **2**:106, 116, 127
"Tribute" (Brutus) **24**:111
"The Tribute" (H. D.) **5**:298, 304
*Tribute to the Angels* (H. D.) **5**:272, 274-75, 283-84, 286-87, 293-97, 308-09, 313, 315
"Trickle Drops" (Whitman) **3**:406
"Tricks with Mirrors" (Atwood) **8**:21-6
"Trickster 1977" (Rose) **13**:232
"Trillium" (Gluck) **16**:171
*Trilogie der Leidenschaft* (Goethe) **5**:250
*Trilogy* (H. D.) **5**:281, 283-86, 292-93, 2960-98, 304-07, 310-15
*Trilogy* (Wakoski) **15**:365
"Trinchera" (Borges) **22**:92
"Trinity Churchyard" (Rukeyser) **12**:225
"Trinity Peace" (Sandburg) **2**:304
"Trio for Two Cats and a Trombone" (Sitwell) **3**:303, 306
"Triolet" (Brooke) **24**:54
*Trionfi* (Petrarch) **8**:224-26, 238, 240, 243, 246, 252, 254, 257, 260, 273-78
"The Triple Fool" (Donne) **1**:125
"The Triple Fool" (Millay) **6**:243
"Triple Time" (Larkin) **21**:227, 236, 242
"Triptych" (Heaney) **18**:246
"El triste" (Borges) **22**:80
"Triste, triste" (Laforgue) **14**:86, 88-9
"Tristesse" (Lamartine) **16**:293
"Tristesse d'Olympio" (Hugo) **17**:64, 76-77, 82, 97
"Tristesse d'un étoile" (Apollinaire) **7**:3
"Les tristesses de la lune" (Baudelaire) **1**:44-5
"Tristia" (Mandelstam) **14**:106
*Tristia* (Mandelstam)
    See *Vtoraya kniga*
*Tristia* (Ovid) **2**:233, 240-42, 244-45, 252-53, 255-59
*Tristibus* (Ovid)
    See *Tristia*
*Tristram* (Robinson) **1**:470-72, 474-75, 481, 489
"Tristram and Iseult" (Arnold) **5**:9, 12, 33-4, 42, 49, 64
*Tristram of Lyonesse* (Swinburne) **24**:307, 309, 310, 313-14, 316, 319, 321-23, 348-50, 352, 355-57
"Tritiya" (Tagore) **8**:415
"Triumph" (Reese) **29**:332
*The Triumph of Achilles* (Gluck) **16**:149, 151-52, 155-57, 159, 163
"Triumph of Charis" (Jonson)
    See *A Celebration of Charis in Ten Lyric Pieces*
*The Triumph of Life* (Shelley) **14**:174, 188, 193, 211
"The Triumph of Time" (Swinburne) **24**:308, 322, 325, 337-38, 342-43
*Triumphal March* (Eliot) **5**:168, 185
*Triumphs* (Petrarch)
    See *Trionfi*
"The Triumphs of Bacchus" (Pushkin) **10**:407
"Trivial Breath" (Wylie) **23**:310
*Trivial Breath* (Wylie) **23**:302, 307-309, 324-25
"Trofeo" (Borges) **22**:93
*Troilus* (Chaucer)
    See *Troilus and Criseyde*
*Troilus and Criseyde* (Chaucer) **19**:6-7, 11, 13, 15, 23, 36-9, 42-3, 60-1, 63, 73-5
*Troilus and Cryseide* (Chaucer)
    See *Troilus and Criseyde*
"Trois Ans après" (Hugo) **17**:83
*Les trois livres du recueil des nouvelles poesies* (Ronsard) **11**:248
*Troisìme livre des odes* (Ronsard) **11**:283

"Trompeten" (Trakl) **20**:250, 254-55
"Troop Train" (Shapiro) **25**:263, 268, 288, 295, 297, 324
"Tropical Birdland" (Alegria) **26**:
"The Tropics in New York" (McKay) **2**:228
"Trostnik" (Lermontov) **18**:304
"A troubadour I traverse all my land" (Brutus) **24**:113
"Trouble in De Kitchen" (Dunbar) **5**:146
"The Trouble is with No and Yes" (Roethke) **15**:277
"The Trouble with Women Is Men" (Nash) **21**:268, 274
"The Troubled Bay" (Cassian) **17**:11, 13
*Troy Park* (Sitwell) **3**:293-94, 298, 301, 303, 307-08, 320
"The Truce of the Bear" (Kipling) **3**:171, 182
"Las truchas" (Forche) **10**:134
"Truck-Garden-Market Day" (Millay) **6**:232
"The True Beatitude" (Brooke) **24**:57
"True Confessional" (Ferlinghetti) **1**:187
"The True Import of Present Dialogue, Black vs. Negro" (Giovanni) **19**:107, 114-15, 139
"True Love" (Olds) **22**:338
"True Night" (Snyder) **21**:300
"True Pearl--Belle of the Lo" (Li Ho) **13**:54
"True Recognition Often Is Refused" (Schwartz) **8**:292
"True Romance" (Kipling) **3**:161
*True Stories* (Atwood) **8**:43
"True Tenderness" (Akhmatova) **2**:14
"The True, the Good, and the Beautiful" (Schwartz) **8**:292
"True Vine" (Wylie) **23**:303, 305, 323
"Truganinny" (Rose) **13**:240
"Trumpet Player: 52nd Street" (Hughes) **1**:241, 247, 249
"The Trusting Heart" (Parker) **28**:362
"Truth" (Ashbery) **26**:
"Truth" (Brooks) **7**:61
"The Truth" (Jimenez)
    See "Paisaje del corozon"
"Truth" (McKay) **2**:215
"The Truth" (Montale) **13**:156
"Truth and Error" (Goethe) **5**:228
"Truth Is Not the Secret of a Few" (Ferlinghetti) **1**:186
"Truth Kills Everybody" (Hughes) **7**:160
"The Truth of the Matter" (Nemerov) **24**:290
"The Truth the Dead Know" (Sexton) **2**:346, 361
*Tryflings* (Ekeloef) **23**:63
"Tsar Sultan" (Pushkin)
    See "Skazka o Tsare Sultane"
*Tsar-devitsa* (Tsvetaeva) **14**:313, 325-26
*The Tsar-Maiden* (Tsvetaeva)
    See *Tsar-devitsa*
*Tsuki ni hoeru* (Hagiwara Sakutaro) **18**:169, 172-73, 175-82
"Tsung-wu's Birthday" (Tu Fu) **9**:324
"Tsurugai Bridge" (Ishikawa)
    See "Tsurugaibashi"
"Tsurugaibashi" (Ishikawa) **10**:213
*Tsygany* (Pushkin) **10**:357-61, 365-66, 369, 371, 386-89, 391-92, 398, 410
"Tú" (Guillen) **23**:134-37
"Il tu" (Montale) **13**:132
"Tú no sabe inglé" (Guillen) **23**:142
"Tu Parles" (Senghor) **25**:250
"tu Te Languis" (Senghor) **25**:249-50
"Tuesday: St. James's Coffee-house: Silliander and Patch" (Montagu) **16**:348
"Tulip" (McGuckian) **27**:79-80, 102
"Tulips" (Page) **12**:176
"Tulips" (Plath) **1**:390, 395, 399-401, 405, 407, 409, 414
*Tulips and Chimneys* (Cummings) **5**:74-5, 77-8, 86, 91, 93-4, 104
"Tulpen" (Celan) **10**:122-23
"Tumbling-Hair" (Cummings) **5**:104
"Tumi o ami" (Tagore) **8**:414

"A Tune for Festive Dances in the Nineteen Sixties" (Merton) **10**:345
"Tunk: A Lecture of Modern Education" (Johnson) **24**:141, 163
"The Tunnel" (Crane) **3**:86, 88-90, 106-07, 110-11
*The Tunnynge of Elynour Rummynge* (Skelton) **25**:330, 332, 338, 342, 347-49, 361-62, 364, 367, 386-88, 390-93
"Il tuo volo" (Montale) **13**:111
"Turin" (Gozzano) **10**:177, 180
"The Turkey in the Straw" (Williams) **7**:400
"Turkeys Observed" (Heaney) **18**:189, 200
"Turkish Verses" (Montagu) **16**:338
"The Turn of the Moon" (Graves) **6**:154, 156
"The Turncoat" (Baraka) **4**:5, 14
"turning" (Clifton) **17**:21
"The Turning" (Levine) **22**:212
"Turning" (Rilke) **2**:280-81
"Turning a Moment to Say So Long" (Ammons) **16**:39
"Turning Fifty" (Wright) **14**:355
"Turning To" (Kumin) **15**:182
"A Turning Wind" (Rukeyser) **12**:213
*A Turning Wind* (Rukeyser) **12**:211-12
*Turns and Movies and Other Tales in Verse* (Aiken) **26**:21, 50, 53
*Turns and Movies The Devine Pilgrim* (Aiken) **26**:
"The Turtle" (Nash) **21**:278
*Turtle Island* (Snyder) **21**:290-300, 306-08, 310, 316-17, 320, 324-25
"Tutecotzimí" (Dario) **15**:92
"Tutto é sciolto" (Joyce) **22**:136
"The Twa Dogs" (Burns) **6**:51, 78, 83-4, 88
"The Twa Herds" (Burns) **6**:85
"Twelfth Night" (Belloc) **24**:49
"Twelfth Night, Next Year, a Weekend in Eternity" (Schwartz) **8**:294
"XII" (Joyce) **22**:136, 138, 145, 164, 169, 171
*The Twelve* (Blok)
    See *Dvenadsat*
"Twelve Articles" (Swift) **9**:260
"The Twelve Dancing Princesses" (Sexton) **2**:365
"Twelve Months After" (Sassoon) **12**:288
*The Twelve-Spoked Wheel Flashing* (Piercy) **29**:311, 313
*Twentieth Century Harlequinade* (Sitwell) **3**:299-300, 302
"20th-century Fox" (Baraka) **4**:11
"XX" (Joyce) **22**:145, 168
"" (Larkin) **21**:242
*Twenty Love Poems and a Despairing Song* (Neruda)
    See *Veinte poemas de amor y una canción desesperada*
*Twenty Love Poems and a Desperate Song* (Neruda)
    See *Veinte poemas de amor y una canción desesperada*
*Twenty Love Poems and a Song of Despair* (Neruda)
    See *Veinte poemas de amor y una canción desesperada*
*Twenty Love Poems and One Song of Despair* (Neruda)
    See *Veinte poemas de amor y una canción desesperada*
*XX Poems* (Larkin) **21**:226, 229
*Twenty Poems* (Neruda)
    See *Veinte poemas de amor y una canción desesperada*
*Twenty Poems* (Trakl) **20**:227
"XXVIII" (Joyce) **22**:145, 154, 159, 162, 169, 172
"28" (Levine) **22**:224
"Twenty-fifth of Vaisakh" (Tagore)
    See "Panchishe vaisakh"
"XXV" (Joyce) **22**:139, 160, 173
*Twenty-Five Poems* (Thomas) **2**:378, 389
"XXIV" (Joyce) **22**:136, 139, 170, 172-73

"Twenty-Four Hokku on a Modern Theme" (Lowell) **13**:66
"Twenty-four Poems" (Schwartz) **8**:302
"Twenty-Four Years" (Thomas) **2**:383
"XXIX" (Joyce) **22**:145, 167, 170, 173
"XXI" (Joyce) **22**:146, 166-68, 170
*Twenty-One Love Poems* (Rich) **5**:384, 395
"XXVII" (Joyce) **22**:145, 156, 170, 172-73
"XXVI" (Joyce) **22**:136, 139, 168, 171, 173
"XXIII" (Joyce) **22**:145, 170
"XXII" (Joyce) **22**:138, 145, 170-71, 173
"Twenty-two Rhymes" (Tu Fu) **9**:326
"Twice" (Rossetti) **7**:267, 275
*Twice or thrice had I loved thee* (Donne)
See *Aire and Angels*
"Twicknam Garden" (Donne) **1**:124, 130, 134
"Twilight" (Apollinaire)
See "Crépuscule"
"Twilight" (Clare) **23**:47
"Twilight" (Kunitz) **19**:147
"The Twilight Bell" (Ishikawa)
See "Kure no kane"
*The Twilight Book* (Neruda)
See *Crepúsculario*
"The Twilight of Freedom" (Mandelstam) **14**:106, 147
"Twilight of the Outward Life" (Viereck) **27**:263
"Twilight Reverie" (Hughes) **1**:255
*Twilight Songs* (Hugo) **17**:45
*The Twin In the Clouds* (Pasternak)
See *Bliznets v tuchakh*
"The Twins" (Bukowski) **18**:4, 22
"Twister" (Stryk) **27**:211
"II" (Joyce) **22**:138, 165-66
"Two Amsterdams" (Ferlinghetti) **1**:183
"The Two April Mornings" (Wordsworth) **4**:374
"The Two Brothers" (Lermontov) **18**:299
"Two Children" (Graves) **6**:156
"Two Children" (Guillen)
See "Dos niños"
"Two Cigarettes" (Pavese)
See "Due sigarette"
"Two days of fever" (Pasolini) **17**:279
"Two Deaths" (Olds) **22**:317
"Two Easter Stanzas" (Lindsay) **23**:282
"Two Egyptian Portrait Masks" (Hayden) **6**:185
"Two English Poems" (Borges) **22**:95
"Two Eskimo Songs" (Hughes) **7**:153, 159
*Two Figures* (Momaday) **25**:201
"Two Figures from the Movies" (Meredith) **28**:187, 210
"The Two Fires" (Atwood) **8**:37
*The Two Fires* (Wright) **14**:341-49, 353-55, 369
*The Two Foscari* (Byron) **16**:103
"Two Generations" (Wright) **14**:344, 354
"Two Girls" (Nemerov) **24**:291
"Two Gun Buster and Trigger Slim" (Walker) **20**:273
"Two Hands" (Sexton) **2**:371
"Two higher mammals" (Piercy) **29**:303
"Two Hours in an Empty Tank" (Brodsky) **9**:2, 4
"Two Hymns" (Ammons) **16**:4
"Two in the Campagna" (Browning) **2**:68
"Two in the Twilight" (Montale)
See "Due nel crepuscolo"
"Two Legends" (Hughes) **7**:159
"Two Little Boots" (Dunbar) **5**:122, 129
"Two Look at Two" (Frost) **1**:194, 229, 231
"Two Lovers" (Eliot) **20**:123
"The Two Lovers" (Marie de France)
See "Les Dous Amanz"
"Two Masks Unearthed in Bulgaria" (Meredith) **28**:182
"Two Night Pieces" (Sitwell) **3**:293
"The Two Offers" (Harper) **21**:194
"Two Old Crows" (Lindsay) **23**:281
"Two Pair" (Nemerov) **24**:302
"The Two Parents" (MacDiarmid) **9**:156, 176
"Two Parted" (Rossetti) **7**:276

"Two Pendants: For the Ears" (Williams) **7**:360, 364, 394
"Two Poems" (Madhubuti) **5**:321
"2 Poems for Black Relocation Centers" (Knight) **14**:46-8
"Two Poets" (Cullen) **20**:68
"Two Preludes" (Swinburne) **24**:323
"Two Rivers" (Emerson) **18**:76, 88-89
"The Two Roads" (Gozzano) **10**:177-78
"Two Scavengers in a Truck, Two Beautiful People in a Mercedes" (Ferlinghetti) **1**:183, 188
"Two Songs" (Rich) **5**:365
"Two Songs from a Play" (Yeats) **20**:315, 319
"Two Songs of a Fool" (Yeats) **20**:304
"Two Speak Together" (Lowell) **13**:96-7
"Two Stories" (Gallagher) **9**:36
"The Two Thieves" (Wordsworth) **4**:374, 388
"Two Tramps in Mud Time" (Frost) **1**:198, 221
"The Two Travellers" (Bryant) **20**:10, 16
"The Two Trees" (Yeats) **20**:317
"221-1424" (San Francisco suicide number Sanchez) **9**:211, 224-25
"Two Views of a Cadaver Room" (Plath) **1**:389
"The Two Voices" (Tennyson) **6**:360
"Two Who Crossed a Line" (He Crosses Cullen) **20**:86
*Two Women, Two Shores* (McGuckian) **27**:95
"Two Years Later" (Yeats) **20**:338
"Two-an'-Six" (McKay) **2**:208-09
"The Two-Days-Old Baby" (Blake)
See "Infant Joy"
*Two-Headed Poems* (Atwood) **8**:43
*Two-Headed Woman* (Clifton) **17**:17-18, 23-24, 26-27, 34-35
"Two-Part Pear Able" (Swenson) **14**:247
*2000* (Neruda) **4**:287
"Two-Volume Novel" (Parker) **28**:352, 359, 352
"Tyaroye" (Senghor) **25**:235
"The Tyger" (Blake) **12**:6-7, 10, 25, 30, 34-5, 59-64
"The Typical American?" (Masters) **1**:343
"Typists" (Page) **12**:173
"Typists in the Phoenix Building" (Wright) **14**:348
*Tyrannus Nix?* (Ferlinghetti) **1**:174
"Tyrian Businesses" (Olson) **19**:280, 283
"Tzu-yeh Song #3" (Li Po) **29**:
"U nog drugikh ne zabyval" (Lermontov) **18**:302
*U samovo morya* (Akhmatova) **2**:15
"U tonkoi pnovoloki nad volnoi ovsov" (Tsvetaeva) **14**:319, 321, 323
"Uber Das Werden im Vergehen" (Holderlin) **4**:147
"Ugolino" (Heaney) **18**:240
"Uh, Philosophy" (Ammons) **16**:6, 13, 36-7
"Ulalume" (Poe) **1**:425-26, 428, 431, 434, 436, 439-40, 442-43, 447, 453
"A Ultima Nau" (Pessoa) **20**:162
"Ultima Ratio Reagan" (Nemerov) **24**:290
"Ultimate Birth" (Aleixandre) **15**:3
"The Ultimate Infidelity" (Gozzano) **10**:180
"The Ultimate Poem Is Abstract" (Stevens) **6**:314
"Ultimatum" (Cullen) **20**:57
"Ultimatum" (Larkin) **21**:224-25
"Ultimatum" (Sassoon) **12**:259
"El último amor" (Aleixandre) **15**:38
"Ultraísmo" (Borges) **22**:93
"Ulysses" (Graves) **6**:130, 137
"Ulysses" (Tennyson) **6**:354, 359, 366, 381, 383-84, 398, 409, 411
"An Umbrella" (Stein) **18**:334
"Umi no ikari" (Ishikawa) **10**:215
"L'umile Italia" (Pasolini) **17**:294
"A un poeta del siglo XIII" (Borges) **22**:82, 85
"A un riche" (Hugo) **17**:94
"Unable to Hate or Love" (Page) **12**:175
"The Unacknowledged Legislator's Dream" (Heaney) **18**:205

"Un'altra risorta" (Gozzano) **10**:185
"Un-American Investigators" (Hughes) **1**:252
*Unattainable Earth* (Milosz)
See *Niobjeta ziemia*
"Unbelief" (Pushkin)
See "Bezverie"
"The Unbeliever" (Bishop) **3**:48
"The Unborn" (Wright) **14**:352
"Unclassified Poem" (Wang Wei) **18**:387
"Unclassified Poems of Ch'in-chou" (Tu Fu) **9**:332
"Uncle Jim" (Cullen) **20**:64
"The Uncle Speaks in the Drawing Room" (Rich) **5**:359, 392
"Unclench Yourself" (Piercy) **29**:310
"Uncollected Poems" (Crane) **3**:90
"The Uncreation" (Pinsky) **27**:164
"Under" (Sandburg) **2**:300
*Under a Soprano Sky* (Sanchez) **9**:238-39, 245
"Under Ben Bulben" (Yeats) **20**:312, 324, 333
"Under Libra" (Merrill) **28**:223, 256
"Under Saturn" (Yeats) **20**:342
"Under Sirius" (Auden) **1**:23
"Under St. Paul's" (Davie) **29**:94
"Under Stars" (Gallagher) **9**:37, 58, 60
*Under Stars* (Gallagher) **9**:37, 42, 54, 58-60
"Under the Bamboo Tree" (Johnson) **24**:151, 170
"Under the Cupola" (Merrill) **28**:251-52
"Under the Earth" (Aleixandre) **15**:20-2
"Under the L.A. Airport" (Ortiz) **17**:229
"Under the Maud Moon" (Kinnell) **26**:247-52, 255, 257, 264, 272
"Under the Mistletoe" (Cullen) **20**:85
"Under the Moon's Reign" (Tomlinson) **17**:336, 349
"Under the Olives" (Graves) **6**:155-56
"Under the Rose" (Rossetti) **7**:266
"Under the Viaduct" (Dove) **6**:110
"Under the Waterfall" (Hardy) **8**:118
"Under Willows" (Rossetti) **7**:285
*Undersong: Chosen Poems Old and New* (Revised Lorde) **12**:153-58
"Understanding but not Forgetting" (Madhubuti) **5**:337-38, 340
"The Undertaking" (Gluck) **16**:126, 128, 142
"Underwear" (Ferlinghetti) **1**:183
*The Under-Wood* (Jonson) **17**:191
*The Under-Wood* (Jonson) **17**:169, 180
*The Under-Wood II* (Jonson) **17**:171, 194-95, 214
*The Under-Wood III* (Jonson) **17**:195
*The Under-Wood IV* (Jonson) **17**:194
*The Under-Wood LVI* (Jonson) **17**:194
*The Under-Wood LVIII* (Jonson) **17**:194
*The Under-Wood LXII* (Jonson) **17**:156
*The Under-Wood LXIV* (Jonson) **17**:156
*The Under-Wood LXIX* (Jonson) **17**:153
*The Under-Wood LXVIII* (Jonson) **17**:156
*The Under-Wood LXX* (Jonson) **17**:164
*The Under-Wood LXXI* (Jonson) **17**:162
*The Under-Wood LXXII* (Jonson) **17**:193
*The Under-Wood LXXVI* (Jonson) **17**:156
*The Under-Wood LXXXVI* (Jonson) **17**:191
*The Under-Wood XIII* (Jonson) **17**:154, 157-59, 211
*The Under-Wood XL* (Jonson) **17**:194
*The Under-Wood XLII* (Jonson) **17**:180
*The Under-Wood XLIV* (Jonson) **17**:194
*The Under-Wood XLV* (Jonson) **17**:181, 189
*The Under-Wood XLVII* (Jonson) **17**:153-54, 208
*The Under-Wood XV* (Jonson) **17**:153, 158, 161-62, 164, 208
*The Under-Wood XVI* (Jonson) **17**:191
*The Under-Wood XXIX* (Jonson) **17**:189
*The Under-Wood XXVI* (Jonson) **17**:153, 172, 192
*The Under-Wood XXXI* (Jonson) **17**:193
*The Under-Wood XXXVII* (Jonson) **17**:153-54
"The Underworld" (Hongo) **23**:199

"Undraped Beauty" (Tagore)
See "Vivasana"
"A une femme" (Hugo) **17**:68
"A une robe rose" (Gautier) **18**:125, 129
*Unedited Books of Poetry* (Jimenez)
See "A Horrible Religious Error"
"The Unending Rose" (Borges) **22**:97
"The Unending Rose" (Borges) **22**:
"Unendurable Love" (Tagore)
See "Asahya bhalobasa"
"The Unequal Fetters" (Finch) **21**:154, 181
"Unequalled Days" (Pasternak)
See "Edinstvennye dni"
"Unexpected Joy" (Blok) **21**:3
"The Unexplorer" (Millay) **6**:235
"The Unfaithful Married Woman" (Garcia
Lorca)
See "La casada infiel"
"The Unfaithful Wife" (Garcia Lorca)
See "La casada infiel"
"Unfinished Ballad" (Wylie) **23**:321
"Unfinished Portrait" (Wylie) **23**:318, 322, 324
"Unfold! Unfold!" (Roethke) **15**:248, 254, 276,
300-03
"The Unfortunate Lover" (Marvell) **10**:265-66,
271, 300, 302
"The Unfortunate One" (Marie de France)
See "Le Chaitivel"
"UnfortunateCoincidence" (Parker) **28**:360
*Ungathered Verse* (Jonson) **17**:161
"Ungratefulnesse" (Herbert) **4**:119, 133-34
"Unidentified Flying Object" (Hayden) **6**:196
"L'Union libre" (Breton) **15**:51, 62
"Unión Soviética" (Guillen) **23**:123, 127
"The Unions at the Front" (Neruda)
See "Los Grernios en el frente"
"A Unison" (Williams) **7**:360
"The United Fruit Company" (Neruda)
See "La United Fruit Company"
"La United Fruit Company" (Neruda) **4**:296
"U.S. 1946 King's X" (Frost) **1**:200
*U.S. One* (Rukeyser) **12**:203-04, 211
"The Universal Andalusia" (Jimenez)
See "El andaluz universal"
*Universal Prayer* (Pope) **26**:311
"Universal Sorrow" (Tagore)
See "Vishvashoka"
"The Universe" (Swenson) **14**:258, 268, 281
"University" (Shapiro) **25**:279, 283, 290, 297-
300, 311, 313, 318
"The Unjustly Punished Child" (Olds) **22**:307
"The Unknown" (Williams) **7**:369
"Unknown Girl in the Maternity Ward"
(Sexton) **2**:349, 355
"The Unknown Neighbor" (Stryk) **27**:201
"Unknown Water" (Wright) **14**:341, 353
"The Unknown Woman" (Blok) **21**:14
"Unnatural Powers" (Jeffers) **17**:118
"The Unpardonable Sin" (Lindsay) **23**:280
"Unregierbarkeit" (Enzensberger) **28**:150
"Unresolved" (Levertov) **11**:198
"The Unreturning" (Owen) **19**:343
"Les uns et les autres" (Verlaine) **2**:416
"An Unsaid Word" (Rich) **5**:359, 393
"The Unseen" (Pinsky) **27**:163
"Unsere Marine" (Heine) **25**:134
"The Unsettled Motorcyclist's Vision of His
Death" (Gunn) **26**:185, 207
"The Unsettled Motorcyclist's Vision of His
Death" (Gunn) **26**:
"Unsleeping City" (Brooklyn Bridge
NocturneGarcia Lorca)
See "Ciudad sin sueño"
"Unsounded" (Rich) **5**:359
"The Unsung Heroes" (Dunbar) **5**:131
"Unsuspecting" (Toomer) **7**:336
"Der Untergand der Titanic" (Enzensberger)
**28**:149-51, 158, 160, 164-66
"Untergang" (Trakl) **20**:234, 264-65, 267, 269
"Untitled" (Swenson) **14**:274, 285
*Unto Dyvers People* (Skelton) **25**:374

"Unto the Whole—How Add?" (Dickinson)
**1**:103
"The Untrustworthy Speaker" (Gluck) **16**:157
"Unwilling Admission" (Wylie) **23**:310
*The Unwritten* (Sikelianos)
See "Agraphon"
"Unylyi kolokola zvon" (Lermontov) **18**:302
"Gli uomini che si voltano" (Montale) **13**:133
"L'uomo di pena" (Pasolini) **17**:261
"Up and Down" (Merrill) **28**:222
"Up and Down" (Smith) **12**:316
"Up at a Villa-Down in the City, as
Distinguished by an Italian Person of
Quality" (Browning) **2**:38
"Up at La Serra" (Tomlinson) **17**:311, 325-26,
341
"Up Branches of Duck River" (Snyder) **21**:297
*Up Country: Poems of New England* (Kumin)
**15**:181-83, 187, 189, 194, 208
"Up Hill" (Rossetti) **7**:261, 298
"The Up Rising" (Duncan) **2**:104
"Upahar" (Tagore) **8**:407
"The Upas Tree" (Pushkin)
See "Anchar"
"An Upbraiding" (Hardy) **8**:93
"Uplands" (Ammons) **16**:31
*Uplands* (Ammons) **16**:22, 28, 46, 61
"Upon a Beautiful Young Nymph Going to
Bed" (Swift)
See "A Beautiful Young Nymph Going to
Bed. Written for the Honour of the Fair
Sex"
"Upon a Child. An Epitaph" (Herrick) **9**:129-31
"Upon a Child That Died" (Herrick) **9**:130-31
"Upon a Comely and Curious Maide"
(Herrick) **9**:129
*Upon a Dead Man's Head* (Skelton) **25**:344
"Upon a fit of Sickness, Anno 1632"
(Bradstreet) **10**:20, 26, 34, 59
"Upon A Mole in Celia's Bosom" (Carew)
**29**:43
"Upon a Ribband" (Carew) **29**:9
"Upon Appleton House" (Marvell) **10**:260, 265-
67, 269, 271-73, 289-91, 294, 298, 303-04,
314-15, 318
"Upon Ben Jonson" (Herrick) **9**:86
"Upon Her Blush" (Herrick) **9**:143
"Upon Himself" (Herrick) **9**:89, 109
"Upon Himselfe Being Buried" (Herrick) **9**:128,
131
"Upon His Kinswoman Mistris Elizabeth
Herrick" (Herrick) **9**:131
"Upon His Last Request to Julia" (Herrick)
**9**:108
"Upon His Returning Home to Pei-hai, I
Respectfully Offer a Farewell Banquet to
Reverend Master Kao Ju-Kuei,
Gentleman of the Tao after He
Transmitted to Me a Register of the
Way" (Li Po) **29**:171
"Upon Julia's Clothes" (Herrick) **9**:135-36
"Upon Julia's Recovery" (Herrick) **9**:102
"Upon Julia's Washing Her Self in the River"
(Herrick) **9**:143
"Upon Meeting Don L. Lee, in a Dream"
(Dove) **6**:104-05, 108
"Upon My Daughter Hannah Wiggin Her
Recovery from a Dangerous Fever"
(Bradstreet) **10**:34
"Upon My Dear and Loving Husband His
Goeing into England" (Bradstreet)
See "To My Dear and Loving Husband His
Goeing into England"
"Upon My Lord Winchilsea's Converting the
Mount in His Garden to a Terras" (Finch)
**21**:176
"Upon My Son Samuel His Going to England,
November 6, 1959" (Bradstreet) **10**:26,
34, 36, 63

"Upon occasion of his Ode of defiance annext
to his Play of the new Inne" (Carew)
See "To Ben Jonson Upon occasion of his
Ode of defiance annext to his play of the
new Inne"
"Upon the Annunciation and Passion" (Donne)
**1**:139
"Upon the Death of King James the Second"
(Finch) **21**:170
"Upon the Death of O.C." (Marvell)
See "Poem upon the Death of O. C."
"Upon the Death of Sir William Twisden"
(Finch) **21**:144
"Upon the Death of the Lord Protector"
(Marvell)
See "Poem upon the Death of O. C."
"Upon the Dolorous Death and Much
Lamentable Chance of the Most
Honourable Earl of Northumberland"
(Skelton) **25**:339, 372
"Upon the Hill and Grove at Billborow"
(Marvell) **10**:269
"Upon the Much Lamented, Master J. Warr"
(Herrick) **9**:129
"Upon the Nipples of Julia's Breast" (Herrick)
**9**:143
"Upon the Roses in Julias Bosome" (Herrick)
**9**:143
"Upon Your Held-Out Hand" (Thomas) **2**:406
"Uptown" (Ginsberg) **4**:47
"The Urals" (Pasternak) **6**:268
"Urania" (Arnold) **5**:43
"An Urban Convalescence" (Merrill) **28**:226,
234, 249, 273
*Urbasi* (Tagore) **8**:403
"Uriel" (Emerson) **18**:69, 79, 88
"The Urn" (Olds) **22**:324
*The Urn* (Bely)
See *Urna*
*Urna* (Bely) **11**:3-4, 6-7, 24, 32-3
"Urvashi" (Tagore) **8**:409
"Us" (Sexton) **2**:352
"The Use of 'Tu'" (Montale) **13**:145
"Used Up" (Sandburg) **2**:303
"Useless" (Atwood) **8**:27
"Usignolo VI" (Pasolini) **17**:266
"Usignolo VII" (Pasolini) **17**:266
*L'usignuolo della Chiesa Cattolica* (Pasolini)
**17**:252, 262, 264-67, 270, 272, 275, 277,
285, 287
"Ustica" (Paz) **1**:355, 360-61
"Uswetakiyawa" (Ondaatje) **28**:338
"Ut Pictura" (Ashbery) **26**:
*Ut Pictura Poesis* (Ashbery) **26**:
"Utopia" (Enzensberger) **28**:159
"Utopias" (Eliot) **20**:123
"Utopie" (Lamartine) **16**:263, 284
"Utsarga" (Tagore) **8**:409
"Uznik" (Lermontov) **18**:304
"V Al'bom" (Lermontov) **18**:302
"V bol'nitse" (Pasternak) **6**:266, 269, 286-87
"V den' Blagoveshchen'ia" (Tsvetaeva) **14**:322
"V. L. Davydovu" (Pushkin) **10**:412
"V lesu" (Pasternak) **6**:280
"V ony dni, ty mne byla kak mat'" (Tsvetaeva)
**14**:321
"V starinny gody zhili-byli" (Lermontov)
**18**:288
"vaalee daancers" (Bissett) **14**:33
"The Vacant Lot" (Brooks) **7**:69
"Vacation" (Shapiro) **25**:310, 316
"Vacation" (Zagajewski) **27**:389
*Vacation Time: Poems for Children* (Giovanni)
**19**:138
"La Vache" (Hugo) **17**:76, 91
"Vacillation" (Yeats) **20**:333
"Vagabonds" (Rimbaud) **3**:261
*Vägvisare till underjorden* (Ekeloef) **23**:62,
68-9, 77-8
"Vain and Careless" (Graves) **6**:141, 150
"Vain Word" (Borges)
See "Vanilocuencia"

"Les vaines danseuses" (Valery) **9**:392
"Vaishnava kavita" (Tagore) **8**:408
"Vaishnava Poetry" (Tagore)
    See "Vaishnava kavita"
"Vaivén" (Paz) **1**:359
*Vala* (Blake)
    See *The Four Zoas: The Torments of Love
    and Jealousy in the Death and
    Judgement of Albion the Ancient Man*
*Vala* (Blake)
    See *The Four Zoas: The Torments of Love
    and Jealousy in the Death and
    Judgement of Albion the Ancient Man*
*Vale* (Viereck) **27**:259, 278
*Vale Ave* (H. D.) **5**:282
"The Vale of Esthwaite" (Wordsworth) **4**:417
"Valediction" (Heaney) **18**:207
"A Valediction: forbidding mourning" (Donne)
    **1**:124, 126, 130, 135
"A Valediction Forbidding Mourning" (Rich)
    **5**:371, 395
"A Valediction: of my name, in the window"
    (Donne) **1**:152
"A Valediction: of the booke" (Donne) **1**:128,
    130
"A Valediction: of weeping" (Donne) **1**:124,
    130, 153
"Valentine" (Ashbery) **26**:145
"A Valentine" (Poe) **1**:445
"Valentine" (Wylie) **23**:332
"Valentine" (Zukofsky) **11**:349
"Valentine Delivered by a Raven" (Gallagher)
    **9**:63
"Valentine I" (Bishop) **3**:36
"Valerik" (Lermontov) **18**:283
"Valley Candle" (Stevens) **6**:338
"The Valley of the Shadow" (Robinson) **1**:490
"The Valley of Unrest" (Poe) **1**:438
"Le vallon" (Lamartine) **16**:268, 276, 283, 290,
    298-301
"Valuable" (Smith) **12**:296
"Values in Use" (Moore) **4**:261
"Valvins" (Valery) **9**:392
"The Vampire" (Baudelaire)
    See "Les métamorphoses du vampire"
"Le Vampire" (Baudelaire)
    See "Les métamorphoses du vampire"
"The Vampire" (Kipling) **3**:166
"Van Winkle" (Crane) **3**:100, 109
"Vanaspati" (Tagore) **8**:415
"Vancouver" (Davie) **29**:109
"Vandracour" (Wordsworth) **4**:399
"Vanilocuencia" (Borges) **22**:72
"Vanishing Point: Urban Indian" (Rose) **13**:232
"Vanitie" (Herbert) **4**:120
"Vanitie I" (Herbert) **4**:132
"The Vanity of All Worldly Things"
    (Bradstreet) **10**:2, 6, 21
"Vanna's Twins" (Rossetti) **7**:291
"Vapor Trail Reflected in the Frog Pond"
    (Kinnell) **26**:263, 290
"Variation and Reflection on a Poem by Rilke"
    (Levertov) **11**:206
"Variation and Reflection on a Theme by
    Rilke" (The Book of Hours Book I Poem
    7Levertov) **11**:203
"Variation on a Theme by Rilke" (Levertov)
    **11**:202
"Variations Calypso and Fugue on a Theme of
    Ella Wheeler Wilcox" (Ashbery) **26**:137,
    155
*Variations on a Sunbeam* (Elytis) **21**:120
"Variations on a Theme" (Cullen) **20**:58, 85
"Variations on a Theme by Rilke" (The Book
    of Hours Book I Poem 4Levertov) **11**:203
"Variations on an Original Theme" (Ashbery)
    **26**:140
"Variations on Two Dicta of William Blake"
    (Duncan) **2**:103
"Variations sur le carnaval de Venise"
    (Gautier) **18**:130

*Various Poems of All Periods* (Valery)
    See *Poésies*
"Various Protestations from Various People"
    (Knight) **14**:52
"Varsha-mangal" (Tagore) **8**:411
"Varshashesh" (Tagore) **8**:411
"Vasanter Kusumer mela" (Tagore) **8**:406
"Vashti" (Harper) **21**:185, 191, 209
"Vasundhara" (Tagore) **8**:408
*Vaudeville for a Princess, and Other Poems*
    (Schwartz) **8**:285, 292-94, 318
"Vecchi versi" (Montale) **13**:108, 157
"La vecchia ubriaca" (Pavese) **13**:214
"A veces me sucede" (Fuertes) **27**:3
*Vecher* (Akhmatova) **2**:3, 5-6, 11, 17
*Vecherny albom* (Tsvetaeva) **14**:305
"Vechernyaya progulka" (Bely) **11**:22
"Vegetable Island" (Page) **12**:178
"Vegetation" (Tagore)
    See "Vanaspati"
"Vegnerà el vero Cristo" (Pasolini) **17**:254
*Veinte poemas de amor y una canción
    desesperada* (Neruda) **4**:276, 282, 284,
    291, 299-305, 307
"Velvet Shoes" (Wylie) **23**:301, 305, 307, 314-
    15, 318-20, 322-23, 330-32
"El vendedor de papeles" (Fuertes) **27**:11
"Vendémiaire" (Apollinaire) **7**:10, 36, 44-6
"vending machine" (Enzensberger) **28**:147
*Venetian Epigrams* (Goethe) **5**:223
*The Venetian Glass Nephew* (Wylie) **23**:322,
    330
"Veni vidi vixi" (Hugo) **17**:64
"Venice" (Pasternak) **6**:276
"Venice" (Tomlinson) **17**:331, 334
"The Venice Poem" (Duncan) **2**:105-06
"Il ventaglio" (Montale) **13**:108, 128-29
"Ventas" (Guillen) **23**:111
"Vento e bandiere" (Montale) **13**:164
"Vento sulla mezzaluna" (Montale) **13**:110
*Vents* (Perse) **23**:209, 211, 213-18, 221, 223,
    232, 234-35, 238-40, 242-43, 247-53, 255,
    257
*Venture of the Infinite Man* (Neruda)
    See *Tentativa del hombre infinito*
"Venus" (Dario) **15**:87
"Vénus anadyomène" (Rimbaud) **3**:255
"Venus and the Ark" (Sexton) **2**:355
*Venus and the Rain* (McGuckian) **27**:77-78, 80-
    81, 93, 95, 100-104
"Venus and the Sun" (McGuckian) **27**:97
"Venus Transiens" (Lowell) **13**:66, 96
"Venus Tying the Wings of Love"
    (McGuckian) **27**:103
"Veracruz" (Hayden) **6**:193-94
"Le Verbe Être" (Breton) **15**:51
"Le verbe marronner à René Depestre"
    (Cesaire) **25**:29, 33
"La verdad" (Jimenez) **7**:202
"Vermächtnis" (Goethe) **5**:248
"Vermeer" (Nemerov) **24**:262, 266, 299
"Vermont" (Carruth) **10**:73-4, 83
"Vernal Equinox" (Lowell) **13**:64
"Vernal Sentiment" (Roethke) **15**:246
"Vers dorés" (Nerval) **13**:181
*Vers et prose* (Mallarme) **4**:207
"Vers l'Arc en ciel" (Breton) **15**:49
"Vers nouveaux et chansons" (Rimbaud) **3**:285
*Verschiedene* (Heine) **25**:129-131
"Verse about a Red Officer" (Tsvetaeva) **14**:313
"Verses about Russia" (Blok) **21**:9
"Verses about the Beautiful Lady" (Blok)
    **21**:2-3, 23
*The Verses about the Beautiful Lady* (Blok)
    See *Stikhi o prekrasnoi dame*
*Verses Address'd to the Imitator of the First
    Satire of the Second Book of Horace*
    (Montagu) **16**:338-41
*Verses and Sonnets* (Belloc) **24**:28-9, 34, 38
"Verses for a Certain Dog" (Parker) **28**:360
"Verses in the Night" (Parker) **28**:362
"Verses on His Own Death" (Swift) **9**:265

"Verses on the Death of Dr. Swift" (Swift)
    **9**:258, 279-82, 294-95, 304, 306-08, 310
"Verses on the Death of T. S. Eliot" (Brodsky)
    See "Stixi na smert T. S. Èliota"
"Verses on the Unknown Soldier"
    (Mandelstam)
    See "Stikhi o neizvestnom soldate"
"Verses to Czechoslovakia" (Tsvetaeva)
    See "Stikhi k Chekhii"
*Verses to the Imitator of Horace* (Montagu)
    See *Verses Address'd to the Imitator of the
    First Satire of the Second Book of
    Horace*
"Verses Upon the Burning of Our House"
    (Bradstreet)
    See "Some Verses Upon the Burning of
    Our House, July 10th, 1666"
"Verses Wrote in a Lady's Ivory Table-book"
    (Swift)
    See "Written in a Lady's Ivory Table-book,
    1698"
"Versi del testamento" (Pasolini) **17**:259
"Versilian Shore" (Montale)
    See "Proda di Versilia"
*Verso la cuna del mondo* (Gozzano) **10**:177,
    184
"Verso la fede" (Gozzano) **10**:184
"Verso Siena" (Montale) **13**:109
*Versts* (Tsvetaeva)
    See *Vyorsty I*
*Versty I* (Tsvetaeva)
    See *Vyorsty I*
*Versty II* (Tsvetaeva)
    See *Vyorsty II*
*Versus* (Nash) **21**:267, 269
*Verteidigung der Wölfe* (Enzensberger) **28**:133-
    38, 140, 143
"Vertigo" (Rich) **5**:360
"Vertue" (Herbert) **4**:100-01, 110, 113, 132-34
"Very late July" (Piercy) **29**:315
"A Very Short Song" (Parker) **28**:346
"Very Tree" (Kunitz) **19**:147, 160
"Vespers" (Gluck) **16**:170
"Vespers" (Lowell) **13**:64, 67, 97
"Vestigia nulla retrorsum" (In Memoriam:
    Rainer Maria Rilke
    1875-1926MacDiarmid) **9**:156, 176
"Les veuves" (Baudelaire) **1**:44, 58-9
"Via Crucis" (Noyes) **27**:136
*La via del refugio* (Gozzano) **10**:179, 184-85,
    188
"Via Portello" (Davie) **29**:95
*Via Unica* (Alegria) **26**:
"Vibratory Description" (McGuckian) **27**:105
"Vice" (Baraka) **4**:15
"Vicissitude" (Gray)
    See "Ode on the Pleasure Arising from
    Vicissitude"
"The Victims" (Olds) **22**:310, 312, 319, 321,
    323
"The Victor Dog" (Merrill) **28**:230
*A Victorian Village* (Reese) **29**:339
"Victoria's Tears" (Browning) **6**:14, 29
"The Victorious Sun" (Aleixandre) **15**:19
*Victory Odes* (Pindar) **19**:378, 386, 390
"La Vida a veces es un río frío y seco"
    (Fuertes) **27**:16
"Viday" (Tagore) **8**:415
"Videshi phul" (Tagore) **8**:415
"La Vie dans la mort" (Gautier) **18**:131-32, 155
"Viennese Waltz" (Wylie) **23**:314, 333
*Viento entero* (Paz) **1**:353, 356, 362-63, 369
"El vientre" (Aleixandre) **15**:34
"Le vierge, le vivace et le bel aujourdhui"
    (Mallarme) **4**:202, 206
"Les Vierges de Verdun" (Hugo) **17**:62, 74
"Vies" (Rimbaud) **3**:261-62
"Vietnam Addenda" (Lorde) **12**:155
"Le vieux saltimbanque" (Baudelaire) **1**:44, 58
"The View" (Holderlin) **4**:178
"The View" (Milosz) **8**:198

"A View across the Roman Campagna"
(Browning) **6**:23
"The View from an Attic Window" (Nemerov)
**24**:270-71
"View from an Empty Chair" (Gallagher) **9**:50
"View from the screen" (Bukowski) **18**:22
"A View of Cracow" (Zagajewski) **27**:381, 385
"A View of Delft" (Zagajewski) **27**:385
"View of Teignmouth in Devonshire" (Lowell)
**13**:67
"A View of the Brooklyn Bridge" (Meredith)
**28**:182, 190
"A View of the Burning" (Merrill) **28**:239
"View of the Pig" (Hughes) **7**:136, 140
"View of the Wilds" (Tu Fu) **9**:332
"View to the North" (Swenson) **14**:288
"Viewing the Waterfall at Mount Lu" (Li Po)
**29**:145
"The Vigil" (Roethke) **15**:263
"Vigil Strange I Kept on the Field One Night"
(Whitman) **3**:378
"Vigilance" (Breton) **15**:50-1
*Vigils* (Sassoon) **12**:258-59, 271
"La vigne et la maison" (Lamartine) **16**:268
"Le vigneron champenois" (Apollinaire) **7**:22
"Vignette" (Kumin) **15**:224
"Vihanger gan" (Tagore) **8**:406
*VIII* (Wylie) **23**:305
"Viking Dublin: Trial Piece" (Heaney) **18**:204
"Villa Adriana" (Rich) **5**:362
"Villa on Chung-nan Mountain" (Wang Wei)
**18**:368
"The Village" (Carruth) **10**:71
"The Village" (Pushkin) **10**:408-09
"The Village Atheist" (Masters) **1**:335
"A Village Edmund" (Gunn) **26**:183
*The Village Minstrel, and Other Poems* (Clare)
**23**:25, 38, 42-4
"Village Mystery" (Wylie) **23**:301
"The Village Wedding" (Sikelianos) **29**:359,
367-68, 373
"The Villagers and Death" (Graves) **6**:142
"A Villequier" (Hugo) **17**:64, 82-83
"Villes" (Rimbaud) **3**:261, 264-65
"Vilota" (Pasolini) **17**:252
"Le vin perdu" (Valery) **9**:388, 390, 396
"The Vindictives" (Frost) **1**:206
"Vine" (Herrick) **9**:100, 109, 137
"Vine en un barco negre" (Guillen) **23**:120, 127
"The Vineyard" (Kipling) **3**:182
*Vingt-cinq poèmes* (Tzara) **27**:223, 227, 233
"Vino, primero, puro" (Jimenez) **7**:187
"Il vino triste" (Pavese) **13**:224
"Vintage" (Hass) **16**:216
"Vinus sai no zenban" (Nishiwaki) **15**:238
*Violent Pastoral* (Merrill) **28**:253
*The Violent Season* (Paz)
See *La estación violenta*
"The Violent Space" (or when your sister
sleeps around for moneyKnight) **14**:39,
41, 43-4, 52
*The Violet of the Night* (Blok) **21**:
"Viper-Man" (Davie) **29**:110
"Virgen de plástico" (Fuertes) **27**:23, 30
"A Virgile" (Hugo) **17**:94-95
"The Virgin Carrying a Lantern" (Stevens)
**6**:310
"The Virgin Mary to the Child Jesus"
(Browning) **6**:29-30
"Virginia" (Eliot) **5**:166
"Virginia" (Lindsay) **23**:280
"The Virginians Are Coming Again" (Lindsay)
**23**:280, 285
"Virgins Plus Curtains Minus Dots" (Loy)
**16**:333
"Virtue" (Herbert)
See "Vertue"
"Virtue" (Wheatley)
See "On Virtue"
"Virtuoso Literature" (Wakoski) **15**:346-47
*Virtuoso Literature for Two and Four Hands*
(Wakoski) **15**:346, 355, 361, 365-66

"Vishvashoka" (Tagore) **8**:417
"A Vision" (Berry) **28**:8-9
"Vision" (Bridges) **28**:63, 88
"The Vision" (Burns) **6**:50
"A Vision" (Clare) **23**:22, 25
"Vision" (Gibran)
See "Ru'ya"
"The Vision" (Masters) **1**:342
"Vision" (Rimbaud) **3**:263
"Vision" (Sassoon) **12**:245
"Vision And Prayer" (Thomas) **2**:382, 387-88,
390
"La Vision des montagnes" (Hugo) **17**:66
"Vision in the Repair Shop" (Graves) **6**:143
"A Vision of India" (Kipling) **3**:190
"Vision of Jubal" (Eliot) **20**:123
"A Vision of Poets" (Browning) **6**:7, 26, 38, 41
"The Vision of Sin" (Tennyson) **6**:359-60, 366,
378
"The Vision of the Archagels" (Brooke) **24**:62,
75-6
*A Vision of the Last Judgment* (Blake) **12**:40-2
"The Visionary" (Bronte) **8**:52
*Les visions* (Lamartine) **16**:266, 269, 287
*Visions of the Daughters of Albion: The Eye
Sees More Than the Heart Knows* (Blake)
**12**:35, 46, 57, 61, 63
"The Visions of the Maid of Orleans"
(Coleridge)
See "Joan of Arc"
"Visit" (Ammons) **16**:54
"The Visit" (Baraka) **4**:17
"The Visit" (Nash) **21**:274
"A visit from the ex" (Piercy) **29**:313
"Visit to Toronto, with Companions" (Atwood)
**8**:40
"The Visitation" (Graves) **6**:172
"Visiting a Dead Man on a Summer Day"
(Piercy) **29**:307
"Visiting Flannery O'Connor's Grave"
(Kumin) **15**:215
"Visiting Hsiang-chi Monastery" (Wang Wei)
**18**:378-80
"Visiting Monk Hsüan" (Wang Wei) **18**:388
"Visiting the Ho Family Again" (Tu Fu) **9**:319
"Visiting the Temple of Gathered Fragrance"
(Wang Wei) **18**:383, 386
"The Visitor" (Forche) **10**:144, 153
"Visits to St. Elizabeth" (Bishop) **3**:47, 56
"Vita Nuova" (Kunitz) **19**:148, 176, 179
*La vita nuova* (Dante) **21**:48-53, 55, 62, 66,
72-6, 86-92, 94
"Vitam quae faciunt beatiorem" (Martial)
**10**:243
"Vitzliputzli" (Heine) **25**:167, 170
*ViVa* (Cummings) **5**:100, 104-07, 110-11
"Vivamus" (Bridges) **28**:59, 63
"Vivasana" (Tagore) **8**:407
*V-Letter and Other Poems* (Shapiro) **25**:262-67,
269, 285, 288, 292, 295, 297, 307, 309, 316,
319, 322
"Vlez besenok v mokroi sherstke"
(Mandelstam) **14**:153-54
"Vnov' Ia Posetil" (Pushkin)
See "Vnov' Ya Posetil"
"Vnov' Ya Posetil" (Pushkin) **10**:384, 414-15
"Vnutri gory bezdeistvuet kumir"
(Mandelstam) **14**:153
"Vocation" (Levertov) **11**:198
"Voce giunta con le folaghe" (Montale) **13**:112
"Voeu à Phebus" (Ronsard) **11**:256
"The Voice" (Arnold) **5**:49
"A Voice" (Atwood) **8**:14
"The Voice" (Brooke) **24**:56, 76
"The Voice" (Hardy) **8**:88, 117-18, 135
"The Voice" (Levine) **22**:225
"The Voice" (Roethke) **15**:275
"Voice Arriving with the Coots" (Montale)
**13**:146, 149
"The Voice as a Girl" (Snyder) **21**:289
"Voice Coming with the Moorhens" (Montale)
See "Voce giunta con le folaghe"

"A Voice from a Chorus" (Blok) **21**:15
"Voice from the Tomb" (Smith) **12**:349
"The Voice of Nature" (Bridges) **28**:67
"The Voice of Rock" (Ginsberg) **4**:55
"The Voice of the Ancient Bard" (Blake) **12**:7
*Voice of the Forest* (Tagore)
See *Banabani*
"Voice of the Past" (Bely)
See "Golos proshlogo"
"The Voice of the People" (Belloc) **24**:42
"The Voice of the People" (Holderlin)
See "Stimme des Volks"
"Voices about the Princess Anemone" (Smith)
**12**:298, 348-49
"Voices from Kansas" (Kumin) **15**:215
"Voices from the Other World" (Merrill) **28**:235,
259
"Voices of the elements" (Enzensberger) **28**:143
"Voices under the Ground" (Ekeloef) **23**:71, 73,
75
"Voicy le temps, Hurault, qui joyeux nous
convie" (Ronsard) **11**:250
"Void in Law" (Browning) **6**:28, 32
"Void Only" (Rexroth) **20**:221
"Voie" (Tzara) **27**:229-31
"La Voix" (Baudelaire) **1**:73
*Les Voix intérieures* (Hugo) **17**:42, 45, 52, 63,
74, 76, 80, 83, 91-92, 96-97
"Volcanic Holiday" (Merrill) **28**:283, 285
*Volcano a Memoir of Hawaii* (Hongo) **23**:204-
206
"The Volcanoes" (Alegria) **26**:
"The Volcanos" (Alegria) **26**:
"An vollen Büschelzweigen" (Goethe) **5**:247
"Vollmondnacht" (Goethe) **5**:247
"Vol'nost': Oda" (Pushkin) **10**:408-09
*Volshebny fonar* (Tsvetaeva) **14**:318
"Volt" (Tzara) **27**:229-31
*Volume Two* (Villa) **22**:347, 353
"Voluntaries" (Emerson) **18**:76-77, 88, 113
"La volupté" (Baudelaire) **1**:71
"Von diesen Stauden" (Celan) **10**:122
*Von Schwelle zu Schwelle* (Celan) **10**:95, 121
"Vooruzhennyi zren'em uzkikh os"
(Mandelstam) **14**:154
"Voracities and Verities Sometimes Are
Interacting" (Moore) **4**:261
"Vorobyev Hills" (Pasternak) **6**:251-54
*Voronezh Notebooks* (Mandelstam) **14**:123,
149-50
"Vorstadt im Föhn" (Trakl) **20**:261
"Vospominanie v Tsarskom Sele" (Pushkin)
**10**:409, 421
"Vostok pobledneuskii, vostok onemesvshii"
(Bely) **11**:32
"A Vow" (Ginsberg) **4**:56
"The Vow" (Kinnell) **26**:286
"The Vow" (Lowell) **13**:86-7
"Vowels 2" (Baraka) **4**:24
"vowl man" (Bissett) **14**:15
"Vox Humana" (Gunn) **26**:200
"Voy hasta Uján" (Guillen) **23**:128
"Le voyage" (Baudelaire) **1**:50, 60, 70, 73-4
"The Voyage" (Jonson) **17**:207
"Le voyage à Cythère" (Baudelaire) **1**:65, 72-3
"Le Voyage de Tours, ou les amoureus Thoinet
et Perrot" (Ronsard) **11**:260-61, 264
"The Voyage of Maeldune" (Tennyson) **6**:359,
369
"Voyage to Cythera" (Baudelaire)
See "Le voyage à Cythère"
*Voyage to the Island of Love* (Behn)
See *Poems upon Several Occasions, with a
Voyage to the Island of Love*
"Voyage to the Moon" (Pinsky) **27**:157
"Voyagers" (Page) **12**:199
"Voyages" (Clampitt) **19**:91
"Voyages" (Crane) **3**:90, 97, 104
*Voyages: A Homage to John Keats* (Clampitt)
**19**:87
"Voyages II" (Crane) **3**:80, 83, 96, 102
"Voyages III" (Crane) **3**:83

"Voyages IV" (Crane) **3**:83
"Voyages V" (Crane) **3**:83
"Le voyageur" (Apollinaire) **7**:48
"Les Voyelles" (Rimbaud) **3**:249, 268, 274
"Vozdushnyi korabl" (Lermontov) **18**:291
*Vozmezdie* (Blok) **21**:10, 17, 25-6, 39, 44
*Vozvrat: Tretiia simfoniia* (Bely) **11**:3, 8-9, 14-17, 22
"Vpon a Ribband" (Carew)
    See "Upon a Ribband"
"Le vrai de la chose" (Laforgue) **14**:76
"Vriksha-ropan" (Tagore) **8**:416
"Vriksha-vandana" (Tagore) **8**:416
*Vrindaban* (Paz) **1**:361-63
"Vse Povtoryayv pervyi stikh" (Tsvetaeva) **14**:329
"Vstrecha" (Pasternak) **6**:280
"Vsye eto bylo bylo bylo" (Blok) **21**:15
*Vtoraia simfoniia: Dramaticheskaia* (Bely) **11**:3-4, 8-11, 13-16, 21, 27, 33
*Vtoraya kniga* (Mandelstam) **14**:106, 113-18, 121-22, 129, 135, 141, 150, 153, 155
"Vue" (Valery) **9**:392
"Vuelta" (Paz) **1**:370-72, 374
*Vuelta* (Paz) **1**:370-71, 374, 376
"La vuelta a America" (Cardenal) **22**:110
"La vuelta a Buenos Aires" (Borges) **22**:94
"Vuelta de paseo" (Garcia Lorca) **3**:139
*VV* (Cummings)
    See *ViVa*
"Vykhozhu odin ja na dorogu" (Lermontov) **18**:303
*Vyorsty I* (Tsvetaeva) **14**:310, 318
*Vyorsty II* (Tsvetaeva) **14**:322
"Vysokaya bolesn" (Pasternak) **6**:265
"Vystrel" (Pushkin) **10**:414
"W. S. Landor" (Moore) **4**:242, 259
"Wadin' in de Crick" (Dunbar) **5**:144
"Wading at Wellfleet" (Bishop) **3**:49, 57
"Waga Uta" (Yosano Akiko) **11**:302, 306
"The Waggon" (Noyes) **27**:
"Wagner" (Brooke) **24**:53, 56, 64, 83
"The Wagoner" (Pavese) **13**:205
"Waialua" (Song)
    See "Easter: Wahiawa, 1959"
"Waikiki" (Brooke) **24**:56, 67, 86
"Wail" (Parker) **28**:360
"Wait" (Kinnell) **26**:292-93
"The Waiting" (Olds) **22**:330, 332, 334, 337, 340
"Waiting" (Reese) **29**:333
"Waiting" (Wright) **14**:341
"Waiting by the Gate" (Bryant) **20**:8
"Waiting for Breakfast" (Larkin) **21**:226-27
"Waiting for It" (Swenson) **14**:263
*Waiting for the King of Spain* (Wakoski) **15**:366
"The Waiting Head" (Sexton) **2**:350
"Waiting Inland" (Kumin) **15**:208
"Wake-Up Niggers" (Madhubuti) **5**:329, 338
"The Waking" (Kinnell) **26**:279
"The Waking" (Roethke) **15**:278, 286
"Waking an Angel" (Levine) **22**:213
"Waking from Drunkenness on a Spring Day" (Li Po) **29**:143
"Waking in a Newly-Build House" (Gunn) **26**:201
"Waking in a Newly-Built House" (Gunn) **26**:211
"Waking in the Blue" (Lowell) **3**:209, 221
"Waking in the Dark" (Rich) **5**:370, 392, 395
*The Waking: Poems, 1933-1953* (Roethke) **15**:249, 261, 263, 282, 284, 309
"Waking this Morning" (Rukeyser) **12**:230
"Waking Up in Streator" (Stryk) **27**:214
"Waldeinsamkeit" (Emerson) **18**:76, 88
"Wales Visitation" (Ginsberg) **4**:74, 93-4
"The Walk" (Hardy) **8**:93
"A Walk in Late Summer" (Roethke) **15**:274
"A Walk in the Country" (Kinnell) **26**:257
"A Walk in the Garden" (Aiken) **26**:
"A Walk on Snow" (Viereck) **27**:260, 277, 282
"Walk on the Moon" (Momaday) **25**:188

"A Walk with Tom Jefferson" (Levine) **22**:225-27
"Walking Down Park" (Giovanni) **19**:140-41, 143
"Walking in Paris" (Sexton) **2**:363
"Walking in the Blue" (Sexton) **2**:350
"Walking into Love" (Piercy) **29**:308, 311
"The Walking Man of Rodin" (Sandburg) **2**:334
"Walking on the Prayerstick" (Rose) **13**:233
"Walking to Bell rock" (Ondaatje) **28**:336-37
"The Wall" (Brooks) **7**:82
"The Wall" (Montale) **13**:148
"Die Wallfahrt nach Kevlaar" (Heine) **25**:145
"Walls" (Hughes) **7**:149
*The Walls Do Not Fall* (H. D.) **5**:272, 274-76, 293-95, 307, 309, 312, 314-15
"The Walrus and the Carpenter" (Carroll) **18**:51-52
"Walt Whitman" (Whitman) **3**:414
"Walter Bradford" (Brooks) **7**:92
"Walter Jenks' Bath" (Meredith) **28**:178, 182, 213
"The Waltz" (Aleixandre) **15**:8, 14
"The Waltzer in the House" (Kunitz) **19**:155
"Wanda" (Vigny) **26**:369, 402
"The Wanderer" (Pushkin) **10**:409
"The Wanderer" (Smith) **12**:326, 349-50, 354
"The Wanderer" (Williams) **7**:374, 382, 394
"A Wanderer" (Zagajewski) **27**:381
"The Wanderer's Song" (Hagiwara Sakutaro)
    See "Hyōhakusha no uta"
"The Wandering Jew" (Robinson) **1**:487
"Wandering on Mount T'ai" (Li Po) **29**:166
"The Wanderings of Cain" (Coleridge) **11**:89, 91
"The Wanderings of Oisin" (Yeats) **20**:353
*The Wanderings of Oisin, and Other Poems* (Yeats) **20**:298, 302, 344, 346
"Wanderschaft" (Trakl) **20**:241
"Wandrers Sturmlied" (Goethe) **5**:237-39
*Wang Stream Collection* (Wang Wei) **18**:367, 370, 385
"Wang-ch'uan Garland" (Wang Wei) **18**:374
"The Want" (Olds) **22**:321, 325-26, 340
*The Want Bone* (Pinsky) **27**:156, 160, 163-64, 169, 172, 174
"Wanting to Die" (Sexton) **2**:364
"Wants" (Larkin) **21**:227, 242, 252
"War" (Levine) **22**:218
"The War Against the Trees" (Kunitz) **19**:175
*War All the Time: Poems, 1981-1984* (Bukowski) **18**:15, 18-19
"The War in the Air" (Nemerov) **24**:290
"War Machine" (Ondaatje) **28**:327-28, 331
"War Pictures" (Lowell) **13**:76
"War Song" (Parker) **28**:356
"War Sonnet" (Meredith) **28**:209
*War Stories Poems about Long Ago and Now* (Nemerov) **24**:287, 289-90
*War Trilogy* (H. D.)
    See *Trilogy*
"The Ward" (Rukeyser) **12**:225
*Ware the Hawk* (Skelton) **25**:335, 338, 354, 377, 377-78, 380-81
"Waring" (Browning) **2**:26
"A Warm Place to Shit" (Bissett) **14**:10
"A Warm Small Rain" (Zagajewski) **27**:394
"Warning" (Hughes) **1**:252
"Warning: Children at Play" (Nemerov) **24**:255
"Warning to Children" (Graves) **6**:139, 143-44, 150
"A Warning to Those Who Live on Mountains" (Day Lewis) **11**:144
"Warnung" (Goethe) **5**:250
"The Warriors of the North" (Hughes) **7**:132, 148
"The Warrior's Prayer" (Dunbar) **5**:134
"The Wars" (Ondaatje) **28**:338
"A Warsaw Gathering" (Zagajewski) **27**:381
"Warum gabst du uns die tiefen Blicke" (Goethe) **5**:246
"Was He Married?" (Smith) **12**:333, 352

"Was I never yet" (Wyatt) **27**:356
"Washerwoman" (Sandburg) **2**:329
"Washington Cathedral" (Shapiro) **25**:286, 318
"Washyuma Motor Hotel" (Ortiz) **17**:227
"A WASP Woman Visits a Black Junkie in Prison" (Knight) **14**:42, 53
"The Wassaile" (Herrick) **9**:104
*The Waste Land* (Eliot) **5**:155-62, 165-67, 173-74, 176, 178-79, 183-89, 191-93, 198, 206-18
*The Waste Land* (Pound) **4**:353
"Waste Paper Basket" (Tagore) **8**:417
"Waste Sonata" (Olds) **22**:325
*Watakushi no Oitach* (Yosano Akiko) **11**:309-11
"The Watch" (Swenson) **14**:250
"Watchers of the Sky" (Noyes) **27**:128
"Watchful, A Tale of Psyche" (Smith) **12**:303-05, 337
"Watching Crow Looking South Towards the Manzano" (Harjo) **27**:64
"Watching Football on TV" (Nemerov) **24**:284
"Watching Shoah in a Hotel Room in America" (Zagajewski) **27**:388, 391
"Watching the Dance" (Merrill) **28**:254
"Watching the Needleboats at San Sabra" (Joyce) **22**:137
"The Water" (Carruth) **10**:71
"Water" (Larkin) **21**:244
"Water" (Lee) **24**:247
"Water" (Lowell) **3**:212, 215
"Water" (Wright) **14**:366
"Water and Marble" (Page) **12**:178
"Water Color" (Verlaine)
    See "Aquarelles"
"The Water Drop" (Elytis) **21**:130
"Water Element Song for Sylvia" (Wakoski) **15**:345
"the water falls in yr mind nd yu get wet tooo" (Bissett) **14**:16, 33
"The Water Hyacinth" (Merrill) **28**:247
*Water Lilies* (Jimenez)
    See *Ninfeas*
"Water Music" (MacDiarmid) **9**:154, 156, 158, 171, 176
"The Water Nymph" (Lermontov)
    See "Rusalka"
"Water of Life" (MacDiarmid) **9**:197-98
"Water Picture" (Swenson) **14**:261, 263; **106**:351
"Water Raining" (Stein) **18**:334, 349
"Water Sign Woman" (Clifton) **17**:29
"Water Sleep" (Wylie) **23**:301
*Water Street* (Merrill) **28**:220, 225, 228, 234, 238, 240, 244, 247-49, 281
"Watercolor of Grantchester Meadows" (Plath) **1**:388
"Watercolors" (Rose) **13**:238
"The Watercourse" (Herbert) **4**:114
"Waterfall" (Heaney) **18**:200
"The Waterfall at Powerscourt" (Davie) **29**:110
"Watergate" (Baraka) **4**:30
"The Watergaw" (MacDiarmid) **9**:156, 160, 196
"Waterlily Fire" (Rukeyser) **12**:221
*Waterlily Fire: Poems, 1935-1962* (Rukeyser) **12**:215-16
"Watermaid" (Okigbo) **7**:232, 239
"The Wattle-tree" (Wright) **14**:344, 353
"A Wave" (Ashbery) **26**:159
"Wave" (Snyder) **21**:304-06, 308
*A Wave* (Ashbery) **26**:169-170
"Wave Song" (Ekeloef) **23**:53-4
"The Wave the Flame the Cloud and the Leopard Speak to the Mind" (Swenson) **14**:247
"Waxworks" (Shapiro) **25**:308, 312
"The Way" (Lowell) **13**:60, 83
"The Way Down" (Kunitz) **19**:149, 155, 178
"Way down the Ravi River" (Kipling) **3**:194
"The Way In" (Tomlinson) **17**:319-20, 326
*The Way In and Other Poems* (Tomlinson) **17**:327, 336, 349, 351-52, 354
"the Way it Was" (Clifton) **17**:23

*Way of All the Earth* (Akhmatova) **2**:16
"The Way of Refuge" (Gozzano)
  See "The Road to Shelter"
*The Way of Refuge* (Gozzano)
  See *La via del refugio*
"The Way of the Wind" (Swinburne) **24**:329
"The Way through the Woods" (Kipling) **3**:171,
  183, 186, 192
"The Way West, Underground" (Snyder) **21**:296
"The Wayfarers" (Brooke) **24**:57
"Way-Out Morgan" (Brooks) **7**:63
*A Wayside Lute* (Reese) **29**:330, 335, 339, 346,
  349, 352-53
*The Wayward and the Seeking: A Collection of
  Writing by Jean Toomer* (Toomer) **7**:341
*We a BadddDDD People* (Sanchez) **9**:204, 206-
  08, 210-13, 216, 218-20, 224-27, 229, 234,
  237-38, 240, 242
"We a BadddDDD People" (for gwendolyn
  brooks/a fo real bad oneSanchez) **9**:209,
  225, 237
"We Are" (Kumin) **15**:183
"We are Alive" (Harjo) **27**:57
"We Are Muslim Women" (Sanchez) **9**:228
"We Are Seven" (Wordsworth) **4**:374, 415, 420,
  428
"We become new" (Piercy) **29**:301
"We Come Back" (Rexroth) **20**:217-18
"We Encounter Nat King Cole as We Invent
  the Future" (Harjo) **27**:65, 72
"We English" (Loy) **16**:320
"We Fought South of the Ramparts" (Li Po)
  **29**:176
"We Free Singers Be" (Knight) **14**:40, 46
"We Have Been Believers" (Walker) **20**:272-
  74, 283, 289
"we live in a hundrid yeer old house" (Bissett)
  **14**:25
"We Lying by Seasand" (Thomas) **2**:404
"We Need th Setting" (Bissett) **14**:10
"We Real Cool" (Brooks) **7**:62, 85, 90
"We Shall Gather Again in Petersburg"
  (Mandelstam) **14**:116, 121, 157
*we sleep inside each other all* (Bissett) **14**:6
"We Stood There Singing" (Kumin) **15**:213
"We Too" (H. D.) **5**:268
*We Walk the Way of the New World*
  (Madhubuti) **5**:326-27, 336, 343, 345-46
"We Wear the Mask" (Dunbar) **5**:124, 130, 132,
  135, 140, 142, 144
"We Were Three" (Alegria) **26**:
"We Who Are Playing" (Lindsay) **23**:286
"The Weak Monk" (Smith) **12**:333
"A Wearied Pilgrim" (Herrick) **9**:108
"The Wearing of the Green" (Davie) **29**:107,
  109, 120
"The Weary Blues" (Hughes) **1**:236, 246, 248,
  261, 269
*The Weary Blues* (Hughes) **1**:236-37, 242, 244-
  46, 248, 258, 260, 262-64, 268-70
"Weary in Well-Doing" (Rossetti) **7**:268
"Weary of the Bitter Ease" (Mallarme)
  See "Las de l'amer repos"
"The Weary Pund o' Tow" (Burns) **6**:78
"The Weather of the World" (Nemerov) **24**:287,
  302
"The Weather-Cock Points South" (Lowell)
  **13**:96
"Weathering Out" (Dove) **6**:111
"Weathers" (Hardy) **8**:124
"Webster Ford" (Masters) **1**:344, 346,348
"The Wedding Photograph" (Smith) **12**:316,
  323
"Wedding Wind" (Larkin) **21**:227, 247
"The Wedding2 **26**:
*The Wedge* (Williams) **7**:370, 402
"Wednesday at the Waldorf" (Swenson) **14**:267,
  276
"Wednesday: The Tete a Tete" (Montagu)
  **16**:348-49
"The Weed" (Bishop) **3**:37, 45, 75
"Weed Puller" (Roethke) **15**:278, 295, 297

"The Weeping Garden" (Pasternak) **6**:268
"The Weeping Saviour" (Browning) **6**:14
"Weggebeizt" (Celan) **10**:106, 111
"Weiß sind die Tulpen" (Celan) **10**:123
"The weight" (Piercy) **29**:313
"Weight" (Tagore)
  See "Bhar"
"Die Weihe" (Heine) **25**:157-61, 163-64
*Die Weise von Liebe und Tod des Cornets
  Christoph Rilke* (Rilke) **2**:266, 268
"Weitere Gründe dafür daB Dichter lügen"
  (Enzensberger) **28**:165
"weiterung" (Enzensberger) **28**:135
"Welcome Aboard the Turbojet Electra"
  (Swenson) **14**:268
"Welcome and Parting" (Goethe)
  See "Willkommen und Abschied"
"Welcome Back, Mr. Knight: Love of My
  Life" (Knight) **14**:46
"Welcome Morning" (Sexton) **2**:372
"The Welcome to Sack" (Herrick) **9**:88, 94, 102
"Welcome to the Caves of Arta" (Graves) **6**:153
"The Well" (Levertov) **11**:168, 205-06
"The Well" (Tomlinson) **17**:341-42
"Well Said Old Mole" (Viereck) **27**:259
"The Well-Beloved" (Hardy) **8**:91
"The Wellspring" (Olds) **22**:338
*The Wellspring* (Olds) **22**:330, 338-39
"Welsh Incident" (Graves) **6**:143, 150
"The Welsh Marches" (Housman) **2**:159, 179
"wer they angels i didnt know" (Bissett) **14**:34
"We're at the Graveyard" (Ondaatje) **28**:327,
  331, 334
"We're few" (Pasternak) **6**:252
"We're Not Learnen to Be Paper Boys" (for
  the young brothas who sell Muhammad
  SpeaksSanchez) **9**:229
"The Wereman" (Atwood) **8**:36
"The Werewolf" (Marie de France)
  See "Bisclavret"
"An Werther" (Goethe) **5**:250-51
*Wessex Poems, and Other Verses* (Hardy) **8**:114,
  123
"The West" (Housman) **2**:167, 191, 199
"West and Away the Wheels of Darkness Roll"
  (Housman) **2**:162
*West Indies, Ltd.: Poemas* (Guillen) **23**:98-99,
  106-107, 114, 133, 137-39
"The West Main Book Store chickens"
  (Piercy) **29**:315
"The West Wind" (Bryant) **20**:4, 40
"West Wind" (Wright) **14**:342, 354
"Westering" (Heaney) **18**:203
"The Western Approaches" (Nemerov) **24**:
*The Western Approaches: Poems, 1973-1975*
  (Nemerov) **24**:275, 284-86, 303
"The Western Front" (Bridges) **28**:77, 81
"Western Song" (Trakl)
  See "Abendländisches Lied"
*West-Östlicher Divan* (Goethe) **5**:223, 225, 229,
  239, 247, 250
"Westport" (Kinnell) **26**:238, 252
"West-Running Brook" (Frost) **1**:203, 218, 220
*West-Running Brook* (Frost) **1**:195, 203, 205,
  213
"Westward" (Clampitt) **19**:95-8
*Westward* (Clampitt) **19**:93, 95-6
"Wet Casements" (Ashbery) **26**:155
"Wha Is That at My Bower-Door" (Burns) **6**:77
"The Whaleboat Struck" (Ammons) **16**:39
*what* (Bissett) **14**:15
*What a Kingdom It Was* (Kinnell) **26**:236, 238-
  39, 252-53, 255, 257, 279, 289
"What a Pretty Net" (Viereck) **27**:259, 179
"What Are Cities For?" (Jeffers) **17**:132
"What Are Years" (Moore) **4**:243
"What can I Tell My Bones?" (Roethke) **15**:264,
  274
"What Did You Buy" (Wylie) **23**:330
"What God Is" (Herrick) **9**:94, 141
"What God Is Like to Him I Serve?"
  (Bradstreet) **10**:34

"What goes up" (Piercy) **29**:315, 317-19, 322
"What Happened" (Duncan) **2**:103
"What Happened Here Before" (Snyder)
  **21**:298, 325
*What Happened When the Hopi Hit New York*
  (Rose) **13**:239
"What Have I Learned" (Snyder) **21**:318
*What I Love* (Elytis) **21**:131
"What I Should Have Said" (Harjo) **27**:56
"What is Life?" (Clare) **23**:40
"What is Most Hoped and/or Most Feared: The
  Judgement" (Piercy) **29**:326
"What It Cost" (Forche) **10**:166
"Lo What It is to Love" (Wyatt) **27**:317, 346
"What Lips My Lips Have Kissed" (Millay)
  **6**:225
"What may it availl me" (Wyatt) **27**:324
"What menythe this?" (Wyatt) **27**:316, 322, 324
*What Moon Drove Me To This?* (Harjo) **27**:64
"What no perdy" (Wyatt) **27**:304, 328
"What of the Night?" (Kunitz) **19**:175-76, 178
*what poetiks* (Bissett) **14**:15
"What rage is this?" (Wyatt) **27**:304
"What Shall I Give My Children?" (Brooks)
  **7**:76
"What? So Soon" (Hughes) **1**:266
"What Stillness Round a God" (Rilke) **2**:275
"What the Bird with the Human Head Knew"
  (Sexton) **2**:372
"What the Light Was Like" (Clampitt) **19**:102
*What the Light Was Like* (Clampitt) **19**:85-7,
  90-1, 93
"What the Moon Saw" (Lindsay) **23**:268
"What the Rattlesnake Said" (Lindsay) **23**:286
"What the Women Said" (Bogan) **12**:110
"What Then?" (Yeats) **20**:342
"What This Mode of Motion Said" (Ammons)
  **16**:20
"What vaileth truth" (Wyatt) **27**:366
"What Virginia Said" (Tomlinson) **17**:353
"What We Come To Know" (Ortiz) **17**:246
"what we dew if thrs anything" (Bissett) **14**:33
"What Were They Like?" (Levertov) **11**:176
"What Why When How Who" (Pinsky) **27**:164
*What Work Is* (Levine) **22**:220-21, 227-28,
  231-32
"What Would Tennessee Williams Have Said"
  (Wakoski) **15**:368
"What Wourde is That" (Wyatt) **27**:314, 342
"Whatever Happened?" (Larkin) **21**:235-36
"Whatever You Say Say Nothing" (Heaney)
  **18**:189, 205
"Whatever You Wish, Lord" (Jimenez) **7**:184
"WHATS HAPPINING OZONE CUM BACK
  WE STILL LOV YU" (Bissett) **14**:32
"What's Meant by Here" (Snyder) **21**:300
*What's O'Clock* (Lowell) **13**:66, 76, 84-5, 91,
  93-4, 97-8
"What's That" (Sexton) **2**:359
"Whe' Fe Do?" (McKay) **2**:222-23
"Wheat-in-the-Ear" (Lowell) **13**:96
"The Wheel" (Cesaire) **25**:17
"The Wheel" (Hayden) **6**:194-95
*The Wheel* (Berry) **28**:16
"The Wheel of Being II" (Carruth) **10**:71
"The Wheel Revolves" (Rexroth) **20**:195
"Wheesht, Wheesht, My Foolish Heart"
  (MacDiarmid) **9**:156, 160
"When All My Five and Country Senses See"
  (Thomas) **2**:392
"When Black Is a Color Because It Follows a
  Grey Day" (Wakoski) **15**:348
"When Coldness Wraps This Suffering Clay"
  (Byron) **16**:89
"When de Co'n Pone's Hot" (Dunbar) **5**:117,
  122
"When Death Came April Twelve 1945"
  (Sandburg) **2**:333
"When First I Saw" (Burns) **6**:78
"When from Afar" (Holderlin) **4**:174, 178
"When God Lets My Body Be" (Cummings)
  **5**:99

"When Guilford Good" (Burns) **6**:78
"When Hair Falls Off and Eyes Blur and"
    (Cummings) **5**:105
"When He Would Have His Verses Read"
    (Herrick) **9**:87, 96, 102, 109, 139, 145
"When I Buy Pictures" (Moore) **4**:251, 266
"When I consider how my light is spent"
    (Milton)
    See "When I consider how my light is
    spent"
"When I Die" (Brooks) **7**:68
"When I Die" (Giovanni) **19**:113
"When I Have Fears That I May Cease to Be"
    (Keats) **1**:314
"When I Nap" (Giovanni) **19**:112
"When I Roved a Young Highlander" (Byron)
    **16**:86
"When I Set Out for Lyonesse" (Hardy) **8**:92,
    112, 115
"When I Was One-and-Twenty" (Housman)
    **2**:161, 192
"When I Watch the Living Meet" (Housman)
    **2**:184
"When in the Gloomiest of Capitals"
    (Akhmatova)
    See "Kogda v mrachneyshey iz stolits"
"When Jemmy First Began to Love" (Behn)
    See "Song to a Scotish Tune (When Jemmy
    First Began to Love)"
"When Lilacs Last in the Dooryard Bloom'd"
    (Whitman) **3**:378, 382, 396-97, 410, 418-
    19, 422
"When Lilacs Last in the Dooryard Bloomed"
    (Whitman) **3**:378, 382, 396-97, 410, 418-
    19, 422
"When Malindy Sings" (Dunbar) **5**:117, 119-
    21, 134, 146
"When Mrs. Martin's Booker T." (Brooks) **7**:67,
    69
"When on my night of life the Dawn shall
    break" (Brooke) **24**:72
*When One Has Lived a Long Time Alone*
    (Kinnell) **26**:285-87, 293
"When Rain Whom Fear" (Cummings) **5**:105
"When Serpents bargain for the Right to
    Squirm" (Cummings) **5**:90, 107
"When Sir Beelzebub" (Sitwell) **3**:303
"When Smoke Stood Up from Ludlow"
    (Housman) **2**:184
"When Summer's End Is Nighing" (Housman)
    **2**:165, 181
"When the Dead Ask My Father about Me"
    (Olds) **22**:323, 326
"When the Lamp Is Shattered" (Shelley)
    **14**:177, 207
"When the Light Falls" (Kunitz) **19**:151, 155
"When the Shy Star" (Joyce)
    See "IV"
*When the Skies Clear* (Pasternak)
    See *Kogda razglyaetsya*
"When the Yellowing Fields Billow"
    (Lermontov) **18**:281
"When They Have Lost" (Day Lewis) **11**:144
"When Under the Icy Eaves" (Masters) **1**:328
"When Unto Nights of Autumn Do Complain"
    (Cummings) **5**:104
"When We with Sappho" (Rexroth) **20**:203, 216
"When We'll Worship Jesus" (Baraka) **4**:29, 39
"When Will I Return" (Brutus) **24**:116
"When You Are Old" (Yeats) **20**:355
"When You Lie Down, the Sea Stands Up"
    (Swenson) **14**:261
"When You Speak to Me" (Gallagher) **9**:36
"When You've Forgotten Sunday" (Brooks)
    **7**:53, 68
"Where Are the War Poets?" (Day Lewis)
    **11**:131
"Where can I go, now it's January?"
    (Mandelstam)
    See "Kuda mne det'sia v etom Ianvare?"

"Where He's Staying Now" (Meredith) **28**:179
"Where Is the Real Non-Resistant?" (Lindsay)
    **23**:281
"Where Knock Is Open Wide" (Roethke)
    **15**:251, 261, 272, 275-76, 278, 298, 300
"Where nothing grows" (Piercy) **29**:313
"Where, O Where?" (Wylie) **23**:324
"Where shall I have at myn owne will"
    (Wyatt) **27**:332, 351-352
"Where Shall the Lover Rest" (Scott) **13**:304
"Where, Tall Girl, Is Your Gypsy Babe"
    (Akhmatova)
    See "Gde, vysokaya, tvoy tsyganyonok"
"Where the Hell Would Chopin Be?"
    (Bukowski) **18**:4
"Where the Picnic Was" (Hardy) **8**:136
"Where the Rainbow Ends" (Lowell) **3**:200,
    207
"Where the Tennis Court Was" (Montale)
    See "Dov'era il tennis"
"Where the Track Vanishes" (Kinnell) **26**:238,
    252
*Where the Wolves Drink* (Tzara) **27**:250
"Where There's a Will There's Velleity"
    (Nash) **21**:265
"Where They So Fondly Go" (Bukowski) **18**:5
"Where We Live Now" (Levine) **22**:214
"Where's Agnes?" (Browning) **6**:24
"Where's the Poker" (Smart) **13**:348
"Whether on Ida's Shady Brow" (Blake) **12**:11
"Which, Being Interpreted, Is as May Be, or,
    Otherwise" (Lowell) **13**:91
"While Blooming Youth" (Prior) **52**:205
"While Drawing in a Churchyard" (Hardy)
    **8**:120-21
"While Sitting in the Tuileries and Facing the
    Slanting Sun" (Swenson) **14**:261, 285
"While the Record Plays" (Illyes) **16**:249, 251
"whilst waiting for" (Bissett) **14**:32
"Whip the World" (MacDiarmid) **9**:187
*Whipperginny* (Graves) **6**:127-28, 131
"The Whipping" (Hayden) **6**:194-96
"The Whirlwind" (Lindsay) **23**:281
"Whiskers, A Philosophical Ode" (Pushkin)
    **10**:407
"whispered to lucifer" (Clifton) **17**:30
"Whispers of Heavenly Death" (Whitman)
    **3**:378
"Whistle and I'll Come tae Ye, My Lad"
    (Burns) **6**:59
"Whistle and I'll Come tae Ye, My Lad"
    (Burns)
    See "Whistle and I'll Come tae Ye, My
    Lad"
"The Whistle Cockade" (Burns) **6**:82
*Whistles and Whistling* (Ishikawa)
    See *Yobuko to kuchibue*
"A Whistling Girl" (Parker) **28**:353, 362
"Whistling Sam" (Dunbar) **5**:122, 146
"White and Green" (Lowell) **13**:60, 69
"White and Violet" (Jimenez) **7**:183
"White April" (Reese) **29**:339
*White April* (Reese) **29**:335-36, 339, 348, 351
"White Arrow" (Toomer) **7**:336
*White Buildings* (Crane) **3**:81, 84, 87, 90
"The White City" (McKay) **2**:211
*The White Doe of Rylstone; or, The Fate of the
    Nortons* (Wordsworth) **4**:394, 402, 407
"White Dwarf" (Ammons) **16**:45
"White Dwarfs" (Ondaatje) **28**:314, 317, 327,
    331-32, 334, 336, 338
*White Flock* (Akhmatova)
    See *Belaya staya*
"White Horses" (Kipling) **3**:183
"The White House" (McKay) **2**:210, 221, 229
"White Lady" (Clifton) **17**:28
"The White Lilies" (Gluck) **16**:170-71
"The White Man's Burden" (Kipling) **3**:192
"White Night" (Wright) **14**:372
"The White Porch" (Song) **21**:331-32, 334, 338,
    340-41, 350
"White Shoulders" (Sandburg) **2**:303

"White Shroud" (Ginsberg) **4**:86, 90
*White Shroud* (Ginsberg) **4**:86-7, 89-90
"The White Snake" (Sexton) **2**:365
"The White Thought" (Smith) **12**:292, 341, 354
"The White Troops" (Brooks) **7**:73
"The White Van" (Tomlinson) **17**:333
"White Wines" (Stein) **18**:341
"The White Witch" (Johnson) **24**:127, 142, 161,
    166
*White-Haired Lover* (Shapiro) **25**:316, 321-22
*The White-Haired Revolver* (Breton)
    See *Le revolver á cheveux blancs*
"The White-Tailed Hornet" (Frost) **1**:221
"The Whitsun Weddings" (Larkin) **21**:228, 230,
    238-39, 255
*The Whitsun Weddings* (Larkin) **21**:224, 227-
    28, 230, 233, 235, 240, 244, 253, 255, 259
"Whitsunday" (Herbert) **4**:118
"Who Among You Knows the Essence of
    Garlic" (Hongo) **23**:196-97
*Who Are We Now?* (Ferlinghetti) **1**:187-88
"Who But the Lord" (Hughes) **1**:241
"Who Cares, Long as It's B-Flat" (Carruth)
    **10**:85
"Who ever comes to shroud me do not harme"
    (Donne)
    See "The Funerall"
"Who has not walked" (Bridges) **28**:83
"Who Hath Herd" (Wyatt) **27**:317
*Who Is the Real Non-Resistant?* (Lindsay)
    **23**:282
"Who is this Who Howls and Mutters?"
    (Smith) **12**:313, 336
"Who Knows" (Dunbar) **5**:130
"Who Know's If the Moon's" (Cummings) **5**:88
"Who list his wealth and ease retain" (Wyatt)
    **27**:368
"Who Made Paul Bunyan" (Sandburg) **2**:327
"Who on Earth" (Kinnell) **26**:287
"Who Said It Was Simple" (Lorde) **12**:153, 157
"Who Shot Eugenie?" (Smith) **12**:333
"Who so list to hount" (Wyatt) **27**:300-01, 303,
    309-10, 323, 329-30, 342-44, 348, 356, 358,
    360, 363, 367
*Who Will Know Us?: New Poems* (Soto) **28**:402
"Who Will Survive America?/Few
    Americans/Very Few Negroes/No
    Crackers at All" (Baraka) **4**:14, 19
"Whoever Finds a Horseshoe" (Mandelstam)
    See "Nashedshij podkovu"
"Wholesome" (Meredith) **28**:208
"Whorls" (Meredith) **28**:198
"Whuchulls" (MacDiarmid) **9**:197-98
"Why Can't I Live Forever?" (Viereck) **27**:258,
    276
"Why Come Ye Nat to Courte?" (Skelton)
    **25**:336-37, 342, 348, 350, 356, 374, 379
"why dew magazines lie" (Bissett) **14**:32
"Why Did I Laugh Tonight" (Keats) **1**:279, 305
"'Why Did I Sketch'" (Hardy) **8**:137
"Why do I" (Smith) **12**:337
"Why Do You Sing My Bird" (Ekeloef) **23**:87
"Why East Wind Chills" (Thomas) **2**:379
"Why I Am a Liberal" (Browning) **2**:66
"Why I Voted the Socialist Ticket" (Lindsay)
    **23**:267, 282, 296
"Why I write not of love" (Jonson)
    See "Why I write not of love"
"Why Some Look Up to Planets and Heroes"
    (Merton) **10**:334
"Why We Die" (Swenson) **14**:247
"Whys/Wise" (Baraka) **4**:40
"Wichita Vortex Sutra" (Ginsberg) **4**:50, 53, 66,
    82, 85
"The Wide Mouth" (Snyder) **21**:292
"The Widow at Windsor" (Kipling) **3**:161, 186-
    87, 191
"Widow La Rue" (Masters) **1**:330, 333
"The Widow o' Windsor" (Kipling)
    See "The Widow at Windsor"
"The Widow of Windsor" (Kipling)
    See "The Widow at Windsor"

"Widower's Tango" (Neruda) **4**:306
"Widowhood or the Home-Coming of Lady Ross" (Smith) **12**:351-52
"Widows" (Baudelaire)
   See "Les veuves"
"The Widow's Lament in Springtime" (Williams) **7**:345, 353, 360, 363
"The Widow's Party" (Kipling) **3**:160
"The Widow's Resolution" (Smart) **13**:347
"Wie wenn am Feiertage ..." (Holderlin) **4**:162, 165-66, 169
"A Wife at Daybreak I Shall Be" (Dickinson) **1**:93
"Wife of Bath's Prologue" (Chaucer)
   See "Prologue to the Wife of Bath's Tale"
"Wife of Bath's Tale" (Chaucer) **19**:13, 15, 29, 33, 60, 63
"Wife to Husband" (Rossetti) **7**:267
"Wife's Tale" (Chaucer)
   See "Wife of Bath's Tale"
"The Wild" (Berry) **28**:14, 37
"Wild Blessings" (Clifton) **17**:29
"Wild Boys of the Road" (Ashbery) **26**:163
"Wild Cherries" (Zagajewski) **27**:389
*Wild Cherry* (Reese) **29**:335-36, 339, 347-48, 351
*Wild Dreams of a New Beginning* (Ferlinghetti) **1**:188
"Wild Flower" (Tagore)
   See "Banaphul"
"WILD FLOWRS ABOVE TH TREE LINE" (Bissett) **14**:20
"Wild Grapes" (Frost) **1**:215
*The Wild Iris* (Gluck) **16**:168, 170-71
"Wild Life Cameo, Early Morn" (Ferlinghetti) **1**:182-83, 188
"Wild Oats" (Larkin) **21**:230, 234, 244, 247
"Wild Orchard" (Williams) **7**:345
*A Wild Patience Has Taken Me This Far: Poems, 1978-1981* (Rich) **5**:385, 389
"Wild Peaches" (Wylie) **23**:301, 305, 314, 329, 333-34
*The Wild Rose Flowers* (Akhmatova)
   See *Shipovnik tsevetyot*
"The Wild Sky" (Rich) **5**:362
"The Wild Swans at Coole" (Yeats) **20**:303, 327
*The Wild Swans at Coole* (Yeats) **20**:304, 310-11, 314, 326, 328
"Wild Water" (Swenson) **14**:283
"Wild Without Love" (McGuckian) **27**:83
"The Wilderness" (Robinson) **1**:459
"Wilderness" (Sandburg) **2**:302
"The Wildflower" (Williams) **7**:382, 386
"Wildflower Plain" (Wright) **14**:342
*Wilf* (Alegria) **26**:
"Wilfred Owen's Photographs" (Hughes) **7**:133
"The Will" (Donne) **1**:126
"The Will" (Merrill) **28**:272
"Will Be" (Pasternak) **6**:252
"Will Boyden Lectures" (Masters) **1**:343
"Will Not Come Back" (Lowell) **3**:226-27
"Will Out of Kindness of Their Hearts a Few Philosophers Tell Me" (Cummings) **5**:93
"Will They Cry When You're Gone, You Bet" (Baraka) **4**:18
*The Will to Change: Poems, 1968-1970* (Rich) **5**:365-67, 370-72, 383, 387-89, 391, 399
"Will Waterproof's Lyrical Monologue" (Tennyson) **6**:360
"Will You Perhaps Consent to Be" (Schwartz) **8**:305
"Willful Homing" (Frost) **1**:197
*William Blake's Prophetic Writing* (Blake) **12**:25
"William Bond" (Blake) **12**:35, 43
*William Carlos Williams: Selected Poems* (Williams) **7**:357
"William H. Herndon" (Masters) **1**:334
"William Marion Reedy" (Masters) **1**:325, 333, 342

"Willie" (Brooks)
   See "To Keorapetse Kgositsile (Willie)"
"Willie Brew'd a Peck o' Maut" (Burns) **6**:76
"Willie Wastle" (Burns) **6**:78, 81; **40**:97
"The Willing Mistress" (Behn) **13**:4, 14-16, 18-20, 29
"Willingly" (Gallagher) **9**:58
*Willingly* (Gallagher) **9**:42-4, 50-1, 53, 56, 58-62
"Willkommen und Abschied" (Goethe) **5**:247, 251
"Willow Waves" (Wang Wei) **18**:364
"Willows" (Stryk) **27**:212-13
"Wilt thou forgive" (Donne)
   See "A Hymne to God the Father"
"Wind" (Hughes) **7**:118, 165
"Wind" (Soto) **28**:370, 373-75, 377-78, 384
"Wind" (Tomlinson) **17**:328
*The Wind among the Reeds* (Yeats) **20**:303, 330
"Wind and Flags" (Montale)
   See "Vento e bandiere"
"Wind and Glacier Voices" (Ortiz) **17**:232
"Wind and Silver" (Lowell) **13**:94-5
"The Wind and Stream" (Bryant) **20**:15
"The Wind and the Rain" (Frost) **1**:196
"Wind at Night" (Zagajewski) **27**:394
"The Wind at Penistone" (Davie) **29**:94, 108, 110
"The Wind Bloweth Where It Listeth" (Cullen) **20**:58
"The Wind Coming Down From" (Ammons) **16**:5
"Wind in Florence" (Brodsky) **9**:14
"Wind is the wall of the year" (Piercy) **29**:314
"Wind on the Crescent" (Lewis)
   See "Vento sulla mezzaluna"
"The Windhover" (Hopkins) **15**:125, 127, 132-33, 144, 160, 168, 169, 171
"The Windhover" (Kinnell) **26**:
*The Winding Stair* (Yeats) **20**:307, 311, 326-28, 330, 333, 335
"The Windmill" (Bridges) **28**:67
"Window" (Hass) **16**:222
"A Window" (Merton)
   See "The Blessed Virgin Mary Compared to a Window"
"Window" (Pinsky) **27**:157, 164, 172
"Window Poems" (Berry) **28**:5, 39
"The Windows" (Apollinaire) **7**:36
"The Windows" (Herbert) **4**:119, 131
"The Windows" (Mallarme)
   See "Les fenêtres"
"Windows in th Straw" (Bissett) **14**:8
"Windows to the Fifth Season" (Elytis) **21**:118
"Windröschen" (Celan) **10**:122
"Winds" (Auden) **1**:23
"The Winds" (Williams) **7**:369
*Winds* (Perse)
   See *Vents*
"The Winds of Orisha" (Lorde) **12**:155
"The Wind's Prophecy" (Hardy) **8**:115-17
"the Wind's Way" (Swinburne) **24**:327
*Windsor Forest* (Pope) **26**:315, 319, 321
"The Windy City" (Sandburg) **2**:306, 308, 314
"The Wine" (Ashbery) **26**:135-136
*Wine from These Grapes* (Millay) **6**:214, 217, 232
"The Wine Menagerie" (Crane) **3**:81, 90
"Wine: Passages 12" (Duncan) **2**:108
"The Winged Horse" (Belloc) **24**:11
"Wingfoot Lake" (Dove) **6**:112
"Wings" (Hughes) **7**:132, 137
"Wings of a God" (Levertov) **11**:176
"Winiter's gone the summer breezes" (Clare) **23**:23
"Winkel im Wald" (Trakl) **20**:232
"Der Winkel von Hahrdt" (Holderlin) **4**:148
"The Winning Argument" (Piercy) **29**:309
"Winning His Way" (Stein) **18**:312-14, 316
"The Winnowers" (Bridges) **28**:66-7
"Wino" (Hughes) **7**:123, 132, 137
"Winston Prairie" (Masters) **1**:343

"Winter" (Celan) **10**:129
"Winter" (Clare) **23**:44-5
"Winter" (Dario)
   See "Invernal"
"Winter" (Giovanni) **19**:116
"Winter" (Hagiwara Sakutaro) **18**:168
"Winter" (Milosz) **8**:210
"Winter" (Wright) **14**:376
"Winter, a Dirge" (Burns) **6**:52
"Winter Encounters" (Tomlinson) **17**:333, 344, 352
"Winter Evening" (Pushkin)
   See "Zimniy Vecher"
"Winter Event" (Cassian) **17**:5
"Winter Festivities" (Pasternak) **6**:266
"Winter Fields" (Clare) **23**:45
"Winter Garden" (Neruda)
   See "Jardín de invierno"
"Winter Holding off the Coast of North America" (Momaday) **25**:219
"Winter in Dunbarton" (Lowell) **3**:218-19
*Winter Love* (H. D.) **5**:299-300
"Winter: My Secret" (Rossetti) **7**:281
"Winter on the River" (Meredith) **28**:198
"A Winter Piece" (Bryant) **20**:18, 35-7, 39
"Winter Piece" (Tomlinson) **17**:325
"A Winter Poem For Tony Weinberger Written on the Occasion of Feeling Very Happy" (Wakoski) **15**:331
"A Winter Scene" (Bryant) **20**:15
"The Winter Ship" (Plath) **1**:389
"Winter Sleep" (Wylie) **23**:309, 329, 332
"Winter Sleepers" (Atwood) **8**:12
"Winter Song" (Owen) **19**:336, 343
"Winter Swan" (Bogan) **12**:95, 106, 122
*A Winter Talent and Other Poems* (Davie) **29**:93-96, 100, 106, 108-09, 112, 117
*Winter Trees* (Plath) **1**:396
"The Winter Twilight Glowing Black and Gold" (Schwartz) **8**:295
"Winter Verse for His Sister" (Meredith) **28**:213
*Winter Words: Various Moods and Metres* (Hardy) **8**:89, 96, 124
"Wintering" (Plath) **1**:410, 412-13
*Wintering Out* (Heaney) **18**:188, 192-95, 199, 202-5, 209-11, 215, 238, 241, 252
*Wintermarchen* (Heine)
   See *Deutschland: Ein Wintermärchen*
"Winternacht" (Trakl) **20**:229
"A Winter's Day" (Dunbar) **5**:126
"The Winter's Night" (Merton) **10**:340, 351
"A Winter's Tale" (Thomas) **2**:382, 385, 402
*Winter's Tale* (Heine)
   See *Deutschland: Ein Wintermärchen*
"Wintry" (Gozzano)
   See "A Wintry Scene"
"A Wintry Scene" (Gozzano) **10**:177-78, 180
"Wintry Sky" (Pasternak) **6**:250
"Wirers" (Sassoon) **12**:267, 285
"Wires" (Tsvetaeva)
   See "Provoda"
"Wiretapping" (Montale)
   See "Intercettazione telefonica"
"Das wirkliche Messer" (Enzensberger) **28**:159-61, 165
"Wisdom" (Parker) **28**:362
"Wisdom Cometh with the Years" (Cullen) **20**:52, 62
"The Wise" (Cullen) **20**:54-55
"Wise Men in Their Bad Hours" (Jeffers) **17**:129
"The Wish" (Lermontov) **18**:277, 295
"Wish: Metamorphosis to Hearldic Emblem" (Atwood) **8**:32, 39
"The Wish to be Generous" (Berry) **28**:43
"The Wish to Escape into Inner Space" (Swenson) **14**:250
"Wishbones" (Wakoski) **15**:332
"Wishes" (Wright) **14**:355
"wishes for sons" (Clifton) **17**:29, 36
"The Wishing Tree" (Heaney) **18**:229, 232
"Witch Burning" (Plath) **1**:394

"Witch Doctor" (Hayden) **6**:186, 196
"Witch Hazel" (Reese) **29**:330
"The Witch of Atlas" (Shelley) **14**:174, 193, 196, 198
"The Witch of Coös" (Frost) **1**:197, 209, 220
"Witches are Flying" (Shapiro) **25**:316
"The Witch's Life" (Sexton) **2**:373
"Witch-Woman" (Lowell) **13**:61, 64
"With a Guitar, to Jane" (Shelley) **14**:177, 189
"With a Rose to Brunhilde" (Lindsay) **23**:286
"With All Deliberate Speed" (Madhubuti) **5**:346
"With Eyes At The Back of Our Heads" (Levertov) **11**:168
*With Eyes at the Back of Our Heads* (Levertov) **11**:168, 205
"With Garments Flowinig" (Clare) **23**:23
"With Happiness Stretch's across the Hills" (Blake) **12**:36
"With Her Lips Only" (Graves) **6**:151
"With Mercy for the Greedy" (Sexton) **2**:346, 348, 351, 370
"With Official Lu Hsiang Passing Hermit Hsiu-Chung's Bower" (Wang Wei) **18**:358
"With Rue My Heart Is Laden" (Housman) **2**:180, 184, 192
"With Scindia to Delhi" (Kipling) **3**:182
"With Seed the Sowers Scatter" (Housman) **2**:180
"With the Caribou" (Kumin) **15**:212, 223
"With the World in My Bloodstream" (Merton) **10**:345
"With Trumpets and Zithers" (Milosz) See "Natrabach i na cytrze"
"With Vengeance Like a Tiger Crawls" (Bukowski) **18**:5
"Without" (Snyder) **21**:297
"Without a Counterpart" (Gunn) **26**:218
"Without Benefit of Declaration" (Hughes) **1**:252
"Without Ceremony" (Hardy) **8**:134-35
"Without End" (Zagajewski) **27**:383
"Without Faith" (Aleixandre) **15**:5
"The Witness" (Tomlinson) **17**:344
*A Witness Tree* (Frost) **1**:196-97, 203, 205-06
"The Witnesses" (Auden) **1**:22
"Wives in the Sere" (Hardy) **8**:90
"Wizards" (Noyes) **27**:135
"Wm. Brazier" (Graves) **6**:143
"Wodwo" (Hughes) **7**:127-28, 155
*Wodwo* (Hughes) **7**:120-23, 133-34, 136-38, 140-42, 150, 157-60, 163, 171-72
"Woefully arrayed" (Skelton) **25**:330
"Wolf" (Mandelstam) **14**:149
"Wolfe Tone" (Heaney) **18**:228, 232
"Wolves Defended against the Lambs" (Enzensberger) **28**:147, 165
"The Woman" (Carruth) **10**:71
"The Woman" (Levertov) **11**:213-14
"A Woman" (Pinsky) **27**:176
"A Woman Alone" (Levertov) **11**:210
"Woman and Tree" (Graves) **6**:149
"A Woman Dead in Her Forties" (Rich) **5**:379-80, 394
"The Woman Hanging From the Thirteenth Floor" (Harjo) **27**:64-65
"A Woman Homer Sung" (Yeats) **20**:329
"A Woman in Heat Wiping Herself" (Olds) **22**:316
"Woman in Orchard" (Wright) **14**:373
"The Woman in the Ordinary" (Piercy) **29**:309
"Woman of Strength" (Tagore) See "Sabala"
*Woman of the River* (Alegria) **26**:
"The Woman of the Sumpul River" (Alegria) **26**:
"Woman Poem" (Giovanni) **19**:108
"A Woman Resurrected" (Gozzano) **10**:177-78
"A Woman Speaks" (Lorde) **12**:160
"Woman to Child" (Wright) **14**:337, 341, 349, 352, 360, 362, 364
"Woman to Man" (Wright) **14**:333, 336-39, 349, 358-60, 363

*Woman to Man* (Wright) **14**:334, 336-38, 341, 345-47, 349, 352, 358, 363, 365-66, 369
"A Woman Waits for Me" (Whitman) **3**:372, 387
"The Woman Who Lived in a Crate" (Stryk) **27**:187
"The Woman Who Raised Goats" (Gallagher) **9**:35-6, 59
"Woman with Girdle" (Sexton) **2**:346, 350
"Woman With the Blue-Ringed Bowl" (McGuckian) **27**:102
"A Woman Young and Old" (Yeats) **20**:327
"The Womanhood" (Brooks) **7**:54
"Woman's Constancy" (Donne) **1**:125
"Woman's Song" (Wright) **14**:349, 352, 364
"Women" (Bogan) **12**:101
"Women" (Rich) **5**:370
"Women" (Swenson) **14**:279
*The Women and the Men* (Giovanni) **19**:114, 124, 128, 130, 137
"The Women at Point Sur" (Jeffers) **17**:130
*The Women at Point Sur* (Jeffers) **17**:107, 109-11, 116, 124, 135, 144-46
"Women like You" (Ondaatje) **28**:314
"The Women of Dan Dance With Swords in Their Hands to Mark the Time When They Were Warriors" (Lorde) **12**:159-60
"the women you are accustomed to" (Clifton) **17**:30
"Women's Tug of War at Lough Arrow" (Gallagher) **9**:37
"The Wonder Castle" (Illyes) **16**:234, 250
"The Wonder Woman" (Giovanni) **19**:107, 110, 112
"The Wonderful Musician" (Sexton) **2**:365
"Wonga Vine" (Wright) **14**:348
"Woodcutting on Lost Mountain" (Gallagher) **9**:60
*The Wooden Pegasus* (Sitwell) **3**:301-02
"The Woodlot" (Clampitt) **19**:89
"The Woodman" (Clare) **23**:13
"Woodnotes" (Emerson) **18**:79, 87-88, 99, 102-3, 108-10
"The Woodpile" (Frost) **1**:220, 222, 226, 228
"Woodrow Wilson" (February, 1924 Jeffers) **17**:107
"Woods" (Berry) **28**:43
"Wooing" (Bridges) **28**:63, 86
"A Word" (Chesterton) **28**:100
"The Word" (Smith) **12**:354
"Word Basket Woman" (Snyder) **21**:326
"The Word 'Beautiful'" (Swenson) **14**:250
"The Word Crys Out" (Ammons) **16**:25
"A Word on the Quick and Modern Poem-Makers" (Bukowski) **18**:5
*Word over All* (Day Lewis) **11**:144, 148
"Words" (Gunn) **26**:212
"Words" (Levine) **22**:219
"The Words" (Montale) See "Le parole"
"Words" (Plath) **1**:409
"Words" (Reese) **29**:336
"Words" (Sexton) **2**:372-73
"Words" (Yeats) **20**:329, 331
"Words for a Wall-Painting" (Shapiro) **25**:304
"Words for Hart Crane" (Lowell) **3**:219, 222
"Words for Maria" (Merrill) **28**:224, 231, 264, 277
"Words for Music Perhaps" (Yeats) **20**:326-29, 331, 333
*Words for Music Perhaps, and Other Poems* (Yeats) **20**:328, 334
"Words for the Hour" (Harper) **21**:190
"Words for the Wind" (Roethke) **15**:263
*Words for the Wind: The Collected Verse of Theodore Roethke* (Roethke) **15**:257, 262-64, 267, 282, 284, 286, 288, 309
*Words in th Fire* (Bissett) **14**:13-14
"Words in the Mourning Time" (Hayden) **6**:197-98
*Words in the Mourning Time* (Hayden) **6**:179, 181-83, 193, 195

"Words of Comfort" (Ammons) **16**:25, 43
"The Words of the Poet" (Aleixandre) **15**:6
"The Words of the Preacher" (Kunitz) **19**:149, 170
"Words on a Windy Day" (Stryk) **27**:212
"Words, Roses, Stars" (Wright) **14**:378-79
"Work" (Hass) **16**:249
"Work Gangs" (Sandburg) **2**:304, 308
"Work in Progress" (MacDiarmid) **9**:199
*Work Is Tiresome* (Pavese) See *Lavorare stanca*
"Work Wearies" (Pavese) See "Lavorare stanca"
*Work Wearies* (Pavese) See *Lavorare stanca*
"A Worker Reads History" (MacDiarmid) **9**:181
"Working on the '58 Willys Pickup" (Snyder) **21**:300
"A Working Party" (Sassoon) **12**:257, 261-62, 277-78, 284
"The Workingman's Drink" (Baudelaire) **1**:47
*Works* (Pope) **26**:359-60
*Works, 1735—Poems on Several Occasions* (Swift) **9**:256
"The Works and Wonders of Almighty Power" (Thomson) **23**:
*Works II* (Pope) **26**:360
*The Works of Aphra Behn* (Behn) **13**:16, 18
*The Works of George Herbert* (Herbert) **4**:107
*The Works of Horace, Translated into Verse* (Smart) **13**:361-62
*The Works of William Blake* (Blake) **12**:51
"The World" (Herbert) **4**:100
"The World" (Milosz) **8**:187, 192, 194, 207, 209
"The World" (Rossetti) **7**:277
"The World" (Smith) **12**:328
"The World" (Tagore) See "Vasundhara"
*World Alone* (Aleixandre) See *Mundo a solas*
"The World and the Child" (Merrill) **28**:249
"The World and the Child" (Wright) **14**:352
"The World and the Quietist" (Arnold) **5**:38, 49
"A World in Crystal" (Illyes) **16**:249
"The World Is a Beautiful Place" (Ferlinghetti) **1**:180, 182-83
"The World Is a Wedding" (Schwartz) **8**:303
"A World Is Everyone" (Ekeloef) **23**:80
"The World Is Full of Remarkable Things" (Baraka) **4**:23-4
"The World of Fantasy the Buddha Saw" (Hagiwara Sakutaro) **18**:178
*The World of Gwendolyn Brooks* (Brooks) **7**:64, 66, 105
*World of the Buddha* (Stryk) **27**:181, 194, 198
"The World Outside" (Levertov) **11**:168, 193
"World Soul" (Bely) **11**:24
"The World State" (Chesterton) **28**:100
*Worldly Hopes* (Ammons) **16**:45-6
"Worlds" (Masters) **1**:333
"Worlds Back of Worlds" (Masters) **1**:343
"The World's Desire" (Masters) **1**:333
"World's End" (Ashbery) **26**:166
"The World's Wonders" (Jeffers) **17**:141
"The World-Soul" (Emerson) **18**:86
*Worleys* (Reese) **29**:339
"The Worms of History" (Graves) **6**:137, 142, 144
"The Wormwood Star" (Milosz) **8**:201, 204
"Worsening Situation" (Ashbery) **26**:124
"The Worst Of It" (Sassoon) **12**:248
*Worthy It Is* (Elytis) See *The Axion Esti*
"Would Jacob Wrestle with a Flabby Angel?" (Viereck) **27**:286
"The Wound" (Gluck) **16**:124, 138, 154
"The Wound" (Gunn) **26**:199, 206-207
"The Wound" (Hardy) **8**:93
"The Wound" (Soto) **28**:375
*The Wound* (Hughes) **7**:155

"The Wounded Wilderness of Morris Graves"
(Ferlinghetti) **1**:165
*Woven Stone* (Ortiz) **17**:244
"The Wraith" (Roethke) **15**:256, 272
"The Wrath of Samson" (Vigny)
See "La colère de Samson"
"A Wreath" (Herbert) **4**:127, 130
"Wreath" (Illyes) **16**:250
"Wreath for the Warm-Eyed" (Merrill) **28**:234
"The Wreck of the Deutschland" (Hopkins)
"The Wreck of the Thresher" (Meredith) **28**:178,
181, 193-94, 200, 206, 213, 215
*The Wreck of the Thresher* (Meredith) **28**:175,
178, 191-95, 209, 211, 213, 215
"Wreckage" (Momaday) **25**:221
"The Wrestler's Heart" (Soto) **28**:394, 399
"The Wretched One" (Marie de France)
See "Le Chaitivel"
"Write It Down" (Ekeloef) **23**:86
"The Writhing Imperfect Earth" (Lindsay)
**23**:281
"Writing" (Nemerov) **24**:259
"Writing in the Dark" (Levertov) **11**:199
"Writing My Feelings" (Li Po) **29**:179
"Writing to Aaron" (Levertov) **11**:208
*Writing Writing* (Duncan) **2**:106
"The Writings Depart" (Breton) **15**:73
"Written aboard a Boat on the Day of Little
Cold Food" (Tu Fu) **9**:320
"Written after Long Rains at My Villa by
Wang Stream" (Wang Wei) **18**:392
"Written by Dr. Swift on His Own Deafness"
(Swift) **9**:295
"Written in a Lady's Ivory Table-book, 1698"
(Swift) **9**:251, 295
"Written in Emerson's Essays" (Arnold) **5**:38,
49
"Written in the Mountains in Early Autumn"
(Wang Wei) **18**:392
"Written on The Door" (Perse) **23**:229
*Written on Water* (Tomlinson) **17**:321-23, 327,
333
*Written on Water* (Tomlinson) **17**:321-23, 327,
333
"The Wrong Kind of Insurance" (Ashbery)
**26**:134
"Wrong Number" (Bukowski) **18**:4
"die würgengel" (Enzensberger) **28**:134
"X" (Shapiro) **25**:
*Xaipe: Seventy-One Poems* (Cummings) **5**:82-3,
86, 107-08
*Xenia* (Martial) **10**:230
*Xenia* (Montale) **13**:132-33, 135-36, 138, 165,
167
"Xenia I" (Montale) **13**:144
"Xenia II" (Montale) **13**:144
"Xenion" (Montale) **13**:133-34
"Xenion" No. 7 (Montale) **13**:134
*Xénophiles* (Breton) **15**:53-4
"Xoanon" (Ekeloef) **23**:67
"XVI" (Shapiro) **25**:285
"XXX" (Joyce) **22**:138, 144-45, 164, 173
*Y and X* (Olson) **19**:318
"Ya que para despedirme" (Juana Ines de la
Cruz) **24**:180
"The Yachts" (Williams) **7**:360, 368
"Yalluh Hammer" (Walker) **20**:273, 275-76,
286, 292
"Yam" (Merrill) **28**:259
"Yama no ugoku hi" (Yosano Akiko) **11**:321
"Yamanote Sen" (Hongo) **23**:197
"Los yaruros" (Cardenal) **22**:132
"Yauvan-svapna" (Tagore) **8**:407
"Yawm mawlidi" (Gibran) **9**:78
"Ye Are Na Mary Morison" (Burns) **6**:99
"Ye Know My Herte" (Wyatt) **27**:314-15
"Ye old mule" (Wyatt) **27**:362
"yeah man?" (Bukowski) **18**:14
"The Year 1812" (Davie) **29**:109
"The Year 1905" (Pasternak)
See "Devyatsat pyaty god"
"Year at Mudstraw" (Forche) **10**:133

"The Year of Mourning" (Jeffers) **17**:141
"The Year of the Double Spring" (Swenson)
**14**:267, 275
"The Years" (Aleixandre) **15**:4
*The Years as Catches* (Duncan) **2**:104, 109
"The Year's Awakening" (Hardy) **8**:105
"Years of Indiscretion" (Ashbery) **26**:115, 124
"A Year's Spinning" (Browning) **6**:32
"A Year's Windfalls" (Rossetti) **7**:262
"Yee Bow" (Masters) **1**:327
"Yell'ham Wood's Story" (Hardy) **8**:91
*The Yellow Heart* (Neruda)
See *El corazón amarillo*
*The Yellow House on the Corner* (Dove) **6**:104-
09, 116, 118, 122
"Yellow Light" (Hongo) **23**:203
*Yellow Light* (Hongo) **23**:195, 197, 202-204
"Yellow Ribbons, Baghdad 1991" (Rose)
**13**:241
"The Yellow Violet" (Bryant) **20**:4, 35, 40
"Yellowhammer's Nest" (Clare) **23**:5
"Yes" (Ferlinghetti) **1**:187
"Yes" (Gallagher) **9**:64-5
"Yes and It's Hopeless" (Ginsberg) **4**:76, 85
"Yes, I am lying in the earth, moving my lips"
(Mandelstam)
See "Da, ia lezhu v zemle . . ."
"Yesterday" (Aleixandre) **15**:5
"Yesterday" (Sitwell) **3**:293
"Yesterday I Was Called Nigger" (Guillen)
See "Ayer me dijeron negro"
"Yestreen I Had a Pint o' Wine" (Burns) **6**:75
"Yet Do I Marvel" (Cullen) **20**:63, 76
"the yeti poet returns to his village to tell his
story" (Clifton) **17**:30
"Les yeux des pauvres" (Baudelaire) **1**:58
"Yeux Glauques" (Pound) **4**:319
*Yevgeny Onegin* (Pushkin) **10**:357-62, 366, 368-
69, 371, 374-83, 386, 391, 400-04, 406, 409
"YgUDuh" (Cummings) **5**:98
"Ylang-Ylang" (McGuckian) **27**:83
"Yo" (Fuertes) **27**:26, 49-50
"Yo persigo una forma" (Dario) **15**:103-04, 119
"Yo soy aquél" (Dario) **15**:97
*Yobuko to kuchibue* (Ishikawa) **10**:211
"Yogisha" (Hagiwara Sakutaro) **18**:168, 179,
183
"Yonder See the Morning Blink" (Housman)
**2**:179
"Yonec" (Marie de France) **22**:241-45, 258,
260-66, 269-72, 274-75, 299-300, 302-03
"York: In Memoriam W. H. Auden" (Brodsky)
**9**:12
*The York Road* (Reese) **29**:339
"You" (Cummings) **5**:105
"You All Are State I Alone Am Moving"
(Viereck) **27**:258
"You All Know the Story of the Other
Woman" (Sexton) **2**:352-53
"You and Me" (Tagore)
See "Tumi o ami"
"You Are" (Swenson) **14**:274, 283-84
*You Are Happy* (Atwood) **8**:25, 27
*You Are Happy* (Atwood) **8**:20-4, 29, 31, 33,
41-2
"You are old Father William" (Carroll) **18**:49
"You Are Waiting" (Aleixandre) **15**:6
"You Asked About My Life; I Send You, Pei
Di, These Lines" (Wang Wei) **18**:391
"You Be Like You" (Celan)
See "Du sei wei du"
"You Bet Travel Is Broadening" (Nash) **21**:273
"You Can Have It" (Levine) **22**:223
*You Can't Get There from Here* (Nash) **21**:274
"You, Dr. Martin" (Sexton) **2**:359, 365
"You Drive in a Circle" (Hughes) **7**:137
"You Frog!" (Hagiwara Sakutaro)
See "You Frog!"
"You Have a Name" (Aleixandre) **15**:5
"You may not see the Nazis" (Brutus) **24**:118
"You Speak No English" (Guillen)
See "Tú no sabe inglé"

"You Talk on Your Telephone; I Talk on Mine"
(Gallagher) **9**:59
"You Think of the Sun That It" (Ammons)
**16**:43
"The Young" (Aleixandre) **15**:5
"Young" (Sexton) **2**:350
"Young Africans" (Brooks) **7**:65, 91, 93
"A Young Birch" (Frost) **1**:200
"The Young British Soldier" (Kipling) **3**:158
*Young Cherry Trees Secured Against Hares*
(Breton) **15**:47
"A Young Child and His Pregnant Mother"
(Schwartz) **8**:282, 302, 304
"The Young Cordwainer" (Graves) **6**:144
*The Young Fate* (Valery)
See *La jeune parque*
"Young Girls" (Page) **12**:176
"Young Heroes" (Brooks) **7**:92-3, 105
"The Young Housewife" (Williams) **7**:348, 363,
378, 409
"Young Love" (Marvell) **10**:303-04
"Young Love" (Williams) **7**:382, 410
"The Young Lovers" (Aleixandre) **15**:4-6
"The Young Mage" (Bogan) **12**:100
"Young Man with Letter" (Ashbery) **26**:125
"A Young Man's Exhortation" (Hardy) **8**:108
"Young Man's Song" (Yeats) **20**:331, 333
"Young Mothers" (Olds) **22**:328
"Young Mothers I" (Olds) **22**:308
"Young Singer" (Hughes) **1**:236, 246
"Young Sorrows"
See "Junge Leiden"
"Young Soul" (Baraka) **4**:9
"Young Sycamore" (Williams) **7**:372-77
"The Young Warrior" (Johnson) **24**:127, 166
"The Youngest Daughter" (Song) **21**:331-32,
350
"Your Birthday in the California Mountains"
(Rexroth) **20**:204
"Your Face on the Dog's Neck" (Sexton) **2**:363
"Your Flight" (Montale)
See "Il tuo volo"
"Your Last Drive" (Hardy) **8**:134
"Your Lead Partner I Hope We've Read the
Same Book" (Nash) **21**:
*Your Native Land, Your Life* (Rich) **5**:387-89
"You're" (Plath) **1**:389-90
"You's Sweet to Yo' Mammy jes de Same"
(Johnson) **24**:141
"Youth" (Akhmatova) **2**:8
"Youth" (Zukofsky) **11**:368
"Youth and Calm" (Arnold) **5**:42, 51
"Youth in Heaven" (Harper) **21**:209
"The Youth of Man" (Arnold) **5**:19, 49
"The Youth of Nature" (Arnold) **5**:19, 42, 49,
51, 59
"The Youth's Magic Horn" (Ashbery) **26**:162
"Ys It Possyble" (Wyatt) **27**:317, 324
*Ysopet* (Marie de France) **22**:258-59
*yu can eat it at th opening* (Bissett) **14**:17
"yu know th creaturs ar ourselvs" (Bissett)
**14**:34
"yu sing" (Bissett) **14**:30
"yu want th music" (Bissett) **14**:34
"Yube no kane" (Ishikawa) **10**:214
"Yūbe no umi" (Ishikawa) **10**:213, 215
"Yugel'skii baron" (Lermontov) **18**:288
"Za Ki Tan Ke Parlay Lot" (Lorde) **12**:155
*Zahme Xenien* (Goethe) **5**:223
"Zakinuv golovu i opustiv glaza" (Tsvetaeva)
**14**:319, 322-23
"Zambesi and Ranee" (Swenson) **14**:277
"Zaporogue" (Apollinaire) **7**:48
"Ein zärtlich jugendlicher Kummer" (Goethe)
**5**:247
"Zauberspruch" (Celan) **10**:124-25
"Zaveshchanije" (Lermontov) **18**:303
"Zaydee" (Levine) **22**:223
"Zeitgedichte" (Heine) **25**:131, 134
*Zeitgedichte* (Heine) **25**:129
*Zeitgehöft* (Celan) **10**:96, 111
"Der Zeitgeist" (Holderlin) **4**:166

"Zen Poems of China and Japan: The Crane's
    Bill" (Stryk) **27**:181
"Zen Poetry" (Stryk) **27**:188
"The Zeppelin Factory" (Dove) **6**:110
"Zero" (Berry) **28**:6
"Zero" (Gallagher) **9**:58
"Zero Hour" (Cardenal)
    See "La hora O"
*Zero Hour and Other Documentary Poems*
    (Cardenal) **22**:117

"Zeroing In" (Levertov) **11**:205
"Zeus over Redeye" (Hayden) **6**:183, 194
"Zhil Na Svete Rytsar' Bednyi" (Pushkin)
    **10**:411
"Zhong feng" (Li Po) **29**:188
"Zikade" (Enzensberger) **28**:139
"Zimniy Vecher" (Pushkin) **10**:381
"Zim-Zizimi" (Hugo) **17**:59
"Znayu" (Bely) **11**:32
*Zoloto v lazuri* (Bely) **11**:3-6, 22, 26, 31-2

"Zone" (Ammons) **16**:6, 28
"Zone" (Apollinaire) **7**:6, 10-12, 14-15, 21, 41,
    44-8
"Zone" (Bogan) **12**:126
"Zoo de verbena" (Fuertes) **27**:16
"Zoo Keeper's Wife" (Plath) **1**:399
*Zovy vremen* (Bely) **11**:31-2
"Zueignung" (Goethe) **5**:257
"Zuleika" (Goethe) **5**:228
*Zvezda* (Bely) **11**:7, 24, 30, 32

ISBN 0-7876-3077-2

90000

174.75